Collins

Collins
French
Dictionary

Collins
French
Dictionary

HarperCollins Publishers
Westerhill Road
Bishopbriggs
Glasgow
G64 2QT
Great Britain

First edition 2007

Reprint 10 9 8 7 6 5 4 3 2 1 0

© HarperCollins Publishers 2007

ISBN 978-0-00-779340-2

www.collins.co.uk

A catalogue record for this book is
available from the British Library

Designed by Mark Thomson

Typeset by Thomas Callan

Printed in Great Britain by
Clays Ltd, St Ives plc

Acknowledgements
We would like to thank those authors and
publishers who kindly gave permission for
copyright material to be used in the Collins
Word Web. We would also like to thank
Times Newspapers Ltd for providing
valuable data.

Table des matières

Contents

Introduction

You may be starting French for the first time, or you may wish to extend your knowledge of the language. Perhaps you want to read and study French books, newspapers and magazines, or perhaps simply have a conversation with French speakers. Whatever the reason, whether you're a student, a tourist or want to use French for business, this is the ideal book to help you understand and communicate. This modern, user-friendly dictionary gives priority to everyday vocabulary and the language of current affairs, business, computing and tourism, and, as in all Collins dictionaries, the emphasis is firmly placed on contemporary language and expressions.

How to use the dictionary
Below you will find an outline of how information is presented in your dictionary. Our aim is to give you the maximum amount of detail in the clearest and most helpful way.

Entries
A typical entry in your dictionary will be made up of the following elements:

Phonetic transcription
Phonetics appear in square brackets immediately after the headword. They are shown using the International Phonetic Alphabet (IPA), and a complete list of the symbols used in this system can be found on pages xii and xiii.

Grammatical information
All words belong to one of the following parts of speech: noun, verb, adjective, adverb, pronoun, article, conjunction, preposition.

Nouns can be singular or plural and, in French, masculine or feminine. Verbs can be transitive, intransitive, reflexive or impersonal. Parts of speech appear in *italics* immediately after the phonetic spelling of the headword. The gender of the translation appears in *italics* immediately following the key element of the translation.

Often a word can have more than one part of speech. Just as the English word **chemical** can be an adjective or a noun, the French word **rose** can be an adjective ("pink") or a feminine noun ("rose"). In the same way the verb **to walk** is sometimes transitive, ie it takes an object ("to walk the dog") and sometimes intransitive, ie it doesn't take an object ("to walk to school"). To help you find the meaning you are looking for quickly and for clarity of presentation, the different part of speech categories are separated by a right facing triangle ▷.

Meaning divisions

Most words have more than one meaning. Take, for example, **punch** which can be, amongst other things, a blow with the fist or an object used for making holes. Other words are translated differently depending on the context in which they are used. The transitive verb **to roll up**, for example, can be translated by "rouler" or "retrousser" depending on what it is you are rolling up. To help you select the most appropriate translation in every context, entries are divided according to meaning. Different meanings are introduced by an "indicator" in *italics* and in brackets. Thus, the examples given above will be shown as follows:

> **punch** *n* (*blow*) coup *m* de poing; (*tool*) poinçon *m*
> **roll up** *vt* (*carpet, cloth, map*) rouler; (*sleeves*) retrousser

Likewise, some words can have a different meaning when used to talk about a specific subject area or field. For example, **bishop**, which we generally use to mean a high-ranking clergyman, is also the name of a chess piece. To show English speakers which translation to use, we have added "subject field labels" in *italics*, starting with a capital letter, and in brackets, in this case (*Chess*):

> **bishop** *n* évêque *m*; (*Chess*) fou *m*

Field labels are often shortened to save space. You will find a complete list of abbreviations used in the dictionary on pages x and xi.

Translations

Most English words have a direct translation in French and vice versa, as shown in the examples given above. Sometimes, however, no exact equivalent exists in the target language. In such cases we have given an approximate equivalent, indicated by the sign ≈. An example is **National Insurance**, the French equivalent of which is "Sécurité Sociale". There is no exact equivalent since the systems of the two countries are quite different:

> **National Insurance** *n* (*Brit*) ≈ Sécurité Sociale

On occasion it is impossible to find even an approximate equivalent. This may be the case, for example, with the names of types of food:

> **mince pie** *n* *sorte de tarte aux fruits secs*

Here the translation (which doesn't exist) is replaced by an explanation. For increased clarity the explanation, or "gloss", is shown in *italics*.

It is often the case that a word, or a particular meaning of a word, cannot be translated in isolation. The translation of **Dutch**, for example, is "hollandais(e), neérlandais(e)". However, the phrase **to go Dutch** is rendered by "partager les frais".

Even an expression as simple as **washing powder** needs a separate translation since it translates as "lessive (en poudre)", not "poudre à laver". This is where your dictionary will prove to be particularly informative and useful since it contains an abundance of compounds, phrases and idiomatic expressions.

Levels of formality and familiarity

In English you instinctively know when to say "I don't have any money" and when to say "I'm broke" or "I'm a bit short of cash". When you are trying to understand someone who is speaking French, however, or when you yourself try to speak French, it is important to know what is polite and what is less so, and what you can say in a relaxed situation but not in a formal context. To help you with this, on the French–English side we have added the label (*inf*) to show that a French meaning or expression is colloquial, while those meanings or expressions which are vulgar are given an exclamation mark (*inf!*), warning you they can cause serious offence. Note also that on the English–French side, translations which are vulgar are followed by an exclamation mark in brackets.

Abréviations   # Abbreviations

abréviation	*ab(b)r*	abbreviation
adjectif, locution adjectivale	*adj*	adjective, adjectival phrase
administration	*Admin*	administration
adverbe, locution adverbiale	*adv*	adverb, adverbial phrase
agriculture	*Agr*	agriculture
anatomie	*Anat*	anatomy
architecture	*Archit*	architecture
article défini	*art déf*	definite article
article indéfini	*art indéf*	indefinite article
automobile	*Aut(o)*	the motor car and motoring
aviation, voyages aériens	*Aviat*	flying, air travel
biologie	*Bio(l)*	biology
botanique	*Bot*	botany
anglais britannique	*Brit*	British English
chimie	*Chem*	chemistry
cinéma	*Ciné, Cine*	cinema
commerce, finance, banque	*Comm*	commerce, finance, banking
informatique	*Comput*	computing
conjonction	*conj*	conjunction
construction	*Constr*	building
nom utilisé comme adjectif	*cpd*	compound element
cuisine	*Culin*	cookery
article défini	*def art*	definite article
déterminant: article; adjectif démonstratif *ou* indéfini etc	*dét*	determiner: article, demonstrative etc
économie	*Écon, Econ*	economics
électricité, électronique	*Élec, Elec*	electricity, electronics
en particulier	*esp*	especially
exclamation, interjection	*excl*	exclamation, interjection
féminin	*f*	feminine
langue familière (! emploi vulgaire)	*fam(!)*	colloquial usage (! particularly offensive)
emploi figuré	*fig*	figurative use
(verbe anglais) dont la particule est inséparable	*fus*	(phrasal verb) where the particle is inseparable
généralement	*gén, gen*	generally
géographie, géologie	*Géo, Geo*	geography, geology
géométrie	*Géom, Geom*	geometry
langue familière (! emploi vulgaire)	*inf(!)*	colloquial usage (! particularly offensive)
infinitif	*infin*	infinitive
informatique	*Inform*	computing
invariable	*inv*	invariable
irrégulier	*irrég, irreg*	irregular
domaine juridique	*Jur*	law

Abréviations

Abbreviations

grammaire, linguistique	*Ling*	grammar, linguistics
masculin	*m*	masculine
mathématiques, algèbre	*Math*	mathematics, calculus
médecine	*Méd, Med*	medical term, medicine
masculin *ou* féminin	*m/f*	masculine *or* feminine
domaine militaire, armée	*Mil*	military matters
musique	*Mus*	music
nom	*n*	noun
navigation, nautisme	*Navig, Naut*	sailing, navigation
nom *ou* adjectif numéral	*num*	numeral noun *or* adjective
	o.s.	oneself
péjoratif	*péj, pej*	derogatory, pejorative
photographie	*Phot(o)*	photography
physiologie	*Physiol*	physiology
pluriel	*pl*	plural
politique	*Pol*	politics
participe passé	*pp*	past participle
préposition	*prép, prep*	preposition
pronom	*pron*	pronoun
psychologie, psychiatrie	*Psych*	psychology, psychiatry
temps du passé	*pt*	past tense
quelque chose	*qch*	
quelqu'un	*qn*	
religion, domaine ecclésiastique	*Rel*	religion
	sb	somebody
enseignement, système scolaire et universitaire	*Scol*	schooling, schools and universities
singulier	*sg*	singular
	sth	something
subjonctif	*sub*	subjunctive
sujet (grammatical)	*su(b)j*	(grammatical) subject
superlatif	*superl*	superlative
techniques, technologie	*Tech*	technical term, technology
télécommunications	*Tél, Tel*	telecommunications
télévision	*TV*	television
typographie	*Typ(o)*	typography, printing
anglais des USA	*US*	American English
verbe (auxiliare)	*vb (aux)*	(auxiliary) verb
verbe intransitif	*vi*	intransitive verb
verbe transitif	*vt*	transitive verb
zoologie	*Zool*	zoology
marque déposée	®	registered trademark
indique une équivalence culturelle	≈	introduces a cultural equivalent

Transcription phonétique

Consonnes		**Consonants**	
poupée	p	*p*u*pp*y	
bombe	b	*b*a*b*y	
tente thermal	t	*t*en*t*	
dinde	d	*d*a*dd*y	
coq qui képi	k	*c*or*k* *k*iss *ch*ord	
gag bague	g	*g*a*g* *g*uess	
sale ce nation	s	*s*o ri*c*e ki*ss*	
zéro rose	z	cou*s*in bu*zz*	
tache chat	ʃ	*sh*eep *s*ugar	
gilet juge	ʒ	plea*s*ure bei*ge*	
	tʃ	*ch*ur*ch*	
	dʒ	*j*udge *g*eneral	
fer phare	f	*f*arm ra*ff*le	
valve	v	*v*ery re*v*	
	θ	*th*in ma*th*s	
	ð	*th*at o*th*er	
lent salle	l	*l*itt*l*e ba*ll*	
rare rentrer	ʀ		
	r	*r*at ra*r*e	
maman femme	m	*m*u*mm*y co*m*b	
non nonne	n	*n*o ra*n*	
agneau vigne	ɲ		
	ŋ	si*ng*ing ba*n*k	
hop!	h	*h*at re*h*eat	
yeux paille pied	j	*y*et	
nouer oui	w	*w*all be*w*ail	
huile lui	ɥ		
	x	lo*ch*	

Divers		**Miscellaneous**	
pour l'anglais: le "r" final se prononce en liaison devant une voyelle	ʳ	in English transcription: final "r" can be pronounced before a vowel	
pour l'anglais: précède la syllabe accentuée	'	in French wordlist: no liaison before aspirate "h"	

NB: p, b, t, d, k, g sont suivis d'une aspiration en anglais.
p, b, t, d, k, g are not aspirated in French.

En règle générale, la prononciation est donnée entre crochets après chaque entrée. Toutefois, du côté anglais-français et dans le cas des expressions composées de deux ou plusieurs mots non réunis par un trait d'union et faisant l'objet d'une entrée séparée, la prononciation doit être cherchée sous chacun des mots constitutifs de l'expression en question.

Phonetic transcription

Voyelles

ici vie lyrique	i i:	
	ɪ	
jouer été	e	
lait jouet merci	ɛ	
plat amour	a æ	
bas pâte	ɑ ɑ:	
	ʌ	
le premier	ə	
beurre peur	œ	
peu deux	ø ə:	
or homme	ɔ	
mot eau gauche	o ɔ:	
genou roue	u	
	u:	
rue urne	y	

Vowels

i i:	heel bead
ɪ	hit pity
e	
ɛ	set tent
a æ	bat apple
ɑ ɑ:	after car calm
ʌ	fun cousin
ə	over above
œ	
ø ə:	urgent fern work
ɔ	wash pot
o ɔ:	born cork
u	full hook
u:	boom shoe
y	

Diphtongues

Diphthongs

ɪə	beer tier
ɛə	tear fair there
eɪ	date plaice day
aɪ	life buy cry
au	owl foul now
əu	low no
ɔɪ	boil boy oily
uə	poor tour

Nasales

Nasal vowels

matin plein	ɛ̃	
brun	œ̃	
sang an dans	ɑ̃	
non pont	ɔ̃	

NB: La mise en équivalence de certains sons n'indique qu'une ressemblance approximative.

The pairing of some vowel sounds only indicates approximate equivalence.

In general, we give the pronunciation of each entry in square brackets after the word in question. However, on the English-French side, where the entry is composed of two or more unhyphenated words, each of which is given elsewhere in this dictionary, you will find the pronunciation of each word in its alphabetical position.

French verb forms

1 Present participle 2 Past participle 3 Present 4 Imperfect 5 Future 6 Conditional
7 Present subjunctive 8 Impératif

acquérir 1 acquérant 2 acquis 3 acquiers,
acquérons, acquièrent 4 acquérais
5 acquerrai 7 acquière

ALLER 1 allant 2 allé 3 vais, vas, va, allons,
allez, vont 4 allais 5 irai 6 irais 7 aille

asseoir 1 asseyant 2 assis 3 assieds,
asseyons, asseyez, asseyent 4 asseyais
5 assiérai 7 asseye

atteindre 1 atteignant 2 atteint 3 atteins,
atteignons 4 atteignais 7 atteigne

AVOIR 1 ayant 2 eu 3 ai, as, a, avons, avez,
ont 4 avais 5 aurai 6 aurais 7 aie, aies, ait,
ayons, ayez, aient

battre 1 battant 2 battu 3 bats, bat, battons
4 battais 7 batte

boire 1 buvant 2 bu 3 bois, buvons, boivent
4 buvais 7 boive

bouillir 1 bouillant 2 bouilli 3 bous,
bouillons 4 bouillais 7 bouille

conclure 1 concluant 2 conclu 3 conclus,
concluons 4 concluais 7 conclue

conduire 1 conduisant 2 conduit 3 conduis,
conduisons 4 conduisais 7 conduise

connaître 1 connaissant 2 connu 3 connais,
connaît, connaissons 4 connaissais
7 connaisse

coudre 1 cousant 2 cousu 3 couds, cousons,
cousez, cousent 4 cousais 7 couse

courir 1 courant 2 couru 3 cours, courons
4 courais 5 courrai 7 coure

couvrir 1 couvrant 2 couvert 3 couvre,
couvrons 4 couvrais 7 couvre

craindre 1 craignant 2 craint 3 crains,
craignons 4 craignais 7 craigne

croire 1 croyant 2 cru 3 crois, croyons,
croient 4 croyais 7 croie

croître 1 croissant 2 crû, crue, crus, crues
3 croîs, croissons 4 croissais 7 croisse

cueillir 1 cueillant 2 cueilli 3 cueille,
cueillons 4 cueillais 5 cueillerai 7 cueille

devoir 1 devant 2 dû, due, dus, dues 3 dois,
devons, doivent 4 devais 5 devrai 7 doive

dire 1 disant 2 dit 3 dis, disons, dites,
disent 4 disais 7 dise

dormir 1 dormant 2 dormi 3 dors, dormons
4 dormais 7 dorme

écrire 1 écrivant 2 écrit 3 écris, écrivons
4 écrivais 7 écrive

ÊTRE 1 étant 2 été 3 suis, es, est, sommes,
êtes, sont 4 étais 5 serai 6 serais 7 sois,
sois, soit, soyons, soyez, soient

FAIRE 1 faisant 2 fait 3 fais, fais, fait,
faisons, faites, font 4 faisais 5 ferai
6 ferais 7 fasse

falloir 2 fallu 3 faut 4 fallait 5 faudra
7 faille

FINIR 1 finissant 2 fini 3 finis, finis, finit,
finissons, finissez, finissent 4 finissais
5 finirai 6 finirais 7 finisse

fuir 1 fuyant 2 fui 3 fuis, fuyons, fuient
4 fuyais 7 fuie

joindre 1 joignant 2 joint 3 joins, joignons
4 joignais 7 joigne

lire 1 lisant 2 lu 3 lis, lisons 4 lisais 7 lise

luire 1 luisant 2 lui 3 luis, luisons 4 luisais
7 luise

maudire 1 maudissant 2 maudit
3 maudis, maudissons 4 maudissait
7 maudisse

mentir 1 mentant 2 menti 3 mens,
mentons 4 mentais 7 mente

mettre 1 mettant 2 mis 3 mets, mettons
4 mettais 7 mette

mourir 1 mourant 2 mort 3 meurs,
mourons, meurent 4 mourais 5 mourrai
7 meure

naître 1 naissant 2 né 3 nais, naît,
naissons 4 naissais 7 naisse

offrir 1 offrant 2 offert 3 offre, offrons
4 offrais 7 offre

PARLER 1 parlant 2 parlé 3 parle, parles,
parle, parlons, parlez, parlent 4 parlais,
parlais, parlait, parlions, parliez, parlaient
5 parlerai, parleras, parlera, parlerons,

parlerez, parleront **6** parlerais, parlerais,
parlerait, parlerions, parleriez, parleraient
7 parle, parles, parle, parlions, parliez,
parlent **8** parle! parlons! parlez!

partir **1** partant **2** parti **3** pars, partons
4 partais **7** parte

plaire **1** plaisant **2** plu **3** plais, plaît,
plaisons **4** plaisais **7** plaise

pleuvoir **1** pleuvant **2** plu **3** pleut, pleuvent
4 pleuvait **5** pleuvra **7** pleuve

pourvoir **1** pourvoyant **2** pourvu
3 pourvois, pourvoyons, pourvoient
4 pourvoyais **7** pourvoie

pouvoir **1** pouvant **2** pu **3** peux, peut,
pouvons, peuvent **4** pouvais **5** pourrai
7 puisse

prendre **1** prenant **2** pris **3** prends,
prenons, prennent **4** prenais **7** prenne

prévoir *like* **voir** **5** prévoirai

RECEVOIR **1** recevant **2** reçu **3** reçois,
reçois, reçoit, recevons, recevez, rerçoivent
4 recevais **5** recevrai **6** recevrais **7** reçoive

RENDRE **1** rendant **2** rendu **3** rends, rends,
rend, rendons, rendez, rendent **4** rendais
5 rendrai **6** rendrais **7** rende

résoudre **1** résolvant **2** résolu **3** résous,
résout, résolvons **4** résolvais **7** résolve

rire **1** riant **2** ri **3** ris, rions **4** riais **7** rie

savoir **1** sachant **2** su **3** sais, savons, savent
4 savais **5** saurai **7** sache **8** sache! sachons!
sachez!

servir **1** servant **2** servi **3** sers, servons
4 servais **7** serve

sortir **1** sortant **2** sorti **3** sors, sortons
4 sortais **7** sorte

souffrir **1** souffrant **2** souffert **3** souffre,
souffrons **4** souffrais **7** souffre

suffire **1** suffisant **2** suffi **3** suffis, suffisons
4 suffisais **7** suffise

suivre **1** suivant **2** suivi **3** suis, suivons
4 suivais **7** suive

taire **1** taisant **2** tu **3** tais, taisons **4** taisais
7 taise

tenir **1** tenant **2** tenu **3** tiens, tenons,
tiennent **4** tenais **5** tiendrai **7** tienne

vaincre **1** vainquant **2** vaincu **3** vaincs,
vainc, vainquons **4** vainquais **7** vainque

valoir **1** valant **2** valu **3** vaux, vaut, valons
4 valais **5** vaudrai **7** vaille

venir **1** venant **2** venu **3** viens, venons,
viennent **4** venais **5** viendrai **7** vienne

vivre **1** vivant **2** vécu **3** vis, vivons **4** vivais
7 vive

voir **1** voyant **2** vu **3** vois, voyons, voient
4 voyais **5** verrai **7** voie

vouloir **1** voulant **2** voulu **3** veux, veut,
voulons, veulent **4** voulais **5** voudrai
7 veuille **8** veuillez!

Les nombres

un (une)	1	one	
deux	2	two	
trois	3	three	
quatre	4	four	
cinq	5	five	
six	6	six	
sept	7	seven	
huit	8	eight	
neuf	9	nine	
dix	10	ten	
onze	11	eleven	
douze	12	twelve	
treize	13	thirteen	
quatorze	14	fourteen	
quinze	15	fifteen	
seize	16	sixteen	
dix-sept	17	seventeen	
dix-huit	18	eighteen	
dix-neuf	19	nineteen	
vingt	20	twenty	
vingt et un (une)	21	twenty-one	
vingt-deux	22	twenty-two	
trente	30	thirty	
quarante	40	forty	
cinquante	50	fifty	
soixante	60	sixty	
soixante-dix	70	seventy	
soixante-et-onze	71	seventy-one	
soixante-douze	72	seventy	
quatre-vingts	80	eighty	
quatre-vingt-un (-une)	81	eighty-one	
quatre-vingt-dix	90	ninety	
cent	100	a hundred, one hundred	
cent un (une)	101	a hundred and one	
deux cents	200	two hundred	
deux cent un (une)	201	two hundred and one	
quatre cents	400	four hundred	
mille	1000	a thousand	
cinq mille	5000	five thousand	
un million	1000000	a million	

Numbers

Les nombres

premier (première), 1er (1ère)
deuxième, 2e or 2ème
troisième, 3e or 3ème
quatrième, 4e or 4ème
cinquième, 5e or 5ème
sixième, 6e or 6ème
septième
huitième
neuvième
dixième
onzième
douzième
treizième
quartorzième
quinzième
seizième
dix-septième
dix-huitième
dix-neuvième
vingtième
vingt-et-unième
vingt-deuxième
trentième
centième
cent-unième
millième

Numbers

first, 1st
second, 2nd
third, 3rd
fourth, 4th
fifth, 5th
sixth, 6th
seventh
eighth
ninth
tenth
eleventh
twelfth
thirteenth
fourteenth
fifteenth
sixteenth
seventeenth
eighteenth
nineteenth
twentieth
twenty-first
twenty-second
thirtieth
hundredth
hundred-and-first
thousandth

L'heure

quelle heure est-il?
   il est ...

minuit
une heure (du matin)
une heure cinq
une heure dix
une heure et quart
une heure vingt-cinq
une heure et demie,
   une heure trente
deux heures moins vingt-cinq,
   une heure trente-cinq
deux heures moins vingt,
   une heure quarante
deux heures moins le quart,
   une heure quarante-cinq
deux heures moins dix,
   une heure cinquante
midi
deux heures (de l'après-midi),
   quatorze heures
sept heures (du soir),
   dix-sept heures

à quelle heure?
à minuit
à sept heures

dans vingt minutes
il y a un quart d'heure

The time

what time is it?
   it's ...

midnight, twelve p.m.
one o'clock (in the morning), one (a.m.)
five past one
ten past one
a quarter past one, one fifteen
twenty-five past one, one twenty-five
half-past one,
   one thirty
twenty-five to two,
   one thirty-five
twenty to two,
   one forty
a quarter to two,
   one forty-five
ten to two,
   one fifty
twelve o'clock, midday, noon
two o'clock (in the afternoon),
   two (p.m.)
seven o'clock (in the evening),
   seven (p.m.)

(at) what time?
at midnight
at seven o'clock

in twenty minutes
fifteen minutes ago

La date

aujourd'hui
demain
après-demain
hier
avant-hier
la veille
le lendemain

le matin
le soir
ce matin
ce soir
cet après-midi
hier matin
hier soir
demain matin
demain soir
dans la nuit du samedi au
  dimanche
il viendra samedi
le samedi
tous les samedis
samedi passé *ou* dernier
samedi prochain
samedi en huit
samedi en quinze
du lundi au samedi
tous les jours
une fois par semaine
une fois par mois
deux fois par semaine
il y a une semaine *ou* huit jours
il y a quinze jours
l'année passée *ou* dernière
dans deux jours
dans huit jours *ou* une semaine
dans quinze jours
le mois prochain
l'année prochaine

quel jour sommes-nous?
le 1er/24 octobre 2007

en 2007
mille neuf cent quatre-vingt seize
44 av. J.-C.
14 apr. J.-C.
au XIXe (siècle)
dans les années trente
il était une fois …

The date

today
tomorrow
the day after tomorrow
yesterday
the day before yesterday
the day before, the previous day
the next *or* following day

morning
evening
this morning
this evening
this afternoon
yesterday morning
yesterday evening
tomorrow morning
tomorrow evening
during Saturday night, during the
  night of Saturday to Sunday
he's coming on Saturday
on Saturdays
every Saturday
last Saturday
next Saturday
a week on Saturday
a fortnight *or* two weeks on Saturday
from Monday to Saturday
every day
once a week
once a month
twice a week
a week ago
a fortnight *or* two weeks ago
last year
in two days
in a week
in a fortnight *or* two weeks
next month
next year

what day is it?
the 1st/24th of October 2007,
  October 1st/24th 2007
in 2007
nineteen ninety-six
44 BC
14 AD
in the nineteenth century
in the thirties
once upon a time …

Aa

a [a] *vb voir* **avoir**

à [a] (*ã+le* = **au**, *ã+les* = **aux**) *prép* **1** (*endroit, situation*) at, in; **être à Paris/au Portugal** to be in Paris/Portugal; **être à la maison/à l'école** to be at home/at school; **à la campagne** in the country; **c'est à 10 m/km/à 20 minutes (d'ici)** it's 10 m/km/20 minutes away

2 (*direction*) to; **aller à Paris/au Portugal** to go to Paris/Portugal; **aller à la maison/à l'école** to go home/to school; **à la campagne** to the country

3 (*temps*): **à 3 heures/minuit** at 3 o'clock/midnight; **au printemps** in the spring; **au mois de juin** in June; **au départ** at the start, at the outset; **à demain/la semaine prochaine!** see you tomorrow/next week!; **visites de 5 heures à 6 heures** visiting from 5 to *ou* till 6 o'clock

4 (*attribution, appartenance*) to; **le livre est à Paul/à lui/à nous** this book is Paul's/his/ours; **donner qch à qn** to give sth to sb; **un ami à moi** a friend of mine; **c'est à moi de le faire** it's up to me to do it

5 (*moyen*) with; **se chauffer au gaz** to have gas heating; **à bicyclette** on a *ou* by bicycle; **à la main/machine** by hand/machine; **à la télévision/la radio** on television/the radio

6 (*provenance*) from; **boire à la bouteille** to drink from the bottle

7 (*caractérisation, manière*): **l'homme aux yeux bleus** the man with the blue eyes; **à la russe** the Russian way; **glace à la framboise** raspberry ice cream

8 (*but, destination*): **tasse à café** coffee cup; **maison à vendre** house for sale; **problème à régler** problem to sort out

9 (*rapport, évaluation, distribution*): **100 km/unités à l'heure** 100 km/units per *ou* an hour; **payé à l'heure** paid by the hour; **cinq à six** five to six

10 (*conséquence, résultat*): **à ce qu'il prétend** according to him; **à leur grande surprise** much to their surprise; **à nous trois nous n'avons pas su le faire** we couldn't do it even between the three of us; **ils sont arrivés à quatre** four of them arrived (together)

abaisser [abese] *vt* to lower, bring down; (*manette*) to pull down; (*fig*) to debase; to humiliate; **s'abaisser** *vi* to go down; (*fig*)

to demean o.s.; **s'~ à faire/à qch** to stoop *ou* descend to doing/to sth

abandon [abãdɔ̃] *nm* abandoning; deserting; giving up; withdrawal; surrender, relinquishing; (*fig*) lack of constraint; relaxed pose *ou* mood; **être à l'~** to be in a state of neglect; **laisser à l'~** to abandon

abandonner [abãdɔne] *vt* to leave, abandon, desert; (*projet, activité*) to abandon, give up; (*Sport*) to retire *ou* withdraw from; (*Inform*) to abort; (*céder*) to surrender, relinquish; **s'abandonner** *vi* to let o.s. go; **s'~ à** (*paresse, plaisirs*) to give o.s. up to; **~ qch à qn** to give sth up to sb

abasourdir [abazurdir] *vt* to stun, stagger

abat-jour [abaʒur] *nm inv* lampshade

abats [aba] *vb voir* **abattre** ▷ *nmpl* (*de bœuf, porc*) offal *sg* (Brit), entrails (US); (*de volaille*) giblets

abattement [abatmã] *nm* (*physique*) enfeeblement; (*moral*) dejection, despondency; (*déduction*) reduction; **~ fiscal** ≈ tax allowance

abattoir [abatwar] *nm* abattoir (Brit), slaughterhouse

abattre [abatr(ə)] *vt* (*arbre*) to cut down, fell; (*mur, maison*) to pull down; (*avion, personne*) to shoot down; (*animal*) to shoot, kill; (*fig: physiquement*) to wear out, tire out; (*: moralement*) to demoralize; **s'abattre** *vi* to crash down; **s'~ sur** (*pluie*) to beat down on; (*: coups, injures*) to rain down on; **~ ses cartes** (*aussi fig*) to lay one's cards on the table; **~ du travail** *ou* **de la besogne** to get through a lot of work

abbaye [abei] *nf* abbey

abbé [abe] *nm* priest; (*d'une abbaye*) abbot; **M l'~** Father

abcès [apsɛ] *nm* abscess

abdiquer [abdike] *vi* to abdicate ▷ *vt* to renounce, give up

abdominal, e, -aux [abdɔminal, -o] *adj* abdominal ▷ *nmpl*: **faire des abdominaux** to do exercises for the stomach muscles

abeille [abɛj] *nf* bee

aberrant, e [abɛrã, -ãt] *adj* absurd

aberration [abɛrasjɔ̃] *nf* aberration

abêtir [abetir] *vt* to make morons (*ou* a moron) of

abîme [abim] *nm* abyss, gulf

abîmer [abime] *vt* to spoil, damage; **s'abîmer** *vi* to get spoilt *ou* damaged; (*fruits*) to spoil; (*tomber*)

to sink, founder; **s'~ les yeux** to ruin one's eyes
ou eyesight
ablation [ablɑsjɔ̃] *nf* removal
aboiement [abwamɑ̃] *nm* bark, barking *no pl*
abois [abwa] *nmpl:* **aux ~** at bay
abolir [abɔliʀ] *vt* to abolish
abominable [abɔminabl(ə)] *adj* abominable
abondance [abɔ̃dɑ̃s] *nf* abundance; (*richesse*)
affluence; **en ~** in abundance
abondant, e [abɔ̃dɑ̃, -ɑ̃t] *adj* plentiful,
abundant, copious
abonder [abɔ̃de] *vi* to abound, be plentiful; **~ en**
to be full of, abound in; **~ dans le sens de qn** to
concur with sb
abonné, e [abɔne] *nm/f* subscriber; season ticket
holder ▷ *adj:* **être ~ à un journal** to subscribe to
ou have a subscription to a periodical; **être ~ au**
téléphone to be on the (tele)phone
abonnement [abɔnmɑ̃] *nm* subscription; (*pour
transports en commun, concerts*) season ticket
abonner [abɔne] *vt:* **s'abonner à** to subscribe to,
take out a subscription to
abord [abɔʀ] *nm:* **être d'un ~ facile** to be
approachable; **être d'un ~ difficile** (*personne*) to
be unapproachable; (*lieu*) to be hard to reach *ou*
difficult to get to; **de prime ~**, **au premier ~** at
first sight; **d'~** *adv* first; **tout d'~** first of all
abordable [abɔʀdabl(ə)] *adj* (*personne*)
approachable; (*marchandise*) reasonably priced;
(*prix*) affordable, reasonable
aborder [abɔʀde] *vi* to land ▷ *vt* (*sujet, difficulté*) to
tackle; (*personne*) to approach; (*rivage etc*) to reach;
(*Navig: attaquer*) to board; (: *heurter*) to collide with
aboutir [abutiʀ] *vi* (*négociations etc*) to succeed;
(*abcès*) to come to a head; **~ à/dans/sur** to end
up at/in/on
aboyer [abwaje] *vi* to bark
abréger [abʀeʒe] *vt* (*texte*) to shorten, abridge;
(*mot*) to shorten, abbreviate; (*réunion, voyage etc*) to
cut short, shorten
abreuver [abʀœve] *vt* to water; (*fig*): **~ qn de** to
shower *ou* swamp sb with; (*injures etc*) to shower
sb with; **s'abreuver** *vi* to drink
abreuvoir [abʀœvwaʀ] *nm* watering place
abréviation [abʀevjɑsjɔ̃] *nf* abbreviation
abri [abʀi] *nm* shelter; **à l'~** under cover; **être/se**
mettre à l'~ to be/get under cover *ou* shelter; **à**
l'~ de sheltered from; (*fig*) safe from
abricot [abʀiko] *nm* apricot
abriter [abʀite] *vt* to shelter; (*loger*) to
accommodate; **s'abriter** *vi* to shelter, take cover
abrupt, e [abʀypt] *adj* sheer, steep; (*ton*) abrupt
abruti, e [abʀyti] *nm/f* (*fam*) idiot, moron
absence [apsɑ̃s] *nf* absence; (*Méd*) blackout;
(*distraction*) mental blank; **en l'~ de** in the
absence of
absent, e [apsɑ̃, -ɑ̃t] *adj* absent; (*chose*) missing,
lacking; (*distrait: air*) vacant, faraway ▷ *nm/f*
absentee
absenter [apsɑ̃te]: **s'absenter** *vi* to take time off
work; (*sortir*) to leave, go out
absolu, e [apsɔly] *adj* absolute; (*caractère*) rigid,

uncompromising ▷ *nm* (*Philosophie*): **l'~** the
Absolute; **dans l'~** in the absolute, in a vacuum
absolument [apsɔlymɑ̃] *adv* absolutely
absorbant, e [apsɔʀbɑ̃, -ɑ̃t] *adj* absorbent;
(*tâche*) absorbing, engrossing
absorber [apsɔʀbe] *vt* to absorb; (*gén Méd: manger,
boire*) to take; (*Écon: firme*) to take over, absorb
abstenir [apstəniʀ]: **s'abstenir** *vi* (*Pol*) to
abstain; **s'~ de qch/de faire** to refrain from
sth/from doing
abstraction [apstʀaksjɔ̃] *nf* abstraction; **faire**
~ de to set *ou* leave aside; **~ faite de ...** leaving
aside ...
abstrait, e [apstʀɛ, -ɛt] *pp de* **abstraire** ▷ *adj*
abstract ▷ *nm:* **dans l'~** in the abstract
absurde [apsyʀd(ə)] *adj* absurd ▷ *nm* absurdity;
(*Philosophie*): **l'~** absurd; **par l'~** ad absurdo
abus [aby] *nm* (*excès*) abuse, misuse; (*injustice*)
abuse; **~ de confiance** breach of trust;
(*détournement de fonds*) embezzlement
abuser [abyze] *vi* to go too far, overstep the mark
▷ *vt* to deceive, mislead; **s'abuser** *vi* (*se méprendre*)
to be mistaken; **~ de** *vt* (*force, droit*) to misuse;
(*alcool*) to take to excess; (*violer, duper*) to take
advantage of
abusif, -ive [abyzif, -iv] *adj* exorbitant; (*punition*)
excessive; (*pratique*) improper
acabit [akabi] *nm:* **du même ~** of the same type
académie [akademi] *nf* (*société*) learned society;
(*école: d'art, de danse*) academy; (*Art: nu*) nude; (*Scol:
circonscription*) ≈ regional education authority;
l'A~ (française) the French Academy; *see note*
acajou [akaʒu] *nm* mahogany
acariâtre [akaʀjɑtʀ(ə)] *adj* sour(-tempered)
(*Brit*), cantankerous
accablant, e [akablɑ̃, -ɑ̃t] *adj* (*témoignage, preuve*)
overwhelming
accablement [akabləmɑ̃] *nm* deep despondency
accabler [akable] *vt* to overwhelm, overcome;
(*témoignage*) to condemn, damn; **~ qn d'injures**
to heap *ou* shower abuse on sb; **~ qn de travail**
to overburden sb with work; **accablé de dettes/**
soucis weighed down with debts/cares
accalmie [akalmi] *nf* lull
accaparer [akapaʀe] *vt* to monopolize; (*travail
etc*) to take up (all) the time *ou* attention of
accéder [aksede]: **~ à** *vt* (*lieu*) to reach; (*fig:
pouvoir*) to accede to; (: *poste*) to attain; (*accorder:
requête*) to grant, accede to
accélérateur [akseleʀatœʀ] *nm* accelerator
accélération [akseleʀɑsjɔ̃] *nf* speeding up;
acceleration
accélérer [akseleʀe] *vt* (*mouvement, travaux*) to
speed up ▷ *vi* (*Auto*) to accelerate
accent [aksɑ̃] *nm* accent; (*inflexions expressives*)
tone (of voice); (*Phonétique, fig*) stress; **aux ~s de**
(*musique*) to the strains of; **mettre l'~ sur** (*fig*) to
stress; **~ aigu/grave/circonflexe** acute/grave/
circumflex accent
accentuer [aksɑ̃tɥe] *vt* (*Ling: orthographe*) to
accent; (: *phonétique*) to stress, accent; (*fig*)
to accentuate, emphasize; (: *effort, pression*)

to increase; **s'accentuer** vi to become more marked ou pronounced

acceptation [akseptasjɔ̃] nf acceptance

accepter [aksepte] vt to accept; (tolérer): ~ **que qn fasse** to agree to sb doing; ~ **de faire** to agree to do

accès [akse] nm (à un lieu, Inform) access; (Méd) attack; (: de toux) fit, bout ▷ nmpl (routes etc) means of access, approaches; **d'~ facile/malaisé** easily/not easily accessible; **donner ~ à** (lieu) to give access to; (carrière) to open the door to; **avoir ~ auprès de qn** to have access to sb; **l'~ aux quais est interdit aux personnes non munies d'un billet** ticket-holders only on platforms, no access to platforms without a ticket; ~ **de colère** fit of anger; ~ **de joie** burst of joy

accessible [aksesibl(ə)] adj accessible; (personne) approachable; (livre, sujet): ~ **à qn** within the reach of sb; (sensible): ~ **à la pitié/l'amour** open to pity/love

accessoire [akseswaʀ] adj secondary, of secondary importance; (frais) incidental ▷ nm accessory; (Théât) prop

accident [aksidɑ̃] nm accident; **par ~** by chance; ~ **de parcours** mishap; ~ **de la route** road accident; ~ **du travail** accident at work; industrial injury ou accident; ~**s de terrain** unevenness of the ground

accidenté, e [aksidɑ̃te] adj damaged ou injured (in an accident); (relief, terrain) uneven; hilly

accidentel, le [aksidɑ̃tɛl] adj accidental

acclamation [aklamɑsjɔ̃] nf: **par ~** (vote) by acclamation; **acclamations** nfpl cheers, cheering sg

acclamer [aklame] vt to cheer, acclaim

acclimater [aklimate] vt to acclimatize; **s'acclimater** vi to become acclimatized

accolade [akɔlad] nf (amicale) embrace; (signe) brace; **donner l'~ à qn** to embrace sb

accommodant, e [akɔmɔdɑ̃, -ɑ̃t] adj accommodating, easy-going

accommoder [akɔmɔde] vt (Culin) to prepare; (points de vue) to reconcile; ~ **qch à** (adapter) to adapt sth to; **s'accommoder de** to put up with; (se contenter de) to make do with; **s'~ à** (s'adapter) to adapt to

accompagnateur, -trice [akɔ̃paɲatœʀ, -tʀis] nm/f (Mus) accompanist; (de voyage) guide; (de voyage organisé) courier; (d'enfants) accompanying adult

accompagner [akɔ̃paɲe] vt to accompany, be ou go ou come with; (Mus) to accompany; **s'accompagner de** to bring, be accompanied by

accompli, e [akɔ̃pli] adj accomplished

accomplir [akɔ̃pliʀ] vt (tâche, projet) to carry out; (souhait) to fulfil; **s'accomplir** vi to be fulfilled

accord [akɔʀ] nm (entente, convention, Ling) agreement; (entre des styles, tons etc) harmony; (consentement) agreement, consent; (Mus) chord; **donner son ~** to give one's agreement; **mettre deux personnes d'~** to make two people come to an agreement, reconcile two people; **se mettre d'~** to come to an agreement (with each other); **être d'~** to agree; **être d'~ avec qn** to agree with sb; **d'~!** OK!, right!; **d'un commun ~** of one accord; ~ **parfait** (Mus) tonic chord

accordéon [akɔʀdeɔ̃] nm (Mus) accordion

accorder [akɔʀde] vt (faveur, délai) to grant; (attribuer): ~ **de l'importance/de la valeur à qch** to attach importance/value to sth; (harmoniser) to match; (Mus) to tune; **s'accorder** vi to get on together; (être d'accord) to agree; (couleurs, caractères) to go together, match; (Ling) to agree; **je vous accorde que …** I grant you that …

accoster [akɔste] vt (Navig) to draw alongside; (personne) to accost ▷ vi (Navig) to berth

accotement [akɔtmɑ̃] nm (de route) verge (Brit), shoulder; ~ **stabilisé/non stabilisé** hard shoulder/soft verge ou shoulder

accouchement [akuʃmɑ̃] nm delivery, (child)birth; (travail) labour (Brit), labor (US); ~ **à terme** delivery at (full) term; ~ **sans douleur** natural childbirth

accoucher [akuʃe] vi to give birth, have a baby; (être en travail) to be in labour (Brit) ou labor (US) ▷ vt to deliver; ~ **d'un garçon** to give birth to a boy

accoucheur [akuʃœʀ] nm: **(médecin) ~** obstetrician

accouder [akude]: **s'accouder** vi: **s'~ à/contre/sur** to rest one's elbows on/against/on; **accoudé à la fenêtre** leaning on the windowsill

accoudoir [akudwaʀ] nm armrest

accoupler [akuple] vt to couple; (pour la reproduction) to mate; **s'accoupler** vi to mate

accourir [akuʀiʀ] vi to rush ou run up

accoutrement [akutʀəmɑ̃] nm (péj) getup (Brit), outfit

accoutumance [akutymɑ̃s] nf (gén) adaptation; (Méd) addiction

accoutumé, e [akutyme] adj (habituel) customary, usual; **comme à l'~e** as is customary ou usual

accoutumer [akutyme] vt: ~ **qn à qch/faire** to accustom sb to sth/to doing; **s'accoutumer à** to get accustomed ou used to

accréditer [akʀedite] vt (nouvelle) to substantiate; ~ **qn (auprès de)** to accredit sb (to)

accroc [akʀo] nm (déchirure) tear; (fig) hitch, snag; **sans ~** without a hitch; **faire un ~ à** (vêtement) to make a tear in, tear; (fig: règle etc) to infringe

accrochage [akʀɔʃaʒ] nm hanging (up); hitching (up); (Auto: minor) collision; (Mil) encounter, engagement; (dispute) clash, brush

accrocher [akʀɔʃe] vt (suspendre): ~ **qch à** to hang sth (up) on; (attacher: remorque) to hitch sth (up) to; (heurter) to catch; to hit; (déchirer): ~ **qch (à)** to catch sth (on); (Mil) to engage; (fig) to catch, attract ▷ vi to stick, get stuck; (fig: pourparlers etc) to hit a snag; (plaire: disque etc) to catch on; **s'accrocher** vi (se disputer) to have a clash ou brush; (ne pas céder) to hold one's own, hang on in (fam); **s'~ à** (rester pris à) to catch on; (agripper, *fig*) to hang on *ou* cling to

accroissement [akʀwasmɑ̃] *nm* increase

accroître [akʀwatʀ(ə)] *vt*, **s'accroître** *vi* to increase

accroupir [akʀupiʀ]: **s'accroupir** *vi* to squat, crouch (down)

accru, e [akʀy] *pp de* **accroître**

accueil [akœj] *nm* welcome; (*endroit*) reception (desk); (: *dans une gare*) information kiosk; **comité/centre d'~** reception committee/centre

accueillant, e [akœjɑ̃, -ɑ̃t] *adj* welcoming, friendly

accueillir [akœjiʀ] *vt* to welcome; (*loger*) to accommodate

acculer [akyle] *vt*: ~ **qn à** *ou* **contre** to drive sb back against; ~ **qn dans** to corner sb in; ~ **qn à** (*faillite*) to drive sb to the brink of

accumuler [akymyle] *vt* to accumulate, amass; **s'accumuler** *vi* to accumulate; to pile up

accusation [akyzasjɔ̃] *nf* (*gén*) accusation; (*Jur*) charge; (*partie*): **l'~** the prosecution; **mettre en ~** to indict; **acte d'~** bill of indictment

accusé, e [akyze] *nm/f* accused; (*prévenu(e)*) defendant ▷ *nm*: ~ **de réception** acknowledgement of receipt

accuser [akyze] *vt* to accuse; (*fig*) to emphasize, bring out; (: *montrer*) to show; **s'accuser** *vi* (*s'accentuer*) to become more marked; ~ **qn de** to accuse sb of; (*Jur*) to charge sb with; ~ **qn/qch de qch** (*rendre responsable*) to blame sb/sth for sth; **s'~ de qch/d'avoir fait qch** to admit sth/having done sth; to blame o.s. for sth/for having done sth; ~ **réception de** to acknowledge receipt of; ~ **le coup** (*aussi fig*) to be visibly affected

acerbe [asɛʀb(ə)] *adj* caustic, acid

acéré, e [aseʀe] *adj* sharp

acharné, e [aʃaʀne] *adj* (*lutte, adversaire*) fierce, bitter; (*travail*) relentless, unremitting

acharner [aʃaʀne]: **s'acharner** *vi*: **s'~ sur** to go at fiercely, hound; **s'~ contre** to set o.s. against; to dog, pursue; (*malchance*) to hound; **s'~ à faire** to try doggedly to do; to persist in doing

achat [aʃa] *nm* buying *no pl*; (*article acheté*) purchase; **faire l'~ de** to buy, purchase; **faire des ~s** to do some shopping, buy a few things

acheminer [aʃmine] *vt* (*courrier*) to forward, dispatch; (*troupes*) to convey, transport; (*train*) to route; **s'~ vers** to head for

acheter [aʃte] *vt* to buy, purchase; (*soudoyer*) to buy, bribe; ~ **qch à** (*marchand*) to buy *ou* purchase sth from; (*ami etc*: *offrir*) to buy sth for; ~ **à crédit** to buy on credit

acheteur, -euse [aʃtœʀ, -øz] *nm/f* buyer; shopper; (*Comm*) buyer; (*Jur*) vendee, purchaser

achever [aʃve] *vt* to complete, finish; (*blessé*) to finish off; **s'achever** *vi* to end

acide [asid] *adj* sour, sharp; (*ton*) acid, biting; (*Chimie*) acid(ic) ▷ *nm* acid

acidulé, e [asidyle] *adj* slightly acid; **bonbons ~s** acid drops (*Brit*), ≈ lemon drops (*US*)

acier [asje] *nm* steel; ~ **inoxydable** stainless steel

aciérie [asjeʀi] *nf* steelworks *sg*

acné [akne] *nf* acne

acolyte [akɔlit] *nm* (*péj*) associate

acompte [akɔ̃t] *nm* deposit; (*versement régulier*) instalment; (*sur somme due*) payment on account; (*sur salaire*) advance; **un ~ de 10 euros** 10 euros on account

à-côté [akote] *nm* side-issue; (*argent*) extra

à-coup [aku] *nm* (*du moteur*) (hic)cough; (*fig*) jolt; **sans ~s** smoothly; **par ~s** by fits and starts

acoustique [akustik] *nf* (*d'une salle*) acoustics *pl*; (*science*) acoustics *sg* ▷ *adj* acoustic

acquéreur [akeʀœʀ] *nm* buyer, purchaser; **se porter/se rendre ~ de qch** to announce one's intention to purchase/to purchase sth

acquérir [akeʀiʀ] *vt* to acquire; (*par achat*) to purchase, acquire; (*valeur*) to gain; (*résultats*) to achieve; **ce que ses efforts lui ont acquis** what his efforts have won *ou* gained (for) him

acquis, e [aki, -iz] *pp de* **acquérir** ▷ *nm* (accumulated) experience; (*avantage*) gain ▷ *adj* (*voir acquérir*) acquired; gained; achieved; **être ~ à** (*plan, idée*) to be in full agreement with; **son aide nous est ~e** we can count on *ou* be sure of his help; **tenir qch pour ~** to take sth for granted

acquit [aki] *vb voir* **acquérir** ▷ *nm* (*quittance*) receipt; **pour ~** received; **par ~ de conscience** to set one's mind at rest

acquitter [akite] *vt* (*Jur*) to acquit; (*facture*) to pay, settle; **s'~ de** to discharge; (*promesse, tâche*) to fulfil (*Brit*), fulfill (*US*), carry out

âcre [ɑkʀ(ə)] *adj* acrid, pungent

acrobate [akʀɔbat] *nm/f* acrobat

acrobatie [akʀɔbasi] *nf* (*art*) acrobatics *sg*; (*exercice*) acrobatic feat; **~ aérienne** aerobatics *sg*

acte [akt(ə)] *nm* act, action; (*Théât*) act; **actes** *nmpl* (*compte-rendu*) proceedings; **prendre ~ de** to note, take note of; **faire ~ de présence** to put in an appearance; **faire ~ de candidature** to submit an application; **~ d'accusation** charge (*Brit*), bill of indictment; **~ de baptême** baptismal certificate; **~ de mariage/naissance** marriage/birth certificate; **~ de vente** bill of sale

acteur [aktœʀ] *nm* actor

actif, -ive [aktif, -iv] *adj* active ▷ *nm* (*Comm*) assets *pl*; (*Ling*) active (voice); (*fig*): **avoir à son ~** to have to one's credit; **actifs** *nmpl* people in employment; **mettre à son ~** to add to one's list of achievements; **l'~ et le passif** assets and liabilities; **prendre une part active à qch** to take an active part in sth; **population active** working population

action [aksjɔ̃] *nf* (*gén*) action; (*Comm*) share; **une bonne/mauvaise ~** a good/an unkind deed; **mettre en ~** to put into action; **passer à l'~** to take action; **sous l'~ de** under the effect of; **l'~ syndicale** (the) union action; **un film d'~** an action film *ou* movie; **~ en diffamation** libel action; **~ de grâce(s)** (*Rel*) thanksgiving

actionnaire [aksjɔnɛʀ] *nm/f* shareholder

actionner [aksjɔne] *vt* to work; to activate; to operate

activer [aktive] vt to speed up; (Chimie) to activate; **s'activer** vi (s'affairer) to bustle about; (se hâter) to hurry up

activité [aktivite] nf activity; **en ~** (volcan) active; (fonctionnaire) in active life; (militaire) on active service

actrice [aktris] nf actress

actualiser [aktɥalize] vt to actualize; (mettre à jour) to bring up to date

actualité [aktɥalite] nf (d'un problème) topicality; (événements): **l'~** current events; **les ~s** (Ciné, TV) the news; **l'~ politique/sportive** the political/ sports ou sporting news; **les ~s télévisées** the television news; **d'~** topical

actuel, le [aktɥel] adj (présent) present; (d'actualité) topical; (non virtuel) actual; **à l'heure ~le** at this moment in time, at the moment

actuellement [aktɥelmã] adv at present, at the present time

acuité [akɥite] nf acuteness

acuponcteur, acupuncteur [akypɔ̃ktœr] nm acupuncturist

acuponcture, acupuncture [akypɔ̃ktyr] nf acupuncture

adaptateur, -trice [adaptatœr, -tris] nm/f adapter

adapter [adapte] vt to adapt; **s'~ (à)** (personne) to adapt (to); (: objet, prise etc) to apply (to); **~ qch à** (approprier) to adapt sth to (fit); **~ qch sur/dans/à** (fixer) to fit sth on/into/to

additif [aditif] nm additional clause; (substance) additive; **~ alimentaire** food additive

addition [adisjɔ̃] nf addition; (au café) bill

additionner [adisjɔne] vt to add (up); **s'additionner** vi to add up; **~ un produit d'eau** to add water to a product

adepte [adept(ə)] nm/f follower

adéquat, e [adekwa, -at] adj appropriate, suitable

adhérent, e [aderã, -ãt] nm/f (de club) member

adhérer [adere] vi (coller) to adhere, stick; **~ à** (coller) to adhere ou stick to; (se rallier à: parti, club) to join; to be a member of; (: opinion, mouvement) to support

adhésif, -ive [adezif, -iv] adj adhesive, sticky ▷ nm adhesive

adhésion [adezjɔ̃] nf (à un club) joining; membership; (à une opinion) support

adieu, x [adjø] excl goodbye ▷ nm farewell; **dire ~ à qn** to say goodbye ou farewell to sb; **dire ~ à qch** (renoncer) to say ou wave goodbye to sth

adjectif [adʒɛktif] nm adjective; **~ attribut** adjectival complement; **~ épithète** attributive adjective

adjoindre [adʒwɛ̃dr(ə)] vt: **~ qch à** to attach sth to; (ajouter) to add sth to; **~ qn à** (personne) to appoint sb as an assistant to; (comité) to appoint sb to, attach sb to; **s'adjoindre** vt (collaborateur etc) to take on, appoint

adjoint, e [adʒwɛ̃, -wɛ̃t] pp de **adjoindre** ▷ nm/f assistant; **directeur ~** assistant manager

adjudant [adʒydã] nm (Mil) warrant officer;

~-chef ≈ warrant officer 1st class (Brit), ≈ chief warrant officer (US)

adjuger [adʒyʒe] vt (prix, récompense) to award; (lors d'une vente) to auction (off); **s'adjuger** vt to take for o.s.; **adjugé!** (vendu) gone!, sold!

adjurer [adʒyre] vt: **~ qn de faire** to implore ou beg sb to do

admettre [admɛtr(ə)] vt (visiteur, nouveau-venu) to admit, let in; (candidat: Scol) to pass; (Tech: gaz, eau, air) to admit; (tolérer) to allow, accept; (reconnaître) to admit, acknowledge; (supposer) to suppose; **j'admets que ...** I admit that ...; **je n'admets pas que tu fasses cela** I won't allow you to do that; **admettons que ...** let's suppose that ...; **admettons** let's suppose so

administrateur, -trice [administratœr, -tris] nm/f (Comm) director; (Admin) administrator; **~ délégué** managing director; **~ judiciaire** receiver

administration [administrasjɔ̃] nf administration; **l'A~** ≈ the Civil Service

administrer [administre] vt (firme) to manage, run; (biens, remède, sacrement etc) to administer

admirable [admirabl(ə)] adj admirable, wonderful

admirateur, -trice [admiratœr, -tris] nm/f admirer

admiration [admirasjɔ̃] nf admiration; **être en ~ devant** to be lost in admiration before

admirer [admire] vt to admire

admis, e [admi, -iz] pp de **admettre**

admissible [admisibl(ə)] adj (candidat) eligible; (comportement) admissible, acceptable; (Jur) receivable

admission [admisjɔ̃] nf admission; **tuyau d'~** intake pipe; **demande d'~** application for membership; **service des ~s** admissions

ADN sigle m (= acide désoxyribonucléique) DNA

adolescence [adɔlesɑ̃s] nf adolescence

adolescent, e [adɔlesɑ̃, -ɑ̃t] nm/f adolescent, teenager

adonner [adɔne]: **s'adonner à** vt (sport) to devote o.s. to; (boisson) to give o.s. over to

adopter [adɔpte] vt to adopt; (projet de loi etc) to pass

adoptif, -ive [adɔptif, -iv] adj (parents) adoptive; (fils, patrie) adopted

adorable [adɔrabl(ə)] adj adorable

adorer [adɔre] vt to adore; (Rel) to worship

adosser [adose] vt: **~ qch à ou contre** to stand sth against; **s'~ à ou contre** to lean with one's back against; **être adossé à ou contre** to be leaning with one's back against

adoucir [adusir] vt (goût, température) to make milder; (avec du sucre) to sweeten; (peau, voix, eau) to soften; (caractère, personne) to mellow; (peine) to soothe, allay; **s'adoucir** vi to become milder; to soften; to mellow

adresse [adres] nf (voir adroit) skill, dexterity; (domicile, Inform) address; **à l'~ de** (pour) for the benefit of

adresser [adrese] vt (lettre: expédier) to send;

(: *écrire l'adresse sur*) to address; (*injure, compliments*) to address; **~ qn à un docteur/bureau** to refer *ou* send sb to a doctor/an office; **~ la parole à qn** to speak to *ou* address sb; **s'adresser à** (*parler à*) to speak to, address; (*s'informer auprès de*) to go and see, go and speak to; (: *bureau*) to enquire at; (*livre, conseil*) to be aimed at

adroit, e [adʀwa, -wat] *adj* (*joueur, mécanicien*) skilful (*Brit*), skillful (*US*), dext(e)rous; (*politicien etc*) shrewd, skilled

ADSL *sigle m* (= *asymmetrical digital subscriber line*) ADSL; **avoir l'~** to have broadband

adulte [adylt(ə)] *nm/f* adult, grown-up ▷ *adj* (*personne, attitude*) adult, grown-up; (*chien, arbre*) fully-grown, mature; **l'âge ~** adulthood; **formation/film pour ~s** adult training/film

adultère [adyltɛʀ] *adj* adulterous ▷ *nm/f* adulterer/adulteress ▷ *nm* (*acte*) adultery

advenir [advəniʀ] *vi* to happen; **qu'est-il advenu de …?** what has become of …?; **quoi qu'il advienne** whatever befalls *ou* happens

adverbe [advɛʀb(ə)] *nm* adverb; **~ de manière** adverb of manner

adversaire [advɛʀsɛʀ] *nm/f* (*Sport, gén*) opponent, adversary; (*Mil*) adversary, enemy

adverse [advɛʀs(ə)] *adj* opposing

aération [aeʀɑsjɔ̃] *nf* airing; (*circulation de l'air*) ventilation; **conduit d'~** ventilation shaft; **bouche d'~** air vent

aérer [aeʀe] *vt* to air; (*fig*) to lighten; **s'aérer** *vi* to get some (fresh) air

aérien, ne [aeʀjɛ̃, -ɛn] *adj* (*Aviat*) air *cpd*, aerial; (*câble, métro*) overhead; (*fig*) light; **compagnie ~ne** airline (company); **ligne ~ne** airline

aérobic [aeʀɔbik] *nf* aerobics *sg*

aérogare [aeʀɔgaʀ] *nf* airport (buildings); (*en ville*) air terminal

aéroglisseur [aeʀɔglisœʀ] *nm* hovercraft

Aéronavale [aeʀɔnaval] *nf* ≈ Fleet Air Arm (*Brit*), ≈ Naval Air Force (*US*)

aérophagie [aeʀɔfaʒi] *nf*: **il fait de l'~** he suffers from abdominal wind

aéroport [aeʀɔpɔʀ] *nm* airport; **~ d'embarquement** departure airport

aéroporté, e [aeʀɔpɔʀte] *adj* airborne, airlifted

aérosol [aeʀɔsɔl] *nm* aerosol

affable [afabl(ə)] *adj* affable

affaiblir [afebliʀ] *vt* to weaken; **s'affaiblir** *vi* to weaken, grow weaker; (*vue*) to grow dim

affaire [afɛʀ] *nf* (*problème, question*) matter; (*criminelle, judiciaire*) case; (*scandaleuse etc*) affair; (*entreprise*) business; (*marché, transaction*) (business) deal, (piece of) business *no pl*; (*occasion intéressante*) good deal; **affaires** *nfpl* affairs; (*activité commerciale*) business *sg*; (*effets personnels*) things, belongings; **tirer qn/se tirer d'~** to get sb/o.s. out of trouble; **ceci fera l'~** this will do (nicely); **avoir ~ à** (*comme adversaire*) to be faced with; (*en contact*) to be dealing with; **tu auras ~ à moi!** (*menace*) you'll have me to contend with!; **c'est une ~ de goût/d'argent** it's a question *ou* matter of taste/money; **c'est l'~ d'une** minute/heure it'll only take a minute/an hour; **ce sont mes ~s** (*cela me concerne*) that's my business; **toutes ~s cessantes** forthwith; **les ~s étrangères** (*Pol*) foreign affairs

affairer [afeʀe]: **s'affairer** *vi* to busy o.s., bustle about

affaisser [afese]: **s'affaisser** *vi* (*terrain, immeuble*) to subside, sink; (*personne*) to collapse

affaler [afale]: **s'affaler** *vi*: **s'~ dans/sur** to collapse *ou* slump into/onto

affamé, e [afame] *adj* starving, famished

affectation [afɛktɑsjɔ̃] *nf* (*voir affecter*) allotment; appointment; posting; (*voir affecté*) affectedness

affecter [afɛkte] *vt* (*émouvoir*) to affect, move; (*feindre*) to affect, feign; (*telle ou telle forme etc*) to take on, assume; **~ qch à** to allocate *ou* allot sth to; **~ qn à** to appoint sb to; (*diplomate*) to post sb to; **~ qch de** (*de coefficient*) to modify sth by

affectif, -ive [afɛktif, -iv] *adj* emotional, affective

affection [afɛksjɔ̃] *nf* affection; (*mal*) ailment; **avoir de l'~ pour** to feel affection for; **prendre en ~** to become fond of

affectionner [afɛksjɔne] *vt* to be fond of

affectueusement [afɛktɥøzmɑ̃] *adv* affectionately

affectueux, -euse [afɛktɥø, -øz] *adj* affectionate

affermir [afɛʀmiʀ] *vt* to consolidate, strengthen

affichage [afiʃaʒ] *nm* billposting, billsticking; (*électronique*) display; **"~ interdit"** "stick no bills", "billsticking prohibited"; **~ à cristaux liquides** liquid crystal display, LCD; **~ numérique** *ou* **digital** digital display

affiche [afiʃ] *nf* poster; (*officielle*) (public) notice; (*Théât*) bill; **être à l'~** (*Théât*) to be on; **tenir l'~** to run

afficher [afiʃe] *vt* (*affiche*) to put up, post up; (*réunion*) to put up a notice about; (*électroniquement*) to display; (*fig*) to exhibit, display; **s'afficher** *vi* (*péj*) to flaunt o.s.; **"défense d'~"** "stick no bills"

affilée [afile]: **d'~** *adv* at a stretch

affiler [afile] *vt* to sharpen

affilier [afilje] *vt*: **s'affilier à** to become affiliated to

affiner [afine] *vt* to refine; **s'affiner** *vi* to become (more) refined

affirmatif, -ive [afiʀmatif, -iv] *adj* affirmative ▷ *nf*: **répondre par l'affirmative** to reply in the affirmative; **dans l'affirmative** (*si oui*) if (the answer is) yes …, if he does (*ou* you do *etc*) …

affirmation [afiʀmɑsjɔ̃] *nf* assertion

affirmer [afiʀme] *vt* (*prétendre*) to maintain, assert; (*autorité etc*) to assert; **s'affirmer** *vi* to assert o.s.; to assert itself

affligé, e [afliʒe] *adj* distressed, grieved; **~ de** (*maladie, tare*) afflicted with

affliger [afliʒe] *vt* (*peiner*) to distress, grieve

affluence [aflyɑ̃s] *nf* crowds *pl*; **heures d'~** rush hour *sg*; **jours d'~** busiest days

affluent [aflyɑ̃] *nm* tributary

affluer [aflye] *vi* (*secours, biens*) to flood in, pour in;

(*sang*) to rush, flow
affolant, e [afɔlɑ̃, -ɑ̃t] *adj* terrifying
affolement [afɔlmɑ̃] *nm* panic
affoler [afɔle] *vt* to throw into a panic; **s'affoler** *vi* to panic
affranchir [afʀɑ̃ʃiʀ] *vt* to put a stamp *ou* stamps on; (*à la machine*) to frank (*Brit*), meter (*US*); (*esclave*) to enfranchise, emancipate; (*fig*) to free, liberate; **s'affranchir de** to free o.s. from; **machine à ~** franking machine, postage meter
affranchissement [afʀɑ̃ʃismɑ̃] *nm* franking (*Brit*), metering (*US*); freeing; (*Postes: prix payé*) postage; **tarifs d'~** postage rates
affréter [afʀete] *vt* to charter
affreux, -euse [afʀø, -øz] *adj* dreadful, awful
affront [afʀɔ̃] *nm* affront
affrontement [afʀɔ̃tmɑ̃] *nm* (*Mil, Pol*) clash, confrontation
affronter [afʀɔ̃te] *vt* to confront, face; **s'affronter** to confront each other
affubler [afyble] *vt* (*péj*): **~ qn de** to rig *ou* deck sb out in; (*surnom*) to attach to sb
affût [afy] *nm* (*de canon*) gun carriage; **à l'~ (de)** (*gibier*) lying in wait (for); (*fig*) on the look-out (for)
affûter [afyte] *vt* to sharpen, grind
afin [afɛ̃]: **~ que** *conj* so that, in order that; **~ de faire** in order to do, so as to do
africain, e [afʀikɛ̃, -ɛn] *adj* African ▷ *nm/f*: **A~, e** African
Afrique [afʀik] *nf*: **l'~** Africa; **l'~ australe/du Nord/du Sud** southern/North/South Africa
agacer [agase] *vt* to pester, tease; (*involontairement*) to irritate, aggravate; (*aguicher*) to excite, lead on
âge [ɑʒ] *nm* age; **quel ~ as-tu?** how old are you?; **une femme d'un certain ~** a middle-aged woman, a woman who is getting on (in years); **bien porter son ~** to wear well; **prendre de l'~** to be getting on (in years), grow older; **limite d'~** age limit; **dispense d'~** special exemption from age limit; **troisième ~** (*période*) retirement; (*personnes âgées*) senior citizens; **l'~ ingrat** the awkward *ou* difficult age; **~ légal** legal age; **~ mental** mental age; **l'~ mûr** maturity, middle age; **~ de raison** age of reason
âgé, e [ɑʒe] *adj* old, elderly; **~ de 10 ans** 10 years old
agence [aʒɑ̃s] *nf* agency, office; (*succursale*) branch; **~ immobilière** estate agent's (office) (*Brit*), real estate office (*US*); **~ matrimoniale** marriage bureau; **~ de placement** employment agency; **~ de publicité** advertising agency; **~ de voyages** travel agency
agencer [aʒɑ̃se] *vt* to put together; (*local*) to arrange, lay out
agenda [aʒɛ̃da] *nm* diary
agenouiller [aʒnuje]: **s'agenouiller** *vi* to kneel (down)
agent [aʒɑ̃] *nm* (*aussi*: **agent de police**) policeman; (*Admin*) official, officer; (*fig: élément, facteur*) agent; **~ d'assurances** insurance broker;

~ de change stockbroker; **~ commercial** sales representative; **~ immobilier** estate agent (*Brit*), realtor (*US*); **~ (secret)** (secret) agent
agglomération [aglɔmeʀɑsjɔ̃] *nf* town; (*Auto*) built-up area; **l'~ parisienne** the urban area of Paris
aggloméré [aglɔmeʀe] *nm* (*bois*) chipboard; (*pierre*) conglomerate
aggraver [agʀave] *vt* to worsen, aggravate; (*Jur: peine*) to increase; **s'aggraver** *vi* to worsen; **~ son cas** to make one's case worse
agile [aʒil] *adj* agile, nimble
agir [aʒiʀ] *vi* (*se comporter*) to behave, act; (*faire quelque chose*) to act, take action; (*avoir de l'effet*) to act; **il s'agit de** it's a matter *ou* question of; it is about; (*il importe que*) we (*ou* you *etc*) must do; **de quoi s'agit-il?** what is it about?
agitation [aʒitɑsjɔ̃] *nf* (hustle and) bustle; (*trouble*) agitation, excitement; (*politique*) unrest, agitation
agité, e [aʒite] *adj* (*remuant*) fidgety, restless; (*troublé*) agitated, perturbed; (*journée*) hectic; (*mer*) rough; (*sommeil*) disturbed, broken
agiter [aʒite] *vt* (*bouteille, chiffon*) to shake; (*bras, mains*) to wave; (*préoccuper, exciter*) to trouble, perturb; **s'agiter** *vi* to bustle about; (*dormeur*) to toss and turn; (*enfant*) to fidget; (*Pol*) to grow restless; **"~ avant l'emploi"** "shake before use"
agneau, x [aɲo] *nm* lamb; (*toison*) lambswool
agonie [agɔni] *nf* mortal agony, death pangs *pl*; (*fig*) death throes *pl*
agrafe [agʀaf] *nf* (*de vêtement*) hook, fastener; (*de bureau*) staple; (*Méd*) clip
agrafer [agʀafe] *vt* to fasten; to staple
agrafeuse [agʀaføz] *nf* stapler
agrandir [agʀɑ̃diʀ] *vt* (*magasin, domaine*) to extend, enlarge; (*trou*) to enlarge, make bigger; (*Photo*) to enlarge, blow up; **s'agrandir** *vi* to be extended; to be enlarged
agrandissement [agʀɑ̃dismɑ̃] *nm* extension; enlargement; (*photographie*) enlargement
agréable [agʀeabl(ə)] *adj* pleasant, nice
agréé, e [agʀee] *adj*: **concessionnaire ~** registered dealer; **magasin ~** registered dealer('s)
agréer [agʀee] *vt* (*requête*) to accept; **~ à** *vt* to please, suit; **veuillez ~ ...** (*formule épistolaire*) yours faithfully
agrégation [agʀegɑsjɔ̃] *nf* highest teaching diploma in France; *see note*
agrégé, e [agʀeʒe] *nm/f* holder of the *agrégation*
agrément [agʀemɑ̃] *nm* (*accord*) consent, approval; (*attraits*) charm, attractiveness; (*plaisir*) pleasure; **voyage d'~** pleasure trip
agrémenter [agʀemɑ̃te] *vt*: **~ (de)** to embellish (with), adorn (with)
agresser [agʀese] *vt* to attack
agresseur [agʀesœʀ] *nm* aggressor
agressif, -ive [agʀesif, -iv] *adj* aggressive
agricole [agʀikɔl] *adj* agricultural, farm *cpd*
agriculteur, -trice [agʀikyltœʀ, -tʀis] *nm/f* farmer

agriculture [agʁikyltyʁ] nf agriculture; farming

agripper [agʁipe] vt to grab, clutch; (pour arracher) to snatch, grab; **s'~ à** to cling (on) to, clutch, grip

agroalimentaire [agʁɔalimɑ̃tɛʁ] adj farming cpd ▷ nm: **l'~** agribusiness

agrumes [agʁym] nmpl citrus fruit(s)

aguerrir [ageʁiʁ] vt to harden; **s'~ (contre)** to become hardened (to)

aguets [agɛ]: **aux ~** adv: **être aux ~** to be on the look-out

aguicher [agiʃe] vt to entice

ahuri, e [ayʁi] adj (stupéfait) flabbergasted; (idiot) dim-witted

ai [e] vb voir **avoir**

aide [ɛd] nm/f assistant ▷ nf assistance, help; (secours financier) aid; **à l'~ de** with the help ou aid of; **aller à l'~ de qn** to go to sb's aid, go to help sb; **venir en ~ à qn** to help sb, come to sb's assistance; **appeler (qn) à l'~** to call for help (from sb); **à l'~!** help!; **~ de camp** nm aide-de-camp; **~ comptable** nm accountant's assistant; **~ électricien** nm electrician's mate; **~ familiale** nf mother's help, ≈ home help; **~ judiciaire** nf legal aid; **~ de laboratoire** nm/f laboratory assistant; **~ ménagère** nf ≈ home help; **~ sociale** nf (assistance) state aid; **~ soignant, e** nm/f auxiliary nurse; **~ technique** nf ≈ VSO (Brit), ≈ Peace Corps (US)

aide-éducateur, -trice [ɛdmedykatœʁ, tʁis] nm/f classroom assistant

aide-mémoire [ɛdmemwaʁ] nm inv (key facts) handbook

aider [ede] vt to help; **~ à qch** to help (towards) sth; **~ qn à faire qch** to help sb to do sth; **s'~ de** (se servir de) to use, make use of

aide-soignant, e [ɛdswaɲɑ̃, ɑ̃t] nm/f auxiliary nurse

aie etc [ɛ] vb voir **avoir**

aïe [aj] excl ouch!

aïeul, e [ajœl] nm/f grandparent, grandfather/grandmother; (ancêtre) forebear

aïeux [ajø] nmpl grandparents; forebears, forefathers

aigle [ɛgl(ə)] nm eagle

aigre [ɛgʁ(ə)] adj sour, sharp; (fig) sharp, cutting; **tourner à l'~** to turn sour

aigre-doux, -douce [ɛgʁədu, -dus] adj (fruit) bitter-sweet; (sauce) sweet and sour

aigreur [ɛgʁœʁ] nf sourness; sharpness; **~s d'estomac** heartburn sg

aigrir [egʁiʁ] vt (personne) to embitter; (caractère) to sour; **s'aigrir** vi to become embittered; to sour; (lait etc) to turn sour

aigu, ë [egy] adj (objet, arête) sharp, pointed; (son, voix) high-pitched, shrill; (note) high(-pitched); (douleur, intelligence) acute, sharp

aiguille [eguij] nf needle; (de montre) hand; **~ à tricoter** knitting needle

aiguiller [eguije] vt (orienter) to direct; (Rail) to shunt

aiguilleur [eguijœʁ] nm: **~ du ciel** air traffic controller

aiguillon [eguijɔ̃] nm (d'abeille) sting; (fig) spur, stimulus

aiguillonner [eguijɔne] vt to spur ou goad on

aiguiser [egize] vt to sharpen, grind; (fig) to stimulate; (: esprit) to sharpen; (: sens) to excite

ail [aj] nm garlic

aile [ɛl] nf wing; (de voiture) wing (Brit), fender (US); (fig) to be in a sorry state; **voler de ses propres ~s** to stand on one's own two feet; **~ libre** hang-glider

aileron [ɛlʁɔ̃] nm (de requin) fin; (d'avion) aileron

ailier [elje] nm (Sport) winger

aille etc [aj] vb voir **aller**

ailleurs [ajœʁ] adv elsewhere, somewhere else; **partout/nulle part ~** everywhere/nowhere else; **d'~** (du reste) moreover, besides; **par ~** adv (d'autre part) moreover, furthermore

aimable [ɛmabl(ə)] adj kind, nice; **vous êtes bien ~** that's very nice ou kind of you, how kind (of you)!

aimant¹ [ɛmɑ̃] nm magnet

aimant², e [ɛmɑ̃, -ɑ̃t] adj loving, affectionate

aimer [eme] vt to love; (d'amitié, affection, par goût) to like; (souhait): **j'aimerais ...** I would like ...; **s'aimer** to love each other; to like each other; **je n'aime pas beaucoup Paul** I don't like Paul much, I don't care much for Paul; **~ faire qch** to like doing sth, like to do sth; **aimeriez-vous que je vous accompagne?** would you like me to come with you?; **j'aimerais (bien) m'en aller** I should (really) like to go; **bien ~ qn/qch** to like sb/sth; **j'aime mieux Paul (que Pierre)** I prefer Paul (to Pierre); **j'aime mieux ou autant vous dire que** I may as well tell you that; **j'aimerais autant ou mieux y aller maintenant** I'd sooner ou rather go now; **j'aime assez aller au cinéma** I quite like going to the cinema

aine [ɛn] nf groin

aîné, e [ene] adj elder, older; (le plus âgé) eldest, oldest ▷ nm/f oldest child ou one, oldest boy ou son/girl ou daughter; **aînés** nmpl (fig: anciens) elders; **il est mon ~ (de 2 ans)** he's (2 years) older than me, he's (2 years) my senior

ainsi [ɛ̃si] adv (de cette façon) like this, in this way, thus; (ce faisant) thus ▷ conj thus, so; **~ que** (comme) (just) as; (et aussi) as well as; **pour ~ dire** so to speak, as it were; **~ donc** and so; **~ soit-il** (Rel) so be it; **et ~ de suite** and so on (and so forth)

aïoli [ajɔli] nm = **ailloli**

air [ɛʁ] nm air; (mélodie) tune; (expression) look, air; (atmosphère, ambiance): **dans l'~** in the air (fig); **prendre de grands ~s (avec qn)** to give o.s. airs (with sb); **en l'~** (up) into the air; **tirer en l'~** to fire shots in the air; **paroles/menaces en l'~** idle words/threats; **prendre l'~** to get some (fresh) air; (avion) to take off; **avoir l'~ triste** to look ou seem sad; **avoir l'~ de qch** to look like sth; **avoir l'~ de faire** to look as though one is doing, appear to be doing; **courant d'~** draught (Brit), draft (US); **le grand ~** the open air; **mal**

de l'~ air-sickness; **tête en l'~** scatterbrain; ~ **comprimé** compressed air; ~ **conditionné** air-conditioning

airbag [ɛʀbag] *nm* airbag

aisance [ɛzɑ̃s] *nf* ease; (*Couture*) easing, freedom of movement; (*richesse*) affluence; **être dans l'~** to be well-off *ou* affluent

aise [ɛz] *nf* comfort ▷ *adj*: **être bien ~ de/que** to be delighted to/that; **aises** *nfpl*: **aimer ses ~s** to like one's (creature) comforts; **prendre ses ~s** to make o.s. comfortable; **frémir d'~** to shudder with pleasure; **être à l'~** *ou* **à son ~** to be comfortable; (*financièrement*) to be comfortably off; **se mettre à l'~** to make o.s. comfortable; **être mal à l'~** *ou* **à son ~** to be uncomfortable; (*gêné*) to be ill at ease; **mettre qn à l'~** to put sb at his (*ou* her) ease; **mettre qn mal à l'~** to make sb feel ill at ease; **à votre ~** please yourself, just as you like; **en faire à son ~** to do as one likes; **en prendre à son ~ avec qch** to be free and easy with sth, do as one likes with sth

aisé, e [eze] *adj* easy; (*assez riche*) well-to-do, well-off

aisselle [ɛsɛl] *nf* armpit

ait [ɛ] *vb voir* **avoir**

ajonc [aʒɔ̃] *nm* gorse *no pl*

ajourner [aʒuʀne] *vt* (*réunion*) to adjourn; (*décision*) to defer, postpone; (*candidat*) to refer; (*conscrit*) to defer

ajouter [aʒute] *vt* to add; ~ **à** (*accroître*) to add to; **s'~ à** to add to; ~ **que** to add that; ~ **foi à** to lend *ou* give credence to

ajusté, e [aʒyste] *adj*: **bien ~** (*robe etc*) close-fitting

ajuster [aʒyste] *vt* (*régler*) to adjust; (*vêtement*) to alter; (*arranger*): ~ **sa cravate** to adjust one's tie; (*coup de fusil*) to aim; (*cible*) to aim at; (*adapter*): ~ **qch à** to fit sth to

alarme [alaʀm(ə)] *nf* alarm; **donner l'~** to give *ou* raise the alarm; **jeter l'~** to cause alarm

alarmer [alaʀme] *vt* to alarm; **s'alarmer** *vi* to become alarmed

alarmiste [alaʀmist(ə)] *adj* alarmist

album [albɔm] *nm* album; ~ **à colorier** colouring book; ~ **de timbres** stamp album

albumine [albymin] *nf* albumin; **avoir** *ou* **faire de l'~** to suffer from albuminuria

alcool [alkɔl] *nm*: **l'~** alcohol; **un ~** a spirit, a brandy; ~ **à brûler** methylated spirits (*Brit*), wood alcohol (*US*); ~ **à 90°** surgical spirit; ~ **camphré** camphorated alcohol; ~ **de prune** *etc* plum *etc* brandy

alcoolique [alkɔlik] *adj, nm/f* alcoholic

alcoolisé, e [alkɔlize] *adj* alcoholic

alcoolisme [alkɔlism(ə)] *nm* alcoholism

alcootest®, alcotest® [alkɔtɛst] *nm* (*objet*) Breathalyser®; (*test*) breath-test; **faire subir l'alco(o)test à qn** to Breathalyse® sb

aléas [alea] *nmpl* hazards

aléatoire [aleatwaʀ] *adj* uncertain; (*Inform, Statistique*) random

alentour [alɑ̃tuʀ] *adv* around (about); **alentours** *nmpl* surroundings; **aux ~s de** in the vicinity *ou* neighbourhood of, around about; (*temps*) around about

alerte [alɛʀt(ə)] *adj* agile, nimble; (*style*) brisk, lively ▷ *nf* alert; warning; **donner l'~** to give the alert; **à la première ~** at the first sign of trouble *ou* danger; ~ **à la bombe** bomb scare

alerter [alɛʀte] *vt* to alert

algèbre [alʒɛbʀ(ə)] *nf* algebra

Alger [alʒe] *n* Algiers

Algérie [alʒeʀi] *nf*: **l'~** Algeria

algérien, ne [alʒeʀjɛ̃, -ɛn] *adj* Algerian ▷ *nm/f*: **A~, ne** Algerian

algue [alg(ə)] *nf* seaweed *no pl*

alibi [alibi] *nm* alibi

aliéné, e [aljene] *nm/f* insane person, lunatic (*péj*)

aligner [aliɲe] *vt* to align, line up; (*idées, chiffres*) to string together; (*adapter*): ~ **qch sur** to bring sth into alignment with; **s'aligner** *vi* (*soldats etc*) to line up; **s'~ sur** (*Pol*) to align o.s. with

aliment [alimɑ̃] *nm* food; ~ **complet** whole food

alimentaire [alimɑ̃tɛʀ] *adj* food *cpd*; (*péj: besogne*) done merely to earn a living; **produits ~s** foodstuffs, foods

alimentation [alimɑ̃tasjɔ̃] *nf* feeding; supplying, supply; (*commerce*) food trade; (*produits*) groceries *pl*; (*régime*) diet; (*Inform*) feed; ~ **(générale)** (general) grocer's; ~ **de base** staple diet; ~ **en feuilles/en continu/en papier** form/stream/sheet feed

alimenter [alimɑ̃te] *vt* to feed; (*Tech*): ~ **(en)** to supply (with), feed (with); (*fig*) to sustain, keep going

alinéa [alinea] *nm* paragraph; **"nouvel ~"** "new line"

aliter [alite]: **s'aliter** *vi* to take to one's bed; **infirme alité** bedridden person *ou* invalid

allaiter [alete] *vt* (*femme*) to (breast-)feed, nurse; (*animal*) to suckle; ~ **au biberon** to bottle-feed

allant [alɑ̃] *nm* drive, go

alléchant, e [aleʃɑ̃, -ɑ̃t] *adj* tempting, enticing

allécher [aleʃe] *vt*: ~ **qn** to make sb's mouth water; to tempt sb, entice sb

allée [ale] *nf* (*de jardin*) path; (*en ville*) avenue, drive; ~ **s et venues** comings and goings

allégé, e [aleʒe] *adj* (*yaourt etc*) low-fat

alléger [aleʒe] *vt* (*voiture*) to make lighter; (*chargement*) to lighten; (*souffrance*) to alleviate, soothe

allègre [alɛgʀ(ə)] *adj* lively, jaunty (*Brit*); (*personne*) gay, cheerful

alléguer [alege] *vt* to put forward (as proof *ou* an excuse)

Allemagne [aləmaɲ] *nf*: **l'~** Germany; **l'~ de l'Est/Ouest** East/West Germany; **l'~ fédérale (RFA)** the Federal Republic of Germany (FRG)

allemand, e [almɑ̃, -ɑ̃d] *adj* German ▷ *nm* (*Ling*) German ▷ *nm/f*: **A~, e** German; **A~ de l'Est/l'Ouest** East/West German

aller [ale] *nm* (*trajet*) outward journey; (*billet*): ~

(simple) single (Brit) ou one-way ticket; **~ (et) retour (AR)** (trajet) return trip ou journey (Brit), round trip (US); (billet) return (Brit) ou round-trip (US) ticket ▷ vi (gén) to go; **~ à** (convenir) to suit; (forme, pointure etc) to fit; **cela me va** (couleur) that suits me; (vêtement) that suits me; that fits me; (projet, disposition) that suits me, that's fine ou OK by me; **~ à la chasse/pêche** to go hunting/fishing; **~ avec** (couleurs, style etc) to go (well) with; **je vais le faire/me fâcher** I'm going to do it/to get angry; **~ voir/chercher qn** to go and see/look for sb; **comment allez-vous?** how are you?; **comment ça va?** how are you?; (affaires etc) how are things?; **ça va? — oui (ça va)!** how are things? — fine!; **pour ~ à** how do I get to; **ça va (comme ça)** that's fine (as it is); **il va bien/mal** he's well/not well, he's fine/ill; **ça va bien/mal** (affaires etc) it's going well/not going well; **tout va bien** everything's fine; **ça ne va pas!** (mauvaise humeur etc) that's not on!, hey, come on!; **ça ne va pas sans difficultés** it's not without difficulties; **~ mieux** to be better; **il y a de leur vie** their lives are at stake; **se laisser ~** to let o.s. go; **s'en aller** vi (partir) to be off, go, leave; (disparaître) to go away; **~ jusqu'à** to go as far as; **ça va de soi, ça va sans dire** that goes without saying; **tu y vas un peu fort** you're going a bit (too) far; **allez!** go on!; come on!; **allons-y!** let's go!; **allez, au revoir!** right ou OK then, bye-bye!

allergique [alɛʀʒik] adj allergic; **~ à** allergic to

alliage [aljaʒ] nm alloy

alliance [aljɑ̃s] nf (Mil, Pol) alliance; (mariage) marriage; (bague) wedding ring; **neveu par ~** nephew by marriage

allier [alje] vt (métaux) to alloy; (Pol, gén) to ally; (fig) to combine; **s'allier** vi to become allies; (éléments, caractéristiques) to combine; **s'~ à** to become allied to ou with

allô [alo] excl hullo, hallo

allocation [alɔkasjɔ̃] nf allowance; **~ (de) chômage** unemployment benefit; **~ (de) logement** rent allowance; **~s familiales** ≈ child benefit no pl; **~s de maternité** maternity allowance

allocution [alɔkysjɔ̃] nf short speech

allonger [alɔ̃ʒe] vt to lengthen, make longer; (étendre: bras, jambe) to stretch (out); (sauce) to spin out, make go further; **s'allonger** vi to get longer; (se coucher) to lie down, stretch out; **~ le pas** to hasten one's step(s)

allouer [alwe] vt: **~ qch à** to allocate sth to, allot sth to

allumage [alymaʒ] nm (Auto) ignition

allume-cigare [alymsigaʀ] nm inv cigar lighter

allumer [alyme] vt (lampe, phare, radio) to put ou switch on; (pièce) to put ou switch the light(s) on in; (feu, bougie, cigare, pipe, gaz) to light; (chauffage) to put on; **s'allumer** vi (lumière, lampe) to come ou go on; **~ (la lumière** ou **l'électricité)** to put on the light

allumette [alymɛt] nf match; (morceau de bois) matchstick; (Culin): **~ au fromage** cheese straw;

~ de sûreté safety match

allure [alyʀ] nf (vitesse) speed; (: à pied) pace; (démarche) walk; (maintien) bearing; (aspect, air) look; **avoir de l'~** to have style ou a certain elegance; **à toute ~** at top ou full speed

allusion [alyzjɔ̃] nf allusion; (sous-entendu) hint; **faire ~ à** to allude ou refer to; to hint at

alors [alɔʀ] adv 1 (à ce moment-là) then, at that time; **il habitait ~ à Paris** he lived in Paris at that time; **jusqu'~** up till ou until then

2 (par conséquent) then; **tu as fini? ~ je m'en vais** have you finished? I'm going then

3 (expressions): **~? quoi de neuf?** well ou so? what's new?; **et ~?** so (what?); **ça ~!** (well) really! ▷ conj: **~ que** 1 (au moment où) when, as; **il est arrivé ~ que je partais** he arrived as I was leaving

2 (pendant que) while, when; **~ qu'il était à Paris, il a visité ...** while ou when he was in Paris, he visited ...

3 (tandis que) whereas, while; **~ que son frère travaillait dur, lui se reposait** while his brother was working hard, HE would rest

alouette [alwɛt] nf (sky)lark

alourdir [aluʀdiʀ] vt to weigh down, make heavy; **s'alourdir** vi to grow heavy ou heavier

aloyau [alwajo] nm sirloin

Alpes [alp(ə)] nfpl: **les ~** the Alps

alphabet [alfabɛ] nm alphabet; (livre) ABC (book), primer

alphabétique [alfabetik] adj alphabetic(al); **par ~ ordre** = in alphabetical order

alphabétiser [alfabetize] vt to teach to read and write; (pays) to eliminate illiteracy in

alpinisme [alpinism(ə)] nm mountaineering, climbing

alpiniste [alpinist(ə)] nm/f mountaineer, climber

Alsace [alzas] nf: **l'~** Alsace

alsacien, ne [alzasjɛ̃, -ɛn] adj Alsatian

altérer [altere] vt (faits, vérité) to falsify, distort; (qualité) to debase, impair; (données) to corrupt; (donner soif à) to make thirsty; **s'altérer** vi to deteriorate; to spoil

altermondialisme [altɛʀmɔ̃djalism] nm anti-globalism

altermondialiste [altɛʀmɔ̃djalist] adj, nm/f anti-globalist

alternateur [altɛʀnatœʀ] nm alternator

alternatif, -ive [altɛʀnatif, -iv] adj alternating ▷ nf alternative

alternativement [altɛʀnativmɑ̃] adv alternately

alterner [altɛʀne] vt to alternate ▷ vi: **~ (avec)** to alternate (with); **(faire) ~ qch avec qch** to alternate sth with sth

Altesse [altɛs] nf Highness

altitude [altityd] nf altitude, height; **à 1000 m d'~** at a height ou an altitude of 1000 m; **en ~** at high altitudes; **perdre/prendre de l'~** to lose/gain height; **voler à haute/basse ~** to fly at a high/low altitude

alto [alto] nm (instrument) viola ▷ nf (contr)alto

aluminium [alyminjɔm] nm aluminium (Brit), aluminum (US)

amabilité [amabilite] nf kindness; **il a eu l'~ de** he was kind ou good enough to

amadouer [amadwe] vt to coax, cajole; (adoucir) to mollify, soothe

amaigrir [amegʀiʀ] vt to make thin ou thinner

amaigrissant, e [amegʀisã, -ãt] adj: **régime ~** slimming (Brit) ou weight-reduction (US) diet

amalgame [amalgam] nm amalgam; (fig: de gens, d'idées) hotch-potch, mixture

amande [amãd] nf (de l'amandier) almond; (de noyau de fruit) kernel; **en ~** (yeux) almond cpd, almond-shaped

amandier [amãdje] nm almond (tree)

amant [amã] nm lover

amarrer [amaʀe] vt (Navig) to moor; (gén) to make fast

amas [ama] nm heap, pile

amasser [amase] vt to amass; **s'amasser** vi to pile up, accumulate; (foule) to gather

amateur [amatœʀ] nm amateur; **en ~** (péj) amateurishly; **musicien/sportif ~** amateur musician/sportsman; **~ de musique/sport** etc music/sport etc lover

amazone [amazɔn] nf horsewoman; **en ~** side-saddle

ambassade [ãbasad] nf embassy; (mission): **en ~** on a mission

ambassadeur, -drice [ãbasadœʀ, -dʀis] nm/f ambassador/ambassadress

ambiance [ãbjãs] nf atmosphere; **il y a de l'~** everyone's having a good time

ambiant, e [ãbjã, -ãt] adj (air, milieu) surrounding; (température) ambient

ambigu, ë [ãbigy] adj ambiguous

ambitieux, -euse [ãbisjø, -øz] adj ambitious

ambition [ãbisjɔ̃] nf ambition

ambulance [ãbylãs] nf ambulance

ambulancier, -ière [ãbylãsje, -jɛʀ] nm/f ambulanceman/woman (Brit), paramedic (US)

ambulant, e [ãbylã, -ãt] adj travelling, itinerant

âme [am] nf soul; **rendre l'~** to give up the ghost; **bonne ~** (aussi ironique) kind soul; **un joueur/tricheur dans l'~** a gambler/cheat through and through; **~ sœur** kindred spirit

amélioration [ameljɔʀasjɔ̃] nf improvement

améliorer [ameljɔʀe] vt to improve; **s'améliorer** vi to improve, get better

aménager [amenaʒe] vt (agencer: espace, local) to fit out; (: terrain) to lay out; (: quartier, territoire) to develop; (installer) to fix up, put in; **ferme aménagée** converted farmhouse

amende [amãd] nf fine; **mettre à l'~** to penalize; **faire ~ honorable** to make amends

amener [amne] vt to bring; (causer) to bring about; (baisser: drapeau, voiles) to strike; **s'amener** vi (fam) to show up, turn up; **~ qn à qch/à faire** to lead sb to sth/to do

amenuiser [amənɥize]: **s'amenuiser** vi to dwindle; (chances) to grow slimmer, lessen

amer, amère [amɛʀ] adj bitter

américain, e [ameʀikɛ̃, -ɛn] adj American ▷ nm (Ling) American (English) ▷ nm/f: **A~, e** American; **en vedette ~e** as a special guest (star)

Amérique [ameʀik] nf America; **l'~ centrale** Central America; **l'~ latine** Latin America; **l'~ du Nord** North America; **l'~ du Sud** South America

amertume [amɛʀtym] nf bitterness

ameublement [amœbləmã] nm furnishing; (meubles) furniture; **articles d'~** furnishings; **tissus d'~** soft furnishings, furnishing fabrics

ameuter [amøte] vt (badauds) to draw a crowd of; (peuple) to rouse, stir up

ami, e [ami] nm/f friend; (amant/maîtresse) boyfriend/girlfriend ▷ adj: **pays/groupe ~** friendly country/group; **être (très) ~ avec qn** to be (very) friendly with sb; **être ~ de l'ordre** to be a lover of order; **un ~ des arts** a patron of the arts; **un ~ des chiens** a dog lover; **petit ~/petite ~e** (fam) boyfriend/girlfriend

amiable [amjabl(ə)]: **à l'~** adv (Jur) out of court; (gén) amicably

amiante [amjãt] nm asbestos

amical, e, -aux [amikal, -o] adj friendly ▷ nf (club) association

amicalement [amikalmã] adv in a friendly way; (formule épistolaire) regards

amidon [amidɔ̃] nm starch

amincir [amɛ̃siʀ] vt (objet) to thin (down); **s'amincir** vi to get thinner ou slimmer; **~ qn** to make sb thinner ou slimmer

amincissant, e [amɛ̃sisã, -ãt] adj slimming

amiral, -aux [amiʀal, -o] nm admiral

amitié [amitje] nf friendship; **prendre en ~** to take a liking to; **faire** ou **présenter ses ~s à qn** to send sb one's best wishes; **~s** (formule épistolaire) (with) best wishes

ammoniaque [amɔnjak] nf ammonia (water)

amnistie [amnisti] nf amnesty

amoindrir [amwɛ̃dʀiʀ] vt to reduce

amollir [amɔliʀ] vt to soften

amonceler [amɔ̃sle] vt: **s'amonceler** to pile ou heap up; (fig) to accumulate

amont [amɔ̃]: **en ~** adv upstream; (sur une pente) uphill; **en ~ de** prép upstream from; uphill from, above

amorce [amɔʀs(ə)] nf (sur un hameçon) bait; (explosif) cap; (tube) primer; (: contenu) priming; (fig: début) beginning(s), start

amorcer [amɔʀse] vt to bait; to prime; (commencer) to begin, start

amorphe [amɔʀf(ə)] adj passive, lifeless

amortir [amɔʀtiʀ] vt (atténuer: choc) to absorb, cushion; (bruit, douleur) to deaden; (Comm: dette) to pay off, amortize; (: mise de fonds, matériel) to write off; **~ un abonnement** to make a season ticket pay (for itself)

amortisseur [amɔʀtisœʀ] nm shock absorber

amour [amuʀ] nm love; (liaison) love affair, love; (statuette etc) cupid; **un ~ de** a lovely little; **faire**

l'~ to make love

amouracher [amuraʃe]: **s'amouracher de** vt (péj) to become infatuated with

amoureux, -euse [amurø, -øz] adj (regard, tempérament) amorous; (vie, problèmes) love cpd; (personne): **~ (de qn)** in love (with sb) ▷ nm/f lover ▷ nmpl courting couple(s); **tomber ~ de qn** to fall in love with sb; **être ~ de qch** to be passionately fond of sth; **un ~ de la nature** a nature lover

amour-propre (pl **amours-propres**) [amurprɔpr(ə)] nm self-esteem

amovible [amɔvibl(ə)] adj removable, detachable

ampère [ɑ̃pɛʀ] nm amp(ere)

amphithéâtre [ɑ̃fiteatʀ(ə)] nm amphitheatre; (d'université) lecture hall ou theatre

ample [ɑ̃pl(ə)] adj (vêtement) roomy, ample; (gestes, mouvement) broad; (ressources) ample; **jusqu'à plus ~ informé** (Admin) until further details are available

amplement [ɑ̃pləmɑ̃] adv amply; **~ suffisant** ample, more than enough

ampleur [ɑ̃plœʀ] nf scale, size; extent, magnitude

amplificateur [ɑ̃plifikatœʀ] nm amplifier

amplifier [ɑ̃plifje] vt (son, oscillation) to amplify; (fig) to expand, increase

ampoule [ɑ̃pul] nf (électrique) bulb; (de médicament) phial; (aux mains, pieds) blister

ampoulé, e [ɑ̃pule] adj (péj) pompous, bombastic

amputer [ɑ̃pyte] vt (Méd) to amputate; (fig) to cut ou reduce drastically; **~ qn d'un bras/pied** to amputate sb's arm/foot

amusant, e [amyzɑ̃, -ɑ̃t] adj (divertissant, spirituel) entertaining, amusing; (comique) funny, amusing

amuse-gueule [amyzgœl] nm inv appetizer, snack

amusement [amyzmɑ̃] nm (voir amusé) amusement; (voir amuser) entertaining, amusing; (jeu etc) pastime, diversion

amuser [amyze] vt (divertir) to entertain, amuse; (égayer, faire rire) to amuse; (détourner l'attention de) to distract; **s'amuser** vi (jouer) to amuse o.s., play; (se divertir) to enjoy o.s., have fun; (fig) to mess around; **s'~ de qch** (trouver comique) to find sth amusing; **s'~ avec** ou **de qn** (duper) to make a fool of sb

amygdale [amidal] nf tonsil; **opérer qn des ~s** to take sb's tonsils out

an [ɑ̃] nm year; **être âgé de** ou **avoir 3 ans** to be 3 (years old); **en l'an 1980** in the year 1980; **le jour de l'an, le premier de l'an, le nouvel an** New Year's Day

analogique [analɔʒik] adj (Logique: raisonnement) analogical; (calculateur, montre etc) analogue; (Inform) analog

analogue [analɔg] adj: **~ (à)** analogous (to), similar (to)

analphabète [analfabɛt] nm/f illiterate

analyse [analiz] nf analysis; (Méd) test; **faire l'~**

de to analyse; **une ~ approfondie** an in-depth analysis; **en dernière ~** in the last analysis; **avoir l'esprit d'~** to have an analytical turn of mind; **~ grammaticale** grammatical analysis, parsing (Scol)

analyser [analize] vt to analyse; (Méd) to test

ananas [anana] nm pineapple

anarchie [anaʀʃi] nf anarchy

anatomie [anatɔmi] nf anatomy

ancêtre [ɑ̃sɛtʀ(ə)] nm/f ancestor; (fig): **l'~ de** the forerunner of

anchois [ɑ̃ʃwa] nm anchovy

ancien, ne [ɑ̃sjɛ̃, -ɛn] adj old; (de jadis, de l'antiquité) ancient; (précédent, ex-) former, old ▷ nm (mobilier ancien): **l'~** antiques pl ▷ nm/f (dans une tribu etc) elder; **un ~ ministre** a former minister; **mon ~ne voiture** my previous car; **être plus ~ que qn dans une maison** to have been in a firm longer than sb; (dans la hiérarchie) to be senior to sb in a firm; **~ combattant** ex-serviceman; **~ (élève)** (Scol) ex-pupil (Brit), alumnus (US)

anciennement [ɑ̃sjɛnmɑ̃] adv formerly

ancienneté [ɑ̃sjɛnte] nf oldness; antiquity; (Admin) (length of) service; seniority

ancre [ɑ̃kʀ(ə)] nf anchor; **jeter/lever l'~** to cast/ weigh anchor; **à l'~** at anchor

ancrer [ɑ̃kʀe] vt (Constr) to anchor; (fig) to fix firmly; **s'ancrer** vi (Navig) to (cast) anchor

Andorre [ɑ̃dɔʀ] nf Andorra

andouille [ɑ̃duj] nf (Culin) sausage made of chitterlings; (fam) clot, nit

âne [ɑn] nm donkey, ass; (péj) dunce, fool

anéantir [aneɑ̃tiʀ] vt to annihilate, wipe out; (fig) to obliterate, destroy; (déprimer) to overwhelm

anémie [anemi] nf anaemia

anémique [anemik] adj anaemic

ânerie [ɑnʀi] nf stupidity; (parole etc) stupid ou idiotic comment etc

anesthésie [anɛstezi] nf anaesthesia; **sous ~** under anaesthetic; **~ générale/locale** general/ local anaesthetic; **faire une ~ locale à qn** to give sb a local anaesthetic

ange [ɑ̃ʒ] nm angel; **être aux ~s** to be over the moon; **~ gardien** guardian angel

angélus [ɑ̃ʒelys] nm angelus; (cloches) evening bells pl

angine [ɑ̃ʒin] nf sore throat, throat infection; **~ de poitrine** angina (pectoris)

anglais, e [ɑ̃glɛ, -ɛz] adj English ▷ nm (Ling) English ▷ nm/f: **A~, e** Englishman/woman; **les A~** the English; **filer à l'~e** to take French leave; **à l'~e** (Culin) boiled

angle [ɑ̃gl(ə)] nm angle; (coin) corner; **~ droit/ obtus/aigu/mort** right/obtuse/acute/dead angle

Angleterre [ɑ̃glətɛʀ] nf: **l'~** England

anglo... [ɑ̃glɔ] préfixe Anglo-, anglo(-)

anglophone [ɑ̃glɔfɔn] adj English-speaking

angoisse [ɑ̃gwas] nf: **l'~** anguish no pl

angoissé, e [ɑ̃gwase] adj anguished; (personne) full of anxieties ou hang-ups (fam)

angoisser [ãgwase] *vt* to harrow, cause anguish to ▷ *vi* to worry, fret

anguille [ãgij] *nf* eel; ~ **de mer** conger (eel); **il y a ~ sous roche** (*fig*) there's something going on, there's something beneath all this

anicroche [anikrɔʃ] *nf* hitch, snag

animal, e, -aux [animal, -o] *adj, nm* animal; ~ **domestique/sauvage** domestic/wild animal

animateur, -trice [animatœr, -tris] *nm/f* (*de télévision*) host; (*de music-hall*) compère; (*de groupe*) leader, organizer; (*Ciné: technicien*) animator

animation [animasjɔ̃] *nf* (*voir animé*) busyness; liveliness; (*Ciné: technique*) animation; **animations** *nfpl* (*activité*) activities; **centre d'~** ≈ community centre

animé, e [anime] *adj* (*rue, lieu*) busy, lively; (*conversation, réunion*) lively, animated; (*opposé à inanimé, aussi Ling*) animate

animer [anime] *vt* (*ville, soirée*) to liven up, enliven; (*mettre en mouvement*) to drive; (*stimuler*) to drive, impel; **s'animer** *vi* to liven up, come to life

anis [ani] *nm* (*Culin*) aniseed; (*Bot*) anise

ankyloser [ãkiloze]: **s'ankyloser** *vi* to get stiff

anneau, x [ano] *nm* ring; (*de chaîne*) link; (*Sport*): **exercices aux ~x** ring exercises

année [ane] *nf* year; **souhaiter la bonne ~ à qn** to wish sb a Happy New Year; **tout au long de l'~** all year long; **d'une ~ à l'autre** from one year to the next; **d'~ en ~** from year to year; **l'~ scolaire/fiscale** the school/tax year

annexe [anɛks(ə)] *adj* (*problème*) related; (*document*) appended; (*salle*) adjoining ▷ *nf* (*bâtiment*) annex(e); (*de document, ouvrage*) annex, appendix; (*jointe à une lettre, un dossier*) enclosure

anniversaire [aniversɛr] *nm* birthday; (*d'un événement, bâtiment*) anniversary ▷ *adj*: **jour ~** anniversary

annonce [anɔ̃s] *nf* announcement; (*signe, indice*) sign; (*aussi*: **annonce publicitaire**) advertisement; (*Cartes*) declaration; ~ **personnelle** personal message; **les petites ~s** the small *ou* classified ads

annoncer [anɔ̃se] *vt* to announce; (*être le signe de*) to herald; (*Cartes*) to declare; **je vous annonce que ...** I wish to tell you that ...; **s'annoncer bien/difficile** *vi* to look promising/difficult; ~ **la couleur** (*fig*) to lay one's cards on the table

annonceur, -euse [anɔ̃sœr, -øz] *nm/f* (*TV, Radio: speaker*) announcer; (*publicitaire*) advertiser

annuaire [anɥɛr] *nm* yearbook, annual; ~ **téléphonique** (telephone) directory, phone book

annuel, le [anɥɛl] *adj* annual, yearly

annuité [anɥite] *nf* annual instalment

annulation [anylasjɔ̃] *nf* cancellation; annulment; quashing, repeal

annuler [anyle] *vt* (*rendez-vous, voyage*) to cancel, call off; (*mariage*) to annul; (*jugement*) to quash (*Brit*), repeal (*US*); (*résultats*) to declare void; (*Math, Physique*) to cancel out; **s'annuler** to cancel each other out

anodin, e [anɔdɛ̃, -in] *adj* harmless; (*sans importance*) insignificant, trivial

anonymat [anɔnima] *nm* anonymity; **garder l'~** to remain anonymous

anonyme [anɔnim] *adj* anonymous; (*fig*) impersonal

anorak [anɔrak] *nm* anorak

anorexie [anɔrɛksi] *nf* anorexia

anormal, e, -aux [anɔrmal, -o] *adj* abnormal; (*insolite*) unusual, abnormal

ANPE *sigle f* (= *Agence nationale pour l'emploi*) national employment agency (*functions include job creation*)

anse [ãs] *nf* handle; (*Géo*) cove

antan [ãtã]: **d'~** *adj* of yesteryear, of long ago

antarctique [ãtarktik] *adj* Antarctic ▷ *nm*: **l'A~** the Antarctic; **le cercle A~** the Antarctic Circle; **l'océan A~** the Antarctic Ocean

antécédent [ãtesedã] *nm* (*Ling*) antecedent; **antécédents** *nmpl* (*Méd etc*) past history *sg*; ~**s professionnels** record, career to date

antenne [ãtɛn] *nf* (*de radio, télévision*) aerial; (*d'insecte*) antenna (*pl* -ae), feeler; (*poste avancé*) outpost; (*petite succursale*) sub-branch; **sur l'~** on the air; **passer à/avoir l'~** to go/be on the air; **deux heures d'~** two hours' broadcasting time; **hors ~** off the air; ~ **chirurgicale** (*Mil*) advance surgical unit

antérieur, e [ãterjœr] *adj* (*d'avant*) previous, earlier; (*de devant*) front; ~ **à** prior *ou* previous to; **passé/futur ~** (*Ling*) past/future anterior

anti... [ãti] *préfixe* anti...

antialcoolique [ãtialkɔlik] *adj* anti-alcohol; **ligue ~** temperance league

antiatomique [ãtiatɔmik] *adj*: **abri ~** fallout shelter

antibiotique [ãtibjɔtik] *nm* antibiotic

antibrouillard [ãtibrujar] *adj*: **phare ~** fog lamp

anticipation [ãtisipasjɔ̃] *nf* anticipation; (*Comm*) payment in advance; **par ~** in anticipation, in advance; **livre/film d'~** science fiction book/film

anticipé, e [ãtisipe] *adj* (*règlement, paiement*) early, in advance; (*joie etc*) anticipated, early; **avec mes remerciements ~s** thanking you in advance *ou* anticipation

anticiper [ãtisipe] *vt* to anticipate, foresee; (*paiement*) to pay *ou* make in advance ▷ *vi* to look *ou* think ahead; (*en racontant*) to jump ahead; (*prévoir*) to anticipate; ~ **sur** to anticipate

anticonceptionnel, le [ãtikɔ̃sɛpsjɔnɛl] *adj* contraceptive

anticorps [ãtikɔr] *nm* antibody

antidote [ãtidɔt] *nm* antidote

antigel [ãtiʒɛl] *nm* antifreeze

antihistaminique [ãtiistaminik] *nm* antihistamine

antillais, e [ãtijɛ, -ɛz] *adj* West Indian

Antilles [ãtij] *nfpl*: **les ~** the West Indies; **les Grandes/Petites ~** the Greater/Lesser Antilles

antilope [ãtilɔp] *nf* antelope

antimite, antimites [ãtimit] *adj, nm*: (*produit*) ~**(s)** mothproofer, moth repellent

antipathique [ɑ̃tipatik] *adj* unpleasant, disagreeable

antipelliculaire [ɑ̃tipelikylɛʀ] *adj* anti-dandruff

antipodes [ɑ̃tipɔd] *nmpl* (*Géo*): **les ~** the antipodes; (*fig*): **être aux ~ de** to be the opposite extreme of

antiquaire [ɑ̃tikɛʀ] *nm/f* antique dealer

antique [ɑ̃tik] *adj* antique; (*très vieux*) ancient, antiquated

antiquité [ɑ̃tikite] *nf* (*objet*) antique; **l'A-** Antiquity; **magasin/marchand d'~s** antique shop/dealer

antirabique [ɑ̃tiʀabik] *adj* rabies *cpd*

antirouille [ɑ̃tiʀuj] *adj inv*: **peinture ~** antirust paint; **traitement ~** rustproofing

antisémite [ɑ̃tisemit] *adj* anti-Semitic

antiseptique [ɑ̃tisɛptik] *adj, nm* antiseptic

antivirus [ɑ̃tiviʀys] *nm* (*Inform*) antivirus (program)

antivol [ɑ̃tivɔl] *adj, nm*: (**dispositif**) **~** antitheft device; (*pour vélo*) padlock

antre [ɑ̃tʀ(ə)] *nm* den, lair

anxiété [ɑ̃ksjete] *nf* anxiety

anxieux, -euse [ɑ̃ksjø, -øz] *adj* anxious, worried; **être ~ de faire** to be anxious to do

AOC *sigle f* (= *Appellation d'origine contrôlée*) *guarantee of quality of wine; see note*

août [u] *nm* August; *voir aussi* **juillet; Assomption**

apaiser [apeze] *vt* (*colère*) to calm, quell, soothe; (*faim*) to appease, assuage; (*douleur*) to soothe; (*personne*) to calm (down), pacify; **s'apaiser** *vi* (*tempête, bruit*) to die down, subside

apanage [apanaʒ] *nm*: **être l'~ de** to be the privilege *ou* prerogative of

aparté [apaʀte] *nm* (*Théât*) aside; (*entretien*) private conversation; **en ~** *adv* in an aside (*Brit*); (*entretien*) in private

apathique [apatik] *adj* apathetic

apatride [apatʀid] *nm/f* stateless person

apercevoir [apɛʀsəvwaʀ] *vt* to see; **s'apercevoir de** *vt* to notice; **s'~ que** to notice that; **sans s'en ~** without realizing *ou* noticing

aperçu, e [apɛʀsy] *pp de* **apercevoir** ▷ *nm* (*vue d'ensemble*) general survey; (*intuition*) insight

apéritif, -ive [apeʀitif, -iv] *adj* which stimulates the appetite ▷ *nm* (*boisson*) aperitif; (*réunion*) (pre-lunch *ou* -dinner) drinks *pl*; **prendre l'~** to have drinks (before lunch *ou* dinner) *ou* an aperitif

à-peu-près [apøpʀɛ] *nm inv* (*péj*) vague approximation

apeuré, e [apœʀe] *adj* frightened, scared

aphte [aft(ə)] *nm* mouth ulcer

apiculture [apikyltyʀ] *nf* beekeeping, apiculture

apitoyer [apitwaje] *vt* to move to pity; **~ qn sur qn/qch** to move sb to pity for sb/over sth; **s'~ (sur qn/qch)** to feel pity *ou* compassion (for sb/over sth)

aplanir [aplaniʀ] *vt* to level; (*fig*) to smooth away, iron out

aplatir [aplatiʀ] *vt* to flatten; **s'aplatir** *vi* to become flatter; (*écrasé*) to be flattened; (*fig*) to lie flat on the ground; (: *fam*) to fall flat on one's face; (: *péj*) to grovel

aplomb [aplɔ̃] *nm* (*équilibre*) balance, equilibrium; (*fig*) self-assurance; (: *péj*) nerve; **d'~** *adv* steady; (*Constr*) plumb

apogée [apɔʒe] *nm* (*fig*) peak, apogee

apologie [apɔlɔʒi] *nf* praise; (*Jur*) vindication

a posteriori [apɔsteʀjɔʀi] *adv* after the event, with hindsight, a posteriori

apostrophe [apɔstʀɔf] *nf* (*signe*) apostrophe; (*appel*) interpellation

apostropher [apɔstʀɔfe] *vt* (*interpeller*) to shout at, address sharply

apothéose [apɔteoz] *nf* pinnacle (of achievement); (*Mus etc*) grand finale

apôtre [apotʀ(ə)] *nm* apostle, disciple

apparaître [apaʀɛtʀ(ə)] *vi* to appear ▷ *vb copule* to appear, seem

apparat [apaʀa] *nm*: **tenue/dîner d'~** ceremonial dress/dinner

appareil [apaʀɛj] *nm* (*outil, machine*) piece of apparatus, device; (*électrique etc*) appliance; (*politique, syndical*) machinery; (*avion*) (aero)plane (*Brit*), (air)plane (*US*), aircraft *inv*; (*téléphonique*) telephone; (*dentier*) brace (*Brit*), braces (*US*); **~ digestif/reproducteur** digestive/reproductive system *ou* apparatus; **l'~ productif** the means of production; **qui est à l'~?** who's speaking?; **dans le plus simple ~** in one's birthday suit; **~ (photographique)** camera; **~ 24 x 36** *ou* **petit format** 35 mm camera

appareiller [apaʀeje] *vi* (*Navig*) to cast off, get under way ▷ *vt* (*assortir*) to match up

appareil-photo [apaʀejfɔto] (*pl* **appareils-photos**) *nm* camera

apparemment [apaʀamɑ̃] *adv* apparently

apparence [apaʀɑ̃s] *nf* appearance; **malgré les ~s** despite appearances; **en ~** apparently, seemingly

apparent, e [apaʀɑ̃, -ɑ̃t] *adj* visible; (*évident*) obvious; (*superficiel*) apparent; **coutures ~es** topstitched seams; **poutres ~es** exposed beams

apparenté, e [apaʀɑ̃te] *adj*: **~ à** related to; (*fig*) similar to

apparition [apaʀisjɔ̃] *nf* appearance; (*surnaturelle*) apparition; **faire son ~** to appear

appartement [apaʀtəmɑ̃] *nm* flat (*Brit*), apartment (*US*)

appartenir [apaʀtəniʀ]: **~ à** *vt* to belong to; (*faire partie de*) to belong to, be a member of; **il lui appartient de** it is up to him to

apparu, e [apaʀy] *pp de* **apparaître**

appât [apɑ] *nm* (*Pêche*) bait; (*fig*) lure, bait

appâter [apɑte] *vt* (*hameçon*) to bait; (*poisson, fig*) to lure, entice

appauvrir [apovʀiʀ] *vt* to impoverish; **s'appauvrir** *vi* to grow poorer, become impoverished

appel [apɛl] *nm* call; (*nominal*) roll call; (: *Scol*) register; (*Mil: recrutement*) call-up; (*Jur*) appeal; **faire ~ à** (*invoquer*) to appeal to; (*avoir recours à*) to call on; (*nécessiter*) to call for, require; **faire** *ou* **interjeter ~** (*Jur*) to appeal, lodge an appeal;

faire l'~ to call the roll; to call the register; **indicatif d'~** call sign; **numéro d'~** (*Tél*) number; **produit d'~** (*Comm*) loss leader; **sans ~** (*fig*) final, irrevocable; **~ d'air** in-draught; **~ d'offres** (*Comm*) invitation to tender; **faire un ~ de phares** to flash one's headlights; **~ (téléphonique)** (tele)phone call

appelé [aple] *nm* (*Mil*) conscript

appeler [aple] *vt* (*Tél*) to call, ring; (*faire venir: médecin etc*) to call, send for; (*fig: nécessiter*) to call for, demand; **~ au secours** to call for help; **~ qn à l'aide** *ou* **au secours** to call to sb to help; **~ qn à un poste/des fonctions** to appoint sb to a post/assign duties to sb; **être appelé à** (*fig*) to be destined to; **~ qn à comparaître** (*Jur*) to summon sb to appear; **en ~ à** to appeal to; **s'appeler: elle s'appelle Gabrielle** her name is Gabrielle, she's called Gabrielle; **comment ça s'appelle?** what is it *ou* that called?

appendice [apɛ̃dis] *nm* appendix

appendicite [apɑ̃disit] *nf* appendicitis

appentis [apɑ̃ti] *nm* lean-to

appesantir [apzɑ̃tiʀ]: **s'appesantir** *vi* to grow heavier; **s'~ sur** (*fig*) to dwell at length on

appétissant, e [apetisɑ̃, -ɑ̃t] *adj* appetizing, mouth-watering

appétit [apeti] *nm* appetite; **couper l'~ à qn** to take away sb's appetite; **bon ~!** enjoy your meal!

applaudir [aplodiʀ] *vt* to applaud ▷ *vi* to applaud, clap; **~ à** *vt* (*décision*) to applaud, commend

applaudissements [aplodismɑ̃] *nmpl* applause *sg*, clapping *sg*

application [aplikasjɔ̃] *nf* application; (*d'une loi*) enforcement; **mettre en ~** to implement

applique [aplik] *nf* wall lamp

appliquer [aplike] *vt* to apply; (*loi*) to enforce; (*donner: gifle, châtiment*) to give; **s'appliquer** *vi* (*élève etc*) to apply o.s.; **s'~ à** (*loi, remarque*) to apply to; **s'~ à faire qch** to apply o.s. to doing sth, take pains to do sth; **s'~ sur** (*coïncider avec*) to fit over

appoint [apwɛ̃] *nm* (extra) contribution *ou* help; **avoir/faire l'~** (*en payant*) to have/give the right change *ou* money; **chauffage d'~** extra heating

appointements [apwɛ̃tmɑ̃] *nmpl* salary *sg*, stipend

apport [apɔʀ] *nm* supply; (*argent, biens etc*) contribution

apporter [apɔʀte] *vt* to bring; (*preuve*) to give, provide; (*modification*) to make; (*remarque*) to contribute, add

apposer [apoze] *vt* to append; (*sceau etc*) to affix

appréciable [apʀesjabl(ə)] *adj* (*important*) appreciable, significant

apprécier [apʀesje] *vt* to appreciate; (*évaluer*) to estimate, assess; **j'~ais que tu ...** I should appreciate (it) if you ...

appréhender [apʀeɑ̃de] *vt* (*craindre*) to dread; (*arrêter*) to apprehend; **~ que** to fear that; **~ de faire** to dread doing

appréhension [apʀeɑ̃sjɔ̃] *nf* apprehension

apprendre [apʀɑ̃dʀ(ə)] *vt* to learn; (*événement,*

résultats) to learn of, hear of; **~ qch à qn** (*informer*) to tell sb (of) sth; (*enseigner*) to teach sb sth; **tu me l'apprends!** that's news to me!; **~ à faire qch** to learn to do sth; **~ à qn à faire qch** to teach sb to do sth

apprenti, e [apʀɑ̃ti] *nm/f* apprentice; (*fig*) novice, beginner

apprentissage [apʀɑ̃tisaʒ] *nm* learning; (*Comm, Scol: période*) apprenticeship; **école** *ou* **centre d'~** training school *ou* centre; **faire l'~ de qch** (*fig*) to be initiated into sth

apprêté, e [apʀete] *adj* (*fig*) affected

apprêter [apʀete] *vt* to dress, finish; **s'apprêter** *vi*: **s'~ à qch/à faire qch** to prepare for sth/for doing sth

appris, e [apʀi, -iz] *pp de* **apprendre**

apprivoiser [apʀivwaze] *vt* to tame

approbation [apʀɔbasjɔ̃] *nf* approval; **digne d'~** (*conduite, travail*) praiseworthy, commendable

approchant, e [apʀɔʃɑ̃, -ɑ̃t] *adj* similar, close; **quelque chose d'~** something similar

approche [apʀɔʃ] *nf* approaching; (*arrivée, attitude*) approach; **approches** *nfpl* (*abords*) surroundings; **à l'~ du bateau/de l'ennemi** as the ship/enemy approached *ou* drew near; **l'~ d'un problème** the approach to a problem; **travaux d'~** (*fig*) manoeuvrings

approcher [apʀɔʃe] *vi* to approach, come near ▷ *vt* (*vedette, artiste*) to come close to, approach; (*rapprocher*): **~ qch (de qch)** to bring *ou* put *ou* move sth near (to sth); **~ de** *vt* to draw near to; (*quantité, moment*) to approach; **s'approcher de** *vt* to approach, go *ou* come *ou* move near to; **approchez-vous** come *ou* go nearer

approfondir [apʀɔfɔ̃diʀ] *vt* to deepen; (*question*) to go further into; **sans ~** without going too deeply into it

approprié, e [apʀɔpʀije] *adj*: **~ (à)** appropriate (to), suited (to)

approprier [apʀɔpʀije] *vt* (*adapter*) adapt; **s'approprier** *vt* to appropriate, take over

approuver [apʀuve] *vt* to agree with; (*autoriser: loi, projet*) to approve, pass; (*trouver louable*) to approve of; **je vous approuve entièrement/ne vous approuve pas** I agree with you entirely/don't agree with you; **lu et approuvé** (read and) approved

approvisionner [apʀɔvizjɔne] *vt* to supply; (*compte bancaire*) to pay funds into; **~ qn en** to supply sb with; **s'approvisionner** *vi*: **s'~ dans un certain magasin/au marché** to shop in a certain shop/at the market; **s'~ en** to stock up with

approximatif, -ive [apʀɔksimatif, -iv] *adj* approximate, rough; (*imprécis*) vague

appt *abr* = **appartement**

appui [apɥi] *nm* support; **prendre ~ sur** to lean on; (*objet*) to rest on; **point d'~** fulcrum; (*fig*) something to lean on; **à l'~ de** (*pour prouver*) in support of; **à l'~** *adv* to support one's argument; **l'~ de la fenêtre** the windowsill, the window ledge

appui-tête, appuie-tête [apɥitɛt] *nm inv* headrest

appuyer [apɥije] *vt* (*poser*): ~ **qch sur/contre/à** to lean *ou* rest sth on/against/on; (*soutenir*: *personne, demande*) to support, back (up) ▷ *vi*: ~ **sur** (*bouton, frein*) to press, push; (*mot, détail*) to stress, emphasize; (*chose*: *peser sur*) to rest (heavily) on, press against; **s'appuyer sur** *vt* to lean on; (*compter sur*) to rely on; **s'~ sur qn** to lean on sb; ~ **contre** (*toucher*: *mur, porte*) to lean *ou* rest against; ~ **à droite** *ou* **sur sa droite** to bear (to the) right; ~ **sur le champignon** to put one's foot down

âpre [ɑpʀ(ə)] *adj* acrid, pungent; (*fig*) harsh; (*lutte*) bitter; ~ **au gain** grasping, greedy

après [apʀɛ] *prép* after ▷ *adv* afterwards; **deux heures** ~ two hours later; ~ **qu'il est parti/avoir fait** after he left/having done; **courir** ~ to run after sb; **crier** ~ **qn** to shout at sb; **être toujours** ~ **qn** (*critiquer etc*) to be always on at sb; ~ **quoi** after which; **d'~** *prép* (*selon*) according to; **d'~ lui** according to him; **d'~ moi** in my opinion; ~ **coup** *adv* after the event, afterwards; ~ **tout** *adv* (*au fond*) after all; **et (puis)** ~? so what?

après-demain [apʀɛdmɛ̃] *adv* the day after tomorrow

après-guerre [apʀɛgɛʀ] *nm* post-war years *pl*; **d'~** *adj* post-war

après-midi [apʀɛmidi] *nm ou f inv* afternoon

après-rasage [apʀɛʀazaʒ] *nm inv*: (**lotion**) ~ after-shave (lotion)

après-shampooing [apʀɛʃɑ̃pwɛ̃] *nm inv* conditioner

après-ski [apʀɛski] *nm inv* (*chaussure*) snow boot; (*moment*) après-ski

après-soleil [apʀɛsɔlej] *adj inv* after-sun *cpd* ▷ *nm* after-sun cream *ou* lotion

à-propos [apʀopo] *nm* (*d'une remarque*) aptness; **faire preuve d'~** to show presence of mind, do the right thing; **avec** ~ suitably, aptly

apte [apt(ə)] *adj*: ~ **à qch/faire qch** capable of sth/doing sth; ~ **(au service)** (*Mil*) fit (for service)

aquarelle [akwaʀɛl] *nf* (*tableau*) watercolour (*Brit*), watercolor (*US*); (*genre*) watercolo(u)rs *pl*, aquarelle

aquarium [akwaʀjɔm] *nm* aquarium

arabe [aʀab] *adj* Arabic; (*désert, cheval*) Arabian; (*nation, peuple*) Arab ▷ *nm* (*Ling*) Arabic ▷ *nm/f*: **A~** Arab

Arabie [aʀabi] *nf*: **l'~** Arabia; **l'~ Saoudite** *ou* **Séoudite** Saudi Arabia

arachide [aʀaʃid] *nf* groundnut (plant); (*graine*) peanut, groundnut

araignée [aʀeɲe] *nf* spider; ~ **de mer** spider crab

arbitraire [aʀbitʀɛʀ] *adj* arbitrary

arbitre [aʀbitʀ(ə)] *nm* (*Sport*) referee; (: *Tennis, Cricket*) umpire; (*fig*) arbiter, judge; (*Jur*) arbitrator

arbitrer [aʀbitʀe] *vt* to referee; to umpire; to arbitrate

arborer [aʀbɔʀe] *vt* to bear, display; (*avec ostentation*) to sport

arbre [aʀbʀ(ə)] *nm* tree; (*Tech*) shaft; ~ **à cames** (*Auto*) camshaft; ~ **fruitier** fruit tree; ~ **généalogique** family tree; ~ **de Noël** Christmas tree; ~ **de transmission** (*Auto*) driveshaft

arbuste [aʀbyst(ə)] *nm* small shrub, bush

arc [aʀk] *nm* (*arme*) bow; (*Géom*) arc; (*Archit*) arch; ~ **de cercle** arc of a circle; **en** ~ **de cercle** *adj* semi-circular

arcade [aʀkad] *nf* arch(way); ~**s** arcade *sg*, arches; ~ **sourcilière** arch of the eyebrows

arcanes [aʀkan] *nmpl* mysteries

arc-boutant (*pl* **arcs-boutants**) [aʀkbutɑ̃] *nm* flying buttress

arceau, x [aʀso] *nm* (*métallique etc*) hoop

arc-en-ciel (*pl* **arcs-en-ciel**) [aʀkɑ̃sjɛl] *nm* rainbow

arche [aʀʃ(ə)] *nf* arch; ~ **de Noé** Noah's Ark

archéologie [aʀkeɔlɔʒi] *nf* arch(a)eology

archéologue [aʀkeɔlɔg] *nm/f* arch(a)eologist

archet [aʀʃɛ] *nm* bow

archevêque [aʀʃəvɛk] *nm* archbishop

archi... [aʀʃi] *préfixe* (*très*) dead, extra

archipel [aʀʃipɛl] *nm* archipelago

architecte [aʀʃitɛkt(ə)] *nm* architect

architecture [aʀʃitɛktyʀ] *nf* architecture

archive [aʀʃiv] *nf* file; **archives** *nfpl* archives

arctique [aʀktik] *adj* Arctic ▷ *nm*: **l'A~** the Arctic; **le cercle A~** the Arctic Circle; **l'océan A~** the Arctic Ocean

ardemment [aʀdamɑ̃] *adv* ardently, fervently

ardent, e [aʀdɑ̃, -ɑ̃t] *adj* (*soleil*) blazing; (*fièvre*) raging; (*amour*) ardent, passionate; (*prière*) fervent

ardeur [aʀdœʀ] *nf* blazing heat; (*fig*) fervour, ardour

ardoise [aʀdwaz] *nf* slate

ardu, e [aʀdy] *adj* arduous, difficult; (*pente*) steep, abrupt

arène [aʀɛn] *nf* arena; (*fig*): **l'~ politique** the political arena; **arènes** *nfpl* bull-ring *sg*

arête [aʀɛt] *nf* (*de poisson*) bone; (*d'une montagne*) ridge; (*Géom etc*) edge (*where two faces meet*)

argent [aʀʒɑ̃] *nm* (*métal*) silver; (*monnaie*) money; (*couleur*) silver; **en avoir pour son** ~ to get value for money; **gagner beaucoup d'~** to earn a lot of money; ~ **comptant** (hard) cash; ~ **liquide** ready money, (ready) cash; ~ **de poche** pocket money

argenté, e [aʀʒɑ̃te] *adj* silver(y); (*métal*) silver-plated

argenterie [aʀʒɑ̃tʀi] *nf* silverware; (*en métal argenté*) silver plate

argentin, e [aʀʒɑ̃tɛ̃, -in] *adj* Argentinian, Argentine ▷ *nm/f*: **A~, e** Argentinian, Argentine

Argentine [aʀʒɑ̃tin] *nf*: **l'~** Argentina, the Argentine

argentique [aʀʒɑ̃tik] *adj* (*appareil-photo*) film *cpd*

argile [aʀʒil] *nf* clay

argot [aʀgo] *nm* slang; *see note*

argotique [aʀgɔtik] *adj* slang *cpd*; (*très familier*) slangy

argument [aʀgymɑ̃] *nm* argument

argumentaire [aʀgymɑ̃tɛʀ] *nm* list of sales points; *(brochure)* sales leaflet

argumenter [aʀgymɑ̃te] *vi* to argue

argus [aʀgys] *nm* guide to second-hand car etc prices

aride [aʀid] *adj* arid

aristocratie [aʀistɔkʀasi] *nf* aristocracy

aristocratique [aʀistɔkʀatik] *adj* aristocratic

arithmétique [aʀitmetik] *adj* arithmetic(al) ▷ *nf* arithmetic

armateur [aʀmatœʀ] *nm* shipowner

armature [aʀmatyʀ] *nf* framework; *(de tente etc)* frame; *(de corset)* bone; *(de soutien-gorge)* wiring

arme [aʀm(ə)] *nf* weapon; *(section de l'armée)* arm; **armes** *nfpl* weapons, arms; *(blason)* (coat of) arms; **les ~s** *(profession)* soldiering *sg*; **à ~s égales** on equal terms; **en ~s** up in arms; **passer par les ~s** to execute (by firing squad); **prendre/présenter les ~s** to take up/present arms; **se battre à l'~ blanche** to fight with blades; **~ à feu** firearm; **~s de destruction massive** weapons of mass destruction

armée [aʀme] *nf* army; **~ de l'air** Air Force; **l'~ du Salut** the Salvation Army; **~ de terre** Army

armement [aʀməmɑ̃] *nm (matériel)* arms *pl*, weapons *pl*; (: *d'un pays*) arms *pl*, armament; *(action d'équiper: d'un navire)* fitting out; **~s nucléaires** nuclear armaments; **course aux ~s** arms race

armer [aʀme] *vt* to arm; *(arme à feu)* to cock; *(appareil-photo)* to wind on; **~ qch de** to fit sth with; *(renforcer)* to reinforce sth with; **~ qn de** to arm ou equip sb with; **s'armer de** to arm o.s. with

armistice [aʀmistis] *nm* armistice; **l'A~** = Remembrance *(Brit)* ou Veterans *(US)* Day

armoire [aʀmwaʀ] *nf* (tall) cupboard; *(penderie)* wardrobe *(Brit)*, closet *(US)*; **~ à pharmacie** medicine chest

armoiries [aʀmwaʀi] *nfpl* coat of arms *sg*

armure [aʀmyʀ] *nf* armour *no pl*, suit of armour

armurier [aʀmyʀje] *nm* gunsmith; *(Mil, d'armes blanches)* armourer

arnaque [aʀnak] *nf*: **de l'~** daylight robbery

arnaquer [aʀnake] *vt* to do *(fam)*, swindle; **se faire ~** to be had *(fam)* ou done

arobase [aʀobaz] *nf (Inform)* "at" symbol, @; **"paul ~ société point fr"** "paul at société dot fr"

aromates [aʀɔmat] *nmpl* seasoning *sg*, herbs (and spices)

aromathérapie [aʀɔmateʀapi] *nf* aromatherapy

aromatisé, e [aʀɔmatize] *adj* flavoured

arôme [aʀom] *nm* aroma; *(d'une fleur etc)* fragrance

arpenter [aʀpɑ̃te] *vt* to pace up and down

arpenteur [aʀpɑ̃tœʀ] *nm* land surveyor

arqué, e [aʀke] *adj* arched; *(jambes)* bow *cpd*, bandy

arrache-pied [aʀaʃpje]: **d'~** *adv* relentlessly

arracher [aʀaʃe] *vt* to pull out; *(page etc)* to tear off, tear out; *(déplanter: légume)* to lift; (: *herbe, souche)* to pull up; *(bras etc: par explosion)* to blow off; (: *par accident)* to tear off; **s'arracher** *vt (article très recherché)* to fight over; **~ qch à qn** to snatch sth from sb; *(fig)* to wring sth out of sb, wrest sth from sb; **~ qn à** *(solitude, rêverie)* to drag sb out of; *(famille etc)* to tear ou wrench sb away from; **se faire ~ une dent** to have a tooth out ou pulled *(US)*; **s'~ de** *(lieu)* to tear o.s. away from; *(habitude)* to force o.s. out of

arraisonner [aʀɛzɔne] *vt* to board and search

arrangeant, e [aʀɑ̃ʒɑ̃, -ɑ̃t] *adj* accommodating, obliging

arrangement [aʀɑ̃ʒmɑ̃] *nm* arrangement

arranger [aʀɑ̃ʒe] *vt* to arrange; *(réparer)* to fix, put right; *(régler)* to settle, sort out; *(convenir à)* to suit, be convenient for; **s'arranger** *vi (se mettre d'accord)* to come to an agreement ou arrangement; *(s'améliorer: querelle, situation)* to be sorted out; *(se débrouiller)*: **s'~ pour que ...** to arrange things so that ...; **je vais m'~** I'll manage; **ça va s'~** it'll sort itself out; **s'~ pour faire** to make sure that ou see to it that one can do

arrestation [aʀɛstasjɔ̃] *nf* arrest

arrêt [aʀɛ] *nm* stopping; *(de bus etc)* stop; *(Jur)* judgment, decision; *(Football)* save; **arrêts** *nmpl (Mil)* arrest *sg*; **être à l'~** to be stopped, have come to a halt; **rester** ou **tomber en ~ devant** to stop short in front of; **sans ~** without stopping, non-stop; *(fréquemment)* continually; **~ d'autobus** bus stop; **~ facultatif** request stop; **~ de mort** capital sentence; **~ de travail** stoppage (of work)

arrêté, e [aʀete] *adj (idées)* firm, fixed ▷ *nm* order, decree; **~ municipal** ≈ bylaw, byelaw

arrêter [aʀete] *vt* to stop; *(chauffage etc)* to turn off, switch off; *(Comm: compte)* to settle; *(Couture: point)* to fasten off; *(fixer: date etc)* to appoint, decide on; *(criminel, suspect)* to arrest; **s'arrêter** *vi* to stop; *(s'interrompre)* to stop o.s.; **~ de faire** to stop doing; **arrête de te plaindre** stop complaining; **ne pas ~ de faire** to keep on doing; **s'~ de faire** to stop doing; **s'~ sur** *(choix, regard)* to fall on

arrhes [aʀ] *nfpl* deposit *sg*

arrière [aʀjɛʀ] *nm* back; *(Sport)* fullback ▷ *adj inv*: **siège/roue ~** back ou rear seat/wheel; **arrières** *nmpl (fig)*: **protéger ses ~s** to protect the rear; **à l'~** *adv* behind, at the back; **en ~** *adv* behind; *(regarder)* back, behind; *(tomber, aller)* backwards; **en ~ de** *prép* behind

arriéré, e [aʀjeʀe] *adj (péj)* backward ▷ *nm (d'argent)* arrears *pl*

arrière-goût [aʀjɛʀgu] *nm* aftertaste

arrière-grand-mère *(pl* **-s)** [aʀjɛʀgʀɑ̃mɛʀ] *nf* great-grandmother

arrière-grand-père *(pl* **arrière-grands-pères)** [aʀjɛʀgʀɑ̃pɛʀ] *nm* great-grandfather

arrière-pays [aʀjɛʀpei] *nm inv* hinterland

arrière-pensée [aʀjɛʀpɑ̃se] *nf* ulterior motive; *(doute)* mental reservation

arrière-plan [aʀjɛʀplɑ̃] *nm* background; **d'~** *adj (Inform)* background *cpd*

arrière-saison [aʀjɛʀsɛzɔ̃] *nf* late autumn
arrière-train [aʀjɛʀtʀɛ̃] *nm* hindquarters *pl*
arrimer [aʀime] *vt* to stow; (*fixer*) to secure, fasten securely
arrivage [aʀivaʒ] *nm* arrival
arrivée [aʀive] *nf* arrival; (*ligne d'arrivée*) finish; **~ d'air/de gaz** air/gas inlet; **courrier à l'~** incoming mail; **à mon ~** when I arrived
arriver [aʀive] *vi* to arrive; (*survenir*) to happen, occur; **j'arrive!** (I'm) just coming!; **il arrive à Paris à 8 h** he gets to *ou* arrives in Paris at 8; **~ à destination** to arrive at one's destination; **~ à** (*atteindre*) to reach; **~ à (faire) qch** (*réussir*) to manage (to do) sth; **~ à échéance** to fall due; **en ~ à faire …** to end up doing …, get to the point of doing …; **il arrive que …** it happens that …; **il lui arrive de faire …** he sometimes does …
arriviste [aʀivist(ə)] *nm/f* go-getter
arrogance [aʀɔgɑ̃s] *nf* arrogance
arrogant, e [aʀɔgɑ̃, -ɑ̃t] *adj* arrogant
arrondir [aʀɔ̃diʀ] *vt* (*forme, objet*) to round; (*somme*) to round off; **s'arrondir** *vi* to become round(ed); **~ ses fins de mois** to supplement one's pay
arrondissement [aʀɔ̃dismɑ̃] *nm* (*Admin*) ≈ district
arroser [aʀoze] *vt* to water; (*victoire etc*) to celebrate (over a drink); (*Culin*) to baste
arrosoir [aʀozwaʀ] *nm* watering can
arsenal, -aux [aʀsənal, -o] *nm* (*Navig*) naval dockyard; (*Mil*) arsenal; (*fig*) gear, paraphernalia
art [aʀ] *nm* art; **avoir l'~ de faire** (*fig: personne*) to have a talent for doing; **les ~s** the arts; **livre/critique d'~** art book/ critic; **objet d'~** objet d'art; **~ dramatique** dramatic art; **~s martiaux** martial arts; **~s et métiers** applied arts and crafts; **~s ménagers** home economics *sg*; **~s plastiques** plastic arts
artère [aʀtɛʀ] *nf* (*Anat*) artery; (*rue*) main road
arthrite [aʀtʀit] *nf* arthritis
artichaut [aʀtiʃo] *nm* artichoke
article [aʀtikl(ə)] *nm* article; (*Comm*) item, article; **faire l'~** (*Comm*) to do one's sales spiel; **faire l'~ de** (*fig*) to sing the praises of; **à l'~ de la mort** at the point of death; **~ défini/indéfini** definite/indefinite article; **~ de fond** (*Presse*) feature article; **~s de bureau** office equipment; **~s de voyage** travel goods *ou* items
articulation [aʀtikylasjɔ̃] *nf* articulation; (*Anat*) joint
articuler [aʀtikyle] *vt* to articulate; **s'articuler (sur)** *vi* (*Anat, Tech*) to articulate (with); **s'~ autour de** (*fig*) to centre around *ou* on, turn on
artifice [aʀtifis] *nm* device, trick
artificiel, le [aʀtifisjɛl] *adj* artificial
artisan [aʀtizɑ̃] *nm* artisan, (self-employed) craftsman; **l'~ de la victoire/du malheur** the architect of victory/of the disaster
artisanal, e, -aux [aʀtizanal, -o] *adj* of *ou* made by craftsmen; (*péj*) cottage industry *cpd*, unsophisticated
artisanat [aʀtizana] *nm* arts and crafts *pl*

artiste [aʀtist(ə)] *nm/f* artist; (*Théât, Mus*) artist, performer; (: *de variétés*) entertainer
artistique [aʀtistik] *adj* artistic
as *vb* [a] *voir* **avoir** ▷ *nm* [ɑs] ace
ascendance [asɑ̃dɑ̃s] *nf* (*origine*) ancestry; (*Astrologie*) ascendant
ascendant, e [asɑ̃dɑ̃, -ɑ̃t] *adj* upward ▷ *nm* influence; **ascendants** *nmpl* ascendants
ascenseur [asɑ̃sœʀ] *nm* lift (*Brit*), elevator (*US*)
ascension [asɑ̃sjɔ̃] *nf* ascent; climb; **l'A~** (*Rel*) the Ascension; (: *jour férié*) Ascension (Day); *see note*; **(île de) l'A~** Ascension Island
aseptisé, e [asɛptize] (*péj*) *adj* sanitized
asiatique [azjatik] *adj* Asian, Asiatic ▷ *nm/f*: **A~** Asian
Asie [azi] *nf*: **l'~** Asia
asile [azil] *nm* (*refuge*) refuge, sanctuary; (*Pol*): **droit d'~** (political) asylum; (*pour malades, vieillards etc*) home; **accorder l'~ politique à qn** to grant *ou* give sb political asylum; **chercher/trouver ~ quelque part** to seek/find refuge somewhere
aspect [aspɛ] *nm* appearance, look; (*fig*) aspect, side; (*Ling*) aspect; **à l'~ de** at the sight of
asperge [aspɛʀʒ(ə)] *nf* asparagus *no pl*
asperger [aspɛʀʒe] *vt* to spray, sprinkle
aspérité [asperite] *nf* excrescence, protruding bit (of rock *etc*)
asphalte [asfalt(ə)] *nm* asphalt
asphyxier [asfiksje] *vt* to suffocate, asphyxiate; (*fig*) to stifle; **mourir asphyxié** to die of suffocation *ou* asphyxiation
aspirateur [aspiʀatœʀ] *nm* vacuum cleaner, hoover®
aspirer [aspiʀe] *vt* (*air*) to inhale; (*liquide*) to suck (up); (*appareil*) to suck *ou* draw up; **~ à** *vt* to aspire to
aspirine [aspiʀin] *nf* aspirin
assagir [asaʒiʀ] *vt*: **s'assagir** *vi* to quieten down, sober down
assaillir [asajiʀ] *vt* to assail, attack; **~ qn de** (*questions*) to assail *ou* bombard sb with
assainir [aseniʀ] *vt* to clean up; (*eau, air*) to purify
assaisonnement [asɛzɔnmɑ̃] *nm* seasoning
assaisonner [asɛzɔne] *vt* to season; **bien assaisonné** highly seasoned
assassin [asasɛ̃] *nm* murderer; assassin
assassiner [asasine] *vt* to murder; (*surtout Pol*) to assassinate
assaut [aso] *nm* assault, attack; **prendre d'~** to (take by) storm, assault; **donner l'~ (à)** to attack; **faire ~ de** (*rivaliser*) to vie with *ou* rival each other in
assécher [aseʃe] *vt* to drain
assemblage [asɑ̃blaʒ] *nm* assembling; (*Menuiserie*) joint; **un ~ de** (*fig*) a collection of; **langage d'~** (*Inform*) assembly language
assemblée [asɑ̃ble] *nf* (*réunion*) meeting; (*public, assistance*) gathering; assembled people; (*Pol*) assembly; (*Rel*): **l'~ des fidèles** the congregation; **l'A~ nationale (AN)** the (French)

National Assembly; *see note*

assembler [asɑ̃ble] *vt* (*joindre, monter*) to assemble, put together; (*amasser*) to gather (together), collect (together); **s'assembler** *vi* to gather, collect

assener, asséner [asene] *vt*: ~ **un coup à qn** to deal sb a blow

assentiment [asɑ̃timɑ̃] *nm* assent, consent; (*approbation*) approval

asseoir [aswaʀ] *vt* (*malade, bébé*) to sit up; (*personne debout*) to sit down; (*autorité, réputation*) to establish; **s'asseoir** *vi* to sit (o.s.) up; to sit (o.s.) down; **faire ~ qn** to ask sb to sit down; **asseyez-vous!, assieds-toi!** sit down!; ~ **qch sur** to build sth on; (*appuyer*) to base sth on

assermenté, e [asɛʀmɑ̃te] *adj* sworn, on oath

asservir [asɛʀviʀ] *vt* to subjugate, enslave

assez [ase] *adv* (*suffisamment*) enough, sufficiently; (*passablement*) rather, quite, fairly; **~!** enough!, that'll do!; **~/pas ~ cuit** well enough done/underdone; **est-il ~ fort/rapide?** is he strong/fast enough?; **il est passé ~ vite** he went past rather *ou* quite *ou* fairly fast; **~ de pain/ livres** enough *ou* sufficient bread/books; **vous en avez ~?** have you got enough?; **en avoir ~ de qch** (*en être fatigué*) to have had enough of sth; **travailler ~** to work (hard) enough

assidu, e [asidy] *adj* assiduous, painstaking; (*régulier*) regular; ~ **auprès de qn** attentive towards sb

assied *etc* [asje] *vb voir* **asseoir**

assiéger [asjeʒe] *vt* to besiege, lay siege to; (*foule, touristes*) to mob, besiege

assiérai *etc* [asjeʀe] *vb voir* **asseoir**

assiette [asjɛt] *nf* plate; (*contenu*) plate(ful); (*équilibre*) seat; (*de colonne*) seating; (*de navire*) trim; ~ **anglaise** assorted cold meats; ~ **creuse** (soup) dish, soup plate; ~ **à dessert** dessert *ou* side plate; ~ **de l'impôt** basis of (tax) assessment; ~ **plate** (dinner) plate

assigner [asiɲe] *vt*: ~ **qch à** to assign *ou* allot sth to; (*valeur, importance*) to attach sth to; (*somme*) to allocate sth to; (*limites*) to set *ou* fix sth to; (*cause, effet*) to ascribe *ou* attribute sth to; ~ **qn à** (*affecter*) to assign sb to; ~ **qn à résidence** (*Jur*) to give sb a compulsory order of residence

assimiler [asimile] *vt* to assimilate, absorb; (*comparer*): ~ **qch/qn à** to liken *ou* compare sth/sb to; **s'assimiler** *vi* (*s'intégrer*) to be assimilated *ou* absorbed; **ils sont assimilés aux infirmières** (*Admin*) they are classed as nurses

assis, e [asi, -iz] *pp de* **asseoir** ▷ *adj* sitting (down), seated ▷ *nf* (*Constr*) course; (*Géo*) stratum (*pl* -a); (*fig*) basis (*pl* bases), foundation; ~ **en tailleur** sitting cross-legged

assises [asiz] *nfpl* (*Jur*) assizes; (*congrès*) (annual) conference

assistance [asistɑ̃s] *nf* (*public*) audience; (*aide*) assistance; **porter** *ou* **prêter ~ à qn** to give sb assistance; **A~ publique** (AP) *public health service*; **enfant de l'A~ (publique)** child in care; ~ **technique** technical aid

assistant, e [asistɑ̃, -ɑ̃t] *nm/f* assistant; (*d'université*) probationary lecturer; **les assistants** *nmpl* (*auditeurs etc*) those present; **~e sociale** social worker

assisté, e [asiste] *adj* (*Auto*) power assisted ▷ *nm/f* person receiving aid from the State

assister [asiste] *vt* to assist; ~ **à** *vt* (*scène, événement*) to witness; (*conférence*) to attend, be (present) at; (*spectacle, match*) to be at, see

association [asɔsjɑsjɔ̃] *nf* association; (*Comm*) partnership; ~ **d'idées/images** association of ideas/images

associé, e [asɔsje] *nm/f* associate; (*Comm*) partner

associer [asɔsje] *vt* to associate; ~ **qn à** (*profits*) to give sb a share of; (*affaire*) to make sb a partner in; (*joie, triomphe*) to include sb in; ~ **qch à** (*joindre, allier*) to combine sth with; **s'associer** *vi* to join together; (*Comm*) to form a partnership ▷ *vt* (*collaborateur*) to take on (as a partner); **s'~ à** to be combined with; (*opinions, joie de qn*) to share in; **s'~ à** *ou* **avec qn pour faire** to join (forces) *ou* join together with sb to do

assoiffé, e [aswafe] *adj* thirsty; (*fig*): ~ **de** (*sang*) thirsting for; (*gloire*) thirsting after

assombrir [asɔ̃bʀiʀ] *vt* to darken; (*fig*) to fill with gloom; **s'assombrir** *vi* to darken; (*devenir nuageux, fig: visage*) to cloud over; (*fig*) to become gloomy

assommer [asɔme] *vt* (*étourdir, abrutir*) to knock out, stun; (*fam: ennuyer*) to bore stiff

Assomption [asɔ̃psjɔ̃] *nf*: **l'~** the Assumption; *see note*

assorti, e [asɔʀti] *adj* matched, matching; **fromages/légumes ~s** assorted cheeses/ vegetables; ~ **à** matching; ~ **de** accompanied with; (*conditions, conseils*) coupled with; **bien/ mal ~** well/ill-matched

assortiment [asɔʀtimɑ̃] *nm* (*choix*) assortment, selection; (*harmonie de couleurs, formes*) arrangement; (*Comm: lot, stock*) selection

assortir [asɔʀtiʀ] *vt* to match; **s'assortir** *vi* to go well together, match; ~ **qch à** to match sth with; ~ **qch de** to accompany sth with; **s'~ de** to be accompanied by

assoupi, e [asupi] *adj* dozing, sleeping; (*fig*) (be)numbed; (*sens*) dulled

assoupir [asupiʀ]: **s'assoupir** *vi* (*personne*) to doze off; (*sens*) to go numb

assouplir [asupliʀ] *vt* to make supple, soften; (*membres, corps*) to limber up, make supple; (*fig*) to relax; (: *caractère*) to soften, make more flexible; **s'assouplir** *vi* to soften; to limber up; to relax; to become more flexible

assouplissant [asuplisɑ̃] *nm* (*fabric*) softener

assourdir [asuʀdiʀ] *vt* (*bruit*) to deaden, muffle; (*bruit*) to deafen

assouvir [asuviʀ] *vt* to satisfy, appease

assujettir [asyʒetiʀ] *vt* to subject, subjugate; (*fixer: planches, tableau*) to fix securely; ~ **qn à** (*règle, impôt*) to subject sb to

assumer [asyme] *vt* (*fonction, emploi*) to assume,

take on; (*accepter: conséquence, situation*) to accept

assurance [asyʀɑ̃s] *nf* (*certitude*) assurance; (*confiance en soi*) (self-)confidence; (*contrat*) insurance (policy); (*secteur commercial*) insurance; **prendre une ~ contre** to take out insurance *ou* an insurance policy against; **~ contre l'incendie** fire insurance; **~ contre le vol** insurance against theft; **société d'~**, **compagnie d'~s** insurance company; **~ maladie (AM)** health insurance; **~ au tiers** third party insurance; **~ tous risques** (*Auto*) comprehensive insurance; **~s sociales (AS)** ≈ National Insurance (Brit), ≈ Social Security (US)

assurance-vie (*pl* **assurances-vie**) [asyʀɑ̃svi] *nf* life assurance *ou* insurance

assuré, e [asyʀe] *adj* (*victoire etc*) certain, sure; (*démarche, voix*) assured, (self-)confident; (*certain*): **~ de** confident of; (*Assurances*) insured ▷ *nm/f* insured (person); **~ social** = member of the National Insurance (Brit) *ou* Social Security (US) scheme

assurément [asyʀemɑ̃] *adv* assuredly, most certainly

assurer [asyʀe] *vt* (*Comm*) to insure; (*stabiliser*) to steady, stabilize; (*victoire etc*) to ensure, make certain; (*frontières, pouvoir*) to make secure; (*service, garde*) to provide, operate; **~ qch à qn** (*garantir*) to secure *ou* guarantee sth for sb; (*certifier*) to assure sb of sth; **~ à qn que** to assure sb that; **je vous assure que non/si** I assure you that that is not the case/is the case; **~ qn de** to assure sb of; **~ ses arrières** (*fig*) to be sure one has something to fall back on; **s'assurer (contre)** *vi* (*Comm*) to insure o.s. (against); **s'~ de/que** (*vérifier*) to make sure of/that; **s'~ (de)** (*aide de qn*) to secure; **s'~ sur la vie** to take out life insurance; **s'~ le concours/la collaboration de qn** to secure sb's aid/collaboration

assureur [asyʀœʀ] *nm* insurance agent; (*société*) insurers *pl*

asthmatique [asmatik] *adj* asthmatic

asthme [asm(ə)] *nm* asthma

asticot [astiko] *nm* maggot

astiquer [astike] *vt* to polish, shine

astre [astʀ(ə)] *nm* star

astreignant, e [astʀɛɲɑ̃, -ɑ̃t] *adj* demanding

astreindre [astʀɛ̃dʀ(ə)] *vt*: **~ qn à qch** to force sth upon sb; **~ qn à faire** to compel *ou* force sb to do; **s'~ à** to compel *ou* force o.s. to

astrologie [astʀɔlɔʒi] *nf* astrology

astronaute [astʀonot] *nm/f* astronaut

astronomie [astʀonɔmi] *nf* astronomy

astuce [astys] *nf* shrewdness, astuteness; (*truc*) trick, clever way; (*plaisanterie*) wisecrack

astucieux, -euse [astysjø, -øz] *adj* shrewd, clever, astute

atelier [atəlje] *nm* workshop; (*de peintre*) studio

athée [ate] *adj* atheistic ▷ *nm/f* atheist

Athènes [atɛn] *n* Athens

athlète [atlɛt] *nm/f* (*Sport*) athlete; (*costaud*) muscleman

athlétisme [atletism(ə)] *nm* athletics *sg*; **faire**

de l'~ to do athletics; **tournoi d'~** athletics meeting

atlantique [atlɑ̃tik] *adj* Atlantic ▷ *nm*: **l'(océan) A~** the Atlantic (Ocean)

atlas [atlɑs] *nm* atlas

atmosphère [atmɔsfɛʀ] *nf* atmosphere

atome [atom] *nm* atom

atomique [atɔmik] *adj* atomic, nuclear; (*usine*) nuclear; (*nombre, masse*) atomic

atomiseur [atɔmizœʀ] *nm* atomizer

atout [atu] *nm* trump; (*fig*) asset; (*: plus fort*) trump card; **"~ pique/trèfle"** "spades/clubs are trumps"

âtre [ɑtʀ(ə)] *nm* hearth

atroce [atʀɔs] *adj* atrocious, horrible

attabler [atable]: **s'attabler** *vi* to sit down at (the) table; **s'~ à la terrasse** to sit down (at a table) on the terrace

attachant, e [ataʃɑ̃, -ɑ̃t] *adj* engaging, likeable

attache [ataʃ] *nf* clip, fastener; (*fig*) tie; **attaches** *nfpl* (*relations*) connections; **à l'~** (*chien*) tied up

attacher [ataʃe] *vt* to tie up; (*étiquette*) to attach, tie on; (*souliers*) to do up ▷ *vi* (*poêle, riz*) to stick; **s'attacher** *vi* (*robe etc*) to do up; **s'~ à** (*par affection*) to become attached to; **s'~ à faire qch** to endeavour to do sth; **~ qch à** to tie *ou* fasten *ou* attach sth to; **~ qn à** (*fig: lier*) to attach sb to; **~ du prix/de l'importance à** to attach great value/attach importance to

attaque [atak] *nf* attack; (*cérébrale*) stroke; (*d'épilepsie*) fit; **être/se sentir d'~** to be/feel on form; **~ à main armée** armed attack

attaquer [atake] *vt* to attack; (*en justice*) to bring an action against, sue; (*travail*) to tackle, set about ▷ *vi* to attack; **s'attaquer à** *vt* to attack; (*épidémie, misère*) to tackle, attack

attardé, e [ataʀde] *adj* (*passants*) late; (*enfant*) backward; (*conceptions*) old-fashioned

attarder [ataʀde]: **s'attarder** *vi* (*sur qch, en chemin*) to linger; (*chez qn*) to stay on

atteindre [atɛ̃dʀ(ə)] *vt* to reach; (*blesser*) to hit; (*contacter*) to reach, contact, get in touch with; (*émouvoir*) to affect

atteint, e [atɛ̃, -ɛ̃t] *pp de* **atteindre** ▷ *adj* (*Méd*): **être ~ de** to be suffering from ▷ *nf* attack; **hors d'~e** out of reach; **porter ~e à** to strike a blow at, undermine

atteler [atle] *vt* (*cheval, bœufs*) to hitch up; (*wagons*) to couple; **s'atteler à** (*travail*) to buckle down to

attelle [atɛl] *nf* splint

attenant, e [atnɑ̃, -ɑ̃t] *adj*: **~ (à)** adjoining

attendant [atɑ̃dɑ̃]: **en ~** *adv* (*dans l'intervalle*) meanwhile, in the meantime

attendre [atɑ̃dʀ(ə)] *vt* to wait for; (*être destiné ou réservé à*) to await, be in store for ▷ *vi* to wait; **je n'attends plus rien (de la vie)** I expect nothing more (from life); **attendez que je réfléchisse** wait while I think; **s'~ à (ce que)** (*escompter*) to expect (that); **je ne m'y attendais pas** I didn't expect that; **ce n'est pas ce à quoi je m'attendais** that's not what I expected; **~ un**

enfant to be expecting a baby; **~ de pied ferme** to wait determinedly; **~ de faire/d'être** to wait until one does/is; **~ que** to wait until; **~ qch de** to expect sth of; **faire ~ qn** to keep sb waiting; **se faire ~** to keep oneself (*ou us etc*) waiting; **en attendant** *adv voir* **attendant**

attendrir [atɑ̃dʀiʀ] *vt* to move (to pity); (*viande*) to tenderize; **s'~ (sur)** to be moved *ou* touched (by)

attendrissant, e [atɑ̃dʀisɑ̃, -ɑ̃t] *adj* moving, touching

attendu, e [atɑ̃dy] *pp de* **attendre** ▷ *adj* long-awaited; (*prévu*) expected ▷ *nm*: **~s** reasons adduced for a judgment; **~ que** *conj* considering that, since

attentat [atɑ̃ta] *nm* (*contre une personne*) assassination attempt; (*contre un bâtiment*) attack; **~ à la bombe** bomb attack; **~ à la pudeur** (*exhibitionnisme*) indecent exposure *no pl*; (*agression*) indecent assault *no pl*; **~ suicide** suicide bombing

attente [atɑ̃t] *nf* wait; (*espérance*) expectation; **contre toute ~** contrary to (all) expectations

attenter [atɑ̃te]: **~ à** *vt* (*liberté*) to violate; **~ à la vie de qn** to make an attempt on sb's life; **~ à ses jours** to make an attempt on one's life

attentif, -ive [atɑ̃tif, -iv] *adj* (*auditeur*) attentive; (*soin*) scrupulous; (*travail*) careful; **~ à** paying attention to; (*devoir*) mindful of; **~ à faire** careful to do

attention [atɑ̃sjɔ̃] *nf* attention; (*prévenance*) attention, thoughtfulness *no pl*; **mériter ~** to be worthy of attention; **porter qch à l'~ de qn** to bring sth to sb's attention; **attirer l'~ de qn sur qch** to draw sb's attention to sth; **faire ~ (à)** to be careful (of); **faire ~ (à ce) que** to be *ou* make sure that; **~! careful!, watch!, watch *ou* mind (Brit) out!; ~, si vous ouvrez cette lettre** (*sanction*) just watch out, if you open that letter; **~, respectez les consignes de sécurité** be sure to observe the safety instructions

attentionné, e [atɑ̃sjɔne] *adj* thoughtful, considerate

atténuer [atenɥe] *vt* to alleviate, ease; (*diminuer*) to lessen; (*amoindrir*) to mitigate the effects of; **s'atténuer** *vi* to ease; (*violence etc*) to abate

atterrer [atere] *vt* to dismay, appal

atterrir [aterir] *vi* to land

atterrissage [aterisaʒ] *nm* landing; **~ sur le ventre/sans visibilité/forcé** belly/blind/forced landing

attestation [atɛstasjɔ̃] *nf* certificate, testimonial; **~ médicale** doctor's certificate

attester [atɛste] *vt* to testify to, vouch for; (*démontrer*) to attest, testify to; **~ que** to testify that

attirail [atiʀaj] *nm* gear; (*péj*) paraphernalia

attirant, e [atiʀɑ̃, -ɑ̃t] *adj* attractive, appealing

attirer [atiʀe] *vt* to attract; (*appâter*) to lure, entice; **~ qn dans un coin/vers soi** to draw sb into a corner/towards one; **~ l'attention de qn** to attract sb's attention; **~ l'attention**

de qn sur qch to draw sb's attention to sth; **~ des ennuis à qn** to make trouble for sb; **s'~ des ennuis** to bring trouble upon o.s., get into trouble

attiser [atize] *vt* (*feu*) to poke (up), stir up; (*fig*) to fan the flame of, stir up

attitré, e [atitʀe] *adj* qualified; (*agréé*) accredited, appointed

attitude [atityd] *nf* attitude; (*position du corps*) bearing

attouchements [atuʃmɑ̃] *nmpl* touching *sg*; (*sexuels*) fondling *sg*, stroking *sg*

attraction [atʀaksjɔ̃] *nf* attraction; (*de cabaret, cirque*) number

attrait [atʀɛ] *nm* appeal, attraction; (*plus fort*) lure; **attraits** *nmpl* attractions; **éprouver de l'~ pour** to be attracted to

attrape-nigaud [atʀapnigo] *nm* con

attraper [atʀape] *vt* to catch; (*habitude, amende*) to get, pick up; (*fam: duper*) to take in (Brit), con

attrayant, e [atʀɛjɑ̃, -ɑ̃t] *adj* attractive

attribuer [atʀibɥe] *vt* (*prix*) to award; (*rôle, tâche*) to allocate, assign; (*imputer*): **~ qch à** to attribute sth to, ascribe sth to, put sth down to; **s'attribuer** *vt* (*s'approprier*) to claim for o.s.

attribut [atʀiby] *nm* attribute; (*Ling*) complement

attrister [atʀiste] *vt* to sadden; **s'~ de qch** to be saddened by sth

attroupement [atʀupmɑ̃] *nm* crowd, mob

attrouper [atʀupe]: **s'attrouper** *vi* to gather

au [o] *prép voir* **à**

aubaine [obɛn] *nf* godsend; (*financière*) windfall; (*Comm*) bonanza

aube [ob] *nf* dawn, daybreak; (*Rel*) alb; **à l'~** at dawn *ou* daybreak; **à l'~ de** (*fig*) at the dawn of

aubépine [obepin] *nf* hawthorn

auberge [obɛʀʒ(ə)] *nf* inn; **~ de jeunesse** youth hostel

aubergine [obɛʀʒin] *nf* aubergine (*Brit*), eggplant (*US*)

aubergiste [obɛʀʒist(ə)] *nm/f* inn-keeper, hotel-keeper

aucun, e [okœ̃, -yn] *adj, pron* no; (*positif*) any ▷ *pron* none; (*positif*) any(one); **il n'y a ~ livre** there isn't any book, there is no book; **je n'en vois ~ qui** ... I can't see any which ..., I (can) see none which ...; **~ homme** no man; **sans ~ doute** without any doubt; **sans ~e hésitation** without hesitation; **plus qu'~ autre** more than any other; **plus qu'~ de ceux qui** ... more than any of those who ...; **en ~e façon** in no way at all; **~ des deux** neither of the two; **~ d'entre eux** none of them; **d'~s** (*certains*) some

aucunement [okynmɑ̃] *adv* in no way, not in the least

audace [odas] *nf* daring, boldness; (*péj*) audacity; **il a eu l'~ de** ... he had the audacity to ...; **vous ne manquez pas d'~!** you're not lacking in nerve *ou* cheek!

audacieux, -euse [odasjø, -øz] *adj* daring, bold

au-delà [odla] *adv* beyond ▷ *nm*: **l'~** the

hereafter; ~ **de** *prép* beyond

au-dessous [odsu] *adv* underneath; below; ~ **de** *prép* under(neath), below; *(limite, somme etc)* below, under; *(dignité, condition)* below

au-dessus [odsy] *adv* above; ~ **de** *prép* above

au-devant [odvã]: ~ **de** *prép*: **aller** ~ **de** to go (out) and meet; *(souhaits de qn)* to anticipate

audience [odjãs] *nf* audience; *(Jur: séance)* hearing; **trouver** ~ **auprès de** to arouse much interest among, get the (interested) attention of

audimat® [odimat] *nm* *(taux d'écoute)* ratings *pl*

audio-visuel, le [odjovizɥɛl] *adj* audio-visual ▷ *nm* *(équipement)* audio-visual aids *pl*; *(méthodes)* audio-visual methods *pl*; **l'**~ radio and television

auditeur, -trice [oditœʀ, -tʀis] *nm/f* *(à la radio)* listener; *(à une conférence)* member of the audience, listener; ~ **libre** unregistered student *(attending lectures)*, auditor (US)

audition [odisjõ] *nf* *(ouïe, écoute)* hearing; *(Jur: de témoins)* examination; *(Mus, Théât: épreuve)* audition

auditoire [oditwaʀ] *nm* audience

auge [oʒ] *nf* trough

augmentation [ogmãtasjõ] *nf* *(action)* increasing; raising; *(résultat)* increase; ~ **(de salaire)** rise (in salary) *(Brit)*, (pay) raise (US)

augmenter [ogmãte] *vt* to increase; *(salaire, prix)* to increase, raise, put up; *(employé)* to increase the salary of, give a (salary) rise *(Brit)* *ou* (pay) raise (US) to ▷ *vi* to increase; ~ **de poids/volume** to gain (in) weight/volume

augure [ogyʀ] *nm* soothsayer, oracle; **de bon/mauvais** ~ of good/ill omen

augurer [ogyʀe] *vt*: ~ **qch de** to foresee sth (coming) from *ou* out of; ~ **bien de** to augur well for

aujourd'hui [oʒuʀdɥi] *adv* today; **aujourd'hui en huit/quinze** a week/two weeks today, a week/two weeks from now; **à dater** *ou* **partir d'aujourd'hui** from today('s date)

aumône [omon] *nf* alms *sg* *(pl inv)*; **faire l'**~ **(à qn)** to give alms (to sb); **faire l'**~ **de qch à qn** *(fig)* to favour sb with sth

aumônier [omonje] *nm* chaplain

auparavant [opaʀavã] *adv* before(hand)

auprès [opʀɛ]: ~ **de** *prép* next to, close to; *(recourir, s'adresser)* to; *(en comparaison de)* compared with, next to; *(dans l'opinion de)* in the opinion of

auquel [okɛl] *pron* *voir* **lequel**

aura *etc* [oʀa] *vb voir* **avoir**

aurai *etc* [oʀe] *vb voir* **avoir**

auréole [oʀeɔl] *nf* halo; *(tache)* ring

aurons *etc* [oʀõ] *vb voir* **avoir**

aurore [`ʀ] *nf* dawn, daybreak; ~ **boréale** northern lights *pl*

ausculter [oskylte] *vt* to sound

aussi [osi] *adv* *(également)* also, too; *(de comparaison)* as ▷ *conj* therefore, consequently; ~ **fort que** as strong as; **lui** ~ *(sujet)* he too; *(objet)* him too; ~ **bien que** *(de même que)* as well as

aussitôt [osito] *adv* straight away, immediately; ~ **que** as soon as; ~ **envoyé** as soon as it is *(ou* was) sent; ~ **fait** no sooner done

austère [ostɛʀ] *adj* austere; *(sévère)* stern

austral, e [ostʀal] *adj* southern; **l'océan A-** the Antarctic Ocean; **les Terres A-es** Antarctica

Australie [ostʀali] *nf*: **l'**~ Australia

australien, ne [ostʀaljɛ̃, -ɛn] *adj* Australian ▷ *nm/f*: **A-, ne** Australian

autant [otã] *adv* so much; *(comparatif)*: ~ **(que)** as much (as); *(nombre)* as many (as); ~ **de** so much *(ou* many); as many *(ou* many); **n'importe qui aurait pu en faire** ~ anyone could have done the same *ou* as much; ~ **partir** we *(ou* you *etc)* may as well leave; ~ **ne rien dire** best not say anything; ~ **dire que ...** one might as well say that ...; **fort** ~ **que courageux** as strong as he is brave; **il n'est pas découragé pour** ~ he isn't discouraged for all that; **pour** ~ **que** *conj* assuming, as long as; **d'**~ *adv* accordingly, in proportion; **d'**~ **plus/mieux (que)** all the more/the better (since)

autel [otɛl] *nm* altar

auteur [otœʀ] *nm* author; **l'**~ **de cette remarque** the person who said that; **droit d'**~ copyright

authenticité [otãtisite] *nf* authenticity

authentique [otãtik] *adj* authentic, genuine

auto [oto] *nf* car; ~**s tamponneuses** bumper cars, dodgems

autobiographie [otobjɔgʀafi] *nf* autobiography

autobronzant [otobʀõzã] *nm* self-tanning cream *(or* lotion *etc)*

autobus [otobys] *nm* bus

autocar [otokaʀ] *nm* coach

autochtone [otɔktɔn] *nm/f* native

autocollant, e [otokɔlã, -ãt] *adj* self-adhesive; *(enveloppe)* self-seal ▷ *nm* sticker

auto-couchettes [otokuʃɛt] *adj inv*: **train** ~ car sleeper train, motorail® train *(Brit)*

autocuiseur [otokwizœʀ] *nm* *(Culin)* pressure cooker

autodéfense [otodefãs] *nf* self-defence; **groupe d'**~ vigilante committee

autodidacte [otodidakt(ə)] *nm/f* self-taught person

auto-école [otoekɔl] *nf* driving school

autographe [otogʀaf] *nm* autograph

automate [otomat] *nm* *(robot)* automaton; *(machine)* (automatic) machine

automatique [otomatik] *adj, nm* automatic; **l'**~ *(Tél)* ≈ direct dialling

automatiquement [otomatikmã] *adv* automatically

automatiser [otomatize] *vt* to automate

automne [otɔn] *nm* autumn *(Brit)*, fall (US)

automobile [otomɔbil] *adj* motor *cpd* ▷ *nf* (motor) car; **l'**~ motoring; *(industrie)* the car *ou* automobile (US) industry

automobiliste [otomɔbilist(ə)] *nm/f* motorist

autonome [otonɔm] *adj* autonomous

autonomie [otonɔmi] *nf* autonomy; *(Pol)* self-government, autonomy; ~ **de vol** range

autopsie [otopsi] *nf* post-mortem

(examination), autopsy

autoradio [ɔtɔradjo] *nf* car radio

autorisation [ɔtɔrizasjɔ̃] *nf* permission, authorization; (*papiers*) permit; **donner à qn l'~ de** to give sb permission to, authorize sb to; **avoir l'~ de faire** to be allowed *ou* have permission to do, be authorized to do

autorisé, e [ɔtɔrize] *adj* (*opinion, sources*) authoritative; (*permis*): **~ à faire** authorized *ou* permitted to do; **dans les milieux ~s** in official circles

autoriser [ɔtɔrize] *vt* to give permission for, authorize; (*fig*) to allow (of), sanction; **~ qn à faire** to give permission to sb to do, authorize sb to do

autoritaire [ɔtɔritɛr] *adj* authoritarian

autorité [ɔtɔrite] *nf* authority; **faire ~** to be authoritative; **~s constituées** constitutional authorities

autoroute [ɔtɔrut] *nf* motorway (*Brit*), expressway (*US*); **~ de l'information** (*Tél*) information highway

auto-stop [ɔtɔstɔp] *nm*: **l'~** hitch-hiking; **faire de l'~** to hitch-hike; **prendre qn en ~** to give sb a lift

auto-stoppeur, -euse [ɔtɔstɔpœr, -øz] *nm/f* hitch-hiker, hitcher (*Brit*)

autour [otur] *adv* around; **~ de** *prép* around; (*environ*) around, about; **tout ~** *adv* all around

autre [otr(ə)] *adj* **1** (*différent*) other, different; **je préférerais un ~ verre** I'd prefer another *ou* a different glass; **d'~s verres** different glasses; **se sentir ~** to feel different; **la difficulté est ~** the difficulty is *ou* lies elsewhere

2 (*supplémentaire*) other; **je voudrais un ~ verre d'eau** I'd like another glass of water

3: **~ chose** something else; **~ part** somewhere else; **d'~ part** on the other hand

▷ *pron* **1**: **un ~** another (one); **nous/vous ~s** us/ you; **d'~s** others; **l'~** the other (one); **les ~s** the others; (*autrui*) others; **l'un et l'~** both of them; **ni l'un ni l'~** neither of them; **se détester l'un/les uns les ~s** to hate each other *ou* one another; **d'une semaine/minute à l'~** from one week/minute *ou* moment to the next; (*incessamment*) any week/minute *ou* moment now; **de temps à ~** from time to time; **entre ~s** among other things

2 (*expressions*): **j'en ai vu d'~s** I've seen worse; **à d'~s!** pull the other one!

autrefois [otrəfwa] *adv* in the past

autrement [otrəmã] *adv* differently; (*d'une manière différente*) in another way; (*sinon*) otherwise; **je n'ai pas pu faire ~** I couldn't do anything else, I couldn't do otherwise; **~ dit** in other words; (*c'est-à-dire*) that is to say

Autriche [otriʃ] *nf*: **l'~** Austria

autrichien, ne [otriʃjɛ̃, -ɛn] *adj* Austrian ▷ *nm/f*: **A~, ne** Austrian

autruche [otryʃ] *nf* ostrich; **faire l'~** (*fig*) to bury one's head in the sand

autrui [otrɥi] *pron* others

auvent [ovã] *nm* canopy

aux [o] *prép voir* **à**

auxiliaire [ɔksiljɛr] *adj, nm/f* auxiliary

auxquels, auxquelles [okɛl] *pron voir* **lequel**

avachi, e [avaʃi] *adj* limp, flabby; (*chaussure, vêtement*) out-of-shape; (*personne*): **~ sur qch** slumped on *ou* across sth

aval [aval] *nm* (*accord*) endorsement, backing; (*Géo*): **en ~** downstream, downriver; (*sur une pente*) downhill; **en ~ de** downstream *ou* downriver from; downhill from

avalanche [avalɑ̃ʃ] *nf* avalanche; **~ poudreuse** powder snow avalanche

avaler [avale] *vt* to swallow

avance [avɑ̃s] *nf* (*de troupes etc*) advance; (*progrès*) progress; (*d'argent*) advance; (*opposé à retard*) lead; being ahead of schedule; **avances** *nfpl* overtures; (*amoureuses*) advances; **une ~ de 300 m/4 h** (*Sport*) a 300 m/4 hour lead; (**être**) **en ~** (to be) early; (*sur un programme*) (to be) ahead of schedule; **on n'est pas en ~!** we're kind of late!; **être en ~ sur qn** to be ahead of sb; **d'~, à l'~, par ~** in advance; **~ (du) papier** (*Inform*) paper advance

avancé, e [avɑ̃se] *adj* advanced; (*travail etc*) well on, well under way; (*fruit, fromage*) overripe ▷ *nf* projection; overhang; **il est ~ pour son âge** he is advanced for his age

avancement [avɑ̃smɑ̃] *nm* (*professionnel*) promotion; (*de travaux*) progress

avancer [avɑ̃se] *vi* to move forward, advance; (*projet, travail*) to make progress; (*être en saillie*) to overhang; to project; (*montre, réveil*) to be fast; (: *d'habitude*) to gain ▷ *vt* to move forward, advance; (*argent*) to advance; (*montre, pendule*) to put forward; (*faire progresser: travail etc*) to advance, move on; **s'avancer** *vi* to move forward, advance; (*fig*) to commit o.s.; (*faire saillie*) to overhang; to project; **j'avance (d'une heure)** I'm (an hour) fast

avant [avɑ̃] *prép* before ▷ *adv*: **trop/plus ~** too far/further forward ▷ *adj inv*: **siège/roue ~** front seat/wheel ▷ *nm* front; (*Sport: joueur*) forward; **~ qu'il parte/de partir** before he leaves/leaving; **~ qu'il (ne) pleuve** before it rains (*ou* rained); **~ tout** (*surtout*) above all; **à l'~** (*dans un véhicule*) in (the) front; **en ~** *adv* forward(s); **en ~ de** *prép* in front of; **aller de l'~** to steam ahead (*fig*), make good progress

avantage [avɑ̃taʒ] *nm* advantage; (*Tennis*): **~ service/dehors** advantage *ou* van (*Brit*) *ou* ad (*US*) in/out; **tirer ~ de** to take advantage of; **vous auriez ~ à faire** you would be well-advised to do, it would be to your advantage to do; **à l'~ de qn** to sb's advantage; **être à son ~** to be at one's best; **~s en nature** benefits in kind; **~s sociaux** fringe benefits

avantager [avɑ̃taʒe] *vt* (*favoriser*) to favour; (*embellir*) to flatter

avantageux, -euse [avɑ̃taʒø, -øz] *adj* attractive; (*intéressant*) attractively priced; (*portrait, coiffure*) flattering; **conditions avantageuses**

favourable terms

avant-bras [avɑ̃bʀa] *nm inv* forearm

avant-coureur [avɑ̃kuʀœʀ] *adj inv* (*bruit etc*) precursory; **signe** ~ advance indication *ou* sign

avant-dernier, -ière [avɑ̃dɛʀnje, -jɛʀ] *adj, nm/f* next to last, last but one

avant-goût [avɑ̃gu] *nm* foretaste

avant-hier [avɑ̃tjɛʀ] *adv* the day before yesterday

avant-première [avɑ̃pʀəmjɛʀ] *nf* (*de film*) preview; **en** ~ as a preview, in a preview showing

avant-projet [avɑ̃pʀɔʒɛ] *nm* preliminary draft

avant-propos [avɑ̃pʀɔpo] *nm* foreword

avant-veille [avɑ̃vɛj] *nf*: **l'**~ two days before

avare [avaʀ] *adj* miserly, avaricious ▷ *nm/f* miser; ~ **de compliments** stingy *ou* sparing with one's compliments

avarié, e [avaʀje] *adj* (*viande, fruits*) rotting, going off (*Brit*); (*Navig: navire*) damaged

avaries [avaʀi] *nfpl* (*Navig*) damage *sg*

avec [avɛk] *prép* with; (*à l'égard de*) to(wards), with ▷ *adv* (*fam*) with it (*ou* him *etc*); ~ **habileté/ lenteur** skilfully/slowly; ~ **eux/ces maladies** with them/these diseases; ~ **ça** (*malgré ça*) for all that; **et** ~ **ça?** (*dans un magasin*) anything *ou* something else?

avenant, e [avnɑ̃, -ɑ̃t] *adj* pleasant ▷ *nm* (*Assurances*) additional clause; **à l'**~ *adv* in keeping

avènement [avɛnmɑ̃] *nm* (*d'un roi*) accession, succession; (*d'un changement*) advent; (*d'une politique, idée*) coming

avenir [avniʀ] *nm*: **l'**~ the future; **à l'**~ in future; **sans** ~ with no future, without a future; **carrière/politicien d'**~ career/politician with prospects *ou* a future

aventure [avɑ̃tyʀ] *nf*: **l'**~ adventure; **une** ~ an adventure; (*amoureuse*) an affair; **partir à l'**~ to go off in search of adventure; (*au hasard*) to go where one's fancy takes one; **roman/film d'**~ adventure story/film

aventurer [avɑ̃tyʀe] *vt* (*somme, réputation, vie*) to stake; (*remarque, opinion*) to venture; **s'aventurer** *vi* to venture; **s'**~ **à faire qch** to venture into sth

aventureux, -euse [avɑ̃tyʀø, -øz] *adj* adventurous, venturesome; (*projet*) risky, chancy

avenue [avny] *nf* avenue

avérer [aveʀe]: **s'avérer** *vr*: **s'**~ **faux/coûteux** to prove (to be) wrong/expensive

averse [avɛʀs(ə)] *nf* shower

averti, e [avɛʀti] *adj* (well-)informed

avertir [avɛʀtiʀ] *vt*: ~ **qn (de qch/que)** to warn sb (of sth/that); (*renseigner*) to inform sb (of sth/ that); ~ **qn de ne pas faire qch** to warn sb not to do sth

avertissement [avɛʀtismɑ̃] *nm* warning

avertisseur [avɛʀtisœʀ] *nm* horn, siren; ~ **(d'incendie)** (fire) alarm

aveu, x [avø] *nm* confession; **passer aux** ~**x** to make a confession; **de l'**~ **de** according to

aveugle [avœgl(ə)] *adj* blind ▷ *nm/f* blind

person; **les** ~**s** the blind; **test en (double)** ~ (double) blind test

aveuglément [avœglemɑ̃] *adv* blindly

aveugler [avœgle] *vt* to blind

aviateur, -trice [avjatœʀ, -tʀis] *nm/f* aviator, pilot

aviation [avjasjɔ̃] *nf* (*secteur commercial*) aviation; (*sport, métier de pilote*) flying; (*Mil*) air force; **terrain d'**~ airfield; ~ **de chasse** fighter force

avide [avid] *adj* eager; (*péj*) greedy, grasping; ~ **de** (*sang etc*) thirsting for; ~ **d'honneurs/d'argent** greedy for honours/money; ~ **de connaître/ d'apprendre** eager to know/learn

avilir [aviliʀ] *vt* to debase

avion [avjɔ̃] *nm* (aero)plane (*Brit*), (air)plane (*US*); **aller (quelque part) en** ~ to go (somewhere) by plane, fly (somewhere); **par** ~ by airmail; ~ **de chasse** fighter; ~ **de ligne** airliner; ~ **à réaction** jet (plane)

aviron [aviʀɔ̃] *nm* oar; (*sport*): **l'**~ rowing

avis [avi] *nm* opinion; (*notification*) notice; (*Comm*): ~ **de crédit/débit** credit/debit advice; **à mon** ~ in my opinion; **je suis de votre** ~ I share your opinion, I am of your opinion; **être d'**~ **que** to be of the opinion that; **changer d'**~ to change one's mind; **sauf** ~ **contraire** unless you hear to the contrary; **sans** ~ **préalable** without notice; **jusqu'à nouvel** ~ until further notice; ~ **de décès** death announcement

avisé, e [avize] *adj* sensible, wise; **être bien/mal** ~ **de faire** to be well-/ill-advised to do

aviser [avize] *vt* (*voir*) to notice, catch sight of; (*informer*): ~ **qn de/que** to advise *ou* inform *ou* notify sb of/that ▷ *vi* to think about things, assess the situation; **s'**~ **de qch/que** to become suddenly aware of sth/that; **s'**~ **de faire** to take it into one's head to do

avocat, e [avɔka, -at] *nm/f* (*Jur*) ≈ barrister (*Brit*), lawyer; (*fig*) advocate, champion ▷ *nm* (*Culin*) avocado (pear); **se faire l'**~ **du diable** to be the devil's advocate; **l'**~ **de la défense/partie civile** the counsel for the defence/plaintiff; ~ **d'affaires** business lawyer; ~ **général** assistant public prosecutor

avoine [avwan] *nf* oats *pl*

avoir [avwaʀ] *nm* assets *pl*, resources *pl*; (*Comm*) credit; ~ **fiscal** tax credit

▷ *vt* **1** (*posséder*) to have; **elle a deux enfants/une belle maison** she has (got) two children/a lovely house; **il a les yeux bleus** he has (got) blue eyes

2 (*éprouver*): **qu'est-ce que tu as?, qu'as-tu?** what's wrong?, what's the matter?; *voir aussi* **faim, peur** *etc*

3 (*âge, dimensions*) to be; **il a 3 ans** he is 3 (years old); **le mur a 3 mètres de haut** the wall is 3 metres high

4 (*fam: duper*) to do, have; **on vous a eu!** you've been done *ou* had!

5: **en** ~ **contre qn** to have a grudge against sb; **en** ~ **assez** to be fed up; **j'en ai pour une demi- heure** it'll take me half an hour; **n'**~ **que faire de qch** to have no use for sth

▷ *vb aux* **1** to have; **~ mangé/dormi** to have eaten/slept; **hier je n'ai pas mangé** I didn't eat yesterday

2 (*avoir+à +infinitif*): **~ à faire qch** to have to do sth; **vous n'avez qu'à lui demander** you only have to ask him; **tu n'as pas à me poser des questions** it's not for you to ask me questions

▷ *vb impers* **1**: **il y a** (+ *singulier*) there is; (+ *pluriel*) there are; **qu'y-a-t-il?, qu'est-ce qu'il y a?** what's the matter?, what is it?; **il doit y ~ une explication** there must be an explanation; **il n'y a qu'à ...** we (*ou* you *etc*) will just have to ...; **il ne peut y en ~ qu'un** there can only be one

2 (*temporel*): **il y a 10 ans** 10 years ago; **il y a 10 ans/longtemps que je le connais** I've known him for 10 years/a long time; **il y a 10 ans qu'il est arrivé** it's 10 years since he arrived

avoisiner [avwazine] *vt* to be near *ou* close to; (*fig*) to border *ou* verge on

avortement [avɔʀtəmɑ̃] *nm* abortion

avorter [avɔʀte] *vi* (*Méd*) to have an abortion; (*fig*) to fail; **faire ~** to abort; **se faire ~** to have an abortion

avoué, e [avwe] *adj* avowed ▷ *nm* (*Jur*) ≈ solicitor (*Brit*), lawyer

avouer [avwe] *vt* (*crime, défaut*) to confess (to) ▷ *vi* (*se confesser*) to confess; (*admettre*) to admit; **~ avoir fait/que** to admit *ou* confess to having done/that; **~ que oui/non** to admit that that is so/not so

avril [avʀil] *nm* April; *voir aussi* **juillet**

axe [aks(ə)] *nm* axis (*pl* axes); (*de roue etc*) axle; **dans l'~ de** directly in line with; (*fig*) main line; **~ routier** trunk road, main road

axer [akse] *vt*: **~ qch sur** to centre sth on

ayons *etc* [ɛjɔ̃] *vb voir* **avoir**

azote [azɔt] *nm* nitrogen

Bb

baba [baba] *adj inv:* **en être ~** (*fam*) to be flabbergasted ▷ *nm:* **~ au rhum** rum baba

babines [babin] *nfpl* chops

babiole [babjɔl] *nf* (*bibelot*) trinket; (*vétille*) trifle

bâbord [babɔR] *nm:* **à** *ou* **par ~** to port, on the port side

baby-foot [babifut] *nm inv* table football

baby-sitting [babisitiŋ] *nm* baby-sitting; **faire du ~** to baby-sit

bac [bak] *nm* (*Scol*) = **baccalauréat**; (*bateau*) ferry; (*récipient*) tub; (: *Photo etc*) tray; (: *Industrie*) tank; **à glace** ice-tray; **à légumes** vegetable compartment *ou* rack

baccalauréat [bakalɔRea] *nm* ≈ A-levels *pl* (*Brit*), ≈ high school diploma (US); *see note*

bâche [baʃ] *nf* tarpaulin, canvas sheet

bachelier, -ière [baʃəlje, -jɛR] *nm/f* holder of the *baccalauréat*

bâcler [bakle] *vt* to botch (up)

badaud, e [bado, -od] *nm/f* idle onlooker

badigeonner [badiʒɔne] *vt* to distemper; to colourwash; (*péj: barbouiller*) to daub; (*Méd*) to paint

badiner [badine] *vi:* **~ avec qch** to treat sth lightly; **ne pas ~ avec qch** not to trifle with sth

baffe [baf] *nf* (*fam*) slap, clout

baffle [bafl(ə)] *nm* baffle (board)

bafouer [bafwe] *vt* to deride, ridicule

bafouiller [bafuje] *vi, vt* to stammer

bâfrer [bafRe] *vi, vt* (*fam*) to guzzle, gobble

bagage [bagaʒ] *nm:* **~s** luggage *sg*, baggage *sg*; **faire ses ~s** to pack (one's bags); **~ littéraire** (stock of) literary knowledge; **~s à main** hand-luggage

bagarre [bagaR] *nf* fight, brawl; **il aime la ~** he loves a fight, he likes fighting

bagarrer [bagare]: **se bagarrer** *vi* to (have a) fight

bagatelle [bagatɛl] *nf* trifle, trifling sum (*ou* matter)

bagne [baɲ] *nm* penal colony; **c'est le ~** (*fig*) it's forced labour

bagnole [baɲɔl] *nf* (*fam*) car, wheels *pl* (*Brit*)

bagout [bagu] *nm* glibness; **avoir du ~** to have the gift of the gab

bague [bag] *nf* ring; **~ de fiançailles** engagement ring; **~ de serrage** clip

baguette [bagɛt] *nf* stick; (*cuisine chinoise*) chopstick; (*de chef d'orchestre*) baton; (*pain*) stick of (French) bread; (*Constr: moulure*) beading; **mener qn à la ~** to rule sb with a rod of iron; **~ magique** magic wand; **~ de sourcier** divining rod; **~ de tambour** drumstick

baie [bɛ] *nf* (*Géo*) bay; (*fruit*) berry; **~ (vitrée)** picture window

baignade [beɲad] *nf* (*action*) bathing; (*bain*) bathe; (*endroit*) bathing place

baigner [beɲe] *vt* (*bébé*) to bath ▷ *vi:* **~ dans son sang** to lie in a pool of blood; **~ dans la brume** to be shrouded in mist; **se baigner** *vi* to go swimming *ou* bathing; (*dans une baignoire*) to have a bath; **ça baigne!** (*fam*) everything's great!

baignoire [beɲwaR] *nf* bath(tub); (*Théât*) ground-floor box

bail, baux [baj, bo] *nm* lease; **donner** *ou* **prendre qch à ~** to lease sth

bâillement [bajmã] *nm* yawn

bâiller [baje] *vi* to yawn; (*être ouvert*) to gape

bâillonner [bajɔne] *vt* to gag

bain [bɛ] *nm* (*dans une baignoire, Photo, Tech*) bath; (*dans la mer, une piscine*) swim; **costume de ~** bathing costume (*Brit*), swimsuit; **prendre un ~** to have a bath; **se mettre dans le ~** (*fig*) to get into (the way of) it *ou* things; **~ de bouche** mouthwash; **~ de foule** walkabout; **~ de pieds** footbath; (*au bord de la mer*) paddle; **~ de siège** hip bath; **~ de soleil** sunbathing *no pl*; **prendre un ~ de soleil** to sunbathe; **~s de mer** sea bathing *sg*; **~s(-douches) municipaux** public baths

bain-marie (*pl* **bains-marie**) [bɛmaRi] *nm* double boiler; **faire chauffer au ~** (*boîte etc*) to immerse in boiling water

baiser [beze] *nm* kiss ▷ *vt* (*main, front*) to kiss; (*fam!*) to screw (!)

baisse [bɛs] *nf* fall, drop; (*Comm*): **"~ sur la viande"** "meat prices down"; **en ~** (*cours, action*) falling; **à la ~** downwards

baisser [bese] *vt* to lower; (*radio, chauffage*) to turn down; (*Auto: phares*) to dip (*Brit*), lower (US) ▷ *vi* to fall, drop, go down; **se baisser** *vi* to bend down

bal [bal] *nm* dance; (*grande soirée*) ball; **~ costumé/masqué** fancy-dress/masked ball; **~ musette** dance (*with accordion accompaniment*)

balade [balad] *nf* walk, stroll; (*en voiture*) drive;

faire une ~ to go for a walk *ou* stroll; to go for a drive

balader [balade] *vt* (*traîner*) to trail around; **se balader** *vi* to go for a walk *ou* stroll; to go for a drive

baladeur [baladœʀ] *nm* personal stereo; **~ numérique** MP3 player

balafre [balafʀ(ə)] *nf* gash, slash; (*cicatrice*) scar

balai [bale] *nm* broom, brush; (*Auto: d'essuie-glace*) blade; (*Mus: de batterie etc*) brush; **donner un coup de ~** to give the floor a sweep; **~ mécanique** carpet sweeper

balai-brosse (*pl* **balais-brosses**) [balɛbʀɔs] *nm* (long-handled) scrubbing brush

balance [balɑ̃s] *nf* (*à plateaux*) scales *pl*; (*de précision*) balance; (*Comm, Pol*): **~ des comptes** *ou* **paiements** balance of payments; (*signe*): **la B~** Libra, the Scales; **être de la B~** to be Libra; **~ commerciale** balance of trade; **~ des forces** balance of power; **~ romaine** steelyard

balancer [balɑ̃se] *vt* to swing; (*lancer*) to fling, chuck; (*renvoyer, jeter*) to chuck out ▷ *vi* to swing; **se balancer** *vi* to swing; (*bateau*) to rock; (*branche*) to sway; **se ~ de qch** (*fam*) not to give a toss about sth

balançoire [balɑ̃swaʀ] *nf* swing; (*sur pivot*) seesaw

balayer [baleje] *vt* (*feuilles etc*) to sweep up, brush up; (*pièce, cour*) to sweep; (*chasser*) to sweep away *ou* aside; (*radar*) to scan; (: *phares*) to sweep across

balayeur, -euse [balɛjœʀ, -øz] *nm/f* road sweeper ▷ *nf* (*engin*) road sweeper

balbutier [balbysje] *vi, vt* to stammer

balcon [balkɔ̃] *nm* balcony; (*Théât*) dress circle

baleine [balɛn] *nf* whale; (*de parapluie*) rib; (*de corset*) bone

balise [baliz] *nf* (*Navig*) beacon, (marker) buoy; (*Aviat*) runway light, beacon; (*Auto, Ski*) sign

baliser [balize] *vt* to mark out (with beacons *ou* lights *etc*)

balivernes [balivɛʀn(ə)] *nfpl* twaddle *sg* (*Brit*), nonsense *sg*

ballant, e [balɑ̃, -ɑ̃t] *adj* dangling

balle [bal] *nf* (*de fusil*) bullet; (*de sport*) ball; (*du blé*) chaff; (*paquet*) bale; (*fam: franc*) franc; **~ perdue** stray bullet

ballerine [balʀin] *nf* ballet dancer; (*chaussure*) pump, ballerina

ballet [balɛ] *nm* ballet; (*fig*): **~ diplomatique** diplomatic to-ings and fro-ings

ballon [balɔ̃] *nm* (*de sport*) ball; (*jouet, Aviat, de bande dessinée*) balloon; (*de vin*) glass; **~ d'essai** (*météorologique*) pilot balloon; (*fig*) feeler(s); **~ de football** football; **~ d'oxygène** oxygen bottle

ballot [balo] *nm* bundle; (*péj*) nitwit

ballottage [balɔtaʒ] *nm* (*Pol*) second ballot

ballotter [balɔte] *vi* to roll around; (*bateau etc*) to toss ▷ *vt* to shake *ou* throw about; to toss; **être ballotté entre** (*fig*) to be shunted between; (: *indécis*) to be torn between

balnéaire [balneɛʀ] *adj* seaside *cpd*

balourd, e [baluʀ, -uʀd(ə)] *adj* clumsy ▷ *nm/f* clodhopper

balustrade [balystʀad] *nf* railings *pl*, handrail

bambin [bɑ̃bɛ̃] *nm* little child

bambou [bɑ̃bu] *nm* bamboo

ban [bɑ̃] *nm* round of applause, cheer; **être/ mettre au ~ de** to be outlawed/to outlaw from; **le ~ et l'arrière-~ de sa famille** every last one of his relatives; **~s (de mariage)** banns, bans

banal, e [banal] *adj* banal, commonplace; (*péj*) trite; **four/moulin ~** village oven/mill

banalité [banalite] *nf* banality; (*remarque*) truism, trite remark

banane [banan] *nf* banana

banc [bɑ̃] *nm* seat, bench; (*de poissons*) shoal; **~ des accusés** dock; **~ d'essai** (*fig*) testing ground; **~ de sable** sandbank; **~ des témoins** witness box; **~ de touche** dugout

bancaire [bɑ̃kɛʀ] *adj* banking, bank *cpd*

bancal, e [bɑ̃kal] *adj* wobbly; (*personne*) bow-legged; (*fig: projet*) shaky

bandage [bɑ̃daʒ] *nm* bandaging; (*pansement*) bandage; **~ herniaire** truss

bande [bɑ̃d] *nf* (*de tissu etc*) strip; (*Méd*) bandage; (*motif, dessin*) stripe; (*Ciné*) film; (*Radio, groupe*) band; (*péj*): **une ~ de** a bunch *ou* crowd of; **par la ~** in a roundabout way; **donner de la ~** to list; **faire ~ à part** to keep to o.s.; **~ dessinée (BD)** strip cartoon (*Brit*), comic strip; **~ magnétique** magnetic tape; **~ passante** (*Inform*) bandwidth; **~ perforée** punched tape; **~ de roulement** (*de pneu*) tread; **~ sonore** sound track; **~ de terre** strip of land; **~ Velpeau®** (*Méd*) crêpe bandage

bandeau, x [bɑ̃do] *nm* headband; (*sur les yeux*) blindfold; (*Méd*) head bandage

bander [bɑ̃de] *vt* to bandage; (*muscle*) to tense; (*arc*) to bend ▷ *vi* (*fam!*) to have a hard on (!); **~ les yeux à qn** to blindfold sb

banderole [bɑ̃dʀɔl] *nf* banderole; (*dans un défilé etc*) streamer

bandit [bɑ̃di] *nm* bandit

banditisme [bɑ̃ditism(ə)] *nm* violent crime, armed robberies *pl*

bandoulière [bɑ̃duljɛʀ] *nf*: **en ~** (slung *ou* worn) across the shoulder

banlieue [bɑ̃ljø] *nf* suburbs *pl*; **quartiers de ~** suburban areas; **trains de ~** commuter trains

banlieusard, e [bɑ̃ljøzaʀ, -aʀd(ə)] *nm/f* suburbanite

bannière [banjɛʀ] *nf* banner

bannir [baniʀ] *vt* to banish

banque [bɑ̃k] *nf* bank; (*activités*) banking; **~ des yeux/du sang** eye/blood bank; **~ d'affaires** merchant bank; **~ de dépôt** deposit bank; **~ de données** (*Inform*) data bank; **~ d'émission** bank of issue

banqueroute [bɑ̃kʀut] *nf* bankruptcy

banquet [bɑ̃kɛ] *nm* (*de club*) dinner; (*de noces*) reception; (*d'apparat*) banquet

banquette [bɑ̃kɛt] *nf* seat

banquier [bɑ̃kje] *nm* banker

banquise [bɑ̃kiz] *nf* ice field

baptême [batɛm] *nm* (*sacrement*) baptism;

(*cérémonie*) christening, baptism; (*d'un navire*) launching; (*d'une cloche*) consecration, dedication; ~ **de l'air** first flight

baptiser [batize] *vt* to christen; to baptize; to launch; to consecrate, dedicate

baquet [bakɛ] *nm* tub, bucket

bar [baʀ] *nm* bar; (*poisson*) bass

baraque [baʀak] *nf* shed; (*fam*) house; ~ **foraine** fairground stand

baraqué, e [baʀake] *adj* well-built, hefty

baraquements [baʀakmɑ̃] *nmpl* huts (*for refugees, workers etc*)

baratin [baʀatɛ̃] *nm* (*fam*) smooth talk, patter

baratiner [baʀatine] *vt* to chat up

barbant, e [baʀbɑ̃, -ɑ̃t] *adj* (*fam*) deadly (boring)

barbare [baʀbaʀ] *adj* barbaric ▷ *nm/f* barbarian

barbarie [baʀbaʀi] *nf* barbarism; (*cruauté*) barbarity

barbe [baʀb(ə)] *nf* beard; (**au nez et**) **à la ~ de qn** (*fig*) under sb's very nose; **quelle ~!** (*fam*) what a drag *ou* bore!; ~ **à papa** candy-floss (*Brit*), cotton candy (*US*)

barbelé [baʀbəle] *nm* barbed wire *no pl*

barber [baʀbe] *vt* (*fam*) to bore stiff

barbiturique [baʀbityʀik] *nm* barbiturate

barboter [baʀbɔte] *vi* to paddle, dabble ▷ *vt* (*fam*) to filch

barbouiller [baʀbuje] *vt* to daub; (*péj: écrire, dessiner*) to scribble; **avoir l'estomac barbouillé** to feel queasy *ou* sick

barbu, e [baʀby] *adj* bearded

barda [baʀda] *nm* (*fam*) kit, gear

barder [baʀde] *vt* (*Culin: rôti, volaille*) to bard ▷ *vi* (*fam*): **ça va ~** sparks will fly

barème [baʀɛm] *nm* scale; (*liste*) table; ~ **des salaires** salary scale

baril [baʀil] *nm* (*tonneau*) barrel; (*de poudre*) keg

bariolé, e [baʀjɔle] *adj* many-coloured, rainbow-coloured

baromètre [baʀɔmɛtʀ(ə)] *nm* barometer; ~ **anéroïde** aneroid barometer

baron [baʀɔ̃] *nm* baron

baroque [baʀɔk] *adj* (*Art*) baroque; (*fig*) weird

barque [baʀk(ə)] *nf* small boat

barquette [baʀkɛt] *nf* small boat-shaped tart; (*récipient: en aluminium*) tub; (: *en bois*) basket

barrage [baʀaʒ] *nm* dam; (*sur route*) roadblock, barricade; ~ **de police** police roadblock

barre [baʀ] *nf* (*de fer etc*) rod; (*Navig*) helm; (*écrite*) line, stroke; (*Danse*) barre; (*niveau*): **la livre a franchi la ~ des 1,70 euros** the pound has broken the 1.70 euros barrier; (*Jur*): **comparaître à la ~** to appear as a witness; **être à** *ou* **tenir la ~** (*Navig*) to be at the helm; **coup de ~** (*fig*): **c'est le coup de ~!** it's daylight robbery!; **j'ai le coup de ~!** I'm all in!; ~ **fixe** (*Gym*) horizontal bar; ~ **de mesure** (*Mus*) bar line; **à mine** crowbar; **~s parallèles/asymétriques** (*Gym*) parallel/asymmetric bars

barreau, x [baʀo] *nm* bar; (*Jur*): **le ~** the Bar

barrer [baʀe] *vt* (*route etc*) to block; (*mot*) to cross out; (*chèque*) to cross (*Brit*); (*Navig*) to steer; **se**

barrer *vi* (*fam*) to clear off

barrette [baʀɛt] *nf* (*pour cheveux*) (hair) slide (*Brit*) *ou* clip (*US*); (*broche*) brooch

barricader [baʀikade] *vt* to barricade; **se ~ chez soi** (*fig*) to lock o.s. in

barrière [baʀjɛʀ] *nf* fence; (*obstacle*) barrier; (*porte*) gate; **la Grande B~** the Great Barrier Reef; ~ **de dégel** (*Admin: on roadsigns*) no heavy vehicles -- road liable to subsidence due to thaw; **~s douanières** trade barriers

barrique [baʀik] *nf* barrel, cask

bar-tabac [baʀtaba] *nm* bar (*which sells tobacco and stamps*)

bas, basse [bɑ, bɑs] *adj* low; (*action*) low, ignoble ▷ *nm* (*vêtement*) stocking; (*partie inférieure*): **le ~ de** the lower part *ou* foot *ou* bottom of ▷ *nf* (*Mus*) bass ▷ *adv* low; (*parler*) softly; **plus ~** lower down; more softly; (*dans un texte*) further on, below; **la tête ~se** with lowered head; (*fig*) with head hung low; **avoir la vue ~se** to be short-sighted; **au ~ mot** at the lowest estimate; **enfant en ~ âge** infant, young child; **en ~** down below; at (*ou* to) the bottom; (*dans une maison*) downstairs; **en ~ de** at the bottom of; **de ~ en haut** upwards; from the bottom to the top; **des hauts et des ~** ups and downs; **un ~ de laine** (*fam: économies*) money under the mattress (*fig*); **mettre ~** *vi* (*animal*) to give birth; **à ~ la dictature!** down with dictatorship!; ~ **morceaux** (*viande*) cheap cuts

basané, e [bazane] *adj* (*teint*) tanned, bronzed; (*foncé: péj*) swarthy

bas-côté [bɑkote] *nm* (*de route*) verge (*Brit*), shoulder (*US*); (*d'église*) (side) aisle

bascule [baskyl] *nf*: (**jeu de**) ~ seesaw; (**balance à**) ~ scales *pl*; **fauteuil à ~** rocking chair; **système à** ~ tip-over device; rocker device

basculer [baskyle] *vi* to fall over, topple (over); (*benne*) to tip up ▷ *vt* (*aussi*: **faire basculer**) to topple over; to tip out, tip up

base [bɑz] *nf* base; (*Pol*): **la ~** the rank and file, the grass roots; (*fondement, principe*) basis (*pl* bases); **jeter les ~s de** to lay the foundations of; **à la ~ de** (*fig*) at the root of; **sur la ~ de** (*fig*) on the basis of; **de ~** basic; **à ~ de café** *etc* coffee *etc* -based; ~ **de données** (*Inform*) database; ~ **de lancement** launching site

baser [bɑze] *vt*: ~ **qch sur** to base sth on; **se ~ sur** (*données, preuves*) to base one's argument on; **être basé à/dans** (*Mil*) to be based at/in

bas-fond [bɑfɔ̃] *nm* (*Navig*) shallow; **bas-fonds** *nmpl* (*fig*) dregs

basilic [bazilik] *nm* (*Culin*) basil

basket [baskɛt], **basket-ball** [basketbol] *nm* basketball

basque [bask(ə)] *adj, nm* (*Ling*) Basque ▷ *nm/f*: **B~** Basque; **le Pays ~** the Basque country

basse [bɑs] *adj f, nf voir* **bas**

basse-cour (*pl* **basses-cours**) [bɑskuʀ] *nf* farmyard; (*animaux*) farmyard animals

bassin [basɛ̃] *nm* (*cuvette*) bowl; (*pièce d'eau*) pond, pool; (*de fontaine, Géo*) basin; (*Anat*) pelvis;

(*portuaire*) dock; **~ houiller** coalfield

bassine [basin] *nf* basin; (*contenu*) bowl, bowlful

basson [basɔ̃] *nm* bassoon

bas-ventre [bavɑ̃tʀ(ə)] *nm* (lower part of the) stomach

bataille [batɑj] *nf* battle; **en ~** (*en travers*) at an angle; (*en désordre*) awry; **~ rangée** pitched battle

bâtard, e [batɑʀ, -aʀd(ə)] *adj* (*enfant*) illegitimate; (*fig*) hybrid ▷ *nm/f* illegitimate child, bastard (*péj*) ▷ *nm* (*Boulangerie*) ≈ Vienna loaf; **chien ~** mongrel

bateau, x [bato] *nm* boat; (*grand*) ship ▷ *adj inv* (*banal, rebattu*) hackneyed; **~ de pêche/à moteur/à voiles** fishing/motor/sailing boat

bateau-mouche [batomuʃ] *nm* (passenger) pleasure boat (*on the Seine*)

bâti, e [bati] *adj* (*terrain*) developed ▷ *nm* (*armature*) frame; (*Couture*) tacking; **bien ~** (*personne*) well-built

batifoler [batifɔle] *vi* to frolic *ou* lark about

bâtiment [batimɑ̃] *nm* building; (*Navig*) ship, vessel; (*industrie*): **le ~** the building trade

bâtir [batiʀ] *vt* to build; (*Couture: jupe, ourlet*) to tack; **fil à ~** (*Couture*) tacking thread

bâtisse [batis] *nf* building

bâton [batɔ̃] *nm* stick; **mettre des ~s dans les roues à qn** to put a spoke in sb's wheel; **à ~s rompus** informally; **~ de rouge (à lèvres)** lipstick; **~ de ski** ski stick

bats [ba] *vb voir* **battre**

battage [bataʒ] *nm* (*publicité*) (hard) plugging

battant, e [batɑ̃, -ɑ̃t] *vb voir* **battre** ▷ *adj*: **pluie ~e** lashing rain ▷ *nm* (*de cloche*) clapper; (*de volets*) shutter, flap; (*de porte*) side; (*fig: personne*) fighter; **porte à double ~** double door; **tambour ~** briskly

battement [batmɑ̃] *nm* (*de cœur*) beat; (*intervalle*) interval (*between classes, trains etc*); **~ de paupières** blinking *no pl* (of eyelids); **un ~ de 10 minutes, 10 minutes de ~** 10 minutes to spare

batterie [batʀi] *nf* (*Mil, Élec*) battery; (*Mus*) drums *pl*, drum kit; **~ de cuisine** kitchen utensils *pl*; (*casseroles etc*) pots and pans *pl*; **une ~ de tests** a string of tests

batteur [batœʀ] *nm* (*Mus*) drummer; (*appareil*) whisk

battre [batʀ(ə)] *vt* to beat; (*pluie, vagues*) to beat *ou* lash against; (*œufs etc*) to beat up, whisk; (*blé*) to thresh; (*cartes*) to shuffle; (*passer au peigne fin*) to scour ▷ *vi* (*cœur*) to beat; (*volets etc*) to bang, rattle; **se battre** *vi* to fight; **~ la mesure** to beat time; **~ en brèche** (*Mil: mur*) to batter; (*fig: théorie*) to demolish; (: *institution etc*) to attack; **~ son plein** to be at its height, be going full swing; **~ pavillon britannique** to fly the British flag; **~ des mains** to clap one's hands; **~ des ailes** to flap its wings; **~ de l'aile** (*fig*) to be in a bad way *ou* in bad shape; **~ la semelle** to stamp one's feet; **~ en retraite** to beat a retreat

baume [bom] *nm* balm

bavard, e [bavaʀ, -aʀd(ə)] *adj* (very) talkative; gossipy

bavarder [bavaʀde] *vi* to chatter; (*indiscrètement*) to gossip; (: *révéler un secret*) to blab

bave [bav] *nf* dribble; (*de chien etc*) slobber, slaver (*Brit*), drool (*US*); (*d'escargot*) slime

baver [bave] *vi* to dribble; to slobber, slaver (*Brit*), drool (*US*); (*encre, couleur*) to run; **en ~** (*fam*) to have a hard time (of it)

baveux, -euse [bavø, -øz] *adj* dribbling; (*omelette*) runny

bavoir [bavwaʀ] *nm* (*de bébé*) bib

bavure [bavyʀ] *nf* smudge; (*fig*) hitch; blunder

bayer [baje] *vi*: **~ aux corneilles** to stand gaping

bazar [bazaʀ] *nm* general store; (*fam*) jumble

bazarder [bazaʀde] *vt* (*fam*) to chuck out

BCBG *sigle adj* (= *bon chic bon genre*) ≈ preppy

BD *sigle f* = **bande dessinée**; (= *base de données*) DB

bd *abr* = **boulevard**

béant, e [beɑ̃, -ɑ̃t] *adj* gaping

béat, e [bea, -at] *adj* showing open-eyed wonder; (*sourire etc*) blissful

béatitude [beatityd] *nf* bliss

beau, bel, belle, beaux [bo, bɛl] *adj* beautiful, lovely; (*homme*) handsome ▷ *nf* (*Sport*) decider ▷ *adv*: **il fait ~** the weather's fine ▷ *nm*: **avoir le sens du ~** to have an aesthetic sense; **le temps est au ~** the weather is set fair; **un ~ geste** (*fig*) a fine gesture; **un ~ salaire** a good salary; **un ~ gâchis/rhume** a fine mess/nasty cold; **en faire/dire de belles** to do/say (some) stupid things; **le ~ monde** high society; **~ parleur** smooth talker; **un ~ jour** one (fine) day; **de plus belle** more than ever, even more; **bel et bien** well and truly; (*vraiment*) really (and truly); **le plus ~ c'est que ...** the best of it is that ...; **c'est du ~!** that's great, that is!; **on a ~ essayer** however hard *ou* no matter how hard we try; **il a ~ jeu de protester** *etc* it's easy for him to protest *etc*; **faire le ~** (*chien*) to sit up and beg

beaucoup [boku] *adv* a lot; **il boit ~** he drinks a lot; **il ne boit pas ~** he doesn't drink much *ou* a lot

2 (*suivi de plus, trop etc*) much, a lot, far; **il est ~ plus grand** he is much *ou* a lot *ou* far taller

3: **~ de** (*nombre*) many, a lot of; (*quantité*) a lot of; **pas ~ de** (*nombre*) not many, not a lot of; (*quantité*) not much, not a lot of; **~ d'étudiants/de touristes** a lot of *ou* many students/tourists; **~ de courage** a lot of courage; **il n'a pas ~ d'argent** he hasn't got much *ou* a lot of money; **il n'y a pas ~ de touristes** there aren't many *ou* a lot of tourists

4: **de ~** by far

▷ *pron*: **~ le savent** lots of people know that

beau-fils (*pl* **beaux-fils**) [bofis] *nm* son-in-law; (*remariage*) stepson

beau-frère (*pl* **beaux-frères**) [bofʀɛʀ] *nm* brother-in-law

beau-père (*pl* **beaux-pères**) [bopɛʀ] *nm* father-in-law; (*remariage*) stepfather

beauté [bote] *nf* beauty; **de toute ~** beautiful; **en ~** *adv* with a flourish, brilliantly

beaux-arts [bozaʀ] *nmpl* fine arts

beaux-parents [bopaʀɑ̃] *nmpl* wife's/husband's family, in-laws

bébé [bebe] *nm* baby

bec [bɛk] *nm* beak, bill; (*de plume*) nib; (*de cafetière etc*) spout; (*de casserole etc*) lip; (*d'une clarinette etc*) mouthpiece; (*fam*) mouth; **clouer le ~ à qn** (*fam*) to shut sb up; **ouvrir le ~** (*fam*) to open one's mouth; **~ de gaz** (street) gaslamp; **~ verseur** pouring lip

bécane [bekan] *nf* (*fam*) bike

bec-de-lièvre (*pl* **becs-de-lièvre**) [bɛkdəljɛvʀ(ə)] *nm* harelip

bêche [bɛʃ] *nf* spade

bêcher [beʃe] *vt* (*terre*) to dig; (*personne: critiquer*) to slate; (*: snober*) to look down on

bécoter [bekɔte]: **se bécoter** *vi* to smooch

becqueter [bɛkte] *vt* (*fam*) to eat

bedaine [bədɛn] *nf* paunch

bedonnant, e [bədɔnɑ̃, -ɑ̃t] *adj* paunchy, potbellied

bée [be] *adj*: **bouche ~** gaping

beffroi [befʀwa] *nm* belfry

bégayer [begeje] *vt, vi* to stammer

bègue [bɛg] *nm/f*: **être ~** to have a stammer

beige [bɛʒ] *adj* beige

beignet [bɛɲɛ] *nm* fritter

bel [bɛl] *adj m voir* **beau**

bêler [bele] *vi* to bleat

belette [bəlɛt] *nf* weasel

belge [bɛlʒ(ə)] *adj* Belgian ▷ *nm/f*: **B~** Belgian; *see note*

Belgique [bɛlʒik] *nf*: **la ~** Belgium

bélier [belje] *nm* ram; (*engin*) (battering) ram; (*signe*): **le B~** Aries, the Ram; **être du B~** to be Aries

belle [bɛl] *adj f, nf voir* **beau**

belle-fille (*pl* **belles-filles**) [bɛlfij] *nf* daughter-in-law; (*remariage*) stepdaughter

belle-mère (*pl* **belles-mères**) [bɛlmɛʀ] *nf* mother-in-law; (*remariage*) stepmother

belle-sœur (*pl* **belles-sœurs**) [bɛlsœʀ] *nf* sister-in-law

belliqueux, -euse [belikø, -øz] *adj* aggressive, warlike

belvédère [bɛlvedɛʀ] *nm* panoramic viewpoint (*or small building there*)

bémol [bemɔl] *nm* (*Mus*) flat

bénédiction [benediksjɔ̃] *nf* blessing

bénéfice [benefis] *nm* (*Comm*) profit; (*avantage*) benefit; **au ~ de** in aid of

bénéficier [benefisje] *vi*: **~ de** to enjoy; (*profiter*) to benefit by *ou* from; (*obtenir*) to get, be given

bénéfique [benefik] *adj* beneficial

bénévole [benevɔl] *adj* voluntary, unpaid

bénin, -igne [benɛ̃, -iɲ] *adj* minor, mild; (*tumeur*) benign

bénir [beniʀ] *vt* to bless

bénit, e [beni, -it] *adj* consecrated; **eau ~e** holy water

benjamin, e [bɛ̃ʒamɛ̃, -in] *nm/f* youngest child; (*Sport*) under-13

benne [bɛn] *nf* skip; (*de téléphérique*) (cable) car; **~ basculante** tipper (*Brit*), dump *ou* dumper truck

BEP *sigle m* (= *Brevet d'études professionnelles*) school-leaving diploma, taken at approx. 18 years

béquille [bekij] *nf* crutch; (*de bicyclette*) stand

berceau, x [bɛʀso] *nm* cradle, crib

bercer [bɛʀse] *vt* to rock, cradle; (*musique etc*) to lull; **~ qn de** (*promesses etc*) to delude sb with

berceur, -euse [bɛʀsœʀ, -øz] *adj* soothing ▷ *nf* (*chanson*) lullaby

béret [beʀɛ] , **béret basque** [beʀɛbask(ə)] *nm* beret

berge [bɛʀʒ(ə)] *nf* bank

berger, -ère [bɛʀʒe, -ɛʀ] *nm/f* shepherd/shepherdess; **~ allemand** (*chien*) alsatian (dog) (*Brit*), German shepherd (dog) (*US*)

berlingot [bɛʀlɛ̃go] *nm* (*emballage*) carton (*pyramid shaped*); (*bonbon*) lozenge

berlue [bɛʀly] *nf*: **j'ai la ~** I must be seeing things

berner [bɛʀne] *vt* to fool

besogne [bəzɔɲ] *nf* work *no pl*, job

besoin [bəzwɛ̃] *nm* need; (*pauvreté*): **le ~** need, want; **le ~ d'argent/de gloire** the need for money/glory; **~s (naturels)** nature's needs; **faire ses ~s** to relieve o.s.; **avoir ~ de qch/faire qch** to need sth/to do sth; **il n'y a pas ~ de (faire)** there is no need to (do); **au ~, si ~ est** if need be; **pour les ~s de la cause** for the purpose in hand

bestial, e, -aux [bɛstjal, -o] *adj* bestial, brutish ▷ *nmpl* cattle

bestiole [bɛstjɔl] *nf* (tiny) creature

bétail [betaj] *nm* livestock, cattle *pl*

bête [bɛt] *nf* animal; (*bestiole*) insect, creature ▷ *adj* stupid, silly; **les ~s** (the) animals; **chercher la petite ~** to nit-pick; **~ noire** pet hate, bugbear (*Brit*); **~ sauvage** wild beast; **~ de somme** beast of burden

bêtement [bɛtmɑ̃] *adv* stupidly; **tout ~** quite simply

bêtise [betiz] *nf* stupidity; (*action, remarque*) stupid thing (to say *ou* do); (*bonbon*) type of mint sweet (*Brit*) *ou* candy (*US*); **faire/dire une ~** to do/say something stupid

béton [betɔ̃] *nm* concrete; (**en**) **~** (*fig: alibi, argument*) cast iron; **~ armé** reinforced concrete; **~ précontraint** prestressed concrete

bétonnière [betɔnjɛʀ] *nf* cement mixer

betterave [bɛtʀav] *nf* (*rouge*) beetroot (*Brit*), beet (*US*); **~ fourragère** mangel-wurzel; **~ sucrière** sugar beet

beugler [bøgle] *vi* to low; (*péj: radio etc*) to blare ▷ *vt* (*péj: chanson etc*) to bawl out

Beur [bœʀ] *adj, nm/f see note*

beurre [bœʀ] *nm* butter; **mettre du ~ dans les épinards** (*fig*) to add a little to the kitty; **~ de cacao** cocoa butter; **~ noir** brown butter (sauce)

beurrer [bœʀe] *vt* to butter

beurrier [bœʀje] *nm* butter dish

beuverie [bœvʀi] *nf* drinking session

bévue [bevy] *nf* blunder

Beyrouth [beʀut] *n* Beirut

biais [bjɛ] *nm* (*moyen*) device, expedient; (*aspect*) angle; (*bande de tissu*) piece of cloth cut on the bias; **en ~, de ~** (*obliquement*) at an angle; (*fig*) indirectly

biaiser [bjeze] *vi* (*fig*) to sidestep the issue

bibelot [biblo] *nm* trinket, curio

biberon [bibʀɔ̃] *nm* (feeding) bottle; **nourrir au ~** to bottle-feed

bible [bibl(ə)] *nf* bible

bibliobus [biblijɔbys] *nm* mobile library van

bibliographie [biblijɔgʀafi] *nf* bibliography

bibliothécaire [biblijɔtekɛʀ] *nm/f* librarian

bibliothèque [biblijɔtɛk] *nf* library; (*meuble*) bookcase; **~ municipale** public library

bic® [bik] *nm* Biro®

bicarbonate [bikaʀbɔnat] *nm*: **~ (de soude)** bicarbonate of soda

biceps [bisɛps] *nm* biceps

biche [biʃ] *nf* doe

bichonner [biʃɔne] *vt* to groom

bicolore [bikɔlɔʀ] *adj* two-coloured (*Brit*), two-colored (*US*)

bicoque [bikɔk] *nf* (*péj*) shack, dump

bicyclette [bisiklɛt] *nf* bicycle

bide [bid] *nm* (*fam: ventre*) belly; (*Théât*) flop

bidet [bide] *nm* bidet

bidon [bidɔ̃] *nm* can ▷ *adj inv* (*fam*) phoney

bidonville [bidɔ̃vil] *nm* shanty town

bidule [bidyl] *nm* (*fam*) thingamajig

bien [bjɛ̃] *nm* **1** (*avantage, profit*): **faire le ~** to do good; **faire du ~ à qn** to do sb good; **ça fait du ~ de faire** it does you good to do; **dire du ~ de** to speak well of; **c'est pour son ~** it's for his own good; **changer en ~** to change for the better; **le ~ public** the public good; **vouloir du ~ à qn** (*vouloir aider*) to have sb's (best) interests at heart; **je te veux du ~** (*pour mettre en confiance*) I don't wish you any harm

2 (*possession, patrimoine*) possession, property; **son ~ le plus précieux** his most treasured possession; **avoir du ~** to have property; **~s (de consommation** *etc*) (consumer *etc*) goods; **~s durables** (consumer) durables

3 (*moral*): **le ~** good; **distinguer le ~ du mal** to tell good from evil

▷ *adv* **1** (*de façon satisfaisante*) well; **elle travaille/mange ~** she works/eats well; **aller** *or* **se porter ~** to be well; **croyant ~ faire, je/il …** thinking I/he was doing the right thing, I/he …

2 (*valeur intensive*) quite; **~ jeune** quite young; **~ assez** quite enough; **~ mieux** (very) much better; **~ du temps/des gens** quite a time/a number of people; **j'espère ~ y aller** I do hope to go; **je veux ~ le faire** (*concession*) I'm quite willing to do it; **il faut ~ le faire** it has to be done; **il y a ~ deux ans** at least two years ago; **il semble ~ que** it really seems that; **peut-être ~** it could well be; **aimer ~** to like; **Paul est ~ venu, n'est-ce pas?** Paul HAS come, hasn't he?; **où peut-il ~ être passé?** where on earth can he have got to?

3 (*conséquence, résultat*): **si ~ que** with the result that; **on verra ~** we'll see; **faire ~ de …** to be right to …

▷ *excl* right!, OK!, fine!; **eh ~!** well!; **(c'est) ~ fait** it serves you (*ou* him *etc*) right!; **~ sûr!, ~ entendu!** certainly!, of course!

▷ *adj inv* **1** (*en bonne forme, à l'aise*): **je me sens ~, je suis ~** I feel fine; **je ne me sens pas ~, je ne suis pas ~** I don't feel well; **on est ~ dans ce fauteuil** this chair is very comfortable

2 (*joli, beau*) good-looking; **tu es ~ dans cette robe** you look good in that dress

3 (*satisfaisant*) good; **elle est ~, cette maison/secrétaire** it's a good house/she's a good secretary; **c'est très ~ (comme ça)** it's fine (like that); **ce n'est pas si ~ que ça** it's not as good *ou* great as all that; **c'est ~?** is that all right?

4 (*moralement*) right; (: *personne*) good, nice; (*respectable*) respectable; **ce n'est pas ~ de …** it's not right to …; **elle est ~, cette femme** she's a nice woman, she's a good sort; **des gens ~** respectable people

5 (*en bons termes*): **être ~ avec qn** to be on good terms with sb

bienséant, e [bjɛ̃seɑ̃, -ɑ̃t] *adj* proper, seemly

bientôt [bjɛ̃to] *adv* soon; **à ~** see you soon

bienveillant, e [bjɛ̃vɛjɑ̃, -ɑ̃t] *adj* kindly

bienvenu, e [bjɛ̃vny] *adj* welcome ▷ *nm/f*: **être le ~/la ~e** to be welcome ▷ *nf*: **souhaiter la ~e à** to welcome; **~e à** welcome to

bière [bjɛʀ] *nf* (*boisson*) beer; (*cercueil*) bier; **~ blonde** lager; **~ brune** brown ale; **~ (à la) pression** draught beer

biffer [bife] *vt* to cross out

bifteck [biftɛk] *nm* steak

bifurquer [bifyʀke] *vi* (*route*) to fork; (*véhicule*) to turn off

bigarré, e [bigaʀe] *adj* multicoloured (*Brit*), multicolored (*US*); (*disparate*) motley

bigorneau, x [bigɔʀno] *nm* winkle

bigot, e [bigo, -ɔt] (*péj*) *adj* bigoted ▷ *nm/f* bigot

bigoudi [bigudi] *nm* curler

bijou, x [biʒu] *nm* jewel

bijouterie [biʒutʀi] *nf* (*magasin*) jeweller's (shop) (*Brit*), jewelry store (*US*); (*bijoux*) jewellery, jewelry

bijoutier, -ière [biʒutje, -jɛʀ] *nm/f* jeweller (*Brit*), jeweler (*US*)

bikini [bikini] *nm* bikini

bilan [bilɑ̃] *nm* (*Comm*) balance sheet(s); (*annuel*) end of year statement; (*fig*) (net) outcome; (: *de victimes*) toll; **faire le ~ de** to assess; to review; **déposer son ~** to file a bankruptcy statement; **~ de santé** (*Méd*) check-up; **~ social** statement of a firm's policies towards its employees

bile [bil] *nf* bile; **se faire de la ~** (*fam*) to worry o.s. sick

bilieux, -euse [biljø, -øz] *adj* bilious; (*fig: colérique*) testy

bilingue [bilɛ̃g] *adj* bilingual

billard [bijaʀ] *nm* billiards *sg*; (*table*) billiard table; **c'est du ~** (*fam*) it's a cinch; **passer sur le ~** (*fam*) to have an (*ou* one's) operation; **~ électrique** pinball

bille [bij] *nf* ball; (*du jeu de billes*) marble; (*de bois*)

log; **jouer aux ~s** to play marbles
billet [bijɛ] nm (aussi: **billet de banque**)
(bank)note; (de cinéma, de bus etc) ticket; (courte
lettre) note; ~ **à ordre** ou **de commerce** (Comm)
promissory note, IOU; ~ **d'avion/de train** plane/
train ticket; ~ **circulaire** round-trip ticket; ~
doux love letter; ~ **de faveur** complimentary
ticket; ~ **de loterie** lottery ticket; ~ **de quai**
platform ticket; ~ **électronique** e-ticket
billetterie [bijɛtri] nf ticket office; (distributeur)
ticket dispenser; (Banque) cash dispenser
billion [biljɔ̃] nm billion (Brit), trillion (US)
billot [bijo] nm block
bimensuel, le [bimɑ̃sɥɛl] adj bimonthly, twice-
monthly
binette [binɛt] nf (outil) hoe
bio [bjo] adj (fam) = **biologique**; (produits, aliments)
organic
biocarburant [bjokarbyrɑ̃] nm biofuel
biochimie [bjɔʃimi] nf biochemistry
biodiversité [bjodivɛrsite] nf biodiversity
bioéthique [bjoetik] nf bioethics sg
biographie [bjografi] nf biography
biologie [bjɔlɔʒi] nf biology
biologique [bjɔlɔʒik] adj biological
biologiste [bjɔlɔʒist(ə)] nm/f biologist
biotechnologie [bjoteknɔlɔʒi] nf biotechnology
bioterrorisme [bjotɛrɔrism] nm bioterrorism
bioterroriste [bjotɛrɔrist] nm/f bioterrorist
Birmanie [birmani] nf: **la ~** Burma
bis, e [bi, biz] adj (couleur) greyish brown ▷ adv
[bis]: **12 ~ 12a** ou A ▷ excl, nm [bis] encore ▷ nf
(baiser) kiss; (vent) North wind; **faire une** ou **la ~e**
à qn to kiss sb
bisannuel, le [bizanɥɛl] adj biennial
biscornu, e [biskɔrny] adj crooked; (bizarre)
weird(-looking)
biscotte [biskɔt] nf (breakfast) rusk
biscuit [biskɥi] nm biscuit (Brit), cookie (US);
(gateau) sponge cake; ~ **à la cuiller** sponge finger
bise [biz] adj f, nf voir **bis**
bisou [bizu] nm (fam) kiss
bissextile [bisɛkstil] adj: **année ~** leap year
bistouri [bisturi] nm lancet
bistro, bistrot [bistro] nm bistro, café
bitume [bitym] nm asphalt
bizarre [bizar] adj strange, odd
blafard, e [blafar, -ard(ə)] adj wan
blague [blag] nf (propos) joke; (farce) trick; **sans ~!**
no kidding!; ~ **à tabac** tobacco pouch
blaguer [blage] vi to joke ▷ vt to tease
blaireau, x [blɛro] nm (Zool) badger; (brosse)
shaving brush
blairer [blɛre] vt: **je ne peux pas le ~** I can't bear
ou stand him
blâme [blɑm] nm blame; (sanction) reprimand
blâmer [blɑme] vt (réprouver) to blame;
(réprimander) to reprimand
blanc, blanche [blɑ̃, blɑ̃ʃ] adj white; (non imprimé)
blank; (innocent) pure ▷ nm/f white, white man/
woman ▷ nm (couleur) white; (linge): **le ~** whites
pl; (espace non écrit) blank; (aussi: **blanc d'œuf**)

(egg-)white; (aussi: **blanc de poulet**) breast,
white meat; (aussi: **vin blanc**) white wine ▷ nf
(Mus) minim (Brit), half-note (US); (fam: drogue)
smack; **d'une voix blanche** in a toneless voice;
aux cheveux ~s white-haired; **le ~ de l'œil** the
white of the eye; **laisser en ~** to leave blank;
chèque en ~ blank cheque; **à ~** adv (chauffer)
white-hot; (tirer, charger) with blanks; **saigner à**
~ to bleed white; **~ cassé** off-white
blancheur [blɑ̃ʃœr] nf whiteness
blanchir [blɑ̃ʃir] vt (gén) to whiten; (linge, fig:
argent) to launder; (Culin) to blanch; (fig: disculper)
to clear ▷ vi to grow white; (cheveux) to go white;
blanchi à la chaux whitewashed
blanchisserie [blɑ̃ʃisri] nf laundry
blason [blazɔ̃] nm coat of arms
blasphème [blasfɛm] nm blasphemy
blazer [blazɛr] nm blazer
blé [ble] nm wheat; ~ **en herbe** wheat on the ear;
~ **noir** buckwheat
bled [blɛd] nm (péj) hole; (en Afrique du Nord): **le ~**
the interior
blême [blɛm] adj pale
blessant, e [blɛsɑ̃, -ɑ̃t] adj hurtful
blessé, e [blese] adj injured ▷ nm/f injured
person, casualty; **un ~ grave, un grand ~** a
seriously injured ou wounded person
blesser [blese] vt to injure; (délibérément: Mil etc)
to wound; (souliers etc, offenser) to hurt; **se blesser**
to injure o.s.; **se ~ au pied** etc to injure one's
foot etc
blessure [blesyr] nf injury; wound
bleu, e [blø] adj blue; (bifteck) very rare ▷ nm
(couleur) blue; (novice) greenhorn; (contusion)
bruise; (vêtement: aussi: **bleus**) overalls pl (Brit),
coveralls pl (US); **avoir une peur ~e** to be
scared stiff; **zone ~e** ≈ restricted parking area;
fromage ~ blue cheese; **au ~** (Culin) au bleu; ~
(de lessive) ≈ blue bag; ~ **de méthylène** (Méd)
methylene blue; ~ **marine/nuit/roi** navy/
midnight/royal blue
bleuet [bløɛ] nm cornflower
bleuté, e [bløte] adj blue-shaded
blinder [blɛ̃de] vt to armour (Brit), armor (US);
(fig) to harden
bloc [blɔk] nm (de pierre etc, Inform) block; (de papier
à lettres) pad; (ensemble) group, block; **serré**
à ~ tightened right down; **en ~** as a whole;
wholesale; **faire ~** to unite; ~ **opératoire**
operating ou theatre block; ~ **sanitaire** toilet
block; ~ **sténo** shorthand notebook
blocage [blɔkaʒ] nm (voir bloquer) blocking;
jamming; freezing; (Psych) hang-up
bloc-notes (pl **blocs-notes**) [blɔknɔt] nm note pad
blocus [blɔkys] nm blockade
blog, blogue [blɔg] nm blog
bloguer [blɔge] vi to blog
blond, e [blɔ̃, -ɔ̃d] adj fair; (plus clair) blond; (sable,
blés) golden ▷ nm/f fair-haired ou blond man/
woman; ~ **cendré** ash blond
bloquer [blɔke] vt (passage) to block; (pièce mobile)
to jam; (crédits, compte) to freeze; (personne,

négociations etc) to hold up; (*regrouper*) to group; ~ **les freins** to jam on the brakes

blottir [blɔtiʀ]: **se blottir** *vi* to huddle up

blouse [bluz] *nf* overall

blouson [bluzɔ̃] *nm* blouson (jacket); ~ **noir** (*fig*) ≈ rocker

blue-jean [bludʒin], **blue-jeans** [bludʒins] *nm* jeans

bluff [blœf] *nm* bluff

bluffer [blœfe] *vi, vt* to bluff

bobard [bɔbaʀ] *nm* (*fam*) tall story

bobine [bɔbin] *nf* (*de fil*) reel; (*de machine à coudre*) spool; (*de machine à écrire*) ribbon; (*Élec*) coil; ~ **(d'allumage)** (*Auto*) coil; ~ **de pellicule** (*Photo*) roll of film

bocal, -aux [bɔkal, -o] *nm* jar

bock [bɔk] *nm* (beer) glass; (*contenu*) glass of beer

body [bɔdi] *nm* body(suit); (*Sport*) leotard

bœuf [bœf, *pl* bø] *nm* ox, steer; (*Culin*) beef; (*Mus: fam*) jam session

bof [bɔf] *excl* (*fam: indifférence*) don't care!; (: *pas terrible*) nothing special

bogue [bɔg] *nf* (*Bot*) husk ▷ *nm* (*Inform*) bug

bohème [bɔɛm] *adj* happy-go-lucky, unconventional

bohémien, ne [bɔemjɛ̃, -ɛn] *adj* Bohemian ▷ *nm/f* gipsy

boire [bwaʀ] *vt* to drink; (*s'imprégner de*) to soak up; ~ **un coup** to have a drink

bois [bwa] *vb voir* **boire** ▷ *nm* wood; (*Zool*) antler; (*Mus*): **les** ~ the woodwind; **de** ~, **en** ~ wooden; ~ **vert** green wood; ~ **mort** deadwood; ~ **de lit** bedstead

boisé, e [bwaze] *adj* woody, wooded

boisson [bwasɔ̃] *nf* drink; **pris de** ~ drunk, intoxicated; ~**s alcoolisées** alcoholic beverages *ou* drinks; ~**s non alcoolisées** soft drinks

boîte [bwat] *nf* box; (*fam: entreprise*) firm, company; **aliments en** ~ canned *ou* tinned (Brit) foods; ~ **de sardines/petits pois** can *ou* tin (Brit) of sardines/peas; **mettre qn en** ~ (*fam*) to have a laugh at sb's expense; ~ **d'allumettes** box of matches; (*vide*) matchbox; ~ **de conserves** can *ou* tin (Brit) (of food); ~ **crânienne** cranium; ~ **à gants** glove compartment; ~ **aux lettres** letter box, mailbox (US); (*Inform*) mailbox; ~ **à musique** musical box; ~ **noire** (*Aviat*) black box; ~ **de nuit** night club; ~ **à ordures** dustbin (Brit), trash can (US); ~ **postale (BP)** PO box; ~ **de vitesses** gear box; ~ **vocale** voice mail

boiter [bwate] *vi* to limp; (*fig*) to wobble; (*raisonnement*) to be shaky

boîtier [bwatje] *nm* case; (*d'appareil-photo*) body; ~ **de montre** watch case

boive *etc* [bwav] *vb voir* **boire**

bol [bɔl] *nm* bowl; (*contenu*): **un** ~ **de café** *etc* a bowl of coffee *etc*; **un** ~ **d'air** a breath of fresh air; **en avoir ras le** ~ (*fam*) to have had a bellyful

bolide [bɔlid] *nm* racing car; **comme un** ~ like a rocket

bombardement [bɔ̃baʀdəmɑ̃] *nm* bombing

bombarder [bɔ̃baʀde] *vt* to bomb; ~ **qn de** (*cailloux, lettres*) to bombard sb with; ~ **qn directeur** to thrust sb into the director's seat

bombe [bɔ̃b] *nf* bomb; (*atomiseur*) (aerosol) spray; (*Équitation*) riding cap; **faire la** ~ (*fam*) to go on a binge; ~ **atomique** atomic bomb; ~ **à retardement** time bomb

bombé, e [bɔ̃be] *adj* rounded; (*mur*) bulging; (*front*) domed; (*route*) steeply cambered

bomber [bɔ̃be] *vi* to bulge; (*route*) to camber ▷ *vt*: ~ **le torse** to swell out one's chest

bon, bonne [bɔ̃, bɔn] *adj* **1** (*agréable, satisfaisant*) good; **un** ~ **repas/restaurant** a good meal/restaurant; **être** ~ **en maths** to be good at maths **2** (*charitable*): **être** ~ **(envers)** to be good (to), to be kind (to); **vous êtes trop** ~ you're too kind **3** (*correct*) right; **le** ~ **numéro/moment** the right number/moment **4** (*souhaits*): ~ **anniversaire** happy birthday; ~ **courage** good luck; ~ **séjour** enjoy your stay; ~ **voyage** have a good trip; ~ **week-end** have a good weekend; ~**ne année** happy New Year; ~**ne chance** good luck; ~**ne fête** happy holiday; ~**ne nuit** good night **5** (*approprié*): ~ **à/pour** fit to/for; ~ **à jeter** fit for the bin; **c'est** ~ **à savoir** that's useful to know; **à quoi** ~ **(...)?** what's the point *ou* use of ...)? **6** (*intensif*): **ça m'a pris deux** ~**nes heures** it took me a good two hours; **un** ~ **nombre de** a good number of **7**: ~ **enfant** *adj inv* accommodating, easy-going; ~**ne femme** (*péj*) woman; **de** ~**ne heure** early; ~ **marché** cheap; ~ **mot** witticism; **pour faire** ~ **poids** ... to make up for it ...; ~ **sens** common sense; ~ **vivant** jovial chap; ~**nes œuvres** charitable works, charities; ~**ne sœur** nun ▷ *nm* **1** (*billet*) voucher; (*aussi:* **bon cadeau**) gift voucher; ~ **de caisse** cash voucher; ~ **d'essence** petrol coupon; ~ **à tirer** pass for press; ~ **du Trésor** Treasury bond **2**: **avoir du** ~ to have its good points; **il y a du** ~ **dans ce qu'il dit** there's some sense in what he says; **pour de** ~ for good ▷ *nm/f*: **un** ~ **à rien** a good-for-nothing ▷ *adv*: **il fait** ~ it's *ou* the weather is fine; **sentir** ~ to smell good; **tenir** ~ to stand firm; **juger** ~ **faire ...** to think fit to do ... ▷ *excl* right!, good!; **ah** ~? really?; ~, **je reste** right, I'll stay; *voir aussi* **bonne**

bonbon [bɔ̃bɔ̃] *nm* (boiled) sweet

bonbonne [bɔ̃bɔn] *nf* demijohn; carboy

bond [bɔ̃] *nm* leap; (*d'une balle*) rebound, ricochet; **faire un** ~ to leap in the air; **d'un seul** ~ in one bound, with one leap; ~ **en avant** (*fig: progrès*) leap forward

bondé, e [bɔ̃de] *adj* packed (full)

bondir [bɔ̃diʀ] *vi* to leap; ~ **de joie** (*fig*) to jump for joy; ~ **de colère** (*fig*) to be hopping mad

bonheur [bɔnœʀ] *nm* happiness; **avoir le** ~ **de** to have the good fortune to; **porter** ~ **(à qn)** to bring (sb) luck; **au petit** ~ haphazardly; **par** ~ fortunately

bonhomie [bɔnɔmi] *nf* good-naturedness

bonhomme [bɔnɔm] (pl **bonshommes**) [bɔ̃zɔm] nm fellow ▷ adj good-natured; **un vieux ~** an old chap; **aller son ~ de chemin** to carry on in one's own sweet way; **~ de neige** snowman

bonifier [bɔnifje]: **se bonifier** vi to improve

boniment [bɔnimɑ̃] nm patter no pl

bonjour [bɔ̃ʒuʀ] excl, nm hello; (selon l'heure) good morning (ou afternoon); **donner** ou **souhaiter le ~ à qn** to bid sb good morning ou afternoon

bonne [bɔn] adj f voir **bon** ▷ nf (domestique) maid; **~ à toute faire** general help; **~ d'enfant** nanny

bonnement [bɔnmɑ̃] adv: **tout ~** quite simply

bonnet [bɔnɛ] nm bonnet, hat; (de soutien-gorge) cup; **~ d'âne** dunce's cap; **~ de bain** bathing cap; **~ de nuit** nightcap

bonsoir [bɔ̃swaʀ] excl good evening

bonté [bɔ̃te] nf kindness no pl; **avoir la ~ de** to be kind ou good enough to

bonus [bɔnys] nm (Assurances) no-claims bonus

bord [bɔʀ] nm (de table, verre, falaise) edge; (de rivière, lac) bank; (de route) side; (de vêtement) edge, border; (de chapeau) brim; **(monter) à ~** (to go) on board; **le commandant de ~/les hommes du ~** the ship's master/crew; **du même ~** (fig) of the same opinion; **au ~ de la mer/route** at the seaside/roadside; **être au ~ des larmes** to be on the verge of tears; **virer de ~** (Navig) to tack; **sur les ~s** (fig) slightly; **de tous ~s** on all sides; **~ du trottoir** kerb (Brit), curb (US)

bordeaux [bɔʀdo] nm Bordeaux ▷ adj inv maroon

bordel [bɔʀdɛl] nm brothel; (fam!) bloody (Brit) ou goddamn (US) mess (!) ▷ excl hell!

bordelais, e [bɔʀdəlɛ, -ɛz] adj of ou from Bordeaux

border [bɔʀde] vt (être le long de) to border, line; (garnir): **~ qch de** to line sth with; to trim sth with; (qn dans son lit) to tuck up

bordereau, x [bɔʀdəʀo] nm docket, slip

bordure [bɔʀdyʀ] nf border; (sur un vêtement) trim(ming), border; **en ~ de** on the edge of

borgne [bɔʀɲ(ə)] adj one-eyed; **hôtel ~** shady hotel; **fenêtre ~** obstructed window

borne [bɔʀn(ə)] nf boundary stone; (aussi: **borne kilométrique**) kilometre-marker, ≈ milestone; **bornes** nfpl (fig) limits; **dépasser les ~s** to go too far; **sans ~(s)** boundless

borné, e [bɔʀne] adj narrow; (obtus) narrow-minded

borner [bɔʀne] vt (délimiter) to limit; (limiter) to confine; **se ~ à faire** to content o.s. with doing; to limit o.s. to doing

Bosnie-Herzégovine [bɔsniɛʀzegɔvin] nf Bosnia-Herzegovina

bosquet [bɔskɛ] nm copse (Brit), grove

bosse [bɔs] nf (de terrain etc) bump; (enflure) lump; (du bossu, du chameau) hump; **avoir la ~ des maths** etc to have a gift for maths etc; **il a roulé sa ~** he's been around

bosser [bɔse] vi (fam) to work; (: dur) to slog (hard) (Brit), slave (away)

bossu, e [bɔsy] nm/f hunchback

botanique [bɔtanik] nf botany ▷ adj botanic(al)

botte [bɔt] nf (soulier) (high) boot; (Escrime) thrust; (gerbe): **~ de paille** bundle of straw; **~ de radis/d'asperges** bunch of radishes/asparagus; **~s de caoutchouc** wellington boots

botter [bɔte] vt to put boots on; (donner un coup de pied à) to kick; (fam): **ça me botte** I fancy that

bottin® [bɔtɛ̃] nm directory

bottine [bɔtin] nf ankle boot

bouc [buk] nm goat; (barbe) goatee; **~ émissaire** scapegoat

boucan [bukɑ̃] nm din, racket

bouche [buʃ] nf mouth; **une ~ à nourrir** a mouth to feed; **les ~s inutiles** the non-productive members of the population; **faire du ~ à ~ à qn** to give sb the kiss of life (Brit), give sb mouth-to-mouth resuscitation; **de ~ à oreille** confidentially; **pour la bonne ~** (pour la fin) till last; **faire venir l'eau à la ~** to make one's mouth water; **~ cousue!** mum's the word!; **~ d'aération** air vent; **~ de chaleur** hot air vent; **~ d'égout** manhole; **~ d'incendie** fire hydrant; **~ de métro** métro entrance

bouché, e [buʃe] adj (flacon etc) stoppered; (temps, ciel) overcast; (carrière) blocked; (péj: personne) thick; (trompette) muted; **avoir le nez ~** to have a blocked(-up) nose

bouchée [buʃe] nf mouthful; **ne faire qu'une ~ de** (fig) to make short work of; **pour une ~ de pain** (fig) for next to nothing; **~s à la reine** chicken vol-au-vents

boucher [buʃe] nm butcher ▷ vt (pour colmater) to stop up; to fill up; (obstruer) to block (up); **se boucher** (tuyau etc) to block up, get blocked up; **se ~ le nez** to hold one's nose

boucherie [buʃʀi] nf butcher's (shop); (métier) butchery; (fig) slaughter, butchery

bouche-trou [buʃtʀu] nm (fig) stop-gap

bouchon [buʃɔ̃] nm (en liège) cork; (autre matière) stopper; (fig: embouteillage) holdup; (Pêche) float; **~ doseur** measuring cap

boucle [bukl(ə)] nf (forme, figure, aussi Inform) loop; (objet) buckle; **~ (de cheveux)** curl; **~ d'oreilles** earring

bouclé, e [bukle] adj curly; (tapis) uncut

boucler [bukle] vt (fermer: ceinture etc) to fasten; (: magasin) to shut; (: terminer) to finish off; (: circuit) to complete; (budget) to balance; (enfermer) to shut away; (: condamné) to lock up; (: quartier) to seal off ▷ vi to curl; **faire ~** (cheveux) to curl; **~ la boucle** (Aviat) to loop the loop

bouclier [buklije] nm shield

bouddhiste [budist(ə)] nm/f Buddhist

bouder [bude] vi to sulk ▷ vt (chose) to turn one's nose up at; (personne) to refuse to have anything to do with

boudin [budɛ̃] nm (Culin) black pudding; (Tech) roll; **~ blanc** white pudding

boue [bu] nf mud

bouée [bwe] nf buoy; (de baigneur) rubber ring; **~ (de sauvetage)** lifebuoy; (fig) lifeline

boueux, -euse [bwø, -øz] adj muddy ▷ nm (fam)

refuse (Brit) ou garbage (US) collector

bouffe [buf] nf (fam) grub, food

bouffée [bufe] nf puff; ~ **de chaleur** (gén) blast of hot air; (Méd) hot flush (Brit) ou flash (US); ~ **de fièvre/de honte** flush of fever/shame; ~ **d'orgueil** fit of pride

bouffer [bufe] vi (fam) to eat; (Couture) to puff out ▷ vt (fam) to eat

bouffi, e [bufi] adj swollen

bougeoir [buʒwaʀ] nm candlestick

bougeotte [buʒɔt] nf: **avoir la** ~ to have the fidgets

bouger [buʒe] vi to move; (dent etc) to be loose; (changer) to alter; (agir) to stir ▷ vt to move; **se bouger** (fam) to move (oneself)

bougie [buʒi] nf candle; (Auto) spark(ing) plug

bougon, ne [bugɔ̃, -ɔn] adj grumpy

bougonner [bugɔne] vi, vt to grumble

bouillabaisse [bujabɛs] nf type of fish soup

bouillant, e [bujɑ̃, -ɑ̃t] adj (qui bout) boiling; (très chaud) boiling (hot); (fig: ardent) hot-headed; ~ **de colère** etc seething with anger etc

bouillie [buji] nf gruel; (de bébé) cereal; **en** ~ (fig) crushed

bouillir [bujiʀ] vi to boil ▷ vt (aussi: **faire bouillir**: Culin) to boil; ~ **de colère** etc to seethe with anger etc

bouilloire [bujwaʀ] nf kettle

bouillon [bujɔ̃] nm (Culin) stock no pl; (bulles, écume) bubble; ~ **de culture** culture medium

bouillonner [bujɔne] vi to bubble; (fig) to bubble up; (torrent) to foam

bouillotte [bujɔt] nf hot-water bottle

boulanger, -ère [bulɑ̃ʒe, -ɛʀ] nm/f baker ▷ nf (femme du boulanger) baker's wife

boulangerie [bulɑ̃ʒʀi] nf bakery, baker's (shop); (commerce) bakery; ~ **industrielle** bakery

boulangerie-pâtisserie (pl **boulangeries-pâtisseries**) [bulɑ̃ʒʀipatisʀi] nf baker's and confectioner's (shop)

boule [bul] nf (gén) ball; (pour jouer) bowl; (de machine à écrire) golf ball; **roulé en** ~ curled up in a ball; **se mettre en** ~ (fig) to fly off the handle, blow one's top; **perdre la** ~ (fig: fam) to go off one's rocker; ~ **de gomme** (bonbon) gum(drop), pastille; ~ **de neige** snowball; **faire** ~ **de neige** (fig) to snowball

bouleau, x [bulo] nm (silver) birch

bouledogue [buldɔg] nm bulldog

boulet [bulɛ] nm (aussi: **boulet de canon**) cannonball; (de bagnard) ball and chain; (charbon) (coal) nut

boulette [bulɛt] nf ball

boulevard [bulvaʀ] nm boulevard

bouleversant, e [bulvɛʀsɑ̃, -ɑ̃t] adj (récit) deeply distressing; (nouvelle) shattering

bouleversement [bulvɛʀsəmɑ̃] nm (politique, social) upheaval

bouleverser [bulvɛʀse] vt (émouvoir) to overwhelm; (causer du chagrin à) to distress; (pays, vie) to disrupt; (papiers, objets) to turn upside down, upset

boulon [bulɔ̃] nm bolt

boulot [bulo] nm (fam: travail) work

boulot, te [bulo, -ɔt] adj plump, tubby

boum [bum] nm bang ▷ nf party

bouquet [bukɛ] nm (de fleurs) bunch (of flowers), bouquet; (de persil etc) bunch; (parfum) bouquet; (fig) crowning piece; **c'est le** ~! that's the last straw!; ~ **garni** (Culin) bouquet garni

bouquin [bukɛ̃] nm (fam) book

bouquiner [bukine] vi (fam) to read

bouquiniste [bukinist(ə)] nm/f bookseller

bourbeux, -euse [buʀbø, -øz] adj muddy

bourbier [buʀbje] nm (quag)mire

bourde [buʀd(ə)] nf (erreur) howler; (gaffe) blunder

bourdon [buʀdɔ̃] nm bumblebee

bourdonner [buʀdɔne] vi to buzz; (moteur) to hum

bourg [buʀ] nm small market town (ou village)

bourgeois, e [buʀʒwa, -waz] adj (péj) ≈ (upper) middle class; bourgeois; (maison etc) very comfortable ▷ nm/f (autrefois) burgher

bourgeoisie [buʀʒwazi] nf ≈ upper middle classes pl; bourgeoisie; **petite** ~ middle classes

bourgeon [buʀʒɔ̃] nm bud

Bourgogne [buʀgɔɲ] nf: **la** ~ Burgundy ▷ nm: **bourgogne** Burgundy (wine)

bourguignon, ne [buʀgiɲɔ̃, -ɔn] adj of ou from Burgundy, Burgundian; **bœuf** ~ bœuf bourguignon

bourlinguer [buʀlɛ̃ge] vi to knock about a lot, get around a lot

bourrade [buʀad] nf shove, thump

bourrage [buʀaʒ] nm (papier) jamming; ~ **de crâne** brainwashing; (Scol) cramming

bourrasque [buʀask(ə)] nf squall

bourratif, -ive [buʀatif, -iv] adj filling, stodgy

bourré, e [buʀe] adj (rempli): ~ **de** crammed full of; (fam: ivre) pickled, plastered

bourreau, x [buʀo] nm executioner; (fig) torturer; ~ **de travail** workaholic, glutton for work

bourrelet [buʀlɛ] nm draught (Brit) ou draft (US) excluder; (de peau) fold ou roll (of flesh)

bourrer [buʀe] vt (pipe) to fill; (poêle) to pack; (valise) to cram (full); ~ **de** to cram (full) with, stuff with; ~ **de coups** to hammer blows on, pummel; ~ **le crâne à qn** to pull the wool over sb's eyes; (endoctriner) to brainwash sb

bourrique [buʀik] nf (âne) ass

bourru, e [buʀy] adj surly, gruff

bourse [buʀs(ə)] nf (subvention) grant; (porte-monnaie) purse; **sans** ~ **délier** without spending a penny; **la B~** the Stock Exchange; **du travail** ≈ trades union council (regional headquarters)

boursier, -ière [buʀsje, -jɛʀ] adj (Comm) Stock Market cpd ▷ nm/f (Scol) grant-holder

boursoufler [buʀsufle] vt to swell up, bloat; **se boursoufler** vi (visage) to swell ou puff up; (peinture) to blister

bous [bu] vb voir **bouillir**

bousculade [buskylad] nf (hâte) rush; (poussée)

crush

bousculer [buskyle] vt to knock over; to knock into; (fig) to push, rush

bouse [buz] nf: ~ **(de vache)** (cow) dung no pl (Brit), manure no pl

bousiller [buzije] vt (fam) to wreck

boussole [busɔl] nf compass

bout [bu] vb voir **bouillir** ▷ nm bit; (extrémité: d'un bâton etc) tip; (: d'une ficelle, table, rue, période) end; **au ~ de** at the end of, after; **au ~ du compte** at the end of the day; **pousser qn à ~** to push sb to the limit (of his patience); **venir à ~ de** to manage to finish (off) ou overcome; **~ à ~** end to end; **à tout ~ de champ** at every turn; **d'un ~ à l'autre, de ~ en ~** from one end to the other; **à ~ portant** at point-blank range; **un ~ de chou** (enfant) a little tot; **~ d'essai** (Ciné etc) screen test; **~ filtre** filter tip

boutade [butad] nf quip, sally

boute-en-train [butɑ̃trɛ̃] nm inv live wire (fig)

bouteille [butɛj] nf bottle; (de gaz butane) cylinder

boutique [butik] nf shop (Brit), store (US); (de grand couturier, de mode) boutique

bouton [butɔ̃] nm (de vêtement, électrique etc) button; (Bot) bud; (sur la peau) spot; (de porte) knob; **~ de manchette** cuff-link; **~ d'or** buttercup

boutonner [butɔne] vt to button up, do up; **se boutonner** to button one's clothes up

boutonnière [butɔnjɛr] nf buttonhole

bouton-pression (pl **boutons-pression**) [butɔ̃presjɔ̃] nm press stud, snap fastener

bouture [butyr] nf cutting; **faire des ~s** to take cuttings

bovin, e [bɔvɛ̃, -in] adj bovine ▷ nm: **~s** cattle

bowling [bolin] nm (tenpin) bowling; (salle) bowling alley

box [bɔks] nm lock-up (garage); (de salle, dortoir) cubicle; (d'écurie) loose-box; (aussi: **box-calf**) box calf; **le ~ des accusés** the dock

boxe [bɔks(ə)] nf boxing

boxeur [bɔksœr] nm boxer

boyaux [bwajo] nmpl (viscères) entrails, guts

BP sigle f = **boîte postale**

bracelet [braslɛ] nm bracelet

braconnier [brakɔnje] nm poacher

brader [brade] vt to sell off, sell cheaply

braderie [bradri] nf clearance sale; (par des particuliers) ≈ car boot sale (Brit), ≈ garage sale (US); (magasin) discount store; (sur marché) cut-price (Brit) ou cut-rate (US) stall

braguette [bragɛt] nf fly, flies pl (Brit), zipper (US)

brailler [braje] vi to bawl, yell ▷ vt to bawl out, yell out

braire [brɛr] vi to bray

braise [brɛz] nf embers pl

brancard [brɑ̃kar] nm (civière) stretcher; (bras, perche) shaft

brancardier [brɑ̃kardje] nm stretcher-bearer

branchages [brɑ̃ʃaʒ] nmpl branches, boughs

branche [brɑ̃ʃ] nf branch; (de lunettes) side (-piece)

branché, e [brɑ̃ʃe] adj (fam) switched-on, trendy ▷ nm/f (fam) trendy

brancher [brɑ̃ʃe] vt to connect (up); (en mettant la prise) to plug in; **~ qn/qch sur** (fig) to get sb/sth launched onto

brandir [brɑ̃dir] vt (arme) to brandish, wield; (document) to flourish, wave

branle [brɑ̃l] nm: **mettre en ~** to set swinging; **donner le ~ à** to set in motion

branle-bas [brɑ̃lba] nm inv commotion

braquer [brake] vi (Auto) to turn (the wheel) ▷ vt (revolver etc): **~ qch sur** to aim sth at, point sth at; (mettre en colère): **~ qn** to antagonize sb, put sb's back up; **~ son regard sur** to fix one's gaze on; **se braquer** vi: **se ~ (contre)** to take a stand (against)

bras [bra] nm arm; (de fleuve) branch ▷ nmpl (fig: travailleurs) labour sg (Brit), labor sg (US); **~ dessus - dessous** arm in arm; **à ~ raccourcis** with fists flying; **à tour de ~** with all one's might; **baisser les ~** to give up; **~ droit** (fig) right hand man; **~ de fer** arm-wrestling; **une partie de ~ de fer** (fig) a trial of strength; **~ de levier** lever arm; **~ de mer** arm of the sea, sound

brasier [brazje] nm blaze, (blazing) inferno; (fig) inferno

bras-le-corps [bralkɔr]: **à ~** adv (a)round the waist

brassard [brasar] nm armband

brasse [bras] nf (nage) breast-stroke; (mesure) fathom; **~ papillon** butterfly(-stroke)

brassée [brase] nf armful; **une ~ de** (fig) a number of

brasser [brase] vt (bière) to brew; (remuer: salade) to toss; (: cartes) to shuffle; (fig) to mix; **~ l'argent/les affaires** to handle a lot of money/ business

brasserie [brasri] nf (restaurant) bar (selling food), brasserie; (usine) brewery

brave [brav] adj (courageux) brave; (bon, gentil) good, kind

braver [brave] vt to defy

bravo [bravo] excl bravo! ▷ nm cheer

bravoure [bravur] nf bravery

break [brɛk] nm (Auto) estate car (Brit), station wagon (US)

brebis [brəbi] nf ewe; **~ galeuse** black sheep

brèche [brɛʃ] nf breach, gap; **être sur la ~** (fig) to be on the go

bredouille [brəduj] adj empty-handed

bredouiller [brəduje] vi, vt to mumble, stammer

bref, brève [brɛf, brɛv] adj short, brief ▷ adv in short ▷ nf (voyelle) short vowel; (information) brief news item; **d'un ton ~** sharply, curtly; **en ~** in short, in brief; **à ~ délai** shortly

Brésil [brezil] nm: **le ~** Brazil

brésilien, ne [breziljɛ̃, -ɛn] adj Brazilian ▷ nm/f: **B~, ne** Brazilian

Bretagne [bʀətaɲ] *nf*: **la ~** Brittany
bretelle [bʀətɛl] *nf* (*de fusil etc*) sling; (*de
vêtement*) strap; (*d'autoroute*) slip road (Brit),
entrance *ou* exit ramp (US); **bretelles** *nfpl*
(*pour pantalon*) braces (Brit), suspenders (US);
~ de contournement (Auto) bypass; **~ de
raccordement** (Auto) access road
breton, ne [bʀətɔ̃, -ɔn] *adj* Breton ▷ *nm* (Ling)
Breton ▷ *nm/f*: **B~, ne** Breton
breuvage [bʀœvaʒ] *nm* beverage, drink
brève [bʀɛv] *adj f, nf voir* **bref**
brevet [bʀəvɛ] *nm* diploma, certificate; **~
(d'invention)** patent; **~ d'apprentissage**
certificate of apprenticeship; **~ (des collèges)**
school certificate, taken at approx. 16 years
breveté, e [bʀəvte] *adj* patented; (*diplômé*)
qualified
bribes [bʀib] *nfpl* bits, scraps; (*d'une conversation*)
snatches; **par ~** piecemeal
bricolage [bʀikɔlaʒ] *nm*: **le ~** do-it-yourself
(jobs); (*péj*) patched-up job
bricole [bʀikɔl] *nf* (*babiole, chose insignifiante*) trifle;
(*petit travail*) small job
bricoler [bʀikɔle] *vi* to do odd jobs; (*en amateur*)
to do DIY jobs; (*passe-temps*) to potter about ▷ *vt*
(*réparer*) to fix up; (*mal réparer*) to tinker with;
(*trafiquer: voiture etc*) to doctor, fix
bricoleur, -euse [bʀikɔlœʀ, -øz] *nm/f*
handyman/woman, DIY enthusiast
bride [bʀid] *nf* bridle; (*d'un bonnet*) string, tie; **à ~
abattue** flat out, hell for leather; **tenir en ~** to
keep in check; **lâcher la ~ à, laisser la ~ sur le
cou à** to give free rein to
bridé, e [bʀide] *adj*: **yeux ~s** slit eyes
bridge [bʀidʒ(ə)] *nm* bridge
brièvement [bʀijɛvmɑ̃] *adv* briefly
brigade [bʀigad] *nf* squad; (Mil) brigade
brigadier [bʀigadje] *nm* (Police) ≈ sergeant; (Mil)
bombardier; corporal
brigandage [bʀigɑ̃daʒ] *nm* robbery
briguer [bʀige] *vt* to aspire to; (*suffrages*) to
canvass
brillamment [bʀijamɑ̃] *adv* brilliantly
brillant, e [bʀijɑ̃, -ɑ̃t] *adj* brilliant; bright;
(*luisant*) shiny, shining ▷ *nm* (*diamant*)
brilliant
briller [bʀije] *vi* to shine
brimer [bʀime] *vt* to harass; to bully
brin [bʀɛ̃] *nm* (*de laine, ficelle etc*) strand; (*fig*): **un
~ de** a bit of; **un ~ mystérieux** *etc* (*fam*) a weeny
bit mysterious *etc*; **~ d'herbe** blade of grass; **~
de muguet** sprig of lily of the valley; **~ de paille**
wisp of straw
brindille [bʀɛ̃dij] *nf* twig
brio [bʀijo] *nm* brilliance; (Mus) brio; **avec ~**
brilliantly, with panache
brioche [bʀijɔʃ] *nf* brioche (bun); (*fam: ventre*)
paunch
brique [bʀik] *nf* brick; (*fam*) 10 000 francs ▷ *adj
inv* brick red
briquer [bʀike] *vt* (*fam*) to polish up
briquet [bʀikɛ] *nm* (*cigarette*) lighter

brise [bʀiz] *nf* breeze
briser [bʀize] *vt* to break; **se briser** *vi* to break
britannique [bʀitanik] *adj* British ▷ *nm/f*: **B~**
Briton, British person; **les B~s** the British
brocante [bʀɔkɑ̃t] *nf* (*objets*) secondhand goods
pl, junk; (*commerce*) secondhand trade; junk
dealing
brocanteur, -euse [bʀɔkɑ̃tœʀ, -øz] *nm/f* junk
shop owner; junk dealer
broche [bʀɔʃ] *nf* brooch; (Culin) spit; (*fiche*) spike,
peg; (Méd) pin; **à la ~** spit-roasted, roasted on
a spit
broché, e [bʀɔʃe] *adj* (*livre*) paper-backed; (*tissu*)
brocaded
brochet [bʀɔʃɛ] *nm* pike *inv*
brochette [bʀɔʃɛt] *nf* skewer; **~ de décorations**
row of medals
brochure [bʀɔʃyʀ] *nf* pamphlet, brochure,
booklet
broder [bʀɔde] *vt* to embroider ▷ *vi*: **~ (sur des
faits *ou* une histoire)** to embroider the facts
broderie [bʀɔdʀi] *nf* embroidery
broncher [bʀɔ̃ʃe] *vi*: **sans ~** without flinching,
without turning a hair
bronches [bʀɔ̃ʃ] *nfpl* bronchial tubes
bronchite [bʀɔ̃ʃit] *nf* bronchitis
bronze [bʀɔ̃z] *nm* bronze
bronzer [bʀɔ̃ze] *vt* to tan ▷ *vi* to get a tan; **se
bronzer** to sunbathe
brosse [bʀɔs] *nf* brush; **donner un coup de
~ à qch** to give sth a brush; **coiffé en ~** with
a crewcut; **~ à cheveux** hairbrush; **~ à dents**
toothbrush; **~ à habits** clothesbrush
brosser [bʀɔse] *vt* (*nettoyer*) to brush; (*fig: tableau
etc*) to paint; to draw; **se brosser** *vt, vi* to brush
one's clothes; **se ~ les dents** to brush one's
teeth; **tu peux te ~!** (*fam*) you can sing for it!
brouette [bʀuɛt] *nf* wheelbarrow
brouhaha [bʀuaa] *nm* hubbub
brouillard [bʀujaʀ] *nm* fog; **être dans le ~** (*fig*) to
be all at sea
brouille [bʀuj] *nf* quarrel
brouiller [bʀuje] *vt* to mix up; to confuse; (Radio)
to cause interference to; (: *délibérément*) to jam;
(*rendre trouble*) to cloud; (*désunir: amis*) to set at
odds; **se brouiller** *vi* (*ciel, vue*) to cloud over;
(*détails*) to become confused; **se ~ (avec)** to fall
out (with); **~ les pistes** to cover one's tracks;
(*fig*) to confuse the issue
brouillon, ne [bʀujɔ̃, -ɔn] *adj* disorganized,
unmethodical ▷ *nm* (first) draft; **cahier de ~**
rough (work) book
broussailles [bʀusaj] *nfpl* undergrowth *sg*
broussailleux, -euse [bʀusajø, -øz] *adj* bushy
brousse [bʀus] *nf*: **la ~** the bush
brouter [bʀute] *vt* to graze on ▷ *vi* to graze;
(Auto) to judder
broutille [bʀutij] *nf* trifle
broyer [bʀwaje] *vt* to crush; **~ du noir** to be
down in the dumps
bru [bʀy] *nf* daughter-in-law
brugnon [bʀyɲɔ̃] *nm* nectarine

bruiner [bʀɥine] vb impers: **il bruine** it's drizzling, there's a drizzle

bruire [bʀɥiʀ] vi (eau) to murmur; (feuilles, étoffe) to rustle

bruit [bʀɥi] nm: **un ~** a noise, a sound; (fig: rumeur) a rumour (Brit), a rumor (US); **le ~** noise; **pas/trop de ~** no/too much noise; **sans ~** without a sound, noiselessly; **faire du ~** to make a noise; **~ de fond** background noise

bruitage [bʀɥitaʒ] nm sound effects pl

brûlant, e [bʀylɑ̃, -ɑ̃t] adj burning (hot); (liquide) boiling (hot); (regard) fiery; (sujet) red-hot

brûlé, e [bʀyle] adj (fig: démasqué) blown; (: homme politique etc) discredited ▷ nm: **odeur de ~** smell of burning

brûle-pourpoint [bʀylpuʀpwɛ̃]: **à ~** adv point-blank

brûler [bʀyle] vt to burn; (eau bouillante) to scald; (consommer: électricité, essence) to use; (feu rouge, signal) to go through (without stopping) ▷ vi to burn; (jeu): **tu brûles** you're getting warm ou hot; **se brûler** to burn o.s.; to scald o.s.; **se ~ la cervelle** to blow one's brains out; **~ les étapes** to make rapid progress; (aller trop vite) to cut corners; **~ (d'impatience) de faire qch** to burn with impatience to do sth, be dying to do sth

brûlure [bʀylyʀ] nf (lésion) burn; (sensation) burning no pl, burning sensation; **~s d'estomac** heartburn sg

brume [bʀym] nf mist

brumeux, -euse [bʀymø, -øz] adj misty; (fig) hazy

brumisateur [bʀymizatœʀ] nm atomizer

brun, e [bʀœ̃, -yn] adj brown; (cheveux, personne) dark ▷ nm (couleur) brown ▷ nf (cigarette) cigarette made of dark tobacco; (bière) ≈ brown ale, ≈ stout

brunch [bʀœntʃ] nm brunch

brunir [bʀyniʀ] vi: **se brunir** to get a tan ▷ vt to tan

brushing [bʀœʃiŋ] nm blow-dry

brusque [bʀysk(ə)] adj (soudain) abrupt, sudden; (rude) abrupt, brusque

brusquer [bʀyske] vt to rush

brut, e [bʀyt] adj raw, crude, rough; (diamant) uncut; (soie, minéral, Inform: données) raw; (Comm) gross ▷ nf brute; **(champagne) ~** brut champagne; **(pétrole) ~** crude (oil)

brutal, e, -aux [bʀytal, -o] adj brutal

brutaliser [bʀytalize] vt to handle roughly, manhandle

Bruxelles [bʀysɛl] n Brussels

bruyamment [bʀɥijamɑ̃] adv noisily

bruyant, e [bʀɥijɑ̃, -ɑ̃t] adj noisy

bruyère [bʀyjɛʀ] nf heather

BTS sigle m (= Brevet de technicien supérieur) vocational training certificate taken at end of two-year higher education course

bu, e [by] pp de **boire**

buccal, e, -aux [bykal, -o] adj: **par voie ~e** orally

bûche [byʃ] nf log; **prendre une ~** (fig) to come a cropper (Brit), fall flat on one's face; **~ de Noël** Yule log

bûcher [byʃe] nm pyre; bonfire ▷ vi (fam: étudier) to swot (Brit), grind (US) ▷ vt to swot up (Brit), cram

bûcheron [byʃʀɔ̃] nm woodcutter

bûcheur, -euse [byʃœʀ, -øz] nm/f (fam: étudiant) swot (Brit), grind (US)

budget [bydʒɛ] nm budget

buée [bɥe] nf (sur une vitre) mist; (de l'haleine) steam

buffet [byfɛ] nm (meuble) sideboard; (de réception) buffet; **~ (de gare)** (station) buffet, snack bar

buffle [byfl(ə)] nm buffalo

buis [bɥi] nm box tree; (bois) box(wood)

buisson [bɥisɔ̃] nm bush

buissonnière [bɥisɔnjɛʀ] adj f: **faire l'école ~** to play truant (Brit), skip school

bulbe [bylb(ə)] nm (Bot, Anat) bulb; (coupole) onion-shaped dome

Bulgarie [bylgaʀi] nf: **la ~** Bulgaria

bulle [byl] adj, nm: **(papier) ~** manil(l)a paper ▷ nf bubble; (de bande dessinée) balloon; (papale) bull; **~ de savon** soap bubble

bulletin [byltɛ̃] nm (communiqué, journal) bulletin; (papier) form; (: de bagages) ticket; (Scol) report; **~ d'informations** news bulletin; **~ météorologique** weather report; **~ de naissance** birth certificate; **~ de salaire** pay slip; **~ de santé** medical bulletin; **~ (de vote)** ballot paper

bureau, x [byʀo] nm (meuble) desk; (pièce, service) office; **~ de change** (foreign) exchange office ou bureau; **~ d'embauche** ≈ job centre; **~ d'études** design office; **~ de location** box office; **~ des objets trouvés** lost property office (Brit), lost and found (US); **~ de placement** employment agency; **~ de poste** post office; **~ de tabac** tobacconist's (shop), smoke shop (US); **~ de vote** polling station

bureaucratie [byʀokʀasi] nf bureaucracy

burin [byʀɛ̃] nm cold chisel; (Art) burin

burlesque [byʀlɛsk(ə)] adj ridiculous; (Littérature) burlesque

bus vb [by] voir **boire** ▷ nm [bys] (véhicule, aussi Inform) bus

busqué, e [byske] adj: **nez ~** hook(ed) nose

buste [byst(ə)] nm (Anat) chest; (: de femme) bust; (sculpture) bust

but [by] vb voir **boire** ▷ nm (cible) target; (fig) goal, aim; (Football etc) goal; **de ~ en blanc** point-blank; **avoir pour ~ de faire** to aim to do; **dans le ~ de** with the intention of

butane [bytan] nm butane; (domestique) calor gas® (Brit), butane

buté, e [byte] adj stubborn, obstinate ▷ nf (Archit) abutment; (Tech) stop

buter [byte] vi: **~ contre** ou **sur** to bump into; (trébucher) to stumble against ▷ vt to antagonize; **se buter** vi to get obstinate, dig in one's heels

butin [bytɛ̃] nm booty, spoils pl; (d'un vol) loot

butiner [bytine] *vi* to gather nectar
butte [byt] *nf* mound, hillock; **être en ~ à** to be
  exposed to
buvais *etc* [byvɛ] *vb voir* **boire**

buvard [byvaʀ] *nm* blotter
buvette [byvɛt] *nf* refreshment room *ou* stall;
  (*comptoir*) bar
buveur, -euse [byvœʀ, -øz] *nm/f* drinker

Cc

c' [s] *pron voir* **ce**

CA *sigle m* = **chiffre d'affaires; conseil d'administration; corps d'armée** ▷ *sigle f* = **chambre d'agriculture**

ça [sa] *pron (pour désigner)* this; (: *plus loin*) that; (*comme sujet indéfini*) it; **ça m'étonne que** it surprises me that; **ça va?** how are you?; how are things?; (*d'accord?*) OK?, all right?; **ça alors!** (*désapprobation*) well!, really!; (*étonnement*) heavens!; **c'est ça** that's right

çà [sa] *adv:* **çà et là** here and there

cabane [kaban] *nf* hut, cabin

cabaret [kabaʀɛ] *nm* night club

cabas [kabɑ] *nm* shopping bag

cabillaud [kabijo] *nm* cod *inv*

cabine [kabin] *nf (de bateau)* cabin; (*de plage*) (beach) hut; (*de piscine etc*) cubicle; (*de camion, train*) cab; (*d'avion*) cockpit; **~ (d'ascenseur)** lift cage; **~ d'essayage** fitting room; **~ de projection** projection room; **~ spatiale** space capsule; **~ (téléphonique)** call *ou* (tele)phone box, (tele)phone booth

cabinet [kabinɛ] *nm (petite pièce)* closet; (*de médecin*) surgery (Brit), office (US); (*de notaire etc*) office; (: *clientèle*) practice; (Pol) cabinet; (*d'un ministre*) advisers *pl*; **cabinets** *nmpl* (w.-c.) toilet *sg*; **~ d'affaires** business consultants' (bureau), business partnership; **~ de toilette** toilet; **~ de travail** study

câble [kɑbl(ə)] *nm* cable; **le ~** (TV) cable television, cablevision (US)

cabosser [kabɔse] *vt* to dent

cabrer [kabʀe]: **se cabrer** *vi (cheval)* to rear up; (*avion*) to nose up; (*fig*) to revolt, rebel; to jib

cabriole [kabʀijɔl] *nf* caper; (*gymnastique etc*) somersault

cacahuète [kakaɥɛt] *nf* peanut

cacao [kakao] *nm* cocoa (powder); (*boisson*) cocoa

cache [kaʃ] *nm* mask, card (*for masking*) ▷ *nf* hiding place

cache-cache [kaʃkaʃ] *nm:* **jouer à ~** to play hide-and-seek

cachemire [kaʃmiʀ] *nm* cashmere ▷ *adj:* **dessin ~** paisley pattern; **le C~** Kashmir

cache-nez [kaʃne] *nm inv* scarf, muffler

cacher [kaʃe] *vt* to hide, conceal; **~ qch à qn** to hide *ou* conceal sth from sb; **se cacher** to hide; to

be hidden *ou* concealed; **il ne s'en cache pas** he makes no secret of it

cachet [kaʃɛ] *nm (comprimé)* tablet; (*sceau: du roi*) seal; (: *de la poste*) postmark; (*rétribution*) fee; (*fig*) style, character

cacheter [kaʃte] *vt* to seal; **vin cacheté** vintage wine

cachette [kaʃɛt] *nf* hiding place; **en ~** on the sly, secretly

cachot [kaʃo] *nm* dungeon

cachotterie [kaʃɔtʀi] *nf* mystery; **faire des ~s** to be secretive

cactus [kaktys] *nm* cactus

cadavre [kadɑvʀ(ə)] *nm* corpse, (dead) body

Caddie® [kadi] *nm* (supermarket) trolley

cadeau, x [kado] *nm* present, gift; **faire un ~ à qn** to give sb a present *ou* gift; **faire ~ de qch à qn** to make a present of sth to sb, give sb sth as a present

cadenas [kadnɑ] *nm* padlock

cadence [kadɑ̃s] *nf* (Mus) cadence; (: *rythme*) rhythm; (*de travail etc*) rate; **cadences** *nfpl* (*en usine*) production rate *sg*; **en ~** rhythmically; in time

cadet, te [kadɛ, -ɛt] *adj* younger; (*le plus jeune*) youngest ▷ *nm/f* youngest child *ou* one, youngest boy *ou* son/girl *ou* daughter; **il est mon ~ de deux ans** he's two years younger than me, he's two years my junior; **les ~s** (Sport) the minors (15–17 years); **le ~ de mes soucis** the least of my worries

cadran [kadʀɑ̃] *nm* dial; **~ solaire** sundial

cadre [kɑdʀ(ə)] *nm* frame; (*environnement*) surroundings *pl*; (*limites*) scope ▷ *nm/f* (Admin) managerial employee, executive ▷ *adj:* **loi ~** outline *ou* blueprint law; **~ moyen/supérieur** (Admin) middle/senior management employee, junior/senior executive; **rayer qn des ~s** to discharge sb; to dismiss sb; **dans le ~ de** (*fig*) within the framework *ou* context of

cadrer [kadʀe] *vi:* **~ avec** to tally *ou* correspond with ▷ *vt* (Ciné, Photo) to frame

cafard [kafaʀ] *nm* cockroach; **avoir le ~** to be down in the dumps, be feeling low

café [kafe] *nm* coffee; (*bistro*) café ▷ *adj inv* coffee *cpd;* **~ crème** coffee with cream; **~ au lait** white coffee; **~ noir** black coffee; **~ en grains** coffee beans; **~ en poudre** instant coffee; **~ tabac** *tobacconist's or newsagent's also serving coffee and spirits*; **~ liégeois** *coffee ice cream with whipped cream*

cafétéria [kafeteʀja] *nf* cafeteria

cafetière [kaftjɛʀ] *nf (pot)* coffee-pot

cafouiller [kafuje] *vi* to get in a shambles; *(machine etc)* to work in fits and starts

cage [kaʒ] *nf* cage; *(des buts)* goal; **en ~** in a cage, caged up *ou* in; **~ d'ascenseur** lift shaft; **~ d'escalier** (stair)well; **~ thoracique** rib cage

cageot [kaʒo] *nm* crate

cagibi [kaʒibi] *nm* shed

cagnotte [kaɲɔt] *nf* kitty

cagoule [kagul] *nf* cowl; hood; *(Ski etc)* cagoule

cahier [kaje] *nm* notebook; *(Typo)* signature; *(revue)*: **~s** journal; **~ de revendications/ doléances** list of claims/grievances; **~ de brouillons** rough book, jotter; **~ des charges** specification; **~ d'exercices** exercise book

cahot [kao] *nm* jolt, bump

caïd [kaid] *nm* big chief, boss

caille [kaj] *nf* quail

cailler [kaje] *vi (lait)* to curdle; *(sang)* to clot; *(fam)* to be cold

caillot [kajo] *nm* (blood) clot

caillou, x [kaju] *nm* (little) stone

caillouteux, -euse [kajutø, -øz] *adj* stony; pebbly

Caire [kɛʀ] *nm*: **le ~** Cairo

caisse [kɛs] *nf* box; *(où l'on met la recette)* cashbox; *(: machine)* till; *(où l'on paye)* cash desk (Brit), checkout counter; *(: au supermarché)* checkout; *(de banque)* cashier's desk; *(Tech)* case, casing; **faire sa ~** *(Comm)* to count the takings; **~ claire** *(Mus)* side drum *ou* snare drum; **~ éclair** express checkout; **~ enregistreuse** cash register; **~ d'épargne** (CE) savings bank; **~ noire** slush fund; **~ de retraite** pension fund; **~ de sortie** checkout; *voir* **grosse**

caissier, -ière [kesje, -jɛʀ] *nm/f* cashier

cajoler [kaʒɔle] *vt* to wheedle, coax; to surround with love and care, make a fuss of

cake [kɛk] *nm* fruit cake

calandre [kalɑ̃dʀ(ə)] *nf* radiator grill; *(machine)* calender, mangle

calanque [kalɑ̃k] *nf* rocky inlet

calcaire [kalkɛʀ] *nm* limestone ▷ *adj (eau)* hard; *(Géo)* limestone *cpd*

calciné, e [kalsine] *adj* burnt to ashes

calcul [kalkyl] *nm* calculation; **le ~** *(Scol)* arithmetic; **~ différentiel/intégral** differential/integral calculus; **~ mental** mental arithmetic; **~ (biliaire)** (gall)stone; **~ (rénal)** (kidney) stone; **d'après mes ~s** by my reckoning

calculateur [kalkylatœʀ] *nm*, **calculatrice** [kalkylatʀis] ▷ *nf* calculator

calculer [kalkyle] *vt* to calculate, work out, reckon; *(combiner)* to calculate; **~ qch de tête** to work sth out in one's head

calculette [kalkylɛt] *nf* (pocket) calculator

cale [kal] *nf (de bateau)* hold; *(en bois)* wedge, chock; **~ sèche** *ou* **de radoub** dry dock

calé, e [kale] *adj (fam)* clever, bright

caleçon [kalsɔ̃] *nm* pair of underpants, trunks *pl*; **~ de bain** bathing trunks *pl*

calembour [kalɑ̃buʀ] *nm* pun

calendrier [kalɑ̃dʀije] *nm* calendar; *(fig)* timetable

calepin [kalpɛ̃] *nm* notebook

caler [kale] *vt* to wedge, chock up; **~ (son moteur/véhicule)** to stall (one's engine/ vehicle); **se ~ dans un fauteuil** to make o.s. comfortable in an armchair

calfeutrer [kalføtʀe] *vt* to (make) draughtproof (Brit) *ou* draftproof (US); **se calfeutrer** *vi* to make o.s. snug and comfortable

calibre [kalibʀ(ə)] *nm (d'un fruit)* grade; *(d'une arme)* bore, calibre (Brit), caliber (US); *(fig)* calibre, caliber

califourchon [kalifuʀʃɔ̃]: **à ~** *adv* astride; **à ~ sur** astride, straddling

câlin, e [kalɛ̃, -in] *adj* cuddly, cuddlesome; tender

câliner [kaline] *vt* to fondle, cuddle

calmant [kalmɑ̃] *nm* tranquillizer, sedative; *(contre la douleur)* painkiller

calme [kalm(ə)] *adj* calm, quiet ▷ *nm* calm(ness), quietness; **sans perdre son ~** without losing one's cool *ou* calmness; **~ plat** *(Navig)* dead calm

calmer [kalme] *vt* to calm (down); *(douleur, inquiétude)* to ease, soothe; **se calmer** *vi* to calm down

calomnie [kalɔmni] *nf* slander; *(écrite)* libel

calomnier [kalɔmnje] *vt* to slander; to libel

calorie [kalɔʀi] *nf* calorie

calotte [kalɔt] *nf (coiffure)* skullcap; *(gifle)* slap; **la ~** *(péj: clergé)* the cloth, the clergy; **~ glaciaire** icecap

calquer [kalke] *vt* to trace; *(fig)* to copy exactly

calvaire [kalvɛʀ] *nm (croix)* wayside cross, calvary; *(souffrances)* suffering, martyrdom

calvitie [kalvisi] *nf* baldness

camarade [kamaʀad] *nm/f* friend, pal; *(Pol)* comrade

camaraderie [kamaʀadʀi] *nf* friendship

cambouis [kɑ̃bwi] *nm* dirty oil *ou* grease

cambrer [kɑ̃bʀe] *vt* to arch; **se cambrer** *vi* to arch one's back; **~ la taille** *ou* **les reins** to arch one's back

cambriolage [kɑ̃bʀijɔlaʒ] *nm* burglary

cambrioler [kɑ̃bʀijɔle] *vt* to burgle (Brit), burglarize (US)

cambrioleur, -euse [kɑ̃bʀijɔlœʀ, -øz] *nm/f* burglar

camelote [kamlɔt] *nf* rubbish, trash, junk

caméra [kameʀa] *nf (Ciné, TV)* camera; *(d'amateur)* cine-camera

caméscope® [kameskɔp] *nm* camcorder

camion [kamjɔ̃] *nm* lorry (Brit), truck; *(plus petit, fermé)* van; *(charge)*: **~ de sable/cailloux** lorry-load (Brit) *ou* truck-load of sand/stones; **~ de dépannage** breakdown (Brit) *ou* tow (US) truck

camion-citerne *(pl camions-citernes)* [kamjɔ̃sitɛʀn(ə)] *nm* tanker

camionnette [kamjɔnɛt] *nf* (small) van

camionneur [kamjɔnœʀ] *nm (entrepreneur)*

haulage contractor (*Brit*), trucker (*US*); (*chauffeur*) lorry (*Brit*) *ou* truck driver; van driver

camisole [kamizɔl] *nf*: ~ **(de force)** straitjacket

camomille [kamɔmij] *nf* camomile; (*boisson*) camomile tea

camoufler [kamufle] *vt* to camouflage; (*fig*) to conceal, cover up

camp [kɑ̃] *nm* camp; (*fig*) side; ~ **de nudistes/vacances** nudist/holiday camp; ~ **de concentration** concentration camp

campagnard, e [kɑ̃paɲaʀ, -aʀd(ə)] *adj* country *cpd* ▷ *nm/f* countryman/woman

campagne [kɑ̃paɲ] *nf* country, countryside; (*Mil, Pol, Comm*) campaign; **en ~** (*Mil*) in the field; **à la ~** in/to the country; **faire ~ pour** to campaign for; **~ électorale** election campaign; **~ de publicité** advertising campaign

camper [kɑ̃pe] *vi* to camp ▷ *vt* (*chapeau etc*) to pull *ou* put on firmly; (*dessin*) to sketch; **se ~ devant** to plant o.s. in front of

campeur, -euse [kɑ̃pœʀ, -øz] *nm/f* camper

camping [kɑ̃piŋ] *nm* camping; (**terrain de**) ~ campsite, camping site; **faire du ~** to go camping; **faire du ~ sauvage** to camp rough

camping-car [kɑ̃piŋkaʀ] *nm* caravanette, camper (*US*)

camping-gaz® [kɑ̃piŋgaz] *nm inv* camp(ing) stove

Canada [kanada] *nm*: **le ~** Canada

canadien, ne [kanadjɛ̃, -ɛn] *adj* Canadian ▷ *nm/f*: **C~, ne** Canadian ▷ *nf* (*veste*) fur-lined jacket

canaille [kanɑj] *nf* (*péj*) scoundrel; (*populace*) riff-raff ▷ *adj* raffish, rakish

canal, -aux [kanal, -o] *nm* canal; (*naturel*) channel; (*Admin*): **par le ~ de** through (the medium of), via; **~ de distribution/télévision** distribution/television channel; **~ de Panama/Suez** Panama/Suez Canal

canalisation [kanalizasjɔ̃] *nf* (*tuyau*) pipe

canaliser [kanalize] *vt* to canalize; (*fig*) to channel

canapé [kanape] *nm* settee, sofa; (*Culin*) canapé, open sandwich

canard [kanaʀ] *nm* duck

canari [kanaʀi] *nm* canary

cancans [kɑ̃kɑ̃] *nmpl* (malicious) gossip *sg*

cancer [kɑ̃sɛʀ] *nm* cancer; (*signe*): **le C~** Cancer, the Crab; **être du C~** to be Cancer; **il a un ~** he has cancer

cancre [kɑ̃kʀ(ə)] *nm* dunce

candeur [kɑ̃dœʀ] *nf* ingenuousness

candidat, e [kɑ̃dida, -at] *nm/f* candidate; (*à un poste*) applicant, candidate

candidature [kɑ̃didatyʀ] *nf* candidacy; application; **poser sa ~** to submit an application, apply; **~ spontanée** unsolicited job application

candide [kɑ̃did] *adj* ingenuous, guileless, naïve

cane [kan] *nf* (female) duck

caneton [kantɔ̃] *nm* duckling

canette [kanɛt] *nf* (*de bière*) (flip-top) bottle; (*de machine à coudre*) spool

canevas [kanva] *nm* (*Couture*) canvas (for tapestry work); (*fig*) framework, structure

caniche [kaniʃ] *nm* poodle

canicule [kanikyl] *nf* scorching heat; midsummer heat, dog days *pl*

canif [kanif] *nm* penknife, pocket knife

canin, e [kanɛ̃, -in] *adj* canine ▷ *nf* canine (tooth), eye tooth

caniveau, x [kanivo] *nm* gutter

canne [kan] *nf* (walking) stick; **~ à pêche** fishing rod; **~ à sucre** sugar cane; **les ~s blanches** (*les aveugles*) the blind

cannelle [kanɛl] *nf* cinnamon

canoë [kanɔe] *nm* canoe; (*sport*) canoeing; **~ (kayak)** kayak

canon [kanɔ̃] *nm* (*arme*) gun; (*Hist*) cannon; (*d'une arme: tube*) barrel; (*fig*) model; (*Mus*) canon ▷ *adj*: **droit ~** canon law; **~ rayé** rifled barrel

canot [kano] *nm* boat, ding(h)y; **~ pneumatique** rubber *ou* inflatable ding(h)y; **~ de sauvetage** lifeboat

canotier [kanɔtje] *nm* boater

cantatrice [kɑ̃tatʀis] *nf* (opera) singer

cantine [kɑ̃tin] *nf* canteen; (*réfectoire d'école*) dining hall

cantique [kɑ̃tik] *nm* hymn

canton [kɑ̃tɔ̃] *nm* district (*consisting of several communes*); *see note*; (*en Suisse*) canton

cantonade [kɑ̃tɔnad]: **à la ~** *adv* to everyone in general; (*crier*) from the rooftops

cantonner [kɑ̃tɔne] *vt* (*Mil*) to billet (*Brit*), quarter; to station; **se ~ dans** to confine o.s. to

cantonnier [kɑ̃tɔnje] *nm* roadmender

canular [kanylaʀ] *nm* hoax

caoutchouc [kautʃu] *nm* rubber; **~ mousse** foam rubber; **en ~** rubber *cpd*

CAP *sigle m* (= *Certificat d'aptitude professionnelle*) vocational training certificate taken at secondary school

cap [kap] *nm* (*Géo*) cape; headland; (*fig*) hurdle; watershed; (*Navig*): **changer de ~** to change course; **mettre le ~ sur** to head *ou* steer for; **doubler** *ou* **passer le ~** (*fig*) to get over the worst; **Le C~** Cape Town; **le ~ de Bonne Espérance** the Cape of Good Hope; **le ~ Horn** Cape Horn; **les îles du C~ Vert** (*aussi*: **le Cap-Vert**) the Cape Verde Islands

capable [kapabl(ə)] *adj* able, capable; **~ de qch/faire** capable of sth/doing; **il est ~ d'oublier** he could easily forget; **spectacle ~ d'intéresser** show likely to be of interest

capacité [kapasite] *nf* (*compétence*) ability; (*Jur, Inform, d'un récipient*) capacity; **~ (en droit)** basic legal qualification

cape [kap] *nf* cape, cloak; **rire sous ~** to laugh up one's sleeve

CAPES [kapɛs] *sigle m* (= *Certificat d'aptitude au professorat de l'enseignement du second degré*) secondary teaching diploma; *see note*

capillaire [kapilɛʀ] *adj* (*soins, lotion*) hair *cpd*; (*vaisseau etc*) capillary; **artiste ~** hair artist *ou* designer

capitaine [kapitɛn] *nm* captain; **~ des pompiers**

fire chief (Brit), fire marshal (US); **~ au long cours** master mariner

capital, e, -aux [kapital, -o] adj major; fundamental; (Jur) capital ▷ nm capital; (fig) stock; asset ▷ nf (ville) capital; (lettre) capital (letter) ▷ nmpl (fonds) capital sg, money sg; **les sept péchés capitaux** the seven deadly sins; **peine ~e** capital punishment; **~ (social)** authorized capital; **~ d'exploitation** working capital

capitalisme [kapitalism(ə)] nm capitalism

capitaliste [kapitalist(ə)] adj, nm/f capitalist

capitonné, e [kapitone] adj padded

caporal, -aux [kapɔral, -o] nm lance corporal

capot [kapo] nm (Auto) bonnet (Brit), hood (US)

capote [kapɔt] nf (de voiture) hood (Brit), top (US); (de soldat) greatcoat; **~ (anglaise)** (fam) rubber, condom

capoter [kapote] vi to overturn; (négociations) to founder

câpre [kɑpʀ(ə)] nf caper

caprice [kapʀis] nm whim, caprice; passing fancy; **caprices** nmpl (de la mode etc) vagaries; **faire un ~** to throw a tantrum; **faire des ~s** to be temperamental

capricieux, -euse [kapʀisjø, -øz] adj capricious; whimsical; temperamental

Capricorne [kapʀikɔrn] nm: **le ~** Capricorn, the Goat; **être du ~** to be Capricorn

capsule [kapsyl] nf (de bouteille) cap; (amorce) primer; cap; (Bot etc, spatiale) capsule

capter [kapte] vt (ondes radio) to pick up; (eau) to harness; (fig) to win, capture

captivant, e [kaptivɑ̃, -ɑ̃t] adj captivating

captivité [kaptivite] nf captivity; **en ~** in captivity

capturer [kaptyʀe] vt to capture, catch

capuche [kapyʃ] nf hood

capuchon [kapyʃɔ̃] nm hood; (de stylo) cap, top

capucine [kapysin] nf (Bot) nasturtium

caquet [kakɛ] nm: **rabattre le ~ à qn** to bring sb down a peg or two

caqueter [kakte] vi (poule) to cackle; (fig) to prattle

car [kaʀ] nm coach (Brit), bus ▷ conj because, for; **~ de police** police van; **~ de reportage** broadcasting ou radio van

carabine [kaʀabin] nf carbine, rifle; **~ à air comprimé** airgun

caractère [kaʀaktɛʀ] nm (gén) character; **en ~s gras** in bold type; **en petits ~s** in small print; **en ~s d'imprimerie** in block capitals; **avoir du ~** to have character; **avoir bon/mauvais ~** to be good-/ill-natured ou tempered; **~ de remplacement** wild card (Inform); **~s/seconde (cps)** characters per second (cps)

caractériel, le [kaʀakterjɛl] adj (enfant) (emotionally) disturbed ▷ nm/f problem child; **troubles ~s** emotional problems

caractérisé, e [kaʀakterize] adj: **c'est une grippe/de l'insubordination ~e** it is a clear(-cut) case of flu/insubordination

caractériser [kaʀakterize] vt to characterize; **se ~ par** to be characterized ou distinguished by

caractéristique [kaʀakteristik] adj, nf characteristic

carafe [kaʀaf] nf decanter; carafe

caraïbe [kaʀaib] adj Caribbean; **les Caraïbes** nfpl the Caribbean (Islands); **la mer des C~s** the Caribbean Sea

carambolage [kaʀɑ̃bɔlaʒ] nm multiple crash, pileup

caramel [kaʀamɛl] nm (bonbon) caramel, toffee; (substance) caramel

carapace [kaʀapas] nf shell

caravane [kaʀavan] nf caravan

caravaning [kaʀavaniŋ] nm caravanning; (emplacement) caravan site

carbone [kaʀbɔn] nm carbon; (feuille) carbon, sheet of carbon paper; (double) carbon (copy)

carbonique [kaʀbɔnik] adj: **gaz ~** carbon dioxide; **neige ~** dry ice

carbonisé, e [kaʀbɔnize] adj charred; **mourir ~** to be burned to death

carburant [kaʀbyʀɑ̃] nm (motor) fuel

carburateur [kaʀbyʀatœʀ] nm carburettor

carcan [kaʀkɑ̃] nm (fig) yoke, shackles pl

carcasse [kaʀkas] nf carcass; (de véhicule etc) shell

cardiaque [kaʀdjak] adj cardiac, heart cpd ▷ nm/f heart patient; **être ~** to have a heart condition

cardigan [kaʀdigɑ̃] nm cardigan

cardiologue [kaʀdjɔlɔg] nm/f cardiologist, heart specialist

carême [kaʀɛm] nm: **le C~** Lent

carence [kaʀɑ̃s] nf incompetence, inadequacy; (manque) deficiency; **~ vitaminique** vitamin deficiency

caresse [kaʀɛs] nf caress

caresser [kaʀese] vt to caress, stroke, fondle; (fig: projet, espoir) to toy with

cargaison [kaʀgɛzɔ̃] nf cargo, freight

cargo [kaʀgo] nm cargo boat, freighter; **~ mixte** cargo and passenger ship

caricature [kaʀikatyʀ] nf caricature; (politique etc) (satirical) cartoon

carie [kaʀi] nf: **la ~ (dentaire)** tooth decay; **une ~** a bad tooth

carillon [kaʀijɔ̃] nm (d'église) bells pl; (de pendule) chimes pl; (de porte): **~ (électrique)** (electric) door chime ou bell

caritatif, -ive [kaʀitatif, -iv] adj charitable

carnassier, -ière [kaʀnasje, -jɛʀ] adj carnivorous ▷ nm carnivore

carnaval [kaʀnaval] nm carnival

carnet [kaʀnɛ] nm (calepin) notebook; (de tickets, timbres etc) book; (d'école) school report; (journal intime) diary; **~ d'adresses** address book; **~ de chèques** cheque book (Brit), checkbook (US); **~ de commandes** order book; **~ de notes** (Scol) (school) report; **~ à souches** counterfoil book

carotte [kaʀɔt] nf (aussi fig) carrot

carpette [kaʀpɛt] nf rug

carré, e [kaʀe] adj square; (fig: franc) straightforward ▷ nm (de terrain, jardin) patch,

plot; (*Navig: salle*) wardroom; (*Math*) square; ~
blanc (*TV*) "adults only" symbol; (*Cartes*): ~ **d'as/
de rois** four aces/kings; **élever un nombre au ~**
to square a number; **mètre/kilomètre** ~ square
metre/kilometre; **de soie** silk headsquare *ou*
headscarf; ~ **d'agneau** loin of lamb

carreau, x [kaʀo] *nm* (*en faïence etc*) (floor) tile,
(wall) tile; (*window*) pane; (*motif*) check, square;
(*Cartes: couleur*) diamonds *pl*; (: *carte*) diamond;
tissu à ~x checked fabric; **papier à ~x** squared
paper

carrefour [kaʀfuʀ] *nm* crossroads *sg*

carrelage [kaʀlaʒ] *nm* tiling; (tiled) floor

carrelet [kaʀlɛ] *nm* (*poisson*) plaice

carrément [kaʀemɑ̃] *adv* (*franchement*) straight
out, bluntly; (*sans détours, sans hésiter*) straight;
(*nettement*) definitely; **il l'a ~ mis à la porte** he
threw him straight out

carrière [kaʀjɛʀ] *nf* (*de roches*) quarry; (*métier*)
career; **militaire de ~** professional soldier;
faire ~ dans to make one's career in

carrossable [kaʀɔsabl(ə)] *adj* suitable for
(motor) vehicles

carrosse [kaʀɔs] *nm* (horse-drawn) coach

carrosserie [kaʀɔsʀi] *nf* body, bodywork *no
pl* (*Brit*); (*activité, commerce*) coachwork (*Brit*),
(car) body manufacturing; **atelier de ~** (*pour
réparations*) body shop, panel beaters' (yard) (*Brit*)

carrure [kaʀyʀ] *nf* build; (*fig*) stature

cartable [kaʀtabl(ə)] *nm* (*d'écolier*) satchel,
(school)bag

carte [kaʀt(ə)] *nf* (*de géographie*) map; (*marine,
du ciel*) chart; (*de fichier, d'abonnement etc, à jouer*)
card; (*au restaurant*) menu; (*aussi:* **carte postale**)
(post)card; (*aussi:* **carte de visite**) (visiting) card;
avoir/donner ~ blanche to have/give carte
blanche *ou* a free hand; **tirer les ~s à qn** to read
sb's cards; **jouer aux ~s** to play cards; **jouer ~s
sur table** (*fig*) to put one's cards on the table; **à
la ~** (*au restaurant*) à la carte; ~ **à circuit imprimé**
printed circuit; ~ **à puce** smartcard; ~ **bancaire**
cash card; **C~ Bleue®** debit card; ~ **de crédit**
credit card; ~ **d'état-major** ≈ Ordnance (*Brit*)
ou Geological (*US*) Survey map; **la ~ grise** (*Auto*)
≈ the (car) registration document; ~ **d'identité**
identity card; ~ **jeune** young person's railcard; ~
perforée punch(ed) card; ~ **routière** road map;
~ **de séjour** residence permit; ~ **SIM** SIM card; ~
téléphonique phonecard; **la ~ verte** (*Auto*) the
green card; **la ~ des vins** the wine list

carter [kaʀtɛʀ] *nm* (*Auto: d'huile*) sump (*Brit*),
oil pan (*US*); (: *de la boîte de vitesses*) casing; (*de
bicyclette*) chain guard

carton [kaʀtɔ̃] *nm* (*matériau*) cardboard; (*boîte*)
(cardboard) box; (*d'invitation*) invitation card;
(*Art*) sketch; cartoon; **en ~** cardboard *cpd*; **faire
un ~** (*au tir*) to have a go at the rifle range; to score
a hit; ~ **à dessin** portfolio

carton-pâte [kaʀtɔ̃pat] *nm* pasteboard; **de ~** (*fig*)
cardboard *cpd*

cartouche [kaʀtuʃ] *nf* cartridge; (*de cigarettes*)
carton

cas [ka] *nm* case; **faire peu de ~/grand ~ de** to
attach little/great importance to; **le ~ échéant**
if need be; **en aucun ~** on no account, under
no circumstances (whatsoever); **au ~ où** in
case; **dans ce ~** in that case; **en ~ de** in case of,
in the event of; **en ~ de besoin** if need be; **en
~ d'urgence** in an emergency; **en ce ~** in that
case; **en tout ~** in any case, at any rate; ~ **de
conscience** matter of conscience; ~ **de force
majeure** case of absolute necessity; (*Assurances*)
act of God; ~ **limite** borderline case; ~ **social**
social problem

casanier, -ière [kazanje, -jɛʀ] *adj* stay-at-home

cascade [kaskad] *nf* waterfall, cascade; (*fig*)
stream, torrent

cascadeur, -euse [kaskadœʀ, -øz] *nm/f*
stuntman/girl

case [kaz] *nf* (*hutte*) hut; (*compartiment*)
compartment; (*pour le courrier*) pigeonhole; (*de
mots croisés, d'échiquier*) square; (*sur un formulaire*) box

caser [kaze] *vt* (*mettre*) to put; (*loger*) to put up;
(*péj*) to find a job for; to marry off; **se caser** *vi*
(*personne*) to settle down

caserne [kazɛʀn(ə)] *nf* barracks

cash [kaʃ] *adv*: **payer ~** to pay cash down

casier [kazje] *nm* (*à journaux etc*) rack; (*de bureau*)
filing cabinet; (: *à cases*) set of pigeonholes;
(*case*) compartment; pigeonhole; (: *à clef*) locker;
(*Pêche*) lobster pot; ~ **à bouteilles** bottle rack; ~
judiciaire police record

casino [kazino] *nm* casino

casque [kask] *nm* helmet; (*chez le coiffeur*)
(hair-)dryer; (*pour audition*) (head-)phones *pl*,
headset; **les C~s bleus** the UN peacekeeping
force

casquette [kaskɛt] *nf* cap

cassant, e [kasɑ̃, -ɑ̃t] *adj* brittle; (*fig*) brusque,
abrupt

cassation [kasasjɔ̃] *nf*: **se pourvoir en ~** to lodge
an appeal; **recours en ~** appeal to the Supreme
Court

casse [kas] *nf* (*pour voitures*): **mettre à la ~** to
scrap, send to the breakers (*Brit*); (*dégâts*): **il y a
eu de la ~** there were a lot of breakages; (*Typo*):
haut/bas de ~ upper/lower case

casse-cou [kasku] *adj inv* daredevil, reckless;
crier ~ à qn to warn sb (*against a risky undertaking*)

casse-croûte [kaskʀut] *nm inv* snack

casse-noisettes [kasnwazɛt] *nm inv*
nutcrackers *pl*

casse-pieds [kaspje] *adj, nm/f inv* (*fam*): **il est ~,
c'est un ~** he's a pain (in the neck)

casser [kase] *vt* to break; (*Admin: gradé*) to
demote; (*Jur*) to quash; (*Comm*): ~ **les prix** to
slash prices; **se casser** *vi* to break; (*fam*) to go,
leave ▷ *vt*: **se ~ la jambe/une jambe** to break
one's leg/a leg; **à tout ~** fantastic, brilliant; **se ~
net** to break clean off

casserole [kasʀɔl] *nf* saucepan; **à la ~** (*Culin*)
braised

casse-tête [kastɛt] *nm inv* (*fig*) brain teaser;
(*difficultés*) headache (*fig*)

cassette [kasɛt] *nf* (*bande magnétique*) cassette; (*coffret*) casket; ~ **numérique** digital compact cassette; ~ **vidéo** video

casseur [kɑsœʀ] *nm* hooligan; rioter

cassis [kasis] *nm* blackcurrant; (*de la route*) dip, bump

cassoulet [kasulɛ] *nm* *sausage and bean hotpot*

cassure [kɑsyʀ] *nf* break, crack

castor [kastɔʀ] *nm* beaver

castrer [kastʀe] *vt* (*mâle*) to castrate; (*femelle*) to spay; (*cheval*) to geld; (*chat, chien*) to doctor (*Brit*), fix (*US*)

catalogue [katalɔg] *nm* catalogue

cataloguer [katalɔge] *vt* to catalogue, list; (*péj*) to put a label on

catalyseur [katalizœʀ] *nm* catalyst

catalytique [katalitik] *adj* catalytic

catastrophe [katastʀɔf] *nf* catastrophe, disaster; **atterrir en** ~ to make an emergency landing; **partir en** ~ to rush away

catch [katʃ] *nm* (all-in) wrestling

catéchisme [kateʃism(ə)] *nm* catechism

catégorie [kategɔʀi] *nf* category; (*Boucherie*): **morceaux de première/deuxième** ~ prime/second cuts

catégorique [kategɔʀik] *adj* categorical

cathédrale [katedʀal] *nf* cathedral

catholique [katɔlik] *adj, nm/f* (Roman) Catholic; **pas très** ~ a bit shady *ou* fishy

catimini [katimini]: **en** ~ *adv* on the sly, on the quiet

cauchemar [koʃmaʀ] *nm* nightmare

cause [koz] *nf* cause; (*Jur*) lawsuit, case; brief; **faire** ~ **commune avec qn** to take sides with sb; **être** ~ **de** to be the cause of; **à** ~ **de** because of, owing to; **pour** ~ **de** on account of; owing to; (**et) pour** ~ and for (a very) good reason; **être en** ~ (*intérêts*) to be at stake; (*personne*) to be involved; (*qualité*) to be in question; **mettre en** ~ to implicate; to call into question; **remettre en** ~ to challenge, call into question; **c'est hors de** ~ it's out of the question; **en tout état de** ~ in any case

causer [koze] *vt* to cause ▷ *vi* to chat, talk

causerie [kozʀi] *nf* talk

causette [kozɛt] *nf*: **faire la** *ou* **un brin de** ~ to have a chat

caution [kosjɔ̃] *nf* guarantee, security; deposit; (*Jur*) bail (bond); (*fig*) backing, support; **payer la** ~ **de qn** to stand bail for sb; **se porter** ~ **pour qn** to stand security for sb; **libéré sous** ~ released on bail; **sujet à** ~ unconfirmed

cautionner [kosjone] *vt* to guarantee; (*soutenir*) to support

cavalcade [kavalkad] *nf* (*fig*) stampede

cavalier, -ière [kavalje, -jɛʀ] *adj* (*désinvolte*) offhand ▷ *nm/f* rider; (*au bal*) partner ▷ *nm* (*Échecs*) knight; **faire** ~ **seul** to go it alone; **allée** *ou* **piste cavalière** riding path

cave [kav] *nf* cellar; (*cabaret*) (cellar) nightclub ▷ *adj*: **yeux** ~**s** sunken eyes; **joues** ~**s** hollow cheeks

caveau, x [kavo] *nm* vault

caverne [kavɛʀn(ə)] *nf* cave

CCP *sigle m* = **compte chèque postal**

CD *sigle m* (= *chemin départemental*) secondary road, ≈ B road (*Brit*); (= *compact disc*) CD; (= *comité directeur*) steering committee; (*Pol*) = **corps diplomatique**

CD-ROM [sedeʀɔm] *nm inv* (= *Compact Disc Read Only Memory*) CD-Rom

CE *sigle f* (= *Communauté européenne*) EC; (*Comm*) = **caisse d'épargne** ▷ *sigle m* (*Industrie*) = **comité d'entreprise**; (*Scol*) = **cours élémentaire**

ce, cette [sə, sɛt] (*devant nm* **cet** + *voyelle ou h aspiré*) (*pl* **ces**) *adj dém* (*proximité*) this; these *pl*; (*non-proximité*) that; those *pl*; **cette maison(-ci/là)** this/that house; **cette nuit** (*qui vient*) tonight; (*passée*) last night
 ▷ *pron* **1**: **c'est** it's, it is; **c'est petit/grand/un livre** it's *ou* it is small/big/a book; **c'est un peintre** he's *ou* he is a painter; **ce sont des peintres** they're *ou* they are painters; **c'est le facteur** *etc* (*à la porte*) it's the postman *etc*; **qui est-ce?** who is it?; (*en désignant*) who is he/she?; **qu'est-ce?** what is it?; **c'est toi qui lui as parlé** it was you who spoke to him
 2: **c'est que: c'est qu'il est lent/qu'il n'a pas faim** the fact is, he's slow/he's not hungry
 3 (*expressions*): **c'est ça** (*correct*) that's it, that's right; **c'est toi qui le dis!** that's what YOU say!; *voir aussi* **c'est-à-dire**; *voir* **-ci**; **est-ce que**; **n'est-ce pas**
 4: **ce qui, ce que** what; (*chose qui*): **il est bête, ce qui me chagrine** he's stupid, which saddens me; **tout ce qui bouge** everything that *ou* which moves; **tout ce que je sais** all I know; **ce dont j'ai parlé** what I talked about; **ce que c'est grand!** it's so big!

ceci [səsi] *pron* this

cécité [sesite] *nf* blindness

céder [sede] *vt* to give up ▷ *vi* (*pont, barrage*) to give way; (*personne*) to give in; ~ **à** to yield to, give in to

cédérom [sedeʀɔm] *nm* CD-ROM

CEDEX [sedɛks] *sigle m* (= *courrier d'entreprise à distribution exceptionnelle*) *accelerated postal service for bulk users*

cédille [sedij] *nf* cedilla

cèdre [sɛdʀ(ə)] *nm* cedar

CEI *sigle f* (= *Communauté des États indépendants*) CIS

ceinture [sɛ̃tyʀ] *nf* belt; (*taille*) waist; (*fig*) ring; belt; circle; ~ **de sauvetage** lifebelt (*Brit*), life preserver (*US*); ~ **de sécurité** safety *ou* seat belt; ~ **(de sécurité) à enrouleur** inertia reel seat belt; ~ **verte** green belt

cela [səla] *pron* that; (*comme sujet indéfini*) it; ~ **m'étonne que** it surprises me that; **quand/où** ~**?** when/where (was that)?

célèbre [selɛbʀ(ə)] *adj* famous

célébrer [selebʀe] *vt* to celebrate; (*louer*) to extol

céleri [sɛlʀi] *nm*: ~**(-rave)** celeriac; ~ **(en branche)** celery

célibat [seliba] *nm* celibacy; bachelor/

spinsterhood

célibataire [selibatɛʀ] *adj* single, unmarried
▷ *nm/f* bachelor/unmarried *ou* single woman;
mère ~ single *ou* unmarried mother

celle, celles [sɛl] *pron voir* **celui**

cellier [selje] *nm* storeroom

cellule [selyl] *nf* (*gén*) cell; ~ **(photo-électrique)**
electronic eye

cellulite [selylit] *nf* cellulite

celui, celle [səlɥi, sɛl] (*mpl* **ceux**, *fpl* **celles**) *pron*
1: ~-**ci/là, celle-ci/là** this one/that one; **ceux-ci, celles-ci** these (ones); **ceux-là, celles-là** those (ones); ~ **de mon frère** my brother's; ~ **du salon/du dessous** the one in (*ou* from) the lounge/below
2: ~ **qui bouge** the one which *ou* that moves;
(*personne*) the one who moves; ~ **que je vois** the one (which *ou* that) I see; (*personne*) the one (whom) I see; ~ **dont je parle** the one I'm talking about
3 (*valeur indéfinie*): ~ **qui veut** whoever wants

cendre [sādʀ(ə)] *nf* ash; ~**s** (*d'un foyer*) ash(es), cinders; (*volcaniques*) ash *sg*; (*d'un défunt*) ashes; **sous la** ~ (*Culin*) in (the) embers

cendrier [sādʀije] *nm* ashtray

cène [sɛn] *nf*: **la** ~ (Holy) Communion; (*Art*) the Last Supper

censé, e [sāse] *adj*: **être** ~ **faire** to be supposed to do

censeur [sāsœʀ] *nm* (*Scol*) deputy head (*Brit*), vice-principal (*US*); (*Ciné, Pol*) censor

censure [sāsyʀ] *nf* censorship

censurer [sāsyʀe] *vt* (*Ciné, Presse*) to censor; (*Pol*) to censure

cent [sā] *num* a hundred, one hundred; **pour** ~ (%) per cent (%); **faire les** ~ **pas** to pace up and down ▷ *nm* (*US, Canada, partie de l'euro etc*) cent

centaine [sātɛn] *nf*: **une** ~ (**de**) about a hundred, a hundred or so; (*Comm*) a hundred; **plusieurs** ~**s (de)** several hundred; **des** ~**s (de)** hundreds (of)

centenaire [sātnɛʀ] *adj* hundred-year-old ▷ *nm/f* centenarian ▷ *nm* (*anniversaire*) centenary

centième [sātjɛm] *num* hundredth

centigrade [sātigʀad] *nm* centigrade

centilitre [sātilitʀ(ə)] *nm* centilitre (*Brit*), centiliter (*US*)

centime [sātim] *nm* centime; ~ **d'euro** euro cent

centimètre [sātimɛtʀ(ə)] *nm* centimetre (*Brit*), centimeter (*US*); (*ruban*) tape measure, measuring tape

central, e, -aux [sātʀal, -o] *adj* central ▷ *nm*: ~ **(téléphonique)** (telephone) exchange ▷ *nf*: ~**e d'achat** (*Comm*) central buying service; ~**e électrique/nucléaire** electric/nuclear power station; ~**e syndicale** group of affiliated trade unions

centre [sātʀ(ə)] *nm* centre (*Brit*), center (*US*); ~ **commercial/sportif/culturel** shopping/sports/arts centre; ~ **aéré** outdoor centre; ~ **d'appels** call centre; ~ **d'apprentissage** training college; ~ **d'attraction** centre of

attraction; ~ **de gravité** centre of gravity; ~ **de loisirs** leisure centre; ~ **d'enfouissement des déchets** landfill site; ~ **hospitalier** hospital complex; ~ **de tri** (*Postes*) sorting office; ~**s nerveux** (*Anat*) nerve centres

centre-ville (*pl* **centres-villes**) [sātʀəvil] *nm* town centre (*Brit*) *ou* center (*US*), downtown (area) (*US*)

centuple [sātypl(ə)] *nm*: **le** ~ **de qch** a hundred times sth; **au** ~ a hundredfold

cep [sɛp] *nm* (*vine*) stock

cèpe [sɛp] *nm* (edible) boletus

cependant [səpādā] *adv* however, nevertheless

céramique [seʀamik] *adj* ceramic ▷ *nf* ceramic; (*art*) ceramics *sg*

cercle [sɛʀkl(ə)] *nm* circle; (*objet*) band, hoop; **décrire un** ~ (*avion*) to circle; (*projectile*) to describe a circle; ~ **d'amis** circle of friends; ~ **de famille** family circle; ~ **vicieux** vicious circle

cercueil [sɛʀkœj] *nm* coffin

céréale [seʀeal] *nf* cereal

cérémonie [seʀemɔni] *nf* ceremony; **cérémonies** *nfpl* (*péj*) fuss *sg*, to-do *sg*

cerf [sɛʀ] *nm* stag

cerfeuil [sɛʀfœj] *nm* chervil

cerf-volant [sɛʀvɔlā] *nm* kite; **jouer au** ~ to fly a kite

cerise [səʀiz] *nf* cherry

cerisier [səʀizje] *nm* cherry (tree)

cerner [sɛʀne] *vt* (*Mil etc*) to surround; (*fig: problème*) to delimit, define

cernes [sɛʀn(ə)] *nfpl* (dark) rings, shadows (under the eyes)

certain, e [sɛʀtɛ̃, -ɛn] *adj* certain; (*sûr*): ~ **(de/que)** certain *ou* sure (of/ that); **d'un** ~ **âge** past one's prime, not so young; **un** ~ **temps** (quite) some time; **sûr et** ~ absolutely certain; ~**s** *pron* some

certainement [sɛʀtɛnmā] *adv* (*probablement*) most probably *ou* likely; (*bien sûr*) certainly, of course

certes [sɛʀt(ə)] *adv* admittedly; of course; indeed (yes)

certificat [sɛʀtifika] *nm* certificate; **C**~ **d'études (primaires)** *former school leaving certificate (taken at the end of primary education)*; **C**~ **de fin d'études secondaires** school leaving certificate

certifier [sɛʀtifje] *vt* to certify, guarantee; ~ **à qn que** to assure sb that, guarantee to sb that; ~ **qch à qn** to guarantee sth to sb

certitude [sɛʀtityd] *nf* certainty

cerveau, x [sɛʀvo] *nm* brain; ~ **électronique** electronic brain

cervelas [sɛʀvəla] *nm* saveloy

cervelle [sɛʀvɛl] *nf* (*Anat*) brain; (*Culin*) brain(s); **se creuser la** ~ to rack one's brains

CES *sigle m* (= *Collège d'enseignement secondaire*) ≈ (junior) secondary school (*Brit*), ≈ junior high school (*US*)

ces [se] *adj dém voir* **ce**

cesse [sɛs]: **sans** ~ *adv* continually, constantly; continuously; **il n'avait de** ~ **que** he would not rest until

cesser [sese] *vt* to stop ▷ *vi* to stop, cease; **~ de faire** to stop doing; **faire ~** (*bruit, scandale*) to put a stop to

cessez-le-feu [seselfø] *nm inv* ceasefire

c'est-à-dire [setadir] *adv* that is (to say); (*demander de préciser*): **c'est-à-dire?** what does that mean?; **c'est-à-dire que ...** (*en conséquence*) which means that ...; (*manière d'excuse*) well, in fact ...

cet [sɛt] *adj dém voir* **ce**

ceux [sø] *pron voir* **celui**

CFC *sigle mpl* (= *chlorofluorocarbures*) CFC

CFDT *sigle f* (= *Confédération française démocratique du travail*) *trade union*

CGT *sigle f* (= *Confédération générale du travail*) *trade union*

chacun, e [ʃakœ̃, -yn] *pron* each; (*indéfini*) everyone, everybody

chagrin, e [ʃagrɛ̃, -in] *adj* morose ▷ *nm* grief, sorrow; **avoir du ~** to be grieved *ou* sorrowful

chagriner [ʃagrine] *vt* to grieve, distress; (*contrarier*) to bother, worry

chahut [ʃay] *nm* uproar

chahuter [ʃayte] *vt* to rag, bait ▷ *vi* to make an uproar

chaîne [ʃɛn] *nf* chain; (*Radio, TV*) channel; (*Inform*) string; **chaînes** *nfpl* (*liens, asservissement*) fetters, bonds; **travail à la ~** production line work; **réactions en ~** chain reactions; **faire la ~** to form a (human) chain; **~ alimentaire** food chain; **~ compacte** music centre; **~ d'entraide** mutual aid association; **~ (haute-fidélité** *ou* **hi-fi)** hi-fi system; **~ (de montage** *ou* **de fabrication)** production *ou* assembly line; **~ (de montagnes)** (mountain) range; **~ de solidarité** solidarity network; **~ (stéréo** *ou* **audio)** stereo (system)

chaînette [ʃɛnɛt] *nf* (small) chain

chair [ʃɛr] *nf* flesh ▷ *adj*: (*couleur*) **~** flesh-coloured; **avoir la ~ de poule** to have goose pimples *ou* goose flesh; **bien en ~** plump, well-padded; **en ~ et en os** in the flesh; **~ à saucisses** sausage meat

chaire [ʃɛr] *nf* (*d'église*) pulpit; (*d'université*) chair

chaise [ʃɛz] *nf* chair; **~ de bébé** high chair; **~ électrique** electric chair; **~ longue** deckchair

châle [ʃal] *nm* shawl

chaleur [ʃalœr] *nf* heat; (*fig*) warmth; fire, fervour (*Brit*), fervor (*US*); heat; **en ~** (*Zool*) on heat

chaleureux, -euse [ʃalœrø, -øz] *adj* warm

chaloupe [ʃalup] *nf* launch; (*de sauvetage*) lifeboat

chalumeau, x [ʃalymo] *nm* blowlamp (*Brit*), blowtorch

chalutier [ʃalytje] *nm* trawler; (*pêcheur*) trawlerman

chamailler [ʃamaje]: **se chamailler** *vi* to squabble, bicker

chambouler [ʃabule] *vt* to disrupt, turn upside down

chambre [ʃabr(ə)] *nf* bedroom; (*Tech*) chamber;

(*Pol*) chamber, house; (*Jur*) court; (*Comm*) chamber; federation; **faire ~ à part** to sleep in separate rooms; **stratège/alpiniste en ~** armchair strategist/mountaineer; **~ à un lit/deux lits** single/twin-bedded room; **~ pour une/deux personne(s)** single/double room; **~ d'accusation** court of criminal appeal; **~ d'agriculture (CA)** *body responsible for the agricultural interests of a département*; **~ à air** (*de pneu*) (inner) tube; **~ d'amis** spare *ou* guest room; **~ de combustion** combustion chamber; **~ de commerce et d'industrie (CCI)** chamber of commerce and industry; **~ à coucher** bedroom; **la C~ des députés** the Chamber of Deputies, ≈ the House (of Commons) (*Brit*), ≈ the House of Representatives (*US*); **~ forte** strongroom; **~ froide** *ou* **frigorifique** cold room; **~ à gaz** gas chamber; **~ d'hôte** ≈ bed and breakfast (in private home); **~ des machines** engine-room; **~ des métiers (CM)** *chamber of commerce for trades*; **~ meublée** bedsit(ter) (*Brit*), furnished room; **~ noire** (*Photo*) dark room

chambrer [ʃabre] *vt* (vin) to bring to room temperature

chameau, x [ʃamo] *nm* camel

chamois [ʃamwa] *nm* chamois ▷ *adj*: (*couleur*) **~** fawn, buff

champ [ʃã] *nm* (aussi Inform) field; (*Photo: aussi*: **dans le champ**) in the picture; **prendre du ~** to draw back; **laisser le ~ libre à qn** to leave sb a clear field; **~ d'action** sphere of operation(s); **~ de bataille** battlefield; **~ de courses** racecourse; **~ d'honneur** field of honour; **~ de manœuvre** (*Mil*) parade ground; **~ de mines** minefield; **~ de tir** shooting *ou* rifle range; **~ visuel** field of vision

champagne [ʃãpaɲ] *nm* champagne

champêtre [ʃãpɛtr(ə)] *adj* country *cpd*, rural

champignon [ʃãpiɲɔ̃] *nm* mushroom; (*terme générique*) fungus; (*fam: accélérateur*) accelerator, gas pedal (*US*); **~ de couche** *ou* **de Paris** button mushroom; **~ vénéneux** toadstool, poisonous mushroom

champion, ne [ʃãpjɔ̃, -ɔn] *adj, nm/f* champion

championnat [ʃãpjɔna] *nm* championship

chance [ʃãs] *nf*: **la ~** luck; **une ~** a stroke *ou* piece of luck *ou* good fortune; (*occasion*) a lucky break; **chances** *nfpl* (*probabilités*) chances; **avoir de la ~** to be lucky; **il a des ~s de gagner** he has a chance of winning; **il y a de fortes ~s pour que Paul soit malade** it's highly probable that Paul is ill; **bonne ~!** good luck!; **encore une ~ que tu viennes!** it's lucky you're coming!; **je n'ai pas de ~** I'm out of luck; (*toujours*) I never have any luck; **donner sa ~ à qn** to give sb a chance

chanceler [ʃãsle] *vi* to totter

chancelier [ʃãsəlje] *nm* (*allemand*) chancellor; (*d'ambassade*) secretary

chanceux, -euse [ʃãsø, -øz] *adj* lucky, fortunate

chandail [ʃãdaj] *nm* (thick) jumper *ou* sweater

Chandeleur [ʃãdlœr] *nf*: **la ~** Candlemas

chandelier [ʃãdəlje] *nm* candlestick; (à plusieurs

branches) candelabra

chandelle [ʃɑ̃dɛl] *nf* (*tallow*) candle; (*Tennis*):
faire une ~ to lob; (*Aviat*): **monter en** ~ to climb
vertically; **tenir la** ~ to play gooseberry; **dîner
aux ~s** candlelight dinner

change [ʃɑ̃ʒ] *nm* (*Comm*) exchange; **opérations
de** ~ (foreign) exchange transactions; **contrôle
des ~s** exchange control; **gagner/perdre au** ~ to
be better/worse off (for it); **donner le** ~ **à qn** (*fig*)
to lead sb up the garden path

changement [ʃɑ̃ʒmɑ̃] *nm* change; ~ **de vitesse**
(*dispositif*) gears *pl*; (*action*) gear change

changer [ʃɑ̃ʒe] *vt* (*modifier*) to change, alter;
(*remplacer, Comm, rhabiller*) to change ▷ *vi* to
change, alter; **se changer** *vi* to change (o.s.); ~
de (*remplacer: adresse, nom, voiture etc*) to change
one's; ~ **de train** to change trains; ~ **d'air** to
get a change of air; ~ **de couleur/direction** to
change colour/direction; ~ **d'idée** to change
one's mind; ~ **de place avec qn** to change places
with sb; ~ **de vitesse** (*Auto*) to change gear; ~
qn/qch de place to move sb/sth to another
place; ~ (**de bus** *etc*) to change (buses *etc*); ~ **qch
en** to change sth into

chanson [ʃɑ̃sɔ̃] *nf* song

chant [ʃɑ̃] *nm* song; (*art vocal*) singing; (*d'église*)
hymn; (*de poème*) canto; (*Tech*): **posé de** *ou* **sur ~**
placed edgeways; ~ **de Noël** Christmas carol

chantage [ʃɑ̃taʒ] *nm* blackmail; **faire du** ~ to use
blackmail; **soumettre qn à un** ~ to blackmail
sb

chanter [ʃɑ̃te] *vt, vi* to sing; ~ **juste/faux** to sing
in tune/out of tune; **si cela lui chante** (*fam*) if
he feels like it *ou* fancies it

chanteur, -euse [ʃɑ̃tœʀ, -øz] *nm/f* singer; ~ **de
charme** crooner

chantier [ʃɑ̃tje] *nm* (building) site; (*sur une route*)
roadworks *pl*; **mettre en** ~ to start work on; ~
naval shipyard

chantilly [ʃɑ̃tiji] *nf voir* **crème**

chantonner [ʃɑ̃tɔne] *vi, vt* to sing to oneself,
hum

chanvre [ʃɑ̃vʀ(ə)] *nm* hemp

chaparder [ʃapaʀde] *vt* to pinch

chapeau, x [ʃapo] *nm* hat; (*Presse*) introductory
paragraph; ~! well done!; ~ **melon** bowler hat; ~
mou trilby; **~x de roues** hub caps

chapelet [ʃaplɛ] *nm* (*Rel*) rosary; (*fig*): **un ~ de** a
string of; **dire son** ~ to tell one's beads

chapelle [ʃapɛl] *nf* chapel; ~ **ardente** chapel of
rest

chapelure [ʃaplyʀ] *nf* (dried) breadcrumbs *pl*

chapiteau, x [ʃapito] *nm* (*Archit*) capital; (*de
cirque*) marquee, big top

chapitre [ʃapitʀ(ə)] *nm* chapter; (*fig*) subject,
matter; **avoir voix au** ~ to have a say in the
matter

chaque [ʃak] *adj* each, every; (*indéfini*) every

char [ʃaʀ] *nm* (*à foin etc*) cart, waggon; (*de carnaval*)
float; ~ (**d'assaut**) tank

charabia [ʃaʀabja] *nm* (*péj*) gibberish,
gobbledygook (*Brit*)

charade [ʃaʀad] *nf* riddle; (*mimée*) charade

charbon [ʃaʀbɔ̃] *nm* coal; ~ **de bois** charcoal

charcuterie [ʃaʀkytʀi] *nf* (*magasin*) pork
butcher's shop and delicatessen; (*produits*)
cooked pork meats *pl*

charcutier, -ière [ʃaʀkytje, -jɛʀ] *nm/f* pork
butcher

chardon [ʃaʀdɔ̃] *nm* thistle

charge [ʃaʀʒ(ə)] *nf* (*fardeau*) load; (*explosif, Élec, Mil,
Jur*) charge; (*rôle, mission*) responsibility; **charges**
nfpl (*du loyer*) service charges; **à la ~ de** (*dépendant
de*) dependent upon, supported by; (*aux frais de*)
chargeable to, payable by; **j'accepte, à ~ de
revanche** I accept, provided I can do the same
for you (in return) one day; **prendre en** ~ to take
charge of; (*véhicule*) to take on; (*dépenses*) to take
care of; ~ **utile** (*Auto*) live load; (*Comm*) payload;
~s sociales social security contributions

chargé [ʃaʀʒe] *adj* (*voiture, animal, personne*) laden;
(*fusil, batterie, caméra*) loaded; (*occupé: emploi du
temps, journée*) busy, full; (*estomac*) heavy, full;
(*langue*) furred; (*décoration, style*) heavy, ornate
▷ *nm*: ~ **d'affaires** chargé d'affaires; ~ **de cours**
≈ lecturer; ~ **de** (*responsable de*) responsible for

chargement [ʃaʀʒəmɑ̃] *nm* (*action*) loading;
charging; (*objets*) load

charger [ʃaʀʒe] *vt* (*voiture, fusil, caméra*) to load;
(*batterie*) to charge ▷ *vi* (*Mil etc*) to charge; **se ~
de** *vt* to see to, take care of; ~ **qn de qch/faire
qch** to give sb the responsibility for sth/of doing
sth; to put sb in charge of sth/doing sth; **se ~
faire qch** to take it upon o.s. to do sth

chariot [ʃaʀjo] *nm* trolley; (*charrette*) waggon; (*de
machine à écrire*) carriage; ~ **élévateur** fork-lift
truck

charité [ʃaʀite] *nf* charity; **faire la** ~ to give to
charity; to do charitable works; **faire la** ~ **à** to
give (something) to; **fête/vente de** ~ fête/sale in
aid of charity

charmant, e [ʃaʀmɑ̃, -ɑ̃t] *adj* charming

charme [ʃaʀm(ə)] *nm* charm; **charmes** *nmpl*
(*appas*) charms; **c'est ce qui en fait le** ~ that is
its attraction; **faire du** ~ to be charming, turn
on the charm; **aller** *ou* **se porter comme un** ~ to
be in the pink

charmer [ʃaʀme] *vt* to charm; **je suis charmé
de ...** I'm delighted to ...

charnel, le [ʃaʀnɛl] *adj* carnal

charnière [ʃaʀnjɛʀ] *nf* hinge; (*fig*) turning-point

charnu, e [ʃaʀny] *adj* fleshy

charpente [ʃaʀpɑ̃t] *nf* frame(work); (*fig*)
structure, framework; (*carrure*) build, frame

charpentier [ʃaʀpɑ̃tje] *nm* carpenter

charpie [ʃaʀpi] *nf*: **en ~** (*fig*) in shreds *ou* ribbons

charrette [ʃaʀɛt] *nf* cart

charrier [ʃaʀje] *vt* to carry (along); to cart, carry
▷ *vi* (*fam*) to exaggerate

charrue [ʃaʀy] *nf* plough (*Brit*), plow (*US*)

charter [tʃaʀtœʀ] *nm* (*vol*) charter flight; (*avion*)
charter plane

chasse [ʃas] *nf* hunting; (*au fusil*) shooting;
(*poursuite*) chase; (*aussi*: **chasse d'eau**) flush; **la**

~ **est ouverte** the hunting season is open; **la** ~ **est fermée** it is the close (Brit) ou closed (US) season; **aller à la** ~ to go hunting; **prendre en** ~, **donner la** ~ **à** to give chase to; **tirer la** ~ **(d'eau)** to flush the toilet, pull the chain; ~ **aérienne** aerial pursuit; ~ **à courre** hunting; ~ **à l'homme** manhunt; ~ **gardée** private hunting grounds pl; ~ **sous-marine** underwater fishing

chasse-neige [ʃasnɛʒ] nm inv snowplough (Brit), snowplow (US)

chasser [ʃase] vt to hunt; (expulser) to chase away ou out, drive away ou out; (dissiper) to chase ou sweep away; to dispel, drive away

chasseur, -euse [ʃasœʀ, -øz] nm/f hunter ▷ nm (avion) fighter; (domestique) page (boy), messenger (boy); ~ **d'images** roving photographer; ~ **de têtes** (fig) headhunter; ~**s alpins** mountain infantry

châssis [ʃasi] nm (Auto) chassis; (cadre) frame; (de jardin) cold frame

chat¹ [ʃa] nm cat; ~ **sauvage** wildcat

chat² [tʃat] nm (Internet) chat

châtaigne [ʃatɛɲ] nf chestnut

châtaignier [ʃatɛɲe] nm chestnut (tree)

châtain [ʃatɛ̃] adj inv chestnut (brown); (personne) chestnut-haired

château, x [ʃato] nm castle; ~ **d'eau** water tower; ~ **fort** stronghold, fortified castle; ~ **de sable** sand castle

châtier [ʃatje] vt to punish, castigate; (fig: style) to polish, refine

châtiment [ʃatimɑ̃] nm punishment, castigation; ~ **corporel** corporal punishment

chaton [ʃatɔ̃] nm (Zool) kitten; (Bot) catkin; (de bague) bezel; stone

chatouiller [ʃatuje] vt to tickle; (l'odorat, le palais) to titillate

chatouilleux, -euse [ʃatujø, -øz] adj ticklish; (fig) touchy, over-sensitive

chatoyer [ʃatwaje] vi to shimmer

châtrer [ʃatʀe] vt (mâle) to castrate; (femelle) to spay; (cheval) to geld; (chat, chien) to doctor (Brit), fix (US); (fig) to mutilate

chatte [ʃat] nf (she-)cat

chatter [tʃate] vi (Internet) to chat

chaud, e [ʃo, -od] adj (gén) warm; (très chaud) hot; (fig: félicitations) hearty; (discussion) heated; **il fait** ~ it's warm; it's hot; **manger** ~ to have something hot to eat; **avoir** ~ to be warm; to be hot; **tenir** ~ to keep hot; **ça me tient** ~ it keeps me warm; **tenir au** ~ to keep in a warm place; **rester au** ~ to stay in the warm

chaudière [ʃodjɛʀ] nf boiler

chaudron [ʃodʀɔ̃] nm cauldron

chauffage [ʃofaʒ] nm heating; ~ **au gaz/à l'électricité/au charbon** gas/electric/solid fuel heating; ~ **central** central heating; ~ **par le sol** underfloor heating

chauffard [ʃofaʀ] nm (péj) reckless driver; road hog; (après un accident) hit-and-run driver

chauffe-eau [ʃofo] nm inv water heater

chauffer [ʃofe] vt to heat ▷ vi to heat up, warm up; (trop chauffer: moteur) to overheat; **se chauffer** vi (se mettre en train) to warm up; (au soleil) to warm o.s.

chauffeur [ʃofœʀ] nm driver; (privé) chauffeur; **voiture avec/sans** ~ chauffeur-driven/self-drive car; ~ **de taxi** taxi driver

chaume [ʃom] nm (du toit) thatch; (tiges) stubble

chaumière [ʃomjɛʀ] nf (thatched) cottage

chaussée [ʃose] nf road(way); (digue) causeway

chausse-pied [ʃospje] nm shoe-horn

chausser [ʃose] vt (bottes, skis) to put on; (enfant) to put shoes on; (soulier) to fit; ~ **du 38/42** to take size 38/42; ~ **grand/bien** to be big/well-fitting; **se chausser** to put one's shoes on

chaussette [ʃosɛt] nf sock

chausson [ʃosɔ̃] nm slipper; (de bébé) bootee; ~ **(aux pommes)** (apple) turnover

chaussure [ʃosyʀ] nf shoe; (commerce): **la** ~ the shoe industry ou trade; ~**s basses** flat shoes; ~**s montantes** ankle boots; ~**s de ski** ski boots

chauve [ʃov] adj bald

chauve-souris (pl **chauves-souris**) [ʃovsuʀi] nf bat

chauvin, e [ʃovɛ̃, -in] adj chauvinistic; jingoistic

chaux [ʃo] nf lime; **blanchi à la** ~ whitewashed

chavirer [ʃaviʀe] vi to capsize, overturn

chef [ʃɛf] nm head, leader; (patron) boss; (de cuisine) chef; **au premier** ~ extremely, to the nth degree; **de son propre** ~ on his ou her own initiative; **général/commandant en** ~ general-/commander-in-chief; ~ **d'accusation** (Jur) charge, count (of indictment); ~ **d'atelier** (shop) foreman; ~ **de bureau** head clerk; ~ **de clinique** senior hospital lecturer; ~ **d'entreprise** company head; ~ **d'équipe** team leader; ~ **d'état** head of state; ~ **de famille** head of the family; ~ **de file** (de parti etc) leader; ~ **de gare** station master; ~ **d'orchestre** conductor (Brit), leader (US); ~ **de rayon** department(al) supervisor; ~ **de service** departmental head

chef-d'œuvre (pl **chefs-d'œuvre**) [ʃɛdœvʀ(ə)] nm masterpiece

chef-lieu (pl **chefs-lieux**) [ʃɛfljø] nm county town

chemin [ʃəmɛ̃] nm path; (itinéraire, direction, trajet) way; **en** ~, ~ **faisant** on the way; ~ **de fer** railway (Brit), railroad (US); **par** ~ **de fer** by rail; **les** ~**s de fer** the railways (Brit), the railroad (US); ~ **de terre** dirt track

cheminée [ʃəmine] nf chimney; (à l'intérieur) chimney piece, fireplace; (de bateau) funnel

cheminement [ʃəminmɑ̃] nm progress; course

cheminot [ʃəmino] nm railwayman (Brit), railroad worker (US)

chemise [ʃəmiz] nf shirt; (dossier) folder; ~ **de nuit** nightdress

chemisier [ʃəmizje] nm blouse

chenal, -aux [ʃənal, -o] nm channel

chêne [ʃɛn] nm oak (tree); (bois) oak

chenil [ʃənil] nm kennels pl

chenille [ʃənij] nf (Zool) caterpillar; (Auto) caterpillar track; **véhicule à** ~**s** tracked vehicle, caterpillar

chèque [ʃɛk] nm cheque (Brit), check (US); **faire/
toucher un ~** to write/cash a cheque; **par ~**
by cheque; **~ barré/sans provision** crossed
(Brit) /bad cheque; **~ en blanc** blank cheque;
~ au porteur cheque to bearer; **~ postal** post
office cheque, ≈ giro cheque (Brit); **~ de voyage**
traveller's cheque

chéquier [ʃekje] nm cheque book (Brit),
checkbook (US)

cher, -ère [ʃɛR] adj (aimé) dear; (coûteux)
expensive, dear ▷ adv: **coûter/payer ~** to cost/
pay a lot ▷ nf: **la bonne chère** good food; **cela
coûte ~** it's expensive, it costs a lot of money;
mon ~, ma chère my dear

chercher [ʃɛRʃe] vt to look for; (gloire etc) to seek; **~
des ennuis/la bagarre** to be looking for trouble/
a fight; **aller ~** to go for, go and fetch; **~ à faire**
to try to do

chercheur, -euse [ʃɛRʃœR, -øz] nm/f researcher,
research worker; **~ de** seeker of; hunter of; **~
d'or** gold digger

chère [ʃɛR] adj f, nf voir **cher**

chéri, e [ʃeri] adj beloved, dear; **(mon) ~** darling

chérir [ʃeRiR] vt to cherish

cherté [ʃɛRte] nf: **la ~ de la vie** the high cost of
living

chétif, -ive [ʃetif, -iv] adj puny, stunted

cheval, -aux [ʃəval, -o] nm horse; (Auto): **~
(vapeur) (CV)** horsepower no pl; **50 chevaux
(au frein)** 50 brake horsepower, 50 b.h.p.;
10 chevaux (fiscaux) 10 horsepower (for tax
purposes); **faire du ~** to ride; **à ~** on horseback; **à
~ sur** astride, straddling; (fig) overlapping; **~
d'arçons** vaulting horse; **~ à bascule** rocking
horse; **~ de bataille** charger; (fig) hobby-horse;
~ de course race horse; **chevaux de bois** (des
manèges) wooden (fairground) horses; (manège)
merry-go-round

chevalet [ʃəvalɛ] nm easel

chevalier [ʃəvalje] nm knight; **~ servant** escort

chevalière [ʃəvaljɛR] nf signet ring

chevalin, e [ʃəvalɛ̃, -in] adj of horses, equine;
(péj) horsy; **boucherie ~e** horse-meat butcher's

chevaucher [ʃəvoʃe] vi (aussi: **se chevaucher**) to
overlap (each other) ▷ vt to be astride, straddle

chevaux [ʃəvo] nmpl voir **cheval**

chevelu, e [ʃəvly] adj with a good head of hair,
hairy (péj)

chevelure [ʃəvlyR] nf hair no pl

chevet [ʃəvɛ] nm: **au ~ de qn** at sb's bedside;
lampe de ~ bedside lamp

cheveu, x [ʃəvø] nm hair ▷ nmpl (chevelure) hair
sg; **avoir les ~x courts/en brosse** to have short
hair/a crew cut; **se faire couper les ~x** to get
ou have one's hair cut; **tiré par les ~x** (histoire)
far-fetched

cheville [ʃəvij] nf (Anat) ankle; (de bois) peg; (pour
enfoncer une vis) plug; **être en ~ avec qn** to be in
cahoots with sb; **~ ouvrière** (fig) kingpin

chèvre [ʃɛvR(ə)] nf (she-)goat; **ménager la ~ et
le chou** to try to please everyone

chevreau, x [ʃəvRo] nm kid

chèvrefeuille [ʃɛvRəfœj] nm honeysuckle

chevreuil [ʃəvRœj] nm roe deer inv; (Culin)
venison

chevronné, e [ʃəvRɔne] adj seasoned,
experienced

chez [ʃe] prép **1** (à la demeure de) at; (: direction) to;
~ qn at/to sb's house ou place; **~ moi** at home;
(direction) home

2 (à l'entreprise de): **il travaille ~ Renault** he
works for Renault, he works at Renault('s)

3 (+profession) at; (: direction) to: **~ le boulanger/
dentiste** at ou to the baker's/dentist's

4 (dans le caractère, l'œuvre de) in; **~ les renards/
Racine** in foxes/Racine; **~ les Français** among
the French; **~ lui, c'est un devoir** for him, it's
a duty

▷ nm inv: **mon ~ moi/ton ~ toi** etc my/your etc
home ou place

chez-soi [ʃeswa] nm inv home

chic [ʃik] adj inv chic, smart; (généreux) nice,
decent ▷ nm stylishness; **avoir le ~ de ou pour**
to have the knack of ou for; **de ~** adv off the cuff;
~! great!, terrific!

chicane [ʃikan] nf (obstacle) zigzag; (querelle)
squabble

chicaner [ʃikane] vi (ergoter): **~ sur** to quibble
about

chiche [ʃiʃ] adj (mesquin) niggardly, mean; (pauvre)
meagre (Brit), meager (US) ▷ excl (en réponse à un
défi) you're on!; **tu n'es pas ~ de lui parler!** you
wouldn't (dare) speak to her!

chichis [ʃiʃi] (fam) nmpl fuss sg

chicorée [ʃikɔRe] nf (café) chicory; (salade) endive;
~ frisée curly endive

chien [ʃjɛ̃] nm dog; (de pistolet) hammer; **temps
de ~** rotten weather; **vie de ~** dog's life; **couché
en ~ de fusil** curled up; **~ d'aveugle** guide dog;
~ de chasse gun dog; **~ de garde** guard dog; **~
policier** police dog; **~ de race** pedigree dog; **~ de
traîneau** husky

chiendent [ʃjɛ̃dɑ̃] nm couch grass

chien-loup (pl **chiens-loups**) [ʃjɛ̃lu] nm wolfhound

chienne [ʃjɛn] nf (she-)dog, bitch

chier [ʃje] vi (fam!) to crap (!), shit (!); **faire ~ qn**
(importuner) to bug sb; (causer des ennuis à) to piss sb
around (!); **se faire ~** (s'ennuyer) to be bored rigid

chiffon [ʃifɔ̃] nm (piece of) rag

chiffonner [ʃifɔne] vt to crumple, crease;
(tracasser) to concern

chiffre [ʃifR(ə)] nm (représentant un nombre) figure;
numeral; (montant, total) total, sum; (d'un code)
code, cipher; **~s romains/arabes** roman/arabic
figures ou numerals; **en ~s ronds** in round
figures; **écrire un nombre en ~s** to write a
number in figures; **~ d'affaires (CA)** turnover; **~
de ventes** sales figures

chiffrer [ʃifRe] vt (dépense) to put a figure to,
assess; (message) to (en)code, cipher ▷ vi: **~ à, se ~
à** to add up to

chignon [ʃiɲɔ̃] nm chignon, bun

Chili [ʃili] nm: **le ~** Chile

chilien, ne [ʃiljɛ̃, -ɛn] adj Chilean ▷ nm/f: **C~, ne**

Chilean
chimie [ʃimi] *nf* chemistry
chimique [ʃimik] *adj* chemical; **produits ~s** chemicals
chimpanzé [ʃɛ̃pɑ̃ze] *nm* chimpanzee
Chine [ʃin] *nf*: **la ~** China; **la ~ libre, la république de ~** the Republic of China, Nationalist China (*Taiwan*)
chine [ʃin] *nm* rice paper; (*porcelaine*) china (*vase*)
chinois, e [ʃinwa, -waz] *adj* Chinese; (*fig: péj*) pernickety, fussy ▷ *nm* (*Ling*) Chinese ▷ *nm/f*: **C~, e** Chinese
chiot [ʃjo] *nm* pup(py)
chiper [ʃipe] *vt* (*fam*) to pinch
chipoter [ʃipɔte] *vi* (*manger*) to nibble; (*ergoter*) to quibble, haggle
chips [ʃips] *nfpl* (*aussi:* **pommes chips**) crisps (*Brit*), (potato) chips (*US*)
chiquenaude [ʃiknod] *nf* flick, flip
chirurgical, e, -aux [ʃiryrʒikal, -o] *adj* surgical
chirurgie [ʃiryrʒi] *nf* surgery; **~ esthétique** cosmetic *ou* plastic surgery
chirurgien [ʃiryrʒjɛ̃] *nm* surgeon; **~ dentiste** dental surgeon
chlore [klɔr] *nm* chlorine
choc [ʃɔk] *nm* impact; shock; crash; (*moral*) shock; (*affrontement*) clash ▷ *adj*: **prix ~** amazing *ou* incredible price/prices; **de ~** (*troupe, traitement*) shock *cpd*; (*patron etc*) high-powered; **~ opératoire/nerveux** post-operative/nervous shock; **~ en retour** return shock; (*fig*) backlash
chocolat [ʃɔkɔla] *nm* chocolate; (*boisson*) (hot) chocolate; **~ chaud** hot chocolate; **~ à cuire** cooking chocolate; **~ au lait** milk chocolate; **~ en poudre** drinking chocolate
chœur [kœr] *nm* (*chorale*) choir; (*Opéra, Théât*) chorus; (*Archit*) choir, chancel; **en ~** in chorus
choisir [ʃwazir] *vt* to choose; (*entre plusieurs*) to choose, select; **~ de faire qch** to choose *ou* opt to do sth
choix [ʃwa] *nm* choice; selection; **avoir le ~** to have the choice; **je n'avais pas le ~** I had no choice; **de premier ~** (*Comm*) class *ou* grade one; **de ~** choice *cpd*, selected; **au ~** as you wish *ou* prefer; **de mon/son ~** of my/his *ou* her choosing
chômage [ʃomaʒ] *nm* unemployment; **mettre au ~** to make redundant, put out of work; **être au ~** to be unemployed *ou* out of work; **~ partiel** short-time working; **~ structurel** structural unemployment; **~ technique** lay-offs *pl*
chômeur, -euse [ʃomœr, -øz] *nm/f* unemployed person, person out of work
chope [ʃɔp] *nf* tankard
choper [ʃɔpe] (*fam*) *vt* (*objet, maladie*) to catch
choquer [ʃɔke] *vt* (*offenser*) to shock; (*commotionner*) to shake (up)
choral, e [kɔral] *adj* choral ▷ *nf* choral society, choir
choriste [kɔrist(ə)] *nm/f* choir member; (*Opéra*) chorus member
chose [ʃoz] *nf* thing ▷ *nm* (*fam: machin*) thingamajig ▷ *adj inv*: **être/se sentir tout ~**

(*bizarre*) to be/feel a bit odd; (*malade*) to be/feel out of sorts; **dire bien des ~s à qn** to give sb's regards to sb; **parler de ~(s) et d'autre(s)** to talk about one thing and another; **c'est peu de ~** it's nothing much
chou, x [ʃu] *nm* cabbage ▷ *adj inv* cute; **mon petit ~** (my) sweetheart; **faire ~ blanc** to draw a blank; **feuille de ~** (*fig: journal*) rag; **~ à la crème** cream bun (*made of choux pastry*); **~ de Bruxelles** Brussels sprout
chouchou, te [ʃuʃu, -ut] *nm/f* (*Scol*) teacher's pet
choucroute [ʃukrut] *nf* sauerkraut; **~ garnie** sauerkraut with cooked meats and potatoes
chouette [ʃwɛt] *nf* owl ▷ *adj* (*fam*) great, smashing
chou-fleur (*pl* **choux-fleurs**) [ʃuflœr] *nm* cauliflower
choyer [ʃwaje] *vt* to cherish; to pamper
chrétien, ne [kretjɛ̃, -ɛn] *adj, nm/f* Christian
Christ [krist] *nm*: **le ~** Christ; **christ** (*crucifix etc*) figure of Christ; **Jésus ~** Jesus Christ
christianisme [kristjanism(ə)] *nm* Christianity
chrome [krom] *nm* chromium; (*revêtement*) chrome, chromium
chromé, e [krome] *adj* chrome-plated, chromium-plated
chronique [krɔnik] *adj* chronic ▷ *nf* (*de journal*) column, page; (*historique*) chronicle; (*Radio, TV*): **la ~ sportive/théâtrale** the sports/theatre review; **la ~ locale** local news and gossip
chronologique [krɔnɔlɔʒik] *adj* chronological
chronomètre [krɔnɔmɛtr(ə)] *nm* stopwatch
chronométrer [krɔnɔmetre] *vt* to time
chrysanthème [krizɑ̃tɛm] *nm* chrysanthemum
chuchotement [ʃyʃɔtmɑ̃] *nm* whisper
chuchoter [ʃyʃɔte] *vt, vi* to whisper
chut *excl* [ʃyt] sh! ▷ *vb* [ʃy] *voir* **choir**
chute [ʃyt] *nf* fall; (*de bois, papier: déchet*) scrap; **la ~ des cheveux** hair loss; **faire une ~ (de 10 m)** to fall (10 m); **~s de pluie/neige** rain/snowfalls; **~ (d'eau)** waterfall; **~ du jour** nightfall; **~ libre** free fall; **~ des reins** small of the back
Chypre [ʃipr] *nm* Cyprus
-ci, ci- [si] *adv voir* **par**; **ci-contre**; **ci-joint** *etc* ▷ *adj dém*: **ce garçon-/-là** this/that boy; **ces femmes-/-là** these/those women
cible [sibl(ə)] *nf* target
ciboulette [sibulɛt] *nf* (small) chive
cicatrice [sikatris] *nf* scar
cicatriser [sikatrize] *vt* to heal; **se cicatriser** to heal (up), form a scar
ci-contre [sikɔ̃tr(ə)] *adv* opposite
ci-dessous [sidəsu] *adv* below
ci-dessus [sidəsy] *adv* above
cidre [sidr(ə)] *nm* cider
Cie *abr* (= *compagnie*) Co
ciel [sjɛl] *nm* sky; (*Rel*) heaven; **ciels** *nmpl* (*Peinture etc*) skies; **cieux** *nmpl* sky *sg*, skies; (*Rel*) heaven *sg*; **à ~ ouvert** open-air; (*mine*) opencast; **tomber du ~** (*arriver à l'improviste*) to appear out of the blue; (*être stupéfait*) to be unable to believe one's eyes; **C~!** good heavens!; **~ de lit** canopy

cierge [sjɛrʒ(ə)] *nm* candle; ~ **pascal** Easter candle

cieux [sjø] *nmpl voir* **ciel**

cigale [sigal] *nf* cicada

cigare [sigar] *nm* cigar

cigarette [sigarɛt] *nf* cigarette; ~ **(à) bout filtre** filter cigarette

ci-gît [siʒi] *adv* here lies

cigogne [sigɔɲ] *nf* stork

ci-inclus, e [siɛ̃kly, -yz] *adj, adv* enclosed

ci-joint, e [siʒwɛ̃, -ɛt] *adj, adv* enclosed; **veuillez trouver** ~ please find enclosed

cil [sil] *nm* (eye)lash

cime [sim] *nf* top; (*montagne*) peak

ciment [simɑ̃] *nm* cement; ~ **armé** reinforced concrete

cimetière [simtjɛr] *nm* cemetery; (*d'église*) churchyard; ~ **de voitures** scrapyard

cinéaste [sineast(ə)] *nm/f* film-maker

cinéma [sinema] *nm* cinema; **aller au** ~ to go to the cinema *ou* pictures *ou* movies; ~ **d'animation** cartoon (film)

cinématographique [sinematɔgrafik] *adj* film *cpd*, cinema *cpd*

cinglant, e [sɛ̃glɑ̃, -ɑ̃t] *adj* (*propos, ironie*) scathing, biting; (*échec*) crushing

cinglé, e [sɛ̃gle] *adj* (*fam*) crazy

cinq [sɛ̃k] *num* five

cinquantaine [sɛ̃kɑ̃tɛn] *nf*: **une** ~ **(de)** about fifty; **avoir la** ~ (*âge*) to be around fifty

cinquante [sɛ̃kɑ̃t] *num* fifty

cinquantenaire [sɛ̃kɑ̃tnɛr] *adj, nm/f* fifty-year-old

cinquième [sɛ̃kjɛm] *num* fifth

cintre [sɛ̃tr(ə)] *nm* coat-hanger; (*Archit*) arch; **plein** ~ semicircular arch

cintré, e [sɛ̃tre] *adj* curved; (*chemise*) fitted, slim-fitting

cirage [siraʒ] *nm* (shoe) polish

circonflexe [sirkɔ̃flɛks(ə)] *adj*: **accent** ~ circumflex accent

circonscription [sirkɔ̃skripsjɔ̃] *nf* district; ~ **électorale** (*d'un député*) constituency; ~ **militaire** military area

circonscrire [sirkɔ̃skrir] *vt* to define, delimit; (*incendie*) to contain; (*propriété*) to mark out; (*sujet*) to define

circonstance [sirkɔ̃stɑ̃s] *nf* circumstance; (*occasion*) occasion; **œuvre de** ~ occasional work; **air de** ~ fitting air; **tête de** ~ appropriate demeanour (*Brit*) *ou* demeanor (*US*); ~**s atténuantes** mitigating circumstances

circuit [sirkɥi] *nm* (*trajet*) tour, (round) trip; (*Élec, Tech*) circuit; ~ **automobile** motor circuit; ~ **de distribution** distribution network; ~ **fermé** closed circuit; ~ **intégré** integrated circuit

circulaire [sirkylɛr] *adj, nf* circular

circulation [sirkylasjɔ̃] *nf* circulation; (*Auto*): **la** ~ (the) traffic; **bonne/mauvaise** ~ good/bad circulation; **mettre en** ~ to put into circulation

circuler [sirkyle] *vi* to drive (along); to walk along; (*train etc*) to run; (*sang, devises*) to circulate;

faire ~ (*nouvelle*) to spread (about), circulate; (*badauds*) to move on

cire [sir] *nf* wax; ~ **à cacheter** sealing wax

ciré [sire] *nm* oilskin

cirer [sire] *vt* to wax, polish

cirque [sirk(ə)] *nm* circus; (*arène*) amphitheatre (*Brit*), amphitheater (*US*); (*Géo*) cirque; (*fig: désordre*) chaos, bedlam; (: *chichis*) carry-on

cisaille [sizaj], **cisailles** *nf(pl)* (gardening) shears *pl*

ciseau, x [sizo] *nm*: ~ **(à bois)** chisel ▷ *nmpl* (pair of) scissors; **sauter en** ~**x** to do a scissors jump; ~ **à froid** cold chisel

ciseler [sizle] *vt* to chisel, carve

citadin, e [sitadɛ̃, -in] *nm/f* city dweller ▷ *adj* town *cpd*, city *cpd*, urban

citation [sitasjɔ̃] *nf* (*d'auteur*) quotation; (*Jur*) summons *sg*; (*Mil: récompense*) mention

cité [site] *nf* town; (*plus grande*) city; ~ **ouvrière** (workers') housing estate; ~ **universitaire** students' residences *pl*

citer [site] *vt* (*un auteur*) to quote (from); (*nommer*) to name; (*Jur*) to summon; ~ **(en exemple)** (*personne*) to hold up (as an example); **je ne veux** ~ **personne** I don't want to name names

citerne [sitɛrn(ə)] *nf* tank

citoyen, ne [sitwajɛ̃, -ɛn] *nm/f* citizen

citron [sitrɔ̃] *nm* lemon; ~ **pressé** (fresh) lemon juice; ~ **vert** lime

citronnade [sitrɔnad] *nf* lemonade

citrouille [sitruj] *nf* pumpkin

civet [sive] *nm* stew; ~ **de lièvre** jugged hare

civière [sivjɛr] *nf* stretcher

civil, e [sivil] *adj* (*Jur, Admin, poli*) civil; (*non militaire*) civilian ▷ *nm* civilian; **en** ~ in civilian clothes; **dans le** ~ in civilian life

civilisation [sivilizasjɔ̃] *nf* civilization

clair, e [klɛr] *adj* light; (*chambre*) light, bright; (*eau, son, fig*) clear ▷ *adv*: **voir** ~ to see clearly ▷ *nm*: **mettre au** ~ (*notes etc*) to tidy up; **tirer qch au** ~ to clear sth up, clarify sth; **bleu** ~ light blue; **pour être** ~ so as to make it plain; **y voir** ~ (*comprendre*) to understand, see; **le plus** ~ **de son temps/argent** the better part of his time/money; **en** ~ (*non codé*) in clear; ~ **de lune** moonlight

clairement [klɛrmɑ̃] *adv* clearly

clairière [klɛrjɛr] *nf* clearing

clairon [klɛrɔ̃] *nm* bugle

claironner [klɛrɔne] *vt* (*fig*) to trumpet, shout from the rooftops

clairsemé, e [klɛrsəme] *adj* sparse

clairvoyant, e [klɛrvwajɑ̃, -ɑ̃t] *adj* perceptive, clear-sighted

clandestin, e [klɑ̃dɛstɛ̃, -in] *adj* clandestine, covert; (*Pol*) underground, clandestine; **passager** ~ stowaway

clapier [klapje] *nm* (rabbit) hutch

clapoter [klapɔte] *vi* to lap

claque [klak] *nf* (*gifle*) slap; (*Théât*) claque ▷ *nm* (*chapeau*) opera hat

claquer [klake] *vi* (*drapeau*) to flap; (*porte*) to bang, slam; (*coup de feu*) to ring out ▷ vt (*porte*) to slam, bang; (*doigts*) to snap; **elle claquait des dents** her teeth were chattering; **se ~ un muscle** to pull *ou* strain a muscle

claquettes [klaket] *nfpl* tap-dancing *sg*

clarinette [klarinet] *nf* clarinet

clarté [klarte] *nf* lightness; brightness; (*d'un son, de l'eau*) clearness; (*d'une explication*) clarity

classe [klas] *nf* class; (*Scol: local*) class(room); (: *leçon*) class; (: *élèves*) class, form; **1ère/2ème ~ 1st/2nd class**; **un (soldat de) deuxième ~** (*Mil: armée de terre*) ≈ private (soldier); (: *armée de l'air*) ≈ aircraftman (*Brit*), ≈ airman basic (*US*); **de ~** luxury *cpd*; **faire ses ~s** (*Mil*) to do one's (recruit's) training; **faire la ~** (*Scol*) to be a *ou* the teacher; to teach; **aller en ~** to go to school; **aller en ~ verte/de neige/de mer** to go to the countryside/skiing/to the seaside with the school; **~ préparatoire** *class which prepares students for the Grandes Écoles entry exams; see note*; **~ sociale** social class; **~ touriste** economy class

classement [klasmã] *nm* classifying; filing; grading; closing; (*rang: Scol*) place; (: *Sport*) placing; (*liste: Scol*) class list (in order of merit); (: *Sport*) placings *pl*; **premier au ~ général** (*Sport*) first overall

classer [klase] *vt* (*idées, livres*) to classify; (*papiers*) to file; (*candidat, concurrent*) to grade; (*personne: juger: péj*) to rate; (*Jur: affaire*) to close; **se ~ premier/dernier** to come first/last; (*Sport*) to finish first/last

classeur [klasœr] *nm* file; (*meuble*) filing cabinet; **~ à feuillets mobiles** ring binder

classique [klasik] *adj* classical; (*habituel*) standard, classic ▷ *nm* classic; classical author; **études ~s** classical studies, classics

clause [kloz] *nf* clause

clavecin [klavsɛ̃] *nm* harpsichord

clavicule [klavikyl] *nf* clavicle, collarbone

clavier [klavje] *nm* keyboard

clé, clef [kle] *nf* key; (*Mus*) clef; (*de mécanicien*) spanner (*Brit*), wrench (*US*) ▷ *adj*: **problème/position ~** key problem/position; **mettre sous ~** to place under lock and key; **prendre la ~ des champs** to run away, make off; **prix ~s en main** (*d'une voiture*) on-the-road price; (*d'un appartement*) price with immediate entry; **~ de sol/de fa/d'ut** treble/bass/alto clef; **livre/film** *etc* **à ~** *book/film etc in which real people are depicted under fictitious names*; **à la ~** (*à la fin*) at the end of it all; **~ anglaise**; **= clé à molette**; **~ de contact** ignition key; **~ à molette** adjustable spanner (*Brit*) *ou* wrench, monkey wrench; **~ USB** USB key; **~ de voûte** keystone

clément, e [klemã, -ãt] *adj* (*temps*) mild; (*indulgent*) lenient

clerc [klɛr] *nm*: **~ de notaire** *ou* **d'avoué** lawyer's clerk

clergé [klɛrʒe] *nm* clergy

cliché [kliʃe] *nm* (*Photo*) negative; print; (*Typo*) (printing) plate; (*Ling*) cliché

client, e [klijã, -ãt] *nm/f* (*acheteur*) customer, client; (*d'hôtel*) guest, patron; (*du docteur*) patient; (*de l'avocat*) client

clientèle [klijãtɛl] *nf* (*du magasin*) customers *pl*, clientèle; (*du docteur, de l'avocat*) practice; **accorder sa ~ à** to give one's custom to; **retirer sa ~ à** to take one's business away from

cligner [kliɲe] *vi*: **~ des yeux** to blink (one's eyes); **~ de l'œil** to wink

clignotant [kliɲɔtã] *nm* (*Auto*) indicator

clignoter [kliɲɔte] *vi* (*étoiles etc*) to twinkle; (*lumière: à intervalles réguliers*) to flash; (: *vaciller*) to flicker; (*yeux*) to blink

climat [klima] *nm* climate

climatisation [klimatizasjɔ̃] *nf* air conditioning

climatisé, e [klimatize] *adj* air-conditioned

clin d'œil [klɛ̃dœj] *nm* wink; **en un clin d'œil** in a flash

clinique [klinik] *adj* clinical ▷ *nf* nursing home, (private) clinic

clinquant, e [klɛ̃kã, -ãt] *adj* flashy

clip [klip] *nm* (*pince*) clip; (*vidéo*) pop (*ou* promotional) video

cliqueter [klikte] *vi* to clash; (*ferraille, clefs, monnaie*) to jangle, jingle; (*verres*) to chink

clochard, e [klɔʃar, -ard(ə)] *nm/f* tramp

cloche [klɔʃ] *nf* (*d'église*) bell; (*fam*) clot; (*chapeau*) cloche (hat); **~ à fromage** cheese-cover

cloche-pied [klɔʃpje]: **à ~** *adv* on one leg, hopping (along)

clocher [klɔʃe] *nm* church tower; (*en pointe*) steeple ▷ *vi* (*fam*) to be *ou* go wrong; **de ~** (*péj*) parochial

cloison [klwazɔ̃] *nf* partition (wall); **~ étanche** (*fig*) impenetrable barrier, brick wall (*fig*)

cloître [klwatr(ə)] *nm* cloister

cloîtrer [klwatre] *vt*: **se cloîtrer** to shut o.s. away; (*Rel*) to enter a convent *ou* monastery

clonage [klɔnaʒ] *nm* cloning

clone [klɔn] *nm* clone

cloner [klɔne] *vt* to clone

cloque [klɔk] *nf* blister

clore [klɔr] *vt* to close; **~ une session** (*Inform*) to log out

clos, e [klo, -oz] *pp de* **clore** ▷ *adj voir* **maison**; **huis**; **vase** ▷ *nm* (enclosed) field

clôture [klotyr] *nf* closure, closing; (*barrière*) enclosure, fence

clôturer [klotyre] *vt* (*terrain*) to enclose, close off; (*festival, débats*) to close

clou [klu] *nm* nail; (*Méd*) boil; **clous** *nmpl* = **passage clouté**; **pneus à ~s** studded tyres; **le ~ du spectacle** the highlight of the show; **~ de girofle** clove

clouer [klue] *vt* to nail down (*ou* up); (*fig*): **~ sur/contre** to pin to/against

clown [klun] *nm* clown; **faire le ~** (*fig*) to clown (about), play the fool

club [klœb] *nm* club

CMU *sigle f* (= *couverture maladie universelle*) *system of free health care for those on low incomes*

CNRS *sigle m* = **Centre national de la recherche scientifique**

coaguler [kɔagyle] [vi, vt]: **se coaguler** vi to coagulate

coasser [kɔase] vi to croak

cobaye [kɔbaj] nm guinea-pig

coca® [kɔka] nm Coke®

cocaïne [kɔkain] nf cocaine

cocasse [kɔkas] adj comical, funny

coccinelle [kɔksinɛl] nf ladybird (Brit), ladybug (US)

cocher [kɔʃe] nm coachman ▷ vt to tick off; (entailler) to notch

cochère [kɔʃɛR] adj f voir **porte**

cochon, ne [kɔʃɔ̃, -ɔn] nm pig ▷ nm/f (péj: sale) (filthy) pig; (: méchant) swine ▷ adj (fam) dirty, smutty; ~ **d'Inde** guinea-pig; ~ **de lait** (Culin) sucking pig

cochonnerie [kɔʃɔnRi] nf (fam: saleté) filth; (: marchandises) rubbish, trash

cocktail [kɔktɛl] nm cocktail; (réception) cocktail party

coco [kɔko] nm voir **noix**; (fam) bloke (Brit), dude (US)

cocorico [kɔkɔRiko] excl, nm cock-a-doodle-do

cocotier [kɔkɔtje] nm coconut palm

cocotte [kɔkɔt] nf (en fonte) casserole; **ma ~** (fam) sweetie (pie); **~ (minute)®** pressure cooker; **~ en papier** paper shape

cocu [kɔky] nm cuckold

code [kɔd] nm code; **se mettre en ~(s)** to dip (Brit) ou dim (US) one's (head)lights; **~ à barres** bar code; **~ de caractère** (Inform) character code; **~ civil** Common Law; **~ machine** machine code; **~ pénal** penal code; **~ postal** (numéro) postcode (Brit), zip code (US); **~ de la route** highway code; **~ secret** cipher

cœur [kœR] nm heart; (Cartes: couleur) hearts pl; (: carte) heart; (Culin): **~ de laitue/d'artichaut** lettuce/artichoke heart; (fig): **~ du débat** heart of the debate; **~ de l'été** height of summer; **~ de la forêt** depths pl of the forest; **affaire de ~** love affair; **avoir bon ~** to be kind-hearted; **avoir mal au ~** to feel sick; **contre** ou **sur son ~** to one's breast; **opérer qn à ~ ouvert** to perform open-heart surgery on sb; **recevoir qn à ~ ouvert** to welcome sb with open arms; **parler à ~ ouvert** to open one's heart; **de tout son ~** with all one's heart; **avoir le ~ gros** ou **serré** to have a heavy heart; **en avoir le ~ net** to be clear in one's own mind (about it); **par ~** by heart; **de bon ~** willingly; **avoir à ~ de faire** to be very keen to do; **cela lui tient à ~** that's (very) close to his heart; **prendre les choses à ~** to take things to heart; **à ~ joie** to one's heart's content; **être de tout ~ avec qn** to be (completely) in accord with sb

coffre [kɔfR(ə)] nm (meuble) chest; (coffre-fort) safe; (d'auto) boot (Brit), trunk (US); **avoir du ~** (fam) to have a lot of puff

coffre-fort (pl **coffres-forts**) [kɔfRəfɔR] nm safe

coffret [kɔfRɛ] nm casket; **~ à bijoux** jewel box

cognac [kɔɲak] nm brandy, cognac

cogner [kɔɲe] vi to knock, bang; **se cogner** vi to bump o.s.

cohérent, e [kɔeRɑ̃, -ɑ̃t] adj coherent

cohorte [kɔɔRt(ə)] nf troop

cohue [kɔy] nf crowd

coi, coite [kwa, kwat] adj: **rester ~** to remain silent

coiffe [kwaf] nf headdress

coiffé, e [kwafe] adj: **bien/mal ~** with tidy/untidy hair; **~ d'un béret** wearing a beret; **~ en arrière** with one's hair brushed ou combed back; **~ en brosse** with a crew cut

coiffer [kwafe] vt (fig) to cover, top; **~ qn** to do sb's hair; **~ qn d'un béret** to put a beret on sb; **se coiffer** vi to do one's hair; to put on a ou one's hat

coiffeur, -euse [kwafœR, -øz] nm/f hairdresser ▷ nf (table) dressing table

coiffure [kwafyR] nf (cheveux) hairstyle, hairdo; (chapeau) hat, headgear no pl; (art): **la ~** hairdressing

coin [kwɛ̃] nm corner; (pour graver) die; (pour coincer) wedge; (poinçon) hallmark; **l'épicerie du ~** the local grocer; **dans le ~** (aux alentours) in the area, around about; locally; **au ~ du feu** by the fireside; **du ~ de l'œil** out of the corner of one's eye; **regard en ~** side(ways) glance; **sourire en ~** half-smile

coincé, e [kwɛse] adj stuck, jammed; (fig: inhibé) inhibited, with hang-ups

coincer [kwɛse] vt to jam; (fam) to catch (out); to nab; **se coincer** vi to get stuck ou jammed

coïncidence [kɔɛsidɑ̃s] nf coincidence

coïncider [kɔɛside] vi: **~ (avec)** to coincide (with); (correspondre: témoignage etc) to correspond ou tally (with)

coing [kwɛ̃] nm quince

col [kɔl] nm (de chemise) collar; (encolure, cou) neck; (de montagne) pass; **~ roulé** polo-neck; **~ de l'utérus** cervix

colère [kɔlɛR] nf anger; **une ~** a fit of anger; **être en ~ (contre qn)** to be angry (with sb); **mettre qn en ~** to make sb angry; **se mettre en ~** to get angry

coléreux, -euse [kɔleRø, -øz] adj, **colérique** [kɔleRik] ▷ adj quick-tempered, irascible

colifichet [kɔlifiʃɛ] nm trinket

colimaçon [kɔlimasɔ̃] nm: **escalier en ~** spiral staircase

colin [kɔlɛ̃] nm hake

colique [kɔlik] nf diarrhoea (Brit), diarrhea (US); (douleurs) colic (pains pl); (fam: personne ou chose ennuyeuse) pain

colis [kɔli] nm parcel; **par ~ postal** by parcel post

collaborateur, -trice [kɔlabɔRatœR, -tRis] nm/f (aussi Pol) collaborator; (d'une revue) contributor

collaborer [kɔlabɔRe] vi to collaborate; (aussi: **collaborer à**) to collaborate on; (revue) to contribute to

collant, e [kɔlɑ̃, -ɑ̃t] adj sticky; (robe etc) clinging, skintight; (péj) clinging ▷ nm (bas) tights pl

collation [kɔlasjɔ̃] nf light meal

colle [kɔl] nf glue; (à papiers peints) (wallpaper)

paste; (*devinette*) teaser, riddle; (*Scol fam*) detention; ~ **forte** superglue®

collecte [kɔlɛkt(ə)] *nf* collection; **faire une** ~ to take up a collection

collectif, -ive [kɔlɛktif, -iv] *adj* collective; (*visite, billet etc*) group *cpd* ▷ *nm*: ~ **budgétaire** mini-budget (*Brit*), mid-term budget; **immeuble** ~ block of flats

collection [kɔlɛksjɔ̃] *nf* collection; (*Édition*) series; **pièce de** ~ collector's item; **faire (la)** ~ **de** to collect; (**toute**) **une** ~ **de ...** (*fig*) a (complete) set of ...

collectionner [kɔlɛksjɔne] *vt* (*tableaux, timbres*) to collect

collectionneur, -euse [kɔlɛksjɔnœʀ, -øz] *nm/f* collector

collectivité [kɔlɛktivite] *nf* group; **la** ~ the community, the collectivity; **les ~s locales** local authorities

collège [kɔlɛʒ] *nm* (*école*) (secondary) school; *see note*; (*assemblée*) body; ~ **électoral** electoral college

collégien, ne [kɔleʒjɛ̃, -ɛn] *nm/f* secondary school pupil (*Brit*), high school student (*US*)

collègue [kɔlɛg] *nm/f* colleague

coller [kɔle] *vt* (*papier, timbre*) to stick (on); (*affiche*) to stick up; (*appuyer, placer contre*): ~ **son front à la vitre** to press one's face to the window; (*enveloppe*) to stick down; (*morceaux*) to stick *ou* glue together; (*fam: mettre, fourrer*) to stick, shove; (*Scol fam*) to keep in, give detention to ▷ *vi* (*être collant*) to be sticky; (*adhérer*) to stick; ~ **qch sur** to stick (*ou* paste *ou* glue) sth on(to); ~ **à** to stick to; (*fig*) to cling to

collet [kɔlɛ] *nm* (*piège*) snare, noose; (*cou*): **prendre qn au** ~ to grab sb by the throat; ~ **monté** *adj inv* straight-laced

collier [kɔlje] *nm* (*bijou*) necklace; (*de chien, Tech*) collar; ~ (**de barbe**), **barbe en** ~ narrow beard along the line of the jaw; ~ **de serrage** choke collar

collimateur [kɔlimatœʀ] *nm*: **être dans le** ~ (*fig*) to be in the firing line; **avoir qn/qch dans le** ~ (*fig*) to have sb/sth in one's sights

colline [kɔlin] *nf* hill

collision [kɔlizjɔ̃] *nf* collision, crash; **entrer en** ~ (**avec**) to collide (with)

colloque [kɔlɔk] *nm* colloquium, symposium

collyre [kɔliʀ] *nm* (*Méd*) eye lotion

colmater [kɔlmate] *vt* (*fuite*) to seal off; (*brèche*) to plug, fill in

colombe [kɔlɔ̃b] *nf* dove

Colombie [kɔlɔ̃bi] *nf*: **la** ~ Colombia

colon [kɔlɔ̃] *nm* settler; (*enfant*) boarder (*in children's holiday camp*)

colonel [kɔlɔnɛl] *nm* colonel; (*de l'armée de l'air*) group captain

colonie [kɔlɔni] *nf* colony; ~ (**de vacances**) holiday camp (*for children*)

colonne [kɔlɔn] *nf* column; **se mettre en** ~ **par deux/quatre** to get into twos/fours; **en** ~ **par deux** in double file; ~ **de secours** rescue party; ~

(**vertébrale**) spine, spinal column

colorant [kɔlɔʀɑ̃] *nm* colo(u)ring

colorer [kɔlɔʀe] *vt* to colour (*Brit*), color (*US*); **se colorer** *vi* to turn red; to blush

colorier [kɔlɔʀje] *vt* to colo(u)r (in); **album à** ~ colouring book

coloris [kɔlɔʀi] *nm* colo(u)r, shade

colporter [kɔlpɔʀte] *vt* to peddle

colza [kɔlza] *nm* rape(seed)

coma [kɔma] *nm* coma; **être dans le** ~ to be in a coma

combat [kɔ̃ba] *vb voir* **combattre** ▷ *nm* fight; fighting *no pl*; ~ **de boxe** boxing match; ~ **de rues** street fighting *no pl*; ~ **singulier** single combat

combattant [kɔ̃batɑ̃] *vb voir* **combattre** ▷ *nm* combatant; (*d'une rixe*) brawler; **ancien** ~ war veteran

combattre [kɔ̃batʀ(ə)] *vi* to fight ▷ *vt* to fight; (*épidémie, ignorance*) to combat

combien [kɔ̃bjɛ̃] *adv* (*quantité*) how much; (*nombre*) how many; (*exclamatif*) how; ~ **de** how much; how many; ~ **de temps** how long, how much time; **c'est** ~?, **ça fait** ~? how much is it?; ~ **coûte/pèse ceci?** how much does this cost/weigh?; **vous mesurez** ~? what size are you?; **ça fait** ~ **en largeur?** how wide is that?

combinaison [kɔ̃binɛzɔ̃] *nf* combination; (*astuce*) device, scheme; (*de femme*) slip; (*d'aviateur*) flying suit; (*d'homme-grenouille*) wetsuit; (*bleu de travail*) boilersuit (*Brit*), coveralls *pl* (*US*)

combine [kɔ̃bin] *nf* trick; (*péj*) scheme, fiddle (*Brit*)

combiné [kɔ̃bine] *nm* (*aussi:* **combiné téléphonique**) receiver; (*Ski*) combination (*event*); (*vêtement de femme*) corselet

combiner [kɔ̃bine] *vt* to combine; (*plan, horaire*) to work out, devise

comble [kɔ̃bl(ə)] *adj* (*salle*) packed (full) ▷ *nm* (*du bonheur, plaisir*) height; **combles** *nmpl* (*Constr*) attic *sg*, loft *sg*; **de fond en** ~ from top to bottom; **pour** ~ **de malchance** to cap it all; **c'est le** ~! that beats everything!, that takes the biscuit! (*Brit*); **sous les** ~**s** in the attic

combler [kɔ̃ble] *vt* (*trou*) to fill in; (*besoin, lacune*) to fill; (*déficit*) to make good; (*satisfaire*) to gratify, fulfil (*Brit*), fulfill (*US*); ~ **qn de joie** to fill sb with joy; ~ **qn d'honneurs** to shower sb with honours

combustible [kɔ̃bystibl(ə)] *adj* combustible ▷ *nm* fuel

comédie [kɔmedi] *nf* comedy; (*fig*) playacting *no pl*; **jouer la** ~ (*fig*) to put on an act; **la C-française**; *see note*; ~ **musicale** musical

comédien, ne [kɔmedjɛ̃, -ɛn] *nm/f* actor/actress; (*comique*) comedy actor/actress, comedian/comedienne; (*fig*) sham

comestible [kɔmɛstibl(ə)] *adj* edible; **comestibles** *nmpl* foods

comique [kɔmik] *adj* (*drôle*) comical; (*Théât*) comic ▷ *nm* (*artiste*) comic, comedian; **le** ~ **de qch** the funny *ou* comical side of sth

comité [kɔmite] nm committee; **petit ~** select group; **~ directeur** management committee; **~ d'entreprise (CE)** works council; **~ des fêtes** festival committee

commandant [kɔmɑ̃dɑ̃] nm (gén) commander, commandant; (Mil: grade) major; (: armée de l'air) squadron leader; (Navig) captain; **~ (de bord)** (Aviat) captain

commande [kɔmɑ̃d] nf (Comm) order; (Inform) command; **commandes** nfpl (Aviat etc) controls; **passer une ~ (de)** to put in an order (for); **sur ~** to order; **~ à distance** remote control; **véhicule à double ~** vehicle with dual controls

commandement [kɔmɑ̃dmɑ̃] nm command; (ordre) command, order; (Rel) commandment

commander [kɔmɑ̃de] vt (Comm) to order; (diriger, ordonner) to command; **~ à** (Mil) to command; (contrôler, maîtriser) to have control over; **~ à qn de faire** to command ou order sb to do

commando [kɔmɑ̃do] nm commando (squad)

comme [kɔm] prép 1 (comparaison) like; **tout ~ son père** just like his father; **fort ~ un bœuf** as strong as an ox; **joli ~ tout** ever so pretty

2 (manière) like; **faites-le ~ ça** do it like this, do it this way; **~ ça ou cela on n'aura pas d'ennuis** that way we won't have any problems; **~ ci, ~ ça** so-so, middling; **~ ça va?** how are things? — OK; **~ on dit** as they say

3 (en tant que) as a; **donner ~ prix** to give as a prize; **travailler ~ secrétaire** to work as a secretary

4: **~ quoi** (d'où il s'ensuit que) which shows that; **il a écrit une lettre ~ quoi il ...** he's written a letter saying that ...

5: **~ il faut** adv properly
▷ adj (correct) proper, correct
▷ conj 1 (ainsi que) as; **elle écrit ~ elle parle** she writes as she talks; **~ si** as if

2 (au moment où, alors que) as; **il est parti ~ j'arrivais** he left as I arrived

3 (parce que, puisque) as, since; **~ il était en retard, il ...** as he was late, he ...
▷ adv: **~ il est fort/c'est bon!** he's so strong/it's so good!; **il est malin ~ c'est pas permis** he's as smart as anything

commémorer [kɔmemɔre] vt to commemorate

commencement [kɔmɑ̃smɑ̃] nm beginning, start, commencement; **commencements** nmpl (débuts) beginnings

commencer [kɔmɑ̃se] vt to begin, start, commence ▷ vi to begin, start, commence; **~ à ou de faire** to begin ou start doing; **~ par qch** to begin with sth; **~ par faire qch** to begin by doing sth

comment [kɔmɑ̃] adv how; **~?** (que dites-vous) (I beg your) pardon?; **~!** what! ▷ nm: **le ~ et le pourquoi** the whys and wherefores; **et ~!** and how!; **~ donc!** of course!; **~ faire?** how will we do it?; **~ se fait-il que ...?** how is it that ...?

commentaire [kɔmɑ̃tɛr] nm comment; remark; **~ (de texte)** (Scol) commentary; **~ sur image** voice-over

commenter [kɔmɑ̃te] vt (jugement, événement) to comment (up)on; (Radio, TV: match, manifestation) to cover, give a commentary on

commérages [kɔmeraʒ] nmpl gossip sg

commerçant, e [kɔmɛrsɑ̃, -ɑ̃t] adj commercial; trading; (rue) shopping cpd; (personne) commercially shrewd ▷ nm/f shopkeeper, trader

commerce [kɔmɛrs(ə)] nm (activité) trade, commerce; (boutique) business; **le petit ~** small shop owners pl, small traders pl; **faire ~ de** to trade in; (fig: péj) to trade on; **chambre de ~** Chamber of Commerce; **livres de ~** (account) books; **vendu dans le ~** sold in the shops; **vendu hors-~** sold directly to the public; **~ en ou de gros/détail** wholesale/retail trade; **~ électronique** e-commerce; **~ équitable** fair trade; **~ intérieur/extérieur** home/foreign trade

commercial, e, -aux [kɔmɛrsjal, -o] adj commercial, trading; (péj) commercial ▷ nm: **les commerciaux** the commercial people

commercialiser [kɔmɛrsjalize] vt to market

commère [kɔmɛr] nf gossip

commettre [kɔmɛtr(ə)] vt to commit; **se commettre** vi to compromise one's good name

commis¹ [kɔmi] nm (de magasin) (shop) assistant (Brit), sales clerk (US); (de banque) clerk; **~ voyageur** commercial traveller (Brit) ou traveler (US)

commis², e [kɔmi, -iz] pp de **commettre**

commissaire [kɔmisɛr] nm (de police) ≈ (police) superintendent (Brit), ≈ (police) captain (US); (de rencontre sportive etc) steward; **~ du bord** (Navig) purser; **~ aux comptes** (Admin) auditor

commissaire-priseur (pl **commissaires-priseurs**) [kɔmisɛrprizœr] nm (official) auctioneer

commissariat [kɔmisarja] nm: **~ (de police)** police station; (Admin) commissionership

commission [kɔmisjɔ̃] nf (comité, pourcentage) commission; (message) message; (course) errand; **commissions** nfpl (achats) shopping sg; **~ d'examen** examining board

commode [kɔmɔd] adj (pratique) convenient, handy; (facile) easy; (air, personne) easy-going; (personne): **pas ~** awkward (to deal with) ▷ nf chest of drawers

commodité [kɔmɔdite] nf convenience

commotion [kɔmɔsjɔ̃] nf: **~ (cérébrale)** concussion

commotionné, e [kɔmɔsjɔne] adj shocked, shaken

commun, e [kɔmœ̃, -yn] adj common; (pièce) communal, shared; (réunion, effort) joint ▷ nf (Admin) commune, ≈ district; (: urbaine) ≈ borough; **communs** nmpl (bâtiments) outbuildings; **cela sort du ~** it's out of the ordinary; **le ~ des mortels** the common run of people; **sans ~e mesure** incomparable; **être ~ à** (chose) to be shared by; **en ~ (faire)** jointly; **mettre en ~** to pool, share; **peu ~** unusual; **d'un ~ accord** of one accord; with one accord

communauté [kɔmynote] *nf* community; (*Jur*): **régime de la** ~ communal estate settlement

commune [kɔmyn] *adj f, nf voir* **commun**

communicatif, -ive [kɔmynikatif, -iv] *adj* (*personne*) communicative; (*rire*) infectious

communication [kɔmynikasjɔ] *nf* communication; ~ **(téléphonique)** (telephone) call; **avoir la** ~ **(avec)** to get *ou* be through (to); **vous avez la** ~ you're through; **donnez-moi la** ~ **avec** put me through to; **mettre qn en** ~ **avec qn** (*en contact*) to put sb in touch with sb; (*au téléphone*) to connect sb with sb; ~ **interurbaine** long-distance call; ~ **en PCV** reverse charge (*Brit*) *ou* collect (*US*) call; ~ **avec préavis** personal call

communier [kɔmynje] *vi* (*Rel*) to receive communion; (*fig*) to be united

communion [kɔmynjɔ] *nf* communion

communiquer [kɔmynike] *vt* (*nouvelle, dossier*) to pass on, convey; (*maladie*) to pass on; (*peur etc*) to communicate; (*chaleur, mouvement*) to transmit ▷ *vi* to communicate; ~ **avec** (*salle*) to communicate with; **se** ~ **à** (*se propager*) to spread to

communisme [kɔmynism(ə)] *nm* communism

communiste [kɔmynist(ə)] *adj, nm/f* communist

commutateur [kɔmytatœʀ] *nm* (*Élec*) (change-over) switch, commutator

compact, e [kɔpakt] *adj* dense; compact

compagne [kɔpaɲ] *nf* companion

compagnie [kɔpaɲi] *nf* (*firme, Mil*) company; (*groupe*) gathering; (*présence*): **la** ~ **de qn** sb's company; **homme/femme de** ~ escort; **tenir** ~ **à qn** to keep sb company; **fausser** ~ **à qn** to give sb the slip, slip *ou* sneak away from sb; **en** ~ **de** in the company of; **Dupont et** ~, **Dupont et Cie** Dupont and Company, Dupont and Co; ~ **aérienne** airline (company)

compagnon [kɔpaɲɔ] *nm* companion; (*autrefois: ouvrier*) craftsman; journeyman

comparable [kɔpaʀabl(ə)] *adj*: ~ **(à)** comparable (to)

comparaison [kɔpaʀɛzɔ] *nf* comparison; (*métaphore*) simile; **en** ~ **(de)** in comparison (with); **par** ~ **(à)** by comparison (with)

comparaître [kɔpaʀɛtʀ(ə)] *vi*: ~ **(devant)** to appear (before)

comparer [kɔpaʀe] *vt* to compare; ~ **qch/qn à** *ou* **et** (*pour choisir*) to compare sth/sb with *ou* and; (*pour établir une similitude*) to compare sth/sb to *ou* and

compartiment [kɔpaʀtimɑ] *nm* compartment

comparution [kɔpaʀysjɔ] *nf* appearance

compas [kɔpa] *nm* (*Géom*) (pair of) compasses *pl*; (*Navig*) compass

compatible [kɔpatibl(ə)] *adj*: ~ **(avec)** compatible (with)

compatir [kɔpatiʀ] *vi*: ~ **(à)** to sympathize (with)

compatriote [kɔpatʀijɔt] *nm/f* compatriot, fellow countryman/woman

compensation [kɔpɑsasjɔ] *nf* compensation; (*Banque*) clearing; **en** ~ in *ou* as compensation

compenser [kɔpɑse] *vt* to compensate for, make up for

compère [kɔpɛʀ] *nm* accomplice; fellow musician *ou* comedian *etc*

compétence [kɔpetɑs] *nf* competence

compétent, e [kɔpetɑ, -ɑt] *adj* (*apte*) competent, capable; (*Jur*) competent

compétition [kɔpetisjɔ] *nf* (*gén*) competition; (*Sport: épreuve*) event; **la** ~ competitive sport; **être en** ~ **avec** to be competing with; **la** ~ **automobile** motor racing

complainte [kɔplɛt] *nf* lament

complaire [kɔplɛʀ]: **se complaire** *vi*: **se** ~ **dans/parmi** to take pleasure in/in being among

complaisance [kɔplɛzɑs] *nf* kindness; (*péj*) indulgence; (: *fatuité*) complacency; **attestation de** ~ certificate produced to oblige a patient *etc*; **pavillon de** ~ flag of convenience

complaisant, e [kɔplɛzɑ, -ɑt] *vb voir* **complaire** ▷ *adj* (*aimable*) kind; obliging; (*péj*) accommodating; (: *fat*) complacent

complément [kɔplemɑ] *nm* complement; (*reste*) remainder; (*Ling*) complement; ~ **d'information** (*Admin*) supplementary *ou* further information; ~ **d'agent** agent; ~ **(d'objet) direct/indirect** direct/indirect object; ~ **(circonstanciel) de lieu/temps** adverbial phrase of place/time; ~ **de nom** possessive phrase

complémentaire [kɔplemɑtɛʀ] *adj* complementary; (*additionnel*) supplementary

complet, -ète [kɔplɛ, -ɛt] *adj* complete; (*plein: hôtel etc*) full ▷ *nm* (*aussi:* **complet-veston**) suit; **au (grand)** ~ all together

complètement [kɔplɛtmɑ] *adv* (*en entier*) completely; (*absolument: fou, faux etc*) absolutely; (*à fond: étudier etc*) fully, in depth

compléter [kɔplete] *vt* (*porter à la quantité voulue*) to complete; (*augmenter*) to complement, supplement; to add to; **se compléter** *vi* (*personnes*) to complement one another; (*collection etc*) to become complete

complexe [kɔplɛks(ə)] *adj* complex ▷ *nm* (*Psych*) complex, hang-up; (*bâtiments*): ~ **hospitalier/industriel** hospital/industrial complex

complexé, e [kɔplɛkse] *adj* mixed-up, hung-up

complication [kɔplikasjɔ] *nf* complexity, intricacy; (*difficulté, ennui*) complication; **complications** *nfpl* (*Méd*) complications

complice [kɔplis] *nm* accomplice

complicité [kɔplisite] *nf* complicity

compliment [kɔplimɑ] *nm* (*louange*) compliment; **compliments** *nmpl* (*félicitations*) congratulations

compliqué, e [kɔplike] *adj* complicated, complex, intricate; (*personne*) complicated

compliquer [kɔplike] *vt* to complicate; **se compliquer** *vi* (*situation*) to become complicated; **se** ~ **la vie** to make life difficult *ou* complicated for o.s

complot [kɔplo] *nm* plot

comportement [kɔpɔʀtəmɑ] *nm* behaviour

(Brit), behavior (US); (Tech: d'une pièce, d'un véhicule) behavio(u)r, performance

comporter [kɔ̃pɔʀte] vt to be composed of, consist of, comprise; (être équipé de) to have; (impliquer) to entail, involve; **se comporter** vi to behave; (Tech) to behave, perform

composant [kɔ̃pozɑ̃] nm component, constituent

composé, e [kɔ̃poze] adj (visage, air) studied; (Bio, Chimie, Ling) compound ▷ nm (Chimie, Ling) compound; **~ de** made up of

composer [kɔ̃poze] vt (musique, texte) to compose; (mélange, équipe) to make up; (faire partie de) to make up, form; (Typo) to (type)set ▷ vi (Scol) to sit ou do a test; (transiger) to come to terms; **se ~ de** to be composed of, be made up of; **~ un numéro** (au téléphone) to dial a number

compositeur, -trice [kɔ̃pozitœʀ, -tʀis] nm/f (Mus) composer; (Typo) compositor, typesetter

composition [kɔ̃pozisjɔ̃] nf composition; (Scol) test; (Typo) (type)setting, composition; **de bonne ~** (accommodant) easy to deal with; **amener qn à ~** to get sb to come to terms; **~ française** (Scol) French essay

composter [kɔ̃pɔste] vt to date-stamp; to punch

compote [kɔ̃pɔt] nf stewed fruit no pl; **~ de pommes** stewed apples

compréhensible [kɔ̃pʀeɑ̃sibl(ə)] adj comprehensible; (attitude) understandable

compréhensif, -ive [kɔ̃pʀeɑ̃sif, -iv] adj understanding

comprendre [kɔ̃pʀɑ̃dʀ(ə)] vt to understand; (se composer de) to comprise, consist of; (inclure) to include; **se faire ~** to make o.s. understood; to get one's ideas across; **mal ~** to misunderstand

compresse [kɔ̃pʀɛs] nf compress

compression [kɔ̃pʀesjɔ̃] nf compression; (d'un crédit etc) reduction

comprimé, e [kɔ̃pʀime] adj: **air ~** compressed air ▷ nm tablet

comprimer [kɔ̃pʀime] vt to compress; (fig: crédit etc) to reduce, cut down

compris, e [kɔ̃pʀi, -iz] pp de **comprendre** ▷ adj (inclus) included; **~?** understood?, is that clear?; **~ entre** (situé) contained between; **la maison ~e/ non ~e, y/non ~ la maison** including/excluding the house; **service ~** service (charge) included; **100 euros tout ~** 100 euros all inclusive ou all-in

compromettre [kɔ̃pʀɔmɛtʀ(ə)] vt to compromise

compromis [kɔ̃pʀɔmi] vb voir **compromettre** ▷ nm compromise

comptabilité [kɔ̃tabilite] nf (activité, technique) accounting, accountancy; (d'une société: comptes) accounts pl, books pl; (: service) accounts office ou department; **~ à partie double** double-entry book-keeping

comptable [kɔ̃tabl(ə)] nm/f accountant ▷ adj accounts cpd, accounting

comptant [kɔ̃tɑ̃] adv: **payer ~** to pay cash; **acheter ~** to buy for cash

compte [kɔ̃t] nm count, counting; (total, montant) count, (right) number; (bancaire, facture) account; **comptes** nmpl accounts, books; (fig) explanation sg; **ouvrir un ~** to open an account; **rendre des ~s à qn** (fig) to be answerable to sb; **faire le ~ de** to count up, make a count of; **tout ~ fait** on the whole; **à ce ~-là** (dans ce cas) in that case; (à ce train-là) at that rate; **en fin de ~** (fig) all things considered, weighing it all up; **au bout du ~** in the final analysis; **à bon ~** at a favourable price; (fig) lightly; **avoir son ~** (fig: fam) to have had it; **pour le ~** de on behalf of; **pour son propre ~** for one's own benefit; **sur le ~ de qn** (à son sujet) about sb; **travailler à son ~** to work for oneself; **mettre qch sur le ~ de qn** (le rendre responsable) to attribute sth to sb; **prendre qch à son ~** to take responsibility for sth; **trouver son ~ à qch** to do well out of sth; **régler un ~** (s'acquitter de qch) to settle an account; (se venger) to get one's own back; **rendre ~ (à qn) de qch** to give (sb) an account of sth; **tenir ~ de qch** to take sth into account; **~ tenu de** taking into account; **~ en banque** bank account; **~ chèque(s)** current account; **~ chèque postal (CCP)** Post Office account; **~ client** (sur bilan) accounts receivable; **~ courant (CC)** current account; **~ de dépôt** deposit account; **~ d'exploitation** operating account; **~ fournisseur** (sur bilan) accounts payable; **~ à rebours** countdown; **~ rendu** account, report; (de film, livre) review; voir aussi **rendre**

compte-gouttes [kɔ̃tgut] nm inv dropper

compter [kɔ̃te] vt to count; (facturer) to charge for; (avoir à son actif, comporter) to have; (prévoir) to allow, reckon; (tenir compte de, inclure) to include; (penser, espérer): **~ réussir/revenir** to expect to succeed/return ▷ vi to count; (être économe) to economize; (être non négligeable) to count, matter; (valoir): **~ pour** to count for; (figurer): **~ parmi** to be ou rank among; **~ sur** to count (up)on; **~ avec qch/qn** to reckon with ou take account of sth/sb; **~ sans qch/qn** to reckon without sth/sb; **sans ~ que** besides which; **à ~ du 10 janvier** (Comm) (as) from 10th January

compteur [kɔ̃tœʀ] nm meter; **~ de vitesse** speedometer

comptine [kɔ̃tin] nf nursery rhyme

comptoir [kɔ̃twaʀ] nm (de magasin) counter; (de café) counter, bar; (colonial) trading post

compulser [kɔ̃pylse] vt to consult

comte, comtesse [kɔ̃t, kɔ̃tɛs] nm/f count/ countess

con, ne [kɔ̃, kɔn] adj (fam!) bloody (Brit) ou damned stupid (!)

concéder [kɔ̃sede] vt to grant; (défaite, point) to concede; **~ que** to concede that

concentré [kɔ̃sɑ̃tʀe] nm concentrate; **~ de tomates** tomato purée

concentrer [kɔ̃sɑ̃tʀe] vt to concentrate; **se concentrer** to concentrate

concept [kɔ̃sɛpt] nm concept

conception [kɔ̃sɛpsjɔ̃] nf conception; (d'une machine etc) design

concerner [kɔ̃sɛʀne] vt to concern; **en ce qui me concerne** as far as I am concerned; **en ce qui concerne ceci** as far as this is concerned, with regard to this

concert [kɔ̃sɛʀ] nm concert; **de ~** adv in unison; together

concerter [kɔ̃sɛʀte] vt to devise; **se concerter** vi (collaborateurs etc) to put our (ou their etc) heads together, consult (each other)

concession [kɔ̃sesjɔ̃] nf concession

concessionnaire [kɔ̃sesjɔnɛʀ] nm/f agent, dealer

concevoir [kɔ̃svwaʀ] vt (idée, projet) to conceive (of); (méthode, plan d'appartement, décoration etc) to plan, design; (enfant) to conceive; **maison bien/ mal conçue** well-/badly-designed ou -planned house

concierge [kɔ̃sjɛʀʒ(ə)] nm/f caretaker; (d'hôtel) head porter

conciliabules [kɔ̃siljabyl] nmpl (private) discussions, confabulations (Brit)

concilier [kɔ̃silje] vt to reconcile; **se ~ qn/ l'appui de qn** to win sb over/sb's support

concis, e [kɔ̃si, -iz] adj concise

concitoyen, ne [kɔ̃sitwajɛ̃, -ɛn] nm/f fellow citizen

concluant, e [kɔ̃klyɑ̃, -ɑ̃t] vb voir **conclure** ▷ adj conclusive

conclure [kɔ̃klyʀ] vt to conclude; (signer: accord, pacte) to enter into; (déduire): **~ qch de qch** to deduce sth from sth; **~ à l'acquittement** to decide in favour of an acquittal; **~ au suicide** to come to the conclusion (ou Jur) to pronounce) that it is a case of suicide; **~ un marché** to clinch a deal; **j'en conclus que** from that I conclude that

conclusion [kɔ̃klyzjɔ̃] nf conclusion; **conclusions** nfpl (Jur) submissions; findings; **en ~** in conclusion

conçois [kɔ̃swa], **conçoive** etc [kɔ̃swav] vb voir **concevoir**

concombre [kɔ̃kɔ̃bʀ(ə)] nm cucumber

concorder [kɔ̃kɔʀde] vi to tally, agree

concourir [kɔ̃kuʀiʀ] vi (Sport) to compete; **~ à** vt (effet etc) to work towards

concours [kɔ̃kuʀ] vb voir **concourir** ▷ nm competition; (Scol) competitive examination; (assistance) aid, help; **recrutement par voie de ~** recruitment by (competitive) examination; **apporter son ~ à** to give one's support to; **~ de circonstances** combination of circumstances; **~ hippique** horse show; voir **hors-concours**

concret, -ète [kɔ̃kʀɛ, -ɛt] adj concrete

concrétiser [kɔ̃kʀetize] vt to realize; **se concrétiser** vi to materialize

conçu, e [kɔ̃sy] pp de **concevoir**

concubinage [kɔ̃kybinaʒ] nm (Jur) cohabitation

concurrence [kɔ̃kyʀɑ̃s] nf competition; **jusqu'à ~ de** up to; **~ déloyale** unfair competition

concurrent, e [kɔ̃kyʀɑ̃, -ɑ̃t] adj competing ▷ nm/f (Sport, Écon etc) competitor; (Scol) candidate

condamner [kɔ̃dane] vt (blâmer) to condemn; (Jur) to sentence; (porte, ouverture) to fill in, block up; (malade) to give up (hope for); (obliger): **~ qn à qch/à faire** to condemn sb to sth/to do; **~ qn à deux ans de prison** to sentence sb to two years' imprisonment; **~ qn à une amende** to impose a fine on sb

condensation [kɔ̃dɑ̃sasjɔ̃] nf condensation

condenser [kɔ̃dɑ̃se]: **se condenser** vi to condense

condisciple [kɔ̃disipl(ə)] nm/f school fellow, fellow student

condition [kɔ̃disjɔ̃] nf condition; **conditions** nfpl (tarif, prix) terms; (circonstances) conditions; **sans ~** adj unconditional ▷ adv unconditionally; **sous ~ que** on condition that; **à ~ de ou que** provided that; **en bonne ~** in good condition; **mettre en ~** (Sport etc) to get fit; (Psych) to condition (mentally); **~s de vie** living conditions

conditionnel, le [kɔ̃disjɔnɛl] adj conditional ▷ nm conditional (tense)

conditionnement [kɔ̃disjɔnmɑ̃] nm (emballage) packaging; (fig) conditioning

conditionner [kɔ̃disjɔne] vt (déterminer) to determine; (Comm: produit) to package; (fig: personne) to condition; **air conditionné** air conditioning; **réflexe conditionné** conditioned reflex

condoléances [kɔ̃dɔleɑ̃s] nfpl condolences

conducteur, -trice [kɔ̃dyktœʀ, -tʀis] adj (Élec) conducting ▷ nm/f (Auto etc) driver; (d'une machine) operator ▷ nm (Élec etc) conductor

conduire [kɔ̃dɥiʀ] vt (véhicule, passager) to drive; (délégation, troupeau) to lead; **se conduire** vi to behave; **~ vers/à** to lead towards/to; **~ qn quelque part** to take sb somewhere; to drive sb somewhere

conduite [kɔ̃dɥit] nf (en auto) driving; (comportement) behaviour (Brit), behavior (US); (d'eau, de gaz) pipe; **sous la ~ de** led by; **~ forcée** pressure pipe; **~ à gauche** left-hand drive; **~ intérieure** saloon (car)

cône [kon] nm cone; **en forme de ~** cone-shaped

confection [kɔ̃fɛksjɔ̃] nf (fabrication) making; (Couture): **la ~** the clothing industry, the rag trade (fam); **vêtement de ~** ready-to-wear ou off-the-peg garment

confectionner [kɔ̃fɛksjɔne] vt to make

conférence [kɔ̃feʀɑ̃s] nf (exposé) lecture; (pourparlers) conference; **~ de presse** press conference; **~ au sommet** summit (conference)

conférencier, -ière [kɔ̃feʀɑ̃sje, -jɛʀ] nm/f lecturer

confesser [kɔ̃fese] vt to confess; **se confesser** vi (Rel) to go to confession

confession [kɔ̃fesjɔ̃] nf confession; (culte: catholique etc) denomination

confiance [kɔ̃fjɑ̃s] nf confidence, trust; faith; **avoir ~ en** to have confidence ou faith in, trust; **faire ~ à** to trust; **en toute ~** with complete confidence; **de ~** trustworthy, reliable; **mettre qn en ~** to win sb's trust; **vote de ~** (Pol) vote of confidence; **inspirer ~ à** to inspire confidence

in; ~ **en soi** self-confidence; *voir* **question**
confiant, e [kɔ̃fjɑ̃, -ɑ̃t] *adj* confident; trusting
confidence [kɔ̃fidɑ̃s] *nf* confidence
confidentiel, le [kɔ̃fidɑ̃sjɛl] *adj* confidential
confier [kɔ̃fje] *vt*: ~ **à qn** (*objet en dépôt, travail etc*) to entrust to sb; (*secret, pensée*) to confide to sb; **se ~ à qn** to confide in sb
confins [kɔ̃fɛ̃] *nmpl*: **aux ~ de** on the borders of
confirmation [kɔ̃firmasjɔ̃] *nf* confirmation
confirmer [kɔ̃firme] *vt* to confirm; ~ **qn dans une croyance/ses fonctions** to strengthen sb in a belief/his duties
confiserie [kɔ̃fizri] *nf* (*magasin*) confectioner's *ou* sweet shop (*Brit*), candy store (*US*); **confiseries** *nfpl* (*bonbons*) confectionery *sg*, sweets, candy *no pl*
confisquer [kɔ̃fiske] *vt* to confiscate
confit, e [kɔ̃fi, -it] *adj*: **fruits ~s** crystallized fruits ▷ *nm*: ~ **d'oie** potted goose
confiture [kɔ̃fityr] *nf* jam; ~ **d'oranges** (orange) marmalade
conflit [kɔ̃fli] *nm* conflict
confondre [kɔ̃fɔ̃dr(ə)] *vt* (*jumeaux, faits*) to confuse, mix up; (*témoin, menteur*) to confound; **se confondre** *vi* to merge; **se ~ en excuses** to offer profuse apologies, apologize profusely; ~ **qch/qn avec qch/qn d'autre** to mistake sth/sb for sth/sb else
confondu, e [kɔ̃fɔ̃dy] *pp de* **confondre** ▷ *adj* (*stupéfait*) speechless, overcome; **toutes catégories ~es** taking all categories together
conforme [kɔ̃fɔrm(ə)] *adj*: ~ **à** (*en accord avec*) in accordance with, in keeping with; (*identique à*) true to; **copie certifiée ~** (*Admin*) certified copy; ~ **à la commande** as per order
conformément [kɔ̃fɔrmemɑ̃] *adv*: ~ **à** in accordance with
conformer [kɔ̃fɔrme] *vt*: ~ **qch à** to model sth on; **se ~ à** to conform to
confort [kɔ̃fɔr] *nm* comfort; **tout ~** (*Comm*) with all mod cons (*Brit*) *ou* modern conveniences
confortable [kɔ̃fɔrtabl(ə)] *adj* comfortable
confrère [kɔ̃frɛr] *nm* colleague; fellow member
confronter [kɔ̃frɔ̃te] *vt* to confront; (*textes*) to compare, collate
confus, e [kɔ̃fy, -yz] *adj* (*vague*) confused; (*embarrassé*) embarrassed
confusion [kɔ̃fyzjɔ̃] *nf* (*voir confus*) confusion; embarrassment; (*voir confondre*) confusion; mixing up; (*erreur*) confusion; ~ **des peines** (*Jur*) concurrency of sentences
congé [kɔ̃ʒe] *nm* (*vacances*) holiday; (*arrêt de travail*) time off *no pl*, leave *no pl*; (*Mil*) leave *no pl*; (*avis de départ*) notice; **en ~** on holiday; off (work); on leave; **semaine/jour de ~** week/day off; **prendre ~ de qn** to take one's leave of sb; **donner son ~ à** to hand *ou* give in one's notice to; ~ **de maladie** sick leave; ~ **de maternité** maternity leave; ~**s payés** paid holiday *ou* leave
congédier [kɔ̃ʒedje] *vt* to dismiss
congélateur [kɔ̃ʒelatœr] *nm* freezer, deep freeze
congeler [kɔ̃ʒle]: **se congeler** *vi* to freeze
congestion [kɔ̃ʒɛstjɔ̃] *nf* congestion; ~

cérébrale stroke; ~ **pulmonaire** congestion of the lungs
congestionner [kɔ̃ʒɛstjɔne] *vt* to congest; (*Méd*) to flush
congrès [kɔ̃grɛ] *nm* congress
conifère [kɔnifɛr] *nm* conifer
conjecture [kɔ̃ʒɛktyr] *nf* conjecture, speculation *no pl*
conjoint, e [kɔ̃ʒwɛ̃, -wɛ̃t] *adj* joint ▷ *nm/f* spouse
conjonction [kɔ̃ʒɔ̃ksjɔ̃] *nf* (*Ling*) conjunction
conjonctivite [kɔ̃ʒɔ̃ktivit] *nf* conjunctivitis
conjoncture [kɔ̃ʒɔ̃ktyr] *nf* circumstances *pl*; **la ~ (économique)** the economic climate *ou* situation
conjugaison [kɔ̃ʒygɛzɔ̃] *nf* (*Ling*) conjugation
conjuguer [kɔ̃ʒyge] *vt* (*Ling*) to conjugate; (*efforts etc*) to combine
conjuration [kɔ̃ʒyrɑsjɔ̃] *nf* conspiracy
conjurer [kɔ̃ʒyre] *vt* (*sort, maladie*) to avert; (*implorer*): ~ **qn de faire qch** to beseech *ou* entreat sb to do sth
connaissance [kɔnɛsɑ̃s] *nf* (*savoir*) knowledge *no pl*; (*personne connue*) acquaintance; (*conscience*) consciousness; **connaissances** *nfpl* knowledge *no pl*; **être sans ~** to be unconscious; **perdre/reprendre ~** to lose/regain consciousness; **à ma/sa ~** to (the best of) my/his knowledge; **faire ~ avec qn** *ou* **la ~ de qn** (*rencontrer*) to meet sb; (*apprendre à connaître*) to get to know sb; **avoir ~ de** to be aware of; **prendre ~ de** (*document etc*) to peruse; **en ~ de cause** with full knowledge of the facts; **de ~** (*personne, visage*) familiar
connaisseur, -euse [kɔnɛsœr, -øz] *nm/f* connoisseur ▷ *adj* expert
connaître [kɔnɛtr(ə)] *vt* to know; (*éprouver*) to experience; (*avoir*) to have; to enjoy; ~ **de nom/vue** to know by name/sight; **se connaître** *vi* to know each other; (*soi-même*) to know o.s.; **ils se sont connus à Genève** they (first) met in Geneva; **s'y ~ en qch** to know about sth
connecter [kɔnɛkte] *vt* to connect; **se ~ à Internet** to log onto the internet
connerie [kɔnri] *nf* (*fam*) (bloody) stupid (*Brit*) *ou* damn-fool (*US*) thing to do *ou* say
connu, e [kɔny] *pp de* **connaître** ▷ *adj* (*célèbre*) well-known
conquérir [kɔ̃kerir] *vt* to conquer, win
conquête [kɔ̃kɛt] *nf* conquest
consacrer [kɔ̃sakre] *vt* (*Rel*): ~ **qch (à)** to consecrate sth (to); (*fig: usage etc*) to sanction, establish; (*employer*): ~ **qch à** to devote *ou* dedicate sth to; **se ~ à qch/faire** to dedicate *ou* devote o.s. to sth/to doing
conscience [kɔ̃sjɑ̃s] *nf* conscience; (*perception*) consciousness; **avoir/prendre ~ de** to be/become aware of; **perdre/reprendre ~** to lose/regain consciousness; **avoir bonne/mauvaise ~** to have a clear/guilty conscience; **en (toute) ~** in all conscience
consciencieux, -euse [kɔ̃sjɑ̃sjø, -øz] *adj* conscientious
conscient, e [kɔ̃sjɑ̃, -ɑ̃t] *adj* conscious; ~ **de**

aware ou conscious of

conscrit [kɔ̃skʀi] nm conscript

consécutif, -ive [kɔ̃sekytif, -iv] adj consecutive; ~ **à** following upon

conseil [kɔ̃sɛj] nm (avis) piece of advice, advice no pl; (assemblée) council; (expert): ~ **en recrutement** recruitment consultant ▷ adj: **ingénieur-~** engineering consultant; **tenir ~** to hold a meeting; to deliberate; **donner un ~ ou des ~s à qn** to give sb (a piece of) advice; **demander ~ à qn** to ask sb's advice; **prendre ~ (auprès de qn)** to take advice (from sb); ~ **d'administration (CA)** board (of directors); ~ **de classe** (Scol) meeting of teachers, parents and class representatives to discuss pupils' progress; ~ **de discipline** disciplinary committee; ~ **général** regional council; see note; ~ **de guerre** court-martial; **le ~ des ministres** ≈ the Cabinet; ~ **municipal (CM)** town council; ~ **régional** regional board of elected representatives; ~ **de révision** recruitment ou draft (US) board

conseiller[1] [kɔ̃seje] vt (personne) to advise; (méthode, action) to recommend, advise; ~ **qch à qn** to recommend sth to sb; ~ **à qn de faire qch** to advise sb to do sth

conseiller[2], **-ère** [kɔ̃seje, -ɛʀ] nm/f adviser; ~ **général** regional councillor; ~ **matrimonial** marriage guidance counsellor; ~ **municipal** town councillor; ~ **d'orientation** (Scol) careers adviser (Brit), (school) counselor (US)

consentement [kɔ̃sɑ̃tmɑ̃] nm consent

consentir [kɔ̃sɑ̃tiʀ] vt: ~ **(à qch/faire)** to agree ou consent (to sth/to doing); ~ **qch à qn** to grant sb sth

conséquence [kɔ̃sekɑ̃s] nf consequence, outcome; **conséquences** nfpl consequences, repercussions; **en ~** (donc) consequently; (de façon appropriée) accordingly; **ne pas tirer à ~** to be unlikely to have any repercussions; **sans ~** unimportant; **de ~** important

conséquent, e [kɔ̃sekɑ̃, -ɑ̃t] adj logical, rational; (fam: important) substantial; **par ~** consequently

conservateur, -trice [kɔ̃sɛʀvatœʀ, -tʀis] adj conservative ▷ nm/f (Pol) conservative; (de musée) curator

conservatoire [kɔ̃sɛʀvatwaʀ] nm academy; (Écologie) conservation area

conserve [kɔ̃sɛʀv(ə)] nf (gén pl) canned ou tinned (Brit) food; ~**s de poisson** canned ou tinned (Brit) fish; **en ~** canned, tinned (Brit); **de ~** (ensemble) in concert; (naviguer) in convoy

conserver [kɔ̃sɛʀve] vt (faculté) to retain, keep; (habitude) to keep up; (amis, livres) to keep; (préserver, Culin) to preserve; **se conserver** vi (aliments) to keep; "~ **au frais**" "store in a cool place"

considérable [kɔ̃sideʀabl(ə)] adj considerable, significant, extensive

considération [kɔ̃sideʀasjɔ̃] nf consideration; (estime) esteem, respect; **considérations** nfpl (remarques) reflections; **prendre en ~** to take into consideration ou account; **ceci mérite ~** this is

worth considering; **en ~ de** given, because of

considérer [kɔ̃sideʀe] vt to consider; (regarder) to consider, study; ~ **qch comme** to regard sth as

consigne [kɔ̃siɲ] nf (Comm) deposit; (de gare) left luggage (office) (Brit), checkroom (US); (punition: Scol) detention; (: Mil) confinement to barracks; (ordre, instruction) instructions pl; ~ **automatique** left-luggage locker; ~**s de sécurité** safety instructions

consigner [kɔ̃siɲe] vt (note, pensée) to record; (marchandises) to deposit; (punir: Mil) to confine to barracks; (: élève) to put in detention; (Comm) to put a deposit on

consistant, e [kɔ̃sistɑ̃, -ɑ̃t] adj thick; solid

consister [kɔ̃siste] vi: ~ **en/dans/à faire** to consist of/in/in doing

consœur [kɔ̃sœʀ] nf (lady) colleague; fellow member

console [kɔ̃sɔl] nf console; ~ **graphique** ou **de visualisation** (Inform) visual display unit, VDU; ~ **de jeux** games console

consoler [kɔ̃sɔle] vt to console; **se ~ (de qch)** to console o.s. (for sth)

consolider [kɔ̃sɔlide] vt to strengthen, reinforce; (fig) to consolidate; **bilan consolidé** consolidated balance sheet

consommateur, -trice [kɔ̃sɔmatœʀ, -tʀis] nm/f (Écon) consumer; (dans un café) customer

consommation [kɔ̃sɔmasjɔ̃] nf consumption; (Jur) consummation; (boisson) drink; ~ **aux 100 km** (Auto) (fuel) consumption per 100 km, ≈ miles per gallon (mpg), ≈ gas mileage (US); **de ~** (biens, société) consumer cpd

consommer [kɔ̃sɔme] vt (personne) to eat ou drink, consume; (voiture, usine, poêle) to use, consume; (Jur) to consummate ▷ vi (dans un café) to (have a) drink

consonne [kɔ̃sɔn] nf consonant

conspirer [kɔ̃spiʀe] vi to conspire, plot; ~ **à** (tendre à) to conspire to

constamment [kɔ̃stamɑ̃] adv constantly

constant, e [kɔ̃stɑ̃, -ɑ̃t] adj constant; (personne) steadfast ▷ nf constant

constat [kɔ̃sta] nm (d'huissier) certified report (by bailiff); (de police) report; (observation) (observed) fact, observation; (affirmation) statement; ~ **(à l'amiable)** (jointly agreed) statement for insurance purposes

constatation [kɔ̃statasjɔ̃] nf noticing; certifying; (remarque) observation

constater [kɔ̃state] vt (remarquer) to note, notice; (Admin, Jur: attester) to certify; (dégâts) to note; ~ **que** (dire) to state that

consterner [kɔ̃stɛʀne] vt to dismay

constipé, e [kɔ̃stipe] adj constipated; (fig) stiff

constitué, e [kɔ̃stitɥe] adj: ~ **de** made up ou composed of; **bien ~** of sound constitution; well-formed

constituer [kɔ̃stitɥe] vt (comité, équipe) to set up, form; (dossier, collection) to put together, build up; (éléments, parties: composer) to make up, constitute; (représenter, être) to constitute; **se ~ prisonnier**

to give o.s. up; **se ~ partie civile** *to bring an independent action for damages*

constitution [kɔ̃stitysjɔ̃] *nf* setting up; building up; (*composition*) composition, make-up; (*santé, Pol*) constitution

constructeur [kɔ̃stʀyktœʀ] *nm* manufacturer, builder

constructif, -ive [kɔ̃stʀyktif, -iv] *adj* (*positif*) constructive

construction [kɔ̃stʀyksjɔ̃] *nf* construction, building

construire [kɔ̃stʀɥiʀ] *vt* to build, construct; **se construire** *vi*: **l'immeuble s'est construit très vite** the building went up *ou* was built very quickly

consul [kɔ̃syl] *nm* consul

consulat [kɔ̃syla] *nm* consulate

consultant, e [kɔ̃syltɑ̃, -ɑ̃t] *adj* consultant

consultation [kɔ̃syltasjɔ̃] *nf* consultation; **consultations** *nfpl* (*Pol*) talks; **être en ~** (*délibération*) to be in consultation; (*médecin*) to be consulting; **aller à la ~** (*Méd*) to go to the surgery (*Brit*) *ou* doctor's office (*US*); **heures de ~** (*Méd*) surgery (*Brit*) *ou* office (*US*) hours

consulter [kɔ̃sylte] *vt* to consult ▷ *vi* (*médecin*) to hold surgery (*Brit*), be in (the office) (*US*); **se consulter** *vi* to confer

consumer [kɔ̃syme] *vt* to consume; **se consumer** *vi* to burn; **se ~ de chagrin/douleur** to be consumed with sorrow/grief

contact [kɔ̃takt] *nm* contact; **au ~ de** (*air, peau*) on contact with; (*gens*) through contact with; **mettre/couper le ~** (*Auto*) to switch on/off the ignition; **entrer en ~** (*fils, objets*) to come into contact, make contact; **se mettre en ~ avec** (*Radio*) to make contact with; **prendre ~ avec** (*relation d'affaires, connaissance*) to get in touch *ou* contact with

contacter [kɔ̃takte] *vt* to contact, get in touch with

contagieux, -euse [kɔ̃taʒjø, -øz] *adj* contagious; infectious

contaminer [kɔ̃tamine] *vt* (*par un virus*) to infect; (*par des radiations*) to contaminate

conte [kɔ̃t] *nm* tale; **~ de fées** fairy tale

contempler [kɔ̃tɑ̃ple] *vt* to contemplate, gaze at

contemporain, e [kɔ̃tɑ̃pɔʀɛ̃, -ɛn] *adj, nm/f* contemporary

contenance [kɔ̃tnɑ̃s] *nf* (*d'un récipient*) capacity; (*attitude*) bearing, attitude; **perdre ~** to lose one's composure; **se donner une ~** to give the impression of composure; **faire bonne ~ (devant)** to put on a bold front (in the face of)

conteneur [kɔ̃tnœʀ] *nm* container; **~ (de bouteilles)** bottle bank

contenir [kɔ̃tniʀ] *vt* to contain; (*avoir une capacité de*) to hold; **se contenir** *vi* (*se retenir*) to control o.s. *ou* one's emotions, contain o.s.

content, e [kɔ̃tɑ̃, -ɑ̃t] *adj* pleased, glad; **~ de** pleased with; **je serais ~ que tu ...** I would be pleased if you ...

contenter [kɔ̃tɑ̃te] *vt* to satisfy, please; (*envie*) to

satisfy; **se ~ de** to content o.s. with

contentieux [kɔ̃tɑ̃sjø] *nm* (*Comm*) litigation; (: *service*) litigation department; (*Pol etc*) contentious issues *pl*

contenu, e [kɔ̃tny] *pp de* **contenir** ▷ *nm* (*d'un bol*) contents *pl*; (*d'un texte*) content

conter [kɔ̃te] *vt* to recount, relate; **en ~ de belles à qn** to tell tall stories to sb

contestable [kɔ̃tɛstabl(ə)] *adj* questionable

contestation [kɔ̃tɛstasjɔ̃] *nf* questioning, contesting; (*Pol*): **la ~** anti-establishment activity, protest

conteste [kɔ̃tɛst(ə)]: **sans ~** *adv* unquestionably, indisputably

contester [kɔ̃tɛste] *vt* to question, contest ▷ *vi* (*Pol*: *gén*) to protest, rebel (against established authority)

contexte [kɔ̃tɛkst(ə)] *nm* context

contigu, ë [kɔ̃tigy] *adj*: **~ (à)** adjacent (to)

continent [kɔ̃tinɑ̃] *nm* continent

continu, e [kɔ̃tiny] *adj* continuous; **(courant) ~** direct current, DC

continuel, le [kɔ̃tinɥɛl] *adj* (*qui se répète*) constant, continual; (*continu*) continuous

continuer [kɔ̃tinɥe] *vt* (*travail, voyage etc*) to continue (with), carry on (with), go on with; (*prolonger: alignement, rue*) to continue ▷ *vi* (*pluie, vie, bruit*) to continue, go on; (*voyageur*) to go on; **se continuer** *vi* to carry on; **~ à** *ou* **de faire** to go on *ou* continue doing

contorsionner [kɔ̃tɔʀsjɔne]: **se contorsionner** *vi* to contort o.s., writhe about

contour [kɔ̃tuʀ] *nm* outline, contour; **contours** *nmpl* (*d'une rivière etc*) windings

contourner [kɔ̃tuʀne] *vt* to bypass, walk *ou* drive) round

contraceptif, -ive [kɔ̃tʀasɛptif, -iv] *adj, nm* contraceptive

contraception [kɔ̃tʀasɛpsjɔ̃] *nf* contraception

contracté, e [kɔ̃tʀakte] *adj* (*muscle*) tense, contracted; (*personne: tendu*) tense, tensed up; **article ~** (*Ling*) contracted article

contracter [kɔ̃tʀakte] *vt* (*muscle etc*) to tense, contract; (*maladie, dette, obligation*) to contract; (*assurance*) to take out; **se contracter** *vi* (*métal, muscles*) to contract

contractuel, le [kɔ̃tʀaktɥɛl] *adj* contractual ▷ *nm/f* (*agent*) traffic warden; (*employé*) contract employee

contradiction [kɔ̃tʀadiksjɔ̃] *nf* contradiction

contradictoire [kɔ̃tʀadiktwaʀ] *adj* contradictory, conflicting; **débat ~** (open) debate

contraignant, e [kɔ̃tʀɛɲɑ̃, -ɑ̃t] *vb voir* **contraindre** ▷ *adj* restricting

contraindre [kɔ̃tʀɛ̃dʀ(ə)] *vt*: **~ qn à faire** to force *ou* compel sb to do

contraint, e [kɔ̃tʀɛ̃, -ɛ̃t] *pp de* **contraindre** ▷ *nf* constraint

contraire [kɔ̃tʀɛʀ] *adj, nm* opposite; **~ à** contrary to; **au ~** *adv* on the contrary

contrarier [kɔ̃tʀaʀje] *vt* (*personne*) to annoy,

bother; (fig) to impede; to thwart, frustrate

contrariété [kɔ̃tʀaʀjete] nf annoyance

contraste [kɔ̃tʀast(ə)] nm contrast

contrat [kɔ̃tʀa] nm contract; (fig: accord, pacte) agreement; ~ **de travail** employment contract

contravention [kɔ̃tʀavɑ̃sjɔ̃] nf (infraction): ~ **à** contravention of; (amende) fine; (PV pour stationnement interdit) parking ticket; **dresser** ~ **à** (automobiliste) to book; to write out a parking ticket for

contre [kɔ̃tʀ(ə)] prép against; (en échange) (in exchange) for; **par** ~ on the other hand

contrebande [kɔ̃tʀəbɑ̃d] nf (trafic) contraband, smuggling; (marchandise) contraband, smuggled goods pl; **faire la** ~ **de** to smuggle

contrebandier, -ière [kɔ̃tʀəbɑ̃dje, -jɛʀ] nm/f smuggler

contrebas [kɔ̃tʀəba]: **en** ~ adv (down) below

contrebasse [kɔ̃tʀəbas] nf (double) bass

contrecarrer [kɔ̃tʀəkaʀe] vt to thwart

contrecœur [kɔ̃tʀəkœʀ]: **à** ~ adv (be)grudgingly, reluctantly

contrecoup [kɔ̃tʀəku] nm repercussions pl; **par** ~ as an indirect consequence

contredire [kɔ̃tʀədiʀ] vt (personne) to contradict; (témoignage, assertion, faits) to refute; **se contredire** vi to contradict o.s.

contrée [kɔ̃tʀe] nf region; land

contrefaçon [kɔ̃tʀəfasɔ̃] nf forgery; ~ **de brevet** patent infringement

contrefaire [kɔ̃tʀəfɛʀ] vt (document, signature) to forge, counterfeit; (personne, démarche) to mimic; (dénaturer: sa voix etc) to disguise

contre-indication [kɔ̃tʀɛ̃dikasjɔ̃] nf contraindication

contre-indiqué, e [kɔ̃tʀɛ̃dike] adj (Méd) contraindicated

contre-jour [kɔ̃tʀəʒuʀ]: **à** ~ adv against the light

contremaître [kɔ̃tʀəmɛtʀ(ə)] nm foreman

contrepartie [kɔ̃tʀəpaʀti] nf compensation; **en** ~ in compensation; in return

contre-pied [kɔ̃tʀəpje] nm (inverse, opposé): **le** ~ **de ...** the exact opposite of ...; **prendre le** ~ **de** to take the opposing view of; to take the opposite course to; **prendre qn à** ~ (Sport) to wrong-foot sb

contre-plaqué [kɔ̃tʀəplake] nm plywood

contrepoids [kɔ̃tʀəpwa] nm counterweight, counterbalance; **faire** ~ to act as a counterbalance

contrepoison [kɔ̃tʀəpwazɔ̃] nm antidote

contrer [kɔ̃tʀe] vt to counter

contresens [kɔ̃tʀəsɑ̃s] nm misinterpretation; (mauvaise traduction) mistranslation; (absurdité) nonsense no pl; **à** ~ adv the wrong way

contretemps [kɔ̃tʀətɑ̃] nm hitch, contretemps; **à** ~ adv (Mus) out of time; (fig) at an inopportune moment

contrevenir [kɔ̃tʀəvniʀ]: ~ **à** vt to contravene

contribuable [kɔ̃tʀibɥabl(ə)] nm/f taxpayer

contribuer [kɔ̃tʀibɥe]: ~ **à** vt to contribute towards

contribution [kɔ̃tʀibysjɔ̃] nf contribution; **les** ~**s** (bureaux) the tax office; **mettre à** ~ to call upon; ~**s directes/indirectes** direct/indirect taxation

contrôle [kɔ̃tʀol] nm checking no pl, check; supervision; monitoring; (test) test, examination; **perdre le** ~ **de son véhicule** to lose control of one's vehicle; ~ **des changes** (Comm) exchange controls; ~ **continu** (Scol) continuous assessment; ~ **d'identité** identity check; ~ **des naissances** birth control; ~ **des prix** price control

contrôler [kɔ̃tʀole] vt (vérifier) to check; (surveiller) to supervise; to monitor, control; (maîtriser, Comm: firme) to control; **se contrôler** vi to control o.s.

contrôleur, -euse [kɔ̃tʀolœʀ, -øz] nm/f (de train) (ticket) inspector; (de bus) (bus) conductor/tress; ~ **de la navigation aérienne**, ~ **aérien** air traffic controller; ~ **financier** financial controller

contrordre [kɔ̃tʀɔʀdʀ(ə)] nm counter-order, countermand; **sauf** ~ unless otherwise directed

controversé, e [kɔ̃tʀovɛʀse] adj (personnage, question) controversial

contusion [kɔ̃tyzjɔ̃] nf bruise, contusion

convaincre [kɔ̃vɛ̃kʀ(ə)] vt: ~ **qn (de qch)** to convince sb (of sth); ~ **qn (de faire)** to persuade sb (to do); ~ **qn de** (Jur: délit) to convict sb of

convalescence [kɔ̃valesɑ̃s] nf convalescence; **maison de** ~ convalescent home

convenable [kɔ̃vnabl(ə)] adj suitable; (décent) acceptable, proper; (assez bon) decent, acceptable, adequate, passable

convenance [kɔ̃vnɑ̃s] nf: **à ma/votre** ~ to my/ your liking; **convenances** nfpl proprieties

convenir [kɔ̃vniʀ] vt to be suitable; ~ **à** to suit; **il convient de** it is advisable to; (bienséant) it is right ou proper to; ~ **de** (bien-fondé de qch) to admit (to), acknowledge; (date, somme etc) to agree upon; ~ **que** (admettre) to admit that, acknowledge the fact that; ~ **de faire qch** to agree to do sth; **il a été convenu que** it has been agreed that; **comme convenu** as agreed

convention [kɔ̃vɑ̃sjɔ̃] nf convention; **conventions** nfpl (convenances) convention sg, social conventions; **de** ~ conventional; ~ **collective** (Écon) collective agreement

conventionné, e [kɔ̃vɑ̃sjɔne] adj (Admin) applying charges laid down by the state

convenu, e [kɔ̃vny] pp de **convenir** ▷ adj agreed

conversation [kɔ̃vɛʀsasjɔ̃] nf conversation; **avoir de la** ~ to be a good conversationalist

convertir [kɔ̃vɛʀtiʀ] vt: ~ **qn (à)** to convert sb (to); ~ **qch en** to convert sth into; **se** ~ **(à)** to be converted (to)

conviction [kɔ̃viksjɔ̃] nf conviction

convier [kɔ̃vje] vt: ~ **qn à** (dîner etc) to (cordially) invite sb to; ~ **qn à faire** to urge sb to do

convive [kɔ̃viv] nm/f guest (at table)

convivial, e [kɔ̃vivjal] adj (Inform) user-friendly

convocation [kɔ̃vɔkasjɔ̃] nf (voir convoquer) convening, convoking; summoning; invitation;

(*document*) notification to attend; summons *sg*

convoi [kɔ̃vwa] *nm* (*de voitures, prisonniers*) convoy; (*train*) train; ~ **(funèbre)** funeral procession

convoiter [kɔ̃vwate] *vt* to covet

convoquer [kɔ̃vɔke] *vt* (*assemblée*) to convene, convoke; (*subordonné, témoin*) to summon; (*candidat*) to ask to attend; ~ **qn (à)** (*réunion*) to invite sb (to attend)

convoyeur [kɔ̃vwajœʀ] *nm* (*Navig*) escort ship; ~ **de fonds** security guard

coopération [kɔɔpeʀasjɔ̃] *nf* co-operation; (*Admin*): **la C~** ≈ Voluntary Service Overseas (*Brit*) *ou* the Peace Corps (*US*) (*done as alternative to military service*)

coopérer [kɔɔpeʀe] *vi*: ~ **(à)** to co-operate (in)

coordonner [kɔɔʀdɔne] *vt* to coordinate

copain, copine [kɔpɛ̃, kɔpin] *nm/f* mate (*Brit*), pal ▷ *adj*: **être ~ avec** to be pally with

copeau, x [kɔpo] *nm* shaving; (*de métal*) turning

copie [kɔpi] *nf* copy; (*Scol*) script, paper; exercise; ~ **certifiée conforme** certified copy; ~ **papier** (*Inform*) hard copy

copier [kɔpje] *vt, vi* to copy; ~ **sur** to copy from

copieur [kɔpjœʀ] *nm* (photo)copier

copieux, -euse [kɔpjø, -øz] *adj* copious, hearty

copine [kɔpin] *nf voir* **copain**

copropriété [kɔpʀɔpʀijete] *nf* co-ownership, joint ownership; **acheter en ~** to buy on a co-ownership basis

coq [kɔk] *nm* cockerel, rooster ▷ *adj inv* (*Boxe*): **poids ~** bantamweight; ~ **de bruyère** grouse; ~ **du village** (*fig: péj*) ladykiller; ~ **au vin** coq au vin

coq-à-l'âne [kɔkalan] *nm inv* abrupt change of subject

coque [kɔk] *nf* (*de noix, mollusque*) shell; (*de bateau*) hull; **à la ~** (*Culin*) (soft-)boiled

coquelicot [kɔkliko] *nm* poppy

coqueluche [kɔklyʃ] *nf* whooping-cough; (*fig*): **être la ~ de qn** to be sb's flavour of the month

coquet, te [kɔkɛ, -ɛt] *adj* appearance-conscious; (*joli*) pretty

coquetier [kɔktje] *nm* egg-cup

coquillage [kɔkijaʒ] *nm* (*mollusque*) shellfish *inv*; (*coquille*) shell

coquille [kɔkij] *nf* shell; (*Typo*) misprint; ~ **de beurre** shell of butter; ~ **d'œuf** *adj* (*couleur*) eggshell; ~ **de noix** nutshell; ~ **St Jacques** scallop

coquin, e [kɔkɛ̃, -in] *adj* mischievous, roguish; (*polisson*) naughty ▷ *nm/f* (*péj*) rascal

cor [kɔʀ] *nm* (*Mus*) horn; (*Méd*): ~ **(au pied)** corn; **réclamer à ~ et à cri** to clamour for; ~ **anglais** cor anglais; ~ **de chasse** hunting horn

corail, -aux [kɔʀaj, -o] *nm* coral *no pl*

Coran [kɔʀɑ̃] *nm*: **le ~** the Koran

corbeau, x [kɔʀbo] *nm* crow

corbeille [kɔʀbɛj] *nf* basket; (*Inform*) recycle bin; (*Bourse*): **la ~** ≈ the floor (of the Stock Exchange); ~ **de mariage** (*fig*) wedding presents *pl*; ~ **à ouvrage** work-basket; ~ **à pain** breadbasket; ~ **à papier** waste paper basket *ou* bin

corbillard [kɔʀbijaʀ] *nm* hearse

corde [kɔʀd(ə)] *nf* rope; (*de violon, raquette, d'arc*) string; (*trame*): **la ~** the thread; (*Athlétisme, Auto*): **la ~** the rails *pl*; **les ~s** (*Boxe*) the ropes; **les (instruments à) ~s** (*Mus*) the strings, the stringed instruments; **semelles de ~** rope soles; **tenir la ~** (*Athlétisme, Auto*) to be in the inside lane; **tomber des ~s** to rain cats and dogs; **tirer sur la ~** to go too far; **la ~ sensible** the right chord; **usé jusqu'à la ~** threadbare; ~ **à linge** washing *ou* clothes line; ~ **lisse** (climbing) rope; ~ **à nœuds** knotted climbing rope; ~ **raide** tightrope; ~ **à sauter** skipping rope; ~**s vocales** vocal cords

cordée [kɔʀde] *nf* (*d'alpinistes*) rope, roped party

cordialement [kɔʀdjalmɑ̃] *adv* cordially, heartily; (*formule épistolaire*) (kind) regards

cordon [kɔʀdɔ̃] *nm* cord, string; ~ **sanitaire/ de police** sanitary/police cordon; ~ **littoral** sandbank, sandbar; ~ **ombilical** umbilical cord

cordonnerie [kɔʀdɔnʀi] *nf* shoe repairer's *ou* mender's (shop)

cordonnier [kɔʀdɔnje] *nm* shoe repairer *ou* mender, cobbler

Corée [kɔʀe] *nf*: **la ~** Korea; **la ~ du Sud/du Nord** South/North Korea; **la République (démocratique populaire) de ~** the (Democratic People's) Republic of Korea

coriace [kɔʀjas] *adj* tough

corne [kɔʀn(ə)] *nf* horn; (*de cerf*) antler; (*de la peau*) callus; ~ **d'abondance** horn of plenty; ~ **de brume** (*Navig*) foghorn

cornée [kɔʀne] *nf* cornea

corneille [kɔʀnɛj] *nf* crow

cornemuse [kɔʀnəmyz] *nf* bagpipes *pl*; **joueur de ~** piper[12]

cornet [kɔʀnɛ] *nm* (paper) cone; (*de glace*) cornet, cone; ~ **à pistons** cornet

corniche [kɔʀniʃ] *nf* (*de meuble, neigeuse*) cornice; (*route*) coast road

cornichon [kɔʀniʃɔ̃] *nm* gherkin

Cornouailles [kɔʀnwaj] *nf(pl)* Cornwall

corporation [kɔʀpɔʀasjɔ̃] *nf* corporate body; (*au Moyen-Âge*) guild

corporel, le [kɔʀpɔʀɛl] *adj* bodily; (*punition*) corporal; **soins ~s** care *sg* of the body

corps [kɔʀ] *nm* (*gén*) body; (*cadavre*) (dead) body; **à son ~ défendant** against one's will; **à ~ perdu** headlong; **perdu ~ et biens** lost with all hands; **prendre ~** to take shape; **faire ~ avec** to be joined to; to form one body with; ~ **d'armée** (*CA*) army corps; ~ **de ballet** corps de ballet; ~ **constitués** (*Pol*) constitutional bodies; **le ~ consulaire** (*CC*) the consular corps; **à ~** *adv* hand-to-hand ▷ *nm* clinch; **le ~ du délit** (*Jur*) corpus delicti; **le ~ diplomatique** (*CD*) the diplomatic corps; **le ~ électoral** the electorate; **le ~ enseignant** the teaching profession; ~ **étranger** (*Méd*) foreign body; ~ **expéditionnaire** task force; ~ **de garde** guardroom; ~ **législatif** legislative body; **le ~ médical** the medical profession

corpulent, e [kɔʀpylɑ̃, -ɑ̃t] *adj* stout (*Brit*),

corpulent

correct, e [kɔʀɛkt] *adj* (*exact*) accurate, correct; (*bienséant, honnête*) correct; (*passable*) adequate

correcteur, -trice [kɔʀɛktœʀ, -tʀis] *nm/f* (*Scol*) examiner, marker; (*Typo*) proofreader

correction [kɔʀɛksjɔ̃] *nf* (*voir corriger*) correction; marking; (*voir correct*) correctness; (*rature, surcharge*) correction, emendation; (*coups*) thrashing; **~ sur écran** (*Inform*) screen editing; **~ (des épreuves)** proofreading

correctionnel, le [kɔʀɛksjɔnɛl] *adj* (*Jur*): **tribunal ~ ≈** criminal court

correspondance [kɔʀɛspɔ̃dɑ̃s] *nf* correspondence; (*de train, d'avion*) connection; **ce train assure la ~ avec l'avion de 10 heures** this train connects with the 10 o'clock plane; **cours par ~** correspondence course; **vente par ~** mail-order business

correspondant, e [kɔʀɛspɔ̃dɑ̃, -ɑ̃t] *nm/f* correspondent; (*Tél*) person phoning (*ou being phoned*)

correspondre [kɔʀɛspɔ̃dʀ(ə)] *vi* (*données, témoignages*) to correspond, tally; (*chambres*) to communicate; **~ à** to correspond to; **~ avec qn** to correspond with sb

corrida [kɔʀida] *nf* bullfight

corridor [kɔʀidɔʀ] *nm* corridor, passage

corrigé [kɔʀiʒe] *nm* (*Scol*) correct version; fair copy

corriger [kɔʀiʒe] *vt* (*devoir*) to correct, mark; (*texte*) to correct, emend; (*erreur, défaut*) to correct, put right; (*punir*) to thrash; **~ qn de** (*défaut*) to cure sb of; **se ~ de** to cure o.s. of

corroborer [kɔʀɔbɔʀe] *vt* to corroborate

corrompre [kɔʀɔ̃pʀ(ə)] *vt* (*dépraver*) to corrupt; (*acheter: témoin etc*) to bribe

corruption [kɔʀypsjɔ̃] *nf* corruption; bribery

corsage [kɔʀsaʒ] *nm* (*d'une robe*) bodice; (*chemisier*) blouse

corsaire [kɔʀsɛʀ] *nm* pirate, corsair; privateer

corse [kɔʀs(ə)] *adj* Corsican ▷ *nm/f*: **C~** Corsican ▷ *nf*: **la C~** Corsica

corsé, e [kɔʀse] *adj* vigorous; (*café etc*) full-flavoured (*Brit*) *ou* -flavored (*US*); (*goût*) full; (*fig*) spicy; tricky

corset [kɔʀsɛ] *nm* corset; (*d'une robe*) bodice; **~ orthopédique** surgical corset

cortège [kɔʀtɛʒ] *nm* procession

cortisone [kɔʀtizɔn] *nf* (*Méd*) cortisone

corvée [kɔʀve] *nf* chore, drudgery *no pl*; (*Mil*) fatigue (duty)

cosmétique [kɔsmetik] *nm* (*pour les cheveux*) hair-oil; (*produit de beauté*) beauty care product

cosmopolite [kɔsmɔpɔlit] *adj* cosmopolitan

cossu, e [kɔsy] *adj* opulent-looking, well-to-do

costaud, e [kɔsto, -od] *adj* strong, sturdy

costume [kɔstym] *nm* (*d'homme*) suit; (*de théâtre*) costume

costumé, e [kɔstyme] *adj* dressed up

cote [kɔt] *nf* (*en Bourse etc*) quotation; quoted value; (*d'un cheval*): **la ~ de** the odds *pl* on; (*d'un candidat etc*) rating; (*mesure: sur une carte*) spot

height; (*: sur un croquis*) dimension; (*de classement*) (classification) mark; reference number; **avoir la ~** to be very popular; **inscrit à la ~** quoted on the Stock Exchange; **~ d'alerte** danger *ou* flood level; **~ mal taillée** (*fig*) compromise; **~ de popularité** popularity rating

coté, e [kɔte] *adj*: **être ~** to be listed *ou* quoted; **être ~ en Bourse** to be quoted on the Stock Exchange; **être bien/mal ~** to be highly/poorly rated

côte [kot] *nf* (*rivage*) coast(line); (*pente*) slope; (*: sur une route*) hill; (*Anat*) rib; (*d'un tricot, tissu*) rib, ribbing *no pl*; **~ à ~** *adv* side by side; **la C~ (d'Azur)** the (French) Riviera; **la C~ d'Ivoire** the Ivory Coast; **~ de porc** pork chop

côté [kote] *nm* (*gén*) side; (*direction*) way, direction; **de chaque ~ (de)** on each side of; **de tous les ~s** from all directions; **de quel ~ est-il parti?** which way *ou* in which direction did he go?; **de ce/de l'autre ~** this/the other way; **d'un ~ ... de l'autre ~ ...** (*alternative*) on (the) one hand ... on the other (hand) ...; **du ~ de** (*provenance*) from; (*direction*) towards; **du ~ de Lyon** (*proximité*) near Lyons; **du ~ gauche** on the left-hand side; **de ~** *adv* sideways; on one side; to one side; aside; **laisser de ~** to leave on one side; **mettre de ~** to put on one side, put aside; **de mon ~** (*quant à moi*) for my part; **à ~** *adv* (right) nearby; beside; next door; (*d'autre part*) besides; **à ~ de** beside; next to; (*fig*) in comparison to; **à ~ (de la cible)** off target, wide (of the mark); **être aux ~s de** to be by the side of

coteau, x [kɔto] *nm* hill

côtelette [kotlɛt] *nf* chop

côtier, -ière [kotje, -jɛʀ] *adj* coastal

cotisation [kɔtizasjɔ̃] *nf* subscription, dues *pl*; (*pour une pension*) contributions *pl*

cotiser [kɔtize] *vi*: **~ (à)** to pay contributions (to); (*à une association*) to subscribe (to); **se cotiser** to club together

coton [kɔtɔ̃] *nm* cotton; **~ hydrophile** cotton wool (*Brit*), absorbent cotton (*US*)

Coton-Tige® [kɔtɔ̃tiʒ] *nm* cotton bud®

côtoyer [kotwaje] *vt* to be close to; (*rencontrer*) to rub shoulders with; (*longer*) to run alongside; (*fig: friser*) to be bordering *ou* verging on

cou [ku] *nm* neck

couchant [kuʃɑ̃] *adj*: **soleil ~** setting sun

couche [kuʃ] *nf* (*strate: gén, Géo*) layer, stratum (*pl -a*); (*de peinture, vernis*) coat; (*de poussière, crème*) layer; (*de bébé*) nappy (*Brit*), diaper (*US*); **~ d'ozone** ozone layer; **couches** *nfpl* (*Méd*) confinement *sg*; **~s sociales** social levels *ou* strata

couché, e [kuʃe] *adj* (*étendu*) lying down; (*au lit*) in bed

coucher [kuʃe] *nm* (*du soleil*) setting ▷ *vt* (*personne*) to put to bed; (*: loger*) to put up; (*objet*) to lay on its side; (*écrire*) to inscribe, couch ▷ *vi* (*dormir*) to sleep, spend the night; **~ avec qn** to sleep with sb, go to bed with sb; **se coucher** *vi* (*pour dormir*) to go to bed; (*pour se reposer*) to lie down; (*soleil*) to

set, go down; **à prendre avant le ~** (*Méd*) take at
night *ou* before going to bed; **~ de soleil** sunset
couchette [kuʃɛt] *nf* couchette; (*de marin*) bunk
coucou [kuku] *nm* cuckoo ▷ *excl* peek-a-boo
coude [kud] *nm* (*Anat*) elbow; (*de tuyau, de la route*)
bend; **~ à ~** *adv* shoulder to shoulder, side by side
coudre [kudʀ(ə)] *vt* (*bouton*) to sew on; (*robe*) to
sew (up) ▷ *vi* to sew
couenne [kwan] *nf* (*de lard*) rind
couette [kwɛt] *nf* duvet, (continental) quilt;
couettes *nfpl* (*cheveux*) bunches
couffin [kufɛ̃] *nm* Moses basket; (straw) basket
couler [kule] *vi* to flow, run; (*fuir: stylo, récipient*) to
leak; (*sombrer: bateau*) to sink ▷ *vt* (*cloche, sculpture*)
to cast; (*bateau*) to sink; (*fig*) to ruin, bring down;
(: *passer*): **~ une vie heureuse** to enjoy a happy
life; **se ~ dans** (*interstice etc*) to slip into; **faire ~**
(*eau*) to run; **faire ~ un bain** to run a bath; **il a
coulé une bielle** (*Auto*) his big end went; **~ de
source** to follow on naturally; **~ à pic** to sink *ou*
go straight to the bottom
couleur [kulœʀ] *nf* colour (*Brit*), color (*US*);
(*Cartes*) suit; **couleurs** *nfpl* (*du teint*) colo(u)r
sg; **les ~s** (*Mil*) the colo(u)rs; **en ~s** (*film*) in
colo(u)r; **télévision en ~s** colo(u)r television;
de ~ (*homme, femme*) colo(u)red; **sous ~ de** on the
pretext of; **de quelle ~** of what colo(u)r
couleuvre [kulœvʀ(ə)] *nf* grass snake
coulisse [kulis] *nf* (*Tech*) runner; **coulisses** *nfpl*
(*Théât*) wings; (*fig*): **dans les ~s** behind the
scenes; **porte à ~** sliding door
coulisser [kulise] *vi* to slide, run
couloir [kulwaʀ] *nm* corridor, passage; (*d'avion*)
aisle; (*de bus*) gangway; (: *sur la route*) bus lane;
(*Sport: de piste*) lane; (*Géo*) gully; **~ aérien** air
corridor *ou* lane; **~ de navigation** shipping lane
coup [ku] *nm* (*heurt, choc*) knock; (*affectif*) blow,
shock; (*agressif*) blow; (*avec arme à feu*) shot; (*de
l'horloge*) chime; stroke; (*Sport*) stroke; blow;
(*fam: fois*) time; (*Échecs*) move; **~ de coude/genou**
nudge (with the elbow)/ with the knee; **à ~s
de hache/marteau** (hitting) with an axe/a
hammer; **~ de tonnerre** clap of thunder; **~ de
sonnette** ring of the bell; **~ de crayon/pinceau**
stroke of the pencil/brush; **donner un ~ de
balai** to sweep up, give the floor a sweep;
donner un ~ de chiffon to go round with the
duster; **avoir le ~** (*fig*) to have the knack; **être
dans le/hors du ~** to be/not to be in on it; **boire
un ~** to have a drink; **d'un seul ~** (*subitement*)
suddenly; (*à la fois*) at one go; in one blow; **du ~**
so (you see); **du premier ~** first time *ou* go, at the
first attempt; **du même ~** at the same time; **à ~
sûr** definitely, without fail; **après ~** afterwards;
~ sur ~ in quick succession; **être sur un ~** to be
on to something; **sur le ~** outright; **sous le ~ de**
(*surprise etc*) under the influence of; **tomber sous
le ~ de la loi** to constitute a statutory offence;
à tous les ~s every time; **il a raté son ~** he
missed his turn; **pour le ~** for once; **~ bas** (*fig*):
donner un ~ bas à qn to hit sb below the belt; **~
de chance** stroke of luck; **~ de chapeau** (*fig*) pat

on the back; **~ de couteau** stab (of a knife); **~
dur** hard blow; **~ d'éclat** (great) feat; **~ d'envoi**
kick-off; **~ d'essai** first attempt; **~ d'état** coup
d'état; **~ de feu** shot; **~ de filet** (*Police*) haul; **~
de foudre** (*fig*) love at first sight; **~ fourré** stab
in the back; **~ franc** free kick; **~ de frein** (sharp)
braking *no pl*; **~ de fusil** rifle shot; **~ de grâce**
coup de grâce; **~ du lapin** (*Auto*) whiplash; **~ de
main**: **donner un coup de main à qn** to give sb
a (helping) hand; **~ de maître** master stroke; **~
d'œil** glance; **~ de pied** kick; **~ de poing** punch;
~ de soleil sunburn *no pl*; **~ de téléphone**
phone call; **~ de tête** (*fig*) (sudden) impulse; **~
de théâtre** (*fig*) dramatic turn of events; **~ de
vent** gust of wind; **en ~ de vent** (*rapidement*) in a
tearing hurry
coupable [kupabl(ə)] *adj* guilty; (*pensée*) guilty,
culpable ▷ *nm/f* (*gén*) culprit; (*Jur*) guilty party; **~
de** guilty of
coupe [kup] *nf* (*verre*) goblet; (*à fruits*) dish; (*Sport*)
cup; (*de cheveux, de vêtement*) cut; (*graphique, plan*)
(cross) section; **être sous la ~ de** to be under the
control of; **faire des ~s sombres dans** to make
drastic cuts in
coupe-papier [kuppapje] *nm inv* paper knife
couper [kupe] *vt* to cut; (*retrancher*) to cut (out),
take out; (*route, courant*) to cut off; (*appétit*) to take
away; (*fièvre*) to take down, reduce; (*vin, cidre*) to
blend; (: *à table*) to dilute (with water) ▷ *vi* to cut;
(*prendre un raccourci*) to take a short-cut; (*Cartes:
diviser le paquet*) to cut; (: *avec l'atout*) to trump; **se
couper** *vi* (*se blesser*) to cut o.s.; (*en témoignant
etc*) to give o.s. away; **~ l'appétit à qn** to spoil
sb's appetite; **~ la parole à qn** to cut sb short; **~
les vivres à qn** to cut off sb's vital supplies; **~
le contact** *ou* **l'allumage** (*Auto*) to turn off the
ignition; **~ les ponts avec qn** to break with
sb; **se faire ~ les cheveux** to have *ou* get one's
hair cut
couple [kupl(ə)] *nm* couple; **~ de torsion** torque
couplet [kuplɛ] *nm* verse
coupole [kupɔl] *nf* dome; cupola
coupon [kupɔ̃] *nm* (*ticket*) coupon; (*de tissu*)
remnant; roll
coupon-réponse (*pl* **coupons-réponses**)
[kupɔ̃ʀepɔ̃s] *nm* reply coupon
coupure [kupyʀ] *nf* cut; (*billet de banque*) note; (*de
journal*) cutting; **~ de courant** power cut
cour [kuʀ] *nf* (*de ferme, jardin*) (court)yard;
(*d'immeuble*) back yard; (*Jur, royale*) court; **faire la
~ à qn** to court sb; **~ d'appel** appeal court (*Brit*),
appellate court (*US*); **~ d'assises** court of assizes,
≈ Crown Court (*Brit*); **~ de cassation** final court
of appeal; **~ des comptes** (*Admin*) revenue court; **~
martiale** court-martial; **~ de récréation** (*Scol*)
schoolyard, playground
courage [kuʀaʒ] *nm* courage, bravery
courageux, -euse [kuʀaʒø, -øz] *adj* brave,
courageous
couramment [kuʀamɑ̃] *adv* commonly; (*parler*)
fluently
courant, e [kuʀɑ̃, -ɑ̃t] *adj* (*fréquent*) common;

(*Comm*, *gén*: *normal*) standard; (*en cours*) current ▷ *nm* current; (*fig*) movement; trend; **être au ~ (de)** (*fait*, *nouvelle*) to know (about); **mettre qn au ~ (de)** (*fait*, *nouvelle*) to tell sb (about); (*nouveau travail etc*) to teach sb the basics (of), brief sb (about); **se tenir au ~ (de)** (*techniques etc*) to keep o.s. up-to-date (on); **dans le ~ de** (*pendant*) in the course of; **~ octobre** *etc* in the course of October *etc*; **le 10 ~** (*Comm*) the 10th inst.; **~ d'air** draught (*Brit*), draft (*US*); **~ électrique** (electric) current, power

courbature [kuʀbatyʀ] *nf* ache

courbe [kuʀb(ə)] *adj* curved ▷ *nf* curve; **~ de niveau** contour line

courber [kuʀbe] *vt* to bend; **~ la tête** to bow one's head; **se courber** *vi* (*branche etc*) to bend, curve; (*personne*) to bend (down)

coureur, -euse [kuʀœʀ, -øz] *nm/f* (*Sport*) runner (*ou* driver); (*péj*) womanizer/manhunter; **~ cycliste/automobile** racing cyclist/driver

courge [kuʀʒ(ə)] *nf* (*Bot*) gourd; (*Culin*) marrow

courgette [kuʀʒɛt] *nf* courgette (*Brit*), zucchini (*US*)

courir [kuʀiʀ] *vi* (*gén*) to run; (*se dépêcher*) to rush; (*fig*: *rumeurs*) to go round; (*Comm*: *intérêt*) to accrue ▷ *vt* (*Sport*: *épreuve*) to compete in; (*risque*) to run; (*danger*) to face; **~ les cafés/bals** to do the rounds of the cafés/ dances; **le bruit court que** the rumour is going round that; **par les temps qui courent** at the present time; **~ après qn** to run after sb, chase (after) sb; **laisser ~** to let things alone; **faire ~ qn** to make sb run around (all over the place); **tu peux (toujours) ~!** you've got a hope!

couronne [kuʀɔn] *nf* crown; (*de fleurs*) wreath, circlet; **~ (funéraire** *ou* **mortuaire)** (funeral) wreath

courons [kuʀɔ̃], **courrai** *etc* [kuʀe] *vb voir* **courir**

courrier [kuʀje] *nm* mail, post; (*lettres à écrire*) letters *pl*; (*rubrique*) column; **qualité ~** letter quality; **long/moyen ~** *adj* (*Aviat*) long-/medium-haul; **~ du cœur** problem page; **~ électronique** electronic mail, E-mail

courroie [kuʀwa] *nf* strap; (*Tech*) belt; **~ de transmission/de ventilateur** driving/fan belt

courrons *etc* [kuʀɔ̃] *vb voir* **courir**

cours [kuʀ] *vb voir* **courir** ▷ *nm* (*leçon*) lesson; class; (*série de leçons*) course; (*cheminement*) course; (*écoulement*) flow; (*avenue*) walk; (*Comm*) rate; price; (*Bourse*) quotation; **donner libre ~ à** to give free expression to; **avoir ~** (*monnaie*) to be legal tender; (*fig*) to be current; (*Scol*) to have a class *ou* lecture; **en ~** (*année*) current; (*travaux*) in progress; **en ~ de route** on the way; **au ~ de** in the course of, during; **le ~ du change** the exchange rate; **~ d'eau** waterway; **~ élémentaire (CE)** 2nd and 3rd years of primary school; **~ moyen (CM)** 4th and 5th years of primary school; **~ préparatoire** ≈ infants' class (*Brit*), ≈ 1st grade (*US*); **~ du soir** night school

course [kuʀs(ə)] *nf* running; (*Sport*: *épreuve*) race; (*trajet*: *du soleil*) course; (: *d'un projectile*) flight;

(: *d'une pièce mécanique*) travel; (*excursion*) outing; climb; (*d'un taxi*, *autocar*) journey, trip; (*petite mission*) errand; **courses** *nfpl* (*achats*) shopping *sg*; (*Hippisme*) races; **faire les** *ou* **ses ~s** to go shopping; **jouer aux ~s** to bet on the races; **à bout de ~** (*épuisé*) exhausted; **~ automobile** car race; **~ de côte** (*Auto*) hill climb; **~ par étapes** *ou* **d'étapes** race in stages; **~ d'obstacles** obstacle race; **~ à pied** walking race; **~ de vitesse** sprint; **~s de chevaux** horse racing

court, e [kuʀ, kuʀt(ə)] *adj* short ▷ *adv* short ▷ *nm*: **~ (de tennis)** (tennis) court; **tourner ~** to come to a sudden end; **couper ~ à** to cut short; **à ~ de** short of; **prendre qn de ~** to catch sb unawares; **pour faire ~** briefly, to cut a long story short; **ça fait ~** that's not very long; **tirer à la ~e paille** to draw lots; **faire la ~e échelle à qn** to give sb a leg up; **~ métrage** (*Ciné*) short (film)

court-circuit (*pl* **courts-circuits**) [kuʀsiʀkɥi] *nm* short-circuit

courtier, -ière [kuʀtje, -jɛʀ] *nm/f* broker

courtiser [kuʀtize] *vt* to court, woo

courtois, e [kuʀtwa, -waz] *adj* courteous

courtoisie [kuʀtwazi] *nf* courtesy

couru, e [kuʀy] *pp de* **courir** ▷ *adj* (*spectacle etc*) popular; **c'est ~ (d'avance)!** (*fam*) it's a safe bet!

cousais *etc* [kuze] *vb voir* **coudre**

couscous [kuskus] *nm* couscous

cousin, e [kuzɛ̃, -in] *nm/f* cousin ▷ *nm* (*Zool*) mosquito; **~ germain** first cousin

coussin [kusɛ̃] *nm* cushion; **~ d'air** (*Tech*) air cushion

cousu, e [kuzy] *pp de* **coudre** ▷ *adj*: **~ d'or** rolling in riches

coût [ku] *nm* cost; **le ~ de la vie** the cost of living

coûtant [kutɑ̃] *adj m*: **au prix ~** at cost price

couteau, x [kuto] *nm* knife; **~ à cran d'arrêt** flick-knife; **~ de cuisine** kitchen knife; **~ à pain** bread knife; **~ de poche** pocket knife

coûter [kute] *vt* to cost ▷ *vi*: **~ à qn** to cost sb a lot; **~ cher** to be expensive; **~ cher à qn** (*fig*) to cost sb dear *ou* dearly; **combien ça coûte?** how much is it?, what does it cost?; **coûte que coûte** at all costs

coûteux, -euse [kutø, -øz] *adj* costly, expensive

coutume [kutym] *nf* custom; **de ~** usual, customary

couture [kutyʀ] *nf* sewing; dress-making; (*points*) seam

couturier [kutyʀje] *nm* fashion designer, couturier

couturière [kutyʀjɛʀ] *nf* dressmaker

couvée [kuve] *nf* brood, clutch

couvent [kuvɑ̃] *nm* (*de sœurs*) convent; (*de frères*) monastery; (*établissement scolaire*) convent (school)

couver [kuve] *vt* to hatch; (*maladie*) to be sickening for ▷ *vi* (*feu*) to smoulder (*Brit*), smolder (*US*); (*révolte*) to be brewing; **~ qn/qch des yeux** to look lovingly at sb/sth; (*convoiter*) to look longingly at sb/sth

couvercle [kuvɛʀkl(ə)] *nm* lid; (*de bombe aérosol etc, qui se visse*) cap, top

couvert, e [kuvɛʀ, -ɛʀt(ə)] *pp de* **couvrir** ▷ *adj* (*ciel*) overcast; (*coiffé d'un chapeau*) wearing a hat ▷ *nm* place setting; (*place à table*) place; (*au restaurant*) cover charge; **couverts** *nmpl* place settings; cutlery *sg*; ~ **de** covered with *ou* in; **bien** ~ (*habillé*) well wrapped up; **mettre le** ~ **to** lay the table; **à** ~ under cover; **sous le** ~ **de** under the shelter of; (*fig*) under cover of

couverture [kuvɛʀtyʀ] *nf* (*de lit*) blanket; (*de bâtiment*) roofing; (*de livre, fig: d'un espion etc, Assurances, Presse*) coverage; **de** ~ (*lettre etc*) covering; ~ **chauffante** electric blanket

couveuse [kuvøz] *nf* (*à poules*) sitter, brooder; (*de maternité*) incubator

couvre-feu, x [kuvʀəfø] *nm* curfew

couvre-lit [kuvʀəli] *nm* bedspread

couvreur [kuvʀœʀ] *nm* roofer

couvrir [kuvʀiʀ] *vt* to cover; (*dominer, étouffer: voix, pas*) to drown out; (*erreur*) to cover up; (*Zool: s'accoupler à*) to cover; **se couvrir** *vi* (*ciel*) to cloud over; (*s'habiller*) to cover up, wrap up; (*se coiffer*) to put on one's hat; (*par une assurance*) to cover o.s.; **se** ~ **de** (*fleurs, boutons*) to become covered in

cow-boy [kɔbɔj] *nm* cowboy

crabe [kʀab] *nm* crab

cracher [kʀaʃe] *vi* to spit ▷ *vt* to spit out; (*fig: lave etc*) to belch (out); ~ **du sang** to spit blood

crachin [kʀaʃɛ̃] *nm* drizzle

crack [kʀak] *nm* (*intellectuel*) whiz kid; (*sportif*) ace; (*poulain*) hot favourite (*Brit*) *ou* favorite (*US*)

craie [kʀɛ] *nf* chalk

craindre [kʀɛ̃dʀ(ə)] *vt* to fear, be afraid of; (*être sensible à: chaleur, froid*) to be easily damaged by; ~ **de/que** to be afraid of/that; **je crains qu'il (ne) vienne** I am afraid he may come

crainte [kʀɛ̃t] *nf* fear; **de** ~ **de/que** for fear of/that

craintif, -ive [kʀɛ̃tif, -iv] *adj* timid

cramoisi, e [kʀamwazi] *adj* crimson

crampe [kʀɑ̃p] *nf* cramp; ~ **d'estomac** stomach cramp

crampon [kʀɑ̃pɔ̃] *nm* (*de semelle*) stud; (*Alpinisme*) crampon

cramponner [kʀɑ̃pɔne]: **se cramponner** *vi*: **se** ~ (**à**) to hang *ou* cling on (to)

cran [kʀɑ̃] *nm* (*entaille*) notch; (*de courroie*) hole; (*courage*) guts *pl*; ~ **d'arrêt/de sûreté** safety catch; ~ **de mire** bead

crâne [kʀɑn] *nm* skull

crâner [kʀɑne] *vi* (*fam*) to swank, show off

crapaud [kʀapo] *nm* toad

crapule [kʀapyl] *nf* villain

craquement [kʀakmɑ̃] *nm* crack, snap; (*du plancher*) creak, creaking *no pl*

craquer [kʀake] *vi* (*bois, plancher*) to creak; (*fil, branche*) to snap; (*couture*) to come apart, burst; (*fig*) to break down, fall apart; (*: être enthousiasmé*) to go wild ▷ *vt*: ~ **une allumette** to strike a match

crasse [kʀas] *nf* grime, filth ▷ *adj* (*fig: ignorance*) crass

crasseux, -euse [kʀasø, øz] *adj* filthy

cravache [kʀavaʃ] *nf* (riding) crop

cravate [kʀavat] *nf* tie

crawl [kʀol] *nm* crawl

crayon [kʀɛjɔ̃] *nm* pencil; (*de rouge à lèvres etc*) stick, pencil; **écrire au** ~ to write in pencil; ~ **à bille** ball-point pen; ~ **de couleur** crayon; ~ **optique** light pen

crayon-feutre (*pl* **crayons-feutres**) [kʀɛjɔ̃føtʀ(ə)] *nm* felt-(tip) pen

créancier, -ière [kʀeɑ̃sje, -jɛʀ] *nm/f* creditor

création [kʀeasjɔ̃] *nf* creation

créature [kʀeatyʀ] *nf* creature

crèche [kʀɛʃ] *nf* (*de Noël*) crib; *see note*; (*garderie*) crèche, day nursery

crédit [kʀedi] *nm* (*gén*) credit; **crédits** *nmpl* funds; **acheter à** ~ to buy on credit *ou* on easy terms; **faire** ~ **à qn** to give sb credit; ~ **municipal** pawnshop; ~ **relais** bridging loan

créditer [kʀedite] *vt*: ~ **un compte (de)** to credit an account (with)

crédule [kʀedyl] *adj* credulous, gullible

créer [kʀee] *vt* to create; (*Théât: pièce*) to produce (for the first time); (*: rôle*) to create

crémaillère [kʀemajɛʀ] *nf* (*Rail*) rack; (*tige crantée*) trammel; **direction à** ~ (*Auto*) rack and pinion steering; **pendre la** ~ to have a house-warming party

crématoire [kʀematwaʀ] *adj*: **four** ~ crematorium

crème [kʀɛm] *nf* cream; (*entremets*) cream dessert ▷ *adj inv* cream; **un** (**café**) ~ = a white coffee; ~ **chantilly** whipped cream, crème Chantilly; ~ **fouettée** whipped cream; ~ **glacée** ice cream; ~ **à raser** shaving cream; ~ **solaire** sun cream

crémerie [kʀɛmʀi] *nf* dairy; (*tearoom*) teashop

crémeux, -euse [kʀemø, -øz] *adj* creamy

créneau, x [kʀeno] *nm* (*de fortification*) crenel(le); (*fig, aussi Comm*) gap, slot; (*Auto*): **faire un** ~ to reverse into a parking space (*between cars alongside the kerb*)

crêpe [kʀɛp] *nf* (*galette*) pancake ▷ *nm* (*tissu*) crêpe; (*de deuil*) black mourning crêpe; (*ruban*) black armband (*ou* hatband *ou* ribbon); **semelle** (**de**) ~ crêpe sole; ~ **de Chine** crêpe de Chine

crêpé, e [kʀepe] *adj* (*cheveux*) backcombed

crêperie [kʀepʀi] *nf* pancake shop *ou* restaurant

crépiter [kʀepite] *vi* to sputter, splutter, crackle

crépu, e [kʀepy] *adj* frizzy, fuzzy

crépuscule [kʀepyskyl] *nm* twilight, dusk

cresson [kʀesɔ̃] *nm* watercress

crête [kʀɛt] *nf* (*de coq*) comb; (*de vague, montagne*) crest

creuser [kʀøze] *vt* (*trou, tunnel*) to dig; (*sol*) to dig a hole in; (*bois*) to hollow out; (*fig*) to go (deeply) into; **ça creuse** that gives you a real appetite; **se** ~ (**la cervelle**) to rack one's brains

creux, -euse [kʀø, -øz] *adj* hollow ▷ *nm* hollow; (*fig: sur graphique etc*) trough; **heures creuses** slack periods; off-peak periods; **le** ~ **de l'estomac** the pit of the stomach

crevaison [krəvɛzɔ̃] nf puncture, flat

crevasse [krəvas] nf (dans le sol) crack, fissure; (de glacier) crevasse; (de la peau) crack

crevé, e [krəve] adj (fam: fatigué) worn out, dead beat

crever [krəve] vt (papier) to tear, break; (tambour, ballon) to burst ▷ vi (pneu) to burst; (automobiliste) to have a puncture (Brit) ou a flat (tire) (US); (abcès, outre, nuage) to burst (open); (fam) to die; **cela lui a crevé un œil** it blinded him in one eye; **~ l'écran** to have real screen presence

crevette [krəvɛt] nf: **~ (rose)** prawn; **~ grise** shrimp

cri [kri] nm cry, shout; (d'animal: spécifique) cry, call; **à grands ~s** at the top of one's voice; **c'est le dernier ~** (fig) it's the latest fashion

criant, e [krijɑ̃, -ɑ̃t] adj (injustice) glaring

criard, e [krijar, -ard(ə)] adj (couleur) garish, loud; (voix) yelling

crible [kribl(ə)] nm riddle; (mécanique) screen, jig; **passer qch au ~** to put sth through a riddle; (fig) to go over sth with a fine-tooth comb

criblé, e [krible] adj: **~ de** riddled with

cric [krik] nm (Auto) jack

crier [krije] vi (pour appeler) to shout, cry (out); (de peur, de douleur etc) to scream, yell; (fig: grincer) to squeal, screech ▷ vt (ordre, injure) to shout (out), yell (out); **sans ~ gare** without warning; **~ grâce** to cry for mercy; **~ au secours** to shout for help

crime [krim] nm crime; (meurtre) murder

criminel, le [kriminɛl] adj criminal ▷ nm/f criminal; murderer; **~ de guerre** war criminal

crin [krɛ̃] nm hair no pl; (fibre) horsehair; **à tous ~s, à tout** ~ diehard, out-and-out

crinière [krinjɛr] nf mane

crique [krik] nf creek, inlet

criquet [krikɛ] nm grasshopper

crise [kriz] nf crisis (pl crises); (Méd) attack; fit; **~ cardiaque** heart attack; **~ de foi** crisis of belief; **~ de foie** bilious attack; **~ de nerfs** attack of nerves

crisper [krispe] vt to tense; (poings) to clench; **se crisper** to tense; to clench; (personne) to get tense

crisser [krise] vi (neige) to crunch; (tissu) to rustle; (pneu) to screech

cristal, -aux [kristal, -o] nm crystal; **crystaux** nmpl (objets) crystal(ware) sg; **~ de plomb** (lead) crystal; **~ de roche** rock-crystal; **cristaux de soude** washing soda sg

cristallin, e [kristalɛ̃, -in] adj crystal-clear ▷ nm (Anat) crystalline lens

critère [kritɛr] nm criterion (pl -ia)

critiquable [kritikabl(ə)] adj open to criticism

critique [kritik] adj critical ▷ nm/f (de théâtre, musique) critic ▷ nf criticism; (Théât etc: article) review; **la ~** (activité) criticism; (personnes) the critics pl

critiquer [kritike] vt (dénigrer) to criticize; (évaluer, juger) to assess, examine (critically)

croasser [krɔase] vi to caw

Croatie [krɔasi] nf: **la ~** Croatia

croc [kro] nm (dent) fang; (de boucher) hook

croc-en-jambe (pl crocs-en-jambe) [krɔkɑ̃jɑ̃b] nm: **faire un ~ à qn** to trip sb up

croche [krɔʃ] nf (Mus) quaver (Brit), eighth note (US); **double ~** semiquaver (Brit), sixteenth note (US)

croche-pied [krɔʃpje] nm = **croc-en-jambe**

crochet [krɔʃɛ] nm hook; (clef) picklock; (détour) detour; (Boxe): **~ du gauche** left hook; (Tricot: aiguille) crochet hook; (: technique) crochet; **crochets** nmpl (Typo) square brackets; **vivre aux ~s de qn** to live ou sponge off sb

crochu, e [krɔʃy] adj hooked; claw-like

crocodile [krɔkɔdil] nm crocodile

croire [krwar] vt to believe; **~ qn honnête** to believe sb (to be) honest; **se ~ fort** to think one is strong; **~ que** to believe ou think that; **vous croyez?** do you think so?; **~ être/faire** to think one is/does; **~ à, ~ en** to believe in

croîs etc [krwa] vb voir **croître**

croisade [krwazad] nf crusade

croisé, e [krwaze] adj (veston) double-breasted ▷ nm (guerrier) crusader ▷ nf (fenêtre) window, casement; **~e d'ogives** intersecting ribs; **à la ~e des chemins** at the crossroads

croisement [krwazmɑ̃] nm (carrefour) crossroads sg; (Bio) crossing; crossbreed

croiser [krwaze] vt (personne, voiture) to pass; (route) to cross, cut across; (Bio) to cross ▷ vi (Navig) to cruise; **~ les jambes/bras** to cross one's legs/fold one's arms; **se croiser** vi (personnes, véhicules) to pass each other; (routes) to cross, intersect; (lettres) to cross (in the post); (regards) to meet; **se ~ les bras** (fig) to twiddle one's thumbs

croisière [krwazjɛr] nf cruise; **vitesse de ~** (Auto etc) cruising speed

croissance [krwasɑ̃s] nf growing, growth; **troubles de la ~** growing pains; **maladie de ~** growth disease; **~ économique** economic growth

croissant, e [krwasɑ̃, -ɑ̃t] vb voir **croître** ▷ adj growing; rising ▷ nm (à manger) croissant; (motif) crescent; **~ de lune** crescent moon

croître [krwatr(ə)] vi to grow; (lune) to wax

croix [krwa] nf cross; **en ~** adj, adv in the form of a cross; **la C~ Rouge** the Red Cross

croque-madame [krɔkmadam] nm inv toasted cheese sandwich with a fried egg on top

croque-monsieur [krɔkməsjø] nm inv toasted ham and cheese sandwich

croquer [krɔke] vt (manger) to crunch; to munch; (dessiner) to sketch ▷ vi to be crisp ou crunchy; **chocolat à ~** plain dessert chocolate

croquis [krɔki] nm sketch

cross [krɔs], **cross-country** [krɔskuntri] (pl -(-countries)) nm cross-country race ou run; cross-country racing ou running

crosse [krɔs] nf (de fusil) butt; (de revolver) grip; (d'évêque) crook, crosier; (de hockey) hockey stick

crotte [krɔt] nf droppings pl; **~!** (fam) damn!

crotté, e [krɔte] adj muddy, mucky

crottin [kʀɔtɛ̃] nm: ~ **(de cheval)** (horse) dung ou manure

crouler [kʀule] vi (s'effondrer) to collapse; (être délabré) to be crumbling

croupe [kʀup] nf croup, rump; **en** ~ pillion

croupir [kʀupiʀ] vi to stagnate

croustillant, e [kʀustijã, -ãt] adj crisp; (fig) spicy

croûte [kʀut] nf crust; (du fromage) rind; (de vol-au-vent) case; (Méd) scab; **en** ~ (Culin) in pastry, in a pie; ~ **aux champignons** mushrooms on toast; ~ **au fromage** cheese on toast no pl; ~ **de pain** (morceau) crust (of bread); ~ **terrestre** earth's crust

croûton [kʀutɔ̃] nm (Culin) crouton; (bout du pain) crust, heel

croyable [kʀwajabl(ə)] adj believable, credible

croyant, e [kʀwajã, -ãt] vb voir **croire** ▷ adj: **être/ ne pas être** ~ to be/not to be a believer ▷ nm/f believer

CRS sigle fpl (= Compagnies républicaines de sécurité) state security police force ▷ sigle m member of the CRS

cru, e [kʀy] pp de **croire** ▷ adj (non cuit) raw; (lumière, couleur) harsh; (description) crude; (paroles, langage: franc) blunt; (: grossier) crude ▷ nm (vignoble) vineyard; (vin) wine ▷ nf (d'un cours d'eau) swelling, rising; **de son (propre)** ~ (fig) of his own devising; **monter à** ~ to ride bareback; **du** ~ local; **en** ~**e** in spate

crû [kʀy] pp de **croître**

cruauté [kʀyote] nf cruelty

cruche [kʀyʃ] nf pitcher, (earthenware) jug

crucifix [kʀysifi] nm crucifix

crucifixion [kʀysifiksjɔ̃] nf crucifixion

crudité [kʀydite] nf crudeness no pl; harshness no pl; **crudités** nfpl (Culin) mixed salads (as hors-d'œuvre)

crue [kʀy] nf voir **cru**

cruel, le [kʀyɛl] adj cruel

crus, crûs etc [kʀy] vb voir **croire; croître**

crustacés [kʀystase] nmpl shellfish

Cuba [kyba] nm: **le** ~ Cuba

cubain, e [kybɛ̃, -ɛn] adj Cuban ▷ nm/f: **C~, e** Cuban

cube [kyb] nm cube; (jouet) brick, building block; **gros** ~ powerful motorbike; **mètre** ~ cubic metre; **2 au** ~ **= 8** 2 cubed is 8; **élever au** ~ to cube

cueillette [kœjɛt] nf picking, gathering; harvest ou crop (of fruit)

cueillir [kœjiʀ] vt (fruits, fleurs) to pick, gather; (fig) to catch

cuiller, cuillère [kɥijɛʀ] nf spoon; ~ **à café** coffee spoon; (Culin) ≈ teaspoonful; ~ **à soupe** soup spoon; (Culin) ≈ tablespoonful

cuillerée [kɥijʀe] nf spoonful; (Culin): ~ **à soupe/ café** tablespoonful/teaspoonful

cuir [kɥiʀ] nm leather; (avant tannage) hide; ~ **chevelu** scalp

cuire [kɥiʀ] vt: **(faire)** ~ (aliments) to cook; (au four) to bake; (poterie) to fire ▷ vi to cook; (picoter) to smart, sting, burn; **bien cuit** (viande) well done; **trop cuit** overdone; **pas assez cuit** underdone; **cuit à point** medium done; done to a turn

cuisant, e [kɥizã, -ãt] vb voir **cuire** ▷ adj (douleur) smarting, burning; (fig: souvenir, échec) bitter

cuisine [kɥizin] nf (pièce) kitchen; (art culinaire) cookery, cooking; (nourriture) cooking, food; **faire la** ~ to cook

cuisiné, e [kɥizine] adj: **plat** ~ ready-made meal ou dish

cuisiner [kɥizine] vt to cook; (fam) to grill ▷ vi to cook

cuisinier, -ière [kɥizinje, -jɛʀ] nm/f cook ▷ nf (poêle) cooker; **cuisinière électrique/à gaz** electric/gas cooker

cuisse [kɥis] nf (Anat) thigh; (Culin) leg

cuisson [kɥisɔ̃] nf cooking; (de poterie) firing

cuit, e [kɥi, -it] pp de **cuire** ▷ nf (fam): **prendre une** ~ to get plastered ou smashed

cuivre [kɥivʀ(ə)] nm copper; **les** ~**s** (Mus) the brass; ~ **rouge** copper; ~ **jaune** brass

cul [ky] nm (fam!) arse (Brit) (!), ass (US) (!), bum (Brit); ~ **de bouteille** bottom of a bottle

culbute [kylbyt] nf somersault; (accidentelle) tumble, fall

culminant, e [kylminã, -ãt] adj: **point** ~ highest point; (fig) height, climax

culminer [kylmine] vi to reach its highest point; to tower

culot [kylo] nm (d'ampoule) cap; (effronterie) cheek, nerve

culotte [kylɔt] nf (de femme) panties pl, knickers pl (Brit); (d'homme) underpants pl; (pantalon) trousers pl (Brit), pants pl (US); ~ **de cheval** riding breeches pl

culpabilité [kylpabilite] nf guilt

culte [kylt(ə)] adj: **livre/film** ~ cult film/book ▷ nm (religion) religion; (hommage, vénération) worship; (protestant) service

cultivateur, -trice [kyltivatœʀ, -tʀis] nm/f farmer

cultivé, e [kyltive] adj (personne) cultured, cultivated

cultiver [kyltive] vt to cultivate; (légumes) to grow, cultivate

culture [kyltyʀ] nf cultivation; growing; (connaissance etc) culture; **(champs de)** ~**s** land(s) under cultivation; ~ **physique** physical training

culturel, le [kyltyʀɛl] adj cultural

culturisme [kyltyʀism(ə)] nm body-building

cumin [kymɛ̃] nm (Culin) cumin

cumuler [kymyle] vt (emplois, honneurs) to hold concurrently; (salaires) to draw concurrently; (Jur: droits) to accumulate

cupide [kypid] adj greedy, grasping

cure [kyʀ] nf (Méd) course of treatment; (Rel) cure, ≈ living; presbytery, ≈ vicarage; **faire une** ~ **de fruits** to go on a fruit cure ou diet; **faire une** ~ **thermale** to take the waters; **n'avoir** ~ **de** to pay no attention to; ~ **d'amaigrissement** slimming course; ~ **de repos** rest cure; ~ **de sommeil** sleep therapy no pl

curé [kyʀe] nm parish priest; **M le** ~ ≈ Vicar

cure-dent [kyʀdã] nm toothpick

cure-pipe [kyʀpip] nm pipe cleaner

curer [kyʀe] vt to clean out; **se ~ les dents** to pick one's teeth

curieusement [kyʀjøzmɑ̃] adv oddly

curieux, -euse [kyʀjø, -øz] adj (étrange) strange, curious; (indiscret) curious, inquisitive; (intéressé) inquiring, curious ▷ nmpl (badauds) onlookers, bystanders

curiosité [kyʀjozite] nf curiosity, inquisitiveness; (objet) curio(sity); (site) unusual feature ou sight

curriculum vitae [kyʀikylɔmvite] nm inv curriculum vitae

curseur [kyʀsœʀ] nm (Inform) cursor; (de règle) slide; (de fermeture-éclair) slider

cutané, e [kytane] adj cutaneous, skin cpd

cuti-réaction [kytiʀeaksjɔ̃] nf (Méd) skin-test

cuve [kyv] nf vat; (à mazout etc) tank

cuvée [kyve] nf vintage

cuvette [kyvɛt] nf (récipient) bowl, basin; (du lavabo) (wash)basin; (des w.-c.) pan; (Géo) basin

CV sigle m (Auto) = **cheval vapeur**; (Admin) = **curriculum vitae**

cyanure [sjanyʀ] nm cyanide

cybercafé [sibɛʀkafe] nm cybercafé

cyberespace [sibɛʀɛspas] nm cyberspace

cybernaute [sibɛʀnot] nm/f Internet user

cyclable [siklabl(ə)] adj: **piste ~** cycle track

cycle [sikl(ə)] nm cycle; (Scol): **premier/second ~** = middle/upper school (Brit), = junior/senior high school (US)

cyclisme [siklism(ə)] nm cycling

cycliste [siklist(ə)] nm/f cyclist ▷ adj cycle cpd; **coureur ~** racing cyclist

cyclomoteur [siklɔmɔtœʀ] nm moped

cyclone [siklon] nm hurricane

cygne [siɲ] nm swan

cylindre [silɛ̃dʀ(ə)] nm cylinder; **moteur à 4 ~s en ligne** straight-4 engine

cylindrée [silɛ̃dʀe] nf (Auto) (cubic) capacity; **une (voiture de) grosse ~** a big-engined car

cymbale [sɛ̃bal] nf cymbal

cynique [sinik] adj cynical

cystite [sistit] nf cystitis

Dd

d' *prép, art voir* **de**

dactylo [daktilo] *nf* (*aussi:* **dactylographe**) typist; (*aussi:* **dactylographie**) typing, typewriting

dactylographier [daktilɔɡʀafje] *vt* to type (out)

dada [dada] *nm* hobby-horse

daigner [deɲe] *vt* to deign

daim [dɛ̃] *nm* (fallow) deer *inv*; (*peau*) buckskin; (*imitation*) suede

dalle [dal] *nf* slab; (*au sol*) paving stone, flag(stone); **que** ~ nothing at all, damn all (Brit)

daltonien, ne [daltɔnjɛ̃, -ɛn] *adj* colour-blind (Brit), color-blind (US)

dam [dam] *nm:* **au grand ~ de** much to the detriment (*ou* annoyance) of

dame [dam] *nf* lady; (*Cartes, Échecs*) queen; **dames** *nfpl* (*jeu*) draughts *sg* (Brit), checkers *sg* (US); **les (toilettes des) ~s** the ladies' (toilets); ~ **de charité** benefactress; ~ **de compagnie** lady's companion

damner [dane] *vt* to damn

dancing [dɑ̃siŋ] *nm* dance hall

Danemark [danmaʀk] *nm:* **le ~** Denmark

danger [dɑ̃ʒe] *nm* danger; **mettre en ~** to endanger, put in danger; **être en ~ de mort** to be in peril of one's life; **être hors de ~** to be out of danger

dangereux, -euse [dɑ̃ʒʀø, -øz] *adj* dangerous

danois, e [danwa, -waz] *adj* Danish ▷ *nm* (Ling) Danish ▷ *nm/f:* **D~, e** Dane

dans [dɑ̃] *prép* **1** (*position*) in; (*à l'intérieur de*) inside; **c'est ~ le tiroir/le salon** it's in the drawer/lounge; ~ **la boîte** *ou* inside the box; **marcher ~ la ville/la rue** to walk about the town/along the street; **je l'ai lu ~ le journal** I read it in the newspaper; **être ~ les meilleurs** to be among *ou* one of the best

2 (*direction*) into; **elle a couru ~ le salon** she ran into the lounge

3 (*provenance*) out of, from; **je l'ai pris ~ le tiroir/salon** I took it out of *ou* from the drawer/lounge; **boire ~ un verre** to drink out of *ou* from a glass

4 (*temps*) in; ~ **deux mois** in two months, in two months' time

5 (*approximation*) about; ~ **les 20 euros** about 20 euros

danse [dɑ̃s] *nf:* **la ~** dancing; (*classique*) (ballet) dancing; **une ~** a dance; ~ **du ventre** belly dancing

danser [dɑ̃se] *vi, vt* to dance

danseur, -euse [dɑ̃sœʀ, -øz] *nm/f* ballet dancer; (*au bal etc*) dancer; (: *cavalier*) partner; ~ **de claquettes** tap-dancer; **en danseuse** (*à vélo*) standing on the pedals

dard [daʀ] *nm* sting (*organ*)

date [dat] *nf* date; **faire ~** to mark a milestone; **de longue ~** *adj* longstanding; ~ **de naissance** date of birth; ~ **limite** deadline; (*d'un aliment:* *aussi:* **date limite de vente**) sell-by date

dater [date] *vt, vi* to date; ~ **de** to date from, go back to; **à ~ de** (as) from

datte [dat] *nf* date

dauphin [dofɛ̃] *nm* (Zool) dolphin; (*du roi*) dauphin; (*fig*) heir apparent

davantage [davɑ̃taʒ] *adv* more; (*plus longtemps*) longer; ~ **de** more; ~ **que** more than

de, d' (*de* + *le* = **du**, *de* + *les* = **des**) *prép* **1** (*appartenance*) of; **le toit de la maison** the roof of the house; **la voiture d'Elisabeth/de mes parents** Elizabeth's/my parents' car

2 (*provenance*) from; **il vient de Londres** he comes from London; **de Londres à Paris** from London to Paris; **elle est sortie du cinéma** she came out of the cinema

3 (*moyen*) with; **je l'ai fait de mes propres mains** I did it with my own two hands

4 (*caractérisation, mesure*): **un mur de brique/bureau d'acajou** a brick wall/mahogany desk; **un billet de 10 euros** a 10 euro note; **une pièce de 2 m de large** *ou* **large de 2 m** a room 2 m wide, a 2m-wide room; **un bébé de 10 mois** a 10-month-old baby; **12 mois de crédit/travail** 12 months' credit/work; **elle est payée 20 euros de l'heure** she's paid 20 euros an hour *ou* per hour; **augmenter de 10 euros** to increase by 10 euros; **trois jours de libres** three free days, three days free; **un verre d'eau** a glass of water; **il mange de tout** he'll eat anything

5 (*rapport*) from; **de quatre à six** from four to six

6 (*de la part de*): **estimé de ses collègues** respected by his colleagues

7 (*cause*): **mourir de faim** to die of hunger; **rouge de colère** red with fury

8 (*vb + de + infin*) to; **il m'a dit de rester** he told me to stay

9 (*en apposition*): **cet imbécile de Paul** that idiot Paul; **le terme de franglais** the term "franglais"

▷ **art 1** (*phrases affirmatives*) some (*souvent omis*); **du vin, de l'eau, des pommes** (some) wine, (some) water, (some) apples; **des enfants sont venus** some children came; **pendant des mois** for months

2 (*phrases interrogatives et négatives*) any; **a-t-il du vin?** has he got any wine?; **il n'a pas de pommes/d'enfants** he hasn't (got) any apples/children, he has no apples/children

dé [de] *nm* (*à jouer*) die *ou* dice; (*aussi*: **dé à coudre**) thimble; **dés** *nmpl* (*jeu*) (game of) dice; **un coup de dés** a throw of the dice; **couper en dés** (*Culin*) to dice

dealer [dilœr] *nm* (*fam*) (drug) pusher

déambuler [deãbyle] *vi* to stroll about

débâcle [debakl(ə)] *nf* rout

déballer [debale] *vt* to unpack

débandade [debãdad] *nf* scattering; (*déroute*) rout

débarbouiller [debarbuje] *vt* to wash; **se débarbouiller** *vi* to wash (one's face)

débarcadère [debarkadɛr] *nm* landing stage (*Brit*), wharf

débardeur [debardœr] *nm* docker, stevedore; (*maillot*) slipover, tank top

débarquer [debarke] *vt* to unload, land ▷ *vi* to disembark; (*fig*) to turn up

débarras [debara] *nm* lumber room; (*placard*) junk cupboard; (*remise*) outhouse; **bon ~!** good riddance!

débarrasser [debarase] *vt* to clear ▷ *vi* (*enlever le couvert*) to clear away; **~ qn de** (*vêtements, paquets*) to relieve sb of; (*habitude, ennemi*) to rid sb of; **~ qch de** (*fouillis etc*) to clear sth of; **se débarrasser de** *vt* to get rid of; to rid o.s. of

débat [deba] *vb voir* **débattre** ▷ *nm* discussion, debate; **débats** *nmpl* (*Pol*) proceedings, debates

débattre [debatr(ə)] *vt* to discuss, debate; **se débattre** *vi* to struggle

débaucher [debofe] *vt* (*licencier*) to lay off, dismiss; (*salarié d'une autre entreprise*) to poach; (*entraîner*) to lead astray, debauch; (*inciter à la grève*) to incite

débile [debil] *adj* weak, feeble; (*fam: idiot*) dim-witted ▷ *nm/f*: **~ mental, e** mental defective

débit [debi] *nm* (*d'un liquide, fleuve*) (rate of) flow; (*d'un magasin*) turnover (of goods); (*élocution*) delivery; (*bancaire*) debit; **avoir un ~ de 10 euros** to be 10 euros in debit; **~ de boissons** drinking establishment; **~ de tabac** tobacconist's (shop) (*Brit*), tobacco *ou* smoke shop (*US*)

débiter [debite] *vt* (*compte*) to debit; (*liquide, gaz*) to yield, produce, give out; (*couper: bois, viande*) to cut up; (*vendre*) to retail; (*péj: paroles etc*) to come out with, churn out

débiteur, -trice [debitœr, -tris] *nm/f* debtor ▷ *adj* in debit; (*compte*) debit *cpd*

déblayer [debleje] *vt* to clear; **~ le terrain** (*fig*) to clear the ground

débloquer [debloke] *vt* (*frein, fonds*) to release; (*prix*) to unfreeze ▷ *vi* (*fam*) to talk rubbish

déboires [debwar] *nmpl* setbacks

déboiser [debwaze] *vt* to clear of trees; (*région*) to deforest; **se déboiser** *vi* (*colline, montagne*) to become bare of trees

déboîter [debwate] *vt* (*Auto*) to pull out; **se ~ le genou** *etc* to dislocate one's knee *etc*

débonnaire [debonɛr] *adj* easy-going, good-natured

débordé, e [deborde] *adj*: **être ~ de** (*travail, demandes*) to be snowed under with

déborder [deborde] *vi* to overflow; (*lait etc*) to boil over ▷ *vt* (*Mil, Sport*) to outflank; **~ (de) qch** (*dépasser*) to extend beyond sth; **~ de** (*joie, zèle*) to be brimming over with *ou* bursting with

débouché [debuʃe] *nm* (*pour vendre*) outlet; (*perspective d'emploi*) opening; (*sortie*) **au ~ de la vallée** where the valley opens out (onto the plain)

déboucher [debuʃe] *vt* (*évier, tuyau etc*) to unblock; (*bouteille*) to uncork, open ▷ *vi*: **~ de** to emerge from, come out of; **~ sur** to come out onto; to open out onto; (*fig*) to arrive at, lead up to

débourser [deburse] *vt* to pay out, lay out

déboussoler [debusole] *vt* to disorientate, disorient

debout [dəbu] *adv*: **être ~** (*personne*) to be standing, stand; (: *levé, éveillé*) to be up (and about); (*chose*) to be upright; **être encore ~** (*fig: en état*) to be still going; to be still standing; to be still up; **mettre qn ~** to get sb to his feet; **mettre qch ~** to stand sth up; **se mettre ~** to get up (on one's feet); **se tenir ~** to stand; **~! **get up!; **cette histoire ne tient pas ~** this story doesn't hold water

déboutonner [debutone] *vt* to undo, unbutton; **se déboutonner** *vi* to come undone *ou* unbuttoned

débraillé, e [debraje] *adj* slovenly, untidy

débrancher [debrãʃe] *vt* (*appareil électrique*) to unplug; (*téléphone, courant électrique*) to disconnect, cut off

débrayage [debrɛjaʒ] *nm* (*Auto*) clutch; (: *action*) disengaging the clutch; (*grève*) stoppage; **faire un double ~** to double-declutch

débrayer [debreje] *vi* (*Auto*) to declutch, disengage the clutch; (*cesser le travail*) to stop work

débris [debri] *nm* (*fragment*) fragment ▷ *nmpl* (*déchets*) pieces, debris *sg*; rubbish *sg* (*Brit*), garbage *sg* (*US*)

débrouillard, e [debrujar, -ard(ə)] *adj* smart, resourceful

débrouiller [debruje] *vt* to disentangle, untangle; (*fig*) to sort out, unravel; **se débrouiller** *vi* to manage

début [deby] *nm* beginning, start; **débuts** *nmpl* beginnings; (*de carrière*) début *sg*; **faire ses ~s** to start out; **au ~** in *ou* at the beginning, at first; **au ~ de** at the beginning *ou* start of; **dès le ~** from the start

débutant, e [debytã, -ãt] *nm/f* beginner, novice

débuter [debyte] vi to begin, start; (faire ses débuts) to start out

deçà [dəsa]: **en ~ de** prép this side of; **en ~** adv on this side

décadence [dekadɑ̃s] nf decadence; decline

décaféiné, e [dekafeine] adj decaffeinated, caffeine-free

décalage [dekalaʒ] nm move forward ou back; shift forward ou back; (écart) gap; (désaccord) discrepancy; **~ horaire** time difference (between time zones), time-lag

décaler [dekale] vt (dans le temps: avancer) to bring forward; (: retarder) to put back; (changer de position) to shift forward ou back; **~ de 10 cm** to move forward ou back by 10 cm; **~ de deux heures** to bring ou move forward two hours; to put back two hours

décalquer [dekalke] vt to trace; (par pression) to transfer

décamper [dekɑ̃pe] vi to clear out ou off

décaper [dekape] vt to strip; (avec abrasif) to scour; (avec papier de verre) to sand

décapiter [dekapite] vt to behead; (par accident) to decapitate; (fig) to cut the top off; (: organisation) to remove the top people from

décapotable [dekapɔtabl(ə)] adj convertible

décapsuleur [dekapsylœʀ] nm bottle-opener

décarcasser [dekaʀkase] vt: **se ~ pour qn/pour faire qch** (fam) to slog one's guts out for sb/to do sth

décédé, e [desede] adj deceased

décéder [desede] vi to die

déceler [desle] vt to discover, detect; (révéler) to indicate, reveal

décembre [desɑ̃bʀ(ə)] nm December; voir aussi juillet

décemment [desamɑ̃] adv decently

décennie [deseni] nf decade

décent, e [desɑ̃, -ɑ̃t] adj decent

déception [desɛpsjɔ̃] nf disappointment

décerner [desɛʀne] vt to award

décès [desɛ] nm death, decease; **acte de ~** death certificate

décevant, e [desvɑ̃, -ɑ̃t] adj disappointing

décevoir [desvwaʀ] vt to disappoint

déchaîner [deʃene] vt (passions, colère) to unleash; (rires etc) to give rise to, arouse; **se déchaîner** vi to be unleashed; (rires) to burst out; (se mettre en colère) to fly into a rage; **se ~ contre qn** to unleash one's fury on sb

déchanter [deʃɑ̃te] vi to become disillusioned

décharge [deʃaʀʒ(ə)] nf (dépôt d'ordures) rubbish tip ou dump; (électrique) electrical discharge; (salve) volley of shots; **à la ~ de** in defence of

décharger [deʃaʀʒe] vt (marchandise, véhicule) to unload; (Élec) to discharge; (arme: neutraliser) to unload; (: faire feu) to discharge, fire; **~ qn de** (responsabilité) to relieve sb of, release sb from; **~ sa colère (sur)** to vent one's anger on; **~ sa conscience** to unburden one's conscience; **se ~ dans** (se déverser) to flow into; **se ~ d'une affaire sur qn** to hand a matter over to sb

décharné, e [deʃaʀne] adj bony, emaciated, fleshless

déchausser [deʃose] vt (personne) to take the shoes off; (skis) to take off; **se déchausser** vi to take off one's shoes; (dent) to come ou work loose

déchéance [deʃeɑ̃s] nf (déclin) degeneration, decay, decline; (chute) fall

déchet [deʃɛ] nm (de bois, tissu etc) scrap; (perte: gén Comm) wastage, waste; **déchets** nmpl (ordures) refuse sg, rubbish sg (Brit), garbage sg (US); **~s radioactifs** radioactive waste

déchiffrer [deʃifʀe] vt to decipher

déchiqueter [deʃikte] vt to tear ou pull to pieces

déchirant, e [deʃiʀɑ̃, -ɑ̃t] adj heart-breaking, heart-rending

déchirement [deʃiʀmɑ̃] nm (chagrin) wrench, heartbreak; (gén pl: conflit) rift, split

déchirer [deʃiʀe] vt to tear, rip; (mettre en morceaux) to tear up; (pour ouvrir) to tear off; (arracher) to tear out; (fig) to tear apart; **se déchirer** vi to tear, rip; **se ~ un muscle/tendon** to tear a muscle/tendon

déchirure [deʃiʀyʀ] nf (accroc) tear, rip; **~ musculaire** torn muscle

déchoir [deʃwaʀ] vi (personne) to lower o.s., demean o.s.; **~ de** to fall from

déchu, e [deʃy] pp de **déchoir** ▷ adj fallen; (roi) deposed

décidé, e [deside] adj (personne, air) determined; **c'est ~** it's decided; **être ~ à faire** to be determined to do

décidément [desidemɑ̃] adv undoubtedly; really

décider [deside] vt: **~ qch** to decide on sth; **~ de faire/que** to decide to do/that; **~ qn (à faire qch)** to persuade ou induce sb (to do sth); **~ de qch** to decide upon sth; (chose) to determine sth; **se décider** vi (personne) to decide, make up one's mind; (problème, affaire) to be resolved; **se ~ à qch** to decide on sth; **se ~ à faire** to decide ou make up one's mind to do; **se ~ pour qch** to decide on ou in favour of sth

décimal, e, -aux [desimal, -o] adj, nf decimal

décimètre [desimɛtʀ(ə)] nm decimetre (Brit), decimeter (US); **double ~** (20 cm) ruler

décisif, -ive [desizif, -iv] adj decisive; (qui l'emporte): **le facteur/l'argument ~** the deciding factor/argument

décision [desizjɔ̃] nf decision; (fermeté) decisiveness, decision; **prendre une ~** to make a decision; **prendre la ~ de faire** to take the decision to do; **emporter** ou **faire la ~** to be decisive

déclaration [deklaʀasjɔ̃] nf declaration; registration; (discours: Pol etc) statement; (compte rendu) report; **fausse ~** misrepresentation; **~ (d'amour)** declaration; **~ de décès** registration of death; **~ de guerre** declaration of war; **~ (d'impôts)** statement of income, tax declaration, ≈ tax return; **~ (de sinistre)** (insurance) claim; **~ de revenus** statement of income

déclarer [deklaʀe] vt to declare, announce;

(*revenus, employés, marchandises*) to declare; (*décès, naissance*) to register; (*vol etc: à la police*) to report; **rien à ~** nothing to declare; **se déclarer** *vi* (*feu, maladie*) to break out; **~ la guerre** to declare war

déclencher [deklɑ̃ʃe] *vt* (*mécanisme etc*) to release; (*sonnerie*) to set off, activate; (*attaque, grève*) to launch; (*provoquer*) to trigger off; **se déclencher** *vi* to release itself; to go off

déclic [deklik] *nm* trigger mechanism; (*bruit*) click

décliner [dekline] *vi* to decline ▷ *vt* (*invitation*) to decline, refuse; (*responsabilité*) to refuse to accept; (*nom, adresse*) to state; (*Ling*) to decline; **se décliner** (*Ling*) to decline

décocher [dekɔʃe] *vt* to hurl; (*flèche, regard*) to shoot

décoiffer [dekwafe] *vt*: **~ qn** to disarrange *ou* mess up sb's hair; to take sb's hat off; **se décoiffer** *vi* to take off one's hat

déçois *etc* [deswa], **déçoive** *etc* [deswav] *vb voir* **décevoir**

décollage [dekɔlaʒ] *nm* (*Aviat, Écon*) takeoff

décoller [dekɔle] *vt* to unstick ▷ *vi* to take off; (*projet, entreprise*) to take off, get off the ground; **se décoller** *vi* to come unstuck

décolleté, e [dekɔlte] *adj* low-necked, low-cut; (*femme*) wearing a low-cut dress ▷ *nm* low neck(line); (*épaules*) (bare) neck and shoulders; (*plongeant*) cleavage

décolorer [dekɔlɔre] *vt* (*tissu*) to fade; (*cheveux*) to bleach, lighten; **se décolorer** *vi* to fade

décombres [dekɔ̃bʀ(ə)] *nmpl* rubble *sg*, debris *sg*

décommander [dekɔmɑ̃de] *vt* to cancel; (*invités*) to put off; **se décommander** *vi* to cancel, cry off

décomposé, e [dekɔ̃poze] *adj* (*pourri*) decomposed; (*visage*) haggard, distorted

décompte [dekɔ̃t] *nm* deduction; (*facture*) breakdown (of an account), detailed account

déconcerter [dekɔ̃sɛrte] *vt* to disconcert, confound

déconfit, e [dekɔ̃fi, -it] *adj* crestfallen, downcast

décongeler [dekɔ̃ʒle] *vt* to thaw (out)

déconner [dekɔne] *vi* (*fam!: en parlant*) to talk (a load of) rubbish (*Brit*) *ou* garbage (*US*); (*: faire des bêtises*) to muck about; **sans ~** no kidding

déconseiller [dekɔ̃seje] *vt*: **~ qch (à qn)** to advise (sb) against sth; **~ à qn de faire** to advise sb against doing; **c'est déconseillé** it's not advised *ou* advisable

déconvenue [dekɔ̃vny] *nf* disappointment

décor [dekɔʀ] *nm* décor; (*paysage*) scenery; **décors** *nmpl* (*Théât*) scenery *sg*, decor *sg*; (*Ciné*) set *sg*; **changement de ~** (*fig*) change of scene; **entrer dans le ~** (*fig*) to run off the road; **en ~ naturel** (*Ciné*) on location

décorateur, -trice [dekɔʀatœʀ, -tʀis] *nm/f* (interior) decorator; (*Ciné*) set designer

décoration [dekɔʀasjɔ̃] *nf* decoration

décorer [dekɔʀe] *vt* to decorate

décortiquer [dekɔʀtike] *vt* to shell; (*riz*) to hull; (*fig*) to dissect

découcher [dekuʃe] *vi* to spend the night away

découdre [dekudʀ(ə)] *vt* (*vêtement, couture*) to unpick, take the stitching out of; (*bouton*) to take off; **se découdre** *vi* to come unstitched; (*bouton*) to come off; **en ~** (*fig*) to fight, do battle

découler [dekule] *vi*: **~ de** to ensue *ou* follow from

découper [dekupe] *vt* (*papier, tissu etc*) to cut up; (*volaille, viande*) to carve; (*détacher: manche, article*) to cut out; **se ~ sur** (*ciel, fond*) to stand out against

décourager [dekuʀaʒe] *vt* to discourage, dishearten; (*dissuader*) to discourage, put off; **se décourager** *vi* to lose heart, become discouraged; **~ qn de faire/de qch** to discourage sb from doing/from sth, put sb off doing/sth

décousu, e [dekuzy] *pp de* **découdre** ▷ *adj* unstitched; (*fig*) disjointed, disconnected

découvert, e [dekuvɛʀ, -ɛʀt(ə)] *pp de* **découvrir** ▷ *adj* (*tête*) bare, uncovered; (*lieu*) open, exposed ▷ *nm* (*bancaire*) overdraft ▷ *nf* discovery; **à ~** *adv* (*Mil*) exposed, without cover; (*fig*) openly ▷ *adj* (*Comm*) overdrawn; **à visage ~** openly; **aller à la ~e de** to go in search of

découvrir [dekuvʀiʀ] *vt* to discover; (*apercevoir*) to see; (*enlever ce qui couvre ou protège*) to uncover; (*montrer, dévoiler*) to reveal; **se découvrir** *vi* to take off one's hat; (*se déshabiller*) to take something off; (*au lit*) to uncover o.s.; (*ciel*) to clear; **se ~ des talents** to find hidden talents in o.s.

décret [dekʀɛ] *nm* decree

décréter [dekʀete] *vt* to decree; (*ordonner*) to order

décrié, e [dekʀije] *adj* disparaged

décrire [dekʀiʀ] *vt* to describe; (*courbe, cercle*) to follow, describe

décrocher [dekʀɔʃe] *vt* (*dépendre*) to take down; (*téléphone*) to take off the hook; (: *pour répondre*): **~ (le téléphone)** to pick up *ou* lift the receiver; (*fig: contrat etc*) to get, land ▷ *vi* to drop out; to switch off; **se décrocher** *vi* (*tableau, rideau*) to fall down

décroître [dekʀwatʀ(ə)] *vi* to decrease, decline, diminish

décrypter [dekʀipte] *vt* to decipher

déçu, e [desy] *pp de* **décevoir** ▷ *adj* disappointed *vi*

décupler [dekyple] *vt, vi* to increase tenfold

dédaigner [dedeɲe] *vt* to despise, scorn; (*négliger*) to disregard, spurn; **~ de faire** to consider it beneath one to do, not deign to do

dédaigneux, -euse [dedɛɲø, -øz] *adj* scornful, disdainful

dédain [dedɛ̃] *nm* scorn, disdain

dédale [dedal] *nm* maze

dedans [dədɑ̃] *adv* inside; (*pas en plein air*) indoors, inside ▷ *nm* inside; **au ~** on the inside; inside; **en ~** (*vers l'intérieur*) inwards; *voir aussi* **là**

dédicacer [dedikase] *vt*: **~ (à qn)** to sign (for sb), autograph (for sb), inscribe (to sb)

dédier [dedje] *vt* to dedicate

dédire [dediʀ]: **se dédire** *vi* to go back on one's word; (*se rétracter*) to retract, recant

dédommagement [dedɔmaʒmɑ̃] *nm* compensation

dédommager [dedɔmaʒe] *vt*: ~ **qn (de)** to compensate sb (for); *(fig)* to repay sb (for)

dédouaner [dedwane] *vt* to clear through customs

dédoubler [deduble] *vt (classe, effectifs)* to split (into two); *(couverture etc)* to unfold; *(manteau)* to remove the lining of; ~ **un train/les trains** to run a relief train/additional trains; **se dédoubler** *vi (Psych)* to have a split personality

déduire [dedɥiʀ] *vt*: ~ **qch (de)** *(ôter)* to deduct sth (from); *(conclure)* to deduce *ou* infer sth (from)

déesse [deɛs] *nf* goddess

défaillance [defajɑ̃s] *nf (syncope)* blackout; *(fatigue)* (sudden) weakness *no pl*; *(technique)* fault, failure; *(morale etc)* weakness; ~ **cardiaque** heart failure

défaillir [defajiʀ] *vi* to faint; to feel faint; *(mémoire etc)* to fail

défaire [defɛʀ] *vt (installation, échafaudage)* to take down, dismantle; *(paquet etc, nœud, vêtement)* to undo; *(bagages)* to unpack; *(ouvrage)* to undo, unpick; *(cheveux)* to take out; **se défaire** *vi* to come undone; **se ~ de** *vt (se débarrasser de)* to get rid of; *(se séparer de)* to part with; ~ **le lit** *(pour changer les draps)* to strip the bed; *(pour se coucher)* to turn back the bedclothes

défait, e [defɛ, -ɛt] *pp de* **défaire** ▷ *adj (visage)* haggard, ravaged ▷ *nf* defeat

défalquer [defalke] *vt* to deduct

défaut [defo] *nm (moral)* fault, failing, defect; *(d'étoffe, métal)* fault, flaw, defect; *(manque, carence)*: ~ **de** lack of; shortage of; *(Inform)* bug; ~ **de la cuirasse** *(fig)* chink in the armour (Brit) *ou* armor (US); **en** ~ at fault; in the wrong; **faire** ~ *(manquer)* to be lacking; **à** ~ *adv* failing that; **à ~ de** for lack *ou* want of; **par** ~ *(Jur)* in his *(ou* her *etc)* absence

défavorable [defavɔʀabl(ə)] *adj* unfavourable (Brit), unfavorable (US)

défavoriser [defavɔʀize] *vt* to put at a disadvantage

défection [defɛksjɔ̃] *nf* defection, failure to give support *ou* assistance; failure to appear; **faire ~** *(d'un parti etc)* to withdraw one's support, leave

défectueux, -euse [defɛktɥø, -øz] *adj* faulty, defective

défendre [defɑ̃dʀ(ə)] *vt* to defend; *(interdire)* to forbid; ~ **à qn qch/de faire** to forbid sb sth/to do; **il est défendu de cracher** spitting (is) prohibited *ou* is not allowed; **c'est défendu** it is forbidden; **se défendre** *vi* to defend o.s.; **il se défend** *(fig)* he can hold his own; **ça se défend** *(fig)* it holds together; **se ~ de/contre** *(se protéger)* to protect o.s. from/against; **se ~ de** *(se garder de)* to refrain from; *(nier)*: **se ~ de vouloir** to deny wanting

défense [defɑ̃s] *nf* defence (Brit), defense (US); *(d'éléphant etc)* tusk; **ministre de la ~** Minister of Defence (Brit), Defence Secretary; **la ~ nationale** defence, the defence of the realm

(Brit); **la ~ contre avions** anti-aircraft defence; **"~ de fumer/cracher"** "no smoking/spitting", "smoking/spitting prohibited"; **prendre la ~ de qn** to stand up for sb; ~ **des consommateurs** consumerism

déférer [defeʀe] *vt (Jur)* to refer; ~ **à** *vt (requête, décision)* to defer to; ~ **qn à la justice** to hand sb over to justice

déferler [defɛʀle] *vi (vagues)* to break; *(fig)* to surge

défi [defi] *nm (provocation)* challenge; *(bravade)* defiance; **mettre qn au ~ de faire qch** to challenge sb to do sth; **relever un ~** to take up *ou* accept a challenge

déficit [defisit] *nm (Comm)* deficit; *(Psych etc: manque)* defect; ~ **budgétaire** budget deficit; **être en ~** to be in deficit

déficitaire [defisitɛʀ] *adj (année, récolte)* bad; **entreprise/budget ~** business/budget in deficit

défier [defje] *vt (provoquer)* to challenge; *(fig)* to defy, brave; **se ~ de** *(se méfier de)* to distrust, mistrust; ~ **qn de faire** to challenge *ou* defy sb to do; ~ **qn à** to challenge sb to; ~ **toute comparaison/concurrence** to be incomparable/unbeatable

défigurer [defigyʀe] *vt* to disfigure; *(boutons etc)* to mar *ou* spoil (the looks of); *(fig: œuvre)* to mutilate, deface

défilé [defile] *nm (Géo)* (narrow) gorge *ou* pass; *(soldats)* parade; *(manifestants)* procession, march; **un ~ de** *(voitures, visiteurs etc)* a stream of

défiler [defile] *vi (troupes)* to march past; *(sportifs)* to parade; *(manifestants)* to march; *(visiteurs)* to pour, stream; **se défiler** *vi (se dérober)* to slip away, sneak off; **faire ~** *(bande, film)* to put on; *(Inform)* to scroll

définir [definiʀ] *vt* to define

définitif, -ive [definitif, -iv] *adj (final)* final, definitive; *(pour longtemps)* permanent, definitive; *(sans appel)* final, definite ▷ *nf*: **en définitive** eventually; *(somme toute)* when all is said and done

définitivement [definitivmɑ̃] *adv* definitively; permanently; definitely

défoncer [defɔ̃se] *vt (caisse)* to stave in; *(porte)* to smash in *ou* down; *(lit, fauteuil)* to burst (the springs of); *(terrain, route)* to rip *ou* plough up; **se défoncer** *vi (se donner à fond)* to give it all one's got

déformer [defɔʀme] *vt* to put out of shape; *(corps)* to deform; *(pensée, fait)* to distort; **se déformer** *vi* to lose its shape

défouler [defule]: **se défouler** *vi (Psych)* to work off one's tensions, release one's pent-up feelings; *(gén)* to unwind, let off steam

défraîchir [defʀeʃiʀ]: **se défraîchir** *vi* to fade; to become shop-soiled

défricher [defʀiʃe] *vt* to clear (for cultivation)

défunt, e [defœ̃, -œ̃t] *adj*: **son ~ père** his late father ▷ *nm/f* deceased

dégagé, e [degaʒe] *adj* clear; *(ton, air)* casual, jaunty

dégagement [degaʒmɑ̃] *nm* emission; freeing;

clearing; (*espace libre*) clearing; passage; clearance; (*Football*) clearance; **voie de** ~ slip road; **itinéraire de** ~ alternative route (*to relieve traffic congestion*)

dégager [degaʒe] *vt* (*exhaler*) to give off, emit; (*délivrer*) to free, extricate; (*Mil: troupes*) to relieve; (*désencombrer*) to clear; (*isoler, mettre en valeur*) to bring out; (*crédits*) to release; **se dégager** *vi* (*odeur*) to emanate, be given off; (*passage, ciel*) to clear; ~ **qn de** (*engagement, parole etc*) to release *ou* free sb from; **se** ~ **de** (*fig: engagement etc*) to get out of; (: *promesse*) to go back on

dégarnir [degaʀniʀ] *vt* (*vider*) to empty, clear; **se dégarnir** *vi* to empty; to be cleaned out *ou* cleared; (*tempes, crâne*) to go bald

dégâts [dega] *nmpl* damage *sg*; **faire des** ~ to damage

dégel [deʒɛl] *nm* thaw; (*fig: des prix etc*) unfreezing

dégeler [deʒle] *vt* to thaw (out); (*fig*) to unfreeze ▷ *vi* to thaw (out); **se dégeler** *vi* (*fig*) to thaw out

dégénérer [deʒeneʀe] *vi* to degenerate; (*empirer*) to go from bad to worse; (*devenir*) : ~ **en** to degenerate into

dégingandé, e [deʒɛ̃gɑ̃de] *adj* gangling, lanky

dégivrer [deʒivʀe] *vt* (*frigo*) to defrost; (*vitres*) to de-ice

dégonflé, e [degɔ̃fle] *adj* (*pneu*) flat; (*fam*) chicken ▷ *nm/f* (*fam*) chicken

dégonfler [degɔ̃fle] *vt* (*pneu, ballon*) to let down, deflate ▷ *vi* (*désenfler*) to go down; **se dégonfler** *vi* (*fam*) to chicken out

dégouliner [deguline] *vi* to trickle, drip; ~ **de** to be dripping with

dégourdi, e [deguʀdi] *adj* smart, resourceful

dégourdir [deguʀdiʀ] *vt* to warm (up); **se** ~ (**les jambes**) to stretch one's legs

dégoût [degu] *nm* disgust, distaste

dégoûtant, e [degutɑ̃, -ɑ̃t] *adj* disgusting

dégoûté, e [degute] *adj* disgusted; ~ **de** sick of

dégoûter [degute] *vt* to disgust; **cela me dégoûte** I find this disgusting *ou* revolting; ~ **qn de qch** to put sb off sth; **se** ~ **de** to get *ou* become sick of

dégrader [degʀade] *vt* (*Mil: officier*) to degrade; (*abîmer*) to damage, deface; (*avilir*) to degrade, debase; **se dégrader** *vi* (*relations, situation*) to deteriorate

dégrafer [degʀafe] *vt* to unclip, unhook, unfasten

degré [dǝgʀe] *nm* degree; (*d'escalier*) step; **brûlure au 1er/2ème** ~ 1st/2nd degree burn; **équation du 1er/2ème** ~ linear/quadratic equation; **le premier** ~ (*Scol*) primary level; **alcool à 90 ~s** surgical spirit; **vin de 10 ~s** 10°wine (*on Gay-Lussac scale*); **par ~(s)** *adv* by degrees, gradually

dégressif, -ive [degʀesif, -iv] *adj* on a decreasing scale, degressive; **tarif** ~ decreasing rate of charge

dégringoler [degʀɛ̃gɔle] *vi* to tumble (down); (*fig: prix, monnaie etc*) to collapse

dégrossir [degʀosiʀ] *vt* (*bois*) to trim; (*fig*) to work out roughly; (: *personne*) to knock the rough edges off

déguenillé, e [degnije] *adj* ragged, tattered

déguerpir [degɛʀpiʀ] *vi* to clear off

dégueulasse [degœlas] *adj* (*fam*) disgusting

dégueuler [degœle] *vi* (*fam*) to puke, throw up

déguisement [degizmɑ̃] *nm* disguise; (*habits: pour s'amuser*) dressing-up clothes; (: *pour tromper*) disguise

déguiser [degize] *vt* to disguise; **se déguiser (en)** *vi* (*se costumer*) to dress up (as); (*pour tromper*) to disguise o.s. (as)

dégustation [degystasjɔ̃] *nf* tasting; sampling; savouring (*Brit*), savoring (*US*); (*séance*): ~ **de vin(s)** wine-tasting

déguster [degyste] *vt* (*vins*) to taste; (*fromages etc*) to sample; (*savourer*) to enjoy, savour (*Brit*), savor (*US*)

dehors [dǝɔʀ] *adv* outside; (*en plein air*) outdoors, outside ▷ *nm* outside ▷ *nmpl* (*apparences*) appearances, exterior *sg*; **mettre** *ou* **jeter** ~ to throw out; **au** ~ outside; (*en apparence*) outwardly; **au** ~ **de** outside; **de** ~ from outside; **en** ~ outside; outwards; **en** ~ **de** apart from

déjà [deʒa] *adv* already; (*auparavant*) before, already; **as-tu** ~ **été en France?** have you been to France before?; **c'est** ~ **pas mal** that's not too bad (at all); **c'est** ~ **quelque chose** (at least) it's better than nothing; **quel nom,** ~? what was the name again?

déjeuner [deʒœne] *vi* to (have) lunch; (*le matin*) to have breakfast ▷ *nm* lunch; (*petit déjeuner*) breakfast; ~ **d'affaires** business lunch

déjouer [deʒwe] *vt* to elude, to foil, thwart

delà [dǝla] *adv*: **par** ~, **en** ~ (**de**), **au** ~ (**de**) beyond

délabrer [delabʀe]: **se délabrer** *vi* to fall into decay, become dilapidated

délacer [delase] *vt* to unlace, undo

délai [delɛ] *nm* (*attente*) waiting period; (*sursis*) extension (of time); (*temps accordé: aussi*: **délais**) time limit; **sans** ~ without delay; **à bref** ~ shortly, very soon; at short notice; **dans les** ~**s** within the time limit; **un** ~ **de 30 jours** a period of 30 days; **comptez un** ~ **de livraison de 10 jours** allow 10 days for delivery

délaisser [delese] *vt* (*abandonner*) to abandon, desert; (*négliger*) to neglect

délasser [delase] *vt* (*reposer*) to relax; (*divertir*) to divert, entertain; **se délasser** *vi* to relax

délavé, e [delave] *adj* faded

délayer [deleje] *vt* (*Culin*) to mix (with water *etc*); (*peinture*) to thin down; (*fig*) to pad out, spin out

delco® [dɛlko] *nm* (*Auto*) distributor; **tête de delco** distributor cap

délecter [delɛkte]: **se délecter** *vi*: **se** ~ **de** to revel *ou* delight in

délégué, e [delege] *adj* delegated ▷ *nm/f* delegate; representative; **ministre** ~ **à** minister with special responsibility for

déléguer [delege] *vt* to delegate

délibéré, e [delibeʀe] *adj* (*conscient*) deliberate; (*déterminé*) determined, resolute; **de propos** ~ (*à* *dessein, exprès*) intentionally

délibérer [delibeʀe] *vi* to deliberate

délicat, e [delika, -at] *adj* delicate; (*plein de tact*) tactful; (*attentionné*) thoughtful; (*exigeant*) fussy, particular; **procédés peu ~s** unscrupulous methods

délicatement [delikatmɑ̃] *adv* delicately; (*avec douceur*) gently

délice [delis] *nm* delight

délicieux, -euse [delisjø, -øz] *adj* (*au goût*) delicious; (*sensation, impression*) delightful

délimiter [delimite] *vt* to delimit

délinquance [delɛ̃kɑ̃s] *nf* criminality; ~ **juvénile** juvenile delinquency

délinquant, e [delɛ̃kɑ̃, -ɑ̃t] *adj, nm/f* delinquent

délirant, e [deliʀɑ̃, -ɑ̃t] *adj* (*Méd: fièvre*) delirious; (*imagination*) frenzied; (*fam: déraisonnable*) crazy

délirer [deliʀe] *vi* to be delirious; (*fig*) to be raving

délit [deli] *nm* (criminal) offence; ~ **de droit commun** violation of common law; ~ **de fuite** failure to stop after an accident; ~ **d'initiés** insider dealing *ou* trading; ~ **de presse** violation of the press laws

délivrer [delivʀe] *vt* (*prisonnier*) to (set) free, release; (*passeport, certificat*) to issue; ~ **qn de** (*ennemis*) to set sb free from, deliver *ou* free sb from; (*fig*) to rid sb of

déloger [deloʒe] *vt* (*locataire*) to turn out; (*objet coincé, ennemi*) to dislodge

déloyal, e, -aux [delwajal, -o] *adj* (*personne, conduite*) disloyal; (*procédé*) unfair

deltaplane® [dɛltaplan] *nm* hang-glider

déluge [delyʒ] *nm* (*biblique*) Flood, Deluge; (*grosse pluie*) downpour, deluge; (*grand nombre*): ~ **de** flood of

déluré, e [delyʀe] *adj* smart, resourceful; (*péj*) forward, pert

demain [dəmɛ̃] *adv* tomorrow; ~ **matin/soir** tomorrow morning/evening; ~ **midi** tomorrow at midday; **à ~!** see you tomorrow!

demande [dəmɑ̃d] *nf* (*requête*) request; (*revendication*) demand; (*Admin, formulaire*) application; (*Écon*): **la ~** demand; **"~s d'emploi"** "situations wanted"; **à la ~ générale** by popular request; ~ **en mariage** (marriage) proposal; **faire sa ~ (en mariage)** to propose (marriage); ~ **de naturalisation** application for naturalization; ~ **de poste** job application

demandé, e [dəmɑ̃de] *adj* (*article etc*): **très ~** (very) much in demand

demander [dəmɑ̃de] *vt* to ask for; (*question: date, heure, chemin*) to ask; (*requérir, nécessiter*) to require, demand; ~ **qch à qn** to ask sb for sth, ask sb sth; **ils demandent deux secrétaires et un ingénieur** they're looking for two secretaries and an engineer; ~ **la main de qn** to ask for sb's hand (in marriage); ~ **pardon à qn** to apologize to sb; ~ **à** *ou* **de voir/faire** to ask to see/ask if one can do; ~ **à qn de faire** to ask sb to do; ~ **que/pourquoi** to ask that/why; **se ~ si/pourquoi** *etc* to wonder if/why *etc*; (*sens purement réfléchi*) to ask o.s. if/why *etc*; **on vous demande au téléphone**

you're wanted on the phone, there's someone for you on the phone; **il ne demande que ça** that's all he wants; **je ne demande pas mieux** I'm asking nothing more; **il ne demande qu'à faire** all he wants is to do

demandeur, -euse [dəmɑ̃dœʀ, -øz] *nm/f*: ~ **d'emploi** job-seeker

démangeaison [demɑ̃ʒɛzɔ̃] *nf* itching

démanger [demɑ̃ʒe] *vi* to itch; **la main me démange** my hand is itching; **l'envie** *ou* **ça me démange de faire** I'm itching to do

démanteler [demɑ̃tle] *vt* to break up; to demolish

démaquillant [demakijɑ̃] *nm* make-up remover

démaquiller [demakije] *vt*: **se démaquiller** to remove one's make-up

démarche [demaʀʃ(ə)] *nf* (*allure*) gait, walk; (*intervention*) step; approach; (*fig: intellectuelle*) thought processes *pl*; approach; **faire** *ou* **entreprendre des ~s** to take action; **faire des ~s auprès de qn** to approach sb

démarcheur, -euse [demaʀʃœʀ, -øz] *nm/f* (*Comm*) door-to-door salesman/woman; (*Pol etc*) canvasser

démarque [demaʀk(ə)] *nf* (*Comm: d'un article*) mark-down

démarrage [demaʀaʒ] *nm* starting *no pl*, start; ~ **en côte** hill start

démarrer [demaʀe] *vt* to start up ▷ *vi* (*conducteur*) to start (up); (*véhicule*) to move off; (*travaux, affaire*) to get moving; (*coureur: accélérer*) to pull away

démarreur [demaʀœʀ] *nm* (*Auto*) starter

démêlant, e [demelɑ̃, -ɑ̃t] *adj*: **baume ~, crème ~e** (hair) conditioner

démêler [demele] *vt* to untangle, disentangle

démêlés [demele] *nmpl* problems

déménagement [demenaʒmɑ̃] *nm* (*du point de vue du locataire etc*) move; (: *du déménageur*) removal (*Brit*), moving (*US*); **entreprise/camion de ~** removal (*Brit*) *ou* moving (*US*) firm/van

déménager [demenaʒe] *vt* (*meubles*) to (re)move ▷ *vi* to move (house)

déménageur [demenaʒœʀ] *nm* removal man (*Brit*), (furniture) mover (*US*); (*entrepreneur*) furniture remover

démener [demne]: **se démener** *vi* to thrash about; (*fig*) to exert o.s.

dément, e [demɑ̃, -ɑ̃t] *vb voir* **démentir** ▷ *adj* (*fou*) mad (*Brit*), crazy; (*fam*) brilliant, fantastic

démentiel, le [demɑ̃sjɛl] *adj* insane

démentir [demɑ̃tiʀ] *vt* (*nouvelle, témoin*) to refute; (*faits etc*) to belie, refute; ~ **que** to deny that; **ne pas se ~** not to fail, keep up

démerder [demɛʀde]: **se démerder** *vi* (*fam!*) to bloody well manage for o.s.

démesuré, e [deməzyʀe] *adj* immoderate, disproportionate

démettre [demɛtʀ(ə)] *vt*: ~ **qn de** (*fonction, poste*) to dismiss sb from; **se ~ (de ses fonctions)** to resign (from) one's duties; **se ~ l'épaule** *etc* to dislocate one's shoulder *etc*

demeurant [dəmœrɑ̃]: **au ~** adv for all that
demeure [dəmœR] nf residence; **dernière ~** (fig) last resting place; **mettre qn en ~ de faire** to enjoin ou order sb to do; **à ~** adv permanently
demeurer [dəmœRe] vi (habiter) to live; (séjourner) to stay; (rester) to remain; **en ~ là** (personne) to leave it at that; (: choses) to be left at that
demi, e [dəmi] adj: **et ~, trois heures/bouteilles et ~es** three and a half hours/bottles, three hours/bottles and a half ▷ nm (bière: = 0.25 litre) ≈ half-pint; (Football) half-back; **il est 2 heures et ~e** it's half past 2; **il est midi et ~** it's half past 12; **~ de mêlée/d'ouverture** (Rugby) scrum/fly half; **à ~** adv half-; **ouvrir à ~** to half-open; **faire les choses à ~** to do things by halves; **à la ~e** (heure) on the half-hour
demi-cercle [dəmisɛRkl(ə)] nm semicircle; **en ~** adj semicircular ▷ adv in a semicircle
demi-douzaine [dəmiduzɛn] nf half-dozen, half a dozen
demi-finale [dəmifinal] nf semifinal
demi-frère [dəmifRɛR] nm half-brother
demi-heure [dəmijœR] nf: **une ~** a half-hour, half an hour
demi-journée [dəmiʒuRne] nf half-day, half a day
demi-litre [dəmilitR(ə)] nm half-litre (Brit), half-liter (US), half a litre ou liter
demi-livre [dəmilivR(ə)] nf half-pound, half a pound
demi-mot [dəmimo]: **à ~** adv without having to spell things out
demi-pension [dəmipɑ̃sjɔ̃] nf half-board; **être en ~** (Scol) to take school meals
demi-pensionnaire [dəmipɑ̃sjɔnɛR] nm/f (Scol) half-boarder
demi-place [dəmiplas] nf half-price; (Transports) half-fare
démis, e [demi, -iz] pp de **démettre** ▷ adj (épaule etc) dislocated
demi-sel [dəmisɛl] adj inv slightly salted
demi-sœur [dəmisœR] nf half-sister
démission [demisjɔ̃] nf resignation; **donner sa ~** to give ou hand in one's notice, hand in one's resignation
démissionner [demisjɔne] vi (de son poste) to resign, give ou hand in one's notice
demi-tarif [dəmitaRif] nm half-price; (Transports) half-fare
demi-tour [dəmituR] nm about-turn; **faire un ~** (Mil etc) to make an about-turn; **faire ~** to turn (and go) back; (Auto) to do a U-turn
démocratie [demɔkRasi] nf democracy; **~ populaire/libérale** people's/liberal democracy
démocratique [demɔkRatik] adj democratic
démodé, e [demɔde] adj old-fashioned
demoiselle [dəmwazɛl] nf (jeune fille) young lady; (célibataire) single lady, maiden lady; **~ d'honneur** bridesmaid
démolir [demɔliR] vt to demolish; (fig: personne) to do for
démon [demɔ̃] nm demon, fiend; evil spirit;

(enfant turbulent) devil, demon; **le ~ du jeu/des femmes** a mania for gambling/women; **le D~** the Devil
démonstration [demɔ̃stRasjɔ̃] nf demonstration; (aérienne, navale) display
démonté, e [demɔ̃te] adj (fig) raging, wild
démonter [demɔ̃te] vt (machine etc) to take down, dismantle; (pneu, porte) to take off; (cavalier) to throw, unseat; (fig: personne) to disconcert; **se démonter** vi (personne) to lose countenance
démontrer [demɔ̃tRe] vt to demonstrate, show
démordre [demɔRdR] vi (aussi: **ne pas démordre de**) to refuse to give up, stick to
démouler [demule] vt (gâteau) to turn out
démuni, e [demyni] adj (sans argent) impoverished; **~ de** without, lacking in
démunir [demyniR] vt: **~ qn de** to deprive sb of; **se ~ de** to part with, give up
dénaturer [denatyRe] vt (goût) to alter (completely); (pensée, fait) to distort, misrepresent
dénicher [deniʃe] vt to unearth
dénier [denje] vt to deny; **~ qch à qn** to deny sb sth
dénigrer [denigRe] vt to denigrate, run down
dénivellation [denivelasjɔ̃] nf, **dénivellement** [denivɛlmɑ̃] ▷ nm difference in level; (pente) ramp; (creux) dip
dénombrer [denɔ̃bRe] vt (compter) to count; (énumérer) to enumerate, list
dénomination [denɔminasjɔ̃] nf designation, appellation
dénommé, e [denɔme] adj: **le ~ Dupont** the man by the name of Dupont
dénoncer [denɔ̃se] vt to denounce; **se dénoncer** vi to give o.s. up, come forward
dénouement [denumɑ̃] nm outcome, conclusion; (Théât) dénouement
dénouer [denwe] vt to unknot, undo
dénoyauter [denwajote] vt to stone; **appareil à ~** stoner
denrée [dɑ̃Re] nf commodity; (aussi: **denrée alimentaire**) food(stuff)
dense [dɑ̃s] adj dense
densité [dɑ̃site] nf denseness; (Physique) density
dent [dɑ̃] nf tooth; **avoir/garder une ~ contre qn** to have/hold a grudge against sb; **se mettre qch sous la ~** to eat sth; **être sur les ~s** to be on one's last legs; **faire ses ~s** to teethe, cut (one's) teeth; **en ~s de scie** serrated; (irrégulier) jagged; **avoir les ~s longues** (fig) to be ruthlessly ambitious; **~ de lait/sagesse** milk/wisdom tooth
dentaire [dɑ̃tɛR] adj dental; **cabinet ~** dental surgery; **école ~** dental school
dentelé, e [dɑ̃tle] adj jagged, indented
dentelle [dɑ̃tɛl] nf lace no pl
dentier [dɑ̃tje] nm denture
dentifrice [dɑ̃tifRis] adj, nm: (**pâte**) **~** toothpaste; **eau ~** mouthwash
dentiste [dɑ̃tist(ə)] nm/f dentist
dentition [dɑ̃tisjɔ̃] nf teeth pl, dentition

dénuder [denyde] *vt* to bare; **se dénuder**
(*personne*) to strip
dénué, e [denɥe] *adj*: **~ de** lacking in; (*intérêt*)
devoid of
dénuement [denymɑ̃] *nm* destitution
déodorant [deɔdɔrɑ̃] *nm* deodorant
déontologie [deɔ̃tɔlɔʒi] *nf* code of ethics;
(*professionnelle*) (professional) code of practice
dépannage [depanaʒ] *nm*: **service/camion de ~**
(*Auto*) breakdown service/truck
dépanner [depane] *vt* (*voiture, télévision*) to fix,
repair; (*fig*) to bail out, help out
dépanneuse [depanøz] *nf* breakdown lorry
(*Brit*), tow truck (*US*)
dépareillé, e [depareje] *adj* (*collection, service*)
incomplete; (*gant, volume, objet*) odd
départ [depar] *nm* leaving *no pl*, departure;
(*Sport*) start; (*sur un horaire*) departure; **à son ~**
when he left; **au ~** (*au début*) initially, at the start;
courrier au ~ outgoing mail
départager [departaʒe] *vt* to decide between
département [departəmɑ̃] *nm* department;
see note
dépassé, e [depɑse] *adj* superseded, outmoded;
(*fig*) out of one's depth
dépasser [depɑse] *vt* (*véhicule, concurrent*) to
overtake; (*endroit*) to pass, go past; (*somme, limite*)
to exceed; (*fig: en beauté etc*) to surpass, outshine;
(*être en saillie sur*) to jut out above (*ou* in front of);
(*dérouter*): **cela me dépasse** it's beyond me ▷ *vi*
(*Auto*) to overtake; (*jupon*) to show; **se dépasser**
vi to excel o.s.
dépaysé, e [depeize] *adj* disorientated
dépaysement [depeizmɑ̃] *nm* disorientation;
change of scenery
dépecer [depəse] *vt* (*boucher*) to joint, cut up;
(*animal*) to dismember
dépêche [depɛʃ] *nf* dispatch; **~ (télégraphique)**
telegram, wire
dépêcher [depeʃe] *vt* to dispatch; **se dépêcher** *vi*
to hurry; **se ~ de faire qch** to hasten to do sth,
hurry (in order) to do sth
dépeindre [depɛ̃dr(ə)] *vt* to depict
dépendance [depɑ̃dɑ̃s] *nf* (*interdépendance*)
dependence *no pl*, dependency; (*bâtiment*)
outbuilding
dépendre [depɑ̃dr(ə)] *vt* (*tableau*) to take down;
~ de *vt* to depend on, to be dependent on;
(*appartenir*) to belong to; **ça dépend** it depends
dépens [depɑ̃] *nmpl*: **aux ~ de** at the expense of
dépense [depɑ̃s] *nf* spending *no pl*, expense,
expenditure *no pl*; (*fig*) consumption; (: *de temps,
de forces*) expenditure; **pousser qn à la ~** to make
sb incur an expense; **~ physique** (physical)
exertion; **~s de fonctionnement** revenue
expenditure; **~s d'investissement** capital
expenditure; **~s publiques** public expenditure
dépenser [depɑ̃se] *vt* to spend; (*gaz, eau*) to use;
(*fig*) to expend, use up; **se dépenser** *vi* (*se fatiguer*)
to exert o.s.
dépensier, -ière [depɑ̃sje, -jɛr] *adj*: **il est ~** he's
a spendthrift

dépérir [deperir] *vi* (*personne*) to waste away;
(*plante*) to wither
dépêtrer [depetre] *vt*: **se ~ de** (*situation*) to
extricate o.s. from
dépeupler [depœple] *vt* to depopulate; **se
dépeupler** *vi* to be depopulated
dépilatoire [depilatwar] *adj* depilatory, hair-
removing
dépister [depiste] *vt* to detect; (*Méd*) to screen;
(*voleur*) to track down; (*poursuivants*) to throw off
the scent
dépit [depi] *nm* vexation, frustration; **en ~ de**
prép in spite of; **en ~ du bon sens** contrary to all
good sense
dépité, e [depite] *adj* vexed, frustrated
déplacé, e [deplase] *adj* (*propos*) out of place,
uncalled-for; **personne ~e** displaced person
déplacement [deplasmɑ̃] *nm* moving; shifting;
transfer; (*voyage*) trip, travelling *no pl* (*Brit*),
traveling *no pl* (*US*); **en ~** away (on a trip); **~ d'air**
displacement of air; **~ de vertèbre** slipped disc
déplacer [deplase] *vt* (*table, voiture*) to move, shift;
(*employé*) to transfer, move; **se déplacer** *vi* (*objet*)
to move; (*organe*) to become displaced; (*personne:
bouger*) to move, walk; (: *voyager*) to travel ▷ *vt*
(*vertèbre etc*) to displace
déplaire [deplɛr] *vi*: **ceci me déplaît** I don't
like this, I dislike this; **il cherche à nous ~** he's
trying to displease us *ou* be disagreeable to us;
se ~ quelque part to dislike it *ou* be unhappy
somewhere
déplaisant, e [deplɛzɑ̃, -ɑ̃t] *vb voir* **déplaire** ▷ *adj*
disagreeable, unpleasant
dépliant [deplijɑ̃] *nm* leaflet
déplier [deplije] *vt* to unfold; **se déplier** *vi*
(*parachute*) to open
déplorer [deplɔre] *vt* (*regretter*) to deplore; (*pleurer
sur*) to lament
déployer [deplwaje] *vt* to open out, spread; (*Mil*)
to deploy; (*montrer*) to display, exhibit
déporter [depɔrte] *vt* (*Pol*) to deport; (*dévier*)
to carry off course; **se déporter** *vi* (*voiture*) to
swerve
déposer [depoze] *vt* (*gén: mettre, poser*) to lay
down, put down, set down; (*à la banque, à la
consigne*) to deposit; (*caution*) to put down;
(*passager*) to drop (off), set down; (*démonter:
serrure, moteur*) to take out; (: *rideau*) to take down;
(*roi*) to depose; (*Admin: faire enregistrer*) to file; to
register ▷ *vi* to form a sediment *ou* deposit; (*Jur*):
~ (contre) to testify *ou* give evidence (against);
se déposer *vi* to settle; **~ son bilan** (*Comm*) to go
into (voluntary) liquidation
dépositaire [depozitɛr] *nm/f* (*Jur*) depository;
(*Comm*) agent; **~ agréé** authorized agent
déposition [depozisjɔ̃] *nf* (*Jur*) deposition
dépôt [depo] *nm* (*à la banque, sédiment*) deposit;
(*entrepôt, réserve*) warehouse, store; (*gare*) depot;
(*prison*) cells *pl*; **~ d'ordures** rubbish (*Brit*)
ou garbage (*US*) dump, tip (*Brit*); **~ de bilan**
(voluntary) liquidation; **~ légal** registration of
copyright

dépotoir [depɔtwaʀ] *nm* dumping ground, rubbish (*Brit*) *ou* garbage (*US*) dump; ~ **nucléaire** nuclear (waste) dump

dépouiller [depuje] *vt* (*animal*) to skin; (*spolier*) to deprive of one's possessions; (*documents*) to go through, peruse; ~ **qn/qch de** to strip sb/sth of; ~ **le scrutin** to count the votes

dépourvu, e [depuʀvy] *adj*: ~ **de** lacking in, without; **au** ~ *adv*: **prendre qn au** ~ to catch sb unawares

déprécier [depʀesje] *vt* to reduce the value of; **se déprécier** *vi* to depreciate

dépression [depʀɛsjɔ̃] *nf* depression; ~ **(nerveuse)** (nervous) breakdown

déprimant, e [depʀimɑ̃, -ɑ̃t] *adj* depressing

déprimer [depʀime] *vt* to depress

depuis [dəpɥi] *prép* **1** (*point de départ dans le temps*) since; **il habite Paris ~ 1983/l'an dernier** he has been living in Paris since 1983/last year; ~ **quand?** since when?; ~ **quand le connaissez-vous?** how long have you known him?; ~ **lors** since then

2 (*temps écoulé*) for; **il habite Paris ~ cinq ans** he has been living in Paris for five years; **je le connais ~ trois ans** I've known him for three years; ~ **combien de temps êtes-vous ici?** how long have you been here?

3 (*lieu*) : **il a plu ~ Metz** it's been raining since Metz; **elle a téléphoné ~ Valence** she rang from Valence

4 (*quantité, rang*) from; ~ **les plus petits jusqu'aux plus grands** from the youngest to the oldest

▷ *adv* (*temps*) since (then); **je ne lui ai pas parlé** ~ I haven't spoken to him since (then); ~ **que** *conj* (ever) since; ~ **qu'il m'a dit ça** (ever) since he said that to me

député, e [depyte] *nm/f* (*Pol*) deputy, ≈ Member of Parliament (*Brit*), ≈ Congressman/woman (*US*)

députer [depyte] *vt* to delegate; ~ **qn auprès de** to send sb (as a representative) to

déraciner [deʀasine] *vt* to uproot

dérailler [deʀaje] *vi* (*train*) to be derailed, go off *ou* jump the rails; (*fam*) to be completely off the track; **faire** ~ to derail

déraisonner [deʀɛzɔne] *vi* to talk nonsense, rave

dérangement [deʀɑ̃ʒmɑ̃] *nm* (*gêne, déplacement*) trouble; (*gastrique etc*) disorder; (*mécanique*) breakdown; **en** ~ (*téléphone*) out of order

déranger [deʀɑ̃ʒe] *vt* (*personne*) to trouble, bother, disturb; (*projets*) to disrupt, upset; (*objets, vêtements*) to disarrange; **se déranger** to put o.s. out; (*se déplacer*) to (take the trouble to) come (*ou* go) out; **est-ce que cela vous dérange si ...?** do you mind if ...?; **ça te dérangerait de faire ...?** would you mind doing ...?; **ne vous dérangez pas** don't go to any trouble; don't disturb yourself

déraper [deʀape] *vi* (*voiture*) to skid; (*personne, semelles, couteau*) to slip; (*fig: économie etc*) to go out of control

dérégler [deʀegle] *vt* (*mécanisme*) to put out of order, cause to break down; (*estomac*) to upset; **se dérégler** *vi* to break down, go wrong

dérider [deʀide] *vt*: **se dérider** *vi* to cheer up

dérision [deʀizjɔ̃] *nf* derision; **tourner en** ~ to deride; **par** ~ in mockery

dérisoire [deʀizwaʀ] *adj* derisory

dérive [deʀiv] *nf* (*de dériveur*) centre-board; **aller à la** ~ (*Navig, fig*) to drift; ~ **des continents** (*Géo*) continental drift

dérivé, e [deʀive] *adj* derived ▷ *nm* (*Ling*) derivative; (*Tech*) by-product ▷ *nf* (*Math*) derivative

dériver [deʀive] *vt* (*Math*) to derive; (*cours d'eau etc*) to divert ▷ *vi* (*bateau*) to drift; ~ **de** to derive from

dermatologue [dɛʀmatɔlɔg] *nm/f* dermatologist

dernier, -ière [dɛʀnje, -jɛʀ] *adj* (*dans le temps, l'espace*) last; (*le plus récent: gén avant n*) latest, last; (*final, ultime: effort*) final; (*échelon, grade*) top, highest ▷ *nm* (*étage*) top floor; **lundi/le mois** ~ last Monday/month; **du** ~ **chic** extremely smart; **le** ~ **cri** the last word (in fashion); **les** ~**s honneurs** the last tribute; **le** ~ **soupir, rendre le** ~ **soupir** to breathe one's last; **en** ~ *adv* last; **ce** ~, **cette dernière** the latter

dernièrement [dɛʀnjɛʀmɑ̃] *adv* recently

dérobé, e [deʀɔbe] *adj* (*porte*) secret, hidden; **à la** ~**e** surreptitiously

dérober [deʀɔbe] *vt* to steal; (*cacher*): ~ **qch à (la vue de) qn** to conceal *ou* hide sth from sb('s view); **se dérober** *vi* (*s'esquiver*) to slip away; (*fig*) to shy away; **se** ~ **sous** (*s'effondrer*) to give way beneath; **se** ~ **à** (*justice, regards*) to hide from; (*obligation*) to shirk

dérogation [deʀɔgasjɔ̃] *nf* (special) dispensation

déroger [deʀɔʒe] : ~ **à** *vt* to go against, depart from

dérouiller [deʀuje] *vt*: **se** ~ **les jambes** to stretch one's legs

déroulement [deʀulmɑ̃] *nm* (*d'une opération etc*) progress

dérouler [deʀule] *vt* (*ficelle*) to unwind; (*papier*) to unroll; **se dérouler** *vi* to unwind; to unroll, come unrolled; (*avoir lieu*) to take place; (*se passer*) to go

dérouter [deʀute] *vt* (*avion, train*) to reroute, divert; (*étonner*) to disconcert, throw (out)

derrière [dɛʀjɛʀ] *adv, prép* behind ▷ *nm* (*d'une maison*) back; (*postérieur*) behind, bottom; **les pattes de** ~ the back legs, the hind legs; **par** ~ from behind; (*fig*) in an underhand way, behind one's back

des [de] *art voir* **de**

dès [dɛ] *prép* from; ~ **que** *conj* as soon as; ~ **à présent** here and now; ~ **son retour** as soon as he was (*ou* is) back; ~ **réception** upon receipt; ~ **lors** *adv* from then on; ~ **lors que** *conj* from the moment (that)

désabusé, e [dezabyze] *adj* disillusioned

désaccord [dezakɔʀ] *nm* disagreement

désaccordé, e [dezakɔʀde] *adj* (*Mus*) out of tune

désaffecté, e [dezafɛkte] *adj* disused
désagréable [dezagʀeable(ə)] *adj* unpleasant, disagreeable
désagréger [dezagʀeʒe]: **se désagréger** *vi* to disintegrate, break up
désagrément [dezagʀemã] *nm* annoyance, trouble *no pl*
désaltérer [dezalteʀe] *vt*: **se désaltérer** to quench one's thirst; **ça désaltère** it's thirst-quenching, it quenches your thirst
désapprobateur, -trice [dezapʀɔbatœʀ, -tʀis] *adj* disapproving
désapprouver [dezapʀuve] *vt* to disapprove of
désarmant, e [dezaʀmã, -ãt] *adj* disarming
désarroi [dezaʀwa] *nm* helplessness, disarray
désastre [dezastʀ(ə)] *nm* disaster
désastreux, -euse [dezastʀø, -øz] *adj* disastrous
désavantage [dezavãtaʒ] *nm* disadvantage; *(inconvénient)* drawback, disadvantage
désavantager [dezavãtaʒe] *vt* to put at a disadvantage
descendre [desãdʀ(ə)] *vt (escalier, montagne)* to go *(ou* come) down; *(valise, paquet)* to take *ou* get down; *(étagère etc)* to lower; *(fam: abattre)* to shoot down; *(: boire)* to knock back ▷ *vi* to go *(ou* come) down; *(passager: s'arrêter)* to get out, alight; *(niveau, température)* to go *ou* come down, fall, drop; *(marée)* to go out; **~ à pied/en voiture** to walk/drive down, go down on foot/by car; **~ de** *(famille)* to be descended from; **~ du train** to get out *ou* off the train; **~ d'un arbre** to climb down from a tree; **~ de cheval** to dismount, get off one's horse; **~ à l'hôtel** to stay at a hotel; **~ dans la rue** *(manifester)* to take to the streets; **~ en ville** to go into town, go down town
descente [desãt] *nf* descent, going down; *(chemin)* way down; *(Ski)* downhill (race); **au milieu de la ~** halfway down; **freinez dans les ~s** use the brakes going downhill; **~ de lit** bedside rug; **~ (de police)** (police) raid
description [dɛskʀipsjɔ̃] *nf* description
désemparé, e [dezãpaʀe] *adj* bewildered, distraught; *(bateau, avion)* crippled
désemplir [dezãpliʀ] *vi*: **ne pas ~** to be always full
déséquilibre [dezekilibʀ(ə)] *nm (position)*: **être en ~** to be unsteady; *(fig: des forces, du budget)* imbalance; *(Psych)* unbalance
déséquilibré, e [dezekilibʀe] *nm/f (Psych)* unbalanced person
déséquilibrer [dezekilibʀe] *vt* to throw off balance
désert, e [dezɛʀ, -ɛʀt(ə)] *adj* deserted ▷ *nm* desert
déserter [dezɛʀte] *vi, vt* to desert
désertique [dezɛʀtik] *adj* desert *cpd*; *(inculte)* barren, empty
désespéré, e [dezɛspeʀe] *adj* desperate; *(regard)* despairing; **état ~** *(Méd)* hopeless condition
désespérer [dezɛspeʀe] *vt* to drive to despair ▷ *vi*: **se désespérer** *vi* to despair; **~ de** to despair of

désespoir [dezɛspwaʀ] *nm* despair; **être** *ou* **faire le ~ de qn** to be the despair of sb; **en ~ de cause** in desperation
déshabiller [dezabije] *vt* to undress; **se déshabiller** *vi* to undress (o.s.)
déshérité, e [dezeʀite] *adj* disinherited ▷ *nm/f*: **les ~s** *(pauvres)* the underprivileged, the deprived
déshériter [dezeʀite] *vt* to disinherit
déshonneur [dezɔnœʀ] *nm* dishonour (Brit), dishonor (US), disgrace
déshydraté, e [dezidʀate] *adj* dehydrated
desiderata [deziderata] *nmpl* requirements
désigner [dezine] *vt (montrer)* to point out, indicate; *(dénommer)* to denote, refer to; *(nommer: candidat etc)* to name, appoint
désinfectant, e [dezɛ̃fɛktã, -ãt] *adj, nm* disinfectant
désinfecter [dezɛ̃fɛkte] *vt* to disinfect
désintégrer [dezɛ̃tegʀe] *vt* to break up; **se désintégrer** *vi* to disintegrate
désintéressé, e [dezɛ̃teʀese] *adj (généreux, bénévole)* disinterested, unselfish
désintéresser [dezɛ̃teʀese] *vt*: **se désintéresser (de)** to lose interest (in)
désintoxication [dezɛ̃tɔksikasjɔ̃] *nf* treatment for alcoholism *(ou* drug addiction); **faire une cure de ~** to have *ou* undergo treatment for alcoholism *(ou* drug addiction)
désinvolte [dezɛ̃vɔlt(ə)] *adj* casual, off-hand
désinvolture [dezɛ̃vɔltyʀ] *nf* casualness
désir [deziʀ] *nm* wish; *(fort, sensuel)* desire
désirer [deziʀe] *vt* to want, wish for; *(sexuellement)* to desire; **je désire ...** *(formule de politesse)* I would like ...; **il désire que tu l'aides** he would like *ou* he wants you to help him; **~ faire** to want *ou* wish to do; **ça laisse à ~** it leaves something to be desired
désister [deziste]: **se désister** *vi* to stand down, withdraw
désobéir [dezɔbeiʀ] *vi*: **~ (à qn/qch)** to disobey (sb/sth)
désobéissant, e [dezɔbeisã, -ãt] *adj* disobedient
désobligeant, e [dezɔbliʒã, -ãt] *adj* disagreeable, unpleasant
désodorisant [dezɔdɔʀizã] *nm* air freshener, deodorizer
désœuvré, e [dezœvʀe] *adj* idle
désolé, e [dezɔle] *adj (paysage)* desolate; **je suis ~** I'm sorry
désoler [dezɔle] *vt* to distress, grieve; **se désoler** *vi* to be upset
désopilant, e [dezɔpilã, -ãt] *adj* screamingly funny, hilarious
désordonné, e [dezɔʀdɔne] *adj* untidy, disorderly
désordre [dezɔʀdʀ(ə)] *nm* disorder(liness), untidiness; *(anarchie)* disorder; **désordres** *nmpl* (Pol) disturbances, disorder *sg*; **en ~** in a mess, untidy
désorienté, e [dezɔʀjãte] *adj* disorientated; *(fig)* bewildered
désormais [dezɔʀmɛ] *adv* in future, from now on

désosser [dezɔse] vt to bone

desquels, desquelles [dekɛl] *prép+pron voir* **lequel**

desséché, e [deseʃe] *adj* dried up

dessécher [deseʃe] vt (*terre, plante*) to dry out, parch; (*peau*) to dry out; (*volontairement: aliments etc*) to dry, dehydrate; (*fig: cœur*) to harden; **se dessécher** vi to dry out; (*peau, lèvres*) to go dry

dessein [desɛ̃] nm design; **dans le ~ de** with the intention of; **à ~** intentionally, deliberately

desserrer [desere] vt to loosen; (*frein*) to release; (*poing, dents*) to unclench; (*objets alignés*) to space out; **ne pas ~ les dents** not to open one's mouth

dessert [deser] vb voir **desservir** ▷ nm dessert, pudding

desserte [desert(ə)] nf (*table*) side table; (*transport*): **la ~ du village est assurée par autocar** there is a coach service to the village; **chemin** ou **voie de ~** service road

desservir [deservir] vt (*ville, quartier*) to serve; (*: voie de communication*) to lead into; (*vicaire: paroisse*) to serve; (*nuire à: personne*) to do a disservice to; (*débarrasser*): **~ (la table)** to clear the table

dessin [desɛ̃] nm (*œuvre, art*) drawing; (*motif*) pattern, design; (*contour*) (out)line; **le ~ industriel** draughtsmanship (*Brit*), draftsmanship (*US*); **~ animé** cartoon (film); **~ humoristique** cartoon

dessinateur, -trice [desinatœr, -tris] nm/ f drawer; (*de bandes dessinées*) cartoonist; (*industriel*) draughtsman (*Brit*), draftsman (*US*); **dessinatrice de mode** fashion designer

dessiner [desine] vt to draw; (*concevoir: carrosserie, maison*) to design; (*robe: taille*) to show off; **se dessiner** vi (*forme*) to be outlined; (*fig: solution*) to emerge

dessous [dəsu] adv underneath, beneath ▷ nm underside; (*étage inférieur*): **les voisins du ~** the downstairs neighbours ▷ nmpl (*sous-vêtements*) underwear sg; (*fig*) hidden aspects; **en ~** underneath; below; (*fig: en catimini*) slyly, on the sly; **par ~** underneath; below; **de ~ le lit** from under the bed; **au-~** adv below; **au-~ de** prép below; (*peu digne de*) beneath; **au-~ de tout** the (absolute) limit; **avoir le ~** to get the worst of it

dessous-de-plat [dəsudpla] nm inv tablemat

dessus [dəsy] adv on top; (*collé, écrit*) on it ▷ nm top; (*étage supérieur*): **les voisins/l'appartement du ~** the upstairs neighbours/flat; **en ~** above; **par ~** adv over it ▷ prép over; **au-~** above; **au-~ de** above; **avoir/prendre le ~** to have/get the upper hand; **reprendre le ~** to get over it; **bras ~ bras dessous** arm in arm; **sens ~ dessous** upside down; voir **ci-**; **là-**

dessus-de-lit [dəsydli] nm inv bedspread

destin [destɛ̃] nm fate; (*avenir*) destiny

destinataire [destinatɛr] nm/f (*Postes*) addressee; (*d'un colis*) consignee; (*d'un mandat*) payee; **aux risques et périls du ~** at owner's risk

destination [destinasjɔ̃] nf (*lieu*) destination; (*usage*) purpose; **à ~ de** (*avion etc*) bound for; (*voyageur*) bound for, travelling to

destinée [destine] nf fate; (*existence, avenir*) destiny

destiner [destine] vt: **~ qn à** (*poste, sort*) to destine sb for; **~ qn/qch à** (*prédestiner*) to mark sb/sth out for; **~ qch à** (*envisager d'affecter*) to intend to use sth for; **~ qch à** (*envisager de donner*) to intend to give sth to sb, intend sb to have sth; (*adresser*) to intend sth for sb; **se ~ à l'enseignement** to intend to become a teacher; **être destiné à** (*sort*) to be destined to + verbe; (*usage*) to be intended ou meant for; (*sort*) to be in store for

destruction [destryksjɔ̃] nf destruction

désuet, -ète [desɥe, -ɛt] adj outdated, outmoded

détachant [detaʃɑ̃] nm stain remover

détachement [detaʃmɑ̃] nm detachment; (*fonctionnaire, employé*): **être en ~** to be on secondment (*Brit*) ou a posting

détacher [detaʃe] vt (*enlever*) to detach, remove; (*délier*) to untie; (*Admin*): **~ qn (auprès de** ou **à)** to send sb on secondment (to) (*Brit*), post sb (to); (*Mil*) to detail; (*vêtement: nettoyer*) to remove the stains from; **se détacher** vi (*tomber*) to come off; to come out; (*se défaire*) to come undone; (*Sport*) to pull ou break away; (*se délier: chien, prisonnier*) to break loose; **se ~ sur** to stand out against; **se ~ de** (*se désintéresser*) to grow away from

détail [detaj] nm detail; (*Comm*): **le ~** retail; **prix de ~** retail price; **au ~** adv (*Comm*) retail; (*: individuellement*) separately; **donner le ~ de** to give a detailed account of; (*compte*) to give a breakdown of; **en ~** in detail

détaillant, e [detajɑ̃, -ɑ̃t] nm/f retailer

détaillé, e [detaje] adj (*récit*) detailed

détailler [detaje] vt to sell retail; to sell separately; (*expliquer*) to explain in detail; to detail; (*examiner*) to look over, examine

détaler [detale] vi (*lapin*) to scamper off; (*fam: personne*) to make off, scarper (*fam*)

détartrant [detartrɑ̃] nm descaling agent (*Brit*), scale remover

détaxer [detakse] vt (*réduire*) to reduce the tax on; (*ôter*) to remove the tax on

détecter [detɛkte] vt to detect

détective [detɛktiv] nm detective; **~ (privé)** private detective ou investigator

déteindre [detɛ̃dr(ə)] vi to fade; (*fig*): **~ sur** to rub off on

détendre [detɑ̃dr(ə)] vt (*fil*) to slacken, loosen; (*personne, atmosphère*) to relax; (*: situation*) to relieve; **se détendre** vi to lose its tension; to relax

détenir [detnir] vt (*fortune, objet, secret*) to be in possession of; (*prisonnier*) to detain; (*record*) to hold; **~ le pouvoir** to be in power

détente [detɑ̃t] nf relaxation; (*Pol*) détente; (*d'une arme*) trigger; (*d'un athlète qui saute*) spring

détention [detɑ̃sjɔ̃] nf (*voir détenir*) possession; detention; holding; **~ préventive** (pre-trial) custody

détenu, e [detny] pp de **détenir** ▷ nm/f prisoner

détergent [detɛrʒɑ̃] *nm* detergent
détériorer [deterjɔre] *vt* to damage; **se détériorer** *vi* to deteriorate
déterminé, e [detɛrmine] *adj* (*résolu*) determined; (*précis*) specific, definite
déterminer [detɛrmine] *vt* (*fixer*) to determine; (*décider*): **~ qn à faire** to decide sb to do; **se ~ à faire** to make up one's mind to do
déterrer [detere] *vt* to dig up
détestable [detɛstabl(ə)] *adj* foul, detestable
détester [detɛste] *vt* to hate, detest
détonner [detɔne] *vi* (*Mus*) to go out of tune; (*fig*) to clash
détour [detur] *nm* detour; (*tournant*) bend, curve; (*fig: subterfuge*) roundabout means; **sans ~** (*fig*) plainly
détourné, e [deturne] *adj* (*sentier, chemin, moyen*) roundabout
détournement [deturnəmɑ̃] *nm* diversion, rerouting; **~ d'avion** hijacking; **~ (de fonds)** embezzlement *ou* misappropriation (of funds); **~ de mineur** corruption of a minor
détourner [deturne] *vt* to divert; (*avion*) to divert, reroute; (: *par la force*) to hijack; (*yeux, tête*) to turn away; (*de l'argent*) to embezzle, misappropriate; **se détourner** to turn away; **~ la conversation** to change the subject; **~ qn de son devoir** to divert sb from his duty; **~ l'attention (de qn)** to distract *ou* divert (sb's) attention
détracteur, -trice [detraktœr, -tris] *nm/f* disparager, critic
détraquer [detrake] *vt* to put out of order; (*estomac*) to upset; **se détraquer** *vi* to go wrong
détrempé, e [detrɑ̃pe] *adj* (*sol*) sodden, waterlogged
détresse [detrɛs] *nf* distress; **en ~** (*avion etc*) in distress; **appel/signal de ~** distress call/signal
détriment [detrimɑ̃] *nm*: **au ~ de** to the detriment of
détritus [detritys] *nmpl* rubbish *sg*, refuse *sg*, garbage *sg* (US)
détroit [detrwa] *nm* strait; **le ~ de Bering** *ou* **Behring** the Bering Strait; **le ~ de Gibraltar** the Straits of Gibraltar; **le ~ du Bosphore** the Bosphorus; **le ~ de Magellan** the Strait of Magellan, the Magellan Strait
détromper [detrɔ̃pe] *vt* to disabuse; **se détromper** *vi*: **détrompez-vous** don't believe it
détruire [detruir] *vt* to destroy; (*fig: santé, réputation*) to ruin; (*documents*) to shred
dette [dɛt] *nf* debt; **~ publique** *ou* **de l'État** national debt
DEUG [døg] *sigle m* = **Diplôme d'études universitaires générales**; *see note*
deuil [dœj] *nm* (*perte*) bereavement; (*période*) mourning; (*chagrin*) grief; **porter le ~** to wear mourning; **prendre le/être en ~** to go into/be in mourning
deux [dø] *num* two; **les ~** both; **ses ~ mains** both his hands, his two hands; **à ~ pas** a short distance away; **tous les ~ mois** every two

months, every other month; **~ points** colon *sg*
deuxième [døzjɛm] *num* second
deuxièmement [døzjɛmmɑ̃] *adv* secondly, in the second place
deux-pièces [døpjɛs] *nm inv* (*tailleur*) two-piece (suit); (*de bain*) two-piece (swimsuit); (*appartement*) two-roomed flat (Brit) *ou* apartment (US)
deux-roues [døru] *nm* two-wheeled vehicle
devais *etc* [dəvɛ] *vb voir* **devoir**
dévaler [devale] *vt* to hurtle down
dévaliser [devalize] *vt* to rob, burgle
dévaloriser [devalɔrize] *vt* to reduce the value of; **se dévaloriser** *vi* to depreciate
dévaluation [devalɥasjɔ̃] *nf* depreciation; (*Écon: mesure*) devaluation
devancer [dəvɑ̃se] *vt* to be ahead of; (*distancer*) to get ahead of; (*arriver avant*) to arrive before; (*prévenir*) to anticipate; **~ l'appel** (*Mil*) to enlist before call-up
devant [dəvɑ̃] *vb voir* **devoir** ▷ *adv* in front; (*à distance: en avant*) ahead ▷ *prép* in front of; ahead of; (*avec mouvement: passer*) past; (*fig*) before, in front of; (: *face à*) faced with, in the face of; (: *vu*) in view of ▷ *nm* front; **prendre les ~s** to make the first move; **de ~** (*roue, porte*) front; **les pattes de ~** the front legs, the forelegs; **par ~** (*boutonner*) at the front; (*entrer*) the front way; **par-~ notaire** in the presence of a notary; **aller au-~ de qn** to go out to meet sb; **aller au-~ de** (*désirs de qn*) to anticipate; **aller au-~ des ennuis** *ou* **difficultés** to be asking for trouble
devanture [dəvɑ̃tyr] *nf* (*façade*) (shop) front; (*étalage*) display; (shop) window
déveine [devɛn] *nf* rotten luck *no pl*
développement [devlɔpmɑ̃] *nm* development
développer [devlɔpe] *vt*: **se développer** *vi* to develop
devenir [dəvnir] *vi* to become; **~ instituteur** to become a teacher; **que sont-ils devenus?** what has become of them?
dévergondé, e [devɛrgɔ̃de] *adj* wild, shameless
déverser [devɛrse] *vt* (*liquide*) to pour (out); (*ordures*) to tip (out); **se ~ dans** (*fleuve, mer*) to flow into
dévêtir [devetir] *vt*: **se dévêtir** *vi* to undress
devez [dəve] *vb voir* **devoir**
déviation [devjasjɔ̃] *nf* deviation; (*Auto*) diversion (Brit), detour (US); **~ de la colonne (vertébrale)** curvature of the spine
dévier [devje] *vt* (*fleuve, circulation*) to divert; (*coup*) to deflect ▷ *vi* to veer (off course); (**faire**) ~ (*projectile*) to deflect; (*véhicule*) to push off course
devin [dəvɛ̃] *nm* soothsayer, seer
deviner [dəvine] *vt* to guess; (*prévoir*) to foretell, foresee; (*apercevoir*) to distinguish
devinette [dəvinɛt] *nf* riddle
devis [dəvi] *nm* estimate, quotation; **~ descriptif/estimatif** detailed/preliminary estimate
dévisager [devizaʒe] *vt* to stare at
devise [dəviz] *nf* (*formule*) motto, watchword;

(*Écon: monnaie*) currency; **devises** *nfpl* (*argent*) currency *sg*

deviser [dəvize] *vi* to converse

dévisser [devise] *vt* to unscrew, undo; **se dévisser** *vi* to come unscrewed

dévoiler [devwale] *vt* to unveil

devoir [dəvwaʀ] *nm* duty; (*Scol*) piece of homework, homework *no pl*; (: *en classe*) exercise ▷ *vt* (*argent, respect*): ~ **qch (à qn)** to owe (sb) sth; (*suivi de l'infinitif: obligation*): **il doit le faire** he has to do it, he must do it; (: *fatalité*): **cela devait arriver un jour** it was bound to happen; (: *intention*): **il doit partir demain** he is (due) to leave tomorrow; (: *probabilité*): **il doit être tard** it must be late; **se faire un ~ de faire qch** to make it one's duty to do sth; **~s de vacances** homework set for the holidays; **se ~ de faire qch** to be duty bound to do sth; **je devrais faire** I ought to *ou* should do; **tu n'aurais pas dû** you ought not to have *ou* shouldn't have; **comme il se doit** (*comme il faut*) as is right and proper

dévolu, e [devɔly] *adj*: ~ **à** allotted to ▷ *nm*: **jeter son ~ sur** to fix one's choice on

dévorer [devɔʀe] *vt* to devour; (*feu, soucis*) to consume; ~ **qn/qch des yeux** *ou* **du regard** (*fig*) to eye sb/sth intently; (: *convoitise*) to eye sb/sth greedily

dévot, e [devo, -ɔt] *adj* devout, pious ▷ *nm/f* devout person; **un faux ~** a falsely pious person

dévotion [devosjɔ̃] *nf* devoutness; **être à la ~ de qn** to be totally devoted to sb; **avoir une ~ pour qn** to worship sb

dévoué, e [devwe] *adj* devoted

dévouement [devumã] *nm* devotion, dedication

dévouer [devwe]: **se dévouer** *vi* (*se sacrifier*): **se ~ (pour)** to sacrifice o.s. (for); (*se consacrer*): **se ~ à** to devote *ou* dedicate o.s. to

dévoyé, e [devwaje] *adj* delinquent

devrai *etc* [dəvʀe] *vb voir* **devoir**

dézipper [dezipe] *vt* (*Inform*) to unzip

diabète [djabɛt] *nm* diabetes *sg*

diabétique [djabetik] *nm/f* diabetic

diable [djabl(ə)] *nm* devil; **une musique du ~** an unholy racket; **il fait une chaleur du ~** it's fiendishly hot; **avoir le ~ au corps** to be the very devil

diabolo [djabɔlo] *nm* (*jeu*) diabolo; (*boisson*) lemonade and fruit cordial; **~(-menthe)** lemonade and mint cordial

diagnostic [djagnɔstik] *nm* diagnosis *sg*

diagnostiquer [djagnɔstike] *vt* to diagnose

diagonal, e, -aux [djagɔnal, -o] *adj, nf* diagonal; **en ~e** diagonally; **lire en ~e** (*fig*) to skim through

diagramme [djagʀam] *nm* chart, graph

dialecte [djalɛkt(ə)] *nm* dialect

dialogue [djalɔg] *nm* dialogue; **~ de sourds** dialogue of the deaf

diamant [djamã] *nm* diamond

diamètre [djamɛtʀ(ə)] *nm* diameter

diapason [djapazɔ̃] *nm* tuning fork; (*fig*): **être/se mettre au ~ (de)** to be/get in tune (with)

diaphragme [djafʀagm(ə)] *nm* (*Anat, Photo*)

diaphragm; (*contraceptif*) diaphragm, cap; **ouverture du ~** (*Photo*) aperture

diapo [djapo], **diapositive** [djapozitiv] *nf* transparency, slide

diarrhée [djaʀe] *nf* diarrhoea (*Brit*), diarrhea (*US*)

dictateur [diktatœʀ] *nm* dictator

dictature [diktatyʀ] *nf* dictatorship

dictée [dikte] *nf* dictation; **prendre sous ~** to take down (*sth dictated*)

dicter [dikte] *vt* to dictate

dictionnaire [diksjɔnɛʀ] *nm* dictionary; **~ géographique** gazetteer

dicton [diktɔ̃] *nm* saying, dictum

dièse [djɛz] *nm* (*Mus*) sharp

diesel [djezɛl] *nm, adj inv* diesel

diète [djɛt] *nf* diet; **être à la ~** to be on a diet

diététique [djetetik] *nf* dietetics *sg* ▷ *adj*: **magasin ~** health food shop (*Brit*) *ou* store (*US*)

dieu, x [djø] *nm* god; **D~** God; **le bon D~** the good Lord; **mon D~!** good heavens!

diffamation [difamasjɔ̃] *nf* slander; (*écrite*) libel; **attaquer qn en ~** to sue sb for slander (*ou* libel)

différé [difeʀe] *adj* (*Inform*): **traitement ~** batch processing; **crédit ~** deferred credit ▷ *nm* (*TV*): **en ~** (pre-)recorded

différemment [difeʀamã] *adv* differently

différence [difeʀɑ̃s] *nf* difference; **à la ~ de** unlike

différencier [difeʀɑ̃sje] *vt* to differentiate; **se différencier** *vi* (*organisme*) to become differentiated; **se ~ de** to differentiate o.s. from; (*être différent*) to differ from

différend [difeʀɑ̃] *nm* difference (of opinion), disagreement

différent, e [difeʀɑ̃, -ɑ̃t] *adj*: ~ **(de)** different (from); **~s objets** different *ou* various objects; **à ~es reprises** on various occasions

différer [difeʀe] *vt* to postpone, put off ▷ *vi*: ~ **(de)** to differ (from); **~ de faire** (*tarder*) to delay doing

difficile [difisil] *adj* difficult; (*exigeant*) hard to please, difficult (to please); **faire le** *ou* **la ~** to be hard to please, be difficult

difficilement [difisilmã] *adv* (*marcher, s'expliquer etc*) with difficulty; **~ lisible/compréhensible** difficult *ou* hard to read/understand

difficulté [difikylte] *nf* difficulty; **en ~** (*bateau, alpiniste*) in trouble *ou* difficulties; **avoir de la ~ à faire** to have difficulty (in) doing

difforme [difɔʀm(ə)] *adj* deformed, misshapen

diffuser [difyze] *vt* (*chaleur, bruit, lumière*) to diffuse; (*émission, musique*) to broadcast; (*nouvelle, idée*) to circulate; (*Comm: livres, journaux*) to distribute

digérer [diʒeʀe] *vt* (*personne*) to digest; (: *machine*) to process; (*fig: accepter*) to stomach, put up with

digestif, -ive [diʒɛstif, -iv] *adj* digestive ▷ *nm* (after-dinner) liqueur

digestion [diʒɛstjɔ̃] *nf* digestion

digne [diɲ] *adj* dignified; **~ de** worthy of; **~ de foi** trustworthy

dignité [diɲite] *nf* dignity

digue [dig] *nf* dike, dyke; (*pour protéger la côte*) sea wall

dilapider [dilapide] *vt* to squander, waste; (*détourner: biens, fonds publics*) to embezzle, misappropriate

dilemme [dilɛm] *nm* dilemma

dilettante [diletãt] *nm/f* dilettante; **en ~** in a dilettantish way

diligence [diliʒãs] *nf* stagecoach, diligence; (*empressement*) despatch; **faire ~** to make haste

diluer [dilɥe] *vt* to dilute

diluvien, ne [dilyvjɛ̃, -ɛn] *adj*: **pluie ~ne** torrential rain

dimanche [dimãʃ] *nm* Sunday; **le ~ des Rameaux/de Pâques** Palm/Easter Sunday; *voir aussi* **lundi**

dimension [dimãsjɔ̃] *nf* (*grandeur*) size; (*gén pl: cotes, Math: de l'espace*) dimension

diminué, e [diminɥe] *adj* (*personne: physiquement*) run-down; (: *mentalement*) less alert

diminuer [diminɥe] *vt* to reduce, decrease; (*ardeur etc*) to lessen; (*personne: physiquement*) to undermine; (*dénigrer*) to belittle ▷ *vi* to decrease, diminish

diminutif [diminytif] *nm* (*Ling*) diminutive; (*surnom*) pet name

diminution [diminysjɔ̃] *nf* decreasing, diminishing

dinde [dɛ̃d] *nf* turkey; (*femme stupide*) goose

dindon [dɛ̃dɔ̃] *nm* turkey

dîner [dine] *nm* dinner ▷ *vi* to have dinner; **~ d'affaires/de famille** business/family dinner

dingue [dɛ̃g] *adj* (*fam*) crazy

dinosaure [dinozɔʀ] *nm* dinosaur

diplomate [diplɔmat] *adj* diplomatic ▷ *nm* diplomat; (*fig: personne habile*) diplomatist; (*Culin: gâteau*) dessert made of sponge cake, candied fruit and custard, ≈ trifle (*Brit*)

diplomatie [diplɔmasi] *nf* diplomacy

diplôme [diplom] *nm* diploma certificate; (*examen*) (diploma) examination

diplômé, e [diplome] *adj* qualified

dire [diʀ] *nm*: **au ~ de** according to; **leurs ~s** what they say ▷ *vt* to say; (*secret, mensonge*) to tell; **~ l'heure/la vérité** to tell the time/the truth; **dis pardon/merci** say sorry/thank you; **~ qch à qn** to tell sb sth; **~ à qn qu'il fasse** *ou* **de faire** to tell sb to do; **~ que** to say that; **on dit que** they say that; **comme on dit** as they say; **on dirait que** it looks (*ou* sounds *etc*) as though; **on dirait du vin** you'd *ou* one would think it was wine; **que dites-vous de** (*penser*) what do you think of; **si cela lui dit** if he feels like it, if he fancies it; **cela ne me dit rien** that doesn't appeal to me; **à vrai ~** truth to tell; **pour ainsi ~** so to speak; **cela va sans ~** that goes without saying; **dis donc!, dites donc!** (*pour attirer l'attention*) hey!; (*au fait*) by the way; **et ~ que …** to think that …; **ceci** *ou* **cela dit** that being said; (*à ces mots*) whereupon; **c'est dit, voilà qui est dit** so that's settled; **il n'y a pas à ~** there's no getting away from it; **c'est ~ si …** that just shows that

…; **c'est beaucoup/peu ~** that's saying a lot/not saying much; **se dire** *vi* (*à soi-même*) to say to oneself; (*se prétendre*): **se ~ malade** *etc* to say (that) one is ill *etc*; **ça se dit … en anglais** that is … in English; **cela ne se dit pas comme ça** you don't say it like that; **se ~ au revoir** to say goodbye (to each other)

direct, e [diʀɛkt] *adj* direct ▷ *nm* (*train*) through train; **en ~** (*émission*) live; **train/bus ~** express train/bus

directement [diʀɛktəmã] *adv* directly

directeur, -trice [diʀɛktœʀ, -tʀis] *nm/f* (*d'entreprise*) director; (*de service*) manager/eress; (*d'école*) head(teacher) (*Brit*), principal (*US*); **comité ~** management *ou* steering committee; **~ général** general manager; **~ de thèse** ≈ PhD supervisor

direction [diʀɛksjɔ̃] *nf* management; conducting; supervision; (*Auto*) steering; (*sens*) direction; **sous la ~ de** (*Mus*) conducted by; **en ~ de** (*avion, train, bateau*) for; **"toutes ~s"** (*Auto*) "all routes"

dirent [diʀ] *vb voir* **dire**

dirigeant, e [diʀiʒã, -ãt] *adj* managerial; (*classes*) ruling ▷ *nm/f* (*d'un parti etc*) leader; (*d'entreprise*) manager, member of the management

diriger [diʀiʒe] *vt* (*entreprise*) to manage, run; (*véhicule*) to steer; (*orchestre*) to conduct; (*recherches, travaux*) to supervise, be in charge of; (*braquer: regard, arme*): **~ sur** to point *ou* level *ou* aim at; (*fig: critiques*): **~ contre** to aim at; **se diriger** *vi* (*s'orienter*) to find one's way; **se ~ vers** *ou* **sur** to make *ou* head for

dis [di], **disais** *etc* [dize] *vb voir* **dire**

discernement [disɛʀnəmã] *nm* discernment, judgment

discerner [disɛʀne] *vt* to discern, make out

discipline [disiplin] *nf* discipline

discipliner [disipline] *vt* to discipline; (*cheveux*) to control

discontinu, e [diskɔ̃tiny] *adj* intermittent; (*bande: sur la route*) broken

discontinuer [diskɔ̃tinɥe] *vi*: **sans ~** without stopping, without a break

discordant, e [diskɔʀdã, -ãt] *adj* discordant; conflicting

discothèque [diskɔtɛk] *nf* (*disques*) record collection; (: *dans une bibliothèque*): **~ (de prêt)** record library; (*boîte de nuit*) disco(thèque)

discours [diskuʀ] *vb voir* **discourir** ▷ *nm* speech; **~ direct/indirect** (*Ling*) direct/indirect *ou* reported speech

discret, -ète [diskʀɛ, -ɛt] *adj* discreet; (*fig: musique, style*) unobtrusive; (: *endroit*) quiet

discrétion [diskʀesjɔ̃] *nf* discretion; **à la ~ de qn** at sb's discretion; in sb's hands; **à ~** (*boisson etc*) unlimited, as much as one wants

discrimination [diskʀiminasjɔ̃] *nf* discrimination; **sans ~** indiscriminately

disculper [diskylpe] *vt* to exonerate

discussion [diskysjɔ̃] *nf* discussion

discutable [diskytabl(ə)] *adj* (*contestable*)

doubtful; (*à débattre*) debatable

discuté, e [diskyte] *adj* controversial

discuter [diskyte] *vt* (*contester*) to question, dispute; (*débattre: prix*) to discuss ▷ *vi* to talk; (*ergoter*) to argue; ~ **de** to discuss

dise *etc* [diz] *vb voir* **dire**

diseuse [dizøz] *nf*: ~ **de bonne aventure** fortune-teller

disgracieux, -euse [disgRasjø, -øz] *adj* ungainly, awkward

disjoindre [disʒwɛ̃dR(ə)] *vt* to take apart; **se disjoindre** *vi* to come apart

disjoncteur [disʒɔ̃ktœR] *nm* (*Élec*) circuit breaker

disloquer [dislɔke] *vt* (*membre*) to dislocate; (*chaise*) to dismantle; (*troupe*) to disperse; **se disloquer** *vi* (*parti, empire*) to break up; **se ~ l'épaule** to dislocate one's shoulder

disons *etc* [dizɔ̃] *vb voir* **dire**

disparaître [dispaRɛtR(ə)] *vi* to disappear; (*à la vue*) to vanish, disappear; to be hidden *ou* concealed; (*être manquant*) to go missing, disappear; (*se perdre: traditions etc*) to die out; (*personne: mourir*) to die; **faire ~** (*objet, tache, trace*) to remove; (*personne*) to get rid of

disparition [dispaRisjɔ̃] *nf* disappearance

disparu, e [dispaRy] *pp de* **disparaître** ▷ *nm/f* missing person; (*défunt*) departed; **être porté ~** to be reported missing

dispensaire [dispɑ̃sɛR] *nm* community clinic

dispenser [dispɑ̃se] *vt* (*donner*) to lavish, bestow; (*exempter*): ~ **qn de** to exempt sb from; **se ~ de** *vt* to avoid, get out of

disperser [dispɛRse] *vt* to scatter; (*fig: son attention*) to dissipate; **se disperser** *vi* to scatter; (*fig*) to dissipate one's efforts

disponibilité [disponibilite] *nf* availability; (*Admin*): **être en ~** to be on leave of absence; **disponibilités** *nfpl* (*Comm*) liquid assets

disponible [disponibl(ə)] *adj* available

dispos [dispo] *adj m*: (**frais et**) **~** fresh (as a daisy)

disposé, e [dispoze] *adj* (*d'une certaine manière*) arranged, laid-out; **bien/mal ~** (*humeur*) in a good/bad mood; **bien/mal ~ pour** *ou* **envers qn** well/badly disposed towards sb; **~ à** (*prêt à*) willing *ou* prepared to

disposer [dispoze] *vt* (*arranger, placer*) to arrange; (*inciter*): ~ **qn à qch/faire qch** to dispose *ou* incline sb towards sth/to do sth ▷ *vi*: **vous pouvez ~** you may leave; **~ de** *vt* to have (at one's disposal); **se ~ à faire** to prepare to do, be about to do

dispositif [dispozitif] *nm* device; (*fig*) system, plan of action; set-up; (*d'un texte de loi*) operative part; **~ de sûreté** safety device

disposition [dispozisjɔ̃] *nf* (*arrangement*) arrangement, layout; (*humeur*) mood; (*tendance*) tendency; **dispositions** *nfpl* (*mesures*) steps, measures; (*préparatifs*) arrangements; (*de loi, testament*) provisions; (*aptitudes*) bent *sg*, aptitude *sg*; **à la ~ de qn** at sb's disposal

disproportionné, e [dispRɔpɔRsjɔne] *adj* disproportionate, out of all proportion

dispute [dispyt] *nf* quarrel, argument

disputer [dispyte] *vt* (*match*) to play; (*combat*) to fight; (*course*) to run; **se disputer** *vi* to quarrel, have a quarrel; (*match, combat, course*) to take place; **~ qch à qn** to fight with sb for *ou* over sth

disquaire [diskɛR] *nm/f* record dealer

disqualifier [diskalifje] *vt* to disqualify; **se disqualifier** *vi* to bring discredit on o.s.

disque [disk(ə)] *nm* (*Mus*) record; (*Inform*) disk, disc; (*forme, pièce*) disc; (*Sport*) discus; **~ compact** compact disc; **~ compact interactif** CD-I®; **~ dur** hard disk; **~ d'embrayage** (*Auto*) clutch plate; **~ laser** compact disc; **~ de stationnement** parking disc; **~ système** system disk

disquette [diskɛt] *nf* diskette, floppy (disk)

disséminer [disemine] *vt* to scatter; (*troupes: sur un territoire*) to disperse

disséquer [diseke] *vt* to dissect

dissertation [disɛRtasjɔ̃] *nf* (*Scol*) essay

dissimuler [disimyle] *vt* to conceal; **se dissimuler** *vi* to conceal o.s.; to be concealed

dissipé, e [disipe] *adj* (*indiscipliné*) unruly

dissiper [disipe] *vt* to dissipate; (*fortune*) to squander, fritter away; **se dissiper** *vi* (*brouillard*) to clear, disperse; (*doutes*) to disappear, melt away; (*élève*) to become undisciplined *ou* unruly

dissolvant, e [disɔlvɑ̃, -ɑ̃t] *vb voir* **dissoudre** ▷ *nm* (*Chimie*) solvent; **~ (gras)** nail polish remover

dissonant, e [disɔnɑ̃, -ɑ̃t] *adj* discordant

dissoudre [disudR(ə)] *vt*: **se dissoudre** *vi* to dissolve

dissuader [disɥade] *vt*: **~ qn de faire/de qch** to dissuade sb from doing/from sth

dissuasion [disɥazjɔ̃] *nf* dissuasion; **force de ~** deterrent power

distance [distɑ̃s] *nf* distance; (*fig: écart*) gap; **à ~** at *ou* from a distance; (*mettre en marche, commander*) by remote control; (**situé**) **à ~** (*Inform*) remote; **tenir qn à ~** to keep sb at a distance; **se tenir à ~** to keep one's distance; **à une ~ de 10 km, à 10 km de ~** 10 km away, at a distance of 10 km; **à deux ans de ~** with a gap of two years; **prendre ses ~s** to space out; **garder ses ~s** to keep one's distance; **tenir la ~** (*Sport*) to cover the distance, last the course; **~ focale** (*Photo*) focal length

distancer [distɑ̃se] *vt* to outdistance, leave behind

distant, e [distɑ̃, -ɑ̃t] *adj* (*réservé*) distant, aloof; (*éloigné*) distant, far away; **~ de** (*lieu*) far away *ou* a long way from; **~ de 5 km (d'un lieu)** 5 km away (from a place)

distendre [distɑ̃dR(ə)] *vt*: **se distendre** *vi* to distend

distillerie [distilRi] *nf* distillery

distinct, e [distɛ̃(kt), distɛ̃kt(ə)] *adj* distinct

distinctement [distɛ̃ktəmɑ̃] *adv* distinctly

distinctif, -ive [distɛ̃ktif, -iv] *adj* distinctive

distingué, e [distɛ̃ge] *adj* distinguished

distinguer [distɛ̃ge] *vt* to distinguish; **se distinguer** *vi* (*s'illustrer*) to distinguish o.s.;

(*différer*): **se ~ (de)** to distinguish o.s. *ou* be
distinguished (from)
distraction [distraksjɔ̃] *nf* (*manque
d'attention*) absent-mindedness; (*oubli*) lapse
(in concentration *ou* attention); (*détente*)
diversion, recreation; (*passe-temps*) distraction,
entertainment
distraire [distrɛr] *vt* (*déranger*) to distract;
(*divertir*) to entertain, divert; (*détourner: somme
d'argent*) to divert, misappropriate; **se distraire** *vi*
to amuse *ou* enjoy o.s.
distrait, e [distrɛ, -ɛt] *pp de* **distraire** ▷ *adj*
absent-minded
distrayant, e [distrɛjɑ̃, -ɑ̃t] *vb voir* **distraire** ▷ *adj*
entertaining
distribuer [distribɥe] *vt* to distribute; to hand
out; (*Cartes*) to deal (out); (*courrier*) to deliver
distributeur [distribytœr] *nm* (*Auto, Comm*)
distributor; (*automatique*) (vending) machine; **~
de billets** (*Rail*) ticket machine; (*Banque*) cash
dispenser
distribution [distribysjɔ̃] *nf* distribution;
(*postale*) delivery; (*choix d'acteurs*) casting;
circuits de ~ (*Comm*) distribution network; **~
des prix** (*Scol*) prize giving
dit, e [di, dit] *pp de* **dire** ▷ *adj* (*fixé*) **le jour ~** the
arranged day; (*surnommé*): **X, ~ Pierrot** X, known
as *ou* called Pierrot
dites [dit] *vb voir* **dire**
divaguer [divage] *vi* to ramble; (*malade*) to rave
divan [divɑ̃] *nm* divan
diverger [divɛrʒe] *vi* to diverge
divers, e [divɛr, -ɛrs(ə)] *adj* (*varié*) diverse,
varied; (*différent*) different, various; (**frais**) **~**
(*Comm*) sundries, miscellaneous (expenses); **"~"**
(*rubrique*) "miscellaneous"
diversifier [divɛrsifje] *vt*: **se diversifier** *vi* to
diversify
diversité [divɛrsite] *nf* diversity, variety
divertir [divɛrtir] *vt* to amuse, entertain; **se
divertir** *vi* to amuse *ou* enjoy o.s.
divertissement [divɛrtismɑ̃] *nm*
entertainment; (*Mus*) divertimento,
divertissement
divin, e [divɛ̃, -in] *adj* divine; (*fig: excellent*)
heavenly, divine
diviser [divize] *vt* (*gén, Math*) to divide; (*morceler,
subdiviser*) to divide (up), split (up); **se ~ en** to
divide into; **~ par** to divide by
division [divizjɔ̃] *nf* (*gén*) division; **~ du travail**
(*Écon*) division of labour
divorce [divɔrs(ə)] *nm* divorce
divorcé, e [divɔrse] *nm/f* divorcee
divorcer [divɔrse] *vi* to get a divorce, get
divorced; **~ de** *ou* **d'avec qn** to divorce sb
divulguer [divylge] *vt* to divulge, disclose
dix [di, dis, diz] *num* ten
dixième [dizjɛm] *num* tenth
dizaine [dizɛn] *nf* (10) ten; (*environ 10*): **une ~ (de)**
about ten, ten or so
do [do] *nm* (*note*) C; (*en chantant la gamme*) do(h)
docile [dɔsil] *adj* docile

dock [dɔk] *nm* dock; (*hangar, bâtiment*) warehouse
docker [dɔkɛr] *nm* docker
docteur [dɔktœr] *nm/f* doctor; **~ en médecine**
doctor of medicine
doctorat [dɔktɔra] *nm*: **~ (d'Université)**
≈ doctorate; **~ d'État** ≈ PhD; **~ de troisième
cycle** ≈ doctorate
doctoresse [dɔktɔrɛs] *nf* lady doctor
doctrine [dɔktrin] *nf* doctrine
document [dɔkymɑ̃] *nm* document
documentaire [dɔkymɑ̃tɛr] *adj, nm*
documentary
documentaliste [dɔkymɑ̃talist(ə)] *nm/f*
archivist; (*Presse, TV*) researcher
documentation [dɔkymɑ̃tasjɔ̃] *nf*
documentation, literature; (*Presse, TV: service*)
research
documenter [dɔkymɑ̃te] *vt*: **se ~ (sur)** to gather
information *ou* material (on *ou* about)
dodo [dɔdo] *nm*: **aller faire ~** to go to beddy-byes
dodu, e [dɔdy] *adj* plump
dogue [dɔg] *nm* mastiff
doigt [dwa] *nm* finger; **à deux ~s de** within an
ace (*Brit*) *ou* an inch of; **un ~ de lait/whisky** a
drop of milk/whisky; **désigner** *ou* **montrer
du ~** to point at; **au ~ et à l'œil** to the letter;
connaître qch sur le bout du ~ to know sth
backwards; **mettre le ~ sur la plaie** (*fig*) to find
the sensitive spot; **~ de pied** toe
doigté [dwate] *nm* (*Mus*) fingering; (*fig: habileté*)
diplomacy, tact
doit etc [dwa] *vb voir* **devoir**
doléances [dɔleɑ̃s] *nfpl* complaints; (*réclamations*)
grievances
dollar [dɔlar] *nm* dollar
domaine [dɔmɛn] *nm* estate, property; (*fig*)
domain, field; **tomber dans le ~ public** (*livre
etc*) to be out of copyright; **dans tous les ~s** in
all areas
domestique [dɔmɛstik] *adj* domestic ▷ *nm/f*
servant, domestic
domestiquer [dɔmɛstike] *vt* to domesticate;
(*vent, marées*) to harness
domicile [dɔmisil] *nm* home, place of residence;
à ~ at home; **élire ~ à** to take up residence
in; **sans ~ fixe** of no fixed abode; **~ conjugal**
marital home; **~ légal** domicile
domicilié, e [dɔmisilje] *adj*: **être ~ à** to have
one's home in *ou* at
dominant, e [dɔminɑ̃, -ɑ̃t] *adj* dominant; (*plus
important*) predominant ▷ *nf* (*caractéristique*)
dominant characteristic; (*couleur*) dominant
colour
dominer [dɔmine] *vt* to dominate; (*passions
etc*) to control, master; (*surpasser*) to outclass,
surpass; (*surplomber*) to tower above, dominate
▷ *vi* to be in the dominant position; **se dominer**
vi to control o.s.
domino [dɔmino] *nm* domino; **dominos** *nmpl*
(*jeu*) dominoes *sg*
dommage [dɔmaʒ] *nm* (*préjudice*) harm, injury;
(*dégâts, pertes*) damage *no pl*; **c'est ~ de faire/que**

it's a shame *ou* pity to do/that; **quel ~!** what a pity *ou* shame!; **~s corporels** physical injury

dommages-intérêts [dɔmaʒ(əz)ɛ̃teʀɛ] *nmpl* damages

dompter [dɔ̃te] *vt* to tame

dompteur, -euse [dɔ̃tœʀ, -øz] *nm/f* trainer; (*de lion*) lion tamer

DOM-ROM [dɔmʀɔm], **DOM-TOM** [dɔmtɔm] *sigle m ou mpl* (= *Département(s) et Régions/Territoire(s) d'outre-mer*) *French overseas departments and regions*

don [dɔ̃] *nm* (*cadeau*) gift; (*charité*) donation; (*aptitude*) gift, talent; **avoir des ~s pour** to have a gift *ou* talent for; **faire ~ de** to make a gift of; **~ en argent** cash donation

donc [dɔ̃k] *conj* therefore, so; (*après une digression*) so, then; (*intensif*): **voilà ~ la solution** so there's the solution; **je disais ~ que ...** as I was saying, ...; **venez ~ dîner à la maison** do come for dinner; **allons ~!** come now!; **faites ~** go ahead

donjon [dɔ̃ʒɔ̃] *nm* keep

donné, e [dɔne] *adj* (*convenu*) given; (*pas cher*) very cheap ▷ *nf* (*Math, Inform, gén*) datum; **c'est ~** it's a gift; **étant ~ ...** given ...

données [dɔne] *nfpl* data

donner [dɔne] *vt* to give; (*vieux habits etc*) to give away; (*spectacle*) to put on; (*film*) to show; **~ qch à qn** to give sb sth, give sth to sb; **~ qch à qn** to give sb sth, give sth to sb; **~ sur** (*fenêtre, chambre*) to look (out) onto; **~ dans** (*piège etc*) to fall into; **faire ~ l'infanterie** (*Mil*) to send in the infantry; **~ l'heure à qn** to tell sb the time; **~ le ton** (*fig*) to set the tone; **~ à penser/entendre que ...** to make one think/give one to understand that ...; **se ~ à fond (à son travail)** to give one's all (to one's work); **se ~ du mal** *ou* **de la peine (pour faire qch)** to go to a lot of trouble (to do sth); **s'en ~ à cœur joie** (*fam*) to have a great time (of it)

dont [dɔ̃] *pron relatif* **1** (*appartenance: objets*) whose, of which; (: *êtres animés*) whose; **la maison ~ le toit est rouge** the house the roof of which is red, the house whose roof is red; **l'homme ~ je connais la sœur** the man whose sister I know **2** (*parmi lesquel(le)s*): **deux livres, ~ l'un est ...** two books, one of which is ...; **il y avait plusieurs personnes, ~ Gabrielle** there were several people, among them Gabrielle; **10 blessés, ~ 2 grièvement** 10 injured, 2 of them seriously **3** (*complément d'adjectif, de verbe*): **le fils ~ il est si fier** the son he's so proud of; **ce ~ je parle** what I'm talking about; **la façon ~ il l'a fait** the way (in which) he did it

doré, e [dɔʀe] *adj* golden; (*avec dorure*) gilt, gilded

dorénavant [dɔʀenavɑ̃] *adv* from now on, henceforth

dorer [dɔʀe] *vt* (*cadre*) to gild; (*faire*) **~** (*Culin*) to brown; (: *gâteau*) to glaze; **se ~ au soleil** to sunbathe; **~ la pilule à qn** to sugar the pill for sb

dorloter [dɔʀlɔte] *vt* to pamper, cosset (*Brit*); **se faire ~** to be pampered *ou* cosseted

dormir [dɔʀmiʀ] *vi* to sleep; (*être endormi*) to be asleep; **~ à poings fermés** to sleep very soundly

dortoir [dɔʀtwaʀ] *nm* dormitory

dorure [dɔʀyʀ] *nf* gilding

dos [do] *nm* back; (*de livre*) spine; **"voir au ~"** "see over"; **robe décolletée dans le ~** low-backed dress; **de ~** from the back, from behind; **~ à ~** back to back; **sur le ~** on one's back; **à ~ de chameau** riding on a camel; **avoir bon ~** to be a good excuse; **se mettre qn à ~** to turn sb against one

dosage [dozaʒ] *nm* mixture

dose [doz] *nf* (*Méd*) dose; **forcer la ~** (*fig*) to overstep the mark

doser [doze] *vt* to measure out; (*mélanger*) to mix in the correct proportions; (*fig*) to expend in the right amounts *ou* proportions; to strike a balance between

dossard [dosaʀ] *nm* number (*worn by competitor*)

dossier [dosje] *nm* (*renseignements, fichier*) file; (*enveloppe*) folder, file; (*de chaise*) back; (*Presse*) feature; **le ~ social/monétaire** (*fig*) the social/financial question; **~ suspendu** suspension file

dot [dɔt] *nf* dowry

doter [dɔte] *vt*: **~ qn/qch de** to equip sb/sth with

douane [dwan] *nf* (*poste, bureau*) customs *pl*; (*taxes*) (customs) duty; **passer la ~** to go through customs; **en ~** (*marchandises, entrepôt*) bonded

douanier, -ière [dwanje, -jɛʀ] *adj* customs *cpd* ▷ *nm* customs officer

double [dubl(ə)] *adj, adv* double ▷ *nm* (2 *fois plus*): **le ~ (de)** twice as much (*ou* many) (as), double the amount (*ou* number) (of); (*autre exemplaire*) duplicate, copy; (*sosie*) double; (*Tennis*) doubles *sg*; **voir ~** to see double; **en ~ (exemplaire)** in duplicate; **faire ~ emploi** to be redundant; **à ~ sens** with a double meaning; **à ~ tranchant** two-edged; **~ carburateur** twin carburettor; **à ~s commandes** dual-control; **~ messieurs/mixte** men's/mixed doubles *sg*; **~ toit** (*de tente*) fly sheet; **~ vue** second sight

double-cliquer [dubl(ə)klike] *vi* (*Inform*) to double-click

doubler [duble] *vt* (*multiplier par 2*) to double; (*vêtement*) to line; (*dépasser*) to overtake, pass; (*film*) to dub; (*acteur*) to stand in for ▷ *vi* to double, increase twofold; **se ~ de** to be coupled with; **~ (la classe)** (*Scol*) to repeat a year; **~ un cap** (*Navig*) to round a cape; (*fig*) to get over a hurdle

doublure [dublyʀ] *nf* lining; (*Ciné*) stand-in

douce [dus] *adj f voir* **doux**

douceâtre [dusɑtʀ(ə)] *adj* sickly sweet

doucement [dusmɑ̃] *adv* gently; (*à voix basse*) softly; (*lentement*) slowly

doucereux, -euse [dusʀø, -øz] *adj* (*péj*) sugary

douceur [dusœʀ] *nf* softness; sweetness; mildness; gentleness; **douceurs** *nfpl* (*friandises*) sweets (*Brit*), candy *sg* (*US*); **en ~** gently

douche [duʃ] *nf* shower; **douches** *nfpl* shower room *sg*; **prendre une ~** to have *ou* take a shower; **~ écossaise** (*fig*): **~ froide** (*fig*) let-down

doucher, -euse [duʃe] *vt*: **~ qn** to give sb a shower; (*mouiller*) to drench sb; (*fig*) to give sb a telling-off; **se doucher** to have *ou* take a shower

doudoune [dudun] *nf* padded jacket; (*fam*) boob

doué, e [dwe] *adj* gifted, talented; **~ de** endowed with; **être ~ pour** to have a gift for

douille [duj] *nf* (*Élec*) socket; (*de projectile*) case

douillet, te [dujɛ, -et] *adj* cosy; (*péj*) soft

douleur [dulœʀ] *nf* pain; (*chagrin*) grief, distress; **ressentir des ~s** to feel pain; **il a eu la ~ de perdre son père** he suffered the grief of losing his father

douloureux, -euse [duluʀø, -øz] *adj* painful

doute [dut] *nm* doubt; **sans ~** *adv* no doubt; (*probablement*) probably; **sans nul** *ou* **aucun ~** without (a) doubt; **hors de ~** beyond doubt; **nul ~ que** there's no doubt that; **mettre en ~** to call into question; **mettre en ~ que** to question whether

douter [dute] *vt* to doubt; **~ de** *vt* (*allié*) to doubt, have (one's) doubts about; (*résultat*) to be doubtful of; **~ que** to doubt whether *ou* if; **j'en doute** I have my doubts; **se ~ de qch/que** to suspect sth/that; **je m'en doutais** I suspected as much; **il ne se doutait de rien** he didn't suspect a thing

douteux, -euse [dutø, -øz] *adj* (*incertain*) doubtful; (*discutable*) dubious, questionable; (*péj*) dubious-looking

Douvres [duvʀ(ə)] *n* Dover

doux, douce [du, dus] *adj* (*lisse, moelleux, pas vif: couleur, non calcaire: eau*) soft; (*sucré, agréable*) sweet; (*peu fort: moutarde etc, clément: climat*) mild; (*pas brusque*) gentle; **en douce** (*partir etc*) on the quiet

douzaine [duzɛn] *nf* (12) dozen; (*environ 12*) **une ~ (de)** a dozen or so, twelve or so

douze [duz] *num* twelve; **les D~** (*membres de la CEE*) the Twelve

douzième [duzjɛm] *num* twelfth

doyen, ne [dwajɛ̃, -ɛn] *nm/f* (*en âge, ancienneté*) most senior member; (*de faculté*) dean

dragée [dʀaʒe] *nf* sugared almond; (*Méd*) (sugar-coated) pill

dragon [dʀagɔ̃] *nm* dragon

draguer [dʀage] *vt* (*rivière: pour nettoyer*) to dredge; (: *pour trouver qch*) to drag; (*fam*) to try and pick up, chat up (*Brit*) ▷ *vi* (*fam*) to try and pick sb up, chat sb up (*Brit*)

dramatique [dʀamatik] *adj* dramatic; (*tragique*) tragic ▷ *nf* (*TV*) (television) drama

dramaturge [dʀamatyʀʒ(ə)] *nm* dramatist, playwright

drame [dʀam] *nm* (*Théât*) drama; (*catastrophe*) drama, tragedy; **~ familial** family drama

drap [dʀa] *nm* (*de lit*) sheet; (*tissu*) woollen fabric; **~ de plage** beach towel

drapeau, x [dʀapo] *nm* flag; **sous les ~x** with the colours (*Brit*) *ou* colors (*US*), in the army

drap-housse (*pl* **draps-housses**) [dʀaus] *nm* fitted sheet

dresser [dʀese] *vt* (*mettre vertical, monter: tente*) to put up, erect; (*fig: liste, bilan, contrat*) to draw up; (*animal*) to train; **se dresser** *vi* (*falaise, obstacle*) to stand; (*avec grandeur, menace*) to tower (up);

(*personne*) to draw o.s. up; **~ l'oreille** to prick up one's ears; **~ la table** to set *ou* lay the table; **~ qn contre qn d'autre** to set sb against sb else; **~ un procès-verbal** *ou* **une contravention à qn** to book sb

drogue [dʀɔg] *nf* drug; **la ~** drugs *pl*; **~ dure/douce** hard/soft drugs *pl*

drogué, e [dʀɔge] *nm/f* drug addict

droguer [dʀɔge] *vt* to drug; (*malade*) to give drugs to; **se droguer** (*aux stupéfiants*) to take drugs; (*péj: de médicaments*) to dose o.s. up

droguerie [dʀɔgʀi] *nf* ≈ hardware shop (*Brit*) *ou* store (*US*)

droguiste [dʀɔgist(ə)] *nm* ≈ keeper (*ou* owner) of a hardware shop *ou* store

droit, e [dʀwa, dʀwat] *adj* (*non courbe*) straight; (*vertical*) upright, straight; (*fig: loyal, franc*) upright, straight(forward); (*opposé à gauche*) right, right-hand ▷ *adv* straight ▷ *nm* (*prérogative, Boxe*) right; (*taxe*) duty, tax; (: *d'inscription*) fee; (*lois, branche*): **le ~** law ▷ *nf* (*Pol*) right (wing); (*ligne*) straight line; **~ au but** *ou* **au fait/cœur** straight to the point/heart; **avoir le ~ de** to be allowed to; **avoir ~ à** to be entitled to; **être en ~ de** to have a *ou* the right to; **faire ~ à** to grant, accede to; **être dans son ~** to be within one's rights; **à bon ~** (*justement*) with good reason; **de quel ~?** by what right?; **à qui de ~** to whom it may concern; **à ~e** on the right; (*direction*) (to the) right; **à ~e de** to the right of; **de ~e, sur votre ~e** on your right; (*Pol*) right-wing; **~ d'auteur** copyright; **~ de cité** (**dans**) (*fig*) to belong (to); **~ coutumier** common law; **~ de regard** right of access *ou* inspection; **~ de réponse** right to reply; **~ de visite** (right of) access; **~ de vote** (right to) vote; **~s d'auteur** royalties; **~s de douane** customs duties; **~s de l'homme** human rights; **~s d'inscription** enrolment *ou* registration fees

droitier, -ière [dʀwatje, -jɛʀ] *nm/f* right-handed person

droiture [dʀwatyʀ] *nf* uprightness, straightness

drôle [dʀol] *adj* (*amusant*) funny, amusing; (*bizarre*) funny, peculiar; **un ~ de ...** (*bizarre*) a strange *ou* funny ...; (*intensif*) an incredible ..., a terrific ...

drôlement [dʀolmã] *adv* funnily; peculiarly; (*très*) terribly, awfully; **il fait ~ froid** it's awfully cold

dromadaire [dʀɔmadɛʀ] *nm* dromedary

dru, e [dʀy] *adj* (*cheveux*) thick, bushy; (*pluie*) heavy ▷ *adv* (*pousser*) thickly; (*tomber*) heavily

du [dy] *art voir* **de**

dû, due [dy] *pp de* **devoir** ▷ *adj* (*somme*) owing, owed; (: *venant à échéance*) due; (*causé par*): **dû à** due to ▷ *nm* due; (*somme*) dues *pl*

duc [dyk] *nm* duke

duchesse [dyʃɛs] *nf* duchess

dûment [dymã] *adv* duly

dune [dyn] *nf* dune

Dunkerque [dœ̃kɛʀk] *n* Dunkirk

duo [dɥo] *nm* (*Mus*) duet; (*fig: couple*) duo, pair

dupe [dyp] *nf* dupe ▷ *adj*: **(ne pas) être ~ de** (not) to be taken in by

duplex [dypleks] *nm* (*appartement*) split-level apartment, duplex; (TV): **émission en ~** link-up

duplicata [dyplikata] *nm* duplicate

duquel [dykɛl] *prép* + *pron voir* **lequel**

dur, e [dyʀ] *adj* (*pierre, siège, travail, problème*) hard; (*lumière, voix, climat*) hard(-climat); (*sévère*) hard, harsh; (*cruel*) hard(-hearted); (*porte, col*) stiff; (*viande*) tough ▷ *adv* hard ▷ *nf*: **à la ~e** rough; **mener la vie ~e à qn** to give sb a hard time; **~ d'oreille** hard of hearing

durant [dyʀɑ̃] *prép* (*au cours de*) during; (*pendant*) for; **~ des mois, des mois ~** for months

durcir [dyʀsiʀ] *vt, vi*: **se durcir** *vi* to harden

durée [dyʀe] *nf* length; (*d'une pile etc*) life; (*déroulement: des opérations etc*) duration; **pour une ~ illimitée** for an unlimited length of time; **de courte ~** (*séjour, répit*) brief, short-term; **de longue ~** (*effet*) long-term; **pile de longue ~** long-life battery

durement [dyʀmɑ̃] *adv* harshly

durer [dyʀe] *vi* to last

dureté [dyʀte] *nf* (*voir dur*) hardness; harshness; stiffness; toughness

durit® [dyʀit] *nf* (car radiator) hose

duvet [dyvɛ] *nm* down; **(sac de couchage en) ~** down-filled sleeping bag

DVD *sigle m* (= *digital versatile disc*) DVD

dynamique [dinamik] *adj* dynamic

dynamisme [dinamism(ə)] *nm* dynamism

dynamite [dinamit] *nf* dynamite

dynamo [dinamo] *nf* dynamo

dyslexie [dislɛksi] *nf* dyslexia, word blindness

Ee

eau, x [o] *nf* water ▷ *nfpl* waters; **prendre l'~**
(*chaussure etc*) to leak, let in water; **prendre les**
~x to take the waters; **faire ~** to leak; **tomber**
à l'~ (*fig*) to fall through; **à l'~ de rose** slushy,
sentimental; **~ bénite** holy water; **~ de Cologne**
eau de Cologne; **~ courante** running water; **~**
distillée distilled water; **~ douce** fresh water;
~ de Javel bleach; **~ lourde** heavy water; **~**
minérale mineral water; **~ oxygénée** hydrogen
peroxide; **~ plate** still water; **~ de pluie**
rainwater; **~ salée** salt water; **~ de toilette**
toilet water; **~x ménagères** dirty water (*from*
washing up etc); **~x territoriales** territorial
waters; **~x usées** liquid waste
eau-de-vie [odvi] (*pl* **eaux-de-vie**) *nf* brandy
eau-forte [ofɔʀt(ə)] (*pl* **eaux-fortes**) *nf* etching
ébahi, e [ebai] *adj* dumbfounded, flabbergasted
ébattre [ebatʀ(ə)]: **s'ébattre** *vi* to frolic
ébaucher [eboʃe] *vt* to sketch out, outline; (*fig*): **~**
un sourire/geste to give a hint of a smile/make
a slight gesture; **s'ébaucher** *vi* to take shape
ébène [ebɛn] *nf* ebony
ébéniste [ebenist(ə)] *nm* cabinetmaker
éberlué, e [ebɛʀlɥe] *adj* astounded,
flabbergasted
éblouir [ebluiʀ] *vt* to dazzle
éborgner [ebɔʀɲe] *vt*: **~ qn** to blind sb in one eye
éboueur [ebwœʀ] *nm* dustman (*Brit*), garbage
man (*US*)
ébouillanter [ebujɑ̃te] *vt* to scald; (*Culin*) to
blanch; **s'ébouillanter** *vi* to scald o.s.
éboulement [ebulmɑ̃] *nm* falling rocks *pl*, rock
fall; (*amas*) heap of boulders *etc*
ébouler [ebule]: **s'ébouler** *vi* to crumble,
collapse
éboulis [ebuli] *nmpl* fallen rocks
ébouriffé, e [eburife] *adj* tousled, ruffled
ébranler [ebrɑ̃le] *vt* to shake; (*rendre instable: mur,*
santé) to weaken; **s'ébranler** *vi* (*partir*) to move off
ébrécher [ebreʃe] *vt* to chip
ébriété [ebrijete] *nf*: **en état d'~** in a state of
intoxication
ébrouer [ebrue]: **s'ébrouer** *vi* (*souffler*) to snort;
(*s'agiter*) to shake o.s.
ébruiter [ebrɥite] *vt*: **s'ébruiter** *vi* to spread
ébullition [ebylisjɔ̃] *nf* boiling point; **en ~**
boiling; (*fig*) in an uproar

écaille [ekaj] *nf* (*de poisson*) scale; (*de coquillage*)
shell; (*matière*) tortoiseshell; (*de roc etc*) flake
écailler [ekaje] *vt* (*poisson*) to scale; (*huître*) to
open; **s'écailler** *vi* to flake *ou* peel (off)
écarlate [ekaʀlat] *adj* scarlet
écarquiller [ekaʀkije] *vt*: **~ les yeux** to stare
wide-eyed
écart [ekaʀ] *nm* gap; (*embardée*) swerve; (*saut*)
sideways leap; (*fig*) departure, deviation; **à l'~**
adv out of the way; **à l'~ de** *prép* away from; (*fig*)
out of; **faire le grand ~** (*Danse, Gymnastique*) to do
the splits; **~ de conduite** misdemeanour
écarté, e [ekaʀte] *adj* (*lieu*) out-of-the-way,
remote; (*ouvert*): **les jambes ~es** legs apart; **les**
bras ~s arms outstretched
écarter [ekaʀte] *vt* (*séparer*) to move apart,
separate; (*éloigner*) to push back, move away;
(*ouvrir: bras, jambes*) to spread, open; (: *rideau*)
to draw (back); (*éliminer: candidat, possibilité*) to
dismiss; (*Cartes*) to discard; **s'écarter** *vi* to part;
(*personne*) to move away; **s'~ de** to wander from
écervelé, e [esɛʀvəle] *adj* scatterbrained,
featherbrained
échafaud [eʃafo] *nm* scaffold
échafaudage [eʃafodaʒ] *nm* scaffolding; (*fig*)
heap, pile
échafauder [eʃafode] *vt* (*plan*) to construct
échalote [eʃalɔt] *nf* shallot
échancrure [eʃɑ̃kʀyʀ] *nf* (*de robe*) scoop neckline;
(*de côte, arête rocheuse*) indentation
échange [eʃɑ̃ʒ] *nm* exchange; **en ~** in exchange;
en ~ de in exchange *ou* return for; **libre ~** free
trade; **~ de lettres/politesses/vues** exchange
of letters/civilities/views; **~s commerciaux**
trade; **~s culturels** cultural exchanges
échanger [eʃɑ̃ʒe] *vt*: **~ qch (contre)** to exchange
sth (for)
échangeur [eʃɑ̃ʒœʀ] *nm* (*Auto*) interchange
échantillon [eʃɑ̃tijɔ̃] *nm* sample
échappement [eʃapmɑ̃] *nm* (*Auto*) exhaust; **~**
libre cutout
échapper [eʃape]: **~ à** *vt* (*gardien*) to escape (from);
(*punition, péril*) to escape; **~ à qn** (*détail, sens*) to
escape sb; (*objet qu'on tient: aussi*: **échapper des**
mains de qn) to slip out of sb's hands; **laisser**
~ to let fall; (*cri etc*) to let out; **s'échapper** *vi* to
escape; **l'~ belle** to have a narrow escape

écharde [eʃaʀd(ə)] nf splinter (of wood)
écharpe [eʃaʀp(ə)] nf scarf; (de maire) sash; (Méd) sling; **prendre en ~** (dans une collision) to hit sideways on
échasse [eʃas] nf stilt
échassier [eʃasje] nm wader
échauffer [eʃofe] vt (métal, moteur) to overheat; (fig: exciter) to fire, excite; **s'échauffer** vi (Sport) to warm up; (discussion) to become heated
échéance [eʃeɑ̃s] nf (d'un paiement: date) settlement date; (: somme due) financial commitment(s); (fig) deadline; **à brève/longue ~** adj short-/long-term ▷ adv in the short/long term
échéant [eʃeɑ̃]: **le cas ~** adv if the case arises
échec [eʃɛk] nm failure; (Échecs): **~ et mat/au roi** checkmate/check; **échecs** nmpl (jeu) chess sg; **mettre en ~** to put in check; **tenir en ~** to hold in check; **faire ~ à** to foil, thwart
échelle [eʃɛl] nf ladder; (fig, d'une carte) scale; **à l'~ de** on the scale of; **sur une grande/petite ~** on a large/small scale; **faire la courte ~ à qn** to give sb a leg up; **~ de corde** rope ladder
échelon [eʃlɔ̃] nm (d'échelle) rung; (Admin) grade
échelonner [eʃlɔne] vt to space out, spread out; **(versement) échelonné** (payment) by instalments
échevelé, e [eʃəvle] adj tousled, dishevelled; (fig) wild, frenzied
échine [eʃin] nf backbone, spine
échiquier [eʃikje] nm chessboard
écho [eko] nm echo; **échos** nmpl (potins) gossip sg, rumours; (Presse: rubrique) "news in brief"; **rester sans ~** (suggestion etc) to come to nothing; **se faire l'~ de** to repeat, spread about
échographie [ekɔgʀafi] nf ultrasound (scan)
échoir [eʃwaʀ] vi (dette) to fall due; (délais) to expire; **~ à** vt to fall to
échouer [eʃwe] vi to fail; (débris etc: sur la plage) to be washed up; (aboutir: personne dans un café etc) to arrive ▷ vt (bateau) to ground; **s'échouer** vi to run aground
échu, e [eʃy] pp de **échoir** ▷ adj due, mature
éclabousser [eklabuse] vt to splash; (fig) to tarnish
éclair [eklɛʀ] nm (d'orage) flash of lightning, lightning no pl; (Photo: de flash) flash; (fig) flash, spark; (gâteau) éclair
éclairage [eklɛʀaʒ] nm lighting
éclaircie [eklɛʀsi] nf bright ou sunny interval
éclaircir [eklɛʀsiʀ] vt to lighten; (fig) to clear up, clarify; (Culin) to thin (down); **s'éclaircir** vi (ciel) to brighten up, clear; (cheveux) to go thin; (situation etc) to become clearer; **s'~ la voix** to clear one's throat
éclaircissement [eklɛʀsismɑ̃] nm clearing up, clarification
éclairer [eklɛʀe] vt (lieu) to light (up); (personne: avec une lampe de poche etc) to light the way for; (fig: instruire) to enlighten; (: rendre compréhensible) to shed light on ▷ vi: **~ mal/bien** to give a poor/good light; **s'éclairer** vi (phare, rue) to light up;

(situation etc) to become clearer; **s'~ à la bougie/l'électricité** to use candlelight/have electric lighting
éclaireur, -euse [eklɛʀœʀ, -øz] nm/f (scout) (boy) scout/(girl) guide ▷ nm (Mil) scout; **partir en ~** to go off to reconnoitre
éclat [ekla] nm (de bombe, de verre) fragment; (du soleil, d'une couleur etc) brightness, brilliance; (d'une cérémonie) splendour; (scandale): **faire un ~** to cause a commotion; **action d'~** outstanding action; **voler en ~s** to shatter; **des ~s de verre** broken glass; flying glass; **~ de rire** burst ou roar of laughter; **~ de voix** shout
éclatant, e [eklatɑ̃, -ɑ̃t] adj brilliant, bright; (succès) resounding; (revanche) devastating
éclater [eklate] vi (pneu) to burst; (bombe) to explode; (guerre, épidémie) to break out; (groupe, parti) to break up; **~ de rire/en sanglots** to burst out laughing/sobbing
éclipse [eklips] nf eclipse
éclipser [eklipse] vt to eclipse; **s'éclipser** vi to slip away
éclore [eklɔʀ] vi (œuf) to hatch; (fleur) to open (out)
écluse [eklyz] nf lock
écœurant, e [ekœʀɑ̃, -ɑ̃t] adj sickening; (gâteau etc) sickly
écœurer [ekœʀe] vt: **~ qn** to make sb feel sick; (fig: démoraliser) to disgust sb
école [ekɔl] nf school; **aller à l'~** to go to school; **faire ~** to collect a following; **les grandes ~s** prestige university-level colleges with competitive entrance examinations; **~ maternelle** nursery school; see note; **~ primaire** primary (Brit) ou grade (US) school; **~ secondaire** secondary (Brit) ou high (US) school; **~ privée/publique** private/state/elementary school; **~ de dessin/danse/musique** art/dancing/music school; **~ hôtelière** catering college; **~ normale (d'instituteurs) (ENI)** primary school teachers' training college; **~ normale supérieure (ENS)** grande école for training secondary school teachers; **~ de secrétariat** secretarial college
écolier, -ière [ekɔlje, -jɛʀ] nm/f schoolboy/girl
écologie [ekɔlɔʒi] nf ecology; (sujet scolaire) environmental studies pl
écologique [ekɔlɔʒik] adj ecological; environmental
écologiste [ekɔlɔʒist(ə)] nm/f ecologist; environmentalist
éconduire [ekɔ̃dɥiʀ] vt to dismiss
économe [ekɔnɔm] adj thrifty ▷ nm/f (de lycée etc) bursar (Brit), treasurer (US)
économie [ekɔnɔmi] nf (vertu) economy, thrift; (gain: d'argent, de temps etc) saving; (science) economics sg; (situation économique) economy; **économies** nfpl (pécule) savings; **faire des ~s** to save up; **une ~ de temps/d'argent** a saving in time/of money; **~ dirigée** planned economy; **~ de marché** market economy
économique [ekɔnɔmik] adj (avantageux) economical; (Écon) economic
économiser [ekɔnɔmize] vt, vi to save

économiseur [ekɔnɔmizœʀ] *nm*: ~ **d'écran** (*Inform*) screen saver

écoper [ekɔpe] *vi* to bale out; (*fig*) to cop it; ~ **(de)** *vt* to get

écorce [ekɔʀs(ə)] *nf* bark; (*de fruit*) peel

écorcher [ekɔʀʃe] *vt* (*animal*) to skin; (*égratigner*) to graze; ~ **une langue** to speak a language brokenly; **s'~ le genou** *etc* to scrape *ou* graze one's knee *etc*

écorchure [ekɔʀʃyʀ] *nf* graze

écossais, e [ekɔsɛ, -ɛz] *adj* Scottish, Scots; (*whisky, confiture*) Scotch; (*écharpe, tissu*) tartan ▷ *nm* (*Ling*) Scots; (: *gaélique*) Gaelic; (*tissu*) tartan (cloth) ▷ *nm/f*: **É~, e** Scot, Scotsman/woman; **les É~** the Scots

Écosse [ekɔs] *nf*: **l'~** Scotland

écosser [ekɔse] *vt* to shell

écoulement [ekulmɑ̃] *nm* (*de faux billets*) circulation; (*de stock*) selling

écouler [ekule] *vt* to dispose of; **s'écouler** *vi* (*eau*) to flow (out); (*foule*) to drift away; (*jours, temps*) to pass (by)

écourter [ekuʀte] *vt* to curtail, cut short

écoute [ekut] *nf* (*Navig: cordage*) sheet; (*Radio, TV*): **temps d'~** (listening *ou* viewing) time; **heure de grande ~** peak listening *ou* viewing time; **prendre l'~** to tune in; **rester à l'~ (de)** to stay tuned in (to); **~s téléphoniques** phone tapping *sg*

écouter [ekute] *vt* to listen to

écouteur [ekutœʀ] *nm* (*Tél*) (additional) earpiece; **écouteurs** *nmpl* (*Radio*) headphones, headset *sg*

écoutille [ekutij] *nf* hatch

écran [ekʀɑ̃] *nm* screen; (*Inform*) screen, VDU; ~ **de fumée/d'eau** curtain of smoke/water; **porter à l'~** (*Ciné*) to adapt for the screen; **le petit ~** television, the small screen

écrasant, e [ekʀazɑ̃, -ɑ̃t] *adj* overwhelming

écraser [ekʀaze] *vt* to crush; (*piéton*) to run over; (*Inform*) to overwrite; **se faire ~** to be run over; **écrase(-toi)!** shut up!; **s'~ (au sol)** to crash; **s'~ contre** to crash into

écrémé, e [ekʀeme] *adj* (*lait*) skimmed

écrevisse [ekʀəvis] *nf* crayfish *inv*

écrier [ekʀije]: **s'écrier** *vi* to exclaim

écrin [ekʀɛ̃] *nm* case, box

écrire [ekʀiʀ] *vt, vi* to write ▷ *vi*: **ça s'écrit comment?** how is it spelt?; ~ **à qn que** to write and tell sb that; **s'écrire** *vi* to write to one another

écrit, e [ekʀi, -it] *pp de* **écrire** ▷ *adj*: **bien/mal ~** well/badly written ▷ *nm* document; (*examen*) written paper; **par ~** in writing

écriteau, x [ekʀito] *nm* notice, sign

écriture [ekʀityʀ] *nf* writing; (*Comm*) entry; **écritures** *nfpl* (*Comm*) accounts, books; **l'É~ (sainte), les É~s** the Scriptures

écrivain [ekʀivɛ̃] *nm* writer

écrou [ekʀu] *nm* nut

écrouer [ekʀue] *vt* to imprison; (*provisoirement*) to remand in custody

écrouler [ekʀule]: **s'écrouler** *vi* to collapse

écru, e [ekʀy] *adj* (*toile*) raw, unbleached; (*couleur*) off-white, écru

écueil [ekœj] *nm* reef; (*fig*) pitfall; stumbling block

éculé, e [ekyle] *adj* (*chaussure*) down-at-heel; (*fig: péj*) hackneyed

écume [ekym] *nf* foam; (*Culin*) scum; ~ **de mer** meerschaum

écumer [ekyme] *vt* (*Culin*) to skim; (*fig*) to plunder ▷ *vi* (*mer*) to foam; (*fig*) to boil with rage

écumoire [ekymwaʀ] *nf* skimmer

écureuil [ekyʀœj] *nm* squirrel

écurie [ekyʀi] *nf* stable

écusson [ekysɔ̃] *nm* badge

écuyer, -ère [ekɥije, -ɛʀ] *nm/f* rider

eczéma [ɛgzema] *nm* eczema

édenté, e [edɑ̃te] *adj* toothless

EDF *sigle f* (= *Électricité de France*) national electricity company

édifice [edifis] *nm* building, edifice

édifier [edifje] *vt* to build, erect; (*fig*) to edify

Édimbourg [edɛ̃buʀ] *n* Edinburgh

éditer [edite] *vt* (*publier*) to publish; (: *disque*) to produce; (*préparer: texte, Inform*) to edit

éditeur, -trice [editœʀ, -tʀis] *nm/f* publisher; editor; ~ **de textes** (*Inform*) text editor

édition [edisjɔ̃] *nf* editing *no pl*; (*série d'exemplaires*) edition; (*industrie du livre*): **l'~** publishing; ~ **sur écran** (*Inform*) screen editing

édredon [edʀədɔ̃] *nm* eiderdown, comforter (*US*)

éducateur, -trice [edykatœʀ, -tʀis] *nm/f* teacher; ~ **spécialisé** specialist teacher

éducatif, -ive [edykatif, -iv] *adj* educational

éducation [edykasjɔ̃] *nf* education; (*familiale*) upbringing; (*manières*) (good) manners *pl*; **bonne/mauvaise ~** good/bad upbringing; **sans ~** bad-mannered, ill-bred; **l'É~ (nationale)** ≈ the Department for Education; ~ **permanente** continuing education; ~ **physique** physical education

édulcorant [edylkɔʀɑ̃] *nm* sweetener

éduquer [edyke] *vt* to educate; (*élever*) to bring up; (*faculté*) to train; **bien/mal éduqué** well/badly brought up

effacé, e [efase] *adj* (*fig*) retiring, unassuming

effacer [efase] *vt* to erase, rub out; (*bande magnétique*) to erase; (*Inform: fichier, fiche*) to delete; **s'effacer** *vi* (*inscription etc*) to wear off; (*pour laisser passer*) to step aside; ~ **le ventre** to pull one's stomach in

effarant, e [efaʀɑ̃, -ɑ̃t] *adj* alarming

effarer [efaʀe] *vt* to alarm

effaroucher [efaʀuʃe] *vt* to frighten *ou* scare away; (*personne*) to alarm

effectif, -ive [efɛktif, -iv] *adj* real; effective ▷ *nm* (*Mil*) strength; (*Scol*) total number of pupils, size; **~s** numbers, strength *sg*; (*Comm*) manpower *sg*; **réduire l'~ de** to downsize

effectivement [efɛktivmɑ̃] *adv* effectively; (*réellement*) actually, really; (*en effet*) indeed

effectuer [efɛktɥe] *vt* (*opération, mission*) to carry out; (*déplacement, trajet*) to make, complete; (*mouvement*) to execute, make; **s'effectuer** *vi* to be carried out

efféminé, e [efemine] *adj* effeminate

effervescent, e [efɛʀvesɑ̃, -ɑ̃t] *adj* (*cachet, boisson*) effervescent; (*fig*) agitated, in a turmoil

effet [efɛ] *nm* (*résultat, artifice*) effect; (*impression*) impression; (*Comm*) bill; (*Jur: d'une loi, d'un jugement*): **avec ~ rétroactif** applied retrospectively; **effets** *nmpl* (*vêtements etc*) things; **~ de style/couleur/lumière** stylistic/colour/lighting effect; **~s de voix** dramatic effects with one's voice; **faire de l'~** (*médicament, menace*) to have an effect, be effective; **sous l'~ de** under the effect of; **donner de l'~ à une balle** (*Tennis*) to put some spin on a ball; **à cet ~** to that end; **en ~** *adv* indeed; **~ (de commerce)** bill of exchange; **~ de serre** greenhouse effect; **~s spéciaux** (*Ciné*) special effects

efficace [efikas] *adj* (*personne*) efficient; (*action, médicament*) effective

efficacité [efikasite] *nf* efficiency; effectiveness

effilocher [efilɔʃe]: **s'effilocher** *vi* to fray

efflanqué, e [eflɑ̃ke] *adj* emaciated

effleurer [eflœʀe] *vt* to brush (against); (*sujet*) to touch upon; (*idée, pensée*): **~ qn** to cross sb's mind

effluves [eflyv] *nmpl* exhalation(s)

effondrer [efɔ̃dʀe]: **s'effondrer** *vi* to collapse

efforcer [efɔʀse]: **s'efforcer de** *vt*: **s'~ de faire** to try hard to do

effort [efɔʀ] *nm* effort; **faire un ~** to make an effort; **faire tous ses ~s** to try one's hardest; **faire l'~ de ...** to make the effort to ...; **sans ~** *adj* effortless ▷ *adv* effortlessly; **~ de mémoire** attempt to remember; **~ de volonté** effort of will

effraction [efʀaksjɔ̃] *nf* breaking-in; **s'introduire par ~ dans** to break into

effrayant, e [efʀɛjɑ̃, -ɑ̃t] *adj* frightening, fearsome; (*sens affaibli*) dreadful

effrayer [efʀeje] *vt* to frighten, scare; (*rebuter*) to put off; **s'effrayer (de)** *vi* to be frightened *ou* scared (by)

effréné, e [efʀene] *adj* wild

effriter [efʀite]: **s'effriter** *vi* to crumble; (*monnaie*) to be eroded; (*valeurs*) to slacken off

effroi [efʀwa] *nm* terror, dread *no pl*

effronté, e [efʀɔ̃te] *adj* insolent

effroyable [efʀwajabl(ə)] *adj* horrifying, appalling

effusion [efyzjɔ̃] *nf* effusion; **sans ~ de sang** without bloodshed

égal, e, -aux [egal, -o] *adj* (*identique, ayant les mêmes droits*) equal; (*plan: surface*) even, level; (*constant: vitesse*) steady; (*équitable*) even ▷ *nm/f* equal; **être ~ à** (*prix, nombre*) to be equal to; **ça m'est ~** it's all the same to me, it doesn't matter to me, I don't mind; **c'est ~, ...** all the same, ...; **sans ~** matchless, unequalled; **à l'~ de** (*comme*) just like; **d'~ à ~** as equals

également [egalmɑ̃] *adv* equally; evenly; steadily; (*aussi*) too, as well

égaler [egale] *vt* to equal

égaliser [egalize] *vt* (*sol, salaires*) to level (out); (*chances*) to equalize ▷ *vi* (*Sport*) to equalize

égalité [egalite] *nf* equality; evenness; steadiness; (*Math*) identity; **être à ~ (de points)** to be level; **~ de droits** equality of rights; **~ d'humeur** evenness of temper

égard [egaʀ] *nm*: **~s** *nmpl* consideration *sg*; **à cet ~** in this respect; **à certains ~s/tous ~s** in certain respects/all respects; **eu ~ à** in view of; **par ~ pour** out of consideration for; **sans ~ pour** without regard for; **à l'~ de** *prép* towards; (*en ce qui concerne*) concerning, as regards

égarement [egaʀmɑ̃] *nm* distraction; aberration

égarer [egaʀe] *vt* (*objet*) to mislay; (*moralement*) to lead astray; **s'égarer** *vi* to get lost, lose one's way; (*objet*) to go astray; (*fig: dans une discussion*) to wander

égayer [egeje] *vt* (*personne*) to amuse; (: *remonter*) to cheer up; (*récit, endroit*) to brighten up, liven up

églantine [eglɑ̃tin] *nf* wild *ou* dog rose

églefin [egləfɛ̃] *nm* haddock

église [egliz] *nf* church

égoïsme [egɔism(ə)] *nm* selfishness, egoism

égoïste [egɔist(ə)] *adj* selfish, egoistic ▷ *nm/f* egoist

égorger [egɔʀʒe] *vt* to cut the throat of

égosiller [egozije]: **s'égosiller** *vi* to shout o.s. hoarse

égout [egu] *nm* sewer; **eaux d'~** sewage

égoutter [egute] *vt* (*linge*) to wring out; (*vaisselle, fromage*) to drain ▷ *vi*: **s'égoutter** *vi* to drip

égouttoir [egutwaʀ] *nm* draining board; (*mobile*) draining rack

égratigner [egʀatiɲe] *vt* to scratch; **s'égratigner** *vi* to scratch o.s.

égratignure [egʀatiɲyʀ] *nf* scratch

Égypte [eʒipt] *nf*: **l'~** Egypt

égyptien, ne [eʒipsjɛ̃, -ɛn] *adj* Egyptian ▷ *nm/f*: **É~, ne** Egyptian

eh [e] *excl* hey!; **eh bien** well

éhonté, e [eɔ̃te] *adj* shameless, brazen (*Brit*)

éjecter [eʒɛkte] *vt* (*Tech*) to eject; (*fam*) to kick *ou* chuck out

élaborer [elabɔʀe] *vt* to elaborate; (*projet, stratégie*) to work out; (*rapport*) to draft

élan [elɑ̃] *nm* (*Zool*) elk, moose; (*Sport: avant le saut*) run up; (*de véhicule*) momentum; (*fig: de tendresse etc*) surge; **prendre son ~/de l'~** to take a run up/gather speed; **perdre son ~** to lose one's momentum

élancé, e [elɑ̃se] *adj* slender

élancement [elɑ̃smɑ̃] *nm* shooting pain

élancer [elɑ̃se]: **s'élancer** *vi* to dash, hurl o.s.; (*fig: arbre, clocher*) to soar (upwards)

élargir [elaʀʒiʀ] *vt* to widen; (*vêtement*) to let out; (*Jur*) to release; **s'élargir** *vi* to widen; (*vêtement*) to stretch

élastique [elastik] *adj* elastic ▷ *nm* (*de bureau*) rubber band; (*pour la couture*) elastic *no pl*

électeur, -trice [elɛktœʀ, -tʀis] *nm/f* elector, voter

élection [elɛksjɔ̃] *nf* election; **élections** *nfpl*
(Pol) election(s); **sa terre/patrie d'~** the
land/country of one's choice; **~ partielle** ≈ by-
election; **~s législatives/présidentielles**
general/presidential election *sg*; *see note*

électorat [elɛktɔʀa] *nm* electorate

électricien, ne [elɛktʀisjɛ̃, -ɛn] *nm/f* electrician

électricité [elɛktʀisite] *nf* electricity; **allumer/
éteindre l'~** to put on/off the light; **~ statique**
static electricity

électrique [elɛktʀik] *adj* electric(al)

électrocuter [elɛktʀɔkyte] *vt* to electrocute

électroménager [elɛktʀɔmenaʒe] *adj*:
appareils ~s domestic (electrical) appliances
▷ *nm*: **l'~** household appliances

électronique [elɛktʀɔnik] *adj* electronic ▷ *nf*
(science) electronics *sg*

électrophone [elɛktʀɔfɔn] *nm* record player

élégance [elegɑ̃s] *nf* elegance

élégant, e [elegɑ̃, -ɑ̃t] *adj* elegant; (solution) neat,
elegant; (attitude, procédé) courteous, civilized

élément [elemɑ̃] *nm* element; (pièce) component,
part; **éléments** *nmpl* elements

élémentaire [elemɑ̃tɛʀ] *adj* elementary; (Chimie)
elemental

éléphant [elefɑ̃] *nm* elephant; **~ de mer**
elephant seal

élevage [ɛlvaʒ] *nm* breeding; (de bovins) cattle
breeding *ou* rearing; (ferme) cattle farm

élévation [elevasjɔ̃] *nf* (gén) elevation; (voir élever)
raising; (voir s'élever) rise

élevé, e [ɛlve] *adj* (prix, sommet) high; (fig: noble)
elevated; **bien/mal ~** well-/ill-mannered

élève [elɛv] *nm/f* pupil; **~ infirmière** student
nurse

élever [ɛlve] *vt* (enfant) to bring up, raise; (bétail,
volaille) to breed; (abeilles) to keep; (hausser: taux,
niveau) to raise; (fig: âme, esprit) to elevate; (édifier:
monument) to put up, erect; **s'élever** *vi* (avion,
alpiniste) to go up; (niveau, température, aussi: cri etc)
to rise; (survenir: difficultés) to arise; **s'~ à** (frais,
dégâts) to amount to, add up to; **s'~ contre** to
rise up against; **~ une protestation/critique**
to raise a protest/make a criticism; **~ qn au
rang de** to raise *ou* elevate sb to the rank of; **~
un nombre au carré/au cube** to square/cube
a number

éleveur, -euse [elvœʀ, -øz] *nm/f* stock breeder

élimé, e [elime] *adj* worn (thin), threadbare

éliminatoire [eliminatwaʀ] *adj* eliminatory;
(Sport) disqualifying ▷ *nf* (Sport) heat

éliminer [elimine] *vt* to eliminate

élire [eliʀ] *vt* to elect; **~ domicile à** to take up
residence in *ou* at

elle [ɛl] *pron* (sujet) she; (: chose) it; (complément)
her; it; **~s** (sujet) they; (complément) them; **~~
même** herself; itself; **~s-mêmes** themselves;
voir **il**

élocution [elɔkysjɔ̃] *nf* delivery; **défaut d'~**
speech impediment

éloge [elɔʒ] *nm* praise *gen no pl*; **faire l'~ de** to
praise

élogieux, -euse [elɔʒjø, -øz] *adj* laudatory, full
of praise

éloigné, e [elwaɲe] *adj* distant, far-off

éloignement [elwaɲmɑ̃] *nm* removal; putting
off; estrangement; (fig: distance) distance

éloigner [elwaɲe] *vt* (objet): **~ qch (de)** to move
ou take sth away (from); (personne): **~ qn (de)** to
take sb away *ou* remove sb (from); (échéance) to
put off, postpone; (soupçons, danger) to ward off;
s'éloigner (de) *vi* (personne) to go away (from);
(véhicule) to move away (from); (affectivement) to
become estranged (from)

élu, e [ely] *pp de* **élire** ▷ *nm/f* (Pol) elected
representative

éluder [elyde] *vt* to evade

Élysée [elize] *nm*: **(le palais de) l'~** the Élysée
palace; *see note*; **les Champs ~s** the Champs
Élysées

émacié, e [emasje] *adj* emaciated

émail, -aux [emaj, -o] *nm* enamel

e-mail [imɛl] *nm* email; **envoyer qch par ~** to
email sth

émaillé, e [emaje] *adj* enamelled; (fig): **~ de**
dotted with

émanciper [emɑ̃sipe] *vt* to emancipate;
s'émanciper (fig) to become emancipated *ou*
liberated

émaner [emane] : **~ de** *vt* to emanate from;
(Admin) to proceed from

emballage [ɑ̃balaʒ] *nm* wrapping; packing;
(papier) wrapping; (carton) packaging

emballer [ɑ̃bale] *vt* to wrap (up); (dans un
carton) to pack (up); (fig: fam) to thrill (to bits);
s'emballer *vi* (moteur) to race; (cheval) to bolt; (fig:
personne) to get carried away

embarcadère [ɑ̃baʀkadɛʀ] *nm* landing stage
(Brit), pier

embarcation [ɑ̃baʀkasjɔ̃] *nf* (small) boat,
(small) craft *inv*

embardée [ɑ̃baʀde] *nf* swerve; **faire une ~** to
swerve

embarquement [ɑ̃baʀkəmɑ̃] *nm* embarkation;
loading; boarding

embarquer [ɑ̃baʀke] *vt* (personne) to embark;
(marchandise) to load; (fam) to cart off; (: arrêter)
to nick ▷ *vi* (passager) to board; (Navig) to ship
water; **s'embarquer** *vi* to board; **s'~ dans** (affaire,
aventure) to embark upon

embarras [ɑ̃baʀa] *nm* (obstacle) hindrance;
(confusion) embarrassment; (ennuis): **être dans
l'~** to be in a predicament *ou* an awkward
position; (gêne financière) to be in difficulties; **~
gastrique** stomach upset

embarrassant, e [ɑ̃baʀasɑ̃, -ɑ̃t] *adj*
cumbersome; embarrassing; awkward

embarrasser [ɑ̃baʀase] *vt* (encombrer) to clutter
(up); (gêner) to hinder, hamper; (fig) to cause
embarrassment to; to put in an awkward
position; **s'embarrasser de** *vi* to burden o.s.
with

embauche [ɑ̃boʃ] *nf* hiring; **bureau d'~** labour
office

embaucher [ābоʃe] vt to take on, hire; **s'embaucher comme** vi to get (o.s.) a job as

embaumer [ābome] vt to embalm; (parfumer) to fill with its fragrance; ~ **la lavande** to be fragrant with (the scent of) lavender

embellie [ābeli] nf bright spell, brighter period

embellir [ābelir] vt to make more attractive; (une histoire) to embellish ▷ vi to grow lovelier ou more attractive

embêtant, e [ābɛtā, -āt] adj annoying

embêtement [ābɛtmā] nm problem, difficulty; **embêtements** nmpl trouble sg

embêter [ābete] vt to bother; **s'embêter** vi (s'ennuyer) to be bored; **ça m'embête** it bothers me; **il ne s'embête pas!** (ironique) he does all right for himself!

emblée [āble]: **d'~** adv straightaway

embobiner [ābobine] vt (enjôler): ~ **qn** to get round sb

emboîter [ābwate] vt to fit together; **s'emboîter dans** to fit into; **s'~ (l'un dans l'autre)** to fit together; ~ **le pas à qn** to follow in sb's footsteps

embonpoint [ābɔ̃pwɛ̃] nm stoutness (Brit), corpulence; **prendre de l'~** to grow stout (Brit) ou corpulent

embouchure [ābuʃyr] nf (Géo) mouth; (Mus) mouthpiece

embourber [āburbe]: **s'embourber** vi to get stuck in the mud; (fig): **s'~ dans** to sink into

embourgeoiser [āburʒwaze]: **s'embourgeoiser** vi to adopt a middle-class outlook

embouteillage [ābutɛjaʒ] nm traffic jam, (traffic) holdup (Brit)

emboutir [ābutir] vt (Tech) to stamp; (heurter) to crash into, ram

embranchement [ābrāʃmā] nm (routier) junction; (classification) branch

embraser [ābraze]: **s'embraser** vi to flare up

embrasser [ābrase] vt to kiss; (sujet, période) to embrace, encompass; (carrière) to embark on; (métier) to go in for, take up; ~ **du regard** to take in (with eyes); **s'embrasser** vi to kiss (each other)

embrasure [ābrazyr] nf: **dans l'~ de la porte** in the door(way)

embrayage [ābrɛjaʒ] nm clutch

embrayer [ābrɛje] vi (Auto) to let in the clutch ▷ vt (fig: affaire) to set in motion; ~ **sur qch** to begin on sth

embrocher [ābroʃe] vt to (put on a) spit (ou skewer)

embrouiller [ābruje] vt (fils) to tangle (up); (fiches, idées, personne) to muddle up; **s'embrouiller** vi to get in a muddle

embruns [ābrœ̃] nmpl sea spray sg

embryon [ābrijɔ̃] nm embryo

embûches [ābyʃ] nfpl pitfalls, traps

embué, e [ābɥe] adj misted up; **yeux ~s de larmes** eyes misty with tears

embuscade [ābyskad] nf ambush; **tendre une ~ à** to lay an ambush for

éméché, e [emeʃe] adj tipsy, merry

émeraude [ɛmrod] nf emerald ▷ adj inv emerald-green

émerger [emɛrʒe] vi to emerge; (faire saillie, aussi fig) to stand out

émeri [ɛmri] nm: **toile** ou **papier** ~ emery paper

émerveillement [emɛrvɛjmā] nm wonderment

émerveiller [emɛrvɛje] vt to fill with wonder; **s'émerveiller de** vi to marvel at

émettre [emɛtr(ə)] vt (son, lumière) to give out, emit; (message etc: Radio) to transmit; (billet, timbre, emprunt, chèque) to issue; (hypothèse, avis) to voice, put forward; (vœu) to express ▷ vi: ~ **sur ondes courtes** to broadcast on short wave

émeus etc [emø] vb voir **émouvoir**

émeute [emøt] nf riot

émietter [emjete] vt (pain, terre) to crumble; (fig) to split up, disperse; **s'émietter** vi (pain, terre) to crumble

émigrer [emigre] vi to emigrate

émincer [emɛ̃se] vt (Culin) to slice thinly

éminent, e [eminā, -āt] adj distinguished

émission [emisjɔ̃] nf (voir émettre) emission; transmission; issue; (Radio, TV) programme, broadcast

emmagasiner [āmagazine] vt to (put into) store; (fig) to store up

emmanchure [āmāʃyr] nf armhole

emmêler [āmele] vt to tangle (up); (fig) to muddle up; **s'emmêler** vi to get into a tangle

emménager [āmenaʒe] vi to move in; ~ **dans** to move into

emmener [āmne] vt to take (with one); (comme otage, capture) to take away; ~ **qn au concert** to take sb to a concert

emmerder [āmɛrde] (fam!) vt to bug, bother; **s'emmerder** vi (s'ennuyer) to be bored stiff; **je t'emmerde!** to hell with you!

emmitoufler [āmitufle] vt to wrap up (warmly); **s'emmitoufler** vi to wrap (o.s.) up (warmly)

émoi [emwa] nm (agitation, effervescence) commotion; (trouble) agitation; **en ~** (sens) excited, stirred

émoticone [emotikon] nm (Inform) smiley

émotif, -ive [emotif, -iv] adj emotional

émotion [emosjɔ̃] nf emotion; **avoir des ~s** (fig) to get a fright; **donner des ~s à** to give a fright to; **sans ~** without emotion, coldly

émousser [emuse] vt to blunt; (fig) to dull

émouvoir [emuvwar] vt (troubler) to stir, affect; (toucher, attendrir) to move; (indigner) to rouse; (effrayer) to disturb, worry; **s'émouvoir** vi to be affected; to be moved; to be roused; to be disturbed ou worried

empailler [āpaje] vt to stuff

empaqueter [āpakte] vt to pack up

emparer [āpare]: **s'emparer de** vt (objet) to seize, grab; (comme otage, Mil) to seize; (peur etc) to take hold of

empâter [āpate]: **s'empâter** vi to thicken out

empêchement [āpɛʃmā] nm (unexpected) obstacle, hitch

empêcher [āpɛʃe] vt to prevent; ~ **qn de faire** to prevent ou stop sb (from) doing; ~ **que qch**

(n')arrive/qn (ne) fasse to prevent sth from happening/sb from doing; **il n'empêche que** nevertheless, be that as it may; **il n'a pas pu s'~ de rire** he couldn't help laughing

empereur [ɑ̃pʀœʀ] *nm* emperor

empester [ɑ̃pɛste] *vt* (*lieu*) to stink out ▷ *vi* to stink, reek; **~ le tabac/le vin** to stink *ou* reek of tobacco/wine

empêtrer [ɑ̃petʀe] *vt*: **s'empêtrer dans** (*fils etc, aussi fig*) to get tangled up in

emphase [ɑ̃faz] *nf* pomposity, bombast; **avec ~** pompously

empiéter [ɑ̃pjete] : **~ sur** *vt* to encroach upon

empiffrer [ɑ̃pifʀe] : **s'empiffrer** *vi* (*péj*) to stuff o.s.

empiler [ɑ̃pile] *vt* to pile (up), stack (up); **s'empiler** *vi* to pile up

empire [ɑ̃piʀ] *nm* empire; (*fig*) influence; **style** E~ Empire style; **sous l'~ de** in the grip of

empirer [ɑ̃piʀe] *vi* to worsen, deteriorate

emplacement [ɑ̃plasmɑ̃] *nm* site; **sur l'~ de** on the site of

emplette [ɑ̃plɛt] *nf*: **faire l'~ de** to purchase; **emplettes** shopping *sg*; **faire des ~s** to go shopping

emplir [ɑ̃pliʀ] *vt* to fill; **s'emplir (de)** *vi* to fill (with)

emploi [ɑ̃plwa] *nm* use; (*Comm, Écon*) **l'~** employment; (*poste*) job, situation; **d'~ facile** easy to use; **le plein ~** full employment; **~ du temps** timetable, schedule

employé, e [ɑ̃plwaje] *nm/f* employee; **~ de bureau/banque** office/bank employee *ou* clerk; **~ de maison** domestic (servant)

employer [ɑ̃plwaje] *vt* (*outil, moyen, méthode, mot*) to use; (*ouvrier, main-d'œuvre*) to employ; **s'~ à qch/ à faire** to apply *ou* devote o.s. to sth/to doing

employeur, -euse [ɑ̃plwajœʀ, -øz] *nm/f* employer

empocher [ɑ̃pɔʃe] *vt* to pocket

empoigner [ɑ̃pwaɲe] *vt* to grab; **s'empoigner** (*fig*) to have a row *ou* set-to

empoisonner [ɑ̃pwazɔne] *vt* to poison; (*empester: air, pièce*) to stink out; (*fam*): **~ qn** to drive sb mad; **s'empoisonner** to poison o.s.; **~ l'atmosphère** (*aussi fig*) to poison the atmosphere; (*aussi*: **il nous empoisonne l'existence**) he's the bane of our life

emporté, e [ɑ̃pɔʀte] *adj* (*personne, caractère*) fiery

emporter [ɑ̃pɔʀte] *vt* to take (with one); (*en dérobant ou enlevant, emmener: blessés, voyageurs*) to take away; (*entraîner*) to carry away *ou* along; (*arracher*) to tear off; (*rivière, vent*) to carry away; (*Mil: position*) to take; (*avantage, approbation*) to win; **s'emporter** *vi* (*de colère*) to fly into a rage, lose one's temper; **la maladie qui l'a emporté** the illness which caused his death; **l'~** to gain victory; **l'~ (sur)** to get the upper hand (of); (*méthode etc*) to prevail (over); **boissons à ~** take-away drinks

empreint, e [ɑ̃pʀɛ̃, -ɛ̃t] *adj*: **~ de** marked with; tinged with ▷ *nf* (*de pied, main*) print; (*fig*) stamp, mark; **~e (digitale)** fingerprint; **~e écologique** carbon footprint

empressé, e [ɑ̃pʀese] *adj* attentive; (*péj*) overanxious to please, overattentive

empressement [ɑ̃pʀɛsmɑ̃] *nm* eagerness

empresser [ɑ̃pʀese] : **s'empresser** *vi*: **s'~ auprès de qn** to surround sb with attentions; **s'~ de faire** to hasten to do

emprise [ɑ̃pʀiz] *nf* hold, ascendancy; **sous l'~ de** under the influence of

emprisonnement [ɑ̃pʀizɔnmɑ̃] *nm* imprisonment

emprisonner [ɑ̃pʀizɔne] *vt* to imprison, jail

emprunt [ɑ̃pʀœ̃] *nm* borrowing *no pl*, loan (*from debtor's point of view*); (*Ling etc*) borrowing; **nom d'~** assumed name; **~ d'État** government *ou* state loan; **~ public à 5%** 5% public loan

emprunté, e [ɑ̃pʀœ̃te] *adj* (*fig*) ill-at-ease, awkward

emprunter [ɑ̃pʀœ̃te] *vt* to borrow; (*itinéraire*) to take, follow; (*style, manière*) to adopt, assume

ému, e [emy] *pp de* **émouvoir** ▷ *adj* excited; touched; moved

en [ɑ̃] *prép* **1** (*endroit, pays*) in; (*direction*) to; **habiter en France/ville** to live in France/town; **aller en France/ville** to go to France/town

2 (*moment, temps*) in; **en été/juin** in summer/June; **en 3 jours/20 ans** in 3 days/20 years

3 (*moyen*) by; **en avion/taxi** by plane/taxi

4 (*composition*) made of; **c'est en verre/coton/laine** it's (made of) glass/cotton/wool; **en metal/plastique** made of metal/plastic; **un collier en argent** a silver necklace; **en deux volumes/une pièce** in two volumes/one piece

5 (*description, état*): **une femme (habillée) en rouge** a woman (dressed) in red; **peindre qch en rouge** to paint sth red; **en T/étoile** T-/star-shaped; **en chemise/chaussettes** in one's shirt sleeves/socks; **en soldat** as a soldier; **en civil** in civilian clothes; **cassé en plusieurs morceaux** broken into several pieces; **en réparation** being repaired, under repair; **en vacances** on holiday; **en bonne santé** healthy, in good health; **en deuil** in mourning; **le même en plus grand** the same but *ou* only bigger

6 (*avec gérondif*) while; on; **en dormant** while sleeping, as one sleeps; **en sortant** on going out, as he *etc* went out; **sortir en courant** to run out; **en apprenant la nouvelle, il s'est évanoui** he fainted at the news *ou* when he heard the news

7 (*matière*): **fort en math** good at maths; **expert en** expert in

8 (*conformité*): **en tant que** as; **en bon politicien, il …** good politician that he is, he …, like a good *ou* true politician, he …; **je te parle en ami** I'm talking to you as a friend

▷ *pron* **1** (*indéfini*): **j'en ai/veux** I have/want some; **en as-tu?** have you got any?; **il n'y en a pas** there isn't/aren't any; **je n'en veux pas** I don't want any; **j'en ai deux** I've got two; **combien y en a-t-il?** how many (of them) are there?; **j'en ai assez** I've got enough (of it *ou* them); (*j'en ai* *marre*) I've had enough; **où en étais-je?** where was I?

2 (*provenance*) from there; **j'en viens** I've come from there

3 (*cause*): **il en est malade/perd le sommeil** he is ill/can't sleep because of it

4 (*de la part de*): **elle en est aimée** she is loved by him (*ou* them *etc*)

5 (*complément de nom, d'adjectif, de verbe*): **j'en connais les dangers** I know its *ou* the dangers; **j'en suis fier/ai besoin** I am proud of it/need it; **il en est ainsi** *ou* **de même pour moi** it's the same for me, same here

ENA [ena] *sigle f* (= *École nationale d'administration*) *grande école for training civil servants*

encadrement [ākadʀəmā] *nm* framing; training; (*de porte*) frame; **~ du crédit** credit restrictions

encadrer [ākadʀe] *vt* (*tableau, image*) to frame; (*fig: entourer*) to surround; (*personnel, soldats etc*) to train; (*Comm: crédit*) to restrict

encaissé, e [ākese] *adj* (*vallée*) steep-sided; (*rivière*) with steep banks

encaisser [ākese] *vt* (*chèque*) to cash; (*argent*) to collect; (*fig: coup, défaite*) to take

encart [ākaʀ] *nm* insert; **~ publicitaire** publicity insert

en-cas [āka] *nm inv* snack

encastré, e [ākastʀe] *adj* (*four, baignoire*) built-in

enceinte [āsɛ̃t] *adj f*: **~ (de six mois)** (six months) pregnant ▷ *nf* (*mur*) wall; (*espace*) enclosure; **~ (acoustique)** speaker

encens [āsā] *nm* incense

encercler [āsɛʀkle] *vt* to surround

enchaîner [āʃene] *vt* to chain up; (*mouvements, séquences*) to link (together) ▷ *vi* to carry on

enchanté, e [āʃāte] *adj* (*ravi*) delighted; (*ensorcelé*) enchanted; **~ (de faire votre connaissance)** pleased to meet you, how do you do?

enchantement [āʃātmā] *nm* delight; (*magie*) enchantment; **comme par ~** as if by magic

enchère [āʃɛʀ] *nf* bid; **faire une ~** to (make a) bid; **mettre/vendre aux ~s** to put up for (sale by)/sell by auction; **les ~s montent** the bids are rising; **faire monter les ~s** (*fig*) to raise the bidding

enchevêtrer [āʃvetʀe] *vt* to tangle (up)

enclencher [āklāʃe] *vt* (*mécanisme*) to engage; (*fig: affaire*) to set in motion; **s'enclencher** *vi* to engage

enclin, e [āklɛ̃, -in] *adj*: **~ à qch/à faire** inclined *ou* prone to sth/to do

enclos [āklo] *nm* enclosure; (*clôture*) fence

enclume [āklym] *nf* anvil

encoche [ākɔʃ] *nf* notch

encoignure [ākɔɲyʀ] *nf* corner

encolure [ākɔlyʀ] *nf* (*tour de cou*) collar size; (*col, cou*) neck

encombrant, e [ākɔ̃bʀā, -āt] *adj* cumbersome, bulky

encombre [ākɔ̃bʀ(ə)]: **sans ~** *adv* without mishap *ou* incident

encombrement [ākɔ̃bʀəmā] *nm* (*d'un lieu*) cluttering (up); (*d'un objet: dimensions*) bulk

encombrer [ākɔ̃bʀe] *vt* to clutter (up); (*gêner*) to hamper; **s'encombrer de** (*bagages etc*) to load *ou* burden o.s. with; **~ le passage** to block *ou* obstruct the way

encontre [ākɔ̃tʀ(ə)]: **à l'~ de** *prép* against, counter to

encore [ākɔʀ] *adv* **1** (*continuation*) still; **il y travaille ~** he's still working on it; **pas ~** not yet

2 (*de nouveau*) again; **j'irai ~ demain** I'll go again tomorrow; **~ une fois** (once) again; **~ un effort** one last effort; **~ deux jours** two more days

3 (*intensif*) even, still; **~ plus fort/mieux** even louder/better, louder/better still; **hier ~** even yesterday; **non seulement ..., mais ~ ...** not only ..., but also ...; **~!** (*insatisfaction*) not again!; **quoi ~?** what now?

4 (*restriction*) even so *ou* then, only; **~ pourrais-je le faire si ...** even so, I might be able to do it if ...; **si ~** if only; **~ que** *conj* although

encouragement [ākuʀaʒmā] *nm* encouragement; (*récompense*) incentive

encourager [ākuʀaʒe] *vt* to encourage; **~ qn à faire qch** to encourage sb to do sth

encourir [ākuʀiʀ] *vt* to incur

encrasser [ākʀase] *vt* to foul up; (*Auto etc*) to soot up

encre [ākʀ(ə)] *nf* ink; **~ de Chine** Indian ink; **~ indélébile** indelible ink; **~ sympathique** invisible ink

encrier [ākʀije] *nm* inkwell

encroûter [ākʀute]: **s'encroûter** *vi* (*fig*) to get into a rut, get set in one's ways

encyclopédie [āsiklɔpedi] *nf* encyclopaedia (*Brit*), encyclopedia (*US*)

endetter [ādete] *vt*: **s'endetter** *vi* to get into debt

endiablé, e [ādjable] *adj* furious; (*enfant*) boisterous

endimanché, e [ādimāʃe] *adj* in one's Sunday best

endive [ādiv] *nf* chicory *no pl*

endoctriner [ādɔktʀine] *vt* to indoctrinate

endommager [ādɔmaʒe] *vt* to damage

endormi, e [ādɔʀmi] *pp de* **endormir** ▷ *adj* (*personne*) asleep; (*fig: indolent, lent*) sluggish; (*engourdi: main, pied*) numb

endormir [ādɔʀmiʀ] *vt* to put to sleep; (*chaleur etc*) to send to sleep; (*Méd: dent, nerf*) to anaesthetize; (*fig: soupçons*) to allay; **s'endormir** *vi* to fall asleep, go to sleep

endosser [ādose] *vt* (*responsabilité*) to take, shoulder; (*chèque*) to endorse; (*uniforme, tenue*) to put on, don

endroit [ādʀwa] *nm* place; (*localité*): **les gens de l'~** the local people; (*opposé à l'envers*) right side; **à cet ~** in this place; **à l'~** right side out; the right way up; (*vêtement*) the right way out; **à l'~ de** *prép* regarding, with regard to; **par ~s** in places

enduire [ādɥiʀ] *vt* to coat; **~ qch de** to coat sth with

enduit, e [ɑ̃dɥi, -it] pp de **enduire** ▷ nm coating
endurance [ɑ̃dyʀɑ̃s] nf endurance
endurant, e [ɑ̃dyʀɑ̃, -ɑ̃t] adj tough, hardy
endurcir [ɑ̃dyʀsiʀ] vt (physiquement) to toughen; (moralement) to harden; **s'endurcir** vi to become tougher; to become hardened
endurer [ɑ̃dyʀe] vt to endure, bear
énergétique [enɛʀʒetik] adj (ressources etc) energy cpd; (aliment) energizing
énergie [enɛʀʒi] nf (Physique) energy; (Tech) power; (fig: physique) energy; (: morale) vigour, spirit; ~ **éolienne/solaire** wind/solar power
énergique [enɛʀʒik] adj energetic; vigorous; (mesures) drastic, stringent
énervant, e [enɛʀvɑ̃, -ɑ̃t] adj irritating
énervé, e [enɛʀve] adj nervy, on edge; (agacé) irritated
énerver [enɛʀve] vt to irritate, annoy; **s'énerver** vi to get excited, get worked up
enfance [ɑ̃fɑ̃s] nf (âge) childhood; (fig) infancy; (enfants) children pl; **c'est l'~ de l'art** it's child's play; **petite ~** infancy; **souvenir/ami d'~** childhood memory/friend; **retomber en ~** to lapse into one's second childhood
enfant [ɑ̃fɑ̃] nm/f child; ~ **adoptif/naturel** adopted/natural child; **bon ~** adj good-natured, easy-going; ~ **de chœur** nm (Rel) altar boy; ~ **prodige** child prodigy; ~ **unique** only child
enfantillage [ɑ̃fɑ̃tijaʒ] nm (péj) childish behaviour no pl
enfantin, e [ɑ̃fɑ̃tɛ̃, -in] adj childlike; (péj) childish; (langage) child cpd
enfer [ɑ̃fɛʀ] nm hell; **allure/bruit d'~** horrendous speed/noise
enfermer [ɑ̃fɛʀme] vt to shut up; (à clef, interner) to lock up; **s'enfermer** to shut o.s. away; **s'~ à clé** to lock o.s. in; **s'~ dans la solitude/le mutisme** to retreat into solitude/silence
enfiévré, e [ɑ̃fjevʀe] adj (fig) feverish
enfiler [ɑ̃file] vt (vêtement): ~ **qch** to slip sth on, slip into sth; (insérer): ~ **qch dans** to stick sth into; (rue, couloir) to take; (perles) to string; (aiguille) to thread; **s'enfiler dans** vi to disappear into
enfin [ɑ̃fɛ̃] adv at last; (en énumérant) lastly; (de restriction, résignation) still; (eh bien) well; (pour conclure) in a word
enflammer [ɑ̃flame] vt to set fire to; (Méd) to inflame; **s'enflammer** vi to catch fire; to become inflamed
enflé, e [ɑ̃fle] adj swollen; (péj: style) bombastic, turgid
enfler [ɑ̃fle] vi to swell (up); **s'enfler** vi to swell
enfoncer [ɑ̃fɔ̃se] vt (clou) to drive in; (faire pénétrer): ~ **qch dans** to push (ou drive) sth into; (forcer: porte) to break open; (: plancher) to cause to cave in; (défoncer: côtes etc) to smash; (fam: surpasser) to lick, beat (hollow) ▷ vi (dans la vase etc) to sink in; (sol, surface porteuse) to give way; **s'enfoncer** vi to sink; **s'~ dans** to sink into; (forêt, ville) to disappear into; ~ **un chapeau sur la tête** to cram ou jam a hat on one's head; ~ **qn**

dans la dette to drag sb into debt
enfouir [ɑ̃fwiʀ] vt (dans le sol) to bury; (dans un tiroir etc) to tuck away; **s'enfouir dans/sous** to bury o.s. in/under
enfourcher [ɑ̃fuʀʃe] vt to mount; ~ **son dada** (fig) to get on one's hobby-horse
enfreindre [ɑ̃fʀɛ̃dʀ(ə)] vt to infringe, break
enfuir [ɑ̃fɥiʀ]: **s'enfuir** vi to run away ou off
enfumer [ɑ̃fyme] vt to smoke out
engageant, e [ɑ̃gaʒɑ̃, -ɑ̃t] adj attractive, appealing
engagement [ɑ̃gaʒmɑ̃] nm taking on, engaging; starting; investing; (promesse) commitment; (Mil: combat) engagement; (: recrutement) enlistment; (Sport) entry; **prendre l'~ de faire** to undertake to do; **sans ~** (Comm) without obligation
engager [ɑ̃gaʒe] vt (embaucher) to take on, engage; (commencer) to start; (lier) to bind, commit; (impliquer, entraîner) to involve; (investir) to invest, lay out; (faire intervenir) to engage; (Sport: concurrents, chevaux) to enter; (inciter): ~ **qn à faire** to urge sb to do; (faire pénétrer): ~ **qch dans** to insert sth into; ~ **qn à qch** to urge sth on sb; **s'engager** vi to get taken on; (Mil) to enlist; (promettre, politiquement) to commit o.s.; (débuter) to start (up); **s'~ à faire** to undertake to do; **s'~ dans** (rue, passage) to enter, turn into; (s'emboîter) to engage ou fit into; (fig: affaire, discussion) to enter into, embark on
engelures [ɑ̃ʒlyʀ] nfpl chilblains
engendrer [ɑ̃ʒɑ̃dʀe] vt to father; (fig) to create, breed
engin [ɑ̃ʒɛ̃] nm machine instrument; vehicle; (péj) gadget; (Aviat: avion) aircraft inv; (: missile) missile; ~ **blindé** armoured vehicle; ~ **(explosif)** (explosive) device; ~**s (spéciaux)** missiles
englober [ɑ̃glɔbe] vt to include
engloutir [ɑ̃glutiʀ] vt to swallow up; (fig: dépenses) to devour; **s'engloutir** vi to be engulfed
engoncé, e [ɑ̃gɔ̃se] adj: ~ **dans** cramped in
engorger [ɑ̃gɔʀʒe] vt to obstruct, block; **s'engorger** vi to become blocked
engouement [ɑ̃gumɑ̃] nm (sudden) passion
engouffrer [ɑ̃gufʀe] vt to swallow up, devour; **s'engouffrer dans** to rush into
engourdir [ɑ̃guʀdiʀ] vt to numb; (fig) to dull, blunt; **s'engourdir** vi to go numb
engrais [ɑ̃gʀɛ] nm manure; ~ **(chimique)** (chemical) fertilizer; ~ **organique/inorganique** organic/inorganic fertilizer
engraisser [ɑ̃gʀese] vt to fatten (up); (terre: fertiliser) to fertilize ▷ vi (péj) to get fat(ter)
engrenage [ɑ̃gʀənaʒ] nm gears pl, gearing; (fig) chain
engueuler [ɑ̃gœle] vt (fam) to bawl at ou out
enhardir [ɑ̃aʀdiʀ]: **s'enhardir** vi to grow bolder
énigme [enigm(ə)] nf riddle
enivrer [ɑ̃nivʀe] vt: **s'enivrer** to get drunk; **s'~ de** (fig) to become intoxicated with
enjambée [ɑ̃ʒɑ̃be] nf stride; **d'une ~** with one stride

enjamber [ãʒãbe] vt to stride over; (pont etc) to span, straddle

enjeu, x [ãʒø] nm stakes pl

enjôler [ãʒole] vt to coax, wheedle

enjoliver [ãʒɔlive] vt to embellish

enjoliveur [ãʒɔlivœʀ] nm (Auto) hub cap

enjoué, e [ãʒwe] adj playful

enlacer [ãlase] vt (étreindre) to embrace, hug; (lianes) to wind round, entwine

enlaidir [ãlediʀ] vt to make ugly ▷ vi to become ugly

enlèvement [ãlεvmã] nm removal; (rapt) abduction, kidnapping; **l'~ des ordures ménagères** refuse collection

enlever [ãlve] vt (ôter: gén) to remove; (: vêtement, lunettes) to take off; (: Méd: organe) to remove; (emporter: ordures etc) to collect, take away; (kidnapper) to abduct, kidnap; (obtenir: prix, contrat) to win; (Mil: position) to take; (morceau de piano etc) to execute with spirit ou brio; (prendre): **~ qch à qn** to take sth (away) from sb; **s'enlever** vi (tache) to come out ou off; **la maladie qui nous l'a enlevé** (euphémisme) the illness which took him from us

enliser [ãlize]: **s'enliser** vi to sink, get stuck; (dialogue etc) to get bogged down

enneigé, e [ãneʒe] adj snowy; (col) snowed-up; (maison) snowed-in

ennemi, e [εnmi] adj hostile; (Mil) enemy cpd ▷ nm/f enemy; **être ~ de** to be strongly averse ou opposed to

ennui [ãnɥi] nm (lassitude) boredom; (difficulté) trouble no pl; **avoir des ~s** to have problems; **s'attirer des ~s** to cause problems for o.s.

ennuyer [ãnɥije] vt to bother; (lasser) to bore; **s'ennuyer** vi to be bored; (s'ennuyer de: regretter) to miss; **si cela ne vous ennuie pas** if it's no trouble to you

ennuyeux, -euse [ãnɥijø, -øz] adj boring, tedious; (agaçant) annoying

énoncé [enɔse] nm terms pl; wording; (Ling) utterance

énoncer [enɔse] vt to say, express; (conditions) to set out, lay down, state

enorgueillir [ãnɔʀgœjiʀ]: **s'enorgueillir de** vt to pride o.s. on; to boast

énorme [enɔʀm(ə)] adj enormous, huge

énormément [enɔʀmemã] adv enormously, tremendously; **~ de neige/gens** an enormous amount of snow/number of people

énormité [enɔʀmite] nf enormity, hugeness; (propos) outrageous remark

enquérir [ãkeʀiʀ]: **s'enquérir de** vt to inquire about

enquête [ãkεt] nf (de journaliste, de police) investigation; (judiciaire, administrative) inquiry; (sondage d'opinion) survey

enquêter [ãkete] vi to investigate; to hold an inquiry; (faire un sondage): **~ (sur)** to do a survey (on), carry out an opinion poll (on)

enquiers, enquière etc [ãkjεʀ] vb voir **enquérir**

enquiquiner [ãkikine] vt to rile, irritate

enraciné, e [ãʀasine] adj deep-rooted

enragé, e [ãʀaʒe] adj (Méd) rabid, with rabies; (furieux) furiously angry; (fig) fanatical; **~ de** wild about

enrageant, e [ãʀaʒã, -ãt] adj infuriating

enrager [ãʀaʒe] vi to be furious, be in a rage; **faire ~ qn** to make sb wild with anger

enrayer [ãʀeje] vt to check, stop; **s'enrayer** vi (arme à feu) to jam

enregistrement [ãʀʒistʀəmã] nm recording; (Admin) registration; **~ des bagages** (à l'aéroport) baggage check-in; **~ magnétique** tape-recording

enregistrer [ãʀʒistʀe] vt (Mus) to record; (Inform) to save; (remarquer, noter) to note, record; (Comm: commande) to note, enter; (fig: mémoriser) to make a mental note of; (Admin) to register; (aussi: **faire enregistrer**: bagages: par train) to register; (: à l'aéroport) to check in

enrhumé, e [ãʀyme] adj: **il est ~** he has a cold

enrhumer [ãʀyme]: **s'enrhumer** vi to catch a cold

enrichir [ãʀiʃiʀ] vt to make rich(er); (fig) to enrich; **s'enrichir** vi to get rich(er)

enrober [ãʀɔbe] vt: **~ qch de** to coat sth with; (fig) to wrap sth up in

enrôler [ãʀole] vt to enlist; **s'enrôler (dans)** vi to enlist (in)

enrouer [ãʀwe]: **s'enrouer** vi to go hoarse

enrouler [ãʀule] vt (fil, corde) to wind (up); **s'enrouler** to coil up; **~ qch autour de** to wind sth (a)round

ensanglanté, e [ãsãglãte] adj covered with blood

enseignant, e [ãsεɲã, -ãt] adj teaching ▷ nm/f teacher

enseigne [ãsεɲ] nf sign ▷ nm: **~ de vaisseau** lieutenant; **à telle ~ que** so much so that; **être logés à la même ~** (fig) to be in the same boat; **~ lumineuse** neon sign

enseignement [ãsεɲmã] nm teaching; **~ ménager** home economics; **~ primaire** primary (Brit) ou grade school (US) education; **~ secondaire** secondary (Brit) ou high school (US) education

enseigner [ãseɲe] vt, vi to teach; **~ qch à qn/à qn que** to teach sb sth/sb that

ensemble [ãsãbl(ə)] adv together ▷ nm (assemblage, Math) set; (totalité): **l'~ du/de la** the whole ou entire; (vêtement féminin) ensemble, suit; (unité, harmonie) unity; (résidentiel) housing development; **aller ~** to go together; **impression/idée d'~** overall ou general impression/idea; **dans l'~** (en gros) on the whole; **dans son ~** overall, in general; **~ vocal/musical** vocal/musical ensemble

ensemencer [ãsmãse] vt to sow

ensevelir [ãsəvliʀ] vt to bury

ensoleillé, e [ãsɔleje] adj sunny

ensommeillé, e [ãsɔmeje] adj sleepy, drowsy

ensorceler [ãsɔʀsəle] vt to enchant, bewitch

ensuite [ãsɥit] adv then, next; (plus tard)

afterwards, later; **~ de quoi** after which
ensuivre [ɑ̃sɥivʀ(ə)]: **s'ensuivre** vi to follow, ensue; **il s'ensuit que ...** it follows that ...; **et tout ce qui s'ensuit** and all that goes with it
entaille [ɑ̃taj] nf (encoche) notch; (blessure) cut; **se faire une ~** to cut o.s.
entamer [ɑ̃tame] vt to start; (hostilités, pourparlers) to open; (fig: altérer) to make a dent in; to damage
entasser [ɑ̃tase] vt (empiler) to pile up, heap up; (tenir à l'étroit) to cram together; **s'entasser** vi to pile up; to cram; **s'~ dans** to cram into
entendre [ɑ̃tɑ̃dʀ(ə)] vt to hear; (comprendre) to understand; (vouloir dire) to mean; (vouloir): **~ être obéi/que** to intend ou mean to be obeyed/that; **j'ai entendu dire que** I've heard (it said) that; **je suis heureux de vous l'~ dire** I'm pleased to hear you say it; **~ parler de** to hear of; **laisser ~ que**, **donner à ~ que** to let it be understood that; **~ raison** to see sense, listen to reason; **qu'est-ce qu'il ne faut pas ~!** whatever next!; **j'ai mal entendu** I didn't catch what was said; **je vous entends très mal** I can hardly hear you; **s'entendre** vi (sympathiser) to get on; (se mettre d'accord) to agree; **s'~ à qch/à faire** (être compétent) to be good at sth/doing; **ça s'entend** (est audible) it's audible; **je m'entends** I mean; **entendons-nous!** let's be clear what we mean
entendu, e [ɑ̃tɑ̃dy] pp de **entendre** ▷ adj (réglé) agreed; (au courant: air) knowing; **étant ~ que** since (it's understood ou agreed that); **(c'est)** **~** all right, agreed; **c'est ~** (concession) all right, granted; **bien ~** of course
entente [ɑ̃tɑ̃t] nf (entre amis, pays) understanding, harmony; (accord, traité) agreement, understanding; **à double ~** (sens) with a double meaning
entériner [ɑ̃teʀine] vt to ratify, confirm
enterrement [ɑ̃tɛʀmɑ̃] nm burying; (cérémonie) funeral, burial; (cortège funèbre) funeral procession
enterrer [ɑ̃teʀe] vt to bury
entêtant, e [ɑ̃tɛtɑ̃, -ɑ̃t] adj heady
en-tête [ɑ̃tɛt] nm heading; (de papier à lettres) letterhead; **papier à ~** headed notepaper
entêté, e [ɑ̃tete] adj stubborn
entêter [ɑ̃tete]: **s'entêter** vi: **s'~ (à faire)** to persist (in doing)
enthousiasme [ɑ̃tuzjasm(ə)] nm enthusiasm; **avec ~** enthusiastically
enthousiasmer [ɑ̃tuzjasme] vt to fill with enthusiasm; **s'~ (pour qch)** to get enthusiastic (about sth)
enthousiaste [ɑ̃tuzjast(ə)] adj enthusiastic
enticher [ɑ̃tiʃe]: **s'enticher de** vt to become infatuated with
entier, -ière [ɑ̃tje, -jɛʀ] adj (non entamé, en totalité) whole; (total, complet): complete; (fig: caractère) unbending, averse to compromise ▷ nm (Math) whole; **en ~** totally; in its entirety; **se donner tout ~ à qch** to devote o.s. completely to sth; **lait ~** full-cream milk; **pain ~** wholemeal bread; **nombre ~** whole number

entièrement [ɑ̃tjɛʀmɑ̃] adv entirely, completely, wholly
entonner [ɑ̃tɔne] vt (chanson) to strike up
entonnoir [ɑ̃tɔnwaʀ] nm (ustensile) funnel; (trou) shell-hole, crater
entorse [ɑ̃tɔʀs(ə)] nf (Méd) sprain; (fig): **~ à la loi/au règlement** infringement of the law/rule; **se faire une ~ à la cheville/au poignet** to sprain one's ankle/wrist
entortiller [ɑ̃tɔʀtije] vt (envelopper): **~ qch dans/avec** to wrap sth in/with; (enrouler): **~ qch autour de** to twist ou wind sth (a)round; (fam): **~ qn** to get (a)round sb; (: duper) to hoodwink sb (Brit), trick sb; **s'entortiller dans** vi (draps) to roll o.s. up in; (fig: réponses) to get tangled up in
entourage [ɑ̃tuʀaʒ] nm circle; family (circle); (d'une vedette etc) entourage; (ce qui enclôt) surround
entouré, e [ɑ̃tuʀe] adj (recherché, admiré) popular; **~ de** surrounded by
entourer [ɑ̃tuʀe] vt to surround; (apporter son soutien à) to rally round; **~ de** to surround with; (trait) to encircle with; **s'entourer de** vi to surround o.s. with; **s'~ de précautions** to take all possible precautions
entracte [ɑ̃tʀakt(ə)] nm interval
entraide [ɑ̃tʀɛd] nf mutual aid ou assistance
entrain [ɑ̃tʀɛ̃] nm spirit; **avec ~** (répondre, travailler) energetically; **faire qch sans ~** to do sth half-heartedly ou without enthusiasm
entraînement [ɑ̃tʀɛnmɑ̃] nm training; (Tech): **~ à chaîne/galet** chain/wheel drive; **manquer d'~** to be unfit; **~ par ergots/friction** (Inform) tractor/friction feed
entraîner [ɑ̃tʀene] vt (tirer: wagons) to pull; (charrier) to carry ou drag along; (Tech) to drive; (emmener: personne) to take (off); (mener à l'assaut, influencer) to lead; (Sport) to train; (impliquer) to entail; (causer) to lead to, bring about; **~ qn à faire** (inciter) to lead sb to do; **s'entraîner** vi (Sport) to train; **s'~ à qch/à faire** to train o.s. for sth/to do
entraîneur [ɑ̃tʀɛnœʀ] nm (Sport) coach, trainer; (Hippisme) trainer
entraver [ɑ̃tʀave] vt (circulation) to hold up; (action, progrès) to hinder, hamper
entre [ɑ̃tʀ(ə)] prép between; (parmi) among(st); **l'un d'~ eux/nous** one of them/us; **le meilleur d'~ eux/nous** the best of them/us; **ils préfèrent rester ~ eux** they prefer to keep to themselves; **~ autres (choses)** among other things; **~ nous, ...** between ourselves ..., between you and me ...; **ils se battent ~ eux** they are fighting among(st) themselves
entrebâillé, e [ɑ̃tʀəbaje] adj half-open, ajar
entrechoquer [ɑ̃tʀəʃɔke]: **s'entrechoquer** vi to knock ou bang together
entrecôte [ɑ̃tʀəkot] nf entrecôte ou rib steak
entrecouper [ɑ̃tʀəkupe] vt: **~ qch de** to intersperse sth with; **~ un récit/voyage de** to interrupt a story/journey with; **s'entrecouper** vi (traits, lignes) to cut across each other

entrecroiser [ɑ̃trəkrwaze] *vt*: **s'entrecroiser** *vi* to intertwine

entrée [ɑ̃tre] *nf* entrance; (*accès: au cinéma etc*) admission; (*billet*) (admission) ticket; (*Culin*) first course; (*Comm: de marchandises*) entry; (*Inform*) entry, input; **entrées** *nfpl*: **avoir ses ~s chez** *ou* **auprès de** to be a welcome visitor to; **d'~** *adv* from the outset; **erreur d'~** input error; **"~ interdite"** "no admittance *ou* entry"; **~ des artistes** stage door; **~ en matière** introduction; **~ principale** main entrance; **~ en scène** entrance; **~ de service** service entrance

entrefaites [ɑ̃trəfɛt]: **sur ces ~** *adv* at this juncture

entrefilet [ɑ̃trəfilɛ] *nm* (*article*) paragraph, short report

entrejambes [ɑ̃trəʒɑ̃b] *nm inv* crotch

entrelacer [ɑ̃trəlase] *vt*: **s'entrelacer** *vi* to intertwine

entremêler [ɑ̃trəmele] *vt*: **~ qch de** to (inter)mingle sth with

entremets [ɑ̃trəmɛ] *nm* (cream) dessert

entremise [ɑ̃trəmiz] *nf* intervention; **par l'~ de** through

entreposer [ɑ̃trəpoze] *vt* to store, put into storage

entrepôt [ɑ̃trəpo] *nm* warehouse

entreprenant, e [ɑ̃trəprənɑ̃, -ɑ̃t] *vb voir* **entreprendre** ▷ *adj* (*actif*) enterprising; (*trop galant*) forward

entreprendre [ɑ̃trəprɑ̃dr(ə)] *vt* (*se lancer dans*) to undertake; (*commencer*) to begin *ou* start (upon); (*personne*) to buttonhole; **~ qn sur un sujet** to tackle sb on a subject; **~ de faire** to undertake to do

entrepreneur [ɑ̃trəprənœr] *nm*: **~ (en bâtiment)** (building) contractor; **~ de pompes funèbres** funeral director, undertaker

entrepris, e [ɑ̃trəpri, -iz] *pp de* **entreprendre** ▷ *nf* (*société*) firm, business; (*action*) undertaking, venture

entrer [ɑ̃tre] *vi* to go (*ou* come) in, enter ▷ *vt* (*Inform*) to input, enter; **(faire) ~ qch dans** to get sth into; **~ dans** (*gén*) to enter; (*pièce*) to go (*ou* come) into, enter; (*club*) to join; (*heurter*) to run into; (*partager: vues, craintes de qn*) to share; (*être une composante de*) to go into; (*faire partie de*) to form part of; **~ au couvent** to enter a convent; **~ à l'hôpital** to go into hospital; **~ dans le système** (*Inform*) to log in; **~ en fureur** to become angry; **~ en ébullition** to start to boil; **~ en scène** to come on stage; **laisser ~ qn/qch** to let sb/sth in; **faire ~** (*visiteur*) to show in

entresol [ɑ̃trəsɔl] *nm* entresol, mezzanine

entre-temps [ɑ̃trətɑ̃] *adv* meanwhile, (in the) meantime

entretenir [ɑ̃trətnir] *vt* to maintain; (*amitié*) to keep alive; (*famille, maîtresse*) to support, keep; **~ qn (de)** to speak to sb (about); **s'entretenir (de)** to converse (about); **~ qn dans l'erreur** to let sb remain in ignorance

entretien [ɑ̃trətjɛ̃] *nm* maintenance; (*discussion*) discussion, talk; (*audience*) interview; **frais d'~** maintenance charges

entrevoir [ɑ̃trəvwar] *vt* (*à peine*) to make out; (*brièvement*) to catch a glimpse of

entrevu, e [ɑ̃trəvy] *pp de* **entrevoir** ▷ *nf* meeting; (*audience*) interview

entrouvert, e [ɑ̃truvɛr, -ɛrt(ə)] *pp de* **entrouvrir** ▷ *adj* half-open

énumérer [enymere] *vt* to list, enumerate

envahir [ɑ̃vair] *vt* to invade; (*inquiétude, peur*) to come over

envahissant, e [ɑ̃vaisɑ̃, -ɑ̃t] *adj* (*péj: personne*) interfering, intrusive

enveloppe [ɑ̃vlɔp] *nf* (*de lettre*) envelope; (*Tech*) casing; outer layer; **mettre sous ~** to put in an envelope; **~ autocollante** self-seal envelope; **~ budgétaire** budget; **~ à fenêtre** window envelope

envelopper [ɑ̃vlɔpe] *vt* to wrap; (*fig*) to envelop, shroud; **s'~ dans un châle/une couverture** to wrap o.s. in a shawl/blanket

envenimer [ɑ̃vnime] *vt* to aggravate; **s'envenimer** *vi* (*plaie*) to fester; (*situation, relations*) to worsen

envergure [ɑ̃vɛrgyr] *nf* (*d'un oiseau, avion*) wingspan; (*fig: étendue*) scope; (*: valeur*) calibre

enverrai *etc* [ɑ̃vɛre] *vb voir* **envoyer**

envers [ɑ̃vɛr] *prép* towards, to ▷ *nm* other side; (*d'une étoffe*) wrong side; **à l'~** upside down; back to front; (*vêtement*) inside out; **~ et contre tous** *ou* **tout** against all opposition

envie [ɑ̃vi] *nf* (*sentiment*) envy; (*souhait*) desire, wish; (*tache sur la peau*) birthmark; (*filet de peau*) hangnail; **avoir ~ de** to feel like; (*désir plus fort*) to want; **avoir ~ de faire** to feel like doing; to want to do; **avoir ~ que** to wish that; **donner à qn l'~ de faire** to make sb want to do; **ça lui fait ~** he would like that

envier [ɑ̃vje] *vt* to envy; **~ qch à qn** to envy sb sth; **n'avoir rien à ~ à** to have no cause to be envious of

envieux, -euse [ɑ̃vjø, -øz] *adj* envious

environ [ɑ̃virɔ̃] *adv*: **~ 3 h/2 km, 3 h/2km ~** (around) about 3 o'clock/2 km, 3 o'clock/2 km or so

environnant, e [ɑ̃virɔnɑ̃, -ɑ̃t] *adj* surrounding

environnement [ɑ̃virɔnmɑ̃] *nm* environment

environs [ɑ̃virɔ̃] *nmpl* surroundings; **aux ~ de** around

envisager [ɑ̃vizaʒe] *vt* (*examiner, considérer*) to view, contemplate; (*avoir en vue*) to envisage; **~ de faire** to consider doing

envoi [ɑ̃vwa] *nm* sending; (*paquet*) parcel, consignment; **~ contre remboursement** (*Comm*) cash on delivery

envoler [ɑ̃vɔle]: **s'envoler** *vi* (*oiseau*) to fly away *ou* off; (*avion*) to take off; (*papier, feuille*) to blow away; (*fig*) to vanish (into thin air)

envoûter [ɑ̃vute] *vt* to bewitch

envoyé, e [ɑ̃vwaje] *nm/f* (*Pol*) envoy; (*Presse*) correspondent ▷ *adj*: **bien ~** (*remarque, réponse*) well-aimed

envoyer [ɑ̃vwaje] *vt* to send; (*lancer*) to hurl,
throw; **~ une gifle/un sourire à qn** to aim a
blow/flash a smile at sb; **~ les couleurs** to run
up the colours; **~ chercher** to send for; **~ par le
fond** (*bateau*) to send to the bottom

épagneul, e [epaɲœl] *nm/f* spaniel

épais, se [epɛ, -ɛs] *adj* thick

épaisseur [epɛsœr] *nf* thickness

épancher [epɑ̃ʃe] *vt* to give vent to; **s'épancher**
vi to open one's heart; (*liquide*) to pour out

épanouir [epanwir]: **s'épanouir** *vi* (*fleur*) to
bloom, open out; (*visage*) to light up; (*fig: se
développer*) to blossom (out); (: *mentalement*) to
open up

épargne [eparɲ(ə)] *nf* saving; **l'~-logement**
property investment

épargner [eparɲe] *vt* to save; (*ne pas tuer ou
endommager*) to spare ▷ *vi* to save; **~ qch à qn** to
spare sb sth

éparpiller [eparpije] *vt* to scatter; (*pour répartir*) to
disperse; (*fig: efforts*) to dissipate; **s'éparpiller** *vi*
to scatter; (*fig*) to dissipate one's efforts

épars, e [epar, -ars(ə)] *adj* (*maisons*) scattered;
(*cheveux*) sparse

épatant, e [epatɑ̃, -ɑ̃t] *adj* (*fam*) super, splendid

épater [epate] *vt* to amaze; (*impressionner*) to
impress

épaule [epol] *nf* shoulder

épauler [epole] *vt* (*aider*) to back up, support;
(*arme*) to raise (to one's shoulder) ▷ *vi* to (take)
aim

épaulette [epolɛt] *nf* (*Mil, d'un veston*) epaulette;
(*de combinaison*) shoulder strap

épave [epav] *nf* wreck

épée [epe] *nf* sword

épeler [eple] *vt* to spell

éperdu, e [epɛrdy] *adj* (*personne*) overcome;
(*sentiment*) passionate; (*fuite*) frantic

éperon [eprɔ̃] *nm* spur

épervier [epɛrvje] *nm* (*Zool*) sparrowhawk;
(*Pêche*) casting net

épi [epi] *nm* (*de blé, d'orge*) ear; **~ de cheveux** tuft
of hair; **stationnement/se garer en ~** parking/
to park at an angle to the kerb

épice [epis] *nf* spice

épicé, e [epise] *adj* highly spiced, spicy; (*fig*)
spicy

épicer [epise] *vt* to spice; (*fig*) to add spice to

épicerie [episri] *nf* (*magasin*) grocer's shop;
(*denrées*) groceries *pl*; **~ fine** delicatessen (shop)

épicier, -ière [episje, -jɛr] *nm/f* grocer

épidémie [epidemi] *nf* epidemic

épiderme [epidɛrm(ə)] *nm* skin, epidermis

épier [epje] *vt* to spy on, watch closely; (*occasion*)
to look out for

épilepsie [epilɛpsi] *nf* epilepsy

épiler [epile] *vt* (*jambes*) to remove the hair from;
(*sourcils*) to pluck; **s'~ les jambes** to remove the
hair from one's legs; **s'~ les sourcils** to pluck
one's eyebrows; **se faire ~** to get unwanted
hair removed; **crème à ~** hair-removing *ou*
depilatory cream; **pince à ~** eyebrow tweezers

épilogue [epilɔg] *nm* (*fig*) conclusion,
dénouement

épiloguer [epilɔge] *vi*: **~ sur** to hold forth on

épinards [epinar] *nmpl* spinach *sg*

épine [epin] *nf* thorn, prickle; (*d'oursin etc*) spine,
prickle; **~ dorsale** backbone

épineux, -euse [epinø, -øz] *adj* thorny, prickly

épingle [epɛ̃gl(ə)] *nf* pin; **tirer son ~ du jeu**
to play one's game well; **tiré à quatre ~s** well
turned-out; **monter qch en ~** to build sth
up, make a thing of sth (*fam*); **~ à chapeau**
hatpin; **~ à cheveux** hairpin; **virage en ~ à
cheveux** hairpin bend; **~ de cravate** tie pin; **~
de nourrice** *ou* **de sûreté** *ou* **double** safety pin,
nappy (*Brit*) *ou* diaper (*US*) pin

épingler [epɛ̃gle] *vt* (*badge, décoration*): **~ qch
sur** to pin sth on(to); (*Couture: tissu, robe*) to pin
together; (*fam*) to catch, nick

épique [epik] *adj* epic

épisode [epizɔd] *nm* episode; **film/roman à ~s**
serialized film/novel, serial

épisodique [epizɔdik] *adj* occasional

éploré, e [eplɔre] *adj* in tears, tearful

épluche-légumes [eplyʃlegym] *nm inv* potato
peeler

éplucher [eplyʃe] *vt* (*fruit, légumes*) to peel;
(*comptes, dossier*) to go over with a fine-tooth
comb

épluchures [eplyʃyr] *nfpl* peelings

éponge [epɔ̃ʒ] *nf* sponge; **passer l'~ (sur)** (*fig*) to
let bygones be bygones (with regard to); **jeter
l'~** (*fig*) to throw in the towel; **~ métallique**
scourer

éponger [epɔ̃ʒe] *vt* (*liquide*) to mop *ou* sponge up;
(*surface*) to sponge; (*fig: déficit*) to soak up, absorb;
s'~ le front to mop one's brow

épopée [epɔpe] *nf* epic

époque [epɔk] *nf* (*de l'histoire*) age, era; (*de l'année,
la vie*) time; **d'~** *adj* (*meuble*) period *cpd*; **à cette ~**
at this (*ou* that) time *ou* period; **faire ~** to make
history

époumoner [epumɔne]: **s'époumoner** *vi* to
shout (*ou* sing) o.s. hoarse

épouse [epuz] *nf* wife

épouser [epuze] *vt* to marry; (*fig: idées*) to
espouse; (: *forme*) to fit

épousseter [epuste] *vt* to dust

époustouflant, e [epustuflɑ̃, -ɑ̃t] *adj* staggering,
mind-boggling

épouvantable [epuvɑ̃tabl(ə)] *adj* appalling,
dreadful

épouvantail [epuvɑ̃taj] *nm* (*à moineaux*)
scarecrow; (*fig*) bog(e)y; bugbear

épouvante [epuvɑ̃t] *nf* terror; **film d'~** horror
film

épouvanter [epuvɑ̃te] *vt* to terrify

époux [epu] *nm* husband ▷ *nmpl*: **les ~** the
(married) couple, the husband and wife

éprendre [eprɑ̃dr(ə)]: **s'éprendre de** *vt* to fall in
love with

épreuve [eprœv] *nf* (*d'examen*) test; (*malheur,
difficulté*) trial, ordeal; (*Photo*) print; (*Typo*) proof;

(*Sport*) event; **à l'~ des balles/du feu** (*vêtement*) bulletproof/fireproof; **à toute ~** unfailing; **mettre à l'~** to put to the test; **~ de force** trial of strength; (*fig*) showdown; **~ de résistance** test of resistance; **~ de sélection** (*Sport*) heat

épris, e [epʀi, -iz] *vb voir* **éprendre** ▷ *adj*: **~ de** in love with

éprouvant, e [epʀuvɑ̃, -ɑ̃t] *adj* trying

éprouver [epʀuve] *vt* (*tester*) to test; (*mettre à l'épreuve*) to put to the test; (*marquer, faire souffrir*) to afflict, distress; (*ressentir*) to experience

éprouvette [epʀuvɛt] *nf* test tube

épuisé, e [epɥize] *adj* exhausted; (*livre*) out of print

épuisement [epɥizmɑ̃] *nm* exhaustion; **jusqu'à ~ des stocks** while stocks last

épuiser [epɥize] *vt* (*fatiguer*) to exhaust, wear *ou* tire out; (*stock, sujet*) to exhaust; **s'épuiser** *vi* to wear *ou* tire o.s. out, exhaust o.s.; (*stock*) to run out

épuisette [epɥizɛt] *nf* landing net; shrimping net

épurer [epyʀe] *vt* (*liquide*) to purify; (*parti, administration*) to purge; (*langue, texte*) to refine

équateur [ekwatœʀ] *nm* equator; **(la république de) l'É-** Ecuador

équation [ekwasjɔ̃] *nf* equation; **mettre en ~** to equate; **~ du premier/second degré** simple/quadratic equation

équerre [ekɛʀ] *nf* (*à dessin*) (set) square; (*pour fixer*) brace; **en ~** at right angles; **à l'~, d'~** straight; **double ~** T-square

équilibre [ekilibʀ(ə)] *nm* balance; (*d'une balance*) equilibrium; **~ budgétaire** balanced budget; **garder/perdre l'~** to keep/lose one's balance; **être en ~** to be balanced; **mettre en ~** to make steady; **avoir le sens de l'~** to be well-balanced

équilibré, e [ekilibʀe] *adj* (*fig*) well-balanced, stable

équilibrer [ekilibʀe] *vt* to balance; **s'équilibrer** *vi* (*poids*) to balance; (*fig: défauts etc*) to balance each other out

équipage [ekipaʒ] *nm* crew; **en grand ~** in great array

équipe [ekip] *nf* team; (*bande: parfois péj*) bunch; **travailler par ~s** to work in shifts; **travailler en ~** to work as a team; **faire ~ avec** to team up with; **~ de chercheurs** research team; **~ de secours** *ou* **de sauvetage** rescue team

équipé, e [ekipe] *adj* (*cuisine etc*) equipped, fitted(-out) ▷ *nf* escapade

équipement [ekipmɑ̃] *nm* equipment; **équipements** *nmpl* amenities, facilities; installations; **biens/dépenses d'~** capital goods/expenditure; **ministère de l'É-** department of public works; **~s sportifs/collectifs** sports/community facilities *ou* resources

équiper [ekipe] *vt* to equip; (*voiture, cuisine*) to equip, fit out; **~ qn/qch de** to equip sb/sth with; **s'équiper** *vi* (*sportif*) to equip o.s., kit o.s. out

équipier, -ière [ekipje, -jɛʀ] *nm/f* team member

équitable [ekitabl(ə)] *adj* fair

équitation [ekitasjɔ̃] *nf* (horse-)riding; **faire de l'~** to go (horse-)riding

équivalent, e [ekivalɑ̃, -ɑ̃t] *adj, nm* equivalent

équivaloir [ekivalwaʀ]: **~ à** *vt* to be equivalent to; (*représenter*) to amount to

équivoque [ekivɔk] *adj* equivocal, ambiguous; (*louche*) dubious ▷ *nf* ambiguity

érable [eʀabl(ə)] *nm* maple

érafler [eʀafle] *vt* to scratch; **s'~ la main/les jambes** to scrape *ou* scratch one's hand/legs

éraflure [eʀaflyʀ] *nf* scratch

éraillé, e [eʀaje] *adj* (*voix*) rasping, hoarse

ère [eʀ] *nf* era; **en l'an 1050 de notre ~** in the year 1050 A.D.

érection [eʀɛksjɔ̃] *nf* erection

éreinter [eʀɛ̃te] *vt* to exhaust, wear out; (*fig: critiquer*) to slate; **s'~ (à faire qch/à qch)** to wear o.s. out (doing sth/with sth)

ériger [eʀiʒe] *vt* (*monument*) to erect; **~ qch en principe/loi** to make sth a principle/law; **s'~ en critique (de)** to set o.s. up as a critic (of)

ermite [ɛʀmit] *nm* hermit

éroder [eʀɔde] *vt* to erode

érotique [eʀɔtik] *adj* erotic

errer [eʀe] *vi* to wander

erreur [eʀœʀ] *nf* mistake, error; (*Inform*) error; (*morale*) ~s *nfpl* errors; **être dans l'~** to be wrong; **induire qn en ~** to mislead sb; **par ~** by mistake; **sauf ~** unless I'm mistaken; **faire ~** to be mistaken; **~ de date** mistake in the date; **~ de fait** error of fact; **~ d'impression** (*Typo*) misprint; **~ judiciaire** miscarriage of justice; **~ de jugement** error of judgment; **~ matérielle** *ou* **d'écriture** clerical error; **~ tactique** tactical error

érudit, e [eʀydi, -it] *adj* erudite, learned ▷ *nm/f* scholar

éruption [eʀypsjɔ̃] *nf* eruption; (*cutanée*) outbreak; (: *boutons*) rash; (*fig: de joie, colère, folie*) outburst

es [ɛ] *vb voir* **être**

ès [ɛs] *prép*: **licencié ès lettres/sciences** ≈ Bachelor of Arts/Science; **docteur ès lettres** ≈ doctor of philosophy, ≈ PhD

escabeau, x [ɛskabo] *nm* (*tabouret*) stool; (*échelle*) stepladder

escadron [ɛskadʀɔ̃] *nm* squadron

escalade [ɛskalad] *nf* climbing *no pl*; (*Pol etc*) escalation

escalader [ɛskalade] *vt* to climb, scale

escale [ɛskal] *nf* (*Navig*) call; (: *port*) port of call; (*Aviat*) stop(over); **faire ~ à** to put in at, call in at; to stop over at; **~ technique** (*Aviat*) refuelling stop

escalier [ɛskalje] *nm* stairs *pl*; **dans l'~** *ou* **les ~s** on the stairs; **descendre l'~** *ou* **les ~s** to go downstairs; **~ mécanique** *ou* **roulant** escalator; **~ de secours** fire escape; **~ de service** backstairs; **~ à vis** *ou* **en colimaçon** spiral staircase

escamoter [ɛskamɔte] *vt* (*esquiver*) to get round,

evade; (faire disparaître) to conjure away; (dérober: portefeuille etc) to snatch; (train d'atterrissage) to retract; (mots) to miss out

escapade [ɛskapad] nf: **faire une ~** to go on a jaunt; (s'enfuir) to run away ou off

escargot [ɛskaʀgo] nm snail

escarpé, e [ɛskaʀpe] adj steep

escarpin [ɛskaʀpɛ̃] nm flat(-heeled) shoe

escient [esjɑ̃] nm: **à bon ~** advisedly

esclaffer [ɛsklafe]: **s'esclaffer** vi to guffaw

esclandre [ɛsklɑ̃dʀ(ə)] nm scene, fracas

esclavage [ɛsklavaʒ] nm slavery

esclave [ɛsklav] nm/f slave; **être ~ de** (fig) to be a slave of

escompte [ɛskɔ̃t] nm discount

escompter [ɛskɔ̃te] vt (Comm) to discount; (espérer) to expect, reckon upon; **~ que** to reckon ou expect that

escorte [ɛskɔʀt(ə)] nf escort; **faire ~ à** to escort

escorter [ɛskɔʀte] vt to escort

escouade [ɛskwad] nf squad; (fig: groupe de personnes) group

escrime [ɛskʀim] nf fencing; **faire de l'~** to fence

escrimer [ɛskʀime]: **s'escrimer** vi: **s'~ à faire** to wear o.s. out doing

escroc [ɛskʀo] nm swindler, con-man

escroquer [ɛskʀoke] vt: **~ qn (de qch)/qch à qn** to swindle sb (out of sth)/sth out of sb

escroquerie [ɛskʀokʀi] nf swindle

espace [ɛspas] nm space; **~ publicitaire** advertising space; **~ vital** living space

espacer [ɛspase] vt to space out; **s'espacer** vi (visites etc) to become less frequent

espadon [ɛspadɔ̃] nm swordfish inv

espadrille [ɛspadʀij] nf rope-soled sandal

Espagne [ɛspaɲ(ə)] nf: **l'~** Spain

espagnol, e [ɛspaɲɔl] adj Spanish ▷ nm (Ling) Spanish ▷ nm/f: **E~, e** Spaniard

espèce [ɛspɛs] nf (Bio, Bot, Zool) species inv; (gén: sorte) sort, kind, type; (péj): **~ de maladroit/de brute!** you clumsy oaf/you brute!; **espèces** nfpl (Comm) cash sg; (Rel) species; **de toute ~** of all kinds ou sorts; **en l'~** adv in the case in point; **payer en ~s** to pay (in) cash; **cas d'~** individual case; **l'~ humaine** humankind

espérance [ɛspeʀɑ̃s] nf hope; **~ de vie** life expectancy

espérer [ɛspeʀe] vt to hope for; **j'espère (bien)** I hope so; **~ que/faire** to hope that/to do; **~ en** to trust in

espiègle [ɛspjɛgl(ə)] adj mischievous

espion, ne [ɛspjɔ̃, -ɔn] nm/f spy; **avion ~** spy plane

espionnage [ɛspjonaʒ] nm espionage, spying; **film/roman d'~** spy film/novel

espionner [ɛspjone] vt to spy (up)on

esplanade [ɛsplanad] nf esplanade

espoir [ɛspwaʀ] nm hope; **l'~ de qch/de faire qch** the hope of sth/of doing sth; **avoir bon ~ que ...** to have high hopes that ...; **garder l'~ que ...** to remain hopeful that ...; **un ~ de la**

boxe/du ski one of boxing's/skiing's hopefuls, one of the hopes of boxing/skiing; **sans ~** adj hopeless

esprit [ɛspʀi] nm (pensée, intellect) mind; (humour, ironie) wit; (mentalité, d'une loi etc, fantôme etc) spirit; **l'~ d'équipe/de compétition** team/competitive spirit; **faire de l'~** to try to be witty; **reprendre ses ~s** to come to; **perdre l'~** to lose one's mind; **avoir bon/mauvais ~** to be of a good/bad disposition; **avoir l'~ à faire qch** to have a mind to do sth; **avoir l'~ critique** to be critical; **~ de contradiction** contrariness; **~ de corps** esprit de corps; **~ de famille** family loyalty; **l'~ malin** (le diable) the Evil One; **~s chagrins** fault-finders

esquimau, de, -x [ɛskimo, -od] adj Eskimo ▷ nm (Ling) Eskimo; (glace): **E~®** ice lolly (Brit), popsicle (US) ▷ nm/f: **E~, de** Eskimo; **chien ~** husky

esquinter [ɛskɛ̃te] vt (fam) to mess up; **s'esquinter** vi: **s'~ à faire qch** to knock o.s. out doing sth

esquisse [ɛskis] nf sketch; **l'~ d'un sourire/changement** a hint of a smile/of change

esquisser [ɛskise] vt to sketch; **s'esquisser** vi (amélioration) to begin to be detectable; **~ un sourire** to give a hint of a smile

esquiver [ɛskive] vt to dodge; **s'esquiver** vi to slip away

essai [esɛ] nm trying; (tentative) attempt, try; (Rugby) try; (Littérature) essay; **essais** nmpl (Auto) trials; **à l'~** on a trial basis; **~ gratuit** (Comm) free trial

essaim [esɛ̃] nm swarm

essayer [eseje] vt (gén) to try; (vêtement, chaussures) to try (on); (restaurant, méthode, voiture) to try (out) ▷ vi to try; **~ de faire** to try ou attempt to do; **s'~ à faire** to try one's hand at doing; **essayez un peu!** (menace) just you try!

essence [esɑ̃s] nf (de voiture) petrol (Brit), gas(oline) (US); (extrait de plante, Philosophie) essence; (espèce: d'arbre) species inv; **prendre de l'~** to get (some) petrol ou gas; **par ~** (essentiellement) essentially; **~ de citron/rose** lemon/rose oil; **~ sans plomb** unleaded petrol; **~ de térébenthine** turpentine

essentiel, le [esɑ̃sjɛl] adj essential ▷ nm: **l'~ d'un discours/d'une œuvre** the essence of a speech/work of art; **emporter l'~** to take the essentials; **c'est l'~** (ce qui importe) that's the main thing; **l'~ de** (la majeure partie) the main part of

essieu, x [esjø] nm axle

essor [esɔʀ] nm (de l'économie etc) rapid expansion; **prendre son ~** (oiseau) to fly off

essorer [esɔʀe] vt (en tordant) to wring (out); (par la force centrifuge) to spin-dry; (salade) to spin; (: en secouant) to shake dry

essoreuse [esɔʀøz] nf mangle, wringer; (à tambour) spin-dryer

essoufflé, e [esufle] adj out of breath, breathless

essouffler [esufle] vt to make breathless; **s'essouffler** vi to get out of breath; (fig: économie) to run out of steam

essuie-glace [esɥiglas] nm windscreen (Brit) ou

windshield (US) wiper

essuyer [esɥije] *vt* to wipe; (*fig: subir*) to suffer; **s'essuyer** (*après le bain*) to dry o.s.; **~ la vaisselle** to dry up, dry the dishes

est [ɛ] *vb voir* **être** ▷ *nm* [ɛst]: **l'~** the east ▷ *adj inv* east; (*région*) east(ern); **à l'~** in the east; (*direction*) to the east, east(wards); **à l'~ de** (to the) east of; **les pays de l'E~** the eastern countries

estampe [ɛstɑ̃p] *nf* print, engraving

est-ce que [ɛskə] *adv*: **~ c'est cher/c'était bon?** is it expensive/was it good?; **quand est-ce qu'il part?** when does he leave?, when is he leaving?; **où est-ce qu'il va?** where's he going?; *voir aussi* **que**

esthéticienne [ɛstetisjɛn] *nf* beautician

esthétique [ɛstetik] *adj* (*sens, jugement*) aesthetic; (*beau*) attractive, aesthetically pleasing ▷ *nf* aesthetics *sg*; **l'~ industrielle** industrial design

estimation [ɛstimasjɔ̃] *nf* valuation; assessment; **d'après mes ~s** according to my calculations

estime [ɛstim] *nf* esteem, regard; **avoir de l'~ pour qn** to think highly of sb

estimer [ɛstime] *vt* (*respecter*) to esteem, hold in high regard; (*expertiser*) to value; (*évaluer*) to assess, estimate; (*penser*): **~ que/être** to consider that/o.s. to be; **s'estimer satisfait/heureux** *vi* to feel satisfied/happy; **j'estime la distance à 10 km** I reckon the distance to be 10 km

estival, e, -aux [ɛstival, -o] *adj* summer *cpd*; **station ~e** (summer) holiday resort

estivant, e [ɛstivã, -ãt] *nm/f* (summer) holiday-maker

estomac [ɛstɔma] *nm* stomach; **avoir mal à l'~** to have stomach ache; **avoir l'~ creux** to have an empty stomach

estomaqué, e [ɛstɔmake] *adj* flabbergasted

estomper [ɛstɔ̃pe] *vt* (*Art*) to shade off; (*fig*) to blur, dim; **s'estomper** *vi* (*sentiments*) to soften; (*contour*) to become blurred

estrade [ɛstrad] *nf* platform, rostrum

estragon [ɛstragɔ̃] *nm* tarragon

estuaire [ɛstɥɛr] *nm* estuary

et [e] *conj* and; **et lui?** what about him?; **et alors?, et (puis) après?** so what?; (*ensuite*) and then?

étable [etabl(ə)] *nf* cowshed

établi, e [etabli] *adj* established ▷ *nm* (work)bench

établir [etablir] *vt* (*papiers d'identité, facture*) to make out; (*liste, programme*) to draw up; (*gouvernement, artisan etc: aider à s'installer*) to set up, establish; (*entreprise, atelier, camp*) to set up; (*réputation, usage, fait, culpabilité, relations*) to establish; (*Sport: record*) to set; **s'établir** vi (*se faire: entente etc*) to be established; **s'~** (à son compte) to set up in business; **s'~ à/près de** to settle in/near

établissement [etablismã] *nm* making out; drawing up; setting up, establishing; (*entreprise, institution*) establishment; **~ de crédit** credit institution; **~ hospitalier** hospital complex; **~**

industriel industrial plant, factory; **~ scolaire** school, educational establishment

étage [etaʒ] *nm* (*d'immeuble*) storey (Brit), story (US), floor; (*de fusée*) stage; (*Géo: de culture, végétation*) level; **au 2ème** ~ on the 2nd (Brit) *ou* 3rd (US) floor; **à l'~** upstairs; **maison à deux ~s** two-storey *ou* -story house; **de bas** ~ *adj* low-born; (*médiocre*) inferior

étagère [etaʒɛr] *nf* (*rayon*) shelf; (*meuble*) shelves *pl*, set of shelves

étai [etɛ] *nm* stay, prop

étain [etɛ̃] *nm* tin; (*Orfèvrerie*) pewter *no pl*

étais *etc* [etɛ] *vb voir* **être**

étal [etal] *nm* stall

étalage [etalaʒ] *nm* display; (*vitrine*) display window; **faire ~ de** to show off, parade

étaler [etale] *vt* (*carte, nappe*) to spread (out); (*peinture, liquide*) to spread; (*échelonner: paiements, dates, vacances*) to spread, stagger; (*exposer: marchandises*) to display; (*richesses, connaissances*) to parade; **s'étaler** vi (*liquide*) to spread out; (*fam*) to come a cropper (Brit), fall flat on one's face; **s'~ sur** (*paiements etc*) to be spread over

étalon [etalɔ̃] *nm* (*mesure*) standard; (*cheval*) stallion; **l'~-or** the gold standard

étanche [etɑ̃ʃ] *adj* (*récipient, aussi fig*) watertight; (*montre, vêtement*) waterproof; **~ à l'air** airtight

étancher [etɑ̃ʃe] *vt* (*liquide*) to stop (flowing); **~ sa soif** to quench *ou* slake one's thirst

étang [etɑ̃] *nm* pond

étant [etɑ̃] *vb voir* **être**; **donné**

étape [etap] *nf* stage; (*lieu d'arrivée*) stopping place; (*Cyclisme*) staging point; **faire ~ à** to stop off at; **brûler les ~s** (*fig*) to cut corners

état [eta] *nm* (*Pol, condition*) state; (*d'un article d'occasion etc*) condition, state; (*liste*) inventory, statement; (*condition: professionnelle*) profession, trade; (*: sociale*) status; **en bon/mauvais** ~ in good/poor condition; **en ~ (de marche)** in (working) order; **remettre en ~** to repair; **hors d'~** out of order; **être en ~/hors d'~ de faire** to be in a state/in no fit state to do; **en tout ~ de cause** in any event; **être dans tous ses ~s** to be in a state; **faire ~ de** (*alléguer*) to put forward; **en ~ d'arrestation** under arrest; **~ de grâce** (*Rel*) state of grace; (*fig*) honeymoon period; **en ~ de grâce** (*fig*) inspired; **en ~ d'ivresse** under the influence of drink; **~ de choses** (*situation*) state of affairs; **~ civil** civil status; (*bureau*) registry office (Brit); **~ d'esprit** frame of mind; **~ des lieux** inventory of fixtures; **~ de santé** state of health; **~ de siège/d'urgence** state of siege/emergency; **~ de veille** (*Psych*) waking state; **~s d'âme** moods; **les É~s barbaresques** the Barbary States; **les É~s du Golfe** the Gulf States; **~s de service** service record *sg*

étatiser [etatize] *vt* to bring under state control

état-major (*pl* **états-majors**) [etamaʒɔr] *nm* (*Mil*) staff; (*d'un parti etc*) top advisers *pl*; (*d'une entreprise*) top management

États-Unis [etazyni] *nmpl*: **les ~ (d'Amérique)** the United States (of America)

étau, x [eto] *nm* vice (Brit), vise (US)

étayer [eteje] *vt* to prop *ou* shore up; (*fig*) to back up

et cætera, et cetera [ɛtsetera], **etc.** *adv* et cetera, and so on, etc

été [ete] *pp de* **être** ▷ *nm* summer; **en ~** in summer

éteindre [etɛ̃dʀ(ə)] *vt* (*lampe, lumière, radio, chauffage*) to turn *ou* switch off; (*cigarette, incendie, bougie*) to put out, extinguish; (*Jur: dette*) to extinguish; **s'éteindre** *vi* to go off; to go out; (*mourir*) to pass away

éteint, e [etɛ̃, -ɛ̃t] *pp de* **éteindre** ▷ *adj* (*fig*) lacklustre, dull; (*volcan*) extinct; **tous feux ~s** (*Auto: rouler*) without lights

étendard [etɑ̃daʀ] *nm* standard

étendre [etɑ̃dʀ(ə)] *vt* (*appliquer: pâte, liquide*) to spread; (*déployer: carte etc*) to spread out; (*sur un fil: lessive, linge*) to hang up *ou* out; (*bras, jambes, par terre: blessé*) to stretch out; (*diluer*) to dilute, thin; (*fig: agrandir*) to extend; (*fam: adversaire*) to floor; **s'étendre** *vi* (*augmenter, se propager*) to spread; (*terrain, forêt etc*): **s'~ jusqu'à/de ... à** to stretch as far as/from ... to; **s'~ (sur)** (*s'allonger*) to stretch out (upon); (*se coucher*) to lie down (on); (*fig: expliquer*) to elaborate *ou* enlarge (upon)

étendu, e [etɑ̃dy] *adj* extensive ▷ *nf* (*d'eau, de sable*) stretch, expanse; (*importance*) extent

éternel, le [etɛʀnɛl] *adj* eternal; **les neiges ~les** perpetual snow

éterniser [etɛʀnize]: **s'éterniser** *vi* to last for ages; (*personne*) to stay for ages

éternité [etɛʀnite] *nf* eternity; **il y a** *ou* **ça fait une ~ que** it's ages since; **de toute ~** from time immemorial

éternuement [etɛʀnymɑ̃] *nm* sneeze

éternuer [etɛʀnɥe] *vi* to sneeze

êtes [ɛt] *vb voir* **être**

éthique [etik] *adj* ethical ▷ *nf* ethics *sg*

ethnie [ɛtni] *nf* ethnic group

éthylisme [etilism(ə)] *nm* alcoholism

étiez [etje] *vb voir* **être**

étinceler [etɛ̃sle] *vi* to sparkle

étincelle [etɛ̃sɛl] *nf* spark

étiqueter [etikte] *vt* to label

étiquette [etikɛt] *vb voir* **étiqueter** ▷ *nf* label; (*protocole*): **l'~** etiquette

étirer [etiʀe] *vt* to stretch; (*ressort*) to stretch out; **s'étirer** *vi* (*personne*) to stretch; (*convoi, route*): **s'~ sur** to stretch out over

étoffe [etɔf] *nf* material, fabric; **avoir l'~ d'un chef** *etc* to be cut out to be a leader *etc*; **avoir de l'~** to be a forceful personality

étoffer [etɔfe] *vt* to flesh out; **s'étoffer** *vi* to fill out

étoile [etwal] *nf* star ▷ *adj*: **danseuse** *ou* **danceur ~** leading dancer; **la bonne/mauvaise ~ de qn** sb's lucky/unlucky star; **à la belle ~** (out) in the open; **~ filante** shooting star; **~ de mer** starfish; **~ polaire** pole star

étoilé, e [etwale] *adj* starry

étonnant, e [etɔnɑ̃, -ɑ̃t] *adj* surprising

étonnement [etɔnmɑ̃] *nm* surprise; **à mon grand ~ ...** to my great surprise *ou* amazement ...

étonner [etɔne] *vt* to surprise; **s'étonner que/de** to be surprised that/at; **cela m'~ait (que)** (*j'en doute*) I'd be (very) surprised (if)

étouffant, e [etufɑ̃, -ɑ̃t] *adj* stifling

étouffé, e [etufe] *adj* (*asphyxie*) suffocated; (*assourdi: cris, rires*) smothered ▷ *nf*: **à l'~e** (*Culin: poisson, légumes*) steamed; (: *viande*) braised

étouffer [etufe] *vt* to suffocate; (*bruit*) to muffle; (*scandale*) to hush up ▷ *vi* to suffocate; (*avoir trop chaud; aussi fig*) to feel stifled; **s'étouffer** *vi* (*en mangeant etc*) to choke

étourderie [etuʀdəʀi] *nf* heedlessness *no pl*; thoughtless blunder; **faute d'~** careless mistake

étourdi, e [etuʀdi] *adj* (*distrait*) scatterbrained, heedless

étourdir [etuʀdiʀ] *vt* (*assommer*) to stun, daze; (*griser*) to make dizzy *ou* giddy

étourdissement [etuʀdismɑ̃] *nm* dizzy spell

étourneau, x [etuʀno] *nm* starling

étrange [etʀɑ̃ʒ] *adj* strange

étranger, -ère [etʀɑ̃ʒe, -ɛʀ] *adj* foreign; (*pas de la famille, non familier*) strange ▷ *nm/f* foreigner; stranger ▷ *nm*: **l'~** foreign countries; **à l'~** abroad; **de l'~** from abroad; **~ à** (*mal connu*) unfamiliar to; (*sans rapport*) irrelevant to

étrangler [etʀɑ̃gle] *vt* to strangle; (*fig: presse, libertés*) to stifle; **s'étrangler** *vi* (*en mangeant etc*) to choke; (*se resserrer*) to make a bottleneck

être [ɛtʀ(ə)] *nm* being; **~ humain** human being ▷ *vb copule* **1** (*état, description*) to be; **il est instituteur** he is *ou* he's a teacher; **vous êtes grand/intelligent/fatigué** you are *ou* you're tall/clever/tired

2 (+à: *appartenir*) to be; **le livre est à Paul** the book is Paul's *ou* belongs to Paul; **c'est à moi/eux** it is *ou* it's mine/theirs

3 (+de: *provenance*): **il est de Paris** he is from Paris; (*appartenance*;): **il est des nôtres** he is one of us

4 (*date*): **nous sommes le 10 janvier** it's the 10th of January (today)

▷ *vi* to be; **je ne serai pas ici demain** I won't be here tomorrow

▷ *vb aux* **1** to have; to be; **~ arrivé/allé** to have arrived/gone; **il est parti** he has left, he has gone

2 (*forme passive*) to be; **~ fait par** to be made by; **il a été promu** he has been promoted

3 (+à +inf: *obligation, but*): **c'est à réparer** it needs repairing; **c'est à essayer** it should be tried; **il est à espérer que ...** it is *ou* it's to be hoped that ...

▷ *vb impers* **1**: **il est** (*avec adjectif*) it is; **il est impossible de le faire** it's impossible to do it

2 (*heure, date*): **il est 10 heures** it is *ou* it's 10 o'clock

3 (*emphatique*): **c'est moi** it's me; **c'est à lui de le faire** it's up to him to do it; *voir aussi* **est-ce que**; **n'est-ce pas**; **c'est-à-dire**; **ce**

étreindre [etʀɛ̃dʀ(ə)] *vt* to clutch, grip;

(*amoureusement, amicalement*) to embrace; **s'étreindre** to embrace

étrenner [etʀene] *vt* to use (*ou* wear) for the first time

étrennes [etʀɛn] *nfpl* (*cadeaux*) New Year's present; (*gratifications*) ≈ Christmas box *sg*, ≈ Christmas bonus

étrier [etʀije] *nm* stirrup

étriqué, e [etʀike] *adj* skimpy

étroit, e [etʀwa, -wat] *adj* narrow; (*vêtement*) tight; (*fig: serré*) close, tight; **à l'~** cramped; **~ d'esprit** narrow-minded

étude [etyd] *nf* studying; (*ouvrage, rapport, Mus*) study; (*de notaire: bureau*) office; (: *charge*) practice; (*Scol: salle de travail*) study room; **études** *nfpl* (*Scol*) studies; **être à l'~** (*projet etc*) to be under consideration; **faire des ~s (de droit/médecine)** to study (law/medicine); **~s secondaires/supérieures** secondary/higher education; **~ de cas** case study; **~ de faisabilité** feasibility study; **~ de marché** (*Écon*) market research

étudiant, e [etydjã, -ãt] *adj, nm/f* student

étudier [etydje] *vt, vi* to study

étui [etɥi] *nm* case

étuve [etyv] *nf* steamroom; (*appareil*) sterilizer

étuvée [etyve]: **à l'~** *adv* braised

eu, eue [y] *pp de* avoir

euh [ø] *excl* er

euro [øʀo] *nm* euro

Euroland [øʀolãd] *nm* Euroland

Europe [øʀɔp] *nf*: **l'~** Europe; **l'~ centrale** Central Europe; **l'~ verte** European agriculture

européen, ne [øʀɔpeẽ, -ɛn] *adj* European ▷ *nm/f*: **E~, ne** European

eus *etc* [y] *vb voir* avoir

eux [ø] *pron* (*sujet*) they; (*objet*) them; **~, ils ont fait ...** THEY did ...

évacuer [evakɥe] *vt* (*salle, région*) to evacuate, clear; (*occupants, population*) to evacuate; (*toxine etc*) to evacuate, discharge

évader [evade]: **s'évader** *vi* to escape

évaluer [evalɥe] *vt* to assess, evaluate

évangile [evãʒil] *nm* gospel; (*texte de la Bible*): **É~** Gospel; **ce n'est pas l'É~** (*fig*) it's not gospel

évanouir [evanwiʀ]: **s'évanouir** *vi* to faint, pass out; (*disparaître*) to vanish, disappear

évanouissement [evanwismã] *nm* (*syncope*) fainting fit; (*Méd*) loss of consciousness

évaporer [evapɔʀe]: **s'évaporer** *vi* to evaporate

évasé, e [evaze] *adj* (*jupe etc*) flared

évasif, -ive [evazif, -iv] *adj* evasive

évasion [evazjõ] *nf* escape; **littérature d'~** escapist literature; **~ des capitaux** (*Écon*) flight of capital; **~ fiscale** tax avoidance

évêché [eveʃe] *nm* (*fonction*) bishopric; (*palais*) bishop's palace

éveil [evɛj] *nm* awakening; **être en ~** to be alert; **mettre qn en ~, donner l'~ à qn** to arouse sb's suspicions; **activités d'~** early-learning activities

éveillé, e [eveje] *adj* awake; (*vif*) alert, sharp

éveiller [eveje] *vt* to (a)waken; **s'éveiller** *vi* to (a)waken; (*fig*) to be aroused

événement [evɛnmã] *nm* event

éventail [evãtaj] *nm* fan; (*choix*) range; **en ~** fanned out; fan-shaped

éventaire [evãtɛʀ] *nm* stall, stand

éventer [evãte] *vt* (*secret, complot*) to uncover; (*avec un éventail*) to fan; **s'éventer** *vi* (*parfum, vin*) to go stale

éventualité [evãtɥalite] *nf* eventuality; possibility; **dans l'~ de** in the event of; **parer à toute ~** to guard against all eventualities

éventuel, le [evãtɥel] *adj* possible

éventuellement [evãtɥelmã] *adv* possibly

évêque [evɛk] *nm* bishop

évertuer [evɛʀtɥe]: **s'évertuer** *vi*: **s'~ à faire** to try very hard to do

éviction [eviksjõ] *nf* ousting, supplanting; (*de locataire*) eviction

évidemment [evidamã] *adv* obviously

évidence [evidãs] *nf* obviousness; (*fait*) obvious fact; **se rendre à l'~** to bow before the evidence; **nier l'~** to deny the evidence; **à l'~** evidently; **de toute ~** quite obviously *ou* evidently; **en ~** conspicuous; **mettre en ~** to bring to the fore

évident, e [evidã, -ãt] *adj* obvious, evident; **ce n'est pas ~** (*cela pose des problèmes*) it's not (all that) straightforward, it's not as simple as all that

évider [evide] *vt* to scoop out

évier [evje] *nm* (kitchen) sink

évincer [evẽse] *vt* to oust, supplant

éviter [evite] *vt* to avoid; **~ de faire/que qch ne se passe** to avoid doing/sth happening; **~ qch à qn** to spare sb sth

évolué, e [evolɥe] *adj* advanced; (*personne*) broad-minded

évoluer [evolɥe] *vi* (*enfant, maladie*) to develop; (*situation, moralement*) to evolve, develop; (*aller et venir: danseur etc*) to move about, circle

évolution [evolysjõ] *nf* development; evolution; **évolutions** *nfpl* movements

évoquer [evɔke] *vt* to call to mind, evoke; (*mentionner*) to mention

exact, e [egzakt] *adj* (*précis*) exact, accurate, precise; (*correct*) correct; (*ponctuel*) punctual; **l'heure ~e** the right *ou* exact time

exactement [ɛgzaktəmã] *adv* exactly, accurately, precisely; correctly; (*c'est cela même*) exactly

ex aequo [ɛgzeko] *adj* equally placed; **classé 1er ~** placed equal first

exagéré, e [ɛgzaʒeʀe] *adj* (*prix etc*) excessive

exagérer [ɛgzaʒeʀe] *vt* to exaggerate ▷ *vi* (*abuser*) to go too far; (*dépasser les bornes*) to overstep the mark; (*déformer les faits*) to exaggerate; **s'exagérer qch** to exaggerate sth

exalter [ɛgzalte] *vt* (*enthousiasmer*) to excite, elate; (*glorifier*) to exalt

examen [ɛgzamẽ] *nm* examination; (*Scol*) exam, examination; **à l'~** (*dossier, projet*) under consideration; (*Comm*) on approval; **~ blanc**

mock exam(ination); **~ de la vue** sight test

examinateur, -trice [ɛgzaminatœʀ, -tʀis] nm/f examiner

examiner [ɛgzamine] vt to examine

exaspérant, e [ɛgzaspeʀɑ̃, -ɑ̃t] adj exasperating

exaspérer [ɛgzaspeʀe] vt to exasperate; (aggraver) to exacerbate

exaucer [ɛgzose] vt (vœu) to grant, fulfil; **~ qn** to grant sb's wishes

excédent [ɛksedɑ̃] nm surplus; **en ~** surplus; **payer 60 euros d'~** (de bagages) to pay 60 euros excess baggage; **~ de bagages** excess baggage; **~ commercial** trade surplus

excéder [ɛksede] vt (dépasser) to exceed; (agacer) to exasperate; **excédé de fatigue** exhausted; **excédé de travail** worn out with work

excellent, e [ɛksɛlɑ̃, -ɑ̃t] adj excellent

excentrique [ɛksɑ̃tʀik] adj eccentric; (quartier) outlying ▷ nm/f eccentric

excepté, e [ɛksɛpte] adj, prép: **les élèves ~s, ~ les élèves** except for ou apart from the pupils; **~ si/ quand** except if/when; **~ que** except that

exception [ɛksɛpsjɔ̃] nf exception; **faire ~** to be an exception; **faire une ~** to make an exception; **sans ~** without exception; **à l'~ de** except for, with the exception of; **d'~** (mesure, loi) special, exceptional

exceptionnel, le [ɛksɛpsjɔnɛl] adj exceptional; (prix) special

exceptionnellement [ɛksɛpsjɔnɛlmɑ̃] adv exceptionally; (par exception) by way of an exception, on this occasion

excès [ɛksɛ] nm surplus ▷ nmpl excesses; **à l'~** (méticuleux, généreux) to excess; **avec ~** to excess; **sans ~** in moderation; **tomber dans l'~ inverse** to go to the opposite extreme; **~ de langage** immoderate language; **~ de pouvoir** abuse of power; **~ de vitesse** speeding no pl, exceeding the speed limit; **~ de zèle** overzealousness no pl

excessif, -ive [ɛksesif, -iv] adj excessive

excitant, e [ɛksitɑ̃, -ɑ̃t] adj exciting ▷ nm stimulant

excitation [ɛksitasjɔ̃] nf (état) excitement

exciter [ɛksite] vt to excite; (café etc) to stimulate; **s'exciter** vi to get excited; **~ qn à** (révolte etc) to incite sb to

exclamation [ɛksklamasjɔ̃] nf exclamation

exclamer [ɛksklame]: **s'exclamer** vi to exclaim

exclure [ɛksklyʀ] vt (faire sortir) to expel; (ne pas compter) to exclude, leave out; (rendre impossible) to exclude, rule out

exclusif, -ive [ɛksklyzif, -iv] adj exclusive; **avec la mission exclusive/dans le but ~ de ...** with the sole mission/aim of ...; **agent ~** sole agent

exclusion [ɛksklyzjɔ̃] nf expulsion; **à l'~ de** with the exclusion ou exception of

exclusivité [ɛksklyzivite] nf exclusiveness; (Comm) exclusive rights pl; **passer en ~** (film) to go on general release

excursion [ɛkskyʀsjɔ̃] nf (en autocar) excursion, trip; (à pied) walk, hike; **faire une ~** to go on an excursion ou a trip; to go on a walk ou hike

excuse [ɛkskyz] nf excuse; **excuses** nfpl apology sg, apologies; **faire des ~s** to apologize; **faire ses ~s** to offer one's apologies; **mot d'~** (Scol) note from one's parent(s) (to explain absence etc); **lettre d'~** letter of apology

excuser [ɛkskyze] vt to excuse; **~ qn de qch** (dispenser) to excuse sb from sth; **s'excuser (de)** to apologize (for); **"excusez-moi"** "I'm sorry"; (pour attirer l'attention) "excuse me"; **se faire ~** to ask to be excused

exécrable [ɛgzekʀabl(ə)] adj atrocious

exécuter [ɛgzekyte] vt (prisonnier) to execute; (tâche etc) to execute, carry out; (Mus: jouer) to perform, execute; (Inform) to run; **s'exécuter** vi to comply

exécutif, -ive [ɛgzekytif, -iv] adj, nm (Pol) executive

exécution [ɛgzekysjɔ̃] nf execution; carrying out; **mettre à ~** to carry out

exemplaire [ɛgzɑ̃plɛʀ] adj exemplary ▷ nm copy

exemple [ɛgzɑ̃pl(ə)] nm example; **par ~** for instance, for example; (valeur intensive) really!; **sans ~** (bêtise, gourmandise etc) unparalleled; **donner l'~** to set an example; **prendre ~ sur** to take as a model; **à l'~ de** just like; **pour l'~** (punir) as an example

exempt, e [ɛgzɑ̃, -ɑ̃t] adj: **~ de** (dispensé de) exempt from; (sans) free from; **~ de taxes** tax-free

exercer [ɛgzɛʀse] vt (pratiquer) to exercise, practise; (faire usage de: prérogative) to exercise; (effectuer: influence, contrôle, pression) to exert; (former) to exercise, train ▷ vi (médecin) to be in practice; **s'exercer** (sportif, musicien) to practise; (se faire sentir: pression etc): **s'~ (sur** ou **contre)** to be exerted (on); **s'~ à faire qch** to train o.s. to do sth

exercice [ɛgzɛʀsis] nm practice; exercising; (tâche, travail) exercise; (Comm, Admin: période) accounting period; **l'~** (sportive etc) exercise; (Mil) drill; **en ~** (juge) in office; (médecin) practising; **dans l'~ de ses fonctions** in the discharge of his duties; **~s d'assouplissement** limbering-up (exercises)

exhaustif, -ive [ɛgzostif, -iv] adj exhaustive

exhiber [ɛgzibe] vt (montrer: papiers, certificat) to present, produce; (péj) to display, flaunt; **s'exhiber** (personne) to parade; (exhibitionniste) to expose o.s.

exhibitionniste [ɛgzibisjɔnist(ə)] nm/f exhibitionist

exhorter [ɛgzɔʀte] vt: **~ qn à faire** to urge sb to do

exigeant, e [ɛgziʒɑ̃, -ɑ̃t] adj demanding; (péj) hard to please

exigence [ɛgziʒɑ̃s] nf demand, requirement

exiger [ɛgziʒe] vt to demand, require

exigu, ë [ɛgzigy] adj cramped, tiny

exil [ɛgzil] nm exile; **en ~** in exile

exiler [ɛgzile] vt to exile; **s'exiler** to go into exile

existence [ɛgzistɑ̃s] nf existence; **dans l'~** in life

exister [ɛgziste] vi to exist; **il existe un/des** there is a/are (some)

exonérer [ɛgzɔneʀe] vt: **~ de** to exempt from

exorbitant, e [εgzɔrbitã, -ãt] adj exorbitant
exorbité, e [εgzɔrbite] adj: **yeux ~s** bulging eyes
exotique [εgzɔtik] adj exotic
expatrier [εkspatrije] vt (argent) to take ou send out of the country; **s'expatrier** to leave one's country
expectative [εkspεktativ] nf: **être dans l'~** to be waiting to see
expédient [εkspedjã] nm (parfois péj) expedient; **vivre d'~s** to live by one's wits
expédier [εkspedje] vt (lettre, paquet) to send; (troupes, renfort) to dispatch; (péj: travail etc) to dispose of, dispatch
expéditeur, -trice [εkspeditœr, -tris] nm/f (Postes) sender
expédition [εkspedisjɔ̃] nf sending; (scientifique, sportive, Mil) expedition; **~ punitive** punitive raid
expérience [εksperjãs] nf (de la vie, des choses) experience; (scientifique) experiment; **avoir de l'~** to have experience, be experienced; **avoir l'~ de** to have experience of; **faire l'~ de qch** to experience sth; **~ de chimie/d'électricité** chemical/electrical experiment
expérimenté, e [εksperimãte] adj experienced
expérimenter [εksperimãte] vt (machine, technique) to test out, experiment with
expert, e [εkspεr, -εrt(ə)] adj: **~ en** expert in **~** nm (spécialiste) expert; **~ en assurances** insurance valuer
expert-comptable (pl **experts-comptables**) [εkspεrkɔ̃tabl(ə)] nm ≈ chartered (Brit) ou certified public (US) accountant
expertise [εkspεrtiz] nf valuation; assessment; valuer's (ou assessor's) report; (Jur) (forensic) examination
expertiser [εkspεrtize] vt (objet de valeur) to value; (voiture accidentée etc) to assess damage to
expier [εkspje] vt to expiate, atone for
expirer [εkspire] vi (prendre fin, littéraire: mourir) to expire; (respirer) to breathe out
explicatif, -ive [εksplikatif, -iv] adj (mot, texte, note) explanatory
explication [εksplikasjɔ̃] nf explanation; (discussion) discussion; **~ de texte** (Scol) critical analysis (of a text)
explicite [εksplisit] adj explicit
expliquer [εksplike] vt to explain; **~ (à qn) comment/que** to point out ou explain (to sb) how/that; **s'expliquer** (se faire comprendre: personne) to explain o.s.; (discuter) to discuss things; (se disputer) to have it out; (comprendre): **je m'explique son retard/absence** I understand his lateness/absence; **son erreur s'explique** one can understand his mistake
exploit [εksplwa] nm exploit, feat
exploitant [εksplwatã] nm farmer
exploitation [εksplwatasjɔ̃] nf exploitation; running; (entreprise): **~ agricole** farming concern
exploiter [εksplwate] vt to exploit; (entreprise, ferme) to run, operate
explorer [εksplɔre] vt to explore

exploser [εksploze] vi to explode, blow up; (engin explosif) to go off; (fig: joie, colère) to burst out, explode; (: personne: de colère) to explode, flare up; **faire ~** (bombe) to explode, detonate; (bâtiment, véhicule) to blow up
explosif, -ive [εksplozif, -iv] adj, nm explosive
explosion [εksplozjɔ̃] nf explosion; **~ de joie/ colère** outburst of joy/rage; **~ démographique** population explosion
exportateur, -trice [εkspɔrtatœr, -tris] adj exporting ▷ nm exporter
exportation [εkspɔrtasjɔ̃] nf export
exporter [εkspɔrte] vt to export
exposant [εkspozã] nm exhibitor; (Math) exponent
exposé, e [εkspoze] nm (écrit) exposé; (oral) talk ▷ adj: **~ au sud** facing south, with a southern aspect; **bien ~** well situated; **très ~** very exposed
exposer [εkspoze] vt (montrer: marchandise) to display; (: peinture) to exhibit, show; (parler de: problème, situation) to explain, expose, set out; (mettre en danger, orienter: maison etc) to expose; **~ qn/qch à** to expose sb/sth to; **~ sa vie** to risk one's life; **s'exposer à** (soleil, danger) to expose o.s. to; (critiques, punition) to lay o.s. open to
exposition [εkspozisjɔ̃] nf (voir exposer) displaying; exhibiting; explanation, exposition; exposure; (voir exposé) aspect, situation; (manifestation) exhibition; (Photo) exposure; (introduction) exposition
exprès¹ [εksprε] adv (délibérément) on purpose; (spécialement) specially; **faire ~ de faire qch** to do sth on purpose
exprès², -esse [εksprεs] adj (ordre, défense) express, formal ▷ adj inv, adv (Postes) express; **envoyer qch en ~** to send sth express
express [εksprεs] adj, nm: **(café) ~** espresso; **(train) ~** fast train
expressément [εksprεsemã] adv expressly, specifically
expressif, -ive [εksprεsif, -iv] adj expressive
expression [εksprεsjɔ̃] nf expression; **réduit à sa plus simple ~** reduced to its simplest terms; **liberté/moyens d'~** freedom/means of expression; **~ toute faite** set phrase
exprimer [εksprime] vt (sentiment, idée) to express; (faire sortir: jus, liquide) to press out; **s'exprimer** vi (personne) to express o.s.
exproprier [εksprɔprije] vt to buy up (ou buy the property of) by compulsory purchase, expropriate
expulser [εkspylse] vt (d'une salle, d'un groupe) to expel; (locataire) to evict; (Football) to send off
exquis, e [εkski, -iz] adj (gâteau, parfum, élégance) exquisite; (personne, temps) delightful
extase [εkstaz] nf ecstasy; **être en ~** to be in raptures
extasier [εkstazje]: **s'extasier** vi: **s'~ sur** to go into raptures over
extension [εkstãsjɔ̃] nf (d'un muscle, ressort) stretching; (Méd): **à l'~** in traction; (fig) extension; expansion

exténuer [εkstenɥe] vt to exhaust
extérieur, e [εksterjœʀ] adj (de dehors: porte, mur
etc) outer, outside; (: commerce, politique) foreign;
(: influences, pressions) external; (au dehors: escalier,
w.-c.) outside; (apparent: calme, gaieté etc) outer
▷ nm (d'une maison, d'un récipient etc) outside,
exterior; (d'une personne: apparence) exterior; (d'un
pays, d'un groupe social): **l'~** the outside world; **à l'~**
(dehors) outside; (fig: à l'étranger) abroad
extérieurement [εksterjœʀmã] adv (de dehors)
on the outside; (en apparence) on the surface
exterminer [εkstεʀmine] vt to exterminate,
wipe out
externat [εkstεʀna] nm day school
externe [εkstεʀn(ə)] adj external, outer ▷ nm/f
(Méd) non-resident medical student, extern (US);
(Scol) day pupil
extincteur [εkstɛ̃ktœʀ] nm (fire) extinguisher
extinction [εkstɛ̃ksjɔ̃] nf extinction; (Jur: d'une
dette) extinguishment; **~ de voix** (Méd) loss of
voice
extorquer [εkstɔʀke] vt (de l'argent, un
renseignement): **~ qch à qn** to extort sth from sb
extra [εkstʀa] adj inv first-rate; (marchandises)
top-quality ▷ nm inv extra help ▷ préfixe extra(-)
extrader [εkstʀade] vt to extradite
extraire [εkstʀεʀ] vt to extract
extrait, e [εkstʀε, -εt] pp de **extraire** ▷ nm (de

plante) extract; (de film, livre) extract, excerpt; **~ de
naissance** birth certificate
extraordinaire [εkstʀaɔʀdinεʀ] adj
extraordinary; (Pol, Admin) special;
ambassadeur ~ ambassador extraordinary;
assemblée ~ extraordinary meeting; **par ~** by
some unlikely chance
extravagant, e [εkstʀavagã, -ãt] adj (personne,
attitude) extravagant; (idée) wild
extraverti, e [εkstʀavεʀti] adj extrovert
extrême [εkstʀεm] adj, nm extreme; (intensif):
d'une ~ simplicité/brutalité extremely
simple/brutal; **d'un ~ à l'autre** from one
extreme to another; **à l'~** in the extreme; **à l'~
rigueur** in the absolute extreme
extrêmement [εkstʀεmmã] adv extremely
extrême-onction (pl **extrêmes-onctions**)
[εkstʀεmɔ̃ksjɔ̃] nf (Rel) last rites pl, Extreme
Unction
Extrême-Orient [εkstʀεmɔʀjã] nm: **l'~** the Far
East
extrémité [εkstʀemite] nf (bout) end; (situation)
straits pl, plight; (geste désespéré) extreme action;
extrémités nfpl (pieds et mains) extremities; **à la
dernière ~** (à l'agonie) on the point of death
exubérant, e [εgzybeʀã, -ãt] adj exuberant
exutoire [εgzytwaʀ] nm outlet, release

Ff

F, f [ɛf] *nm inv* F, f ▷ *abr* = **féminin**; (= *franc*) fr.;
(= *Fahrenheit*) F; (= *frère*) Br(o).; (= *femme*) W;
(*appartement*): **un F2/F3** a 2-/3-roomed flat (Brit)
ou apartment (US); **F comme François** F for
Frederick (Brit) *ou* Fox (US)

fa [fa] *nm inv* (*Mus*) F; (*en chantant la gamme*) fa

fable [fabl(ə)] *nf* fable; (*mensonge*) story, tale

fabricant [fabʀikɑ̃] *nm* manufacturer, maker

fabrication [fabʀikasjɔ̃] *nf* manufacture,
making

fabrique [fabʀik] *nf* factory

fabriquer [fabʀike] *vt* to make; (*industriellement*)
to manufacture, make; (*construire: voiture*) to
manufacture, build; (: *maison*) to build; (*fig:
inventer: histoire, alibi*) to make up; (*fam*): **qu'est-ce
qu'il fabrique?** what is he up to?; **~ en série** to
mass-produce

fabulation [fabylasjɔ̃] *nf* (*Psych*) fantasizing

fac [fak] *abr f* (*fam*: = **faculté**) Uni (Brit *fam*)
≈ college (US)

façade [fasad] *nf* front, façade; (*fig*) façade

face [fas] *nf* face; (*fig: aspect*) side ▷ *adj*: **le côté
~** heads; **perdre/sauver la ~** to lose/save face;
regarder qn en ~ to look sb in the face; **la
maison/le trottoir d'en ~** the house/pavement
opposite; **en ~ de** *prép* opposite; (*fig*) in front
of; **de ~** *adv* from the front; face on; **~ à** *prép*
facing; (*fig*) faced with, in the face of; **faire ~ à**
to face; **faire ~ à la demande** (*Comm*) to meet
the demand; **~ à ~** *adv* facing each other ▷ *nm
inv* encounter

fâché, e [faʃe] *adj* angry; (*désolé*) sorry

fâcher [faʃe] *vt* to anger; **se fâcher** *vi* to get
angry; **se ~ avec** (*se brouiller*) to fall out with

fâcheux, -euse [faʃø, -øz] *adj* unfortunate,
regrettable

facile [fasil] *adj* easy; (*accommodant*) easy-going

facilement [fasilmɑ̃] *adv* easily

facilité [fasilite] *nf* easiness; (*disposition, don*)
aptitude; (*moyen, occasion, possibilité*): **il a la ~ de
rencontrer les gens** he has every opportunity
to meet people; **facilités** *nfpl* facilities; (*Comm*)
terms; **~s de crédit** credit terms; **~s de
paiement** easy terms

faciliter [fasilite] *vt* to make easier

façon [fasɔ̃] *nf* (*manière*) way; (*d'une robe etc*)
making-up; cut; (: *main-d'œuvre*) labour (Brit),

labor (US); (*imitation*): **châle ~ cachemire**
cashmere-style shawl; **façons** *nfpl* (*péj*) fuss
sg; **faire des ~s** (*péj: être affecté*) to be affected;
(: *faire des histoires*) to make a fuss; **de quelle ~?**
(in) what way?; **sans ~** *adv* without fuss ▷ *adj*
unaffected; **d'une autre ~** in another way; **en
aucune ~** in no way; **de ~ à so as to**; **de ~ à ce
que, de (telle) ~ que** so that; **de toute ~** anyway,
in any case; (**c'est une**) **~ de parler** it's a way of
putting it; **travail à ~** tailoring

façonner [fasɔne] *vt* (*fabriquer*) to manufacture;
(*travailler: matière*) to shape, fashion; (*fig*) to
mould, shape

facteur, -trice [faktœʀ, -tʀis] *nm/f* postman/
woman (Brit), mailman/woman (US) ▷ *nm* (*Math,
gén*) factor; **~ d'orgues** organ builder; **~ de
pianos** piano maker; **~ rhésus** rhesus factor

factice [faktis] *adj* artificial

faction [faksjɔ̃] *nf* (*groupe*) faction; (*Mil*) guard *ou*
sentry (duty); watch; **en ~** on guard; standing
watch

facture [faktyʀ] *nf* (*à payer: gén*) bill; (: *Comm*)
invoice; (*d'un artisan, artiste*) technique,
workmanship

facturer [faktyʀe] *vt* to invoice

facultatif, -ive [fakyltatif, -iv] *adj* optional;
(*arrêt de bus*) request *cpd*

faculté [fakylte] *nf* (*intellectuelle, d'université*)
faculty; (*pouvoir, possibilité*) power

fade [fad] *adj* insipid

fagot [fago] *nm* (*de bois*) bundle of sticks

faible [fɛbl(ə)] *adj* weak; (*voix, lumière, vent*) faint;
(*élève, copie*) poor; (*rendement, intensité, revenu etc*)
low ▷ *nm* weak point; (*pour quelqu'un*) weakness,
soft spot; **~ d'esprit** feeble-minded

faiblesse [fɛblɛs] *nf* weakness

faiblir [feblir] *vi* to weaken; (*lumière*) to dim;
(*vent*) to drop

faïence [fajɑ̃s] *nf* earthenware *no pl*; (*objet*) piece
of earthenware

faignant, e [fɛɲɑ̃, -ɑ̃t] *nm/f* = **fainéant, e**

faille [faj] *vb voir* **falloir** ▷ *nf* (*Géo*) fault; (*fig*) flaw,
weakness

faillir [fajiʀ] *vi*: **j'ai failli tomber/lui dire**
I almost *ou* nearly fell/told him; **~ à une
promesse/un engagement** to break a promise/
an agreement

faillite [fajit] *nf* bankruptcy; (*échec: d'une politique etc*) collapse; **être en ~** to be bankrupt; **faire ~** to go bankrupt

faim [fɛ̃] *nf* hunger; (*fig*): **~ d'amour/de richesse** hunger *ou* yearning for love/wealth; **avoir ~** to be hungry; **rester sur sa ~** (*aussi fig*) to be left wanting more

fainéant, e [fɛneɑ̃, -ɑ̃t] *nm/f* idler, loafer

faire [fɛʀ] *vt* **1** (*fabriquer, être l'auteur de*) to make; (*produire*) to produce; (*construire: maison, bateau*) to build; **~ du vin/une offre/un film** to make wine/an offer/a film; **~ du bruit** to make a noise

2 (*effectuer: travail, opération*) to do; **que faites-vous?** (*quel métier etc*) what do you do?; (*quelle activité: au moment de la question*) what are you doing?; **que ~?** what are we going to do?, what can be done (about it)?; **~ la lessive/le ménage** to do the washing/the housework

3 (*études*) to do; (*sport, musique*) to play; **~ du droit/du français** to do law/French; **~ du rugby/piano** to play rugby/the piano; **~ du cheval/du ski** to go riding/skiing

4 (*visiter*): **~ les magasins** to go shopping; **~ l'Europe** to tour *ou* do Europe

5 (*simuler*): **~ le malade/l'ignorant** to act the invalid/the fool

6 (*transformer, avoir un effet sur*): **~ de qn un frustré/avocat** to make sb frustrated/a lawyer; **ça ne me fait rien** (*m'est égal*) I don't care *ou* mind; (*me laisse froid*) it has no effect on me; **ça ne fait rien** it doesn't matter; **~ que** (*impliquer*) to mean that

7 (*calculs, prix, mesures*): **deux et deux font quatre** two and two are *ou* make four; **ça fait 10 m/15 euros** it's 10 m/15 euros; **je vous le fais 10 euros** I'll let you have it for 10 euros

8 (*vb+de*): **qu'a-t-il fait de sa valise/de sa sœur?** what has he done with his case/his sister?

9: ne ~ que: il ne fait que critiquer (*sans cesse*) all he (ever) does is criticize; (*seulement*) he's only criticizing

10 (*dire*) to say; **vraiment? fit-il** really? he said

11 (*maladie*) to have; **~ du diabète/de la tension** to have diabetes *sg*/high blood pressure

▷ *vi* **1** (*agir, s'y prendre*) to act, do; **il faut ~ vite** we (*ou* you *etc*) must act quickly; **comment a-t-il fait pour?** how did he manage to?; **faites comme chez vous** make yourself at home; **je n'ai pas pu ~ autrement** there was nothing else I could do

2 (*paraître*) to look; **~ vieux/démodé** to look old/old-fashioned; **ça fait bien** it looks good; **tu fais jeune dans cette robe** that dress makes you look young(er)

3 (*remplaçant un autre verbe*) to do; **ne le casse pas comme je l'ai fait** don't break it as I did; **je peux le voir? -- faites!** can I see it? -- please do!; **remets-le en place -- je viens de le ~** put it back in its place -- I just have (done)

▷ *vb impers* **1: il fait beau** *etc* the weather is fine *etc*; *voir aussi* **jour**; **froid** *etc*

2 (*temps écoulé, durée*): **ça fait deux ans qu'il est parti** it's two years since he left; **ça fait deux ans qu'il y est** he's been there for two years

▷ *vb aux* **1: ~** (*+infinitif: action directe*) to make; **~ tomber/bouger qch** to make sth fall/move; **~ démarrer un moteur/chauffer de l'eau** to start up an engine/heat some water; **cela fait dormir** it makes you sleep; **~ travailler les enfants** to make the children work *ou* get the children to work; **il m'a fait traverser la rue** he helped me to cross the road

2 (*indirectement, par un intermédiaire*): **~ réparer qch** to get *ou* have sth repaired; **~ punir les enfants** to have the children punished; **il m'a fait ouvrir la porte** he got me to open the door; **se faire** *vi* **2** (*vin, fromage*) to mature

2: cela se fait beaucoup/ne se fait pas it's done a lot/not done

3 (*+nom ou pron*): **se ~ une jupe** to make o.s. a skirt; **se ~ des amis** to make friends; **se ~ du souci** to worry; **se ~ des illusions** to delude o.s.; **se ~ beaucoup d'argent** to make a lot of money; **il ne s'en fait pas** he doesn't worry

4 (*+adj: devenir*): **se ~ vieux** to be getting old; (*délibérément*): **se ~ beau** to do o.s. up

5: se ~ à (*s'habituer*) to get used to; **je n'arrive pas à me ~ à la nourriture/au climat** I can't get used to the food/climate

6 (*+infinitif*): **se ~ examiner la vue/opérer** to have one's eyes tested/have an operation; **se ~ couper les cheveux** to get one's hair cut; **il va se ~ tuer/punir** he's going to get himself killed/get (himself) punished; **il s'est fait aider** he got somebody to help him; **il s'est fait aider par Simon** he got Simon to help him; **se ~ ~ un vêtement** to get a garment made for o.s.

7 (*impersonnel*): **comment se fait-il/faisait-il que?** how is it/was it that?; **il peut se ~ que nous utilisions ...** it's possible that we could use ...

faire-part [fɛʀpaʀ] *nm inv* announcement (*of birth, marriage etc*)

faisable [fəzabl(ə)] *adj* feasible

faisan, e [fəzɑ̃, -an] *nm/f* pheasant

faisandé, e [fəzɑ̃de] *adj* high (*bad*); (*fig péj*) corrupt, decadent

faisceau, x [fɛso] *nm* (*de lumière etc*) beam; (*de branches etc*) bundle

faisons *etc* [fəzɔ̃] *vb voir* **faire**

fait[1] [fɛ] *vb voir* **faire** ▷ *nm* (*événement*) event, occurrence; (*réalité, donnée*) fact; **le ~ que/de manger** the fact that/of eating; **être le ~ de** (*causé par*) to be the work of; **être au ~ (de)** to be informed (of); **mettre qn au ~** to inform sb, put sb in the picture; **au ~** (*à propos*) by the way; **en venir au ~** to get to the point; **de ~** *adj* (*opposé à: de droit*) de facto ▷ *adv* in fact; **du ~ de ceci/qu'il a menti** because of *ou* on account of this/his having lied; **de ce ~** therefore, for this reason; **en ~** in fact; **en ~ de repas** by way of a meal; **prendre ~ et cause pour qn** to support sb, side with sb; **prendre qn sur le ~** to catch sb in the act; **dire à qn son** ~ to give sb a piece of one's mind; **hauts ~s** (exploits) exploits; **~ d'armes** feat of arms; **~ divers** (short) news item; **les ~s et gestes de qn** sb's actions ou doings

fait², e [fɛ, fɛt] pp de **faire** ▷ adj (mûr: fromage, melon) ripe; (maquillé: yeux) made-up; (vernis: ongles) painted, polished; **un homme ~** a grown man; **tout(e) ~(e)** (préparé à l'avance) ready-made; **c'en est ~ de notre tranquillité** that's the end of our peace; **c'est bien ~ (pour lui** ou **eux** etc) it serves him (ou them etc) right

faîte [fɛt] nm top; (fig) pinnacle, height

faites [fɛt] vb voir **faire**

faitout [fetu] nm stewpot

falaise [falɛz] nf cliff

falloir [falwaʀ] vb impers: **il faut faire les lits** we (ou you etc) have to ou must make the beds; **il faut que je fasse les lits** I have to ou must make the beds; **il a fallu qu'il parte** he had to leave; **il faudrait qu'elle rentre** she ought to go home; **il va ~ 10 euros** we'll (ou I'll etc) need 10 euros; **il doit ~ du temps** that must take time; **il vous faut tourner à gauche après l'église** you have to turn left past the church; **nous avons ce qu'il (nous) faut** we have what we need; **il faut qu'il ait oublié** he must have forgotten; **il a fallu qu'il l'apprenne** he would have to hear about it; **il ne fallait pas** (pour remercier) you shouldn't have (done); **faut le faire!** (it) takes some doing! ▷ vi: **s'en falloir: il s'en est fallu de 10 euros/5 minutes** we (ou they etc) were 10 euros short/5 minutes late (ou early); **il s'en faut de beaucoup qu'il soit ...** he is far from being ...; **il s'en est fallu de peu que cela n'arrive** it very nearly happened; **ou peu s'en faut** or just about, or as good as; **comme il faut** adj proper ▷ adv properly

falsifier [falsifje] vt to falsify

famé, e [fame] adj: **mal ~** disreputable, of ill repute

famélique [famelik] adj half-starved

fameux, -euse [famø, -øz] adj (illustre: parfois péj) famous; (bon: repas, plat etc) first-rate, first-class; (intensif): **un ~ problème** etc a real problem etc; **pas ~** not great, not much good

familial, e, -aux [familjal, -o] adj family cpd ▷ nf (Auto) family estate car (Brit), station wagon (US)

familiarité [familjaʀite] nf familiarity; informality; **familiarités** nfpl familiarities; **~ avec** (sujet, science) familiarity with

familier, -ière [familje, -jɛʀ] adj (connu, impertinent) familiar; (dénotant une certaine intimité) informal, friendly; (Ling) informal, colloquial ▷ nm regular (visitor)

famille [famij] nf family; **il a de la ~ à Paris** he has relatives in Paris

famine [famin] nf famine

fana [fana] adj, nm/f (fam) = **fanatique**

fanatique [fanatik] adj: **~ (de)** fanatical (about) ▷ nm/f fanatic

fanatisme [fanatism(ə)] nm fanaticism

faner [fane]: **se faner** vi to fade

fanfare [fɑ̃faʀ] nf (orchestre) brass band; (musique) fanfare; **en ~** (avec bruit) noisily

fanfaron, ne [fɑ̃faʀɔ̃, -ɔn] nm/f braggart

fantaisie [fɑ̃tezi] nf (spontanéité) fancy, imagination; (caprice) whim; extravagance; (Mus) fantasia ▷ adj: **bijou (de) ~** (piece of) costume jewellery (Brit) ou jewelry (US); **pain (de) ~** fancy bread

fantaisiste [fɑ̃tezist(ə)] adj (péj) unorthodox, eccentric ▷ nm/f (de music-hall) variety artist ou entertainer

fantasme [fɑ̃tasm(ə)] nm fantasy

fantasque [fɑ̃task(ə)] adj whimsical, capricious; fantastic

fantastique [fɑ̃tastik] adj fantastic

fantôme [fɑ̃tom] nm ghost, phantom

faon [fɑ̃] nm fawn (deer)

FAQ abr f (= foire aux questions) FAQ pl (= frequently asked questions)

farce [faʀs(ə)] nf (viande) stuffing; (blague) (practical) joke; (Théât) farce; **faire une ~ à qn** to play a (practical) joke on sb; **~s et attrapes** jokes and novelties

farcir [faʀsiʀ] vt (viande) to stuff; (fig): **~ qch de** to stuff sth with; **se farcir** (fam): **je me suis farci la vaisselle** I've got stuck ou landed with the washing-up

fardeau, x [faʀdo] nm burden

farder [faʀde] vt to make up; (vérité) to disguise; **se farder** to make o.s. up

farfelu, e [faʀfəly] adj wacky (fam), hare-brained

farine [faʀin] nf flour; **~ de blé** wheatflour; **~ de maïs** cornflour (Brit), cornstarch (US); **~ lactée** (pour bouillie) baby cereal

farineux, -euse [faʀinø, -øz] adj (sauce, pomme) floury ▷ nmpl (aliments) starchy foods

farouche [faʀuʃ] adj shy, timid; (sauvage) savage, wild; (violent) fierce

fart [faʀ(t)] nm (ski) wax

fascicule [fasikyl] nm volume

fascination [fasinasjɔ̃] nf fascination

fasciner [fasine] vt to fascinate

fascisme [faʃism(ə)] nm fascism

fasse etc [fas] vb voir **faire**

faste [fast(ə)] nm splendour (Brit), splendor (US) ▷ adj: **c'est un jour ~** it's his (ou our etc) lucky day

fastidieux, -euse [fastidjø, -øz] adj tedious, tiresome

fastueux, -euse [fastɥø, -øz] adj sumptuous, luxurious

fatal, e [fatal] adj fatal; (inévitable) inevitable

fatalité [fatalite] nf (destin) fate; (coïncidence) fateful coincidence; (caractère inévitable) inevitability

fatidique [fatidik] adj fateful

fatigant, e [fatigɑ̃, -ɑ̃t] adj tiring; (agaçant) tiresome

fatigue [fatig] nf tiredness, fatigue; (détérioration) fatigue; **les ~s du voyage** the wear and tear of the journey

fatigué, e [fatige] adj tired

fatiguer [fatige] vt to tire, make tired; (Tech) to

put a strain on, strain; *(fig: importuner)* to wear out ▷ *vi (moteur)* to labour *(Brit)*, labor *(US)*, strain; **se fatiguer** *vi* to get tired; to tire o.s. (out); **se ~ à faire qch** to tire o.s. out doing sth

fatras [fatʀa] *nm* jumble, hotchpotch

faubourg [fobuʀ] *nm* suburb

fauché, e [foʃe] *adj (fam)* broke

faucher [foʃe] *vt (herbe)* to cut; *(champs, blés)* to reap; *(fig)* to cut down; to mow down; *(fam: voler)* to pinch, nick

faucille [fosij] *nf* sickle

faucon [fokɔ̃] *nm* falcon, hawk

faudra *etc* [fodʀa] *vb voir* **falloir**

faufiler [fofile] *vt* to tack, baste; **se faufiler** *vi*: **se ~ dans** to edge one's way into; **se ~ parmi/entre** to thread one's way among/between

faune [fon] *nf (Zool)* wildlife, fauna; *(fig péj)* set, crowd ▷ *nm* faun; **~ marine** marine (animal) life

faussaire [fosɛʀ] *nm/f* forger

fausse [fos] *adj f voir* **faux**

faussement [fosmɑ̃] *adv (accuser)* wrongly, wrongfully; *(croire)* falsely, erroneously

fausser [fose] *vt (objet)* to bend, buckle; *(fig)* to distort; **~ compagnie à qn** to give sb the slip

faut [fo] *vb voir* **falloir**

faute [fot] *nf (erreur)* mistake, error; *(péché, manquement)* misdemeanour; *(Football etc)* offence; *(Tennis)* fault; *(responsabilité)*: **par la ~ de** through the fault of, because of; **c'est de sa/ma ~** it's his/my fault; **être en ~** to be in the wrong; **prendre qn en ~** to catch sb out; **~ de** *(temps, argent)* for *ou* through lack of; **~ de mieux** for want of anything *ou* something better; **sans ~** *adv* without fail; **~ de frappe** typing error; **~ d'inattention** careless mistake; **~ d'orthographe** spelling mistake; **~ professionnelle** professional misconduct *no pl*

fauteuil [fotœj] *nm* armchair; **~ à bascule** rocking chair; **~ club** (big) easy chair; **~ d'orchestre** seat in the front stalls *(Brit) ou* the orchestra *(US)*; **~ roulant** wheelchair

fauteur [fotœʀ] *nm*: **~ de troubles** trouble-maker

fautif, -ive [fotif, -iv] *adj (incorrect)* incorrect, inaccurate; *(responsable)* at fault, in the wrong; *(coupable)* guilty ▷ *nm/f* culprit

fauve [fov] *nm* wildcat; *(peintre)* Fauve ▷ *adj (couleur)* fawn

faux¹ [fo] *nf* scythe

faux², fausse [fo, fos] *adj (inexact)* wrong; *(piano, voix)* out of tune; *(falsifié)* fake, forged; *(sournois, postiche)* false ▷ *adv (Mus)* out of tune ▷ *nm (copie)* fake, forgery; *(opposé au vrai)*: **le ~** falsehood; **le ~ numéro/la fausse clé** the wrong number/key; **faire fausse route** to go the wrong way; **faire ~ bond à qn** to let sb down; **~ ami** *(Ling)* faux ami; **~ col** detachable collar; **~ départ** *(Sport, fig)* false start; **~ frais** *nmpl* extras, incidental expenses; **~ frère** *(fig péj)* false friend; **~ mouvement** awkward movement; **~ nez** false nose; **~ nom** assumed name; **~ pas** tripping *no pl*; *(fig)* faux

pas; **~ témoignage** *(délit)* perjury; **fausse alerte** false alarm; **fausse clé** skeleton key; **fausse couche** *(Méd)* miscarriage; **fausse joie** vain joy; **fausse note** wrong note

faux-filet [fofilɛ] *nm* sirloin

faux-monnayeur [fomɔnɛjœʀ] *nm* counterfeiter, forger

faveur [favœʀ] *nf* favour *(Brit)*, favor *(US)*; **traitement de ~** preferential treatment; **à la ~ de** under cover of; *(grâce à)* thanks to; **en ~ de** favo(u)r of

favorable [favɔʀabl(ə)] *adj* favo(u)rable

favori, te [favɔʀi, -it] *adj, nm/f* favo(u)rite

favoriser [favɔʀize] *vt* to favour *(Brit)*, favor *(US)*

fax [faks] *nm* fax

faxer *vt* to fax

FB *abr (= franc belge)* BF, FB

fébrile [febʀil] *adj* feverish, febrile; **capitaux ~s** *(Écon)* hot money

fécond, e [fekɔ̃, -ɔ̃d] *adj* fertile

féconder [fekɔ̃de] *vt* to fertilize

fécondité [fekɔ̃dite] *nf* fertility

fécule [fekyl] *nf* potato flour

féculent [fekylɑ̃] *nm* starchy food

fédéral, e, -aux [federal, -o] *adj* federal

fée [fe] *nf* fairy

féerique [feʀik] *adj* magical, fairytale *cpd*

feignant, e [fɛɲɑ̃, -ɑ̃t] *nm/f* = **fainéant, e**

feindre [fɛ̃dʀ(ə)] *vt* to feign ▷ *vi* to dissemble; **~ de faire** to pretend to do

feint, e [fɛ̃, fɛ̃t] *pp de* **feindre** ▷ *adj* feigned ▷ *nf (Sport: escrime)* feint; (: *Football, Rugby)* dummy *(Brit)*, fake *(US)*; *(fam: ruse)* sham

fêler [fele] *vt* to crack

félicitations [felisitasjɔ̃] *nfpl* congratulations

féliciter [felisite] *vt*: **~ qn (de)** to congratulate sb (on)

félin, e [felɛ̃, -in] *adj* feline ▷ *nm* (big) cat

fêlure [felyʀ] *nf* crack

femelle [fəmɛl] *adj (aussi Élec, Tech)* female ▷ *nf* female

féminin, e [feminɛ̃, -in] *adj* feminine; *(sexe)* female; *(équipe, vêtements etc)* women's; *(parfois péj: homme)* effeminate ▷ *nm (Ling)* feminine

féministe [feminist(ə)] *adj, nf* feminist

femme [fam] *nf* woman; *(épouse)* wife; **être très ~** to be very much a woman; **devenir ~** to attain womanhood; **~ d'affaires** businesswoman; **~ de chambre** chambermaid; **~ fatale** femme fatale; **~ au foyer** housewife; **~ d'intérieur** (real) homemaker; **~ de ménage** domestic help, cleaning lady; **~ du monde** society woman; **~-objet** sex object; **~ de tête** determined, intellectual woman

fémur [femyʀ] *nm* femur, thighbone

fendre [fɑ̃dʀ(ə)] *vt (couper en deux)* to split; *(fissurer)* to crack; *(fig: traverser)* to cut through; to push one's way through; **se fendre** *vi* to crack

fenêtre [fənɛtʀ(ə)] *nf* window; **~ à guillotine** sash window

fenouil [fənuj] *nm* fennel

fente [fɑ̃t] *nf* slit; *(fissure)* crack

féodal, e, -aux [feɔdal, -o] *adj* feudal
fer [fɛʀ] *nm* iron; (*de cheval*) shoe; **fers** *nmpl*
(*Méd*) forceps; **mettre aux ~s** (*enchaîner*) to put
in chains; **au ~ rouge** with a red-hot iron;
santé/main de ~ iron constitution/hand; **~ à
cheval** horseshoe; **en ~ à cheval** (*fig*) horseshoe-
shaped; **~ forgé** wrought iron; **~ à friser** curling
tongs; **~ de lance** spearhead; **~ (à repasser)**
iron; **~ à souder** soldering iron
fer-blanc [fɛʀblɑ̃] *nm* tin(plate)
férié, e [feʀje] *adj*: **jour ~** public holiday
ferions *etc* [fəʀjɔ̃] *vb voir* **faire**
ferme [fɛʀm(ə)] *adj* firm ▷ *adv* (*travailler etc*) hard;
(*discuter*) ardently ▷ *nf* (*exploitation*) farm; (*maison*)
farmhouse; **tenir ~** to stand firm
fermé, e [fɛʀme] *adj* closed, shut; (*gaz, eau etc*)
off; (*fig: personne*) uncommunicative; (: *milieu*)
exclusive
fermenter [fɛʀmɑ̃te] *vi* to ferment
fermer [fɛʀme] *vt* to close, shut; (*cesser
l'exploitation de*) to close down, shut down; (*eau,
lumière, électricité, robinet*) to put off, turn off;
(*aéroport, route*) to close ▷ *vi* to close, shut; to close
down, shut down; **se fermer** *vi* (*yeux*) to close,
shut; (*fleur, blessure*) to close up; **~ à clef** to lock;
~ au verrou to bolt; **~ les yeux (sur qch)** (*fig*) to
close one's eyes (to sth); **se ~ à** (*pitié, amour*) to
close one's heart *ou* mind to
fermeté [fɛʀməte] *nf* firmness
fermeture [fɛʀmətyʀ] *nf* closing; shutting;
closing *ou* shutting down; putting *ou* turning
off; (*dispositif*) catch; fastening, fastener; **heure
de ~** (*Comm*) closing time; **jour de ~** (*Comm*) day
on which the shop (*etc*) is closed; **~ éclair®** *ou* **à
glissière** zip (fastener) (*Brit*), zipper; *voir* **fermer**
fermier, -ière [fɛʀmje, -jɛʀ] *nm/f* farmer ▷ *nf*
(*femme de fermier*) farmer's wife ▷ *adj*: **beurre/
cidre ~** farm butter/cider
fermoir [fɛʀmwaʀ] *nm* clasp
féroce [feʀɔs] *adj* ferocious, fierce
ferons *etc* [fəʀɔ̃] *vb voir* **faire**
ferraille [fɛʀaj] *nf* scrap iron; **mettre à la ~** to
scrap; **bruit de ~** clanking
ferrer [fɛʀe] *vt* (*cheval*) to shoe; (*chaussure*) to nail;
(*canne*) to tip; (*poisson*) to strike
ferronnerie [fɛʀɔnʀi] *nf* ironwork; **~ d'art**
wrought iron work
ferroviaire [fɛʀɔvjɛʀ] *adj* rail *cpd*, railway *cpd*
(*Brit*), railroad *cpd* (*US*)
ferry [fɛʀe], **ferry-boat** [fɛʀebot] *nm* ferry
fertile [fɛʀtil] *adj* fertile; **~ en incidents**
eventful, packed with incidents
féru, e [feʀy] *adj*: **~ de** with a keen interest in
fervent, e [fɛʀvɑ̃, -ɑ̃t] *adj* fervent
fesse [fɛs] *nf* buttock; **les ~s** the bottom *sg*, the
buttocks
fessée [fese] *nf* spanking
festin [fɛstɛ̃] *nm* feast
festival [fɛstival] *nm* festival
festivités [fɛstivite] *nfpl* festivities,
merrymaking *sg*
festoyer [fɛstwaje] *vi* to feast

fêtard [fɛtaʀ] *nm* (*péj*) high liver, merrymaker
fête [fɛt] *nf* (*religieuse*) feast; (*publique*) holiday;
(*en famille etc*) celebration; (*kermesse*) fête, fair,
festival; (*du nom*) feast day, name day; **faire la
~** to live it up; **faire ~ à qn** to give sb a warm
welcome; **se faire une ~ de** to look forward to;
to enjoy; **ça va être sa ~!** (*fam*) he's going to get
it!; **jour de ~** holiday; **les ~s (de fin d'année)**
the festive season; **la salle/le comité des ~s** the
village hall/festival committee; **la ~ des Mères/
Pères** Mother's/Father's Day; **~ de charité**
charity fair *ou* fête; **~ foraine** (fun)fair; **la ~ de la
musique**; *see note*; **~ mobile** movable feast (day);
la F~ Nationale the national holiday
fêter [fete] *vt* to celebrate; (*personne*) to have a
celebration for
feu¹ [fø] *adj inv*: **~ son père** his late father
feu², x [fø] *nm* (*gén*) fire; (*signal lumineux*) light;
(*de cuisinière*) ring; (*sensation de brûlure*) burning
(sensation); **feux** *nmpl* fire *sg*; (*Auto*) (traffic)
lights; **tous ~x éteints** (*Navig, Auto*) without
lights; **au ~!** (*incendie*) fire!; **à ~ doux/vif** over a
slow/brisk heat; **à petit ~** (*Culin*) over a gentle
heat; (*fig*) slowly; **faire ~** to fire; **ne pas faire
long ~** (*fig*) not to last long; **commander le ~**
(*Mil*) to give the order to (open) fire; **tué au
~** (*Mil*) killed in action; **mettre à ~** (*fusée*) to
fire off; **pris entre deux ~x** caught in the
crossfire; **en ~** on fire; **être tout ~ tout flamme
(pour)** (*passion*) to be aflame with passion (for);
(*enthousiasme*) to be fired with enthusiasm (for);
prendre ~ to catch fire; **mettre le ~ à** to set fire
to, set on fire; **faire du ~** to make a fire; **avez-
vous du ~?** (*pour cigarette*) have you (got) a light?;
~ rouge/vert/orange (*Auto*) red/green/amber
(*Brit*) *ou* yellow (*US*) light; **donner le ~ vert à
qch/qn** (*fig*) to give sth/sb the go-ahead *ou* green
light; **~ arrière** (*Auto*) rear light; **~ d'artifice**
firework; (*spectacle*) fireworks *pl*; **~ de camp**
campfire; **~ de cheminée** chimney fire; **~ de
joie** bonfire; **~ de paille** (*fig*) flash in the pan; **~x
de brouillard** (*Auto*) fog lights *ou* lamps; **~x de
croisement** (*Auto*) dipped (*Brit*) *ou* dimmed (*US*)
headlights; **~x de position** (*Auto*) sidelights;
~x de route (*Auto*) headlights (on full (*Brit*) *ou*
high (*US*) beam); **~x de stationnement** parking
lights
feuillage [fœjaʒ] *nm* foliage, leaves *pl*
feuille [fœj] *nf* (*d'arbre*) leaf; **~ (de papier)** sheet
(of paper); **rendre ~ blanche** (*Scol*) to give in a
blank paper; **~ d'or/de métal** gold/metal leaf; **~
de chou** (*péj: journal*) rag; **~ d'impôts** tax form;
~ de maladie medical expenses claim form;
~ morte dead leaf; **~ de paye** pay slip; **~ de
présence** attendance sheet; **~ de température**
temperature chart; **~ de vigne** (*Bot*) vine leaf;
(*sur statue*) fig leaf; **~ volante** loose sheet
feuillet [fœjɛ] *nm* leaf, page
feuilleté, e [fœjte] *adj* (*Culin*) flaky; (*verre*)
laminated
feuilleter [fœjte] *vt* (*livre*) to leaf through
feuilleton [fœjtɔ̃] *nm* serial

feutre [føtʀ(ə)] nm felt; (*chapeau*) felt hat; (*stylo*) felt-tip(ped pen)

feutré, e [føtʀe] adj feltlike; (*pas, voix*) muffled

fève [fɛv] nf broad bean; (*dans la galette des Rois*) charm (*hidden in cake eaten on Twelfth Night*)

février [fevʀije] nm February; *voir aussi* **juillet**

FF abr (= *franc français*) FF

FFF abr = **Fédération française de football**

fiable [fjabl(ə)] adj reliable

fiançailles [fjɑ̃saj] nfpl engagement *sg*

fiancé, e [fjɑ̃se] nm/f fiancé (fiancée) ▷ adj: **être ~ (à)** to be engaged (to)

fiancer [fjɑ̃se]: **se fiancer** vi: **se ~ (avec)** to become engaged (to)

fibre [fibʀ(ə)] nf fibre, fiber (US); **avoir la ~ paternelle/militaire** to be a born father/soldier; **~ optique** optical fibre *ou* fiber; **~ de verre** fibreglass (Brit), fiberglass (US), glass fibre *ou* fiber

ficeler [fisle] vt to tie up

ficelle [fisɛl] nf string *no pl*; (*morceau*) piece *ou* length of string; (*pain*) stick of French bread; **ficelles** nfpl (*fig*) strings; **tirer sur la ~** (*fig*) to go too far

fiche [fiʃ] nf (*carte*) (index) card; (*formulaire*) form; (*Élec*) plug; **~ de paye** pay slip; **~ signalétique** (*Police*) identification card; **~ technique** data sheet, specification *ou* spec sheet

ficher [fiʃe] vt (*dans un fichier*) to file; (: *Police*) to put on file; (*fam*) to do; (: *donner*) to give; (: *mettre*) to stick *ou* shove; (*planter*): **~ qch dans** to stick *ou* drive sth into; **~ qn à la porte** (*fam*) to chuck sb out; **fiche(-moi) le camp** (*fam*) clear off; **fiche-moi la paix** (*fam*) leave me alone; **se ~ dans** (*s'enfoncer*) to get stuck in, embed itself in; **se ~ de** (*fam*) to make fun of; not to care about

fichier [fiʃje] nm (*gén, Inform*) file; (*à cartes*) card index; **~ actif** *ou* **en cours d'utilisation** (*Inform*) active file; **~ d'adresses** mailing list; **~ d'archives** (*Inform*) archive file

fichu, e [fiʃy] pp de **ficher** (*fam*) ▷ adj (*fam: fini, inutilisable*) bust, done for; (: *intensif*) wretched, darned ▷ nm (*foulard*) (head)scarf; **être ~ de** to be capable of; **mal ~** feeling lousy; useless; **bien ~** great

fictif, -ive [fiktif, -iv] adj fictitious

fiction [fiksjɔ̃] nf fiction; (*fait imaginé*) invention

fidèle [fidɛl] adj: **~ (à)** faithful (to) ▷ nm/f (Rel): **les ~s** the faithful; (*à l'église*) the congregation

fidélité [fidelite] nf faithfulness

fier¹ [fje]: **se ~ à** vt to trust

fier², fière [fjɛʀ] adj proud; **~ de** proud of; **avoir fière allure** to cut a fine figure

fierté [fjɛʀte] nf pride

fièvre [fjɛvʀ(ə)] nf fever; **avoir de la ~/39 de ~** to have a high temperature/a temperature of 39°C; **~ typhoïde** typhoid fever

fiévreux, -euse [fjevʀø, -øz] adj feverish

figé, e [fiʒe] adj (*manières*) stiff; (*société*) rigid; (*sourire*) set

figer [fiʒe] vt to congeal; (*fig: personne*) to freeze, root to the spot; **se figer** vi to congeal; to freeze;

(*institutions etc*) to become set, stop evolving

fignoler [fiɲɔle] vt to put the finishing touches to

figue [fig] nf fig

figuier [figje] nm fig tree

figurant, e [figyʀɑ̃, -ɑ̃t] nm/f (Théât) walk-on; (Ciné) extra

figure [figyʀ] nf (*visage*) face; (*image, tracé, forme, personnage*) figure; (*illustration*) picture, diagram; **faire ~ de** to look like; **faire bonne ~** to put up a good show; **faire triste ~** to be a sorry sight; **~ de rhétorique** figure of speech

figuré, e [figyʀe] adj (*sens*) figurative

figurer [figyʀe] vi to appear ▷ vt to represent; **se ~ que** to imagine that; **figurez-vous que ...** would you believe that ...?

fil [fil] nm (*brin, fig: d'une histoire*) thread; (*du téléphone*) cable, wire; (*textile de lin*) linen; (*d'un couteau: tranchant*) edge; **au ~ des années** with the passing of the years; **au ~ de l'eau** with the stream *ou* current; **de ~ en aiguille** one thing leading to another; **ne tenir qu'à un ~** (*vie, réussite etc*) to hang by a thread; **donner du ~ à retordre à qn** to make life difficult for sb; **donner/recevoir un coup de ~** to make/get a phone call; **~ à coudre** (sewing) thread *ou* yarn; **~ dentaire** dental floss; **~ électrique** electric wire; **~ de fer** wire; **~ de fer barbelé** barbed wire; **~ à pêche** fishing line; **~ à plomb** plumb line; **~ à souder** soldering wire

filament [filamɑ̃] nm (*Élec*) filament; (*de liquide*) trickle, thread

filandreux, -euse [filɑ̃dʀø, -øz] adj stringy

filature [filatyʀ] nf (*fabrique*) mill; (*policière*) shadowing *no pl*, tailing *no pl*; **prendre qn en ~** to shadow *ou* tail sb

file [fil] nf line; **~ (d'attente)** queue (Brit), line (US); **prendre la ~** to join the (end of the) queue *ou* line; **prendre la ~ de droite** (Auto) to move into the right-hand lane; **se mettre en ~** to form a line; (Auto) to get into lane; **stationner en double ~** (Auto) to double-park; **à la ~** adv (*d'affilée*) in succession; (*à la suite*) one after another; **à la** *ou* **en ~ indienne** in single file

filer [file] vt (*tissu, toile, verre*) to spin; (*dérouler: câble etc*) to pay *ou* let out; (*prendre en filature*) to shadow, tail; (*fam: donner*): **~ qch à qn** to slip sb sth ▷ vi (*bas, maille, liquide, pâte*) to run; (*aller vite*) to fly past *ou* by; (*fam: partir*) to make off; **~ à l'anglaise** to take French leave; **~ doux** to behave o.s., toe the line; **~ un mauvais coton** to be in a bad way

filet [filɛ] nm net; (Culin) fillet; (*d'eau, de sang*) trickle; **tendre un ~** (*police*) to set a trap; **~ (à bagages)** (Rail) luggage rack; **~ (à provisions)** string bag

filial, e, -aux [filjal, -o] adj filial ▷ nf (Comm) subsidiary; affiliate

filière [filjɛʀ] nf: **passer par la ~** to go through the (administrative) channels; **suivre la ~** to work one's way up (through the hierarchy)

filiforme [filifɔʀm(ə)] adj spindly; threadlike

filigrane [filigʀan] nm (*d'un billet, timbre*)

watermark; **en ~** (fig) showing just beneath the surface

fille [fij] nf girl; (opposé à fils) daughter; **vieille ~** old maid; **~ de joie** prostitute; **~ de salle** waitress

fillette [fijɛt] nf (little) girl

filleul, e [fijœl] nm/f godchild, godson (goddaughter)

film [film] nm (pour photo) (roll of) film; (œuvre) film, picture, movie; (couche) film; **~ muet/parlant** silent/talking picture ou movie; **~ alimentaire** clingfilm; **~ d'amour/ d'animation/d'horreur** romantic/animated/ horror film; **~ comique** comedy; **~ policier** thriller

filon [filɔ̃] nm vein, lode; (fig) lucrative line, money-spinner

fils [fis] nm son; **~ de famille** moneyed young man; **~ à papa** (péj) daddy's boy

filtre [filtʀ(ə)] nm filter; **"~ ou sans ~?"** (cigarettes) "tipped or plain?"; **~ à air** air filter

filtrer [filtʀe] vt to filter; (fig: candidats, visiteurs) to screen ▷ vi to filter (through)

fin¹ [fɛ̃] nf end; **fins** nfpl (but) ends; **à (la) ~ mai**, **~ mai** at the end of May; **en ~ de semaine** at the end of the week; **prendre ~** to come to an end; **toucher à sa ~** to be drawing to a close; **mettre ~ à** to put an end to; **mener à bonne ~** to bring to a successful conclusion; **à cette ~** to this end; **à toutes ~s utiles** for your information; **à la ~** in the end, eventually; (pej) endless ▷ adv endlessly; **~ de non-recevoir** (Jur, Admin) objection; **~ de section** (de ligne d'autobus) (fare) stage

fin², e [fɛ̃, fin] adj (papier, couche, fil) thin; (cheveux, poudre, pointe, visage) fine; (taille) neat, slim; (esprit, remarque) subtle; shrewd ▷ adv (moudre, couper) finely ▷ nm: **vouloir jouer au plus ~ (avec qn)** to try to outsmart sb ▷ nf (alcool) liqueur brandy; **c'est ~!** (ironique) how clever!; **~ prêt/soûl** quite ready/drunk; **un ~ gourmet** a gourmet; **un ~ tireur** a crack shot; **avoir la vue/l'ouïe ~e** to have sharp eyes/ears, have keen eyesight/ hearing; **or/linge/vin ~** fine gold/linen/wine; **le ~ fond de** the very depths of; **le ~ mot de** the real story behind; **la ~e fleur de** the flower of; **une ~e mouche** (fig) a sly customer; **~es herbes** mixed herbs

final, e [final] adj, nf final ▷ nm (Mus) finale; **quarts de ~** quarter finals; **8èmes/16èmes de ~** 2nd/1st round (in 5 round knock-out competition)

finalement [finalmɑ̃] adv finally, in the end; (après tout) after all

finance [finɑ̃s] nf finance; **finances** nfpl (situation financière) finances; (activités financières) finance sg; **moyennant ~** for a fee ou consideration

financer [finɑ̃se] vt to finance

financier, -ière [finɑ̃sje, -jɛʀ] adj financial ▷ nm financier

finaud, e [fino, -od] adj wily

finesse [finɛs] nf thinness; fineness; neatness,

slimness; subtlety; shrewdness; **finesses** nfpl (subtilités) niceties; finer points

fini, e [fini] adj finished; (Math) finite; (intensif): **un menteur ~** a liar through and through ▷ nm (d'un objet manufacturé) finish

finir [finiʀ] vt to finish ▷ vi to finish, end; **~ quelque part** to end ou finish up somewhere; **~ de faire** to finish doing; (cesser) to stop doing; **~ par faire** to end ou finish up doing; **il finit par m'agacer** he's beginning to get on my nerves; **~ en pointe/tragédie** to end in a point/in tragedy; **en ~ avec** to be ou have done with; **à n'en plus ~** (route, discussions) never-ending; **il va mal ~** he will come to a bad end; **c'est bientôt fini?** (reproche) have you quite finished?

finition [finisjɔ̃] nf finishing; finish

finlandais, e [fɛ̃lɑ̃dɛ, -ɛz] adj Finnish ▷ nm/f: **F~, e** Finn

Finlande [fɛ̃lɑ̃d] nf: **la ~** Finland

fiole [fjɔl] nf phial

firme [fiʀm(ə)] nf firm

fis [fi] vb voir **faire**

fisc [fisk] nm tax authorities pl, ≈ Inland Revenue (Brit), ≈ Internal Revenue Service (US)

fiscal, e, -aux [fiskal, -o] adj tax cpd, fiscal

fiscalité [fiskalite] nf tax system; (charges) taxation

fissure [fisyʀ] nf crack

fissurer [fisyʀe] vt: **se fissurer** vi to crack

fiston [fistɔ̃] nm (fam) son, lad

fit [fi] vb voir **faire**

fixation [fiksɑsjɔ̃] nf fixing; fastening; setting; (de ski) binding; (Psych) fixation

fixe [fiks(ə)] adj fixed; (emploi) steady, regular ▷ nm (salaire) basic salary; **à heure ~** at a set time; **menu à prix ~** set menu

fixé, e [fikse] adj (heure, jour) appointed; **être ~ (sur)** to have made up one's mind (about); to know for certain (about)

fixer [fikse] vt (attacher): **~ qch (à/sur)** to fix ou fasten sth (to/onto); (déterminer) to fix, set; (Chimie, Photo) to fix; (poser son regard sur) to look hard at, stare at; **se fixer** (s'établir) to settle down; **~ son choix sur qch** to decide on sth; **se ~ sur** (attention) to focus on

flacon [flakɔ̃] nm bottle

flageoler [flaʒɔle] vi to have knees like jelly

flageolet [flaʒɔlɛ] nm (Mus) flageolet; (Culin) dwarf kidney bean

flagrant, e [flagʀɑ̃, -ɑ̃t] adj flagrant, blatant; **en ~ délit** in the act, in flagrante delicto

flair [flɛʀ] nm sense of smell; (fig) intuition

flairer [flɛʀe] vt (humer) to sniff (at); (détecter) to scent

flamand, e [flamɑ̃, -ɑ̃d] adj Flemish ▷ nm (Ling) Flemish ▷ nm/f: **F~, e** Fleming; **les F~s** the Flemish

flamant [flamɑ̃] nm flamingo

flambant [flɑ̃bɑ̃] adv: **~ neuf** brand new

flambé, e [flɑ̃be] adj (Culin) flambé ▷ nf blaze; (fig) flaring-up, explosion

flambeau, x [flɑ̃bo] nm (flaming) torch; **se**

passer le ~ (fig) to hand down the (ou a) tradition

flambée [flãbe] nf (feu) blaze; (Comm): **~ des prix** (sudden) shooting up of prices

flamber [flãbe] vi to blaze (up) ▷ vt (poulet) to singe; (aiguille) to sterilize

flamboyer [flãbwaje] vi to blaze (up); (fig) to flame

flamme [flam] nf flame; (fig) fire, fervour; **en ~s** on fire, ablaze

flan [flã] nm (Culin) custard tart ou pie

flanc [flã] nm side; (Mil) flank; **à ~ de colline** on the hillside; **prêter le ~ à** (fig) to lay o.s. open to

flancher [flãʃe] vi (cesser de fonctionner) to fail, pack up; (armée) to quit

flanelle [flanɛl] nf flannel

flâner [flɑne] vi to stroll

flânerie [flɑnʀi] nf stroll

flanquer [flãke] vt to flank; (fam: jeter): **~ par terre/à la porte** to fling to the ground/chuck out; (: donner): **~ la frousse à qn** to put the wind up sb, give sb an awful fright

flaque [flak] nf (d'eau) puddle; (d'huile, de sang etc) pool

flash (pl **-es**) [flaʃ] nm (Photo) flash; **~ (d'information)** newsflash

flasque [flask(ə)] adj flabby ▷ nf (flacon) flask

flatter [flate] vt to flatter; (caresser) to stroke; **se ~ de qch** to pride o.s. on sth

flatterie [flatʀi] nf flattery

flatteur, -euse [flatœʀ, -øz] adj flattering ▷ nm/f flatterer

fléau, x [fleo] nm scourge, curse; (de balance) beam; (pour le blé) flail

flèche [flɛʃ] nf arrow; (de clocher) spire; (de grue) jib; (trait d'esprit, critique) shaft; **monter en ~** (fig) to soar, rocket; **partir en ~** (fig) to be off like a shot; **à ~ variable** (avion) swing-wing cpd

fléchette [fleʃɛt] nf dart; **fléchettes** nfpl (jeu) darts sg

fléchir [fleʃiʀ] vt (corps, genou) to bend; (fig) to sway, weaken ▷ vi (poutre) to sag, bend; (fig) to weaken, flag; (: baisser: prix) to fall off

flemmard, e [flemaʀ, -aʀd(ə)] nm/f lazybones sg, loafer

flemme [flɛm] nf (fam): **j'ai la ~ de le faire** I can't be bothered

flétrir [fletʀiʀ] vt to wither; (stigmatiser) to condemn (in the most severe terms); **se flétrir** vi to wither

fleur [flœʀ] nf flower; (d'un arbre) blossom; **être en ~** (arbre) to be in blossom; **tissu à ~s** flowered ou flowery fabric; **la (fine) ~ de** (fig) the flower of; **être ~ bleue** to be soppy ou sentimental; **à ~ de terre** just above the ground; **faire une ~ à qn** to do sb a favour (Brit) ou favor (US); **~ de lis** fleur-de-lis

fleuri, e [flœʀi] adj in flower ou bloom; surrounded by flowers; (fig: style) flowery; (: teint) glowing

fleurir [flœʀiʀ] vi (rose) to flower; (arbre) to blossom; (fig) to flourish ▷ vt (tombe) to put flowers on; (chambre) to decorate with flowers

fleuriste [flœʀist(ə)] nm/f florist

fleuve [flœv] nm river; **roman-~** saga; **discours-~** interminable speech

flexible [flɛksibl(ə)] adj flexible

flic [flik] nm (fam: péj) cop

flipper nm [flipœʀ] pinball (machine) ▷ vi [flipe] (fam: être déprimé) to feel down, be on a downer; (: être exalté) to freak out

flirter [flœʀte] vi to flirt

flocon [flɔkɔ̃] nm flake; (de laine etc: boulette) flock; **~s d'avoine** oat flakes, porridge oats

flopée [flɔpe] nf: **une ~ de** loads of

floraison [flɔʀezɔ̃] nf flowering; blossoming; flourishing; voir **fleurir**

flore [flɔʀ] nf flora

florissant, e [flɔʀisã, -ãt] vb voir **fleurir** ▷ adj flourishing; (santé, teint, mine) blooming

flot [flo] nm flood, stream; (marée) flood tide; **flots** nmpl (de la mer) waves; **être à ~** (Navig) to be afloat; (fig) to be on an even keel; **à ~s** (couler) in torrents; **entrer à ~s** to stream ou pour in

flottant, e [flɔtã, -ãt] adj (vêtement) loose(-fitting); (cours, barème) floating

flotte [flɔt] nf (Navig) fleet; (fam) water; rain

flottement [flɔtmã] nm (fig) wavering, hesitation; (Écon) floating

flotter [flɔte] vi to float; (nuage, odeur) to drift; (drapeau) to fly; (vêtements) to hang loose ▷ vb impers (fam: pleuvoir): **il flotte** it's raining ▷ vt to float; **faire ~** to float

flotteur [flɔtœʀ] nm float

flou, e [flu] adj fuzzy, blurred; (fig) woolly (Brit), vague; (non ajusté: robe) loose(-fitting)

fluctuation [flyktɥasjɔ̃] nf fluctuation

fluet, te [flɥɛ, -ɛt] adj thin, slight; (voix) thin

fluide [flɥid] adj fluid; (circulation etc) flowing freely ▷ nm fluid; (force) (mysterious) power

fluor [flyɔʀ] nm fluorine

fluorescent, e [flyɔʀesã, -ãt] adj fluorescent

flûte [flyt] nf (aussi: **flûte traversière**) flute; (verre) flute glass; (pain) long loaf; **petite ~** piccolo; **~!** drat it!; **~ (à bec)** recorder; **~ de Pan** panpipes pl

flux [fly] nm incoming tide; (écoulement) flow; **le ~ et le re~** the ebb and flow

FM sigle f (= frequency modulation) FM

foc [fɔk] nm jib

foi [fwa] nf faith; **sous la ~ du serment** under ou on oath; **ajouter ~ à** to lend credence to; **faire ~** (prouver) to be evidence; **digne de ~** reliable; **sur la ~ de** on the word ou strength of; **être de bonne/mauvaise ~** to be in good faith/not to be in good faith; **ma ~!** well!

foie [fwa] nm liver; **~ gras** foie gras

foin [fwɛ̃] nm hay; **faire les ~s** to make hay; **faire du ~** (fam) to kick up a row

foire [fwaʀ] nf fair; (fête foraine) (fun) fair; (fig: désordre, confusion) bear garden; **~ aux questions** (Internet) frequently asked questions; **faire la ~** to whoop it up; **~ (exposition)** trade fair

fois [fwa] nf time; **une/deux ~** once/twice; **trois/vingt ~** three/twenty times; **deux ~ deux** twice two; **deux/quatre ~ plus grand (que)**

twice/four times as big (as); **une ~** (*passé*) once; (*futur*) sometime; **une (bonne) ~ pour toutes** once and for all; **encore une ~** again, once more; **il était une ~** once upon a time; **une ~ que c'est fait** once it's done; **une ~ parti** once he (*ou* I *etc*) had left; **des ~** (*parfois*) sometimes; **si des ~ ...** (*fam*) if ever ...; **non mais des ~!** (*fam*) (now) look here!; **à la ~** (*ensemble*) (all) at once; **à la ~ grand et beau** both tall and handsome

foison [fwazɔ̃] *nf*: **une ~ de** an abundance of; **à ~** *adv* in plenty

foisonner [fwazɔne] *vi* to abound; **~ en** *ou* **de** to abound in

fol [fɔl] *adj m voir* **fou**

folie [fɔli] *nf* (*d'une décision, d'un acte*) madness, folly; (*état*) madness, insanity; (*acte*) folly; **la ~ des grandeurs** delusions of grandeur; **faire des ~s** (*en dépenses*) to be extravagant

folklorique [fɔlklɔrik] *adj* folk *cpd*; (*fam*) weird

folle [fɔl] *adj f, nf voir* **fou**

follement [fɔlmɑ̃] *adv* (*très*) madly, wildly

foncé, e [fɔ̃se] *adj* dark; **bleu ~** dark blue

foncer [fɔ̃se] *vt* to make darker; (*Culin: moule etc*) to line ▷ *vi* to go darker; (*fam: aller vite*) to tear *ou* belt along; **~ sur** to charge at

foncier, -ière [fɔ̃sje, -jɛʀ] *adj* (*honnêteté etc*) basic, fundamental; (*malhonnêteté*) deep-rooted; (*Comm*) real estate *cpd*

fonction [fɔ̃ksjɔ̃] *nf* (*rôle, Math, Ling*) function; (*emploi, poste*) post, position; **fonctions** *nfpl* (*professionnelles*) duties; **entrer en ~s** to take up one's post *ou* duties; to take up office; **voiture de ~** company car; **être ~ de** (*dépendre de*) to depend on; **en ~ de** (*par rapport à*) according to; **faire ~ de** to serve as; **la ~ publique** the state *ou* civil (*Brit*) service

fonctionnaire [fɔ̃ksjɔnɛʀ] *nm/f* state employee *ou* official; (*dans l'administration*) ≈ civil servant (*Brit*)

fonctionner [fɔ̃ksjɔne] *vi* to work, function; (*entreprise*) to operate, function; **faire ~** to work, operate

fond [fɔ̃] *nm voir aussi* **fonds**; (*d'un récipient, trou*) bottom; (*d'une salle, scène*) back; (*d'un tableau, décor*) background; (*opposé à la forme*) content; (*petite quantité*) **un ~ de verre** a drop; (*Sport*) **le ~** long distance (running); **course/épreuve de ~** long-distance race/trial; **au ~ de** at the bottom of; at the back of; **aller au ~ des choses** to get to the root of things; **le ~ de sa pensée** his (*ou* her) true thoughts *ou* feelings; **envoyer par le ~** (*Navig: couler*) to sink, scuttle; **à ~** *adv* (*connaître, soutenir*) thoroughly; (*appuyer, visser*) right down *ou* home; **à ~ (de train)** *adv* (*fam*) full tilt; **dans le ~, au ~** *adv* (*en somme*) basically, really; **de ~ en comble** *adv* from top to bottom; **~ sonore** background noise; background music; **~ de teint** foundation

fondamental, e, -aux [fɔ̃damɑ̃tal, -o] *adj* fundamental

fondant, e [fɔ̃dɑ̃, -ɑ̃t] *adj* (*neige*) melting; (*poire*) that melts in the mouth; (*chocolat*) fondant

fondateur, -trice [fɔ̃datœʀ, -tʀis] *nm/f* founder; **membre ~** founder (*Brit*) *ou* founding (*US*) member

fondation [fɔ̃dasjɔ̃] *nf* founding; (*établissement*) foundation; **fondations** *nfpl* (*d'une maison*) foundations; **travail de ~** foundation works *pl*

fondé, e [fɔ̃de] *adj* (*accusation etc*) well-founded ▷ *nm*: **~ de pouvoir** authorized representative; **mal ~** unfounded; **être ~ à croire** to have grounds for believing *ou* good reason to believe

fondement [fɔ̃dmɑ̃] *nm* (*derrière*) behind; **fondements** *nmpl* foundations; **sans ~** *adj* (*rumeur etc*) groundless, unfounded

fonder [fɔ̃de] *vt* to found; (*fig*): **~ qch sur** to base sth on; **se ~ sur** (*personne*) to base o.s. on; **~ un foyer** (*se marier*) to set up home

fonderie [fɔ̃dʀi] *nf* smelting works *sg*

fondre [fɔ̃dʀ(ə)] *vt* to melt; (*dans l'eau: sucre, sel*) to dissolve; (*fig: mélanger*) to merge, blend ▷ *vi* to melt; to dissolve; (*fig*) to melt away; (*se précipiter*): **~ sur** to swoop down on; **se fondre** *vi* (*se combiner, se confondre*) to merge into each other; to dissolve; **~ en larmes** to dissolve into tears

fonds [fɔ̃] *nm* (*de bibliothèque*) collection; (*Comm*): **~ (de commerce)** business; (*fig*): **~ de probité** *etc* fund of integrity *etc* ▷ *nmpl* (*argent*) funds; **à ~ perdus** *adv* with little or no hope of getting the money back; **être en ~** to be in funds; **mise de ~** investment, (capital) outlay; **F~ monétaire international (FMI)** International Monetary Fund (IMF); **~ de roulement** *nm* float

fondu, e [fɔ̃dy] *adj* (*beurre, neige*) melted; (*métal*) molten ▷ *nm* (*Ciné*): **~ (enchaîné)** dissolve ▷ *nf* (*Culin*) fondue

font [fɔ̃] *vb voir* **faire**

fontaine [fɔ̃tɛn] *nf* fountain; (*source*) spring

fonte [fɔ̃t] *nf* melting; (*métal*) cast iron; **la ~ des neiges** the (spring) thaw

foot [fut], **football** [futbol] *nm* football, soccer

footballeur, -euse [futbolœr, -øz] *nm/f* footballer (*Brit*), football *ou* soccer player

footing [futiŋ] *nm* jogging; **faire du ~** to go jogging

for [fɔr] *nm*: **dans** *ou* **en son ~ intérieur** in one's heart of hearts

forain, e [fɔrɛ̃, -ɛn] *adj* fairground *cpd* ▷ *nm* (*marchand*) stallholder; (*acteur etc*) fairground entertainer

forçat [fɔrsa] *nm* convict

force [fɔrs(ə)] *nf* strength; (*puissance: surnaturelle etc*) power; (*Physique, Mécanique*) force; **forces** *nfpl* (*physiques*) strength *sg*; (*Mil*) forces; (*effectifs*): **d'importantes ~s de police** large contingents of police; **avoir de la ~** to be strong; **être à bout de ~** to have no strength left; **à la ~ du poignet** (*fig*) by the sweat of one's brow; **à ~ de faire** by dint of doing; **arriver en ~** (*nombreux*) to arrive in force; **cas de ~ majeure** case of absolute necessity; (*Assurances*) act of God; **~ de la nature** natural force; **de ~** *adv* forcibly, by force; **de toutes mes/ses ~s** with all my/his strength; **par la ~** using force; **par la ~ des**

choses/d'habitude by force of circumstances/
habit; **à toute ~** (*absolument*) at all costs; **faire
~ de rames/voiles** to ply the oars/cram on sail;
être de ~ à faire to be up to doing; **de première
~** first class; **la ~ armée** (*les troupes*) the army;
~ d'âme fortitude; **~ de frappe** strike force; **~
d'inertie** force of inertia; **la ~ publique** the
authorities responsible for public order; **~s
d'intervention** (*Mil, Police*) peace-keeping force
sg; **les ~s de l'ordre** the police

forcé, e [fɔʀse] *adj* forced; (*bain*) unintended;
(*inevitable*): **c'est ~!** it's inevitable!, it HAS to be!

forcément [fɔʀsemã] *adv* necessarily;
inevitably; (*bien sûr*) of course

forcené, e [fɔʀsəne] *adj* frenzied ▷ *nm/f* maniac

forcer [fɔʀse] *vt* (*contraindre*): **~ qn à faire** to force
sb to do; (*porte, serrure, plante*) to force; (*moteur, voix*)
to strain ▷ *vi* (*Sport*) to overtax o.s.; **se ~ à faire
qch** to force o.s. to do sth; **~ la dose/l'allure** to
overdo it/increase the pace; **~ l'attention/le
respect** to command attention/respect; **~ la
consigne** to bypass orders

forcir [fɔʀsiʀ] *vi* (*grossir*) to broaden out; (*vent*) to
freshen

forer [fɔʀe] *vt* to drill, bore

forestier, -ière [fɔʀɛstje, -jɛʀ] *adj* forest *cpd*

forêt [fɔʀɛ] *nf* forest; **Office National des F~s**
(*Admin*) ≈ Forestry Commission (*Brit*), ≈ National
Forest Service (*US*); **la F~ Noire** the Black Forest

forfait [fɔʀfɛ] *nm* (*Comm*) fixed *ou* set price; all-
in deal *ou* price; (*crime*) infamy; **déclarer ~** to
withdraw; **gagner par ~** to win by a walkover;
travailler à ~ to work for a lump sum

forfaitaire [fɔʀfɛtɛʀ] *adj* set; inclusive

forge [fɔʀʒ(ə)] *nf* forge, smithy

forger [fɔʀʒe] *vt* to forge; (*fig: personnalité*) to
form; (: *prétexte*) to contrive, make up

forgeron [fɔʀʒəʀɔ̃] *nm* (black)smith

formaliser [fɔʀmalize]: **se formaliser** *vi*: **se ~
(de)** to take offence (at)

formalité [fɔʀmalite] *nf* formality

format [fɔʀma] *nm* size; **petit ~** small size;
(*Photo*) 35 mm (film)

formater [fɔʀmate] *vt* (*disque*) to format; **non
formaté** unformatted

formation [fɔʀmasjɔ̃] *nf* forming; (*éducation*)
training; (*Mus*) group; (*Mil, Aviat, Géo*) formation;
la ~ permanente *ou* **continue** continuing
education; **la ~ professionnelle** vocational
training

forme [fɔʀm(ə)] *nf* (*gén*) form; (*d'un objet*) shape,
form; **formes** *nfpl* (*bonnes manières*) proprieties;
(*d'une femme*) figure *sg*; **en ~ de poire** pear-
shaped, in the shape of a pear; **sous ~ de** in the
form of; in the guise of; **sous ~ de cachets** in
the form of tablets; **être en (bonne** *ou* **pleine)
~, avoir la ~** (*Sport etc*) to be on form; **en bonne
et due ~** in due form; **pour la ~** for the sake
of form; **sans autre ~ de procès** (*fig*) without
further ado; **prendre ~** to take shape

formel, le [fɔʀmɛl] *adj* (*preuve, décision*) definite,
positive; (*logique*) formal

formellement [fɔʀmɛlmã] *adv* (*interdit*) strictly

former [fɔʀme] *vt* (*gén*) to form; (*éduquer: soldat,
ingénieur etc*) to train; **se former** to form; to train

formidable [fɔʀmidabl(ə)] *adj* tremendous

formulaire [fɔʀmylɛʀ] *nm* form

formule [fɔʀmyl] *nf* (*gén*) formula; (*formulaire*)
form; **selon la ~ consacrée** as one says; **~ de
politesse** polite phrase; (*en fin de lettre*) letter
ending

formuler [fɔʀmyle] *vt* (*émettre: réponse, vœux*) to
formulate; (*expliciter: sa pensée*) to express

fort, e [fɔʀ, fɔʀt(ə)] *adj* strong; (*intensité,
rendement*) high, great; (*corpulent*) large; (*doué*):
être ~ (en) to be good (at) ▷ *adv* (*serrer, frapper*)
hard; (*sonner*) loud(ly); (*beaucoup*) greatly, very
much; (*très*) very ▷ *nm* (*édifice*) fort; (*point fort*)
strong point, forte; (*gén pl: personne, pays*): **le ~, les
~s** the strong; **c'est un peu ~!** it's a bit much!;
à plus ~e raison even more so, all the more
reason; **avoir ~ à faire avec qn** to have a hard
job with sb; **se faire ~ de faire** to claim one can
do; **~ bien/peu** very well/few; **au plus ~ de** (*au
milieu de*) in the thick of, at the height of; **~e tête**
rebel

forteresse [fɔʀtəʀɛs] *nf* fortress

fortifiant [fɔʀtifjã] *nm* tonic

fortifier [fɔʀtifje] *vt* to strengthen, fortify; (*Mil*)
to fortify; **se fortifier** *vi* (*personne, santé*) to grow
stronger

fortiori [fɔʀtjɔʀi]: **à ~** *adv* all the more so

fortuit, e [fɔʀtɥi, -it] *adj* fortuitous, chance *cpd*

fortune [fɔʀtyn] *nf* fortune; **faire ~** to make
one's fortune; **de ~** *adj* makeshift; (*compagnon*)
chance *cpd*

fortuné, e [fɔʀtyne] *adj* wealthy, well-off

fosse [fos] *nf* (*grand trou*) pit; (*tombe*) grave; **la
~ aux lions/ours** the lions' den/bear pit; **~
commune** common *ou* communal grave; **~
(d'orchestre)** (orchestra) pit; **~ à purin** cesspit;
~ septique septic tank; **~s nasales** nasal fossae

fossé [fose] *nm* ditch; (*fig*) gulf, gap

fossette [fosɛt] *nf* dimple

fossile [fosil] *nm* fossil ▷ *adj* fossilized, fossil *cpd*

fossoyeur [foswajœʀ] *nm* gravedigger

fou, fol, folle [fu, fɔl] *adj* mad, crazy; (*déréglé
etc*) wild, erratic; (*mèche*) stray; (*herbe*) wild;
(*fam: extrême, très grand*) terrific, tremendous
▷ *nm/f* madman/woman ▷ *nm* (*du roi*) jester,
fool; (*Échecs*) bishop; **~ à lier, ~ furieux (folle
furieuse)** raving mad; **être ~ de** to be mad *ou*
crazy about; (*chagrin, joie, colère*) to be wild with;
faire le ~ to play *ou* act the fool; **avoir le ~ rire** to
have the giggles

foudre [fudʀ(ə)] *nf* lightning; **foudres** *nfpl* (*fig:
colère*) wrath *sg*

foudroyant, e [fudʀwajã, -ãt] *adj* devastating;
(*maladie, poison*) violent

foudroyer [fudʀwaje] *vt* to strike down; **~ qn du
regard** to look daggers at sb; **il a été foudroyé**
he was struck by lightning

fouet [fwɛ] *nm* whip; (*Culin*) whisk; **de plein ~**
adv head on

fouetter [fwete] *vt* to whip; to whisk
fougère [fuʒɛʀ] *nf* fern
fougue [fug] *nf* ardour (Brit), ardor (US), spirit
fougueux, -euse [fugø, -øz] *adj* fiery, ardent
fouille [fuj] *nf* search; **fouilles** *nfpl* (*archéologiques*) excavations; **passer à la ~** to be searched
fouiller [fuje] *vt* to search; (*creuser*) to dig; (: *archéologue*) to excavate; (*approfondir: étude etc*) to go into ▷ *vi* (*archéologue*) to excavate; **~ dans/ parmi** to rummage in/among
fouillis [fuji] *nm* jumble, muddle
fouiner [fwine] *vi* (*péj*): **~ dans** to nose around *ou* about in
foulard [fulaʀ] *nm* scarf
foule [ful] *nf* crowd; **une ~ de** masses of; **venir en ~** to come in droves
foulée [fule] *nf* stride; **dans la ~ de** on the heels of
fouler [fule] *vt* to press; (*sol*) to tread upon; **se fouler** *vi* to overexert o.s.; **se ~ la cheville** to sprain one's ankle; **~ aux pieds** to trample underfoot
foulure [fulyʀ] *nf* sprain
four [fuʀ] *nm* oven; (*de potier*) kiln; (*Théât: échec*) flop; **allant au ~** ovenproof
fourbe [fuʀb(ə)] *adj* deceitful
fourbu, e [fuʀby] *adj* exhausted
fourche [fuʀʃ(ə)] *nf* pitchfork; (*de bicyclette*) fork
fourchette [fuʀʃɛt] *nf* fork; (*Statistique*) bracket, margin
fourgon [fuʀgɔ̃] *nm* van; (*Rail*) wag(g)on; **~ mortuaire** hearse
fourgonnette [fuʀgɔnɛt] *nf* (delivery) van
fourmi [fuʀmi] *nf* ant; **avoir des ~s** (*fig*) to have pins and needles
fourmilière [fuʀmiljɛʀ] *nf* ant-hill; (*fig*) hive of activity
fourmiller [fuʀmije] *vi* to swarm; **~ de** to be teeming with, be swarming with
fournaise [fuʀnɛz] *nf* blaze; (*fig*) furnace, oven
fourneau, x [fuʀno] *nm* stove
fournée [fuʀne] *nf* batch
fourni, e [fuʀni] *adj* (*barbe, cheveux*) thick; (*magasin*): **bien ~ (en)** well stocked (with)
fournir [fuʀniʀ] *vt* to supply; (*preuve, exemple*) to provide, supply; (*effort*) to put in; **~ qch à qn** to supply sth to sb, supply *ou* provide sb with sth; **~ qn en** (*Comm*) to supply sb with; **se ~ chez** to shop at
fournisseur, -euse [fuʀnisœʀ, -øz] *nm/f* supplier; (*Internet*): **~ d'accès à Internet** (Internet) service provider
fourniture [fuʀnityʀ] *nf* supply(ing); **fournitures** *nfpl* supplies; **~s de bureau** office supplies, stationery; **~s scolaires** school stationery
fourrage [fuʀaʒ] *nm* fodder
fourré, e [fuʀe] *adj* (*bonbon, chocolat*) filled; (*manteau, botte*) fur-lined ▷ *nm* thicket
fourrer [fuʀe] *vt* (*fam*): **~ qch dans** to stick *ou* shove sth into; **se ~ dans/sous** to get into/ under; **se ~ dans** (*une mauvaise situation*) to land

o.s. in
fourre-tout [fuʀtu] *nm inv* (*sac*) holdall; (*péj*) junk room (*ou* cupboard); (*fig*) rag-bag
fourrière [fuʀjɛʀ] *nf* pound
fourrure [fuʀyʀ] *nf* fur; (*sur l'animal*) coat; **manteau/col de ~** fur coat/collar
fourvoyer [fuʀvwaje]: **se fourvoyer** *vi* to go astray, stray; **se ~ dans** to stray into
foutre [futʀ(ə)] *vt* (*fam!*) = **ficher**; (*fam*)
foutu, e [futy] *adj* (*fam!*) = **fichu**
foyer [fwaje] *nm* (*de cheminée*) hearth; (*fig*) seat, centre; (*famille*) family; (*domicile*) home; (*local de réunion*) (social) club; (*résidence*) hostel; (*salon*) foyer; (*Optique, Photo*) focus; **lunettes à double ~** bi-focal glasses
fracas [fʀaka] *nm* din; crash
fracassant, e [fʀakasɑ̃, -ɑ̃t] *adj* sensational, staggering
fracasser [fʀakase] *vt* to smash; **se fracasser contre** *ou* **sur** to crash against
fraction [fʀaksjɔ̃] *nf* fraction
fractionner [fʀaksjone] *vt* to divide (up), split (up)
fracture [fʀaktyʀ] *nf* fracture; **~ du crâne** fractured skull; **~ de la jambe** broken leg
fracturer [fʀaktyʀe] *vt* (*coffre, serrure*) to break open; (*os, membre*) to fracture
fragile [fʀaʒil] *adj* fragile, delicate; (*fig*) frail
fragilité [fʀaʒilite] *nf* fragility
fragment [fʀagmɑ̃] *nm* (*d'un objet*) fragment, piece; (*d'un texte*) passage, extract
fraîche [fʀɛʃ] *adj f voir* **frais**
fraîcheur [fʀɛʃœʀ] *nf* coolness; freshness; *voir* **frais**
fraîchir [fʀɛʃiʀ] *vi* to get cooler; (*vent*) to freshen
frais, fraîche [fʀɛ, fʀɛʃ] *adj* (*air, eau, accueil*) cool; (*petit pois, œufs, nouvelles, couleur, troupes*) fresh; **le voilà ~!** he's in a (right) mess! ▷ *adv* (*récemment*) newly, fresh(ly); **il fait ~** it's cool; **servir ~** chill before serving, serve chilled ▷ *nm*: **mettre au ~** to put in a cool place; **prendre le ~** to take a breath of cool air ▷ *nmpl* (*débours*) expenses; (*Comm*) costs; charges; **faire des ~** to spend; to go to a lot of expense; **faire les ~ de** to bear the brunt of; **faire les ~ de la conversation** (*parler*) to do most of the talking; (*en être le sujet*) to be the topic of conversation; **il en a été pour ses ~** he could have spared himself the trouble; **rentrer dans ses ~** to recover one's expenses; **~ de déplacement** travel(ling) expenses; **~ d'entretien** upkeep; **~ généraux** overheads; **~ de scolarité** school fees, tuition (US)
fraise [fʀɛz] *nf* strawberry; (*Tech*) countersink (bit); (*de dentiste*) drill; **~ des bois** wild strawberry
framboise [fʀɑ̃bwaz] *nf* raspberry
franc, franche [fʀɑ̃, fʀɑ̃ʃ] *adj* (*personne*) frank, straightforward; (*visage*) open; (*net: refus, couleur*) clear; (: *coupure*) clean; (*intensif*) downright; (*exempt*): **~ de port** post free, postage paid; (*zone, port*) free; (*boutique*) duty-free ▷ *adv*: **parler ~** to be frank *ou* candid ▷ *nm* franc

français, e [fʀɑ̃sɛ, -ɛz] adj French ▷ nm (Ling) French ▷ nm/f: **F~, e** Frenchman/woman; **les F~** the French

France [fʀɑ̃s] nf: **la ~** France; **en ~** in France; **~ 2, ~ 3** public-sector television channels; note

franche [fʀɑ̃ʃ] adj f voir **franc**

franchement [fʀɑ̃ʃmɑ̃] adv frankly; clearly; (tout à fait) downright ▷ excl well, really!; voir **franc**

franchir [fʀɑ̃ʃiʀ] vt (obstacle) to clear, get over; (seuil, ligne, rivière) to cross; (distance) to cover

franchise [fʀɑ̃ʃiz] nf frankness; (douanière, d'impôt) exemption; (Assurances) excess; (Comm) franchise; **~ de bagages** baggage allowance

franc-maçon (pl **francs-maçons**) [fʀɑ̃masɔ̃] nm Freemason

franco [fʀɑ̃ko] adv (Comm): **~ (de port)** postage paid

francophone [fʀɑ̃kɔfɔn] adj French-speaking ▷ nm/f French speaker

franc-parler [fʀɑ̃paʀle] nm inv outspokenness

frange [fʀɑ̃ʒ] nf fringe; (cheveux) fringe (Brit), bangs (US)

frangipane [fʀɑ̃ʒipan] nf almond paste

franquette [fʀɑ̃kɛt]: **à la bonne ~** adv without any fuss

frappant, e [fʀapɑ̃, -ɑ̃t] adj striking

frappé, e [fʀape] adj (Culin) iced; **~ de panique** panic-stricken; **~ de stupeur** thunderstruck, dumbfounded

frapper [fʀape] vt to hit, strike; (étonner) to strike; (monnaie) to strike, stamp; **se frapper** vi (s'inquiéter) to get worked up; **~ à la porte** to knock at the door; **~ dans ses mains** to clap one's hands; **~ du poing sur** to bang one's fist on; **~ un grand coup** (fig) to strike a blow

frasques [fʀask(ə)] nfpl escapades; **faire des ~** to get up to mischief

fraternel, le [fʀatɛʀnɛl] adj brotherly, fraternal

fraternité [fʀatɛʀnite] nf brotherhood

fraude [fʀod] nf fraud; (Scol) cheating; **passer qch en ~** to smuggle sth in (ou out); **~ fiscale** tax evasion

frauder [fʀode] vi, vt to cheat; **~ le fisc** to evade paying tax(es)

frauduleux, -euse [fʀodylø, -øz] adj fraudulent

frayer [fʀeje] vt to open up, clear ▷ vi to spawn; (fréquenter): **~ avec** to mix ou associate with; **se ~ un passage dans** to clear o.s. a path through, force one's way through

frayeur [fʀejœʀ] nf fright

fredonner [fʀədɔne] vt to hum

freezer [fʀizœʀ] nm freezing compartment

frein [fʀɛ̃] nm brake; **mettre un ~ à** (fig) to put a brake on, check; **sans ~** (sans limites) unchecked; **~ à main** handbrake; **~ moteur** engine braking; **~s à disques** disc brakes; **~s à tambour** drum brakes

freiner [fʀene] vi to brake ▷ vt (progrès etc) to check

frêle [fʀɛl] adj frail, fragile

frelon [fʀəlɔ̃] nm hornet

frémir [fʀemiʀ] vi (de froid, de peur) to tremble,

shiver; (de joie) to quiver; (eau) to (begin to) bubble

frêne [fʀɛn] nm ash (tree)

frénétique [fʀenetik] adj frenzied, frenetic

fréquemment [fʀekamɑ̃] adv frequently

fréquent, e [fʀekɑ̃, -ɑ̃t] adj frequent

fréquentation [fʀekɑ̃tasjɔ̃] nf frequenting; seeing; **fréquentations** nfpl company sg

fréquenté, e [fʀekɑ̃te] adj: **très ~** (very) busy; **mal ~** patronized by disreputable elements

fréquenter [fʀekɑ̃te] vt (lieu) to frequent; (personne) to see; **se fréquenter** to see a lot of each other

frère [fʀɛʀ] nm brother ▷ adj: **partis/pays ~s** sister parties/countries

fresque [fʀɛsk(ə)] nf (Art) fresco

fret [fʀɛ] nm freight

frétiller [fʀetije] vi to wriggle; to quiver; **~ de la queue** to wag its tail

fretin [fʀətɛ̃] nm: **le menu ~** the small fry

friable [fʀijabl(ə)] adj crumbly

friand, e [fʀijɑ̃, -ɑ̃d] adj: **~ de** very fond of ▷ nm (Culin) small minced-meat (Brit) ou ground-meat (US) pie; (: sucré) small almond cake

friandise [fʀijɑ̃diz] nf sweet

fric [fʀik] nm (fam) cash, bread

friche [fʀiʃ]: **en ~** adj, adv (lying) fallow

friction [fʀiksjɔ̃] nf (massage) rub, rub-down; (chez le coiffeur) scalp massage; (Tech, fig) friction

frictionner [fʀiksjɔne] vt to rub (down); to massage

frigidaire® [fʀiʒidɛʀ] nm refrigerator

frigide [fʀiʒid] adj frigid

frigo [fʀigo] nm (= frigidaire) fridge

frigorifique [fʀigɔʀifik] adj refrigerating

frileux, -euse [fʀilø, -øz] adj sensitive to (the) cold; (fig) overcautious

frime [fʀim] nf (fam): **c'est de la ~** it's all put on; **pour la ~** just for show

frimer [fʀime] vi to put on an act

frimousse [fʀimus] nf (sweet) little face

fringale [fʀɛ̃gal] nf: **avoir la ~** to be ravenous

fringant, e [fʀɛ̃gɑ̃, -ɑ̃t] adj dashing

fringues [fʀɛ̃g] nfpl (fam) clothes, gear no pl

fripé, e [fʀipe] adj crumpled

fripon, ne [fʀipɔ̃, -ɔn] adj roguish, mischievous ▷ nm/f rascal, rogue

fripouille [fʀipuj] nf scoundrel

frire [fʀiʀ] vt (aussi: **faire frire**) ▷ vi to fry

frisé, e [fʀize] adj curly, curly-haired ▷ nf: **(chicorée) ~e** curly endive

frisson [fʀisɔ̃], **frissonnement** [fʀisɔnmɑ̃] nm shudder, shiver; quiver

frissonner [fʀisɔne] vi (personne) to shudder, shiver; (feuilles) to quiver

frit, e [fʀi, fʀit] pp de **frire** ▷ adj fried ▷ nf: **(pommes) ~es** chips (Brit), French fries

friteuse [fʀitøz] nf chip pan (Brit), deep (fat) fryer

friture [fʀityʀ] nf (huile) (deep) fat; (plat): **~ (de poissons)** fried fish; (Radio) crackle, crackling no pl; **fritures** nfpl (aliments frits) fried food sg

frivole [fʀivɔl] adj frivolous

froid, e [fʀwa, fʀwad] *adj* cold ▷ *nm* cold; (*absence de sympathie*) coolness *no pl*; **il fait ~** it's cold; **avoir ~** to be cold; **prendre ~** to catch a chill *ou* cold; **à ~** *adv* (*démarrer*) (from) cold; (**pendant**) **les grands ~s** (in) the depths of winter, (during) the cold season; **jeter un ~** (*fig*) to cast a chill; **être en ~ avec** to be on bad terms with; **battre ~ à qn** to give sb the cold shoulder

froidement [fʀwadmɑ̃] *adv* (*accueillir*) coldly; (*décider*) coolly

froideur [fʀwadœʀ] *nf* coolness *no pl*

froisser [fʀwase] *vt* to crumple (up), crease; (*fig*) to hurt, offend; **se froisser** *vi* to crumple, crease; to take offence (*Brit*) *ou* offense (*US*); **se ~ un muscle** to strain a muscle

frôler [fʀole] *vt* to brush against; (*projectile*) to skim past; (*fig*) to come within a hair's breadth of, come very close to

fromage [fʀɔmaʒ] *nm* cheese; **~ blanc** soft white cheese; **~ de tête** pork brawn

froment [fʀɔmɑ̃] *nm* wheat

froncer [fʀɔ̃se] *vt* to gather; **~ les sourcils** to frown

frondaisons [fʀɔ̃dɛzɔ̃] *nfpl* foliage *sg*

front [fʀɔ̃] *nm* forehead, brow; (*Mil, Météorologie, Pol*) front; **avoir le ~ de faire** to have the effrontery to do; **de ~** *adv* (*se heurter*) head-on; (*rouler*) together (2 or 3 abreast); (*simultanément*) at once; **faire ~ à** to face up to; **~ de mer** (sea) front

frontalier, -ière [fʀɔ̃talje, -jɛʀ] *adj* border *cpd*, frontier *cpd* ▷ *nm/f*: (**travailleurs**) **~s** workers who cross the border to go to work, commuters from across the border

frontière [fʀɔ̃tjɛʀ] *nf* (*Géo, Pol*) frontier, border; (*fig*) frontier, boundary

frotter [fʀɔte] *vi* to rub, scrape ▷ *vt* to rub; (*pour nettoyer*) to rub (up); (: *avec une brosse*) to scrub; **~ une allumette** to strike a match; **se ~ à qn** to cross swords with sb; **se ~ à qch** to come up against sth; **se ~ les mains** (*fig*) to rub one's hands (gleefully)

fructifier [fʀyktifje] *vi* to yield a profit; **faire ~** to turn to good account

fructueux, -euse [fʀyktɥø, -øz] *adj* fruitful; profitable

frugal, e, -aux [fʀygal, -o] *adj* frugal

fruit [fʀɥi] *nm* fruit *gen no pl*; **~s de mer** (*Culin*) seafood(s); **~s secs** dried fruit *sg*

fruité, e [fʀɥite] *adj* (*vin*) fruity

fruitier, -ière [fʀɥitje, -jɛʀ] *adj*: **arbre ~** fruit tree ▷ *nm/f* fruiterer (*Brit*), fruit merchant (*US*)

fruste [fʀyst(ə)] *adj* unpolished, uncultivated

frustrer [fʀystʀe] *vt* to frustrate; (*priver*): **~ qn de qch** to deprive sb of sth

FS *abr* (= *franc suisse*) FS, SF

fuel [fjul], **fuel-oil** [fjulɔjl] *nm* fuel oil; (*pour chauffer*) heating oil

fugace [fygas] *adj* fleeting

fugitif, -ive [fyʒitif, -iv] *adj* (*lueur, amour*) fleeting; (*prisonnier etc*) runaway ▷ *nm/f* fugitive, runaway

fugue [fyg] *nf* (*d'un enfant*) running away *no pl*; (*Mus*) fugue; **faire une ~** to run away, abscond

fuir [fɥiʀ] *vt* to flee from; (*éviter*) to shun ▷ *vi* to run away; (*gaz, robinet*) to leak

fuite [fɥit] *nf* flight; (*écoulement*) leak, leakage; (*divulgation*) leak; **être en ~** to be on the run; **mettre en ~** to put to flight; **prendre la ~** to take flight

fulgurant, e [fylgyʀɑ̃, -ɑ̃t] *adj* lightning *cpd*, dazzling

fulminer [fylmine] *vi*: **~ (contre)** to thunder forth (against)

fumé, e [fyme] *adj* (*Culin*) smoked; (*verre*) tinted ▷ *nf* smoke; **partir en ~** to go up in smoke

fumer [fyme] *vi* to smoke; (*liquide*) to steam ▷ *vt* to smoke; (*terre, champ*) to manure

fûmes [fym] *vb voir* **être**

fumet [fyme] *nm* aroma

fumeur, -euse [fymœʀ, -øz] *nm/f* smoker; (**compartiment**) **~s** smoking compartment

fumeux, -euse [fymø, -øz] *adj* (*péj*) woolly (*Brit*), hazy

fumier [fymje] *nm* manure

fumiste [fymist(ə)] *nm* (*ramoneur*) chimney sweep ▷ *nm/f* (*péj: paresseux*) shirker; (*charlatan*) phoney

funèbre [fynɛbʀ(ə)] *adj* funeral *cpd*; (*fig*) doleful; funereal

funérailles [fyneʀaj] *nfpl* funeral *sg*

funeste [fynɛst(ə)] *adj* disastrous; deathly

fur [fyʀ]: **au ~ et à mesure** *adv* as one goes along; **au ~ et à mesure que** as; **au ~ et à mesure de leur progression** as they advance (*ou* advanced)

furet [fyʀɛ] *nm* ferret

fureter [fyʀte] *vi* (*péj*) to nose about

fureur [fyʀœʀ] *nf* fury; (*passion*): **~ de** passion for; **faire ~** to be all the rage

furibond, e [fyʀibɔ̃, -ɔ̃d] *adj* livid, absolutely furious

furie [fyʀi] *nf* fury; (*femme*) shrew, vixen; **en ~** (*mer*) raging

furieux, -euse [fyʀjø, -øz] *adj* furious

furoncle [fyʀɔ̃kl(ə)] *nm* boil

furtif, -ive [fyʀtif, -iv] *adj* furtive

fus [fy] *vb voir* **être**

fusain [fyzɛ̃] *nm* (*Bot*) spindle-tree; (*Art*) charcoal

fuseau, x [fyzo] *nm* (*pantalon*) (ski-)pants *pl*; (*pour filer*) spindle; **en ~** (*jambes*) tapering; (*colonne*) bulging; **~ horaire** time zone

fusée [fyze] *nf* rocket; **~ éclairante** flare

fuser [fyze] *vi* (*rires etc*) to burst forth

fusible [fyzibl(ə)] *nm* (*Élec: fil*) fuse wire; (: *fiche*) fuse

fusil [fyzi] *nm* (*de guerre, à canon rayé*) rifle, gun; (*de chasse, à canon lisse*) shotgun, gun; **~ à deux coups** double-barrelled rifle *ou* shotgun; **~ sous-marin** spear-gun

fusillade [fyzijad] *nf* gunfire *no pl*, shooting *no pl*; (*combat*) gun battle

fusiller [fyzije] *vt* to shoot; **~ qn du regard** to look daggers at sb

fusil-mitrailleur (*pl* **fusils-mitrailleurs**) [fyzimitʀajœʀ] *nm* machine gun

fusionner [fyzjɔne] *vi* to merge

fut [fy] *vb voir* **être**
fût [fy] *vb voir* **être** ▷ *nm* (*tonneau*) barrel, cask; (*de canon*) stock; (*d'arbre*) bole, trunk; (*de colonne*) shaft
futé, e [fyte] *adj* crafty
futile [fytil] *adj* (*inutile*) futile; (*frivole*) frivolous

futur, e [fytyʀ] *adj, nm* future; **son ~ époux** her husband-to-be; **au ~** (*Ling*) in the future
fuyant, e [fɥijɑ̃, -ɑ̃t] *vb voir* **fuir** ▷ *adj* (*regard etc*) evasive; (*lignes etc*) receding; (*perspective*) vanishing
fuyard, e [fɥijaʀ, -aʀd(ə)] *nm/f* runaway

Gg

gâcher [gɑʃe] *vt* (*gâter*) to spoil, ruin; (*gaspiller*) to waste; (*plâtre*) to temper; (*mortier*) to mix

gâchis [gɑʃi] *nm* (*désordre*) mess; (*gaspillage*) waste *no pl*

gadoue [gadu] *nf* sludge

gaffe [gaf] *nf* (*instrument*) boat hook; (*fam: erreur*) blunder; **faire ~** (*fam*) to watch out

gage [gaʒ] *nm* (*dans un jeu*) forfeit; (*fig: de fidélité*) token; **gages** *nmpl* (*salaire*) wages; (*garantie*) guarantee *sg*; **mettre en ~** to pawn; **laisser en ~** to leave as security

gageure [gaʒyʀ] *nf*: **c'est une ~** it's attempting the impossible

gagnant, e [gaɲɑ̃, -ɑ̃t] *adj*: **billet/numéro ~** winning ticket/number ▷ *adv*: **jouer ~** (*aux courses*) to be bound to win ▷ *nm/f* winner

gagne-pain [gaɲpɛ̃] *nm inv* job

gagner [gaɲe] *vt* (*concours, procès, pari*) to win; (*somme d'argent, revenu*) to earn; (*aller vers, atteindre*) to reach; (*s'emparer de*) to overcome; (*envahir*) to spread to; (*se concilier*): **~ qn** to win sb over ▷ *vi* to win; (*fig*) to gain; **~ du temps/de la place** to gain time/save space; **~ sa vie** to earn one's living; **~ du terrain** (*aussi fig*) to gain ground; **~ qn de vitesse** to outstrip sb; (*aussi fig*): **~ à faire** (*s'en trouver bien*) to be better off doing; **il y gagne** it's in his interest, it's to his advantage

gai, e [ge] *adj* cheerful; (*livre, pièce de théâtre*) light-hearted; (*un peu ivre*) merry

gaiement [gemɑ̃] *adv* cheerfully

gaieté [gete] *nf* cheerfulness; **gaietés** *nfpl* (*souvent ironique*) delights; **de ~ de cœur** with a light heart

gaillard, e [gajaʀ, -aʀd(ə)] *adj* (*robuste*) sprightly; (*grivois*) bawdy, ribald ▷ *nm/f* (*strapping*) fellow/wench

gain [gɛ̃] *nm* (*revenu*) earnings *pl*; (*bénéfice: gén pl*) profits *pl*; (*au jeu: gén pl*) winnings *pl*; (*fig: de temps, place*) saving; (: *avantage*) benefit; (: *lucre*) gain; **avoir ~ de cause** to win the case; (*fig*) to be proved right; **obtenir ~ de cause** (*fig*) to win out

gaine [gɛn] *nf* (*corset*) girdle; (*fourreau*) sheath; (*de fil électrique etc*) outer covering

gala [gala] *nm* official reception; **soirée de ~** gala evening

galant, e [galɑ̃, -ɑ̃t] *adj* (*courtois*) courteous, gentlemanly; (*entreprenant*) flirtatious, gallant; (*aventure, poésie*) amorous; **en ~e compagnie** (*homme*) with a lady friend; (*femme*) with a gentleman friend

galère [galɛʀ] *nf* galley

galérer [galeʀe] *vi* (*fam*) to work hard, slave (away)

galerie [galʀi] *nf* gallery; (*Théât*) circle; (*de voiture*) roof rack; (*fig: spectateurs*) audience; **~ marchande** shopping mall; **~ de peinture** (*private*) art gallery

galet [galɛ] *nm* pebble; (*Tech*) wheel; **galets** *nmpl* pebbles, shingle *sg*

galette [galɛt] *nf* (*gâteau*) flat pastry cake; (*crêpe*) savoury pancake; **la ~ des Rois** *cake traditionally eaten on Twelfth Night*

galipette [galipɛt] *nf*: **faire des ~s** to turn somersaults

Galles [gal] *nfpl*: **le pays de ~** Wales

gallois, e [galwa, -waz] *adj* Welsh ▷ *nm* (*Ling*) Welsh ▷ *nm/f*: **G~, e** Welshman(-woman)

galon [galɔ̃] *nm* (*Mil*) stripe; (*décoratif*) piece of braid; **prendre du ~** to be promoted

galop [galo] *nm* gallop; **au ~** at a gallop; **~ d'essai** (*fig*) trial run

galoper [galɔpe] *vi* to gallop

galopin [galɔpɛ̃] *nm* urchin, ragamuffin

gambader [gɑ̃bade] *vi* to skip *ou* frisk about

gamin, e [gamɛ̃, -in] *nm/f* kid ▷ *adj* mischievous, playful

gamme [gam] *nf* (*Mus*) scale; (*fig*) range

gammé, e [game] *adj*: **croix ~e** swastika

gang [gɑ̃g] *nm* gang

gant [gɑ̃] *nm* glove; **prendre des ~s** (*fig*) to handle the situation with kid gloves; **relever le ~** (*fig*) to take up the gauntlet; **~ de crin** massage glove; **~ de toilette** (*face*) flannel (*Brit*), face cloth; **~s de boxe** boxing gloves; **~s de caoutchouc** rubber gloves

garage [gaʀaʒ] *nm* garage; **~ à vélos** bicycle shed

garagiste [gaʀaʒist(ə)] *nm/f* (*propriétaire*) garage owner; (*mécanicien*) garage mechanic

garantie [gaʀɑ̃ti] *nf* guarantee, warranty; (*gage*) security, surety; **(bon de) ~** guarantee *ou* warranty slip; **~ de bonne exécution** performance bond

garantir [gaʀɑ̃tiʀ] *vt* to guarantee; (*protéger*): **~ de** to protect from; **je vous garantis que** I can assure you that; **garanti pure laine/2 ans** guaranteed pure wool/for 2 years

garce [gaʀs(ə)] *nf* (*péj*) bitch

garçon [gaʀsɔ̃] *nm* boy; (*célibataire*) bachelor; (*jeune homme*) boy, lad; (*aussi:* **garçon de café**) waiter; ~ **boucher/coiffeur** butcher's/ hairdresser's assistant; ~ **de courses** messenger; ~ **d'écurie** stable lad; ~ **manqué** tomboy

garçonnière [gaʀsɔnjɛʀ] *nf* bachelor flat

garde [gaʀd(ə)] *nm* (*de prisonnier*) guard; (*de domaine etc*) warden; (*soldat, sentinelle*) guardsman ⊳ *nf* guarding; looking after; (*soldats, Boxe, Escrime*) guard; (*faction*) watch; (*d'une arme*) hilt; (*Typo: aussi:* **page** *ou* **feuille de garde**) flyleaf; (*: collée*) endpaper; **de** ~ *adj, adv* on duty; **monter la** ~ to stand guard; **être sur ses** ~**s** to be on one's guard; **mettre en** ~ to warn; **mise en** ~ warning; **prendre** ~ (**à**) to be careful (of); **avoir la** ~ **des enfants** (*après divorce*) to have custody of the children; ~ **champêtre** *nm* rural policeman; ~ **du corps** *nm* bodyguard; ~ **d'enfants** *nf* child minder; ~ **forestier** *nm* forest warden; ~ **mobile** *nm, nf* mobile guard; ~ **des Sceaux** *nm* ≈ Lord Chancellor (*Brit*), ≈ Attorney General (*US*); ~ **à vue** *nf* (*Jur*) ≈ police custody

garde-à-vous [gaʀdavu] *nm inv:* **être/se mettre au** ~ to be at/stand to attention; ~ (**fixe**)**!** (*Mil*) attention!

garde-barrière (*pl* **gardes-barrière(s)**) [gaʀdəbaʀjɛʀ] *nm/f* level-crossing keeper

garde-boue [gaʀdəbu] *nm inv* mudguard

garde-chasse (*pl* **gardes-chasse(s)**) [gaʀdəʃas] *nm* gamekeeper

garde-malade (*pl* **gardes-malade(s)**) [gaʀdəmalad] *nf* home nurse

garde-manger [gaʀdmɑ̃ʒe] *nm inv* (*boîte*) meat safe; (*placard*) pantry, larder

garder [gaʀde] *vt* (*conserver*) to keep; (*: sur soi: vêtement, chapeau*) to keep on; (*surveiller: enfants*) to look after; (*: immeuble, lieu, prisonnier*) to guard; **se garder** *vi* (*aliment: se conserver*) to keep; **se** ~ **faire** to be careful not to do; ~ **le lit/la chambre** to stay in bed/indoors; ~ **le silence** to keep silent *ou* quiet; ~ **la ligne** to keep one's figure; ~ **à vue** to keep in custody; **pêche/chasse gardée** private fishing/hunting (ground)

garderie [gaʀdəʀi] *nf* day nursery, crèche

garde-robe [gaʀdəʀɔb] *nf* wardrobe

gardien, ne [gaʀdjɛ̃, -ɛn] *nm/f* (*garde*) guard; (*de prison*) warder; (*de domaine, réserve*) warden; (*de musée etc*) attendant; (*de phare, cimetière*) keeper; (*d'immeuble*) caretaker; (*fig*) guardian; ~ **de but** goalkeeper; ~ **de nuit** night watchman; ~ **de la paix** policeman

gare [gaʀ] *nf* (railway) station, train station (*US*) ⊳ *excl:* ~ **à ...** mind ...!, watch out for ...!; ~ **à ne pas ...** mind you don't ...; ~ **à toi!** watch out!; **sans crier** ~ without warning; ~ **maritime** harbour station; ~ **routière** coach (*Brit*) *ou* bus station; (*de camions*) haulage (*Brit*) *ou* trucking (*US*) depot; ~ **de triage** marshalling yard

garer [gaʀe] *vt* to park; **se garer** to park; (*pour laisser passer*) to draw into the side

gargariser [gaʀgaʀize]: **se gargariser** *vi* to gargle; **se** ~ **de** (*fig*) to revel in

gargote [gaʀgɔt] *nf* cheap restaurant, greasy spoon (*fam*)

gargouille [gaʀguj] *nf* gargoyle

gargouiller [gaʀguje] *vi* (*estomac*) to rumble; (*eau*) to gurgle

garnement [gaʀnəmɑ̃] *nm* rascal, scallywag

garni, e [gaʀni] *adj* (*plat*) served with vegetables (*and chips, pasta or rice*) ⊳ *nm* (*appartement*) furnished accommodation *no pl* (*Brit*) *ou* accommodations *pl* (*US*)

garnison [gaʀnizɔ̃] *nf* garrison

garniture [gaʀnityʀ] *nf* (*Culin: légumes*) vegetables *pl*; (*: persil etc*) garnish; (*: farce*) filling; (*décoration*) trimming; (*protection*) fittings *pl*; ~ **de cheminée** mantelpiece ornaments *pl*; ~ **de frein** (*Auto*) brake lining; ~ **intérieure** (*Auto*) interior trim; ~ **périodique** sanitary towel (*Brit*) *ou* napkin (*US*)

gars [gɑ] *nm* lad; (*type*) guy

Gascogne [gaskɔɲ] *nf:* **la** ~ Gascony

gas-oil [gazɔjl] *nm* diesel oil

gaspiller [gaspije] *vt* to waste

gastronome [gastʀɔnɔm] *nm/f* gourmet

gastronomie [gastʀɔnɔmi] *nf* gastronomy

gastronomique [gastʀɔnɔmik] *adj:* **menu** ~ gourmet menu

gâteau, x [gɑto] *nm* cake ⊳ *adj inv* (*fam: trop indulgent*): **papa-/maman-**~ doting father/ mother; ~ **d'anniversaire** birthday cake/; ~ **de riz** ≈ rice pudding; ~ **sec** biscuit

gâter [gɑte] *vt* to spoil; **se gâter** *vi* (*dent, fruit*) to go bad; (*temps, situation*) to change for the worse

gâterie [gɑtʀi] *nf* little treat

gâteux, -euse [gɑtø, -øz] *adj* senile

gauche [goʃ] *adj* left, left-hand; (*maladroit*) awkward, clumsy ⊳ *nf* (*Pol*) left (wing); (*Boxe*) left; **à** ~ on the left; (*direction*) (to the) left; **à** ~ **de** (on *ou* to the) left of; **à la** ~ **de** to the left of; **sur votre** ~ on your left; **de** ~ (*Pol*) left-wing

gaucher, -ère [goʃe, -ɛʀ] *adj* left-handed

gauchiste [goʃist(ə)] *adj, nm/f* leftist

gaufre [gofʀ(ə)] *nf* (*pâtisserie*) waffle; (*de cire*) honeycomb

gaufrette [gofʀɛt] *nf* wafer

gaulois, e [golwa, -waz] *adj* Gallic; (*grivois*) bawdy ⊳ *nm/f:* **G~, e** Gaul

gaver [gave] *vt* to force-feed; (*fig*): ~ **de** to cram with, fill up with; (*personne*): **se** ~ **de** to stuff o.s. with

gaz [gɑz] *nm inv* gas; **mettre les** ~ (*Auto*) to put one's foot down; **chambre/masque à** ~ gas chamber/mask; ~ **en bouteille** bottled gas; ~ **butane** Calor gas® (*Brit*), butane gas; ~ **carbonique** carbon dioxide; ~ **hilarant** laughing gas; ~ **lacrymogène** tear gas; ~ **naturel** natural gas; ~ **de ville** town gas (*Brit*), manufactured domestic gas

gaze [gɑz] *nf* gauze

gazer [gɑze] *vt* to gas ▷ *vi* (*fam*) to be going *ou* working well

gazette [gazɛt] *nf* news sheet

gazeux, -euse [gazø, -øz] *adj* gaseous; (*eau*) sparkling; (*boisson*) fizzy

gazoduc [gazɔdyk] *nm* gas pipeline

gazon [gazɔ̃] *nm* (*herbe*) turf, grass; (*pelouse*) lawn

gazouiller [gazuje] *vi* (*oiseau*) to chirp; (*enfant*) to babble

GDF *sigle m* (= *Gaz de France*) national gas company

geai [ʒɛ] *nm* jay

géant, e [ʒeɑ̃, -ɑ̃t] *adj* gigantic, giant; (*Comm*) giant-size ▷ *nm/f* giant

geindre [ʒɛ̃dʀ(ə)] *vi* to groan, moan

gel [ʒɛl] *nm* frost; (*de l'eau*) freezing; (*fig: des salaires, prix*) freeze; freezing; (*produit de beauté*) gel; ~ **douche** shower gel

gélatine [ʒelatin] *nf* gelatine

gelé, e [ʒəle] *adj* frozen ▷ *nf* jelly; (*gel*) frost; ~ **blanche** hoarfrost, white frost

geler [ʒəle] *vt, vi* to freeze; **il gèle** it's freezing

gélule [ʒelyl] *nf* capsule

gelures [ʒəlyʀ] *nfpl* frostbite *sg*

Gémeaux [ʒemo] *nmpl*: **les** ~ Gemini, the Twins; **être des** ~ to be Gemini

gémir [ʒemiʀ] *vi* to groan, moan

gênant, e [ʒɛnɑ̃, -ɑ̃t] *adj* (*objet*) awkward, in the way; (*histoire, personne*) embarrassing

gencive [ʒɑ̃siv] *nf* gum

gendarme [ʒɑ̃daʀm(ə)] *nm* gendarme

gendarmerie [ʒɑ̃daʀməʀi] *nf* military police force in countryside and small towns; their police station or barracks

gendre [ʒɑ̃dʀ(ə)] *nm* son-in-law

gêné, e [ʒene] *adj* embarrassed; (*dépourvu d'argent*) short (of money)

gêner [ʒene] *vt* (*incommoder*) to bother; (*encombrer*) to hamper; (*bloquer le passage*) to be in the way of; (*déranger*) to bother; (*embarrasser*): ~ **qn** to make sb feel ill-at-ease; **se gêner** to put o.s. out; **ne vous gênez pas!** (*ironique*) go right ahead!, don't mind me!; **je vais me** ~! (*ironique*) why should I care?

général, e, -aux [ʒeneʀal, -o] *adj, nm* general ▷ *nf*: (*répétition*) ~**e** final dress rehearsal; **en** ~ usually, in general; **à la satisfaction** ~**e** to everyone's satisfaction

généralement [ʒeneʀalmɑ̃] *adv* generally

généraliser [ʒeneʀalize] *vt, vi* to generalize; **se généraliser** *vi* to become widespread

généraliste [ʒeneʀalist(ə)] *nm/f* (*Méd*) general practitioner, GP

génération [ʒeneʀasjɔ̃] *nf* generation

généreux, -euse [ʒeneʀø, -øz] *adj* generous

générique [ʒeneʀik] *adj* generic ▷ *nm* (*Ciné, TV*) credits *pl*, credit titles *pl*

générosité [ʒeneʀozite] *nf* generosity

genêt [ʒənɛ] *nm* (*Bot*) broom *no pl*

génétique [ʒenetik] *adj* genetic ▷ *nf* genetics *sg*

Genève [ʒənɛv] *n* Geneva

génial, e, -aux [ʒenjal, -o] *adj* of genius; (*fam*) fantastic, brilliant

génie [ʒeni] *nm* genius; (*Mil*): **le** ~ ≈ the

Engineers *pl*; **avoir du** ~ to have genius; ~ **civil** civil engineering; ~ **génétique** genetic engineering

genièvre [ʒənjɛvʀ(ə)] *nm* (*Bot*) juniper (tree); (*boisson*) Dutch gin; **grain de** ~ juniper berry

génisse [ʒenis] *nf* heifer; **foie de** ~ ox liver

génital, e, -aux [ʒenital, -o] *adj* genital

génois, e [ʒenwa, -waz] *adj* Genoese ▷ *nf* (*gâteau*) ≈ sponge cake

genou, x [ʒnu] *nm* knee; **à** ~**x** on one's knees; **se mettre à** ~**x** to kneel down

genre [ʒɑ̃ʀ] *nm* (*espèce, sorte*) kind, type, sort; (*allure*) manner; (*Ling*) gender; (*Art*) genre; (*Zool etc*) genus; **se donner du** ~ to give o.s. airs; **avoir bon** ~ to have style; **avoir mauvais** ~ to be ill-mannered

gens [ʒɑ̃] *nmpl* (*f in some phrases*) people *pl*; **les** ~ **d'Église** the clergy; **les** ~ **du monde** society people; ~ **de maison** domestics

gentil, le [ʒɑ̃ti, -ij] *adj* kind; (*enfant: sage*) good; (*sympa: endroit etc*) nice; **c'est très** ~ **à vous** it's very kind *ou* good *ou* nice of you

gentillesse [ʒɑ̃tijɛs] *nf* kindness

gentiment [ʒɑ̃timɑ̃] *adv* kindly

géo *abr* (= *géographie*) geography

géographie [ʒeɔgʀafi] *nf* geography

geôlier [ʒolje] *nm* jailer

géologie [ʒeɔlɔʒi] *nf* geology

géomètre [ʒeɔmɛtʀ(ə)] *nm*: (**arpenteur-**)~ (land) surveyor

géométrie [ʒeɔmetʀi] *nf* geometry; **à** ~ **variable** (*Aviat*) swing-wing

géométrique [ʒeɔmetʀik] *adj* geometric

géranium [ʒeʀanjɔm] *nm* geranium

gérant, e [ʒeʀɑ̃, -ɑ̃t] *nm/f* manager/manageress; ~ **d'immeuble** managing agent

gerbe [ʒɛʀb(ə)] *nf* (*de fleurs, d'eau*) spray; (*de blé*) sheaf; (*fig*) shower, burst

gercé, e [ʒɛʀse] *adj* chapped

gerçure [ʒɛʀsyʀ] *nf* crack

gérer [ʒeʀe] *vt* to manage

germain, e [ʒɛʀmɛ̃, -ɛn] *adj*: **cousin** ~ first cousin

germe [ʒɛʀm(ə)] *nm* germ

germer [ʒɛʀme] *vi* to sprout; (*semence, aussi fig*) to germinate

geste [ʒɛst(ə)] *nm* gesture; move; motion; **il fit un** ~ **de la main pour m'appeler** he signed to me to come over, he waved me over; **ne faites pas un** ~ (*ne bougez pas*) don't move

gestion [ʒɛstjɔ̃] *nf* management; ~ **des disques** (*Inform*) housekeeping; ~ **de fichier(s)** (*Inform*) file management

ghetto [geto] *nm* ghetto

gibet [ʒibɛ] *nm* gallows *pl*

gibier [ʒibje] *nm* (*animaux*) game; (*fig*) prey

giboulée [ʒibule] *nf* sudden shower

gicler [ʒikle] *vi* to spurt, squirt

gifle [ʒifl(ə)] *nf* slap (in the face)

gifler [ʒifle] *vt* to slap (in the face)

gigantesque [ʒigɑ̃tɛsk(ə)] *adj* gigantic

gigogne [ʒigɔɲ] *adj*: **lits** ~**s** truckle (*Brit*) *ou* trundle (US) beds; **tables/poupées ~s** nest of tables/dolls

gigot [ʒigo] nm leg (of mutton ou lamb)

gigoter [ʒigɔte] vi to wriggle (about)

gilet [ʒilɛ] nm waistcoat; (pull) cardigan; (de corps) vest; **~ pare-balles** bulletproof jacket; **~ de sauvetage** life jacket

gin [dʒin] nm gin

gingembre [ʒɛ̃ʒɑ̃bR(ə)] nm ginger

girafe [ʒiRaf] nf giraffe

giratoire [ʒiRatwaR] adj: **sens ~** roundabout

girofle [ʒiRɔfl(ə)] nm: **clou de ~** clove

girouette [ʒiRwet] nf weather vane ou cock

gitan, e [ʒitɑ̃, -an] nm/f gipsy

gîte [ʒit] nm home; shelter; (du lièvre) form; **~ (rural)** (country) holiday cottage ou apartment

givre [ʒivR(ə)] nm (hoar)frost

givré, e [ʒivRe] adj: **citron ~/orange ~e** lemon/orange sorbet (served in fruit skin)

glace [glas] nf ice; (crème glacée) ice cream; (verre) sheet of glass; (miroir) mirror; (de voiture) window; **glaces** nfpl (Géo) ice sheets, ice sg; **de ~** (fig: accueil, visage) frosty, icy; **rester de ~** to remain unmoved

glacé, e [glase] adj icy; (boisson) iced

glacer [glase] vt to freeze; (boisson) to chill, ice; (gâteau) to ice (Brit), frost (US); (papier, tissu) to glaze; (fig): **~ qn** to chill sb; (fig) to make sb's blood run cold

glacial, e [glasjal] adj icy

glacier [glasje] nm (Géo) glacier; (marchand) ice-cream maker

glacière [glasjɛR] nf icebox

glaçon [glasɔ̃] nm icicle; (pour boisson) ice cube

glaïeul [glajœl] nm gladiola

glaise [glez] nf clay

gland [glɑ̃] nm (de chêne) acorn; (décoration) tassel; (Anat) glans

glande [glɑ̃d] nf gland

glander [glɑ̃de] vi (fam) to fart around (Brit) (!), screw around (US) (!)

glauque [glok] adj dull blue-green

glissade [glisad] nf (par jeu) slide; (chute) slip; (dérapage) skid; **faire des ~s** to slide

glissant, e [glisɑ̃, -ɑ̃t] adj slippery

glissement [glismɑ̃] nm sliding; (fig) shift; **~ de terrain** landslide

glisser [glise] vi (avancer) to glide ou slide along; (coulisser, tomber) to slide; (déraper) to slip; (être glissant) to be slippery ▷ vt: **~ qch sous/dans/à** to slip sth under/into/to; **~ sur** (fig: détail etc) to skate over; **se ~ dans/entre** to slip into/between

global, e, -aux [glɔbal, -o] adj overall

globe [glɔb] nm globe; **sous ~** under glass; **~ oculaire** eyeball; **le ~ terrestre** the globe

globule [glɔbyl] nm (du sang): **~ blanc/rouge** white/red corpuscle

globuleux, -euse [glɔbylø, -øz] adj: **yeux ~** protruding eyes

gloire [glwaR] nf glory; (mérite) distinction, credit; (personne) celebrity

glorieux, -euse [glɔRjø, -øz] adj glorious

gloussement [glusmɑ̃] nm (de poule) cluck; (rire) chuckle

glousser [gluse] vi to cluck; (rire) to chuckle

glouton, ne [glutɔ̃, -ɔn] adj gluttonous, greedy

gluant, e [glyɑ̃, -ɑ̃t] adj sticky, gummy

glucose [glykoz] nm glucose

glycine [glisin] nf wisteria

GO sigle fpl (= grandes ondes) LW ▷ sigle m (= gentil organisateur) title given to leaders on Club Méditerranée holidays; extended to refer to easy-going leader of any group

go [go]: **tout de go** adv straight out

goal [gol] nm goalkeeper

gobelet [gɔblɛ] nm (en métal) tumbler; (en plastique) beaker; (à dés) cup

gober [gɔbe] vt to swallow

godasse [gɔdas] nf (fam) shoe

godet [gɔdɛ] nm pot; (Couture) unpressed pleat

goéland [gɔelɑ̃] nm (sea)gull

goélette [gɔelɛt] nf schooner

gogo [gɔgo] nm (péj) mug, sucker; **à ~** adv galore

goguenard, e [gɔgnaR, -aRd(ə)] adj mocking

goinfre [gwɛ̃fR(ə)] nm glutton

golf [gɔlf] nm (jeu) golf; (terrain) golf course; **~ miniature** crazy ou miniature golf

golfe [gɔlf(ə)] nm gulf; bay; **le ~ d'Aden** the Gulf of Aden; **le ~ de Gascogne** the Bay of Biscay; **le ~ du Lion** the Gulf of Lions; **le ~ Persique** the Persian Gulf

gomme [gɔm] nf (à effacer) rubber (Brit), eraser; (résine) gum; **boule** ou **pastille de ~** throat pastille

gommer [gɔme] vt (effacer) to rub out (Brit), erase; (enduire de gomme) to gum

gond [gɔ̃] nm hinge; **sortir de ses ~s** (fig) to fly off the handle

gondoler [gɔ̃dɔle]: **se gondoler** vi to warp, buckle; (fam: rire) to hoot with laughter; to be in stitches

gonflé, e [gɔ̃fle] adj swollen; (ventre) bloated; (fam: culotté): **être ~** to have a nerve

gonfler [gɔ̃fle] vt (pneu, ballon) to inflate, blow up; (nombre, importance) to inflate ▷ vi (pied etc) to swell (up); (Culin: pâte) to rise

gonfleur [gɔ̃flœR] nm air pump

gonzesse [gɔ̃zɛs] nf (fam) chick, bird (Brit)

goret [gɔRɛ] nm piglet

gorge [gɔRʒ(ə)] nf (Anat) throat; (poitrine) breast; (Géo) gorge; (rainure) groove; **avoir mal à la ~** to have a sore throat; **avoir la ~ serrée** to have a lump in one's throat

gorgé, e [gɔRʒe] adj: **~ de** filled with; (eau) saturated with ▷ nf mouthful; sip; gulp; **boire à petites/grandes ~es** to take little sips/big gulps

gorille [gɔRij] nm gorilla; (fam) bodyguard

gosier [gozje] nm throat

gosse [gɔs] nm/f kid

goudron [gudRɔ̃] nm (asphalte) tar(mac) (Brit), asphalt; (du tabac) tar

goudronner [gudRɔne] vt to tar(mac) (Brit), asphalt

gouffre [gufR(ə)] nm abyss, gulf

goujat [guʒa] *nm* boor

goulot [gulo] *nm* neck; **boire au ~** to drink from the bottle

goulu, e [guly] *adj* greedy

gourd, e [guʀ, guʀd(ə)] *adj* numb (with cold); *(fam)* oafish

gourde [guʀd(ə)] *nf (récipient)* flask; *(fam)* (clumsy) clot *ou* oaf

gourdin [guʀdɛ̃] *nm* club, bludgeon

gourer [guʀe] *(fam)*: **se gourer** *vi* to boob

gourmand, e [guʀmɑ̃, -ɑ̃d] *adj* greedy

gourmandise [guʀmɑ̃diz] *nf* greed; *(bonbon)* sweet *(Brit)*, piece of candy *(US)*

gourmet [guʀmɛ] *nm* epicure

gourmette [guʀmɛt] *nf* chain bracelet

gousse [gus] *nf (de vanille etc)* pod; **~ d'ail** clove of garlic

goût [gu] *nm* taste; *(fig: appréciation)* taste, liking; **le (bon) ~** good taste; **de bon ~** in good taste, tasteful; **de mauvais ~** in bad taste, tasteless; **avoir bon/mauvais ~** *(aliment)* to taste nice/nasty; *(personne)* to have good/bad taste; **avoir du/manquer de ~** to have/lack taste; **avoir du ~ pour** to have a liking for; **prendre ~ à** to develop a taste *ou* a liking for

goûter [gute] *vt (essayer)* to taste; *(apprécier)* to enjoy ▷ *vi* to have (afternoon) tea ▷ *nm* (afternoon) tea; **~ à** to taste, sample; **~ de** to have a taste of; **~ d'enfants/d'anniversaire** children's tea/birthday party

goutte [gut] *nf* drop; *(Méd)* gout; *(alcool)* nip *(Brit)*, tot *(Brit)*, drop *(US)*; **gouttes** *nfpl (Méd)* drops; **~ à ~** *adv* a drop at a time; **tomber ~ à ~** to drip

goutte-à-goutte [gutagut] *nm inv (Méd)* drip; **alimenter au ~** to drip-feed

gouttelette [gutlɛt] *nf* droplet

gouttière [gutjɛʀ] *nf* gutter

gouvernail [guvɛʀnaj] *nm* rudder; *(barre)* helm, tiller

gouvernant, e [guvɛʀnɑ̃, -ɑ̃t] *adj* ruling *cpd* ▷ *nf* housekeeper; *(d'un enfant)* governess

gouvernement [guvɛʀnəmɑ̃] *nm* government

gouverner [guvɛʀne] *vt* to govern; *(diriger)* to steer; *(fig)* to control

grâce [gʀas] *nf* grace; *(faveur)* favour; *(Jur)* pardon; **grâces** *nfpl (Rel)* grace *sg*; **de bonne/mauvaise ~** with (a) good/bad grace; **dans les bonnes ~s de qn** in favour with sb; **faire ~ à qn de qch** to spare sb sth; **rendre ~(s) à** to give thanks to; **demander ~** to beg for mercy; **droit de ~** right of reprieve; **recours en ~** plea for pardon; **~ à** *prép* thanks to

gracier [gʀasje] *vt* to pardon

gracieux, -euse [gʀasjø, -øz] *adj (charmant, élégant)* graceful; *(aimable)* gracious, kind; **à titre ~** free of charge

grade [gʀad] *nm (Mil)* rank; *(Scol)* degree; **monter en ~** to be promoted

gradin [gʀadɛ̃] *nm (dans un théâtre)* tier; *(de stade)* step; **gradins** *nmpl (de stade)* terracing *no pl (Brit)*, standing area; **en ~s** terraced

gradué, e [gʀadɥe] *adj (exercices)* graded (for difficulty); *(thermomètre, verre)* graduated

graduel, le [gʀadɥɛl] *adj* gradual; progressive

graduer [gʀadɥe] *vt (effort etc)* to increase gradually; *(règle, verre)* to graduate

graffiti [gʀafiti] *nmpl* graffiti

grain [gʀɛ̃] *nm (gén)* grain; *(de chapelet)* bead; *(Navig)* squall; *(averse)* heavy shower; *(fig: petite quantité)*: **un ~ de** a touch of; **~ de beauté** beauty spot; **~ de café** coffee bean; **~ de poivre** peppercorn; **~ de poussière** speck of dust; **~ de raisin** grape

graine [gʀɛn] *nf* seed; **mauvaise ~** *(mauvais sujet)* bad lot; **une ~ de voyou** a hooligan in the making

graissage [gʀɛsaʒ] *nm* lubrication, greasing

graisse [gʀɛs] *nf* fat; *(lubrifiant)* grease; **~ saturée** saturated fat

graisser [gʀɛse] *vt* to lubricate, grease; *(tacher)* to make greasy

graisseux, -euse [gʀɛsø, -øz] *adj* greasy; *(Anat)* fatty

grammaire [gʀamɛʀ] *nf* grammar

grammatical, e, -aux [gʀamatikal, -o] *adj* grammatical

gramme [gʀam] *nm* gramme

grand, e [gʀɑ̃, gʀɑ̃d] *adj (haut)* tall; *(gros, vaste, large)* big, large; *(long)* long; *(sens abstraits)* great ▷ *adv*: **~ ouvert** wide open; **un ~ buveur** a heavy drinker; **un ~ homme** a great man; **son ~ frère** his big *ou* older brother; **avoir ~ besoin de** to be in dire *ou* desperate need of; **il est ~ temps de** it's high time to; **il est assez ~ pour** he's big *ou* old enough to; **voir ~** to think big; **en ~** on a large scale; **au ~ air** in the open (air); **les ~s blessés/brûlés** the severely injured/burned; **de ~ matin** at the crack of dawn; **~ écart** splits *pl*; **~ ensemble** housing scheme; **~ jour** broad daylight; **~ livre** *(Comm)* ledger; **~ magasin** department store; **~ malade** very sick person; **~ public** general public; **~e personne** grown-up; **~e surface** hypermarket, superstore; **~es écoles** *prestige university-level colleges with competitive entrance examinations; see note*; **~es lignes** *(Rail)* main lines; **~es vacances** summer holidays

grand-chose [gʀɑ̃ʃoz] *nm/f inv*: **pas ~** not much

Grande-Bretagne [gʀɑ̃dbʀətaɲ] *nf*: **la ~** (Great) Britain; **en ~** in (Great) Britain

grandeur [gʀɑ̃dœʀ] *nf (dimension)* size; *(fig: ampleur, importance)* magnitude; *(: gloire, puissance)* greatness; **~ nature** *adj* life-size

grandiose [gʀɑ̃djoz] *adj (paysage, spectacle)* imposing

grandir [gʀɑ̃diʀ] *vi (enfant, arbre)* to grow; *(bruit, hostilité)* to increase, grow ▷ *vt*: **~ qn** *(vêtement, chaussure)* to make sb look taller; *(fig)* to make sb grow in stature

grand-mère *(pl* **grand(s)-mères** *)* [gʀɑ̃mɛʀ] *nf* grandmother

grand-messe [gʀɑ̃mɛs] *nf* high mass

grand-peine [gʀɑ̃pɛn]: **à ~** *adv* with (great) difficulty

grand-père (*pl* **grands-pères**) [grɑ̃pɛr] *nm* grandfather

grand-route [grɑ̃rut] *nf* main road

grands-parents [grɑ̃parɑ̃] *nmpl* grandparents

grange [grɑ̃ʒ] *nf* barn

granit, granite [granit] *nm* granite

graphique [grafik] *adj* graphic ▷ *nm* graph

grappe [grap] *nf* cluster; **~ de raisin** bunch of grapes

gras, se [grɑ, grɑs] *adj* (*viande, soupe*) fatty; (*personne*) fat; (*surface, main, cheveux*) greasy; (*terre*) sticky; (*toux*) loose, phlegmy; (*rire*) throaty; (*plaisanterie*) coarse; (*crayon*) soft-lead; (*Typo*) bold ▷ *nm* (*Culin*) fat; **faire la ~se matinée** to have a lie-in (*Brit*), sleep late; **matière ~se** fat (content)

grassement [grɑsmɑ̃] *adv* (*généreusement*): **~ payé** handsomely paid; (*grossièrement: rire*) coarsely

grassouillet, te [grɑsujɛ, -ɛt] *adj* podgy, plump

gratifiant, e [gratifjɑ̃, -ɑ̃t] *adj* gratifying, rewarding

gratin [gratɛ̃] *nm* (*Culin*) cheese- (*ou* crumb-)topped dish; (: *croûte*) topping; **au ~** au gratin; **tout le ~ parisien** all the best people of Paris

gratiné [gratine] *adj* (*Culin*) au gratin; (*fam*) hellish ▷ *nf* (*soupe*) onion soup au gratin

gratis [gratis] *adv, adj* free

gratitude [gratityd] *nf* gratitude

gratte-ciel [gratsjɛl] *nm inv* skyscraper

gratte-papier [gratpapje] *nm inv* (*péj*) penpusher

gratter [grate] *vt* (*frotter*) to scrape; (*enlever*) to scrape off; (*bras, bouton*) to scratch; **se gratter** to scratch o.s.

gratuit, e [gratɥi, -ɥit] *adj* (*entrée*) free; (*billet*) free, complimentary; (*fig*) gratuitous

gravats [grava] *nmpl* rubble *sg*

grave [grav] *adj* (*dangereux: maladie, accident*) serious, bad; (*sérieux: sujet, problème*) serious, grave; (*personne, air*) grave, solemn; (*voix, son*) deep, low-pitched ▷ *nm* (*Mus*) low register; **ce n'est pas ~!** it's all right, don't worry; **blessé ~** seriously injured person

gravement [gravmɑ̃] *adv* seriously; badly; gravely

graver [grave] *vt* (*plaque, nom*) to engrave; (*CD, DVD*) to burn; (*fig*): **~ qch dans son esprit/sa mémoire** to etch sth in one's mind/memory

gravier [gravje] *nm* (loose) gravel *no pl*

gravillons [gravijɔ̃] *nmpl* gravel *sg*, loose chippings *ou* gravel

gravir [gravir] *vt* to climb (up)

gravité [gravite] *nf* (*voir grave*) seriousness; gravity; (*Physique*) gravity

graviter [gravite] *vi*: **~ autour de** to revolve around

gravure [gravyr] *nf* engraving; (*reproduction*) print; plate

gré [gre] *nm*: **à son ~** *adj* to his liking ▷ *adv* as he pleases; **au ~ de** according to, following; **contre le ~ de qn** against sb's will; **de son (plein) ~ de** one's own free will; **de ~ ou de force** whether one likes it or not; **de bon ~** willingly; **bon ~**

mal ~ like it or not; willy-nilly; **de ~ à ~** (*Comm*) by mutual agreement; **savoir (bien) ~ à qn de qch** to be (most) grateful to sb for sth

grec, grecque [grɛk] *adj* Greek; (*classique: vase etc*) Grecian ▷ *nm* (*Ling*) Greek ▷ *nm/f*: **G~, G~que** Greek

Grèce [grɛs] *nf*: **la ~** Greece

greffe [grɛf] *nf* graft; transplant ▷ *nm* (*Jur*) office

greffer [grefe] *vt* (*Bot, Méd: tissu*) to graft; (*Méd: organe*) to transplant

greffier [grefje] *nm* clerk of the court

grêle [grɛl] *adj* (very) thin ▷ *nf* hail

grêler [grele] *vb impers*: **il grêle** it's hailing ▷ *vt*: **la région a été grêlée** the region was damaged by hail

grêlon [grelɔ̃] *nm* hailstone

grelot [grəlo] *nm* little bell

grelotter [grəlɔte] *vi* (*trembler*) to shiver

grenade [grənad] *nf* (*explosive*) grenade; (*Bot*) pomegranate; **~ lacrymogène** teargas grenade

grenadine [grənadin] *nf* grenadine

grenat [grəna] *adj inv* dark red

grenier [grənje] *nm* (*de maison*) attic; (*de ferme*) loft

grenouille [grənuj] *nf* frog

grès [grɛ] *nm* (*roche*) sandstone; (*poterie*) stoneware

grésiller [grezije] *vi* to sizzle; (*Radio*) to crackle

grève [grɛv] *nf* (*d'ouvriers*) strike; (*plage*) shore; **se mettre en/faire ~** to go on/be on strike; **~ bouchon** partial strike (*in key areas of a company*); **~ de la faim** hunger strike; **~ perlée** go-slow (*Brit*), slowdown (*US*); **~ sauvage** wildcat strike; **~ de solidarité** sympathy strike; **~ surprise** lightning strike; **~ sur le tas** sit down strike; **~ tournante** strike by rota; **~ du zèle** work-to-rule (*Brit*), slowdown (*US*)

gréviste [grevist(ə)] *nm/f* striker

gribouiller [gribuje] *vt* to scribble, scrawl ▷ *vi* to doodle

grièvement [grijɛvmɑ̃] *adv* seriously

griffe [grif] *nf* claw; (*fig*) signature; (: *d'un couturier, parfumeur*) label, signature

griffer [grife] *vt* to scratch

griffonner [grifɔne] *vt* to scribble

grignoter [griɲɔte] *vt, vi* to nibble

gril [gril] *nm* steak *ou* grill pan

grillade [grijad] *nf* grill

grillage [grijaʒ] *nm* (*treillis*) wire netting; (*clôture*) wire fencing

grille [grij] *nf* (*portail*) (metal) gate; (*clôture*) railings *pl*; (*d'égout*) (metal) grate; (*fig*) grid

grille-pain [grijpɛ̃] *nm inv* toaster

griller [grije] *vt* (*aussi*: **faire griller**: *pain*) to toast; (: *viande*) to grill (*Brit*), broil (*US*); (: *café*) to roast; (*fig: ampoule etc*) to burn out, blow; **~ un feu rouge** to jump the lights (*Brit*), run a stoplight (*US*) ▷ *vi* (*brûler*) to be roasting

grillon [grijɔ̃] *nm* (*Zool*) cricket

grimace [grimas] *nf* grimace; (*pour faire rire*): **faire des ~s** to pull *ou* make faces

grimper [grɛ̃pe] *vi, vt* to climb ▷ *nm*: **le ~** (*Sport*) rope-climbing; ~ **à/sur** to climb (up)/climb onto

grincer [gʀɛ̃se] *vi* (*porte, roue*) to grate; (*plancher*) to creak; ~ **des dents** to grind one's teeth

grincheux, -euse [gʀɛ̃ʃø, -øz] *adj* grumpy

grippe [gʀip] *nf* flu, influenza; **avoir la** ~ to have (the) flu; **prendre qn/qch en** ~ (*fig*) to take a sudden dislike to sb/sth; ~ **aviaire** bird flu

grippé, e [gʀipe] *adj*: **être** ~ to have (the) flu; (*moteur*) to have seized up (*Brit*) *ou* jammed

gris, e [gʀi, gʀiz] *adj* grey (*Brit*), gray (*US*); (*ivre*) tipsy ▷ *nm* (*couleur*) grey (*Brit*), gray (*US*); **il fait** ~ it's a dull *ou* grey day; **faire ~e mine** to look miserable *ou* morose; **faire ~e mine à qn** to give sb a cool reception

grisaille [gʀizaj] *nf* greyness (*Brit*), grayness (*US*), dullness

griser [gʀize] *vt* to intoxicate; **se ~ de** (*fig*) to become intoxicated with

grisonner [gʀizɔne] *vi* to be going grey (*Brit*) *ou* gray (*US*)

grisou [gʀizu] *nm* firedamp

grive [gʀiv] *nf* (*Zool*) thrush

grivois, e [gʀivwa, -waz] *adj* saucy

Groenland [gʀɔɛnlɑ̃d] *nm*: **le** ~ Greenland

grogner [gʀɔɲe] *vi* to growl; (*fig*) to grumble

grognon, ne [gʀɔɲɔ̃, -ɔn] *adj* grumpy, grouchy

groin [gʀwɛ̃] *nm* snout

grommeler [gʀɔmle] *vi* to mutter to o.s.

gronder [gʀɔ̃de] *vi* (*canon, moteur, tonnerre*) to rumble; (*animal*) to growl; (*fig: révolte*) to be brewing ▷ *vt* to scold

groom [gʀum] *nm* page, bellhop (*US*)

gros, se [gʀo, gʀos] *adj* big, large; (*obèse*) fat; (*problème, quantité*) great; (*travaux, dégâts*) extensive; (*large: trait, fil*) thick, heavy ▷ *adv*: **risquer/gagner** ~ to risk/win a lot ▷ *nm* (*Comm*): **le** ~ the wholesale business; **écrire** ~ to write in big letters; **prix de** ~ wholesale price; **par** ~ **temps/-se mer** in rough weather/heavy seas; **le** ~ **de** the main body of; (*du travail etc*) the bulk of; **en avoir** ~ **sur le cœur** to be upset; **en** ~ roughly; (*Comm*) wholesale; ~ **intestin** large intestine; ~ **lot** jackpot; ~ **mot** coarse word, vulgarity; ~ **œuvre** shell (of building); ~ **plan** (*Photo*) close-up; ~ **porteur** wide-bodied aircraft, jumbo (jet); ~ **sel** cooking salt; ~ **titre** headline; **-se caisse** big drum

groseille [gʀozɛj] *nf*: ~ **(rouge)/(blanche)** red/white currant; ~ **à maquereau** gooseberry

grosse [gʀos] *adj f voir* **gros** ▷ *nf* (*Comm*) gross

grossesse [gʀosɛs] *nf* pregnancy; ~ **nerveuse** phantom pregnancy

grosseur [gʀosœʀ] *nf* size; fatness; (*tumeur*) lump

grossier, -ière [gʀosje, -jɛʀ] *adj* coarse; (*travail*) rough; crude; (*évident: erreur*) gross

grossièrement [gʀosjɛʀmɑ̃] *adv* coarsely; roughly; crudely; (*en gros*) roughly

grossièreté [gʀosjɛʀte] *nf* coarseness; rudeness

grossir [gʀosiʀ] *vi* (*personne*) to put on weight; (*fig*) to grow, get bigger; (*rivière*) to swell ▷ *vt* to increase; (*exagérer*) to exaggerate; (*au microscope*) to magnify, enlarge; (*vêtement*): ~ **qn** to make sb look fatter

grossiste [gʀosist(ə)] *nm/f* wholesaler

grosso modo [gʀosomɔdo] *adv* roughly

grotesque [gʀɔtɛsk(ə)] *adj* grotesque

grotte [gʀɔt] *nf* cave

grouiller [gʀuje] *vi* (*foule*) to mill about; (*fourmis*) to swarm about; ~ **de** to be swarming with

groupe [gʀup] *nm* group; **cabinet de** ~ group practice; **médecine de** ~ group practice; ~ **électrogène** generator; ~ **de parole** support group; ~ **de pression** pressure group; ~ **sanguin** blood group; ~ **scolaire** school complex

groupement [gʀupmɑ̃] *nm* grouping; (*groupe*) group; ~ **d'intérêt économique (GIE)** = trade association

grouper [gʀupe] *vt* to group; (*ressources, moyens*) to pool; **se grouper** to get together

grue [gʀy] *nf* crane; **faire le pied de** ~ (*fam*) to hang around (waiting), kick one's heels (*Brit*)

grumeaux [gʀymo] *nmpl* (*Culin*) lumps

guenilles [gənij] *nfpl* rags

guenon [gənɔ̃] *nf* female monkey

guépard [gepaʀ] *nm* cheetah

guêpe [gɛp] *nf* wasp

guêpier [gepje] *nm* (*fig*) trap

guère [gɛʀ] *adv* (*avec adjectif, adverbe*): **ne … ~** hardly; (*avec verbe*): **ne … ~** (*tournure négative*) much; hardly ever; (*very*) long; **il n'y a ~ que/de** there's hardly anybody (*ou* anything) but/hardly any

guéridon [geʀidɔ̃] *nm* pedestal table

guérilla [geʀija] *nf* guerrilla warfare

guérillero [geʀijeʀo] *nm* guerrilla

guérir [geʀiʀ] *vt* (*personne, maladie*) to cure; (*membre, plaie*) to heal ▷ *vi* (*personne*) to recover, be cured; (*plaie, chagrin*) to heal; ~ **de** to be cured of, recover from; ~ **qn de** to cure sb of

guérison [geʀizɔ̃] *nf* curing; healing; recovery

guérisseur, -euse [geʀisœʀ, -øz] *nm/f* healer

guerre [gɛʀ] *nf* war; (*méthode*): ~ **atomique/de tranchées** atomic/trench warfare *no pl*; **en** ~ at war; **faire la** ~ **à** to wage war against; **de** ~ **lasse** (*fig*) tired of fighting *ou* resisting; **de bonne** ~ fair and square; ~ **civile/mondiale** civil/world war; ~ **froide/sainte** cold/holy war; ~ **d'usure** war of attrition

guerrier, -ière [geʀje, -jɛʀ] *adj* warlike ▷ *nm/f* warrior

guet [gɛ] *nm*: **faire le** ~ to be on the watch *ou* look-out

guet-apens (*pl* **guets-apens**) [gɛtapɑ̃] *nm* ambush

guetter [gete] *vt* (*épier*) to watch (intently); (*attendre*) to watch (out) for; (*: pour surprendre*) to be lying in wait for

gueule [gœl] *nf* mouth; (*fam: visage*) mug; (*: bouche*) gob (!), mouth; **ta ~!** (*fam*) shut up!; ~ **de bois** (*fam*) hangover

gueuler [gœle] *vi* (*fam*) to bawl

gueuleton [gœltɔ̃] *nm* (*fam*) blowout (*Brit*), big meal

gui [gi] nm mistletoe

guichet [giʃɛ] nm (de bureau, banque) counter, window; (d'une porte) wicket, hatch; **les ~s** (à la gare, au théâtre) the ticket office; **jouer à ~s fermés** to play to a full house

guide [gid] nm guide; (livre) guide(book) ▷ nf (fille scout) (girl) guide (Brit), girl scout (US); **guides** nfpl (d'un cheval) reins

guider [gide] vt to guide

guidon [gidɔ̃] nm handlebars pl

guignol [giɲɔl] nm ≈ Punch and Judy show; (fig) clown

guillemets [gijmɛ] nmpl: **entre ~** in inverted commas ou quotation marks; **~ de répétition** ditto marks

guillotiner [gijɔtine] vt to guillotine

guindé, e [gɛ̃de] adj stiff, starchy

guirlande [giʀlɑ̃d] nf garland; (de papier) paper chain; **~ lumineuse** lights pl, fairy lights pl (Brit); **~ de Noël** tinsel no pl

guise [giz] nf: **à votre ~** as you wish ou please; **en ~ de** by way of

guitare [gitaʀ] nf guitar

gym [ʒim] nf (exercices) gym

gymnase [ʒimnɑz] nm gym(nasium)

gymnaste [ʒimnast(ə)] nm/f gymnast

gymnastique [ʒimnastik] nf gymnastics sg; (au réveil etc) keep-fit exercises pl; **~ corrective** remedial gymnastics

gynécologie [ʒinekɔlɔʒi] nf gynaecology (Brit), gynecology (US)

gynécologique [ʒinekɔlɔʒik] adj gynaecological (Brit), gynecological (US)

gynécologue [ʒinekɔlɔg] nm/f gynaecologist (Brit), gynecologist (US)

Hh

habile [abil] *adj* skilful; *(malin)* clever
habileté [abilte] *nf* skill, skilfulness; cleverness
habillé, e [abije] *adj* dressed; *(chic)* dressy; *(Tech)*: ~ **de** covered with; encased in
habillement [abijmā] *nm* clothes *pl*; *(profession)* clothing industry
habiller [abije] *vt* to dress; *(fournir en vêtements)* to clothe; **s'habiller** to dress (o.s.); *(se déguiser, mettre des vêtements chic)* to dress up; **s'~ de/en** to dress in/dress up as; **s'~ chez/à** to buy one's clothes from/at
habit [abi] *nm* outfit; **habits** *nmpl* *(vêtements)* clothes; ~ **(de soirée)** tails *pl*; evening dress; **prendre l'~** *(Rel: entrer en religion)* to enter (holy) orders
habitant, e [abitā, -āt] *nm/f* inhabitant; *(d'une maison)* occupant, occupier; **loger chez l'~** to stay with the locals
habitation [abitasjō] *nf* living; *(demeure)* residence, home; *(maison)* house; **~s à loyer modéré (HLM)** low-rent, state-owned housing, ≈ council housing *sg* *(Brit)*, ≈ public housing units *(US)*
habiter [abite] *vt* to live in; *(sentiment)* to dwell in ▷ *vi*: ~ **à/dans** to live in *ou* at/in; ~ **chez** *ou* **avec qn** to live with sb; ~ **16 rue Montmartre** to live at number 16 rue Montmartre; ~ **rue Montmartre** to live in rue Montmartre
habitude [abityd] *nf* habit; **avoir l'~ de faire** to be in the habit of doing; **avoir l'~ des enfants** to be used to children; **prendre l'~ de faire qch** to get into the habit of doing sth; **perdre une ~** to get out of a habit; **d'~** usually; **comme d'~** as usual; **par ~** out of habit
habitué, e [abitye] *adj*: **être ~ à** to be used *ou* accustomed to ▷ *nm/f* regular visitor; *(client)* regular (customer)
habituel, le [abityɛl] *adj* usual
habituer [abitye] *vt*: ~ **qn à** to get sb used to; **s'habituer à** to get used to
'hache [aʃ] *nf* axe
'hacher [aʃe] *vt* *(viande)* to mince *(Brit)*, grind *(US)*; *(persil)* to chop; ~ **menu** to mince *ou* grind finely; to chop finely
'hachis [aʃi] *nm* mince *no pl* *(Brit)*, hamburger meat *(US)*; ~ **de viande** minced *(Brit)* *ou* ground *(US)* meat

'hachisch [aʃiʃ] *nm* hashish
'hachoir [aʃwar] *nm* chopper; (meat) mincer *(Brit)* *ou* grinder *(US)*; *(planche)* chopping board
'hagard, e [agar, -ard(ə)] *adj* wild, distraught
'haie [ɛ] *nf* hedge; *(Sport)* hurdle; *(fig: rang)* line, row; **200 m ~s** 200 m hurdles; ~ **d'honneur** guard of honour
'haillons [ajō] *nmpl* rags
'haine [ɛn] *nf* hatred
'haïr [air] *vt* to detest, hate; **se 'haïr** to hate each other
'hâlé, e [ale] *adj* (sun)tanned, sunburnt
haleine [alɛn] *nf* breath; **perdre ~** to get out of breath; **à perdre ~** until one is gasping for breath; **avoir mauvaise ~** to have bad breath; **reprendre ~** to get one's breath back; **hors d'~** out of breath; **tenir en ~** to hold spellbound; *(en attente)* to keep in suspense; **de longue ~** *adj* long-term
'haleter [alte] *vi* to pant
'hall [ol] *nm* hall
'halle [al] *nf* (covered) market; **'halles** *nfpl* central food market *sg*
hallucinant, e [alysinā, -āt] *adj* staggering
hallucination [alysinasjō] *nf* hallucination
'halte [alt(ə)] *nf* stop, break; *(escale)* stopping place; *(Rail)* halt ▷ *excl* stop!; **faire ~** to stop
haltère [altɛr] *nm* *(à boules, disques)* dumbbell, barbell; **(poids et) ~s** weightlifting
haltérophilie [alterofili] *nf* weightlifting
'hamac [amak] *nm* hammock
'hamburger [āburgœr] *nm* hamburger
'hameau, x [amo] *nm* hamlet
hameçon [amsō] *nm* (fish) hook
'hamster [amstɛr] *nm* hamster
'hanche [āʃ] *nf* hip
'hand-ball [ādbal] *nm* handball
'handicapé, e [ādikape] *adj* handicapped ▷ *nm/f* physically *(ou* mentally) handicapped person; ~ **moteur** spastic
'hangar [āgar] *nm* shed; *(Aviat)* hangar
'hanneton [antō] *nm* cockchafer
'hanter [āte] *vt* to haunt
'hantise [ātiz] *nf* obsessive fear
'happer [ape] *vt* to snatch; *(train etc)* to hit
'haras [ara] *nm* stud farm
'harassant, e [arasā, -āt] *adj* exhausting

'harcèlement ['aʀsɛlmɑ̃] nm harassment; ~ **sexuel** sexual harassment

'harceler ['aʀsəle] vt (Mil, Chasse) to harass, harry; (importuner) to plague

'hardi, e ['aʀdi] adj bold, daring

'hareng ['aʀɑ̃] nm herring

'hargne ['aʀɲ(ə)] nf aggressivity, aggressiveness

'hargneux, -euse ['aʀɲø, -øz] adj (propos, personne) belligerent, aggressive; (chien) fierce

'haricot ['aʀiko] nm bean; ~ **blanc/rouge** haricot/kidney bean; ~ **vert** French (Brit) ou green bean

harmonica [aʀmɔnika] nm mouth organ

harmonie [aʀmɔni] nf harmony

harmonieux, -euse [aʀmɔnjø, -øz] adj harmonious

'harnacher ['aʀnaʃe] vt to harness

'harnais ['aʀnɛ] nm harness

'harpe ['aʀp(ə)] nf harp

'harponner ['aʀpɔne] vt to harpoon; (fam) to collar

'hasard ['azaʀ] nm: **le ~** chance, fate; **un ~** a coincidence; (aubaine, chance) a stroke of luck; **au ~** (sans but) aimlessly; (à l'aveuglette) at random, haphazardly; **par ~** by chance; **comme par ~** as if by chance; **à tout ~** on the off chance; (en cas de besoin) just in case

'hasarder ['azaʀde] vt (mot) to venture; (fortune) to risk; **se ~ à faire** to risk doing, venture to do

'hâte ['ɑt] nf haste; **à la ~** hurriedly, hastily; **en ~** posthaste, with all possible speed; **avoir ~ de** to be eager ou anxious to

'hâter ['ɑte] vt to hasten; **se 'hâter** to hurry; **se ~ de** to hurry ou hasten to

'hâtif, -ive ['ɑtif, -iv] adj (travail) hurried; (décision) hasty; (légume) early

'hausse ['os] nf rise, increase; (de fusil) backsight adjuster; **à la ~** upwards; **en ~** rising

'hausser ['ose] vt to raise; ~ **les épaules** to shrug (one's shoulders); **se ~ sur la pointe des pieds** to stand (up) on tiptoe ou tippy-toe (US)

'haut, e ['o, 'ot] adj high; (grand) tall; (son, voix) high(-pitched) ▷ adv high ▷ nm top (part); **de 3 m de ~, ~ de 3 m** 3 m high, 3 m in height; **en ~e montagne** high up in the mountains; **en ~ lieu** in high places; **à ~e voix, (tout) ~** aloud, out loud; **des ~s et des bas** ups and downs; **du ~ de** from the top of; **tomber de ~** to fall from a height; (fig) to have one's hopes dashed; **dire qch bien ~** to say sth plainly; **prendre qch de (très) ~** to react haughtily to sth; **traiter qn de ~** to treat sb with disdain; **de ~ en bas** from top to bottom; downwards; ~ **en couleur** (chose) highly coloured; (personne) **un personnage ~ en couleur** a colourful character; **plus ~** higher up, further up; (dans un texte) above; (parler) louder; **en ~** up above; at (ou to) the top; (dans une maison) upstairs; **en ~ de** at the top of; ~ **les mains!** hands up!, stick 'em up!; **la ~e couture/coiffure** haute couture/coiffure; ~ **débit** (Inform) broadband; ~**e fidélité** hi-fi, high fidelity; **la ~e finance** high finance; ~**e trahison** high treason

'hautain, e ['otɛ̃, -ɛn] adj (personne, regard) haughty

'hautbois ['obwa] nm oboe

'haut-de-forme (pl **'hauts-de-forme**) ['odfɔʀm(ə)] nm top hat

'hauteur ['otœʀ] nf height; (Géo) height, hill; (fig) loftiness; haughtiness; **à ~ de** up to (the level of); **à ~ des yeux** at eye level; **à la ~ de** (sur la même ligne) level with; by; (fig) equal to; **à la ~** (fig) up to it, equal to the task

'haut-fourneau (pl **'hauts-fourneaux**) ['ofuʀno] nm blast ou smelting furnace

'haut-le-cœur ['olkœʀ] nm inv retch, heave

'haut-parleur (pl **-s**) ['opaʀlœʀ] nm (loud)speaker

'havre ['avʀ(ə)] nm haven

'Haye ['ɛ] n: **la ~** the Hague

'hayon ['ɛjɔ̃] nm tailgate

hebdo [ɛbdo] nm (fam) weekly

hebdomadaire [ɛbdɔmadɛʀ] adj, nm weekly

hébergement [ebɛʀʒəmɑ̃] nm accommodation, lodging; taking in

héberger [ebɛʀʒe] vt to accommodate, lodge; (réfugiés) to take in

hébergeur [ebɛʀʒœʀ] nm (Internet) host

hébété, e [ebete] adj dazed

hébreu, x [ebʀø] adj m, nm Hebrew

hécatombe [ekatɔ̃b] nf slaughter

hectare [ɛktaʀ] nm hectare, 10,000 square metres

'hein ['ɛ̃] excl eh?; (sollicitant l'approbation): **tu m'approuves, ~?** so I did the right thing then?; **Paul est venu, ~?** Paul came, did he?; **que fais-tu, ~?** hey! what are you doing?

'hélas ['elas] excl alas! ▷ adv unfortunately

'héler ['ele] vt to hail

hélice [elis] nf propeller

hélicoptère [elikɔptɛʀ] nm helicopter

helvétique [ɛlvetik] adj Swiss

hématome [ematom] nm haematoma

hémicycle [emisikl(ə)] nm semicircle; (Pol): **l'~** the benches (in French parliament)

hémisphère [emisfɛʀ] nf: ~ **nord/sud** northern/ southern hemisphere

hémorragie [emɔʀaʒi] nf bleeding no pl, haemorrhage (Brit), hemorrhage (US); ~ **cérébrale** cerebral haemorrhage; ~ **interne** internal bleeding ou haemorrhage

hémorroïdes [em`id] nfpl piles, haemorrhoids (Brit), hemorrhoids (US)

'hennir ['eniʀ] vi to neigh, whinny

'hennissement ['enismɑ̃] nm neighing, whinnying

hépatite [epatit] nf hepatitis, liver infection

herbe [ɛʀb(ə)] nf grass; (Culin, Méd) herb; **en ~** unripe; (fig) budding; **touffe/brin d'~** clump/ blade of grass

herbicide [ɛʀbisid] nm weed-killer

herboriste [ɛʀbɔʀist(ə)] nm/f herbalist

'hère ['ɛʀ] nm: **pauvre ~** poor wretch

héréditaire [eʀeditɛʀ] adj hereditary

'hérisser ['eʀise] vt: ~ **qn** (fig) to ruffle sb; **se**

'hérisser vi to bristle, bristle up

'hérisson ['eʀisɔ̃] nm hedgehog

héritage [eʀitaʒ] nm inheritance; (fig) heritage; (: legs) legacy; **faire un (petit) ~** to come into (a little) money

hériter [eʀite] vi: **~ de qch (de qn)** to inherit sth (from sb); **~ de qn** to inherit sb's property

héritier, -ière [eʀitje, -jɛʀ] nm/f heir/heiress

hermétique [ɛʀmetik] adj (à l'air) airtight; (à l'eau) watertight; (fig: écrivain, style) abstruse; (: visage) impenetrable

hermine [ɛʀmin] nf ermine

'hernie ['ɛʀni] nf hernia

héroïne [eʀɔin] nf heroine; (drogue) heroin

héroïque [eʀɔik] adj heroic

'héron ['eʀɔ̃] nm heron

'héros ['eʀo] nm hero

hésitant, e [ezitɑ̃, -ɑ̃t] adj hesitant

hésitation [ezitasjɔ̃] nf hesitation

hésiter [ezite] vi: **~ (à faire)** to hesitate (to do); **~ sur qch** to hesitate over sth

hétéroclite [eteʀɔklit] adj heterogeneous; (objets) sundry

hétérogène [eteʀɔʒɛn] adj heterogeneous

hétérosexuel, le [eteʀɔsɛkɥɛl] adj heterosexual

'hêtre ['ɛtʀ(ə)] nm beech

heure [œʀ] nf hour; (Scol) period; (moment, moment fixé) time; **c'est l'~** it's time; **pourriez-vous me donner l'~, s'il vous plaît?** could you tell me the time, please?; **quelle ~ est-il?** what time is it?; **2 ~s (du matin)** 2 o'clock (in the morning); **à la bonne ~!** (parfois ironique) splendid!; **être à l'~** to be on time; (montre) to be right; **le bus passe à l'~** the bus runs on the hour; **mettre à l'~** to set right; **100 km à l'~** ≈ 60 miles an ou per hour; **à toute ~** at any time; **24 ~s sur 24** round the clock, 24 hours a day; **à l'~ qu'il est** at this time (of day); (fig) now; **à l'~ actuelle** at the present time; **sur l'~** at once; **pour l'~** for the time being; **d'~ en ~** from one hour to the next; (régulièrement) hourly; **d'une ~ à l'autre** from hour to hour; **de bonne ~** early; **deux ~s de marche/travail** two hours' walking/work; **une ~ d'arrêt** an hour's break ou stop; **~ d'été** summer time (Brit), daylight saving time (US); **~ de pointe** rush hour; **~s de bureau** office hours; **~s supplémentaires** overtime sg

heureusement [œʀøzmɑ̃] adv (par bonheur) fortunately, luckily; **~ que ...** it's a good job that ..., fortunately ...

heureux, -euse [œʀø, -øz] adj happy; (chanceux) lucky, fortunate; (judicieux) felicitous, fortunate; **être ~ de qch** to be pleased ou happy about sth; **être ~ de faire/que** to be pleased ou happy to do/that; **s'estimer ~ de qch/que** to consider o.s. fortunate with sth/that; **encore ~ que ...** just as well that ...

'heurt ['œʀ] nm (choc) collision; **'heurts** nmpl (fig) clashes

'heurter ['œʀte] vt (mur) to strike, hit; (personne) to collide with; (fig) to go against, upset; **se 'heurter** (couleurs, tons) to clash; **se ~ à** to collide

with; (fig) to come up against; **~ qn de front** to clash head-on with sb

hexagone [ɛgzagɔn] nm hexagon; (la France) France (because of its roughly hexagonal shape)

hiberner [ibɛʀne] vi to hibernate

'hibou, x ['ibu] nm owl

'hideux, -euse ['idø, -øz] adj hideous

hier [jɛʀ] adv yesterday; **~ matin/soir/midi** yesterday morning/evening/at midday; **toute la journée d'~** all day yesterday; **toute la matinée d'~** all yesterday morning

'hiérarchie ['jeʀaʀʃi] nf hierarchy

'hi-fi ['ifi] nf inv hi-fi

hilare [ilaʀ] adj mirthful

hindou, e [ɛ̃du] adj, nm/f Hindu; (Indien) Indian

hippique [ipik] adj equestrian, horse cpd

hippisme [ipism(ə)] nm (horse-)riding

hippodrome [ipodʀom] nm racecourse

hippopotame [ipɔpɔtam] nm hippopotamus

hirondelle [iʀɔ̃dɛl] nf swallow

hirsute [iʀsyt] adj (personne) hairy; (barbe) shaggy; (tête) tousled

'hisser ['ise] vt to hoist, haul up; **se 'hisser sur** to haul o.s. up onto

histoire [istwaʀ] nf (science, événements) history; (anecdote, récit, mensonge) story; (affaire) business no pl; (chichis: gén pl) fuss no pl; **histoires** nfpl (ennuis) trouble sg; **l'~ de France** French history, the history of France; **l'~ sainte** biblical history; **une ~ de** (fig) a question of

historique [istɔʀik] adj historical; (important) historic ▷ nm (exposé, récit): **faire l'~ de** to give the background to

'hit-parade ['itpaʀad] nm: **le ~** the charts

hiver [ivɛʀ] nm winter; **en ~** in winter

hivernal, e, -aux [ivɛʀnal, -o] adj (de l'hiver) winter cpd; (comme en hiver) wintry

hiverner [ivɛʀne] vi to winter

HLM sigle m ou f (= habitations à loyer modéré) low-rent, state-owned housing; **un(e) ~** ≈ a council flat (ou house) (Brit), ≈ a public housing unit (US)

'hobby ['ɔbi] nm hobby

'hocher ['ɔʃe] vt: **~ la tête** to nod; (signe négatif ou dubitatif) to shake one's head

'hochet ['ɔʃe] nm rattle

'hockey ['ɔkɛ] nm: **~ (sur glace/gazon)** (ice/field) hockey

'hold-up ['ɔldœp] nm inv hold-up

'hollandais, e ['ɔlɑ̃dɛ, -ɛz] adj Dutch ▷ nm (Ling) Dutch ▷ nm/f: **'Hollandais, e** Dutchman/woman; **les 'Hollandais** the Dutch

'Hollande ['ɔlɑ̃d] nf: **la ~** Holland ▷ nm: **'hollande** (fromage) Dutch cheese

'homard ['ɔmaʀ] nm lobster

homéopathique [ɔmeɔpatik] adj homoeopathic

homicide [ɔmisid] nm murder ▷ nm/f murderer/eress; **~ involontaire** manslaughter

hommage [ɔmaʒ] nm tribute; **hommages** nmpl: **présenter ses ~s** to pay one's respects; **rendre ~ à** to pay tribute ou homage to; **en ~ de** as a token of; **faire ~ de qch à qn** to present sb with sth

homme [ɔm] nm man; (espèce humaine): **l'~** man,

mankind; ~ **d'affaires** businessman; ~ **des cavernes** caveman; ~ **d'Église** churchman, clergyman; ~ **d'État** statesman; ~ **de loi** lawyer; ~ **de main** hired man; ~ **de paille** stooge; ~ **politique** politician; **l'~ de la rue** the man in the street; ~ **à tout faire** odd-job man

homme-grenouille (*pl* **hommes-grenouilles**) [ɔmgʀənuj] *nm* frogman

homogène [ɔmɔʒɛn] *adj* homogeneous

homologue [ɔmɔlɔg] *nm/f* counterpart, opposite number

homologué, e [ɔmɔlɔge] *adj* (*Sport*) officially recognized, ratified; (*tarif*) authorized

homonyme [ɔmɔnim] *nm* (*Ling*) homonym; (*d'une personne*) namesake

homosexuel, le [ɔmɔsɛksɥɛl] *adj* homosexual

'**Hongrie** [ɔ̃gʀi] *nf*: **la ~** Hungary

'**hongrois, e** [ɔ̃gʀwa, -waz] *adj* Hungarian ▷ *nm* (*Ling*) Hungarian ▷ *nm/f*: '**Hongrois, e** Hungarian

honnête [ɔnɛt] *adj* (*intègre*) honest; (*juste, satisfaisant*) fair

honnêtement [ɔnɛtmɑ̃] *adv* honestly

honnêteté [ɔnɛtte] *nf* honesty

honneur [ɔnœʀ] *nm* honour; (*mérite*): **l'~ lui revient** the credit is his; **à qui ai-je l'~?** to whom have I the pleasure of speaking?; **"j'ai l'~ de ..."** "I have the honour of ..."; **en l'~ de** (*personne*) in honour of; (*événement*) on the occasion of; **faire ~ à** (*engagements*) to honour; (*famille, professeur*) to be a credit to; (*fig: repas etc*) to do justice to; **être à l'~** to be in the place of honour; **être en ~** to be in favour; **membre d'~** honorary member; **table d'~** top table

honorable [ɔnɔʀabl(ə)] *adj* worthy, honourable; (*suffisant*) decent

honoraire [ɔnɔʀɛʀ] *adj* honorary; **honoraires** *nmpl* fees; **professeur ~** professor emeritus

honorer [ɔnɔʀe] *vt* to honour; (*faire honneur à*) to do credit to; ~ **qn de** to honour sb with; **s'honorer de** to pride o.s. upon

honorifique [ɔnɔʀifik] *adj* honorary

'**honte** [ɔ̃t] *nf* shame; **avoir ~ de** to be ashamed of; **faire ~ à qn** to make sb (feel) ashamed

'**honteux, -euse** [ɔ̃tø, -øz] *adj* ashamed; (*conduite, acte*) shameful, disgraceful

hôpital, -aux [ɔpital, -o] *nm* hospital

'**hoquet** [ɔkɛ] *nm* hiccough; **avoir le ~** to have (the) hiccoughs

'**hoqueter** [ɔkte] *vi* to hiccough

horaire [ɔʀɛʀ] *adj* hourly ▷ *nm* timetable, schedule; **horaires** *nmpl* (*heures de travail*) hours; ~ **flexible** *ou* **mobile** *ou* **à la carte** *ou* **souple** flex(i)time

horizon [ɔʀizɔ̃] *nm* horizon; (*paysage*) landscape, view; **sur l'~** on the skyline *ou* horizon

horizontal, e, -aux [ɔʀizɔ̃tal, -o] *adj* horizontal ▷ *nf*: **à l'~e** on the horizontal

horloge [ɔʀlɔʒ] *nf* clock; **l'~ parlante** the speaking clock; ~ **normande** grandfather clock; ~ **physiologique** biological clock

horloger, -ère [ɔʀlɔʒe, -ɛʀ] *nm/f* watchmaker; clockmaker

'**hormis** [ɔʀmi] *prép* save

horoscope [ˋskɔp] *nm* horoscope

horreur [ɔʀœʀ] *nf* horror; **avoir ~ de** to loathe, detest; **quelle ~!** how awful!; **cela me fait ~** I find that awful

horrible [ɔʀibl(ə)] *adj* horrible

horrifier [ɔʀifje] *vt* to horrify

horripiler [ɔʀipile] *vt* to exasperate

'**hors** [ɔʀ] *prép* except (for); ~ **de** out of; ~ **ligne** (*Inform*) off line; ~ **pair** outstanding; ~ **de propos** inopportune; ~ **série** (*sur mesure*) made-to-order; (*exceptionnel*) exceptional; ~ **service** (**HS**), ~ **d'usage** out of service; **être ~ de soi** to be beside o.s.

'**hors-bord** [ɔʀbɔʀ] *nm inv* outboard motor; (*canot*) speedboat (with outboard motor)

'**hors-d'œuvre** [ɔʀdœvʀ(ə)] *nm inv* hors d'œuvre

'**hors-jeu** [ɔʀʒø] *nm inv* being offside *no pl*

'**hors-la-loi** [ɔʀlalwa] *nm inv* outlaw

hors-taxe [ɔʀtaks] *adj* (*sur une facture, prix*) excluding VAT; (*boutique, marchandises*) duty-free

hortensia [ɔʀtɑ̃sja] *nm* hydrangea

hospice [ɔspis] *nm* (*de vieillards*) home; (*asile*) hospice

hospitalier, -ière [ɔspitalje, -jɛʀ] *adj* (*accueillant*) hospitable; (*Méd: service, centre*) hospital *cpd*

hospitaliser [ɔspitalize] *vt* to take (*ou* send) to hospital, hospitalize

hospitalité [ɔspitalite] *nf* hospitality

hostie [ɔsti] *nf* host; (*Rel*)

hostile [ɔstil] *adj* hostile

hostilité [ɔstilite] *nf* hostility; **hostilités** *nfpl* hostilities

hôte [ot] *nm* (*maître de maison*) host; (*client*) patron; (*fig*) inhabitant, occupant ▷ *nm/f* (*invité*) guest; ~ **payant** paying guest

hôtel [otɛl] *nm* hotel; **aller à l'~** to stay in a hotel; ~ (**particulier**) (*private*) mansion; ~ **de ville** town hall

hôtelier, -ière [otəlje, -jɛʀ] *adj* hotel *cpd* ▷ *nm/f* hotelier, hotel-keeper

hôtellerie [otɛlʀi] *nf* (*profession*) hotel business; (*auberge*) inn

hôtesse [otɛs] *nf* hostess; ~ **de l'air** flight attendant; ~ (**d'accueil**) receptionist

'**hotte** [ɔt] *nf* (*panier*) basket (*carried on the back*); (*de cheminée*) hood; ~ **aspirante** cooker hood

'**houblon** [ublɔ̃] *nm* (*Bot*) hop; (*pour la bière*) hops *pl*

'**houille** [uj] *nf* coal; ~ **blanche** hydroelectric power

'**houle** [ul] *nf* swell

'**houleux, -euse** [ulø, -øz] *adj* heavy, swelling; (*fig*) stormy, turbulent

'**hourra** [uʀa] *nm* cheer ▷ *excl* hurrah!

'**houspiller** [uspije] *vt* to scold

'**housse** [us] *nf* cover; (*pour protéger provisoirement*) dust cover; (*pour recouvrir à neuf*) loose *ou* stretch cover; ~ (**penderie**) hanging wardrobe

'**houx** [u] *nm* holly

hovercraft [ovœʀkʀaft] *nm* hovercraft
'**hublot** ['yblo] *nm* porthole
'**huche** ['yʃ] *nf*: ~ **à pain** bread bin
'**huer** ['ɥe] *vt* to boo; *(hibou, chouette)* to hoot
huile [ɥil] *nf* oil; *(Art)* oil painting; *(fam)* bigwig;
  mer d'~ *(très calme)* glassy sea, sea of glass;
  faire tache d'~ *(fig)* to spread; ~ **d'arachide**
  groundnut oil; ~ **essentielle** essential oil; ~ **de**
  foie de morue cod-liver oil; ~ **de ricin** castor oil;
  ~ **solaire** suntan oil; ~ **de table** salad oil
huiler [ɥile] *vt* to oil
huileux, -euse [ɥilø, -øz] *adj* oily
huis [ɥi] *nm*: **à ~ clos** in camera
huissier [ɥisje] *nm* usher; *(Jur)* ≈ bailiff
'**huit** ['ɥi(t)] *num* eight; **samedi en ~** a week on
  Saturday; **dans ~ jours** in a week('s time)
'**huitaine** ['ɥitɛn] *nf*: **une ~ de** about eight, eight
  or so; **une ~ de jours** a week or so
'**huitième** ['ɥitjɛm] *num* eighth
huître [ɥitʀ(ə)] *nf* oyster
humain, e [ymɛ̃, -ɛn] *adj* human; *(compatissant)*
  humane ▷ *nm* human (being)
humanitaire [ymanitɛʀ] *adj* humanitarian
humanité [ymanite] *nf* humanity
humble [œ̃bl(ə)] *adj* humble
humecter [ymɛkte] *vt* to dampen; **s'~ les lèvres**
  to moisten one's lips
'**humer** ['yme] *vt* to inhale; *(pour sentir)* to smell
humeur [ymœʀ] *nf* mood; *(tempérament)* temper;
  (irritation) bad temper; **de bonne/mauvaise ~** in
  a good/bad mood; **être d'~ à faire qch** to be in
  the mood for doing sth
humide [ymid] *adj* *(linge)* damp; *(main, yeux)*
  moist; *(climat, chaleur)* humid; *(saison, route)* wet
humilier [ymilje] *vt* to humiliate; **s'~ devant qn**
  to humble o.s. before sb
humilité [ymilite] *nf* humility
humoristique [ymɔʀistik] *adj* humorous;
  humoristic
humour [ymuʀ] *nm* humour; **avoir de l'~** to

have a sense of humour; ~ **noir** sick humour
'**huppé, e** ['ype] *adj* crested; *(fam)* posh
'**hurlement** ['yʀləmɑ̃] *nm* howling *no pl*, howl;
  yelling *no pl*, yell
'**hurler** ['yʀle] *vi* to howl, yell; *(fig: vent)* to howl;
  (: couleurs etc) to clash; ~ **à la mort** *(chien)* to bay
  at the moon
hurluberlu [yʀlybɛʀly] *nm* *(péj)* crank ▷ *adj*
  cranky
'**hutte** ['yt] *nf* hut
hybride [ibʀid] *adj* hybrid
hydratant, e [idʀatɑ̃, -ɑ̃t] *adj* *(crème)*
  moisturizing
hydraulique [idʀolik] *adj* hydraulic
hydravion [idʀavjɔ̃] *nm* seaplane, hydroplane
hydrogène [idʀɔʒɛn] *nm* hydrogen
hydroglisseur [idʀɔglisœʀ] *nm* hydroplane
hyène [jɛn] *nf* hyena
hygiène [iʒjɛn] *nf* hygiene; ~ **intime** personal
  hygiene
hygiénique [iʒenik] *adj* hygienic
hymne [imn(ə)] *nm* hymn; ~ **national** national
  anthem
hyperlien [ipɛʀljɛ̃] *nm* *(Inform)* hyperlink
hypermarché [ipɛʀmaʀʃe] *nm* hypermarket
hypermétrope [ipɛʀmetʀɔp] *adj* long-sighted
hypertension [ipɛʀtɑ̃sjɔ̃] *nf* high blood
  pressure, hypertension
hypertexte [ipɛʀtɛkst] *nm* *(Inform)* hypertext
hypnose [ipnoz] *nf* hypnosis
hypnotiser [ipnotize] *vt* to hypnotize
hypnotiseur [ipnotizœʀ] *nm* hypnotist
hypocrisie [ipɔkʀizi] *nf* hypocrisy
hypocrite [ipɔkʀit] *adj* hypocritical ▷ *nm/f*
  hypocrite
hypothèque [ipɔtɛk] *nf* mortgage
hypothèse [ipɔtɛz] *nf* hypothesis; **dans l'~ où**
  assuming that
hystérique [isteʀik] *adj* hysterical

I i

iceberg [isbɛʀg] *nm* iceberg

ici [isi] *adv* here; **jusqu'~** as far as this; *(temporel)* until now; **d'~ là** by then; *(en attendant)* in the meantime; **d'~ peu** before long

icône [ikon] *nf (aussi Inform)* icon

idéal, e, -aux [ideal, -o] *adj* ideal ▷ *nm* ideal; *(système de valeurs)* ideals *pl*

idéaliste [idealist(ə)] *adj* idealistic ▷ *nm/f* idealist

idée [ide] *nf* idea; *(illusion)*: **se faire des ~s** to imagine things, get ideas into one's head; **avoir dans l'~ que** to have an idea that; **mon ~, c'est que ...** I suggest that ..., I think that ...; **à l'~ de/que** at the idea of/that, at the thought of/that; **je n'ai pas la moindre ~** I haven't the faintest idea; **avoir ~ que** to have an idea that; **avoir des ~s larges/étroites** to be broad-/narrow-minded; **venir à l'~ de qn** to occur to sb; **en voilà des ~s!** the very idea!; **~ fixe** idée fixe, obsession; **~s noires** black *ou* dark thoughts; **~s reçues** accepted ideas *ou* wisdom

identifiant [idɑ̃tifjɑ̃] *nm (Inform)* login

identifier [idɑ̃tifje] *vt* to identify; **~ qch/qn à** to identify sth/sb with; **s'~ avec** *ou* **à qn/qch** *(héros etc)* to identify with sb/sth

identique [idɑ̃tik] *adj*: **~ (à)** identical (to)

identité [idɑ̃tite] *nf* identity; **~ judiciaire** *(Police)* ≈ Criminal Records Office

idiot, e [idjo, idjɔt] *adj* idiotic ▷ *nm/f* idiot

idiotie [idjɔsi] *nf* idiocy; *(propos)* idiotic remark

idole [idɔl] *nf* idol

if [if] *nm* yew

igloo [iglu] *nm* igloo

ignare [iɲaʀ] *adj* ignorant

ignoble [iɲɔbl(ə)] *adj* vile

ignorant, e [iɲɔʀɑ̃, -ɑ̃t] *adj* ignorant ▷ *nm/f*: **faire l'~** to pretend one doesn't know; **~ de** ignorant of, not aware of; **~ en** ignorant of, knowing nothing of

ignorer [iɲɔʀe] *vt (ne pas connaître)* not to know, be unaware *ou* ignorant of; *(être sans expérience de: plaisir, guerre etc)* not to know about, have no experience of; *(bouder: personne)* to ignore; **j'ignore comment/si** I do not know how/if; **~ que** to be unaware that, not to know that; **je n'ignore pas que ...** I'm not forgetting that ..., I'm not unaware that ...; **je l'ignore** I don't know

il [il] *pron* he; *(animal, chose, en tournure impersonnelle)* it, NB: *en anglais les navires et les pays sont en général assimilés aux femelles, et les bébés aux choses, si le sexe n'est pas spécifié*; **ils** they; **il neige** it's snowing; *voir aussi* **avoir**

île [il] *nf* island; **les Î~s** the West Indies; **l'~ de Beauté** Corsica; **l'~ Maurice** Mauritius; **les ~s anglo-normandes** the Channel Islands; **les ~s Britanniques** the British Isles; **les ~s Cocos** *ou* **Keeling** the Cocos *ou* Keeling Islands; **les ~s Cook** the Cook Islands; **les ~s Scilly** the Scilly Isles, the Scillies; **les ~s Shetland** the Shetland Islands, Shetland; **les ~s Sorlingues**; **= les îles Scilly**; **les ~s Vierges** the Virgin Islands

illégal, e, -aux [ilegal, -o] *adj* illegal, unlawful *(Admin)*

illégitime [ileʒitim] *adj* illegitimate; *(optimisme, sévérité)* unjustified, unwarranted

illettré, e [iletʀe] *adj, nm/f* illiterate

illimité, e [ilimite] *adj (immense)* boundless, unlimited; *(congé, durée)* indefinite, unlimited

illisible [ilizibl(ə)] *adj* illegible; *(roman)* unreadable

illogique [ilɔʒik] *adj* illogical

illumination [ilyminɑsjɔ̃] *nf* illumination, floodlighting; *(inspiration)* flash of inspiration; **illuminations** *nfpl* illuminations, lights

illuminer [ilymine] *vt* to light up; *(monument, rue: pour une fête)* to illuminate, floodlight; **s'illuminer** *vi* to light up

illusion [ilyzjɔ̃] *nf* illusion; **se faire des ~s** to delude o.s.; **faire ~** to delude *ou* fool people; **~ d'optique** optical illusion

illusionniste [ilyzjɔnist(ə)] *nm/f* conjuror

illustration [ilystʀasjɔ̃] *nf* illustration; *(d'un ouvrage: photos)* illustrations *pl*

illustre [ilystʀ(ə)] *adj* illustrious, renowned

illustré, e [ilystʀe] *adj* illustrated ▷ *nm* illustrated magazine; *(pour enfants)* comic

illustrer [ilystʀe] *vt* to illustrate; **s'illustrer** to become famous, win fame

îlot [ilo] *nm* small island, islet; *(de maisons)* block; *(petite zone)*: **un ~ de verdure** an island of greenery, a patch of green

ils [il] *pron voir* **il**

image [imaʒ] *nf (gén)* picture; *(comparaison,*

ressemblance, Optique) image; **~ de** picture *ou*
image of; **~ d'Épinal** (social) stereotype; **~ de
marque** brand image; (*d'une personne*) (public)
image; (*d'une entreprise*) corporate image; **~
pieuse** holy picture
imagé, e [imaʒe] *adj* full of imagery
imaginaire [imaʒinɛʀ] *adj* imaginary
imagination [imaʒinasjɔ̃] *nf* imagination;
(*chimère*) fancy, imagining; **avoir de l'~** to be
imaginative, have a good imagination
imaginer [imaʒine] *vt* to imagine; (*croire*):
qu'allez-vous ~ là? what on earth are you
thinking of?; (*inventer: expédient, mesure*) to devise,
think up; **s'imaginer** *vt* (*se figurer: scène etc*) to
imagine, picture; **s'~ à 60 ans** to picture *ou*
imagine o.s. at 60; **s'~ que** to imagine that;
s'~ pouvoir faire qch to think one can do sth;
j'imagine qu'il a voulu plaisanter I suppose
he was joking; **~ de faire** (*se mettre dans l'idée de*) to
dream up the idea of doing
imbattable [ɛ̃batabl(ə)] *adj* unbeatable
imbécile [ɛ̃besil] *adj* idiotic ▷ *nm/f* idiot; (*Méd*)
imbecile
imbécillité [ɛ̃besilite] *nf* idiocy; imbecility;
idiotic action (*ou* remark *etc*)
imbiber [ɛ̃bibe] *vt*: **~ qch de** to moisten *ou* wet
sth with; **s'imbiber de** to become saturated
with; **imbibé(e) d'eau** (*chaussures, étoffe*)
saturated; (*terre*) waterlogged
imbu, e [ɛ̃by] *adj*: **~ de** full of; **~ de soi-même/sa
supériorité** full of oneself/one's superiority
imbuvable [ɛ̃byvabl(ə)] *adj* undrinkable
imitateur, -trice [imitatœʀ, -tʀis] *nm/f*
(*gén*) imitator; (*Music-Hall: d'une personnalité*)
impersonator
imitation [imitasjɔ̃] *nf* imitation;
impersonation; **sac ~ cuir** bag in imitation *ou*
simulated leather; **à l'~ de** in imitation of
imiter [imite] *vt* to imitate; (*personne*) to imitate,
impersonate; (*contrefaire: signature, document*) to
forge, copy; (*ressembler à*) to look like; **il se leva et
je l'imitai** he got up and I did likewise
immaculé, e [imakyle] *adj* spotless,
immaculate; **l'I~e Conception** (*Rel*) the
Immaculate Conception
immangeable [ɛ̃mãʒabl(ə)] *adj* inedible,
uneatable
immatriculation [imatʀikylasjɔ̃] *nf*
registration
immatriculer [imatʀikyle] *vt* to register; **faire/
se faire ~** to register; **voiture immatriculée
dans la Seine** car with a Seine registration
(number)
immédiat, e [imedja, -at] *adj* immediate ▷ *nm*:
dans l'~ for the time being; **dans le voisinage ~
de** in the immediate vicinity of
immédiatement [imedjatmã] *adv* immediately
immense [imãs] *adj* immense
immerger [imɛʀʒe] *vt* to immerse, submerge;
(*câble etc*) to lay under water; (*déchets*) to dump at
sea; **s'immerger** *vi* (*sous-marin*) to dive, submerge
immeuble [imœbl(ə)] *nm* building ▷ *adj* (*Jur*)

immovable, real; **~ locatif** block of rented
flats (*Brit*), rental building (*US*); **~ de rapport**
investment property
immigration [imigʀasjɔ̃] *nf* immigration
immigré, e [imigʀe] *nm/f* immigrant
imminent, e [iminã, -ãt] *adj* imminent,
impending
immiscer [imise]: **s'immiscer** *vi*: **s'~ dans** to
interfere in *ou* with
immobile [imɔbil] *adj* still, motionless; (*pièce
de machine*) fixed; (*fig*) unchanging; **rester/se
tenir ~** to stay/keep still
immobilier, -ière [imɔbilje, -jɛʀ] *adj* property
cpd, in real property ▷ *nm*: **l'~** the property *ou* the
real estate business
immobiliser [imɔbilize] *vt* (*gén*) to immobilize;
(*circulation, véhicule, affaires*) to bring to a standstill;
s'immobiliser (*personne*) to stand still; (*machine,
véhicule*) to come to a halt *ou* a standstill
immonde [imɔ̃d] *adj* foul; (*sale: ruelle, taudis*)
squalid
immoral, e, -aux [imɔʀal, -o] *adj* immoral
immortel, le [imɔʀtɛl] *adj* immortal ▷ *nf* (*Bot*)
everlasting (flower)
immuable [imɥabl(ə)] *adj* (*inébranlable*)
immutable; (*qui ne change pas*) unchanging;
(*personne*): **~ dans ses convictions** immoveable
(in one's convictions)
immunisé, e [im(m)ynize] *adj*: **~ contre**
immune to
immunité [imynite] *nf* immunity; **~
diplomatique** diplomatic immunity; **~
parlementaire** parliamentary privilege
impact [ɛ̃pakt] *nm* impact; **point d'~** point of
impact
impair, e [ɛ̃pɛʀ] *adj* odd ▷ *nm* faux pas, blunder;
numéros ~s odd numbers
impardonnable [ɛ̃paʀdɔnabl(ə)] *adj*
unpardonable, unforgivable; **vous êtes ~
d'avoir fait cela** it's unforgivable of you to have
done that
imparfait, e [ɛ̃paʀfɛ, -ɛt] *adj* imperfect ▷ *nm*
(*Ling*) imperfect (tense)
impartial, e, -aux [ɛ̃paʀsjal, -o] *adj* impartial,
unbiased
impasse [ɛ̃pas] *nf* dead-end, cul-de-sac; (*fig*)
deadlock; **être dans l'~** (*négociations*) to have
reached deadlock; **~ budgétaire** budget deficit
impassible [ɛ̃pasibl(ə)] *adj* impassive
impatience [ɛ̃pasjãs] *nf* impatience
impatient, e [ɛ̃pasjã, -ãt] *adj* impatient; **~ de
faire qch** keen *ou* impatient to do sth
impatienter [ɛ̃pasjãte] *vt* to irritate, annoy;
s'impatienter *vi* to get impatient; **s'~ de/contre**
to lose patience at/with, grow impatient at/with
impeccable [ɛ̃pekabl(ə)] *adj* faultless,
impeccable; (*propre*) spotlessly clean; (*chic*)
impeccably dressed; (*fam*) smashing
impensable [ɛ̃pãsabl(ə)] *adj* unthinkable,
unbelievable
imper [ɛ̃pɛʀ] *nm* (*imperméable*) mac
impératif, -ive [ɛ̃peʀatif, -iv] *adj* imperative;

(Jur) mandatory ▷ nm (Ling) imperative;
impératifs nmpl requirements; demands
impératrice [ɛ̃peratris] nf empress
imperceptible [ɛ̃pɛrsɛptibl(ə)] adj
imperceptible
impérial, e, -aux [ɛ̃perjal, -o] adj imperial ▷ nf
upper deck; **autobus à ~e** double-decker bus
impérieux, -euse [ɛ̃perjø, -øz] adj (caractère, ton)
imperious; (obligation, besoin) pressing, urgent
impérissable [ɛ̃perisabl(ə)] adj undying,
imperishable
imperméable [ɛ̃pɛrmeabl(ə)] adj waterproof;
(Géo) impermeable; (fig): **~ à** impervious to ▷ nm
raincoat; **~ à l'air** airtight
impertinent, e [ɛ̃pɛrtinɑ̃, -ɑ̃t] adj impertinent
imperturbable [ɛ̃pɛrtyrbabl(ə)] adj (personne)
imperturbable; (sang-froid) unshakeable; **rester
~** to remain unruffled
impétueux, -euse [ɛ̃petɥø, -øz] adj fiery
impitoyable [ɛ̃pitwajabl(ə)] adj pitiless,
merciless
implanter [ɛ̃plɑ̃te] vt (usine, industrie, usage) to
establish; (colons etc) to settle; (idée, préjugé) to
implant; **s'implanter dans** vi to be established
in; to settle in; to become implanted in
impliquer [ɛ̃plike] vt to imply; **~ qn (dans)** to
implicate sb (in)
impoli, e [ɛ̃pɔli] adj impolite, rude
impopulaire [ɛ̃pɔpylɛr] adj unpopular
importance [ɛ̃pɔrtɑ̃s] nf importance; **avoir de
l'~** to be important; **sans ~** unimportant; **d'~**
important, considerable; **quelle ~?** what does
it matter?
important, e [ɛ̃pɔrtɑ̃, -ɑ̃t] adj important; (en
quantité) considerable, sizeable; (: gamme, dégâts)
extensive; (péj: airs, ton) self-important ▷ nm: **l'~**
the important thing
importateur, -trice [ɛ̃pɔrtatœr, -tris] adj
importing ▷ nm/f importer; **pays ~ de blé**
wheat-importing country
importation [ɛ̃pɔrtasjɔ̃] nf import;
introduction; (produit) import
importer [ɛ̃pɔrte] vt (Comm) to import; (maladies,
plantes) to introduce ▷ vi (être important) to
matter; **~ à qn** to matter to sb; **il importe de**
it is important to; **il importe qu'il fasse** he
must do, it is important that he should do;
peu m'importe I don't mind, I don't care; **peu
importe** it doesn't matter; **peu importe (que)**
it doesn't matter (if); **peu importe le prix** never
mind the price; *voir aussi* **n'importe**
importun, e [ɛ̃pɔrtœ̃, -yn] adj irksome,
importunate; (arrivée, visite) inopportune, ill-
timed ▷ nm intruder
importuner [ɛ̃pɔrtyne] vt to bother
imposable [ɛ̃pozabl(ə)] adj taxable
imposant, e [ɛ̃pozɑ̃, -ɑ̃t] adj imposing
imposer [ɛ̃poze] vt (taxer) to tax; (Rel): **~ les
mains** to lay on hands; **~ qch à qn** to impose
sth on sb; **s'imposer** vi (être nécessaire) to be
imperative; (montrer sa proéminence) to stand
out, emerge; (artiste: se faire connaître) to win

recognition, come to the fore; **en ~** to be
imposing; **en ~ à** to impress; **ça s'impose** it's
essential, it's vital
impossibilité [ɛ̃pɔsibilite] nf impossibility;
être dans l'~ de faire to be unable to do, find it
impossible to do
impossible [ɛ̃pɔsibl(ə)] adj impossible ▷ nm: **l'~**
the impossible; **~ à faire** impossible to do; **il
m'est ~ de le faire** it is impossible for me to do
it, I can't possibly do it; **faire l'~ (pour que)** to
do one's utmost (so that); **si, par ~ ...** if, by some
miracle ...
imposteur [ɛ̃pɔstœr] nm impostor
impôt [ɛ̃po] nm tax; (taxes) taxation, taxes pl;
impôts nmpl (contributions) (income) tax sg; **payer
1000 euros d'~s** to pay 1,000 euros in tax; **~
direct/indirect** direct/indirect tax; **~ sur le
chiffre d'affaires** tax on turnover; **~ foncier**
land tax; **~ sur la fortune** wealth tax; **~ sur les
plus-values** capital gains tax; **~ sur le revenu**
income tax; **~ sur le RPP** personal income tax;
~ sur les sociétés tax on companies; **~s locaux**
rates, local taxes (US), ≈ council tax (Brit)
impotent, e [ɛ̃pɔtɑ̃, -ɑ̃t] adj disabled
impraticable [ɛ̃pratikabl(ə)] adj (projet)
impracticable, unworkable; (piste) impassable
imprécis, e [ɛ̃presi, -iz] adj (contours, souvenir)
imprecise, vague; (tir) inaccurate, imprecise
imprégner [ɛ̃preɲe] vt (tissu, tampon): **~ (de)** to
soak ou impregnate (with); (lieu, air): **~ (de)** to fill
(with); (amertume, ironie) to pervade; **s'imprégner
de** vi to become impregnated with; to be filled
with; (fig) to absorb
imprenable [ɛ̃prənabl(ə)] adj (forteresse)
impregnable; **vue ~** unimpeded outlook
impresario [ɛ̃presarjo] nm manager, impresario
impression [ɛ̃presjɔ̃] nf impression; (d'un
ouvrage, tissu) printing; (Photo) exposure; **faire
bonne ~** to make a good impression; **donner
une ~ de/l'~ que** to give the impression of/that;
avoir l'~ de/que to have the impression of/that;
faire ~ to make an impression; **~s de voyage**
impressions of one's journey
impressionnant, e [ɛ̃presjɔnɑ̃, -ɑ̃t] adj
impressive; upsetting
impressionner [ɛ̃presjɔne] vt (frapper) to
impress; (troubler) to upset; (Photo) to expose
imprévisible [ɛ̃previzibl(ə)] adj unforeseeable;
(réaction, personne) unpredictable
imprévoyant, e [ɛ̃prevwajɑ̃, -ɑ̃t] adj lacking in
foresight; (en matière d'argent) improvident
imprévu, e [ɛ̃prevy] adj unforeseen, unexpected
▷ nm unexpected incident; **l'~** the unexpected;
en cas d'~ if anything unexpected happens;
sauf ~ barring anything unexpected
imprimante [ɛ̃primɑ̃t] nf (Inform) printer; **~ à
bulle d'encre** bubblejet printer; **~ à jet d'encre**
ink-jet printer; **~ à laser** laser printer; **~ (ligne
par) ligne** line printer; **~ à marguerite** daisy-
wheel printer
imprimé [ɛ̃prime] nm (formulaire) printed form;
(Postes) printed matter no pl; (tissu) printed fabric;

un ~ à fleurs/pois (*tissu*) a floral/polka-dot print
imprimer [ɛ̃pʀime] *vt* to print; (*Inform*) to print
(out); (*apposer: visa, cachet*) to stamp; (*empreinte etc*) to imprint; (*publier*) to publish; (*communiquer: mouvement, impulsion*) to impart, transmit
imprimerie [ɛ̃pʀimʀi] *nf* printing; (*établissement*) printing works *sg*; (*atelier*) printing house, printery
imprimeur [ɛ̃pʀimœʀ] *nm* printer; **~-éditeur/-libraire** printer and publisher/bookseller
impromptu, e [ɛ̃pʀɔ̃pty] *adj* impromptu; (*départ*) sudden
impropre [ɛ̃pʀɔpʀ(ə)] *adj* inappropriate; **~ à** unsuitable for
improviser [ɛ̃pʀɔvize] *vt, vi* to improvize; **s'improviser** (*secours, réunion*) to be improvized; **s'~ cuisinier** to (decide to) act as cook; **~ qn cuisinier** to get sb to act as cook
improviste [ɛ̃pʀɔvist(ə)]: **à l'~** *adv* unexpectedly, without warning
imprudence [ɛ̃pʀydɑ̃s] *nf* carelessness *no pl*; imprudence *no pl*; act of carelessness; (:) foolish *ou* unwise action
imprudent, e [ɛ̃pʀydɑ̃, -ɑ̃t] *adj* (*conducteur, geste, action*) careless; (*remarque*) unwise, imprudent; (*projet*) foolhardy
impudent, e [ɛ̃pydɑ̃, -ɑ̃t] *adj* impudent
impudique [ɛ̃pydik] *adj* shameless
impuissant, e [ɛ̃pɥisɑ̃, -ɑ̃t] *adj* helpless; (*sans effet*) ineffectual; (*sexuellement*) impotent ▷ *nm* impotent man; **~ à faire qch** powerless to do sth
impulsif, -ive [ɛ̃pylsif, -iv] *adj* impulsive
impulsion [ɛ̃pylsjɔ̃] *nf* (*Élec, instinct*) impulse; (*élan, influence*) impetus
impunément [ɛ̃pynemɑ̃] *adv* with impunity
inabordable [inabɔʀdabl(ə)] *adj* (*lieu*) inaccessible; (*cher*) prohibitive
inacceptable [inaksɛptabl(ə)] *adj* unacceptable
inaccessible [inaksesibl(ə)] *adj* inaccessible; (*objectif*) unattainable; (*insensible*) : **~ à** impervious to
inachevé, e [inaʃve] *adj* unfinished
inactif, -ive [inaktif, -iv] *adj* inactive, idle
inadapté, e [inadapte] *adj* (*Psych: adulte, enfant*) maladjusted ▷ *nm/f* (*péj: adulte: asocial*) misfit; **~ à** not adapted to, unsuited to
inadéquat, e [inadekwa, wat] *adj* inadequate
inadmissible [inadmisibl(ə)] *adj* inadmissible
inadvertance [inadvɛʀtɑ̃s]: **par ~** *adv* inadvertently
inaltérable [inalteʀabl(ə)] *adj* (*matière*) stable; (*fig*) unchanging; **~ à** unaffected by; **couleur ~ (au lavage/à la lumière)** fast colour/fade-resistant colour
inanimé, e [inanime] *adj* (*matière*) inanimate; (*évanoui*) unconscious; (*sans vie*) lifeless
inanition [inanisjɔ̃] *nf*: **tomber d'~** to faint with hunger (and exhaustion)
inaperçu, e [inapɛʀsy] *adj*: **passer ~** to go unnoticed
inapte [inapt(ə)] *adj*: **~ à** incapable of; (*Mil*) unfit for

inattaquable [inatakabl(ə)] *adj* (*Mil*) unassailable; (*texte, preuve*) irrefutable
inattendu, e [inatɑ̃dy] *adj* unexpected ▷ *nm*: **l'~** the unexpected
inattentif, -ive [inatɑ̃tif, -iv] *adj* inattentive; **~ à** (*dangers, détails*) heedless of
inattention [inatɑ̃sjɔ̃] *nf* inattention; (*inadvertance*): **une minute d'~** a minute of inattention, a minute's carelessness; **par ~** inadvertently; **faute d'~** careless mistake
inauguration [inɔgyʀasjɔ̃] *nf* unveiling; opening; **discours/cérémonie d'~** inaugural speech/ceremony
inaugurer [inɔgyʀe] *vt* (*monument*) to unveil; (*exposition, usine*) to open; (*fig*) to inaugurate
inavouable [inavwabl(ə)] *adj* undisclosable; (*honteux*) shameful
incalculable [ɛ̃kalkylabl(ə)] *adj* incalculable; **un nombre ~ de** countless numbers of
incandescence [ɛ̃kɑ̃desɑ̃s] *nf* incandescence; **en ~** incandescent, white-hot; **porter à ~** to heat white-hot; **lampe/manchon à ~** incandescent lamp/(gas) mantle
incapable [ɛ̃kapabl(ə)] *adj* incapable; **~ de faire** incapable of doing; (*empêché*) unable to do
incapacité [ɛ̃kapasite] *nf* incapability; (*Jur*) incapacity; **être dans l'~ de faire** to be unable to do; **~ permanente/de travail** permanent/industrial disablement; **~ électorale** ineligibility to vote
incarcérer [ɛ̃kaʀseʀe] *vt* to incarcerate
incarné, e [ɛ̃kaʀne] *adj* incarnate; (*ongle*) ingrown
incarner [ɛ̃kaʀne] *vt* to embody, personify; (*Théât*) to play; (*Rel*) to incarnate; **s'incarner dans** *vi* (*Rel*) to be incarnate in
incassable [ɛ̃kasabl(ə)] *adj* unbreakable
incendiaire [ɛ̃sɑ̃djɛʀ] *adj* incendiary; (*fig: discours*) inflammatory ▷ *nm/f* fire-raiser, arsonist
incendie [ɛ̃sɑ̃di] *nm* fire; **~ criminel** arson *no pl*; **~ de forêt** forest fire
incendier [ɛ̃sɑ̃dje] *vt* (*mettre le feu à*) to set fire to, set alight; (*brûler complètement*) to burn down
incertain, e [ɛ̃sɛʀtɛ̃, -ɛn] *adj* uncertain; (*temps*) uncertain, unsettled; (*imprécis: contours*) indistinct, blurred
incertitude [ɛ̃sɛʀtityd] *nf* uncertainty
incessamment [ɛ̃sesamɑ̃] *adv* very shortly
incident [ɛ̃sidɑ̃] *nm* incident; **~ de frontière** border incident; **~ de parcours** minor hitch *ou* setback; **~ technique** technical difficulties *pl*, technical hitch
incinérer [ɛ̃sineʀe] *vt* (*ordures*) to incinerate; (*mort*) to cremate
incisif, -ive [ɛ̃sizif, -iv] *adj* incisive, cutting ▷ *nf* incisor
inciter [ɛ̃site] *vt*: **~ qn à (faire) qch** to prompt *ou* encourage sb to do sth; (*à la révolte etc*) to incite sb to do sth
inclinable [ɛ̃klinabl(ə)] *adj* (*dossier etc*) tilting; **siège à dossier ~** reclining seat

inclinaison [ɛ̃klinɛzɔ̃] nf (déclivité: d'une route etc) incline; (: d'un toit) slope; (état penché: d'un mur) lean; (: de la tête) tilt; (: d'un navire) list

inclination [ɛ̃klinasjɔ̃] nf (penchant) inclination, tendency; **montrer de l'~ pour les sciences** etc to show an inclination for the sciences etc; **~s égoïstes/altruistes** egoistic/altruistic tendencies; **~ de (la) tête** nod (of the head); **~ (de buste)** bow

incliner [ɛ̃kline] vt (bouteille) to tilt; (tête) to incline; (inciter): **~ qn à qch/à faire** to encourage sb towards sth/to do ▷ vi: **~ à qch/à faire** (tendre à, pencher pour) to incline towards sth/doing, tend towards sth/to do; **s'incliner** vi (route) to slope; (toit) to be sloping; **s'~ (devant)** to bow (before)

inclure [ɛ̃klyʀ] vt to include; (joindre à un envoi) to enclose; **jusqu'au 10 mars inclus** until 10th March inclusive

incognito [ɛ̃kɔɲito] adv incognito ▷ nm: **garder l'~** to remain incognito

incohérent, e [ɛ̃kɔeʀɑ̃, -ɑ̃t] adj inconsistent; incoherent

incollable [ɛ̃kɔlabl(ə)] adj (riz) that does not stick; (fam: personne): **il est ~** he's got all the answers

incolore [ɛ̃kɔlɔʀ] adj colourless

incommoder [ɛ̃kɔmɔde] vt: **~ qn** to bother ou inconvenience sb; (embarrasser) to make sb feel uncomfortable ou ill at ease

incomparable [ɛ̃kɔ̃paʀabl(ə)] adj not comparable; (inégalable) incomparable, matchless

incompatible [ɛ̃kɔ̃patibl(ə)] adj incompatible

incompétent, e [ɛ̃kɔ̃petɑ̃, -ɑ̃t] adj (ignorant) inexpert; (incapable) incompetent, not competent

incomplet, -ète [ɛ̃kɔ̃plɛ, -ɛt] adj incomplete

incompréhensible [ɛ̃kɔ̃pʀeɑ̃sibl(ə)] adj incomprehensible

incompris, e [ɛ̃kɔ̃pʀi, -iz] adj misunderstood

inconcevable [ɛ̃kɔ̃svabl(ə)] adj (conduite etc) inconceivable; (mystère) incredible

inconciliable [ɛ̃kɔ̃siljabl(ə)] adj irreconcilable

inconditionnel, le [ɛ̃kɔ̃disjɔnɛl] adj unconditional; (partisan) unquestioning ▷ nm/f (partisan) unquestioning supporter

inconfort [ɛ̃kɔ̃fɔʀ] nm lack of comfort, discomfort

inconfortable [ɛ̃kɔ̃fɔʀtabl(ə)] adj uncomfortable

incongru, e [ɛ̃kɔ̃gʀy] adj unseemly; (remarque) ill-chosen, incongruous

inconnu, e [ɛ̃kɔny] adj unknown; (sentiment, plaisir) new, strange ▷ nm/f stranger; unknown person (ou artist etc) ▷ nm: **l'~** the unknown ▷ nf (Math) unknown; (fig) unknown factor

inconsciemment [ɛ̃kɔ̃sjamɑ̃] adv unconsciously

inconscient, e [ɛ̃kɔ̃sjɑ̃, -ɑ̃t] adj unconscious; (irréfléchi) reckless ▷ nm (Psych): **l'~** the subconscious, the unconscious; **~ de** unaware of

inconsidéré, e [ɛ̃kɔ̃sideʀe] adj ill-considered

inconsistant, e [ɛ̃kɔ̃sistɑ̃, -ɑ̃t] adj flimsy, weak; (crème etc) runny

inconsolable [ɛ̃kɔ̃sɔlabl(ə)] adj inconsolable

incontestable [ɛ̃kɔ̃tɛstabl(ə)] adj unquestionable, indisputable

incontinent, e [ɛ̃kɔ̃tinɑ̃, -ɑ̃t] adj (Méd) incontinent ▷ adv (tout de suite) forthwith

incontournable [ɛ̃kɔ̃tuʀnabl(ə)] adj unavoidable

incontrôlable [ɛ̃kɔ̃tʀolabl(ə)] adj unverifiable

inconvenant, e [ɛ̃kɔ̃vnɑ̃, -ɑ̃t] adj unseemly, improper

inconvénient [ɛ̃kɔ̃venjɑ̃] nm (d'une situation, d'un projet) disadvantage, drawback; (d'un remède, changement etc) risk, inconvenience; **si vous n'y voyez pas d'~** if you have no objections; **y a-t-il un ~ à ...?** (risque) isn't there a risk in ...?; (objection) is there any objection to ...?

incorporer [ɛ̃kɔʀpɔʀe] vt: **~ (à)** to mix in (with); (paragraphe etc): **~ (dans)** to incorporate (in); (territoire, immigrants): **~ (dans)** to incorporate (into); (Mil: appeler) to recruit, call up; (: affecter): **~ qn dans** to enlist sb into

incorrect, e [ɛ̃kɔʀɛkt] adj (impropre, inconvenant) improper; (défectueux) faulty; (inexact) incorrect; (impoli) impolite; (déloyal) underhand

incorrigible [ɛ̃kɔʀiʒibl(ə)] adj incorrigible

incrédule [ɛ̃kʀedyl] adj incredulous; (Rel) unbelieving

increvable [ɛ̃kʀəvabl(ə)] adj (pneu) puncture-proof; (fam) tireless

incriminer [ɛ̃kʀimine] vt (personne) to incriminate; (action, conduite) to bring under attack; (bonne foi, honnêteté) to call into question; **livre/article incriminé** offending book/article

incroyable [ɛ̃kʀwajabl(ə)] adj incredible, unbelievable

incruster [ɛ̃kʀyste] vt (Art): **~ qch dans/qch de** to inlay sth into/sth with; (radiateur etc) to coat with scale ou fur; **s'incruster** vi (invité) to take root; (radiateur etc) to become coated with scale ou fur; **s'~ dans** (corps étranger, caillou) to become embedded in

inculpé, e [ɛ̃kylpe] nm/f accused

inculper [ɛ̃kylpe] vt: **~ (de)** to charge (with)

inculquer [ɛ̃kylke] vt: **~ qch à** to inculcate sth in, instil sth into

inculte [ɛ̃kylt(ə)] adj uncultivated; (esprit, peuple) uncultured; (barbe) unkempt

Inde [ɛ̃d] nf: **l'~** India

indécent, e [ɛ̃desɑ̃, -ɑ̃t] adj indecent

indéchiffrable [ɛ̃deʃifʀabl(ə)] adj indecipherable

indécis, e [ɛ̃desi, -iz] adj indecisive; (perplexe) undecided

indéfendable [ɛ̃defɑ̃dabl(ə)] adj indefensible

indéfini, e [ɛ̃defini] adj (imprécis, incertain) undefined; (illimité, Ling) indefinite

indéfiniment [ɛ̃definimɑ̃] adv indefinitely

indéfinissable [ɛ̃definisabl(ə)] adj indefinable

indélébile [ɛ̃delebil] adj indelible

indélicat, e [ɛ̃delika, -at] adj tactless; (malhonnête) dishonest

indemne [ɛ̃dɛmn(ə)] adj unharmed

indemniser [ɛ̃dɛmnize] vt: **~ qn (de)** to compensate sb (for); **se faire ~** to get compensation

indemnité [ɛ̃dɛmnite] *nf* (*dédommagement*)
compensation *no pl*; (*allocation*) allowance;
~ **de licenciement** redundancy payment;
~ **de logement** housing allowance; ~
parlementaire ≈ MP's (*Brit*) *ou* Congressman's
(*US*) salary

indépendamment [ɛ̃depɑ̃damɑ̃] *adv*
independently; ~ **de** independently of;
(*abstraction faite de*) irrespective of; (*en plus de*) over
and above

indépendance [ɛ̃depɑ̃dɑ̃s] *nf* independence; ~
matérielle financial independence

indépendant, e [ɛ̃depɑ̃dɑ̃, -ɑ̃t] *adj* independent;
~ **de** independent of; **chambre ~e** room with
private entrance; **travailleur** ~ self-employed
worker

indescriptible [ɛ̃dɛskʀiptibl(ə)] *adj*
indescribable

indésirable [ɛ̃deziʀabl(ə)] *adj* undesirable

indestructible [ɛ̃dɛstʀyktibl(ə)] *adj*
indestructible; (*marque, impression*) indelible

indétermination [ɛ̃detɛʀminasjɔ̃] *nf*
indecision, indecisiveness

indéterminé, e [ɛ̃detɛʀmine] *adj* unspecified;
indeterminate; indeterminable

index [ɛ̃dɛks] *nm* (*doigt*) index finger; (*d'un livre
etc*) index; **mettre à l'~** to blacklist

indexé, e [ɛ̃dɛkse] *adj* (*Écon*): ~ (**sur**) index-
linked (to)

indicateur [ɛ̃dikatœʀ] *nm* (*Police*) informer;
(*livre*) guide; (: *liste*) directory; (*Tech*) gauge;
indicator; (*Écon*) indicator ▷ *adj*: **poteau** ~
signpost; **tableau** ~ indicator (board); ~ **des
chemins de fer** railway timetable; ~ **de
direction** (*Auto*) indicator; ~ **immobilier**
property gazette; ~ **de niveau** level, gauge; ~
de pression pressure gauge; ~ **de rues** street
directory; ~ **de vitesse** speedometer

indicatif, -ive [ɛ̃dikatif, -iv] *adj*: **à titre** ~ for
(your) information ▷ *nm* (*Ling*) indicative; (*d'une
émission*) theme *ou* signature tune; (*Tél*) dialling
code; ~ **d'appel** (*Radio*) call sign

indication [ɛ̃dikasjɔ̃] *nf* indication;
(*renseignement*) information *no pl*; **indications** *nfpl*
(*directives*) instructions; ~ **d'origine** (*Comm*) place
of origin

indice [ɛ̃dis] *nm* (*marque, signe*) indication, sign;
(*Police: lors d'une enquête*) clue; (*Jur: présomption*)
piece of evidence; (*Science, Écon, Tech*) index;
(*Admin*) grading; rating; ~ **du coût de la vie**
cost-of-living index; ~ **inférieur** subscript; ~
d'octane octane rating; ~ **des prix** price index;
~ **de traitement** salary grading

indicible [ɛ̃disibl(ə)] *adj* inexpressible

indien, ne [ɛ̃djɛ̃, -ɛn] *adj* Indian ▷ *nm/f*: **I~, ne**
(*d'Amérique*) Native American; (*d'Inde*) Indian

indifféremment [ɛ̃diferamɑ̃] *adv* (*sans distinction*)
equally; indiscriminately

indifférence [ɛ̃diferɑ̃s] *nf* indifference

indifférent, e [ɛ̃diferɑ̃, -ɑ̃t] *adj* (*peu intéressé*)
indifferent; ~ **à** (*insensible à*) indifferent to,

unconcerned about; (*peu intéressant pour*)
indifferent to; immaterial to; **ça m'est** ~ (**que
...**) it doesn't matter to me (whether ...)

indigence [ɛ̃diʒɑ̃s] *nf* poverty; **être dans l'**~ to
be destitute

indigène [ɛ̃diʒɛn] *adj* native, indigenous; (*de la
région*) local ▷ *nm/f* native

indigeste [ɛ̃diʒɛst(ə)] *adj* indigestible

indigestion [ɛ̃diʒɛstjɔ̃] *nf* indigestion *no pl*;
avoir une ~ to have indigestion

indigne [ɛ̃diɲ] *adj*: ~ (**de**) unworthy (of)

indigner [ɛ̃diɲe] *vt* to make indignant;
s'indigner (de/contre) *vi* to be (*ou* become)
indignant (at)

indiqué, e [ɛ̃dike] *adj* (*date, lieu*) given, appointed;
(*adéquat*) appropriate, suitable; (*conseillé*)
advisable; (*remède, traitement*) appropriate

indiquer [ɛ̃dike] *vt* (*désigner*): ~ **qch/qn à qn** to
point sth/sb out to sb; (*pendule, aiguille*) to show;
(*étiquette, plan*) to show, indicate; (*faire connaître*:
médecin, lieu): ~ **qch/qn à qn** to tell sb of sth/sb;
(*renseigner sur*) to point out, tell; (*déterminer: date,
lieu*) to give, state; (*dénoter*) to indicate, point to;
~ **du doigt** to point out; ~ **de la main** to indicate
with one's hand; ~ **du regard** to glance towards
ou in the direction of; **pourriez-vous m'**~ **les
toilettes/l'heure?** could you direct me to the
toilets/tell me the time?

indirect, e [ɛ̃diʀɛkt] *adj* indirect

indiscipliné, e [ɛ̃disipline] *adj* undisciplined;
(*fig*) unmanageable

indiscret, -ète [ɛ̃diskʀɛ, -ɛt] *adj* indiscreet

indiscutable [ɛ̃diskytabl(ə)] *adj* indisputable

indispensable [ɛ̃dispɑ̃sabl(ə)] *adj* indispensable,
essential; ~ **à qn/pour faire qch** essential for
sb/to do sth

indisposé, e [ɛ̃dispoze] *adj* indisposed, unwell

indisposer [ɛ̃dispoze] *vt* (*incommoder*) to upset;
(*déplaire à*) to antagonize

indistinct, e [ɛ̃distɛ̃, -ɛ̃kt(ə)] *adj* indistinct

indistinctement [ɛ̃distɛ̃ktəmɑ̃] *adv* (*voir,
prononcer*) indistinctly; (*sans distinction*) without
distinction, indiscriminately

individu [ɛ̃dividy] *nm* individual

individuel, le [ɛ̃dividɥɛl] *adj* (*gén*) individual;
(*opinion, livret, contrôle, avantages*) personal;
chambre ~le single room; **maison ~le** detached
house; **propriété ~le** personal *ou* private
property

indolore [ɛ̃dɔlɔʀ] *adj* painless

indomptable [ɛ̃dɔ̃tabl(ə)] *adj* untameable; (*fig*)
invincible, indomitable

Indonésie [ɛ̃donezi] *nf*: **l'**~ Indonesia

indu, e [ɛ̃dy] *adj*: **à des heures ~es** at an ungodly
hour

induire [ɛ̃dɥiʀ] *vt*: ~ **qch de** to induce sth from; ~
qn en erreur to lead sb astray, mislead sb

indulgent, e [ɛ̃dylʒɑ̃, -ɑ̃t] *adj* (*parent, regard*)
indulgent; (*juge, examinateur*) lenient

industrialisé, e [ɛ̃dystʀijalize] *adj*
industrialized

industrie [ɛ̃dystʀi] *nf* industry; ~ **automobile/**

textile car/textile industry; **~ du spectacle** entertainment business

industriel, le [ɛ̃dystʀijɛl] *adj* industrial; (*produit industriellement: pain etc*) mass-produced, factory-produced ▷ *nm* industrialist; (*fabricant*) manufacturer

inébranlable [inebʀɑ̃labl(ə)] *adj* (*masse, colonne*) solid; (*personne, certitude, foi*) steadfast, unwavering

inédit, e [inedi, -it] *adj* (*correspondance etc*) (hitherto) unpublished; (*spectacle, moyen*) novel, original

ineffaçable [inefasabl(ə)] *adj* indelible

inefficace [inefikas] *adj* (*remède, moyen*) ineffective; (*machine, employé*) inefficient

inégal, e, -aux [inegal, -o] *adj* unequal; (*irrégulier*) uneven

inégalable [inegalabl(e)] *adj* matchless

inégalé, e [inegale] *adj* unmatched, unequalled

inégalité [inegalite] *nf* inequality; unevenness *no pl*; **~ de deux hauteurs** difference *ou* disparity between two heights; **~s de terrain** uneven ground

inépuisable [inepɥizabl(ə)] *adj* inexhaustible

inerte [inɛʀt(ə)] *adj* lifeless; (*apathique*) passive, inert; (*Physique, Chimie*) inert

inespéré, e [inɛspeʀe] *adj* unhoped-for, unexpected

inestimable [inɛstimabl(e)] *adj* priceless; (*fig: bienfait*) invaluable

inévitable [inevitabl(ə)] *adj* unavoidable; (*fatal, habituel*) inevitable

inexact, e [inɛgzakt] *adj* inaccurate, inexact; (*non ponctuel*) unpunctual

inexcusable [inɛkskyzabl(ə)] *adj* inexcusable, unforgivable

inexplicable [inɛksplikabl(ə)] *adj* inexplicable

in extremis [inɛkstʀemis] *adv* at the last minute ▷ *adj* last-minute; (*testament*) death bed *cpd*

infaillible [ɛ̃fajibl(ə)] *adj* infallible; (*instinct*) infallible, unerring

infâme [ɛ̃fɑm] *adj* vile

infarctus [ɛ̃faʀktys] *nm*: **~ (du myocarde)** coronary (thrombosis)

infatigable [ɛ̃fatigabl(ə)] *adj* tireless, indefatigable

infect, e [ɛ̃fɛkt] *adj* vile, foul; (*repas, vin*) revolting, foul

infecter [ɛ̃fɛkte] *vt* (*atmosphère, eau*) to contaminate; (*Méd*) to infect; **s'infecter** *vi* to become infected *ou* septic

infection [ɛ̃fɛksjɔ̃] *nf* infection

inférieur, e [ɛ̃feʀjœʀ] *adj* lower; (*en qualité, intelligence*) inferior ▷ *nm/f* inferior; **~ à** (*somme, quantité*) less *ou* smaller than; (*moins bon que*) inferior to; (*tâche: pas à la hauteur de*) unequal to

infernal, e, -aux [ɛ̃fɛʀnal, -o] *adj* (*chaleur, rythme*) infernal; (*méchanceté, complot*) diabolical

infidèle [ɛ̃fidɛl] *adj* unfaithful; (*Rel*) infidel

infiltrer [ɛ̃filtʀe]: **s'infiltrer** *vi*: **s'~ dans** to penetrate into; (*liquide*) to seep into; (*fig: noyauter*) to infiltrate

infime [ɛ̃fim] *adj* minute, tiny; (*inférieur*) lowly

infini, e [ɛ̃fini] *adj* infinite ▷ *nm* infinity; **à l'~** (*Math*) to infinity; (*discourir*) ad infinitum, endlessly; (*agrandir, varier*) infinitely; (*à perte de vue*) endlessly (into the distance)

infiniment [ɛ̃finimɑ̃] *adv* infinitely; **~ grand/ petit** (*Math*) infinitely great/infinitessimal

infinité [ɛ̃finite] *nf*: **une ~ de** an infinite number of

infinitif, -ive [ɛ̃finitif, -iv] *adj, nm* infinitive

infirme [ɛ̃fiʀm(ə)] *adj* disabled ▷ *nm/f* disabled person; **~ de guerre** war cripple; **~ du travail** industrially disabled person

infirmerie [ɛ̃fiʀməʀi] *nf* sick bay

infirmier, -ière [ɛ̃fiʀmje, -jɛʀ] *nm/f* nurse ▷ *adj*: **élève ~** student nurse; **infirmière chef** sister; **infirmière diplômée** registered nurse; **infirmière visiteuse** visiting nurse, = district nurse (*Brit*)

infirmité [ɛ̃fiʀmite] *nf* disability

inflammable [ɛ̃flamabl(ə)] *adj* (in)flammable

inflation [ɛ̃flɑsjɔ̃] *nf* inflation; **~ rampante/ galopante** creeping/galloping inflation

infliger [ɛ̃fliʒe] *vt*: **~ qch (à qn)** to inflict sth (on sb); (*amende, sanction*) to impose sth (on sb)

influençable [ɛ̃flyɑ̃sabl(ə)] *adj* easily influenced

influence [ɛ̃flyɑ̃s] *nf* influence; (*d'un médicament*) effect

influencer [ɛ̃flyɑ̃se] *vt* to influence

influent, e [ɛ̃flyɑ̃, -ɑ̃t] *adj* influential

informateur, -trice [ɛ̃fɔʀmatœʀ, -tʀis] *nm/f* informant

informaticien, ne [ɛ̃fɔʀmatisjɛ̃, -ɛn] *nm/f* computer scientist

information [ɛ̃fɔʀmasjɔ̃] *nf* (*renseignement*) piece of information; (*Presse, TV: nouvelle*) item of news; (*diffusion de renseignements, Inform*) information; (*Jur*) inquiry, investigation; **informations** *nfpl* (TV) news *sg*; **voyage d'~** fact-finding trip; **agence d'~** news agency; **journal d'~** quality (Brit) *ou* serious newspaper

informatique [ɛ̃fɔʀmatik] *nf* (*technique*) data processing; (*science*) computer science ▷ *adj* computer *cpd*

informatiser [ɛ̃fɔʀmatize] *vt* to computerize

informe [ɛ̃fɔʀm(ə)] *adj* shapeless

informer [ɛ̃fɔʀme] *vt*: **~ qn (de)** to inform sb (of) ▷ *vi* (*Jur*): **~ contre qn/sur qch** to initiate inquiries about sb/sth; **s'informer (sur)** to inform o.s. (about); **s'~ (de qch/si)** to inquire *ou* find out (about sth/whether *ou* if)

infos [ɛ̃fo] *nfpl* (= **informations**) news

infraction [ɛ̃fʀaksjɔ̃] *nf* offence; **~ à** violation *ou* breach of; **être en ~** to be in breach of the law

infranchissable [ɛ̃fʀɑ̃ʃisabl(ə)] *adj* impassable; (*fig*) insuperable

infrarouge [ɛ̃fʀaʀuʒ] *adj, nm* infrared

infrastructure [ɛ̃fʀastʀyktyʀ] *nf* (*d'une route etc*) substructure; (*Aviat, Mil*) ground installations *pl*; (*touristique etc*) facilities *pl*

infuser [ɛ̃fyze] *vt* (*aussi:* **faire infuser**: *thé*) to brew; (: *tisane*) to infuse ▷ *vi* to brew; to infuse; **laisser**

~ (to leave) to brew

infusion [ɛ̃fyzjɔ̃] *nf* (*tisane*) infusion, herb tea

ingénier [ɛ̃ʒenje]: **s'ingénier** *vi*: **s'~ à faire** to strive to do

ingénierie [ɛ̃ʒeniʀi] *nf* engineering

ingénieur [ɛ̃ʒenjœʀ] *nm* engineer; **~ agronome/ chimiste** agricultural/chemical engineer; **~ conseil** consulting engineer; **~ du son** sound engineer

ingénieux, -euse [ɛ̃ʒenjø, -øz] *adj* ingenious, clever

ingénu, e [ɛ̃ʒeny] *adj* ingenuous, artless ▷ *nf* (*Théât*) ingénue

ingérer [ɛ̃ʒeʀe]: **s'ingérer** *vi*: **s'~ dans** to interfere in

ingrat, e [ɛ̃gʀa, -at] *adj* (*personne*) ungrateful; (*sol*) poor; (*travail, sujet*) arid, thankless; (*visage*) unprepossessing

ingrédient [ɛ̃gʀedjɑ̃] *nm* ingredient

ingurgiter [ɛ̃gyʀʒite] *vt* to swallow; **faire ~ qch à qn** to make sb swallow sth; (*fig: connaissances*) to force sth into sb

inhabitable [inabitabl(ə)] *adj* uninhabitable

inhabité, e [inabite] *adj* (*régions*) uninhabited; (*maison*) unoccupied

inhabituel, le [inabityɛl] *adj* unusual

inhibition [inibisjɔ̃] *nf* inhibition

inhumain, e [inymɛ̃, -ɛn] *adj* inhuman

inhumation [inymasjɔ̃] *nf* interment, burial

inhumer [inyme] *vt* to inter, bury

inimaginable [inimaʒinabl(ə)] *adj* unimaginable

ininterrompu, e [inɛ̃teʀɔ̃py] *adj* (*file, série*) unbroken; (*flot, vacarme*) uninterrupted, non-stop; (*effort*) unremitting, continuous

initial, e, -aux [inisjal, -o] *adj, nf* initial; **initiales** *nfpl* initials

initialiser [inisjalize] *vt* to initialize

initiation [inisjasjɔ̃] *nf* initiation

initiative [inisjativ] *nf* initiative; **prendre l'~ de qch/de faire** to take the initiative for sth/of doing; **avoir de l'~** to have initiative, show enterprise; **esprit/qualités d'~** spirit/qualities of initiative; **à** *ou* **sur l'~ de qn** on sb's initiative; **de sa propre ~** on one's own initiative

initier [inisje] *vt* to initiate; **~ qn à** to initiate sb into; (*faire découvrir: art, jeu*) to introduce sb to; **s'initier à** *vi* (*métier, profession, technique*) to become initiated into

injecté, e [ɛ̃ʒɛkte] *adj*: **yeux ~s de sang** bloodshot eyes

injecter [ɛ̃ʒɛkte] *vt* to inject

injection [ɛ̃ʒɛksjɔ̃] *nf* injection; **à ~** (*Auto*) fuel injection *cpd*

injure [ɛ̃ʒyʀ] *nf* insult, abuse *no pl*

injurier [ɛ̃ʒyʀje] *vt* to insult, abuse

injurieux, -euse [ɛ̃ʒyʀjø, -øz] *adj* abusive, insulting

injuste [ɛ̃ʒyst(ə)] *adj* unjust, unfair

injustice [ɛ̃ʒystis] *nf* injustice

inlassable [ɛ̃lɑsabl(ə)] *adj* tireless, indefatigable

inné, e [ine] *adj* innate, inborn

innocent, e [inɔsɑ̃, -ɑ̃t] *adj* innocent ▷ *nm/f* innocent person; **faire l'~** to play *ou* come the innocent

innocenter [inɔsɑ̃te] *vt* to clear, prove innocent

innombrable [inɔ̃bʀabl(ə)] *adj* innumerable

innommable [inɔmabl(ə)] *adj* unspeakable

innover [inɔve] *vi*: **~ en matière d'art** to break new ground in the field of art

inoccupé, e [inɔkype] *adj* unoccupied

inodore [inɔdɔʀ] *adj* (*gaz*) odourless; (*fleur*) scentless

inoffensif, -ive [inɔfɑ̃sif, -iv] *adj* harmless, innocuous

inondation [inɔ̃dɑsjɔ̃] *nf* flooding *no pl*; (*torrent, eau*) flood

inonder [inɔ̃de] *vt* to flood; (*fig*) to inundate, overrun; **~ de** (*fig*) to flood *ou* swamp with

inopiné, e [inɔpine] *adj* unexpected, sudden

inopportun, e [inɔpɔʀtœ̃, -yn] *adj* ill-timed, untimely; inappropriate; (*moment*) inopportune

inoubliable [inublijabl(ə)] *adj* unforgettable

inouï, e [inwi] *adj* unheard-of, extraordinary

inox [inɔks] *adj, nm* (= *inoxydable*) stainless (steel)

inqualifiable [ɛ̃kalifjabl(ə)] *adj* unspeakable

inquiet, -ète [ɛ̃kjɛ, -ɛt] *adj* (*par nature*) anxious; (*momentanément*) worried; **~ de qch/au sujet de qn** worried about sth/sb

inquiétant, e [ɛ̃kjetɑ̃, -ɑ̃t] *adj* worrying, disturbing

inquiéter [ɛ̃kjete] *vt* to worry, disturb; (*harceler*) to harass; **s'inquiéter** to worry, become anxious; **s'~ de** to worry about; (*s'enquérir de*) to inquire about

inquiétude [ɛ̃kjetyd] *nf* anxiety; **donner de l'~** *ou* **des ~s à** to worry; **avoir de l'~** *ou* **des ~s au sujet de** to feel anxious *ou* worried about

insaisissable [ɛ̃sezisabl(ə)] *adj* elusive

insalubre [ɛ̃salybʀ(ə)] *adj* unhealthy, insalubrious

insatisfait, e [ɛ̃satisfɛ, -ɛt] *adj* (*non comblé*) unsatisfied; (: *passion, envie*) unfulfilled; (*mécontent*) dissatisfied

inscription [ɛ̃skʀipsjɔ̃] *nf* (*sur un mur, écriteau etc*) inscription; (*à une institution: voir s'inscrire*) enrolment; registration

inscrire [ɛ̃skʀiʀ] *vt* (*marquer: sur son calepin etc*) to note *ou* write down; (: *sur un mur, une affiche etc*) to write; (: *dans la pierre, le métal*) to inscribe; (*mettre: sur une liste, un budget etc*) to put down; (*enrôler: soldat*) to enlist; **~ qn à** (*club, école etc*) to enrol sb at; **s'inscrire** *vi* (*pour une excursion etc*) to put one's name down; **s'~ (à)** (*club, parti*) to join; (*université*) to register *ou* enrol (at); (*examen, concours*) to register *ou* enter (for); **s'~ dans** (*se situer: négociations etc*) to come within the scope of; **s'~ en faux contre** to deny (strongly); (*Jur*) to challenge

insecte [ɛ̃sɛkt(ə)] *nm* insect

insecticide [ɛ̃sɛktisid] *nm* insecticide

insensé, e [ɛ̃sɑ̃se] *adj* insane, mad

insensibiliser [ɛ̃sɑ̃sibilize] *vt* to anaesthetize; (*à une allergie*) to desensitize; **~ à qch** (*fig*) to cause to become insensitive to sth

insensible [ɛ̃sɑ̃sibl(ə)] *adj* (*nerf, membre*) numb; (*dur, indifférent*) insensitive; (*imperceptible*) imperceptible

inséparable [ɛ̃separabl(ə)] *adj*: ~ **(de)** inseparable (from) ▷ *nmpl*: **~s** (*oiseaux*) lovebirds

insigne [ɛ̃siɲ] *nm* (*d'un parti, club*) badge ▷ *adj* distinguished; **insignes** *nmpl* (*d'une fonction*) insignia *pl*

insignifiant, e [ɛ̃siɲifjɑ̃, -ɑ̃t] *adj* insignificant; (*somme, affaire, détail*) trivial, insignificant

insinuer [ɛ̃sinɥe] *vt* to insinuate, imply; **s'insinuer dans** *vi* to seep into; (*fig*) to worm one's way into, creep into

insipide [ɛ̃sipid] *adj* insipid

insister [ɛ̃siste] *vi* to insist; (*s'obstiner*) to keep on; ~ **sur** (*détail, note*) to stress; ~ **pour qch/pour faire qch** to be insistent about sth/about doing sth

insolation [ɛ̃sɔlasjɔ̃] *nf* (*Méd*) sunstroke *no pl*; (*ensoleillement*) period of sunshine

insolent, e [ɛ̃sɔlɑ̃, -ɑ̃t] *adj* insolent

insolite [ɛ̃sɔlit] *adj* strange, unusual

insomnie [ɛ̃sɔmni] *nf* insomnia *no pl*, sleeplessness *no pl*; **avoir des ~s** to suffer from insomnia

insonoriser [ɛ̃sɔnɔrize] *vt* to soundproof

insouciant, e [ɛ̃susjɑ̃, -ɑ̃t] *adj* carefree; (*imprévoyant*) heedless

insoumis, e [ɛ̃sumi, -iz] *adj* (*caractère, enfant*) rebellious, refractory; (*contrée, tribu*) unsubdued; (*Mil: soldat*) absent without leave ▷ *nm* (*Mil: soldat*) absentee

insoupçonnable [ɛ̃supsɔnabl(ə)] *adj* above suspicion

insoupçonné, e [ɛ̃supsɔne] *adj* unsuspected

insoutenable [ɛ̃sutnabl(ə)] *adj* (*argument*) untenable; (*chaleur*) unbearable

inspecter [ɛ̃spɛkte] *vt* to inspect

inspecteur, -trice [ɛ̃spɛktœr, -tris] *nm/f* inspector; (*des assurances*) assessor; ~ **d'Académie** (regional) director of education; ~ **(de l'enseignement) primaire** primary school inspector; ~ **des finances** ≈ tax inspector (*Brit*), ≈ Internal Revenue Service agent (*US*); ~ **(de police)** (police) inspector

inspection [ɛ̃spɛksjɔ̃] *nf* inspection

inspirer [ɛ̃spire] *vt* (*gén*) to inspire ▷ *vi* (*aspirer*) to breathe in; **s'inspirer de** (*artiste*) to draw one's inspiration from; (*tableau*) to be inspired by; ~ **qch à qn** (*œuvre, project, action*) to inspire sb with sth; (*dégoût, crainte, horreur*) to fill sb with sth; **ça ne m'inspire pas** I'm not keen on the idea

instable [ɛ̃stabl(ə)] *adj* (*meuble, équilibre*) unsteady; (*population, temps*) unsettled; (*paix, régime, caractère*) unstable

installation [ɛ̃stalasjɔ̃] *nf* installation; putting in *ou* up; fitting out; settling in; (*appareils etc*) fittings *pl*, installations *pl*; **installations** *nfpl* (*industrielles*) plant *sg*; (*de loisirs*) facilities

installer [ɛ̃stale] *vt* (*loger*): ~ **qn** to get sb settled, install sb; (*asseoir, coucher*) to settle (down); (*placer*) to put, place; (*meuble*) to put in; (*rideau, étagère, tente*) to put up; (*gaz, électricité etc*) to put in, install; (*appartement*) to fit out; (*aménager*): ~ **une salle de bains dans une pièce** to fit out a room with a bathroom suite; **s'installer** *vi* (*s'établir: artisan, dentiste etc*) to set o.s. up; (*se loger*): **s'~ à l'hôtel/chez qn** to move into a hotel/in with sb; (*emménager*) to settle in; (*sur un siège, à un emplacement*) to settle (down); (*fig: maladie, grève*) to take a firm hold *ou* grip

instance [ɛ̃stɑ̃s] *nf* (*Jur: procédure*) (legal) proceedings *pl*; (*autorité*) authority; **instances** *nfpl* (*prières*) entreaties; **affaire en ~** matter pending; **courrier en ~** mail ready for posting; **être en ~ de divorce** to be awaiting a divorce; **train en ~ de départ** train on the point of departure; **tribunal de première ~** court of first instance; **en seconde ~** on appeal

instant [ɛ̃stɑ̃] *nm* moment, instant; **dans un ~** in a moment; **à l'~** this instant; **je l'ai vu à l'~** I've just this minute seen him, I saw him a moment ago; **à l'~ (même) où** at the (very) moment that *ou* when, (just) as; **à chaque ~**, **à tout ~** at any moment; constantly; **pour l'~** for the moment, for the time being; **par ~s** at times; **de tous les ~s** perpetual; **dès l'~ où** *ou* **que ...** from the moment when ..., since that moment when ...

instantané, e [ɛ̃stɑ̃tane] *adj* (*lait, café*) instant; (*explosion, mort*) instantaneous ▷ *nm* snapshot

instar [ɛ̃star]: **à l'~ de** *prép* following the example of, like

instaurer [ɛ̃stɔre] *vt* to institute; **s'instaurer** *vi* to set o.s. up; (*collaboration etc*) to be established

instinct [ɛ̃stɛ̃] *nm* instinct; **d'~** (*spontanément*) instinctively; ~ **grégaire** herd instinct; ~ **de conservation** instinct of self-preservation

instinctivement [ɛ̃stɛ̃ktivmɑ̃] *adv* instinctively

instit [ɛ̃stit] (*fam*) *nm/f* (primary school) teacher

instituer [ɛ̃stitɥe] *vt* to institute, set up; **s'~ défenseur d'une cause** to set o.s up as defender of a cause

institut [ɛ̃stity] *nm* institute; ~ **de beauté** beauty salon; ~ **médico-légal** mortuary; **I-universitaire de technologie (IUT)** technical college

instituteur, -trice [ɛ̃stitytœr, -tris] *nm/f* (primary (*Brit*) *ou* grade (*US*) school) teacher

institution [ɛ̃stitysjɔ̃] *nf* institution; (*collège*) private school

instructif, -ive [ɛ̃stryktif, -iv] *adj* instructive

instruction [ɛ̃stryksjɔ̃] *nf* (*enseignement, savoir*) education; (*Jur*) (preliminary) investigation and hearing; (*directive*) instruction; (*Admin: document*) directive; **instructions** *nfpl* instructions; (*mode d'emploi*) directions, instructions; ~ **civique** civics *sg*; ~ **primaire/publique** primary/public education; ~ **religieuse** religious instruction; ~ **professionnelle** vocational training

instruire [ɛ̃strɥir] *vt* (*élèves*) to teach; (*recrues*) to train; (*Jur: affaire*) to conduct the investigation for; **s'instruire** to educate o.s.; **s'~ auprès de qn de qch** (*s'informer*) to find sth out from sb; **~ qn de qch** (*informer*) to inform *ou* advise sb of sth; **~ contre qn** (*Jur*) to investigate sb

instruit, e [ɛ̃strɥi, -it] *pp de* **instruire** ▷ *adj* educated

instrument [ɛ̃strymɑ̃] *nm* instrument; **~ à cordes/vent** stringed/wind instrument; **~ de mesure** measuring instrument; **~ de musique** musical instrument; **~ de travail** (working) tool

insu [ɛ̃sy] *nm*: **à l'~ de qn** without sb knowing

insubmersible [ɛ̃sybmɛrsibl(ə)] *adj* unsinkable

insuffisant, e [ɛ̃syfizɑ̃, -ɑ̃t] *adj* insufficient; (*élève, travail*) inadequate

insulaire [ɛ̃sylɛr] *adj* island *cpd*; (*attitude*) insular

insuline [ɛ̃sylin] *nf* insulin

insulte [ɛ̃sylt(ə)] *nf* insult

insulter [ɛ̃sylte] *vt* to insult

insupportable [ɛ̃sypɔrtabl(ə)] *adj* unbearable

insurger [ɛ̃syrʒe]: **s'insurger** *vi*: **s'~ (contre)** to rise up *ou* rebel (against)

insurmontable [ɛ̃syrmɔ̃tabl(ə)] *adj* (*difficulté*) insuperable; (*aversion*) unconquerable

insurrection [ɛ̃syrɛksjɔ̃] *nf* insurrection, revolt

intact, e [ɛ̃takt] *adj* intact

intangible [ɛ̃tɑ̃ʒibl(ə)] *adj* intangible; (*principe*) inviolable

intarissable [ɛ̃tarisabl(ə)] *adj* inexhaustible

intégral, e, -aux [ɛ̃tegral, -o] *adj* complete ▷ *nf* (*Math*) integral; (*œuvres complètes*) complete works

intégralement [ɛ̃tegralmɑ̃] *adv* in full, fully

intégralité [ɛ̃tegralite] *nf* (*d'une somme, d'un revenu*) whole (*ou* full) amount; **dans son ~** in its entirety

intégrant, e [ɛ̃tegrɑ̃, -ɑ̃t] *adj*: **faire partie ~e de** to be an integral part of, be part and parcel of

intègre [ɛ̃tɛgr(ə)] *adj* perfectly honest, upright

intégrer [ɛ̃tegre] *vt*: **~ qch à** *ou* **dans** to integrate sth into; **s'~ à** *ou* **dans** to become integrated into

intégrisme [ɛ̃tegrism(ə)] *nm* fundamentalism

intellectuel, le [ɛ̃telɛktɥel] *adj, nm/f* intellectual; (*péj*) highbrow

intelligence [ɛ̃teliʒɑ̃s] *nf* intelligence; (*compréhension*): **l'~ de** the understanding of; (*complicité*): **regard d'~** glance of complicity, meaningful *ou* knowing look; (*accord*): **vivre en bonne ~ avec qn** to be on good terms with sb; **intelligences** *nfpl* (*Mil, fig*) secret contacts; **être d'~** to have an understanding; **~ artificielle** artificial intelligence (A.I.)

intelligent, e [ɛ̃teliʒɑ̃, -ɑ̃t] *adj* intelligent; (*capable*): **~ en affaires** competent in business

intelligible [ɛ̃teliʒibl(ə)] *adj* intelligible

intempéries [ɛ̃tɑ̃peri] *nfpl* bad weather *sg*

intempestif, -ive [ɛ̃tɑ̃pɛstif, -iv] *adj* untimely

intenable [ɛ̃tnabl(ə)] *adj* unbearable

intendant, e [ɛ̃tɑ̃dɑ̃, -ɑ̃t] *nm/f* (*Mil*) quartermaster; (*Scol*) bursar; (*d'une propriété*) steward

intense [ɛ̃tɑ̃s] *adj* intense

intensif, -ive [ɛ̃tɑ̃sif, -iv] *adj* intensive; **cours ~** crash course; **~ en main-d'œuvre** labour-

intensive; **~ en capital** capital-intensive

intenter [ɛ̃tɑ̃te] *vt*: **~ un procès contre** *ou* **à qn** to start proceedings against sb

intention [ɛ̃tɑ̃sjɔ̃] *nf* intention; (*Jur*) intent; **avoir l'~ de faire** to intend to do, have the intention of doing; **dans l'~ de faire qch** with a view to doing sth; **à l'~ de** *prép* for; (*renseignement*) for the benefit *ou* information of; (*film, ouvrage*) aimed at; **à cette ~** with this aim in view; **sans ~** unintentionally; **faire qch sans mauvaise ~** to do sth without ill intent; **agir dans une bonne ~** to act with good intentions

intentionné, e [ɛ̃tɑ̃sjɔne] *adj*: **bien ~** well-meaning *ou* -intentioned; **mal ~** ill-intentioned

interactif, -ive [ɛ̃teraktif, -iv] *adj* (*aussi Inform*) interactive

intercalaire [ɛ̃terkalɛr] *adj, nm*: (**feuillet**) **~** insert; (**fiche**) **~** divider

intercaler [ɛ̃terkale] *vt* to insert; **s'intercaler entre** *vi* to come in between; to slip in between

intercepter [ɛ̃tersepte] *vt* to intercept; (*lumière, chaleur*) to cut off

interchangeable [ɛ̃terʃɑ̃ʒabl(ə)] *adj* interchangeable

interclasse [ɛ̃terklas] *nm* (*Scol*) break (between classes)

interdiction [ɛ̃terdiksjɔ̃] *nf* ban; **~ de faire qch** ban on doing sth; **~ de séjour** (*Jur*) order banning ex-prisoner from frequenting specified places

interdire [ɛ̃terdir] *vt* to forbid; (*Admin: stationnement, meeting, passage*) to ban, prohibit; (*: journal, livre*) to ban; **~ qch à qn** to forbid sb sth; **~ à qn de faire** to forbid sb to do, prohibit sb from doing; (*empêchement*) to prevent *ou* preclude sb from doing; **s'interdire qch** *vi* (*éviter*) to refrain *ou* abstain from sth; (*se refuser*): **il s'interdit d'y penser** he doesn't allow himself to think about it

interdit, e [ɛ̃terdi, -it] *pp de* **interdire** ▷ *adj* (*stupéfait*) taken aback; (*défendu*) forbidden, prohibited ▷ *nm* interdict, prohibition; **film ~ aux moins de 18/13 ans** ≈ 18-/PG-rated film; **sens ~** one way; **stationnement ~** no parking; **~ de chéquier** having cheque book facilities suspended; **~ de séjour** subject to an "interdiction de séjour"

intéressant, e [ɛ̃teresɑ̃, -ɑ̃t] *adj* interesting; **faire l'~** to draw attention to o.s.

intéressé, e [ɛ̃terese] *adj* (*parties*) involved, concerned; (*amitié, motifs*) self-interested ▷ *nm*: **l'~** the interested party; **les ~s** those concerned *ou* involved

intéresser [ɛ̃terese] *vt* to interest; (*toucher*) to be of interest *ou* concern to; (*Admin: concerner*) to affect, concern; (*Comm: travailleur*) to give a share in the profits to; (*: partenaire*) to interest (in the business); **s'intéresser à** *vi* to take an interest in, be interested in; **~ qn à qch** to get sb interested in sth

intérêt [ɛ̃terɛ] *nm* (*aussi Comm*) interest; (*égoïsme*) self-interest; **porter de l'~ à qn** to take an interest in sb; **agir par ~** to act out of self-interest; **avoir des ~s dans** (Comm) to have a financial interest ou a stake in; **avoir ~ à faire** to do well to do; **il y a ~ à ...** it would be a good thing to ...; **~ composé** compound interest

intérieur, e [ɛ̃terjœr] adj (mur, escalier, poche) inside; (commerce, politique) domestic; (cour, calme, vie) inner; (navigation) inland ▷ nm (d'une maison, d'un récipient etc) inside; (d'un pays, aussi: décor, mobilier) interior; (Pol): **l'I~** (the Department of) the Interior, ≈ the Home Office (Brit); **à l'~ (de)** inside; (fig) within; **de l'~** (fig) from the inside; **en ~** (Ciné) in the studio; **vêtement d'~** indoor garment

intérieurement [ɛ̃terjœrmɑ̃] adv inwardly

intérim [ɛ̃terim] nm (période) interim period; (travail) temping; **agence d'~** temping agency; **assurer l'~ (de)** to deputize (for); **président par ~** interim president; **travailler en ~** to temp

intérimaire [ɛ̃terimɛr] adj temporary, interim ▷ nm/f (secrétaire etc) temporary, temp (Brit); (suppléant) deputy

interlocuteur, -trice [ɛ̃terlɔkytœr, -tris] nm/f speaker; (Pol): **~ valable** valid representative; **son ~** the person he ou she was speaking to

interloquer [ɛ̃terlɔke] vt to take aback

intermède [ɛ̃termɛd] nm interlude

intermédiaire [ɛ̃termedjɛr] adj intermediate; middle; half-way ▷ nm/f intermediary; (Comm) middleman; **sans ~** directly; **par l'~ de** through

interminable [ɛ̃terminabl(ə)] adj never-ending

intermittence [ɛ̃termitɑ̃s] nf: **par ~** intermittently, sporadically

internat [ɛ̃terna] nm (Scol) boarding school

international, e, -aux [ɛ̃ternasjɔnal, -o] adj, nm/f international

interne [ɛ̃tern(ə)] adj internal ▷ nm/f (Scol) boarder; (Méd) houseman (Brit), intern (US)

interner [ɛ̃terne] vt (Pol) to intern; (Méd) to confine to a mental institution

Internet [ɛ̃ternɛt] nm: **l'~** the Internet

interpeller [ɛ̃terpele] vt (appeler) to call out to; (apostropher) to shout at; (Police) to take in for questioning; (Pol) to question; **s'interpeller** vi to exchange insults

interphone [ɛ̃terfɔn] nm intercom

interposer [ɛ̃terpoze] vt to interpose; **s'interposer** vi to intervene; **par personnes interposées** through a third party

interprétation [ɛ̃terpretasjɔ̃] nf interpretation

interprète [ɛ̃terprɛt] nm/f interpreter; (porte-parole) spokesman

interpréter [ɛ̃terprete] vt to interpret

interrogateur, -trice [ɛ̃terɔgatœr, -tris] adj questioning, inquiring ▷ nm/f (Scol) (oral) examiner

interrogatif, -ive [ɛ̃terɔgatif, -iv] adj (Ling) interrogative

interrogation [ɛ̃terɔgasjɔ̃] nf question; (Scol) (written ou oral) test

interrogatoire [ɛ̃terɔgatwar] nm (Police) questioning no pl; (Jur) cross-examination, interrogation

interroger [ɛ̃terɔʒe] vt to question; (Inform) to search; (Scol: candidat) to test; **~ qn (sur qch)** to question sb (about sth); **~ qn du regard** to look questioningly at sb, give sb a questioning look; **s'~ sur qch** to ask o.s. about sth, ponder (about) sth

interrompre [ɛ̃terɔ̃pr(ə)] vt (gén) to interrupt; (travail, voyage) to break off, interrupt; **s'interrompre** vi to break off

interrupteur [ɛ̃teryptœr] nm switch

interruption [ɛ̃terypsjɔ̃] nf interruption; **sans ~** without a break; **~ de grossesse** termination of pregnancy; **~ volontaire de grossesse** voluntary termination of pregnancy, abortion

intersection [ɛ̃terseksjɔ̃] nf intersection

interstice [ɛ̃terstis] nm crack, slit

interurbain [ɛ̃teryrbɛ̃] (Tél) nm long-distance call service ▷ adj long-distance

intervalle [ɛ̃terval] nm (espace) space; (de temps) interval; **dans l'~** in the meantime; **à deux mois d'~** after a space of two months; **à ~s rapprochés** at close intervals; **par ~s** at intervals

intervenir [ɛ̃tervənir] vi (gén) to intervene; (survenir) to take place; (faire une conférence) to give a talk ou lecture; **~ auprès de/en faveur de qn** to intervene with/on behalf of sb; **la police a dû ~** police had to step in ou intervene; **les médecins ont dû ~** the doctors had to operate

intervention [ɛ̃tervɑ̃sjɔ̃] nf intervention; (conférence) talk, paper; **~ (chirurgicale)** operation

intervertir [ɛ̃tervertir] vt to invert (the order of), reverse

interview [ɛ̃tervju] nf interview

interviewer [ɛ̃tervjuve] vt to interview ▷ nm [ɛ̃tervjuvœr] (journaliste) interviewer

intestin, e [ɛ̃testɛ̃, -in] adj internal ▷ nm intestine; **~ grêle** small intestine

intime [ɛ̃tim] adj intimate; (vie, journal) private; (convictions) inmost; (dîner, cérémonie) held among friends, quiet ▷ nm/f close friend

intimider [ɛ̃timide] vt to intimidate

intimité [ɛ̃timite] nf intimacy; (vie privée) privacy; private life; **dans l'~** in private; (sans formalités) with only a few friends, quietly

intitulé [ɛ̃tityle] nm title

intolérable [ɛ̃tɔlerabl(ə)] adj intolerable

intox [ɛ̃tɔks] (fam) nf brainwashing

intoxication [ɛ̃tɔksikasjɔ̃] nf poisoning no pl; (toxicomanie) drug addiction; (fig) brainwashing; **~ alimentaire** food poisoning

intoxiquer [ɛ̃tɔksike] vt to poison; (fig) to brainwash; **s'intoxiquer** to poison o.s.

intraduisible [ɛ̃traduizibl(ə)] adj untranslatable; (fig) inexpressible

intraitable [ɛ̃trɛtabl(ə)] adj inflexible, uncompromising

intranet [ɛ̃tranɛt] nm intranet

intransigeant, e [ɛ̃trɑ̃ziʒɑ̃, -ɑ̃t] adj intransigent; (morale, passion) uncompromising

intransitif, -ive [ɛ̃trɑ̃zitif, -iv] adj (Ling)

intransitive

intrépide [ɛ̃tʀepid] *adj* dauntless, intrepid

intrigue [ɛ̃tʀig] *nf* intrigue; (*scénario*) plot

intriguer [ɛ̃tʀige] *vi* to scheme ▷ *vt* to puzzle, intrigue

intrinsèque [ɛ̃tʀɛ̃sɛk] *adj* intrinsic

introduction [ɛ̃tʀɔdyksjɔ̃] *nf* introduction; **paroles/chapitre d'~** introductory words/chapter; **lettre/mot d'~** letter/note of introduction

introduire [ɛ̃tʀɔdɥiʀ] *vt* to introduce; (*visiteur*) to show in; (*aiguille, clef*): **~ qch dans** to insert *ou* introduce sth into; (*personne*): **~ à qch** to introduce to sth; (: *présenter*): **~ qn à qn/dans un club** to introduce sb to sb/to a club; **s'introduire** *vi* (*techniques, usages*) to be introduced; **s'~ dans** to gain entry into; to get o.s. accepted into; (*eau, fumée*) to get into; **~ au clavier** to key in

introuvable [ɛ̃tʀuvabl(ə)] *adj* which cannot be found; (*Comm*) unobtainable

introverti, e [ɛ̃tʀɔvɛʀti] *nm/f* introvert

intrus, e [ɛ̃tʀy, -yz] *nm/f* intruder

intrusion [ɛ̃tʀyzjɔ̃] *nf* intrusion; (*ingérence*) interference

intuition [ɛ̃tɥisjɔ̃] *nf* intuition; **avoir une ~** to have a feeling; **avoir l'~ de qch** to have an intuition of sth; **avoir de l'~** to have intuition

inusable [inyzabl(ə)] *adj* hard-wearing

inusité, e [inyzite] *adj* rarely used

inutile [inytil] *adj* useless; (*superflu*) unnecessary

inutilement [inytilmɑ̃] *adv* needlessly

inutilisable [inytilizabl(ə)] *adj* unusable

invalide [ɛ̃valid] *adj* disabled ▷ *nm/f*: **~ de guerre** disabled ex-serviceman; **~ du travail** industrially disabled person

invariable [ɛ̃vaʀjabl(ə)] *adj* invariable

invasion [ɛ̃vazjɔ̃] *nf* invasion

invectiver [ɛ̃vɛktive] *vt* to hurl abuse at ▷ *vi*: **~ contre** to rail against

invendable [ɛ̃vɑ̃dabl(ə)] *adj* unsaleable, unmarketable

invendu, e [ɛ̃vɑ̃dy] *adj* unsold ▷ *nm* return; **invendus** *nmpl* unsold goods

inventaire [ɛ̃vɑ̃tɛʀ] *nm* inventory; (*Comm*: *liste*) stocklist; (: *opération*) stocktaking *no pl*; (*fig*) survey; **faire un ~** to make an inventory; (*Comm*) to take stock; **faire *ou* procéder à l'~** to take stock

inventer [ɛ̃vɑ̃te] *vt* to invent; (*subterfuge*) to devise, invent; (*histoire, excuse*) to make up, invent; **~ de faire** to hit on the idea of doing

inventeur, -trice [ɛ̃vɑ̃tœʀ, -tʀis] *nm/f* inventor

inventif, -ive [ɛ̃vɑ̃tif, -iv] *adj* inventive

invention [ɛ̃vɑ̃sjɔ̃] *nf* invention; (*imagination, inspiration*) inventiveness

inverse [ɛ̃vɛʀs(ə)] *adj* (*ordre*) reverse; (*sens*) opposite; (*rapport*) inverse ▷ *nm* reverse; inverse; **en proportion ~** in inverse proportion; **dans le sens ~ des aiguilles d'une montre** anti-clockwise; **en sens ~** in (*ou* from) the opposite direction; **à l'~** conversely

inversement [ɛ̃vɛʀsəmɑ̃] *adv* conversely

inverser [ɛ̃vɛʀse] *vt* to reverse, invert; (*Élec*) to reverse

investigation [ɛ̃vɛstigasjɔ̃] *nf* investigation, inquiry

investir [ɛ̃vɛstiʀ] *vt* to invest; **s'investir** *vi* (*Psych*) to involve o.s.; **~ qn de** to vest *ou* invest sb with

investissement [ɛ̃vɛstismɑ̃] *nm* investment; (*Psych*) involvement

investiture [ɛ̃vɛstityʀ] *nf* investiture; (*à une élection*) nomination

invétéré, e [ɛ̃vetere] *adj* (*habitude*) ingrained; (*bavard, buveur*) inveterate

invisible [ɛ̃vizibl(ə)] *adj* invisible; (*fig: personne*) not available

invitation [ɛ̃vitasjɔ̃] *nf* invitation; **à/sur l'~ de qn** at/on sb's invitation; **carte/lettre d'~** invitation card/letter

invité, e [ɛ̃vite] *nm/f* guest

inviter [ɛ̃vite] *vt* to invite; **~ qn à faire qch** to invite sb to do sth; (*chose*) to induce *ou* tempt sb to do sth

invivable [ɛ̃vivabl(ə)] *adj* unbearable, impossible

involontaire [ɛ̃vɔlɔ̃tɛʀ] *adj* (*mouvement*) involuntary; (*insulte*) unintentional; (*complice*) unwitting

invoquer [ɛ̃vɔke] *vt* (*Dieu, muse*) to call upon, invoke; (*prétexte*) to put forward (as an excuse); (*témoignage*) to call upon; (*loi, texte*) to refer to; **~ la clémence de qn** to beg sb *ou* appeal to sb for clemency

invraisemblable [ɛ̃vʀɛsɑ̃blabl(ə)] *adj* unlikely, improbable; (*bizarre*) incredible

iode [jɔd] *nm* iodine

irai *etc* [iʀe] *vb voir* **aller**

Irak [iʀak] *nm*: **l'~** Iraq *ou* Irak

irakien, ne [iʀakjɛ̃, -ɛn] *adj* Iraqi ▷ *nm/f*: **I~, ne** Iraqi

Iran [iʀɑ̃] *nm*: **l'~** Iran

iranien, ne [iʀanjɛ̃, -ɛn] *adj* Iranian ▷ *nm* (*Ling*) Iranian ▷ *nm/f*: **I~, ne** Iranian

irascible [iʀasibl(ə)] *adj* short-tempered, irascible

irions *etc* [iʀjɔ̃] *vb voir* **aller**

iris [iʀis] *nm* iris

irlandais, e [iʀlɑ̃dɛ, -ɛz] *adj, nm* (*Ling*) Irish ▷ *nm/f*: **I~, e** Irishman/woman; **les I~** the Irish

Irlande [iʀlɑ̃d] *nf*: **l'~** (*pays*) Ireland; (*état*) the Irish Republic, the Republic of Ireland, Eire; **~ du Nord** Northern Ireland, Ulster; **~ du Sud** Southern Ireland, Irish Republic, Eire; **la mer d'~** the Irish Sea

ironie [iʀɔni] *nf* irony

ironique [iʀɔnik] *adj* ironical

ironiser [iʀɔnize] *vi* to be ironical

irons *etc* [iʀɔ̃] *vb voir* **aller**

irradier [iʀadje] *vi* to radiate ▷ *vt* to irradiate

irraisonné, e [iʀezɔne] *adj* irrational, unreasoned

irrationnel, le [iʀasjɔnɛl] *adj* irrational

irréalisable [iʀealizabl(ə)] *adj* unrealizable; (*projet*) impracticable

irrécupérable [iʀekypeʀabl(ə)] *adj*

unreclaimable, beyond repair; (*personne*) beyond
redemption *ou* recall
irréductible [iʀedyktibl(ə)] *adj* indomitable,
implacable; (*Math: fraction, équation*) irreducible
irréel, le [iʀeɛl] *adj* unreal
irréfléchi, e [iʀefleʃi] *adj* thoughtless
irrégularité [iʀegylaʀite] *nf* irregularity;
unevenness *no pl*
irrégulier, -ière [iʀegylje, -jɛʀ] *adj* irregular;
(*surface, rythme, écriture*) uneven, irregular; (*élève,
athlète*) erratic
irrémédiable [iʀemedjabl(ə)] *adj* irreparable
irremplaçable [iʀɑ̃plasabl(ə)] *adj* irreplaceable
irréparable [iʀepaʀabl(ə)] *adj* beyond repair,
irreparable; (*fig*) irreparable
irréprochable [iʀepʀɔʃabl(ə)] *adj* irreproachable,
beyond reproach; (*tenue, toilette*) impeccable
irrésistible [iʀezistibl(ə)] *adj* irresistible; (*preuve,
logique*) compelling
irrésolu, e [iʀezɔly] *adj* irresolute
irrespectueux, -euse [iʀɛspɛktɥø, -øz] *adj*
disrespectful
irrespirable [iʀɛspiʀabl(ə)] *adj* unbreathable;
(*fig*) oppressive, stifling
irresponsable [iʀɛspɔ̃sabl(ə)] *adj* irresponsible
irriguer [iʀige] *vt* to irrigate
irritable [iʀitabl(ə)] *adj* irritable
irriter [iʀite] *vt* (*agacer*) to irritate, annoy; (*Méd:
enflammer*) to irritate; **s'~ contre qn/de qch** to
get annoyed *ou* irritated with sb/at sth
irruption [iʀypsjɔ̃] *nf* irruption *no pl*; **faire ~
dans** to burst into
Islam [islam] *nm* Islam
islamique [islamik] *adj* Islamic
islamiste [islamist(ə)] *adj, nm/f* Islamic
Islande [islɑ̃d] *nf*: **l'~** Iceland

isolant, e [izɔlɑ̃, -ɑ̃t] *adj* insulating; (*insonorisant*)
soundproofing ▷ *nm* insulator
isolation [izɔlasjɔ̃] *nf* insulation; **~ acoustique/
thermique** sound/thermal insulation
isolé, e [izɔle] *adj* isolated; (*Élec*) insulated
isoler [izɔle] *vt* to isolate; (*prisonnier*) to put in
solitary confinement; (*ville*) to cut off, isolate;
(*Élec*) to insulate
isoloir [izɔlwaʀ] *nm* polling booth
Israël [isʀaɛl] *nm*: **l'~** Israel
israélien, ne [isʀaeljɛ̃, -ɛn] *adj* Israeli ▷ *nm/f*: **I~,
ne** Israeli
israélite [isʀaelit] *adj* Jewish; (*dans l'Ancien
Testament*) Israelite ▷ *nm/f*: **I~** Jew/Jewess;
Israelite
issu, e [isy] *adj*: **~ de** descended from; (*fig*)
stemming from ▷ *nf* (*ouverture, sortie*) exit;
(*solution*) way out, solution; (*dénouement*)
outcome; **à l'~e de** at the conclusion *ou* close of;
rue sans ~e dead end, no through road (*Brit*), no
outlet (*US*); **~e de secours** emergency exit
Italie [itali] *nf*: **l'~** Italy
italien, ne [italjɛ̃, -ɛn] *adj* Italian ▷ *nm* (*Ling*)
Italian ▷ *nm/f*: **I~, ne** Italian
italique [italik] *nm*: **en ~(s)** in italics
itinéraire [itineʀɛʀ] *nm* itinerary, route
IUT *sigle m* = **Institut universitaire de technologie**
IVG *sigle f* (= *interruption volontaire de grossesse*)
abortion
ivoire [ivwaʀ] *nm* ivory
ivre [ivʀ(ə)] *adj* drunk; **~ de** (*colère*) wild with;
(*bonheur*) drunk *ou* intoxicated with; **~ mort** dead
drunk
ivresse [ivʀɛs] *nf* drunkenness; (*euphorie*)
intoxication
ivrogne [ivʀɔɲ] *nm/f* drunkard

Jj

j' [ʒ] *pron voir* **je**

jacasser [ʒakase] *vi* to chatter

jacinthe [ʒasɛ̃t] *nf* hyacinth; **~ des bois** bluebell

jadis [ʒadis] *adv* in times past, formerly

jaillir [ʒajiʀ] *vi (liquide)* to spurt out, gush out; *(lumière)* to flood out; *(fig)* to rear up; to burst out

jais [ʒɛ] *nm* jet; **(d'un noir) de ~** jet-black

jalousie [ʒaluzi] *nf* jealousy; *(store)* (venetian) blind

jaloux, -ouse [ʒalu, -uz] *adj* jealous; **être ~ de qn/qch** to be jealous of sb/sth

jamais [ʒamɛ] *adv* never; *(sans négation)* ever; **ne ... ~** never; **~ de la vie!** never!; **si ~ ...** if ever ...; **à (tout) ~, pour ~** for ever, for ever and ever

jambe [ʒɑ̃b] *nf* leg; **à toutes ~s** as fast as one's legs can carry one

jambon [ʒɑ̃bɔ̃] *nm* ham

jambonneau, x [ʒɑ̃bɔno] *nm* knuckle of ham

jante [ʒɑ̃t] *nf* (wheel) rim

janvier [ʒɑ̃vje] *nm* January; *voir aussi* **juillet**

Japon [ʒapɔ̃] *nm*: **le ~** Japan

japonais, e [ʒapɔnɛ, -ɛz] *adj* Japanese ▷ *nm (Ling)* Japanese ▷ *nm/f*: **J~, e** Japanese

japper [ʒape] *vi* to yap, yelp

jaquette [ʒakɛt] *nf (de cérémonie)* morning coat; *(de femme)* jacket; *(de livre)* dust cover, (dust) jacket

jardin [ʒaʀdɛ̃] *nm* garden; **~ d'acclimatation** zoological gardens *pl*; **~ botanique** botanical gardens *pl*; **~ d'enfants** nursery school; **~ potager** vegetable garden; **~ public** (public) park, public gardens *pl*; **~ suspendus** hanging gardens; **~ zoologique** zoological gardens

jardinage [ʒaʀdinaʒ] *nm* gardening

jardiner [ʒaʀdine] *vi* to garden, do some gardening

jardinier, -ière [ʒaʀdinje, -jɛʀ] *nm/f* gardener ▷ *nf (de fenêtre)* window box; **jardinière d'enfants** nursery school teacher; **jardinière (de légumes)** *(Culin)* mixed vegetables

jargon [ʒaʀgɔ̃] *nm (charabia)* gibberish; *(publicitaire, scientifique etc)* jargon

jarret [ʒaʀɛ] *nm* back of knee; *(Culin)* knuckle, shin

jarretelle [ʒaʀtɛl] *nf* suspender (Brit), garter (US)

jarretière [ʒaʀtjɛʀ] *nf* garter

jaser [ʒaze] *vi* to chatter, prattle; *(indiscrètement)* to gossip

jatte [ʒat] *nf* basin, bowl

jauge [ʒoʒ] *nf (capacité)* capacity, tonnage; *(instrument)* gauge; **~ (de niveau) d'huile** dipstick

jaune [ʒon] *adj, nm* yellow ▷ *nm/f* Asiatic; *(briseur de grève)* blackleg ▷ *adv (fam)*: **rire ~** to laugh on the other side of one's face; **~ d'œuf** (egg) yolk

jaunir [ʒoniʀ] *vi, vt* to turn yellow

jaunisse [ʒonis] *nf* jaundice

Javel [ʒavɛl] *nf voir* **eau**

javelot [ʒavlo] *nm* javelin; *(Sport)*: **faire du ~** to throw the javelin

J.-C. *abr* = **Jésus-Christ**

je, j' [ʒ(ə)] *pron* I

jean [dʒin] *nm* jeans *pl*

Jésus-Christ [ʒezykʀi(st)] *n* Jesus Christ; **600 avant/après ~ ou J.-C.** 600 B.C./A.D.

jet¹ [ʒɛ] *nm (lancer)* throwing *no pl*, throw; *(jaillissement)* jet; spurt; *(de tuyau)* nozzle; *(fig)*: **premier ~** *(ébauche)* rough outline; **arroser au ~** to hose; **d'un (seul) ~** *(d'un seul coup)* at (*ou* in) one go; **du premier ~** at the first attempt *ou* shot; **~ d'eau** spray; *(fontaine)* fountain

jet² [dʒɛt] *nm (avion)* jet

jetable [ʒətabl(ə)] *adj* disposable

jetée [ʒəte] *nf* jetty; pier

jeter [ʒəte] *vt (gén)* to throw; *(se défaire de)* to throw away *ou* out; *(son, lueur etc)* to give out; **~ qch à qn** to throw sth to sb; *(de façon agressive)* to throw sth at sb; *(Navig)*: **~ l'ancre** to cast anchor; **~ un coup d'œil (à)** to take a look (at); **~ les bras en avant/la tête en arrière** to throw one's arms forward/one's head back(ward); **~ l'effroi parmi** to spread fear among; **~ un sort à qn** to cast a spell on sb; **~ qn dans la misère** to reduce sb to poverty; **~ qn dehors/en prison** to throw sb out/into prison; **~ l'éponge** *(fig)* to throw in the towel; **~ des fleurs à qn** *(fig)* to say lovely things to sb; **~ la pierre à qn** *(accuser, blâmer)* to accuse sb; **se ~ sur** to throw o.s. onto; **se ~ dans** *(fleuve)* to flow into; **se ~ par la fenêtre** to throw o.s. out of the window; **se ~ à l'eau** *(fig)* to take the plunge

jeton [ʒətɔ̃] *nm (au jeu)* counter; *(de téléphone)* token; **~s de présence** (director's) fees

jette *etc* [ʒɛt] *vb voir* **jeter**

jeu, x [ʒø] nm (divertissement, Tech: d'une pièce) play; (défini par des règles, Tennis: partie, Football etc: façon de jouer) game; (Théât etc) acting; (fonctionnement) working, interplay; (série d'objets, jouet) set; (Cartes) hand; (au casino): **le ~** gambling; **cacher son ~** (fig) to keep one's cards hidden, conceal one's hand; **c'est un ~ d'enfant!** (fig) it's child's play!; **en ~** at stake; at work; (Football) in play; **remettre en ~** to throw in; **entrer/mettre en ~** to come/bring into play; **par ~** (pour s'amuser) for fun; **d'entrée de ~** (tout de suite, dès le début) from the outset; **entrer dans le ~/le ~ de qn** (fig) to play the game/sb's game; **jouer gros ~** to play for high stakes; **se piquer/se prendre au ~** to get excited over/get caught up in the game; **~ d'arcade** video game; **~ de boules** game of bowls; (endroit) bowling pitch; (boules) set of bowls; **~ de cartes** card game; (paquet) pack of cards; **~ de construction** building set; **~ d'échecs** chess set; **~ d'écritures** (Comm) paper transaction; **~ électronique** electronic game; **~ de hasard** game of chance; **~ de mots** pun; **le ~ de l'oie** snakes and ladders sg; **~ d'orgue(s)** organ stop; **~ de patience** puzzle; **~ de physionomie** facial expressions pl; **~ de société** parlour game; **~ télévisé** television game; **~ vidéo** computer game; **~x de lumière** lighting effects; **J~x olympiques (JO)** Olympic Games

jeudi [ʒødi] nm Thursday; **~ saint** Maundy Thursday; voir aussi **lundi**

jeun [ʒɛn̄]: **à ~** adv on an empty stomach

jeune [ʒœn] adj young ▷ adv: **faire/s'habiller ~** to look/dress young; **les ~s** young people, the young; **~ fille** nf girl; **~ homme** nm young man; **~ loup** nm (Pol, Écon) young go-getter; **~ premier** leading man; **~s gens** nmpl young people; **~s mariés** nmpl newly weds

jeûne [ʒøn] nm fast

jeunesse [ʒœnɛs] nf youth; (aspect) youthfulness; (jeunes) young people pl, youth

joaillerie [ʒɔajʀi] nf jewel trade; jewellery (Brit), jewelry (US)

joaillier, -ière [ʒɔaje, -jɛʀ] nm/f jeweller (Brit), jeweler (US)

jogging [dʒɔgiŋ] nm tracksuit (Brit), sweatsuit (US); **faire du ~** to jog, go jogging

joie [ʒwa] nf joy

joindre [ʒwɛ̄dʀ(ə)] vt to join; **~ qch à** (à une lettre) to enclose sth with; (à un mail) to attach sth to; (contacter) to contact, get in touch with; **~ les mains/talons** to put one's hands/heels together; **~ les deux bouts** (fig: du mois) to make ends meet; **se joindre** (mains etc) to come together; **se ~ à qn** to join sb; **se ~ à qch** to join in sth

joint, e [ʒwɛ̄, -ɛ̄t] pp de **joindre** ▷ adj: **~ (à)** (lettre, paquet) attached (to), enclosed (with); **pièce ~e** (de lettre) enclosure; (de mail) attachment ▷ nm joint; (ligne) join; (de ciment etc) pointing no pl; **chercher/trouver le ~** (fig) to look for/come up with the answer; **~ de cardan** cardan joint; **~ de culasse** cylinder head gasket; **~ de robinet**

washer; **~ universel** universal joint

joker [ʒɔkɛʀ] nm (Cartes) joker; (Inform): **(caractère) ~** wild card

joli, e [ʒɔli] adj pretty, attractive; **une ~e somme/situation** a nice little sum/situation; **un ~ gâchis** etc a nice mess etc; **c'est du ~!** that's very nice!; **tout ça, c'est bien ~ mais ...** that's all very well but ...

jonc [ʒɔ̄] nm (bul)rush; (bague, bracelet) band

jonction [ʒɔ̄ksjɔ̄] nf joining; **(point de) ~** (de routes) junction; (de fleuves) confluence; **opérer une ~** (Mil etc) to rendez-vous

jongleur, -euse [ʒɔ̄glœʀ, -øz] nm/f juggler

jonquille [ʒɔ̄kij] nf daffodil

Jordanie [ʒɔʀdani] nf: **la ~** Jordan

joue [ʒu] nf cheek; **mettre en ~** to take aim at

jouer [ʒwe] vt (partie, carte, coup, Mus: morceau) to play; (somme d'argent, réputation) to stake, wager; (pièce, rôle) to perform; (film) to show; (simuler: sentiment) to affect, feign ▷ vi to play; (Théât, Ciné) to act, perform; (bois, porte: se voiler) to warp; (clef, pièce: avoir du jeu) to be loose; (entrer ou être en jeu) to come into play, come into it; **~ sur** (miser) to gamble on; **~ de** (Mus) to play; **~ du couteau/des coudes** to use knives/one's elbows; **~ à** (jeu, sport, roulette) to play; **~ au héros** to act ou play the hero; **~ avec** (risquer) to gamble with; **se ~ de** (difficultés) to make light of; **se ~ de qn** to deceive ou dupe sb; **~ un tour à qn** to play a trick on sb; **~ la comédie** (fig) to put on an act, put it on; **~ aux courses** to back horses, bet on horses; **~ à la baisse/hausse** (Bourse) to play for a fall/rise; **~ serré** to play a close game; **~ de malchance** to be dogged with ill-luck; **~ sur les mots** to play with words; **à toi/nous de ~** it's your/our go ou turn

jouet [ʒwɛ] nm toy; **être le ~ de** (illusion etc) to be the victim of

joueur, -euse [ʒwœʀ, -øz] nm/f player ▷ adj (enfant, chat) playful; **être beau/mauvais ~** to be a good/bad loser

joufflu, e [ʒufly] adj chubby(-cheeked)

joug [ʒu] nm yoke

jouir [ʒwiʀ]: **~ de** vt to enjoy

jouissance [ʒwisɑ̄s] nf pleasure; (Jur) use

joujou [ʒuʒu] nm (fam) toy

jour [ʒuʀ] nm day; (opposé à la nuit) day, daytime; (clarté) daylight; (fig: aspect): **sous un ~ favourable/nouveau** in a favourable/new light; (ouverture) opening; (Couture) openwork no pl; **au ~ le ~** from day to day; **de nos ~s** these days, nowadays; **tous les ~s** every day; **de ~ en ~** day by day; **d'un ~ à l'autre** from one day to the next; **du ~ au lendemain** overnight; **il fait ~** it's daylight; **en plein ~** in broad daylight; **au ~** in daylight; **au petit ~** at daybreak; **au grand ~** (fig) in the open; **mettre au ~** to uncover, disclose; **être à ~** to be up to date; **mettre à ~** to bring up to date, update; **mise à ~** updating; **donner le ~ à** to give birth to; **voir le ~** to be born; **se faire ~** (fig) to become clear; **~ férié** public holiday; **le ~ J** D-day; **~ ouvrable** working day

journal, -aux [ʒuʀnal, -o] nm (news)paper; (personnel) journal, diary; ~ **de bord** log; ~ **de mode** fashion magazine; **le J~ officiel (de la République française) (JO)** bulletin giving details of laws and official announcements; ~ **parlé/télévisé** radio/television news sg

journalier, -ière [ʒuʀnalje, -jɛʀ] adj daily; (banal) everyday ▷ nm day labourer

journalisme [ʒuʀnalism(ə)] nm journalism

journaliste [ʒuʀnalist(ə)] nm/f journalist

journée [ʒuʀne] nf day; **la ~ continue** the 9 to 5 working day (with short lunch break)

journellement [ʒuʀnɛlmã] adv (tous les jours) daily; (souvent) every day

joyau, x [ʒwajo] nm gem, jewel

joyeux, -euse [ʒwajø, -øz] adj joyful, merry; ~ **Noël!** Merry ou Happy Christmas!; **joyeuses Pâques!** Happy Easter!; ~ **anniversaire!** many happy returns!

jubiler [ʒybile] vi to be jubilant, exult

jucher [ʒyʃe] vt: ~ **qch sur** to perch sth (up)on ▷ vi (oiseau): ~ **sur** to perch (up)on; **se ~ sur** to perch o.s. (up)on

judas [ʒyda] nm (trou) spy-hole

judiciaire [ʒydisjɛʀ] adj judicial

judicieux, -euse [ʒydisjø, -øz] adj judicious

judo [ʒydo] nm judo

juge [ʒyʒ] nm judge; ~ **d'instruction** examining (Brit) ou committing (US) magistrate; ~ **de paix** justice of the peace; ~ **de touche** linesman

jugé [ʒyʒe] nm: **au ~** adv by guesswork

jugement [ʒyʒmã] nm judgment; (Jur: au pénal) sentence; (: au civil) decision; ~ **de valeur** value judgment

jugeote [ʒyʒɔt] nf (fam) gumption

juger [ʒyʒe] vt to judge ▷ nm: **au ~** by guesswork; ~ **qn/qch satisfaisant** to consider sb/sth (to be) satisfactory; ~ **que** to think ou consider that; ~ **bon de faire** to consider it a good idea to do, see fit to do; ~ **de** vt to judge; **jugez de ma surprise** imagine my surprise

juif, -ive [ʒɥif, -iv] adj Jewish ▷ nm/f: **J~, ive** Jew/ Jewess ou Jewish woman

juillet [ʒɥijɛ] nm July; **le premier ~** the first of July (Brit), July first (US); **le deux/onze ~** the second/eleventh of July, July second/eleventh; **il est venu le 5 ~** he came on 5th July ou July 5th; **en ~** in July; **début/fin ~** at the beginning/end of July; see note

juin [ʒɥɛ̃] nm June; voir aussi **juillet**

jumeau, -elle, -x [ʒymo, -ɛl] adj, nm/f twin; **maisons jumelles** semidetached houses

jumelage [ʒymlaʒ] nm twinning

jumeler [ʒymle] vt to twin; **roues jumelées** double wheels; **billets de loterie jumelés** double series lottery tickets; **pari jumelé** double bet

jumelle [ʒymɛl] adj f, nf voir **jumeau** ▷ vb voir **jumeler**

jument [ʒymã] nf mare

jungle [ʒɔ̃gl(ə)] nf jungle

jupe [ʒyp] nf skirt

jupon [ʒypɔ̃] nm waist slip ou petticoat

juré, e [ʒyʀe] nm/f juror ▷ adj: **ennemi ~** sworn ou avowed enemy

jurer [ʒyʀe] vt (obéissance etc) to swear, vow ▷ vi (dire des jurons) to swear, curse; (dissoner): ~ **(avec)** to clash (with); (s'engager): ~ **de faire/que** to swear ou vow to do/that; (affirmer): ~ **que** to swear ou vouch that; ~ **de qch** (s'en porter garant) to swear to sth; **ils ne jurent que par lui** they swear by him; **je vous jure!** honestly!

juridique [ʒyʀidik] adj legal

juron [ʒyʀɔ̃] nm curse, swearword

jury [ʒyʀi] nm (Jur) jury; (Scol) board (of examiners), jury

jus [ʒy] nm juice; (de viande) gravy, (meat) juice; ~ **de fruits** fruit juice; ~ **de raisin/tomates** grape/tomato juice

jusque [ʒysk(ə)]: **jusqu'à** prép (endroit) as far as, (up) to; (moment) until, till; (limite) up to; ~ **sur/dans** up to, as far as; (y compris) even on/in; ~ **vers** until about; **jusqu'à ce que** conj until; ~**là** (temps) until then; (espace) up to there; **jusqu'ici** (temps) until now; (espace) up to here; **jusqu'à présent** until now, so far

justaucorps [ʒystokɔʀ] nm inv (Danse, Sport) leotard

juste [ʒyst(ə)] adj (équitable) just, fair; (légitime) just, justified; (exact, vrai) right; (étroit, insuffisant) tight ▷ adv right; tight; (chanter) in tune; (seulement) just; ~ **assez/au-dessus** just enough/above; **pouvoir tout ~ faire** to be only just able to do; **au ~** exactly, actually; **comme de ~** of course, naturally; **le ~ milieu** the happy medium; **à ~ titre** rightfully

justement [ʒystəmã] adv rightly; justly; (précisément): **c'est ~ ce qu'il fallait faire** that's just ou precisely what needed doing

justesse [ʒystɛs] nf (précision) accuracy; (d'une remarque) aptness; (d'une opinion) soundness; **de ~** just, by a narrow margin

justice [ʒystis] nf (équité) fairness, justice; (Admin) justice; **rendre la ~** to dispense justice; **traduire en ~** to bring before the courts; **obtenir ~** to obtain justice; **rendre ~ à qn** to do sb justice; **se faire ~** to take the law into one's own hands; (se suicider) to take one's life

justicier, -ière [ʒystisje, -jɛʀ] nm/f judge, righter of wrongs

justificatif, -ive [ʒystifikatif, -iv] adj (document etc) supporting ▷ nm supporting proof

justifier [ʒystifje] vt to justify; ~ **de** vt to prove; **non justifié** unjustified; **justifié à droite/ gauche** ranged right/left

juteux, -euse [ʒytø, -øz] adj juicy

juvénile [ʒyvenil] adj young, youthful

Kk

K, k [kɑ] *nm inv* K, k ▷ *abr* (= *kilo*) kg; **K comme Kléber** K for King

K 7 [kasɛt] *nf* cassette

kaki [kaki] *adj inv* khaki

kangourou [kɑ̃guru] *nm* kangaroo

karaté [kaʀate] *nm* karate

karting [kaʀtiŋ] *nm* go-carting, karting

kascher [kaʃɛʀ] *adj inv* kosher

képi [kepi] *nm* kepi

kermesse [kɛʀmɛs] *nf* bazaar, (charity) fête; village fair

kidnapper [kidnape] *vt* to kidnap

kilo [kilo] *nm* kilo

kilogramme [kilɔgʀam] *nm* kilogramme (*Brit*), kilogram (*US*)

kilométrage [kilɔmetraʒ] *nm* number of kilometres travelled, ≈ mileage

kilomètre [kilɔmɛtʀ(ə)] *nm* kilometre (*Brit*), kilometer (*US*); **~s-heure** kilometres per hour

kilométrique [kilɔmetʀik] *adj* (*distance*) in kilometres; **compteur ~** ≈ mileage indicator

kinésithérapeute [kineziteʀapøt] *nm/f* physiotherapist

kiosque [kjɔsk(ə)] *nm* kiosk, stall; (*Tél etc*) *telephone and/or videotext information service*; **~ à journaux** newspaper kiosk

kir [kiʀ] *nm* kir (*white wine with blackcurrant liqueur*)

kit [kit] *nm* kit; **~ piéton** *ou* **mains libres** hands-free kit; **en ~** in kit form

kiwi [kiwi] *nm* (*Zool*) kiwi; (*Bot*) kiwi (fruit)

klaxon [klaksɔn] *nm* horn

klaxonner [klaksɔne] *vi, vt* to hoot (*Brit*), honk (one's horn) (*US*)

km *abr* (= *kilomètre*) km

km/h *abr* = **kilomètres/heure**

K.-O. [kao] *adj inv* (knocked) out, out for the count

Kosovo [kɔsɔvo] *nm*: **le ~** Kosovo

k-way® [kawɛ] *nm* (lightweight nylon) cagoule

kyste [kist(ə)] *nm* cyst

Ll

l' [l] *art déf voir* **le**

la [la] *art déf, pron voir* **le** ▷ *nm* (*Mus*) A; (*en chantant la gamme*) la

là [la] *adv voir aussi* **-ci; celui** there; (*ici*) here; (*dans le temps*) then; **est-ce que Catherine est là?** is Catherine there (*ou* here)?; **c'est là que** this is where; **là où** where; **de là** (*fig*) hence; **par là** (*fig*) by that; **tout est là** (*fig*) that's what it's all about

là-bas [labɑ] *adv* there

label [labɛl] *nm* stamp, seal

labeur [labœʀ] *nm* toil *no pl*, toiling *no pl*

labo [labo] *nm* (= *laboratoire*) lab

laboratoire [labɔʀatwaʀ] *nm* laboratory; **~ de langues/d'analyses** language/(medical) analysis laboratory

laborieux, -euse [labɔʀjø, -øz] *adj* (*tâche*) laborious; **classes laborieuses** working classes

labour [labuʀ] *nm* ploughing *no pl* (*Brit*), plowing *no pl* (*US*); **labours** *nmpl* (*champs*) ploughed fields; **cheval de ~** plough- *ou* cart-horse; **bœuf de ~** ox

labourer [labuʀe] *vt* to plough (*Brit*), plow (*US*); (*fig*) to make deep gashes *ou* furrows in

labyrinthe [labiʀɛ̃t] *nm* labyrinth, maze

lac [lak] *nm* lake; **le ~ Léman** Lake Geneva; **les Grands L~s** the Great Lakes; *voir aussi* **lacs**

lacer [lase] *vt* to lace *ou* do up

lacérer [laseʀe] *vt* to tear to shreds

lacet [lasɛ] *nm* (*de chaussure*) lace; (*de route*) sharp bend; (*piège*) snare; **chaussures à ~s** lace-up *ou* lacing shoes

lâche [lɑʃ] *adj* (*poltron*) cowardly; (*desserré*) loose, slack; (*morale, mœurs*) lax ▷ *nm/f* coward

lâcher [lɑʃe] *nm* (*de ballons, oiseaux*) release ▷ *vt* to let go of; (*ce qui tombe, abandonner*) to drop; (*oiseau, animal: libérer*) to release, set free; (*fig: mot, remarque*) to let slip, come out with; (*Sport: distancer*) to leave behind ▷ *vi* (*fil, amarres*) to break, give way; (*freins*) to fail; **~ les amarres** (*Navig*) to cast off (the moorings); **~ prise** to let go

lâcheté [lɑʃte] *nf* cowardice; (*bassesse*) lowness

lacrymogène [lakʀimɔʒɛn] *adj*: **grenade/gaz ~** tear gas grenade/tear gas

lacté, e [lakte] *adj* milk *cpd*

lacune [lakyn] *nf* gap

là-dedans [ladədɑ̃] *adv* inside (there), in it; (*fig*) in that

là-dessous [ladsu] *adv* underneath, under there; (*fig*) behind that

là-dessus [ladsy] *adv* on there; (*fig*) at that point; (: *à ce sujet*) about that

ladite [ladit] *adj voir* **ledit**

lagune [lagyn] *nf* lagoon

là-haut [lao] *adv* up there

laïc [laik] *adj, nm/f* = **laïque**

laid, e [lɛ, lɛd] *adj* ugly; (*fig: acte*) mean, cheap

laideur [lɛdœʀ] *nf* ugliness *no pl*; meanness *no pl*

lainage [lɛnaʒ] *nm* woollen garment; (*étoffe*) woollen material

laine [lɛn] *nf* wool; **~ peignée** worsted (wool); **~ à tricoter** knitting wool; **~ de verre** glass wool; **~ vierge** new wool

laïque [laik] *adj* lay, civil; (*Scol*) state *cpd* (*as opposed to private and Roman Catholic*) ▷ *nm/f* layman(-woman)

laisse [lɛs] *nf* (*de chien*) lead, leash; **tenir en ~** to keep on a lead *ou* leash

laisser [lɛse] *vt* to leave ▷ *vb aux*: **~ qn faire** to let sb do; **se ~ exploiter** to let o.s. be exploited; **se ~ aller** to let o.s. go; **~ qn tranquille** to let *ou* leave sb alone; **laisse-toi faire** let me (*ou* him) do it; **rien ne laisse penser que ...** there is no reason to think that ...; **cela ne laisse pas de surprendre** nonetheless it is surprising

laisser-aller [leseale] *nm* carelessness, slovenliness

laissez-passer [lesepɑse] *nm inv* pass

lait [lɛ] *nm* milk; **frère/sœur de ~** foster brother/sister; **~ écrémé/concentré/condensé** skimmed/concentrated/evaporated milk; **~ en poudre** powdered milk, milk powder; **~ de chèvre/vache** goat's/cow's milk; **~ maternel** mother's milk; **~ démaquillant/de beauté** cleansing/beauty lotion

laitage [lɛtaʒ] *nm* milk product

laiterie [lɛtʀi] *nf* dairy

laitier, -ière [letje, -jɛʀ] *adj* dairy ▷ *nm/f* milkman (dairywoman)

laiton [lɛtɔ̃] *nm* brass

laitue [lety] *nf* lettuce

laïus [lajys] *nm* (*péj*) spiel

lambeau, x [lɑ̃bo] *nm* scrap; **en ~x** in tatters, tattered

lambris [lɑ̃bʀi] *nm* panelling *no pl*

lame [lam] nf blade; (vague) wave; (lamelle) strip; ~ **de fond** ground swell no pl; ~ **de rasoir** razor blade

lamelle [lamɛl] nf (lame) small blade; (morceau) sliver; (de champignon) gill; **couper en ~s** to slice thinly

lamentable [lamɑ̃tabl(ə)] adj (déplorable) appalling; (pitoyable) pitiful

lamenter [lamɑ̃te]: **se lamenter** vi: **se ~ (sur)** to moan (over)

lampadaire [lɑ̃padɛR] nm (de salon) standard lamp; (dans la rue) street lamp

lampe [lɑ̃p(ə)] nf lamp; (Tech) valve; ~ **à alcool** spirit lamp; ~ **à bronzer** sunlamp; ~ **de poche** torch (Brit), flashlight (US); ~ **à souder** blowlamp; ~ **témoin** warning light

lampion [lɑ̃pjɔ̃] nm Chinese lantern

lance [lɑ̃s] nf spear; ~ **d'arrosage** garden hose; ~ **à eau** water hose; ~ **d'incendie** fire hose

lancée [lɑ̃se] nf: **être/continuer sur sa ~** to be under way/keep going

lancement [lɑ̃smɑ̃] nm launching no pl, launch; **offre de ~** introductory offer

lance-pierres [lɑ̃spjɛR] nm inv catapult

lancer [lɑ̃se] nm (Sport) throwing no pl, throw; (Pêche) rod and reel fishing ▷ vt to throw; (émettre, projeter) to throw out, send out; (produit, fusée, bateau, artiste) to launch; (injure) to hurl, fling; (proclamation, mandat d'arrêt) to issue; (emprunt) to float; (moteur) to send roaring away; ~ **qch à qn** to throw sth to sb; (de façon agressive) to throw sth at sb; ~ **un cri** ou **un appel** to shout ou call out; **se lancer** vi (prendre de l'élan) to build up speed; (se précipiter): **se ~ sur** ou **contre** to rush at; **se ~ dans** (discussion) to launch into; (aventure) to embark on; (les affaires, la politique) to go into; ~ **du poids** nm putting the shot

lancinant, e [lɑ̃sinɑ̃, -ɑ̃t] adj (regrets etc) haunting; (douleur) shooting

landau [lɑ̃do] nm pram (Brit), baby carriage (US)

lande [lɑ̃d] nf moor

langage [lɑ̃ɡaʒ] nm language; ~ **d'assemblage** (Inform) assembly language; ~ **du corps** body language; ~ **évolué/machine** (Inform) high-level/machine language; ~ **de programmation** (Inform) programming language

langouste [lɑ̃ɡust(ə)] nf crayfish inv

langoustine [lɑ̃ɡustin] nf Dublin Bay prawn

langue [lɑ̃ɡ] nf (Anat, Culin) tongue; (Ling) language; (bande): ~ **de terre** spit of land; **tirer la ~ (à)** to stick out one's tongue (at); **donner sa ~ au chat** to give up, give in; **de ~ française** French-speaking; ~ **maternelle** native language, mother tongue; ~ **verte** slang; ~ **vivante** modern language

langueur [lɑ̃ɡœR] nf languidness

languir [lɑ̃ɡiR] vi to languish; (conversation) to flag; **se languir** vi to be languishing; **faire ~ qn** to keep sb waiting

lanière [lanjɛR] nf (de fouet) lash; (de valise, bretelle) strap

lanterne [lɑ̃tɛRn(ə)] nf (portable) lantern; (électrique) light, lamp; (de voiture) (side)light; ~ **rouge** (fig) tail-ender; ~ **vénitienne** Chinese lantern

laper [lape] vt to lap up

lapidaire [lapidɛR] adj stone cpd; (fig) terse

lapin [lapɛ̃] nm rabbit; (fourrure) cony; **coup du ~** rabbit punch; **poser un ~ à qn** to stand sb up; ~ **de garenne** wild rabbit

Laponie [laponi] nf: **la ~** Lapland

laps [laps] nm: ~ **de temps** space of time, time no pl

laque [lak] nf lacquer; (brute) shellac; (pour cheveux) hair spray ▷ nm lacquer; piece of lacquer ware

laquelle [lakɛl] pron voir **lequel**

larcin [laRsɛ̃] nm theft

lard [laR] nm (graisse) fat; (bacon) (streaky) bacon

lardon [laRdɔ̃] nm (Culin) piece of chopped bacon; (fam: enfant) kid

large [laRʒ(ə)] adj wide; broad; (fig) generous ▷ adv: **calculer/voir ~** to allow extra/think big ▷ nm (largeur): **5 m de ~** 5 m wide ou in width; (mer): **le ~** the open sea; **en ~** adv sideways; **au ~ de** off; ~ **d'esprit** broad-minded; **ne pas en mener ~** to have one's heart in one's boots

largement [laRʒəmɑ̃] adv widely; (de loin) greatly; (amplement, au minimum) easily; (sans compter: donner etc) generously

largesse [laRʒɛs] nf generosity; **largesses** nfpl liberalities

largeur [laRʒœR] nf (qu'on mesure) width; (impression visuelle) wideness, width; breadth; broadness

larguer [laRɡe] vt to drop; (fam: se débarrasser de) to get rid of; ~ **les amarres** to cast off (the moorings)

larme [laRm(ə)] nf tear; (fig): **une ~ de** a drop of; **en ~s** in tears; **pleurer à chaudes ~s** to cry one's eyes out, cry bitterly

larmoyer [laRmwaje] vi (yeux) to water; (se plaindre) to whimper

larvé, e [laRve] adj (fig) latent

laryngite [laRɛ̃ʒit] nf laryngitis

las, lasse [lɑ, lɑs] adj weary

laser [lazeR] nm: (rayon) ~ laser (beam); **chaîne** ou **platine ~** compact disc (player); **disque ~** compact disc

lasse [lɑs] adj f voir **las**

lasser [lɑse] vt to weary, tire; **se ~ de** to grow weary ou tired of

latéral, e, aux [lateRal, -o] adj side cpd, lateral

latin, e [latɛ̃, -in] adj Latin ▷ nm (Ling) Latin ▷ nm/f: **L~, e** Latin; **j'y perds mon ~** it's all Greek to me

latitude [latityd] nf latitude; (fig): **avoir la ~ de faire** to be left free ou be at liberty to do; **à 48° de ~ Nord** at latitude 48° North; **sous toutes les ~s** (fig) world-wide, throughout the world

latte [lat] nf lath, slat; (de plancher) board

lauréat, e [loRea, -at] nm/f winner

laurier [loRje] nm (Bot) laurel; (Culin) bay leaves pl; **lauriers** nmpl (fig) laurels

lavable [lavabl(ə)] adj washable

lavabo [lavabo] *nm* washbasin; **lavabos** *nmpl* toilet *sg*

lavage [lavaʒ] *nm* washing *no pl*, wash; **~ d'estomac/d'intestin** stomach/intestinal wash; **~ de cerveau** brainwashing *no pl*

lavande [lavɑ̃d] *nf* lavender

lave [lav] *nf* lava *no pl*

lave-linge [lavlɛ̃ʒ] *nm inv* washing machine

laver [lave] *vt* to wash; (*tache*) to wash off; (*fig: affront*) to avenge; **se laver** to have a wash, wash; **se ~ les mains/dents** to wash one's hands/clean one's teeth; **~ la vaisselle/le linge** to wash the dishes/clothes; **~ qn de** (*accusation*) to clear sb of

laverie [lavʀi] *nf:* **~ (automatique)** launderette

lavette [lavɛt] *nf* (*chiffon*) dish cloth; (*brosse*) dish mop; (*fam: homme*) wimp, drip

laveur, -euse [lavœʀ, -øz] *nm/f* cleaner

lave-vaisselle [lavvɛsɛl] *nm inv* dishwasher

lavoir [lavwaʀ] *nm* wash house; (*bac*) washtub

laxatif, -ive [laksatif, -iv] *adj, nm* laxative

layette [lɛjɛt] *nf* layette

le, l', la [l(ə)] (*pl* **les**) *art déf* **1** the; **le livre/la pomme/l'arbre** the book/the apple/the tree; **les étudiants** the students

2 (*noms abstraits*): **le courage/l'amour/la jeunesse** courage/love/youth

3 (*indiquant la possession*): **se casser la jambe** *etc* to break one's leg *etc*; **levez la main** put your hand up; **avoir les yeux gris/le nez rouge** to have grey eyes/a red nose

4 (*temps*): **le matin/soir** in the morning/evening; mornings/evenings; **le jeudi** *etc* (*d'habitude*) on Thursdays *etc*; (*ce jeudi-là etc*) on (the) Thursday; **nous venons le 3 décembre** (*parlé*) we're coming on the 3rd of December *ou* on December the 3rd; (*écrit*) we're coming (on) 3rd *ou* 3 December

5 (*distribution, évaluation*) a, an; **trois euros le mètre/kilo** three euros a *ou* per metre/kilo; **le tiers/quart de** a third/quarter of

▷ *pron* **1** (*personne: mâle*) him; (*: femelle*) her; (*: pluriel*) them; **je le/la/les vois** I can see him/her/them

2 (*animal, chose: singulier*) it; (*: pluriel*) them; **je le** (*ou* **la**) **vois** I can see it; **je les vois** I can see them

3 (*remplaçant une phrase*): **je ne le savais pas** I didn't know (about it); **il était riche et ne l'est plus** he was once rich but no longer is

lécher [leʃe] *vt* to lick; (*laper: lait, eau*) to lick *ou* lap up; (*finir, polir*) to over-refine; **~ les vitrines** to go window-shopping; **se ~ les doigts/lèvres** to lick one's fingers/lips

lèche-vitrines [lɛʃvitʀin] *nm inv:* **faire du ~** to go window-shopping

leçon [ləsɔ̃] *nf* lesson; **faire la ~** to teach; **faire la ~ à** (*fig*) to give a lecture to; **~s de conduite** driving lessons; **~s particulières** private lessons *ou* tuition *sg* (*Brit*)

lecteur, -trice [lɛktœʀ, -tʀis] *nm/f* reader; (*d'université*) (foreign language) assistant (*Brit*), (foreign) teaching assistant (*US*) ▷ *nm* (*Tech*): **~ de cassettes** cassette player; **~ de CD/DVD**

(*Inform: d'ordinateur*) CD/DVD drive; (*de salon*) CD/DVD player; **~ MP3** MP3 player

lecture [lɛktyʀ] *nf* reading

ledit [lədi], **ladite** [ladit] (*mpl* **lesdits**) [ledi] (*fpl* **lesdites**) [ledit] *adj* the aforesaid

légal, e, -aux [legal, -o] *adj* legal

légaliser [legalize] *vt* to legalize

légalité [legalite] *nf* legality, lawfulness; **être dans/sortir de la ~** to be within/step outside the law

légendaire [leʒɑ̃dɛʀ] *adj* legendary

légende [leʒɑ̃d] *nf* (*mythe*) legend; (*de carte, plan*) key, legend; (*de dessin*) caption

léger, -ère [leʒe, -ɛʀ] *adj* light; (*bruit, retard*) slight; (*boisson, parfum*) weak; (*couche, étoffe*) thin; (*superficiel*) thoughtless; (*volage*) free and easy; flighty; (*peu sérieux*) lightweight; **blessé ~** slightly injured person; **à la légère** *adv* (*parler, agir*) rashly, thoughtlessly

légèrement [leʒɛʀmɑ̃] *adv* lightly; thoughtlessly, rashly; **~ plus grand** slightly bigger

légèreté [leʒɛʀte] *nf* lightness; thoughtlessness

législatif, -ive [leʒislatif, -iv] *adj* legislative; **législatives** *nfpl* general election *sg*

légitime [leʒitim] *adj* (*Jur*) lawful, legitimate; (*enfant*) legitimate; (*fig*) rightful, legitimate; **en état de ~ défense** in self-defence

legs [lɛg] *nm* legacy

léguer [lege] *vt:* **~ qch à qn** (*Jur*) to bequeath sth to sb; (*fig*) to hand sth down *ou* pass sth on to sb

légume [legym] *nm* vegetable; **~s verts** green vegetables; **~s secs** pulses

lendemain [lɑ̃dmɛ̃] *nm:* **le ~** the next *ou* following day; **le ~ matin/soir** the next *ou* following morning/evening; **le ~ de** the day after; **au ~ de** in the days following; in the wake of; **penser au ~** to think of the future; **sans ~** short-lived; **de beaux ~s** bright prospects; **des ~s qui chantent** a rosy future

lent, e [lɑ̃, lɑ̃t] *adj* slow

lentement [lɑ̃tmɑ̃] *adv* slowly

lenteur [lɑ̃tœʀ] *nf* slowness *no pl*; **lenteurs** *nfpl* (*actions, décisions lentes*) slowness *sg*

lentille [lɑ̃tij] *nf* (*Optique*) lens *sg*; (*Bot*) lentil; **~ d'eau** duckweed; **~s de contact** contact lenses

léopard [leɔpaʀ] *nm* leopard

lèpre [lɛpʀ(ə)] *nf* leprosy

lequel, laquelle [ləkɛl, lakɛl] (*mpl* **lesquels**, *fpl* **lesquelles**) (*à + lequel = auquel, de + lequel = duquel*) *pron* **1** (*interrogatif*) which, which one

2 (*relatif: personne: sujet*) who; (*: objet, après préposition*) whom; (*sujet: possessif*) whose; (*: chose*) which; **je l'ai proposé au directeur, ~ est d'accord** I suggested it to the director, who agrees; **la femme à laquelle j'ai acheté mon chien** the woman from whom I bought my dog; **le pont sur ~ nous sommes passés** the bridge (over) which we crossed; **un homme sur la compétence duquel on peut compter** a man whose competence one can count on

▷ *adj:* **auquel cas** in which case

les [le] *art déf, pron voir* **le**
lesbienne [lɛsbjɛn] *nf* lesbian
lesdits [ledi], **lesdites** [ledit] *adj voir* **ledit**
léser [leze] *vt* to wrong; (*Méd*) to injure
lésiner [lezine] *vt*: ~ (**sur**) to skimp (on)
lésion [lezjɔ̃] *nf* lesion, damage *no pl*; **~s**
cérébrales brain damage
lesquels, lesquelles [lekɛl] *pron voir* **lequel**
lessive [lesiv] *nf* (*poudre*) washing powder; (*linge*)
washing *no pl*, wash; (*opération*) washing *no pl*;
faire la ~ to do the washing
lessiver [lesive] *vt* to wash
lest [lɛst] *nm* ballast; **jeter** *ou* **lâcher du ~** (*fig*) to
make concessions
leste [lɛst(ə)] *adj* (*personne, mouvement*) sprightly,
nimble; (*désinvolte: manières*) offhand; (*osé:
plaisanterie*) risqué
lettre [lɛtʀ(ə)] *nf* letter; **lettres** *nfpl* (*étude, culture*)
literature *sg*; (*Scol*) arts (subjects); **à la ~** (*au sens
propre*) literally; (*ponctuellement*) to the letter; **en
~s majuscules** *ou* **capitales** in capital letters,
in capitals; **en toutes ~s** in words, in full; **~ de
change** bill of exchange; **~ piégée** letter bomb;
~ de voiture (aérienne) (air) waybill, (air) bill of
lading; **~s de noblesse** pedigree
leucémie [løsemi] *nf* leukaemia
leur [lœʀ] *adj poss* their; **~ maison** their house;
~s amis their friends; **à ~ approche** as they
came near; **à ~ vue** at the sight of them
▷ *pron* **1** (*objet indirect*) (to) them; **je ~ ai dit la
vérité** I told them the truth; **je le ~ ai donné** I
gave it to them, I gave them it
2 (*possessif*): **le (la) ~**, **les ~s** theirs
leurre [lœʀ] *nm* (*appât*) lure; (*fig*) delusion;
(*: piège*) snare
leurrer [lœʀe] *vt* to delude, deceive
leurs [lœʀ] *adj voir* **leur**
levain [ləvɛ̃] *nm* leaven; **sans ~** unleavened
levé, e [ləve] *adj*: **être ~** to be up ▷ *nm*: **~ de
terrain** land survey; **à mains ~es** (*vote*) by a
show of hands; **au pied ~** at a moment's notice
levée [ləve] *nf* (*Postes*) collection; (*Cartes*) trick;
~ de boucliers general outcry; **~ du corps**
*collection of the body from house of the deceased, before
funeral*; **~ d'écrou** release from custody; **~ de
terre** levee; **~ de troupes** levy
lever [ləve] *vt* (*vitre, bras etc*) to raise; (*soulever de
terre, supprimer: interdiction, siège*) to lift; (*: difficulté*)
to remove; (*séance*) to close; (*impôts, armée*) to
levy; (*Chasse: lièvre*) to start; (*: perdrix*) to flush;
(*fam: fille*) to pick up ▷ *vi* (*Culin*) to rise ▷ *nm*: **au
~** on getting up; **se lever** *vi* to get up; (*soleil*)
to rise; (*jour*) to break; (*brouillard*) to lift; **levez-
vous!, lève-toi!** stand up!, get up!; **ça va se ~**
the weather will clear; **~ du jour** daybreak; **~
du rideau** (*Théât*) curtain; **~ de rideau** (*pièce*)
curtain raiser; **~ de soleil** sunrise
levier [ləvje] *nm* lever; **faire ~ sur** to lever up (*ou*
off); **~ de changement de vitesse** gear lever
lèvre [lɛvʀ(ə)] *nf* lip; **lèvres** *nfpl* (*d'une plaie*)
edges; **petites/grandes ~s** labia minora/
majora; **du bout des ~s** half-heartedly

lévrier [levʀije] *nm* greyhound
levure [ləvyʀ] *nf* yeast; **~ chimique** baking
powder
lexique [lɛksik] *nm* vocabulary, lexicon;
(*glossaire*) vocabulary
lézard [lezaʀ] *nm* lizard; (*peau*) lizard skin
lézarde [lezaʀd(ə)] *nf* crack
liaison [ljɛzɔ̃] *nf* (*rapport*) connection, link; (*Rail,
Aviat etc*) link; (*relation: d'amitié*) friendship;
(*: d'affaires*) relationship; (*: amoureuse*) affair;
(*Culin, Phonétique*) liaison; **entrer/être en ~ avec**
to get/be in contact with; **~ radio** radio contact;
~ (de transmission de données) (*Inform*) data
link
liane [ljan] *nf* creeper
liant, e [ljɑ̃, -ɑ̃t] *adj* sociable
liasse [ljas] *nf* wad, bundle
Liban [libɑ̃] *nm*: **le ~** (the) Lebanon
libanais [libanɛ, -ɛz] *adj* Lebanese ▷ *nm/f*: **L~, e**
Lebanese
libeller [libele] *vt* (*chèque, mandat*): **~ (au nom de)**
to make out (to); (*lettre*) to word
libellule [libelyl] *nf* dragonfly
libéral, e, -aux [liberal, -o] *adj, nm/f* liberal; **les
professions ~es** the professions
libérer [libere] *vt* (*délivrer*) to free, liberate;
(*: moralement, Psych*) to liberate; (*relâcher: prisonnier*)
to release; (*: soldat*) to discharge; (*dégager: gaz,
cran d'arrêt*) to release; (*Écon: échanges commerciaux*)
to ease restrictions on; **se libérer** (*de rendez-
vous*) to try and be free, get out of previous
engagements; **~ qn de** (*liens, dette*) to free sb
from; (*promesse*) to release sb from
liberté [libɛʀte] *nf* freedom; (*loisir*) free time;
libertés *nfpl* (*privautés*) liberties; **mettre/être
en ~ provisoire/surveillée/
conditionnelle** on bail/probation/parole;
~ d'association right of association; **~ de
conscience** freedom of conscience; **~ du culte**
freedom of worship; **~ d'esprit** independence of
mind; **~ d'opinion** freedom of thought; **~ de la
presse** freedom of the press; **~ de réunion** right
to hold meetings; **~ syndicale** union rights
pl; **~s individuelles** personal freedom *sg*; **~s
publiques** civil rights
libraire [libʀɛʀ] *nm/f* bookseller
librairie [libʀeʀi] *nf* bookshop
libre [libʀ(ə)] *adj* free; (*route*) clear; (*place etc*)
vacant, free; (*fig: propos, manières*) open; (*Scol*)
private and Roman Catholic (*as opposed to
"laïque"*); **de ~** (*place*) free; **~ de qch/de faire**
free from sth/to do; **vente ~** (*Comm*) unrestricted
sale; **~ arbitre** free will; **~ concurrence** free-
market economy; **~ entreprise** free enterprise
libre-échange [libʀeʃɑ̃ʒ] *nm* free trade
libre-service [libʀəsɛʀvis] *nm inv* (*magasin*) self-
service store; (*restaurant*) self-service restaurant
Libye [libi] *nf*: **la ~** Libya
licence [lisɑ̃s] *nf* (*permis*) permit; (*diplôme*)
(first) degree; *see note*; (*liberté*) liberty; (*poétique,
orthographique*) licence (Brit), license (US); (*des
mœurs*) licentiousness; **~ ès lettres/en droit**

arts/law degree

licencié, e [lisɑ̃sje] *nm/f* (*Scol*): **~ ès lettres/en droit** = Bachelor of Arts/Law, arts/law graduate; (*Sport*) permit-holder

licenciement [lisɑ̃simɑ̃] *nm* dismissal; redundancy; laying off *no pl*

licencier [lisɑ̃sje] *vt* (*renvoyer*) to dismiss; (*débaucher*) to make redundant; to lay off

licite [lisit] *adj* lawful

lie [li] *nf* dregs *pl*, sediment

lié, e [lje] *adj*: **très ~ avec** (*fig*) very friendly with *ou* close to; **~ par** (*serment, promesse*) bound by; **avoir partie ~e (avec qn)** to be involved (with sb)

liège [ljɛʒ] *nm* cork

lien [ljɛ̃] *nm* (*corde, fig: affectif, culturel*) bond; (*rapport*) link, connection; (*analogie*) link; **~ de parenté** family tie

lier [lje] *vt* (*attacher*) to tie up; (*joindre*) to link up; (*fig: unir, engager*) to bind; (*Culin*) to thicken; **~ qch à** (*attacher*) to tie sth to; (*associer*) to link sth to; **~ conversation (avec)** to strike up a conversation (with); **se ~ avec** to make friends with

lierre [ljɛʀ] *nm* ivy

liesse [ljɛs] *nf*: **être en ~** to be jubilant

lieu, x [ljø] *nm* place; **lieux** *nmpl* (*locaux*) premises; (*endroit: d'un accident etc*) scene *sg*; **en ~ sûr** in a safe place; **en haut ~** in high places; **vider** *ou* **quitter les ~x** to leave the premises; **arriver/être sur les ~x** to arrive/be on the scene; **en premier ~** in the first place; **en dernier ~** lastly; **avoir ~** to take place; **avoir ~ de faire** to have grounds *ou* good reason for doing; **tenir ~ de** to take the place of; (*servir de*) to serve as; **donner ~ à** to give rise to, give cause for; **au ~ de** instead of; **au ~ qu'il y aille** instead of him going; **~ commun** commonplace; **~ géométrique** locus; **~ de naissance** place of birth

lieu-dit (*pl* **lieux-dits**) [ljødi] *nm* locality

lieutenant [ljøtnɑ̃] *nm* lieutenant; **~ de vaisseau** (*Navig*) lieutenant

lièvre [ljɛvʀ(ə)] *nm* hare; (*coureur*) pacemaker; **lever un ~** (*fig*) to bring up a prickly subject

ligament [ligamɑ̃] *nm* ligament

ligne [liɲ] *nf* (*gén*) line; (*Transports: liaison*) service; (*: trajet*) route; (*silhouette*): **garder la ~** to keep one's figure; **en ~** (*Inform*) on line; **en ~ droite** as the crow flies; **"à la ~"** "new paragraph"; **entrer en ~ de compte** to be taken into account; to come into it; **~ de but/médiane** goal/halfway line; **~ d'arrivée/de départ** finishing/starting line; **~ de conduite** course of action; **~ directrice** guiding line; **~ fixe** (*Tél*) fixed line (phone); **~ d'horizon** skyline; **~ de mire** line of sight; **~ de touche** touchline

ligné, e [liɲe] *adj*: **papier ~** ruled paper ▷ *nf* (*race, famille*) line, lineage; (*postérité*) descendants *pl*

ligoter [ligɔte] *vt* to tie up

ligue [lig] *nf* league

liguer [lige]: **se liguer** *vi* to form a league; **se ~ contre** (*fig*) to combine against

lilas [lila] *nm* lilac

limace [limas] *nf* slug

limande [limɑ̃d] *nf* dab

lime [lim] *nf* (*Tech*) file; (*Bot*) lime; **~ à ongles** nail file

limer [lime] *vt* (*bois, métal*) to file (down); (*ongles*) to file; (*fig: prix*) to pare down

limier [limje] *nm* (*Zool*) bloodhound; (*détective*) sleuth

limitation [limitasjɔ̃] *nf* limitation, restriction; **sans ~ de temps** with no time limit; **~ des naissances** birth control; **~ de vitesse** speed limit

limite [limit] *nf* (*de terrain*) boundary; (*partie ou point extrême*) limit; **dans la ~ de** within the limits of; **à la ~** (*au pire*) if the worst comes (*ou* came) to the worst; **sans ~s** (*bêtise, richesse, pouvoir*) limitless, boundless; **vitesse/charge ~** maximum speed/load; **cas ~** borderline case; **date ~** deadline; **date ~ de vente/consommation** sell-by/best-before date; **prix ~** upper price limit; **~ d'âge** maximum age, age limit

limiter [limite] *vt* (*restreindre*) to limit, restrict; (*délimiter*) to border, form the boundary of; **se ~ (à qch/à faire)** (*personne*) to limit *ou* confine o.s. (to sth/to doing sth); **se ~ à** (*chose*) to be limited to

limitrophe [limitʀɔf] *adj* border *cpd*; **~ de** bordering on

limoger [limɔʒe] *vt* to dismiss

limon [limɔ̃] *nm* silt

limonade [limɔnad] *nf* lemonade (*Brit*), (lemon) soda (*US*)

lin [lɛ̃] *nm* (*Bot*) flax; (*tissu, toile*) linen

linceul [lɛ̃sœl] *nm* shroud

linge [lɛ̃ʒ] *nm* (*serviettes etc*) linen; (*pièce de tissu*) cloth; (*aussi:* **linge de corps**) underwear; (*aussi:* **linge de toilette**) towel; (*lessive*) washing; **~ sale** dirty linen

lingerie [lɛ̃ʒʀi] *nf* lingerie, underwear

lingot [lɛ̃go] *nm* ingot

linguistique [lɛ̃ɡɥistik] *adj* linguistic ▷ *nf* linguistics *sg*

lion, ne [ljɔ̃, ljɔn] *nm/f* lion (lioness); (*signe*): **le L~** Leo, the Lion; **être du L~** to be Leo; **~ de mer** sea lion

lionceau, x [ljɔ̃so] *nm* lion cub

liqueur [likœʀ] *nf* liqueur

liquidation [likidasjɔ̃] *nf* liquidation; (*Comm*) clearance (sale); **~ judiciaire** compulsory liquidation

liquide [likid] *adj* liquid ▷ *nm* liquid; (*Comm*): **en ~** in ready money *ou* cash

liquider [likide] *vt* (*société, biens, témoin gênant*) to liquidate; (*compte, problème*) to settle; (*Comm: articles*) to clear, sell off

liquidités [likidite] *nfpl* (*Comm*) liquid assets

lire [liʀ] *nf* (*monnaie*) lira ▷ *vt, vi* to read; **~ qch à qn** to read sth (out) to sb

lis *vb* [li] *voir* **lire** ▷ *nm* [lis] = **lys**

lisible [lizibl(ə)] *adj* legible; (*digne d'être lu*) readable

lisière [lizjɛʀ] *nf* (*de forêt*) edge; (*de tissu*) selvage
lisons [lizɔ̃] *vb voir* **lire**
lisse [lis] *adj* smooth
liste [list(ə)] *nf* list; (*Inform*) listing; **faire la ~ de** to list, make out a list of; ~ **d'attente** waiting list; ~ **civile** civil list; ~ **électorale** electoral roll; ~ **de mariage** wedding (present) list; ~ **noire** hit list
listing [listiŋ] *nm* (*Inform*) listing; **qualité** ~ draft quality
lit [li] *nm* (*gén*) bed; **faire son** ~ to make one's bed; **aller/se mettre au** ~ to go to/get into bed; **chambre avec un grand** ~ room with a double bed; **prendre le** ~ to take to one's bed; **d'un premier** ~ (*Jur*) of a first marriage; ~ **de camp** camp bed (*Brit*), cot (*US*); ~ **d'enfant** cot (*Brit*), crib (*US*)
literie [litʀi] *nf* bedding; (*linge*) bedding, bedclothes *pl*
litière [litjɛʀ] *nf* litter
litige [litiʒ] *nm* dispute; **en** ~ in contention
litre [litʀ(ə)] *nm* litre; (*récipient*) litre measure
littéraire [liteʀɛʀ] *adj* literary
littéral, e, -aux [liteʀal, -o] *adj* literal
littérature [liteʀatyʀ] *nf* literature
littoral, e, -aux [litɔʀal, -o] *adj* coastal ▷ *nm* coast
liturgie [lityʀʒi] *nf* liturgy
livide [livid] *adj* livid, pallid
livraison [livʀɛzɔ̃] *nf* delivery; ~ **à domicile** home delivery (service)
livre [livʀ(ə)] *nm* book; (*imprimerie etc*): **le** ~ the book industry ▷ *nf* (*poids, monnaie*) pound; **traduire qch à** ~ **ouvert** to translate sth off the cuff *ou* at sight; ~ **blanc** official report (*on war, natural disaster etc, prepared by independent body*); ~ **de bord** (*Navig*) logbook; ~ **de comptes** account(s) book; ~ **de cuisine** cookery book (*Brit*), cookbook; ~ **de messe** mass *ou* prayer book; ~ **d'or** visitors' book; ~ **de poche** paperback (*small and cheap*); ~ **sterling** pound sterling; ~ **verte** green pound
livré, e [livʀe] *nf* livery ▷ *adj*: ~ **à** (*l'anarchie etc*) given over to; ~ **à soi-même** left to oneself *ou* one's own devices
livrer [livʀe] *vt* (*Comm*) to deliver; (*otage, coupable*) to hand over; (*secret, information*) to give away; **se** ~ **à** (*se confier*) to confide in; (*se rendre*) to give o.s. up to; (*s'abandonner à: débauche etc*) to give o.s. up *ou* over to; (*faire: pratiques, actes*) to indulge in; (*travail*) to be engaged in, engage in; (*: sport*) to practise; (*: enquête*) to carry out; ~ **bataille** to give battle
livret [livʀɛ] *nm* booklet; (*d'opéra*) libretto; ~ **de caisse d'épargne** (*savings*) bank-book; ~ **de famille** (*official*) family record book; ~ **scolaire** (*school*) report book
livreur, -euse [livʀœʀ, -øz] *nm/f* delivery boy *ou* man/girl *ou* woman
local, e, -aux [lɔkal, -o] *adj* local ▷ *nm* (*salle*) premises *pl* ▷ *nmpl* premises
localiser [lɔkalize] *vt* (*repérer*) to locate, place; (*limiter*) to localize, confine

localité [lɔkalite] *nf* locality
locataire [lɔkatɛʀ] *nm/f* tenant; (*de chambre*) lodger
location [lɔkasjɔ̃] *nf* (*par le locataire*) renting; (*par l'usager: de voiture etc*) hiring (*Brit*), renting (*US*); (*par le propriétaire*) renting out, letting; hiring out (*Brit*); (*de billets, places*) booking; (*bureau*) booking office; **"~ de voitures"** "car hire (*Brit*) *ou* rental (*US*)"
locomotive [lɔkɔmɔtiv] *nf* locomotive, engine; (*fig*) pacesetter, pacemaker
locution [lɔkysjɔ̃] *nf* phrase
loge [lɔʒ] *nf* (*Théât: d'artiste*) dressing room; (*: de spectateurs*) box; (*de concierge, franc-maçon*) lodge
logement [lɔʒmɑ̃] *nm* flat (*Brit*), apartment (*US*); accommodation *no pl* (*Brit*), accommodations *pl* (*US*); **le** ~ housing; **chercher un** ~ to look for a flat *ou* apartment, look for accommodation(s); **construire des ~s bon marché** to build cheap housing *sg*; **crise du** ~ housing shortage; ~ **de fonction** (*Admin*) company flat *ou* apartment, accommodation(s) provided with one's job
loger [lɔʒe] *vt* to accommodate ▷ *vi* to live; **se loger: trouver à se** ~ to find accommodation; **se** ~ **dans** (*balle, flèche*) to lodge itself in
logeur, -euse [lɔʒœʀ, -øz] *nm/f* landlord (landlady)
logiciel [lɔʒisjɛl] *nm* (*Inform*) piece of software
logique [lɔʒik] *adj* logical ▷ *nf* logic; **c'est** ~ it stands to reason
logis [lɔʒi] *nm* home; abode, dwelling
logo [lɔgo], **logotype** [lɔgɔtip] *nm* logo
loi [lwa] *nf* law; **faire la** ~ to lay down the law; **les ~s de la mode** (*fig*) the dictates of fashion; **proposition de** ~ (*private member's*) bill; **projet de** ~ (*government*) bill
loin [lwɛ̃] *adv* far; (*dans le temps: futur*) a long way off; (*: passé*) a long time ago; **plus** ~ further; **moins** ~ **(que)** not as far (as); ~ **de** far from; ~ **d'ici** a long way from here; **pas** ~ **de 100 euros** not far off 100 euros; **au** ~ far off; **de** ~ *adv* from a distance; (*fig: de beaucoup*) by far; **il vient de** ~ he's come a long way; he comes from a long way away; **de** ~ **en** ~ here and there; (*de temps en temps*) (every) now and then; ~ **de là** (*au contraire*) far from it
lointain, e [lwɛ̃tɛ̃, -ɛn] *adj* faraway, distant; (*dans le futur, passé*) distant, far-off; (*cause, parent*) remote, distant ▷ *nm*: **dans le** ~ in the distance
loir [lwaʀ] *nm* dormouse
loisir [lwaziʀ] *nm*: **heures de** ~ spare time; **loisirs** *nmpl* leisure *sg*; (*activités*) leisure activities; **avoir le** ~ **de faire** to have the time *ou* opportunity to do; **(tout) à** ~ (*en prenant son temps*) at leisure; (*autant qu'on le désire*) at one's pleasure
londonien, ne [lɔ̃dɔnjɛ̃, -ɛn] *adj* London *cpd*, of London ▷ *nm/f*: **L~, ne** Londoner
Londres [lɔ̃dʀ(ə)] *n* London
long, longue [lɔ̃, lɔ̃g] *adj* long ▷ *adv*: **en savoir** ~ to know a great deal ▷ *nm*: **de 3 m de** ~ 3 m long, 3 m in length ▷ *nf*: **à la longue** in the end; **faire** ~ **feu** to fizzle out; **ne pas faire** ~ **feu** not to last

long; **au ~ cours** (Navig) ocean cpd, ocean-going; **de longue date** adj long-standing; **longue durée** adj long-term; **de longue haleine** adj long-term; **être ~ à faire** to take a long time to do; **en ~** adv lengthwise, lengthways; **(tout) le ~ de** (all) along; **tout au ~ de** (année, vie) throughout; **de ~ en large** (marcher) to and fro, up and down; **en ~ et en large** (fig) in every detail

longer [lɔ̃ʒe] vt to go (ou walk ou drive) along(side); (mur, route) to border

longiligne [lɔ̃ʒiliɲ] adj long-limbed

longitude [lɔ̃ʒityd] nf longitude; **à 45° de ~ ouest** at 45° longitude west

longtemps [lɔ̃tɑ̃] adv (for) a long time, (for) long; **ça ne va pas durer ~** it won't last long; **avant ~** before long; **pour/pendant ~** for a long time; **je n'en ai pas pour ~** I shan't be long; **mettre ~ à faire** to take a long time to do; **il en a pour ~** he'll be a long time; **il y a ~ que je travaille** I have been working (for) a long time; **il n'y a pas ~ que je l'ai rencontré** it's not long since I met him

longue [lɔ̃g] adj f voir **long**

longuement [lɔ̃gmɑ̃] adv (longtemps: parler, regarder) for a long time; (en détail: expliquer, raconter) at length

longueur [lɔ̃gœʀ] nf length; **longueurs** nfpl (fig: d'un film etc) tedious parts; **sur une ~ de 10 km** for ou over 10 km; **en ~** adv lengthwise, lengthways; **tirer en ~** to drag on; **à ~ de journée** all day long; **d'une ~** (gagner) by a length; **~ d'onde** wavelength

longue-vue [lɔ̃gvy] nf telescope

look [luk] (fam) nm look, image

lopin [lɔpɛ̃] nm: **~ de terre** patch of land

loque [lɔk] nf (personne) wreck; **loques** nfpl (habits) rags; **être** ou **tomber en ~s** to be in rags

loquet [lɔkɛ] nm latch

lorgner [lɔʀɲe] vt to eye; (convoiter) to have one's eye on

lors [lɔʀ] : **~ de** prép (au moment de) at the time of; (pendant) during; **~ même que** even though

lorsque [lɔʀsk(ə)] conj when, as

losange [lɔzɑ̃ʒ] nm diamond; (Géom) lozenge; **en ~** diamond-shaped

lot [lo] nm (part) share; (de loterie) prize; (fig: destin) fate, lot; (Comm, Inform) batch; **~ de consolation** consolation prize

loterie [lɔtʀi] nf lottery; (tombola) raffle; **L~ nationale** French national lottery

loti, e [lɔti] adj: **bien/mal ~** well-/badly off, lucky/unlucky

lotion [losjɔ̃] nf lotion; **~ après rasage** after-shave (lotion); **~ capillaire** hair lotion

lotissement [lɔtismɑ̃] nm (groupe de maisons, d'immeubles) housing development; (parcelle) (building) plot, lot

loto [lɔto] nm lotto

lotte [lɔt] nf (Zool: de rivière) burbot; (: de mer) monkfish

louable [lwabl(ə)] adj (appartement, garage)

rentable; (action, personne) praiseworthy, commendable

louange [lwɑ̃ʒ] nf: **à la ~ de** in praise of; **louanges** nfpl praise sg

loubar, loubard [lubaʀ] nm (fam) lout

louche [luʃ] adj shady, dubious ▷ nf ladle

loucher [luʃe] vi to squint; (fig): **~ sur** to have one's (beady) eye on

louer [lwe] vt (maison: propriétaire) to let, rent (out); (: locataire) to rent; (voiture etc) to hire out (Brit), rent (out); to hire (Brit), rent; (réserver) to book; (faire l'éloge de) to praise; "**à ~**" "to let" (Brit), "for rent" (US); **~ qn de** to praise sb for; **se ~ de** to congratulate o.s. on

loup [lu] nm wolf; (poisson) bass; (masque) (eye) mask; **jeune ~** young go-getter; **~ de mer** (marin) old seadog

loupe [lup] nf magnifying glass; **~ de noyer** burr walnut; **à la ~** (fig) in minute detail

louper [lupe] vt (fam: manquer) to miss; (: gâcher) to mess up, bungle

lourd, e [luʀ, luʀd(ə)] adj heavy; (chaleur, temps) sultry; (fig: personne, style) heavy-handed ▷ adv: **peser ~** to be heavy; **~ de** (menaces) charged with; (conséquences) fraught with; **artillerie/industrie ~e** heavy artillery/industry

lourdaud, e [luʀdo, -od] adj oafish

lourdement [luʀdəmɑ̃] adv heavily; **se tromper ~** to make a big mistake

lourdeur [luʀdœʀ] nf heaviness; **~ d'estomac** indigestion no pl

loutre [lutʀ(ə)] nf otter; (fourrure) otter skin

louveteau, x [luvto] nm (Zool) wolf-cub; (scout) cub (scout)

louvoyer [luvwaje] vi (Navig) to tack; (fig) to hedge, evade the issue

loyal, e, -aux [lwajal, -o] adj (fidèle) loyal, faithful; (fair-play) fair

loyauté [lwajote] nf loyalty, faithfulness; fairness

loyer [lwaje] nm rent; **~ de l'argent** interest rate

lu, e [ly] pp de **lire**

lubie [lybi] nf whim, craze

lubrifiant [lybʀifjɑ̃] nm lubricant

lubrifier [lybʀifje] vt to lubricate

lubrique [lybʀik] adj lecherous

lucarne [lykaʀn(ə)] nf skylight

lucide [lysid] adj (conscient) lucid, conscious; (perspicace) clear-headed

lucratif, -ive [lykʀatif, -iv] adj lucrative; profitable; **à but non ~** non profit-making

lueur [lɥœʀ] nf (chatoyante) glimmer no pl; (métallique, mouillée) gleam no pl; (rougeoyante) glow no pl; (pâle) (faint) light; (fig) spark; (: d'espérance) glimmer, gleam

luge [lyʒ] nf sledge (Brit), sled (US); **faire de la ~** to sledge (Brit), sled (US), toboggan

lugubre [lygybʀ(ə)] adj gloomy; dismal

lui [lɥi] pp de **luire**
▷ pron **1** (objet indirect: mâle) (to) him; (: femelle) (to) her; (: chose, animal) (to) it; **je ~ ai parlé** I have spoken to him (ou to her); **il ~ a offert un**

cadeau he gave him (*ou* her) a present; **je le ~ ai donné** I gave it to him (*ou* her)

2 (*après préposition, comparatif: personne*) him; (*: chose, animal*) it; **elle est contente de ~** she is pleased with him; **je la connais mieux que ~** I know her better than he does; **cette voiture est à ~** this car belongs to him, this is HIS car

3 (*sujet, forme emphatique*) he; **~, il est à Paris** HE is in Paris; **c'est ~ qui l'a fait** HE did it

luire [lчiʀ] *vi* (*gén*) to shine, gleam; (*surface mouillée*) to glisten; (*reflets chauds, cuivrés*) to glow

lumière [lymjɛʀ] *nf* light; **lumières** *nfpl* (*d'une personne*) knowledge *sg*, wisdom *sg*; **à la ~ de** by the light of; (*fig: événements*) in the light of; **fais de la ~** let's have some light, give us some light; **faire (toute) la ~ sur** (*fig*) to clarify (completely); **mettre en ~** (*fig*) to highlight; **~ du jour/soleil** day/sunlight

luminaire [lyminɛʀ] *nm* lamp, light

lumineux, -euse [lyminø, -øz] *adj* (*émettant de la lumière*) luminous; (*éclairé*) illuminated; (*ciel, journée, couleur*) bright; (*relatif à la lumière: rayon etc*) of light, light *cpd*; (*fig: regard*) radiant

lunatique [lynatik] *adj* whimsical, temperamental

lundi [lœdi] *nm* Monday; **on est ~** it's Monday; **le ~ 20 août** Monday 20th August; **il est venu ~** he came on Monday; **le(s) ~(s)** on Mondays; **à ~!** see you (on) Monday!; **~ de Pâques** Easter Monday; **~ de Pentecôte** Whit Monday (*Brit*)

lune [lyn] *nf* moon; **pleine/nouvelle ~** full/new moon; **être dans la ~** (*distrait*) to have one's head in the clouds; **~ de miel** honeymoon

lunette [lynɛt] *nf*: **~s** *nfpl* glasses, spectacles; (*protectrices*) goggles; **~ d'approche** telescope; **~ arrière** (*Auto*) rear window; **~s noires** dark

glasses; **~s de soleil** sunglasses

lus *etc* [ly] *vb voir* **lire**

lustre [lystʀ(ə)] *nm* (*de plafond*) chandelier; (*fig: éclat*) lustre

lustrer [lystʀe] *vt*: **~ qch** (*faire briller*) to make sth shine; (*user*) to make sth shiny

lut [ly] *vb voir* **lire**

luth [lyt] *nm* lute

lutin [lytɛ̃] *nm* imp, goblin

lutte [lyt] *nf* (*conflit*) struggle; (*Sport*): **la ~** wrestling; **de haute ~** after a hard-fought struggle; **~ des classes** class struggle; **~ libre** (*Sport*) all-in wrestling

lutter [lyte] *vi* to fight, struggle; (*Sport*) to wrestle

luxe [lyks(ə)] *nm* luxury; **un ~ de** (*détails, précautions*) a wealth of; **de ~** *adj* luxury *cpd*

Luxembourg [lyksɑ̃buʀ] *nm*: **le ~** Luxembourg

luxembourgeois, e [lyksɑ̃buʀʒwa, -waz] *adj* of *ou* from Luxembourg ▷ *nm/f*: **L~, e** inhabitant *ou* native of Luxembourg

luxer [lykse] *vt*: **se ~ l'épaule** to dislocate one's shoulder

luxueux, -euse [lyksɥø, -øz] *adj* luxurious

luxure [lyksyʀ] *nf* lust

luxuriant, e [lyksyʀjɑ̃, -ɑ̃t] *adj* luxuriant, lush

lycée [lise] *nm* (*state*) secondary (*Brit*) *ou* high (*US*) school; **~ technique** technical secondary *ou* high school; *see note*

lycéen, ne [liseɛ̃, -ɛn] *nm/f* secondary school pupil

lyophilisé, e [ljɔfilize] *adj* freeze-dried

lyrique [liʀik] *adj* lyrical; (*Opéra*) lyric; **artiste ~** opera singer; **comédie ~** comic opera; **théâtre ~** opera house (*for light opera*)

lys [lis] *nm* lily

Mm

M, m [ɛm] *nm inv* M, m ▷ *abr* = **majeur; masculin;
mètre; Monsieur;** (= *million*) M; **M comme
Marcel** M for Mike
m' [m] *pron voir* **me**
ma [ma] *adj poss voir* **mon**
macaron [makaʀɔ̃] *nm* (*gâteau*) macaroon;
(*insigne*) (round) badge
macaroni [makaʀɔni] *nm*, **macaronis** *nmpl*
macaroni *sg;* **~(s) au gratin** macaroni cheese
(*Brit*), macaroni and cheese (*US*)
macédoine [masedwan] *nf:* **~ de fruits** fruit
salad; **~ de légumes** mixed vegetables *pl*
macérer [maseʀe] *vi, vt* to macerate
mâcher [mɑʃe] *vt* to chew; **ne pas ~ ses mots**
not to mince one's words; **~ le travail à qn** (*fig*)
to spoon-feed sb, do half sb's work for him
machin [maʃɛ̃] *nm* (*fam*) thingamajig, thing;
(*personne*): **M~** what's-his-name
machinal, e, -aux [maʃinal, -o] *adj* mechanical,
automatic
machinalement [maʃinalmɑ̃] *adv*
mechanically, automatically
machination [maʃinasjɔ̃] *nf* scheming, frame-
up
machine [maʃin] *nf* machine; (*locomotive; de
navire etc*) engine; (*fig: rouages*) machinery; (*fam:
personne*): **M~** what's-her-name; **faire ~ arrière**
(*Navig*) to go astern; (*fig*) to back-pedal; **~ à laver/
coudre/tricoter** washing/sewing/knitting
machine; **~ à écrire** typewriter; **~ à sous** fruit
machine; **~ à vapeur** steam engine
macho [matʃo] (*fam*) *nm* male chauvinist
mâchoire [mɑʃwaʀ] *nf* jaw; **~ de frein** brake
shoe
mâchonner [mɑʃone] *vt* to chew (at)
maçon [masɔ̃] *nm* bricklayer; (*constructeur*)
builder
maçonnerie [masɔnʀi] *nf* (*murs: de brique*)
brickwork; (: *de pierre*) masonry, stonework;
(*activité*) bricklaying; building; **~ de béton**
concrete
maculer [makyle] *vt* to stain; (*Typo*) to mackle
Madame [madam] (*pl* **Mesdames**) [medam]
nf: **~ X** Mrs X; **occupez-vous de ~/Monsieur/
Mademoiselle** please serve this lady/
gentleman/(young) lady; **bonjour ~/Monsieur/
Mademoiselle** good morning; (*ton déférent*)

good morning Madam/Sir/Madam; (*le nom
est connu*) good morning Mrs X/Mr X/Miss
X; **~/Monsieur/Mademoiselle!** (*pour appeler*)
excuse me!; (*ton déférent*) Madam/Sir/Miss!;
~/Monsieur/Mademoiselle (*sur lettre*) Dear
Madam/Sir/Madam; **chère ~/cher Monsieur/
chère Mademoiselle** Dear Mrs X/Mr X/Miss X;
~ la Directrice the director; the manageress;
the head teacher; **Mesdames** Ladies
madeleine [madlɛn] ·*nf* madeleine, ≈ sponge
finger cake
Mademoiselle [madmwazɛl] (*pl*
Mesdemoiselles) [medmwazɛl] *nf* Miss; *voir
aussi* **Madame**
Madère [madɛʀ] *nf* Madeira ▷ *nm:* **madère**
Madeira (wine)
magasin [magazɛ̃] *nm* (*boutique*) shop; (*entrepôt*)
warehouse; (*d'arme, appareil-photo*) magazine; **en
~** (*Comm*) in stock; **faire les ~s** to go (a)round the
shops, do the shops; **~ d'alimentation** grocer's
(shop) (*Brit*), grocery store (*US*)
magazine [magazin] *nm* magazine
Maghreb [magʀɛb] *nm:* **le ~** the Maghreb,
North(-West) Africa
maghrébin, e [magʀebɛ̃, -in] *adj* of *ou* from the
Maghreb ▷ *nm/f:* **M~, e** North African, Maghrebi
magicien, ne [maʒisjɛ̃, -ɛn] *nm/f* magician
magie [maʒi] *nf* magic; **~ noire** black magic
magique [maʒik] *adj* (*occulte*) magic; (*fig*)
magical
magistral, e, -aux [maʒistʀal, -o] *adj* (*œuvre,
adresse*) masterly; (*ton*) authoritative; (*gifle etc*)
sound, resounding; (*ex cathedra*): **enseignement
~** lecturing, lectures *pl;* **cours ~** lecture
magistrat [maʒistʀa] *nm* magistrate
magnat [magna] *nm* tycoon, magnate
magnétique [maɲetik] *adj* magnetic
magnétiser [maɲetize] *vt* to magnetize; (*fig*) to
mesmerize, hypnotize
magnétophone [maɲetofɔn] *nm* tape recorder;
~ à cassettes cassette recorder
magnétoscope [maɲetɔskɔp] *nm:* **~ (à cassette)**
video (recorder)
magnifique [maɲifik] *adj* magnificent
magot [mago] *nm* (*argent*) pile (of money);
(*économies*) nest egg
magouille [maguj] *nf* (*fam*) scheming

magret [magʀɛ] nm: ~ **de canard** duck breast
mai [mɛ] nm May; see note; voir aussi **juillet**
maigre [mɛgʀ(ə)] adj (very) thin, skinny; (viande)
lean; (fromage) low-fat; (végétation) thin, sparse;
(fig) poor, meagre, skimpy ▷ adv: **faire ~** not to
eat meat; **jours ~s** days of abstinence, fish days
maigreur [mɛgʀœʀ] nf thinness
maigrir [megʀiʀ] vi to get thinner, lose weight
▷ vt: ~ **qn** (vêtement) to make sb look slim(mer)
mail [mɛl] nm email
maille [maj] nf (boucle) stitch; (ouverture) hole
(in the mesh); **avoir ~ à partir avec qn** to have
a brush with sb; ~ **à l'endroit/à l'envers** knit
one/purl one; (boucle) plain/purl stitch
maillet [majɛ] nm mallet
maillon [majɔ̃] nm link
maillot [majo] nm (aussi: **maillot de corps**) vest;
(de danseur) leotard; (de sportif) jersey; ~ **de bain**
bathing costume (Brit), swimsuit; (d'homme)
bathing trunks pl; ~ **deux pièces** two-piece
swimsuit, bikini; ~ **jaune** yellow jersey
main [mɛ̃] nf hand; **la ~ dans la ~** hand in hand;
à deux ~s with both hands; **à une ~** with one
hand; **à la ~** (tenir, avoir) in one's hand; (faire,
tricoter etc) by hand; **se donner la ~** to hold
hands; **donner ou tendre la ~ à qn** to hold out
one's hand to sb; **se serrer la ~** to shake hands;
serrer la ~ à qn to shake hands with sb; **sous la**
~ to ou at hand; **haut les ~s!** hands up!; **à ~ levée**
(Art) freehand; **à ~s levées** (voter) with a show
of hands; **attaque à ~ armée** armed attack; **à**
~ **droite/gauche** to the right/left; **à remettre**
en ~s propres to be delivered personally; **de**
première ~ (renseignement) first-hand; (Comm:
voiture etc) with only one previous owner; **faire**
~ **basse sur** to help o.s. to; **mettre la dernière**
~ **à** to put the finishing touches to; **mettre la**
~ **à la pâte** (fig) to lend a hand; **avoir/passer**
la ~ (Cartes) to lead/hand over the lead; **s'en**
laver les ~s (fig) to wash one's hands of it; **se**
faire/perdre la ~ to get one's hand in/lose one's
touch; **avoir qch bien en ~** to have got the hang
of sth; **en un tour de ~** (fig) in the twinkling of
an eye; ~ **courante** handrail
main-d'œuvre [mɛ̃dœvʀ(ə)] nf manpower,
labour (Brit), labor (US)
main-forte [mɛ̃fɔʀt(ə)] nf: **prêter ~ à qn** to come
to sb's assistance
mainmise [mɛ̃miz] nf seizure; (fig): **avoir la ~**
sur to have a grip ou stranglehold on
mains-libres [mɛ̃libʀ] adj inv (téléphone, kit)
hands-free
maint, e [mɛ̃, mɛ̃t] adj many a; ~**s** many; **à ~es**
reprises time and (time) again
maintenant [mɛ̃tnɑ̃] adv now; (actuellement)
nowadays
maintenir [mɛ̃tniʀ] vt (retenir, soutenir) to support;
(contenir: foule etc) to keep in check, hold back;
(conserver) to maintain, uphold; (affirmer) to
maintain; **se maintenir** vi (paix, temps) to hold;
(préjugé) to persist; (malade) to remain stable
maintien [mɛ̃tjɛ̃] nm maintaining, upholding;

(attitude) bearing; ~ **de l'ordre** maintenance of
law and order
maire [mɛʀ] nm mayor
mairie [meʀi] nf (endroit) town hall;
(administration) town council
mais [mɛ] conj but; ~ **non!** of course not!; ~ **enfin**
but after all; (indignation) look here!; ~ **encore?**
is that all?
maïs [mais] nm maize (Brit), corn (US)
maison [mɛzɔ̃] nf (bâtiment) house; (chez-soi)
home; (Comm) firm; (famille): **ami de la ~** friend
of the family ▷ adj inv (Culin) home-made; (: au
restaurant) made by the chef; (Comm) in-house,
own; (fam) first-rate; **à la ~** at home; (direction)
home; ~ **d'arrêt** (short-stay) prison; ~ **centrale**
prison; ~ **close** brothel; ~ **de correction**
= remand home (Brit), ≈ reformatory (US); ~ **de**
la culture ≈ arts centre; ~ **des jeunes** ≈ youth
club; ~ **mère** parent company; ~ **de passe**; =
maison close; ~ **de repos** convalescent home;
~ **de retraite** old people's home; ~ **de santé**
mental home
maisonnée [mɛzɔne] nf household, family
maisonnette [mɛzɔnɛt] nf small house
maître, -esse [mɛtʀ(ə), mɛtʀɛs] nm/
f master (mistress); (Scol) teacher,
schoolmaster(-mistress) ▷ nm (peintre etc)
master; (titre): **M~ (Mᵉ)** Maître, term of address for
lawyers etc ▷ nf (amante) mistress ▷ adj (principal,
essentiel) main; **maison de ~** family seat; **être**
~ **de** (soi-même, situation) to be in control of;
se rendre ~ de (pays, ville) to gain control of;
(situation, incendie) to bring under control; **être**
passé ~ dans l'art de to be a (past) master in
the art of; **une maîtresse femme** a forceful
woman; ~ **d'armes** fencing master; ~ **auxiliaire**
(MA) (Scol) temporary teacher; ~ **chanteur**
blackmailer; ~ **de chapelle** choirmaster; ~ **de**
conférences ≈ senior lecturer (Brit), ≈ assistant
professor (US); ~/**maîtresse d'école** teacher,
schoolmaster(-mistress); ~ **d'hôtel** (domestique)
butler; (d'hôtel) head waiter; ~ **de maison** host;
~ **nageur** lifeguard; ~ **d'œuvre** (Constr) project
manager; ~ **d'ouvrage** (Constr) client; ~ **queux**
chef; **maîtresse de maison** hostess; (ménagère)
housewife
maîtrise [mɛtʀiz] nf (aussi: **maîtrise de soi**) self-
control; (habileté) skill, mastery; (suprématie)
mastery, command; (diplôme) ≈ master's degree;
see note; (chefs d'équipe) supervisory staff
maîtriser [mɛtʀize] vt (cheval, incendie) to (bring
under) control; (sujet) to master; (émotion) to
control; **se maîtriser** to control o.s.
majestueux, -euse [maʒɛstɥø, -øz] adj majestic
majeur, e [maʒœʀ] adj (important) major; (Jur) of
age; (fig) adult ▷ nm/f (Jur) person who has come
of age ou attained his (ou her) majority ▷ nm
(doigt) middle finger; **en ~e partie** for the most
part; **la ~e partie de** the major part of
majoration [maʒɔʀasjɔ̃] nf increase
majorer [maʒɔʀe] vt to increase
majoritaire [maʒɔʀitɛʀ] adj majority cpd;

système/scrutin ~ majority system/ballot
majorité [maʒɔʀite] *nf* (*gén*) majority; (*parti*)
party in power; **en** ~ (*composé etc*) mainly
majuscule [maʒyskyl] *adj, nf*: (**lettre**) ~ capital
(letter)
mal, maux [mal, mo] *nm* (*opposé au bien*) evil;
(*tort, dommage*) harm; (*douleur physique*) pain, ache;
(*maladie*) illness, sickness *no pl*; (*difficulté, peine*)
trouble; (*souffrance morale*) pain ▷ *adv* badly ▷ *adj*:
c'est ~ (**de faire**) it's bad *ou* wrong (to do); **être**
~ to be uncomfortable; **être** ~ **avec qn** to be on
bad terms with sb; **être au plus** ~ (*malade*) to
be very bad; (*brouillé*) to be at daggers drawn; **il**
comprend ~ he has difficulty in understanding;
il a ~ **compris** he misunderstood; ~ **tourner** to
go wrong; **dire/penser du** ~ **de** to speak/think
ill of; **ne vouloir de** ~ **à personne** to wish
nobody any ill; **il n'a rien fait de** ~ he has done
nothing wrong; **avoir du** ~ **à faire qch** to have
trouble doing sth; **se donner du** ~ **pour faire**
qch to go to a lot of trouble to do sth; **ne voir**
aucun ~ **à** to see no harm in, see nothing wrong
in; **craignant** ~ **faire** fearing he *etc* was doing
the wrong thing; **sans penser** *ou* **songer à** ~
without meaning any harm; **faire du** ~ **à qn** to
hurt sb; to harm sb; **se faire** ~ to hurt o.s.; **se**
faire ~ **au pied** to hurt one's foot; **ça fait** ~ it
hurts; **j'ai** ~ (**ici**) it hurts (here); **j'ai** ~ **au dos**
my back aches, I've got a pain in my back; **avoir**
~ **à la tête/à la gorge** to have a headache/a sore
throat; **avoir** ~ **aux dents/à l'oreille** to have
toothache/earache; **avoir le** ~ **de l'air** to be
airsick; **avoir le** ~ **du pays** to be homesick; ~ **de**
mer seasickness; ~ **de la route** carsickness; ~
en point *adj inv* in a bad state; **maux de ventre**
stomach ache *sg*; *voir aussi* **cœur**
malade [malad] *adj* ill, sick; (*poitrine, jambe*)
bad; (*plante*) diseased; (*fig: entreprise, monde*)
ailing ▷ *nm/f* invalid, sick person; (*à l'hôpital etc*)
patient; **tomber** ~ to fall ill; **être** ~ **du cœur**
to have heart trouble *ou* a bad heart; **grand** ~
seriously ill person; ~ **mental** mentally sick *ou*
ill person
maladie [maladi] *nf* (*spécifique*) disease, illness;
(*mauvaise santé*) illness, sickness; (*fig: manie*)
mania; **être rongé par la** ~ to be wasting away
(through illness); ~ **d'Alzheimer** Alzheimer's
disease; ~ **de peau** skin disease
maladif, -ive [maladif, -iv] *adj* sickly; (*curiosité,*
besoin) pathological
maladresse [maladʀɛs] *nf* clumsiness *no pl*;
(*gaffe*) blunder
maladroit, e [maladʀwa, -wat] *adj* clumsy
malaise [malez] *nm* (*Méd*) feeling of faintness;
feeling of discomfort; (*fig*) uneasiness, malaise;
avoir un ~ to feel faint *ou* dizzy
malaisé, e [maleze] *adj* difficult
malaria [malaʀja] *nf* malaria
malaxer [malakse] *vt* (*pétrir*) to knead; (*mêler*)
to mix
malchance [malʃɑ̃s] *nf* misfortune, ill luck *no pl*;
par ~ unfortunately; **quelle** ~! what bad luck!

malchanceux, -euse [malʃɑ̃sø, -øz] *adj* unlucky
mâle [mɑl] *adj* (*Élec, Tech*) male; (*viril: voix, traits*)
manly ▷ *nm* male
malédiction [malediksjɔ̃] *nf* curse
malencontreux, -euse [malɑ̃kɔ̃tʀø, -øz] *adj*
unfortunate, untoward
malentendant, e [malɑ̃tɑ̃dɑ̃, -ɑ̃t] *nm/f*: **les** ~**s**
the hard of hearing
malentendu [malɑ̃tɑ̃dy] *nm* misunderstanding
malfaçon [malfasɔ̃] *nf* fault
malfaisant, e [malfəzɑ̃, -ɑ̃t] *adj* evil, harmful
malfaiteur [malfɛtœʀ] *nm* lawbreaker,
criminal; (*voleur*) thief
malfamé, e [malfame] *adj* disreputable, of ill
repute
malgache [malgaʃ] *adj* Malagasy, Madagascan
▷ *nm* (*Ling*) Malagasy ▷ *nm/f*: **M**~ Malagasy,
Madagascan
malgré [malgʀe] *prép* in spite of, despite; ~ **tout**
adv in spite of everything
malhabile [malabil] *adj* clumsy
malheur [malœʀ] *nm* (*situation*) adversity,
misfortune; (*événement*) misfortune; (: *plus fort*)
disaster, tragedy; **par** ~ unfortunately; **quel** ~!
what a shame *ou* pity!; **faire un** ~ (*fam: un éclat*)
to do something desperate; (: *avoir du succès*) to be
a smash hit
malheureusement [malœʀøzmɑ̃] *adv*
unfortunately
malheureux, -euse [malœʀø, -øz] *adj* (*triste*)
unhappy, miserable; (*infortuné, regrettable*)
unfortunate; (*malchanceux*) unlucky; (*insignifiant*)
wretched ▷ *nm/f* (*infortuné, misérable*) poor soul;
(*indigent, miséreux*) unfortunate creature; **les** ~ the
destitute; **avoir là main malheureuse** (*au jeu*)
to be unlucky; (*tout casser*) to be ham-fisted
malhonnête [malɔnɛt] *adj* dishonest
malhonnêteté [malɔnɛtte] *nf* dishonesty;
rudeness *no pl*
malice [malis] *nf* mischievousness; (*méchanceté*):
par ~ out of malice *ou* spite; **sans** ~ guileless
malicieux, -euse [malisjø, -øz] *adj* mischievous
malin, -igne [malɛ̃, -iɲ] *adj* (*futé*: *f gén* **maline**)
smart, shrewd; (: *sourire*) knowing; (*Méd,*
influence) malignant; **faire le** ~ to show off;
éprouver un ~ **plaisir à** to take malicious
pleasure in
malingre [malɛ̃gʀ(ə)] *adj* puny
malle [mal] *nf* trunk; (*Auto*): ~ (**arrière**) boot
(*Brit*), trunk (*US*)
mallette [malɛt] *nf* (*valise*) (small) suitcase;
(*aussi*: **mallette de voyage**) overnight case; (*pour*
documents) attaché case
malmener [malməne] *vt* to manhandle; (*fig*) to
give a rough ride to
malodorant, e [malɔdɔʀɑ̃, -ɑ̃t] *adj* foul-smelling
malotru [malɔtʀy] *nm* lout, boor
malpoli, e [malpoli] *nm/f* rude individual
malpropre [malpʀɔpʀ(ə)] *adj* (*personne, vêtement*)
dirty; (*travail*) slovenly; (*histoire, plaisanterie*)
unsavoury (*Brit*), unsavory (*US*), smutty;
(*malhonnête*) dishonest

malsain, e [malsɛ̃, -ɛn] *adj* unhealthy

malt [malt] *nm* malt; **pur ~** (*whisky*) malt (whisky)

Malte [malt(ə)] *nf* Malta

maltraiter [maltʀete] *vt* (*brutaliser*) to manhandle, ill-treat; (*critiquer, éreinter*) to slate (*Brit*), roast

malveillance [malvɛjɑ̃s] *nf* (*animosité*) ill will; (*intention de nuire*) malevolence; (*Jur*) malicious intent *no pl*

malversation [malvɛʀsasjɔ̃] *nf* embezzlement, misappropriation (of funds)

mal-vivre [malvivʀ] *nm inv* malaise

maman [mamɑ̃] *nf* mum(my) (*Brit*), mom (*US*)

mamelle [mamɛl] *nf* teat

mamelon [mamlɔ̃] *nm* (*Anat*) nipple; (*colline*) knoll, hillock

mamie [mami] *nf* (*fam*) granny

mammifère [mamifɛʀ] *nm* mammal

mammouth [mamut] *nm* mammoth

manche [mɑ̃ʃ] *nf* (*de vêtement*) sleeve; (*d'un jeu, tournoi*) round; (*Géo*): **la M~** the (English) Channel ▷ *nm* (*d'outil, casserole*) handle; (*de pelle, pioche etc*) shaft; (*de violon, guitare*) neck; (*fam*) clumsy oaf; **faire la ~** to pass the hat; **~ à air** *nf* (*Aviat*) wind-sock; **~ à balai** *nm* broomstick; (*Aviat, Inform*) joystick

manchette [mɑ̃ʃɛt] *nf* (*de chemise*) cuff; (*coup*) forearm blow; (*titre*) headline

manchot [mɑ̃ʃo] *nm* one-armed man; armless man; (*Zool*) penguin

mandarine [mɑ̃daʀin] *nf* mandarin (orange), tangerine

mandat [mɑ̃da] *nm* (*postal*) postal *ou* money order; (*d'un député etc*) mandate; (*procuration*) power of attorney, proxy; (*Police*) warrant; **~ d'amener** summons *sg*; **~ d'arrêt** warrant for arrest; **~ de dépôt** committal order; **~ de perquisition** (*Police*) search warrant

mandataire [mɑ̃datɛʀ] *nm/f* (*représentant, délégué*) representative; (*Jur*) proxy

manège [manɛʒ] *nm* riding school; (*à la foire*) roundabout (*Brit*), merry-go-round; (*fig*) game, ploy; **faire un tour de ~** to go for a ride on a *ou* the roundabout *etc*; **~ (de chevaux de bois)** roundabout (*Brit*), merry-go-round

manette [manɛt] *nf* lever, tap; **~ de jeu** (*Inform*) joystick

mangeable [mɑ̃ʒabl(ə)] *adj* edible, eatable

mangeoire [mɑ̃ʒwaʀ] *nf* trough, manger

manger [mɑ̃ʒe] *vt* to eat; (*ronger: rouille etc*) to eat into *ou* away; (*utiliser, consommer*) to eat up ▷ *vi* to eat

mangeur, -euse [mɑ̃ʒœʀ, -øz] *nm/f* eater

mangue [mɑ̃g] *nf* mango

maniable [manjabl(ə)] *adj* (*outil*) handy; (*voiture, voilier*) easy to handle; manoeuvrable (*Brit*), maneuverable (*US*); (*fig: personne*) easily influenced, manipulable

maniaque [manjak] *adj* (*pointilleux, méticuleux*) finicky, fussy; (*atteint de manie*) suffering from a mania ▷ *nm/f* maniac

manie [mani] *nf* mania; (*tic*) odd habit

manier [manje] *vt* to handle; **se manier** *vi* (*fam*) to get a move on

maniéré, e [manjeʀe] *adj* affected

manière [manjɛʀ] *nf* (*façon*) way, manner; (*genre, style*) style; **manières** *nfpl* (*attitude*) manners; (*chichis*) fuss *sg*; **de ~ à** so as to; **de telle ~ que** in such a way that; **de cette ~** in this way *ou* manner; **d'une ~ générale** generally speaking, as a general rule; **de toute ~** in any case; **d'une certaine ~** in a (certain) way; **faire des ~s** to put on airs; **employer la ~ forte** to use strong-arm tactics

manif [manif] *nf* (*manifestation*) demo

manifestant, e [manifɛstɑ̃, -ɑ̃t] *nm/f* demonstrator

manifestation [manifɛstasjɔ̃] *nf* (*de joie, mécontentement*) expression, demonstration; (*symptôme*) outward sign; (*fête etc*) event; (*Pol*) demonstration

manifeste [manifɛst(ə)] *adj* obvious, evident ▷ *nm* manifesto

manifester [manifɛste] *vt* (*volonté, intentions*) to show, indicate; (*joie, peur*) to express, show ▷ *vi* (*Pol*) to demonstrate; **se manifester** *vi* (*émotion*) to show *ou* express itself; (*difficultés*) to arise; (*symptômes*) to appear; (*témoin etc*) to come forward

manigance [manigɑ̃s] *nf* scheme

manigancer [manigɑ̃se] *vt* to plot, devise

manipulation [manipylasjɔ̃] *nf* handling; manipulation

manipuler [manipyle] *vt* to handle; (*fig*) to manipulate

manivelle [manivɛl] *nf* crank

mannequin [mankɛ̃] *nm* (*Couture*) dummy; (*Mode*) model

manœuvre [manœvʀ(ə)] *nf* (*gén*) manoeuvre (*Brit*), maneuver (*US*) ▷ *nm* (*ouvrier*) labourer (*Brit*), laborer (*US*)

manœuvrer [manœvʀe] *vt* to manoeuvre (*Brit*), maneuver (*US*); (*levier, machine*) to operate; (*personne*) to manipulate ▷ *vi* to manoeuvre *ou* maneuver

manoir [manwaʀ] *nm* manor *ou* country house

manque [mɑ̃k] *nm* (*insuffisance*): **~ de** lack of; (*vide*) emptiness, gap; (*Méd*) withdrawal; **manques** *nmpl* (*lacunes*) faults, defects; **par ~ de** for want of; **~ à gagner** loss of profit *ou* earnings

manqué [mɑ̃ke] *adj* failed; **garçon ~** tomboy

manquer [mɑ̃ke] *vi* (*faire défaut*) to be lacking; (*être absent*) to be missing; (*échouer*) to fail ▷ *vt* to miss ▷ *vb impers*: **il (nous) manque encore 10 euros** we are still 10 euros short; **il manque des pages (au livre)** there are some pages missing *ou* some pages are missing (from the book); **l'argent qui leur manque** the money they need *ou* are short of; **le pied/la voix lui manqua** he missed his footing/his voice failed him; **~ à qn** (*absent etc*): **il/cela me manque** I miss him/that; **~ à** *vt* (*règles etc*) to be in breach of, fail to observe; **~ de** *vt* to lack; (*Comm*) to be out of (stock of); **ne pas ~ de faire: il n'a pas manqué de le dire** he certainly said it; **~ (de) faire: il a manqué (de) se tuer** he very nearly got killed; **il ne manquerait plus qu'il fasse** all we need now is for him to do; **je n'y manquerai pas** leave it to me, I'll definitely do it

mansarde [mɑ̃saʀd(ə)] *nf* attic

mansardé, e [mɑ̃saʀde] *adj* attic *cpd*

manteau, x [mɑ̃to] *nm* coat; **~ de cheminée** mantelpiece; **sous le ~** (*fig*) under cover

manucure [manykyʀ] *nf* manicurist

manuel, le [manɥɛl] *adj* manual ▷ *nm/f* manually gifted pupil (*as opposed to intellectually gifted*) ▷ *nm* (*ouvrage*) manual, handbook

manufacture [manyfaktyʀ] *nf* (*établissement*) factory; (*fabrication*) manufacture

manufacturé, e [manyfaktyʀe] *adj* manufactured

manuscrit, e [manyskʀi, -it] *adj* handwritten ▷ *nm* manuscript

manutention [manytɑ̃sjɔ̃] *nf* (*Comm*) handling; (*local*) storehouse

mappemonde [mapmɔ̃d] *nf* (*plane*) map of the world; (*sphère*) globe

maquereau, x [makʀo] *nm* mackerel *inv*; (*fam: proxénète*) pimp

maquette [makɛt] *nf* (*d'un décor, bâtiment, véhicule*) (scale) model; (*Typo*) mockup; (: *d'une page illustrée, affiche*) paste-up; (: *prêt à la réproduction*) artwork

maquillage [makijaʒ] *nm* making up; faking; (*produits*) make-up

maquiller [makije] *vt* (*personne, visage*) to make up; (*truquer: passeport, statistique*) to fake; (: *voiture volée*) to do over (*respray etc*); **se maquiller** to make o.s. up

maquis [maki] *nm* (*Géo*) scrub; (*fig*) tangle; (*Mil*) maquis, underground fighting *no pl*

maraîcher, -ère [maʀeʃe, maʀeʃɛʀ] *adj*: **cultures maraîchères** market gardening *sg* ▷ *nm/f* market gardener

marais [maʀɛ] *nm* marsh, swamp; **~ salant** saltworks

marasme [maʀasm(ə)] *nm* (*Pol, Écon*) stagnation, sluggishness; (*accablement*) dejection, depression

marathon [maʀatɔ̃] *nm* marathon

maraudeur, -euse [maʀodœʀ, -øz] *nm/f* marauder; prowler

marbre [maʀbʀ(ə)] *nm* (*pierre, statue*) marble; (*d'une table, commode*) marble top; (*Typo*) stone, bed; **rester de ~** to remain stonily indifferent

marc [maʀ] *nm* (*de raisin, pommes*) marc; **~ de café** coffee grounds *pl ou* dregs *pl*

marchand, e [maʀʃɑ̃, -ɑ̃d] *nm/f* shopkeeper, tradesman(-woman); (*au marché*) stallholder; (*spécifique*): **~ de cycles/tapis** bicycle/carpet dealer; **~ de charbon/vins** coal/wine merchant ▷ *adj*: **prix/valeur ~(e)** market price/value; **qualité ~e** standard quality; **~ en gros/au détail** wholesaler/retailer; **~ de biens** real estate agent; **~ de canons** (*péj*) arms dealer; **~ de couleurs** ironmonger (*Brit*), hardware dealer (*US*); **~/e de fruits** fruiterer (*Brit*), fruit seller (*US*); **~/e de journaux** newsagent; **~/e de légumes** greengrocer (*Brit*), produce dealer (*US*); **~/e de poisson** fishmonger (*Brit*), fish seller (*US*); **~/e de(s) quatre-saisons** costermonger (*Brit*), street vendor (selling fresh fruit and vegetables); **~ de sable** (*fig*) sandman; **~ de tableaux** art dealer

marchander [maʀʃɑ̃de] *vt* (*article*) to bargain *ou* haggle over; (*éloges*) to be sparing with ▷ *vi* to bargain, haggle

marchandise [maʀʃɑ̃diz] *nf* goods *pl*, merchandise *no pl*

marche [maʀʃ(ə)] *nf* (*d'escalier*) step; (*activité*) walking; (*promenade, trajet, allure*) walk; (*démarche*) walk, gait; (*Mil etc, Mus*) march; (*fonctionnement*) running; (*progression*) progress; course; **à une heure de ~** an hour's walk (away); **ouvrir/ fermer la ~** to lead the way/bring up the rear; **dans le sens de la ~** (*Rail*) facing the engine; **en ~** (*monter etc*) while the vehicle is moving *ou* in motion; **mettre en ~** to start; **remettre qch en ~** to set *ou* start sth going again; **se mettre en ~** (*personne*) to get moving; (*machine*) to start; **~ arrière** (*Auto*) reverse (gear); **faire ~ arrière** (*Auto*) to reverse; (*fig*) to backtrack, back-pedal; **~ à suivre** (correct) procedure; (*sur notice*) (step by step) instructions *pl*

marché [maʀʃe] *nm* (*lieu, Comm, Écon*) market; (*ville*) trading centre; (*transaction*) bargain, deal; **par-dessus le ~** into the bargain; **faire son ~** to do one's shopping; **mettre le ~ en main à qn** to tell sb to take it or leave it; **~ au comptant** (*Bourse*) spot market; **~ aux fleurs** flower market; **~ noir** black market; **faire du ~ noir** to buy and sell on the black market; **~ aux puces** flea market; **~ à terme** (*Bourse*) forward market; **~ du travail** labour market

marchepied [maʀʃəpje] *nm* (*Rail*) step; (*Auto*) running board; (*fig*) stepping stone

marcher [maʀʃe] *vi* to walk; (*Mil*) to march; (*aller: voiture, train, affaires*) to go; (*prospérer*) to go well; (*fonctionner*) to work, run; (*fam*) to go along, agree; (: *croire naïvement*) to be taken in; **~ sur** to walk on; (*mettre le pied sur*) to step on *ou* in; (*Mil*) to march upon; **~ dans** (*herbe etc*) to walk on *ou* in; (*flaque*) to step in; **faire ~ qn** (*pour rire*) to pull sb's leg; (*pour tromper*) to lead sb up the garden path

marcheur, -euse [maʀʃœʀ, -øz] *nm/f* walker

mardi [maʀdi] *nm* Tuesday; **M~ gras** Shrove Tuesday; *voir aussi* **lundi**

mare [maʀ] *nf* pond; **~ de sang** pool of blood

marécage [maʀekaʒ] *nm* marsh, swamp

marécageux, -euse [maʀekaʒø, -øz] *adj* marshy, swampy

maréchal, -aux [maʀeʃal, -o] *nm* marshal; **~ des logis** (*Mil*) sergeant

maréchal-ferrant (*pl* **maréchaux-ferrants**) [maʀeʃalferɑ̃, maʀeʃo-] *nm* blacksmith

marée [maʀe] *nf* tide; (*poissons*) fresh (sea) fish; **~ haute/basse** high/low tide; **~ montante/ descendante** rising/ebb tide; **~ noire** oil slick

marelle [maʀɛl] *nf*: **(jouer à) la ~** (to play) hopscotch

margarine [maʀgaʀin] *nf* margarine

marge [maʀʒ(ə)] *nf* margin; **en ~** in the margin; **en ~ de** (*fig*) on the fringe of; (*en dehors de*) cut off from; (*qui se rapporte à*) connected with; **~ bénéficiaire** profit margin, mark-up; **~ de sécurité** safety margin

marginal, e, -aux [maʀʒinal, -o] *adj* marginal ▷ *nm/f* dropout

marguerite [maʀgəʀit] *nf* marguerite, (oxeye) daisy

mari [maʀi] *nm* husband

mariage [maʀjaʒ] *nm* (*union, état, fig*) marriage; (*noce*) wedding; **~ civil/religieux** registry office (*Brit*) *ou* civil/church wedding; **un ~ de raison/d'amour** a marriage of convenience/a love match; **~ blanc** unconsummated marriage; **~ en blanc** white wedding

marié, e [maʀje] *adj* married ▷ *nm/f* (bride)groom/bride; **les ~s** the bride and groom; **les (jeunes) ~s** the newly-weds

marier [maʀje] *vt* to marry; (*fig*) to blend; **se ~ (avec)** to marry, get married (to); (*fig*) to blend (with)

marin, e [maʀɛ̃, -in] *adj* sea *cpd*, marine ▷ *nm* sailor ▷ *nf* navy; (*Art*) seascape; (*couleur*) navy (blue); **avoir le pied ~** to be a good sailor; (*garder son équilibre*) to have one's sea legs; **~e de guerre** navy; **~e marchande** merchant navy; **~e à voiles** sailing ships *pl*

marine [maʀin] *adj f, nf voir* **marin** ▷ *adj inv* navy (blue) ▷ *nm* (*Mil*) marine

mariner [maʀine] *vi, vt* to marinate, marinade

marionnette [maʀjɔnɛt] *nf* puppet

maritalement [maʀitalmɑ̃] *adv*: **vivre ~** to live together (as husband and wife)

maritime [maʀitim] *adj* sea *cpd*, maritime; (*ville*) coastal, seaside; (*droit*) shipping, maritime

marmelade [maʀməlad] *nf* (*compote*) stewed fruit, compote; **~ d'oranges** (orange) marmalade; **en ~** (*fig*) crushed (to a pulp)

marmite [maʀmit] *nf* (cooking-)pot

marmonner [maʀmɔne] *vt, vi* to mumble, mutter

marmot [maʀmo] *nm* (*fam*) brat

marmotter [maʀmɔte] *vt* (*prière*) to mumble, mutter

Maroc [maʀɔk] *nm*: **le ~** Morocco

marocain, e [maʀɔkɛ̃, -ɛn] *adj* Moroccan ▷ *nm/f*: **M~, e** Moroccan

maroquinerie [maʀɔkinʀi] *nf* (*industrie*) leather craft; (*commerce*) leather shop; (*articles*) fine leather goods *pl*

marquant, e [maʀkɑ̃, -ɑ̃t] *adj* outstanding

marque [maʀk(ə)] *nf* mark; (*Sport, Jeu*) score; (*Comm: de produits*) brand, make; (: *de disques*) label; (*insigne: d'une fonction*) badge; (*fig*): **~ d'affection** token of affection; **~ de joie** sign of joy; **à vos ~s!** (*Sport*) on your marks!; **de ~** *adj* (*Comm*) brand-name *cpd*; proprietary; (*fig*) high-class; (: *personnage, hôte*) distinguished; **produit de ~** quality product; **~ déposée** registered trademark; **~ de fabrique** trademark

marquer [maʀke] *vt* to mark; (*inscrire*) to write down; (*bétail*) to brand; (*Sport: but etc*) to score; (: *joueur*) to mark; (*accentuer: taille etc*) to emphasize; (*manifester: refus, intérêt*) to show ▷ *vi* (*événement, personnalité*) to stand out, be outstanding; (*Sport*) to score; **~ qn de son influence/empreinte** to have an influence/leave its impression on sb; **~ un temps d'arrêt** to pause momentarily; **~ le pas** (*fig*) to mark time; **il a marqué ce jour-là d'une pierre blanche** that was a red-letter day for him; **~ les points** (*tenir la marque*) to keep the score

marqueterie [maʀkətʀi] *nf* inlaid work, marquetry

marquis, e [maʀki, -iz] *nm/f* marquis *ou* marquess (marchioness) ▷ *nf* (*auvent*) glass canopy *ou* awning

marraine [maʀɛn] *nf* godmother; (*d'un navire, d'une rose etc*) namer

marrant, e [maʀɑ̃, -ɑ̃t] *adj* (*fam*) funny

marre [maʀ] *adv* (*fam*): **en avoir ~ de** to be fed up with

marrer [maʀe]: **se marrer** *vi* (*fam*) to have a (good) laugh

marron, ne [maʀɔ̃, -ɔn] *nm* (*fruit*) chestnut ▷ *adj inv* brown ▷ *adj* (*péj*) crooked; (: *faux*) bogus; **~s glacés** marrons glacés

marronnier [maʀɔnje] *nm* chestnut (tree)

mars [maʀs] *nm* March; *voir aussi* **juillet**

Marseille [maʀsɛj] *n* Marseilles

marsouin [maʀswɛ̃] *nm* porpoise

marteau, x [maʀto] *nm* hammer; (*de porte*) knocker; **~ pneumatique** pneumatic drill

marteau-piqueur (*pl* **marteaux-piqueurs**) [maʀtopikœʀ] *nm* pneumatic drill

marteler [maʀtəle] *vt* to hammer; (*mots, phrases*) to rap out

martien, ne [maʀsjɛ̃, -ɛn] *adj* Martian, of *ou* from Mars

martyr, e [maʀtiʀ] *nm/f* martyr ▷ *adj* martyred; **enfants ~s** battered children

martyre [maʀtiʀ] *nm* martyrdom; (*fig: sens affaibli*) agony, torture; **souffrir le ~** to suffer agonies

martyriser [maʀtiʀize] *vt* (*Rel*) to martyr; (*fig*) to bully; (: *enfant*) to batter

mascara [maskaʀa] *nm* mascara

masculin, e [maskylɛ̃, -in] *adj* masculine; (*sexe, population*) male; (*équipe, vêtements*) men's; (*viril*) manly ▷ *nm* masculine

masochiste [mazɔʃist(ə)] *adj* masochistic ▷ *nm/f* masochist

masque [mask(ə)] *nm* mask; **~ de beauté** face pack; **~ à gaz** gas mask; **~ de plongée** diving mask

masquer [maske] *vt* (*cacher: porte, goût*) to hide, conceal; (*dissimuler: vérité, projet*) to mask, obscure

massacre [masakʀ(ə)] *nm* massacre, slaughter; **jeu de ~** (*fig*) wholesale slaughter

massacrer [masakʀe] *vt* to massacre, slaughter;

(fig: adversaire) to slaughter; (: texte etc) to murder
massage [masaʒ] nm massage
masse [mas] nf mass; (péj): **la ~** the masses pl;
(Élec) earth; (maillet) sledgehammer; **masses**
nfpl masses; **une ~ de**, **des ~s de** (fam) masses
ou loads of; **en ~** adv (en bloc) in bulk; (en foule)
en masse ▷ adj (exécutions, production) mass cpd;
~ monétaire (Écon) money supply; **~ salariale**
(Comm) wage(s) bill
masser [mase] vt (assembler) to gather; (pétrir) to
massage; **se masser** vi to gather
masseur, -euse [masœʀ, -øz] nm/f (personne)
masseur(-euse) ▷ nm (appareil) massager
massif, -ive [masif, -iv] adj (porte) solid,
massive; (visage) heavy, large; (bois, or) solid;
(dose) massive; (déportations etc) mass cpd ▷ nm
(montagneux) massif; (de fleurs) clump, bank
massue [masy] nf club, bludgeon ▷ adj inv:
argument ~ sledgehammer argument
mastic [mastik] nm (pour vitres) putty; (pour fentes)
filler
mastiquer [mastike] vt (aliment) to chew,
masticate; (fente) to fill; (vitre) to putty
mat, e [mat] adj (couleur, métal) mat(t); (bruit, son)
dull ▷ adj inv (Échecs): **être ~** to be checkmate
mât [mɑ] nm (Navig) mast; (poteau) pole, post
match [matʃ] nm match; **~ nul** draw, tie (US);
faire ~ nul to draw (Brit), tie (US); **~ aller** first
leg; **~ retour** second leg, return match
matelas [matla] nm mattress; **~ pneumatique**
air bed ou mattress; **~ à ressorts** spring ou
interior-sprung mattress
matelassé, e adj padded; (tissu) quilted
matelot [matlo] nm sailor, seaman
mater [mate] vt (personne) to bring to heel,
subdue; (révolte) to put down; (fam) to watch,
look at
matérialiser [materjalize]: **se matérialiser** vi to
materialize
matérialiste [materjalist(ə)] adj materialistic
▷ nm/f materialist
matériau, x [materjo] nm material; **matériaux**
nmpl material(s); **~x de construction** building
materials
matériel, le [materjɛl] adj material; (organisation,
aide, obstacle) practical; (fig: péj: personne)
materialistic ▷ nm equipment no pl; (de camping
etc) gear no pl; (Inform) hardware; **il n'a pas le
temps ~ de le faire** he doesn't have the time
(needed) to do it; **~ d'exploitation** (Comm) plant;
~ roulant rolling stock
maternel, le [matɛrnɛl] adj (amour, geste)
motherly, maternal; (grand-père, oncle) maternal
▷ nf (aussi: **école maternelle**) (state) nursery
school
maternité [matɛrnite] nf (établissement)
maternity hospital; (état de mère) motherhood,
maternity; (grossesse) pregnancy
mathématique [matematik] adj mathematical
mathématiques [matematik] nfpl
mathematics sg
maths [mat] nfpl maths (Brit), math (US)

matière [matjɛʀ] nf (Physique) matter; (Comm,
Tech) material; matter no pl; (fig: d'un livre etc)
subject matter; (Scol) subject; **en ~ de** as regards;
donner ~ à to give cause to; **~ plastique** plastic;
~s fécales faeces; **~s grasses** fat (content) sg; **~s
premières** raw materials
Matignon [matiɲɔ̃] nm: (**l'hôtel) ~** the French
Prime Minister's residence; see note
matin [matɛ̃] nm, adv morning; **le ~** (pendant le
matin) in the morning; **demain ~** tomorrow
morning; **le lendemain ~** (the) next morning;
du ~ au soir from morning till night; **une
heure du ~** one o'clock in the morning; **de
grand** ou **bon ~** early in the morning
matinal, e, -aux [matinal, -o] adj (toilette,
gymnastique) morning cpd; (de bonne heure) early;
être ~ (personne) to be up early; (: habituellement) to
be an early riser
matinée [matine] nf morning; (spectacle)
matinée, afternoon performance
matou [matu] nm tom(cat)
matraque [matrak] nf (de malfaiteur) cosh (Brit),
club; (de policier) truncheon (Brit), billy (US)
matricule [matrikyl] nf (aussi: **registre
matricule**) roll, register ▷ nm (aussi: **numéro
matricule**: Mil) regimental number; (: Admin)
reference number
matrimonial, e, -aux [matrimɔnjal, -o] adj
marital, marriage cpd
maudire [modir] vt to curse
maudit, e [modi, -it] adj (fam: satané) blasted,
confounded
maugréer [mogree] vi to grumble
maussade [mosad] adj (air, personne) sullen; (ciel,
temps) dismal
mauvais, e [mɔvɛ, -ɛz] adj bad; (méchant,
malveillant) malicious, spiteful; (faux): **le ~
numéro** the wrong number ▷ nm: **le ~** the bad
side ▷ adv: **il fait ~** the weather is bad; **sentir ~**
to have a nasty smell, smell bad ou nasty; **la mer
est ~e** the sea is rough; **~ coucheur** awkward
customer; **~ coup** (fig) criminal venture; **~
garçon** tough; **~ pas** tight spot; **~ plaisant**
hoaxer; **~ traitements** ill treatment sg; **~e
herbe** weed; **~e langue** gossip, scandalmonger
(Brit); **~e passe** difficult situation; (période)
bad patch; **~e tête** rebellious ou headstrong
customer
mauve [mov] adj (couleur) mauve ▷ nf (Bot)
mallow
maux [mo] nmpl voir **mal**
maximal, e, -aux [maksimal, -o] adj maximal
maximum [maksimɔm] adj, nm maximum;
atteindre un/son ~ to reach a/his peak; **au ~** adv
(le plus possible) to the full; as much as one can;
(tout au plus) at the (very) most ou maximum
mayonnaise [majɔnɛz] nf mayonnaise
mazout [mazut] nm (fuel) oil; **chaudière/poêle
à ~** oil-fired boiler/stove
me, m' [m(ə)] pron me; (réfléchi) myself
mec [mɛk] nm (fam) guy, bloke (Brit)
mécanicien, ne [mekanisjɛ̃, -ɛn] nm/f

mechanic; (*Rail*) (train *ou* engine) driver; ~
navigant *ou* **de bord** (*Aviat*) flight engineer
mécanique [mekanik] *adj* mechanical ▷ *nf*
(*science*) mechanics *sg*; (*technologie*) mechanical
engineering; (*mécanisme*) mechanism;
engineering; works *pl*; **ennui** ~ engine trouble
no pl; **s'y connaître en** ~ to be mechanically
minded; ~ **hydraulique** hydraulics *sg*; ~
ondulatoire wave mechanics *sg*
mécanisme [mekanism(ə)] *nm* mechanism; ~
des taux de change exchange rate mechanism
méchamment [meʃamã] *adv* nastily,
maliciously; spitefully; viciously
méchanceté [meʃãste] *nf* (*d'une personne, d'une
parole*) nastiness, maliciousness, spitefulness;
(*parole, action*) nasty *ou* spiteful *ou* malicious
remark (*ou* action)
méchant, e [meʃã, -ãt] *adj* nasty, malicious,
spiteful; (*enfant: pas sage*) naughty; (*animal*)
vicious; (*avant le nom: péjorative*) nasty
mèche [mɛʃ] *nf* (*de lampe, bougie*) wick; (*d'un
explosif*) fuse; (*Méd*) pack, dressing; (*de vilebrequin,
perceuse*) bit; (*de dentiste*) drill; (*de fouet*) lash; (*de
cheveux*) lock; **se faire faire des ~s** (*chez le coiffeur*)
to have one's hair streaked, have highlights
put in one's hair; **vendre la** ~ to give the game
away; **de** ~ **avec** in league with
méchoui [meʃwi] *nm whole sheep barbecue*
méconnaissable [mekɔnɛsabl(ə)] *adj*
unrecognizable
méconnaître [mekɔnɛtʀ(ə)] *vt* (*ignorer*) to be
unaware of; (*mésestimer*) to misjudge
mécontent, e [mekɔ̃tã, -ãt] *adj*: ~ **(de)**
(*insatisfait*) discontented *ou* dissatisfied *ou*
displeased (with); (*contrarié*) annoyed (at) ▷ *nm/f*
malcontent, dissatisfied person
mécontentement [mekɔ̃tãtmã] *nm*
dissatisfaction, discontent, displeasure;
annoyance
médaille [medaj] *nf* medal
médaillon [medajɔ̃] *nm* (*portrait*) medallion;
(*bijou*) locket; (*Culin*) médaillon; **en** ~ *adj* (*carte
etc*) inset
médecin [medsɛ̃] *nm* doctor; ~ **du bord**
(*Navig*) ship's doctor; ~ **généraliste** general
practitioner, GP; ~ **légiste** forensic scientist
(*Brit*), medical examiner (*US*); ~ **traitant** family
doctor, GP
médecine [medsin] *nf* medicine; ~ **générale**
general medicine; ~ **infantile** paediatrics
sg (*Brit*), pediatrics *sg* (*US*); ~ **légale** forensic
medicine; ~ **préventive** preventive medicine; ~
du travail occupational *ou* industrial medicine;
~**s parallèles** *ou* **douces** alternative medicine
médiatique [medjatik] *adj* media *cpd*
médiatisé, e [medjatize] *adj* reported in the
media; **ce procès a été très** ~ (*péj*) this trial was
turned into a media event
médical, e, -aux [medikal, -o] *adj* medical;
visiteur *ou* **délégué** ~ medical rep *ou*
representative
médicament [medikamã] *nm* medicine, drug

médiéval, e, -aux [medjeval, -o] *adj* medieval
médiocre [medjɔkʀ(ə)] *adj* mediocre, poor
médire [mediʀ] *vi*: ~ **de** to speak ill of
médisance [medizãs] *nf* scandalmongering
no pl (*Brit*), mud-slinging *no pl*; (*propos*) piece of
scandal *ou* malicious gossip
méditer [medite] *vt* (*approfondir*) to meditate
on, ponder (over); (*combiner*) to meditate ▷ *vi* to
meditate; ~ **de faire** to contemplate doing, plan
to do
Méditerranée [mediteʀane] *nf*: **la (mer)** ~ the
Mediterranean (Sea)
méditerranéen, ne [mediteʀaneɛ̃, -ɛn] *adj*
Mediterranean ▷ *nm/f*: **M~, ne** Mediterranean
méduse [medyz] *nf* jellyfish
meeting [mitiŋ] *nm* (*Pol, Sport*) rally, meeting; ~
d'aviation air show
méfait [mefɛ] *nm* (*faute*) misdemeanour,
wrongdoing; **méfaits** *nmpl* (*ravages*) ravages
méfiance [mefjãs] *nf* mistrust, distrust
méfiant, e [mefjã, -ãt] *adj* mistrustful,
distrustful
méfier [mefje]: **se méfier** *vi* to be wary; (*faire
attention*) to be careful; **se** ~ **de** *vt* to mistrust,
distrust, be wary of; to be careful about
mégarde [megaʀd(ə)] *nf*: **par** ~ accidentally; (*par
erreur*) by mistake
mégère [meʒɛʀ] *nf* (*péj: femme*) shrew
mégot [mego] *nm* cigarette end *ou* butt
meilleur, e [mɛjœʀ] *adj, adv* better; (*valeur
superlative*) best ▷ *nm*: **le** ~ (*celui qui ...*) the best
(one); (*ce qui ...*) the best ▷ *nf*: **la** ~ (*celui qui ...*) the best (one);
le ~ **des deux** the better of the two; **de** ~**e heure**
earlier; ~ **marché** cheaper
mélancolie [melãkɔli] *nf* melancholy, gloom
mélancolique [melãkɔlik] *adj* melancholy,
gloomy
mélange [melãʒ] *nm* (*opération*) mixing;
blending; (*résultat*) mixture; blend; **sans** ~
unadulterated
mélanger [melãʒe] *vt* (*substances*) to mix; (*vins,
couleurs*) to blend; (*mettre en désordre, confondre*)
to mix up, muddle (up); **se mélanger** (*liquides,
couleurs*) to blend, mix
mélasse [melas] *nf* treacle, molasses *sg*
mêlée [mele] *nf* (*bataille, cohue*) mêlée, scramble;
(*lutte, conflit*) tussle, scuffle; (*Rugby*) scrum(mage)
mêler [mele] *vt* (*substances, odeurs, races*) to mix;
(*embrouiller*) to muddle (up), mix up; **se mêler** to
mix; (*se joindre, s'allier*) to mingle; **se** ~ **à** (*personne*)
to join; to mix with; (: *odeurs etc*) to mingle with;
se ~ **de** (*personne*) to meddle with, interfere
in; **mêle-toi de tes affaires!** mind your own
business!; ~ **à** *ou* **avec** *ou* **de** to mix with; to
mingle with; ~ **qn à** (*affaire*) to get sb mixed up
ou involved in
mélodie [melɔdi] *nf* melody
mélodieux, -euse [melɔdjø, -øz] *adj* melodious,
tuneful
melon [məlɔ̃] *nm* (*Bot*) (honeydew) melon;
(*aussi*: **chapeau melon**) bowler (hat); ~ **d'eau**
watermelon

membre [mɑ̃bʀ(ə)] *nm* (*Anat*) limb; (*personne, pays, élément*) member ▷ *adj* member; **être ~ de** to be a member of; **~ (viril)** (*male*) organ

mémé [meme] *nf* (*fam*) granny; (: *vieille femme*) old dear

même [mɛm] *adj* **1** (*avant le nom*) same; **en ~ temps** at the same time; **ils ont les ~s goûts** they have the same *ou* similar tastes
2 (*après le nom: renforcement*): **il est la loyauté ~** he is loyalty itself; **ce sont ses paroles/celles-là ~** they are his very words/the very ones
▷ *pron*: **le (la) ~** the same one
▷ *adv* **1** (*renforcement*): **il n'a ~ pas pleuré** he didn't even cry; **~ lui l'a dit** even HE said it; **ici ~** at this very place; **~ si** even if
2: **à ~:** **à ~ la bouteille** straight from the bottle; **à ~ la peau** next to the skin; **être à ~ de faire** to be in a position to do, be able to do; **mettre qn à ~ de faire** to enable sb to do
3: **de ~** likewise; **faire de ~** to do likewise *ou* the same; **lui de ~** so does (*ou* did *ou* is) he; **de ~ que** just as; **il en va de ~ pour** the same goes for

mémo [memo] (*fam*) *nm* memo

mémoire [memwaʀ] *nf* memory ▷ *nm* (*Admin, Jur*) memorandum; (*Scol*) dissertation, paper; **avoir la ~ des visages/chiffres** to have a (good) memory for faces/figures; **n'avoir aucune ~** to have a terrible memory; **avoir de la ~** to have a good memory; **à la ~ de** to the *ou* in memory of; **pour ~** *adv* for the record; **de ~** *adv* from memory; **de ~ d'homme** in living memory; **mettre en ~** (*Inform*) to store; **~ morte** ROM; **~ vive** RAM

mémorable [memɔʀabl(ə)] *adj* memorable

menace [mənas] *nf* threat; **~ en l'air** empty threat

menacer [mənase] *vt* to threaten; **~ qn de qch/de faire qch** to threaten sb with sth/to do sth

ménage [menaʒ] *nm* (*travail*) housekeeping, housework; (*couple*) (married) couple; (*famille, Admin*) household; **faire le ~** to do the housework; **faire des ~s** to work as a cleaner (*in private homes*); **monter son ~** to set up house; **se mettre en ~ (avec)** to set up house (with); **heureux en ~** happily married; **faire bon ~ avec** to get on well with; **~ de poupée** doll's kitchen set; **~ à trois** love triangle

ménagement [menaʒmɑ̃] *nm* care and attention; **ménagements** *nmpl* (*égards*) consideration *sg*, attention *sg*

ménager¹ [menaʒe] *vt* (*traiter avec mesure*) to handle with tact; (*traiter considérablement*); (*utiliser*) to use with care; (: *avec économie*) to use sparingly; (*prendre soin de*) to take (great) care of, look after; (*organiser*) to arrange; (*installer*) to put in; to make; **se ménager** to look after o.s.; **~ qch à qn** (*réserver*) to have sth in store for sb

ménager², -ère [menaʒe, -ɛʀ] *adj* household *cpd*, domestic ▷ *nf* (*femme*) housewife; (*couverts*) canteen (of cutlery)

mendiant, e [mɑ̃djɑ̃, -ɑ̃t] *nm/f* beggar

mendier [mɑ̃dje] *vi* to beg ▷ *vt* to beg (for); (*fig: éloges, compliments*) to fish for

mener [məne] *vt* to lead; (*enquête*) to conduct; (*affaires*) to manage, conduct, run ▷ *vi*: **~ (à la marque)** to lead, be in the lead; **~ à/dans** (*emmener*) to take to/into; **~ qch à bonne fin** *ou* **à terme** *ou* **à bien** to see sth through (to a successful conclusion), complete sth successfully

meneur, -euse [mənœʀ, -øz] *nm/f* leader; (*péj: agitateur*) ringleader; **~ d'hommes** born leader; **~ de jeu** host, quizmaster (*Brit*)

méningite [menɛ̃ʒit] *nf* meningitis *no pl*

ménopause [menɔpoz] *nf* menopause

menotte [mənɔt] *nf* (*langage enfantin*) handie; **menottes** *nfpl* handcuffs; **passer les ~s à** to handcuff

mensonge [mɑ̃sɔ̃ʒ] *nm*: **le ~** lying *no pl*; **un ~** a lie

mensonger, -ère [mɑ̃sɔ̃ʒe, -ɛʀ] *adj* false

mensualité [mɑ̃sɥalite] *nf* (*somme payée*) monthly payment; (*somme perçue*) monthly salary

mensuel, le [mɑ̃sɥɛl] *adj* monthly ▷ *nm/f* (*employé*) employee paid monthly ▷ *nm* (*Presse*) monthly

mensurations [mɑ̃syʀasjɔ̃] *nfpl* measurements

mental, e, -aux [mɑ̃tal, -o] *adj* mental

mentalité [mɑ̃talite] *nf* mentality

menteur, -euse [mɑ̃tœʀ, -øz] *nm/f* liar

menthe [mɑ̃t] *nf* mint; **~ (à l'eau)** peppermint cordial

mention [mɑ̃sjɔ̃] *nf* (*note*) note, comment; (*Scol*): **~ (très) bien/passable** (*very*) good/satisfactory pass; **faire ~ de** to mention; **"rayer la ~ inutile"** "delete as appropriate"

mentionner [mɑ̃sjɔne] *vt* to mention

mentir [mɑ̃tiʀ] *vi* to lie

menton [mɑ̃tɔ̃] *nm* chin

menu, e [məny] *adj* (*mince*) thin; (*petit*) tiny; (*frais, difficulté*) minor ▷ *adv* (*couper, hacher*) very fine ▷ *nm* menu; **par le ~** (*raconter*) in minute detail; **~ touristique** popular *ou* tourist menu; **~e monnaie** small change

menuiserie [mənɥizʀi] *nf* (*travail*) joinery, carpentry; (*d'amateur*) woodwork; (*local*) joiner's workshop; (*ouvrages*) woodwork *no pl*

menuisier [mənɥizje] *nm* joiner, carpenter

méprendre [mepʀɑ̃dʀ(ə)]: **se méprendre** *vi*: **se méprendre sur** to be mistaken about

mépris, e [mepʀi, -iz] *pp de* **méprendre** ▷ *nm* (*dédain*) contempt, scorn; (*indifférence*): **le ~ de** contempt *ou* disregard for; **au ~ de** regardless of, in defiance of

méprisable [mepʀizabl(ə)] *adj* contemptible, despicable

méprisant, e [mepʀizɑ̃, -ɑ̃t] *adj* contemptuous, scornful

méprise [mepʀiz] *nf* mistake, error; (*malentendu*) misunderstanding

mépriser [mepʀize] *vt* to scorn, despise; (*gloire, danger*) to scorn, spurn

mer [mɛʀ] *nf* sea; (*marée*) tide; **~ fermée** inland sea; **en ~** at sea; **prendre la ~** to put out to sea; **en haute** *ou* **pleine ~** off shore, on the open sea; **la ~ Adriatique** the Adriatic (Sea); **la ~ des Antilles** *ou* **des Caraïbes** the Caribbean (Sea); **la ~ Baltique** the Baltic (Sea); **la ~ Caspienne** the Caspian Sea; **la ~ de Corail** the Coral Sea; **la ~ Égée** the Aegean (Sea); **la ~ Ionienne** the Ionian Sea; **la ~ Morte** the Dead Sea; **la ~ Noire** the Black Sea; **la ~ du Nord** the North Sea; **la ~ Rouge** the Red Sea; **la ~ des Sargasses** the Sargasso Sea; **les ~s du Sud** the South Seas; **la ~ Tyrrhénienne** the Tyrrhenian Sea

mercenaire [mɛʀsənɛʀ] *nm* mercenary

mercerie [mɛʀsəʀi] *nf* (*Couture*) haberdashery (*Brit*), notions *pl* (*US*); (*boutique*) haberdasher's (shop) (*Brit*), notions store (*US*)

merci [mɛʀsi] *excl* thank you ▷ *nf*: **à la ~ de qn/qch** at sb's mercy/the mercy of sth; **~ beaucoup** thank you very much; **~ de** *ou* **pour** thank you for; **sans ~** *adj* merciless ▷ *adv* mercilessly

mercredi [mɛʀkʀədi] *nm* Wednesday; **~ des Cendres** Ash Wednesday; *voir aussi* **lundi**

mercure [mɛʀkyʀ] *nm* mercury

merde [mɛʀd(ə)] (*fam!*) *nf* shit (!) ▷ *excl* (bloody) hell (!)

mère [mɛʀ] *nf* mother ▷ *adj inv* mother *cpd*; **~ célibataire** single parent, unmarried mother

merguez [mɛʀgɛz] *nf* spicy North African sausage

méridional, e, -aux [meʀidjɔnal, -o] *adj* southern; (*du midi de la France*) Southern (French) ▷ *nm/f* Southerner

meringue [məʀɛ̃g] *nf* meringue

mérite [meʀit] *nm* merit; **le ~ (de ceci) lui revient** the credit (for this) is his

mériter [meʀite] *vt* to deserve; **~ de réussir** to deserve to succeed; **il mérite qu'on fasse ...** he deserves people to do ...

merlan [mɛʀlɑ̃] *nm* whiting

merle [mɛʀl(ə)] *nm* blackbird

merveille [mɛʀvɛj] *nf* marvel, wonder; **faire ~** *ou* **des ~s** to work wonders; **à ~** perfectly, wonderfully

merveilleux, -euse [mɛʀvɛjø, -øz] *adj* marvellous, wonderful

mes [me] *adj poss voir* **mon**

mésange [mezɑ̃ʒ] *nf* tit(mouse); **~ bleue** bluetit

mésaventure [mezavɑ̃tyʀ] *nf* misadventure, misfortune

Mesdames [medam] *nfpl voir* **Madame**

Mesdemoiselles [medmwazɛl] *nfpl voir* **Mademoiselle**

mesquin, e [mɛskɛ̃, -in] *adj* mean, petty

mesquinerie [mɛskinʀi] *nf* meanness *no pl*, pettiness *no pl*

message [mesaʒ] *nm* message; **~ d'erreur** (*Inform*) error message; **~ électronique** (*Inform*) email; **~ publicitaire** ad, advertisement; **~ téléphoné** telegram dictated by telephone

messager, -ère [mesaʒe, -ɛʀ] *nm/f* messenger

messagerie [mesaʒʀi] *nf*: **~ électronique** electronic mail, email; **~ rose** *lonely hearts and contact service on videotext*; **~s aériennes/ maritimes** air freight/shipping service *sg*; **~s de presse** press distribution service; **~ vocale** voice mail

messe [mɛs] *nf* mass; **aller à la ~** to go to mass; **~ de minuit** midnight mass; **faire des ~s basses** (*fig, péj*) to mutter

Messieurs [mesjø] *nmpl voir* **Monsieur**

mesure [məzyʀ] *nf* (*évaluation, dimension*) measurement; (*étalon, récipient, contenu*) measure; (*Mus: cadence*) time, tempo; (: *division*) bar; (*retenue*) moderation; (*disposition*) measure, step; **unité/système de ~** unit/system of measurement; **sur ~** (*costume*) made-to-measure; (*fig*) personally adapted; **à la ~ de** (*fig: personne*) worthy of; (*chambre etc*) on the same scale as; **dans la ~ où** insofar as, inasmuch as; **dans une certaine ~** to some *ou* a certain extent; **à ~ que** as; **en ~** (*Mus*) in time *ou* tempo; **être en ~ de** to be in a position to; **dépasser la ~** (*fig*) to overstep the mark

mesurer [məzyʀe] *vt* to measure; (*juger*) to weigh up, assess; (*limiter*) to limit, ration; (*modérer*) to moderate; (*proportionner*): **~ qch à** to match sth to, gear sth to; **se ~ avec** to have a confrontation with; to tackle; **il mesure 1 m 80** he's 1 m 80 tall

met [mɛ] *vb voir* **mettre**

métal, -aux [metal, -o] *nm* metal

métallique [metalik] *adj* metallic

météo [meteo] *nf* (*bulletin*) (weather) forecast; (*service*) ≈ Met Office (*Brit*), ≈ National Weather Service (*US*)

météorologie [meteɔʀɔlɔʒi] *nf* (*étude*) meteorology; (*service*) ≈ Meteorological Office (*Brit*), ≈ National Weather Service (*US*)

méthode [metɔd] *nf* method; (*livre, ouvrage*) manual, tutor

méticuleux, -euse [metikylø, -øz] *adj* meticulous

métier [metje] *nm* (*profession: gén*) job; (: *manuel*) trade; (: *artisanal*) craft; (*technique, expérience*) (acquired) skill *ou* technique; (*aussi*: **métier à tisser**) (weaving) loom; **être du ~** to be in the trade *ou* profession

métis, se [metis] *adj, nm/f* half-caste, half-breed

métrage [metʀaʒ] *nm* (*de tissu*) length; (*Ciné*) footage, length; **long/moyen/court ~** feature *ou* full-length/medium-length/short film

mètre [mɛtʀ(ə)] *nm* metre (*Brit*), meter (*US*); (*règle*) (metre *ou* meter) rule; (*ruban*) tape measure; **~ carré/cube** square/cubic metre *ou* meter

métrique [metʀik] *adj* metric ▷ *nf* metrics *sg*

métro [metʀo] *nm* underground (*Brit*), subway (*US*)

métropole [metʀɔpɔl] *nf* (*capitale*) metropolis; (*pays*) home country

mets [mɛ] *nm* dish ▷ *vb voir* **mettre**

metteur [metœʀ] *nm*: **~ en scène** (*Théât*) producer; (*Ciné*) director; **~ en ondes** (*Radio*) producer

mettre [mɛtʀ(ə)] *vt* **1** (*placer*) to put; **~ en bouteille/en sac** to bottle/put in bags *ou* sacks; **~ qch à la poste** to post sth (*Brit*), mail sth (*US*); **~ en examen (pour)** to charge (with) (*Brit*), indict

(for) (US); ~ **une note gaie/amusante** to inject
a cheerful/an amusing note; ~ **qn debout/assis**
to help sb up *ou* to their feet/help sb to sit down
2 (*vêtements: revêtir*) to put on; (*: porter*) to wear;
mets ton gilet put your cardigan on; **je ne
mets plus mon manteau** I no longer wear my
coat
3 (*faire fonctionner: chauffage, électricité*) to put on;
(*: reveil, minuteur*) to set; (*installer: gaz, eau*) to put
in, lay on; ~ **en marche** to start up
4 (*consacrer*): ~ **du temps/deux heures à faire
qch** to take time/two hours to do sth; **y ~ du
sien** to pull one's weight
5 (*noter, écrire*) to say, put (down); **qu'est-ce qu'il
a mis sur la carte?** what did he say *ou* write on
the card?; **mettez au pluriel ...** put ... into the
plural
6 (*supposer*): **mettons que ...** let's suppose *ou* say
that ...
7 (*faire + vb*): **faire ~ le gaz/l'électricité** to have
gas/electricity put in *ou* installed; **se mettre** *vi*
1 (*se placer*): **vous pouvez vous ~ là** you can sit
(*ou* stand) there; **où ça se met?** where does it
go?; **se ~ au lit** to get into bed; **se ~ au piano** to
sit down at the piano; **se ~ à l'eau** to get into the
water; **se ~ de l'encre sur les doigts** to get ink
on one's fingers
2 (*s'habiller*): **se ~ en maillot de bain** to get into
ou put on a swimsuit; **n'avoir rien à se ~** to have
nothing to wear
3 (*dans rapports*): **se ~ bien/mal avec qn** to get
on the right/wrong side of sb; **se ~ qn à dos** to
get on sb's bad side; **se ~ avec qn** (*prendre parti*) to
side with sb; (*faire équipe*) to team up with sb; (*en
ménage*) to move in with sb
4: **se ~ à** to begin, start; **se ~ à faire** to begin
ou start doing *ou* to do; **se ~ au piano** to start
learning the piano; **se ~ au régime** to go on a
diet; **se ~ au travail/à l'étude** to get down to
work/one's studies; **il est temps de s'y ~** it's
time we got down to it *ou* got on with it

meuble [mœbl(ə)] *nm* (*objet*) piece of furniture;
(*ameublement*) furniture *no pl* ▷ *adj* (*terre*) loose,
friable; (Jur): **biens ~s** movables

meublé [mœble] *nm* (*pièce*) furnished room;
(*appartement*) furnished flat (Brit) *ou* apartment (US)

meubler [mœble] *vt* to furnish; (*fig*): ~ **qch (de)**
to fill sth (with); **se meubler** to furnish one's
house

meuf [mœf] *nf* (*fam*) woman

meugler [møgle] *vi* to low, moo

meule [møl] *nf* (*à broyer*) millstone; (*à aiguiser*)
grindstone; (*à polir*) buff wheel; (*de foin, blé*) stack;
(*de fromage*) round

meunier, -ière [mønje, -jɛʀ] *nm* miller ▷ *nf*
miller's wife ▷ *adj f* (Culin) meunière

meurtre [mœʀtʀ(ə)] *nm* murder

meurtrier, -ière [mœʀtʀije, -jɛʀ] *adj* (*arme,
épidémie, combat*) deadly; (*accident*) fatal; (*carrefour,
route*) lethal; (*fureur, instincts*) murderous ▷ *nm/f*
murderer(-ess) ▷ *nf* (*ouverture*) loophole

meurtrir [mœʀtʀiʀ] *vt* to bruise; (*fig*) to wound

meurtrissure [mœʀtʀisyʀ] *nf* bruise; (*fig*) scar

meus *etc* [mœ] *vb voir* **mouvoir**

meute [møt] *nf* pack

mexicain, e [mɛksikɛ̃, -ɛn] *adj* Mexican ▷ *nm/f*:
M~, e Mexican

Mexico [mɛksiko] *n* Mexico City

Mexique [mɛksik] *nm*: **le ~** Mexico

Mgr *abr* = **Monseigneur**

mi [mi] *nm* (*Mus*) E; (*en chantant la gamme*) mi

miauler [mjole] *vi* to miaow

mi-bas [miba] *nm inv* knee-length sock

miche [miʃ] *nf* round *ou* cob loaf

mi-chemin [miʃmɛ̃]: **à ~** *adv* halfway, midway

mi-clos, e [miklo, -kloz] *adj* half-closed

micro [mikʀo] *nm* mike, microphone; ~ **cravate**
lapel mike

microbe [mikʀɔb] *nm* germ, microbe

micro-onde [mikʀoɔ̃d] *nf*: **four à ~s** microwave
oven

micro-ordinateur [mikʀɔɔʀdinatœʀ] *nm*
microcomputer

microscope [mikʀɔskɔp] *nm* microscope; **au ~**
under *ou* through the microscope

microscopique [mikʀɔskɔpik] *adj* microscopic

midi [midi] *nm* (*milieu du jour*) midday, noon;
(*moment du déjeuner*) lunchtime; (*sud*) south; (*: de
la France*): **le M~** the South (of France), the Midi;
à ~ at 12 (o'clock) *ou* midday *ou* noon; **tous les ~s**
every lunchtime; **le repas de ~** lunch; **en plein
~** (right) in the middle of the day; (*sud*) facing
south

mie [mi] *nf* inside (of the loaf)

miel [mjɛl] *nm* honey; **être tout ~** (*fig*) to be all
sweetness and light

mielleux, -euse [mjɛlø, -øz] *adj* (*péj*) sugary,
honeyed

mien, ne [mjɛ̃, mjɛn] *adj, pron*: **le (la) ~(ne), les
~s** mine; **les ~s** (*ma famille*) my family

miette [mjɛt] *nf* (*de pain, gâteau*) crumb; (*fig: de
la conversation etc*) scrap; **en ~s** (*fig*) in pieces *ou* bits

mieux [mjø] *adv* **1** (*d'une meilleure façon*): ~
(**que**) better (than); **elle travaille/mange
~** she works/eats better; **aimer ~** to prefer;
j'attendais ~ de vous I expected better of you;
elle va ~ she is better; **de ~ en ~** better and better
2 (*de la meilleure façon*) best; **ce que je sais le ~**
what I know best; **les livres les ~ faits** the best
made books
3 (*intensif*): **vous feriez ~ de faire ...** you would
be better to do ...; **crier à qui ~ ~** to try to shout
each other down
▷ *adj* **1** (*plus à l'aise, en meilleure forme*) better; **se
sentir ~** to feel better
2 (*plus satisfaisant*) better; **c'est ~ ainsi** it's better
like this; **c'est le ~ des deux** it's the better of
the two; **le/la ~, les ~** the best; **demandez-lui,
c'est le ~** ask him, it's the best thing
3 (*plus joli*) better-looking; (*plus gentil*) nicer; **il est
~ que son frère** (*plus beau*) he's better-looking
than his brother; (*plus gentil*) he's nicer than
his brother; **il est ~ sans moustache** he looks
better without a moustache

4: au ~ at best; **au ~ avec** on the best of terms
with; **pour le ~** for the best; **qui ~ est** even
better, better still
▷ *nm* **1** (*progrès*) improvement
2: de mon/ton ~ as best I/you can (*ou* could);
faire de son ~ to do one's best; **du ~ qu'il peut**
the best he can; **faute de ~** for lack *ou* want of
anything better, failing anything better

mièvre [mjɛvʀ(ə)] *adj* sickly sentimental

mignon, ne [miɲɔ̃, -ɔn] *adj* sweet, cute

migraine [migʀɛn] *nf* headache; migraine

mijoter [miʒɔte] *vt* (*préparer avec soin*)
to cook lovingly; (*affaire, projet*) to plot, cook up
▷ *vi* to simmer

mil [mil] *num* = **mille**

milieu, x [miljø] *nm* (*centre*) middle; (*fig*) middle
course *ou* way; (*aussi*: **juste milieu**) happy
medium; (*Bio, Géo*) environment; (*entourage
social*) milieu; (*familial*) background; circle;
(*pègre*): **le ~** the underworld; **au ~ de** in the
middle of; **au beau** *ou* **en plein ~ (de)** right in
the middle (of); **~ de terrain** (*Football*: *joueur*)
midfield player; (*: joueurs*) midfield

militaire [militɛʀ] *adj* military ▷ *nm*
serviceman; **service ~** military service

militant, e [militɑ̃, -ɑ̃t] *adj, nm/f* militant

militer [milite] *vi* to be a militant; **~ pour/
contre** to militate in favour of/against

mille [mil] *num* a *ou* one thousand ▷ *nm* (*mesure*):
~ (marin) nautical mile; **mettre dans le ~** to hit
the bull's-eye; (*fig*) to be bang on (target)

millefeuille [milfœj] *nm* cream *ou* vanilla slice

millénaire [milenɛʀ] *nm* millennium ▷ *adj*
thousand-year-old; (*fig*) ancient

mille-pattes [milpat] *nm inv* centipede

millésimé, e [milezime] *adj* vintage *cpd*

millet [mijɛ] *nm* millet

milliard [miljaʀ] *nm* milliard, thousand million
(*Brit*), billion (*US*)

milliardaire [miljaʀdɛʀ] *nm/f* multimillionaire
(*Brit*), billionaire (*US*)

millier [milje] *nm* thousand; **un ~ (de)** a
thousand or so, about a thousand; **par ~s** in
(their) thousands, by the thousand

milligramme [miligʀam] *nm* milligramme
(*Brit*), milligram (*US*)

millimètre [milimɛtʀ(ə)] *nm* millimetre (*Brit*),
millimeter (*US*)

million [miljɔ̃] *nm* million; **deux ~s de** two
million; **riche à ~s** worth millions

millionnaire [miljɔnɛʀ] *nm/f* millionaire

mime [mim] *nm/f* (*acteur*) mime(r); (*imitateur*)
mimic ▷ *nm* (*art*) mime, miming

mimer [mime] *vt* to mime; (*singer*) to mimic,
take off

mimique [mimik] *nf* (funny) face; (*signes*)
gesticulations *pl*, sign language *no pl*

minable [minabl(ə)] *adj* (*personne*) shabby(-
looking); (*travail*) pathetic

mince [mɛ̃s] *adj* thin; (*personne, taille*) slim; (*fig*:
profit, connaissances) slight, small; (*: prétexte*) weak
▷ *excl*: **~ (alors)!** darn it!

minceur [mɛ̃sœʀ] *nf* thinness slimness,
slenderness

mincir [mɛ̃siʀ] *vi* to get slimmer *ou* thinner

mine [min] *nf* (*physionomie*) expression, look;
(*extérieur*) exterior, appearance; (*de crayon*) lead;
(*gisement, exploitation, explosif*) mine; **mines** *nfpl*
(*péj*) simpering airs; **les M~s** (*Admin*) *the national
mining and geological service, the government vehicle
testing department*; **avoir bonne ~** (*personne*) to
look well; (*ironique*) to look an utter idiot; **avoir
mauvaise ~** to look unwell; **faire ~ de faire** to
make a pretence of doing; **ne pas payer de ~**
to be not much to look at; **~ de rien** *adv* with a
casual air; although you wouldn't think so; **~
de charbon** coal mine; **~ à ciel ouvert** opencast
(*Brit*) *ou* open-air (*US*) mine

miner [mine] *vt* (*saper*) to undermine, erode;
(*Mil*) to mine

minerai [minʀɛ] *nm* ore

minéral, e, -aux [mineʀal, -o] *adj* mineral;
(*Chimie*) inorganic ▷ *nm* mineral

minéralogique [mineʀalɔʒik] *adj*
mineralogical; **plaque ~** number (*Brit*) *ou* license
(*US*) plate; **numéro ~** registration (*Brit*) *ou*
license (*US*) number

minet, te [minɛ, -ɛt] *nm/f* (*chat*) pussy-cat; (*péj*)
young trendy

mineur, e [minœʀ] *adj* minor ▷ *nm/f* (*Jur*) minor
▷ *nm* (*travailleur*) miner; (*Mil*) sapper; **~ de fond**
face worker

miniature [minjatyʀ] *adj, nf* miniature

minibus [minibys] *nm* minibus

mini-cassette [minikasɛt] *nf* cassette (recorder)

minier, -ière [minje, -jɛʀ] *adj* mining

mini-jupe [miniʒyp] *nf* mini-skirt

minimal, e, -aux [minimal, -o] *adj* minimum

minime [minim] *adj* minor, minimal ▷ *nm/f*
(*Sport*) junior

minimiser [minimize] *vt* to minimize; (*fig*) to
play down

minimum [minimɔm] *adj, nm* minimum; **au
~** at the very least; **~ vital** (*salaire*) living wage;
(*niveau de vie*) subsistance level

ministère [ministɛʀ] *nm* (*cabinet*) government;
(*département*) ministry (*Brit*), department; (*Rel*)
ministry; **~ public** (*Jur*) Prosecution, State
Prosecutor

ministre [ministʀ(ə)] *nm* minister (*Brit*),
secretary; (*Rel*) minister; **~ d'État** senior
minister *ou* secretary

Minitel® [minitɛl] *nm videotext terminal and service*

minoritaire [minɔʀitɛʀ] *adj* minority *cpd*

minorité [minɔʀite] *nf* minority; **être en ~** to be
in the *ou* a minority; **mettre en ~** (*Pol*) to defeat

minuit [minɥi] *nm* midnight

minuscule [minyskyl] *adj* minute, tiny ▷ *nf*:
(**lettre**) **~** small letter

minute [minyt] *nf* minute; (*Jur*: *original*) minute,
draft ▷ *excl* just a minute!, hang on!; **à la ~**
(*présent*) (just) this instant; (*passé*) there and
then; **entrecôte** *ou* **steak ~** minute steak

minuter [minyte] *vt* to time

minuterie [minytʀi] *nf* time switch
minutieux, -euse [minysjø, -øz] *adj (personne)*
meticulous; *(inspection)* minutely detailed;
(travail) requiring painstaking attention to detail
mirabelle [miʀabɛl] *nf (fruit)* (cherry) plum; *(eau-de-vie)* plum brandy
miracle [miʀakl(ə)] *nm* miracle
mirage [miʀaʒ] *nm* mirage
mire [miʀ] *nf (d'un fusil)* sight; *(TV)* test card;
point de ~ target; *(fig)* focal point; **ligne de ~**
line of sight
miroir [miʀwaʀ] *nm* mirror
miroiter [miʀwate] *vi* to sparkle, shimmer;
faire ~ qch à qn to paint sth in glowing colours
for sb, dangle sth in front of sb's eyes
mis, e [mi, miz] *pp de* **mettre** ▷ *adj (couvert, table)*
set, laid; *(personne)*: **bien ~** well dressed ▷ *nf*
(argent: au jeu) stake; *(tenue)* clothing; attire;
être de ~e to be acceptable *ou* in season; **~e en
bouteilles** bottling; **~e en examen** charging,
indictment; **~e à feu** blast-off; **~e de fonds**
capital outlay; **~e à jour** *(Inform)* update; **~e à
mort** kill; **~e à pied** *(d'un employé)* suspension;
lay-off; **~e sur pied** *(d'une affaire, entreprise)*
setting up; **~e en plis** set; **~e au point** *(Photo)*
focusing; *(fig)* clarification; **~e à prix** reserve
(*Brit*) *ou* upset price; **~e en scène** production
mise [miz] *adj f, nf voir* **mis**
miser [mize] *vt (enjeu)* to stake, bet; **~ sur** *vt
(cheval, numéro)* to bet on; *(fig)* to bank on *ou* count on
misérable [mizeʀabl(ə)] *adj (lamentable,
malheureux)* pitiful, wretched; *(pauvre)* poverty-
stricken; *(insignifiant, mesquin)* miserable ▷ *nm/f*
wretch; *(miséreux)* poor wretch
misère [mizɛʀ] *nf (pauvreté)* (extreme) poverty,
destitution; **misères** *nfpl (malheurs)* woes,
miseries; *(ennuis)* little troubles; **être dans la ~**
to be destitute *ou* poverty-stricken; **salaire de ~**
starvation wage; **faire des ~s à qn** to torment
sb; **~ noire** utter destitution, abject poverty
missile [misil] *nm* missile
mission [misjɔ̃] *nf* mission; **partir en ~** *(Admin,
Pol)* to go on an assignment
missionnaire [misjɔnɛʀ] *nm/f* missionary
mit [mi] *vb voir* **mettre**
mité, e [mite] *adj* moth-eaten
mi-temps [mitɑ̃] *nf inv (Sport: période)* half;
(: pause) half-time; **à ~** *adj, adv* part-time
miteux, -euse [mitø, -øz] *adj* seedy, shabby
mitigé, e [mitiʒe] *adj (conviction, ardeur)*
lukewarm; *(sentiments)* mixed
mitonner [mitɔne] *vt (préparer)* to cook with
loving care; *(fig)* to cook up quietly
mitoyen, ne [mitwajɛ̃, -ɛn] *adj* common, party
cpd; **maisons ~nes** semi-detached houses; *(plus
de deux)* terraced (*Brit*) *ou* row (*US*) houses
mitrailler [mitʀaje] *vt* to machine-gun; *(fig:
photographier)* to snap away at; **~ qn de** to pelt *ou*
bombard sb with
mitraillette [mitʀajɛt] *nf* submachine gun
mitrailleuse [mitʀajøz] *nf* machine gun
mi-voix [mivwa]: **à ~** *adv* in a low *ou* hushed voice

mixage [miksaʒ] *nm (Ciné)* (sound) mixing
mixer, mixeur [miksœʀ] *nm (Culin)* (food) mixer
mixte [mikst(ə)] *adj (gén)* mixed; *(Scol)* mixed,
coeducational; **à usage ~** dual-purpose;
cuisinière ~ combined gas and electric cooker;
équipe ~ combined team
mixture [mikstyʀ] *nf* mixture; *(fig)* concoction
MJC *sigle f* (= *maison des jeunes et de la culture*)
community arts centre and youth club
Mlle *(pl -s)* *abr* = **Mademoiselle**
MM *abr* = **Messieurs**; *voir* **Monsieur**
Mme *(pl -s)* *abr* = **Madame**
mobile [mɔbil] *adj* mobile; *(amovible)* loose,
removable; *(pièce de machine)* moving; *(élément de
meuble etc)* movable ▷ *nm (motif)* motive; *(œuvre
d'art)* mobile; *(Physique)* moving object *ou* body;
(téléphone) ~ mobile (phone) (*Brit*), cell (phone)
(US)
mobilier, -ière [mɔbilje, -jɛʀ] *adj (Jur)* personal
▷ *nm (meubles)* furniture; **valeurs mobilières**
transferable securities; **vente mobilière** sale of
personal property *ou* chattels
mobiliser [mɔbilize] *vt (Mil, gén)* to mobilize
mobylette® [mɔbilɛt] *nf* moped
mocassin [mɔkasɛ̃] *nm* moccasin
moche [mɔʃ] *adj (fam: laid)* ugly; *(: mauvais,
méprisable)* rotten
modalité [mɔdalite] *nf* form, mode; **modalités**
nfpl (d'un accord etc) clauses, terms; **~s de
paiement** methods of payment
mode [mɔd] *nf* fashion; *(commerce)* fashion trade
ou industry ▷ *nm (manière)* form, mode, method;
(Ling) mood; *(Inform, Mus)* mode; **travailler
dans la ~** to be in the fashion business; **à la ~**
fashionable, in fashion; **~ dialogué** *(Inform)*
interactive *ou* conversational mode; **~ d'emploi**
directions *pl* (for use); **~ de vie** way of life
modèle [mɔdɛl] *adj* model ▷ *nm* model; *(qui
pose: de peintre)* sitter; *(type)* type; *(gabarit,
patron)* pattern; **~ courant** *ou* **de série** *(Comm)*
production model; **~ déposé** registered design;
~ réduit small-scale model
modeler [mɔdle] *vt (Art)* to model, mould;
(vêtement, érosion) to mould, shape; **~ qch sur/
d'après** to model sth on
modem [mɔdɛm] *nm (Inform)* modem
modéré, e [mɔdeʀe] *adj, nm/f* moderate
modérer [mɔdeʀe] *vt* to moderate; **se modérer**
vi to restrain o.s
moderne [mɔdɛʀn(ə)] *adj* modern ▷ *nm (Art)*
modern style; *(ameublement)* modern furniture
moderniser [mɔdɛʀnize] *vt* to modernize
modeste [mɔdɛst(ə)] *adj* modest; *(origine)*
humble, lowly
modestie [mɔdɛsti] *nf* modesty; **fausse ~** false
modesty
modifier [mɔdifje] *vt* to modify, alter; *(Ling)* to
modify; **se modifier** *vi* to alter
modique [mɔdik] *adj (salaire, somme)* modest
modiste [mɔdist(ə)] *nf* milliner
module [mɔdyl] *nm* module
moelle [mwal] *nf* marrow; *(fig)* pith, core; **~**

épinière spinal chord

moelleux, -euse [mwalø, -øz] *adj* soft; (*au goût, à l'ouïe*) mellow; (*gracieux, souple*) smooth

mœurs [mœʀ] *nfpl* (*conduite*) morals; (*manières*) manners; (*pratiques sociales*) habits; (*mode de vie*) life style *sg*; (*d'une espèce animale*) behaviour *sg* (Brit), behavior *sg* (US); **femme de mauvaises ~** loose woman; **passer dans les ~** to become the custom; **contraire aux bonnes ~** contrary to proprieties

mohair [mɔɛʀ] *nm* mohair

moi [mwa] *pron* me; (*emphatique*): **~, je ...** for my part, I ..., I myself ... ▷ *nm inv* (*Psych*) ego, self; **à ~!** (*à l'aide*) help (me)!

moi-même [mwamɛm] *pron* myself; (*emphatique*) I myself

moindre [mwɛ̃dʀ(ə)] *adj* lesser; lower; **le (la) ~, les ~s** the least; the slightest; **le (la) ~ de** the least of; **c'est la ~ des choses** it's nothing at all

moine [mwan] *nm* monk, friar

moineau, x [mwano] *nm* sparrow

moins [mwɛ̃] *adv* **1** (*comparatif*): **~ (que)** less (than); **~ grand que** less tall than, not as tall as; **il a trois ans de ~ que moi** he's three years younger than me; **il est ~ intelligent que moi** he's not as clever as me, he's less clever than me; **~ je travaille, mieux je me porte** the less I work, the better I feel
2 (*superlatif*): **le ~** (the) least; **c'est ce que j'aime le ~** it's what I like (the) least; **le(la) ~ doué(e)** the least gifted; **au ~, du ~** at least; **pour le ~** at the very least
3: **~ de** (*quantité*) less (than); (*nombre*) fewer (than); **~ de sable/d'eau** less sand/water; **~ de livres/gens** fewer books/people; **~ de deux ans** less than two years; **~ de midi** not yet midday
4: **de ~, en ~: 100 euros/3 jours de ~** 100 euros/3 days less; **trois livres en ~** three books fewer; three books too few; **de l'argent en ~** less money; **le soleil en ~** but for the sun, minus the sun; **de ~ en ~** less and less; **en ~ de deux** in a flash *ou* a trice
5: **à ~ de, à ~ que** unless; **à ~ de faire** unless we do (*ou* he does *etc*); **à ~ que tu ne fasses** unless you do; **à ~ d'un accident** barring any accident ▷ *prép*: **quatre ~ deux** four minus two; **dix heures ~ cinq** five to ten; **il fait ~ cinq** it's five (degrees) below (freezing), it's minus five; **il est ~ cinq** it's five to ▷ *nm* (*signe*) minus sign

mois [mwa] *nm* month; (*salaire, somme dû*) (*monthly*) pay *ou* salary; **treizième ~, double ~** extra month's salary

moisi, e [mwazi] *adj* mouldy (Brit), moldy (US), mildewed ▷ *nm* mould, mold, mildew; **odeur de ~** musty smell

moisir [mwaziʀ] *vi* to go mouldy (Brit) *ou* moldy (US); (*fig*) to rot; (*personne*) to hang about ▷ *vt* to make mouldy *ou* moldy

moisissure [mwazisyʀ] *nf* mould *no pl* (Brit), mold *no pl* (US)

moisson [mwasɔ̃] *nf* harvest; (*époque*) harvest

(*time*); (*fig*): **faire une ~ de** to gather a wealth of

moissonner [mwasɔne] *vt* to harvest, reap; (*fig*) to collect

moissonneur, -euse [mwasɔnœʀ, -øz] *nm/f* harvester, reaper ▷ *nf* (*machine*) harvester

moite [mwat] *adj* (*peau, mains*) sweaty, sticky; (*atmosphère*) muggy

moitié [mwatje] *nf* half; (*épouse*): **sa ~** his better half; **la ~** half; **la ~ de** half (of), half the amount (*ou* number) of; **la ~ du temps/des gens** half the time/the people; **à la ~ de** halfway through; **~ moins grand** half as tall; **~ plus long** half as long again, longer by half; **à ~** half (*avant le verbe*), half- (*avant l'adjectif*); **à ~ prix** (at) half price, half-price; **de ~ by half; **~ ~** half-and-half

moka [mɔka] *nm* (*café*) mocha coffee; (*gâteau*) mocha cake

mol [mɔl] *adj m voir* **mou**

molaire [mɔlɛʀ] *nf* molar

molester [mɔlɛste] *vt* to manhandle, maul (about)

molle [mɔl] *adj f voir* **mou**

mollement [mɔlmɑ̃] *adv* softly; (*péj*) sluggishly; (*protester*) feebly

mollet [mɔlɛ] *nm* calf ▷ *adj m*: **œuf ~** soft-boiled egg

molletonné, e [mɔltɔne] *adj* (*gants etc*) fleece-lined

mollir [mɔliʀ] *vi* (*jambes*) to give way; (*Navig: vent*) to drop, die down; (*fig: personne*) to relent; (: *courage*) to fail, flag

mollusque [mɔlysk(ə)] *nm* (*Zool*) mollusc; (*fig: personne*) lazy lump

môme [mom] *nm/f* (*fam: enfant*) brat; (: *fille*) bird (Brit), chick

moment [mɔmɑ̃] *nm* moment; (*occasion*): **profiter du ~** to take (advantage of) the opportunity; **ce n'est pas le ~** this is not the right time; **à un certain ~** at some point; **à un ~ donné** at a certain point; **à quel ~?** when exactly?; **au même ~** at the same time; (*instant*) at the same moment; **pour un bon ~** for a good while; **pour le ~** for the moment, for the time being; **au ~ de** at the time of; **au ~ où** as; at a time when; **à tout ~** at any time *ou* moment; (*continuellement*) constantly, continually; **en ce ~** at the moment; (*aujourd'hui*) at present; **sur le ~** at the time; **par ~s** now and then, at times; **d'un ~ à l'autre** any time (now); **du ~ où *ou* que** seeing that, since; **n'avoir pas un ~ à soi** not to have a minute to oneself

momentané, e [mɔmɑ̃tane] *adj* temporary, momentary

momentanément [mɔmɑ̃tanemɑ̃] *adv* for a moment, for a while

momie [mɔmi] *nf* mummy

mon [mɔ̃], **ma** [ma] (*pl* **mes**) [me] *adj poss* my

Monaco [mɔnako] *nm*: **le ~** Monaco

monarchie [mɔnaʀʃi] *nf* monarchy

monastère [mɔnastɛʀ] *nm* monastery

monceau, x [mɔ̃so] *nm* heap

mondain, e [mɔ̃dɛ̃, -ɛn] *adj* (*soirée, vie*) society *cpd*; (*obligations*) social; (*peintre, écrivain*) fashionable;

(*personne*) society *cpd* ▷ *nm/f* society man/woman, socialite ▷ *nf*: **la Mondaine, la police ~e** ≈ the vice squad

monde [mɔ̃d] *nm* world; (*personnes mondaines*): **le ~** (high) society; (*milieu*): **être du même ~** to move in the same circles; (*gens*): **il y a du ~** (*beaucoup de gens*) there are a lot of people; (*quelques personnes*) there are some people; **y a-t-il du ~ dans le salon?** is there anybody in the lounge?; **beaucoup/peu de ~** many/few people; **le meilleur** *etc* **du ~** the best *etc* in the world; **mettre au ~** to bring into the world; **pas le moins du ~** not in the least; **se faire un ~ de qch** to make a great deal of fuss about sth; **tour du ~** round-the-world trip; **homme/femme du ~** society man/woman

mondial, e, -aux [mɔ̃djal, -o] *adj* (*population*) world *cpd*; (*influence*) world-wide

mondialement [mɔ̃djalmɑ̃] *adv* throughout the world

monégasque [mɔnegask(ə)] *adj* Monegasque, of *ou* from Monaco ▷ *nm/f*: **M~** Monegasque

monétaire [mɔnetɛʀ] *adj* monetary

moniteur, -trice [mɔnitœʀ, -tʀis] *nm/f* (*Sport*) instructor (instructress); (*de colonie de vacances*) supervisor ▷ *nm* (*écran*) monitor; **~ cardiaque** cardiac monitor; **~ d'auto-école** driving instructor

monnaie [mɔnɛ] *nf* (*pièce*) coin; (*Écon: gén: moyen d'échange*) currency; (*petites pièces*): **avoir de la ~** to have (some) change; **faire de la ~** to get (some) change; **avoir/faire la ~ de 20 euros** to have change of/get change for 20 euros; **faire** *ou* **donner à qn la ~ de 20 euros** to give sb change for 20 euros, change 20 euros for sb; **rendre à qn la ~ (sur 20 euros)** to give sb the change (from *ou* out of 20 euros); **servir de ~ d'échange** (*fig*) to be used as a bargaining counter *ou* as bargaining counters; **payer en ~ de singe** to fob (sb) off with empty promises; **c'est ~ courante** it's a common occurrence; **~ légale** legal tender

monnayer [mɔneje] *vt* to convert into cash; (*talent*) to capitalize on

monologue [mɔnɔlɔg] *nm* monologue, soliloquy; **~ intérieur** stream of consciousness

monologuer [mɔnɔlɔge] *vi* to soliloquize

monopole [mɔnɔpɔl] *nm* monopoly

monotone [mɔnɔtɔn] *adj* monotonous

Monsieur [məsjø] (*pl* **Messieurs** [mesjø]) *nm* (*titre*) Mr; (*homme quelconque*): **un/le monsieur** a/the gentleman; *voir aussi* **Madame**

monstre [mɔ̃stʀ(ə)] *nm* monster ▷ *adj* (*fam: effet, publicité*) massive; **un travail ~** a fantastic amount of work; an enormous job; **~ sacré** superstar

monstrueux, -euse [mɔ̃stʀyø, -øz] *adj* monstrous

mont [mɔ̃] *nm*: **par ~s et par vaux** up hill and down dale; **le M~ Blanc** Mont Blanc; **~ de Vénus** mons veneris

montage [mɔ̃taʒ] *nm* putting up; (*d'un bijou*) mounting, setting; (*d'une machine etc*) assembly;

(*Photo*) photomontage; (*Ciné*) editing; **~ sonore** sound editing

montagnard, e [mɔ̃taɲaʀ, -aʀd(ə)] *adj* mountain *cpd* ▷ *nm/f* mountain-dweller

montagne [mɔ̃taɲ] *nf* (*cime*) mountain; (*région*): **la ~** the mountains *pl*; **la haute ~** the high mountains; **les ~s Rocheuses** the Rocky Mountains, the Rockies; **~s russes** big dipper *sg*, switchback *sg*

montagneux, -euse [mɔ̃taɲø, -øz] *adj* mountainous; hilly

montant, e [mɔ̃tɑ̃, -ɑ̃t] *adj* (*mouvement, marée*) rising; (*chemin*) uphill; (*robe, corsage*) high-necked ▷ *nm* (*somme, total*) (sum) total, (total) amount; (*de fenêtre*) upright; (*de lit*) post

monte-charge [mɔ̃tʃaʀʒ(ə)] *nm inv* goods lift, hoist

montée [mɔ̃te] *nf* rising, rise; (*escalade*) ascent, climb; (*chemin*) way up; (*côte*) hill; **au milieu de la ~** halfway up; **le moteur chauffe dans les ~s** the engine overheats going uphill

Monténégro [mɔ̃tenegʀo] *nm*: **le ~** Montenegro

monter [mɔ̃te] *vt* (*escalier, côte*) to go (*ou* come) up; (*valise, paquet*) to take (*ou* bring) up; (*cheval*) to mount; (*femelle*) to cover, serve; (*tente, échafaudage*) to put up; (*machine*) to assemble; (*bijou*) to mount, set; (*Couture*) to sew on; (: *manche*) to set in; (*Ciné*) to edit; (*Théât*) to put on, stage; (*société, coup etc*) to set up; (*fournir, équiper*) to equip ▷ *vi* to go (*ou* come) up; (*avion, voiture*) to climb, go up; (*chemin, niveau, température, voix, prix*) to go up, rise; (*brouillard, bruit*) to rise, come up; (*passager*) to get on; (*à cheval*): **~ bien/mal** to ride well/badly; **~ à cheval/bicyclette** to get on *ou* mount a horse/bicycle; (*faire du cheval etc*) to ride (a horse), to (ride a) bicycle; **~ à pied/en voiture** to walk/ drive up, go up on foot/by car; **~ dans le train/l'avion** to get into the train/plane, board the train/plane; **~ sur** to climb up onto; **~ sur** *ou* **à un arbre/une échelle** to climb (up) a tree/ladder; **~ à bord** to (get on) board; **~ à la tête de qn** to go to sb's head; **~ sur les planches** to go on the stage; **~ en grade** to be promoted; **se monter** (*s'équiper*) to equip o.s., get kitted out (*Brit*); **se ~ à** (*frais etc*) to add up to, come to; **~ qn contre qn** to set sb against sb; **~ la tête à qn** to give sb ideas

montgolfière [mɔ̃gɔlfjɛʀ] *nf* hot-air balloon

montre [mɔ̃tʀ(ə)] *nf* watch; (*ostentation*): **pour la ~** for show; **~ en main** exactly, to the minute; **faire ~ de** to show, display; **contre la ~** (*Sport*) against the clock; **~ de plongée** diver's watch

montre-bracelet (*pl* **montres-bracelets**) [mɔ̃tʀəbʀaslɛ] *nf* wrist watch

montrer [mɔ̃tʀe] *vt* to show; **se montrer** to appear; **~ qch à qn** to show sb sth; **~ qch du doigt** to point to sth, point one's finger at sth; **se ~ intelligent** to prove (to be) intelligent

monture [mɔ̃tyʀ] *nf* (*bête*) mount; (*d'une bague*) setting; (*de lunettes*) frame

monument [mɔnymɑ̃] *nm* monument; **~ aux morts** war memorial

moquer [mɔke]: **se ~ de** vt to make fun of, laugh at; (fam: se désintéresser de) not to care about; (tromper): **se ~ de qn** to take sb for a ride

moquerie [mɔkʀi] nf mockery no pl

moquette [mɔkɛt] nf fitted carpet, wall-to-wall carpeting no pl

moqueur, -euse [mɔkœʀ, -øz] adj mocking

moral, e, -aux [mɔʀal, -o] adj moral ▷ nm morale ▷ nf (conduite) morals pl (règles), moral code, ethic; (valeurs) moral standards pl, morality; (science) ethics sg, moral philosophy; (conclusion: d'une fable etc) moral; **au ~, sur le plan ~** morally; **avoir le ~ à zéro** to be really down; **faire la ~e à** to lecture, preach at

moralité [mɔʀalite] nf (d'une action, attitude) morality; (conduite) morals pl; (conclusion, enseignement) moral

morceau, x [mɔʀso] nm piece, bit; (d'une œuvre) passage, extract; (Mus) piece; (Culin: de viande) cut; **mettre en ~x** to pull to pieces ou bits

morceler [mɔʀsəle] vt to break up, divide up

mordant, e [mɔʀdɑ̃, -ɑ̃t] adj scathing, cutting; (froid) biting ▷ nm (dynamisme, énergie) spirit; (fougue) bite, punch

mordiller [mɔʀdije] vt to nibble at, chew at

mordre [mɔʀdʀ(ə)] vt to bite; (lime, vis) to bite into ▷ vi (poisson) to bite; **~ dans** to bite into; **~ sur** (fig) to go over into, overlap into; **~ à qch** (comprendre, aimer) to take to; **~ à l'hameçon** to bite, rise to the bait

mordu, e [mɔʀdy] pp de mordre ▷ adj (amoureux) smitten ▷ nm/f: **un ~ du jazz/de la voile** a jazz/sailing fanatic ou buff

morfondre [mɔʀfɔ̃dʀ(ə)]: **se morfondre** vi to mope

morgue [mɔʀg(ə)] nf (arrogance) haughtiness; (lieu: de la police) morgue; (: à l'hôpital) mortuary

morne [mɔʀn(ə)] adj (personne, visage) glum, gloomy; (temps, vie) dismal, dreary

morose [mɔʀoz] adj sullen, morose; (marché) sluggish

mors [mɔʀ] nm bit

morse [mɔʀs(ə)] nm (Zool) walrus; (Tél) Morse (code)

morsure [mɔʀsyʀ] nf bite

mort¹ [mɔʀ] nf death; **se donner la ~** to take one's own life; **de ~** (silence, pâleur) deathly; **blessé à ~** fatally wounded ou injured; **à la vie, à la ~** for better, for worse; **~ clinique** brain death; **~ subite du nourrisson, ~ au berceau** cot death

mortalité [mɔʀtalite] nf mortality, death rate

mortel, le [mɔʀtɛl] adj (poison etc) deadly, lethal; (accident, blessure) fatal; (Rel: danger, frayeur) mortal; (fig: froid) deathly; (: ennui, soirée) deadly (boring) ▷ nm/f mortal

mortier [mɔʀtje] nm (gén) mortar

mort-né, e [mɔʀne] adj (enfant) stillborn; (fig) abortive

mortuaire [mɔʀtyɛʀ] adj funeral cpd; **avis ~s** death announcements, intimations; **chapelle ~** mortuary chapel; **couronne ~** (funeral) wreath; **domicile ~** house of the deceased; **drap ~** pall

morue [mɔʀy] nf (Zool) cod inv; (Culin: salée) salt-cod

mosaïque [mɔzaik] nf (Art) mosaic; (fig) patchwork

Moscou [mɔsku] n Moscow

mosquée [mɔske] nf mosque

mot [mo] nm word; (message) line, note; (bon mot etc) saying; **le ~ de la fin** the last word; **~ à ~** adj, adv word for word; **~ pour ~** word for word, verbatim; **sur ou à ces ~s** with these words; **en un ~** in a word; **à ~s couverts** in veiled terms; **prendre qn au ~** to take sb at his word; **se donner le ~** to send the word round; **avoir son ~ à dire** to have a say; **~ d'ordre** watchword; **~ de passe** password; **~s croisés** crossword (puzzle) sg

motard [mɔtaʀ] nm biker; (policier) motorcycle cop

motel [mɔtɛl] nm motel

moteur, -trice [mɔtœʀ, -tʀis] adj (Anat, Physiol) motor; (Tech) driving; (Auto): **à 4 roues motrices** 4-wheel drive ▷ nm engine, motor; (fig) mover, mainspring; **à ~** power-driven, motor cpd; **~ à deux temps** two-stroke engine; **~ à explosion** internal combustion engine; **~ à réaction** jet engine; **~ de recherche** search engine; **~ thermique** heat engine

motif [mɔtif] nm (cause) motive; (décoratif) design, pattern, motif; (d'un tableau) subject, motif; (Mus) figure, motif; **motifs** nmpl (Jur) grounds pl; **sans ~** adj groundless

motivation [mɔtivasjɔ̃] nf motivation

motiver [mɔtive] vt (justifier) to justify, account for; (Admin, Jur, Psych) to motivate

moto [mɔto] nf (motor)bike; **~ verte ou de trial** trail (Brit) ou dirt (US) bike

motocyclette [mɔtɔsiklɛt] nf motorbike, motorcycle

motocycliste [mɔtɔsiklist(ə)] nm/f motorcyclist

motorisé, e [mɔtɔʀize] adj (troupe) motorized; (personne) having one's own transport

motrice [mɔtʀis] adj f voir moteur

motte [mɔt] nf: **~ de terre** lump of earth, clod (of earth); **~ de gazon** turf, sod; **~ de beurre** lump of butter

mou, mol, molle [mu, mɔl] adj soft; (péj: visage, traits) flabby; (: geste) limp; (: personne) sluggish; (: résistance, protestations) feeble ▷ nm (homme mou) wimp; (abats) lights pl, lungs pl; (de la corde): **avoir du ~** to be slack; **donner du ~** to slacken, loosen; **avoir les jambes molles** to be weak at the knees

mouche [muʃ] nf fly; (Escrime) button; (de taffetas) patch; **prendre la ~** to go into a huff; **faire ~** to score a bull's-eye

moucher [muʃe] vt (enfant) to blow the nose of; (chandelle) to snuff (out); **se moucher** to blow one's nose

moucheron [muʃʀɔ̃] nm midge

mouchoir [muʃwaʀ] nm handkerchief, hanky; ~ **en papier** tissue, paper hanky

moudre [mudʀ(ə)] vt to grind

moue [mu] nf pout; **faire la** ~ to pout; (fig) to pull a face

mouette [mwɛt] nf (sea)gull

moufle [mufl(ə)] nf (gant) mitt(en); (Tech) pulley block

mouillé, e [muje] adj wet

mouiller [muje] vt (humecter) to wet, moisten; (tremper): ~ **qn/qch** to make sb/sth wet; (Culin: ragoût) to add stock ou wine to; (couper, diluer) to water down; (mine etc) to lay ▷ vi (Navig) to lie ou be at anchor; **se mouiller** to get wet; (fam) to commit o.s; to get (o.s.) involved; ~ **l'ancre** to drop ou cast anchor

moulant, e [mulɑ̃, -ɑ̃t] adj figure-hugging

moule [mul] vb voir **moudre** ▷ nf (mollusque) mussel ▷ nm (creux, Culin) mould (Brit), mold (US); (modèle plein) cast; ~ **à gâteau** nm cake tin (Brit) ou pan (US); ~ **à gaufre** nm waffle iron; ~ **à tarte** nm pie ou flan dish

moulent [mul] vb voir **moudre**; **mouler**

mouler [mule] vt (brique) to mould (Brit), mold (US); (statue) to cast; (visage, bas-relief) to make a cast of; (lettre) to shape with care; (vêtement) to hug, fit closely round; ~ **qch sur** (fig) to model sth on

moulin [mulɛ̃] nm mill; (fam) engine; ~ **à café** coffee mill; ~ **à eau** watermill; ~ **à légumes** (vegetable) shredder; ~ **à paroles** (fig) chatterbox; ~ **à poivre** pepper mill; ~ **à prières** prayer wheel; ~ **à vent** windmill

moulinet [mulinɛ] nm (de treuil) winch; (de canne à pêche) reel; (mouvement): **faire des** ~**s avec qch** to whirl sth around

moulinette® [mulinɛt] nf (vegetable) shredder

moulu, e [muly] pp de **moudre** ▷ adj (café) ground

mourant, e [muʀɑ̃, -ɑ̃t] vb voir **mourir** ▷ adj dying ▷ nm/f dying man/woman

mourir [muʀiʀ] vi to die; (civilisation) to die out; ~ **assassiné** to be murdered; ~ **de froid/faim/ vieillesse** to die of exposure/hunger/old age; ~ **de faim/d'ennui** (fig) to be starving/be bored to death; ~ **d'envie de faire** to be dying to do; **s'ennuyer à** ~ to be bored to death

mousse [mus] nf (Bot) moss; (écume: sur eau, bière) froth, foam; (: shampooing) lather; (de champagne) bubbles pl; (Culin) mousse; (en caoutchouc etc) foam ▷ nm (Navig) ship's boy; **bain de** ~ bubble bath; **bas** ~ stretch stockings; **balle** ~ rubber ball; ~ **carbonique** (fire-fighting) foam; ~ **de nylon** nylon foam; (tissu) stretch nylon; ~ **à raser** shaving foam

mousseline [muslin] nf (Textiles) muslin; chiffon; **pommes** ~ (Culin) creamed potatoes

mousser [muse] vi to foam; to lather

mousseux, -euse [musø, -øz] adj (chocolat) frothy; (eau) foamy, frothy; (vin) sparkling ▷ nm: (**vin**) ~ sparkling wine

mousson [musɔ̃] nf monsoon

moustache [mustaʃ] nf moustache; **moustaches** nfpl (d'animal) whiskers pl

moustachu, e [mustaʃy] adj wearing a moustache

moustiquaire [mustikɛʀ] nf (rideau) mosquito net; (chassis) mosquito screen

moustique [mustik] nm mosquito

moutarde [mutaʀd(ə)] nf mustard ▷ adj inv mustard(-coloured)

mouton [mutɔ̃] nm (Zool, péj) sheep inv; (peau) sheepskin; (Culin) mutton

mouvement [muvmɑ̃] nm (gen, aussi: mécanisme) movement; (ligne courbe) contours pl; (fig: tumulte, agitation) activity, bustle; (: impulsion) impulse; reaction; (geste) gesture; (Mus: rythme) tempo; **en** ~ in motion; on the move; **mettre qch en** ~ to set sth in motion, set sth going; ~ **d'humeur** fit ou burst of temper; ~ **d'opinion** trend of (public) opinion; **le** ~ **perpétuel** perpetual motion

mouvementé, e [muvmɑ̃te] adj (vie, poursuite) eventful; (réunion) turbulent

mouvoir [muvwaʀ] vt (levier, membre) to move; (machine) to drive; **se mouvoir** to move

moyen, ne [mwajɛ̃, -ɛn] adj average; (tailles, prix) medium; (de grandeur moyenne) medium-sized ▷ nm (façon) means sg, way ▷ nf average; (Statistique) mean; (Scol: à l'examen) pass mark; (Auto) average speed; **moyens** nmpl (capacités) means; **au** – **de** by means of; **y a-t-il** – **de ...?** is it possible to ...?, can one ...?; **par quel** ~? how?, which way?, by which means?; **par tous les** ~**s** by every possible means, every possible way; **avec les** ~**s du bord** (fig) with what's available ou what comes to hand; **employer les grands** ~**s** to resort to drastic measures; **par ses propres** ~**s** all by oneself; **en** ~**ne** on (an) average; **faire la** ~**ne** to work out the average; ~ **de locomotion/ d'expression** means of transport/expression; ~ **âge** Middle Ages; ~ **de transport** means of transport; ~**ne d'âge** average age; ~**ne entreprise** (Comm) medium-sized firm

moyennant [mwajɛnɑ̃] prép (somme) for; (service, conditions) in return for; (travail, effort) with

Moyen-Orient [mwajɛnɔʀjɑ̃] nm: **le** ~ the Middle East

moyeu, x [mwajø] nm hub

MSF sigle mpl = **Médecins sans frontières**

MST sigle f (= maladie sexuellement transmissible) STD (= sexually transmitted disease)

mû, mue [my] pp de **mouvoir**

muer [mɥe] vi (oiseau, mammifère) to moult (Brit), molt (US); (serpent) to slough (its skin); (jeune garçon): **il mue** his voice is breaking; **se** ~ **en** to transform into

muet, te [mɥɛ, -ɛt] adj dumb; (fig): ~ **d'admiration** etc speechless with admiration etc; (joie, douleur, Ciné) silent; (Ling: lettre) silent, mute; (carte) blank ▷ nm/f mute ▷ nm: **le** ~ (Ciné) the silent cinema ou (esp US) movies

mufle [myfl(ə)] *nm* muzzle; (*goujat*) boor ▷ *adj* boorish

mugir [myʒiʀ] *vi* (*bœuf*) to bellow; (*vache*) to low, moo; (*fig*) to howl

muguet [mygɛ] *nm* (Bot) lily of the valley; (Méd) thrush

mule [myl] *nf* (Zool) (she-)mule

mulet [mylɛ] *nm* (Zool) (he-)mule; (*poisson*) mullet

multinational, e, -aux [myltinasjɔnal, -o] *adj, nf* multinational

multiple [myltipl(ə)] *adj* multiple, numerous; (*varié*) many, manifold ▷ *nm* (Math) multiple

multiplication [myltiplikasjɔ̃] *nf* multiplication

multiplier [myltiplije] *vt* to multiply; **se multiplier** *vi* to multiply; (*fig: personne*) to be everywhere at once

municipal, e, -aux [mynisipal, -o] *adj* municipal; town *cpd*

municipalité [mynisipalite] *nf* (*corps municipal*) town council, corporation; (*commune*) town, municipality

munir [myniʀ] *vt*: ~ **qn/qch de** to equip sb/sth with; **se ~ de** to provide o.s. with

munitions [mynisjɔ̃] *nfpl* ammunition *sg*

mur [myʀ] *nm* wall; (*fig*) stone *ou* brick wall; **faire le ~** (*interne, soldat*) to jump the wall; **~ du son** sound barrier

mûr, e [myʀ] *adj* ripe; (*personne*) mature ▷ *nf* (*de la ronce*) blackberry; (*du mûrier*) mulberry

muraille [myʀaj] *nf* (high) wall

mural, e, -aux [myʀal, -o] *adj* wall *cpd* ▷ *nm* (Art) mural

mûre [myʀ] *nf voir* **mûr**

muret [myʀɛ] *nm* low wall

mûrir [myʀiʀ] *vi* (*fruit, blé*) to ripen; (*abcès, furoncle*) to come to a head; (*fig: idée, personne*) to mature; (*projet*) to develop ▷ *vt* (*fruit, blé*) to ripen; (*personne*) to (make) mature; (*pensée, projet*) to nurture

murmure [myʀmyʀ] *nm* murmur; **murmures** *nmpl* (*plaintes*) murmurings, mutterings

murmurer [myʀmyʀe] *vi* to murmur; (*se plaindre*) to mutter, grumble

muscade [myskad] *nf* (*aussi*: **noix muscade**) nutmeg

muscat [myska] *nm* (*raisin*) muscat grape; (*vin*) muscatel (wine)

muscle [myskl(ə)] *nm* muscle

musclé, e [myskle] *adj* (*personne, corps*) muscular; (*fig: politique, régime etc*) strong-arm *cpd*

museau, x [myzo] *nm* muzzle

musée [myze] *nm* museum; (*de peinture*) art gallery

museler [myzle] *vt* to muzzle

muselière [myzəljɛʀ] *nf* muzzle

musette [myzɛt] *nf* (*sac*) lunch bag ▷ *adj inv* (*orchestre etc*) accordion *cpd*

musical, e, -aux [myzikal, -o] *adj* musical

music-hall [myzikol] *nm* variety theatre; (*genre*) variety

musicien, ne [myzisjɛ̃, -ɛn] *adj* musical ▷ *nm/f* musician

musique [myzik] *nf* music; (*fanfare*) band; **faire de la ~** to make music; (*jouer d'un instrument*) to play an instrument; **~ de chambre** chamber music; **~ de fond** background music

musulman, e [myzylmɑ̃, -an] *adj, nm/f* Moslem, Muslim

mutation [mytasjɔ̃] *nf* (Admin) transfer; (Bio) mutation

muter [myte] *vt* (Admin) to transfer

mutilé, e [mytile] *nm/f* disabled person (*through loss of limbs*); **~ de guerre** disabled ex-serviceman; **grand ~** severely disabled person

mutiler [mytile] *vt* to mutilate, maim; (*fig*) to mutilate, deface

mutin, e [mytɛ̃, -in] *adj* (*enfant, air, ton*) mischievous, impish ▷ *nm/f* (Mil, Navig) mutineer

mutinerie [mytinʀi] *nf* mutiny

mutisme [mytism(ə)] *nm* silence

mutuel, le [mytɥɛl] *adj* mutual ▷ *nf* mutual benefit society

myope [mjɔp] *adj* short-sighted

myosotis [mjozɔtis] *nm* forget-me-not

myrtille [miʀtij] *nf* bilberry (Brit), blueberry (US), whortleberry

mystère [mistɛʀ] *nm* mystery

mystérieux, -euse [misteʀjø, -øz] *adj* mysterious

mystifier [mistifje] *vt* to fool, take in; (*tromper*) to mystify

mythe [mit] *nm* myth

mythologie [mitɔlɔʒi] *nf* mythology

Nn

n' [n] adv voir **ne**

nacre [nakʀ(ə)] nf mother-of-pearl

nage [naʒ] nf swimming; (manière) style of swimming, stroke; **traverser/s'éloigner à la ~** to swim across/away; **en ~** bathed in perspiration; **~ indienne** sidestroke; **~ libre** freestyle; **~ papillon** butterfly

nageoire [naʒwaʀ] nf fin

nager [naʒe] vi to swim; (fig: ne rien comprendre) to be all at sea; **~ dans** to be swimming in; (vêtements) to be lost in; **~ dans le bonheur** to be overjoyed

nageur, -euse [naʒœʀ, -øz] nm/f swimmer

naguère [nagɛʀ] adv (il y a peu de temps) not long ago; (autrefois) formerly

naïf, -ïve [naif, naiv] adj naïve

nain, e [nɛ̃, nɛn] adj, nm/f dwarf

naissance [nɛsɑ̃s] nf birth; **donner ~ à** to give birth to; (fig) to give rise to; **prendre ~** to originate; **aveugle de ~** born blind; **Français de ~** French by birth; **à la ~ des cheveux** at the roots of the hair; **lieu de ~** place of birth

naître [nɛtʀ(ə)] vi to be born; (conflit, complications): **~ de** to arise from, be born out of; **~ à** (amour, poésie) to awaken to; **je suis né en 1960** I was born in 1960; **il naît plus de filles que de garçons** there are more girls born than boys; **faire ~** (fig) to give rise to, arouse

naïveté [naivte] nf naivety

nana [nana] nf (fam: fille) bird (Brit), chick

nantir [nɑ̃tiʀ] vt: **~ qn de** to provide sb with; **les nantis** (péj) the well-to-do

nappe [nap] nf tablecloth; (fig) sheet; layer; **~ de mazout** oil slick; **~ (phréatique)** water table

napperon [napʀɔ̃] nm table-mat; **~ individuel** place mat

narcodollars [naʀkodɔlaʀ] nmpl drug money no pl

narguer [naʀge] vt to taunt

narine [naʀin] nf nostril

narquois, e [naʀkwa, -waz] adj derisive, mocking

natal, e [natal] adj native

natalité [natalite] nf birth rate

natation [natasjɔ̃] nf swimming; **faire de la ~** to go swimming (regularly)

natif, -ive [natif, -iv] adj native

nation [nasjɔ̃] nf nation; **les N~s unies (NU)** the United Nations (UN)

national, e, -aux [nasjɔnal, -o] adj national ▷ nf: **(route) ~e** ≈ A road (Brit), ≈ state highway (US); **obsèques ~es** state funeral

nationaliser [nasjɔnalize] vt to nationalize

nationalisme [nasjɔnalism(ə)] nm nationalism

nationalité [nasjɔnalite] nf nationality; **de ~ française** of French nationality

natte [nat] nf (tapis) mat; (cheveux) plait

naturaliser [natyʀalize] vt to naturalize; (empailler) to stuff

nature [natyʀ] nf nature ▷ adj, adv (Culin) plain, without seasoning or sweetening; (café, thé: sans lait) black; (: sans sucre) without sugar; **payer en ~** to pay in kind; **peint d'après ~** painted from life; **être de ~ à faire qch** (propre à) to be the sort of thing (ou person) to do sth; **~ morte** still-life

naturel, le [natyʀɛl] adj natural ▷ nm naturalness; (caractère) disposition, nature; (autochtone) native; (aussi: **au naturel**: Culin) in water; in its own juices

naturellement [natyʀɛlmɑ̃] adv naturally; (bien sûr) of course

naufrage [nofʀaʒ] nm (ship)wreck; (fig) wreck; **faire ~** to be shipwrecked

nauséabond, e [nozeabɔ̃, -ɔ̃d] adj foul, nauseous

nausée [noze] nf nausea; **avoir la ~** to feel sick; **avoir des ~s** to have waves of nausea, feel nauseous ou sick

nautique [notik] adj nautical, water cpd; **sports ~s** water sports

naval, e [naval] adj naval

navet [navɛ] nm turnip; (péj) third-rate film

navette [navɛt] nf shuttle; (en car etc) shuttle (service); **faire la ~ (entre)** to go to and fro (between), shuttle (between); **~ spatiale** space shuttle

navigateur [navigatœʀ] nm (Navig) seafarer, sailor; (Aviat) navigator; (Inform) browser

navigation [navigasjɔ̃] nf navigation, sailing; (Comm) shipping; **compagnie de ~** shipping company; **~ spatiale** space navigation

naviguer [navige] vi to navigate, sail

navire [naviʀ] nm ship; **~ de guerre** warship; **~ marchand** merchantman

navrer [navʀe] vt to upset, distress; **je suis**

navré (de/de faire/que) I'm so sorry (for/for doing/that)

ne, n' [n(ə)] *adv voir* **pas**; **plus**; **jamais** *etc*; *(explétif) non traduit*

né, e [ne] *pp de* **naître**; **né en 1960** born in 1960; **née Scott** née Scott; **né(e) de ... et de ...** son/daughter of ... and of ...; **né d'une mère française** having a French mother; **né pour commander** born to lead ▷ *adj*: **un comédien né** a born comedian

néanmoins [neãmwɛ̃] *adv* nevertheless, yet

néant [neã] *nm* nothingness; **réduire à ~** to bring to nought; *(espoir)* to dash

nécessaire [neseseʀ] *adj* necessary ▷ *nm* necessary; *(sac)* kit; **faire le ~** to do the necessary; **n'emporter que le strict ~** to take only what is strictly necessary; **~ de couture** sewing kit; **~ de toilette** toilet bag; **~ de voyage** overnight bag

nécessité [nesesite] *nf* necessity; **se trouver dans la ~ de faire qch** to find it necessary to do sth; **par ~** out of necessity

nécessiter [nesesite] *vt* to require

nécrologique [nekʀɔlɔʒik] *adj*: **article ~** obituary; **rubrique ~** obituary column

nectar [nɛktaʀ] *nm* nectar

néerlandais, e [neɛʀlɑ̃dɛ, -ɛz] *adj* Dutch, of the Netherlands ▷ *nm (Ling)* Dutch ▷ *nm/f*: **N~, e** Dutchman/woman; **les N~** the Dutch

nef [nɛf] *nf (d'église)* nave

néfaste [nefast(ə)] *adj* baneful; ill-fated

négatif, -ive [negatif, iv] *adj* negative ▷ *nm (Photo)* negative

négligé, e [negliʒe] *adj (en désordre)* slovenly ▷ *nm (tenue)* negligee

négligeable [negliʒabl(ə)] *adj* insignificant, negligible

négligent, e [negliʒã, -ãt] *adj* careless; *(Jur etc)* negligent

négliger [negliʒe] *vt (épouse, jardin)* to neglect; *(tenue)* to be careless about; *(avis, précautions)* to disregard, overlook; **~ de faire** to fail to do, not bother to do; **se négliger** to neglect o.s

négoce [negɔs] *nm* trade

négociant [negɔsjã] *nm* merchant

négociation [negɔsjasjɔ̃] *nf* negotiation; **~s collectives** collective bargaining *sg*

négocier [negɔsje] *vi, vt* to negotiate

nègre [nɛgʀ(ə)] *nm (péj)* Negro; *(péj: écrivain)* ghost writer ▷ *adj (péj)* Negro

neige [nɛʒ] *nf* snow; **battre les œufs en ~** *(Culin)* to whip *ou* beat the egg whites until stiff; **~ carbonique** dry ice; **~ fondue** *(par terre)* slush; *(qui tombe)* sleet; **~ poudreuse** powdery snow

neiger [neʒe] *vi* to snow

nénuphar [nenyfaʀ] *nm* water-lily

néon [neɔ̃] *nm* neon

néo-zélandais, e [neozelãdɛ, -ɛz] *adj* New Zealand *cpd* ▷ *nm/f*: **N~, e** New Zealander

nerf [nɛʀ] *nm* nerve; *(fig)* spirit; *(: forces)* stamina; **nerfs** *nmpl* nerves; **être** *ou* **vivre sur les ~s** to

live on one's nerves; **être à bout de ~s** to be at the end of one's tether; **passer ses ~s sur qn** to take it out on sb

nerveux, -euse [nɛʀvø, -øz] *adj* nervous; *(cheval)* highly-strung; *(voiture)* nippy, responsive; *(tendineux)* sinewy

nervosité [nɛʀvozite] *nf* nervousness; *(émotivité)* excitability

nervure [nɛʀvyʀ] *nf (de feuille)* vein; *(Archit, Tech)* rib

n'est-ce pas [nɛspɑ] *adv* isn't it?, won't you? *etc (selon le verbe qui précède)*; **c'est bon, n'est-ce pas?** it's good, isn't it?; **il a peur, n'est-ce pas?** he's afraid, isn't he?; **n'est-ce pas que c'est bon?** don't you think it's good?; **lui, n'est-ce pas, il peut se le permettre** he, of course, can afford to do that, can't he?

net, nette [nɛt] *adj (sans équivoque, distinct)* clear; *(photo)* sharp; *(évident)* definite; *(propre)* neat, clean; *(Comm: prix, salaire, poids)* net ▷ *adv (refuser)* flatly ▷ *nm*: **mettre au ~** to copy out; **s'arrêter ~** to stop dead; **la lame a cassé ~** the blade snapped clean through; **faire place nette** to make a clean sweep; **~ d'impôt** tax free

Net [nɛt] *nm (Internet)*: **le ~** the Net

nettement [nɛtmã] *adv (distinctement)* clearly; *(évidemment)* definitely; *(avec comparatif, superlatif)*: **~ mieux** definitely *ou* clearly better

netteté [nɛtte] *nf* clearness

nettoyage [nɛtwajaʒ] *nm* cleaning; **~ à sec** dry cleaning

nettoyer [nɛtwaje] *vt* to clean; *(fig)* to clean out

neuf¹ [nœf] *num* nine

neuf², neuve [nœf, n v] *adj* new ▷ *nm*: **repeindre à ~** to redecorate; **remettre à ~** to do up (as good as new), refurbish; **n'acheter que du ~** to buy everything new; **quoi de ~?** what's new?

neutre [nøtʀ(ə)] *adj, nm (Ling)* neutral

neuve [nœv] *adj f voir* **neuf**

neuvième [nœvjɛm] *num* ninth

neveu, x [nəvø] *nm* nephew

névrosé, e [nevʀoze] *adj, nm/f* neurotic

nez [ne] *nm* nose; **rire au ~ de qn** to laugh in sb's face; **avoir du ~** to have flair; **avoir le ~ fin** to have foresight; **~ à ~ avec** face to face with; **à vue de ~** roughly

ni [ni] *conj*: **ni l'un ni l'autre ne sont** *ou* **n'est** neither one nor the other is; **il n'a rien dit ni fait** he hasn't said or done anything

niais, e [njɛ, -ɛz] *adj* silly, thick

niche [niʃ] *nf (du chien)* kennel; *(de mur)* recess, niche; *(farce)* trick

nicher [niʃe] *vi* to nest; **se ~ dans** *(personne: se blottir)* to snuggle into; *(: se cacher)* to hide in; *(objet)* to lodge itself in

nid [ni] *nm* nest; *(fig: repaire etc)* den, lair; **~ d'abeilles** *(Couture, Textile)* honeycomb stitch; **~ de poule** pothole

nièce [njɛs] *nf* niece

nier [nje] *vt* to deny

nigaud, e [nigo, -od] *nm/f* booby, fool

Nil [nil] *nm:* **le ~** the Nile
n'importe [nɛ̃pɔʀt(ə)] *adv:* **n'importe!** no
matter!; **n'importe qui/quoi/où** anybody/
anything/anywhere; **n'importe quoi!** (*fam:*
désapprobation) what rubbish!; **n'importe**
quand any time; **n'importe quel/quelle**
any; **n'importe lequel/laquelle** any (one);
n'importe comment (*sans soin*) carelessly;
n'importe comment, il part ce soir he's
leaving tonight in any case
niveau, x [nivo] *nm* level; (*des élèves, études*)
standard; **au ~ de** at the level of; (*personne*) on
a level with; **de ~ (avec)** level (with); **le ~ de la**
mer sea level; **~ (à bulle)** spirit level; **~ (d'eau)**
water level; **~ de vie** standard of living
niveler [nivle] *vt* to level
NN *abr* (= *nouvelle norme*) *revised standard of hotel*
classification
noble [nɔbl(ə)] *adj* noble; (*de qualité: métal etc*)
precious ▷ *nm/f* noble(man/-woman)
noblesse [nɔblɛs] *nf* (*classe sociale*) nobility; (*d'une*
action etc) nobleness
noce [nɔs] *nf* wedding; (*gens*) wedding party (*ou*
guests pl); **il l'a épousée en secondes ~s** she
was his second wife; **faire la ~** (*fam*) to go on a
binge; **~s d'or/d'argent/de diamant** golden/
silver/diamond wedding
nocif, -ive [nɔsif, -iv] *adj* harmful, noxious
nocturne [nɔktyʀn(ə)] *adj* nocturnal ▷ *nf* (*Sport*)
floodlit fixture; (*d'un magasin*) late opening
Noël [nɔɛl] *nm* Christmas; **la (fête de) ~**
Christmas time
nœud [nø] *nm* (*de corde, du bois, Navig*) knot; (*ruban*)
bow; (*fig: liens*) bond, tie; (: *d'une question*) crux;
(*Théât etc*) **le ~ de l'action** the web of events;
~ coulant noose; **~ gordien** Gordian knot; **~**
papillon bow tie
noir, e [nwaʀ] *adj* black; (*obscur, sombre*) dark
▷ *nm/f* black man/woman ▷ *nm:* **dans le ~** in
the dark ▷ *nf* (*Mus*) crotchet (*Brit*), quarter note
(*US*); **il fait ~** it is dark; **au ~** *adv* (*acheter, vendre*)
on the black market; **travail au ~**
moonlighting
noircir [nwaʀsiʀ] *vt, vi* to blacken
noisette [nwazɛt] *nf* hazelnut; (*morceau: de beurre*
etc) small knob ▷ *adj* (*yeux*) hazel
noix [nwa] *nf* walnut; (*fam*) twit; (*Culin*): **une**
~ de beurre a knob of butter; **à la ~** (*fam*)
worthless; **~ de cajou** cashew nut; **~ de coco**
coconut; **~ muscade** nutmeg; **~ de veau** (*Culin*)
round fillet of veal
nom [nɔ̃] *nm* name; (*Ling*) noun; **connaître**
qn de ~ to know sb by name; **au ~ de** in the
name of; **~ d'une pipe** *ou* **d'un chien!** (*fam*) for
goodness' sake!; **~ de Dieu!** (*fam!*) bloody hell!
(*Brit*), my God!; **~ commun/propre** common/
proper noun; **~ composé** (*Ling*) compound noun;
~ déposé trade name; **~ d'emprunt** assumed
name; **~ de famille** surname; **~ de fichier** file
name; **~ de jeune fille** maiden name
nomade [nɔmad] *adj* nomadic ▷ *nm/f* nomad
nombre [nɔ̃bʀ(ə)] *nm* number; **venir en ~** to

come in large numbers; **depuis ~ d'années** for
many years; **ils sont au ~ de trois** there are
three of them; **au ~ de mes amis** among my
friends; **sans ~** countless; **(bon) ~ de** (*beaucoup*,
plusieurs) a (large) number of; **~ premier/entier**
prime/whole number
nombreux, -euse [nɔ̃bʀø, -øz] *adj* many,
numerous; (*avec nom sg: foule etc*) large; **peu ~** few;
small; **de ~ cas** many cases
nombril [nɔ̃bʀi] *nm* navel
nommer [nɔme] *vt* (*baptiser*) to name, give a
name to; (*qualifier*) to call; (*mentionner*) to name,
give the name of; (*élire*) to appoint, nominate;
se nommer: il se nomme Pascal his name's
Pascal, he's called Pascal
non [nɔ̃] *adv* (*réponse*) no; (*suivi d'un adjectif, adverbe*)
not; **Paul est venu, ~?** Paul came, didn't he?;
répondre *ou* **dire que ~** to say no; **~ pas que** not
that; **~ plus: moi non plus** neither do I, I don't
either; **je préférerais que ~** I would prefer not;
il se trouve que ~ perhaps not; **je pense que**
~ I don't think so; **~ mais!** well really!; **~ mais**
des fois! you must be joking!; **~ alcoolisé** nonalcoholic; **~ loin/seulement** not far/only
nonante [nɔnɑ̃t] *num* (*Belgique, Suisse*) ninety
nonchalant, e [nɔ̃ʃalɑ̃, -ɑ̃t] *adj* nonchalant,
casual
non-fumeur [nɔ̃fymœʀ] *nm* non-smoker
non-sens [nɔ̃sɑ̃s] *nm* absurdity
nord [nɔʀ] *nm* North ▷ *adj* northern; north; **au ~**
(*situation*) in the north; (*direction*) to the north; **au**
~ de north of, to the north of; **perdre le ~** to lose
one's way (*fig*)
nord-est [nɔʀɛst] *nm* North-East
nord-ouest [nɔʀwɛst] *nm* North-West
normal, e, -aux [nɔʀmal, -o] *adj* normal ▷ *nf:* **la**
~e the norm, the average
normalement [nɔʀmalmɑ̃] *adv* (*en général*)
normally; (*comme prévu*): **~, il le fera demain** he
should be doing it tomorrow, he's supposed to
do it tomorrow
normand, e [nɔʀmɑ̃, -ɑ̃d] *adj* (*de Normandie*)
Norman ▷ *nm/f:* **N~, e** (*de Normandie*) Norman
Normandie [nɔʀmɑ̃di] *nf:* **la ~** Normandy
norme [nɔʀm(ə)] *nf* norm; (*Tech*) standard
Norvège [nɔʀvɛʒ] *nf:* **la ~** Norway
norvégien, ne [nɔʀveʒjɛ̃, -ɛn] *adj* Norwegian
▷ *nm* (*Ling*) Norwegian ▷ *nm/f:* **N~, ne**
Norwegian
nos [no] *adj poss voir* **notre**
nostalgie [nɔstalʒi] *nf* nostalgia
nostalgique [nɔstalʒik] *adj* nostalgic
notable [nɔtabl(ə)] *adj* notable, noteworthy;
(*marqué*) noticeable, marked ▷ *nm* prominent
citizen
notaire [nɔtɛʀ] *nm* notary; solicitor
notamment [nɔtamɑ̃] *adv* in particular, among
others
note [nɔt] *nf* (*écrite, Mus*) note; (*Scol*) mark (*Brit*),
grade; (*facture*) bill; **prendre des ~s** to take
notes; **prendre ~ de** to note; (*par écrit*) to note,
write down; **dans la ~** exactly right; **forcer la**

~ to exaggerate; **une ~ de tristesse/de gaieté** a
sad/happy note; **~ de service** memorandum

noté, e [nɔte] *adj*: **être bien/mal ~** *(employé etc)* to
have a good/bad record

noter [nɔte] *vt (écrire)* to write down, note;
(remarquer) to note, notice; *(Scol, Admin: donner une
appréciation)* to mark, give a grade to; **notez bien
que …** (please) note that …

notice [nɔtis] *nf* summary, short article;
(brochure): **~ explicative** explanatory leaflet,
instruction booklet

notifier [nɔtifje] *vt*: **~ qch à qn** to notify sb of
sth, notify sth to sb

notion [nosjɔ̃] *nf* notion, idea; **notions** *nfpl*
(rudiments) rudiments

notoire [nɔtwaʀ] *adj* widely known; *(en mal)*
notorious; **le fait est ~** the fact is common
knowledge

notre, nos [nɔtʀ(ə), no] *adj poss* our

nôtre [notʀ(ə)] *adj* ours ▷ *pron*: **le/la ~** ours; **les
~s** ours; *(alliés etc)* our own people; **soyez des ~s**
join us

nouer [nwe] *vt* to tie, knot; *(fig: alliance etc)*
to strike up; **~ la conversation** to start a
conversation; **se nouer** *vi*: **c'est là où l'intrigue
se noue** it's at that point that the strands of the
plot come together; **ma gorge se noua** a lump
came to my throat

noueux, -euse [nwø, -øz] *adj* gnarled

nouille [nuj] *nf (fam)* noodle *(Brit)*, fathead;
nouilles *nfpl (pâtes)* noodles; pasta *sg*

nourrice [nuʀis] *nf* ≈ baby-minder; *(autrefois)*
wet-nurse

nourrir [nuʀiʀ] *vt* to feed; *(fig: espoir)* to harbour,
nurse; **logé nourri** with board and lodging; **~
au sein** to breast-feed; **se ~ de légumes** to live
on vegetables

nourrissant, e [nuʀisɑ̃, -ɑ̃t] *adj* nourishing,
nutritious

nourrisson [nuʀisɔ̃] *nm (unweaned)* infant

nourriture [nuʀityʀ] *nf* food

nous [nu] *pron (sujet)* we; *(objet)* us

nous-mêmes [numɛm] *pron* ourselves

nouveau, nouvel, -elle, x [nuvo, -ɛl] *adj* new;
(original) novel ▷ *nm/f* new pupil *(ou* employee)
▷ *nm*: **il y a du ~** there's something new ▷ *nf*
(piece of) news *sg*; *(Littérature)* short story;
nouvelles *nfpl (Presse, TV)* news; **de ~ à ~** again;
je suis sans nouvelles de lui I haven't heard
from him; **Nouvel An** New Year; **~ venu,
nouvelle venue** newcomer; **~x mariés** newly-
weds; **nouvelle vague** new wave

nouveau-né, e [nuvone] *nm/f* newborn (baby)

nouveauté [nuvote] *nf* novelty; *(chose nouvelle)*
innovation, something new; *(Comm)* new film
(ou book *ou* creation *etc)*

nouvel *adj m*, **nouvelle** *adj f*, *nf* [nuvɛl] *voir*
nouveau

Nouvelle-Calédonie [nuvɛlkaledɔni] *nf*: **la ~**
New Caledonia

nouvellement [nuvɛlmɑ̃] *adv (arrivé etc)* recently,
newly

Nouvelle-Zélande [nuvɛlzelɑ̃d] *nf*: **la ~** New
Zealand

novembre [nɔvɑ̃bʀ(ə)] *nm* November; *see note*;
voir aussi **juillet**

novice [nɔvis] *adj* inexperienced ▷ *nm/f* novice

noyade [nwajad] *nf* drowning *no pl*

noyau, x [nwajo] *nm (de fruit)* stone; *(Bio, Physique)*
nucleus; *(Élec, Géo, fig: centre)* core; *(fig: d'artistes
etc)* group; *(: de résistants etc)* cell

noyauter [nwajote] *vt (Pol)* to infiltrate

noyer [nwaje] *nm* walnut (tree); *(bois)* walnut
▷ *vt* to drown; *(fig)* to flood; to submerge; *(Auto:
moteur)* to flood; **se noyer** to be drowned, drown;
(suicide) to drown o.s.; **~ son chagrin** to drown
one's sorrows; **~ le poisson** to duck the issue

nu, e [ny] *adj* naked *(membres)* naked, bare;
(chambre, fil, plaine) bare ▷ *nm (Art)* nude; **le nu
intégral** total nudity; **se mettre nu** to strip;
mettre à nu to bare

nuage [nɥaʒ] *nm* cloud; **être dans les ~s** *(distrait)*
to have one's head in the clouds; **~ de lait** drop
of milk

nuageux, -euse [nɥaʒø, -øz] *adj* cloudy

nuance [nɥɑ̃s] *nf (de couleur, sens)* shade; **il y
a une ~ (entre)** there's a slight difference
(between); **une ~ de tristesse** a tinge of
sadness

nuancer [nɥɑ̃se] *vt (pensée, opinion)* to qualify

nucléaire [nykleɛʀ] *adj* nuclear ▷ *nm* nuclear
power

nudiste [nydist(ə)] *adj*, *nm/f* nudist

nuée [nɥe] *nf*: **une ~ de** a cloud *ou* host *ou* swarm
of

nues [ny] *nfpl*: **tomber des ~** to be taken aback;
porter qn aux ~ to praise sb to the skies

nuire [nɥiʀ] *vi* to be harmful; **~ à** to harm, do
damage to

nuisible [nɥizibl(ə)] *adj* harmful; **(animal) ~**
pest

nuit [nɥi] *nf* night; **payer sa ~** to pay for one's
overnight accommodation; **il fait ~** it's dark;
cette ~ *(hier)* last night; *(aujourd'hui)* tonight;
de ~ *(vol, service)* night *cpd*; **~ blanche** sleepless
night; **~ de noces** wedding night; **~ de Noël**
Christmas Eve

nul, nulle [nyl] *adj (aucun)* no; *(minime)* nil, nonexistent; *(non valable)* null; *(péj)* useless, hopeless
▷ *pron* none, no one; **résultat ~, match ~** draw;
nulle part *adv* nowhere

nullement [nylmɑ̃] *adv* by no means

nullité [nylite] *nf* nullity; *(péj)* hopelessness;
(: personne) hopeless individual, nonentity

numérique [nymeʀik] *adj* numerical; *(Inform)*
digital

numéro [nymeʀo] *nm* number; *(spectacle)*
act, turn; **faire** *ou* **composer un ~** to dial
a number; **~ d'identification personnel**
personal identification number (PIN); **~
d'immatriculation** *ou* **minéralogique** *ou* **de
police** registration *(Brit)* ou license (US)
number; **~ de téléphone** (tele)phone number;
~ vert ≈ Freefone® number *(Brit)*, ≈ toll-free

number (US)
numéroter [nymeʀɔte] *vt* to number
nu-pieds [nypje] *nm inv* sandal ▷ *adj inv* barefoot
nuque [nyk] *nf* nape of the neck

nu-tête [nytɛt] *adj inv* bareheaded
nutritif, -ive [nytʀitif, -iv] *adj* nutritional;
  (*aliment*) nutritious, nourishing
nylon [nilɔ̃] *nm* nylon

Oo

oasis [ɔazis] *nf ou m* oasis
obéir [ɔbeiʀ] *vi* to obey; **~ à** to obey; *(moteur, véhicule)* to respond to
obéissance [ɔbeisãs] *nf* obedience
obéissant, e [ɔbeisã, -ãt] *adj* obedient
obèse [ɔbɛz] *adj* obese
obésité [ɔbezite] *nf* obesity
objecter [ɔbʒɛkte] *vt (prétexter)* to plead, put forward as an excuse; **~ qch à** *(argument)* to put forward sth against; **~ (à qn) que** to object (to sb) that
objecteur [ɔbʒɛktœʀ] *nm*: **~ de conscience** conscientious objector
objectif, -ive [ɔbʒɛktif, -iv] *adj* objective ▷ *nm (Optique, Photo)* lens *sg*; *(Mil: fig)* objective; **~ grand angulaire/à focale variable** wide-angle/zoom lens
objection [ɔbʒɛksjõ] *nf* objection; **~ de conscience** conscientious objection
objectivité [ɔbʒɛktivite] *nf* objectivity
objet [ɔbʒɛ] *nm (chose)* object; *(d'une discussion, recherche)* subject; **être** *ou* **faire l'~ de** *(discussion)* to be the subject of; *(soins)* to be given *ou* shown; **sans ~** *adj* purposeless; *(sans fondement)* groundless; **~ d'art** objet d'art; **~s personnels** personal items; **~s de toilette** toiletries; **~s trouvés** lost property *sg* (Brit), lost-and-found *sg* (US); **~s de valeur** valuables
obligation [ɔbligasjõ] *nf* obligation; *(gén pl: devoir)* duty; *(Comm)* bond, debenture; **sans ~ d'achat** with no obligation (to buy); **être dans l'~ de faire** to be obliged to do; **avoir l'~ de faire** to be under an obligation to do; **~s familiales** family obligations *ou* responsibilities; **~s militaires** military obligations *ou* duties
obligatoire [ɔbligatwaʀ] *adj* compulsory, obligatory
obligatoirement [ɔbligatwaʀmã] *adv* compulsorily; *(fatalement)* necessarily
obligé, e [ɔbliʒe] *adj (redevable)*: **être très ~ à qn** to be most obliged to sb; *(contraint)*: **je suis (bien) ~ (de le faire)** I have to (do it); *(nécessaire: conséquence)* necessary; **c'est ~!** it's inevitable!
obligeance [ɔbliʒãs] *nf*: **avoir l'~ de** to be kind *ou* good enough to
obligeant, e [ɔbliʒã, -ãt] *adj* obliging; kind
obliger [ɔbliʒe] *vt (contraindre)*: **~ qn à faire** to

force *ou* oblige sb to do; *(Jur: engager)* to bind; *(rendre service à)* to oblige
oblique [ɔblik] *adj* oblique; **regard ~** sidelong glance; **en ~** *adv* diagonally
obliquer [ɔblike] *vi*: **~ vers** to turn off towards
oblitérer [ɔbliteʀe] *vt (timbre-poste)* to cancel; *(Méd: canal, vaisseau)* to obstruct
obnubiler [ɔbnybile] *vt* to obsess
obscène [ɔpsɛn] *adj* obscene
obscur, e [ɔpskyʀ] *adj (sombre)* dark; *(fig: raisons)* obscure; *(: sentiment, malaise)* vague; *(: personne, vie)* humble, lowly
obscurcir [ɔpskyʀsiʀ] *vt* to darken; *(fig)* to obscure; **s'obscurcir** *vi* to grow dark
obscurité [ɔpskyʀite] *nf* darkness; **dans l'~** in the dark, in darkness; *(anonymat, médiocrité)* in obscurity
obsédé, e [ɔpsede] *nm/f* fanatic; **~(e) sexuel(le)** sex maniac
obséder [ɔpsede] *vt* to obsess, haunt
obsèques [ɔpsɛk] *nfpl* funeral *sg*
observateur, -trice [ɔpsɛʀvatœʀ, -tʀis] *adj* observant, perceptive ▷ *nm/f* observer
observation [ɔpsɛʀvasjõ] *nf* observation; *(d'un règlement etc)* observance; *(commentaire)* observation, remark; *(reproche)* reproof; **en ~** *(Méd)* under observation
observatoire [ɔpsɛʀvatwaʀ] *nm* observatory; *(lieu élevé)* observation post, vantage point
observer [ɔpsɛʀve] *vt (regarder)* to observe, watch; *(examiner)* to examine; *(scientifiquement, aussi: règlement, jeûne etc)* to observe; *(surveiller)* to watch; *(remarquer)* to observe, notice; **faire ~ qch à qn** *(dire)* to point out sth to sb; **s'observer** *vi (se surveiller)* to keep a check on o.s.
obsession [ɔpsesjõ] *nf* obsession; **avoir l'~ de** to have an obsession with
obstacle [ɔpstakl(ə)] *nm* obstacle; *(Équitation)* jump, hurdle; **faire ~ à** *(lumière)* to block out; *(projet)* to hinder, put obstacles in the path of; **~s antichars** tank defences
obstiné, e [ɔpstine] *adj* obstinate
obstiner [ɔpstine]: **s'obstiner** *vi* to insist, dig one's heels in; **s'~ à faire** to persist (obstinately) in doing; **s'~ sur qch** to keep working at sth, labour away at sth
obstruer [ɔpstʀye] *vt* to block, obstruct;

s'obstruer vi to become blocked
obtenir [ɔptəniʀ] vt to obtain, get; (total) to
arrive at, reach; (résultat) to achieve, obtain; ~ **de**
pouvoir faire to obtain permission to do; ~ **qch**
à qn to obtain sth for sb; ~ **de qn qu'il fasse** to
get sb to agree to do(ing)
obturateur [ɔptyʀatœʀ] nm (Photo) shutter; ~ **à**
rideau focal plane shutter
obus [ɔby] nm shell; ~ **explosif** high-explosive
shell; ~ **incendiaire** incendiary device, fire
bomb
occasion [ɔkazjɔ̃] nf (aubaine, possibilité)
opportunity; (circonstance) occasion; (Comm:
article non neuf) secondhand buy; (: acquisition
avantageuse) bargain; **à plusieurs ~s** on several
occasions; **à la première ~** at the first ou earliest
opportunity; **avoir l'~ de faire** to have the
opportunity to do; **être l'~ de** to occasion, give
rise to; **à l'~** adv sometimes, on occasions; (un
jour) some time; **à l'~ de** on the occasion of; **d'~**
adj, adv secondhand
occasionnel, le [ɔkazjɔnɛl] adj (fortuit) chance
cpd; (non régulier) occasional; (: travail) casual
occasionnellement [ɔkazjɔnɛlmɑ̃] adv
occasionally, from time to time
occasionner [ɔkazjɔne] vt to cause, bring about;
~ **qch à qn** to cause sb sth
occident [ɔksidɑ̃] nm: **l'O~** the West
occidental, e, -aux [ɔksidɑ̃tal, -o] adj western;
(Pol) Western ▷ nm/f Westerner
occupation [ɔkypasjɔ̃] nf occupation; **l'O~** the
Occupation (of France)
occupé, e [ɔkype] adj (Mil, Pol) occupied;
(personne: affairé, pris) busy; (esprit: absorbé)
occupied; (place, sièges) taken; (toilettes, ligne)
engaged
occuper [ɔkype] vt to occupy; (poste, fonction) to
hold; (main-d'œuvre) to employ; **s'~ (à qch)** to
occupy o.s ou keep o.s. busy (with sth); **s'~ de**
(être responsable de) to be in charge of; (se charger de:
affaire) to take charge of, deal with; (: clients etc) to
attend to; (s'intéresser à, pratiquer: politique etc) to be
involved in; **ça occupe trop de place** it takes up
too much room
occurrence [ɔkyʀɑ̃s] nf: **en l'~** in this case
océan [ɔseɑ̃] nm ocean; **l'~ Indien** the Indian
Ocean
octante [ɔktɑ̃t] num (Belgique, Suisse) eighty
octet [ɔktɛ] nm byte
octobre [ɔktɔbʀ(ə)] nm October; voir aussi **juillet**
octroyer [ɔktʀwaje] vt: ~ **qch à qn** to grant sth to
sb, grant sb sth
oculiste [ɔkylist(ə)] nm/f eye specialist, oculist
odeur [ɔdœʀ] nf smell
odieux, -euse [ɔdjø, -øz] adj odious, hateful
odorant, e [ɔdɔʀɑ̃, -ɑ̃t] adj sweet-smelling,
fragrant
odorat [ɔdɔʀa] nm (sense of) smell; **avoir l'~ fin**
to have a keen sense of smell
œil [œj] (pl **yeux**) [jø] nm eye; **avoir un ~ poché**
ou **au beurre noir** to have a black eye; **à l'~** (fam)
for free; **à l'~ nu** with the naked eye; **tenir qn**
à l'~ to keep an eye ou a watch on sb; **avoir l'~ à**
to keep an eye on; **faire de l'~ à qn** to make eyes
at sb; **voir qch d'un bon/mauvais ~** to view
sth in a favourable/an unfavourable light; **à l'~**
vif with a lively expression; **à mes/ses yeux** in
my/his eyes; **de ses propres yeux** with his own
eyes; **fermer les yeux (sur)** (fig) to turn a blind
eye (to); **les yeux fermés** (aussi fig) with one's
eyes shut; **fermer l'~** to get a moment's sleep;
~ **pour ~, dent pour dent** an eye for an eye, a
tooth for a tooth; **pour les beaux yeux de qn**
(fig) for love of sb; ~ **de verre** glass eye
œillères [œjɛʀ] nfpl blinkers (Brit), blinders (US);
avoir des ~ (fig) to be blinkered, wear blinders
œillet [œjɛ] nm (Bot) carnation; (trou) eyelet
œuf [œf] nm egg; **étouffer dans l'~** to nip in
the bud; ~ **à la coque/dur/mollet** boiled/hard-
boiled/soft-boiled egg; ~ **au plat/poché** fried/
poached egg; ~**s brouillés** scrambled eggs; ~ **de**
Pâques Easter egg; ~ **à repriser** darning egg
œuvre [œvʀ(ə)] nf (tâche) task, undertaking;
(ouvrage achevé, livre, tableau etc) work; (ensemble
de la production artistique) works pl; (organisation
charitable) charity ▷ nm (d'un artiste) works pl;
(Constr): **le gros ~** the shell; **œuvres** nfpl (actes)
deeds, works; **être/se mettre à l'~** to be at/get
(down) to work; **mettre en ~** (moyens) to make
use of; (plan, loi, projet etc) to implement; ~ **d'art**
work of art; **bonnes ~s** good works ou deeds; ~**s**
de bienfaisance charitable works
offense [ɔfɑ̃s] nf (affront) insult; (Rel: péché)
transgression, trespass
offenser [ɔfɑ̃se] vt to offend, hurt; (principes,
Dieu) to offend against; **s'offenser de** vi to take
offence (Brit) ou offense (US) at
offert, e [ɔfɛʀ, -ɛʀt(ə)] pp de **offrir**
office [ɔfis] nm (charge) office; (agence) bureau,
agency; (Rel) service ▷ nm ou f (pièce) pantry;
faire ~ de to act as; to do duty as; **d'~** adv
automatically; **bons ~s** (Pol) good offices; ~ **du**
tourisme tourist bureau
officiel, le [ɔfisjɛl] adj, nm/f official
officier [ɔfisje] nm officer ▷ vi (Rel) to officiate; ~
de l'état-civil registrar; ~ **ministériel** member
of the legal profession; ~ **de police** = police
officer
officieux, -euse [ɔfisjø, -øz] adj unofficial
offrande [ɔfʀɑ̃d] nf offering
offre [ɔfʀ(ə)] vb voir **offrir** ▷ nf offer; (aux enchères)
bid; (Admin: soumission) tender; (Écon): **l'~** supply;
~ **d'emploi** job advertised; **"~s d'emploi"**
"situations vacant"; ~ **publique d'achat (OPA)**
takeover bid; ~**s de service** offer of service
offrir [ɔfʀiʀ] vt: ~ **(à qn)** to offer (to sb); (faire
cadeau) to give (to sb); **s'offrir** vi (se présenter:
occasion, paysage) to present itself ▷ vt (se payer:
vacances, voiture) to treat o.s. to; ~ **(à qn) de faire**
qch to offer to do sth (for sb); ~ **à boire à qn**
to offer sb a drink; **s'~ à faire qch** to offer ou
volunteer to do sth; **s'~ comme guide/en otage**
to offer one's services as (a) guide/offer o.s. as (a)
hostage; **s'~ aux regards** (personne) to expose o.s.

to the public gaze

offusquer [ɔfyske] *vt* to offend; **s'offusquer de** to take offence (*Brit*) *ou* offense (*US*) at, be offended by

OGM *sigle m* GMO

oie [wa] *nf* (*Zool*) goose; ~ **blanche** (*fig*) young innocent

oignon [ɔɲɔ̃] *nm* (*Culin*) onion; (*de tulipe etc*: *bulbe*) bulb; (*Méd*) bunion; **ce ne sont pas tes ~s** (*fam*) that's none of your business

oiseau, x [wazo] *nm* bird; ~ **de proie** bird of prey

oisif, -ive [wazif, -iv] *adj* idle ▷ *nm/f* (*péj*) man/ lady of leisure

oléoduc [ɔleɔdyk] *nm* (oil) pipeline

olive [ɔliv] *nf* (*Bot*) olive ▷ *adj inv* olive-green

olivier [ɔlivje] *nm* olive (tree); (*bois*) olive (wood)

OLP *sigle f* (= *Organisation de libération de la Palestine*) PLO

olympique [ɔlɛ̃pik] *adj* Olympic

ombragé, e [ɔ̃braʒe] *adj* shaded, shady

ombrageux, -euse [ɔ̃braʒø, -øz] *adj* (*cheval*) skittish, nervous; (*personne*) touchy, easily offended

ombre [ɔ̃br(ə)] *nf* (*espace non ensoleillé*) shade; (*ombre portée, tache*) shadow; **à l'~** in the shade; (*fam: en prison*) behind bars; **à l'~ de** in the shade of; (*tout près de, fig*) in the shadow of; **tu me fais de l'~** you're in my light; **ça nous donne de l'~** it gives us (some) shade; **il n'y a pas l'~ d'un doute** there's not the shadow of a doubt; **dans l'~** in the shade; **vivre dans l'~** (*fig*) to live in obscurity; **laisser dans l'~** (*fig*) to leave in the dark; ~ **à paupières** eye shadow; ~ **portée** shadow; ~**s chinoises** (*spectacle*) shadow show *sg*

ombrelle [ɔ̃brɛl] *nf* parasol, sunshade

omelette [ɔmlɛt] *nf* omelette; ~ **baveuse** runny omelette; ~ **au fromage/au jambon** cheese/ ham omelette; ~ **aux herbes** omelette with herbs; ~ **norvégienne** baked Alaska

omettre [ɔmɛtr(ə)] *vt* to omit, leave out; ~ **de faire** to fail *ou* omit to do

omnibus [ɔmnibys] *nm* slow *ou* stopping train

omoplate [ɔmɔplat] *nf* shoulder blade

on [ɔ̃] *pron* **1** (*indéterminé*) you, one; **on peut le faire ainsi** you *ou* one can do it like this, it can be done like this; **on dit que ...** they say that ..., it is said that ..

2 (*quelqu'un*): **on les a attaqués** they were attacked; **on vous demande au téléphone** there's a phone call for you, you're wanted on the phone; **on frappe à la porte** someone's knocking at the door

3 (*nous*) we; **on va y aller demain** we're going tomorrow

4 (*les gens*) they; **autrefois, on croyait ...** they used to believe ..

5: **on ne peut plus** *adv*: **on ne peut plus stupide** as stupid as can be

oncle [ɔ̃kl(ə)] *nm* uncle

onctueux, -euse [ɔ̃ktɥø, -øz] *adj* creamy, smooth; (*fig*) smooth, unctuous

onde [ɔ̃d] *nf* (*Physique*) wave; **sur l'~** on the

waters; **sur les ~s** on the radio; **mettre en ~s** to produce for the radio; ~ **de choc** shock wave; ~**s courtes (OC)** short wave *sg*; **petites ~s (PO)**, ~**s moyennes (OM)** medium wave *sg*; **grandes ~s (GO)**, ~**s longues (OL)** long wave *sg*; ~**s sonores** sound waves

ondée [ɔ̃de] *nf* shower

on-dit [ɔ̃di] *nm inv* rumour

onduler [ɔ̃dyle] *vi* to undulate; (*cheveux*) to wave

onéreux, -euse [ɔnerø, -øz] *adj* costly; **à titre ~** in return for payment

ongle [ɔ̃gl(ə)] *nm* (*Anat*) nail; **manger** *ou* **ronger ses ~s** to bite one's nails; **se faire les ~s** to do one's nails

ont [ɔ̃] *vb voir* **avoir**

ONU [ɔny] *sigle f* (= *Organisation des Nations unies*) UN(O)

onze [ɔ̃z] *num* eleven

onzième [ɔ̃zjɛm] *num* eleventh

OPA *sigle f* = **offre publique d'achat**

opaque [ɔpak] *adj* (*vitre, verre*) opaque; (*brouillard, nuit*) impenetrable

opéra [ɔpera] *nm* opera; (*édifice*) opera house

opérateur, -trice [ɔperatœr, -tris] *nm/f* operator; ~ **(de prise de vues)** cameraman

opération [ɔperasjɔ̃] *nf* operation; (*Comm*) dealing; **salle/table d'~** operating theatre/ table; ~ **de sauvetage** rescue operation; ~ **à cœur ouvert** open-heart surgery *no pl*

opératoire [ɔperatwar] *adj* (*manœuvre, méthode*) operating; (*choc etc*) post-operative

opérer [ɔpere] *vt* (*Méd*) to operate on; (*faire, exécuter*) to carry out, make ▷ *vi* (*remède: faire effet*) to act, work; (*procéder*) to proceed; (*Méd*) to operate; **s'opérer** *vi* (*avoir lieu*) to occur, take place; **se faire** ~ to have an operation; **se faire** ~ **des amygdales/du cœur** to have one's tonsils out/have a heart operation

opérette [ɔperɛt] *nf* operetta, light opera

ophtalmologie [ɔftalmɔlɔʒi] *nf* ophthalmology

opiner [ɔpine] *vi*: ~ **de la tête** to nod assent ▷ *vt*: ~ **à** to consent to

opinion [ɔpinjɔ̃] *nf* opinion; **l'~ (publique)** public opinion; **avoir bonne/mauvaise ~ de** to have a high/low opinion of

opportun, e [ɔpɔrtœ̃, -yn] *adj* timely, opportune; **en temps ~** at the appropriate time

opportuniste [ɔpɔrtynist(ə)] *adj, nm/f* opportunist

opposant, e [ɔpozɑ̃, -ɑ̃t] *adj* opposing ▷ *nm/f* opponent

opposé, e [ɔpoze] *adj* (*direction, rive*) opposite; (*faction*) opposing; (*couleurs*) contrasting; (*opinions, intérêts*) conflicting; (*contre*): ~ **à** opposed to, against ▷ *nm*: **l'~** the other *ou* opposite side (*ou* direction); (*contraire*) the opposite; **être ~ à** to be opposed to; **à l'~** (*fig*) on the other hand; **à l'~ de** on the other *ou* opposite side from; (*fig*) contrary to, unlike

opposer [ɔpoze] *vt* (*meubles, objets*) to place opposite each other; (*personnes, armées, équipes*) to oppose; (*couleurs, termes, tons*) to contrast;

(*comparer: livres, avantages*) to contrast; ~ **qch à** (*comme obstacle, défense*) to set sth against; (*comme objection*) to put sth forward against; (*en contraste*) to set sth opposite; to match sth with; **s'opposer** *vi* (*sens réciproque*) to conflict; to clash; to face each other; to contrast; **s'~ à** (*interdire, empêcher*) to oppose; (*tenir tête à*) to rebel against; **sa religion s'y oppose** it's against his religion; **s'~ à ce que qn fasse** to be opposed to sb's doing

opposition [ɔpozisjɔ̃] *nf* opposition; **par ~** in contrast; **par ~ à** as opposed to, in contrast with; **entrer en ~ avec** to come into conflict with; **être en ~ avec** (*idées, conduite*) to be at variance with; **faire ~ à un chèque** to stop a cheque

oppressant, e [ɔpresɑ̃, -ɑ̃t] *adj* oppressive

oppresser [ɔprese] *vt* to oppress; **se sentir oppressé** to feel breathless

oppression [ɔpresjɔ̃] *nf* oppression; (*malaise*) feeling of suffocation

opprimer [ɔprime] *vt* (*asservir: peuple, faibles*) to oppress; (*étouffer: liberté, opinion*) to suppress, stifle; (*chaleur etc*) to suffocate, oppress

opter [ɔpte] *vi*: ~ **pour** to opt for; ~ **entre** to choose between

opticien, ne [ɔptisjɛ̃, -ɛn] *nm/f* optician

optimisme [ɔptimism(ə)] *nm* optimism

optimiste [ɔptimist(ə)] *adj* optimistic ▷ *nm/f* optimist

option [ɔpsjɔ̃] *nf* option; (*Auto: supplément*) optional extra; **matière à ~** (*Scol*) optional subject (*Brit*), elective (*US*); **prendre une ~ sur** to take (out) an option on; ~ **par défaut** (*Inform*) default (option)

optique [ɔptik] *adj* (*nerf*) optic; (*verres*) optical ▷ *nf* (*Photo: lentilles etc*) optics *pl*; (*science, industrie*) optics *sg*; (*fig: manière de voir*) perspective

opulent, e [ɔpylɑ̃, -ɑ̃t] *adj* wealthy, opulent; (*formes, poitrine*) ample, generous

or [ɔr] *nm* gold ▷ *conj* now, but; **d'or** (*fig*) golden; **en or** gold *cpd*; (*occasion*) golden; **un mari/ enfant en or** a treasure; **une affaire en or** (*achat*) a real bargain; (*commerce*) a gold mine; **plaqué or** gold-plated; **or noir** black gold

orage [ɔraʒ] *nm* (thunder)storm

orageux, -euse [ɔraʒø, -øz] *adj* stormy

oral, e, -aux [ɔral, -o] *adj* (*déposition, promesse*) oral, verbal; (*Méd*): **par voie ~e** by mouth, orally ▷ *nm* (*Scol*) oral

orange [ɔrɑ̃ʒ] *adj inv, nf* orange; ~ **sanguine** blood orange; ~ **pressée** freshly-squeezed orange juice

orangé, e [ɔrɑ̃ʒe] *adj* orangey, orange-coloured

orangeade [ɔrɑ̃ʒad] *nf* orangeade

oranger [ɔrɑ̃ʒe] *nm* orange tree

orateur [ɔratœr] *nm* speaker; orator

orbite [ɔrbit] *nf* (*Anat*) (eye-)socket; (*Physique*) orbit; **mettre sur ~** to put into orbit; (*fig*) to launch; **dans l'~ de** (*fig*) within the sphere of influence of

orchestre [ɔrkɛstr(ə)] *nm* orchestra; (*de jazz, danse*) band; (*places*) stalls *pl* (*Brit*), orchestra (*US*)

orchestrer [ɔrkɛstre] *vt* (*Mus*) to orchestrate;

(*fig*) to mount, stage-manage

orchidée [ɔrkide] *nf* orchid

ordinaire [ɔrdinɛr] *adj* ordinary; (*coutumier: maladresse etc*) usual; (*de tous les jours*) everyday; (*modèle, qualité*) standard ▷ *nm* ordinary; (*menus*) everyday fare ▷ *nf* (*essence*) ≈ two-star (petrol) (*Brit*), ≈ regular (gas) (*US*); **d'~** usually, normally; **à l'~** usually, ordinarily

ordinateur [ɔrdinatœr] *nm* computer; **mettre sur ~** to computerize, put on computer; ~ **de bureau** desktop computer; ~ **individuel** *ou* **personnel** personal computer; ~ **portable** laptop (computer)

ordonnance [ɔrdɔnɑ̃s] *nf* organization; (*groupement, disposition*) layout; (*Méd*) prescription; (*Jur*) order; (*Mil*) orderly, batman (*Brit*); **d'~** (*Mil*) regulation *cpd*; **officier d'~** aide-de-camp

ordonné, e [ɔrdɔne] *adj* tidy, orderly; (*Math*) ordered ▷ *nf* (*Math*) Y-axis, ordinate

ordonner [ɔrdɔne] *vt* (*agencer*) to organize, arrange; (: *meubles, appartement*) to lay out, arrange; (*donner un ordre*): ~ **à qn de faire** to order sb to do; (*Math*) (to arrange in) order; (*Rel*) to ordain; (*Méd*) to prescribe; (*Jur*) to order; **s'ordonner** *vi* (*faits*) to organize themselves

ordre [ɔrdr(ə)] *nm* (*gén*) order; (*propreté et soin*) orderliness, tidiness; (*association professionnelle, honorifique*) association; (*Comm*): **à l'~ de** payable to; (*nature*): **d'~ pratique** of a practical nature; **ordres** *nmpl* (*Rel*) holy orders; **avoir de l'~** to be tidy *ou* orderly; **mettre en ~** to tidy (up), put in order; **mettre bon ~ à** to put to rights, sort out; **procéder par ~** to take things one at a time; **être aux ~s de qn/sous les ~s de qn** to be at sb's disposal/under sb's command; **rappeler qn à l'~** to call sb to order; **jusqu'à nouvel ~** until further notice; **dans le même ~ d'idées** in this connection; **par ~ d'entrée en scène** in order of appearance; **un ~ de grandeur** some idea of the size (*ou* amount) of; **de premier ~** first-rate; ~ **de grève** strike call; ~ **du jour** (*d'une réunion*) agenda; (*Mil*) order of the day; **à l'~ du jour** on the agenda; (*fig*) topical; (*Mil: citer*) in dispatches; ~ **de mission** (*Mil*) orders *pl*; ~ **public** law and order; ~ **de route** marching orders *pl*

ordure [ɔrdyr] *nf* filth; (*propos, écrit*) obscenity, (piece of) filth; **ordures** *nfpl* (*balayures, déchets*) rubbish *sg*, refuse *sg*; ~**s ménagères** household refuse

oreille [ɔrɛj] *nf* (*Anat*) ear; (*de marmite, tasse*) handle; (*Tech: d'un écrou*) wing; **avoir de l'~** to have a good ear (for music); **avoir l'~ fine** to have good *ou* sharp ears; **l'~ basse** crestfallen, dejected; **se faire tirer l'~** to take a lot of persuading; **dire qch à l'~ de qn** to have a word in sb's ear (about sth)

oreiller [ɔreje] *nm* pillow

oreillons [ɔrɛjɔ̃] *nmpl* mumps *sg*

ores [ɔr]: **d'~ et déjà** *adv* already

orfèvrerie [ɔrfɛvrəri] *nf* (*art, métier*) goldsmith's (*ou* silversmith's) trade; (*ouvrage*) (silver *ou* gold) plate

organe [ɔʀgan] *nm* organ; (*véhicule, instrument*) instrument; (*voix*) voice; (*porte-parole*) representative, mouthpiece; **~s de commande** (*Tech*) controls; **~s de transmission** (*Tech*) transmission system *sg*

organigramme [ɔʀganigʀam] *nm* (*hiérarchique, structure*) organization chart; (*des opérations*) flow chart

organique [ɔʀganik] *adj* organic

organisateur, -trice [ɔʀganizatœʀ, -tʀis] *nm/f* organizer

organisation [ɔʀganizasjɔ̃] *nf* organization; **O~ des Nations unies (ONU)** United Nations (Organization) (UN, UNO); **O~ mondiale de la santé (OMS)** World Health Organization (WHO); **O~ du traité de l'Atlantique Nord (OTAN)** North Atlantic Treaty Organization (NATO)

organiser [ɔʀganize] *vt* to organize; (*mettre sur pied: service etc*) to set up; **s'organiser** *vi* to get organized

organisme [ɔʀganism(ə)] *nm* (*Bio*) organism; (*corps humain*) body; (*Admin, Pol etc*) body, organism

organiste [ɔʀganist(ə)] *nm/f* organist

orgasme [ɔʀgasm(ə)] *nm* orgasm, climax

orge [ɔʀʒ(ə)] *nf* barley

orgue [ɔʀg(ə)] *nm* organ; **orgues** *nfpl* organ *sg*; **~ de Barbarie** barrel *ou* street organ

orgueil [ɔʀgœj] *nm* pride

orgueilleux, -euse [ɔʀgœjø, -øz] *adj* proud

Orient [ɔʀjɑ̃] *nm*: **l'~** the East, the Orient

oriental, e, -aux [ɔʀjɑ̃tal, -o] *adj* oriental, eastern; (*frontière*) eastern ▷ *nm/f*: **O~, e** Oriental

orientation [ɔʀjɑ̃tasjɔ̃] *nf* positioning; adjustment; orientation; direction; (*d'une maison etc*) aspect; (*d'un journal*) leanings *pl*; **avoir le sens de l'~** to have a (good) sense of direction; **course d'~** orienteering exercise; **~ professionnelle** careers advice *ou* guidance; (*service*) careers advisory service

orienté, e [ɔʀjɑ̃te] *adj* (*fig: article, journal*) slanted; **bien/mal ~** (*appartement*) well/badly positioned; **~ au sud** facing south, with a southern aspect

orienter [ɔʀjɑ̃te] *vt* (*situer*) to position; (*placer, disposer: pièce mobile*) to adjust, position; (*tourner*) to direct, turn; (*voyageur, touriste, recherches*) to direct; (*fig: élève*) to orientate; **s'orienter** *vi* (*se repérer*) to find one's bearings; **s'~ vers** (*fig*) to turn towards

origan [ɔʀigɑ̃] *nm* oregano

originaire [ɔʀiʒinɛʀ] *adj* original; **être ~ de** (*pays, lieu*) to be a native of; (*provenir de*) to originate from; to be native to

original, e, -aux [ɔʀiʒinal, -o] *adj* original; (*bizarre*) eccentric ▷ *nm/f* (*fam: excentrique*) eccentric; (: *fantaisiste*) joker ▷ *nm* (*document etc, Art*) original; (*dactylographie*) top copy

origine [ɔʀiʒin] *nf* origin; (*d'un message, appel téléphonique*) source; (*d'une révolution, réussite*) root; **origines** *nfpl* (*d'une personne*) origins; **d'~** of origin; (*pneus etc*) original; (*bureau postal*)

dispatching; **d'~ française** of French origin; **dès l'~** at *ou* from the outset; **à l'~** originally; **avoir son ~ dans** to have its origins in, originate in

originel, le [ɔʀiʒinɛl] *adj* original

orme [ɔʀm(ə)] *nm* elm

ornement [ɔʀnəmɑ̃] *nm* ornament; (*fig*) embellishment, adornment; **~s sacerdotaux** vestments

orner [ɔʀne] *vt* to decorate, adorn; **~ qch de** to decorate sth with

ornière [ɔʀnjɛʀ] *nf* rut; (*fig*): **sortir de l'~** (*routine*) to get out of the rut; (*impasse*) to get out of a spot

orphelin, e [ɔʀfəlɛ̃, -in] *adj* orphan(ed) ▷ *nm/f* orphan; **~ de père/mère** fatherless/motherless

orphelinat [ɔʀfəlina] *nm* orphanage

orteil [ɔʀtɛj] *nm* toe; **gros ~** big toe

orthographe [ɔʀtɔgʀaf] *nf* spelling

ortie [ɔʀti] *nf* (stinging) nettle; **~ blanche** white dead-nettle

os [ɔs] *nm* bone; **sans os** (*Boucherie*) off the bone, boned; **os à moelle** marrowbone

osciller [ɔsile] *vi* (*pendule*) to swing; (*au vent etc*) to rock; (*Tech*) to oscillate; (*fig*): **~ entre** to waver *ou* fluctuate between

osé, e [oze] *adj* daring, bold

oseille [ozɛj] *nf* sorrel

oser [oze] *vi, vt* to dare; **~ faire** to dare (to) do

osier [ozje] *nm* (*Bot*) willow; **d'~, en ~** wicker(work) *cpd*

ossature [ɔsatyʀ] *nf* (*Anat: squelette*) frame, skeletal structure; (: *du visage*) bone structure; (*fig*) framework

osseux, -euse [ɔsø, -øz] *adj* bony; (*tissu, maladie, greffe*) bone *cpd*

ostensible [ɔstɑ̃sibl(ə)] *adj* conspicuous

otage [ɔtaʒ] *nm* hostage; **prendre qn comme ~** to take sb hostage

OTAN [ɔtɑ̃] *sigle f* (= *Organisation du traité de l'Atlantique Nord*) NATO

otarie [ɔtaʀi] *nf* sea-lion

ôter [ote] *vt* to remove; (*soustraire*) to take away; **~ qch à qn** to take sth (away) from sb; **~ qch de** to remove sth from; **six ôté de dix égale quatre** six from ten equals *ou* is four

otite [ɔtit] *nf* ear infection

ou [u] *conj* or; **ou ... ou** either ... or; **ou bien** or (else)

où [u] *pron relatif* **1** (*position, situation*) where, that (*souvent omis*); **la chambre où il était** the room (that) he was in, the room where he was; **la ville où je l'ai rencontré** the town where I met him; **la pièce d'où il est sorti** the room he came out of; **le village d'où je viens** the village I come from; **les villes par où il est passé** the towns he went through

2 (*temps, état*) that (*souvent omis*); **le jour où il est parti** the day (that) he left; **au prix où c'est** at the price it is

▷ *adv* **1** (*interrogation*) where; **où est-il/va-t-il?** where is he/is he going?; **par où?** which way?;

d'où vient que ...? how come ...?
2 (*position*) where; **je sais où il est** I know where he is; **où que l'on aille** wherever you go

ouate [wat] *nf* cotton wool (*Brit*), cotton (*US*); (*bourre*) padding, wadding; ~ **(hydrophile)** cotton wool (*Brit*), (absorbent) cotton (*US*)

oubli [ubli] *nm* (*acte*): **l'~ de** forgetting; (*étourderie*) forgetfulness *no pl*; (*négligence*) omission, oversight; (*absence de souvenirs*) oblivion; ~ **de soi** self-effacement, self-negation

oublier [ublije] *vt* (*gén*) to forget; (*ne pas voir: erreurs etc*) to miss; (*ne pas mettre: virgule, nom*) to leave out, forget; (*laisser quelque part: chapeau etc*) to leave behind; **s'oublier** *vi* to forget o.s.; (*enfant, animal*) to have an accident (*euphemism*); ~ **l'heure** to forget (about) the time

oubliettes [ublijɛt] *nfpl* dungeon *sg*; **(jeter) aux ~** (*fig*) (to put) completely out of mind

ouest [wɛst] *nm* west ▷ *adj inv* west; (*région*) western; **à l'~** in the west, (to the) west, westwards; **à l'~ de** (to the) west of; **vent d'~** westerly wind

ouf [uf] *excl* phew!

oui [wi] *adv* yes; **répondre (par) ~** to answer yes; **mais ~, bien sûr** yes, of course; **je pense que ~** I think so; **pour un ~ ou pour un non** for no apparent reason

ouï-dire [widiR]: **par ~** *adv* by hearsay

ouïe [wi] *nf* hearing; **ouïes** *nfpl* (*de poisson*) gills; (*de violon*) sound-hole *sg*

ouragan [uRagã] *nm* hurricane; (*fig*) storm

ourlet [uRlɛ] *nm* hem; (*de l'oreille*) rim; **faire un ~ à** to hem

ours [uRs] *nm* bear; ~ **brun/blanc** brown/polar bear; ~ **marin** fur seal; ~ **mal léché** uncouth fellow; ~ **(en peluche)** teddy (bear)

oursin [uRsɛ̃] *nm* sea urchin

ourson [uRsɔ̃] *nm* (bear-)cub

ouste [ust(ə)] *excl* hop it!

outil [uti] *nm* tool

outiller [utije] *vt* (*ouvrier, usine*) to equip

outrage [utRaʒ] *nm* insult; **faire subir les derniers ~s à** (*femme*) to ravish; ~ **aux bonnes mœurs** (*Jur*) outrage to public decency; ~ **à magistrat** (*Jur*) contempt of court; ~ **à la pudeur** (*Jur*) indecent behaviour *no pl*

outrager [utRaʒe] *vt* to offend gravely; (*fig: contrevenir à*) to outrage, insult

outrance [utRãs] *nf* excessiveness *no pl*, excess; **à ~** *adv* excessively, to excess

outre [utR(ə)] *nf* goatskin, water skin ▷ *prép* besides ▷ *adv*: **passer ~** to carry on regardless; **passer ~ à** to disregard, take no notice of; **en ~** besides, moreover; ~ **que** apart from the fact that; ~ **mesure** immoderately; unduly

outre-Atlantique [utRatlãtik] *adv* across the Atlantic

outre-Manche [utRəmãʃ] *adv* across the Channel

outre-mer [utRəmɛR] *adv* overseas; **d'~** overseas

outrepasser [utRəpase] *vt* to go beyond, exceed

ouvert, e [uvɛR, -ɛRt(ə)] *pp de* **ouvrir** ▷ *adj* open; (*robinet, gaz etc*) on; **à bras ~s** with open arms

ouvertement [uvɛRtəmã] *adv* openly

ouverture [uvɛRtyR] *nf* opening; (*Mus*) overture; (*Pol*): **l'~** the widening of the political spectrum; (*Photo*): ~ **(du diaphragme)** aperture; **ouvertures** *nfpl* (*propositions*) overtures; ~ **d'esprit** open-mindedness; **heures d'~** (*Comm*) opening hours; **jours d'~** (*Comm*) days of opening

ouvrable [uvRabl(ə)] *adj*: **jour ~** working day, weekday; **heures ~s** business hours

ouvrage [uvRaʒ] *nm* (*tâche, de tricot etc, Mil*) work *no pl*; (*objet: Couture, Art*) (piece of) work; (*texte, livre*) work; **panier** *ou* **corbeille à ~** work basket; ~ **d'art** (*Génie Civil*) bridge *ou* tunnel *etc*

ouvragé, e [uvRaʒe] *adj* finely embroidered (*ou* worked *ou* carved)

ouvre-boîte, ouvre-boîtes [uvRəbwat] *nm inv* tin (*Brit*) *ou* can opener

ouvre-bouteille, ouvre-bouteilles [uvRəbutɛj] *nm inv* bottle-opener

ouvreuse [uvRøz] *nf* usherette

ouvrier, -ière [uvRije, -jɛR] *nm/f* worker ▷ *nf* (*Zool*) worker (bee) ▷ *adj* working-class; (*problèmes, conflit*) industrial, labour *cpd* (*Brit*), labor *cpd* (*US*); (*revendications*) workers'; **classe ouvrière** working class; ~ **agricole** farmworker; ~ **qualifié** skilled worker; ~ **spécialisé (OS)** semiskilled worker; ~ **d'usine** factory worker

ouvrir [uvRiR] *vt* (*gén*) to open; (*brèche, passage*) to open up; (*commencer l'exploitation de, créer*) to open (up); (*eau, électricité, chauffage, robinet*) to turn on; (*Méd: abcès*) to open up, cut open ▷ *vi* to open; to open up; (*Cartes*): ~ **à trèfle** to open in clubs; **s'ouvrir** *vi* to open; **s'~ à** (*art etc*) to open one's mind to; **s'~ à qn (de qch)** to open one's heart to sb (about sth); **s'~ les veines** to slash *ou* cut one's wrists; ~ **sur** to open onto; ~ **l'appétit à qn** to whet sb's appetite; ~ **des horizons** to open up new horizons; ~ **l'esprit** to broaden one's horizons; ~ **une session** (*Inform*) to log in

ovaire [ovɛR] *nm* ovary

ovale [oval] *adj* oval

OVNI [ovni] *sigle m* (= *objet volant non identifié*) UFO

oxyder [ɔkside]: **s'oxyder** *vi* to become oxidized

oxygéné, e [ɔksiʒene] *adj*: **eau ~e** hydrogen peroxide; **cheveux ~s** bleached hair

oxygène [ɔksiʒɛn] *nm* oxygen; (*fig*): **cure d'~** fresh air cure

ozone [ozɔn] *nm* ozone; **trou dans la couche d'~** hole in the ozone layer

Pp

pacifique [pasifik] *adj* (*personne*) peaceable; (*intentions, coexistence*) peaceful ▷ *nm*: **le P~, l'océan P~** the Pacific (Ocean)

pack [pak] *nm* pack

pacotille [pakɔtij] *nf* (*péj*) cheap goods *pl*; **de ~** cheap

PACS [paks] *sigle m* (= *pacte civil de solidarité*) ≈ civil partnership

pacser [pakse]: **se pacser** *vi* ≈ to form a civil partnership

pacte [pakt(ə)] *nm* pact, treaty

pagaie [pagɛ] *nf* paddle

pagaille [pagaj] *nf* mess, shambles *sg*; **il y en a en ~** there are loads *ou* heaps of them

pagayer [pageje] *vi* to paddle

page [paʒ] *nf* page; (*passage: d'un roman*) passage ▷ *nm* page (boy); **mettre en ~** layout; **à la ~** (*fig*) up-to-date; **~ d'accueil** (*Inform*) home page; **~ blanche** blank page; **~ de garde** endpaper; **~ Web** (*Inform*) web page

paiement [pɛmɑ̃] *nm* = **payement**

païen, ne [pajɛ̃, -ɛn] *adj, nm/f* pagan, heathen

paillasson [pajasɔ̃] *nm* doormat

paille [paj] *nf* straw; (*défaut*) flaw; **être sur la ~** to be ruined; **~ de fer** steel wool

paillette [pajɛt] *nf* speck, flake; **paillettes** *nfpl* (*décoratives*) sequins, spangles; **lessive en ~s** soapflakes *pl*

pain [pɛ̃] *nm* (*substance*) bread; (*unité*) loaf (of bread); (*morceau*): **~ de cire** *etc* bar of wax *etc*; (*Culin*): **~ de poisson/légumes** fish/vegetable loaf; **petit ~** (bread) roll; **~ bis/complet** brown/wholemeal (*Brit*) *ou* wholewheat (*US*) bread; **~ de campagne** farmhouse bread; **~ d'épice** ≈ gingerbread; **~ de mie** sandwich loaf; **~ perdu** French toast; **~ de seigle** rye bread; **~ de sucre** sugar loaf

pair, e [pɛʀ] *adj* (*nombre*) even ▷ *nm* peer; **aller de ~ (avec)** to go hand in hand *ou* together (with); **au ~** (*Finance*) at par; **valeur au ~** par value; **jeune fille au ~** au pair

paire [pɛʀ] *nf* pair; **une ~ de lunettes/tenailles** a pair of glasses/pincers; **faire la ~**: **les deux font la paire** they are two of a kind

paisible [pezibl(ə)] *adj* peaceful, quiet

paître [pɛtʀ(ə)] *vi* to graze

paix [pɛ] *nf* peace; (*fig*) peacefulness, peace; **faire la ~ avec** to make peace with; **avoir la ~** to have peace (and quiet)

Pakistan [pakistɑ̃] *nm*: **le ~** Pakistan

palace [palas] *nm* luxury hotel

palais [palɛ] *nm* palace; (*Anat*) palate; **le P~ Bourbon** *the seat of the French National Assembly*; **le P~ de l'Élysée** the Élysée Palace; **~ des expositions** exhibition centre; **le P~ de Justice** the Law Courts *pl*

pâle [pɑl] *adj* pale; (*fig*): **une ~ imitation** a pale imitation; **bleu ~** pale blue; **~ de colère** white *ou* pale with anger

Palestine [palɛstin] *nf*: **la ~** Palestine

palet [palɛ] *nm* disc; (*Hockey*) puck

paletot [palto] *nm* (short) coat

palette [palɛt] *nf* palette; (*de produits*) range

pâleur [pɑlœʀ] *nf* paleness

palier [palje] *nm* (*d'escalier*) landing; (*fig*) level, plateau; (: *phase stable*) levelling (*Brit*) *ou* leveling (*US*) off, new level; (*Tech*) bearing; **nos voisins de ~** our neighbo(u)rs across the landing (*Brit*) *ou* the hall (*US*); **en ~** *adv* level; **par ~s** in stages

pâlir [pɑliʀ] *vi* to turn *ou* go pale; (*couleur*) to fade; **faire ~ qn** (*de jalousie*) to make sb green (with envy)

palissade [palisad] *nf* fence

pallier [palje] *vt*: **~ à** *vt* to offset, make up for

palmarès [palmaʀɛs] *nm* record (of achievements); (*Scol*) prize list; (*Sport*) list of winners

palme [palm(ə)] *nf* (*Bot*) palm leaf; (*symbole*) palm; (*de plongeur*) flipper; **~s (académiques)** *decoration for services to education*

palmé, e [palme] *adj* (*pattes*) webbed

palmier [palmje] *nm* palm tree

pâlot, te [pɑlo, -ɔt] *adj* pale, peaky

palourde [paluʀd(ə)] *nf* clam

palper [palpe] *vt* to feel, finger

palpitant, e [palpitɑ̃, -ɑ̃t] *adj* thrilling, gripping

palpiter [palpite] *vi* (*cœur, pouls*) to beat; (: *plus fort*) to pound, throb; (*narines, chair*) to quiver

paludisme [palydism(ə)] *nm* malaria

pamphlet [pɑ̃flɛ] *nm* lampoon, satirical tract

pamplemousse [pɑ̃pləmus] *nm* grapefruit

pan [pɑ̃] *nm* section, piece; (*côté: d'un prisme, d'une tour*) side, face ▷ *excl* bang!; **~ de chemise** shirt

tail; ~ **de mur** section of wall

panache [panaʃ] nm plume; (fig) spirit, panache

panaché, e [panaʃe] adj: **œillet** ~ variegated carnation; **glace** ~**e** mixed ice cream; **salade** ~**e** mixed salad; **bière** ~**e** shandy

pancarte [pãkaʀt(ə)] nf sign, notice; (dans un défilé) placard

pancréas [pãkʀeɑs] nm pancreas

pané, e [pane] adj fried in breadcrumbs

panier [panje] nm basket; (à diapositives) magazine; **mettre au** ~ to chuck away; ~ **de crabes: c'est un panier de crabes** (fig) they're constantly at one another's throats; ~ **percé** (fig) spendthrift; ~ **à provisions** shopping basket; ~ **à salade** (Culin) salad shaker; (Police) paddy wagon, police van

panier-repas (pl **paniers-repas**) [panjeʀ(ə)pɑ] nm packed lunch

panique [panik] adj panicky ▷ nf panic

paniquer [panike] vi to panic

panne [pan] nf (d'un mécanisme, moteur) breakdown; **être/tomber en** ~ to have broken down/break down; **être en** ~ **d'essence** ou **en** ~ **sèche** to have run out of petrol (Brit) ou gas (US); **mettre en** ~ (Navig) to bring to; ~ **d'électricité** ou **de courant** power ou electrical failure

panneau, x [pano] nm (écriteau) sign, notice; (de boiserie, de tapisserie etc) panel; **tomber dans le** ~ (fig) to walk into the trap; ~ **d'affichage** notice (Brit) ou bulletin (US) board; ~ **électoral** board for election poster; ~ **indicateur** signpost; ~ **publicitaire** hoarding (Brit), billboard (US); ~ **de signalisation** roadsign; ~ **solaire** solar panel

panoplie [panɔpli] nf (jouet) outfit; (d'armes) display; (fig) array

panorama [panɔʀama] nm (vue) all-round view, panorama; (peinture) panorama; (fig: étude complète) complete overview

panse [pãs] nf paunch

pansement [pãsmã] nm dressing, bandage; ~ **adhésif** sticking plaster (Brit), bandaid® (US)

panser [pãse] vt (plaie) to dress, bandage; (bras) to put a dressing on, bandage; (cheval) to groom

pantacourt [pãtakuʀ] nm cropped trousers pl

pantalon [pãtalɔ̃] nm trousers pl (Brit), pants pl (US), pair of trousers ou pants; ~ **de ski** ski pants pl

panthère [pãtɛʀ] nf panther

pantin [pãtɛ̃] nm (jouet) jumping jack; (péj: personne) puppet

pantois [pãtwa] adj m: **rester** ~ to be flabbergasted

pantoufle [pãtufl(ə)] nf slipper

paon [pã] nm peacock

papa [papa] nm dad(dy)

pape [pap] nm pope

paperasse [papʀas] nf (péj) bumf no pl, papers pl; forms pl

paperasserie [papʀasʀi] nf (péj) red tape no pl; paperwork no pl

papeterie [papetʀi] nf (fabrication du papier) paper-making (industry); (usine) paper mill; (magasin)

stationer's (shop (Brit)); (articles) stationery

papetier, -ière [paptje, -jɛʀ] nm/f paper-maker; stationer

papi [papi] nm (fam) granddad

papier [papje] nm paper; (feuille) sheet ou piece of paper; (article) article; (écrit officiel) document; **papiers** nmpl (aussi: **papiers d'identité**) (identity) papers; **sur le** ~ (théoriquement) on paper; **noircir du** ~ to write page after page; ~ **couché/glacé** art/glazed paper; ~ **(d')aluminium** aluminium (Brit) ou aluminum (US) foil, tinfoil; ~ **d'Arménie** incense paper; ~ **bible** India ou bible paper; ~ **de brouillon** rough ou scrap paper; ~ **bulle** manil(l)a paper; ~ **buvard** blotting paper; ~ **calque** tracing paper; ~ **carbone** carbon paper; ~ **collant** Sellotape® (Brit), Scotch tape® (US), sticky tape; ~ **en continu** continuous stationery; ~ **à dessin** drawing paper; ~ **d'emballage** wrapping paper; ~ **gommé** gummed paper; ~ **hygiénique** toilet paper; ~ **journal** newsprint; (pour emballer) newspaper; ~ **à lettres** writing paper, notepaper; ~ **mâché** papier-mâché; ~ **machine** typing paper; ~ **peint** wallpaper; ~ **pelure** India paper; ~ **à pliage accordéon** fanfold paper; ~ **de soie** tissue paper; ~ **thermique** thermal paper; ~ **de tournesol** litmus paper; ~ **de verre** sandpaper

papillon [papijɔ̃] nm butterfly; (fam: contravention) (parking) ticket; (Tech: écrou) wing ou butterfly nut; ~ **de nuit** moth

papillote [papijɔt] nf (pour cheveux) curlpaper; (de gigot) (paper) frill

papoter [papɔte] vi to chatter

paquebot [pakbo] nm liner

pâquerette [pakʀɛt] nf daisy

Pâques [pak] nm, nfpl: **faire ses** ~ to do one's Easter duties; **l'île de** ~ Easter Island

paquet [pakɛ] nm packet; (colis) parcel; (ballot) bundle; (dans négociations) package (deal); (fig: tas): ~ **de** pile ou heap of; **paquets** nmpl (bagages) bags; **mettre le** ~ (fam) to give one's all; ~ **de mer** big wave

paquet-cadeau (pl **paquets-cadeaux**) [pakɛkado] nm gift-wrapped parcel

par [paʀ] prép by; **finir** etc ~ to end etc with; ~ **amour** out of love; **passer** ~ **Lyon/la côte** to go via ou through Lyons/along by the coast; ~ **la fenêtre** (jeter, regarder) out of the window; **trois** ~ **jour/personne** three a ou per day/head; **deux** ~ **deux** two at a time; (marcher etc) in twos; ~ **où?** which way?; ~ **ici** this way; (dans le coin) round here; ~-**ci**, ~-**là** here and there

parabolique [paʀabɔlik] adj parabolic; **antenne** ~ satellite dish

parachever [paʀaʃve] vt to perfect

parachute [paʀaʃyt] nm parachute

parachutiste [paʀaʃytist(ə)] nm/f parachutist; (Mil) paratrooper

parade [paʀad] nf (spectacle, défilé) parade; (Escrime, Boxe) parry; (ostentation): **faire** ~ **de** to display, show off; (défense, riposte): **trouver la** ~ **à une attaque** to find the answer to an attack;

de ~ adj ceremonial; (superficiel) superficial, outward

paradis [paʀadi] nm heaven, paradise; **P~ terrestre** (Rel) Garden of Eden; (fig) heaven on earth

paradoxe [paʀadɔks(ə)] nm paradox

paraffine [paʀafin] nf paraffin; paraffin wax

parages [paʀaʒ] nmpl (Navig) waters; **dans les ~ (de)** in the area ou vicinity (of)

paragraphe [paʀagʀaf] nm paragraph

paraître [paʀɛtʀ(ə)] vb copule to seem, look, appear ▷ vi to appear; (être visible) to appear; (Presse, Édition) to be published, come out, appear; (briller) to show off; **laisser ~ qch** to let (sth) show ▷ vb impers: **il paraît que** it seems ou appears that; **il me paraît que** it seems to me that; **il paraît absurde de** it seems absurd to; **il ne paraît pas son âge** he doesn't look his age; **~ en justice** to appear before the court(s); **~ en scène/en public/à l'écran** to appear on stage/in public/on the screen

parallèle [paʀalɛl] adj parallel; (police, marché) unofficial; (société, énergie) alternative ▷ nm (comparaison): **faire un ~ entre** to draw a parallel between; (Géo) parallel ▷ nf parallel (line); **en ~** in parallel; **mettre en ~** (choses opposées) to compare; (choses semblables) to parallel

paralyser [paʀalize] vt to paralyze

paramédical, e, -aux [paʀamedikal, -o] adj paramedical

paraphrase [paʀafʀɑz] nf paraphrase

parapluie [paʀaplɥi] nm umbrella; **~ atomique** ou **nucléaire** nuclear umbrella; **~ pliant** telescopic umbrella

parasite [paʀazit] nm parasite ▷ adj (Bot, Bio) parasitic(al); **parasites** nmpl (Tél) interference sg

parasol [paʀasɔl] nm parasol, sunshade

paratonnerre [paʀatɔnɛʀ] nm lightning conductor

paravent [paʀavɑ̃] nm folding screen; (fig) screen

parc [paʀk] nm (public) park, gardens pl; (de château etc) grounds pl; (pour le bétail) pen, enclosure; (d'enfant) playpen; (Mil: entrepôt) depot; (ensemble d'unités) stock; (de voitures etc) fleet; **~ d'attractions** amusement park; **~ automobile** (d'un pays) number of cars on the roads; **~ à huîtres** oyster bed; **~ à thème** theme park; **~ national** national park; **~ naturel** nature reserve; **~ de stationnement** car park; **~ zoologique** zoological gardens pl

parcelle [paʀsɛl] nf fragment, scrap; (de terrain) plot, parcel

parce que [paʀsk(ə)] conj because

parchemin [paʀʃəmɛ̃] nm parchment

parcmètre [paʀkmɛtʀ(ə)], **parcomètre** [paʀkɔmɛtʀ(ə)] nm parking meter

parcourir [paʀkuʀiʀ] vt (trajet, distance) to cover; (article, livre) to skim ou glance through; (lieu) to go all over, travel up and down; (frisson, vibration) to run through; **~ des yeux** to run one's eye over

parcours [paʀkuʀ] vb voir **parcourir** ▷ nm (trajet)

journey; (itinéraire) route; (Sport: terrain) course; (: tour) round; run; lap; **~ du combattant** assault course

par-dessous [paʀdəsu] prép, adv under(neath)

pardessus [paʀdəsy] nm overcoat

par-dessus [paʀdəsy] prép over (the top of) ▷ adv over (the top); **~ le marché** on top of it all

par-devant [paʀdəvɑ̃] prép in the presence of, before ▷ adv at the front; round the front

pardon [paʀdɔ̃] nm forgiveness no pl ▷ excl (excuses) (I'm) sorry; (pour interpeller etc) excuse me; (demander de répéter) (I beg your) pardon? (Brit), pardon me? (US)

pardonner [paʀdɔne] vt to forgive; **~ qch à qn** to forgive sb for sth; **qui ne pardonne pas** (maladie, erreur) fatal

paré, e [paʀe] adj ready, prepared

pare-balles [paʀbal] adj inv bulletproof

pare-brise [paʀbʀiz] nm inv windscreen (Brit), windshield (US)

pare-chocs [paʀʃɔk] nm inv bumper (Brit), fender (US)

pareil, le [paʀɛj] adj (identique) the same, alike; (similaire) similar; (tel): **un courage/livre ~** such courage/a book, courage/a book like this; **de ~s livres** such books ▷ adv: **habillés ~** dressed the same (way), dressed alike; **faire ~** to do the same (thing); **j'en veux un ~** I'd like one just like it; **rien de ~** no (ou any) such thing, nothing (ou anything) like it; **ses ~s** one's fellow men; one's peers; **ne pas avoir son (sa) ~(le)** to be second to none; **~ à** the same as; similar to; **sans ~** unparalleled, unequalled; **c'est du ~ au même** it comes to the same thing, it's six (of one) and half-a-dozen (of the other); **en ~ cas** in such a case; **rendre la ~le à qn** to pay sb back in his own coin

parent, e [paʀɑ̃, -ɑ̃t] nm/f: **un/une ~/e** a relative ou relation ▷ adj: **être ~ de** to be related to; **parents** nmpl (père et mère) parents; (famille, proches) relatives, relations; **~ unique** lone parent; **~s par alliance** relatives ou relations by marriage; **~s en ligne directe** blood relations

parenté [paʀɑ̃te] nf (lien) relationship; (personnes) relatives pl, relations pl

parenthèse [paʀɑ̃tɛz] nf (ponctuation) bracket, parenthesis; (Math) bracket; (digression) parenthesis, digression; **ouvrir/fermer la ~** to open/close brackets; **entre ~s** in brackets; (fig) incidentally

parer [paʀe] vt to adorn; (Culin) to dress, trim; (éviter) to ward off; **~ à** (danger) to ward off; (inconvénient) to deal with; **se ~ de** (fig: qualité, titre) to assume; **~ à toute éventualité** to be ready for every eventuality; **~ au plus pressé** to attend to what's most urgent

paresse [paʀɛs] nf laziness

paresseux, -euse [paʀɛsø, -øz] adj lazy; (fig) slow, sluggish ▷ nm (Zool) sloth

parfaire [paʀfɛʀ] vt to perfect, complete

parfait, e [paʀfɛ, -ɛt] pp de **parfaire** ▷ adj perfect ▷ nm (Ling) perfect (tense); (Culin) parfait ▷ excl fine, excellent

parfaitement [paʀfɛtmɑ̃] adv perfectly ▷ excl (most) certainly

parfois [paʀfwa] adv sometimes

parfum [paʀfœ̃] nm (produit) perfume, scent; (odeur: de fleur) scent, fragrance; (: de tabac, vin) aroma; (goût: de glace, milk-shake) flavour (Brit), flavor (US)

parfumé, e [paʀfyme] adj (fleur, fruit) fragrant; (papier à lettres etc) scented; (femme) wearing perfume ou scent, perfumed; (aromatisé): ~ **au café** coffee-flavoured (Brit) ou -flavored (US)

parfumer [paʀfyme] vt (odeur, bouquet) to perfume; (mouchoir) to put scent ou perfume on; (crème, gâteau) to flavour (Brit), flavor (US); **se parfumer** to put on (some) perfume ou scent; (d'habitude) to use perfume ou scent

parfumerie [paʀfymʀi] nf (commerce) perfumery; (produits) perfumes; (boutique) perfume shop (Brit) ou store (US)

pari [paʀi] nm bet, wager; (Sport) bet; ~ **mutuel urbain (PMU)** system of betting on horses

parier [paʀje] vt to bet; **j'aurais parié que si/ non** I'd have said he (ou you etc) would/wouldn't

Paris [paʀi] n Paris

parisien, ne [paʀizjɛ̃, -ɛn] adj Parisian; (Géo, Admin) Paris cpd ▷ nm/f: **P~, ne** Parisian

parjure [paʀʒyʀ] nm (faux serment) false oath, perjury; (violation de serment) breach of oath, perjury ▷ nm/f perjurer

parking [paʀkiŋ] nm (lieu) car park (Brit), parking lot (US)

parlant, e [paʀlɑ̃, -ɑ̃t] adj (fig) graphic, vivid; (: comparaison, preuve) eloquent; (Ciné) talking ▷ adv: **généralement** ~ generally speaking

parlement [paʀləmɑ̃] nm parliament; **le P~ européen** the European Parliament

parlementaire [paʀləmɑ̃tɛʀ] adj parliamentary ▷ nm/f (député) ≈ Member of Parliament (Brit) ou Congress (US); parliamentarian; (négociateur) negotiator, mediator

parlementer [paʀləmɑ̃te] vi (ennemis) to negotiate, parley; (s'entretenir, discuter) to argue at length, have lengthy talks

parler [paʀle] nm speech; dialect ▷ vi to speak, talk; (avouer) to talk; ~ **(à qn) de** to talk ou speak (to sb) about; ~ **pour qn** (intercéder) to speak for sb; ~ **en l'air** to say the first thing that comes into one's head; ~ **le/en français** to speak French/in French; ~ **affaires** to talk business; ~ **en dormant/du nez** to talk in one's sleep/through one's nose; **sans** ~ **de** (fig) not to mention, to say nothing of; **tu parles!** you must be joking!; **n'en parlons plus!** let's forget it!

parloir [paʀlwaʀ] nm (d'une prison, d'un hôpital) visiting room; (Rel) parlour (Brit), parlor (US)

parmi [paʀmi] prép among(st)

paroi [paʀwa] nf wall; (cloison) partition; ~ **rocheuse** rock face

paroisse [paʀwas] nf parish

parole [paʀɔl] nf (faculté): **la** ~ speech; (mot, promesse) word; (Rel): **la bonne** ~ the word of God;

paroles nfpl (Mus) words, lyrics; **tenir** ~ to keep one's word; **avoir la** ~ to have the floor; **n'avoir qu'une** ~ to be true to one's word; **donner la** ~ **à qn** to hand over to sb; **prendre la** ~ to speak; **demander la** ~ to ask for permission to speak; **perdre la** ~ to lose the power of speech; (fig) to lose one's tongue; **je le crois sur** ~ I'll take his word for it, I'll take him at his word; **temps de** ~ (TV, Radio etc) discussion time; **ma** ~! my word!, good heavens!; ~ **d'honneur** word of honour (Brit) ou honor (US)

parquer [paʀke] vt (voiture, matériel) to park; (bestiaux) to pen (in ou up); (prisonniers) to pack in

parquet [paʀkɛ] nm (parquet) floor; (Jur: bureau) public prosecutor's office; **le ~ (général)** (magistrats) ≈ the Bench

parrain [paʀɛ̃] nm godfather; (d'un navire) namer; (d'un nouvel adhérent) sponsor, proposer

parrainer [paʀene] vt (nouvel adhérent) to sponsor, propose; (entreprise) to promote, sponsor

pars [paʀ] vb voir **partir**

parsemer [paʀsəme] vt (feuilles, papiers) to be scattered over; ~ **qch de** to scatter sth with

part [paʀ] vb voir **partir** ▷ nf (qui revient à qn) share; (fraction, partie) part; (de gâteau, fromage) portion; (Finance) (non-voting) share; **prendre** ~ **à** (débat etc) to take part in; (soucis, douleur de qn) to share in; **faire** ~ **de qch à qn** to announce sth to sb, inform sb of sth; **pour ma** ~ as for me, as far as I'm concerned; **à** ~ **entière** adj full; **de la** ~ **de** (au nom de) on behalf of; (donné par) from; **c'est de la** ~ **de qui?** (au téléphone) who's calling ou speaking (please)?; **de toute(s) ~(s)** from all sides ou quarters; **de** ~ **et d'autre** on both sides, on either side; **de** ~ **en** ~ right through; **d'une** ~ ... **d'autre** ~ on the one hand ... on the other hand; **nulle/autre/quelque** ~ nowhere/ elsewhere/somewhere; **à** ~ adv separately; (de côté) aside ▷ prép apart from, except for ▷ adj exceptional, special; **pour une large** ou **bonne** ~ to a great extent; **prendre qch en bonne/ mauvaise** ~ to take sth well/badly; **faire la** ~ **des choses** to make allowances; **faire la** ~ **du feu** (fig) to cut one's losses; **faire la** ~ **(trop) belle à qn** to give sb more than his (ou her) share

partage [paʀtaʒ] nm voir **partager** sharing (out) no pl, share-out; sharing; dividing up; (Pol: de suffrages) share; **recevoir qch en** ~ to receive sth as one's share (ou lot); **sans** ~ undivided

partager [paʀtaʒe] vt to share; (distribuer, répartir) to share (out); (morceler, diviser) to divide (up); **se partager** vt (héritage etc) to share between themselves (ou ourselves etc)

partance [paʀtɑ̃s]: **en** ~ adv outbound, due to leave; **en** ~ **pour** (bound) for

partenaire [paʀtənɛʀ] nm/f partner; ~**s sociaux** management and workforce

parterre [paʀtɛʀ] nm (de fleurs) (flower) bed, border; (Théât) stalls pl

parti [paʀti] nm (Pol) party; (décision) course of action; (personne à marier) match; **tirer** ~ **de** to take advantage of, turn to good account;

prendre le ~ de faire to make up one's mind to do, resolve to do; **prendre le ~ de qn** to stand up for sb, side with sb; **prendre ~ (pour/contre)** to take sides *ou* a stand (for/against); **prendre son ~ de** to come to terms with; **~ pris** bias

partial, e, -aux [paʀsjal, -o] *adj* biased, partial

participant, e [paʀtisipɑ̃, -ɑ̃t] *nm/f* participant; (*à un concours*) entrant; (*d'une société*) member

participation [paʀtisipasjɔ̃] *nf* participation; sharing; (*Comm*) interest; **la ~ aux bénéfices** profit-sharing; **la ~ ouvrière** worker participation; **"avec la ~ de ..."** "featuring ..."

participer [paʀtisipe]: **~ à** *vt* (*course, réunion*) to take part in; (*profits etc*) to share in; (*frais etc*) to contribute to; (*entreprise: financièrement*) to cooperate in; (*chagrin, succès de qn*) to share (in); **~ de** *vt* to partake of.

particularité [paʀtikylaʀite] *nf* particularity; (*distinctive*) characteristic, feature

particulier, -ière [paʀtikylje, -jɛʀ] *adj* (*personnel, privé*) private; (*spécial*) special, particular; (*caractéristique*) characteristic, distinctive; (*spécifique*) particular ▷ *nm* (*individu: Admin*) private individual; **"~ vend ..."** (*Comm*) "for sale privately ...", "for sale by owner ..." (*US*); **~ à** peculiar to; **en ~** *adv* (*surtout*) in particular, particularly; (*à part*) separately; (*en privé*) in private

particulièrement [paʀtikyljɛʀmɑ̃] *adv* particularly

partie [paʀti] *nf* (*gén*) part; (*profession, spécialité*) field, subject; (*Jur etc: protagonistes*) party; (*de cartes, tennis etc*) game; (*fig: lutte, combat*) struggle, fight; **une ~ de campagne/de pêche** an outing in the country/a fishing party *ou* trip; **en ~** *adv* partly, in part; **faire ~ de** to belong to; (*chose*) to be part of; **prendre qn à ~** to take sb to task; (*malmener*) to set on sb; **en grande ~** largely, in the main; **ce n'est que ~ remise** it will be for another time *ou* the next time; **avoir ~ liée avec qn** to be in league with sb; **~ civile** (*Jur*) party claiming damages in a criminal case

partiel, le [paʀsjɛl] *adj* partial ▷ *nm* (*Scol*) class exam

partir [paʀtiʀ] *vi* (*gén*) to go; (*quitter*) to go, leave; (*s'éloigner*) to go (*ou* drive *etc*) away *ou* off; (*moteur*) to start; (*pétard*) to go off; (*bouchon*) to come out; (*bouton*) to come off; **~ de** (*lieu: quitter*) to leave; (: *commencer à*) to start from; (*date*) to run *ou* start from; **~ pour/à** (*lieu, pays etc*) to leave for/go off to; **à ~ de** from

partisan, e [paʀtizɑ̃, -an] *nm/f* partisan; (*d'un parti, régime etc*) supporter ▷ *adj* (*lutte, querelle*) partisan, one-sided; **être ~ de qch/faire** to be in favour (*Brit*) *ou* favor (*US*) of sth/doing

partition [paʀtisjɔ̃] *nf* (*Mus*) score

partout [paʀtu] *adv* everywhere; **~ où il allait** everywhere *ou* wherever he went; **trente ~** (*Tennis*) thirty all

paru [paʀy] *pp de* **paraître**

parure [paʀyʀ] *nf* (*bijoux etc*) finery *no pl*; jewellery *no pl* (*Brit*), jewelry *no pl* (*US*); (*assortiment*) set

parution [paʀysjɔ̃] *nf* publication, appearance

parvenir [paʀvəniʀ]: **~ à** *vt* (*atteindre*) to reach; (*obtenir, arriver à*) to attain; (*réussir*): **~ à faire** to manage to do, succeed in doing; **faire ~ qch à qn** to have sth sent to sb

pas¹ [pɑ] *adv* **1** (*en corrélation avec ne, non etc*) not; **il ne pleure ~** (*habituellement*) he does not *ou* doesn't cry; (*maintenant*) he's not *ou* isn't crying; **je ne mange ~ de viande** I don't *ou* do not eat meat; **il n'a ~ pleuré/ne pleurera ~** he did not *ou* didn't/will not *ou* won't cry; **ils n'ont ~ de voiture/d'enfants** they haven't got a car/any children, they have no car/children; **il m'a dit de ne ~ le faire** he told me not to do it; **non ~ que ...** not that ..

2 (*employé sans ne etc*): **~ moi** not me, not I, I don't (*ou* can't *etc*); **elle travaille, (mais) lui ~ ou ~ lui** she works but he doesn't *ou* does not; **une pomme ~ mûre** an apple which isn't ripe; **~ plus tard qu'hier** only yesterday; **~ du tout** not at all; **~ de sucre, merci** no sugar, thanks; **ceci est à vous ou ~?** is this yours or not?, is this yours or isn't it?

3: **~ mal** (*joli: personne, maison*) not bad; **~ mal fait** not badly done *ou* made; **comment ça va? -- ~ mal** how are things? -- not bad; **~ mal de** quite a lot of

pas² [pɑ] *nm* (*allure, mesure*) pace; (*démarche*) tread; (*enjambée, Danse, fig: étape*) step; (*bruit*) (foot)step; (*trace*) footprint; (*allure*) pace; (*d'un cheval*) walk; (*mesure*) pace; (*Tech: de vis, d'écrou*) thread; **~ à ~** step by step; **au ~** at a walking pace; **de ce ~** (*à l'instant même*) straightaway, at once; **marcher à grands ~** to stride along; **mettre qn au ~** to bring sb to heel; **au ~ gymnastique/de course** at a jog trot/at a run; **à ~ de loup** stealthily; **faire les cent ~** to pace up and down; **faire les premiers ~** to make the first move; **retourner** *ou* **revenir sur ses ~** to retrace one's steps; **se tirer d'un mauvais ~** to get o.s. out of a tight spot; **sur le ~ de la porte** on the doorstep; **le ~ de Calais** (*détroit*) the Straits *pl* of Dover; **~ de porte** (*fig*) key money

passage [pɑsaʒ] *nm* (*fait de passer*) *voir* **passer**; (*lieu, prix de la traversée, extrait de livre etc*) passage; (*chemin*) way; (*itinéraire*): **sur le ~ du cortège** along the route of the procession; **"laissez/n'obstruez pas le ~"** "keep clear/do not obstruct"; **au ~** (*en passant*) as I (*ou* he *etc*) went by; **de ~** (*touristes*) passing through; (*amants etc*) casual; **~ clouté** pedestrian crossing; **"~ interdit"** "no entry"; **~ à niveau** level (*Brit*) *ou* grade (*US*) crossing; **"~ protégé"** *right of way over secondary road(s) on your right*; **~ souterrain** subway (*Brit*), underpass; **~ à tabac** beating-up; **~ à vide** (*fig*) bad patch

passager, -ère [pɑsaʒe, -ɛʀ] *adj* passing; (*hôte*) short-stay *cpd*; (*oiseau*) migratory ▷ *nm/f* passenger; **~ clandestin** stowaway

passant, e [pɑsɑ̃, -ɑ̃t] *adj* (*rue, endroit*) busy ▷ *nm/f* passer-by ▷ *nm* (*pour ceinture etc*) loop; **en ~**: **remarquer qch en passant** to notice sth in passing

passe [pɑs] nf (Sport, magnétique) pass; (Navig) channel ▷ nm (passe-partout) master ou skeleton key; **être en ~ de faire** to be on the way to doing; **être dans une mauvaise ~** (fig) to be going through a bad patch; **être dans une bonne ~** (fig) to be in a healthy situation; **~ d'armes** (fig) heated exchange

passé, e [pɑse] adj (événement, temps) past; (couleur, tapisserie) faded; (précédent): **dimanche ~** last Sunday ▷ prép after ▷ nm past; (Ling) past (tense); **il est ~ midi** ou **midi ~** it's gone (Brit) ou past twelve; **~ de mode** out of fashion; **~ composé** perfect (tense); **~ simple** past historic

passe-partout [pɑspɑʀtu] nm inv master ou skeleton key ▷ adj inv all-purpose

passeport [pɑspɔʀ] nm passport

passer [pɑse] vi (se rendre, aller) to go; (voiture, piétons: défiler) to pass (by), go by; (faire une halte rapide: facteur, laitier etc) to come, call; (: pour rendre visite) to call ou drop in; (courant, air, lumière, franchir un obstacle etc) to get through; (accusé, projet de loi): **~ devant** to come before; (film, émission) to be on; (temps, jours) to pass, go by; (liquide, café) to go through; (être digéré, avalé) to go down; (couleur, papier) to fade; (mode) to die out; (douleur) to pass, go away; (Cartes) to pass; (Scol) to go up (to the next class); (devenir): **~ président** to be appointed ou become president ▷ vt (frontière, rivière etc) to cross; (douane) to go through; (examen) to sit, take; (visite médicale etc) to have; (journée, temps) to spend; (donner): **~ qch à qn** to pass sth to sb; to give sb sth; (transmettre): **~ qch à qn** to pass sth on to sb; (enfiler: vêtement) to slip on; (faire entrer, mettre): **(faire) ~ qch dans/par** to get sth into/through; (café) to pour the water on; (thé, soupe) to strain; (film, pièce) to show, put on; (disque) to play, put on; (marché, accord) to agree on; (tolérer): **~ qch à qn** to let sb get away with sth; **se passer** vi (avoir lieu: scène, action) to take place; (se dérouler: entretien etc) to go; (arriver): **que s'est-il passé?** what happened?; (s'écouler: semaine etc) to pass, go by; **se ~ de** vt to go ou do without; **se ~ les mains sous l'eau/de l'eau sur le visage** to put one's hands under the tap/run water over one's face; **en passant** in passing; **~ par** to go through; **passez devant/par ici** go in front/this way; **~ sur** vt (faute, détail inutile) to pass over; **~ dans les mœurs/l'usage** to become the custom/normal usage; **~ avant qch/qn** (fig) to come before sth/sb; **laisser ~** (air, lumière, personne) to let through; (occasion) to let slip, miss; (erreur) to overlook; **faire ~** (message) to get over ou across; **faire ~ à qn le goût de qch** to cure sb of his (ou her) taste for sth; **~ à la radio/fouille** to be X-rayed/searched; **~ à la radio/télévision** to be on the radio/on television; **~ à table** to sit down to eat; **~ au salon** to go through to ou into the sitting room; **~ à l'opposition** to go over to the opposition; **~ aux aveux** to confess, make a confession; **~ à l'action** to go into action; **~ pour riche** to be taken for a rich man; **il passait**

pour avoir he was said to have; **faire ~ qn/qch pour** to make sb/sth out to be; **passe encore de le penser, mais de le dire!** it's one thing to think it, but to say it!; **passons!** let's say no more (about it); **et j'en passe!** and that's not all!; **~ en seconde, ~ la seconde** (Auto) to change into second; **~ qch en fraude** to smuggle sth in (ou out); **~ la main par la portière** to stick one's hand out of the door; **~ le balai/l'aspirateur** to sweep up/hoover; **~ commande/la parole à qn** to hand over to sb; **je vous passe M. X** (je vous mets en communication avec lui) I'm putting you through to Mr X; (je lui passe l'appareil) here is Mr X, I'll hand you over to Mr X; **~ prendre** to (come and) collect

passerelle [pɑsʀɛl] nf footbridge; (de navire, avion) gangway; (Navig): **~ (de commandement)** bridge

passe-temps [pɑstɑ̃] nm inv pastime

passible [pɑsibl(ə)] adj: **~ de** liable to

passif, -ive [pɑsif, -iv] adj passive ▷ nm (Ling) passive; (Comm) liabilities pl

passion [pɑsjɔ̃] nf passion; **avoir la ~ de** to have a passion for; **fruit de la ~** passion fruit

passionnant, e [pɑsjɔnɑ̃, -ɑ̃t] adj fascinating

passionné, e [pɑsjɔne] adj (personne, tempérament) passionate; (description) impassioned ▷ nm/f: **c'est un ~ d'échecs** he's a chess fanatic; **être ~ de** ou **pour qch** to have a passion for sth

passionner [pɑsjɔne] vt (personne) to fascinate, grip; (débat, discussion) to inflame; **se ~ pour** to take an avid interest in; to have a passion for

passoire [pɑswaʀ] nf sieve; (à légumes) colander; (à thé) strainer

pastèque [pɑstɛk] nf watermelon

pasteur [pɑstœʀ] nm (protestant) minister, pastor

pasteurisé, e [pɑstœʀize] adj pasteurized

pastille [pɑstij] nf (à sucer) lozenge, pastille; (de papier etc) (small) disc; **~s pour la toux** cough drops ou lozenges

patate [patat] nf spud; **~ douce** sweet potato

patauger [patoʒe] vi (pour s'amuser) to splash about; (avec effort) to wade about; (fig) to flounder; **~ dans** (en marchant) to wade through

pâte [pɑt] nf (à tarte) pastry; (à pain) dough; (à frire) batter; (substance molle) paste; cream; **pâtes** nfpl (macaroni etc) pasta sg; **fromage à ~ dure/molle** hard/soft cheese; **~ d'amandes** almond paste; **~ brisée** shortcrust (Brit) ou pie crust (US) pastry; **~ à choux/feuilletée** choux/puff ou flaky (Brit) pastry; **~ de fruits** crystallized fruit no pl; **~ à modeler** modelling clay, Plasticine® (Brit); **~ à papier** paper pulp

pâté [pɑte] nm (charcuterie: terrine) pâté; (tache) ink blot; (de sable) sandpie; **~ (en croûte)** ≈ meat pie; **~ de foie** liver pâté; **~ de maisons** block (of houses)

pâtée [pɑte] nf mash, feed

patente [patɑ̃t] nf (Comm) trading licence (Brit) ou license (US)

paternel, le [patɛʀnɛl] adj (amour, soins) fatherly; (ligne, autorité) paternal

pâteux, -euse [patø, -øz] *adj* thick; pasty; **avoir la bouche** *ou* **langue pâteuse** to have a furred (*Brit*) *ou* coated tongue

pathétique [patetik] *adj* pathetic, moving

patience [pasjɑ̃s] *nf* patience; **être à bout de ~** to have run out of patience; **perdre/prendre ~** to lose (one's)/have patience

patient, e [pasjɑ̃, -ɑ̃t] *adj, nm/f* patient

patienter [pasjɑ̃te] *vi* to wait

patin [patɛ̃] *nm* skate; (*sport*) skating; (*de traîneau, luge*) runner; (*pièce de tissu*) cloth pad (*used as slippers to protect polished floor*); **~ (de frein)** brake block; **~s (à glace)** (ice) skates; **~s à roulettes** roller skates

patinage [patinaʒ] *nm* skating; **~ artistique/de vitesse** figure/speed skating

patiner [patine] *vi* to skate; (*embrayage*) to slip; (*roue, voiture*) to spin; **se patiner** *vi* (*meuble, cuir*) to acquire a sheen, become polished

patineur, -euse [patinœr, -øz] *nm/f* skater

patinoire [patinwar] *nf* skating rink, (ice) rink

pâtir [patir] **~ de** *vt* to suffer because of

pâtisserie [patisri] *nf* (*boutique*) cake shop; (*métier*) confectionery; (*à la maison*) pastry- *ou* cake-making, baking; **pâtisseries** *nfpl* (*gâteaux*) pastries, cakes

pâtissier, -ière [patisje, -jɛr] *nm/f* pastrycook; confectioner

patois [patwa] *nm* dialect, patois

patraque [patrak] (*fam*) *adj* peaky, off-colour

patrie [patri] *nf* homeland

patrimoine [patrimwan] *nm* inheritance, patrimony; (*culture*) heritage; **~ génétique** *ou* **héréditaire** genetic inheritance

patriotique [patrijotik] *adj* patriotic

patron, ne [patrɔ̃, -ɔn] *nm/f* (*chef*) boss, manager(-ess); (*propriétaire*) owner, proprietor(-tress); (*employeur*) employer; (*Méd*) ≈ senior consultant; (*Rel*) patron saint ▷ *nm* (*Couture*) pattern; **~ de thèse** supervisor (of postgraduate thesis)

patronat [patrɔna] *nm* employers *pl*

patronner [patrɔne] *vt* to sponsor, support

patrouille [patruj] *nf* patrol

patte [pat] *nf* (*jambe*) leg; (*pied: de chien, chat*) paw; (: *d'oiseau*) foot; (*languette*) strap; (: *de poche*) flap; (*favoris*): **~s (de lapin)** (short) sideburns; **à ~s d'éléphant** *adj* (*pantalon*) flared; **~s de mouche** (*fig*) spidery scrawl *sg*; **~s d'oie** (*fig*) crow's feet

pâturage [patyraʒ] *nm* pasture

paume [pom] *nf* palm

paumé, e [pome] *nm/f* (*fam*) drop-out

paumer [pome] *vt* (*fam*) to lose

paupière [popjɛr] *nf* eyelid

pause [poz] *nf* (*arrêt*) break; (*en parlant, Mus*) pause; **~ de midi** lunch break

pauvre [povr(ə)] *adj* poor ▷ *nm/f* poor man/woman; **les ~s** the poor; **~ en calcium** low in calcium

pauvreté [povrəte] *nf* (*état*) poverty

pavaner [pavane]: **se pavaner** *vi* to strut about

pavé, e [pave] *adj* (*cour*) paved; (*rue*) cobbled ▷ *nm* (*bloc*) paving stone; cobblestone; (*pavage*) paving; (*bifteck*) slab of steak; (*fam: livre*) hefty tome; **être sur le ~** (*sans domicile*) to be on the streets; (*sans emploi*) to be out of a job; **~ numérique** (*Inform*) keypad

pavillon [pavijɔ̃] *nm* (*de banlieue*) small (detached) house; (*kiosque*) lodge; pavilion; (*d'hôpital*) ward; (*Mus: de cor etc*) bell; (*Anat: de l'oreille*) pavilion, pinna; (*Navig*) flag; **~ de complaisance** flag of convenience

pavoiser [pavwaze] *vt* to deck with flags ▷ *vi* to put out flags; (*fig*) to rejoice, exult

pavot [pavo] *nm* poppy

payant, e [pɛjɑ̃, -ɑ̃t] *adj* (*spectateurs etc*) paying; (*billet*) that you pay for, to be paid for; (*fig: entreprise*) profitable; **c'est ~** you have to pay, there is a charge

paye [pɛj] *nf* pay, wages *pl*

payer [peje] *vt* (*créancier, employé, loyer*) to pay; (*achat, réparations, fig: faute*) to pay for ▷ *vi* to pay; (*métier*) to pay, be well-paid; (*effort, tactique etc*) to pay off; **être bien/mal payé** to be well/badly paid; **il me l'a fait ~ 10 euros** he charged me 10 euros for it; **~ qn de** (*ses efforts, peines*) to reward sb for; **~ qch à qn** to buy sth for sb, buy sb sth; **ils nous ont payé le voyage** they paid for our trip; **~ de sa personne** to give of oneself; **~ d'audace** to act with great daring; **~ cher qch** to pay dear(ly) for sth; **cela ne paie pas de mine** it doesn't look much; **se ~ qch** to buy o.s. sth; **se ~ de mots** to shoot one's mouth off; **se ~ la tête de qn** to take the mickey out of sb (*Brit*), make a fool of sb; (*duper*) to take sb for a ride

pays [pei] *nm* (*territoire, habitants*) country, land; (*région*) region; (*village*) village; **du ~** *adj* local; **le ~ de Galles** Wales

paysage [peizaʒ] *nm* landscape

paysan, ne [peizɑ̃, -an] *nm/f* countryman/-woman; farmer; (*péj*) peasant ▷ *adj* country *cpd*, farming, farmers'

Pays-Bas [peiba] *nmpl*: **les ~** the Netherlands

PC *sigle m* (*Pol*) = **parti communiste**; (*Inform*: = *personal computer*) PC; (= *prêt conventionné*) type of loan for house purchase; (*Constr*) = **permis de construire**; (*Mil*) = **poste de commandement**

PDA *sigle m* (= *personal digital assistant*) PDA

PDG *sigle m* = **président directeur général**

péage [peaʒ] *nm* toll; (*endroit*) tollgate; **pont à ~** toll bridge

peau, x [po] *nf* skin; (*cuir*): **gants de ~** leather gloves; **être bien/mal dans sa ~** to be at ease/odds with oneself; **se mettre dans la ~ de qn** to put o.s. in sb's place *ou* shoes; **faire ~ neuve** (*se renouveler*) to change one's image; **~ de chamois** (*chiffon*) chamois leather, shammy; **~ d'orange** orange peel

Peau-Rouge [poruʒ] *nm/f* Red Indian, red skin

péché [peʃe] *nm* sin; **~ mignon** weakness

pêche [pɛʃ] *nf* (*poissons pêchés*) catch; (*fruit*) peach; **aller à la ~** to go fishing; **avoir la ~** (*fam*) to be on (top) form; **~ à la ligne** (*en rivière*) angling; **~ sous-marine** deep-sea fishing

pêcher [peʃe] vi (Rel) to sin; (fig: personne) to err; (: chose) to be flawed; ~ **contre la bienséance** to break the rules of good behaviour

pêcher [peʃe] nm peach tree ▷ vi to go fishing; (en rivière) to go angling ▷ vt (attraper) to catch, land; (chercher) to fish for; ~ **au chalut** to trawl

pêcheur, -eresse [peʃœr, peʃrɛs] nm/f sinner

pêcheur [peʃœr] nm voir **pêcher** fisherman; angler; ~ **de perles** pearl diver

pécule [pekyl] nm savings pl, nest egg; (d'un détenu) earnings pl (paid on release)

pédagogie [pedagɔʒi] nf educational methods pl, pedagogy

pédagogique [pedagɔʒik] adj educational; **formation** ~ teacher training

pédale [pedal] nf pedal; **mettre la ~ douce** to soft-pedal

pédalo [pedalo] nm pedalo, pedal-boat

pédant, e [pedã, -ãt] adj (péj) pedantic ▷ nm/f pedant

pédestre [pedɛstʀ(ə)] adj: **tourisme** ~ hiking; **randonnée** ~ (activité) rambling; (excursion) ramble

pédiatre [pedjatʀ(ə)] nm/f paediatrician (Brit), pediatrician ou pediatrist (US), child specialist

pédicure [pedikyʀ] nm/f chiropodist

pègre [pɛgʀ(ə)] nf underworld

peignais etc [peɲɛ] vb voir **peindre**

peigne [peɲ] vb voir **peindre**; **peigner** ▷ nm comb

peigner [peɲe] vt to comb (the hair of); **se peigner** to comb one's hair

peignoir [peɲwaʀ] nm dressing gown; ~ **de bain** bathrobe; ~ **de plage** beach robe

peindre [pɛ̃dʀ(ə)] vt to paint; (fig) to portray, depict

peine [pɛn] nf (affliction) sorrow, sadness no pl; (mal, effort) trouble no pl, effort; (difficulté) difficulty; (punition, châtiment) punishment; (Jur) sentence; **faire de la ~ à qn** to distress ou upset sb; **prendre la ~ de faire** to go to the trouble of doing; **se donner de la ~** to make an effort; **ce n'est pas la ~ de faire** there's no point in doing, it's not worth doing; **ce n'est pas la ~ que vous fassiez** there's no point (in) you doing; **avoir de la ~ à faire** to have difficulty doing; **donnez-vous** ou **veuillez-vous donner la ~ d'entrer** please do come in; **c'est ~ perdue** it's a waste of time (and effort); **à ~** adv scarcely, hardly, barely; **à ~ ... que** hardly ... than; **c'est à ~ si ...** it's (ou it was) a job to ...; **sous ~:** **sous peine d'être puni** for fear of being punished; **défense d'afficher sous ~ d'amende** billposters will be fined; ~ **capitale** capital punishment; ~ **de mort** death sentence ou penalty

peiner [pene] vi to work hard; to struggle; (moteur, voiture) to labour (Brit), labor (US) ▷ vt to grieve, sadden

peintre [pɛ̃tʀ(ə)] nm painter; ~ **en bâtiment** house painter, painter and decorator; ~ **d'enseignes** signwriter

peinture [pɛ̃tyʀ] nf painting; (couche de couleur, couleur) paint; (surfaces peintes: aussi: **peintures**) paintwork; **je ne peux pas le voir en** ~ I can't stand the sight of him; ~ **mate/brillante** matt/gloss paint; **"~ fraîche"** "wet paint"

péjoratif, -ive [peʒɔʀatif, -iv] adj pejorative, derogatory

pelage [pəlaʒ] nm coat, fur

pêle-mêle [pɛlmɛl] adv higgledy-piggledy

peler [pəle] vt, vi to peel

pèlerin [pɛlʀɛ̃] nm pilgrim

pèlerinage [pɛlʀinaʒ] nm (voyage) pilgrimage; (lieu) place of pilgrimage, shrine

pelle [pɛl] nf shovel; (d'enfant, de terrassier) spade; ~ **à gâteau** cake slice; ~ **mécanique** mechanical digger

pellicule [pelikyl] nf film; **pellicules** nfpl (Méd) dandruff sg

pelote [pəlɔt] nf (de fil, laine) ball; (d'épingles) pin cushion; ~ **basque** pelota

peloton [pəlɔtɔ̃] nm (groupe: de personnes) group; (: de pompiers, gendarmes) squad; (: Sport) pack; (de laine) ball; ~ **d'exécution** firing squad

pelotonner [pəlɔtɔne]: **se pelotonner** vi to curl (o.s.) up

pelouse [pəluz] nf lawn; (Hippisme) spectating area inside racetrack

peluche [pəlyʃ] nf (bit of) fluff; **animal en** ~ soft toy, fluffy animal

pelure [pəlyʀ] nf peeling, peel no pl; ~ **d'oignon** onion skin

pénal, e, -aux [penal, -o] adj penal

pénalité [penalite] nf penalty

penaud, e [pəno, -od] adj sheepish, contrite

penchant [pɑ̃ʃɑ̃] nm: **un ~ à faire/à qch** a tendency to do/to sth; **un ~ pour qch** a liking ou fondness for sth

pencher [pɑ̃ʃe] vi to tilt, lean over ▷ vt to tilt; **se pencher** vi to lean over; (se baisser) to bend down; **se ~ sur** to bend over; (fig: problème) to look into; **se ~ au dehors** to lean out; ~ **pour** to be inclined to favour (Brit) ou favor (US)

pendaison [pɑ̃dɛzɔ̃] nf hanging

pendant, e [pɑ̃dɑ̃, -ãt] adj hanging (out); (Admin, Jur) pending ▷ nm counterpart; matching piece ▷ prép during; **faire ~ à** to match; to be the counterpart of; ~ **que** while; **~s d'oreilles** drop ou pendant earrings

pendentif [pɑ̃dɑ̃tif] nm pendant

penderie [pɑ̃dʀi] nf wardrobe; (placard) walk-in cupboard

pendre [pɑ̃dʀ(ə)] vt, vi to hang; **se ~ (à)** (se suicider) to hang o.s. (on); ~ **à** to hang (down) from; ~ **qch à** (mur) to hang sth (up) on; (plafond) to hang sth (up) from; **se ~ à** (se suspendre) to hang from

pendule [pɑ̃dyl] nf clock ▷ nm pendulum

pénétrer [penetʀe] vi to come ou get in ▷ vt to penetrate; ~ **dans** to enter; (froid, projectile) to penetrate; (: air, eau) to come into, get into; (mystère, secret) to fathom; **se ~ de qch** to get sth firmly set in one's mind

pénible [penibl(ə)] adj (astreignant) hard; (affligeant) painful; (personne, caractère) tiresome;

il m'est ~ de ... I'm sorry to ...

péniblement [peniblamā] *adv* with difficulty

péniche [peniʃ] *nf* barge; **~ de débarquement** landing craft *inv*

pénicilline [penisilin] *nf* penicillin

péninsule [penēsyl] *nf* peninsula

pénis [penis] *nm* penis

pénitence [penitās] *nf* (*repentir*) penitence; (*peine*) penance; (*punition, châtiment*) punishment; **mettre un enfant en ~** ≈ to make a child stand in the corner; **faire ~** to do a penance

pénitencier [penitāsje] *nm* prison, penitentiary (US)

pénombre [penɔ̄bʀ(ə)] *nf* half-light

pensée [pāse] *nf* thought; (*démarche, doctrine*) thinking *no pl*; (*Bot*) pansy; **se représenter qch par la ~** to conjure up a mental picture of sth; **en ~** in one's mind

penser [pāse] *vi* to think ▷ *vt* to think; (*concevoir: problème, machine*) to think out; **~ à** to think of; (*songer à: ami, vacances*) to think of *ou* about; (*réfléchir à: problème, offre*): **~ à qch** to think about sth, think sth over; **~ à faire qch** to think of doing sth; **~ faire qch** to be thinking of doing sth, intend to do sth; **faire ~ à** to remind one of; **n'y pensons plus** let's forget it; **vous n'y pensez pas!** don't let it bother you!; **sans ~ à mal** without meaning any harm; **je le pense aussi** I think so too; **je pense que oui/non** I think so/don't think so

pensif, -ive [pāsif, -iv] *adj* pensive, thoughtful

pension [pāsjɔ̄] *nf* (*allocation*) pension; (*prix du logement*) board and lodging, bed and board; (*maison particulière*) boarding house; (*hôtel*) guesthouse, hotel; (*école*) boarding school; **prendre ~ chez** to take board and lodging at; **prendre qn en ~** to take sb (in) as a lodger; **mettre en ~** to send to boarding school; **~ alimentaire** (*d'étudiant*) living allowance; (*de divorcée*) maintenance allowance; alimony; **~ complète** full board; **~ de famille** boarding house, guesthouse; **~ de guerre/d'invalidité** war/disablement pension

pensionnaire [pāsjɔnɛʀ] *nm/f* boarder; guest

pensionnat [pāsjɔna] *nm* boarding school

pente [pāt] *nf* slope; **en ~** *adj* sloping

Pentecôte [pātkot] *nf*: **la ~** Whitsun (*Brit*), Pentecost; (*dimanche*) Whitsunday (*Brit*); **lundi de ~** Whit Monday (*Brit*)

pénurie [penyʀi] *nf* shortage; **~ de main-d'œuvre** undermanning

pépé [pepe] *nm* (*fam*) grandad

pépin [pepē] *nm* (*Bot: graine*) pip; (*fam: ennui*) snag, hitch; (*: parapluie*) brolly (*Brit*), umbrella

pépinière [pepinjɛʀ] *nf* nursery; (*fig*) nest, breeding-ground

perçant, e [pɛʀsā, -āt] *adj* (*vue, regard, yeux*) sharp, keen; (*cri, voix*) piercing, shrill

percée [pɛʀse] *nf* (*trouée*) opening; (*Mil, Comm: fig*) breakthrough; (*Sport*) break

perce-neige [pɛʀsənɛʒ] *nm ou f inv* snowdrop

percepteur [pɛʀsɛptœʀ] *nm* tax collector

perception [pɛʀsɛpsjɔ̄] *nf* perception; (*d'impôts etc*) collection; (*bureau*) tax (collector's) office

percer [pɛʀse] *vt* to pierce; (*ouverture etc*) to make; (*mystère, énigme*) to penetrate ▷ *vi* to come through; (*réussir*) to break through; **~ une dent** to cut a tooth

perceuse [pɛʀsøz] *nf* drill; **~ à percussion** hammer drill

percevoir [pɛʀsəvwaʀ] *vt* (*distinguer*) to perceive, detect; (*taxe, impôt*) to collect; (*revenu, indemnité*) to receive

perche [pɛʀʃ(ə)] *nf* (*Zool*) perch; (*bâton*) pole; **~ à son** (sound) boom

percher [pɛʀʃe] *vt*: **~ qch sur** to perch sth on ▷ *vi*: **se percher** *vi* (*oiseau*) to perch

perchoir [pɛʀʃwaʀ] *nm* perch; (*fig*) presidency of the French National Assembly

perçois *etc* [pɛʀswa] *vb voir* **percevoir**

percolateur [pɛʀkɔlatœʀ] *nm* percolator

perçu, e [pɛʀsy] *pp de* **percevoir**

percussion [pɛʀkysjɔ̄] *nf* percussion

percuter [pɛʀkyte] *vt* to strike; (*véhicule*) to crash into ▷ *vi*: **~ contre** to crash into

perdant, e [pɛʀdā, -āt] *nm/f* loser ▷ *adj* losing

perdre [pɛʀdʀ(ə)] *vt* to lose; (*gaspiller: temps, argent*) to waste; (*: occasion*) to waste, miss; (*personne: moralement etc*) to ruin ▷ *vi* to lose; (*sur une vente etc*) to lose out; (*récipient*) to leak; **se perdre** *vi* (*s'égarer*) to get lost, lose one's way; (*fig: se gâter*) to go to waste; (*disparaître*) to disappear, vanish; **il ne perd rien pour attendre** it can wait, it'll keep

perdrix [pɛʀdʀi] *nf* partridge

perdu, e [pɛʀdy] *pp de* **perdre** ▷ *adj* (*enfant, cause, objet*) lost; (*isolé*) out-of-the-way; (*Comm: emballage*) non-returnable; (*récolte etc*) ruined; (*malade*): **il est ~** there's no hope left for him; **à vos moments ~s** in your spare time

père [pɛʀ] *nm* father; **pères** *nmpl* (*ancêtres*) forefathers; **de ~ en fils** from father to son; **~ de famille** father; family man; **mon ~** (*Rel*) Father; **le ~ Noël** Father Christmas

perfection [pɛʀfɛksjɔ̄] *nf* perfection; **à la ~** *adv* to perfection

perfectionné, e [pɛʀfɛksjɔne] *adj* sophisticated

perfectionner [pɛʀfɛksjɔne] *vt* to improve, perfect; **se ~ en anglais** to improve one's English

perforatrice [pɛʀfɔʀatʀis] *nf voir* **perforateur**

perforer [pɛʀfɔʀe] *vt* to perforate, punch a hole *ou* holes in; (*ticket, bande, carte*) to punch

performant, e [pɛʀfɔʀmā, -āt] *adj* (*Écon: produit, entreprise*) high-return *cpd*; (*Tech: appareil, machine*) high-performance *cpd*

perfusion [pɛʀfyzjɔ̄] *nf* perfusion; **faire une ~ à qn** to put sb on a drip

péricliter [peʀiklite] *vi* to go downhill

péril [peʀil] *nm* peril; **au ~ de sa vie** at the risk of his life; **à ses risques et ~s** at his (*ou* her) own risk

périmé, e [peʀime] *adj* (out)dated; (*Admin*) out-of-date, expired

périmètre [peʀimɛtʀ(ə)] *nm* perimeter

période [peʀjɔd] *nf* period

périodique [peʀjɔdik] *adj* (*phases*) periodic; (*publication*) periodical; (*Math: fraction*) recurring ▷ *nm* periodical; **garniture** *ou* **serviette ~** sanitary towel (*Brit*) *ou* napkin (*US*)

péripéties [peʀipesi] *nfpl* events, episodes

périphérique [peʀifeʀik] *adj* (*quartiers*) outlying; (*Anat, Tech*) peripheral; (*station de radio*) operating from a neighbouring country ▷ *nm* (*Inform*) peripheral; (*Auto*): (**boulevard**) ~ ring road (*Brit*), beltway (*US*)

périple [peʀipl(ə)] *nm* journey

périr [peʀiʀ] *vi* to die, perish

périssable [peʀisabl(ə)] *adj* perishable

perle [pɛʀl(ə)] *nf* pearl; (*de plastique, métal, sueur*) bead; (*personne, chose*) gem, treasure; (*erreur*) gem, howler

permanence [pɛʀmanɑ̃s] *nf* permanence; (*local*) (duty) office, strike headquarters; (*service des urgences*) emergency service; (*Scol*) study room; **assurer une ~** (*service public, bureaux*) to operate *ou* maintain a basic service; **être de ~** to be on call *ou* duty; **en ~** *adv* (*toujours*) permanently; (*continûment*) continuously

permanent, e [pɛʀmanɑ̃, -ɑ̃t] *adj* permanent; (*spectacle*) continuous; (*armée, comité*) standing ▷ *nf* perm ▷ *nm/f* (*d'un syndicat, parti*) paid official

perméable [pɛʀmeabl(ə)] *adj* (*terrain*) permeable; **~ à** (*fig*) receptive *ou* open to

permettre [pɛʀmɛtʀ(ə)] *vt* to allow, permit; **~ à qn de faire/qch** to allow sb to do/sth; **se ~ de faire qch** to take the liberty of doing sth; **permettez!** excuse me!

permis, e [pɛʀmi, -iz] *pp de* **permettre** ▷ *nm* permit, licence (*Brit*), license (*US*); **~ de chasse** hunting permit; **~ (de conduire)** (driving) licence (*Brit*), (driver's) license (*US*); **~ de construire** planning permission (*Brit*), building permit (*US*); **~ d'inhumer** burial certificate; **~ poids lourds** ≈ HGV (driving) licence (*Brit*), ≈ class E (driver's) license (*US*); **~ de séjour** residence permit; **~ de travail** work permit

permission [pɛʀmisjɔ̃] *nf* permission; (*Mil*) leave; (: *papier*) pass; **en ~** on leave; **avoir la ~ de faire** to have permission to do, be allowed to do

permuter [pɛʀmyte] *vt* to change around, permutate ▷ *vi* to change, swap

Pérou [peʀu] *nm:* **le ~** Peru

perpétuel, le [pɛʀpetɥɛl] *adj* perpetual; (*Admin etc*) permanent; for life

perpétuité [pɛʀpetɥite] *nf:* **à ~** *adj, adv* for life; **être condamné à ~** to be sentenced to life imprisonment, receive a life sentence

perplexe [pɛʀplɛks(ə)] *adj* perplexed, puzzled

perquisitionner [pɛʀkizisjɔne] *vi* to carry out a search

perron [pɛʀɔ̃] *nm* steps *pl* (*in front of mansion etc*)

perroquet [pɛʀɔkɛ] *nm* parrot

perruche [pɛʀyʃ] *nf* budgerigar (*Brit*), budgie (*Brit*), parakeet (*US*)

perruque [pɛʀyk] *nf* wig

persan, e [pɛʀsɑ̃, -an] *adj* Persian ▷ *nm* (*Ling*) Persian

persécuter [pɛʀsekyte] *vt* to persecute

persévérer [pɛʀseveʀe] *vi* to persevere; **~ à croire que** to continue to believe that

persiennes [pɛʀsjɛn] *nfpl* (slatted) shutters

persil [pɛʀsi] *nm* parsley

Persique [pɛʀsik] *adj:* **le golfe ~** the (Persian) Gulf

persistant, e [pɛʀsistɑ̃, -ɑ̃t] *adj* persistent; (*feuilles*) evergreen; **à feuillage ~** evergreen

persister [pɛʀsiste] *vi* to persist; **~ à faire qch** to persist in doing sth

personnage [pɛʀsɔnaʒ] *nm* (*notable*) personality; figure; (*individu*) character, individual; (*Théât*) character; (*Peinture*) figure

personnalité [pɛʀsɔnalite] *nf* personality; (*personnage*) prominent figure

personne [pɛʀsɔn] *nf* person ▷ *pron* nobody, no one; (*quelqu'un*) anybody, anyone; **personnes** *nfpl* people *pl*; **il n'y a ~** there's nobody in *ou* there, there isn't anybody in *ou* there; **10 euros par ~** 10 euros per person *ou* a head; **en ~** personally, in person; **~ âgée** elderly person; **~ à charge** (*Jur*) dependent; **~ morale** *ou* **civile** (*Jur*) legal entity

personnel, le [pɛʀsɔnɛl] *adj* personal; (*égoïste: personne*) selfish, self-centred; (*idée, opinion*): **j'ai des idées ~les à ce sujet** I have my own ideas about that ▷ *nm* personnel, staff; **service du ~** personnel department

personnellement [pɛʀsɔnɛlmɑ̃] *adv* personally

perspective [pɛʀspɛktiv] *nf* (*Art*) perspective; (*vue, coup d'œil*) view; (*point de vue*) viewpoint, angle; (*chose escomptée, envisagée*) prospect; **en ~** in prospect

perspicace [pɛʀspikas] *adj* clear-sighted, gifted with *ou* showing insight

perspicacité [pɛʀspikasite] *nf* insight, perspicacity

persuader [pɛʀsɥade] *vt:* **~ qn (de/de faire)** to persuade sb (of/to do); **j'en suis persuadé** I'm quite sure *ou* convinced (of it)

persuasif, -ive [pɛʀsɥazif, -iv] *adj* persuasive

perte [pɛʀt(ə)] *nf* loss; (*de temps*) waste; (*fig: morale*) ruin; **pertes** *nfpl* losses; **à ~** (*Comm*) at a loss; **à ~ de vue** as far as the eye can (*ou* could) see; (*fig*) interminably; **en pure ~** for absolutely nothing; **courir à sa ~** to be on the road to ruin; **être en ~ de vitesse** (*fig*) to be losing momentum; **avec ~ et fracas** forcibly; **~ de chaleur** heat loss; **~ sèche** dead loss; **~s blanches** (vaginal) discharge *sg*

pertinemment [pɛʀtinamɑ̃] *adv* to the point; (*savoir*) perfectly well, full well

pertinent, e [pɛʀtinɑ̃, -ɑ̃t] *adj* (*remarque*) apt, pertinent, relevant; (*analyse*) discerning, judicious

perturbation [pɛʀtyʀbasjɔ̃] *nf* (*dans un service public*) disruption; (*agitation, trouble*) perturbation; **~ (atmosphérique)** atmospheric disturbance

perturber [pɛʀtyʀbe] *vt* to disrupt; (*Psych*) to perturb, disturb

pervers, e [pɛʀvɛʀ, -ɛʀs(ə)] *adj* perverted, depraved; (*malfaisant*) perverse

pervertir [pɛʀvɛʀtiʀ] *vt* to pervert

pesant, e [pəzɑ̃, -ɑ̃t] *adj* heavy; (*fig*) burdensome ▷ *nm*: **valoir son ~ de** to be worth one's weight in

pèse-personne [pɛzpɛʀsɔn] *nm* (bathroom) scales *pl*

peser [pəze] *vt* to weigh; (*considérer, comparer*) to weigh up ▷ *vi* to be heavy; (*fig*) to carry weight; **~ sur** (*levier, bouton*) to press, push; (*fig: accabler*) to lie heavy on; (: *influencer*) to influence; **~ à qn** to weigh heavy on sb

pessimisme [pesimism(ə)] *nm* pessimism

pessimiste [pesimist(ə)] *adj* pessimistic ▷ *nm/f* pessimist

peste [pɛst(ə)] *nf* plague; (*fig*) pest, nuisance

pester [pɛste] *vi*: **~ contre** to curse

pétale [petal] *nm* petal

pétanque [petɑ̃k] *nf* type of bowls; *see note*

pétarader [petaʀade] *vi* to backfire

pétard [petaʀ] *nm* (*feu d'artifice*) banger (*Brit*), firecracker; (*de cotillon*) cracker; (*Rail*) detonator

péter [pete] *vi* (*fam: casser, sauter*) to burst; to bust; (*fam!*) to fart (!)

pétillant, e [petijɑ̃, -ɑ̃t] *adj* sparkling

pétiller [petije] *vi* (*flamme, bois*) to crackle; (*mousse, champagne*) to bubble; (*pierre, métal*) to glisten; (*yeux*) to sparkle; (*fig*): **~ d'esprit** to sparkle with wit

petit, e [pəti, -it] *adj* (*gén*) small; (*main, objet, colline, en âge: enfant*) small, little; (*mince, fin: personne, taille, pluie*) slight; (*voyage*) short, little; (*bruit etc*) faint, slight; (*mesquin*) mean; (*peu important*) minor ▷ *nm/f* (*petit enfant*) little one, child; **petits** *nmpl* (*d'un animal*) young *pl*; **faire des ~s** to have kittens (*ou* puppies *etc*); **en ~** in miniature; **mon ~** son; little one; **ma ~e** dear; little one; **pauvre ~** poor little thing; **la classe des ~s** the infant class; **pour ~s et grands** for children and adults; **les tout-~s** the little ones, the tiny tots; **~ à** bit by bit, gradually; **~(e) ami/e** boyfriend/girlfriend; **les ~es annonces** the small ads; **~ déjeuner** breakfast; **~ doigt** little finger; **le ~ écran** the small screen; **~ four** petit four; **~ pain** (bread) roll; **~e monnaie** small change; **~e vérole** smallpox; **~s pois** petit pois *pl*, garden peas; **~es gens** people of modest means

petite-fille (*pl* **petites-filles**) [pətitfij] *nf* granddaughter

petit-fils (*pl* **petits-fils**) [pətifis] *nm* grandson

pétition [petisjɔ̃] *nf* petition; **faire signer une ~** to get up a petition

petits-enfants [pətizɑ̃fɑ̃] *nmpl* grandchildren

petit-suisse (*pl* **petits-suisses**) [pətisɥis] *nm* *small individual pot of cream cheese*

pétrin [petʀɛ̃] *nm* kneading-trough; (*fig*): **dans le ~** in a jam *ou* fix

pétrir [petʀiʀ] *vt* to knead

pétrole [petʀɔl] *nm* oil; (*aussi*: **pétrole lampant**) paraffin (*Brit*), kerosene (*US*)

pétrolier, -ière [petʀɔlje, -jɛʀ] *adj* oil *cpd*; (*pays*) oil-producing ▷ *nm* (*navire*) oil tanker; (*financier*) oilman; (*technicien*) petroleum engineer

P et T *sigle fpl* = **postes et télécommunications**

peu [pø] *adv* **1** (*modifiant verbe, adjectif, adverbe*): **il boit ~** he doesn't drink (very) much; **il est ~ bavard** he's not very talkative; **~ avant/après** shortly before/afterwards; **pour ~ qu'il fasse** if he should do, if by any chance he does

2 (*modifiant nom*): **~ de**: **~ de gens/d'arbres** few *ou* not (very) many people/trees; **il a ~ d'espoir** he hasn't (got) much hope, he has little hope; **pour ~ de temps** for (only) a short while; **à ~ de frais** for very little cost

3: **~ à ~** little by little; **à ~ près** just about, more or less; **à ~ près 10 kg/10 euros** approximately 10 kg/10 euros

▷ *nm* **1**: **le ~ de gens qui** the few people who; **le ~ de sable qui** what little sand, the little sand which

2: **un ~** a little; **un petit ~** a little bit; **un ~ d'espoir** a little hope; **elle est un ~ bavarde** she's rather talkative; **un ~ plus/moins de** slightly more/less (*ou* fewer) than; **pour un ~ il ...**, **un ~ plus et il ...** he very nearly *ou* all but ...; **essayez un ~!** have a go!, just try it!

▷ *pron*: **~ le savent** few know (it); **avant** *ou* **sous ~** shortly, before long; **depuis ~** for a short *ou* little while; (*au passé*) a short *ou* little while ago; **de ~** (only) just; **c'est ~ de chose** it's nothing; **il est de ~ mon cadet** he's just a little *ou* bit younger than me

peuple [pœpl(ə)] *nm* people; (*masse*): **un ~ de vacanciers** a crowd of holiday-makers; **il y a du ~** there are a lot of people

peupler [pœple] *vt* (*pays, région*) to populate; (*étang*) to stock; (*hommes, poissons*) to inhabit; (*fig: imagination, rêves*) to fill; **se peupler** *vi* (*ville, région*) to become populated; (*fig: s'animer*) to fill (up), be filled

peuplier [pøplije] *nm* poplar (tree)

peur [pœʀ] *nf* fear; **avoir ~** (**de/de faire/que**) to be frightened *ou* afraid (of/of doing/that); **prendre ~** to take fright; **faire ~ à** to frighten; **de ~ de/que** for fear of/that; **j'ai ~ qu'il ne soit trop tard** I'm afraid it might be too late; **j'ai ~ qu'il (ne) vienne (pas)** I'm afraid he may (not) come

peureux, -euse [pœʀø, -øz] *adj* fearful, timorous

peut [pø] *vb voir* **pouvoir**

peut-être [pøtɛtʀ(ə)] *adv* perhaps, maybe; **~ que** perhaps, maybe; **~ bien qu'il fera/est** he may well do/be

phare [faʀ] *nm* (*en mer*) lighthouse; (*d'aéroport*) beacon; (*de véhicule*) headlight, headlamp (*Brit*) ▷ *adj*: **produit ~** leading product; **se mettre en ~s**, **mettre ses ~s** to put on one's headlights; **~s de recul** reversing (*Brit*) *ou* back-up (*US*) lights

pharmacie [faʀmasi] *nf* (*science*) pharmacology; (*magasin*) chemist's (*Brit*), pharmacy; (*officine*) dispensary; (*produits*) pharmaceuticals *pl*; (*armoire*) medicine chest *ou* cupboard, first-aid cupboard

pharmacien, ne [faʀmasjɛ̃, -ɛn] nm/f
pharmacist, chemist (Brit)
phénomène [fenɔmɛn] nm phenomenon;
(monstre) freak
philatélie [filateli] nf philately, stamp collecting
philosophe [filɔzɔf] nm/f philosopher ▷ adj
philosophical
philosophie [filɔzɔfi] nf philosophy
phobie [fɔbi] nf phobia
phonétique [fɔnetik] adj phonetic ▷ nf
phonetics sg
phoque [fɔk] nm seal; (fourrure) sealskin
phosphorescent, e [fɔsfɔʀesɑ̃, -ɑ̃t] adj
luminous
photo [fɔto] nf (photographie) photo ▷ adj:
appareil/pellicule ~ camera/film; **en ~** in ou on
a photo; **prendre en ~** to take a photo of; **aimer
la/faire de la ~** to like taking/take photos; **~ en
couleurs** colour photo; **~ d'identité** passport
photo
photocopie [fɔtɔkɔpi] nf (procédé) photocopying;
(document) photocopy
photocopier [fɔtɔkɔpje] vt to photocopy
photocopieur [fɔtɔkɔpjœʀ] nm,
photocopieuse [fɔtɔkɔpjøz] ▷ nf (photo)copier
photographe [fɔtɔgʀaf] nm/f photographer
photographie [fɔtɔgʀafi] nf (procédé, technique)
photography; (cliché) photograph; **faire de la ~**
to do photography as a hobby; (comme métier) to
be a photographer
photographier [fɔtɔgʀafje] vt to photograph,
take
phrase [fʀɑz] nf (Ling) sentence; (propos, Mus)
phrase; **phrases** nfpl (péj) flowery language sg
physicien, ne [fizisjɛ̃, -ɛn] nm/f physicist
physionomie [fizjɔnɔmi] nf face; (d'un paysage
etc) physiognomy
physique [fizik] adj physical ▷ nm physique ▷ nf
physics sg; **au ~** physically
physiquement [fizikmɑ̃] adv physically
piailler [pjaje] vi to squawk
pianiste [pjanist(ə)] nm/f pianist
piano [pjano] nm piano; **~ à queue** grand piano
pianoter [pjanɔte] vi to tinkle away (at the
piano); (tapoter): **~ sur** to drum one's fingers on
pic [pik] nm (instrument) pick(axe); (montagne)
peak; (Zool) woodpecker; **à ~** adv vertically; (fig)
just at the right time; **couler à ~** (bateau) to go
straight down; **~ à glace** ice pick
pichet [piʃɛ] nm jug
picorer [pikɔʀe] vt to peck
picoter [pikɔte] vt (oiseau) to peck ▷ vi (irriter) to
smart, prickle
pie [pi] nf magpie; (fig) chatterbox ▷ adj inv:
cheval ~ piebald; **vache ~** black and white cow
pièce [pjɛs] nf (d'un logement) room; (Théât) play;
(de mécanisme, machine) part; (de monnaie) coin;
(Couture) patch; (document) document; (de drap,
fragment, d'une collection) piece; (de bétail) head;
mettre en ~s to smash to pieces; **deux euros ~**
two euros each; **vendre à la ~** to sell separately
ou individually; **travailler/payer à la ~** to do

piecework/pay piece rate; **de toutes ~s: c'est
inventé de toutes pièces** it's a complete
fabrication; **un maillot une ~** a one-piece
swimsuit; **un deux–~s cuisine** a two-room(ed)
flat (Brit) ou apartment (US) with kitchen; **tout
d'une ~** (personne: franc) blunt; (: sans souplesse)
inflexible; **~ à conviction** exhibit; **~ d'eau**
ornamental lake ou pond; **~ d'identité: avez-
vous une pièce d'identité?** have you got any
(means of) identification?; **~ jointe** (Inform)
attachment; **~ montée** tiered cake; **~ de
rechange** spare (part); **~ de résistance** pièce
de résistance; (plat) main dish; **~s détachées**
spares, (spare) parts; **en ~s détachées** (à monter)
in kit form; **~s justificatives** supporting
documents
pied [pje] nm foot; (de verre) stem; (de table) leg;
(de lampe) base; (plante) plant; **~s nus** barefoot;
à ~ on foot; **à ~ sec** without getting one's feet
wet; **à ~ d'œuvre** ready to start (work); **au ~
de la lettre** literally; **au ~ levé** at a moment's
notice; **de ~ en cap** from head to foot; **en ~**
(portrait) full-length; **avoir ~** to be able to touch
the bottom, not to be out of one's depth; **avoir
le ~ marin** to be a good sailor; **perdre ~** to lose
one's footing; (fig) to get out of one's depth; **sur
~** (Agr) on the stalk, uncut; (debout, rétabli) up
and about; **mettre sur ~** (entreprise) to set up;
mettre à ~ to suspend; to lay off; **mettre qn
au ~ du mur** to get sb with his (ou her) back to
the wall; **sur le ~ de guerre** ready for action;
sur un ~ d'égalité on an equal footing; **sur ~
d'intervention** on stand-by; **faire du ~ à qn**
(prévenir) to give sb a (warning) kick; (galamment)
to play footsie with sb; **mettre les ~s quelque
part** to set foot somewhere; **faire des ~s et des
mains** (fig) to move heaven and earth, pull out
all the stops; **c'est le ~!** (fam) it's terrific!; **se
lever du bon ~/du ~ gauche** to get out of bed on
the right/wrong side; **~ de lit** footboard; **~ de
nez: faire un pied de nez à** to thumb one's nose
at; **~ de vigne** vine
pied-noir (pl **pieds-noirs**) [pjenwaʀ] nm
Algerian-born Frenchman
piège [pjɛʒ] nm trap; **prendre au ~** to trap
piéger [pjeʒe] vt (animal, fig) to trap; (avec une
bombe) to booby-trap; **lettre/voiture piégée**
letter-/car-bomb
piercing [pjɛʀsiŋ] nm piercing
pierre [pjɛʀ] nf stone; **première ~** (d'un édifice)
foundation stone; **mur de ~s sèches** drystone
wall; **faire d'une ~ deux coups** to kill two
birds with one stone; **~ à briquet** flint; **~ fine**
semiprecious stone; **~ ponce** pumice stone; **~
de taille** freestone no pl; **~ tombale** tombstone,
gravestone; **~ de touche** touchstone
pierreries [pjɛʀʀi] nfpl gems, precious stones
piétiner [pjetine] vi (trépigner) to stamp (one's
foot); (marquer le pas) to stand about; (fig) to be at
a standstill ▷ vt to trample on
piéton, ne [pjetɔ̃, -ɔn] nm/f pedestrian ▷ adj
pedestrian cpd

piétonnier, -ière [pjetɔnje, -jɛʀ] *adj* pedestrian *cpd*

pieu, x [pjø] *nm* (*piquet*) post; (*pointu*) stake; (*fam: lit*) bed

pieuvre [pjœvʀ(ə)] *nf* octopus

pieux, -euse [pjø, -øz] *adj* pious

piffer [pife] *vt* (*fam*): **je ne peux pas le ~** I can't stand him

pigeon [piʒ3] *nm* pigeon; **~ voyageur** homing pigeon

piger [piʒe] *vi* (*fam*) to get it ▷ *vt* (*fam*) to get, understand

pigiste [piʒist(ə)] *nm/f* (*typographe*) typesetter on piecework; (*journaliste*) freelance journalist (*paid by the line*)

pignon [piɲ3] *nm* (*de mur*) gable; (*d'engrenage*) cog(wheel), gearwheel; (*graine*) pine kernel; **avoir ~ sur rue** (*fig*) to have a prosperous business

pile [pil] *nf* (*tas, pilier*) pile; (*Élec*) battery ▷ *adj*: **le côté ~** tails ▷ *adv* (*net, brusquement*) dead; (*à temps, à point nommé*) just at the right time; **à deux heures ~** at two on the dot; **jouer à ~ ou face** to toss up (for it); **~ ou face?** heads or tails?

piler [pile] *vt* to crush, pound

pilier [pilje] *nm* (*colonne, support*) pillar; (*personne*) mainstay; (*Rugby*) prop (forward)

piller [pije] *vt* to pillage, plunder, loot

pilote [pilɔt] *nm* pilot; (*de char, voiture*) driver ▷ *adj* pilot *cpd*; **usine/ferme ~** experimental factory/farm; **~ de chasse/d'essai/de ligne** fighter/test/airline pilot; **~ de course** racing driver

piloter [pilɔte] *vt* (*navire*) to pilot; (*avion*) to fly; (*automobile*) to drive; (*fig*): **~ qn** to guide sb round

pilule [pilyl] *nf* pill; **prendre la ~** to be on the pill; **~ du lendemain** morning-after pill

piment [pimã] *nm* (*Bot*) pepper, capsicum; (*fig*) spice, piquancy; **~ rouge** (*Culin*) chilli

pimenté, e [pimãte] *adj* hot and spicy

pimpant, e [pɛ̃pã, -ãt] *adj* spruce

pin [pɛ̃] *nm* pine (tree); (*bois*) pine(wood)

pinard [pinaʀ] *nm* (*fam*) (cheap) wine, plonk (*Brit*)

pince [pɛ̃s] *nf* (*outil*) pliers *pl*; (*de homard, crabe*) pincer, claw; (*Couture: pli*) dart; **~ à sucre/glace** sugar/ice tongs *pl*; **~ à épiler** tweezers *pl*; **~ à linge** clothes peg (*Brit*) *ou* pin (*US*); **~ universelle** (universal) pliers *pl*; **~s de cycliste** bicycle clips

pincé, e [pɛ̃se] *adj* (*air*) stiff; (*mince: bouche*) pinched ▷ *nf*: **une ~e de** a pinch of

pinceau, x [pɛ̃so] *nm* (paint)brush

pincer [pɛ̃se] *vt* to pinch; (*Mus: cordes*) to pluck; (*Couture*) to dart, put darts in; (*fam*) to nab; **se ~ le doigt** to squeeze *ou* nip one's finger; **se ~ le nez** to hold one's nose

pinède [pinɛd] *nf* pinewood, pine forest

pingouin [pɛ̃gwɛ̃] *nm* penguin

ping-pong [piŋpɔ̃g] *nm* table tennis

pingre [pɛ̃gʀ(ə)] *adj* niggardly

pinson [pɛ̃s3] *nm* chaffinch

pintade [pɛ̃tad] *nf* guinea-fowl

pioche [pjɔʃ] *nf* pickaxe

piocher [pjɔʃe] *vt* to dig up (with a pickaxe);

(*fam*) to swot (*Brit*) *ou* grind (*US*) at; **~ dans** to dig into

pion, ne [pj3, pjɔn] *nm/f* (*Scol: péj*) student paid to supervise schoolchildren ▷ *nm* (*Échecs*) pawn; (*Dames*) piece, draught (*Brit*), checker (*US*)

pionnier [pjɔnje] *nm* pioneer

pipe [pip] *nf* pipe; **fumer la** *ou* **une ~** to smoke a pipe; **~ de bruyère** briar pipe

pipeau, x [pipo] *nm* (reed-)pipe

piquant, e [pikã, -ãt] *adj* (*barbe, rosier etc*) prickly; (*saveur, sauce*) hot, pungent; (*fig: description, style*) racy; (*: mordant, caustique*) biting ▷ *nm* (*épine*) thorn, prickle; (*de hérisson*) quill, spine; (*fig*) spiciness, spice

pique [pik] *nf* (*arme*) pike; (*fig*): **envoyer** *ou* **lancer des ~s à qn** to make cutting remarks to sb ▷ *nm* (*Cartes: couleur*) spades *pl*; (*: carte*) spade

pique-nique [piknik] *nm* picnic

pique-niquer [piknike] *vi* to (have a) picnic

piquer [pike] *vt* (*percer*) to prick; (*Méd*) to give an injection to; (*: animal blessé etc*) to put to sleep; (*insecte, fumée, ortie*) to sting; (*: poivre*) to burn; (*: froid*) to bite; (*Couture*) to machine (stitch); (*intérêt etc*) to arouse; (*fam: prendre*) to pick up; (*: voler*) to pinch; (*: arrêter*) to nab; (*planter*): **~ qch dans** to stick sth into; (*fixer*): **~ qch à** *ou* **sur** to pin sth onto ▷ *vi* (*oiseau, avion*) to go into a dive; (*saveur*) to be pungent; to be sour; **se piquer** (*avec une aiguille*) to prick o.s.; (*se faire une piqûre*) to inject o.s.; (*se vexer*) to get annoyed; **se ~ de faire** to pride o.s. on doing; **~ sur** to swoop down on; to head straight for; **~ du nez** (*avion*) to go into a nose-dive; **~ une tête** (*plonger*) to dive headfirst; **~ un galop/un cent mètres** to break into a gallop/put on a sprint; **~ une crise** to throw a fit; **~ au vif** (*fig*) to sting

piquet [pikɛ] *nm* (*pieu*) post, stake; (*de tente*) peg; **mettre un élève au ~** to make a pupil stand in the corner; **~ de grève** (strike) picket; **~ d'incendie** fire-fighting squad

piqûre [pikyʀ] *nf* (*d'épingle*) prick; (*d'ortie*) sting; (*de moustique*) bite; (*Méd*) injection, shot (*US*); (*Couture*) (straight) stitch; straight stitching; (*de ver*) hole; (*tache*) (spot of) mildew; **faire une ~ à qn** to give sb an injection

pirate [piʀat] *adj* pirate *cpd* ▷ *nm* pirate; (*fig: escroc*) crook, shark; (*Inform*) hacker; **~ de l'air** hijacker

pirater [piʀate] *vi* (*Inform*) to hack ▷ *vt* (*Inform*) to hack into

pire [piʀ] *adj* (*comparatif*) worse; (*superlatif*): **le (la) ~ ...** the worst ... ▷ *nm*: **le ~ (de)** the worst (of)

pis [pi] *nm* (*de vache*) udder; (*pire*): **le ~** the worst ▷ *adj, adv* worse; **qui ~ est** what is worse; **au ~ aller** if the worst comes to the worst, at worst

piscine [pisin] *nf* (swimming) pool; **~ couverte** indoor (swimming) pool

pissenlit [pisãli] *nm* dandelion

pistache [pistaʃ] *nf* pistachio (nut)

piste [pist(ə)] *nf* (*d'un animal, sentier*) track, trail; (*indice*) lead; (*de stade, de magnétophone: de cirque*) ring; (*de danse*) floor; (*de patinage*) rink; (*de ski*) run; (*Aviat*) runway; **~ cavalière** bridle path; **~ cyclable** cycle track, bikeway (*US*); **~ sonore** sound track

pistolet [pistɔlɛ] *nm* (*arme*) pistol, gun; (*à peinture*) spray gun; **~ à bouchon/air comprimé** popgun/airgun; **~ à eau** water pistol

pistolet-mitrailleur (*pl* **pistolets-mitrailleurs**) [pistɔlɛmitRajœR] *nm* submachine gun

piston [pistɔ̃] *nm* (*Tech*) piston; (*Mus*) valve; (*fig: appui*) string-pulling

pistonner [pistɔne] *vt* (*candidat*) to pull strings for

piteux, -euse [pitø, -øz] *adj* pitiful, sorry (*avant le nom*); **en ~ état** in a sorry state

pitié [pitje] *nf* pity; **sans ~** *adj* pitiless, merciless; **faire ~** to inspire pity; **il me fait ~** I pity him, I feel sorry for him; **avoir ~ de** (*compassion*) to pity, feel sorry for; (*merci*) to have pity *ou* mercy on; **par ~!** for pity's sake!

pitoyable [pitwajabl(ə)] *adj* pitiful

pitre [pitr(ə)] *nm* clown

pitrerie [pitRəRi] *nf* tomfoolery *no pl*

pittoresque [pitɔRɛsk(ə)] *adj* picturesque; (*expression, détail*) colourful (*Brit*), colorful (*US*)

pivot [pivo] *nm* pivot; (*d'une dent*) post

pivoter [pivɔte] *vi* (*fauteuil*) to swivel; (*porte*) to revolve; **~ sur ses talons** to swing round

pizza [pidza] *nf* pizza

PJ *sigle f* = **police judiciaire** ▷ *sigle fpl* (= *pièces jointes*) encl

placard [plakaR] *nm* (*armoire*) cupboard; (*affiche*) poster, notice; (*Typo*) galley; **~ publicitaire** display advertisement

place [plas] *nf* (*emplacement, situation, classement*) place; (*de ville, village*) square; (*Écon*): **financière/boursière** money/stock market; (*espace libre*) room, space; (*de parking*) space; (*siège: de train, cinéma, voiture*) seat; (*prix: au cinéma etc*) price; (: *dans un bus, taxi*) fare; (*emploi*) job; **en ~** (*mettre*) in its place; **de ~ en ~, par ~s** here and there, in places; **sur ~** on the spot; **faire ~ à** to give way to; **faire de la ~ à** to make room for; **ça prend de la ~** it takes up a lot of room *ou* space; **prendre ~** to take one's place; **remettre qn à sa ~** to put sb in his (*ou* her) place; **ne pas rester** *ou* **tenir en ~** to be always on the go; **à la ~ de** in place of, instead of; **une quatre ~s** (*Auto*) a four-seater; **il y a 20 ~s assises/debout** there are 20 seats/there is standing room for 20; **~ forte** fortified town; **~ d'honneur** place (*ou* seat) of honour (*Brit*) *ou* honor (*US*)

placé, e [plase] *adj* (*Hippisme*) placed; **haut ~** (*fig*) high-ranking; **être bien/mal ~** to be well/badly placed; (*spectateur*) to have a good/bad seat; **être bien/mal ~ pour faire** to be in/not to be in a position to do

placement [plasmɑ̃] *nm* placing; (*Finance*) investment; **agence** *ou* **bureau de ~** employment agency

placer [plase] *vt* to place, put; (*convive, spectateur*) to seat; (*capital, argent*) to place, invest; (*dans la conversation*) to put *ou* get in; **~ qn chez** to get sb a

job at (*ou* with); **se ~ au premier rang** to go and stand (*ou* sit) in the first row

plafond [plafɔ̃] *nm* ceiling

plage [plaʒ] *nf* beach; (*station*) (seaside) resort; (*fig*) band, bracket; (*de disque*) track, band; **~ arrière** (*Auto*) parcel *ou* back shelf

plagiat [plaʒja] *nm* plagiarism

plaid [plɛd] *nm* (tartan) car rug, lap robe (*US*)

plaider [plede] *vi* (*avocat*) to plead; (*plaignant*) to go to court, litigate ▷ *vt* to plead; **~ pour** (*fig*) to speak for

plaidoyer [plɛdwaje] *nm* (*Jur*) speech for the defence (*Brit*) *ou* defense (*US*); (*fig*) plea

plaie [plɛ] *nf* wound

plaignant, e [plɛɲɑ̃, -ɑ̃t] *vb voir* **plaindre** ▷ *nm/f* plaintiff

plaindre [plɛ̃dR(ə)] *vt* to pity, feel sorry for; **se plaindre** *vi* (*gémir*) to moan; (*protester, rouspéter*): **se ~ (à qn) (de)** to complain (to sb) (about); (*souffrir*): **se ~ de** to complain of

plaine [plɛn] *nf* plain

plain-pied [plɛ̃pje]: **de ~** *adv* at street-level; (*fig*) straight; **de ~ (avec)** on the same level (as)

plaint, e [plɛ̃, -ɛ̃t] *pp de* **plaindre** ▷ *nf* (*gémissement*) moan, groan; (*doléance*) complaint; **porter ~e** to lodge a complaint

plaire [plɛR] *vi* to be a success, be successful; to please; **~ à: cela me plaît** I like it; **essayer de ~ à qn** (*en étant serviable etc*) to try and please sb; **elle plaît aux hommes** she's a success with men, men like her; **se ~ quelque part** to like being somewhere, like it somewhere; **se ~ à faire** to take pleasure in doing; **ce qu'il vous plaira** what(ever) you like *ou* wish; **s'il vous plaît** please

plaisance [plɛzɑ̃s] *nf* (*aussi:* **navigation de plaisance**) (pleasure) sailing, yachting

plaisant, e [plɛzɑ̃, -ɑ̃t] *adj* pleasant; (*histoire, anecdote*) amusing

plaisanter [plɛzɑ̃te] *vi* to joke ▷ *vt* (*personne*) to tease, make fun of; **pour ~** for a joke; **on ne plaisante pas avec cela** that's no joking matter; **tu plaisantes!** you're joking *ou* kidding!

plaisanterie [plɛzɑ̃tRi] *nf* joke; joking *no pl*

plaise *etc* [plɛz] *vb voir* **plaire**

plaisir [pleziR] *nm* pleasure; **faire ~ à qn** (*délibérément*) to be nice to sb, please sb; (*cadeau, nouvelle etc*): **ceci me fait ~** I'm delighted *ou* very pleased with this; **prendre ~ à/à faire** to take pleasure in/in doing; **j'ai le ~ de ...** it is with great pleasure that I ...; **M. et Mme X ont le ~ de vous faire part de ...** M. and Mme X are pleased to announce ...; **se faire un ~ de faire qch** to be (only too) pleased to do sth; **faites-moi le ~ de ...** would you mind ..., would you be kind enough to ...; **à ~** freely; for the sake of it; **au ~ (de vous revoir)** (I hope to) see you again; **pour le** *ou* **pour son** *ou* **par ~** for pleasure

plaît [plɛ] *vb voir* **plaire**

plan, e [plɑ̃, -an] *adj* flat ▷ *nm* plan; (*Géom*) plane; (*fig*) level, plane; (*Ciné*) shot; **au premier/second ~** in the foreground/middle distance; **à**

l'arrière ~ in the background; **mettre qch au premier** ~ (*fig*) to consider sth to be of primary importance; **sur le ~ sexuel** sexually, as far as sex is concerned; **laisser/rester en ~** to abandon/be abandoned; ~ **d'action** plan of action; ~ **directeur** (*Écon*) master plan; ~ **d'eau** lake; pond; ~ **de travail** work-top, work surface; ~ **de vol** (*Aviat*) flight plan

planche [plɑ̃ʃ] *nf* (*pièce de bois*) plank, (wooden) board; (*illustration*) plate; (*de salades, radis, poireaux*) bed; (*d'un plongeoir*) (diving) board; **les ~s** (*Théât*) the boards; **en ~s** *adj* wooden; **faire la ~** (*dans l'eau*) to float on one's back; **avoir du pain sur la ~** to have one's work cut out; ~ **à découper** chopping board; ~ **à dessin** drawing board; ~ **à pain** breadboard; ~ **à repasser** ironing board; ~ (**à roulettes**) (*planche*) skateboard; (*sport*) skateboarding; ~ **de salut** (*fig*) sheet anchor; ~ **à voile** (*planche*) windsurfer, sailboard; (*sport*) windsurfing

plancher [plɑ̃ʃe] *nm* floor; (*planches*) floorboards *pl*; (*fig*) minimum level ▷ *vi* to work hard

planer [plane] *vi* (*oiseau, avion*) to glide; (*fumée, vapeur*) to float, hover; (*drogué*) to be (on a) high; ~ **sur** (*fig*) to hang over; to hover above

planète [planɛt] *nf* planet

planeur [planœR] *nm* glider

planification [planifikasjɔ̃] *nf* (*economic*) planning

planifier [planifje] *vt* to plan

planning [planiŋ] *nm* programme (*Brit*), program (*US*), schedule; ~ **familial** family planning

planque [plɑ̃k] *nf* (*fam: combine, filon*) cushy (*Brit*) *ou* easy number; (: *cachette*) hideout

plant [plɑ̃] *nm* seedling, young plant

plante [plɑ̃t] *nf* plant; ~ **d'appartement** house *ou* pot plant; ~ **du pied** sole (of the foot); ~ **verte** house plant

planter [plɑ̃te] *vt* (*plante*) to plant; (*enfoncer*) to hammer *ou* drive in; (*tente*) to put up, pitch; (*drapeau, échelle, décors*) to put up; (*fam: mettre*) to dump; (: *abandonner*) : ~ **là** to ditch; **se planter** *vi* (*fam: se tromper*) to get it wrong; (*ordinateur*) to crash; ~ **qch dans** to hammer *ou* drive sth into; to stick sth into; **se ~ dans** to sink into; to get stuck in; **se ~ devant** to plant o.s. in front of

planteur, -euse [plɑ̃tyRø, -øz] *adj* (*repas*) copious, lavish; (*femme*) buxom

plaque [plak] *nf* plate; (*de verre*) sheet; (*de verglas, d'eczéma*) patch; (*dentaire*) plaque; (*avec inscription*) plaque; ~ (**minéralogique** *ou* **de police** *ou* **d'immatriculation**) number (*Brit*) *ou* license (*US*) plate; ~ **de beurre** slab of butter; ~ **chauffante** hotplate; ~ **de chocolat** bar of chocolate; ~ **de cuisson** hob; ~ **d'identité** identity disc; ~ **tournante** (*fig*) centre (*Brit*), center (*US*)

plaqué, e [plake] *adj*: ~ **or/argent** gold-/silver-plated ▷ *nm*: ~ **or/argent** gold/silver plate; ~ **acajou** with a mahogany veneer

plaquer [plake] *vt* (*bijou*) to plate; (*bois*) to veneer;

(*aplatir*): ~ **qch sur/contre** to make sth stick *ou* cling to; (*Rugby*) to bring down; (*fam: laisser tomber*) to drop, ditch; **se ~ contre** to flatten o.s. against; ~ **qn contre** to pin sb to

plaquette [plakɛt] *nf* tablet; (*de chocolat*) bar; (*de beurre*) slab, packet; (*livre*) small volume; (*Méd: de pilules, gélules*) pack, packet; ~ **de frein** (*Auto*) brake pad

plastique [plastik] *adj* plastic ▷ *nm* plastic ▷ *nf* plastic arts *pl*; (*d'une statue*) modelling

plastiquer [plastike] *vt* to blow up

plat, e [pla, -at] *adj* flat; (*fade: vin*) flat-tasting, insipid; (*personne, livre*) dull ▷ *nm* (*récipient, Culin*) dish; (*d'un repas*): **le premier ~** the first course; (*partie plate*): **le ~ de la main** the flat of the hand; (: *d'une route*) flat (part); **à ~ ventre** *adv* face down; (*tomber*) flat on one's face; **à ~** *adj* (*pneu, batterie*) flat; (*fam: fatigué*) dead beat, tired out; ~ **cuisiné** pre-cooked meal (*ou* dish); ~ **du jour** dish of the day; ~ **principal** *ou* **de résistance** main course; ~**s préparés** convenience food(s)

platane [platan] *nm* plane tree

plateau, x [plato] *nm* (*support*) tray; (*d'une table*) top; (*d'une balance*) pan; (*Géo*) plateau; (*de tourne-disques*) turntable; (*Ciné*) set; (*TV*): **nous avons deux journalistes sur le ~ ce soir** we have two journalists with us tonight; ~ **à fromages** cheeseboard

plate-bande (*pl* **plates-bandes**) [platbɑ̃d] *nf* flower bed

plate-forme (*pl* **plates-formes**) [platfɔRm(ə)] *nf* platform; ~ **de forage/pétrolière** drilling/oil rig

platine [platin] *nm* platinum ▷ *nf* (*d'un tourne-disque*) turntable; ~ **disque/cassette** record/cassette deck; ~ **laser** *ou* **compact-disc** compact disc (player)

plâtre [plɑtR(ə)] *nm* (*matériau*) plaster; (*statue*) plaster statue; (*Méd*) (plaster) cast; **plâtres** *nmpl* plasterwork *sg*; **avoir un bras dans le ~** to have an arm in plaster

plein, e [plɛ̃, -ɛn] *adj* full; (*porte, roue*) solid; (*chienne, jument*) big (with young) ▷ *nm*: **faire le ~ (d'essence)** to fill up (with petrol (*Brit*) *ou* gas (*US*)) ▷ *prép*: **avoir de l'argent ~ les poches** to have loads of money; ~ **de** full of; **avoir les mains ~es** to have one's hands full; **à ~es mains** (*ramasser*) in handfuls; (*empoigner*) firmly; **à ~ régime** at maximum revs; (*fig*) at full speed; **à ~ temps** full-time; **en ~ air** in the open air; **jeux en ~ air** outdoor games; **en ~e mer** on the open sea; **en ~ soleil** in direct sunlight; **en ~e nuit/rue** in the middle of the night/street; **en ~ milieu** right in the middle; **en ~ jour** in broad daylight; **les ~s** the downstrokes (*in handwriting*); **faire le ~ des voix** to get the maximum number of votes possible; **en ~ sur** right on; **en avoir ~ le dos** (*fam*) to have had it up to here

pleurer [plœRe] *vi* to cry; (*yeux*) to water ▷ *vt* to mourn (for); ~ **sur** *vt* to lament (over), bemoan; ~ **de rire** to laugh till one cries

pleurnicher [plœRniʃe] *vi* to snivel, whine

pleurs [plœR] *nmpl*: **en ~** in tears

pleut [plø] *vb voir* **pleuvoir**
pleuvait *etc* [pløvɛ] *vb voir* **pleuvoir**
pleuvoir [pløvwaʀ] *vb impers* to rain ▷ *vi* (*fig*): ~
(**sur**) to shower down (upon), be showered upon;
il pleut it's raining; **il pleut des cordes** *ou* **à**
verse *ou* **à torrents** it's pouring (down), it's
raining cats and dogs
pli [pli] *nm* fold; (*de jupe*) pleat; (*de pantalon*) crease;
(*aussi*: **faux pli**) crease; (*enveloppe*) envelope;
(*lettre*) letter; (*Cartes*) trick; **prendre le ~ de faire**
to get into the habit of doing; **ça ne fait pas un**
~! don't you worry!; ~ **d'aisance** inverted pleat
pliant, e [plijã, -ãt] *adj* folding ▷ *nm* folding
stool, campstool
plier [plije] *vt* to fold; (*pour ranger*) to fold up;
(*table pliante*) to fold down; (*genou, bras*) to bend
▷ *vi* to bend; (*fig*) to yield; **se ~ à** to submit to; ~
bagages (*fig*) to pack up (and go)
plinthe [plɛ̃t] *nf* skirting board
plisser [plise] *vt* (*chiffonner: papier, étoffe*) to
crease; (*rider: front*) to furrow, wrinkle; (: *bouche*)
to pucker; (*jupe*) to put pleats in; **se plisser** *vi*
(*vêtement, étoffe*) to crease
plomb [plɔ̃] *nm* (*métal*) lead; (*d'une cartouche*)
(lead) shot; (*Pêche*) sinker; (*sceau*) (lead) seal;
(*Élec*) fuse; **de ~** (*soleil*) blazing; **sans ~** (*essence*)
unleaded; **sommeil de ~** heavy *ou* very deep
sleep; **mettre à ~** to plumb
plombage [plɔ̃baʒ] *nm* (*de dent*) filling
plomberie [plɔ̃bʀi] *nf* plumbing
plombier [plɔ̃bje] *nm* plumber
plonge [plɔ̃ʒ] *nf*: **faire la ~** to be a washer-up
(*Brit*) *ou* dishwasher (*person*)
plongeant, e [plɔ̃ʒã, -ãt] *adj* (*vue*) from above; (*tir,*
décolleté) plunging
plongée [plɔ̃ʒe] *nf* (*Sport*) diving *no pl*; (: *sans*
scaphandre) skin diving; (*de sous-marin*)
submersion, dive; **en ~** (*sous-marin*) submerged;
(*prise de vue*) high angle
plongeoir [plɔ̃ʒwaʀ] *nm* diving board
plongeon [plɔ̃ʒɔ̃] *nm* dive
plonger [plɔ̃ʒe] *vi* to dive ▷ *vt*: ~ **qch dans** to
plunge sth into; ~ **dans un sommeil profond**
to sink straight into a deep sleep; ~ **qn dans**
l'embarras to throw sb into a state of confusion
plongeur, -euse [plɔ̃ʒœʀ, -øz] *nm/f* diver; (*de café*)
washer-up (*Brit*), dishwasher (*person*)
ployer [plwaje] *vt* to bend ▷ *vi* to bend; (*plancher*)
to sag
plu [ply] *pp de* **plaire**; **pleuvoir**
pluie [plɥi] *nf* rain; (*averse, ondée*): **une ~ brève**
a shower; (*fig*): ~ **de** shower of; **une ~ fine** fine
rain; **retomber en ~** to shower down; **sous la ~**
in the rain
plume [plym] *nf* feather; (*pour écrire*) (pen) nib;
(*fig*) pen; **dessin à la ~** pen and ink drawing
plupart [plypaʀ]: **la ~** *pron* the majority, most
(of them); **la ~ des** most, the majority of; **la ~**
du temps/d'entre nous most of the time/of us;
pour la ~ *adv* for the most part, mostly
pluriel [plyʀjɛl] *nm* plural; **au ~** in the plural
plus¹ [ply] *vb voir* **plaire**

plus² [ply] *adv* **1** (*forme négative*): **ne** ... ~ no more,
no longer; **je n'ai ~ d'argent** I've got no more
money *ou* no money left; **il ne travaille ~** he's
no longer working, he doesn't work any more
2 [ply, plyz] (+*voyelle: comparatif*) more, ...+er;
(*superlatif*): **le ~** the most, the ...+est; ~ **grand/**
intelligent (que) bigger/more intelligent
(than); **le ~ grand/intelligent** the biggest/most
intelligent; **tout au ~** at the very most
3 [plys] (*davantage*) more; **il travaille ~ (que)**
he works more (than); ~ **il travaille, ~ il est**
heureux the more he works, the happier he is;
~ **de pain** more bread; ~ **de 10 personnes/trois**
heures/quatre kilos more than *ou* over 10
people/three hours/four kilos; **trois heures de**
~ **que** three hours more than; ~ **de minuit** after
ou past midnight; **de ~** what's more, moreover;
il a trois ans de ~ que moi he's three years older
than me; **trois kilos en ~** three kilos more; **en ~**
de in addition to; **de ~ en ~** more and more; **en**
~ **de cela** ... what is more ...; ~ **ou moins** more
or less; **ni ~ ni moins** no more, no less; **sans ~**
(but) no more than that, (but) that's all; **qui ~**
est what is more
▷ *prép* [plys]: **quatre ~ deux** four plus two
plusieurs [plyzjœʀ] *adj, pron* several; **ils sont ~**
there are several of them
plus-value [plyvaly] *nf* (*d'un bien*) appreciation;
(*bénéfice*) capital gain; (*budgétaire*) surplus
plut [ply] *vb voir* **plaire**; **pleuvoir**
plutôt [plyto] *adv* rather; **je ferais ~ ceci** I'd
rather *ou* sooner do this; **fais ~ comme ça** try
this way instead; ~ **que (de) faire** rather than *ou*
instead of doing
pluvieux, -euse [plyvjø, -øz] *adj* rainy, wet
PME *sigle fpl* = **petites et moyennes entreprises**
PMU *sigle m* = **pari mutuel urbain**; (*café*) betting
agency; *see note*
PNB *sigle m* (= *produit national brut*) GNP
pneu [pnø] *nm* (*de roue*) tyre (*Brit*), tire (*US*);
(*message*) letter sent by pneumatic tube
pneumonie [pnømɔni] *nf* pneumonia
poche [pɔʃ] *nf* pocket; (*déformation*): **faire**
une/des ~(s) to bag; (*sous les yeux*) bag, pouch;
(*Zool*) pouch ▷ *nm* (*livre de poche*) (pocket-size)
paperback; **de ~** pocket *cpd*; **en être de sa ~** to be
out of pocket; **c'est dans la ~** it's in the bag
pocher [pɔʃe] *vt* (*Culin*) to poach; (*Art*) to sketch
▷ *vi* (*vêtement*) to bag
pochette [pɔʃɛt] *nf* (*de timbres*) wallet, envelope;
(*d'aiguilles etc*) case; (*sac: de femme*) clutch bag,
purse; (: *d'homme*) bag; (*sur veston*) breast pocket;
(*mouchoir*) breast pocket handkerchief; ~
d'allumettes book of matches; ~ **de disque**
record sleeve; ~ **surprise** lucky bag
podcast [pɔdkast] *nm* (*Inform*) podcast
podcaster [pɔdkaste] *vi* (*Inform*) to podcast
poêle [pwal] *nm* stove ▷ *nf*: ~ (**à frire**) frying pan
poème [pɔɛm] *nm* poem
poésie [pɔezi] *nf* (*poème*) poem; (*art*): **la ~** poetry
poète [pɔɛt] *nm* poet; (*fig*) dreamer ▷ *adj* poetic
poids [pwa] *nm* weight; (*Sport*) shot; **vendre au ~**

to sell by weight; **de ~** adj (argument etc) weighty;
prendre du ~ to put on weight; **faire le ~** (fig)
to measure up; **~ plume/mouche/coq/moyen**
(Boxe) feather/fly/bantam/middleweight; **~
et haltères** weight lifting sg; **~ lourd** (Boxe)
heavyweight; (camion: aussi: **PL**) (big) lorry (Brit),
truck (US); (: Admin) large goods vehicle (Brit),
truck (US); **~ mort** dead weight; **~ utile** net
weight

poignant, e [pwaɲɑ̃, -ɑ̃t] adj poignant,
harrowing

poignard [pwaɲaʀ] nm dagger

poignarder [pwaɲaʀde] vt to stab, knife

poigne [pwaɲ] nf grip; (fig) firm-handedness; **à
~** firm-handed

poignée [pwaɲe] nf (de sel etc, fig) handful; (de
couvercle, porte) handle; **~ de main** handshake

poignet [pwaɲɛ] nm (Anat) wrist; (de chemise) cuff

poil [pwal] nm (Anat) hair; (de pinceau, brosse)
bristle; (de tapis, tissu) strand; (pelage) coat;
(ensemble des poils): **avoir du ~ sur la poitrine** to
have hair(s) on one's chest, have a hairy chest; **à
~** adj (fam) starkers; **au ~** adj (fam) hunky-dory;
de tout ~ of all kinds; **être de bon/mauvais ~**
to be in a good/bad mood; **~ à gratter** itching
powder

poilu, e [pwaly] adj hairy

poinçon [pwɛ̃sɔ̃] nm awl; bodkin; (marque)
hallmark

poinçonner [pwɛ̃sɔne] vt (marchandise) to stamp;
(bijou etc) to hallmark; (billet, ticket) to clip, punch

poing [pwɛ̃] nm fist; **dormir à ~s fermés** to
sleep soundly

point [pwɛ̃] vb voir **poindre** ▷ nm (marque, signe)
dot; (: de ponctuation) full stop, period (US);
(moment, de score etc, fig: question) point; (endroit)
spot; (Couture, Tricot) stitch ▷ adv = **pas**; **ne ... ~**
not (at all); **faire le ~** (Navig) to take a bearing,
(fig) to take stock (of the situation); **faire le ~ sur**
to review; **en tout ~** in every respect; **sur le ~ de
faire** (just) about to do; **au ~ que, à tel ~ que** so
much so that; **mettre au ~** (mécanisme, procédé) to
develop; (appareil-photo) to focus; (affaire) to settle;
à ~ (Culin) just right; (: viande) medium; **à ~
(nommé)** just at the right time; **~ de croix/tige/
chaînette** (Couture) cross/stem/chain stitch; **~
mousse/jersey** (Tricot) garter/stocking stitch;
~ de départ/d'arrivée/d'arrêt departure/
arrival/stopping point; **~ chaud** (Mil, Pol) hot
spot; **~ de chute** landing place; (fig) stopping-
off point; **~ (de côté)** stitch (pain); **~ culminant**
summit; (fig) height, climax; **~ d'eau** spring,
water point; **~ d'exclamation** exclamation
mark; **~ faible** weak spot; **~ final** full stop,
period (US); **~ d'interrogation** question mark;
~ mort (Finance) break-even point; **au ~ mort**
(Auto) in neutral; (affaire, entreprise) at a standstill;
~ noir (sur le visage) blackhead; (Auto) accident
black spot; **~ de non-retour** point of no return;
~ de repère landmark; (dans le temps) point of
reference; **~ de vente** retail outlet; **~ de vue**
viewpoint; (fig: opinion) point of view; **du ~ de**

vue de from the point of view of; **~s cardinaux**
points of the compass, cardinal points; **~s de
suspension** suspension points

pointe [pwɛ̃t] nf point; (de la côte) headland;
(allusion) dig; sally; (fig): **une ~ d'ail/d'accent** a
touch ou hint of garlic/of an accent; **pointes** nfpl
(Danse) points, point shoes; **être à la ~ de** (fig)
to be in the forefront of; **faire ou pousser une
~ jusqu'à ...** to press on as far as ...; **sur la ~ des
pieds** on tiptoe; **en ~** adv ▷ adj pointed, tapered; **de ~** adj (technique etc)
leading; (vitesse) maximum, top; **heures/jours
de ~** peak hours/days; **faire du 180 en ~** (Auto)
to have a top ou maximum speed of 180; **faire
des ~s** (Danse) to dance on points; **~ d'asperge**
asparagus tip; **~ de courant** surge (of current);
~ de vitesse burst of speed

pointer [pwɛ̃te] vt (cocher) to tick off; (employés
etc) to check in; (diriger: canon, longue-vue, doigt):
~ vers qch to point at sth; (Mus: note) to dot
▷ vi (employé) to clock in ou on; (pousses) to come
through; (jour) to break; **~ les oreilles** (chien) to
prick up its ears

pointillé [pwɛ̃tije] nm (trait) dotted line; (Art)
stippling no pl

pointilleux, -euse [pwɛ̃tijø, -øz] adj particular,
pernickety

pointu, e [pwɛ̃ty] adj pointed; (clou) sharp; (voix)
shrill; (analyse) precise

pointure [pwɛ̃tyʀ] nf size

point-virgule (pl **points-virgules**) [pwɛ̃viʀgyl]
nm semi-colon

poire [pwaʀ] nf pear; (fam: péj) mug; **~
électrique** (pear-shaped) switch; **~ à injections**
syringe

poireau, x [pwaʀo] nm leek

poireauter [pwaʀote] vi (fam) to hang about
(waiting)

poirier [pwaʀje] nm pear tree; (Sport): **faire le ~**
to do a headstand

pois [pwa] nm (Bot) pea; (sur une étoffe) dot, spot;
à ~ (cravate etc) spotted, polka-dot cpd; **~ chiche**
chickpea; **~ de senteur** sweet pea; **~ cassés**
split peas

poison [pwazɔ̃] nm poison

poisse [pwas] nf rotten luck

poisseux, -euse [pwasø, -øz] adj sticky

poisson [pwasɔ̃] nm fish gen inv; **les P~s** (signe)
Pisces, the Fish; **être des P~s** to be Pisces;
pêcher ou prendre du ~ ou des ~s to fish; **~
d'avril** April fool; (blague) April fool's day trick;
see note; **~ rouge** goldfish

poissonnerie [pwasɔnʀi] nf fishmonger's (Brit),
fish store (US)

poissonnier, -ière [pwasɔnje, -jɛʀ] nm/f
fishmonger (Brit), fish merchant (US) ▷ nf
(ustensile) fish kettle

poitrine [pwatʀin] nf (Anat) chest; (seins) bust,
bosom; (Culin) breast; **~ de bœuf** brisket

poivre [pwavʀ(ə)] nm pepper; **~ en grains/
moulu** whole/ground pepper; **~ de cayenne**
cayenne (pepper); **~ et sel** adj (cheveux) pepper-

and-salt

poivron [pwavʀɔ̃] *nm* pepper, capsicum; ~ **vert/ rouge** green/red pepper

polaire [pɔlɛʀ] *adj* polar

polar [pɔlaʀ] *(fam)* *nm* detective novel

pôle [pol] *nm* (*Géo, Élec*) pole; **le ~ Nord/Sud** the North/South Pole; ~ **d'attraction** (*fig*) centre of attraction

poli, e [pɔli] *adj* polite; (*lisse*) smooth; polished

police [pɔlis] *nf* police; (*discipline*): **assurer la ~ de** *ou* **dans** to keep order in; **peine de simple ~** *sentence given by a magistrates' or police court*; ~ **(d'assurance)** (insurance) policy; ~ **(de caractères)** (*Typo, Inform*) font, typeface; ~ **judiciaire (PJ)** ≈ Criminal Investigation Department (CID) (*Brit*), ≈ Federal Bureau of Investigation (FBI) (*US*); ~ **des mœurs** ≈ vice squad; ~ **secours** ≈ emergency services *pl*

policier, -ière [pɔlisje, -jɛʀ] *adj* police *cpd* ▷ *nm* policeman; (*aussi*: **roman policier**) detective novel

polio [pɔljo] *nf* (*aussi*: **poliomyélite**) polio ▷ *nm/f* (*aussi*: **poliomyélitique**) polio patient *ou* case

poliomyélite [pɔljɔmjelit] *nf* poliomyelitis

poliomyélitique [pɔljɔmjelitik] *nm/f* polio patient *ou* case

polir [pɔliʀ] *vt* to polish

polisson, ne [pɔlisɔ̃, -ɔn] *adj* naughty

politesse [pɔlitɛs] *nf* politeness; **politesses** *nfpl* (exchange of) courtesies; **rendre une ~ à qn** to return sb's favour (*Brit*) *ou* favor (*US*)

politicien, ne [pɔlitisjɛ̃, -ɛn] *adj* political ▷ *nm/f* politician

politique [pɔlitik] *adj* political ▷ *nf* (*science, activité*) politics *sg*; (*principes, tactique*) policy, policies *pl* ▷ *nm* (*politicien*) politician; ~ **étrangère/intérieure** foreign/domestic policy

pollen [pɔlɛn] *nm* pollen

polluant, e [pɔlɥɑ̃, -ɑ̃t] *adj* polluting ▷ *nm* polluting agent, pollutant

polluer [pɔlɥe] *vt* to pollute

pollution [pɔlysjɔ̃] *nf* pollution

polo [pɔlo] *nm* (*sport*) polo; (*tricot*) polo shirt

Pologne [pɔlɔɲ] *nf*: **la ~** Poland

polonais, e [pɔlɔnɛ, -ɛz] *adj* Polish ▷ *nm* (*Ling*) Polish ▷ *nm/f*: **P~, e** Pole

poltron, ne [pɔltʀɔ̃, -ɔn] *adj* cowardly

polycopier [pɔlikɔpje] *vt* to duplicate

Polynésie [pɔlinezi] *nf*: **la ~** Polynesia; **la ~ française** French Polynesia

polyvalent, e [pɔlivalɑ̃, -ɑ̃t] *adj* (*vaccin*) polyvalent; (*personne*) versatile; (*salle*) multi-purpose ▷ *nm* ≈ tax inspector

pommade [pɔmad] *nf* ointment, cream

pomme [pɔm] *nf* (*Bot*) apple; (*boule décorative*) knob; (*pomme de terre*): **steak ~s (frites)** steak and chips (*Brit*) *ou* (French) fries (*US*); **tomber dans les ~s** (*fam*) to pass out; ~ **d'Adam** Adam's apple; **~s allumettes** French fries (*thin-cut*); ~ **d'arrosoir** (sprinkler) rose; ~ **de pin** pine *ou* fir cone; ~ **de terre** potato; **~s vapeur** boiled potatoes

pommeau, x [pɔmo] *nm* (*boule*) knob; (*de selle*) pommel

pommette [pɔmɛt] *nf* cheekbone

pommier [pɔmje] *nm* apple tree

pompe [pɔ̃p] *nf* pump; (*faste*) pomp (and ceremony); ~ **à eau/essence** water/petrol pump; ~ **à huile** oil pump; ~ **à incendie** fire engine (*apparatus*); **~s funèbres** undertaker's *sg*, funeral parlour *sg* (*Brit*), mortician's *sg* (*US*)

pomper [pɔ̃pe] *vt* to pump; (*évacuer*) to pump out; (*aspirer*) to pump up; (*absorber*) to soak up ▷ *vi* to pump

pompeux, -euse [pɔ̃pø, -øz] *adj* pompous

pompier [pɔ̃pje] *nm* fireman ▷ *adj m* (*style*) pretentious, pompous

pompiste [pɔ̃pist(ə)] *nm/f* petrol (*Brit*) *ou* gas (*US*) pump attendant

poncer [pɔ̃se] *vt* to sand (down)

ponctuation [pɔ̃ktɥasjɔ̃] *nf* punctuation

ponctuel, le [pɔ̃ktɥɛl] *adj* (*à l'heure, Tech*) punctual; (*fig: opération etc*) one-off, single; (*scrupuleux*) punctilious, meticulous

pondéré, e [pɔ̃deʀe] *adj* level-headed, composed

pondre [pɔ̃dʀ(ə)] *vt* to lay; (*fig*) to produce ▷ *vi* to lay

poney [pɔnɛ] *nm* pony

pont [pɔ̃] *nm* bridge; (*Auto*): ~ **arrière/avant** rear/front axle; (*Navig*) deck; **faire le ~** to take the extra day off; *see note*; **faire un ~ d'or à qn** to offer sb a fortune to take a job; ~ **aérien** airlift; ~ **basculant** bascule bridge; ~ **d'envol** flight deck; ~ **élévateur** hydraulic ramp; ~ **de graissage** ramp (*in garage*); ~ **à péage** tollbridge; ~ **roulant** travelling crane; ~ **suspendu** suspension bridge; ~ **tournant** swing bridge; **P~s et Chaussées** highways department

pont-levis (*pl* **ponts-levis**) [pɔ̃lvi] *nm* drawbridge

pop [pɔp] *adj inv* pop ▷ *nm*: **le ~** pop (music)

populace [pɔpylas] *nf* (*péj*) rabble

populaire [pɔpylɛʀ] *adj* popular; (*manifestation*) mass *cpd*, of the people; (*milieux, clientèle*) working-class; (*Ling: mot etc*) used by the lower classes (of society)

popularité [pɔpylaʀite] *nf* popularity

population [pɔpylasjɔ̃] *nf* population; ~ **active/ agricole** working/farming population

populeux, -euse [pɔpylø, -øz] *adj* densely populated

porc [pɔʀ] *nm* (*Zool*) pig; (*Culin*) pork; (*peau*) pigskin

porcelaine [pɔʀsəlɛn] *nf* (*substance*) porcelain, china; (*objet*) piece of china(ware)

porc-épic (*pl* **porcs-épics**) [pɔʀkepik] *nm* porcupine

porche [pɔʀʃ(ə)] *nm* porch

porcherie [pɔʀʃəʀi] *nf* pigsty

pore [pɔʀ] *nm* pore

porno [pɔʀno] *adj* porno ▷ *nm* porn

port [pɔʀ] *nm* (*Navig*) harbour (*Brit*), harbor (*US*), port; (*ville, Inform*) port; (*de l'uniforme etc*) wearing; (*pour lettre*) postage; (*pour colis, aussi*:

posture) carriage; **~ de commerce/de pêche** commercial/fishing port; **arriver à bon ~** to arrive safe and sound; **~ d'arme** (*Jur*) carrying of a firearm; **~ d'attache** (*Navig*) port of registry; (*fig*) home base; **~ d'escale** port of call; **~ franc** free port

portable [pɔʀtabl(ə)] *adj* (*vêtement*) wearable; (*portatif*) portable cell (US)

portail [pɔʀtaj] *nm* gate; (*de cathédrale*) portal

portant, e [pɔʀtɑ̃, -ɑ̃t] *adj* (*murs*) structural, supporting; (*roues*) running; **bien/mal ~** in good/poor health

portatif, -ive [pɔʀtatif, -iv] *adj* portable

porte [pɔʀt(ə)] *nf* door; (*de ville, forteresse, Ski*) gate; **mettre à la ~** to throw out; **prendre la ~** to leave, go away; **à ma/sa ~** (*tout près*) on my/his (*ou* her) doorstep; **~ (d'embarquement)** (*Aviat*) (departure) gate; **~ d'entrée** front door; **~ à ~** *nm* door-to-door selling; **~ de secours** emergency exit; **~ de service** service entrance

porté, e [pɔʀte] *adj*: **être ~ à faire qch** to be apt to do sth, tend to do sth; **être ~ sur qch** to be partial to sth

porte-avions [pɔʀtavjɔ̃] *nm inv* aircraft carrier

porte-bagages [pɔʀtbagaʒ] *nm inv* luggage rack (*ou* basket *etc*)

porte-bonheur [pɔʀtbɔnœʀ] *nm inv* lucky charm

porte-clefs [pɔʀtəkle] *nm inv* key ring

porte-documents [pɔʀtdɔkymɑ̃] *nm inv* attaché *ou* document case

portée [pɔʀte] *nf* (*d'une arme*) range; (*fig: importance*) impact, import; (: *capacités*) scope, capability; (*de chatte etc*) litter; (*Mus*) stave, staff; **à/hors de ~ (de)** within/out of reach (of); **à ~ de (la) main** within (arm's) reach; **à ~ de voix** within earshot; **à la ~ de qn** (*fig*) at sb's level, within sb's capabilities; **à la ~ de toutes les bourses** to suit every pocket, within everyone's means

porte-fenêtre (*pl* **portes-fenêtres**) [pɔʀtfənɛtʀ(ə)] *nf* French window

portefeuille [pɔʀtəfœj] *nm* wallet; (*Pol, Bourse*) portfolio; **faire un lit en ~** to make an apple-pie bed

portemanteau, x [pɔʀtmɑ̃to] *nm* coat rack

porte-monnaie [pɔʀtmɔne] *nm inv* purse

porte-parole [pɔʀtpaʀɔl] *nm inv* spokesperson

porter [pɔʀte] *vt* (*charge ou sac etc, aussi: fœtus*) to carry; (*sur soi: vêtement, barbe, bague*) to wear; (*fig: responsabilité etc*) to bear, carry; (*inscription, marque, titre, patronyme: arbre: fruits, fleurs*) to bear; (*jugement*) to pass; (*apporter*): **~ qch quelque part/à qn** to take sth somewhere/to sb; (*inscrire*): **~ qch sur** to put sth down on; to enter sth in ▷ *vi* (*voix, regard, canon*) to carry; (*coup, argument*) to hit home; **se porter** *vi* (*se sentir*): **se ~ bien/mal** to be well/unwell; (*aller*): **se ~ vers** to go towards; **~ sur** (*peser*) to rest on; (*accent*) to fall on; (*conférence etc*) to concern; (*heurter*) to strike; **être porté à faire** to be apt *ou* inclined to do; **elle portait le nom de Rosalie** she was called Rosalie; **~ qn au**

pouvoir to bring sb to power; **~ bonheur à qn** to bring sb luck; **~ qn à croire** to lead sb to believe; **~ son âge** to look one's age; **~ un toast** to drink a toast; **~ de l'argent au crédit d'un compte** to credit an account with some money; **se ~ partie civile** *to associate in a court action with the public prosecutor*; **se ~ garant de qch** to guarantee sth, vouch for sth; **se ~ candidat à la députation** ≈ to stand for Parliament (*Brit*), ≈ run for Congress (*US*); **se faire ~ malade** to report sick; **~ la main à son chapeau** to raise one's hand to one's hat; **~ son effort sur** to direct one's efforts towards; **~ un fait à la connaissance de qn** to bring a fact to sb's attention *ou* notice

porteur, -euse [pɔʀtœʀ, -øz] *adj* (*Comm*) strong, promising; (*nouvelle, chèque etc*): **être ~ de** to be the bearer of ▷ *nm/f* (*de messages*) bearer ▷ *nm* (*de bagages*) porter; (*Comm: de chèque*) bearer; (: *d'actions*) holder; **(avion) gros ~** wide-bodied aircraft, jumbo (jet)

porte-voix [pɔʀtəvwa] *nm inv* megaphone, loudhailer (*Brit*)

portier [pɔʀtje] *nm* doorman, commissionnaire (*Brit*)

portière [pɔʀtjɛʀ] *nf* door

portillon [pɔʀtijɔ̃] *nm* gate

portion [pɔʀsjɔ̃] *nf* (*part*) portion, share; (*partie*) portion, section

porto [pɔʀto] *nm* port (wine)

portrait [pɔʀtʀɛ] *nm* portrait; (*photographie*) photograph; (*fig*): **elle est le ~ de sa mère** she's the image of her mother

portrait-robot [pɔʀtʀɛʀɔbo] *nm* Identikit® *ou* Photo-fit ® (*Brit*) picture

portuaire [pɔʀtɥɛʀ] *adj* port *cpd*, harbour *cpd* (*Brit*), harbor *cpd* (*US*)

portugais, e [pɔʀtygɛ, -ɛz] *adj* Portuguese ▷ *nm* (*Ling*) Portuguese ▷ *nm/f*: **P~, e** Portuguese

Portugal [pɔʀtygal] *nm*: **le ~** Portugal

pose [poz] *nf* (*de moquette*) laying; (*de rideaux, papier peint*) hanging; (*attitude, d'un modèle*) pose; (*Photo*) exposure

posé, e [poze] *adj* calm, unruffled

poser [poze] *vt* (*déposer*): **~ qch (sur)/qn à** to put sth down (on)/drop sb at; (*placer*): **~ qch sur/quelque part** to put sth on/somewhere; (*installer: moquette, carrelage*) to lay; (*rideaux, papier peint*) to hang; (*Math: chiffre*) to put (down); (*question*) to ask; (*principe, conditions*) to lay *ou* set down; (*problème*) to formulate; (*difficulté*) to pose; (*personne: mettre en valeur*) to give standing to ▷ *vi* (*modèle*) to pose; to sit; **se poser** (*oiseau, avion*) to land; (*question*) to arise; **se ~ en** to pass o.s. off as, pose as; **~ son** *ou* **un regard sur qn/qch** to turn one's gaze on sb/sth; **~ sa candidature** to apply; (*Pol*) to put o.s. up for election

positif, -ive [pozitif, -iv] *adj* positive

position [pozisjɔ̃] *nf* position; **prendre ~** (*fig*) to take a stand

posologie [pozɔlɔʒi] *nf* directions *pl* for use, dosage

posséder [posede] *vt* to own, possess; (*qualité,*

talent) to have, possess; (*bien connaître: métier, langue*) to have mastered, have a thorough knowledge of; (*sexuellement, aussi: suj: colère*) to possess; (*fam: duper*) to take in

possession [pɔsesjɔ̃] *nf* ownership *no pl*; possession; (*aussi*: **être/entrer en possession de qch**) to be in/take possession of sth

possibilité [pɔsibilite] *nf* possibility; **possibilités** *nfpl* (*moyens*) means; (*potentiel*) potential *sg*; **avoir la ~ de faire** to be in a position to do; to have the opportunity to do

possible [pɔsibl(ə)] *adj* possible; (*projet, entreprise*) feasible ▷ *nm*: **faire son ~** to do all one can, do one's utmost; (**ce n'est**) **pas ~!** impossible!; **le plus/moins de livres ~** as many/few books as possible; **dès que ~** as soon as possible; **gentil** *etc* **au ~** as nice *etc* as it is possible to be

postal, e, -aux [pɔstal, -o] *adj* postal, post office *cpd*; **sac ~** mailbag, postbag

poste [pɔst(ə)] *nf* (*service*) post, postal service; (*administration, bureau*) post office ▷ *nm* (*fonction, Mil*) post; (*Tél*) extension; (*de radio etc*) set; (*de budget*) item; **postes** *nfpl* post office *sg*; **P~s télécommunications et télédiffusion (PTT)** *postal and telecommunications service*; **agent** *ou* **employé des ~s** post office worker; **mettre à la ~** to post; **~ de commandement (PC)** *nm* (*Mil etc*) headquarters; **~ de contrôle** *nm* checkpoint; **~ de douane** *nm* customs post; **~ émetteur** *nm* transmitting set; **~ d'essence** *nm* filling station; **~ d'incendie** *nm* fire point; **~ de péage** *nm* tollgate; **~ de pilotage** *nm* cockpit; **~ (de police)** *nm* police station; **~ de radio** *nm* radio set; **~ restante (PR)** *nf* poste restante (*Brit*), general delivery (*US*); **~ de secours** *nm* first-aid post; **~ de télévision** *nm* television set; **~ de travail** *nm* work station

poster *vt* [pɔste] to post ▷ *nm* [pɔstɛʀ] poster; **se poster** to position o.s

postérieur, e [pɔsteʀjœʀ] *adj* (*date*) later; (*partie*) back ▷ *nm* (*fam*) behind

posthume [pɔstym] *adj* posthumous

postulant, e [pɔstylɑ̃, -ɑ̃t] *nm/f* (*candidat*) applicant; (*Rel*) postulant

postuler [pɔstyle] *vt* (*emploi*) to apply for, put in for

posture [pɔstyʀ] *nf* posture, position; (*fig*) position

pot [po] *nm* jar, pot; (*en plastique, carton*) carton; (*en métal*) tin; (*fam*): **avoir du ~** to be lucky; **boire** *ou* **prendre un ~** (*fam*) to have a drink; **découvrir le ~ aux roses** to find out what's been going on; **~ catalytique** catalytic converter; **~ (de chambre)** (chamber)pot; **~ d'échappement** exhaust pipe; **~ de fleurs** plant pot, flowerpot; (*plante*) pot plant; **~ à tabac** tobacco jar

potable [pɔtabl(ə)] *adj* (*fig: boisson*) drinkable; (: *travail, devoir*) decent; **eau (non) ~** (not) drinking water

potage [pɔtaʒ] *nm* soup

potager, -ère [pɔtaʒe, -ɛʀ] *adj* (*plante*) edible, vegetable *cpd*; (**jardin**) **~** kitchen *ou* vegetable

garden

pot-au-feu [pɔtofø] *nm inv* (beef) stew; (*viande*) stewing beef ▷ *adj* (*fam: personne*) stay-at-home

pot-de-vin (*pl* **pots-de-vin**) [podvɛ̃] *nm* bribe

pote [pɔt] *nm* (*fam*) mate (*Brit*), pal

poteau, x [pɔto] *nm* post; **~ de départ/arrivée** starting/finishing post; **~ (d'exécution)** execution post, stake; **~ indicateur** signpost; **~ télégraphique** telegraph pole; **~x (de but)** goal-posts

potelé, e [pɔtle] *adj* plump, chubby

potence [pɔtɑ̃s] *nf* gallows *sg*; **en ~** T-shaped

potentiel, le [pɔtɑ̃sjɛl] *adj, nm* potential

poterie [pɔtʀi] *nf* (*fabrication*) pottery; (*objet*) piece of pottery

potier [pɔtje] *nm* potter

potins [pɔtɛ̃] *nmpl* gossip *sg*

potiron [pɔtiʀɔ̃] *nm* pumpkin

pou, x [pu] *nm* louse

poubelle [pubɛl] *nf* (dust)bin

pouce [pus] *nm* thumb; **se tourner** *ou* **se rouler les ~s** (*fig*) to twiddle one's thumbs; **manger sur le ~** to eat on the run, snatch something to eat

poudre [pudʀ(ə)] *nf* powder; (*fard*) (face) powder; (*explosif*) gunpowder; **en ~**: **café en poudre** instant coffee; **savon en ~** soap powder; **lait en ~** dried *ou* powdered milk; **~ à canon** gunpowder; **~ à éternuer** sneezing powder; **~ à récurer** scouring powder; **~ de riz** face powder

poudreux, -euse [pudʀø, -øz] *adj* dusty; (*neige*) powdery, powder *cpd*

poudrier [pudʀije] *nm* (powder) compact

pouffer [pufe] *vi*: **~ (de rire)** to snigger; to giggle

poulailler [pulaje] *nm* henhouse; (*Théât*): **le ~** the gods *sg*

poulain [pulɛ̃] *nm* foal; (*fig*) protégé

poule [pul] *nf* (*Zool*) hen; (*Culin*) (boiling) fowl; (*Sport*) (round-robin) tournament; (*Rugby*) group; (*fam*) bird (*Brit*), chick, broad (*US*); (*prostituée*) tart; **~ d'eau** moorhen; **~ mouillée** coward; **~ pondeuse** laying hen, layer; **~ au riz** chicken and rice

poulet [pulɛ] *nm* chicken; (*fam*) cop

poulie [puli] *nf* pulley

pouls [pu] *nm* pulse; (*Anat*): **prendre le ~ de qn** to take sb's pulse

poumon [pumɔ̃] *nm* lung; **~ d'acier** *ou* **artificiel** iron *ou* artificial lung

poupe [pup] *nf* stern; **en ~** astern

poupée [pupe] *nf* doll; **jouer à la ~** to play with one's doll (*ou* dolls); **de ~** (*très petit*): **jardin de ~** doll's garden, pocket-handkerchief-sized garden

pouponnière [pupɔnjɛʀ] *nf* crèche, day nursery

pour [puʀ] *prép* for ▷ *nm*: **le ~ et le contre** the pros and cons; **~ faire** (so as) to do, in order to do; **~ avoir fait** for having done; **~ que** so that, in order that; **~ moi** (*à mon avis, pour ma part*) for my part, personally; **~ riche qu'il soit** rich though he may be; **~ 20 euros d'essence** 20 euros' worth of petrol; **~ cent** per cent; **~ ce qui est de** as for; **y être ~ quelque chose** to have something to do with it

pourboire [puʀbwaʀ] *nm* tip

pourcentage [puʀsɑ̃taʒ] *nm* percentage; **travailler au ~** to work on commission

pourchasser [puʀʃase] *vt* to pursue

pourparlers [puʀpaʀle] *nmpl* talks, negotiations; **être en ~ avec** to be having talks with

pourpre [puʀpʀ(ə)] *adj* crimson

pourquoi [puʀkwa] *adv, conj* why ▷ *nm inv*: **le ~ (de)** the reason (for)

pourrai *etc* [puʀe] *vb voir* **pouvoir**

pourri, e [puʀi] *adj* rotten; *(roche, pierre)* crumbling; *(temps, climat)* filthy, foul ▷ *nm*: **sentir le ~** to smell rotten

pourriel [puʀjel] *nm* (*Inform*) spam

pourrir [puʀiʀ] *vi* to rot; *(fruit)* to go rotten *ou* bad; *(fig: situation)* to deteriorate ▷ *vt* to rot; *(fig: corrompre: personne)* to corrupt; *(: gâter: enfant)* to spoil thoroughly

pourriture [puʀityʀ] *nf* rot

pourrons *etc* [puʀɔ̃] *vb voir* **pouvoir**

poursuite [puʀsɥit] *nf* pursuit, chase; **poursuites** *nfpl* (*Jur*) legal proceedings; **(course) ~** track race; *(fig)* chase

poursuivre [puʀsɥivʀ(ə)] *vt* to pursue, chase (after); *(relancer)* to hound, harry; *(obséder)* to haunt; *(Jur)* to bring proceedings against, prosecute; *(: au civil)* to sue; *(but)* to strive towards; *(voyage, études)* to carry on with, continue ▷ *vi* to carry on, go on; **se poursuivre** *vi* to go on, continue

pourtant [puʀtɑ̃] *adv* yet; **mais ~** but nevertheless, but even so; **c'est ~ facile** (and) yet it's easy

pourtour [puʀtuʀ] *nm* perimeter

pourvoir [puʀvwaʀ] *nm* (*Comm*) supply ▷ *vt*: **~ qch/qn de** to equip sth/sb with ▷ *vi*: **~ à** to provide for; *(emploi)* to fill; **se pourvoir** *vi* (*Jur*): **se ~ en cassation** to take one's case to the Court of Appeal

pourvoyeur, -euse [puʀvwajœʀ, -øz] *nm/f* supplier

pourvu, e [puʀvy] *pp de* **pourvoir** ▷ *adj*: **~ de** equipped with; **~ que** *conj* *(si)* provided that, so long as; *(espérons que)* let's hope (that)

pousse [pus] *nf* growth; *(bourgeon)* shoot

poussé, e [puse] *adj* sophisticated, advanced; *(moteur)* souped-up

poussée [puse] *nf* thrust; *(coup)* push; *(Méd)* eruption; *(fig)* upsurge

pousser [puse] *vt* to push; *(acculer)* to drive sb to do sth; *(moteur, voiture)* to drive hard; *(émettre: cri etc)* to give; *(stimuler)* to urge on; to drive hard; *(poursuivre)* to carry on; *(inciter)*: **~ qn à faire qch** to urge *ou* press sb to do sth ▷ *vi* to push; *(croître)* to grow; *(aller)*: **~ plus loin** to push on a bit further; **se pousser** *vi* to move over; **faire ~** *(plante)* to grow; **~ le dévouement** *etc* **jusqu'à ...** to take devotion *etc* as far as ...

poussette [pusɛt] *nf* (*voiture d'enfant*) pushchair (*Brit*), stroller (*US*)

poussière [pusjɛʀ] *nf* dust; *(grain)* speck of dust; **et des ~s** *(fig)* and a bit; **~ de charbon** coaldust

poussiéreux, -euse [pusjeʀø, -øz] *adj* dusty

poussin [pusɛ̃] *nm* chick

poutre [putʀ(ə)] *nf* beam; *(en fer, ciment armé)* girder; **~s apparentes** exposed beams

pouvoir [puvwaʀ] *nm* power; *(Pol: dirigeants)*: **le ~** those in power; **les ~s publics** the authorities; **avoir ~ de faire** *(autorisation)* to have (the) authority to do; *(droit)* to have the right to do; **~ absolu** absolute power; **~ absorbant** absorbency; **~ d'achat** purchasing power; **~ calorifique** calorific value

▷ *vb semi-aux* **1** *(être en état de)* can, be able to; **je ne peux pas le réparer** I can't *ou* I am not able to repair it; **déçu de ne pas ~ le faire** disappointed not to be able to do it

2 *(avoir la permission)* can, may, be allowed to; **vous pouvez aller au cinéma** you can *ou* may go to the pictures

3 *(probabilité, hypothèse)* may, might, could; **il a pu avoir un accident** he may *ou* might *ou* could have had an accident; **il aurait pu le dire!** he might *ou* could have said (so)!

4 *(expressions)*: **tu ne peux pas savoir!** you have no idea!; **tu peux le dire!** you can say that again!

▷ *vb impers* may, might, could; **il peut arriver que** it may *ou* might *ou* could happen that; **il pourrait pleuvoir** it might rain

▷ *vt* **1** can, be able to; **j'ai fait tout ce que j'ai pu** I did all I could; **je n'en peux plus** *(épuisé)* I'm exhausted; *(à bout)* I can't take any more

2 *(vb +adj ou adv comparatif)*: **je me porte on ne peut mieux** I'm absolutely fine, I couldn't be better; **elle est on ne peut plus gentille** she couldn't be nicer, she's as nice as can be; **se pouvoir** *vi*: **il se peut que** it may *ou* might be that; **cela se pourrait** that's quite possible

prairie [pʀeʀi] *nf* meadow

praline [pʀalin] *nf* *(bonbon)* sugared almond; *(au chocolat)* praline

praticable [pʀatikabl(ə)] *adj* *(route etc)* passable, practicable; *(projet)* practicable

pratiquant, e [pʀatikɑ̃, -ɑ̃t] *adj* practising (*Brit*), practicing (*US*)

pratique [pʀatik] *nf* practice ▷ *adj* practical; *(commode: horaire etc)* convenient; *(: outil)* handy, useful; **dans la ~** in (actual) practice; **mettre en ~** to put into practice

pratiquement [pʀatikmɑ̃] *adv* *(dans la pratique)* in practice; *(pour ainsi dire)* practically, virtually

pratiquer [pʀatike] *vt* to practise (*Brit*), practice (*US*); *(Sport etc)* to go in for, play; *(appliquer: méthode, théorie)* to apply; *(intervention, opération)* to carry out; *(ouverture, abri)* to make ▷ *vi* (*Rel*) to be a churchgoer

pré [pʀe] *nm* meadow

préalable [pʀealabl(ə)] *adj* preliminary; **condition ~ (de)** precondition (for), prerequisite (for); **sans avis ~** without prior *ou* previous notice; **au ~** first, beforehand

préambule [pʀeɑ̃byl] *nm* preamble; (*fig*) prelude; **sans ~** straight away

préau, x [pʀeo] *nm* (*d'une cour d'école*) covered playground; (*d'un monastère, d'une prison*) inner courtyard

préavis [pʀeavi] *nm* notice; **~ de congé** notice; **communication avec ~** (*Tél*) personal *ou* person-to-person call

précaution [pʀekosjɔ̃] *nf* precaution; **avec ~** cautiously; **prendre des** *ou* **ses ~s** to take precautions; **par ~** as a precaution; **pour plus de ~** to be on the safe side; **~s oratoires** carefully phrased remarks

précédemment [pʀesedamɑ̃] *adv* before, previously

précédent, e [pʀesedɑ̃, -ɑ̃t] *adj* previous ▷ *nm* precedent; **sans ~** unprecedented; **le jour ~** the day before, the previous day

précéder [pʀesede] *vt* to precede; (*marcher ou rouler devant*) to be in front of; (*arriver avant*) to get ahead of

précepteur, -trice [pʀeseptœʀ, -tʀis] *nm/f* (*private*) tutor

prêcher [pʀeʃe] *vt, vi* to preach

précieux, -euse [pʀesjø, -øz] *adj* precious; (*collaborateur, conseils*) invaluable; (*style, écrivain*) précieux, precious

précipice [pʀesipis] *nm* drop, chasm; (*fig*) abyss; **au bord du ~** at the edge of the precipice

précipitamment [pʀesipitamɑ̃] *adv* hurriedly, hastily

précipitation [pʀesipitasjɔ̃] *nf* (*hâte*) haste; **~s (atmosphériques)** precipitation *sg*

précipité, e [pʀesipite] *adj* (*respiration*) fast; (*pas*) hurried; (*départ*) hasty

précipiter [pʀesipite] *vt* (*faire tomber*): **~ qn/qch du haut de** to throw *ou* hurl sb/sth off *ou* from; (*hâter: marche*) to quicken; (*: départ*) to hasten; **se précipiter** *vi* (*événements*) to move faster; (*respiration*) to speed up; **se ~ sur/vers** to rush at/towards; **se ~ au-devant de qn** to throw o.s. before sb

précis, e [pʀesi, -iz] *adj* precise; (*tir, mesures*) accurate, precise ▷ *nm* handbook

précisément [pʀesizemɑ̃] *adv* precisely; **ma vie n'est pas ~ distrayante** my life is not exactly entertaining

préciser [pʀesize] *vt* (*expliquer*) to be more specific about, clarify; (*spécifier*) to state, specify; **se préciser** *vi* to become clear(er)

précision [pʀesizjɔ̃] *nf* precision; accuracy; (*détail*) point *ou* detail (*made clear or to be clarified*); **précisions** *nfpl* further details

précoce [pʀekɔs] *adj* early; (*enfant*) precocious; (*calvitie*) premature

préconçu, e [pʀekɔ̃sy] *adj* preconceived

préconiser [pʀekɔnize] *vt* to advocate

prédécesseur [pʀedesesœʀ] *nm* predecessor

prédilection [pʀedileksjɔ̃] *nf*: **avoir une ~ pour** to be partial to; **de ~** favourite (*Brit*), favorite (*US*)

prédire [pʀediʀ] *vt* to predict

prédominer [pʀedɔmine] *vi* to predominate;

(*avis*) to prevail

préface [pʀefas] *nf* preface

préfecture [pʀefɛktyʀ] *nf* prefecture; *see note*; **~ de police** police headquarters

préférable [pʀefeʀabl(ə)] *adj* preferable

préféré, e [pʀefeʀe] *adj, nm/f* favourite (*Brit*), favorite (*US*)

préférence [pʀefeʀɑ̃s] *nf* preference; **de ~** preferably; **de** *ou* **par ~ à** in preference to, rather than; **donner la ~ à qn** to give preference to sb; **par ordre de ~** in order of preference; **obtenir la ~ sur** to have preference over

préférer [pʀefeʀe] *vt*: **~ qn/qch (à)** to prefer sb/sth (to), like sb/sth better (than); **~ faire** to prefer to do; **je préférerais du thé** I would rather have tea, I'd prefer tea

préfet [pʀefɛ] *nm* prefect; **~ de police** ≈ Chief Constable (*Brit*), ≈ Police Commissioner (*US*)

préhistorique [pʀeistɔʀik] *adj* prehistoric

préjudice [pʀeʒydis] *nm* (*matériel*) loss; (*moral*) harm *no pl*; **porter ~ à** to harm, be detrimental to; **au ~ de** at the expense of

préjugé [pʀeʒyʒe] *nm* prejudice; **avoir un ~ contre** to be prejudiced against; **bénéficier d'un ~ favorable** to be viewed favourably

préjuger [pʀeʒyʒe]: **~ de** *vt* to prejudge

prélasser [pʀelase]: **se prélasser** *vi* to lounge

prélèvement [pʀelɛvmɑ̃] *nm* deduction; withdrawal; **faire un ~ de sang** to take a blood sample

prélever [pʀelve] *vt* (*échantillon*) to take; **~ (sur)** (*argent*) to deduct (from); (*: sur son compte*) to withdraw (from)

prématuré, e [pʀematyʀe] *adj* premature; (*retraite*) early ▷ *nm* premature baby

premier, -ière [pʀəmje, -jɛʀ] *adj* first; (*branche, marche, grade*) bottom; (*fig: fondamental*) basic; prime; (*en importance*) first, foremost ▷ *nm* (*premier étage*) first (*Brit*) *ou* second (*US*) floor ▷ *nf* (*Auto*) first (gear); (*Rail, Aviat etc*) first class; (*Scol: classe*) penultimate school year (*age 16–17*); (*Théât*) first night; (*Ciné*) première; (*exploit*) first; **au ~ abord** at first sight; **au** *ou* **du ~ coup** at the first attempt *ou* go; **de ~ ordre** first-class, first-rate; **de première qualité, de ~ choix** best *ou* top quality; **de première importance** of the highest importance; **de première nécessité** absolutely essential; **le ~ venu** the first person to come along; **jeune ~** leading man; **le ~ de l'an** New Year's Day; **enfant du ~ lit** child of a first marriage; **en ~ lieu** in the first place; **~ âge** (*d'un enfant*) the first three months (of life); **P~ Ministre** Prime Minister

premièrement [pʀəmjɛʀmɑ̃] *adv* firstly

prémonition [pʀemɔnisjɔ̃] *nf* premonition

prémunir [pʀemyniʀ]: **se prémunir** *vi*: **se ~ contre** to protect o.s. from, guard against

prenant, e [pʀənɑ̃, -ɑ̃t] *vb voir* **prendre** ▷ *adj* absorbing, engrossing

prénatal, e [pʀenatal] *adj* (*Méd*) antenatal; (*allocation*) maternity *cpd*

prendre [pʀɑ̃dʀ(ə)] *vt* to take; (*aller chercher*) to

get, fetch; (se procurer) to get; (réserver: place) to book; (acquérir: du poids, de la valeur) to put on, gain; (malfaiteur, poisson) to catch; (passager) to pick up; (personnel, aussi: couleur, goût) to take on; (locataire) to take in; (traiter: enfant, problème) to handle; (voix, ton) to put on; (prélever: pourcentage, argent) to take off; (ôter): **~ qch à** to take sth from; (coincer): **se ~ les doigts dans** to get one's fingers caught in ▷ vi (liquide, ciment) to set; (greffe, vaccin) to take; (mensonge) to be successful; (feu: foyer) to go; (: incendie) to start; (allumette) to light; (se diriger): **~ à gauche** to turn (to the) left; **~ son origine** ou **sa source** (mot, rivière) to have its source; **~ qn pour** to take sb for; **se ~ pour** to think one is; **~ sur soi de faire qch** to take it upon o.s. to do sth; **~ qn en sympathie/horreur** to get to like/ loathe sb; **à tout ~** all things considered; **s'en ~ à** (agresser) to set about; (passer sa colère sur) to take it out on; (critiquer) to attack; (remettre en question) to challenge; **se ~ d'amitié/d'affection pour** to befriend/become fond of; **s'y ~** (procéder) to set about it; **s'y ~ à l'avance** to see to it in advance; **s'y ~ à deux fois** to try twice, make two attempts

preneur [pʀənœʀ] nm: **être ~** to be willing to buy; **trouver ~** to find a buyer

preniez [pʀənje] vb voir **prendre**

prenne etc [pʀɛn] vb voir **prendre**

prénom [pʀenɔ̃] nm first name

préoccupation [pʀeɔkypasjɔ̃] nf (souci) concern; (idée fixe) preoccupation

préoccuper [pʀeɔkype] vt (tourmenter, tracasser) to concern; (absorber, obséder) to preoccupy; **se ~ de qch** to be concerned about sth; to show concern about sth

préparatifs [pʀepaʀatif] nmpl preparations

préparation [pʀepaʀasjɔ̃] nf preparation; (Scol) piece of homework

préparer [pʀepaʀe] vt to prepare; (café, repas) to make; (examen) to prepare for; (voyage, entreprise) to plan; **se préparer** vi (orage, tragédie) to brew, be in the air; **se ~ (à qch/à faire)** to prepare (o.s.) ou get ready (for sth/to do); **~ qch à qn** (surprise etc) to have sth in store for sb; **~ qn à qch** (nouvelle etc) to prepare sb for sth

prépondérant, e [pʀepɔ̃deʀɑ̃, -ɑ̃t] adj major, dominating; **voix ~e** casting vote

préposé, e [pʀepoze] adj: **~ à** in charge of ▷ nm/f (gén: employé) employee; (Admin: facteur) postman/ woman (Brit), mailman/woman (US); (de la douane etc) official; (de vestiaire) attendant

préposition [pʀepozisjɔ̃] nf preposition

près [pʀɛ] adv near, close; **~ de** prép near (to), close to; (environ) nearly, almost; **~ d'ici** near here; **de ~** adv closely; **à cinq kg ~** to within about five kg; **à cela ~ que** apart from the fact that; **je ne suis pas ~ de lui pardonner** I'm nowhere near ready to forgive him; **on n'est pas à un jour ~** one day (either way) won't make any difference, we're not going to quibble over the odd day

présage [pʀezaʒ] nm omen

présager [pʀezaʒe] vt (prévoir) to foresee;

(annoncer) to portend

presbyte [pʀɛsbit] adj long-sighted (Brit), far-sighted (US)

presbytère [pʀɛsbiteʀ] nm presbytery

prescription [pʀɛskʀipsjɔ̃] nf (instruction) order, instruction; (Méd, Jur) prescription

prescrire [pʀɛskʀiʀ] vt to prescribe; **se prescrire** vi (Jur) to lapse

présence [pʀezɑ̃s] nf presence; (au bureau etc) attendance; **en ~** face to face; **en ~ de** in (the) presence of; (fig) in the face of; **faire acte de ~** to put in a token appearance; **~ d'esprit** presence of mind

présent, e [pʀezɑ̃, -ɑ̃t] adj, nm present; (Admin, Comm): **la ~e lettre/loi** this letter/law ▷ nm/f: **les ~s** (personnes) those present ▷ nf (Comm: lettre) **la ~e** this letter; **à ~** now, at present; **dès à ~** here and now; **jusqu'à ~** up till now, until now; **à ~ que** now that

présentation [pʀezɑ̃tasjɔ̃] nf presentation; introduction; (allure) appearance

présenter [pʀezɑ̃te] vt to present; (invité, candidat) to introduce; (félicitations, condoléances) to offer; (montrer: billet, pièce d'identité) to show, produce; (faire inscrire: candidat) to put forward; (soumettre) to submit ▷ vi: **~ mal/bien** to have an unattractive/a pleasing appearance; **se présenter** vi (sur convocation) to report, come; (se faire connaître) to come forward; (à une élection) to stand; (occasion) to arise; **se ~ à un examen** to sit an exam; **se ~ bien/mal** to look good/not too good

préservatif [pʀezɛʀvatif] nm condom, sheath

préserver [pʀezɛʀve] vt: **~ de** (protéger) to protect from; (sauver) to save from

président [pʀezidɑ̃] nm (Pol) president; (d'une assemblée, Comm) chairman; **~ directeur général (PDG)** chairman and managing director (Brit), chairman and president (US); **~ du jury** (Jur) foreman of the jury; (d'examen) chief examiner

présidentiel, le [pʀezidɑ̃sjɛl] adj presidential; **présidentielles** nfpl presidential election(s)

présider [pʀezide] vt to preside over; (dîner) to be the guest of honour (Brit) ou honor (US) at; **~ à** vt to direct; to govern

présomptueux, -euse [pʀezɔ̃ptɥø, -øz] adj presumptuous

presque [pʀɛsk(ə)] adv almost, nearly; **~ rien** hardly anything; **~ pas** hardly (at all); **~ pas de** hardly any; **personne, ou ~** next to nobody, hardly anyone; **la ~ totalité (de)** almost ou nearly all

presqu'île [pʀɛskil] nf peninsula

pressant, e [pʀesɑ̃, -ɑ̃t] adj urgent; (personne) insistent; **se faire ~** to become insistent

presse [pʀɛs] nf press; (affluence): **heures de ~** busy times; **sous ~** gone to press; **mettre sous ~** to send to press; **avoir une bonne/mauvaise ~** to have a good/bad press; **~ féminine** women's magazines pl; **~ d'information** quality newspapers pl

pressé, e [pʀese] adj in a hurry; (air) hurried;

(besogne) urgent ▷ *nm*: **aller au plus ~** to see to first things first; **être ~ de faire qch** to be in a hurry to do sth; **orange ~e** freshly squeezed orange juice

pressentiment [pʀesɑ̃timɑ̃] *nm* foreboding, premonition

pressentir [pʀesɑ̃tiʀ] *vt* to sense; *(prendre contact avec)* to approach

presse-papiers [pʀɛspapje] *nm inv* paperweight

presser [pʀese] *vt (fruit, éponge)* to squeeze; *(interrupteur, bouton)* to press, push; *(allure, affaire)* to speed up; *(débiteur etc)* to press; *(inciter)*: **~ qn de faire** to urge *ou* press sb to do ▷ *vi* to be urgent; **se presser** *(se hâter)* to hurry (up); *(se grouper)* to crowd; **rien ne presse** there's no hurry; **se ~ contre qn** to squeeze up against sb; **~ le pas** to quicken one's step; **~ qn entre ses bras** to squeeze sb tight

pressing [pʀesiŋ] *nm (repassage)* steam-pressing; *(magasin)* dry-cleaner's

pression [pʀesjɔ̃] *nf* pressure; *(bouton)* press stud (*Brit*), snap fastener; **faire ~ sur** to put pressure on; **sous ~** pressurized, under pressure; *(fig)* keyed up; **~ artérielle** blood pressure

prestance [pʀɛstɑ̃s] *nf* presence, imposing bearing

prestataire [pʀɛstatɛʀ] *nm/f* person receiving benefits; *(Comm)*: **~ de services** provider of services

prestation [pʀɛstasjɔ̃] *nf (allocation)* benefit; *(d'une assurance)* cover *no pl*; *(d'une entreprise)* service provided; *(d'un joueur, artiste)* performance; **~ de serment** taking the oath; **~ de service** provision of a service; **~s familiales** ≈ child benefit

prestidigitateur, -trice [pʀɛstidiʒitatœʀ, -tʀis] *nm/f* conjurer

prestige [pʀɛstiʒ] *nm* prestige

prestigieux, -euse [pʀɛstiʒjø, -øz] *adj* prestigious

présumer [pʀezyme] *vt*: **~ que** to presume *ou* assume that; **~ de** to overrate; **~ qn coupable** to presume sb guilty

prêt, e [pʀɛ, pʀɛt] *adj* ready ▷ *nm* lending *no pl*; *(somme prêtée)* loan; **~ à faire** ready to do; **~ à tout** ready for anything; **~ sur gages** pawnbroking *no pl*

prêt-à-porter *(pl* **prêts-à-porter)** [pʀɛtapɔʀte] *nm* ready-to-wear *ou* off-the-peg (*Brit*) clothes *pl*

prétendre [pʀetɑ̃dʀ(ə)] *vt (affirmer)*: **~ que** to claim that; *(avoir l'intention de)*: **~ faire qch** to mean *ou* intend to do sth; **~ à** *vt (droit, titre)* to lay claim to

prétendu, e [pʀetɑ̃dy] *adj (supposé)* so-called

prétentieux, -euse [pʀetɑ̃sjø, -øz] *adj* pretentious

prétention [pʀetɑ̃sjɔ̃] *nf* pretentiousness; *(exigence, ambition)* claim; **sans ~** unpretentious

prêter [pʀete] *vt (livres, argent)*: **~ qch (à)** to lend sth (to); *(supposer)*: **~ à qn** *(caractère, propos)* to attribute to sb ▷ *vi*: **se prêter** *(tissu, cuir)* to give; **~ à** *(commentaires etc)* to be open to, give rise to;

se ~ à to lend o.s. *(ou* itself) to; *(manigances etc)* to go along with; **~ assistance à** to give help to; **~ attention** to pay attention; **~ serment** to take the oath; **~ l'oreille** to listen

prétexte [pʀetɛkst(ə)] *nm* pretext, excuse; **sous aucun ~** on no account; **sous (le) ~ que/de** on the pretext that/of

prétexter [pʀetɛkste] *vt* to give as a pretext *ou* an excuse

prêtre [pʀɛtʀ(ə)] *nm* priest

preuve [pʀœv] *nf* proof; *(indice)* proof, evidence *no pl*; **jusqu'à ~ du contraire** until proved otherwise; **faire ~ de** to show; **faire ses ~s** to prove o.s. *(ou* itself); **~ matérielle** material evidence

prévaloir [pʀevalwaʀ] *vi* to prevail; **se ~ de** *vt* to take advantage of; *(tirer vanité de)* to pride o.s. on

prévenant, e [pʀevnɑ̃, -ɑ̃t] *adj* thoughtful, kind

prévenir [pʀevniʀ] *vt (éviter)* to avoid, prevent; *(anticiper)* to anticipate; **~ qn (de)** *(avertir)* to warn sb (about); *(informer)* to tell *ou* inform sb (about); **~ qn contre** *(influencer)* to prejudice sb against

préventif, -ive [pʀevɑ̃tif, -iv] *adj* preventive

prévention [pʀevɑ̃sjɔ̃] *nf* prevention; *(préjugé)* prejudice; *(Jur)* custody, detention; **~ routière** road safety

prévenu, e [pʀevny] *nm/f (Jur)* defendant, accused

prévision [pʀevizjɔ̃] *nf*: **~s** predictions; *(météorologiques, économiques)* forecast *sg*; **en ~ de** in anticipation of; **~s météorologiques** *ou* **du temps** weather forecast *sg*

prévoir [pʀevwaʀ] *vt (deviner)* to foresee; *(s'attendre à)* to expect, reckon on; *(prévenir)* to anticipate; *(organiser)* to plan; *(préparer, réserver)* to allow; **prévu pour quatre personnes** designed for four people; **prévu pour 10 h** scheduled for 10 o'clock

prévoyant, e [pʀevwajɑ̃, -ɑ̃t] *vb voir* **prévoir** ▷ *adj* gifted with *(ou* showing) foresight, far-sighted

prévu, e [pʀevy] *pp de* **prévoir**

prier [pʀije] *vi* to pray ▷ *vt (Dieu)* to pray to; *(implorer)* to beg; *(demander)*: **~ qn de faire** to ask sb to do; *(inviter)*: **~ qn à dîner** to invite sb to dinner; **se faire ~** to need coaxing *ou* persuading; **je vous en prie** *(allez-y)* please do; *(de rien)* don't mention it; **je vous prie de faire** please (would you) do

prière [pʀijɛʀ] *nf* prayer; *(demande instante)* plea, entreaty; **"~ de faire ..."** "please do ..."

primaire [pʀimɛʀ] *adj* primary; *(péj: personne)* simple-minded; *(: idées)* simplistic ▷ *nm (Scol)* primary education

prime [pʀim] *nf (bonification)* bonus; *(subside)* allowance; *(Comm: cadeau)* free gift; *(Assurances, Bourse)* premium ▷ *adj*: **de ~ abord** at first glance; **~ de risque** danger money *no pl*; **~ de transport** travel allowance

primer [pʀime] *vt (l'emporter sur)* to prevail over; *(récompenser)* to award a prize to ▷ *vi* to dominate, prevail

primeur [pʀimœʀ] *nf*: **avoir la ~ de** to be the first to hear (*ou* see *etc*); **primeurs** *nfpl* (*fruits, légumes*) early fruits and vegetables; **marchand de ~** greengrocer (*Brit*), produce dealer (*US*)

primevère [pʀimvɛʀ] *nf* primrose

primitif, -ive [pʀimitif, -iv] *adj* primitive; (*originel*) original ▷ *nm/f* primitive

primordial, e, -aux [pʀimɔʀdjal, -o] *adj* essential, primordial

prince [pʀɛ̃s] *nm* prince; **~ charmant** Prince Charming; **~ de Galles** *nm inv* (*tissu*) check cloth; **~ héritier** crown prince

princesse [pʀɛ̃sɛs] *nf* princess

principal, e, -aux [pʀɛ̃sipal, -o] *adj* principal, main ▷ *nm* (*Scol*) head (teacher) (*Brit*), principal (*US*); (*essentiel*) main thing ▷ *nf* (*Ling*): **(proposition) ~e** main clause

principe [pʀɛ̃sip] *nm* principle; **partir du ~ que** to work on the principle *ou* assumption that; **pour le ~** on principle, for the sake of it; **de ~** *adj* (*hostilité*) automatic; (*accord*) in principle; **par ~** on principle; **en ~** (*habituellement*) as a rule; (*théoriquement*) in principle

printemps [pʀɛ̃tɑ̃] *nm* spring; **au ~** in spring

priorité [pʀijɔʀite] *nf* (*Auto*): **avoir la ~ (sur)** to have right of way (over); **~ à droite** right of way to vehicles coming from the right; **en ~** as a (matter of) priority

pris, e [pʀi, pʀiz] *pp de* **prendre** ▷ *adj* (*place*) taken; (*billets*) sold; (*journée, mains*) full; (*personne*) busy; (*crème, ciment*) set; (*Méd: enflammé*): **avoir le nez/la gorge ~(e)** to have a stuffy nose/a bad throat; (*saisi*): **être ~ de peur/de fatigue** to be stricken with fear/overcome with fatigue

prise [pʀiz] *nf* (*d'une ville*) capture; (*Pêche, Chasse*) catch; (*de judo ou catch, point d'appui ou pour empoigner*) hold; (*Élec: fiche*) plug; (: *femelle*) socket; (: *au mur*) point; **en ~** (*Auto*) in gear; **être aux ~s avec** to be grappling with; to be battling with; **lâcher ~** to let go; **donner ~ à** (*fig*) to give rise to; **avoir ~ sur qn** to have a hold over sb; **~ en charge** (*taxe*) pick-up charge; (*par la sécurité sociale*) undertaking to reimburse costs; **~ de contact** initial meeting, first contact; **~ de courant** power point; **~ d'eau** water (supply) point; tap; **~ multiple** adaptor; **~ d'otages** hostage-taking; **~ à partie** (*Jur*) action against a judge; **~ de sang** blood test; **~ de son** sound recording; **~ de tabac** pinch of snuff; **~ de terre** earth; **~ de vue** (*photo*) shot; (*action*): **~ de vue(s)** filming, shooting

priser [pʀize] *vt* (*tabac, héroïne*) to take; (*estimer*) to prize, value ▷ *vi* to take snuff

prison [pʀizɔ̃] *nf* prison; **aller/être en ~** to go to/be in prison *ou* jail; **faire de la ~** to serve time; **être condamné à cinq ans de ~** to be sentenced to five years' imprisonment *ou* five years in prison

prisonnier, -ière [pʀizɔnje, -jɛʀ] *nm/f* prisoner ▷ *adj* captive; **faire qn ~** to take sb prisoner

prit [pʀi] *vb voir* **prendre**

privé, e [pʀive] *adj* private; (*dépourvu*): **~ de** without, lacking; **en ~, dans le ~** in private

priver [pʀive] *vt*: **~ qn de** to deprive sb of; **se ~ de**

to go *ou* do without; **ne pas se ~ de faire** not to refrain from doing

privilège [pʀivilɛʒ] *nm* privilege

prix [pʀi] *nm* (*valeur*) price; (*récompense, Scol*) prize; **mettre à ~** to set a reserve (*Brit*) *ou* an upset (*US*) price on; **au ~ fort** at a very high price; **acheter qch à ~ d'or** to pay a (small) fortune for sth; **hors de ~** exorbitantly priced; **à aucun ~** not at any price; **à tout ~** at all costs; **grand ~** (*Sport*) Grand Prix; **~ d'achat/de vente/de revient** purchasing/selling/cost price; **~ conseillé** manufacturer's recommended price (MRP)

probable [pʀɔbabl(ə)] *adj* likely, probable

probablement [pʀɔbabləmɑ̃] *adv* probably

probant, e [pʀɔbɑ̃, -ɑ̃t] *adj* convincing

problème [pʀɔblɛm] *nm* problem

procédé [pʀɔsede] *nm* (*méthode*) process; (*comportement*) behaviour *no pl* (*Brit*), behavior *no pl* (*US*)

procéder [pʀɔsede] *vi* to proceed; to behave; **~ à** *vt* to carry out

procès [pʀɔsɛ] *nm* (*Jur*) trial; (: *poursuites*) proceedings *pl*; **être en ~ avec** to be involved in a lawsuit with; **faire le ~ de qn/qch** (*fig*) to put sb/sth on trial; **sans autre forme de ~** without further ado

processus [pʀɔsesys] *nm* process

procès-verbal, -aux [pʀɔsɛvɛʀbal, -o] *nm* (*constat*) statement; (*aussi*: **PV**): **avoir un ~** to get a parking ticket; to be booked; (*de réunion*) minutes *pl*

prochain, e [pʀɔʃɛ̃, -ɛn] *adj* next; (*proche*) impending; near ▷ *nm* fellow man; **la ~e fois/ semaine ~e** next time/week; **à la ~e!** (*fam*): **à la ~e fois** see you!, till the next time!; **un ~ jour** (some day) soon

prochainement [pʀɔʃɛnmɑ̃] *adv* soon, shortly

proche [pʀɔʃ] *adj* nearby; (*dans le temps*) imminent; close at hand; (*parent, ami*) close; **proches** *nmpl* (*parents*) close relatives, next of kin; (*amis*): **l'un de ses ~s** one of those close to him (*ou* her); **être ~ (de)** to be near, be close (to); **de ~ en ~** gradually

proclamer [pʀɔklame] *vt* to proclaim; (*résultat d'un examen*) to announce

procuration [pʀɔkyʀasjɔ̃] *nf* proxy; power of attorney; **voter par ~** to vote by proxy

procurer [pʀɔkyʀe] *vt* (*fournir*): **~ qch à qn** to get *ou* obtain sth for sb; (*causer: plaisir etc*): **~ qch à qn** to bring *ou* give sb sth; **se procurer** *vt* to get

procureur [pʀɔkyʀœʀ] *nm* public prosecutor; **~ général** public prosecutor (*in appeal court*)

prodige [pʀɔdiʒ] *nm* (*miracle, merveille*) marvel, wonder; (*personne*) prodigy

prodiguer [pʀɔdige] *vt* (*argent, biens*) to be lavish with; (*soins, attentions*): **~ qch à qn** to lavish sth on sb

producteur, -trice [pʀɔdyktœʀ, -tʀis] *adj*: **~ de blé** wheat-producing; (*Ciné*): **société productrice** film *ou* movie company ▷ *nm/f* producer

productif, -ive [pʀɔdyktif, -iv] *adj* productive

production [pʀɔdyksjɔ̃] nf (gén) production; (rendement) output; (produits) products pl, goods pl; (œuvres): **la ~ dramatique du XVIIe siècle** the plays of the 17th century

productivité [pʀɔdyktivite] nf productivity

produire [pʀɔdɥiʀ] vt, vi to produce; **se produire** vi (acteur) to perform, appear; (événement) to happen, occur

produit, e [pʀɔdɥi, -it] pp de **produire** ▷ nm (gén) product; **~ d'entretien** cleaning product; **~ national brut (PNB)** gross national product (GNP); **~ net** net profit; **~ pour la vaisselle** washing-up (Brit) ou dish-washing (US) liquid; **~ des ventes** income from sales; **~s agricoles** farm produce sg; **~s alimentaires** foodstuffs; **~s de beauté** beauty products, cosmetics

prof [pʀɔf] nm (fam: = professeur) teacher; professor; lecturer

profane [pʀɔfan] adj (Rel) secular; (ignorant, non initié) uninitiated ▷ nm/f layman

proférer [pʀɔfeʀe] vt to utter

professeur, e [pʀɔfesœʀ] nm/f teacher; (titulaire d'une chaire) professor; **~ (de faculté)** (university) lecturer

profession [pʀɔfesjɔ̃] nf (libérale) profession; (gén) occupation; **faire ~ de** (opinion, religion) to profess; **de ~** by profession; **"sans ~"** "unemployed"; (femme mariée) "housewife"

professionnel, le [pʀɔfesjɔnɛl] adj professional ▷ nm/f professional; (ouvrier qualifié) skilled worker

profil [pʀɔfil] nm profile; (d'une voiture) line, contour; **de ~** in profile

profit [pʀɔfi] nm (avantage) benefit, advantage; (Comm, Finance) profit; **au ~ de** in aid of; **tirer** ou **retirer ~ de** to profit from; **mettre à ~** to take advantage of; to turn to good account; **~s et pertes** (Comm) profit and loss(es)

profitable [pʀɔfitabl(ə)] adj beneficial; profitable

profiter [pʀɔfite] vi: **~ de** to take advantage of; to make the most of; **~ de ce que ...** to take advantage of the fact that ...; **~ à** to be of benefit to, benefit; to be profitable to

profond, e [pʀɔfɔ̃, -ɔ̃d] adj deep; (méditation, mépris) profound; **peu ~** (eau, vallée, puits) shallow; (coupure) superficial; **au plus ~ de** in the depths of, at the (very) bottom of; **la France ~e** the heartlands of France

profondément [pʀɔfɔ̃demɑ̃] adv deeply; profoundly

profondeur [pʀɔfɔ̃dœʀ] nf depth

progéniture [pʀɔʒenityʀ] nf offspring inv

programme [pʀɔgʀam] nm programme (Brit), program (US); (TV, Radio) program(me)s pl; (Scol) syllabus, curriculum; (Inform) program; **au ~ de ce soir** (TV) among tonight's program(me)s

programmer [pʀɔgʀame] vt (TV, Radio) to put on, show; (organiser, prévoir) to schedule; (Inform) to program

programmeur, -euse [pʀɔgʀamœʀ, -øz] nm/f (computer) programmer

progrès [pʀɔgʀɛ] nm progress no pl; **faire des/ être en ~** to make/be making progress

progresser [pʀɔgʀese] vi to progress; (troupes etc) to make headway ou progress

progressif, -ive [pʀɔgʀesif, -iv] adj progressive

prohiber [pʀɔibe] vt to prohibit, ban

proie [pʀwa] nf prey no pl; **être la ~ de** to fall prey to; **être en ~ à** (doutes, sentiment) to be prey to; (douleur, mal) to be suffering

projecteur [pʀɔʒɛktœʀ] nm projector; (de théâtre, cirque) spotlight

projectile [pʀɔʒɛktil] nm missile; (d'arme) projectile, bullet (ou shell etc)

projection [pʀɔʒɛksjɔ̃] nf projection; showing; **conférence avec ~s** lecture with slides (ou a film)

projet [pʀɔʒɛ] nm plan; (ébauche) draft; **faire des ~s** to make plans; **~ de loi** bill

projeter [pʀɔʒte] vt (envisager) to plan; (film, photos) to project; (passer) to show; (ombre, lueur) to throw, cast, project; (jeter) to throw up (ou off ou out); **~ de faire qch** to plan to do sth

prolétaire [pʀɔletɛʀ] adj, nm/f proletarian

prolongement [pʀɔlɔ̃ʒmɑ̃] nm extension; **prolongements** nmpl (fig) repercussions, effects; **dans le ~ de** running on from

prolonger [pʀɔlɔ̃ʒe] vt (débat, séjour) to prolong; (délai, billet, rue) to extend; (chose) to be a continuation ou an extension of; **se prolonger** vi to go on

promenade [pʀɔmnad] nf walk (ou drive ou ride); **faire une ~** to go for a walk; **une ~ (à pied)/en voiture/à vélo** a walk/drive/(bicycle) ride

promener [pʀɔmne] vt (personne, chien) to take out for a walk; (fig) to carry around; to trail round; (doigts, regard): **~ qch sur** to run sth over; **se promener** vi (à pied) to go for (ou be out for) a walk; (en voiture) to go for (ou be out for) a drive; (fig): **se ~ sur** to wander over

promesse [pʀɔmɛs] nf promise; **~ d'achat** commitment to buy

promettre [pʀɔmɛtʀ(ə)] vt to promise ▷ vi (récolte, arbre) to look promising; (enfant, musicien) to be promising; **se ~ de faire** to resolve ou mean to do; **~ à qn de faire** to promise sb that one will do

promiscuité [pʀɔmiskɥite] nf crowding; lack of privacy

promontoire [pʀɔmɔ̃twaʀ] nm headland

promoteur, -trice [pʀɔmɔtœʀ, -tʀis] nm/f (instigateur) instigator, promoter; **~ (immobilier)** property developer (Brit), real estate promoter (US)

promotion [pʀɔmɔsjɔ̃] nf (avancement) promotion; (Scol) year (Brit), class; **en ~** (Comm) on promotion, on (special) offer

promouvoir [pʀɔmuvwaʀ] vt to promote

prompt, e [pʀɔ̃, pʀɔ̃t] adj swift, rapid; (intervention, changement) sudden; **~ à faire qch** quick to do sth

prôner [pʀone] vt (louer) to laud, extol; (préconiser) to advocate, commend

pronom [prɔnɔ̃] nm pronoun
prononcer [prɔnɔ̃se] vt (son, mot, jugement) to
pronounce; (dire) to utter; (allocution) to deliver
▷ vi (Jur) to deliver ou give a verdict; ~ **bien/mal**
to have good/poor pronunciation; **se prononcer**
vi to reach a decision, give a verdict; **se ~ sur** to
give an opinion on; **se ~ contre** to come down
against; **ça se prononce comment?** how do
you pronounce this?
prononciation [prɔnɔ̃sjasjɔ̃] nf pronunciation
pronostic [prɔnɔstik] nm (Méd) prognosis; (fig:
aussi: **pronostics**) forecast
propagande [prɔpagɑ̃d] nf propaganda; **faire
de la ~ pour qch** to plug ou push sth
propager [prɔpaʒe] vt to spread; **se propager** vi
to spread; (Physique) to be propagated
prophète [prɔfɛt], **prophétesse** [prɔfetɛs] nm/f
prophet(ess)
prophétie [prɔfesi] nf prophecy
propice [prɔpis] adj favourable (Brit), favorable
(US)
proportion [prɔpɔrsjɔ̃] nf proportion; **il n'y a
aucune ~ entre le prix demandé et le prix réel**
the asking price bears no relation to the real
price; **à ~ de** proportionally to, in proportion
to; **en ~ (de)** in proportion (to); **hors de ~** out of
proportion; **toute(s) ~(s) gardée(s)** making due
allowance(s)
propos [prɔpo] nm (paroles) talk no pl, remark;
(intention, but) intention, aim; (sujet): **à quel ~?**
what about?; **à ~ de** about, regarding; **à tout ~**
for no reason at all; **à ce ~** on that subject, in this
connection; **à ~** adv by the way; (opportunément)
(just) at the right moment; **hors de ~, mal à ~**
adv at the wrong moment
proposer [prɔpoze] vt (suggérer): **~ qch (à qn)/de
faire** to suggest sth (to sb)/doing, propose sth (to
sb)/(to) do; (offrir): **~ qch à qn/de faire** to offer sb
sth/to do; (candidat) to nominate, put forward;
(loi, motion) to propose; **se ~ (pour faire)** to offer
one's services (to do); **se ~ de faire** to intend ou
propose to do
proposition [prɔpozisjɔ̃] nf suggestion;
proposal; offer; (Ling) clause; **sur la ~ de** at the
suggestion of; **~ de loi** private bill
propre [prɔpr(ə)] adj clean; (net) neat, tidy; (qui
ne salit pas: chien, chat) house-trained; (: enfant)
toilet-trained; (fig: honnête) honest; (possessif)
own; (sens) literal; (particulier): **~ à** peculiar to,
characteristic of; (approprié): **~ à** suitable ou
appropriate for; (de nature à): **~ à faire** likely
to do, that will do ▷ nm: **recopier au ~** to
make a fair copy of; (particularité): **le ~ de** the
peculiarity of, the distinctive feature of; **au ~**
(Ling) literally; **appartenir à qn en ~** to belong
to sb (exclusively); **~ à rien** nm/f (péj) good-for-
nothing
proprement [prɔprəmɑ̃] adv cleanly; neatly,
tidily; **à ~ parler** strictly speaking; **le village ~
dit** the actual village, the village itself
propreté [prɔprəte] nf cleanliness, cleanness;
neatness, tidiness

propriétaire [prɔprijetɛr] nm/f owner; (d'hôtel
etc) proprietor(-tress), owner; (pour le locataire)
landlord(-lady); **~ (immobilier)** house-owner;
householder; **~ récoltant** grower; **~ (terrien)**
landowner
propriété [prɔprijete] nf (droit) ownership;
(objet, immeuble etc) property gen no pl; (villa)
residence, property; (terres) property gen no pl,
land gen no pl; (qualité, Chimie, Math) property;
(correction) appropriateness, suitability; **~
artistique et littéraire** artistic and literary
copyright; **~ industrielle** patent rights pl
propulser [prɔpylse] vt (missile) to propel;
(projeter) to hurl, fling
proroger [prɔrʒe] vt to put back, defer; (prolonger)
to extend; (assemblée) to adjourn, prorogue
proscrire [prɔskrir] vt (bannir) to banish;
(interdire) to ban, prohibit
prose [proz] nf prose (style)
prospecter [prɔspɛkte] vt to prospect; (Comm)
to canvass
prospectus [prɔspɛktys] nm (feuille) leaflet;
(dépliant) brochure, leaflet
prospère [prɔspɛr] adj prosperous; (santé,
entreprise) thriving, flourishing
prospérer [prɔspere] vi to thrive
prosterner [prɔstɛrne]: **se prosterner** vi to bow
low, prostrate o.s
prostituée [prɔstitɥe] nf prostitute
prostitution [prɔstitysjɔ̃] nf prostitution
protecteur, -trice [prɔtɛktœr, -tris] adj
protective; (air, ton: péj) patronizing ▷ nm/f
(défenseur) protector; (des arts) patron
protection [prɔtɛksjɔ̃] nf protection; (d'un
personnage influent: aide) patronage; **écran de ~**
protective screen; **~ civile** state-financed civilian
rescue service; **~ maternelle et infantile (PMI)**
social service concerned with child welfare
protéger [prɔteʒe] vt to protect; (aider, patronner:
personne, arts) to be a patron of; (: carrière) to
further; **se ~ de/contre** to protect o.s. from
protège-slip [prɔtɛʒslip] nm panty liner
protéine [prɔtein] nf protein
protestant, e [prɔtɛstɑ̃, -ɑ̃t] adj, nm/f Protestant
protestation [prɔtɛstasjɔ̃] nf (plainte) protest;
(déclaration) protestation, profession
protester [prɔtɛste] vi: **~ (contre)** to protest
(against ou about); **~ de** (son innocence, sa loyauté)
to protest
prothèse [prɔtɛz] nf artificial limb, prosthesis;
~ dentaire (appareil) denture; (science) dental
engineering
protocole [prɔtɔkɔl] nm protocol; (fig) etiquette;
~ d'accord draft treaty; **~ opératoire** (Méd)
operating procedure
proue [pru] nf bow(s pl), prow
prouesse [pruɛs] nf feat
prouver [pruve] vt to prove
provenance [prɔvnɑ̃s] nf origin; (de mot,
coutume) source; **avion en ~ de** plane (arriving)
from
provenir [prɔvnir]: **~ de** vt to come from;

(*résulter de*) to be due to, be the result of
proverbe [pʀɔvɛʀb(ə)] *nm* proverb
province [pʀɔvɛ̃s] *nf* province
proviseur [pʀɔvizœʀ] *nm* ≈ head (teacher) (Brit), ≈ principal (US)
provision [pʀɔvizjɔ̃] *nf* (*réserve*) stock, supply; (*avance: à un avocat, avoué*) retainer, retaining fee; (*Comm*) funds *pl* (in account); reserve; **provisions** *nfpl* (*vivres*) provisions, food *no pl*; **faire ~ de** to stock up with; **placard** *ou* **armoire à ~s** food cupboard
provisoire [pʀɔvizwaʀ] *adj* temporary; (*Jur*) provisional; **mise en liberté ~** release on bail
provisoirement [pʀɔvizwaʀmɑ̃] *adv* temporarily, for the time being
provocant, e [pʀɔvɔkɑ̃, -ɑ̃t] *adj* provocative
provoquer [pʀɔvɔke] *vt* (*défier*) to provoke; (*causer*) to cause, bring about; (*: curiosité*) to arouse, give rise to; (*: aveux*) to prompt, elicit; (*inciter*): **~ qn à** to incite sb to
proxénète [pʀɔksenɛt] *nm* procurer
proximité [pʀɔksimite] *nf* nearness, closeness, proximity; (*dans le temps*) imminence, closeness; **à ~** near *ou* close by; **à ~ de** near (to), close to
prudemment [pʀydamɑ̃] *adv* (*voir* **prudent**) carefully; cautiously; prudently; wisely, sensibly
prudence [pʀydɑ̃s] *nf* carefulness; caution; prudence; **avec ~** carefully; cautiously; wisely; **par (mesure de) ~** as a precaution
prudent, e [pʀydɑ̃, -ɑ̃t] *adj* (*pas téméraire*) careful, cautious, prudent; (*: en général*) safety-conscious; (*sage, conseillé*) wise, sensible; (*réservé*) cautious; **ce n'est pas ~** it's risky; it's not sensible; **soyez ~** take care, be careful
prune [pʀyn] *nf* plum
pruneau, x [pʀyno] *nm* prune
prunelle [pʀynɛl] *nf* pupil; (*œil*) eye; (*Bot*) sloe; (*eau de vie*) sloe gin
prunier [pʀynje] *nm* plum tree
PS *sigle m* ≈ **parti socialiste**; (= *post-scriptum*) PS
psaume [psom] *nm* psalm
pseudonyme [psødɔnim] *nm* (*gén*) fictitious name; (*d'écrivain*) pseudonym, pen name; (*de comédien*) stage name
psychanalyse [psikanaliz] *nf* psychoanalysis
psychiatre [psikjatʀ] *nm/f* psychiatrist
psychiatrique [psikjatʀik] *adj* psychiatric; (*hôpital*) mental, psychiatric
psychique [psiʃik] *adj* psychological
psychologie [psikɔlɔʒi] *nf* psychology
psychologique [psikɔlɔʒik] *adj* psychological
psychologue [psikɔlɔg] *nm/f* psychologist; **être ~** (*fig*) to be a good psychologist
pu [py] *pp de* **pouvoir**
puanteur [pɥɑ̃tœʀ] *nf* stink, stench
pub [pyb] *nf* (*fam*) ≈ **publicité**; **la ~** advertising
public, -ique [pyblik] *adj* public; (*école, instruction*) state *cpd*; (*scrutin*) open ▷ *nm* public; (*assistance*) audience; **en ~** in public; **le grand ~** the general public
publicitaire [pyblisitɛʀ] *adj* advertising *cpd*; (*film, voiture*) publicity *cpd*; (*vente*) promotional

▷ *nm* adman; **rédacteur ~** copywriter
publicité [pyblisite] *nf* (*méthode, profession*) advertising; (*annonce*) advertisement; (*révélations*) publicity
publier [pyblije] *vt* to publish; (*nouvelle*) to publicize, make public
publique [pyblik] *adj f voir* **public**
puce [pys] *nf* flea; (*Inform*) chip; (**marché aux**) **~s** flea market *sg*; **mettre la ~ à l'oreille de qn** to give sb something to think about
pudeur [pydœʀ] *nf* modesty
pudique [pydik] *adj* (*chaste*) modest; (*discret*) discreet
puer [pɥe] (*péj*) *vi* to stink ▷ *vt* to stink of, reek of
puéricultrice [pɥeʀikyltʀis] *nf* ≈ nursery nurse
puéril, e [pɥeʀil] *adj* childish
puis [pɥi] *vb voir* **pouvoir** ▷ *adv* (*ensuite*) then; (*dans une énumération*) next; (*en outre*): **et ~** and (then); **et ~ (après** *ou* **quoi)?** so (what)?
puiser [pɥize] *vt*: **~ (dans)** to draw (from); **~ dans qch** to dip into sth
puisque [pɥisk(ə)] *conj* since; (*valeur intensive*): **~ je te le dis!** I'm telling you!
puissance [pɥisɑ̃s] *nf* power; **en ~** *adj* potential; **deux (à la) ~ cinq** two to the power (of) five
puissant, e [pɥisɑ̃, -ɑ̃t] *adj* powerful
puisse *etc* [pɥis] *vb voir* **pouvoir**
puits [pɥi] *nm* well; **~ artésien** artesian well; **~ de mine** mine shaft; **~ de science** fount of knowledge
pull [pyl], **pull-over** [pylɔvœʀ] *nm* sweater, jumper (Brit)
pulluler [pylyle] *vi* to swarm; (*fig: erreurs*) to abound, proliferate
pulpe [pylp(ə)] *nf* pulp
pulvérisateur [pylveʀizatœʀ] *nm* spray
pulvériser [pylveʀize] *vt* (*solide*) to pulverize; (*liquide*) to spray; (*fig: anéantir: adversaire*) to pulverize; (*: record*) to smash, shatter; (*: argument*) to demolish
punaise [pynɛz] *nf* (*Zool*) bug; (*clou*) drawing pin (Brit), thumb tack (US)
punch [pɔ̃ʃ] *nm* (*boisson*) punch [pœnʃ] (*Boxe*) punching ability; (*fig*) punch
punir [pyniʀ] *vt* to punish; **~ qn de qch** to punish sb for sth
punition [pynisjɔ̃] *nf* punishment
pupille [pypij] *nf* (*Anat*) pupil ▷ *nm/f* (*enfant*) ward; **~ de l'État** child in care; **~ de la Nation** war orphan
pupitre [pypitʀ(ə)] *nm* (*Scol*) desk; (*Rel*) lectern; (*de chef d'orchestre*) rostrum; **~ de commande** control panel
pur, e [pyʀ] *adj* pure; (*vin*) undiluted; (*whisky*) neat; (*intentions*) honourable (Brit), honorable (US) ▷ *nm* (*personne*) hard-liner; **en ~e perte** fruitlessly, to no avail
purée [pyʀe] *nf*: **~ (de pommes de terre)** ≈ mashed potatoes *pl*; **~ de marrons** chestnut purée; **~ de pois** (*fig*) peasoup(er)
purement [pyʀmɑ̃] *adv* purely
purgatoire [pyʀgatwaʀ] *nm* purgatory

purger [pyrʒe] *vt* (*radiateur*) to flush (out), drain; (*circuit hydraulique*) to bleed; (*Méd, Pol*) to purge; (*Jur: peine*) to serve

purin [pyrɛ̃] *nm* liquid manure

pur-sang [pyrsɑ̃] *nm inv* thoroughbred, pure-bred

pus [py] *vb voir* **pouvoir** ▷ *nm* pus

putain [pytɛ̃] *nf* (*fam!*) whore (!); **ce/cette ~ de ...** this bloody (*Brit*) *ou* goddamn (*US*) ... (!)

puzzle [pœzl(ə)] *nm* jigsaw (puzzle)

PV *sigle m* = **procès-verbal**

pyjama [piʒama] *nm* pyjamas *pl*, pair of pyjamas

pyramide [piramid] *nf* pyramid

Pyrénées [pirene] *nfpl*: **les ~** the Pyrenees

Qq

QI *sigle m* (= *quotient intellectuel*) IQ
quadragénaire [kadʀaʒenɛʀ] *nm/f* (*de quarante ans*) forty-year-old; (*de quarante à cinquante ans*) man/woman in his/her forties
quadriller [kadʀije] *vt* (*papier*) to mark out in squares; (*Police: ville, région etc*) to keep under tight control, be positioned throughout
quadruple [k(w)adʀypl(ə)] *nm*: **le ~ de** four times as much as
quadruplés, -ées [k(w)adʀyple] *nm/fpl* quadruplets, quads
quai [ke] *nm* (*de port*) quay; (*de gare*) platform; (*de cours d'eau, canal*) embankment; **être à ~** (*navire*) to be alongside; (*train*) to be in the station; **le Q~ d'Orsay** *offices of the French Ministry for Foreign Affairs*; **le Q~ des Orfèvres** *central police headquarters*
qualification [kalifikasjɔ̃] *nf* qualification
qualifié, e [kalifje] *adj* qualified; (*main d'œuvre*) skilled
qualifier [kalifje] *vt* to qualify; (*appeler*): **~ qch/ qn de** to describe sth/sb as; **se qualifier** *vi* (*Sport*) to qualify; **être qualifié pour** to be qualified for
qualité [kalite] *nf* quality; (*titre, fonction*) position; **en ~ de** in one's capacity as; **ès ~s** in an official capacity; **avoir ~ pour** to have authority to; **de ~** *adj* quality *cpd*; **rapport ~- prix** value (for money)
quand [kɑ̃] *conj, adv* when; **~ je serai riche** when I'm rich; **~ même** (*cependant, pourtant*) nevertheless; (*tout de même*) all the same; really; **~ bien même** even though
quant [kɑ̃]: **~ à** *prép* (*pour ce qui est de*) as for, as to; (*au sujet de*) regarding
quant-à-soi [kɑ̃taswa] *nm*: **rester sur son ~** to remain aloof
quantité [kɑ̃tite] *nf* quantity, amount; (*Science*) quantity; (*grand nombre*): **une** *ou* **des ~(s) de** a great deal of; a lot of; **en grande ~** in large quantities; **en ~s industrielles** in vast amounts; **du travail en ~** a great deal of work; **~ de** many
quarantaine [kaʀɑ̃tɛn] *nf* (*isolement*) quarantine; (*âge*): **avoir la ~** to be around forty; (*nombre*): **une ~ (de)** forty or so, about forty; **mettre en ~** to put into quarantine; (*fig*) to send to Coventry (*Brit*), ostracize
quarante [kaʀɑ̃t] *num* forty

quart [kaʀ] *nm* (*fraction*) quarter; (*surveillance*) watch; (*partie*): **un ~ de poulet/fromage** a chicken quarter/a quarter of a cheese; **un ~ de beurre** a quarter kilo of butter, ≈ a half pound of butter; **un ~ de vin** a quarter litre of wine; **une livre un ~** *ou* **et ~** one and a quarter pounds; **le ~ de** a quarter of; **~ d'heure** quarter of an hour; **deux heures et** *ou* **un ~** (a) quarter past two, (a) quarter after two (*US*); **il est le ~** it's (a) quarter past *ou* after (*US*); **une heure moins le ~** (a) quarter to one, (a) quarter of one (*US*); **il est moins le ~** it's (a) quarter to; **être de/prendre le ~** to keep/take the watch; **~ de tour** quarter turn; **au ~ de tour** (*fig*) straight off; **~s de finale** (*Sport*) quarter finals
quartier [kaʀtje] *nm* (*de ville*) district, area; (*de bœuf, de la lune*) quarter; (*de fruit, fromage*) piece; **quartiers** *nmpl* (*Mil, Blason*) quarters; **cinéma/ salle de ~** local cinema/hall; **avoir ~ libre** to be free; (*Mil*) to have leave from barracks; **ne pas faire de ~** to spare no one, give no quarter; **~ commerçant/résidentiel** shopping/residential area; **~ général (QG)** headquarters (HQ)
quartz [kwaʀts] *nm* quartz
quasi [kazi] *adv* almost, nearly ▷ *préfixe*: **~- certitude** near certainty
quasiment [kazimɑ̃] *adv* almost, very nearly
quatorze [katɔʀz(ə)] *num* fourteen
quatre [katʀ(ə)] *num* four; **à ~ pattes** on all fours; **tiré à ~ épingles** dressed up to the nines; **faire les ~ cent coups** to be a bit wild; **se mettre en ~ pour qn** to go out of one's way for sb; **~ à ~** (*monter, descendre*) four at a time; **à ~ mains** (*jouer*) four-handed
quatre-vingt-dix [katʀəvɛ̃dis] *num* ninety
quatre-vingts [katʀəvɛ̃] *num* eighty
quatre-vingt-un *num* eighty-one
quatrième [katʀijɛm] *num* fourth
quatuor [kwatɥɔʀ] *nm* quartet(te)
que [kə] *conj* **1** (*introduisant complétive*) that; **il sait ~ tu es là** he knows (that) you're here; **je veux ~ tu acceptes** I want you to accept; **il a dit ~ oui** he said he would (*ou* it was *etc*)
2 (*reprise d'autres conjonctions*): **quand il rentrera et qu'il aura mangé** when he gets back and (when) he has eaten; **si vous y allez ou ~ vous …** if you go there or if you …

3 (en tête de phrase: hypothèse, souhait etc): **qu'il le veuille ou non** whether he likes it or not; **qu'il fasse ce qu'il voudra!** let him do as he pleases!
4 (but): **tenez-le qu'il ne tombe pas** hold it so (that) it doesn't fall
5 (après comparatif) than; as; voir aussi **plus; aussi; autant** etc
6 (seulement): **ne ... ~** only; **il ne boit ~ de l'eau** he only drinks water
7 (temps): **elle venait à peine de sortir qu'il se mit à pleuvoir** she had just gone out when it started to rain, no sooner had she gone out than it started to rain; **il y a quatre ans qu'il est parti** it is four years since he left, he left four years ago
▷ pron (exclamation): **qu'il** ou **qu'est-ce qu'il est bête/court vite!** he's so silly!/he runs so fast!; **~ de livres!** what a lot of books!
▷ pron **1** (relatif: personne) whom; (: chose) that, which; **l'homme ~ je vois** the man (whom) I see; **le livre ~ tu vois** the book (that ou which) you see; **un jour ~ j'étais ...** a day when I was ..
2 (interrogatif) what; **~ fais-tu?, qu'est-ce ~ tu fais?** what are you doing?; **qu'est-ce ~ c'est?** what is it?, what's that?; **~ faire?** what can one do?; **~ préfères-tu, celui-ci ou celui-là?** which (one) do you prefer, this one or that one?
Québec [kebɛk] n (ville) Quebec ▷ nm: **le ~** Quebec (Province)
québécois, e [kebekwa, -waz] adj Quebec cpd ▷ nm (Ling) Quebec French ▷ nm/f: **Q~, e** Quebecois, Quebec(k)er
quel, quelle [kɛl] adj **1** (interrogatif: personne) who; (: chose) what; which; **~ est cet homme?** who is this man?; **~ est ce livre?** what is this book?; **~ livre/homme?** what book/man?; (parmi un certain choix) which book/man?; **~s acteurs préférez-vous?** which actors do you prefer?; **dans ~s pays êtes-vous allé?** which ou what countries did you go to?
2 (exclamatif): **~le surprise/coïncidence!** what a surprise/coincidence!
3: **~(le) que soit le coupable** whoever is guilty; **~ que soit votre avis** whatever your opinion (may be)
quelconque [kɛlkɔ̃k] adj (médiocre) indifferent, poor; (sans attrait) ordinary, plain; (indéfini): **un ami/prétexte ~** some friend/pretext or other; **un livre ~ suffira** any book will do; **pour une raison ~** for some reason (or other)
quelque [kɛlkə] adj **1** some; a few; (tournure interrogative) any; **~ espoir** some hope; **il a ~s amis** he has a few ou some friends; **a-t-il ~s amis?** has he any friends?; **les ~s livres qui** the few books which; **20 kg et ~(s)** a bit over 20 kg; **il habite à ~ distance d'ici** he lives some distance ou way (away) from here
2: **~ ... que** whatever, whichever; **~ livre qu'il choisisse** whatever (ou whichever) book he chooses; **par ~ temps qu'il fasse** whatever the weather
3: **~ chose** something; (tournure interrogative)

anything; **~ chose d'autre** something else; anything else; **y être pour ~ chose** to have something to do with it; **faire ~ chose à qn** to have an effect on sb, do something to sb; **~ part** somewhere; anywhere; **en ~ sorte** as it were
▷ adv **1** (environ): **~ 100 mètres** some 100 metres
2: **~ peu** rather, somewhat
quelquefois [kɛlkəfwa] adv sometimes
quelques-uns, --unes [kɛlkəzœ̃, -yn] pron some, a few; **~ des lecteurs** some of the readers
quelqu'un [kɛlkœ̃] pron someone, somebody; (tournure interrogative ou négative+) anyone ou anybody; **quelqu'un d'autre** someone ou somebody else; anybody else
quémander [kemɑ̃de] vt to beg for
qu'en dira-t-on [kɑ̃diratɔ̃] nm inv: **le qu'en dira-t-on** gossip, what people say
querelle [kərɛl] nf quarrel; **chercher ~ à qn** to pick a quarrel with sb
quereller [kərele]: **se quereller** vi to quarrel
qu'est-ce que [kɛskə] voir que
qu'est-ce qui [kɛski] voir qui
question [kɛstjɔ̃] nf (gén) question; (fig) matter; issue; **il a été ~ de** we (ou they) spoke about; **il est ~ de les emprisonner** there's talk of them being jailed; **c'est une ~ de temps** it's a matter ou question of time; **de quoi est-il ~?** what is it about?; **il n'en est pas ~** there's no question of it; **en ~** in question; **hors de ~** out of the question; **je ne me suis jamais posé la ~** I've never thought about it; **(re)mettre en ~** (autorité, science) to question; **poser la ~ de confiance** (Pol) to ask for a vote of confidence; **~ piège** (d'apparence facile) trick question; (pour nuire) loaded question; **~ subsidiaire** tiebreaker
questionnaire [kɛstjɔnɛr] nm questionnaire
questionner [kɛstjɔne] vt to question
quête [kɛt] nf (collecte) collection; (recherche) quest, search; **faire la ~** (à l'église) to take the collection; (artiste) to pass the hat round; **se mettre en ~ de qch** to go in search of sth
quetsche [kwɛtʃ(ə)] nf damson
queue [kø] nf tail; (fig: du classement) bottom; (: de poêle) handle; (: de fruit, feuille) stalk; (: de train, colonne, file) rear; (file: de personnes) queue (Brit), line (US); **en ~ (de train)** at the rear (of the train); **faire la ~** to queue (up) (Brit), line up (US); **se mettre à la ~** to join the queue ou line; **histoire sans ~ ni tête** cock and bull story; **à la ~ leu leu** in single file; (fig) one after the other; **~ de cheval** ponytail; **~ de poisson: faire une queue de poisson à qn** (Auto) to cut in front of sb; **finir en ~ de poisson** (film) to come to an abrupt end
qui [ki] pron (personne) who; (avec préposition) whom; (chose, animal) which, that; (interrogatif indirect: sujet): **je me demande ~ est là?** I wonder who is there?; (: objet): **elle ne sait à ~ se plaindre** she doesn't know who to complain to ou to whom to complain; **qu'est-ce ~ est sur la table?** what is on the table?; **à ~ est ce sac?** whose bag is this?; **à ~ parlais-tu?** who were

you talking to?, to whom were you talking?;
chez ~ allez-vous? whose house are you going
to?; **amenez ~ vous voulez** bring who(ever) you
like; **~ est-ce ~ ...?** who?; **~ est-ce que ...?** who?;
whom?; **~ que ce soit** whoever it may be
quiche [kiʃ] *nf* quiche; **~ lorraine** quiche
Lorraine
quiconque [kikɔ̃k] *pron* (*celui qui*) whoever,
anyone who; (*n'importe qui, personne*) anyone,
anybody
quiétude [kjetyd] *nf* (*d'un lieu*) quiet, tranquillity;
(*d'une personne*) peace (of mind), serenity; **en
toute ~** in complete peace; (*mentale*) with
complete peace of mind
quille [kij] *nf* ninepin, skittle (Brit); (Navig: *d'un
bateau*) keel; **(jeu de) ~s** ninepins *sg*, skittles *sg*
(Brit)
quincaillerie [kɛ̃kajʀi] *nf* (*ustensiles, métier*)
hardware, ironmongery (Brit); (*magasin*)
hardware shop *ou* store (US), ironmonger's (Brit)
quincaillier, -ière [kɛ̃kaje, -jɛʀ] *nm/f* hardware
dealer, ironmonger (Brit)
quinquagénaire [kɛ̃kaʒenɛʀ] *nm/f* (*de cinquante
ans*) fifty-year old; (*de cinquante à soixante ans*)
man/woman in his/her fifties
quinquennat [kɛ̃kena] *nm* *five year term of office (of
French President)*
quintal, -aux [kɛ̃tal, -o] *nm* quintal (100 kg)
quinte [kɛ̃t] *nf*: **~ (de toux)** coughing fit
quintuple [kɛ̃typl(ə)] *nm*: **le ~ de** five times as
much as
quintuplés, -ées [kɛ̃typle] *nm/fpl* quintuplets,
quins
quinzaine [kɛ̃zɛn] *nf*: **une ~ (de)** about fifteen,
fifteen or so; **une ~ (de jours)** (*deux semaines*) a
fortnight (Brit), two weeks; **~ publicitaire** *ou*
commerciale (two-week) sale
quinze [kɛ̃z] *num* fifteen; **demain en ~** a
fortnight (Brit) *ou* two weeks tomorrow; **dans
~ jours** in a fortnight('s time) (Brit), in two
weeks(' time)

quiproquo [kipʀɔko] *nm* (*méprise sur une
personne*) mistake; (*malentendu sur un sujet*)
misunderstanding; (*Théât*) (case of) mistaken
identity
quittance [kitɑ̃s] *nf* (*reçu*) receipt; (*facture*) bill
quitte [kit] *adj*: **être ~ envers qn** to be no longer
in sb's debt; (*fig*) to be quits with sb; **être ~ de**
(*obligation*) to be clear of; **en être ~ à bon compte**
to have got off lightly; **~ à faire** even if it means
doing; **~ ou double** (*jeu*) double or quits; (*fig*):
c'est du ~ ou double it's a big risk
quitter [kite] *vt* to leave; (*espoir, illusion*) to give
up; (*vêtement*) to take off; **se quitter** (*couples,
interlocuteurs*) to part; **ne quittez pas** (*au téléphone*)
hold the line; **ne pas ~ qn d'une semelle** to
stick to sb like glue
qui-vive [kiviv] *nm inv*: **être sur le ~** to be on the
alert
quoi [kwa] *pron* (*interrogatif*) what; **~ de neuf** *ou*
de nouveau? what's new *ou* the news?; **as-tu
de ~ écrire?** have you anything to write with?;
il n'a pas de ~ se l'acheter he can't afford it, he
hasn't got the money to buy it; **il y a de ~ être
fier** that's something to be proud of; **"il n'y a
pas de ~"** "(please) don't mention it", "not at
all"; **~ qu'il arrive** whatever happens; **~ qu'il
en soit** be that as it may; **~ que ce soit** anything
at all; **en ~ puis-je vous aider?** how can I help
you?; **à ~ bon?** what's the use *ou* point?; **et puis
~ encore!** what(ever) next!; **~ faire?** what's to be
done?; **sans ~** (*ou sinon*) otherwise
quoique [kwak(ə)] *conj* (al)though
quote-part [kɔtpaʀ] *nf* share
quotidien, ne [kɔtidjɛ̃, -ɛn] *adj* (*journalier*) daily;
(*banal*) ordinary, everyday ▷ *nm* (*journal*) daily
(paper); (*vie quotidienne*) daily life, day-to-day
existence; **les grands ~s** the big (national)
dailies
quotidiennement [kɔtidjɛnmɑ̃] *adv* daily, every
day

Rr

rab [ʀab] (*fam*), **rabiot** [ʀabjo] *nm* extra, more
rabâcher [ʀabɑʃe] *vi* to harp on ▷ *vt* keep on repeating
rabais [ʀabɛ] *nm* reduction, discount; **au ~** at a reduction *ou* discount
rabaisser [ʀabese] *vt* (*rabattre*) to reduce; (*dénigrer*) to belittle
rabat-joie [ʀabaʒwa] *nm/f inv* killjoy (Brit), spoilsport
rabattre [ʀabatʀ(ə)] *vt* (*couvercle, siège*) to pull down; (*col*) to turn down; (*couture*) to stitch down; (*gibier*) to drive; (*somme d'un prix*) to deduct, take off; (*orgueil, prétentions*) to humble; (*Tricot*) to decrease; **se rabattre** *vi* (*bords, couvercle*) to fall shut; (*véhicule, coureur*) to cut in; **se ~ sur** (*accepter*) to fall back on
rabbin [ʀabɛ̃] *nm* rabbi
râblé, e [ʀɑble] *adj* broad-backed, stocky
rabot [ʀabo] *nm* plane
rabougri, e [ʀabugʀi] *adj* stunted
rabrouer [ʀabʀue] *vt* to snub, rebuff
racaille [ʀakɑj] *nf* (*péj*) rabble, riffraff
raccommoder [ʀakɔmɔde] *vt* to mend, repair; (*chaussette etc*) to darn; (*fam: réconcilier: amis, ménage*) to bring together again; **se ~ (avec)** (*fam*) to patch it up (with)
raccompagner [ʀakɔ̃paɲe] *vt* to take *ou* see back
raccord [ʀakɔʀ] *nm* link; **~ de maçonnerie** pointing *no pl*; **~ de peinture** join; touch-up
raccorder [ʀakɔʀde] *vt* to join (up), link up; (*pont etc*) to connect, link; **se ~ à** to join up with; (*fig: se rattacher à*) to tie in with; **~ au réseau du téléphone** to connect to the telephone service
raccourci [ʀakuʀsi] *nm* short cut; **en ~** in brief
raccourcir [ʀakuʀsiʀ] *vt* to shorten ▷ *vi* (*vêtement*) to shrink
raccrocher [ʀakʀɔʃe] *vt* (*tableau, vêtement*) to hang back up; (*récepteur*) to put down; (*fig: affaire*) to save ▷ *vi* (*Tél*) to hang up, ring off; **se ~ à** to cling to, hang on to; **ne raccrochez pas** (*Tél*) hold on, don't hang up
race [ʀas] *nf* race; (*d'animaux, fig: espèce*) breed; (*ascendance, origine*) stock, race; **de ~** *adj* purebred, pedigree
rachat [ʀaʃa] *nm* buying; buying back; redemption; atonement
racheter [ʀaʃte] *vt* (*article perdu*) to buy another;

(*davantage*): **~ du lait/trois œufs** to buy more milk/another three eggs *ou* three more eggs; (*après avoir vendu*) to buy back; (*d'occasion*) to buy; (*Comm: part, firme*) to buy up; (*: pension, rente*) to redeem; (*Rel: pécheur*) to redeem; (*: péché*) to atone for, expiate; (*mauvaise conduite, oubli, défaut*) to make up for; **se racheter** (*Rel*) to redeem o.s.; (*gén*) to make amends, make up for it
racial, e, -aux [ʀasjal, -o] *adj* racial
racine [ʀasin] *nf* root; (*fig: attache*) roots *pl*; **~ carrée/cubique** square/cube root; **prendre ~** (*fig*) to take root; to put down roots
raciste [ʀasist(ə)] *adj, nm/f* racist, racialist
racket [ʀaket] *nm* racketeering *no pl*
raclée [ʀɑkle] *nf* (*fam*) hiding, thrashing
racler [ʀɑkle] *vt* (*os, plat*) to scrape; (*tache, boue*) to scrape off; (*fig: instrument*) to scrape on; (*chose: frotter contre*) to scrape (against)
racoler [ʀakɔle] *vt* (*attirer: prostituée*) to solicit; (*: parti, marchand*) to tout for; (*attraper*) to pick up
racontars [ʀakɔ̃taʀ] *nmpl* stories, gossip *sg*
raconter [ʀakɔ̃te] *vt*: **~ (à qn)** (*décrire*) to relate (to sb), tell (sb) about; (*dire*) to tell (sb)
racorni, e [ʀakɔʀni] *adj* hard(ened)
radar [ʀadaʀ] *nm* radar; **système ~** radar system; **écran ~** radar screen
rade [ʀad] *nf* (*natural*) harbour; **en ~ de Toulon** in Toulon harbour; **rester en ~** (*fig*) to be left stranded
radeau, x [ʀado] *nm* raft; **~ de sauvetage** life raft
radiateur [ʀadjatœʀ] *nm* radiator, heater; (*Auto*) radiator; **~ électrique/à gaz** electric/gas heater *ou* fire
radiation [ʀadjasjɔ̃] *nf* (*d'un nom etc*) striking off *no pl*; (*Physique*) radiation
radical, e, -aux [ʀadikal, -o] *adj* radical ▷ *nm* (*Ling*) stem; (*Math*) root sign; (*Pol*) radical
radier [ʀadje] *vt* to strike off
radieux, -euse [ʀadjø, -øz] *adj* (*visage, personne*) radiant; (*journée, soleil*) brilliant, glorious
radin, e [ʀadɛ̃, -in] *adj* (*fam*) stingy
radio [ʀadjo] *nf* radio; (*Méd*) X-ray ▷ *nm* (*personne*) radio operator; **à la ~** on the radio; **avoir la ~** to have a radio; **passer à la ~** to be on the radio; **se faire faire une ~/une ~ des poumons** to have an X-ray/a chest X-ray

radioactif, -ive [Radjɔaktif, -iv] adj radioactive

radiocassette [Radjɔkaset] nf cassette radio

radiodiffuser [Radjɔdifyze] vt to broadcast

radiographie [Radjɔgrafi] nf radiography; (photo) X-ray photograph, radiograph

radiophonique [Radjɔfɔnik] adj: **programme/émission/jeu** ~ radio programme/broadcast/game

radio-réveil [Radjɔrevej] nm clock radio

radis [Radi] nm radish; ~ **noir** horseradish no pl

radoter [Radɔte] vi to ramble on

radoucir [Radusir]: **se radoucir** vi (se réchauffer) to become milder; (se calmer) to calm down; to soften

rafale [Rafal] nf (vent) gust (of wind); (de balles, d'applaudissements) burst; ~ **de mitrailleuse** burst of machine-gun fire

raffermir [Rafermir] vt: **se raffermir** vi (tissus, muscle) to firm up; (fig) to strengthen

raffiner [Rafine] vt to refine

raffinerie [Rafinri] nf refinery

raffoler [Rafɔle]: ~ **de** vt to be very keen on

rafistoler [Rafistɔle] vt (fam) to patch up

rafle [Rafl(ə)] nf (de police) roundup, raid

rafler [Rafle] vt (fam) to swipe, nick

rafraîchir [Rafreʃir] vt (atmosphère, température) to cool (down); (aussi: **mettre à rafraîchir**) to chill; (air, eau) to freshen up; (: boisson) to refresh; (fig: rénover) to brighten up ▷ vi: **mettre du vin/une boisson à** ~ to chill wine/a drink; **se rafraîchir** to grow cooler; to freshen up; (personne: en buvant etc) to refresh o.s.; ~ **la mémoire à qn** to refresh sb's memory

rafraîchissant, e [Rafreʃisã, -ãt] adj refreshing

rafraîchissement [Rafreʃismã] nm cooling; (boisson) cool drink; **rafraîchissements** nmpl (boissons, fruits etc) refreshments

rage [Raʒ] nf (Méd): **la** ~ rabies; (fureur) rage, fury; **faire** ~ to rage; ~ **de dents** (raging) toothache

ragot [Rago] nm (fam) malicious gossip no pl

ragoût [Ragu] nm (plat) stew

raide [Red] adj (tendu) taut, tight; (escarpé) steep; (droit: cheveux) straight; (ankylosé, dur, guindé) stiff; (fam: cher) steep, stiff; (: sans argent) flat broke; (osé, licencieux) daring ▷ adv (en pente) steeply; ~ **mort** stone dead

raideur [Redœr] nf steepness; stiffness

raidir [Redir] vt (muscles) to stiffen; (câble) to pull taut, tighten; **se raidir** vi to stiffen; to become taut; (personne: se crisper) to tense up; (: devenir intransigeant) to harden

raie [Re] nf (Zool) skate, ray; (rayure) stripe; (des cheveux) parting

raifort [Refɔr] nm horseradish

rail [Raj] nm (barre d'acier) rail; (chemins de fer) railways pl (Brit), railroads pl (US); **les** ~**s** (la voie ferrée) the rails, the track sg; **par** ~ by rail; ~ **conducteur** live ou conductor rail

railler [Raje] vt to scoff at, jeer at

rainure [Renyr] nf groove; slot

raisin [Rezɛ̃] nm (aussi: **raisins**) grapes pl; (variété): ~ **blanc/noir** white (ou green)/black grape; ~

muscat muscat grape; ~**s secs** raisins

raison [Rezɔ̃] nf reason; **avoir** ~ to be right; **donner** ~ **à qn** (personne) to agree with sb; (fait) to prove sb right; **avoir** ~ **de qn/qch** to get the better of sb/sth; **se faire une** ~ to learn to live with it; **perdre la** ~ to become insane; (fig) to take leave of one's senses; **recouvrer la** ~ to come to one's senses; **ramener qn à la** ~ to make sb see sense; **demander** ~ **à qn de** (affront etc) to demand satisfaction from sb for; **entendre** ~ to listen to reason, see reason; **plus que de** ~ too much, more than is reasonable; ~ **de plus** all the more reason; **à plus forte** ~ all the more so; **en** ~ **de** (à cause de) because of; (à proportion de) in proportion to; **à** ~ **de** at the rate of; ~ **d'État** reason of state; ~ **d'être** raison d'être; ~ **sociale** corporate name

raisonnable [Rezɔnabl(ə)] adj reasonable, sensible

raisonnement [Rezɔnmã] nm reasoning; arguing; argument

raisonner [Rezɔne] vi (penser) to reason; (argumenter, discuter) to argue ▷ vt (personne) to reason with; (attitude: justifier) to reason out; **se raisonner** to reason with oneself

rajeunir [Raʒœnir] vt (coiffure, robe): ~ **qn** to make sb look younger; (cure etc) to rejuvenate; (fig: rafraîchir) to brighten up; (: moderniser) to give a new look to; (: en recrutant) to inject new blood into ▷ vi (personne) to become (ou look) younger; (entreprise, quartier) to be modernized

rajouter [Raʒute] vt (commentaire) to add; ~ **du sel/un œuf** to add some more salt/another egg; ~ **que** to add that; **en** ~ to lay it on thick

rajuster [Raʒyste] vt (vêtement) to straighten, tidy; (salaires) to adjust; (machine) to readjust; **se rajuster** to tidy ou straighten o.s. up

ralenti [Ralãti] nm: **au** ~ (Ciné) in slow motion; (fig) at a slower pace; **tourner au** ~ (Auto) to tick over, idle

ralentir [Ralãtir] vt, vi: **se ralentir** vi to slow down

râler [Rale] vi to groan; (fam) to grouse, moan (and groan)

rallier [Ralje] vt (rassembler) to rally; (rejoindre) to rejoin; (gagner à sa cause) to win over; **se** ~ **à** (avis) to come over ou round to

rallonge [Ralɔ̃ʒ] nf (de table) (extra) leaf; (argent etc) extra no pl; (Élec) extension (cable ou flex); (fig: de crédit etc) extension

rallonger [Ralɔ̃ʒe] vt to lengthen

rallye [Rali] nm rally; (Pol) march

ramassage [Ramasaʒ] nm: ~ **scolaire** school bus service

ramassé, e [Ramase] adj (trapu) squat, stocky; (concis: expression etc) compact

ramasser [Ramase] vt (objet tombé ou par terre: fam) to pick up; (recueillir) to collect; (récolter) to gather; (: pommes de terre) to lift; **se ramasser** vi (sur soi-même) to huddle up; to crouch

ramassis [Ramasi] nm (péj: de gens) bunch; (: de choses) jumble

rambarde [ʀɑ̃baʀd(ə)] *nf* guardrail
rame [ʀam] *nf* (*aviron*) oar; (*de métro*) train; (*de papier*) ream; **~ de haricots** bean support; **faire force de ~s** to row hard
rameau, x [ʀamo] *nm* (*small*) branch; (*fig*) branch; **les R~x** (*Rel*) Palm Sunday *sg*
ramener [ʀamne] *vt* to bring back; (*reconduire*) to take back; (*rabattre: couverture, visière*): **~ qch sur** to pull sth back over; **~ qch à** (*réduire à, Math*) to reduce sth to; **~ qn à la vie/raison** to bring sb back to life/bring sb to his (*ou* her) senses; **se ramener** *vi* (*fam*) to roll *ou* turn up; **se ~ à** (*se réduire à*) to come *ou* boil down to
ramer [ʀame] *vi* to row
ramollir [ʀamɔliʀ] *vt* to soften; **se ramollir** *vi* (*os, tissus*) to get (*ou* go) soft; (*beurre, asphalte*) to soften
ramoner [ʀamɔne] *vt* (*cheminée*) to sweep; (*pipe*) to clean
rampe [ʀɑ̃p] *nf* (*d'escalier*) banister(s *pl*); (*dans un garage, d'un terrain*) ramp; (*Théât*): **la ~** the footlights *pl*; (*lampes: lumineuse, de balisage*) floodlights *pl*; **passer la ~** (*toucher le public*) to get across to the audience; **~ de lancement** launching pad
ramper [ʀɑ̃pe] *vi* (*reptile, animal*) to crawl; (*plante*) to creep
rancard [ʀɑ̃kaʀ] *nm* (*fam*) date; tip
rancart [ʀɑ̃kaʀ] *nm*: **mettre au ~** (*article, projet*) to scrap; (*personne*) to put on the scrapheap
rance [ʀɑ̃s] *adj* rancid
rancœur [ʀɑ̃kœʀ] *nf* rancour (*Brit*), rancor (*US*), resentment
rançon [ʀɑ̃sɔ̃] *nf* ransom; (*fig*): **la ~ du succès** *etc* the price of success *etc*
rancune [ʀɑ̃kyn] *nf* grudge, rancour (*Brit*), rancor (*US*); **garder ~ à qn (de qch)** to bear sb a grudge (for sth); **sans ~!** no hard feelings!
rancunier, -ière [ʀɑ̃kynje, -jɛʀ] *adj* vindictive, spiteful
randonnée [ʀɑ̃dɔne] *nf* ride; (*à pied*) walk, ramble; hike, hiking *no pl*
rang [ʀɑ̃] *nm* (*rangée*) row; (*de perles*) row, string, rope; (*grade, condition sociale, classement*) rank; **rangs** *nmpl* (*Mil*) ranks; **se mettre en ~s/sur un ~** to get into *ou* form rows/a line; **sur trois ~s** (lined up) three deep; **se mettre en ~s par quatre** to form fours *ou* rows of four; **se mettre sur les ~s** (*fig*) to get into the running; **au premier ~** in the first row; (*fig*) ranking first; **rentrer dans le ~** to get into line; **au ~ de** (*au nombre de*) among (the ranks of); **avoir ~ de** to hold the rank of
rangé, e [ʀɑ̃ʒe] *adj* (*sérieux*) orderly, steady
rangée [ʀɑ̃ʒe] *nf* row
ranger [ʀɑ̃ʒe] *vt* (*classer, grouper*) to order, arrange; (*mettre à sa place*) to put away; (*voiture dans la rue*) to park; (*mettre de l'ordre dans*) to tidy up; (*arranger, disposer: en cercle etc*) to arrange; (*fig: classer*): **~ qn/qch parmi** to rank sb/sth among; **se ranger** *vi* (*se placer, se disposer: autour d'une table etc*) to take one's place, sit round; (*véhicule, conducteur: s'écarter*) to pull over; (*: s'arrêter*) to pull in; (*piéton*)

to step aside; (*s'assagir*) to settle down; **se ~ à** (*avis*) to come round to, fall in with
ranimer [ʀanime] *vt* (*personne évanouie*) to bring round; (*revigorer: forces, courage*) to restore; (*réconforter: troupes etc*) to kindle new life in; (*douleur, souvenir*) to revive; (*feu*) to rekindle
rap [ʀap] *nm* rap (music)
rapace [ʀapas] *nm* bird of prey ▷ *adj* (*péj*) rapacious, grasping; **~ diurne/nocturne** diurnal/nocturnal bird of prey
râpe [ʀɑp] *nf* (*Culin*) grater; (*à bois*) rasp
râper [ʀɑpe] *vt* (*Culin*) to grate; (*gratter, racler*) to rasp
rapetisser [ʀaptise] *vt*: **~ qch** to shorten sth; to make sth look smaller ▷ *vi*: **se rapetisser** *vi* to shrink
rapide [ʀapid] *adj* fast; (*prompt*) quick; (*intelligence*) quick ▷ *nm* express (train); (*de cours d'eau*) rapid
rapidement [ʀapidmɑ̃] *adv* fast; quickly
rapiécer [ʀapjese] *vt* to patch
rappel [ʀapɛl] *nm* (*d'un ambassadeur, Mil*) recall; (*Théât*) curtain call; (*Méd: vaccination*) booster; (*Admin: de salaire*) back pay *no pl*; (*d'une aventure, d'un nom*) reminder; (*de limitation de vitesse: sur écriteau*) speed limit sign (*reminder*); (*Tech*) return; (*Navig*) sitting out; (*Alpinisme: aussi: **rappel de corde***) abseiling *no pl*, roping down *no pl*; abseil; **~ à l'ordre** call to order
rappeler [ʀaple] *vt* (*pour faire revenir, retéléphoner*) to call back; (*ambassadeur, Mil*) to recall; (*acteur*) to call back (onto the stage); (*faire se souvenir*): **~ qch à qn** to remind sb of sth; **se rappeler** *vt* (*se souvenir de*) to remember, recall; **~ qn à la vie** to bring sb back to life; **~ qn à la décence** to recall sb to a sense of decency; **ça rappelle la Provence** it's reminiscent of Provence, it reminds you of Provence; **se ~ que...** to remember that...
rapport [ʀapɔʀ] *nm* (*compte rendu*) report; (*profit*) yield, return; revenue; (*lien, analogie*) relationship; (*corrélation*) connection; (*proportion: Math, Tech*) ratio; **rapports** *nmpl* (*entre personnes, pays*) relations; **avoir ~ à** to have something to do with, concern; **être en ~ avec** (*idée de corrélation*) to be related to; **être/se mettre en ~ avec qn** to be/get in touch with sb; **par ~ à** (*comparé à*) in relation to; (*à propos de*) with regard to; **sous le ~ de** from the point of view of; **sous tous (les) ~s** in all respects; **~s (sexuels)** (sexual) intercourse *sg*; **~ qualité-prix** value (for money)
rapporter [ʀapɔʀte] *vt* (*rendre, ramener*) to bring back; (*apporter davantage*) to bring more; (*Couture*) to sew on; (*investissement*) to yield; (*: activité*) to bring in; (*relater*) to report; (*Jur: annuler*) to revoke ▷ *vi* (*investissement*) to give a good return *ou* yield; (*activité*) to be very profitable; (*péj: moucharder*) to tell; **~ qch à** (*fig: rattacher*) to relate sth to; **se ~ à** (*correspondre à*) to relate to; **s'en ~ à** to rely on
rapporteur, -euse [ʀapɔʀtœʀ, -øz] *nm/f* (*de procès, commission*) reporter; (*péj*) telltale ▷ *nm* (*Géom*) protractor

rapprochement [ʀapʀɔʃmɑ̃] *nm* (*réconciliation: de nations, familles*) reconciliation; (*analogie, rapport*) parallel

rapprocher [ʀapʀɔʃe] *vt* (*chaise d'une table*): ~ **qch (de)** to bring sth closer (to); (*deux objets*) to bring closer together; (*réunir*) to bring together; (*comparer*) to establish a parallel between; **se rapprocher** *vi* to draw closer *ou* nearer; (*fig: familles, pays*) to come together; to come closer together; **se ~ de** to come closer to; (*présenter une analogie avec*) à ~ close to

rapt [ʀapt] *nm* abduction

raquette [ʀaket] *nf* (*de tennis*) racket; (*de ping-pong*) bat; (*à neige*) snowshoe

rare [ʀaʀ] *adj* rare; (*cheveux, herbe*) sparse; **il est ~ que** it's rare that, it's unusual that; **se faire ~** to become scarce; (*fig: personne*) to make oneself scarce

rarement [ʀaʀmɑ̃] *adv* rarely, seldom

ras, e [ʀɑ, ʀɑz] *adj* (*tête, cheveux*) close-cropped; (*poil, herbe*) short; (*mesure, cuillère*) level ▷ *adv* short; **faire table ~e** to make a clean sweep; **en ~e campagne** in open country; **à ~ bords** to the brim; **au ~ de** level with; **en avoir ~ le bol** (*fam*) to be fed up; **~ du cou** *adj* (*pull, robe*) crew-neck

rasade [ʀɑzad] *nf* glassful

raser [ʀɑze] *vt* (*barbe, cheveux*) to shave off; (*menton, personne*) to shave; (*fam: ennuyer*) to bore; (*démolir*) to raze (to the ground); (*frôler*) to graze, skim; **se raser** to shave; (*fam*) to be bored (to tears)

rasoir [ʀɑzwaʀ] *nm* razor; ~ **électrique** electric shaver *ou* razor; ~ **mécanique** *ou* **de sûreté** safety razor

rassasier [ʀasazje] *vt* to satisfy; **être rassasié** (*dégoûté*) to be sated; to have had more than enough

rassemblement [ʀasɑ̃bləmɑ̃] *nm* (*groupe*) gathering; (*Pol*) union; association; (*Mil*): **le ~** parade

rassembler [ʀasɑ̃ble] *vt* (*réunir*) to assemble, gather; (*regrouper, amasser*) to gather together, collect; **se rassembler** *vi* to gather; **~ ses idées/ses esprits/son courage** to collect one's thoughts/gather one's wits/screw up one's courage

rassis, e [ʀasi, -iz] *adj* (*pain*) stale

rassurer [ʀasyʀe] *vt* to reassure; **se rassurer** to be reassured; **rassure-toi** don't worry

rat [ʀa] *nm* rat; ~ **d'hôtel** hotel thief; ~ **musqué** muskrat

rate [ʀat] *nf* female rat; (*Anat*) spleen

raté, e [ʀate] *adj* (*tentative*) unsuccessful, failed ▷ *nm/f* failure ▷ *nm* misfiring *no pl*

râteau, x [ʀɑto] *nm* rake

rater [ʀate] *vi* (*ne pas partir: coup de feu*) to fail to go off; (*affaire, projet etc*) to go wrong, fail ▷ *vt* (*cible, train, occasion*) to miss; (*démonstration, plat*) to spoil; (*examen*) to fail; **~ son coup** to fail, not to bring it off

ration [ʀasjɔ̃] *nf* ration; (*fig*) share; ~ **alimentaire** food intake

ratisser [ʀatise] *vt* (*allée*) to rake; (*feuilles*) to rake up; (*armée, police*) to comb; ~ **large** to cast one's net wide

RATP *sigle f* (= *Régie autonome des transports parisiens*) Paris transport authority

rattacher [ʀataʃe] *vt* (*animal, cheveux*) to tie up again; (*incorporer: Admin etc*): ~ **qch à** to join sth to, unite sth with; (*fig: relier*): ~ **qch à** to link sth with, relate sth to; (: *lier*): ~ **qn à** to bind *ou* tie sb to; **se ~ à** (*fig: avoir un lien avec*) to be linked (*ou* connected) with

rattrapage [ʀatʀapaʒ] *nm* (*Scol*) remedial classes *pl*; (*Écon*) catching up

rattraper [ʀatʀape] *vt* (*fugitif*) to recapture; (*retenir, empêcher de tomber*) to catch (hold of); (*atteindre, rejoindre*) to catch up with; (*réparer: erreur*) to make up for; **se rattraper** *vi* (*regagner: du temps*) to make up for lost time; (: *de l'argent etc*) to make good one's losses; (*réparer une gaffe etc*) to make up for it; **se ~ (à)** (*se raccrocher*) to stop o.s. falling (by catching hold of); ~ **son retard/le temps perdu** to make up (for) lost time

rature [ʀatyʀ] *nf* deletion, erasure

rauque [ʀok] *adj* raucous; hoarse

ravages [ʀavaʒ] *nmpl* ravages; **faire des ~** to wreak havoc; (*fig: séducteur*) to break hearts

ravaler [ʀavale] *vt* (*mur, façade*) to restore; (*déprécier*) to lower; (*avaler de nouveau*) to swallow again; ~ **sa colère/son dégoût** to stifle one's anger/swallow one's distaste

ravi, e [ʀavi] *adj* delighted; **être ~ de/que** to be delighted with/that

ravigoter [ʀavigɔte] *vt* (*fam*) to buck up

ravin [ʀavɛ̃] *nm* gully, ravine

ravir [ʀaviʀ] *vt* (*enchanter*) to delight; (*enlever*): ~ **qch à qn** to rob sb of sth; **à ~** *adv* delightfully, beautifully; **être beau à ~** to be ravishingly beautiful

raviser [ʀavize] *vt*: **se raviser** *vi* to change one's mind

ravissant, e [ʀavisɑ̃, -ɑ̃t] *adj* delightful

ravisseur, -euse [ʀavisœʀ, -øz] *nm/f* abductor, kidnapper

ravitaillement [ʀavitajmɑ̃] *nm* resupplying; refuelling; (*provisions*) supplies *pl*; **aller au ~** to go for fresh supplies; ~ **en vol** (*Aviat*) in-flight refuelling

ravitailler [ʀavitaje] *vt* to resupply; (*véhicule*) to refuel; **se ravitailler** *vi* to get fresh supplies

raviver [ʀavive] *vt* (*feu*) to rekindle, revive; (*douleur*) to revive; (*couleurs*) to brighten up

rayé, e [ʀeje] *adj* (*à rayures*) striped; (*éraflé*) scratched

rayer [ʀeje] *vt* (*érafler*) to scratch; (*barrer*) to cross *ou* score out; (*d'une liste: radier*) to cross *ou* strike off

rayon [ʀejɔ̃] *nm* (*de soleil etc*) ray; (*Géom*) radius; (*de roue*) spoke; (*étagère*) shelf; (*de grand magasin*) department; (*fig: domaine*) responsibility, concern; (*de ruche*) (honey)comb; **dans un ~ de** within a radius of; **rayons** *nmpl* (*radiothérapie*) radiation; ~ **d'action** range; ~ **de braquage** (*Auto*) turning circle; ~ **laser** laser beam; ~ **de**

soleil sunbeam, ray of sunlight *ou* sunshine; **~s X** X-rays

rayonnement [ʀɛjɔnmɑ̃] *nm* radiation; *(fig: éclat)* radiance; *(: influence)* influence

rayonner [ʀɛjɔne] *vi (chaleur, énergie)* to radiate; *(fig: émotion)* to shine forth; *(: visage)* to be radiant; *(avenues, axes)* to radiate; *(touriste)* to go touring *(from one base)*

rayure [ʀejyʀ] *nf (motif)* stripe; *(éraflure)* scratch; *(rainure, d'un fusil)* groove; **à ~s** striped

raz-de-marée [ʀɑdmaʀe] *nm inv* tidal wave

ré [ʀe] *nm (Mus)* D; *(en chantant la gamme)* re

réacteur [ʀeaktœʀ] *nm* jet engine; **~ nucléaire** nuclear reactor

réaction [ʀeaksjɔ̃] *nf* reaction; **par ~** jet-propelled; **avion/moteur à ~** jet (plane)/jet engine; **~ en chaîne** chain reaction

réadapter [ʀeadapte] *vt* to readjust; *(Méd)* to rehabilitate; **se ~ (à)** to readjust (to)

réagir [ʀeaʒiʀ] *vi* to react

réalisateur, -trice [ʀealizatœʀ, -tʀis] *nm/f (TV, Ciné)* director

réalisation [ʀealizasjɔ̃] *nf* carrying out; realization; fulfilment; achievement; production; *(œuvre)* production, work; *(création)* creation

réaliser [ʀealize] *vt (projet, opération)* to carry out, realize; *(rêve, souhait)* to realize, fulfil; *(exploit)* to achieve; *(achat, vente)* to make; *(film)* to produce; *(se rendre compte de, Comm: bien, capital)* to realize; **se réaliser** *vi* to be realized

réaliste [ʀealist(ə)] *adj* realistic; *(peintre, roman)* realist ▷ *nm/f* realist

réalité [ʀealite] *nf* reality; **en ~** in (actual) fact; **dans la ~** in reality; **~ virtuelle** virtual reality

réanimation [ʀeanimasjɔ̃] *nf* resuscitation; **service de ~** intensive care unit

rébarbatif, -ive [ʀebaʀbatif, -iv] *adj* forbidding; *(style)* off-putting *(Brit)*, crabbed

rebattu, e [ʀəbaty] *pp de* **rebattre** ▷ *adj* hackneyed

rebelle [ʀəbɛl] *nm/f* rebel ▷ *adj (troupes)* rebel; *(enfant)* rebellious; *(mèche etc)* unruly; **~ à qch** unamenable to sth; **~ à faire** unwilling to do

rebeller [ʀəbele] *: se rebeller* *vi* to rebel

rebondi, e [ʀəbɔ̃di] *adj (ventre)* rounded; *(joues)* chubby, well-rounded

rebondir [ʀəbɔ̃diʀ] *vi (ballon: au sol)* to bounce; *(: contre un mur)* to rebound; *(fig: procès, action, conversation)* to get moving again, be suddenly revived

rebondissement [ʀəbɔ̃dismɑ̃] *nm* new development

rebord [ʀəbɔʀ] *nm* edge

rebours [ʀəbuʀ] **: à ~** *adv* the wrong way

rebrousser [ʀəbʀuse] *vt (cheveux, poils)* to brush back, brush up; **~ chemin** to turn back

rebut [ʀəby] *nm*: **mettre au ~** to scrap, discard

rebutant, e [ʀəbytɑ̃, -ɑ̃t] *adj (travail, démarche)* off-putting, disagreeable

rebuter [ʀəbyte] *vt* to put off

récalcitrant, e [ʀekalsitʀɑ̃, -ɑ̃t] *adj* refractory,

recalcitrant

recaler [ʀəkale] *vt (Scol)* to fail

récapituler [ʀekapityle] *vt* to recapitulate; *(résumer)* to sum up

receler [ʀəsəle] *vt (produit d'un vol)* to receive; *(malfaiteur)* to harbour; *(fig)* to conceal

receleur, -euse [ʀəsəlœʀ, -øz] *nm/f* receiver

récemment [ʀesamɑ̃] *adv* recently

recensement [ʀəsɑ̃smɑ̃] *nm* census; inventory

recenser [ʀəsɑ̃se] *vt (population)* to take a census of; *(inventorier)* to make an inventory of; *(dénombrer)* to list

récent, e [ʀesɑ̃, -ɑ̃t] *adj* recent

récépissé [ʀesepise] *nm* receipt

récepteur, -trice [ʀeseptœʀ, -tʀis] *adj* receiving ▷ *nm* receiver; **~ (de radio)** radio set *ou* receiver

réception [ʀesepsjɔ̃] *nf* receiving *no pl*; *(d'une marchandise, commande)* receipt; *(accueil)* reception, welcome; *(bureau)* reception (desk); *(réunion mondaine)* reception, party; *(pièces)* reception rooms *pl*; *(Sport: après un saut)* landing; *(du ballon)* catching *no pl*; **jour/heures de ~** day/hours for receiving visitors *(ou* students *etc)*

réceptionniste [ʀesepsjɔnist(ə)] *nm/f* receptionist

recette [ʀəsɛt] *nf (Culin)* recipe; *(fig)* formula, recipe; *(Comm)* takings *pl*; *(Admin: bureau)* tax *ou* revenue office; **recettes** *nfpl (Comm: rentrées)* receipts; **faire ~** *(spectacle, exposition)* to be a winner

receveur, -euse [ʀəsvœʀ, -øz] *nm/f (des contributions)* tax collector; *(des postes)* postmaster/mistress; *(d'autobus)* conductor/conductress; *(Méd: de sang, organe)* recipient

recevoir [ʀəsvwaʀ] *vt* to receive; *(lettre, prime)* to receive, get; *(client, patient, représentant)* to see; *(jour, soleil: pièce)* to get; *(Scol: candidat)* to pass ▷ *vi* to receive visitors; to give parties; to see patients *etc*; **se recevoir** *vi (athlète)* to land; **~ qn à dîner** to invite sb to dinner; **il reçoit de huit à 10** he's at home from eight to 10, he will see visitors from eight to 10; *(docteur, dentiste etc)* he sees patients from eight to 10; **être reçu (à un examen)** to pass; **être bien/mal reçu** to be well/badly received

rechange [ʀəʃɑ̃ʒ] **: de ~** *adj (pièces, roue)* spare; *(fig: solution)* alternative; **des vêtements de ~** a change of clothes

réchapper [ʀeʃape] **: ~ de** *ou* **à** *vt (accident, maladie)* to come through; **va-t-il en ~?** is he going to get over it?, is he going to come through (it)?

recharge [ʀəʃaʀʒ(ə)] *nf* refill

rechargeable [ʀəʃaʀʒabl(ə)] *adj* refillable; rechargeable

recharger [ʀəʃaʀʒe] *vt (camion, fusil, appareil-photo)* to reload; *(briquet, stylo)* to refill; *(batterie)* to recharge

réchaud [ʀeʃo] *nm* (portable) stove, plate-warmer

réchauffer [ʀeʃofe] *vt (plat)* to reheat; *(mains, personne)* to warm; **se réchauffer** *vi* to get warmer; **se ~ les doigts** to warm (up) one's fingers

rêche [Rɛʃ] *adj* rough

recherche [RəʃɛRʃ(ə)] *nf* (*action*): **la ~ de** the search for; (*raffinement*) affectedness, studied elegance; (*scientifique etc*): **la ~** research; **recherches** *nfpl* (*de la police*) investigations; (*scientifiques*) research *sg*; **être/se mettre à la ~ de** to be/go in search of

recherché, e [RəʃɛRʃe] *adj* (*rare, demandé*) much sought-after; (*entouré: acteur, femme*) in demand; (*raffiné*) studied, affected

rechercher [RəʃɛRʃe] *vt* (*objet égaré, personne*) to look for, search for; (*témoins, coupable, main-d'œuvre*) to look for; (*causes d'un phénomène, nouveau procédé*) to try to find; (*bonheur etc, l'amitié de qn*) to seek; **"~ et remplacer"** (*Inform*) "find and replace"

rechigner [Rəʃiɲe] *vi*: **~ (à)** to balk (at)

rechute [Rəʃyt] *nf* (*Méd*) relapse; (*dans le péché, le vice*) lapse; **faire une ~** to have a relapse

récidiver [Residive] *vi* to commit a second (*ou* subsequent) offence; (*fig*) to do it again

récif [Resif] *nm* reef

récipient [Resipjã] *nm* container

réciproque [ResipRɔk] *adj* reciprocal ▷ *nf*: **la ~** (*l'inverse*) the converse

récit [Resi] *nm* (*action de narrer*) telling; (*conte, histoire*) story

récital [Resital] *nm* recital

réciter [Resite] *vt* to recite

réclamation [Reklamasjɔ̃] *nf* complaint; **réclamations** *nfpl* (*bureau*) complaints department *sg*

réclame [Reklam] *nf*: **la ~** advertising; **une ~** an ad(vertisement), an advert (*Brit*); **faire de la ~ (pour qch/qn)** to advertise (sth/sb); **article en ~** special offer

réclamer [Reklame] *vt* (*aide, nourriture etc*) to ask for; (*revendiquer: dû, part, indemnité*) to claim, demand; (*nécessiter*) to demand, require ▷ *vi* to complain; **se ~ de** to give as one's authority; to claim filiation with

réclusion [Reklyzjɔ̃] *nf* imprisonment; **~ à perpétuité** life imprisonment

recoin [Rəkwɛ̃] *nm* nook, corner; (*fig*) hidden recess

reçois *etc* [Rəswa] *vb voir* **recevoir**

récolte [Rekɔlt(ə)] *nf* harvesting, gathering; (*produits*) harvest, crop; (*fig*) crop, collection; (: *d'observations*) findings

récolter [Rekɔlte] *vt* to harvest, gather (in); (*fig*) to get

recommandé [Rəkɔmɑ̃de] *nm* (*méthode etc*) recommended; (*Postes*): **en ~** by registered mail

recommander [Rəkɔmɑ̃de] *vt* to recommend; (*qualités etc*) to commend; (*Postes*) to register; **~ qch à qn** to recommend sth to sb; **~ à qn de faire** to recommend sb to do; **~ qn auprès de qn** *ou* **à qn** to recommend sb to sb; **il est recommandé de faire ...** it is recommended that one does ...; **se ~ à qn** to commend o.s. to sb; **se ~ de qn** to give sb's name as a reference

recommencer [Rəkɔmɑ̃se] *vt* (*reprendre: lutte, séance*) to resume, start again; (*refaire: travail, explications*) to start afresh, start (over) again; (*récidiver: erreur*) to make again ▷ *vi* to start again; (*récidiver*) to do it again; **~ à faire** to start doing again; **ne recommence pas!** don't do that again!

récompense [Rekɔ̃pɑ̃s] *nf* reward; (*prix*) award; **recevoir qch en ~** to get sth as a reward, be rewarded with sth

récompenser [Rekɔ̃pɑ̃se] *vt*: **~ qn (de** *ou* **pour)** to reward sb (for)

réconcilier [Rekɔ̃silje] *vt* to reconcile; **~ qn avec qn** to reconcile sb with sb; **~ qn avec qch** to reconcile sb to sth; **se réconcilier (avec)** to be reconciled (with)

reconduire [Rəkɔ̃dɥiR] *vt* (*raccompagner*) to take *ou* see back; (: *à la porte*) to show out; (: *à son domicile*) to see home, take home; (*Jur, Pol: renouveler*) to renew

réconfort [Rekɔ̃fɔR] *nm* comfort

réconforter [Rekɔ̃fɔRte] *vt* (*consoler*) to comfort; (*revigorer*) to fortify

reconnaissance [Rəkɔnɛsɑ̃s] *nf* recognition; acknowledgement; (*gratitude*) gratitude, gratefulness; (*Mil*) reconnaissance, recce; **en ~** (*Mil*) on reconnaissance; **~ de dette** acknowledgement of a debt, IOU

reconnaissant, e [Rəkɔnɛsɑ̃, -ɑ̃t] *vb voir* **reconnaître** ▷ *adj* grateful; **je vous serais ~ de bien vouloir** I should be most grateful if you would (kindly)

reconnaître [RəkɔnɛtR(ə)] *vt* to recognize; (*Mil: lieu*) to reconnoitre; (*Jur: enfant, dette, droit*) to acknowledge; **~ que** to admit *ou* acknowledge that; **~ qn/qch à** (*l'identifier grâce à*) to recognize sb/sth by; **~ à qn: je lui reconnais certaines qualités** I recognize certain qualities in him; **se ~ quelque part** (*s'y retrouver*) to find one's way around (a place)

reconnu, e [R(ə)kɔny] *pp de* **reconnaître** ▷ *adj* (*indiscuté, connu*) recognized

reconstituant, e [Rəkɔ̃stitɥɑ̃, -ɑ̃t] *adj* (*régime*) strength-building ▷ *nm* tonic, pick-me-up

reconstituer [Rəkɔ̃stitɥe] *vt* (*monument ancien*) to recreate, build a replica of; (*fresque, vase brisé*) to piece together, reconstitute; (*événement, accident*) to reconstruct; (*fortune, patrimoine*) to rebuild; (*Bio: tissus etc*) to regenerate

reconstruction [Rəkɔ̃stRyksjɔ̃] *nf* rebuilding, reconstruction

reconstruire [Rəkɔ̃stRɥiR] *vt* to rebuild, reconstruct

reconvertir [Rəkɔ̃vɛRtiR] *vt* (*usine*) to reconvert; (*personnel, troupes etc*) to redeploy; **se ~ dans** (*un métier, une branche*) to move into, be redeployed into

record [RəkɔR] *nm, adj* record; **~ du monde** world record

recoupement [Rəkupmɑ̃] *nm*: **faire un ~** *ou* **des ~s** to cross-check; **par ~** by cross-checking

recouper [Rəkupe] *vt* (*tranche*) to cut again;

(*vêtement*) to recut ▷ *vi* (*Cartes*) to cut again; **se recouper** *vi* (*témoignages*) to tie *ou* match up

recourber [ʀəkuʀbe] *vt* (*branche, tige de métal*) to bend

recourir [ʀəkuʀiʀ] *vi* (*courir de nouveau*) to run again; (*refaire une course*) to race again; **~ à** *vt* (*ami, agence*) to turn *ou* appeal to; (*force, ruse, emprunt*) to resort to, have recourse to

recours [ʀəkuʀ] *vb voir* **recourir** ▷ *nm* (*Jur*) appeal; **avoir ~ à**; = **recourir à**; **dernier ~** as a last resort; **sans ~** final; with no way out; **~ en grâce** plea for clemency (*ou pardon*)

recouvrer [ʀəkuvʀe] *vt* (*vue, santé etc*) to recover, regain; (*impôts*) to collect; (*créance*) to recover

recouvrir [ʀəkuvʀiʀ] *vt* (*couvrir à nouveau*) to re-cover; (*couvrir entièrement: aussi fig*) to cover; (*cacher, masquer*) to conceal, hide; **se recouvrir** (*se superposer*) to overlap

récréation [ʀekʀeasjɔ̃] *nf* recreation, entertainment; (*Scol*) break

récrier [ʀekʀije]: **se récrier** *vi* to exclaim

récriminations [ʀekʀiminɑsjɔ̃] *nfpl* remonstrations, complaints

recroqueviller [ʀəkʀɔkvije]: **se recroqueviller** *vi* (*feuilles*) to curl *ou* shrivel up; (*personne*) to huddle up

recru, e [ʀəkʀy] *adj*: **~ de fatigue** exhausted ▷ *nf* recruit

recrudescence [ʀəkʀydesɑ̃s] *nf* fresh outbreak

recruter [ʀəkʀyte] *vt* to recruit

rectangle [ʀɛktɑ̃gl(ə)] *nm* rectangle

rectangulaire [ʀɛktɑ̃gylɛʀ] *adj* rectangular

rectificatif, -ive [ʀɛktifikatif, -iv] *adj* corrected ▷ *nm* correction

rectifier [ʀɛktifje] *vt* (*tracé, virage*) to straighten; (*calcul, adresse*) to correct; (*erreur, faute*) to rectify, put right

rectiligne [ʀɛktiliɲ] *adj* straight; (*Géom*) rectilinear

recto [ʀɛkto] *nm* front (*of a sheet of paper*)

reçu, e [ʀəsy] *pp de* **recevoir** ▷ *adj* (*admis, consacré*) accepted ▷ *nm* (*Comm*) receipt

recueil [ʀəkœj] *nm* collection

recueillir [ʀəkœjiʀ] *vt* to collect; (*voix, suffrages*) to win; (*accueillir: réfugiés, chat*) to take in; **se recueillir** *vi* to gather one's thoughts; to meditate

recul [ʀəkyl] *nm* retreat; recession; decline; (*d'arme à feu*) recoil, kick; **avoir un mouvement de ~** to recoil, start back; **prendre du ~** to stand back; **avec le ~** with the passing of time, in retrospect

reculé, e [ʀəkyle] *adj* remote

reculer [ʀəkyle] *vi* to move back, back away; (*Auto*) to reverse, back (up); (*fig: civilisation, épidémie*) to (be on the) decline; (: *se dérober*) to shrink back ▷ *vt* to move back; to reverse, back (up); (*fig: échéance, limites*) to extend; (: *date, décision*) to postpone; **~ devant** (*danger, difficulté*) to shrink from; **~ pour mieux sauter** (*fig*) to postpone the evil day

reculons [ʀəkylɔ̃]: **à ~** *adv* backwards

récupérer [ʀekypeʀe] *vt* (*rentrer en possession de*) to recover, get back; (: *forces*) to recover; (*déchets etc*) to salvage (for reprocessing); (*remplacer: journée, heures de travail*) to make up; (*délinquant etc*) to rehabilitate; (*Pol*) to bring into line ▷ *vi* to recover

récurer [ʀekyʀe] *vt* to scour; **poudre à ~** scouring powder

récuser [ʀekyze] *vt* to challenge; **se récuser** to decline to give an opinion

recycler [ʀəsikle] *vt* (*Scol*) to reorientate; (*employés*) to retrain; (*matériau*) to recycle; **se recycler** to retrain; to go on a retraining course

rédacteur, -trice [ʀedaktœʀ, -tʀis] *nm/f* (*journaliste*) writer; subeditor; (*d'ouvrage de référence*) editor, compiler; **~ en chef** chief editor; **~ publicitaire** copywriter

rédaction [ʀedaksjɔ̃] *nf* writing; (*rédacteurs*) editorial staff; (*bureau*) editorial office(s); (*Scol: devoir*) essay, composition

redemander [ʀədmɑ̃de] *vt* (*renseignement*) to ask again for; (*nourriture*): **~ de** to ask for more (*ou* another); (*objet prêté*): **~ qch** to ask for sth back

redescendre [ʀədesɑ̃dʀ(ə)] *vi* (*à nouveau*) to go back down; (*après la montée*) to go down (again) ▷ *vt* (*pente etc*) to go down

redevance [ʀədvɑ̃s] *nf* (*Tél*) rental charge; (*TV*) licence (*Brit*) *ou* license (*US*) fee

rédiger [ʀediʒe] *vt* to write; (*contrat*) to draw up

redire [ʀədiʀ] *vt* to repeat; **trouver à ~ à** to find fault with

redonner [ʀədɔne] *vt* (*restituer*) to give back, return; (*du courage, des forces*) to restore

redoubler [ʀəduble] *vi* (*tempête, violence*) to intensify, get even stronger *ou* fiercer *etc*; (*Scol*) to repeat a year ▷ *vt* (*Scol: classe*) to repeat; (*Ling: lettre*) to double; **le vent redouble de violence** the wind is blowing twice as hard

redoutable [ʀədutabl(ə)] *adj* formidable, fearsome

redouter [ʀədute] *vt* to fear; (*appréhender*) to dread; **~ de faire** to dread doing

redressement [ʀədʀɛsmɑ̃] *nm* (*de l'économie etc*) putting right; **maison de ~** reformatory; **~ fiscal** repayment of back taxes

redresser [ʀədʀese] *vt* (*arbre, mât*) to set upright, right; (*pièce tordue*) to straighten out; (*Aviat, Auto*) to straighten up; (*situation, économie*) to put right; **se redresser** *vi* (*objet penché*) to right itself; to straighten up; (*personne*) to sit (*ou* stand) up; to sit (*ou* stand) up straight; (*fig: pays, situation*) to recover; **~ (les roues)** (*Auto*) to straighten up

réduction [ʀedyksjɔ̃] *nf* reduction; **en ~** *adv* in miniature, scaled-down

réduire [ʀedɥiʀ] *vt* (*gén, Culin, Math*) to reduce; (*prix, dépenses*) to cut, reduce; (*carte*) to scale down, reduce; (*Méd: fracture*) to set; **~ qn/qch à** to reduce sb/sth to; **se ~ à** (*revenir à*) to boil down to; **se ~ en** (*se transformer en*) to be reduced to; **en être réduit à** to be reduced to

réduit, e [ʀedɥi, -it] *pp de* **réduire** ▷ *adj* (*prix, tarif, échelle*) reduced; (*mécanisme*) scaled-down;

(*vitesse*) reduced ▷ *nm* tiny room; recess

rééducation [ʀeedykɑsjɔ̃] *nf* (*d'un membre*) re-education; (*de délinquants, d'un blessé*) rehabilitation; **- de la parole** speech therapy; **centre de ~** physiotherapy *ou* physical therapy (US) centre

réel, le [ʀeɛl] *adj* real ▷ *nm*: **le ~** reality

réellement [ʀeɛlmɑ̃] *adv* really

réexpédier [ʀeɛkspedje] *vt* (*à l'envoyeur*) to return, send back; (*au destinataire*) to send on, forward

refaire [ʀəfɛʀ] *vt* (*faire de nouveau, recommencer*) to do again; (*réparer, restaurer*) to do up; **se refaire** *vi* (*en argent*) to make up one's losses; **se ~ une santé** to recuperate; **se ~ à qch** (*se réhabituer à*) to get used to sth again

réfection [ʀefɛksjɔ̃] *nf* repair; **en ~** under repair

réfectoire [ʀefɛktwaʀ] *nm* refectory

référence [ʀefeʀɑ̃s] *nf* reference; **références** *nfpl* (*recommandations*) reference *sg*; **faire ~ à** to refer to; **ouvrage de ~** reference work; **ce n'est pas une ~** (*fig*) that's no recommendation

référer [ʀefeʀe]: **se ~ à** *vt* to refer to; **en ~ à qn** to refer the matter to sb

refermer [ʀəfɛʀme] *vt* to close again, shut again

refiler [ʀəfile] *vt* (*fam*): **~ qch à qn** to palm (Brit) *ou* fob sth off on sb; to pass sth on to sb

réfléchi, e [ʀefleʃi] *adj* (*caractère*) thoughtful; (*action*) well-thought-out; (*Ling*) reflexive

réfléchir [ʀefleʃiʀ] *vt* to reflect ▷ *vi* to think; **~ à** *ou* **sur** to think about; **c'est tout réfléchi** my mind's made up

reflet [ʀəflɛ] *nm* reflection; (*sur l'eau etc*) sheen *no pl*, glint; **reflets** *nmpl* gleam *sg*

refléter [ʀəflete] *vt* to reflect; **se refléter** *vi* to be reflected

réflexe [ʀeflɛks(ə)] *adj, nm* reflex; **~ conditionné** conditioned reflex

réflexion [ʀeflɛksjɔ̃] *nf* (*de la lumière etc, pensée*) reflection; (*fait de penser*) thought; (*remarque*) remark; **réflexions** *nfpl* (*méditations*) thought *sg*, reflection *sg*; **sans ~** without thinking; **~ faite**, **à la ~** après réflexion, on reflection; **délai de ~** cooling-off period; **groupe de ~** think tank

réflexologie [ʀeflɛksɔlɔʒi] *nf* reflexology

refluer [ʀəflye] *vi* to flow back; (*foule*) to surge back

reflux [ʀəfly] *nm* (*de la mer*) ebb; (*fig*) backward surge

réforme [ʀefɔʀm(ə)] *nf* reform; (*Mil*) declaration of unfitness for service; discharge (*on health grounds*); (*Rel*): **la R~** the Reformation

réformer [ʀefɔʀme] *vt* to reform; (*Mil: recrue*) to declare unfit for service; (: *soldat*) to discharge, invalid out; (*matériel*) to scrap

refouler [ʀəfule] *vt* (*envahisseurs*) to drive back, repulse; (*liquide*) to force back; (*fig*) to suppress; (*Psych*) to repress

refrain [ʀəfʀɛ̃] *nm* (*Mus*) refrain, chorus; (*air, fig*) tune

refréner, réfréner [ʀəfʀene, ʀefʀene] *vt* to curb, check

réfrigérateur [ʀefʀiʒeʀatœʀ] *nm* refrigerator;

~-congélateur fridge-freezer

refroidir [ʀəfʀwadiʀ] *vt* to cool; (*fig*) to have a cooling effect on ▷ *vi* to cool (down); **se refroidir** *vi* (*prendre froid*) to catch a chill; (*temps*) to get cooler *ou* colder; (*fig*) to cool (off)

refroidissement [ʀəfʀwadismɑ̃] *nm* cooling; (*grippe etc*) chill

refuge [ʀəfyʒ] *nm* refuge; (*pour piétons*) (traffic) island; **demander ~ à qn** to ask sb for refuge

réfugié, e [ʀefyʒje] *adj, nm/f* refugee

réfugier [ʀefyʒje]: **se réfugier** *vi* to take refuge

refus [ʀəfy] *nm* refusal; **ce n'est pas de ~** I won't say no, it's very welcome

refuser [ʀəfyze] *vt* to refuse; (*Scol: candidat*) to fail ▷ *vi* to refuse; **~ qch à qn/de faire** to refuse sb sth/to do; **~ du monde** to have to turn people away; **se ~ à qch** *ou* **à faire qch** to refuse to do sth; **il ne se refuse rien** he doesn't stint himself; **se ~ à qn** to refuse sb

réfuter [ʀefyte] *vt* to refute

regagner [ʀəɡaɲe] *vt* (*argent, faveur*) to win back; (*lieu*) to get back to; **~ le temps perdu** to make up for lost time; **~ du terrain** to regain ground

regain [ʀəɡɛ̃] *nm* (*herbe*) second crop of hay; (*renouveau*): **~ de qch** renewed sth

régal [ʀeɡal] *nm* treat; **un ~ pour les yeux** a pleasure *ou* delight to look at

régaler [ʀeɡale] *vt*: **~ qn** to treat sb to a delicious meal; **~ qn de** to treat sb to; **se régaler** *vi* to have a delicious meal; (*fig*) to enjoy o.s

regard [ʀəɡaʀ] *nm* (*coup d'œil*) look, glance; (*expression*) look (in one's eye); **parcourir/menacer du ~** to cast an eye over/look threateningly at; **au ~ de** (*loi, morale*) from the point of view of; **en ~** (*vis à vis*) opposite; **en ~ de** in comparison with

regardant, e [ʀəɡaʀdɑ̃, -ɑ̃t] *adj*: **très/peu ~ (sur)** quite fussy/very free (about); (*économe*) very tight-fisted/quite generous (with)

regarder [ʀəɡaʀde] *vt* (*examiner, observer, lire*) to look at; (*film, télévision, match*) to watch; (*envisager: situation, avenir*) to view; (*considérer: son intérêt etc*) to be concerned with; (*être orienté vers*): **~ (vers)** to face; (*concerner*) to concern ▷ *vi* to look; **~ à** *vt* (*dépense, qualité, détails*) to be fussy with *ou* over; **~ à faire** to hesitate to do; **dépenser sans ~** to spend freely; **~ qn/qch comme** to regard sb/sth as; **~ (qch) dans le dictionnaire** to look (sth up) in the dictionary; **~ par la fenêtre** to look out of the window; **cela me regarde** it concerns me, it's my business

régie [ʀeʒi] *nf* (*Comm, Industrie*) state-owned company; (*Théât, Ciné*) production; (*Radio, TV*) control room; **la ~ de l'État** state control

regimber [ʀəʒɛ̃be] *vi* to balk, jib

régime [ʀeʒim] *nm* (*Pol Géo*) régime; (*Admin: carcéral, fiscal etc*) system; (*Méd*) diet; (*Tech*) (engine) speed; (*fig*) rate, pace; (*de bananes, dattes*) bunch; **se mettre au/suivre un ~** to go on/be on a diet; **~ sans sel** salt-free diet; **à bas/haut ~** (*Auto*) at low/high revs; **à plein ~** flat out, at full speed; **~ matrimonial** marriage settlement

régiment [ReʒimÃ] *nm* (*Mil: unité*) regiment; (*fig: fam*): **un ~ de** an army of; **un copain de ~** a pal from military service *ou* (one's) army days

région [Reʒjɔ̃] *nf* region; **la ~ parisienne** the Paris area

régional, e, -aux [Reʒjɔnal, -o] *adj* regional

régir [Reʒiʀ] *vt* to govern

régisseur [Reʒisœʀ] *nm* (*d'un domaine*) steward; (*Ciné, TV*) assistant director; (*Théât*) stage manager

registre [RəʒistR(ə)] *nm* (*livre*) register; logbook; ledger; (*Mus, Ling*) register; (*d'orgue*) stop; **~ de comptabilité** ledger; **~ de l'état civil** register of births, marriages and deaths

réglage [Reglaʒ] *nm* (*d'une machine*) adjustment; (*d'un moteur*) tuning

réglé, e [Regle] *adj* well-ordered; stable, steady; (*papier*) ruled; (*arrangé*) settled

règle [Regl(ə)] *nf* (*instrument*) ruler; (*loi, prescription*) rule; **règles** *nfpl* (*Physiol*) period *sg*; **avoir pour ~ de** to make it a rule that *ou* to; **en ~** (*papiers d'identité*) in order; **être/se mettre en ~** to be/put o.s. straight with the authorities; **en ~ générale** as a (general) rule; **être la ~** to be the rule; **être de ~** to be usual; **~ à calcul** slide rule; **~ de trois** (*Math*) rule of three

règlement [Reglemã] *nm* settling; (*paiement*) settlement; (*arrêté*) regulation; (*règles, statuts*) regulations *pl*, rules *pl*; **~ à la commande** cash with order; **~ de compte(s)** settling of scores; **~ en espèces/par chèque** payment in cash/by cheque; **~ intérieur** (*Scol*) school rules *pl*; (*Admin*) by-laws *pl*; **~ judiciaire** compulsory liquidation

réglementaire [ReglemãtɛR] *adj* conforming to the regulations; (*tenue, uniforme*) regulation *cpd*

réglementation [Reglemãtasjɔ̃] *nf* regulation, control; (*règlements*) regulations *pl*

réglementer [Reglemãte] *vt* to regulate, control

régler [Regle] *vt* (*mécanisme, machine*) to regulate, adjust; (*moteur*) to tune; (*thermostat etc*) to set, adjust; (*emploi du temps etc*) to organize, plan; (*question, conflit, facture, dette*) to settle; (*fournisseur*) to settle up with, pay; (*papier*) to rule; **~ qch sur** to model sth on; **~ son compte** to sort sb out, settle sb; **~ un compte** to settle a score with sb

réglisse [Reglis] *nf ou m* liquorice; **bâton de ~** liquorice stick

règne [Rɛɲ] *nm* (*d'un roi etc, fig*) reign; (*Bio*): **le ~ végétal/animal** the vegetable/animal kingdom

régner [Reɲe] *vi* (*roi*) to rule, reign; (*fig*) to reign

regorger [RəgɔRʒe] *vi* to overflow; **~ de** to overflow with, be bursting with

regret [RəgRɛ] *nm* regret; **à ~** with regret; **avec ~** regretfully; **être au ~ de devoir/ne pas pouvoir faire** to regret to have to/that one is unable to do; **j'ai le ~ de vous informer que ...** I regret to inform you that ...

regrettable [RəgRɛtabl(ə)] *adj* regrettable

regretter [RəgRɛte] *vt* to regret; (*personne*) to miss; **~ d'avoir fait** to regret doing; **~ que** to regret that, be sorry that; **non, je regrette** no, I'm sorry

regrouper [RəgRupe] *vt* (*grouper*) to group together; (*contenir*) to include, comprise; **se regrouper** *vi* to gather (together)

régulier, -ière [Regylje, -jɛR] *adj* (*gén*) regular; (*vitesse, qualité*) steady; (*répartition, pression*) even; (*Transports: ligne, service*) scheduled, regular; (*légal, réglementaire*) lawful, in order; (*fam: correct*) straight, on the level

régulièrement [RegyljɛRmã] *adv* regularly; steadily; evenly; normally

rehausser [Rəose] *vt* to heighten, raise; (*fig*) to set off, enhance

rein [Rɛ̃] *nm* kidney; **reins** *nmpl* (*dos*) back *sg*; **avoir mal aux ~s** to have backache; **~ artificiel** kidney machine

reine [Rɛn] *nf* queen

reine-claude [Rɛnklod] *nf* greengage

réinscriptible [Reɛ̃skriptibl] *adj* (*CD, DVD*) rewritable

réinsertion [Reɛ̃sɛRsjɔ̃] *nf* rehabilitation

réintégrer [Reɛ̃tegre] *vt* (*lieu*) to return to; (*fonctionnaire*) to reinstate

rejaillir [RəʒajiR] *vi* to splash up; **~ sur** to splash up onto; (*fig*) to rebound on; to fall upon

rejet [Rəʒɛ] *nm* (*action, aussi Méd*) rejection; (*Poésie*) enjambement, rejet; (*Bot*) shoot

rejeter [Rəʒte] *vt* (*relancer*) to throw back; (*vomir*) to bring *ou* throw up; (*écarter*) to reject; (*déverser*) to throw out, discharge; (*reporter*): **~ un mot à la fin d'une phrase** to transpose a word to the end of a sentence; **se ~ sur qch** (*accepter faute de mieux*) to fall back on sth; **~ la tête/les épaules en arrière** to throw one's head/pull one's shoulders back; **~ la responsabilité de qch sur qn** to lay the responsibility for sth at sb's door

rejoindre [RəʒwɛdR(ə)] *vt* (*famille, régiment*) to rejoin, return to; (*lieu*) to get (back) to; (*route etc*) to meet, join; (*rattraper*) to catch up (with); **se rejoindre** *vi* to meet; **je te rejoins au café** I'll see *ou* meet you at the café

réjouir [Reʒwiʀ] *vt* to delight; **se réjouir** *vi* to be delighted; **se ~ de qch/de faire** to be delighted about sth/to do; **se ~ que** to be delighted that

réjouissances [Reʒwisãs] *nfpl* (*joie*) rejoicing *sg*; (*fête*) festivities, merry-making *sg*

relâche [Rəlɑʃ]: **faire ~** (*navire*) to put into port; (*Ciné*) to be closed; **c'est le jour de ~** (*Ciné*) it's closed today; **sans ~** *adv* without respite *ou* a break

relâché, e [Rəlɑʃe] *adj* loose, lax

relâcher [Rəlɑʃe] *vt* (*ressort, prisonnier*) to release; (*étreinte, cordes*) to loosen; (*discipline*) to relax ▷ *vi* (*Navig*) to put into port; **se relâcher** *vi* to loosen; (*discipline*) to become slack *ou* lax; (*élève etc*) to slacken off

relais [Rəlɛ] *nm* (*Sport*): (**course de**) **~** relay (race); (*Radio, TV*) relay; (*intermédiaire*) go-between; **équipe de ~** = shift team; (*Sport*) relay team; **prendre le ~ (de)** to take over (from); **~ de poste** post house, coaching inn; **~ routier** = transport café (*Brit*), = truck stop (*US*)

relancer [Rəlãse] *vt* (*balle*) to throw back (again);

(*moteur*) to restart; (*fig*) to boost, revive; (*personne*):
~ **qn** to pester sb; to get on to sb again
relatif, -ive [Rəlatif, -iv] *adj* relative
relation [Rəlɑsjɔ̃] *nf* (*récit*) account, report;
(*rapport*) relation(ship); **relations** *nfpl* (*rapports*)
relations; relationship; (*connaissances*)
connections; **être/entrer en ~(s) avec** to be
in contact *ou* be dealing/get in contact with;
mettre qn en ~(s) avec to put sb in touch with;
~s internationales international relations;
~s publiques public relations; **~s (sexuelles)**
sexual relations, (sexual) intercourse *sg*
relaxer [Rəlakse] *vt* to relax; (*Jur*) to discharge;
se relaxer *vi* to relax
relayer [Rəleje] *vt* (*collaborateur, coureur etc*) to
relieve, take over from; (*Radio, TV*) to relay; **se**
relayer (*dans une activité*) to take it in turns
reléguer [Rəlege] *vt* to relegate; ~ **au second**
plan to push into the background
relent [Rəlɑ̃], **relents** *nm(pl)* stench *sg*
relevé, e [Rəlve] *adj* (*bord de chapeau*) turned-up;
(*manches*) rolled-up; (*fig: style*) elevated; (*: sauce*)
highly-seasoned ▷ *nm* (*lecture*) reading; (*de cotes*)
plotting; (*liste*) statement; list; (*facture*) account;
~ **de compte** bank statement; **~ d'identité**
bancaire (RIB) (bank) account number
relève [Rəlɛv] *nf* relief; (*équipe*) relief team (*ou*
troops *pl*); **prendre la ~** to take over
relever [Rəlve] *vt* (*statue, meuble*) to stand up
again; (*personne tombée*) to help up; (*vitre, plafond,*
niveau de vie) to raise; (*pays, économie, entreprise*)
to put back on its feet; (*col*) to turn up; (*style,*
conversation) to elevate; (*plat, sauce*) to season;
(*sentinelle, équipe*) to relieve; (*souligner: fautes,*
points) to pick out; (*constater: traces etc*) to find,
pick up; (*répliquer à: remarque*) to react to, reply
to; (*: défi*) to accept, take up; (*noter: adresse etc*) to
take down, note; (*: plan*) to sketch; (*: cotes etc*) to
plot; (*compteur*) to read; (*ramasser: cahiers, copies*)
to collect, take in ▷ *vi* (*jupe, bord*) to ride up; **~ de**
vt (*maladie*) to be recovering from; (*être du ressort*
de) to be a matter for; (*Admin: dépendre de*) to come
under; (*fig*) to pertain to; **se relever** *vi* (*se remettre*
debout) to get up; (*fig*): **se ~ (de)** to recover (from);
~ **qn de** (*vœux*) to release sb from; (*fonctions*) to
relieve sb of; **~ la tête** to look up; to hold up
one's head
relief [Rəljɛf] *nm* relief; (*de pneu*) tread pattern;
reliefs *nmpl* (*restes*) remains; **en ~** in relief;
(*photographie*) three-dimensional; **mettre en ~**
(*fig*) to bring out, highlight
relier [Rəlje] *vt* to link up; (*livre*) to bind; ~ **qch**
à to link sth to; **livre relié cuir** leather-bound
book
religieux, -euse [Rəliʒjø, -øz] *adj* religious ▷ *nm*
monk ▷ *nf* nun; (*gâteau*) cream bun
religion [Rəliʒjɔ̃] *nf* religion; (*piété, dévotion*) faith;
entrer en ~ to take one's vows
relire [Rəlir] *vt* (*à nouveau*) to reread, read again;
(*vérifier*) to read over; **se relire** to read through
what one has written
reliure [Rəljyr] *nf* binding; (*art, métier*): **la ~** book-

binding
reluire [Rəlɥir] *vi* to gleam
remanier [Rəmanje] *vt* to reshape, recast; (*Pol*)
to reshuffle
remarquable [Rəmarkabl(ə)] *adj* remarkable
remarque [Rəmark(ə)] *nf* remark; (*écrite*) note
remarquer [Rəmarke] *vt* (*voir*) to notice; (*dire*):
~ **que** to remark that; **se ~** to be noticeable; **se**
faire ~ to draw attention to o.s.; **faire ~ (à qn)**
que to point out (to sb) that; **faire ~ qch (à qn)**
to point sth out (to sb); **remarquez, ...** mark
you, ..., mind you, ...
rembourrer [Rɑ̃bure] *vt* to stuff; (*dossier,*
vêtement, souliers) to pad
remboursement [Rɑ̃bursəmɑ̃] *nm* repayment;
envoi contre ~ cash on delivery
rembourser [Rɑ̃burse] *vt* to pay back, repay
remède [Rəmɛd] *nm* (*médicament*) medicine;
(*traitement, fig*) remedy, cure; **trouver un ~ à**
(*Méd, fig*) to find a cure for
remémorer [Rəmemɔre]: **se remémorer** *vt* to
recall, recollect
remerciements [Rəmɛrsimɑ̃] *nmpl* thanks;
(**avec**) **tous mes ~** (with) grateful *ou* many
thanks
remercier [Rəmɛrsje] *vt* to thank; (*congédier*) to
dismiss; ~ **qn de/d'avoir fait** to thank sb for/for
having done; **non, je vous remercie** no thank
you
remettre [Rəmɛtr(ə)] *vt* (*vêtement*): ~ **qch** to
put sth back on, put sth on again; (*replacer*): ~
qch quelque part to put sth back somewhere;
(*ajouter*): ~ **du sel/un sucre** to add more salt/
another lump of sugar; (*rétablir: personne*): ~ **qn** to
set sb back on his (*ou* her) feet; (*rendre, restituer*): ~
qch à qn to give sth back to sb, return sth to sb;
(*donner, confier: paquet, argent*): ~ **qch à qn** to hand
sth over to sb, deliver sth to sb; (*prix, décoration*):
~ **qch à qn** to present sb with sth; (*ajourner*): ~
qch (à) to postpone sth *ou* put sth off (until);
se remettre *vi* to get better, recover; **se ~ de** to
recover from, get over; **s'en ~ à** to leave it (up)
to; **se ~ à faire/qch** to start doing/sth again; ~
une pendule à l'heure to put a clock right; ~
un moteur/une machine en marche to get an
engine/a machine going again; ~ **en état/en**
ordre to repair/sort out; ~ **en cause/question**
to challenge/question again; ~ **sa démission** to
hand in one's notice; ~ **qch à neuf** to make sth
as good as new; ~ **qn à sa place** (*fig*) to put sb in
his (*ou* her) place
remis, e [Rəmi, -iz] *pp de* **remettre** ▷ *nf* delivery;
presentation; (*rabais*) discount; (*local*) shed; ~
en marche/en ordre starting up again/sorting
out; ~ **en cause/question** calling into question/
challenging; ~ **de fonds** remittance; ~ **en jeu**
(*Football*) throw-in; ~ **à neuf** restoration; ~ **de**
peine remission of sentence
remontant [Rəmɔ̃tɑ̃] *nm* tonic, pick-me-up
remonte-pente [Rəmɔ̃tpɑ̃t] *nm* ski lift, (ski) tow
remonter [Rəmɔ̃te] *vi* (*à nouveau*) to go back up;
(*à cheval*) to remount; (*après une descente*) to go up

(again); (*en voiture*) to get back in; (*jupe*) to ride up ▷ *vt* (*pente*) to go up; (*fleuve*) to sail (*ou* swim *etc*) up; up; (*manches, pantalon*) to roll up; (*col*) to turn up; (*niveau, limite*) to raise; (*fig: personne*) to buck up; (*moteur, meuble*) to put back together, reassemble; (*garde-robe etc*) to renew, replenish; (*montre, mécanisme*) to wind up; ~ **le moral à qn** to raise sb's spirits; ~ **à** (*dater de*) to date *ou* go back to; ~ **en voiture** to get back into the car

remontrance [Rəmɔ̃tRɑ̃s] *nf* reproof, reprimand

remontrer [Rəmɔ̃tRe] *vt* (*montrer de nouveau*): ~ **qch (à qn)** to show sth again (to sb); (*fig*): **en ~ à** to prove one's superiority over

remords [RəmɔR] *nm* remorse *no pl*; **avoir des ~** to feel remorse, be conscience-stricken

remorque [RəmɔRk(ə)] *nf* trailer; **prendre/être en ~** to tow/be on tow; **être à la ~** (*fig*) to tag along (behind)

remorquer [RəmɔRke] *vt* to tow

remorqueur [RəmɔRkœR] *nm* tug(boat)

remous [Rəmu] *nm* (*d'un navire*) (back)wash *no pl*; (*de rivière*) swirl, eddy *pl*; (*fig*) stir *sg*

remparts [Rɑ̃paR] *nmpl* walls, ramparts

remplaçant, e [Rɑ̃plasɑ̃, -ɑ̃t] *nm/f* replacement, substitute, stand-in; (*Théât*) understudy; (*Scol*) supply (*Brit*) *ou* substitute (*US*) teacher

remplacement [Rɑ̃plasmɑ̃] *nm* replacement; (*job*) replacement work *no pl*; (*suppléance: Scol*) supply (*Brit*) *ou* substitute (*US*) teacher; **assurer le ~ de qn** (*remplaçant*) to stand in *ou* substitute for sb; **faire des ~s** (*professeur*) to do supply *ou* substitute teaching; (*médecin*) to do locum work

remplacer [Rɑ̃plase] *vt* to replace; (*prendre temporairement la place de*) to stand in for; (*tenir lieu de*) to take the place of, act as a substitute for; ~ **qch/qn par** to replace sth/sb with

rempli, e [Rɑ̃pli] *adj* (*emploi du temps*) full, busy; ~ **de** full of, filled with

remplir [Rɑ̃pliR] *vt* to fill (up); (*questionnaire*) to fill out *ou* up; (*obligations, fonction, condition*) to fulfil; **se remplir** *vi* to fill up; ~ **qch de** to fill sth with

remporter [Rɑ̃pɔRte] *vt* (*marchandise*) to take away; (*fig*) to win, achieve

remuant, e [Rəmɥɑ̃, -ɑ̃t] *adj* restless

remue-ménage [Rəmymenaʒ] *nm inv* commotion

remuer [Rəmɥe] *vt* to move; (*café, sauce*) to stir ▷ *vi* to move; (*fig: opposants*) to show signs of unrest; **se remuer** *vi* to move; (*se démener*) to stir o.s.; (*fam*) to get a move on

rémunérer [RemyneRe] *vt* to remunerate, pay

renard [RənaR] *nm* fox

renchérir [Rɑ̃ʃeRiR] *vi* to become more expensive; (*fig*): ~ **(sur)** to add something (to)

rencontre [Rɑ̃kɔ̃tR(ə)] *nf* (*de cours d'eau*) confluence; (*de véhicules*) collision; (*entrevue, congrès, match etc*) meeting; (*imprévue*) encounter; **faire la ~ de qn** to meet sb; **aller à la ~ de qn** to go and meet sb; **amours de ~** casual love affairs

rencontrer [Rɑ̃kɔ̃tRe] *vt* to meet; (*mot, expression*) to come across; (*difficultés*) to meet with; **se rencontrer** to meet; (*véhicules*) to collide

rendement [Rɑ̃dmɑ̃] *nm* (*d'un travailleur, d'une machine*) output; (*d'une culture*) yield; (*d'un investissement*) return; **à plein ~** at full capacity

rendez-vous [Rɑ̃devu] *nm* (*rencontre*) appointment; (: *d'amoureux*) date; (*lieu*) meeting place; **donner ~ à qn** to arrange to meet sb; **recevoir sur ~** to have an appointment system; **fixer un ~ à qn** to give sb an appointment; **avoir/prendre ~ (avec)** to have/make an appointment (with); **prendre ~ chez le médecin** to make an appointment with the doctor; ~ **spatial** *ou* **orbital** docking (in space)

rendre [Rɑ̃dR(ə)] *vt* (*livre, argent etc*) to give back, return; (*otages, visite, politesse, Jur: verdict*) to return; (*honneurs*) to pay; (*sang, aliments*) to bring up; (*sons: instrument*) to produce, make; (*exprimer, traduire*) to render; (*jugement*) to pronounce, render; (*faire devenir*): ~ **qn célèbre/qch possible** to make sb famous/sth possible; **se rendre** *vi* (*capituler*) to surrender, give o.s. up; (*aller*): **se ~ quelque part** to go somewhere; **se ~ à** (*arguments etc*) to bow to; (*ordres*) to comply with; **se ~ compte de qch** to realize sth; ~ **la vue/la santé à qn** to restore sb's sight/health; ~ **la liberté à qn** to set sb free; ~ **la monnaie à qn** to give change; **se ~ insupportable/ malade** to become unbearable/make o.s. ill

rênes [REn] *nfpl* reins

renfermé, e [Rɑ̃fERme] *adj* (*fig*) withdrawn ▷ *nm*: **sentir le ~** to smell stuffy

renfermer [Rɑ̃fERme] *vt* to contain; **se renfermer (sur soi-même)** to withdraw into o.s

renflouer [Rɑ̃flue] *vt* to refloat; (*fig*) to set back on its (*ou* his/her *etc*) feet (again)

renfoncement [Rɑ̃fɔ̃smɑ̃] *nm* recess

renforcer [Rɑ̃fɔRse] *vt* to reinforce; ~ **qn dans ses opinions** to confirm sb's opinion

renfort [Rɑ̃fɔR]: ~**s** *nmpl* reinforcements; **en ~** as a back-up; **à grand ~ de** with a great deal of

renfrogné, e [Rɑ̃fRɔɲe] *adj* sullen, scowling

rengaine [Rɑ̃gEn] *nf* (*péj*) old tune

renier [Rənje] *vt* (*parents*) to disown, repudiate; (*engagements*) to go back on; (*foi*) to renounce

renifler [Rənifle] *vi* to sniff ▷ *vt* (*tabac*) to sniff up; (*odeur*) to sniff

renne [REn] *nm* reindeer *inv*

renom [Rənɔ̃] *nm* reputation; (*célébrité*) renown; **vin de grand ~** celebrated *ou* highly renowned wine

renommé, e [R(ə)nɔme] *adj* celebrated, renowned ▷ *nf* fame

renoncer [Rənɔ̃se] *vi*: ~ **à** *vt* to give up; ~ **à faire** to give up the idea of doing; **j'y renonce!** I give up!

renouer [Rənwe] *vt* (*cravate etc*) to retie; (*fig: conversation, liaison*) to renew, resume; ~ **avec** (*tradition*) to revive; (*habitude*) to take up again; ~ **avec qn** to take up with sb again

renouvelable [R(ə)nuvlabl(ə)] *adj* (*contrat, bail, énergie*) renewable; (*expérience*) which can be renewed

renouveler [Rənuvle] *vt* to renew; (*exploit, méfait*) to repeat; **se renouveler** *vi* (*incident*) to recur, happen again, be repeated; (*cellules etc*) to be renewed *ou* replaced; (*artiste, écrivain*) to try something new

renouvellement [ʀ(ə)nuvɛlmɑ̃] *nm* renewal; recurrence

rénover [ʀenɔve] *vt* (*immeuble*) to renovate, do up; (*meuble*) to restore; (*enseignement*) to reform; (*quartier*) to redevelop

renseignement [ʀɑ̃sɛɲmɑ̃] *nm* information *no pl*, piece of information; (*Mil*) intelligence *no pl*; **prendre des ~s sur** to make inquiries about, ask for information about; **(guichet des)~s** information desk; **(service des)~s** (*Tél*) directory inquiries (*Brit*), information (*US*); **service de ~s** (*Mil*) intelligence service; **les ~s généraux** ≈ the secret police

renseigner [ʀɑ̃seɲe] *vt*: **~ qn (sur)** to give information to sb (about); **se renseigner** *vi* to ask for information, make inquiries

rentabilité [ʀɑ̃tabilite] *nf* profitability; cost-effectiveness; (*d'un investissement*) return; **seuil de ~** break-even point

rentable [ʀɑ̃tabl(ə)] *adj* profitable; cost-effective

rente [ʀɑ̃t] *nf* income; (*pension*) pension; (*titre*) government stock *ou* bond; **~ viagère** life annuity

rentrée [ʀɑ̃tʀe] *nf*: **~ (d'argent)** cash *no pl* coming in; **la ~ (des classes)** the start of the new school year; **la ~ (parlementaire)** the reopening *ou* reassembly of parliament; **faire sa ~** (*artiste, acteur*) to make a comeback

rentrer [ʀɑ̃tʀe] *vi* (*entrer de nouveau*) to go (*ou* come) back in; (*entrer*) to go (*ou* come) in; (*revenir chez soi*) to go (*ou* come) (back) home; (*air, clou: pénétrer*) to go in; (*revenu, argent*) to come in ▷ *vt* (*foins*) to bring in; (*véhicule*) to put away; (*chemise dans pantalon etc*) to tuck in; (*griffes*) to draw in; (*train d'atterrissage*) to raise; (*fig: larmes, colère etc*) to hold back; **~ le ventre** to pull in one's stomach; **~ dans** to go (*ou* come) back into; to go (*ou* come) into; (*famille, patrie*) to go back *ou* return to; (*heurter*) to crash into; (*appartenir à*) to be included in; (*: catégorie etc*) to fall into; **~ dans l'ordre** to get back to normal; **~ dans ses frais** to recover one's expenses (*ou* initial outlay)

renverse [ʀɑ̃vɛʀs(ə)]: **à la ~** *adv* backwards

renverser [ʀɑ̃vɛʀse] *vt* (*faire tomber: chaise, verre*) to knock over, overturn; (*piéton*) to knock down; (*liquide, contenu*) to spill, upset; (*retourner: verre, image*) to turn upside down, invert; (*: ordre des mots etc*) to reverse; (*fig: gouvernement etc*) to overthrow; (*stupéfier*) to bowl over, stagger; **se renverser** *vi* to fall over; to overturn; to spill; **se ~ (en arrière)** to lean back; **~ la tête/le corps (en arrière)** to tip one's head back/throw oneself back; **~ la vapeur** (*fig*) to change course

renvoi [ʀɑ̃vwa] *nm* dismissal; return; reflection; postponement; (*référence*) cross-reference; (*éructation*) belch

renvoyer [ʀɑ̃vwaje] *vt* to send back; (*congédier*) to dismiss; (*Tennis*) to return; (*lumière*) to reflect; (*son*) to echo; (*ajourner*): **~ qch (à)** to postpone sth

(until); **~ qch à qn** (*rendre*) to return sth to sb; **~ qn à** (*fig*) to refer sb to

repaire [ʀəpɛʀ] *nm* den

répandre [ʀepɑ̃dʀ(ə)] *vt* (*renverser*) to spill; (*étaler, diffuser*) to spread; (*lumière*) to shed; (*chaleur, odeur*) to give off; **se répandre** *vi* to spill; to spread; **se ~ en** (*injures etc*) to pour out

répandu, e [ʀepɑ̃dy] *pp de* **répandre** ▷ *adj* (*opinion, usage*) widespread

réparateur, -trice [ʀepaʀatœʀ, -tʀis] *nm/f* repairer

réparation [ʀepaʀasjɔ̃] *nf* repairing *no pl*, repair; **en ~** (*machine etc*) under repair; **demander à qn ~ de** (*offense etc*) to ask sb to make amends for

réparer [ʀepaʀe] *vt* to repair; (*fig: offense*) to make up for, atone for; (*: oubli, erreur*) to put right

repartie [ʀəpaʀti] *nf* retort; **avoir de la ~** to be quick at repartee

repartir [ʀəpaʀtiʀ] *vi* to set off again; to leave again; (*fig*) to get going again, pick up again; **~ à zéro** to start from scratch (again)

répartir [ʀepaʀtiʀ] *vt* (*pour attribuer*) to share out; (*pour disperser, disposer*) to divide up; (*poids, chaleur*) to distribute; (*étaler: dans le temps*): **~ sur** to spread over; (*classer, diviser*): **~ en** to divide into, split up into; **se répartir** *vt* (*travail, rôles*) to share out between themselves

répartition [ʀepaʀtisjɔ̃] *nf* sharing out; dividing up; distribution

repas [ʀəpɑ] *nm* meal; **à l'heure des ~** at mealtimes

repassage [ʀəpasaʒ] *nm* ironing

repasser [ʀəpase] *vi* to come (*ou* go) back ▷ *vt* (*vêtement, tissu*) to iron; (*examen*) to retake, resit; (*film*) to show again; (*lame*) to sharpen; (*leçon, rôle: revoir*) to go over (again); (*plat, pain*): **~ qch à qn** to pass sth back to sb

repêcher [ʀəpeʃe] *vt* (*noyé*) to recover the body of, fish out; (*fam: candidat*) to pass (*by inflating marks*); to give a second chance to

repentir [ʀəpɑ̃tiʀ] *nm* repentance; **se repentir** *vi*: **se ~ (de)** to repent (of)

répercussions [ʀepɛʀkysjɔ̃] *nfpl* repercussions

répercuter [ʀepɛʀkyte] *vt* (*réfléchir, renvoyer: son, voix*) to reflect; (*faire transmettre: consignes, charges etc*) to pass on; **se répercuter** *vi* (*bruit*) to reverberate; (*fig*): **se ~ sur** to have repercussions on

repère [ʀəpɛʀ] *nm* mark; (*monument etc*) landmark; **(point de) ~** point of reference

repérer [ʀəpeʀe] *vt* (*erreur, connaissance*) to spot; (*abri, ennemi*) to locate; **se repérer** *vi* to get one's bearings; **se faire ~** to be spotted

répertoire [ʀepɛʀtwaʀ] *nm* (*liste*) (alphabetical) list; (*carnet*) index notebook; (*Inform*) directory; (*de carnet*) thumb index; (*indicateur*) directory, index; (*d'un théâtre, artiste*) repertoire

répéter [ʀepete] *vt* to repeat; (*préparer: leçon*) ▷ *aussi vi* to learn, go over; (*Théât*) to rehearse; **se répéter** (*redire*) to repeat o.s.; (*se reproduire*) to be repeated, recur

répétition [ʀepetisjɔ̃] *nf* repetition; (*Théât*)

rehearsal; **répétitions** nfpl (leçons) private coaching sg; **armes à ~** repeater weapons; **~ générale** final dress rehearsal

répit [ʀepi] nm respite; **sans ~** without letting up

replier [ʀəplije] vt (rabattre) to fold down ou over; **se replier** vi (armée) to withdraw, fall back; **se ~ sur soi-même** to withdraw into oneself

réplique [ʀeplik] nf (repartie, fig) reply; (objection) retort; (Théât) line; (copie) replica; **donner la ~ à** to play opposite; **sans ~** adj no-nonsense; irrefutable

répliquer [ʀeplike] vi to reply; (avec impertinence) to answer back; (riposter) to retaliate

répondeur [ʀepɔ̃dœʀ] nm answering machine

répondre [ʀepɔ̃dʀ(ə)] vi to answer, reply; (freins, mécanisme) to respond; **~ à** vt to reply to, answer; (avec impertinence): **~ à qn** to answer sb back; (invitation, convocation) to reply to; (affection, salut) to return; (provocation: mécanisme etc) to respond to; (correspondre à: besoin) to answer; (: conditions) to meet; (: description) to match; **~ que** to answer ou reply that; **~ de** to answer for

réponse [ʀepɔ̃s] nf answer, reply; **avec ~ payée** (Postes) reply-paid, post-paid (US); **avoir ~ à tout** to have an answer for everything; **en ~ à** in reply to; **carte-/bulletin-~** reply card/slip

reportage [ʀəpɔʀtaʒ] nm (bref) report; (écrit: documentaire) story; article; (en direct) commentary; (genre, activité): **le ~** reporting

reporter nm [ʀəpɔʀtɛʀ] reporter ▷ vt [ʀəpɔʀte] (total): **~ qch sur** to carry sth forward ou over to; (ajourner): **~ qch (à)** to postpone sth (until); (transférer): **~ qch sur** to transfer sth to; **se ~ à** (époque) to think back to; (document) to refer to

repos [ʀəpo] nm rest; (fig) peace (and quiet); (mental) peace of mind; (Mil): **~!** (stand) at ease!; **en ~** at rest; **au ~** at rest; (soldat) at ease; **de tout ~** safe

reposant, e [ʀ(ə)pozɑ̃, -ɑ̃t] adj restful; (sommeil) refreshing

reposer [ʀəpoze] vt (verre, livre) to put down; (rideaux, carreaux) to put back; (délasser) to rest; (problème) to reformulate ▷ vi (liquide, pâte) to settle, rest; (personne): **ici repose ...** here lies ...; **~ sur** to be built on; (fig) to rest on; **se reposer** vi to rest; **se ~ sur qn** to rely on sb

repoussant, e [ʀəpusɑ̃, -ɑ̃t] adj repulsive

repousser [ʀəpuse] vi to grow again ▷ vt to repel, repulse; (offre) to turn down, reject; (tiroir, personne) to push back; (différer) to put back

reprendre [ʀəpʀɑ̃dʀ(ə)] vt (prisonnier, ville) to recapture; (objet prêté, donné) to take back; (chercher): **je viendrai te ~ à 4 h** I'll come and fetch you ou I'll come back for you at 4; (se resservir de): **~ du pain/un œuf** to take (ou eat) more bread/another egg; (Comm: article usagé) to take back; (firme, entreprise) to take over; (travail, promenade) to resume; (emprunter: argument, idée) to take up, use; (refaire: article etc) to go over again; (jupe etc) to alter; (émission, pièce) to put on again;

(réprimander) to tell off; (corriger) to correct ▷ vi (classes, pluie) to start (up) again; (activités, travaux, combats) to resume, start (up) again; (affaires, industrie) to pick up; (dire): **reprit-il** he went on; **se reprendre** (se ressaisir) to recover, pull o.s. together; **s'y ~** to make another attempt; **~ des forces** to recover one's strength; **~ courage** to take new heart; **~ ses habitudes/sa liberté** to get back into one's old habits/regain one's freedom; **~ la route** to resume one's journey, set off again; **~ connaissance** to come to, regain consciousness; **~ haleine** ou **son souffle** to get one's breath back; **~ la parole** to speak again

représailles [ʀəpʀezaj] nfpl reprisals, retaliation sg

représentant, e [ʀəpʀezɑ̃tɑ̃, -ɑ̃t] nm/f representative

représentation [ʀəpʀezɑ̃tasjɔ̃] nf representation; performing; (symbole, image) representation; (spectacle) performance; (Comm): **la ~** commercial travelling; sales representation; **frais de ~** (d'un diplomate) entertainment allowance

représenter [ʀəpʀezɑ̃te] vt to represent; (donner: pièce, opéra) to perform; **se représenter** vt (se figurer) to imagine; to visualize ▷ vi: **se ~ à** (Pol) to stand ou run again at; (Scol) to resit

répression [ʀepʀesjɔ̃] nf voir **réprimer** suppression; repression; (Pol): **la ~** repression; **mesures de ~** repressive measures

réprimer [ʀepʀime] vt (émotions) to suppress; (peuple etc) repress

repris, e [ʀəpʀi, -iz] pp de **reprendre** ▷ nm: **~ de justice** ex-prisoner, ex-convict

reprise [ʀəpʀiz] nf (recommencement) resumption; (économique) recovery; (TV) repeat; (Ciné) rerun; (Boxe etc) round; (Auto) acceleration no pl; (Comm) trade-in, part exchange; (de location) sum asked for any extras or improvements made to the property; (raccommodage) darn; mend; **la ~ des hostilités** the resumption of hostilities; **à plusieurs ~s** on several occasions, several times

repriser [ʀəpʀize] vt to darn; to mend; **aiguille/coton à ~** darning needle/thread

reproche [ʀəpʀɔʃ] nm (remontrance) reproach; **ton/air de ~** reproachful tone/look; **faire des ~s à qn** to reproach sb; **faire ~ à qn de qch** to reproach sb for sth; **sans ~(s)** beyond ou above reproach

reprocher [ʀəpʀɔʃe] vt: **~ qch à qn** to reproach ou blame sb for sth; **~ qch à** (machine, théorie) to have sth against; **se ~ qch/d'avoir fait qch** to blame o.s for sth/for doing sth

reproduction [ʀəpʀɔdyksjɔ̃] nf reproduction; **~ interdite** all rights (of reproduction) reserved

reproduire [ʀəpʀɔdɥiʀ] vt to reproduce; **se reproduire** vi (Bio) to reproduce; (recommencer) to recur, re-occur

réprouver [ʀepʀuve] vt to reprove

reptile [ʀɛptil] nm reptile

repu, e [ʀəpy] pp de **repaître** ▷ adj satisfied, sated

république [ʀepyblik] nf republic; **R~**

arabe du Yémen Yemen Arab Republic; **R~ Centrafricaine** Central African Republic; **R~ de Corée** South Korea; **R~ dominicaine** Dominican Republic; **R~ d'Irlande** Irish Republic, Eire; **R~ populaire de Chine** People's Republic of China; **R~ populaire démocratique de Corée** Democratic People's Republic of Korea; **R~ populaire du Yémen** People's Democratic Republic of Yemen

répugnant, e [Repyɲɑ̃, -ɑ̃t] *adj* repulsive, loathsome

répugner [Repyɲe]: **~ à** *vt*: **~ à qn** to repel *ou* disgust sb; **~ à faire** to be loath *ou* reluctant to do

réputation [Repytɑsjɔ̃] *nf* reputation; **avoir la ~ d'être ...** to have a reputation for being ...; **connaître qn/qch de ~** to know sb/sth by repute; **de ~ mondiale** world-renowned

réputé, e [Repyte] *adj* renowned; **être ~ pour** to have a reputation for, be renowned for

requérir [RɑkeRiR] *vt* (*nécessiter*) to require, call for; (*au nom de la loi*) to call upon; (*Jur: peine*) to call for, demand

requête [Rɑkɛt] *nf* request, petition; (*Jur*) petition

requin [Rɑkɛ̃] *nm* shark

requis, e [Rɑki, -iz] *pp de* **requérir** ▷ *adj* required

RER *sigle m* (= *Réseau express régional*) *Greater Paris high speed train service*

rescapé, e [Rɛskape] *nm/f* survivor

rescousse [Rɛskus] *nf*: **aller à la ~ de qn** to go to sb's aid *ou* rescue; **appeler qn à la ~** to call on sb for help

réseau, x [Rezo] *nm* network

réservation [RezɛRvɑsjɔ̃] *nf* reservation; booking

réserve [RezɛRv(ə)] *nf* (*retenue*) reserve; (*entrepôt*) storeroom; (*restriction, aussi: d'Indiens*) reservation; (*de pêche, chasse*) preserve; (*restrictions*): **faire des ~s** to have reservations; **officier de ~** reserve officer; **sous toutes ~s** with all reserve; (*dire*) with reservations; **sous ~ de** subject to; **sans ~** *adv* unreservedly; **en ~** in reserve; **de ~** (*provisions etc*) in reserve

réservé, e [RezɛRve] *adj* (*discret*) reserved; (*chasse, pêche*) private; **~ à** *ou* **pour** reserved for

réserver [RezɛRve] *vt* (*gén*) to reserve; (*chambre, billet etc*) to book, reserve; (*mettre de côté, garder*): **~ qch pour** *ou* **à** to keep *ou* save sth for; **~ qch à qn** to reserve (*ou* book) sth for sb; (*fig: destiner*) to have sth in store for sb; **se ~ le droit de faire** to reserve the right to do

réservoir [RezɛRvwaR] *nm* tank

résidence [Rezidɑ̃s] *nf* residence; **~ principale/secondaire** main/second home; **~ universitaire** hall of residence; **(en) ~ surveillée** (under) house arrest

résidentiel, le [Rezidɑ̃sjɛl] *adj* residential

résider [Rezide] *vi*: **~ à** *ou* **dans** *ou* **en** to reside in; **~ dans** (*fig*) to lie in

résidu [Rezidy] *nm* residue *no pl*

résigner [Reziɲe] *vt* to relinquish, resign; **se résigner** *vi*: **se ~ (à qch/à faire)** to resign o.s. (to

sth/to doing)

résilier [Rezilje] *vt* to terminate

résistance [Rezistɑ̃s] *nf* resistance; (*de réchaud, bouilloire: fil*) element

résistant, e [Rezistɑ̃, -ɑ̃t] *adj* (*personne*) robust, tough; (*matériau*) strong, hard-wearing ▷ *nm/f* (*patriote*) Resistance worker *ou* fighter

résister [Reziste] *vi* to resist; **~ à** *vt* (*assaut, tentation*) to resist; (*effort, souffrance*) to withstand; (*matériau, plante*) to stand up to, withstand; (*personne: désobéir à*) to stand up to, oppose

résolu, e [Rezɔly] *pp de* **résoudre** ▷ *adj* (*ferme*) resolute; **être ~ à qch/faire** to be set upon sth/doing

résolution [Rezɔlysjɔ̃] *nf* solving; (*fermeté, décision, Inform*) resolution; **prendre la ~ de** to make a resolution to

résonner [Rezɔne] *vi* (*cloche, pas*) to reverberate, resound; (*salle*) to be resonant; **~ de** to resound with

résorber [RezɔRbe]: **se résorber** *vi* (*Méd*) to be resorbed; (*fig*) to be absorbed

résoudre [RezudR(ə)] *vt* to solve; **~ qn à faire qch** to get sb to make up his (*ou* her) mind to do sth; **~ de faire** to resolve to do; **se ~ à faire** to bring o.s. to do

respect [Rɛspɛ] *nm* respect; **tenir en ~** to keep at bay

respecter [Rɛspɛkte] *vt* to respect; **faire ~** to enforce; **le lexicographe qui se respecte** (*fig*) any self-respecting lexicographer

respectueux, -euse [Rɛspɛktɥø, -øz] *adj* respectful; **~ de** respectful of

respiration [RɛspiRɑsjɔ̃] *nf* breathing *no pl*; **faire une ~ complète** to breathe in and out; **retenir sa ~** to hold one's breath; **~ artificielle** artificial respiration

respirer [RɛspiRe] *vi* to breathe; (*fig: se reposer*) to get one's breath, have a break; (: *être soulagé*) to breathe again ▷ *vt* to breathe (in), inhale; (*manifester: santé, calme etc*) to exude

resplendir [Rɛsplɑ̃diR] *vi* to shine; (*fig*): **~ (de)** to be radiant (with)

responsabilité [Rɛspɔ̃sabilite] *nf* responsibility; (*légale*) liability; **refuser la ~ de** to deny responsibility (*ou* liability) for; **prendre ses ~s** to assume responsibility for one's actions; **~ civile** civil liability; **~ pénale/ morale/collective** criminal/moral/collective responsibility

responsable [Rɛspɔ̃sabl(ə)] *adj* responsible ▷ *nm/ f* (*du ravitaillement etc*) person in charge; (*de parti, syndicat*) official; **~ de** responsible for; (*légalement: de dégâts etc*) liable for; (*chargé de*) in charge of, responsible for

resquiller [Rɛskije] *vi* (*au cinéma, au stade*) to get in on the sly; (*dans le train*) to fiddle a free ride

ressaisir [RɑseziR]: **se ressaisir** *vi* to regain one's self-control; (*équipe sportive*) to rally

ressasser [Rɑsase] *vt* (*remâcher*) to keep turning over; (*redire*) to keep trotting out

ressemblance [Rɑsɑ̃blɑ̃s] *nf* (*visuelle*)

resemblance, similarity, likeness; (:*Art*)
likeness; (*analogie, trait commun*) similarity
ressemblant, e [Rəsãblã, -ãt] *adj* (*portrait*)
lifelike, true to life
ressembler [Rəsãble]: ~ **à** *vt* to be like, resemble;
(*visuellement*) to look like; **se ressembler** *vi* to be
(*ou* look) alike
ressemeler [Rəsəmle] *vt* to (re)sole
ressentiment [Rəsãtimã] *nm* resentment
ressentir [RəsãtiR] *vt* to feel; **se ~ de** to feel (*ou*
show) the effects of
resserrer [RəseRe] *vt* (*pores*) to close; (*nœud,
boulon*) to tighten (up); (*fig: liens*) to strengthen;
se resserrer *vi* (*route, vallée*) to narrow; (*liens*)
to strengthen; **se ~ (autour de)** to draw closer
(around), to close in (on)
resservir [RəseRviR] *vi* to do *ou* serve again ▷ *vt*:
~ **qch (à qn)** to serve sth up again (to sb); ~ **de
qch (à qn)** to give (sb) a second helping of sth; ~
qn (d'un plat) to give sb a second helping (of a
dish); **se ~ de** (*plat*) to take a second helping of;
(*outil etc*) to use again
ressort [RəsɔR] *vb voir* **ressortir** ▷ *nm* (*pièce*)
spring; (*force morale*) spirit; (*recours*): **en dernier
~** as a last resort; (*compétence*): **être du ~ de** to fall
within the competence of
ressortir [RəsɔRtiR] *vi* to go (*ou* come) out
(again); (*contraster*) to stand out; ~ **de** (*résulter
de*): **il ressort de ceci que** it emerges from this
that; ~ **à** (*Jur*) to come under the jurisdiction of;
(*Admin*) to be the concern of; **faire ~** (*fig: souligner*)
to bring out
ressortissant, e [RəsɔRtisã, -ãt] *nm/f* national
ressource [RəsuRs(ə)] *nf*: **avoir la ~ de** to have
the possibility of; **ressources** *nfpl* resources;
(*fig*) possibilities; **leur seule ~ était de** the
only course open to them was to; **~s d'énergie**
energy resources
ressusciter [Resysite] *vt* to resuscitate, restore to
life; (*fig*) to revive, bring back ▷ *vi* to rise (from
the dead); (*fig: pays*) to come back to life
restant, e [Restã, -ãt] *adj* remaining ▷ *nm*: **le ~
(de)** the remainder (of); **un ~ de** (*de trop*) some
leftover; (*vestige*) a remnant *ou* last trace of
restaurant [RestɔRã] *nm* restaurant; **manger
au ~** to eat out; ~ **d'entreprise** staff canteen *ou*
cafeteria (*US*); ~ **universitaire (RU)** university
refectory *ou* cafeteria (*US*)
restauration [RestɔRasjɔ̃] *nf* restoration;
(*hôtellerie*) catering; ~ **rapide** fast food
restaurer [RestɔRe] *vt* to restore; **se restaurer** *vi*
to have something to eat
reste [Rest(ə)] *nm* (*restant*): **le ~ (de)** the rest (of);
(*de trop*): **un ~ (de)** some leftover; (*vestige*): **un ~
de** a remnant *ou* last trace of; (*Math*) remainder;
restes *nmpl* leftovers; (*d'une cité etc, dépouille
mortelle*) remains; **avoir du temps de ~** to have
time to spare; **ne voulant pas être en ~** not
wishing to be outdone; **partir sans attendre** *ou*
demander son ~ (*fig*) to leave without waiting
to hear more; **du ~, au ~** *adv* besides, moreover;
pour le ~, quant au ~ *adv* as for the rest

rester [Reste] *vi* (*dans un lieu, un état, une position*) to
stay, remain; (*subsister*) to remain, be left; (*durer*)
to last, live on ▷ *vb impers*: **il reste du pain/deux
œufs** there's some bread/there are two eggs left
(over); **il reste du temps/10 minutes** there's
some time/there are 10 minutes left; **il me
reste assez de temps** I have enough time left;
voilà tout ce qui (me) reste that's all I've got
left; **ce qui reste à faire** what remains to be
done; **ce qui me reste à faire** what remains
for me to do; **(il) reste à savoir/établir si ...** it
remains to be seen/established if *ou* whether ...;
il n'en reste pas moins que ... the fact remains
that ..., it's nevertheless a fact that ...; **en ~ à**
(*stade, menaces*) to go no further than, only go as
far as; **restons-en là** let's leave it at that; **~ sur
une impression** to retain an impression; **y ~: il
a failli y rester** he nearly met his end
restituer [Restitɥe] *vt* (*objet, somme*): **~ qch (à qn)**
to return *ou* restore sth (to sb); (*énergie*) to release;
(*son*) to reproduce
restreindre [RestRɛ̃dR(ə)] *vt* to restrict, limit;
se restreindre (*dans ses dépenses etc*) to cut down;
(*champ de recherches*) to narrow
restriction [RestRiksjɔ̃] *nf* restriction; (*condition*)
qualification; **restrictions** *nfpl* (*mentales*)
reservations; **sans ~** *adv* unreservedly
résultat [Rezylta] *nm* result; (*conséquence*)
outcome *no pl*, result; (*d'élection etc*) results
pl; **résultats** *nmpl* (*d'une enquête*) findings; **~s
sportifs** sports results
résulter [Rezylte]: **~ de** *vt* to result from, be the
result of; **il résulte de ceci que ...** the result of
this is that ...
résumé [Rezyme] *nm* summary, résumé; **faire
le ~ de** to summarize; **en ~** *adv* in brief; (*pour
conclure*) to sum up
résumer [Rezyme] *vt* (*texte*) to summarize;
(*récapituler*) to sum up; (*fig*) to epitomize, typify;
se résumer *vi* (*personne*) to sum up (one's ideas);
se ~ à to come down to
résurrection [RezyRɛksjɔ̃] *nf* resurrection; (*fig*)
revival
rétablir [RetabliR] *vt* to restore, re-establish;
(*personne: traitement*): **~ qn** to restore sb to health,
help sb recover; (*Admin*): **~ qn dans son emploi/
ses droits** to reinstate sb in his post/restore sb's
rights; **se rétablir** *vi* (*guérir*) to recover; (*silence,
calme*) to return, be restored; (*Gym etc*): **se ~ (sur)**
to pull o.s. up (onto)
rétablissement [Retablismã] *nm* restoring;
recovery; pull-up
retaper [Rətape] *vt* (*maison, voiture etc*) to do up;
(*fam: revigorer*) to buck up; (*redactylographier*) to
retype
retard [RətaR] *nm* (*d'une personne attendue*) lateness
no pl; (*sur l'horaire, un programme, une échéance*)
delay; (*fig: scolaire, mental etc*) backwardness;
être en ~ (*pays*) to be backward; (*dans paiement,
travail*) to be behind; **en ~ (de deux heures)**
(two hours) late; **avoir un ~ de deux km** (*Sport*)
to be two km behind; **rattraper son ~** to catch

up; **avoir du ~** to be late; (*sur un programme*) to be behind (schedule); **prendre du ~** (*train, avion*) to be delayed; (*montre*) to lose (time); **sans ~** *adv* without delay; **~ à l'allumage** (*Auto*) retarded spark; **~ scolaire** backwardness at school

retardataire [ʀətaʀdatɛʀ] *adj* late; (*enfant, idées*) backward ▷ *nm/f* latecomer; backward child

retardement [ʀətaʀdəmɑ̃] *nm*: **à ~** *adj* delayed action *cpd*; **bombe à ~** time bomb

retarder [ʀətaʀde] *vt* (*sur un horaire*): **~ qn (d'une heure)** to delay sb (an hour); (*sur un programme*): **~ qn (de trois mois)** to set sb back *ou* delay sb (three months); (*départ, date*): **~ qch (de deux jours)** to put sth back (two days), delay sth (for *ou* by two days); (*horloge*) to put back ▷ *vi* (*montre*) to be slow; (*: habituellement*) to lose (time); **je retarde (d'une heure)** I'm (an hour) slow

retenir [ʀətniʀ] *vt* (*garder, retarder*) to keep, detain; (*maintenir: objet qui glisse, fig: colère, larmes, rire*) to hold back; (*: objet suspendu*) to hold; (*: chaleur, odeur*) to retain; (*fig: empêcher d'agir*): **~ qn (de faire)** to hold sb back (from doing); (*se rappeler*) to retain; (*réserver*) to reserve; (*accepter*) to accept; (*prélever*): **~ qch (sur)** to deduct sth (from); **se retenir** (*euphémisme*) to hold on; (*se raccrocher*): **se ~ à** to hold onto; (*se contenir*): **se ~ de faire** to restrain o.s. from doing; **~ son souffle** *ou* **haleine** to hold one's breath; **~ qn à dîner** to ask sb to stay for dinner; **je pose trois et je retiens deux** put down three and carry two

retentir [ʀətɑ̃tiʀ] *vi* to ring out; (*salle*): **~ de** to ring *ou* resound with; **~ sur** *vt* (*fig*) to have an effect upon

retentissant, e [ʀətɑ̃tisɑ̃, -ɑ̃t] *adj* resounding; (*fig*) impact-making

retentissement [ʀətɑ̃tismɑ̃] *nm* (*retombées*) repercussions *pl*; effect, impact

retenu, e [ʀətny] *pp de* **retenir** ▷ *adj* (*place*) reserved; (*personne: empêché*) held up; (*propos: contenu, discret*) restrained ▷ *nf* (*prélèvement*) deduction; (*Math*) number to carry over; (*Scol*) detention; (*modération*) (self-)restraint; (*réserve*) reserve, reticence; (*Auto*) tailback

réticence [ʀetisɑ̃s] *nf* reticence *no pl*, reluctance *no pl*; **sans ~** without hesitation

réticent, e [ʀetisɑ̃, -ɑ̃t] *adj* reticent, reluctant

rétine [ʀetin] *nf* retina

retiré, e [ʀətiʀe] *adj* (*solitaire*) secluded; (*éloigné*) remote

retirer [ʀətiʀe] *vt* to withdraw; (*vêtement, lunettes*) to take off, remove; (*enlever*): **~ qch à qn** to take sth from sb; (*extraire*): **~ qn/qch de** to take sb away from/sth out of, remove sb/sth from; (*reprendre: bagages, billets*) to collect, pick up; **~ des avantages de** to derive advantages from; **se retirer** *vi* (*partir, reculer*) to withdraw; (*prendre sa retraite*) to retire; **se ~ de** to withdraw from; to retire from

retombées [ʀətɔ̃be] *nfpl* (*radioactives*) fallout *sg*; (*fig*) fallout; spin-offs

retomber [ʀətɔ̃be] *vi* (*à nouveau*) to fall again; (*rechuter*): **~ malade/dans l'erreur** to fall ill

again/fall back into error; (*atterrir: après un saut etc*) to land; (*tomber, redescendre*) to fall back; (*pendre*) to fall, hang (down); (*échoir*): **~ sur qn** to fall on sb

rétorquer [ʀetɔʀke] *vt*: **~ (à qn) que** to retort (to sb) that

retouche [ʀətuʃ] *nf* touching up *no pl*; alteration; **faire une ~** *ou* **des ~s à** to touch up

retoucher [ʀətuʃe] *vt* (*photographie, tableau*) to touch up; (*texte, vêtement*) to alter

retour [ʀətuʀ] *nm* return; **au ~** (*en arrivant*) when we (*ou* they *etc*) get (*ou* got) back; (*en route*) on the way back; **pendant le ~** on the way *ou* journey back; **à mon/ton ~** on my/your return; **au ~ de** on the return of; **être de ~ (de)** to be back (from); **de ~ à .../chez moi** back at .../back home; **en ~** *adv* in return; **par ~ du courrier** by return of post; **par un juste ~ des choses** by a favourable twist of fate; **match ~** return match; **~ en arrière** (*Ciné*) flashback; (*mesure*) backward step; **~ de bâton** kickback; **~ de chariot** carriage return; **~ à l'envoyeur** (*Postes*) return to sender; **~ de flamme** backfire; **~ (automatique) à la ligne** (*Inform*) wordwrap; **~ de manivelle** (*fig*) backfire; **~ offensif** renewed attack; **~ aux sources** (*fig*) return to basics

retourner [ʀətuʀne] *vt* (*dans l'autre sens: matelas, crêpe*) to turn (over); (*: caisse*) to turn upside down; (*: sac, vêtement*) to turn inside out; (*fig: argument*) to turn back; (*en remuant: terre, sol, foin*) to turn over; (*émouvoir: personne*) to shake; (*renvoyer, restituer*): **~ qch à qn** to return sth to sb ▷ *vi* (*aller, revenir*): **~ quelque part/à** to go back *ou* return somewhere/to; **~ à** (*état, activité*) to return to, go back to; **se retourner** *vi* to turn over; (*tourner la tête*) to turn round; **s'en ~** to go back; **se retourner contre** (*fig*) to turn against; **savoir de quoi il retourne** to know what it is all about; **~ sa veste** (*fig*) to turn one's coat; **~ en arrière** *ou* **sur ses pas** to turn back, retrace one's steps; **~ aux sources** to go back to basics

retrait [ʀətʀɛ] *nm voir* **retirer** withdrawal; collection; *voir* **se retirer** withdrawal; (*rétrécissement*) shrinkage; **en ~** *adj* set back; **écrire en ~** to indent; **~ du permis (de conduire)** disqualification from driving (*Brit*), revocation of driver's license (*US*)

retraite [ʀətʀɛt] *nf* (*d'une armée, Rel, refuge*) retreat; (*d'un employé*) retirement; (*revenu*) (retirement) pension; **être/mettre à la ~** to be retired/ pension off *ou* retire; **prendre sa ~** to retire; **~ anticipée** early retirement; **~ aux flambeaux** torchlight tattoo

retraité, e [ʀətʀete] *adj* retired ▷ *nm/f* (old age) pensioner

retrancher [ʀətʀɑ̃ʃe] *vt* (*passage, détails*) to take out, remove; (*nombre, somme*): **~ qch de** to take *ou* deduct sth from; (*couper*) to cut off; **se ~ derrière/dans** to entrench o.s. behind/in; (*fig*) to take refuge behind/in

retransmettre [ʀətʀɑ̃smɛtʀ(ə)] *vt* (*Radio*) to broadcast, relay; (*TV*) to show

rétrécir [ʀetʀesiʀ] vt (vêtement) to take in ▷ vi to shrink; **se rétrécir** vi to narrow

rétribution [ʀetʀibysjɔ̃] nf payment

rétro [ʀetʀo] adj inv old-style ▷ nm (rétroviseur) (rear-view) mirror; **la mode ~** the nostalgia vogue

rétrograde [ʀetʀogʀad] adj reactionary, backward-looking

rétroprojecteur [ʀetʀopʀoʒɛktœʀ] nm overhead projector

rétrospectif, -ive [ʀetʀospɛktif, -iv] adj, nf retrospective

rétrospectivement [ʀetʀospɛktivmɑ̃] adv in retrospect

retrousser [ʀətʀuse] vt to roll up; (fig: nez) to wrinkle; (: lèvres) to curl

retrouvailles [ʀətʀuvaj] nfpl reunion sg

retrouver [ʀətʀuve] vt (fugitif, objet perdu) to find; (occasion) to find again; (calme, santé) to regain; (reconnaître: expression, style) to recognize; (revoir) to see again; (rejoindre) to meet (again), join; **se retrouver** vi to meet; (s'orienter) to find one's way; **se ~ quelque part** to find o.s. somewhere; to end up somewhere; **se ~ seul/sans argent** to find o.s. alone/with no money; **se ~ dans** (calculs, dossiers, désordre) to make sense of; **s'y ~** (rentrer dans ses frais) to break even

rétroviseur [ʀetʀovizœʀ] nm (rear-view) mirror

réunion [ʀeynjɔ̃] nf bringing together; joining; (séance) meeting

réunir [ʀeyniʀ] vt (convoquer) to call together; (rassembler) to gather together; (cumuler) to combine; (rapprocher) to bring together (again), reunite; (rattacher) to join (together); **se réunir** vi (se rencontrer) to meet; (s'allier) to unite

réussi, e [ʀeysi] adj successful

réussir [ʀeysiʀ] vi to succeed, be successful; (à un examen) to pass; (plante, culture) to thrive, do well ▷ vt to make a success of; to bring off; **~ à faire** to succeed in doing; **~ à qn** to go right for sb; (aliment) to agree with sb; **le travail/le mariage lui réussit** work/married life agrees with him

réussite [ʀeysit] nf success; (Cartes) patience

revaloir [ʀəvalwaʀ] vt: **je vous revaudrai cela** I'll repay you some day; (en mal) I'll pay you back for this

revanche [ʀəvɑ̃ʃ] nf revenge; **prendre sa ~ (sur)** to take one's revenge (on); **en ~** (par contre) on the other hand; (en compensation) in return

rêve [ʀɛv] nm dream; (activité psychique): **le ~** dreaming; **paysage/silence de ~** dreamlike landscape/silence; **~ éveillé** daydreaming no pl, daydream

revêche [ʀəvɛʃ] adj surly, sour-tempered

réveil [ʀevɛj] nm (d'un dormeur) waking up no pl; (fig) awakening; (pendule) alarm (clock); **au ~** when I (ou you etc) wake (ou woke) up, on waking (up); **sonner le ~** (Mil) to sound the reveille

réveille-matin [ʀevɛjmatɛ̃] nm inv alarm clock

réveiller [ʀeveje] vt (personne) to wake up; (fig) to awaken, revive; **se réveiller** vi to wake up; (fig) to be revived, reawaken

réveillon [ʀevɛjɔ̃] nm Christmas Eve; (de la Saint-Sylvestre) New Year's Eve; Christmas Eve (ou New Year's Eve) party ou dinner

réveillonner [ʀevɛjone] vi to celebrate Christmas Eve (ou New Year's Eve)

révélateur, -trice [ʀevelatœʀ, -tʀis] adj: **~ (de qch)** revealing (sth) ▷ nm (Photo) developer

révéler [ʀevele] vt (gén) to reveal; (divulguer) to disclose, reveal; (dénoter) to reveal, show; (faire connaître au public): **~ qn/qch** to make sb/sth widely known, bring sb/sth to the public's notice; **se révéler** vi to be revealed, reveal itself; **se ~ facile/faux** to prove (to be) easy/false; **se ~ cruel/un allié sûr** to show o.s. to be cruel/a trustworthy ally

revenant, e [ʀəvnɑ̃, -ɑ̃t] nm/f ghost

revendeur, -euse [ʀəvɑ̃dœʀ, -øz] nm/f (détaillant) retailer; (d'occasions) secondhand dealer

revendication [ʀəvɑ̃dikasjɔ̃] nf claim, demand; **journée de ~** day of action (in support of one's claims)

revendiquer [ʀəvɑ̃dike] vt to claim, demand; (responsabilité) to claim ▷ vi to agitate in favour of one's claims

revendre [ʀəvɑ̃dʀ(ə)] vt (d'occasion) to resell; (détailler) to sell; (vendre davantage de): **~ du sucre/ un foulard/deux bagues** to sell more sugar/ another scarf/another two rings; **à ~** adv (en abondance) to spare

revenir [ʀəvniʀ] vi to come back; (Culin): **faire ~ to brown**; (coûter): **~ cher/à 100 euros (à qn)** to cost (sb) a lot/100 euros; **~ à** (études, projet) to return to, go back to; (équivaloir à) to amount to; **~ à qn** (rumeur, nouvelle) to get back to sb, reach sb's ears; (part, honneur) to go to sb, be sb's; (souvenir, nom) to come back to sb; **~ de** (fig: maladie, étonnement) to recover from; **~ sur** (question, sujet) to go back over; (engagement) to go back on; **~ à la charge** to return to the attack; **~ à soi** to come round; **n'en pas ~**: **je n'en reviens** I can't get over it; **~ sur ses pas** to retrace one's steps; **cela revient à dire que/au même** it amounts to saying that/to the same thing; **~ de loin** (fig) to have been at death's door

revenu, e [ʀəvny] pp de **revenir** ▷ nm income; (de l'État) revenue; (d'un capital) yield; **revenus** nmpl income sg; **~ national brut** gross national income

rêver [ʀeve] vi, vt to dream; (rêvasser) to (day)dream; **~ de** (voir en rêve) to dream of ou about; **~ qch/de faire** to dream of sth/of doing; **~ à** to dream of

réverbère [ʀevɛʀbɛʀ] nm street lamp ou light

réverbérer [ʀevɛʀbeʀe] vt to reflect

révérence [ʀeveʀɑ̃s] nf (vénération) reverence; (salut: d'homme) bow; (: de femme) curtsey

rêverie [ʀɛvʀi] nf daydreaming no pl, daydream

revers [ʀəvɛʀ] nm (de feuille, main) back; (d'étoffe) wrong side; (de pièce, médaille) back, reverse; (Tennis, Ping-Pong) backhand; (de veston) lapel; (de pantalon) turn-up; (fig: échec) setback; **~ de fortune** reverse of fortune; **d'un ~ de main**

with the back of one's hand; **le ~ de la médaille** (*fig*) the other side of the coin; **prendre à ~** (*Mil*) to take from the rear

revêtement [Rəvetmɑ̃] *nm* (*de paroi*) facing; (*des sols*) flooring; (*de chaussée*) surface; (*de tuyau etc*: *enduit*) coating

revêtir [Rəvetir] *vt* (*habit*) to don, put on; (*fig*) to take on; **~ qn de** to dress sb in; (*fig*) to endow *ou* invest sb with; **~ qch de** to cover sth with; (*fig*) to cloak sth in; **~ d'un visa** to append a visa to

rêveur, -euse [REvœR, -øz] *adj* dreamy ▷ *nm/f* dreamer

revient [Rəvjɛ̃] *vb voir* **revenir** ▷ *nm*: **prix de ~** cost price

revigorer [Rəvigɔre] *vt* to invigorate, revive, buck up

revirement [RəviRmɑ̃] *nm* change of mind; (*d'une situation*) reversal

réviser [Revize] *vt* (*texte, Scol: matière*) to revise; (*comptes*) to audit; (*machine, installation, moteur*) to overhaul, service; (*Jur: procès*) to review

révision [Revizjɔ̃] *nf* revision; auditing *no pl*; overhaul, servicing *no pl*; review; **conseil de ~** (*Mil*) recruiting board; **faire ses ~s** (*Scol*) to do one's revision (*Brit*), revise (*Brit*), review (*US*); **la ~ des 10 000 km** (*Auto*) the 10,000 km service

revivre [RəvivR(ə)] *vi* (*reprendre des forces*) to come alive again; (*traditions*) to be revived ▷ *vt* (*épreuve, moment*) to relive; **faire ~** (*mode, institution, usage*) to bring back to life

revoir [RəvwaR] *vt* to see again; (*réviser*) to revise (*Brit*), review (*US*) ▷ *nm*: **au ~** goodbye; **dire au ~ à qn** to say goodbye to sb; **se revoir** (*amis*) to meet (again), see each other again

révoltant, e [Revɔltɑ̃, -ɑ̃t] *adj* revolting

révolte [Revɔlt(ə)] *nf* rebellion, revolt

révolter [Revɔlte] *vt* to revolt, outrage; **se révolter** *vi*: **se ~ (contre)** to rebel (against); **se ~ (à)** to be outraged (by)

révolu, e [Revɔly] *adj* past; (*Admin*): **âgé de 18 ans ~s** over 18 years of age; **après trois ans ~s** when three full years have passed

révolution [Revɔlysjɔ̃] *nf* revolution; **être en ~** (*pays etc*) to be in revolt; **la ~ industrielle** the industrial revolution

révolutionnaire [RevɔlysjɔnɛR] *adj, nm/f* revolutionary

revolver [RevɔlvɛR] *nm* gun; (*à barillet*) revolver

révoquer [Revɔke] *vt* (*fonctionnaire*) to dismiss, remove from office; (*arrêt, contrat*) to revoke

revu, e [Rəvy] *pp de* **revoir** ▷ *nf* (*inventaire, examen*) review; (*Mil: défilé*) review, march past; (: *inspection*) inspection, review; (*périodique*) review, magazine; (*pièce satirique*) revue; (*de music-hall*) variety show; **passer en ~** to review, inspect; (*fig*) to review; **~ de (la) presse** press review

rez-de-chaussée [Redʃose] *nm inv* ground floor

RF *sigle f* = **République française**

Rhin [Rɛ̃] *nm*: **le ~** the Rhine

rhinocéros [RinɔseRɔs] *nm* rhinoceros

Rhône [Ron] *nm*: **le ~** the Rhone

rhubarbe [RybaRb(ə)] *nf* rhubarb

rhum [Rɔm] *nm* rum

rhumatisme [Rymatism(ə)] *nm* rheumatism *no pl*

rhume [Rym] *nm* cold; **~ de cerveau** head cold; **le ~ des foins** hay fever

ri [Ri] *pp de* **rire**

riant, e [Rjɑ̃, -ɑ̃t] *vb voir* **rire** ▷ *adj* smiling, cheerful; (*campagne, paysage*) pleasant

ricaner [Rikane] *vi* (*avec méchanceté*) to snigger; (*bêtement, avec gêne*) to giggle

riche [Riʃ] *adj* (*gén*) rich; (*personne, pays*) rich, wealthy; **~ en** rich in; **~ de** full of; rich in

richesse [Riʃɛs] *nf* wealth; (*fig*) richness; **richesses** *nfpl* wealth *sg*; treasures; **~ en vitamines** high vitamin content

ricochet [Rikɔʃɛ] *nm* rebound; bounce; **faire ~** to rebound, bounce; (*fig*) to rebound; **faire des ~s** to skip stones; **par ~** *adv* on the rebound; (*fig*) as an indirect result

rictus [Riktys] *nm* grin, (snarling) grimace

ride [Rid] *nf* wrinkle; (*fig*) ripple

rideau, x [Rido] *nm* curtain; **tirer/ouvrir les ~x** to draw/open the curtains; **~ de fer** metal shutter; (*Pol*): **le ~ de fer** the Iron Curtain

rider [Ride] *vt* to wrinkle; (*fig*) to ripple, ruffle the surface of; **se rider** *vi* to become wrinkled

ridicule [Ridikyl] *adj* ridiculous ▷ *nm* ridiculousness *no pl*; **le ~** ridicule; (*travers: gén pl*) absurdities *pl*; **tourner en ~** to ridicule

ridiculiser [Ridikylize] *vt* to ridicule; **se ridiculiser** to make a fool of o.s

rien [Rjɛ̃] *pron* **1**: **(ne) ...** ~ nothing; (*tournure négative*) anything; **qu'est-ce que vous avez? — ~** what have you got? — nothing; **il n'a ~ dit/ fait** he said/did nothing, he hasn't said/done anything; **il n'a ~** (*n'est pas blessé*) he's all right; **ça ne fait ~** it doesn't matter; **il n'y est pour ~** he's got nothing to do with it

2 (*quelque chose*): **a-t-il jamais ~ fait pour nous?** has he ever done anything for us?

3: **~ de**: **~ d'intéressant** nothing interesting; **~ d'autre** nothing else; **~ du tout** nothing at all; **il n'a ~ d'un champion** he's no champion, there's nothing of the champion about him

4: **~ que** just, only; nothing but; **~ que pour lui faire plaisir** only *ou* just to please him; **~ que la vérité** nothing but the truth; **~ que cela** that alone

▷ *excl*: **de ~!** not at all!, don't mention it!; **il n'en est ~!** nothing of the sort!; **~ à faire!** it's no good!, it's no use!

▷ *nm*: **un petit ~** (*cadeau*) a little something; **des ~s** trivia *pl*; **un ~ de** a hint of; **en un ~ de temps** in no time at all; **avoir peur d'un ~** to be frightened of the slightest thing

rieur, -euse [RjœR, -øz] *adj* cheerful

rigide [Riʒid] *adj* stiff; (*fig*) rigid; (*moralement*) strict

rigole [Rigɔl] *nf* (*conduit*) channel; (*filet d'eau*) rivulet

rigoler [Rigɔle] *vi* (*rire*) to laugh; (*s'amuser*) to have (some) fun; (*plaisanter*) to be joking *ou* kidding

rigolo, ote [ʀigɔlo, -ɔt] *adj* (*fam*) funny ▷ *nm/f*
comic; (*péj*) fraud, phoney
rigoureusement [ʀiguʀøzmɑ̃] *adv* rigorously; ~
vrai/interdit strictly true/forbidden
rigoureux, -euse [ʀiguʀø, -øz] *adj* (*morale*)
rigorous, strict; (*personne*) stern, strict; (*climat,
châtiment*) rigorous, harsh, severe; (*interdiction,
neutralité*) strict; (*preuves, analyse, méthode*) rigorous
rigueur [ʀigœʀ] *nf* rigour (*Brit*), rigor (*US*);
strictness; harshness; **"tenue de soirée de ~"**
"evening dress (to be worn)"; **être de ~** to be
the usual thing, be the rule; **à la ~** at a pinch;
possibly; **tenir ~ à qn de qch** to hold sth against
sb
rillettes [ʀijɛt] *nfpl* ≈ potted meat *sg*
rime [ʀim] *nf* rhyme; **n'avoir ni ~ ni raison** to
have neither rhyme nor reason
rinçage [ʀɛ̃saʒ] *nm* rinsing (out); (*opération*) rinse
rincer [ʀɛ̃se] *vt* to rinse; (*récipient*) to rinse out; **se
~ la bouche** to rinse one's mouth out
ring [ʀiŋ] *nm* (boxing) ring; **monter sur le ~**
(*aussi fig*) to enter the ring; (: *faire carrière de boxeur*)
to take up boxing
ringard, e [ʀɛ̃gaʀ, -aʀd(ə)] *adj* (*péj*) old-fashioned
rions [ʀjɔ̃] *vb voir* **rire**
riposter [ʀipɔste] *vi* to retaliate ▷ *vt*: **~ que** to
retort that; **~ à** *vt* to counter; to reply to
ripper [ʀipe] *vt* (*Inform*) to rip
rire [ʀiʀ] *vi* to laugh; (*se divertir*) to have fun;
(*plaisanter*) to joke ▷ *nm* laugh; **le ~** laughter; **~
de** *vt* to laugh at; **se ~ de** to make light of; **tu
veux ~!** you must be joking!; **~ aux éclats/aux
larmes** to roar with laughter/laugh until one
cries; **~ jaune** to force oneself to laugh; **~ sous
cape** to laugh up one's sleeve; **~ au nez de qn** to
laugh in sb's face; **pour ~** (*pas sérieusement*) for a
joke *ou* a laugh
risée [ʀize] *nf*: **être la ~ de** to be the laughing
stock of
risible [ʀizibl(ə)] *adj* laughable, ridiculous
risque [ʀisk(ə)] *nm* risk; **l'attrait du ~** the lure
of danger; **prendre des ~s** to take risks; **à ses ~s
et périls** at his own risk; **au ~ de** at the risk of; **~
d'incendie** fire risk; **~ calculé** calculated risk
risqué, e [ʀiske] *adj* risky; (*plaisanterie*) risqué,
daring
risquer [ʀiske] *vt* to risk; (*allusion, question*) to
venture, hazard; **tu risques qu'on te renvoie**
you risk being dismissed; **ça ne risque rien** it's
quite safe; **~ de: il risque de se tuer** he could
get *ou* risks getting himself killed; **il a risqué
de se tuer** he almost got himself killed; **ce qui
risque de se produire** what might *ou* could well
happen; **il ne risque pas de recommencer**
there's no chance of him doing that again; **se
risquer dans** (*s'aventurer*) to venture into; **se
risquer à faire** (*tenter*) to dare to do; **~ le tout
pour le tout** to risk the lot
rissoler [ʀisɔle] *vi, vt*: (**faire**) ~ to brown
ristourne [ʀistuʀn(ə)] *nf* rebate; discount
rite [ʀit] *nm* rite; (*fig*) ritual
rivage [ʀivaʒ] *nm* shore

rival, e, -aux [ʀival, -o] *adj, nm/f* rival; **sans ~** *adj*
unrivalled
rivaliser [ʀivalize] *vi*: **~ avec** to rival, vie with;
(*être comparable*) to hold its own against, compare
with; **~ avec qn de** (*élégance etc*) to vie with *ou*
rival sb in
rivalité [ʀivalite] *nf* rivalry
rive [ʀiv] *nf* shore; (*de fleuve*) bank
riverain, e [ʀivʀɛ̃, -ɛn] *adj* riverside *cpd*; lakeside
cpd; roadside *cpd* ▷ *nm/f* riverside (*ou* lakeside)
resident; local *ou* roadside resident
rivet [ʀivɛ] *nm* rivet
rivière [ʀivjɛʀ] *nf* river; **~ de diamants** diamond
rivière
rixe [ʀiks(ə)] *nf* brawl, scuffle
riz [ʀi] *nm* rice; **~ au lait** ≈ rice pudding
rizière [ʀizjɛʀ] *nf* paddy field
RMI *sigle m* (= *revenu minimum d'insertion*) ≈ income
support (*Brit*), ≈ welfare (*US*)
RN *sigle f* = **route nationale**
robe [ʀɔb] *nf* dress; (*de juge, d'ecclésiastique*) robe;
(*de professeur*) gown; (*pelage*) coat; **~ de soirée/de
mariée** evening/wedding dress; **~ de baptême**
christening robe; **~ de chambre** dressing gown;
~ de grossesse maternity dress
robinet [ʀɔbinɛ] *nm* tap, faucet (*US*); **~ du gaz**
gas tap; **~ mélangeur** mixer tap
robot [ʀɔbo] *nm* robot; **~ de cuisine** food
processor
robuste [ʀɔbyst(ə)] *adj* robust, sturdy
robustesse [ʀɔbystɛs] *nf* robustness, sturdiness
roc [ʀɔk] *nm* rock
rocade [ʀɔkad] *nf* (*Auto*) bypass
rocaille [ʀɔkaj] *nf* (*pierres*) loose stones *pl*; (*terrain*)
rocky *ou* stony ground; (*jardin*) rockery, rock
garden ▷ *adj* (*style*) rocaille
roche [ʀɔʃ] *nf* rock
rocher [ʀɔʃe] *nm* rock; (*Anat*) petrosal bone
rocheux, -euse [ʀɔʃø, -øz] *adj* rocky; **les
(montagnes) Rocheuses** the Rockies, the Rocky
Mountains
rock [ʀɔk], **rock and roll** [ʀɔkɛnʀɔl] *nm* (*musique*)
rock(-'n'-roll); (*danse*) rock
rodage [ʀɔdaʒ] *nm* running in (*Brit*), breaking in
(*US*); **en ~** (*Auto*) running *ou* breaking in
roder [ʀɔde] *vt* (*moteur, voiture*) to run in (*Brit*),
break in (*US*); **~ un spectacle** to iron out the
initial problems of a show
rôder [ʀode] *vi* to roam *ou* wander about; (*de façon
suspecte*) to lurk (about *ou* around)
rôdeur, -euse [ʀodœʀ, -øz] *nm/f* prowler
rogne [ʀɔɲ] *nf*: **être en ~** to be mad *ou* in a
temper; **se mettre en ~** to get mad *ou* in a
temper
rogner [ʀɔɲe] *vt* to trim; (*fig*) to whittle down; **~
sur** (*fig*) to cut down *ou* back on
rognons [ʀɔɲɔ̃] *nmpl* kidneys
roi [ʀwa] *nm* king; **les R~s mages** the Three Wise
Men, the Magi; **le jour** *ou* **la fête des R~s**, **les
R~s** Twelfth Night; *see note*
rôle [ʀol] *nm* role; (*contribution*) part
rollers [ʀɔlœʀ] *nmpl* Rollerblades®

romain, e [ʀɔmɛ̃, -ɛn] *adj* Roman ▷ *nm/f*: **R~, e**
Roman ▷ *nf* (*Culin*) cos (lettuce)

roman, e [ʀɔmɑ̃, -an] *adj* (*Archit*) Romanesque;
(*Ling*) Romance *cpd*, Romanic ▷ *nm* novel; ~
d'amour love story; ~ **d'espionnage** spy novel
ou story; ~ **noir** thriller; ~ **policier** detective
novel

romance [ʀɔmɑ̃s] *nf* ballad

romancer [ʀɔmɑ̃se] *vt* to romanticize

romancier, -ière [ʀɔmɑ̃sje, -jɛʀ] *nm/f* novelist

romanesque [ʀɔmanɛsk(ə)] *adj* (*fantastique*)
fantastic; storybook *cpd*; (*sentimental*) romantic;
(*Littérature*) novelistic

roman-feuilleton (*pl* **romans-feuilletons**)
[ʀɔmɑ̃fœjtɔ̃] *nm* serialized novel

romanichel, le [ʀɔmaniʃɛl] *nm/f* gipsy

romantique [ʀɔmɑ̃tik] *adj* romantic

romarin [ʀɔmaʀɛ̃] *nm* rosemary

rompre [ʀɔ̃pʀ(ə)] *vt* to break; (*entretien, fiançailles*)
to break off ▷ *vi* (*fiancés*) to break it off; **se**
rompre *vi* to break; (*Méd*) to burst, rupture; **se**
~ **les os** *ou* **le cou** to break one's neck; ~ **avec** to
break with; **à tout** ~ *adv* wildly; **applaudir à**
tout ~ to bring down the house, applaud wildly;
~ **la glace** (*fig*) to break the ice; **rompez (les**
rangs)! (*Mil*) dismiss!, fall out!

rompu, e [ʀɔ̃py] *pp de* **rompre** ▷ *adj* (*fourbu*)
exhausted, worn out; ~ **à** with wide experience
of; inured to

ronce [ʀɔ̃s] *nf* (*Bot*) bramble branch; (*Menuiserie*):
~ **de noyer** burr walnut; **ronces** *nfpl* brambles,
thorns

ronchonner [ʀɔ̃ʃɔne] *vi* (*fam*) to grouse, grouch

rond, e [ʀɔ̃, ʀɔ̃d] *adj* round; (*joues, mollets*) well-
rounded; (*fam: ivre*) tight; (*sincère, décidé*): **être**
~ **en affaires** to be on the level in business, do
an honest deal ▷ *nm* (*cercle*) ring; (*fam: sou*): **je**
n'ai plus un ~ I haven't a penny left ▷ *nf* (*gén:*
de surveillance) rounds *pl*, patrol; (*danse*) round
(dance); (*Mus*) semibreve (*Brit*), whole note (*US*)
▷ *adv*: **tourner** ~ (*moteur*) to run smoothly; **ça ne**
tourne pas ~ (*fig*) there's something not quite
right about it; **pour faire un compte** ~ to make
(it) a round figure, to round (it) off; **avoir le dos**
~ to be round-shouldered; **en** ~ (*s'asseoir, danser*)
in a ring; **à la ~e** (*alentour*): **à 10 km à la ~e** for 10
km round; (*à chacun son tour*): **passer qch à la ~e**
to pass sth (a)round; **faire des ~s de jambe** to
bow and scrape; ~ **de serviette** napkin ring

rondelet, te [ʀɔ̃dlɛ, -ɛt] *adj* plump; (*fig: somme*)
tidy; (*: bourse*) well-lined, fat

rondelle [ʀɔ̃dɛl] *nf* (*Tech*) washer; (*tranche*) slice,
round

rondement [ʀɔ̃dmɑ̃] *adv* (*avec décision*) briskly;
(*loyalement*) frankly

rondin [ʀɔ̃dɛ̃] *nm* log

rond-point (*pl* **ronds-points**) [ʀɔ̃pwɛ̃] *nm*
roundabout (*Brit*), traffic circle (*US*)

ronflant, e [ʀɔ̃flɑ̃, -ɑ̃t] *adj* (*péj*) high-flown, grand

ronflement [ʀɔ̃fləmɑ̃] *nm* snore, snoring *no pl*

ronfler [ʀɔ̃fle] *vi* to snore; (*moteur, poêle*) to hum;
(*: plus fort*) to roar

ronger [ʀɔ̃ʒe] *vt* to gnaw (at); (*vers, rouille*) to eat
into; ~ **son frein** to champ (at) the bit; (*fig*): **se**
~ **de souci, se** ~ **les sangs** to worry o.s. sick, fret;
se ~ **les ongles** to bite one's nails

rongeur, -euse [ʀɔ̃ʒœʀ, -øz] *nm/f* rodent

ronronner [ʀɔ̃ʀɔne] *vi* to purr

rosace [ʀozas] *nf* (*vitrail*) rose window, rosace;
(*motif: de plafond etc*) rose

rosbif [ʀɔsbif] *nm*: **du** ~ roasting beef; (*cuit*) roast
beef; **un** ~ a joint of (roasting) beef

rose [ʀoz] *nf* rose; (*vitrail*) rose window ▷ *adj*
pink; ~ **bonbon** *adj inv* candy pink; ~ **des vents**
compass card

rosé, e [ʀoze] *adj* pinkish; (*vin*) ~ rosé (wine)

roseau, x [ʀozo] *nm* reed

rosée [ʀoze] *adj f voir* **rosé** ▷ *nf*: **goutte de** ~
dewdrop

rosette [ʀozɛt] *nf* rosette (*gen of the Légion*
d'honneur)

rosier [ʀozje] *nm* rosebush, rose tree

rosse [ʀɔs] *nf* (*péj: cheval*) nag ▷ *adj* nasty, vicious

rossignol [ʀɔsiɲɔl] *nm* (*Zool*) nightingale;
(*crochet*) picklock

rot [ʀo] *nm* belch; (*de bébé*) burp

rotatif, -ive [ʀɔtatif, -iv] *adj* rotary ▷ *nf* rotary
press

rotation [ʀɔtasjɔ̃] *nf* rotation; (*fig*) rotation,
swap-around; (*renouvellement*) turnover; **par** ~ on
a rota (*Brit*) *ou* rotation (*US*) basis; ~ **des cultures**
crop rotation; ~ **des stocks** stock turnover

roter [ʀɔte] *vi* (*fam*) to burp, belch

rôti [ʀoti] *nm*: **du** ~ roasting meat; (*cuit*) roast
meat; **un** ~ **de bœuf/porc** a joint of (roasting)
beef/pork

rotin [ʀɔtɛ̃] *nm* rattan (cane); **fauteuil en** ~ cane
(arm)chair

rôtir [ʀotiʀ] *vt* (*aussi:* **faire rôtir**) to roast ▷ *vi* to
roast; **se** ~ **au soleil** to bask in the sun

rôtisserie [ʀotisʀi] *nf* (*restaurant*) steakhouse;
(*comptoir, magasin*) roast meat counter (*ou* shop)

rôtissoire [ʀotiswaʀ] *nf* (roasting) spit

rotule [ʀɔtyl] *nf* kneecap, patella

roturier, -ière [ʀɔtyʀje, -jɛʀ] *nm/f* commoner

rouage [ʀwaʒ] *nm* cog(wheel), gearwheel; (*de*
montre) part; (*fig*) cog; **rouages** *nmpl* (*fig*) internal
structure *sg*

roucouler [ʀukule] *vi* to coo; (*fig: péj*) to warble;
(*: amoureux*) to bill and coo

roue [ʀu] *nf* wheel; **faire la** ~ (*paon*) to spread *ou*
fan its tail; (*Gym*) to do a cartwheel; **descendre**
en ~ **libre** to freewheel *ou* coast down; **pousser**
à la ~ to put one's shoulder to the wheel; **grande**
~ (*à la foire*) big wheel; ~ **à aubes** paddle wheel; ~
dentée cogwheel; ~ **de secours** spare wheel

roué, e [ʀwe] *adj* wily

rouer [ʀwe] *vt*: ~ **qn de coups** to give sb a
thrashing

rouge [ʀuʒ] *adj, nm/f* red ▷ *nm* red; (*fard*) rouge;
(*vin*) ~ red wine; **passer au** ~ (*signal*) to go red;
(*automobiliste*) to go through a red light; **porter**
au ~ (*métal*) to bring to red heat; **sur la liste**
~ (*Tél*) ex-directory (*Brit*), unlisted (*US*); ~ **de**

honte/colère red with shame/anger; **se fâcher tout/voir ~** to blow one's top/see red; **~ (à lèvres)** lipstick

rouge-gorge [ʀuʒɡɔʀʒ(ə)] nm robin (redbreast)

rougeole [ʀuʒɔl] nf measles sg

rougeoyer [ʀuʒwaje] vi to glow red

rouget [ʀuʒɛ] nm mullet

rougeur [ʀuʒœʀ] nf redness; (du visage) red face; **rougeurs** nfpl (Méd) red blotches

rougir [ʀuʒiʀ] vi (de honte, timidité) to blush, flush; (de plaisir, colère) to flush; (fraise, tomate) to go ou turn red; (ciel) to redden

rouille [ʀuj] adj inv rust-coloured, rusty ▷ nf rust; (Culin) spicy (Provençal) sauce served with fish dishes

rouillé, e [ʀuje] adj rusty

rouiller [ʀuje] vt to rust ▷ vi to rust, go rusty; **se rouiller** vi to rust; (fig: mentalement) to become rusty; (: physiquement) to grow stiff

roulant, e [ʀulɑ̃, -ɑ̃t] adj (meuble) on wheels; (surface, trottoir) moving; **matériel ~** (Rail) rolling stock; **personnel ~** (Rail) train crews pl

rouleau, x [ʀulo] nm (de papier, tissu, pièces de monnaie, Sport) roll; (de machine à écrire) roller, platen; (à mise en plis, à peinture, vague) roller; **être au bout du ~** (fig) to be at the end of the line; **~ compresseur** steamroller; **~ à pâtisserie** rolling pin; **~ de pellicule** roll of film

roulement [ʀulmɑ̃] nm (bruit) rumbling no pl, rumble; (rotation) rotation; turnover; (: de capitaux) circulation; **par ~** on a rota (Brit) ou rotation (US) basis; **~ (à billes)** ball bearings pl; **~ de tambour** drum roll; **~ d'yeux** roll(ing) of the eyes

rouler [ʀule] vt to roll; (papier, tapis) to roll up; (Culin: pâte) to roll out; (fam) to do, con ▷ vi (bille, boule) to roll; (voiture, train) to go, run; (automobiliste) to drive; (cycliste) to ride; (bateau) to roll; (tonnerre) to rumble, roll; (dégringoler): **~ en bas de** to roll down; **~ sur** (conversation) to turn on; **se ~ dans** (boue) to roll in; (couverture) to roll o.s. (up) in; **~ dans la farine** (fam) to con; **~ les épaules/hanches** to sway one's shoulders/wiggle one's hips; **~ les "r"** to roll one's r's; **~ sur l'or** to be rolling in money, be rolling in it; **~ (sa bosse)** to go places

roulette [ʀulɛt] nf (de table, fauteuil) castor; (de pâtissier) pastry wheel; (jeu): **la ~** roulette; **à ~s** on castors; **la ~ russe** Russian roulette

roulis [ʀuli] nm roll(ing)

roulotte [ʀulɔt] nf caravan

roumain, e [ʀumɛ̃, -ɛn] adj Rumanian, Romanian ▷ nm (Ling) Rumanian, Romanian ▷ nm/f: **R~, e** Rumanian, Romanian

Roumanie [ʀumani] nf: **la ~** Rumania, Romania

rouquin, e [ʀukɛ̃, -in] nm/f (péj) redhead

rouspéter [ʀuspete] vi (fam) to moan, grouse

rousse [ʀus] adj f voir **roux**

roussir [ʀusiʀ] vt to scorch ▷ vi (feuilles) to go ou turn brown; (Culin): **faire ~** to brown

route [ʀut] nf road; (fig: chemin) way; (itinéraire, parcours) route; (fig: voie) road, path; **par (la) ~** by road; **il y a trois heures de ~** it's a three-hour

ride ou journey; **en ~** adv on the way; **en ~!** let's go!; **en cours de ~** en route; **mettre en ~** to start up; **se mettre en ~** to set off; **faire ~ vers** to head towards; **faire fausse ~** (fig) to be on the wrong track; **~ nationale (RN)** ≈ A-road (Brit), ≈ state highway (US)

routier, -ière [ʀutje, -jɛʀ] adj road cpd ▷ nm (camionneur) (long-distance) lorry (Brit) ou truck driver; (restaurant) ≈ transport café (Brit), ≈ truck stop (US); (scout) ≈ rover; (cycliste) road racer ▷ nf (voiture) touring car; **vieux ~** old stager; **carte routière** road map

routine [ʀutin] nf routine; **visite/contrôle de ~** routine visit/check

routinier, -ière [ʀutinje, -jɛʀ] adj (péj: travail) humdrum, routine; (: personne) addicted to routine

rouvrir [ʀuvʀiʀ] vt, vi to reopen, open again; **se rouvrir** vi (blessure) to open up again

roux, rousse [ʀu, ʀus] adj red; (personne) red-haired ▷ nm/f redhead ▷ nm (Culin) roux

royal, e, -aux [ʀwajal, -o] adj royal; (fig) fit for a king, princely; blissful; thorough

royaume [ʀwajom] nm kingdom; (fig) realm; **le ~ des cieux** the kingdom of heaven

Royaume-Uni [ʀwajomyni] nm: **le ~** the United Kingdom

royauté [ʀwajote] nf (dignité) kingship; (régime) monarchy

RPR sigle m (= Rassemblement pour la République) political party

ruban [ʀybɑ̃] nm (gén) ribbon; (pour ourlet, couture) binding; (de téléscripteur etc) tape; (d'acier) strip; **~ adhésif** adhesive tape; **~ carbone** carbon ribbon

rubéole [ʀybeɔl] nf German measles sg, rubella

rubis [ʀybi] nm ruby; (Horlogerie) jewel; **payer ~ sur l'ongle** to pay cash on the nail

rubrique [ʀybʀik] nf (titre, catégorie) heading, rubric; (Presse: article) column

ruche [ʀyʃ] nf hive

rude [ʀyd] adj (barbe, toile) rough; (métier, tâche) hard, tough; (climat) severe, harsh; (bourru) harsh, rough; (fruste) rugged, tough; (fam) jolly good; **être mis à ~ épreuve** to be put through the mill

rudement [ʀydmɑ̃] adv (tomber, frapper) hard; (traiter, reprocher) harshly; (fam: très) terribly; (: beaucoup) terribly hard

rudimentaire [ʀydimɑ̃tɛʀ] adj rudimentary, basic

rudiments [ʀydimɑ̃] nmpl rudiments; basic knowledge sg; basic principles

rudoyer [ʀydwaje] vt to treat harshly

rue [ʀy] nf street; **être/jeter qn à la ~** to be on the streets/throw sb out onto the street

ruée [ʀɥe] nf rush; **la ~ vers l'or** the gold rush

ruelle [ʀɥɛl] nf alley(way)

ruer [ʀɥe] vi (cheval) to kick out; **se ruer** vi: **~ sur** to pounce on; **se ~ vers/dans/hors de** to rush ou dash towards/into/out of; **~ dans les brancards** to become rebellious

rugby [ʀygbi] nm rugby (football); **~ à treize/**

quinze rugby league/union
rugir [ʀyʒiʀ] *vi* to roar
rugueux, -euse [ʀygø, -øz] *adj* rough
ruine [ʀɥin] *nf* ruin; **ruines** *nfpl* ruins; **tomber en ~** to fall into ruin(s)
ruiner [ʀɥine] *vt* to ruin
ruineux, -euse [ʀɥinø, -øz] *adj* terribly expensive to buy (*ou* run), ruinous; extravagant
ruisseau, x [ʀɥiso] *nm* stream, brook; (*caniveau*) gutter; (*fig*): **~x de larmes/sang** floods of tears/streams of blood
ruisseler [ʀɥisle] *vi* to stream; **~ (d'eau)** to be streaming (with water); **~ de lumière** to stream with light
rumeur [ʀymœʀ] *nf* (*bruit confus*) rumbling; hubbub *no pl*; (*protestation*) murmur(ing); (*nouvelle*) rumour (Brit), rumor (US)
ruminer [ʀymine] *vt* (*herbe*) to ruminate; (*fig*) to ruminate on *ou* over, chew over ▷ *vi* (*vache*) to chew the cud, ruminate
rupture [ʀyptyʀ] *nf* (*de câble, digue*) breaking; (*de tendon*) rupture, tearing; (*de négociations etc*)

breakdown; (*de contrat*) breach; (*séparation, désunion*) break-up, split; **en ~ de ban** at odds with authority; **en ~ de stock** (*Comm*) out of stock
rural, e, -aux [ʀyʀal, -o] *adj* rural, country *cpd* ▷ *nmpl*: **les ruraux** country people
ruse [ʀyz] *nf*: **la ~** cunning, craftiness; trickery; **une ~** a trick, a ruse; **par ~** by trickery
rusé, e [ʀyze] *adj* cunning, crafty
russe [ʀys] *adj* Russian ▷ *nm* (*Ling*) Russian ▷ *nm/f*: **R~** Russian
Russie [ʀysi] *nf*: **la ~** Russia; **la ~ blanche** White Russia; **la ~ soviétique** Soviet Russia
rustine [ʀystin] *nf* repair patch (*for bicycle inner tube*)
rustique [ʀystik] *adj* rustic; (*plante*) hardy
rustre [ʀystʀ(ə)] *nm* boor
rutilant, e [ʀytilɑ̃, -ɑ̃t] *adj* gleaming
rythme [ʀitm(ə)] *nm* rhythm; (*vitesse*) rate; (: *de la vie*) pace, tempo; **au ~ de 10 par jour** at the rate of 10 a day
rythmé, e [ʀitme] *adj* rhythmic(al)

Ss

s' [s] *pron voir* **se**

SA *sigle f* = **société anonyme**; (= *Son Altesse*) HH

sa [sa] *adj possessif voir* **son**

sable [sabl(ə)] *nm* sand; **~s mouvants** quicksand(s)

sablé [sable] *adj* (*allée*) sandy ▷ *nm* shortbread biscuit; **pâte ~e** (*Culin*) shortbread dough

sabler [sable] *vt* to sand; (*contre le verglas*) to grit; **~ le champagne** to drink champagne

sablier [sablije] *nm* hourglass; (*de cuisine*) egg timer

sablonneux, -euse [sablɔnø, -øz] *adj* sandy

saborder [sabɔʀde] *vt* (*navire*) to scuttle; (*fig*) to wind up, shut down

sabot [sabo] *nm* clog; (*de cheval, bœuf*) hoof; **~ (de Denver)** (wheel) clamp; **~ de frein** brake shoe

saboter [sabote] *vt* (*travail, morceau de musique*) to botch, make a mess of; (*machine, installation, négociation etc*) to sabotage

sac [sak] *nm* bag; (*à charbon etc*) sack; (*pillage*) sack(ing); **mettre à ~** to sack; **~ à provisions/de voyage** shopping/travelling bag; **~ de couchage** sleeping bag; **~ à dos** rucksack; **~ à main** handbag; **~ de plage** beach bag

saccadé, e [sakade] *adj* jerky

saccager [sakaʒe] *vt* (*piller*) to sack, lay waste; (*dévaster*) to create havoc in, wreck

saccharine [sakaʀin] *nf* saccharin(e)

sacerdoce [sasɛʀdɔs] *nm* priesthood; (*fig*) calling, vocation

sache *etc* [saʃ] *vb voir* **savoir**

sachet [saʃɛ] *nm* (small) bag; (*de lavande, poudre, shampooing*) sachet; **thé en ~s** tea bags; **~ de thé** tea bag

sacoche [sakɔʃ] *nf* (*gén*) bag; (*de bicyclette*) saddlebag; (*du facteur*) (post)bag; (*d'outils*) toolbag

sacquer [sake] *vt* (*fam: candidat, employé*) to sack; (: *réprimander, mal noter*) to plough

sacre [sakʀ(ə)] *nm* coronation; consecration

sacré, e [sakʀe] *adj* sacred; (*fam: satané*) blasted; (: *fameux*): **un ~ ...** a heck of a ...; (*Anat*) sacral

sacrement [sakʀəmɑ̃] *nm* sacrament; **les derniers ~s** the last rites

sacrifice [sakʀifis] *nm* sacrifice; **faire le ~ de** to sacrifice

sacrifier [sakʀifje] *vt* to sacrifice; **~ à** *vt* to conform to; **se sacrifier** to sacrifice o.s; **articles sacrifiés** (*Comm*) items sold at rock-bottom *ou* give-away prices

sacristie [sakʀisti] *nf* sacristy; (*culte protestant*) vestry

sadique [sadik] *adj* sadistic ▷ *nm/f* sadist

safran [safʀɑ̃] *nm* saffron

sage [saʒ] *adj* wise; (*enfant*) good ▷ *nm* wise man; sage

sage-femme [saʒfam] *nf* midwife

sagesse [saʒɛs] *nf* wisdom

Sagittaire [saʒitɛʀ] *nm*: **le ~** Sagittarius, the Archer; **être du ~** to be Sagittarius

Sahara [saaʀa] *nm*: **le ~** the Sahara (Desert); **le ~ occidental** (*pays*) Western Sahara

saignant, e [sɛɲɑ̃, -ɑ̃t] *adj* (*viande*) rare; (*blessure, plaie*) bleeding

saignée [seɲe] *nf* (*Méd*) bleeding *no pl*, bloodletting *no pl*; (*Anat*): **la ~ du bras** the bend of the arm; (*fig: Mil*) heavy losses *pl*; (: *prélèvement*) savage cut

saigner [seɲe] *vi* to bleed ▷ *vt* to bleed; (*animal*) to bleed to death; **~ qn à blanc** (*fig*) to bleed sb white; **~ du nez** to have a nosebleed

saillie [saji] *nf* (*sur un mur etc*) projection; (*trait d'esprit*) witticism; (*accouplement*) covering, serving; **faire ~** to project, stick out; **en ~, formant ~** projecting, overhanging

saillir [sajiʀ] *vi* to project, stick out; (*veine, muscle*) to bulge ▷ *vt* (*Élevage*) to cover, serve

sain, e [sɛ̃, sɛn] *adj* healthy; (*dents, constitution*) healthy, sound; (*lectures*) wholesome; **~ et sauf** safe and sound, unharmed; **~ d'esprit** sound in mind, sane

saindoux [sɛ̃du] *nm* lard

saint, e [sɛ̃, sɛ̃t] *adj* holy; (*fig*) saintly ▷ *nm/f* saint; **la S~e Vierge** the Blessed Virgin

sainteté [sɛ̃te] *nf* holiness; saintliness

Saint-Sylvestre [sɛ̃silvɛstʀ(ə)] *nf*: **la ~** New Year's Eve

sais *etc* [sɛ] *vb voir* **savoir**

saisie [sezi] *nf* seizure; **à la ~** (*texte*) being keyed; **~ (de données)** (data) capture

saisir [seziʀ] *vt* to take hold of, grab; (*fig: occasion*) to seize; (*comprendre*) to grasp; (*entendre*) to get, catch; (*émotions*) to take hold of, come over; (*Inform*) to capture, keyboard; (*Culin*) to fry quickly; (*Jur: biens, publication*) to seize;

(: *juridiction*): **~ un tribunal d'une affaire** to submit *ou* refer a case to a court; **se ~ de** *vt* to seize; **être saisi** (*frappé de*) to be overcome

saisissant, e [sezisã, -ãt] *adj* startling, striking; (*froid*) biting

saison [sɛzɔ̃] *nf* season; **la belle/mauvaise ~** the summer/winter months; **être de ~** to be in season; **en/hors ~** in/out of season; **haute/ basse/morte ~** high/low/slack season; **la ~ des pluies/des amours** the rainy/mating season

saisonnier, -ière [sɛzɔnje, -jɛʀ] *adj* seasonal ▷ *nm* (*travailleur*) seasonal worker; (*vacancier*) seasonal holidaymaker

sait [sɛ] *vb voir* **savoir**

salade [salad] *nf* (Bot) lettuce *etc* (*generic term*); (*Culin*) (green) salad; (*fam*) tangle, muddle; **salades** *nfpl* (*fam*): **raconter des ~s** to tell tales (*fam*); **haricots en ~** bean salad; **~ de concombres** cucumber salad; **~ de fruits** fruit salad; **~ niçoise** salade niçoise; **~ russe** Russian salad; **~ de tomates** tomato salad; **~ verte** green salad

saladier [saladje] *nm* (salad) bowl

salaire [salɛʀ] *nm* (*annuel, mensuel*) salary; (*hebdomadaire, journalier*) pay, wages *pl*; (*fig*) reward; **~ de base** basic salary (*ou* wage); **~ de misère** starvation wage; **~ minimum interprofessionnel de croissance (SMIC)** index-linked guaranteed minimum wage

salami [salami] *nm* salami *no pl*, salami sausage

salarié, e [salarje] *adj* salaried; wage-earning ▷ *nm/f* salaried employee; wage-earner

salaud [salo] *nm* (*fam!*) sod (!), bastard (!)

sale [sal] *adj* dirty; (*fig: avant le nom*) nasty

salé, e [sale] *adj* (*liquide, saveur*) salty; (*Culin*) salted, salt *cpd*; (*fig*) spicy, juicy; (: *note, facture*) steep, stiff ▷ *nm* (*porc salé*) salt pork; **petit ~** ≈ boiling bacon

saler [sale] *vt* to salt

saleté [salte] *nf* (*état*) dirtiness; (*crasse*) dirt, filth; (*tache etc*) dirt *no pl*, something dirty, dirty mark; (*fig: tour*) filthy trick; (: *chose sans valeur*) rubbish *no pl*; (: *obscénité*) filth *no pl*; (: *microbe etc*) bug; **vivre dans la ~** to live in squalor

salière [saljɛʀ] *nf* saltcellar

salin, e [salɛ̃, -in] *adj* saline ▷ *nf* saltworks *sg*

salir [saliʀ] *vt* to (make) dirty; (*fig*) to soil the reputation of; **se salir** to get dirty

salissant, e [salisã, -ãt] *adj* (*tissu*) which shows the dirt; (*métier*) dirty, messy

salle [sal] *nf* room; (*d'hôpital*) ward; (*de restaurant*) dining room; (*d'un cinéma*) auditorium; (: *public*) audience; **faire ~ comble** to have a full house; **~ d'armes** (*pour l'escrime*) arms room; **~ d'attente** waiting room; **~ de bain(s)** bathroom; **~ de bal** ballroom; **~ de cinéma** cinema; **~ de classe** classroom; **~ commune** (*d'hôpital*) ward; **~ de concert** concert hall; **~ de consultation** consulting room (Brit), office (US); **~ de danse** dance hall; **~ de douches** shower-room; **~ d'eau** shower-room; **~ d'embarquement** (*à l'aéroport*) departure lounge; **~ d'exposition**

showroom; **~ de jeux** games room; playroom; **~ des machines** engine room; **~ à manger** dining room; (*mobilier*) dining room suite; **~ obscure** cinema (Brit), movie theater (US); **~ d'opération** (*d'hôpital*) operating theatre; **~ des professeurs** staffroom; **~ de projection** film theatre; **~ de séjour** living room; **~ de spectacle** theatre; cinema; **~ des ventes** saleroom

salon [salɔ̃] *nm* lounge, sitting room; (*mobilier*) lounge suite; (*exposition*) exhibition, show; (*mondain, littéraire*) salon; **~ de coiffure** hairdressing salon; **~ de discussion** (Inform) chatroom; **~ de thé** tearoom

salope [salɔp] *nf* (*fam!*) bitch (!)

saloperie [salɔpʀi] *nf* (*fam!*) filth *no pl*; dirty trick, rubbish *no pl*

salopette [salɔpɛt] *nf* dungarees *pl*; (*d'ouvrier*) overall(s)

salsifis [salsifi] *nm* salsify, oyster plant

salubre [salybʀ(ə)] *adj* healthy, salubrious

saluer [salɥe] *vt* (*pour dire bonjour, fig*) to greet; (*pour dire au revoir*) to take one's leave; (Mil) to salute

salut [saly] *nm* (*sauvegarde*) safety; (Rel) salvation; (*geste*) wave; (*parole*) greeting; (Mil) salute ▷ *excl* (*fam: pour dire bonjour*) hi (there); (: *pour dire au revoir*) see you!, bye!

salutations [salytɑsjɔ̃] *nfpl* greetings; **recevez mes ~ distinguées** *ou* **respectueuses** yours faithfully

samedi [samdi] *nm* Saturday; *voir aussi* **lundi**

SAMU [samy] *sigle m* (= *service d'assistance médicale d'urgence*) ≈ ambulance (service) (Brit), ≈ paramedics (US)

sanction [sɑ̃ksjɔ̃] *nf* sanction; (*fig*) penalty; **prendre des ~s contre** to impose sanctions on

sanctionner [sɑ̃ksjɔne] *vt* (*loi, usage*) to sanction; (*punir*) to punish

sandale [sɑ̃dal] *nf* sandal; **~s à lanières** strappy sandals

sandwich [sɑ̃dwitʃ] *nm* sandwich; **pris en ~** sandwiched

sang [sɑ̃] *nm* blood; **en ~** covered in blood; **jusqu'au ~** (*mordre, pincer*) till the blood comes; **se faire du mauvais ~** to fret, get in a state

sang-froid [sɑ̃fʀwa] *nm* calm, sangfroid; **garder/perdre/reprendre son ~** to keep/lose/ regain one's cool; **de ~** in cold blood

sanglant, e [sɑ̃glɑ̃, -ɑ̃t] *adj* bloody, covered in blood; (*combat*) bloody; (*fig: reproche, affront*) cruel

sangle [sɑ̃gl(ə)] *nf* strap; **sangles** *nfpl* (*pour lit etc*) webbing

sanglier [sɑ̃glije] *nm* (wild) boar

sanglot [sɑ̃glo] *nm* sob

sangloter [sɑ̃glɔte] *vi* to sob

sangsue [sɑ̃sy] *nf* leech

sanguin, e [sɑ̃gɛ̃, -in] *adj* blood *cpd*; (*fig*) fiery ▷ *nf* (Art) red pencil drawing

sanguinaire [sɑ̃ginɛʀ] *adj* (*animal, personne*) bloodthirsty; (*lutte*) bloody

sanitaire [sanitɛʀ] *adj* health *cpd*; **sanitaires** *nmpl* (*salle de bain et w.-c.*) bathroom *sg*;

installation/appareil ~ bathroom plumbing/
appliance

sans [sã] *prép* without; **~ qu'il s'en aperçoive**
without him *ou* his noticing; **~ scrupules**
unscrupulous; **~ manches** sleeveless

sans-abri [sãzabʀi] *nmpl* homeless

sans-emploi [sãzãplwa] *nmpl* jobless

sans-gêne [sãʒɛn] *adj inv* inconsiderate ▷ *nm inv*
(*attitude*) lack of consideration

santé [sãte] *nf* health; **avoir une ~ de fer** to be
bursting with health; **être en bonne ~** to be in
good health, be healthy; **boire à la ~ de qn** to
drink (to) sb's health; **"à la ~ de"** "here's to"; **à
ta** *ou* **votre ~!** cheers!; **service de ~** (*dans un port
etc*) quarantine service; **la ~ publique** public
health

saoudien, ne [saudjɛ̃, -ɛn] *adj* Saudi (Arabian)
▷ *nm/f:* **S~, ne** Saudi (Arabian)

saoul, e [su, sul] *adj* = **soûl, e**

saper [sape] *vt* to undermine, sap; **se saper** *vi*
(*fam*) to dress

sapeur-pompier [sapœʀpɔ̃pje] *nm* fireman

saphir [safiʀ] *nm* sapphire; (*d'électrophone*)
needle, sapphire

sapin [sapɛ̃] *nm* fir (tree); (*bois*) fir; **~ de Noël**
Christmas tree

sarcastique [saʀkastik] *adj* sarcastic

sarcler [saʀkle] *vt* to weed

Sardaigne [saʀdɛɲ] *nf:* **la ~** Sardinia

sardine [saʀdin] *nf* sardine; **~s à l'huile**
sardines in oil

SARL [saʀl] *sigle f* = **société à responsabilité
limitée**

sarrasin [saʀazɛ̃] *nm* buckwheat

sas [sas] *nm* (*de sous-marin, d'engin spatial*) airlock;
(*d'écluse*) lock

satané, e [satane] *adj* (*fam*) confounded

satellite [satelit] *nm* satellite; **pays ~** satellite
country

satin [satɛ̃] *nm* satin

satire [satiʀ] *nf* satire; **faire la ~** to satirize

satirique [satiʀik] *adj* satirical

satisfaction [satisfaksjɔ̃] *nf* satisfaction; **à ma
grande ~** to my great satisfaction; **obtenir ~** to
obtain *ou* get satisfaction; **donner ~ (à)** to give
satisfaction (to)

satisfaire [satisfɛʀ] *vt* to satisfy; **se satisfaire
de** to be satisfied *ou* content with; **~ à** *vt*
(*engagement*) to fulfil; (*revendications, conditions*) to
satisfy, meet

satisfaisant, e [satisfəzɑ̃, -ɑ̃t] *vb voir* **satisfaire**
▷ *adj* satisfactory; (*qui fait plaisir*) satisfying

satisfait, e [satisfɛ, -ɛt] *pp de* **satisfaire** ▷ *adj*
satisfied; **~ de** happy *ou* satisfied with

saturer [satyʀe] *vt* to saturate; **~ qn/qch de** to
saturate sb/sth with

sauce [sos] *nf* sauce; (*avec un rôti*) gravy; **en ~** in a
sauce; **~ blanche** white sauce; **~ chasseur** sauce
chasseur; **~ tomate** tomato sauce

saucière [sosjɛʀ] *nf* sauceboat; gravy boat

saucisse [sosis] *nf* sausage

saucisson [sosisɔ̃] *nm* (slicing) sausage; **~ à l'ail**
garlic sausage

sauf¹ [sof] *prép* except; **~ si** (*à moins que*) unless; **~
avis contraire** unless you hear to the contrary; **~
empêchement** barring (any) problems; **~
erreur** if I'm not mistaken; **~ imprévu** unless
anything unforeseen arises, barring accidents

sauf², sauve [sof, sov] *adj* unharmed, unhurt;
(*fig: honneur*) intact, saved; **laisser la vie sauve à
qn** to spare sb's life

sauge [soʒ] *nf* sage

saugrenu, e [sogʀəny] *adj* preposterous,
ludicrous

saule [sol] *nm* willow (tree); **~ pleureur** weeping
willow

saumon [somɔ̃] *nm* salmon *inv* ▷ *adj inv* salmon
(pink)

saumure [somyʀ] *nf* brine

saupoudrer [supudʀe] *vt:* **~ qch de** to sprinkle
sth with

saur [sɔʀ] *adj m:* **hareng ~** smoked *ou* red herring,
kipper

saurai *etc* [sɔʀe] *vb voir* **savoir**

saut [so] *nm* jump; (*discipline sportive*) jumping;
faire un ~ to (make a) jump *ou* leap; **faire un ~
chez qn** to pop over to sb's (place); **au ~ du lit**
on getting out of bed; **~ en hauteur/longueur**
high/long jump; **~ à la corde** skipping; **~
de page/ligne** (*Inform*) page/line break; **~ en
parachute** parachuting *no pl*; **~ à la perche** pole
vaulting; **~ à l'élastique** bungee jumping; **~
périlleux** somersault

saute [sot] *nf:* **~ de vent/température** sudden
change of wind direction/in the temperature;
avoir des ~s d'humeur to have sudden changes
of mood

sauter [sote] *vi* to jump, leap; (*exploser*) to blow
up, explode; (*: fusibles*) to blow; (*se rompre*) to snap,
burst; (*se détacher*) to pop out (*ou* off) ▷ *vt* to jump
(over), leap (over); (*fig: omettre*) to skip, miss
(out); **faire ~** to blow up; to burst open; (*Culin*) to
sauté; **~ à pieds joints/à cloche-pied** to make a
standing jump/to hop; **~ en parachute** to make
a parachute jump; **~ à la corde** to skip; **~ de joie**
to jump for joy; **~ de colère** to be hopping with
rage *ou* hopping mad; **~ au cou de qn** to fly into
sb's arms; **~ aux yeux** to be quite obvious; **~ au
plafond** (*fig*) to hit the roof

sauterelle [sotʀɛl] *nf* grasshopper

sautiller [sotije] *vi* to hop; to skip

sauvage [sovaʒ] *adj* (*gén*) wild; (*peuplade*) savage;
(*farouche*) unsociable; (*barbare*) wild, savage; (*non
officiel*) unauthorized, unofficial ▷ *nm/f* savage;
(*timide*) unsociable type, recluse

sauve [sov] *adj f voir* **sauf**

sauvegarde [sovgaʀd(ə)] *nf* safeguard; **sous la
~ de** under the protection of; **disquette/fichier
de ~** (*Inform*) backup disk/file

sauvegarder [sovgaʀde] *vt* to safeguard; (*Inform:
enregistrer*) to save; (*: copier*) to back up

sauve-qui-peut [sovkipø] *nm inv* stampede, mad
rush ▷ *excl* run for your life!

sauver [sove] *vt* to save; (*porter secours à*) to rescue;

(*récupérer*) to salvage, rescue; **se sauver** *vi* (*s'enfuir*) to run away; (*fam: partir*) to be off; **~ qn de** to save sb from; **~ la vie à qn** to save sb's life; **~ les apparences** to keep up appearances

sauvetage [sovtaʒ] *nm* rescue; **~ en montagne** mountain rescue; **ceinture de ~** lifebelt (*Brit*), life preserver (*US*); **brassière** *ou* **gilet de ~** lifejacket (*Brit*), life preserver (*US*)

sauveteur [sovtœʀ] *nm* rescuer

sauvette [sovɛt]: **à la ~** *adv* (*vendre*) without authorization; (*se marier etc*) hastily, hurriedly; **vente à la ~** (*unauthorized*) street trading, (street) peddling

sauveur [sovœʀ] *nm* saviour (*Brit*), savior (*US*)

savais *etc* [save] *vb voir* **savoir**

savamment [savamã] *adv* (*avec érudition*) learnedly; (*habilement*) skilfully, cleverly

savant, e [savã, -ãt] *adj* scholarly, learned; (*calé*) clever ▷ *nm* scientist; **animal ~** performing animal

saveur [savœʀ] *nf* flavour (*Brit*), flavor (*US*); (*fig*) savour (*Brit*), savor (*US*)

savoir [savwaʀ] *vt* to know; (*être capable de*): **il sait nager** he knows how to swim, he can swim ▷ *nm* knowledge; **se savoir** (*être connu*) to be known; **se savoir malade/incurable** to know that one is ill/incurably ill; **il est petit: tu ne peux pas ~!** you won't believe how small he is!; **vous n'êtes pas sans ~ que** you are not *ou* will not be unaware of the fact that; **je crois ~ que** ... I believe that ..., I think I know that ...; **je n'en sais rien** I (really) don't know; **à ~ (que)** that is, namely; **faire ~ qch à qn** to inform sb about sth, let sb know sth; **pas que je sache** not as far as I know; **sans le ~** *adv* unknowingly, unwittingly; **en ~ long** to know a lot

savon [savõ] *nm* (*produit*) soap; (*morceau*) bar *ou* tablet of soap; (*fam*): **passer un ~ à qn** to give sb a good dressing-down

savonner [savɔne] *vt* to soap

savonnette [savɔnɛt] *nf* bar *ou* tablet of soap

savons [savõ] *vb voir* **savoir**

savourer [savuʀe] *vt* to savour (*Brit*), savor (*US*)

savoureux, -euse [savuʀø, -øz] *adj* tasty; (*fig*) spicy, juicy

saxo [saksɔ], **saxophone** [saksɔfɔn] *nm* sax(ophone)

scabreux, -euse [skabʀø, -øz] *adj* risky; (*indécent*) improper, shocking

scandale [skãdal] *nm* scandal; (*tapage*): **faire du ~** to make a scene, create a disturbance; **faire ~** to scandalize people; **au grand ~ de ...** to the great indignation of ...

scandaleux, -euse [skãdalø, -øz] *adj* scandalous, outrageous

scandinave [skãdinav] *adj* Scandinavian ▷ *nm/f*: **S~** Scandinavian

Scandinavie [skãdinavi] *nf*: **la ~** Scandinavia

scaphandre [skafãdʀ(ə)] *nm* (*de plongeur*) diving suit; (*de cosmonaute*) spacesuit; **~ autonome** aqualung

scarabée [skaʀabe] *nm* beetle

scarlatine [skaʀlatin] *nf* scarlet fever

scarole [skaʀɔl] *nf* endive

sceau, x [so] *nm* seal; (*fig*) stamp, mark; **sous le ~ du secret** under the seal of secrecy

scélérat, e [selera, -at] *nm/f* villain, blackguard ▷ *adj* villainous, blackguardly

sceller [sele] *vt* to seal

scénario [senaʀjo] *nm* (*Ciné*) screenplay, script; (*: idée, plan*) scenario; (*fig*) pattern; scenario

scène [sɛn] *nf* (*gén*) scene; (*estrade, fig: théâtre*) stage; **entrer en ~** to come on stage; **mettre en ~** (*Théât*) to stage; (*Ciné*) to direct; (*fig*) to present, introduce; **sur le devant de la ~** (*en pleine actualité*) in the forefront; **porter à la ~** to adapt for the stage; **faire une ~ (à qn)** to make a scene (with sb); **~ de ménage** domestic fight *ou* scene

sceptique [sɛptik] *adj* sceptical ▷ *nm/f* sceptic

schéma [ʃema] *nm* (*diagramme*) diagram, sketch; (*fig*) outline

schématique [ʃematik] *adj* diagrammatic(al), schematic; (*fig*) oversimplified

sciatique [sjatik] *adj*: **nerf ~** sciatic nerve ▷ *nf* sciatica

scie [si] *nf* saw; (*fam: rengaine*) catch-tune; (*: personne*) bore; **~ à bois** wood saw; **~ circulaire** circular saw; **~ à découper** fretsaw; **~ à métaux** hacksaw; **~ sauteuse** jigsaw

sciemment [sjamã] *adv* knowingly, wittingly

science [sjãs] *nf* science; (*savoir*) knowledge; (*savoir-faire*) art, skill; **~s économiques** economics; **~s humaines/sociales** social sciences; **~s naturelles** natural science *sg*, biology *sg*; **~s po** political studies

science-fiction [sjãsfiksjõ] *nf* science fiction

scientifique [sjãtifik] *adj* scientific ▷ *nm/f* (*savant*) scientist; (*étudiant*) science student

scier [sje] *vt* to saw; (*retrancher*) to saw off

scierie [siʀi] *nf* sawmill

scinder [sɛde] *vt*: **se scinder** *vi* to split (up)

scintiller [sɛtije] *vi* to sparkle

scission [sisjõ] *nf* split

sciure [sjyʀ] *nf*: **~ (de bois)** sawdust

sclérose [skleʀoz] *nf* sclerosis; (*fig*) ossification; **~ en plaques (SEP)** multiple sclerosis (MS)

scolaire [skɔlɛʀ] *adj* school *cpd*; (*péj*) schoolish; **l'année ~** the school year; (*à l'université*) the academic year; **en âge ~** of school age

scolariser [skɔlaʀize] *vt* to provide with schooling (*ou* schools)

scolarité [skɔlaʀite] *nf* schooling; **frais de ~** school fees (*Brit*), tuition (*US*)

scooter [skutœʀ] *nm* (motor) scooter

score [skɔʀ] *nm* score; (*électoral etc*) result

scorpion [skɔʀpjõ] *nm* (*signe*): **le S~** Scorpio, the Scorpion; **être du S~** to be Scorpio

scotch [skɔtʃ] *nm* (*whisky*) scotch, whisky; (*adhésif*) Sellotape® (*Brit*), Scotch tape® (*US*)

scout, e [skut] *adj, nm* scout

script [skʀipt(ə)] *nm* printing; (*Ciné*) (shooting) script

scrupule [skʀypyl] *nm* scruple; **être sans ~s** to be unscrupulous; **se faire un ~ de qch** to have scruples ou qualms about doing sth

scruter [skʀyte] vt to search, scrutinize; (l'obscurité) to peer into; (motifs, comportement) to examine, scrutinize

scrutin [skʀytɛ̃] nm (vote) ballot; (ensemble des opérations) poll; ~ **proportionnel/majoritaire** election on a proportional/majority basis; ~ **à deux tours** poll with two ballots ou rounds; ~ **de liste** list system

sculpter [skylte] vt to sculpt; (érosion) to carve

sculpteur [skyltœʀ] nm sculptor

sculpture [skyltyʀ] nf sculpture; ~ **sur bois** wood carving

SDF sigle m (= sans domicile fixe) homeless person; **les** ~ the homeless

se, s' [s(ə)] pron **1** (emploi réfléchi) oneself; (: masc) himself; (: fém) herself; (: sujet non humain) itself; (: pl) themselves; **se voir comme l'on est** to see o.s. as one is
2 (réciproque) one another, each other; **ils s'aiment** they love one another ou each other
3 (passif): **cela se répare facilement** it is easily repaired
4 (possessif): **se casser la jambe/laver les mains** to break one's leg/wash one's hands

séance [seɑ̃s] nf (d'assemblée, récréative) meeting, session; (de tribunal) sitting, session; (musicale, Ciné, Théât) performance; **ouvrir/lever la** ~ to open/close the meeting; ~ **tenante** forthwith

seau, x [so] nm bucket, pail; ~ **à glace** ice bucket

sec, sèche [sɛk, sɛʃ] adj dry; (raisins, figues) dried; (cœur, personne: insensible) hard, cold; (maigre, décharné) spare, lean; (réponse, ton) sharp, curt; (démarrage) sharp, sudden ▷ nm: **tenir au** ~ to keep in a dry place ▷ adv hard; (démarrer) sharply; **boire** ~ to be a heavy drinker; **je le bois** ~ I drink it straight ou neat; **à pied** ~ without getting one's feet wet; **à** ~ adj dried up; (à court d'argent) broke

sécateur [sekatœʀ] nm secateurs pl (Brit), shears pl, pair of secateurs ou shears

sèche [sɛʃ] adj f voir **sec** ▷ nf (fam) cigarette, fag (Brit)

sèche-cheveux [sɛʃʃəvø] nm inv hair-drier

sèche-linge [sɛʃlɛ̃ʒ] nm inv drying cabinet

sèchement [sɛʃmɑ̃] adv (frapper etc) sharply; (répliquer etc) drily, sharply

sécher [seʃe] vt to dry; (dessécher: peau, blé) to dry (out); (: étang) to dry up; (bois) to season; (fam: classe, cours) to skip, miss ▷ vi to dry; to dry out; to dry up; (fam: candidat) to be stumped; **se sécher** (après le bain) to dry o.s.

sécheresse [seʃʀɛs] nf dryness; (absence de pluie) drought

séchoir [seʃwaʀ] nm drier

second, e [s(ə)gɔ̃, -ɔ̃d] adj second ▷ nm (assistant) second in command; (étage) second floor (Brit), third floor (US); (Navig) first mate ▷ nf second; (Scol) ≈ fifth form (Brit), ≈ tenth grade (US); **en** ~ (en second rang) in second place; **voyager en ~e** to travel second-class; **doué de ~e vue** having (the gift of) second sight; **trouver son** ~ **souffle** (Sport, fig) to get one's second wind; **être dans un état** ~ to be in a daze (ou trance); **de ~e main** second-hand

secondaire [s(ə)gɔ̃dɛʀ] adj secondary

seconder [s(ə)gɔ̃de] vt to assist; (favoriser) to back

secouer [s(ə)kwe] vt to shake; (passagers) to rock; (traumatiser) to shake (up); **se secouer** (chien) to shake itself; (fam: se démener) to shake o.s. up; ~ **la poussière d'un tapis** to shake the dust off a carpet; ~ **la tête** to shake one's head

secourir [s(ə)kuʀiʀ] vt (aller sauver) to (go and) rescue; (prodiguer des soins à) to help, assist; (venir en aide à) to assist, aid

secourisme [s(ə)kuʀism(ə)] nm (premiers soins) first aid; (sauvetage) life saving

secouriste [s(ə)kuʀist(ə)] nm/f first-aid worker

secours [s(ə)kuʀ] vb voir **secourir** ▷ nm help, aid, assistance ▷ nmpl aid sg; **cela lui a été d'un grand** ~ this was a great help to him; **au** ~! help!; **appeler au** ~ to shout ou call for help; **appeler qn à son** ~ to call sb to one's assistance; **porter** ~ **à qn** to give sb assistance, help sb; **les premiers** ~ first aid sg; **le** ~ **en montagne** mountain rescue

secousse [s(ə)kus] nf jolt, bump; (électrique) shock; (fig: psychologique) jolt, shock; ~ **sismique** ou **tellurique** earth tremor

secret, -ète [səkʀɛ, -ɛt] adj secret; (fig: renfermé) reticent, reserved ▷ nm secret; (discrétion absolue): **le** ~ secrecy; **en** ~ in secret, secretly; **au** ~ in solitary confinement; ~ **de fabrication** trade secret; ~ **professionnel** professional secrecy

secrétaire [səkʀetɛʀ] nm/f secretary ▷ nm (meuble) writing desk, secretaire; ~ **d'ambassade** embassy secretary; ~ **de direction** private ou personal secretary; ~ **d'État** ≈ junior minister; ~ **général (SG)** Secretary-General; (Comm) company secretary; ~ **de mairie** town clerk; ~ **médicale** medical secretary; ~ **de rédaction** sub-editor

secrétariat [s(ə)kʀetaʀja] nm (profession) secretarial work; (bureau: d'entreprise, d'école) (secretary's) office; (: d'organisation internationale) secretariat; (Pol etc: fonction) secretaryship, office of Secretary

secteur [sɛktœʀ] nm sector; (Admin) district; (Élec): **branché sur le** ~ plugged into the mains (supply); **fonctionne sur pile et** ~ battery or mains operated; **le** ~ **privé/public** (Écon) the private/public sector; **le** ~ **primaire/tertiaire** the primary/tertiary sector

section [sɛksjɔ̃] nf section; (de parcours d'autobus) fare stage; (Mil: unité) platoon; ~ **rythmique** rhythm section

sectionner [sɛksjɔne] vt to sever; **se sectionner** vi to be severed

sécu [seky] nf (fam: = sécurité sociale) ≈ dole (Brit), ≈ Welfare (US)

séculaire [sekylɛʀ] adj secular; (très vieux) age-old

sécuriser [sekyʀize] vt to give a sense of security to

sécurité [sekyʀite] nf security; (absence de danger)

safety; **impression de** ~ sense of security;
la ~ internationale international security;
système de ~ security (*ou* safety) system; **être
en** ~ to be safe; **la ~ de l'emploi** job security; **la
~ routière** road safety; **la ~ sociale** ≈ (the) Social
Security (*Brit*), ≈ (the) Welfare (*US*)
sédentaire [sedɑ̃tɛʀ] *adj* sedentary
séduction [sedyksjɔ̃] *nf* seduction; (*charme*,
attrait) appeal, charm
séduire [seduiʀ] *vt* to charm; (*femme: abuser de*) to
seduce; (*chose*) to appeal to
séduisant, e [seduizɑ̃, -ɑ̃t] *vb voir* **séduire** ▷ *adj*
(*femme*) seductive; (*homme, offre*) very attractive
ségrégation [segʀegɑsjɔ̃] *nf* segregation
seigle [sɛgl(ə)] *nm* rye
seigneur [sɛɲœʀ] *nm* lord; **le S~** the Lord
sein [sɛ̃] *nm* breast; (*entrailles*) womb; **au ~ de**
prép (*équipe, institution*) within; (*flots, bonheur*) in
the midst of; **donner le ~ à** (*bébé*) to feed (at the
breast); to breast-feed; **nourrir au ~** to breast-
feed
séisme [seism(ə)] *nm* earthquake
seize [sɛz] *num* sixteen
seizième [sɛzjɛm] *num* sixteenth
séjour [seʒuʀ] *nm* stay; (*pièce*) living room
séjourner [seʒuʀne] *vi* to stay
sel [sɛl] *nm* salt; (*fig*) wit; spice; **~ de cuisine/de
table** cooking/table salt; **~ gemme** rock salt; **~s
de bain** bathsalts
sélection [selɛksjɔ̃] *nf* selection; **faire/opérer
une ~ parmi** to make a selection from among;
épreuve de ~ (*Sport*) trial (for selection); **~
naturelle** natural selection; **~ professionnelle**
professional recruitment
sélectionner [selɛksjɔne] *vt* to select
self [sɛlf] *nm* (*fam*) self-service
self-service [sɛlfsɛʀvis] *adj* self-service ▷ *nm*
self-service (restaurant); (*magasin*) self-service
shop
selle [sɛl] *nf* saddle; **selles** *nfpl* (*Méd*) stools;
aller à la ~ (*Méd*) to have a bowel movement; **se
mettre en ~** to mount, get into the saddle
seller [sele] *vt* to saddle
sellette [selɛt] *nf*: **être sur la ~** to be on the
carpet (*fig*)
selon [səlɔ̃] *prép* according to; (*en se conformant
à*) in accordance with; **~ moi** as I see it; **~ que**
according to, depending on whether
semaine [səmɛn] *nf* week; (*salaire*) week's wages
ou pay, weekly wages *ou* pay; **en ~** during the
week, on weekdays; **à la petite ~** from day to
day; **la ~ sainte** Holy Week
semblable [sɑ̃blabl(ə)] *adj* similar; (*de ce genre*):
de ~s mésaventures such mishaps ▷ *nm* fellow
creature *ou* man; **~ à** similar to, like
semblant [sɑ̃blɑ̃] *nm*: **un ~ de vérité** a
semblance of truth; **faire ~ (de faire)** to pretend
(to do)
sembler [sɑ̃ble] *vb copule* to seem ▷ *vb impers*: **il
semble (bien) que/inutile de** it (really) seems
ou appears that/useless to; **il me semble (bien)
que** it (really) seems to me that, I (really) think

that; **il me semble le connaître** I think *ou*
I've a feeling I know him; **~ être** to seem to
be; **comme bon lui semble** as he sees fit; **me
semble-t-il, à ce qu'il me semble** it seems to
me, to my mind
semelle [səmɛl] *nf* sole; (*intérieure*) insole, inner
sole; **battre la ~** to stamp one's feet (to keep
them warm); (*fig*) to hang around (waiting); **~s
compensées** platform soles
semence [səmɑ̃s] *nf* (*graine*) seed; (*clou*) tack
semer [səme] *vt* to sow; (*fig: éparpiller*) to scatter;
(*confusion*) to spread; (: *poursuivants*) to lose, shake
off; **~ la discorde parmi** to sow discord among;
semé de (*difficultés*) riddled with
semestre [səmɛstʀ(ə)] *nm* half-year; (*Scol*)
semester
séminaire [seminɛʀ] *nm* seminar; (*Rel*)
seminary
semi-remorque [səmiʀəmɔʀk(ə)] *nf* trailer ▷ *nm*
articulated lorry (Brit), semi(trailer) (US)
semoule [səmul] *nf* semolina; **~ de riz** ground
rice
sempiternel, le [sɛ̃pitɛʀnɛl] *adj* eternal, never-
ending
sénat [sena] *nm* senate; *see note*
sénateur [senatœʀ] *nm* senator
sens [sɑ̃] *vb voir* **sentir** ▷ *nm* [sɑ̃s] (*Physiol, instinct*)
sense; (*signification*) meaning, sense; (*direction*)
direction, way ▷ *nmpl* (*sensualité*) senses;
reprendre ses ~ to regain consciousness; **avoir
le ~ des affaires/de la mesure** to have business
sense/a sense of moderation; **ça n'a pas de ~**
that doesn't make (any) sense; **en dépit du
bon ~** contrary to all good sense; **tomber sous
le ~** to stand to reason, be perfectly obvious; **en
un ~, dans un ~** in a way; **en ce ~ que** in the
sense that; **à mon ~** to my mind; **dans le ~ des
aiguilles d'une montre** clockwise; **dans le ~
de la longueur/largeur** lengthways/widthways;
dans le mauvais ~ the wrong way; in the
wrong direction; **bon ~** good sense; **~ commun**
common sense; **~ dessus dessous** upside down;
~ interdit, ~ unique one-way street
sensass [sɑ̃sas] *adj* (*fam*) fantastic
sensation [sɑ̃sasjɔ̃] *nf* sensation; **faire ~**
to cause a sensation, create a stir; **à ~** (*péj*)
sensational
sensationnel, le [sɑ̃sasjɔnɛl] *adj* sensational
sensé, e [sɑ̃se] *adj* sensible
sensibiliser [sɑ̃sibilize] *vt* to sensitize; **~ qn (à)**
to make sb sensitive (to)
sensibilité [sɑ̃sibilite] *nf* sensitivity; (*affectivité*,
émotivité) sensitivity, sensibility
sensible [sɑ̃sibl(ə)] *adj* sensitive; (*aux sens*)
perceptible; (*appréciable: différence, progrès*)
appreciable, noticeable; (*quartier*) problem *cpd*; **~
à** sensitive to
sensiblement [sɑ̃sibləmɑ̃] *adv* (*notablement*)
appreciably, noticeably; (*à peu près*): **ils ont ~ le
même poids** they weigh approximately the
same
sensiblerie [sɑ̃sibləʀi] *nf* sentimentality;

squeamishness

sensuel, le [sãsɥɛl] *adj* sensual; sensuous

sentence [sãtãs] *nf* (*jugement*) sentence; (*adage*) maxim

sentier [sãtje] *nm* path

sentiment [sãtimã] *nm* feeling; (*conscience, impression*): **avoir le ~ de/que** to be aware of/have the feeling that; **recevez mes ~s respectueux** yours faithfully; **faire du ~** (*péj*) to be sentimental; **si vous me prenez par les ~s** if you appeal to my feelings

sentimental, e, -aux [sãtimãtal, -o] *adj* sentimental; (*vie, aventure*) love *cpd*

sentinelle [sãtinɛl] *nf* sentry; **en ~** standing guard; (*soldat: en faction*) on sentry duty

sentir [sãtiʀ] *vt* (*par l'odorat*) to smell; (*par le goût*) to taste; (*au toucher, fig*) to feel; (*répandre une odeur de*) to smell of; (: *ressemblance*) to smell like; (*avoir la saveur de*) to taste of; to taste like; (*fig: dénoter, annoncer*) to be indicative of; to smack of; to foreshadow ▷ *vi* to smell; **~ mauvais** to smell bad; **se ~ bien** to feel good; **se ~ mal** (*être indisposé*) to feel unwell *ou* ill; **se ~ le courage/la force de faire** to feel brave/strong enough to do; **ne plus se ~ de joie** to be beside o.s. with joy; **il ne peut pas le ~** (*fam*) he can't stand him

séparation [sepaʀasjõ] *nf* separation; (*cloison*) division, partition; **~ de biens** division of property (*in marriage settlement*); **~ de corps** legal separation

séparé, e [sepaʀe] *adj* (*appartements, pouvoirs*) separate; (*époux*) separated; **~ de** separate from; separated from

séparément [sepaʀemã] *adv* separately

séparer [sepaʀe] *vt* (*gén*) to separate; (*divergences etc*) to divide; to drive apart; (: *différences, obstacles*) to stand between; (*détacher*): **~ qch de** to pull sth (off) from; (*dissocier*) to distinguish between; (*diviser*): **~ qch par** to divide sth (up) with; **~ une pièce en deux** to divide a room into two; **se séparer** (*époux*) to separate, part; (*prendre congé: amis etc*) to part, leave each other; (*adversaires*) to separate; (*se diviser: route, tige etc*) to divide; (*se détacher*): **se ~ (de)** to split off (from); to come off; **se ~ de** (*époux*) to separate *ou* part from; (*employé, objet personnel*) to part with

sept [sɛt] *num* seven

septante [sɛptãt] *num* (*Belgique, Suisse*) seventy

septembre [sɛptãbʀ(ə)] *nm* September; *voir aussi* **juillet**

septennat [sɛptena] *nm* seven-year term (of office)

septentrional, e, -aux [sɛptãtʀijɔnal, -o] *adj* northern

septicémie [sɛptisemi] *nf* blood poisoning, septicaemia

septième [sɛtjɛm] *num* seventh; **être au ~ ciel** to be on cloud nine

septique [sɛptik] *adj*: **fosse ~** septic tank

sépulture [sepyltyʀ] *nf* burial; (*tombeau*) burial place, grave

séquelles [sekɛl] *nfpl* after-effects; (*fig*) aftermath *sg*; consequences

séquestrer [sekɛstʀe] *vt* (*personne*) to confine illegally; (*biens*) to impound

serai *etc* [səʀe] *vb voir* **être**

serein, e [səʀɛ̃, -ɛn] *adj* serene; (*jugement*) dispassionate

serez [səʀe] *vb voir* **être**

sergent [sɛʀʒã] *nm* sergeant

série [seʀi] *nf* (*de questions, d'accidents, TV*) series *inv*; (*de clés, casseroles, outils*) set; (*catégorie: Sport*) rank; class; **en ~** in quick succession; (*Comm*) mass *cpd*; **de ~** *adj* standard; **hors ~** (*Comm*) custom-built; (*fig*) outstanding; **imprimante ~** (*Inform*) serial printer; **soldes de fin de ~s** end of line special offers; **~ noire** *nm* (*crime*) thriller ▷ *nf* (*suite de malheurs*) run of bad luck

sérieusement [seʀjøzmã] *adv* seriously; reliably; responsibly; **il parle ~** he's serious, he means it; **~?** are you serious?, do you mean it?

sérieux, -euse [seʀjø, -øz] *adj* serious; (*élève, employé*) reliable, responsible; (*client, maison*) reliable, dependable; (*offre, proposition*) genuine, serious; (*grave, sévère*) serious, solemn; (*maladie, situation*) serious, grave; (*important*) considerable ▷ *nm* seriousness; reliability; **ce n'est pas ~** (*raisonnable*) that's not on; **garder son ~** to keep a straight face; **manquer de ~** not to be very responsible (*ou* reliable); **prendre qch/qn au ~** to take sth/sb seriously

serin [səʀɛ̃] *nm* canary

seringue [səʀɛ̃g] *nf* syringe

serions *etc* [səʀjõ] *vb voir* **être**

serment [sɛʀmã] *nm* (*juré*) oath; (*promesse*) pledge, vow; **prêter ~** to take the *ou* an oath; **faire le ~ de** to take a vow to, swear to; **sous ~** on *ou* under oath

sermon [sɛʀmõ] *nm* sermon; (*péj*) sermon, lecture

séronégatif, -ive [seʀonegatif, -iv] *adj* HIV negative

séropositif, -ive [seʀopozitif, -iv] *adj* HIV positive

serpent [sɛʀpã] *nm* snake; **~ à sonnettes** rattlesnake; **~ monétaire (européen)** (European) monetary snake

serpenter [sɛʀpãte] *vi* to wind

serpillière [sɛʀpijɛʀ] *nf* floorcloth

serre [sɛʀ] *nf* (*Agr*) greenhouse; **~ chaude** hothouse; **~ froide** unheated greenhouse

serré, e [seʀe] *adj* (*tissu*) closely woven; (*réseau*) dense; (*écriture*) close; (*habits*) tight; (*fig: lutte, match*) tight, close-fought; (*passagers etc*) (tightly) packed; (*café*) strong ▷ *adv*: **jouer ~** to play it close, play a close game; **écrire ~** to write a cramped hand; **avoir la gorge ~e** to have a lump in one's throat

serrer [seʀe] *vt* (*tenir*) to grip *ou* hold tight; (*comprimer, coincer*) to squeeze; (*poings, mâchoires*) to clench; (*vêtement*) to be too tight for; to fit tightly; (*rapprocher*) to close up, move closer together; (*ceinture, nœud, frein, vis*) to tighten ▷ *vi*: **~ à droite** to keep to the right; to move into the right-hand lane; **se serrer** (*se rapprocher*) to squeeze up; **se ~ contre qn** to huddle up to sb; **se ~ les coudes** to stick together, back one another up; **se ~ la ceinture** to tighten one's belt; **~ la main à qn** to shake sb's hand; **~ qn dans ses bras** to hug sb, clasp sb in one's arms; **~ la gorge à qn** (*chagrin*) to bring a lump to sb's throat; **~ les dents** to clench ou grit one's teeth; **~ qn de près** to follow close behind sb; **~ le trottoir** to hug the kerb; **~ sa droite** to keep well to the right; **~ la vis à qn** to crack down harder on sb; **~ les rangs** to close ranks

serrure [seʀyʀ] *nf* lock

serrurier [seʀyʀje] *nm* locksmith

sers, sert [seʀ] *vb voir* **servir**

servante [seʀvɑ̃t] *nf* (maid)servant

serveur, -euse [seʀvœʀ, -øz] *nm/f* waiter (waitress) ▷ *nm* (*Inform*) server ▷ *adj*: **centre ~** (*Inform*) service centre

serviable [seʀvjabl(ə)] *adj* obliging, willing to help

service [seʀvis] *nm* (*gén*) service; (*série de repas*): **premier ~** first sitting; (*pourboire*) service (charge); (*assortiment de vaisselle*) set, service; (*linge de table*) set; (*bureau: de la vente etc*) department, section; (*travail*): **pendant le ~** on duty; **services** *nmpl* (*travail, Écon*) services, inclusive/exclusive of service; **faire le ~** to serve; **être en ~ chez qn** (*domestique*) to be in sb's service; **être au ~ de** (*patron, patrie*) to be in the service of; **être au ~ de qn** (*collaborateur, voiture*) to be at sb's service; **porte de ~** tradesman's entrance; **rendre ~ à** to help; **il aime rendre ~** he likes to help; **rendre un ~ à qn** to do sb a favour; **heures de ~** hours of duty; **être de ~** to be on duty; **reprendre du ~** to get back into action; **avoir 25 ans de ~** to have completed 25 years' service; **être/mettre en ~** to be in/put into service ou operation; **hors ~** not in use; out of order; **~ à thé/café** tea/coffee set ou service; **~ après-vente (SAV)** after-sales service; **en ~ commandé** on an official assignment; **~ funèbre** funeral service; **~ militaire** military service; *see note*; **~ d'ordre** police (ou stewards) in charge of maintaining order; **~s publics** public services, (public) utilities; **~s secrets** secret service *sg*; **~s sociaux** social services

serviette [seʀvjɛt] *nf* (*de table*) (table) napkin, serviette; (*de toilette*) towel; (*porte-documents*) briefcase; **~ éponge** terry towel; **~ hygiénique** sanitary towel

servir [seʀviʀ] *vt* (*gén*) to serve; (*dîneur: au restaurant*) to wait on; (*client: au magasin*) to serve, attend to; (*fig: aider*): **~ qn** to aid sb; to serve sb's interests; to stand sb in good stead; (*Comm: rente*) to pay ▷ *vi* (*Tennis*) to serve; (*Cartes*) to deal; (*être militaire*) to serve; **~ qch à qn** to serve sb with sth, help sb to sth; **qu'est-ce que je vous sers?** what can I get you?; **se servir** (*prendre d'un plat*) to help o.s.; (*s'approvisionner*): **se ~ chez** to shop at; **se ~ de** (*plat*) to help o.s. to; (*voiture, outil, relations*) to use; **~ à qn** (*diplôme, livre*) to be of use to sb; **ça m'a servi pour faire** it was useful to me when

I did; I used it to do; **~ à qch/à faire** (*outil etc*) to be used for sth/for doing; **ça peut ~** it may come in handy; **à quoi cela sert-il (de faire)?** what's the use (of doing)?; **cela ne sert à rien** it's no use; **~ (à qn) de ...** to serve as ... (for sb); **~ à dîner (à qn)** to serve dinner (to sb)

serviteur [seʀvitœʀ] *nm* servant

ses [se] *adj possessif voir* **son**

set [sɛt] *nm* set; (*napperon*) placemat; **~ de table** set of placemats

seuil [sœj] *nm* doorstep; (*fig*) threshold; **sur le ~ de la maison** in the doorway of his house, on his doorstep; **au ~ de** (*fig*) on the threshold ou brink ou edge of; **~ de rentabilité** (*Comm*) breakeven point

seul, e [sœl] *adj* (*sans compagnie*) alone; (*avec nuance affective: isolé*) lonely; (*unique*): **un ~ livre** only one book, a single book; **le ~ livre** the only book; **~ ce livre, ce livre ~** this book alone, only this book; **d'un ~ coup** (*soudainement*) all at once; (*à la fois*) at one blow ▷ *adv* (*vivre*) alone, on one's own; **parler tout ~** to talk to oneself; **faire qch (tout) ~** to do sth (all) on one's own ou (all) by oneself ▷ *nm, nf*: **il en reste un(e) ~(e)** there's only one left; **pas un(e) ~(e)** not a single; **à lui (tout) ~** single-handed, on his own; **~ à ~** in private

seulement [sœlmɑ̃] *adv* (*pas davantage*): **~ cinq, cinq ~** only five; (*exclusivement*): **~ eux** only them, them alone; (*pas avant*): **~ hier/à 10h** only yesterday/at 10 o'clock; (*mais, toutefois*): **il consent, ~ il demande des garanties** he agrees, only he wants guarantees; **non ~ ... mais aussi** ou **encore** not only ... but also

sève [sɛv] *nf* sap

sévère [seveʀ] *adj* severe

sévices [sevis] *nmpl* (physical) cruelty *sg*, ill treatment *sg*

sévir [seviʀ] *vi* (*punir*) to use harsh measures, crack down; (*fléau*) to rage, be rampant; **~ contre** (*abus*) to deal ruthlessly with, crack down on

sevrer [səvʀe] *vt* to wean; (*fig*): **~ qn de** to deprive sb of

sexe [sɛks(ə)] *nm* sex; (*organe mâle*) member

sexuel, le [sɛksɥɛl] *adj* sexual; **acte ~** sex act

seyant, e [sɛjɑ̃, -ɑ̃t] *vb voir* **seoir** ▷ *adj* becoming

shampooing [ʃɑ̃pwɛ̃] *nm* shampoo; **se faire un ~** to shampoo one's hair; **~ colorant** (colour) rinse; **~ traitant** medicated shampoo

short [ʃɔʀt] *nm* (pair of) shorts *pl*

si [si] *nm* (*Mus*) B; (*en chantant la gamme*) ti ▷ *adv* **1** (*oui*) yes; **"Paul n'est pas venu"** ‹ **"si!"** "Paul hasn't come" ‹ "Yes he has!"; **je vous assure que si** I assure you he did/she is *etc* **2** (*tellement*) so; **si gentil/rapidement** so kind/ fast; (*tant et*) **si bien que** so much so that; **si rapide qu'il soit** however fast he may be ▷ *conj* **if**; **si tu veux** if you want; **je me demande si** I wonder if ou whether; **si j'étais toi** if I were you; **si seulement** if only; **si ce n'est que** apart from; **une des plus belles, si ce n'est la plus belle** one of the most beautiful, if not THE most beautiful; **s'il est aimable, eux par contre** ... while *ou* whereas he's nice, they (on the other hand) ...

Sicile [sisil] *nf*: **la ~** Sicily

sida [sida] *nm* (= *syndrome immuno-déficitaire acquis*) AIDS *sg*

sidéré, e [sideRe] *adj* staggered

sidérurgie [sideRyRʒi] *nf* steel industry

siècle [sjɛkl(ə)] *nm* century; (*époque*): **le ~ des lumières/de l'atome** the age of enlightenment/atomic age; (*Rel*): **le ~** the world

siège [sjɛʒ] *nm* seat; (*d'entreprise*) head office; (*d'organisation*) headquarters *pl*; (*Mil*) siege; **lever le ~** to raise the siege; **mettre le ~ devant** to besiege; **présentation par le ~** (*Méd*) breech presentation; **~ avant/arrière** (*Auto*) front/back seat; **~ baquet** bucket seat; **~ social** registered office

siéger [sjeʒe] *vi* (*assemblée, tribunal*) to sit; (*résider, se trouver*) to lie, be located

sien, ne [sjɛ̃, sjɛn] *pron*: **le(la) ~(ne), les ~s(~nes)** his; hers; (*d'une chose*) its; **y mettre du ~** to pull one's weight; **faire des ~nes** (*fam*) to be up to one's (usual) tricks; **les ~s** (*sa famille*) one's family

sieste [sjɛst(ə)] *nf* (afternoon) snooze *ou* nap, siesta; **faire la ~** to have a snooze *ou* nap

sifflement [sifləmɑ̃] *nm* whistle, whistling *no pl*; wheezing *no pl*; hissing *no pl*

siffler [sifle] *vi* (*gén*) to whistle; (*avec un sifflet*) to blow (on) one's whistle; (*en respirant*) to wheeze; (*serpent, vapeur*) to hiss ▷ *vt* (*chanson*) to whistle; (*chien etc*) to whistle for; (*fille*) to whistle at; (*pièce, orateur*) to hiss, boo; (*faute*) to blow one's whistle at; (*fin du match, départ*) to blow one's whistle for; (*fam: verre, bouteille*) to guzzle, knock back (Brit)

sifflet [siflɛ] *nm* whistle; **sifflets** *nmpl* (*de mécontentement*) whistles, boos; **coup de ~** whistle

siffloter [siflɔte] *vi, vt* to whistle

sigle [sigl(ə)] *nm* acronym, (set of) initials *pl*

signal, -aux [siɲal, -o] *nm* (*signe convenu, appareil*) signal; (*indice, écriteau*) sign; **donner le ~ de** to give the signal for; **~ d'alarme** alarm signal; **~ d'alerte/de détresse** warning/distress signal; **~ horaire** time signal; **~ optique/sonore** warning light/sound; **signaux (lumineux)** (*Auto*) traffic signals; **signaux routiers** road signs; (*lumineux*) traffic lights

signalement [siɲalmɑ̃] *nm* description, particulars *pl*

signaler [siɲale] *vt* to indicate; to announce; to report; (*être l'indice de*) to indicate; (*faire remarquer*): **~ qch à qn/à qn que** to point out sth to sb/to sb that; (*appeler l'attention sur*): **~ qn à la police** to bring sb to the notice of the police; **se ~ par** to distinguish o.s. by; **se ~ à l'attention de qn** to attract sb's attention

signature [siɲatyR] *nf* signature; (*action*) signing

signe [siɲ] *nm* sign; (*Typo*) mark; **ne pas donner ~ de vie** to give no sign of life; **c'est bon ~** it's a good sign; **c'est ~ que** it's a sign that; **faire un ~ de la main/tête** to give a sign with one's hand/shake one's head; **faire ~ à qn** (*fig*) to get in touch with sb; **faire ~ à qn d'entrer** to motion (to) sb to come in; **en ~ de** as a sign *ou* mark of; **le ~ de la croix** the sign of the Cross; **~ de ponctuation** punctuation mark; **~ du zodiaque** sign of the zodiac; **~s particuliers** distinguishing marks

signer [siɲe] *vt* to sign; **se signer** *vi* to cross o.s.

significatif, -ive [siɲifikatif, -iv] *adj* significant

signification [siɲifikasjɔ̃] *nf* meaning

signifier [siɲifje] *vt* (*vouloir dire*) to mean, signify; (*faire connaître*): **~ qch (à qn)** to make sth known (to sb); (*Jur*): **~ qch à qn** to serve notice of sth on sb

silence [silɑ̃s] *nm* silence; (*Mus*) rest; **garder le ~ (sur qch)** to keep silent (about sth), say nothing (about sth); **passer sous ~** to pass over (in silence); **réduire au ~** to silence

silencieux, -euse [silɑ̃sjø, -øz] *adj* quiet, silent ▷ *nm* silencer (Brit), muffler (US)

silex [silɛks] *nm* flint

silhouette [silwɛt] *nf* outline, silhouette; (*lignes, contour*) outline; (*figure*) figure

silicium [silisjɔm] *nm* silicon; **plaquette de ~** silicon chip

sillage [sijaʒ] *nm* wake; (*fig*) trail; **dans le ~ de** (*fig*) in the wake of

sillon [sijɔ̃] *nm* (*d'un champ*) furrow; (*de disque*) groove

sillonner [sijɔne] *vt* (*creuser*) to furrow; (*traverser*) to cross, criss-cross

simagrées [simagRe] *nfpl* fuss *sg*; airs and graces

similaire [similɛR] *adj* similar

similicuir [similikɥiR] *nm* imitation leather

similitude [similityd] *nf* similarity

simple [sɛ̃pl(ə)] *adj* (*gén*) simple; (*non multiple*) single; **simples** *nmpl* (*Méd*) medicinal plants; **~ messieurs** *nm* (*Tennis*) men's singles *sg*; **un ~ particulier** an ordinary citizen; **une ~ formalité** a mere formality; **cela varie du ~ au double** it can double, it can double the price *etc*; **dans le plus ~ appareil** in one's birthday suit; **~ course** *adj* single; **~ d'esprit** *nm/f* simpleton; **~ soldat** private

simplicité [sɛ̃plisite] *nf* simplicity; **en toute ~** quite simply

simplifier [sɛ̃plifje] *vt* to simplify

simulacre [simylakR(ə)] *nm* enactment; (*péj*): **un ~ de** a pretence of, a sham

simuler [simyle] *vt* to sham, simulate

simultané, e [simyltane] *adj* simultaneous

sincère [sɛ̃sɛR] *adj* sincere; genuine; heartfelt; **mes ~s condoléances** my deepest sympathy

sincèrement [sɛ̃sɛRmɑ̃] *adv* sincerely; genuinely

sincérité [sɛ̃seRite] *nf* sincerity; **en toute ~** in all sincerity

sine qua non [sinekwanɔn] *adj*: **condition ~** indispensable condition

singe [sɛ̃ʒ] *nm* monkey; (*de grande taille*) ape

singer [sɛ̃ʒe] vt to ape, mimic
singeries [sɛ̃ʒʀi] nfpl antics; (simagrées) airs and graces
singulariser [sɛ̃gylaʀize] vt to mark out; **se singulariser** to call attention to o.s.
singularité [sɛ̃gylaʀite] nf peculiarity
singulier, -ière [sɛ̃gylje, -jɛʀ] adj remarkable, singular; (Ling) singular ▷ nm singular
sinistre [sinistʀ(ə)] adj sinister; (intensif): **un ~ imbécile** an incredible idiot ▷ nm (incendie) blaze; (catastrophe) disaster; (Assurances) damage (giving rise to a claim)
sinistré, e [sinistʀe] adj disaster-stricken ▷ nm/f disaster victim
sinon [sinɔ̃] conj (autrement, sans quoi) otherwise, or else; (sauf) except, other than; (si ce n'est) if not
sinueux, -euse [sinɥø, -øz] adj winding; (fig) tortuous
sinus [sinys] nm (Anat) sinus; (Géom) sine
sinusite [sinyzit] nf sinusitis, sinus infection
siphon [sifɔ̃] nm (tube, d'eau gazeuse) siphon; (d'évier etc) U-bend
sirène [siʀɛn] nf siren; **~ d'alarme** fire alarm; (pendant la guerre) air-raid siren
sirop [siʀo] nm (à diluer: de fruit etc) syrup, cordial (Brit); (boisson) fruit drink; (pharmaceutique) syrup, mixture; **~ de menthe** mint syrup ou cordial; **~ contre la toux** cough syrup ou mixture
siroter [siʀote] vt to sip
sismique [sismik] adj seismic
site [sit] nm (paysage, environnement) setting; (d'une ville etc: emplacement) site; **~ (pittoresque)** beauty spot; **~s touristiques** places of interest; **~s naturels/historiques** natural/historic sites; **~ web** (Inform) website
sitôt [sito] adv: **~ parti** as soon as he etc had left; **~ après** straight after; **pas de ~** not for a long time; **~ (après) que** as soon as
situation [sitɥasjɔ̃] nf (gén) situation; (d'un édifice, d'une ville) situation, position; (emplacement) location; **être en ~ de faire qch** to be in a position to do sth; **~ de famille** marital status
situé, e [sitɥe] adj: **bien ~** well situated, in a good location; **~ à/près de** situated at/near
situer [sitɥe] vt to site, situate; (en pensée) to set, place; **se situer** vi: **se ~ à/près de** to be situated at/near
six [sis] num six
sixième [sizjɛm] num sixth; **en ~** (Scol: classe) first form (Brit), sixth grade (US)
skaï® [skaj] nm ≈ Leatherette®
ski [ski] nm (objet) ski; (sport) skiing; **faire du ~** to ski; **~ alpin** Alpine skiing; **~ court** short ski; **~ évolutif** short ski method; **~ de fond** cross-country skiing; **~ nautique** water-skiing; **~ de piste** downhill skiing; **~ de randonnée** cross-country skiing
skier [skje] vi to ski
skieur, -euse [skjœʀ, -øz] nm/f skier
slip [slip] nm (sous-vêtement) underpants pl, pants pl (Brit), briefs pl; (de bain: d'homme) (bathing ou

swimming) trunks pl; (: du bikini) (bikini) briefs pl ou bottoms pl
slogan [slɔgɑ̃] nm slogan
SMIC [smik] sigle m = **salaire minimum interprofessionnel de croissance**; see note
smicard, e [smikaʀ, -aʀd(ə)] nm/f minimum wage earner
smoking [smɔkiŋ] nm dinner ou evening suit
SMS sigle m = **short message service**; (message) text (message)
SNC abr = **service non compris**
SNCF sigle f (= Société nationale des chemins de fer français) French railways
snob [snɔb] adj snobbish ▷ nm/f snob
snobisme [snɔbism(ə)] nm snobbery
sobre [sɔbʀ(ə)] adj temperate, abstemious; (élégance, style) restrained, sober; **~ de** (gestes, compliments) sparing of
sobriquet [sɔbʀikɛ] nm nickname
social, e, -aux [sɔsjal, -o] adj social
socialisme [sɔsjalism(ə)] nm socialism
socialiste [sɔsjalist(ə)] adj, nm/f socialist
société [sɔsjete] nf society; (d'abeilles, de fourmis) colony; (sportive) club; (Comm) company; **la bonne ~** polite society; **se plaire dans la ~ de** to enjoy the society of; **l'archipel de la S~** the Society Islands; **la ~ d'abondance/de consommation** the affluent/consumer society; **~ par actions** joint stock company; **~ anonyme (SA)** ≈ limited company (Ltd) (Brit), ≈ incorporated company (Inc.) (US); **~ d'investissement à capital variable (SICAV)** ≈ investment trust (Brit), ≈ mutual fund (US); **~ à responsabilité limitée (SARL)** type of limited liability company (with non-negotiable shares); **~ savante** learned society; **~ de services** service company
sociologie [sɔsjɔlɔʒi] nf sociology
socle [sɔkl(ə)] nm (de colonne, statue) plinth, pedestal; (de lampe) base
socquette [sɔkɛt] nf ankle sock
sœur [sœʀ] nf sister; (religieuse) nun, sister; **~ Élisabeth** (Rel) Sister Elizabeth; **~ de lait** foster sister
soi [swa] pron oneself; **cela va de ~** that ou it goes without saying, it stands to reason
soi-disant [swadizɑ̃] adj inv so-called ▷ adv supposedly
soie [swa] nf silk; (de porc, sanglier: poil) bristle
soierie [swaʀi] nf (industrie) silk trade; (tissu) silk
soif [swaf] nf thirst; (fig): **~ de** thirst ou craving for; **avoir ~** to be thirsty; **donner ~ à qn** to make sb thirsty
soigné, e [swaɲe] adj (tenue) well-groomed, neat; (travail) careful, meticulous; (fam) whopping; stiff
soigner [swaɲe] vt (malade, maladie: docteur) to treat; (: infirmière, mère) to nurse, look after; (blessé) to tend; (travail, détails) to take care over; (jardin, chevelure, invités) to look after
soigneux, -euse [swaɲø, -øz] adj (propre) tidy, neat; (méticuleux) painstaking, careful; **~ de**

careful with

soi-même [swamɛm] *pron* oneself

soin [swɛ̃] *nm* (*application*) care; (*propreté, ordre*) tidiness, neatness; (*responsabilité*): **le ~ de qch** the care of sth; **soins** *nmpl* (*à un malade, blessé*) treatment *sg*, medical attention *sg*; (*attentions, prévenance*) care and attention *sg*; (*hygiène*) care *sg*; **~s de la chevelure/de beauté** hair/beauty care; **~s du corps/ménage** care of one's body/ the home; **avoir** *ou* **prendre ~ de** to take care of, look after; **avoir** *ou* **prendre ~ de faire** to take care to do; **faire qch avec (grand) ~** to do sth (very) carefully; **sans ~** *adj* careless; untidy; **les premiers ~s** first aid *sg*; **aux bons ~s de** c/o, care of; **être aux petits ~s pour qn** to wait on sb hand and foot, see to sb's every need; **confier qn aux ~s de qn** to hand sb over to sb's care

soir [swaʀ] *nm, adv* evening; **le ~** in the evening(s); **ce ~** this evening, tonight; **à ce ~!** see you this evening (*ou* tonight)!; **la veille au ~** the previous evening; **sept/dix heures du ~** seven in the evening/ten at night; **le repas/ journal du ~** the evening meal/newspaper; **dimanche ~** Sunday evening; **hier ~** yesterday evening; **demain ~** tomorrow evening, tomorrow night

soirée [swaʀe] *nf* evening; (*réception*) party; **donner en ~** (*film, pièce*) to give an evening performance of

soit [swa] *vb voir* **être** ▷ *conj* (*à savoir*) namely, to wit; (*ou*): **~ ... ~** either ... or ▷ *adv* so be it, very well; **~ un triangle ABC** let ABC be a triangle; **~ que ... ~ que** *ou* **ou que** whether ... or whether

soixantaine [swasɑ̃tɛn] *nf*: **une ~ (de)** sixty or so, about sixty; **avoir la ~** to be around sixty

soixante [swasɑ̃t] *num* sixty

soixante-dix [swasɑ̃tdis] *num* seventy

soja [sɔʒa] *nm* soya; (*graines*) soya beans *pl*; **germes de ~** beansprouts

sol [sɔl] *nm* ground; (*de logement*) floor; (*revêtement*) flooring *no pl*; (*territoire, Agr, Géo*) soil; (*Mus*) G; (: *en chantant la gamme*) so(h)

solaire [sɔlɛʀ] *adj* solar, sun *cpd*

soldat [sɔlda] *nm* soldier; **S~ inconnu** Unknown Warrior *ou* Soldier; **~ de plomb** tin *ou* toy soldier

solde [sɔld(ə)] *nf* pay ▷ *nm* (*Comm*) balance; **soldes** *nmpl ou nfpl* (*Comm*) sales; (*articles*) sale goods; **à la ~ de qn** (*péj*) in sb's pay; **~ créditeur/ débiteur** credit/debit balance; **~ à payer** balance outstanding; **en ~** at sale price; **aux ~s** at the sales

solder [sɔlde] *vt* (*compte*) to settle; (*marchandise*) to sell at sale price, sell off; **se ~ par** (*fig*) to end in; **article soldé (à) 10 euros** item reduced to 10 euros

sole [sɔl] *nf* sole *inv* (*fish*)

soleil [sɔlɛj] *nm* sun; (*lumière*) sun(light); (*temps ensoleillé*) sun(shine); (*feu d'artifice*) Catherine wheel; (*d'acrobate*) grand circle; (*Bot*) sunflower; **il y a** *ou* **il fait du ~** it's sunny; **au ~** in the sun; **en plein ~** in full sun; **le ~ levant/couchant** the rising/setting sun; **le ~ de minuit** the midnight sun

solennel, le [sɔlanɛl] *adj* solemn; ceremonial

solfège [sɔlfɛʒ] *nm* rudiments *pl* of music; (*exercices*) ear training *no pl*

solidaire [sɔlidɛʀ] *adj* (*personnes*) who stand together, who show solidarity; (*pièces mécaniques*) interdependent; (*Jur: engagement*) binding on all parties; (: *débiteurs*) jointly liable; **être ~ de** (*collègues*) to stand by; (*mécanisme*) to be bound up with, be dependent on

solidarité [sɔlidaʀite] *nf* (*entre personnes*) solidarity; (*de mécanisme, phénomènes*) interdependence; **par ~ (avec)** (*cesser le travail etc*) in sympathy (with)

solide [sɔlid] *adj* solid; (*mur, maison, meuble*) solid, sturdy; (*connaissances, argument*) sound; (*personne*) robust, sturdy; (*estomac*) strong ▷ *nm* solid; **avoir les reins ~s** (*fig*) to be in a good financial position; to have sound financial backing

soliste [sɔlist(ə)] *nm/f* soloist

solitaire [sɔlitɛʀ] *adj* (*sans compagnie*) solitary, lonely; (*isolé*) solitary, isolated, lone; (*lieu*) lonely ▷ *nm/f* recluse; loner ▷ *nm* (*diamant, jeu*) solitaire

solitude [sɔlityd] *nf* loneliness; (*paix*) solitude

solive [sɔliv] *nf* joist

solliciter [sɔlisite] *vt* (*personne*) to appeal to; (*emploi, faveur*) to seek; (*moteur*) to prompt; (*occupations, attractions etc*): **~ qn** to appeal to sb's curiosity *etc*; to entice sb; to make demands on sb's time; **~ qn de faire** to appeal to sb *ou* request sb to do

sollicitude [sɔlisityd] *nf* concern

soluble [sɔlybl(ə)] *adj* (*sucre, cachet*) soluble; (*problème etc*) soluble, solvable

solution [sɔlysjɔ̃] *nf* solution; **~ de continuité** gap, break; **~ de facilité** easy way out

solvable [sɔlvabl(ə)] *adj* solvent

sombre [sɔ̃bʀ(ə)] *adj* dark; (*fig*) sombre, gloomy; (*sinistre*) awful, dreadful

sombrer [sɔ̃bʀe] *vi* (*bateau*) to sink, go down; **~ corps et biens** to go down with all hands; **~ dans** (*misère, désespoir*) to sink into

sommaire [sɔmɛʀ] *adj* (*simple*) basic; (*expéditif*) summary ▷ *nm* summary; **faire le ~ de** to make a summary of, summarize; **exécution ~** summary execution

sommation [sɔmasjɔ̃] *nf* (*Jur*) summons *sg*; (*avant de faire feu*) warning

somme [sɔm] *nf* (*Math*) sum; (*fig*) amount; (*argent*) sum, amount ▷ *nm*: **faire un ~** to have a (short) nap; **faire la ~ de** to add up; **en ~**, **~ toute** *adv* all in all

sommeil [sɔmɛj] *nm* sleep; **avoir ~** to be sleepy; **avoir le ~ léger** to be a light sleeper; **en ~** (*fig*) dormant

sommeiller [sɔmeje] *vi* to doze; (*fig*) to lie dormant

sommer [sɔme] *vt*: **~ qn de faire** to command *ou* order sb to do; (*Jur*) to summon sb to do

sommes [sɔm] *vb voir* **être**; *voir aussi* **somme**

sommet [sɔmɛ] *nm* top; (*d'une montagne*) summit, top; (*fig: de la perfection, gloire*) height; (*Géom:*

d'angle) vertex; (*conférence*) summit (conference)

sommier [sɔmje] *nm* bed base, bedspring (US); (*Admin: registre*) register; **~ à ressorts** (interior sprung) divan base (*Brit*), box spring (US); **~ à lattes** slatted bed base

somnambule [sɔmnɑ̃byl] *nm/f* sleepwalker

somnifère [sɔmnifɛʀ] *nm* sleeping drug; (*comprimé*) sleeping pill *ou* tablet

somnoler [sɔmnɔle] *vi* to doze

somptueux, -euse [sɔ̃ptɥø, -øz] *adj* sumptuous; (*cadeau*) lavish

son¹ [sɔ̃], **sa** [sa] (*pl* **ses**) [se] *adj possessif* (*antécédent humain mâle*) his; (: *femelle*) her; (: *valeur indéfinie*) one's, his (her); (: *non humain*) its; *voir* **il**

son² [sɔ̃] *nm* sound; (*de blé etc*) bran; **~ et lumière** *adj inv* son et lumière

sondage [sɔ̃daʒ] *nm* (*de terrain*) boring, drilling; (*de mer, atmosphère*) sounding; probe; (*enquête*) survey, sounding out of opinion; **~ (d'opinion)** (opinion) poll

sonde [sɔ̃d] *nf* (*Navig*) lead *ou* sounding line; (*Météorologie*) sonde; (*Méd*) probe; catheter; (*d'alimentation*) feeding tube; (*Tech*) borer, driller; (*de forage, sondage*) drill; (*pour fouiller etc*) probe; **~ à avalanche** pole (*for probing snow and locating victims*); **~ spatiale** probe

sonder [sɔ̃de] *vt* (*Navig*) to sound; (*atmosphère, plaie, bagages etc*) to probe; (*Tech*) to bore, drill; (*fig: personne*) to sound out; (: *opinion*) to probe; **~ le terrain** (*fig*) to see how the land lies

songe [sɔ̃ʒ] *nm* dream

songer [sɔ̃ʒe] *vi* to dream; **~ à** (*rêver à*) to muse over, think over; (*penser à*) to think of; (*envisager*) to contemplate, think of, consider; **~ que** to consider that; to think that

songeur, -euse [sɔ̃ʒœʀ, -øz] *adj* pensive; **ça me laisse ~** that makes me wonder

sonnant, e [sɔnɑ̃, -ɑ̃t] *adj*: **en espèces ~es et trébuchantes** in coin of the realm; **à huit heures ~es** on the stroke of eight

sonné, e [sɔne] *adj* (*fam*) cracked; (*passé*): **il est midi ~** it's gone twelve; **il a quarante ans bien ~s** he's well into his forties

sonner [sɔne] *vi* (*retentir*) to ring; (*donner une impression*) to sound ▷ *vt* (*cloche*) to ring; (*glas, tocsin*) to sound; (*portier, infirmière*) to ring for; (*messe*) to ring the bell for; (*fam: choc, coup*) to knock out; **~ du clairon** to sound the bugle; **~ bien/mal/creux** to sound good/bad/hollow; **~ faux** (*instrument*) to sound out of tune; (*rire*) to ring false; **~ les heures** to strike the hours; **minuit vient de ~** midnight has just struck; **~ chez qn** to ring sb's doorbell, ring at sb's door

sonnerie [sɔnʀi] *nf* (*son*) ringing; (*sonnette*) bell; (*mécanisme d'horloge*) striking mechanism; (*de téléphone portable*) ringtone; **~ d'alarme** alarm bell; **~ de clairon** bugle call

sonnette [sɔnɛt] *nf* bell; **~ d'alarme** alarm bell; **~ de nuit** night-bell

sono [sɔno] *nf* (= *sonorisation*) PA (system); (*d'une discothèque*) sound system

sonore [sɔnɔʀ] *adj* (*voix*) sonorous, ringing; (*salle,*

métal) resonant; (*ondes, film, signal*) sound *cpd*; (*Ling*) voiced; **effets ~s** sound effects

sonorisation [sɔnɔʀizasjɔ̃] *nf* (*installations*) public address system; (*d'une discothèque*) sound system

sonorité [sɔnɔʀite] *nf* (*de piano, violon*) tone; (*de voix, mot*) sonority; (*d'une salle*) resonance; acoustics *pl*

sont [sɔ̃] *vb voir* **être**

sophistiqué, e [sɔfistike] *adj* sophisticated

sorbet [sɔʀbɛ] *nm* water ice, sorbet

sorcellerie [sɔʀsɛlʀi] *nf* witchcraft *no pl*, sorcery *no pl*

sorcier, -ière [sɔʀsje, -jɛʀ] *nm/f* sorcerer (witch *ou* sorceress) ▷ *adj*: **ce n'est pas ~** (*fam*) it's as easy as pie

sordide [sɔʀdid] *adj* sordid; squalid

sornettes [sɔʀnɛt] *nfpl* twaddle *sg*

sort [sɔʀ] *vb voir* **sortir** ▷ *nm* (*fortune, destinée*) fate; (*condition, situation*) lot; (*magique*): **jeter un ~** to cast a spell; **un coup du ~** a blow dealt by fate; **le ~ en est jeté** the die is cast; **tirer au ~** to draw lots; **tirer qch au ~** to draw lots for sth

sorte [sɔʀt(ə)] *vb voir* **sortir** ▷ *nf* sort, kind; **une ~ de** a sort of; **de la ~** *adv* in that way; **en quelque ~** in a way; **de ~ à** so as to, in order to; **de (telle) ~ que, en ~ que** (*de manière que*) so that; (*si bien que*) so much so that; **faire en ~ que** to see to it that

sortie [sɔʀti] *nf* (*issue*) way out, exit; (*Mil*) sortie; (*fig: verbale*) outburst; sally; (: *parole incongrue*) odd remark; (*d'un gaz, de l'eau*) outlet; (*promenade*) outing; (*le soir: au restaurant etc*) night out; (*de produits*) export; (*de capitaux*) outflow; (*Comm: somme*): **~s** items of expenditure; outgoings; (*Inform*) output; (*d'imprimante*) printout; **à sa ~** as he went out *ou* left; **à la ~ de l'école/l'usine** (*moment*) after school/work; when school/the factory comes out; (*lieu*) at the school/factory gates; **à la ~ de ce nouveau modèle** when this new model comes (*ou* came) out, when they bring (*ou* brought) out this new model; **~ de bain** (*vêtement*) bathrobe; **"~ de camions"** "vehicle exit"; **~ papier** hard copy; **~ de secours** emergency exit

sortilège [sɔʀtilɛʒ] *nm* (magic) spell

sortir [sɔʀtiʀ] *vi* (*gén*) to come out; (*partir, se promener, aller au spectacle etc*) to go out; (*bourgeon, plante, numéro gagnant*) to come up ▷ *vt* (*gén*) to take out; (*produit, ouvrage, modèle*) to bring out; (*boniments, incongruités*) to come out with; (*Inform*) to output; (: *sur papier*) to print out; (*fam: expulser*) to throw out ▷ *nm*: **au ~ de l'hiver/l'enfance** as winter/childhood nears its end; **~ qch de** to take sth out of; **~ qn d'embarras** to get sb out of trouble; **~ de** (*gén*) to leave; (*endroit*) to go (*ou* come) out of, leave; (*rainure etc*) to come out of; (*maladie*) to get over; (*époque*) to get through; (*cadre, compétence*) to be outside; (*provenir de: famille etc*) to come from; **~ de table** to leave the table; **~ du système** (*Inform*) to log out; **~ de ses gonds** (*fig*) to fly off the handle; **se ~ de** (*affaire, situation*) to get out of; **s'en ~** (*malade*) to pull through;

(*d'une difficulté etc*) to come through all right; to get through, be able to manage

sosie [sɔzi] *nm* double

sot, sotte [so, sɔt] *adj* silly, foolish ▷ *nm/f* fool

sottise [sɔtiz] *nf* silliness *no pl*, foolishness *no pl*; (*propos, acte*) silly *ou* foolish thing (to do *ou* say)

sou [su] *nm*: **près de ses ~s** tight-fisted; **sans le ~** penniless; **~ à ~** penny by penny; **pas un ~ de bon sens** not a scrap *ou* an ounce of good sense; **de quatre ~s** worthless

soubresaut [subʀəso] *nm* (*de peur etc*) start; (*cahot: d'un véhicule*) jolt

souche [suʃ] *nf* (*d'arbre*) stump; (*de carnet*) counterfoil (Brit), stub; **dormir comme une ~** to sleep like a log; **de vieille ~** of old stock

souci [susi] *nm* (*inquiétude*) worry; (*préoccupation*) concern; (*Bot*) marigold; **se faire du ~** to worry; **avoir (le) ~ de** to have concern for; **par ~ de** for the sake of, out of concern for

soucier [susje]: **se ~ de** *vt* to care about

soucieux, -euse [susjø, -øz] *adj* concerned, worried; **~ de** concerned about; **peu ~ de/que** caring little about/whether

soucoupe [sukup] *nf* saucer; **~ volante** flying saucer

soudain, e [sudɛ̃, -ɛn] *adj* (*douleur, mort*) sudden ▷ *adv* suddenly, all of a sudden

soude [sud] *nf* soda

souder [sude] *vt* (*avec fil à souder*) to solder; (*par soudure autogène*) to weld; (*fig*) to bind *ou* knit together; to fuse (together); **se souder** *vi* (*os*) to knit (together)

soudoyer [sudwaje] *vt* (*péj*) to bribe, buy over

soudure [sudyʀ] *nf* soldering; welding; (*joint*) soldered joint; weld; **faire la ~** (Comm) to fill a gap; (*fig: assurer une transition*) to bridge the gap

souffert, e [sufɛʀ, -ɛʀt(ə)] *pp de* **souffrir**

souffle [sufl(ə)] *nm* (*en expirant*) breath; (*en soufflant*) puff, blow; (*respiration*) breathing; (*d'explosion, de ventilateur*) blast; (*du vent*) blowing; (*fig*) inspiration; **retenir son ~** to hold one's breath; **avoir du/manquer de ~** to have a lot of puff/be short of breath; **être à bout de ~** to be out of breath; **avoir le ~ court** to be short-winded; **un ~ d'air** *ou* **de vent** a breath of air, a puff of wind; **~ au cœur** (Méd) heart murmur

soufflé, e [sufle] *adj* (Culin) soufflé; (*fam: ahuri, stupéfié*) staggered ▷ *nm* (Culin) soufflé

souffler [sufle] *vi* (*gén*) to blow; (*haleter*) to puff (and blow) ▷ *vt* (*feu, bougie*) to blow out; (*chasser: poussière etc*) to blow away; (*Tech: verre*) to blow; (*explosion*) to destroy (with its blast); (*dire*): **~ qch à qn** to whisper sth to sb; (*fam: voler*): **~ qch à qn** to pinch sth from sb; **~ son rôle à qn** to prompt sb; **ne pas ~ mot** not to breathe a word; **laisser ~ qn** (*fig*) to give sb a breather

soufflet [sufle] *nm* (*instrument*) bellows *pl*; (*entre wagons*) vestibule; (*Couture*) gusset; (*gifle*) slap (in the face)

souffleur, -euse [suflœʀ, -øz] *nm/f* (Théât) prompter; (Tech) glass-blower

souffrance [sufʀɑ̃s] *nf* suffering; **en ~**

(*marchandise*) awaiting delivery; (*affaire*) pending

souffrant, e [sufʀɑ̃, -ɑ̃t] *adj* unwell

souffre-douleur [sufʀədulœʀ] *nm inv* whipping boy (Brit), butt, underdog

souffrir [sufʀiʀ] *vi* to suffer; (*éprouver des douleurs*) to be in pain ▷ *vt* to suffer, endure; (*supporter*) to bear, stand; (*admettre: exception etc*) to allow *ou* admit of; **~ de** (*maladie, froid*) to suffer from; **~ des dents** to have trouble with one's teeth; **ne pas pouvoir ~ qch/que ...** not to be able to endure *ou* bear sth/that ...; **faire ~ qn** (*personne*) to make sb suffer; (: *dents, blessure etc*) to hurt sb

soufre [sufʀ(ə)] *nm* sulphur (Brit), sulfur (US)

souhait [swɛ] *nm* wish; **tous nos ~s de** good wishes *ou* our best wishes for; **riche** *etc* **à ~** as rich *etc* as one could wish; **à vos ~s!** bless you!

souhaitable [swɛtabl(ə)] *adj* desirable

souhaiter [swete] *vt* to wish for; **~ le bonjour à qn** to bid sb good day; **~ la bonne année à qn** to wish sb a happy New Year; **il est à ~ que** it is to be hoped that

souiller [suje] *vt* to dirty, soil; (*fig*) to sully, tarnish

soûl, e [su, sul] *adj* drunk; (*fig*): **~ de musique/ plaisirs** drunk with music/pleasure ▷ *nm*: **tout son ~** to one's heart's content

soulagement [sulaʒmɑ̃] *nm* relief

soulager [sulaʒe] *vt* to relieve; **~ qn de** to relieve sb of

soûler [sule] *vt*: **~ qn** to get sb drunk; (*boisson*) to make sb drunk; (*fig*) to make sb's head spin *ou* reel; **se soûler** to get drunk; **se ~ de** (*fig*) to intoxicate o.s with

soulever [sulve] *vt* to lift; (*vagues, poussière*) to send up; (*peuple*) to stir up (to revolt); (*enthousiasme*) to arouse; (*question, débat, protestations, difficultés*) to raise; **se soulever** *vi* (*peuple*) to rise up; (*personne couchée*) to lift o.s. up; (*couvercle etc*) to lift; **cela me soulève le cœur** it makes me feel sick

soulier [sulje] *nm* shoe; **~s bas** low-heeled shoes; **~s plats/à talons** flat/heeled shoes

souligner [suliɲe] *vt* to underline; (*fig*) to emphasize, stress

soumettre [sumɛtʀ(ə)] *vt* (*pays*) to subject, subjugate; (*rebelles*) to put down, subdue; **~ qn/qch à** to subject sb/sth to; **~ qch à qn** (*projet etc*) to submit sth to sb; **se ~ (à)** (*se rendre, obéir*) to submit (to); **se ~ à** (*formalités etc*) to submit to; (*régime etc*) to submit o.s. to

soumis, e [sumi, -iz] *pp de* **soumettre** ▷ *adj* submissive; **revenus ~ à l'impôt** taxable income

soumission [sumisjɔ̃] *nf* (*voir se soumettre*) submission; (*docilité*) submissiveness; (Comm) tender

soupape [supap] *nf* valve; **~ de sûreté** safety valve

soupçon [supsɔ̃] *nm* suspicion; (*petite quantité*): **un ~ de** a hint *ou* touch of; **avoir ~ de** to suspect; **au dessus de tout ~** above (all) suspicion

soupçonner [supsɔne] *vt* to suspect; **~ qn de**

qch/d'être to suspect sb of sth/of being

soupçonneux, -euse [supsɔnø, -øz] *adj* suspicious

soupe [sup] *nf* soup; **~ au lait** *adj inv* quick-tempered; **~ à l'oignon/de poisson** onion/fish soup; **~ populaire** soup kitchen

souper [supe] *vi* to have supper ▷ *nm* supper; **avoir soupé de** (*fam*) to be sick and tired of

soupeser [supəze] *vt* to weigh in one's hand(s), feel the weight of; (*fig*) to weigh up

soupière [supjɛʀ] *nf* (soup) tureen

soupir [supiʀ] *nm* sigh; (*Mus*) crotchet rest (*Brit*), quarter note rest (*US*); **rendre le dernier ~** to breathe one's last

soupirail, -aux [supiʀaj, -o] *nm* (small) basement window

soupirer [supiʀe] *vi* to sigh; **~ après qch** to yearn for sth

souple [supl(ə)] *adj* supple; (*col*) soft; (*fig: règlement, caractère*) flexible; (: *démarche, taille*) lithe, supple

souplesse [suplɛs] *nf* suppleness; flexibility

source [suʀs(ə)] *nf* (*point d'eau*) spring; (*d'un cours d'eau, fig*) source; **prendre sa ~ à/dans** (*cours d'eau*) to have its source at/in; **tenir qch de bonne ~/de ~ sûre** to have sth on good authority/from a reliable source; **~ thermale/d'eau minérale** hot *ou* thermal/mineral spring

sourcil [suʀsij] *nm* (eye)brow

sourciller [suʀsije] *vi*: **sans ~** without turning a hair *ou* batting an eyelid

sourd, e [suʀ, suʀd(ə)] *adj* deaf; (*bruit, voix*) muffled; (*couleur*) muted; (*douleur*) dull; (*lutte*) silent, hidden; (*Ling*) voiceless ▷ *nm/f* deaf person; **être ~ à** to be deaf to

sourdine [suʀdin] *nf* (*Mus*) mute; **en ~** *adv* softly, quietly; **mettre une ~ à** (*fig*) to tone down

sourd-muet, sourde-muette [suʀmyɛ, suʀdmyɛt] *adj* deaf-and-dumb ▷ *nm/f* deaf-mute

souriant, e [suʀjã, -ãt] *vb voir* **sourire** ▷ *adj* cheerful

souricière [suʀisjɛʀ] *nf* mousetrap; (*fig*) trap

sourire [suʀiʀ] *nm* smile ▷ *vi* to smile; **~ à qn** to smile at sb; (*fig*) to appeal to sb; (: *chance*) to smile on sb; **faire un ~ à qn** to give sb a smile; **garder le ~** to keep smiling

souris [suʀi] *nf* (*aussi Inform*) mouse

sournois, e [suʀnwa, -waz] *adj* deceitful, underhand

sous [su] *prép* (*gén*) under; **~ la pluie/le soleil** in the rain/sunshine; **~ mes yeux** before my eyes; **~ terre** *adj, adv* underground; **~ vide** *adj, adv* vacuum-packed; **~ l'influence/l'action de** under the influence of/by the action of; **~ antibiotiques/perfusion** on antibiotics/a drip; **~ cet angle/ce rapport** from this angle/in this respect; **~ peu** *adv* shortly, before long

sous-bois [subwa] *nm inv* undergrowth

souscrire [suskʀiʀ]: **~ à** *vt* to subscribe to

sous-directeur, -trice [sudiʀɛktœʀ, -tʀis] *nm/f* assistant manager/manageress, submanager/

manageress

sous-entendre [suzãtãdʀ(ə)] *vt* to imply, infer

sous-entendu, e [suzãtãdy] *adj* implied; (*Ling*) understood ▷ *nm* innuendo, insinuation

sous-estimer [suzɛstime] *vt* to underestimate

sous-jacent, e [suʒasã, -ãt] *adj* underlying

sous-louer [sulwe] *vt* to sublet

sous-marin, e [sumaʀɛ̃, -in] *adj* (*flore, volcan*) submarine; (*navigation, pêche, explosif*) underwater ▷ *nm* submarine

sous-officier [suzɔfisje] *nm* ≈ non-commissioned officer (NCO)

sous-produit [supʀɔdɥi] *nm* by-product; (*fig: péj*) pale imitation

sous-pull [supul] *nm* thin poloneck sweater

soussigné, e [susiɲe] *adj*: **je ~** I the undersigned

sous-sol [susɔl] *nm* basement; (*Géo*) subsoil

sous-titre [sutitʀ(ə)] *nm* subtitle

soustraction [sustʀaksjɔ̃] *nf* subtraction

soustraire [sustʀɛʀ] *vt* to subtract, take away; (*dérober*): **~ qch à qn** to remove sth from sb; **~ qn à** (*danger*) to shield sb from; **se ~ à** (*autorité, obligation, devoir*) to elude, escape from

sous-traitant [sutʀɛtã] *nm* subcontractor

sous-traiter [sutʀɛte] *vt, vi* to subcontract

sous-vêtement [suvɛtmã] *nm* undergarment, item of underwear; **sous-vêtements** *nmpl* underwear *sg*

soutane [sutan] *nf* cassock, soutane

soute [sut] *nf* hold; **~ à bagages** baggage hold

soutenir [sutniʀ] *vt* to support; (*assaut, choc, regard*) to stand up to, withstand; (*intérêt, effort*) to keep up; (*assurer*): **~ que** to maintain that; **se soutenir** (*dans l'eau etc*) to hold o.s. up; (*être soutenable: point de vue*) to be tenable; (*s'aider mutuellement*) to stand by each other; **~ la comparaison avec** to bear *ou* stand comparison with; **~ le regard de qn** to be able to look sb in the face

soutenu, e [sutny] *pp de* **soutenir** ▷ *adj* (*efforts*) sustained, unflagging; (*style*) elevated; (*couleur*) strong

souterrain, e [sutɛʀɛ̃, -ɛn] *adj* underground; (*fig*) subterranean ▷ *nm* underground passage

soutien [sutjɛ̃] *nm* support; **apporter son ~ à** to lend one's support to; **~ de famille** breadwinner

soutien-gorge (*pl* **soutiens-gorge**) [sutjɛ̃gɔʀʒ(ə)] *nm* bra; (*de maillot de bain*) top

soutirer [sutiʀe] *vt*: **~ qch à qn** to squeeze *ou* get sth out of sb

souvenir [suvniʀ] *nm* (*réminiscence*) memory; (*cadeau*) souvenir, keepsake; (*de voyage*) souvenir ▷ *vb*: **se ~ de** *vt* to remember; **se ~ que** to remember that; **garder le ~ de** to retain the memory of; **en ~ de** in memory *ou* remembrance of; **avec mes affectueux/meilleurs ~s, ...** with love from, .../regards, ...

souvent [suvã] *adv* often; **peu ~** seldom, infrequently; **le plus ~** more often than not, most often

souverain, e [suvʀɛ̃, -ɛn] *adj* sovereign; (*fig: mépris*) supreme ▷ *nm/f* sovereign, monarch

soyeux, -euse [swajø, -øz] *adj* silky

soyons *etc* [swajɔ̃] *vb voir* **être**

spacieux, -euse [spasjø, -øz] *adj* spacious; roomy

spaghettis [spageti] *nmpl* spaghetti *sg*

sparadrap [sparadRa] *nm* adhesive *ou* sticking (Brit) plaster, bandaid® (US)

spatial, e, -aux [spasjal, -o] *adj* (*Aviat*) space *cpd*; (*Psych*) spatial

speaker, ine [spikœR, -kRin] *nm/f* announcer

spécial, e, -aux [spesjal, -o] *adj* special; (*bizarre*) peculiar

spécialement [spesjalmã] *adv* especially, particularly; (*tout exprès*) specially; **pas ~** not particularly

spécialiser [spesjalize]: **se spécialiser** *vi* to specialize

spécialiste [spesjalist(ə)] *nm/f* specialist

spécialité [spesjalite] *nf* speciality; (*Scol*) special field; **~ pharmaceutique** patent medicine

spécifier [spesifje] *vt* to specify, state

spécimen [spesimɛn] *nm* specimen; (*revue etc*) specimen *ou* sample copy

spectacle [spɛktakl(ə)] *nm* (*tableau, scène*) sight; (*représentation*) show; (*industrie*) show business, entertainment; **se donner en ~** (*péj*) to make a spectacle *ou* an exhibition of o.s; **pièce/revue à grand ~** spectacular (play/revue); **au ~ de ...** at the sight of ...

spectaculaire [spɛktakylɛR] *adj* spectacular

spectateur, -trice [spɛktatœR, -tRis] *nm/f* (*Ciné etc*) member of the audience; (*Sport*) spectator; (*d'un événement*) onlooker, witness

spéculer [spekyle] *vi* to speculate; **~ sur** (*Comm*) to speculate in; (*réfléchir*) to speculate on; (*tabler sur*) to bank *ou* rely on

spéléologie [speleɔlɔʒi] *nf* (*étude*) speleology; (*activité*) potholing

sperme [spɛRm(ə)] *nm* semen, sperm

sphère [sfɛR] *nf* sphere

spirale [spiRal] *nf* spiral; **en ~** in a spiral

spirituel, le [spiRitɥɛl] *adj* spiritual; (*fin, piquant*) witty; **musique ~le** sacred music; **concert ~** concert of sacred music

splendide [splãdid] *adj* splendid, magnificent

sponsoriser [spɔ̃sɔRize] *vt* to sponsor

spontané, e [spɔ̃tane] *adj* spontaneous

spontanéité [spɔ̃taneite] *nf* spontaneity

sport [spɔR] *nm* sport ▷ *adj inv* (*vêtement*) casual; (*fair-play*) sporting; **faire du ~** to do sport; **~ individuel/d'équipe** individual/team sport; **~ de combat** combative sport; **~s d'hiver** winter sports

sportif, -ive [spɔRtif, -iv] *adj* (*journal, association, épreuve*) sports *cpd*; (*allure, démarche*) athletic; (*attitude, esprit*) sporting; **les résultats ~s** the sports results

spot [spɔt] *nm* (*lampe*) spot(light); (*annonce*): **~ (publicitaire)** commercial (break)

square [skwaR] *nm* public garden(s)

squelette [skəlɛt] *nm* skeleton

squelettique [skəletik] *adj* scrawny; (*fig*) skimpy

SRAS *sigle m* (= *syndrome respiratoire aigu sévère*) SARS

stabiliser [stabilize] *vt* to stabilize; (*terrain*) to consolidate

stable [stabl(ə)] *adj* stable, steady

stade [stad] *nm* (*Sport*) stadium; (*phase, niveau*) stage

stage [staʒ] *nm* training period; training course; (*d'avocat stagiaire*) articles *pl*; **~ en entreprise** work experience placement

stagiaire [staʒjɛR] *nm/f, adj* trainee (*cpd*)

stagner [stagne] *vi* to stagnate

stalle [stal] *nf* stall, box

stand [stãd] *nm* (*d'exposition*) stand; (*de foire*) stall; **~ de tir** (*à la foire, Sport*) shooting range; **~ de ravitaillement** pit

standard [stãdaR] *adj inv* standard ▷ *nm* (*type, norme*) standard; (*téléphonique*) switchboard

standardiste [stãdaRdist(ə)] *nm/f* switchboard operator

standing [stãdiŋ] *nm* standing; **immeuble de grand ~** block of luxury flats (Brit), condo(minium) (US)

starter [staRtɛR] *nm* (*Auto*) choke; (*Sport: personne*) starter; **mettre le ~** to pull out the choke

station [stɑsjɔ̃] *nf* station; (*de bus*) stop; (*de villégiature*) resort; (*posture*): **la ~ debout** standing, an upright posture; **~ balnéaire** seaside resort; **~ de graissage** lubrication bay; **~ de lavage** carwash; **~ de ski** ski resort; **~ de sports d'hiver** winter sports resort; **~ de taxis** taxi rank (Brit) *ou* stand (US); **~ thermale** thermal spa; **~ de travail** workstation

stationnement [stasjɔnmã] *nm* parking; **zone de ~ interdit** no parking area; **~ alterné** parking on alternate sides

stationner [stasjɔne] *vi* to park

station-service [stasjɔ̃sɛRvis] *nf* service station

statistique [statistik] *nf* (*science*) statistics *sg*; (*rapport, étude*) statistic ▷ *adj* statistical; **statistiques** *nfpl* (*données*) statistics *pl*

statue [staty] *nf* statue

statu quo [statykwo] *nm* status quo

statut [staty] *nm* status; **statuts** *nmpl* (*Jur, Admin*) statutes

statutaire [statytɛR] *adj* statutory

Sté *abr* (= *société*) soc

steak [stɛk] *nm* steak shorthand; **prendre en sténo** to take down in shorthand

sténographie [stenɔgrafi] *nf* shorthand; **prendre en ~** to take down in shorthand

stéréo *nf* (*aussi*: **stéréophonie**) stereo; **émission en ~** stereo broadcast ▷ *adj* (*aussi*: **stéréophonique**) stereo

stéréophonie [stereɔfɔni] *nf* stereo(phony); **émission en ~** stereo broadcast

stéréophonique [stereɔfɔnik] *adj* stereo(phonic)

stérile [steRil] *adj* sterile; (*terre*) barren; (*fig*) fruitless, futile

stérilet [steRilɛ] *nm* coil, loop

stériliser [steRilize] *vt* to sterilize

stigmates [stigmat] *nmpl* scars, marks; (*Rel*) stigmata *pl*

stimulant, e [stimylã, -ãt] *adj* stimulating ▷ *nm* (*Méd*) stimulant; (*fig*) stimulus, incentive

stimuler [stimyle] *vt* to stimulate

stipuler [stipyle] *vt* to stipulate, specify

stock [stɔk] *nm* stock; **en ~** in stock

stocker [stɔke] *vt* to stock; (*déchets*) to store

stop [stɔp] *nm* (*Auto: écriteau*) stop sign; (: *signal*) brake-light; (*dans un télégramme*) stop ▷ *excl* stop!

stopper [stɔpe] *vt* to stop, halt; (*Couture*) to mend ▷ *vi* to stop, halt

store [stɔʀ] *nm* blind; (*de magasin*) shade, awning

strabisme [stʀabism(ə)] *nm* squint(ing)

strapontin [stʀapɔ̃tɛ̃] *nm* jump *ou* foldaway seat

Strasbourg [stʀazbuʀ] *n* Strasbourg

stratégie [stʀateʒi] *nf* strategy

stratégique [stʀateʒik] *adj* strategic

stress [stʀɛs] *nm inv* stress

stressant, e [stʀɛsã, -ãt] *adj* stressful

stresser [stʀɛse] *vt* to stress, cause stress in

strict, e [stʀikt(ə)] *adj* strict; (*tenue, décor*) severe, plain; **son droit le plus ~** his most basic right; **dans le plus ~e intimité** strictly in private; **le ~ nécessaire/minimum** the bare essentials/minimum

strident, e [stʀidã, -ãt] *adj* shrill, strident

strophe [stʀɔf] *nf* verse, stanza

structure [stʀyktyʀ] *nf* structure; **~s d'accueil/touristiques** reception/tourist facilities

studieux, -euse [stydjø, -øz] *adj* (*élève*) studious; (*vacances*) study *cpd*

studio [stydjo] *nm* (*logement*) studio flat (*Brit*) *ou* apartment (*US*); (*d'artiste, TV etc*) studio

stupéfait, e [stypefɛ, -ɛt] *adj* astonished

stupéfiant, e [stypefjã, -ãt] *adj* stunning, astonishing ▷ *nm* (*Méd*) drug, narcotic

stupéfier [stypefje] *vt* to stupefy; (*étonner*) to stun, astonish

stupeur [stypœʀ] *nf* (*inertie, insensibilité*) stupor; (*étonnement*) astonishment, amazement

stupide [stypid] *adj* stupid; (*hébété*) stunned

stupidité [stypidite] *nf* stupidity *no pl*; (*propos, action*) stupid thing (to say *ou* do)

style [stil] *nm* style; **meuble/robe de ~** piece of period furniture/period dress; **~ de vie** lifestyle

stylé, e [stile] *adj* well-trained

styliste [stilist(ə)] *nm/f* designer; stylist

stylo [stilo] *nm*: **~ (à encre)** (fountain) pen; **~ (à) bille** ballpoint pen

su, e [sy] *pp de* **savoir** ▷ *nm*: **au su de** with the knowledge of

suave [sɥav] *adj* (*odeur*) sweet; (*voix*) suave, smooth; (*coloris*) soft, mellow

subalterne [sybaltɛʀn(ə)] *adj* (*employé, officier*) junior; (*rôle*) subordinate, subsidiary ▷ *nm/f* subordinate, inferior

subconscient [sypkɔ̃sjã] *nm* subconscious

subir [sybiʀ] *vt* (*affront, dégâts, mauvais traitements*) to suffer; (*influence, charme*) to be under, be subjected to; (*traitement, opération, châtiment*) to undergo; (*personne*) to suffer, be subjected to

subit, e [sybi, -it] *adj* sudden

subitement [sybitmã] *adv* suddenly, all of a sudden

subjectif, -ive [sybʒɛktif, -iv] *adj* subjective

subjonctif [sybʒɔ̃ktif] *nm* subjunctive

subjuguer [sybʒyge] *vt* to subjugate

submerger [sybmɛʀʒe] *vt* to submerge; (*foule*) to engulf; (*fig*) to overwhelm

subordonné, e [sybɔʀdɔne] *adj, nm/f* subordinate; **~ à** (*personne*) subordinate to; (*résultats etc*) subject to, depending on

subrepticement [sybʀɛptismã] *adv* surreptitiously

subside [sypsid] *nm* grant

subsidiaire [sypsidjɛʀ] *adj* subsidiary; **question ~** deciding question

subsister [sybziste] *vi* (*rester*) to remain, subsist; (*vivre*) to live; (*survivre*) to live on

substance [sypstãs] *nf* substance; **en ~** in substance

substituer [sypstitɥe] *vt*: **~ qn/qch à** to substitute sb/sth for; **se ~ à qn** (*représenter*) to substitute for sb; (*évincer*) to substitute o.s. for sb

substitut [sypstity] *nm* (*Jur*) deputy public prosecutor; (*succédané*) substitute

subterfuge [syptɛʀfyʒ] *nm* subterfuge

subtil, e [syptil] *adj* subtle

subtiliser [syptilize] *vt*: **~ qch (à qn)** to spirit sth away (from sb)

subvenir [sybvəniʀ]: **~ à** *vt* to meet

subvention [sybvãsjɔ̃] *nf* subsidy, grant

subventionner [sybvãsjɔne] *vt* to subsidize

suc [syk] *nm* (*Bot*) sap; (*de viande, fruit*) juice; **~s gastriques** gastric juices

succédané [syksedane] *nm* substitute

succéder [syksede]: **~ à** *vt* (*directeur, roi etc*) to succeed; (*venir après: dans une série*) to follow, succeed; **se succéder** *vi* (*accidents, années*) to follow one another

succès [syksɛ] *nm* success; **avec ~** successfully; **sans ~** unsuccessfully; **avoir du ~** to be a success, be successful; **à ~** successful; **livre à ~** bestseller; **~ de librairie** bestseller; **~ (féminins)** conquests

successeur [syksesœʀ] *nm* successor

successif, -ive [syksesif, -iv] *adj* successive

succession [syksesjɔ̃] *nf* (*série, Pol*) succession; (*Jur: patrimoine*) estate, inheritance; **prendre la ~ de** (*directeur*) to succeed, take over from; (*entreprise*) to take over

succomber [sykɔ̃be] *vi* to die, succumb; (*fig*): **~ à** to give way to, succumb to

succulent, e [sykylã, -ãt] *adj* succulent

succursale [sykyʀsal] *nf* branch; **magasin à ~s multiples** chain *ou* multiple store

sucer [syse] *vt* to suck

sucette [sysɛt] *nf* (*bonbon*) lollipop; (*de bébé*) dummy (*Brit*), comforter, pacifier (*US*)

sucre [sykʀ(ə)] *nm* (*substance*) sugar; (*morceau*) lump of sugar, sugar lump *ou* cube; **~ de canne/betterave** cane/beet sugar; **~ en morceaux/cristallisé/en poudre** lump *ou* cube/

granulated/caster sugar; **~ glace** icing sugar; **~ d'orge** barley sugar

sucré, e [sykʀe] *adj* (*produit alimentaire*) sweetened; (*au goût*) sweet; (*péj*) sugary, honeyed

sucrer [sykʀe] *vt* (*thé, café*) to sweeten, put sugar in; **~ qn** to put sugar in sb's tea (*ou* coffee *etc*); **se sucrer** to help o.s. to sugar, have some sugar; (*fam*) to line one's pocket(s)

sucrerie [sykʀəʀi] *nf* (*usine*) sugar refinery; **sucreries** *nfpl* (*bonbons*) sweets, sweet things

sucrier, -ière [sykʀije, -jɛʀ] *adj* (*industrie*) sugar *cpd*; (*région*) sugar-producing ▷ *nm* (*fabricant*) sugar producer; (*récipient*) sugar bowl *ou* basin

sud [syd] *nm*: **le ~** the south ▷ *adj inv* south; (*côte*) south, southern; **au ~** (*situation*) in the south; (*direction*) to the south; **au ~ de** (to the) south of

sud-africain, e [sydafʀikɛ̃, -ɛn] *adj* South African ▷ *nm/f*: **Sud-Africain, e** South African

sud-américain, e [sydamerikɛ̃, -ɛn] *adj* South American ▷ *nm/f*: **Sud-Américain, e** South American

sud-est [sydɛst] *nm, adj inv* south-east

sud-ouest [sydwɛst] *nm, adj inv* south-west

Suède [sɥɛd] *nf*: **la ~** Sweden

suédois, e [sɥedwa, -waz] *adj* Swedish ▷ *nm* (*Ling*) Swedish ▷ *nm/f*: **S~, e** Swede

suer [sɥe] *vi* to sweat; (*suinter*) to ooze ▷ *vt* (*fig*) to exude; **~ à grosses gouttes** to sweat profusely

sueur [sɥœʀ] *nf* sweat; **en ~** sweating, in a sweat; **avoir des ~s froides** to be in a cold sweat

suffire [syfiʀ] *vi* (*être assez*): **~ (à qn/pour qch/ pour faire)** to be enough *ou* sufficient (for sb/for sth/to do); (*satisfaire*): **cela lui suffit** he's content with this, this is enough for him; **se suffire** *vi* to be self-sufficient; **cela suffit pour les irriter/qu'ils se fâchent** it's enough to annoy them/for them to get angry; **il suffit d'une négligence/qu'on oublie pour que ...** it only takes one act of carelessness/one only needs to forget for ...; **ça suffit!** that's enough!, that'll do!

suffisamment [syfizamɑ̃] *adv* sufficiently, enough; **~ de** sufficient, enough

suffisant, e [syfizɑ̃, -ɑ̃t] *adj* (*temps, ressources*) sufficient; (*résultats*) satisfactory; (*vaniteux*) self-important, bumptious

suffixe [syfiks(ə)] *nm* suffix

suffoquer [syfɔke] *vt* to choke, suffocate; (*stupéfier*) to stagger, astound ▷ *vi* to choke, suffocate; **~ de colère/d'indignation** to choke with anger/indignation

suffrage [syfʀaʒ] *nm* (*Pol: voix*) vote; (: *méthode*): **~ universel/direct/indirect** universal/direct/ indirect suffrage; (*du public etc*) approval *no pl*; **~s exprimés** valid votes

suggérer [sygʒeʀe] *vt* to suggest; **~ que/de faire** to suggest that/doing

suggestion [sygʒɛstjɔ̃] *nf* suggestion

suicide [sɥisid] *nm* suicide ▷ *adj*: **opération ~** suicide mission

suicider [sɥiside]: **se suicider** *vi* to commit suicide

suie [sɥi] *nf* soot

suinter [sɥɛ̃te] *vi* to ooze

suis [sɥi] *vb voir* **être; suivre**

suisse [sɥis] *adj* Swiss ▷ *nm* (*bedeau*) ≈ verger ▷ *nm/f*: **S~** Swiss *pl inv* ▷ *nf*: **la S~** Switzerland; **la S~ romande/allemande** French-speaking/ German-speaking Switzerland; **~ romand** Swiss French

Suissesse [sɥisɛs] *nf* Swiss (woman *ou* girl)

suite [sɥit] *nf* (*continuation: d'énumération etc*) rest, remainder; (: *de feuilleton*) continuation; (: *second film etc sur le même thème*) sequel; (*série: de maisons, succès*): **une ~ de** a series *ou* succession of; (*Math*) series *sg*; (*conséquence*) result; (*ordre, liaison logique*) coherence; (*appartement, Mus*) suite; (*escorte*) retinue, suite; **suites** *nfpl* (*d'une maladie etc*) effects; **prendre la ~ de** (*directeur etc*) to succeed, take over from; **donner ~ à** (*requête, projet*) to follow up; **faire ~ à** to follow; **(faisant) ~ à votre lettre du** further to your letter of the; **sans ~** *adj* incoherent, disjointed ▷ *adv* incoherently, disjointedly; **de ~** *adv* (*d'affilée*) in succession; (*immédiatement*) at once; **par la ~** afterwards, subsequently; **à la ~** *adv* one after the other; **à la ~ de** (*derrière*) behind; (*en conséquence de*) following; **par ~ de** owing to, as a result of; **avoir de la ~ dans les idées** to show great singleness of purpose; **attendre la ~ des événements** to (wait and see) what happens

suivant, e [sɥivɑ̃, -ɑ̃t] *vb voir* **suivre** ▷ *adj* next, following; (*ci-après*): **l'exercice ~** the following exercise ▷ *prép* (*selon*) according to; **~ que** according to whether; **au ~!** next!

suivi, e [sɥivi] *pp de* **suivre** ▷ *adj* (*régulier*) regular; (*Comm: article*) in general production; (*cohérent*) consistent; coherent ▷ *nm* follow-up; **très/peu ~** (*cours*) well-/poorly-attended; (*mode*) widely/ not widely adopted; (*feuilleton etc*) widely/not widely followed

suivre [sɥivʀ(ə)] *vt* (*gén*) to follow; (*Scol: cours*) to attend; (: *leçon*) to follow, attend to; (: *programme*) to keep up with; (*Comm: article*) to continue to stock ▷ *vi* to follow; (*élève: écouter*) to attend, pay attention; (: *assimiler le programme*) to keep up, follow; **se suivre** (*accidents, personnes, voitures etc*) to follow one after the other; (*raisonnement*) to be coherent; **~ des yeux** to follow with one's eyes; **faire ~** (*lettre*) to forward; **~ son cours** (*enquête etc*) to run *ou* take its course; **"à ~"** "to be continued"

sujet, te [syʒɛ, -ɛt] *adj*: **être ~ à** (*accidents*) to be prone to; (*vertige etc*) to be liable *ou* subject to ▷ *nm/f* (*d'un souverain*) subject ▷ *nm* subject; **un ~ de dispute/discorde/mécontentement** a cause for argument/dissension/dissatisfaction; **c'est à quel ~?** what is it about?; **avoir ~ de se plaindre** to have cause for complaint; **au ~ de** *prép* about; **~ à caution** *adj* questionable; **~ de conversation** topic *ou* subject of conversation; **~ d'examen** (*Scol*) examination question; examination paper; **~ d'expérience** (*Bio etc*) experimental subject

summum [sɔmɔm] *nm*: **le ~ de** the height of

super [sypɛʀ] *adj inv* great, fantastic ▷ *nm*
(= *supercarburant*) ≈ 4-star (Brit), ≈ premium (US)

superbe [sypɛʀb(ə)] *adj* magnificent, superb ▷ *nf*
arrogance

supercherie [sypɛʀʃəʀi] *nf* trick, trickery *no pl*;
(*fraude*) fraud

supérette [sypeʀɛt] *nf* minimarket

superficie [sypɛʀfisi] *nf* (surface) area; (*fig*)
surface

superficiel, le [sypɛʀfisjɛl] *adj* superficial

superflu, e [sypɛʀfly] *adj* superfluous ▷ *nm:* **le ~**
the superfluous

supérieur, e [sypeʀjœʀ] *adj* (*lèvre, étages, classes*)
upper; (*plus élevé: température, niveau*): **~ (à)** higher
(than); (*meilleur: qualité, produit*): **~ (à)** superior
(to); (*excellent, hautain*) superior ▷ *nm/f* superior;
Mère ~e Mother Superior; **à l'étage ~** on the
next floor up; **~ en nombre** superior in number

supériorité [sypeʀjɔʀite] *nf* superiority

superlatif [sypɛʀlatif] *nm* superlative

supermarché [sypɛʀmaʀʃe] *nm* supermarket

superposer [sypɛʀpoze] *vt* to superpose;
(*meubles, caisses*) to stack; (*faire chevaucher*) to
superimpose; **se superposer** (*images, souvenirs*) to
be superimposed; **lits superposés** bunk beds

superproduction [sypɛʀpʀɔdyksjɔ̃] *nf* (*film*)
spectacular

superpuissance [sypɛʀpɥisɑ̃s] *nf* superpower

superstitieux, -euse [sypɛʀstisjø, -øz] *adj*
superstitious

superviser [sypɛʀvize] *vt* to supervise

supplanter [syplɑ̃te] *vt* to supplant

suppléance [sypleɑ̃s] *nf* (*poste*) supply post (Brit),
substitute teacher's post (US)

suppléant, e [sypleɑ̃, -ɑ̃t] *adj* (*juge, fonctionnaire*)
deputy *cpd*; (*professeur*) supply *cpd* (Brit),
substitute *cpd* (US) ▷ *nm/f* deputy; supply *ou*
substitute teacher; **médecin ~** locum

suppléer [syplee] *vt* (*ajouter: mot manquant etc*)
to supply, provide; (*compenser: lacune*) to fill in;
(*: défaut*) to make up for; (*remplacer: professeur*)
to stand in for; (*: juge*) to deputize for; **~ à** *vt* to
make up for; to substitute for

supplément [syplemɑ̃] *nm* supplement; **un ~
de travail** extra *ou* additional work; **un ~ de
frites** *etc* an extra portion of chips *etc*; **un ~ de
10 euros** a supplement of 10 euros, an extra *ou*
additional 10 euros; **ceci est en ~** (*au menu etc*)
this is extra, there is an extra charge for this; **~
d'information** additional information

supplémentaire [syplemɑ̃tɛʀ] *adj* additional,
further; (*train, bus*) relief *cpd*, extra

supplication [syplikasjɔ̃] *nf* (*Rel*) supplication;
supplications *nfpl* (*adjurations*) pleas, entreaties

supplice [syplis] *nm* (*peine corporelle*) torture *no pl*;
form of torture; (*douleur physique, morale*) torture,
agony; **être au ~** to be in agony

supplier [syplije] *vt* to implore, beseech

support [sypɔʀ] *nm* support; (*pour livre, outils*)
stand; **~ audio-visuel** audio-visual aid; **~
publicitaire** advertising medium

supportable [sypɔʀtabl(ə)] *adj* (*douleur,*

température) bearable; (*procédé, conduite*) tolerable

supporter *nm* [sypɔʀtɛʀ] supporter, fan ▷ *vt*
[sypɔʀte] (*poids, poussée, Sport: concurrent, équipe*) to
support; (*conséquences, épreuve*) to bear, endure;
(*défauts, personne*) to tolerate, put up with; (*chose:
chaleur etc*) to withstand; (*personne: chaleur, vin*)
to take

supposer [sypoze] *vt* to suppose; (*impliquer*) to
presuppose; **en supposant** *ou* **à ~ que** supposing
(that)

suppositoire [sypozitwaʀ] *nm* suppository

suppression [sypʀesjɔ̃] *nf* (*voir supprimer*)
removal; deletion; cancellation; suppression

supprimer [sypʀime] *vt* (*cloison, cause, anxiété*)
to remove; (*clause, mot*) to delete; (*congés, service
d'autobus etc*) to cancel; (*publication, article*) to
suppress; (*emplois, privilèges, témoin gênant*) to do
away with; **~ qch à qn** to deprive sb of sth

suprême [sypʀɛm] *adj* supreme

sur¹ [syʀ] *prép* **1** (*position*) on; (*pardessus*) over; (*au-
dessus*) above; **pose-le ~ la table** put it on the
table; **je n'ai pas d'argent ~ moi** I haven't any
money on me

2 (*direction*) towards; **en allant ~ Paris** going
towards Paris; **~ votre droite** on *ou* to your right

3 (*à propos de*) on, about; **un livre/une
conférence ~ Balzac** a book/lecture on *ou* about
Balzac

4 (*proportion, mesures*) out of; by; **un ~ 10** one in 10;
(*Scol*) one out of 10; **~ 20, deux sont venus** out of
20, two came; **4 m ~ 2** 4 m by 2; **avoir accident ~
accident** to have one accident after another

5 (*cause*): **~ sa recommandation** on *ou* at his
recommendation; **~ son invitation** at his
invitation

6: **~ ce** *adv* whereupon; **~ ce, il faut que je vous
quitte** and now I must leave you

sur², e [syʀ] *adj* sour

sûr, e [syʀ] *adj* sure, certain; (*digne de confiance*)
reliable; (*sans danger*) safe; **peu ~** unreliable; **~ de
qch** sure *ou* certain of sth; **être ~ de qn** to be sure
of sb; **~ et certain** absolutely certain; **~ de soi**
self-assured, self-confident; **le plus ~ est de** the
safest thing is to

surcharge [syʀʃaʀʒ(ə)] *nf* (*de passagers,
marchandises*) excess load; (*de détails, d'ornements*)
overabundance, excess; (*correction*) alteration;
(*Postes*) surcharge; **prendre des passagers en
~** to take on excess *ou* extra passengers; **~ de
bagages** excess luggage; **~ de travail** extra work

surcharger [syʀʃaʀʒe] *vt* to overload; (*timbre-
poste*) to surcharge; (*décoration*) to overdo

surchoix [syʀʃwa] *adj inv* top-quality

surclasser [syʀklase] *vt* to outclass

surcroît [syʀkʀwa] *nm:* **~ de qch** additional sth;
par *ou* **de ~** moreover; **en ~** in addition

surdité [syʀdite] *nf* deafness; **atteint de ~
totale** profoundly deaf

surélever [syʀelve] *vt* to raise, heighten

sûrement [syʀmɑ̃] *adv* reliably; safely, securely;
(*certainement*) certainly; **~ pas** certainly not

surenchère [syʀɑ̃ʃɛʀ] *nf* (*aux enchères*) higher

bid; (sur prix fixe) overbid; (fig) overstatement; outbidding tactics pl; **~ de violence** build-up of violence; **~ électorale** political (ou electoral) one-upmanship

surenchérir [syRɑ̃ʃeRiR] vi to bid higher; to raise one's bid; (fig) to try and outbid each other

surent [syR] vb voir **savoir**

surestimer [syRɛstime] vt (tableau) to overvalue; (possibilité, personne) to overestimate

sûreté [syRte] nf (voir sûr) reliability; safety; (Jur) guaranty; surety; **mettre en ~** to put in a safe place; **pour plus de ~** as an extra precaution; to be on the safe side; **la ~ de l'État** State security; **la S~ (nationale)** division of the Ministère de l'Intérieur heading all police forces except the gendarmerie and the Paris préfecture de police

surf [sœRf] nm surfing; **faire du ~** to go surfing

surface [syRfas] nf surface; (superficie) surface area; **faire ~** to surface; **en ~** adv near the surface; (fig) superficially; **la pièce fait 100 m² de ~** the room has a surface area of 100m²; **~ de réparation** (Sport) penalty area; **~ porteuse** ou **de sustentation** (Aviat) aerofoil

surfait, e [syRfɛ, -ɛt] adj overrated

surfer [sœRfe] vi to surf; **~ sur Internet** to surf the Internet

surgelé, e [syRʒəle] adj (deep-)frozen

surgir [syRʒiR] vi (personne, véhicule) to appear suddenly; (jaillir) to shoot up; (montagne etc) to rise up, loom up; (fig: problème, conflit) to arise

surhumain, e [syRymɛ̃, -ɛn] adj superhuman

sur-le-champ [syRləʃɑ̃] adv immediately

surlendemain [syRlɑ̃dmɛ̃] nm: **le ~ (soir)** two days later (in the evening); **le ~ de** two days after

surmenage [syRmənaʒ] nm overwork; **le ~ intellectuel** mental fatigue

surmener [syRməne] vt: **se surmener** vi to overwork

surmonter [syRmɔ̃te] vt (coupole etc) to surmount, top; (vaincre) to overcome, surmount

surnaturel, le [syRnatyRɛl] adj, nm supernatural

surnom [syRnɔ̃] nm nickname

surnombre [syRnɔ̃bR(ə)] nm: **être en ~** to be too many (ou one too many)

surpeuplé, e [syRpœple] adj overpopulated

surplace [syRplas] nm: **faire du ~** to mark time

surplomber [syRplɔ̃be] vi to be overhanging ▷ vt to overhang; (dominer) to tower above

surplus [syRply] nm (Comm) surplus; (reste): **~ de bois** wood left over; **au ~** moreover; **~ américains** American army surplus sg

surprenant, e [syRpRənɑ̃, -ɑ̃t] vb voir **surprendre** ▷ adj amazing

surprendre [syRpRɑ̃dR(ə)] vt (étonner, prendre à l'improviste) to amaze, surprise; (secret) to discover; (tomber sur: intrus etc) to catch; (fig) to detect; to chance ou happen upon; (clin d'œil) to intercept; (conversation) to overhear; (orage, nuit etc) to catch out, take by surprise; **la vigilance/ bonne foi de qn** to catch sb out/betray sb's good faith; **se ~ à faire** to catch ou find o.s. doing

surpris, e [syRpRi, -iz] pp de **surprendre** ▷ adj: **~**

(de/que) amazed ou surprised (at/that)

surprise [syRpRiz] nf surprise; **faire une ~ à qn** to give sb a surprise; **voyage sans ~s** uneventful journey; **par ~** adv by surprise

surprise-partie [syRpRizpaRti] nf party

sursaut [syRso] nm start, jump; **~ de** (énergie, indignation) sudden fit ou burst of; **en ~** adv with a start

sursauter [syRsote] vi (give a) start, jump

sursis [syRsi] nm (Jur: gén) suspended sentence; (à l'exécution capitale, aussi fig) reprieve; (Mil): **~ (d'appel** ou **d'incorporation)** deferment; **condamné à cinq mois (de prison) avec ~** given a five-month suspended (prison) sentence

surtaxe [syRtaks(ə)] nf surcharge

surtout [syRtu] adv (avant tout, d'abord) above all; (spécialement, particulièrement) especially; **il aime le sport, ~ le football** he likes sport, especially football; **cet été, il a ~ fait de la pêche** this summer he went fishing more than anything (else); **~ pas d'histoires!** no fuss now!; **~, ne dites rien!** whatever you do – don't say anything!; **~ pas!** certainly ou definitely not!; **~ que** ... especially as ...

surveillance [syRvejɑ̃s] nf watch; (Police, Mil) surveillance; **sous ~ médicale** under medical supervision; **la ~ du territoire** internal security; voir aussi **DST**

surveillant, e [syRvejɑ̃, -ɑ̃t] nm/f (de prison) warder; (Scol) monitor; (de travaux) supervisor, overseer

surveiller [syRveje] vt (enfant, élèves, bagages) to watch, keep an eye on; (malade) to watch over; (prisonnier, suspect) to keep (a) watch on; (territoire, bâtiment) to (keep) watch over; (travaux, cuisson) to supervise; (Scol: examen) to invigilate; **se surveiller** to keep a check ou watch on o.s.; **son langage/sa ligne** to watch one's language/ figure

survenir [syRvəniR] vi (incident, retards) to occur, arise; (événement) to take place; (personne) to appear, arrive

survêt [syRvɛt], **survêtement** [syRvɛtmɑ̃] nm tracksuit (Brit), sweat suit (US)

survie [syRvi] nf survival; (Rel) afterlife; **équipement de ~** survival equipment; **une ~ de quelques mois** a few more months of life

survivant, e [syRvivɑ̃, -ɑ̃t] vb voir **survivre** ▷ nm/f survivor

survivre [syRvivR(ə)] vi to survive; **~ à** vt (accident etc) to survive; (personne) to outlive; **la victime a peu de chance de ~** the victim has little hope of survival

survoler [syRvɔle] vt to fly over; (fig: livre) to skim through; (: question, problèmes) to skim over

survolté, e [syRvɔlte] adj (Élec) stepped up, boosted; (fig) worked up

sus [sy(s)]: **en ~ de** prép in addition to, over and above; **en ~** in addition; **~ à** excl: **~ au tyran!** at the tyrant! vb [sy] voir **savoir**

susceptible [sysɛptibl(ə)] adj touchy, sensitive; **~ d'amélioration** ou **d'être amélioré** that can be improved, open to improvement; ~ **de faire** (*capacité*) able to do; (*probabilité*) liable to do

susciter [sysite] *vt* (*admiration*) to arouse; (*obstacles, ennuis*): ~ **(à qn)** to create (for sb)

suspect, e [syspɛ(kt), -ɛkt(ə)] *adj* suspicious; (*témoignage, opinions, vin etc*) suspect ▷ *nm/f* suspect; **peu ~ de** most unlikely to be suspected of

suspecter [syspɛkte] *vt* to suspect; (*honnêteté de qn*) to question, have one's suspicions about; ~ **qn d'être/d'avoir fait qch** to suspect sb of being/having done sth

suspendre [syspɑ̃dʀ(ə)] *vt* (*accrocher: vêtement*): ~ **qch (à)** to hang sth up (on); (*fixer: lustre etc*): ~ **qch à** to hang sth from; (*interrompre, démettre*) to suspend; (*remettre*) to defer; **se ~ à** to hang from

suspendu, e [syspɑ̃dy] *pp de* **suspendre** ▷ *adj* (*accroché*): ~ **à** hanging on (*ou* from); (*perché*): ~ **au-dessus de** suspended over; (*Auto*): **bien/mal** ~ with good/poor suspension; **être ~ aux lèvres de qn** to hang upon sb's every word

suspens [syspɑ̃]: **en ~** *adv* (*affaire*) in abeyance; **tenir en ~** to keep in suspense

suspense [syspɑ̃s] *nm* suspense

suspension [syspɑ̃sjɔ̃] *nf* suspension; deferment; (*Auto*) suspension; (*lustre*) pendant light fitting; **en ~** in suspension, suspended; ~ **d'audience** adjournment

sut [sy] *vb voir* **savoir**

suture [sytyʀ] *nf*: **point de ~** stitch

svelte [svɛlt(ə)] *adj* slender, svelte

SVP *sigle* (= *s'il vous plaît*) please

sweat [swit] *nm* (*fam*) sweatshirt

sweat-shirt [switʃœrt] (*pl* -**s**) *nm* sweatshirt

syllabe [silab] *nf* syllable

symbole [sɛ̃bɔl] *nm* symbol

symbolique [sɛ̃bɔlik] *adj* symbolic; (*geste, offrande*) token *cpd*; (*salaire, dommages-intérêts*) nominal

symboliser [sɛ̃bɔlize] *vt* to symbolize

symétrique [simetʀik] *adj* symmetrical

sympa [sɛ̃pa] *adj inv* (= *sympathique*) nice; friendly; good

sympathie [sɛ̃pati] *nf* (*inclination*) liking; (*affinité*) fellow feeling; (*condoléances*) sympathy; **accueillir avec ~** (*projet*) to receive favourably;

avoir de la ~ pour qn to like sb, have a liking for sb; **témoignages de ~** expressions of sympathy; **croyez à toute ma ~** you have my deepest sympathy

sympathique [sɛ̃patik] *adj* (*personne, figure*) nice, friendly, likeable; (*geste*) friendly; (*livre*) good; (*déjeuner*) nice; (*réunion, endroit*) pleasant, nice

sympathisant, e [sɛ̃patizɑ̃, -ɑ̃t] *nm/f* sympathizer

sympathiser [sɛ̃patize] *vi* (*voisins etc: s'entendre*) to get on (*Brit*) *ou* along (*US*) (well); (: *se fréquenter*) to socialize, see each other; ~ **avec** to get on *ou* along (well) with, to see, socialize with

symphonie [sɛ̃fɔni] *nf* symphony

symptôme [sɛ̃ptom] *nm* symptom

synagogue [sinagɔg] *nf* synagogue

syncope [sɛ̃kɔp] *nf* (*Méd*) blackout; (*Mus*) syncopation; **tomber en ~** to faint, pass out

syndic [sɛ̃dik] *nm* managing agent

syndical, e, -aux [sɛ̃dikal, -o] *adj* (trade-)union *cpd*; **centrale ~e** group of affiliated trade unions

syndicaliste [sɛ̃dikalist(ə)] *nm/f* trade unionist

syndicat [sɛ̃dika] *nm* (*d'ouvriers, employés*) (trade(s)) union; (*autre association d'intérêts*) union, association; ~ **d'initiative (SI)** tourist office *ou* bureau; ~ **patronal** employers' syndicate, federation of employers; ~ **de propriétaires** association of property owners

syndiqué, e [sɛ̃dike] *adj* belonging to a (trade) union; **non ~** non-union

syndiquer [sɛ̃dike]: **se syndiquer** *vi* to form a trade union; (*adhérer*) to join a trade union

synonyme [sinɔnim] *adj* synonymous ▷ *nm* synonym; ~ **de** synonymous with

syntaxe [sɛ̃taks(ə)] *nf* syntax

synthèse [sɛ̃tɛz] *nf* synthesis; **faire la ~ de** to synthesize

synthétique [sɛ̃tetik] *adj* synthetic

Syrie [siʀi] *nf*: **la ~** Syria

systématique [sistematik] *adj* systematic

système [sistɛm] *nm* system; **le ~ D** resourcefulness; ~ **décimal** decimal system; ~ **expert** expert system; ~ **d'exploitation** (*Inform*) operating system; ~ **immunitaire** immune system; ~ **métrique** metric system; ~ **solaire** solar system

Tt

t' [t(ə)] *pron voir* **te**

ta [ta] *adj poss voir* **ton**

tabac [taba] *nm* tobacco; (*aussi*: **débit** *ou* **bureau de tabac**) tobacconist's (shop) ▷ *adj inv*: **(couleur)** ~ buff, tobacco *cpd*; **passer qn à** ~ to beat sb up; **faire un** ~ (*fam*) to be a big hit; ~ **blond/brun** light/dark tobacco; ~ **gris** shag; ~ **à priser** snuff

tabagisme [tabaʒism(ə)] *nm* nicotine addiction; ~ **passif** passive smoking

tabasser [tabase] *vt* to beat up

table [tabl(ə)] *nf* table; **avoir une bonne** ~ to keep a good table; **à** ~! dinner *etc* is ready!; **se mettre à** ~ to sit down to eat; (*fig: fam*) to come clean; **mettre** *ou* **dresser/desservir la** ~ to lay *ou* set/clear the table; **faire** ~ **rase de** to make a clean sweep of; ~ **basse** coffee table; ~ **de cuisson** (*à l'électricité*) hotplate; (*au gas*) gas ring; ~ **d'écoute** wire-tapping set; ~ **d'harmonie** sounding board; ~ **d'hôte** set menu; ~ **de lecture** turntable; ~ **des matières** (table of) contents *pl*; ~ **de multiplication** multiplication table; ~ **des négociations** negotiating table; ~ **de nuit** *ou* **de chevet** bedside table; ~ **ronde** (*débat*) round table; ~ **roulante** (tea) trolley; ~ **de toilette** washstand; ~ **traçante** (*Inform*) plotter

tableau, x [tablo] *nm* (*Art*) painting; (*reproduction, fig*) picture; (*panneau*) board; (*schéma*) table, chart; ~ **d'affichage** notice board; ~ **de bord** dashboard; (*Aviat*) instrument panel; ~ **de chasse** tally; ~ **de contrôle** console, control panel; ~ **de maître** masterpiece; ~ **noir** blackboard

tabler [table] *vi*: ~ **sur** to count *ou* bank on

tablette [tablɛt] *nf* (*planche*) shelf; ~ **de chocolat** bar of chocolate

tableur [tablœʀ] *nm* (*Inform*) spreadsheet

tablier [tablije] *nm* apron; (*de pont*) roadway; (*de cheminée*) (flue-)shutter

tabou, e [tabu] *adj, nm* taboo

tabouret [tabuʀɛ] *nm* stool

tac [tak] *nm*: **du** ~ **au** ~ tit for tat

tache [taʃ] *nf* (*saleté*) stain, mark; (*Art: de couleur, lumière*) spot; splash, patch; **faire** ~ **d'huile** to spread, gain ground; ~ **de rousseur** *ou* **de son** freckle; ~ **de vin** (*sur la peau*) strawberry mark

tâche [taʃ] *nf* task; **travailler à la** ~ to do piecework

tacher [taʃe] *vt* to stain, mark; (*fig*) to sully, stain; **se tacher** *vi* (*fruits*) to become marked

tâcher [taʃe] *vi*: ~ **de faire** to try to do, endeavour (*Brit*) *ou* endeavor (*US*) to do

tacheté, e [taʃte] *adj*: ~ **de** speckled *ou* spotted with

tacot [tako] *nm* (*péj: voiture*) banger (*Brit*), clunker (*US*)

tact [takt] *nm* tact; **avoir du** ~ to be tactful, have tact

tactique [taktik] *adj* tactical ▷ *nf* (*technique*) tactics *nsg*; (*plan*) tactic

taie [tɛ] *nf*: ~ **(d'oreiller)** pillowslip, pillowcase

taille [taj] *nf* cutting; pruning; (*milieu du corps*) waist; (*hauteur*) height; (*grandeur*) size; **de** ~ **à faire** capable of doing; **de** ~ *adj* sizeable; **quelle** ~ **faites-vous?** what size are you?

taille-crayon, taille-crayons [tajkʀɛjɔ̃] *nm inv* pencil sharpener

tailler [taje] *vt* (*pierre, diamant*) to cut; (*arbre, plante*) to prune; (*vêtement*) to cut out; (*crayon*) to sharpen; **se tailler** *vt* (*ongles, barbe*) to trim, cut; (*fig: réputation*) to gain, win ▷ *vi* (*fam: s'enfuir*) to beat it; ~ **dans** (*chair, bois*) to cut into; ~ **grand/petit** to be on the large/small side

tailleur [tajœʀ] *nm* (*couturier*) tailor; (*vêtement*) suit, costume; **en** ~ (*assis*) cross-legged; ~ **de diamants** diamond-cutter

taillis [taji] *nm* copse

taire [tɛʀ] *vt* to keep to o.s., conceal ▷ *vi*: **faire** ~ **qn** to make sb be quiet; (*fig*) to silence sb; **se taire** *vi* (*s'arrêter de parler*) to fall silent, stop talking; (*ne pas parler*) to be silent *ou* quiet; (*s'abstenir de s'exprimer*) to keep quiet; (*bruit, voix*) to disappear; **tais-toi!, taisez-vous!** be quiet!

talc [talk] *nm* talc, talcum powder

talent [talɑ̃] *nm* talent; **avoir du** ~ to be talented, have talent

talkie-walkie [tɔkiwɔki] *nm* walkie-talkie

taloche [talɔʃ] *nf* (*fam: claque*) slap; (*Tech*) plaster float

talon [talɔ̃] *nm* heel; (*de chèque, billet*) stub, counterfoil (*Brit*); ~**s plats/aiguilles** flat/stiletto heels; **être sur les** ~**s de qn** to be on sb's heels; **tourner les** ~**s** to turn on one's heel; **montrer les** ~**s** (*fig*) to show a clean pair of heels

talonner [talɔne] vt to follow hard behind; (fig) to hound; (Rugby) to heel

talus [taly] nm embankment; **~ de remblai/ déblai** embankment/excavation slope

tambour [tãbuʀ] nm (Mus, also Tech) drum; (musicien) drummer; (porte) revolving door(s pl); **sans ~ ni trompette** unobtrusively

tambourin [tãbuʀɛ̃] nm tambourine

tambouriner [tãbuʀine] vi: **~ contre** to drum against ou on

tamis [tami] nm sieve

Tamise [tamiz] nf: **la ~** the Thames

tamisé, e [tamize] adj (fig) subdued, soft

tampon [tãpɔ̃] nm (de coton, d'ouate) pad; (aussi: **tampon hygiénique** ou **périodique**) tampon; (amortisseur, Inform: aussi: **mémoire tampon**) buffer; (bouchon) plug, stopper; (cachet, timbre) stamp; (Chimie) buffer; **~ buvard** blotter; **~ encreur** inking pad; **~ (à récurer)** scouring pad

tamponner [tãpɔne] vt (timbres) to stamp; (heurter) to crash ou ram into; (essuyer) to mop up; **se tamponner** (voitures) to crash (into each other)

tamponneuse [tãpɔnøz] adj f: **autos ~s** dodgems, bumper cars

tandem [tãdɛm] nm tandem; (fig) duo, pair

tandis [tãdi]: **~ que** conj while

tanguer [tãge] vi to pitch (and toss)

tanière [tanjɛʀ] nf lair, den

tanné, e [tane] adj weather-beaten

tanner [tane] vt to tan

tant [tã] adv so much; **~ de** (sable, eau) so much; (gens, livres) so many; **~ que** conj as long as; **~ que** (comparatif) as much as; **~ mieux** that's great; so much the better; **~ mieux pour lui** good for him; **~ pis** too bad; **un ~ soit peu** a little bit; (même un peu) (even) remotely; **~ bien que mal** as well as can be expected; **s'en faut** far from it, not by a long way

tante [tãt] nf aunt

tantôt [tãto] adv (parfois): **~ ... ~** now ... now; (cet après-midi) this afternoon

taon [tã] nm horsefly, gadfly

tapage [tapaʒ] nm uproar, din; (fig) fuss, row; **~ nocturne** (Jur) disturbance of the peace (at night)

tapageur, -euse [tapaʒœʀ, -øz] adj (bruyant: enfants etc) noisy; (toilette) loud, flashy; (publicité) obtrusive

tape [tap] nf slap

tape-à-l'œil [tapalœj] adj inv flashy, showy

taper [tape] vt (personne) to clout; (porte) to bang, slam; (dactylographier) to type (out); (Inform) to key(board); (fam: emprunter): **~ qn de 10 euros** to touch sb for 10 euros, cadge 10 euros off sb ▷ vi (soleil) to beat down; **se taper** vt (fam: travail) to get landed with; (: boire, manger) to down; **~ sur qn** to thump sb; (fig) to run sb down; **~ sur qch** (clou etc) to hit sth; (table etc) to bang on sth; **~ à** (porte etc) to knock on; **~ dans** (se servir) to dig into; **~ des mains/pieds** to clap one's hands/stamp one's feet; **~ (à la machine)** to type

tapi, e [tapi] adj: **~ dans/derrière** (blotti) crouching ou cowering in/behind; (caché) hidden away in/behind

tapis [tapi] nm carpet; (de table) cloth; **mettre sur le ~** (fig) to bring up for discussion; **aller au ~** (Boxe) to go down; **envoyer au ~** (Boxe) to floor; **~ roulant** conveyor belt; **~ de sol** (de tente) groundsheet; **~ de souris** (Inform) mouse mat

tapisser [tapise] vt (avec du papier peint) to paper; (recouvrir): **~ qch (de)** to cover sth (with)

tapisserie [tapisʀi] nf (tenture, broderie) tapestry; (: travail) tapestry-making; (: ouvrage) tapestry work; (papier peint) wallpaper; (fig): **faire ~** to sit out, be a wallflower

tapissier, -ière [tapisje, -jɛʀ] nm/f: **~-décorateur** upholsterer and decorator

tapoter [tapɔte] vt to pat, tap

taquin, e [takɛ̃, -in] adj teasing

taquiner [takine] vt to tease

tarabiscoté, e [taʀabiskɔte] adj over-ornate, fussy

tard [taʀ] adv late; **au plus ~** at the latest; **plus ~ later (on)** ▷ nm: **sur le ~** (à une heure avancée) late in the day; (vers la fin de la vie) late in life

tarder [taʀde] vi (chose) to be a long time coming; (personne): **~ à faire** to delay doing; **il me tarde d'être** I am longing to be; **sans (plus) ~** without (further) delay

tardif, -ive [taʀdif, -iv] adj (heure, repas, fruit) late; (talent, goût) late in developing

taré, e [taʀe] nm/f cretin

tarif [taʀif] nm (liste) price list, tariff (Brit); (barème) rate, rates pl, tariff (Brit); (: de taxis etc) fares pl; **voyager à plein ~/à ~ réduit** to travel at full/reduced fare

tarir [taʀiʀ] vi to dry up, run dry ▷ vt to dry up

tarte [taʀt(ə)] nf tart; **~ aux pommes/à la crème** apple/custard tart

tartine [taʀtin] nf slice of bread (and butter (ou jam)); **~ de miel** slice of bread and honey; **~ beurrée** slice of bread and butter

tartiner [taʀtine] vt to spread; **fromage à ~** cheese spread

tartre [taʀtʀ(ə)] nm (des dents) tartar; (de chaudière) fur, scale

tas [ta] nm heap, pile; (fig): **un ~ de** heaps of, lots of; **en ~** in a heap ou pile; **dans le ~** (fig) in the crowd; among them; **formé sur le ~** trained on the job

tasse [tas] nf cup; **boire la ~** (en se baignant) to swallow a mouthful; **~ à café/thé** coffee/teacup

tassé, e [tase] adj: **bien ~** (café etc) strong

tasser [tase] vt (terre, neige) to pack down; (entasser): **~ qch dans** to cram sth into; **se tasser** vi (terrain) to settle; (personne: avec l'âge) to shrink; (fig) to sort itself out, settle down

tâter [tate] vt to feel; (fig) to sound out; **~ de** (prison etc) to have a taste of; **se tâter** (hésiter) to be in two minds; **~ le terrain** (fig) to test the ground

tatillon, ne [tatijɔ̃, -ɔn] adj pernickety

tâtonnement [tatɔnmã] nm: **par ~s** (fig) by trial and error

tâtonner [tatɔne] vi to grope one's way along;

(fig) to grope around (in the dark)

tâtons [tatɔ̃]: **à ~** *adv*: **chercher/avancer à ~** to grope around for/grope one's way forward

tatouage [tatwaʒ] *nm* tattooing; *(dessin)* tattoo

tatouer [tatwe] *vt* to tattoo

taudis [todi] *nm* hovel, slum

taule [tol] *nf (fam)* nick (Brit), jail

taupe [top] *nf* mole; *(peau)* moleskin

taureau, x [tɔro] *nm* bull; *(signe)*: **le T~** Taurus, the Bull; **être du T~** to be Taurus

tauromachie [tʼmaʃi] *nf* bullfighting

taux [to] *nm* rate; *(d'alcool)* level; **~ d'escompte** discount rate; **~ d'intérêt** interest rate; **~ de mortalité** mortality rate

taxe [taks(ə)] *nf* tax; *(douanière)* duty; **toutes ~s comprises (TTC)** inclusive of tax; **~ de base** *(Tél)* unit charge; **~ de séjour** tourist tax; **~ à** *ou* **sur la valeur ajoutée (TVA)** value added tax (VAT)

taxer [takse] *vt (personne)* to tax; *(produit)* to put a tax on, tax; **~ qn de qch** *(qualifier)* to call sb sth; *(accuser)* to accuse sb of sth, tax sb with sth

taxi [taksi] *nm* taxi

Tchécoslovaquie [tʃekɔslɔvaki] *nf*: **la ~** Czechoslovakia

tchèque [tʃɛk] *adj* Czech ▷ *nm (Ling)* Czech ▷ *nm/ f*: **T~** Czech; **la République ~** the Czech Republic

Tchétchénie [tʃetʃeni] *nf*: **la ~** Chechnya

te, t' [t(ə)] *pron* you; *(réfléchi)* yourself

technicien, ne [tɛknisjɛ̃, -ɛn] *nm/f* technician

technico-commercial, e, -aux [tɛknikokɔmɛrsjal, -o] *adj*: **agent ~** sales technician

technique [tɛknik] *adj* technical ▷ *nf* technique

techniquement [tɛknikmɑ̃] *adv* technically

techno [tɛkno] *nf (fam: Mus)*: **la (musique) ~** techno (music); *(fam)* = **technologie**

technologie [tɛknɔlɔʒi] *nf* technology

technologique [tɛknɔlɔʒik] *adj* technological

teck [tɛk] *nm* teak

tee-shirt [tiʃœrt] *nm* T-shirt, tee-shirt

teindre [tɛ̃dR(ə)] *vt* to dye; **se ~ (les cheveux)** to dye one's hair

teint, e [tɛ̃, tɛ̃t] *pp de* **teindre** ▷ *adj* dyed ▷ *nm (du visage: permanent)* complexion, colouring (Brit), coloring (US); *(momentané)* colour (Brit), color (US) ▷ *nf* shade, colour, color; *(fig: petite dose)*: **une ~e de** a hint of; **grand ~** *adj inv* colourfast; **bon ~** *adj inv (couleur)* fast; *(tissu)* colourfast; *(personne)* staunch, firm

teinté, e [tɛ̃te] *adj (verres)* tinted; *(bois)* stained; **~ acajou** mahogany-stained; **~ de** *(fig)* tinged with

teinter [tɛ̃te] *vt* to tint; *(bois)* to stain; *(fig: d'ironie etc)* to tinge

teinture [tɛ̃tyR] *nf* dyeing; *(substance)* dye; *(Méd)*: **~ d'iode** tincture of iodine

teinturerie [tɛ̃tyRRi] *nf* dry cleaner's

teinturier, -ière [tɛ̃tyRje, -jɛR] *nm/f* dry cleaner

tel, telle [tɛl] *adj (pareil)* such; *(comme)*: **~ un/des ...** like a/like ...; *(indéfini)* such-and-such a, a given; *(intensif)*: **un ~/de ~s ...** such (a)/such ...; **rien de ~** nothing like it, no such thing; **~ que**

conj like, such as; **~ quel** as it is *ou* stands *(ou* was *etc)*

télé [tele] *nf (télévision)* TV, telly (Brit); **à la ~** on TV *ou* telly

télécabine [telekabin] *nm, nf* telecabine, gondola

télécarte [telekart(ə)] *nf* phonecard

téléchargeable [teleʃarʒabl] *adj* downloadable

téléchargement [teleʃarʒemɑ̃] *nm (action)* downloading; *(fichier)* download

télécommande [telekɔmɑ̃d] *nf* remote control

télécopie [telekɔpi] *nf* fax, telefax

télécopieur [telekɔpjœr] *nm* fax (machine)

télédistribution [teledistRibysjɔ̃] *nf* cable TV

téléférique [teleferik] *nm* = **téléphérique**

télégramme [telegram] *nm* telegram

télégraphier [telegrafje] *vt* to telegraph, cable

téléguider [telegide] *vt* to operate by remote control, radio-control

téléjournal, -aux [teleʒurnal, -o] *nm* television news magazine programme

télématique [telematik] *nf* telematics *nsg* ▷ *adj* telematic

téléobjectif [teleɔbʒɛktif] *nm* telephoto lens *nsg*

télépathie [telepati] *nf* telepathy

téléphérique [teleferik] *nm* cable-car

téléphone [telefɔn] *nm* telephone; **avoir le ~** to be on the (tele)phone; **au ~** on the phone; **~ arabe** bush telegraph; **~ à carte** cardphone; **~ avec appareil photo** cameraphone; **~ mobile** *ou* **portable** mobile (phone) (Brit), cell (phone) (US); **~ rouge** hotline; **~ sans fil** cordless (tele)phone

téléphoner [telefɔne] *vt* to telephone ▷ *vi* to telephone; to make a phone call; **~ à** to phone up, ring up, call up

téléphonie [telefɔni] *nf* telephony

téléphonique [telefɔnik] *adj* telephone *cpd*, phone *cpd*; **cabine ~** call box (Brit), (tele)phone box (Brit) *ou* booth; **conversation/appel ~** (tele)phone conversation/call

téléréalité [telerealite] *nf* reality TV

télescope [telɛskɔp] *nm* telescope

télescoper [telɛskɔpe] *vt* to smash up; **se télescoper** *(véhicules)* to collide, crash into each other

téléscripteur [teleskriptœr] *nm* teleprinter

télésiège [telesjɛʒ] *nm* chairlift

téléski [teleski] *nm* ski-tow; **~ à archets** T-bar tow; **~ à perche** button lift

téléspectateur, -trice [telespɛktatœr, -tris] *nm/f* (television) viewer

télévente [televɑ̃t] *nf* telesales

téléviseur [televizœr] *nm* television set

télévision [televizjɔ̃] *nf* television; **(poste de) ~** television (set); **avoir la ~** to have a television; **à la ~** on television; **~ par câble/satellite** cable/ satellite television

télex [telɛks] *nm* telex

telle [tɛl] *adj f voir* **tel**

tellement [tɛlmɑ̃] *adv (tant)* so much; *(si)* so; **~ plus grand (que)** so much bigger (than); **~ de** *(sable, eau)* so much; *(gens, livres)* so many; **il**

s'est endormi ~ il était fatigué he was so tired (that) he fell asleep; **pas ~** not really; **pas ~ fort/lentement** not (all) that strong/slowly; **il ne mange pas ~** he doesn't eat (all that) much

téméraire [temerɛʀ] adj reckless, rash

témérité [temerite] nf recklessness, rashness

témoignage [temwaɲaʒ] nm (Jur: déclaration) testimony no pl, evidence no pl; (: faits) evidence no pl; (gén: rapport, récit) account; (fig: d'affection etc) token, mark; expression

témoigner [temwaɲe] vt (manifester: intérêt, gratitude) to show ▷ vi (Jur) to testify, give evidence; **~ que** to testify that; (fig: démontrer) to reveal that, testify to the fact that; **~ de** vt (confirmer) to bear witness to, testify to

témoin [temwɛ̃] nm witness; (fig) testimony; (Sport) baton; (Constr) telltale ▷ adj control cpd, test cpd; **~ le fait que …** (as) witness the fact that …; **appartement~** show flat (Brit), model apartment (US); **être ~ de** (voir) to witness; **prendre à ~** to call to witness; **~ à charge** witness for the prosecution; **T~ de Jehovah** Jehovah's Witness; **~ de moralité** character reference; **~ oculaire** eyewitness

tempe [tɑ̃p] nf (Anat) temple

tempérament [tɑ̃peʀamɑ̃] nm temperament, disposition; (santé) constitution; **à ~** (vente) on deferred (payment) terms; (achat) by instalments, hire purchase cpd; **avoir du ~** to be hot-blooded

température [tɑ̃peʀatyʀ] nf temperature; **prendre la ~ de** to take the temperature of; (fig) to gauge the feeling of; **avoir** ou **faire de la ~** to be running ou have a temperature

tempéré, e [tɑ̃peʀe] adj temperate

tempête [tɑ̃pɛt] nf storm; **~ de sable/neige** sand/snowstorm; **vent de ~** gale

temple [tɑ̃pl(ə)] nm temple; (protestant) church

temporaire [tɑ̃pɔʀɛʀ] adj temporary

temps [tɑ̃] nm (atmosphérique) weather; (durée) time; (époque) time, times pl; (Ling) tense; (Mus) beat; (Tech) stroke; **les ~ changent/sont durs** times are changing/hard; **il fait beau/mauvais ~** the weather is fine/bad; **avoir le ~/tout le ~/juste le ~** to have time/plenty of time/just enough time; **avoir fait son ~** (fig) to have had its (ou his etc) day; **en ~ de paix/guerre** in peacetime/wartime; **en ~ utile** ou **voulu** in due time ou course; **de ~ en ~, de ~ à autre** from time to time, now and again; **en même ~** at the same time; **à ~** (partir, arriver) in time; **à plein/mi~** adv, adj full-/part-time; **à ~ partiel** adv, adj part-time; **dans le ~** at one time; **de tout ~** always; **du ~ que** at the time when, in the days when; **dans le** ou **du** ou **au ~ où** at the time when; **pendant ce ~** in the meantime; **~ d'accès** (Inform) access time; **~ d'arrêt** pause, halt; **~ mort** (Sport) stoppage (time); (Comm) slack period; **~ partagé** (Inform) time-sharing; **~ réel** (Inform) real time

tenable [tənabl(ə)] adj bearable

tenace [tənas] adj tenacious, persistent

tenailler [tənaje] vt (fig) to torment, torture

tenailles [tənaj] nfpl pincers

tenais etc [t(ə)nɛ] vb voir **tenir**

tenancier, -ière [tənɑ̃sje, -jɛʀ] nm/f (d'hôtel, de bistro) manager (manageress)

tenant, e [tənɑ̃, -ɑ̃t] adj f voir **séance** ▷ nm/f (Sport): **~ du titre** title-holder ▷ nm: **d'un seul ~** in one piece; **les ~s et les aboutissants** (fig) the ins and outs

tendance [tɑ̃dɑ̃s] nf (opinions) leanings pl, sympathies pl; (inclination) tendency; (évolution) trend; **~ à la hausse/baisse** upward/downward trend; **avoir ~ à** to have a tendency to, tend to

tendeur [tɑ̃dœʀ] nm (de vélo) chain-adjuster; (de câble) wire-strainer; (de tente) runner; (attache) elastic strap

tendre [tɑ̃dʀ(ə)] adj (viande, légumes) tender; (bois, roche, couleur) soft; (affectueux) tender, loving ▷ vt (élastique, peau) to stretch, draw tight; (muscle) to tense; (donner): **~ qch à qn** to hold sth out to sb; to offer sb sth; (fig: piège) to set, lay; (tapisserie): **tendu de soie** hung with silk, with silk hangings; **se tendre** vi (corde) to tighten; (relations) to become strained; **~ à qch/à faire** to tend towards sth/to do; **~ l'oreille** to prick up one's ears; **~ la main/le bras** to hold out one's hand/stretch out one's arm; **~ la perche à qn** (fig) to throw sb a line

tendrement [tɑ̃dʀəmɑ̃] adv tenderly, lovingly

tendresse [tɑ̃dʀɛs] nf tenderness; **tendresses** nfpl (caresses etc) tenderness no pl, caresses

tendu, e [tɑ̃dy] pp de **tendre** ▷ adj tight; tensed; strained

ténèbres [tenɛbʀ(ə)] nfpl darkness nsg

teneur [tənœʀ] nf content, substance; (d'une lettre) terms pl, content; **~ en cuivre** copper content

tenir [təniʀ] vt to hold; (magasin, hôtel) to run; (promesse) to keep ▷ vi to hold; (neige, gel) to last; (survivre) to survive; **se tenir** vi (avoir lieu) to be held, take place; (être: personne) to stand; **se ~ droit** to stand up (ou sit up) straight; **bien se ~** to behave well; **se ~ à qch** to hold on to sth; **s'en ~ à qch** to confine o.s. to sth; to stick to sth; **~ à** vt to be attached to, care about (ou for); (avoir pour cause) to be due to, stem from; **~ à faire** to want to do, be keen to do; **~ à ce que qn fasse qch** to be anxious that sb should do sth; **~ de** vt to partake of; (ressembler à) to take after; **ça ne tient qu'à lui** it is entirely up to him; **~ qn pour** to take sb for; **~ qch de qn** (histoire) to have heard ou learnt sth from sb; (qualité, défaut) to have inherited ou got sth from sb; **~ les comptes** to keep the books; **~ un rôle** to play a part; **~ de la place** to take up space ou room; **~ l'alcool** to be able to hold a drink; **~ le coup** to hold out; **~ bon** to stand ou hold fast; **~ trois jours/deux mois** (résister) to hold out ou last three days/two months; **~ au chaud/à l'abri** keep hot/under shelter ou cover; **~ prêt** to have ready; **~ sa langue** (fig) to hold one's tongue; **tiens (ou tenez), voilà le stylo** there's the pen!;

tiens, Alain! look, here's Alain!; **tiens?** (*surprise*) really?; **tiens-toi bien!** (*pour informer*) brace yourself!, take a deep breath!

tennis [tenis] *nm* tennis; (*aussi:* **court de tennis**) tennis court ▷ *nmpl ou fpl* (*aussi:* **chaussures de tennis**) tennis *ou* gym shoes; **~ de table** table tennis

tennisman [tenisman] *nm* tennis player

tension [tɑ̃sjɔ̃] *nf* tension; (*fig: des relations, de la situation*) tension; (: *concentration, effort*) strain; (*Méd*) blood pressure; **faire** *ou* **avoir de la ~** to have high blood pressure; **~ nerveuse/raciale** nervous/racial tension

tentation [tɑ̃tasjɔ̃] *nf* temptation

tentative [tɑ̃tativ] *nf* attempt, bid; **~ d'évasion** escape bid; **~ de suicide** suicide attempt

tente [tɑ̃t] *nf* tent; **~ à oxygène** oxygen tent

tenter [tɑ̃te] *vt* (*éprouver, attirer*) to tempt; (*essayer*): **~ qch/de faire** to attempt *ou* try sth/to do; **être tenté de** to be tempted to; **~ sa chance** to try one's luck

tenture [tɑ̃tyʀ] *nf* hanging

tenu, e [təny] *pp de* **tenir** ▷ *adj* (*maison, comptes*): **bien ~** well-kept; (*obligé*): **~ de faire** under an obligation to do ▷ *nf* (*action de tenir*) running; keeping; holding; (*vêtements*) clothes *pl*, gear; (*allure*) dress *no pl*, appearance; (*comportement*) manners *pl*, behaviour (*Brit*), behavior (*US*); **être en ~e** to be dressed (up); **se mettre en ~e** to dress (up); **en grande ~e** in full dress; **en petite ~e** scantily dressed *ou* clad; **avoir de la ~e** to have good manners; (*journal*) to have a high standard; **~e de combat** combat gear *ou* dress; **~e de pompier** fireman's uniform; **~e de route** (*Auto*) road-holding; **~e de soirée** evening dress; **~e de sport/voyage** sports/travelling clothes *pl ou* gear *no pl*

TER *abr m* (= *Train Régional Express*) *local train*

ter [tɛʀ] *adj*: **16 ~ 16b** *ou* B

térébenthine [teʀebɑ̃tin] *nf*: (**essence de**) **~** (oil of) turpentine

tergal® [tɛʀɡal] *nm* Terylene®

terme [tɛʀm(ə)] *nm* term; (*fin*) end; **être en bons/mauvais ~s avec qn** to be on good/bad terms with sb; **vente/achat à ~** (*Comm*) forward sale/purchase; **au ~ de** at the end of; **en d'autres ~s** in other words; **moyen ~** (*solution intermédiaire*) middle course; **à court/long ~** *adj* short-/long-term *ou* -range ▷ *adv* in the short/long term; **à ~** *adj* (*Méd*) full-term ▷ *adv* sooner or later, eventually; (*Méd*) at term; **avant ~** (*Méd*) ▷ *adj* premature ▷ *adv* prematurely; **mettre un ~ à** to put an end *ou* a stop to; **toucher à son ~** to be nearing its end

terminaison [tɛʀminɛzɔ̃] *nf* (*Ling*) ending

terminal, e, -aux [tɛʀminal, -o] *adj* (*partie, phase*) final; (*Méd*) terminal ▷ *nm* terminal ▷ *nf* (*Scol*) ≈ sixth form *ou* year (*Brit*), ≈ twelfth grade (*US*)

terminer [tɛʀmine] *vt* to end; (*travail, repas*) to finish; **se terminer** *vi* to end; **se ~ par** to end with

terne [tɛʀn(ə)] *adj* dull

ternir [tɛʀniʀ] *vt* to dull; (*fig*) to sully, tarnish; **se ternir** *vi* to become dull

terrain [tɛʀɛ̃] *nm* (*sol, fig*) ground; (*Comm*) land *no pl*, plot (of land); (: *à bâtir*) site; **sur le ~** (*fig*) on the field; **~ de football/rugby** football/rugby pitch (*Brit*) *ou* field (*US*); **~ d'atterrissage** landing strip; **~ d'aviation** airfield; **~ de camping** campsite; **un ~ d'entente** an area of agreement; **~ de golf** golf course; **~ de jeu** playground; (*Sport*) games field; **~ de sport** sports ground; **~ vague** waste ground *no pl*

terrasse [tɛʀas] *nf* terrace; (*de café*) pavement area, terrasse; **à la ~** (*café*) outside

terrasser [tɛʀase] *vt* (*adversaire*) to floor, bring down; (*maladie etc*) to lay low

terre [tɛʀ] *nf* (*gén, aussi Élec*) earth; (*substance*) soil, earth; (*opposé à mer*) land *no pl*; (*contrée*) land; **terres** *nfpl* (*terrains*) lands, land *nsg*; **travail de la ~** work on the land; **en ~** (*pipe, poterie*) clay *cpd*; **mettre en ~** (*plante etc*) to plant; (*personne: enterrer*) to bury; **à** *ou* **par ~** (*mettre, être*) on the ground (*ou* floor); (*jeter, tomber*) to the ground, down; **~ à ~** *adj inv* down-to-earth, matter-of-fact; **la T~ Adélie** Adélie Coast *ou* Land; **~ de bruyère** (heath-)peat; **~ cuite** earthenware; terracotta; **la ~ ferme** dry land, terra firma; **la T~ de Feu** Tierra del Fuego; **~ glaise** clay; **la T~ promise** the Promised Land; **la T~ Sainte** the Holy Land

terreau [tɛʀo] *nm* compost

terre-plein [tɛʀplɛ̃] *nm* platform

terrer [tɛʀe]: **se terrer** *vi* to hide away; to go to ground

terrestre [tɛʀɛstʀ(ə)] *adj* (*surface*) earth's, of the earth; (*Bot, Zool, Mil*) land *cpd*; (*Rel*) earthly, worldly

terreur [tɛʀœʀ] *nf* terror *no pl*, fear

terrible [tɛʀibl(ə)] *adj* terrible, dreadful; (*fam: fantastique*) terrific

terrien, ne [tɛʀjɛ̃, -ɛn] *adj*: **propriétaire ~** landowner ▷ *nm/f* countryman/woman, man/woman of the soil; (*non martien etc*) earthling; (*non marin*) landsman

terrier [tɛʀje] *nm* burrow, hole; (*chien*) terrier

terrifier [tɛʀifje] *vt* to terrify

terrine [tɛʀin] *nf* (*récipient*) terrine; (*Culin*) pâté

territoire [tɛʀitwaʀ] *nm* territory; **T~ des Afars et des Issas** French Territory of Afars and Issas

terroir [tɛʀwaʀ] *nm* (*Agr*) soil; (*région*) region; **accent du ~** country *ou* rural accent

terroriser [tɛʀɔʀize] *vt* to terrorize

terrorisme [tɛʀɔʀism(ə)] *nm* terrorism

terroriste [tɛʀɔʀist(ə)] *nm/f* terrorist

tertiaire [tɛʀsjɛʀ] *adj* tertiary ▷ *nm* (*Écon*) tertiary sector, service industries *pl*

tertre [tɛʀtʀ(ə)] *nm* hillock, mound

tes [te] *adj poss voir* **ton**

tesson [tesɔ̃] *nm*: **~ de bouteille** piece of broken bottle

test [tɛst] *nm* test; **~ de grossesse** pregnancy test

testament [tɛstamɑ̃] *nm* (*Jur*) will; (*fig*) legacy;

(*Rel*): **T~** Testament; **faire son ~** to make one's will

tester [tɛste] *vt* to test

testicule [tɛstikyl] *nm* testicle

tétanos [tetanos] *nm* tetanus

têtard [tɛtaʀ] *nm* tadpole

tête [tɛt] *nf* head; (*cheveux*) hair *no pl*; (*visage*) face; (*longueur*): **gagner d'une (courte) ~** to win by a (short) head; (*Football*) header; **de ~** *adj* (*wagon etc*) front *cpd*; (*concurrent*) leading ▷ *adv* (*calculer*) in one's head, mentally; **par ~** (*par personne*) per head; **se mettre en ~ que** to get it into one's head that; **se mettre en ~ de faire** to take it into one's head to do; **prendre la ~ de qch** to take the lead in sth; **perdre la ~** (*fig*: *s'affoler*) to lose one's head; (: *devenir fou*) to go off on one's head; **ça ne va pas, la ~?** (*fam*) are you crazy?; **tenir ~ à qn** to stand up to *ou* defy sb; **la ~ en bas** with one's head down; **la ~ la première** (*tomber*) head-first; **la ~ basse** hanging one's head; **avoir la ~ dure** (*fig*) to be thickheaded; **faire une ~** (*Football*) to head the ball; **faire la ~** (*fig*) to sulk; **en ~** (*Sport*) in the lead; at the front *ou* head; **de la ~ aux pieds** from head to toe; **~ d'affiche** (*Théât etc*) top of the bill; **~ de bétail** head *inv* of cattle; **~ brûlée** desperado; **~ chercheuse** homing device; **~ d'enregistrement** recording head; **~ d'impression** printhead; **~ de lecture** (playback) head; **~ de ligne** (*Transports*) start of the line; **~ de liste** (*Pol*) chief candidate; **~ de mort** skull and crossbones; **~ de pont** (*Mil*) bridge- *ou* beachhead; **~ de série** (*Tennis*) seeded player, seed; **~ de Turc** (*fig*) whipping boy (*Brit*), butt; **~ de veau** (*Culin*) calf's head

tête-à-queue [tɛtakø] *nm inv*: **faire un ~** to spin round

téter [tete] *vt*: **~ (sa mère)** to suck at one's mother's breast, feed

tétine [tetin] *nf* teat; (*sucette*) dummy (*Brit*), pacifier (*US*)

têtu, e [tety] *adj* stubborn, pigheaded

texte [tɛkst(ə)] *nm* text; (*Scol*: *d'un devoir*) subject, topic; **apprendre son ~** (*Théât*) to learn one's lines; **un ~ de loi** the wording of a law

textile [tɛkstil] *adj* textile *cpd* ▷ *nm* textile; (*industrie*) textile industry

Texto® [tɛksto] *nm* text (message)

texto [tɛksto] (*fam*) *adj* word for word

texture [tɛkstyʀ] *nf* texture; (*fig*: *d'un texte, livre*) feel

TGV *sigle m* = **train à grande vitesse**

thaïlandais, e [tailɑ̃dɛ, -ɛz] *adj* Thai

Thaïlande [tailɑ̃d] *nf*: **la ~** Thailand

thé [te] *nm* tea; (*réunion*) tea party; **prendre le ~** to have tea; **~ au lait/citron** tea with milk/lemon

théâtral, e, -aux [teatʀal, -o] *adj* theatrical

théâtre [teatʀ(ə)] *nm* theatre; (*techniques, genre*) drama, theatre; (*activité*) stage, theatre; (*œuvres*) plays *pl*, dramatic works *pl*; (*fig*: *lieu*): **le ~ de** the scene of; (*péj*) histrionics *pl*, playacting; **faire du ~** (*en professionnel*) to be on the stage; (*en amateur*) to do some acting; **~ filmé** filmed stage productions *pl*

théière [tejɛʀ] *nf* teapot

thème [tɛm] *nm* theme; (*Scol*: *traduction*) prose (composition); **~ astral** birth chart

théologie [teɔlɔʒi] *nf* theology

théorie [teɔʀi] *nf* theory; **en ~** in theory

théorique [teɔʀik] *adj* theoretical

thérapie [teʀapi] *nf* therapy; **~ de groupe** group therapy

thermal, e, -aux [tɛʀmal, -o] *adj* thermal; **station ~e** spa; **cure ~e** water cure

thermes [tɛʀm(ə)] *nmpl* thermal baths; (*romains*) thermae *pl*

thermomètre [tɛʀmɔmɛtʀ(ə)] *nm* thermometer

thermos® [tɛʀmos] *nm ou nf*: **(bouteille) thermos** vacuum *ou* Thermos® flask (*Brit*) *ou* bottle (*US*)

thermostat [tɛʀmɔsta] *nm* thermostat

thèse [tɛz] *nf* thesis

thon [tɔ̃] *nm* tuna (fish)

thym [tɛ̃] *nm* thyme

tibia [tibja] *nm* shin; (*os*) shinbone, tibia

TIC *sigle fpl* (= *technologies de l'information et de la communication*) ICT *sg*

tic [tik] *nm* tic, (nervous) twitch; (*de langage etc*) mannerism

ticket [tikɛ] *nm* ticket; **~ de caisse** till receipt; **~ modérateur** *patient's contribution towards medical costs*; **~ de quai** platform ticket; **~ repas** luncheon voucher

tic-tac [tiktak] *nm inv* tick-tock

tiède [tjɛd] *adj* (*bière etc*) lukewarm; (*thé, café etc*) tepid; (*bain, accueil, sentiment*) lukewarm; (*vent, air*) mild, warm ▷ *adv*: **boire ~** to drink things lukewarm

tiédir [tjediʀ] *vi* (*se réchauffer*) to grow warmer; (*refroidir*) to cool

tien, tienne [tjɛ̃, tjɛn] *pron*: **le ~ (la ~ne), les ~s (~nes)** yours; **à la ~ne!** cheers!

tiens [tjɛ̃] *vb, excl voir* **tenir**

tierce [tjɛʀs(ə)] *adj f, nf voir* **tiers**

tiercé [tjɛʀse] *nm system of forecast betting giving first three horses*

tiers, tierce [tjɛʀ, tjɛʀs(ə)] *adj* third ▷ *nm* (*Jur*) third party; (*fraction*) third ▷ *nf* (*Mus*) third; (*Cartes*) tierce; **une tierce personne** a third party; **assurance au ~** third-party insurance; **le ~ monde** the third world; **~ payant** *direct payment by insurers of medical expenses*; **~ provisionnel** *interim payment of tax*

tifs [tif] (*fam*) *nmpl* hair

tige [tiʒ] *nf* stem; (*baguette*) rod

tignasse [tiɲas] *nf* (*péj*) shock *ou* mop of hair

tigre [tigʀ(ə)] *nm* tiger

tigré, e [tigʀe] *adj* (*rayé*) striped; (*tacheté*) spotted

tigresse [tigʀɛs] *nf* tigress

tilleul [tijœl] *nm* lime (tree), linden (tree); (*boisson*) lime(-blossom) tea

timbale [tɛ̃bal] *nf* (metal) tumbler; **timbales** *nfpl* (*Mus*) timpani, kettledrums

timbre [tɛ̃bʀ(ə)] *nm* (*tampon*) stamp; (*aussi*:

timbre-poste) (postage) stamp; (cachet de la poste) postmark; (sonnette) bell; (Mus: de voix, instrument) timbre, tone; ~ **anti-tabac** nicotine patch; ~ **dateur** date stamp

timbré, e [tɛ̃bʀe] adj (enveloppe) stamped; (voix) resonant; (fam: fou) cracked, nuts

timide [timid] adj (emprunté) shy, timid; (timoré) timid, timorous

timidement [timidmɑ̃] adv shyly; timidly

timidité [timidite] nf shyness; timidity

tintamarre [tɛ̃tamaʀ] nm din, uproar

tinter [tɛ̃te] vi to ring, chime; (argent, clés) to jingle

tique [tik] nf tick (insect)

tir [tiʀ] nm (sport) shooting; (fait ou manière de tirer) firing no pl; (Football) shot; (stand) shooting gallery; ~ **d'obus/de mitraillette** shell/machine gun fire; ~ **à l'arc** archery; ~ **de barrage** barrage fire; ~ **au fusil** (rifle) shooting; ~ **au pigeon** (d'argile) clay pigeon shooting

tirage [tiʀaʒ] nm (action) printing; (Photo) print; (Inform) printout; (de journal) circulation; (de livre) (print-)run; edition; (de cheminée) draught (Brit), draft (US); (de loterie) draw; (fig: désaccord) friction; ~ **au sort** drawing lots

tirailler [tiʀaje] vt to pull at, tug at; (fig) to gnaw at ▷ vi to fire at random

tire [tiʀ] nf: **vol à la** ~ pickpocketing

tiré [tiʀe] adj (visage, traits) drawn ▷ nm (Comm) drawee; ~ **par les cheveux** far-fetched; ~ **à part** off-print

tire-au-flanc [tiʀoflɑ̃] nm inv (péj) skiver

tire-bouchon [tiʀbuʃɔ̃] nm corkscrew

tirelire [tiʀliʀ] nf moneybox

tirer [tiʀe] vt (gén) to pull; (extraire): ~ **qch de** to take ou pull sth out of; to get sth out of; to extract sth from; (tracer: ligne, trait) to draw, trace; (fermer: volet, porte, trappe) to pull to, close; (: rideau) to draw; (choisir: carte, conclusion, aussi Comm: chèque) to draw; (en faisant feu: balle, coup) to fire; (: animal) to shoot; (journal, livre, photo) to print; (Football: corner etc) to take ▷ vi (faire feu) to fire; (faire du tir, Football) to shoot; (cheminée) to draw; **se tirer** vi (fam) to push off; (aussi): **s'en tirer** to pull through; ~ **sur** (corde, poignée) to pull on ou at; (faire feu sur) to shoot ou fire at; (pipe) to draw on; (fig: avoisiner) to verge ou border on; ~ **six mètres** (Navig) to draw six metres of water; ~ **son nom de** to take ou get its name from; ~ **la langue** to stick out one's tongue; ~ **qn de** (embarras etc) to help ou get sb out of; ~ **à l'arc/la carabine** to shoot with a bow and arrow/with a rifle; ~ **en longueur** to drag on; ~ **à sa fin** to be drawing to an end; ~ **les cartes** to read ou tell the cards

tiret [tiʀɛ] nm dash; (en fin de ligne) hyphen

tireur [tiʀœʀ] nm gunman; (Comm) drawer; **bon** ~ good shot; ~ **d'élite** marksman; ~ **de cartes** fortuneteller

tiroir [tiʀwaʀ] nm drawer

tiroir-caisse [tiʀwaʀkɛs] nm till

tisane [tizan] nf herb tea

tisonnier [tizɔnje] nm poker

tisser [tise] vt to weave

tisserand, e [tisʀɑ̃, -ɑ̃d] nm/f weaver

tissu¹ [tisy] nm fabric, material, cloth no pl; (fig) fabric; (Anat, Bio) tissue; ~ **de mensonges** web of lies

tissu², e [tisy] adj: ~ **de** woven through with

tissu-éponge [tisyepɔ̃ʒ] nm (terry) towelling no pl

titre [titʀ(ə)] nm (gén) title; (de journal) headline; (diplôme) qualification; (Comm) security; (Chimie) titre; **en** ~ (champion, responsable) official, recognized; **à juste** ~ with just cause, rightly; **à quel** ~? on what grounds?; **à aucun** ~ on no account; **au même** ~ (que) in the same way (as); **au** ~ **de la coopération** etc in the name of cooperation etc; **à** ~ **d'exemple** as an ou by way of an example; **à** ~ **exceptionnel** exceptionally; **à** ~ **d'information** for (your) information; **à** ~ **gracieux** free of charge; **à** ~ **d'essai** on a trial basis; **à** ~ **privé** in a private capacity; ~ **courant** running head; ~ **de propriété** title deed; ~ **de transport** ticket

tituber [titybe] vi to stagger ou reel (along)

titulaire [titylɛʀ] adj (Admin) appointed, with tenure ▷ nm (Admin) incumbent; **être** ~ **de** to hold

TNT sigle m (= Trinitrotoluène) TNT ▷ sigle f (= Télévision numérique terrestre) digital television

toast [tost] nm slice ou piece of toast; (de bienvenue) (welcoming) toast; **porter un** ~ **à qn** to propose ou drink a toast to sb

toboggan [tɔbɔgɑ̃] nm toboggan; (jeu) slide; (Auto) flyover (Brit), overpass (US); ~ **de secours** (Aviat) escape chute

toc [tɔk] nm: **en** ~ imitation cpd

tocsin [tɔksɛ̃] nm alarm (bell)

toge [tɔʒ] nf toga; (de juge) gown

tohu-bohu [tɔybɔy] nm (désordre) confusion; (tumulte) commotion

toi [twa] pron you; ~, **tu l'as fait?** did YOU do it?

toile [twal] nf (matériau) cloth no pl; (bâche) piece of canvas; (tableau) canvas; **grosse** ~ canvas; **tisser sa** ~ (araignée) to spin its web; ~ **d'araignée** spider's web; (au plafond etc: à enlever) cobweb; ~ **cirée** oilcloth; ~ **émeri** emery cloth; ~ **de fond** (fig) backdrop; ~ **de jute** hessian; ~ **de lin** linen; ~ **de tente** canvas

toilette [twalɛt] nf wash; (s'habiller et se préparer) getting ready, washing and dressing; (habits) outfit; dress no pl; **toilettes** nfpl toilet nsg; **les** ~**s des dames/messieurs** the ladies'/gents' (toilets) (Brit), the ladies'/men's (rest)room (US); **faire sa** ~ to have a wash, get washed; **faire la** ~ **de** (animal) to groom; (voiture etc) to clean, wash; (texte) to tidy up; **articles de** ~ toiletries; ~ **intime** personal hygiene

toi-même [twamɛm] pron yourself

toiser [twaze] vt to eye up and down

toison [twazɔ̃] nf (de mouton) fleece; (cheveux) mane

toit [twa] nm roof; ~ **ouvrant** sun roof

toiture [twatyʀ] nf roof

tôle [tol] nf sheet metal no pl; (plaque) steel (ou iron) sheet; **tôles** nfpl (carosserie) bodywork nsg (Brit), body nsg; panels; **~ d'acier** sheet steel no pl; **~ ondulée** corrugated iron

tolérable [tɔleʀabl(ə)] adj tolerable, bearable

tolérant, e [tɔleʀɑ̃, -ɑ̃t] adj tolerant

tolérer [tɔleʀe] vt to tolerate; (Admin: hors taxe etc) to allow

tollé [tɔle] nm: **un ~ (de protestations)** a general outcry

tomate [tɔmat] nf tomato

tombe [tɔ̃b] nf (sépulture) grave; (avec monument) tomb

tombeau, x [tɔ̃bo] nm tomb; **à ~ ouvert** at breakneck speed

tombée [tɔ̃be] nf: **à la ~ du jour** ou **de la nuit** at the close of day, at nightfall

tomber [tɔ̃be] vi to fall ▷ vt: **~ la veste** to slip off one's jacket; **laisser ~** to drop; **~ sur** vt (rencontrer) to come across; (attaquer) to set about; **~ de fatigue/sommeil** to drop from exhaustion/be falling asleep on one's feet; **~ à l'eau** (fig: projet etc) to fall through; **~ en panne** to break down; **~ juste** (opération, calcul) to come out right; **~ en ruine** to fall into ruins; **ça tombe bien/mal** (fig) that's come at the right/wrong time; **il est bien/mal tombé** (fig) he's been lucky/unlucky

tombola [tɔ̃bɔla] nf tombola

tome [tɔm] nm volume

ton¹, ta (pl **tes**) [tɔ̃, ta, te] adj poss your

ton² [tɔ̃] nm (gén) tone; (Mus) key; (couleur) shade, tone; (de la voix: hauteur) pitch; **donner le ~** to set the tone; **élever** ou **hausser le ~** to raise one's voice; **de bon ~** in good taste; **si vous le prenez sur ce ~** if you're going to take it like that; **~ sur ~** in matching shades

tonalité [tɔnalite] nf (au téléphone) dialling tone; (Mus) tonality; (: ton) key; (fig) tone

tondeuse [tɔ̃døz] nf (à gazon) (lawn)mower; (du coiffeur) clippers pl; (pour la tonte) shears pl

tondre [tɔ̃dr(ə)] vt (pelouse, herbe) to mow; (haie) to cut, clip; (mouton, toison) to shear; (cheveux) to crop

tongs [tɔg] nfpl flip-flops (Brit), thongs (US)

tonifier [tɔnifje] vt (air, eau) to invigorate; (peau, organisme) to tone up

tonique [tɔnik] adj fortifying; (personne) dynamic ▷ nm, nf tonic

tonne [tɔn] nf metric ton, tonne

tonneau, x [tɔno] nm (à vin, cidre) barrel; (Navig) ton; **faire des ~x** (voiture, avion) to roll over

tonnelle [tɔnɛl] nf bower, arbour (Brit), arbor (US)

tonner [tɔne] vi to thunder; (parler avec véhémence): **~ contre qn/qch** to inveigh against sb/sth; **il tonne** it is thundering, there's some thunder

tonnerre [tɔnɛʀ] nm thunder; **coup de ~** (fig) thunderbolt, bolt from the blue; **un ~ d'applaudissements** thunderous applause; **du ~** adj (fam) terrific

tonte [tɔ̃t] nf shearing

tonton [tɔ̃tɔ̃] nm uncle

tonus [tɔnys] nm (des muscles) tone; (d'une personne) dynamism

top [tɔp] nm: **au troisième ~** at the third stroke ▷ adj: **~ secret** top secret ▷ excl go!

topinambour [tɔpinɑ̃buʀ] nm Jerusalem artichoke

topo [tɔpo] nm (discours, exposé) talk; (fam) spiel

toque [tɔk] nf (de fourrure) fur hat; **~ de jockey/juge** jockey's/judge's cap; **~ de cuisinier** chef's hat

toqué, e [tɔke] adj (fam) touched, cracked

torche [tɔʀʃ(ə)] nf torch; **se mettre en ~** (parachute) to candle

torchon [tɔʀʃɔ̃] nm cloth, duster; (à vaisselle) tea towel ou cloth

tordre [tɔʀdʀ(ə)] vt (chiffon) to wring; (barre, fig: visage) to twist; **se tordre** vi (barre) to bend; (roue) to twist, buckle; (ver, serpent) to writhe; **se ~ le pied/bras** to twist one's foot/arm; **se ~ de douleur/rire** to writhe in pain/be doubled up with laughter

tordu, e [tɔʀdy] pp de **tordre** ▷ adj (fig) warped, twisted

tornade [tɔʀnad] nf tornado

torpille [tɔʀpij] nf torpedo

torréfier [tɔʀefje] vt to roast

torrent [tɔʀɑ̃] nm torrent, mountain stream; (fig): **un ~ de** a torrent ou flood of; **il pleut à ~s** the rain is lashing down

torsade [tɔʀsad] nf twist; (Archit) cable moulding (Brit) ou molding (US)

torse [tɔʀs(ə)] nm torso; (poitrine) chest

tort [tɔʀ] nm (défaut) fault; (préjudice) wrong no pl; **torts** nmpl (Jur) fault nsg; **avoir ~** to be wrong; **être dans son ~** to be in the wrong; **donner ~ à qn** to lay the blame on sb; (fig) to prove sb wrong; **causer du ~ à** to harm; to be harmful ou detrimental to; **en ~** in the wrong, at fault; **à ~** wrongly; **à ~ ou à raison** rightly or wrongly; **à ~ et à travers** wildly

torticolis [tɔʀtikɔli] nm stiff neck

tortiller [tɔʀtije] vt (corde, mouchoir) to twist; (doigts) to twiddle; **se tortiller** vi to wriggle, squirm

tortionnaire [tɔʀsjɔnɛʀ] nm torturer

tortue [tɔʀty] nf tortoise; (fig) slowcoach (Brit), slowpoke (US)

tortueux, -euse [tɔʀtɥø, -øz] adj (rue) twisting; (fig) tortuous

torture [tɔʀtyʀ] nf torture

torturer [tɔʀtyʀe] vt to torture; (fig) to torment

tôt [to] adv early; **~ ou tard** sooner or later; **si ~** so early; (déjà) so soon; **au plus ~** at the earliest, as soon as possible; **plus ~** earlier; **il eut ~ fait de faire ...** he soon did ...

total, e, -aux [tɔtal, -o] adj, nm total; **au ~** in total ou all; (fig) all in all; **faire le ~** to work out the total

totalement [tɔtalmɑ̃] adv totally, completely

totaliser [tɔtalize] vt to total (up)

totalitaire [tɔtalitɛʀ] adj totalitarian

totalité [tɔtalite] nf: **la ~ de: la totalité des**

élèves all (of) the pupils; **la ~ de la population/
classe** the whole population/class; **en ~** entirely
toubib [tubib] *nm (fam)* doctor
touchant, e [tuʃɑ̃, -ɑ̃t] *adj* touching
touche [tuʃ] *nf (de piano, de machine à écrire)* key;
(de violon) fingerboard; *(de télécommande etc)* key,
button; *(Peinture etc)* stroke, touch; *(fig: de couleur,
nostalgie)* touch, hint; *(Rugby)* line-out; *(Football:
aussi:* **remise en touche)** throw-in; *(aussi:* **ligne
de touche)** touch-line; *(Escrime)* hit; **en ~** in *(ou
into)* touch; **avoir une drôle de ~** to look a sight;
~ de commande/de fonction/de retour *(Inform)*
control/function/return key; **à effleurement**
ou **sensitive** touch-sensitive control *ou* key
toucher [tuʃe] *nm* touch ▷ *vt* to touch; *(palper)* to
feel; *(atteindre: d'un coup de feu etc)* to hit; *(affecter)*
to touch, affect; *(concerner)* to concern, affect;
(contacter) to reach, contact; *(recevoir: récompense)*
to receive, get; *(: salaire)* to draw, get; *(chèque)* to
cash; *(aborder: problème, sujet)* to touch on; **au ~** to
the touch; by the feel; **se toucher** *(être en contact)*
to touch; **~ à** to touch; *(modifier)* to touch, tamper
ou meddle with; *(traiter de, concerner)* to have to do
with, concern; **je vais lui en ~ un mot** I'll have
a word with him about it; **~ au but** *(fig)* to near
one's goal; **~ à sa fin** to be drawing to a close
touffe [tuf] *nf* tuft
touffu, e [tufy] *adj* thick, dense; *(fig)* complex,
involved
toujours [tuʒuR] *adv* always; *(encore)* still;
(constamment) forever; **depuis ~** always; **essaie
~** (you can) try anyway; **pour ~** forever; **~ est-il
que** the fact remains that; **~ plus** more and
more
toupet [tupɛ] *nm* quiff (Brit), tuft; *(fam)* nerve,
cheek (Brit)
toupie [tupi] *nf* (spinning) top
tour [tuR] *nf* tower; *(immeuble)* high-rise block
(Brit) *ou* building (US), tower block (Brit); *(Échecs)*
castle, rook ▷ *nm* *(excursion: à pied)* stroll, walk;
(: en voiture etc) run, ride; *(: plus long)* trip; *(Sport:
aussi:* **tour de piste)** lap; *(d'être servi ou de jouer etc,
tournure, de vis ou clef)* turn; *(de roue etc)* revolution;
(circonférence) **de 3 m de ~** 3 m round, with a
circumference *ou* girth of 3 m; *(Pol: aussi:* **tour de
scrutin)** ballot; *(ruse, de prestidigitation, de cartes)*
trick; *(de potier)* wheel; *(à bois, métaux)* lathe; **faire
le ~ de** to go (a)round; *(à pied)* to walk (a)round;
(fig) to review; **faire le ~ de l'Europe** to tour
Europe; **faire un ~** to go for a walk; *(en voiture etc)*
to go for a ride; **faire 2 ~s** to go (a)round twice;
(hélice etc) to turn *ou* revolve twice; **fermer à
double ~** *vi* to double-lock the door; **c'est au ~
de Renée** it's Renée's turn; **à ~ de rôle, ~ à ~** in
turn; **~ de bras** with all one's strength; *(fig)*
non-stop, relentlessly; **~ de taille/tête** waist/
head measurement; **~ de chant** song recital; **~
de contrôle** *nf* control tower; **le T~ de France**
the Tour de France; *see note;* **~ de garde** spell of
duty; **~ d'horizon** *(fig)* general survey; **~ de lit**
valance; **~ de main** dexterity, knack; **en un ~
de main** (as) quick as a flash; **~ de passe-passe**

trick, sleight of hand; **~ de reins** sprained back
tourbe [tuRb(ə)] *nf* peat
tourbillon [tuRbijɔ̃] *nm* whirlwind; *(d'eau)*
whirlpool; *(fig)* whirl, swirl
tourbillonner [tuRbijɔne] *vi* to whirl, swirl;
(objet, personne) to whirl *ou* twirl round
tourelle [tuRɛl] *nf* turret
tourisme [tuRism(ə)] *nm* tourism; **agence de
~** tourist agency; **avion/voiture de ~** private
plane/car; **faire du ~** to do some sightseeing,
go touring
touriste [tuRist(ə)] *nm/f* tourist
touristique [tuRistik] *adj* tourist *cpd*; *(région)*
touristic *(péj)*, with tourist appeal
tourment [tuRmɑ̃] *nm* torment
tourmenter [tuRmɑ̃te] *vt* to torment; **se
tourmenter** *vi* to fret, worry o.s.
tournage [tuRnaʒ] *nm (d'un film)* shooting
tournant, e [tuRnɑ̃, -ɑ̃t] *adj (feu, scène)* revolving;
(chemin) winding; *(escalier)* spiral *cpd*; *(mouvement)*
circling ▷ *nm (de route)* bend (Brit), curve (US); *(fig)*
turning point; *voir* **plaque; grève**
tournebroche [tuRnəbRɔʃ] *nm* roasting spit
tourne-disque [tuRnədisk(ə)] *nm* record player
tournée [tuRne] *nf (du facteur etc)* round; *(d'artiste,
politicien)* tour; *(au café)* round (of drinks); **faire la
~ de** to go (a)round
tournemain [tuRnəmɛ̃]: **en un ~** *adv* in a flash
tourner [tuRne] *vt* to turn; *(sauce, mélange)* to stir;
(contourner) to get (a)round; *(Ciné)* to shoot; to
make ▷ *vi* to turn; *(moteur)* to run; *(compteur)* to
tick away; *(lait etc)* to turn (sour); *(fig: chance, vie)*
to turn out; **se tourner** *vi* to turn (a)round; **se ~
vers** to turn to; to turn towards; **bien ~** to turn
out well; **~ autour de** to go (a)round; *(planète)*
to revolve (a)round; *(péj)* to hang (a)round; **~
autour du pot** *(fig)* to go (a)round in circles; **~
à/en** to turn into; **~ à la pluie/au rouge** to turn
rainy/red; **~ en ridicule** to ridicule; **~ le dos à**
(mouvement) to turn one's back on; *(position)* to
have one's back to; **~ court** to come to a sudden
end; **se ~ les pouces** to twiddle one's thumbs; **~
la tête** to look away; **~ la tête à qn** *(fig)* to go to
sb's head; **~ de l'œil** to pass out; **~ la page** *(fig)* to
turn the page
tournesol [tuRnəsɔl] *nm* sunflower
tournevis [tuRnəvis] *nm* screwdriver
tourniquet [tuRnikɛ] *nm (pour arroser)* sprinkler;
(portillon) turnstile; *(présentoir)* revolving stand,
spinner; *(Chirurgie)* tourniquet
tournoi [tuRnwa] *nm* tournament
tournoyer [tuRnwaje] *vi (oiseau)* to wheel
(a)round; *(fumée)* to swirl (a)round
tournure [tuRnyR] *nf (Ling: syntaxe)* turn of
phrase; form; *(: d'une phrase)* phrasing; *(évolution)*:
la ~ de qch the way sth is developing; *(aspect)*: **la
~ de** the look of; **la ~ des événements** the turn
of events; **prendre ~** to take shape
tourte [tuRt(ə)] *nf* pie
tourterelle [tuRtəRɛl] *nf* turtledove
tous [tu] *adj* [tus] ▷ *pron voir* **tout**
Toussaint [tusɛ̃] *nf*: **la ~** All Saints' Day

tousser [tuse] *vi* to cough

tout, e [tu, tut] (*mpl* **tous**, *fpl* **-es**) *adj* **1** (*avec article singulier*) all; ~ **le lait** all the milk; ~**e la nuit** all night, the whole night; ~ **le livre** the whole book; ~ **un pain** a whole loaf; ~ **le temps** all the time, the whole time; **c'est** ~ **le contraire** it's quite the opposite; **c'est ~e une affaire** *ou* **histoire** it's quite a business, it's a whole rigmarole

2 (*avec article pluriel*) every; all; **tous les livres** all the books; ~**es les nuits** every night; ~**es les fois** every time; ~**es les trois/deux semaines** every third/other *ou* second week, every three/two weeks; **tous les deux** both *ou* each of us (*ou* them *ou* you); ~**es les trois** all three of us (*ou* them *ou* you)

3 (*sans article*): **à ~ âge** at any age; **pour ~e nourriture, il avait ...** his only food was ...; **de tous côtés, de ~es parts** from everywhere, from every side

▷ *pron* everything, all; **il a ~ fait** he's done everything; **je les vois tous** I can see them all *ou* all of them; **nous y sommes tous allés** all of us went, we all went; **c'est ~** that's all; **en ~** in all; **en ~ et pour ~** all in all; ~ **ce qu'il sait** all he knows; **c'était ~ ce qu'il y a de chic** it was the last word *ou* the ultimate in chic

▷ *nm* whole; **le ~** all of it (*ou* them); **le ~ est de ...** the main thing is to ...; **pas du ~** not at all; **elle a ~ d'une mère/d'une intrigante** she's a real *ou* true mother/schemer; **du ~ au ~** utterly

▷ *adv* **1** (*très, complètement*) very; **~près** *ou* **à côté** very near; **le ~ premier** the very first; ~ **seul** all alone; **il était ~ rouge** he was really *ou* all red; **parler ~ bas** to speak very quietly; **le livre ~ entier** the whole book; ~ **en haut** right at the top; ~ **droit** straight ahead

2: ~ **en** while; ~ **en travaillant** while working, as he *etc* works

3: ~ **d'abord** first of all; ~ **à coup** suddenly; ~ **à fait** absolutely; ~ **à fait!** exactly!; ~ **à l'heure** a short while ago; (*futur*) in a short while, shortly; **à ~ à l'heure!** see you later!; **il répondit ~ court que non** he just answered no (and that was all); ~ **de même** all the same; ~ **le monde** everybody; ~ **ou rien** all or nothing; ~ **simplement** quite simply; ~ **de suite** immediately, straight away

toutefois [tutfwa] *adv* however

toux [tu] *nf* cough

toxicomane [tɔksikɔman] *nm/f* drug addict

toxique [tɔksik] *adj* toxic, poisonous

trac [tʀak] *nm* nerves *pl*; (*Théât*) stage fright; **avoir le ~** to get an attack of nerves; to have stage fright; **tout à ~** all of a sudden

tracasser [tʀakase] *vt* to worry, bother; (*harceler*) to harass; **se tracasser** *vi* to worry o.s., fret

trace [tʀas] *nf* (*empreintes*) tracks *pl*; (*marques, aussi fig*) mark; (*restes, vestige*) trace; (*indice*) sign; (*aussi*: **suivre à la trace**) to track; **~s de pas** footprints

tracé [tʀase] *nm* (*contour*) line; (*plan*) layout

tracer [tʀase] *vt* to draw; (*mot*) to trace; (*piste*) to open up; (*fig: chemin*) to show

tract [tʀakt] *nm* tract, pamphlet; (*publicitaire*) handout

tractations [tʀaktasjɔ̃] *nfpl* dealings, bargaining *nsg*

tracteur [tʀaktœʀ] *nm* tractor

traction [tʀaksjɔ̃] *nf* traction; (*Gym*) pull-up; ~ **avant/arrière** front-wheel/rear-wheel drive; ~ **électrique** electric(al) traction *ou* haulage

tradition [tʀadisjɔ̃] *nf* tradition

traditionnel, le [tʀadisjɔnɛl] *adj* traditional

traducteur, -trice [tʀadyktœʀ, -tʀis] *nm/f* translator

traduction [tʀadyksjɔ̃] *nf* translation

traduire [tʀadɥiʀ] *vt* to translate; (*exprimer*) to render, convey; **se ~ par** to find expression in; ~ **en français** to translate into French; ~ **en justice** to bring before the courts

trafic [tʀafik] *nm* traffic; ~ **d'armes** arms dealing; ~ **de drogue** drug peddling

trafiquant, e [tʀafikɑ̃, -ɑ̃t] *nm/f* trafficker; dealer

trafiquer [tʀafike] *vt* (*péj*) to doctor, tamper with ▷ *vi* to traffic, be engaged in trafficking

tragédie [tʀaʒedi] *nf* tragedy

tragique [tʀaʒik] *adj* tragic ▷ *nm*: **prendre qch au ~** to make a tragedy out of sth

trahir [tʀaiʀ] *vt* to betray; (*fig*) to give away, reveal; **se trahir** to betray o.s., give o.s. away

trahison [tʀaizɔ̃] *nf* betrayal; (*Jur*) treason

train [tʀɛ̃] *nm* (*Rail*) train; (*allure*) pace; (*fig: ensemble*) set; **être en ~ de faire qch** to be doing sth; **mettre qch en ~** to get sth under way; **mettre qn en ~** to put sb in good spirits; **se mettre en ~** (*commencer*) to get started; (*faire de la gymnastique*) to warm up; **se sentir en ~** to feel in good form; **aller bon ~** to make good progress; ~ **avant/arrière** front-wheel/rear-wheel axle unit; ~ **à grande vitesse (TGV)** high-speed train; ~ **d'atterrissage** undercarriage; ~ **autos-couchettes** car-sleeper train; ~ **électrique** (*jouet*) (electric) train set; ~ **de pneus** set of tyres *ou* tires; ~ **de vie** style of living

traîne [tʀɛn] *nf* (*de robe*) train; **être à la ~** to be in tow; (*en arrière*) to lag behind; (*en désordre*) to be lying around

traîneau, x [tʀɛno] *nm* sleigh, sledge

traînée [tʀɛne] *nf* streak, trail; (*péj*) slut

traîner [tʀene] *vt* (*remorque*) to pull; (*enfant, chien*) to drag *ou* trail along; (*maladie*): **il traîne un rhume depuis l'hiver** he has a cold which has been dragging on since winter ▷ *vi* (*être en désordre*) to lie around; (*marcher lentement*) to dawdle (along); (*vagabonder*) to hang about; (*agir lentement*) to idle about; (*durer*) to drag on; **se traîner** *vi* (*ramper*) to crawl along; (*marcher avec difficulté*) to drag o.s. along; (*durer*) to drag on; ~ **par terre** to crawl (on the ground); ~ **qn au cinéma** to drag sb to the cinema; ~ **les pieds** to drag one's feet; ~ **par terre** to trail on the ground; ~ **en longueur** to drag out

train-train [tʀɛ̃tʀɛ̃] *nm* humdrum routine

traire [tʀɛʀ] *vt* to milk

trait, e [tʀɛ, -ɛt] *pp de* **traire** ▷ *nm* (*ligne*) line;
(*de dessin*) stroke; (*caractéristique*) feature, trait;
(*flèche*) dart, arrow; shaft; **traits** *nmpl* (*du visage*)
features; **d'un ~** (*boire*) in one gulp; **de ~** *adj*
(*animal*) draught (*Brit*), draft (*US*); **avoir ~ à** to
concern; **~ pour ~** line for line; **~ de caractère**
characteristic, trait; **~ d'esprit** flash of wit; **~ de
génie** brainwave; **~ d'union** hyphen; (*fig*) link

traitant, e [tʀɛtɑ̃, -ɑ̃t] *adj*: **votre médecin ~**
your usual *ou* family doctor; **shampooing ~**
medicated shampoo; **crème ~e** conditioning
cream, conditioner

traite [tʀɛt] *nf* (*Comm*) draft; (*Agr*) milking;
(*trajet*) stretch; **d'une (seule) ~** without
stopping (once); **la ~ des noirs** the slave trade;
la ~ des blanches the white slave trade

traité [tʀete] *nm* treaty

traitement [tʀɛtmɑ̃] *nm* treatment; processing;
(*salaire*) salary; **suivre un ~** to undergo
treatment; **mauvais ~** ill-treatment; **~ de
données** *ou* **de l'information** (*Inform*) data
processing; **~ hormono-supplétif** hormone
replacement therapy; **~ par lots** (*Inform*) batch
processing; **~ de texte** (*Inform*) word processing

traiter [tʀete] *vt* (*gén*) to treat; (*Tech: matériaux*) to
process, treat; (*Inform*) to process; (*affaire*) to deal
with, handle; (*qualifier*): **~ qn d'idiot** to call sb a
fool ▷ *vi* to deal; **~ de** *vt* to deal with; **bien/mal
~** to treat well/ill-treat

traiteur [tʀetœʀ] *nm* caterer

traître, -esse [tʀɛtʀ(ə), -tʀɛs] *adj* (*dangereux*)
treacherous ▷ *nm* traitor; **prendre qn en ~** to
make an insidious attack on sb

trajectoire [tʀaʒɛktwaʀ] *nf* trajectory, path

trajet [tʀaʒɛ] *nm* journey; (*itinéraire*) route; (*fig*)
path, course

trame [tʀam] *nf* (*de tissu*) weft; (*fig*) framework;
texture; (*Typo*) screen

tramer [tʀame] *vt* to plot, hatch

trampoline [tʀɑ̃pɔlin], **trampolino** [tʀɑ̃pɔlino]
nm trampoline; (*Sport*) trampolining

tramway [tʀamwɛ] *nm* tram(way); (*voiture*)
tram(car) (*Brit*), streetcar (*US*)

tranchant, e [tʀɑ̃ʃɑ̃, -ɑ̃t] *adj* sharp; (*fig: personne*)
peremptory; (: *couleurs*) striking ▷ *nm* (*d'un
couteau*) cutting edge; (*de la main*) edge; **à double
~** (*argument, procédé*) double-edged

tranche [tʀɑ̃ʃ] *nf* (*morceau*) slice; (*arête*) edge;
(*partie*) section; (*série*) block; (*d'impôts, revenus etc*)
bracket; (*loterie*) issue; **~ d'âge** age bracket; **~ (de
silicium)** wafer

tranché, e [tʀɑ̃ʃe] *adj* (*couleurs*) distinct, sharply
contrasted; (*opinions*) clear-cut, definite ▷ *nf*
trench

trancher [tʀɑ̃ʃe] *vt* to cut, sever; (*fig: résoudre*)
to settle ▷ *vi* to be decisive; (*entre deux choses*) to
settle the argument; **~ avec** to contrast sharply
with

tranquille [tʀɑ̃kil] *adj* calm, quiet; (*enfant, élève*)
quiet; (*rassuré*) easy in one's mind, with one's
mind at rest; **se tenir ~** (*enfant*) to be quiet; **avoir
la conscience ~** to have an easy conscience;

laisse-moi/laisse-ça ~ leave me/it alone

tranquillisant, e [tʀɑ̃kilizɑ̃, -ɑ̃t] *adj* (*nouvelle*)
reassuring ▷ *nm* tranquillizer

tranquillité [tʀɑ̃kilite] *nf* quietness, peace (and
quiet); **en toute ~** with complete peace of mind;
~ d'esprit peace of mind

transat [tʀɑ̃zat] *nm* deckchair ▷ *nf* = **course
transatlantique**

transborder [tʀɑ̃sbɔʀde] *vt* to tran(s)ship

transcription [tʀɑ̃skʀipsjɔ̃] *nf* transcription

transférer [tʀɑ̃sfeʀe] *vt* to transfer

transfert [tʀɑ̃sfɛʀ] *nm* transfer

transformation [tʀɑ̃sfɔʀmasjɔ̃] *nf*
transformation; (*Rugby*) conversion; **industries
de ~** processing industries

transformer [tʀɑ̃sfɔʀme] *vt* to transform, alter
("*alter*" *implique un changement moins radical*); (*matière
première, appartement, Rugby*) to convert; **~ en** to
transform into; to turn into; to convert into; **se
transformer** *vi* to be transformed; to alter

transfusion [tʀɑ̃sfyzjɔ̃] *nf*: **~ sanguine** blood
transfusion

transgénique [tʀɑ̃sʒenik] *adj* transgenic

transgresser [tʀɑ̃sgʀese] *vt* to contravene,
disobey

transi, e [tʀɑ̃zi] *adj* numb (with cold), chilled to
the bone

transiger [tʀɑ̃ziʒe] *vi* to compromise, come to
an agreement; **~ sur** *ou* **avec qch** to compromise
on sth

transistor [tʀɑ̃zistɔʀ] *nm* transistor

transit [tʀɑ̃zit] *nm* transit; **de ~** transit *cpd*; **en
~** in transit

transiter [tʀɑ̃zite] *vi* to pass in transit

transitif, -ive [tʀɑ̃zitif, -iv] *adj* transitive

transition [tʀɑ̃zisjɔ̃] *nf* transition; **de ~**
transitional

transitoire [tʀɑ̃zitwaʀ] *adj* (*mesure, gouvernement*)
transitional, provisional; (*fugitif*) transient

translucide [tʀɑ̃slysid] *adj* translucent

transmettre [tʀɑ̃smɛtʀ(ə)] *vt* (*passer*): **~ qch à qn**
to pass sth on to sb; (*Tech, Tél, Méd*) to transmit;
(*TV, Radio: retransmettre*) to broadcast

transmission [tʀɑ̃smisjɔ̃] *nf* transmission,
passing on; (*Auto*) transmission; **transmissions**
nfpl (*Mil*) ≈ signals corps *nsg*; **~ de données**
(*Inform*) data transmission; **~ de pensée** thought
transmission

transparent, e [tʀɑ̃spaʀɑ̃, -ɑ̃t] *adj* transparent

transpercer [tʀɑ̃spɛʀse] *vt* to go through, pierce

transpiration [tʀɑ̃spiʀasjɔ̃] *nf* perspiration

transpirer [tʀɑ̃spiʀe] *vi* to perspire; (*information,
nouvelle*) to come to light

transplantation [tʀɑ̃splɑ̃tasjɔ̃] *nf* transplant

transplanter [tʀɑ̃splɑ̃te] *vt* (*Méd, Bot*) to
transplant; (*personne*) to uproot, move

transport [tʀɑ̃spɔʀ] *nm* transport; (*émotions*):
~ de colère fit of rage; **~ de joie** transport
of delight; **~ de voyageurs/marchandises**
passenger/goods transportation; **~s en
commun** public transport *nsg*; **~s routiers**
haulage (*Brit*), trucking (*US*)

transporter [trɑ̃spɔrte] vt to carry, move; (Comm) to transport, convey; (fig): ~ **qn (de joie)** to send sb into raptures; **se ~ quelque part** (fig) to let one's imagination carry one away (somewhere)

transporteur [trɑ̃spɔrtœr] nm haulage contractor (Brit), trucker (US)

transvaser [trɑ̃svaze] vt to decant

transversal, e, -aux [trɑ̃svɛrsal, -o] adj transverse, cross(-); (route etc) cross-country; (mur, chemin, rue) running at right angles; (Auto): **axe ~** main cross-country road (Brit) ou highway (US)

trapèze [trapɛz] nm (Géom) trapezium; (au cirque) trapeze

trappe [trap] nf (de cave, grenier) trap door; (piège) trap

trapu, e [trapy] adj squat, stocky

traquenard [traknar] nm trap

traquer [trake] vt to track down; (harceler) to hound

traumatiser [tromatize] vt to traumatize

travail, -aux [travaj, -o] nm (gén) work; (tâche, métier) work no pl, job; (Écon, Méd) labour (Brit), labor (US); (Inform) job ▷ nmpl (de réparation, agricoles etc) work nsg; (sur route) roadworks; (de construction) building (work) nsg; **être/entrer en ~** (Méd) to be in/go into labour; **être sans ~** (employé) to be out of work, be unemployed; **~ d'intérêt général (TIG)** ≈ community service; **~ (au) noir** moonlighting; **~ posté** shiftwork; **travaux des champs** farmwork nsg; **travaux dirigés (TD)** (Scol) supervised practical work nsg; **travaux forcés** hard labour nsg; **travaux manuels** (Scol) handicrafts; **travaux ménagers** housework nsg; **travaux pratiques (TP)** (gén) practical work; (en laboratoire) lab work (Brit), lab (US); **travaux publics (TP)** ≈ public works nsg

travailler [travaje] vi to work; (bois) to warp ▷ vt (bois, métal) to work; (pâte) to knead; (objet d'art, discipline, fig: influencer) to work on; **cela le travaille** it is on his mind; **~ la terre** to work the land; **~ son piano** to do one's piano practice; **~ à** to work on; (fig: contribuer à) to work towards; **~ à faire** to endeavour (Brit) ou endeavor (US) to do

travailleur, -euse [travajœr, -øz] adj hard-working ▷ nm/f worker; **~ de force** labourer (Brit), laborer (US); **~ intellectuel** non-manual worker; **~ social** social worker; **travailleuse familiale** home help

travailliste [travajist(ə)] adj ≈ Labour cpd ▷ nm/f member of the Labour party

travers [travɛr] nm fault, failing; **en ~ (de)** across; **au ~ (de)** through; **de ~** adj askew ▷ adv sideways; (fig) the wrong way; **à ~** through; **regarder de ~** (fig) to look askance at

traverse [travɛrs(ə)] nf (de voie ferrée) sleeper; **chemin de ~** shortcut

traversée [travɛrse] nf crossing

traverser [travɛrse] vt (gén) to cross; (ville, tunnel, aussi: percer, fig) to go through; (ligne, trait) to run across

traversin [travɛrsɛ̃] nm bolster

travesti [travɛsti] nm (costume) fancy dress; (artiste de cabaret) female impersonator, drag artist; (pervers) transvestite

trébucher [trebyʃe] vi: **~ (sur)** to stumble (over), trip (over)

trèfle [trɛfl(ə)] nm (Bot) clover; (Cartes: couleur) clubs pl; (: carte) club; **~ à quatre feuilles** four-leaf clover

treille [trɛj] nf (tonnelle) vine arbour (Brit) ou arbor (US); (vigne) climbing vine

treillis [trɛji] nm (métallique) wire-mesh; (toile) canvas; (Mil: tenue) combat uniform; (pantalon) combat trousers pl

treize [trɛz] num thirteen

treizième [trɛzjɛm] num thirteenth; see note

tréma [trema] nm diaeresis

tremblement [trɑ̃bləmɑ̃] nm trembling no pl, shaking no pl, shivering no pl; **~ de terre** earthquake

trembler [trɑ̃ble] vi to tremble, shake; **~ de** (froid, fièvre) to shiver ou tremble with; (peur) to shake ou tremble with; **~ pour qn** to fear for sb

trémousser [tremuse]: **se trémousser** vi to jig about, wriggle about

trempe [trɑ̃p] nf (fig): **de cette/sa ~** of this/his calibre (Brit) ou caliber (US)

trempé, e [trɑ̃pe] adj soaking (wet), drenched; (Tech): **acier ~** tempered steel

tremper [trɑ̃pe] vt to soak, drench; (aussi: **faire tremper, mettre à tremper**) to soak; (plonger): **~ qch dans** to dip sth in(to) ▷ vi to soak; (fig): **~ dans** to be involved ou have a hand in; **se tremper** vi to have a quick dip; **se faire ~** to get soaked ou drenched

trempette [trɑ̃pɛt] nf: **faire ~** to go paddling

tremplin [trɑ̃plɛ̃] nm springboard; (Ski) ski jump

trentaine [trɑ̃tɛn] nf (âge): **avoir la ~** to be around thirty; **une ~ (de)** thirty or so, about thirty

trente [trɑ̃t] num thirty; **voir ~-six chandelles** (fig) to see stars; **être/se mettre sur son ~ et un** to be/get dressed to kill; **~-trois tours** nm long-playing record, LP

trentième [trɑ̃tjɛm] num thirtieth

trépidant, e [trepidɑ̃, -ɑ̃t] adj (fig: rythme) pulsating; (: vie) hectic

trépied [trepje] nm (d'appareil) tripod; (meuble) trivet

trépigner [trepiɲe] vi to stamp (one's feet)

très [trɛ] adv very; **~ beau/bien** very beautiful/well; **~ critiqué** much criticized; **~ industrialisé** highly industrialized; **j'ai ~ faim** I'm very hungry

trésor [trezɔr] nm treasure; (Admin) finances pl; (d'une organisation) funds pl; **~ (public) (TP)** public revenue; (service) public revenue office

trésorerie [trezɔrri] nf (fonds) funds pl; (gestion) accounts pl; (bureaux) accounts department; (poste) treasurership; **difficultés de ~** cash problems, shortage of cash ou funds; **~ générale (TG)** local government finance office

trésorier, -ière [tʀezɔʀje, -jɛʀ] *nm/f* treasurer
tressaillir [tʀesajiʀ] *vi* (*de peur etc*) to shiver,
shudder; (*de joie*) to quiver
tressauter [tʀesote] *vi* to start, jump
tresse [tʀɛs] *nf* (*de cheveux*) braid, plait; (*cordon,
galon*) braid
tresser [tʀese] *vt* (*cheveux*) to braid, plait; (*fil, jonc*)
to plait; (*corbeille*) to weave; (*corde*) to twist
tréteau, x [tʀeto] *nm* trestle; **les ~x** (*fig: Théât*)
the boards
treuil [tʀœj] *nm* winch
trêve [tʀɛv] *nf* (*Mil, Pol*) truce; (*fig*) respite; **sans
~** unremittingly; **~ de ...** enough of this ...; **les
États de la T~** the Trucial States
tri [tʀi] *nm* (*voir trier*) sorting (out) *no pl*; selection;
screening; (*Inform*) sort; (*Postes: action*) sorting;
(*: bureau*) sorting office
triangle [tʀijɑ̃gl(ə)] *nm* triangle; **~ isocèle/
équilatéral** isosceles/equilateral triangle; **~
rectangle** right-angled triangle
triangulaire [tʀijɑ̃gylɛʀ] *adj* triangular
tribord [tʀibɔʀ] *nm*: **à ~** to starboard, on the
starboard side
tribu [tʀiby] *nf* tribe
tribunal, -aux [tʀibynal, -o] *nm* (*Jur*) court; (*Mil*)
tribunal; **~ de police/pour enfants** police/
juvenile court; **~ d'instance (TI)** ≈ magistrates'
court (*Brit*), ≈ district court (*US*); **~ de grande
instance (TGI)** ≈ High Court (*Brit*), ≈ Supreme
Court (*US*)
tribune [tʀibyn] *nf* (*estrade*) platform, rostrum;
(*débat*) forum; (*d'église, de tribunal*) gallery; (*de
stade*) stand; **~ libre** (*Presse*) opinion column
tribut [tʀiby] *nm* tribute
tributaire [tʀibytɛʀ] *adj*: **être ~ de** to be
dependent on; (*Géo*) to be a tributary of
tricher [tʀiʃe] *vi* to cheat
tricheur, -euse [tʀiʃœʀ, -øz] *nm/f* cheat
tricolore [tʀikɔlɔʀ] *adj* three-coloured (*Brit*),
three-colored (*US*); (*français: drapeau*) red, white
and blue; (*: équipe etc*) French
tricot [tʀiko] *nm* (*technique, ouvrage*) knitting *no pl*;
(*tissu*) knitted fabric; (*vêtement*) jersey, sweater; **~
de corps** vest (*Brit*), undershirt (*US*)
tricoter [tʀikɔte] *vt* to knit; **machine/aiguille à
~** knitting machine/needle (*Brit*) *ou* pin (*US*)
trictrac [tʀiktʀak] *nm* backgammon
tricycle [tʀisikl(ə)] *nm* tricycle
triennal, e, -aux [tʀiɛnal, -o] *adj* (*prix, foire,
élection*) three-yearly; (*charge, mandat, plan*) three-
year
trier [tʀije] *vt* (*classer*) to sort (out); (*choisir*) to
select; (*visiteurs*) to screen; (*Postes, Inform*) to sort
trimestre [tʀimɛstʀ(ə)] *nm* (*Scol*) term; (*Comm*)
quarter
trimestriel, le [tʀimɛstʀijɛl] *adj* quarterly; (*Scol*)
end-of-term
tringle [tʀɛ̃gl(ə)] *nf* rod
trinquer [tʀɛ̃ke] *vi* to clink glasses; (*fam*) to cop
it; **~ à qch/la santé de qn** to drink to sth/sb
triomphe [tʀijɔ̃f] *nm* triumph; **être reçu/porté
en ~** to be given a triumphant welcome/be

carried shoulder-high in triumph
triompher [tʀijɔ̃fe] *vi* to triumph; **~ de** to
triumph over, overcome
tripes [tʀip] *nfpl* (*Culin*) tripe *nsg*; (*fam*) guts
triple [tʀipl(ə)] *adj* (*à trois éléments*) triple; (*trois
fois plus grand*) treble ▷ *nm*: **le ~ (de)** (*comparaison*)
three times as much (as); **en ~ exemplaire** in
triplicate; **~ saut** (*Sport*) triple jump
tripler [tʀiple] *vi, vt* to triple, treble, increase
threefold
triplés, -ées [tʀiple] *nm/fpl* triplets
tripoter [tʀipɔte] *vt* to fiddle with, finger ▷ *vi*
(*fam*) to rummage about
triste [tʀist(ə)] *adj* sad; (*péj*): **~ personnage/
affaire** sorry individual/affair; **c'est pas ~!** (*fam*)
it's something else!
tristesse [tʀistɛs] *nf* sadness
trivial, e, -aux [tʀivjal, -o] *adj* coarse, crude;
(*commun*) mundane
troc [tʀɔk] *nm* (*Écon*) barter; (*transaction*)
exchange, swap
troène [tʀɔɛn] *nm* privet
trognon [tʀɔɲɔ̃] *nm* (*de fruit*) core; (*de légume*) stalk
trois [tʀwɑ] *num* three
troisième [tʀwazjɛm] *num* third; **le ~ âge** the
years of retirement
trois quarts [tʀwakaʀ] *nmpl*: **les ~ de** three-
quarters of
trombe [tʀɔ̃b] *nf* waterspout; **des ~s d'eau** a
downpour; **en ~** (*arriver, passer*) like a whirlwind
trombone [tʀɔ̃bɔn] *nm* (*Mus*) trombone; (*de
bureau*) paper clip; **~ à coulisse** slide trombone
trompe [tʀɔ̃p] *nf* (*d'éléphant*) trunk; (*Mus*)
trumpet, horn; **~ d'Eustache** Eustachian tube;
~s utérines Fallopian tubes
tromper [tʀɔ̃pe] *vt* to deceive; (*fig: espoir, attente*)
to disappoint; (*vigilance, poursuivants*) to elude; **se
tromper** *vi* to make a mistake, be mistaken; **se
tromper de voiture/jour** to take the wrong car/
get the day wrong; **se ~ de 3 cm/20 euros** to be
out by 3 cm/20 euros
tromperie [tʀɔ̃pʀi] *nf* deception, trickery *no pl*
trompette [tʀɔ̃pɛt] *nf* trumpet; **en ~** (*nez*)
turned-up
trompeur, -euse [tʀɔ̃pœʀ, -øz] *adj* deceptive,
misleading
tronc [tʀɔ̃] *nm* (*Bot, Anat*) trunk; (*d'église*)
collection box; **~ d'arbre** tree trunk; **~ commun**
(*Scol*) common-core syllabus; **~ de cône**
truncated cone
tronçon [tʀɔ̃sɔ̃] *nm* section
tronçonner [tʀɔ̃sɔne] *vt* (*arbre*) to saw up; (*pierre*)
to cut up
trône [tʀon] *nm* throne; **monter sur le ~** to
ascend the throne
trop [tʀo] *adv* too; (*avec verbe*) too much; (*aussi:
trop nombreux) too many; (*aussi:* **trop souvent**)
too often; **~ peu (nombreux)** too few; **~
longtemps** (for) too long; **~ de** (*nombre*) too
many; (*quantité*) too much; **de ~, en ~**: **des livres
en trop** a few books too many, a few extra books;
du lait en ~ too much milk; **trois livres/cinq**

euros de ~ three books too many/five euros too much

tropical, e, -aux [tʀɔpikal, -o] *adj* tropical

tropique [tʀɔpik] *nm* tropic; **tropiques** *nmpl* tropics; **~ du Cancer/Capricorne** Tropic of Cancer/Capricorn

trop-plein [tʀɔplɛ̃] *nm* (*tuyau*) overflow *ou* outlet (pipe); (*liquide*) overflow

troquer [tʀɔke] *vt*: **~ qch contre** to barter *ou* trade sth for; (*fig*) to swap sth for

trot [tʀo] *nm* trot; **aller au ~** to trot along; **partir au ~** to set off at a trot

trotter [tʀɔte] *vi* to trot; (*fig*) to scamper along (*ou* about)

trotteuse [tʀɔtøz] *nf* (*de montre*) second hand

trottinette [tʀɔtinɛt] *nf* (child's) scooter

trottoir [tʀɔtwaʀ] *nm* pavement (*Brit*), sidewalk (*US*); **faire le ~** (*péj*) to walk the streets; **~ roulant** moving pavement (*Brit*) *ou* walkway

trou [tʀu] *nm* hole; (*fig*) gap; (*Comm*) deficit; **~ d'aération** (air) vent; **~ d'air** air pocket; **~ de mémoire** blank, lapse of memory; **~ noir** black hole; **~ de la serrure** keyhole

troublant, e [tʀublɑ̃, -ɑ̃t] *adj* disturbing

trouble [tʀubl(ə)] *adj* (*liquide*) cloudy; (*image, mémoire*) indistinct, hazy; (*affaire*) shady, murky ▷ *adv* indistinctly ▷ *nm* (*désarroi*) distress, agitation; (*émoi sensuel*) turmoil, agitation; (*embarras*) confusion; (*zizanie*) unrest, discord; **troubles** *nmpl* (*Pol*) disturbances, troubles, unrest *nsg*; (*Méd*) trouble *nsg*, disorders; **~s de la personnalité** personality problems; **~s de la vision** eye trouble

trouble-fête [tʀubləfɛt] *nm/f inv* spoilsport

troubler [tʀuble] *vt* (*embarrasser*) to confuse, disconcert; (*émouvoir*) to agitate; to disturb; to perturb; (*perturber: ordre etc*) to disrupt, disturb; (*liquide*) to make cloudy; **se troubler** *vi* (*personne*) to become flustered *ou* confused; **~ l'ordre public** to cause a breach of the peace

trouer [tʀue] *vt* to make a hole (*ou* holes) in; (*fig*) to pierce

trouille [tʀuj] *nf* (*fam*): **avoir la ~** to be scared stiff, be scared out of one's wits

troupe [tʀup] *nf* (*Mil*) troop; (*groupe*) troop, group; **la ~** (*Mil: l'armée*) the army; (*: les simples soldats*) the troops *pl*; **~ (de théâtre)** (theatrical) company; **~s de choc** shock troops

troupeau, x [tʀupo] *nm* (*de moutons*) flock; (*de vaches*) herd

trousse [tʀus] *nf* case, kit; (*d'écolier*) pencil case; (*de docteur*) instrument case; **aux ~s de** (*fig*) on the heels *ou* tail of; **~ à outils** toolkit; **~ de toilette** toilet *ou* sponge (*Brit*) bag

trousseau, x [tʀuso] *nm* (*de mariée*) trousseau; **~ de clefs** bunch of keys

trouvaille [tʀuvaj] *nf* find; (*fig: idée, expression etc*) brainwave

trouver [tʀuve] *vt* to find; (*rendre visite*): **aller/venir ~ qn** to go/come and see sb; **je trouve que** I find *ou* think that; **~ à boire/critiquer** to find something to drink/criticize; **~ asile/refuge**

to find refuge/shelter; **se trouver** *vi* (*être*) to be; (*être soudain*) to find o.s.; **se ~ être/avoir** to happen to be/have; **il se trouve que** it happens that, it turns out that; **se ~ bien** to feel well; **se ~ mal** to pass out

truand [tʀyɑ̃] *nm* villain, crook

truander [tʀyɑ̃de] *vi* (*fam*) to cheat, do

truc [tʀyk] *nm* (*astuce*) way, device; (*de cinéma, prestidigitateur*) trick effect; (*chose*) thing; (*machin*) thingumajig, whatsit (*Brit*); **avoir le ~** to have the knack; **c'est pas son** (*ou* **mon** *etc*) **~** (*fam*) it's not really his (*ou* my *etc*) thing

truelle [tʀyɛl] *nf* trowel

truffe [tʀyf] *nf* truffle; (*nez*) nose

truffé, e [tʀyfe] *adj*: **~ de** (*fig*) peppered with; (*fautes*) riddled with; (*pièges*) bristling with

truie [tʀɥi] *nf* sow

truite [tʀɥit] *nf* trout *inv*

truquage [tʀykaʒ] *nm* fixing; (*Ciné*) special effects *pl*

truquer [tʀyke] *vt* (*élections, serrure, dés*) to fix; (*Ciné*) to use special effects in

TSVP *abr* (= *tournez s'il vous plaît*) PTO

TTC *abr* = **toutes taxes comprises**

tu¹ [ty] *pron* you ▷ *nm*: **employer le tu** to use the "tu" form

tu², e [ty] *pp de* **taire**

tuba [tyba] *nm* (*Mus*) tuba; (*Sport*) snorkel

tube [tyb] *nm* tube; (*de canalisation, métallique etc*) pipe; (*chanson, disque*) hit song *ou* record; **~ digestif** alimentary canal, digestive tract; **~ à essai** test tube

tuberculose [tybɛʀkyloz] *nf* tuberculosis, TB

tuer [tɥe] *vt* to kill; **se tuer** (*se suicider*) to kill o.s.; (*dans un accident*) to be killed; **se ~ au travail** (*fig*) to work o.s. to death

tuerie [tyʀi] *nf* slaughter *no pl*, massacre

tue-tête [tytɛt]: **à ~** *adv* at the top of one's voice

tueur [tɥœʀ] *nm* killer; **~ à gages** hired killer

tuile [tɥil] *nf* tile; (*fam*) spot of bad luck, blow

tulipe [tylip] *nf* tulip

tuméfié, e [tymefje] *adj* puffy, swollen

tumeur [tymœʀ] *nf* growth, tumour (*Brit*), tumor (*US*)

tumulte [tymylt(ə)] *nm* commotion, hubbub

tumultueux, -euse [tymyltɥø, -øz] *adj* stormy, turbulent

tunique [tynik] *nf* tunic; (*de femme*) smock, tunic

Tunisie [tynizi] *nf*: **la ~** Tunisia

tunisien, ne [tynizjɛ̃, -ɛn] *adj* Tunisian ▷ *nm/f*: **T~, ne** Tunisian

tunnel [tynɛl] *nm* tunnel; **le ~ sous la Manche** the Channel Tunnel, the Chunnel

turbulences [tyʀbylɑ̃s] *nfpl* (*Aviat*) turbulence *sg*

turbulent, e [tyʀbylɑ̃, -ɑ̃t] *adj* boisterous, unruly

turc, turque [tyʀk(ə)] *adj* Turkish; (*w.-c.*) seatless ▷ *nm* (*Ling*) Turkish ▷ *nm/f*: **T~, Turque** Turk/Turkish woman; **à la turque** *adv* (*assis*) cross-legged

turf [tyʀf] *nm* racing

turfiste [tyʀfist(ə)] *nm/f* racegoer

Turquie [tyʀki] *nf*: **la ~** Turkey

turquoise [tyʀkwaz] *nf, adj inv* turquoise

tus *etc* [ty] *vb voir* **taire**

tutelle [tytɛl] *nf* (*Jur*) guardianship; (*Pol*) trusteeship; **sous la ~ de** (*fig*) under the supervision of

tuteur, -trice [tytœʀ, -tʀis] *nm/f* (*Jur*) guardian; (*de plante*) stake, support

tutoyer [tytwaje] *vt*: **~ qn** to address sb as "tu"

tuyau, x [tɥijo] *nm* pipe; (*flexible*) tube; (*fam: conseil*) tip; (: *mise au courant*) gen *no pl*; **~ d'arrosage** hosepipe; **~ d'échappement** exhaust pipe; **~ d'incendie** fire hose

tuyauterie [tɥijotʀi] *nf* piping *no pl*

TVA *sigle f* = **taxe à** *ou sur la valeur ajoutée*

tympan [tɛ̃pɑ̃] *nm* (*Anat*) eardrum

type [tip] *nm* type; (*personne, chose: représentant*) classic example, epitome; (*fam*) chap, guy ▷ *adj* typical, standard; **avoir le ~ nordique** to be Nordic-looking

typé, e [tipe] *adj* ethnic (*euph*)

typique [tipik] *adj* typical

tyran [tiʀɑ̃] *nm* tyrant

tyrannique [tiʀanik] *adj* tyrannical

tzigane [dzigan] *adj* gipsy, tzigane ▷ *nm/f* (Hungarian) gipsy, Tzigane

Uu

UEM *sigle f* (= *Union économique et monétaire*) EMU
ulcère [ylsɛʀ] *nm* ulcer; **~ à l'estomac** stomach ulcer
ulcérer [ylseʀe] *vt* (*Méd*) to ulcerate; (*fig*) to sicken, appal
ultérieur, e [ylteʀjœʀ] *adj* later, subsequent; **remis à une date ~e** postponed to a later date
ultérieurement [ylteʀjœʀmɑ̃] *adv* later
ultime [yltim] *adj* final
UMP *sigle f* (= *Union pour un mouvement populaire*) *political party*
un, une [œ̃, yn] *art indéf* a; (*devant voyelle*) an; **un garçon/vieillard** a boy/an old man; **une fille** a girl
▷ *pron* one; **l'un des meilleurs** one of the best; **l'un ..., l'autre** (the) one ..., the other; **les uns ..., les autres** some ..., others; **l'un et l'autre** both (of them); **l'un ou l'autre** either (of them); **l'un l'autre, les uns les autres** each other, one another; **pas un seul** not a single one; **un par un** one by one
▷ *num* one; **une pomme seulement** one apple only
▷ *nf*: **la une** (*Presse*) the front page
unanime [ynanim] *adj* unanimous; **ils sont ~s (à penser que)** they are unanimous (in thinking that)
unanimité [ynanimite] *nf* unanimity; **à l'~** unanimously; **faire l'~** to be approved unanimously
uni, e [yni] *adj* (*ton, tissu*) plain; (*surface*) smooth, even; (*famille*) close(-knit); (*pays*) united
unifier [ynifje] *vt* to unite, unify; (*systèmes*) to standardize, unify; **s'unifier** *vi* to become united
uniforme [ynifɔʀm(ə)] *adj* (*mouvement*) regular, uniform; (*surface, ton*) even; (*objets, maisons*) uniform; (*fig: vie, conduite*) unchanging ▷ *nm* uniform; **être sous l'~** (*Mil*) to be serving
uniformiser [ynifɔʀmize] *vt* to make uniform; (*systèmes*) to standardize
union [ynjɔ̃] *nf* union; **~ conjugale** union of marriage; **~ de consommateurs** consumers' association; **~ libre** free love; **l'U~ des Républiques socialistes soviétiques (URSS)** the Union of Soviet Socialist Republics (USSR); **l'U~ soviétique** the Soviet Union

unique [ynik] *adj* (*seul*) only; (*le même*): **un prix/système** ~ a single price/system; (*exceptionnel*) unique; **ménage à salaire** ~ one-salary family; **route à voie** ~ single-lane road; **fils/fille** ~ only son/daughter, only child; **~ en France** the only one of its kind in France
uniquement [ynikmɑ̃] *adv* only, solely; (*juste*) only, merely
unir [yniʀ] *vt* (*nations*) to unite; (*éléments, couleurs*) to combine; (*en mariage*) to unite, join together; **~ qch à** to unite sth with; to combine sth with; **s'unir** *vi* to unite; (*en mariage*) to be joined together; **s'~ à** *ou* **avec** to unite with
unitaire [yniteʀ] *adj* unitary; (*Pol*) unitarian; **prix** ~ unit price
unité [ynite] *nf* (*harmonie, cohésion*) unity; (*Comm, Mil, de mesure, Math*) unit; **~ centrale** central processing unit; **~ de valeur** (*university*) course, credit
univers [ynivɛʀ] *nm* universe
universel, le [ynivɛʀsɛl] *adj* universal; (*esprit*) all-embracing
universitaire [ynivɛʀsiteʀ] *adj* university *cpd*; (*diplôme, études*) academic, university *cpd* ▷ *nm/f* academic
université [ynivɛʀsite] *nf* university
urbain, e [yʀbɛ̃, -ɛn] *adj* urban, city *cpd*, town *cpd*; (*poli*) urbane
urbanisme [yʀbanism(ə)] *nm* town planning
urgence [yʀʒɑ̃s] *nf* urgency; (*Méd etc*) emergency; **d'~** *adj* emergency *cpd* ▷ *adv* as a matter of urgency; **en cas d'~** in case of emergency; **service des ~s** emergency service
urgent, e [yʀʒɑ̃, -ɑ̃t] *adj* urgent
urine [yʀin] *nf* urine
urinoir [yʀinwaʀ] *nm* (public) urinal
urne [yʀn(ə)] *nf* (*électorale*) ballot box; (*vase*) urn; **aller aux ~s** (*voter*) to go to the polls
urticaire [yʀtikɛʀ] *nf* nettle rash, urticaria
us [ys] *nmpl*: **us et coutumes** (habits and) customs
USA *sigle mpl* (= *United States of America*) USA
usage [yzaʒ] *nm* (*emploi, utilisation*) use; (*coutume*) custom; (*éducation*) (good) manners *pl*, (good) breeding; (*Ling*): **l'~** usage; **faire ~ de** (*pouvoir, droit*) to exercise; **avoir l'~ de** to have the use of; **à l'~** *adv* with use; **à l'~ de** (*pour*) for (use of); **en**

~ in use; **hors d'~** out of service; **à ~ interne** to be taken; **à ~ externe** for external use only

usagé, e [yzaʒe] *adj* (*usé*) worn; (*d'occasion*) used

usager, -ère [yzaʒe, -ɛʀ] *nm/f* user

usé, e [yze] *adj* worn (down *ou* out *ou* away); ruined; (*banal*) hackneyed

user [yze] *vt* (*outil*) to wear down; (*vêtement*) to wear out; (*matière*) to wear away; (*consommer: charbon etc*) to use; (*fig: santé*) to ruin; (: *personne*) to wear out; **s'user** *vi* to wear; to wear out; (*fig*) to decline; **s'~ à la tâche** to wear o.s. out with work; **~ de** *vt* (*moyen, procédé*) to use, employ; (*droit*) to exercise

usine [yzin] *nf* factory; **~ atomique** nuclear power plant; **~ à gaz** gasworks *sg*; **~ marémotrice** tidal power station

usité, e [yzite] *adj* in common use, common; **peu ~** rarely used

ustensile [ystɑ̃sil] *nm* implement; **~ de cuisine** kitchen utensil

usuel, le [yzɥɛl] *adj* everyday, common

usure [yzyʀ] *nf* wear; worn state; (*de l'usurier*) usury; **avoir qn à l'~** to wear sb down; **~ normale** fair wear and tear

utérus [yteʀys] *nm* uterus, womb

utile [ytil] *adj* useful; **~ à qn/qch** of use to sb/sth

utilisation [ytilizɑsjɔ̃] *nf* use

utiliser [ytilize] *vt* to use

utilitaire [ytilitɛʀ] *adj* utilitarian; (*objets*) practical ▷ *nm* (*Inform*) utility

utilité [ytilite] *nf* usefulness *no pl*; use; **jouer les ~s** (*Théât*) to play bit parts; **reconnu d'~ publique** state-approved; **c'est d'une grande ~** it's extremely useful; **il n'y a aucune ~ à ...** there's no use in ...

utopie [ytɔpi] *nf* (*idée, conception*) utopian idea *ou* view; (*société etc idéale*) utopia

Vv

va [va] *vb voir* **aller**

vacance [vakɑ̃s] *nf* (*Admin*) vacancy; **vacances**
nfpl holiday(s) *pl* (*Brit*), vacation *sg* (*US*); **les
grandes ~s** the summer holidays *ou* vacation;
prendre des/ses ~s to take a holiday *ou*
vacation/one's holiday(s) *ou* vacation; **aller en
~s** to go on holiday *ou* vacation

vacancier, -ière [vakɑ̃sje, -jɛʀ] *nm/f*
holidaymaker (*Brit*), vacationer (*US*)

vacant, e [vakɑ̃, -ɑ̃t] *adj* vacant

vacarme [vakaʀm(ə)] *nm* row, din

vaccin [vaksɛ̃] *nm* vaccine; (*opération*) vaccination

vaccination [vaksinasjɔ̃] *nf* vaccination

vacciner [vaksine] *vt* to vaccinate; (*fig*) to make
immune; **être vacciné** (*fig*) to be immune

vache [vaʃ] *nf* (*Zool*) cow; (*cuir*) cowhide ▷ *adj*
(*fam*) rotten, mean; **~ à eau** (canvas) water bag;
(manger de la) ~ enragée (to go through) hard
times; **~ à lait** (*péj*) mug, sucker; **~ laitière** dairy
cow; **période des ~s maigres** lean times *pl*, lean
period

vachement [vaʃmɑ̃] *adv* (*fam*) damned, really

vacherie [vaʃʀi] *nf* (*fam*) meanness *no pl*; (*action*)
dirty trick; (*propos*) nasty remark

vaciller [vasije] *vi* to sway, wobble; (*bougie,
lumière*) to flicker; (*fig*) to be failing, falter; **~ dans
ses réponses** to falter in one's replies; **~ dans
ses résolutions** to waver in one's resolutions

va-et-vient [vaevjɛ̃] *nm inv* (*de pièce mobile*) to and
fro (*ou* up and down) movement; (*de personnes,
véhicules*) comings and goings *pl*, to-ings and fro-
ings *pl*; (*Élec*) two-way switch

vagabond, e [vagabɔ̃, -ɔ̃d] *adj* wandering;
(*imagination*) roaming, roving ▷ *nm* (*rôdeur*)
tramp, vagrant; (*voyageur*) wanderer

vagabonder [vagabɔ̃de] *vi* to roam, wander

vagin [vaʒɛ̃] *nm* vagina

vague [vag] *nf* wave ▷ *adj* vague; (*regard*)
faraway; (*manteau, robe*) loose(-fitting);
(*quelconque*): **un ~ bureau/cousin** some office/
cousin or other ▷ *nm*: **être dans le ~** to be rather
in the dark; **rester dans le ~** to keep things
rather vague; **regarder dans le ~** to gaze into
space; **~ à l'âme** *nm* vague melancholy; **~
d'assaut** *nf* (*Mil*) wave of assault; **~ de chaleur**
nf heatwave; **~ de fond** *nf* ground swell; **~ de
froid** *nf* cold spell

vaillant, e [vajɑ̃, -ɑ̃t] *adj* (*courageux*) brave,
gallant; (*robuste*) vigorous, hale and hearty;
n'avoir plus un sou ~ to be penniless

vaille [vaj] *vb voir* **valoir**

vain, e [vɛ̃, vɛn] *adj* vain; **en ~** *adv* in vain

vaincre [vɛ̃kʀ(ə)] *vt* to defeat; (*fig*) to conquer,
overcome

vaincu, e [vɛ̃ky] *pp de* **vaincre** ▷ *nm/f* defeated
party

vainqueur [vɛ̃kœʀ] *nm* victor; (*Sport*) winner
▷ *adj m* victorious

vais [vɛ] *vb voir* **aller**

vaisseau, x [vɛso] *nm* (*Anat*) vessel; (*Navig*) ship,
vessel; **~ spatial** spaceship

vaisselier [vɛsəlje] *nm* dresser

vaisselle [vɛsɛl] *nf* (*service*) crockery; (*plats etc
à laver*) (dirty) dishes *pl*; **faire la ~** to do the
washing-up (*Brit*) *ou* the dishes

val [val] (*pl* **vaux** *ou* **-s**) *nm* valley

valable [valabl(ə)] *adj* valid; (*acceptable*) decent,
worthwhile

valent *etc* [val] *vb voir* **valoir**

valet [valɛ] *nm* valet; (*péj*) lackey; (*Cartes*) jack,
knave (*Brit*); **~ de chambre** manservant, valet; **~
de ferme** farmhand; **~ de pied** footman

valeur [valœʀ] *nf* (*gén*) value; (*mérite*) worth,
merit; (*Comm: titre*) security; **mettre en ~**
(*bien*) to exploit; (*terrain, région*) to develop; (*fig*)
to highlight; to show off to advantage; **avoir
de la ~** to be valuable; **prendre de la ~** to
go up *ou* gain in value; **sans ~** worthless; **~
absolue** absolute value; **~ d'échange** exchange
value; **~ nominale** face value; **~s mobilières**
transferable securities

valide [valid] *adj* (*en bonne santé*) fit, well;
(*indemne*) able-bodied, fit; (*valable*) valid

valider [valide] *vt* to validate

valions *etc* [valjɔ̃] *vb voir* **valoir**

valise [valiz] *nf* (suit)case; **faire sa ~** to pack
one's (suit)case; **la ~ (diplomatique)** the
diplomatic bag

vallée [vale] *nf* valley

vallon [valɔ̃] *nm* small valley

vallonné, e [valɔne] *adj* undulating

valoir [valwaʀ] *vi* (*être valable*) to hold, apply ▷ *vt*
(*prix, valeur, effort*) to be worth; (*causer*): **~ qch à qn**
to earn sb sth; **se valoir** to be of equal merit; (*péj*)

to be two of a kind; **faire ~** (*droits, prérogatives*) to assert; (*domaine, capitaux*) to exploit; **faire ~ que** to point out that; **se faire ~** to make the most of o.s.; **à ~** on account; **à ~ sur** to be deducted from; **vaille que vaille** somehow or other; **cela ne me dit rien qui vaille** I don't like the look of it at all; **ce climat ne me vaut rien** this climate doesn't suit me; **la peine** to be worth the trouble, be worth it; **~ mieux: il vaut mieux se taire** it's better to say nothing; **il vaut mieux que je fasse/comme ceci** it's better if I do/like this; **ça ne vaut rien** it's worthless; **que vaut ce candidat?** how good is this applicant?

valse [vals(ə)] *nf* waltz; **c'est la ~ des étiquettes** the prices don't stay the same from one moment to the next

valu, e [valy] *pp de* **valoir**

vandalisme [vɑ̃dalism(ə)] *nm* vandalism

vanille [vanij] *nf* vanilla; **glace à la ~** vanilla ice cream

vanité [vanite] *nf* vanity

vaniteux, -euse [vanitø, -øz] *adj* vain, conceited

vanne [van] *nf* gate; (*fam: remarque*) dig, (nasty) crack; **lancer une ~ à qn** to have a go at sb (*Brit*), knock sb

vannerie [vanʀi] *nf* basketwork

vantard, e [vɑ̃taʀ, -aʀd(ə)] *adj* boastful

vanter [vɑ̃te] *vt* to speak highly of, vaunt; **se vanter** *vi* to boast, brag; **se ~ de** to pride o.s. on; (*péj*) to boast of

vapeur [vapœʀ] *nf* steam; (*émanation*) vapour (*Brit*), vapor (*US*), fumes *pl*; (*brouillard, buée*) haze; **vapeurs** *nfpl* (*bouffées*) vapours, vapors; **à ~** steam-powered, steam *cpd*; **à toute ~** full steam ahead; (*fig*) at full tilt; **renverser la ~** to reverse engines; (*fig*) to backtrack, backpedal; **cuit à la ~ steamed**

vaporeux, -euse [vapɔʀø, -øz] *adj* (*flou*) hazy, misty; (*léger*) filmy, gossamer *cpd*

vaporisateur [vapɔʀizatœʀ] *nm* spray

vaporiser [vapɔʀize] *vt* (*Chimie*) to vaporize; (*parfum etc*) to spray

varappe [vaʀap] *nf* rock climbing

vareuse [vaʀøz] *nf* (*blouson*) pea jacket; (*d'uniforme*) tunic

variable [vaʀjabl(ə)] *adj* variable; (*temps, humeur*) changeable; (*Tech: à plusieurs positions etc*) adaptable; (*Ling*) inflectional; (*divers: résultats*) varied, various ▷ *nf* (*Inform, Math*) variable

varice [vaʀis] *nf* varicose vein

varicelle [vaʀisɛl] *nf* chickenpox

varié, e [vaʀje] *adj* varied; (*divers*) various; **hors-d'œuvre ~s** selection of hors d'œuvres

varier [vaʀje] *vi* to vary; (*temps, humeur*) to change ▷ *vt* to vary

variété [vaʀjete] *nf* variety; **spectacle de ~s** variety show

variole [vaʀjɔl] *nf* smallpox

vas [va] *vb voir* **aller**; **~-y!** [vazi] go on!

vase [vaz] *nm* vase ▷ *nf* silt, mud; **en ~ clos** in isolation; **~ de nuit** chamberpot; **~s communicants** communicating vessels

vaseux, -euse [vazø, -øz] *adj* silty, muddy; (*fig: confus*) woolly, hazy; (: *fatigué*) peaky; (: *étourdi*) woozy

vasistas [vazistas] *nm* fanlight

vaste [vast(ə)] *adj* vast, immense

vaudrai *etc* [vodʀe] *vb voir* **valoir**

vaurien, ne [voʀjɛ̃, -ɛn] *nm/f* good-for-nothing, guttersnipe

vaut [vo] *vb voir* **valoir**

vautour [votuʀ] *nm* vulture

vautrer [votʀe]: **se vautrer** *vi*: **se ~ dans** to wallow in; **se ~ sur** to sprawl on

vaux [vo] *pl de* **val** ▷ *vb voir* **valoir**

va-vite [vavit]: **à la ~** *adv* in a rush

VDQS *sigle m* (= *vin délimité de qualité supérieure*) *label guaranteeing quality of wine*

veau, x [vo] *nm* (*Zool*) calf; (*Culin*) veal; (*peau*) calfskin; **tuer le ~ gras** to kill the fatted calf

vécu, e [veky] *pp de* **vivre** ▷ *adj* real(-life)

vedette [vədɛt] *nf* (*artiste etc*) star; (*canot*) patrol boat; launch; **avoir la ~** to top the bill, get star billing; **mettre qn en ~** (*Ciné etc*) to give sb the starring role; (*fig*) to push sb into the limelight; **voler la ~ à qn** to steal the show from sb

végétal, e, -aux [veʒetal, -o] *adj* vegetable ▷ *nm* vegetable, plant

végétalien, ne [veʒetaljɛ̃, -ɛn] *adj, nm/f* vegan

végétarien, ne [veʒetaʀjɛ̃, -ɛn] *adj, nm/f* vegetarian

végétation [veʒetasjɔ̃] *nf* vegetation; **végétations** *nfpl* (*Méd*) adenoids

véhicule [veikyl] *nm* vehicle; **~ utilitaire** commercial vehicle

veille [vɛj] *nf* (*garde*) watch; (*Psych*) wakefulness; (*jour*): **la ~** the day before, the previous day; **la ~ au soir** the previous evening; **la ~ de** the day before; **à la ~ de** on the eve of; **l'état de ~** the waking state

veillée [veje] *nf* (*soirée*) evening; (*réunion*) evening gathering; **~ d'armes** night before combat; (*fig*) vigil; **~ (mortuaire)** watch

veiller [veje] *vi* (*rester debout*) to stay *ou* sit up; (*ne pas dormir*) to be awake; (*être de garde*) to be on watch; (*être vigilant*) to be watchful ▷ *vt* (*malade, mort*) to watch over, sit up with; **~ à** *vt* to attend to, see to; **~ à ce que** to make sure that, see to it that; **~ sur** *vt* to keep a watch *ou* an eye on

veilleur [vɛjœʀ] *nm*: **~ de nuit** night watchman

veilleuse [vɛjøz] *nf* (*lampe*) night light; (*Auto*) sidelight; (*flamme*) pilot light; **en ~** *adj* (*lampe*) dimmed; (*fig: affaire*) shelved, set aside

veinard, e [venaʀ, -aʀd(ə)] *nm/f* (*fam*) lucky devil

veine [vɛn] *nf* (*Anat, du bois etc*) vein; (*filon*) vein, seam; (*fam: chance*): **avoir de la ~** to be lucky; (*inspiration*) inspiration

véliplanchiste [veliplɑ̃ʃist(ə)] *nm/f* windsurfer

vélo [velo] *nm* bike, cycle; **faire du ~** to go cycling

vélomoteur [velomotœʀ] *nm* moped

velours [vəluʀ] *nm* velvet; **~ côtelé** corduroy

velouté, e [vəlute] *adj* (*au toucher*) velvety; (*à la vue*) soft, mellow; (*au goût*) smooth, mellow ▷ *nm*: **~ d'asperges/de tomates** cream of asparagus/

tomato soup

velu, e [vəly] *adj* hairy

venais *etc* [vənɛ] *vb voir* **venir**

venaison [vənɛzɔ̃] *nf* venison

vendange [vɑ̃dɑ̃ʒ] *nf* (*opération, période: aussi:* **vendanges**) grape harvest; (*raisins*) grape crop, grapes *pl*

vendanger [vɑ̃dɑ̃ʒe] *vi* to harvest the grapes

vendeur, -euse [vɑ̃dœʀ, -øz] *nm/f* (*de magasin*) shop *ou* sales assistant (*Brit*), sales clerk (*US*); (*Comm*) salesman/woman ▷ *nm* (*Jur*) vendor, seller; ~ **de journaux** newspaper seller

vendre [vɑ̃dʀ(ə)] *vt* to sell; ~ **qch à qn** to sell sb sth; **cela se vend à la douzaine** these are sold by the dozen; **"à ~"** "for sale"

vendredi [vɑ̃dʀədi] *nm* Friday; **V~ saint** Good Friday; *voir aussi* **lundi**

vénéneux, -euse [venenø, -øz] *adj* poisonous

vénérien, ne [venerjɛ̃, -ɛn] *adj* venereal

vengeance [vɑ̃ʒɑ̃s] *nf* vengeance *no pl*, revenge *no pl*; (*acte*) act of vengeance *ou* revenge

venger [vɑ̃ʒe] *vt* to avenge; **se venger** *vi* to avenge o.s.; (*par rancune*) to take revenge; **se ~ de qch** to avenge o.s. for sth; to take one's revenge for sth; **se ~ de qn** to take revenge on sb; **se ~ sur** to wreak vengeance upon; to take revenge on *ou* through; to take it out on

venimeux, -euse [vənimø, -øz] *adj* poisonous, venomous; (*fig: haineux*) venomous, vicious

venin [vənɛ̃] *nm* venom, poison; (*fig*) venom

venir [vəniʀ] *vi* to come; ~ **de** to come from; ~ **de faire: je viens d'y aller/de le voir** I've just been there/seen him; **s'il vient à pleuvoir** if it should rain, if it happens to rain; **en ~ à faire: j'en viens à croire que** I am coming to believe that; **où veux-tu en ~?** what are you getting at?; **il en est venu à mendier** he has been reduced to begging; **en ~ aux mains** to come to blows; **les années/générations à ~** the years/generations to come; **il me vient une idée** an idea has just occurred to me; **il me vient des soupçons** I'm beginning to be suspicious; **je te vois ~** I know what you're after; **faire ~** (*docteur, plombier*) to call (out); **d'où vient que ...?** how is it that ...?; ~ **au monde** to come into the world

vent [vɑ̃] *nm* wind; **il y a du ~** it's windy; **c'est du ~** it's all hot air; **au ~** to windward; **sous le ~** to leeward; **avoir le ~ debout/arrière** to head into the wind/have the wind astern; **dans le ~** (*fam*) trendy; **prendre le ~** (*fig*) to see which way the wind blows; **avoir ~ de** to get wind of; **contre ~s et marées** come hell or high water

vente [vɑ̃t] *nf* sale; **la ~** (*activité*) selling; (*secteur*) sales *pl*; **mettre en ~** to put on sale; (*objets personnels*) to put up for sale; ~ **de charité** jumble (*Brit*) *ou* rummage (*US*) sale; ~ **par correspondance (VPC)** mail-order selling; ~ **aux enchères** auction sale

venteux, -euse [vɑ̃tø, -øz] *adj* windswept, windy

ventilateur [vɑ̃tilatœʀ] *nm* fan

ventiler [vɑ̃tile] *vt* to ventilate; (*total, statistiques*) to break down

ventouse [vɑ̃tuz] *nf* (*ampoule*) cupping glass; (*de caoutchouc*) suction pad; (*Zool*) sucker

ventre [vɑ̃tʀ(ə)] *nm* (*Anat*) stomach; (*fig*) belly; **prendre du ~** to be getting a paunch; **avoir mal au ~** to have (a) stomach ache

ventriloque [vɑ̃tʀilɔk] *nm/f* ventriloquist

venu, e [vəny] *pp de* **venir** ▷ *adj*: **être mal ~ à** *ou* **de faire** to have no grounds for doing, be in no position to do; **mal ~** ill-timed, unwelcome; **bien ~** timely, welcome ▷ *nf* coming

ver [vɛʀ] *nm* worm; (*des fruits etc*) maggot; (*du bois*) woodworm *no pl*; ~ **blanc** May beetle grub; ~ **luisant** glow-worm; ~ **à soie** silkworm; ~ **solitaire** tapeworm; ~ **de terre** earthworm

verbaliser [vɛʀbalize] *vi* (*Police*) to book *ou* report an offender; (*Psych*) to verbalize

verbe [vɛʀb(ə)] *nm* (*Ling*) verb; (*voix*): **avoir le ~ sonore** to have a sonorous tone (of voice); (*expression*): **la magie du ~** the magic of language *ou* the word; (*Rel*): **le V~** the Word

verdâtre [vɛʀdɑtʀ(ə)] *adj* greenish

verdict [vɛʀdik(t)] *nm* verdict

verdir [vɛʀdiʀ] *vi, vt* to turn green

verdure [vɛʀdyʀ] *nf* (*arbres, feuillages*) greenery; (*légumes verts*) green vegetables *pl*, greens *pl*

véreux, -euse [verø, -øz] *adj* worm-eaten; (*malhonnête*) shady, corrupt

verge [vɛʀʒ(ə)] *nf* (*Anat*) penis; (*baguette*) stick, cane

verger [vɛʀʒe] *nm* orchard

verglacé, e [vɛʀglase] *adj* icy, iced-over

verglas [vɛʀgla] *nm* (black) ice

vergogne [vɛʀgɔɲ]: **sans ~** *adv* shamelessly

véridique [veridik] *adj* truthful

vérification [verifikasjɔ̃] *nf* checking *no pl*, check; ~ **d'identité** identity check

vérifier [verifje] *vt* to check; (*corroborer*) to confirm, bear out; **se vérifier** *vi* to be confirmed *ou* verified

véritable [veritabl(ə)] *adj* real; (*ami, amour*) true; **un ~ désastre** an absolute disaster

vérité [verite] *nf* truth; (*d'un portrait*) lifelikeness; (*sincérité*) truthfulness, sincerity; **en ~, à la ~** to tell the truth

vermeil, le [vɛʀmɛj] *adj* bright red, ruby red ▷ *nm* (*substance*) vermeil

vermine [vɛʀmin] *nf* vermin *pl*

vermoulu, e [vɛʀmuly] *adj* worm-eaten, with woodworm

verni, e [vɛʀni] *adj* varnished; glazed; (*fam*) lucky; **cuir ~** patent leather; **souliers ~s** patent (leather) shoes

vernir [vɛʀniʀ] *vt* (*bois, tableau, ongles*) to varnish; (*poterie*) to glaze

vernis [vɛʀni] *nm* (*enduit*) varnish; glaze; (*fig*) veneer; ~ **à ongles** nail varnish (*Brit*) *ou* polish

vernissage [vɛʀnisaʒ] *nm* varnishing; glazing; (*d'une exposition*) preview

vérole [verɔl] *nf* (*variole*) smallpox; (*fam: syphilis*) pox

verrai *etc* [veʀe] *vb voir* **voir**

verre [vɛʀ] *nm* glass; (*de lunettes*) lens *sg*; **verres**

nmpl (lunettes) glasses; **boire** *ou* **prendre un ~** to have a drink; **~ à vin/à liqueur** wine/liqueur glass; **~ à dents** tooth mug; **~ dépoli** frosted glass; **~ de lampe** lamp glass *ou* chimney; **~ de montre** watch glass; **~ à pied** stemmed glass; **~s de contact** contact lenses; **~s fumés** tinted lenses

verrerie [vɛʀʀi] *nf (fabrique)* glassworks *sg*; *(activité)* glass-making, glass-working; *(objets)* glassware

verrière [vɛʀjɛʀ] *nf (grand vitrage)* window; *(toit vitré)* glass roof

verrons *etc* [vɛʀɔ̃] *vb voir* **voir**

verrou [veʀu] *nm (targette)* bolt; *(fig)* constriction; **mettre le ~** to bolt the door; **mettre qn sous les ~s** to put sb behind bars

verrouillage [veʀujaʒ] *nm (dispositif)* locking mechanism; *(Auto):* **~ central** *ou* **centralisé** central locking

verrouiller [veʀuje] *vt* to bolt; to lock; *(Mil: brèche)* to close

verrue [veʀy] *nf* wart; *(plantaire)* verruca; *(fig)* eyesore

vers [vɛʀ] *nm* line ▷ *nmpl (poésie)* verse *sg* ▷ *prép (en direction de)* toward(s); *(près de)* around (about); *(temporel)* about, around

versant [vɛʀsɑ̃] *nm* slopes *pl*, side

versatile [vɛʀsatil] *adj* fickle, changeable

verse [vɛʀs(ə)]: **à ~** *adv*: **il pleut à ~** it's pouring (with rain)

Verseau [vɛʀso] *nm*: **le ~** Aquarius, the water-carrier; **être du ~** to be Aquarius

versement [vɛʀsəmɑ̃] *nm* payment; *(sur un compte)* deposit, remittance; **en trois ~s** in three instalments

verser [vɛʀse] *vt (liquide, grains)* to pour; *(larmes, sang)* to shed; *(argent)* to pay; *(soldat: affecter):* **~ qn dans** to assign sb to ▷ *vi (véhicule)* to overturn; *(fig):* **~ dans** to lapse into; **~ à un compte** to pay into an account

verset [vɛʀsɛ] *nm* verse; versicle

version [vɛʀsjɔ̃] *nf* version; *(Scol)* translation *(into the mother tongue)*; **film en ~ originale** film in the original language

verso [vɛʀso] *nm* back; **voir au ~** see over(leaf)

vert, e [vɛʀ, vɛʀt(ə)] *adj* green; *(vin)* young; *(vigoureux)* sprightly; *(cru)* forthright ▷ *nm* green; **dire des ~es (et des pas mûres)** to say some pretty spicy things; **il en a vu des ~es** he's seen a thing or two; **~ bouteille** *adj inv* bottle-green; **~ d'eau** *adj inv* sea-green; **~ pomme** *adj inv* apple-green

vertèbre [vɛʀtɛbʀ(ə)] *nf* vertebra

vertement [vɛʀtəmɑ̃] *adv (réprimander)* sharply

vertical, e, -aux [vɛʀtikal, -o] *adj, nf* vertical; **à la ~e** *adv* vertically

verticalement [vɛʀtikalmɑ̃] *adv* vertically

vertige [vɛʀtiʒ] *nm (peur du vide)* vertigo; *(étourdissement)* dizzy spell; *(fig)* fever; **ça me donne le ~** it makes me dizzy; *(fig)* it makes my head spin *ou* reel

vertigineux, -euse [vɛʀtiʒinø, -øz] *adj*

(hausse, vitesse) breathtaking; *(altitude, gorge)* breathtakingly high *(ou* deep)

vertu [vɛʀty] *nf* virtue; **une ~** a saint, a paragon of virtue; **avoir la ~ de faire** to have the virtue of doing; **en ~ de** *prép* in accordance with

vertueux, -euse [vɛʀtɥø, -øz] *adj* virtuous

verve [vɛʀv(ə)] *nf* witty eloquence; **être en ~** to be in brilliant form

verveine [vɛʀvɛn] *nf (Bot)* verbena, vervain; *(infusion)* verbena tea

vésicule [vezikyl] *nf* vesicle; **~ biliaire** gall-bladder

vessie [vesi] *nf* bladder

veste [vɛst(ə)] *nf* jacket; **~ droite/croisée** single-/double-breasted jacket; **retourner sa ~** *(fig)* to change one's colours

vestiaire [vɛstjɛʀ] *nm (au théâtre etc)* cloakroom; *(de stade etc)* changing-room *(Brit)*, locker-room *(US)*; *(métallique):* **(armoire) ~** locker

vestibule [vɛstibyl] *nm* hall

vestige [vɛstiʒ] *nm (objet)* relic; *(fragment)* trace; *(fig)* remnant, vestige; **vestiges** *nmpl (d'une ville)* remains; *(d'une civilisation, du passé)* remnants, relics

vestimentaire [vɛstimɑ̃tɛʀ] *adj (dépenses)* clothing; *(détail)* of dress; *(élégance)* sartorial

veston [vɛstɔ̃] *nm* jacket

vêtement [vɛtmɑ̃] *nm* garment, item of clothing; *(Comm):* **le ~** the clothing industry; **vêtements** *nmpl* clothes; **~s de sport** sportswear *sg*, sports clothes

vétérinaire [veteʀinɛʀ] *adj* veterinary ▷ *nm/f* vet, veterinary surgeon *(Brit)*, veterinarian *(US)*

vêtir [vetiʀ] *vt* to clothe, dress; **se vêtir** to dress (o.s.)

veto [veto] *nm* veto; **droit de ~** right of veto; **mettre** *ou* **opposer un ~ à** to veto

vêtu, e [vety] *pp de* **vêtir** ▷ *adj*: **~ de** dressed in, wearing; **chaudement ~** warmly dressed

vétuste [vetyst(ə)] *adj* ancient, timeworn

veuf, veuve [vœf, v v] *adj* widowed ▷ *nm* widower ▷ *nf* widow

veuille [vœj], **veuillez** *etc* [vœje] *vb voir* **vouloir**

veule [vøl] *adj* spineless

veuve [vœv] *adj f, nf voir* **veuf**

veux [vø] *vb voir* **vouloir**

vexant, e [vɛksɑ̃, -ɑ̃t] *adj (contrariant)* annoying; *(blessant)* upsetting

vexations [vɛksasjɔ̃] *nfpl* humiliations

vexer [vɛkse] *vt* to hurt, upset; **se vexer** *vi* to be hurt, get upset

viable [vjabl(ə)] *adj* viable

viaduc [vjadyk] *nm* viaduct

viager, -ère [vjaʒe, -ɛʀ] *adj*: **rente viagère** life annuity ▷ *nm*: **mettre en ~** to sell in return for a life annuity

viande [vjɑ̃d] *nf* meat

vibrer [vibʀe] *vi* to vibrate; *(son, voix)* to be vibrant; *(fig)* to be stirred; **faire ~** to (cause to) vibrate; to stir, thrill

vice [vis] *nm* vice; *(défaut)* fault; **~ caché** *(Comm)* latent *ou* inherent defect; **~ de forme** legal flaw *ou* irregularity

vichy [viʃi] *nm* (*toile*) gingham; (*eau*) Vichy water; **carottes V~** boiled carrots

vicié, e [visje] *adj* (*air*) polluted, tainted; (*Jur*) invalidated

vicieux, -euse [visjø, -øz] *adj* (*pervers*) dirty(-minded); (*méchant*) nasty; (*fautif*) incorrect, wrong

vicinal, e, -aux [visinal, -o] *adj*: **chemin ~** byroad, byway

victime [viktim] *nf* victim; (*d'accident*) casualty; **être (la) ~ de** to be the victim of; **être ~ d'une attaque/d'un accident** to suffer a stroke/be involved in an accident

victoire [viktwaʀ] *nf* victory

victuailles [viktɥaj] *nfpl* provisions

vidange [vidɑ̃ʒ] *nf* (*d'un fossé, réservoir*) emptying; (*Auto*) oil change; (*de lavabo: bonde*) waste outlet; **vidanges** *nfpl* (*matières*) sewage *sg*; **faire la ~** (*Auto*) to change the oil, do an oil change; **tuyau de ~** drainage pipe

vidanger [vidɑ̃ʒe] *vt* to empty; **faire ~ la voiture** to have the oil changed in one's car

vide [vid] *adj* empty ▷ *nm* (*Physique*) vacuum; (*espace*) (empty) space, gap; (*sous soi: dans une falaise etc*) drop; (*futilité, néant*) void; **~ de** empty of; (*de sens etc*) devoid of; **sous ~** *adv* in a vacuum; **emballé sous ~** vacuum-packed; **regarder dans le ~** to stare into space; **avoir peur du ~** to be afraid of heights; **parler dans le ~** to waste one's breath; **faire le ~** (*dans son esprit*) to make one's mind go blank; **faire le ~ autour de qn** to isolate sb; **à ~** *adv* (*sans occupants*) empty; (*sans charge*) unladen; (*Tech*) without gripping *ou* being in gear

vidéo [video] *nf, adj inv* video; **~ inverse** reverse video

vidéoclip [videoklip] *nm* music video

vidéoclub [videoklœb] *nm* video club

vidéoconférence *nf* videoconference

vide-ordures [vidɔʀdyʀ] *nm inv* (rubbish) chute

vidéothèque [videotɛk] *nf* video library

vide-poches [vidpɔʃ] *nm inv* tidy; (*Auto*) glove compartment

vider [vide] *vt* to empty; (*Culin: volaille, poisson*) to gut, clean out; (*régler: querelle*) to settle; (*fatiguer*) to wear out; (*fam: expulser*) to throw out, chuck out; **se vider** *vi* to empty; **~ les lieux** to quit *ou* vacate the premises

videur [vidœʀ] *nm* (*de boîte de nuit*) bouncer

vie [vi] *nf* life; **être en ~** to be alive; **sans ~** lifeless; **à ~** for life; **membre à ~** life member; **dans la ~ courante** in everyday life; **avoir la ~ dure** to have nine lives; to die hard; **mener la ~ dure à qn** to make life a misery for sb

vieil [vjɛj] *adj m voir* **vieux**

vieillard [vjɛjaʀ] *nm* old man; **les ~s** old people, the elderly

vieille [vjɛj] *adj f, nf voir* **vieux**

vieilleries [vjɛjʀi] *nfpl* old things *ou* stuff *sg*

vieillesse [vjɛjɛs] *nf* old age; (*vieillards*): **la ~** the old *pl*, the elderly *pl*

vieillir [vjejiʀ] *vi* (*prendre de l'âge*) to grow old; (*population, vin*) to age; (*doctrine, auteur*) to become dated ▷ *vt* to age; **il a beaucoup vieilli** he has aged a lot; **se vieillir** to make o.s. older

vieillissement [vjejismɑ̃] *nm* growing old; ageing

Vienne [vjɛn] *n* (*en Autriche*) Vienna

vienne [vjɛn], **viens** *etc* [vjɛ̃] *vb voir* **venir**

viens [vjɛ̃] *vb voir* **venir**

vierge [vjɛʀʒ(ə)] *adj* virgin; (*film*) blank; (*page*) clean, blank; (*jeune fille*): **être ~** to be a virgin ▷ *nf* virgin; (*signe*): **la V~** Virgo, the Virgin; **être de la V~** to be Virgo; **~ de** (*sans*) free from, unsullied by

Viêtnam, Vietnam [vjɛtnam] *nm*: **le ~** Vietnam; **le ~ du Nord/du Sud** North/South Vietnam

vietnamien, ne [vjɛtnamjɛ̃, -ɛn] *adj* Vietnamese ▷ *nm* (*Ling*) Vietnamese ▷ *nm/f*: **V~, ne** Vietnamese; **V~, ne du Nord/Sud** North/South Vietnamese

vieux, vieil, vieille [vjø, vjɛj] *adj* old ▷ *nm/f* old man/woman ▷ *nmpl*: **les ~** the old, old people; (*fam: parents*) the old folk *ou* ones; **un petit ~** a little old man; **mon ~/ma vieille** (*fam*) old man/girl; **pauvre ~** poor old soul; **prendre un coup de ~** to put years on; **se faire ~** to make o.s. look older; **un ~ de la vieille** one of the old brigade; **~ garçon** *nm* bachelor; **~ jeu** *adj inv* old-fashioned; **~ rose** *adj inv* old rose; **vieil or** *adj inv* old gold; **vieille fille** *nf* spinster

vif, vive [vif, viv] *adj* (*animé*) lively; (*alerte*) sharp, quick; (*brusque*) sharp, brusque; (*aigu*) sharp; (*lumière, couleur*) brilliant; (*air*) crisp; (*vent, émotion*) keen; (*froid*) bitter; (*fort: regret, déception*) great, deep; (*vivant*): **brûlé ~** burnt alive; **eau vive** running water; **de vive voix** personally; **piquer qn au ~** to cut sb to the quick; **tailler dans le ~** to cut into the living flesh; **à ~** (*plaie*) open; **avoir les nerfs à ~** to be on edge; **sur le ~** (*Art*) from life; **entrer dans le ~ du sujet** to get to the very heart of the matter

vigne [viɲ] *nf* (*plante*) vine; (*plantation*) vineyard; **~ vierge** Virginia creeper

vigneron [viɲʀɔ̃] *nm* wine grower

vignette [viɲɛt] *nf* (*motif*) vignette; (*de marque*) manufacturer's label *ou* seal; (*petite illustration*) (small) illustration; (*Admin*) ≈ (road) tax disc (*Brit*), ≈ license plate sticker (*US*); (: *sur médicament*) price label (*on medicines for reimbursement by Social Security*)

vignoble [viɲɔbl(ə)] *nm* (*plantation*) vineyard; (*vignes d'une région*) vineyards *pl*

vigoureux, -euse [viguʀø, -øz] *adj* vigorous, robust

vigueur [vigœʀ] *nf* vigour (*Brit*), vigor (*US*); **être/entrer en ~** to be in/come into force; **en ~** current

vil, e [vil] *adj* vile, base; **à ~ prix** at a very low price

vilain, e [vilɛ̃, -ɛn] *adj* (*laid*) ugly; (*affaire, blessure*) nasty; (*pas sage: enfant*) naughty ▷ *nm* (*paysan*) villein, villain; **ça va tourner au ~** things are going to turn nasty; **~ mot** bad word

villa [vila] *nf* (detached) house

village [vilaʒ] *nm* village; ~ **de toile** tent village; ~ **de vacances** holiday village

villageois, e [vilaʒwa, -waz] *adj* village *cpd* ▷ *nm/f* villager

ville [vil] *nf* town; (*importante*) city; (*administration*): **la** ~ ≈ the Corporation, ≈ the (town) council; **aller en** ~ to go to town; **habiter en** ~ to live in town; ~ **jumelée** twin town; ~ **nouvelle** new town

villégiature [vileʒjatyʀ] *nf* (*séjour*) holiday; (*lieu*) (holiday) resort

vin [vɛ̃] *nm* wine; **avoir le** ~ **gai/triste** to get happy/miserable after a few drinks; ~ **blanc/rosé/rouge** white/rosé/red wine; ~ **d'honneur** reception; (*with wine and snacks*); ~ **de messe** altar wine; ~ **ordinaire** *ou* **de table** table wine; ~ **de pays** local wine; *voir aussi* **AOC; VDQS**

vinaigre [vinɛgʀ(ə)] *nm* vinegar; **tourner au** ~ (*fig*) to turn sour; ~ **de vin/d'alcool** wine/spirit vinegar

vinaigrette [vinɛgʀɛt] *nf* vinaigrette, French dressing

vindicatif, -ive [vɛ̃dikatif, -iv] *adj* vindictive

vineux, -euse [vinø, -øz] *adj* win(e)y

vingt [vɛ̃, vɛ̃t] (+*voyelle following 2nd pron*) *num* twenty; ~-**quatre heures sur ~-quatre** twenty-four hours a day, round the clock

vingtaine [vɛ̃tɛn] *nf*: **une** ~ **(de)** around twenty, twenty or so

vingtième [vɛ̃tjɛm] *num* twentieth

vinicole [vinikɔl] *adj* (*production*) wine *cpd*; (*région*) wine-growing

vins *etc* [vɛ̃] *vb voir* **venir**

vinyle [vinil] *nm* vinyl

viol [vjɔl] *nm* (*d'une femme*) rape; (*d'un lieu sacré*) violation

violacé, e [vjɔlase] *adj* purplish, mauvish

violemment [vjɔlamɑ̃] *adv* violently

violence [vjɔlɑ̃s] *nf* violence; **violences** *nfpl* acts of violence; **faire** ~ **à qn** to do violence to sb; **se faire** ~ to force o.s

violent, e [vjɔlɑ̃, -ɑ̃t] *adj* violent; (*remède*) drastic; (*besoin, désir*) intense, urgent

violer [vjɔle] *vt* (*femme*) to rape; (*sépulture*) to desecrate, violate; (*loi, traité*) to violate

violet, te [vjɔlɛ, -ɛt] *adj, nm* purple, mauve ▷ *nf* (*fleur*) violet

violon [vjɔlɔ̃] *nm* violin; (*dans la musique folklorique etc*) fiddle; (*fam: prison*) lock-up; **premier** ~ first violin; ~ **d'Ingres** (artistic) hobby

violoncelle [vjɔlɔ̃sɛl] *nm* cello

violoniste [vjɔlɔnist(ə)] *nm/f* violinist, violin-player; (*folklorique etc*) fiddler

vipère [vipɛʀ] *nf* viper, adder

virage [viʀaʒ] *nm* (*d'un véhicule*) turn; (*d'une route, piste*) bend; (*Chimie*) change in colour (*Brit*) *ou* color (*US*); (*de cuti-réaction*) positive reaction; (*Photo*) toning; (*fig: Pol*) about-turn; **prendre un** ~ to go into a bend, take a bend; ~ **sans visibilité** blind bend

virée [viʀe] *nf* (*courte*) run; (: *à pied*) walk; (*longue*)

trip; hike, walking tour

virement [viʀmɑ̃] *nm* (*Comm*) transfer; ~ **bancaire** (bank) credit transfer, ≈ (bank) giro transfer (*Brit*); ~ **postal** Post office credit transfer, ≈ Girobank® transfer (*Brit*)

virent [viʀ] *vb voir* **voir**

virer [viʀe] *vt* (*Comm*): ~ **qch (sur)** to transfer sth (into); (*Photo*) to tone; (*fam: renvoyer*) to sack, boot out ▷ *vi* to turn; (*Chimie*) to change colour (*Brit*) *ou* color (*US*); (*cuti-réaction*) to come up positive; (*Photo*) to tone; ~ **au bleu** to turn blue; ~ **de bord** to tack; (*fig*) to change tack; ~ **sur l'aile** to bank

virevolter [viʀvɔlte] *vi* to twirl around

virgule [viʀgyl] *nf* comma; (*Math*) point; **quatre** ~ **deux** four point two; ~ **flottante** floating decimal

viril, e [viʀil] *adj* (*propre à l'homme*) masculine; (*énergique, courageux*) manly, virile

virtuel, le [viʀtɥɛl] *adj* potential; (*théorique*) virtual

virtuose [viʀtɥoz] *nm/f* (*Mus*) virtuoso; (*gén*) master

virus [viʀys] *nm* virus

vis *vb* [vi] *voir* **voir; vivre** ▷ *nf* [vis] screw; ~ **à tête plate/ronde** flat-headed/round-headed screw; ~ **platinées** (*Auto*) (contact) points; ~ **sans fin** worm, endless screw

visa [viza] *nm* (*sceau*) stamp; (*validation de passeport*) visa; ~ **de censure** (censor's) certificate

visage [vizaʒ] *nm* face; **à** ~ **découvert** (*franchement*) openly

vis-à-vis [vizavi] *adv* face to face ▷ *nm* person opposite; house *etc* opposite; ~ **de** *prép* opposite; (*fig*) towards, vis-à-vis; **en** ~ facing *ou* opposite each other; **sans** ~ (*immeuble*) with an open outlook

viscéral, e, -aux [viseʀal, -o] *adj* (*fig*) deep-seated, deep-rooted

visée [vize] *nf* (*avec une arme*) aiming; (*Arpentage*) sighting; **visées** *nfpl* (*intentions*) designs; **avoir des ~s sur qn/qch** to have designs on sb/sth

viser [vize] *vi* to aim ▷ *vt* to aim at; (*concerner*) to be aimed *ou* directed at; (*apposer un visa sur*) to stamp, visa; ~ **à qch/faire** to aim at sth/at doing *ou* to do

viseur [vizœʀ] *nm* (*d'arme*) sights *pl*; (*Photo*) viewfinder

visibilité [vizibilite] *nf* visibility; **sans** ~ (*pilotage, virage*) blind *cpd*

visible [vizibl(ə)] *adj* visible; (*disponible*): **est-il ~?** can he see me?, will he see visitors?

visière [vizjɛʀ] *nf* (*de casquette*) peak; (*qui s'attache*) eyeshade

vision [vizjɔ̃] *nf* vision; (*sens*) (eye)sight, vision; (*fait de voir*): **la** ~ **de** the sight of; **première** ~ (*Ciné*) first showing

visionneuse [vizjɔnøz] *nf* viewer

visite [vizit] *nf* visit; (*visiteur*) visitor; (*touristique: d'un musée etc*) tour; (*Comm: de représentant*) call; (*expertise, d'inspection*) inspection; (*médicale, à domicile*) visit, call; **la** ~ (*Méd*) medical examination; (*Mil: d'entrée*) medicals *pl*;

(: *quotidienne*) sick parade; **faire une ~ à qn** to call on sb, pay sb a visit; **rendre ~ à qn** to visit sb, pay sb a visit; **être en ~ (chez qn)** to be visiting (sb); **heures de ~** (*hôpital, prison*) visiting hours; **le droit de ~** (*Jur: aux enfants*) right of access, access; **~ de douane** customs inspection *ou* examination; **~ guidée** guided tour

visiter [vizite] *vt* to visit; (*musée, ville*) to visit, go round

visiteur, -euse [vizitœr, -øz] *nm/f* visitor; **~ des douanes** customs inspector; **~ médical** medical rep(resentative); **~ de prison** prison visitor

vison [vizɔ̃] *nm* mink

visser [vise] *vt*: **~ qch** (*fixer, serrer*) to screw sth on

visuel, le [vizɥɛl] *adj* visual

vit [vi] *vb voir* **vivre; voir**

vital, e, -aux [vital, -o] *adj* vital

vitamine [vitamin] *nf* vitamin

vite [vit] *adv* (*rapidement*) quickly, fast; (*sans délai*) quickly; soon; **faire ~** (*agir rapidement*) to act fast; (*se dépêcher*) to be quick; **ce sera ~ fini** this will soon be finished; **viens ~** come quick(ly)

vitesse [vitɛs] *nf* speed; (*Auto: dispositif*) gear; **faire de la ~** to drive fast *ou* at speed; **prendre qn de ~** to outstrip sb, get ahead of sb; **prendre de la ~** to pick up *ou* gather speed; **à toute ~** at full *ou* top speed; **en perte de ~** (*avion*) losing lift; (*fig*) losing momentum; **changer de ~** (*Auto*) to change gear; **~ acquise** momentum; **~ de croisière** cruising speed; **~ de pointe** top speed; **~ du son** speed of sound

viticole [vitikɔl] *adj* (*industrie*) wine *cpd*; (*région*) wine-growing

viticulteur [vitikyltœr] *nm* wine grower

vitrage [vitraʒ] *nm* (*cloison*) glass partition; (*toit*) glass roof; (*rideau*) net curtain

vitrail, -aux [vitraj, -o] *nm* stained-glass window

vitre [vitr(ə)] *nf* (*window*) pane; (*de portière, voiture*) window

vitré, e [vitre] *adj* glass *cpd*

vitrer [vitre] *vt* to glaze

vitreux, -euse [vitrø, -øz] *adj* vitreous; (*terne*) glassy

vitrine [vitrin] *nf* (*devanture*) (shop) window; (*étalage*) display; (*petite armoire*) display cabinet; **en ~** in the window, on display; **~ publicitaire** display case, showcase

vivable [vivabl(ə)] *adj* (*personne*) livable-with; (*endroit*) fit to live in

vivace *adj* [vivas] (*arbre, plante*) hardy; (*fig*) enduring ▷ *adv* [vivatʃe] (*Mus*) vivace

vivacité [vivasite] *nf* (*voir vif*) liveliness, vivacity; sharpness; brilliance

vivant, e [vivɑ̃, -ɑ̃t] *vb voir* **vivre** ▷ *adj* (*qui vit*) living, alive; (*animé*) lively; (*preuve, exemple*) living; (*langue*) modern ▷ *nm*: **du ~ de qn** in sb's lifetime; **les ~s et les morts** the living and the dead

vive [viv] *adj f voir* **vif** ▷ *vb voir* **vivre** ▷ *excl*: **~ le roi!** long live the king!; **~ les vacances!** hurrah for the holidays!

vivement [vivmɑ̃] *adv* vivaciously; sharply ▷ *excl*: **~ les vacances!** I can't wait for the holidays!, roll on the holidays!

vivier [vivje] *nm* (*au restaurant etc*) fish tank; (*étang*) fishpond

vivifiant, e [vivifjɑ̃, -ɑ̃t] *adj* invigorating

vivions [vivjɔ̃] *vb voir* **vivre**

vivoter [vivote] *vi* (*personne*) to scrape a living, get by; (*fig: affaire etc*) to struggle along

vivre [vivr(ə)] *vi, vt* to live ▷ *nm*: **le ~ et le logement** board and lodging; **vivres** *nmpl* provisions, food supplies; **il vit encore** he is still alive; **se laisser ~** to take life as it comes; **ne plus ~** (*être anxieux*) to live on one's nerves; **il a vécu** (*eu une vie aventureuse*) he has seen life; **ce régime a vécu** this regime has had its day; **être facile à ~** to be easy to get on with; **faire ~ qn** (*pourvoir à sa subsistance*) to provide (a living) for sb; **~ mal** (*chichement*) to have a meagre existence; **~ de** (*salaire etc*) to live on

vlan [vlɑ̃] *excl* wham!, bang!

VO *sigle f* (*Ciné*) = **version originale**; **voir un film en VO** to see a film in its original language

vocable [vɔkabl(ə)] *nm* term

vocabulaire [vɔkabylɛr] *nm* vocabulary

vocation [vɔkasjɔ̃] *nf* vocation, calling; **avoir la ~** to have a vocation

vociférer [vɔsifere] *vi, vt* to scream

vœu, x [vø] *nm* wish; (*à Dieu*) vow; **faire ~ de** to take a vow of; **avec tous nos ~x** with every good wish *ou* our best wishes; **meilleurs ~x** best wishes; (*sur une carte*) "Season's Greetings"; **~x de bonheur** best wishes for your future happiness; **~x de bonne année** best wishes for the New Year

vogue [vɔg] *nf* fashion, vogue; **en ~** in fashion, in vogue

voguer [vɔge] *vi* to sail

voici [vwasi] *prép* (*pour introduire, désigner*) here is; (*+ sg*) here are; (*+ pl*): **et ~ que ...** and now it (*ou* he) ...; **il est parti ~ trois ans** he left three years ago; **~ une semaine que je l'ai vue** it's a week since I've seen her; **me ~** here I am; *voir aussi* **voilà**

voie [vwa] *vb voir* **voir** ▷ *nf* way; (*Rail*) track, line; (*Auto*) lane; **par ~ buccale** *ou* **orale** orally; **par ~ rectale** rectally; **suivre la ~ hiérarchique** to go through official channels; **ouvrir/montrer la ~** to open up/show the way; **être en bonne ~** to be shaping *ou* going well; **mettre qn sur la ~** to put sb on the right track; **être en ~ d'achèvement/de rénovation** to be nearing completion/in the process of renovation; **à ~ étroite** narrow-gauge; **à ~ unique** single-track; **route à deux/trois ~s** two/three-lane road; **par la ~ aérienne/maritime** by air/sea; **~ d'eau** (*Navig*) leak; **~ express** expressway; **~ de fait** (*Jur*) assault (and battery); **~ ferrée** track; railway line (*Brit*), railroad (*US*); **par ~ ferrée** by rail, by railroad; **~ de garage** (*Rail*) siding; **la ~ lactée** the Milky Way; **~ navigable** waterway; **~ prioritaire** (*Auto*) road with right of way; **~**

privée private road; **la ~ publique** the public highway

voilà [vwala] *prép (en désignant)* there is; *(+ sg)* there are; *(+ pl)*: **les ~ ou voici** here *ou* there they are; **en ~ ou voici un** here's one, there's one; *~ ou* **voici deux ans** two years ago; **~ ou voici deux ans que** it's two years since; **et ~!** there we are!; **~ tout** that's all; **"~ ou voici"** *(en offrant etc)* "there *ou* here you are"

voile [vwal] *nm* veil; *(tissu léger)* net ▷ *nf* sail; *(sport)* sailing; **prendre le ~** to take the veil; **mettre à la ~** to make way under sail; **~ du palais** *nm* soft palate, velum; **~ au poumon** *nm* shadow on the lung

voiler [vwale] *vt* to veil; *(Photo)* to fog; *(fausser: roue)* to buckle; *(: bois)* to warp; **se voiler** *vi (lune, regard)* to mist over; *(ciel)* to grow hazy; *(voix)* to become husky; *(roue, disque)* to buckle; *(planche)* to warp; **se ~ la face** to hide one's face

voilier [vwalje] *nm* sailing ship; *(de plaisance)* sailing boat

voilure [vwalyʁ] *nf (de voilier)* sails *pl*; *(d'avion)* aerofoils *pl* (Brit), airfoils *pl* (US); *(de parachute)* canopy

voir [vwaʁ] *vi, vt* to see; **se voir**: **se ~ critiquer/ transformer** to be criticized/transformed; **cela se voit** *(cela arrive)* it happens; *(c'est visible)* that's obvious, it shows; **~ à faire qch** to see to it that sth is done; **~ loin** *(fig)* to be far-sighted; **~ venir** *(fig)* to wait and see; **faire ~ qch à qn** to show sb sth; **en faire ~ à qn** *(fig)* to give sb a hard time; **ne pas pouvoir ~ qn** *(fig)* not to be able to stand sb; **regardez ~** just look; **montrez ~** show (me); **dites ~** tell me; **voyons!** let's see now; *(indignation etc)* come (along) now!; **c'est à ~!** we'll see!; **c'est ce qu'on va ~!** we'll see about that!; **avoir quelque chose à ~ avec** to have something to do with; **ça n'a rien à ~ avec lui** that has nothing to do with him

voire [vwaʁ] *adv* indeed; nay; or even

voisin, e [vwazɛ̃, -in] *adj (proche)* neighbouring (Brit), neighboring (US); *(contigu)* next; *(ressemblant)* connected ▷ *nm/f* neighbo(u)r; *(de table, de dortoir etc)* person next to me *(ou* him *etc)*; **~ de palier** neighbo(u)r across the landing (Brit) *ou* hall (US)

voisinage [vwazinaʒ] *nm (proximité)* proximity; *(environs)* vicinity; *(quartier, voisins)* neighbourhood (Brit), neighborhood (US); **relations de bon ~** neighbo(u)rly terms

voiture [vwatyʁ] *nf* car; *(wagon)* coach, carriage; **en ~!** all aboard!; **~ à bras** handcart; **~ d'enfant** pram (Brit), baby carriage (US); **~ d'infirme** invalid carriage; **~ de sport** sports car

voix [vwa] *nf* voice; *(Pol)* vote; **la ~ de la conscience/raison** the voice of conscience/ reason; **à haute ~** aloud; **à ~ basse** in a low voice; **faire la grosse ~** to speak gruffly; **avoir de la ~** to have a good voice; **rester sans ~** to be speechless; **~ de basse/ténor** *etc* bass/tenor *etc* voice; **à deux/quatre ~** *(Mus)* in two/four parts; **avoir ~ au chapitre** to have a say in the matter;

mettre aux ~ to put to the vote; **~ off** voice-over

vol [vɔl] *nm (mode de locomotion)* flying; *(trajet, voyage, groupe d'oiseaux)* flight; *(mode d'appropriation)* theft, stealing; *(larcin)* theft; **à ~ d'oiseau** as the crow flies; **au ~**: **attraper qch au vol** to catch sth as it flies past; **saisir une remarque au ~** to pick up a passing remark; **prendre son ~** to take flight; **de haut ~** *(fig)* of the highest order; **en ~** in flight; **~ avec effraction** breaking and entering *no pl*, break-in; **~ à l'étalage** shoplifting *no pl*; **~ libre** hang-gliding; **~ à main armée** armed robbery; **~ de nuit** night flight; **~ plané** *(Aviat)* glide, gliding *no pl*; **~ à la tire** pickpocketing *no pl*; **~ à voile** gliding

volage [vɔlaʒ] *adj* fickle

volaille [vɔlaj] *nf (oiseaux)* poultry *pl*; *(viande)* poultry *no pl*; *(oiseau)* fowl

volant, e [vɔlɑ̃, -ɑ̃t] *adj voir* **feuille** *etc* ▷ *nm (d'automobile)* (steering) wheel; *(de commande)* wheel; *(objet lancé)* shuttlecock; *(jeu)* battledore and shuttlecock; *(bande de tissu)* flounce; *(feuillet détachable)* tear-off portion; **le personnel ~**, **les ~s** *(Aviat)* the flight staff; **~ de sécurité** *(fig)* reserve, margin, safeguard

volcan [vɔlkɑ̃] *nm* volcano; *(fig: personne)* hothead

volée [vɔle] *nf (groupe d'oiseaux)* flight, flock; *(Tennis)* volley; **~ de coups/de flèches** volley of blows/arrows; **à la ~**: **rattraper à la volée** to catch in midair; **lancer à la ~** to fling about; **semer à la ~** to (sow) broadcast; **à toute ~** *(sonner les cloches)* vigorously; *(lancer un projectile)* with full force; **de haute ~** *(fig)* of the highest order

voler [vɔle] *vi (avion, oiseau, fig)* to fly; *(voleur)* to steal ▷ *vt (objet)* to steal; *(personne)* to rob; **~ en éclats** to smash to smithereens; **~ de ses propres ailes** *(fig)* to stand on one's own two feet; **~ au vent** to fly in the wind; **~ qch à qn** to steal sth from sb

volet [vɔlɛ] *nm (de fenêtre)* shutter; *(Aviat)* flap; *(de feuillet, document)* section; *(fig: d'un plan)* facet; **trié sur le ~** hand-picked

voleur, -euse [vɔlœʁ, -øz] *nm/f* thief ▷ *adj* thieving; **"au ~!"** "stop thief!"

volière [vɔljɛʁ] *nf* aviary

volley [vɔlɛ], **volley-ball** [vɔlɛbol] *nm* volleyball

volontaire [vɔlɔ̃tɛʁ] *adj (acte, activité)* voluntary; *(délibéré)* deliberate; *(caractère, personne: décidé)* self-willed ▷ *nm/f* volunteer

volonté [vɔlɔ̃te] *nf (faculté de vouloir)* will; *(énergie, fermeté)* will(power); *(souhait, désir)* wish; **se servir/boire à ~** to take/drink as much as one likes; **bonne ~** goodwill, willingness; **mauvaise ~** lack of goodwill, unwillingness

volontiers [vɔlɔ̃tje] *adv (de bonne grâce)* willingly; *(avec plaisir)* willingly, gladly; *(habituellement, souvent)* readily, willingly; **"~"** "with pleasure", "I'd be glad to"

volt [vɔlt] *nm* volt

volte-face [vɔltəfas] *nf inv* about-turn; *(fig)* about-turn, U-turn; **faire ~** to do an about-turn; to do a U-turn

voltige [vɔltiʒ] *nf (Équitation)* trick riding; *(au*

cirque) acrobatics *sg*; (*Aviat*) (aerial) acrobatics *sg*;
numéro de haute ~ acrobatic act
voltiger [vɔltiʒe] *vi* to flutter (about)
volubile [vɔlybil] *adj* voluble
volume [vɔlym] *nm* volume; (*Géom: solide*) solid
volumineux, -euse [vɔlyminø, -øz] *adj*
voluminous, bulky
volupté [vɔlypte] *nf* sensual delight *ou* pleasure
vomi [vɔmi] *nm* vomit
vomir [vɔmiʀ] *vi* to vomit, be sick ▷ *vt* to vomit,
bring up; (*fig*) to belch out, spew out; (*exécrer*) to
loathe, abhor
vomissements [vɔmismã] *nmpl* (*action*)
vomiting *no pl*; **des ~** vomit *sg*
vont [vɔ̃] *vb voir* **aller**
vorace [vɔʀas] *adj* voracious
vos [vo] *adj poss voir* **votre**
vote [vɔt] *nm* vote; **~ par correspondance/
procuration** postal/proxy vote; **~ à main levée**
vote by show of hands; **~ secret, ~ à bulletins
secrets** secret ballot
voter [vɔte] *vi* to vote ▷ *vt* (*loi, décision*) to vote for
votre [vɔtʀ(ə)] (*pl* **vos**) [vo] *adj poss* your
vôtre [votʀ(ə)] *pron*: **le ~, la ~, les ~s** yours; **les ~s**
(*fig*) your family *ou* folks; **à la ~** (*toast*) your (good)
health!
voudrai *etc* [vudʀe] *vb voir* **vouloir**
voué, e [vwe] *adj*: **~ à** doomed to, destined for
vouer [vwe] *vt*: **~ qch à** (*Dieu/un saint*) to dedicate
sth to; **~ sa vie/son temps à** (*étude, cause etc*)
to devote one's life/time to; **~ une haine/
amitié éternelle à qn** to vow undying hatred/
friendship to sb
vouloir [vulwaʀ] *nm*: **le bon ~ de qn** sb's
goodwill; sb's pleasure
▷ *vt* **1** (*exiger, désirer*) to want; **~ faire/que qn
fasse** to want to do/sb to do; **voulez-vous du
thé?** would you like *ou* do you want some tea?;
~ qch à qn to wish sth for sb; **que me veut-il?**
what does he want with me?; **que veux-tu
que je te dise?** what do you want me to say?;
sans le ~ (*involontairement*) without meaning to,
unintentionally; **je voudrais ceci/to do** I would
ou I'd like this/to do; **le hasard a voulu que ...** as
fate would have it, ...; **la tradition veut
que ...** tradition demands that ...; **... qui se veut
moderne** ... which purports to be modern
2 (*consentir*): **je veux bien** (*bonne volonté*) I'll be
happy to; (*concession*) fair enough, that's fine;
oui, si on veut (*en quelque sorte*) yes, if you like;
comme tu veux as you wish; (*en quelque sorte*)
if you like; **veuillez attendre** please wait;
veuillez agréer ... (*formule épistolaire*) yours
faithfully
3: **en ~** (*être ambitieux*) to be out to win; **en ~ à qn**
to bear sb a grudge; **je lui en veux d'avoir fait
ça** I resent his having done that; **s'en ~ (de)** to
be annoyed with o.s. (for); **il en veut à mon
argent** he's after my money
4: **~ de** to want; **la compagnie ne veut plus de
lui** the firm doesn't want him any more; **elle ne
veut pas de son aide** she doesn't want his help

5: **~ dire** to mean
voulu, e [vuly] *pp de* **vouloir** ▷ *adj* (*requis*)
required, requisite; (*délibéré*) deliberate,
intentional
vous [vu] *pron* you; (*objet indirect*) (to) you; (*réfléchi*)
yourself; (*réciproque*) each other ▷ *nm*: **employer
le ~** (*vouvoyer*) to use the "vous" form; **~-même**
yourself; **~-mêmes** yourselves
voûte [vut] *nf* vault; **la ~ céleste** the vault of
heaven; **~ du palais** (*Anat*) roof of the mouth; **~
plantaire** arch (of the foot)
voûter [vute] *vt* (*Archit*) to arch, vault; **se voûter**
vi (*dos, personne*) to become stooped
vouvoyer [vuvwaje] *vt*: **~ qn** to address sb as
"vous"
voyage [vwajaʒ] *nm* journey, trip; (*fait de voyager*):
le ~ travel(ling); **partir/être en ~** to go off/be
away on a journey *ou* trip; **faire un ~** to go on
ou make a trip *ou* journey; **faire bon ~** to have a
good journey; **les gens du ~** travelling people; **~
d'agrément/d'affaires** pleasure/business trip; **
~ de noces** honeymoon; **~ organisé** package
tour
voyager [vwajaʒe] *vi* to travel
voyageur, -euse [vwajaʒœʀ, -øz] *nm/f* traveller;
(*passager*) passenger ▷ *adj* (*tempérament*) nomadic,
wayfaring; **~ (de commerce)** commercial
traveller
voyant, e [vwajã, -ãt] *adj* (*couleur*) loud, gaudy
▷ *nm/f* (*personne qui voit*) sighted person ▷ *nm*
(*signal*) (warning) light ▷ *nf* clairvoyant
voyelle [vwajɛl] *nf* vowel
voyons *etc* [vwajɔ̃] *vb voir* **voir**
voyou [vwaju] *nm* lout, hoodlum; (*enfant*)
guttersnipe
vrac [vʀak]: **en ~** *adv* higgledy-piggledy; (*Comm*)
in bulk
vrai, e [vʀɛ] *adj* (*véridique: récit, faits*) true; (*non
factice, authentique*) real ▷ *nm*: **le ~** the truth; **à ~
dire** to tell the truth; **il est ~ que** it is true that;
être dans le ~ to be right
vraiment [vʀɛmã] *adv* really
vraisemblable [vʀɛsãblabl(ə)] *adj* (*plausible*)
likely, plausible; (*probable*) likely, probable
vraisemblablement [vʀɛsãblabləmã] *adv* in all
likelihood, very likely
vraisemblance [vʀɛsãblãs] *nf* likelihood,
plausibility; (*romanesque*) verisimilitude; **selon
toute ~** in all likelihood
vrille [vʀij] *nf* (*de plante*) tendril; (*outil*) gimlet;
(*spirale*) spiral; (*Aviat*) spin
vrombir [vʀɔ̃biʀ] *vi* to hum
VRP *sigle m* (= *voyageur, représentant, placier*) (sales)
rep
VTT *sigle m* (= *vélo tout-terrain*) mountain bike
vu¹ [vy] *prép* (*en raison de*) in view of; **vu que** in
view of the fact that
vu², e¹ [vy] *pp de* **voir** ▷ *adj*: **bien/mal vu** (*personne*)
well/poorly thought of; (*conduite*) good/bad
form ▷ *nm*: **au vu et au su de tous** openly and
publicly; **ni vu ni connu** what the eye doesn't
see ...!, no one will be any the wiser; **c'est tout**

vu it's a foregone conclusion

vue² [vy] *nf* (*fait de voir*): **la ~ de** the sight of; (*sens, faculté*) (eye)sight; (*panorama, image, photo*) view; (*spectacle*) sight; **vues** *nfpl* (*idées*) views; (*dessein*) designs; **perdre la ~** to lose one's (eye)sight; **perdre de ~** to lose sight of; **à la ~ de tous** in full view of everybody; **hors de ~** out of sight; **à première ~** at first sight; **connaître de ~** to know by sight; **à ~** (*Comm*) at sight; **tirer à ~** to shoot on sight; **à ~ d'œil** *adv* visibly; (*à première vue*) at a quick glance; **avoir ~ sur** to have a view of; **en ~** (*visible*) in sight; (*Comm*) in the public eye; **avoir qch en ~** (*intentions*) to have one's sights on sth; **en ~ de faire** with the intention of doing, with a view to doing; **~ d'ensemble** overall view; **~ de l'esprit** theoretical view

vulgaire [vylgɛʀ] *adj* (*grossier*) vulgar, coarse; (*trivial*) commonplace, mundane; (*péj: quelconque*): **de ~s touristes/chaises de cuisine** common tourists/kitchen chairs; (*Bot, Zool: non latin*) common

vulgariser [vylgaʀize] *vt* to popularize

vulnérable [vylneʀabl(ə)] *adj* vulnerable

Ww

wagon [vagɔ̃] *nm* (*de voyageurs*) carriage; (*de marchandises*) truck, wagon

wagon-lit (*pl* **wagons-lits**) [vagɔ̃li] *nm* sleeper, sleeping car

wagon-restaurant (*pl* **wagons-restaurants**) [vagɔ̃ʀɛstɔʀɑ̃] *nm* restaurant *ou* dining car

wallon, ne [walɔ̃, -ɔn] *adj* Walloon ▷ *nm* (*Ling*) Walloon ▷ *nm/f*: **W~, ne** Walloon

waters [watɛʀ] *nmpl* toilet *sg*, loo *sg* (Brit)

watt [wat] *nm* watt

WC [vese] *nmpl* toilet *sg*, lavatory *sg*

Web [wɛb] *nm inv*: **le ~** the (World Wide) Web

webcam [wɛbkam] *nf* webcam

webmaster [-mastœʀ], **webmestre** [-mɛstʀ] *nm/f* webmaster

week-end [wikɛnd] *nm* weekend

western [wɛstɛʀn] *nm* western

whisky (*pl* **whiskies**) [wiski] *nm* whisky

WWW *sigle m*: **World Wide Web** WWW

Xx

xénophobe [gzenɔfɔb] *adj* xenophobic ▷ *nm/f* xenophobe

xérès [gzeʀɛs] *nm* sherry
xylophone [ksilɔfɔn] *nm* xylophone

Yy

y [i] *adv* (*à cet endroit*) there; (*dessus*) on it (*ou* them); (*dedans*) in it (*ou* them) ▷ *pron* (about *ou* on *ou* of) it (*vérifier la syntaxe du verbe employé*); **j'y pense** I'm thinking about it; *voir aussi* **aller; avoir**

yacht [jɔt] *nm* yacht

yaourt [jauʀt] *nm* yoghurt

yeux [jø] *nmpl de* **œil**

yoga [jɔga] *nm* yoga

yoghourt [jɔguʀt] *nm* = **yaourt**

yougoslave [jugɔslav] *adj* Yugoslav(ian) ▷ *nm/f*: **Y~** Yugoslav(ian)

Yougoslavie [jugɔslavi] *nf*: **la ~** Yugoslavia

Zz

zapper [zape] *vi* to zap

zapping [zapiŋ] *nm*: **faire du** ~ to flick through the channels

zébré, e [zebre] *adj* striped, streaked

zèbre [zɛbʀ(ə)] *nm* (*Zool*) zebra

zélé, e [zele] *adj* zealous

zèle [zɛl] *nm* diligence, assiduousness; **faire du** ~ (*péj*) to be over-zealous

zéro [zeʀo] *nm* zero, nought (*Brit*); **au-dessous de** ~ below zero (Centigrade), below freezing; **partir de** ~ to start from scratch; **réduire à** ~ to reduce to nothing; **trois (buts) à** ~ three (goals to) nil

zeste [zɛst(ə)] *nm* peel, zest; **un** ~ **de citron** a piece of lemon peel

zézayer [zezeje] *vi* to have a lisp

zigzag [zigzag] *nm* zigzag

zigzaguer [zigzage] *vi* to zigzag (along)

zinc [zɛ̃g] *nm* (*Chimie*) zinc; (*comptoir*) bar, counter

zipper [zipe] *vt* (*Inform*) to zip

zizanie [zizani] *nf*: **semer la** ~ to stir up ill-feeling

zizi [zizi] *nm* (*fam*) willy (*Brit*), peter (*US*)

zodiaque [zɔdjak] *nm* zodiac

zona [zona] *nm* shingles *sg*

zone [zon] *nf* zone, area; (*quartiers*): **la** ~ the slum belt; **de seconde** ~ (*fig*) second-rate; ~ **d'action** (*Mil*) sphere of activity; ~ **bleue** ≈ restricted parking area; ~ **d'extension** *ou* **d'urbanisation** urban development area; ~ **franche** free zone; ~ **industrielle (ZI)** industrial estate; ~ **piétonne** pedestrian precinct; ~ **résidentielle** residential area; ~ **tampon** buffer zone

zoo [zoo] *nm* zoo

zoologie [zɔɔlɔʒi] *nf* zoology

zoologique [zɔɔlɔʒik] *adj* zoological

zut [zyt] *excl* dash (it)! (*Brit*), nuts! (*US*)

Aa

A, a¹ [eɪ] *n* (*letter*) A, a *m*; (*Scol*: *mark*) A; (*Mus*) la *m*; **A for Andrew, A for Able** (*US*) A comme Anatole; **A shares** *npl* (*Brit Stock Exchange*) actions *fpl* prioritaires

a² [eɪ, ə] (*before vowel and silent h* **an**) *indef art* **1** un(e); **a book** un livre; **an apple** une pomme; **she's a doctor** elle est médecin

2 (*instead of the number "one"*) un(e); **a year ago** il y a un an; **a hundred/thousand** *etc* **pounds** cent/mille *etc* livres

3 (*in expressing ratios, prices etc*): **three a day/week** trois par jour/semaine; **10 km an hour** 10 km à l'heure; **£5 a person** 5£ par personne; **30p a kilo** 30p le kilo

A2 *n* (*Brit*: *Scol*) deuxième partie de l'examen équivalent au baccalauréat

A.A. *n abbr* (*Brit*: = *Automobile Association*) ≈ ACF *m*; (*US*: = *Associate in/of Arts*) diplôme universitaire; (= *Alcoholics Anonymous*) AA; (= *anti-aircraft*) AA

A.A.A. *n abbr* (= *American Automobile Association*) ≈ ACF *m*; (*Brit*) = **Amateur Athletics Association**

aback [ə'bæk] *adv*: **to be taken ~** être décontenancé(e)

abandon [ə'bændən] *vt* abandonner ▷ *n* abandon *m*; **to ~ ship** évacuer le navire

abate [ə'beɪt] *vi* s'apaiser, se calmer

abattoir ['æbətwɑːʳ] *n* (*Brit*) abattoir *m*

abbey ['æbɪ] *n* abbaye *f*

abbot ['æbət] *n* père supérieur

abbreviation [əbriːvɪ'eɪʃən] *n* abréviation *f*

abdicate ['æbdɪkeɪt] *vt, vi* abdiquer

abdomen ['æbdəmən] *n* abdomen *m*

abduct [æb'dʌkt] *vt* enlever

aberration [æbə'reɪʃən] *n* anomalie *f*; **in a moment of mental ~** dans un moment d'égarement

abide [ə'baɪd] *vt* souffrir, supporter; **I can't ~ it/him** je ne le supporte pas

▶ **abide by** *vt fus* observer, respecter

ability [ə'bɪlɪtɪ] *n* compétence *f*; capacité *f*; (*skill*) talent *m*; **to the best of my ~** de mon mieux

abject ['æbdʒɛkt] *adj* (*poverty*) sordide; (*coward*) méprisable; **an ~ apology** les excuses les plus plates

ablaze [ə'bleɪz] *adj* en feu, en flammes; **~ with light** resplendissant de lumière

able ['eɪbl] *adj* compétent(e); **to be ~ to do sth** pouvoir faire qch, être capable de faire qch

able-bodied ['eɪbl'bɔdɪd] *adj* robuste; **~ seaman** (*Brit*) matelot breveté

ably ['eɪblɪ] *adv* avec compétence *or* talent, habilement

abnormal [æb'nɔːməl] *adj* anormal(e)

aboard [ə'bɔːd] *adv* à bord ▷ *prep* à bord de; (*train*) dans

abode [ə'bəud] *n* (*old*) demeure *f*; (*Law*): **of no fixed ~** sans domicile fixe

abolish [ə'bɔlɪʃ] *vt* abolir

abolition [æbə'lɪʃən] *n* abolition *f*

aborigine [æbə'rɪdʒɪnɪ] *n* aborigène *m/f*

abort [ə'bɔːt] *vt* (*Med*) faire avorter; (*Comput, fig*) abandonner

abortion [ə'bɔːʃən] *n* avortement *m*; **to have an ~** se faire avorter

abortive [ə'bɔːtɪv] *adj* manqué(e)

about [ə'baut] *adv* **1** (*approximately*) environ, à peu près; **~ a hundred/thousand** *etc* environ cent/mille *etc*, une centaine (de)/un millier (de) *etc*; **it takes ~ 10 hours** ça prend environ *or* à peu près 10 heures; **at ~ 2 o'clock** vers 2 heures; **I've just ~ finished** j'ai presque fini

2 (*referring to place*) çà et là, de-ci de-là; **to run ~** courir çà et là; **to walk ~** se promener, aller et venir; **is Paul ~?** (*Brit*) est-ce que Paul est là?; **it's ~ here** c'est par ici, c'est dans les parages; **they left all their things lying ~** ils ont laissé traîner toutes leurs affaires

3: **to be ~ to do sth** être sur le point de faire qch; **I'm not ~ to do all that for nothing** (*inf*) je ne vais quand même pas faire tout ça pour rien

4 (*opposite*): **it's the other way ~** (*Brit*) c'est l'inverse ▷ *prep* **1** (*relating to*) au sujet de, à propos de; **a book ~ London** un livre sur Londres; **what is it ~?** de quoi s'agit-il?; **we talked ~ it** nous en avons parlé; **do something ~ it!** faites quelque chose!; **what** *or* **how ~ doing this?** et si nous faisions ceci?

2 (*referring to place*) dans; **to walk ~ the town** se promener dans la ville

above [ə'bʌv] *adv* au-dessus ▷ *prep* au-dessus de; (*more than*) plus de; **mentioned ~** mentionné ci-dessus; **costing ~ £10** coûtant plus de 10 livres; **~ all** par-dessus tout, surtout

aboveboard [ə'bʌv'bɔːd] *adj* franc (franche),

loyal(e); honnête

abrasive [ə'breɪzɪv] *adj* abrasif(-ive); (*fig*) caustique, agressif(-ive)

abreast [ə'brest] *adv* de front; **to keep ~ of** se tenir au courant de

abroad [ə'brɔːd] *adv* à l'étranger; **there is a rumour ~ that ...** (*fig*) le bruit court que ...

abrupt [ə'brʌpt] *adj* (*steep, blunt*) abrupt(e); (*sudden, gruff*) brusque

abruptly [ə'brʌptlɪ] *adv* (*speak, end*) brusquement

abscess ['æbsɪs] *n* abcès *m*

absence ['æbsəns] *n* absence *f*; **in the ~ of** (*person*) en l'absence de; (*thing*) faute de

absent ['æbsənt] *adj* absent(e); **~ without leave (AWOL)** (*Mil*) en absence irrégulière

absentee [æbsən'tiː] *n* absent(e)

absent-minded ['æbsənt'maɪndɪd] *adj* distrait(e)

absolute ['æbsəluːt] *adj* absolu(e)

absolutely [æbsə'luːtlɪ] *adv* absolument

absolve [əb'zɔlv] *vt*: **to ~ sb (from)** (*sin etc*) absoudre qn (de); **to ~ sb from** (*oath*) délier qn de

absorb [əb'zɔːb] *vt* absorber; **to be ~ed in a book** être plongé(e) dans un livre

absorbent cotton [əb'zɔːbənt-] *n* (*US*) coton *m* hydrophile

absorbing [əb'zɔːbɪŋ] *adj* absorbant(e); (*book, film etc*) captivant(e)

abstain [əb'steɪn] *vi*: **to ~ (from)** s'abstenir (de)

abstract ['æbstrækt] *adj* abstrait(e) ▷ *n* (*summary*) résumé *m* ▷ *vt* [æb'strækt] extraire

absurd [əb'səːd] *adj* absurde

abundance [ə'bʌndəns] *n* abondance *f*

abundant [ə'bʌndənt] *adj* abondant(e)

abuse *n* [ə'bjuːs] (*insults*) insultes *fpl*, injures *fpl*; (*ill-treatment*) mauvais traitements *mpl*; (*of power etc*) abus *m* ▷ *vt* [ə'bjuːz] (*insult*) insulter; (*ill-treat*) malmener; (*power etc*) abuser de; **to be open to ~** se prêter à des abus

abusive [ə'bjuːsɪv] *adj* grossier(-ière), injurieux(-euse)

abysmal [ə'bɪzməl] *adj* exécrable; (*ignorance etc*) sans bornes

abyss [ə'bɪs] *n* abîme *m*, gouffre *m*

AC *n abbr* (*US*) = **athletic club**

academic [ækə'demɪk] *adj* universitaire; (*person: scholarly*) intellectuel(-le); (*pej: issue*) oiseux(-euse), purement théorique ▷ *n* universitaire *m/f*; **~ freedom** liberté *f* académique

academic year *n* (*University*) année *f* universitaire; (*Scol*) année scolaire

academy [ə'kædəmɪ] *n* (*learned body*) académie *f*; (*school*) collège *m*; **military/naval ~** école militaire/navale; **~ of music** conservatoire *m*

accelerate [æk'seləreɪt] *vt, vi* accélérer

acceleration [ækselə'reɪʃən] *n* accélération *f*

accelerator [æk'seləreɪtə] *n* (*Brit*) accélérateur *m*

accent ['æksent] *n* accent *m*

accept [ək'sept] *vt* accepter

acceptable [ək'septəbl] *adj* acceptable

acceptance [ək'septəns] *n* acceptation *f*; **to**

meet with general ~ être favorablement accueilli par tous

access ['æksɛs] *n* accès *m* ▷ *vt* (*Comput*) accéder à; **to have ~ to** (*information, library etc*) avoir accès à, pouvoir utiliser *or* consulter; (*person*) avoir accès auprès de; **the burglars gained ~ through a window** les cambrioleurs sont entrés par une fenêtre

accessible [æk'sɛsəbl] *adj* accessible

accessory [æk'sɛsərɪ] *n* accessoire *m*; **toilet accessories** (*Brit*) articles *mpl* de toilette; **~ to** (*Law*) accessoire à

accident ['æksɪdənt] *n* accident *m*; (*chance*) hasard *m*; **to meet with** *or* **to have an ~** avoir un accident; **I've had an ~** j'ai eu un accident; **~s at work** accidents du travail; **by ~** (*by chance*) par hasard; (*not deliberately*) accidentellement

accidental [æksɪ'dɛntl] *adj* accidentel(le)

accidentally [æksɪ'dɛntəlɪ] *adv* accidentellement

Accident and Emergency Department *n* (*Brit*) service *m* des urgences

accident insurance *n* assurance *f* accident

accident-prone ['æksɪdənt'prəun] *adj* sujet(te) aux accidents

acclaim [ə'kleɪm] *vt* acclamer ▷ *n* acclamations *fpl*

accommodate [ə'kɔmədeɪt] *vt* loger, recevoir; (*oblige, help*) obliger; (*car etc*) contenir; (*adapt*): **to ~ one's plans to** adapter ses projets à

accommodating [ə'kɔmədeɪtɪŋ] *adj* obligeant(e), arrangeant(e)

accommodation, (*US*) **accommodations** [əkɔmə'deɪʃən(z)] *n(pl)* logement *m*; **he's found ~** il a trouvé à se loger; **"~ to let"** (*Brit*) "appartement *or* studio *etc* à louer"; **they have ~ for 500** ils peuvent recevoir 500 personnes, il y a de la place pour 500 personnes; **the hall has seating ~ for 600** (*Brit*) la salle contient 600 places assises

accompaniment [ə'kʌmpənɪmənt] *n* accompagnement *m*

accompany [ə'kʌmpənɪ] *vt* accompagner

accomplice [ə'kʌmplɪs] *n* complice *m/f*

accomplish [ə'kʌmplɪʃ] *vt* accomplir

accomplishment [ə'kʌmplɪʃmənt] *n* (*skill: gen pl*) talent *m*; (*completion*) accomplissement *m*; (*achievement*) réussite *f*

accord [ə'kɔːd] *n* accord *m* ▷ *vt* accorder; **of his own ~** de son plein gré; **with one ~** d'un commun accord

accordance [ə'kɔːdəns] *n*: **in ~ with** conformément à

according [ə'kɔːdɪŋ]: **~ to** (*prep*) selon; **~ to plan** comme prévu

accordingly [ə'kɔːdɪŋlɪ] *adv* (*appropriately*) en conséquence; (*as a result*) par conséquent

accordion [ə'kɔːdɪən] *n* accordéon *m*

account [ə'kaunt] *n* (*Comm*) compte *m*; (*report*) compte rendu, récit *m*; **accounts** *npl* (*Comm: records*) comptabilité *f*, comptes; **"~ payee only"** (*Brit*) "chèque non endossable"; **to keep an ~ of**

noter; **to bring sb to ~ for sth/for having done
sth** amener qn à rendre compte de qch/d'avoir
fait qch; **by all ~s** au dire de tous; **of little ~** de
peu d'importance; **of no ~** sans importance;
on ~ en acompte; **to buy sth on ~** acheter qch à
crédit; **on no ~** en aucun cas; **on ~ of** à cause de;
to take into ~, take ~ of tenir compte de
▶ **account for** vt fus (explain) expliquer, rendre
compte de; (represent) représenter; **all the
children were ~ed for** aucun enfant ne
manquait; **four people are still not ~ed for** on
n'a toujours pas retrouvé quatre personnes
accountable [ə'kaʊntəbl] adj: **~ (for/to)**
responsable (de/devant)
accountancy [ə'kaʊntənsɪ] n comptabilité f
accountant [ə'kaʊntənt] n comptable m/f
account number n numéro m de compte
accrue [ə'kru:] vi s'accroître; (mount up)
s'accumuler; **to ~ to** s'ajouter à; **~d interest**
intérêt couru
accumulate [ə'kju:mjuleɪt] vt accumuler,
amasser ▷ vi s'accumuler, s'amasser
accuracy ['ækjurəsɪ] n exactitude f, précision f
accurate ['ækjurɪt] adj exact(e), précis(e); (device)
précis
accurately ['ækjurɪtlɪ] adv avec précision
accusation [ækju'zeɪʃən] n accusation f
accuse [ə'kju:z] vt: **to ~ sb (of sth)** accuser qn
(de qch)
accused [ə'kju:zd] n (Law) accusé(e)
accustom [ə'kʌstəm] vt accoutumer, habituer;
to ~ o.s. to sth s'habituer à qch
accustomed [ə'kʌstəmd] adj (usual) habituel(le);
~ to habitué(e) or accoutumé(e) à
ace [eɪs] n as m; **within an ~ of** (Brit) à deux
doigts or un cheveu de
ache [eɪk] n mal m, douleur f ▷ vi (be sore) faire
mal, être douloureux(-euse); (yearn): **to ~ to
do sth** mourir d'envie de faire qch; **I've got
stomach ~** or (US) **a stomach ~** j'ai mal à
l'estomac; **my head ~s** j'ai mal à la tête; **I'm
aching all over** j'ai mal partout
achieve [ə'tʃi:v] vt (aim) atteindre; (victory, success)
remporter, obtenir; (task) accomplir
achievement [ə'tʃi:vmənt] n exploit m, réussite
f; (of aims) réalisation f
acid ['æsɪd] adj, n acide (m)
acid rain n pluies fpl acides
acknowledge [ək'nɔlɪdʒ] vt (also: **acknowledge
receipt of**) accuser réception de; (fact)
reconnaître
acknowledgement [ək'nɔlɪdʒmənt] n (of letter)
accusé m de réception; **acknowledgements** (in
book) remerciements mpl
acne ['æknɪ] n acné m
acorn ['eɪkɔ:n] n gland m
acoustic [ə'ku:stɪk] adj acoustique
acoustics [ə'ku:stɪks] n, npl acoustique f
acquaint [ə'kweɪnt] vt: **to ~ sb with sth** mettre
qn au courant de qch; **to be ~ed with** (person)
connaître; (fact) savoir
acquaintance [ə'kweɪntəns] n connaissance f;

to make sb's ~ faire la connaissance de qn
acquire [ə'kwaɪə*] vt acquérir
acquisition [ækwɪ'zɪʃən] n acquisition f
acquit [ə'kwɪt] vt acquitter; **to ~ o.s. well** s'en
tirer très honorablement
acre ['eɪkə*] n acre f (= 4047 m²)
acrid ['ækrɪd] adj (smell) âcre; (fig) mordant(e)
acrobat ['ækrəbæt] n acrobate m/f
acronym ['ækrənɪm] n acronyme m
across [ə'krɔs] prep (on the other side) de l'autre
côté de; (crosswise) en travers de ▷ adv de l'autre
côté; en travers; **to walk ~** (the road) traverser
(la route); **to run/swim ~** traverser en courant/à
la nage; **to take sb ~ the road** faire traverser
la route à qn; **a road ~ the wood** une route qui
traverse le bois; **the lake is 12 km ~** le lac fait 12
km de large; **~ from** en face de; **to get sth ~ (to
sb)** faire comprendre qch (à qn)
acrylic [ə'krɪlɪk] adj, n acrylique (m)
act [ækt] n acte m, action f; (Theat: part of play)
acte; (: of performer) numéro m; (Law) loi f ▷ vi
agir; (Theat) jouer; (pretend) jouer la comédie ▷ vt
(role) jouer, tenir; **~ of God** (Law) catastrophe
naturelle; **to catch sb in the ~** prendre qn sur
le fait or en flagrant délit; **it's only an ~** c'est du
cinéma; **to ~ Hamlet** (Brit) tenir or jouer le rôle
d'Hamlet; **to ~ the fool** (Brit) faire l'idiot; **to ~
as** servir de; **it ~s as a deterrent** cela a un effet
dissuasif; **~ing in my capacity as chairman, I
...** en ma qualité de président, je ...
▶ **act on** vt: **to ~ on sth** agir sur la base de qch
▶ **act out** vt (event) raconter en mimant;
(fantasies) réaliser
▶ **act up** (inf) vi (person) se conduire mal; (knee,
back, injury) jouer des tours; (machine) être
capricieux(-ieuse)
acting ['æktɪŋ] adj suppléant(e), par intérim ▷ n
(of actor) jeu m; (activity): **to do some ~** faire du
théâtre (or du cinéma); **he is the ~ manager** il
remplace (provisoirement) le directeur
action ['ækʃən] n action f; (Mil) combat(s) m(pl);
(Law) procès m, action en justice; **to bring an
~ against sb** (Law) poursuivre qn en justice,
intenter un procès contre qn; **killed in ~** (Mil)
tué au champ d'honneur; **out of ~** hors de
combat; (machine etc) hors d'usage; **to take ~**
agir, prendre des mesures; **to put a plan into ~**
mettre un projet à exécution
action replay n (Brit TV) ralenti m
activate ['æktɪveɪt] vt (mechanism) actionner,
faire fonctionner; (Chem, Physics) activer
active ['æktɪv] adj actif(-ive); (volcano) en
activité; **to play an ~ part in** jouer un rôle actif
dans
actively ['æktɪvlɪ] adv activement; (discourage)
vivement
activist ['æktɪvɪst] n activiste m/f
activity [æk'tɪvɪtɪ] n activité f
activity holiday n vacances actives
actor ['æktə*] n acteur m
actress ['æktrɪs] n actrice f
actual ['æktjuəl] adj réel(le), véritable; (emphatic

use) lui-même (elle-même)

actually [ˈæktjuəlɪ] *adv* réellement, véritablement; (*in fact*) en fait

acupuncture [ˈækjupʌŋktʃəʳ] *n* acuponcture *f*

acute [əˈkjuːt] *adj* aigu(ë); (*mind, observer*) pénétrant(e)

A.D. *adv abbr* (= *Anno Domini*) ap. J.-C. ▷ *n abbr* (*US Mil*) = **active duty**

ad [æd] *n abbr* = **advertisement**

adamant [ˈædəmənt] *adj* inflexible

adapt [əˈdæpt] *vt* adapter ▷ *vi*: **to ~ (to)** s'adapter (à)

adaptable [əˈdæptəbl] *adj* (*device*) adaptable; (*person*) qui s'adapte facilement

adapter, adaptor [əˈdæptəʳ] *n* (*Elec*) adaptateur *m*; (*for several plugs*) prise *f* multiple

add [æd] *vt* ajouter; (*figures: also:* **to add up**) additionner ▷ *vi*: **to ~ to** (*increase*) ajouter à, accroître
  ▶ **add on** *vt* ajouter ▷ *vi* (*fig*): **it doesn't ~ up** cela ne rime à rien
  ▶ **add up to** *vt fus* (*Math*) s'élever à; (*fig: mean*) signifier; **it doesn't ~ up to much** ça n'est pas grand'chose

adder [ˈædəʳ] *n* vipère *f*

addict [ˈædɪkt] *n* toxicomane *m/f*; (*fig*) fanatique *m/f*; **heroin ~** héroïnomane *m/f*; **drug ~** drogué(e) *m/f*

addicted [əˈdɪktɪd] *adj*: **to be ~ to** (*drink, drugs*) être adonné(e) à; (*fig: football etc*) être un(e) fanatique de

addiction [əˈdɪkʃən] *n* (*Med*) dépendance *f*

addictive [əˈdɪktɪv] *adj* qui crée une dépendance

addition [əˈdɪʃən] *n* (*adding up*) addition *f*; (*thing added*) ajout *m*; **in ~** de plus, de surcroît; **in ~ to** en plus de

additional [əˈdɪʃənl] *adj* supplémentaire

additive [ˈædɪtɪv] *n* additif *m*

address [əˈdrɛs] *n* adresse *f*; (*talk*) discours *m*, allocution *f* ▷ *vt* adresser; (*speak to*) s'adresser à; **my ~ is ...** mon adresse, c'est ...; **form of ~** titre *m*; **what form of ~ do you use for ...?** comment s'adresse-t-on à ...?; **to ~ (o.s. to) sth** (*problem, issue*) aborder qch; **absolute/relative ~** (*Comput*) adresse absolue/relative

address book *n* carnet *m* d'adresses

adept [ˈædɛpt] *adj*: **~ at** expert(e) à *or* en

adequate [ˈædɪkwɪt] *adj* (*enough*) suffisant(e); (*satisfactory*) satisfaisant(e); **to feel ~ to the task** se sentir à la hauteur de la tâche

adhere [ədˈhɪəʳ] *vi*: **to ~ to** adhérer à; (*fig: rule, decision*) se tenir à

adhesive [ədˈhiːzɪv] *adj* adhésif(-ive) ▷ *n* adhésif *m*

adhesive tape *n* (*Brit*) ruban *m* adhésif; (*US Med*) sparadrap *m*

ad hoc [ædˈhɔk] *adj* (*decision*) de circonstance; (*committee*) ad hoc

adjacent [əˈdʒeɪsənt] *adj* adjacent(e), contigu(ë); **~ to** adjacent à

adjective [ˈædʒɛktɪv] *n* adjectif *m*

adjoining [əˈdʒɔɪnɪŋ] *adj* voisin(e), adjacent(e),

attenant(e) ▷ *prep* voisin de, adjacent à

adjourn [əˈdʒəːn] *vt* ajourner ▷ *vi* suspendre la séance; lever la séance; clore la session; (*go*) se retirer; **to ~ a meeting till the following week** reporter une réunion à la semaine suivante; **they ~ed to the pub** (*Brit inf*) ils ont filé au pub

adjust [əˈdʒʌst] *vt* (*machine*) ajuster, régler; (*prices, wages*) rajuster ▷ *vi*: **to ~ (to)** s'adapter (à)

adjustable [əˈdʒʌstəbl] *adj* réglable

adjustment [əˈdʒʌstmənt] *n* (*of machine*) ajustage *m*, réglage *m*; (*of prices, wages*) rajustement *m*; (*of person*) adaptation *f*

ad-lib [ædˈlɪb] *vt, vi* improviser ▷ *n* improvisation *f* ▷ *adv*: **ad lib** à volonté, à discrétion

administer [ədˈmɪnɪstəʳ] *vt* administrer; (*justice*) rendre

administration [ədmɪnɪsˈtreɪʃən] *n* (*management*) administration *f*; (*government*) gouvernement *m*

administrative [ədˈmɪnɪstrətɪv] *adj* administratif(-ive)

administrator [ədˈmɪnɪstreɪtəʳ] *n* administrateur(-trice)

admiral [ˈædmərəl] *n* amiral *m*

Admiralty [ˈædmərəltɪ] *n* (*Brit: also:* **Admiralty Board**) ministère *m* de la Marine

admiration [ædməˈreɪʃən] *n* admiration *f*

admire [ədˈmaɪəʳ] *vt* admirer

admirer [ədˈmaɪərəʳ] *n* (*fan*) admirateur(-trice)

admission [ədˈmɪʃən] *n* admission *f*; (*to exhibition, night club etc*) entrée *f*; (*confession*) aveu *m*; **"~ free", "free ~"** "entrée libre"; **by his own ~** de son propre aveu

admission charge *n* droits *mpl* d'admission

admit [ədˈmɪt] *vt* laisser entrer; admettre; (*agree*) reconnaître, admettre; (*crime*) reconnaître avoir commis; **"children not ~ted"** "entrée interdite aux enfants"; **this ticket ~s two** ce billet est valable pour deux personnes; **I must ~ that ...** je dois admettre *or* reconnaître que ...
  ▶ **admit of** *vt fus* admettre, permettre
  ▶ **admit to** *vt fus* reconnaître, avouer

admittance [ədˈmɪtəns] *n* admission *f*, (droit *m* d')entrée *f*; **"no ~"** "défense d'entrer"

admittedly [ədˈmɪtɪdlɪ] *adv* il faut en convenir

ado [əˈduː] *n*: **without (any) more ~** sans plus de cérémonies

adolescence [ædəuˈlɛsns] *n* adolescence *f*

adolescent [ædəuˈlɛsnt] *adj, n* adolescent(e)

adopt [əˈdɔpt] *vt* adopter

adopted [əˈdɔptɪd] *adj* adoptif(-ive), adopté(e)

adoption [əˈdɔpʃən] *n* adoption *f*

adore [əˈdɔːʳ] *vt* adorer

adorn [əˈdɔːn] *vt* orner

Adriatic [eɪdrɪˈætɪk]

Adriatic Sea *n*: **the Adriatic (Sea)** la mer Adriatique, l'Adriatique *f*

adrift [əˈdrɪft] *adv* à la dérive; **to come ~** (*boat*) aller à la dérive; (*wire, rope, fastening etc*) se défaire

adult [ˈædʌlt] *n* adulte *m/f* ▷ *adj* (*grown-up*) adulte; (*for adults*) pour adultes

adult education *n* éducation *f* des adultes

adultery [ə'dʌltəri] *n* adultère *m*
advance [əd'vɑ:ns] *n* avance *f* ▷ *vt* avancer
▷ *vi* s'avancer; **in** ~ en avance, d'avance; **to
make ~s to sb** (*gen*) faire des propositions à qn;
(*amorously*) faire des avances à qn; ~ **booking**
location *f*; ~ **notice**, ~ **warning** préavis *m*; (*verbal*)
avertissement *m*; **do I need to book in** ~? est-ce
qu'il faut réserver à l'avance?
advanced [əd'vɑ:nst] *adj* avancé(e); (*Scol: studies*)
supérieur(e); ~ **in years** d'un âge avancé
advantage [əd'vɑ:ntɪdʒ] *n* (*also Tennis*) avantage
m; **to take** ~ **of** (*person*) exploiter; (*opportunity*)
profiter de; **it's to our** ~ c'est notre intérêt; **it's
to our** ~ **to** ... nous avons intérêt à ...
advent ['ædvənt] *n* avènement *m*, venue *f*; **A~**
(*Rel*) avent *m*
adventure [əd'ventʃə'] *n* aventure *f*
adventurous [əd'ventʃərəs] *adj*
aventureux(-euse)
adverb ['ædvə:b] *n* adverbe *m*
adversary ['ædvəsəri] *n* adversaire *m/f*
adverse ['ædvə:s] *adj* adverse; (*effect*)
négatif(-ive); (*weather, publicity*) mauvais(e);
(*wind*) contraire; ~ **to** hostile à; **in** ~
circumstances dans l'adversité
advert ['ædvə:t] *n abbr* (*Brit*) = **advertisement**
advertise ['ædvətaiz] *vi* faire de la publicité
or de la réclame; (*in classified ads etc*) mettre
une annonce ▷ *vt* faire de la publicité *or* de la
réclame pour; (*in classified ads etc*) mettre une
annonce pour vendre; **to** ~ **for** (*staff*) recruter par
(voie d')annonce
advertisement [əd'və:tɪsmənt] *n* (*Comm*)
publicité *f*, réclame *f*; (*in classified ads etc*)
annonce *f*
advertiser ['ædvətaizə'] *n* annonceur *m*
advertising ['ædvətaiziŋ] *n* publicité *f*
advice [əd'vais] *n* conseils *mpl*; (*notification*)
avis *m*; **a piece of** ~ un conseil; **to ask** (**sb**)
for ~ demander conseil (à qn); **to take legal** ~
consulter un avocat
advisable [əd'vaizəbl] *adj* recommandable,
indiqué(e)
advise [əd'vaiz] *vt* conseiller; **to** ~ **sb of sth**
aviser *or* informer qn de qch; **to** ~ **against sth/
doing sth** déconseiller qch/conseiller de ne pas
faire qch; **you would be well/ill ~d to go** vous
feriez mieux d'y aller/de ne pas y aller, vous
auriez intérêt à y aller/à ne pas y aller
adviser, advisor [əd'vaizə'] *n* conseiller(-ère)
advisory [əd'vaizəri] *adj* consultatif(-ive); **in an**
~ **capacity** à titre consultatif
advocate *n* ['ædvəkɪt] (*lawyer*) avocat (plaidant);
(*upholder*) défenseur *m*, avocat(e) ▷ *vt* ['ædvəkeit]
recommander, prôner; **to be an** ~ **of** être
partisan(e) de
Aegean [i:'dʒi:ən] *n, adj*: **the** ~ **(Sea)** la mer Égée,
l'Égée *f*
aerial ['ɛəriəl] *n* antenne *f* ▷ *adj* aérien(ne)
aerobics [ɛə'rəubiks] *n* aérobic *m*
aeroplane ['ɛərəplein] *n* (*Brit*) avion *m*
aerosol ['ɛərəsɔl] *n* aérosol *m*

aesthetic [ɪs'θɛtɪk] *adj* esthétique
afar [ə'fɑ:'] *adv*: **from** ~ de loin
affair [ə'fɛə'] *n* affaire *f*; (*also:* **love affair**) liaison
f, aventure *f*; **affairs** (*business*) affaires
affect [ə'fɛkt] *vt* affecter; (*subj: disease*) atteindre
affected [ə'fɛktɪd] *adj* affecté(e)
affection [ə'fɛkʃən] *n* affection *f*
affectionate [ə'fɛkʃənɪt] *adj* affectueux(-euse)
affinity [ə'fɪnɪti] *n* affinité *f*
afflict [ə'flɪkt] *vt* affliger
affluence ['æfluəns] *n* aisance *f*, opulence *f*
affluent ['æfluənt] *adj* opulent(e); (*person, family,
surroundings*) aisé(e), riche; **the** ~ **society** la
société d'abondance
afford [ə'fɔ:d] *vt* (*goods etc*) avoir les moyens
d'acheter *or* d'entretenir; (*behaviour*) se
permettre; (*provide*) fournir, procurer; **can we** ~
a car? avons-nous de quoi acheter *or* les moyens
d'acheter une voiture?; **I can't** ~ **the time** je n'ai
vraiment pas le temps
affordable [ə'fɔ:dəbl] *adj* abordable
Afghanistan [æf'gænistæn] *n* Afghanistan *m*
afloat [ə'fləut] *adj* à flot ▷ *adv*: **to stay** ~
surnager; **to keep/get a business** ~ maintenir à
flot/lancer une affaire
afoot [ə'fut] *adv*: **there is something** ~ il se
prépare quelque chose
afraid [ə'freid] *adj* effrayé(e); **to be** ~ **of** *or* **to**
avoir peur de; **I am** ~ **that** je crains que + *sub*; **I'm**
~ **so/not** oui/non, malheureusement
Africa ['æfrikə] *n* Afrique *f*
African ['æfrikən] *adj* africain(e) ▷ *n* Africain(e)
African-American ['æfrikənə'merikən] *adj* afro-
américain(e) ▷ *n* Afro-Américain(e)
after ['ɑ:ftə'] *prep, adv* après ▷ *conj* après que,
après avoir *or* être + *pp*; ~ **dinner** après (le)
dîner; **the day** ~ **tomorrow** après demain; **it's
quarter** ~ **two** (*US*) il est deux heures et quart; ~
having done/~ he left après avoir fait/ après son
départ; **to name sb** ~ **sb** donner à qn le nom de
qn; **to ask** ~ **sb** demander des nouvelles de qn;
what/who are you ~? que/qui cherchez-vous?;
the police are ~ **him** la police est à ses trousses;
~ **you!** après vous!; ~ **all** après tout
after-effects ['ɑ:ftərɪfɛkts] *npl* (*of disaster,
radiation, drink etc*) répercussions *fpl*; (*of illness*)
séquelles *fpl*, suites *fpl*
aftermath ['ɑ:ftəmɑ:θ] *n* conséquences *fpl*; **in
the** ~ **of** dans les mois *or* années *etc* qui suivirent,
au lendemain de
afternoon ['ɑ:ftə'nu:n] *n* après-midi *m or f*; **good
~!** bonjour!; (*goodbye*) au revoir!
afters ['ɑ:ftəz] *n* (*Brit inf: dessert*) dessert *m*
after-sales service [ɑ:ftə'seilz-] *n* service *m*
après-vente, SAV *m*
after-shave ['ɑ:ftəʃeiv], **after-shave lotion** *n*
lotion *f* après-rasage
aftersun ['ɑ:ftəsʌn], **aftersun cream,
aftersun lotion** *n* après-soleil *m inv*
afterthought ['ɑ:ftəθɔ:t] *n*: **I had an** ~ il m'est
venu une idée après coup
afterwards ['ɑ:ftəwədz], (*US*) **afterward** ['ɑ:

ftəwəd] *adv* après

again [ə'gɛn] *adv* de nouveau, encore (une fois); **to do sth ~** refaire qch; **not ... ~** ne ... plus; **~ and ~** à plusieurs reprises; **he's opened it ~** il l'a rouvert, il l'a de nouveau *or* l'a encore ouvert; **now and ~** de temps à autre

against [ə'gɛnst] *prep* contre; (*compared to*) par rapport à; **a blue background** sur un fond bleu; **(as) ~** (Brit) contre

age [eɪdʒ] *n* âge *m* ▷ *vt, vi* vieillir; **what ~ is he?** quel âge a-t-il?; **he is 20 years of ~** il a 20 ans; **under ~** mineur(e); **to come of ~** atteindre sa majorité; **it's been ~s since I saw you** ça fait une éternité que je ne t'ai pas vu

aged ['eɪdʒd] *adj* âgé(e); **~ 10** âgé de 10 ans; **the ~** ['eɪdʒɪd] ▷ *npl* les personnes âgées

age group *n* tranche *f* d'âge; **the 40 to 50 ~** la tranche d'âge des 40 à 50 ans

age limit *n* limite *f* d'âge

agency ['eɪdʒənsɪ] *n* agence *f*; **through** *or* **by the ~ of** par l'entremise *or* l'action de

agenda [ə'dʒɛndə] *n* ordre *m* du jour; **on the ~** à l'ordre du jour

agent ['eɪdʒənt] *n* agent *m*; (*firm*) concessionnaire *m*

aggravate ['ægrəveɪt] *vt* (*situation*) aggraver; (*annoy*) exaspérer, agacer

aggression [ə'grɛʃən] *n* agression *f*

aggressive [ə'grɛsɪv] *adj* agressif(-ive)

agile ['ædʒaɪl] *adj* agile

agitate ['ædʒɪteɪt] *vt* rendre inquiet(-ète) *or* agité(e) ▷ *vi* faire de l'agitation (politique); **to ~ for** faire campagne pour

AGM *n abbr* (= *annual general meeting*) AG *f*

ago [ə'gəu] *adv*: **two days ~** il y a deux jours; **not long ~** il n'y a pas longtemps; **as long ~ as 1960** déjà en 1960; **how long ~?** il y a combien de temps (de cela)?

agony ['ægənɪ] *n* (*pain*) douleur *f* atroce; (*distress*) angoisse *f*; **to be in ~** souffrir le martyre

agree [ə'griː] *vt* (*price*) convenir de ▷ *vi*: **to ~ with** (*person*) être d'accord avec; (*statements etc*) concorder avec; (*Ling*) s'accorder avec; **to ~ to do** accepter de *or* consentir à faire; **to ~ to sth** consentir à qch; **to ~ that** (*admit*) convenir *or* reconnaître que; **it was ~d that ...** il a été convenu que ...; **they ~ on this** ils sont d'accord sur ce point; **they ~d on going/a price** ils se mirent d'accord pour y aller/sur un prix; **garlic doesn't ~ with me** je ne supporte pas l'ail

agreeable [ə'griːəbl] *adj* (*pleasant*) agréable; (*willing*) consentant(e), d'accord; **are you ~ to this?** est-ce que vous êtes d'accord?

agreed [ə'griːd] *adj* (*time, place*) convenu(e); **to be ~** être d'accord

agreement [ə'griːmənt] *n* accord *m*; **in ~** d'accord; **by mutual ~** d'un commun accord

agricultural [ægrɪ'kʌltʃərəl] *adj* agricole

agriculture ['ægrɪkʌltʃəʳ] *n* agriculture *f*

aground [ə'graund] *adv*: **to run ~** s'échouer

ahead [ə'hɛd] *adv* en avant; devant; **go right** *or* **straight ~** (*direction*) allez tout droit; **go ~!**

(*permission*) allez-y!; **~ of** devant; (*fig: schedule etc*) en avance sur; **~ of time** en avance; **they were (right) ~ of us** ils nous précédaient (de peu), ils étaient (juste) devant nous

aid [eɪd] *n* aide *f*; (*device*) appareil *m* ▷ *vt* aider; **with the ~ of** avec l'aide de; **in ~ of** en faveur de; **to ~ and abet** (*Law*) se faire le complice de

aide [eɪd] *n* (*person*) assistant(e)

AIDS [eɪdz] *n abbr* (= *acquired immune* (*or immuno-*) *deficiency syndrome*) SIDA *m*

ailing ['eɪlɪŋ] *adj* (*person*) souffreteux(euse); (*economy*) malade

ailment ['eɪlmənt] *n* affection *f*

aim [eɪm] *vt*: **to ~ sth (at)** (*gun, camera*) braquer *or* pointer qch (sur); (*missile*) lancer qch (à *or* contre *or* en direction de); (*remark, blow*) destiner *or* adresser qch (à) ▷ *vi* (*also*: **to take aim**) viser ▷ *n* (*objective*) but *m*; (*skill*): **his ~ is bad** il vise mal; **to ~ at** viser; (*fig*) viser (à); avoir pour but *or* ambition; **to ~ to do** avoir l'intention de faire

aimless ['eɪmlɪs] *adj* sans but

ain't [eɪnt] (*inf*) = **am not**; **aren't**; **isn't**

air [ɛəʳ] *n* air *m* ▷ *vt* aérer; (*idea, grievance, views*) mettre sur le tapis; (*knowledge*) faire étalage de ▷ *cpd* (*currents, attack etc*) aérien(ne); **to throw sth into the ~** (*ball etc*) jeter qch en l'air; **by ~** par avion; **to be on the ~** (Radio, TV: *programme*) être diffusé(e); (: *station*) émettre

airbag ['ɛəbæg] *n* airbag *m*

airbed ['ɛəbɛd] *n* (Brit) matelas *m* pneumatique

airborne ['ɛəbɔːn] *adj* (*plane*) en vol; (*troops*) aéroporté(e); (*particles*) dans l'air; **as soon as the plane was ~** dès que l'avion eut décollé

air-conditioned ['ɛəkən'dɪʃənd] *adj* climatisé(e), à air conditionné

air conditioning [-kən'dɪʃnɪŋ] *n* climatisation *f*

aircraft ['ɛəkrɑːft] *n inv* avion *m*

aircraft carrier *n* porte-avions *m inv*

airfield ['ɛəfiːld] *n* terrain *m* d'aviation

Air Force *n* Armée *f* de l'air

air freshener [-'frɛʃnəʳ] *n* désodorisant *m*

airgun ['ɛəgʌn] *n* fusil *m* à air comprimé

air hostess *n* (Brit) hôtesse *f* de l'air

airing cupboard *n* (Brit) placard qui contient la chaudière et dans lequel on met le linge à sécher

air letter *n* (Brit) aérogramme *m*

airlift ['ɛəlɪft] *n* pont aérien

airline ['ɛəlaɪn] *n* ligne aérienne, compagnie aérienne

airliner ['ɛəlaɪnəʳ] *n* avion *m* de ligne

airmail ['ɛəmeɪl] *n*: **by ~** par avion

air mile *n* air mile *m*

airplane ['ɛəpleɪn] *n* (US) avion *m*

airport ['ɛəpɔːt] *n* aéroport *m*

air raid *n* attaque aérienne

airsick ['ɛəsɪk] *adj*: **to be ~** avoir le mal de l'air

airspace ['ɛəspeɪs] *n* espace *m* aérien

airstrip ['ɛəstrɪp] *n* terrain *m* d'atterrissage

air terminal *n* aérogare *f*

airtight ['ɛətaɪt] *adj* hermétique

air-traffic controller *n* aiguilleur *m* du ciel

airy ['ɛərɪ] *adj* bien aéré(e); (*manners*) dégagé(e)

aisle [aɪl] n (of church: central) allée f centrale; (: side) nef f latérale, bas-côté m; (in theatre, supermarket) allée; (on plane) couloir m

aisle seat n place f côté couloir

ajar [ə'dʒɑːʳ] adj entrouvert(e)

akin [ə'kɪn] adj: ~ **to** semblable à, du même ordre que

à la carte [ælæ'kɑːt] adv à la carte

alarm [ə'lɑːm] n alarme f ▷ vt alarmer

alarm call n coup m de fil pour réveiller; **could I have an ~ at 7 am, please?** pouvez-vous me réveiller à 7 heures, s'il vous plaît?

alarm clock n réveille-matin m inv, réveil m

alarmed [ə'lɑːmd] adj (frightened) alarmé(e); (protected by an alarm) protégé(e) par un système d'alarme; **to become ~** prendre peur

alarming [ə'lɑːmɪŋ] adj alarmant(e)

alas [ə'læs] excl hélas

Albania [æl'beɪnɪə] n Albanie f

albeit [ɔːl'biːɪt] conj bien que + sub, encore que + sub

album ['ælbəm] n album m

alcohol ['ælkəhɔl] n alcool m

alcohol-free ['ælkəhɔlfriː] adj sans alcool

alcoholic [ælkə'hɔlɪk] adj, n alcoolique (m/f)

alcove ['ælkəuv] n alcôve f

ale [eɪl] n bière f

alert [ə'ləːt] adj alerte, vif (vive); (watchful) vigilant(e) ▷ n alerte f ▷ vt alerter; **to ~ sb (to sth)** attirer l'attention de qn (sur qch); **to ~ sb to the dangers of sth** avertir qn des dangers de qch; **on the ~** sur le qui-vive; (Mil) en état d'alerte

algebra ['ældʒɪbrə] n algèbre m

Algeria [æl'dʒɪərɪə] n Algérie f

Algerian [æl'dʒɪərɪən] adj algérien(ne) ▷ n Algérien(ne)

Algiers [æl'dʒɪəz] n Alger

alias ['eɪlɪəs] adv alias ▷ n faux nom, nom d'emprunt

alibi ['ælɪbaɪ] n alibi m

alien ['eɪlɪən] n (from abroad) étranger(-ère); (from outer space) extraterrestre ▷ adj: ~ **(to)** étranger(-ère) (à)

alienate ['eɪlɪəneɪt] vt aliéner; (subj: person) s'aliéner

alight [ə'laɪt] adj, adv en feu ▷ vi mettre pied à terre; (passenger) descendre; (bird) se poser

align [ə'laɪn] vt aligner

alike [ə'laɪk] adj semblable, pareil(le) ▷ adv de même; **to look ~** se ressembler

alimony ['ælɪmənɪ] n (payment) pension f alimentaire

alive [ə'laɪv] adj vivant(e); (active) plein(e) de vie; ~ **with** grouillant(e) de; ~ **to** sensible à

all [ɔːl] adj (singular) tout(e); (plural) tous (toutes); ~ **day** toute la journée; ~ **night** toute la nuit; ~ **men** tous les hommes; ~ **five** tous les cinq; ~ **the food** toute la nourriture; ~ **the books** tous les livres; ~ **the time** tout le temps; ~ **his life** toute sa vie

▷ pron **1** tout; **I ate it ~**, **I ate ~ of it** j'ai tout mangé; ~ **of us went** nous y sommes tous allés; ~ **of the boys went** tous les garçons y sont allés;

is that ~? c'est tout?; (in shop) ce sera tout?

2 (in phrases): **above ~** surtout, par-dessus tout; **after ~** après tout; **at ~**: **not at all** (in answer to question) pas du tout; (in answer to thanks) je vous en prie!; **I'm not at ~ tired** je ne suis pas du tout fatigué(e); **anything at ~ will do** n'importe quoi fera l'affaire; ~ **in ~** tout bien considéré, en fin de compte

▷ adv: ~ **alone** tout(e) seul(e); **it's not as hard as ~ that** ce n'est pas si difficile que ça; ~ **the more/the better** d'autant plus/mieux; ~ **but** presque, pratiquement; **to be ~ in** (Brit inf) être complètement à plat; **the score is 2 ~** le score est de 2 partout

Allah ['ælə] n Allah m

allegation [ælɪ'geɪʃən] n allégation f

allege [ə'lɛdʒ] vt alléguer, prétendre; **he is ~d to have said** il aurait dit

alleged [ə'lɛdʒd] adj prétendu(e)

allegedly [ə'lɛdʒɪdlɪ] adv à ce que l'on prétend, paraît-il

allegiance [ə'liːdʒəns] n fidélité f, obéissance f

allergic [ə'ləːdʒɪk] adj: ~ **to** allergique à; **I'm ~ to penicillin** je suis allergique à la pénicilline

allergy ['ælədʒɪ] n allergie f

alleviate [ə'liːvɪeɪt] vt soulager, adoucir

alley ['ælɪ] n ruelle f; (in garden) allée f

alliance [ə'laɪəns] n alliance f

allied ['ælaɪd] adj allié(e)

alligator ['ælɪgeɪtəʳ] n alligator m

all-in ['ɔːlɪn] adj, adv (Brit: charge) tout compris

all-night ['ɔːl'naɪt] adj ouvert(e) or qui dure toute la nuit

allocate ['æləkeɪt] vt (share out) répartir, distribuer; **to ~ sth to** (duties) assigner or attribuer qch à; (sum, time) allouer qch à; **to ~ sth for** affecter qch à

allot [ə'lɔt] vt (share out) répartir, distribuer; **to ~ sth to** (time) allouer qch à; (duties) assigner qch à; **in the ~ted time** dans le temps imparti

allotment [ə'lɔtmənt] n (share) part f; (garden) lopin m de terre (loué à la municipalité)

all-out ['ɔːlaut] adj (effort etc) total(e)

allow [ə'lau] vt (practice, behaviour) permettre, autoriser; (sum to spend etc) accorder, allouer; (sum, time estimated) compter, prévoir; (claim, goal) admettre; (concede): **to ~ that** convenir que; **to ~ sb to do** permettre à qn de faire, autoriser qn à faire; **he is ~ed to ...** on lui permet de ...; **smoking is not ~ed** il est interdit de fumer; **we must ~ three days for the journey** il faut compter trois jours pour le voyage

▷ **allow for** vt fus tenir compte de

allowance [ə'lauəns] n (money received) allocation f; (: from parent etc) subside m; (: for expenses) indemnité f; (US: pocket money) argent m de poche; (Tax) somme f déductible du revenu imposable, abattement m; **to make ~s for** (person) essayer de comprendre; (thing) tenir compte de

alloy ['ælɔɪ] n alliage m

all right adv (feel, work) bien; (as answer) d'accord

all-rounder [ɔːˈraʊndəʳ] n (Brit): **to be a good ~** être doué(e) en tout

all-time [ˈɔːltaɪm] adj (record) sans précédent, absolu(e)

ally [ˈælaɪ] n allié m ▷ vt [əˈlaɪ]: **to ~ o.s. with** s'allier avec

almighty [ɔːlˈmaɪtɪ] adj tout(e)-puissant(e); (tremendous) énorme

almond [ˈɑːmənd] n amande f

almost [ˈɔːlməʊst] adv presque; **he ~ fell** il a failli tomber

alone [əˈləʊn] adj, adv seul(e); **to leave sb ~** laisser qn tranquille; **to leave sth ~** ne pas toucher à qch; **let ~ ...** sans parler de ...; encore moins ...

along [əˈlɒŋ] prep le long de ▷ adv: **is he coming ~ with us?** vient-il avec nous?; **he was hopping/ limping ~** il venait or avançait en sautillant/ boitant; **~ with** avec, en plus de; (person) en compagnie de; **all ~** (all the time) depuis le début

alongside [əˈlɒŋˈsaɪd] prep (along) le long de; (beside) à côté de ▷ adv bord à bord; côte à côte; **we brought our boat ~** (of a pier, shore etc) nous avons accosté

aloof [əˈluːf] adj distant(e) ▷ adv à distance, à l'écart; **to stand ~** se tenir à l'écart or à distance

aloud [əˈlaud] adv à haute voix

alphabet [ˈælfəbɛt] n alphabet m

alphabetical [ælfəˈbɛtɪkl] adj alphabétique; **in ~ order** par ordre alphabétique

alpine [ˈælpaɪn] adj alpin(e), alpestre; **~ hut** cabane f or refuge m de montagne; **~ pasture** pâturage m (de montagne); **~ skiing** ski alpin

Alps [ælps] npl: **the ~** les Alpes fpl

already [ɔːlˈrɛdɪ] adv déjà

alright [ˈɔːlˈraɪt] adv (Brit) = **all right**

Alsatian [ælˈseɪʃən] adj alsacien(ne), d'Alsace ▷ n Alsacien(ne); (Brit: dog) berger allemand

also [ˈɔːlsəʊ] adv aussi

altar [ˈɔltəʳ] n autel m

alter [ˈɔltəʳ] vt, vi changer

alteration [ɔltəˈreɪʃən] n changement m, modification f; **alterations** npl (Sewing) retouches fpl; (Archit) modifications fpl; **timetable subject to ~** horaires sujets à modifications

alternate adj [ɔlˈtəːnɪt] alterné(e), alternant(e), alternatif(-ive); (US) = **alternative** ▷ vi [ˈɔltə-neɪt] alterner; **to ~ with** alterner avec; **on ~ days** un jour sur deux, tous les deux jours

alternative [ɔlˈtəːnətɪv] adj (solution, plan) autre, de remplacement; (energy) doux (douce); (lifestyle) parallèle ▷ n (choice) alternative f; (other possibility) autre possibilité f; **~ medicine** médecine alternative, médecine douce

alternatively [ɔlˈtəːnətɪvlɪ] adv: **~ one could ...** une autre or l'autre solution serait de ...

alternator [ˈɔltəˈneɪtəʳ] n (Aut) alternateur m

although [ɔːlˈðəʊ] conj bien que + sub

altitude [ˈæltɪtjuːd] n altitude f

alto [ˈæltəʊ] n (female) contralto m; (male) haute-contre f

altogether [ɔːltəˈgɛðəʳ] adv entièrement, tout à fait; (on the whole) tout compte fait; (in all) en tout; **how much is that ~?** ça fait combien en tout?

aluminium [æljuˈmɪnɪəm], (US) **aluminum** [əˈluːmɪnəm] n aluminium m

always [ˈɔːlweɪz] adv toujours

Alzheimer's [ˈæltshaɪməz], **Alzheimer's disease** n maladie f d'Alzheimer

AM abbr = **amplitude modulation** ▷ n abbr (= Assembly Member) député m au Parlement gallois

am [æm] vb see **be**

a.m. adv abbr (= ante meridiem) du matin

amalgamate [əˈmælgəmeɪt] vt, vi fusionner

amass [əˈmæs] vt amasser

amateur [ˈæmətəʳ] n amateur m ▷ adj (Sport) amateur inv; **~ dramatics** le théâtre amateur

amateurish [ˈæmətərɪʃ] adj (pej) d'amateur, un peu amateur

amaze [əˈmeɪz] vt stupéfier; **to be ~d (at)** être stupéfait(e) (de)

amazed [əˈmeɪzd] adj stupéfait(e)

amazement [əˈmeɪzmənt] n surprise f, étonnement m

amazing [əˈmeɪzɪŋ] adj étonnant(e), incroyable; (bargain, offer) exceptionnel(le)

Amazon [ˈæməzən] n (Geo, Mythology) Amazone f ▷ cpd amazonien(ne), de l'Amazone; **the ~ basin** le bassin de l'Amazone; **the ~ jungle** la forêt amazonienne

ambassador [æmˈbæsədəʳ] n ambassadeur m

amber [ˈæmbəʳ] n ambre m; **at ~** (Brit Aut) à l'orange

ambiguous [æmˈbɪgjuəs] adj ambigu(ë)

ambition [æmˈbɪʃən] n ambition f

ambitious [æmˈbɪʃəs] adj ambitieux(-euse)

ambulance [ˈæmbjuləns] n ambulance f; **call an ~!** appelez une ambulance!

ambush [ˈæmbuʃ] n embuscade f ▷ vt tendre une embuscade à

amen [ˈɑːˈmɛn] excl amen

amenable [əˈmiːnəbl] adj: **~ to** (advice etc) disposé(e) à écouter or suivre; **~ to the law** responsable devant la loi

amend [əˈmɛnd] vt (law) amender; (text) corriger; (habits) réformer ▷ vi s'amender, se corriger; **to make ~s** réparer ses torts, faire amende honorable

amendment [əˈmɛndmənt] n (to law) amendement m; (to text) correction f

amenities [əˈmiːnɪtɪz] npl aménagements mpl, équipements mpl

America [əˈmɛrɪkə] n Amérique f

American [əˈmɛrɪkən] adj américain(e) ▷ n Américain(e)

American football n (Brit) football m américain

amiable [ˈeɪmɪəbl] adj aimable, affable

amicable [ˈæmɪkəbl] adj amical(e); (Law) à l'amiable

amid [əˈmɪd], **amidst** [əˈmɪdst] prep parmi, au milieu de

amiss [ə'mɪs] *adj, adv*: **there's something ~** il y a quelque chose qui ne va pas *or* qui cloche; **to take sth ~** prendre qch mal *or* de travers

ammonia [ə'məunɪə] *n* (*gas*) ammoniac *m*; (*liquid*) ammoniaque *f*

ammunition [æmju'nɪʃən] *n* munitions *fpl*; (*fig*) arguments *mpl*

amnesty [ˈæmnɪstɪ] *n* amnistie *f*; **to grant an ~ to** accorder une amnistie à

amok [ə'mɔk] *adv*: **to run ~** être pris(e) d'un accès de folie furieuse

among [ə'mʌŋ], **amongst** [ə'mʌŋst] *prep* parmi, entre

amorous [ˈæmərəs] *adj* amoureux(-euse)

amount [ə'maunt] *n* (*sum of money*) somme *f*; (*total*) montant *m*; (*quantity*) quantité *f*; nombre *m* ▷ *vi*: **to ~ to** (*total*) s'élever à; (*be same as*) équivaloir à, revenir à; **this ~s to a refusal** cela équivaut à un refus; **the total ~** (*of money*) le montant total

amp [æmp], **ampère** [ˈæmpɛəʳ] *n* ampère *m*; **a 13 ~ plug** une fiche de 13 A

ample [ˈæmpl] *adj* ample, spacieux(-euse); (*enough*): **this is ~** c'est largement suffisant; **to have ~ time/room** avoir bien assez de temps/place, avoir largement le temps/la place

amplifier [ˈæmplɪfaɪəʳ] *n* amplificateur *m*

amputate [ˈæmpjuteɪt] *vt* amputer

Amtrak [ˈæmtræk] (*US*) *n société mixte de transports ferroviaires interurbains pour voyageurs*

amuse [ə'mju:z] *vt* amuser; **to ~ o.s. with sth/by doing sth** se divertir avec qch/à faire qch; **to be ~d at** être amusé par; **he was not ~d** il n'a pas apprécié

amusement [ə'mju:zmənt] *n* amusement *m*; (*pastime*) distraction *f*

amusement arcade *n* salle *f* de jeu

amusement park *n* parc *m* d'attractions

amusing [ə'mju:zɪŋ] *adj* amusant(e), divertissant(e)

an [æn, ən, n] *indef art see* **a**

anaemia, (*US*) **anemia** [ə'ni:mɪə] *n* anémie *f*

anaemic, (*US*) **anemic** [ə'ni:mɪk] *adj* anémique

anaesthetic, (*US*) **anesthetic** [ænɪs'θetɪk] *adj, n* anesthésique *m*; **under the ~** sous anesthésie; **local/general ~** anesthésie locale/générale

analogue, analog [ˈænəlɔg] *adj* (*watch, computer*) analogique

analogy [ə'nælədʒɪ] *n* analogie *f*; **to draw an ~ between** établir une analogie entre

analyse, (*US*) **analyze** [ˈænəlaɪz] *vt* analyser

analysis (*pl* **analyses**) [ə'næləsɪs, -si:z] *n* analyse *f*; **in the last ~** en dernière analyse

analyst [ˈænəlɪst] *n* (*political analyst etc*) analyste *m/f*; (*US*) psychanalyste *m/f*

analyze [ˈænəlaɪz] *vt* (*US*) = **analyse**

anarchist [ˈænəkɪst] *adj, n* anarchiste (*m/f*)

anarchy [ˈænəkɪ] *n* anarchie *f*

anatomy [ə'nætəmɪ] *n* anatomie *f*

ancestor [ˈænsɪstəʳ] *n* ancêtre *m*, aïeul *m*

anchor [ˈæŋkəʳ] *n* ancre *f* ▷ *vi* (*also*: **to drop anchor**) jeter l'ancre, mouiller ▷ *vt* mettre à

l'ancre; (*fig*): **to ~ sth to** fixer qch à; **to weigh ~** lever l'ancre

anchovy [ˈæntʃəvɪ] *n* anchois *m*

ancient [ˈeɪnʃənt] *adj* ancien(ne), antique; (*person*) d'un âge vénérable; (*car*) antédiluvien(ne); **~ monument** monument *m* historique

ancillary [æn'sɪlərɪ] *adj* auxiliaire

and [ænd] *conj* et; **~ so on** et ainsi de suite; **try ~ come** tâchez de venir; **come ~ sit here** venez vous asseoir ici; **he talked ~ talked** il a parlé pendant des heures; **better ~ better** de mieux en mieux; **more ~ more** de plus en plus

Andorra [æn'dɔ:rə] *n* (principauté *f* d')Andorre *f*

anemia *etc* [ə'ni:mɪə] *n* (*US*) = **anaemia** *etc*

anesthetic [ænɪs'θetɪk] *n, adj* (*US*) = **anaesthetic**

anew [ə'nju:] *adv* à nouveau

angel [ˈeɪndʒəl] *n* ange *m*

anger [ˈæŋgəʳ] *n* colère *f* ▷ *vt* mettre en colère, irriter

angina [æn'dʒaɪnə] *n* angine *f* de poitrine

angle [ˈæŋgl] *n* angle *m* ▷ *vi*: **to ~ for** (*trout*) pêcher; (*compliments*) chercher, quêter; **from their ~** de leur point de vue

angler [ˈæŋgləʳ] *n* pêcheur(-euse) à la ligne

Anglican [ˈæŋglɪkən] *adj, n* anglican(e)

angling [ˈæŋglɪŋ] *n* pêche *f* à la ligne

Anglo- [ˈæŋgləu] *prefix* anglo(-)

angrily [ˈæŋgrɪlɪ] *adv* avec colère

angry [ˈæŋgrɪ] *adj* en colère, furieux(-euse); (*wound*) enflamé(e); **to be ~ with sb/at sth** être furieux contre qn/de qch; **to get ~** se fâcher, se mettre en colère; **to make sb ~** mettre qn en colère

anguish [ˈæŋgwɪʃ] *n* angoisse *f*

animal [ˈænɪməl] *n* animal *m* ▷ *adj* animal(e)

animate *vt* [ˈænɪmeɪt] animer ▷ *adj* [ˈænɪmɪt] animé(e), vivant(e)

animated [ˈænɪmeɪtɪd] *adj* animé(e)

animation [ænɪ'meɪʃən] *n* (*of person*) entrain *m*; (*of street, Cine*) animation *f*

aniseed [ˈænɪsi:d] *n* anis *m*

ankle [ˈæŋkl] *n* cheville *f*

ankle socks *npl* socquettes *fpl*

annex [ˈæneks] *n* (*Brit: also*: **annexe**) annexe *f* ▷ *vt* [ə'neks] annexer

anniversary [ænɪ'və:sərɪ] *n* anniversaire *m*

announce [ə'nauns] *vt* annoncer; (*birth, death*) faire part de; **he ~d that he wasn't going** il a déclaré qu'il n'irait pas

announcement [ə'naunsmənt] *n* annonce *f*; (*for births etc: in newspaper*) avis *m* de faire-part; (: *letter, card*) faire-part *m*; **I'd like to make an ~** j'ai une communication à faire

announcer [ə'naunsəʳ] *n* (*Radio, TV: between programmes*) speaker(ine); (: *in a programme*) présentateur(-trice)

annoy [ə'nɔɪ] *vt* agacer, ennuyer, contrarier; **to be ~ed (at sth/with sb)** être en colère *or* irrité (contre qch/qn); **don't get ~ed!** ne vous fâchez pas!

annoyance [ə'nɔɪəns] *n* mécontentement *m*,

contrariété f

annoying [əˈnɔɪɪŋ] adj agaçant(e), contrariant(e)

annual [ˈænjuəl] adj annuel(le) ▷ n (Bot) plante annuelle; (book) album m

annually [ˈænjuəlɪ] adv annuellement

annul [əˈnʌl] vt annuler; (law) abroger

annum [ˈænəm] n see per

anonymous [əˈnɒnɪməs] adj anonyme; **to remain ~** garder l'anonymat

anorak [ˈænəræk] n anorak m

anorexia [ænəˈrɛksɪə] n (also: **anorexia nervosa**) anorexie f

anorexic [ænəˈrɛksɪk] adj, n anorexique (m/f)

another [əˈnʌðəʳ] adj: **~ book** (one more) un autre livre, encore un livre, un livre de plus; (a different one) un autre livre ▷ pron un(e) autre, encore un(e), un(e) de plus; **~ drink?** encore un verre?; **in ~ five years** dans cinq ans; see also **one**

answer [ˈɑːnsəʳ] n réponse f; (to problem) solution f ▷ vi répondre ▷ vt (reply to) répondre à; (problem) résoudre; (prayer) exaucer; **in ~ to your letter** suite à or en réponse à votre lettre; **to ~ the phone** répondre (au téléphone); **to ~ the bell** or **the door** aller or venir ouvrir (la porte)
  ▶ **answer back** vi répondre, répliquer
  ▶ **answer for** vt fus répondre de, se porter garant de; (crime, one's actions) répondre de
  ▶ **answer to** vt fus (description) répondre or correspondre à

answerable [ˈɑːnsərəbl] adj: **~ (to sb/for sth)** responsable (devant qn/de qch); **I am ~ to no-one** je n'ai de comptes à rendre à personne

answering machine [ˈɑːnsərɪŋ-] n répondeur m

answerphone [ˈɑːnsərfəʊn] n (esp Brit) répondeur m (téléphonique)

ant [ænt] n fourmi f

antagonism [ænˈtægənɪzəm] n antagonisme m

antagonize [ænˈtægənaɪz] vt éveiller l'hostilité de, contrarier

Antarctic [æntˈɑːktɪk] adj antarctique, austral(e) ▷ n: **the ~** l'Antarctique m

antelope [ˈæntɪləʊp] n antilope f

antenatal [ˈæntɪˈneɪtl] adj prénatal(e)

antenatal clinic n service m de consultation prénatale

antenna (pl **-e**) [ænˈtɛnə, -niː] n antenne f

anthem [ˈænθəm] n motet m; **national ~** hymne national

anthology [ænˈθɒlədʒɪ] n anthologie f

anthrax [ˈænθræks] n anthrax m

anthropology [ænθrəˈpɒlədʒɪ] n anthropologie f

anti [ˈæntɪ] prefix anti-

anti-aircraft [ˈæntɪˈɛəkrɑːft] adj antiaérien(ne)

antibiotic [ˈæntɪbaɪˈɒtɪk] n antibiotique m

antibody [ˈæntɪbɒdɪ] n anticorps m

anticipate [ænˈtɪsɪpeɪt] vt s'attendre à, prévoir; (wishes, request) aller au devant de, devancer; **this is worse than I ~d** c'est pire que je ne pensais; **as ~d** comme prévu

anticipation [æntɪsɪˈpeɪʃən] n attente f; **thanking you in ~** en vous remerciant d'avance, avec mes remerciements anticipés

anticlimax [ˈæntɪˈklaɪmæks] n déception f

anticlockwise [ˈæntɪˈklɒkwaɪz] (Brit) adv dans le sens inverse des aiguilles d'une montre

antics [ˈæntɪks] npl singeries fpl

antidepressant [ˈæntɪdɪˈprɛsnt] n antidépresseur m

antidote [ˈæntɪdəʊt] n antidote m, contrepoison m

antifreeze [ˈæntɪfriːz] n antigel m

anti-globalization [æntɪglʊbəlaɪˈzeɪʃən] n antimondialisation f

antihistamine [æntɪˈhɪstəmɪn] n antihistaminique m

antiperspirant [ˈæntɪˈpəːspɪrənt] n déodorant m

antiquated [ˈæntɪkweɪtɪd] adj vieilli(e), suranné(e), vieillot(te)

antique [ænˈtiːk] n (ornament) objet m d'art ancien; (furniture) meuble ancien ▷ adj ancien(ne); (pre-mediaeval) antique

antique dealer n antiquaire m/f

antique shop n magasin m d'antiquités

anti-Semitism [ˈæntɪˈsɛmɪtɪzəm] n antisémitisme m

antiseptic [æntɪˈsɛptɪk] adj, n antiseptique (m)

antisocial [ˈæntɪˈsəʊʃəl] adj (unfriendly) peu liant(e), insociable; (against society) antisocial(e)

antlers [ˈæntləz] npl bois mpl, ramure f

anvil [ˈænvɪl] n enclume f

anxiety [æŋˈzaɪətɪ] n anxiété f; (keenness): **~ to do** grand désir or impatience f de faire

anxious [ˈæŋkʃəs] adj (très) inquiet(-ète); (always worried) anxieux(-euse); (worrying) angoissant(e); (keen): **~ to do/that** qui tient beaucoup à faire/à ce que + sub; impatient(e) de faire/que + sub; **I'm very ~ about you** je me fais beaucoup de souci pour toi

any [ˈɛnɪ] adj **1** (in questions etc: singular) du, de l', de la; (: plural) des; **do you have ~ butter/children/ink?** avez-vous du beurre/des enfants/de l'encre?
2 (with negative) de, d'; **I don't have ~ money/ books** je n'ai pas d'argent/de livres; **without ~ difficulty** sans la moindre difficulté
3 (no matter which) n'importe quel(le); (each and every) tout(e), chaque; **choose ~ book you like** vous pouvez choisir n'importe quel livre; **~ teacher you ask will tell you** n'importe quel professeur vous le dira
4 (in phrases): **in ~ case** de toute façon; **~ day now** d'un jour à l'autre; **at ~ moment** à tout moment, d'un instant à l'autre; **at ~ rate** en tout cas; **~ time** n'importe quand; **he might come (at) ~ time** il pourrait venir n'importe quand; **come (at) ~ time** venez quand vous voulez
  ▷ pron **1** (in questions etc) en; **have you got ~?** est-ce que vous en avez?; **can ~ of you sing?** est-ce que parmi vous il y en a qui savent chanter?
2 (with negative) en; **I don't have ~ (of them)** je n'en ai pas, je n'en ai aucun
3 (no matter which one(s)) n'importe lequel (or laquelle); (anybody) n'importe qui; **take ~ of those books (you like)** vous pouvez prendre

n'importe lequel de ces livres
▷ *adv* **1** *(in questions etc)*: **do you want ~ more soup/sandwiches?** voulez-vous encore de la soupe/des sandwichs?; **are you feeling ~ better?** est-ce que vous vous sentez mieux? **2** *(with negative)*: **I can't hear him ~ more** je ne l'entends plus; **don't wait ~ longer** n'attendez pas plus longtemps

anybody ['ɛnɪbɒdɪ] *pron* n'importe qui; *(in interrogative sentences)* quelqu'un; *(in negative sentences)*: **I don't see ~** je ne vois personne; **if ~ should phone ...** si quelqu'un téléphone ...

anyhow ['ɛnɪhau] *adv* quoi qu'il en soit; *(haphazardly)* n'importe comment; **do it ~ you like** faites-le comme vous voulez; **she leaves things just ~** elle laisse tout traîner; **I shall go ~** j'irai de toute façon

anyone ['ɛnɪwʌn] *pron* = **anybody**

anything ['ɛnɪθɪŋ] *pron (no matter what)* n'importe quoi; *(in questions)* quelque chose; *(with negative)* ne ... rien; **I don't want ~** je ne veux rien; **can you see ~?** tu vois quelque chose?; **if ~ happens to me ...** s'il m'arrive quoi que ce soit ...; **you can say ~ you like** vous pouvez dire ce que vous voulez; **~ will do** n'importe quoi fera l'affaire; **he'll eat ~** il mange de tout; **~ else?** *(in shop)* avec ceci?; **it can cost ~ between £15 and £20** *(Brit)* ça peut coûter dans les 15 à 20 livres

anytime ['ɛnɪtaɪm] *adv (at any moment)* d'un moment à l'autre; *(whenever)* n'importe quand

anyway ['ɛnɪweɪ] *adv* de toute façon; **~, I couldn't come even if I wanted to** de toute façon, je ne pouvais pas venir même si je le voulais; **I shall go ~** j'irai quand même; **why are you phoning, ~?** au fait, pourquoi tu me téléphones?

anywhere ['ɛnɪwɛə^r] *adv* n'importe où; *(in interrogative sentences)* quelque part; *(in negative sentences)*: **I can't see him ~** je ne le vois nulle part; **can you see him ~?** tu le vois quelque part?; **put the books down ~** pose les livres n'importe où; **~ in the world** *(no matter where)* n'importe où dans le monde

apart [ə'pɑːt] *adv (to one side)* à part; de côté; à l'écart; *(separately)* séparément; **to take/pull ~** démonter; **10 miles/a long way ~** à 10 miles/très éloignés l'un de l'autre; **they are living ~** ils sont séparés; **~ from** *(prep)* à part, excepté

apartheid [ə'pɑːteɪt] *n* apartheid *m*

apartment [ə'pɑːtmənt] *n (US)* appartement *m*, logement *m*; *(room)* chambre *f*

apartment building *n (US)* immeuble *m*; maison divisée en appartements

apathy ['æpəθɪ] *n* apathie *f*, indifférence *f*

ape [eɪp] *n (grand)* singe ▷ *vt* singer

aperitif [ə'pɛrɪtɪf] *n* apéritif *m*

aperture ['æpətʃuə^r] *n* orifice *m*, ouverture *f*; *(Phot)* ouverture (du diaphragme)

APEX ['eɪpɛks] *n abbr (Aviat: = advance purchase excursion)* APEX *m*

apex ['eɪpɛks] *n* sommet *m*

apologetic [əpɒlə'dʒɛtɪk] *adj (tone, letter)*

d'excuse; **to be very ~ about** s'excuser vivement de

apologize [ə'pɒlədʒaɪz] *vi*: **to ~ (for sth to sb)** s'excuser (de qch auprès de qn), présenter des excuses (à qn pour qch)

apology [ə'pɒlədʒɪ] *n* excuses *fpl*; **to send one's apologies** envoyer une lettre *or* un mot d'excuse, s'excuser (de ne pas pouvoir venir); **please accept my apologies** vous voudrez bien m'excuser

apostle [ə'pɒsl] *n* apôtre *m*

apostrophe [ə'pɒstrəfɪ] *n* apostrophe *f*

appal, *(US)* **appall** [ə'pɔːl] *vt* consterner, atterrer; horrifier

appalling [ə'pɔːlɪŋ] *adj* épouvantable; *(stupidity)* consternant(e); **she's an ~ cook** c'est une très mauvaise cuisinière

apparatus [æpə'reɪtəs] *n* appareil *m*, dispositif *m*; *(in gymnasium)* agrès *mpl*

apparel [ə'pærl] *n (US)* habillement *m*, confection *f*

apparent [ə'pærənt] *adj* apparent(e); **it is ~ that** il est évident que

apparently [ə'pærəntlɪ] *adv* apparemment

appeal [ə'piːl] *vi (Law)* faire *or* interjeter appel
▷ *n (Law)* appel *m*; *(request)* appel; prière *f*; *(charm)* attrait *m*, charme *m*; **to ~ for** demander (instamment); implorer; **to ~ to** *(beg)* faire appel à; *(be attractive)* plaire à; **to ~ to sb for mercy** implorer la pitié de qn, prier *or* adjurer qn d'avoir pitié; **it doesn't ~ to me** cela ne m'attire pas; **right of ~** droit *m* de recours

appealing [ə'piːlɪŋ] *adj (attractive)* attrayant(e); *(touching)* attendrissant(e)

appear [ə'pɪə^r] *vi* apparaître, se montrer; *(Law)* comparaître; *(publication)* paraître, sortir, être publié(e); *(seem)* paraître, sembler; **it would ~ that** il semble que; **to ~ in Hamlet** jouer dans Hamlet; **to ~ on TV** passer à la télé

appearance [ə'pɪərəns] *n* apparition *f*; parution *f*; *(look, aspect)* apparence *f*, aspect *m*; **to put in** *or* **make an ~** faire acte de présence; *(Theat)*: **by order of ~** par ordre d'entrée en scène; **to keep up ~s** sauver les apparences; **to all ~s** selon toute apparence

appease [ə'piːz] *vt* apaiser, calmer

appendices [ə'pɛndɪsiːz] *npl of* **appendix**

appendicitis [əpɛndɪ'saɪtɪs] *n* appendicite *f*

appendix *(pl* **appendices)** [ə'pɛndɪks, -siːz] *n* appendice *m*; **to have one's ~ out** se faire opérer de l'appendicite

appetite ['æpɪtaɪt] *n* appétit *m*; **that walk has given me an ~** cette promenade m'a ouvert l'appétit

appetizer ['æpɪtaɪzə^r] *n (food)* amuse-gueule *m*; *(drink)* apéritif *m*

applaud [ə'plɔːd] *vt, vi* applaudir

applause [ə'plɔːz] *n* applaudissements *mpl*

apple ['æpl] *n* pomme *f*; *(also:* **apple tree)** pommier *m*; **it's the ~ of my eye** j'y tiens comme à la prunelle de mes yeux

apple pie *n* tarte *f* aux pommes

appliance [ə'plaɪəns] *n* appareil *m*; **electrical ~s** l'électroménager *m*

applicable [ə'plɪkəbl] *adj* applicable; **the law is ~ from January** la loi entre en vigueur au mois de janvier; **to be ~ to** (*relevant*) valoir pour

applicant ['æplɪkənt] *n*: ~ **(for)** (*Admin: for benefit etc*) demandeur(-euse) (de); (*for post*) candidat(e) (à)

application [æplɪ'keɪʃən] *n* application *f*; (*for a job, a grant etc*) demande *f*; candidature *f*; **on** ~ sur demande

application form *n* formulaire *m* de demande

applied [ə'plaɪd] *adj* appliqué(e); ~ **arts** *npl* arts décoratifs

apply [ə'plaɪ] *vt*: **to ~ (to)** (*paint, ointment*) appliquer (sur); (*law, etc*) appliquer (à) ▷ *vi*: **to ~ to** (*ask*) s'adresser à; (*be suitable for, relevant to*) s'appliquer à, être valable pour; **to ~ (for)** (*permit, grant*) faire une demande (en vue d'obtenir); (*job*) poser sa candidature (pour), faire une demande d'emploi (concernant); **to ~ the brakes** actionner les freins, freiner; **to ~ o.s. to** s'appliquer à

appoint [ə'pɔɪnt] *vt* (*to post*) nommer, engager; (*date, place*) fixer, désigner

appointment [ə'pɔɪntmənt] *n* (*to post*) nomination *f*; (*job*) poste *m*; (*arrangement to meet*) rendez-vous *m*; **to have an ~** avoir un rendez-vous; **to make an ~ (with)** prendre rendez-vous (avec); **I'd like to make an ~** je voudrais prendre rendez-vous; **"~s (vacant)"** (*Press*) "offres d'emploi"; **by ~** sur rendez-vous

appraisal [ə'preɪzl] *n* évaluation *f*

appreciate [ə'priːʃɪeɪt] *vt* (*like*) apprécier, faire cas de; (*be grateful for*) être reconnaissant(e) de; (*assess*) évaluer; (*be aware of*) comprendre, se rendre compte de ▷ *vi* (*Finance*) prendre de la valeur; **I ~ your help** je vous remercie pour votre aide

appreciation [əpriːʃɪ'eɪʃən] *n* appréciation *f*; (*gratitude*) reconnaissance *f*; (*Finance*) hausse *f*, valorisation *f*

appreciative [ə'priːʃɪətɪv] *adj* (*person*) sensible; (*comment*) élogieux(-euse)

apprehension [æprɪ'hɛnʃən] *n* appréhension *f*, inquiétude *f*

apprehensive [æprɪ'hɛnsɪv] *adj* inquiet(-ète), appréhensif(-ive)

apprentice [ə'prɛntɪs] *n* apprenti *m* ▷ *vt*: **to be ~d to** être en apprentissage chez

apprenticeship [ə'prɛntɪʃɪp] *n* apprentissage *m*; **to serve one's ~** faire son apprentissage

approach [ə'prəʊtʃ] *vi* approcher ▷ *vt* (*come near*) approcher de; (*ask, apply to*) s'adresser à; (*subject, passer-by*) aborder ▷ *n* approche *f*; accès *m*, abord *m*; démarche *f* (*auprès de qn*); démarche *f* (*intellectuelle*); **to ~ sb about sth** aller *or* venir voir qn pour qch

approachable [ə'prəʊtʃəbl] *adj* accessible

appropriate *adj* [ə'prəʊprɪɪt] (*tool etc*) qui convient, approprié(e); (*moment, remark*) opportun(e) ▷ *vt* [ə'prəʊprɪeɪt] (*take*)

s'approprier; (*allot*): **to ~ sth for** affecter qch à; ~ **for** *or* **to** approprié à; **it would not be ~ for me to comment** il ne me serait pas approprié de commenter

approval [ə'pruːvəl] *n* approbation *f*; **to meet with sb's ~** (*proposal etc*) recueillir l'assentiment de qn; **on ~** (*Comm*) à l'examen

approve [ə'pruːv] *vt* approuver
▶ **approve of** *vt fus* (*thing*) approuver; (*person*): **they don't ~ of her** ils n'ont pas bonne opinion d'elle

approximate [ə'prɒksɪmɪt] *adj* approximatif(-ive) ▷ *vt* [ə'prɒksɪmeɪt] se rapprocher de; être proche de

approximately [ə'prɒksɪmətlɪ] *adv* approximativement

Apr. *abbr* = **April**

apricot ['eɪprɪkɒt] *n* abricot *m*

April ['eɪprəl] *n* avril *m*; ~ **fool!** poisson d'avril!; *for phrases see also* **July**

April Fools' Day *n* le premier avril; *voir article*

apron ['eɪprən] *n* tablier *m*; (*Aviat*) aire *f* de stationnement

apt [æpt] *adj* (*suitable*) approprié(e); (*able*): ~ **(at)** doué(e) (pour); apte (à); (*likely*): ~ **to do** susceptible de faire; ayant tendance à faire

aquarium [ə'kwɛərɪəm] *n* aquarium *m*

Aquarius [ə'kwɛərɪəs] *n* le Verseau; **to be ~** être du Verseau

Arab ['ærəb] *n* Arabe *m/f* ▷ *adj* arabe

Arabia [ə'reɪbɪə] *n* Arabie *f*

Arabian [ə'reɪbɪən] *adj* arabe

Arabic ['ærəbɪk] *adj*, *n* arabe (*m*)

arbitrary ['ɑːbɪtrərɪ] *adj* arbitraire

arbitration [ɑːbɪ'treɪʃən] *n* arbitrage *m*; **the dispute went to ~** le litige a été soumis à arbitrage

arc [ɑːk] *n* arc *m*

arcade [ɑː'keɪd] *n* arcade *f*; (*passage with shops*) passage *m*, galerie *f*; (*with games*) salle *f* de jeu

arch [ɑːtʃ] *n* arche *f*; (*of foot*) cambrure *f*, voûte *f* plantaire ▷ *vt* arquer, cambrer ▷ *adj* malicieux(-euse) ▷ *prefix*: ~(-) achevé(e); par excellence; **pointed ~** ogive *f*

archaeologist [ɑːkɪ'ɒlədʒɪst] *n* archéologue *m/f*

archaeology, (*US*) **archeology** [ɑːkɪ'ɒlədʒɪ] *n* archéologie *f*

archbishop [ɑːtʃ'bɪʃəp] *n* archevêque *m*

archeology [ɑːkɪ'ɒlədʒɪ] (*US*) = **archaeology**

archery ['ɑːtʃərɪ] *n* tir *m* à l'arc

architect ['ɑːkɪtɛkt] *n* architecte *m*

architectural [ɑːkɪ'tɛktʃərəl] *adj* architectural(e)

architecture ['ɑːkɪtɛktʃə'] *n* architecture *f*

archive ['ɑːkaɪv] *n* (*often pl*) archives *fpl*

archives ['ɑːkaɪvz] *npl* archives *fpl*

Arctic ['ɑːktɪk] *adj* arctique ▷ *n*: **the ~** l'Arctique *m*

ardent ['ɑːdənt] *adj* fervent(e)

are [ɑː'] *vb see* **be**

area ['ɛərɪə] *n* (*Geom*) superficie *f*; (*zone*) région *f*; (: *smaller*) secteur *m*; (*in room*) coin *m*; (*knowledge, research*) domaine *m*; **the London ~** la région

Londonienne

area code (US) n (Tel) indicatif m de zone

arena [ə'riːnə] n arène f

aren't [ɑːnt] = **are not**

Argentina [ɑːdʒən'tiːnə] n Argentine f

Argentinian [ɑːdʒən'tɪnɪən] adj argentin(e) ▷ n Argentin(e)

arguably ['ɑːgjuəblɪ] adv: **it is ~ ...** on peut soutenir que c'est ...

argue ['ɑːgjuː] vi (quarrel) se disputer; (reason) argumenter ▷ vt (debate: case, matter) débattre; **to ~ about sth (with sb)** se disputer (avec qn) au sujet de qch; **to ~ that** objecter or alléguer que, donner comme argument que

argument ['ɑːgjumənt] n (quarrel) dispute f, discussion f; (reasons) argument m; (debate) discussion, controverse f; **~ for/against** argument pour/contre

argumentative [ɑːgju'mɛntətɪv] adj ergoteur(-euse), raisonneur(-euse)

Aries ['ɛərɪz] n le Bélier; **to be ~** être du Bélier

arise (pt **arose**, pp **-n**) [ə'raɪz, ə'rəuz, ə'rɪzn] vi survenir, se présenter; **to ~ from** résulter de; **should the need ~** en cas de besoin

aristocrat ['ærɪstəkræt] n aristocrate m/f

arithmetic [ə'rɪθmətɪk] n arithmétique f

ark [ɑːk] n: **Noah's A~** l'Arche f de Noé

arm [ɑːm] n bras m ▷ vt armer; **arms** npl (weapons, Heraldry) armes fpl; **~ in ~** bras dessus bras dessous

armaments ['ɑːməmənts] npl (weapons) armement m

armchair ['ɑːmtʃɛər] n fauteuil m

armed [ɑːmd] adj armé(e)

armed forces npl: **the ~** les forces armées

armed robbery n vol m à main armée

armour, (US) **armor** ['ɑːmər] n armure f; (also: **armour-plating**) blindage m; (Mil: tanks) blindés mpl

armoured car, (US) **armored car** ['ɑːməd-] n véhicule blindé

armpit ['ɑːmpɪt] n aisselle f

armrest ['ɑːmrɛst] n accoudoir m

army ['ɑːmɪ] n armée f

A road n (Brit) ≈ route nationale

aroma [ə'rəumə] n arôme m

aromatherapy [ərəumə'θɛrəpɪ] n aromathérapie f

arose [ə'rəuz] pt of **arise**

around [ə'raund] adv (tout) autour; (nearby) dans les parages ▷ prep autour de; (near) près de; (fig: about) environ; (: date, time) vers; **is he ~?** est-il dans les parages or là?

arouse [ə'rauz] vt (sleeper) éveiller; (curiosity, passions) éveiller, susciter; (anger) exciter

arrange [ə'reɪndʒ] vt arranger; (programme) arrêter, convenir de ▷ vi: **we have ~d for a car to pick you up** nous avons prévu qu'une voiture vienne vous prendre; **it was ~d that ...** il a été convenu que ..., il a été décidé que ...; **to ~ to do sth** prévoir de faire qch

arrangement [ə'reɪndʒmənt] n arrangement

m; **to come to an ~ (with sb)** se mettre d'accord (avec qn); **home deliveries by ~** livraison à domicile sur demande; **arrangements** npl (plans etc) arrangements mpl, dispositions fpl; **I'll make ~s for you to be met** je vous enverrai chercher

array [ə'reɪ] n (of objects) déploiement m, étalage m; (Math, Comput) tableau m

arrears [ə'rɪəz] npl arriéré m; **to be in ~ with one's rent** devoir un arriéré de loyer, être en retard pour le paiement de son loyer

arrest [ə'rɛst] vt arrêter; (sb's attention) retenir, attirer ▷ n arrestation f; **under ~** en état d'arrestation

arrival [ə'raɪvl] n arrivée f; (Comm) arrivage m; (person) arrivant(e); **new ~** nouveau venu/ nouvelle venue; (baby) nouveau-né(e)

arrive [ə'raɪv] vi arriver

▷ **arrive at** vt fus (decision, solution) parvenir à

arrogance ['ærəgəns] n arrogance f

arrogant ['ærəgənt] adj arrogant(e)

arrow ['ærəu] n flèche f

arse [ɑːs] n (Brit inf!) cul m (!)

arson ['ɑːsn] n incendie criminel

art [ɑːt] n art m; (craft) métier m; **work of ~** œuvre f d'art; **Arts** npl (Scol) les lettres fpl

art college n école f des beaux-arts

artery ['ɑːtərɪ] n artère f

art gallery n musée m d'art; (saleroom) galerie f de peinture

arthritis [ɑː'θraɪtɪs] n arthrite f

artichoke ['ɑːtɪtʃəuk] n artichaut m; **Jerusalem ~** topinambour m

article ['ɑːtɪkl] n article m; (Brit Law: training): **articles** npl ≈ stage m; **~s of clothing** vêtements mpl

articulate [adj ɑː'tɪkjulɪt, vb ɑː'tɪkjuleɪt] adj (person) qui s'exprime clairement et aisément; (speech) bien articulé(e), prononcé(e) clairement ▷ vi articuler, parler distinctement ▷ vt articuler

articulated lorry [ɑː'tɪkjuleɪtɪd-] n (Brit) (camion m) semi-remorque m

artificial [ɑːtɪ'fɪʃəl] adj artificiel(le)

artificial respiration n respiration artificielle

artist ['ɑːtɪst] n artiste m/f

artistic [ɑː'tɪstɪk] adj artistique

artistry ['ɑːtɪstrɪ] n art m, talent m

art school n ≈ école f des beaux-arts

as [æz] conj **1** (time: moment) comme, alors que; à mesure que; (: duration) tandis que; **he came in as I was leaving** il est arrivé comme je partais; **as the years went by** à mesure que les années passaient; **as from tomorrow** à partir de demain

2 (since, because) comme, puisque; **he left early as he had to be home by 10** comme il or puisqu'il devait être de retour avant 10h, il est parti de bonne heure

3 (referring to manner, way) comme; **do as you wish** faites comme vous voudrez; **as she said** comme elle disait

▷ adv **1** (in comparisons): **as big as** aussi grand

que; **twice as big as** deux fois plus grand que; **big as it is** si grand que ce soit; **much as I like them, I ...** je les aime bien, mais je ...; **as much** or **many as** autant que; **as much money/many books as** autant d'argent/de livres que; **as soon as** dès que

2 (*concerning*): **as for** or **to that** quant à cela, pour ce qui est de cela

3: **as if** or **though** comme si; **he looked as if he was ill** il avait l'air d'être malade; *see also* **long; such; well**

▷ *prep* (*in the capacity of*) en tant que, en qualité de; **he works as a driver** il travaille comme chauffeur; **as chairman of the company, he ...** en tant que président de la société, il ...; **dressed up as a cowboy** déguisé en cowboy; **he gave me it as a present** il me l'a offert, il m'en a fait cadeau

a.s.a.p. *abbr* = **as soon as possible**
asbestos [æz'bɛstəs] *n* asbeste *m*, amiante *m*
ascend [ə'sɛnd] *vt* gravir
ascent [ə'sɛnt] *n* (*climb*) ascension *f*
ascertain [æsə'teɪn] *vt* s'assurer de, vérifier; établir
ash [æʃ] *n* (*dust*) cendre *f*; (*also:* **ash tree**) frêne *m*
ashamed [ə'ʃeɪmd] *adj* honteux(-euse), confus(e); **to be ~ of** avoir honte de; **to be ~ (of o.s.) for having done** avoir honte d'avoir fait
ashore [ə'ʃɔːʳ] *adv* à terre; **to go ~** aller à terre, débarquer
ashtray ['æʃtreɪ] *n* cendrier *m*
Ash Wednesday *n* mercredi *m* des Cendres
Asia ['eɪʃə] *n* Asie *f*
Asian ['eɪʃən] *n* (*from Asia*) Asiatique *m/f*; (*Brit: from Indian subcontinent*) Indo-Pakistanais(-e) ▷ *adj* asiatique; indo-pakistanais(-e)
aside [ə'saɪd] *adv* de côté; à l'écart ▷ *n* aparté *m*; **~ from** *prep* à part, excepté
ask [ɑːsk] *vt* demander; (*invite*) inviter; **to ~ sb sth/to do sth** demander à qn qch/de faire qch; **to ~ sb the time** demander l'heure à qn; **to ~ sb about sth** questionner qn au sujet de qch; se renseigner auprès de qn au sujet de qch; **to ~ about the price** s'informer du prix, se renseigner au sujet du prix; **to ~ (sb) a question** poser une question (à qn); **to ~ sb out to dinner** inviter qn au restaurant
▸ **ask after** *vt fus* demander des nouvelles de
▸ **ask for** *vt fus* demander; **it's just ~ing for trouble** or **for it** ce serait chercher des ennuis
asking price ['ɑːskɪŋ-] *n* prix demandé
asleep [ə'sliːp] *adj* endormi(e); **to be ~** dormir, être endormi(e); **to fall ~** s'endormir
AS level *n abbr* (= *Advanced Subsidiary level*) première partie de l'examen équivalent au baccalauréat
asparagus [əs'pærəgəs] *n* asperges *fpl*
aspect ['æspɛkt] *n* aspect *m*; (*direction in which a building etc faces*) orientation *f*, exposition *f*
aspire [əs'paɪəʳ] *vi*: **to ~ to** aspirer à
aspirin ['æsprɪn] *n* aspirine *f*
ass [æs] *n* âne *m*; (*inf*) imbécile *m/f*; (*US inf!*) cul *m* (!)

assailant [ə'seɪlənt] *n* agresseur *m*; assaillant *m*
assassin [ə'sæsɪn] *n* assassin *m*
assassinate [ə'sæsɪneɪt] *vt* assassiner
assassination [əsæsɪ'neɪʃən] *n* assassinat *m*
assault [ə'sɔːlt] *n* (*Mil*) assaut *m*; (*gen: attack*) agression *f*; (*Law*): **~ (and battery)** voies *fpl* de fait, coups *mpl* et blessures *fpl* ▷ *vt* attaquer; (*sexually*) violenter
assemble [ə'sɛmbl] *vt* assembler ▷ *vi* s'assembler, se rassembler
assembly [ə'sɛmblɪ] *n* (*meeting*) rassemblement *m*; (*parliament*) assemblée *f*; (*construction*) assemblage *m*
assembly line *n* chaîne *f* de montage
assent [ə'sɛnt] *n* assentiment *m*, consentement *m* ▷ *vi*: **to ~ (to sth)** donner son assentiment (à qch), consentir (à qch)
assert [ə'sɜːt] *vt* affirmer, déclarer; établir; (*authority*) faire valoir; (*innocence*) protester de; **to ~ o.s.** s'imposer
assertion [ə'sɜːʃən] *n* assertion *f*, affirmation *f*
assess [ə'sɛs] *vt* évaluer, estimer; (*tax, damages*) établir or fixer le montant de; (*property etc: for tax*) calculer la valeur imposable de; (*person*) juger la valeur de
assessment [ə'sɛsmənt] *n* évaluation *f*, estimation *f*; (*of tax*) fixation *f*; (*of property*) calcul *m* de la valeur imposable; (*judgment*): **~ (of)** jugement *m* or opinion *f* (sur)
assessor [ə'sɛsəʳ] *n* expert *m* (*en matière d'impôt et d'assurance*)
asset ['æsɛt] *n* avantage *m*, atout *m*; (*person*) atout; **assets** *npl* (*Comm*) capital *m*; avoir(s) *m*(*pl*); actif *m*
assign [ə'saɪn] *vt* (*date*) fixer, arrêter; **to ~ sth to** (*task*) assigner qch à; (*resources*) affecter qch à; (*cause, meaning*) attribuer qch à
assignment [ə'saɪnmənt] *n* (*task*) mission *f*; (*homework*) devoir *m*
assist [ə'sɪst] *vt* aider, assister; (*injured person etc*) secourir
assistance [ə'sɪstəns] *n* aide *f*, assistance *f*; secours *mpl*
assistant [ə'sɪstənt] *n* assistant(e), adjoint(e); (*Brit: also:* **shop assistant**) vendeur(-euse)
associate [*adj, n* ə'səuʃɪɪt, *vb* ə'səuʃɪeɪt] *adj, n* associé(e) ▷ *vt* associer ▷ *vi*: **to ~ with sb** fréquenter qn; **~ director** directeur adjoint; **~d company** société affiliée
association [əsəusɪ'eɪʃən] *n* association *f*; **in ~ with** en collaboration avec
assorted [ə'sɔːtɪd] *adj* assorti(e); **in ~ sizes** en plusieurs tailles
assortment [ə'sɔːtmənt] *n* assortiment *m*; (*of people*) mélange *m*
assume [ə'sjuːm] *vt* supposer; (*responsibilities etc*) assumer; (*attitude, name*) prendre, adopter
assumption [ə'sʌmpʃən] *n* supposition *f*, hypothèse *f*; (*of power*) assomption *f*, prise *f*; **on the ~ that** dans l'hypothèse où; (*on condition that*) à condition que
assurance [ə'ʃuərəns] *n* assurance *f*; **I can give**

you no ~s je ne peux rien vous garantir

assure [əˈʃʊəʳ] vt assurer

asterisk [ˈæstərɪsk] n astérisque m

asthma [ˈæsmə] n asthme m

astonish [əˈstɒnɪʃ] vt étonner, stupéfier

astonished [əˈstɒnɪʃd] adj étonné(e); **to be ~ at** être étonné(e) de

astonishing [əˈstɒnɪʃɪŋ] adj étonnant(e), stupéfiant(e); **I find it ~ that ...** je trouve incroyable que ...+sub

astonishment [əˈstɒnɪʃmənt] n (grand) étonnement, stupéfaction f

astound [əˈstaʊnd] vt stupéfier, sidérer

astray [əˈstreɪ] adv: **to go ~** s'égarer; (fig) quitter le droit chemin; **to lead ~** (morally) détourner du droit chemin; **to go ~ in one's calculations** faire fausse route dans ses calculs

astride [əˈstraɪd] adv à cheval ▷ prep à cheval sur

astrology [əsˈtrɒlədʒɪ] n astrologie f

astronaut [ˈæstrənɔːt] n astronaute m/f

astronomer [əsˈtrɒnəməʳ] n astronome m

astronomical [æstrəˈnɒmɪkl] adj astronomique

astronomy [əsˈtrɒnəmɪ] n astronomie f

astute [əsˈtjuːt] adj astucieux(-euse), malin(-igne)

asylum [əˈsaɪləm] n asile m; **to seek political ~** demander l'asile politique

asylum seeker [-siːkəʳ] n demandeur(-euse) d'asile

at [æt] prep **1** (referring to position, direction) à; **at the top** au sommet; **at home/school** à la maison or chez soi/à l'école; **at the baker's** à la boulangerie, chez le boulanger; **to look at sth** regarder qch

2 (referring to time): **at 4 o'clock** à 4 heures; **at Christmas** à Noël; **at night** la nuit; **at times** par moments, parfois

3 (referring to rates, speed etc) à; **at £1 a kilo** une livre le kilo; **two at a time** deux à la fois; **at 50 km/h** à 50 km/h; **at full speed** à toute vitesse

4 (referring to manner): **at a stroke** d'un seul coup; **at peace** en paix

5 (referring to activity): **to be at work** (in the office etc) être au travail; (working) travailler; **to play at cowboys** jouer aux cowboys; **to be good at sth** être bon en qch

6 (referring to cause): **shocked/surprised/ annoyed at sth** choqué par/étonné de/agacé par qch; **I went at his suggestion** j'y suis allé sur son conseil

7 (@ symbol) arobase f

ate [eɪt] pt of **eat**

atheist [ˈeɪθɪɪst] n athée m/f

Athens [ˈæθɪnz] n Athènes

athlete [ˈæθliːt] n athlète m/f

athletic [æθˈlɛtɪk] adj athlétique

athletics [æθˈlɛtɪks] n athlétisme m

Atlantic [ətˈlæntɪk] adj atlantique ▷ n: **the ~ (Ocean)** l'(océan m) Atlantique m

atlas [ˈætləs] n atlas m

A.T.M. n abbr (= Automated Telling Machine) guichet m automatique

atmosphere [ˈætməsfɪəʳ] n (air) atmosphère f; (fig: of place etc) atmosphère, ambiance f

atom [ˈætəm] n atome m

atom bomb n bombe f atomique

atomic [əˈtɒmɪk] adj atomique

atomic bomb n bombe f atomique

atomizer [ˈætəmaɪzəʳ] n atomiseur m

atone [əˈtəʊn] vi: **to ~ for** expier, racheter

atrocious [əˈtrəʊʃəs] adj (very bad) atroce, exécrable

atrocity [əˈtrɒsɪtɪ] n atrocité f

attach [əˈtætʃ] vt (gen) attacher; (document, letter) joindre; (employee, troops) affecter; **to be ~ed to sb/sth** (to like) être attaché à qn/qch; **the ~ed letter** la lettre ci-jointe

attaché case n mallette f, attaché-case m

attachment [əˈtætʃmənt] n (tool) accessoire m; (Comput) fichier m joint; (love): **~ (to)** affection f (pour), attachement m (à)

attack [əˈtæk] vt attaquer; (task etc) s'attaquer à ▷ n attaque f; **heart ~** crise f cardiaque

attacker [əˈtækəʳ] n attaquant m; agresseur m

attain [əˈteɪn] vt (also: **to attain to**) parvenir à, atteindre; (knowledge) acquérir

attempt [əˈtɛmpt] n tentative f ▷ vt essayer, tenter; **~ed theft etc** (Law) tentative de vol etc; **to make an ~ on sb's life** attenter à la vie de qn; **he made no ~ to help** il n'a rien fait pour m'aider or l'aider etc

attempted [əˈtɛmptɪd] adj: **~ murder/suicide** tentative f de meurtre/suicide

attend [əˈtɛnd] vt (course) suivre; (meeting, talk) assister à; (school, church) aller à, fréquenter; (patient) soigner, s'occuper de; **to ~ (up)on** servir; être au service de

▶ **attend to** vt fus (needs, affairs etc) s'occuper de; (customer) s'occuper de, servir

attendance [əˈtɛndəns] n (being present) présence f; (people present) assistance f

attendant [əˈtɛndənt] n employé(e); gardien(ne) ▷ adj concomitant(e), qui accompagne or s'ensuit

attention [əˈtɛnʃən] n attention f; **attentions** attentions fpl, prévenances fpl ▷ excl (Mil) garde-à-vous!; **at ~** (Mil) au garde-à-vous; **for the ~ of** (Admin) à l'attention de; **it has come to my ~ that ...** je constate que ...

attentive [əˈtɛntɪv] adj attentif(-ive); (kind) prévenant(e)

attest [əˈtɛst] vi: **to ~ to** témoigner de attester (de)

attic [ˈætɪk] n grenier m, combles mpl

attitude [ˈætɪtjuːd] n (behaviour) attitude f, manière f; (posture) pose f, attitude; (view): **~ (to)** attitude (envers)

attorney [əˈtəːnɪ] n (US: lawyer) avocat m; (having proxy) mandataire m; **power of ~** procuration f

Attorney General n (Brit) ≈ procureur général; (US) ≈ garde m des Sceaux, ministre m de la Justice

attract [əˈtrækt] vt attirer

attraction [əˈtrækʃən] n (gen pl: pleasant things)

attraction f, attrait m; (Physics) attraction; (fig: towards sb, sth) attirance f
attractive [ə'træktɪv] adj séduisant(e), attrayant(e)
attribute ['ætrɪbjuːt] n attribut m ▷ vt [ə'trɪbjuːt]: **to ~ sth to** attribuer qch à
attrition [ə'trɪʃən] n: **war of ~** guerre f d'usure
aubergine ['əubəʒiːn] n aubergine f
auburn ['ɔːbən] adj auburn inv, châtain roux inv
auction ['ɔːkʃən] n (also: **sale by auction**) vente f aux enchères ▷ vt (also: **to sell by auction**) vendre aux enchères; (also: **to put up for auction**) mettre aux enchères
auctioneer [ɔːkʃə'nɪəʳ] n commissaire-priseur m
audible ['ɔːdɪbl] adj audible
audience ['ɔːdɪəns] n (people) assistance f, public m; (on radio) auditeurs mpl; (at theatre) spectateurs mpl; (interview) audience f
audiovisual [ɔːdɪəu'vɪzjuəl] adj audio-visuel(le); **~ aids** supports or moyens audiovisuels
audit ['ɔːdɪt] n vérification f des comptes, apurement m ▷ vt vérifier, apurer
audition [ɔː'dɪʃən] n audition f ▷ vi auditionner
auditor ['ɔːdɪtəʳ] n vérificateur m des comptes
auditorium [ɔːdɪ'tɔːrɪəm] n auditorium m, salle f de concert or de spectacle
Aug. abbr = **August**
augur ['ɔːgəʳ] vt (be a sign of) présager, annoncer ▷ vi: **it ~s well** c'est bon signe or de bon augure, cela s'annonce bien
August ['ɔːgəst] n août m; for phrases see also **July**
august [ɔː'gʌst] adj majestueux(-euse), imposant(e)
aunt [ɑːnt] n tante f
auntie, aunty ['ɑːntɪ] n diminutive of **aunt**
au pair ['əu'pɛəʳ] n (also: **au pair girl**) jeune fille f au pair
aura ['ɔːrə] n atmosphère f; (of person) aura f
auspicious [ɔːs'pɪʃəs] adj de bon augure, propice
austerity [ɔs'tɛrɪtɪ] n austérité f
Australia [ɔs'treɪlɪə] n Australie f
Australian [ɔs'treɪlɪən] adj australien(ne) ▷ n Australien(ne)
Austria ['ɔstrɪə] n Autriche f
Austrian ['ɔstrɪən] adj autrichien(ne) ▷ n Autrichien(ne)
authentic [ɔː'θɛntɪk] adj authentique
author ['ɔːθəʳ] n auteur m
authoritarian [ɔːθɔrɪ'tɛərɪən] adj autoritaire
authoritative [ɔː'θɔrɪtətɪv] adj (account) digne de foi; (study, treatise) qui fait autorité; (manner) autoritaire
authority [ɔː'θɔrɪtɪ] n autorité f; (permission) autorisation (formelle); **the authorities** les autorités fpl, l'administration f; **to have ~ to do sth** être habilité à faire qch
authorize ['ɔːθəraɪz] vt autoriser
auto ['ɔːtəu] n (US) auto f, voiture f
autobiography [ɔːtəbaɪ'ɔgrəfɪ] n autobiographie f
autograph ['ɔːtəgrɑːf] n autographe m ▷ vt signer, dédicacer

automated ['ɔːtəmeɪtɪd] adj automatisé(e)
automatic [ɔːtə'mætɪk] adj automatique ▷ n (gun) automatique m; (washing machine) lave-linge m automatique; (car) voiture f à transmission automatique
automatically [ɔːtə'mætɪklɪ] adv automatiquement
automation [ɔːtə'meɪʃən] n automatisation f
automobile ['ɔːtəməbiːl] n (US) automobile f
autonomous [ɔː'tɔnəməs] adj autonome
autonomy [ɔː'tɔnəmɪ] n autonomie f
autumn ['ɔːtəm] n automne m
auxiliary [ɔːg'zɪlɪərɪ] adj, n auxiliaire (m/f)
avail [ə'veɪl] vt: **to ~ o.s. of** user de; profiter de ▷ n: **to no ~** sans résultat, en vain, en pure perte
availability [əveɪlə'bɪlɪtɪ] n disponibilité f
available [ə'veɪləbl] adj disponible; **every ~ means** tous les moyens possibles or à sa (or notre etc) disposition; **is the manager ~?** est-ce que le directeur peut (me) recevoir?; (on phone) pourrais-je parler au directeur?; **to make sth ~ to sb** mettre qch à la disposition de qn
avalanche ['ævəlɑːnʃ] n avalanche f
Ave. abbr = **avenue**
avenge [ə'vɛndʒ] vt venger
avenue ['ævənjuː] n avenue f; (fig) moyen m
average ['ævərɪdʒ] n moyenne f ▷ adj moyen(ne) ▷ vt (a certain figure) atteindre or faire etc en moyenne; **on ~** en moyenne; **above/below (the) ~** au-dessus/en-dessous de la moyenne
▷ **average out** vi: **to ~ out at** représenter en moyenne, donner une moyenne de
averse [ə'vəːs] adj: **to be ~ to sth/doing** éprouver une forte répugnance envers qch/à faire; **I wouldn't be ~ to a drink** un petit verre ne serait pas de refus, je ne dirais pas non à un petit verre
avert [ə'vəːt] vt (danger) prévenir, écarter; (one's eyes) détourner
aviary ['eɪvɪərɪ] n volière f
avid ['ævɪd] adj avide
avocado [ævə'kɑːdəu] n (Brit: also: **avocado pear**) avocat m
avoid [ə'vɔɪd] vt éviter
await [ə'weɪt] vt attendre; **~ing attention/ delivery** (Comm) en souffrance; **long ~ed** tant attendu(e)
awake [ə'weɪk] (pt awoke) [ə'wəuk] (pp awoken) [ə'wəukən] adj éveillé(e); (fig) en éveil ▷ vt éveiller ▷ vi s'éveiller; **~ to** conscient de; **to be ~** être réveillé(e); **he was still ~** il ne dormait pas encore
awakening [ə'weɪknɪŋ] n réveil m
award [ə'wɔːd] n (for bravery) récompense f; (prize) prix m; (Law: damages) dommages-intérêts mpl ▷ vt (prize) décerner; (Law: damages) accorder
aware [ə'wɛəʳ] adj: **~ of** (conscious) conscient(e) de; (informed) au courant de; **to become ~ of/that** prendre conscience de/que; se rendre compte de/que; **politically/socially ~** sensibilisé(e) aux or ayant pris conscience des problèmes politiques/sociaux; **I am fully ~ that** je me rends parfaitement compte que

awareness [ə'wɛənɪs] *n* conscience *f*,
connaissance *f*; **to develop people's ~ (of)**
sensibiliser le public (à)

away [ə'weɪ] *adv* (au) loin; (*movement*): **she went
~** (au) loin; (*movement*): **she went
~** elle est partie ▷ *adj* (*not in, not here*) absent(e);
far ~ (au) loin; **two kilometres ~** à (une distance
de) deux kilomètres, à deux kilomètres de
distance; **two hours ~ by car** à deux heures de
voiture *or* de route; **the holiday was two weeks
~** il restait deux semaines jusqu'aux vacances; **~
from** loin de; **he's ~ for a week** il est parti (pour)
une semaine; **he's ~ in Milan** il est (parti) à
Milan; **to take sth ~ from sb** prendre qch à qn;
to take sth ~ from sth (*subtract*) ôter qch de qch;
to work/pedal ~ travailler/pédaler à cœur joie;
to fade ~ (*colour*) s'estomper; (*sound*) s'affaiblir

away game *n* (*Sport*) match *m* à l'extérieur

awe [ɔː] *n* respect mêlé de crainte, effroi mêlé
d'admiration

awe-inspiring ['ɔːɪnspaɪərɪŋ], **awesome** ['ɔː
səm] *adj* impressionnant(e)

awesome ['ɔːsəm] (*US*) *adj* (*inf: excellent*) génial(e)

awful ['ɔːfəl] *adj* affreux(-euse); **an ~ lot of**
énormément de

awfully ['ɔːfəlɪ] *adv* (*very*) terriblement, vraiment

awkward ['ɔːkwəd] *adj* (*clumsy*) gauche,
maladroit(e); (*inconvenient*) peu pratique;
(*embarrassing*) gênant; **I can't talk just now, it's
a bit ~** je ne peux pas parler tout de suite, c'est
un peu difficile

awning ['ɔːnɪŋ] *n* (*of tent*) auvent *m*; (*of shop*) store
m; (*of hotel etc*) marquise *f* (de toile)

awoke [ə'wəuk] *pt of* **awake**

awoken [ə'wəukən] *pp of* **awake**

axe, (*US*) **ax** [æks] *n* hache *f* ▷ *vt* (*employee*)
renvoyer; (*project etc*) abandonner; (*jobs*)
supprimer; **to have an ~ to grind** (*fig*) prêcher
pour son saint

axes ['æksiːz] *npl of* **axis**

axis (*pl* **axes**) ['æksɪs, -siːz] *n* axe *m*

axle ['æksl] *n* (*also:* **axle-tree**) essieu *m*

ay, aye [aɪ] *excl* (*yes*) oui ▷ *n*: **the ay(e)s** les oui

azalea [ə'zeɪlɪə] *n* azalée *f*

Bb

B, b [biː] *n* (*letter*) B, b *m*; (*Scol: mark*) B; (*Mus*): **B** si *m*; **B for Benjamin** (*US*): **B for Baker** B comme Berthe; **B road** *n* (*Brit Aut*) route départementale

B.A. *abbr* = **British Academy**; (*Scol*) = **Bachelor of Arts**

babble ['bæbl] *vi* babiller ▷ *n* babillage *m*

baby ['beɪbɪ] *n* bébé *m*

baby carriage *n* (*US*) voiture *f* d'enfant

baby food *n* aliments *mpl* pour bébé(s)

baby-sit ['beɪbɪsɪt] *vi* garder les enfants

baby-sitter ['beɪbɪsɪtə'] *n* baby-sitter *m/f*

baby wipe *n* lingette *f* (*pour bébé*)

bachelor ['bætʃələ'] *n* célibataire *m*; **B~ of Arts/Science (BA/BSc)** ≈ licencié(e) ès *or* en lettres/sciences; **B~ of Arts/Science degree (BA/BSc)** *n* ≈ licence *f* ès *or* en lettres/sciences; *voir article*

back [bæk] *n* (*of person, horse*) dos *m*; (*of hand*) dos, revers *m*; (*of house*) derrière *m*; (*of car, train*) arrière *m*; (*of chair*) dossier *m*; (*of page*) verso *m*; (*of crowd*): **can the people at the ~ hear me properly?** est-ce que les gens du fond peuvent m'entendre?; (*Football*) arrière *m*; **to have one's ~ to the wall** (*fig*) être au pied du mur; **to break the ~ of a job** (*Brit*) faire le gros d'un travail; **~ to front** à l'envers ▷ *vt* (*financially*) soutenir (financièrement); (*candidate: also*: **back up**) soutenir, appuyer; (*horse: at races*) parier *or* miser sur; (*car*) (faire) reculer ▷ *vi* reculer; (*car etc*) faire marche arrière ▷ *adj* (*in compounds*) de derrière, à l'arrière; **~ seat/wheel** (*Aut*) siège *m*/ roue *f* arrière *inv*; **~ payments/rent** arriéré *m* de paiements/loyer; **~ garden/room** jardin/pièce sur l'arrière; **to take a ~ seat** (*fig*) se contenter d'un second rôle, être relégué(e) au second plan ▷ *adv* (*not forward*) en arrière; (*returned*): **he's ~** il est rentré, il est de retour; **when will you be ~?** quand seras-tu de retour?; **he ran ~** il est revenu en courant; (*restitution*): **throw the ball ~** renvoie la balle; **can I have it ~?** puis-je le ravoir?, peux-tu me le rendre?; (*again*): **he called ~** il a rappelé

▶ **back down** *vi* rabattre de ses prétentions

▶ **back on to** *vt fus*: **the house ~s on to the golf course** la maison donne derrière sur le terrain de golf

▶ **back out** *vi* (*of promise*) se dédire

▶ **back up** *vt* (*person*) soutenir; (*Comput*) faire une copie de sauvegarde de

backache ['bækeɪk] *n* mal *m* au dos

backbencher [bæk'bɛntʃə'] (*Brit*) *n* membre *du* parlement sans portefeuille

backbone ['bækbəun] *n* colonne vertébrale, épine dorsale; **he's the ~ of the organization** c'est sur lui que repose l'organisation

backdate [bæk'deɪt] *vt* (*letter*) antidater; **~d pay rise** augmentation *f* avec effet rétroactif

back door *n* porte *f* de derrière

backfire [bæk'faɪə'] *vi* (*Aut*) pétarader; (*plans*) mal tourner

backgammon ['bækgæmən] *n* trictrac *m*

background ['bækgraund] *n* arrière-plan *m*; (*of events*) situation *f*, conjoncture *f*; (*basic knowledge*) éléments *mpl* de base; (*experience*) formation *f* ▷ *cpd* (*noise, music*) de fond; **~ reading** lecture(s) générale(s) (sur un sujet); **family ~** milieu familial

backhand ['bækhænd] *n* (*Tennis: also*: **backhand stroke**) revers *m*

backhander ['bæk'hændə'] *n* (*Brit: bribe*) pot-de-vin *m*

backing ['bækɪŋ] *n* (*fig*) soutien *m*, appui *m*; (*Comm*) soutien (financier); (*Mus*) accompagnement *m*

backlash ['bæklæʃ] *n* contre-coup *m*, répercussion *f*

backlog ['bæklɔg] *n*: **~ of work** travail *m* en retard

back number *n* (*of magazine etc*) vieux numéro

backpack ['bækpæk] *n* sac *m* à dos

backpacker ['bækpækə'] *n* randonneur(-euse)

back pain *n* mal *m* de dos

back pay *n* rappel *m* de salaire

backside ['bæksaɪd] *n* (*inf*) derrière *m*, postérieur *m*

backslash ['bækslæʃ] *n* barre oblique inversée

backstage [bæk'steɪdʒ] *adv* dans les coulisses

backstroke ['bækstrəuk] *n* dos crawlé

backup ['bækʌp] *adj* (*train, plane*) supplémentaire, de réserve; (*Comput*) de sauvegarde ▷ *n* (*support*) appui *m*, soutien *m*; (*Comput: also*: **backup file**) sauvegarde *f*

backward ['bækwəd] *adj* (*movement*) en arrière; (*measure*) rétrograde; (*person, country*) arriéré(e), attardé(e); (*shy*) hésitant(e); **~ and forward**

movement mouvement de va-et-vient
backwards ['bækwədz] *adv* (*move, go*) en
arrière; (*read a list*) à l'envers, à rebours; (*fall*)
à la renverse; (*walk*) à reculons; (*in time*) en
arrière, vers le passé; **to know sth ~** *or* (*US*) **~
and forwards** (*inf*) connaître qch sur le bout des
doigts
backwater ['bækwɔːtəʳ] *n* (*fig*) coin reculé; bled
perdu
backyard [bæk'jɑːd] *n* arrière-cour *f*
bacon ['beɪkən] *n* bacon *m*, lard *m*
bacteria [bæk'tɪərɪə] *npl* bactéries *fpl*
bad [bæd] *adj* mauvais(e); (*child*) vilain(e);
(*mistake, accident*) grave; (*meat, food*) gâté(e),
avarié(e); **his ~ leg** sa jambe malade; **to go ~**
(*meat, food*) se gâter; (*milk*) tourner; **to have a
~ time of it** traverser une mauvaise passe; **I
feel ~ about it** (*guilty*) j'ai un peu mauvaise
conscience; **~ debt** créance douteuse; **in ~ faith**
de mauvaise foi
bade [bæd] *pt of* **bid**
badge [bædʒ] *n* insigne *m*; (*of policeman*) plaque *f*;
(*stick-on, sew-on*) badge *m*
badger ['bædʒəʳ] *n* blaireau *m* ▷ *vt* harceler
badly ['bædlɪ] *adv* (*work, dress etc*) mal; **to reflect
~ on sb** donner une mauvaise image de qn; **~
wounded** grièvement blessé; **he needs it** – il
en a absolument besoin; **things are going ~** les
choses vont mal; **~ off** (*adj, adv*) dans la gêne
bad-mannered ['bæd'mænəd] *adj* mal élevé(e)
badminton ['bædmɪntən] *n* badminton *m*
bad-tempered ['bæd'tɛmpəd] *adj* (*by nature*)
ayant mauvais caractère; (*on one occasion*) de
mauvaise humeur
baffle ['bæfl] *vt* (*puzzle*) déconcerter
bag [bæg] *n* sac *m*; (*of hunter*) gibecière *f*, chasse
f ▷ *vt* (*inf: take*) empocher; s'approprier; (*Tech*)
mettre en sacs; **~s of** (*inf: lots of*) des tas de; **to
pack one's ~s** faire ses valises or bagages; **~s
under the eyes** poches *fpl* sous les yeux
baggage ['bægɪdʒ] *n* bagages *mpl*
baggage allowance *n* franchise *f* de bagages
baggage reclaim *n* (*at airport*) livraison *f* des
bagages
baggy ['bægɪ] *adj* avachi(e), qui fait des poches
bagpipes ['bægpaɪps] *npl* cornemuse *f*
bail [beɪl] *n* caution *f* ▷ *vt* (*prisoner: also*: **grant bail
to**) mettre en liberté sous caution; (*boat: also*: **bail
out**) écoper; **to be released on ~** être libéré(e)
sous caution; *see* **bale**
  ▶ **bail out** *vt* (*prisoner*) payer la caution de
bailiff ['beɪlɪf] *n* huissier *m*
bait [beɪt] *n* appât *m* ▷ *vt* appâter; (*fig: tease*)
tourmenter
bake [beɪk] *vt* (*faire*) cuire au four ▷ *vi* (*bread
etc*) cuire (au four); (*make cakes etc*) faire de la
pâtisserie
baked beans [beɪkt-] *npl* haricots blancs à la
sauce tomate
baked potato *n* pomme *f* de terre en robe des
champs
baker ['beɪkəʳ] *n* boulanger *m*

bakery ['beɪkərɪ] *n* boulangerie *f*; boulangerie
industrielle
baking ['beɪkɪŋ] *n* (*process*) cuisson *f*
baking powder *n* levure *f* (chimique)
balance ['bæləns] *n* équilibre *m*; (*Comm: sum*)
solde *m*; (*remainder*) reste *m*; (*scales*) balance *f* ▷ *vt*
mettre or faire tenir en équilibre; (*pros and cons*)
peser; (*budget*) équilibrer; (*account*) balancer;
(*compensate*) compenser, contrebalancer; **~ of
trade/payments** balance commerciale/des
comptes or paiements; **~ carried forward** solde
m à reporter; **~ brought forward** solde reporté;
to ~ the books arrêter les comptes, dresser le
bilan
balanced ['bælənst] *adj* (*personality, diet*)
équilibré(e); (*report*) objectif(-ive)
balance sheet *n* bilan *m*
balcony ['bælkənɪ] *n* balcon *m*; **do you have a
room with a ~?** avez-vous une chambre avec
balcon?
bald [bɔːld] *adj* chauve; (*tyre*) lisse
bale [beɪl] *n* balle *f*, ballot *m*
  ▶ **bale out** *vi* (*airplane*) sauter en parachute ▷ *vt*
(*Naut: water, boat*) écoper
ball [bɔːl] *n* boule *f*; (*football*) ballon *m*; (*for tennis,
golf*) balle *f*; (*dance*) bal *m*; **to play ~** jouer au
ballon (or à la balle); (*fig*) coopérer; **to be on the
~** (*fig: competent*) être à la hauteur; (: *alert*) être
éveillé(e), être vif (vive); **to start the ~ rolling**
(*fig*) commencer; **the ~ is in their court** (*fig*) la
balle est dans leur camp
ballast ['bæləst] *n* lest *m*
ball bearings *n* roulement *m* à billes
ballerina [bælə'riːnə] *n* ballerine *f*
ballet ['bæleɪ] *n* ballet *m*; (*art*) danse *f* (classique)
ballet dancer *n* danseur(-euse) de ballet
ballet shoe *n* chausson *m* de danse
balloon [bə'luːn] *n* ballon *m*; (*in comic strip*) bulle
f ▷ *vi* gonfler
ballot ['bælət] *n* scrutin *m*
ballot paper *n* bulletin *m* de vote
ballpoint ['bɔːlpɔɪnt], **ballpoint pen** *n* stylo *m*
à bille
ballroom ['bɔːlrum] *n* salle *f* de bal
Baltic [bɔːltɪk] *adj, n*: **the ~ (Sea)** la (mer)
Baltique
bamboo [bæm'buː] *n* bambou *m*
ban [bæn] *n* interdiction *f* ▷ *vt* interdire; **he was
~ned from driving** (*Brit*) on lui a retiré le permis
(de conduire)
banana [bə'nɑːnə] *n* banane *f*
band [bænd] *n* bande *f*; (*at a dance*) orchestre *m*;
(*Mil*) musique *f*, fanfare *f*
  ▶ **band together** *vi* se liguer
bandage ['bændɪdʒ] *n* bandage *m*, pansement
m ▷ *vt* (*wound, leg*) mettre un pansement or un
bandage sur; (*person*) mettre un pansement or un
bandage à
Band-Aid® ['bændeɪd] *n* (*US*) pansement
adhésif
B. & B. *n abbr* = **bed and breakfast**
bandit ['bændɪt] *n* bandit *m*

bandy-legged ['bændɪ'lɛgɪd] *adj* aux jambes arquées

bang [bæŋ] *n* détonation *f*; (*of door*) claquement *m*; (*blow*) coup (violent) ▷ *vt* frapper (violemment); (*door*) claquer ▷ *vi* détoner; claquer ▷ *adv*: **to be ~ on time** (*Brit inf*) être à l'heure pile; **to ~ at the door** cogner à la porte; **to ~ into sth** se cogner contre qch

Bangladesh [bæŋglə'dɛʃ] *n* Bangladesh *m*

Bangladeshi [bæŋglə'dɛʃɪ] *adj* du Bangladesh ▷ *n* habitant(e) du Bangladesh

bangle ['bæŋgl] *n* bracelet *m*

bangs [bæŋz] *npl* (*US: fringe*) frange *f*

banish ['bænɪʃ] *vt* bannir

banister ['bænɪstər] *n*, **banisters** ['bænɪstəz] ▷ *npl* rampe *f* (d'escalier)

banjo (*pl* **-es** *or* **-s**) ['bændʒəu] *n* banjo *m*

bank [bæŋk] *n* banque *f*; (*of river, lake*) bord *m*, rive *f*; (*of earth*) talus *m*, remblai *m* ▷ *vi* (*Aviat*) virer sur l'aile; (*Comm*): **they ~ with Pitt's** leur banque *or* banquier est Pitt's

▶ **bank on** *vt fus* miser *or* tabler sur

bank account *n* compte *m* en banque

bank balance *n* solde *m* bancaire.

bank card (*Brit*) *n* carte *f* d'identité bancaire

bank charges *npl* (*Brit*) frais *mpl* de banque

banker ['bæŋkər] *n* banquier *m*; **~'s card** (*Brit*) carte *f* d'identité bancaire; **~'s order** (*Brit*) ordre *m* de virement

bank holiday *n* (*Brit*) jour férié (*où les banques sont fermées*); *voir article*

banking ['bæŋkɪŋ] *n* opérations *fpl* bancaires; profession *f* de banquier

bank manager *n* directeur *m* d'agence (bancaire)

banknote ['bæŋknəut] *n* billet *m* de banque

bank rate *n* taux *m* de l'escompte

bankrupt ['bæŋkrʌpt] *n* failli(e) ▷ *adj* en faillite; **to go ~** faire faillite

bankruptcy ['bæŋkrʌptsɪ] *n* faillite *f*

bank statement *n* relevé *m* de compte

banner ['bænər] *n* bannière *f*

bannister ['bænɪstər] *n*, **bannisters** ['bænɪstəz] ▷ *npl* = **banister; banisters**

banquet ['bæŋkwɪt] *n* banquet *m*, festin *m*

baptism ['bæptɪzəm] *n* baptême *m*

baptize [bæp'taɪz] *vt* baptiser

bar [bɑːr] *n* (*pub*) bar *m*; (*counter*) comptoir *m*, bar; (*rod: of metal etc*) barre *f*; (*of window etc*) barreau *m*; (*of chocolate*) tablette *f*, plaque *f*; (*fig: obstacle*) obstacle *m*; (*prohibition*) mesure *f* d'exclusion; (*Mus*) mesure *f* ▷ *vt* (*road*) barrer; (*window*) munir de barreaux; (*person*) exclure; (*activity*) interdire; **~ of soap** savonnette *f*; **behind ~s** (*prisoner*) derrière les barreaux; **the B~** (*Law*) le barreau; **~ none** sans exception

barbaric [bɑː'bærɪk] *adj* barbare

barbecue ['bɑːbɪkjuː] *n* barbecue *m*

barbed wire ['bɑːbd-] *n* fil *m* de fer barbelé

barber ['bɑːbər] *n* coiffeur *m* (pour hommes)

barber's ['bɑːbəz], (*US*) **barber's shop**, **barber shop** *n* salon *m* de coiffure (pour hommes); **to go to the barber's** aller chez le coiffeur

bar code *n* code *m* à barres, code-barre *m*

bare [bɛər] *adj* nu(e) ▷ *vt* mettre à nu, dénuder; (*teeth*) montrer; **the ~ essentials** le strict nécessaire

bareback ['bɛəbæk] *adv* à cru, sans selle

barefaced ['bɛəfeɪst] *adj* impudent(e), effronté(e)

barefoot ['bɛəfut] *adj*, *adv* nu-pieds, (les) pieds nus

barely ['bɛəlɪ] *adv* à peine

bargain ['bɑːgɪn] *n* (*transaction*) marché *m*; (*good buy*) affaire *f*, occasion *f* ▷ *vi* (*haggle*) marchander; (*negotiate*) négocier, traiter; **into the ~** par-dessus le marché

▶ **bargain for** *vt fus* (*inf*): **he got more than he ~ed for!** il en a eu pour son argent!

barge [bɑːdʒ] *n* péniche *f*

▶ **barge in** *vi* (*walk in*) faire irruption; (*interrupt talk*) intervenir mal à propos

▶ **barge into** *vt fus* rentrer dans

bark [bɑːk] *n* (*of tree*) écorce *f*; (*of dog*) aboiement *m* ▷ *vi* aboyer

barley ['bɑːlɪ] *n* orge *f*

barley sugar *n* sucre *m* d'orge

barmaid ['bɑːmeɪd] *n* serveuse *f* (de bar), barmaid *f*

barman ['bɑːmən] (*irreg*) *n* serveur *m* (de bar), barman *m*

bar meal *n* repas *m* de bistrot; **to go for a ~** aller manger au bistrot

barn [bɑːn] *n* grange *f*

barometer [bə'rɔmɪtər] *n* baromètre *m*

baron ['bærən] *n* baron *m*; **the press/oil ~s** les magnats *mpl or* barons *mpl* de la presse/du pétrole

baroness ['bærənɪs] *n* baronne *f*

barracks ['bærəks] *npl* caserne *f*

barrage ['bærɑːʒ] *n* (*Mil*) tir *m* de barrage; (*dam*) barrage *m*; (*of criticism*) feu *m*

barrel ['bærəl] *n* tonneau *m*; (*of gun*) canon *m*

barren ['bærən] *adj* stérile; (*hills*) aride

barrette [bə'rɛt] (*US*) *n* barrette *f*

barricade [bærɪ'keɪd] *n* barricade *f* ▷ *vt* barricader

barrier ['bærɪər] *n* barrière *f*; (*Brit: also*: **crash barrier**) rail *m* de sécurité

barring ['bɑːrɪŋ] *prep* sauf

barrister ['bærɪstər] *n* (*Brit*) avocat (plaidant); *voir article*

barrow ['bærəu] *n* (*cart*) charrette *f* à bras

bartender ['bɑːtɛndər] *n* (*US*) serveur *m* (de bar), barman *m*

barter ['bɑːtər] *n* échange *m*, troc *m* ▷ *vt*: **to ~ sth for** échanger qch contre

base [beɪs] *n* base *f* ▷ *vt* (*troops*): **to be ~d at** être basé(e) à; (*opinion, belief*): **to ~ sth on** baser *or* fonder qch sur ▷ *adj* vil(e), bas(se); **coffee-~d** à base de café; **a Paris-~d firm** une maison opérant de Paris *or* dont le siège est à Paris; **I'm ~d in London** je suis basé(e) à Londres

baseball ['beɪsbɔːl] *n* base-ball *m*

baseball cap *n* casquette *f* de base-ball

Basel [bɑːl] n = **Basle**

basement ['beɪsmənt] n sous-sol m

bases ['beɪsiːz] npl of **basis** ['beɪsɪz] ▷ npl of **base**

bash [bæʃ] vt (inf) frapper, cogner ▷ n: **I'll have a ~ (at it)** (Brit inf) je vais essayer un coup; **~ed in** adj enfoncé(e), défoncé(e)

  ▸ **bash up** vt (inf: car) bousiller; (: Brit: person) tabasser

bashful ['bæʃful] adj timide; modeste

basic ['beɪsɪk] adj (precautions, rules) élémentaire; (principles, research) fondamental(e); (vocabulary, salary) de base; (minimal) réduit(e) au minimum, rudimentaire

basically ['beɪsɪklɪ] adv (in fact) en fait; (essentially) fondamentalement

basics ['beɪsɪks] npl: **the ~** l'essentiel m

basil ['bæzl] n basilic m

basin ['beɪsn] n (vessel, also Geo) cuvette f, bassin m; (Brit: for food) bol m; (: bigger) saladier m; (also: **washbasin**) lavabo m

basis (pl **bases**) ['beɪsɪs, -siːz] n base f; **on a part-time/trial ~** à temps partiel/à l'essai; **on the ~ of what you've said** d'après or compte tenu de ce que vous dites

bask [bɑːsk] vi: **to ~ in the sun** se chauffer au soleil

basket ['bɑːskɪt] n corbeille f; (with handle) panier m

basketball ['bɑːskɪtbɔːl] n basket-ball m

Basle [bɑːl] n Bâle

Basque [bæsk] adj basque ▷ n: Basque m/f; **the ~ Country** le Pays basque

bass [beɪs] n (Mus) basse f

bass drum n grosse caisse f

bassoon [bə'suːn] n basson m

bastard ['bɑːstəd] n enfant naturel(le), bâtard(e); (inf!) salaud m (!)

bat [bæt] n chauve-souris f; (for baseball etc) batte f; (Brit: for table tennis) raquette f ▷ vt: **he didn't ~ an eyelid** il n'a pas sourcillé or bronché; **off one's own ~** de sa propre initiative

batch [bætʃ] n (of bread) fournée f; (of papers) liasse f; (of applicants, letters) paquet m; (of work) monceau m; (of goods) lot m

bated ['beɪtɪd] adj: **with ~ breath** en retenant son souffle

bath (pl **-s**) [bɑːθ, bɑːðz] n bain m; (bathtub) baignoire f ▷ vt baigner, donner un bain à; **to have a ~** prendre un bain; see also **baths**

bathe [beɪð] vi se baigner ▷ vt baigner; (wound etc) laver

bathing ['beɪðɪŋ] n baignade f

bathing costume, (US) **bathing suit** n maillot m (de bain)

bathrobe ['bɑːθrəub] n peignoir m de bain

bathroom ['bɑːθrum] n salle f de bains

baths [bɑːðz] npl (Brit: also: **swimming baths**) piscine f

bath towel n serviette f de bain

bathtub ['bɑːθtʌb] n baignoire f

baton ['bætən] n bâton m; (Mus) baguette f; (club) matraque f

batter ['bætər] vt battre ▷ n pâte f à frire

battered ['bætəd] adj (hat, pan) cabossé(e); **~ wife/child** épouse/enfant maltraité(e) or martyr(e)

battery ['bætərɪ] n (for torch, radio) pile f; (Aut, Mil) batterie f

battery farming n élevage m en batterie

battle ['bætl] n bataille f, combat m ▷ vi se battre, lutter; **that's half the ~** (fig) c'est déjà bien; **it's a** or **we're fighting a losing ~** (fig) c'est perdu d'avance, c'est peine perdue

battlefield ['bætlfiːld] n champ m de bataille

battleship ['bætlʃɪp] n cuirassé m

Bavaria [bə'vɛərɪə] n Bavière f

bawl [bɔːl] vi hurler, brailler

bay [beɪ] n (of sea) baie f; (Brit: for parking) place f de stationnement; (: for loading) aire f de chargement; (horse) bai(e) m/f; **B~ of Biscay** golfe m de Gascogne; **to hold sb at ~** tenir qn à distance or en échec

bay leaf n laurier m

bazaar [bə'zɑːr] n (shop, market) bazar m; (sale) vente f de charité

BBC n abbr (= British Broadcasting Corporation) office de la radiodiffusion et télévision britannique

B.C. adv abbr (= before Christ) av. J.-C. ▷ abbr (Canada) = **British Columbia**

be [biː] (pt **was**, **were**, pp **been**) aux vb **1** (with present participle: forming continuous tenses): **what are you doing?** que faites-vous?; **they're coming tomorrow** ils viennent demain; **I've been waiting for you for 2 hours** je t'attends depuis 2 heures

2 (with pp: forming passives) être; **to be killed** être tué(e); **the box had been opened** la boîte avait été ouverte; **he was nowhere to be seen** on ne le voyait nulle part

3 (in tag questions): **it was fun, wasn't it?** c'était drôle, n'est-ce pas?; **he's good-looking, isn't he?** il est beau, n'est-ce pas?; **she's back, is she?** elle est rentrée, n'est-ce pas or alors?

4 (+to +infinitive): **the house is to be sold** (necessity) la maison doit être vendue; (future) la maison va être vendue; **he's not to open it** il ne doit pas l'ouvrir; **am I to understand that ...?** dois-je comprendre que ...?; **he was to have come yesterday** il devait venir hier

5 (possibility, supposition): **if I were you, I ...** à votre place, je ..., si j'étais vous, je ...

▷ vb + complement **1** (gen) être; **I'm English** je suis anglais(e); **I'm tired** je suis fatigué(e); **I'm hot/cold** j'ai chaud/froid; **he's a doctor** il est médecin; **be careful/good/quiet!** faites attention/soyez sages/taisez-vous!; **2 and 2 are 4** 2 et 2 font 4

2 (of health) aller; **how are you?** comment allez-vous?; **I'm better now** je vais mieux maintenant; **he's fine now** il va bien maintenant; **he's very ill** il est très malade

3 (of age) avoir; **how old are you?** quel âge avez-vous?; **I'm sixteen (years old)** j'ai seize ans

4 (cost) coûter; **how much was the meal?** combien a coûté le repas?; **that'll be £5, please**

ça fera 5 livres, s'il vous plaît; **this shirt is £17** cette chemise coûte 17 livres
▷ vi **1** (*exist, occur etc*) être, exister; **the prettiest girl that ever was** la fille la plus jolie qui ait jamais existé; **is there a God?** y a-t-il un dieu?; **be that as it may** quoi qu'il en soit; **so be it** soit
2 (*referring to place*) être, se trouver; **I won't be here tomorrow** je ne serai pas là demain; **Edinburgh is in Scotland** Édimbourg est or se trouve en Écosse
3 (*referring to movement*) aller; **where have you been?** où êtes-vous allé(s)?
▷ impers vb **1** (*referring to time*) être; **it's 5 o'clock** il est 5 heures; **it's the 28th of April** c'est le 28 avril
2 (*referring to distance*): **it's 10 km to the village** le village est à 10 km
3 (*referring to the weather*) faire; **it's too hot/cold** il fait trop chaud/froid; **it's windy today** il y a du vent aujourd'hui
4 (*emphatic*): **it's me/the postman** c'est moi/le facteur; **it was Maria who paid the bill** c'est Maria qui a payé la note
beach [biːtʃ] *n* plage *f* ▷ *vt* échouer
beacon [ˈbiːkən] *n* (*lighthouse*) fanal *m*; (*marker*) balise *f*; (*also*: **radio beacon**) radiophare *m*
bead [biːd] *n* perle *f*; (*of dew, sweat*) goutte *f*; **beads** *npl* (*necklace*) collier *m*
beak [biːk] *n* bec *m*
beaker [ˈbiːkər] *n* gobelet *m*
beam [biːm] *n* (*Archit*) poutre *f*; (*of light*) rayon *m*; (*Radio*) faisceau *m* radio ▷ *vi* rayonner; **to drive on full** or **main** or (US) **high ~** rouler en pleins phares
bean [biːn] *n* haricot *m*; (*of coffee*) grain *m*
beansprouts [ˈbiːnsprauts] *npl* pousses *fpl* or germes *mpl* de soja
bear [beər] (*pt* **bore**, *pp* **borne**) [bɔːʳ, bɔːn] *n* ours *m*; (*Stock Exchange*) baissier *m* ▷ *vt* porter; (*endure*) supporter; (*traces, signs*) porter; (*Comm: interest*) rapporter ▷ *vi*: **to ~ right/left** obliquer à droite/gauche, se diriger vers la droite/gauche; **to ~ the responsibility of** assumer la responsabilité de; **to ~ comparison with** soutenir la comparaison avec; **I can't ~ him** je ne peux pas le supporter or souffrir; **to bring pressure to ~ on sb** faire pression sur qn
▶ **bear out** *vt* (*theory, suspicion*) confirmer
▶ **bear up** *vi* supporter, tenir le coup; **he bore up well** il a tenu le coup
▶ **bear with** *vt fus* (*sb's moods, temper*) supporter; **~ with me a minute** un moment, s'il vous plaît
beard [biəd] *n* barbe *f*
bearded [ˈbiədid] *adj* barbu(e)
bearer [ˈbeərər] *n* porteur *m*; (*of passport etc*) titulaire *m/f*
bearing [ˈbeəriŋ] *n* maintien *m*, allure *f*; (*connection*) rapport *m*; (*Tech*): **(ball) bearings** *npl* roulement *m* (à billes); **to take a ~** faire le point; **to find one's ~s** s'orienter
beast [biːst] *n* bête *f*; (*inf: person*) brute *f*
beastly [ˈbiːstli] *adj* infect(e)
beat [biːt] *n* battement *m*; (*Mus*) temps *m*,

mesure *f*; (*of policeman*) ronde *f* ▷ *vt, vi* (*pt* -, *pp* **-en**) battre; **off the ~en track** hors des chemins or sentiers battus; **to ~ it** (*inf*) ficher le camp; **to ~ about the bush** tourner autour du pot; **that ~s everything!** c'est le comble!
▶ **beat down** *vt* (*door*) enfoncer; (*price*) faire baisser; (*seller*) faire descendre ▷ *vi* (*rain*) tambouriner; (*sun*) taper
▶ **beat off** *vt* repousser
▶ **beat up** *vt* (*eggs*) battre; (*inf: person*) tabasser
beating [ˈbiːtiŋ] *n* raclée *f*
beautiful [ˈbjuːtiful] *adj* beau (belle)
beautifully [ˈbjuːtifli] *adv* admirablement
beauty [ˈbjuːti] *n* beauté *f*; **the ~ of it is that ...** le plus beau, c'est que ...
beauty parlour, (US) **beauty parlor** [-ˈpɑːlər] *n* institut *m* de beauté
beauty salon *n* institut *m* de beauté
beauty spot *n* (*on skin*) grain *m* de beauté; (*Brit Tourism*) site naturel (d'une grande beauté)
beaver [ˈbiːvər] *n* castor *m*
became [biˈkeim] *pt of* **become**
because [biˈkɔz] *conj* parce que; **~ of** (*prep*) à cause de
beck [bek] *n*: **to be at sb's ~ and call** être à l'entière disposition de qn
beckon [ˈbekən] *vt* (*also*: **beckon to**) faire signe (de venir) à
become [biˈkʌm] *vi* devenir; **to ~ fat/thin** grossir/maigrir; **to ~ angry** se mettre en colère; **it became known that** on apprit que; **what has ~ of him?** qu'est-il devenu?
becoming [biˈkʌmiŋ] *adj* (*behaviour*) convenable, bienséant(e); (*clothes*) seyant(e)
bed [bed] *n* lit *m*; (*of flowers*) parterre *m*; (*of coal, clay*) couche *f*; (*of sea, lake*) fond *m*; **to go to ~** aller se coucher
▶ **bed down** *vi* se coucher
bed and breakfast *n* (*terms*) chambre et petit déjeuner; (*place*) ≈ chambre *f* d'hôte; *voir article*
bedclothes [ˈbedkləuðz] *npl* couvertures *fpl* et draps *mpl*
bedding [ˈbediŋ] *n* literie *f*
bed linen *n* draps *mpl* de lit (et taies *fpl* d'oreillers), literie *f*
bedraggled [biˈdrægld] *adj* dépenaillé(e), les vêtements en désordre
bedridden [ˈbedridn] *adj* cloué(e) au lit
bedroom [ˈbedrum] *n* chambre *f* (à coucher)
bedside [ˈbedsaid] *n*: **at sb's ~** au chevet de qn ▷ *cpd* (*book, lamp*) de chevet
bedside lamp *n* lampe *f* de chevet
bedside table *n* table *f* de chevet
bedsit [ˈbedsit], **bedsitter** [ˈbedsitər] *n* (*Brit*) chambre meublée, studio *m*
bedspread [ˈbedspred] *n* couvre-lit *m*, dessus-de-lit *m*
bedtime [ˈbedtaim] *n*: **it's ~** c'est l'heure de se coucher
bee [biː] *n* abeille *f*; **to have a ~ in one's bonnet (about sth)** être obnubilé(e) (par qch)
beech [biːtʃ] *n* hêtre *m*

beef [bi:f] n bœuf m; **roast** ~ rosbif m
▶ **beef up** vt (inf: support) renforcer; (: essay)
étoffer
beefburger ['bi:fbə:gəʳ] n hamburger m
beehive ['bi:haɪv] n ruche f
beeline ['bi:laɪn] n: **to make a ~ for** se diriger
tout droit vers
been [bi:n] pp of **be**
beer [bɪəʳ] n bière f
beer garden n (Brit) jardin m d'un pub (où l'on peut
emmener ses consommations)
beet [bi:t] n (vegetable) betterave f; (US: also: **red
beet**) betterave (potagère)
beetle ['bi:tl] n scarabée m, coléoptère m
beetroot ['bi:tru:t] n (Brit) betterave f
before [bɪ'fɔ:ʳ] prep (of time) avant; (of space)
devant ▷ conj avant que + sub; avant de ▷ adv
avant; ~ **going** avant de partir; ~ **she goes**
avant qu'elle (ne) parte; **the week** ~ la semaine
précédente or d'avant; **I've seen it** ~ je l'ai déjà
vu; **I've never seen it** ~ c'est la première fois
que je le vois
beforehand [bɪ'fɔ:hænd] adv au préalable, à
l'avance
beg [bɛg] vi mendier ▷ vt mendier; (favour)
quémander, solliciter; (forgiveness, mercy etc)
demander; (entreat) supplier; **to ~ sb to do
sth** supplier qn de faire qch; **I ~ your pardon**
(apologising) excusez-moi; (: not hearing) pardon?;
that ~s the question of ... cela soulève la
question de ..., cela suppose réglée la question de
...; see also **pardon**
began [bɪ'gæn] pt of **begin**
beggar ['bɛgəʳ] n (also: **beggarman,
beggarwoman**) mendiant(e)
begin [bɪ'gɪn] (pt **began**, pp **begun**) [bɪ'gɪn, -'gæn,
-'gʌn] vt, vi commencer; **to ~ doing** or **to do sth**
commencer à faire qch; ~**ning (from) Monday**
à partir de lundi; **I can't ~ to thank you** je ne
saurais vous remercier; **to ~ with** d'abord, pour
commencer
beginner [bɪ'gɪnəʳ] n débutant(e)
beginning [bɪ'gɪnɪŋ] n commencement m, début
m; **right from the** ~ dès le début
begun [bɪ'gʌn] pp of **begin**
behalf [bɪ'hɑ:f] n: **on** ~ **of** (US): **in** ~ **of**
(representing) de la part de; au nom de; (for benefit
of) pour le compte de; **on my/his** ~ de ma/sa part
behave [bɪ'heɪv] vi se conduire, se comporter;
(well: also: **behave o.s.**) se conduire bien or
comme il faut
behaviour, (US) **behavior** [bɪ'heɪvjəʳ] n
comportement m, conduite f
behead [bɪ'hɛd] vt décapiter
behind [bɪ'haɪnd] prep derrière; (time) en retard
sur; (supporting): **to be** ~ **sb** soutenir qn ▷ adv
derrière; en retard ▷ n derrière m; ~ **the scenes**
dans les coulisses; **to leave sth** ~ (forget) oublier
de prendre qch; **to be** ~ **(schedule) with sth** être
en retard dans qch
behold [bɪ'həuld] vt (irreg: like **hold**) apercevoir,
voir

beige [beɪʒ] adj beige
Beijing ['beɪ'dʒɪŋ] n Pékin
being ['bi:ɪŋ] n être m; **to come into** ~ prendre
naissance
Beirut [beɪ'ru:t] n Beyrouth
Belarus [bɛlə'rus] n Biélorussie f, Bélarus m
belated [bɪ'leɪtɪd] adj tardif(-ive)
belch [bɛltʃ] vi avoir un renvoi, roter ▷ vt (also:
belch out: smoke etc) vomir, cracher
Belgian ['bɛldʒən] adj belge, de Belgique ▷ n
Belge m/f
Belgium ['bɛldʒəm] n Belgique f
belie [bɪ'laɪ] vt démentir; (give false impression of)
occulter
belief [bɪ'li:f] n (opinion) conviction f; (trust, faith)
foi f; (acceptance as true) croyance f; **it's beyond** ~
c'est incroyable; **in the** ~ **that** dans l'idée que
believe [bɪ'li:v] vt, vi croire, estimer; **to** ~ **in** (God)
croire en; (ghosts, method) croire à; **I don't** ~ **in
corporal punishment** je ne suis pas partisan
des châtiments corporels; **he is ~d to be abroad**
il serait à l'étranger
believer [bɪ'li:vəʳ] n (in idea, activity) partisan(e); ~
in partisan(e) de; (Rel) croyant(e)
belittle [bɪ'lɪtl] vt déprécier, rabaisser
bell [bɛl] n cloche f; (small) clochette f, grelot
m; (on door) sonnette f; (electric) sonnerie f; **that
rings a** ~ (fig) cela me rappelle qch
bellboy ['bɛlbɔɪ], (US) **bellhop** ['bɛlhɔp] n groom
m, chasseur m
belligerent [bɪ'lɪdʒərənt] adj (at war)
belligérant(e); (fig) agressif(-ive)
bellow ['bɛləu] vi (bull) meugler; (person) brailler
▷ vt (orders) hurler
bell pepper n (esp US) poivron m
belly ['bɛlɪ] n ventre m
belly button n (inf) nombril m
belong [bɪ'lɔŋ] vi: **to** ~ **to** appartenir à; (club etc)
faire partie de; **this book ~s here** ce livre va ici,
la place de ce livre est ici
belongings [bɪ'lɔŋɪŋz] npl affaires fpl,
possessions fpl; **personal** ~ effets personnels
beloved [bɪ'lʌvɪd] adj (bien-)aimé(e), chéri(e) ▷ n
bien-aimé(e)
below [bɪ'ləu] prep sous, au-dessous de ▷ adv en
dessous; en contre-bas; **see** ~ voir plus bas or
plus loin ci-dessous; **temperatures** ~ **normal**
températures inférieures à la normale
belt [bɛlt] n ceinture f; (Tech) courroie f ▷ vt
(thrash) donner une raclée à ▷ vi (Brit inf) filer (à
toutes jambes); **industrial** ~ zone industrielle
▶ **belt out** vt (song) chanter à tue-tête or à pleins
poumons
▶ **belt up** vi (Brit inf) la boucler
beltway ['bɛltweɪ] n (US Aut) route f de ceinture;
(: motorway) périphérique m
bemused [bɪ'mju:zd] adj médusé(e)
bench [bɛntʃ] n banc m; (in workshop) établi m; **the
B~** (Law: judges) la magistrature, la Cour
bend [bɛnd] (pt, pp **bent**) [bɛnt] vt courber; (leg,
arm) plier ▷ vi se courber ▷ n (Brit: in road) virage
m, tournant m; (in pipe, river) coude m

▶ **bend down** vi se baisser

▶ **bend over** vi se pencher

beneath [bɪ'niːθ] prep sous, au-dessous de; (unworthy of) indigne de ▷ adv dessous, au-dessous, en bas

benefactor ['benɪfæktə'] n bienfaiteur m

beneficial [benɪ'fɪʃəl] adj: ~ (**to**) salutaire (pour), bénéfique (à)

benefit ['benɪfɪt] n avantage m, profit m; (allowance of money) allocation f ▷ vt faire du bien à, profiter à ▷ vi: **he'll ~ from it** cela lui fera du bien, il y gagnera or s'en trouvera bien

Benelux ['benɪlʌks] n Bénélux m

benevolent [bɪ'nevələnt] adj bienveillant(e)

benign [bɪ'naɪn] adj (person, smile) bienveillant(e), affable; (Med) bénin(-igne)

bent [bent] pt, pp of **bend** ▷ n inclination f, penchant m ▷ adj (wire, pipe) coudé(e); (inf: dishonest) véreux(-euse); **to be ~ on** être résolu(e) à

bequest [bɪ'kwest] n legs m

bereaved [bɪ'riːvd] n: **the ~** la famille du disparu ▷ adj endeuillé(e)

beret ['bereɪ] n béret m

Berlin [bəː'lɪn] n Berlin; **East/West ~** Berlin Est/Ouest

berm [bəːm] n (US Aut) accotement m

Bermuda [bəː'mjuːdə] n Bermudes fpl

Bern [bəːn] n Berne

berry ['berɪ] n baie f

berserk [bə'səːk] adj: **to go ~** être pris(e) d'une rage incontrôlable; se déchaîner

berth [bəːθ] n (bed) couchette f; (for ship) poste m d'amarrage, mouillage m ▷ vi (in harbour) venir à quai; (at anchor) mouiller; **to give sb a wide ~** (fig) éviter qn

beseech (pt, pp besought) [bɪ'siːtʃ, -'sɔːt] vt implorer, supplier

beset (pt, pp ~-) [bɪ'set] vt assaillir ▷ adj: ~ **with** semé(e) de

beside [bɪ'saɪd] prep à côté de; (compared with) par rapport à; **that's ~ the point** ça n'a rien à voir; **to be ~ o.s. (with anger)** être hors de soi

besides [bɪ'saɪdz] adv en outre, de plus ▷ prep en plus de; (except) excepté

besiege [bɪ'siːdʒ] vt (town) assiéger; (fig) assaillir

best [best] adj meilleur(e) ▷ adv le mieux; **the ~ part of** (quantity) le plus clair de, la plus grande partie de; **at ~** au mieux; **to make the ~ of sth** s'accommoder de qch (du mieux que l'on peut); **to do one's ~** faire de son mieux; **to the ~ of my knowledge** pour autant que je sache; **to the ~ of my ability** du mieux que je pourrai; **he's not exactly patient at the ~ of times** il n'est jamais spécialement patient; **the ~ thing to do is ... le** mieux, c'est de ...

best-before date n date f de limite d'utilisation or de consommation

best man (irreg) n garçon m d'honneur

bestow [bɪ'stəu] vt accorder; (title) conférer

bestseller ['best'selə'] n best-seller m, succès m de librairie

bet [bet] n pari m ▷ vt, vi (pt, pp ~ or -**ted**) parier; **it's a safe ~** (fig) il y a de fortes chances; **to ~ sb sth** parier qch à qn

betray [bɪ'treɪ] vt trahir

better ['betə'] adj meilleur(e) ▷ adv mieux ▷ vt améliorer ▷ n: **to get the ~ of** triompher de, l'emporter sur; **a change for the ~** une amélioration; **I had ~ go** il faut que je m'en aille; **you had ~ do it** vous feriez mieux de le faire; **he thought ~ of it** il s'est ravisé; **to get ~** (Med) aller mieux; (improve) s'améliorer; **that's ~!** c'est mieux!; ~ **off** adj plus à l'aise financièrement; (fig) **you'd be ~ off this way** vous vous en trouveriez mieux ainsi, ce serait mieux or plus pratique ainsi

betting ['betɪŋ] n paris mpl

betting shop n (Brit) bureau m de paris

between [bɪ'twiːn] prep entre ▷ adv au milieu, dans l'intervalle; **the road ~ here and London** la route d'ici à Londres; **we only had 5 ~ us** nous n'en avions que 5 en tout

beverage ['bevərɪdʒ] n boisson f (gén sans alcool)

beware [bɪ'weə'] vt, vi: **to ~ (of)** prendre garde (à); **"~ of the dog"** "(attention) chien méchant"

bewildered [bɪ'wɪldəd] adj dérouté(e), ahuri(e)

beyond [bɪ'jɔnd] prep (in space, time) au-delà de; (exceeding) au-dessus de ▷ adv au-delà; ~ **doubt** hors de doute; ~ **repair** irréparable

bias ['baɪəs] n (prejudice) préjugé m, parti pris; (preference) prévention f

biased, biassed ['baɪəst] adj partial(e), montrant un parti pris; **to be bias(s)ed against** avoir un préjugé contre

bib [bɪb] n bavoir m, bavette f

Bible ['baɪbl] n Bible f

bicarbonate of soda [baɪ'kɑːbənɪt-] n bicarbonate m de soude

biceps ['baɪseps] n biceps m

bicker ['bɪkə'] vi se chamailler

bicycle ['baɪsɪkl] n bicyclette f

bicycle pump n pompe f à vélo

bid [bɪd] n offre f; (at auction) enchère f; (attempt) tentative f ▷ vi (pt, pp ~-) faire une enchère or offre ▷ vt (pt **bade**) [bæd] (pp -**den**) ['bɪdn] faire une enchère or offre de; **to ~ sb good day** souhaiter le bonjour à qn

bidder ['bɪdə'] n: **the highest ~** le plus offrant

bidding ['bɪdɪŋ] n enchères fpl

bide [baɪd] vt: **to ~ one's time** attendre son heure

bidet ['biːdeɪ] n bidet m

bifocals [baɪ'fəuklz] npl lunettes fpl à double foyer

big [bɪg] adj (in height: person, building, tree) grand(e); (in bulk, amount: person, parcel, book) gros(se); **to do things in a ~ way** faire les choses en grand

bigheaded ['bɪg'hedɪd] adj prétentieux(-euse)

bigot ['bɪgət] n fanatique m/f, sectaire m/f

bigoted ['bɪgətɪd] adj fanatique, sectaire

bigotry ['bɪgətrɪ] n fanatisme m, sectarisme m

big toe n gros orteil

big top n grand chapiteau

bike [baɪk] n vélo m, bécane f
bike lane n piste f cyclable
bikini [bɪˈkiːnɪ] n bikini m
bilateral [baɪˈlætərl] adj bilatéral(e)
bilingual [baɪˈlɪŋgwəl] adj bilingue
bill [bɪl] n note f, facture f; (in restaurant) addition f, note f; (Pol) projet m de loi; (US: banknote) billet m (de banque); (notice) affiche f; (of bird) bec m; (Theat): **on the** ~ à l'affiche ▷ vt (item) facturer; (customer) remettre la facture à; **may I have the ~ please?** (est-ce que je peux avoir) l'addition, s'il vous plaît?; **put it on my** ~ mettez-le sur mon compte; **"post no ~s"** "défense d'afficher"; **to fit** or **fill the** ~ (fig) faire l'affaire; ~ **of exchange** lettre f de change; ~ **of lading** connaissement m; ~ **of sale** contrat m de vente
billboard [ˈbɪlbɔːd] (US) n panneau m d'affichage
billet [ˈbɪlɪt] n cantonnement m (chez l'habitant) ▷ vt (troops) cantonner
billfold [ˈbɪlfəuld] n (US) portefeuille m
billiards [ˈbɪljədz] n (jeu m de) billard m
billion [ˈbɪljən] n (Brit) billion m (million de millions); (US) milliard m
bimbo [ˈbɪmbəu] n (inf) ravissante idiote f
bin [bɪn] n boîte f; (Brit: also: **dustbin, litter bin**) poubelle f; (for coal) coffre m
bind (pt, pp **bound**) [baɪnd, baund] vt attacher; (book) relier; (oblige) obliger, contraindre ▷ n (inf: nuisance) scie f
▶ **bind over** vt (Law) mettre en liberté conditionnelle
▶ **bind up** vt (wound) panser; **to be bound up in** (work, research etc) être complètement absorbé par, être accroché par; **to be bound up with** (person) être accroché à
binding [ˈbaɪndɪŋ] n (of book) reliure f ▷ adj (contract) qui constitue une obligation
binge [bɪndʒ] n (inf): **to go on a** ~ faire la bringue
bingo [ˈbɪŋgəu] n sorte de jeu de loto pratiqué dans des établissements publics
binoculars [bɪˈnɔkjuləz] npl jumelles fpl [baɪə-] prefix
biochemistry [baɪəˈkemɪstrɪ] n biochimie f
biodegradable [ˈbaɪəudɪˈɡreɪdəbl] adj biodégradable
biography [baɪˈɔɡrəfɪ] n biographie f
biological [baɪəˈlɔdʒɪkl] adj biologique
biology [baɪˈɔlədʒɪ] n biologie f
biometric [baɪəˈmetrɪk] adj biométrique
birch [bəːtʃ] n bouleau m
bird [bəːd] n oiseau m; (Brit inf: girl) nana f
bird flu n grippe f aviaire
bird of prey n oiseau m de proie
bird's-eye view [ˈbəːdzaɪ-] n vue f à vol d'oiseau; (fig) vue d'ensemble or générale
bird watcher [-wɔtʃəʳ] n ornithologue m/f amateur
birdwatching [ˈbəːdwɔtʃɪŋ] n ornithologie f (d'amateur)
Biro® [ˈbaɪərəu] n stylo m à bille
birth [bəːθ] n naissance f; **to give** ~ **to** donner naissance à, mettre au monde; (subj: animal) mettre bas
birth certificate n acte m de naissance
birth control n (policy) limitation f des naissances; (methods) méthode(s) contraceptive(s)
birthday [ˈbəːθdeɪ] n anniversaire m ▷ cpd (cake, card etc) d'anniversaire
birthmark [ˈbəːθmɑːk] n envie f, tache f de vin
birthplace [ˈbəːθpleɪs] n lieu m de naissance
birth rate n (taux m de) natalité f
biscuit [ˈbɪskɪt] n (Brit) biscuit m; (US) petit pain au lait
bisect [baɪˈsekt] vt couper or diviser en deux
bishop [ˈbɪʃəp] n évêque m; (Chess) fou m
bistro [ˈbiːstrəu] n petit restaurant m, bistrot m
bit [bɪt] pt of **bite** ▷ n morceau m; (Comput) bit m, élément m binaire; (of tool) mèche f; (of horse) mors m; **a** ~ **of** un peu de; **a** ~ **mad/dangerous** un peu fou/risqué; ~ **by** ~ petit à petit; **to come to** ~**s** (break) tomber en morceaux, se déglinguer; **bring all your** ~**s and pieces** apporte toutes tes affaires; **to do one's** ~ y mettre du sien
bitch [bɪtʃ] n (dog) chienne f; (inf!) salope f (!), garce f
bite [baɪt] vt, vi (pt **bit**, pp **bitten**) [bɪt, ˈbɪtn] mordre; (insect) piquer ▷ n morsure f; (insect bite) piqûre f; (mouthful) bouchée f; **let's have a** ~ (**to eat**) mangeons un morceau; **to** ~ **one's nails** se ronger les ongles
bitten [ˈbɪtn] pp of **bite**
bitter [ˈbɪtəʳ] adj amer(-ère); (criticism) cinglant(e); (icy: weather, wind) glacial(e) ▷ n (Brit: beer) bière f (à forte teneur en houblon); **to the** ~ **end** jusqu'au bout
bitterness [ˈbɪtənɪs] n amertume f; goût amer
bizarre [bɪˈzɑːʳ] adj bizarre
black [blæk] adj noir(e) ▷ n (colour) noir m; (person): **B**~ noir(e) ▷ vt (shoes) cirer; (Brit Industry) boycotter; **to give sb a** ~ **eye** pocher l'œil à qn, faire un œil au beurre noir à qn; **there it is in** ~ **and white** (fig) c'est écrit noir sur blanc; **to be in the** ~ (in credit) avoir un compte créditeur; ~ **and blue** (bruised) couvert(e) de bleus
▶ **black out** vi (faint) s'évanouir
blackberry [ˈblækbərɪ] n mûre f
blackbird [ˈblækbəːd] n merle m
blackboard [ˈblækbɔːd] n tableau noir
black coffee n café noir
blackcurrant [ˈblækkʌrənt] n cassis m
blacken [ˈblækn] vt noircir
black ice n verglas m
blackleg [ˈblækleɡ] n (Brit) briseur m de grève, jaune m
blacklist [ˈblæklɪst] n liste noire ▷ vt mettre sur la liste noire
blackmail [ˈblækmeɪl] n chantage m ▷ vt faire chanter, soumettre au chantage
black market n marché noir
blackout [ˈblækaut] n panne f d'électricité; (in wartime) black-out m; (TV) interruption f d'émission; (fainting) syncope f
black pepper n poivre noir

black pudding n boudin (noir)
Black Sea n: **the ~** la mer Noire
black sheep n brebis galeuse
blacksmith ['blæksmɪθ] n forgeron m
black spot n (Aut) point noir
bladder ['blædə'] n vessie f
blade [bleɪd] n lame f; (of oar) plat m; (of propeller) pale f; **a ~ of grass** un brin d'herbe
blame [bleɪm] n faute f, blâme m ▷ vt: **to ~ sb/ sth for sth** attribuer à qn/qch la responsabilité de qch; reprocher qch à qn/qch; **who's to ~?** qui est le fautif or coupable or responsable?; **I'm not to ~** ce n'est pas ma faute
bland [blænd] adj affable; (taste, food) doux (douce), fade
blank [blæŋk] adj blanc (blanche); (look) sans expression, dénué(e) d'expression ▷ n espace m vide, blanc m; (cartridge) cartouche f à blanc; **his mind was a ~** il avait la tête vide; **we drew a ~** (fig) nous n'avons abouti à rien
blanket ['blæŋkɪt] n couverture f; (of snow, cloud) couche f ▷ adj (statement, agreement) global(e), de portée générale; **to give ~ cover** (insurance policy) couvrir tous les risques
blare [blɛə'] vi (brass band, horns, radio) beugler
blast [blɑːst] n explosion f; (shock wave) souffle m; (of air, steam) bouffée f ▷ vt faire sauter or exploser ▷ excl (Brit inf) zut!; **(at) full ~** (play music etc) à plein volume
  ▶ **blast off** vi (Space) décoller
blast-off ['blɑːstɒf] n (Space) lancement m
blatant ['bleɪtənt] adj flagrant(e), criant(e)
blaze [bleɪz] n (fire) incendie m; (flames: of fire, sun etc) embrasement m; (: in hearth) flamme f, flambée f; (fig) flamboiement m ▷ vi (fire) flamber; (fig) flamboyer, resplendir ▷ vt: **to ~ a trail** (fig) montrer la voie; **in a ~ of publicity** à grand renfort de publicité
blazer ['bleɪzə'] n blazer m
bleach [bliːtʃ] n (also: **household bleach**) eau f de Javel ▷ vt (linen) blanchir
bleached [bliːtʃt] adj (hair) oxygéné(e), décoloré(e)
bleachers ['bliːtʃəz] npl (US Sport) gradins mpl (en plein soleil)
bleak [bliːk] adj morne, désolé(e); (weather) triste, maussade; (smile) lugubre; (prospect, future) morose
bleat [bliːt] n bêlement m ▷ vi bêler
bled [bled] pt, pp of **bleed**
bleed (pt, pp **bled**) [bliːd, bled] vt saigner; (brakes, radiator) purger ▷ vi saigner; **my nose is ~ing** je saigne du nez
bleeper ['bliːpə'] n (of doctor etc) bip m
blemish ['blemɪʃ] n défaut m; (on reputation) tache f
blend [blend] n mélange m ▷ vt mélanger ▷ vi (colours etc: also: **blend in**) se mélanger, se fondre, s'allier
blender ['blendə'] n (Culin) mixeur m
bless (pt, pp **-ed** or **blest**) [bles, blest] vt bénir; **to be ~ed with** avoir le bonheur de jouir de or

d'avoir; **~ you!** (after sneeze) à tes souhaits!
blessing ['blesɪŋ] n bénédiction f; (godsend) bienfait m; **to count one's ~s** s'estimer heureux; **it was a ~ in disguise** c'est un bien pour un mal
blew [bluː] pt of **blow**
blight [blaɪt] n (of plants) rouille f ▷ vt (hopes etc) anéantir, briser
blimey ['blaɪmɪ] excl (Brit inf) mince alors!
blind [blaɪnd] adj aveugle ▷ n (for window) store m ▷ vt aveugler; **to turn a ~ eye (on or to)** fermer les yeux (sur); **the blind** npl les aveugles mpl
blind alley n impasse f
blind corner n (Brit) virage m sans visibilité
blindfold ['blaɪndfəʊld] n bandeau m ▷ adj, adv les yeux bandés ▷ vt bander les yeux à
blindly ['blaɪndlɪ] adv aveuglément
blindness ['blaɪndnɪs] n cécité f; (fig) aveuglement m
blind spot n (Aut etc) angle m aveugle; (fig) angle mort
blink [blɪŋk] vi cligner des yeux; (light) clignoter ▷ n: **the TV's on the ~** (inf) la télé ne va pas tarder à nous lâcher
blinkers ['blɪŋkəz] npl œillères fpl
bliss [blɪs] n félicité f, bonheur m sans mélange
blister ['blɪstə'] n (on skin) ampoule f, cloque f; (on paintwork) boursouflure f ▷ vi (paint) se boursoufler, se cloquer
blizzard ['blɪzəd] n blizzard m, tempête f de neige
bloated ['bləʊtɪd] adj (face) bouffi(e); (stomach, person) gonflé(e)
blob [blɒb] n (drop) goutte f; (stain, spot) tache f
block [blɒk] n bloc m; (in pipes) obstruction f; (toy) cube m; (of buildings) pâté m (de maisons) ▷ vt bloquer; (fig) faire obstacle à; (Comput) grouper; **the sink is ~ed** l'évier est bouché; **~ of flats** (Brit) immeuble (locatif); **3 ~s from here** à trois rues d'ici; **mental ~** blocage m; **~ and tackle** (Tech) palan m
  ▶ **block up** vt boucher
blockade [blɔ'keɪd] n blocus m ▷ vt faire le blocus de
blockage ['blɔkɪdʒ] n obstruction f
blockbuster ['blɔkbʌstə'] n (film, book) grand succès
block capitals npl majuscules fpl d'imprimerie
block letters npl majuscules fpl
blog [blɒg] n blog m, blogue m ▷ vi blogger
bloke [bləʊk] n (Brit inf) type m
blond, blonde [blɒnd] adj, n blond(e)
blood [blʌd] n sang m
blood donor n donneur(-euse) de sang
blood group n groupe sanguin
bloodhound ['blʌdhaʊnd] n limier m
blood poisoning n empoisonnement m du sang
blood pressure n tension (artérielle); **to have high/low ~** faire de l'hypertension/ l'hypotension
bloodshed ['blʌdʃed] n effusion f de sang, carnage m
bloodshot ['blʌdʃɒt] adj: **~ eyes** yeux injectés de

sang

blood sports *npl* sports *mpl* sanguinaires

bloodstream ['blʌdstriːm] *n* sang *m*, système sanguin

blood test *n* analyse *f* de sang

bloodthirsty ['blʌdθəːstɪ] *adj* sanguinaire

blood transfusion *n* transfusion *f* de sang

blood type *n* groupe sanguin

blood vessel *n* vaisseau sanguin

bloody ['blʌdɪ] *adj* sanglant(e); (*Brit inf!*): **this ~ … ce foutu …, ce putain de … (!) ▷ *adv*: ~ strong/ good** (*Brit: inf!*) vachement or sacrément fort/bon

bloody-minded ['blʌdɪ'maɪndɪd] *adj* (*Brit inf*) contrariant(e), obstiné(e)

bloom [bluːm] *n* fleur *f*; (*fig*) épanouissement *m* ▷ *vi* être en fleur; (*fig*) s'épanouir; être florissant(e)

blossom ['blɔsəm] *n* fleur(s) *f(pl)* ▷ *vi* être en fleurs; (*fig*) s'épanouir; **to ~ into** (*fig*) devenir

blot [blɔt] *n* tache *f* ▷ *vt* tacher; (*ink*) sécher; **to be a ~ on the landscape** gâcher le paysage; **to ~ one's copy book** (*fig*) faire un impair

▶ **blot out** *vt* (*memories*) effacer; (*view*) cacher, masquer; (*nation, city*) annihiler

blotchy ['blɔtʃɪ] *adj* (*complexion*) couvert(e) de marbrures

blotting paper ['blɔtɪŋ-] *n* buvard *m*

blouse [blauz] *n* (*feminine garment*) chemisier *m*, corsage *m*

blow [bləu] (*pt* **blew**, *pp* **-n**) [bluː, bləun] *n* coup *m* ▷ *vi* souffler ▷ *vt* (*glass*) souffler; (*instrument*) jouer de; (*fuse*) faire sauter; **to ~ one's nose** se moucher; **to ~ a whistle** siffler; **to come to ~s** en venir aux coups

▶ **blow away** *vi* s'envoler ▷ *vt* chasser, faire s'envoler

▶ **blow down** *vt* faire tomber, renverser

▶ **blow off** *vi* s'envoler ▷ *vt* (*hat*) emporter; (*ship*): **to ~ off course** faire dévier

▶ **blow out** *vi* (*fire, flame*) s'éteindre; (*tyre*) éclater; (*fuse*) sauter

▶ **blow over** *vi* s'apaiser

▶ **blow up** *vi* exploser, sauter ▷ *vt* faire sauter; (*tyre*) gonfler; (*Phot*) agrandir

blow-dry ['bləudraɪ] *n* (*hairstyle*) brushing *m* ▷ *vt* faire un brushing à

blowlamp ['bləulæmp] *n* (*Brit*) chalumeau *m*

blown [bləun] *pp* of **blow**

blow-out ['bləuaut] *n* (*of tyre*) éclatement *m*; (*Brit: inf: big meal*) gueuleton *m*

blowtorch ['bləutɔːtʃ] *n* chalumeau *m*

blue [bluː] *adj* bleu(e); (*depressed*) triste; ~ **film/ joke** film *m*/histoire *f* pornographique; (**only**) **once in a ~ moon** tous les trente-six du mois; **out of the ~** (*fig*) à l'improviste, sans qu'on s'y attende

bluebell ['bluːbɛl] *n* jacinthe *f* des bois

blueberry ['bluːbərɪ] *n* myrtille *f*, airelle *f*

bluebottle ['bluːbɔtl] *n* mouche *f* à viande

blue cheese *n* (*fromage*) bleu *m*

blueprint ['bluːprɪnt] *n* bleu *m*; (*fig*) projet *m*, plan directeur

blues [bluːz] *npl*: **the ~** (*Mus*) le blues; **to have the ~** (*inf: feeling*) avoir le cafard

bluff [blʌf] *vi* bluffer ▷ *n* bluff *m*; (*cliff*) promontoire *m*, falaise *f* ▷ *adj* (*person*) bourru(e), brusque; **to call sb's ~** mettre qn au défi d'exécuter ses menaces

blunder ['blʌndər] *n* gaffe *f*, bévue *f* ▷ *vi* faire une gaffe or une bévue; **to ~ into sb/sth** buter contre qn/qch

blunt [blʌnt] *adj* (*knife*) émoussé(e), peu tranchant(e); (*pencil*) mal taillé(e); (*person*) brusque, ne mâchant pas ses mots ▷ *vt* émousser; ~ **instrument** (*Law*) instrument contondant

blur [bləːr] *n* (*shape*): **to become a ~** devenir flou ▷ *vt* brouiller, rendre flou(e)

blurred [bləːd] *adj* flou(e)

blush [blʌʃ] *vi* rougir ▷ *n* rougeur *f*

blusher ['blʌʃər] *n* rouge *m* à joues

blustery ['blʌstərɪ] *adj* (*weather*) à bourrasques

boar [bɔːr] *n* sanglier *m*

board [bɔːd] *n* (*wooden*) planche *f*; (*on wall*) panneau *m*; (*for chess etc*) plateau *m*; (*cardboard*) carton *m*; (*committee*) conseil *m*, comité *m*; (*in firm*) conseil d'administration; (*Naut, Aviat*): **on ~** à bord ▷ *vt* (*ship*) monter à bord de; (*train*) monter dans; **full ~** (*Brit*) pension complète; **half ~** (*Brit*) demi-pension *f*; ~ **and lodging** (*n*) chambre *f* avec pension; **with ~ and lodging** logé nourri; **above ~** (*fig*) régulier(-ère); **across the ~** (*fig: adv*) systématiquement; (*: adj*) de portée générale; **to go by the ~** (*hopes, principles*) être abandonné(e); (*be unimportant*) compter pour rien, n'avoir aucune importance

▶ **board up** *vt* (*door*) condamner (*au moyen de planches, de tôle*)

boarder ['bɔːdər] *n* pensionnaire *m/f*; (*Scol*) interne *m/f*, pensionnaire

board game *n* jeu *m* de société

boarding card ['bɔːdɪŋ-] *n* (*Aviat, Naut*) carte *f* d'embarquement

boarding house ['bɔːdɪŋ-] *n* pension *f*

boarding pass ['bɔːdɪŋ-] *n* (*Brit*) = **boarding card**

boarding school ['bɔːdɪŋ-] *n* internat *m*, pensionnat *m*

board room *n* salle *f* du conseil d'administration

boast [bəust] *vi*: **to ~ (about or of)** se vanter (de) ▷ *vt* s'enorgueillir de ▷ *n* vantardise *f*; sujet *m* d'orgueil or de fierté

boat [bəut] *n* bateau *m*; (*small*) canot *m*; barque *f*; **to go by ~** aller en bateau; **to be in the same ~** (*fig*) être logé à la même enseigne

bob [bɔb] *vi* (*boat, cork on water: also*: **bob up and down**) danser, se balancer ▷ *n* (*Brit inf*) = **shilling**

▶ **bob up** *vi* surgir ou apparaître brusquement

bobby ['bɔbɪ] *n* (*Brit inf*) ≈ agent *m* (de police)

bobby pin ['bɔbɪ-] *n* (*US*) pince *f* à cheveux

bobsleigh ['bɔbsleɪ] *n* bob *m*

bode [bəud] *vi*: **to ~ well/ill (for)** être de bon/ mauvais augure (pour)

bodily ['bɔdɪlɪ] *adj* corporel(le); (*pain, comfort*) physique; (*needs*) matériel(le) ▷ *adv* (*carry, lift*) dans ses bras

body ['bɔdɪ] n corps m; (of car) carrosserie f; (of plane) fuselage m; (also: **body stocking**) body m, justaucorps m; (fig: society) organe m, organisme m; (: quantity) ensemble m, masse f; (of wine) corps; **ruling ~** organe directeur; **in a ~** en masse, ensemble; (speak) comme un seul et même homme

body-building ['bɔdɪbɪldɪŋ] n body-building m, culturisme m

bodyguard ['bɔdɪgɑ:d] n garde m du corps

bodywork ['bɔdɪwə:k] n carrosserie f

bog [bɔg] n tourbière f ▷ vt: **to get ~ged down (in)** (fig) s'enliser (dans)

bogus ['bəugəs] adj bidon inv; fantôme

boil [bɔɪl] vt (faire) bouillir ▷ vi bouillir ▷ n (Med) furoncle m; **to come to the** or (US) **a ~** bouillir; **to bring to the** or (US) **a ~** porter à ébullition

▶ **boil down** vi (fig): **to ~ down to** se réduire or ramener à

▶ **boil over** vi déborder

boiled egg n œuf m à la coque

boiler ['bɔɪlə'] n chaudière f

boiling ['bɔɪlɪŋ] adj: **I'm ~ (hot)** (inf) je crève de chaud

boiling point n point m d'ébullition

boisterous ['bɔɪstərəs] adj bruyant(e), tapageur(-euse)

bold [bəuld] adj hardi(e), audacieux(-euse); (pej) effronté(e); (outline, colour) franc (franche), tranché(e), marqué(e)

bollard ['bɔləd] n (Naut) bitte f d'amarrage; (Brit Aut) borne lumineuse or de signalisation

bolt [bəult] n verrou m; (with nut) boulon m ▷ adv: **~ upright** droit(e) comme un piquet ▷ vt (door) verrouiller; (food) engloutir ▷ vi se sauver, filer (comme une flèche); **a ~ from the blue** (horse) s'emballer; (fig) un coup de tonnerre dans un ciel bleu

bomb [bɔm] n bombe f ▷ vt bombarder

bombard [bɔm'bɑ:d] vt bombarder

bomb disposal n: **~ unit** section f de déminage; **~ expert** artificier m

bomber ['bɔmə'] n caporal m d'artillerie; (Aviat) bombardier m; (terrorist) poseur m de bombes

bombing ['bɔmɪŋ] n bombardement m

bomb scare n alerte f à la bombe

bombshell ['bɔmʃɛl] n obus m; (fig) bombe f

bond [bɔnd] n lien m; (binding promise) engagement m, obligation f; (Finance) obligation; **bonds** npl (chains) chaînes fpl; **in ~** (of goods) en entrepôt

bondage ['bɔndɪdʒ] n esclavage m

bone [bəun] n os m; (of fish) arête f ▷ vt désosser; ôter les arêtes de

bone-dry ['bəun'draɪ] adj absolument sec (sèche)

bone idle adj fainéant(e)

bone marrow n moelle osseuse

bonfire ['bɔnfaɪə'] n feu m (de joie); (for rubbish) feu

bonnet ['bɔnɪt] n bonnet m; (Brit: of car) capot m

bonus ['bəunəs] n (money) prime f; (advantage) avantage m

bony ['bəunɪ] adj (arm, face: Med: tissue) osseux(-euse); (thin: person) squelettique; (meat) plein(e) d'os; (fish) plein d'arêtes

boo [bu:] excl hou!, peuh! ▷ vt huer ▷ n huée f

booby trap ['bu:bɪ-] n guet-apens m

book [buk] n livre m; (of stamps, tickets etc) carnet m; (Comm): **books** npl comptes mpl, comptabilité f ▷ vt (ticket) prendre; (seat, room) réserver; (driver) dresser un procès-verbal à; (football player) prendre le nom de, donner un carton à; **I ~ed a table in the name of ...** j'ai réservé une table au nom de ...; **to keep the ~s** tenir la comptabilité; **by the ~** à la lettre, selon les règles; **to throw the ~ at sb** passer un savon à qn

▶ **book in** vi (Brit: at hotel) prendre sa chambre

▶ **book up** vt réserver; **all seats are ~ed up** tout est pris, c'est complet; **the hotel is ~ed up** l'hôtel est complet

bookcase ['bukkeɪs] n bibliothèque f (meuble)

booking ['bukɪŋ] n (Brit) réservation f; **I confirmed my ~ by fax/email** j'ai confirmé ma réservation par fax/e-mail

booking office n (Brit) bureau m de location

book-keeping ['buk'ki:pɪŋ] n comptabilité f

booklet ['buklɪt] n brochure f

bookmaker ['bukmeɪkə'] n bookmaker m

bookmark ['bukmɑ:k] n (for book) marque-page m; (Comput) signet m

bookseller ['buksɛlə'] n libraire m/f

bookshelf ['bukʃɛlf] n (single) étagère f (à livres); (bookcase) bibliothèque f; **bookshelves** rayons mpl (de bibliothèque)

bookshop ['bukʃɔp], **bookstore** n librairie f

book store ['bukstɔ:'] n = **bookshop**

boom [bu:m] n (noise) grondement m; (in prices, population) forte augmentation; (busy period) boom m, vague f de prospérité ▷ vi gronder; prospérer

boon [bu:n] n bénédiction f, grand avantage

boost [bu:st] n stimulant m, remontant m ▷ vt stimuler; **to give a ~ to sb's spirits** or **to sb** remonter le moral à qn

booster ['bu:stə'] n (TV) amplificateur m (de signal); (Elec) survolteur m; (also: **booster rocket**) booster m; (Med: vaccine) rappel m

boot [bu:t] n botte f; (for hiking) chaussure f (de marche); (ankle boot) bottine f; (Brit: of car) coffre m ▷ vt (Comput) lancer, mettre en route; **to ~** (in addition) par-dessus le marché, en plus; **to give sb the ~** (inf) flanquer qn dehors, virer qn

booth [bu:ð] n (at fair) baraque (foraine); (of telephone etc) cabine f; (also: **voting booth**) isoloir m

booze [bu:z] (inf) n boissons fpl alcooliques, alcool m ▷ vi boire, picoler

border ['bɔ:də'] n bordure f; bord m; (of a country) frontière f; **the B~s** la région frontière entre l'Écosse et l'Angleterre

▶ **border on** vt fus être voisin(e) de, toucher à

borderline ['bɔ:dəlaɪn] n (fig) ligne f de démarcation ▷ adj: **~ case** cas m limite

bore [bɔ:'] pt of **bear** ▷ vt (person) ennuyer, raser;

(*hole*) percer; (*well, tunnel*) creuser ▷ n (*person*) raseur(-euse); (*boring thing*) barbe f; (*of gun*) calibre m

bored ['bɔːd] *adj*: **to be ~** s'ennuyer; **he's ~ to tears** or **to death** or **stiff** il s'ennuie à mourir

boredom ['bɔːdəm] *n* ennui m

boring ['bɔːrɪŋ] *adj* ennuyeux(-euse)

born [bɔːn] *adj*: **to be ~** naître; **I was ~ in 1960** je suis né en 1960; **~ blind** aveugle de naissance; **a ~ comedian** un comédien-né

borne [bɔːn] *pp of* **bear**

borough ['bʌrə] *n* municipalité f

borrow ['bɔrəu] *vt*: **to ~ sth (from sb)** emprunter qch (à qn); **may I ~ your car?** est-ce que je peux vous emprunter votre voiture?

Bosnian ['bɒznɪən] *adj* bosniaque, bosnien(ne) ▷ n Bosniaque m/f, Bosnien(ne)

bosom ['buzəm] *n* poitrine f; (*fig*) sein m

boss [bɒs] *n* patron(ne) ▷ vt (*also*: **boss about, boss around**) mener à la baguette

bossy ['bɒsɪ] *adj* autoritaire

bosun ['bəusn] *n* maître m d'équipage

botany ['bɒtənɪ] *n* botanique f

botch [bɒtʃ] *vt* (*also*: **botch up**) saboter, bâcler

both [bəuθ] *adj* les deux, l'un(e) et l'autre ▷ pron: **~ (of them)** les deux, tous (toutes) (les) deux, l'un(e) et l'autre; **~ of us went, we ~ went** nous y sommes allés tous les deux ▷ adv: **~ A and B** A et B; **they sell ~ the fabric and the finished curtains** ils vendent (et) le tissu et les rideaux (finis), ils vendent à la fois le tissu et les rideaux (finis)

bother ['bɒðəʳ] *vt* (*worry*) tracasser; (*needle, bait*) importuner, ennuyer; (*disturb*) déranger ▷ vi (*also*: **bother o.s.**) se tracasser, se faire du souci ▷ n (*trouble*) ennuis mpl; **it is a ~ to have to do** c'est vraiment ennuyeux d'avoir à faire ▷ excl zut!; **to ~ doing** prendre la peine de faire; **I'm sorry to ~ you** excusez-moi de vous déranger; **please don't ~** ne vous dérangez pas; **don't ~** ce n'est pas la peine; **it's no ~** aucun problème

bottle ['bɒtl] *n* bouteille f; (*baby's*) biberon m; (*of perfume, medicine*) flacon m ▷ vt mettre en bouteille(s); **~ of wine/milk** bouteille de vin/lait; **wine/milk ~** bouteille à vin/lait
▸ **bottle up** *vt* refouler, contenir

bottle bank *n* conteneur m (de bouteilles)

bottleneck ['bɒtlnɛk] *n* (*in traffic*) bouchon m; (*in production*) goulet m d'étranglement

bottle-opener ['bɒtləupnəʳ] *n* ouvre-bouteille m

bottom ['bɒtəm] *n* (*of container, sea etc*) fond m; (*buttocks*) derrière m; (*of page, list*) bas m; (*of chair*) siège m; (*of mountain, tree, hill*) pied m ▷ adj (*shelf, step*) du bas; **to get to the ~ of sth** (*fig*) découvrir le fin fond de qch

bough [bau] *n* branche f, rameau m

bought [bɔːt] *pt, pp of* **buy**

boulder ['bəuldəʳ] *n* gros rocher (*gén lisse, arrondi*)

bounce [bauns] *vi* (*ball*) rebondir; (*cheque*) être refusé (*étant sans provision*); (*also*: **to bounce forward/out etc**) bondir, s'élancer ▷ vt faire rebondir ▷ n (*rebound*) rebond m; **he's got plenty**

of **~** (*fig*) il est plein d'entrain or d'allant

bouncer ['baunsəʳ] *n* (*inf: at dance, club*) videur m

bound [baund] *pt, pp of* **bind** ▷ n (*gen pl*) limite f; (*leap*) bond m ▷ vi (*leap*) bondir ▷ vt (*limit*) borner ▷ adj: **to be ~ to do sth** (*obliged*) être obligé(e) or avoir obligation de faire qch; **he's ~ to fail** (*likely*) il est sûr d'échouer, son échec est inévitable or assuré; **~ by** (*law, regulation*) engagé(e) par; **~ for** à destination de; **out of ~s** dont l'accès est interdit

boundary ['baundrɪ] *n* frontière f

bouquet ['bukeɪ] *n* bouquet m

bourbon ['buəbən] *n* (*US: also:* **bourbon whiskey**) bourbon m

bout [baut] *n* période f; (*of malaria etc*) accès m, crise f, attaque f; (*Boxing etc*) combat m, match m

boutique [buːˈtiːk] *n* boutique f

bow[1] [bəu] *n* nœud m; (*weapon*) arc m; (*Mus*) archet m

bow[2] [bau] *n* (*with body*) révérence f, inclination f (*du buste or corps*); (*Naut: also:* **bows**) proue f ▷ vi faire une révérence, s'incliner; (*yield*): **to ~ to** or **before** s'incliner devant, se soumettre à; **to ~ to the inevitable** accepter l'inévitable or l'inéluctable

bowels [bauəlz] *npl* intestins mpl; (*fig*) entrailles fpl

bowl [bəul] *n* (*for eating*) bol m; (*for washing*) cuvette f; (*ball*) boule f; (*of pipe*) fourneau m ▷ vi (*Cricket*) lancer (la balle)
▸ **bowl over** *vt* (*fig*) renverser

bow-legged ['bəuˈlɛgɪd] *adj* aux jambes arquées

bowler ['bəuləʳ] *n* joueur m de boules; (*Cricket*) lanceur m (*de la balle*); (*Brit: also:* **bowler hat**) (chapeau m) melon m

bowling ['bəulɪŋ] *n* (*game*) jeu m de boules, jeu de quilles

bowling alley *n* bowling m

bowling green *n* terrain m de boules (*gazonné et carré*)

bowls [bəulz] *n* (jeu m de) boules fpl

bow tie [bəu-] *n* nœud m papillon

box [bɒks] *n* boîte f; (*also:* **cardboard box**) carton m; (*crate*) caisse f; (*Theat*) loge f ▷ vt mettre en boîte; (*Sport*) boxer avec ▷ vi boxer, faire de la boxe

boxer ['bɒksəʳ] *n* (*person*) boxeur m; (*dog*) boxer m

boxer shorts ['bɒksəʃɔːts] *npl* caleçon m

boxing ['bɒksɪŋ] *n* (*sport*) boxe f

Boxing Day *n* (*Brit*) le lendemain de Noël; *voir article*

boxing gloves *npl* gants mpl de boxe

boxing ring *n* ring m

box office *n* bureau m de location

box room *n* débarras m; chambrette f

boy [bɔɪ] *n* garçon m

boy band *n* boys band m

boycott ['bɔɪkɒt] *n* boycottage m ▷ vt boycotter

boyfriend ['bɔɪfrɛnd] *n* (petit) ami

boyish ['bɔɪɪʃ] *adj* d'enfant, de garçon; **to look ~** (*man: appear youthful*) faire jeune

BR *abbr* = **British Rail**

bra [brɑː] *n* soutien-gorge m

brace [breɪs] n (support) attache f, agrafe f; (Brit: also: **braces**: on teeth) appareil m (dentaire); (tool) vilebrequin m; (Typ: also: **brace bracket**) accolade f ▷ vt (support) consolider, soutenir; **braces** npl (Brit: for trousers) bretelles fpl; **to ~ o.s.** (fig) se préparer mentalement

bracelet ['breɪslɪt] n bracelet m

bracing ['breɪsɪŋ] adj tonifiant(e), tonique

bracket ['brækɪt] n (Tech) tasseau m, support m; (group) classe f, tranche f; (also: **brace bracket**) accolade f; (also: **round bracket**) parenthèse f; (also: **square bracket**) crochet m ▷ vt mettre entre parenthèses; (fig: also: **bracket together**) regrouper; **income ~** tranche f des revenus; **in ~s** entre parenthèses or crochets

brag [bræg] vi se vanter

braid [breɪd] n (trimming) galon m; (of hair) tresse f, natte f

brain [breɪn] n cerveau m; **brains** npl (intellect, food) cervelle f; **he's got ~s** il est intelligent

brainwash ['breɪnwɒʃ] vt faire subir un lavage de cerveau à

brainwave ['breɪnweɪv] n idée f de génie

brainy ['breɪnɪ] adj intelligent(e), doué(e)

braise [breɪz] vt braiser

brake [breɪk] n frein m ▷ vt, vi freiner

brake light n feu m de stop

bran [bræn] n son m

branch [brɑːntʃ] n branche f; (Comm) succursale f; (: of bank) agence f; (of association) section locale ▷ vi bifurquer

▶ **branch off** vi (road) bifurquer

▶ **branch out** vi diversifier ses activités; **to ~ out into** étendre ses activités à

brand [brænd] n marque (commerciale) ▷ vt (cattle) marquer (au fer rouge); (fig: pej): **to ~ sb a communist** etc traiter or qualifier qn de communiste etc

brand name n nom m de marque

brand-new ['brænd'njuː] adj tout(e) neuf (neuve), flambant neuf (neuve)

brandy ['brændɪ] n cognac m, fine f

brash [bræʃ] adj effronté(e)

brass [brɑːs] n cuivre m (jaune), laiton m; **the ~** (Mus) les cuivres

brass band n fanfare f

brat [bræt] n (pej) mioche m/f, môme m/f

brave [breɪv] adj courageux(-euse), brave ▷ n guerrier indien ▷ vt braver, affronter

bravery ['breɪvərɪ] n bravoure f, courage m

brawl [brɔːl] n rixe f, bagarre f ▷ vi se bagarrer

brazen ['breɪzn] adj impudent(e), effronté(e) ▷ vt: **to ~ it out** payer d'effronterie, crâner

brazier ['breɪzɪəʳ] n brasero m

Brazil [brə'zɪl] n Brésil m

Brazilian [brə'zɪljən] adj brésilien(ne) ▷ n Brésilien(ne)

breach [briːtʃ] vt ouvrir une brèche dans ▷ n (gap) brèche f; (estrangement) brouille f; (breaking): **~ of contract** rupture f de contrat; **~ of the peace** attentat m à l'ordre public; **~ of trust** abus m de confiance

bread [brɛd] n pain m; (inf: money) fric m; **~ and butter** (n) tartines (beurrées); (fig) subsistance f; **to earn one's daily ~** gagner son pain; **to know which side one's ~ is buttered (on)** savoir où est son avantage or intérêt

breadbin ['brɛdbɪn] n (Brit) boîte f or huche f à pain

breadbox ['brɛdbɒks] n (US) boîte f or huche f à pain

breadcrumbs ['brɛdkrʌmz] npl miettes fpl de pain; (Culin) chapelure f, panure f

breadline ['brɛdlaɪn] n: **to be on the ~** être sans le sou or dans l'indigence

breadth [brɛtθ] n largeur f

breadwinner ['brɛdwɪnəʳ] n soutien m de famille

break [breɪk] (pt **broke**, pp **broken**) [brəuk, 'brəukən] vt casser, briser; (promise) rompre; (law) violer ▷ vi se casser, se briser; (promise) tourner; (storm) éclater; (day) se lever ▷ n (gap) brèche f; (fracture) cassure f; (rest) interruption f, arrêt m; (: short) pause f; (: at school) récréation f; (chance) chance f, occasion f favorable; **to ~ one's leg** etc se casser la jambe etc; **to ~ a record** battre un record; **to ~ the news to sb** annoncer la nouvelle à qn; **to ~ with sb** rompre avec qn; **to ~ even** vi rentrer dans ses frais; **to ~ free** or **loose** vi se dégager, s'échapper; **to take a ~** (few minutes) faire une pause, s'arrêter cinq minutes; (holiday) prendre un peu de repos; **without a ~** sans interruption, sans arrêt

▶ **break down** vt (door etc) enfoncer; (resistance) venir à bout de; (figures, data) décomposer, analyser ▷ vi s'effondrer; (Med) faire une dépression (nerveuse); (Aut) tomber en panne; **my car has broken down** ma voiture est en panne

▶ **break in** vt (horse etc) dresser ▷ vi (burglar) entrer par effraction; (interrupt) interrompre

▶ **break into** vt fus (house) s'introduire or pénétrer par effraction dans

▶ **break off** vi (speaker) s'interrompre; (branch) se rompre ▷ vt (talks, engagement) rompre

▶ **break open** vt (door etc) forcer, fracturer

▶ **break out** vi éclater, se déclarer; (prisoner) s'évader; **to ~ out in spots** se couvrir de boutons

▶ **break through** vi: **the sun broke through** le soleil a fait son apparition ▷ vt fus (defences, barrier) franchir; (crowd) se frayer un passage à travers

▶ **break up** vi (partnership) cesser, prendre fin; (marriage) se briser; (crowd, meeting) se séparer; (ship) se disloquer; (line) couper; **the line's** or **you're ~ing up** ça coupe ▷ vt fracasser, casser; (fight etc) interrompre, faire cesser; (marriage) désunir

breakage ['breɪkɪdʒ] n casse f; **to pay for ~s** payer la casse

breakdown ['breɪkdaun] n (Aut) panne f; (in communications, marriage) rupture f; (Med: also: **nervous breakdown**) dépression (nerveuse); (of figures) ventilation f, répartition f

breakdown truck, (US) **breakdown van** n dépanneuse f

breaker ['breɪkə^r] n brisant m

breakfast ['brɛkfəst] n petit déjeuner m; **what time is ~?** le petit déjeuner est à quelle heure?

break-in ['breɪkɪn] n cambriolage m

breaking and entering n (Law) effraction f

breakthrough ['breɪkθru:] n percée f

breakwater ['breɪkwɔ:tə^r] n brise-lames m inv, digue f

breast [brɛst] n (of woman) sein m; (chest) poitrine f; (of chicken, turkey) blanc m

breast-feed ['brɛstfi:d] vt, vi (irreg: like **feed**) allaiter

breast-stroke ['brɛststrəuk] n brasse f

breath [brɛθ] n haleine f, souffle m; **to go out for a ~ of air** sortir prendre l'air; **to take a deep ~** respirer à fond; **out of ~** à bout de souffle, essoufflé(e)

Breathalyser® ['brɛθəlaɪzə^r] (Brit) n alcootest m

breathe [bri:ð] vt, vi respirer; **I won't ~ a word about it** je n'en soufflerai pas mot, je n'en dirai rien à personne

▸ **breathe in** vi inspirer ▷ vt aspirer

▸ **breathe out** vt, vi expirer

breather ['bri:ðə^r] n moment m de repos or de répit

breathing ['bri:ðɪŋ] n respiration f

breathless ['brɛθlɪs] adj essoufflé(e), haletant(e), oppressé(e); **~ with excitement** le souffle coupé par l'émotion

breathtaking ['brɛθteɪkɪŋ] adj stupéfiant(e), à vous couper le souffle

breath test n alcootest m

bred [brɛd] pt, pp of **breed**

breed [bri:d] (pt, pp **bred**) [brɛd] vt élever, faire l'élevage de; (fig: hate, suspicion) engendrer ▷ vi se reproduire ▷ n race f, variété f

breeding ['bri:dɪŋ] n reproduction f; élevage m; (upbringing) éducation f

breeze [bri:z] n brise f

breezy ['bri:zɪ] adj (day, weather) venteux(-euse); (manner) désinvolte; (person) jovial(e)

brevity ['brɛvɪtɪ] n brièveté f

brew [bru:] vt (tea) faire infuser; (beer) brasser; (plot) tramer, préparer ▷ vi (tea) infuser; (beer) fermenter; (fig) se préparer, couver

brewery ['bru:ərɪ] n brasserie f (fabrique)

bribe [braɪb] n pot-de-vin m ▷ vt acheter; soudoyer; **to ~ sb to do sth** soudoyer qn pour qu'il fasse qch

bribery ['braɪbərɪ] n corruption f

bric-a-brac ['brɪkəbræk] n bric-à-brac m

brick [brɪk] n brique f

bricklayer ['brɪkleɪə^r] n maçon m

bridal ['braɪdl] adj nuptial(e); **~ party** noce f

bride [braɪd] n mariée f, épouse f

bridegroom ['braɪdgru:m] n marié m, époux m

bridesmaid ['braɪdzmeɪd] n demoiselle f d'honneur

bridge [brɪdʒ] n pont m; (Naut) passerelle f (de commandement); (of nose) arête f; (Cards, Dentistry) bridge m ▷ vt (river) construire un pont sur; (gap) combler

bridle ['braɪdl] n bride f ▷ vt refréner, mettre la bride à; (horse) brider

bridle path n piste or allée cavalière

brief [bri:f] adj bref (brève) ▷ n (Law) dossier m, cause f; (gen) tâche f ▷ vt mettre au courant; (Mil) donner des instructions à; **briefs** npl slip m; **in ~ ...** (en) bref ...

briefcase ['bri:fkeɪs] n serviette f; porte-documents m inv

briefing ['bri:fɪŋ] n instructions fpl; (Press) briefing m

briefly ['bri:flɪ] adv brièvement; (visit) en coup de vent; **to glimpse ~** entrevoir

brigadier [brɪgə'dɪə^r] n brigadier général

bright [braɪt] adj brillant(e); (room, weather) clair(e); (person: clever) intelligent(e), doué(e); (: cheerful) gai(e); (idea) génial(e); (colour) vif (vive); **to look on the ~ side** regarder le bon côté des choses

brighten ['braɪtn] (also: **brighten up**) vt (room) éclaircir; égayer ▷ vi s'éclaircir; (person) retrouver un peu de sa gaieté

brilliance ['brɪljəns] n éclat m; (fig: of person) brio m

brilliant ['brɪljənt] adj brillant(e); (light, sunshine) éclatant(e); (inf: great) super

brim [brɪm] n bord m

brine [braɪn] n eau salée; (Culin) saumure f

bring [brɪŋ] (pt, pp **brought**) [brɪŋ, brɔ:t] vt (thing) apporter; (person) amener; **to ~ sth to an end** mettre fin à qch; **I can't ~ myself to fire him** je ne peux me résoudre à le mettre à la porte

▸ **bring about** vt provoquer, entraîner

▸ **bring back** vt rapporter; (person) ramener

▸ **bring down** vt (lower) abaisser; (shoot down) abattre; (government) faire s'effondrer

▸ **bring forward** vt avancer; (Book-Keeping) reporter

▸ **bring in** vt (person) faire entrer; (object) rentrer; (Pol: legislation) introduire; (Law: verdict) rendre; (produce: income) rapporter

▸ **bring off** vt (task, plan) réussir, mener à bien; (deal) mener à bien

▸ **bring on** vt (illness, attack) provoquer; (player, substitute) amener

▸ **bring out** vt sortir; (meaning) faire ressortir, mettre en relief; (new product, book) sortir

▸ **bring round, bring to** vt (unconscious person) ranimer

▸ **bring up** vt élever; (carry up) monter; (question) soulever; (food: vomit) vomir, rendre

brink [brɪŋk] n bord m; **on the ~ of doing** sur le point de faire, à deux doigts de faire; **she was on the ~ of tears** elle était au bord des larmes

brisk [brɪsk] adj vif (vive); (abrupt) brusque; (trade etc) actif(-ive); **to go for a ~ walk** se promener d'un bon pas; **business is ~** les affaires marchent (bien)

bristle ['brɪsl] n poil m ▷ vi se hérisser; **bristling with** hérissé(e) de

Brit [brɪt] *n abbr* (*inf*: = British person) Britannique *m/f*

Britain ['brɪtən] *n* (*also*: **Great Britain**) la Grande-Bretagne; **in ~** en Grande-Bretagne

British ['brɪtɪʃ] *adj* britannique ▷ *npl*: **the ~** les Britanniques *mpl*

British Isles *npl*: **the ~** les îles *fpl* Britanniques

British Rail *n* compagnie ferroviaire britannique, ≈ SNCF f

Briton ['brɪtən] *n* Britannique *m/f*

Brittany ['brɪtənɪ] *n* Bretagne f

brittle ['brɪtl] *adj* cassant(e), fragile

broach [brəʊtʃ] *vt* (*subject*) aborder

B road *n* (*Brit*) ≈ route départementale

broad [brɔːd] *adj* large; (*distinction*) général(e); (*accent*) prononcé(e) ▷ *n* (*US inf*) nana f; **~ hint** allusion transparente; **in ~ daylight** en plein jour; **the ~ outlines** les grandes lignes

broadband ['brɔːdbænd] *n* transmission f à haut débit

broad bean *n* fève f

broadcast ['brɔːdkɑːst] (*pt, pp* -) *n* émission f ▷ *vt* (*Radio*) radiodiffuser; (*TV*) téléviser ▷ *vi* émettre

broaden ['brɔːdn] *vt* élargir; **to ~ one's mind** élargir ses horizons ▷ *vi* s'élargir

broadly ['brɔːdlɪ] *adv* en gros, généralement

broad-minded ['brɔːd'maɪndɪd] *adj* large d'esprit

broccoli ['brɒkəlɪ] *n* brocoli *m*

brochure ['brəʊʃjʊəʳ] *n* prospectus *m*, dépliant *m*

broil [brɔɪl] (*US*) *vt* rôtir

broke [brəʊk] *pt of* **break** ▷ *adj* (*inf*) fauché(e); **to go ~** (*business*) faire faillite

broken ['brəʊkn] *pp of* **break** ▷ *adj* (*stick, leg etc*) cassé(e); (*machine*: *also*: **broken down**) fichu(e); (*promise, vow*) rompu(e); **a ~ marriage** un couple dissocié; **a ~ home** un foyer désuni; **in ~ French/English** dans un français/anglais approximatif *or* hésitant

broken-hearted ['brəʊkn'hɑːtɪd] *adj* (ayant) le cœur brisé

broker ['brəʊkəʳ] *n* courtier *m*

brolly ['brɒlɪ] *n* (*Brit inf*) pépin *m*, parapluie *m*

bronchitis [brɒŋ'kaɪtɪs] *n* bronchite f

bronze [brɒnz] *n* bronze *m*

brooch [brəʊtʃ] *n* broche f

brood [bruːd] *n* couvée f ▷ *vi* (*hen, storm*) couver; (*person*) méditer (sombrement), ruminer

broom [brum] *n* balai *m*; (*Bot*) genêt *m*

broomstick ['brumstɪk] *n* manche *m* à balai

Bros. *abbr* (*Comm*: = brothers) Frères

broth [brɔθ] *n* bouillon *m* de viande et de légumes

brothel ['brɔθl] *n* maison close, bordel *m*

brother ['brʌðəʳ] *n* frère *m*

brother-in-law ['brʌðərɪn'lɔːʳ] *n* beau-frère *m*

brought [brɔːt] *pt, pp of* **bring**

brow [brau] *n* front *m*; (*rare*: *gen*: *eyebrow*) sourcil *m*; (*of hill*) sommet *m*

brown [braun] *adj* brun(e), marron *inv*; (*hair*) châtain *inv*; (*tanned*) bronzé(e); (*rice, bread, flour*) complet(-ète) ▷ *n* (*colour*) brun *m*, marron *m* ▷ *vt*

brunir; (*Culin*) faire dorer, faire roussir; **to go ~** (*person*) bronzer; (*leaves*) jaunir

brown bread *n* pain *m* bis

Brownie ['braunɪ] *n* jeannette f éclaireuse (cadette)

brown paper *n* papier *m* d'emballage, papier kraft

brown rice *n* riz *m* complet

brown sugar *n* cassonade f

browse [brauz] *vi* (*in shop*) regarder (*sans acheter*); (*among books*) bouquiner, feuilleter les livres; (*animal*) paître; **to ~ through a book** feuilleter un livre

browser ['brauzəʳ] *n* (*Comput*) navigateur *m*

bruise [bruːz] *n* bleu *m*, ecchymose f, contusion f ▷ *vt* contusionner, meurtrir ▷ *vi* (*fruit*) se taler, se meurtrir; **to ~ one's arm** se faire un bleu au bras

brunette [bruː'nɛt] *n* (*femme*) brune

brunt [brʌnt] *n*: **the ~ of** (*attack, criticism etc*) le plus gros de

brush [brʌʃ] *n* brosse f; (*for painting*) pinceau *m*; (*for shaving*) blaireau *m*; (*quarrel*) accrochage *m*, prise f de bec ▷ *vt* brosser; (*also*: **brush past**, **brush against**) effleurer, frôler; **to have a ~ with sb** s'accrocher avec qn; **to have a ~ with the police** avoir maille à partir avec la police

▶ **brush aside** *vt* écarter, balayer

▶ **brush up** *vt* (*knowledge*) rafraîchir, réviser

brushwood ['brʌʃwud] *n* broussailles *fpl*, taillis *m*

Brussels ['brʌslz] *n* Bruxelles

Brussels sprout [-spraut] *n* chou *m* de Bruxelles

brutal ['bruːtl] *adj* brutal(e)

brute [bruːt] *n* brute f ▷ *adj*: **by ~ force** par la force

B.Sc. *n abbr* = **Bachelor of Science**

BSE *n abbr* (= bovine spongiform encephalopathy) ESB f, BSE f

bubble ['bʌbl] *n* bulle f ▷ *vi* bouillonner, faire des bulles; (*sparkle, fig*) pétiller

bubble bath *n* bain moussant

bubble gum *n* chewing-gum *m*

bubblejet printer ['bʌbldʒɛt-] *n* imprimante f à bulle d'encre

buck [bʌk] *n* mâle *m* (d'un lapin, lièvre, daim etc); (*US inf*) dollar *m* ▷ *vi* ruer, lancer une ruade; **to pass the ~ (to sb)** se décharger de la responsabilité (sur qn)

▶ **buck up** *vi* (*cheer up*) reprendre du poil de la bête, se remonter ▷ *vt*: **to ~ one's ideas up** se reprendre

bucket ['bʌkɪt] *n* seau *m* ▷ *vi* (*Brit inf*): **the rain is ~ing (down)** il pleut à verse

Buckingham Palace ['bʌkɪŋhəm-] *n* le palais de Buckingham; *voir article*

buckle ['bʌkl] *n* boucle f ▷ *vt* (*belt etc*) boucler, attacher ▷ *vi* (*warp*) tordre, gauchir; (: *wheel*) se voiler

▶ **buckle down** *vi* s'y mettre

bud [bʌd] *n* bourgeon *m*; (*of flower*) bouton *m* ▷ *vi* bourgeonner; (*flower*) éclore

Buddhism ['budɪzəm] n bouddhisme m

Buddhist ['budɪst] adj bouddhiste ▷ n
Bouddhiste m/f

budding ['bʌdɪŋ] adj (flower) en bouton; (poet etc)
en herbe; (passion etc) naissant(e)

buddy ['bʌdɪ] n (US) copain m

budge [bʌdʒ] vt faire bouger ▷ vi bouger

budgerigar ['bʌdʒərɪgɑːʳ] n perruche f

budget ['bʌdʒɪt] n budget m ▷ vi: **to ~ for sth**
inscrire qch au budget; **I'm on a tight ~** je dois
faire attention à mon budget

budgie ['bʌdʒɪ] n = **budgerigar**

buff [bʌf] adj (couleur f) chamois m ▷ n (inf:
enthusiast) mordu(e)

buffalo (pl - or -es) ['bʌfələu] n (Brit) buffle m; (US)
bison m

buffer ['bʌfəʳ] n tampon m; (Comput) mémoire f
tampon

buffet n ['bufeɪ] (food Brit: bar) buffet m ▷ vt ['bʌfɪt]
gifler, frapper; secouer, ébranler

buffet car n (Brit Rail) voiture-bar f

bug [bʌg] n (bedbug etc) punaise f; (esp US: any
insect) insecte m, bestiole f; (fig: germ) virus m,
microbe m; (spy device) dispositif m d'écoute
(électronique), micro clandestin; (Comput:
of program) erreur f; (: of equipment) défaut m
▷ vt (room) poser des micros dans; (inf: annoy)
embêter; **I've got the travel ~** (fig) j'ai le virus
du voyage

buggy ['bʌgɪ] n poussette f

bugle ['bjuːgl] n clairon m

build [bɪld] n (of person) carrure f, charpente f ▷ vt
(pt, pp **built**) [bɪlt] construire, bâtir
▶ **build on** vt fus (fig) tirer parti de, partir de
▶ **build up** vt accumuler, amasser; (business)
développer; (reputation) bâtir

builder ['bɪldəʳ] n entrepreneur m

building ['bɪldɪŋ] n (trade) construction f;
(structure) bâtiment m, construction; (: residential,
offices) immeuble m

building site n chantier m (de construction)

building society n (Brit) société f de crédit
immobilier; voir article

built [bɪlt] pt, pp of **build**

built-in ['bɪlt'ɪn] adj (cupboard) encastré(e); (device)
incorporé(e); intégré(e)

built-up ['bɪlt'ʌp] adj: **~ area** agglomération
(urbaine); zone urbanisée

bulb [bʌlb] n (Bot) bulbe m, oignon m; (Elec)
ampoule f

Bulgaria [bʌl'gɛərɪə] n Bulgarie f

Bulgarian [bʌl'gɛərɪən] adj bulgare ▷ n Bulgare
m/f; (Ling) bulgare m

bulge [bʌldʒ] n renflement m, gonflement m; (in
birth rate, sales) brusque augmentation f ▷ vi faire
saillie; présenter un renflement; (pocket, file): **to
be bulging with** être plein(e) à craquer de

bulimia [bə'lɪmɪə] n boulimie f

bulimic [bju:'lɪmɪk] adj, n boulimique m/f

bulk [bʌlk] n masse f, volume m; **in ~** (Comm) en
gros, en vrac; **the ~ of** la plus grande or grosse
partie de

bulky ['bʌlkɪ] adj volumineux(-euse),
encombrant(e)

bull [bul] n taureau m; (male elephant, whale) mâle
m; (Stock Exchange) haussier m; (Rel) bulle f

bulldog ['buldɔg] n bouledogue m

bulldozer ['buldəuzəʳ] n bulldozer m

bullet ['bulɪt] n balle f (de fusil etc)

bulletin ['bulɪtɪn] n bulletin m, communiqué m;
(also: **news bulletin**) (bulletin d')informations fpl

bulletin board n (Comput) messagerie f
(électronique)

bulletproof ['bulɪtpru:f] adj à l'épreuve des
balles; **~ vest** gilet m pare-balles

bullfight ['bulfaɪt] n corrida f, course f de
taureaux

bullfighter ['bulfaɪtəʳ] n torero m

bullfighting ['bulfaɪtɪŋ] n tauromachie f

bullion ['buljən] n or m or argent m en lingots

bullock ['bulək] n bœuf m

bullring ['bulrɪŋ] n arène f

bull's-eye ['bulzaɪ] n centre m (de la cible)

bully ['bulɪ] n brute f, tyran m ▷ vt tyranniser,
rudoyer; (frighten) intimider

bum [bʌm] n (inf: Brit: backside) derrière m; (: esp
US: tramp) vagabond(e), traîne-savates m/f inv;
(: idler) glandeur m
▶ **bum around** vi (inf) vagabonder

bumblebee ['bʌmblbi:] n bourdon m

bump [bʌmp] n (blow) coup m, choc m; (jolt)
cahot m; (on road etc, on head) bosse f ▷ vt heurter,
cogner; (car) emboutir
▶ **bump along** vi avancer en cahotant
▶ **bump into** vt fus rentrer dans, tamponner; (inf:
meet) tomber sur

bumper ['bʌmpəʳ] n pare-chocs m inv ▷ adj: **~
crop/harvest** récolte/moisson exceptionnelle

bumper cars npl (US) autos tamponneuses

bumpy ['bʌmpɪ] adj (road) cahoteux(-euse);
it was a ~ flight/ride on a été secoués dans
l'avion/la voiture

bun [bʌn] n (cake) petit gâteau m; (bread) petit pain
au lait; (of hair) chignon m

bunch [bʌntʃ] n (of flowers) bouquet m; (of keys)
trousseau m; (of bananas) régime m; (of people)
groupe m; **bunches** npl (in hair) couettes fpl; **~ of
grapes** grappe f de raisin

bundle ['bʌndl] n paquet m ▷ vt (also: **bundle
up**) faire un paquet de; (put): **to ~ sth/sb into**
fourrer or enfourner qch/qn dans
▶ **bundle off** vt (person) faire sortir (en toute
hâte); expédier
▶ **bundle out** vt éjecter, sortir (sans
ménagements)

bungalow ['bʌŋgələu] n bungalow m

bungee jumping ['bʌndʒi:'dʒʌmpɪŋ] n saut m à
l'élastique

bungle ['bʌŋgl] vt bâcler, gâcher

bunion ['bʌnjən] n oignon m (au pied)

bunk [bʌŋk] n couchette f; (Brit inf): **to do a ~**
mettre les bouts or les voiles
▶ **bunk off** vi (Brit inf: Scol) sécher (les cours); **I'll ~
off at 3 o'clock this afternoon** je vais mettre les

bouts or les voiles à 3 heures cet après-midi
bunk beds *npl* lits superposés
bunker ['bʌŋkəʳ] *n* (*coal store*) soute *f* à charbon;
(*Mil, Golf*) bunker *m*
bunny ['bʌnɪ] *n* (*also*: **bunny rabbit**) lapin *m*
bunting ['bʌntɪŋ] *n* pavoisement *m*, drapeaux
mpl
buoy [bɔɪ] *n* bouée *f*
▸ **buoy up** *vt* faire flotter; (*fig*) soutenir, épauler
buoyant ['bɔɪənt] *adj* (*ship*) flottable; (*carefree*)
gai(e), plein(e) d'entrain; (*Comm: market, economy*)
actif(-ive); (*: prices, currency*) soutenu(e)
burden ['bə:dn] *n* fardeau *m*, charge *f* ▷ *vt*
charger; (*oppress*) accabler, surcharger; **to be a ~
to sb** être un fardeau pour qn
bureau (*pl* **-x**) ['bjʊərəu, -z] *n* (*Brit: writing desk*)
bureau *m*, secrétaire *m*; (*US: chest of drawers*)
commode *f*; (*office*) bureau, office *m*
bureaucracy [bjuə'rɔkrəsɪ] *n* bureaucratie *f*
bureaucrat ['bjuərəkræt] *n* bureaucrate *m/f*,
rond-de-cuir *m*
bureau de change [-də'ʃɑ̃ʒ] (*pl* **bureaux de
change**) *n* bureau *m* de change
bureaux ['bjuərəuz] *npl of* **bureau**
burger ['bə:gəʳ] *n* hamburger *m*
burglar ['bə:gləʳ] *n* cambrioleur *m*
burglar alarm *n* sonnerie *f* d'alarme
burglary ['bə:glərɪ] *n* cambriolage *m*
Burgundy ['bə:gəndɪ] *n* Bourgogne *f*
burial ['berɪəl] *n* enterrement *m*
burly ['bə:lɪ] *adj* de forte carrure, costaud(e)
Burma ['bə:mə] *n* Birmanie *f*; *see also* **Myanmar**
burn [bə:n] *vt, vi* (*pt, pp* **-ed** *or* **-t**) [bə:nt] brûler ▷ *n*
brûlure *f*; **the cigarette ~t a hole in her dress**
la cigarette a fait un trou dans sa robe; **I've ~t
myself!** je me suis brûlé(e)!
▸ **burn down** *vt* incendier, détruire par le feu
▸ **burn out** *vt* (*writer etc*): **to ~ o.s. out** s'user (à
force de travailler)
burner ['bə:nəʳ] *n* brûleur *m*
burning ['bə:nɪŋ] *adj* (*building, forest*) en flammes;
(*issue, question*) brûlant(e); (*ambition*) dévorant(e)
Burns' Night [bə:nz-] *n* fête écossaise à la mémoire du
poète Robert Burns; voir article
burnt [bə:nt] *pt, pp of* **burn**
burp [bə:p] (*inf*) *n* rot *m* ▷ *vi* roter
burrow ['bʌrəu] *n* terrier *m* ▷ *vt* creuser ▷ *vi*
(*rabbit*) creuser un terrier; (*rummage*) fouiller
bursary ['bə:sərɪ] *n* (*Brit*) bourse *f* (d'études)
burst [bə:st] (*pt, pp* **-**) *vt* faire éclater; (*river:
banks etc*) rompre ▷ *vi* éclater; (*tyre*) crever ▷ *n*
explosion *f*; (*also*: **burst pipe**) fuite *f* (*due à une
rupture*); **a ~ of enthusiasm/energy** un accès
d'enthousiasme/d'énergie; **~ of laughter**
éclat *m* de rire; **a ~ of applause** une salve
d'applaudissement; **a ~ of gunfire** une rafale de
tir; **a ~ of speed** une pointe de vitesse; **~ blood
vessel** rupture *f* de vaisseau sanguin; **the river
has ~ its banks** le cours d'eau est sorti de son lit;
to ~ into flames s'enflammer soudainement;
to ~ out laughing éclater de rire; **to ~ into
tears** fondre en larmes; **to ~ open** (*vi*) s'ouvrir

violemment or soudainement; **to be ~ing with**
(*container*) être plein(e) (à craquer) de, regorger
de; (*fig*) être débordant(e) de
▸ **burst into** *vt fus* (*room etc*) faire irruption dans
▸ **burst out of** *vt fus* sortir précipitamment de
bury ['berɪ] *vt* enterrer; **to ~ one's face in one's
hands** se couvrir le visage de ses mains; **to
~ one's head in the sand** (*fig*) pratiquer la
politique de l'autruche; **to ~ the hatchet** (*fig*)
enterrer la hache de guerre
bus (*pl* **-es**) [bʌs, 'bʌsɪz] *n* autobus *m*
bus conductor *n* receveur(-euse) *m/f* de bus
bush [buʃ] *n* buisson *m*; (*scrub land*) brousse *f*; **to
beat about the ~** tourner autour du pot
bushy ['buʃɪ] *adj* broussailleux(-euse), touffu(e)
busily ['bɪzɪlɪ] *adv*: **to be ~ doing sth** s'affairer à
faire qch
business ['bɪznɪs] *n* (*matter, firm*) affaire *f*; (*trading*)
affaires *fpl*; (*job, duty*) travail *m*; **to be away on ~**
être en déplacement d'affaires; **I'm here on ~** je
suis là pour affaires; **he's in the insurance ~** il
est dans les assurances; **to do ~ with sb** traiter
avec qn; **it's none of my ~** cela ne me regarde
pas, ce ne sont pas mes affaires; **he means ~** il
ne plaisante pas, il est sérieux
business class *n* (*on plane*) classe *f* affaires
businesslike ['bɪznɪslaɪk] *adj* sérieux(-euse),
efficace
businessman ['bɪznɪsmən] (*irreg*) *n* homme *m*
d'affaires
business trip *n* voyage *m* d'affaires
businesswoman ['bɪznɪswumən] (*irreg*) *n*
femme *f* d'affaires
busker ['bʌskəʳ] *n* (*Brit*) artiste ambulant(e)
bus pass *n* carte *f* de bus
bus shelter *n* abribus *m*
bus station *n* gare routière
bus stop *n* arrêt *m* d'autobus
bust [bʌst] *n* buste *m*; (*measurement*) tour *m* de
poitrine ▷ *adj* (*inf: broken*) fichu(e), fini(e) ▷ *vt*
(*inf: Police: arrest*) pincer; **to go ~** faire faillite
bustle ['bʌsl] *n* remue-ménage *m*, affairement *m*
▷ *vi* s'affairer, se démener
bustling ['bʌslɪŋ] *adj* (*person*) affairé(e); (*town*)
très animé(e)
busy ['bɪzɪ] *adj* occupé(e); (*shop, street*) très
fréquenté(e); (*US: telephone, line*) occupé ▷ *vt*: **to
~ o.s.** s'occuper; **he's a ~ man** (*normally*) c'est un
homme très pris; (*temporarily*) il est très pris
busybody ['bɪzɪbɔdɪ] *n* mouche *f* du coche, âme *f*
charitable
busy signal *n* (*US*) tonalité *f* occupé *inv*
but [bʌt] *conj* mais; **I'd love to come, ~ I'm
busy** j'aimerais venir mais je suis occupé; **he's
not English – French** il n'est pas anglais mais
français; **~ that's far too expensive!** mais c'est
bien trop cher!
▷ *prep* (*apart from, except*) sauf, excepté; **nothing ~**
rien d'autre que; **we've had nothing ~ trouble**
nous n'avons eu que des ennuis; **no-one ~ him
can do it** lui seul peut le faire; **who ~ a lunatic
would do such a thing?** qui sinon un fou

ferait une chose pareille?; **~ for you/your help** sans toi/ton aide; **anything ~ that** tout sauf or excepté ça, tout mais pas ça; **the last ~ one** (Brit) l'avant-dernier(-ère)
▷ adv (just, only) ne … que; **she's ~ a child** elle n'est qu'une enfant; **had I ~ known** si seulement j'avais su; **I can ~ try** je peux toujours essayer; **all ~ finished** pratiquement terminé; **anything ~ finished** tout sauf fini, très loin d'être fini

butcher ['butʃə^r] n boucher m ▷ vt massacrer; (cattle etc for meat) tuer

butcher's ['butʃə^rz], **butcher's shop** n boucherie f

butler ['bʌtlə^r] n maître m d'hôtel

butt [bʌt] n (cask) gros tonneau; (thick end) (gros) bout; (of gun) crosse f; (of cigarette) mégot m; (Brit fig: target) cible f ▷ vt donner un coup de tête à
▶ **butt in** vi (interrupt) interrompre

butter ['bʌtə^r] n beurre m ▷ vt beurrer

buttercup ['bʌtəkʌp] n bouton m d'or

butterfly ['bʌtəflaɪ] n papillon m; (Swimming: also: **butterfly stroke**) brasse f papillon

buttocks ['bʌtəks] npl fesses fpl

button ['bʌtn] n bouton m; (US: badge) pin m ▷ vt (also: **button up**) boutonner ▷ vi se boutonner

buttress ['bʌtrɪs] n contrefort m

buy [baɪ] (pt, pp **bought**) [bɔːt] vt acheter; (Comm: company) (r)acheter ▷ n achat m; **that was a good/bad ~** c'était un bon/mauvais achat; **to ~ sb sth/sth from sb** acheter qch à qn; **to ~ sb a drink** offrir un verre or à boire à qn; **can I ~ you a drink?** je vous offre un verre?; **where can I ~ some postcards?** où est-ce que je peux acheter des cartes postales?
▶ **buy back** vt racheter
▶ **buy in** vt (Brit: goods) acheter, faire venir
▶ **buy into** vt fus (Brit Comm) acheter des actions de
▶ **buy off** vt (bribe) acheter
▶ **buy out** vt (partner) désintéresser; (business) racheter
▶ **buy up** vt acheter en bloc, rafler

buyer ['baɪə^r] n acheteur(-euse) m/f; **~'s market** marché m favorable aux acheteurs

buzz [bʌz] n bourdonnement m; (inf: phone call): **to give sb a ~** passer un coup de fil à qn ▷ vi bourdonner ▷ vt (call on intercom) appeler; (with buzzer) sonner; (Aviat: plane, building) raser; **my head is ~ing** j'ai la tête qui bourdonne
▶ **buzz off** vi (inf) s'en aller, ficher le camp

buzzer ['bʌzə^r] n timbre m électrique

buzz word n (inf) mot m à la mode or dans le vent

by [baɪ] prep **1** (referring to cause, agent) par, de; **killed by lightning** tué par la foudre; **surrounded by a fence** entouré d'une barrière; **a painting by Picasso** un tableau de Picasso

2 (referring to method, manner, means): **by bus/car** en autobus/voiture; **by train** par le or en train; **to pay by cheque** payer par chèque; **by moonlight/candlelight** à la lueur de la lune/ d'une bougie; **by saving hard, he …** à force d'économiser, il …

3 (via, through) par; **we came by Dover** nous sommes venus par Douvres

4 (close to, past) à côté de; **the house by the school** la maison à côté de l'école; **a holiday by the sea** des vacances au bord de la mer; **she sat by his bed** elle était assise à son chevet; **she went by me** elle est passée à côté de moi; **I go by the post office every day** je passe devant la poste tous les jours

5 (with time: not later than) avant; (: during): **by daylight** à la lumière du jour; **by night** la nuit, de nuit; **by 4 o'clock** avant 4 heures; **by this time tomorrow** d'ici demain à la même heure; **by the time I got here it was too late** lorsque je suis arrivé il était déjà trop tard

6 (amount) à; **by the kilo/metre** au kilo/au mètre; **paid by the hour** payé à l'heure; **to increase etc by the hour** augmenter etc d'heure en heure

7 (Math: measure): **to divide/multiply by 3** diviser/multiplier par 3; **a room 3 metres by 4** une pièce de 3 mètres sur 4; **it's broader by a metre** c'est plus large d'un mètre; **the bullet missed him by inches** la balle est passée à quelques centimètres de lui; **one by one** un à un; **little by little** petit à petit, peu à peu

8 (according to) d'après, selon; **it's 3 o'clock by my watch** il est 3 heures à ma montre; **it's all right by me** ça ne m'ai rien contre

9: (all) **by oneself** etc tout(e) seul(e)
▷ adv **1** see **go**; **pass** etc
2: **by and by** un peu plus tard, bientôt; **by and large** dans l'ensemble

bye ['baɪ], **bye-bye** ['baɪ'baɪ] excl au revoir!, salut!

bye-law ['baɪlɔː] n = **by-law**

by-election ['baɪɪlɛkʃən] n (Brit) élection (législative) partielle

bygone ['baɪɡɔn] adj passé(e) ▷ n: **let ~s be ~s** passons l'éponge, oublions le passé

by-law ['baɪlɔː] n arrêté municipal

bypass ['baɪpɑːs] n rocade f; (Med) pontage m ▷ vt éviter

by-product ['baɪprɔdʌkt] n sous-produit m, dérivé m; (fig) conséquence f secondaire, retombée f

bystander ['baɪstændə^r] n spectateur(-trice), badaud(e)

byte [baɪt] n (Comput) octet m

byword ['baɪwəːd] n: **to be a ~ for** être synonyme de (fig)

Cc

C¹, c¹ [siː] *n* (*letter*) C, c *m*; (*Scol: mark*) C; (*Mus*): **C** do
m; **C for Charlie** C comme Célestin

C² *abbr* (= *Celsius, centigrade*) C

c² *abbr* (= *century*) s.; (= *circa*) v.; (*US etc*) = **cent(s)**

CA *n abbr* = **Central America**; (*Brit*) = **chartered
accountant** ▷ *abbr* (*US*) = **California**

cab [kæb] *n* taxi *m*; (*of train, truck*) cabine *f*; (*horse-
drawn*) fiacre *m*

cabaret ['kæbəreɪ] *n* attractions *fpl*; (*show*)
spectacle *m* de cabaret

cabbage ['kæbɪdʒ] *n* chou *m*

cabin ['kæbɪn] *n* (*house*) cabane *f*, hutte *f*; (*on ship*)
cabine *f*; (*on plane*) compartiment *m*

cabin crew *n* (*Aviat*) équipage *m*

cabin cruiser *n* yacht *m* (à moteur)

cabinet ['kæbɪnɪt] *n* (*Pol*) cabinet *m*; (*furniture*)
petit meuble à tiroirs et rayons; (*also:* **display
cabinet**) vitrine *f*, petite armoire vitrée

cabinet minister *n* ministre *m* (membre du cabinet)

cable ['keɪbl] *n* câble *m* ▷ *vt* câbler, télégraphier

cable car ['keɪblkaːʳ] *n* téléphérique *m*

cable television *n* télévision *f* par câble

cache [kæʃ] *n* cachette *f*; **a ~ of food** *etc* un dépôt
secret de provisions *etc*, une cachette contenant
des provisions *etc*

cackle ['kækl] *vi* caqueter

cactus (*pl* **cacti**) ['kæktəs, -taɪ] *n* cactus *m*

cadet [kə'dɛt] *n* (*Mil*) élève *m* officier; **police ~**
élève agent de police

cadge [kædʒ] *vt* (*inf*) se faire donner; **to ~ a meal
(off sb)** se faire inviter à manger (par qn)

Caesarean, (*US*) **Cesarean** [siː'zɛərɪən] *adj*: **~
(section)** césarienne *f*

café ['kæfeɪ] *n* ≈ café(-restaurant) *m* (sans alcool)

cafeteria [kæfɪ'tɪərɪə] *n* cafétéria *f*

caffeine ['kæfiːn] *n* caféine *f*

cage [keɪdʒ] *n* cage *f* ▷ *vt* mettre en cage

cagey ['keɪdʒɪ] *adj* (*inf*) réticent(e), méfiant(e)

cagoule [kə'guːl] *n* K-way® *m*

Cairo ['kaɪərəu] *n* le Caire

cajole [kə'dʒəul] *vt* couvrir de flatteries *or* de
gentillesses

cake [keɪk] *n* gâteau *m*; **~ of soap** savonnette *f*;
it's a piece of ~ (*inf*) c'est un jeu d'enfant; **he
wants to have his ~ and eat it (too)** (*fig*) il veut
tout avoir

caked [keɪkt] *adj*: **~ with** raidi(e) par, couvert(e)

d'une croûte de

calcium ['kælsɪəm] *n* calcium *m*

calculate ['kælkjuleɪt] *vt* calculer; (*estimate:
chances, effect*) évaluer

▶ **calculate on** *vt fus*: **to ~ on sth/on doing sth**
compter sur qch/faire qch

calculation [kælkju'leɪʃən] *n* calcul *m*

calculator ['kælkjuleɪtəʳ] *n* machine *f* à calculer,
calculatrice *f*

calendar ['kæləndəʳ] *n* calendrier *m*

calendar year *n* année civile

calf (*pl* **calves**) [kaːf, kaːvz] *n* (*of cow*) veau *m*; (*of
other animals*) petit *m*; (*also:* **calfskin**) veau *m*,
vachette *f*; (*Anat*) mollet *m*

calibre, (*US*) **caliber** ['kælɪbəʳ] *n* calibre *m*

call [kɔːl] *vt* (*gen, also Tel*) appeler; (*announce: flight*)
annoncer; (*meeting*) convoquer; (*strike*) lancer ▷ *vi*
appeler; (*visit: also:* **call in, call round**) passer ▷ *n*
(*shout*) appel *m*, cri *m*; (*summons: for flight etc, fig:
lure*) appel; (*visit*) visite *f*; (*also:* **telephone call**)
coup *m* de téléphone; communication *f*; **to be
on ~** être de permanence; **to be ~ed** s'appeler;
she's ~ed Suzanne elle s'appelle Suzanne;
who is ~ing? (*Tel*) qui est à l'appareil?; **London
~ing** (*Radio*) ici Londres; **please give me a ~ at 7**
appelez-moi à 7 heures; **to make a ~** téléphoner,
passer un coup de fil; **can I make a ~ from
here?** est-ce que je peux téléphoner d'ici?; **to
pay a ~ on sb** rendre visite à qn, passer voir qn;
there's not much ~ for these items ces articles
ne sont pas très demandés

▶ **call at** *vt fus* (*ship*) faire escale à; (*train*) s'arrêter
à

▶ **call back** *vi* (*return*) repasser; (*Tel*) rappeler ▷ *vt*
(*Tel*) rappeler; **can you ~ back later?** pouvez-
vous rappeler plus tard?

▶ **call for** *vt fus* (*demand*) demander; (*fetch*) passer
prendre

▶ **call in** *vt* (*doctor, expert, police*) appeler, faire
venir

▶ **call off** *vt* annuler; **the strike was ~ed off**
l'ordre de grève a été rapporté

▶ **call on** *vt fus* (*visit*) rendre visite à, passer voir;
(*request*): **to ~ on sb to do** inviter qn à faire

▶ **call out** *vi* pousser un cri *or* des cris ▷ *vt* (*doctor,
police, troops*) appeler

▶ **call up** *vt* (*Mil*) appeler, mobiliser; (*Tel*) appeler

call box ['kɔːlbɒks] n (Brit) cabine f téléphonique

call centre, (US) **call center** n centre m d'appels

caller ['kɔːlə'] n (Tel) personne f qui appelle; (visitor) visiteur m; **hold the line, ~!** (Tel) ne quittez pas, Monsieur (or Madame)!

call girl n call-girl f

call-in ['kɔːlɪn] n (US Radio, TV) programme m à ligne ouverte

calling ['kɔːlɪŋ] n vocation f; (trade, occupation) état m

calling card n (US) carte f de visite

callous ['kæləs] adj dur(e), insensible

calm [kɑːm] adj calme ▷ n calme m ▷ vt calmer, apaiser
  ▸ **calm down** vi se calmer, s'apaiser ▷ vt calmer, apaiser

calmly ['kɑːmlɪ] adv calmement, avec calme

Calor gas® ['kælə'-] n (Brit) butane m, butagaz® m

calorie ['kælərɪ] n calorie f; **low ~ product** produit m pauvre en calories

calves [kɑːvz] npl of **calf**

camber ['kæmbə'] n (of road) bombement m

Cambodia [kæm'bəudɪə] n Cambodge m

camcorder ['kæmkɔːdə'] n caméscope m

came [keɪm] pt of **come**

camel ['kæməl] n chameau m

camera ['kæmərə] n appareil-photo m; (Cine, TV) caméra f; **35mm ~** appareil 24 x 36 or petit format; **in ~** à huis clos, en privé

cameraman ['kæmərəmæn] (irreg) n caméraman m

camera phone n téléphone m avec appareil photo

camouflage ['kæməflɑːʒ] n camouflage m ▷ vt camoufler

camp [kæmp] n camp m ▷ vi camper ▷ adj (man) efféminé(e)

campaign [kæm'peɪn] n (Mil, Pol) campagne f ▷ vi (also fig) faire campagne; **to ~ for/against** militer pour/contre

campaigner [kæm'peɪnə'] n: **~ for** partisan(e) de; **~ against** opposant(e) à

camp bed ['kæmp'bed] n (Brit) lit m de camp

camper ['kæmpə'] n campeur(-euse); (vehicle) camping-car m

camping ['kæmpɪŋ] n camping m; **to go ~** faire du camping

camping gas® n butane m

campsite ['kæmpsaɪt] n (terrain m de) camping m

campus ['kæmpəs] n campus m

can¹ [kæn] n (of milk, oil, water) bidon m; (tin) boîte f (de conserve) ▷ vt mettre en conserve; **a ~ of beer** une canette de bière; **he had to carry the ~** (Brit inf) on lui a fait porter le chapeau; see also **keyword**

can² [kæn] (negative **-not, -'t**, conditional and pt **could**) aux vb 1 (be able to) pouvoir; **you ~ do it if you try** vous pouvez le faire si vous essayez; **I ~'t hear you** je ne t'entends pas
2 (know how to) savoir; **I ~ swim/play tennis/**

drive je sais nager/jouer au tennis/conduire; **~ you speak French?** parlez-vous français?
3 (may) pouvoir; **~ I use your phone?** puis-je me servir de votre téléphone?
4 (expressing disbelief, puzzlement etc): **it ~'t be true!** ce n'est pas possible!; **what ~ he want?** qu'est-ce qu'il peut bien vouloir?
5 (expressing possibility, suggestion etc): **he could be in the library** il est peut-être dans la bibliothèque; **she could have been delayed** il se peut qu'elle ait été retardée; **they could have forgotten** ils ont pu oublier

Canada ['kænədə] n Canada m

Canadian [kə'neɪdɪən] adj canadien(ne) ▷ n Canadien(ne)

canal [kə'næl] n canal m

canary [kə'nɛərɪ] n canari m, serin m

cancel ['kænsəl] vt annuler; (train) supprimer; (party, appointment) décommander; (cross out) barrer, rayer; (stamp) oblitérer; (cheque) faire opposition à; **I would like to ~ my booking** je voudrais annuler ma réservation
  ▸ **cancel out** vt annuler; **they ~ each other out** ils s'annulent

cancellation [kænsə'leɪʃən] n annulation f; suppression f; oblitération f; (Tourism) réservation annulée, client etc qui s'est décommandé

Cancer ['kænsə'] n (Astrology) le Cancer; **to be ~** être du Cancer

cancer ['kænsə'] n cancer m

candid ['kændɪd] adj (très) franc (franche), sincère

candidate ['kændɪdeɪt] n candidat(e)

candle ['kændl] n bougie f; (of tallow) chandelle f; (in church) cierge m

candlelight ['kændllaɪt] n: **by ~** à la lumière d'une bougie; (dinner) aux chandelles

candlestick ['kændlstɪk] n (also: **candle holder**) bougeoir m; (bigger, ornate) chandelier m

candour, (US) **candor** ['kændə'] n (grande) franchise or sincérité

candy ['kændɪ] n sucre candi; (US) bonbon m

candy bar (US) n barre f chocolatée

candyfloss ['kændɪflɒs] n (Brit) barbe f à papa

cane [keɪn] n canne f; (for baskets, chairs etc) rotin m ▷ vt (Brit Scol) administrer des coups de bâton à

canister ['kænɪstə'] n boîte f (gén en métal); (of gas) bombe f

cannabis ['kænəbɪs] n (drug) cannabis m; (cannabis plant) chanvre indien

canned ['kænd] adj (food) en boîte, en conserve; (inf: music) enregistré(e); (Brit inf: drunk) bourré(e); (US inf: worker) mis(e) à la porte

cannon (pl - or **-s**) ['kænən] n (gun) canon m

cannot ['kænɒt] = **can not**

canoe [kə'nuː] n pirogue f; (Sport) canoë m

canoeing [kə'nuːɪŋ] n (sport) canoë m

canon ['kænən] n (clergyman) chanoine m; (standard) canon m

can-opener [-'əupnə'] n ouvre-boîte m

canopy ['kænəpɪ] n baldaquin m; dais m

can't [kɑːnt] = **can not**

canteen [kæn'tiːn] n (eating place) cantine f; (Brit: of cutlery) ménagère f

canter ['kæntər] n petit galop ▷ vi aller au petit galop

canvas ['kænvəs] n (gen) toile f; **under ~** (camping) sous la tente; (Naut) toutes voiles dehors

canvass ['kænvəs] vi (Pol): **to ~ for** faire campagne pour ▷ vt (Pol: district) faire la tournée électorale dans; (: person) solliciter le suffrage de; (Comm: district) prospecter; (citizens, opinions) sonder

canyon ['kænjən] n cañon m, gorge (profonde)

cap [kæp] n casquette f; (for swimming) bonnet m de bain; (of pen) capuchon m; (of bottle) capsule f; (Brit: contraceptive: also: **Dutch cap**) diaphragme m; (Football) sélection f pour l'équipe nationale ▷ vt capsuler; (outdo) surpasser; (put limit on) plafonner; **~ped with** coiffé(e) de; **and to ~ it all, he** ... (Brit) pour couronner le tout, il ...

capability [keɪpə'bɪlɪtɪ] n aptitude f, capacité f

capable ['keɪpəbl] adj capable; **~ of** (interpretation etc) susceptible de

capacity [kə'pæsɪtɪ] n (of container) capacité f, contenance f; (ability) aptitude f; **filled to ~ plein(e)**; **in his ~ as** en sa qualité de; **in an advisory ~** à titre consultatif; **to work at full ~** travailler à plein rendement

cape [keɪp] n (garment) cape f; (Geo) cap m

caper ['keɪpər] n (Culin: gen pl) câpre f; (prank) farce f

capital ['kæpɪtl] n (also: **capital city**) capitale f; (money) capital m; (also: **capital letter**) majuscule f

capital gains tax n impôt m sur les plus-values

capitalism ['kæpɪtəlɪzəm] n capitalisme m

capitalist ['kæpɪtəlɪst] adj, n capitaliste m/f

capitalize ['kæpɪtəlaɪz] vt (provide with capital) financer
  ▶ **capitalize on** vt fus (fig) profiter de

capital punishment n peine capitale

Capitol ['kæpɪtl] n: **the ~** le Capitole; voir article

Capricorn ['kæprɪkɔːn] n le Capricorne; **to be ~** être du Capricorne

capsize [kæp'saɪz] vt faire chavirer ▷ vi chavirer

capsule ['kæpsjuːl] n capsule f

captain ['kæptɪn] n capitaine m ▷ vt commander, être le capitaine de

caption ['kæpʃən] n légende f

captive ['kæptɪv] adj, n captif(-ive)

captivity [kæp'tɪvɪtɪ] n captivité f

capture ['kæptʃər] vt (prisoner, animal) capturer; (town) prendre; (attention) capter; (Comput) saisir ▷ n capture f; (of data) saisie f de données

car [kɑːr] n voiture f, auto f; (US Rail) wagon m, voiture; **by ~** en voiture

carafe [kə'ræf] n carafe f

caramel ['kærəməl] n caramel m

carat ['kærət] n carat m; **18 ~ gold** or m à 18 carats

caravan ['kærəvæn] n caravane f

caravan site n (Brit) camping m pour caravanes

carbohydrate [kɑːbəʊ'haɪdreɪt] n hydrate m de carbone; (food) féculent m

carbon ['kɑːbən] n carbone m

carbon dioxide [-daɪ'ɒksaɪd] n gaz m carbonique, dioxyde m de carbone

carbon monoxide [-mɔ'nɒksaɪd] n oxyde m de carbone

carbon paper n papier m carbone

car boot sale n marché aux puces où des particuliers vendent des objets entreposés dans le coffre de leur voiture.

carburettor, (US) **carburetor** [kɑː'bjuːrɛtər] n carburateur m

card [kɑːd] n carte f; (material) carton m; (membership card) carte d'adhérent; **to play ~s** jouer aux cartes

cardboard ['kɑːdbɔːd] n carton m

card game n jeu m de cartes

cardiac ['kɑːdɪæk] adj cardiaque

cardigan ['kɑːdɪgən] n cardigan m

cardinal ['kɑːdɪnl] adj cardinal(e); (importance) capital(e) ▷ n cardinal m

card index n fichier m (alphabétique)

cardphone ['kɑːdfəʊn] n téléphone m à carte (magnétique)

care [kɛər] n soin m, attention f; (worry) souci m ▷ vi: **to ~ about** (feel interest for) se soucier de, s'intéresser à; (person: love) être attaché(e) à; **in sb's ~** à la garde de qn, confié à qn; **~ of** (on letter) chez; **"with ~"** "fragile"; **to take ~ (to do)** faire attention (à faire); **to take ~ of** (vt) s'occuper de; **the child has been taken into ~** l'enfant a été placé en institution; **would you ~ to/for ...?** voulez-vous ...?; **I wouldn't ~ to do it** je n'aimerais pas le faire; **I don't ~** ça m'est bien égal, peu m'importe; **I couldn't ~ less** cela m'est complètement égal, je m'en fiche complètement
  ▶ **care for** vt fus s'occuper de; (like) aimer

career [kə'rɪər] n carrière f ▷ vi (also: **career along**) aller à toute allure

career woman (irreg) n femme ambitieuse

carefree ['kɛəfriː] adj sans souci, insouciant(e)

careful ['kɛəful] adj soigneux(-euse); (cautious) prudent(e); **(be) ~!** (fais) attention!; **to be ~ with one's money** regarder à la dépense

carefully ['kɛəfəlɪ] adv avec soin, soigneusement; prudemment

caregiver ['kɛəgɪvər] (US) n (professional) travailleur social; (unpaid) personne qui s'occupe d'un proche qui est malade

careless ['kɛəlɪs] adj négligent(e); (heedless) insouciant(e)

carelessness ['kɛəlɪsnɪs] n manque m de soin, négligence f; insouciance f

carer ['kɛərər] n (professional) travailleur social; (unpaid) personne qui s'occupe d'un proche qui est malade

caress [kə'rɛs] n caresse f ▷ vt caresser

caretaker ['kɛəteɪkər] n gardien(ne), concierge m/f

car-ferry ['kɑːfɛrɪ] n (on sea) ferry(-boat) m; (on river) bac m

cargo (pl **-es**) ['kɑːgəʊ] n cargaison f, chargement m

car hire n (Brit) location f de voitures
Caribbean [kærɪˈbiːən] adj, n: **the ~ (Sea)** la mer des Antilles or des Caraïbes
caring [ˈkɛərɪŋ] adj (person) bienveillant(e); (society, organization) humanitaire
carnation [kaːˈneɪʃən] n œillet m
carnival [ˈkaːnɪvl] n (public celebration) carnaval m; (US: funfair) fête foraine
carol [ˈkærəl] n: **(Christmas) ~** chant m de Noël
carousel [kærəˈsɛl] n (for luggage) carrousel m; (US) manège m
carp [kaːp] n (fish) carpe f
 ▸ **carp at** vt fus critiquer
car park (Brit) n parking m, parc m de stationnement
carpenter [ˈkaːpɪntəʳ] n charpentier m; (joiner) menuisier m
carpentry [ˈkaːpɪntrɪ] n charpenterie f, métier m de charpentier; (woodwork: at school etc) menuiserie f
carpet [ˈkaːpɪt] n tapis m ▸ vt recouvrir (d'un tapis); **fitted ~** (Brit) moquette f
carpet sweeper [-ˈswiːpəʳ] n balai m mécanique
car phone n téléphone m de voiture
car rental n (US) location f de voitures
carriage [ˈkærɪdʒ] n (Brit Rail) wagon m; (horse-drawn) voiture f; (of goods) transport m; (: cost) port m; (of typewriter) chariot m; (bearing) maintien m, port m; **~ forward** port dû; **~ free** franco de port; **~ paid** (en) port payé
carriageway [ˈkærɪdʒweɪ] n (Brit: part of road) chaussée f
carrier [ˈkærɪəʳ] n transporteur m, camionneur m; (company) entreprise f de transport; (Med) porteur(-euse); (Naut) porte-avions m inv
carrier bag n (Brit) sac m en papier or en plastique
carrot [ˈkærət] n carotte f
carry [ˈkærɪ] vt (subj: person) porter; (: vehicle) transporter; (a motion, bill) voter, adopter; (Math: figure) retenir; (Comm: interest) rapporter; (involve: responsibilities etc) comporter, impliquer; (Med: disease) être porteur de ▸ vi (sound) porter; **to get carried away** (fig) s'emballer, s'enthousiasmer; **this loan carries 10% interest** ce prêt est à 10% (d'intérêt)
 ▸ **carry forward** vt (gen, Book-Keeping) reporter
 ▸ **carry on** vi (continue) continuer; (inf: make a fuss) faire des histoires ▸ vt (conduct: business) diriger; (: conversation) entretenir; (continue: business, conversation) continuer; **to ~ on with sth/doing** continuer qch/à faire
 ▸ **carry out** vt (orders) exécuter; (investigation) effectuer; (idea, threat) mettre à exécution
carrycot [ˈkærɪkɔt] n (Brit) porte-bébé m
carry-on [ˈkærɪˈɔn] n (inf: fuss) histoires fpl; (: annoying behaviour) cirque m, cinéma m
cart [kaːt] n charrette f ▸ vt (inf) transporter
carton [ˈkaːtən] n (box) carton m; (of yogurt) pot m (en carton); (of cigarettes) cartouche f
cartoon [kaːˈtuːn] n (Press) dessin m (humoristique); (satirical) caricature f; (comic strip) bande dessinée; (Cine) dessin animé

cartridge [ˈkaːtrɪdʒ] n (for gun, pen) cartouche f; (for camera) chargeur m; (music tape) cassette f; (of record player) cellule f
carve [kaːv] vt (meat: also: **carve up**) découper; (wood, stone) tailler, sculpter
carving [ˈkaːvɪŋ] n (in wood etc) sculpture f
carving knife n couteau m à découper
car wash n station f de lavage (de voitures)
case [keɪs] n cas m; (Law) affaire f, procès m; (box) caisse f, boîte f; (for glasses) étui m; (Brit: also: **suitcase**) valise f; (Typ): **lower/upper ~** minuscule f/majuscule f; **to have a good ~** avoir de bons arguments; **there's a strong ~ for reform** il y aurait lieu d'engager une réforme; **in ~ of** en cas de; **in ~ he** au cas où il; **just in ~** à tout hasard; **in any ~** en tout cas, de toute façon
cash [kæʃ] n argent m; (Comm) (argent m) liquide m, numéraire m; liquidités fpl; (: in payment) argent comptant, espèces fpl ▸ vt encaisser; **to pay (in) ~** payer (en argent) comptant or en espèces; **~ with order/on delivery** (Comm) payable or paiement à la commande/livraison; **to be short of ~** être à court d'argent; **I haven't got any ~** je n'ai pas de liquide
 ▸ **cash in** vt (insurance policy etc) toucher
 ▸ **cash in on** vt fus profiter de
cashback [ˈkæʃbæk] n (discount) remise f; (at supermarket etc) retrait m (à la caisse)
cashbook [ˈkæʃbuk] n livre m de caisse
cash card n carte f de retrait
cash desk n (Brit) caisse f
cash dispenser n distributeur m automatique de billets
cashew [kæˈʃuː] n (also: **cashew nut**) noix f de cajou
cashier [kæˈʃɪəʳ] n caissier(-ère) ▸ vt (Mil) destituer, casser
cashmere [ˈkæʃmɪəʳ] n cachemire m
cash point n distributeur m automatique de billets
cash register n caisse enregistreuse
casing [ˈkeɪsɪŋ] n revêtement (protecteur), enveloppe (protectrice)
casino [kəˈsiːnəu] n casino m
casket [ˈkaːskɪt] n coffret m; (US: coffin) cercueil m
casserole [ˈkæsərəul] n (pot) cocotte f; (food) ragoût m (en cocotte)
cassette [kæˈsɛt] n cassette f
cassette player n lecteur m de cassettes
cassette recorder n magnétophone m à cassettes
cast [kaːst] (vb: pt, pp ~) vt (throw) jeter; (shadow: lit) projeter; (: fig) jeter; (glance) jeter; (shed) perdre; se dépouiller de; (metal) couler, fondre ▸ n (Theat) distribution f; (mould) moule m; (also: **plaster cast**) plâtre m; **to ~ sb as Hamlet** attribuer à qn le rôle d'Hamlet; **to ~ one's vote** voter, exprimer son suffrage; **to ~ doubt on** jeter un doute sur
 ▸ **cast aside** vt (reject) rejeter
 ▸ **cast off** vi (Naut) larguer les amarres; (Knitting) arrêter les mailles ▸ vt (Knitting) arrêter

▶ **cast on** (Knitting) vt monter ▷ vi monter les mailles

castanets [kæstə'nɛts] npl castagnettes fpl

castaway ['kɑːstəweɪ] n naufragé(e)

caster sugar ['kɑːstə-] n (Brit) sucre m semoule

casting vote ['kɑːstɪŋ-] n (Brit) voix prépondérante (pour départager)

cast-iron ['kɑːstaɪən] adj (lit) de or en fonte; (fig: will) de fer; (alibi) en béton

cast iron n fonte f

castle ['kɑːsl] n château m; (fortress) château-fort m; (Chess) tour f

castor ['kɑːstə-r] n (wheel) roulette f

castor oil n huile f de ricin

castrate [kæs'treɪt] vt châtrer

casual ['kæʒjul] adj (by chance) de hasard, fait(e) au hasard, fortuit(e); (irregular: work etc) temporaire; (unconcerned) désinvolte; ~ **wear** vêtements mpl sport inv

casually ['kæʒjulɪ] adv avec désinvolture, négligemment; (by chance) fortuitement

casualty ['kæʒjultɪ] n accidenté(e), blessé(e); (dead) victime f, mort(e); (Brit: Med: department) urgences fpl; **heavy casualties** lourdes pertes

cat [kæt] n chat m

Catalan ['kætəlæn] adj catalan(e)

catalogue, (US) **catalog** ['kætəlɔg] n catalogue m ▷ vt cataloguer

catalyst ['kætəlɪst] n catalyseur m

catalytic converter [kætə'lɪtɪkkən'vəːtə-r] n pot m catalytique

catapult ['kætəpʌlt] n lance-pierres m inv, fronde f; (History) catapulte f

cataract ['kætərækt] n (also Med) cataracte f

catarrh [kə'tɑː-r] n rhume m chronique, catarrhe f

catastrophe [kə'tæstrəfɪ] n catastrophe f

catch [kætʃ] (pt, pp **caught** [kɔːt]) vt (ball, train, thief, cold) attraper; (person: by surprise) prendre, surprendre; (understand) saisir; (get entangled) accrocher ▷ vi (fire) prendre; (get entangled) s'accrocher ▷ n (fish etc) prise f; (thief etc) capture f; (hidden problem) attrape f; (Tech) loquet m; cliquet m; **to ~ sb's attention** or **eye** attirer l'attention de qn; **to ~ fire** prendre feu; **to ~ sight of** apercevoir; **to play ~** jouer à chat; (with ball) jouer à attraper le ballon

▶ **catch on** vi (become popular) prendre; (understand): **to ~ on (to sth)** saisir (qch)

▶ **catch out** vt (Brit: fig: with trick question) prendre en défaut

▶ **catch up** vi (with work) se rattraper, combler son retard ▷ vt (also: **catch up with**) rattraper

catching ['kætʃɪŋ] adj (Med) contagieux(-euse)

catchment area ['kætʃmənt-] n (Brit Scol) aire f de recrutement; (Geo) bassin m hydrographique

catch phrase n slogan m, expression toute faite

catchy ['kætʃɪ] adj (tune) facile à retenir

category ['kætɪgərɪ] n catégorie f

cater ['keɪtə-r] vi: **to ~ for** (Brit: needs) satisfaire, pourvoir à; (: readers, consumers) s'adresser à, pourvoir aux besoins de; (Comm: parties etc) préparer des repas pour

caterer ['keɪtərə-r] n traiteur m; fournisseur m

catering ['keɪtərɪŋ] n restauration f; approvisionnement m, ravitaillement m

caterpillar ['kætəpɪlə-r] n chenille f ▷ cpd (vehicle) à chenille; ~ **track** n chenille f

cathedral [kə'θiːdrəl] n cathédrale f

Catholic ['kæθəlɪk] (Rel) adj catholique ▷ n catholique m/f

catholic ['kæθəlɪk] adj (wide-ranging) éclectique; universel(le); libéral(e)

cattle ['kætl] npl bétail m, bestiaux mpl

catty ['kætɪ] adj méchant(e)

catwalk ['kætwɔːk] n passerelle f; (for models) podium m (de défilé de mode)

caucus ['kɔːkəs] n (US Pol) comité électoral (pour désigner des candidats); voir article; (Brit Pol: group) comité local (d'un parti politique)

caught [kɔːt] pt, pp of **catch**

cauliflower ['kɔlɪflauə-r] n chou-fleur m

cause [kɔːz] n cause f ▷ vt causer; **there is no ~ for concern** il n'y a pas lieu de s'inquiéter; **to ~ sth to be done** faire faire qch; **to ~ sb to do sth** faire faire qch à qn

caution ['kɔːʃən] n prudence f; (warning) avertissement m ▷ vt avertir, donner un avertissement à

cautious ['kɔːʃəs] adj prudent(e)

cavalry ['kævəlrɪ] n cavalerie f

cave [keɪv] n caverne f, grotte f ▷ vi: **to go caving** faire de la spéléo(logie)

▶ **cave in** vi (roof etc) s'effondrer

caveman ['keɪvmæn] (irreg) n homme m des cavernes

caviar, caviare ['kævɪɑː-r] n caviar m

cavity ['kævɪtɪ] n cavité f; (Med) carie f

CB n abbr (= Citizens' Band (Radio)) CB f; (Brit: = Companion of (the Order of) the Bath) titre honorifique

CBI n abbr (= Confederation of British Industry) ≈ CNPF m (= Conseil national du patronat français)

cc abbr (= cubic centimetre) cm³; (on letter etc) = **carbon copy**

CCTV n abbr = **closed-circuit television**

CD n abbr (= compact disc) CD m; (Mil: Brit) = **Civil Defence (Corps)**; (: US) = **Civil Defense** ▷ abbr (Brit: = Corps Diplomatique) CD

CD burner n graveur m de CD

CD player n platine f laser

CD-ROM [siːdiː'rɔm] n abbr (= compact disc read-only memory) CD-ROM m inv

CD writer n graveur m de CD

cease [siːs] vt, vi cesser

ceasefire ['siːsfaɪə-r] n cessez-le-feu m

ceaseless ['siːslɪs] adj incessant(e), continuel(le)

cedar ['siːdə-r] n cèdre m

ceilidh ['keɪlɪ] n bal m folklorique écossais or irlandais

ceiling ['siːlɪŋ] n (also fig) plafond m

celebrate ['sɛlɪbreɪt] vt, vi célébrer

celebrated ['sɛlɪbreɪtɪd] adj célèbre

celebration [sɛlɪ'breɪʃən] n célébration f

celebrity [sɪ'lɛbrɪtɪ] n célébrité f

celery ['sɛlərɪ] n céleri m (en branches)

cell [sɛl] *n* (*gen*) cellule *f*; (*Elec*) élément *m* (*de pile*)

cellar ['sɛlər] *n* cave *f*

cello ['tʃɛləʊ] *n* violoncelle *m*

Cellophane® ['sɛləfeɪn] *n* cellophane® *f*

cellphone ['sɛlfəʊn] *n* (téléphone *m*) portable *m*, mobile *m*

Celsius ['sɛlsɪəs] *adj* Celsius *inv*

Celt [kɛlt, sɛlt] *n* Celte *m/f*

Celtic ['kɛltɪk, 'sɛltɪk] *adj* celte, celtique ▷ *n* (*Ling*) celtique *m*

cement [sə'mɛnt] *n* ciment *m* ▷ *vt* cimenter

cement mixer *n* bétonnière *f*

cemetery ['sɛmɪtrɪ] *n* cimetière *m*

censor ['sɛnsər] *n* censeur *m* ▷ *vt* censurer

censorship ['sɛnsəʃɪp] *n* censure *f*

censure ['sɛnʃər] *vt* blâmer, critiquer

census ['sɛnsəs] *n* recensement *m*

cent [sɛnt] *n* (*unit of dollar, euro*) cent *m* (= *un centième du dollar, de l'euro*); *see also* **per**

centenary [sɛn'tiːnərɪ], (*US*) **centennial** [sɛn'tɛnɪəl] *n* centenaire *m*

center ['sɛntər] *n*, *vt* (*US*) = **centre** [sɛntɪ] *prefix*

centigrade ['sɛntɪɡreɪd] *adj* centigrade

centimetre, (*US*) **centimeter** ['sɛntɪmiːtər] *n* centimètre *m*

centipede ['sɛntɪpiːd] *n* mille-pattes *m inv*

central ['sɛntrəl] *adj* central(e)

Central America *n* Amérique centrale

central heating *n* chauffage central

central reservation *n* (*Brit Aut*) terre-plein central

centre, (*US*) **center** ['sɛntər] *n* centre *m* ▷ *vt* centrer; (*Phot*) cadrer; (*concentrate*): **to ~ (on)** centrer (sur)

centre-forward ['sɛntə'fɔːwəd] *n* (*Sport*) avant-centre *m*

centre-half ['sɛntə'hɑːf] *n* (*Sport*) demi-centre *m*

century ['sɛntjʊrɪ] *n* siècle *m*; **in the twentieth ~** au vingtième siècle

CEO *n abbr* (*US*) = **chief executive officer**

ceramic [sɪ'ræmɪk] *adj* céramique

cereal ['siːrɪəl] *n* céréale *f*

ceremony ['sɛrɪmənɪ] *n* cérémonie *f*; **to stand on ~** faire des façons

certain ['sɜːtən] *adj* certain(e); **to make ~ of** s'assurer de; **for ~** certainement, sûrement

certainly ['sɜːtənlɪ] *adv* certainement

certainty ['sɜːtəntɪ] *n* certitude *f*

certificate [sə'tɪfɪkɪt] *n* certificat *m*

certify ['sɜːtɪfaɪ] *vt* certifier; (*award diploma to*) conférer un diplôme *etc* à; (*declare insane*) déclarer malade mental(e) ▷ *vi*: **to ~ to** attester

cervical ['sɜːvɪkl] *adj*: **~ cancer** cancer *m* du col de l'utérus; **~ smear** frottis vaginal

cervix ['sɜːvɪks] *n* col *m* de l'utérus

cf. *abbr* (= *compare*) cf., voir

CFC *n abbr* (= *chlorofluorocarbon*) CFC *m*

ch. *abbr* (= *chapter*) chap

chafe [tʃeɪf] *vt* irriter, frotter contre ▷ *vi* (*fig*): **to ~ against** se rebiffer contre, regimber contre

chain [tʃeɪn] *n* (*gen*) chaîne *f* ▷ *vt* (*also*: **chain up**) enchaîner, attacher (avec une chaîne)

chain reaction *n* réaction *f* en chaîne

chain-smoke ['tʃeɪnsməʊk] *vi* fumer cigarette sur cigarette

chain store *n* magasin *m* à succursales multiples

chair [tʃɛər] *n* chaise *f*; (*armchair*) fauteuil *m*; (*of university*) chaire *f*; (*of meeting*) présidence *f* ▷ *vt* (*meeting*) présider; **the ~** (*US*: *electric chair*) la chaise électrique

chairlift ['tʃɛəlɪft] *n* télésiège *m*

chairman ['tʃɛəmən] (*irreg*) *n* président *m*

chairperson ['tʃɛəpɜːsn] (*irreg*) *n* président(e)

chairwoman ['tʃɛəwʊmən] (*irreg*) *n* présidente *f*

chalet ['ʃæleɪ] *n* chalet *m*

chalk [tʃɔːk] *n* craie *f*

▶ **chalk up** *vt* écrire à la craie; (*fig*: *success etc*) remporter

challenge ['tʃælɪndʒ] *n* défi *m* ▷ *vt* défier; (*statement, right*) mettre en question, contester; **to ~ sb to a fight/game** inviter qn à se battre/à jouer (*sous forme d'un défi*); **to ~ sb to do** mettre qn au défi de faire

challenging ['tʃælɪndʒɪŋ] *adj* (*task, career*) qui représente un défi or une gageure; (*tone, look*) de défi, provocateur(-trice)

chamber ['tʃeɪmbər] *n* chambre *f*; (*Brit Law*: *gen pl*) cabinet *m*; **~ of commerce** chambre de commerce

chambermaid ['tʃeɪmbəmeɪd] *n* femme *f* de chambre

chamber music *n* musique *f* de chambre

champagne [ʃæm'peɪn] *n* champagne *m*

champion ['tʃæmpɪən] *n* (*also of cause*) champion(ne) ▷ *vt* défendre

championship ['tʃæmpɪənʃɪp] *n* championnat *m*

chance [tʃɑːns] *n* (*luck*) hasard *m*; (*opportunity*) occasion *f*, possibilité *f*; (*hope, likelihood*) chance *f*; (*risk*) risque *m* ▷ *vt* (*risk*) risquer; (*happen*): **to ~ to do** faire par hasard ▷ *adj* fortuit(e), de hasard; **there is little ~ of his coming** il est peu probable *or* il y a peu de chances qu'il vienne; **to take a ~** prendre un risque; **it's the ~ of a lifetime** c'est une occasion unique; **by ~** par hasard; **to ~ doing sth** se risquer à faire qch; **to ~ it** risquer le coup, essayer

▶ **chance on, chance upon** *vt fus* (*person*) tomber sur, rencontrer par hasard; (*thing*) trouver par hasard

chancellor ['tʃɑːnsələr] *n* chancelier *m*

Chancellor of the Exchequer [-ɪks'tʃɛkər] (*Brit*) *n* chancelier *m* de l'Échiquier

chandelier [ʃændə'lɪər] *n* lustre *m*

change [tʃeɪndʒ] *vt* (*alter, replace*: *Comm*: *money*) changer; (*switch, substitute*: *hands, trains, clothes, one's name etc*) changer de; (*transform*): **to ~ sb into** changer *or* transformer qn en ▷ *vi* (*gen*) changer; (*change clothes*) se changer; (*be transformed*): **to ~ into** se changer *or* transformer en ▷ *n* changement *m*; (*money*) monnaie *f*; **to ~ gear** (*Aut*) changer de vitesse; **to ~ one's mind** changer d'avis; **she ~d into an old skirt** elle (s'est changée et) a enfilé une vieille jupe; **a ~ of clothes** des vêtements de rechange; **for a ~** pour changer; **small ~** petite monnaie; **to give sb ~ for** or **of £10** faire à qn la monnaie de 10 livres; **do you have ~ for £10?** vous avez la monnaie de 10 livres?; **where can I ~ some money?** où est-ce que je peux changer de l'argent?; **keep the ~!** gardez la monnaie!

▸ **change over** vi (swap) échanger; (change: drivers etc) changer; (change sides: players etc) changer de côté; **to ~ over from sth to sth** passer de qch à qch

changeable ['tʃeɪndʒəbl] adj (weather) variable; (person) d'humeur changeante

change machine n distributeur m de monnaie

changeover ['tʃeɪndʒəʊvəʳ] n (to new system) changement m, passage m

changing ['tʃeɪndʒɪŋ] adj changeant(e)

changing room n (Brit: in shop) salon m d'essayage; (: Sport) vestiaire m

channel ['tʃænl] n (TV) chaîne f; (waveband, groove, fig: medium) canal m; (of river, sea) chenal m ▷ vt canaliser; (fig: interest, energies): **to ~ into** diriger vers; **through the usual ~s** en suivant la filière habituelle; **green/red ~** (Customs) couloir m or sortie f "rien à déclarer"/"marchandises à déclarer"; **the (English) C~** la Manche

channel-hopping ['tʃænl'hɔpɪŋ] n (TV) zapping m

Channel Islands npl: **the ~** les îles fpl Anglo-Normandes

Channel Tunnel n: **the ~** le tunnel sous la Manche

chant [tʃɑːnt] n chant m; mélopée f; (Rel) psalmodie f ▷ vt chanter, scander; psalmodier

chaos ['keɪɔs] n chaos m

chaotic [keɪ'ɔtɪk] adj chaotique

chap [tʃæp] n (Brit inf: man) type m; (term of address): **old ~** mon vieux ▷ vt (skin) gercer, crevasser

chapel ['tʃæpl] n chapelle f

chaplain ['tʃæplɪn] n aumônier m

chapped [tʃæpt] adj (skin, lips) gercé(e)

chapter ['tʃæptəʳ] n chapitre m

char [tʃɑːʳ] vt (burn) carboniser ▷ vi (Brit: cleaner) faire des ménages ▷ n (Brit) = **charlady**

character ['kærɪktəʳ] n caractère m; (in novel, film) personnage m; (eccentric person) numéro m, phénomène m; **a person of good ~** une personne bien

characteristic ['kærɪktə'rɪstɪk] adj, n caractéristique (f)

characterize ['kærɪktəraɪz] vt caractériser; **to ~ (as)** définir (comme)

charcoal ['tʃɑːkəul] n charbon m de bois; (Art) charbon

charge [tʃɑːdʒ] n (accusation) accusation f; (Law) inculpation f; (cost) prix (demandé); (of gun, battery, Mil: attack) charge f ▷ vt (gun, battery, Mil: enemy) charger; (customer, sum) faire payer ▷ vi (gen with: up, along etc) foncer; **charges** npl (costs) frais mpl; (Brit Tel): **to reverse the ~s** téléphoner en PCV; **bank/labour ~s** frais mpl de banque/main-d'œuvre; **is there a ~?** doit-on payer?; **there's no ~** c'est gratuit, on ne fait pas payer;

extra ~ supplément m; **to take ~ of** se charger de; **to be in ~ of** être responsable de, s'occuper de; **to ~ in/out** entrer/sortir en trombe; **to ~ down/up** dévaler/ grimper à toute allure; **to ~ sb (with)** (Law) inculper qn (de); **to have ~ of sb** avoir la charge de qn; **they ~d us £10 for the meal** ils nous ont fait payer le repas 10 livres, ils nous ont compté 10 livres pour le repas; **how much do you ~ for this repair?** combien demandez-vous pour cette réparation?; **to ~ an expense (up) to sb** mettre une dépense sur le compte de qn; **~ it to my account** facturez-le sur mon compte

charge card n carte f de client (émise par un grand magasin)

charger ['tʃɑːdʒəʳ] n (also: **battery charger**) chargeur m; (old: warhorse) cheval m de bataille

charismatic [kærɪz'mætɪk] adj charismatique

charity ['tʃærɪtɪ] n charité f; (organization) institution f charitable or de bienfaisance, œuvre f (de charité)

charity shop n (Brit) boutique vendant des articles d'occasion au profit d'une organisation caritative

charm [tʃɑːm] n charme m; (on bracelet) breloque f ▷ vt charmer, enchanter

charming ['tʃɑːmɪŋ] adj charmant(e)

chart [tʃɑːt] n tableau m, diagramme m; graphique m; (map) carte marine; (weather chart) carte f du temps ▷ vt dresser or établir la carte de; (sales, progress) établir la courbe de; **charts** npl (Mus) hit-parade m; **to be in the ~s** (record, pop group) figurer au hit-parade

charter ['tʃɑːtəʳ] vt (plane) affréter ▷ n (document) charte f; **on ~** (plane) affrété(e)

chartered accountant ['tʃɑːtəd-] n (Brit) expert-comptable m

charter flight n charter m

chase [tʃeɪs] vt poursuivre, pourchasser; (also: **chase away**) chasser ▷ n poursuite f, chasse f

▸ **chase down** vt (US) = **chase up**

▸ **chase up** vt (Brit: person) relancer; (: information) rechercher

chasm ['kæzəm] n gouffre m, abîme m

chat [tʃæt] vi (also: **have a chat**) bavarder, causer; (on Internet) chatter ▷ n conversation f

▸ **chat up** vt (Brit inf: girl) baratiner

chat room n (Internet) salon m de discussion

chat show n (Brit) talk-show m

chatter ['tʃætəʳ] vi (person) bavarder, papoter ▷ n bavardage m, papotage m; **my teeth are ~ing** je claque des dents

chatterbox ['tʃætəbɔks] n moulin m à paroles, babillard(e)

chatty ['tʃætɪ] adj (style) familier(-ière); (person) enclin(e) à bavarder or au papotage

chauffeur ['ʃəufəʳ] n chauffeur m (de maître)

chauvinist ['ʃəuvɪnɪst] n (also: **male chauvinist**) phallocrate m, macho m; (nationalist) chauvin(e)

cheap [tʃiːp] adj bon marché inv, pas cher (chère); (reduced: ticket) à prix réduit; (: fare) réduit(e); (joke) facile, d'un goût douteux; (poor quality) à bon marché, de qualité médiocre ▷ adv à bon marché, pour pas cher; **~er** adj moins cher (chère); **can you recommend a ~ hotel/ restaurant, please?** pourriez-vous m'indiquer un hôtel/restaurant bon marché?

cheap day return n billet m d'aller et retour réduit (valable pour la journée)

cheaply ['tʃiːplɪ] adv à bon marché, à bon compte

cheat [tʃiːt] vi tricher; (in exam) copier ▷ vt tromper, duper; (rob): **to ~ sb out of sth** escroquer qch à qn ▷ n tricheur(-euse) m/f; escroc m; (trick) duperie f, tromperie f
▶ **cheat on** vt fus tromper

Chechnya [tʃɪtʃˈnjaː] n Tchétchénie f

check [tʃɛk] vt vérifier; (passport, ticket) contrôler; (halt) enrayer; (restrain) maîtriser ▷ vi (official etc) se renseigner ▷ n vérification f; contrôle m; (curb) frein m; (Brit: bill) addition f; (US = **cheque**); (pattern: gen pl) carreaux mpl ▷ adj (also: **checked**: pattern, cloth) à carreaux; **to ~ with sb** demander à qn; **to keep a ~ on sb/sth** surveiller qn/qch
▶ **check in** vi (in hotel) remplir sa fiche (d'hôtel); (at airport) se présenter à l'enregistrement ▷ vt (luggage) (faire) enregistrer
▶ **check off** vt (tick off) cocher
▶ **check out** vi (in hotel) régler sa note ▷ vt (luggage) retirer; (investigate: story) vérifier; (person) prendre des renseignements sur
▶ **check up** vi: **to ~ up (on sth)** vérifier (qch); **to ~ up on sb** se renseigner sur le compte de qn

checkbook ['tʃɛkbʊk] n (US) = **chequebook**

checked ['tʃɛkt] adj (pattern, cloth) à carreaux

checkered ['tʃɛkəd] adj (US) = **chequered**

checkers ['tʃɛkəz] n (US) jeu m de dames

check-in ['tʃɛkɪn] n (also: **check-in desk**: at airport) enregistrement m

checking account ['tʃɛkɪŋ-] n (US) compte courant

checklist ['tʃɛklɪst] n liste f de contrôle

checkmate ['tʃɛkmeɪt] n échec et mat m

checkout ['tʃɛkaʊt] n (in supermarket) caisse f

checkpoint ['tʃɛkpɔɪnt] n contrôle m

checkroom ['tʃɛkruːm] (US) n consigne f

checkup ['tʃɛkʌp] n (Med) examen médical, check-up m

cheddar ['tʃɛdəʳ] n (also: **cheddar cheese**) cheddar m

cheek [tʃiːk] n joue f; (impudence) toupet m, culot m; **what a ~!** quel toupet!

cheekbone ['tʃiːkbəʊn] n pommette f

cheeky ['tʃiːkɪ] adj effronté(e), culotté(e)

cheep [tʃiːp] n (of bird) piaulement m ▷ vi piauler

cheer [tʃɪəʳ] vt acclamer, applaudir; (gladden) réjouir, réconforter ▷ vi applaudir ▷ n (gen pl) acclamations fpl, applaudissements mpl; bravos mpl, hourras mpl; **~s!** à la vôtre!
▶ **cheer on** vt encourager (par des cris etc)
▶ **cheer up** vi se dérider, reprendre courage ▷ vt remonter le moral à or de, dérider, égayer

cheerful ['tʃɪəful] adj gai(e), joyeux(-euse)

cheerio [tʃɪərɪˈəu] excl (Brit) salut!, au revoir!

cheerleader ['tʃɪəliːdəʳ] n membre d'un groupe de majorettes qui chantent et dansent pour soutenir leur équipe pendant les matchs de football américain

cheese [tʃiːz] n fromage m

cheeseboard ['tʃiːzbɔːd] n plateau m à fromages; (with cheese on it) plateau m de fromages

cheeseburger ['tʃiːzbəːgəʳ] n cheeseburger m

cheesecake ['tʃiːzkeɪk] n tarte f au fromage

cheetah ['tʃiːtə] n guépard m

chef [ʃɛf] n chef (cuisinier)

chemical ['kɛmɪkl] adj chimique ▷ n produit m chimique

chemist ['kɛmɪst] n (Brit: pharmacist) pharmacien(ne); (scientist) chimiste m/f

chemistry ['kɛmɪstrɪ] n chimie f

chemist's ['kɛmɪsts], **chemist's shop** n (Brit) pharmacie f

cheque, (US) **check** [tʃɛk] n chèque m; **to pay by ~** payer par chèque

chequebook, (US) **checkbook** ['tʃɛkbuk] n chéquier m, carnet m de chèques

cheque card n (Brit) carte f (d'identité) bancaire

chequered, (US) **checkered** ['tʃɛkəd] adj (fig) varié(e)

cherish ['tʃɛrɪʃ] vt chérir; (hope etc) entretenir

cherry ['tʃɛrɪ] n cerise f; (also: **cherry tree**) cerisier m

chess [tʃɛs] n échecs mpl

chessboard ['tʃɛsbɔːd] n échiquier m

chest [tʃɛst] n poitrine f; (box) coffre m, caisse f; **to get sth off one's ~** (inf) vider son sac

chestnut ['tʃɛsnʌt] n châtaigne f; (also: **chestnut tree**) châtaignier m; (colour) châtain m ▷ adj (hair) châtain inv; (horse) alezan

chest of drawers n commode f

chew [tʃuː] vt mâcher

chewing gum ['tʃuːɪŋ-] n chewing-gum m

chic [ʃiːk] adj chic inv, élégant(e)

chick [tʃɪk] n poussin m; (inf) pépée f

chicken ['tʃɪkɪn] n poulet m; (inf: coward) poule mouillée
▶ **chicken out** vi (inf) se dégonfler

chickenpox ['tʃɪkɪnpɔks] n varicelle f

chickpea ['tʃɪkpiː] n pois m chiche

chicory ['tʃɪkərɪ] n chicorée f; (salad) endive f

chief [tʃiːf] n chef m ▷ adj principal(e); **C~ of Staff** (Mil) chef d'État-major

chief executive, (US) **chief executive officer** n directeur(-trice) général(e)

chiefly ['tʃiːflɪ] adv principalement, surtout

chiffon ['ʃɪfɔn] n mousseline f de soie

chilblain ['tʃɪlbleɪn] n engelure f

child (pl **-ren**) [tʃaɪld, 'tʃɪldrən] n enfant m/f

child abuse n maltraitance f d'enfants; (sexual) abus mpl sexuels sur des enfants

child benefit n (Brit) ≈ allocations familiales

childbirth ['tʃaɪldbə:θ] n accouchement m

childcare ['tʃaɪldkɛəʳ] n (for working parents) garde f des enfants (pour les parents qui travaillent)

childhood ['tʃaɪldhud] n enfance f

childish ['tʃaɪldɪʃ] adj puéril(e), enfantin(e)

childlike ['tʃaɪldlaɪk] adj innocent(e), pur(e)

child minder n (Brit) garde f d'enfants

children ['tʃɪldrən] npl of **child**

Chile ['tʃɪlɪ] n Chili m
chill [tʃɪl] n (of water) froid m; (of air) fraîcheur f; (Med) refroidissement m, coup m de froid ▷ adj froid(e), glacial(e) ▷ vt (person) faire frissonner; refroidir; (Culin) mettre au frais, rafraîchir; "**serve ~ed**" "à servir frais"
  ▶ **chill out** vi (inf: esp US) se relaxer
chilli, chili ['tʃɪlɪ] n piment m (rouge)
chilly ['tʃɪlɪ] adj froid(e), glacé(e); (sensitive to cold) frileux(-euse); **to feel ~** avoir froid
chime [tʃaɪm] n carillon m ▷ vi carillonner, sonner
chimney ['tʃɪmnɪ] n cheminée f
chimney sweep n ramoneur m
chimpanzee [tʃɪmpæn'zi:] n chimpanzé m
chin [tʃɪn] n menton m
China ['tʃaɪnə] n Chine f
china ['tʃaɪnə] n (material) porcelaine f; (crockery) (vaisselle f en) porcelaine
Chinese [tʃaɪ'ni:z] adj chinois(e) ▷ n (pl inv) Chinois(e); (Ling) chinois m
chink [tʃɪŋk] n (opening) fente f, fissure f; (noise) tintement m
chip [tʃɪp] n (gen pl: Culin: Brit) frite f; (: US: also: **potato chip**) chip m; (of wood) copeau m; (of glass, stone) éclat m; (also: **microchip**) puce f; (in gambling) fiche f ▷ vt (cup, plate) ébrécher; **when the ~s are down** (fig) au moment critique
  ▶ **chip in** vi (inf) mettre son grain de sel
chip shop n (Brit) friterie f; voir article
chiropodist [kɪ'rɔpədɪst] n (Brit) pédicure m/f
chirp [tʃə:p] n pépiement m, gazouillis m; (of crickets) stridulation f ▷ vi pépier, gazouiller; chanter, striduler
chisel ['tʃɪzl] n ciseau m
chit [tʃɪt] n mot m, note f
chitchat ['tʃɪttʃæt] n bavardage m, papotage m
chivalry ['ʃɪvəlrɪ] n chevalerie f; esprit m chevaleresque
chives [tʃaɪvz] npl ciboulette f, civette f
chlorine ['klɔ:ri:n] n chlore m
choc-ice ['tʃɔkaɪs] n (Brit) esquimau® m
chock-a-block ['tʃɔkə'blɔk], **chock-full** [tʃɔk'ful] adj plein(e) à craquer
chocolate ['tʃɔklɪt] n chocolat m
choice [tʃɔɪs] n choix m ▷ adj de choix; **by** or **from ~** par choix; **a wide ~** un grand choix
choir ['kwaɪə'] n chœur m, chorale f
choirboy ['kwaɪəbɔɪ] n jeune choriste m, petit chanteur
choke [tʃəuk] vi étouffer ▷ vt étrangler; étouffer; (block) boucher, obstruer ▷ n (Aut) starter m
cholesterol [kə'lɛstərɔl] n cholestérol m
choose (pt **chose**, pp **chosen**) [tʃu:z, tʃəuz, 'tʃəuzn] vt choisir ▷ vi: **to ~ between** choisir entre; **to ~ from** choisir parmi; **to ~ to do** décider de faire, juger bon de faire
choosy ['tʃu:zɪ] adj: (**to be**) **~** (faire le) difficile
chop [tʃɔp] vt (wood) couper (à la hache); (Culin: also: **chop up**) couper (fin), émincer, hacher (en morceaux) ▷ n coup m (de hache, du tranchant de la main); (Culin) côtelette f; **to get the ~** (Brit inf:

project) tomber à l'eau; (: person: be sacked) se faire renvoyer
  ▶ **chop down** vt (tree) abattre
  ▶ **chop off** vt trancher
chopper ['tʃɔpə'] n (helicopter) hélicoptère m, hélico m
choppy ['tʃɔpɪ] adj (sea) un peu agité(e)
chopsticks ['tʃɔpstɪks] npl baguettes fpl
chord [kɔ:d] n (Mus) accord m
chore [tʃɔ:'] n travail m de routine; **household ~s** travaux mpl du ménage
chortle ['tʃɔ:tl] vi glousser
chorus ['kɔ:rəs] n chœur m; (repeated part of song, also fig) refrain m
chose [tʃəuz] pt of **choose**
chosen ['tʃəuzn] pp of **choose**
chowder ['tʃaudə'] n soupe f de poisson
Christ [kraɪst] n Christ m
christen ['krɪsn] vt baptiser
christening ['krɪsnɪŋ] n baptême m
Christian ['krɪstɪən] adj, n chrétien(ne)
Christianity [krɪstɪ'ænɪtɪ] n christianisme m
Christian name n prénom m
Christmas ['krɪsməs] n Noël m or f; **happy** or **merry ~!** joyeux Noël!
Christmas card n carte f de Noël
Christmas carol n chant m de Noël
Christmas Day n le jour de Noël
Christmas Eve n la veille de Noël; la nuit de Noël
Christmas pudding n (esp Brit) Christmas m pudding
Christmas tree n arbre m de Noël
chrome [krəum] n chrome m
chromium ['krəumɪəm] n chrome m; (also: **chromium plating**) chromage m
chronic ['krɔnɪk] adj chronique; (fig: liar, smoker) invétéré(e)
chronicle ['krɔnɪkl] n chronique f
chronological [krɔnə'lɔdʒɪkl] adj chronologique
chrysanthemum [krɪ'sænθəməm] n chrysanthème m
chubby ['tʃʌbɪ] adj potelé(e), rondelet(te)
chuck [tʃʌk] vt (inf) lancer, jeter; (Brit: also: **chuck up**: job) lâcher; (: person) plaquer
  ▶ **chuck out** vt (inf: person) flanquer dehors or à la porte; (: rubbish etc) jeter
chuckle ['tʃʌkl] vi glousser
chug [tʃʌg] vi faire teuf-teuf; souffler
chum [tʃʌm] n copain (copine)
chunk [tʃʌŋk] n gros morceau; (of bread) quignon m
church [tʃə:tʃ] n église f; **the C~ of England** l'Église anglicane
churchyard ['tʃə:tʃjɑ:d] n cimetière m
churn [tʃə:n] n (for butter) baratte f; (also: **milk churn**) (grand) bidon à lait
  ▶ **churn out** vt débiter
chute [ʃu:t] n goulotte f; (also: **rubbish chute**) vide-ordures m inv; (Brit: children's slide) toboggan m
chutney ['tʃʌtnɪ] n chutney m
CIA n abbr (= Central Intelligence Agency) CIA f

CID *n abbr* (= *Criminal Investigation Department*) ≈ P.J. *f*
cider ['saɪdə'] *n* cidre *m*
cigar [sɪ'gɑ:'] *n* cigare *m*
cigarette [sɪgə'rɛt] *n* cigarette *f*
cigarette case *n* étui *m* à cigarettes
cigarette end *n* mégot *m*
cigarette lighter *n* briquet *m*
Cinderella [sɪndə'rɛlə] *n* Cendrillon
cine-camera ['sɪnɪ'kæmərə] *n* (*Brit*) caméra *f*
cinema ['sɪnəmə] *n* cinéma *m*
cinnamon ['sɪnəmən] *n* cannelle *f*
circle ['sə:kl] *n* cercle *m*; (*in cinema*) balcon *m*
▷ *vi* faire ou décrire des cercles ▷ *vt* (*surround*)
entourer, encercler; (*move round*) faire le tour de,
tourner autour de
circuit ['sə:kɪt] *n* circuit *m*; (*lap*) tour *m*
circuitous [sə:'kjuɪtəs] *adj* indirect(e), qui fait
un détour
circular ['sə:kjulə'] *adj* circulaire ▷ *n* circulaire *f*;
(*as advertisement*) prospectus *m*
circulate ['sə:kjuleɪt] *vi* circuler ▷ *vt* faire
circuler
circulation [sə:kju'leɪʃən] *n* circulation *f*; (*of
newspaper*) tirage *m*
circumflex ['sə:kəmflɛks] *n* (*also:* **circumflex
accent**) accent *m* circonflexe
circumstances ['sə:kəmstənsɪz] *npl*
circonstances *fpl*; (*financial condition*) moyens *mpl*,
situation financière; **in** *or* **under the** ~ dans
ces conditions; **under no** ~ en aucun cas, sous
aucun prétexte
circus ['sə:kəs] *n* cirque *m*; (*also:* **Circus**: *in place
names*) place *f*
CIS *n abbr* (= *Commonwealth of Independent States*)
CEI *f*
cistern ['sɪstən] *n* réservoir *m* (d'eau); (*in toilet*)
réservoir de la chasse d'eau
cite [saɪt] *vt* citer
citizen ['sɪtɪzn] *n* (*Pol*) citoyen(ne); (*resident*): **the
~s of this town** les habitants de cette ville
citizenship ['sɪtɪznʃɪp] *n* citoyenneté *f*; (*Brit*: *Scol*)
≈ éducation *f* civique
citrus fruits ['sɪtrəs-] *npl* agrumes *mpl*
city ['sɪtɪ] *n* (grande) ville *f*; **the C~** la Cité de
Londres (*centre des affaires*)
city centre *n* centre ville *m*
city technology college *n* (*Brit*) établissement
m d'enseignement technologique (*situé dans un
quartier défavorisé*)
civic ['sɪvɪk] *adj* civique; (*authorities*) municipal(e)
civic centre *n* (*Brit*) centre administratif
(municipal)
civil ['sɪvɪl] *adj* civil(e); (*polite*) poli(e), civil(e)
civil engineer *n* ingénieur civil
civilian [sɪ'vɪlɪən] *adj*, *n* civil(e)
civilization [sɪvɪlaɪ'zeɪʃən] *n* civilisation *f*
civilized ['sɪvɪlaɪzd] *adj* civilisé(e); (*fig*) où
règnent les bonnes manières, empreint(e) d'une
courtoisie de bon ton
civil law *n* code civil; (*study*) droit civil
civil rights *npl* droits *mpl* civiques
civil servant *n* fonctionnaire *m/f*

Civil Service *n* fonction publique,
administration *f*
civil war *n* guerre civile
CJD *n abbr* (= *Creutzfeldt-Jakob disease*) MCJ *f*
clad [klæd] *adj*: ~ **(in)** habillé(e) de, vêtu(e) de
claim [kleɪm] *vt* (*rights etc*) revendiquer;
(*compensation*) réclamer; (*assert*) déclarer,
prétendre ▷ *vi* (*for insurance*) faire une déclaration
de sinistre ▷ *n* revendication *f*; prétention
f; (*right*) droit *m*; (*for expenses*) note *f* de frais;
(**insurance**) ~ demande *f* d'indemnisation,
déclaration *f* de sinistre; **to put in a ~ for** (*pay rise
etc*) demander
claimant ['kleɪmənt] *n* (*Admin, Law*) requérant(e)
claim form *n* (*gen*) formulaire *m* de demande
clairvoyant [klɛə'vɔɪənt] *n* voyant(e), extra-
lucide *m/f*
clam [klæm] *n* palourde *f*
▶ **clam up** *vi* (*inf*) la boucler
clamber ['klæmbə'] *vi* grimper, se hisser
clammy ['klæmɪ] *adj* humide et froid(e) (au
toucher), moite
clamour, (*US*) **clamor** ['klæmə'] *n* (*noise*)
clameurs *fpl*; (*protest*) protestations bruyantes
▷ *vi*: **to ~ for sth** réclamer qch à grands cris
clamp [klæmp] *n* crampon *m*; (*on workbench*) valet
m; (*on car*) sabot *m* de Denver ▷ *vt* attacher; (*car*)
mettre un sabot à
▶ **clamp down on** *vt fus* sévir contre, prendre des
mesures draconiennes à l'égard de
clan [klæn] *n* clan *m*
clang [klæŋ] *n* bruit *m* or fracas *m* métallique ▷ *vi*
émettre un bruit *or* fracas métallique
clap [klæp] *vi* applaudir ▷ *vt*: **to ~ (one's hands)**
battre des mains ▷ *n* claquement *m*; tape *f*; **a ~ of
thunder** un coup de tonnerre
clapping ['klæpɪŋ] *n* applaudissements *mpl*
claret ['klærət] *n* (vin *m* de) bordeaux *m* (rouge)
clarify ['klærɪfaɪ] *vt* clarifier
clarinet [klærɪ'nɛt] *n* clarinette *f*
clarity ['klærɪtɪ] *n* clarté *f*
clash [klæʃ] *n* (*sound*) choc *m*, fracas *m*; (*with police*)
affrontement *m*; (*fig*) conflit *m* ▷ *vi* se heurter;
être *or* entrer en conflit; (*colours*) jurer; (*dates,
events*) tomber en même temps
clasp [klɑ:sp] *n* (*of necklace, bag*) fermoir *m* ▷ *vt*
serrer, étreindre
class [klɑ:s] *n* (*gen*) classe *f*; (*group, category*)
catégorie *f* ▷ *vt* classer, classifier
classic ['klæsɪk] *adj* classique ▷ *n* (*author, work*)
classique *m*; (*race etc*) classique *f*
classical ['klæsɪkl] *adj* classique
classification [klæsɪfɪ'keɪʃən] *n* classification *f*
classified ['klæsɪfaɪd] *adj* (*information*)
secret(-ète); ~ **ads** petites annonces
classify ['klæsɪfaɪ] *vt* classifier, classer
classmate ['klɑ:smeɪt] *n* camarade *m/f* de classe
classroom ['klɑ:srum] *n* (salle *f* de) classe *f*
classroom assistant *n* assistant(-e) d'éducation
classy ['klɑ:sɪ] (*inf*) *adj* classe (*inf*)
clatter ['klætə'] *n* cliquetis *m* ▷ *vi* cliqueter
clause [klɔ:z] *n* clause *f*; (*Ling*) proposition *f*

claustrophobic [klɔːstrəˈfəubɪk] adj (person)
claustrophobe; (place) où l'on se sent
claustrophobe

claw [klɔː] n griffe f; (of bird of prey) serre f; (of
lobster) pince f ▷ vt griffer; déchirer

clay [kleɪ] n argile f

clean [kliːn] adj propre; (clear, smooth) net(te);
(record, reputation) sans tache; (joke, story)
correct(e) ▷ vt nettoyer ▷ adv: **he ~ forgot** il a
complètement oublié; **to come ~** (inf: admit guilt)
se mettre à table; **to ~ one's teeth** se laver les
dents; **~ driving licence** or (US) **record** permis où
n'est portée aucune indication de contravention
▶ **clean off** vt enlever
▶ **clean out** vt nettoyer (à fond)
▶ **clean up** vt nettoyer; (fig) remettre de l'ordre
dans ▷ vi (fig: make profit): **to ~ up on** faire son
beurre avec

clean-cut [ˈkliːnˈkʌt] adj (man) soigné; (situation
etc) bien délimité(e), net(te), clair(e)

cleaner [ˈkliːnəʳ] n (person) nettoyeur(-euse),
femme f de ménage; (also: **dry cleaner**)
teinturier(-ière); (product) détachant m

cleaner's [ˈkliːnəʳz] n (also: **dry cleaner's**)
teinturier m

cleaning [ˈkliːnɪŋ] n nettoyage m

cleanliness [ˈklɛnlɪnɪs] n propreté f

cleanse [klɛnz] vt nettoyer; purifier

cleanser [ˈklɛnzəʳ] n détergent m; (for face)
démaquillant m

clean-shaven [ˈkliːnˈʃeɪvn] adj rasé(e) de près

cleansing department [ˈklɛnzɪŋ-] n (Brit)
service m de voirie

clear [klɪəʳ] adj clair(e); (glass, plastic)
transparent(e); (road, way) libre, dégagé(e);
(profit, majority) net(te); (conscience) tranquille;
(skin) frais (fraîche); (sky) dégagé(e) ▷ vt (road)
dégager, déblayer; (table) débarrasser; (room
etc: of people) faire évacuer; (woodland) défricher;
(cheque) compenser; (Comm: goods) liquider; (Law:
suspect) innocenter; (obstacle) franchir or sauter
sans heurter ▷ vi (weather) s'éclaircir; (fog) se
dissiper ▷ adv: **~ of** à distance de, à l'écart de
▷ n: **to be in the ~** (out of debt) être dégagé(e) de
toute dette; (out of suspicion) être lavé(e) de tout
soupçon; (out of danger) être hors de danger; **to
~ the table** débarrasser la table, desservir; **to ~
one's throat** s'éclaircir la gorge; **to ~ a profit**
faire un bénéfice net; **to make o.s. ~** se faire
bien comprendre; **to make it ~ to sb that ...**
bien faire comprendre à qn que ...; **I have a ~ day
tomorrow** (Brit) je n'ai rien de prévu demain; **to
keep ~ of sb/sth** éviter qn/qch
▶ **clear away** vt (things, clothes etc) enlever, retirer;
to ~ away the dishes débarrasser la table
▶ **clear off** vi (inf: leave) dégager
▶ **clear up** vi s'éclaircir, se dissiper ▷ vt ranger,
mettre en ordre; (mystery) éclaircir, résoudre

clearance [ˈklɪərəns] n (removal) déblayage
m; (free space) dégagement m; (permission)
autorisation f

clear-cut [ˈklɪəˈkʌt] adj précis(e), nettement

défini(e)

clearing [ˈklɪərɪŋ] n (in forest) clairière f; (Brit
Banking) compensation f, clearing m

clearing bank n (Brit) banque f qui appartient à
une chambre de compensation

clearly [ˈklɪəlɪ] adv clairement; (obviously) de
toute évidence

clearway [ˈklɪəweɪ] n (Brit) route f à
stationnement interdit

clef [klɛf] n (Mus) clé f

cleft [klɛft] n (in rock) crevasse f, fissure f

clementine [ˈklɛməntaɪn] n clémentine f

clench [klɛntʃ] vt serrer

clergy [ˈkləːdʒɪ] n clergé m

clergyman [ˈkləːdʒɪmən] (irreg) n
ecclésiastique m

clerical [ˈklɛrɪkl] adj de bureau, d'employé de
bureau; (Rel) clérical(e), du clergé

clerk [klɑːk] (US) [kləːrk] n (Brit) employé(e) de
bureau; (US: salesman/woman) vendeur(-euse); **C~
of Court** (Law) greffier m (du tribunal)

clever [ˈklɛvəʳ] adj (intelligent) intelligent(e);
(skilful) habile, adroit(e); (device, arrangement)
ingénieux(-euse), astucieux(-euse)

cliché [ˈkliːʃeɪ] n cliché m

click [klɪk] vi faire un bruit sec or un déclic;
(Comput) cliquer ▷ vt: **to ~ one's tongue** faire
claquer sa langue; **to ~ one's heels** claquer des
talons; **to ~ on an icon** cliquer sur une icône

client [ˈklaɪənt] n client(e)

cliff [klɪf] n falaise f

climate [ˈklaɪmɪt] n climat m

climate change n changement m climatique

climax [ˈklaɪmæks] n apogée m, point
culminant; (sexual) orgasme m

climb [klaɪm] vi grimper, monter; (plane) prendre
de l'altitude ▷ vt (stairs) monter; (mountain)
escalader; (tree) grimper à ▷ n montée f, escalade
f; **to ~ over a wall** passer par dessus un mur
▶ **climb down** vi (re)descendre; (Brit fig) rabattre
de ses prétentions

climb-down [ˈklaɪmdaun] n (Brit) reculade f

climber [ˈklaɪməʳ] n (also: **rock climber**)
grimpeur(-euse), varappeur(-euse); (plant)
plante grimpante

climbing [ˈklaɪmɪŋ] n (also: **rock climbing**)
escalade f, varappe f

clinch [klɪntʃ] vt (deal) conclure, sceller

cling (pt, pp clung) [klɪŋ, klʌŋ] vi: **to ~ (to)** se
cramponner (à), s'accrocher (à); (clothes) coller
(à)

Clingfilm® [ˈklɪŋfɪlm] n film m alimentaire

clinic [ˈklɪnɪk] n clinique f; centre médical;
(session: Med) consultation(s) f(pl), séance(s) f(pl);
(Sport) séance(s) de perfectionnement

clinical [ˈklɪnɪkl] adj clinique; (fig) froid(e)

clink [klɪŋk] vi tinter, cliqueter

clip [klɪp] n (for hair) barrette f; (also: **paper clip**)
trombone m; (Brit: also: **bulldog clip**) pince f
de bureau; (holding hose etc) collier m or bague f
(métallique) de serrage; (TV, Cinema) clip m ▷ vt
(also: **clip together**: papers) attacher; (hair, nails)

couper; (*hedge*) tailler

clippers ['klɪpəz] *npl* tondeuse *f*; (*also*: **nail clippers**) coupe-ongles *m inv*

clipping ['klɪpɪŋ] *n* (*from newspaper*) coupure *f* de journal

cloak [kləuk] *n* grande cape ▷ *vt* (*fig*) masquer, cacher

cloakroom ['kləukrum] *n* (*for coats etc*) vestiaire *m*; (*Brit*: W.C.) toilettes *fpl*

clock [klɔk] *n* (*large*) horloge *f*; (*small*) pendule *f*; **round the ~** (*work etc*) vingt-quatre heures sur vingt-quatre; **to sleep round the ~** or the **~ round** faire le tour du cadran; **30,000 on the ~** (*Brit Aut*) 30 000 milles au compteur; **to work against the ~** faire la course contre la montre
 ▶ **clock in** or **on** (*Brit*) *vi* (*with card*) pointer (en arrivant); (*start work*) commencer à travailler
 ▶ **clock off** or **out** (*Brit*) *vi* (*with card*) pointer (en partant); (*leave work*) quitter le travail
 ▶ **clock up** *vt* (*miles, hours etc*) faire

clockwise ['klɔkwaɪz] *adv* dans le sens des aiguilles d'une montre

clockwork ['klɔkwə:k] *n* rouages *mpl*, mécanisme *m*; (*of clock*) mouvement *m* (d'horlogerie) ▷ *adj* (*toy, train*) mécanique

clog [klɔg] *n* sabot *m* ▷ *vt* boucher, encrasser ▷ *vi* (*also*: **clog up**) se boucher, s'encrasser

cloister ['klɔɪstə^r] *n* cloître *m*

clone [kləun] *n* clone *m* ▷ *vt* cloner

close[1] [kləus] *adj* (*near*): **~ (to)** près (de), proche (de); (*writing, texture*) serré(e); (*contact, link, watch*) étroit(e); (*examination*) attentif(-ive), minutieux(-euse); (*contest*) très serré(e); (*weather*) lourd(e), étouffant(e); (*room*) mal aéré(e) ▷ *adv* près, à proximité; **~ to** (*prep*) près de; **~ by**, **~ at hand** (*adj, adv*) tout(e) près; **how ~ is Edinburgh to Glasgow?** combien de kilomètres y-a-t-il entre Édimbourg et Glasgow?; **a ~ friend** un ami intime; **to have a ~ shave** (*fig*) l'échapper belle; **at ~ quarters** tout près, à côté

close[2] [kləuz] *vt* fermer; (*bargain, deal*) conclure ▷ *vi* (*shop etc*) fermer; (*lid, door etc*) se fermer; (*end*) se terminer, se conclure ▷ *n* (*end*) conclusion *f*; **to bring sth to a ~** mettre fin à qch; **what time do you ~?** à quelle heure fermez-vous?
 ▶ **close down** *vt*, *vi* fermer (*définitivement*)
 ▶ **close in** *vi* (*hunters*) approcher; (*night, fog*) tomber; **the days are closing in** les jours raccourcissent; **to ~ in on sb** cerner qn
 ▶ **close off** *vt* (*area*) boucler

closed [kləuzd] *adj* (*shop etc*) fermé(e); (*road*) fermé à la circulation

closed shop *n* organisation *f* qui n'admet que des travailleurs syndiqués

close-knit ['kləus'nɪt] *adj* (*family, community*) très uni(e)

closely ['kləuslɪ] *adv* (*examine, watch*) de près; **we are ~ related** nous sommes proches parents; **a ~ guarded secret** un secret bien gardé

closet ['klɔzɪt] *n* (*cupboard*) placard *m*, réduit *m*

close-up ['kləusʌp] *n* gros plan

closing time *n* heure *f* de fermeture

closure ['kləuʒə^r] *n* fermeture *f*

clot [klɔt] *n* (*of blood, milk*) caillot *m*; (*inf: person*) ballot *m* ▷ *vi* (*blood*) former des caillots; (: *external bleeding*) se coaguler

cloth [klɔθ] *n* (*material*) tissu *m*, étoffe *f*; (*Brit*: *also*: **tea cloth**) torchon *m*; lavette *f*; (*also*: **tablecloth**) nappe *f*

clothe [kləuð] *vt* habiller, vêtir

clothes [kləuðz] *npl* vêtements *mpl*, habits *mpl*; **to put one's ~ on** s'habiller; **to take one's ~ off** enlever ses vêtements

clothes brush *n* brosse *f* à habits

clothes line *n* corde *f* (à linge)

clothes peg, (US) **clothes pin** *n* pince *f* à linge

clothing ['kləuðɪŋ] *n* = **clothes**

cloud [klaud] *n* nuage *m* ▷ *vt* (*liquid*) troubler; **to ~ the issue** brouiller les cartes; **every ~ has a silver lining** (*proverb*) à quelque chose malheur est bon (*proverbe*)
 ▶ **cloud over** *vi* se couvrir; (*fig*) s'assombrir

cloudburst ['klaudbə:st] *n* violente averse

cloudy ['klaudɪ] *adj* nuageux(-euse), couvert(e); (*liquid*) trouble

clout [klaut] *n* (*blow*) taloche *f*; (*fig*) pouvoir *m* ▷ *vt* flanquer une taloche à

clove [kləuv] *n* clou *m* de girofle; **a ~ of garlic** une gousse d'ail

clover ['kləuvə^r] *n* trèfle *m*

clown [klaun] *n* clown *m* ▷ *vi* (*also*: **clown about, clown around**) faire le clown

cloying ['klɔɪɪŋ] *adj* (*taste, smell*) écœurant(e)

club [klʌb] *n* (*society*) club *m*; (*weapon*) massue *f*, matraque *f*; (*also*: **golf club**) club ▷ *vt* matraquer ▷ *vi*: **to ~ together** s'associer; **clubs** *npl* (*Cards*) trèfle *m*

club class *n* (*Aviat*) classe *f* club

clubhouse ['klʌbhaus] *n* pavillon *m*

cluck [klʌk] *vi* glousser

clue [klu:] *n* indice *m*; (*in crosswords*) définition *f*; **I haven't a ~** je n'en ai pas la moindre idée

clump [klʌmp] *n*: **~ of trees** bouquet *m* d'arbres

clumsy ['klʌmzɪ] *adj* (*person*) gauche, maladroit(e); (*object*) malcommode, peu maniable

clung [klʌŋ] *pt*, *pp of* **cling**

cluster ['klʌstə^r] *n* (*petit*) groupe; (*of flowers*) grappe *f* ▷ *vi* se rassembler

clutch [klʌtʃ] *n* (*Aut*) embrayage *m*; (*grasp*): **~es** étreinte *f*, prise *f* ▷ *vt* (*grasp*) agripper; (*hold tightly*) serrer fort; (*hold on to*) se cramponner à

clutter ['klʌtə^r] *vt* (*also*: **clutter up**) encombrer ▷ *n* désordre *m*, fouillis *m*

cm *abbr* (= *centimetre*) cm

CND *n abbr* = **Campaign for Nuclear Disarmament**

Co. *abbr* = **company, county**

c/o *abbr* = *care of* c/o, aux bons soins de

coach [kəutʃ] *n* (*bus*) autocar *m*; (*horse-drawn*) diligence *f*; (*of train*) voiture *f*, wagon *m*; (*Sport*: *trainer*) entraîneur(-euse); (*school*: *tutor*) répétiteur(-trice) ▷ *vt* (*Sport*) entraîner; (*student*)

donner des leçons particulières à
coach station (Brit) n gare routière
coach trip n excursion f en car
coal [kəul] n charbon m
coal face n front m de taille
coalfield ['kəulfi:ld] n bassin houiller
coalition [kəuə'lɪʃən] n coalition f
coalman ['kəulmən] (irreg) n charbonnier m,
marchand m de charbon
coal mine n mine f de charbon
coarse [kɔ:s] adj grossier(-ère), rude; (vulgar)
vulgaire
coast [kəust] n côte f ▷ vi (car, cycle) descendre en
roue libre
coastal ['kəustl] adj côtier(-ère)
coastguard ['kəustgɑ:d] n garde-côte m
coastline ['kəustlaɪn] n côte f, littoral m
coat [kəut] n manteau m; (of animal) pelage m,
poil m; (of paint) couche f ▷ vt couvrir, enduire; ~
of arms n blason m, armoiries fpl
coat hanger n cintre m
coating ['kəutɪŋ] n couche f, enduit m
coax [kəuks] vt persuader par des cajoleries
cob [kɔb] n see **corn**
cobbled ['kɔbld] adj pavé(e)
cobbler ['kɔblə'] n cordonnier m
cobbles, cobblestones ['kɔblz, 'kɔblstəunz] npl
pavés (ronds)
cobweb ['kɔbwɛb] n toile f d'araignée
cocaine [kə'keɪn] n cocaïne f
cock [kɔk] n (rooster) coq m; (male bird) mâle m ▷ vt
(gun) armer; **to ~ one's ears** (fig) dresser l'oreille
cockerel ['kɔkərl] n jeune coq m
cockle ['kɔkl] n coque f
cockney ['kɔknɪ] n cockney m/f (habitant
des quartiers populaires de l'East End de Londres),
≈ faubourien(ne)
cockpit ['kɔkpɪt] n (in aircraft) poste m de pilotage,
cockpit m
cockroach ['kɔkrəutʃ] n cafard m, cancrelat m
cocktail ['kɔkteɪl] n cocktail m; **prawn ~** (US):
shrimp ~ cocktail de crevettes
cocktail cabinet n (meuble-)bar m
cocktail party n cocktail m
cocoa ['kəukəu] n cacao m
coconut ['kəukənʌt] n noix f de coco
C.O.D. abbr = **cash on delivery**; (US) = **collect on
delivery**
cod [kɔd] n morue fraîche, cabillaud m
code [kəud] n code m; (Tel: area code) indicatif
m; ~ **of behaviour** règles fpl de conduite; ~ **of
practice** déontologie f
cod-liver oil ['kɔdlɪvər-] n huile f de foie de
morue
coeducational ['kəuɛdju'keɪʃənl] adj mixte
coercion [kəu'ə:ʃən] n contrainte f
coffee ['kɔfɪ] n café m; **white ~** (US): ~ **with
cream** (café-)crème m
coffee bar n (Brit) café m
coffee bean n grain m de café
coffee break n pause-café f
coffee maker n cafetière f

coffeepot ['kɔfɪpɔt] n cafetière f
coffee shop n café m
coffee table n (petite) table basse
coffin ['kɔfɪn] n cercueil m
cog [kɔg] n (wheel) roue dentée; (tooth) dent f
(d'engrenage)
cogent ['kəudʒənt] adj puissant(e),
convaincant(e)
cognac ['kɔnjæk] n cognac m
coherent [kəu'hɪərənt] adj cohérent(e)
coil [kɔɪl] n rouleau m, bobine f; (one loop) anneau
m, spire f; (of smoke) volute f; (contraceptive) stérilet
m ▷ vt enrouler
coin [kɔɪn] n pièce f (de monnaie) ▷ vt (word)
inventer
coinage ['kɔɪnɪdʒ] n monnaie f, système m
monétaire
coinbox ['kɔɪnbɔks] n (Brit) cabine f téléphonique
coincide [kəuɪn'saɪd] vi coïncider
coincidence [kəu'ɪnsɪdəns] n coïncidence f
Coke® [kəuk] n coca m
coke [kəuk] n (coal) coke m
colander ['kɔləndə'] n passoire f (à légumes)
cold [kəuld] adj froid(e) ▷ n froid m; (Med) rhume
m; **it's ~** il fait froid; **to be ~** (person) avoir froid;
to catch ~ prendre or attraper froid; **to catch a
~** s'enrhumer, attraper un rhume; **in ~ blood** de
sang-froid; **to have ~ feet** avoir froid aux pieds;
(fig) avoir la frousse or la trouille; **to give sb the
~ shoulder** battre froid à qn
cold sore n bouton m de fièvre
coleslaw ['kəulslɔ:] n sorte de salade de chou cru
colic ['kɔlɪk] n colique(s) f(pl)
collaborate [kə'læbəreɪt] vi collaborer
collapse [kə'læps] vi s'effondrer, s'écrouler;
(Med) avoir un malaise ▷ n effondrement m,
écroulement m; (of government) chute f
collapsible [kə'læpsəbl] adj pliant(e),
télescopique
collar ['kɔlə'] n (of coat, shirt) col m; (for dog) collier
m; (Tech) collier, bague f ▷ vt (inf: person) pincer
collarbone ['kɔləbəun] n clavicule f
collateral [kə'lætərl] n nantissement m
colleague ['kɔli:g] n collègue m/f
collect [kə'lɛkt] vt rassembler; (pick up) ramasser;
(as a hobby) collectionner; (Brit: call for) (passer)
prendre; (mail) faire la levée de, ramasser; (money
owed) encaisser; (donations, subscriptions) recueillir
▷ vi (people) se rassembler; (dust, dirt) s'amasser;
to ~ one's thoughts réfléchir, réunir ses
idées; ~ **on delivery (COD)** (US Comm) payable
or paiement à la livraison; **to call ~** (US Tel)
téléphoner en PCV
collection [kə'lɛkʃən] n collection f; (of mail) levée
f; (for money) collecte f, quête f
collective [kə'lɛktɪv] adj collectif(-ive) ▷ n
collectif m
collector [kə'lɛktə'] n collectionneur m; (of taxes)
percepteur m; (of rent, cash) encaisseur m; ~'s
item or **piece** pièce f de collection
college ['kɔlɪdʒ] n collège m; (of technology,
agriculture etc) institut m; **to go to ~** faire des

études supérieures; **~ of education** ≈ école normale

collide [kə'laɪd] *vi*: **to ~ (with)** entrer en collision (avec)

colliery ['kɔlɪərɪ] *n* (*Brit*) mine *f* de charbon, houillère *f*

collision [kə'lɪʒən] *n* collision *f*, heurt *m*; **to be on a ~ course** aller droit à la collision; (*fig*) aller vers l'affrontement

colloquial [kə'ləukwɪəl] *adj* familier(-ère)

cologne [kə'ləun] *n* (*also*: **eau de cologne**) eau *f* de cologne

colon ['kəulən] *n* (*sign*) deux-points *mpl*; (*Med*) côlon *m*

colonel ['kə:nl] *n* colonel *m*

colonial [kə'ləunɪəl] *adj* colonial(e)

colony ['kɔlənɪ] *n* colonie *f*

colour, (*US*) **color** ['kʌlə*] *n* couleur *f* ▷ *vt* colorer; (*dye*) teindre; (*paint*) peindre; (*with crayons*) colorier; (*news*) fausser, exagérer ▷ *vi* (*blush*) rougir ▷ *cpd* (*film, photograph, television*) en couleur; **colours** *npl* (*of party, club*) couleurs *fpl*; **I'd like a different ~** je le voudrais dans un autre coloris ▶ **colour in** *vt* colorier

colour bar, (*US*) **color bar** *n* discrimination raciale (*dans un établissement etc*)

colour-blind, (*US*) **color-blind** ['kʌləblaɪnd] *adj* daltonien(ne)

coloured, (*US*) **colored** ['kʌləd] *adj* coloré(e); (*photo*) en couleur

colour film, (*US*) **color film** *n* (*for camera*) pellicule *f* (en) couleur

colourful, (*US*) **colorful** ['kʌləful] *adj* coloré(e), vif (vive); (*personality*) pittoresque, haut(e) en couleurs

colouring, (*US*) **coloring** ['kʌlərɪŋ] *n* colorant *m*; (*complexion*) teint *m*

colour scheme, (*US*) **color scheme** *n* combinaison *f* de(s) couleur(s)

colour television, (*US*) **color television** *n* télévision *f* (en) couleur

colt [kəult] *n* poulain *m*

column ['kɔləm] *n* colonne *f*; (*fashion column, sports column etc*) rubrique *f*; **the editorial ~** l'éditorial *m*

columnist ['kɔləmnɪst] *n* rédacteur(-trice) d'une rubrique

coma ['kəumə] *n* coma *m*

comb [kəum] *n* peigne *m* ▷ *vt* (*hair*) peigner; (*area*) ratisser, passer au peigne fin

combat ['kɔmbæt] *n* combat *m* ▷ *vt* combattre, lutter contre

combination [kɔmbɪ'neɪʃən] *n* (*gen*) combinaison *f*

combine [kəm'baɪn] *vt* combiner ▷ *vi* s'associer; (*Chem*) se combiner ▷ *n* ['kɔmbaɪn] association *f*; (*Econ*) trust *m*; (*also*: **combine harvester**) moissonneuse-batteuse(-lieuse) *f*; **to ~ sth with sth** (*one quality with another*) joindre *ou* allier qch à qch; **a ~d effort** un effort conjugué

combine harvester *n* moissonneuse-batteuse(-lieuse) *f*

come (*pt* **came**, *pp* **-**) [kʌm, keɪm] *vi* **1** (*movement towards*) venir; **to ~ running** arriver en courant; **he's ~ here to work** il est venu ici pour travailler; **~ with me** suivez-moi; **to ~ into sight** *or* **view** apparaître

2 (*arrive*) arriver; **to ~ home** rentrer (chez soi *or* à la maison); **we've just ~ from Paris** nous arrivons de Paris; **coming!** j'arrive!

3 (*reach*): **to ~ to** (*decision etc*) parvenir à, arriver à; **the bill came to £40** la note s'est élevée à 40 livres; **if it ~s to it** s'il le faut, dans le pire des cas

4 (*occur*): **an idea came to me** il m'est venu une idée; **what might ~ of it** ce qui pourrait en résulter, ce qui pourrait advenir *or* se produire

5 (*be, become*): **to ~ loose/undone** se défaire/desserrer; **I've ~ to like him** j'ai fini par bien l'aimer

6 (*inf: sexually*) jouir

▶ **come about** *vi* se produire, arriver

▶ **come across** *vt fus* rencontrer par hasard, tomber sur ▷ *vi*: **to ~ across well/badly** faire une bonne/mauvaise impression

▶ **come along** *vi* (*Brit: pupil, work*) faire des progrès, avancer; **~ along!** viens!; allons!, allez!

▶ **come apart** *vi* s'en aller en morceaux; se détacher

▶ **come away** *vi* partir, s'en aller; (*become detached*) se détacher

▶ **come back** *vi* revenir; (*reply*): **can I ~ back to you on that one?** est-ce qu'on peut revenir là-dessus plus tard?

▶ **come by** *vt fus* (*acquire*) obtenir, se procurer

▶ **come down** *vi* descendre; (*prices*) baisser; (*buildings*) s'écrouler; (: *be demolished*) être démoli(e)

▶ **come forward** *vi* s'avancer; (*make o.s. known*) se présenter, s'annoncer

▶ **come from** *vt fus* (*source*) venir de; (*place*) venir de, être originaire de

▶ **come in** *vi* entrer; (*train*) arriver; (*fashion*) entrer en vogue; (*on deal etc*) participer

▶ **come in for** *vt fus* (*criticism etc*) être l'objet de

▶ **come into** *vt fus* (*money*) hériter de

▶ **come off** *vi* (*button*) se détacher; (*attempt*) réussir

▶ **come on** *vi* (*lights, electricity*) s'allumer; (*central heating*) se mettre en marche; (*pupil, work, project*) faire des progrès, avancer; **~ on!** viens!; allons!, allez!

▶ **come out** *vi* sortir; (*sun*) se montrer; (*book*) paraître; (*stain*) s'enlever; (*strike*) cesser le travail, se mettre en grève

▶ **come over** *vt fus*: **I don't know what's ~ over him!** je ne sais pas ce qui lui a pris!

▶ **come round** *vi* (*after faint, operation*) revenir à soi, reprendre connaissance

▶ **come through** *vi* (*survive*) s'en sortir; (*telephone call*): **the call came through** l'appel est bien parvenu

▶ **come to** *vi* revenir à soi ▷ *vt* (*add up to: amount*): **how much does it ~ to?** ça fait combien?

▶ **come under** vt fus (heading) se trouver sous; (influence) subir

▶ **come up** vi monter; (sun) se lever; (problem) se poser; (event) survenir; (in conversation) être soulevé

▶ **come up against** vt fus (resistance, difficulties) rencontrer

▶ **come up to** vt fus arriver à; **the film didn't ~ up to our expectations** le film nous a déçu

▶ **come up with** vt fus (money) fournir; **he came up with an idea** il a eu une idée, il a proposé quelque chose

▶ **come upon** vt fus tomber sur

comeback ['kʌmbæk] n (Theat) rentrée f; (reaction) réaction f; (response) réponse f

comedian [kə'miːdɪən] n (comic) comique m; (Theat) comédien m

comedy ['kɔmɪdɪ] n comédie f; (humour) comique m

comet ['kɔmɪt] n comète f

comeuppance [kʌm'ʌpəns] n: **to get one's ~** recevoir ce qu'on mérite

comfort ['kʌmfət] n confort m, bien-être m; (solace) consolation f, réconfort m ▷ vt consoler, réconforter

comfortable ['kʌmfətəbl] adj confortable; (person) à l'aise; (financially) aisé(e); (patient) dont l'état est stationnaire; **I don't feel very ~ about it** cela m'inquiète un peu

comfortably ['kʌmfətəblɪ] adv (sit) confortablement; (live) à l'aise

comfort station n (US) toilettes fpl

comic ['kɔmɪk] adj (also: **comical**) comique ▷ n (person) comique m; (Brit: magazine: for children) magazine m de bandes dessinées or de BD; (: for adults) illustré m

comic book (US) n (for children) magazine m de bandes dessinées or de BD; (for adults) illustré m

comic strip n bande dessinée

coming ['kʌmɪŋ] n arrivée f ▷ adj (next) prochain(e); (future) à venir; **in the ~ weeks** dans les prochaines semaines

comma ['kɔmə] n virgule f

command [kə'mɑːnd] n ordre m, commandement m; (Mil: authority) commandement; (mastery) maîtrise f; (Comput) commande f ▷ vt (troops) commander; (be able to get) (pouvoir) disposer de, avoir à sa disposition; (deserve) avoir droit à; **to ~ sb to do** donner l'ordre or commander à qn de faire; **to have/ take ~ of** avoir/prendre le commandement de; **to have at one's ~** (money, resources etc) disposer de

commandeer [kɔmən'dɪər] vt réquisitionner (par la force)

commander [kə'mɑːndər] n chef m; (Mil) commandant m

commando [kə'mɑːndəu] n commando m; membre m d'un commando

commemorate [kə'mɛməreɪt] vt commémorer

commence [kə'mɛns] vt, vi commencer

commend [kə'mɛnd] vt louer; (recommend) recommander

commensurate [kə'mɛnʃərɪt] adj: **~ with/to** en rapport avec/selon

comment ['kɔment] n commentaire m ▷ vi faire des remarques or commentaires; **to ~ on** faire des remarques sur; **to ~ that** faire remarquer que; **"no ~"** "je n'ai rien à déclarer"

commentary ['kɔməntərɪ] n commentaire m; (Sport) reportage m (en direct)

commentator ['kɔmənteɪtər] n commentateur m; (Sport) reporter m

commerce ['kɔməːs] n commerce m

commercial [kə'məːʃəl] adj commercial(e) ▷ n (Radio, TV) annonce f publicitaire, spot m (publicitaire)

commercial break n (Radio, TV) spot m (publicitaire)

commiserate [kə'mɪzəreɪt] vi: **to ~ with sb** témoigner de la sympathie pour qn

commission [kə'mɪʃən] n (committee, fee) commission f; (order for work of art etc) commande f ▷ vt (Mil) nommer (à un commandement); (work of art) commander, charger un artiste de l'exécution de; **out of ~** (Naut) hors de service; (machine) hors service; **I get 10% ~** je reçois une commission de 10%; **~ of inquiry** (Brit) commission d'enquête

commissionaire [kəmɪʃə'nɛər] n (Brit: at shop, cinema etc) portier m (en uniforme)

commissioner [kə'mɪʃənər] n membre m d'une commission; (Police) préfet m (de police)

commit [kə'mɪt] vt (act) commettre; (resources) consacrer; (to sb's care) confier (à); **to ~ o.s. (to do)** s'engager (à faire); **to ~ suicide** se suicider; **to ~ to writing** coucher par écrit; **to ~ sb for trial** traduire qn en justice

commitment [kə'mɪtmənt] n engagement m; (obligation) responsabilité(s) (fpl)

committee [kə'mɪtɪ] n comité m; commission f; **to be on a ~** siéger dans un comité or une commission)

commodity [kə'mɔdɪtɪ] n produit m, marchandise f, article m; (food) denrée f

common ['kɔmən] adj (gen) commun(e); (usual) courant(e) ▷ n terrain communal; **in ~** en commun; **in ~ use** d'un usage courant; **it's ~ knowledge that** il est bien connu or notoire que; **to the ~ good** pour le bien de tous, dans l'intérêt général

commoner ['kɔmənər] n roturier(-ière)

common law n droit coutumier

commonly ['kɔmənlɪ] adv communément, généralement; couramment

Common Market n Marché commun

commonplace ['kɔmənpleɪs] adj banal(e), ordinaire

commonroom ['kɔmənrum] n salle commune; (Scol) salle des professeurs

Commons ['kɔmənz] npl (Brit Pol): **the (House of) ~** la chambre des Communes

common sense n bon sens

Commonwealth ['kɔmənwɛlθ] n: **the ~** le Commonwealth; voir article

commotion [kə'məʊʃən] n désordre m, tumulte m

communal ['kɔmju:nl] adj (life) communautaire; (for common use) commun(e)

commune ['kɔmju:n] n (group) communauté f ▷ vi [kə'mju:n]: **to ~ with** (nature) converser intimement avec; communier avec

communicate [kə'mju:nɪkeɪt] vt communiquer, transmettre ▷ vi: **to ~ (with)** communiquer (avec)

communication [kəmju:nɪ'keɪʃən] n communication f

communication cord n (Brit) sonnette f d'alarme

communion [kə'mju:nɪən] n (also: **Holy Communion**) communion f

communism ['kɔmjunɪzəm] n communisme m

communist ['kɔmjunɪst] adj, n communiste m/f

community [kə'mju:nɪtɪ] n communauté f

community centre, (US) **community center** n foyer socio-éducatif, centre m de loisirs

community chest n (US) fonds commun

community service n ≈ travail m d'intérêt général, TIG m

commutation ticket [kɔmju'teɪʃən-] n (US) carte f d'abonnement

commute [kə'mju:t] vi faire le trajet journalier (de son domicile à un lieu de travail assez éloigné) ▷ vt (Law) commuer; (Math: terms etc) opérer la commutation de

commuter [kə'mju:tə'] n banlieusard(e) (qui fait un trajet journalier pour se rendre à son travail)

compact adj [kəm'pækt] compact(e) ▷ n ['kɔmpækt] contrat m, entente f; (also: **powder compact**) poudrier m

compact disc n disque compact

compact disc player n lecteur m de disques compacts

companion [kəm'pænjən] n compagnon (compagne)

companionship [kəm'pænjənʃɪp] n camaraderie f

company ['kʌmpənɪ] n (also Comm, Mil, Theat) compagnie f; **he's good ~** il est d'une compagnie agréable; **we have ~** nous avons de la visite; **to keep sb ~** tenir compagnie à qn; **to part ~ with** se séparer de; **Smith and C~** Smith et Compagnie

company car n voiture f de fonction

company director n administrateur(-trice)

company secretary n (Brit Comm) secrétaire général (d'une société)

comparable ['kɔmpərəbl] adj comparable

comparative [kəm'pærətɪv] adj (study) comparatif(-ive); (relative) relatif(-ive)

comparatively [kəm'pærətɪvlɪ] adv (relatively) relativement

compare [kəm'pɛə'] vt: **to ~ sth/sb with** or **to** comparer qch/qn avec or à ▷ vi: **to ~ (with)** se comparer (à); être comparable (à); **how do the prices ~?** comment sont les prix?, est-ce que les prix sont comparables?; **~d with** or **to** par

rapport à

comparison [kəm'pærɪsn] n comparaison f; **in ~ (with)** en comparaison (de)

compartment [kəm'pɑ:tmənt] n (also Rail) compartiment m; **a non-smoking ~** un compartiment non-fumeurs

compass ['kʌmpəs] n boussole f; **compasses** npl (Math) compas m; **within the ~ of** dans les limites de

compassion [kəm'pæʃən] n compassion f, humanité f

compassionate [kəm'pæʃənɪt] adj accessible à la compassion, au cœur charitable et bienveillant; **on ~ grounds** pour raisons personnelles or de famille

compatible [kəm'pætɪbl] adj compatible

compel [kəm'pɛl] vt contraindre, obliger

compelling [kəm'pɛlɪŋ] adj (fig: argument) irrésistible

compensate ['kɔmpənseɪt] vt indemniser, dédommager ▷ vi: **to ~ for** compenser

compensation [kɔmpən'seɪʃən] n compensation f; (money) dédommagement m, indemnité f

compere ['kɔmpɛə'] n présentateur(-trice), animateur(-trice)

compete [kəm'pi:t] vi (take part) concourir; (vie): **to ~ (with)** rivaliser (avec), faire concurrence (à)

competent ['kɔmpɪtənt] adj compétent(e), capable

competition [kɔmpɪ'tɪʃən] n (contest) compétition f, concours m; (Econ) concurrence f; **in ~ with** en concurrence avec

competitive [kəm'pɛtɪtɪv] adj (Econ) concurrentiel(le); (sports) de compétition; (person) qui a l'esprit de compétition

competitor [kəm'pɛtɪtə'] n concurrent(e)

complacency [kəm'pleɪsnsɪ] n contentement m de soi, autosatisfaction f

complacent [kəm'pleɪsnt] adj (trop) content(e) de soi

complain [kəm'pleɪn] vi: **to ~ (about)** se plaindre (de); (in shop etc) réclamer (au sujet de)
▷ **complain of** vt fus (Med) se plaindre de

complaint [kəm'pleɪnt] n plainte f; (in shop etc) réclamation f; (Med) affection f

complement ['kɔmplɪmənt] n complément m; (esp of ship's crew etc) effectif complet ▷ vt (enhance) compléter

complementary [kɔmplɪ'mɛntərɪ] adj complémentaire

complete [kəm'pli:t] adj complet(-ète); (finished) achevé(e) ▷ vt achever, parachever; (set, group) compléter; (a form) remplir

completely [kəm'pli:tlɪ] adv complètement

completion [kəm'pli:ʃən] n achèvement m; (of contract) exécution f; **to be nearing ~** être presque terminé

complex ['kɔmplɛks] adj complexe ▷ n (Psych, buildings etc) complexe m

complexion [kəm'plɛkʃən] n (of face) teint m; (of event etc) aspect m, caractère m

compliance [kəm'plaɪəns] n (submission) docilité

f; (agreement): ~ **with** le fait de se conformer à; **in ~ with** en conformité avec, conformément à
complicate ['kɔmplɪkeɪt] vt compliquer
complicated ['kɔmplɪkeɪtɪd] adj compliqué(e)
complication [kɔmplɪ'keɪʃən] n complication f
compliment n ['kɔmplɪmənt] compliment m ▷ vt ['kɔmplɪmɛnt] complimenter; **compliments** npl compliments mpl, hommages mpl; vœux mpl; **to pay sb a** ~ faire or adresser un compliment à qn; **to** ~ **sb** (**on sth/on doing sth**) féliciter qn (pour qch/de faire qch)
complimentary [kɔmplɪ'mɛntərɪ] adj flatteur(-euse); (free) à titre gracieux
complimentary ticket n billet m de faveur
comply [kəm'plaɪ] vi: **to** ~ **with** se soumettre à, se conformer à
component [kəm'pəunənt] adj composant(e), constituant(e) ▷ n composant m, élément m
compose [kəm'pəuz] vt composer; (form): **to be ~d of** se composer de; **to** ~ **o.s.** se calmer, se maîtriser; **to** ~ **one's features** prendre une contenance
composed [kəm'pəuzd] adj calme, posé(e)
composer [kəm'pəuzə'] n (Mus) compositeur m
composition [kɔmpə'zɪʃən] n composition f
composure [kəm'pəuʒə'] n calme m, maîtrise f de soi
compound ['kɔmpaund] n (Chem, Ling) composé m; (enclosure) enclos m, enceinte f ▷ adj composé(e); (fracture) compliqué(e) ▷ vt [kəm'paund] (fig: problem etc) aggraver
compound fracture n fracture compliquée
compound interest n intérêt composé
comprehend [kɔmprɪ'hɛnd] vt comprendre
comprehension [kɔmprɪ'hɛnʃən] n compréhension f
comprehensive [kɔmprɪ'hɛnsɪv] adj (très) complet(-ète); ~ **policy** (Insurance) assurance f tous risques
comprehensive [kɔmprɪ'hɛnsɪv], **comprehensive school** n (Brit) école secondaire non sélective avec libre circulation d'une section à l'autre, ≈ CES m
compress vt [kəm'prɛs] comprimer; (text, information) condenser ▷ n ['kɔmprɛs] (Med) compresse f
comprise [kəm'praɪz] vt (also: **be comprised of**) comprendre; (constitute) constituer, représenter
compromise ['kɔmprəmaɪz] n compromis m ▷ vt compromettre ▷ vi transiger, accepter un compromis ▷ cpd (decision, solution) de compromis
compulsion [kəm'pʌlʃən] n contrainte f, force f; **under** ~ sous la contrainte
compulsive [kəm'pʌlsɪv] adj (Psych) compulsif(-ive); (book, film etc) captivant(e); **he's a** ~ **smoker** c'est un fumeur invétéré
compulsory [kəm'pʌlsərɪ] adj obligatoire
computer [kəm'pju:tə'] n ordinateur m; (mechanical) calculatrice f
computer game n jeu m vidéo
computer-generated [kəm'pju:tə'dʒɛnəreɪtɪd] adj de synthèse

computerize [kəm'pju:təraɪz] vt (data) traiter par ordinateur; (system, office) informatiser
computer programmer n programmeur(-euse)
computer programming n programmation f
computer science n informatique f
computer studies npl informatique f
computing [kəm'pju:tɪŋ] n informatique f
comrade ['kɔmrɪd] n camarade m/f
con [kɔn] vt duper; (cheat) escroquer ▷ n escroquerie f; **to** ~ **sb into doing sth** tromper qn pour lui faire faire qch
conceal [kən'si:l] vt cacher, dissimuler
concede [kən'si:d] vt concéder ▷ vi céder
conceit [kən'si:t] n vanité f, suffisance f, prétention f
conceited [kən'si:tɪd] adj vaniteux(-euse), suffisant(e)
conceive [kən'si:v] vt, vi concevoir; **to** ~ **of sth/of doing sth** imaginer qch/de faire qch
concentrate ['kɔnsəntreɪt] vi se concentrer ▷ vt concentrer
concentration [kɔnsən'treɪʃən] n concentration f
concentration camp n camp m de concentration
concept ['kɔnsɛpt] n concept m
concern [kən'sə:n] n affaire f; (Comm) entreprise f, firme f; (anxiety) inquiétude f, souci m ▷ vt (worry) inquiéter; (involve) concerner; (relate to) se rapporter à; **to be ~ed** (**about**) s'inquiéter (de), être inquiet(-ète) (au sujet de); **"to whom it may ~"** "à qui de droit"; **as far as I am ~ed** en ce qui me concerne; **to be ~ed with** (person: involved with) s'occuper de; **the department ~ed** (under discussion) le service en question; (involved) le service concerné
concerning [kən'sə:nɪŋ] prep en ce qui concerne, à propos de
concert ['kɔnsət] n concert m; **in** ~ à l'unisson, en chœur; ensemble
concerted [kən'sə:tɪd] adj concerté(e)
concert hall n salle f de concert
concerto [kən'tʃə:təu] n concerto m
concession [kən'sɛʃən] n (compromise) concession f; (reduced price) réduction f; **tax** ~ dégrèvement fiscal; **"~s"** tarif réduit
concise [kən'saɪs] adj concis(e)
conclude [kən'klu:d] vt conclure ▷ vi (speaker) conclure; (events): **to** ~ (**with**) se terminer (par)
conclusion [kən'klu:ʒən] n conclusion f; **to come to the ~ that** (en) conclure que
conclusive [kən'klu:sɪv] adj concluant(e), définitif(-ive)
concoct [kən'kɔkt] vt confectionner, composer
concoction [kən'kɔkʃən] n (food, drink) mélange m
concourse ['kɔnkɔ:s] n (hall) hall m, salle f des pas perdus; (crowd) affluence f; multitude f
concrete ['kɔnkri:t] n béton m ▷ adj concret(-ète); (Constr) en béton
concur [kən'kə:'] vi être d'accord
concurrently [kən'kʌrntlɪ] adv simultanément
concussion [kən'kʌʃən] n (Med) commotion

(cérébrale)

condemn [kən'dɛm] vt condamner

condensation [kɔndɛn'seɪʃən] n condensation f

condense [kən'dɛns] vi se condenser ▷ vt condenser

condensed milk [kən'dɛnst-] n lait concentré (sucré)

condition [kən'dɪʃən] n condition f; (disease) maladie f ▷ vt déterminer, conditionner; **in good/poor ~** en bon/mauvais état; **a heart ~** une maladie cardiaque; **weather ~s** conditions fpl météorologiques; **on ~ that** à condition que + sub, à condition de

conditional [kən'dɪʃənl] adj conditionnel(le); **to be ~ upon** dépendre de

conditioner [kən'dɪʃənər] n (for hair) baume démêlant; (for fabrics) assouplissant m

condo ['kɔndəu] n (US inf) = **condominium**

condolences [kən'dəulənsɪz] npl condoléances fpl

condom ['kɔndəm] n préservatif m

condominium [kɔndə'mɪnɪəm] n (US: building) immeuble m (en copropriété); (: rooms) appartement m (dans un immeuble en copropriété)

condone [kən'dəun] vt fermer les yeux sur, approuver (tacitement)

conducive [kən'dju:sɪv] adj: **~ to** favorable à, qui contribue à

conduct n ['kɔndʌkt] conduite f ▷ vt [kən'dʌkt] conduire; (manage) mener, diriger; (Mus) diriger; **to ~ o.s.** se conduire, se comporter

conductor [kən'dʌktər] n (of orchestra) chef m d'orchestre; (on bus) receveur m; (US: on train) chef m de train; (Elec) conducteur m

conductress [kən'dʌktrɪs] n (on bus) receveuse f

cone [kəun] n cône m; (for ice-cream) cornet m; (Bot) pomme f de pin, cône

confectioner [kən'fɛkʃənər] n (of cakes) pâtissier(-ière); (of sweets) confiseur(-euse); **~'s (shop)** confiserie(-pâtisserie) f

confectionery [kən'fɛkʃənrɪ] n (sweets) confiserie f; (cakes) pâtisserie f

confer [kən'fə:r] vt: **to ~ sth on** conférer qch à ▷ vi conférer, s'entretenir; **to ~ (with sb about sth)** s'entretenir (de qch avec qn)

conference ['kɔnfərns] n conférence f; **to be in ~** être en réunion or en conférence

confess [kən'fɛs] vt confesser, avouer ▷ vi (admit sth) avouer; (Rel) se confesser

confession [kən'fɛʃən] n confession f

confetti [kən'fɛtɪ] n confettis mpl

confide [kən'faɪd] vi: **to ~ in** s'ouvrir à, se confier à

confidence ['kɔnfɪdns] n confiance f; (also: **self-confidence**) assurance f, confiance en soi; (secret) confidence f; **to have (every) ~ that** être certain que; **motion of no ~** motion f de censure; **in ~ (speak, write)** en confidence, confidentiellement; **to tell sb sth in strict ~** dire qch à qn en toute confidence

confidence trick n escroquerie f

confident ['kɔnfɪdənt] adj (self-assured) sûr(e) de soi; (sure) sûr

confidential [kɔnfɪ'dɛnʃəl] adj confidentiel(le); (secretary) particulier(-ère)

confine [kən'faɪn] vt limiter, borner; (shut up) confiner, enfermer; **to ~ o.s. to doing sth/to sth** se contenter de faire qch/se limiter à qch

confined [kən'faɪnd] adj (space) restreint(e), réduit(e)

confinement [kən'faɪnmənt] n emprisonnement m, détention f; (Mil) consigne f (au quartier); (Med) accouchement m

confines ['kɔnfaɪnz] npl confins mpl, bornes fpl

confirm [kən'fə:m] vt (report, Rel) confirmer; (appointment) ratifier

confirmation [kɔnfə'meɪʃən] n confirmation f; ratification f

confirmed [kən'fə:md] adj invétéré(e), incorrigible

confiscate ['kɔnfɪskeɪt] vt confisquer

conflict n ['kɔnflɪkt] conflit m, lutte f ▷ vi [kən'flɪkt] être or entrer en conflit; (opinions) s'opposer, se heurter

conflicting [kən'flɪktɪŋ] adj contradictoire

conform [kən'fɔ:m] vi: **to ~ (to)** se conformer (à)

confound [kən'faund] vt confondre; (amaze) rendre perplexe

confront [kən'frʌnt] vt (two people) confronter; (enemy, danger) affronter, faire face à; (problem) faire face à

confrontation [kɔnfrən'teɪʃən] n confrontation f

confuse [kən'fju:z] vt (person) troubler; (situation) embrouiller; (one thing with another) confondre

confused [kən'fju:zd] adj (person) dérouté(e), désorienté(e); (situation) embrouillé(e)

confusing [kən'fju:zɪŋ] adj peu clair(e), déroutant(e)

confusion [kən'fju:ʒən] n confusion f

congeal [kən'dʒi:l] vi (oil) se figer; (blood) se coaguler

congenial [kən'dʒi:nɪəl] adj sympathique, agréable

congested [kən'dʒɛstɪd] adj (Med) congestionné(e); (fig) surpeuplé(e); congestionné; bloqué(e); (telephone lines) encombré(e)

congestion [kən'dʒɛstʃən] n (Med) congestion f; (fig: traffic) encombrement m

congratulate [kən'grætjuleɪt] vt: **to ~ sb (on)** féliciter qn (de)

congratulations [kəngrætju'leɪʃənz] npl: **~ (on)** félicitations fpl (pour) ▷ excl: **~!** (toutes mes) félicitations!

congregate ['kɔŋgrɪgeɪt] vi se rassembler, se réunir

congregation [kɔŋgrɪ'geɪʃən] n assemblée f (des fidèles)

congress ['kɔŋgrɛs] n congrès m; (Pol): **C-** Congrès m; voir article

congressman ['kɔŋgrɛsmən] (irreg) n membre m du Congrès

congresswoman ['kɔŋɡrɛswumən] (*irreg*) *n*
membre *m* du Congrès

conifer ['kɔnɪfə'] *n* conifère *m*

conjugate ['kɔndʒuɡeɪt] *vt* conjuguer

conjugation [kɔndʒə'ɡeɪʃən] *n* conjugaison *f*

conjunction [kən'dʒʌŋkʃən] *n* conjonction *f*; **in
~ with** (conjointement) avec

conjunctivitis [kəndʒʌŋktɪ'vaɪtɪs] *n*
conjonctivite *f*

conjure ['kʌndʒə'] *vt* faire apparaître (par la
prestidigitation) [kən'dʒuə'] conjurer, supplier
▷ *vi* faire des tours de passe-passe
▶ **conjure up** *vt* (*ghost, spirit*) faire apparaître;
(*memories*) évoquer

conjurer ['kʌndʒərə'] *n* prestidigitateur *m*,
illusionniste *m/f*

conman ['kɔnmæn] (*irreg*) *n* escroc *m*

connect [kə'nɛkt] *vt* joindre, relier; (*Elec*)
connecter; (*Tel: caller*) mettre en connexion;
(: *subscriber*) brancher; (*fig*) établir un rapport
entre, faire un rapprochement entre ▷ *vi* (*train*):
to ~ with assurer la correspondance avec; **to
be ~ed with** avoir un rapport avec; (*have dealings
with*) avoir des rapports avec, être en relation
avec; **I am trying to ~ you** (*Tel*) j'essaie d'obtenir
votre communication

connecting flight *n* (vol *m* de) correspondance *f*

connection [kə'nɛkʃən] *n* relation *f*, lien *m*; (*Elec*)
connexion *f*; (*Tel*) communication *f*; (*train etc*)
correspondance *f*; **in ~ with** à propos de; **what is
the ~ between them?** quel est le lien entre eux?;
business ~s relations d'affaires; **to miss/get
one's ~** (*train etc*) rater/avoir sa correspondance

connive [kə'naɪv] *vi*: **to ~ at** se faire le complice
de

conquer ['kɔŋkə'] *vt* conquérir; (*feelings*) vaincre,
surmonter

conquest ['kɔŋkwɛst] *n* conquête *f*

cons [kɔnz] *npl see* **convenience; pro**

conscience ['kɔnʃəns] *n* conscience *f*; **in all ~** en
conscience

conscientious [kɔnʃɪ'ɛnʃəs] *adj*
consciencieux(-euse); (*scruple, objection*) de
conscience

conscious ['kɔnʃəs] *adj* conscient(e); (*deliberate:
insult, error*) délibéré(e); **to become ~ of sth/that**
prendre conscience de qch/que

consciousness ['kɔnʃəsnɪs] *n* conscience *f*;
(*Med*) connaissance *f*; **to lose/regain ~** perdre/
reprendre connaissance

conscript ['kɔnskrɪpt] *n* conscrit *m*

consecutive [kən'sɛkjutɪv] *adj* consécutif(-ive);
on three ~ occasions trois fois de suite

consensus [kən'sɛnsəs] *n* consensus *m*; **the ~ (of
opinion)** le consensus (d'opinion)

consent [kən'sɛnt] *n* consentement *m* ▷ *vi*: **to ~
(to)** consentir (à); **age of ~** âge nubile (légal); **by
common ~** d'un commun accord

consequence ['kɔnsɪkwəns] *n* suites *fpl*,
conséquence *f*; (*significance*) importance *f*; **in ~** en
conséquence, par conséquent

consequently ['kɔnsɪkwəntlɪ] *adv* par

conséquent, donc

conservation [kɔnsə'veɪʃən] *n* préservation *f*,
protection *f*; (*also*: **nature conservation**) défense
f de l'environnement; **energy ~** économies *fpl*
d'énergie

conservative [kən'sə:vətɪv] *adj*
conservateur(-trice); (*cautious*) prudent(e)

Conservative [kən'sə:vətɪv] *adj, n* (*Brit Pol*)
conservateur(-trice); **the ~ Party** le parti
conservateur

conservatory [kən'sə:vətrɪ] *n* (*room*) jardin *m*
d'hiver; (*Mus*) conservatoire *m*

conserve [kən'sə:v] *vt* conserver, préserver;
(*supplies, energy*) économiser ▷ *n* confiture *f*,
conserve *f* (de fruits)

consider [kən'sɪdə'] *vt* (*study*) considérer,
réfléchir à; (*take into account*) penser à, prendre en
considération; (*regard, judge*) considérer, estimer;
to ~ doing sth envisager de faire qch; **~ yourself
lucky** estimez-vous heureux; **all things ~ed**
(toute) réflexion faite

considerable [kən'sɪdərəbl] *adj* considérable

considerably [kən'sɪdərəblɪ] *adv* nettement

considerate [kən'sɪdərɪt] *adj* prévenant(e),
plein(e) d'égards

consideration [kənsɪdə'reɪʃən] *n* considération
f; (*reward*) rétribution *f*, rémunération *f*; **out of ~
for** par égard pour; **under ~** à l'étude; **my first
~ is my family** ma famille passe avant tout le
reste

considering [kən'sɪdərɪŋ] *prep*: **~ (that)** étant
donné (que)

consign [kən'saɪn] *vt* expédier, livrer

consignment [kən'saɪnmənt] *n* arrivage *m*,
envoi *m*

consist [kən'sɪst] *vi*: **to ~ of** consister en, se
composer de

consistency [kən'sɪstənsɪ] *n* (*thickness*)
consistance *f*; (*fig*) cohérence *f*

consistent [kən'sɪstənt] *adj* logique,
cohérent(e); **~ with** compatible avec, en accord
avec

consolation [kɔnsə'leɪʃən] *n* consolation *f*

console¹ [kən'səul] *vt* consoler

console² ['kɔnsəul] *n* console *f*

consonant ['kɔnsənənt] *n* consonne *f*

conspicuous [kən'spɪkjuəs] *adj* voyant(e),
qui attire l'attention; **to make o.s. ~** se faire
remarquer

conspiracy [kən'spɪrəsɪ] *n* conspiration *f*,
complot *m*

constable ['kʌnstəbl] *n* (*Brit*) ≈ agent *m* de police,
gendarme *m*; **chief ~** ≈ préfet *m* de police

constabulary [kən'stæbjulərɪ] *n* ≈ police *f*,
gendarmerie *f*

constant ['kɔnstənt] *adj* constant(e);
incessant(e)

constantly ['kɔnstəntlɪ] *adv* constamment, sans
cesse

constipated ['kɔnstɪpeɪtɪd] *adj* constipé(e)

constipation [kɔnstɪ'peɪʃən] *n* constipation *f*

constituency [kən'stɪtjuənsɪ] *n* (*Pol: area*)

circonscription électorale; (: *electors*) électorat *m*; *voir* article

constituent [kən'stɪtjuənt] *n* électeur(-trice); (*part*) élément constitutif, composant *m*

constitute ['kɔnstɪtjuːt] *vt* constituer

constitution [kɔnstɪ'tjuːʃən] *n* constitution *f*

constitutional [kɔnstɪ'tjuːʃnl] *adj* constitutionnel(le)

constraint [kən'streɪnt] *n* contrainte *f*; (*embarrassment*) gêne *f*

construct [kən'strʌkt] *vt* construire

construction [kən'strʌkʃən] *n* construction *f*; (*fig: interpretation*) interprétation *f*; **under ~** (*building etc*) en construction

constructive [kən'strʌktɪv] *adj* constructif(-ive)

consul ['kɔnsl] *n* consul *m*

consulate ['kɔnsjulɪt] *n* consulat *m*

consult [kən'sʌlt] *vt* consulter; **to ~ sb (about sth)** consulter qn (à propos de qch)

consultant [kən'sʌltənt] *n* (*Med*) médecin consultant; (*other specialist*) consultant *m*, (expert-)conseil *m* ▷ *cpd*: **~ engineer** *n* ingénieur-conseil *m*; **~ paediatrician ~** pédiatre *m*; **legal/management ~** conseiller *m* juridique/en gestion

consultation [kɔnsəl'teɪʃən] *n* consultation *f*; **in ~ with** en consultation avec

consulting room [kən'sʌltɪŋ-] *n* (*Brit*) cabinet *m* de consultation

consume [kən'sjuːm] *vt* consommer; (*subj: flames, hatred, desire*) consumer; **to be ~d with hatred** être dévoré par la haine; **to be ~d with desire** brûler de désir

consumer [kən'sjuːmər] *n* consommateur(-trice); (*of electricity, gas etc*) usager *m*

consumer goods *npl* biens *mpl* de consommation

consumer society *n* société *f* de consommation

consummate ['kɔnsʌmeɪt] *vt* consommer

consumption [kən'sʌmpʃən] *n* consommation *f*; **not fit for human ~** non comestible

cont. *abbr* (= *continued*) suite

contact ['kɔntækt] *n* contact *m*; (*person*) connaissance *f*, relation *f* ▷ *vt* se mettre en contact or en rapport avec; **to be in ~ with sb/sth** être en contact avec qn/qch; **business ~s** relations *fpl* d'affaires, contacts *mpl*

contact lenses *npl* verres *mpl* de contact

contagious [kən'teɪdʒəs] *adj* contagieux(-euse)

contain [kən'teɪn] *vt* contenir; **to ~ o.s.** se contenir, se maîtriser

container [kən'teɪnər] *n* récipient *m*; (*for shipping etc*) conteneur *m*

contaminate [kən'tæmɪneɪt] *vt* contaminer

cont'd *abbr* (= *continued*) suite

contemplate ['kɔntəmpleɪt] *vt* contempler; (*consider*) envisager

contemporary [kən'tempərərɪ] *adj* contemporain(e); (*design, wallpaper*) moderne ▷ *n* contemporain(e)

contempt [kən'tempt] *n* mépris *m*, dédain *m*; **~**

of court (*Law*) outrage *m* à l'autorité de la justice

contemptuous [kən'temptjuəs] *adj* dédaigneux(-euse), méprisant(e)

contend [kən'tend] *vt*: **to ~ that** soutenir or prétendre que ▷ *vi*: **to ~ with** (*compete*) rivaliser avec; (*struggle*) lutter avec; **to have to ~ with** (*be faced with*) avoir affaire à, être aux prises avec

contender [kən'tendər] *n* prétendant(e); candidat(e)

content [kən'tent] *adj* content(e), satisfait(e) ▷ *vt* contenter, satisfaire ▷ *n* ['kɔntent] contenu *m*; (*of fat, moisture*) teneur *f*; **contents** *npl* (*of container etc*) contenu *m*; (**table of**) **~s** table *f* des matières; **to be ~ with** se contenter de; **to ~ o.s. with sth/with doing sth** se contenter de qch/de faire qch

contented [kən'tentɪd] *adj* content(e), satisfait(e)

contention [kən'tenʃən] *n* dispute *f*, contestation *f*; (*argument*) assertion *f*, affirmation *f*; **bone of ~** sujet *m* de discorde

contest *n* ['kɔntest] combat *m*, lutte *f*; (*competition*) concours *m* ▷ *vt* [kən'test] contester, discuter; (*compete for*) disputer; (*Law*) attaquer

contestant [kən'testənt] *n* concurrent(e); (*in fight*) adversaire *m/f*

context ['kɔntekst] *n* contexte *m*; **in/out of ~** dans le/hors contexte

continent ['kɔntɪnənt] *n* continent *m*; **the C~** (*Brit*) l'Europe continentale; **on the C~** en Europe (continentale)

continental [kɔntɪ'nentl] *adj* continental(e) ▷ *n* (*Brit*) Européen(ne) (continental(e))

continental breakfast *n* café (or thé) complet

continental quilt *n* (*Brit*) couette *f*

contingency [kən'tɪndʒənsɪ] *n* éventualité *f*, événement imprévu

continual [kən'tɪnjuəl] *adj* continuel(le)

continually [kən'tɪnjuəlɪ] *adv* continuellement, sans cesse

continuation [kəntɪnju'eɪʃən] *n* continuation *f*; (*after interruption*) reprise *f*; (*of story*) suite *f*

continue [kən'tɪnjuː] *vi* continuer ▷ *vt* continuer; (*start again*) reprendre; **to be ~d** (*story*) à suivre; **~d on page 10** suite page 10

continuity [kɔntɪ'njuːɪtɪ] *n* continuité *f*; (*TV*) enchaînement *m*; (*Cine*) script *m*

continuous [kən'tɪnjuəs] *adj* continu(e), permanent(e); (*Ling*) progressif(-ive); **~ performance** (*Cine*) séance permanente; **~ stationery** (*Comput*) papier *m* en continu

continuous assessment (*Brit*) *n* contrôle continu

continuously [kən'tɪnjuəslɪ] *adv* (*repeatedly*) continuellement; (*uninterruptedly*) sans interruption

contort [kən'tɔːt] *vt* tordre, crisper

contour ['kɔntuər] *n* contour *m*, profil *m*; (*also:* **contour line**) courbe *f* de niveau

contraband ['kɔntrəbænd] *n* contrebande *f* ▷ *adj* de contrebande

contraception [kɔntrə'sepʃən] *n* contraception *f*

contraceptive [kɒntrəˈsɛptɪv] *adj* contraceptif(-ive), anticonceptionnel(le) ▷ *n* contraceptif *m*

contract [*n, cpd* ˈkɒntrækt, *vb* kənˈtrækt] *n* contrat *m* ▷ *cpd* (*price, date*) contractuel(le); (*work*) à forfait ▷ *vi* (*become smaller*) se contracter, se resserrer ▷ *vt* contracter; (*Comm*): **to ~ to do sth** s'engager (par contrat) à faire qch; **~ of employment/service** contrat de travail/de service

  ▶ **contract in** *vi* s'engager (par contrat); (*Brit Admin*) s'affilier au régime de retraite complémentaire

  ▶ **contract out** *vi* se dégager; (*Brit Admin*) opter pour la non-affiliation au régime de retraite complémentaire

contraction [kənˈtrækʃən] *n* contraction *f*; (*Ling*) forme contractée

contractor [kənˈtræktəʳ] *n* entrepreneur *m*

contradict [kɒntrəˈdɪkt] *vt* contredire; (*be contrary to*) démentir, être en contradiction avec

contradiction [kɒntrəˈdɪkʃən] *n* contradiction *f*; **to be in ~ with** contredire, être en contradiction avec

contraflow [ˈkɒntrəfləu] *n* (*Aut*): **~ lane** voie *f* à contresens; **there's a ~ system in operation on ...** une voie a été mise en sens inverse sur ...

contraption [kənˈtræpʃən] *n* (*pej*) machin *m*, truc *m*

contrary¹ [ˈkɒntrərɪ] *adj* contraire, opposé(e) ▷ *n* contraire *m*; **on the ~** au contraire; **unless you hear to the ~** sauf avis contraire; **~ to what we thought** contrairement à ce que nous pensions

contrary² [kənˈtrɛərɪ] *adj* (*perverse*) contrariant(e), entêté(e)

contrast *n* [ˈkɒntrɑːst] contraste *m* ▷ *vt* [kənˈtrɑːst] mettre en contraste, contraster; **in ~ to** *or* **with** contrairement à, par opposition à

contravene [kɒntrəˈviːn] *vt* enfreindre, violer, contrevenir à

contribute [kənˈtrɪbjuːt] *vi* contribuer ▷ *vt*: **to ~ £10/an article to** donner 10 livres/un article à; **to ~ to** (*gen*) contribuer à; (*newspaper*) collaborer à; (*discussion*) prendre part à

contribution [kɒntrɪˈbjuːʃən] *n* contribution *f*; (*Brit: for social security*) cotisation *f*; (*to publication*) article *m*

contributor [kənˈtrɪbjutəʳ] *n* (*to newspaper*) collaborateur(-trice); (*of money, goods*) donateur(-trice)

contrive [kənˈtraɪv] *vt* combiner, inventer ▷ *vi*: **to ~ to do** s'arranger pour faire, trouver le moyen de faire

control [kənˈtrəul] *vt* (*process, machinery*) commander; (*temper*) maîtriser; (*disease*) enrayer; (*check*) contrôler ▷ *n* maîtrise *f*; (*power*) autorité *f*; **controls** *npl* (*of machine etc*) commandes *fpl*; (*on radio*) boutons *mpl* de réglage; **to take ~ of** se rendre maître de; (*Comm*) acquérir une participation majoritaire dans; **to be in ~ of** être maître de, maîtriser; (*in charge of*) être responsable de; **to ~ o.s.** se contrôler;

everything is under ~ j'ai (*or* il a *etc*) la situation en main; **the car went out of ~** j'ai (*or* il a *etc*) perdu le contrôle du véhicule; **beyond our ~** indépendant(e) de notre volonté

control panel *n* (*on aircraft, ship, TV etc*) tableau *m* de commandes

control room *n* (*Naut Mil*) salle *f* des commandes; (*Radio, TV*) régie *f*

control tower *n* (*Aviat*) tour *f* de contrôle

controversial [kɒntrəˈvəːʃl] *adj* discutable, controversé(e)

controversy [ˈkɒntrəvəːsɪ] *n* controverse *f*, polémique *f*

convalesce [kɒnvəˈlɛs] *vi* relever de maladie, se remettre (d'une maladie)

convector [kənˈvɛktəʳ] *n* radiateur *m* à convection, appareil *m* de chauffage par convection

convene [kənˈviːn] *vt* convoquer, assembler ▷ *vi* se réunir, s'assembler

convenience [kənˈviːnɪəns] *n* commodité *f*; **at your ~** quand *or* comme cela vous convient; **at your earliest ~** (*Comm*) dans les meilleurs délais, le plus tôt possible; **all modern ~s, all mod cons** (*Brit*) avec tout le confort moderne, tout confort

convenient [kənˈviːnɪənt] *adj* commode; **if it is ~ to you** si cela vous convient, si cela ne vous dérange pas

convent [ˈkɒnvənt] *n* couvent *m*

convention [kənˈvɛnʃən] *n* convention *f*; (*custom*) usage *m*

conventional [kənˈvɛnʃənl] *adj* conventionnel(le)

convent school *n* couvent *m*

conversant [kənˈvəːsnt] *adj*: **to be ~ with** s'y connaître en; être au courant de

conversation [kɒnvəˈseɪʃən] *n* conversation *f*

converse [ˈkɒnvəːs] *n* contraire *m*, inverse *m* ▷ *vi* [kənˈvəːs]: **to ~ (with sb about sth)** s'entretenir (avec qn de qch)

conversely [kɒnˈvəːslɪ] *adv* inversement, réciproquement

conversion [kənˈvəːʃən] *n* conversion *f*; (*Brit: of house*) transformation *f*, aménagement *m*; (*Rugby*) transformation *f*

convert *vt* [kənˈvəːt] (*Rel, Comm*) convertir; (*alter*) transformer; (*house*) aménager; (*Rugby*) transformer ▷ *n* [ˈkɒnvəːt] converti(e)

convertible [kənˈvəːtəbl] *adj* convertible ▷ *n* (*voiture f*) décapotable *f*

convey [kənˈveɪ] *vt* transporter; (*thanks*) transmettre; (*idea*) communiquer

conveyor belt [kənˈveɪəʳ-] *n* convoyeur *m* tapis roulant

convict *vt* [kənˈvɪkt] déclarer (*or* reconnaître) coupable ▷ *n* [ˈkɒnvɪkt] forçat *m*, convict *m*

conviction [kənˈvɪkʃən] *n* (*Law*) condamnation *f*; (*belief*) conviction *f*

convince [kənˈvɪns] *vt* convaincre, persuader; **to ~ sb (of sth/that)** persuader qn (de qch/que)

convinced [kənˈvɪnst] *adj*: **~ of/that**

convaincu(e) de/que

convincing [kən'vɪnsɪŋ] *adj* persuasif(-ive), convaincant(e)

convoluted ['kɔnvəlu:tɪd] *adj* (*shape*) tarabiscoté(e); (*argument*) compliqué(e)

convoy ['kɔnvɔɪ] *n* convoi *m*

convulse [kən'vʌls] *vt* ébranler; **to be ~d with laughter** se tordre de rire

cook [kuk] *vt* (*faire*) cuire ▷ *vi* cuire; (*person*) faire la cuisine ▷ *n* cuisinier(-ière)
  ▶ **cook up** *vt* (*inf: excuse, story*) inventer

cookbook ['kukbuk] *n* livre *m* de cuisine

cooker ['kukə^r] *n* cuisinière *f*

cookery ['kukərɪ] *n* cuisine *f*

cookery book *n* (*Brit*) = **cookbook**

cookie ['kukɪ] *n* (*US*) biscuit *m*, petit gâteau sec

cooking ['kukɪŋ] *n* cuisine *f* ▷ *cpd* (*apples, chocolate*) à cuire; (*utensils, salt*) de cuisine

cool [ku:l] *adj* frais (fraîche); (*not afraid*) calme; (*unfriendly*) froid(e); (*impertinent*) effronté(e); (*inf: trendy*) cool *inv* (*inf*); (*: great*) super *inv* (*inf*) ▷ *vt, vi* rafraîchir, refroidir; **it's ~** (*weather*) il fait frais; **to keep sth ~** *or* **in a ~ place** garder *or* conserver qch au frais
  ▶ **cool down** *vi* refroidir; (*fig: person, situation*) se calmer
  ▶ **cool off** *vi* (*become calmer*) se calmer; (*lose enthusiasm*) perdre son enthousiasme

coop [ku:p] *n* poulailler *m* ▷ *vt:* **to ~ up** (*fig*) cloîtrer, enfermer

cooperate [kəu'ɔpəreɪt] *vi* coopérer, collaborer

cooperation [kəuɔpə'reɪʃən] *n* coopération *f*, collaboration *f*

cooperative [kəu'ɔpərətɪv] *adj* coopératif(-ive) ▷ *n* coopérative *f*

coordinate *vt* [kəu'ɔ:dɪneɪt] coordonner ▷ *n* [kəu'ɔdɪnət] (*Math*) coordonnée *f*; **coordinates** *npl* (*clothes*) ensemble *m*, coordonnés *mpl*

co-ownership ['kəu'əunəʃɪp] *n* copropriété *f*

cop [kɔp] *n* (*inf*) flic *m*

cope [kəup] *vi* s'en sortir, tenir le coup; **to ~ with** (*problem*) faire face à; (*take care of*) s'occuper de

copper ['kɔpə^r] *n* cuivre *m*; (*Brit: inf: policeman*) flic *m*; **coppers** *npl* petite monnaie

copy ['kɔpɪ] *n* copie *f*; (*book etc*) exemplaire *m*; (*material: for printing*) copie ▷ *vt* copier; (*imitate*) imiter; **rough ~** (*gen*) premier jet; (*Scol*) brouillon *m*; **fair ~** version définitive; propre *m*; **to make good ~** (*Press*) faire un bon sujet d'article
  ▶ **copy out** *vt* copier

copyright ['kɔpɪraɪt] *n* droit *m* d'auteur, copyright *m*; **~ reserved** tous droits (de reproduction) réservés

coral ['kɔrəl] *n* corail *m*

cord [kɔ:d] *n* corde *f*; (*fabric*) velours côtelé; whipcord *m*; corde *f*; (*Elec*) cordon *m* (d'alimentation), fil *m* (électrique); **cords** *npl* (*trousers*) pantalon *m* de velours côtelé

cordial ['kɔ:dɪəl] *adj* cordial(e), chaleureux(-euse) ▷ *n* sirop *m*; cordial *m*

cordless ['kɔ:dlɪs] *adj* sans fil

cordon ['kɔ:dn] *n* cordon *m*

▶ **cordon off** *vt* (*area*) interdire l'accès à; (*crowd*) tenir à l'écart

corduroy ['kɔ:dərɔɪ] *n* velours côtelé

core [kɔ:^r] *n* (*of fruit*) trognon *m*, cœur *m*; (*Tech: also of earth*) noyau *m*; cœur ▷ *vt* enlever le trognon *or* le cœur de; **rotten to the ~** complètement pourri

coriander [kɔrɪ'ændə^r] *n* coriandre *f*

cork [kɔ:k] *n* (*material*) liège *m*; (*of bottle*) bouchon *m*

corkscrew ['kɔ:kskru:}] *n* tire-bouchon *m*

corn [kɔ:n] *n* (*Brit: wheat*) blé *m*; (*US: maize*) maïs *m*; (*on foot*) cor *m*; **~ on the cob** (*Culin*) épi *m* de maïs au naturel

corned beef ['kɔ:nd-] *n* corned-beef *m*

corner ['kɔ:nə^r] *n* coin *m*; (*in road*) tournant *m*, virage *m*; (*Football: also:* **corner kick**) corner *m* ▷ *vt* (*trap: prey*) acculer; (*fig*) coincer; (*Comm: market*) accaparer ▷ *vi* prendre un virage; **to cut ~s** (*fig*) prendre des raccourcis

corner shop (*Brit*) *n* magasin *m* du coin

cornerstone ['kɔ:nəstəun] *n* pierre *f* angulaire

cornet ['kɔ:nɪt] *n* (*Mus*) cornet *m* à pistons; (*Brit: of ice-cream*) cornet (de glace)

cornflakes ['kɔ:nfleɪks] *npl* cornflakes *mpl*

cornflour ['kɔ:nflauə^r] *n* (*Brit*) farine *f* de maïs, maïzena® *f*

cornstarch ['kɔ:nstɑ:tʃ] *n* (*US*) farine *f* de maïs, maïzena® *f*

Cornwall ['kɔ:nwəl] *n* Cornouailles *f*

corny ['kɔ:nɪ] *adj* (*inf*) rebattu(e), galvaudé(e)

coronary ['kɔrənərɪ] *n:* **~ (thrombosis)** infarctus *m* (du myocarde), thrombose *f* coronaire

coronation [kɔrə'neɪʃən] *n* couronnement *m*

coroner ['kɔrənə^r] *n* coroner *m*, *officier de police judiciaire chargé de déterminer les causes d'un décès*

corporal ['kɔ:pərl] *n* caporal *m*, brigadier *m* ▷ *adj:* **~ punishment** châtiment corporel

corporate ['kɔ:pərɪt] *adj* (*action, ownership*) en commun; (*Comm*) de la société

corporation [kɔ:pə'reɪʃən] *n* (*of town*) municipalité *f*, conseil municipal; (*Comm*) société *f*

corps [kɔ:^r] (*pl* **~**) [kɔ:z] *n* corps *m*; **the diplomatic ~** le corps diplomatique; **the press ~** la presse

corpse [kɔ:ps] *n* cadavre *m*

correct [kə'rɛkt] *adj* (*accurate*) correct(e), exact(e); (*proper*) correct, convenable ▷ *vt* corriger; **you are ~** vous avez raison

correction [kə'rɛkʃən] *n* correction *f*

correspond [kɔrɪs'pɔnd] *vi* correspondre; **to ~ to sth** (*be equivalent to*) correspondre à qch

correspondence [kɔrɪs'pɔndəns] *n* correspondance *f*

correspondence course *n* cours *m* par correspondance

correspondent [kɔrɪs'pɔndənt] *n* correspondant(e)

corresponding [kɔrɪs'pɔndɪŋ] *adj* correspondant(e)

corridor ['kɔrɪdɔ:^r] *n* couloir *m*, corridor *m*

corrode [kə'rəud] *vt* corroder, ronger ▷ *vi* se

corroder

corrugated ['kɔrəgeɪtɪd] *adj* plissé(e); ondulé(e)

corrugated iron *n* tôle ondulée

corrupt [kə'rʌpt] *adj* corrompu(e); (*Comput*) altéré(e) ▷ *vt* corrompre; (*Comput*) altérer; ~ **practices** (*dishonesty, bribery*) malversation *f*

corruption [kə'rʌpʃən] *n* corruption *f*; (*Comput*) altération *f* (de données)

Corsica ['kɔ:sɪkə] *n* Corse *f*

cosmetic [kɔz'mɛtɪk] *n* produit *m* de beauté, cosmétique *m* ▷ *adj* (*preparation*) cosmétique; (*fig: reforms*) symbolique, superficiel(le)

cosmetic surgery *n* chirurgie *f* esthétique

cosmopolitan [kɔzmə'pɔlɪtn] *adj* cosmopolite

cost [kɔst] (*pt, pp* -) *n* coût *m* ▷ *vi* coûter ▷ *vt* établir *or* calculer le prix de revient de; **costs** *npl* (*Comm*) frais *mpl*; (*Law*) dépens *mpl*; **how much does it** ~? combien ça coûte?; **it** ~**s £5/too much** cela coûte 5 livres/trop cher; **what will it** ~ **to have it repaired?** combien cela coûtera de le faire réparer?; **to** ~ **sb time/effort** demander du temps/un effort à qn; **it** ~ **him his life/job** ça lui a coûté la vie/son emploi; **at all** ~**s** coûte que coûte, à tout prix

co-star ['kəustɑ:ʳ] *n* partenaire *m/f*

cost-effective ['kɔstɪ'fɛktɪv] *adj* rentable

costly ['kɔstlɪ] *adj* coûteux(-euse)

cost of living ['kɔstəv'lɪvɪŋ] *n* coût *m* de la vie ▷ *adj*: ~ **allowance** indemnité *f* de vie chère; ~ **index** indice *m* du coût de la vie

cost price *n* (*Brit*) prix coûtant *or* de revient

costume ['kɔstju:m] *n* costume *m*; (*lady's suit*) tailleur *m*; (*Brit: also:* **swimming costume**) maillot *m* (de bain)

costume jewellery *n* bijoux *mpl* de fantaisie

cosy, (*US*) **cozy** ['kəuzɪ] *adj* (*room, bed*) douillet(te); (*scarf, gloves*) bien chaud(e); (*atmosphere*) chaleureux(-euse); **to be** ~ (*person*) être bien (au chaud)

cot [kɔt] *n* (*Brit: child's*) lit *m* d'enfant, petit lit; (*US: campbed*) lit de camp

cottage ['kɔtɪdʒ] *n* petite maison (à la campagne), cottage *m*

cottage cheese *n* fromage blanc (*maigre*)

cotton ['kɔtn] *n* coton *m*; (*thread*) fil *m* (de coton); ~ **dress** *etc* robe *etc* en *or* de coton

▶ **cotton on** *vi* (*inf*): **to** ~ **on (to sth)** piger (qch)

cotton bud (*Brit*) *n* coton-tige ® *m*

cotton candy (*US*) *n* barbe *f* à papa

cotton wool *n* (*Brit*) ouate *f*, coton *m* hydrophile

couch [kautʃ] *n* canapé *m*; divan *m*; (*doctor's*) table *f* d'examen; (*psychiatrist's*) divan ▷ *vt* formuler, exprimer

couchette [ku:'ʃɛt] *n* couchette *f*

cough [kɔf] *vi* tousser ▷ *n* toux *f*; **I've got a** ~ j'ai la toux

cough mixture, cough syrup *n* sirop *m* pour la toux

cough sweet *n* pastille *f* pour *or* contre la toux

could [kud] *pt of* **can²**

couldn't ['kudnt] = **could not**

council ['kaunsl] *n* conseil *m*; **city** *or* **town** ~

conseil municipal; **C~ of Europe** Conseil de l'Europe

council estate *n* (*Brit*) (quartier *m or* zone *f* de) logements loués à/par la municipalité

council house *n* (*Brit*) maison *f* (à loyer modéré) louée par la municipalité

councillor, (*US*) **councilor** ['kaunsləʳ] *n* conseiller(-ère)

council tax *n* (*Brit*) impôts locaux

counsel ['kaunsl] *n* conseil *m*; (*lawyer*) avocat(e) ▷ *vt*: **to** ~ **(sb to do sth)** conseiller (à qn de faire qch); ~ **for the defence/the prosecution** (avocat de la) défense/avocat du ministère public

counselling, (*US*) **counseling** ['kaunslɪŋ] *n* (*Psych*) aide psychosociale

counsellor, (*US*) **counselor** ['kaunsləʳ] *n* conseiller(-ère); (*US Law*) avocat *m*

count [kaunt] *vt, vi* compter ▷ *n* compte *m*; (*nobleman*) comte *m*; **to** ~ **(up) to 10** compter jusqu'à 10; **to keep** ~ **of sth** tenir le compte de qch; **not** ~**ing the children** sans compter les enfants; **10** ~**ing him** 10 avec lui, 10 en le comptant; **to** ~ **the cost of** établir le coût de; **it** ~**s for very little** cela n'a pas beaucoup d'importance; ~ **yourself lucky** estimez-vous heureux

▶ **count in** *vt* (*inf*): **to** ~ **sb in on sth** inclure qn dans qch

▶ **count on** *vt fus* compter sur; **to** ~ **on doing sth** compter faire qch

▶ **count up** *vt* compter, additionner

countdown ['kauntdaun] *n* compte *m* à rebours

countenance ['kauntɪnəns] *n* expression *f* ▷ *vt* approuver

counter ['kauntəʳ] *n* comptoir *m*; (*in post office, bank*) guichet *m*; (*in game*) jeton *m* ▷ *vt* aller à l'encontre de, opposer; (*blow*) parer ▷ *adv*: ~ **to** à l'encontre de; contrairement à; **to buy under the** ~ (*fig*) acheter sous le manteau *or* en sous-main; **to** ~ **sth with sth/by doing sth** contrer *or* riposter à qch par qch/en faisant qch

counteract ['kauntər'ækt] *vt* neutraliser, contrebalancer

counterclockwise ['kauntə'klɔkwaɪz] (*US*) *adv* en sens inverse des aiguilles d'une montre

counterfeit ['kauntəfɪt] *n* faux *m*, contrefaçon *f* ▷ *vt* contrefaire ▷ *adj* faux (fausse)

counterfoil ['kauntəfɔɪl] *n* talon *m*, souche *f*

counterpart ['kauntəpɑ:t] *n* (*of document etc*) double *m*; (*of person*) homologue *m/f*

countess ['kauntɪs] *n* comtesse *f*

countless ['kauntlɪs] *adj* innombrable

country ['kʌntrɪ] *n* pays *m*; (*native land*) patrie *f*; (*as opposed to town*) campagne *f*; (*region*) région *f*, pays; **in the** ~ à la campagne; **mountainous** ~ pays de montagne, région montagneuse

country and western, country and western music *n* musique *f* country

country dancing *n* (*Brit*) danse *f* folklorique

country house *n* manoir *m*, (petit) château

countryman ['kʌntrɪmən] (*irreg*) *n* (*national*)

compatriote *m*; (*rural*) habitant *m* de la campagne, campagnard *m*

countryside ['kʌntrɪsaɪd] *n* campagne *f*

county ['kauntɪ] *n* comté *m*

coup [kuː'] (*pl* **-s**) [kuːz] *n* (*achievement*) beau coup; (*also*: **coup d'état**) coup d'État

couple ['kʌpl] *n* couple *m* ▷ *vt* (*carriages*) atteler; (*Tech*) coupler; (*ideas, names*) associer; **a ~ of** (*two*) deux; (*a few*) deux ou trois

coupon ['kuːpɔn] *n* (*voucher*) bon *m* de réduction; (*detachable form*) coupon *m* détachable, coupon-réponse *m*; (*Finance*) coupon

courage ['kʌrɪdʒ] *n* courage *m*

courageous [kə'reɪdʒəs] *adj* courageux(-euse)

courgette [kuə'ʒɛt] *n* (*Brit*) courgette *f*

courier ['kurɪə'] *n* messager *m*, courrier *m*; (*for tourists*) accompagnateur(-trice)

course [kɔːs] *n* cours *m*; (*of ship*) route *f*; (*for golf*) terrain *m*; (*part of meal*) plat *m*; **first ~** entrée *f*; **of ~** (*adv*) bien sûr; **(no,) of ~ not!** bien sûr que non!, évidemment que non!; **in the ~ of** au cours de; **in the ~ of the next few days** au cours des prochains jours; **in due ~** en temps utile or voulu; **~ (of action)** parti *m*, ligne *f* de conduite; **the best ~ would be to ...** le mieux serait de ...; **we have no other ~ but to ...** nous n'avons pas d'autre solution que de ...; **~ of lectures** série *f* de conférences; **~ of treatment** (*Med*) traitement *m*

court [kɔːt] *n* cour *f*; (*Law*) cour, tribunal *m*; (*Tennis*) court *m* ▷ *vt* (*woman*) courtiser, faire la cour à; (*fig: favour, popularity*) rechercher; (: *death, disaster*) courir après, flirter avec; **out of ~** (*Law: settle*) à l'amiable; **to take to ~** actionner or poursuivre en justice; **~ of appeal** cour d'appel

courteous ['kə:tɪəs] *adj* courtois(e), poli(e)

courtesy ['kə:təsɪ] *n* courtoisie *f*, politesse *f*; **(by) ~ of** avec l'aimable autorisation de

courtesy bus, courtesy coach *n* navette gratuite

court-house ['kɔ:thaus] *n* (*US*) palais *m* de justice

courtier ['kɔ:tɪə'] *n* courtisan *m*, dame *f* de cour

court martial (*pl* **courts martial**) *n* cour martiale, conseil *m* de guerre

courtroom ['kɔ:trum] *n* salle *f* de tribunal

courtyard ['kɔ:tja:d] *n* cour *f*

cousin ['kʌzn] *n* cousin(e); **first ~** cousin(e) germain(e)

cove [kəuv] *n* petite baie, anse *f*

covenant ['kʌvənənt] *n* contrat *m*, engagement *m* ▷ *vt*: **to ~ £200 per year to a charity** s'engager à verser 200 livres par an à une œuvre de bienfaisance

cover ['kʌvə'] *vt* couvrir; (*Press: report on*) faire un reportage sur; (*feelings, mistake*) cacher; (*include*) englober; (*discuss*) traiter ▷ *n* (*of book, Comm*) couverture *f*; (*of pan*) couvercle *m*; (*over furniture*) housse *f*; (*shelter*) abri *m*; **covers** *npl* (*on bed*) couvertures; **to take ~** se mettre à l'abri; **under ~** à l'abri; **under ~ of darkness** à la faveur de la nuit; **under separate ~** (*Comm*) sous pli séparé;

£10 will ~ everything 10 livres suffiront (pour tout payer)

▶ **cover up** *vt* (*person, object*): **to ~ up (with)** couvrir (de); (*fig: truth, facts*) occulter ▷ *vi*: **to ~ up for sb** (*fig*) couvrir qn

coverage ['kʌvərɪdʒ] *n* (*in media*) reportage *m*; (*Insurance*) couverture *f*

cover charge *n* couvert *m* (*supplément à payer*)

covering ['kʌvərɪŋ] *n* couverture *f*, enveloppe *f*

covering letter, (*US*) **cover letter** *n* lettre explicative

cover note *n* (*Insurance*) police *f* provisoire

covert ['kʌvət] *adj* (*threat*) voilé(e), caché(e); (*attack*) indirect(e); (*glance*) furtif(-ive)

cover-up ['kʌvərʌp] *n* tentative *f* pour étouffer une affaire

covet ['kʌvɪt] *vt* convoiter

cow [kau] *n* vache *f* ▷ *cpd* femelle ▷ *vt* effrayer, intimider

coward ['kauəd] *n* lâche *m/f*

cowardice ['kauədɪs] *n* lâcheté *f*

cowardly ['kauədlɪ] *adj* lâche

cowboy ['kaubɔɪ] *n* cow-boy *m*

cower ['kauə'] *vi* se recroqueviller; trembler

coy [kɔɪ] *adj* faussement effarouché(e) or timide

cozy ['kəuzɪ] *adj* (*US*) = **cosy**

CPA *n abbr* (*US*) = **certified public accountant**

crab [kræb] *n* crabe *m*

crab apple *n* pomme *f* sauvage

crack [kræk] *n* (*split*) fente *f*, fissure *f*; (*in cup, bone*) fêlure *f*; (*in wall*) lézarde *f*; (*noise*) craquement *m*, coup (sec); (*joke*) plaisanterie *f*; (*inf: attempt*): **to have a ~ (at sth)** essayer (qch); (*Drugs*) crack *m* ▷ *vt* fendre, fissurer; fêler; lézarder; (*whip*) faire claquer; (*nut*) casser; (*problem*) résoudre, trouver la clef de; (*code*) déchiffrer ▷ *cpd* (*athlete*) de première classe, d'élite; **to ~ jokes** (*inf*) raconter des blagues; **to get ~ing** (*inf*) s'y mettre, se magner

▶ **crack down on** *vt fus* (*crime*) sévir contre, réprimer; (*spending*) mettre un frein à

▶ **crack up** *vi* être au bout de son rouleau, flancher

cracked [krækt] *adj* (*cup, bone*) fêlé(e); (*broken*) cassé(e); (*wall*) lézardé(e); (*surface*) craquelé(e); (*inf*) toqué(e), timbré(e)

cracker ['krækə'] *n* (*also*: **Christmas cracker**) pétard *m*; (*biscuit*) biscuit (salé), craquelin *m*; **a ~ of a ...** (*Brit inf*) un(e) ... formidable; **he's ~s** (*Brit inf*) il est cinglé

crackle ['krækl] *vi* crépiter, grésiller

cradle ['kreɪdl] *n* berceau *m* ▷ *vt* (*child*) bercer; (*object*) tenir dans ses bras

craft [krɑ:ft] *n* métier (artisanal); (*cunning*) ruse *f*, astuce *f*; (*boat: pl inv*) embarcation *f*, barque *f*; (*plane: pl inv*) appareil *m*

craftsman (*irreg*) ['krɑ:ftsmən] (*irreg*) *n* artisan *m* ouvrier (qualifié)

craftsmanship ['krɑ:ftsmənʃɪp] *n* métier *m*, habileté *f*

crafty ['krɑ:ftɪ] *adj* rusé(e), malin(-igne), astucieux(-euse)

crag [kræg] n rocher escarpé

cram [kræm] vt (fill): **to ~ sth with** bourrer qch de; (put): **to ~ sth into** fourrer qch dans ▷ vi (for exams) bachoter

cramp [kræmp] n crampe f ▷ vt gêner, entraver; **I've got ~ in my leg** j'ai une crampe à la jambe

cramped [kræmpt] adj à l'étroit, très serré(e)

cranberry ['krænbəri] n canneberge f

crane [kreɪn] n grue f ▷ vt, vi: **to ~ forward, to ~ one's neck** allonger le cou

crank [kræŋk] n manivelle f; (person) excentrique m/f

cranny ['kræni] n see **nook**

crap [kræp] n (inf!: nonsense) conneries fpl (!); (: excrement) merde f (!); **the party was ~** la fête était merdique (!); **to have a ~** chier (!)

crash [kræʃ] n (noise) fracas m; (of car, plane) collision f; (of business) faillite f; (Stock Exchange) krach m ▷ vt (plane) écraser ▷ vi (plane) s'écraser; (two cars) se percuter, s'emboutir; (business) s'effondrer; **to ~ into** se jeter or se fracasser contre; **he ~ed the car into a wall** il s'est écrasé contre un mur avec sa voiture

crash course n cours intensif

crash helmet n casque (protecteur)

crash landing n atterrissage forcé or en catastrophe

crate [kreɪt] n cageot m; (for bottles) caisse f

cravat [krə'væt] n foulard (noué autour du cou)

crave [kreɪv] vt, vi: **to ~ (for)** désirer violemment, avoir un besoin physiologique de, avoir une envie irrésistible de

crawl [krɔːl] vi ramper; (vehicle) avancer au pas ▷ n (Swimming) crawl m; **to ~ on one's hands and knees** aller à quatre pattes; **to ~ to sb** (inf) faire de la lèche à qn

crayfish ['kreɪfɪʃ] n (pl inv: freshwater) écrevisse f; (saltwater) langoustine f

crayon ['kreɪən] n crayon m (de couleur)

craze [kreɪz] n engouement m

crazy ['kreɪzɪ] adj fou (folle); **to go ~** devenir fou; **to be ~ about sb/sth** (inf) être fou de qn/qch

creak [kriːk] vi (hinge) grincer; (floor, shoes) craquer

cream [kriːm] n crème f ▷ adj (colour) crème inv; **whipped ~** crème fouettée
▶ **cream off** vt (fig) prélever

cream cake n (petit) gâteau à la crème

cream cheese n fromage m à la crème, fromage blanc

creamy ['kriːmɪ] adj crémeux(-euse)

crease [kriːs] n pli m ▷ vt froisser, chiffonner ▷ vi se froisser, se chiffonner

create [kriː'eɪt] vt créer; (impression, fuss) faire

creation [kriː'eɪʃən] n création f

creative [kriː'eɪtɪv] adj créatif(-ive)

creator [kriː'eɪtə'] n créateur(-trice)

creature ['kriːtʃə'] n créature f

crèche [krɛʃ] n garderie f, crèche f

credence ['kriːdns] n croyance f, foi f

credentials [krɪ'dɛnʃlz] npl (references) références fpl; (identity papers) pièce f d'identité; (letters of reference) pièces justificatives

credibility [krɛdɪ'bɪlɪtɪ] n crédibilité f

credible ['krɛdɪbl] adj digne de foi, crédible

credit ['krɛdɪt] n crédit m; (recognition) honneur m; (Scol) unité f de valeur ▷ vt (Comm) créditer; (believe: also: **give credit to**) ajouter foi à, croire; **credits** npl (Cine) générique m; **to be in ~** (person, bank account) être créditeur(-trice); **on ~** à crédit; **to one's ~** à son honneur, à son actif; **to take the ~ for** s'attribuer le mérite de; **it does him ~** cela lui fait honneur; **to ~ sb with** (fig) prêter or attribuer à qn; **to ~ £5 to sb** créditer (le compte de) qn de 5 livres

credit card n carte f de crédit; **do you take ~s?** acceptez-vous les cartes de crédit?

creditor ['krɛdɪtə'] n créancier(-ière)

creed [kriːd] n croyance f; credo m, principes mpl

creek [kriːk] n (inlet) crique f, anse f; (US: stream) ruisseau m, petit cours d'eau

creep (pt, pp **crept**) [kriːp, krɛpt] vi ramper; (silently) se faufiler, se glisser; (plant) grimper ▷ n (inf: flatterer) lèche-botte m; **he's a ~** c'est un type puant; **it gives me the ~s** cela me fait froid dans le dos; **to ~ up on sb** s'approcher furtivement de qn

creeper ['kriːpə'] n plante grimpante

creepy ['kriːpɪ] adj (frightening) qui fait frissonner, qui donne la chair de poule

cremate [krɪ'meɪt] vt incinérer

crematorium (pl **crematoria**) [krɛmə'tɔːrɪəm, -'tɔːrɪə] n four m crématoire

crepe [kreɪp] n crêpe m

crepe bandage n (Brit) bande f Velpeau®

crept [krɛpt] pt, pp of **creep**

crescent ['krɛsnt] n croissant m; (street) rue f (en arc de cercle)

cress [krɛs] n cresson m

crest [krɛst] n crête f; (of helmet) cimier m; (of coat of arms) timbre m

crestfallen ['krɛstfɔːlən] adj déconfit(e), découragé(e)

Crete ['kriːt] n Crète f

crevice ['krɛvɪs] n fissure f, lézarde f, fente f

crew [kruː] n équipage m; (Cine) équipe f (de tournage); (gang) bande f

crew-cut ['kruːkʌt] n: **to have a ~** avoir les cheveux en brosse

crew-neck ['kruːnɛk] n col ras

crib [krɪb] n lit m d'enfant; (for baby) berceau m ▷ vt (inf) copier

crick [krɪk] n crampe f; **~ in the neck** torticolis m

cricket ['krɪkɪt] n (insect) grillon m, cri-cri m inv; (game) cricket m

cricketer ['krɪkɪtə'] n joueur m de cricket

crime [kraɪm] n crime m; **minor ~** délit mineur, infraction mineure

criminal ['krɪmɪnl] adj, n criminel(le)

crimson ['krɪmzn] adj cramoisi(e)

cringe [krɪndʒ] vi avoir un mouvement de recul; (fig) s'humilier, ramper

crinkle ['krɪŋkl] vt froisser, chiffonner

cripple ['krɪpl] n boiteux(-euse), infirme m/f ▷ vt (person) estropier, paralyser; (ship, plane) immobiliser; (*production, exports*) paralyser; **~d with rheumatism** perclus(e) de rhumatismes

crisis (*pl* **crises**) ['kraɪsɪs, -siːz] *n* crise *f*

crisp [krɪsp] *adj* croquant(e); (*weather*) vif (vive); (*manner etc*) brusque

crisps [krɪsps] (*Brit*) *npl* (pommes *fpl*) chips *fpl*

crispy [krɪspɪ] *adj* croustillant(e)

crisscross ['krɪskrɔs] *adj* entrecroisé(e), en croisillons ▷ *vt* sillonner; **~ pattern** croisillons *mpl*

criterion (*pl* **criteria**) [kraɪ'tɪərɪən, -'tɪərɪə] *n* critère *m*

critic ['krɪtɪk] *n* critique *m/f*

critical ['krɪtɪkl] *adj* critique; **to be ~ of sb/sth** critiquer qn/qch

critically ['krɪtɪklɪ] *adv* (*examine*) d'un œil critique; (*speak*) sévèrement; **~ ill** gravement malade

criticism ['krɪtɪsɪzəm] *n* critique *f*

criticize ['krɪtɪsaɪz] *vt* critiquer

croak [krəuk] *vi* (*frog*) coasser; (*raven*) croasser

Croat ['krəuæt] *adj, n* = **Croatian**

Croatia [krəu'eɪʃə] *n* Croatie *f*

Croatian [krəu'eɪʃən] *adj* croate ▷ *n* Croate *m/f*; (*Ling*) croate *m*

crochet ['krəuʃeɪ] *n* travail *m* au crochet

crockery ['krɔkərɪ] *n* vaisselle *f*

crocodile ['krɔkədaɪl] *n* crocodile *m*

crocus ['krəukəs] *n* crocus *m*

croft [krɔft] *n* (*Brit*) petite ferme

croissant ['krwasɑ̃] *n* croissant *m*

crony ['krəunɪ] *n* copain (copine)

crook [kruk] *n* escroc *m*; (*of shepherd*) houlette *f*

crooked ['krukɪd] *adj* courbé(e), tordu(e); (*action*) malhonnête

crop [krɔp] *n* (*produce*) culture *f*; (*amount produced*) récolte *f*; (*riding crop*) cravache *f*; (*of bird*) jabot *m* ▷ *vt* (*hair*) tondre; (*animals: grass*) brouter
  ▶ **crop up** *vi* surgir, se présenter, survenir

cross [krɔs] *n* croix *f*; (*Biol*) croisement *m* ▷ *vt* (*street etc*) traverser; (*arms, legs, Biol*) croiser; (*cheque*) barrer; (*thwart: person, plan*) contrarier ▷ *vi*: **the boat ~es from ... to ...** le bateau fait la traversée de ... à ... ▷ *adj* en colère, fâché(e); **to ~ o.s.** se signer, faire le signe de (la) croix; **we have a ~ed line** (*Brit: on telephone*) il y a des interférences; **they've got their lines ~ed** (*fig*) il y a un malentendu entre eux; **to be/get ~ with sb (about sth)** être en colère/(se) fâcher contre qn (à propos de qch)
  ▶ **cross off** *or* **out** *vt* barrer, rayer
  ▶ **cross over** *vi* traverser

crossbar ['krɔsbɑːʳ] *n* barre transversale

cross-Channel ferry ['krɔs'tʃænl-] *n* ferry *m* qui fait la traversée de la Manche

cross-country ['krɔs'kʌntrɪ], **cross-country race** *n* cross(-country) *m*

cross-examine ['krɔsɪg'zæmɪn] *vt* (*Law*) faire subir un examen contradictoire à

cross-eyed ['krɔsaɪd] *adj* qui louche

crossfire ['krɔsfaɪəʳ] *n* feux croisés

crossing ['krɔsɪŋ] *n* croisement *m*, carrefour *m*; (*sea passage*) traversée *f*; (*also*: **pedestrian crossing**) passage clouté; **how long does the ~ take?** combien de temps dure la traversée?

crossing guard (*US*) *n* contractuel qui fait traverser la rue aux enfants

cross-purposes ['krɔs'pəːpəsɪz] *npl*: **to be at ~ with sb** comprendre qn de travers; **we're (talking) at ~** on ne parle pas de la même chose

cross-reference ['krɔs'rɛfrəns] *n* renvoi *m*, référence *f*

crossroads ['krɔsrəudz] *n* carrefour *m*

cross section *n* (*Biol*) coupe transversale; (*in population*) échantillon *m*

crosswalk ['krɔswɔːk] *n* (*US*) passage clouté

crosswind ['krɔswɪnd] *n* vent *m* de travers

crossword ['krɔswəːd] *n* mots *mpl* croisés

crotch [krɔtʃ] *n* (*of garment*) entrejambe *m*; (*Anat*) entrecuisse *m*

crouch [krautʃ] *vi* s'accroupir; (*hide*) se tapir; (*before springing*) se ramasser

crouton ['kruːtɔn] *n* croûton *m*

crow [krəu] *n* (*bird*) corneille *f*; (*of cock*) chant *m* du coq, cocorico *m* ▷ *vi* (*cock*) chanter; (*fig*) pavoiser, chanter victoire

crowbar ['krəubɑːʳ] *n* levier *m*

crowd [kraud] *n* foule *f* ▷ *vt* bourrer, remplir ▷ *vi* affluer, s'attrouper, s'entasser; **~s of people** une foule de gens

crowded ['kraudɪd] *adj* bondé(e), plein(e); **~ with** plein de

crown [kraun] *n* couronne *f*; (*of head*) sommet *m* de la tête, calotte crânienne; (*of hat*) fond *m*; (*of hill*) sommet *m* ▷ *vt* (*also tooth*) couronner

crown jewels *npl* joyaux *mpl* de la Couronne

crow's-feet ['krəuzfiːt] *npl* pattes *fpl* d'oie (*fig*)

crucial ['kruːʃl] *adj* crucial(e), décisif(-ive); (*also*: **crucial to**) essentiel(le) à

crucifix ['kruːsɪfɪks] *n* crucifix *m*

crucifixion [kruːsɪ'fɪkʃən] *n* crucifiement *m*, crucifixion *f*

crude [kruːd] *adj* (*materials*) brut(e); non raffiné(e); (*basic*) rudimentaire, sommaire; (*vulgar*) cru(e), grossier(-ière) ▷ *n* (*also*: **crude oil**) (pétrole *m*) brut *m*

cruel ['kruəl] *adj* cruel(le)

cruelty ['kruəltɪ] *n* cruauté *f*

cruise [kruːz] *n* croisière *f* ▷ *vi* (*ship*) croiser; (*car*) rouler; (*aircraft*) voler; (*taxi*) être en maraude

cruiser ['kruːzəʳ] *n* croiseur *m*

crumb [krʌm] *n* miette *f*

crumble ['krʌmbl] *vt* émietter ▷ *vi* s'émietter; (*plaster etc*) s'effriter; (*land, earth*) s'ébouler; (*building*) s'écrouler, crouler; (*fig*) s'effondrer

crumbly ['krʌmblɪ] *adj* friable

crumpet ['krʌmpɪt] *n* petite crêpe (épaisse)

crumple ['krʌmpl] *vt* froisser, friper

crunch [krʌntʃ] *vt* croquer; (*underfoot*) faire craquer, écraser; faire crisser ▷ *n* (*fig*) instant *m* or moment *m* critique, moment de vérité

crunchy ['krʌntʃɪ] *adj* croquant(e), croustillant(e)

crusade [kruː'seɪd] *n* croisade *f* ▷ *vi* (*fig*): **to ~ for/against** partir en croisade pour/contre

crush [krʌʃ] n (crowd) foule f, cohue f; (love): **to have a ~ on sb** avoir le béguin pour qn; (drink): **lemon ~** citron pressé ▷ vt écraser; (crumple) froisser; (grind, break up: garlic, ice) piler; (: grapes) presser; (hopes) anéantir

crust [krʌst] n croûte f

crusty ['krʌstɪ] adj (bread) croustillant(e); (inf: person) revêche, bourru(e); (: remark) irrité(e)

crutch [krʌtʃ] n béquille f; (Tech) support m; (also: **crotch**) entrejambe m

crux [krʌks] n point crucial

cry [kraɪ] vi pleurer; (shout: also: **cry out**) crier ▷ n cri m; **why are you ~ing?** pourquoi pleures-tu?; **to ~ for help** appeler à l'aide; **she had a good ~** elle a pleuré un bon coup; **it's a far ~ from …** (fig) on est loin de …
  ▶ **cry off** vi se dédire; se décommander
  ▶ **cry out** vi (call out, shout) pousser un cri ▷ vt crier

cryptic ['krɪptɪk] adj énigmatique

crystal ['krɪstl] n cristal m

crystal-clear ['krɪstl'klɪəʳ] adj clair(e) comme de l'eau de roche

CSA n abbr = **Confederate States of America**; (Brit: = Child Support Agency) organisme pour la protection des enfants de parents séparés, qui contrôle le versement des pensions alimentaires.

CTC n abbr (Brit) = **city technology college**

cub [kʌb] n petit m (d'un animal); (also: **cub scout**) louveteau m

Cuba ['kjuːbə] n Cuba m

cube [kjuːb] n cube m ▷ vt (Math) élever au cube

cubic ['kjuːbɪk] adj cubique; **~ metre** etc mètre m etc cube; **~ capacity** (Aut) cylindrée f

cubicle ['kjuːbɪkl] n (in hospital) box m; (at pool) cabine f

cuckoo ['kukuː] n coucou m

cuckoo clock n (pendule f à) coucou m

cucumber ['kjuːkʌmbəʳ] n concombre m

cuddle ['kʌdl] vt câliner, caresser ▷ vi se blottir l'un contre l'autre

cue [kjuː] n queue f de billard; (Theat etc) signal m

cuff [kʌf] n (Brit: of shirt, coat etc) poignet m, manchette f; (US: on trousers) revers m; (blow) gifle f ▷ vt gifler; **off the ~** (adv) à l'improviste

cufflinks ['kʌflɪŋks] n boutons m de manchette

cuisine [kwɪˈziːn] n cuisine f, art m culinaire

cul-de-sac ['kʌldəsæk] n cul-de-sac m, impasse f

cull [kʌl] vt sélectionner; (kill selectively) pratiquer l'abattage sélectif de ▷ n (of animals) abattage sélectif

culminate ['kʌlmɪneɪt] vi: **to ~ in** finir or se terminer par; (lead to) mener à

culmination [kʌlmɪˈneɪʃən] n point culminant

culottes [kjuːˈlɔts] npl jupe-culotte f

culprit ['kʌlprɪt] n coupable m/f

cult [kʌlt] n culte m

cultivate ['kʌltɪveɪt] vt (also fig) cultiver

cultivation [kʌltɪˈveɪʃən] n culture f

cultural ['kʌltʃərəl] adj culturel(le)

culture ['kʌltʃəʳ] n (also fig) culture f

cultured ['kʌltʃəd] adj cultivé(e) (fig)

cumbersome ['kʌmbəsəm] adj encombrant(e), embarrassant(e)

cumin ['kʌmɪn] n (spice) cumin m

cunning ['kʌnɪŋ] n ruse f, astuce f ▷ adj rusé(e), malin(-igne); (clever: device, idea) astucieux(-euse)

cup [kʌp] n tasse f; (prize, event) coupe f; (of bra) bonnet m; **a ~ of tea** une tasse de thé

cupboard ['kʌbəd] n placard m

cup final n (Brit Football) finale f de la coupe

cup tie ['kʌptaɪ] n (Brit Football) match m de coupe

curate ['kjuərɪt] n vicaire m

curator [kjuəˈreɪtəʳ] n conservateur m (d'un musée etc)

curb [kəːb] vt refréner, mettre un frein à; (expenditure) limiter, juguler ▷ n (fig) frein m; (US) bord m du trottoir

curdle ['kəːdl] vi (se) cailler

cure [kjuəʳ] vt guérir; (Culin: salt) saler; (: smoke) fumer; (: dry) sécher ▷ n remède m; **to be ~d of sth** être guéri de qch

curfew ['kəːfjuː] n couvre-feu m

curiosity [kjuərɪˈɔsɪtɪ] n curiosité f

curious ['kjuərɪəs] adj curieux(-euse); **I'm ~ about him** il m'intrigue

curl [kəːl] n boucle f (de cheveux); (of smoke etc) volute f ▷ vt, vi boucler; (tightly) friser
  ▶ **curl up** vi s'enrouler; (person) se pelotonner

curler ['kəːləʳ] n bigoudi m, rouleau m; (Sport) joueur(-euse) de curling

curly ['kəːlɪ] adj bouclé(e); (tightly curled) frisé(e)

currant ['kʌrnt] n raisin m de Corinthe, raisin sec; (fruit) groseille f

currency ['kʌrnsɪ] n monnaie f; **foreign ~** devises étrangères, monnaie étrangère; **to gain ~** (fig) s'accréditer

current ['kʌrnt] n courant m ▷ adj (common) courant(e); (tendency, price, event) actuel(le); **direct/alternating ~** (Elec) courant continu/alternatif; **the ~ issue of a magazine** le dernier numéro d'un magazine; **in ~ use** d'usage courant

current account n (Brit) compte courant

current affairs npl (questions fpl d')actualité f

currently ['kʌrntlɪ] adv actuellement

curriculum (pl **-s** or **curricula**) [kəˈrɪkjuləm, -lə] n programme m d'études

curriculum vitae [-ˈviːtaɪ] n curriculum vitae (CV) m

curry ['kʌrɪ] n curry m ▷ vt: **to ~ favour with** chercher à gagner la faveur or à s'attirer les bonnes grâces de; **chicken ~** curry de poulet, poulet m au curry

curry powder n poudre f de curry

curse [kəːs] vi jurer, blasphémer ▷ vt maudire ▷ n (spell) malédiction f; (problem, scourge) fléau m; (swearword) juron m

cursor ['kəːsəʳ] n (Comput) curseur m

cursory ['kəːsərɪ] adj superficiel(le), hâtif(-ive)

curt [kəːt] adj brusque, sec(-sèche)

curtail [kəːˈteɪl] vt (visit etc) écourter; (expenses etc) réduire

curtain ['kəːtn] n rideau m; **to draw the ~s**

(*together*) fermer *or* tirer les rideaux; (*apart*) ouvrir les rideaux

curtsey, curtsy ['kə:tsɪ] *n* révérence *f* ▷ *vi* faire une révérence

curve [kə:v] *n* courbe *f*; (*in the road*) tournant *m*, virage *m* ▷ *vt* courber ▷ *vi* se courber; (*road*) faire une courbe

curved [kə:vd] *adj* courbe

cushion ['kuʃən] *n* coussin *m* ▷ *vt* (*seat*) rembourrer; (*fall, shock*) amortir

custard ['kʌstəd] *n* (*for pouring*) crème anglaise

custody ['kʌstədɪ] *n* (*of child*) garde *f*; (*for offenders*) détention préventive; **to take sb into ~** placer qn en détention préventive; **in the ~ of** sous la garde de

custom ['kʌstəm] *n* coutume *f*, usage *m*; (*Law*) droit coutumier, coutume; (*Comm*) clientèle *f*

customary ['kʌstəmərɪ] *adj* habituel(le); **it is ~ to do it** l'usage veut qu'on le fasse

customer ['kʌstəmə*r*] *n* client(e); **he's an awkward ~** (*inf*) ce n'est pas quelqu'un de facile

customized ['kʌstəmaɪzd] *adj* personnalisé(e); (*car etc*) construit(e) sur commande

custom-made ['kʌstəm'meɪd] *adj* (*clothes*) fait(e) sur mesure; (*other goods: also*: **custom-built**) hors série, fait(e) sur commande

customs ['kʌstəmz] *npl* douane *f*; **to go through (the) ~** passer la douane

customs officer *n* douanier *m*

cut [kʌt] (*pt, pp* **~**) *vt* couper; (*meat*) découper; (*shape, make*) tailler; couper; creuser; graver; (*reduce*) réduire; (*inf: lecture, appointment*) manquer ▷ *vi* couper; (*intersect*) se couper ▷ *n* (*gen*) coupure *f*; (*of clothes*) coupe *f*; (*of jewel*) taille *f*; (*in salary etc*) réduction *f*; (*of meat*) morceau *m*; **to ~ teeth** (*baby*) faire ses dents; **to ~ a tooth** percer une dent; **to ~ one's finger** se couper le doigt; **to get one's hair ~** se faire couper les cheveux; **I've ~ myself** je me suis coupé; **to ~ sth short** couper court à qch; **to ~ sb dead** ignorer (complètement) qn

▶ **cut back** *vt* (*plants*) tailler; (*production, expenditure*) réduire

▶ **cut down** *vt* (*tree*) abattre; (*reduce*) réduire; **to ~ sb down to size** (*fig*) remettre qn à sa place

▶ **cut down on** *vt fus* réduire

▶ **cut in** *vi* (*interrupt: conversation*): **to ~ in (on)** couper la parole (à); (*Aut*) faire une queue de poisson

▶ **cut off** *vt* couper; (*fig*) isoler; **we've been ~ off** (*Tel*) nous avons été coupés

▶ **cut out** *vt* (*picture etc*) découper; (*remove*) supprimer

▶ **cut up** *vt* découper

cutback ['kʌtbæk] *n* réduction *f*

cute [kju:t] *adj* mignon(ne), adorable; (*clever*) rusé(e), astucieux(-euse)

cutlery ['kʌtlərɪ] *n* couverts *mpl*; (*trade*) coutellerie *f*

cutlet ['kʌtlɪt] *n* côtelette *f*

cutout ['kʌtaut] *n* coupe-circuit *m inv*; (*paper figure*) découpage *m*

cut-price ['kʌt'praɪs], (*US*) **cut-rate** ['kʌt'reɪt] *adj* au rabais, à prix réduit

cut-throat ['kʌtθrəut] *n* assassin *m* ▷ *adj*: **~ competition** concurrence *f* sauvage

cutting ['kʌtɪŋ] *adj* tranchant(e), coupant(e); (*fig*) cinglant(e) ▷ *n* (*Brit: from newspaper*) coupure *f* (de journal); (*from plant*) bouture *f*; (*Rail*) tranchée *f*; (*Cine*) montage *m*

CV *n abbr* = **curriculum vitae**

cwt *abbr* = **hundredweight**

cyanide ['saɪənaɪd] *n* cyanure *m*

cyberspace ['saɪbəspeɪs] *n* cyberespace *m*

cycle ['saɪkl] *n* cycle *m*; (*bicycle*) bicyclette *f*, vélo *m* ▷ *vi* faire de la bicyclette

cycle hire *n* location *f* de vélos

cycle lane, cycle path *n* piste *f* cyclable

cycling ['saɪklɪŋ] *n* cyclisme *m*; **to go on a ~ holiday** (*Brit*) faire du cyclotourisme

cyclist ['saɪklɪst] *n* cycliste *m/f*

cyclone ['saɪkləun] *n* cyclone *m*

cygnet ['sɪgnɪt] *n* jeune cygne *m*

cylinder ['sɪlɪndə*r*] *n* cylindre *m*

cymbals ['sɪmblz] *npl* cymbales *fpl*

cynic ['sɪnɪk] *n* cynique *m/f*

cynical ['sɪnɪkl] *adj* cynique

cynicism ['sɪnɪsɪzəm] *n* cynisme *m*

Cypriot ['sɪprɪət] *adj* cypriote, chypriote ▷ *n* Cypriote *m/f*, Chypriote *m/f*

Cyprus ['saɪprəs] *n* Chypre *f*

cyst [sɪst] *n* kyste *m*

cystitis [sɪs'taɪtɪs] *n* cystite *f*

czar [zɑ:*r*] *n* tsar *m*

Czech [tʃɛk] *adj* tchèque ▷ *n* Tchèque *m/f*; (*Ling*) tchèque *m*

Czechoslovak [tʃɛkə'sləuvæk] *adj, n* = **Czechoslovakian**

Czechoslovakia [tʃɛkəslə'vækɪə] *n* Tchécoslovaquie *f*

Czechoslovakian [tʃɛkəslə'vækɪən] *adj* tchécoslovaque ▷ *n* Tchécoslovaque *m/f*

Czech Republic *n*: **the ~** la République tchèque

Dd

D¹, d² [di:] *n* (*letter*) D, d *m*; (*Mus*): **D** ré *m*; **D for David** (*US*): **D for Dog** D comme Désirée

D² *abbr* (*US Pol*) = **democrat; democratic**

d² *abbr* (*Brit: old*) = **penny**

dab [dæb] *vt* (*eyes, wound*) tamponner; (*paint, cream*) appliquer (par petites touches *or* rapidement); **a ~ of paint** un petit coup de peinture

dabble ['dæbl] *vi*: **to ~ in** faire *or* se mêler *or* s'occuper un peu de

dad, daddy [dæd, 'dædɪ] *n* papa *m*

daffodil ['dæfədɪl] *n* jonquille *f*

daft [dɑːft] *adj* (*inf*) idiot(e), stupide; **to be ~ about** être toqué(e) *or* mordu(e) de

dagger ['dægəʳ] *n* poignard *m*; **to be at ~s drawn with sb** être à couteaux tirés avec qn; **to look ~s at sb** foudroyer qn du regard

daily ['deɪlɪ] *adj* quotidien(ne), journalier(-ière)
▷ *n* quotidien *m*; (*Brit: servant*) femme *f* de ménage (*à la journée*) ▷ *adv* tous les jours; **twice ~** deux fois par jour

dainty ['deɪntɪ] *adj* délicat(e), mignon(ne)

dairy ['dɛərɪ] *n* (*shop*) crémerie *f*, laiterie *f*; (*on farm*) laiterie ▷ *adj* laitier(-ière)

dairy produce *n* produits laitiers

dairy products *npl* produits laitier

daisy ['deɪzɪ] *n* pâquerette *f*

dale [deɪl] *n* vallon *m*

dam [dæm] *n* (*wall*) barrage *m*; (*water*) réservoir *m*, lac *m* de retenue ▷ *vt* endiguer

damage ['dæmɪdʒ] *n* dégâts *mpl*, dommages *mpl*; (*fig*) tort *m* ▷ *vt* endommager, abîmer; (*fig*) faire du tort à; **damages** *npl* (*Law*) dommages-intérêts *mpl*; **to pay £5000 in ~s** payer 5000 livres de dommages- intérêts; **~ to property** dégâts matériels

damn [dæm] *vt* condamner; (*curse*) maudire ▷ *n* (*inf*): **I don't give a ~** je m'en fous ▷ *adj* (*inf: also:* **damned**): **this ~ ...** ce sacré *or* foutu ...; **~ (it)!** zut!

damning ['dæmɪŋ] *adj* (*evidence*) accablant(e)

damp [dæmp] *adj* humide ▷ *n* humidité *f* ▷ *vt* (*also:* **dampen**: *cloth, rag*) humecter; (: *enthusiasm etc*) refroidir

damson ['dæmzən] *n* prune *f* de Damas

dance [dɑːns] *n* danse *f*; (*ball*) bal *m* ▷ *vi* danser; **to ~ about** sautiller, gambader

dance floor *n* piste *f* de danse

dance hall *n* salle *f* de bal, dancing *m*

dancer ['dɑːnsəʳ] *n* danseur(-euse)

dancing ['dɑːnsɪŋ] *n* danse *f*

dandelion ['dændɪlaɪən] *n* pissenlit *m*

dandruff ['dændrəf] *n* pellicules *fpl*

D & T *n abbr* (*Brit: Scol*) = **design and technology**

Dane [deɪn] *n* Danois(e)

danger ['deɪndʒəʳ] *n* danger *m*; **~!** (*on sign*) danger!; **there is a ~ of fire** il y a (un) risque d'incendie; **in ~** en danger; **he was in ~ of falling** il risquait de tomber; **out of ~** hors de danger

dangerous ['deɪndʒrəs] *adj* dangereux(-euse)

dangle ['dæŋgl] *vt* balancer; (*fig*) faire miroiter ▷ *vi* pendre, se balancer

Danish ['deɪnɪʃ] *adj* danois(e) ▷ *n* (*Ling*) danois *m*

dare [dɛəʳ] *vt*: **to ~ sb to do** défier qn *or* mettre qn au défi de faire ▷ *vi*: **to ~ (to) do sth** oser faire qch; **I ~n't tell him** (*Brit*) je n'ose pas le lui dire; **I ~ say he'll turn up** il est probable qu'il viendra

daring ['dɛərɪŋ] *adj* hardi(e), audacieux(-euse) ▷ *n* audace *f*, hardiesse *f*

dark [dɑːk] *adj* (*night, room*) obscur(e), sombre; (*colour, complexion*) foncé(e), sombre; (*fig*) sombre ▷ *n*: **in the ~** dans le noir; **to be in the ~ about** (*fig*) ignorer tout de; **after ~** après la tombée de la nuit; **it is/is getting ~** il fait nuit/commence à faire nuit

darken ['dɑːkn] *vt* obscurcir, assombrir ▷ *vi* s'obscurcir, s'assombrir

dark glasses *npl* lunettes noires

darkness ['dɑːknɪs] *n* obscurité *f*

darkroom ['dɑːkrum] *n* chambre noire

darling ['dɑːlɪŋ] *adj, n* chéri(e)

darn [dɑːn] *vt* repriser

dart [dɑːt] *n* fléchette *f*; (*in sewing*) pince *f* ▷ *vi*: **to ~ towards** (*also:* **make a dart towards**) se précipiter *or* s'élancer vers; **to ~ away/along** partir/passer comme une flèche

dartboard ['dɑːtbɔːd] *n* cible *f* (de jeu de fléchettes)

darts [dɑːts] *n* jeu *m* de fléchettes

dash [dæʃ] *n* (*sign*) tiret *m*; (*small quantity*) goutte *f*, larme *f* ▷ *vt* (*throw*) jeter *or* lancer violemment; (*hopes*) anéantir ▷ *vi*: **to ~ towards** (*also:* **make a dash towards**) se précipiter *or* se ruer vers; **a ~ of soda** un peu d'eau gazeuse

▸ **dash away** *vi* partir à toute allure
dashboard ['dæʃbɔːd] *n* (*Aut*) tableau *m* de bord
dashing ['dæʃɪŋ] *adj* fringant(e)
▸ **dash off** *vi* = **dash away**
data ['deɪtə] *npl* données *fpl*
database ['deɪtəbeɪs] *n* base *f* de données
data processing *n* traitement *m* (électronique)
de l'information
date [deɪt] *n* date *f*; (*with sb*) rendez-vous *m*;
(*fruit*) datte *f* ▷ *vt* dater; (*person*) sortir avec;
what's the ~ today? quelle date sommes-nous
aujourd'hui?; **~ of birth** date de naissance;
closing ~ date de clôture; **to ~** (*adv*) à ce jour;
out of ~ périmé(e); **up to ~** à la page, mis(e) à
jour, moderne; **to bring up to ~** (*correspondence*,
information) mettre à jour; (*method*) moderniser;
(*person*) mettre au courant; **letter ~d 5th July** *or*
(*US*) **July 5th** lettre (datée) du 5 juillet
dated ['deɪtɪd] *adj* démodé(e)
date rape *n* viol *m* (à l'issue d'un rendez-vous galant)
daub [dɔːb] *vt* barbouiller
daughter ['dɔːtər] *n* fille *f*
daughter-in-law ['dɔːtərɪnlɔː] *n* belle-fille *f*,
bru *f*
daunting ['dɔːntɪŋ] *adj* décourageant(e),
intimidant(e)
dawdle ['dɔːdl] *vi* traîner, lambiner; **to ~ over**
one's work traînasser *or* lambiner sur son
travail
dawn [dɔːn] *n* aube *f*, aurore *f* ▷ *vi* (*day*) se lever,
poindre; (*fig*) naître, se faire jour; **at ~** à l'aube;
from ~ to dusk du matin au soir; **it ~ed on him**
that ... il lui vint à l'esprit que ...
day [deɪ] *n* jour *m*; (*as duration*) journée *f*; (*period
of time, age*) époque *f*, temps *m*; **the ~ before**
la veille, le jour précédent; **the ~ after, the**
following ~ le lendemain, le jour suivant; **the**
~ before yesterday avant-hier; **the ~ after**
tomorrow après-demain; **(on) the ~ that** ... le
jour où ...; **~ by ~** jour après jour; **by ~** de jour;
paid by the ~ payé(e) à la journée; **these ~s, in**
the present ~ de nos jours, à l'heure actuelle
daybreak ['deɪbreɪk] *n* point *m* du jour
day-care centre ['deɪkɛə-] *n* (*for elderly etc*) centre
m d'accueil de jour; (*for children*) garderie *f*
daydream ['deɪdriːm] *n* rêverie *f* ▷ *vi* rêver (tout
éveillé)
daylight ['deɪlaɪt] *n* (lumière *f* du) jour *m*
day return *n* (*Brit*) billet *m* d'aller-retour (*valable
pour la journée*)
daytime ['deɪtaɪm] *n* jour *m*, journée *f*
day-to-day ['deɪtə'deɪ] *adj* (*routine, expenses*)
journalier(-ière); **on a ~ basis** au jour le jour
day trip *n* excursion *f* (d'une journée)
daze [deɪz] *vt* (*drug*) hébéter; (*blow*) étourdir ▷ *n*:
in a ~ hébété(e), étourdi(e)
dazed [deɪzd] *adj* abruti(e)
dazzle ['dæzl] *vt* éblouir, aveugler
dazzling ['dæzlɪŋ] *adj* (*light*) aveuglant(e),
éblouissant(e); (*fig*) éblouissant(e)
DC *abbr* (*Elec*) = **direct current**; (*US*) = **District of**
Columbia

D-day ['diːdeɪ] *n* le jour J
dead [dɛd] *adj* mort(e); (*numb*) engourdi(e),
insensible; (*battery*) à plat ▷ *adv* (*completely*)
absolument, complètement; (*exactly*) juste; **the**
dead *npl* les morts; **he was shot ~** il a été tué
d'un coup de revolver; **~ on time** à l'heure pile;
~ tired éreinté(e), complètement fourbu(e); **to**
stop ~ s'arrêter pile *or* net; **the line is ~** (*Tel*) la
ligne est coupée
deaden [dɛdn] *vt* (*blow, sound*) amortir; (*make
numb*) endormir, rendre insensible
dead end *n* impasse *f*
dead heat *n* (*Sport*): **to finish in a ~** terminer ex
aequo
deadline ['dɛdlaɪn] *n* date *f* or heure *f* limite; **to**
work to a ~ avoir des délais stricts à respecter
deadlock ['dɛdlɔk] *n* impasse *f*; (*fig*)
dead loss *n* (*inf*): **to be a ~** (*person*) n'être bon
(bonne à rien); (*thing*) ne rien valoir
deadly ['dɛdlɪ] *adj* mortel(le); (*weapon*)
meurtrier(-ière); **~ dull** ennuyeux(-euse) à
mourir, mortellement ennuyeux
deadpan ['dɛdpæn] *adj* impassible; (*humour*)
pince-sans-rire *inv*
Dead Sea *n*: **the ~** la mer Morte
deaf [dɛf] *adj* sourd(e); **to turn a ~ ear to sth**
faire la sourde oreille à qch
deafen ['dɛfn] *vt* rendre sourd(e); (*fig*) assourdir
deafening ['dɛfnɪŋ] *adj* assourdissant(e)
deaf-mute ['dɛfmjuːt] *n* sourd/e-muet/te
deafness ['dɛfnɪs] *n* surdité *f*
deal [diːl] *n* affaire *f*, marché *m* ▷ *vt* (*pt, pp* **-t**)
[dɛlt] (*blow*) porter; (*cards*) donner, distribuer; **to**
strike a ~ with sb faire *or* conclure un marché
avec qn; **it's a ~!** (*inf*) marché conclu!, tope-là!,
topez-là!; **he got a bad ~ from them** ils ont
mal agi envers lui; **he got a fair ~ from them**
ils ont agi loyalement envers lui; **a good ~** (*a lot*)
beaucoup; **a good ~ of, a great ~ of** beaucoup de,
énormément de
▸ **deal in** *vt fus* (*Comm*) faire le commerce de, être
dans le commerce de
▸ **deal with** *vt fus* (*Comm*) traiter avec; (*handle*)
s'occuper *or* se charger de; (*be about: book etc*)
traiter de
dealer ['diːlər] *n* (*Comm*) marchand *m*; (*Cards*)
donneur *m*
dealings ['diːlɪŋz] *npl* (*in goods, shares*) opérations
fpl, transactions *fpl*; (*relations*) relations *fpl*,
rapports *mpl*
dealt [dɛlt] *pt, pp of* **deal**
dean [diːn] *n* (*Rel, Brit Scol*) doyen *m*; (*US Scol*)
conseiller principal (conseillère principale)
d'éducation
dear [dɪər] *adj* cher (chère); (*expensive*) cher,
coûteux(-euse) ▷ *n*: **my ~** mon cher (ma chère)
▷ *excl*: **~ me!** mon Dieu!; **D~ Sir/Madam** (*in
letter*) Monsieur/Madame; **D~ Mr/Mrs X** Cher
Monsieur/Chère Madame X
dearly ['dɪəlɪ] *adv* (*love*) tendrement; (*pay*) cher
death [dɛθ] *n* mort *f*; (*Admin*) décès *m*
death certificate *n* acte *m* de décès

deathly ['dεθlı] *adj* de mort ▷ *adv* comme la mort
death penalty *n* peine *f* de mort
death rate *n* taux *m* de mortalité
death sentence *n* condamnation *f* à mort
death toll *n* nombre *m* de morts
debase [dı'beıs] *vt* (*currency*) déprécier, dévaloriser; (*person*) abaisser, avilir
debatable [dı'beıtəbl] *adj* discutable, contestable; **it is ~ whether ...** il est douteux que ...
debate [dı'beıt] *n* discussion *f*, débat *m* ▷ *vt* discuter, débattre ▷ *vi* (*consider*): **to ~ whether** se demander si
debit ['dεbıt] *n* débit *m* ▷ *vt*: **to ~ a sum to sb** *or* **to sb's account** porter une somme au débit de qn, débiter qn d'une somme
debit card *n* carte *f* de paiement
debris ['dεbri:] *n* débris *mpl*, décombres *mpl*
debt [dεt] *n* dette *f*; **to be in ~** avoir des dettes, être endetté(e); **bad ~** créance *f* irrécouvrable
debtor ['dεtə'] *n* débiteur(-trice)
debut ['deıbju:] *n* début(s) *m(pl)*
Dec. *abbr* (= *December*) déc
decade ['dεkeıd] *n* décennie *f*, décade *f*
decadence ['dεkədəns] *n* décadence *f*
decaf ['di:kæf] *n* (*inf*) déca *m*
decaffeinated [dı'kæfıneıtıd] *adj* décaféiné(e)
decanter [dı'kæntə'] *n* carafe *f*
decay [dı'keı] *n* (*of food, wood etc*) décomposition *f*, pourriture *f*; (*of building*) délabrement *m*; (*fig*) déclin *m*; (*also*: **tooth decay**) carie *f* (dentaire) ▷ *vi* (*rot*) se décomposer, pourrir; (: *teeth*) se carier; (*fig: city, district, building*) se délabrer; (: *civilization*) décliner; (: *system*) tomber en ruine
deceased [dı'si:st] *n*: **the ~** le (la) défunt(e)
deceit [dı'si:t] *n* tromperie *f*, supercherie *f*
deceitful [dı'si:tful] *adj* trompeur(-euse)
deceive [dı'si:v] *vt* tromper; **to ~ o.s.** s'abuser
December [dı'sεmbə'] *n* décembre *m*; *for phrases see also* **July**
decency ['di:sənsı] *n* décence *f*
decent ['di:sənt] *adj* (*proper*) décent(e), convenable; **they were very ~ about it** ils se sont montrés très chics
deception [dı'sεpʃən] *n* tromperie *f*
deceptive [dı'sεptıv] *adj* trompeur(-euse)
decide [dı'saıd] *vt* (*subj: person*) décider; (*question, argument*) trancher, régler ▷ *vi* se décider, décider; **to ~ to do/that** décider de faire/que; **to ~ on** décider, se décider pour; **to ~ on doing** décider de faire; **to ~ against doing** décider de ne pas faire
decided [dı'saıdıd] *adj* (*resolute*) résolu(e), décidé(e); (*clear, definite*) net(te), marqué(e)
decidedly [dı'saıdıdlı] *adv* résolument; incontestablement, nettement
deciduous [dı'sıdjuəs] *adj* à feuilles caduques
decimal ['dεsıməl] *adj* décimal(e) ▷ *n* décimale *f*; **to three ~ places** (jusqu')à la troisième décimale
decimal point *n* ≈ virgule *f*
decipher [dı'saıfə'] *vt* déchiffrer

decision [dı'sıʒən] *n* décision *f*; **to make a ~** prendre une décision
decisive [dı'saısıv] *adj* décisif(-ive); (*influence*) décisif, déterminant(e); (*manner, person*) décidé(e), catégorique; (*reply*) ferme, catégorique
deck [dεk] *n* (*Naut*) pont *m*; (*of cards*) jeu *m*; (*record deck*) platine *f*; (*of bus*): **top ~** impériale *f*; **to go up on ~** monter sur le pont; **below ~** dans l'entrepont
deckchair ['dεktʃεə'] *n* chaise longue
declaration [dεklə'reıʃən] *n* déclaration *f*
declare [dı'klεə'] *vt* déclarer
decline [dı'klaın] *n* (*decay*) déclin *m*; (*lessening*) baisse *f* ▷ *vt* refuser, décliner ▷ *vi* décliner; (*business*) baisser; **~ in living standards** baisse du niveau de vie; **to ~ to do sth** refuser (poliment) de faire qch
decoder [di:'kəudə'] *n* (*Comput, TV*) décodeur *m*
decorate ['dεkəreıt] *vt* (*adorn, give a medal to*) décorer; (*paint and paper*) peindre et tapisser
decoration [dεkə'reıʃən] *n* (*medal etc, adornment*) décoration *f*
decorator ['dεkəreıtə'] *n* peintre *m* en bâtiment
decoy ['di:kɔı] *n* piège *m*; **they used him as a ~ for the enemy** ils se sont servis de lui pour attirer l'ennemi
decrease *n* ['di:kri:s] diminution *f* ▷ *vt, vi* [di:'kri:s] diminuer; **to be on the ~** diminuer, être en diminution
decree [dı'kri:] *n* (*Pol, Rel*) décret *m*; (*Law*) arrêt *m*, jugement *m* ▷ *vt*: **to ~ (that)** décréter (que), ordonner (que); **~ absolute** jugement définitif (de divorce); **~ nisi** jugement provisoire de divorce
dedicate ['dεdıkeıt] *vt* consacrer; (*book etc*) dédier
dedicated ['dεdıkeıtıd] *adj* (*person*) dévoué(e); (*Comput*) spécialisé(e), dédié(e); **~ word processor** station *f* de traitement de texte
dedication [dεdı'keıʃən] *n* (*devotion*) dévouement *m*; (*in book*) dédicace *f*
deduce [dı'dju:s] *vt* déduire, conclure
deduct [dı'dʌkt] *vt*: **to ~ sth (from)** déduire qch (de), retrancher qch (de); (*from wage etc*) prélever qch (sur), retenir qch (sur)
deduction [dı'dʌkʃən] *n* (*deducting, deducing*) déduction *f*; (*from wage etc*) prélèvement *m*, retenue *f*
deed [di:d] *n* action *f*, acte *m*; (*Law*) acte notarié, contrat *m*; **~ of covenant** (acte *m* de) donation *f*
deem [di:m] *vt* (*formal*) juger, estimer; **to ~ it wise to do** juger bon de faire
deep [di:p] *adj* (*water, sigh, sorrow, thoughts*) profond(e); (*voice*) grave ▷ *adv*: **~ in snow** recouvert(e) d'une épaisse couche de neige; **spectators stood 20 ~** il y avait 20 rangs de spectateurs; **knee-~ in water** dans l'eau jusqu'aux genoux; **4 metres ~** de 4 mètres de profondeur; **how ~ is the water?** l'eau a quelle profondeur?; **he took a ~ breath** il inspira profondément, il prit son souffle
deepen [di:pn] *vt* (*hole*) approfondir ▷ *vi* s'approfondir; (*darkness*) s'épaissir

deepfreeze ['diːp'friːz] n congélateur m ▷ vt surgeler

deep-fry ['diːp'fraɪ] vt faire frire (dans une friteuse)

deeply ['diːplɪ] adv profondément; (dig) en profondeur; (regret, interested) vivement

deep-sea ['diːp'siː] adj: ~ **diver** plongeur sous-marin; ~ **diving** plongée sous-marine; ~ **fishing** pêche hauturière

deep-seated ['diːp'siːtɪd] adj (belief) profondément enraciné(e)

deer [dɪəʳ] n (pl inv): **the** ~ les cervidés mpl; (Zool): (**red**) ~ cerf m; (**fallow**) ~ daim m; (**roe**) ~ chevreuil m

deerskin ['dɪəskɪn] n peau f de daim

deface [dɪ'feɪs] vt dégrader; barbouiller rendre illisible

default [dɪ'fɔːlt] vi (Law) faire défaut; (gen) manquer à ses engagements ▷ n (Comput: also: **default value**) valeur f par défaut; **by** ~ (Law) par défaut, par contumace; (Sport) par forfait; **to** ~ **on a debt** ne pas s'acquitter d'une dette

defeat [dɪ'fiːt] n défaite f ▷ vt (team, opponents) battre; (fig: plans, efforts) faire échouer

defect ['diːfɛkt] n défaut m ▷ vi [dɪ'fɛkt]: **to** ~ **to the enemy/the West** passer à l'ennemi/l'Ouest; **physical** ~ malformation f, vice m de conformation; **mental** ~ anomalie or déficience mentale

defective [dɪ'fɛktɪv] adj défectueux(-euse)

defence, (US) **defense** [dɪ'fɛns] n défense f; **in** ~ **of** pour défendre; **witness for the** ~ témoin m à décharge; **the Ministry of D~** (US): **the Department of Defense** le ministère de la Défense nationale

defenceless [dɪ'fɛnslɪs] adj sans défense

defend [dɪ'fɛnd] vt défendre; (decision, action, opinion) justifier, défendre

defendant [dɪ'fɛndənt] n défendeur(-deresse); (in criminal case) accusé(e), prévenu(e)

defender [dɪ'fɛndəʳ] n défenseur m

defense [dɪ'fɛns] n (US) = **defence**

defensive [dɪ'fɛnsɪv] adj défensif(-ive) ▷ n défensive f; **on the** ~ sur la défensive

defer [dɪ'fəːʳ] vt (postpone) différer, ajourner ▷ vi (submit): **to** ~ **to sb/sth** déférer à qn/qch, s'en remettre à qn/qch

defiance [dɪ'faɪəns] n défi m; **in** ~ **of** au mépris de

defiant [dɪ'faɪənt] adj provocant(e), de défi; (person) rebelle, intraitable

deficiency [dɪ'fɪʃənsɪ] n (lack) insuffisance f; (: Med) carence f; (flaw) faiblesse f; (Comm) déficit m, découvert m

deficient [dɪ'fɪʃənt] adj (inadequate) insuffisant(e); (defective) défectueux(-euse); **to be** ~ **in** manquer de

deficit ['dɛfɪsɪt] n déficit m

define [dɪ'faɪn] vt définir

definite ['dɛfɪnɪt] adj (fixed) défini(e), (bien) déterminé(e); (clear, obvious) net(te), manifeste; (Ling) défini(e); (certain) sûr(e); **he was** ~ **about it**

il a été catégorique; il était sûr de son fait

definitely ['dɛfɪnɪtlɪ] adv sans aucun doute

definition [dɛfɪ'nɪʃən] n définition f; (clearness) netteté f

deflate [diː'fleɪt] vt dégonfler; (pompous person) rabattre le caquet à; (Econ) provoquer la déflation de; (: prices) faire tomber or baisser

deflect [dɪ'flɛkt] vt détourner, faire dévier

deformed [dɪ'fɔːmd] adj difforme

defraud [dɪ'frɔːd] vt frauder; **to** ~ **sb of sth** soutirer qch malhonnêtement à qn; escroquer qch à qn; frustrer qn de qch

defrost [diː'frɔst] vt (fridge) dégivrer; (frozen food) décongeler

deft [dɛft] adj adroit(e), preste

defunct [dɪ'fʌŋkt] adj défunt(e)

defuse [diː'fjuːz] vt désamorcer

defy [dɪ'faɪ] vt défier; (efforts etc) résister à; **it defies description** cela défie toute description

degenerate vi [dɪ'dʒɛnəreɪt] dégénérer ▷ adj [dɪ'dʒɛnərɪt] dégénéré(e)

degree [dɪ'griː] n degré m; (Scol) diplôme m (universitaire); **10 ~s below (zero)** 10 degrés au-dessous de zéro; **a (first)** ~ **in maths** (Brit) une licence en maths; **a considerable** ~ **of risk** un considérable facteur or élément de risque; **by** ~**s** (gradually) par degrés; **to some** ~, **to a certain** ~ jusqu'à un certain point, dans une certaine mesure

dehydrated [diːhaɪ'dreɪtɪd] adj déshydraté(e); (milk, eggs) en poudre

de-ice ['diː'aɪs] vt (windscreen) dégivrer

de-icer ['diː'aɪsəʳ] n dégivreur m

deign [deɪn] vi: **to** ~ **to do** daigner faire

dejected [dɪ'dʒɛktɪd] adj abattu(e), déprimé(e)

delay [dɪ'leɪ] vt (journey, operation) retarder, différer; (traveller, train) retarder; (payment) différer ▷ vi s'attarder ▷ n délai m, retard m; **to be ~ed** être en retard; **without** ~ sans délai, sans tarder

delectable [dɪ'lɛktəbl] adj délicieux(-euse)

delegate n ['dɛlɪgɪt] délégué(e) ▷ vt ['dɛlɪgeɪt] déléguer; **to** ~ **sth to sb/sb to do sth** déléguer qch à qn/qn pour faire qch

delete [dɪ'liːt] vt rayer, supprimer; (Comput) effacer

deli ['dɛlɪ] n épicerie fine

deliberate adj [dɪ'lɪbərɪt] (intentional) délibéré(e); (slow) mesuré(e) ▷ vi [dɪ'lɪbəreɪt] délibérer, réfléchir

deliberately [dɪ'lɪbərɪtlɪ] adv (on purpose) exprès, délibérément

delicacy ['dɛlɪkəsɪ] n délicatesse f; (choice food) mets fin or délicat, friandise f

delicate ['dɛlɪkɪt] adj délicat(e)

delicatessen [dɛlɪkə'tɛsn] n épicerie fine

delicious [dɪ'lɪʃəs] adj délicieux(-euse), exquis(e)

delight [dɪ'laɪt] n (grande) joie, grand plaisir ▷ vt enchanter; **she's a** ~ **to work with** c'est un plaisir de travailler avec elle; **a** ~ **to the eyes** un régal or plaisir pour les yeux; **to take** ~ **in** prendre grand plaisir à; **to be the** ~ **of** faire les délices or la joie de

delighted [dɪ'laɪtɪd] adj: ~ **(at** or **with sth)** ravi(e) (de qch); **to be ~ to do sth/that** être enchanté(e) or ravi(e) de faire qch/que; **I'd be ~** j'en serais enchanté or ravi

delightful [dɪ'laɪtful] adj (person) absolument charmant(e), adorable; (meal, evening) merveilleux(-euse)

delinquent [dɪ'lɪŋkwənt] adj, n délinquant(e)

delirious [dɪ'lɪrɪəs] adj (Med: fig) délirant(e); **to be ~** délirer

deliver [dɪ'lɪvəʳ] vt (mail) distribuer; (goods) livrer; (message) remettre; (speech) prononcer; (warning, ultimatum) lancer; (free) délivrer; (Med: baby) mettre au monde; (: woman) accoucher; **to ~ the goods** (fig) tenir ses promesses

delivery [dɪ'lɪvərɪ] n (of mail) distribution f; (of goods) livraison f; (of speaker) élocution f; (Med) accouchement m; **to take ~ of** prendre livraison de

delude [dɪ'lu:d] vt tromper, leurrer; **to ~ o.s.** se leurrer, se faire des illusions

delusion [dɪ'lu:ʒən] n illusion f; **to have ~s of grandeur** être un peu mégalomane

de luxe [də'lʌks] adj de luxe

delve [dɛlv] vi: **to ~ into** fouiller dans

demand [dɪ'mɑ:nd] vt réclamer, exiger; (need) exiger, requérir ▷ n exigence f; (claim) revendication f; (Econ) demande f; **to ~ sth (from** or **of sb)** exiger qch (de qn), réclamer qch (à qn); **in ~** demandé(e), recherché(e); **on ~** sur demande

demanding [dɪ'mɑ:ndɪŋ] adj (person) exigeant(e); (work) astreignant(e)

demean [dɪ'mi:n] vt: **to ~ o.s.** s'abaisser

demeanour, (US) **demeanor** [dɪ'mi:nəʳ] n comportement m; maintien m

demented [dɪ'mɛntɪd] adj dément(e), fou (folle)

demise [dɪ'maɪz] n décès m

demister [di:'mɪstəʳ] n (Brit Aut) dispositif m anti-buée inv

demo ['dɛməu] n abbr (inf) = **demonstration**; (protest) manif f; (Comput) démonstration f

democracy [dɪ'mɔkrəsɪ] n démocratie f

democrat ['dɛməkræt] n démocrate m/f

democratic [dɛmə'krætɪk] adj démocratique; **the D~ Party** (US) le parti démocrate

demolish [dɪ'mɔlɪʃ] vt démolir

demolition [dɛmə'lɪʃən] n démolition f

demon ['di:mən] n démon m ▷ cpd: **a ~ squash player** un crack en squash; **a ~ driver** un fou du volant

demonstrate ['dɛmənstreɪt] vt démontrer, prouver; (show) faire une démonstration de ▷ vi: **to ~ (for/against)** manifester (en faveur de/contre)

demonstration [dɛmən'streɪʃən] n démonstration f; (Pol etc) manifestation f; **to hold a ~** (Pol etc) organiser une manifestation, manifester

demonstrator ['dɛmənstreɪtəʳ] n (Pol etc) manifestant(e); (Comm: sales person)

vendeur(-euse); (: car, computer etc) modèle m de démonstration

demote [dɪ'məut] vt rétrograder

demure [dɪ'mjuəʳ] adj sage, réservé(e), d'une modestie affectée

den [dɛn] n (of lion) tanière f; (room) repaire m

denial [dɪ'naɪəl] n (of accusation) démenti m; (of rights, guilt, truth) dénégation f

denim ['dɛnɪm] n jean m; **denims** npl (blue-)jeans mpl

Denmark ['dɛnmɑ:k] n Danemark m

denomination [dɪnɔmɪ'neɪʃən] n (money) valeur f; (Rel) confession f; culte m

denounce [dɪ'nauns] vt dénoncer

dense [dɛns] adj dense; (inf: stupid) obtus(e), dur(e) or lent(e) à la comprenette

densely ['dɛnslɪ] adv: ~ **wooded** couvert(e) d'épaisses forêts; ~ **populated** à forte densité (de population), très peuplé(e)

density ['dɛnsɪtɪ] n densité f

dent [dɛnt] n bosse f ▷ vt (also: **make a dent in**) cabosser; **to make a ~ in** (fig) entamer

dental ['dɛntl] adj dentaire

dental floss [-flɔs] n fil m dentaire

dental surgeon n (chirurgien(ne)) dentiste

dental surgery n cabinet m de dentiste

dentist ['dɛntɪst] n dentiste m/f; ~'**s surgery** (Brit) cabinet m de dentiste

dentures ['dɛntʃəz] npl dentier msg

deny [dɪ'naɪ] vt nier; (refuse) refuser; (disown) renier; **he denies having said it** il nie l'avoir dit

deodorant [di:'əudərənt] n désodorisant m, déodorant m

depart [dɪ'pɑ:t] vi partir; **to ~ from** (leave) quitter, partir de; (fig: differ from) s'écarter de

department [dɪ'pɑ:tmənt] n (Comm) rayon m; (Scol) section f; (Pol) ministère m, département m; **that's not my ~** (fig) ce n'est pas mon domaine or ma compétence, ce n'est pas mon rayon; **D~ of State** (US) Département d'État

department store n grand magasin

departure [dɪ'pɑ:tʃəʳ] n départ m; (fig): ~ **from** écart m par rapport à; **a new ~** une nouvelle voie

departure lounge n salle f de départ

depend [dɪ'pɛnd] vi: **to ~ (up)on** dépendre de; (rely on) compter sur; (financially) dépendre (financièrement) de, être à la charge de; **it ~s** cela dépend; ~**ing on the result ...** selon le résultat ...

dependable [dɪ'pɛndəbl] adj sûr(e), digne de confiance

dependant [dɪ'pɛndənt] n personne f à charge

dependent [dɪ'pɛndənt] adj: **to be ~ (on)** dépendre (de) ▷ n = **dependant**

depict [dɪ'pɪkt] vt (in picture) représenter; (in words) (dé)peindre, décrire

depleted [dɪ'pli:tɪd] adj (considérablement) réduit(e) or diminué(e)

deport [dɪ'pɔ:t] vt déporter, expulser

deposit [dɪ'pɔzɪt] n (Chem, Comm, Geo) dépôt m; (of ore, oil) gisement m; (part payment) arrhes fpl, acompte m; (on bottle etc) consigne f; (for hired *goods etc*) cautionnement *m*, garantie *f* ▷ *vt* déposer; (*valuables*) mettre *or* laisser en dépôt; **to put down a ~ of £50** verser 50 livres d'arrhes *or* d'acompte; laisser 50 livres en garantie

deposit account *n* compte *m* sur livret

depot ['dɛpəu] *n* dépôt *m*; (US: Rail) gare *f*

depreciate [dɪ'priːʃɪeɪt] *vt* déprécier ▷ *vi* se déprécier, se dévaloriser

depress [dɪ'prɛs] *vt* déprimer; (*press down*) appuyer sur, abaisser; (*wages etc*) faire baisser

depressed [dɪ'prɛst] *adj* (*person*) déprimé(e), abattu(e); (*area*) en déclin, touché(e) par le sous-emploi; (*Comm: market, trade*) maussade; **to get ~** se démoraliser, se laisser abattre

depressing [dɪ'prɛsɪŋ] *adj* déprimant(e)

depression [dɪ'prɛʃən] *n* (*Econ*) dépression *f*

deprivation [dɛprɪ'veɪʃən] *n* privation *f*; (*loss*) perte *f*

deprive [dɪ'praɪv] *vt*: **to ~ sb of** priver qn de

deprived [dɪ'praɪvd] *adj* déshérité(e)

dept. *abbr* (= *department*) dép, dépt

depth [dɛpθ] *n* profondeur *f*; **in the ~s of** au fond de; au cœur de; au plus profond de; **to be in the ~s of despair** être au plus profond du désespoir; **at a ~ of 3 metres** à 3 mètres de profondeur; **to be out of one's ~** (*Brit: swimmer*) ne plus avoir pied; (*fig*) être dépassé(e), nager; **to study sth in ~** étudier qch en profondeur

deputize ['dɛpjutaɪz] *vi*: **to ~ for** assurer l'intérim de

deputy ['dɛpjutɪ] *n* (*replacement*) suppléant(e), intérimaire *m/f*; (*second in command*) adjoint(e); (*Pol*) député *m*; (*US: also:* **deputy sheriff**) shérif adjoint ▷ *adj*: **~ chairman** vice-président *m*; **~ head** (*Scol*) directeur(-trice) adjoint(e), sous-directeur(-trice); **~ leader** (*Brit Pol*) vice-président(e), secrétaire adjoint(e)

derail [dɪ'reɪl] *vt* faire dérailler; **to be ~ed** dérailler

deranged [dɪ'reɪndʒd] *adj*: **to be (mentally) ~** avoir le cerveau dérangé

derby ['dəːrbɪ] *n* (US) (chapeau *m*) melon *m*

derelict ['dɛrɪlɪkt] *adj* abandonné(e), à l'abandon

derisory [dɪ'raɪsərɪ] *adj* (*sum*) dérisoire; (*smile, person*) moqueur(-euse), railleur(-euse)

derive [dɪ'raɪv] *vt*: **to ~ sth from** tirer qch de; trouver qch dans ▷ *vi*: **to ~ from** provenir de, dériver de

derogatory [dɪ'rɔgətərɪ] *adj* désobligeant(e), péjoratif(-ive)

descend [dɪ'sɛnd] *vt, vi* descendre; **to ~ from** descendre de, être issu(e) de; **to ~ to** s'abaisser à; **in ~ing order of importance** par ordre d'importance décroissante

▶ **descend on** *vt fus* (*enemy, angry person*) tomber *or* sauter sur; (*misfortune*) s'abattre sur; (*gloom, silence*) envahir; **visitors ~ed (up)on us** des gens sont arrivés chez nous à l'improviste

descendant [dɪ'sɛndənt] *n* descendant(e)

descent [dɪ'sɛnt] *n* descente *f*; (*origin*) origine *f*

describe [dɪs'kraɪb] *vt* décrire

description [dɪs'krɪpʃən] *n* description *f*; (*sort*)

sorte *f*, espèce *f*; **of every ~** de toutes sortes

desecrate ['dɛsɪkreɪt] *vt* profaner

desert [*n* 'dɛzət, *vb* dɪ'zəːt] *n* désert *m* ▷ *vt* déserter, abandonner ▷ *vi* (*Mil*) déserter

deserted [dɪ'zəːtɪd] *adj* désert(e)

deserter [dɪ'zəːtəʳ] *n* déserteur *m*

desertion [dɪ'zəːʃən] *n* désertion *f*

desert island *n* île déserte

deserve [dɪ'zəːv] *vt* mériter

deserving [dɪ'zəːvɪŋ] *adj* (*person*) méritant(e); (*action, cause*) méritoire

design [dɪ'zaɪn] *n* (*sketch*) plan *m*, dessin *m*; (*layout, shape*) conception *f*, ligne *f*; (*pattern*) dessin, motif(s) *m(pl)*; (*of dress, car*) modèle *m*; (*art*) design *m*, stylisme *m*; (*intention*) dessein *m* ▷ *vt* dessiner; (*plan*) concevoir; **to have ~s on** avoir des visées sur; **well-~ed** *adj* bien conçu(e); **industrial ~** esthétique industrielle

design and technology *n* (*Brit: Scol*) technologie *f*

designate *vt* ['dɛzɪgneɪt] désigner ▷ *adj* ['dɛzɪgnɪt] désigné(e)

designer [dɪ'zaɪnəʳ] *n* (*Archit, Art*) dessinateur(-trice); (*Industry*) concepteur *m*, designer *m*; (*Fashion*) styliste *m/f*

desirable [dɪ'zaɪərəbl] *adj* (*property, location, purchase*) attrayant(e); **it is ~ that** il est souhaitable que

desire [dɪ'zaɪəʳ] *n* désir *m* ▷ *vt* désirer, vouloir; **to ~ to do sth/that** désirer faire qch/que

desk [dɛsk] *n* (*in office*) bureau *m*; (*for pupil*) pupitre *m*; (*Brit: in shop, restaurant*) caisse *f*; (*in hotel, at airport*) réception *f*

desk-top publishing ['dɛsktɔp-] *n* publication assistée par ordinateur, PAO *f*

desolate ['dɛsəlɪt] *adj* désolé(e)

despair [dɪs'pɛəʳ] *n* désespoir *m* ▷ *vi*: **to ~ of** désespérer de; **to be in ~** être au désespoir

despatch [dɪs'pætʃ] *n, vt* = **dispatch**

desperate ['dɛspərɪt] *adj* désespéré(e); (*fugitive*) prêt(e) à tout; (*measures*) désespéré, extrême; **to be ~ for sth/to do sth** avoir désespérément besoin de qch/de faire qch; **we are getting ~** nous commençons à désespérer

desperately ['dɛspərɪtlɪ] *adv* désespérément; (*very*) terriblement, extrêmement; **~ ill** très gravement malade

desperation [dɛspə'reɪʃən] *n* désespoir *m*; **in (sheer) ~** en désespoir de cause

despicable [dɪs'pɪkəbl] *adj* méprisable

despise [dɪs'paɪz] *vt* mépriser, dédaigner

despite [dɪs'paɪt] *prep* malgré, en dépit de

despondent [dɪs'pɔndənt] *adj* découragé(e), abattu(e)

dessert [dɪ'zəːt] *n* dessert *m*

dessertspoon [dɪ'zəːtspuːn] *n* cuiller *f* à dessert

destination [dɛstɪ'neɪʃən] *n* destination *f*

destined ['dɛstɪnd] *adj*: **to be ~ to do sth** être destiné(e) à faire qch; **~ for London** à destination de Londres

destiny ['dɛstɪnɪ] *n* destinée *f*, destin *m*

destitute ['dɛstɪtjuːt] *adj* indigent(e), dans le

dénuement; **~ of** dépourvu(e) or dénué(e) de

destroy [dɪs'trɔɪ] vt détruire; (*injured horse*) abattre; (*dog*) faire piquer

destroyer [dɪs'trɔɪəʳ] n (Naut) contre-torpilleur m

destruction [dɪs'trʌkʃən] n destruction f

destructive [dɪs'trʌktɪv] adj destructeur(-trice)

detach [dɪ'tætʃ] vt détacher

detached [dɪ'tætʃt] adj (*attitude*) détaché(e)

detached house n pavillon m maison(nette) (individuelle)

detachment [dɪ'tætʃmənt] n (Mil) détachement m; (*fig*) détachement, indifférence f

detail ['di:teɪl] n détail m; (Mil) détachement m ▷ vt raconter en détail, énumérer; (Mil): **to ~ sb (for)** affecter qn (à), détacher qn (pour); **in ~** en détail; **to go into ~(s)** entrer dans les détails

detailed ['di:teɪld] adj détaillé(e)

detain [dɪ'teɪn] vt retenir; (*in captivity*) détenir; (*in hospital*) hospitaliser

detect [dɪ'tɛkt] vt déceler, percevoir; (Med, Police) dépister; (Mil, Radar, Tech) détecter

detection [dɪ'tɛkʃən] n découverte f; (Med, Police) dépistage m; (Mil, Radar, Tech) détection f; **to escape ~** échapper aux recherches, éviter d'être découvert(e); (*mistake*) passer inaperçu(e); **crime ~** le dépistage des criminels

detective [dɪ'tɛktɪv] n agent m de la sûreté, policier m; **private ~** détective privé

detective story n roman policier

detention [dɪ'tɛnʃən] n détention f; (Scol) retenue f, consigne f

deter [dɪ'təːʳ] vt dissuader

detergent [dɪ'təːdʒənt] n détersif m, détergent m

deteriorate [dɪ'tɪərɪəreɪt] vi se détériorer, se dégrader

determination [dɪtəːmɪ'neɪʃən] n détermination f

determine [dɪ'təːmɪn] vt déterminer; **to ~ to do** résoudre de faire, se déterminer à faire

determined [dɪ'təːmɪnd] adj (*person*) déterminé(e), décidé(e); (*quantity*) déterminé, établi(e); (*effort*) très gros(se); **~ to do** bien décidé à faire

deterrent [dɪ'tɛrənt] n effet m de dissuasion; force f de dissuasion; **to act as a ~** avoir un effet dissuasif

detest [dɪ'tɛst] vt détester, avoir horreur de

detonate ['dɛtəneɪt] vi exploser ▷ vt faire exploser or détoner

detour ['di:tuəʳ] n détour m; (US Aut: *diversion*) déviation f

detract [dɪ'trækt] vt: **to ~ from** (*quality, pleasure*) diminuer; (*reputation*) porter atteinte à

detriment ['dɛtrɪmənt] n: **to the ~ of** au détriment de, au préjudice de; **without ~ to** sans porter atteinte or préjudice à, sans conséquences fâcheuses pour

detrimental [dɛtrɪ'mɛntl] adj: **~ to** préjudiciable or nuisible à

devaluation [dɪvælju'eɪʃən] n dévaluation f

devastate ['dɛvəsteɪt] vt dévaster; **he was ~d by the news** cette nouvelle lui a porté un coup terrible

devastating ['dɛvəsteɪtɪŋ] adj dévastateur(-trice); (*news*) accablant(e)

develop [dɪ'vɛləp] vt (*gen*) développer; (*disease*) commencer à souffrir de; (*habit*) contracter; (*resources*) mettre en valeur, exploiter; (*land*) aménager ▷ vi se développer; (*situation, disease: evolve*) évoluer; (*facts, symptoms: appear*) se manifester, se produire; **can you ~ this film?** pouvez-vous développer cette pellicule?; **to ~ a taste for sth** prendre goût à qch; **to ~ into** devenir

developer [dɪ'vɛləpəʳ] n (Phot) révélateur m; (*of land*) promoteur m; (*also:* **property developer**) promoteur immobilier

developing country [dɪ'vɛləpɪŋ-] n pays m en voie de développement

development [dɪ'vɛləpmənt] n développement m; (*of land*) exploitation f; (*new fact, event*) rebondissement m, fait(s) nouveau(x)

device [dɪ'vaɪs] n (*scheme*) moyen m, expédient m; (*apparatus*) appareil m, dispositif m; **explosive ~** engin explosif

devil ['dɛvl] n diable m; démon m

devious ['di:vɪəs] adj (*means*) détourné(e); (*person*) sournois(e), dissimulé(e)

devise [dɪ'vaɪz] vt imaginer, concevoir

devoid [dɪ'vɔɪd] adj: **~ of** dépourvu(e) de, dénué(e) de

devolution [di:və'lu:ʃən] n (Pol) décentralisation f

devote [dɪ'vəut] vt: **to ~ sth to** consacrer qch à

devoted [dɪ'vəutɪd] adj dévoué(e); **to be ~ to** être dévoué(e) or très attaché(e) à; (*book etc*) être consacré(e) à

devotee [dɛvəu'ti:] n (Rel) adepte m/f; (Mus, Sport) fervent(e)

devotion [dɪ'vəuʃən] n dévouement m, attachement m; (Rel) dévotion f, piété f

devour [dɪ'vauəʳ] vt dévorer

devout [dɪ'vaut] adj pieux(-euse), dévot(e)

dew [dju:] n rosée f

diabetes [daɪə'bi:ti:z] n diabète m

diabetic [daɪə'bɛtɪk] n diabétique m/f ▷ adj (*person*) diabétique; (*chocolate, jam*) pour diabétiques

diabolical [daɪə'bɔlɪkl] adj diabolique; (*inf: dreadful*) infernal(e), atroce

diagnose [daɪəg'nəuz] vt diagnostiquer

diagnosis (*pl* **diagnoses**) [daɪəg'nəusɪs, -si:z] n diagnostic m

diagonal [daɪ'ægənl] adj diagonal(e) ▷ n diagonale f

diagram ['daɪəgræm] n diagramme m, schéma m

dial ['daɪəl] n cadran m ▷ vt (*number*) faire, composer; **to ~ a wrong number** faire un faux numéro; **can I ~ London direct?** puis-je or est-ce-que je peux avoir Londres par l'automatique?

dialect ['daɪəlɛkt] n dialecte m

dialling code ['daɪəlɪŋ-], (US) **dial code** n indicatif m (téléphonique); **what's the ~ for Paris?** quel est l'indicatif de Paris?

dialling tone ['daɪəlɪŋ-], (US) **dial tone** n
tonalité f

dialogue, (US) **dialog** ['daɪəlɔg] n dialogue m

diameter [daɪ'æmɪtəʳ] n diamètre m

diamond ['daɪəmənd] n diamant m; (shape)
losange m; **diamonds** npl (Cards) carreau m

diaper ['daɪəpəʳ] n (US) couche f

diaphragm ['daɪəfræm] n diaphragme m

diarrhoea, (US) **diarrhea** [daɪə'riːə] n diarrhée f

diary ['daɪərɪ] n (daily account) journal m; (book)
agenda m; **to keep a ~** tenir un journal

dice [daɪs] n (pl inv) dé m ▷ vt (Culin) couper en dés
or en cubes

dictate [vb dɪk'teɪt, n 'dɪkteɪt] vt dicter ▷ vi: **to
~ to** (person) imposer sa volonté à, régenter; **I
won't be ~d to** je n'ai d'ordres à recevoir de
personne ▷ n injonction f

dictation [dɪk'teɪʃən] n dictée f; **at ~ speed** à une
vitesse de dictée

dictator [dɪk'teɪtəʳ] n dictateur m

dictatorship [dɪk'teɪtəʃɪp] n dictature f

dictionary ['dɪkʃənrɪ] n dictionnaire m

did [dɪd] pt of **do**

didn't ['dɪdnt] = **did not**

die [daɪ] n (pl **dice**) dé m (pl **-s**) coin m; matrice f;
étampe f ▷ vi mourir; **to ~ of** or **from** mourir de;
to be dying être mourant(e); **to be dying for
sth** avoir une envie folle de qch; **to be dying to
do sth** mourir d'envie de faire qch
 ▶ **die away** vi s'éteindre
 ▶ **die down** vi se calmer, s'apaiser
 ▶ **die out** vi disparaître, s'éteindre

diesel ['diːzl] n (vehicle) diesel m; (also: **diesel oil**)
carburant m diesel, gas-oil m

diesel engine n moteur m diesel

diet ['daɪət] n alimentation f; (restricted food)
régime m ▷ vi (also: **be on a diet**) suivre un
régime; **to live on a ~ of** se nourrir de

differ ['dɪfəʳ] vi: **to ~ from sth** (be different) être
différent(e) de qch, différer de qch; **to ~ from
sb over sth** ne pas être d'accord avec qn au sujet
de qch

difference ['dɪfrəns] n différence f; (quarrel)
différend m, désaccord m; **it makes no ~ to me**
cela m'est égal, cela m'est indifférent; **to settle
one's ~s** résoudre la situation

different ['dɪfrənt] adj différent(e)

differentiate [dɪfə'rɛnʃɪeɪt] vt différencier
 ▷ vi se différencier; **to ~ between** faire une
différence entre

differently ['dɪfrəntlɪ] adv différemment

difficult ['dɪfɪkəlt] adj difficile; **~ to understand**
difficile à comprendre

difficulty ['dɪfɪkəltɪ] n difficulté f; **to have
difficulties with** avoir des ennuis or problèmes
avec; **to be in ~** avoir des difficultés, avoir des
problèmes

diffident ['dɪfɪdənt] adj qui manque de confiance
or d'assurance, peu sûr(e) de soi

dig [dɪg] vt (pt, pp **dug**) [dʌg] (hole) creuser;
(garden) bêcher ▷ n (prod) coup m de coude; (fig:
remark) coup de griffe or de patte; (Archaeology)

fouille f; **to ~ into** (snow, soil) creuser; **to ~ into
one's pockets for sth** fouiller dans ses poches
pour chercher or prendre qch; **to ~ one's nails
into** enfoncer ses ongles dans
 ▶ **dig in** vi (also: **dig o.s. in**: Mil) se retrancher;
(: fig) tenir bon, se braquer; (inf: eat) attaquer (un
repas or un plat etc) ▷ vt (compost) bien mélanger
à la bêche; (knife, claw) enfoncer; **to ~ in one's
heels** (fig) se braquer, se buter
 ▶ **dig out** vt (survivors, car from snow) sortir or
dégager (à coups de pelles or pioches)
 ▶ **dig up** vt déterrer

digest vt [daɪ'dʒɛst] digérer ▷ n ['daɪdʒɛst]
sommaire m, résumé m

digestion [dɪ'dʒɛstʃən] n digestion f

digit ['dɪdʒɪt] n (number) chiffre m (de o à 9); (finger)
doigt m

digital ['dɪdʒɪtl] adj (system, recording, radio)
numérique, digital(e); (watch) à affichage
numérique or digital

digital camera n appareil m photo numérique

digital TV n télévision f numérique

dignified ['dɪgnɪfaɪd] adj digne

dignity ['dɪgnɪtɪ] n dignité f

digress [daɪ'grɛs] vi: **to ~ from** s'écarter de,
s'éloigner de

digs [dɪgz] npl (Brit inf) piaule f, chambre meublée

dilapidated [dɪ'læpɪdeɪtɪd] adj délabré(e)

dilemma [daɪ'lɛmə] n dilemme m; **to be in a ~**
être pris dans un dilemme

diligent ['dɪlɪdʒənt] adj appliqué(e), assidu(e)

dill [dɪl] n aneth m

dilute [daɪ'luːt] vt diluer ▷ adj dilué(e)

dim [dɪm] adj (light, eyesight) faible; (memory,
outline) vague, indécis(e); (room) sombre; (inf:
stupid) borné(e), obtus(e) ▷ vt (light) réduire,
baisser; (US Aut) mettre en code, baisser; **to take
a ~ view of sth** voir qch d'un mauvais œil

dime [daɪm] n (US) pièce f de 10 cents

dimension [daɪ'mɛnʃən] n dimension f

diminish [dɪ'mɪnɪʃ] vt, vi diminuer

diminutive [dɪ'mɪnjutɪv] adj minuscule, tout(e)
petit(e) ▷ n (Ling) diminutif m

dimmer ['dɪməʳ] n (also: **dimmer switch**)
variateur m; **dimmers** npl (US Aut: dipped
headlights) phares mpl, code inv; (parking lights) feux
mpl de position

dimple ['dɪmpl] n fossette f

din [dɪn] n vacarme m ▷ vt: **to ~ sth into sb** (inf)
enfoncer qch dans la tête or la caboche de qn

dine [daɪn] vi dîner

diner ['daɪnəʳ] n (person) dîneur(-euse); (Rail) =
dining car; (US: eating place) petit restaurant

dinghy ['dɪŋgɪ] n youyou m; (inflatable) canot m
pneumatique; (also: **sailing dinghy**) voilier m,
dériveur m

dingy ['dɪndʒɪ] adj miteux(-euse), minable

dining car ['daɪnɪŋ-] n (Brit) voiture-restaurant f,
wagon-restaurant m

dining room ['daɪnɪŋ-] n salle f à manger

dining table ['daɪnɪŋ-] n table f de (la) salle à
manger

dinner ['dɪnə^r] *n* (*evening meal*) dîner *m*; (*lunch*) déjeuner *m*; (*public*) banquet *m*; **~'s ready!** à table!

dinner jacket *n* smoking *m*

dinner party *n* dîner *m*

dinner time *n* (*evening*) heure *f* du dîner; (*midday*) heure du déjeuner

dinosaur ['daɪnəsɔː^r] *n* dinosaure *m*

dip [dɪp] *n* (*slope*) déclivité *f*; (*in sea*) baignade *f*, bain *m*; (*Culin*) ≈ sauce *f* ▷ *vt* tremper, plonger; (*Brit Aut: lights*) mettre en code, baisser ▷ *vi* plonger

diploma [dɪ'pləʊmə] *n* diplôme *m*

diplomacy [dɪ'pləʊməsɪ] *n* diplomatie *f*

diplomat ['dɪpləmæt] *n* diplomate *m*

diplomatic [dɪplə'mætɪk] *adj* diplomatique; **to break off ~ relations (with)** rompre les relations diplomatiques (avec)

dipstick ['dɪpstɪk] *n* (*Brit Aut*) jauge *f* de niveau d'huile

dipswitch ['dɪpswɪtʃ] *n* (*Brit Aut*) commutateur *m* de code

dire [daɪə^r] *adj* (*poverty*) extrême; (*awful*) affreux(-euse)

direct [daɪ'rɛkt] *adj* direct(e); (*manner, person*) direct, franc (franche) ▷ *vt* (*tell way*) diriger, orienter; (*letter, remark*) adresser; (*Cine, TV*) réaliser; (*Theat*) mettre en scène; (*order*): **to ~ sb to do sth** ordonner à qn de faire qch ▷ *adv* directement; **can you ~ me to ...?** pouvez-vous m'indiquer le chemin de ...?

direct debit *n* (*Brit Banking*) prélèvement *m* automatique

direction [dɪ'rɛkʃən] *n* direction *f*; (*Theat*) mise *f* en scène; (*Cine, TV*) réalisation *f*; **directions** *npl* (*to a place*) indications *fpl*; **~s for use** mode *m* d'emploi; **to ask for ~s** demander sa route *or* son chemin; **sense of ~** sens *m* de l'orientation; **in the ~ of** dans la direction de, vers

directly [dɪ'rɛktlɪ] *adv* (*in straight line*) directement, tout droit; (*at once*) tout de suite, immédiatement

director [dɪ'rɛktə^r] *n* directeur *m*; (*board member*) administrateur *m*; (*Theat*) metteur *m* en scène; (*Cine, TV*) réalisateur(-trice); **D~ of Public Prosecutions** (*Brit*) ≈ procureur général

directory [dɪ'rɛktərɪ] *n* annuaire *m*; (*also:* **street directory**) indicateur *m* de rues; (*also:* **trade directory**) annuaire du commerce; (*Comput*) répertoire *m*

directory enquiries, (*US*) **directory assistance** *n* (*Tel: service*) renseignements *mpl*

dirt [dəːt] *n* saleté *f*; (*mud*) boue *f*; **to treat sb like ~** traiter qn comme un chien

dirt-cheap ['dəːt'tʃiːp] *adj* (ne) coûtant presque rien

dirty ['dəːtɪ] *adj* sale; (*joke*) cochon(ne) ▷ *vt* salir; **~ story** histoire cochonne; **~ trick** coup tordu

disability [dɪsə'bɪlɪtɪ] *n* invalidité *f*, infirmité *f*

disabled [dɪs'eɪbld] *adj* handicapé(e); (*maimed*) mutilé(e); (*through illness, old age*) impotent(e)

disadvantage [dɪsəd'vɑːntɪdʒ] *n* désavantage *m*,

inconvénient *m*

disagree [dɪsə'griː] *vi* (*differ*) ne pas concorder; (*be against, think otherwise*): **to ~ (with)** ne pas être d'accord (avec); **garlic ~s with me** l'ail ne me convient pas, je ne supporte pas l'ail

disagreeable [dɪsə'griːəbl] *adj* désagréable

disagreement [dɪsə'griːmənt] *n* désaccord *m*, différend *m*

disallow ['dɪsə'lau] *vt* rejeter, désavouer; (*Brit Football: goal*) refuser

disappear [dɪsə'pɪə^r] *vi* disparaître

disappearance [dɪsə'pɪərəns] *n* disparition *f*

disappoint [dɪsə'pɔɪnt] *vt* décevoir

disappointed [dɪsə'pɔɪntɪd] *adj* déçu(e)

disappointing [dɪsə'pɔɪntɪŋ] *adj* décevant(e)

disappointment [dɪsə'pɔɪntmənt] *n* déception *f*

disapproval [dɪsə'pruːvəl] *n* désapprobation *f*

disapprove [dɪsə'pruːv] *vi*: **to ~ of** désapprouver

disarm [dɪs'ɑːm] *vt* désarmer

disarmament [dɪs'ɑːməmənt] *n* désarmement *m*

disarray [dɪsə'reɪ] *n* désordre *m*, confusion *f*; **in ~** (*troops*) en déroute; (*thoughts*) embrouillé(e); (*clothes*) en désordre; **to throw into ~** semer la confusion *or* le désordre dans (*or* parmi)

disaster [dɪ'zɑːstə^r] *n* catastrophe *f*, désastre *m*

disastrous [dɪ'zɑːstrəs] *adj* désastreux(-euse)

disband [dɪs'bænd] *vt* démobiliser; disperser ▷ *vi* se séparer; se disperser

disbelief ['dɪsbə'liːf] *n* incrédulité *f*; **in ~** avec incrédulité

disc [dɪsk] *n* disque *m*; (*Comput*) = **disk**

discard [dɪs'kɑːd] *vt* (*old things*) se débarrasser de, mettre au rencart *or* au rebut; (*fig*) écarter, renoncer à

discern [dɪ'səːn] *vt* discerner, distinguer

discerning [dɪ'səːnɪŋ] *adj* judicieux(-euse), perspicace

discharge *vt* [dɪs'tʃɑːdʒ] (*duties*) s'acquitter de; (*settle: debt*) s'acquitter de, régler; (*waste etc*) déverser; décharger; (*Elec, Med*) émettre; (*patient*) renvoyer (chez lui); (*employee, soldier*) congédier, licencier; (*defendant*) relaxer, élargir ▷ *n* ['dɪstʃɑːdʒ] (*Elec, Med*) émission *f*; (*also:* **vaginal discharge**) pertes blanches; (*dismissal*) renvoi *m*; licenciement *m*; élargissement *m*; **to ~ one's gun** faire feu; **~d bankrupt** failli(e), réhabilité(e)

discipline ['dɪsɪplɪn] *n* discipline *f* ▷ *vt* discipliner; (*punish*) punir; **to ~ o.s. to do sth** s'imposer *or* s'astreindre à une discipline pour faire qch

disc jockey *n* disque-jockey *m* (DJ)

disclaim [dɪs'kleɪm] *vt* désavouer, dénier

disclose [dɪs'kləuz] *vt* révéler, divulguer

disclosure [dɪs'kləuʒə^r] *n* révélation *f*, divulgation *f*

disco ['dɪskəu] *n abbr* discothèque *f*

discoloured, (*US*) **discolored** [dɪs'kʌləd] *adj* décoloré(e), jauni(e)

discomfort [dɪs'kʌmfət] *n* malaise *m*, gêne *f*; (*lack of comfort*) manque *m* de confort

disconcert [dɪskən'sə:t] vt déconcerter, décontenancer

disconnect [dɪskə'nɛkt] vt détacher; (Elec, Radio) débrancher; (gas, water) couper

discontent [dɪskən'tɛnt] n mécontentement m

discontented [dɪskən'tɛntɪd] adj mécontent(e)

discontinue [dɪskən'tɪnju:] vt cesser, interrompre; **"~d"** (Comm) "fin de série"

discord ['dɪskɔ:d] n discorde f, dissension f; (Mus) dissonance f

discount n ['dɪskaunt] remise f, rabais m ▷ vt [dɪs'kaunt] (report etc) ne pas tenir compte de; **to give sb a ~ on sth** faire une remise or un rabais à qn sur qch; **~ for cash** escompte f au comptant; **at a ~** avec une remise or réduction, au rabais

discourage [dɪs'kʌrɪdʒ] vt décourager; (dissuade, deter) dissuader, décourager

discover [dɪs'kʌvəʳ] vt découvrir

discovery [dɪs'kʌvərɪ] n découverte f

discredit [dɪs'krɛdɪt] vt (idea) mettre en doute; (person) discréditer ▷ n discrédit m

discreet [dɪ'skri:t] adj discret(-ète)

discrepancy [dɪ'skrɛpənsɪ] n divergence f, contradiction f

discretion [dɪ'skrɛʃən] n discrétion f; **at the ~ of** à la discrétion de; **use your own ~** à vous de juger

discriminate [dɪ'skrɪmɪneɪt] vi: **to ~ between** établir une distinction entre, faire la différence entre; **to ~ against** pratiquer une discrimination contre

discriminating [dɪ'skrɪmɪneɪtɪŋ] adj qui a du discernement

discrimination [dɪskrɪmɪ'neɪʃən] n discrimination f; (judgment) discernement m; **racial/sexual ~** discrimination raciale/sexuelle

discuss [dɪ'skʌs] vt discuter de; (debate) discuter

discussion [dɪ'skʌʃən] n discussion f; **under ~** en discussion

disdain [dɪs'deɪn] n dédain m

disease [dɪ'zi:z] n maladie f

disembark [dɪsɪm'bɑ:k] vt, vi débarquer

disentangle [dɪsɪn'tæŋgl] vt démêler

disfigure [dɪs'fɪgəʳ] vt défigurer

disgrace [dɪs'greɪs] n honte f; (disfavour) disgrâce f ▷ vt déshonorer, couvrir de honte

disgraceful [dɪs'greɪsful] adj scandaleux(-euse), honteux(-euse)

disgruntled [dɪs'grʌntld] adj mécontent(e)

disguise [dɪs'gaɪz] n déguisement m ▷ vt déguiser; (voice) déguiser, contrefaire; (feelings etc) masquer, dissimuler; **in ~** déguisé(e); **to ~ o.s. as** se déguiser en; **there's no disguising the fact that ...** on ne peut pas se dissimuler que ...

disgust [dɪs'gʌst] n dégoût m, aversion f ▷ vt dégoûter, écœurer

disgusted [dɪs'gʌstɪd] adj dégoûté(e), écœuré(e)

disgusting [dɪs'gʌstɪŋ] adj dégoûtant(e), révoltant(e)

dish [dɪʃ] n plat m; **to do** or **wash the ~es** faire la vaisselle

▶ **dish out** vt distribuer

▶ **dish up** vt servir; (facts, statistics) sortir, débiter

dishcloth ['dɪʃklɔθ] n (for drying) torchon m; (for washing) lavette f

dishearten [dɪs'hɑ:tn] vt décourager

dishevelled, (US) **disheveled** [dɪ'ʃɛvəld] adj ébouriffé(e), décoiffé(e), débraillé(e)

dishonest [dɪs'ɔnɪst] adj malhonnête

dishonour, (US) **dishonor** [dɪs'ɔnəʳ] n déshonneur m

dishonourable, (US) **dishonorable** [dɪs'ɔnərəbl] adj déshonorant(e)

dishtowel ['dɪʃtauəl] n (US) torchon m (à vaisselle)

dishwasher ['dɪʃwɔʃəʳ] n lave-vaisselle m; (person) plongeur(-euse)

disillusion [dɪsɪ'lu:ʒən] vt désabuser, désenchanter ▷ n désenchantement m; **to become ~ed (with)** perdre ses illusions (en ce qui concerne)

disinfect [dɪsɪn'fɛkt] vt désinfecter

disinfectant [dɪsɪn'fɛktənt] n désinfectant m

disintegrate [dɪs'ɪntɪgreɪt] vi se désintégrer

disinterested [dɪs'ɪntrəstɪd] adj désintéressé(e)

disjointed [dɪs'dʒɔɪntɪd] adj décousu(e), incohérent(e)

disk [dɪsk] n (Comput) disquette f; **single-/double-sided ~** disquette une face/double face

disk drive n lecteur m de disquette

diskette [dɪs'kɛt] n (Comput) disquette f

dislike [dɪs'laɪk] n aversion f, antipathie f ▷ vt ne pas aimer; **to take a ~ to sb/sth** prendre qn/qch en grippe; **I ~ the idea** l'idée me déplaît

dislocate ['dɪsləkeɪt] vt disloquer, déboîter; (services etc) désorganiser; **he has ~d his shoulder** il s'est disloqué l'épaule

dislodge [dɪs'lɔdʒ] vt déplacer, faire bouger; (enemy) déloger

disloyal [dɪs'lɔɪəl] adj déloyal(e)

dismal ['dɪzml] adj (gloomy) lugubre, maussade; (very bad) lamentable

dismantle [dɪs'mæntl] vt démonter; (fort, warship) démanteler

dismay [dɪs'meɪ] n consternation f ▷ vt consterner; **much to my ~** à ma grande consternation, à ma grande inquiétude

dismiss [dɪs'mɪs] vt congédier, renvoyer; (idea) écarter; (Law) rejeter ▷ vi (Mil) rompre les rangs

dismissal [dɪs'mɪsl] n renvoi m

dismount [dɪs'maunt] vi mettre pied à terre

disobedient [dɪsə'bi:dɪənt] adj désobéissant(e), indiscipliné(e)

disobey [dɪsə'beɪ] vt désobéir à; (rule) transgresser, enfreindre

disorder [dɪs'ɔ:dəʳ] n désordre m; (rioting) désordres mpl; (Med) troubles mpl

disorderly [dɪs'ɔ:dəlɪ] adj (room) en désordre; (behaviour, retreat, crowd) désordonné(e)

disorganized [dɪs'ɔ:gənaɪzd] adj désorganisé(e)

disorientated [dɪs'ɔ:rɪenteɪtɪd] adj désorienté(e)

disown [dɪs'əun] vt renier

disparaging [dɪs'pærɪdʒɪŋ] adj désobligeant(e);

to be ~ about sb/sth faire des remarques
désobligeantes sur qn/qch
dispassionate [dɪsˈpæʃənət] *adj* calme, froid(e),
impartial(e), objectif(-ive)
dispatch [dɪsˈpætʃ] *vt* expédier, envoyer; (*deal
with: business*) régler, en finir avec ▷ *n* envoi *m*,
expédition *f*; (*Mil, Press*) dépêche *f*
dispel [dɪsˈpɛl] *vt* dissiper, chasser
dispense [dɪsˈpɛns] *vt* distribuer, administrer;
(*medicine*) préparer (et vendre); **to ~ sb from**
dispenser qn de
  ▶ **dispense with** *vt fus* se passer de; (*make
unnecessary*) rendre superflu(e)
dispenser [dɪsˈpɛnsər] *n* (*device*) distributeur *m*
dispensing chemist [dɪsˈpɛnsɪŋ-] *n* (*Brit*)
pharmacie *f*
disperse [dɪsˈpəːs] *vt* disperser; (*knowledge*)
disséminer ▷ *vi* se disperser
dispirited [dɪsˈpɪrɪtɪd] *adj* découragé(e),
déprimé(e)
displace [dɪsˈpleɪs] *vt* déplacer
display [dɪsˈpleɪ] *n* (*of goods*) étalage *m*; affichage
m; (*Comput: information*) visualisation *f*; (*: device*)
visuel *m*; (*of feeling*) manifestation *f*; (*pej*)
ostentation *f*; (*show, spectacle*) spectacle *m*;
(*military display*) parade *f* militaire ▷ *vt* montrer;
(*goods*) mettre à l'étalage, exposer; (*results,
departure times*) afficher; (*pej*) faire étalage de; **on
~** (*exhibits*) exposé(e), exhibé(e); (*goods*) à l'étalage
displease [dɪsˈpliːz] *vt* mécontenter, contrarier;
~d with mécontent(e) de
displeasure [dɪsˈplɛʒər] *n* mécontentement *m*
disposable [dɪsˈpəuzəbl] *adj* (*pack etc*) jetable;
(*income*) disponible; **~ nappy** (*Brit*) couche *f* à
jeter, couche-culotte *f*
disposal [dɪsˈpəuzl] *n* (*of rubbish*) évacuation *f*,
destruction *f*; (*of property etc: by selling*) vente *f*; (*: by
giving away*) cession *f*; (*availability, arrangement*)
disposition *f*; **at one's ~** à sa disposition; **to put
sth at sb's ~** mettre qch à la disposition de qn
dispose [dɪsˈpəuz] *vt* disposer ▷ *vi*: **to ~ of**
(*time, money*) disposer de; (*unwanted goods*) se
débarrasser de, se défaire de; (*Comm: stock*)
écouler, vendre; (*problem*) expédier
disposed [dɪsˈpəuzd] *adj*: **~ to do** disposé(e) à faire
disposition [dɪspəˈzɪʃən] *n* disposition *f*;
(*temperament*) naturel *m*
disproportionate [dɪsprəˈpɔːʃənət] *adj*
disproportionné(e)
disprove [dɪsˈpruːv] *vt* réfuter
dispute [dɪsˈpjuːt] *n* discussion *f*; (*also*: **industrial
dispute**) conflit *m* ▷ *vt* (*question*) contester;
(*matter*) discuter; (*victory*) disputer; **to be in** *or*
under ~ (*matter*) être en discussion; (*territory*) être
contesté(e)
disqualify [dɪsˈkwɔlɪfaɪ] *vt* (*Sport*) disqualifier; **to
~ sb for sth/from doing** (*status, situation*) rendre
qn inapte à qch/à faire; (*authority*) signifier à qn
l'interdiction de faire; **to ~ sb (from driving)**
(*Brit*) retirer à qn son permis (de conduire)
disquiet [dɪsˈkwaɪət] *n* inquiétude *f*, trouble *m*
disregard [dɪsrɪˈgɑːd] *vt* ne pas tenir compte

de ▷ *n* (*indifference*): **~ (for)** (*feelings*) indifférence
f (pour), insensibilité *f* (à); (*danger, money*)
mépris *m* (pour)
disrepair [ˈdɪsrɪˈpɛər] *n* mauvais état; **to fall into
~** (*building*) tomber en ruine; (*street*) se dégrader
disreputable [dɪsˈrɛpjutəbl] *adj* (*person*) de
mauvaise réputation, peu recommandable;
(*behaviour*) déshonorant(e); (*area*) mal famé(e),
louche
disrespectful [dɪsrɪˈspɛktful] *adj*
irrespectueux(-euse)
disrupt [dɪsˈrʌpt] *vt* (*plans, meeting, lesson*)
perturber, déranger
disruption [dɪsˈrʌpʃən] *n* perturbation *f*,
dérangement *m*
dissatisfaction [dɪssætɪsˈfækʃən] *n*
mécontentement *m*, insatisfaction *f*
dissatisfied [dɪsˈsætɪsfaɪd] *adj*: **~ (with)**
insatisfait(e) (de)
dissect [dɪˈsɛkt] *vt* disséquer; (*fig*) disséquer,
éplucher
dissent [dɪˈsɛnt] *n* dissentiment *m*, différence *f*
d'opinion
dissertation [dɪsəˈteɪʃən] *n* (*Scol*) mémoire *m*
disservice [dɪsˈsəːvɪs] *n*: **to do sb a ~** rendre un
mauvais service à qn; desservir qn
dissimilar [dɪˈsɪmɪlər] *adj*: **~ (to)** dissemblable (à),
différent(e) (de)
dissipate [ˈdɪsɪpeɪt] *vt* dissiper; (*energy, efforts*)
disperser
dissolute [ˈdɪsəluːt] *adj* débauché(e), dissolu(e)
dissolve [dɪˈzɔlv] *vt* dissoudre ▷ *vi* se dissoudre,
fondre; (*fig*) disparaître; **to ~ in(to) tears** fondre
en larmes
distance [ˈdɪstns] *n* distance *f*; **what's the ~ to
London?** à quelle distance se trouve Londres?;
it's within walking ~ on peut y aller à pied; **in
the ~** au loin
distant [ˈdɪstnt] *adj* lointain(e), éloigné(e);
(*manner*) distant(e), froid(e)
distaste [dɪsˈteɪst] *n* dégoût *m*
distasteful [dɪsˈteɪstful] *adj* déplaisant(e),
désagréable
distended [dɪsˈtɛndɪd] *adj* (*stomach*) dilaté(e)
distil, (*US*) **distill** [dɪsˈtɪl] *vt* distiller
distillery [dɪsˈtɪlərɪ] *n* distillerie *f*
distinct [dɪsˈtɪŋkt] *adj* distinct(e); (*clear*)
marqué(e); **as ~ from** par opposition à, en
contraste avec
distinction [dɪsˈtɪŋkʃən] *n* distinction *f*; (*in exam*)
mention *f* très bien; **to draw a ~ between** faire
une distinction entre; **a writer of ~** un écrivain
réputé
distinctive [dɪsˈtɪŋktɪv] *adj* distinctif(-ive)
distinguish [dɪsˈtɪŋgwɪʃ] *vt* distinguer ▷ *vi*: **to
~ between** (*concepts*) distinguer entre, faire une
distinction entre; **to ~ o.s.** se distinguer
distinguished [dɪsˈtɪŋgwɪʃt] *adj* (*eminent, refined*)
distingué(e); (*career*) remarquable, brillant(e)
distinguishing [dɪsˈtɪŋgwɪʃɪŋ] *adj* (*feature*)
distinctif(-ive), caractéristique
distort [dɪsˈtɔːt] *vt* déformer

distract [dɪsˈtrækt] vt distraire, déranger

distracted [dɪsˈtræktɪd] adj (not concentrating) distrait(e); (worried) affolé(e)

distraction [dɪsˈtrækʃən] n distraction f, dérangement m; **to drive sb to ~** rendre qn fou (folle)

distraught [dɪsˈtrɔːt] adj éperdu(e)

distress [dɪsˈtrɛs] n détresse f; (pain) douleur f ▷ vt affliger; **in ~** (ship) en perdition; (plane) en détresse; **~ed area** (Brit) zone sinistrée

distressing [dɪsˈtrɛsɪŋ] adj douloureux(-euse), pénible, affligeant(e)

distribute [dɪsˈtrɪbjuːt] vt distribuer

distribution [dɪstrɪˈbjuːʃən] n distribution f

distributor [dɪsˈtrɪbjutəʳ] n (gen: Tech) distributeur m; (Comm) concessionnaire m/f

district [ˈdɪstrɪkt] n (of country) région f; (of town) quartier m; (Admin) district m

district attorney n (US) ≈ procureur m de la République

district nurse n (Brit) infirmière visiteuse

distrust [dɪsˈtrʌst] n méfiance f, doute m ▷ vt se méfier de

disturb [dɪsˈtəːb] vt troubler; (inconvenience) déranger; **sorry to ~ you** excusez-moi de vous déranger

disturbance [dɪsˈtəːbəns] n dérangement m; (political etc) troubles mpl; (by drunks etc) tapage m; **to cause a ~** troubler l'ordre public; **~ of the peace** (Law) tapage injurieux or nocturne

disturbed [dɪsˈtəːbd] adj (worried, upset) agité(e), troublé(e); **to be emotionally ~** avoir des problèmes affectifs

disturbing [dɪsˈtəːbɪŋ] adj troublant(e), inquiétant(e)

disuse [dɪsˈjuːs] n: **to fall into ~** tomber en désuétude

disused [dɪsˈjuːzd] adj désaffecté(e)

ditch [dɪtʃ] n fossé m; (for irrigation) rigole f ▷ vt (inf) abandonner; (person) plaquer

dither [ˈdɪðəʳ] vi hésiter

ditto [ˈdɪtəu] adv idem

dive [daɪv] n plongeon m; (of submarine) plongée f; (Aviat) piqué m; (pej: café, bar etc) bouge m ▷ vi plonger; **to ~ into** (bag etc) plonger la main dans; (place) se précipiter dans

diver [ˈdaɪvəʳ] n plongeur m

diverse [daɪˈvəːs] adj divers(e)

diversion [daɪˈvəːʃən] n (Brit Aut) déviation f; (distraction, Mil) diversion f

diversity [daɪˈvəːsɪtɪ] n diversité f, variété f

divert [daɪˈvəːt] vt (Brit: traffic) dévier; (plane) dérouter; (train, river) détourner; (amuse) divertir

divide [dɪˈvaɪd] vt diviser; (separate) séparer ▷ vi se diviser; **to ~ (between or among)** répartir or diviser (entre); **40 ~d by 5** 40 divisé par 5
  ▶ **divide out** vt: **to ~ out (between or among)** distribuer or répartir (entre)

divided highway (US) n route f à quatre voies

dividend [ˈdɪvɪdɛnd] n dividende m

divine [dɪˈvaɪn] adj divin(e) ▷ vt (future) prédire; (truth) deviner, entrevoir; (water, metal) détecter

la présence de (par l'intermédiaire de la radiesthésie)

diving [ˈdaɪvɪŋ] n plongée (sous-marine)

diving board n plongeoir m

divinity [dɪˈvɪnɪtɪ] n divinité f; (as study) théologie f

division [dɪˈvɪʒən] n division f; (Brit: Football) division f; (separation) séparation f; (Comm) service m; (Brit: Pol) vote m; (also: **division of labour**) division du travail

divorce [dɪˈvɔːs] n divorce m ▷ vt divorcer d'avec

divorced [dɪˈvɔːst] adj divorcé(e)

divorcee [dɪvɔːˈsiː] n divorcé(e)

DIY adj, n abbr (Brit) = **do-it-yourself**

dizzy [ˈdɪzɪ] adj (height) vertigineux(-euse); **to make sb ~** donner le vertige à qn; **I feel ~** la tête me tourne, j'ai la tête qui tourne

DJ n abbr = **disc jockey**

DNA n abbr (= deoxyribonucleic acid) ADN m

DNA fingerprinting [-ˈfɪŋɡəprɪntɪŋ] n technique f des empreintes génétiques

do abbr (= ditto) d

do [duː] (pt **did**, pp **done**) n (inf: party etc) soirée f, fête f; (: formal gathering) réception f
▷ vb **1** (in negative constructions) non traduit; **I don't understand** je ne comprends pas
2 (to form questions) non traduit; **didn't you know?** vous ne le saviez pas?; **what do you think?** qu'en pensez-vous?; **why didn't you come?** pourquoi n'êtes-vous pas venu?
3 (for emphasis, in polite expressions): **people do make mistakes sometimes** on peut toujours se tromper; **she does seem rather late** je trouve qu'elle est bien en retard; **do sit down/help yourself** asseyez-vous/servez-vous je vous en prie; **do take care!** faites bien attention à vous!; **I DO wish I could go** j'aimerais tant y aller; **but I DO like it!** mais si, je l'aime!
4 (used to avoid repeating vb): **she swims better than I do** elle nage mieux que moi; **do you agree? — yes, I do/no I don't** vous êtes d'accord? — oui/non; **she lives in Glasgow — so do I** elle habite Glasgow — moi aussi; **he didn't like it and neither did we** il n'a pas aimé ça, et nous non plus; **who broke it? — I did** qui l'a cassé? — c'est moi; **he asked me to help him and I did** il m'a demandé de l'aider, et c'est ce que j'ai fait
5 (in question tags): **you like him, don't you?** vous l'aimez bien, n'est-ce pas?; **he laughed, didn't he?** il a ri, n'est-ce pas?; **I don't know him, do I?** je ne crois pas le connaître
▷ vt **1** (gen: carry out, perform etc) faire; (visit: city, museum) faire, visiter; **what are you doing tonight?** qu'est-ce que vous faites ce soir?; **what do you do?** (job) que faites-vous dans la vie?; **what did he do with the cat?** qu'a-t-il fait du chat?; **what can I do for you?** que puis-je faire pour vous?; **to do the cooking/washing-up** faire la cuisine/la vaisselle; **to do one's teeth/hair/nails** se brosser les dents/se coiffer/se faire les ongles
2 (Aut etc: distance) faire; (: speed) faire du; **we've**

done **200 km already** nous avons déjà fait 200 km; **the car was doing 100** la voiture faisait du 100 (à l'heure); **he can do 100 in that car** il peut faire du 100 (à l'heure) dans cette voiture-là ▷ vi **1** (act, behave) faire; **do as I do** faites comme moi

2 (get on, fare) marcher; **the firm is doing well** l'entreprise marche bien; **he's doing well/ badly at school** ça marche bien/mal pour lui à l'école; **how do you do?** comment allez-vous?; (on being introduced) enchanté(e)!

3 (suit) aller; **will it do?** est-ce que ça ira?

4 (be sufficient) suffire, aller; **will £10 do?** est-ce que 10 livres suffiront?; **that'll do** ça suffit, ça ira; **that'll do!** (in annoyance) ça va or suffit comme ça!; **to make do (with)** se contenter (de)

▸ **do away with** vt fus abolir; (kill) supprimer

▸ **do for** vt fus (Brit inf: clean for) faire le ménage chez

▸ **do up** vt (laces, dress) attacher; (buttons) boutonner; (zip) fermer; (renovate: room) refaire; (: house) remettre à neuf; **to do o.s. up** se faire beau (belle)

▸ **do with** vt fus (need): **I could do with a drink/some help** quelque chose à boire/un peu d'aide ne serait pas de refus; **it could do with a wash** ça ne lui ferait pas de mal d'être lavé; (be connected with): **that has nothing to do with you** cela ne vous concerne pas; **I won't have anything to do with it** je ne veux pas m'en mêler; **what has that got to do with it?** quel est le rapport?, qu'est-ce que cela vient faire là-dedans?

▸ **do without** vi s'en passer; **if you're late for tea then you'll do without** si vous êtes en retard pour le dîner il faudra vous en passer ▷ vt fus se passer de; **I can do without a car** je peux me passer de voiture

dock [dɔk] n dock m; (wharf) quai m; (Law) banc m des accusés ▷ vi se mettre à quai; (Space) s'arrimer ▷ vt: **they ~ed a third of his wages** ils lui ont retenu or décompté un tiers de son salaire; **docks** npl (Naut) docks

docker ['dɔkər] n docker m

dockyard ['dɔkjɑːd] n chantier m de construction navale

doctor ['dɔktər] n médecin m, docteur m; (PhD etc) docteur ▷ vt (cat) couper; (interfere with: food) altérer; (: drink) frelater; (: text, document) arranger; **~'s office** (US) cabinet m de consultation; **call a ~!** appelez un docteur or un médecin!

Doctor of Philosophy n (degree) doctorat m; (person) titulaire m/f d'un doctorat

document ['dɔkjumənt] n document m ▷ vt ['dɔkjument] documenter

documentary [dɔkju'mɛntərɪ] adj, n documentaire (m)

documentation [dɔkjumən'teɪʃən] n documentation f

dodge [dɔdʒ] n truc m; combine f ▷ vt esquiver, éviter ▷ vi faire un saut de côté; (Sport) faire une esquive; **to ~ out of the way** s'esquiver;

to ~ through the traffic se faufiler or faire de savantes manœuvres entre les voitures

dodgems ['dɔdʒemz] npl (Brit) autos tamponneuses

dodgy ['dɔdʒɪ] adj (inf: uncertain) douteux(-euse); (: shady) louche

doe [dəu] n (deer) biche f; (rabbit) lapine f

does [dʌz] vb see **do**

doesn't ['dʌznt] = **does not**

dog [dɔg] n chien(ne) ▷ vt (follow closely) suivre de près, ne pas lâcher d'une semelle; (fig: memory etc) poursuivre, harceler; **to go to the ~s** (nation etc) aller à vau-l'eau

dog collar n collier m de chien; (fig) faux-col m d'ecclésiastique

dog-eared ['dɔgɪəd] adj corné(e)

dogged ['dɔgɪd] adj obstiné(e), opiniâtre

doggy bag ['dɔgɪ-] n petit sac pour emporter les restes

dogsbody ['dɔgzbɔdɪ] n (Brit) bonne f à tout faire, tâcheron m

doings ['duːɪŋz] npl activités fpl

do-it-yourself ['duːɪtjɔː'self] n bricolage m

doldrums ['dɔldrəmz] npl: **to be in the ~** avoir le cafard; être dans le marasme

dole [dəul] n (Brit: payment) allocation f de chômage; **on the ~** au chômage

▸ **dole out** vt donner au compte-goutte

doll [dɔl] n poupée f

▸ **doll up** vt: **to ~ o.s. up** se faire beau (belle)

dollar ['dɔlər] n dollar m

dolphin ['dɔlfɪn] n dauphin m

dome [dəum] n dôme m

domestic [də'mɛstɪk] adj (duty, happiness) familial(e); (policy, affairs, flight) intérieur(e); (news) national(e); (animal) domestique

domesticated [də'mɛstɪkeɪtɪd] adj domestiqué(e); (pej) d'intérieur; **he's very ~** il participe volontiers aux tâches ménagères; question ménage, il est très organisé

dominant ['dɔmɪnənt] adj dominant(e)

dominate ['dɔmɪneɪt] vt dominer

domineering [dɔmɪ'nɪərɪŋ] adj dominateur(-trice), autoritaire

dominion [də'mɪnɪən] n domination f; territoire m; dominion m

domino ['dɔmɪnəu] (pl -es) n domino m

dominoes ['dɔmɪnəuz] n (game) dominos mpl

don [dɔn] n (Brit) professeur m d'université ▷ vt revêtir

donate [də'neɪt] vt faire don de, donner

donation [də'neɪʃən] n donation f, don m

done [dʌn] pp of **do**

donkey ['dɔŋkɪ] n âne m

donor ['dəunər] n (of blood etc) donneur(-euse); (to charity) donateur(-trice)

donor card n carte f de don d'organes

don't [dəunt] = **do not**

donut ['dəunʌt] (US) n = **doughnut**

doodle ['duːdl] n griffonnage m, gribouillage m ▷ vi griffonner, gribouiller

doom [duːm] n (fate) destin m; (ruin) ruine f ▷ vt: **to be ~ed to failure** être voué(e) à l'échec

door [dɔːʳ] n porte f; (Rail, car) portière f; **to go from ~ to ~** aller de porte en porte

doorbell ['dɔːbɛl] n sonnette f

door handle n poignée f de porte; (of car) poignée de portière

doorknob ['dɔːnɔb] n poignée f or bouton m de porte

doorman ['dɔːmən] (irreg) n (in hotel) portier m; (in block of flats) concierge m

doormat ['dɔːmæt] n paillasson m

doorstep ['dɔːstɛp] n pas m de (la) porte, seuil m

doorway ['dɔːweɪ] n (embrasure f de) porte f

dope [dəup] n (inf: drug) drogue f; (: person) andouille f; (: information) tuyaux mpl, rancards mpl ▷ vt (horse etc) doper

dormant ['dɔːmənt] adj assoupi(e), en veilleuse; (rule, law) inappliqué(e)

dormitory ['dɔːmɪtrɪ] n (Brit) dortoir m; (US: hall of residence) résidence f universitaire

dormouse (pl **dormice**) ['dɔːmaus, -maɪs] n loir m

DOS [dɔs] n abbr (= disk operating system) DOS m

dosage ['dəusɪdʒ] n dose f; dosage m; (on label) posologie f

dose [dəus] n dose f; (Brit: bout) attaque f ▷ vt: **to ~ o.s.** se bourrer de médicaments; **a ~ of flu** une belle or bonne grippe

dosh [dɔʃ] (inf) n fric m

doss house ['dɔs-] n (Brit) asile m de nuit

dot [dɔt] n point m; (on material) pois m ▷ vt: **~ted with** parsemé(e) de; **on the ~** à l'heure tapante

dotcom [dɔt'kɔm] n point com m, pointcom m

dotted line ['dɔtɪd-] n ligne pointillée; (Aut) ligne discontinue; **to sign on the ~** signer à l'endroit indiqué or sur la ligne pointillée; (fig) donner son consentement

double ['dʌbl] adj double ▷ adv (fold) en deux; (twice): **to cost ~ (sth)** coûter le double (de qch) or deux fois plus (que qch) ▷ n double m; (Cine) doublure f ▷ vt doubler; (fold) plier en deux ▷ vi doubler; (have two uses): **to ~ as** servir aussi de; **~ five two six (5526)** (Brit Tel) cinquante-cinq – vingt-six; **it's spelt with a – "l"** ça s'écrit avec deux "l"; **on the ~**, **at the ~** au pas de course
  ▶ **double back** vi (person) revenir sur ses pas
  ▶ **double up** vi (bend over) se courber, se plier; (share room) partager la chambre

double bass n contrebasse f

double bed n grand lit

double-breasted ['dʌbl'brɛstɪd] adj croisé(e)

double-check ['dʌbl'tʃɛk] vt, vi revérifier

double-click ['dʌbl'klɪk] vi (Comput) double-cliquer

double-cross ['dʌbl'krɔs] vt doubler, trahir

double-decker ['dʌbl'dɛkəʳ] n autobus m à impériale

double glazing n (Brit) double vitrage m

double room n chambre f pour deux

doubles ['dʌblz] n (Tennis) double m

double yellow lines npl (Brit: Aut) double bande jaune marquant l'interdiction de stationner

doubly ['dʌblɪ] adv doublement, deux fois plus

doubt [daut] n doute m ▷ vt douter de; **no ~** sans doute; **without (a) ~** sans aucun doute; **beyond ~** adv indubitablement ▷ adj indubitable; **to ~ that** douter que + sub; **I ~ it very much** j'en doute fort

doubtful ['dautful] adj douteux(-euse); (person) incertain(e); **to be ~ about sth** avoir des doutes sur qch, ne pas être convaincu de qch; **I'm a bit ~** je n'en suis pas certain or sûr

doubtless ['dautlɪs] adv sans doute, sûrement

dough [dəu] n pâte f; (inf: money) fric m, pognon m

doughnut ['dəunʌt], (US) **donut** n beignet m

dove [dʌv] n colombe f

Dover ['dəuvəʳ] n Douvres

dovetail ['dʌvteɪl] n: **~ joint** assemblage m à queue d'aronde ▷ vi (fig) concorder

dowdy ['daudɪ] adj démodé(e), mal fagoté(e)

down [daun] n (fluff) duvet m; (hill) colline (dénudée) ▷ adv en bas, vers le bas; (on the ground) par terre ▷ prep en bas de; (along) le long de ▷ vt (enemy) abattre; (inf: drink) siffler; **to fall ~** tomber; **she's going ~ to Bristol** elle descend à Bristol; **to write sth ~** écrire qch; **~ there** là-bas (en bas), là au fond; **~ here** ici en bas; **the price of meat is ~** le prix de la viande a baissé; **I've got it ~ in my diary** c'est inscrit dans mon agenda; **to pay £2 ~** verser 2 livres d'arrhes or en acompte; **England is two goals ~** l'Angleterre a deux buts de retard; **to walk ~ a hill** descendre une colline; **to run ~ the street** descendre la rue en courant; **to ~ tools** (Brit) cesser le travail; **~ with X!** à bas X!

down-and-out ['daunəndaut] n (tramp) clochard(e)

down-at-heel ['daunət'hiːl] adj (fig) miteux(-euse)

downcast ['daunkɑːst] adj démoralisé(e)

downfall ['daunfɔːl] n chute f; ruine f

downhearted ['daun'hɑːtɪd] adj découragé(e)

downhill ['daun'hɪl] adv (face, look) en aval, vers l'aval; (roll, go) vers le bas, en bas ▷ n (Ski: also: **downhill race**) descente f; **to go ~** descendre; (business) péricliter, aller à vau-l'eau

Downing Street ['daunɪŋ-] n (Brit): **10 ~** résidence du Premier ministre; voir article

download ['daunləud] n téléchargement m ▷ vt (Comput) télécharger

down payment n acompte m

downpour ['daunpɔːʳ] n pluie torrentielle, déluge m

downright ['daunraɪt] adj (lie etc) effronté(e); (refusal) catégorique

downsize [daun'saɪz] vt réduire l'effectif de

Down's syndrome [daunz-] n mongolisme m, trisomie f; **a Down's syndrome baby** un bébé mongolien or trisomique

downstairs ['daun'stɛəz] adv (on or to ground floor) au rez-de-chaussée; (on or to floor below) à l'étage inférieur; **to come ~, to go ~** descendre (l'escalier)

downstream ['daunstriːm] adv en aval

down-to-earth ['dauntuˈəːθ] adj terre à terre inv

downtown ['daun'taun] *adv* en ville ▷ *adj* (US): ~ **Chicago** le centre commerçant de Chicago

down under *adv* en Australie *or* Nouvelle Zélande

downward ['daunwəd] *adj, adv* vers le bas; **a ~ trend** une tendance à la baisse, une diminution progressive

downwards ['daunwədz] *adv* vers le bas

dowry ['dauri] *n* dot *f*

doz. *abbr* = **dozen**

doze [dəuz] *vi* sommeiller
  ▶ **doze off** *vi* s'assoupir

dozen ['dʌzn] *n* douzaine *f*; **a ~ books** une douzaine de livres; **8op a ~** 8op la douzaine; **~s of** des centaines de

Dr. *abbr* (= *doctor*) Dr; (*in street names*) = **drive**

drab [dræb] *adj* terne, morne

draft [drɑːft] *n* (*of letter, school work*) brouillon *m*; (*of literary work*) ébauche *f*; (*of contract, document*) version *f* préliminaire; (*Comm*) traite *f*; (*US Mil*) contingent *m*; (: *call-up*) conscription *f* ▷ *vt* faire le brouillon de; (*document, report*) rédiger une version préliminaire de; (*Mil: send*) détacher; *see also* **draught**

drag [dræg] *vt* traîner; (*river*) draguer ▷ *vi* traîner ▷ *n* (*Aviat, Naut*) résistance *f*; (*inf*) casse-pieds *m/f*; (*women's clothing*): **in ~** (-en) travesti; **to ~ and drop** (*Comput*) glisser-poser
  ▶ **drag away** *vt*: **to ~ away (from)** arracher *or* emmener de force (de)
  ▶ **drag on** *vi* s'éterniser

dragon ['drægn] *n* dragon *m*

dragonfly ['drægənflai] *n* libellule *f*

drain [drein] *n* égout *m*; (*on resources*) saignée *f* ▷ *vt* (*land, marshes*) drainer, assécher; (*vegetables*) égoutter; (*reservoir etc*) vider ▷ *vi* (*water*) s'écouler; **to feel ~ed (of energy** *or* **emotion)** être miné(e)

drainage ['dreinidʒ] *n* (*system*) système *m* d'égouts; (*act*) drainage *m*

draining board (US) ['dreinin-], **drainboard** ['dreinbɔːd] *n* égouttoir *m*

drainpipe ['dreinpaip] *n* tuyau *m* d'écoulement

drama ['drɑːmə] *n* (*art*) théâtre *m*, art *m* dramatique; (*play*) pièce *f*; (*event*) drame *m*

dramatic [drə'mætik] *adj* (*Theat*) dramatique; (*impressive*) spectaculaire

dramatist ['dræmətist] *n* auteur *m* dramatique

dramatize ['dræmətaiz] *vt* (*events etc*) dramatiser; (*adapt*) adapter pour la télévision (*or* pour l'écran)

drank [dræŋk] *pt of* **drink**

drape [dreip] *vt* draper; **drapes** *npl* (US) rideaux *mpl*

drastic ['dræstik] *adj* (*measures*) d'urgence, énergique; (*change*) radical(e)

draught, (US) **draft** [drɑːft] *n* courant *m* d'air; (*of chimney*) tirage *m*; (*Naut*) tirant *m* d'eau; **on ~** (*beer*) à la pression

draught beer *n* bière *f* (à la) pression

draughtboard ['drɑːftbɔːd] *n* (Brit) damier *m*

draughts [drɑːfts] *n* (Brit: *game*) (jeu *m* de) dames *fpl*

draughtsman, (US) **draftsman** ['drɑːftsmən] (*irreg*) *n* dessinateur(-trice) (industriel(le))

draw [drɔː] (*vb: pt* **drew**, *pp* **-n**) [druː, drɔːn] *vt* tirer; (*picture*) dessiner; (*attract*) attirer; (*line, circle*) tracer; (*money*) toucher; (*wages*) toucher; (*comparison, distinction*): **to ~ (between)** faire (entre) ▷ *vi* (*Sport*) faire match nul ▷ *n* match nul; (*lottery*) loterie *f*; (: *picking of ticket*) tirage *m* au sort; **to ~ to a close** toucher à *or* tirer à sa fin; **to ~ near** *vi* s'approcher; approcher
  ▶ **draw back** *vi* (*move back*): **to ~ back (from)** reculer (de)
  ▶ **draw in** *vi* (Brit: *car*) s'arrêter le long du trottoir (: *train*) entrer en gare *or* dans la station
  ▶ **draw on** *vt* (*resources*) faire appel à; (*imagination, person*) avoir recours à, faire appel à
  ▶ **draw out** *vi* (*lengthen*) s'allonger ▷ *vt* (*money*) retirer
  ▶ **draw up** *vi* (*stop*) s'arrêter ▷ *vt* (*document*) établir, dresser; (*plan*) formuler, dessiner; (*chair*) approcher

drawback ['drɔːbæk] *n* inconvénient *m*, désavantage *m*

drawbridge ['drɔːbridʒ] *n* pont-levis *m*

drawer [drɔːʳ] *n* tiroir *m* ['drɔːəʳ] (*of cheque*) tireur *m*

drawing ['drɔːiŋ] *n* dessin *m*

drawing board *n* planche *f* à dessin

drawing pin *n* (Brit) punaise *f*

drawing room *n* salon *m*

drawl [drɔːl] *n* accent traînant

drawn [drɔːn] *pp of* **draw** ▷ *adj* (*haggard*) tiré(e), crispé(e)

dread [dred] *n* épouvante *f*, effroi *m* ▷ *vt* redouter, appréhender

dreadful ['dredful] *adj* épouvantable, affreux(-euse)

dream [driːm] *n* rêve *m* ▷ *vt, vi* (*pt, pp* **-ed** *or* **-t**) [dremt] rêver; **to have a ~ about sb/sth** rêver à qn/qch; **sweet ~s!** faites de beaux rêves!
  ▶ **dream up** *vt* inventer

dreamer ['driːməʳ] *n* rêveur(-euse)

dreamt [dremt] *pt, pp of* **dream**

dreamy ['driːmi] *adj* (*absent-minded*) rêveur(-euse)

dreary ['driəri] *adj* triste; monotone

dredge [dredʒ] *vt* draguer
  ▶ **dredge up** *vt* draguer; (*fig: unpleasant facts*) (faire) ressortir

dregs [dregz] *npl* lie *f*

drench [drentʃ] *vt* tremper; **~ed to the skin** trempé(e) jusqu'aux os

dress [dres] *n* robe *f*; (*clothing*) habillement *m*, tenue *f* ▷ *vt* habiller; (*wound*) panser; (*food*) préparer ▷ *vi*: **she ~es very well** elle s'habille très bien; **to ~ o.s., to get ~ed** s'habiller; **to ~ a shop window** faire l'étalage *or* la vitrine
  ▶ **dress up** *vi* s'habiller; (*in fancy dress*) se déguiser

dress circle *n* (Brit) premier balcon

dresser ['dresəʳ] *n* (*Theat*) habilleur(-euse); (*also*: **window dresser**) étalagiste *m/f*; (*furniture*) vaisselier *m*; (: US) coiffeuse *f*, commode *f*

dressing ['dresiŋ] *n* (*Med*) pansement *m*; (*Culin*)

sauce f, assaisonnement m

dressing gown n (Brit) robe f de chambre

dressing room n (Theat) loge f; (Sport) vestiaire m

dressing table n coiffeuse f

dressmaker ['drɛsmeɪkəʳ] n couturière f

dress rehearsal n (répétition f) générale f

drew [druː] pt of **draw**

dribble ['drɪbl] vi tomber goutte à goutte; (baby) baver ▷ vt (ball) dribbler

dried [draɪd] adj (fruit, beans) sec (sèche); (eggs, milk) en poudre

drier ['draɪəʳ] n = **dryer**

drift [drɪft] n (of current etc) force f; direction f; (of sand etc) amoncellement m; (of snow) rafale f; coulée f; (: on ground) congère f; (general meaning) sens général ▷ vi (boat) aller à la dérive, dériver; (sand, snow) s'amonceler, s'entasser; **to let things ~** laisser les choses aller à la dérive; **to ~ apart** (friends, lovers) s'éloigner l'un de l'autre; **I get** or **catch your ~** je vois en gros ce que vous voulez dire

driftwood ['drɪftwud] n bois flotté

drill [drɪl] n perceuse f; (bit) foret m; (of dentist) roulette f, fraise f; (Mil) exercice m ▷ vt percer; (troops) entraîner; (pupils: in grammar) faire faire des exercices à ▷ vi (for oil) faire un or des forage(s)

drink [drɪŋk] n boisson f; (alcoholic) verre m ▷ vt, vi (pt **drank**, pp **drunk**) [dræŋk, drʌŋk] boire; **to have a ~** boire quelque chose, boire un verre; **a ~ of water** un verre d'eau; **would you like a ~?** tu veux boire quelque chose?; **we had ~s before lunch** on a pris l'apéritif

▶ **drink in** vt (fresh air) inspirer profondément; (story) avaler, ne pas perdre une miette de; (sight) se remplir la vue de

drink-driving ['drɪŋk'draɪvɪŋ] n conduite f en état d'ivresse

drinker ['drɪŋkəʳ] n buveur(-euse)

drinking water n eau f potable

drip [drɪp] n (drop) goutte f; (sound: of water etc) bruit m de l'eau qui tombe goutte à goutte; (Med: device) goutte-à-goutte m inv; (: liquid) perfusion f; (inf: person) lavette f, nouille f ▷ vi tomber goutte à goutte; (tap) goutter; (washing) s'égoutter; (wall) suinter

drip-dry ['drɪp'draɪ] adj (shirt) sans repassage

dripping ['drɪpɪŋ] n graisse f de rôti ▷ adj: **~ wet** trempé(e)

drive [draɪv] (pt **drove**, pp **-n**) [drəuv, 'drɪvn] n promenade f or trajet m en voiture; (also: **driveway**) allée f; (energy) dynamisme m, énergie f; (Psych) besoin m; pulsion f; (push) effort (concerté); campagne f; (Sport) drive m; (Tech) entraînement m; traction f; transmission f; (Comput: also: **disk drive**) lecteur m de disquette ▷ vt conduire; (nail) enfoncer; (push) chasser, pousser; (Tech: motor) actionner; entraîner ▷ vi (be at the wheel) conduire; (travel by car) aller en voiture; **to go for a ~** aller faire une promenade en voiture; **it's 3 hours' ~ from London** Londres est à 3 heures de route; **left-/right-**

hand ~ (Aut) conduite f à gauche/droite; **front-/rear-wheel ~** (Aut) traction f avant/arrière; **to ~ sb to (do) sth** pousser or conduire qn à (faire) qch; **to ~ sb mad** rendre qn fou (folle)

▶ **drive at** vt fus (fig: intend, mean) vouloir dire, en venir à

▶ **drive on** vi poursuivre sa route, continuer; (after stopping) reprendre sa route, repartir ▷ vt (incite, encourage) inciter

▶ **drive out** vt (force out) chasser

drive-by ['draɪvbaɪ] n (also: **drive-by shooting**) tentative d'assassinat par coups de feu tirés d'une voiture

drive-in ['draɪvɪn] adj, n (esp US) drive-in m

drivel ['drɪvl] n (inf) idioties fpl, imbécillités fpl

driven ['drɪvn] pp of **drive**

driver ['draɪvəʳ] n conducteur(-trice); (of taxi, bus) chauffeur m

driver's license n (US) permis m de conduire

driveway ['draɪvweɪ] n allée f

driving ['draɪvɪŋ] adj: **~ rain** n pluie battante ▷ n conduite f

driving instructor n moniteur m d'auto-école

driving lesson n leçon f de conduite

driving licence n (Brit) permis m de conduire

driving school n auto-école f

driving test n examen m du permis de conduire

drizzle ['drɪzl] n bruine f, crachin m ▷ vi bruiner

drool [druːl] vi baver; **to ~ over sb/sth** (fig) baver d'admiration or être en extase devant qn/qch

droop [druːp] vi (flower) commencer à se faner; (shoulders, head) tomber

drop [drɔp] n (of liquid) goutte f; (fall) baisse f; (: in salary) réduction f; (also: **parachute drop**) saut m; (of cliff) dénivellation f; à-pic m ▷ vt laisser tomber; (voice, eyes, price) baisser; (passenger) déposer ▷ vi (wind, temperature, price, voice) tomber; (numbers, attendance) diminuer; **drops** npl (Med) gouttes; **cough ~s** pastilles fpl pour la toux; **a ~ of 10%** une baisse or réduction de 10%; **to ~ anchor** jeter l'ancre; **to ~ sb a line** mettre un mot à qn

▶ **drop in** vi (inf: visit): **to ~ in (on)** faire un saut (chez), passer (chez)

▶ **drop off** vi (sleep) s'assoupir ▷ vt (passenger) déposer; **to ~ sb off** déposer qn

▶ **drop out** vi (withdraw) se retirer; (student etc) abandonner, décrocher

dropout ['drɔpaut] n (from society) marginal(e); (from university) drop-out m/f, dropé(e)

dropper ['drɔpəʳ] n (Med etc) compte-gouttes m inv

droppings ['drɔpɪŋz] npl crottes fpl

drought [draut] n sécheresse f

drove [drəuv] pt of **drive** ▷ n: **~s of people** une foule de gens

drown [draun] vt noyer; (also: **drown out**: sound) couvrir, étouffer ▷ vi se noyer

drowsy ['drauzɪ] adj somnolent(e)

drug [drʌg] n médicament m; (narcotic) drogue f ▷ vt droguer; **to be on ~s** se droguer; **he's on ~s** il se drogue; (Med) il est sous médication

drug addict n toxicomane m/f

drug dealer n revendeur(-euse) de drogue

druggist ['drʌgɪst] n (US) pharmacien(ne)-droguiste

drugstore ['drʌgstɔːʳ] n (US) pharmacie-droguerie f, drugstore m

drum [drʌm] n tambour m; (for oil, petrol) bidon m ▷ vt: **to ~ one's fingers on the table** pianoter or tambouriner sur la table; **drums** npl (Mus) batterie f

▶ **drum up** vt (enthusiasm, support) susciter, rallier

drummer ['drʌməʳ] n (joueur m de) tambour m

drunk [drʌŋk] pp of **drink** ▷ adj ivre, soûl(e) ▷ n (also: **drunkard**) ivrogne m/f; **to get ~** s'enivrer, se soûler

drunken ['drʌŋkən] adj ivre, soûl(e); (rage, stupor) ivrogne, d'ivrogne; **~ driving** conduite f en état d'ivresse

dry [draɪ] adj sec (sèche); (day) sans pluie; (humour) pince-sans-rire; (uninteresting) aride, rébarbatif(-ive) ▷ vt sécher; (clothes) faire sécher ▷ vi sécher; **on ~ land** sur la terre ferme; **to ~ one's hands/hair/eyes** se sécher les mains/les cheveux/les yeux

▶ **dry off** vi, vt sécher

▶ **dry up** vi (river, supplies) se tarir; (: speaker) sécher, rester sec

dry-cleaner's ['draɪ'kliːnəz] n teinturerie f

dry-cleaning ['draɪ'kliːnɪŋ] n (process) nettoyage m à sec

dryer ['draɪəʳ] n (tumble-dryer) sèche-linge m inv; (for hair) sèche-cheveux m inv

dryness ['draɪnɪs] n sécheresse f

dry rot n pourriture sèche (du bois)

DSS n abbr (Brit) = **Department of Social Security**

DTP n abbr (= desktop publishing) PAO f

dual ['djuəl] adj double

dual carriageway n (Brit) route f à quatre voies

dual-purpose ['djuəl'pəːpəs] adj à double emploi

dubbed [dʌbd] adj (Cine) doublé(e); (nicknamed) surnommé(e)

dubious ['djuːbɪəs] adj hésitant(e), incertain(e); (reputation, company) douteux(-euse); (also: **I'm very dubious about it**) j'ai des doutes sur la question, je n'en suis pas sûr du tout

duchess ['dʌtʃɪs] n duchesse f

duck [dʌk] n canard m ▷ vi se baisser vivement, baisser subitement la tête ▷ vt plonger dans l'eau

duckling ['dʌklɪŋ] n caneton m

duct [dʌkt] n conduite f, canalisation f; (Anat) conduit m

dud [dʌd] n (shell) obus non éclaté; (object, tool): **it's a ~** c'est de la camelote, ça ne marche pas ▷ adj (Brit: cheque) sans provision; (: note, coin) faux (fausse)

due [djuː] adj (money, payment) dû (due); (expected) attendu(e); (fitting) qui convient ▷ n dû m ▷ adv: **~ north** droit vers le nord; **dues** npl (for club, union) cotisation f; (in harbour) droits mpl (de port); **~ to** (because of) en raison de; (caused by) dû à; **in ~ course** en temps utile or voulu; (in the end) finalement; **the rent is ~ on the 30th** il faut payer le loyer le 30; **the train is ~ at 8 a.m.** le train est attendu à 8 h; **she is ~ back tomorrow** elle doit rentrer demain; **he is ~ £10** on lui doit 10 livres; **I am ~ 6 days' leave** j'ai droit à 6 jours de congé; **to give sb his** or **her ~** être juste envers qn

duel ['djuəl] n duel m

duet [djuːˈɛt] n duo m

duffel bag, duffle bag ['dʌfl-] n sac marin

duffel coat, duffle coat ['dʌfl-] n duffel-coat m

dug [dʌg] pt, pp of **dig**

duke [djuːk] n duc m

dull [dʌl] adj (boring) ennuyeux(-euse); (slow) borné(e); (not bright) morne, terne; (sound, pain) sourd(e); (weather, day) gris(e), maussade; (blade) émoussé(e) ▷ vt (pain, grief) atténuer; (mind, senses) engourdir

duly ['djuːlɪ] adv (on time) en temps voulu; (as expected) comme il se doit

dumb [dʌm] adj muet(te); (stupid) bête; **to be struck ~** (fig) rester abasourdi(e), être sidéré(e)

dumbfounded [dʌmˈfaʊndɪd] adj sidéré(e)

dummy ['dʌmɪ] n (tailor's model) mannequin m; (mock-up) factice m, maquette f; (Sport) feinte f; (Brit: for baby) tétine f ▷ adj faux (fausse), factice

dump [dʌmp] n tas m d'ordures; (also: **rubbish dump**) décharge (publique); (Mil) dépôt m; (Comput) listage m (de la mémoire); (inf: place) trou m ▷ vt (put down) déposer; déverser; (get rid of) se débarrasser de; (Comput) lister; (Comm: goods) vendre à perte (sur le marché extérieur); **to be (down) in the ~s** (inf) avoir le cafard, broyer du noir

dumpling ['dʌmplɪŋ] n boulette f (de pâte)

dumpy ['dʌmpɪ] adj courtaud(e), boulot(te)

dunce [dʌns] n âne m, cancre m

dune [djuːn] n dune f

dung [dʌŋ] n fumier m

dungarees [dʌŋgəˈriːz] npl bleu(s) m(pl); (for child, woman) salopette f

dungeon ['dʌndʒən] n cachot m

duplex ['djuːplɛks] n (US: also: **duplex apartment**) duplex m

duplicate ['djuːplɪkət] n double m, copie exacte; (copy of letter etc) duplicata m ▷ adj (copy) en double ▷ vt ['djuːplɪkeɪt] faire un double de; (on machine) polycopier; **in ~** en deux exemplaires, en double; **~ key** double m de la (or d'une) clé

durable ['djuərəbl] adj durable; (clothes, metal) résistant(e), solide

duration [djuəˈreɪʃən] n durée f

during ['djuərɪŋ] prep pendant, au cours de

dusk [dʌsk] n crépuscule m

dust [dʌst] n poussière f ▷ vt (furniture) essuyer, épousseter; (cake etc): **to ~ with** saupoudrer de

▶ **dust off** vt (also fig) dépoussiérer

dustbin ['dʌstbɪn] n (Brit) poubelle f

duster ['dʌstəʳ] n chiffon m

dustman ['dʌstmən] (irreg) n (Brit) boueux m, éboueur m

dustpan ['dʌstpæn] n pelle f à poussière

dusty ['dʌstɪ] adj poussiéreux(-euse)

Dutch [dʌtʃ] adj hollandais(e), néerlandais(e) ▷ n

(*Ling*) hollandais *m*, néerlandais *m* ▷ *adv*: **to go
~** or **dutch** (*inf*) partager les frais; **the Dutch** *npl*
les Hollandais, les Néerlandais

Dutchman ['dʌtʃmən] (*irreg*) *n* Hollandais *m*

Dutchwoman ['dʌtʃwumən] (*irreg*) *n*
Hollandaise *f*

duty ['dju:tɪ] *n* devoir *m*; (*tax*) droit *m*, taxe *f*;
duties *npl* fonctions *fpl*; **to make it one's ~ to
do sth** se faire un devoir de faire qch; **to pay ~
on sth** payer un droit *or* une taxe sur qch; **on ~**
de service; (*at night etc*) de garde; **off ~** libre, pas
de service *or* de garde

duty-free ['dju:tɪ'fri:] *adj* exempté(e) de douane,
hors-taxe; **~ shop** boutique *f* hors-taxe

duvet ['du:veɪ] *n* (*Brit*) couette *f*

DVD *n abbr* (= *digital versatile or video disc*) DVD *m*

DVD burner *n* graveur *m* de DVD

DVD player *n* lecteur *m* de DVD

DVD writer *n* graveur *m* de DVD

dwarf (*pl* **dwarves**) [dwɔːf, dwɔːvz] *n* nain(e) ▷ *vt*
écraser

dwell (*pt, pp* **dwelt**) [dwɛl, dwɛlt] *vi* demeurer
▶ **dwell on** *vt fus* s'étendre sur

dwelt [dwɛlt] *pt, pp of* **dwell**

dwindle ['dwɪndl] *vi* diminuer, décroître

dye [daɪ] *n* teinture *f* ▷ *vt* teindre; **hair ~**
teinture pour les cheveux

dying ['daɪɪŋ] *adj* mourant(e), agonisant(e)

dyke [daɪk] *n* (*embankment*) digue *f*

dynamic [daɪ'næmɪk] *adj* dynamique

dynamite ['daɪnəmaɪt] *n* dynamite *f* ▷ *vt*
dynamiter, faire sauter à la dynamite

dynamo ['daɪnəməu] *n* dynamo *f*

dyslexia [dɪs'lɛksɪə] *n* dyslexie *f*

dyslexic [dɪs'lɛksɪk] *adj*, *n* dyslexique *m/f*

Ee

E¹, e [iː] *n* (*letter*) E, e *m*; (*Mus*): **E** mi *m*; **E for Edward** (*US*): **E for Easy** E comme Eugène

E² *abbr* (= *east*) E ▷ *n abbr* (*Drugs*) = **ecstasy**

each [iːtʃ] *adj* chaque ▷ *pron* chacun(e); **~ one** chacun(e); **~ other** l'un l'autre; **they hate ~ other** ils se détestent (mutuellement); **you are jealous of ~ other** vous êtes jaloux l'un de l'autre; **~ day** chaque jour, tous les jours; **they have 2 books** ~ ils ont 2 livres chacun; **they cost £5** ~ ils coûtent 5 livres (la) pièce; **~ of us** chacun(e) de nous

eager ['iːɡəʳ] *adj* (*person, buyer*) empressé(e); (*lover*) ardent(e), passionné(e); (*keen: pupil, worker*) enthousiaste; **to be ~ to do sth** (*impatient*) brûler de faire qch; (*keen*) désirer vivement faire qch; **to be ~ for** (*event*) désirer vivement; (*vengeance, affection, information*) être avide de

eagle ['iːɡl] *n* aigle *m*

ear [ɪəʳ] *n* oreille *f*; (*of corn*) épi *m*; **up to one's ~s in debt** endetté(e) jusqu'au cou

earache ['ɪəreɪk] *n* mal *m* aux oreilles

eardrum ['ɪədrʌm] *n* tympan *m*

earl [əːl] *n* comte *m*

earlier ['əːlɪəʳ] *adj* (*date etc*) plus rapproché(e); (*edition etc*) plus ancien(ne), antérieur(e) ▷ *adv* plus tôt

early ['əːlɪ] *adv* tôt, de bonne heure; (*ahead of time*) en avance; (*near the beginning*) au début ▷ *adj* précoce, qui se manifeste (*or* se fait) tôt *or* de bonne heure; (*Christians, settlers*) premier(-ière); (*reply*) rapide; (*death*) prématuré(e); (*work*) de jeunesse; **to have an ~ night/start** se coucher/partir tôt *or* de bonne heure; **take the ~ train** prenez le premier train; **in the ~** *or* **~ in the spring/19th century** au début *or* commencement du printemps/19ème siècle; **you're ~!** tu es en avance!; **~ in the morning** tôt le matin; **she's in her ~ forties** elle a un peu plus de quarante ans *or* de la quarantaine; **at your earliest convenience** (*Comm*) dans les meilleurs délais

early retirement *n* retraite anticipée

earmark ['ɪəmɑːk] *vt*: **to ~ sth for** réserver *or* destiner qch à

earn [əːn] *vt* gagner; (*Comm: yield*) rapporter; **to ~ one's living** gagner sa vie; **this ~ed him much praise, he ~ed much praise for this** ceci lui

a valu de nombreux éloges; **he's ~ed his rest/reward** il mérite *or* a bien mérité *or* a bien gagné son repos/sa récompense

earnest ['əːnɪst] *adj* sérieux(-euse) ▷ *n* (*also*: **earnest money**) acompte *m*, arrhes *fpl*; **in ~** (*adv*) sérieusement, pour de bon

earnings ['əːnɪŋz] *npl* salaire *m*; gains *mpl*; (*of company etc*) profits *mpl*, bénéfices *mpl*

earphones ['ɪəfəunz] *npl* écouteurs *mpl*

earplugs ['ɪəplʌgz] *npl* boules *fpl* Quiès®; (*to keep out water*) protège-tympans *mpl*

earring ['ɪərɪŋ] *n* boucle *f* d'oreille

earshot ['ɪəʃɔt] *n*: **out of/within ~** hors de portée/à portée de voix

earth [əːθ] *n* (*gen, also Brit Elec*) terre *f*; (*of fox etc*) terrier *m* ▷ *vt* (*Brit Elec*) relier à la terre

earthenware ['əːθnwɛəʳ] *n* poterie *f*; faïence *f* ▷ *adj* de *or* en faïence

earthquake ['əːθkweɪk] *n* tremblement *m* de terre, séisme *m*

earthy ['əːθɪ] *adj* (*fig*) terre à terre *inv*, truculent(e)

ease [iːz] *n* facilité *f*, aisance *f*; (*comfort*) bien-être *m* ▷ *vt* (*soothe: mind*) tranquilliser; (*reduce: pain, problem*) atténuer; (*: tension*) réduire; (*loosen*) relâcher, détendre; (*help pass*): **to ~ sth in/out** faire pénétrer/sortir qch délicatement *or* avec douceur, faciliter la pénétration/la sortie de qch ▷ *vi* (*situation*) se détendre; **with ~** sans difficulté, aisément; **life of ~** vie oisive; **at ~** à l'aise; (*Mil*) au repos

▶ **ease off, ease up** *vi* diminuer; (*slow down*) ralentir; (*relax*) se détendre

easel ['iːzl] *n* chevalet *m*

easily ['iːzɪlɪ] *adv* facilement; (*by far*) de loin

east [iːst] *n* est *m* ▷ *adj* (*wind*) d'est; (*side*) est *inv* ▷ *adv* à l'est, vers l'est; **the E~** l'Orient *m*; (*Pol*) les pays *mpl* de l'Est

eastbound ['iːstbaund] *adj* en direction de l'est; (*carriageway*) est *inv*

Easter ['iːstəʳ] *n* Pâques *fpl* ▷ *adj* (*holidays*) de Pâques, pascal(e)

Easter egg *n* œuf *m* de Pâques

easterly ['iːstəlɪ] *adj* d'est

eastern ['iːstən] *adj* de l'est, oriental(e); **E~ Europe** l'Europe de l'Est; **the E~ bloc** (*Pol*) les pays *mpl* de l'est

Easter Sunday *n* le dimanche de Pâques

eastward ['i:stwəd], **eastwards** ['i:stwədz] adv vers l'est, à l'est

easy ['i:zɪ] adj facile; (manner) aisé(e) ▷ adv: **to take it** or **things ~** (rest) ne pas se fatiguer; (not worry) ne pas (trop) s'en faire; **to have an ~ life** avoir la vie facile; **payment on ~ terms** (Comm) facilités fpl de paiement; **that's easier said than done** c'est plus facile à dire qu'à faire, c'est vite dit; **I'm ~** (inf) ça m'est égal

easy chair n fauteuil m

easy-going ['i:zɪ'gəʊɪŋ] adj accommodant(e), facile à vivre

eat (pt **ate**, pp **-en**) [i:t, eɪt, 'i:tn] vt, vi manger; **can we have something to ~?** est-ce qu'on peut manger quelque chose?
▸ **eat away** vt (sea) saper, éroder; (acid) ronger, corroder
▸ **eat away at, eat into** vt fus ronger, attaquer
▸ **eat out** vi manger au restaurant
▸ **eat up** vt (food) finir (de manger); **it ~s up electricity** ça bouffe du courant, ça consomme beaucoup d'électricité

eaten ['i:tn] pp of **eat**

eaves [i:vz] npl avant-toit m

eavesdrop ['i:vzdrɔp] vi: **to ~ (on)** écouter de façon indiscrète

ebb [ɛb] n reflux m ▷ vi refluer; (fig: also: **ebb away**) décliner; **the ~ and flow** le flux et le reflux; **to be at a low ~** (fig) être bien bas(se), ne pas aller bien fort

ebony ['ɛbənɪ] n ébène f

e-book ['i:buk] n livre m électronique

e-business ['i:bɪznɪs] n (company) entreprise f électronique; (commerce) commerce m électronique

ECB n abbr (= European Central Bank) BCE f (= Banque centrale européenne)

eccentric [ɪk'sɛntrɪk] adj, n excentrique m/f

echo ['ɛkəʊ] (pl **-es**) n écho m ▷ vt répéter; faire chorus avec ▷ vi résonner; faire écho

eclipse [ɪ'klɪps] n éclipse f ▷ vt éclipser

eco-friendly [i:kəʊ'frɛndlɪ] adj non nuisible à or qui ne nuit pas à l'environnement

ecological [i:kə'lɔdʒɪkəl] adj écologique

ecology [ɪ'kɔlədʒɪ] n écologie f

e-commerce [i:kɔmə:s] n commerce m électronique

economic [i:kə'nɔmɪk] adj économique; (profitable) rentable

economical [i:kə'nɔmɪkl] adj économique; (person) économe

economics [i:kə'nɔmɪks] n (Scol) économie f politique ▷ npl (of project etc) côté m or aspect m économique

economist [ɪ'kɔnəmɪst] n économiste m/f

economize [ɪ'kɔnəmaɪz] vi économiser, faire des économies

economy [ɪ'kɔnəmɪ] n économie f; **economies of scale** économies d'échelle

economy class n (Aviat) classe f touriste

economy class syndrome n syndrome m de la classe économique

economy size n taille f économique

ecstasy ['ɛkstəsɪ] n extase f; (Drugs) ecstasy m; **to go into ecstasies over** s'extasier sur

ecstatic [ɛks'tætɪk] adj extatique, en extase

eczema ['ɛksɪmə] n eczéma m

edge [ɛdʒ] n bord m; (of knife etc) tranchant m, fil m ▷ vt border ▷ vi: **to ~ forward** avancer petit à petit; **to ~ away from** s'éloigner furtivement de; **on ~** (fig) crispé(e), tendu(e); **to have the ~ on** (fig) l'emporter (de justesse) sur, être légèrement meilleur que

edgeways ['ɛdʒweɪz] adv latéralement; **he couldn't get a word in ~** il ne pouvait se placer un mot

edgy ['ɛdʒɪ] adj crispé(e), tendu(e)

edible ['ɛdɪbl] adj comestible; (meal) mangeable

Edinburgh ['ɛdɪnbərə] n Édimbourg

edit ['ɛdɪt] vt (text, book) éditer; (report) préparer; (film) monter; (broadcast) réaliser; (magazine) diriger; (newspaper) être le rédacteur or la rédactrice en chef de

edition [ɪ'dɪʃən] n édition f

editor ['ɛdɪtər] n (of newspaper) rédacteur(-trice), rédacteur(-trice) en chef; (of sb's work) éditeur(-trice); (also: **film editor**) monteur(-euse); **political/ foreign ~** rédacteur politique/au service étranger

editorial [ɛdɪ'tɔ:rɪəl] adj de la rédaction, éditorial(e) ▷ n éditorial m; **the ~ staff** la rédaction

educate ['ɛdjukeɪt] vt (teach) instruire; (bring up) éduquer; **~d at ...** qui a fait ses études à ...

educated ['ɛdjukeɪtɪd] adj (person) cultivé(e)

education [ɛdju'keɪʃən] n éducation f; (studies) études fpl; (teaching) enseignement m, instruction f; (at university: subject etc) pédagogie f; **primary** or (US) **elementary/secondary ~** instruction f primaire/secondaire

educational [ɛdju'keɪʃənl] adj pédagogique; (institution) scolaire; (useful) instructif(-ive); (game, toy) éducatif(-ive); **~ technology** technologie f de l'enseignement

eel [i:l] n anguille f

eerie ['ɪərɪ] adj inquiétant(e), spectral(e), surnaturel(le)

effect [ɪ'fɛkt] n effet m ▷ vt effectuer; **effects** npl (Theat) effets mpl; (property) effets, affaires fpl; **to take ~** (Law) entrer en vigueur, prendre effet; (drug) agir, faire son effet; **to put into ~** (plan) mettre en application or à exécution; **to have an ~ on sb/sth** avoir or produire un effet sur qn/qch; **in ~** en fait; **his letter is to the ~ that ...** sa lettre nous apprend que ...

effective [ɪ'fɛktɪv] adj efficace; (striking: display, outfit) frappant(e), qui produit or fait de l'effet; (actual) véritable; **to become ~** (Law) entrer en vigueur, prendre effet; **~ date** date f d'effet or d'entrée en vigueur

effectively [ɪ'fɛktɪvlɪ] adv efficacement; (strikingly) d'une manière frappante, avec beaucoup d'effet; (in reality) effectivement, en fait

effectiveness [ɪ'fɛktɪvnɪs] n efficacité f
effeminate [ɪ'fɛmɪnɪt] adj efféminé(e)
effervescent [ɛfə'vɛsnt] adj effervescent(e)
efficiency [ɪ'fɪʃənsɪ] n efficacité f; (of machine, car) rendement m
efficient [ɪ'fɪʃənt] adj efficace; (machine, car) d'un bon rendement
efficiently [ɪ'fɪʃəntlɪ] adv efficacement
effort ['ɛfət] n effort m; **to make an ~ to do sth** faire or fournir un effort pour faire qch
effortless ['ɛfətlɪs] adj sans effort, aisé(e); (achievement) facile
effusive [ɪ'fjuːsɪv] adj (person) expansif(-ive); (welcome) chaleureux(-euse)
e.g. adv abbr (= exempli gratia) par exemple, p. ex.
egg [ɛg] n œuf m; **hard-boiled/soft-boiled ~** œuf dur/à la coque
▶ **egg on** vt pousser
eggcup ['ɛgkʌp] n coquetier m
egg plant ['ɛgplɑːnt] (US) n aubergine f
eggshell ['ɛgʃɛl] n coquille f d'œuf ▷ adj (colour) blanc cassé inv
egg white n blanc m d'œuf
egg yolk n jaune m d'œuf
ego ['iːgəu] n (self-esteem) amour-propre m; (Psych) moi m
egotism ['ɛgəutɪzəm] n égotisme m
egotist ['ɛgəutɪst] n égocentrique m/f
Egypt ['iːdʒɪpt] n Égypte f
Egyptian [ɪ'dʒɪpʃən] adj égyptien(ne) ▷ n Égyptien(ne)
eiderdown ['aɪdədaun] n édredon m
Eiffel Tower ['aɪfəl-] n tour f Eiffel
eight [eɪt] num huit
eighteen [eɪ'tiːn] num dix-huit
eighteenth [eɪ'tiːnθ] num dix-huitième
eighth [eɪtθ] num huitième
eightieth ['eɪtɪɪθ] num quatre-vingtième
eighty ['eɪtɪ] num quatre-vingt(s)
Eire ['ɛərə] n République f d'Irlande
either ['aɪðəʳ] adj l'un ou l'autre; (both, each) chaque ▷ pron: **~ (of them)** l'un ou l'autre ▷ adv non plus ▷ conj: **~ good or bad** ou bon ou mauvais, soit bon soit mauvais; **I haven't seen ~ one or the other** je n'ai vu ni l'un ni l'autre; **on ~ side** de chaque côté; **I don't like ~** je n'aime ni l'un ni l'autre; **no, I don't ~** moi non plus; **which bike do you want? — ~ will do** quel vélo voulez-vous? — n'importe lequel; **answer with ~ yes or no** répondez par oui ou par non
eject [ɪ'dʒɛkt] vt (tenant etc) expulser; (object) éjecter ▷ vi (pilot) s'éjecter
elaborate [adj ɪ'læbərɪt, vb ɪ'læbəreɪt] adj compliqué(e), recherché(e), minutieux(-euse) ▷ vt élaborer ▷ vi entrer dans les détails
elastic [ɪ'læstɪk] adj, n élastique (m)
elastic band n (Brit) élastique m
elated [ɪ'leɪtɪd] adj transporté(e) de joie
elation [ɪ'leɪʃən] n (grande) joie, allégresse f
elbow ['ɛlbəu] n coude m ▷ vt: **to ~ one's way through the crowd** se frayer un passage à travers la foule (en jouant des coudes)

elder ['ɛldəʳ] adj aîné(e) ▷ n (tree) sureau m; **one's ~s** ses aînés
elderly ['ɛldəlɪ] adj âgé(e) ▷ npl: **the ~** les personnes âgées
eldest ['ɛldɪst] adj, n: **the ~ (child)** l'aîné(e) (des enfants)
elect [ɪ'lɛkt] vt élire; (choose): **to ~ to do** choisir de faire ▷ adj: **the president ~** le président désigné
election [ɪ'lɛkʃən] n élection f; **to hold an ~** procéder à une élection
electioneering [ɪlɛkʃə'nɪərɪŋ] n propagande électorale, manœuvres électorales
elector [ɪ'lɛktəʳ] n électeur(-trice)
electoral [ɪ'lɛktərəl] adj électoral(e)
electorate [ɪ'lɛktərɪt] n électorat m
electric [ɪ'lɛktrɪk] adj électrique
electrical [ɪ'lɛktrɪkl] adj électrique
electric blanket n couverture chauffante
electric fire n (Brit) radiateur m électrique
electrician [ɪlɛk'trɪʃən] n électricien m
electricity [ɪlɛk'trɪsɪtɪ] n électricité f; **to switch on/off the ~** rétablir/couper le courant
electric shock n choc m or décharge f électrique
electrify [ɪ'lɛktrɪfaɪ] vt (Rail) électrifier; (audience) électriser
electronic [ɪlɛk'trɔnɪk] adj électronique
electronic mail n courrier m électronique
electronics [ɪlɛk'trɔnɪks] n électronique f
elegance ['ɛlɪgəns] n élégance f
elegant ['ɛlɪgənt] adj élégant(e)
element ['ɛlɪmənt] n (gen) élément m; (of heater, kettle etc) résistance f
elementary [ɛlɪ'mɛntərɪ] adj élémentaire; (school, education) primaire
elementary school n (US) école f primaire; voir article
elephant ['ɛlɪfənt] n éléphant m
elevate ['ɛlɪveɪt] vt élever
elevation [ɛlɪ'veɪʃən] n élévation f; (height) altitude f
elevator ['ɛlɪveɪtəʳ] n (in warehouse etc) élévateur m, monte-charge m inv; (US: lift) ascenseur m
eleven [ɪ'lɛvn] num onze
elevenses [ɪ'lɛvnzɪz] npl (Brit) ≈ pause-café f
eleventh [ɪ'lɛvnθ] num onzième; **at the ~ hour** (fig) à la dernière minute
elicit [ɪ'lɪsɪt] vt: **to ~ (from)** obtenir (de); tirer (de)
eligible ['ɛlɪdʒəbl] adj éligible; (for membership) admissible; **an ~ young man** un beau parti; **to be ~ for sth** remplir les conditions requises pour qch; **~ for a pension** ayant droit à la retraite
eliminate [ɪ'lɪmɪneɪt] vt éliminer
elm [ɛlm] n orme m
elongated ['iːlɔŋgeɪtɪd] adj étiré(e), allongé(e)
elope [ɪ'ləup] vi (lovers) s'enfuir (ensemble)
eloquent ['ɛləkwənt] adj éloquent(e)
else [ɛls] adv d'autre; **something ~** quelque chose d'autre, autre chose; **somewhere ~** ailleurs, autre part; **everywhere ~** partout ailleurs; **everyone ~** tous les autres; **nothing ~** rien d'autre; **is there anything ~ I can do?**

est-ce que je peux faire quelque chose d'autre?; **where** ~? à quel autre endroit?; **little** ~ pas grand-chose d'autre

elsewhere [ɛls'wɛəʳ] *adv* ailleurs, autre part

elude [ɪ'lu:d] *vt* échapper à; *(question)* éluder

elusive [ɪ'lu:sɪv] *adj* insaisissable; *(answer)* évasif(-ive)

emaciated [ɪ'meɪsɪeɪtɪd] *adj* émacié(e), décharné(e)

email ['i:meɪl] *n abbr* (= *electronic mail*) (e-)mail *m*, courriel *m* ▷ *vt*: **to ~ sb** envoyer un (e-)mail *or* un courriel à qn

email account *n* compte *m* (e-)mail

email address *n* adresse *f* (e-)mail *or* électronique

emancipate [ɪ'mænsɪpeɪt] *vt* émanciper

embankment [ɪm'bæŋkmənt] *n* (*of road, railway*) remblai *m*, talus *m*; (*of river*) berge *f*, quai *m*; (*dyke*) digue *f*

embargo [ɪm'bɑ:gəu] (*pl* **-es**) *n* (*Comm, Naut*) embargo *m*; (*prohibition*) interdiction *f* ▷ *vt* frapper d'embargo, mettre l'embargo sur; **to put an ~ on sth** mettre l'embargo sur qch

embark [ɪm'bɑ:k] *vi* embarquer; **to ~ on** (s')embarquer à bord de *or* sur ▷ *vt* embarquer; **to ~ on** (*journey etc*) commencer, entreprendre; (*fig*) se lancer *or* s'embarquer dans

embarkation [ɛmbɑ:'keɪʃən] *n* embarquement *m*

embarrass [ɪm'bærəs] *vt* embarrasser, gêner

embarrassed [ɪm'bærəst] *adj* gêné(e); **to be ~** être gêné(e)

embarrassing [ɪm'bærəsɪŋ] *adj* gênant(e), embarrassant(e)

embarrassment [ɪm'bærəsmənt] *n* embarras *m*, gêne *f*; (*embarrassing thing, person*) source *f* d'embarras

embassy ['ɛmbəsɪ] *n* ambassade *f*; **the French E~** l'ambassade de France

embellish [ɪm'bɛlɪʃ] *vt* embellir; enjoliver

embers ['ɛmbəz] *npl* braise *f*

embezzle [ɪm'bɛzl] *vt* détourner

embezzlement [ɪm'bɛzlmənt] *n* détournement *m* (de fonds)

embitter [ɪm'bɪtəʳ] *vt* aigrir; envenimer

embody [ɪm'bɔdɪ] *vt* (*features*) réunir, comprendre; (*ideas*) formuler, exprimer

embossed [ɪm'bɔst] *adj* repoussé(e), gaufré(e); **~ with** où figure(nt) en relief

embrace [ɪm'breɪs] *vt* embrasser, étreindre; (*include*) embrasser, couvrir, comprendre ▷ *vi* s'embrasser, s'étreindre ▷ *n* étreinte *f*

embroider [ɪm'brɔɪdəʳ] *vt* broder; (*fig: story*) enjoliver

embroidery [ɪm'brɔɪdərɪ] *n* broderie *f*

embryo ['ɛmbrɪəu] *n* (*also fig*) embryon *m*

emerald ['ɛmərəld] *n* émeraude *f*

emerge [ɪ'mə:dʒ] *vi* apparaître; (*from room, car*) surgir; (*from sleep, imprisonment*) sortir; **it ~s that** (*Brit*) il ressort que

emergency [ɪ'mə:dʒənsɪ] *n* (*crisis*) cas *m* d'urgence; (*Med*) urgence *f*; **in an ~** en cas d'urgence; **state of ~** état *m* d'urgence

emergency brake (*US*) *n* frein *m* à main

emergency exit *n* sortie *f* de secours

emergency landing *n* atterrissage forcé

emergency room *n* (*US: Med*) urgences *fpl*

emergency services *npl*: **the ~** (*fire, police, ambulance*) les services *mpl* d'urgence

emery board ['ɛmərɪ-] *n* lime *f* à ongles (*en carton émerisé*)

emigrate ['ɛmɪgreɪt] *vi* émigrer

emigration [ɛmɪ'greɪʃən] *n* émigration *f*

eminent ['ɛmɪnənt] *adj* éminent(e)

emissions [ɪ'mɪʃənz] *npl* émissions *fpl*

emit [ɪ'mɪt] *vt* émettre

emotion [ɪ'məuʃən] *n* sentiment *m*; (*as opposed to reason*) émotion *f*, sentiments

emotional [ɪ'məuʃənl] *adj* (*person*) émotif(-ive), très sensible; (*needs*) affectif(-ive); (*scene*) émouvant(e); (*tone, speech*) qui fait appel aux sentiments

emotive [ɪ'məutɪv] *adj* émotif(-ive); **~ power** capacité *f* d'émouvoir *or* de toucher

emperor ['ɛmpərəʳ] *n* empereur *m*

emphasis (*pl* **-ases**) ['ɛmfəsɪs, -si:z] *n* accent *m*; **to lay** *or* **place ~ on sth** (*fig*) mettre l'accent sur, insister sur; **the ~ is on reading** la lecture tient une place primordiale, on accorde une importance particulière à la lecture

emphasize ['ɛmfəsaɪz] *vt* (*syllable, word, point*) appuyer *or* insister sur; (*feature*) souligner, accentuer

emphatic [ɛm'fætɪk] *adj* (*strong*) énergique, vigoureux(-euse); (*unambiguous, clear*) catégorique

empire ['ɛmpaɪəʳ] *n* empire *m*

employ [ɪm'plɔɪ] *vt* employer; **he's ~ed in a bank** il est employé de banque, il travaille dans une banque

employee [ɪmplɔɪ'i:] *n* employé(e)

employer [ɪm'plɔɪəʳ] *n* employeur(-euse)

employment [ɪm'plɔɪmənt] *n* emploi *m*; **to find ~** trouver un emploi *or* du travail; **without ~** au chômage, sans emploi; **place of ~** lieu *m* de travail

employment agency *n* agence *f* or bureau *m* de placement

empower [ɪm'pauəʳ] *vt*: **to ~ sb to do** autoriser *or* habiliter qn à faire

empress ['ɛmprɪs] *n* impératrice *f*

emptiness ['ɛmptɪnɪs] *n* vide *m*; (*of area*) aspect *m* désertique

empty ['ɛmptɪ] *adj* vide; (*street, area*) désert(e); (*threat, promise*) en l'air, vain(e) ▷ *n* (*bottle*) bouteille *f* vide ▷ *vt* vider ▷ *vi* se vider; (*liquid*) s'écouler; **on an ~ stomach** à jeun; **to ~ into** (*river*) se jeter dans, se déverser dans

empty-handed ['ɛmptɪ'hændɪd] *adj* les mains vides

EMU *n abbr* (= *European Monetary Union*) UME *f*

emulate ['ɛmjuleɪt] *vt* rivaliser avec, imiter

emulsion [ɪ'mʌlʃən] *n* émulsion *f*; (*also:* **emulsion paint**) peinture mate

enable [ɪ'neɪbl] *vt*: **to ~ sb to do** permettre à qn

de faire, donner à qn la possibilité de faire
enamel [ɪ'næməl] n émail m; (also: **enamel paint**) (peinture f) laque f
enchant [ɪn'tʃɑːnt] vt enchanter
enchanting [ɪn'tʃɑːntɪŋ] adj ravissant(e), enchanteur(-eresse)
encl. abbr (on letters etc: = enclosed) ci-joint(e); (= enclosure) PJ f
enclose [ɪn'kləuz] vt (land) clôturer; (space, object) entourer; (letter etc): **to ~ (with)** joindre (à); **please find ~d** veuillez trouver ci-joint
enclosure [ɪn'kləuʒəʳ] n enceinte f; (in letter etc) annexe f
encompass [ɪn'kʌmpəs] vt encercler, entourer; (include) contenir, inclure
encore [ɔŋ'kɔːʳ] excl, n bis (m)
encounter [ɪn'kauntəʳ] n rencontre f ▷ vt rencontrer
encourage [ɪn'kʌrɪdʒ] vt encourager; (industry, growth) favoriser; **to ~ sb to do sth** encourager qn à faire qch
encouragement [ɪn'kʌrɪdʒmənt] n encouragement m
encouraging [ɪn'kʌrɪdʒɪŋ] adj encourageant(e)
encroach [ɪn'krəutʃ] vi: **to ~ (up)on** empiéter sur
encyclopaedia, encyclopedia [ɛnsaɪkləu'piːdɪə] n encyclopédie f
end [ɛnd] n fin f; (of table, street, rope etc) bout m, extrémité f; (of pointed object) pointe f; (of town) bout; (Sport) côté m ▷ vt terminer; (also: **bring to an end, put an end to**) mettre fin à ▷ vi se terminer, finir; **from ~ to ~** d'un bout à l'autre; **to come to an ~** prendre fin; **to be at an ~** être fini(e), être terminé(e); **in the ~** finalement; **on ~** (object) debout, dressé(e); **to stand on ~** (hair) se dresser sur la tête; **for 5 hours on ~** durant 5 heures d'affilée or de suite; **for hours on ~** pendant des heures (et des heures); **at the ~ of the day** (Brit fig) en fin de compte; **to this ~, with this ~ in view** à cette fin, dans ce but
▶ **end up** vi: **to ~ up in** (condition) finir or se terminer par; (place) finir or aboutir à
endanger [ɪn'deɪndʒəʳ] vt mettre en danger; **an ~ed species** une espèce en voie de disparition
endearing [ɪn'dɪərɪŋ] adj attachant(e)
endeavour, (US) **endeavor** [ɪn'dɛvəʳ] n effort m; (attempt) tentative f ▷ vt: **to ~ to do** tenter or s'efforcer de faire
ending ['ɛndɪŋ] n dénouement m, conclusion f; (Ling) terminaison f
endive ['ɛndaɪv] n (curly) chicorée f; (smooth, flat) endive f
endless ['ɛndlɪs] adj sans fin, interminable; (patience, resources) inépuisable, sans limites; (possibilities) illimité(e)
endorse [ɪn'dɔːs] vt (cheque) endosser; (approve) appuyer, approuver, sanctionner
endorsement [ɪn'dɔːsmənt] n (approval) appui m, aval m; (signature) endossement m; (Brit: on driving licence) contravention f (portée au permis de conduire)
endurance [ɪn'djuərəns] n endurance f
endure [ɪn'djuəʳ] vt (bear) supporter, endurer ▷ vi

(last) durer
enemy ['ɛnəmɪ] adj, n ennemi(e); **to make an ~ of sb** se faire un(e) ennemi(e) de qn, se mettre qn à dos
energetic [ɛnə'dʒɛtɪk] adj énergique; (activity) très actif(-ive), qui fait se dépenser (physiquement)
energy ['ɛnədʒɪ] n énergie f; **Department of E~** ministère m de l'Énergie
enforce [ɪn'fɔːs] vt (law) appliquer, faire respecter
engage [ɪn'geɪdʒ] vt engager; (Mil) engager le combat avec; (lawyer) prendre ▷ vi (Tech) s'enclencher, s'engrener; **to ~ in** se lancer dans; **to ~ sb in conversation** engager la conversation avec qn
engaged [ɪn'geɪdʒd] adj (Brit: busy, in use) occupé(e); (betrothed) fiancé(e); **to get ~** se fiancer; **the line's ~** la ligne est occupée; **he is ~ in research/a survey** il fait de la recherche/une enquête
engaged tone n (Brit Tel) tonalité f occupé inv
engagement [ɪn'geɪdʒmənt] n (undertaking) obligation f, engagement m; (appointment) rendez-vous m inv; (to marry) fiançailles fpl; (Mil) combat m; **I have a previous ~** j'ai déjà un rendez-vous, je suis déjà pris(e)
engagement ring n bague f de fiançailles
engaging [ɪn'geɪdʒɪŋ] adj engageant(e), attirant(e)
engine ['ɛndʒɪn] n (Aut) moteur m; (Rail) locomotive f
engine driver n (Brit: of train) mécanicien m
engineer [ɛndʒɪ'nɪəʳ] n ingénieur m; (Brit: repairer) dépanneur m; (Navy, US Rail) mécanicien m; **civil/mechanical ~** ingénieur des Travaux Publics or des Ponts et Chaussées/mécanicien
engineering [ɛndʒɪ'nɪərɪŋ] n engineering m, ingénierie f; (of bridges, ships) génie m; (of machine) mécanique f ▷ cpd: **~ works** or **factory** atelier m de construction mécanique
England ['ɪŋglənd] n Angleterre f
English ['ɪŋglɪʃ] adj anglais(e) ▷ n (Ling) anglais m; **the ~** (npl) les Anglais; **an ~ speaker** un anglophone
English Channel n: **the ~** la Manche
Englishman ['ɪŋglɪʃmən] (irreg) n Anglais m
Englishwoman ['ɪŋglɪʃwumən] (irreg) n Anglaise f
engrave [ɪn'greɪv] vt graver
engraving [ɪn'greɪvɪŋ] n gravure f
engrossed [ɪn'grəust] adj: **~ in** absorbé(e) par, plongé(e) dans
engulf [ɪn'gʌlf] vt engloutir
enhance [ɪn'hɑːns] vt rehausser, mettre en valeur; (position) améliorer; (reputation) accroître
enjoy [ɪn'dʒɔɪ] vt aimer, prendre plaisir à; (have benefit of: health, fortune) jouir de; (: success) connaître; **to ~ o.s.** s'amuser
enjoyable [ɪn'dʒɔɪəbl] adj agréable
enjoyment [ɪn'dʒɔɪmənt] n plaisir m
enlarge [ɪn'lɑːdʒ] vt accroître; (Phot) agrandir

▷ vi: **to ~ on** (*subject*) s'étendre sur

enlargement [ɪnˈlɑːdʒmənt] n (*Phot*) agrandissement m

enlighten [ɪnˈlaɪtn] vt éclairer

enlightened [ɪnˈlaɪtnd] adj éclairé(e)

enlightenment [ɪnˈlaɪtnmənt] n édification f; éclaircissements mpl; (*History*): **the E~** ≈ le Siècle des lumières

enlist [ɪnˈlɪst] vt recruter; (*support*) s'assurer ▷ vi s'engager; **~ed man** (*US Mil*) simple soldat m

enmity [ˈɛnmɪtɪ] n inimitié f

enormous [ɪˈnɔːməs] adj énorme

enough [ɪˈnʌf] adj: **~ time/books** assez or suffisamment de temps/livres ▷ adv: **big ~** assez or suffisamment grand ▷ pron: **have you got ~?** (en) avez-vous assez?; **will five be ~?** est-ce que cinq suffiront?, est-ce qu'il y en aura assez avec cinq?; **~ to eat** assez à manger; **that's ~!** ça suffit!, assez!; **that's ~, thanks** cela suffit or c'est assez, merci; **I've had ~!** je n'en peux plus!; **I've had ~ of him** j'en ai assez de lui; **he has not worked ~** il n'a pas assez or suffisamment travaillé, il n'a pas travaillé assez or suffisamment; **~! assez!**, ça suffit!; **it's hot ~ (as it is)!** il fait assez chaud comme ça!; **he was kind ~ to lend me the money** il a eu la gentillesse de me prêter l'argent; **... which, funnily** or **oddly ~ ...** qui, chose curieuse, ...

enquire [ɪnˈkwaɪəʳ] vt, vi = **inquire**

enquiry [ɪnˈkwaɪərɪ] n = **inquiry**

enrage [ɪnˈreɪdʒ] vt mettre en fureur or en rage, rendre furieux(-euse)

enrich [ɪnˈrɪtʃ] vt enrichir

enrol, (*US*) **enroll** [ɪnˈrəul] vt inscrire ▷ vi s'inscrire

enrolment, (*US*) **enrollment** [ɪnˈrəulmənt] n inscription f

en route [ɔnˈruːt] adv en route, en chemin; **~ for** or **to** en route vers, à destination de

en suite [ˈɔnswiːt] adj: **with ~ bathroom** avec salle de bains en attenante

ensure [ɪnˈʃuəʳ] vt assurer, garantir; **to ~ that** s'assurer que

entail [ɪnˈteɪl] vt entraîner, nécessiter

entangle [ɪnˈtæŋgl] vt emmêler, embrouiller; **to become ~d in sth** (*fig*) se laisser entraîner or empêtrer dans qch

enter [ˈɛntəʳ] vt (*room*) entrer dans, pénétrer dans; (*club, army*) entrer à; (*profession*) embrasser; (*competition*) s'inscrire à or pour; (*sb for a competition*) (faire) inscrire; (*write down*) inscrire, noter; (*Comput*) entrer, introduire ▷ vi entrer

▶ **enter for** vt fus s'inscrire à, se présenter pour or à

▶ **enter into** vt fus (*explanation*) se lancer dans; (*negotiations*) entamer; (*debate*) prendre part à; (*agreement*) conclure

▶ **enter on** vt fus commencer

▶ **enter up** vt inscrire

▶ **enter upon** vt fus = **enter on**

enterprise [ˈɛntəpraɪz] n (*company, undertaking*) entreprise f; (*initiative*) (esprit m d')initiative

f; **free ~** libre entreprise; **private ~** entreprise privée

enterprising [ˈɛntəpraɪzɪŋ] adj entreprenant(e), dynamique; (*scheme*) audacieux(-euse)

entertain [ɛntəˈteɪn] vt amuser, distraire; (*invite*) recevoir (à dîner); (*idea, plan*) envisager

entertainer [ɛntəˈteɪnəʳ] n artiste m/f de variétés

entertaining [ɛntəˈteɪnɪŋ] adj amusant(e), distrayant(e) ▷ n: **to do a lot of ~** beaucoup recevoir

entertainment [ɛntəˈteɪnmənt] n (*amusement*) distraction f, divertissement m, amusement m; (*show*) spectacle m

enthralled [ɪnˈθrɔːld] adj captivé(e)

enthusiasm [ɪnˈθuːzɪæzəm] n enthousiasme m

enthusiast [ɪnˈθuːzɪæst] n enthousiaste m/f; **a jazz etc ~** un fervent or passionné du jazz etc

enthusiastic [ɪnθuːzɪˈæstɪk] adj enthousiaste; **to be ~ about** être enthousiasmé(e) par

entire [ɪnˈtaɪəʳ] adj (tout) entier(-ère)

entirely [ɪnˈtaɪəlɪ] adv entièrement, complètement

entirety [ɪnˈtaɪərətɪ] n: **in its ~** dans sa totalité

entitle [ɪnˈtaɪtl] vt (*allow*): **to ~ sb to do** donner (le) droit à qn de faire; **to ~ sb to sth** donner droit à qch à qn

entitled [ɪnˈtaɪtld] adj (*book*) intitulé(e); **to be ~ to do** avoir le droit de faire

entrance n [ˈɛntrns] entrée f ▷ vt [ɪnˈtrɑːns] enchanter, ravir; **where's the ~?** où est l'entrée?; **to gain ~ to** (*university etc*) être admis à

entrance examination n examen m d'entrée or d'admission

entrance fee n (*to museum etc*) prix m d'entrée; (*to join club etc*) droit m d'inscription

entrance ramp n (*US Aut*) bretelle f d'accès

entrant [ˈɛntrnt] n (*in race etc*) participant(e), concurrent(e); (*Brit: in exam*) candidat(e)

entrenched [ɛnˈtrɛntʃt] adj retranché(e)

entrepreneur [ˈɔntrəprəˈnəːʳ] n entrepreneur m

entrust [ɪnˈtrʌst] vt: **to ~ sth to** confier qch à

entry [ˈɛntrɪ] n entrée f; (*in register, diary*) inscription f; (*in ledger*) écriture f; **"no ~"** "défense d'entrer", "entrée interdite"; (*Aut*) "sens interdit"; **single/double ~ book-keeping** comptabilité f en partie simple/double

entry form n feuille f d'inscription

entry phone n (*Brit*) interphone m (à l'entrée d'un immeuble)

envelop [ɪnˈvɛləp] vt envelopper

envelope [ˈɛnvələup] n enveloppe f

envious [ˈɛnvɪəs] adj envieux(-euse)

environment [ɪnˈvaɪərnmənt] n (*social, moral*) milieu m; (*natural world*): **the ~** l'environnement m; **Department of the E~** (*Brit*) ministère de l'Équipement et de l'Aménagement du territoire

environmental [ɪnvaɪərnˈmɛntl] adj (*of surroundings*) du milieu; (*issue, disaster*) écologique; **~ studies** (*in school etc*) écologie f

environmentally [ɪnvaɪərnˈmɛntlɪ] adv: **~ sound/friendly** qui ne nuit pas à l'environnement

envisage [ɪn'vɪzɪdʒ] vt (imagine) envisager; (foresee) prévoir

envoy ['ɛnvɔɪ] n envoyé(e); (diplomat) ministre m plénipotentiaire

envy ['ɛnvɪ] n envie f ▷ vt envier; **to ~ sb sth** envier qch à qn

epic ['ɛpɪk] n épopée f ▷ adj épique

epidemic [ɛpɪ'dɛmɪk] n épidémie f

epilepsy ['ɛpɪlɛpsɪ] n épilepsie f

epileptic [ɛpɪ'lɛptɪk] adj, n épileptique m/f

epileptic fit [ɛpɪ'lɛptɪk-] n crise f d'épilepsie

episode ['ɛpɪsəʊd] n épisode m

epitome [ɪ'pɪtəmɪ] n (fig) quintessence f, type m

epitomize [ɪ'pɪtəmaɪz] vt (fig) illustrer, incarner

equal ['iːkwl] adj égal(e) ▷ n égal(e) ▷ vt égaler; **~ to** (task) à la hauteur de; **~ to doing** de taille à or capable de faire

equality [iː'kwɔlɪtɪ] n égalité f

equalize ['iːkwəlaɪz] vt, vi (Sport) égaliser

equally ['iːkwəlɪ] adv également; (share) en parts égales; (treat) de la même façon; (pay) autant; (just as) tout aussi; **they are ~ clever** ils sont tout aussi intelligents

equanimity [ɛkwə'nɪmɪtɪ] n égalité f d'humeur

equate [ɪ'kweɪt] vt: **to ~ sth with** comparer qch à; assimiler qch à; **to ~ sth to** mettre qch en équation avec; égaler qch à

equation [ɪ'kweɪʃən] n (Math) équation f

equator [ɪ'kweɪtəʳ] n équateur m

equilibrium [iːkwɪ'lɪbrɪəm] n équilibre m

equip [ɪ'kwɪp] vt équiper; **to ~ sb/sth with** équiper or munir qn/qch de; **he is well ~ped for the job** il a les compétences or les qualités requises pour ce travail

equipment [ɪ'kwɪpmənt] n équipement m; (electrical etc) appareillage m, installation f

equities ['ɛkwɪtɪz] npl (Brit Comm) actions cotées en Bourse

equivalent [ɪ'kwɪvəlnt] adj équivalent(e) ▷ n équivalent m; **to be ~ to** équivaloir à, être équivalent(e) à

ER abbr (Brit: = Elizabeth Regina) la reine Élisabeth; (US: Med: = emergency room) urgences fpl

era ['ɪərə] n ère f, époque f

eradicate [ɪ'rædɪkeɪt] vt éliminer

erase [ɪ'reɪz] vt effacer

eraser [ɪ'reɪzəʳ] n gomme f

erect [ɪ'rɛkt] adj droit(e) ▷ vt construire; (monument) ériger, élever; (tent etc) dresser

erection [ɪ'rɛkʃən] n (Physiol) érection f; (of building) construction f; (of machinery etc) installation f

ERM n abbr (= Exchange Rate Mechanism) mécanisme m des taux de change

erode [ɪ'rəʊd] vt éroder; (metal) ronger

erosion [ɪ'rəʊʒən] n érosion f

erotic [ɪ'rɔtɪk] adj érotique

errand ['ɛrnd] n course f, commission f; **to run ~s** faire des courses; **~ of mercy** mission f de charité, acte m charitable

erratic [ɪ'rætɪk] adj irrégulier(-ière), inconstant(e)

error ['ɛrəʳ] n erreur f; **typing/spelling ~** faute f de frappe/d'orthographe; **in ~** par erreur, par méprise; **~s and omissions excepted** sauf erreur ou omission

erupt [ɪ'rʌpt] vi entrer en éruption; (fig) éclater, exploser

eruption [ɪ'rʌpʃən] n éruption f; (of anger, violence) explosion f

escalate ['ɛskəleɪt] vi s'intensifier; (costs) monter en flèche

escalator ['ɛskəleɪtəʳ] n escalier roulant

escapade [ɛskə'peɪd] n fredaine f; équipée f

escape [ɪ'skeɪp] n évasion f, fuite f; (of gas etc) fuite; (Tech) échappement m ▷ vi s'échapper, fuir; (from jail) s'évader; (fig) s'en tirer, en réchapper; (leak) fuir; s'échapper ▷ vt échapper à; **to ~ from** (person) échapper à; (place) s'échapper de; (fig) fuir; **to ~ to** (another place) fuir à, s'enfuir à; **to ~ to safety** se réfugier dans or gagner un endroit sûr; **to ~ notice** passer inaperçu(e); **his name ~s me** son nom m'échappe

escapism [ɪ'skeɪpɪzəm] n évasion f (fig)

escort vt [ɪ'skɔːt] escorter ▷ n ['ɛskɔːt] (Mil) escorte f; (to dance etc): **her ~** son compagnon or cavalier; **his ~** sa compagne

Eskimo ['ɛskɪməʊ] adj esquimau(de), eskimo ▷ n Esquimau(de); (Ling) esquimau m

especially [ɪ'spɛʃlɪ] adv (particularly) particulièrement; (above all) surtout

espionage ['ɛspɪənɑːʒ] n espionnage m

Esquire [ɪ'skwaɪəʳ] n (Brit: abbr **Esq.**): **J. Brown, ~** Monsieur J. Brown

essay ['ɛseɪ] n (Scol) dissertation f; (Literature) essai m; (attempt) tentative f

essence ['ɛsns] n essence f; (Culin) extrait m; **in ~** en substance; **speed is of the ~** l'essentiel, c'est la rapidité

essential [ɪ'sɛnʃl] adj essentiel(le); (basic) fondamental(e); **essentials** npl éléments essentiels; **it is ~ that** il est essentiel or primordial que

essentially [ɪ'sɛnʃlɪ] adv essentiellement

establish [ɪ'stæblɪʃ] vt établir; (business) fonder, créer; (one's power etc) asseoir, affermir

established [ɪ'stæblɪʃt] adj bien établi(e)

establishment [ɪ'stæblɪʃmənt] n établissement m; (founding) création f; (institution) établissement; **the E~** les pouvoirs établis; l'ordre établi

estate [ɪ'steɪt] n (land) domaine m, propriété f; (Law) biens mpl, succession f; (Brit: also: **housing estate**) lotissement m

estate agent n (Brit) agent immobilier

estate car n (Brit) break m

esteem [ɪ'stiːm] n estime f ▷ vt estimer; apprécier; **to hold sb in high ~** tenir qn en haute estime

esthetic [ɪs'θɛtɪk] adj (US) = **aesthetic**

estimate [n 'ɛstɪmət, vb 'ɛstɪmeɪt] n estimation f; (Comm) devis m ▷ vt estimer ▷ vi (Brit Comm): **to ~ for** estimer, faire une estimation de; (bid *for*) faire un devis pour; **to give sb an ~ of** faire *or* donner un devis à qn pour; **at a rough ~** approximativement

estimation [ɛstɪ'meɪʃən] *n* opinion *f*; estime *f*; **in my ~** à mon avis, selon moi

estranged [ɪs'treɪndʒd] *adj* (*couple*) séparé(e); (*husband, wife*) dont on s'est séparé(e)

etc *abbr* (= *et cetera*) etc

eternal [ɪ'tə:nl] *adj* éternel(le)

eternity [ɪ'tə:nɪtɪ] *n* éternité *f*

ethical ['ɛθɪkl] *adj* moral(e)

ethics ['ɛθɪks] *n* éthique *f* ▷ *npl* moralité *f*

Ethiopia [i:θɪ'əupɪə] *n* Éthiopie *f*

ethnic ['ɛθnɪk] *adj* ethnique; (*clothes, food*) folklorique, exotique, *propre aux minorités ethniques non-occidentales*

ethnic minority *n* minorité *f* ethnique

ethos ['i:θɒs] *n* (*système m de*) valeurs *fpl*

e-ticket ['i:tɪkɪt] *n* billet *m* électronique

etiquette ['ɛtɪkɛt] *n* convenances *fpl*, étiquette *f*

EU *n abbr* (= *European Union*) UE *f*

euro ['juərəu] *n* (*currency*) euro *m*

Euroland ['juərəulænd] *n* Euroland *m*

Europe ['juərəp] *n* Europe *f*

European [juərə'pi:ən] *adj* européen(ne) ▷ *n* Européen(ne)

European Community *n* Communauté européenne

European Union *n* Union européenne

Eurostar® ['juərəusta:ʳ] *n* Eurostar® *m*

evacuate [ɪ'vækjueɪt] *vt* évacuer

evade [ɪ'veɪd] *vt* échapper à; (*question etc*) éluder; (*duties*) se dérober à

evaluate [ɪ'væljueɪt] *vt* évaluer

evaporate [ɪ'væpəreɪt] *vi* s'évaporer; (*fig: hopes, fear*) s'envoler; (*anger*) se dissiper ▷ *vt* faire évaporer

evaporated milk [ɪ'væpəreɪtɪd-] *n* lait condensé (non sucré)

evasion [ɪ'veɪʒən] *n* dérobade *f*; (*excuse*) faux-fuyant *m*

eve [i:v] *n*: **on the ~ of** à la veille de

even ['i:vn] *adj* (*level, smooth*) régulier(-ière); (*equal*) égal(e); (*number*) pair(e) ▷ *adv* même; **~ if** même si + *indic*; **~ though** quand (bien) même + *cond*, alors même que + *cond*; **~ more** encore plus; **~ faster** encore plus vite; **~ so** quand même; **not ~** pas même; **~ he was there** même lui était là; **~ on Sundays** même le dimanche; **to break ~** s'y retrouver, équilibrer ses comptes; **to get ~ with sb** prendre sa revanche sur qn

▶ **even out** *vi* s'égaliser

evening ['i:vnɪŋ] *n* soir *m*; (*as duration, event*) soirée *f*; **in the ~** le soir; **this ~** ce soir; **tomorrow/yesterday ~** demain/hier soir

evening class *n* cours *m* du soir

evening dress *n* (*man's*) tenue *f* de soirée, smoking *m*; (*woman's*) robe *f* de soirée

event [ɪ'vɛnt] *n* événement *m*; (*Sport*) épreuve *f*; **in the course of ~s** par la suite; **in the ~ of** en cas de; **in the ~** en réalité, en fait; **at all ~s** (*Brit*): **in any ~** en tout cas, de toute manière

eventful [ɪ'vɛntful] *adj* mouvementé(e)

eventual [ɪ'vɛntʃuəl] *adj* final(e)

eventuality [ɪvɛntʃu'ælɪtɪ] *n* possibilité *f*, éventualité *f*

eventually [ɪ'vɛntʃuəlɪ] *adv* finalement

ever ['ɛvəʳ] *adv* jamais; (*at all times*) toujours; (*in questions*): **why ~ not?** mais enfin, pourquoi pas?; **the best ~** le meilleur qu'on ait jamais vu; **have you ~ seen it?** l'as-tu déjà vu?, as-tu eu l'occasion *or* t'est-il arrivé de le voir?; **did you ~ meet him?** est-ce qu'il vous est arrivé de le rencontrer?; **have you ~ been there?** y êtes-vous déjà allé?; **for ~** pour toujours; **hardly ~** ne ... presque jamais; **~ since** (*as adv*) depuis; (*as conj*) depuis que; **~ so pretty** si joli; **thank you ~ so much** merci mille fois

evergreen ['ɛvəgri:n] *n* arbre *m* à feuilles persistantes

everlasting [ɛvə'lɑ:stɪŋ] *adj* éternel(le)

every ['ɛvrɪ] *adj* 1 (*each*) chaque; **~ one of them** tous (sans exception); **~ shop in town was closed** tous les magasins en ville étaient fermés 2 (*all possible*) tous (toutes) les; **I gave you ~ assistance** j'ai fait tout mon possible pour vous aider; **I have ~ confidence in him** j'ai entièrement *or* pleinement confiance en lui; **we wish you ~ success** nous vous souhaitons beaucoup de succès 3 (*showing recurrence*) tous les; **~ day** tous les jours, chaque jour; **~ other car** une voiture sur deux; **~ other/third day** tous les deux/trois jours; **~ now and then** de temps en temps

everybody ['ɛvrɪbɔdɪ] *pron* = **everyone**

everyday ['ɛvrɪdeɪ] *adj* (*expression*) courant(e), d'usage courant; (*use*) courant; (*clothes, life*) de tous les jours; (*occurrence, problem*) quotidien(ne)

everyone ['ɛvrɪwʌn] *pron* tout le monde, tous *pl*; **~ knows about it** tout le monde le sait; **~ else** tous les autres

everything ['ɛvrɪθɪŋ] *pron* tout; **~ is ready** tout est prêt; **he did ~ possible** il a fait tout son possible

everywhere ['ɛvrɪwɛəʳ] *adv* partout; **~ you go you meet ...** où qu'on aille on rencontre ...

evict [ɪ'vɪkt] *vt* expulser

eviction [ɪ'vɪkʃən] *n* expulsion *f*

evidence ['ɛvɪdns] *n* (*proof*) preuve(s) *f(pl)*; (*of witness*) témoignage *m*; (*sign*): **to show ~ of** donner des signes de; **to give ~** témoigner, déposer; **in ~** (*obvious*) en évidence; en vue

evident ['ɛvɪdnt] *adj* évident(e)

evidently ['ɛvɪdntlɪ] *adv* de toute évidence; (*apparently*) apparemment

evil ['i:vl] *adj* mauvais(e) ▷ *n* mal *m*

evoke [ɪ'vəuk] *vt* évoquer; (*admiration*) susciter

evolution [i:və'lu:ʃən] *n* évolution *f*

evolve [ɪ'vɔlv] *vt* élaborer ▷ *vi* évoluer, se transformer

ewe [ju:] *n* brebis *f*

ex [ɛks] *n* (*inf*): **my ex** mon ex

ex- [ɛks] *prefix* (*former: husband, president etc*) ex-; (*out of*): **the price ~works** le prix départ usine

exact [ɪg'zækt] *adj* exact(e) ▷ *vt*: **to ~ sth (from)** (*signature, confession*) extorquer qch (à); (*apology*) exiger qch (de)

exacting [ɪg'zæktɪŋ] *adj* exigeant(e); (*work*) fatigant(e)

exactly [ɪg'zæktlɪ] *adv* exactement; **~!** parfaitement!, précisément!

exaggerate [ɪg'zædʒəreɪt] *vt, vi* exagérer

exaggeration [ɪgzædʒə'reɪʃən] *n* exagération *f*

exalted [ɪg'zɔːltɪd] *adj* (*rank*) élevé(e); (*person*) haut placé(e); (*elated*) exalté(e)

exam [ɪg'zæm] *n abbr* (*Scol*) = **examination**

examination [ɪgzæmɪ'neɪʃən] *n* (*Scol, Med*) examen *m*; **to take** *or* **sit an ~** (*Brit*) passer un examen; **the matter is under ~** la question est à l'examen

examine [ɪg'zæmɪn] *vt* (*gen*) examiner; (*Scol, Law: person*) interroger; (*inspect: machine, premises*) inspecter; (*passport*) contrôler; (*luggage*) fouiller

examiner [ɪg'zæmɪnə'] *n* examinateur(-trice)

example [ɪg'zɑːmpl] *n* exemple *m*; **for ~** par exemple; **to set a good/bad ~** donner le bon/ mauvais exemple

exasperate [ɪg'zɑːspəreɪt] *vt* exaspérer, agacer

exasperated [ɪg'zɑːspəreɪtɪd] *adj* exaspéré(e)

exasperation [ɪgzɑːspə'reɪʃən] *n* exaspération *f*, irritation *f*

excavate ['ɛkskəveɪt] *vt* (*site*) fouiller, excaver; (*object*) mettre au jour

excavation [ɛkskə'veɪʃən] *n* excavation *f*

exceed [ɪk'siːd] *vt* dépasser; (*one's powers*) outrepasser

exceedingly [ɪk'siːdɪŋlɪ] *adv* extrêmement

excel [ɪk'sɛl] *vi* exceller ▷ *vt* surpasser; **to ~ o.s.** se surpasser

excellence ['ɛksələns] *n* excellence *f*

excellent ['ɛksələnt] *adj* excellent(e)

except [ɪk'sɛpt] *prep* (*also*: **except for, excepting**) sauf, excepté, à l'exception de ▷ *vt* excepter; **~ if/when** sauf si/quand; **~ that** excepté que, si ce n'est que

exception [ɪk'sɛpʃən] *n* exception *f*; **to take ~ to** s'offusquer de; **with the ~ of** à l'exception de

exceptional [ɪk'sɛpʃənl] *adj* exceptionnel(le)

exceptionally [ɪk'sɛpʃənəlɪ] *adv* exceptionnellement

excerpt ['ɛksəːpt] *n* extrait *m*

excess [ɪk'sɛs] *n* excès *m*; **in ~ of** plus de

excess baggage *n* excédent *m* de bagages

excess fare *n* supplément *m*

excessive [ɪk'sɛsɪv] *adj* excessif(-ive)

exchange [ɪks'tʃeɪndʒ] *n* échange *m*; (*also*: **telephone exchange**) central *m* ▷ *vt*: **to ~ (for)** échanger (contre); **could I ~ this, please?** est-ce que je peux échanger ceci, s'il vous plaît?; **in ~ for** en échange de; **foreign ~** (*Comm*) change *m*

exchange rate *n* taux *m* de change

excise *n* ['ɛksaɪz] taxe *f* ▷ *vt* [ɛk'saɪz] exciser

excite [ɪk'saɪt] *vt* exciter

excited [ɪk'saɪtəd] *adj* (tout (toute) excité(e); **to get ~** s'exciter

excitement [ɪk'saɪtmənt] *n* excitation *f*

exciting [ɪk'saɪtɪŋ] *adj* passionnant(e)

exclaim [ɪk'skleɪm] *vi* s'exclamer

exclamation [ɛksklə'meɪʃən] *n* exclamation *f*

exclamation mark, (*US*) **exclamation point** *n* point *m* d'exclamation

exclude [ɪk'skluːd] *vt* exclure

excluding [ɪk'skluːdɪŋ] *prep*: **~ VAT** la TVA non comprise

exclusion [ɪk'skluːʒən] *n* exclusion *f*; **to the ~ of** à l'exclusion de

exclusion zone *n* zone interdite

exclusive [ɪk'skluːsɪv] *adj* exclusif(-ive); (*club, district*) sélect(e); (*item of news*) en exclusivité ▷ *adv* (*Comm*) exclusivement, non inclus; **~ of VAT** TVA non comprise; **~ of postage** (les) frais de poste non compris; **from 1st to 15th March ~** du 1er au 15 mars exclusivement *or* exclu; **~ rights** (*Comm*) exclusivité *f*

exclusively [ɪk'skluːsɪvlɪ] *adv* exclusivement

excruciating [ɪk'skruːʃɪeɪtɪŋ] *adj* (*pain*) atroce, déchirant(e); (*embarrassing*) pénible

excursion [ɪk'skəːʃən] *n* excursion *f*

excuse *n* [ɪk'skjuːs] excuse *f* ▷ *vt* [ɪk'skjuːz] (*forgive*) excuser; (*justify*) excuser, justifier; **to ~ sb from** (*activity*) dispenser qn de; **~ me!** excusez-moi!, pardon!; **now if you will ~ me, ...** maintenant, si vous (le) permettez ...; **to make ~s for sb** trouver des excuses à qn; **to ~ o.s. for sth/for doing sth** s'excuser de/d'avoir fait qch

ex-directory ['ɛksdɪ'rɛktərɪ] *adj* (*Brit*) sur la liste rouge

execute ['ɛksɪkjuːt] *vt* exécuter

execution [ɛksɪ'kjuːʃən] *n* exécution *f*

executive [ɪg'zɛkjutɪv] *n* (*person*) cadre *m*; (*managing group*) bureau *m*; (*Pol*) exécutif *m* ▷ *adj* exécutif(-ive); (*position, job*) de cadre; (*secretary*) de direction; (*offices*) de la direction; (*car, plane*) de fonction

exemplify [ɪg'zɛmplɪfaɪ] *vt* illustrer

exempt [ɪg'zɛmpt] *adj*: **~ from** exempté(e) *or* dispensé(e) de ▷ *vt*: **to ~ sb from** exempter *or* dispenser qn de

exercise ['ɛksəsaɪz] *n* exercice *m* ▷ *vt* exercer; (*patience etc*) faire preuve de; (*dog*) promener ▷ *vi* (*also*: **to take exercise**) prendre de l'exercice

exercise book *n* cahier *m*

exert [ɪg'zəːt] *vt* exercer, employer; (*strength, force*) employer; **to ~ o.s.** se dépenser

exertion [ɪg'zəːʃən] *n* effort *m*

exhale [ɛks'heɪl] *vt* (*breathe out*) expirer; exhaler ▷ *vi* expirer

exhaust [ɪg'zɔːst] *n* (*also*: **exhaust fumes**) gaz *mpl* d'échappement; (*also*: **exhaust pipe**) tuyau *m* d'échappement ▷ *vt* épuiser; **to ~ o.s.** s'épuiser

exhausted [ɪg'zɔːstɪd] *adj* épuisé(e)

exhaustion [ɪg'zɔːstʃən] *n* épuisement *m*; **nervous ~** fatigue nerveuse

exhaustive [ɪg'zɔːstɪv] *adj* très complet(-ète)

exhibit [ɪg'zɪbɪt] *n* (*Art*) objet exposé, pièce exposée; (*Law*) pièce à conviction ▷ *vt* (*Art*) exposer; (*courage, skill*) faire preuve de

exhibition [ɛksɪ'bɪʃən] *n* exposition *f*; **~ of**

temper manifestation *f* de colère
exhilarating [ɪgˈzɪləreɪtɪŋ] *adj* grisant(e), stimulant(e)
ex-husband [ˈɛksˈhʌzbənd] *n* ex-mari *m*
exile [ˈɛksaɪl] *n* exil *m*; (*person*) exilé(e) ▷ *vt* exiler; **in ~** en exil
exist [ɪgˈzɪst] *vi* exister
existence [ɪgˈzɪstəns] *n* existence *f*; **to be in ~** exister
existing [ɪgˈzɪstɪŋ] *adj* (*laws*) existant(e); (*system, regime*) actuel(le)
exit [ˈɛksɪt] *n* sortie *f* ▷ *vi* (*Comput, Theat*) sortir; **where's the ~?** où est la sortie?
exit poll *n* sondage *m* (*fait à la sortie de l'isoloir*)
exit ramp *n* (*US Aut*) bretelle *f* d'accès
exodus [ˈɛksədəs] *n* exode *m*
exonerate [ɪgˈzɔnəreɪt] *vt*: **to ~ from** disculper de
exotic [ɪgˈzɔtɪk] *adj* exotique
expand [ɪkˈspænd] *vt* (*area*) agrandir; (*quantity*) accroître; (*influence etc*) étendre ▷ *vi* (*population, production*) s'accroître; (*trade, etc*) se développer, s'accroître; (*gas, metal*) se dilater, dilater; **to ~ on** (*notes, story etc*) développer
expanse [ɪkˈspæns] *n* étendue *f*
expansion [ɪkˈspænʃən] *n* (*territorial, economic*) expansion *f*; (*of trade, influence etc*) développement *m*; (*of production*) accroissement *m*; (*of population*) croissance *f*; (*of gas, metal*) expansion, dilatation *f*
expect [ɪkˈspɛkt] *vt* (*anticipate*) s'attendre à, s'attendre à ce que+*sub*; (*count on*) compter sur, escompter; (*hope for*) espérer; (*require*) demander, exiger; (*suppose*) supposer; (*await: also baby*) attendre ▷ *vi*: **to be ~ing** (*pregnant woman*) être enceinte; **to ~ sb to do** (*anticipate*) s'attendre à ce que qn fasse; (*demand*) attendre de qn qu'il fasse; **to ~ to do sth** penser *or* compter faire qch, s'attendre à faire qch; **as ~ed** comme prévu; **I ~ so** je crois que oui, je crois bien
expectancy [ɪksˈpɛktənsɪ] *n* attente *f*; **life ~** espérance *f* de vie
expectant [ɪkˈspɛktənt] *adj* qui attend (quelque chose); **~ mother** future maman
expectation [ɛkspɛkˈteɪʃən] *n* (*hope*) attente *f*, espérance(s) *f(pl)*; (*belief*) attente; **in ~ of** dans l'attente de, en prévision de; **against** *or* **contrary to all ~(s)** contre toute attente, contrairement à ce qu'on attendait; **to come** *or* **live up to sb's ~s** répondre à l'attente *or* aux espérances de qn
expedient [ɪkˈspiːdɪənt] *adj* indiqué(e), opportun(e), commode ▷ *n* expédient *m*
expedition [ɛkspəˈdɪʃən] *n* expédition *f*
expel [ɪkˈspɛl] *vt* chasser, expulser; (*Scol*) renvoyer, exclure
expend [ɪkˈspɛnd] *vt* consacrer; (*use up*) dépenser
expenditure [ɪkˈspɛndɪtʃəʳ] *n* (*act of spending*) dépense *f*; (*money spent*) dépenses *fpl*
expense [ɪkˈspɛns] *n* (*high cost*) coût *m*; (*spending*) dépense *f*, frais *mpl*; **expenses** *npl* frais *mpl*; dépenses; **to go to the ~ of** faire la dépense de; **at great/little ~** à grands/peu de frais; **at the ~**

of aux frais de; (*fig*) aux dépens de
expense account *n* (*note f de*) frais *mpl*
expensive [ɪkˈspɛnsɪv] *adj* cher (chère), coûteux(-euse); **to be ~** coûter cher; **it's too ~** ça coûte trop cher; **~ tastes** goûts *mpl* de luxe
experience [ɪkˈspɪərɪəns] *n* expérience *f* ▷ *vt* connaître; (*feeling*) éprouver; **to know by ~** savoir par expérience
experienced [ɪkˈspɪərɪənst] *adj* expérimenté(e)
experiment [ɪkˈspɛrɪmənt] *n* expérience *f* ▷ *vi* faire une expérience; **to ~ with** expérimenter; **to perform** *or* **carry out an ~** faire une expérience; **as an ~** à titre d'expérience
experimental [ɪksperɪˈmɛntl] *adj* expérimental(e)
expert [ˈɛkspəːt] *adj* expert(e) ▷ *n* expert *m*; **~ in** *or* **at doing sth** spécialiste de qch; **an ~ on sth** un spécialiste de qch; **~ witness** (*Law*) expert *m*
expertise [ɛkspəːˈtiːz] *n* (*grande*) compétence
expire [ɪkˈspaɪəʳ] *vi* expirer
expiry [ɪkˈspaɪərɪ] *n* expiration *f*
expiry date *n* date *f* d'expiration; (*on label*) à utiliser avant ...
explain [ɪkˈspleɪn] *vt* expliquer
▸ **explain away** *vt* justifier, excuser
explanation [ɛkspləˈneɪʃən] *n* explication *f*; **to find an ~ for sth** trouver une explication à qch
explanatory [ɪkˈsplænətrɪ] *adj* explicatif(-ive)
explicit [ɪkˈsplɪsɪt] *adj* explicite; (*definite*) formel(le)
explode [ɪkˈspləud] *vi* exploser ▷ *vt* faire exploser; (*fig: theory*) démolir; **to ~ a myth** détruire un mythe
exploit *n* [ˈɛksplɔɪt] exploit *m* ▷ *vt* [ɪkˈsplɔɪt] exploiter
exploitation [ɛksplɔɪˈteɪʃən] *n* exploitation *f*
exploratory [ɪkˈsplɔrətrɪ] *adj* (*fig: talks*) préliminaire; **~ operation** (*Med*) intervention *f* (à visée) exploratrice
explore [ɪkˈsplɔːʳ] *vt* explorer; (*possibilities*) étudier, examiner
explorer [ɪkˈsplɔːrəʳ] *n* explorateur(-trice)
explosion [ɪkˈspləuʒən] *n* explosion *f*
explosive [ɪkˈspləusɪv] *adj* explosif(-ive) ▷ *n* explosif *m*
exponent [ɪkˈspəunənt] *n* (*of school of thought etc*) interprète *m*, représentant *m*; (*Math*) exposant *m*
export *vt* [ɛkˈspɔːt] exporter ▷ *n* [ˈɛkspɔːt] exportation *f* ▷ *cpd* [ˈɛkspɔːt] d'exportation
exporter [ɛkˈspɔːtəʳ] *n* exportateur *m*
expose [ɪkˈspəuz] *vt* exposer; (*unmask*) démasquer, dévoiler; **to ~ o.s.** (*Law*) commettre un outrage à la pudeur
exposed [ɪkˈspəuzd] *adj* (*land, house*) exposé(e); (*Elec: wire*) à nu; (*pipe, beam*) apparent(e)
exposure [ɪkˈspəuʒəʳ] *n* exposition *f*; (*publicity*) couverture *f*; (*Phot: speed*) (*temps m de*) pose *f*; (*: shot*) pose; **suffering from ~** (*Med*) souffrant des effets du froid et de l'épuisement; **to die of ~** (*Med*) mourir de froid
exposure meter *n* posemètre *m*
express [ɪkˈsprɛs] *adj* (*definite*) formel(le),

exprès(-esse); (Brit: letter etc) exprès inv ▷ n (train)
rapide m ▷ adv (send) exprès ▷ vt exprimer; **to ~
o.s.** s'exprimer

expression [ɪk'sprɛʃən] n expression f

expressly [ɪk'sprɛslɪ] adv expressément,
formellement

expressway [ɪk'sprɛsweɪ] n (US) voie f express (à
plusieurs files)

exquisite [ɛk'skwɪzɪt] adj exquis(e)

extend [ɪk'stɛnd] vt (visit, street) prolonger;
(deadline) reporter, remettre; (building) agrandir;
(offer) présenter, offrir; (Comm: credit) accorder;
(hand, arm) tendre ▷ vi (land) s'étendre

extension [ɪk'stɛnʃən] n (of visit, street)
prolongation f; (of building) agrandissement
m; (building) annexe f; (to wire, table) rallonge
f; (telephone: in offices) poste m; (: in private house)
téléphone m supplémentaire; **~ 3718** (Tel) poste
3718

extension cable, extension lead n (Elec)
rallonge f

extensive [ɪk'stɛnsɪv] adj étendu(e), vaste;
(damage, alterations) considérable; (inquiries)
approfondi(e); (use) largement répandu(e)

extensively [ɪk'stɛnsɪvlɪ] adv (altered, damaged
etc) considérablement; **he's travelled ~** il a
beaucoup voyagé

extent [ɪk'stɛnt] n étendue f; (degree: of damage,
loss) importance f; **to some ~** dans une certaine
mesure; **to a certain ~** dans une certaine
mesure, jusqu'à un certain point; **to a large ~**
en grande partie; **to the ~ of ...** au point de ...;
to what ~? dans quelle mesure?, jusqu'à quel
point?; **to such an ~ that ...** à tel point que ...

extenuating [ɪk'stɛnjueɪtɪŋ] adj: **~
circumstances** circonstances atténuantes

exterior [ɛk'stɪərɪəʳ] adj extérieur(e) ▷ n
extérieur m

external [ɛk'stə:nl] adj externe ▷ n: **the ~s** les
apparences fpl; **for ~ use only** (Med) à usage
externe

extinct [ɪk'stɪŋkt] adj (volcano) éteint(e); (species)
disparu(e)

extinction [ɪk'stɪŋkʃən] n extinction f

extinguish [ɪk'stɪŋgwɪʃ] vt éteindre

extort [ɪk'stɔ:t] vt: **to ~ sth (from)** extorquer
qch (à)

extortionate [ɪk'stɔ:ʃnɪt] adj exorbitant(e)

extra ['ɛkstrə] adj supplémentaire, de plus ▷ adv
(in addition) en plus ▷ n supplément m; (perk) à-

coté m; (Cine, Theat) figurant(e); **wine will cost
~** le vin sera en supplément; **~ large sizes** très
grandes tailles

extract vt [ɪk'strækt] extraire; (tooth) arracher;
(money, promise) soutirer ▷ n ['ɛkstrækt] extrait m

extracurricular ['ɛkstrəkə'rɪkjuləʳ] adj (Scol)
parascolaire

extradite ['ɛkstrədaɪt] vt extrader

extramarital ['ɛkstrə'mærɪtl] adj
extraconjugal(e)

extramural ['ɛkstrə'mjuərl] adj hors-faculté inv

extraordinary [ɪk'strɔ:dnrɪ] adj extraordinaire;
the ~ thing is that ... le plus étrange or
étonnant c'est que ...

extravagance [ɪk'strævəgəns] n (excessive
spending) prodigalités fpl; (thing bought) folie f,
dépense excessive

extravagant [ɪk'strævəgənt] adj extravagant(e);
(in spending: person) prodigue, dépensier(-ière);
(: tastes) dispendieux(-euse)

extreme [ɪk'stri:m] adj, n extrême (m); **the ~
left/right** (Pol) l'extrême gauche f/droite f; **~s
of temperature** différences fpl extrêmes de
température

extremely [ɪk'stri:mlɪ] adv extrêmement

extremist [ɪk'stri:mɪst] adj, n extrémiste m/f

extricate ['ɛkstrɪkeɪt] vt: **to ~ sth (from)**
dégager qch (de)

extrovert ['ɛkstrəvə:t] n extraverti(e)

ex-wife ['ɛkswaɪf] n ex-femme f

eye [aɪ] n œil m; (of needle) trou m, chas m ▷ vt
examiner; **as far as the ~ can see** à perte de
vue; **to keep an ~ on** surveiller; **to have an ~ for
sth** avoir l'œil pour qch; **in the public ~** en vue;
with an ~ to doing sth (Brit) en vue de faire qch;
there's more to this than meets the ~ ce n'est
pas aussi simple que cela paraît

eyeball ['aɪbɔ:l] n globe m oculaire

eyebrow ['aɪbrau] n sourcil m

eye drops ['aɪdrɔps] npl gouttes fpl pour les yeux

eyelash ['aɪlæʃ] n cil m

eyelid ['aɪlɪd] n paupière f

eyeliner ['aɪlaɪnəʳ] n eye-liner m

eye-opener ['aɪəupnəʳ] n révélation f

eye shadow ['aɪʃædəu] n ombre f à paupières

eyesight ['aɪsaɪt] n vue f

eyesore ['aɪsɔ:ʳ] n horreur f, chose f qui dépare
or enlaidit

eye witness n témoin m oculaire

F¹, f [ɛf] *n* (*letter*) F, f *m*; (*Mus*): **F** fa *m*; **F for Frederick** (*US*): **F for Fox** F comme François

F² *abbr* (= *Fahrenheit*) F

fable ['feɪbl] *n* fable *f*

fabric ['fæbrɪk] *n* tissu *m* ▷ *cpd*: **~ ribbon** (*for typewriter*) ruban *m* (en) tissu

fabulous ['fæbjuləs] *adj* fabuleux(-euse); (*inf: super*) formidable, sensationnel(le)

face [feɪs] *n* visage *m*, figure *f*; (*expression*) air *m*; grimace *f*; (*of clock*) cadran *m*; (*of cliff*) paroi *f*; (*of mountain*) face *f*; (*of building*) façade *f*; (*side, surface*) face *f* ▷ *vt* faire face à; (*facts etc*) accepter; **~ down** (*person*) à plat ventre; (*card*) face en dessous; **to lose/save ~** perdre/sauver la face; **to pull a ~** faire une grimace; **in the ~ of** (*difficulties etc*) face à, devant; **on the ~ of it** à première vue; **~ to ~** face à face
  ▶ **face up to** *vt fus* faire face à, affronter

face cloth *n* (*Brit*) gant *m* de toilette

face cream *n* crème *f* pour le visage

face lift *n* lifting *m*; (*of façade etc*) ravalement *m*, retapage *m*

face pack *n* (*Brit*) masque *m* (de beauté)

face powder *n* poudre *f* (pour le visage)

face value ['feɪs'vælju:] *n* (*of coin*) valeur nominale; **to take sth at ~** (*fig*) prendre qch pour argent comptant

facial ['feɪʃl] *adj* facial(e) ▷ *n* soin complet du visage

facilitate [fə'sɪlɪteɪt] *vt* faciliter

facilities [fə'sɪlɪtɪz] *npl* installations *fpl*, équipement *m*; **credit ~** facilités de paiement

facility [fə'sɪlɪtɪ] *n* facilité *f*

facing ['feɪsɪŋ] *prep* face à, en face de ▷ *n* (*of wall etc*) revêtement *m*; (*Sewing*) revers *m*

facsimile [fæk'sɪmɪlɪ] *n* (*exact replica*) facsimilé *m*; (*also:* **facsimile machine**) télécopieur *m*; (*transmitted document*) télécopie *f*

fact [fækt] *n* fait *m*; **in ~** en fait; **to know for a ~ that ...** savoir pertinemment que ...

faction ['fækʃən] *n* faction *f*

factor ['fæktə'] *n* facteur *m*; (*of sun cream*) indice *m* (de protection); (*Comm*) factor *m*, société *f* d'affacturage; (: *agent*) dépositaire *m/f* ▷ *vi* faire du factoring; **safety ~** facteur de sécurité; **I'd like a ~ 15 suntan lotion** je voudrais une crème solaire d'indice 15

factory ['fæktərɪ] *n* usine *f*, fabrique *f*

factual ['fæktjuəl] *adj* basé(e) sur les faits

faculty ['fækltɪ] *n* faculté *f*; (*US: teaching staff*) corps enseignant

fad [fæd] *n* (*personal*) manie *f*; (*craze*) engouement *m*

fade [feɪd] *vi* se décolorer, passer; (*light, sound*) s'affaiblir, disparaître; (*flower*) se faner
  ▶ **fade away** *vi* (*sound*) s'affaiblir
  ▶ **fade in** *vt* (*picture*) ouvrir en fondu; (*sound*) monter progressivement
  ▶ **fade out** *vt* (*picture*) fermer en fondu; (*sound*) baisser progressivement

fag [fæg] *n* (*Brit inf: cigarette*) clope *f*; (: *chore*): **what a ~!** quelle corvée!; (*US inf: homosexual*) pédé *m*

Fahrenheit ['fɑːrənhaɪt] *n* Fahrenheit *m inv*

fail [feɪl] *vt* (*exam*) échouer à; (*candidate*) recaler; (*subj: courage, memory*) faire défaut à ▷ *vi* échouer; (*supplies*) manquer; (*eyesight, health, light: also:* **be failing**) baisser, s'affaiblir; (*brakes*) lâcher; **to ~ to do sth** (*neglect*) négliger de *or* ne pas faire qch; (*be unable*) ne pas arriver *or* parvenir à faire qch; **without ~** à coup sûr; sans faute

failing ['feɪlɪŋ] *n* défaut *m* ▷ *prep* faute de; **~ that** à défaut, sinon

failure ['feɪljə'] *n* échec *m*; (*person*) raté(e); (*mechanical etc*) défaillance *f*; **his ~ to turn up** le fait de n'être pas venu *or* qu'il ne soit pas venu

faint [feɪnt] *adj* faible; (*recollection*) vague; (*mark*) à peine visible; (*smell, breeze, trace*) léger(-ère) ▷ *n* évanouissement *m* ▷ *vi* s'évanouir; **to feel ~** défaillir

faintest ['feɪntɪst] *adj*: **I haven't the ~ idea** je n'en ai pas la moindre idée

faintly ['feɪntlɪ] *adv* faiblement; (*vaguely*) vaguement

fair [fɛə'] *adj* équitable, juste; (*reasonable*) correct(e), honnête; (*hair*) blond(e); (*skin, complexion*) pâle, blanc (blanche); (*weather*) beau (belle); (*good enough*) assez bon(ne); (*sizeable*) considérable ▷ *adv*: **to play ~** jouer franc jeu ▷ *n* foire *f*; (*Brit: funfair*) fête (foraine); (*also:* **trade fair**) foire(-exposition) commerciale; **it's not ~!** ce n'est pas juste!; **a ~ amount of** une quantité considérable de

fairground ['fɛəɡraund] *n* champ *m* de foire

fair-haired [fɛə'hɛəd] *adj* (*person*) aux cheveux

clairs, blond(e)

fairly ['fɛəlɪ] *adv* (*justly*) équitablement; (*quite*) assez; **I'm ~ sure** j'en suis quasiment *or* presque sûr

fairness ['fɛənɪs] *n* (*of trial etc*) justice *f*, équité *f*; (*of person*) sens *m* de la justice; **in all ~** en toute justice

fair trade *n* commerce *m* équitable

fairway ['fɛəweɪ] *n* (*Golf*) fairway *m*

fairy ['fɛərɪ] *n* fée *f*

fairy tale *n* conte *m* de fées

faith [feɪθ] *n* foi *f*; (*trust*) confiance *f*; (*sect*) culte *m*, religion *f*; **to have ~ in sb/sth** avoir confiance en qn/qch

faithful ['feɪθful] *adj* fidèle

faithfully ['feɪθfəlɪ] *adv* fidèlement; **yours ~** (*Brit: in letters*) veuillez agréer l'expression de mes salutations les plus distinguées

fake [feɪk] *n* (*painting etc*) faux *m*; (*photo*) trucage *m*; (*person*) imposteur *m* ⊳ *adj* faux (fausse) ⊳ *vt* (*emotions*) simuler; (*painting*) faire un faux de; (*photo*) truquer; (*story*) fabriquer; **his illness is a ~** sa maladie est une comédie *or* de la simulation

falcon ['fɔːlkən] *n* faucon *m*

fall [fɔːl] *n* chute *f*; (*decrease*) baisse *f*; (*US: autumn*) automne *m* ⊳ *vi* (*pt* **fell**, *pp* **-en**) [fɛl, 'fɔːlən] tomber; (*price, temperature, dollar*) baisser; **falls** *npl* (*waterfall*) chute *f* d'eau, cascade *f*; **to ~ flat** (*vi: on one's face*) tomber de tout son long, s'étaler; (*joke*) tomber à plat; (*plan*) échouer; **to ~ short of** (*sb's expectations*) ne pas répondre à; **a ~ of snow** (*Brit*) une chute de neige

▶ **fall apart** *vi* (*object*) tomber en morceaux; (*inf: emotionally*) craquer

▶ **fall back** *vi* reculer, se retirer

▶ **fall back on** *vt fus* se rabattre sur; **to have something to ~ back on** (*money etc*) avoir quelque chose en réserve; (*job etc*) avoir une solution de rechange

▶ **fall behind** *vi* prendre du retard

▶ **fall down** *vi* (*person*) tomber; (*building*) s'effondrer, s'écrouler

▶ **fall for** *vt fus* (*trick*) se laisser prendre à; (*person*) tomber amoureux(-euse) de

▶ **fall in** *vi* s'effondrer; (*Mil*) se mettre en rangs

▶ **fall in with** *vt fus* (*sb's plans etc*) accepter

▶ **fall off** *vi* tomber; (*diminish*) baisser, diminuer

▶ **fall out** *vi* (*friends etc*) se brouiller; (*hair, teeth*) tomber

▶ **fall over** *vi* tomber (par terre)

▶ **fall through** *vi* (*plan, project*) tomber à l'eau

fallacy ['fæləsɪ] *n* erreur *f*, illusion *f*

fallen ['fɔːlən] *pp of* **fall**

fallout ['fɔːlaut] *n* retombées (radioactives)

fallow ['fæləu] *adj* en jachère; en friche

false [fɔːls] *adj* faux (fausse); **under ~ pretences** sous un faux prétexte

false alarm *n* fausse alerte

false teeth *npl* (*Brit*) fausses dents, dentier *m*

falter ['fɔːltər] *vi* chanceler, vaciller

fame [feɪm] *n* renommée *f*, renom *m*

familiar [fə'mɪlɪər] *adj* familier(-ière); **to be ~**

with sth connaître qch; **to make o.s. ~ with sth** se familiariser avec qch; **to be on ~ terms with sb** bien connaître qn

familiarize [fə'mɪlɪəraɪz] *vt* familiariser; **to ~ o.s. with** se familiariser avec

family ['fæmɪlɪ] *n* famille *f*

family doctor *n* médecin *m* de famille

family planning *n* planning familial

famine ['fæmɪn] *n* famine *f*

famished ['fæmɪʃt] *adj* affamé(e); **I'm ~!** (*inf*) je meurs de faim!

famous ['feɪməs] *adj* célèbre

famously ['feɪməslɪ] *adv* (*get on*) fameusement, à merveille

fan [fæn] *n* (*folding*) éventail *m*; (*Elec*) ventilateur *m*; (*person*) fan *m*, admirateur(-trice); (*Sport*) supporter *m/f* ⊳ *vt* éventer; (*fire, quarrel*) attiser

▶ **fan out** *vi* se déployer (en éventail)

fanatic [fə'nætɪk] *n* fanatique *m/f*

fan belt *n* courroie *f* de ventilateur

fan club *n* fan-club *m*

fancy ['fænsɪ] *n* (*whim*) fantaisie *f*, envie *f*; (*imagination*) imagination *f* ⊳ *adj* (*luxury*) de luxe; (*elaborate: jewellery, packaging*) fantaisie *inv*; (*showy*) tape-à-l'œil *inv*; (*pretentious: words*) recherché(e) ⊳ *vt* (*feel like, want*) avoir envie de; (*imagine*) imaginer; **to take a ~ to** se prendre d'affection pour; s'enticher de; **it took** *or* **caught my ~** ça m'a plu; **when the ~ takes him** quand ça lui prend; **to ~ that ...** se figurer *or* s'imaginer que ...; **he fancies her** elle lui plaît

fancy dress *n* déguisement *m*, travesti *m*

fancy-dress ball [fænsɪ'drɛs-] *n* bal masqué *or* costumé

fang [fæŋ] *n* croc *m*; (*of snake*) crochet *m*

fan heater *n* (*Brit*) radiateur soufflant

fantasize ['fæntəsaɪz] *vi* fantasmer

fantastic [fæn'tæstɪk] *adj* fantastique

fantasy ['fæntəsɪ] *n* imagination *f*, fantaisie *f*; (*unreality*) fantasme *m*

fanzine ['fænziːn] *n* fanzine *m*

FAQ *n abbr* (= *frequently asked question*) FAQ *f inv*, faq *f inv* ⊳ *abbr* (= *free alongside quay*) FLQ

far [fɑːʳ] *adj* (*distant*) lointain(e), éloigné(e) ⊳ *adv* loin; **the ~ side/end** l'autre côté/bout; **the ~ left/right** (*Pol*) l'extrême gauche *f*/droite *f*; **is it ~ to London?** est-ce qu'on est loin de Londres?; **it's not ~ (from here)** ce n'est pas loin (d'ici); **~ away, ~ off** au loin, dans le lointain; **~ better** beaucoup mieux; **~ from** loin de; **by ~** de loin, de beaucoup; **as ~ back as the 13th century** dès le 13e siècle; **go as ~ as the bridge** allez jusqu'au pont; **as ~ as I know** pour autant que je sache; **how ~ is it to ...?** combien y a-t-il jusqu'à ...?; **as ~ as possible** dans la mesure du possible; **how ~ have you got with your work?** où en êtes-vous dans votre travail?

faraway ['fɑːrəweɪ] *adj* lointain(e); (*look*) absent(e)

farce [fɑːs] *n* farce *f*

fare [fɛəʳ] *n* (*on trains, buses*) prix *m* du billet; (*in taxi*) prix de la course; (*passenger in taxi*) client *m*;

(food) table f, chère f ▷ vi se débrouiller; **half ~** demi-tarif; **full ~** plein tarif

Far East n: **the ~** l'Extrême-Orient m

farewell [fɛə'wɛl] excl, n adieu m ▷ cpd *(party etc)* d'adieux

farm [fɑːm] n ferme f ▷ vt cultiver
▶ **farm out** vt *(work etc)* distribuer

farmer ['fɑːmə'] n fermier(-ière), cultivateur(-trice)

farmhand ['fɑːmhænd] n ouvrier(-ière) agricole

farmhouse ['fɑːmhaus] n (maison f de) ferme f

farming ['fɑːmɪŋ] n agriculture f; *(of animals)* élevage m; **intensive ~** culture intensive; **sheep ~** élevage du mouton

farmland ['fɑːmlænd] n terres cultivées or arables

farm worker n = **farmhand**

farmyard ['fɑːmjɑːd] n cour f de ferme

far-reaching ['fɑː'riːtʃɪŋ] adj d'une grande portée

fart [fɑːt] *(inf!)* n pet m ▷ vi péter

farther ['fɑːðə'] adv plus loin ▷ adj plus éloigné(e), plus lointain(e)

farthest ['fɑːðɪst] superlative of **far**

fascinate ['fæsɪneɪt] vt fasciner, captiver

fascinating ['fæsɪneɪtɪŋ] adj fascinant(e)

fascination [fæsɪ'neɪʃən] n fascination f

fascism ['fæʃɪzəm] n fascisme m

fascist ['fæʃɪst] adj, n fasciste m/f

fashion ['fæʃən] n mode f; *(manner)* façon f, manière f ▷ vt façonner; **in ~** à la mode; **out of ~** démodé(e); **in the Greek ~** à la grecque; **after a ~** *(finish, manage etc)* tant bien que mal

fashionable ['fæʃnəbl] adj à la mode

fashion show n défilé m de mannequins or de mode

fast [fɑːst] adj rapide; *(clock)*: **to be ~** avancer; *(dye, colour)* grand or bon teint inv ▷ adv vite, rapidement; *(stuck, held)* solidement ▷ n jeûne m ▷ vi jeûner; **my watch is 5 minutes ~** ma montre avance de 5 minutes; **~ asleep** profondément endormi; **as ~ as I can** aussi vite que je peux; **to make a boat ~** *(Brit)* amarrer un bateau

fasten ['fɑːsn] vt attacher, fixer; *(coat)* attacher, fermer ▷ vi se fermer, s'attacher
▶ **fasten on, fasten upon** vt fus *(idea)* se cramponner à

fastener ['fɑːsnə'], **fastening** ['fɑːsnɪŋ] n fermeture f, attache f; *(Brit: zip fastener)* fermeture éclair® inv or à glissière

fast food n fast food m, restauration f rapide

fastidious [fæs'tɪdɪəs] adj exigeant(e), difficile

fat [fæt] adj gros(se) ▷ n graisse f; *(on meat)* gras m; *(for cooking)* matière grasse; **to live off the ~ of the land** vivre grassement

fatal ['feɪtl] adj *(mistake)* fatal(e); *(injury)* mortel(le)

fatality [fə'tælɪtɪ] n *(road death etc)* victime f, décès m

fatally ['feɪtəlɪ] adv fatalement; *(injured)* mortellement

fate [feɪt] n destin m; *(of person)* sort m; **to meet one's ~** trouver la mort

fateful ['feɪtful] adj fatidique

father ['fɑːðə'] n père m

Father Christmas n le Père Noël

father-in-law ['fɑːðərɪnlɔː] n beau-père m

fatherly ['fɑːðəlɪ] adj paternel(le)

fathom ['fæðəm] n brasse f (= 1828 mm) ▷ vt *(mystery)* sonder, pénétrer

fatigue [fə'tiːg] n fatigue f; *(Mil)* corvée f; **metal ~** fatigue du métal

fatten ['fætn] vt, vi engraisser

fattening ['fætnɪŋ] adj *(food)* qui fait grossir; **chocolate is ~** le chocolat fait grossir

fatty ['fætɪ] adj *(food)* gras(se) ▷ n *(inf)* gros (grosse)

fatuous ['fætjuəs] adj stupide

faucet ['fɔːsɪt] n *(US)* robinet m

fault [fɔːlt] n faute f; *(defect)* défaut m; *(Geo)* faille f ▷ vt trouver des défauts à, prendre en défaut; **it's my ~** c'est de ma faute; **to find ~ with** trouver à redire or à critiquer à; **at ~** fautif(-ive), coupable; **to a ~** à l'excès

faulty ['fɔːltɪ] adj défectueux(-euse)

fauna ['fɔːnə] n faune f

favour, *(US)* **favor** ['feɪvə'] n faveur f; *(help)* service m ▷ vt *(proposition)* être en faveur de; *(pupil etc)* favoriser; *(team, horse)* donner gagnant; **to do sb a ~** rendre un service à qn; **in ~ of** en faveur de; **to be in ~ of sth/of doing sth** être partisan de qch/de faire qch; **to find ~ with sb** trouver grâce aux yeux de qn

favourable, *(US)* **favorable** ['feɪvrəbl] adj favorable; *(price)* avantageux(-euse)

favourite, *(US)* **favorite** ['feɪvrɪt] adj, n favori(te)

fawn [fɔːn] n *(deer)* faon m ▷ adj *(also:* **fawn-coloured)** fauve ▷ vi: **to ~ (up)on** flatter servilement

fax [fæks] n *(document)* télécopie f; *(machine)* télécopieur m ▷ vt envoyer par télécopie

FBI n abbr *(US: = Federal Bureau of Investigation)* FBI m

fear [fɪə'] n crainte f, peur f ▷ vt craindre ▷ vi: **to ~ for** craindre pour; **to ~ that** craindre que; **~ of heights** vertige m; **for ~ of** de peur que + sub or de + infinitive

fearful ['fɪəful] adj craintif(-ive); *(sight, noise)* affreux(-euse), épouvantable; **to be ~ of** avoir peur de, craindre

fearless ['fɪəlɪs] adj intrépide, sans peur

feasible ['fiːzəbl] adj faisable, réalisable

feast [fiːst] n festin m, banquet m; *(Rel: also:* **feast day)** fête f ▷ vi festoyer; **to ~ on** se régaler de

feat [fiːt] n exploit m, prouesse f

feather ['fɛðə'] n plume f ▷ vt: **to ~ one's nest** *(fig)* faire sa pelote ▷ cpd *(bed etc)* de plumes

feature ['fiːtʃə'] n caractéristique f; *(article)* chronique f, rubrique f ▷ vt *(film)* avoir pour vedette(s) ▷ vi figurer (en bonne place); **features** npl *(of face)* traits mpl; **a (special) ~ on sth/sb** un reportage sur qch/qn; **it ~d prominently in ...** cela a figuré en bonne place sur or dans ...

feature film n long métrage

Feb. abbr *(= February)* fév

February ['fɛbruərı] n février m; *for phrases see also* **July**

fed [fɛd] *pt, pp of* **feed**

federal ['fɛdərəl] *adj* fédéral(e)

federation [fɛdə'reɪʃən] n fédération f

fed up [fɛd'ʌp] *adj*: **to be ~ (with)** en avoir marre *or* plein le dos (de)

fee [fi:] n rémunération f; *(of doctor, lawyer)* honoraires mpl; *(of school, college etc)* frais mpl de scolarité; *(for examination)* droits mpl; **entrance/ membership ~** droit d'entrée/d'inscription; **for a small ~** pour une somme modique

feeble ['fi:bl] *adj* faible; *(attempt, excuse)* pauvre; *(joke)* piteux(-euse)

feed [fi:d] n *(of baby)* tétée f; *(of animal)* nourriture f, pâture f; *(on printer)* mécanisme m d'alimentation ▷ vt *(pt, pp* **fed)** [fɛd] *(person)* nourrir; *(Brit: baby: breastfeed)* allaiter; (*: with bottle)* donner le biberon à; *(horse etc)* donner à manger à; *(machine)* alimenter; *(data etc)*: **to ~ sth into** enregistrer qch dans
  ▶ **feed back** vt *(results)* donner en retour
  ▶ **feed on** vt *fus* se nourrir de

feedback ['fi:dbæk] n *(Elec)* effet m Larsen; *(from person)* réactions fpl

feel [fi:l] n *(sensation)* sensation f; *(impression)* impression f ▷ vt *(pt, pp* **felt)** [fɛlt] *(touch)* toucher; *(explore)* tâter, palper; *(cold, pain)* sentir; *(grief, anger)* ressentir, éprouver; *(think, believe)*: **to ~ (that)** trouver que; **I ~ that you ought to do it** il me semble que vous devriez le faire; **to ~ hungry/cold** avoir faim/froid; **to ~ lonely/ better** se sentir seul/mieux; **I don't ~ well** je ne me sens pas bien; **to ~ sorry for** avoir pitié de; **it ~s soft** c'est doux au toucher; **it ~s colder here** je trouve qu'il fait plus froid ici; **it ~s like velvet** on dirait du velours, ça ressemble au velours; **to ~ like** *(want)* avoir envie de; **to ~ about** *or* **around** fouiller, tâtonner; **to get the ~ of sth** *(fig)* s'habituer à qch

feeler ['fi:lə'] n *(of insect)* antenne f; *(fig)*: **to put out a ~** *or* **~s** tâter le terrain

feeling ['fi:lɪŋ] n *(physical)* sensation f; *(emotion, impression)* sentiment m; **to hurt sb's ~s** froisser qn; **~s ran high about it** cela a déchaîné les passions; **what are your ~s about the matter?** quel est votre sentiment sur cette question?; **my ~ is that ...** j'estime que ...; **I have a ~ that ...** j'ai l'impression que ...

feet [fi:t] npl *of* **foot**

feign [feɪn] vt feindre, simuler

fell [fɛl] *pt of* **fall** ▷ vt *(tree)* abattre ▷ n *(Brit: mountain)* montagne f; (*: moorland)*: **the ~s** la lande ▷ *adj*: **with one ~ blow** d'un seul coup

fellow ['fɛləu] n type m; *(comrade)* compagnon m; *(of learned society)* membre m; *(of university)* universitaire m/f *(membre du conseil)* ▷ *cpd*: **their ~ prisoners/students** leurs camarades prisonniers/étudiants; **his ~ workers** ses collègues mpl *(de travail)*

fellow citizen n concitoyen(ne)

fellow countryman *(irreg)* n compatriote m

fellow men npl semblables mpl

fellowship ['fɛləuʃɪp] n *(society)* association f; *(comradeship)* amitié f, camaraderie f; *(Scol)* sorte de bourse universitaire

felony ['fɛlənɪ] n crime m, forfait m

felt [fɛlt] *pt, pp of* **feel** ▷ n feutre m

felt-tip ['fɛlttɪp-] n *(also:* **felt-tip pen)** stylo-feutre m

female ['fi:meɪl] n *(Zool)* femelle f; *(pej: woman)* bonne femme ▷ *adj* *(Biol, Elec)* femelle; *(sex, character)* féminin(e); *(vote etc)* des femmes; *(child etc)* du sexe féminin; **male and ~ students** étudiants et étudiantes

feminine ['fɛmɪnɪn] *adj* féminin(e) ▷ n féminin m

feminist ['fɛmɪnɪst] n féministe m/f

fence [fɛns] n barrière f; *(Sport)* obstacle m; *(inf: person)* receleur(-euse) ▷ vt *(also:* **fence in)** clôturer ▷ vi faire de l'escrime; **to sit on the ~** *(fig)* ne pas se mouiller

fencing ['fɛnsɪŋ] n *(sport)* escrime m

fend [fɛnd] vi: **to ~ for o.s.** se débrouiller (tout seul)
  ▶ **fend off** vt *(attack etc)* parer; *(questions)* éluder

fender ['fɛndə'] n garde-feu m inv; *(on boat)* défense f; *(US: of car)* aile f

fennel ['fɛnl] n fenouil m

ferment vi [fə'mɛnt] fermenter ▷ n ['fə:mɛnt] *(fig)* agitation f, effervescence f

fern [fə:n] n fougère f

ferocious [fə'rəuʃəs] *adj* féroce

ferret ['fɛrɪt] n furet m
  ▶ **ferret about, ferret around** vi fureter
  ▶ **ferret out** vt dénicher

ferry ['fɛrɪ] n *(small)* bac m; *(large: also:* **ferryboat)** ferry-(boat m) m ▷ vt transporter; **to ~ sth/sb across** *or* **over** faire traverser qch/qn

fertile ['fə:taɪl] *adj* fertile; *(Biol)* fécond(e); **~ period** période f de fécondité

fertilize ['fə:tɪlaɪz] vt fertiliser; *(Biol)* féconder

fertilizer ['fə:tɪlaɪzə'] n engrais m

fester ['fɛstə'] vi suppurer

festival ['fɛstɪvəl] n *(Rel)* fête f; *(Art, Mus)* festival m

festive ['fɛstɪv] *adj* de fête; **the ~ season** *(Brit: Christmas)* la période des fêtes

festivities [fɛs'tɪvɪtɪz] npl réjouissances fpl

festoon [fɛs'tu:n] vt: **to ~ with** orner de

fetch [fɛtʃ] vt aller chercher; *(Brit: sell for)* rapporter; **how much did it ~?** ça a atteint quel prix?
  ▶ **fetch up** vi *(Brit)* se retrouver

fête [feɪt] n fête f, kermesse f

fetus ['fi:təs] n *(US)* = **foetus**

feud [fju:d] n querelle f, dispute f ▷ vi se quereller, se disputer; **a family ~** une querelle de famille

fever ['fi:və'] n fièvre f; **he has a ~** il a de la fièvre

feverish ['fi:vərɪʃ] *adj* fiévreux(-euse), fébrile

few [fju:] *adj* *(not many)* peu de ▷ *pron* peu; **~ succeed** il y en a peu qui réussissent, (bien) peu réussissent; **they were ~** ils étaient peu (nombreux), il y en avait peu; **a ~ (***as adj***)** quelques; (*as pron*) quelques-uns(-unes); **I know a ~** j'en connais quelques-uns; **quite a ~ ...** (*adj*) un certain nombre de ..., pas mal de ...; **in the next ~ days** dans les jours qui viennent; **in the past ~ days** ces derniers jours; **every ~ days/ months** tous les deux ou trois jours/mois; **a ~ more ...** encore quelques ..., quelques ... de plus

fewer ['fju:ər] *adj* moins de ▷ *pron* moins; **they are ~ now** il y en a moins maintenant, ils sont moins (nombreux) maintenant

fewest ['fju:ɪst] *adj* le moins nombreux

fiancé [fɪ'ɑ̃:ŋseɪ] *n* fiancé *m*

fiancée [fɪ'ɑ̃:ŋseɪ] *n* fiancée *f*

fiasco [fɪ'æskəu] *n* fiasco *m*

fib [fɪb] *n* bobard *m*

fibre, (US) **fiber** ['faɪbər] *n* fibre *f*

fibreglass, (US) **Fiberglass®** ['faɪbəglɑ:s] *n* fibre *f* de verre

fickle ['fɪkl] *adj* inconstant(e), volage, capricieux(-euse)

fiction ['fɪkʃən] *n* romans *mpl*, littérature *f* romanesque; (*invention*) fiction *f*

fictional ['fɪkʃənl] *adj* fictif(-ive)

fictitious [fɪk'tɪʃəs] *adj* fictif(-ive), imaginaire

fiddle ['fɪdl] *n* (*Mus*) violon *m*; (*cheating*) combine *f*; escroquerie *f* ▷ *vt* (*Brit: accounts*) falsifier, maquiller; **tax ~** fraude fiscale, combine *f* pour échapper au fisc; **to work a ~** traficoter
▶ **fiddle with** *vt fus* tripoter

fidelity [fɪ'dɛlɪtɪ] *n* fidélité *f*

fidget ['fɪdʒɪt] *vi* se trémousser, remuer

field [fi:ld] *n* champ *m*; (*fig*) domaine *m*, champ; (*Sport: ground*) terrain *m*; (*Comput*) champ, zone *f*; **to lead the ~** (*Sport, Comm*) dominer; **the children had a ~ day** (*fig*) c'était un grand jour pour les enfants

field marshal *n* maréchal *m*

fieldwork ['fi:ldwə:k] *n* travaux *mpl* pratiques (*or* recherches *fpl*) sur le terrain

fiend [fi:nd] *n* démon *m*

fierce [fɪəs] *adj* (*look, animal*) féroce, sauvage; (*wind, attack, person*) (très) violent(e); (*fighting, enemy*) acharné(e)

fiery ['faɪərɪ] *adj* ardent(e), brûlant(e), fougueux(-euse)

fifteen [fɪf'ti:n] *num* quinze

fifteenth [fɪf'ti:nθ] *num* quinzième

fifth [fɪfθ] *num* cinquième

fiftieth ['fɪftɪɪθ] *num* cinquantième

fifty ['fɪftɪ] *num* cinquante

fifty-fifty ['fɪftɪ'fɪftɪ] *adv* moitié-moitié; **to share ~ with sb** partager moitié-moitié avec qn ▷ *adj*: **to have a ~ chance (of success)** avoir une chance sur deux de réussir

fig [fɪg] *n* figue *f*

fight [faɪt] (*pt, pp* **fought**) [fɔ:t] *n* (*between persons*) bagarre *f*; (*argument*) dispute *f*; (*Mil*) combat *m*; (*against cancer etc*) lutte *f* ▷ *vt* se battre contre; (*cancer, alcoholism, emotion*) combattre, lutter contre; (*election*) se présenter à; (*Law: case*) défendre ▷ *vi* se battre; (*argue*) se disputer; (*fig*):

to ~ (for/against) lutter (pour/contre)
▶ **fight back** *vi* rendre les coups; (*after illness*) reprendre le dessus ▷ *vt* (*tears*) réprimer
▶ **fight off** *vt* repousser; (*disease, sleep, urge*) lutter contre

fighter ['faɪtər] *n* lutteur *m*; (*fig: plane*) chasseur *m*

fighting ['faɪtɪŋ] *n* combats *mpl*; (*brawls*) bagarres *fpl*

figment ['fɪgmənt] *n*: **a ~ of the imagination** une invention

figurative ['fɪgjurətɪv] *adj* figuré(e)

figure ['fɪgər] *n* (*Drawing, Geom*) figure *f*; (*number*) chiffre *m*; (*body, outline*) silhouette *f*; (*person's shape*) ligne *f*, formes *fpl*; (*person*) personnage *m* ▷ *vt* (*US: think*) supposer ▷ *vi* (*appear*) figurer; (*US: make sense*) s'expliquer; **public ~** personnalité *f*; **~ of speech** figure *f* de rhétorique
▶ **figure on** *vt fus* (*US*): **to ~ on doing** compter faire
▶ **figure out** *vt* (*understand*) arriver à comprendre; (*plan*) calculer

figurehead ['fɪgəhɛd] *n* (*Naut*) figure *f* de proue; (*pej*) prête-nom *m*

file [faɪl] *n* (*tool*) lime *f*; (*dossier*) dossier *m*; (*folder*) dossier, chemise *f*; (: *binder*) classeur *m*; (*Comput*) fichier *m*; (*row*) file *f* ▷ *vt* (*nails, wood*) limer; (*papers*) classer; (*Law: claim*) faire enregistrer; déposer ▷ *vi*: **to ~ in/out** entrer/sortir l'un derrière l'autre; **to ~ past** défiler devant; **to ~ a suit against sb** (*Law*) intenter un procès à qn

filing cabinet *n* classeur *m* (*meuble*)

Filipino [fɪlɪ'pi:nəu] *adj* philippin(e) ▷ *n* (*person*) Philippin(e); (*Ling*) tagalog *m*

fill [fɪl] *vt* remplir; (*vacancy*) pourvoir à ▷ *n*: **to eat one's ~** manger à sa faim; **to ~ with** remplir de
▶ **fill in** *vt* (*hole*) boucher; (*form*) remplir; (*details, report*) compléter
▶ **fill out** *vt* (*form, receipt*) remplir
▶ **fill up** *vt* remplir ▷ *vi* (*Aut*) faire le plein; **~ it up, please** (*Aut*) le plein, s'il vous plaît

fillet ['fɪlɪt] *n* filet *m* ▷ *vt* préparer en filets

fillet steak *n* filet *m* de bœuf, tournedos *m*

filling ['fɪlɪŋ] *n* (*Culin*) garniture *f*, farce *f*; (*for tooth*) plombage *m*

filling station *n* station-service *f*, station *f* d'essence

film [fɪlm] *n* film *m*; (*Phot*) pellicule *f*, film; (*of powder, liquid*) couche *f*, pellicule ▷ *vt* (*scene*) filmer ▷ *vi* tourner; **I'd like a 36-exposure ~** je voudrais une pellicule de 36 poses

film star *n* vedette *f* de cinéma

filter ['fɪltər] *n* filtre *m* ▷ *vt* filtrer

filter lane *n* (*Brit Aut: at traffic lights*) voie *f* de dégagement; (: *on motorway*) voie *f* de sortie

filter tip *n* bout *m* filtre

filth [fɪlθ] *n* saleté *f*

filthy ['fɪlθɪ] *adj* sale, dégoûtant(e); (*language*) ordurier(-ière), grossier(-ière)

fin [fɪn] *n* (*of fish*) nageoire *f*; (*of shark*) aileron *m*; (*of diver*) palme *f*

final ['faɪnl] *adj* final(e), dernier(-ière); (*decision, answer*) définitif(-ive) ▷ *n* (*Brit Sport*) finale *f*;

finals *npl* (Scol) examens *mpl* de dernière année; (US Sport) finale *f*; **~ demand** (on invoice etc) dernier rappel

finale [fɪ'nɑːlɪ] *n* finale *m*

finalist ['faɪnəlɪst] *n* (Sport) finaliste *m/f*

finalize ['faɪnəlaɪz] *vt* mettre au point

finally ['faɪnəlɪ] *adv* (eventually) enfin, finalement; (lastly) en dernier lieu; (irrevocably) définitivement

finance [faɪ'næns] *n* finance *f* ▷ *vt* financer; **finances** *npl* finances *fpl*

financial [faɪ'nænʃəl] *adj* financier(-ière); **~ statement** bilan *m*, exercice financier

financial year *n* année *f* budgétaire

find [faɪnd] *vt* (pt, pp **found**) [faʊnd] trouver; (lost object) retrouver ▷ *n* trouvaille *f*, découverte *f*; **to ~ sb guilty** (Law) déclarer qn coupable; **to ~ (some) difficulty in doing sth** avoir du mal à faire qch
▶ **find out** *vt* se renseigner sur; (truth, secret) découvrir; (person) démasquer ▷ *vi*: **to ~ out about** (make enquiries) se renseigner sur; (by chance) apprendre

findings ['faɪndɪŋz] *npl* (Law) conclusions *fpl*, verdict *m*; (of report) constatations *fpl*

fine [faɪn] *adj* (weather) beau (belle); (excellent) excellent(e); (thin, subtle, not coarse) fin(e); (acceptable) bien ▷ *adv* (well) très bien; (small) fin, finement ▷ *n* (Law) amende *f*; contravention *f* ▷ *vt* (Law) condamner à une amende; donner une contravention à; **he's ~** il va bien; **the weather is ~** il fait beau; **you're doing ~** c'est bien, vous vous débrouillez bien; **to cut it ~** calculer un peu juste

fine arts *npl* beaux-arts *mpl*

finery ['faɪnərɪ] *n* parure *f*

finger ['fɪŋgəʳ] *n* doigt *m* ▷ *vt* palper, toucher; **index ~** index *m*

fingernail ['fɪŋgəneɪl] *n* ongle *m* (de la main)

fingerprint ['fɪŋgəprɪnt] *n* empreinte digitale ▷ *vt* (person) prendre les empreintes digitales de

fingertip ['fɪŋgətɪp] *n* bout *m* du doigt; (fig): **to have sth at one's ~s** avoir qch à sa disposition; (knowledge) savoir qch sur le bout du doigt

finish ['fɪnɪʃ] *n* fin *f*; (Sport) arrivée *f*; (polish etc) finition *f* ▷ *vt* finir, terminer ▷ *vi* finir, se terminer; (session) s'achever; **to ~ doing sth** finir de faire qch; **to ~ third** arriver *or* terminer troisième; **when does the show ~?** quand est-ce que le spectacle se termine?
▶ **finish off** *vt* finir, terminer; (kill) achever
▶ **finish up** *vi*, *vt* finir

finishing line ['fɪnɪʃɪŋ-] *n* ligne *f* d'arrivée

finite ['faɪnaɪt] *adj* fini(e); (verb) conjugué(e)

Finland ['fɪnlənd] *n* Finlande *f*

Finn [fɪn] *n* Finnois(e), Finlandais(e)

Finnish ['fɪnɪʃ] *adj* finnois(e), finlandais(e) ▷ *n* (Ling) finnois *m*

fir [fəːʳ] *n* sapin *m*

fire ['faɪəʳ] *n* feu *m*; (accidental) incendie *m*; (heater) radiateur *m* ▷ *vt* (discharge): **to ~ a gun** tirer un coup de feu; (fig: interest) enflammer, animer;

(inf: dismiss) mettre à la porte, renvoyer ▷ *vi* (shoot) tirer, faire feu ▷ *cpd*: **~ hazard, ~ risk: that's a fire hazard** *or* **risk** cela présente un risque d'incendie; **~!** au feu!; **on ~** en feu; **to set ~ to sth, set sth on ~** mettre le feu à qch; **insured against ~** assuré contre l'incendie

fire alarm *n* avertisseur *m* d'incendie

firearm ['faɪərɑːm] *n* arme *f* à feu

fire brigade *n* (régiment *m* de sapeurs-)pompiers *mpl*

fire department *n* (US) = **fire brigade**

fire engine *n* (Brit) pompe *f* à incendie

fire escape *n* escalier *m* de secours

fire exit *n* issue *f* *or* sortie *f* de secours

fire extinguisher *n* extincteur *m*

fireman (irreg) ['faɪəmən] *n* pompier *m*

fireplace ['faɪəpleɪs] *n* cheminée *f*

fireside ['faɪəsaɪd] *n* foyer *m*, coin *m* du feu

fire station *n* caserne *f* de pompiers

fire truck *n* (US) = **fire engine**

firewall ['faɪəwɔːl] *n* (Internet) pare-feu *m*

firewood ['faɪəwud] *n* bois *m* de chauffage

fireworks ['faɪəwəːks] *npl* (display) feu(x) *m(pl)* d'artifice

firing squad *n* peloton *m* d'exécution

firm [fəːm] *adj* ferme ▷ *n* compagnie *f*, firme *f*; **it is my ~ belief that …** je crois fermement que …

firmly ['fəːmlɪ] *adv* fermement

first [fəːst] *adj* premier(-ière) ▷ *adv* (before other people) le premier, la première; (before other things) en premier, d'abord; (when listing reasons etc) en premier lieu, premièrement; (in the beginning) au début ▷ *n* (person: in race) premier(-ière); (Brit Scol) mention *f* très bien; (Aut) première *f*; **the ~ of January** le premier janvier; **at ~** au commencement, au début; **~ of all** tout d'abord, pour commencer; **in the ~ instance** en premier lieu; **I'll do it ~ thing tomorrow** je le ferai tout de suite demain matin

first aid *n* premiers secours *or* soins

first-aid kit [fəːst'eɪd-] *n* trousse *f* à pharmacie

first-class ['fəːst'klɑːs] *adj* (ticket etc) de première classe; (excellent) excellent(e), exceptionnel(le); (post) en tarif prioritaire

first-hand ['fəːst'hænd] *adj* de première main

first lady *n* (US) femme *f* du président

firstly ['fəːstlɪ] *adv* premièrement, en premier lieu

first name *n* prénom *m*

first-rate ['fəːst'reɪt] *adj* excellent(e)

fiscal ['fɪskl] *adj* fiscal(e)

fiscal year *n* exercice financier

fish [fɪʃ] *n* (pl inv) poisson *m*; poissons *mpl* ▷ *vt*, *vi* pêcher; **to ~ a river** pêcher dans une rivière; **~ and chips** poisson frit et frites

fisherman (irreg) ['fɪʃəmən] *n* pêcheur *m*

fish farm *n* établissement *m* piscicole

fish fingers *npl* (Brit) bâtonnets *mpl* de poisson (congelés)

fishing ['fɪʃɪŋ] *n* pêche *f*; **to go ~** aller à la pêche

fishing boat ['fɪʃɪŋ-] *n* barque *f* de pêche

fishing line ['fɪʃɪŋ-] *n* ligne *f* (de pêche)

fishing rod ['fɪʃɪŋ-] n canne f à pêche
fishing tackle ['fɪʃɪŋ-] n attirail m de pêche
fishmonger ['fɪʃmʌŋgə'] n (Brit) marchand m de poisson
fishmonger's ['fɪʃmʌŋgəz], **fishmonger's shop** n (Brit) poissonnerie f
fish slice n (Brit) pelle f à poisson
fish sticks npl (US) = **fish fingers**
fishy ['fɪʃɪ] adj (inf) suspect(e), louche
fist [fɪst] n poing m
fit [fɪt] adj (Med, Sport) en (bonne) forme; (proper) convenable; approprié(e) ▷ vt (subj: clothes) aller à; (adjust) ajuster; (put in, attach) installer, poser; adapter; (equip) équiper, garnir, munir; (suit) convenir à ▷ vi (clothes) aller; (parts) s'adapter; (in space, gap) entrer, s'adapter ▷ n (Med) accès m, crise f; (of anger) accès; (of hysterics, jealousy) crise; **~ to** (ready to) en état de; **~ for** (worthy) digne de; (capable) apte à; **to keep ~** se maintenir en forme; **this dress is a tight/good ~** cette robe est un peu juste/(me) va très bien; **a ~ of coughing** une quinte de toux; **to have a ~** (Med) faire or avoir une crise; (inf) piquer une crise; **by ~s and starts** par à-coups
▶ **fit in** vi (add up) cadrer; (integrate) s'intégrer; (to new situation) s'adapter
▶ **fit out** vt (Brit: also: **fit up**) équiper
fitful ['fɪtful] adj intermittent(e)
fitment ['fɪtmənt] n meuble encastré, élément m
fitness ['fɪtnɪs] n (Med) forme f physique; (of remark) à-propos m, justesse f
fitted ['fɪtɪd] adj (jacket, shirt) ajusté(e)
fitted carpet ['fɪtɪd-] n moquette f
fitted kitchen ['fɪtɪd-] n (Brit) cuisine équipée
fitted sheet ['fɪtɪd-] n drap-housse m
fitter ['fɪtə'] n monteur m; (Dressmaking) essayeur(-euse)
fitting ['fɪtɪŋ] adj approprié(e) ▷ n (of dress) essayage m; (of piece of equipment) pose f, installation f
fitting room n (in shop) cabine f d'essayage
fittings ['fɪtɪŋz] npl installations fpl
five [faɪv] num cinq
fiver ['faɪvə'] n (inf: Brit) billet m de cinq livres; (: US) billet de cinq dollars
fix [fɪks] vt (date, amount etc) fixer; (sort out) arranger; (mend) réparer; (make ready: meal, drink) préparer; (inf: game etc) truquer ▷ n: **to be in a ~** être dans le pétrin
▶ **fix up** vt (meeting) arranger; **to ~ sb up with sth** faire avoir qch à qn
fixation [fɪk'seɪʃən] n (Psych) fixation f; (fig) obsession f
fixed [fɪkst] adj (prices etc) fixe; **there's a ~ charge** il y a un prix forfaitaire; **how are you ~ for money?** (inf) question fric, ça va?
fixture ['fɪkstʃə'] n installation f (fixe); (Sport) rencontre f (au programme)
fizzy ['fɪzɪ] adj pétillant(e), gazeux(-euse)
flabbergasted ['flæbəgɑːstɪd] adj sidéré(e), ahuri(e)
flabby ['flæbɪ] adj mou (molle)

flag [flæg] n drapeau m; (also: **flagstone**) dalle f ▷ vi faiblir; fléchir; **~ of convenience** pavillon m de complaisance
▶ **flag down** vt héler, faire signe (de s'arrêter) à
flagpole ['flægpəul] n mât m
flagship ['flægʃɪp] n vaisseau m amiral; (fig) produit m vedette
flair [flɛə'] n flair m
flak [flæk] n (Mil) tir antiaérien; (inf: criticism) critiques fpl
flake [fleɪk] n (of rust, paint) écaille f; (of snow, soap powder) flocon m ▷ vi (also: **flake off**) s'écailler
flamboyant [flæm'bɔɪənt] adj flamboyant(e), éclatant(e); (person) haut(e) en couleur
flame [fleɪm] n flamme f
flamingo [flə'mɪŋgəu] n flamant m (rose)
flammable ['flæməbl] adj inflammable
flan [flæn] n (Brit) tarte f
flank [flæŋk] n flanc m ▷ vt flanquer
flannel ['flænl] n (Brit: also: **face flannel**) gant m de toilette; (fabric) flanelle f; (Brit inf) baratin m; **flannels** npl pantalon m de flanelle
flap [flæp] n (of pocket, envelope) rabat m ▷ vt (wings) battre (de) ▷ vi (sail, flag) claquer; (inf: also: **be in a flap**) paniquer
flare [flɛə'] n (signal) signal lumineux; (Mil) fusée éclairante; (in skirt etc) évasement m; **flares** npl (trousers) pantalon m à pattes d'éléphant
▶ **flare up** vi s'embraser; (fig: person) se mettre en colère, s'emporter; (: revolt) éclater
flash [flæʃ] n éclair m; (also: **news flash**) flash m (d'information); (Phot) flash ▷ vt (switch on) allumer (brièvement); (direct): **to ~ sth at** braquer qch sur; (flaunt) étaler, exhiber; (send: message) câbler; (smile) lancer ▷ vi briller; jeter des éclairs; (light on ambulance etc) clignoter; **a ~ of lightning** un éclair; **in a ~** en un clin d'œil; **to ~ one's headlights** faire un appel de phares; **he ~ed by** or **past** il passa (devant nous) comme un éclair
flashback ['flæʃbæk] n flashback m, retour m en arrière
flashbulb ['flæʃbʌlb] n ampoule f de flash
flashcube ['flæʃkjuːb] n cube-flash m
flashlight ['flæʃlaɪt] n lampe f de poche
flashy ['flæʃɪ] adj (pej) tape-à-l'œil inv, tapageur(-euse)
flask [flɑːsk] n flacon m, bouteille f; (Chem) ballon m; (also: **vacuum flask**) bouteille f thermos®
flat [flæt] adj plat(e); (tyre) dégonflé(e), à plat; (beer) éventé(e); (battery) à plat; (denial) catégorique; (Mus) bémol inv; (: voice) faux (fausse) ▷ n (Brit: apartment) appartement m; (Aut) crevaison f, pneu crevé; (Mus) bémol m; **~ out** (work) sans relâche; (race) à fond; **~ rate of pay** (Comm) salaire m fixe
flatly ['flætlɪ] adv catégoriquement
flatten ['flætn] vt (also: **flatten out**) aplatir; (crop) coucher; (house, city) raser
flatter ['flætə'] vt flatter
flattering ['flætərɪŋ] adj flatteur(-euse); (clothes etc) seyant(e)

flattery ['flætərɪ] n flatterie f
flaunt [flɔːnt] vt faire étalage de
flavour, (US) **flavor** ['fleɪvəʳ] n goût m, saveur f; (of ice cream etc) parfum m ▷ vt parfumer, aromatiser; **vanilla--ed** à l'arôme de vanille, vanillé(e); **what ~s do you have?** quels parfums avez-vous?; **to give** or **add ~ to** donner du goût à, relever
flavouring, (US) **flavoring** ['fleɪvərɪŋ] n arôme m (synthétique)
flaw [flɔː] n défaut m
flawless ['flɔːlɪs] adj sans défaut
flax [flæks] n lin m
flea [fliː] n puce f
flea market n marché m aux puces
fleck [flɛk] n (of dust) particule f; (of mud, paint, colour) tacheture f, moucheture f ▷ vt tacher, éclabousser; **brown ~ed with white** brun moucheté de blanc
fled [flɛd] pt, pp of **flee**
flee (pt, pp **fled**) [fliː, flɛd] vt fuir, s'enfuir de ▷ vi fuir, s'enfuir
fleece [fliːs] n (of sheep) toison f; (top) (laine f) polaire f ▷ vt (col) (inf) voler, filouter
fleet [fliːt] n flotte f; (of lorries, cars etc) parc m; convoi m
fleeting ['fliːtɪŋ] adj fugace, fugitif(-ive); (visit) très bref (brève)
Flemish ['flɛmɪʃ] adj flamand(e) ▷ n (Ling) flamand m; **the ~** (npl) les Flamands
flesh [flɛʃ] n chair f
flesh wound [-wuːnd] n blessure superficielle
flew [fluː] pt of **fly**
flex [flɛks] n fil m or câble m électrique (souple) ▷ vt (knee) fléchir; (muscles) tendre
flexibility [flɛksɪ'bɪlɪtɪ] n flexibilité f
flexible ['flɛksəbl] adj flexible; (person, schedule) souple
flexitime ['flɛksɪtaɪm], (US) **flextime** ['flɛkstaɪm] n horaire m variable or à la carte
flick [flɪk] n petit coup; (with finger) chiquenaude f ▷ vt donner un petit coup à; (switch) appuyer sur
▶ **flick through** vt fus feuilleter
flicker ['flɪkəʳ] vi (light, flame) vaciller ▷ n vacillement m; **a ~ of light** une brève lueur
flier ['flaɪəʳ] n aviateur m
flies [flaɪz] npl of **fly**
flight [flaɪt] n vol m; (escape) fuite f; (also: **flight of steps**) escalier m; **to take ~** prendre la fuite; **to put to ~** mettre en fuite
flight attendant n steward m, hôtesse f de l'air
flight deck n (Aviat) poste m de pilotage; (Naut) pont m d'envol
flimsy ['flɪmzɪ] adj peu solide; (clothes) trop léger(-ère); (excuse) pauvre, mince
flinch [flɪntʃ] vi tressaillir; **to ~ from** se dérober à, reculer devant
fling [flɪŋ] vt (pt, pp **flung**) [flʌŋ] jeter, lancer ▷ n (love affair) brève liaison, passade f
flint [flɪnt] n silex m; (in lighter) pierre f (à briquet)
flip [flɪp] n chiquenaude f ▷ vt (throw) donner une chiquenaude à; (switch) appuyer sur; (US:

pancake) faire sauter; **to ~ sth over** retourner qch ▷ vi: **to ~ for sth** (US) jouer qch à pile ou face
▶ **flip through** vt fus feuilleter
flip-flops ['flɪpflɔps] npl (esp Brit) tongs fpl
flippant ['flɪpənt] adj désinvolte, irrévérencieux(-euse)
flipper ['flɪpəʳ] n (of animal) nageoire f; (for swimmer) palme f
flirt [fləːt] vi flirter ▷ n flirteur(-euse)
float [fləut] n flotteur m; (in procession) char m; (sum of money) réserve f ▷ vi flotter; (bather) flotter, faire la planche ▷ vt faire flotter; (loan, business, idea) lancer
flock [flɔk] n (of sheep) troupeau m; (of birds) vol m; (of people) foule f
flog [flɔg] vt fouetter
flood [flʌd] n inondation f; (of letters, refugees etc) flot m ▷ vt inonder; (Aut: carburettor) noyer ▷ vi (place) être inondé; (people): **to ~ into** envahir; **to ~ the market** (Comm) inonder le marché; **in ~ en crue
flooding ['flʌdɪŋ] n inondation f
floodlight ['flʌdlaɪt] n projecteur m ▷ vt éclairer aux projecteurs, illuminer
floor [flɔːʳ] n sol m; (storey) étage m; (of sea, valley) fond m; (fig: at meeting): **the ~** l'assemblée f, les membres mpl de l'assemblée ▷ vt (knock down) terrasser; (baffle) désorienter; **on the ~** par terre; **ground ~** (US): **first ~** rez-de-chaussée m; **first ~** (US): **second ~** premier étage; **top ~** dernier étage; **what ~ is it on?** c'est à quel étage?; **to have the ~** (speaker) avoir la parole
floorboard ['flɔːbɔːd] n planche f (du plancher)
flooring ['flɔːrɪŋ] n sol m; (wooden) plancher m; (material to make floor) matériau(x) m(pl) pour planchers; (covering) revêtement m de sol
floor show n spectacle m de variétés
flop [flɔp] n fiasco m ▷ vi (fail) faire fiasco; (fall) s'affaler, s'effondrer
floppy ['flɔpɪ] adj lâche, flottant(e) ▷ n (Comput: also: **floppy disk**) disquette f; **~ hat** chapeau m à bords flottants
flora ['flɔːrə] n flore f
floral ['flɔːrl] adj floral(e); (dress) à fleurs
florid ['flɔrɪd] adj (complexion) fleuri(e); (style) plein(e) de fioritures
florist ['flɔrɪst] n fleuriste m/f
florist's ['flɔrɪsts], **florist's shop** n magasin m or boutique f de fleuriste
flotation [fləu'teɪʃən] n (of shares) émission f; (of company) lancement m (en Bourse)
flounder ['flaundəʳ] n (Zool) flet m ▷ vi patauger
flour ['flauə'] n farine f
flourish ['flʌrɪʃ] vi prospérer ▷ vt brandir ▷ n (gesture) moulinet m; (decoration) fioriture f; (of trumpets) fanfare f
flout [flaut] vt se moquer de, faire fi de
flow [fləu] n (of water, traffic etc) écoulement m; (tide, influx) flux m; (of orders, letters etc) flot m; (of blood, Elec) circulation f; (of river) courant m ▷ vi couler; (traffic) s'écouler; (robes, hair) flotter
flow chart, flow diagram n organigramme m

flower ['flauə^r] n fleur f ▷ vi fleurir; **in ~** en fleur
flower bed n plate-bande f
flowerpot ['flauəpɒt] n pot m (à fleurs)
flowery ['flauərɪ] adj fleuri(e)
flown [fləun] pp of **fly**
fl. oz. abbr = **fluid ounce**
flu [fluː] n grippe f
fluctuate ['flʌktjueɪt] vi varier, fluctuer
fluent ['fluːənt] adj (speech, style) coulant(e),
aisé(e); **he's a ~ speaker/reader** il s'exprime/
lit avec aisance or facilité; **he speaks ~
French, he's ~ in French** il parle le français
couramment
fluff [flʌf] n duvet m; (on jacket, carpet) peluche f
fluffy ['flʌfɪ] adj duveteux(-euse); (jacket, carpet)
pelucheux(-euse); (toy) en peluche
fluid ['fluːɪd] n fluide m; (in diet) liquide m ▷ adj
fluide
fluid ounce n (Brit) = 0.028 l; 0.05 pints
fluke [fluːk] n coup m de veine
flung [flʌŋ] pt, pp of **fling**
fluorescent [fluəˈrɛsnt] adj fluorescent(e)
fluoride ['fluəraɪd] n fluor m
flurry ['flʌrɪ] n (of snow) rafale f, bourrasque f; **a
~ of activity** un affairement soudain; **a ~ of
excitement** une excitation soudaine
flush [flʌʃ] n (on face) rougeur f; (fig: of youth etc)
éclat m; (of blood) afflux m ▷ vt nettoyer à grande
eau; (also: **flush out**) débusquer ▷ vi rougir ▷ adj
(inf) en fonds; (level): **~ with** au ras de, de niveau
avec; **to ~ the toilet** tirer la chasse (d'eau); **hot
~es** (Med) bouffées fpl de chaleur
flushed ['flʌʃt] adj (tout(e)) rouge
flustered ['flʌstəd] adj énervé(e)
flute [fluːt] n flûte f
flutter ['flʌtə^r] n (of panic, excitement) agitation f;
(of wings) battement m ▷ vi (bird) battre des ailes,
voleter; (person) aller et venir dans une grande
agitation
flux [flʌks] n: **in a state of ~** fluctuant sans cesse
fly [flaɪ] (pt **flew**, pp **flown**) [fluː, fləun] n (insect)
mouche f; (on trousers: also: **flies**) braguette f ▷ vt
(plane) piloter; (passengers, cargo) transporter (par
avion); (distance) parcourir ▷ vi voler; (passengers)
aller en avion; (escape) s'enfuir, fuir; (flag) se
déployer; **to ~ open** s'ouvrir brusquement; **to ~
off the handle** s'énerver, s'emporter
▶ **fly away, fly off** vi s'envoler
▶ **fly in** vi (plane) atterrir; **he flew in yesterday** il
est arrivé hier (par avion)
▶ **fly out** vi partir (par avion)
fly-drive ['flaɪdraɪv] n formule f avion plus
voiture
flying ['flaɪɪŋ] n (activity) aviation f; (action) vol
m ▷ adj: **~ visit** visite f éclair inv; **with ~ colours**
haut la main; **he doesn't like ~** il n'aime pas
voyager en avion
flying saucer n soucoupe volante
flying start n: **to get off to a ~** faire un excellent
départ
flyover ['flaɪəuvə^r] n (Brit: overpass) pont routier,
saut-de-mouton m (Canada)

flysheet ['flaɪʃiːt] n (for tent) double toit m
FM abbr (Brit Mil) = **field marshal**; (Radio:
= frequency modulation) FM
foal [fəul] n poulain m
foam [fəum] n écume f; (on beer) mousse f; (also:
foam rubber) caoutchouc m mousse; (also:
plastic foam) mousse cellulaire or de plastique
▷ vi (liquid) écumer; (soapy water) mousser
fob [fɒb] n (also: **watch fob**) chaîne f, ruban m
▷ vt: **to ~ sb off with sth** refiler qch à qn
focal point n foyer m; (fig) centre m de
l'attention, point focal
focus ['fəukəs] n (pl **-es**) foyer m; (of interest) centre
m ▷ vt (field glasses etc) mettre au point; (light rays)
faire converger ▷ vi: **to ~ (on)** (with camera) régler
la mise au point (sur); (with eyes) fixer son regard
(sur); (fig: concentrate) se concentrer; **out of/in ~**
(picture) flou(e)/net(te); (camera) pas au point/au
point
fodder ['fɒdə^r] n fourrage m
foe [fəu] n ennemi m
foetus, (US) **fetus** ['fiːtəs] n fœtus m
fog [fɒg] n brouillard m
foggy ['fɒgɪ] adj: **it's ~** il y a du brouillard
fog lamp, (US) **fog light** n (Aut) phare m antibrouillard
foil [fɔɪl] vt déjouer, contrecarrer ▷ n feuille f
de métal; (kitchen foil) papier m d'alu(minium);
(Fencing) fleuret m; **to act as a ~ to** (fig) servir de
repoussoir or de faire-valoir à
fold [fəuld] n (bend, crease) pli m; (Agr) parc m à
moutons; (fig) bercail m ▷ vt plier; **to ~ one's
arms** croiser les bras
▶ **fold up** vi (map etc) se plier, se replier; (business)
fermer boutique ▷ vt (map etc) plier, replier
folder ['fəuldə^r] n (for papers) chemise f; (: binder)
classeur m; (brochure) dépliant m; (Comput)
dossier m
folding ['fəuldɪŋ] adj (chair, bed) pliant(e)
foliage ['fəulɪɪdʒ] n feuillage m
folk [fəuk] npl gens mpl ▷ cpd folklorique; **folks**
npl (inf: parents) famille f, parents mpl
folklore ['fəuklɔː^r] n folklore m
folk music n musique f folklorique; (contemporary)
musique folk, folk m
folk song ['fəuksɔŋ] n chanson f folklorique;
(contemporary) chanson folk inv
follow ['fɒləu] vt suivre ▷ vi suivre; (result)
s'ensuivre; **to ~ sb's advice** suivre les conseils
de qn; **I don't quite ~ you** je ne vous suis plus;
to ~ in sb's footsteps emboîter le pas à qn; (fig)
suivre les traces de qn; **it ~s that ...** de ce fait, il
s'ensuit que ...; **to ~ suit** (fig) faire de même
▶ **follow out** vt (idea, plan) poursuivre, mener à
terme
▶ **follow through** vt = **follow out**
▶ **follow up** vt (victory) tirer parti de; (letter, offer)
donner suite à; (case) suivre
follower ['fɒləuə^r] n disciple m/f, partisan(e)
following ['fɒləuɪŋ] adj suivant(e) ▷ n partisans
mpl, disciples mpl
follow-up ['fɒləuʌp] n suite f; (on file, case) suivi m

folly ['fɒlɪ] *n* inconscience *f*; sottise *f*; (*building*) folie *f*

fond [fɒnd] *adj* (*memory, look*) tendre, affectueux(-euse); (*hopes, dreams*) un peu fou (folle); **to be ~ of** aimer beaucoup

fondle ['fɒndl] *vt* caresser

font [fɒnt] *n* (*Rel*) fonts baptismaux; (*Typ*) police *f* de caractères

food [fu:d] *n* nourriture *f*

food mixer *n* mixeur *m*

food poisoning *n* intoxication *f* alimentaire

food processor *n* robot *m* de cuisine

food stamp *n* (*US*) bon *m* de nourriture (*pour indigents*)

foodstuffs ['fu:dstʌfs] *npl* denrées *fpl* alimentaires

fool [fu:l] *n* idiot(e); (*History: of king*) bouffon *m*, fou *m*; (*Culin*) mousse *f* de fruits ▷ *vt* berner, duper ▷ *vi* (*also:* **fool around**) faire l'idiot *or* l'imbécile; **to make a ~ of sb** (*ridicule*) ridiculiser qn; (*trick*) avoir *or* duper qn; **to make a ~ of o.s.** se couvrir de ridicule; **you can't ~ me** vous (ne) me la ferez pas, on (ne) me la fait pas
▶ **fool about, fool around** *vi* (*pej: waste time*) traînailler, glandouiller; (: *behave foolishly*) faire l'idiot *or* l'imbécile

foolhardy ['fu:lhɑ:dɪ] *adj* téméraire, imprudent(e)

foolish ['fu:lɪʃ] *adj* idiot(e), stupide; (*rash*) imprudent(e)

foolproof ['fu:lpru:f] *adj* (*plan etc*) infaillible

foot (*pl* **feet**) [fut, fi:t] *n* pied *m*; (*of animal*) patte *f*; (*measure*) pied (= 30.48 cm; 12 inches) ▷ *vt* (*bill*) casquer, payer; **on ~** à pied; **to find one's feet** (*fig*) s'acclimater; **to put one's ~ down** (*Aut*) appuyer sur le champignon; (*say no*) s'imposer

footage ['futɪdʒ] *n* (*Cine: length*) = métrage *m*; (: *material*) séquences *fpl*

foot-and-mouth [futənd'mauθ], **foot-and-mouth disease** *n* fièvre aphteuse

football ['futbɔ:l] *n* (*ball*) ballon *m* (de football); (*sport: Brit*) football *m*; (: *US*) football américain

footballer ['futbɔ:lə*r*] *n* (*Brit*) = **football player**

football match *n* (*Brit*) match *m* de foot(ball)

football player *n* footballeur(-euse), joueur(-euse) de football; (*US*) joueur(-euse) de football américain

football pools *npl* (*US*) = loto *m* sportif, = pronostics *mpl* (sur les matchs de football)

footbrake ['futbreɪk] *n* frein *m* à pédale

footbridge ['futbrɪdʒ] *n* passerelle *f*

foothills ['futhɪlz] *npl* contreforts *mpl*

foothold ['futhəuld] *n* prise *f* (de pied)

footing ['futɪŋ] *n* (*fig*) position *f*; **to lose one's ~** perdre pied; **on an equal ~** sur pied d'égalité

footlights ['futlaɪts] *npl* rampe *f*

footnote ['futnəut] *n* note *f* (en bas de page)

footpath ['futpɑ:θ] *n* sentier *m*; (*in street*) trottoir *m*

footprint ['futprɪnt] *n* trace *f* (de pied)

footstep ['futstep] *n* pas *m*

footwear ['futwɛə*r*] *n* chaussures *fpl*

for [fɔ:*r*] *prep* **1** (*indicating destination, intention,*

purpose) pour; **the train ~ London** le train pour (*or* à destination de) Londres; **he left ~ Rome** il est parti pour Rome; **he went ~ the paper** il est allé chercher le journal; **is this ~ me?** c'est pour moi?; **it's time ~ lunch** c'est l'heure du déjeuner; **what's it ~?** ça sert à quoi?; **what ~?** (*why*) pourquoi?; (*to what end*) pour quoi faire?, à quoi bon?; **~ sale** à vendre; **to pray ~ peace** prier pour la paix

2 (*on behalf of, representing*) pour; **the MP ~ Hove** le député de Hove; **to work ~ sb/sth** travailler pour qn/qch; **I'll ask him ~ you** je vais lui demander pour toi; **G ~ George** G comme Georges

3 (*because of*) pour; **~ this reason** pour cette raison; **~ fear of being criticized** de peur d'être critiqué

4 (*with regard to*) pour; **it's cold ~ July** il fait froid pour juillet; **a gift ~ languages** un don pour les langues

5 (*in exchange for*): **I sold it ~ £5** je l'ai vendu 5 livres; **to pay 50 pence ~ a ticket** payer un billet 50 pence

6 (*in favour of*) pour; **are you ~ or against us?** êtes-vous pour ou contre nous?; **I'm all ~ it** je suis tout à fait pour; **vote ~ X** votez pour X

7 (*referring to distance*) pendant, sur; **there are roadworks ~ 5 km** il y a des travaux sur *or* pendant 5 km; **we walked ~ miles** nous avons marché pendant des kilomètres

8 (*referring to time*) pendant; depuis; pour; **he was away ~ 2 years** il a été absent pendant 2 ans; **she will be away ~ a month** elle sera absente (pendant) un mois; **it hasn't rained ~ 3 weeks** ça fait 3 semaines qu'il ne pleut pas, il ne pleut pas depuis 3 semaines; **I have known her ~ years** je la connais depuis des années; **can you do it ~ tomorrow?** est-ce que tu peux le faire pour demain?

9 (*with infinitive clauses*): **it is not ~ me to decide** ce n'est pas à moi de décider; **it would be best ~ you to leave** le mieux serait que vous partiez; **there is still time ~ you to do it** vous avez encore le temps de le faire; **~ this to be possible ...** pour que cela soit possible ..

10 (*in spite of*): **~ all that** malgré cela, néanmoins; **~ all his work/ef-ts** malgré tout son travail/ tous ses efforts; **~ all his complaints, he's very fond of her** il a beau se plaindre, il l'aime beaucoup
▷ *conj* (*since, as: formal*) car

forage ['fɒrɪdʒ] *n* fourrage *m* ▷ *vi* fourrager, fouiller

foray ['fɒreɪ] *n* incursion *f*

forbid (*pt* **forbad(e)**, *pp* **-den**) [fə'bɪd, -'bæd, -'bɪdn] *vt* défendre, interdire; **to ~ sb to do** défendre *or* interdire à qn de faire

forbidden [fə'bɪdn] *adj* défendu(e)

forbidding [fə'bɪdɪŋ] *adj* d'aspect *or* d'allure sévère *or* sombre

force [fɔ:s] *n* force *f* ▷ *vt* forcer; (*push*) pousser (de force); **Forces** *npl*: **the F~s** (*Brit Mil*) les forces armées; **to ~ o.s. to do** se forcer à faire; **to ~ sb**

to do sth forcer qn à faire qch; **in ~** (*being used: rule, law, prices*) en vigueur; (*in large numbers*) en force; **to come into ~** entrer en vigueur; **a ~ 5 wind** un vent de force 5; **the sales ~** (*Comm*) la force de vente; **to join ~s** unir ses forces
▶ **force back** *vt* (*crowd, enemy*) repousser; (*tears*) refouler
▶ **force down** *vt* (*food*) se forcer à manger

forced [fɔːst] *adj* forcé(e)
force-feed ['fɔːsfiːd] *vt* nourrir de force
forceful ['fɔːsful] *adj* énergique
forcibly ['fɔːsəblɪ] *adv* par la force, de force; (*vigorously*) énergiquement
ford [fɔːd] *n* gué *m* ▷ *vt* passer à gué
fore [fɔːʳ] *n*: **to the ~** en évidence; **to come to the ~** se faire remarquer
forearm ['fɔːrɑːm] *n* avant-bras *m inv*
foreboding [fɔːˈbəudɪŋ] *n* pressentiment *m* (néfaste)
forecast ['fɔːkɑːst] *n* prévision *f*; (*also:* **weather forecast**) prévisions *fpl* météorologiques, météo *f* ▷ *vt* (*irreg: like* **cast**) prévoir
forecourt ['fɔːkɔːt] *n* (*of garage*) devant *m*
forefinger ['fɔːfɪŋgəʳ] *n* index *m*
forefront ['fɔːfrʌnt] *n*: **in the ~ of** au premier rang *or* plan de
foregone ['fɔːgɔn] *adj*: **it's a ~ conclusion** c'est à prévoir, c'est couru d'avance
foreground ['fɔːgraund] *n* premier plan ▷ *cpd* (*Comput*) prioritaire
forehead ['fɔrɪd] *n* front *m*
foreign ['fɔrɪn] *adj* étranger(-ère); (*trade*) extérieur(e); (*travel*) à l'étranger
foreign currency *n* devises étrangères
foreigner ['fɔrɪnəʳ] *n* étranger(-ère)
foreign exchange *n* (*system*) change *m*; (*money*) devises *fpl*
Foreign Office *n* (*Brit*) ministère *m* des Affaires étrangères
Foreign Secretary *n* (*Brit*) ministre *m* des Affaires étrangères
foreleg ['fɔːlɛg] *n* patte *f* de devant, jambe antérieure
foreman (*irreg*) ['fɔːmən] *n* (*in construction*) contremaître *m*; (*Law: of jury*) président *m* (du jury)
foremost ['fɔːməust] *adj* le (la) plus en vue, premier(-ière) ▷ *adv*: **first and ~** avant tout, tout d'abord
forename ['fɔːneɪm] *n* prénom *m*
forensic [fəˈrɛnsɪk] *adj*: **~ medicine** médecine légale; **~ expert** expert *m* de la police, expert légiste
forerunner ['fɔːrʌnəʳ] *n* précurseur *m*
foresee (*pt* **foresaw**, *pp* **-n**) [fɔːˈsiː, -ˈsɔː, -ˈsiːn] *vt* prévoir
foreseeable [fɔːˈsiːəbl] *adj* prévisible
foreseen [fɔːˈsiːn] *pp of* **foresee**
foreshadow [fɔːˈʃædəu] *vt* présager, annoncer, laisser prévoir
foresight ['fɔːsaɪt] *n* prévoyance *f*
forest ['fɔrɪst] *n* forêt *f*

forestry ['fɔrɪstrɪ] *n* sylviculture *f*
foretaste ['fɔːteɪst] *n* avant-goût *m*
foretell (*pt, pp* **foretold**) [fɔːˈtɛl, -ˈtəuld] *vt* prédire
foretold [fɔːˈtəuld] *pt, pp of* **foretell**
forever [fəˈrɛvəʳ] *adv* pour toujours; (*fig: endlessly*) continuellement
foreword ['fɔːwəːd] *n* avant-propos *m inv*
forfeit ['fɔːfɪt] *n* prix *m*, rançon *f* ▷ *vt* perdre; (*one's life, health*) payer de
forgave [fəˈgeɪv] *pt of* **forgive**
forge [fɔːdʒ] *n* forge *f* ▷ *vt* (*signature*) contrefaire; (*wrought iron*) forger; **to ~ documents/a will** fabriquer de faux papiers/un faux testament; **to ~ money** (*Brit*) fabriquer de la fausse monnaie
▶ **forge ahead** *vi* pousser de l'avant, prendre de l'avance
forged [fɔːdʒd] *adj* faux (fausse)
forger ['fɔːdʒəʳ] *n* faussaire *m*
forgery ['fɔːdʒərɪ] *n* faux *m*, contrefaçon *f*
forget (*pt* **forgot**, *pp* **forgotten**) [fəˈgɛt, -ˈgɔt, -ˈgɔtn] *vt, vi* oublier; **to ~ to do sth** oublier de faire qch; **to ~ about sth** (*accidentally*) oublier qch; (*on purpose*) ne plus penser à qch; **I've forgotten my key/passport** j'ai oublié ma clé/mon passeport
forgetful [fəˈgɛtful] *adj* distrait(e), étourdi(e); **~ of** oublieux(-euse) de
forget-me-not [fəˈgɛtmɪnɔt] *n* myosotis *m*
forgive (*pt* **forgave**, *pp* **-n**) [fəˈgɪv, -ˈgeɪv, -ˈgɪvn] *vt* pardonner; **to ~ sb for sth/for doing sth** pardonner qch à qn/à qn de faire qch
forgiveness [fəˈgɪvnɪs] *n* pardon *m*
forgo (*pt* **forwent**, *pp* **-ne**) [fɔːˈgəu, -ˈwɛnt, -ˈgɔn] *vt* = **forego**
forgot [fəˈgɔt] *pt of* **forget**
forgotten [fəˈgɔtn] *pp of* **forget**
fork [fɔːk] *n* (*for eating*) fourchette *f*; (*for gardening*) fourche *f*; (*of roads*) bifurcation *f*; (*of railways*) embranchement *m* ▷ *vi* (*road*) bifurquer
▶ **fork out** (*inf: pay*) *vt* allonger, se fendre de ▷ *vi* casquer
fork-lift truck ['fɔːklɪft-] *n* chariot élévateur
forlorn [fəˈlɔːn] *adj* (*person*) délaissé(e); (*deserted*) abandonné(e); (*hope, attempt*) désespéré(e)
form [fɔːm] *n* forme *f*; (*Scol*) classe *f*; (*questionnaire*) formulaire *m* ▷ *vt* former; (*habit*) contracter; **in the ~ of** sous forme de; **to ~ part of sth** faire partie de qch; **to be on good ~** (*Sport: fig*) être en forme; **on top ~** en pleine forme
formal ['fɔːməl] *adj* (*offer, receipt*) en bonne et due forme; (*person*) cérémonieux(-euse), à cheval sur les convenances; (*occasion, dinner*) officiel(le); (*garden*) à la française; (*Art, Philosophy*) formel(le); (*clothes*) de soirée
formality [fɔːˈmælɪtɪ] *n* formalité *f*, cérémonie(s) *f(pl)*
formally ['fɔːməlɪ] *adv* officiellement; formellement; cérémonieusement
format ['fɔːmæt] *n* format *m* ▷ *vt* (*Comput*) formater
formation [fɔːˈmeɪʃən] *n* formation *f*
formative ['fɔːmətɪv] *adj*: **~ years** années *fpl*

d'apprentissage (fig) or de formation (d'un enfant,
d'un adolescent)

former ['fɔːməʳ] adj ancien(ne); (before n)
précédent(e); **the ~ ... the latter** le premier ... le
second, celui-là ... celui-ci; **the ~ president** l'ex-
président; **the ~ Yugoslavia/Soviet Union** l'ex
Yougoslavie/Union Soviétique

formerly ['fɔːməlɪ] adv autrefois

formidable ['fɔːmɪdəbl] adj redoutable

formula ['fɔːmjulə] n formule f; **F~ One** (Aut)
Formule un

forsake (pt **forsook**, pp **-n**) [fə'seɪk, -'suk, -'seɪkən]
vt abandonner

fort [fɔːt] n fort m; **to hold the ~** (fig) assurer la
permanence

forte ['fɔːtɪ] n (point) fort m

forth [fɔːθ] adv en avant; **to go back and ~** aller
et venir; **and so ~** et ainsi de suite

forthcoming [fɔːθ'kʌmɪŋ] adj qui va paraître or
avoir lieu prochainement; (character) ouvert(e),
communicatif(-ive); (available) disponible

forthright ['fɔːθraɪt] adj franc (franche),
direct(e)

forthwith ['fɔːθ'wɪθ] adv sur le champ

fortieth ['fɔːtɪɪθ] num quarantième

fortify ['fɔːtɪfaɪ] vt (city) fortifier; (person)
remonter

fortitude ['fɔːtɪtjuːd] n courage m, force f d'âme

fortnight ['fɔːtnaɪt] n (Brit) quinzaine f, quinze
jours mpl; **it's a ~ since ...** il y a quinze jours
que ...

fortnightly ['fɔːtnaɪtlɪ] adj bimensuel(le) ▷ adv
tous les quinze jours

fortress ['fɔːtrɪs] n forteresse f

fortunate ['fɔːtʃənɪt] adj heureux(-euse); (person)
chanceux(-euse); **to be ~** avoir de la chance; **it is
~ that** c'est une chance que, il est heureux que

fortunately ['fɔːtʃənɪtlɪ] adv heureusement, par
bonheur

fortune ['fɔːtʃən] n chance f; (wealth) fortune f;
to make a ~ faire fortune

fortune-teller ['fɔːtʃəntɛləʳ] n diseuse f de bonne
aventure

forty ['fɔːtɪ] num quarante

forum ['fɔːrəm] n forum m, tribune f

forward ['fɔːwəd] adj (movement, position) en
avant, vers l'avant; (not shy) effronté(e); (in
time) en avance; (Comm: delivery, sales, exchange) à
terme ▷ adv (also: **forwards**) en avant ▷ n (Sport)
avant m ▷ vt (letter) faire suivre; (parcel, goods)
expédier; (fig) promouvoir, favoriser; **to look ~
to sth** attendre qch avec impatience; **to move
~** avancer; **"please ~"** "prière de faire suivre"; **~
planning** planification f à long terme

forwarding address n adresse f de réexpédition

forward slash n barre f oblique

fossil ['fɔsl] adj, n fossile m; **~ fuel** combustible m
fossile

foster ['fɔstəʳ] vt (encourage) encourager,
favoriser; (child) élever (sans adopter)

foster child n enfant élevé dans une famille d'accueil

foster parent n parent qui élève un enfant sans

l'adopter

fought [fɔːt] pt, pp of **fight**

foul [faul] adj (weather, smell, food) infect(e);
(language) ordurier(-ière); (deed) infâme ▷ n
(Football) faute f ▷ vt (dirty) salir, encrasser;
(football player) commettre une faute sur;
(entangle: anchor, propeller) emmêler; **he's got a ~
temper** il a un caractère de chien

foul play n (Sport) jeu déloyal; (Law) acte
criminel; **~ is not suspected** la mort (or
l'incendie etc) n'a pas de causes suspectes, on
écarte l'hypothèse d'un meurtre (or d'un acte
criminel)

found [faund] pt, pp of **find** ▷ vt (establish) fonder

foundation [faun'deɪʃən] n (act) fondation f;
(base) fondement m; (also: **foundation cream**)
fond m de teint; **foundations** npl (of building)
fondations fpl; **to lay the ~s** (fig) poser les
fondements

founder ['faundəʳ] n fondateur m ▷ vi couler,
sombrer

foundry ['faundrɪ] n fonderie f

fountain ['fauntɪn] n fontaine f

fountain pen n stylo m (à encre)

four [fɔːʳ] num quatre; **on all ~s** à quatre pattes

four-letter word ['fɔːlɛtə-] n obscénité f, gros
mot

four-poster ['fɔː'pəustəʳ] n (also: **four-poster bed**)
lit m à baldaquin

fourteen ['fɔː'tiːn] num quatorze

fourteenth ['fɔː'tiːnθ] num quatorzième

fourth ['fɔːθ] num quatrième ▷ n (Aut: also: **fourth
gear**) quatrième f

four-wheel drive ['fɔːwiːl-] n (Aut: car) voiture f
à quatre roues motrices; **with ~** à quatre roues
motrices

fowl [faul] n volaille f

fox [fɔks] n renard m ▷ vt mystifier

foyer ['fɔɪeɪ] n (in hotel) vestibule m; (Theat)
foyer m

fraction ['frækʃən] n fraction f

fracture ['fræktʃəʳ] n fracture f ▷ vt fracturer

fragile ['frædʒaɪl] adj fragile

fragment ['frægmənt] n fragment m

fragrance ['freɪgrəns] n parfum m

fragrant ['freɪgrənt] adj parfumé(e), odorant(e)

frail [freɪl] adj fragile, délicat(e); (person) frêle

frame [freɪm] n (of building) charpente f; (of human,
animal) charpente, ossature f; (of picture) cadre m;
(of door, window) encadrement m, chambranle m;
(of spectacles: also: **frames**) monture f ▷ vt (picture)
encadrer; (theory, plan) construire, élaborer; **to
~ sb** (inf) monter un coup contre qn; **~ of mind**
disposition f d'esprit

framework ['freɪmwəːk] n structure f

France [frɑːns] n la France; **in ~** en France

franchise ['fræntʃaɪz] n (Pol) droit m de vote;
(Comm) franchise f

frank [fræŋk] adj franc (franche) ▷ vt (letter)
affranchir

frankly ['fræŋklɪ] adv franchement

frantic ['fræntɪk] adj (hectic) frénétique; (need,

desire) effréné(e); *(distraught)* hors de soi

fraternity [frə'tə:nɪtɪ] *n (club)* communauté *f*, confrérie *f*; *(spirit)* fraternité *f*

fraud [frɔːd] *n* supercherie *f*, fraude *f*, tromperie *f*; *(person)* imposteur *m*

fraught [frɔːt] *adj (tense: person)* très tendu(e); *(: situation)* pénible; **~ with** *(difficulties etc)* chargé(e) de, plein(e) de

fray [freɪ] *n* bagarre *f*; *(Mil)* combat *m* ▷ *vt* effilocher ▷ *vi* s'effilocher; **tempers were ~ed** les gens commençaient à s'énerver; **her nerves were ~ed** elle était à bout de nerfs

freak [friːk] *(eccentric person)* phénomène *m*; *(unusual event)* hasard *m* extraordinaire; *(pej: fanatic)*: **health food ~** fana *m/f* or obsédé(e) de l'alimentation saine ▷ *adj (storm)* exceptionnel(le); *(accident)* bizarre
 ▶ **freak out** *vi (inf: drop out)* se marginaliser; *(: on drugs)* se défoncer

freckle ['frɛkl] *n* tache *f* de rousseur

free [friː] *adj* libre; *(gratis)* gratuit(e); *(liberal)* généreux(-euse), large ▷ *vt (prisoner etc)* libérer; *(jammed object or person)* dégager; **is this seat ~?** la place est libre?; **to give sb a ~ hand** donner carte blanche à qn; **~ and easy** sans façon, décontracté(e); **admission ~** entrée libre; **~ (of charge)** gratuitement

freedom ['friːdəm] *n* liberté *f*

Freefone® ['friːfəun] *n* numéro vert

free-for-all ['friːfərɔːl] *n* mêlée générale

free gift *n* prime *f*

freehold ['friːhəuld] *n* propriété foncière libre

free kick *n (Sport)* coup franc

freelance ['friːlɑːns] *adj (journalist etc)* indépendant(e), free-lance *inv*; *(work)* en free-lance ▷ *adv* en free-lance

freely ['friːlɪ] *adv* librement; *(liberally)* libéralement

freemason ['friːmeɪsn] *n* franc-maçon *m*

Freepost® ['friːpəust] *n (Brit)* port payé

free-range ['friː'reɪndʒ] *adj (egg)* de ferme; *(chicken)* fermier

free trade *n* libre-échange *m*

freeway ['friːweɪ] *n (US)* autoroute *f*

free will *n* libre arbitre *m*; **of one's own ~** de son plein gré

freeze [friːz] *(pt* **froze***, pp* **frozen***)* [frəuz, 'frəuzn] *vi* geler ▷ *vt* geler; *(food)* congeler; *(prices, salaries)* bloquer, geler ▷ *n* gel *m*; *(of prices, salaries)* blocage *m*
 ▶ **freeze over** *vi (river)* geler; *(windscreen)* se couvrir de givre or de glace
 ▶ **freeze up** *vi* geler

freeze-dried ['friːzdraɪd] *adj* lyophilisé(e)

freezer ['friːzəʳ] *n* congélateur *m*

freezing ['friːzɪŋ] *adj*: **~ (cold)** *(room etc)* glacial(e); *(person, hands)* gelé(e), glacé(e) ▷ *n*: **3 degrees below ~** 3 degrés au-dessous de zéro; **it's ~** il fait un froid glacial

freezing point *n* point *m* de congélation

freight [freɪt] *n (goods)* fret *m*, cargaison *f*; *(money charged)* fret, prix *m* du transport; **~ forward** port

dû; **~ inward** port payé par le destinataire

freight train *n (US)* train *m* de marchandises

French [frɛntʃ] *adj* français(e) ▷ *n (Ling)* français *m*; **the ~** *(npl)* les Français; **what's the ~ (word) for ...?** comment dit-on ... en français?

French bean *n (Brit)* haricot vert

French bread *n* pain *m* français

French dressing *n (Culin)* vinaigrette *f*

French fried potatoes, *(US)* **French fries** *npl* (pommes de terre *fpl)* frites *fpl*

French horn *n (Mus)* cor *m* (d'harmonie)

French kiss *n* baiser profond

French loaf *n* ≈ pain *m*, ≈ parisien *m*

Frenchman *(irreg)* ['frɛntʃmən] *n* Français *m*

French stick *n* ≈ baguette *f*

French window *n* porte-fenêtre *f*

Frenchwoman *(irreg)* ['frɛntʃwumən] *n* Française *f*

frenzy ['frɛnzɪ] *n* frénésie *f*

frequency ['friːkwənsɪ] *n* fréquence *f*

frequent *adj* ['friːkwənt] fréquent(e) ▷ *vt* [frɪ'kwɛnt] fréquenter

frequently ['friːkwəntlɪ] *adv* fréquemment

fresh [frɛʃ] *adj* frais (fraîche); *(new)* nouveau (nouvelle); *(cheeky)* familier(-ière), culotté(e); **to make a ~ start** prendre un nouveau départ

freshen ['frɛʃən] *vi (wind, air)* fraîchir
 ▶ **freshen up** *vi* faire un brin de toilette

fresher ['frɛʃəʳ] *n (Brit University: inf)* bizuth *m*, étudiant(e) de première année

freshly ['frɛʃlɪ] *adv* nouvellement, récemment

freshman *(US: irreg)* ['frɛʃmən] *n* = **fresher**

freshness ['frɛʃnɪs] *n* fraîcheur *f*

freshwater ['frɛʃwɔːtəʳ] *adj (fish)* d'eau douce

fret [frɛt] *vi* s'agiter, se tracasser

friar ['fraɪəʳ] *n* moine *m*, frère *m*

friction ['frɪkʃən] *n* friction *f*, frottement *m*

Friday ['fraɪdɪ] *n* vendredi *m*; *for phrases see also* **Tuesday**

fridge [frɪdʒ] *n (Brit)* frigo *m*, frigidaire® *m*

fried [fraɪd] *pt, pp of* **fry** ▷ *adj* frit(e); **~ egg** œuf *m* sur le plat

friend [frɛnd] *n* ami(e); **to make ~s with** se lier (d'amitié) avec

friendly ['frɛndlɪ] *adj* amical(e); *(kind)* sympathique, gentil(le); *(place)* accueillant(e); *(Pol: country)* ami(e) ▷ *n (also:* **friendly match)** match amical; **to be ~ with** être ami(e) avec; **to be ~ to** être bien disposé(e) à l'égard de

friendship ['frɛndʃɪp] *n* amitié *f*

fries [fraɪz] *(esp US) npl* = **French fried potatoes**

frieze [friːz] *n* frise *f*, bordure *f*

frigate ['frɪgɪt] *n (Naut: modern)* frégate *f*

fright [fraɪt] *n* peur *f*, effroi *m*; **to give sb a ~** faire peur à qn; **to take ~** prendre peur, s'effrayer; **she looks a ~** elle a l'air d'un épouvantail

frighten ['fraɪtn] *vt* effrayer, faire peur à
 ▶ **frighten away, frighten off** *vt (birds, children etc)* faire fuir, effaroucher

frightened ['fraɪtnd] *adj*: **to be ~ (of)** avoir peur (de)

frightening ['fraɪtnɪŋ] *adj* effrayant(e)

frightful ['fraɪtful] adj affreux(-euse)
frigid ['frɪdʒɪd] adj frigide
frill [frɪl] n (of dress) volant m; (of shirt) jabot m; **without ~s** (fig) sans manières
fringe [frɪndʒ] n (Brit: of hair) frange f; (edge: of forest etc) bordure f; (fig): **on the ~** en marge
fringe benefits npl avantages sociaux or en nature
Frisbee® ['frɪzbɪ] n Frisbee® m
frisk [frɪsk] vt fouiller
fritter ['frɪtər] n beignet m
▶ **fritter away** vt gaspiller
frivolous ['frɪvələs] adj frivole
frizzy ['frɪzɪ] adj crépu(e)
fro [frəu] adv see **to**
frock [frɔk] n robe f
frog [frɔg] n grenouille f; **to have a ~ in one's throat** avoir un chat dans la gorge
frogman (irreg) ['frɔgmən] n homme-grenouille m
frolic ['frɔlɪk] n ébats mpl ▷ vi folâtrer, batifoler
from [frɔm] prep **1** (indicating starting place, origin etc) de; **where do you come ~?, where are you ~?** d'où venez-vous?; **where has he come ~?** d'où arrive-t-il?; **~ London to Paris** de Londres à Paris; **to escape ~ sb/sth** échapper à qn/qch; **a letter/telephone call ~ my sister** une lettre/un appel de ma sœur; **to drink ~ the bottle** boire à (même) la bouteille; **tell him ~ me that ...** dites-lui de ma part que ...
2 (indicating time) (à partir) de; **~ one o'clock to** or **until** or **till two** d'une heure à deux heures; **~ January (on)** à partir de janvier
3 (indicating distance) de; **the hotel is one kilometre ~ the beach** l'hôtel est à un kilomètre de la plage
4 (indicating price, number etc) de; **prices range ~ £10 to £50** les prix varient entre 10 livres et 50 livres; **the interest rate was increased ~ 9% to 10%** le taux d'intérêt est passé de 9% à 10%
5 (indicating difference) de; **he can't tell red ~ green** il ne peut pas distinguer le rouge du vert; **to be different ~ sb/sth** être différent de qn/qch
6 (because of, on the basis of): **~ what he says** d'après ce qu'il dit; **weak ~ hunger** affaibli par la faim
front [frʌnt] n (of house, dress) devant m; (of coach, train) avant m; (of book) couverture f; (promenade: also: **sea front**) bord m de mer; (Mil, Pol, Meteorology) front m; (fig: appearances) contenance f, façade f ▷ adj de devant; (page, row) premier(-ière), (seat, wheel) avant inv ▷ vi: **to ~ onto sth** donner sur qch; **in ~ (of)** devant
frontage ['frʌntɪdʒ] n façade f; (of shop) devanture f
front door n porte f d'entrée; (of car) portière f avant
frontier ['frʌntɪər] n frontière f
front page n première page
front room n (Brit) pièce f de devant, salon m
front-wheel drive ['frʌntwiːl-] n traction f avant
frost [frɔst] n gel m, gelée f; (also: **hoarfrost**)

givre m
frostbite ['frɔstbaɪt] n gelures fpl
frosted ['frɔstɪd] adj (glass) dépoli(e); (esp US: cake) glacé(e)
frosting ['frɔstɪŋ] n (esp US: on cake) glaçage m
frosty ['frɔstɪ] adj (window) couvert(e) de givre; (weather, welcome) glacial(e)
froth [frɔθ] n mousse f; écume f
frown [fraun] n froncement m de sourcils ▷ vi froncer les sourcils
▶ **frown on** vt (fig) désapprouver
froze [frəuz] pt of **freeze**
frozen ['frəuzn] pp of **freeze** ▷ adj (food) congelé(e); (very cold: person; Comm: assets) gelé(e)
fruit [fruːt] n (pl inv) fruit m
fruiterer ['fruːtərər] n fruitier m, marchand(e) de fruits; **~'s (shop)** fruiterie f
fruitful ['fruːtful] adj fructueux(-euse); (plant, soil) fécond(e)
fruition [fruː'ɪʃən] n: **to come to ~** se réaliser
fruit juice n jus m de fruit
fruit machine n (Brit) machine f à sous
fruit salad n salade f de fruits
frustrate [frʌs'treɪt] vt frustrer; (plot, plans) faire échouer
frustrated [frʌs'treɪtɪd] adj frustré(e)
fry (pt, pp **fried**) [fraɪ, -d] vt (faire) frire ▷ n: **small ~** le menu fretin
frying pan ['fraɪɪŋ-] n poêle f (à frire)
ft. abbr = **foot**; **feet**
fudge [fʌdʒ] n (Culin) sorte de confiserie à base de sucre, de beurre et de lait ▷ vt (issue, problem) esquiver
fuel [fjuəl] n (for heating) combustible m; (for engine) carburant m
fuel oil n mazout m
fuel tank n cuve f à mazout, citerne f; (in vehicle) réservoir m de or à carburant
fugitive ['fjuːdʒɪtɪv] n fugitif(-ive)
fulfil, (US) **fulfill** [ful'fɪl] vt (function, condition) remplir; (order) exécuter; (wish, desire) satisfaire, réaliser
fulfilment, (US) **fulfillment** [ful'fɪlmənt] n (of wishes) réalisation f
full [ful] adj plein(e); (details, hotel, bus) complet(-ète); (price) fort(e), normal(e); (busy: day) chargé(e); (skirt) ample, large ▷ adv: **to know ~ well** savoir fort bien que; **~ (up)** (hotel etc) complet(-ète); **I'm ~ (up)** j'ai bien mangé; **~ employment/fare** plein emploi/tarif; **a ~ two hours** deux bonnes heures; **at ~ speed** à toute vitesse; **in ~** (reproduce, quote, pay) intégralement; (write name etc) en toutes lettres
full-length ['ful'leŋθ] adj (portrait) en pied; (coat) long(ue); **~ film** long métrage
full moon n pleine lune
full-scale ['fulskeɪl] adj (model) grandeur nature inv; (search, retreat) complet(-ète), total(e)
full stop n point m
full-time ['ful'taɪm] adj, adv (work) à plein temps ▷ n (Sport) fin f du match
fully ['fulɪ] adv entièrement, complètement; (at least): **~ as big** au moins aussi grand

fully-fledged ['fʊlɪ'flɛdʒd] *adj* (*teacher, barrister*) diplômé(e); (*citizen, member*) à part entière

fumble ['fʌmbl] *vi* fouiller, tâtonner ▷ *vt* (*ball*) mal réceptionner, cafouiller
▶ **fumble with** *vt fus* tripoter

fume [fjuːm] *vi* (*rage*) rager

fumes [fjuːmz] *npl* vapeurs *fpl*, émanations *fpl*

fun [fʌn] *n* amusement *m*, divertissement *m*; **to have ~** s'amuser; **for ~** pour rire; **it's not much ~** ce n'est pas très drôle *or* amusant; **to make ~ of** se moquer de

function ['fʌŋkʃən] *n* fonction *f*; (*reception, dinner*) cérémonie *f*, soirée officielle ▷ *vi* fonctionner; **to ~ as** faire office de

functional ['fʌŋkʃənl] *adj* fonctionnel(le)

fund [fʌnd] *n* caisse *f*, fonds *m*; (*source, store*) source *f*, mine *f*; **funds** *npl* (*money*) fonds *mpl*

fundamental [fʌndə'mɛntl] *adj* fondamental(e); **fundamentals** *npl* principes *mpl* de base

funeral ['fjuːnərəl] *n* enterrement *m*, obsèques *fpl* (*more formal occasion*)

funeral director *n* entrepreneur *m* des pompes funèbres

funeral parlour [-'pɑːlə^r] *n* (*Brit*) dépôt *m* mortuaire

funeral service *n* service *m* funèbre

funfair ['fʌnfɛə^r] *n* (*Brit*) fête (foraine)

fungus (*pl* **fungi**) ['fʌŋgəs, -gaɪ] *n* champignon *m*; (*mould*) moisissure *f*

funnel ['fʌnl] *n* entonnoir *m*; (*of ship*) cheminée *f*

funny ['fʌnɪ] *adj* amusant(e), drôle; (*strange*) curieux(-euse), bizarre

fur [fəː^r] *n* fourrure *f*; (*Brit: in kettle etc*) (dépôt *m* de) tartre *m*

fur coat *n* manteau *m* de fourrure

furious ['fjuərɪəs] *adj* furieux(-euse); (*effort*) acharné(e); **to be ~ with sb** être dans une fureur noire contre qn

furlong ['fəːlɔŋ] *n* = 201.17 m (*terme d'hippisme*)

furnace ['fəːnɪs] *n* fourneau *m*

furnish ['fəːnɪʃ] *vt* meubler; (*supply*) fournir; **~ed flat** *or* (*US*) **apartment** meublé *m*

furnishings ['fəːnɪʃɪŋz] *npl* mobilier *m*, articles *mpl* d'ameublement

furniture ['fəːnɪtʃə^r] *n* meubles *mpl*, mobilier *m*; **piece of ~** meuble *m*

furrow ['fʌrəu] *n* sillon *m*

furry ['fəːrɪ] *adj* (*animal*) à fourrure; (*toy*) en peluche

further ['fəːðə^r] *adj* supplémentaire, autre; nouveau (nouvelle) ▷ *adv* plus loin; (*more*) davantage; (*moreover*) de plus ▷ *vt* faire avancer *or* progresser, promouvoir; **how much ~ is it?** quelle distance *or* combien reste-t-il à parcourir?; **until ~ notice** jusqu'à nouvel ordre *or* avis; **~ to your letter of ...** (*Comm*) suite à votre lettre du ...

further education *n* enseignement *m* postscolaire (*recyclage, formation professionnelle*)

furthermore [fəːðə'mɔː^r] *adv* de plus, en outre

furthest ['fəːðɪst] *superlative of* **far**

fury ['fjuərɪ] *n* fureur *f*

fuse, (*US*) **fuze** [fjuːz] *n* fusible *m*; (*for bomb etc*) amorce *f*, détonateur *m* ▷ *vt, vi* (*metal*) fondre; (*fig*) fusionner; (*Brit: Elec*): **to ~ the lights** faire sauter les fusibles *or* les plombs; **a ~ has blown** un fusible a sauté

fuse box *n* boîte *f* à fusibles

fusion ['fjuːʒən] *n* fusion *f*

fuss [fʌs] *n* (*anxiety, excitement*) chichis *mpl*, façons *fpl*; (*commotion*) tapage *m*; (*complaining, trouble*) histoire(s) *f(pl)* ▷ *vi* faire des histoires ▷ *vt* (*person*) embêter; **to make a ~** faire des façons (*or* des histoires); **to make a ~ of sb** dorloter qn
▶ **fuss over** *vt fus* (*person*) dorloter

fussy ['fʌsɪ] *adj* (*person*) tatillon(ne), difficile, chichiteux(-euse); (*dress, style*) tarabiscoté(e); **I'm not ~** (*inf*) ça m'est égal

future ['fjuːtʃə^r] *adj* futur(e) ▷ *n* avenir *m*; (*Ling*) futur *m*; **futures** *npl* (*Comm*) opérations *fpl* à terme; **in (the) ~** à l'avenir; **in the near/immediate ~** dans un avenir proche/immédiat

fuze [fjuːz] *n, vt, vi* (*US*) = **fuse**

fuzzy ['fʌzɪ] *adj* (*Phot*) flou(e); (*hair*) crépu(e)

FYI *abbr* = **for your information**

Gg

G¹, g [dʒiː] n (letter) G, g m; (Mus): **G** sol m; **G for George** G comme Gaston

G² n abbr (Brit Scol: = good) b (= bien); (US Cine: = general (audience)) ≈ tous publics; (Pol: = G8) G8 m

g. abbr (= gram) g; (= gravity) g

gabble ['gæbl] vi bredouiller; jacasser

gable ['geɪbl] n pignon m

gadget ['gædʒɪt] n gadget m

Gaelic ['geɪlɪk] adj, n (Ling) gaélique (m)

gag [gæg] n (on mouth) bâillon m; (joke) gag m ▷ vt (prisoner etc) bâillonner ▷ vi (choke) étouffer

gaiety ['geɪtɪ] n gaieté f

gain [geɪn] n (improvement) gain m; (profit) gain, profit m ▷ vt gagner ▷ vi (watch) avancer; **to ~ from/by** gagner de/à; **to ~ on sb** (catch up) rattraper qn; **to ~ 3lbs (in weight)** prendre 3 livres; **to ~ ground** gagner du terrain

gal. abbr = **gallon**

gala ['gɑːlə] n gala m; **swimming ~** grand concours de natation

galaxy ['gæləksɪ] n galaxie f

gale [geɪl] n coup m de vent; **~ force 10** vent m de force 10

gallant ['gælənt] adj vaillant(e), brave; (towards ladies) empressé(e), galant(e)

gall bladder ['gɔːl-] n vésicule f biliaire

gallery ['gælərɪ] n galerie f; (also: **art gallery**) musée m; (: private) galerie; (for spectators) tribune f; (: in theatre) dernier balcon

gallon ['gæln] n gallon m (Brit = 4.543 l; US = 3.785 l), = 8 pints

gallop ['gæləp] n galop m ▷ vi galoper; **~ing inflation** inflation galopante

gallows ['gæləuz] n potence f

gallstone ['gɔːlstəun] n calcul m (biliaire)

galore [gə'lɔːʳ] adv en abondance, à gogo

Gambia ['gæmbɪə] n Gambie f

gambit ['gæmbɪt] n (fig): (opening) **~** manœuvre f stratégique

gamble ['gæmbl] n pari m, risque calculé ▷ vt, vi jouer; **to ~ on the Stock Exchange** jouer en or à la Bourse; **to ~ on** (fig) miser sur

gambler ['gæmbləʳ] n joueur m

gambling ['gæmblɪŋ] n jeu m

game [geɪm] n jeu m; (event) match m; (of tennis, chess, cards) partie f; (Hunting) gibier m ▷ adj brave; (willing): **to be ~ (for)** être prêt(e) (à or pour); **a**

~ of football/tennis une partie de football/ tennis; **big ~** gros gibier; **games** npl (Scol) sport m; (sport event) jeux

gamekeeper ['geɪmkiːpəʳ] n garde-chasse m

games console ['geɪmz-] n console f de jeux vidéo

game show ['geɪmʃəu] n jeu télévisé

gammon ['gæmən] n (bacon) quartier m de lard fumé; (ham) jambon fumé or salé

gamut ['gæmət] n gamme f

gang [gæŋ] n bande f, groupe m; (of workmen) équipe f
▷ **gang up** vi: **to ~ up on sb** se liguer contre qn

gangster ['gæŋstəʳ] n gangster m, bandit m

gangway ['gæŋweɪ] n passerelle f; (Brit: of bus) couloir central

gaol [dʒeɪl] n, vt (Brit) = **jail**

gap [gæp] n trou m; (in time) intervalle m; (fig) lacune f; vide m; (difference): **~ (between)** écart m (entre)

gape [geɪp] vi (person) être or rester bouche bée; (hole, shirt) être ouvert(e)

gaping ['geɪpɪŋ] adj (hole) béant(e)

gap year n année que certains étudiants prennent pour voyager ou pour travailler avant d'entrer à l'université

garage ['gærɑːʒ] n garage m

garage sale n vide-grenier m

garbage ['gɑːbɪdʒ] n (US: rubbish) ordures fpl, détritus mpl; (inf: nonsense) âneries fpl

garbage can n (US) poubelle f, boîte f à ordures

garbage collector n (US) éboueur m

garbled ['gɑːbld] adj déformé(e), faussé(e)

garden ['gɑːdn] n jardin m ▷ vi jardiner; **gardens** npl (public) jardin public; (private) parc m

garden centre (Brit) n pépinière f, jardinerie f

gardener ['gɑːdnəʳ] n jardinier m

gardening ['gɑːdnɪŋ] n jardinage m

gargle ['gɑːgl] vi se gargariser ▷ n gargarisme m

garish ['gɛərɪʃ] adj criard(e), voyant(e)

garland ['gɑːlənd] n guirlande f; couronne f

garlic ['gɑːlɪk] n ail m

garment ['gɑːmənt] n vêtement m

garnish ['gɑːnɪʃ] (Culin) vt garnir ▷ n décoration f

garrison ['gærɪsn] n garnison f ▷ vt mettre en garnison, stationner

garter ['gɑːtəʳ] n jarretière f; (US: suspender) jarretelle f

gas [gæs] n gaz m; (used as anaesthetic): **to be given** ~ se faire endormir; (US: gasoline) essence f ▷ vt asphyxier; (Mil) gazer; **I can smell** ~ ça sent le gaz
gas cooker n (Brit) cuisinière f à gaz
gas cylinder n bouteille f de gaz
gas fire n (Brit) radiateur m à gaz
gash [gæʃ] n entaille f; (on face) balafre f ▷ vt taillader; balafrer
gasket ['gæskɪt] n (Aut) joint m de culasse
gas mask n masque m à gaz
gas meter n compteur m à gaz
gasoline ['gæsəliːn] n (US) essence f
gasp [gɑːsp] n halètement m; (of shock etc): **she gave a small** ~ **of pain** la douleur lui coupa le souffle ▷ vi haleter; (fig) avoir le souffle coupé
▶ **gasp out** vt (say) dire dans un souffle or d'une voix entrecoupée
gas pedal n (US) accélérateur m
gas ring n brûleur m
gas station n (US) station-service f
gas tank n (US Aut) réservoir m d'essence
gas tap n bouton m (de cuisinière à gaz); (on pipe) robinet m à gaz
gastric ['gæstrɪk] adj gastrique
gate [geɪt] n (of garden) portail m; (of field, at level crossing) barrière f; (of building, town, at airport) porte f; (of lock) vanne f
gateau (pl -x) ['gætəu, -z] n gros gâteau à la crème
gatecrash ['geɪtkræʃ] vt s'introduire sans invitation dans
gateway ['geɪtweɪ] n porte f
gather ['gæðəʳ] vt (flowers, fruit) cueillir; (pick up) ramasser; (assemble: objects) rassembler; (: people) réunir; (: information) recueillir; (understand) comprendre; (Sewing) froncer ▷ vi (assemble) se rassembler; (dust) s'amasser; (clouds) s'amonceler; **to** ~ **(from/that)** conclure or déduire (de/que); **as far as I can** ~ d'après ce que je comprends; **to** ~ **speed** prendre de la vitesse
gathering ['gæðərɪŋ] n rassemblement m
gaudy ['gɔːdɪ] adj voyant(e)
gauge [geɪdʒ] n (standard measure) calibre m; (Rail) écartement m; (instrument) jauge f ▷ vt jauger; (fig: sb's capabilities, character) juger de; **to** ~ **the right moment** calculer le moment propice; **petrol** ~ (US): **gas** ~ jauge d'essence
gaunt [gɔːnt] adj décharné(e); (grim, desolate) désolé(e)
gauntlet ['gɔːntlɪt] n (fig): **to throw down the** ~ jeter le gant; **to run the** ~ **through an angry crowd** se frayer un passage à travers une foule hostile or entre deux haies de manifestants etc hostiles
gauze [gɔːz] n gaze f
gave [geɪv] pt of **give**
gay [geɪ] adj (homosexual) homosexuel(le); (slightly old-fashioned: cheerful) gai(e), réjoui(e); (colour) gai, vif (vive)
gaze [geɪz] n regard m fixe ▷ vi: **to** ~ **at** (vt) fixer du regard

gazump [gə'zʌmp] vi (Brit) revenir sur une promesse de vente pour accepter un prix plus élevé
GB n abbr = **Great Britain**
GCE n abbr (Brit) = **General Certificate of Education**
GCSE n abbr (Brit: = General Certificate of Secondary Education) examen passé à l'âge de 16 ans sanctionnant les connaissances de l'élève; **she's got eight** ~**s** elle a réussi dans huit matières aux épreuves du GCSE
gear [gɪəʳ] n matériel m, équipement m; (Tech) engrenage m; (Aut) vitesse f ▷ vt (fig: adapt) adapter; **top** or (US) **high/low** ~ quatrième (or cinquième)/première vitesse; **in** ~ en prise; **out of** ~ au point mort; **our service is** ~**ed to meet the needs of the disabled** notre service répond de façon spécifique aux besoins des handicapés
▶ **gear up** vi: **to** ~ **up (to do)** se préparer (à faire)
gear box n boîte f de vitesse
gear lever n levier m de vitesse
gear shift (US) n = **gear lever**
gear stick (Brit) n = **gear lever**
geese [giːs] npl of **goose**
gel [dʒel] n gelée f; (Chem) colloïde m
gem [dʒem] n pierre précieuse
Gemini ['dʒemɪnaɪ] n les Gémeaux mpl; **to be** ~ être des Gémeaux
gender ['dʒendəʳ] n genre m; (person's sex) sexe m
gene [dʒiːn] n (Biol) gène m
general ['dʒenərl] n général m ▷ adj général(e); **in** ~ en général; **the** ~ **public** le grand public; ~ **audit** (Comm) vérification annuelle
general anaesthetic, (US) **general anesthetic** n anesthésie générale
general delivery n poste restante
general election n élection(s) législative(s)
generalize ['dʒenrəlaɪz] vi généraliser
general knowledge n connaissances générales
generally ['dʒenrəlɪ] adv généralement
general practitioner n généraliste m/f
general store n épicerie f
generate ['dʒenəreɪt] vt engendrer; (electricity) produire
generation [dʒenə'reɪʃən] n génération f; (of electricity etc) production f
generator ['dʒenəreɪtəʳ] n générateur m
generosity [dʒenə'rɔsɪtɪ] n générosité f
generous ['dʒenərəs] adj généreux(-euse); (copious) copieux(-euse)
genetic [dʒɪ'netɪk] adj génétique; ~ **engineering** ingénierie m génétique; ~ **fingerprinting** système m d'empreinte génétique
genetically modified adj (food etc) génétiquement modifié(e)
genetics [dʒɪ'netɪks] n génétique f
Geneva [dʒɪ'niːvə] n Genève; **Lake** ~ le lac Léman
genial ['dʒiːnɪəl] adj cordial(e), chaleureux(-euse); (climate) clément(e)
genitals ['dʒenɪtlz] npl organes génitaux
genius ['dʒiːnɪəs] n génie m
gent [dʒent] n abbr (Brit inf) = **gentleman**
genteel [dʒen'tiːl] adj de bon ton, distingué(e)
gentle ['dʒentl] adj doux (douce); (breeze, touch)

léger(-ère)

gentleman (*irreg*) ['dʒɛntlmən] *n* monsieur *m*; (*well-bred man*) gentleman *m*; **~'s agreement** gentleman's agreement *m*

gently ['dʒɛntlɪ] *adv* doucement

gentry ['dʒɛntrɪ] *n* petite noblesse

gents [dʒɛnts] *n* W.-C. *mpl* (pour hommes)

genuine ['dʒɛnjuɪn] *adj* véritable, authentique; (*person, emotion*) sincère

genuinely ['dʒɛnjuɪnlɪ] *adv* sincèrement, vraiment

geographic [dʒɪə'græfɪk], **geographical** [dʒɪə'græfɪkl] *adj* géographique

geography [dʒɪ'ɔgrəfɪ] *n* géographie *f*

geology [dʒɪ'ɔlədʒɪ] *n* géologie *f*

geometric [dʒɪə'mɛtrɪk], **geometrical** [dʒɪə'mɛtrɪkl] *adj* géométrique

geometry [dʒɪ'ɔmətrɪ] *n* géométrie *f*

geranium [dʒɪ'reɪnɪəm] *n* géranium *m*

geriatric [dʒɛrɪ'ætrɪk] *adj* gériatrique ▷ *n* patient(e) gériatrique

germ [dʒə:m] *n* (*Med*) microbe *m*; (*Biol: fig*) germe *m*

German ['dʒə:mən] *adj* allemand(e) ▷ *n* Allemand(e); (*Ling*) allemand *m*

German measles *n* rubéole *f*

Germany ['dʒə:mənɪ] *n* Allemagne *f*

gesture ['dʒɛstjər] *n* geste *m*; **as a ~ of friendship** en témoignage d'amitié

get [gɛt] (*pt, pp* **got**, *pp* **gotten**) (US) *vi* **1** (*become, be*) devenir; **to ~ old/tired** devenir vieux/fatigué, vieillir/se fatiguer; **to ~ drunk** s'enivrer; **to ~ ready/washed/shaved** *etc* se préparer/laver/raser *etc*; **to ~ killed** se faire tuer; **to ~ dirty** se salir; **to ~ married** se marier; **when do I ~ paid?** quand est-ce que je serai payé?; **it's ~ting late** il se fait tard

2 (*go*): **to ~ to/from** aller à/de; **to ~ home** rentrer chez soi; **how did you ~ here?** comment es-tu arrivé ici?; **he got across the bridge/under the fence** il a traversé le pont/est passé au-dessous de la barrière

3 (*begin*) commencer *or* se mettre à; **to ~ to know sb** apprendre à connaître qn; **I'm ~ting to like him** je commence à l'apprécier; **let's ~ going** *or* **started** allons-y

4 (*modal aux vb*): **you've got to do it** il faut que vous le fassiez; **I've got to tell the police** je dois le dire à la police

▷ *vt* **1**: **to ~ sth done** (*do*) faire qch; (*have done*) faire faire qch; **to ~ sth/sb ready** préparer qch/qn; **to ~ one's hair cut** se faire couper les cheveux; **to ~ the car going** *or* **to go** (faire) démarrer la voiture; **to ~ sb to do sth** faire faire qch à qn; **to ~ sb drunk** enivrer qn

2 (*obtain: money, permission, results*) obtenir, avoir; (*buy*) acheter; (*find: job, flat*) trouver; (*fetch: person, doctor, object*) aller chercher; **to ~ sth for sb** procurer qch à qn; **~ me Mr Jones, please** (*on phone*) passez-moi Mr Jones, s'il vous plaît; **can I ~ you a drink?** est-ce que je peux vous servir à boire?

3 (*receive: present, letter*) recevoir, avoir; (*acquire:*

reputation) avoir; (*prize*) obtenir; **what did you ~ for your birthday?** qu'est-ce que tu as eu pour ton anniversaire?; **how much did you ~ for the painting?** combien avez-vous vendu le tableau?

4 (*catch*) prendre, saisir, attraper; (*hit: target etc*) atteindre; **to ~ sb by the arm/throat** prendre *or* saisir *or* attraper qn par le bras/à la gorge; **~ him!** arrête-le!; **the bullet got him in the leg** la balle l'a atteint à la jambe; **he really ~s me!** il me porte sur les nerfs!

5 (*take, move*): **to ~ sth to sb** faire parvenir qch à qn; **do you think we'll ~ it through the door?** on arrivera à le faire passer par la porte?; **I'll ~ you there somehow** je me débrouillerai pour t'y emmener

6 (*catch, take: plane, bus etc*) prendre; **where do I ~ the train for Birmingham?** où prend-on le train pour Birmingham?

7 (*understand*) comprendre, saisir; (*hear*) entendre; **I've got it!** j'ai compris!; **I don't ~ your meaning** je ne vois *or* comprends pas ce que vous voulez dire; **I didn't ~ your name** je n'ai pas entendu votre nom

8 (*have, possess*): **to have got** avoir; **how many have you got?** vous en avez combien?

9 (*illness*) avoir; **I've got a cold** j'ai le rhume; **she got pneumonia and died** elle a fait une pneumonie et elle en est morte

▶ **get about** *vi* se déplacer; (*news*) se répandre

▶ **get across** *vt*: **to ~ across (to)** (*message, meaning*) faire passer (à) ▷ *vi*: **to ~ across (to)** (*speaker*) se faire comprendre (par)

▶ **get along** *vi* (*agree*) s'entendre; (*depart*) s'en aller; (*manage*) = **get by**

▶ **get at** *vt fus* (*attack*) s'en prendre à; (*reach*) attraper, atteindre; **what are you ~ting at?** à quoi voulez-vous en venir?

▶ **get away** *vi* partir, s'en aller; (*escape*) s'échapper

▶ **get away with** *vt fus* (*punishment*) en être quitte pour; (*crime etc*) se faire pardonner

▶ **get back** *vi* (*return*) rentrer ▷ *vt* récupérer, recouvrer; **to ~ back to** (*start again*) retourner *or* revenir à; (*contact again*) recontacter; **when do we ~ back?** quand serons-nous de retour?

▶ **get back at** *vt fus* (*inf*): **to ~ back at sb** rendre la monnaie de sa pièce à qn

▶ **get by** *vi* (*pass*) passer; (*manage*) se débrouiller; **I can ~ by in Dutch** je me débrouille en hollandais

▶ **get down** *vi, vt fus* descendre ▷ *vt* descendre; (*depress*) déprimer

▶ **get down to** *vt fus* (*work*) se mettre à (faire); **to ~ down to business** passer aux choses sérieuses

▶ **get in** *vi* entrer; (*arrive home*) rentrer; (*train*) arriver ▷ *vt* (*bring in: harvest*) rentrer; (: *coal*) faire rentrer; (: *supplies*) faire des provisions de

▶ **get into** *vt fus* entrer dans; (*car, train etc*) monter dans; (*clothes*) mettre, enfiler, endosser; **to ~ into bed/a rage** se mettre au lit/en colère

▶ **get off** *vi* (*from train etc*) descendre; (*depart: person, car*) s'en aller; (*escape*) s'en tirer ▷ *vt* (*remove: clothes, stain*) enlever; (*send off*) expédier; (*have as leave: day, time*): **we got 2 days off** nous avons eu 2 jours de congé ▷ *vt fus* (*train, bus*) descendre de; **where do I ~ off?** où est-ce que je dois descendre?; **to ~ off to a good start** (*fig*) prendre un bon départ

▶ **get on** *vi* (*at exam etc*) se débrouiller; (*agree*): **to ~ on (with)** s'entendre (avec); **how are you ~ting on?** comment ça va? ▷ *vt fus* monter dans; (*horse*) monter sur

▶ **get on to** *vt fus* (*Brit: deal with: problem*) s'occuper de; (*contact: person*) contacter

▶ **get out** *vi* sortir; (*of vehicle*) descendre; (*news etc*) s'ébruiter ▷ *vt* sortir

▶ **get out of** *vt fus* sortir de; (*duty etc*) échapper à, se soustraire à

▶ **get over** *vt fus* (*illness*) se remettre de ▷ *vt* (*communicate: idea etc*) communiquer; (*finish*): **let's ~ it over (with)** finissons-en

▶ **get round** *vi*: **to ~ round to doing sth** se mettre (finalement) à faire qch ▷ *vt fus* contourner; (*fig: person*) entortiller

▶ **get through** *vi* (*Tel*) avoir la communication; **to ~ through to sb** atteindre qn ▷ *vt fus* (*finish: work, book*) finir, terminer

▶ **get together** *vi* se réunir ▷ *vt* rassembler

▶ **get up** *vi* (*rise*) se lever ▷ *vt fus* monter

▶ **get up to** *vt fus* (*reach*) arriver à; (*prank etc*) faire

getaway ['gɛtəweɪ] *n* fuite *f*

geyser ['giːzəʳ] *n* chauffe-eau *m inv*; (*Geo*) geyser *m*

Ghana ['gɑːnə] *n* Ghana *m*

ghastly ['gɑːstlɪ] *adj* atroce, horrible; (*pale*) livide, blême

gherkin ['gəːkɪn] *n* cornichon *m*

ghetto ['gɛtəu] *n* ghetto *m*

ghetto blaster [-blɑːstəʳ] *n* (*inf*) gros radiocassette

ghost [gəust] *n* fantôme *m*, revenant *m* ▷ *vt* (*sb else's book*) écrire

giant ['dʒaɪənt] *n* géant(e) ▷ *adj* géant(e), énorme; **~ (size) packet** paquet géant

gibberish ['dʒɪbərɪʃ] *n* charabia *m*

giblets ['dʒɪblɪts] *npl* abats *mpl*

Gibraltar [dʒɪˈbrɔːltəʳ] *n* Gibraltar *m*

giddy ['gɪdɪ] *adj* (*dizzy*): **to be (or feel) ~** avoir le vertige; (*height*) vertigineux(-euse); (*thoughtless*) sot(te), étourdi(e)

gift [gɪft] *n* cadeau *m*, présent *m*; (*donation, talent*) don *m*; (*Comm: also*: **free gift**) cadeau(-réclame) *m*; **to have a ~ for sth** avoir des dons pour *or* le don de qch

gifted ['gɪftɪd] *adj* doué(e)

gift shop, (*US*) **gift store** *n* boutique *f* de cadeaux

gift token, **gift voucher** *n* chèque-cadeau *m*

gig [gɪg] *n* (*inf: concert*) concert *m*

gigabyte ['dʒɪgəbaɪt] *n* gigaoctet *m*

gigantic [dʒaɪˈgæntɪk] *adj* gigantesque

giggle ['gɪgl] *vi* pouffer, ricaner sottement ▷ *n* petit rire sot, ricanement *m*

gill [dʒɪl] *n* (*measure*) = 0.25 pints (Brit = 0.148 l; US = 0.118 l)

gills [gɪlz] *npl* (*of fish*) ouïes *fpl*, branchies *fpl*

gilt [gɪlt] *n* dorure *f* ▷ *adj* doré(e)

gilt-edged ['gɪltɛdʒd] *adj* (*stocks, securities*) de premier ordre

gimmick ['gɪmɪk] *n* truc *m*; **sales ~** offre promotionnelle

gin [dʒɪn] *n* gin *m*

ginger ['dʒɪndʒəʳ] *n* gingembre *m*

▶ **ginger up** *vt* secouer; animer

ginger ale, **ginger beer** *n* boisson gazeuse au gingembre

gingerbread ['dʒɪndʒəbrɛd] *n* pain *m* d'épices

gingerly ['dʒɪndʒəlɪ] *adv* avec précaution

gipsy ['dʒɪpsɪ] *n* = **gypsy**

giraffe [dʒɪˈrɑːf] *n* girafe *f*

girder ['gəːdəʳ] *n* poutrelle *f*

girl [gəːl] *n* fille *f*, fillette *f*; (*young unmarried woman*) jeune fille; (*daughter*) fille; **an English ~** une jeune Anglaise; **a little English ~** une petite Anglaise

girl band *n* girls band *m*

girlfriend ['gəːlfrɛnd] *n* (*of girl*) amie *f*; (*of boy*) petite amie

Girl Guide *n* (*Brit*) éclaireuse *f*; (*Roman Catholic*) guide *f*

girlish ['gəːlɪʃ] *adj* de jeune fille

Girl Scout *n* (*US*) = **Girl Guide**

giro ['dʒaɪrəu] *n* (*bank giro*) virement *m* bancaire; (*post office giro*) mandat *m*

gist [dʒɪst] *n* essentiel *m*

give [gɪv] (*pt* **gave**, *pp* -**n**) [geɪv, 'gɪvn] *n* (*of fabric*) élasticité *f* ▷ *vt* donner ▷ *vi* (*break*) céder; (*stretch: fabric*) se prêter; **to ~ sb sth**, **~ sth to sb** donner qch à qn; (*gift*) offrir qch à qn; (*message*) transmettre qch à qn; **to ~ sb a call/kiss** appeler/embrasser qn; **to ~ a cry/sigh** pousser un cri/un soupir; **how much did you ~ for it?** combien (l')avez-vous payé?; **12 o'clock, ~ or take a few minutes** midi, à quelques minutes près; **to ~ way** céder; (*Brit Aut*) donner la priorité

▶ **give away** *vt* donner; (*give free*) faire cadeau de; (*betray*) donner, trahir; (*disclose*) révéler; (*bride*) conduire à l'autel

▶ **give back** *vt* rendre

▶ **give in** *vi* céder ▷ *vt* donner

▶ **give off** *vt* dégager

▶ **give out** *vt* (*food etc*) distribuer; (*news*) annoncer ▷ *vi* (*be exhausted: supplies*) s'épuiser; (*fail*) lâcher

▶ **give up** *vi* renoncer ▷ *vt* renoncer à; **to ~ up smoking** arrêter de fumer; **to ~ o.s. up** se rendre

given ['gɪvn] *pp of* **give** ▷ *adj* (*fixed: time, amount*) donné(e), déterminé(e) ▷ *conj*: **~ the circumstances ...** étant donné les circonstances ..., vu les circonstances ...; **~ that ...** étant donné que ...

glacier ['glæsɪəʳ] *n* glacier *m*

glad [glæd] *adj* content(e); **to be ~ about sth/ that** être heureux(-euse) *or* bien content de qch/ que; **I was ~ of his help** j'étais bien content de (pouvoir compter sur) son aide *or* qu'il m'aide

gladly ['glædlɪ] adv volontiers
glamorous ['glæmərəs] adj (person) séduisant(e); (job) prestigieux(-euse)
glamour, (US) **glamor** ['glæmə^r] n éclat m, prestige m
glance [glɑːns] n coup m d'œil ▷ vi: **to ~ at** jeter un coup d'œil à
▶ **glance off** vt fus (bullet) ricocher sur
glancing ['glɑːnsɪŋ] adj (blow) oblique
gland [glænd] n glande f
glare [glɛə^r] n (of anger) regard furieux; (of light) lumière éblouissante; (of publicity) feux mpl ▷ vi briller d'un éclat aveuglant; **to ~ at** lancer un regard or des regards furieux à
glaring ['glɛərɪŋ] adj (mistake) criant(e), qui saute aux yeux
glass [glɑːs] n verre m; (also: **looking glass**) miroir m; **glasses** npl (spectacles) lunettes fpl
glasshouse ['glɑːshaus] n serre f
glassware ['glɑːswɛə^r] n verrerie f
glaze [gleɪz] vt (door) vitrer; (pottery) vernir; (Culin) glacer ▷ n vernis m; (Culin) glaçage m
glazed [gleɪzd] adj (eye) vitreux(-euse); (pottery) verni(e); (tiles) vitrifié(e)
glazier ['gleɪzɪə^r] n vitrier m
gleam [gliːm] n lueur f ▷ vi luire, briller; **a ~ of hope** une lueur d'espoir
glean [gliːn] vt (information) recueillir
glee [gliː] n joie f
glen [glɛn] n vallée f
glib [glɪb] adj qui a du bagou; facile
glide [glaɪd] vi glisser; (Aviat, bird) planer ▷ n glissement m; vol plané
glider ['glaɪdə^r] n (Aviat) planeur m
gliding ['glaɪdɪŋ] n (Aviat) vol m à voile
glimmer ['glɪmə^r] vi luire ▷ n lueur f
glimpse [glɪmps] n vision passagère, aperçu m ▷ vt entrevoir, apercevoir; **to catch a ~ of** entrevoir
glint [glɪnt] n éclair m ▷ vi étinceler
glisten ['glɪsn] vi briller, luire
glitter ['glɪtə^r] vi scintiller, briller ▷ n scintillement m
gloat [gləut] vi: **to ~ (over)** jubiler (à propos de)
global ['gləubl] adj (world-wide) mondial(e); (overall) global(e)
globalization [gləublaɪz'eɪʃən] n mondialisation f
global warming [-'wɔːmɪŋ] n réchauffement m de la planète
globe [gləub] n globe m
gloom [gluːm] n obscurité f; (sadness) tristesse f, mélancolie f
gloomy ['gluːmɪ] adj (person) morose; (place, outlook) sombre; **to feel ~** avoir or se faire des idées noires
glorious ['glɔːrɪəs] adj glorieux(-euse); (beautiful) splendide
glory ['glɔːrɪ] n gloire f; splendeur f ▷ vi: **to ~ in** se glorifier de
gloss [glɔs] n (shine) brillant m, vernis m; (also: **gloss paint**) peinture brillante or laquée

▶ **gloss over** vt fus glisser sur
glossary ['glɔsərɪ] n glossaire m, lexique m
glossy ['glɔsɪ] adj brillant(e), luisant(e) ▷ n (also: **glossy magazine**) revue f de luxe
glove [glʌv] n gant m
glove compartment n (Aut) boîte f à gants, vide-poches m inv
glow [gləu] vi rougeoyer; (face) rayonner; (eyes) briller ▷ n rougeoiement m
glower ['glauə^r] vi lancer des regards mauvais
glucose ['gluːkəus] n glucose m
glue [gluː] n colle f ▷ vt coller
glum [glʌm] adj maussade, morose
glut [glʌt] n surabondance f ▷ vt rassasier; (market) encombrer
glutton ['glʌtn] n glouton(ne); **a ~ for work** un bourreau de travail
GM abbr (= genetically modified) génétiquement modifié(e)
gm abbr (= gram) g
GMO n abbr (= genetically modified organism) OGM m
GMT abbr (= Greenwich Mean Time) GMT
gnat [næt] n moucheron m
gnaw [nɔː] vt ronger
go [gəu] (pt **went**, pp **gone**) [wɛnt, gɔn] vi aller; (depart) partir, s'en aller; (work) marcher; (break) céder; (time) passer; (be sold): **to go for £10** se vendre 10 livres; (become): **to go pale/mouldy** pâlir/moisir ▷ n (pl **goes**); **to have a go (at)** essayer (de faire); **to be on the go** être en mouvement; **whose go is it?** à qui est-ce de jouer?; **to go by car/on foot** aller en voiture/à pied; **he's going to do it** il va le faire, il est sur le point de le faire; **to go for a walk** aller se promener; **to go dancing/shopping** aller danser/faire les courses; **to go looking for sb/sth** aller or partir à la recherche de qn/qch; **to go to sleep** s'endormir; **to go and see sb, go to see sb** aller voir qn; **how is it going?** comment ça marche?; **how did it go?** comment est-ce que ça s'est passé?; **to go round the back/by the shop** passer par derrière/devant le magasin; **my voice has gone** j'ai une extinction de voix; **the cake is all gone** il n'y a plus de gâteau; **I'll take whatever is going** (Brit) je prendrai ce qu'il y a (or ce que vous avez); **... to go** (US: food) ... à emporter
▶ **go about** vi (also: **go around**) aller çà et là; (rumour) se répandre ▷ vt fus: **how do I go about this?** comment dois-je m'y prendre (pour faire ceci)?; **to go about one's business** s'occuper de ses affaires
▶ **go after** vt fus (pursue) poursuivre, courir après; (job, record etc) essayer d'obtenir
▶ **go against** vt fus (be unfavourable to) être défavorable à; (be contrary to) être contraire à
▶ **go ahead** vi (make progress) avancer; (take place) avoir lieu; (get going) y aller
▶ **go along** vi aller, avancer ▷ vt fus longer, parcourir; **as you go along (with your work)** au fur et à mesure (de votre travail); **to go along with** (accompany) accompagner; (agree with: idea)

être d'accord sur; (: *person*) suivre

▶ **go away** vi partir, s'en aller

▶ **go back** vi rentrer; revenir; (*go again*) retourner

▶ **go back on** vt fus (*promise*) revenir sur

▶ **go by** vi (*years, time*) passer, s'écouler ▷ vt fus s'en tenir à; (*believe*) en croire

▶ **go down** vi descendre; (*number, price, amount*) baisser; (*ship*) couler; (*sun*) se coucher ▷ vt fus descendre; **that should go down well with him** (*fig*) ça devrait lui plaire

▶ **go for** vt fus (*fetch*) aller chercher; (*like*) aimer; (*attack*) s'en prendre à; attaquer

▶ **go in** vi entrer

▶ **go in for** vt fus (*competition*) se présenter à; (*like*) aimer

▶ **go into** vt fus entrer dans; (*investigate*) étudier, examiner; (*embark on*) se lancer dans

▶ **go off** vi partir, s'en aller; (*food*) se gâter; (*milk*) tourner; (*bomb*) sauter; (*alarm clock*) sonner; (*alarm*) se déclencher; (*lights etc*) s'éteindre; (*event*) se dérouler ▷ vt fus ne plus aimer, ne plus avoir envie de; **the gun went off** le coup est parti; **to go off to sleep** s'endormir; **the party went off well** la fête s'est bien passée *or* était très réussie

▶ **go on** vi continuer; (*happen*) se passer; (*lights*) s'allumer ▷ vt fus (*be guided by: evidence etc*) se fonder sur; **to go on doing** continuer à faire; **what's going on here?** qu'est-ce qui se passe ici?

▶ **go on at** vt fus (*nag*) tomber sur le dos de

▶ **go on with** vt fus poursuivre, continuer

▶ **go out** vi sortir; (*fire, light*) s'éteindre; (*tide*) descendre; **to go out with sb** sortir avec qn

▶ **go over** vi (*ship*) chavirer ▷ vt fus (*check*) revoir, vérifier; **to go over sth in one's mind** repasser qch dans son esprit

▶ **go past** vt fus: **to go past sth** passer devant qch

▶ **go round** vi (*circulate: news, rumour*) circuler; (*revolve*) tourner; (*suffice*) suffire (pour tout le monde); (*visit*): **to go round to sb's** passer chez qn; aller chez qn; (*make a detour*): **to go round (by)** faire un détour (par)

▶ **go through** vt fus (*town etc*) traverser; (*search through*) fouiller; (*suffer*) subir; (*examine: list, book*) lire *or* regarder en détail, éplucher; (*perform: lesson*) réciter; (: *formalities*) remplir; (: *programme*) exécuter

▶ **go through with** vt fus (*plan, crime*) aller jusqu'au bout de

▶ **go under** vi (*sink: also fig*) couler; (: *person*) succomber

▶ **go up** vi monter; (*price*) augmenter ▷ vt fus gravir; (*also*: **go up in flames**) flamber, s'enflammer brusquement

▶ **go with** vt fus aller avec

▶ **go without** vt fus se passer de

goad [gəʊd] vt aiguillonner

go-ahead ['gəʊəhɛd] adj dynamique, entreprenant(e) ▷ n feu vert

goal [gəʊl] n but m

goalkeeper ['gəʊlkiːpəʳ] n gardien m de but

goal-post [gəʊlpəʊst] n poteau m de but

goat [gəʊt] n chèvre f

gobble ['gɒbl] vt (*also*: **gobble down, gobble up**) engloutir

go-between ['gəʊbɪtwiːn] n médiateur m

god [gɒd] n dieu m; **G-** Dieu

godchild ['gɒdtʃaɪld] n filleul(e)

goddaughter ['gɒddɔːtəʳ] n filleule f

goddess ['gɒdɪs] n déesse f

godfather ['gɒdfɑːðəʳ] n parrain m

god-forsaken ['gɒdfəseɪkən] adj maudit(e)

godmother ['gɒdmʌðəʳ] n marraine f

godsend ['gɒdsɛnd] n aubaine f

godson ['gɒdsʌn] n filleul m

goggles ['gɒglz] npl (*for skiing etc*) lunettes (protectrices); (*for swimming*) lunettes de piscine

going ['gəʊɪŋ] n (*conditions*) état m du terrain ▷ adj: **the ~ rate** le tarif (en vigueur); **a ~ concern** une affaire prospère; **it was slow ~** les progrès étaient lents, ça n'avançait pas vite

gold [gəʊld] n or m ▷ adj en or; (*reserves*) d'or

golden ['gəʊldən] adj (*made of gold*) en or; (*gold in colour*) doré(e)

goldfish ['gəʊldfɪʃ] n poisson m rouge

goldmine ['gəʊldmaɪn] n mine f d'or

gold-plated ['gəʊld'pleɪtɪd] adj plaqué(e) or inv

goldsmith ['gəʊldsmɪθ] n orfèvre m

golf [gɒlf] n golf m

golf ball n balle f de golf; (*on typewriter*) boule f

golf club n club m de golf; (*stick*) club m, crosse f de golf

golf course n terrain m de golf

golfer ['gɒlfəʳ] n joueur(-euse) de golf

gone [gɒn] pp of **go** ▷ adj parti(e)

gong [gɒŋ] n gong m

good [gʊd] adj bon(ne); (*kind*) gentil(le); (*child*) sage; (*weather*) beau (belle) ▷ n bien m; **goods** npl marchandise f, articles mpl; (*Comm etc*) marchandises; **~!** bon!, très bien!; **to be ~ at** être bon en; **to be ~ for** être bon pour; **it's ~ for you** c'est bon pour vous; **it's a ~ thing you were there** heureusement que vous étiez là; **she is ~ with children/her hands** elle sait bien s'occuper des enfants/sait se servir de ses mains; **to feel ~** se sentir bien; **it's ~ to see you** ça me fait plaisir de vous voir, je suis content de vous voir; **he's up to no ~** il prépare quelque mauvais coup; **it's no ~ complaining** cela ne sert à rien de se plaindre; **to make ~** (*deficit*) combler; (*losses*) compenser; **for the common ~** dans l'intérêt commun; **for ~** (*for ever*) pour de bon, une fois pour toutes; **would you be ~ enough to ...?** auriez-vous la bonté *or* l'amabilité de ...?; **that's very ~ of you** c'est très gentil de votre part; **is this any ~?** (*will it do?*) est-ce que ceci fera l'affaire?, est-ce que cela peut vous rendre service?; (*what's it like?*) qu'est-ce que ça vaut?; **~s and chattels** biens mpl et effets mpl; **a ~ deal (of)** beaucoup (de); **a ~ many** beaucoup (de); **~ morning/afternoon!** bonjour!; **~ evening!** bonsoir!; **~ night!** bonsoir!; (*on going to bed*) bonne nuit!

goodbye [gud'baɪ] *excl* au revoir!; **to say ~ to sb** dire au revoir à qn

Good Friday *n* Vendredi saint

good-looking ['gud'lukɪŋ] *adj* beau (belle), bien inv

good-natured ['gud'neɪtʃəd] *adj* (*person*) qui a un bon naturel; (*discussion*) enjoué(e)

goodness ['gudnɪs] *n* (*of person*) bonté *f*; **for ~ sake!** je vous en prie!; **~ gracious!** mon Dieu!

goods train *n* (*Brit*) train *m* de marchandises

goodwill [gud'wɪl] *n* bonne volonté; (*Comm*) réputation *f* (auprès de la clientèle)

goose (*pl* **geese**) [guːs, giːs] *n* oie *f*

gooseberry ['guzbərɪ] *n* groseille *f* à maquereau; **to play ~** (*Brit*) tenir la chandelle

goose bumps, goose pimples *npl* chair *f* de poule

gooseflesh ['guːsflɛʃ] *n*, **goosepimples** ['guː spɪmplz] ▷ *npl* chair *f* de poule

gore [gɔːʳ] *vt* encorner ▷ *n* sang *m*

gorge [gɔːdʒ] *n* gorge *f* ▷ *vt*: **to ~ o.s. (on)** se gorger (de)

gorgeous ['gɔːdʒəs] *adj* splendide, superbe

gorilla [gə'rɪlə] *n* gorille *m*

gorse [gɔːs] *n* ajoncs *mpl*

gory ['gɔːrɪ] *adj* sanglant(e)

gosh [gɒʃ] *excl* (*inf*) mince alors!

go-slow ['gəu'sləu] *n* (*Brit*) grève perlée

gospel ['gɒspl] *n* évangile *m*

gossip ['gɒsɪp] *n* (*chat*) bavardages *mpl*; (*malicious*) commérage *m*, cancans *mpl*; (*person*) commère *f* ▷ *vi* bavarder; cancaner, faire des commérages; **a piece of ~** un ragot, un racontar

gossip column *n* (*Press*) échos *mpl*

got [gɒt] *pt, pp of* **get**

gotten ['gɒtn] (*US*) *pp of* **get**

gourmet ['guəmeɪ] *n* gourmet *m*, gastronome *m/f*

gout [gaut] *n* goutte *f*

govern ['gʌvən] *vt* (*gen*: *Ling*) gouverner; (*influence*) déterminer

governess ['gʌvənɪs] *n* gouvernante *f*

government ['gʌvnmənt] *n* gouvernement *m*; (*Brit*: *ministers*) ministère *m* ▷ *cpd* de l'État

governor ['gʌvənəʳ] *n* (*of colony, state, bank*) gouverneur *m*; (*of school, hospital etc*) administrateur(-trice); (*Brit*: *of prison*) directeur(-trice)

gown [gaun] *n* robe *f*; (*of teacher, Brit*: *of judge*) toge *f*

GP *n abbr* (*Med*) = **general practitioner; who's your GP?** qui est votre médecin traitant?

GPS *n abbr* (= *global positioning system*) GPS *m*

grab [græb] *vt* saisir, empoigner; (*property, power*) se saisir de ▷ *vi*: **to ~ at** essayer de saisir

grace [greɪs] *n* grâce *f* ▷ *vt* (*honour*) honorer; (*adorn*) orner; **5 days' ~** un répit de 5 jours; **to say ~** dire la bénédicité; (*after meal*) dire les grâces; **with a good/bad ~** de bonne/mauvaise grâce; **his sense of humour is his saving ~** il se rachète par son sens de l'humour

graceful ['greɪsful] *adj* gracieux(-euse), élégant(e)

gracious ['greɪʃəs] *adj* (*kind*) charmant(e), bienveillant(e); (*elegant*) plein(e) d'élégance, d'une grande élégance; (*formal: pardon etc*) miséricordieux(-euse) ▷ *excl*: **(good) ~!** mon Dieu!

grade [greɪd] *n* (*Comm*: *quality*) qualité *f*; (*size*) calibre *m*; (*type*) catégorie *f*; (*in hierarchy*) grade *m*, échelon *m*; (*Scol*) note *f*; (*US*: *school class*) classe *f*; (: *gradient*) pente *f* ▷ *vt* classer; (*by size*) calibrer; graduer; **to make the ~** (*fig*) réussir

grade crossing *n* (*US*) passage *m* à niveau

grade school *n* (*US*) école *f* primaire

gradient ['greɪdɪənt] *n* inclinaison *f*, pente *f*; (*Geom*) gradient *m*

gradual ['grædjuəl] *adj* graduel(le), progressif(-ive)

gradually ['grædjuəlɪ] *adv* peu à peu, graduellement

graduate *n* ['grædjuɪt] diplômé(e) d'université; (*US*: *of high school*) diplômé(e) de fin d'études ▷ *vi* ['grædjueɪt] obtenir un diplôme d'université (or de fin d'études)

graduation [grædju'eɪʃən] *n* cérémonie *f* de remise des diplômes

graffiti [grə'fiːtɪ] *npl* graffiti *mpl*

graft [grɑːft] *n* (*Agr, Med*) greffe *f*; (*bribery*) corruption *f* ▷ *vt* greffer; **hard ~** (*Brit*: *inf*) boulot acharné

grain [greɪn] *n* (*single piece*) grain *m*; (*no pl*: *cereals*) céréales *fpl*; (*US*: *corn*) blé *m*; (*of wood*) fibre *f*; **it goes against the ~** cela va à l'encontre de sa (or ma *etc*) nature

gram [græm] *n* gramme *m*

grammar ['græməʳ] *n* grammaire *f*

grammar school *n* (*Brit*) ≈ lycée *m*

grammatical [grə'mætɪkl] *adj* grammatical(e)

gramme [græm] *n* = **gram**

gran [græn] (*inf*) *n* (*Brit*) mamie *f* (*inf*), mémé *f* (*inf*); **my ~** (*young child speaking*) ma mamie or mémé; (*older child or adult speaking*) ma grand-mère

grand [grænd] *adj* magnifique, splendide; (*terrific*) magnifique, formidable; (*gesture etc*) noble ▷ *n* (*inf*: *thousand*) mille livres *fpl* (or dollars *mpl*)

grandad ['grændæd] (*inf*) *n* = **granddad**

grandchild (*pl* **-ren**) ['græntʃaɪld, 'græntʃɪldrən] *n* petit-fils *m*, petite-fille *f*; **grandchildren** *npl* petits-enfants

granddad ['grændæd] *n* (*inf*) papy *m* (*inf*), papi *m* (*inf*), pépé *m* (*inf*); **my ~** (*young child speaking*) mon papy or papi or pépé; (*older child or adult speaking*) mon grand-père

granddaughter ['grændɔːtəʳ] *n* petite-fille *f*

grandfather ['grændfɑːðəʳ] *n* grand-père *m*

grandma ['grænmɑː] *n* (*inf*) = **gran**

grandmother ['grænmʌðəʳ] *n* grand-mère *f*

grandpa ['grænpɑː] *n* (*inf*) = **granddad**

grandparents ['grændpɛərənts] *npl* grands-parents *mpl*

grand piano *n* piano *m* à queue

Grand Prix ['grã:'pri:] n (Aut) grand prix automobile

grandson ['grænsʌn] n petit-fils m

grandstand ['grændstænd] n (Sport) tribune f

granite ['grænɪt] n granit m

granny ['grænɪ] n (inf) = **gran**

grant [grɑ:nt] vt accorder; (a request) accéder à; (admit) concéder ▷ n (Scol) bourse f; (Admin) subside m, subvention f; **to take sth for ~ed** considérer qch comme acquis; **to take sb for ~ed** considérer qn comme faisant partie du décor; **to ~ that** admettre que

granulated ['grænjuleɪtɪd] adj: **~ sugar** sucre m en poudre

grape [greɪp] n raisin m; **a bunch of ~s** une grappe de raisin

grapefruit ['greɪpfru:t] n pamplemousse m

graph [grɑ:f] n graphique m, courbe f

graphic ['græfɪk] adj graphique; (vivid) vivant(e)

graphics ['græfɪks] n (art) arts mpl graphiques; (process) graphisme m ▷ npl (drawings) illustrations fpl

grapple ['græpl] vi: **to ~ with** être aux prises avec

grasp [grɑ:sp] vt saisir, empoigner; (understand) saisir, comprendre ▷ n (grip) prise f; (fig) compréhension f, connaissance f; **to have sth within one's ~** avoir qch à sa portée; **to have a good ~ of sth** (fig) bien comprendre qch
▶ **grasp at** vt fus (rope etc) essayer de saisir; (fig: opportunity) sauter sur

grasping ['grɑ:spɪŋ] adj avide

grass [grɑ:s] n herbe f; (lawn) gazon m; (Brit inf: informer) mouchard(e); (: ex-terrorist) balanceur(-euse)

grasshopper ['grɑ:shɔpə'] n sauterelle f

grass roots npl (fig) base f

grate [greɪt] n grille f de cheminée ▷ vi grincer ▷ vt (Culin) râper

grateful ['greɪtful] adj reconnaissant(e)

grater ['greɪtə'] n râpe f

gratifying ['grætɪfaɪɪŋ] adj agréable, satisfaisant(e)

grating ['greɪtɪŋ] n (iron bars) grille f ▷ adj (noise) grinçant(e)

gratitude ['grætɪtju:d] n gratitude f

gratuity [grə'tju:ɪtɪ] n pourboire m

grave [greɪv] n tombe f ▷ adj grave, sérieux(-euse)

gravel ['grævl] n gravier m

gravestone ['greɪvstəun] n pierre tombale

graveyard ['greɪvjɑ:d] n cimetière m

gravity ['grævɪtɪ] n (Physics) gravité f; pesanteur f; (seriousness) gravité, sérieux m

gravy ['greɪvɪ] n jus m (de viande), sauce f (au jus de viande)

gray [greɪ] adj (US) = **grey**

graze [greɪz] vi paître, brouter ▷ vt (touch lightly) frôler, effleurer; (scrape) écorcher ▷ n écorchure f

grease [gri:s] n (fat) graisse f; (lubricant) lubrifiant m ▷ vt graisser; lubrifier; **to ~ the skids** (US: fig) huiler les rouages

greaseproof paper ['gri:spru:f-] n (Brit) papier sulfurisé

greasy ['gri:sɪ] adj gras(se), graisseux(-euse); (hands, clothes) graisseux; (Brit: road, surface) glissant(e)

great [greɪt] adj grand(e); (heat, pain etc) très fort(e), intense; (inf) formidable; **they're ~ friends** ils sont très amis, ce sont de grands amis; **we had a ~ time** nous nous sommes bien amusés; **it was ~!** c'était fantastique or super!; **the ~ thing is that ...** ce qu'il y a de vraiment bien c'est que ...

Great Britain n Grande-Bretagne f

great-grandfather [greɪt'grænfɑ:ðə'] n arrière-grand-père m

great-grandmother [greɪt'grænmʌðə'] n arrière-grand-mère f

greatly ['greɪtlɪ] adv très, grandement; (with verbs) beaucoup

greatness ['greɪtnɪs] n grandeur f

Greece [gri:s] n Grèce f

greed [gri:d] n (also: **greediness**) avidité f; (for food) gourmandise f

greedy ['gri:dɪ] adj avide; (for food) gourmand(e)

Greek [gri:k] adj grec (grecque) ▷ n Grec (Grecque); (Ling) grec m; **ancient/modern ~** grec classique/moderne

green [gri:n] adj vert(e); (inexperienced) (bien) jeune, naïf(-ive); (ecological: product etc) écologique ▷ n (colour) vert m; (on golf course) green m; (stretch of grass) pelouse f; (also: **village green**) ≈ place f du village; **greens** npl (vegetables) légumes verts; **to have ~ fingers** or (US) **a ~ thumb** (fig) avoir le pouce vert; **G~** (Pol) écologiste m/f; **the G~ Party** le parti écologiste

green belt n (round town) ceinture verte

green card n (Aut) carte verte; (US: work permit) permis m de travail

greenery ['gri:nərɪ] n verdure f

greengage ['gri:ngeɪdʒ] n reine-claude f

greengrocer ['gri:ngrəusə'] n (Brit) marchand m de fruits et légumes

greengrocer's ['gri:ngrəusə' z], **greengrocer's shop** n magasin m de fruits et légumes

greenhouse ['gri:nhaus] n serre f

greenhouse effect n: **the ~** l'effet m de serre

greenhouse gas n gaz m contribuant à l'effet de serre

greenish ['gri:nɪʃ] adj verdâtre

Greenland ['gri:nlənd] n Groenland m

green salad n salade verte

greet [gri:t] vt accueillir

greeting ['gri:tɪŋ] n salutation f; **Christmas/birthday ~s** souhaits mpl de Noël/de bon anniversaire

greeting card, greetings card n carte f de vœux

gregarious [grə'gɛərɪəs] adj grégaire; sociable

grenade [grə'neɪd] n (also: **hand grenade**) grenade f

grew [gru:] pt of **grow**

grey, (US) **gray** [greɪ] adj gris(e); (dismal) sombre; **to go ~** (commencer à) grisonner

grey-haired, (US) **gray-haired** [greɪˈhɛəd] *adj* aux cheveux gris

greyhound [ˈɡreɪhaund] *n* lévrier *m*

grid [ɡrɪd] *n* grille *f*; (*Elec*) réseau *m*; (*US Aut*) intersection *f* (*matérialisée par des marques au sol*)

gridlock [ˈɡrɪdlɔk] *n* (*traffic jam*) embouteillage *m*

gridlocked [ˈɡrɪdlɔk t] *adj*: **to be ~** (*roads*) être bloqué par un embouteillage; (*talks etc*) être suspendu

grief [ɡriːf] *n* chagrin *m*, douleur *f*; **to come to ~** (*plan*) échouer; (*person*) avoir un malheur

grievance [ˈɡriːvəns] *n* doléance *f*, grief *m*; (*cause for complaint*) grief

grieve [ɡriːv] *vi* avoir du chagrin; se désoler ▷ *vt* faire de la peine à, affliger; **to ~ for sb** pleurer qn; **to ~ at** se désoler de; pleurer

grievous [ˈɡriːvəs] *adj* grave, cruel(le); **~ bodily harm** (*Law*) coups *mpl* et blessures *fpl*

grill [ɡrɪl] *n* (*on cooker*) gril *m*; (*also*: **mixed grill**) grillade(s) *f(pl)*; (*also*: **grillroom**) rôtisserie *f* ▷ *vt* (*Brit*) griller; (*inf: question*) interroger longuement, cuisiner

grille [ɡrɪl] *n* grillage *m*; (*Aut*) calandre *f*

grillroom [ˈɡrɪlrum] *n* rôtisserie *f*

grim [ɡrɪm] *adj* sinistre, lugubre; (*serious, stern*) sévère

grimace [ɡrɪˈmeɪs] *n* grimace *f* ▷ *vi* grimacer, faire une grimace

grime [ɡraɪm] *n* crasse *f*

grin [ɡrɪn] *n* large sourire *m* ▷ *vi* sourire; **to ~ (at)** faire un grand sourire (à)

grind [ɡraɪnd] (*pt, pp* **ground**) [ɡraund] *vt* écraser; (*coffee, pepper etc*) moudre; (*US: meat*) hacher; (*make sharp*) aiguiser; (*polish: gem, lens*) polir ▷ *vi* (*car gears*) grincer ▷ *n* (*work*) corvée *f*; **to ~ one's teeth** grincer des dents; **to ~ to a halt** (*vehicle*) s'arrêter dans un grincement de freins; (*fig*) s'arrêter, s'immobiliser; **the daily ~** (*inf*) le train-train quotidien

grip [ɡrɪp] *n* (*handclasp*) poigne *f*; (*control*) prise *f*; (*handle*) poignée *f*; (*holdall*) sac *m* de voyage ▷ *vt* saisir, empoigner; (*viewer, reader*) captiver; **to come to ~s with** se colleter avec, en venir aux prises avec; **to ~ the road** (*Aut*) adhérer à la route; **to lose one's ~** lâcher prise; (*fig*) perdre les pédales, être dépassé(e)

gripping [ˈɡrɪpɪŋ] *adj* prenant(e), palpitant(e)

grisly [ˈɡrɪzlɪ] *adj* sinistre, macabre

gristle [ˈɡrɪsl] *n* cartilage *m* (*de poulet etc*)

grit [ɡrɪt] *n* gravillon *m*; (*courage*) cran *m* ▷ *vt* (*road*) sabler; **to ~ one's teeth** serrer les dents; **to have a piece of ~ in one's eye** avoir une poussière *or* saleté dans l'œil

grits [ɡrɪts] *npl* (*US*) gruau *m* de maïs

groan [ɡrəun] *n* (*of pain*) gémissement *m*; (*of disapproval, dismay*) grognement *m* ▷ *vi* gémir; grogner

grocer [ˈɡrəusəʳ] *n* épicier *m*

groceries [ˈɡrəusərɪz] *npl* provisions *fpl*

grocer's [ˈɡrəusəz], **grocer's shop**, **grocery** [ˈɡrəusərɪ] *n* épicerie *f*

groin [ɡrɔɪn] *n* aine *f*

groom [ɡruːm] *n* (*for horses*) palefrenier *m*; (*also*: **bridegroom**) marié *m* ▷ *vt* (*horse*) panser; (*fig*): **to ~ sb for** former qn pour

groove [ɡruːv] *n* sillon *m*, rainure *f*

grope [ɡrəup] *vi* tâtonner; **to ~ for** chercher à tâtons

gross [ɡrəus] *adj* grossier(-ière); (*Comm*) brut(e) ▷ *n* (*pl inv: twelve dozen*) grosse *f* ▷ *vt* (*Comm*): **to ~ £500,000** gagner 500 000 livres avant impôt

grossly [ˈɡrəuslɪ] *adv* (*greatly*) très, grandement

grotesque [ɡrəˈtɛsk] *adj* grotesque

grotto [ˈɡrɔtəu] *n* grotte *f*

grotty [ˈɡrɔtɪ] *adj* (*Brit inf*) minable

ground [ɡraund] *pt, pp of* **grind** ▷ *n* sol *m*, terre *f*; (*land*) terrain *m*, terres *fpl*; (*Sport*) terrain; (*reason: gen pl*) raison *f*; (*US: also*: **ground wire**) terre *f* ▷ *vt* (*plane*) empêcher de décoller, retenir au sol; (*US Elec*) équiper d'une prise de terre, mettre à la terre ▷ *vi* (*ship*) s'échouer ▷ *adj* (*coffee etc*) moulu(e); (*US: meat*) haché(e); **grounds** *npl* (*gardens etc*) parc *m*, domaine *m*; (*of coffee*) marc *m*; **on the ~, to the ~** par terre; **below ~** sous terre; **to gain/lose ~** gagner/perdre du terrain; **common ~** terrain d'entente; **he covered a lot of ~ in his lecture** sa conférence a traité un grand nombre de questions *or* la question en profondeur

ground cloth *n* (*US*) = **groundsheet**

ground floor *n* (*Brit*) rez-de-chaussée *m*

grounding [ˈɡraundɪŋ] *n* (*in education*) connaissances *fpl* de base

groundless [ˈɡraundlɪs] *adj* sans fondement

groundsheet [ˈɡraundʃiːt] *n* (*Brit*) tapis *m* de sol

ground staff *n* équipage *m* au sol

groundwork [ˈɡraundwəːk] *n* préparation *f*

group [ɡruːp] *n* groupe *m* ▷ *vt* (*also*: **group together**) grouper ▷ *vi* (*also*: **group together**) se grouper

grouse [ɡraus] *n* (*pl inv: bird*) grouse *f* (*sorte de coq de bruyère*) ▷ *vi* (*complain*) rouspéter, râler

grove [ɡrəuv] *n* bosquet *m*

grovel [ˈɡrɔvl] *vi* (*fig*): **to ~ (before)** ramper (devant)

grow (*pt* **grew**, *pp* **~n**) [ɡrəu, ɡruː, ɡrəun] *vi* (*plant*) pousser, croître; (*person*) grandir; (*increase*) augmenter, se développer; (*become*) devenir; **to ~ rich/weak** s'enrichir/s'affaiblir ▷ *vt* cultiver, faire pousser; (*hair, beard*) laisser pousser

▶ **grow apart** *vi* (*fig*) se détacher (l'un de l'autre)

▶ **grow away from** *vt fus* (*fig*) s'éloigner de

▶ **grow on** *vt fus*: **that painting is ~ing on me** je finirai par aimer ce tableau

▶ **grow out of** *vt fus* (*clothes*) devenir trop grand pour; (*habit*) perdre (avec le temps); **he'll ~ out of it** ça lui passera

▶ **grow up** *vi* grandir

grower [ˈɡrəuəʳ] *n* producteur *m*; (*Agr*) cultivateur(-trice)

growing [ˈɡrəuɪŋ] *adj* (*fear, amount*) croissant(e), grandissant(e); **~ pains** (*Med*) fièvre *f* de croissance; (*fig*) difficultés *fpl* de croissance

growl [ɡraul] *vi* grogner

grown [grəun] *pp of* **grow** ▷ *adj* adulte
grown-up ['grəun'ʌp] *n* adulte *m/f*, grande personne
growth [grəuθ] *n* croissance *f*, développement *m*; (*what has grown*) pousse *f*; poussée *f*; (*Med*) grosseur *f*, tumeur *f*
grub [grʌb] *n* larve *f*; (*inf: food*) bouffe *f*
grubby ['grʌbɪ] *adj* crasseux(-euse)
grudge [grʌdʒ] *n* rancune *f* ▷ *vt*: **to ~ sb sth** (*in giving*) donner qch à qn à contre-cœur; (*resent*) reprocher qch à qn; **to bear sb a ~ (for)** garder rancune *or* en vouloir à qn (de); **he ~s spending** il rechigne à dépenser
gruelling, (US) **grueling** ['gruəlɪŋ] *adj* exténuant(e)
gruesome ['gru:səm] *adj* horrible
gruff [grʌf] *adj* bourru(e)
grumble ['grʌmbl] *vi* rouspéter, ronchonner
grumpy ['grʌmpɪ] *adj* grincheux(-euse)
grunt [grʌnt] *vi* grogner ▷ *n* grognement *m*
G-string ['dʒi:strɪŋ] *n* (*garment*) cache-sexe *m inv*
guarantee [gærən'ti:] *n* garantie *f* ▷ *vt* garantir; **he can't ~ (that) he'll come** il n'est pas absolument certain de pouvoir venir
guard [gɑːd] *n* garde *f*, surveillance *f*; (*squad: Boxing, Fencing*) garde *f*; (*one man*) garde *m*; (*Brit Rail*) chef *m* de train; (*safety device: on machine*) dispositif *m* de sûreté; (*also:* **fireguard**) garde-feu *m inv* ▷ *vt* garder, surveiller; (*protect*): **to ~ sb/sth (against** *or* **from)** protéger qn/qch (contre); **to be on one's ~** (*fig*) être sur ses gardes
▶ **guard against** *vi*: **to ~ against doing sth** se garder de faire qch
guarded ['gɑːdɪd] *adj* (*fig*) prudent(e)
guardian ['gɑːdɪən] *n* gardien(ne); (*of minor*) tuteur(-trice)
guard's van ['gɑːdz-] *n* (*Brit Rail*) fourgon *m*
guerrilla [gə'rɪlə] *n* guérillero *m*
guess [ges] *vi* deviner ▷ *vt* deviner; (*estimate*) évaluer; (US) croire, penser ▷ *n* supposition *f*, hypothèse *f*; **to take** *or* **have a ~** essayer de deviner; **to keep sb ~ing** laisser qn dans le doute *or* l'incertitude, tenir qn en haleine
guesswork ['geswə:k] *n* hypothèse *f*; **I got the answer by ~** j'ai deviné la réponse
guest [gest] *n* invité(e); (*in hotel*) client(e); **be my ~** faites comme chez vous
guest house ['gesthaus] *n* pension *f*
guest room *n* chambre *f* d'amis
guffaw [gʌ'fɔ:] *n* gros rire *m* ▷ *vi* pouffer de rire
guidance ['gaɪdəns] *n* (*advice*) conseils *mpl*; **under the ~ of** conseillé(e) *or* encadré(e) par, sous la conduite de; **vocational ~** orientation professionnelle; **marriage ~** conseils conjugaux
guide [gaɪd] *n* (*person*) guide *m/f*; (*book*) guide *m*; (*also:* **Girl Guide**) éclaireuse *f*; (*Roman Catholic*) guide *f* ▷ *vt* guider; **to be ~d by sb/sth** se laisser guider par qn/qch; **is there an English-speaking ~?** est-ce que l'un des guides parle anglais?
guidebook ['gaɪdbuk] *n* guide *m*; **do you have a ~ in English?** est-ce que vous avez un guide en anglais?
guide dog *n* chien *m* d'aveugle
guided tour *n* visite guidée; **what time does the ~ start?** la visite guidée commence à quelle heure?
guidelines ['gaɪdlaɪnz] *npl* (*advice*) instructions générales, conseils *mpl*
guild [gɪld] *n* (*History*) corporation *f*; (*sharing interests*) cercle *m*, association *f*
guillotine ['gɪləti:n] *n* guillotine *f*; (*for paper*) massicot *m*
guilt [gɪlt] *n* culpabilité *f*
guilty ['gɪltɪ] *adj* coupable; **to plead ~/not ~** plaider coupable/non coupable; **to feel ~ about doing sth** avoir mauvaise conscience à faire qch
guinea pig ['gɪnɪ-] *n* cobaye *m*
guise [gaɪz] *n* aspect *m*, apparence *f*
guitar [gɪ'tɑːʳ] *n* guitare *f*
guitarist [gɪ'tɑːrɪst] *n* guitariste *m/f*
gulf [gʌlf] *n* golfe *m*; (*abyss*) gouffre *m*; **the (Persian) G~** le golfe Persique
gull [gʌl] *n* mouette *f*
gullible ['gʌlɪbl] *adj* crédule
gully ['gʌlɪ] *n* ravin *m*; ravine *f*; couloir *m*
gulp [gʌlp] *vi* avaler sa salive; (*from emotion*) avoir la gorge serrée, s'étrangler ▷ *vt* (*also:* **gulp down**) avaler ▷ *n* (*of drink*) gorgée *f*; **at one ~** d'un seul coup
gum [gʌm] *n* (*Anat*) gencive *f*; (*glue*) colle *f*; (*sweet*) boule *f* de gomme; (*also:* **chewing-gum**) chewing-gum *m* ▷ *vt* coller
gumboots ['gʌmbu:ts] *npl* (*Brit*) bottes *fpl* en caoutchouc
gun [gʌn] *n* (*small*) revolver *m*, pistolet *m*; (*rifle*) fusil *m*, carabine *f*; (*cannon*) canon *m* ▷ *vt* (*also:* **gun down**) abattre; **to stick to one's ~s** (*fig*) ne pas en démordre
gunboat ['gʌnbəut] *n* canonnière *f*
gunfire ['gʌnfaɪəʳ] *n* fusillade *f*
gunman (*irreg*) ['gʌnmən] *n* bandit armé
gunpoint ['gʌnpɔɪnt] *n*: **at ~** sous la menace du pistolet (*or* fusil)
gunpowder ['gʌnpaudəʳ] *n* poudre *f* à canon
gunshot ['gʌnʃɔt] *n* coup *m* de feu; **within ~** à portée de fusil
gurgle ['gə:gl] *n* gargouillis *m* ▷ *vi* gargouiller
gush [gʌʃ] *n* jaillissement *m*, jet *m* ▷ *vi* jaillir; (*fig*) se répandre en effusions
gust [gʌst] *n* (*of wind*) rafale *f*; (*of smoke*) bouffée *f*
gusto ['gʌstəu] *n* enthousiasme *m*
gut [gʌt] *n* intestin *m*, boyau *m*; (*Mus etc*) boyau ▷ *vt* (*poultry, fish*) vider; (*building*) ne laisser que les murs de; **guts** *npl* (*Anat*) boyaux *mpl*; (*inf: courage*) cran *m*; **to hate sb's ~s** ne pas pouvoir voir qn en peinture *or* sentir qn
gutter ['gʌtəʳ] *n* (*of roof*) gouttière *f*; (*in street*) caniveau *m*; (*fig*) ruisseau *m*
guy [gaɪ] *n* (*inf: man*) type *m*; (*also:* **guyrope**) corde *f*; (*figure*) effigie de Guy Fawkes
Guy Fawkes' Night [gaɪ'fɔ:ks-] *n* *voir article*
guzzle ['gʌzl] *vi* s'empiffrer ▷ *vt* avaler gloutonnement

gym [dʒɪm] *n* (*also*: **gymnasium**) gymnase *m*;
(*also*: **gymnastics**) gym *f*

gymnasium [dʒɪm'neɪzɪəm] *n* gymnase *m*

gymnast ['dʒɪmnæst] *n* gymnaste *m/f*

gymnastics [dʒɪm'næstɪks] *n*, *npl* gymnastique *f*

gym shoes *npl* chaussures *fpl* de gym(nastique)

gynaecologist, (*US*) **gynecologist**
[gaɪnɪ'kɔlədʒɪst] *n* gynécologue *m/f*

gypsy ['dʒɪpsɪ] *n* gitan(e), bohémien(ne) ▷ *cpd*: ~
caravan *n* roulotte *f*

Hh

haberdashery [hæbə'dæʃərɪ] *n* (Brit) mercerie *f*

habit ['hæbɪt] *n* habitude *f*; (costume: Rel) habit *m*; (for riding) tenue *f* d'équitation; **to get out of/into the ~ of doing sth** perdre/prendre l'habitude de faire qch

habitat ['hæbɪtæt] *n* habitat *m*

habitual [hə'bɪtjuəl] *adj* habituel(le); (drinker, liar) invétéré(e)

hack [hæk] *vt* hacher, tailler ▷ *n* (cut) entaille *f*; (blow) coup *m*; (pej: writer) nègre *m*; (old horse) canasson *m*

hacker ['hækər] *n* (Comput) pirate *m* (informatique); (: enthusiast) passionné(e) *m/f* des ordinateurs

hackneyed ['hæknɪd] *adj* usé(e), rebattu(e)

had [hæd] *pt, pp of* **have**

haddock (pl - or -s) ['hædək] *n* églefin *m*; **smoked ~ haddock** *m*

hadn't ['hædnt] = **had not**

haemorrhage, (US) **hemorrhage** ['hɛmərɪdʒ] *n* hémorragie *f*

haemorrhoids, (US) **hemorrhoids** ['hɛmərɔɪdz] *npl* hémorroïdes *fpl*

haggle ['hægl] *vi* marchander; **to ~ over** chicaner sur

Hague [heɪg] *n*: **The ~** La Haye

hail [heɪl] *n* grêle *f* ▷ *vt* (call) héler; (greet) acclamer ▷ *vi* grêler; (originate): **he ~s from Scotland** il est originaire d'Écosse

hailstone ['heɪlstəun] *n* grêlon *m*

hair [hɛər] *n* cheveux *mpl*; (on body) poils *mpl*, pilosité *f*; (of animal) pelage *m*; (single hair: on head) cheveu *m*; (: on body, of animal) poil *m*; **to do one's ~** se coiffer

hairband ['hɛəbænd] *n* (elasticated) bandeau *m*; (plastic) serre-tête *m*

hairbrush ['hɛəbrʌʃ] *n* brosse *f* à cheveux

haircut ['hɛəkʌt] *n* coupe *f* (de cheveux)

hairdo ['hɛəduː] *n* coiffure *f*

hairdresser ['hɛədrɛsər] *n* coiffeur(-euse)

hairdresser's ['hɛədrɛsəz] *n* salon *m* de coiffure, coiffeur *m*

hair dryer ['hɛədraɪər] *n* sèche-cheveux *m*, séchoir *m*

hair gel *n* gel *m* pour cheveux

hairgrip ['hɛəgrɪp] *n* pince *f* à cheveux

hairnet ['hɛənɛt] *n* résille *f*

hairpiece ['hɛəpiːs] *n* postiche *m*

hairpin ['hɛəpɪn] *n* épingle *f* à cheveux

hairpin bend, (US) **hairpin curve** *n* virage *m* en épingle à cheveux

hair-raising ['hɛəreɪzɪŋ] *adj* à (vous) faire dresser les cheveux sur la tête

hair removing cream *n* crème *f* dépilatoire

hair spray *n* laque *f* (pour les cheveux)

hairstyle ['hɛəstaɪl] *n* coiffure *f*

hairy ['hɛərɪ] *adj* poilu(e), chevelu(e); (inf: frightening) effrayant(e)

hake (pl - or -s) [heɪk] *n* colin *m*, merlu *m*

half [hɑːf] *n* (pl **halves**) [hɑːvz] moitié *f*; (of beer: also: **half pint**) ≈ demi *m*; (Rail, bus: also: **half fare**) demi-tarif *m*; (Sport: of match) mi-temps *f*; (: of ground) moitié (du terrain) ▷ *adj* demi(e) ▷ *adv* (à) moitié, à demi; **~ an hour** une demi-heure; **~ a dozen** une demi-douzaine; **~ a pound** une demi-livre, ≈ 250 g; **two and a ~** deux et demi; **a week and a ~** une semaine et demie; **~ (of it)** la moitié; **~ (of)** la moitié de; **~ the amount of** la moitié de; **to cut sth in ~** couper qch en deux; **~ past three** trois heures et demie; **~ empty/closed** à moitié vide/fermé; **to go halves (with sb)** se mettre de moitié avec qn

half board *n* (Brit: in hotel) demi-pension *f*

half-brother ['hɑːfbrʌðər] *n* demi-frère *m*

half-caste ['hɑːfkɑːst] *n* (pej) métis(se)

half day *n* demi-journée *f*

half fare *n* demi-tarif *m*

half-hearted ['hɑːf'hɑːtɪd] *adj* tiède, sans enthousiasme

half-hour [hɑːf'auər] *n* demi-heure *f*

half-mast ['hɑːf'mɑːst] *n*: **at ~** (flag) en berne, à mi-mât

halfpenny ['heɪpnɪ] *n* demi-penny *m*

half-price ['hɑːf'praɪs] *adj* à moitié prix ▷ *adv* (also: **at half-price**) à moitié prix

half term *n* (Brit Scol) vacances *fpl* (de demi-trimestre)

half-time [hɑːf'taɪm] *n* mi-temps *f*

halfway ['hɑːf'weɪ] *adv* à mi-chemin; **to meet sb ~** (fig) parvenir à un compromis avec qn; **~ through sth** au milieu de qch

hall [hɔːl] *n* salle *f*; (entrance way: big) hall *m*; (small) entrée *f*; (US: corridor) couloir *m*; (mansion) château *m*, manoir *m*

hallmark ['hɔːlmɑːk] n poinçon m; (fig) marque f
hallo [hə'ləu] excl = **hello**
hall of residence n (Brit) pavillon m or résidence f universitaire
Hallowe'en, Halloween ['hæləu'iːn] n veille f de la Toussaint; voir article
hallucination [həluːsɪ'neɪʃən] n hallucination f
hallway ['hɔːlweɪ] n (entrance) vestibule m; (corridor) couloir m
halo ['heɪləu] n (of saint etc) auréole f; (of sun) halo m
halt [hɔːlt] n halte f, arrêt m ▷ vt faire arrêter; (progress etc) interrompre ▷ vi faire halte, s'arrêter; **to call a ~ to sth** (fig) mettre fin à qch
halve [hɑːv] vt (apple etc) partager or diviser en deux; (reduce by half) réduire de moitié
halves [hɑːvz] npl of **half**
ham [hæm] n jambon m; (inf: also: **radio ham**) radio-amateur m; (also: **ham actor**) cabotin(e)
hamburger ['hæmbəːgəʳ] n hamburger m
hamlet ['hæmlɪt] n hameau m
hammer ['hæməʳ] n marteau m ▷ vt (nail) enfoncer; (fig) éreinter, démolir ▷ vi (at door) frapper à coups redoublés; **to ~ a point home to sb** faire rentrer qch dans la tête de qn
▶ **hammer out** vt (metal) étendre au marteau; (fig: solution) élaborer
hammock ['hæmək] n hamac m
hamper ['hæmpəʳ] vt gêner ▷ n panier m (d'osier)
hamster ['hæmstəʳ] n hamster m
hamstring ['hæmstrɪŋ] n (Anat) tendon m du jarret
hand [hænd] n main f; (of clock) aiguille f; (handwriting) écriture f; (at cards) jeu m; (measurement: of horse) paume f; (worker) ouvrier(-ière) ▷ vt passer, donner; **to give sb a ~** donner un coup de main à qn; **at ~** à portée de la main; **in ~** (situation) en main; (work) en cours; **we have the situation in ~** nous avons la situation bien en main; **to be on ~** (person) être disponible; (emergency services) se tenir prêt(e) (à intervenir); **to ~** (information etc) sous la main, à portée de la main; **to force sb's ~** forcer la main à qn; **to have a free ~** avoir carte blanche; **to have sth in one's ~** tenir qch à la main; **on the one ~ ...**, **on the other ~** d'une part ..., d'autre part
▶ **hand down** vt passer; (tradition, heirloom) transmettre; (US: sentence, verdict) prononcer
▶ **hand in** vt remettre
▶ **hand out** vt distribuer
▶ **hand over** vt remettre; (powers etc) transmettre
▶ **hand round** vt (Brit: information) faire circuler; (: chocolates etc) faire passer
handbag ['hændbæg] n sac m à main
hand baggage n = **hand luggage**
handbook ['hændbuk] n manuel m
handbrake ['hændbreɪk] n frein m à main
handcuffs ['hændkʌfs] npl menottes fpl
handful ['hændful] n poignée f
handicap ['hændɪkæp] n handicap m ▷ vt

handicaper; mentally/physically ~ped handicapé(e) mentalement/physiquement
handicraft ['hændɪkrɑːft] n travail m d'artisanat, technique artisanale
handiwork ['hændɪwəːk] n ouvrage m; **this looks like his ~** (pej) ça a tout l'air d'être son œuvre
handkerchief ['hæŋkətʃɪf] n mouchoir m
handle ['hændl] n (of door etc) poignée f; (of cup etc) anse f; (of knife etc) manche m; (of saucepan) queue f; (for winding) manivelle f ▷ vt toucher, manier; (deal with) s'occuper de; (treat: people) prendre; **"~ with care"** "fragile"; **to fly off the ~** s'énerver
handlebar ['hændlbɑːʳ] n, **handlebars** ['hændlbɑːz] ▷ npl guidon m
hand luggage ['hændlʌgɪdʒ] n bagages mpl à main; **one item of ~** un bagage à main
handmade ['hændmeɪd] adj fait(e) à la main
handout ['hændaut] n (money) aide f, don m; (leaflet) prospectus m; (press handout) communiqué m de presse; (at lecture) polycopié m
handrail ['hændreɪl] n (on staircase etc) rampe f, main courante
handset ['hændset] n (Tel) combiné m
hands-free [hændz'friː] adj mains libres inv ▷ n (also: **hands-free kit**) kit m mains libres inv
handshake ['hændʃeɪk] n poignée f de main; (Comput) établissement m de la liaison
handsome ['hænsəm] adj beau (belle); (gift) généreux(-euse); (profit) considérable
handwriting ['hændraɪtɪŋ] n écriture f
handy ['hændɪ] adj (person) adroit(e); (close at hand) sous la main; (convenient) pratique; **to come in ~** être (or s'avérer) utile
hang (pt, pp **hung**) [hæŋ, hʌŋ] vt accrocher; (criminal) (pt, pp **-ed**) pendre ▷ vi pendre; (hair, drapery) tomber ▷ n: **to get the ~ of (doing) sth** (inf) attraper le coup pour faire qch
▶ **hang about, hang around** vi flâner, traîner
▶ **hang back** vi (hesitate): **to ~ back (from doing)** être réticent(e) (pour faire)
▶ **hang down** vi pendre
▶ **hang on** vi (wait) attendre ▷ vt fus (depend on) dépendre de; **to ~ on to** (keep hold of) ne pas lâcher; (keep) garder
▶ **hang out** vt (washing) étendre (dehors) ▷ vi pendre; (inf: live) habiter, percher; (: spend time) traîner
▶ **hang round** vi = **hang around**
▶ **hang together** vi (argument etc) se tenir, être cohérent(e)
▶ **hang up** vi (Tel) raccrocher ▷ vt (coat, painting etc) accrocher, suspendre; **to ~ up on sb** (Tel) raccrocher au nez de qn
hangar ['hæŋəʳ] n hangar m
hanger ['hæŋəʳ] n cintre m, portemanteau m
hanger-on [hæŋər'ɔn] n parasite m
hang-gliding ['hæŋglaɪdɪŋ] n vol m libre or sur aile delta
hangover ['hæŋəuvəʳ] n (after drinking) gueule f de bois
hang-up ['hæŋʌp] n complexe m

hanker ['hæŋkə^r] vi: **to ~ after** avoir envie de
hankie, hanky ['hæŋkɪ] n abbr = **handkerchief**
haphazard [hæp'hæzəd] adj fait(e) au hasard, fait(e) au petit bonheur
happen ['hæpən] vi arriver, se passer, se produire; **what's ~ing?** que se passe-t-il?; **she ~ed to be free** il s'est trouvé (or se trouvait) qu'elle était libre; **if anything ~ed to him** s'il lui arrivait quoi que ce soit; **as it ~s** justement
▸ **happen on, happen upon** vt fus tomber sur
happening ['hæpnɪŋ] n événement m
happily ['hæpɪlɪ] adv heureusement; (cheerfully) joyeusement
happiness ['hæpɪnɪs] n bonheur m
happy ['hæpɪ] adj heureux(-euse); **~ with** (arrangements etc) satisfait(e) de; **to be ~ to do** faire volontiers; **yes, I'd be ~ to** oui, avec plaisir or (bien) volontiers; **~ birthday!** bon anniversaire!; **~ Christmas/New Year!** joyeux Noël/bonne année!
happy-go-lucky ['hæpɪɡəʊ'lʌkɪ] adj insouciant(e)
happy hour n l'heure f de l'apéritif, heure pendant laquelle les consommations sont à prix réduit
harass ['hærəs] vt accabler, tourmenter
harassment ['hærəsmənt] n tracasseries fpl; **sexual ~** harcèlement sexuel
harbour, (US) **harbor** ['hɑːbə^r] n port m ▷ vt héberger, abriter; (hopes, suspicions) entretenir; **to ~ a grudge against sb** en vouloir à qn
hard [hɑːd] adj dur(e); (question, problem) difficile; (facts, evidence) concret(-ète) ▷ adv (work) dur; (think, try) sérieusement; **to look ~ at** regarder fixement; (thing) regarder de près; **to drink ~** boire sec; **~ luck!** pas de veine!; **no ~ feelings!** sans rancune!; **to be ~ of hearing** être dur(e) d'oreille; **to be ~ done by** être traité(e) injustement; **to be ~ on sb** être dur(e) avec qn; **I find it ~ to believe that ...** je n'arrive pas à croire que ...
hardback ['hɑːdbæk] n livre relié
hardboard ['hɑːdbɔːd] n Isorel® m
hard cash n espèces fpl
hard disk n (Comput) disque dur
harden ['hɑːdn] vt durcir; (steel) tremper; (fig) endurcir ▷ vi (substance) durcir
hard-headed [hɑːd'hɛdɪd] adj réaliste; décidé(e)
hard labour n travaux forcés
hardly ['hɑːdlɪ] adv (scarcely) à peine; (harshly) durement; **it's ~ the case** ce n'est guère le cas; **~ anywhere/ever** presque nulle part/jamais; **I can ~ believe it** j'ai du mal à le croire
hardship ['hɑːdʃɪp] n (difficulties) épreuves fpl; (deprivation) privations fpl
hard shoulder n (Brit Aut) accotement stabilisé
hard-up [hɑːd'ʌp] adj (inf) fauché(e)
hardware ['hɑːdwɛə^r] n quincaillerie f; (Comput, Mil) matériel m
hardware shop, (US) **hardware store** n quincaillerie f
hard-wearing [hɑːd'wɛərɪŋ] adj solide
hard-working [hɑːd'wəːkɪŋ] adj

travailleur(-euse), consciencieux(-euse)
hardy ['hɑːdɪ] adj robuste; (plant) résistant(e) au gel
hare [hɛə^r] n lièvre m
hare-brained ['hɛəbreɪnd] adj farfelu(e), écervelé(e)
harm [hɑːm] n mal m; (wrong) tort m ▷ vt (person) faire du mal or du tort à; (thing) endommager; **to mean no ~** ne pas avoir de mauvaises intentions; **there's no ~ in trying** on peut toujours essayer; **out of ~'s way** à l'abri du danger, en lieu sûr
harmful ['hɑːmful] adj nuisible
harmless [hɑːmlɪs] adj inoffensif(-ive)
harmony ['hɑːmənɪ] n harmonie f
harness ['hɑːnɪs] n harnais m ▷ vt (horse) harnacher; (resources) exploiter
harp [hɑːp] n harpe f ▷ vi: **to ~ on about** revenir toujours sur
harrowing ['hærəʊɪŋ] adj déchirant(e)
harsh [hɑːʃ] adj (hard) dur(e); (severe) sévère; (rough: surface) rugueux(-euse); (unpleasant: sound) discordant(e); (: light) cru(e); (: taste) âpre
harvest ['hɑːvɪst] n (of corn) moisson f; (of fruit) récolte f; (of grapes) vendange f ▷ vi, vt moissonner; récolter; vendanger
has [hæz] vb see **have**
hash [hæʃ] n (Culin) hachis m; (fig: mess) gâchis m ▷ n abbr (inf) = **hashish**
hasn't ['hæznt] = **has not**
hassle ['hæsl] n (inf: fuss) histoire(s) f(pl)
haste [heɪst] n hâte f, précipitation f; **in ~** à la hâte, précipitamment
hasten ['heɪsn] vt hâter, accélérer ▷ vi se hâter, s'empresser; **I ~ to add that ...** je m'empresse d'ajouter que ...
hastily ['heɪstɪlɪ] adv à la hâte; (leave) précipitamment
hasty ['heɪstɪ] adj (decision, action) hâtif(-ive); (departure, escape) précipité(e)
hat [hæt] n chapeau m
hatch [hætʃ] n (Naut: also: **hatchway**) écoutille f; (Brit: also: **service hatch**) passe-plats m inv ▷ vi éclore ▷ vt faire éclore; (fig: scheme) tramer, ourdir
hatchback ['hætʃbæk] n (Aut) modèle m avec hayon arrière
hatchet ['hætʃɪt] n hachette f
hate [heɪt] vt haïr, détester ▷ n haine f; **to ~ to do** or **doing** détester faire; **I ~ to trouble you, but ...** désolé de vous déranger, mais ...
hateful ['heɪtful] adj odieux(-euse), détestable
hatred ['heɪtrɪd] n haine f
haughty ['hɔːtɪ] adj hautain(e), arrogant(e)
haul [hɔːl] vt traîner, tirer; (by lorry) camionner; (Naut) haler ▷ n (of fish) prise f; (of stolen goods etc) butin m
haulage ['hɔːlɪdʒ] n transport routier
haulier ['hɔːlɪə^r], (US) **hauler** ['hɔːlə^r] n transporteur (routier), camionneur m
haunch [hɔːntʃ] n hanche f; **~ of venison** cuissot m de chevreuil

haunt [hɔːnt] vt (subj: ghost, fear) hanter; (: person) fréquenter ▷ n repaire m

haunted ['hɔːntɪd] adj (castle etc) hanté(e); (look) égaré(e), hagard(e)

have [hæv] (pt, pp **had**) aux vb **1** (gen) avoir; être; **to ~ eaten/slept** avoir mangé/dormi; **to ~ arrived/gone** être arrivé(e)/allé(e); **he has been promoted** il a eu une promotion; **having finished** or **when he had finished, he left** quand il a eu fini, il est parti; **we'd already eaten** nous avions déjà mangé

2 (in tag questions): **you've done it, ~n't you?** vous l'avez fait, n'est-ce pas?

3 (in short answers and questions): **no I ~n't!/yes we ~!** mais non!/mais si!; **so I ~!** ah oui!, oui c'est vrai!; **I've been there before, ~ you?** j'y suis déjà allé, et vous?

▷ modal aux vb (be obliged): **to ~ (got) to do sth** devoir faire qch, être obligé(e) de faire qch; **she has (got) to do it** elle doit le faire, il faut qu'elle le fasse; **you ~n't to tell her** vous n'êtes pas obligé de le lui dire; (must not) ne le lui dites surtout pas; **do you ~ to book?** il faut réserver?

▷ vt **1** (possess) avoir; **he has (got) blue eyes/dark hair** il a les yeux bleus/les cheveux bruns

2 (referring to meals etc): **to ~ breakfast** prendre le petit déjeuner; **to ~ dinner/lunch** dîner/déjeuner; **to ~ a drink** prendre un verre; **to ~ a cigarette** fumer une cigarette

3 (receive) avoir, recevoir; (obtain) avoir; **may I ~ your address?** puis-je avoir votre adresse?; **you can ~ it for £5** vous pouvez l'avoir pour 5 livres; **I must ~ it for tomorrow** il me le faut pour demain; **to ~ a baby** avoir un bébé

4 (maintain, allow): **I won't ~ it!** ça ne se passera pas comme ça!; **we can't ~ that** nous ne tolérerons pas ça

5 (by sb else): **to ~ sth done** faire faire qch; **to ~ one's hair cut** se faire couper les cheveux; **to ~ sb do sth** faire faire qch à qn

6 (experience, suffer) avoir; **to ~ a cold/flu** avoir un rhume/la grippe; **to ~ an operation** se faire opérer; **she had her bag stolen** elle s'est fait voler son sac

7 (+noun): **to ~ a swim/walk** nager/se promener; **to ~ a bath/shower** prendre un bain/une douche; **let's ~ a look** regardons; **to ~ a meeting** se réunir; **to ~ a party** organiser une fête; **let me ~ a try** laissez-moi essayer

8 (inf: dupe) avoir; **he's been had** il s'est fait avoir or rouler

▶ **have out** vt: **to ~ it out with sb** (settle a problem etc) s'expliquer (franchement) avec qn

haven ['heɪvn] n port m; (fig) havre m

haven't ['hævnt] = **have not**

havoc ['hævək] n ravages mpl, dégâts mpl; **to play ~ with** (fig) désorganiser complètement; détraquer

Hawaii [hə'waɪiː] n (îles fpl) Hawaï m

hawk [hɔːk] n faucon m ▷ vt (goods for sale) colporter

hawthorn ['hɔːθɔːn] n aubépine f

hay [heɪ] n foin m

hay fever n rhume m des foins

haystack ['heɪstæk] n meule f de foin

haywire ['heɪwaɪər] adj (inf): **to go ~** perdre la tête; mal tourner

hazard ['hæzəd] n (risk) danger m, risque m; (chance) hasard m, chance f ▷ vt risquer, hasarder; **to be a health/fire ~** présenter un risque pour la santé/d'incendie; **to ~ a guess** émettre or hasarder une hypothèse

hazardous ['hæzədəs] adj hasardeux(-euse), risqué(e)

hazard warning lights npl (Aut) feux mpl de détresse

haze [heɪz] n brume f

hazel [heɪzl] n (tree) noisetier m ▷ adj (eyes) noisette inv

hazelnut ['heɪzlnʌt] n noisette f

hazy ['heɪzɪ] adj brumeux(-euse); (idea) vague; (photograph) flou(e)

he [hiː] pron il; **it is he who ...** c'est lui qui ...; **here he is** le voici; **he-bear** etc ours etc mâle

head [hɛd] n tête f; (leader) chef m; (of school) directeur(-trice); (of secondary school) proviseur m ▷ vt (list) être en tête de; (group, company) être à la tête de; **heads** pl (on coin) (le côté) face; **~s or tails** pile ou face; **~ first** la tête la première; **~ over heels in love** follement or éperdument amoureux(-euse); **to ~ the ball** faire une tête; **10 euros a** or **per ~** 10 euros par personne; **to sit at the ~ of the table** présider la tablée; **to have a ~ for business** avoir des dispositions pour les affaires; **to have no ~ for heights** être sujet(te) au vertige; **to come to a ~** (fig: situation etc) devenir critique

▶ **head for** vt fus se diriger vers; (disaster) aller à

▶ **head off** vt (threat, danger) détourner

headache ['hɛdeɪk] n mal m de tête; **to have a ~** avoir mal à la tête

headdress ['hɛddrɛs] n coiffure f

heading ['hɛdɪŋ] n titre m; (subject title) rubrique f

headlamp ['hɛdlæmp] (Brit) n = **headlight**

headland ['hɛdlənd] n promontoire m, cap m

headlight ['hɛdlaɪt] n phare m

headline ['hɛdlaɪn] n titre m

headlong ['hɛdlɔŋ] adv (fall) la tête la première; (rush) tête baissée

headmaster [hɛd'mɑːstər] n directeur m, proviseur m

headmistress [hɛd'mɪstrɪs] n directrice f

head office n siège m, bureau m central

head-on [hɛd'ɔn] adj (collision) de plein fouet

headphones ['hɛdfəunz] npl casque m (à écouteurs)

headquarters ['hɛdkwɔːtəz] npl (of business) bureau or siège central; (Mil) quartier général

headrest ['hɛdrɛst] n appui-tête m

headroom ['hɛdrum] n (in car) hauteur f de plafond; (under bridge) hauteur limite; dégagement m

headscarf ['hɛdskɑːf] (pl **headscarves**) [-skɑːvz] n foulard m

headset ['hɛdsɛt] n = **headphones**

headstrong ['hɛdstrɒŋ] adj têtu(e), entêté(e)

headteacher [hɛd'tiːtʃəʳ] n directeur(-trice); (of secondary school) proviseur m

head waiter n maître m d'hôtel

headway ['hɛdweɪ] n: **to make ~** avancer, faire des progrès

headwind ['hɛdwɪnd] n vent m contraire

heady ['hɛdɪ] adj capiteux(-euse), enivrant(e)

heal [hiːl] vt, vi guérir

health [hɛlθ] n santé f; **Department of H~** (Brit, US) ≈ ministère m de la Santé

health care n services médicaux

health centre n (Brit) centre m de santé

health food n aliment(s) naturel(s)

health food shop n magasin m diététique

Health Service n: **the ~** (Brit) ≈ la Sécurité Sociale

healthy ['hɛlθɪ] adj (person) en bonne santé; (climate, food, attitude etc) sain(e)

heap [hiːp] n tas m, monceau m ▷ vt (also: **heap up**) entasser, amonceler; **she ~ed her plate with cakes** elle a chargé son assiette de gâteaux; **~s (of)** (inf: lots) des tas (de); **to ~ favours/praise/ gifts etc on sb** combler qn de faveurs/d'éloges/de cadeaux etc

hear (pt, pp **-d**) [hɪəʳ, həːd] vt entendre; (news) apprendre; (lecture) assister à, écouter ▷ vi entendre; **to ~ about** entendre parler de; (have news of) avoir des nouvelles de; **did you ~ about the move?** tu es au courant du déménagement?; **to ~ from sb** recevoir des nouvelles de qn; **I've never ~d of that book** je n'ai jamais entendu parler de ce livre

▶ **hear out** vt écouter jusqu'au bout

heard [həːd] pt, pp of **hear**

hearing ['hɪərɪŋ] n (sense) ouïe f; (of witnesses) audition f; (of a case) audience f; (of committee) séance f; **to give sb a ~** (Brit) écouter ce que qn a à dire

hearing aid n appareil m acoustique

hearsay ['hɪəseɪ] n on-dit mpl, rumeurs fpl; **by ~** adv par ouï-dire

hearse [həːs] n corbillard m

heart [hɑːt] n cœur m; **hearts** npl (Cards) cœur; **at ~** au fond; **by ~** (learn, know) par cœur; **to have a weak ~** avoir le cœur malade, avoir des problèmes de cœur; **to lose/take ~** perdre/ prendre courage; **to set one's ~ on sth/on doing sth** vouloir absolument qch/faire qch; **the ~ of the matter** le fond du problème

heart attack n crise f cardiaque

heartbeat ['hɑːtbiːt] n battement m de cœur

heartbreaking ['hɑːtbreɪkɪŋ] adj navrant(e), déchirant(e)

heartbroken ['hɑːtbrəukən] adj: **to be ~** avoir beaucoup de chagrin

heartburn ['hɑːtbəːn] n brûlures fpl d'estomac

heart disease n maladie f cardiaque

heart failure n (Med) arrêt m du cœur

heartfelt ['hɑːtfɛlt] adj sincère

hearth [hɑːθ] n foyer m, cheminée f

heartily ['hɑːtɪlɪ] adv chaleureusement; (laugh)

de bon cœur; (eat) de bon appétit; **to agree ~** être entièrement d'accord; **to be ~ sick of** (Brit) en avoir ras le bol de

heartless ['hɑːtlɪs] adj (person) sans cœur, insensible; (treatment) cruel(le)

hearty ['hɑːtɪ] adj chaleureux(-euse); (appetite) solide; (dislike) cordial(e); (meal) copieux(-euse)

heat [hiːt] n chaleur f; (fig) ardeur f; feu m; (Sport: also: **qualifying heat**) éliminatoire f; (Zool): **in** or **on ~** (Brit) en chaleur ▷ vt chauffer

▶ **heat up** vi (liquid) chauffer; (room) se réchauffer ▷ vt réchauffer

heated ['hiːtɪd] adj chauffé(e); (fig) passionné(e), échauffé(e), excité(e)

heater ['hiːtəʳ] n appareil m de chauffage; radiateur m; (in car) chauffage m; (water heater) chauffe-eau m

heath [hiːθ] n (Brit) lande f

heather ['hɛðəʳ] n bruyère f

heating ['hiːtɪŋ] n chauffage m

heatstroke ['hiːtstrəuk] n coup m de chaleur

heatwave ['hiːtweɪv] n vague f de chaleur

heave [hiːv] vt soulever (avec effort) ▷ vi se soulever; (retch) avoir des haut-le-cœur ▷ n (push) poussée f; **to ~ a sigh** pousser un gros soupir

heaven ['hɛvn] n ciel m, paradis m; (fig) paradis; **~ forbid!** surtout pas!; **thank ~!** Dieu merci!; **for ~`s sake!** (pleading) je vous en prie!; (protesting) mince alors!

heavenly ['hɛvnlɪ] adj céleste, divin(e)

heavily ['hɛvɪlɪ] adv lourdement; (drink, smoke) beaucoup; (sleep, sigh) profondément

heavy ['hɛvɪ] adj lourd(e); (work, rain, user, eater) gros(se); (drinker, smoker) grand(e); (schedule, week) chargé(e); **it's too ~** c'est trop lourd; **it's ~ going** ça ne va pas tout seul, c'est pénible

heavy goods vehicle n (Brit) poids lourd m

heavyweight ['hɛvɪweɪt] n (Sport) poids lourd

Hebrew ['hiːbruː] adj hébraïque ▷ n (Ling) hébreu m

Hebrides ['hɛbrɪdiːz] npl: **the ~** les Hébrides fpl

heckle ['hɛkl] vt interpeller (un orateur)

hectare ['hɛktɑːʳ] n (Brit) hectare m

hectic ['hɛktɪk] adj (schedule) très chargé(e); (day) mouvementé(e); (activity) fiévreux(-euse); (lifestyle) trépidant(e)

he'd [hiːd] = **he would**; **he had**

hedge [hɛdʒ] n haie f ▷ vi se dérober ▷ vt: **to ~ one's bets** (fig) se couvrir; **as a ~ against inflation** pour se prémunir contre l'inflation

▶ **hedge in** vt entourer d'une haie

hedgehog ['hɛdʒhɒg] n hérisson m

heed [hiːd] vt (also: **take heed of**) tenir compte de, prendre garde à

heedless ['hiːdlɪs] adj insouciant(e)

heel [hiːl] n talon m ▷ vt (shoe) retalonner; **to bring to ~** (dog) faire venir à ses pieds; (fig: person) rappeler à l'ordre; **to take to one's ~s** prendre ses jambes à son cou

hefty ['hɛftɪ] adj (person) costaud(e); (parcel) lourd(e); (piece, price) gros(se)

heifer ['hɛfəʳ] n génisse f

height [haɪt] n (of person) taille f, grandeur f; (of object) hauteur f; (of plane, mountain) altitude f; (high ground) hauteur f, éminence f; (fig: of glory, fame, power) sommet m; (: of luxury, stupidity) comble m; **at the ~ of summer** au cœur de l'été; **what ~ are you?** combien mesurez-vous?, quelle est votre taille?; **of average ~** de taille moyenne; **to be afraid of ~s** être sujet(te) au vertige; **it's the ~ of fashion** c'est le dernier cri

heighten ['haɪtn] vt hausser, surélever; (fig) augmenter

heir [ɛəʳ] n héritier m

heiress ['ɛərɛs] n héritière f

heirloom ['ɛəluːm] n meuble m (or bijou m or tableau m) de famille

held [hɛld] pt, pp of **hold**

helicopter ['hɛlɪkɔptəʳ] n hélicoptère m

hell [hɛl] n enfer m; **a ~ of a ...** (inf) un(e) sacré(e) ...; **oh ~!** (inf) merde!

he'll [hiːl] = **he will; he shall**

hellish ['hɛlɪʃ] adj infernal(e)

hello [hə'ləu] excl bonjour!; (to attract attention) hé!; (surprise) tiens!

helm [hɛlm] n (Naut) barre f

helmet ['hɛlmɪt] n casque m

help [hɛlp] n aide f; (cleaner etc) femme f de ménage; (assistant etc) employé(e) ▷ vt, vi aider; **~!** au secours!; **~ yourself** servez-vous; **can you ~ me?** pouvez-vous m'aider?; **can I ~ you?** (in shop) vous désirez?; **with the ~ of** (person) avec l'aide de; (tool etc) à l'aide de; **to be of ~ to sb** être utile à qn; **to ~ sb (to) do sth** aider qn à faire qch; **I can't ~ ~ saying** je ne peux pas m'empêcher de dire; **he can't ~ it** il n'y peut rien
▶ **help out** vi aider ▷ vt: **to ~ sb out** aider qn

helper ['hɛlpəʳ] n aide m/f, assistant(e)

helpful ['hɛlpful] adj serviable, obligeant(e); (useful) utile

helping ['hɛlpɪŋ] n portion f

helpless ['hɛlplɪs] adj impuissant(e); (baby) sans défense

helpline ['hɛlplaɪn] n service m d'assistance téléphonique; ≈ numéro vert

hem [hɛm] n ourlet m ▷ vt ourler
▶ **hem in** vt cerner; **to feel ~med in** (fig) avoir l'impression d'étouffer, se sentir oppressé(e) or écrasé(e)

hemisphere ['hɛmɪsfɪəʳ] n hémisphère m

hemorrhage ['hɛmərɪdʒ] n (US) = **haemorrhage**

hemorrhoids ['hɛmərɔɪdz] npl (US) = **haemorrhoids**

hen [hɛn] n poule f; (female bird) femelle f

hence [hɛns] adv (therefore) d'où, de là; **2 years ~** d'ici 2 ans

henceforth [hɛns'fɔːθ] adv dorénavant

hen night, hen party n soirée f entre filles (avant le mariage de l'une d'elles)

hepatitis [hɛpə'taɪtɪs] n hépatite f

her [həːʳ] pron (direct) la, l' + vowel or h mute; (indirect) lui; (stressed, after prep) elle ▷ adj son (sa), ses pl; **I see ~** je la vois; **give ~ a book** donne-lui un livre; **after ~** après elle; see also **me; my**

herald ['hɛrəld] n héraut m ▷ vt annoncer

heraldry ['hɛrəldrɪ] n héraldique f; (coat of arms) blason m

herb [həːb] n herbe f; **herbs** npl fines herbes

herbal ['həːbl] adj à base de plantes

herbal tea n tisane f

herd [həːd] n troupeau m; (of wild animals, swine) troupeau, troupe f ▷ vt (drive: animals, people) mener, conduire; (gather) rassembler; **~ed together** parqués (comme du bétail)

here [hɪəʳ] adv ici; (time) alors ▷ excl tiens!, tenez!; **~!** (present) présent!; **~ is, ~ are** voici; **~'s my sister** voici ma sœur; **~ he/she is** la (voici; **~ she comes** la voici qui vient; **come ~!** viens ici!; **~ and there** ici et là

hereafter [hɪər'ɑːftəʳ] adv après, plus tard; ci-après ▷ n: **the ~** l'au-delà m

hereby [hɪə'baɪ] adv (in letter) par la présente

hereditary [hɪ'rɛdɪtrɪ] adj héréditaire

heresy ['hɛrəsɪ] n hérésie f

heritage ['hɛrɪtɪdʒ] n héritage m, patrimoine m; **our national ~** notre patrimoine national

hermit ['həːmɪt] n ermite m

hernia ['həːnɪə] n hernie f

hero ['hɪərəu] (pl -es) n héros m

heroic [hɪ'rəuɪk] adj héroïque

heroin ['hɛrəuɪn] n héroïne f (drogue)

heroine ['hɛrəuɪn] n héroïne f (femme)

heron ['hɛrən] n héron m

herring ['hɛrɪŋ] n hareng m

hers [həːz] pron le (la) sien(ne), les siens (siennes); **a friend of ~** un(e) ami(e) à elle, un(e) de ses ami(e)s; see also **mine¹**

herself [həː'sɛlf] pron (reflexive) se; (emphatic) elle-même; (after prep) elle; see also **oneself**

he's [hiːz] = **he is; he has**

hesitant ['hɛzɪtənt] adj hésitant(e), indécis(e); **to be ~ about doing sth** hésiter à faire qch

hesitate ['hɛzɪteɪt] vi: **to ~ (about/to do)** hésiter (sur/à faire)

hesitation [hɛzɪ'teɪʃən] n hésitation f; **I have no ~ in saying (that) ...** je n'hésiterais pas à dire (que) ...

heterosexual ['hɛtərəu'sɛksjuəl] adj, n hétérosexuel(le)

hexagon ['hɛksəgən] n hexagone m

hey [heɪ] excl hé!

heyday ['heɪdeɪ] n: **the ~ of** l'âge m d'or de, les beaux jours de

HGV n abbr = **heavy goods vehicle**

hi [haɪ] excl salut!; (to attract attention) hé!

hiatus [haɪ'eɪtəs] n trou m, lacune f; (Ling) hiatus m

hibernate ['haɪbəneɪt] vi hiberner

hiccough, hiccup ['hɪkʌp] vi hoqueter ▷ n hoquet m; **to have (the) ~s** avoir le hoquet

hid [hɪd] pt of **hide**

hidden ['hɪdn] pp of **hide** ▷ adj: **there are no ~ extras** absolument tout est compris dans le prix; **~ agenda** intentions non déclarées

hide [haɪd] (pt **hid**, pp **hidden**) [hɪd, 'hɪdn] n (skin) peau f ▷ vt cacher; (feelings, truth) dissimuler; **to**

~ **sth from sb** cacher qch à qn ▷ vi: **to ~ (from sb)** se cacher (de qn)

hide-and-seek ['haɪdən'siːk] n cache-cache m

hideous ['hɪdɪəs] adj hideux(-euse), atroce

hiding ['haɪdɪŋ] n (beating) volée f de coups; **to be in ~** (concealed) se tenir caché(e)

hierarchy ['haɪərɑːkɪ] n hiérarchie f

hi-fi ['haɪfaɪ] adj, n abbr (= high fidelity) hi-fi f inv

high [haɪ] adj haut(e); (speed, respect, number) grand(e); (price) élevé(e); (wind) fort(e), violent(e); (voice) aigu(ë); (inf: person: on drugs) défoncé(e), fait(e); (: on drink) soûl(e), bourré(e); (Brit Culin: meat, game) faisandé(e); (: spoilt) avarié(e) ▷ adv haut, en haut ▷ n (weather) zone f de haute pression; **exports have reached a new ~** les exportations ont atteint un nouveau record; **20 m ~** haut(e) de 20 m; **to pay a ~ price for sth** payer cher pour qch; ~ **in the air** haut dans le ciel

highbrow ['haɪbrau] adj, n intellectuel(le)

highchair ['haɪtʃɛəʳ] n (child's) chaise haute

high-class ['haɪ'klɑːs] adj (neighbourhood, hotel) chic inv, de grand standing; (performance etc) de haut niveau

higher education n études supérieures

high-handed [haɪ'hændɪd] adj très autoritaire; très cavalier(-ière)

high-heeled [haɪ'hiːld] adj à hauts talons

high heels npl talons hauts, hauts talons

high jump n (Sport) saut m en hauteur

highlands ['haɪləndz] npl région montagneuse; **the H~** (in Scotland) les Highlands mpl

highlight ['haɪlaɪt] n (fig: of event) point culminant ▷ vt (emphasize) faire ressortir, souligner; **highlights** npl (in hair) reflets mpl

highlighter ['haɪlaɪtəʳ] n (pen) surligneur (lumineux)

highly ['haɪlɪ] adv extrêmement, très; (unlikely) fort; (recommended, skilled, qualified) hautement; ~ **paid** très bien payé(e); **to speak ~ of** dire beaucoup de bien de

highly strung adj nerveux(-euse), toujours tendu(e)

highness ['haɪnɪs] n hauteur f; **His/Her H~** son Altesse f

high-pitched [haɪ'pɪtʃt] adj aigu(ë)

high-rise ['haɪraɪz] n (also: **high-rise block, high-rise building**) tour f (d'habitation)

high school n lycée m; (US) établissement m d'enseignement supérieur; voir article

high season n (Brit) haute saison

high street n (Brit) grand-rue f

high-tech ['haɪ'tɛk] (inf) adj de pointe

highway ['haɪweɪ] n (Brit) route f; (US) route nationale; **the information ~** l'autoroute f de l'information

Highway Code n (Brit) code m de la route

hijack ['haɪdʒæk] vt détourner (par la force) ▷ n (also: **hijacking**) détournement m (d'avion)

hijacker ['haɪdʒækəʳ] n auteur m d'un détournement d'avion, pirate m de l'air

hike [haɪk] vi faire des excursions à pied ▷ n excursion f à pied, randonnée f; (inf: in prices etc) augmentation f ▷ vt (inf) augmenter

hiker ['haɪkəʳ] n promeneur(-euse), excursionniste m/f

hiking ['haɪkɪŋ] n excursions fpl à pied, randonnée f

hilarious [hɪ'lɛərɪəs] adj (behaviour, event) désopilant(e)

hill [hɪl] n colline f; (fairly high) montagne f; (on road) côte f

hillside ['hɪlsaɪd] n (flanc m de) coteau m

hill walking ['hɪl'wɔːkɪŋ] n randonnée f de basse montagne

hilly ['hɪlɪ] adj vallonné(e), montagneux(-euse); (road) à fortes côtes

hilt [hɪlt] n (of sword) garde f; **to the ~** (fig: support) à fond

him [hɪm] pron (direct) le, l' + vowel or h mute; (stressed, indirect, after prep) lui; **I see ~** je le vois; **give ~ a book** donne-lui un livre; **after ~** après lui; see also **me**

himself [hɪm'sɛlf] pron (reflexive) se; (emphatic) lui-même; (after prep) lui; see also **oneself**

hind [haɪnd] adj de derrière ▷ n biche f

hinder ['hɪndəʳ] vt gêner, (delay) retarder; (prevent): **to ~ sb from doing** empêcher qn de faire

hindrance ['hɪndrəns] n gêne f, obstacle m

hindsight ['haɪndsaɪt] n bon sens après coup; **with (the benefit of) ~** avec du recul, rétrospectivement

Hindu ['hɪnduː] n Hindou(e)

Hinduism ['hɪnduɪzəm] n (Rel) hindouisme m

hinge [hɪndʒ] n charnière f ▷ vi (fig): **to ~ on** dépendre de

hint [hɪnt] n allusion f; (advice) conseil m; (clue) indication f ▷ vt: **to ~ that** insinuer que ▷ vi: **to ~ at** faire une allusion à; **to drop a ~** faire une allusion or insinuation; **give me a ~** (clue) mettez-moi sur la voie, donnez-moi une indication

hip [hɪp] n hanche f; (Bot) fruit m de l'églantier or du rosier

hippie, hippy ['hɪpɪ] n hippie m/f

hippo ['hɪpəu] (pl **-s**) n hippopotame m

hippopotamus [hɪpə'pɔtəməs] **-es** or **hippopotami** [hɪpə'pɔtəmaɪ] (pl n hippopotame m

hippy ['hɪpɪ] n = **hippie**

hire ['haɪəʳ] vt (Brit: car, equipment) louer; (worker) embaucher, engager ▷ n location f; **for ~** à louer; (taxi) libre; **on ~** en location; **I'd like to ~ a car** je voudrais louer une voiture
  ▶ **hire out** vt louer

hire car, hired car ['haɪəd-] n (Brit) voiture f de location

hire purchase n (Brit) achat m (or vente f) à tempérament or crédit; **to buy sth on ~** acheter qch en location-vente

his [hɪz] pron le (la) sien(ne), les siens (siennes) ▷ adj son (sa), ses pl; **this is ~** c'est à lui, c'est le sien; **a friend of ~** un(e) de ses ami(e)s, un(e) ami(e) à lui; *see also* **mine'**; *see also* **my**

Hispanic [hɪs'pænɪk] *adj* (*in US*) hispano-américain(e) ▷ *n* Hispano-Américain(e)

hiss [hɪs] *vi* siffler ▷ *n* sifflement *m*

historian [hɪ'stɔːrɪən] *n* historien(ne)

historic [hɪ'stɔrɪk], **historical** [hɪ'stɔrɪkl] *adj* historique

history ['hɪstərɪ] *n* histoire *f*; **medical ~** (*of patient*) passé médical

hit [hɪt] *vt* (*pt, pp* **~**) frapper; (*knock against*) cogner; (*reach: target*) atteindre, toucher; (*collide with: car*) entrer en collision avec, heurter; (*fig: affect*) toucher; (*find*) tomber sur ▷ *n* coup *m*; (*success*) coup réussi; succès *m*; (*song*) chanson *f* à succès, tube *m*; (*to website*) visite *f*; (*on search engine*) résultat *m* de recherche; **to ~ it off with sb** bien s'entendre avec qn; **to ~ the headlines** être à la une des journaux; **to ~ the road** (*inf*) se mettre en route

▸ **hit back** *vi*: **to ~ back at sb** prendre sa revanche sur qn

▸ **hit on** *vt fus* (*answer*) trouver (par hasard); (*solution*) tomber sur (par hasard)

▸ **hit out at** *vt fus* envoyer un coup à; (*fig*) attaquer

▸ **hit upon** *vt fus* = **hit on**

hit-and-run driver ['hɪtænd'rʌn-] *n* chauffard *m*

hitch [hɪtʃ] *vt* (*fasten*) accrocher, attacher; (*also:* **hitch up**) remonter d'une saccade ▷ *vi* faire de l'autostop ▷ *n* (*knot*) nœud *m*; (*difficulty*) anicroche *f*, contretemps *m*; **to ~ a lift** faire du stop; **technical ~** incident *m* technique

▸ **hitch up** *vt* (*horse, cart*) atteler; *see also* **hitch**

hitch-hike ['hɪtʃhaɪk] *vi* faire de l'auto-stop

hitch-hiker ['hɪtʃhaɪkəʳ] *n* auto-stoppeur(-euse)

hitch-hiking ['hɪtʃhaɪkɪŋ] *n* auto-stop *m*, stop *m* (*inf*)

hi-tech ['haɪtɛk] *adj* de pointe ▷ *n* high-tech *m*

hitherto [hɪðə'tuː] *adv* jusqu'ici, jusqu'à présent

hitman ['hɪtmæn] (*irreg*) *n* (*inf*) tueur *m* à gages

HIV *n abbr* (= *human immunodeficiency virus*) HIV *m*, VIH *m*; **~-negative/positive** séronégatif(-ive)/positif(-ive)

hive [haɪv] *n* ruche *f*; **the shop was a ~ of activity** (*fig*) le magasin était une véritable ruche

▸ **hive off** *vt* (*inf*) mettre à part, séparer

HMS *abbr* (*Brit*) = **His (or Her) Majesty's Ship**

hoard [hɔːd] *n* (*of food*) provisions *fpl*, réserves *fpl*; (*of money*) trésor *m* ▷ *vt* amasser

hoarding ['hɔːdɪŋ] *n* (*Brit*) panneau *m* d'affichage *or* publicitaire

hoarse [hɔːs] *adj* enroué(e)

hoax [həuks] *n* canular *m*

hob [hɔb] *n* plaque chauffante

hobble ['hɔbl] *vi* boitiller

hobby ['hɔbɪ] *n* passe-temps favori

hobo ['həubəu] *n* (*US*) vagabond *m*

hockey ['hɔkɪ] *n* hockey *m*

hockey stick *n* crosse *f* de hockey

hog [hɔg] *n* porc (châtré) ▷ *vt* (*fig*) accaparer; **to go the whole ~** aller jusqu'au bout

Hogmanay [hɔgmə'neɪ] *n* réveillon *m* du jour de l'An, Saint-Sylvestre *f*; *voir article*

hoist [hɔɪst] *n* palan *m* ▷ *vt* hisser

hold [həuld] (*pt, pp* **held**) [hɛld] *vt* tenir; (*contain*) contenir; (*meeting*) tenir; (*keep back*) retenir; (*believe*) maintenir; considérer; (*possess*) avoir; détenir ▷ *vi* (*withstand pressure*) tenir (bon); (*be valid*) valoir; (*on telephone*) attendre ▷ *n* prise *f*; (*fig*) influence *f*; (*Naut*) cale *f*; **to catch** *or* **get (a) ~ of** saisir; **to get ~ of** (*find*) trouver; **to get ~ of o.s.** se contrôler; **~ the line!** (*Tel*) ne quittez pas!; **to ~ one's own** (*fig*) (bien) se défendre; **to ~ office** (*Pol*) avoir un portefeuille; **to ~ firm** *or* **fast** tenir bon; **he ~s the view that ...** il pense *or* estime que ..., d'après lui ...; **to ~ sb responsible for sth** tenir qn pour responsable de qch

▸ **hold back** *vt* retenir; (*secret*) cacher; **to ~ sb back from doing sth** empêcher qn de faire qch

▸ **hold down** *vt* (*person*) maintenir à terre; (*job*) occuper

▸ **hold forth** *vi* pérorer

▸ **hold off** *vt* tenir à distance ▷ *vi*: **if the rain ~s off** s'il ne pleut pas, s'il ne se met pas à pleuvoir

▸ **hold on** *vi* tenir bon; (*wait*) attendre; **~ on!** (*Tel*) ne quittez pas!; **to ~ on to sth** (*grasp*) se cramponner à qch; (*keep*) conserver *or* garder qch

▸ **hold out** *vt* offrir ▷ *vi* (*resist*): **to ~ out (against)** résister (devant), tenir bon (devant)

▸ **hold over** *vt* (*meeting etc*) ajourner, reporter

▸ **hold up** *vt* (*raise*) lever; (*support*) soutenir; (*delay*) retarder; (*: traffic*) ralentir; (*rob*) braquer

holdall ['həuldɔːl] *n* (*Brit*) fourre-tout *m inv*

holder ['həuldəʳ] *n* (*container*) support *m*; (*of ticket, record*) détenteur(-trice); (*of office, title, passport etc*) titulaire *m/f*

holding ['həuldɪŋ] *n* (*share*) intérêts *mpl*; (*farm*) ferme *f*

hold-up ['həuldʌp] *n* (*robbery*) hold-up *m*; (*delay*) retard *m*; (*Brit: in traffic*) embouteillage *m*

hole [həul] *n* trou *m* ▷ *vt* trouer, faire un trou dans; **~ in the heart** (*Med*) communication *f* interventriculaire; **to pick ~s (in)** (*fig*) chercher des poux (dans)

▸ **hole up** *vi* se terrer

holiday ['hɔlədɪ] *n* (*Brit: vacation*) vacances *fpl*; (*day off*) jour *m* de congé; (*public*) jour férié; **to be on ~** être en vacances; **I'm here on ~** je suis ici en vacances; **tomorrow is a ~** demain c'est fête on a congé demain

holiday camp *n* (*Brit: for children*) colonie *f* de vacances; (*also:* **holiday centre**) camp *m* de vacances

holiday job *n* (*Brit*) boulot *m* (*inf*) de vacances

holiday-maker ['hɔlədɪmeɪkəʳ] *n* (*Brit*) vacancier(-ière)

holiday resort *n* centre *m* de villégiature *or* de vacances

Holland ['hɔlənd] *n* Hollande *f*

hollow ['hɔləu] *adj* creux(-euse); (*fig*) faux (fausse) ▷ *n* creux *m*; (*in land*) dépression *f* (de terrain), cuvette *f* ▷ *vt*: **to ~ out** creuser, évider

holly ['hɔlɪ] *n* houx *m*

holocaust ['hɔləkɔːst] n holocauste m

holster ['həulstə^r] n étui m de revolver

holy ['həulı] adj saint(e); (bread, water) bénit(e); (ground) sacré(e)

Holy Ghost, Holy Spirit n Saint-Esprit m

homage ['hɔmɪdʒ] n hommage m; **to pay ~ to** rendre hommage à

home [həum] n foyer m, maison f; (country) pays natal, patrie f; (institution) maison ▷ adj de famille; (Econ, Pol) national(e), intérieur(e); (Sport: team) qui reçoit; (: match, win) sur leur (or notre) terrain ▷ adv chez soi, à la maison; au pays natal; (right in: nail etc) à fond; **at ~** chez soi, à la maison; **to go** (or **come**) **~** rentrer (chez soi), rentrer à la maison (or au pays); **I'm going ~ on Tuesday** je rentre mardi; **make yourself at ~** faites comme chez vous; **near my ~** près de chez moi

▶ **home in on** vt fus (missile) se diriger automatiquement vers or sur

home address n domicile permanent

homeland ['həumlænd] n patrie f

homeless ['həumlɪs] adj sans foyer, sans abri; **the homeless** npl les sans-abri mpl

homely ['həumlı] adj (plain) simple, sans prétention; (welcoming) accueillant(e)

home-made [həum'meɪd] adj fait(e) à la maison

home match n match m à domicile

Home Office n (Brit) ministère m de l'Intérieur

homeopathy etc [həumɪ'ɔpəθɪ] (US) = **homoeopathy** etc

home owner ['həuməunə^r] n propriétaire occupant

home page n (Comput) page f d'accueil

home rule n autonomie f

Home Secretary n (Brit) ministre m de l'Intérieur

homesick ['həumsɪk] adj: **to be ~** avoir le mal du pays; (missing one's family) s'ennuyer de sa famille

home town n ville natale

homeward ['həumwəd] adj (journey) du retour ▷ adv = **homewards**

homework ['həumwə:k] n devoirs mpl

homicide ['hɔmɪsaɪd] n (US) homicide m

homoeopathic, (US) **homeopathic** [həumɪə'pæθɪk] adj (medicine) homéopathique; (doctor) homéopathe

homoeopathy, (US) **homeopathy** [həumɪ'ɔpəθɪ] n homéopathie f

homogeneous [hɔməu'dʒiːnɪəs] adj homogène

homosexual [hɔməu'sɛksjuəl] adj, n homosexuel(le)

honest ['ɔnɪst] adj honnête; (sincere) franc (franche); **to be quite ~ with you ...** à dire vrai ...

honestly ['ɔnɪstlɪ] adv honnêtement; franchement

honesty ['ɔnɪstɪ] n honnêteté f

honey ['hʌnɪ] n miel m; (inf: darling) chéri(e)

honeycomb ['hʌnɪkəum] n rayon m de miel; (pattern) nid m d'abeilles, motif alvéolé ▷ vt (fig): **to ~ with** cribler de

honeymoon ['hʌnɪmuːn] n lune f de miel, voyage m de noces; **we're on ~** nous sommes en voyage de noces

honeysuckle ['hʌnɪsʌkl] n chèvrefeuille m

Hong Kong ['hɔŋ'kɔŋ] n Hong Kong

honk [hɔŋk] n (Aut) coup m de klaxon ▷ vi klaxonner

honorary ['ɔnərərɪ] adj honoraire; (duty, title) honorifique; **~ degree** diplôme m honoris causa

honour, (US) **honor** ['ɔnə^r] vt honorer ▷ n honneur m; **in ~ of** en l'honneur de; **to graduate with ~s** obtenir sa licence avec mention

honourable, (US) **honorable** ['ɔnərəbl] adj honorable (US)

honours degree ['ɔnəz-] n (Scol) ≈ licence f avec mention

hood [hud] n capuchon m; (of cooker) hotte f; (Brit Aut) capote f; (US Aut) capot m; (inf) truand m

hoodie ['hudɪ] n (top) sweat m à capuche

hoof (pl **-s** or **hooves**) [huːf, huːvz] n sabot m

hook [huk] n crochet m; (on dress) agrafe f; (for fishing) hameçon m ▷ vt accrocher; (dress) agrafer; **off the ~** (Tel) décroché; **~ and eye** agrafe; **by ~ or by crook** de gré ou de force, coûte que coûte; **to be ~ed (on)** (inf) être accroché(e) (par); (person) être dingue (de)

▶ **hook up** vt (Radio, TV etc) faire un duplex entre

hooligan ['huːlɪgən] n voyou m

hoop [huːp] n cerceau m; (of barrel) cercle m

hoot [huːt] vi (Brit: Aut) klaxonner; (siren) mugir; (owl) hululer ▷ vt (jeer at) huer ▷ n huée f; coup m de klaxon; mugissement m; hululement m; **to ~ with laughter** rire aux éclats

hooter ['huːtə^r] n (Brit Aut) klaxon m; (Naut, factory) sirène f

Hoover® ['huːvə^r] n (Brit) aspirateur m ▷ vt: **to hoover** (room) passer l'aspirateur dans; (carpet) passer l'aspirateur sur

hooves [huːvz] npl of **hoof**

hop [hɔp] vi sauter; (on one foot) sauter à cloche-pied; (bird) sautiller ▷ n saut m

hope [həup] vt, vi espérer ▷ n espoir m; **I ~ so** je l'espère; **I ~ not** j'espère que non

hopeful ['həupful] adj (person) plein(e) d'espoir; (situation) prometteur(-euse), encourageant(e); **I'm ~ that she'll manage to come** j'ai bon espoir qu'elle pourra venir

hopefully ['həupfulɪ] adv (expectantly) avec espoir, avec optimisme; (one hopes) avec un peu de chance; **~, they'll come back** espérons bien qu'ils reviendront

hopeless ['həuplɪs] adj désespéré(e), sans espoir; (useless) nul(le)

hops [hɔps] npl houblon m

horizon [hə'raɪzn] n horizon m

horizontal [hɔrɪ'zɔntl] adj horizontal(e)

hormone ['hɔːməun] n hormone f

horn [hɔːn] n corne f; (Mus) cor m; (Aut) klaxon m

hornet ['hɔːnɪt] n frelon m

horoscope ['hɔrəskəup] n horoscope m

horrendous [hə'rɛndəs] adj horrible,

affreux(-euse)

horrible ['hɒrɪbl] *adj* horrible, affreux(-euse)

horrid ['hɒrɪd] *adj* (*person*) détestable; (*weather, place, smell*) épouvantable

horrific [hɒ'rɪfɪk] *adj* horrible

horrify ['hɒrɪfaɪ] *vt* horrifier

horrifying ['hɒrɪfaɪɪŋ] *adj* horrifiant(e)

horror ['hɒrə'] *n* horreur *f*

horror film *n* film *m* d'épouvante

hors d'œuvre [ɔ:'də:vrə] *n* hors d'œuvre *m*

horse [hɔ:s] *n* cheval *m*

horseback ['hɔ:sbæk]: **on ~** (*adj, adv*) à cheval

horse chestnut *n* (*nut*) marron *m* (d'Inde); (*tree*) marronnier *m* (d'Inde)

horseman ['hɔ:smən] (*irreg*) *n* cavalier *m*

horsepower ['hɔ:spauə'] *n* puissance *f* (en chevaux); (*unit*) cheval-vapeur *m* (CV)

horse-racing ['hɔ:sreɪsɪŋ] *n* courses *fpl* de chevaux

horseradish ['hɔ:srædɪʃ] *n* raifort *m*

horse riding *n* (*Brit*) équitation *f*

horseshoe ['hɔ:ʃu:] *n* fer *m* à cheval

hose [həuz] *n* (*also*: **hosepipe**) tuyau *m*; (*also*: **garden hose**) tuyau d'arrosage

▶ **hose down** *vt* laver au jet

hosepipe ['həuzpaɪp] *n* tuyau *m*; (*in garden*) tuyau d'arrosage; (*for fire*) tuyau d'incendie

hospitable ['hɒspɪtəbl] *adj* hospitalier(-ière)

hospital ['hɒspɪtl] *n* hôpital *m*; **in ~** (US): **in the ~** à l'hôpital; **where's the nearest ~?** où est l'hôpital le plus proche?

hospitality [hɒspɪ'tælɪti] *n* hospitalité *f*

host [həust] *n* hôte *m*; (*in hotel etc*) patron *m*; (*TV, Radio*) présentateur(-trice), animateur(-trice); (*large number*): **a ~ of** une foule de; (*Rel*) hostie *f* ▷ *vt* (*TV programme*) présenter, animer

hostage ['hɒstɪdʒ] *n* otage *m*

hostel ['hɒstl] *n* foyer *m*; (*also*: **youth hostel**) auberge *f* de jeunesse

hostess ['həustɪs] *n* hôtesse *f*; (*Brit*: *also*: **air hostess**) hôtesse de l'air; (*TV, Radio*) animatrice *f*; (*in nightclub*) entraîneuse *f*

hostile ['hɒstaɪl] *adj* hostile

hostility [hɒ'stɪlɪti] *n* hostilité *f*

hot [hɒt] *adj* chaud(e); (*as opposed to only warm*) très chaud; (*spicy*) fort(e); (*fig: contest*) acharné(e); (*topic*) brûlant(e); (*temper*) violent(e), passionné(e); **to be ~** (*person*) avoir chaud; (*thing*) être (très) chaud; (*weather*) faire chaud

▶ **hot up** (*Brit inf*) *vi* (*situation*) devenir tendu(e); (*party*) s'animer ▷ *vt* (*pace*) accélérer, forcer; (*engine*) gonfler

hotbed ['hɒtbɛd] *n* (*fig*) foyer *m*, pépinière *f*

hot dog *n* hot-dog *m*

hotel [həu'tɛl] *n* hôtel *m*

hothouse ['hɒthaus] *n* serre chaude

hotline ['hɒtlaɪn] *n* (*Pol*) téléphone *m* rouge, ligne directe

hotly ['hɒtlɪ] *adv* passionnément, violemment

hotplate ['hɒtpleɪt] *n* (*on cooker*) plaque chauffante

hotpot ['hɒtpɒt] *n* (*Brit Culin*) ragoût *m*

hot-water bottle [hɒt'wɔ:tə-] *n* bouillotte *f*

hound [haund] *vt* poursuivre avec acharnement ▷ *n* chien courant; **the ~s** la meute

hour ['auə'] *n* heure *f*; **at 30 miles an ~** ≈ à 50 km à l'heure; **lunch ~** heure du déjeuner; **to pay sb by the ~** payer qn à l'heure

hourly ['auəlɪ] *adj* toutes les heures; (*rate*) horaire; **~ paid** *adj* payé(e) à l'heure

house *n* [haus] (*pl* **-s**) ['hauzɪz] maison *f*; (*Pol*) chambre *f*; (*Theat*) salle *f*; auditoire *m* ▷ *vt* [hauz] (*person*) loger, héberger; **at** (*or* **to**) **my ~** chez moi; **the H~ of Commons/of Lords** (*Brit*) la Chambre des communes/des lords; *voir article*; **the H~ (of Representatives)** (US) la Chambre des représentants; *voir article*; **on the ~** (*fig*) aux frais de la maison

house arrest *n* assignation *f* à domicile

houseboat ['hausbəut] *n* bateau (aménagé en habitation)

housebound ['hausbaund] *adj* confiné(e) chez soi

housebreaking ['hausbreɪkɪŋ] *n* cambriolage *m* (avec effraction)

household ['haushəuld] *n* (*Admin etc*) ménage *m*; (*people*) famille *f*, maisonnée *f*; **~ name** nom connu de tout le monde

householder ['haushəuldə'] *n* propriétaire *m/f*; (*head of house*) chef *m* de famille

housekeeper ['hauski:pə'] *n* gouvernante *f*

housekeeping ['hauski:pɪŋ] *n* (*work*) ménage *m*; (*also*: **housekeeping money**) argent *m* du ménage; (*Comput*) gestion *f* (des disques)

house-warming ['hauswɔ:mɪŋ] *n* (*also*: **house-warming party**) pendaison *f* de crémaillère

housewife (*irreg*) ['hauswaɪf] *n* ménagère *f*; femme *f* au foyer

house wine *n* cuvée *f* maison *or* du patron

housework ['hauswə:k] *n* (travaux *mpl* du) ménage *m*

housing ['hauzɪŋ] *n* logement *m* ▷ *cpd* (*problem, shortage*) de *or* du logement

housing development, (*Brit*) **housing estate** *n* (*blocks of flats*) cité *f*; (*houses*) lotissement *m*

hovel ['hɒvl] *n* taudis *m*

hover ['hɒvə'] *vi* planer; **to ~ round sb** rôder *or* tourner autour de qn

hovercraft ['hɒvəkrɑ:ft] *n* aéroglisseur *m*, hovercraft *m*

how [hau] *adv* comment; **~ are you?** comment allez-vous?; **~ do you do?** bonjour; (*on being introduced*) enchanté(e); **~ far is it to ...?** combien y a-t-il jusqu'à ...?; **~ long have you been here?** depuis combien de temps êtes-vous là?; **~ lovely/awful!** que *or* comme c'est joli/affreux!; **~ many/much?** combien?; **~ much time/many people?** combien de temps/gens?; **~ much does it cost?** ça coûte combien?; **~ old are you?** quel âge avez-vous?; **~ tall is he?** combien mesure-t-il?; **~ is school?** ça va à l'école?; **~ was the film?** comment était le film?; **~'s life?** (*inf*) comment ça va?; **~ about a drink?** si on buvait quelque chose?; **~ is it that ...?** comment se fait-il que

... + *sub*?

however [hau'ɛvər] *conj* pourtant, cependant ▷ *adv* de quelque façon *or* manière que + *sub*; (+ *adjective*) quelque *or* si ... que + *sub*; (*in questions*) comment; **~ I do it** de quelque manière que je m'y prenne; **~ cold it is** même s'il fait très froid; **~ did you do it?** comment y êtes-vous donc arrivé?

howl [haul] *n* hurlement *m* ▷ *vi* hurler; (*wind*) mugir

H.P. *n abbr* (*Brit*) = **hire purchase**

h.p. *abbr* (*Aut*) = **horsepower**

HQ *n abbr* (= *headquarters*) QG *m*

hr *abbr* (= *hour*) h

hrs *abbr* (= *hours*) h

HTML *n abbr* (= *hypertext markup language*) HTML *m*

hub [hʌb] *n* (*of wheel*) moyeu *m*; (*fig*) centre *m*, foyer *m*

hubcap [hʌbkæp] *n* (*Aut*) enjoliveur *m*

huddle ['hʌdl] *vi*: **to ~ together** se blottir les uns contre les autres

hue [hju:] *n* teinte *f*, nuance *f*; **~ and cry** *n* tollé (général), clameur *f*

huff [hʌf] *n*: **in a ~** fâché(e); **to take the ~** prendre la mouche

hug [hʌg] *vt* serrer dans ses bras; (*shore, kerb*) serrer ▷ *n* étreinte *f*; **to give sb a ~** serrer qn dans ses bras

huge [hju:dʒ] *adj* énorme, immense

hulk [hʌlk] *n* (*ship*) vieux rafiot; (*car, building*) carcasse *f*; (*person*) mastodonte *m*, malabar *m*

hull [hʌl] *n* (*of ship*) coque *f*; (*of nuts*) coque; (*of peas*) cosse *f*

hullo [hə'ləu] *excl* = **hello**

hum [hʌm] *vt* (*tune*) fredonner ▷ *vi* fredonner; (*insect*) bourdonner; (*plane, tool*) vrombir ▷ *n* fredonnement *m*; bourdonnement *m*; vrombissement *m*

human ['hju:mən] *adj* humain(e) ▷ *n* (*also:* **human being**) être humain

humane [hju:'meɪn] *adj* humain(e), humanitaire

humanitarian [hju:mænɪ'tɛərɪən] *adj* humanitaire

humanity [hju:'mænɪtɪ] *n* humanité *f*

human rights *npl* droits *mpl* de l'homme

humble ['hʌmbl] *adj* humble, modeste ▷ *vt* humilier

humdrum ['hʌmdrʌm] *adj* monotone, routinier(-ière)

humid ['hju:mɪd] *adj* humide

humidity [hju:'mɪdɪtɪ] *n* humidité *f*

humiliate [hju:'mɪlɪeɪt] *vt* humilier

humiliating [hju:'mɪlɪeɪtɪŋ] *adj* humiliant(e)

humiliation [hju:mɪlɪ'eɪʃən] *n* humiliation *f*

hummus ['huməs] *n* houm(m)ous *m*

humorous ['hju:mərəs] *adj* humoristique; (*person*) plein(e) d'humour

humour, (*US*) **humor** ['hju:mər] *n* humour *m*; (*mood*) humeur *f* ▷ *vt* (*person*) faire plaisir à; se prêter aux caprices de; **sense of ~** sens *m* de l'humour; **to be in a good/bad ~** être de bonne/

mauvaise humeur

hump [hʌmp] *n* bosse *f*

hunch [hʌntʃ] *n* bosse *f*; (*premonition*) intuition *f*; **I have a ~ that** j'ai (comme une vague) idée que

hunchback ['hʌntʃbæk] *n* bossu(e)

hunched [hʌntʃt] *adj* arrondi(e), voûté(e)

hundred ['hʌndrəd] *num* cent; **about a ~ people** une centaine de personnes; **~s of** des centaines de; **I'm a ~ per cent sure** j'en suis absolument certain

hundredth [-ɪdθ] *num* centième

hundredweight ['hʌndrɪdweɪt] *n* (*Brit*) =50.8 *kg*; 112 *lb*; (*US*) = 45.3 *kg*; 100 *lb*

hung [hʌŋ] *pt, pp of* **hang**

Hungarian [hʌŋ'gɛərɪən] *adj* hongrois(e) ▷ *n* Hongrois(e); (*Ling*) hongrois *m*

Hungary ['hʌŋgərɪ] *n* Hongrie *f*

hunger ['hʌŋgər] *n* faim *f* ▷ *vi*: **to ~ for** avoir faim de, désirer ardemment

hungry ['hʌŋgrɪ] *adj* affamé(e); **to be ~** avoir faim; **~ for** (*fig*) avide de

hunk [hʌŋk] *n* gros morceau; (*inf*: *man*) beau mec

hunt [hʌnt] *vt* (*seek*) chercher; (*criminal*) pourchasser; (*Sport*) chasser ▷ *vi* (*search*): **to ~ for** chercher (partout); (*Sport*) chasser ▷ *n* (*Sport*) chasse *f*

▶ **hunt down** *vt* pourchasser

hunter ['hʌntər] *n* chasseur *m*; (*Brit*: *horse*) cheval *m* de chasse

hunting ['hʌntɪŋ] *n* chasse *f*

hurdle ['hə:dl] *n* (*for fences*) claie *f*; (*Sport*) haie *f*; (*fig*) obstacle *m*

hurl [hə:l] *vt* lancer (avec violence); (*abuse, insults*) lancer

hurrah, hurray [hu'rɑ:, hu'reɪ] *excl* hourra!

hurricane ['hʌrɪkən] *n* ouragan *m*

hurried ['hʌrɪd] *adj* pressé(e), précipité(e); (*work*) fait(e) à la hâte

hurriedly ['hʌrɪdlɪ] *adv* précipitamment, à la hâte

hurry ['hʌrɪ] *n* hâte *f*, précipitation *f* ▷ *vi* se presser, se dépêcher ▷ *vt* (*person*) faire presser, faire se dépêcher; (*work*) presser; **to be in a ~** être pressé(e); **to do sth in a ~** faire qch en vitesse; **to ~ in/out** entrer/sortir précipitamment; **to ~ home** se dépêcher de rentrer

▶ **hurry along** *vi* marcher d'un pas pressé

▶ **hurry away, hurry off** *vi* partir précipitamment

▶ **hurry up** *vi* se dépêcher

hurt [hə:t] (*pt, pp ~*) *vt* (*cause pain to*) faire mal à; (*injure, fig*) blesser; (*damage: business, interests etc*) nuire à; faire du tort à ▷ *vi* faire mal ▷ *adj* blessé(e); **my arm ~s** j'ai mal au bras; **I ~ my arm** je me suis fait mal au bras; **to ~ o.s.** se faire mal; **where does it ~?** où avez-vous mal?, où est-ce que ça vous fait mal?

hurtful ['hə:tful] *adj* (*remark*) blessant(e)

hurtle ['hə:tl] *vt* lancer (de toutes ses forces) ▷ *vi*: **to ~ past** passer en trombe; **to ~ down** dégringoler

husband ['hʌzbənd] *n* mari *m*

hush [hʌʃ] n calme m, silence m ▷ vt faire taire;
~! chut!
▶ **hush up** vt (fact) étouffer
husk [hʌsk] n (of wheat) balle f; (of rice, maize)
enveloppe f; (of peas) cosse f
husky ['hʌskɪ] adj (voice) rauque; (burly)
costaud(e) ▷ n chien m esquimau or de traîneau
hustle ['hʌsl] vt pousser, bousculer ▷ n
bousculade f; ~ **and bustle** n tourbillon m
(d'activité)
hut [hʌt] n hutte f; (shed) cabane f
hutch [hʌtʃ] n clapier m
hyacinth ['haɪəsɪnθ] n jacinthe f
hydrant ['haɪdrənt] n prise f d'eau; (also: **fire
hydrant**) bouche f d'incendie
hydraulic [haɪ'drɔːlɪk] adj hydraulique
hydroelectric ['haɪdrəʊɪ'lɛktrɪk] adj hydro-
électrique
hydrofoil ['haɪdrəfɔɪl] n hydrofoil m
hydrogen ['haɪdrədʒən] n hydrogène m
hyena [haɪ'iːnə] n hyène f

hygiene ['haɪdʒiːn] n hygiène f
hygienic [haɪ'dʒiːnɪk] adj hygiénique
hymn [hɪm] n hymne m; cantique m
hype [haɪp] n (inf) matraquage m publicitaire or
médiatique
hypermarket ['haɪpəmɑːkɪt] (Brit) n
hypermarché m
hypertext ['haɪpətɛkst] n (Comput) hypertexte m
hyphen ['haɪfn] n trait m d'union
hypnotize ['hɪpnətaɪz] vt hypnotiser
hypocrisy [hɪ'pɔkrɪsɪ] n hypocrisie f
hypocrite ['hɪpəkrɪt] n hypocrite m/f
hypocritical [hɪpə'krɪtɪkl] adj hypocrite
hypothesis (pl **hypotheses**) [haɪ'pɔθɪsɪs, -siːz] n
hypothèse f
hysterical [hɪ'stɛrɪkl] adj hystérique; (funny)
hilarant(e); **to become** ~ avoir une crise de nerfs
hysterics [hɪ'stɛrɪks] npl (violente) crise de nerfs
(laughter) crise de rire; **to be in/have** ~ (anger,
panic) avoir une crise de nerfs; (laughter) attraper
un fou rire

I i

I [aɪ] *pron* je; (*before vowel*) j'; (*stressed*) moi ▷ *abbr* (= *island, isle*) I

ice [aɪs] *n* glace *f*; (*on road*) verglas *m* ▷ *vt* (*cake*) glacer; (*drink*) faire rafraîchir ▷ *vi* (*also*: **ice over**) geler; (*also*: **ice up**) se givrer; **to put sth on ~** (*fig*) mettre qch en attente

iceberg ['aɪsbə:g] *n* iceberg *m*; **the tip of the ~** (*also fig*) la partie émergée de l'iceberg

icebox ['aɪsbɔks] *n* (*US*) réfrigérateur *m*; (*Brit*) compartiment *m* à glace; (*insulated box*) glacière *f*

ice cream *n* glace *f*

ice cube *n* glaçon *m*

iced [aɪst] *adj* (*drink*) frappé(e); (*coffee, tea, also cake*) glacé(e)

ice hockey *n* hockey *m* sur glace

Iceland ['aɪslənd] *n* Islande *f*

Icelander ['aɪsləndə^r] *n* Islandais(e)

Icelandic [aɪs'lændɪk] *adj* islandais(e) ▷ *n* (*Ling*) islandais *m*

ice lolly *n* (*Brit*) esquimau *m*

ice rink *n* patinoire *f*

ice skating ['aɪsskeɪtɪŋ] *n* patinage *m* (sur glace)

icicle ['aɪsɪkl] *n* glaçon *m* (*naturel*)

icing ['aɪsɪŋ] *n* (*Aviat etc*) givrage *m*; (*Culin*) glaçage *m*

icing sugar *n* (*Brit*) sucre *m* glace

icon ['aɪkɔn] *n* icône *f*

ICT *n abbr* (*Brit: Scol: = information and communications technology*) TIC *fpl*

icy ['aɪsɪ] *adj* glacé(e); (*road*) verglacé(e); (*weather, temperature*) glacial(e)

I'd [aɪd] = **I would; I had**

ID card *n* carte *f* d'identité

idea [aɪ'dɪə] *n* idée *f*; **good ~!** bonne idée!; **to have an ~ that ...** avoir idée que ...; **I have no ~** je n'ai pas la moindre idée

ideal [aɪ'dɪəl] *n* idéal *m* ▷ *adj* idéal(e)

ideally [aɪ'dɪəlɪ] *adv* (*preferably*) dans l'idéal; (*perfectly*): **he is ~ suited to the job** il est parfait pour ce poste; **~ the book should have ...** l'idéal serait que le livre ait ...

identical [aɪ'dɛntɪkl] *adj* identique

identification [aɪdɛntɪfɪ'keɪʃən] *n* identification *f*; **means of ~** pièce *f* d'identité

identify [aɪ'dɛntɪfaɪ] *vt* identifier ▷ *vi*: **to ~ with** s'identifier à

Identikit® [aɪ'dɛntɪkɪt] *n*: **Identikit (picture)** portrait-robot *m*

identity [aɪ'dɛntɪtɪ] *n* identité *f*

identity card *n* carte *f* d'identité

identity theft *n* usurpation *f* d'identité

ideology [aɪdɪ'ɔlədʒɪ] *n* idéologie *f*

idiom ['ɪdɪəm] *n* (*language*) langue *f*, idiome *m*; (*phrase*) expression *f* idiomatique; (*style*) style *m*

idiosyncrasy [ɪdɪəu'sɪŋkrəsɪ] *n* particularité *f*, caractéristique *f*

idiot ['ɪdɪət] *n* idiot(e), imbécile *m/f*

idiotic [ɪdɪ'ɔtɪk] *adj* idiot(e), bête, stupide

idle ['aɪdl] *adj* (*doing nothing*) sans occupation, désœuvré(e); (*lazy*) oisif(-ive), paresseux(-euse); (*unemployed*) au chômage; (*machinery*) au repos; (*question, pleasures*) vain(e), futile ▷ *vi* (*engine*) tourner au ralenti; **to lie ~** être arrêté, ne pas fonctionner

▸ **idle away** *vt*: **to ~ away one's time** passer son temps à ne rien faire

idol ['aɪdl] *n* idole *f*

idolize ['aɪdəlaɪz] *vt* idolâtrer, adorer

idyllic [ɪ'dɪlɪk] *adj* idyllique

i.e. *abbr* (= *id est: that is*) c. à d., c'est-à-dire

if [ɪf] *conj* si ▷ *n*: **there are a lot of ifs and buts** il y a beaucoup de si *mpl* et de mais *mpl*; **I'd be pleased if you could do it** je serais très heureux si vous pouviez le faire; **if necessary** si nécessaire, le cas échéant; **if so** si c'est le cas; **if not** sinon; **if only I could!** si seulement je pouvais!; **if only he were here** si seulement il était là; **if only to show him my gratitude** ne serait-ce que pour lui témoigner ma gratitude; *see also* **as; even**

ignite [ɪg'naɪt] *vt* mettre le feu à, enflammer ▷ *vi* s'enflammer

ignition [ɪg'nɪʃən] *n* (*Aut*) allumage *m*; **to switch on/off the ~** mettre/couper le contact

ignition key *n* (*Aut*) clé *f* de contact

ignorance ['ɪgnərəns] *n* ignorance *f*; **to keep sb in ~ of sth** tenir qn dans l'ignorance de qch

ignorant ['ɪgnərənt] *adj* ignorant(e); **to be ~ of** (*subject*) ne rien connaître en; (*events*) ne pas être au courant de

ignore [ɪg'nɔː^r] *vt* ne tenir aucun compte de; (*mistake*) ne pas relever; (*person: pretend to not see*) faire semblant de ne pas reconnaître; (: *pay no attention to*) ignorer

ill [ɪl] *adj* (*sick*) malade; (*bad*) mauvais(e) ▷ *n* mal *m* ▷ *adv*: **to speak/think ~ of sb** dire/penser du mal de qn; **to be taken ~** tomber malade

I'll [aɪl] = **I will; I shall**

ill-advised [ɪləd'vaɪzd] *adj* (*decision*) peu judicieux(-euse); (*person*) malavisé(e)

ill-at-ease [ɪlət'iːz] *adj* mal à l'aise

illegal [ɪ'liːgl] *adj* illégal(e)

illegible [ɪ'ledʒɪbl] *adj* illisible

illegitimate [ɪlɪ'dʒɪtɪmət] *adj* illégitime

ill-fated [ɪl'feɪtɪd] *adj* malheureux(-euse); (*day*) néfaste

ill feeling *n* ressentiment *m*, rancune *f*

ill health *n* mauvaise santé

illiterate [ɪ'lɪtərət] *adj* illettré(e); (*letter*) plein(e) de fautes

ill-mannered [ɪl'mænəd] *adj* impoli(e), grossier(-ière)

illness ['ɪlnɪs] *n* maladie *f*

ill-treat [ɪl'triːt] *vt* maltraiter

illuminate [ɪ'luːmɪneɪt] *vt* (*room, street*) éclairer; (*for special effect*) illuminer; **~d sign** enseigne lumineuse

illumination [ɪluːmɪ'neɪʃən] *n* éclairage *m*; illumination *f*

illusion [ɪ'luːʒən] *n* illusion *f*; **to be under the ~ that** avoir l'illusion que

illustrate ['ɪləstreɪt] *vt* illustrer

illustration [ɪlə'streɪʃən] *n* illustration *f*

ill will *n* malveillance *f*

I'm [aɪm] = **I am**

image ['ɪmɪdʒ] *n* image *f*; (*public face*) image de marque

imagery ['ɪmɪdʒərɪ] *n* images *fpl*

imaginary [ɪ'mædʒɪnərɪ] *adj* imaginaire

imagination [ɪmædʒɪ'neɪʃən] *n* imagination *f*

imaginative [ɪ'mædʒɪnətɪv] *adj* imaginatif(-ive); (*person*) plein(e) d'imagination

imagine [ɪ'mædʒɪn] *vt* s'imaginer; (*suppose*) imaginer, supposer

imbalance [ɪm'bæləns] *n* déséquilibre *m*

imitate ['ɪmɪteɪt] *vt* imiter

imitation [ɪmɪ'teɪʃən] *n* imitation *f*

immaculate [ɪ'mækjulət] *adj* impeccable; (*Rel*) immaculé(e)

immaterial [ɪmə'tɪərɪəl] *adj* sans importance, insignifiant(e)

immature [ɪmə'tjuər] *adj* (*fruit*) qui n'est pas mûr(e); (*person*) qui manque de maturité

immediate [ɪ'miːdɪət] *adj* immédiat(e)

immediately [ɪ'miːdɪətlɪ] *adv* (*at once*) immédiatement; **~ next to** juste à côté de

immense [ɪ'mɛns] *adj* immense, énorme

immerse [ɪ'məːs] *vt* immerger, plonger; **to ~ sth in** plonger qch dans; **to be ~d in** (*fig*) être plongé dans

immersion heater [ɪ'məːʃən-] *n* (*Brit*) chauffe-eau *m* électrique

immigrant ['ɪmɪgrənt] *n* immigrant(e); (*already established*) immigré(e)

immigration [ɪmɪ'greɪʃən] *n* immigration *f*

imminent ['ɪmɪnənt] *adj* imminent(e)

immoral [ɪ'mɔrl] *adj* immoral(e)

immortal [ɪ'mɔːtl] *adj, n* immortel(le)

immune [ɪ'mjuːn] *adj*: **~ (to)** immunisé(e) (contre)

immune system *n* système *m* immunitaire

immunity [ɪ'mjuːnɪtɪ] *n* immunité *f*; **diplomatic ~** immunité diplomatique

immunize ['ɪmjunaɪz] *vt* immuniser

impact ['ɪmpækt] *n* choc *m*, impact *m*; (*fig*) impact

impair [ɪm'pɛər] *vt* détériorer, diminuer

impart [ɪm'pɑːt] *vt* (*make known*) communiquer, transmettre; (*bestow*) confier, donner

impartial [ɪm'pɑːʃl] *adj* impartial(e)

impassable [ɪm'pɑːsəbl] *adj* infranchissable; (*road*) impraticable

impassive [ɪm'pæsɪv] *adj* impassible

impatience [ɪm'peɪʃəns] *n* impatience *f*

impatient [ɪm'peɪʃənt] *adj* impatient(e); **to get** *or* **grow ~** s'impatienter

impatiently [ɪm'peɪʃəntlɪ] *adv* avec impatience

impeccable [ɪm'pɛkəbl] *adj* impeccable, parfait(e)

impede [ɪm'piːd] *vt* gêner

impediment [ɪm'pɛdɪmənt] *n* obstacle *m*; (*also*: **speech impediment**) défaut *m* d'élocution

impending [ɪm'pɛndɪŋ] *adj* imminent(e)

imperative [ɪm'pɛrətɪv] *adj* nécessaire; (*need*) urgent(e), pressant(e); (*tone*) impérieux(-euse) ▷ *n* (*Ling*) impératif *m*

imperfect [ɪm'pəːfɪkt] *adj* imparfait(e); (*goods etc*) défectueux(-euse) ▷ *n* (*Ling: also*: **imperfect tense**) imparfait *m*

imperial [ɪm'pɪərɪəl] *adj* impérial(e); (*Brit: measure*) légal(e)

impersonal [ɪm'pəːsənl] *adj* impersonnel(le)

impersonate [ɪm'pəːsəneɪt] *vt* se faire passer pour; (*Theat*) imiter

impertinent [ɪm'pəːtɪnənt] *adj* impertinent(e), insolent(e)

impervious [ɪm'pəːvɪəs] *adj* imperméable; (*fig*): **~ to** insensible à; inaccessible à

impetuous [ɪm'pɛtjuəs] *adj* impétueux(-euse), fougueux(-euse)

impetus ['ɪmpətəs] *n* impulsion *f*; (*of runner*) élan *m*

impinge [ɪm'pɪndʒ]: **to ~ on** *vt fus* (*person*) affecter, toucher; (*rights*) empiéter sur

implant [ɪm'plɑːnt] *vt* (*Med*) implanter; (*fig: idea, principle*) inculquer

implement *n* ['ɪmplɪmənt] outil *m*, instrument *m*; (*for cooking*) ustensile *m* ▷ *vt* ['ɪmplɪment] exécuter, mettre à effet

implicate ['ɪmplɪkeɪt] *vt* impliquer, compromettre

implication [ɪmplɪ'keɪʃən] *n* implication *f*; **by ~** indirectement

implicit [ɪm'plɪsɪt] *adj* implicite; (*complete*) absolu(e), sans réserve

imply [ɪm'plaɪ] *vt* (*hint*) suggérer, laisser entendre; (*mean*) indiquer, supposer

impolite [ɪmpə'laɪt] *adj* impoli(e)

import *vt* [ɪm'pɔːt] importer ▷ *n* ['ɪmpɔːt] (*Comm*)

importation f; (*meaning*) portée f, signification f
▷ *cpd* ['ɪmpɔːt] (*duty, licence etc*) d'importation
importance [ɪm'pɔːtns] n importance f; **to be of
great/little** ~ avoir beaucoup/peu d'importance
important [ɪm'pɔːtnt] *adj* important(e); **it
is** ~ **that** il importe que, il est important que;
it's not ~ c'est sans importance, ce n'est pas
important
importer [ɪm'pɔːtər] n importateur(-trice)
impose [ɪm'pəuz] *vt* imposer ▷ *vi*: **to** ~ **on sb**
abuser de la gentillesse de qn
imposing [ɪm'pəuzɪŋ] *adj* imposant(e),
impressionnant(e)
imposition [ɪmpə'zɪʃən] n (*of tax etc*) imposition
f; **to be an** ~ **on** (*person*) abuser de la gentillesse
or la bonté de
impossible [ɪm'pɔsɪbl] *adj* impossible; **it is** ~ **for
me to leave** il m'est impossible de partir
impotent ['ɪmpətnt] *adj* impuissant(e)
impound [ɪm'paund] *vt* confisquer, saisir
impoverished [ɪm'pɔvərɪʃt] *adj* pauvre,
appauvri(e)
impractical [ɪm'præktɪkl] *adj* pas pratique;
(*person*) qui manque d'esprit pratique
impregnable [ɪm'pregnəbl] *adj* (*fortress*)
imprenable; (*fig*) inattaquable, irréfutable
impress [ɪm'pres] *vt* impressionner, faire
impression sur; (*mark*) imprimer, marquer; **to** ~
sth on sb faire bien comprendre qch à qn
impressed [ɪm'prest] *adj* impressionné(e)
impression [ɪm'preʃən] n impression f; (*of stamp,
seal*) empreinte f; (*imitation*) imitation f; **to
make a good/bad** ~ **on sb** faire bonne/mauvaise
impression sur qn; **to be under the** ~ **that** avoir
l'impression que
impressionist [ɪm'preʃənɪst] n impressionniste
m/f
impressive [ɪm'presɪv] *adj* impressionnant(e)
imprint ['ɪmprɪnt] n empreinte f; (*Publishing*)
notice f; (: *label*) nom m (de collection or
d'éditeur)
imprison [ɪm'prɪzn] *vt* emprisonner, mettre en
prison
imprisonment [ɪm'prɪznmənt] n
emprisonnement m; (*period*): **to sentence sb to
10 years'** ~ condamner qn à 10 ans de prison
improbable [ɪm'prɔbəbl] *adj* improbable; (*excuse*)
peu plausible
improper [ɪm'prɔpər] *adj* (*wrong*) incorrect(e);
(*unsuitable*) déplacé(e), de mauvais goût; (*indecent*)
indécent(e); (*dishonest*) malhonnête
improve [ɪm'pruːv] *vt* améliorer ▷ *vi*
s'améliorer; (*pupil etc*) faire des progrès
▶ **improve on, improve upon** *vt fus* (*offer*)
enchérir sur
improvement [ɪm'pruːvmənt] n amélioration
f; (*of pupil etc*) progrès m; **to make ~s to** apporter
des améliorations à
improvise ['ɪmprəvaɪz] *vt, vi* improviser
impudent ['ɪmpjudnt] *adj* impudent(e)
impulse ['ɪmpʌls] n impulsion f; **on** ~
impulsivement, sur un coup de tête

impulsive [ɪm'pʌlsɪv] *adj* impulsif(-ive)
in [ɪn] *prep* **1** (*indicating place, position*) dans; **in the
house/the fridge** dans la maison/le frigo; **in
the garden** dans le or au jardin; **in town** en
ville; **in the country** à la campagne; **in school**
à l'école; **in here/there** ici/là
2 (*with place names: of town, region, country*): **in
London** à Londres; **in England** en Angleterre;
in Japan au Japon; **in the United States** aux
États-Unis
3 (*indicating time: during*): **in spring** au printemps;
in summer en été; **in May/2005** en mai/2005;
in the afternoon (dans) l'après-midi; **at 4
o'clock in the afternoon** à 4 heures de l'après-
midi
4 (*indicating time: in the space of*) en; (: *future*) dans;
I did it in 3 hours/days je l'ai fait en 3 heures/
jours; **I'll see you in 2 weeks** or **in 2 weeks'
time** je te verrai dans 2 semaines; **once in a
hundred years** une fois tous les cent ans
5 (*indicating manner etc*) à; **in a loud/soft voice**
à voix haute/basse; **in pencil** au crayon; **in
writing** par écrit; **in French** en français; **to pay
in dollars** payer en dollars; **the boy in the blue
shirt** le garçon à or avec la chemise bleue
6 (*indicating circumstances*): **in the sun** au soleil;
in the shade à l'ombre; **in the rain** sous la
pluie; **a change in policy** un changement de
politique
7 (*indicating mood, state*): **in tears** en larmes; **in
anger** sous le coup de la colère; **in despair** au
désespoir; **in good condition** en bon état; **to
live in luxury** vivre dans le luxe
8 (*with ratios, numbers*): **1 in 10 households, 1
household in 10** 1 ménage sur 10; **20 pence
in the pound** 20 pence par livre sterling; **they
lined up in twos** ils se mirent en rangs (deux)
par deux; **in hundreds** par centaines
9 (*referring to people, works*) chez; **the disease
is common in children** c'est une maladie
courante chez les enfants; **in (the works
of) Dickens** chez Dickens, dans (l'œuvre de)
Dickens
10 (*indicating profession etc*) dans; **to be in
teaching** être dans l'enseignement
11 (*after superlative*) de; **the best pupil in the
class** le meilleur élève de la classe
12 (*with present participle*): **in saying this** en
disant ceci
▷ *adv*: **to be in** (*person: at home, work*) être là; (*train,
ship, plane*) être arrivé(e); (*in fashion*) être à la
mode; **to ask sb in** inviter qn à entrer; **to run/
limp etc in** entrer en courant/boitant *etc*; **their
party is in** leur parti est au pouvoir
▷ *n*: **the ins and outs (of)** (*of proposal, situation etc*)
les tenants et aboutissants (de)
in. *abbr* = **inch; inches**
inability [ɪnə'bɪlɪtɪ] n incapacité f; ~ **to pay**
incapacité de payer
inaccurate [ɪn'ækjurət] *adj* inexact(e); (*person*)
qui manque de précision
inadequate [ɪn'ædɪkwət] *adj* insuffisant(e),

inadéquat(e)

inadvertently [ɪnəd'vəːtntlɪ] *adv* par mégarde

inadvisable [ɪnəd'vaɪzəbl] *adj* à déconseiller; **it is ~ to** il est déconseillé de

inane [ɪ'neɪn] *adj* inepte, stupide

inanimate [ɪn'ænɪmət] *adj* inanimé(e)

inappropriate [ɪnə'prəʊprɪət] *adj* inopportun(e), mal à propos; (*word, expression*) impropre

inarticulate [ɪnɑː'tɪkjʊlət] *adj* (*person*) qui s'exprime mal; (*speech*) indistinct(e)

inasmuch [ɪnəz'mʌtʃ] *adv*: **~ as** vu que, en ce sens que

inaugurate [ɪ'nɔːgjʊreɪt] *vt* inaugurer; (*president, official*) investir de ses fonctions

inauguration [ɪnɔːgjʊ'reɪʃən] *n* inauguration *f*; investiture *f*

inborn [ɪn'bɔːn] *adj* (*feeling*) inné(e); (*defect*) congénital(e)

inbred [ɪn'brɛd] *adj* inné(e), naturel(le); (*family*) consanguin(e)

Inc. *abbr* = **incorporated**

incapable [ɪn'keɪpəbl] *adj*: **~ (of)** incapable (de)

incapacitate [ɪnkə'pæsɪteɪt] *vt*: **to ~ sb from doing** rendre qn incapable de faire

incense *n* ['ɪnsɛns] encens *m* ▷ *vt* [ɪn'sɛns] (*anger*) mettre en colère

incentive [ɪn'sɛntɪv] *n* encouragement *m*, raison *f* de se donner de la peine

incessant [ɪn'sɛsnt] *adj* incessant(e)

incessantly [ɪn'sɛsntlɪ] *adv* sans cesse, constamment

inch [ɪntʃ] *n* pouce *m* (=25 mm; 12 *in a foot*); **within an ~ of** à deux doigts de; **he wouldn't give an ~** (*fig*) il n'a pas voulu céder d'un pouce
▷ **inch forward** *vi* avancer petit à petit

incidence ['ɪnsɪdns] *n* (*of crime, disease*) fréquence *f*

incident ['ɪnsɪdnt] *n* incident *m*; (*in book*) péripétie *f*

incidental [ɪnsɪ'dɛntl] *adj* accessoire; (*unplanned*) accidentel(le); **~ to** qui accompagne; **~ expenses** faux frais *mpl*

incidentally [ɪnsɪ'dɛntəlɪ] *adv* (*by the way*) à propos

inclination [ɪnklɪ'neɪʃən] *n* inclination *f*; (*desire*) envie *f*

incline [*n* 'ɪnklaɪn, *vb* ɪn'klaɪn] *n* pente *f*, plan incliné ▷ *vt* incliner ▷ *vi* (*surface*) s'incliner; **to ~ to** avoir tendance à; **to be ~d to do** (*want to*) être enclin(e) à faire; (*have a tendency to do*) avoir tendance à faire; **to be well ~d towards sb** être bien disposé(e) à l'égard de qn

include [ɪn'kluːd] *vt* inclure, comprendre; **service is/is not ~d** le service est compris/n'est pas compris

including [ɪn'kluːdɪŋ] *prep* y compris; **~ service** service compris

inclusion [ɪn'kluːʒən] *n* inclusion *f*

inclusive [ɪn'kluːsɪv] *adj* inclus(e), compris(e); **~ of tax** taxes comprises; **£50 ~ of all surcharges** 50 livres tous frais compris

income ['ɪnkʌm] *n* revenu *m*; (*from property etc*) rentes *fpl*; **gross/net ~** revenu brut/net; **~ and expenditure account** compte *m* de recettes et de dépenses

income support *n* (*Brit*) ≈ revenu *m* minimum d'insertion, RMI *m*

income tax *n* impôt *m* sur le revenu

incoming ['ɪnkʌmɪŋ] *adj* (*passengers, mail*) à l'arrivée; (*government, tenant*) nouveau (nouvelle); **~ tide** marée montante

incompatible [ɪnkəm'pætɪbl] *adj* incompatible

incompetence [ɪn'kɔmpɪtns] *n* incompétence *f*, incapacité *f*

incompetent [ɪn'kɔmpɪtnt] *adj* incompétent(e), incapable

incomplete [ɪnkəm'pliːt] *adj* incomplet(-ète)

incongruous [ɪn'kɔŋgruəs] *adj* peu approprié(e); (*remark, act*) incongru(e), déplacé(e)

inconsiderate [ɪnkən'sɪdərət] *adj* (*action*) inconsidéré(e); (*person*) qui manque d'égards

inconsistency [ɪnkən'sɪstənsɪ] *n* (*of actions etc*) inconséquence *f*; (*of work*) irrégularité *f*; (*of statement etc*) incohérence *f*

inconsistent [ɪnkən'sɪstnt] *adj* qui manque de constance; (*work*) irrégulier(-ière); (*statement*) peu cohérent(e); **~ with** en contradiction avec

inconspicuous [ɪnkən'spɪkjuəs] *adj* qui passe inaperçu(e); (*colour, dress*) discret(-ète); **to make o.s. ~** ne pas se faire remarquer

inconvenience [ɪnkən'viːnjəns] *n* inconvénient *m*; (*trouble*) dérangement *m* ▷ *vt* déranger; **don't ~ yourself** ne vous dérangez pas

inconvenient [ɪnkən'viːnjənt] *adj* malcommode; (*time, place*) mal choisi(e), qui ne convient pas; (*visitor*) importun(e); **that time is very ~ for me** c'est un moment qui ne me convient pas du tout

incorporate [ɪn'kɔːpəreɪt] *vt* incorporer; (*contain*) contenir ▷ *vi* fusionner; (*two firms*) se constituer en société

incorporated [ɪn'kɔːpəreɪtɪd] *adj*: **~ company** (*US*) ≈ société *f* anonyme

incorrect [ɪnkə'rɛkt] *adj* incorrect(e); (*opinion, statement*) inexact(e)

increase *n* ['ɪnkriːs] augmentation *f* ▷ *vi, vt* [ɪn'kriːs] augmenter; **an ~ of 5%** une augmentation de 5%; **to be on the ~** être en augmentation

increasing [ɪn'kriːsɪŋ] *adj* croissant(e)

increasingly [ɪn'kriːsɪŋlɪ] *adv* de plus en plus

incredible [ɪn'krɛdɪbl] *adj* incroyable

incredibly [ɪn'krɛdɪblɪ] *adv* incroyablement

incubator ['ɪnkjubeɪtəʳ] *n* incubateur *m*; (*for babies*) couveuse *f*

incumbent [ɪn'kʌmbənt] *adj*: **it is ~ on him to ...** il lui appartient de ... ▷ *n* titulaire *m/f*

incur [ɪn'kəːʳ] *vt* (*expenses*) encourir; (*anger, risk*) s'exposer à; (*debt*) contracter; (*loss*) subir

indebted [ɪn'dɛtɪd] *adj*: **to be ~ to sb (for)** être redevable à qn (de)

indecent [ɪn'diːsnt] *adj* indécent(e), inconvenant(e)

indecent assault *n* (*Brit*) attentat *m* à la pudeur

indecent exposure *n* outrage *m* public à la

pudeur

indecisive [ɪndɪ'saɪsɪv] adj indécis(e); (discussion) peu concluant(e)

indeed [ɪn'di:d] adv (confirming, agreeing) en effet, effectivement; (for emphasis) vraiment; (furthermore) d'ailleurs; **yes ~!** certainement!

indefinitely [ɪn'dɛfɪnɪtlɪ] adv (wait) indéfiniment; (speak) vaguement, avec imprécision

indemnity [ɪn'dɛmnɪtɪ] n (insurance) assurance f, garantie f; (compensation) indemnité f

independence [ɪndɪ'pɛndns] n indépendance f

Independence Day n (US) fête de l'Indépendance américaine; voir article

independent [ɪndɪ'pɛndnt] adj indépendant(e); (radio) libre; **to become ~** s'affranchir

independent school n (Brit) école privée

index ['ɪndɛks] n (pl -es) (in book) index m; (: in library etc) catalogue m (pl **indices**) ['ɪndɪsi:z] (ratio, sign) indice m

index card n fiche f

index finger n index m

index-linked ['ɪndɛks'lɪŋkt], (US) **indexed** ['ɪndɛkst] adj indexé(e) (sur le coût de la vie etc)

India ['ɪndɪə] n Inde f

Indian ['ɪndɪən] adj indien(ne) ▷ n Indien(ne); (**American**) ~ Indien(ne) (d'Amérique)

Indian Ocean n: **the ~** l'océan Indien

indicate ['ɪndɪkeɪt] vt indiquer ▷ vi (Brit Aut): **to ~ left/right** mettre son clignotant à gauche/à droite

indication [ɪndɪ'keɪʃən] n indication f, signe m

indicative [ɪn'dɪkətɪv] adj indicatif(-ive); **to be ~ of sth** être symptomatique de qch ▷ n (Ling) indicatif m

indicator ['ɪndɪkeɪtə^r] n (sign) indicateur m; (Aut) clignotant m

indices ['ɪndɪsi:z] npl of **index**

indict [ɪn'daɪt] vt accuser

indictment [ɪn'daɪtmənt] n accusation f

indifference [ɪn'dɪfrəns] n indifférence f

indifferent [ɪn'dɪfrənt] adj indifférent(e); (poor) médiocre, quelconque

indigenous [ɪn'dɪdʒɪnəs] adj indigène

indigestion [ɪndɪ'dʒɛstʃən] n indigestion f, mauvaise digestion

indignant [ɪn'dɪgnənt] adj: **~ (at sth/with sb)** indigné(e) (de qch/contre qn)

indignity [ɪn'dɪgnɪtɪ] n indignité f, affront m

indirect [ɪndɪ'rɛkt] adj indirect(e)

indiscreet [ɪndɪ'skri:t] adj indiscret(-ète); (rash) imprudent(e)

indiscriminate [ɪndɪ'skrɪmɪnət] adj (person) qui manque de discernement; (admiration) aveugle; (killings) commis(e) au hasard

indispensable [ɪndɪ'spɛnsəbl] adj indispensable

indisputable [ɪndɪ'spju:təbl] adj incontestable, indiscutable

individual [ɪndɪ'vɪdjuəl] n individu m ▷ adj individuel(le); (characteristic) particulier(-ière), original(e)

individually [ɪndɪ'vɪdjuəlɪ] adv

individuellement

indoctrination [ɪndɔktrɪ'neɪʃən] n endoctrinement m

Indonesia [ɪndə'ni:zɪə] n Indonésie f

indoor ['ɪndɔ:^r] adj d'intérieur; (plant) d'appartement; (swimming pool) couvert(e); (sport, games) pratiqué(e) en salle

indoors [ɪn'dɔ:z] adv à l'intérieur; (at home) à la maison

induce [ɪn'dju:s] vt (persuade) persuader; (bring about) provoquer; (labour) déclencher; **to ~ sb to do sth** inciter or pousser qn à faire qch

inducement [ɪn'dju:smənt] n incitation f; (incentive) but m; (pej: bribe) pot-de-vin m

indulge [ɪn'dʌldʒ] vt (whim) céder à, satisfaire; (child) gâter ▷ vi: **to ~ in sth** (luxury) s'offrir qch, se permettre qch; (fantasies etc) se livrer à qch

indulgence [ɪn'dʌldʒəns] n fantaisie f (que l'on s'offre); (leniency) indulgence f

indulgent [ɪn'dʌldʒənt] adj indulgent(e)

industrial [ɪn'dʌstrɪəl] adj industriel(le); (injury) du travail; (dispute) ouvrier(-ière)

industrial action n action revendicative

industrial estate n (Brit) zone industrielle

industrialist [ɪn'dʌstrɪəlɪst] n industriel m

industrial park n (US) zone industrielle

industrious [ɪn'dʌstrɪəs] adj travailleur(-euse)

industry ['ɪndəstrɪ] n industrie f; (diligence) zèle m, application f

inebriated [ɪ'ni:brɪeɪtɪd] adj ivre

inedible [ɪn'ɛdɪbl] adj immangeable; (plant etc) non comestible

ineffective [ɪnɪ'fɛktɪv], **ineffectual** [ɪnɪ'fɛktʃuəl] adj inefficace; incompétent(e)

inefficient [ɪnɪ'fɪʃənt] adj inefficace

inequality [ɪnɪ'kwɔlɪtɪ] n inégalité f

inescapable [ɪnɪ'skeɪpəbl] adj inéluctable, inévitable

inevitable [ɪn'ɛvɪtəbl] adj inévitable

inevitably [ɪn'ɛvɪtəblɪ] adv inévitablement, fatalement

inexpensive [ɪnɪk'spɛnsɪv] adj bon marché inv

inexperienced [ɪnɪk'spɪərɪənst] adj inexpérimenté(e); **to be ~ in sth** manquer d'expérience dans qch

inexplicable [ɪnɪk'splɪkəbl] adj inexplicable

infallible [ɪn'fælɪbl] adj infaillible

infamous ['ɪnfəməs] adj infâme, abominable

infancy ['ɪnfənsɪ] n petite enfance, bas âge; (fig) enfance, débuts mpl

infant ['ɪnfənt] n (baby) nourrisson m; (young child) petit(e) enfant

infantry ['ɪnfəntrɪ] n infanterie f

infant school n (Brit) classes fpl préparatoires (entre 5 et 7 ans)

infatuated [ɪn'fætjueɪtɪd] adj: **~ with** entiché(e) de; **to become ~ (with sb)** s'enticher (de qn)

infatuation [ɪnfætju'eɪʃən] n toquade f; engouement m

infect [ɪn'fɛkt] vt (wound) infecter; (person, blood) contaminer; (fig pej) corrompre; **~ed with** (illness) atteint(e) de; **to become ~ed** (wound) s'infecter

infection [ɪnˈfɛkʃən] n infection f; (contagion) contagion f
infectious [ɪnˈfɛkʃəs] adj infectieux(-euse); (also fig) contagieux(-euse)
infer [ɪnˈfəːʳ] vt: **to ~ (from)** conclure (de), déduire (de)
inferior [ɪnˈfɪərɪəʳ] adj inférieur(e); (goods) de qualité inférieure ▷ n inférieur(e); (in rank) subalterne m/f; **to feel ~** avoir un sentiment d'infériorité
inferiority [ɪnfɪərɪˈɔrətɪ] n infériorité f
infertile [ɪnˈfəːtaɪl] adj stérile
infertility [ɪnfəˈtɪlɪtɪ] n infertilité f, stérilité f
infested [ɪnˈfɛstɪd] adj: **~ (with)** infesté(e) (de)
in-fighting [ˈɪnfaɪtɪŋ] n querelles fpl internes
infinite [ˈɪnfɪnɪt] adj infini(e); (time, money) illimité(e)
infinitely [ˈɪnfɪnɪtlɪ] adv infiniment
infinitive [ɪnˈfɪnɪtɪv] n infinitif m
infinity [ɪnˈfɪnɪtɪ] n infinité f; (also Math) infini m
infirmary [ɪnˈfəːmərɪ] n hôpital m; (in school, factory) infirmerie f
inflamed [ɪnˈfleɪmd] adj enflammé(e)
inflammable [ɪnˈflæməbl] adj (Brit) inflammable
inflammation [ɪnfləˈmeɪʃən] n inflammation f
inflatable [ɪnˈfleɪtəbl] adj gonflable
inflate [ɪnˈfleɪt] vt (tyre, balloon) gonfler; (fig: exaggerate) grossir, gonfler; (: increase) gonfler
inflation [ɪnˈfleɪʃən] n (Econ) inflation f
inflationary [ɪnˈfleɪʃənərɪ] adj inflationniste
inflexible [ɪnˈflɛksɪbl] adj inflexible, rigide
inflict [ɪnˈflɪkt] vt: **to ~ on** infliger à sans infliger de douleurs
influence [ˈɪnfluəns] n influence f ▷ vt influencer; **under the ~ of** sous l'effet de; **under the ~ of alcohol** en état d'ébriété
influential [ɪnfluˈɛnʃl] adj influent(e)
influenza [ɪnfluˈɛnzə] n grippe f
influx [ˈɪnflʌks] n afflux m
info (inf) [ˈɪnfəu] n (= information) renseignements mpl
infomercial [ˈɪnfəuməːʃl] (US) n (for product) publi-information f; (Pol) émission où un candidat présente son programme électoral
inform [ɪnˈfɔːm] vt: **to ~ sb (of)** informer or avertir qn (de) ▷ vi: **to ~ on sb** dénoncer qn, informer contre qn; **to ~ sb about** renseigner qn sur, mettre qn au courant de
informal [ɪnˈfɔːml] adj (person, manner, party) simple, sans cérémonie; (visit, discussion) dénué(e) de formalités; (announcement, invitation) non officiel(le); (colloquial) familier(-ère); **"dress ~"** "tenue de ville"
informality [ɪnfɔːˈmælɪtɪ] n simplicité f, absence f de cérémonie; caractère non officiel
informant [ɪnˈfɔːmənt] n informateur(-trice)
information [ɪnfəˈmeɪʃən] n information(s) f(pl); renseignements mpl; (knowledge) connaissances fpl; **to get ~ on** se renseigner sur; **a piece of ~** un renseignement; **for your ~** à titre d'information
information desk n accueil m

information office n bureau m de renseignements
information technology n informatique f
informative [ɪnˈfɔːmətɪv] adj instructif(-ive)
informer [ɪnˈfɔːməʳ] n dénonciateur(-trice); (also: **police informer**) indicateur(-trice)
infra-red [ɪnfrəˈrɛd] adj infrarouge
infrastructure [ˈɪnfrəstrʌktʃəʳ] n infrastructure f
infrequent [ɪnˈfriːkwənt] adj peu fréquent(e), rare
infringe [ɪnˈfrɪndʒ] vt enfreindre ▷ vi: **to ~ on** empiéter sur
infringement [ɪnˈfrɪndʒmənt] n: **~ (of)** infraction f (à)
infuriate [ɪnˈfjuərɪeɪt] vt mettre en fureur
infuriating [ɪnˈfjuərɪeɪtɪŋ] adj exaspérant(e)
ingenious [ɪnˈdʒiːnjəs] adj ingénieux(-euse)
ingenuity [ɪndʒɪˈnjuːɪtɪ] n ingéniosité f
ingenuous [ɪnˈdʒɛnjuəs] adj franc (franche), ouvert(e)
ingot [ˈɪŋgət] n lingot m
ingrained [ɪnˈgreɪnd] adj enraciné(e)
ingratiate [ɪnˈgreɪʃɪeɪt] vt: **to ~ o.s. with** s'insinuer dans les bonnes grâces de, se faire bien voir de
ingredient [ɪnˈgriːdɪənt] n ingrédient m; (fig) élément m
inhabit [ɪnˈhæbɪt] vt habiter
inhabitant [ɪnˈhæbɪtnt] n habitant(e)
inhale [ɪnˈheɪl] vt inhaler; (perfume) respirer; (smoke) avaler ▷ vi (breathe in) aspirer; (in smoking) avaler la fumée
inhaler [ɪnˈheɪləʳ] n inhalateur m
inherent [ɪnˈhɪərənt] adj: **~ (in or to)** inhérent(e) (à)
inherit [ɪnˈhɛrɪt] vt hériter (de)
inheritance [ɪnˈhɛrɪtəns] n héritage m; (fig): **the situation that was his ~ as president** la situation dont il a hérité en tant que président; **law of ~** droit m de la succession
inhibit [ɪnˈhɪbɪt] vt (Psych) inhiber; (growth) freiner; **to ~ sb from doing** empêcher or retenir qn de faire
inhibition [ɪnhɪˈbɪʃən] n inhibition f
inhuman [ɪnˈhjuːmən] adj inhumain(e)
initial [ɪˈnɪʃl] adj initial(e) ▷ n initiale f ▷ vt parafer; **initials** npl initiales fpl; (as signature) parafe m
initially [ɪˈnɪʃəlɪ] adv initialement, au début
initiate [ɪˈnɪʃɪeɪt] vt (start) entreprendre; amorcer; (enterprise) lancer; (person) initier; **to ~ sb into a secret** initier qn à un secret; **to ~ proceedings against sb** (Law) intenter une action à qn, engager des poursuites contre qn
initiative [ɪˈnɪʃətɪv] n initiative f; **to take the ~** prendre l'initiative
inject [ɪnˈdʒɛkt] vt (liquid, fig: money) injecter; (person): **to ~ sb with sth** faire une piqûre de qch à qn
injection [ɪnˈdʒɛkʃən] n injection f, piqûre f; **to have an ~** se faire faire une piqûre
injure [ˈɪndʒəʳ] vt blesser; (wrong) faire du tort à;

(*damage*: *reputation etc*) compromettre; (*feelings*) heurter; **to ~ o.s.** se blesser

injured ['ɪndʒəd] *adj* (*person, leg etc*) blessé(e); (*tone, feelings*) offensé(e); **~ party** (*Law*) partie lésée

injury ['ɪndʒərɪ] *n* blessure *f*; (*wrong*) tort *m*; **to escape without ~** s'en sortir sain et sauf

injury time *n* (*Sport*) arrêts *mpl* de jeu

injustice [ɪn'dʒʌstɪs] *n* injustice *f*; **you do me an ~** vous êtes injuste envers moi

ink [ɪŋk] *n* encre *f*

ink-jet printer ['ɪŋkdʒet-] *n* imprimante *f* à jet d'encre

inkling ['ɪŋklɪŋ] *n* soupçon *m*, vague idée *f*

inlaid ['ɪnleɪd] *adj* incrusté(e); (*table etc*) marqueté(e)

inland *adj* ['ɪnlənd] intérieur(e) ▷ *adv* [ɪn'lænd] à l'intérieur, dans les terres; **~ waterways** canaux *mpl* et rivières *fpl*

Inland Revenue *n* (*Brit*) fisc *m*

in-laws ['ɪnlɔːz] *npl* beaux-parents *mpl*; belle famille

inlet ['ɪnlet] *n* (*Geo*) crique *f*

inmate ['ɪnmeɪt] *n* (*in prison*) détenu(e); (*in asylum*) interné(e)

inn [ɪn] *n* auberge *f*

innate [ɪ'neɪt] *adj* inné(e)

inner ['ɪnə'] *adj* intérieur(e)

inner city *n* centre *m* urbain (*souffrant souvent de délabrement, d'embouteillages etc*)

inner-city ['ɪnə'sɪtɪ] *adj* (*schools, problems*) de quartiers déshérités

inner tube *n* (*of tyre*) chambre *f* à air

inning ['ɪnɪŋ] *n* (*US: Baseball*) tour *m* de batte; **innings** *npl* (*Cricket*) tour de batte; (*Brit fig*): **he has had a good ~** il (en) a bien profité

innocence ['ɪnəsns] *n* innocence *f*

innocent ['ɪnəsnt] *adj* innocent(e)

innocuous [ɪ'nɔkjuəs] *adj* inoffensif(-ive)

innovation [ɪnəu'veɪʃən] *n* innovation *f*

innovative ['ɪnəu'veɪtɪv] *adj* novateur(-trice); (*product*) innovant(e)

innuendo [ɪnju'ɛndəu] (*pl* **-es**) *n* insinuation *f*, allusion (malveillante)

innumerable [ɪ'njuːmrəbl] *adj* innombrable

in-patient ['ɪnpeɪʃənt] *n* malade hospitalisé(e)

input ['ɪnput] *n* (*contribution*) contribution *f*; (*resources*) ressources *fpl*; (*Elec*) énergie *f*, puissance *f*; (*of machine*) consommation *f*; (*Comput*) entrée *f* (de données); (: *data*) données *fpl* ▷ *vt* (*Comput*) introduire, entrer

inquest ['ɪnkwest] *n* enquête (criminelle); (*coroner's*) enquête judiciaire

inquire [ɪn'kwaɪə'] *vi* demander ▷ *vt* demander, s'informer de; **to ~ about** s'informer de, se renseigner sur; **to ~ when/where/whether** demander quand/où/si

▶ **inquire after** *vt fus* demander des nouvelles de

▶ **inquire into** *vt fus* faire une enquête sur

inquiry [ɪn'kwaɪərɪ] *n* demande *f* de renseignements; (*Law*) enquête *f*, investigation *f*; **"inquiries"** "renseignements"; **to hold an ~ into sth** enquêter sur qch

inquisitive [ɪn'kwɪzɪtɪv] *adj* curieux(-euse)

ins. *abbr* = **inches**

insane [ɪn'seɪn] *adj* fou (folle); (*Med*) aliéné(e)

insanity [ɪn'sænɪtɪ] *n* folie *f*; (*Med*) aliénation (mentale)

inscription [ɪn'skrɪpʃən] *n* inscription *f*; (*in book*) dédicace *f*

inscrutable [ɪn'skruːtəbl] *adj* impénétrable

insect ['ɪnsekt] *n* insecte *m*

insecticide [ɪn'sektɪsaɪd] *n* insecticide *m*

insect repellent *n* crème *f* anti-insectes

insecure [ɪnsɪ'kjuə'] *adj* (*person*) anxieux(-euse); (*job*) précaire; (*building etc*) peu sûr(e)

insecurity [ɪnsɪ'kjuərɪtɪ] *n* insécurité *f*

insensitive [ɪn'sensɪtɪv] *adj* insensible

insert *vt* [ɪn'səːt] insérer ▷ *n* ['ɪnsəːt] insertion *f*

insertion [ɪn'səːʃən] *n* insertion *f*

in-service ['ɪn'səːvɪs] *adj* (*training*) continu(e); (*course*) d'initiation; de perfectionnement; de recyclage

inshore [ɪn'ʃɔː'] *adj* côtier(-ière) ▷ *adv* près de la côte; vers la côte

inside ['ɪn'saɪd] *n* intérieur *m*; (*of road: Brit*) côté *m* gauche (*de la route*); (: *US, Europe etc*) côté droit (*de la route*) ▷ *adj* intérieur(e) ▷ *adv* à l'intérieur, dedans ▷ *prep* à l'intérieur de; (*of time*): **~ 10 minutes** en moins de 10 minutes; **insides** *npl* (*inf*) intestins *mpl*; **~ information** renseignements *mpl* à la source; **~ story** histoire racontée par un témoin; **to go ~** rentrer

inside lane *n* (*Aut: in Britain*) voie *f* de gauche; (: *in US, Europe*) voie *f* de droite

inside out *adv* à l'envers; (*know*) à fond; **to turn sth ~** retourner qch

insider dealing, insider trading *n* (*Stock Exchange*) délit *m* d'initiés

insight ['ɪnsaɪt] *n* perspicacité *f*; (*glimpse, idea*) aperçu *m*; **to gain (an) ~ into** parvenir à comprendre

insignificant [ɪnsɪg'nɪfɪknt] *adj* insignifiant(e)

insincere [ɪnsɪn'sɪə'] *adj* hypocrite

insinuate [ɪn'sɪnjueɪt] *vt* insinuer

insist [ɪn'sɪst] *vi* insister; **to ~ on doing** insister pour faire; **to ~ on sth** exiger qch; **to ~ that** insister pour que + *sub*; (*claim*) maintenir *or* soutenir que

insistent [ɪn'sɪstənt] *adj* insistant(e), pressant(e); (*noise, action*) ininterrompu(e)

insole ['ɪnsəul] *n* semelle intérieure; (*fixed part of shoe*) première *f*

insolent ['ɪnsələnt] *adj* insolent(e)

insolvent [ɪn'sɔlvənt] *adj* insolvable; (*bankrupt*) en faillite

insomnia [ɪn'sɔmnɪə] *n* insomnie *f*

inspect [ɪn'spekt] *vt* inspecter; (*Brit: ticket*) contrôler

inspection [ɪn'spekʃən] *n* inspection *f*; (*Brit: of tickets*) contrôle *m*

inspector [ɪn'spektə'] *n* inspecteur(-trice); (*Brit: on buses, trains*) contrôleur(-euse)

inspiration [ɪnspə'reɪʃən] *n* inspiration *f*

inspire [ɪnˈspaɪəʳ] vt inspirer
inspiring [ɪnˈspaɪərɪŋ] adj inspirant(e)
instability [ɪnstəˈbɪlɪtɪ] n instabilité f
install, (US) **instal** [ɪnˈstɔːl] vt installer
installation [ɪnstəˈleɪʃən] n installation f
instalment, (US) **installment** [ɪnˈstɔːlmənt] n
(payment) acompte m, versement partiel; (of TV
serial etc) épisode m; **in ~s** (pay) à tempérament;
(receive) en plusieurs fois
instance [ˈɪnstəns] n exemple m; **for ~** par
exemple; **in many ~s** dans bien des cas; **in that
~** dans ce cas; **in the first ~** tout d'abord, en
premier lieu
instant [ˈɪnstənt] n instant m ▷ adj immédiat(e),
urgent(e); (coffee, food) instantané(e), en poudre;
the 10th ~ le 10 courant
instantly [ˈɪnstəntlɪ] adv immédiatement, tout
de suite
instant messaging n messagerie f instantanée
instead [ɪnˈstɛd] adv au lieu de cela; **~ of** au lieu
de; **~ of sb** à la place de qn
instep [ˈɪnstɛp] n cou-de-pied m; (of shoe)
cambrure f
instigate [ˈɪnstɪɡeɪt] vt (rebellion, strike, crime)
inciter à; (new ideas etc) susciter
instil [ɪnˈstɪl] vt: **to ~ (into)** inculquer (à);
(courage) insuffler (à)
instinct [ˈɪnstɪŋkt] n instinct m
instinctive [ɪnˈstɪŋktɪv] adj instinctif(-ive)
institute [ˈɪnstɪtjuːt] n institut m ▷ vt instituer,
établir; (inquiry) ouvrir; (proceedings) entamer
institution [ɪnstɪˈtjuːʃən] n institution f;
(school) établissement m (scolaire); (for care)
établissement (psychiatrique etc)
instruct [ɪnˈstrʌkt] vt instruire, former; **to ~ sb
in sth** enseigner qch à qn; **to ~ sb to do** charger
qn or ordonner à qn de faire
instruction [ɪnˈstrʌkʃən] n instruction f;
instructions npl (orders) directives fpl; **~s for use**
mode m d'emploi
instructor [ɪnˈstrʌktəʳ] n professeur m; (for skiing,
driving) moniteur m
instrument [ˈɪnstrəmənt] n instrument m
instrumental [ɪnstruˈmɛntl] adj (Mus)
instrumental(e); **to be ~ in sth/in doing sth**
contribuer à qch/à faire qch
instrument panel n tableau m de bord
insufficient [ɪnsəˈfɪʃənt] adj insuffisant(e)
insular [ˈɪnsjuləʳ] adj insulaire; (outlook) étroit(e);
(person) aux vues étroites
insulate [ˈɪnsjuleɪt] vt isoler; (against sound)
insonoriser
insulation [ɪnsjuˈleɪʃən] n isolation f; (against
sound) insonorisation f
insulin [ˈɪnsjulɪn] n insuline f
insult n [ˈɪnsʌlt] insulte f, affront m ▷ vt [ɪnˈsʌlt]
insulter, faire un affront à
insulting [ɪnˈsʌltɪŋ] adj insultant(e),
injurieux(-euse)
insurance [ɪnˈʃuərəns] n assurance f; **fire/life
~** assurance-incendie/-vie; **to take out ~
(against)** s'assurer (contre)

insurance company n compagnie f or société f
d'assurances
insurance policy n police f d'assurance
insure [ɪnˈʃuəʳ] vt assurer; **to ~ (o.s.) against**
(fig) parer à; **to ~ sb/sb's life** assurer qn/la vie
de qn; **to be ~d for £5000** être assuré(e) pour
5000 livres
intact [ɪnˈtækt] adj intact(e)
intake [ˈɪnteɪk] n (Tech) admission f; (consumption)
consommation f; (Brit Scol): **an ~ of 200 a year**
200 admissions par an
integral [ˈɪntɪɡrəl] adj (whole) intégral(e); (part)
intégrant(e)
integrate [ˈɪntɪɡreɪt] vt intégrer ▷ vi s'intégrer
integrity [ɪnˈtɛɡrɪtɪ] n intégrité f
intellect [ˈɪntəlɛkt] n intelligence f
intellectual [ɪntəˈlɛktjuəl] adj, n intellectuel(le)
intelligence [ɪnˈtɛlɪdʒəns] n intelligence f; (Mil)
informations fpl, renseignements mpl
Intelligence Service n services mpl de
renseignements
intelligent [ɪnˈtɛlɪdʒənt] adj intelligent(e)
intend [ɪnˈtɛnd] vt (gift etc): **to ~ sth for** destiner
qch à; **to ~ to do** avoir l'intention de faire
intense [ɪnˈtɛns] adj intense; (person)
véhément(e)
intensely [ɪnˈtɛnslɪ] adv intensément; (moving)
profondément
intensify [ɪnˈtɛnsɪfaɪ] vt intensifier
intensity [ɪnˈtɛnsɪtɪ] n intensité f
intensive [ɪnˈtɛnsɪv] adj intensif(-ive)
intensive care n: **to be in ~** être en réanimation
intensive care unit n service m de réanimation
intent [ɪnˈtɛnt] n intention f ▷ adj attentif(-ive),
absorbé(e); **to all ~s and purposes** en fait,
pratiquement; **to be ~ on doing sth** être (bien)
décidé à faire qch
intention [ɪnˈtɛnʃən] n intention f
intentional [ɪnˈtɛnʃənl] adj intentionnel(le),
délibéré(e)
intently [ɪnˈtɛntlɪ] adv attentivement
interact [ɪntərˈækt] vi avoir une action
réciproque; (people) communiquer
interaction [ɪntərˈækʃən] n interaction f
interactive [ɪntərˈæktɪv] adj (group)
interactif(-ive); (Comput) interactif,
conversationnel(le)
intercept [ɪntəˈsɛpt] vt intercepter; (person)
arrêter au passage
interchange n [ˈɪntətʃeɪndʒ] (exchange) échange
m; (on motorway) échangeur m ▷ vt [ɪntəˈtʃeɪndʒ]
échanger; mettre à la place l'un(e) de l'autre
interchangeable [ɪntəˈtʃeɪndʒəbl] adj
interchangeable
intercom [ˈɪntəkɔm] n interphone m
intercourse [ˈɪntəkɔːs] n rapports mpl; **sexual ~**
rapports sexuels
interest [ˈɪntrɪst] n intérêt m; (Comm: stake, share)
participation f, intérêts mpl ▷ vt intéresser;
compound/simple ~ intérêt composé/simple;
British ~s in the Middle East les intérêts
britanniques au Moyen-Orient; **his main ~ is ...**

ce qui l'intéresse le plus est ...

interested ['ɪntrɪstɪd] *adj* intéressé(e); **to be ~ in** sth s'intéresser à qch; **I'm ~ in going** ça m'intéresse d'y aller

interesting ['ɪntrɪstɪŋ] *adj* intéressant(e)

interest rate *n* taux *m* d'intérêt

interface ['ɪntəfeɪs] *n* (*Comput*) interface *f*

interfere [ɪntə'fɪəʳ] *vi*: **to ~ in** (*quarrel*) s'immiscer dans; (*other people's business*) se mêler de; **to ~ with** (*object*) tripoter, toucher à; (*plans*) contrecarrer; (*duty*) être en conflit avec; **don't ~** mêlez-vous de vos affaires

interference [ɪntə'fɪərəns] *n* (*gen*) ingérence *f*; (*Physics*) interférence *f*; (*Radio, TV*) parasites *mpl*

interim ['ɪntərɪm] *adj* provisoire; (*post*) intérimaire ▷ *n*: **in the ~** dans l'intérim

interior [ɪn'tɪərɪəʳ] *n* intérieur *m* ▷ *adj* intérieur(e); (*minister, department*) de l'intérieur

interior decorator, interior designer *n* décorateur(-trice) d'intérieur

interior design *n* architecture *f* d'intérieur

interjection [ɪntə'dʒɛkʃən] *n* interjection *f*

interlock [ɪntə'lɔk] *vi* s'enclencher ▷ *vt* enclencher

interlude ['ɪntəluːd] *n* intervalle *m*; (*Theat*) intermède *m*

intermediate [ɪntə'miːdɪət] *adj* intermédiaire; (*Scol: course, level*) moyen(ne)

intermission [ɪntə'mɪʃən] *n* pause *f*; (*Theat, Cine*) entracte *m*

intern *vt* [ɪn'təːn] interner ▷ *n* ['ɪntəːn] (*US*) interne *m/f*

internal [ɪn'təːnl] *adj* interne; (*dispute, reform etc*) intérieur(e); **~ injuries** lésions *fpl* internes

internally [ɪn'təːnəlɪ] *adv* intérieurement; **"not to be taken ~"** "pour usage externe"

Internal Revenue Service *n* (*US*) fisc *m*

international [ɪntə'næʃənl] *adj* international(e) ▷ *n* (*Brit Sport*) international *m*

Internet [ɪntə'nɛt] *n*: **the ~** l'Internet *m*

Internet café *n* cybercafé *m*

Internet Service Provider *n* fournisseur *m* d'accès à Internet

Internet user *n* internaute *m/f*

interplay ['ɪntəpleɪ] *n* effet *m* réciproque, jeu *m*

interpret [ɪn'təːprɪt] *vt* interpréter ▷ *vi* servir d'interprète

interpretation [ɪntəːprɪ'teɪʃən] *n* interprétation *f*

interpreter [ɪn'təːprɪtəʳ] *n* interprète *m/f*; **could you act as an ~ for us?** pourriez-vous nous servir d'interprète?

interrelated [ɪntərɪ'leɪtɪd] *adj* en corrélation, en rapport étroit

interrogate [ɪn'tɛrəugeɪt] *vt* interroger; (*suspect etc*) soumettre à un interrogatoire

interrogation [ɪntɛrəu'geɪʃən] *n* interrogation *f*; (*by police*) interrogatoire *m*

interrogative [ɪntə'rɔgətɪv] *adj* interrogateur(-trice) ▷ *n* (*Ling*) interrogatif *m*

interrupt [ɪntə'rʌpt] *vt, vi* interrompre

interruption [ɪntə'rʌpʃən] *n* interruption *f*

intersect [ɪntə'sɛkt] *vt* couper, croiser; (*Math*) intersecter ▷ *vi* se croiser, se couper; s'intersecter

intersection [ɪntə'sɛkʃən] *n* intersection *f*; (*of roads*) croisement *m*

intersperse [ɪntə'spəːs] *vt*: **to ~ with** parsemer de

interstate ['ɪntəsteɪt] (*US*) *n* autoroute *f* (qui relie plusieurs États)

intertwine [ɪntə'twaɪn] *vt* entrelacer ▷ *vi* s'entrelacer

interval ['ɪntəvl] *n* intervalle *m*; (*Brit: Theat*) entracte *m*; (: *Sport*) mi-temps *f*; **bright ~s** (*in weather*) éclaircies *fpl*; **at ~s** par intervalles

intervene [ɪntə'viːn] *vi* (*time*) s'écouler (entre-temps); (*event*) survenir; (*person*) intervenir

intervention [ɪntə'vɛnʃən] *n* intervention *f*

interview ['ɪntəvjuː] *n* (*Radio, TV*) interview *f*; (*for job*) entrevue *f* ▷ *vt* interviewer, avoir une entrevue avec

interviewer ['ɪntəvjuəʳ] *n* (*Radio, TV*) interviewer *m*

intestine [ɪn'tɛstɪn] *n* intestin *m*; **large ~** gros intestin; **small ~** intestin grêle

intimacy ['ɪntɪməsɪ] *n* intimité *f*

intimate *adj* ['ɪntɪmət] intime; (*friendship*) profond(e); (*knowledge*) approfondi(e) ▷ *vt* ['ɪntɪmeɪt] suggérer, laisser entendre; (*announce*) faire savoir

intimidate [ɪn'tɪmɪdeɪt] *vt* intimider

intimidating [ɪn'tɪmɪdeɪtɪŋ] *adj* intimidant(e)

into ['ɪntu] *prep* dans; **~ pieces/French** en morceaux/français; **to change pounds ~ dollars** changer des livres en dollars; **3 ~ 9 goes 3** 9 divisé par 3 donne 3; **she's ~ opera** c'est une passionnée d'opéra

intolerant [ɪn'tɔlərnt] *adj*: **~ (of)** intolérant(e) (de); (*Med*) intolérant (à)

intoxicated [ɪn'tɔksɪkeɪtɪd] *adj* ivre

intractable [ɪn'træktəbl] *adj* (*child, temper*) indocile, insoumis(e); (*problem*) insoluble; (*illness*) incurable

intranet [ɪn'trənɛt] *n* intranet *m*

intransitive [ɪn'trænsɪtɪv] *adj* intransitif(-ive)

intravenous [ɪntrə'viːnəs] *adj* intraveineux(-euse)

in-tray ['ɪntreɪ] *n* courrier *m* "arrivée"

intricate ['ɪntrɪkət] *adj* complexe, compliqué(e)

intrigue [ɪn'triːg] *n* intrigue *f* ▷ *vt* intriguer ▷ *vi* intriguer, comploter

intriguing [ɪn'triːgɪŋ] *adj* fascinant(e)

intrinsic [ɪn'trɪnsɪk] *adj* intrinsèque

introduce [ɪntrə'djuːs] *vt* introduire; (*TV show etc*) présenter; **to ~ sb (to sb)** présenter qn (à qn); **to ~ sb to** (*pastime, technique*) initier qn à; **may I ~ ...?** je vous présente ...

introduction [ɪntrə'dʌkʃən] *n* introduction *f*; (*of person*) présentation *f*; (*to new experience*) initiation *f*; **a letter of ~** une lettre de recommandation

introductory [ɪntrə'dʌktərɪ] *adj* préliminaire, introductif(-ive); **~ remarks** remarques *fpl* liminaires; **an ~ offer** une offre de lancement

intrude [ɪn'tru:d] vi (person) être importun(e); **to ~ on** or **into** (conversation etc) s'immiscer dans; **am I intruding?** est-ce que je vous dérange?
intruder [ɪn'tru:də\] n intrus(e)
intuition [ɪntju:'ɪʃən] n intuition f
inundate ['ɪnʌndeɪt] vt: **to ~ with** inonder de
invade [ɪn'veɪd] vt envahir
invalid n ['ɪnvəlɪd] malade m/f; (with disability) invalide m/f ▷ adj [ɪn'vælɪd] (not valid) invalide, non valide
invaluable [ɪn'væljuəbl] adj inestimable, inappréciable
invariably [ɪn'veərɪəblɪ] adv invariablement; **she is ~ late** elle est toujours en retard
invasion [ɪn'veɪʒən] n invasion f
invent [ɪn'vɛnt] vt inventer
invention [ɪn'vɛnʃən] n invention f
inventive [ɪn'vɛntɪv] adj inventif(-ive)
inventor [ɪn'vɛntə\] n inventeur(-trice)
inventory ['ɪnvəntrɪ] n inventaire m
invert [ɪn'və:t] vt intervertir; (cup, object) retourner
inverted commas [ɪn'və:tɪd-] npl (Brit) guillemets mpl
invest [ɪn'vɛst] vt investir; (endow): **to ~ sb with sth** conférer qch à qn ▷ vi faire un investissement, investir; **to ~ in** placer de l'argent or investir dans; (fig: acquire) s'offrir, faire l'acquisition de
investigate [ɪn'vɛstɪgeɪt] vt étudier, examiner; (crime) faire une enquête sur
investigation [ɪnvɛstɪ'geɪʃən] n examen m; (of crime) enquête f, investigation f
investigator [ɪn'vɛstɪgeɪtə\] n investigateur(-trice); **private ~** détective privé
investment [ɪn'vɛstmənt] n investissement m, placement m
investor [ɪn'vɛstə\] n épargnant(e); (shareholder) actionnaire m/f
invigilator [ɪn'vɪdʒɪleɪtə\] n (Brit) surveillant m (d'examen)
invigorating [ɪn'vɪgəreɪtɪŋ] adj vivifiant(e), stimulant(e)
invisible [ɪn'vɪzɪbl] adj invisible
invitation [ɪnvɪ'teɪʃən] n invitation f; **by ~ only** sur invitation; **at sb's ~** à la demande de qn
invite [ɪn'vaɪt] vt inviter; (opinions etc) demander; (trouble) chercher; **to ~ sb (to do)** inviter qn (à faire); **to ~ sb to dinner** inviter qn à dîner
▶ **invite out** vt inviter (à sortir)
▶ **invite over** vt inviter (chez soi)
inviting [ɪn'vaɪtɪŋ] adj engageant(e), attrayant(e); (gesture) encourageant(e)
invoice ['ɪnvɔɪs] n facture f ▷ vt facturer; **to ~ sb for goods** facturer des marchandises à qn
involuntary [ɪn'vɔləntrɪ] adj involontaire
involve [ɪn'vɔlv] vt (entail) impliquer; (concern) concerner; (require) nécessiter; **to ~ sb in** (theft etc) impliquer qn dans; (activity, meeting) faire participer qn à
involved [ɪn'vɔlvd] adj (complicated) complexe; **to be ~ in** (take part) participer à; (be engrossed) être

plongé(e) dans; **to feel ~** se sentir concerné(e); **to become ~** (in love etc) s'engager
involvement [ɪn'vɔlvmənt] n (personal role) rôle m; (participation) participation f; (enthusiasm) enthousiasme m; (of resources, funds) mise f en jeu
inward ['ɪnwəd] adj (movement) vers l'intérieur; (thought, feeling) profond(e), intime ▷ adv = **inwards**
inwards ['ɪnwədz] adv vers l'intérieur
I/O abbr (Comput: = input/output) E/S
iodine ['aɪəʊdi:n] n iode m
IOM abbr = **Isle of Man**
iota [aɪ'əʊtə] n (fig) brin m, grain m
IOU n abbr (= I owe you) reconnaissance f de dette
IQ n abbr (= intelligence quotient) Q.I. m
IRA n abbr (= Irish Republican Army) IRA f; (US) = **individual retirement account**
Iran [ɪ'rɑ:n] n Iran m
Iranian [ɪ'reɪnɪən] adj iranien(ne) ▷ n Iranien(ne); (Ling) iranien m
Iraq [ɪ'rɑ:k] n Irak m
Iraqi [ɪ'rɑ:kɪ] adj irakien(ne) ▷ n Irakien(ne)
irate [aɪ'reɪt] adj courroucé(e)
Ireland ['aɪələnd] n Irlande f; **Republic of ~** République f d'Irlande
iris, irises ['aɪrɪs, -ɪz] n iris m
Irish ['aɪrɪʃ] adj irlandais(e) ▷ npl: **the ~** les Irlandais ▷ n (Ling) irlandais m; **the Irish** npl les Irlandais
Irishman ['aɪrɪʃmən] (irreg) n Irlandais m
Irish Sea n: **the ~** la mer d'Irlande
Irishwoman ['aɪrɪʃwumən] (irreg) n Irlandaise f
iron ['aɪən] n fer m; (for clothes) fer m à repasser ▷ adj de or en fer ▷ vt (clothes) repasser; **irons** npl (chains) fers mpl, chaînes fpl
▶ **iron out** vt (crease) faire disparaître au fer; (fig) aplanir; faire disparaître
ironic [aɪ'rɔnɪk], **ironical** [aɪ'rɔnɪkl] adj ironique
ironically [aɪ'rɔnɪklɪ] adv ironiquement
ironing ['aɪənɪŋ] n (activity) repassage m; (clothes: ironed) linge repassé; (: to be ironed) linge à repasser
ironing board n planche f à repasser
ironmonger ['aɪənmʌŋgə\] n (Brit) quincaillier m; **~'s (shop)** quincaillerie f
irony ['aɪrənɪ] n ironie f
irrational [ɪ'ræʃənl] adj irrationnel(le); (person) qui n'est pas rationnel
irregular [ɪ'regjulə\] adj irrégulier(-ière); (surface) inégal(e); (action, event) peu orthodoxe
irrelevant [ɪ'reləvənt] adj sans rapport, hors de propos
irresistible [ɪrɪ'zɪstɪbl] adj irrésistible
irrespective [ɪrɪ'spɛktɪv]: **~ of** prep sans tenir compte de
irresponsible [ɪrɪ'spɔnsɪbl] adj (act) irréfléchi(e); (person) qui n'a pas le sens des responsabilités
irrigate ['ɪrɪgeɪt] vt irriguer
irrigation [ɪrɪ'geɪʃən] n irrigation f
irritable ['ɪrɪtəbl] adj irritable
irritate ['ɪrɪteɪt] vt irriter
irritating ['ɪrɪteɪtɪŋ] adj irritant(e)

irritation [ɪrɪ'teɪʃən] *n* irritation *f*

IRS *n abbr* (US) = **Internal Revenue Service**

is [ɪz] *vb see* **be**

ISDN *n abbr* (= *Integrated Services Digital Network*) RNIS *m*

Islam ['ɪzlɑːm] *n* Islam *m*

Islamic [ɪz'lɑːmɪk] *adj* islamique; **~ fundamentalists** intégristes *mpl* musulmans

island ['aɪlənd] *n* île *f*; (*also*: **traffic island**) refuge *m* (pour piétons)

islander ['aɪləndə'] *n* habitant(e) d'une île, insulaire *m/f*

isle [aɪl] *n* île *f*

isn't ['ɪznt] = **is not**

isolate ['aɪsəleɪt] *vt* isoler

isolated ['aɪsəleɪtɪd] *adj* isolé(e)

isolation [aɪsə'leɪʃən] *n* isolement *m*

ISP *n abbr* = **Internet Service Provider**

Israel ['ɪzreɪl] *n* Israël *m*

Israeli [ɪz'reɪlɪ] *adj* israélien(ne) ▷ *n* Israélien(ne)

issue ['ɪʃuː] *n* question *f*, problème *m*; (*outcome*) résultat *m*, issue *f*; (*of banknotes*) émission *f*; (*of newspaper*) numéro *m*; (*of book*) publication *f*, parution *f*; (*offspring*) descendance *f* ▷ *vt* (*rations, equipment*) distribuer; (*orders*) donner; (*statement*) publier, faire; (*certificate, passport*) délivrer; (*book*) faire paraître; publier; (*banknotes, cheques, stamps*) émettre, mettre en circulation ▷ *vi*: **to ~ from** provenir de; **at ~** en jeu, en cause; **to avoid the ~** éluder le problème; **to take ~ with sb (over sth)** exprimer son désaccord avec qn (sur qch); **to make an ~ of sth** faire de qch un problème; **to confuse** *or* **obscure the ~** embrouiller la question

IT *n abbr* = **information technology**

it [ɪt] *pron* **1** (*specific: subject*) il (elle); (: *direct object*) le (la, l'); (: *indirect object*) lui; **it's on the table** c'est *or* il (*or* elle) est sur la table; **I can't find it** je n'arrive pas à le trouver; **give it to me** donne-le-moi

2 (*after prep*): **about/from/of it** en; **I spoke to him about it** je lui en ai parlé; **what did you learn from it?** qu'est-ce que vous en avez retiré?;

I'm proud of it j'en suis fier; **I've come from it** j'en viens; **in/to it** y; **put the book in it** mettez-y le livre; **it's on it** c'est dessus; **he agreed to it** il y a consenti; **did you go to it?** (*party, concert etc*) est-ce que vous y êtes allé(s)?; **above it, over it** (au-)dessus; **below it, under it** (en-)dessous; **in front of/behind it** devant/derrière

3 (*impersonal*) il; ce, cela, ça; **it's raining** il pleut; **it's Friday tomorrow** demain, c'est vendredi *or* nous sommes, vendredi; **it's 6 o'clock** il est 6 heures; **how far is it?** — **it's 10 miles** c'est loin? — c'est à 10 miles; **it's 2 hours by train** c'est à 2 heures de train; **who is it?** — **it's me** qui est-ce? — c'est moi

Italian [ɪ'tæljən] *adj* italien(ne) ▷ *n* Italien(ne); (*Ling*) italien *m*

italic [ɪ'tælɪk] *adj* italique

italics [ɪ'tælɪks] *npl* italique *m*

Italy ['ɪtəlɪ] *n* Italie *f*

itch [ɪtʃ] *n* démangeaison *f* ▷ *vi* (*person*) éprouver des démangeaisons; (*part of body*) démanger; **I'm ~ing to do** l'envie me démange de faire

itchy ['ɪtʃɪ] *adj* qui démange; **my back is ~** j'ai le dos qui me démange

it'd ['ɪtd] = **it would**; **it had**

item ['aɪtəm] *n* (*gen*) article *m*; (*on agenda*) question *f*, point *m*; (*in programme*) numéro *m*; (*also*: **news item**) nouvelle *f*; **~s of clothing** articles vestimentaires

itemize ['aɪtəmaɪz] *vt* détailler, spécifier

itinerary [aɪ'tɪnərərɪ] *n* itinéraire *m*

it'll ['ɪtl] = **it will**; **it shall**

its [ɪts] *adj* son (sa), ses *pl* ▷ *pron* le (la) sien(ne), les siens (siennes)

it's [ɪts] = **it is**; **it has**

itself [ɪt'self] *pron* (*reflexive*) se; (*emphatic*) lui-même (elle-même)

ITV *n abbr* (*Brit*: = *Independent Television*) chaîne de télévision commerciale

IUD *n abbr* = **intra-uterine device**

I've [aɪv] = **I have**

ivory ['aɪvərɪ] *n* ivoire *m*

ivy ['aɪvɪ] *n* lierre *m*

J j

jab [dʒæb] vt: **to ~ sth into** enfoncer or planter qch dans ▷ n coup m; (Med: inf) piqûre f

jack [dʒæk] n (Aut) cric m; (Bowls) cochonnet m; (Cards) valet m
  ▶**jack in** vt (inf) laisser tomber
  ▶**jack up** vt soulever (au cric)

jackal ['dʒækl] n chacal m

jacket ['dʒækɪt] n veste f, veston m; (of boiler etc) enveloppe f; (of book) couverture f, jaquette f

jacket potato n pomme f de terre en robe des champs

jackknife ['dʒæknaɪf] n couteau m de poche ▷ vi: **the lorry ~d** la remorque (du camion) s'est mise en travers

jack plug n (Brit) jack m

jackpot ['dʒækpɔt] n gros lot

Jacuzzi® [dʒə'kuːzɪ] n jacuzzi® m

jaded ['dʒeɪdɪd] adj éreinté(e), fatigué(e)

jagged ['dʒægɪd] adj dentelé(e)

jail [dʒeɪl] n prison f ▷ vt emprisonner, mettre en prison

jail sentence n peine f de prison

jam [dʒæm] n confiture f; (of shoppers etc) cohue f; (also: **traffic jam**) embouteillage m ▷ vt (passage etc) encombrer, obstruer; (mechanism, drawer etc) bloquer, coincer; (Radio) brouiller ▷ vi (mechanism, sliding part) se coincer, se bloquer; (gun) s'enrayer; **to be in a ~** (inf) être dans le pétrin; **to get sb out of a ~** (inf) sortir qn du pétrin; **to ~ sth into** (stuff) entasser or comprimer qch dans; (thrust) enfoncer qch dans; **the telephone lines are ~med** les lignes (téléphoniques) sont encombrées

Jamaica [dʒə'meɪkə] n Jamaïque f

jam jar n pot m à confiture

jammed [dʒæmd] adj (window etc) coincé(e)

jam-packed [dʒæm'pækt] adj: **~ (with)** bourré(e) (de)

jangle ['dʒæŋgl] vi cliqueter

janitor ['dʒænɪtər] n (caretaker) concierge m

January ['dʒænjuərɪ] n janvier m; for phrases see also **July**

Japan [dʒə'pæn] n Japon m

Japanese [dʒæpə'niːz] adj japonais(e) ▷ n (pl inv) Japonais(e); (Ling) japonais m

jar [dʒɑːr] n (stone, earthenware) pot m; (glass) bocal m ▷ vi (sound) produire un son grinçant or discordant; (colours etc) détonner, jurer ▷ vt (shake) ébranler, secouer

jargon ['dʒɑːgən] n jargon m

jaundice ['dʒɔːndɪs] n jaunisse f

javelin ['dʒævlɪn] n javelot m

jaw [dʒɔː] n mâchoire f

jay [dʒeɪ] n geai m

jaywalker ['dʒeɪwɔːkər] n piéton indiscipliné

jazz [dʒæz] n jazz m
  ▶**jazz up** vt animer, égayer

jealous ['dʒeləs] adj jaloux(-ouse)

jealousy ['dʒeləsɪ] n jalousie f

jeans [dʒiːnz] npl jean m

jeer [dʒɪər] vi: **to ~ (at)** huer; se moquer cruellement (de), railler

Jehovah's Witness [dʒɪ'həuvəz-] n témoin m de Jéhovah

Jello® ['dʒeləu] (US) n gelée f

jelly ['dʒelɪ] n (dessert) gelée f; (US: jam) confiture f

jellyfish ['dʒelɪfɪʃ] n méduse f

jeopardize ['dʒepədaɪz] vt mettre en danger or péril

jeopardy ['dʒepədɪ] n: **in ~** en danger or péril

jerk [dʒəːk] n secousse f, saccade f; (of muscle) spasme m; (inf) pauvre type m ▷ vt (shake) donner une secousse à; (pull) tirer brusquement ▷ vi (vehicles) cahoter

jersey ['dʒəːzɪ] n tricot m; (fabric) jersey m

Jesus ['dʒiːzəs] n Jésus m; **~ Christ** Jésus-Christ

jet [dʒet] n (of gas, liquid) jet m; (Aut) gicleur m; (Aviat) avion m à réaction, jet m

jet-black ['dʒet'blæk] adj (d'un noir) de jais

jet engine n moteur m à réaction

jet lag n décalage m horaire

jet-ski vi faire du jet-ski or scooter des mers

jettison ['dʒetɪsn] vt jeter par-dessus bord

jetty ['dʒetɪ] n jetée f, digue f

Jew [dʒuː] n Juif m

jewel ['dʒuːəl] n bijou m, joyau m; (in watch) rubis m

jeweller, (US) **jeweler** ['dʒuːələr] n bijoutier(-ière), joaillier m

jeweller's, jeweller's shop n (Brit) bijouterie f, joaillerie f

jewellery, (US) **jewelry** ['dʒuːəlrɪ] n bijoux mpl

Jewess ['dʒuːɪs] n Juive f

Jewish ['dʒuːɪʃ] adj juif (juive)

jibe [dʒaɪb] *n* sarcasme *m*

jiffy ['dʒɪfɪ] *n* (*inf*): **in a ~** en un clin d'œil

jigsaw ['dʒɪgsɔ:] *n* (*also*: **jigsaw puzzle**) puzzle *m*; (*tool*) scie sauteuse

jilt [dʒɪlt] *vt* laisser tomber, plaquer

jingle ['dʒɪŋgl] *n* (*advertising jingle*) couplet *m* publicitaire ▷ *vi* cliqueter, tinter

jinx [dʒɪŋks] *n* (*inf*) (mauvais) sort

jitters ['dʒɪtəz] *npl* (*inf*): **to get the ~** avoir la trouille *or* la frousse

job [dʒɔb] *n* (*chore, task*) travail *m*, tâche *f*; (*employment*) emploi *m*, poste *m*, place *f*; **a part-time/full-time ~** un emploi à temps partiel/à plein temps; **he's only doing his ~** il fait son boulot; **it's a good ~ that ...** c'est heureux *or* c'est une chance que ... +*sub*; **just the ~!** (c'est) juste *or* exactement ce qu'il faut!

job centre ['dʒɔbsentə'] (*Brit*) *n* ≈ ANPE *f*, ≈ Agence nationale pour l'emploi

jobless ['dʒɔblɪs] *adj* sans travail, au chômage ▷ *npl*: **the ~** les sans-emploi *m inv*, les chômeurs *mpl*

jockey ['dʒɔkɪ] *n* jockey *m* ▷ *vi*: **to ~ for position** manœuvrer pour être bien placé

jog [dʒɔg] *vt* secouer ▷ *vi* (*Sport*) faire du jogging; **to ~ along** cahoter; trotter; **to ~ sb's memory** rafraîchir la mémoire de qn

jogging ['dʒɔgɪŋ] *n* jogging *m*

join [dʒɔɪn] *vt* (*put together*) unir, assembler; (*become member of*) s'inscrire à; (*meet*) rejoindre, retrouver; (*queue*) se joindre à ▷ *vi* (*roads, rivers*) se rejoindre, se rencontrer ▷ *n* raccord *m*; **will you ~ us for dinner?** vous dînerez bien avec nous?; **I'll ~ you later** je vous rejoindrai plus tard; **to ~ forces (with)** s'associer (à)

▶ **join in** *vi* se mettre à la partie ▷ *vt fus* se mêler à

▶ **join up** *vi* (*meet*) se rejoindre; (*Mil*) s'engager

joiner ['dʒɔɪnə'] (*Brit*) *n* menuisier *m*

joint [dʒɔɪnt] *n* (*Tech*) jointure *f*; joint *m*; (*Anat*) articulation *f*, jointure *f*; (*Brit Culin*) rôti *m*; (*inf*: *place*) boîte *f*; (*of cannabis*) joint ▷ *adj* commun(e); (*committee*) mixte, paritaire; (*winner*) ex aequo; **~ responsibility** coresponsabilité *f*

joint account *n* compte joint

jointly ['dʒɔɪntlɪ] *adv* ensemble, en commun

joke [dʒəuk] *n* plaisanterie *f*; (*also*: **practical joke**) farce *f* ▷ *vi* plaisanter; **to play a ~ on** jouer un tour à, faire une farce à

joker ['dʒəukə'] *n* plaisantin *m*, blagueur(-euse); (*Cards*) joker *m*

jolly ['dʒɔlɪ] *adj* gai(e), enjoué(e); (*enjoyable*) amusant(e), plaisant(e) ▷ *adv* (*Brit inf*) rudement, drôlement ▷ *vt* (*Brit*): **to ~ sb along** amadouer qn, convaincre *or* entraîner qn à force d'encouragements; **~ good!** (*Brit*) formidable!

jolt [dʒəult] *n* cahot *m*, secousse *f*; (*shock*) choc *m* ▷ *vt* cahoter, secouer

Jordan ['dʒɔ:dən] *n* (*country*) Jordanie *f*; (*river*) Jourdain *m*

jostle ['dʒɔsl] *vt* bousculer, pousser ▷ *vi* jouer des coudes

jot [dʒɔt] *n*: **not one ~** pas un brin

▶ **jot down** *vt* inscrire rapidement, noter

jotter ['dʒɔtə'] *n* (*Brit*) cahier *m* (de brouillon); bloc-notes *m*

journal ['dʒə:nl] *n* journal *m*

journalism ['dʒə:nəlɪzəm] *n* journalisme *m*

journalist ['dʒə:nəlɪst] *n* journaliste *m/f*

journey ['dʒə:nɪ] *n* voyage *m*; (*distance covered*) trajet *m* ▷ *vi* voyager; **the ~ takes two hours** le trajet dure deux heures; **a 5-hour ~** un voyage de 5 heures; **how was your ~?** votre voyage s'est bien passé?

joy [dʒɔɪ] *n* joie *f*

joyful ['dʒɔɪful], **joyous** ['dʒɔɪəs] *adj* joyeux(-euse)

joyrider ['dʒɔɪraɪdə'] *n* voleur(-euse) de voiture (*qui fait une virée dans le véhicule volé*)

joy stick ['dʒɔɪstɪk] *n* (*Aviat*) manche *m* à balai; (*Comput*) manche à balai, manette *f* (de jeu)

JP *n abbr* = **Justice of the Peace**

Jr *abbr* = **junior**

jubilant ['dʒu:bɪlnt] *adj* triomphant(e), réjoui(e)

judge [dʒʌdʒ] *n* juge *m* ▷ *vt* juger; (*estimate: weight, size etc*) apprécier; (*consider*) estimer ▷ *vi*: **judging** *or* **to ~ by his expression** d'après son expression; **as far as I can ~** autant que je puisse en juger

judgment, judgement ['dʒʌdʒmənt] *n* jugement *m*; (*punishment*) châtiment *m*; **in my ~** à mon avis; **to pass ~ on** (*Law*) prononcer un jugement (sur)

judicial [dʒu:'dɪʃl] *adj* judiciaire; (*fair*) impartial(e)

judiciary [dʒu:'dɪʃɪərɪ] *n* (pouvoir *m*) judiciaire *m*

judo ['dʒu:dəu] *n* judo *m*

jug [dʒʌg] *n* pot *m*, cruche *f*

juggernaut ['dʒʌgənɔ:t] *n* (*Brit: huge truck*) mastodonte *m*

juggle ['dʒʌgl] *vi* jongler

juggler ['dʒʌglə'] *n* jongleur *m*

juice [dʒu:s] *n* jus *m*; (*inf: petrol*): **we've run out of ~** c'est la panne sèche

juicy ['dʒu:sɪ] *adj* juteux(-euse)

jukebox ['dʒu:kbɔks] *n* juke-box *m*

July [dʒu:'laɪ] *n* juillet *m*; **the first of ~** le premier juillet; (**on**) **the eleventh of ~** le onze juillet; **in the month of ~** au mois de juillet; **at the beginning/end of ~** au début/à la fin (du mois) de juillet, début/fin juillet; **in the middle of ~** au milieu (du mois) de juillet, à la mi-juillet; **during ~** pendant le mois de juillet; **in ~ of next year** en juillet de l'année prochaine; **each** *or* **every ~** tous les ans *or* chaque année en juillet; **~ was wet this year** il a beaucoup plu cette année en juillet

jumble ['dʒʌmbl] *n* fouillis *m* ▷ *vt* (*also*: **jumble up, jumble together**) mélanger, brouiller

jumble sale *n* (*Brit*) vente *f* de charité

jumbo ['dʒʌmbəu] *adj* (*also*: **jumbo jet**) (avion) gros porteur (à réaction); **~ size** format maxi *or* extra-grand

jump [dʒʌmp] *vi* sauter, bondir; (*with fear etc*)

sursauter; (*increase*) monter en flèche ▷ *vt*
sauter, franchir ▷ *n* saut *m*, bond *m*; (*with fear
etc*) sursaut *m*; (*fence*) obstacle *m*; **to ~ the queue**
(*Brit*) passer avant son tour
  ▶ **jump about** *vi* sautiller
  ▶ **jump at** *vt fus* (*fig*) sauter sur; **he ~ed at the
  offer** il s'est empressé d'accepter la proposition
  ▶ **jump down** *vi* sauter (pour descendre)
  ▶ **jump up** *vi* se lever (d'un bond)
jumper ['dʒʌmpəʳ] *n* (*Brit: pullover*) pull-over
m; (*US: pinafore dress*) robe-chasuble *f*; (*Sport*)
sauteur(-euse)
jump leads, (*US*) **jumper cables** *npl* câbles *mpl*
de démarrage
jumpy ['dʒʌmpɪ] *adj* nerveux(-euse), agité(e)
Jun. *abbr* = **June; junior**
junction ['dʒʌŋkʃən] *n* (*Brit: of roads*) carrefour *m*;
(*of rails*) embranchement *m*
juncture ['dʒʌŋktʃəʳ] *n*: **at this ~** à ce moment-là,
sur ces entrefaites
June [dʒuːn] *n* juin *m*; *for phrases see also* **July**
jungle ['dʒʌŋɡl] *n* jungle *f*
junior ['dʒuːnɪəʳ] *adj, n*: **he's ~ to me (by two
years), he's my ~ (by two years)** il est mon
cadet (de deux ans), il est plus jeune que moi
(de deux ans); **he's ~ to me** (*seniority*) il est en
dessous de moi (dans la hiérarchie), j'ai plus
d'ancienneté que lui
junior high school *n* (*US*) ≈ collège *m*
d'enseignement secondaire; *see also* **high school**
junior school *n* (*Brit*) école *f* primaire
junk [dʒʌŋk] *n* (*rubbish*) camelote *f*; (*cheap
goods*) bric-à-brac *m inv*; (*ship*) jonque *f* ▷ *vt* (*inf*)
abandonner, mettre au rancart
junk food *n* snacks vite prêts (*sans valeur nutritive*)
junkie ['dʒʌŋkɪ] *n* (*inf*) junkie *m*, drogué(e)
junk mail *n* prospectus *mpl*; (*Comput*) messages
mpl publicitaires

junk shop *n* (boutique *f* de) brocanteur *m*
Junr *abbr* = **junior**
Jupiter ['dʒuːpɪtəʳ] *n* (*planet*) Jupiter *f*
jurisdiction [dʒuərɪs'dɪkʃən] *n* juridiction *f*; **it
falls** or **comes within/outside our ~** cela est/
n'est pas de notre compétence or ressort
juror ['dʒuərəʳ] *n* juré *m*
jury ['dʒuərɪ] *n* jury *m*
just [dʒʌst] *adj* juste ▷ *adv*: **he's ~ done it/left**
il vient de le faire/partir; **~ as I expected**
exactement or précisément comme je m'y
attendais; **~ right/two o'clock** exactement or
juste ce qu'il faut/deux heures; **we were ~ going**
nous partions; **I was ~ about to phone** j'allais
téléphoner; **~ as he was leaving** au moment or à
l'instant précis où il partait; **~ before/enough/
here** juste avant/assez/là; **it's ~ me/a mistake**
ce n'est que moi/(rien) qu'une erreur; **~ missed/
caught** manqué/attrapé de justesse; **~ listen
to this!** écoutez un peu ça!; **~ ask someone the
way** vous n'avez qu'à demander votre chemin à
quelqu'un; **it's ~ as good** c'est (vraiment) aussi
bon; **she's ~ as clever as you** elle est tout aussi
intelligente que vous; **it's ~ as well that you
...** heureusement que vous ...; **not ~ now** pas
tout de suite; **~ a minute!, ~ one moment!** un
instant (s'il vous plaît)!
justice ['dʒʌstɪs] *n* justice *f*; (*US: judge*) juge *m* de
la Cour suprême; **Lord Chief J~** (*Brit*) premier
président de la cour d'appel; **this photo doesn't
do you ~** cette photo ne vous avantage pas
Justice of the Peace *n* juge *m* de paix
justification [dʒʌstɪfɪ'keɪʃən] *n* justification *f*
justify ['dʒʌstɪfaɪ] *vt* justifier; **to be justified in
doing sth** être en droit de faire qch
jut [dʒʌt] *vi* (*also:* **jut out**) dépasser, faire saillie
juvenile ['dʒuːvənaɪl] *adj* juvénile; (*court, books*)
pour enfants ▷ *n* adolescent(e)

K, k [keɪ] *n* (*letter*) K, k *m*; **K for King** K comme Kléber ▷ *abbr* (= *one thousand*) K; (*Brit*: = *Knight*) titre honorifique

kangaroo [kæŋgə'ru:] *n* kangourou *m*

karaoke [ka:rə'əukɪ] *n* karaoké *m*

karate [kə'ra:tɪ] *n* karaté *m*

kebab [kə'bæb] *n* kebab *m*

keel [ki:l] *n* quille *f*; **on an even ~** (*fig*) à flot
▶ **keel over** *vi* (*Naut*) chavirer, dessaler; (*person*) tomber dans les pommes

keen [ki:n] *adj* (*eager*) plein(e) d'enthousiasme; (*interest, desire, competition*) vif (vive); (*eye, intelligence*) pénétrant(e); (*edge*) effilé(e); **to be ~ to do** *or* **on doing sth** désirer vivement faire qch, tenir beaucoup à faire qch; **to be ~ on sth/sb** aimer beaucoup qch/qn; **I'm not ~ on going** je ne suis pas très chaud pour y aller, je n'ai pas très envie d'y aller

keep [ki:p] (*pt, pp* **kept**) [kɛpt] *vt* (*retain, preserve*) garder; (*hold back*) retenir; (*shop, accounts, promise, diary*) tenir; (*support*) entretenir, assurer la subsistance de; (*a promise*) tenir; (*chickens, bees, pigs etc*) élever ▷ *vi* (*food*) se conserver; (*remain: in a certain state or place*) rester ▷ *n* (*of castle*) donjon *m*; (*food etc*) **enough for his ~** assez pour (assurer) sa subsistance; **to ~ doing sth** (*continue*) continuer à faire qch; (*repeatedly*) ne pas arrêter de faire qch; **to ~ sb from doing/sth from happening** empêcher qn de faire *or* que qn (ne) fasse/que qch (n')arrive; **to ~ sb happy/a place tidy** faire que qn soit content/qu'un endroit reste propre; **to ~ sb waiting** faire attendre qn; **to ~ an appointment** ne pas manquer un rendez-vous; **to ~ a record of sth** prendre note de qch; **to ~ sth to o.s.** garder qch pour soi, tenir qch secret; **to ~ sth from sb** cacher qch à qn; **to ~ time** (*clock*) être à l'heure, ne pas retarder; **for ~s** (*inf*) pour de bon, pour toujours
▶ **keep away** *vt*: **to ~ sth/sb away from sb** tenir qch/qn éloigné de qn ▷ *vi*: **to ~ away (from)** ne pas s'approcher (de)
▶ **keep back** *vt* (*crowds, tears, money*) retenir; (*conceal: information*): **to ~ sth back from sb** cacher qch à qn ▷ *vi* rester en arrière
▶ **keep down** *vt* (*control: prices, spending*) empêcher d'augmenter, limiter; (*retain: food*) garder ▷ *vi* (*person*) rester assis(e); rester par terre

▶ **keep in** *vt* (*invalid, child*) garder à la maison; (*Scol*) consigner ▷ *vi* (*inf*): **to ~ in with sb** rester en bons termes avec qn
▶ **keep off** *vt* (*dog, person*) éloigner ▷ *vi* ne pas s'approcher; **if the rain ~s off** s'il ne pleut pas; **~ your hands off!** pas touche! (*inf*); **"~ off the grass"** "pelouse interdite"
▶ **keep on** *vi* continuer; **to ~ on doing** continuer à faire; **don't ~ on about it!** arrête (d'en parler)!
▶ **keep out** *vt* empêcher d'entrer ▷ *vi* (*stay out*) rester en dehors; **"~ out"** "défense d'entrer"
▶ **keep up** *vi* (*fig: in comprehension*) suivre ▷ *vt* continuer, maintenir; **to ~ up with sb** (*in work etc*) se maintenir au même niveau que qn; (*in race etc*) aller aussi vite que qn

keeper ['ki:pər] *n* gardien(ne)

keep-fit [ki:p'fɪt] *n* gymnastique *f* (d'entretien)

keeping ['ki:pɪŋ] *n* (*care*) garde *f*; **in ~ with** en harmonie avec

keepsake ['ki:pseɪk] *n* souvenir *m*

kennel ['kɛnl] *n* niche *f*; **kennels** *npl* (*for boarding*) chenil *m*

Kenya ['kɛnjə] *n* Kenya *m*

kept [kɛpt] *pt, pp of* **keep**

kerb [kə:b] *n* (*Brit*) bordure *f* du trottoir

kernel ['kə:nl] *n* amande *f*; (*fig*) noyau *m*

kerosene ['kɛrəsi:n] *n* kérosène *m*

ketchup ['kɛtʃəp] *n* ketchup *m*

kettle ['kɛtl] *n* bouilloire *f*

key [ki:] *n*; clé *f*; (*of piano, typewriter*) touche *f*; (*on map*) légende *f* ▷ *adj* (*factor, role, area*) clé *inv* ▷ *cpd* (-)clé ▷ *vt* (*also*: **key in**: *text*) saisir; **can I have my ~?** je peux avoir ma clé?; **a ~ issue** un problème fondamental

keyboard ['ki:bɔ:d] *n* clavier *m* ▷ *vt* (*text*) saisir

keyed up [ki:d'ʌp] *adj*: **to be (all) ~** être surexcité(e)

keyhole ['ki:həul] *n* trou *m* de la serrure

keyhole surgery *n* chirurgie très minutieuse où l'incision est minimale

keynote ['ki:nəut] *n* (*Mus*) tonique *f*; (*fig*) note dominante

keyring ['ki:rɪŋ] *n* porte-clés *m*

kg *abbr* (= *kilogram*) K

khaki ['ka:kɪ] *adj, n* kaki *m*

kick [kɪk] *vt* donner un coup de pied à ▷ *vi* (*horse*) ruer ▷ *n* coup *m* de pied; (*of rifle*) recul *m*; (*inf*:

thrill): **he does it for ~s** il le fait parce que ça l'excite, il le fait pour le plaisir; **to ~ the habit** (*inf*) arrêter

▸ **kick around** *vi* (*inf*) traîner

▸ **kick off** *vi* (*Sport*) donner le coup d'envoi

kick-off ['kɪkɔf] *n* (*Sport*) coup *m* d'envoi

kid [kɪd] *n* (*inf: child*) gamin(e), gosse *m/f*; (*animal, leather*) chevreau *m* ▸ *vi* (*inf*) plaisanter, blaguer

kidnap ['kɪdnæp] *vt* enlever, kidnapper

kidnapper ['kɪdnæpə^r] *n* ravisseur(-euse)

kidnapping ['kɪdnæpɪŋ] *n* enlèvement *m*

kidney ['kɪdnɪ] *n* (*Anat*) rein *m*; (*Culin*) rognon *m*

kidney bean *n* haricot *m* rouge

kill [kɪl] *vt* tuer; (*fig*) faire échouer; détruire; supprimer ▸ *n* mise *f* à mort; **to ~ time** tuer le temps

▸ **kill off** *vt* exterminer; (*fig*) éliminer

killer ['kɪlə^r] *n* tueur(-euse); (*murderer*) meurtrier(-ière)

killing ['kɪlɪŋ] *n* meurtre *m*; (*of group of people*) tuerie *f*, massacre *m*; (*inf*): **to make a ~** se remplir les poches, réussir un beau coup ▸ *adj* (*inf*) tordant(e)

killjoy ['kɪldʒɔɪ] *n* rabat-joie *m inv*

kiln [kɪln] *n* four *m*

kilo ['ki:ləu] *n* kilo *m*

kilobyte ['ki:ləubaɪt] *n* (*Comput*) kilo-octet *m*

kilogram, kilogramme ['kɪləugræm] *n* kilogramme *m*

kilometre, (*US*) **kilometer** ['kɪləmi:tə^r] *n* kilomètre *m*

kilowatt ['kɪləuwɔt] *n* kilowatt *m*

kilt [kɪlt] *n* kilt *m*

kin [kɪn] *n see* **next-of-kin**; **kith**

kind [kaɪnd] *adj* gentil(le), aimable ▸ *n* sorte *f*, espèce *f*; (*species*) genre *m*; **would you be ~ enough to …?**, **would you be so ~ as to …?** auriez-vous la gentillesse *or* l'obligeance de …?; **it's very ~ of you (to do)** c'est très aimable à vous (de faire); **to be two of a ~** se ressembler; **in ~** (*Comm*) en nature; (*fig*): **to repay sb in ~** rendre la pareille à qn; **~ of** (*inf: rather*) plutôt; **a ~ of** une sorte de; **what ~ of …?** quelle sorte de …?

kindergarten ['kɪndəga:tn] *n* jardin *m* d'enfants

kind-hearted [kaɪnd'ha:tɪd] *adj* bon (bonne)

kindle ['kɪndl] *vt* allumer, enflammer

kindly ['kaɪndlɪ] *adj* bienveillant(e), plein(e) de gentillesse ▸ *adv* avec bonté; **will you ~ …** auriez-vous la bonté *or* l'obligeance de …; **he didn't take it ~** il l'a mal pris

kindness ['kaɪndnɪs] *n* (*quality*) bonté *f*, gentillesse *f*

king [kɪŋ] *n* roi *m*

kingdom ['kɪŋdəm] *n* royaume *m*

kingfisher ['kɪŋfɪʃə^r] *n* martin-pêcheur *m*

king-size ['kɪŋsaɪz], **king-sized** ['kɪŋsaɪzd] *adj* (*cigarette*) (format) extra-long (longue)

king-size bed, king-sized bed *n* grand lit (*de 1,95 m de large*)

kiosk ['ki:ɔsk] *n* kiosque *m*; (*Brit: also:* **telephone kiosk**) cabine *f* (téléphonique); (*also:* **newspaper kiosk**) kiosque à journaux

kipper ['kɪpə^r] *n* hareng fumé et salé

kiss [kɪs] *n* baiser *m* ▸ *vt* embrasser; **to ~ (each other)** s'embrasser; **to ~ sb goodbye** dire au revoir à qn en l'embrassant

kiss of life *n* (*Brit*) bouche à bouche *m*

kit [kɪt] *n* équipement *m*, matériel *m*; (*set of tools etc*) trousse *f*; (*for assembly*) kit *m*; **tool ~** nécessaire *m* à outils

▸ **kit out** *vt* (*Brit*) équiper

kitchen ['kɪtʃɪn] *n* cuisine *f*

kitchen sink *n* évier *m*

kite [kaɪt] *n* (*toy*) cerf-volant *m*; (*Zool*) milan *m*

kitten ['kɪtn] *n* petit chat, chaton *m*

kitty ['kɪtɪ] *n* (*money*) cagnotte *f*

kiwi ['ki:wi:] *n* (*also:* **kiwi fruit**) kiwi *m*

km *abbr* (= *kilometre*) km

km/h *abbr* (= *kilometres per hour*) km/h

knack [næk] *n*: **to have the ~ (of doing)** avoir le coup (pour faire); **there's a ~** il y a un coup à prendre *or* une combine

knapsack ['næpsæk] *n* musette *f*

knead [ni:d] *vt* pétrir

knee [ni:] *n* genou *m*

kneecap ['ni:kæp] *n* rotule *f* ▸ *vt* tirer un coup de feu dans la rotule de

kneel (*pt, pp* **knelt**) [ni:l, nɛlt] *vi* (*also:* **kneel down**) s'agenouiller

knelt [nɛlt] *pt, pp of* **kneel**

knew [nju:] *pt of* **know**

knickers ['nɪkəz] *npl* (*Brit*) culotte *f* (de femme)

knife [naɪf] *n* (*pl* **knives**) [naɪvz] couteau *m* ▸ *vt* poignarder, frapper d'un coup de couteau; **~, fork and spoon** couvert *m*

knight [naɪt] *n* chevalier *m*; (*Chess*) cavalier *m*

knighthood ['naɪthud] *n* chevalerie *f*; (*title*): **to get a ~** être fait chevalier

knit [nɪt] *vt* tricoter; (*fig*): **to ~ together** unir ▸ *vi* tricoter; (*broken bones*) se ressouder; **to ~ one's brows** froncer les sourcils

knitting ['nɪtɪŋ] *n* tricot *m*

knitting needle *n* aiguille *f* à tricoter

knitwear ['nɪtwɛə^r] *n* tricots *mpl*, lainages *mpl*

knives [naɪvz] *npl of* **knife**

knob [nɔb] *n* bouton *m*; (*Brit*): **a ~ of butter** une noix de beurre

knock [nɔk] *vt* frapper; (*bump into*) heurter; (*make: hole etc*): **to ~ a hole in** faire un trou dans, trouer; (*force: nail etc*): **to ~ a nail into** enfoncer un clou dans; (*fig: col*) dénigrer ▸ *vi* (*engine*) cogner; (*at door etc*): **to ~ at/on** frapper à/sur ▸ *n* coup *m*; **he ~ed at the door** il frappa à la porte

▸ **knock down** *vt* renverser; (*price*) réduire

▸ **knock off** *vi* (*inf: finish*) s'arrêter (de travailler) ▸ *vt* (*vase, object*) faire tomber; (*inf: steal*) piquer; (*fig: from price etc*): **to ~ off £10** faire une remise de 10 livres

▸ **knock out** *vt* assommer; (*Boxing*) mettre k.-o.; (*in competition*) éliminer

▸ **knock over** *vt* (*object*) faire tomber; (*pedestrian*) renverser

knocker ['nɔkə^r] *n* (*on door*) heurtoir *m*

knockout ['nɔkaut] *n* (*Boxing*) knock-out *m*, K.-

O. *m*; **~ competition** (*Brit*) compétition *f* avec épreuves éliminatoires

knot [nɔt] *n* (*gen*) nœud *m* ▷ *vt* nouer; **to tie a ~** faire un nœud

know [nəu] *vt* (*pt* **knew**, *pp* **-n**) [njuː, nəun] savoir; (*person, place*) connaître; **to ~ that** savoir que; **to ~ how to do** savoir faire; **to ~ how to swim** savoir nager; **to ~ about/of sth** (*event*) être au courant de qch; (*subject*) connaître qch; **to get to ~ sth** (*fact*) apprendre qch; (*place*) apprendre à connaître qch; **I don't ~** je ne sais pas; **I don't ~ him** je ne le connais pas; **do you ~ where I can ...?** savez-vous où je peux ...?; **to ~ right from wrong** savoir distinguer le bon du mauvais; **as far as I ~ ...** à ma connaissance ..., autant que je sache ...

know-all ['nəuɔːl] *n* (*Brit pej*) je-sais-tout *m/f*

know-how ['nəuhau] *n* savoir-faire *m*, technique *f*, compétence *f*

knowing ['nəuɪŋ] *adj* (*look etc*) entendu(e)

knowingly ['nəuɪŋlɪ] *adv* (*on purpose*) sciemment; (*smile, look*) d'un air entendu

know-it-all ['nəuɪtɔːl] *n* (*US*) = **know-all**

knowledge ['nɔlɪdʒ] *n* connaissance *f*; (*learning*) connaissances, savoir *m*; **to have no ~ of** ignorer; **not to my ~** pas à ma connaissance; **without my ~** à mon insu; **to have a working ~ of French** se débrouiller en français; **it is common ~ that ...** chacun sait que ...; **it has come to my ~ that ...** j'ai appris que ...

knowledgeable ['nɔlɪdʒəbl] *adj* bien informé(e)

known [nəun] *pp of* **know** ▷ *adj* (*thief, facts*) notoire; (*expert*) célèbre

knuckle ['nʌkl] *n* articulation *f* (des phalanges), jointure *f*
  ▶ **knuckle down** *vi* (*inf*) s'y mettre
  ▶ **knuckle under** *vi* (*inf*) céder

koala [kəuˈɑːlə] *n* (*also*: **koala bear**) koala *m*

Koran [kɔˈrɑːn] *n* Coran *m*

Korea [kəˈrɪə] *n* Corée *f*; **North/South ~** Corée du Nord/Sud

Korean [kəˈrɪən] *adj* coréen(ne) ▷ *n* Coréen(ne)

kosher ['kəuʃər] *adj* kascher *inv*

Kosovar, Kosovan ['kɔsəvaːr, 'kɔsəvən] *adj* kosovar(e)

Kosovo ['kɔsɔvəu] *n* Kosovo *m*

Kuwait [kuˈweɪt] *n* Koweït *m*

Ll

L *abbr* (= *lake, large*) L; (= *left*) g; (*Brit Aut*: = *learner*) signale un conducteur débutant

l. *abbr* (= *litre*) l

lab [læb] *n abbr* (= *laboratory*) labo *m*

label ['leɪbl] *n* étiquette *f*; (*brand: of record*) marque *f* ▷ *vt* étiqueter; **to ~ sb a ...** qualifier qn de ...

labor *etc* ['leɪbə^r] (*US*) = **labour** *etc*

laboratory [lə'bɔrətərɪ] *n* laboratoire *m*

Labor Day *n* (*US, Canada*) fête *f* du travail (*le premier lundi de septembre*); *voir article*

Labour ['leɪbə^r] *n* (*Brit Pol: also:* **the Labour Party**) le parti travailliste, les travaillistes *mpl*

labour, (*US*) **labor** ['leɪbə^r] *n* (*work*) travail *m*; (*workforce*) main-d'œuvre *f*; (*Med*) travail, accouchement *m* ▷ *vi*: **to ~ (at)** travailler dur (à), peiner (sur) ▷ *vt*: **to ~ a point** insister sur un point; **in ~** (*Med*) en travail

laboured, (*US*) **labored** ['leɪbəd] *adj* lourd(e), laborieux(-euse); (*breathing*) difficile, pénible; (*style*) lourd, embarrassé(e)

labourer, (*US*) **laborer** ['leɪbərə^r] *n* manœuvre *m*; **farm ~** ouvrier *m* agricole

lace [leɪs] *n* dentelle *f*; (*of shoe etc*) lacet *m* ▷ *vt* (*shoe: also:* **lace up**) lacer; (*drink*) arroser, corser

lack [læk] *n* manque *m* ▷ *vt* manquer de; **through** or **for ~ of** faute de, par manque de; **to be ~ing** manquer, faire défaut; **to be ~ing in** manquer de

lacquer ['lækə^r] *n* laque *f*

lacy ['leɪsɪ] *adj* (*made of lace*) en dentelle; (*like lace*) comme de la dentelle, qui ressemble à de la dentelle

lad [læd] *n* garçon *m*, gars *m*; (*Brit: in stable etc*) lad *m*

ladder ['lædə^r] *n* échelle *f*; (*Brit: in tights*) maille filée *f* ▷ *vt, vi* (*Brit: tights*) filer

laden ['leɪdn] *adj*: **~ (with)** chargé(e) (de); **fully ~** (*truck, ship*) en pleine charge

ladle ['leɪdl] *n* louche *f*

lady ['leɪdɪ] *n* dame *f*; **"ladies and gentlemen ..."** "Mesdames (et) Messieurs ..."; **young ~** jeune fille *f*; (*married*) jeune femme *f*; **L~ Smith** lady Smith; **the ladies' (room)** les toilettes *fpl* des dames; **a ~ doctor** une doctoresse, une femme médecin

ladybird ['leɪdɪbə:d], (*US*) **ladybug** ['leɪdɪbʌg] *n* coccinelle *f*

ladylike ['leɪdɪlaɪk] *adj* distingué(e)

ladyship ['leɪdɪʃɪp] *n*: **your L~** Madame la comtesse (*or* la baronne *etc*)

lag [læg] *n* retard *m* ▷ *vi* (*also:* **lag behind**) rester en arrière, traîner; (*fig*) rester à la traîne ▷ *vt* (*pipes*) calorifuger

lager ['lɑ:gə^r] *n* bière blonde

lagoon [lə'gu:n] *n* lagune *f*

laid [leɪd] *pt, pp of* **lay**

laid back *adj* (*inf*) relaxe, décontracté(e)

laid up *adj* alité(e)

lain [leɪn] *pp of* **lie**

lake [leɪk] *n* lac *m*

lamb [læm] *n* agneau *m*

lamb chop *n* côtelette *f* d'agneau

lame [leɪm] *adj* (*also fig*) boiteux(-euse); **~ duck** (*fig*) canard boiteux

lament [lə'mɛnt] *n* lamentation *f* ▷ *vt* pleurer, se lamenter sur

laminated ['læmɪneɪtɪd] *adj* laminé(e); (*windscreen*) (en verre) feuilleté

lamp [læmp] *n* lampe *f*

lamppost ['læmppəust] *n* (*Brit*) réverbère *m*

lampshade ['læmpʃeɪd] *n* abat-jour *m inv*

lance [lɑ:ns] *n* lance *f* ▷ *vt* (*Med*) inciser

land [lænd] *n* (*as opposed to sea*) terre *f* (ferme); (*country*) pays *m*; (*soil*) terre; (*piece of land*) terrain *m*; (*estate*) terre(s), domaine(s) *m(pl)* ▷ *vi* (*from ship*) débarquer; (*Aviat*) atterrir; (*fig: fall*) (re)tomber ▷ *vt* (*passengers, goods*) débarquer; (*obtain*) décrocher; **to go/travel by ~** se déplacer par voie de terre; **to own ~** être propriétaire foncier; **to ~ on one's feet** (*also fig*) retomber sur ses pieds; **to ~ sb with sth** (*inf*) coller qch à qn ▶ **land up** *vi* atterrir, (*finir par*) se retrouver

landfill site ['lændfɪl-] *n* centre *m* d'enfouissement des déchets

landing ['lændɪŋ] *n* (*from ship*) débarquement *m*; (*Aviat*) atterrissage *m*; (*of staircase*) palier *m*

landing card *n* carte *f* de débarquement

landing strip *n* piste *f* d'atterrissage

landlady ['lændleɪdɪ] *n* propriétaire *f*, logeuse *f*; (*of pub*) patronne *f*

landlocked ['lændlɔkt] *adj* entouré(e) de terre(s), sans accès à la mer

landlord ['lændlɔ:d] *n* propriétaire *m*, logeur *m*;

(*of pub etc*) patron *m*

landmark ['lændmɑːk] *n* (point *m* de) repère *m*;
to be a ~ (*fig*) faire date *or* époque

landowner ['lændəʊnə^r] *n* propriétaire foncier
or terrien

landscape ['lænskeɪp] *n* paysage *m*

landscape architect, landscape gardener *n*
paysagiste *m/f*

landslide ['lændslaɪd] *n* (*Geo*) glissement *m* (de
terrain); (*fig: Pol*) raz-de-marée (électoral)

lane [leɪn] *n* (*in country*) chemin *m*; (*in town*) ruelle
f; (*Aut: of road*) voie *f*; (*: line of traffic*) file *f*; (*in race*)
couloir *m*; **shipping ~** route *f* maritime *or* de
navigation

language ['læŋgwɪdʒ] *n* langue *f*; (*way one speaks*)
langage *m*; **what ~s do you speak?** quelles
langues parlez-vous?; **bad ~** grossièretés *fpl*,
langage grossier

language laboratory *n* laboratoire *m* de
langues

language school *n* école *f* de langue

lank [læŋk] *adj* (*hair*) raide et terne

lanky ['læŋkɪ] *adj* grand(e) et maigre,
efflanqué(e)

lantern ['læntn] *n* lanterne *f*

lap [læp] *n* (*of track*) tour *m* (de piste); (*of body*): **in**
or **on one's ~** sur les genoux ▷ *vt* (*also*: **lap up**)
laper ▷ *vi* (*waves*) clapoter
▶ **lap up** *vt* (*fig*) boire comme du petit-lait, se
gargariser de; (*: lies etc*) gober

lapel [lə'pɛl] *n* revers *m*

Lapland ['læplænd] *n* Laponie *f*

lapse [læps] *n* défaillance *f*; (*in behaviour*) écart *m*
(de conduite) ▷ *vi* (*Law*) cesser d'être en vigueur;
(*contract*) expirer; (*pass*) être périmé; (*subscription*)
prendre fin; **to ~ into bad habits** prendre
de mauvaises habitudes; **~ of time** laps *m* de
temps, intervalle *m*; **a ~ of memory** un trou de
mémoire

laptop ['læptɔp], **laptop computer** *n*
portable *m*

larceny ['lɑːsənɪ] *n* vol *m*

larch [lɑːtʃ] *n* mélèze *m*

lard [lɑːd] *n* saindoux *m*

larder ['lɑːdə^r] *n* garde-manger *m inv*

large [lɑːdʒ] *adj* grand(e); (*person, animal*) gros
(grosse); **to make ~r** agrandir; **a ~ number of
people** beaucoup de gens; **by and ~** en général;
on a ~ scale sur une grande échelle; **at ~** (*free*)
en liberté; (*generally*) en général; pour la plupart;
see also **by**

largely ['lɑːdʒlɪ] *adv* en grande partie; (*principally*)
surtout

large-scale ['lɑːdʒ'skeɪl] *adj* (*map, drawing etc*) à
grande échelle; (*fig*) important(e)

lark [lɑːk] *n* (*bird*) alouette *f*; (*joke*) blague *f*, farce *f*
▶ **lark about** *vi* faire l'idiot, rigoler

laryngitis [lærɪn'dʒaɪtɪs] *n* laryngite *f*

lasagne [lə'zænjə] *n* lasagne *f*

laser ['leɪzə^r] *n* laser *m*

laser printer *n* imprimante *f* laser

lash [læʃ] *n* coup *m* de fouet; (*also*: **eyelash**) cil *m*

▷ *vt* fouetter; (*tie*) attacher
▶ **lash down** *vt* attacher; amarrer; arrimer ▷ *vi*
(*rain*) tomber avec violence
▶ **lash out** *vi*: **to ~ out** (**at** *or* **against sb/sth**)
attaquer violemment (qn/qch); **to ~ out (on sth)**
(*inf: spend*) se fendre (de qch)

lass [læs] (*Brit*) *n* (jeune) fille *f*

lasso [læ'suː] *n* lasso *m* ▷ *vt* prendre au lasso

last [lɑːst] *adj* dernier(-ière) ▷ *adv* en dernier;
(*most recently*) la dernière fois; (*finally*) finalement
▷ *vi* durer; **~ week** la semaine dernière; **~ night**
(*evening*) hier soir; (*night*) la nuit dernière; **at ~**
enfin; **~ but one** avant-dernier(-ière); **the ~
time** la dernière fois; **it ~s (for) 2 hours** ça dure
2 heures

last-ditch ['lɑːst'dɪtʃ] *adj* ultime, désespéré(e)

lasting ['lɑːstɪŋ] *adj* durable

lastly ['lɑːstlɪ] *adv* en dernier lieu, pour finir

last-minute ['lɑːstmɪnɪt] *adj* de dernière minute

latch [lætʃ] *n* loquet *m*
▶ **latch onto** *vt fus* (*cling to: person, group*)
s'accrocher à; (*idea*) se mettre en tête

late [leɪt] *adj* (*not on time*) en retard; (*far on in day
etc*) tardif(-ive); (*: edition, delivery*) dernier(-ière);
(*recent*) récent(e), dernier; (*former*) ancien(ne);
(*dead*) défunt(e) ▷ *adv* tard; (*behind time, schedule*)
en retard; **to be ~** avoir du retard; **to be 10
minutes ~** avoir 10 minutes de retard; **sorry
I'm ~** désolé d'être en retard; **it's too ~** il est trop
tard; **to work ~** travailler tard; **~ in life** sur le
tard, à un âge avancé; **of ~** dernièrement; **in ~
May** vers la fin (du mois) de mai, fin mai; **the ~
Mr X** feu M. X

latecomer ['leɪtkʌmə^r] *n* retardataire *m/f*

lately ['leɪtlɪ] *adv* récemment

later ['leɪtə^r] *adj* (*date etc*) ultérieur(e); (*version etc*)
plus récent(e) ▷ *adv* plus tard; **~ on today** plus
tard dans la journée

latest ['leɪtɪst] *adj* tout(e) dernier(-ière); **the ~
news** les dernières nouvelles; **at the ~** au plus
tard

lathe [leɪð] *n* tour *m*

lather ['lɑːðə^r] *n* mousse *f* (de savon) ▷ *vt*
savonner ▷ *vi* mousser

Latin ['lætɪn] *n* latin *m* ▷ *adj* latin(e)

Latin America *n* Amérique latine

Latin American *adj* latino-américain(e),
d'Amérique latine ▷ *n* Latino-Américain(e)

latitude ['lætɪtjuːd] *n* (*also fig*) latitude *f*

latter ['lætə^r] *adj* deuxième, dernier(-ière) ▷ *n*:
the ~ ce dernier, celui-ci

latterly ['lætəlɪ] *adv* dernièrement, récemment

laudable ['lɔːdəbl] *adj* louable

laugh [lɑːf] *n* rire *m* ▷ *vi* rire; **(to do sth) for a ~**
(faire qch) pour rire
▶ **laugh at** *vt fus* se moquer de; (*joke*) rire de
▶ **laugh off** *vt* écarter *or* rejeter par une
plaisanterie *or* par une boutade

laughable ['lɑːfəbl] *adj* risible, ridicule

laughing stock *n*: **the ~ of** la risée de

laughter ['lɑːftə^r] *n* rire *m*; (*of several people*) rires
mpl

launch [lɔːntʃ] n lancement m; (boat) chaloupe f; (also: **motor launch**) vedette f ▷ vt (ship, rocket, plan) lancer
▶ **launch into** vt fus se lancer dans
▶ **launch out** vi: **to ~ out (into)** se lancer (dans)
launder ['lɔːndəʳ] vt laver; (fig: money) blanchir
Launderette® [lɔːn'drɛt], (US) **Laundromat®** ['lɔːndrəmæt] n laverie f (automatique)
laundry ['lɔːndrɪ] n (clothes) linge m; (business) blanchisserie f; (room) buanderie f; **to do the ~** faire la lessive
laurel ['lɔrl] n laurier m; **to rest on one's ~s** se reposer sur ses lauriers
lava ['lɑːvə] n lave f
lavatory ['lævətərɪ] n toilettes fpl
lavender ['lævəndəʳ] n lavande f
lavish ['lævɪʃ] adj (amount) copieux(-euse); (meal) somptueux(-euse); (hospitality) généreux(-euse); (person: giving freely): **~ with** prodigue de ▷ vt: **to ~ sth on sb** prodiguer qch à qn; (money) dépenser qch sans compter pour qn
law [lɔː] n loi f; (science) droit m; **against the ~** contraire à la loi; **to study ~** faire du droit; **to go to ~** (Brit) avoir recours à la justice; **~ and order** (n) l'ordre public
law-abiding ['lɔːəbaɪdɪŋ] adj respectueux(-euse) des lois
law court n tribunal m, cour f de justice
lawful ['lɔːful] adj légal(e), permis(e)
lawless ['lɔːlɪs] adj (action) illégal(e); (place) sans loi
lawn [lɔːn] n pelouse f
lawnmower ['lɔːnməuəʳ] n tondeuse f à gazon
lawn tennis n tennis m
law school n faculté f de droit
lawsuit ['lɔːsuːt] n procès m; **to bring a ~ against** engager des poursuites contre
lawyer ['lɔːjəʳ] n (consultant, with company) juriste m; (for sales, wills etc) ≈ notaire m; (partner, in court) ≈ avocat m
lax [læks] adj relâché(e)
laxative ['læksətɪv] n laxatif m
lay [leɪ] pt of **lie** ▷ adj laïque; (not expert) profane ▷ vt (pt, pp **laid**) [leɪd] poser, mettre; (eggs) pondre; (trap) tendre; (plans) élaborer; **to ~ the table** mettre la table; **to ~ the facts/one's proposals before sb** présenter les faits/ses propositions à qn; **to get laid** (inf!) baiser (!), se faire baiser (!)
▶ **lay aside, lay by** vt mettre de côté
▶ **lay down** vt poser; (rules etc) établir; **to ~ down the law** (fig) faire la loi
▶ **lay in** vt accumuler, s'approvisionner en
▶ **lay into** vi (inf: attack) tomber sur; (: scold) passer une engueulade à
▶ **lay off** vt (workers) licencier
▶ **lay on** vt (water, gas) mettre, installer; (provide: meal etc) fournir; (paint) étaler
▶ **lay out** vt (design) dessiner, concevoir; (display) disposer; (spend) dépenser
▶ **lay up** vt (store) amasser; (car) remiser; (ship) désarmer; (illness) forcer à s'aliter

layabout ['leɪəbaut] n fainéant(e)
lay-by ['leɪbaɪ] n (Brit) aire f de stationnement (sur le bas-côté)
layer ['leɪəʳ] n couche f
layman ['leɪmən] (irreg) n (Rel) laïque m; (non-expert) profane m
layout ['leɪaut] n disposition f, plan m, agencement m; (Press) mise f en page
laze [leɪz] vi paresser
lazy ['leɪzɪ] adj paresseux(-euse)
lb. abbr (weight) = **pound**
lead¹ [liːd] (pt, pp **led**) [lɛd] n (front position) tête f; (distance, time ahead) avance f; (clue) piste f; (Elec) fil m; (for dog) laisse f; (Theat) rôle principal ▷ vt mener, conduire; (induce) amener; (be leader of) être à la tête de; (Sport) être en tête de; (orchestra: Brit) être le premier violon de; (: US) diriger ▷ vi (Sport) mener, être en tête; **to ~ to** (road, pipe) mener à, conduire à; (result in) conduire à; aboutir à; **to ~ sb astray** détourner qn du droit chemin; **to be in the ~** (Sport: in race) mener, être en tête; (: in match) mener (à la marque); **to take the ~** (Sport) passer en tête, prendre la tête; mener; (fig) prendre l'initiative; **to ~ sb to believe that ...** amener qn à croire que ...; **to ~ sb to do sth** amener qn à faire qch; **to ~ the way** montrer le chemin
▶ **lead away** vt emmener
▶ **lead back** vt ramener
▶ **lead off** vi (in game etc) commencer
▶ **lead on** vt (tease) faire marcher; **to ~ sb on to** (induce) amener qn à
▶ **lead up to** vt conduire à; (in conversation) en venir à
lead² [lɛd] n (metal) plomb m; (in pencil) mine f
leaded petrol n essence f au plomb
leaden ['lɛdn] adj de or en plomb
leader ['liːdəʳ] n (of team) chef m; (of party etc) dirigeant(e), leader m; (Sport: in league) leader; (: in race) coureur m de tête; (in newspaper) éditorial m; **they are ~s in their field** (fig) ils sont à la pointe du progrès dans leur domaine; **the L~ of the House** (Brit) le chef de la majorité ministérielle
leadership ['liːdəʃɪp] n (position) direction f; **under the ~ of ...** sous la direction de ...; **qualities of ~** qualités fpl de chef or de meneur
lead-free ['lɛdfriː] adj sans plomb
leading ['liːdɪŋ] adj de premier plan; (main) principal(e); (in race) de tête; **a ~ question** une question tendancieuse; **~ role** rôle prépondérant or de premier plan
leading lady n (Theat) vedette (féminine)
leading light n (person) sommité f, personnalité f de premier plan
leading man (irreg) n (Theat) vedette (masculine)
lead singer [liːd-] n (in pop group) (chanteur m) vedette f
leaf (pl **leaves**) [liːf, liːvz] n feuille f; (of table) rallonge f; **to turn over a new ~** (fig) changer de conduite or d'existence; **to take a ~ out of sb's book** (fig) prendre exemple sur qn

▶ **leaf through** vt (book) feuilleter

leaflet ['li:flɪt] n prospectus m, brochure f; (Pol, Rel) tract m

league [li:g] n ligue f; (Football) championnat m; (measure) lieue f; **to be in ~ with** avoir partie liée avec, être de mèche avec

leak [li:k] n (out: also fig) fuite f; (in) infiltration f ▷ vi (pipe, liquid etc) fuir; (shoes) prendre l'eau; (ship) faire eau ▷ vt (liquid) répandre; (information) divulguer

▶ **leak out** vi fuir; (information) être divulgué(e)

lean [li:n] (pt, pp **-ed** or **-t**) [lɛnt] adj maigre ▷ n (of meat) maigre m ▷ vt: **to ~ sth on** appuyer qch sur ▷ vi (slope) pencher; (rest): **to ~ against** s'appuyer contre; être appuyé(e) contre; **to ~ on** s'appuyer sur

▶ **lean back** vi se pencher en arrière

▶ **lean forward** vi se pencher en avant

▶ **lean out** vi: **to ~ out (of)** se pencher au dehors (de)

▶ **lean over** vi se pencher

leaning ['li:nɪŋ] adj penché(e) ▷ n: ~ **(towards)** penchant m (pour); **the L~ Tower of Pisa** la tour penchée de Pise

leant [lɛnt] pt, pp of **lean**

leap [li:p] n bond m, saut m ▷ vi (pt, pp **-ed** or **-t**) [lɛpt] bondir, sauter; **to ~ at an offer** saisir une offre

▶ **leap up** vi (person) faire un bond; se lever d'un bond

leapfrog ['li:pfrɔg] n jeu m de saute-mouton

leapt [lɛpt] pt, pp of **leap**

leap year n année f bissextile

learn (pt, pp **-ed** or **-t**) [lə:n, -t] vt, vi apprendre; **to ~ (how) to do sth** apprendre à faire qch; **we were sorry to ~ that ...** nous avons appris avec regret que ...; **to ~ about sth** (Scol) étudier qch; (hear, read) apprendre qch

learned ['lə:nɪd] adj érudit(e), savant(e)

learner ['lə:nə'] n débutant(e); (Brit: also: **learner driver**) (conducteur(-trice)) débutant(e)

learning ['lə:nɪŋ] n savoir m

learnt [lə:nt] pp of **learn**

lease [li:s] n bail m ▷ vt louer à bail; **on ~** en location

▶ **lease back** vt vendre en cession-bail

leash [li:ʃ] n laisse f

least [li:st] adj: **the ~** (+noun) le (la) plus petit(e), le (la) moindre; (smallest amount of) le moins de ▷ pron: **(the) ~** le moins ▷ adv (+verb) le moins; (+adj): **the ~** le (la) moins; **the ~ money** le moins d'argent; **the ~ expensive** le (la) moins cher (chère); **the ~ possible effort** le moins d'effort possible; **at ~** au moins; (or rather) du moins; **you could at ~ have written** tu aurais au moins pu écrire; **not in the ~** pas le moins du monde

leather ['lɛðə'] n cuir m ▷ cpd en or de cuir; ~ **goods** maroquinerie f

leave [li:v] (vb: pt, pp **left**) [lɛft] vt laisser; (go away from) quitter; (forget) oublier ▷ vi partir, s'en aller ▷ n (time off) congé m; (Mil, also: consent) permission f; **what time does the train/bus ~?**
le train/le bus part à quelle heure?; **to ~ sth to sb** (money etc) laisser qch à qn; **to be left** rester; **there's some milk left over** il reste du lait; **to ~ school** quitter l'école, terminer sa scolarité; **~ it to me!** laissez-moi faire!, je m'en occupe!; **on ~** en permission; **to take one's ~ of** prendre congé de; **~ of absence** n congé exceptionnel; (Mil) permission spéciale

▶ **leave behind** vt (also fig) laisser; (opponent in race) distancer; (forget) laisser, oublier

▶ **leave off** vt (cover, lid, heating) ne pas (re)mettre; (light) ne pas (r)allumer, laisser éteint(e); (Brit inf: stop): **to ~ off (doing sth)** s'arrêter (de faire qch)

▶ **leave on** vt (coat etc) garder, ne pas enlever; (lid) laisser dessus; (light, fire, cooker) laisser allumé(e)

▶ **leave out** vt oublier, omettre

leaves [li:vz] npl of **leaf**

Lebanon ['lɛbənən] n Liban m

lecherous ['lɛtʃərəs] adj lubrique

lecture ['lɛktʃə'] n conférence f; (Scol) cours (magistral) ▷ vi donner des cours; enseigner ▷ vt (scold) sermonner, réprimander; **to ~ on** faire un cours (or son cours) sur; **to give a ~ (on)** faire une conférence (sur), faire un cours (sur)

lecture hall n amphithéâtre m

lecturer ['lɛktʃərə'] n (speaker) conférencier(-ière); (Brit: at university) professeur m (d'université), prof m/f de fac (inf); **assistant ~** (Brit) ≈ assistant(e); **senior ~** (Brit) ≈ chargé(e) d'enseignement

lecture theatre n = **lecture hall**

led [lɛd] pt, pp of **lead¹**

ledge [lɛdʒ] n (of window, on wall) rebord m; (of mountain) saillie f, corniche f

ledger ['lɛdʒə'] n registre m, grand livre

leech [li:tʃ] n sangsue f

leek [li:k] n poireau m

leer [lɪə'] vi: **to ~ at sb** regarder qn d'un air mauvais or concupiscent, lorgner qn

leeway ['li:weɪ] n (fig): **to make up ~** rattraper son retard; **to have some ~** avoir une certaine liberté d'action

left [lɛft] pt, pp of **leave** ▷ adj gauche ▷ adv à gauche ▷ n gauche f; **there are two ~** il en reste deux; **on the ~**, **to the ~** à gauche; **the L~** (Pol) la gauche

left-hand ['lɛfthænd] adj: **the ~ side** la gauche, le côté gauche

left-hand drive ['lɛfthænd-] n (Brit) conduite f à gauche; (vehicle) véhicule m avec la conduite à gauche

left-handed [lɛft'hændɪd] adj gaucher(-ère); (scissors etc) pour gauchers

left-luggage [lɛft'lʌgɪdʒ], **left-luggage office** n (Brit) consigne f

left-luggage locker [lɛft'lʌgɪdʒ-] n (Brit) (casier m à) consigne f automatique

left-overs ['lɛftəuvəz] npl restes mpl

left wing n (Mil, Sport) aile f gauche; (Pol) gauche f

left-wing ['lɛft'wɪŋ] adj (Pol) de gauche

leg [lɛg] n jambe f; (of animal) patte f; (of furniture) pied m; (Culin: of chicken) cuisse f; (of journey) étape *f*; **1st/2nd ~** (*Sport*) match *m* aller/retour; (*of journey*) 1ère/2ème étape; **~ of lamb** (*Culin*) gigot *m* d'agneau; **to stretch one's ~s** se dégourdir les jambes

legacy ['lɛɡəsɪ] *n* (*also fig*) héritage *m*, legs *m*

legal ['li:ɡl] *adj* (*permitted by law*) légal(e); (*relating to law*) juridique; **to take ~ action** or **proceedings against sb** poursuivre qn en justice

legal holiday (*US*) *n* jour férié

legalize ['li:ɡəlaɪz] *vt* légaliser

legally ['li:ɡəlɪ] *adv* légalement; **~ binding** juridiquement contraignant(e)

legal tender *n* monnaie légale

legend ['lɛdʒənd] *n* légende *f*

legendary ['lɛdʒəndərɪ] *adj* légendaire

leggings ['lɛɡɪŋz] *npl* caleçon *m*

legible ['lɛdʒəbl] *adj* lisible

legislation [lɛdʒɪs'leɪʃən] *n* législation *f*; **a piece of ~** un texte de loi

legislative ['lɛdʒɪslətɪv] *adj* législatif(-ive)

legislature ['lɛdʒɪslətʃər] *n* corps législatif

legitimate [lɪ'dʒɪtɪmət] *adj* légitime

leg-room ['lɛɡruːm] *n* place *f* pour les jambes

leisure ['lɛʒər] *n* (*free time*) temps libre, loisirs *mpl*; **at ~** (*tout*) à loisir; **at your ~** (*later*) à tête reposée

leisure centre *n* (*Brit*) centre *m* de loisirs

leisurely ['lɛʒəlɪ] *adj* tranquille, fait(e) sans se presser

lemon ['lɛmən] *n* citron *m*

lemonade [lɛmə'neɪd] *n* (*fizzy*) limonade *f*

lemon tea *n* thé *m* au citron

lend (*pt, pp* **lent**) [lɛnd, lɛnt] *vt*: **to ~ sth (to sb)** prêter qch (à qn); **could you ~ me some money?** pourriez-vous me prêter de l'argent?; **to ~ a hand** donner un coup de main

length [lɛŋθ] *n* longueur *f*; (*section: of road, pipe etc*) morceau *m*, bout *m*; **~ of time** durée *f*; **what ~ is it?** quelle longueur fait-il?; **it is 2 metres in ~** cela fait 2 mètres de long; **to fall full ~** tomber de tout son long; **at ~** (*at last*) enfin, à la fin; (*lengthily*) longuement; **to go to any ~(s) to do sth** faire n'importe quoi pour faire qch, ne reculer devant rien pour faire qch

lengthen ['lɛŋθn] *vt* allonger, prolonger ▷ *vi* s'allonger

lengthways ['lɛŋθweɪz] *adv* dans le sens de la longueur, en long

lengthy ['lɛŋθɪ] *adj* (très) long (longue)

lenient ['li:nɪənt] *adj* indulgent(e), clément(e)

lens [lɛnz] *n* lentille *f*; (*of spectacles*) verre *m*; (*of camera*) objectif *m*

Lent [lɛnt] *n* carême *m*

lent [lɛnt] *pt, pp of* **lend**

lentil ['lɛntl] *n* lentille *f*

Leo ['li:əu] *n* le Lion; **to be ~** être du Lion

leopard ['lɛpəd] *n* léopard *m*

leotard ['li:əta:d] *n* justaucorps *m*

leprosy ['lɛprəsɪ] *n* lèpre *f*

lesbian ['lɛzbɪən] *n* lesbienne *f* ▷ *adj* lesbien(ne)

less [lɛs] *adj* moins de ▷ *pron, adv* moins ▷ *prep*: **~ tax/10% discount** avant impôt/moins 10%

de remise; **~ than that/you** moins que cela/vous; **~ than half** moins de la moitié; **~ than one/a kilo/3 metres** moins de un/d'un kilo/de 3 mètres; **~ than ever** moins que jamais; **~ and ~** de moins en moins; **the ~ he works ...** moins il travaille ...

lessen ['lɛsn] *vi* diminuer, s'amoindrir, s'atténuer ▷ *vt* diminuer, réduire, atténuer

lesser ['lɛsər] *adj* moindre; **to a ~ extent** or **degree** à un degré moindre

lesson ['lɛsn] *n* leçon *f*; **a maths ~** une leçon or un cours de maths; **to give ~s in** donner des cours de; **to teach sb a ~** (*fig*) donner une bonne leçon à qn; **it taught him a ~** (*fig*) cela lui a servi de leçon

let (*pt, pp* ~) [lɛt] *vt* laisser; (*Brit: lease*) louer; **to ~ sb do sth** laisser qn faire qch; **to ~ sb know sth** faire savoir qch à qn, prévenir qn de qch; **he ~ me go** il m'a laissé partir; **~ the water boil and ... faites bouillir l'eau et ...; **to ~ go** lâcher prise; **to ~ go of sth, to ~ sth go** lâcher qch; **~'s go** allons-y; **~ him come** qu'il vienne; **"to ~"** (*Brit*) "à louer"

▶ **let down** *vt* (*lower*) baisser; (*dress*) rallonger; (*hair*) défaire; (*Brit: tyre*) dégonfler; (*disappoint*) décevoir

▶ **let go** *vi* lâcher prise ▷ *vt* lâcher

▶ **let in** *vt* laisser entrer; (*visitor etc*) faire entrer; **what have you ~ yourself in for?** à quoi t'es-tu engagé?

▶ **let off** *vt* (*allow to leave*) laisser partir; (*not punish*) ne pas punir; (*taxi driver, bus driver*) déposer; (*firework etc*) faire partir; (*bomb*) faire exploser; (*smell etc*) dégager; **to ~ off steam** (*fig: inf*) se défouler, décharger sa rate or bile

▶ **let on** *vi* (*inf*): **to ~ on that ....** révéler que ..., dire que ...

▶ **let out** *vt* laisser sortir; (*dress*) élargir; (*scream*) laisser échapper; (*Brit: rent out*) louer

▶ **let up** *vi* diminuer, s'arrêter

lethal ['li:θl] *adj* mortel(le), fatal(e); (*weapon*) meurtrier(-ère)

letter ['lɛtər] *n* lettre *f*; **letters** *npl* (*Literature*) lettres; **small/capital ~** minuscule *f*/majuscule *f*; **~ of credit** lettre *f* de crédit

letter bomb *n* lettre piégée

letterbox ['lɛtəbɒks] *n* (*Brit*) boîte *f* aux or à lettres

lettering ['lɛtərɪŋ] *n* lettres *fpl*; caractères *mpl*

lettuce ['lɛtɪs] *n* laitue *f*, salade *f*

let-up ['lɛtʌp] *n* répit *m*, détente *f*

leukaemia, (*US*) **leukemia** [lu:'ki:mɪə] *n* leucémie *f*

level ['lɛvl] *adj* (*flat*) plat(e), plan(e), uni(e); (*horizontal*) horizontal(e) ▷ *n* niveau *m*; (*flat place*) terrain plat; (*also*: **spirit level**) niveau à bulle ▷ *vt* niveler, aplanir; (*gun*) pointer, braquer; (*accusation*): **to ~ (against)** lancer or porter (contre) ▷ *vi* (*inf*): **to ~ with sb** être franc (franche) avec qn; **"A" ~s** (*npl: Brit*) ≈ baccalauréat *m*; **"O" ~s** *npl* (*Brit: formerly*) examens passés à l'âge de 16 ans sanctionnant les connaissances de l'élève, ≈ brevet *m* des collèges; **a ~ spoonful** (*Culin*) une cuillerée rase; **to be ~ with** être au même niveau que; **to draw ~ with** (team) arriver à égalité de points avec, égaliser avec; arriver au même classement que; (runner, car) arriver à la hauteur de, rattraper; **on the ~** à l'horizontale; (fig: honest) régulier(-ière)

▶ **level off, level out** vi (prices etc) se stabiliser ▷ vt (ground) aplanir, niveler

level crossing n (Brit) passage m à niveau

level-headed ['lɛvl'hɛdɪd] adj équilibré(e)

lever ['li:vəʳ] n levier m ▷ vt: **to ~ up/out** soulever/extraire au moyen d'un levier

leverage ['li:vərɪdʒ] n (influence): **~ (on or with)** prise f (sur)

levy ['lɛvɪ] n taxe f, impôt m ▷ vt (tax) lever; (fine) infliger

lewd [lu:d] adj obscène, lubrique

liability [laɪə'bɪlətɪ] n responsabilité f; (handicap) handicap m

liable ['laɪəbl] adj (subject): **~ to** sujet(te) à, passible de; (responsible): **~ (for)** responsable (de); (likely): **~ to do** susceptible de faire; **to be ~ to a fine** être passible d'une amende

liaise [li:'eɪz] vi: **to ~ with** assurer la liaison avec

liaison [li:'eɪzɔn] n liaison f

liar ['laɪəʳ] n menteur(-euse)

libel ['laɪbl] n diffamation f; (document) écrit m diffamatoire ▷ vt diffamer

liberal ['lɪbərl] adj libéral(e); (generous): **~ with** prodigue de, généreux(-euse) avec ▷ n: **L~** (Pol) libéral(e)

Liberal Democrat n (Brit) libéral(e)-démocrate m/f

liberate ['lɪbəreɪt] vt libérer

liberation [lɪbə'reɪʃən] n libération f

liberty ['lɪbətɪ] n liberté f; **to be at ~** (criminal) être en liberté; **at ~ to do** libre de faire; **to take the ~ of** prendre la liberté de, se permettre de

Libra ['li:brə] n la Balance; **to be ~** être de la Balance

librarian [laɪ'brɛərɪən] n bibliothécaire m/f

library ['laɪbrərɪ] n bibliothèque f

libretto [lɪ'brɛtəu] n livret m

Libya ['lɪbɪə] n Libye f

lice [laɪs] npl of **louse**

licence, (US) **license** ['laɪsns] n autorisation f, permis m; (Comm) licence f; (Radio, TV) redevance f; (also: **driving licence**: US: also: **driver's license**) permis m (de conduire); (excessive freedom) licence; **import ~** licence d'importation; **produced under ~** fabriqué(e) sous licence

licence number n (Brit Aut) numéro m d'immatriculation

license ['laɪsns] n (US) = **licence** ▷ vt donner une licence à; (car) acheter la vignette de; délivrer la vignette de

licensed ['laɪsnst] adj (for alcohol) patenté(e) pour la vente des spiritueux, qui a une patente de débit de boissons; (car) muni(e) de la vignette

license plate n (US Aut) plaque f minéralogique

licensing hours (Brit) npl heures fpl d'ouvertures (des pubs)

lick [lɪk] vt lécher; (inf: defeat) écraser, flanquer une piquette or raclée à ▷ n coup m de langue; **a ~ of paint** un petit coup de peinture; **to ~ one's lips** (fig) se frotter les mains

licorice ['lɪkərɪs] n = **liquorice**

lid [lɪd] n couvercle m; (eyelid) paupière f; **to take the ~ off sth** (fig) exposer or étaler qch au grand jour

lie [laɪ] n mensonge m ▷ vi (pt, pp **-d**) (tell lies) mentir (pt **lay**, pp **lain**) [leɪ, leɪn] (rest) être étendu(e) or allongé(e) or couché(e); (in grave) être enterré(e), reposer; (object: be situated) se trouver, être; **to ~ low** (fig) se cacher, rester caché(e); **to tell ~s** mentir

▶ **lie about, lie around** vi (things) traîner; (Brit: person) traînasser, flemmarder

▶ **lie back** vi se renverser en arrière

▶ **lie down** vi se coucher, s'étendre

▶ **lie up** vi (hide) se cacher

Liechtenstein ['lɪktənstaɪn] n Liechtenstein m

lie-down ['laɪdaun] n (Brit): **to have a ~** s'allonger, se reposer

lie-in ['laɪɪn] n (Brit): **to have a ~** faire la grasse matinée

lieutenant [lɛf'tɛnənt] (US) [lu:'tɛnənt] n lieutenant m

life (pl **lives**) [laɪf, laɪvz] n vie f; **to come to ~** (fig) s'animer ▷ cpd de vie; de la vie; à vie; **true to ~** réaliste, fidèle à la réalité; **to paint from ~** peindre d'après nature; **to be sent to prison for ~** être condamné(e) (à la réclusion criminelle) à perpétuité; **country/city ~** la vie à la campagne/à la ville

life assurance n (Brit) = **life insurance**

lifebelt ['laɪfbɛlt] n (Brit) bouée f de sauvetage

lifeboat ['laɪfbəut] n canot m or chaloupe f de sauvetage

lifebuoy ['laɪfbɔɪ] n bouée f de sauvetage

lifeguard ['laɪfgɑ:d] n surveillant m de baignade

life insurance n assurance-vie f

life jacket n gilet m or ceinture f de sauvetage

lifeless ['laɪflɪs] adj sans vie, inanimé(e); (dull) qui manque de vie or de vigueur

lifelike ['laɪflaɪk] adj qui semble vrai(e) or vivant(e), ressemblant(e); (painting) réaliste

lifelong ['laɪflɔŋ] adj de toute une vie, de toujours

life preserver [-prɪ'zə:vəʳ] n (US) gilet m or ceinture f de sauvetage

life-saving ['laɪfseɪvɪŋ] n sauvetage m

life sentence n condamnation f à vie or à perpétuité

life-size ['laɪfsaɪz], **life-sized** ['laɪfsaɪzd] adj grandeur nature inv

life span n (durée f de) vie f

lifestyle ['laɪfstaɪl] n style m de vie

life-support system n (Med) respirateur artificiel

lifetime ['laɪftaɪm] n: **in his ~** de son vivant; **the chance of a ~** la chance de ma (or sa etc) vie, une occasion unique

lift [lɪft] vt soulever, lever; (end) supprimer,

lever; (steal) prendre, voler ▷ vi (fog) se lever ▷ n
(Brit: elevator) ascenseur m; **to give sb a ~** (Brit)
emmener or prendre qn en voiture; **can you give
me a ~ to the station?** pouvez-vous m'emmener
à la gare?
 ▶ **lift off** vi (rocket, helicopter) décoller
 ▶ **lift out** vt sortir; (troops, evacuees etc) évacuer
par avion or hélicoptère
 ▶ **lift up** vt soulever
lift-off ['lɪftɔf] n décollage m
light [laɪt] n lumière f; (daylight) lumière, jour m;
(lamp) lampe f; (Aut: rear light) feu m; (: headlamp)
phare m; (for cigarette etc): **have you got a ~?** avez-
vous du feu? ▷ vt (pt, pp **-ed**, pt, pp **lit**) [lɪt] (candle,
cigarette, fire) allumer; (room) éclairer ▷ adj (room,
colour) clair(e); (not heavy, also fig) léger(-ère); (not
strenuous) peu fatigant(e) ▷ adv (travel) avec peu
de bagages; **lights** npl (traffic lights) feux mpl; **to
turn the ~ on/off** allumer/éteindre; **to cast**
or **shed** or **throw ~ on** éclaircir; **to come to ~**
être dévoilé(e) or découvert(e); **in the ~ of** à la
lumière de; étant donné; **to make ~ of sth** (fig)
prendre qch à la légère, faire peu de cas de qch
 ▶ **light up** vi s'allumer; (face) s'éclairer; (smoke)
allumer une cigarette or une pipe etc ▷ vt
(illuminate) éclairer, illuminer
light bulb n ampoule f
lighten ['laɪtn] vi s'éclairer ▷ vt (light up) éclairer;
(make lighter) éclaircir; (make less heavy) alléger
lighter ['laɪtəʳ] n (also: **cigarette lighter**) briquet
m; (: in car) allume-cigare m inv; (boat) péniche f
light-headed [laɪt'hɛdɪd] adj étourdi(e),
écervelé(e)
light-hearted [laɪt'hɑːtɪd] adj gai(e),
joyeux(-euse), enjoué(e)
lighthouse ['laɪthaus] n phare m
lighting ['laɪtɪŋ] n éclairage m; (in theatre)
éclairages
lightly ['laɪtlɪ] adv légèrement; **to get off ~** s'en
tirer à bon compte
lightness ['laɪtnɪs] n clarté f; (in weight) légèreté f
lightning ['laɪtnɪŋ] n foudre f; (flash) éclair m
lightning conductor, (US) **lightning rod** n
paratonnerre m
light pen n crayon m optique
lightweight ['laɪtweɪt] adj (suit) léger(-ère) ▷ n
(Boxing) poids léger
like [laɪk] vt aimer (bien) ▷ prep comme ▷ adj
semblable, pareil(le) ▷ n: **the ~** un(e) pareil(le)
or semblable; **le (la) pareil(le)**; (pej) (d')autres
du même genre or acabit; **his ~s and dislikes**
ses goûts mpl or préférences fpl; **I would ~, I'd ~**
je voudrais, j'aimerais; **would you ~ a coffee?**
voulez-vous du café?; **to be/look ~ sb/sth**
ressembler à qn/qch; **what's he ~?** comment
est-il?; **what's the weather ~?** quel temps fait-
il?; **what does it look ~?** de quoi est-ce que ça
a l'air?; **what does it taste ~?** quel goût est-ce
que ça a?; **that's just ~ him** c'est bien de lui, ça
lui ressemble; **something ~ that** quelque chose
comme ça; **do it ~ this** fais-le comme ceci; **I feel
~ a drink** je boirais bien quelque chose; **if you ~**

si vous voulez; **it's nothing ~ ...** ce n'est pas du
tout comme ...; **there's nothing ~ ...** il n'y a rien
de tel que ...
likeable ['laɪkəbl] adj sympathique, agréable
likelihood ['laɪklɪhud] n probabilité f; **in all ~**
selon toute vraisemblance
likely ['laɪklɪ] adj (result, outcome) probable; (excuse)
plausible; **he's ~ to leave** il va sûrement partir,
il risque fort de partir; **not ~!** (inf) pas de danger!
likeness ['laɪknɪs] n ressemblance f
likewise ['laɪkwaɪz] adv de même, pareillement
liking ['laɪkɪŋ] n (for person) affection f; (for thing)
penchant m, goût m; **to take a ~ to sb** se prendre
d'amitié pour qn; **to be to sb's ~** être au goût de
qn, plaire à qn
lilac ['laɪlək] n lilas m ▷ adj lilas inv
Lilo® ['laɪləu] n matelas m pneumatique
lily ['lɪlɪ] n lis m; **~ of the valley** muguet m
limb [lɪm] n membre m; **to be out on a ~** (fig) être
isolé(e)
limber ['lɪmbəʳ]: **to ~ up** vi se dégourdir, se
mettre en train
limbo ['lɪmbəu] n: **to be in ~** (fig) être tombé(e)
dans l'oubli
lime [laɪm] n (tree) tilleul m; (fruit) citron vert,
lime f; (Geo) chaux f
limelight ['laɪmlaɪt] n: **in the ~** (fig) en vedette,
au premier plan
limerick ['lɪmərɪk] n petit poème humoristique
limestone ['laɪmstəun] n pierre f à chaux; (Geo)
calcaire m
limit ['lɪmɪt] n limite f ▷ vt limiter; **weight/
speed ~** limite de poids/de vitesse
limited ['lɪmɪtɪd] adj limité(e), restreint(e); **~
edition** édition f à tirage limité; **to be ~ to** se
limiter à, ne concerner que
limited company, limited liability company n
(Brit) ≈ société f anonyme
limousine ['lɪməziːn] n limousine f
limp [lɪmp] n: **to have a ~** boiter ▷ vi boiter ▷ adj
mou (molle)
limpet ['lɪmpɪt] n patelle f; **like a ~** (fig) comme
une ventouse
line [laɪn] n (gen) ligne f; (stroke) trait m; (wrinkle)
ride f; (rope) corde f; (wire) fil m; (of poem) vers
m; (row, series) rangée f; (of people) file f, queue f;
(railway track) voie f; (Comm: series of goods) article(s)
m(pl), ligne de produits; (work) métier m ▷ vt:
to ~ (with) (clothes) doubler (de); (box) garnir or
tapisser (de); (subj: trees, crowd) border; **to stand
in ~** (US) faire la queue; **to cut in ~** (US) passer
avant son tour; **in his ~ of business** dans sa
partie, dans son rayon; **on the right ~s** sur la
bonne voie; **a new ~ in cosmetics** une nouvelle
ligne de produits de beauté; **hold the ~ please**
(Brit Tel) ne quittez pas; **to be in ~ for sth** (fig)
être en lice pour qch; **in ~ with** en accord avec,
en conformité avec; **in a ~** aligné(e); **to bring
sth into ~ with sth** aligner qch sur qch; **to
draw the ~ at (doing) sth** (fig) se refuser à (faire)
qch; ne pas tolérer or admettre (qu'on fasse) qch;
to take the ~ that ... être d'avis or de l'opinion

que …

▶ **line up** vi s'aligner, se mettre en rang(s); (in queue) faire la queue ▷ vt aligner; (event) prévoir; (find) trouver; **to have sb/sth ~d up** avoir qn/qch en vue or de prévu(e)

linear ['lɪnɪəʳ] adj linéaire

lined [laɪnd] adj (paper) réglé(e); (face) marqué(e), ridé(e); (clothes) doublé(e)

linen ['lɪnɪn] n linge m (de corps or de maison); (cloth) lin m

liner ['laɪnəʳ] n (ship) paquebot m de ligne; (for bin) sac-poubelle m

linesman ['laɪnzmən] (irreg) n (Tennis) juge m de ligne; (Football) juge de touche

line-up ['laɪnʌp] n (US: queue) file f; (also: **police line-up**) parade f d'identification; (Sport) (composition f de l')équipe f

linger ['lɪŋgəʳ] vi s'attarder; traîner; (smell, tradition) persister

lingerie ['lænʒəriː] n lingerie f

linguist ['lɪŋgwɪst] n linguiste m/f; **to be a good ~** être doué(e) pour les langues

linguistic [lɪŋ'gwɪstɪk] adj linguistique

linguistics [lɪŋ'gwɪstɪks] n linguistique f

lining ['laɪnɪŋ] n doublure f; (Tech) revêtement m; (: of brakes) garniture f

link [lɪŋk] n (connection) lien m, rapport m; (Internet) lien; (of a chain) maillon m ▷ vt relier, lier, unir; **links** npl (Golf) (terrain m de) golf m; **rail ~** liaison f ferroviaire

▶ **link up** vt relier ▷ vi (people) se rejoindre; (companies etc) s'associer

lino ['laɪnəu] n = **linoleum**

linoleum [lɪ'nəuliəm] n linoléum m

lion ['laɪən] n lion m

lioness ['laɪənɪs] n lionne f

lip [lɪp] n lèvre f; (of cup etc) rebord m; (insolence) insolences fpl

liposuction ['lɪpəusʌkʃən] n liposuccion f

lipread ['lɪpriːd] vi (irreg: like **read**) lire sur les lèvres

lip salve [-sælv] n pommade f pour les lèvres, pommade rosat

lip service n: **to pay ~ to sth** ne reconnaître le mérite de qch que pour la forme or qu'en paroles

lipstick ['lɪpstɪk] n rouge m à lèvres

liqueur [lɪ'kjuəʳ] n liqueur f

liquid ['lɪkwɪd] n liquide m ▷ adj liquide

liquidize ['lɪkwɪdaɪz] vt (Brit Culin) passer au mixer

liquidizer ['lɪkwɪdaɪzəʳ] n (Brit Culin) mixer m

liquor ['lɪkəʳ] n spiritueux m, alcool m

liquorice ['lɪkərɪs] n (Brit) réglisse m

liquor store (US) n magasin m de vins et spiritueux

Lisbon ['lɪzbən] n Lisbonne f

lisp [lɪsp] n zézaiement m ▷ vi zézayer

list [lɪst] n liste f; (of ship) inclinaison f ▷ vt (write down) inscrire; (make list of) faire la liste de; (enumerate) énumérer; (Comput) lister ▷ vi (ship) gîter, donner de la bande; **shopping ~** liste des courses

listed building ['lɪstɪd-] n (Archit) monument classé

listen ['lɪsn] vi écouter; **to ~ to** écouter

listener ['lɪsnəʳ] n auditeur(-trice)

listless ['lɪstlɪs] adj indolent(e), apathique

lit [lɪt] pt, pp of **light**

liter ['liːtəʳ] n (US) = **litre**

literacy ['lɪtərəsɪ] n degré m d'alphabétisation, fait m de savoir lire et écrire; (Brit: Scol) enseignement m de la lecture et de l'écriture

literal ['lɪtərl] adj littéral(e)

literally ['lɪtrəlɪ] adv littéralement; (really) réellement

literary ['lɪtərərɪ] adj littéraire

literate ['lɪtərət] adj qui sait lire et écrire; (educated) instruit(e)

literature ['lɪtrɪtʃəʳ] n littérature f; (brochures etc) copie f publicitaire, prospectus mpl

lithe [laɪð] adj agile, souple

litigation [lɪtɪ'geɪʃən] n litige m; contentieux m

litre, (US) **liter** ['liːtəʳ] n litre m

litter ['lɪtəʳ] n (rubbish) détritus mpl; (dirtier) ordures fpl; (young animals) portée f ▷ vt éparpiller; laisser des détritus dans; **~ed with** jonché(e) de, couvert(e) de

litter bin n (Brit) poubelle f

little ['lɪtl] adj (small) petit(e); (not much): **~ milk** peu de lait ▷ adv peu; **a ~** un peu (de); **a ~ milk** un peu de lait; **a ~ bit** un peu; **for a ~ while** pendant un petit moment; **with ~ difficulty** sans trop de difficulté; **as ~ as possible** le moins possible; **~ by ~** petit à petit, peu à peu; **to make ~ of** faire peu de cas de

little finger n auriculaire m, petit doigt

live[1] [laɪv] adj (animal) vivant(e), en vie; (wire) sous tension; (broadcast) (transmis(e)) en direct; (issue) d'actualité, brûlant(e); (unexploded) non explosé(e); **~ ammunition** munitions fpl de combat

live[2] [lɪv] vi vivre; (reside) vivre, habiter; **to ~ in London** habiter (à) Londres; **where do you ~?** où habitez-vous?

▶ **live down** vt faire oublier (avec le temps)

▶ **live in** vi être logé(e) et nourri(e); être interne

▶ **live off** vt (land, fish etc) vivre de; (pej: parents etc) vivre aux crochets de

▶ **live on** vt fus (food) vivre de ▷ vi survivre; **to ~ on £50 a week** vivre avec 50 livres par semaine

▶ **live out** vi (Brit: students) être externe ▷ vt: **to ~ out one's days** or **life** passer sa vie

▶ **live together** vi vivre ensemble, cohabiter

▶ **live up** vt: **to ~ it up** (inf) faire la fête; mener la grande vie

▶ **live up to** vt fus se montrer à la hauteur de

livelihood ['laɪvlɪhud] n moyens mpl d'existence

lively ['laɪvlɪ] adj vif (vive), plein(e) d'entrain; (place, book) vivant(e)

liven up ['laɪvn-] vt (room etc) égayer; (discussion, evening) animer ▷ vi s'animer

liver ['lɪvəʳ] n foie m

lives [laɪvz] npl of **life**

livestock ['laɪvstɔk] n cheptel m, bétail m

livid ['lɪvɪd] *adj* livide, blafard(e); *(furious)* furieux(-euse), furibond(e)

living ['lɪvɪŋ] *adj* vivant(e), en vie ▷ *n*: **to earn** or **make a ~** gagner sa vie; **within ~ memory** de mémoire d'homme

living conditions *npl* conditions *fpl* de vie

living room *n* salle *f* de séjour

living standards *npl* niveau *m* de vie

living wage *n* salaire *m* permettant de vivre (décemment)

lizard ['lɪzəd] *n* lézard *m*

load [ləud] *n* *(weight)* poids *m*; *(thing carried)* chargement *m*, charge *f*; *(Elec, Tech)* charge ▷ *vt*: **to ~ (with)** *(also: load up: lorry, ship)* charger (de); *(gun, camera)* charger (avec); *(Comput)* charger; **a ~ of**, **~s of** *(fig)* un or des tas de, des masses de; **to talk a ~ of rubbish** *(inf)* dire des bêtises

loaded ['ləudɪd] *adj* *(dice)* pipé(e); *(question)* insidieux(-euse); *(inf: rich)* bourré(e) de fric; *(: drunk)* bourré

loaf *(pl loaves)* [ləuf, ləuvz] *n* pain *m*, miche *f* ▷ *vi* *(also: loaf about, loaf around)* fainéanter, traîner

loan [ləun] *n* prêt *m* ▷ *vt* prêter; **on ~** prêté(e), en prêt; **public ~** emprunt public

loath [ləuθ] *adj*: **to be ~ to do** répugner à faire

loathe [ləuð] *vt* détester, avoir en horreur

loaves [ləuvz] *npl of* **loaf**

lobby ['lɔbɪ] *n* hall *m*, entrée *f*; *(Pol)* groupe *m* de pression, lobby *m* ▷ *vt* faire pression sur

lobster ['lɔbstə^r] *n* homard *m*

local ['ləukl] *adj* local(e) ▷ *n* *(Brit: pub)* pub *m* or café *m* du coin; **the locals** *npl* les gens *mpl* du pays or du coin

local anaesthetic, *(US)* **local anesthetic** *n* anesthésie locale

local authority *n* collectivité locale, municipalité *f*

local call *n* *(Tel)* communication urbaine

local government *n* administration locale or municipale

locality [ləu'kælɪtɪ] *n* région *f*, environs *mpl*; *(position)* lieu *m*

locally ['ləukəlɪ] *adv* localement; dans les environs or la région

locate [ləu'keɪt] *vt* *(find)* trouver, repérer; *(situate)* situer; **to be ~d in** être situé à or en

location [ləu'keɪʃən] *n* emplacement *m*; **on ~** *(Cine)* en extérieur

loch [lɔx] *n* lac *m*, loch *m*

lock [lɔk] *n* *(of door, box)* serrure *f*; *(of canal)* écluse *f*; *(of hair)* mèche *f*, boucle *f* ▷ *vt* *(with key)* fermer à clé; *(immobilize)* bloquer ▷ *vi* *(door etc)* fermer à clé; *(wheels)* se bloquer; **~ stock and barrel** *(fig)* en bloc; **on full ~** *(Brit Aut)* le volant tourné à fond
▶ **lock away** *vt* *(valuables)* mettre sous clé; *(criminal)* mettre sous les verrous, enfermer
▶ **lock in** *vt* enfermer
▶ **lock out** *vt* enfermer dehors; *(on purpose)* mettre à la porte; *(: workers)* lock-outer
▶ **lock up** *vt* *(person)* enfermer; *(house)* fermer à clé ▷ *vi* tout fermer (à clé)

locker ['lɔkə^r] *n* casier *m*; *(in station)* consigne *f* automatique

locker-room ['lɔkə'ru:m] *(US)* *n* *(Sport)* vestiaire *m*

locket ['lɔkɪt] *n* médaillon *m*

locksmith ['lɔksmɪθ] *n* serrurier *m*

lock-up ['lɔkʌp] *n* *(prison)* prison *f*; *(cell)* cellule *f* provisoire; *(also: lock-up garage)* box *m*

locomotive [ləukə'məutɪv] *n* locomotive *f*

locum ['ləukəm] *n* *(Med)* suppléant(e) de médecin *etc*

lodge [lɔdʒ] *n* pavillon *m* (de gardien); *(also: hunting lodge)* pavillon de chasse; *(Freemasonry)* loge *f* ▷ *vi* *(person)*: **to ~ with** être logé(e) chez, être en pension chez; *(bullet)* se loger ▷ *vt* *(appeal etc)* présenter; déposer; **to ~ a complaint** porter plainte; **to ~ (itself) in/between** se loger dans/entre

lodger ['lɔdʒə^r] *n* locataire *m/f*; *(with room and meals)* pensionnaire *m/f*

lodging ['lɔdʒɪŋ] *n* logement *m*; *see also* **board**

lodgings ['lɔdʒɪŋz] *npl* chambre *f*, meublé *m*

loft [lɔft] *n* grenier *m*; *(apartment)* grenier aménagé (en appartement) *(gén dans ancien entrepôt ou fabrique)*

lofty ['lɔftɪ] *adj* élevé(e); *(haughty)* hautain(e); *(sentiments, aims)* noble

log [lɔg] *n* *(of wood)* bûche *f*; *(Naut)* livre *m* or journal *m* de bord; *(of car)* ≈ carte grise ▷ *n abbr* (= *logarithm*) log *m* ▷ *vt* enregistrer
▶ **log in**, **log on** *vi* *(Comput)* ouvrir une session, entrer dans le système
▶ **log off**, **log out** *vi* *(Comput)* clore une session, sortir du système

logbook ['lɔgbuk] *n* *(Naut)* livre *m* or journal *m* de bord; *(Aviat)* carnet *m* de vol; *(of lorry driver)* carnet de route; *(of movement of goods etc)* registre *m*; *(of car)* ≈ carte grise

loggerheads ['lɔgəhɛdz] *npl*: **at ~ (with)** à couteaux tirés (avec)

logic ['lɔdʒɪk] *n* logique *f*

logical ['lɔdʒɪkl] *adj* logique

logo ['ləugəu] *n* logo *m*

loin [lɔɪn] *n* *(Culin)* filet *m*, longe *f*; **loins** *npl* reins *mpl*

Loire [lwa:] *n*: **the (River) ~** la Loire

loiter ['lɔɪtə^r] *vi* s'attarder; **to ~ (about)** traîner, musarder; *(pej)* rôder

loll [lɔl] *vi* *(also: loll about)* se prélasser, fainéanter

lollipop ['lɔlɪpɔp] *n* sucette *f*

lollipop man/lady *(Brit: irreg)* *n* contractuel(le) qui fait traverser la rue aux enfants; *voir article*

lolly ['lɔlɪ] *n* *(inf: ice)* esquimau *m*; *(: lollipop)* sucette *f*; *(: money)* fric *m*

London ['lʌndən] *n* Londres

Londoner ['lʌndənə^r] *n* Londonien(ne)

lone [ləun] *adj* solitaire

loneliness ['ləunlɪnɪs] *n* solitude *f*, isolement *m*

lonely ['ləunlɪ] *adj* seul(e); *(childhood etc)* solitaire; *(place)* solitaire, isolé(e)

long [lɔŋ] *adj* long (longue) ▷ *adv* longtemps ▷ *n*: **the ~ and the short of it is that ...** *(fig)* le fin mot de l'histoire c'est que ... ▷ *vi*: **to ~ for**

sth/to do sth avoir très envie de qch/de faire qch, attendre qch avec impatience/attendre avec impatience de faire qch; **he had ~ understood that ...** il avait compris depuis longtemps que ...; **how ~ is this river/course?** quelle est la longueur de ce fleuve/la durée de ce cours?; **6 metres ~ (long)** de 6 mètres; **6 months ~** qui dure 6 mois, de 6 mois; **all night ~** toute la nuit; **he no ~er comes** il ne vient plus; **I can't stand it any ~er** je ne peux plus le supporter; **~ before** longtemps avant; **before ~** (+ *future*) avant peu, dans peu de temps; (+ *past*) peu de temps après; **~ ago** il y a longtemps; **don't be ~!** fais vite!, dépêche-toi!; **I shan't be ~** je n'en ai pas pour longtemps; **at ~ last** enfin; **in the ~ run** à la longue; finalement; **so** *or* **as ~ as** à condition que + *sub*

long-distance [lɔŋ'dɪstəns] *adj* (*race*) de fond; (*call*) interurbain(e)

longer ['lɔŋgəʳ] *adv see* **long**

longhand ['lɔŋhænd] *n* écriture normale *or* courante

long-haul ['lɔŋhɔ:l] *adj* (*flight*) long-courrier

longing ['lɔŋɪŋ] *n* désir *m*, envie *f*; (*nostalgia*) nostalgie *f* ▷ *adj* plein(e) d'envie *or* de nostalgie

longitude ['lɔŋgɪtju:d] *n* longitude *f*

long jump *n* saut *m* en longueur

long-life [lɔŋ'laɪf] *adj* (*batteries etc*) longue durée *inv*; (*milk*) longue conservation

long-lost ['lɔŋlɒst] *adj* perdu(e) depuis longtemps

long-range ['lɔŋ'reɪndʒ] *adj* à longue portée; (*weather forecast*) à long terme

long-sighted ['lɔŋ'saɪtɪd] *adj* (*Brit*) presbyte; (*fig*) prévoyant(e)

long-standing ['lɔŋ'stændɪŋ] *adj* de longue date

long-suffering [lɔŋ'sʌfərɪŋ] *adj* empreint(e) d'une patience résignée; extrêmement patient(e)

long-term ['lɔŋtə:m] *adj* à long terme

long wave *n* (*Radio*) grandes ondes, ondes longues

long-winded [lɔŋ'wɪndɪd] *adj* intarissable, interminable

loo [lu:] *n* (*Brit inf*) w.-c *mpl*, petit coin

look [lʊk] *vi* regarder; (*seem*) sembler, paraître, avoir l'air; (*building etc*): **to ~ south/on to the sea** donner au sud/sur la mer ▷ *n* regard *m*; (*appearance*) air *m*, allure *f*, aspect *m*; **looks** *npl* (*good looks*) physique *m*, beauté *f*; **to ~ like** ressembler à; **it ~s like him** on dirait que c'est lui; **it ~s about 4 metres long** je dirais que ça fait 4 mètres de long; **it ~s all right to me** ça me paraît bien; **to have a ~** regarder; **to have a ~ at sth** jeter un coup d'œil à qch; **to have a ~ for sth** chercher qch; **to ~ ahead** regarder devant soi; (*fig*) envisager l'avenir; **~ (here)!** (*annoyance*) écoutez!

▸ **look after** *vt fus* s'occuper de, prendre soin de; (*luggage etc: watch over*) garder, surveiller

▸ **look around** *vi* regarder autour de soi

▸ **look at** *vt fus* regarder; (*problem etc*) examiner

▸ **look back** *vi*: **to ~ back at sth/sb** se retourner pour regarder qch/qn; **to ~ back on** (*event, period*) évoquer, repenser à

▸ **look down on** *vt fus* (*fig*) regarder de haut, dédaigner

▸ **look for** *vt fus* chercher; **we're ~ing for a hotel/restaurant** nous cherchons un hôtel/restaurant

▸ **look forward to** *vt fus* attendre avec impatience; **I'm not ~ing forward to it** cette perspective ne me réjouit guère; **~ing forward to hearing from you** (*in letter*) dans l'attente de vous lire

▸ **look in** *vi*: **to ~ in on sb** passer voir qn

▸ **look into** *vt fus* (*matter, possibility*) examiner, étudier

▸ **look on** *vi* regarder (en spectateur)

▸ **look out** *vi* (*beware*): **to ~ out (for)** prendre garde (à), faire attention (à); **~ out!** attention!

▸ **look out for** *vt fus* (*seek*) être à la recherche de; (*try to spot*) guetter

▸ **look over** *vt* (*essay*) jeter un coup d'œil à; (*town, building*) visiter (rapidement); (*person*) jeter un coup d'œil à; examiner de la tête aux pieds

▸ **look round** *vt fus* (*house, shop*) faire le tour de ▷ *vi* (*turn*) regarder derrière soi, se retourner; **to ~ round for sth** chercher qch

▸ **look through** *vt fus* (*papers, book*) examiner; (: *briefly*) parcourir; (*telescope*) regarder à travers

▸ **look to** *vt fus* veiller à; (*rely on*) compter sur

▸ **look up** *vi* lever les yeux; (*improve*) s'améliorer ▷ *vt* (*word*) chercher; (*friend*) passer voir

▸ **look up to** *vt fus* avoir du respect pour

lookout ['lʊkaʊt] *n* (*tower etc*) poste *m* de guet; (*person*) guetteur *m*; **to be on the ~ (for)** guetter

loom [lu:m] *n* métier *m* à tisser ▷ *vi* (*also*: **loom up**) surgir; (*event*) paraître imminent(e); (*threaten*) menacer

loony ['lu:nɪ] *adj, n* (*inf*) timbré(e), cinglé(e) *m/f*

loop [lu:p] *n* boucle *f*; (*contraceptive*) stérilet *m* ▷ *vt*: **to ~ sth round sth** passer qch autour de qch

loophole ['lu:phəʊl] *n* (*fig*) porte *f* de sortie; échappatoire *f*

loose [lu:s] *adj* (*knot, screw*) desserré(e); (*stone*) branlant(e); (*clothes*) vague, ample, lâche; (*hair*) dénoué(e), épars(e); (*not firmly fixed*) pas solide; (*animal*) en liberté, échappé(e); (*life*) dissolu(e); (*morals, discipline*) relâché(e); (*thinking*) peu rigoureux(-euse), vague; (*translation*) approximatif(-ive) ▷ *n*: **to be on the ~** être en liberté ▷ *vt* (*free: animal*) lâcher; (: *prisoner*) relâcher, libérer; (*slacken*) détendre, relâcher; desserrer; défaire; donner du mou à; donner du ballant à; (*Brit: arrow*) tirer; **~ connection** (*Elec*) mauvais contact; **to be at a ~ end** *or* (*US*) **at ~ ends** (*fig*) ne pas trop savoir quoi faire; **to tie up ~ ends** (*fig*) mettre au point *or* régler les derniers détails

loose change *n* petite monnaie

loose chippings [-'tʃɪpɪŋz] *npl* (*on road*) gravillons *mpl*

loosely ['lu:slɪ] *adv* sans serrer; (*imprecisely*)

approximativement

loosen ['lu:sn] *vt* desserrer, relâcher, défaire
▸ **loosen up** *vi* (*before game*) s'échauffer; (*inf: relax*) se détendre, se laisser aller

loot [lu:t] *n* butin *m* ▷ *vt* piller

lop-sided ['lɔp'saɪdɪd] *adj* de travers, asymétrique

lord [lɔːd] *n* seigneur *m*; **L~ Smith** lord Smith; **the L~** (*Rel*) le Seigneur; **my L~** (*to noble*) Monsieur le comte/le baron; (*to judge*) Monsieur le juge; (*to bishop*) Monseigneur; **good L~!** mon Dieu!

Lords ['lɔːdz] *npl* (*Brit: Pol*): **the (House of) ~** (*Brit*) la Chambre des Lords

lordship ['lɔːdʃɪp] *n* (*Brit*): **your L~** Monsieur le comte (*or* le baron *or* le Juge)

lore [lɔːʳ] *n* tradition(s) *f(pl)*

lorry ['lɔrɪ] *n* (*Brit*) camion *m*

lorry driver *n* (*Brit*) camionneur *m*, routier *m*

lose (*pt, pp* **lost**) [lu:z, lɔst] *vt* perdre; (*opportunity*) manquer, perdre; (*pursuers*) distancer, semer ▷ *vi* perdre; **I've lost my wallet/passport** j'ai perdu mon portefeuille/passeport; **to ~** (*time*) (*clock*) retarder; **to ~ no time (in doing sth)** ne pas perdre de temps (à faire qch); **to get lost** (*vi: person*) se perdre; **my watch has got lost** ma montre est perdue
▸ **lose out** *vi* être perdant(e)

loser ['lu:zəʳ] *n* perdant(e); **to be a good/bad ~** être beau/mauvais joueur

loss [lɔs] *n* perte *f*; **to cut one's ~es** limiter les dégâts; **to make a ~** enregistrer une perte; **to sell sth at a ~** vendre qch à perte; **to be at a ~** être perplexe *or* embarrassé(e); **to be at a ~ to do** se trouver incapable de faire

lost [lɔst] *pt, pp* of **lose** ▷ *adj* perdu(e); **to get ~** (*vi*) se perdre; **I'm ~** je me suis perdu; **~ in thought** perdu dans ses pensées; **~ and found property** (*n: US*) objets trouvés; **~ and found** (*n: US*) (bureau *m* des) objets trouvés

lost property *n* (*Brit*) objets trouvés; **~ office** *or* **department** (bureau *m* des) objets trouvés

lot [lɔt] *n* (*at auctions, set*) lot *m*; (*destiny*) sort *m*, destinée *f*; **the ~** (*everything*) le tout; (*everyone*) tous *mpl*, toutes *fpl*; **a ~** beaucoup; **a ~ of** beaucoup de; **~s of** des tas de; **to draw ~s (for sth)** tirer (qch) au sort

lotion ['ləʊʃən] *n* lotion *f*

lottery ['lɔtərɪ] *n* loterie *f*

loud [laʊd] *adj* bruyant(e), sonore; (*voice*) fort(e); (*condemnation etc*) vigoureux(-euse); (*gaudy*) voyant(e), tapageur(-euse) ▷ *adv* (*speak etc*) fort; **out ~** tout haut

loud-hailer [laʊd'heɪləʳ] *n* porte-voix *m inv*

loudly ['laʊdlɪ] *adv* fort, bruyamment

loudspeaker [laʊd'spiːkəʳ] *n* haut-parleur *m*

lounge [laʊndʒ] *n* salon *m*; (*of airport*) salle *f*; (*Brit: also: **lounge bar***) (salle de) café *m or* bar *m* ▷ *vi* (*also: **lounge about, lounge around***) se prélasser, paresser

lounge suit *n* (*Brit*) complet *m*; (*: on invitation*) "tenue de ville"

louse (*pl* **lice**) [laʊs, laɪs] *n* pou *m*
▸ **louse up** [lauz-] *vt* (*inf*) gâcher

lousy ['laʊzɪ] (*inf*) *adj* (*bad quality*) infect(e), moche; **I feel ~** je suis mal fichu(e)

lout [laʊt] *n* rustre *m*, butor *m*

lovable ['lʌvəbl] *adj* très sympathique; adorable

love [lʌv] *n* amour *m* ▷ *vt* aimer; (*caringly, kindly*) aimer beaucoup; **I ~ chocolate** j'adore le chocolat; **to ~ to do** aimer beaucoup *or* adorer faire; **I'd ~ to come** cela me ferait très plaisir (de venir); **"15 ~"** (*Tennis*) "15 à rien *or* zéro"; **to be/fall in ~ with** être/tomber amoureux(-euse) de; **to make ~** faire l'amour; **~ at first sight** le coup de foudre; **to send one's ~ to sb** adresser ses amitiés à qn; **~ from Anne, ~, Anne** affectueusement, Anne; **I ~ you** je t'aime

love affair *n* liaison (amoureuse)

love life *n* vie sentimentale

lovely ['lʌvlɪ] *adj* (*pretty*) ravissant(e); (*friend, wife*) charmant(e); (*holiday, surprise*) très agréable, merveilleux(-euse); **we had a ~ time** c'était vraiment très bien, nous avons eu beaucoup de plaisir

lover ['lʌvəʳ] *n* amant *m*; (*person in love*) amoureux(-euse); (*amateur*): **a ~ of** un(e) ami(e) de, un(e) amoureux(-euse) de

loving ['lʌvɪŋ] *adj* affectueux(-euse), tendre, aimant(e)

low [ləʊ] *adj* bas (basse); (*quality*) mauvais(e), inférieur(e) ▷ *adv* bas ▷ *n* (*Meteorology*) dépression *f* ▷ *vi* (*cow*) mugir; **to feel ~** se sentir déprimé(e); **he's very ~** (*ill*) il est bien bas *or* très affaibli; **to turn (down)** (*vt*) baisser; **to be ~ on** (*supplies etc*) être à court de; **to reach a new** *or* **an all-time ~** tomber au niveau le plus bas

low-alcohol [ləʊ'ælkəhɔl] *adj* à faible teneur en alcool, peu alcoolisé(e)

low-calorie ['ləʊ'kælərɪ] *adj* hypocalorique

low-cut ['ləʊkʌt] *adj* (*dress*) décolleté(e)

lower *adj* ['ləʊəʳ] inférieur(e) ▷ *vt* baisser; (*resistance*) diminuer ▷ *vi* ['laʊəʳ] (*person*): **to ~ at sb** jeter un regard mauvais *or* noir à qn; (*sky, clouds*) être menaçant; **to ~ o.s. to** s'abaisser à

lower sixth (*Brit*) *n* (*Scol*) première *f*

low-fat ['ləʊ'fæt] *adj* maigre

lowland, lowlands ['ləʊlənd(z)] *n(pl)* plaine(s) *f(pl)*

lowly ['ləʊlɪ] *adj* humble, modeste

loyal ['lɔɪəl] *adj* loyal(e), fidèle

loyalty ['lɔɪəltɪ] *n* loyauté *f*, fidélité *f*

loyalty card *n* carte *f* de fidélité

lozenge ['lɔzɪndʒ] *n* (*Med*) pastille *f*; (*Geom*) losange *m*

L-plates ['ɛlpleɪts] *npl* (*Brit*) plaques *fpl* (obligatoires) d'apprenti conducteur

Lt *abbr* (= *lieutenant*) Lt.

Ltd *abbr* (*Comm: company:* = *limited*) ≈ S.A.

lubricant ['lu:brɪkənt] *n* lubrifiant *m*

lubricate ['lu:brɪkeɪt] *vt* lubrifier, graisser

luck [lʌk] *n* chance *f*; **bad ~** malchance *f*, malheur *m*; **to be in ~** avoir de la chance; **to be out of ~** ne pas avoir de chance; **good ~!** bonne

chance!; **bad** or **hard** or **tough** ~! pas de chance!
luckily ['lʌkɪlɪ] adv heureusement, par bonheur
lucky ['lʌkɪ] adj (person) qui a de la chance;
(coincidence) heureux(-euse); (number etc) qui porte
bonheur
lucrative ['lu:krətɪv] adj lucratif(-ive), rentable,
qui rapporte
ludicrous ['lu:dɪkrəs] adj ridicule, absurde
lug [lʌg] vt traîner, tirer
luggage ['lʌgɪdʒ] n bagages mpl; **our ~ hasn't
arrived** nos bagages ne sont pas arrivés; **could
you send someone to collect our ~?** pourriez-
vous envoyer quelqu'un chercher nos bagages?
luggage rack n (in train) porte-bagages m inv
(: made of string) filet m à bagages; (on car) galerie f
lukewarm ['lu:kwɔ:m] adj tiède
lull [lʌl] n accalmie f; (in conversation) pause f ▷ vt:
to ~ sb to sleep bercer qn pour qu'il s'endorme;
to be ~ed into a false sense of security
s'endormir dans une fausse sécurité
lullaby ['lʌləbaɪ] n berceuse f
lumbago [lʌm'beɪgəu] n lumbago m
lumber ['lʌmbəʳ] n (wood) bois m de charpente;
(junk) bric-à-brac m inv ▷ vt (Brit inf): **to ~ sb
with sth/sb** coller or refiler qch/qn à qn ▷ vi
(also: **lumber about, lumber along**) marcher
pesamment
lumberjack ['lʌmbədʒæk] n bûcheron m
luminous ['lu:mɪnəs] adj lumineux(-euse)
lump [lʌmp] n morceau m; (in sauce) grumeau
m; (swelling) grosseur f ▷ vt (also: **lump together**)
réunir, mettre en tas
lump sum n somme globale or forfaitaire
lumpy ['lʌmpɪ] adj (sauce) qui a des grumeaux;
(bed) défoncé(e), peu confortable
lunar ['lu:nəʳ] adj lunaire
lunatic ['lu:nətɪk] n fou (folle), dément(e) ▷ adj
fou (folle), dément(e)
lunch [lʌntʃ] n déjeuner m ▷ vi déjeuner; **it is his

~ hour** c'est l'heure où il déjeune; **to invite sb
to** or **for ~** inviter qn à déjeuner
lunch break, lunch hour n pause f de midi,
heure f du déjeuner
luncheon ['lʌntʃən] n déjeuner m
luncheon meat n sorte de saucisson
luncheon voucher n chèque-repas m, ticket-
repas m
lunchtime ['lʌntʃtaɪm] n: **it's ~** c'est l'heure du
déjeuner
lung [lʌŋ] n poumon m
lunge [lʌndʒ] vi (also: **lunge forward**) faire
un mouvement brusque en avant; **to ~ at sb**
envoyer or assener un coup à qn
lurch [lə:tʃ] vi vaciller, tituber ▷ n écart m
brusque, embardée f; **to leave sb in the ~** laisser
qn se débrouiller or se dépêtrer tout(e) seul(e)
lure [luəʳ] n (attraction) attrait m, charme m;
(in hunting) appât m, leurre m ▷ vt attirer or
persuader par la ruse
lurid ['luərɪd] adj affreux(-euse), atroce
lurk [lə:k] vi se tapir, se cacher
luscious ['lʌʃəs] adj succulent(e), appétissant(e)
lush [lʌʃ] adj luxuriant(e)
lust [lʌst] n (sexual) désir (sexuel); (Rel) luxure f;
(fig): ~ **for** soif f de
▶ **lust after** vt fus convoiter, désirer
lusty ['lʌstɪ] adj vigoureux(-euse), robuste
Luxembourg ['lʌksəmbə:g] n Luxembourg m
luxurious [lʌg'zjuərɪəs] adj luxueux(-euse)
luxury ['lʌkʃərɪ] n luxe m ▷ cpd de luxe
Lycra® ['laɪkrə] n Lycra® m
lying ['laɪɪŋ] n mensonge(s) m(pl) ▷ adj (statement,
story) mensonger(-ère), faux (fausse); (person)
menteur(-euse)
Lyons ['ljɔ̃] n Lyon
lyric ['lɪrɪk] adj lyrique
lyrical ['lɪrɪkl] adj lyrique
lyrics ['lɪrɪks] npl (of song) paroles fpl

Mm

m. *abbr* (= *metre*) m; (= *million*) M; (= *mile*) mi
M.A. *n abbr* (*Scol*) = **Master of Arts** ▷ *abbr* (*US*)
= **military academy**; (*US*) = **Massachusetts**
ma [mɑ:] (*inf*) *n* maman *f*
mac [mæk] *n* (*Brit*) imper(méable *m*) *m*
macaroni [mækə'rəʊnɪ] *n* macaronis *mpl*
Macedonia [mæsɪ'dəʊnɪə] *n* Macédoine *f*
Macedonian [mæsɪ'dəʊnɪən] *adj*
macédonien(ne) ▷ *n* Macédonien(ne); (*Ling*)
macédonien *m*
machine [mə'ʃi:n] *n* machine *f* ▷ *vt* (*dress etc*)
coudre à la machine; (*Tech*) usiner
machine gun *n* mitrailleuse *f*
machine language *n* (*Comput*) langage *m*
machine
machinery [mə'ʃi:nərɪ] *n* machinerie *f*,
machines *fpl*; (*fig*) mécanisme(s) *m(pl)*
machine washable *adj* (*garment*) lavable en
machine
macho ['mætʃəʊ] *adj* macho *inv*
mackerel ['mækrl] *n* (*pl inv*) maquereau *m*
mackintosh ['mækɪntɔʃ] *n* (*Brit*) imperméable *m*
mad [mæd] *adj* fou (folle); (*foolish*) insensé(e);
(*angry*) furieux(-euse); **yes ~** oui; **to go ~** ▷ devenir fou; **to
be ~ (keen) about** *or* **on sth** (*inf*) être follement
passionné de qch, être fou de qch
Madagascar [mædə'gæskə^r] *n* Madagascar *m*
madam ['mædəm] *n* madame *f*; **yes ~** oui
Madame; **M~ Chairman** Madame la Présidente
mad cow disease *n* maladie *f* des vaches folles
madden ['mædn] *vt* exaspérer
made [meɪd] *pt, pp* of **make**
Madeira [mə'dɪərə] *n* (*Geo*) Madère *f*; (*wine*)
madère *m*
made-to-measure ['meɪdtə'mɛʒə^r] *adj* (*Brit*)
fait(e) sur mesure
made-up ['meɪdʌp] *adj* (*story*) inventé(e),
fabriqué(e)
madly ['mædlɪ] *adv* follement; **~ in love**
éperdument amoureux(-euse)
madman ['mædmən] (*irreg*) *n* fou *m*, aliéné *m*
madness ['mædnɪs] *n* folie *f*
Madrid [mə'drɪd] *n* Madrid
Mafia ['mæfɪə] *n* maf(f)ia *f*
mag [mæg] *n abbr* (*Brit inf*: = *magazine*) magazine *m*
magazine [mægə'zi:n] *n* (*Press*) magazine *m*,
revue *f*; (*Radio, TV*) magazine; (*Mil: store*) dépôt *m*,

arsenal *m*; (*of firearm*) magasin *m*
maggot ['mægət] *n* ver *m*, asticot *m*
magic ['mædʒɪk] *n* magie *f* ▷ *adj* magique
magical ['mædʒɪkl] *adj* magique; (*experience,
evening*) merveilleux(-euse)
magician [mə'dʒɪʃən] *n* magicien(ne)
magistrate ['mædʒɪstreɪt] *n* magistrat *m*; juge
m; **~s' court** (*Brit*) ≈ tribunal *m* d'instance
magnet ['mægnɪt] *n* aimant *m*
magnetic [mæg'nɛtɪk] *adj* magnétique
magnificent [mæg'nɪfɪsnt] *adj* superbe,
magnifique; (*splendid: robe, building*)
somptueux(-euse), magnifique
magnify ['mægnɪfaɪ] *vt* grossir; (*sound*) amplifier
magnifying glass ['mægnɪfaɪɪŋ-] *n* loupe *f*
magnitude ['mægnɪtju:d] *n* ampleur *f*
magpie ['mægpaɪ] *n* pie *f*
mahogany [mə'hɔgənɪ] *n* acajou *m* ▷ *cpd* en
(bois d')acajou
maid [meɪd] *n* bonne *f*; (*in hotel*) femme *f* de
chambre; **old ~** (*pej*) vieille fille
maiden ['meɪdn] *n* jeune fille *f* ▷ *adj* (*aunt etc*)
non mariée; (*speech, voyage*) inaugural(e)
maiden name *n* nom *m* de jeune fille
mail [meɪl] *n* poste *f*; (*letters*) courrier *m* ▷ *vt*
envoyer (par la poste); **by ~** par la poste
mailbox ['meɪlbɔks] *n* (*US: also Comput*) boîte *f*
aux lettres
mailing list ['meɪlɪŋ-] *n* liste *f* d'adresses
mailman ['meɪlmæn] (*irreg*) *n* (*US*) facteur *m*
mail-order ['meɪlɔ:də^r] *n* vente *f* or achat *m* par
correspondance ▷ *cpd*: **~ firm** *or* **house** maison *f*
de vente par correspondance
maim [meɪm] *vt* mutiler
main [meɪn] *adj* principal(e) ▷ *n* (*pipe*) conduite
principale, canalisation *f*; **the ~s** (*Elec*) le
secteur; **the ~ thing** l'essentiel *m*; **in the ~** dans
l'ensemble
main course *n* (*Culin*) plat *m* de résistance
mainframe ['meɪnfreɪm] *n* (*also*: **mainframe
computer**) (gros) ordinateur, unité centrale
mainland ['meɪnlənd] *n* continent *m*
mainly ['meɪnlɪ] *adv* principalement, surtout
main road *n* grand axe, route nationale
mainstay ['meɪnsteɪ] *n* (*fig*) pilier *m*
mainstream ['meɪnstri:m] *n* (*fig*) courant
principal

main street n rue f principale

maintain [meɪn'teɪn] vt entretenir; (continue) maintenir, préserver; (affirm) soutenir; **to ~ that ...** soutenir que ...

maintenance ['meɪntənəns] n entretien m; (Law: alimony) pension f alimentaire

maisonette [meɪzə'nɛt] n (Brit) appartement m en duplex

maize [meɪz] n (Brit) maïs m

majestic [mə'dʒɛstɪk] adj majestueux(-euse)

majesty ['mædʒɪstɪ] n majesté f; (title): **Your M~** Votre Majesté

major ['meɪdʒə'] n (Mil) commandant m ▷ adj (important) important(e); (most important) principal(e); (Mus) majeur(e) ▷ vi (US Scol): **to ~ (in)** se spécialiser (en); **a ~ operation** (Med) une grosse opération

Majorca [mə'jɔːkə] n Majorque f

majority [mə'dʒɔrɪtɪ] n majorité f ▷ cpd (verdict, holding) majoritaire

make [meɪk] vt (pt, pp **made**) [meɪd] faire; (manufacture) faire, fabriquer; (earn) gagner; (decision) prendre; (friend) se faire; (speech) faire, prononcer; (cause to be): **to ~ sb sad** etc rendre qn triste etc; (force): **to ~ sb do sth** obliger qn à faire qch, faire faire qch à qn; (equal): **2 and 2 ~ 4** 2 et 2 font 4 ▷ n (manufacture) fabrication f; (brand) marque f; **to ~ the bed** faire le lit; **to ~ a fool of sb** (ridicule) ridiculiser qn; (trick) avoir or duper qn; **to ~ a profit** faire un or des bénéfice(s); **to ~ a loss** essuyer une perte; **to ~ it** (in time etc) y arriver; (succeed) réussir; **what time do you ~ it?** quelle heure avez-vous?; **I ~ it £249** d'après mes calculs ça fait 249 livres; **to be made of** être en; **to ~ good** vi (succeed) faire son chemin, réussir ▷ vt (deficit) combler; (losses) compenser; **to ~ do with** se contenter de; se débrouiller avec
▸ **make for** vt fus (place) se diriger vers
▸ **make off** vi filer
▸ **make out** vt (write out: cheque) faire; (decipher) déchiffrer; (understand) comprendre; (see) distinguer; (claim, imply) prétendre, vouloir faire croire; **to ~ out a case for sth** présenter des arguments solides en faveur de qch
▸ **make over** vt (assign): **to ~ over (to)** céder (à), transférer (au nom de)
▸ **make up** vt (invent) inventer, imaginer; (constitute) constituer; (parcel, bed) faire ▷ vi se réconcilier; (with cosmetics) se maquiller, se farder; **to be made up of** se composer de
▸ **make up for** vt fus compenser; (lost time) rattraper

make-believe ['meɪkbɪliːv] n: **a world of ~** un monde de chimères or d'illusions; **it's just ~** c'est de la fantaisie; c'est une illusion

makeover ['meɪkəʊvə'] n (by beautician) soins mpl de maquillage; (change of image) changement m d'image

maker ['meɪkə'] n fabricant m; (of film, programme) réalisateur(-trice)

makeshift ['meɪkʃɪft] adj provisoire, improvisé(e)

make-up ['meɪkʌp] n maquillage m

making ['meɪkɪŋ] n (fig): **in the ~** en formation or gestation; **to have the ~s of** (actor, athlete) avoir l'étoffe de

malaria [mə'lɛərɪə] n malaria f, paludisme m

Malaysia [mə'leɪzɪə] n Malaisie f

male [meɪl] n (Biol, Elec) mâle m ▷ adj (sex, attitude) masculin(e); (animal) mâle; (child etc) du sexe masculin; **~ and female students** étudiants et étudiantes

malevolent [mə'lɛvələnt] adj malveillant(e)

malfunction [mæl'fʌŋkʃən] n fonctionnement défectueux

malice ['mælɪs] n méchanceté f, malveillance f

malicious [mə'lɪʃəs] adj méchant(e), malveillant(e); (Law) avec intention criminelle

malignant [mə'lɪgnənt] adj (Med) malin(-igne)

mall [mɔːl] n (also: **shopping mall**) centre commercial

mallet ['mælɪt] n maillet m

malnutrition [mælnjuː'trɪʃən] n malnutrition f

malpractice [mæl'præktɪs] n faute professionnelle; négligence f

malt [mɔːlt] n malt m ▷ cpd (whisky) pur malt

Malta ['mɔːltə] n Malte f

Maltese [mɔːl'tiːz] adj maltais(e) ▷ n (pl inv) Maltais(e); (Ling) maltais m

mammal ['mæml] n mammifère m

mammoth ['mæməθ] n mammouth m ▷ adj géant(e), monstre

man (pl men) [mæn, mɛn] n homme m; (Sport) joueur m; (Chess) pièce f; (Draughts) pion m ▷ vt (Naut: ship) garnir d'hommes; (machine) assurer le fonctionnement de; (Mil: gun) servir; (: post) être de service à; **an old ~** un vieillard; **~ and wife** mari et femme

manage ['mænɪdʒ] vi se débrouiller; (succeed) y arriver, réussir ▷ vt (business) gérer; (team, operation) diriger; (control: ship) manier, manœuvrer; (: person) savoir s'y prendre avec; (device, things to do, carry etc) arriver à se débrouiller avec, s'en tirer avec; **to ~ to do** se débrouiller pour faire; (succeed) réussir à faire

manageable ['mænɪdʒəbl] adj maniable; (task etc) faisable; (number) raisonnable

management ['mænɪdʒmənt] n (running) administration f, direction f; (people in charge: of business, firm) dirigeants mpl, cadres mpl; (: of hotel, shop, theatre) direction; **"under new ~"** "changement de gérant", "changement de propriétaire"

manager ['mænɪdʒə'] n (of business) directeur m; (of institution etc) administrateur m; (of department, unit) responsable m/f, chef m; (of hotel etc) gérant m; (Sport) manager m; (of artist) impresario m; **sales ~** responsable or chef des ventes

manageress [mænɪdʒə'rɛs] n directrice f; (of hotel etc) gérante f

managerial [mænɪ'dʒɪərɪəl] adj directorial(e); (skills) de cadre, de gestion; **~ staff** cadres mpl

managing director ['mænɪdʒɪŋ-] n directeur général

mandarin ['mændərɪn] n (also: **mandarin orange**) mandarine f; (person) mandarin m

mandate ['mændeɪt] n mandat m

mandatory ['mændətərɪ] adj obligatoire; (powers etc) mandataire

mane [meɪn] n crinière f

maneuver [mə'nu:və^r] (US) = **manoeuvre**

manfully ['mænfəlɪ] adv vaillamment

mangetout ['mɒnʒ'tu:] n mange-tout m inv

mangle ['mæŋgl] vt déchiqueter; mutiler ▷ n essoreuse f; calandre f

mango (pl **-es**) ['mæŋgəu] n mangue f

mangy ['meɪndʒɪ] adj galeux(-euse)

manhandle ['mænhændl] vt (mistreat) maltraiter, malmener; (move by hand) manutentionner

manhole ['mænhəul] n trou m d'homme

manhood ['mænhud] n (age) âge m d'homme; (manliness) virilité f

man-hour ['mænauə^r] n heure-homme f, heure f de main-d'œuvre

manhunt ['mænhʌnt] n chasse f à l'homme

mania ['meɪnɪə] n manie f

maniac ['meɪnɪæk] n maniaque m/f; (fig) fou (folle)

manic ['mænɪk] adj maniaque

manicure ['mænɪkjuə^r] n manucure f ▷ vt (person) faire les mains à

manifest ['mænɪfest] vt manifester ▷ adj manifeste, évident(e) ▷ n (Aviat, Naut) manifeste m

manifesto [mænɪ'festəu] n (Pol) manifeste m

manipulate [mə'nɪpjuleɪt] vt manipuler; (system, situation) exploiter

mankind [mæn'kaɪnd] n humanité f, genre humain

manly ['mænlɪ] adj viril(e)

man-made ['mæn'meɪd] adj artificiel(le); (fibre) synthétique

manner ['mænə^r] n manière f, façon f; (behaviour) attitude f, comportement m; **manners** npl: (good) ~s (bonnes) manières; **bad ~s** mauvaises manières; **all ~ of** toutes sortes de

mannerism ['mænərɪzəm] n particularité f de langage (or de comportement), tic m

manoeuvre, (US) **maneuver** [mə'nu:və^r] vt (move) manœuvrer; (manipulate: person) manipuler; (: situation) exploiter ▷ n manœuvre f; **to ~ sb into doing sth** manipuler qn pour lui faire faire qch

manor ['mænə^r] n (also: **manor house**) manoir m

manpower ['mænpauə^r] n main-d'œuvre f

mansion ['mænʃən] n château m, manoir m

manslaughter ['mænslɔ:tə^r] n homicide m involontaire

mantelpiece ['mæntlpi:s] n cheminée f

manual ['mænjuəl] adj manuel(le) ▷ n manuel m

manufacture [mænju'fæktʃə^r] vt fabriquer ▷ n fabrication f

manufacturer [mænju'fæktʃərə^r] n fabricant m

manure [mə'njuə^r] n fumier m; (artificial) engrais m

manuscript ['mænjuskrɪpt] n manuscrit m

many ['menɪ] adj beaucoup de, de nombreux(-euses) ▷ pron beaucoup, un grand nombre; **how ~?** combien?; **a great ~** un grand nombre (de); **too ~ difficulties** trop de difficultés; **twice as ~** deux fois plus; **~ a ...** bien des ..., plus d'un(e) ...

map [mæp] n carte f; (of town) plan m ▷ vt dresser la carte de; **can you show it to me on the ~?** pouvez-vous me l'indiquer sur la carte?
 ▶ **map out** vt tracer; (fig: task) planifier; (career, holiday) organiser, préparer (à l'avance); (: essay) faire le plan de

maple ['meɪpl] n érable m

mar [mɑ:^r] vt gâcher, gâter

marathon ['mærəθən] n marathon m ▷ adj: **a ~ session** une séance-marathon

marble ['mɑ:bl] n marbre m; (toy) bille f; **marbles** npl (game) billes

March [mɑ:tʃ] n mars m

march [mɑ:tʃ] vi marcher au pas; (demonstrators) défiler ▷ n marche f; (demonstration) manifestation f; **to ~ out of/into** etc sortir de/entrer dans etc (de manière décidée ou impulsive)

mare [mɛə^r] n jument f

margarine [mɑ:dʒə'ri:n] n margarine f

margin ['mɑ:dʒɪn] n marge f

marginal ['mɑ:dʒɪnl] adj marginal(e); **~ seat** (Pol) siège disputé

marginally ['mɑ:dʒɪnəlɪ] adv très légèrement, sensiblement

marigold ['mærɪgəuld] n souci m

marijuana [mærɪ'wɑ:nə] n marijuana f

marina [mə'ri:nə] n marina f

marinade n [mærɪ'neɪd] marinade f ▷ vt ['mærɪneɪd] = **marinate**

marinate ['mærɪneɪt] vt (faire) mariner

marine [mə'ri:n] adj marin(e) ▷ n fusilier marin; (US) marine m

marital ['mærɪtl] adj matrimonial(e)

marital status n situation f de famille

maritime ['mærɪtaɪm] adj maritime

marjoram ['mɑ:dʒərəm] n marjolaine f

mark [mɑ:k] n marque f; (of skid etc) trace f; (Brit Scol) note f; (Sport) cible f; (currency) mark m; (Brit Tech): **M~ 2/3** 2ème/3ème série f or version f; (oven temperature): **(gas) ~ 4** thermostat m 4 ▷ vt (also Sport: player) marquer; (stain) tacher; (Brit Scol) corriger, noter; (also: **punctuation marks**) signes mpl de ponctuation; **to ~ time** marquer le pas; **to be quick off the ~ (in doing)** (fig) ne pas perdre de temps (pour faire); **up to the ~** (in efficiency) à la hauteur
 ▶ **mark down** vt (prices, goods) démarquer, réduire le prix de
 ▶ **mark off** vt (tick off) cocher, pointer
 ▶ **mark out** vt désigner
 ▶ **mark up** vt (price) majorer

marked [mɑ:kt] adj (obvious) marqué(e), net(te)

marker ['mɑ:kə^r] n (sign) jalon m; (bookmark) signet m

market ['mɑːkɪt] n marché m ▷ vt (Comm) commercialiser; **to be on the ~** être sur le marché; **on the open ~** en vente libre; **to play the ~** jouer à la or spéculer en Bourse

market garden n (Brit) jardin maraîcher

marketing ['mɑːkɪtɪŋ] n marketing m

marketplace ['mɑːkɪtpleɪs] n place f du marché; (Comm) marché m

market research n étude f de marché

marksman ['mɑːksmən] (irreg) n tireur m d'élite

marmalade ['mɑːməleɪd] n confiture f d'oranges

maroon [mə'ruːn] vt: **to be ~ed** être abandonné(e); (fig) être bloqué(e) ▷ adj (colour) bordeaux inv

marquee [mɑːˈkiː] n chapiteau m

marriage ['mærɪdʒ] n mariage m

marriage certificate n extrait m d'acte de mariage

married ['mærɪd] adj marié(e); (life, love) conjugal(e)

marrow ['mærəu] n (of bone) moelle f; (vegetable) courge f

marry ['mærɪ] vt épouser, se marier avec; (subj: father, priest etc) marier ▷ vi (also: **get married**) se marier

Mars [mɑːz] n (planet) Mars f

Marseilles [mɑːˈseɪ] n Marseille

marsh [mɑːʃ] n marais m, marécage m

marshal ['mɑːʃl] n maréchal m; (US: fire, police) ≈ capitaine m; (for demonstration, meeting) membre m du service d'ordre ▷ vt rassembler

marshy ['mɑːʃɪ] adj marécageux(-euse)

martyr ['mɑːtər] n martyr(e) ▷ vt martyriser

martyrdom ['mɑːtədəm] n martyre m

marvel ['mɑːvl] n merveille f ▷ vi: **to ~ (at)** s'émerveiller (de)

marvellous, (US) **marvelous** ['mɑːvləs] adj merveilleux(-euse)

Marxism ['mɑːksɪzəm] n marxisme m

Marxist ['mɑːksɪst] adj, n marxiste (m/f)

marzipan ['mɑːzɪpæn] n pâte f d'amandes

mascara [mæs'kɑːrə] n mascara m

mascot ['mæskət] n mascotte f

masculine ['mæskjulɪn] adj masculin(e) ▷ n masculin m

mash [mæʃ] vt (Culin) faire une purée de

mashed potato n, **mashed potatoes** npl purée f de pommes de terre

mask [mɑːsk] n masque m ▷ vt masquer

mason ['meɪsn] n (also: **stonemason**) maçon m; (also: **freemason**) franc-maçon m

masonry ['meɪsnrɪ] n maçonnerie f

masquerade [mæskə'reɪd] n bal masqué; (fig) mascarade f ▷ vi: **to ~ as** se faire passer pour

mass [mæs] n multitude f, masse f; (Physics) masse; (Rel) messe f ▷ cpd (communication) de masse; (unemployment) massif(-ive) ▷ vi se masser; **masses** npl: **the ~es** les masses; **~es of** (inf) des tas de; **to go to ~** aller à la messe

massacre ['mæsəkər] n massacre m ▷ vt massacrer

massage ['mæsɑːʒ] n massage m ▷ vt masser

massive ['mæsɪv] adj énorme, massif(-ive)

mass media npl mass-media mpl

mass-produce ['mæsprə'djuːs] vt fabriquer en série

mass production n fabrication f en série

mast [mɑːst] n mât m; (Radio, TV) pylône m

master ['mɑːstər] n maître m; (in secondary school) professeur m; (in primary school) instituteur m; (title for boys): **M~ X** Monsieur X ▷ vt maîtriser; (learn) apprendre à fond; (understand) posséder parfaitement or à fond; **~ of ceremonies (MC)** n maître des cérémonies; **M~ of Arts/Science (MA/MSc)** (n) ≈ titulaire m/f d'une maîtrise (en lettres/science); **M~ of Arts/Science degree (MA/MSc)** (n) ≈ maîtrise f

masterly ['mɑːstəlɪ] adj magistral(e)

mastermind ['mɑːstəmaɪnd] n esprit supérieur ▷ vt diriger, être le cerveau de

masterpiece ['mɑːstəpiːs] n chef-d'œuvre m

master plan n stratégie f d'ensemble

mastery ['mɑːstərɪ] n maîtrise f; connaissance parfaite

masturbate ['mæstəbeɪt] vi se masturber

mat [mæt] n petit tapis; (also: **doormat**) paillasson m; (also: **tablemat**) set m de table ▷ adj = **matt**

match [mætʃ] n allumette f; (game) match m, partie f; (fig) égal(e); mariage m; parti m ▷ vt (also: **match up**) assortir; (go well with) aller bien avec, s'assortir à; (equal) égaler, valoir ▷ vi être assorti(e); **to be a good ~** être bien assorti(e) ▷ **match up** vt assortir

matchbox ['mætʃbɔks] n boîte f d'allumettes

matching ['mætʃɪŋ] adj assorti(e)

mate [meɪt] n camarade m f de travail; (inf) copain (copine); (animal) partenaire m/f, mâle (femelle); (in merchant navy) second m ▷ vi s'accoupler ▷ vt accoupler

material [mə'tɪərɪəl] n (substance) matière f, matériau m; (cloth) tissu m, étoffe f; (information, data) données fpl ▷ adj matériel(le); (relevant: evidence) pertinent(e); (important) essentiel(le); **materials** npl (equipment) matériaux mpl; **reading ~** de quoi lire, de la lecture

materialize [mə'tɪərɪəlaɪz] vi se matérialiser, se réaliser

maternal [mə'tɜːnl] adj maternel(le)

maternity [mə'tɜːnɪtɪ] n maternité f ▷ cpd de maternité, de grossesse

maternity dress n robe f de grossesse

maternity hospital n maternité f

maternity leave n congé m de maternité

math [mæθ] n (US: = mathematics) maths fpl

mathematical [mæθə'mætɪkl] adj mathématique

mathematician [mæθəmə'tɪʃən] n mathématicien(ne)

mathematics [mæθə'mætɪks] n mathématiques fpl

maths [mæθs] n abbr (Brit: = mathematics) maths fpl

matinée ['mætɪneɪ] n matinée f

mating call n appel m du mâle
matrices ['meɪtrɪsi:z] npl of **matrix**
matriculation [mətrɪkju'leɪʃən] n inscription f
matrimonial [mætrɪ'məunɪəl] adj matrimonial(e), conjugal(e)
matrimony ['mætrɪmənɪ] n mariage m
matrix (pl **matrices**) ['meɪtrɪks, 'meɪtrɪsi:z] n matrice f
matron ['meɪtrən] n (in hospital) infirmière-chef f; (in school) infirmière f
matt [mæt] adj mat(e)
matted ['mætɪd] adj emmêlé(e)
matter ['mætəʳ] n question f; (Physics) matière f, substance f; (content) contenu m, fond m; (Med: pus) pus m ▷ vi importer; **matters** npl (affairs, situation) la situation; **it doesn't** ~ cela n'a pas d'importance; (I don't mind) cela ne fait rien; **what's the** ~? qu'est-ce qu'il y a?, qu'est-ce qui ne va pas?; **no** ~ **what** quoi qu'il arrive; **that's another** ~ c'est une autre affaire; **as a** ~ **of course** tout naturellement; **as a** ~ **of fact** en fait; **it's a** ~ **of habit** c'est une question d'habitude; **printed** ~ imprimés mpl; **reading** ~ (Brit) de quoi lire, de la lecture
matter-of-fact ['mætərəv'fækt] adj terre à terre, neutre
mattress ['mætrɪs] n matelas m
mature [mə'tjuəʳ] adj mûr(e); (cheese) fait(e); (wine) arrive(e) à maturité ▷ vi mûrir; (cheese, wine) se faire
mature student n étudiant(e) plus âgé(e) que la moyenne
maturity [mə'tjuərɪtɪ] n maturité f
maul [mɔːl] vt lacérer
mauve [məuv] adj mauve
max abbr = **maximum**
maximize ['mæksɪmaɪz] vt (profits etc, chances) maximiser
maximum ['mæksɪməm] (pl **maxima**) ['mæksɪmə] adj maximum ▷ n maximum m
May [meɪ] n mai m; for phrases see also **July**
may [meɪ] (conditional **might**) vi (indicating possibility): **he** ~ **come** il se peut qu'il vienne; (be allowed to): ~ **I smoke?** puis-je fumer?; (wishes): ~ **God bless you!** (que) Dieu vous bénisse!; ~ **I sit here?** vous permettez que je m'assoie ici?; **he might be there** il pourrait bien y être, il se pourrait qu'il y soit; **you** ~ **as well go** vous feriez aussi bien d'y aller; **I might as well go** je ferais aussi bien d'y aller, autant y aller; **you might like to try** vous pourriez (peut-être) essayer
maybe ['meɪbi:] adv peut-être; ~ **he'll** ... peut-être qu'il ...; ~ **not** peut-être pas
May Day n le Premier mai
mayday ['meɪdeɪ] n S.O.S m
mayhem ['meɪhɛm] n grabuge m
mayonnaise [meɪə'neɪz] n mayonnaise f
mayor [mɛəʳ] n maire m
mayoress ['mɛərɛs] n (female mayor) maire m; (wife of mayor) épouse f du maire
maze [meɪz] n labyrinthe m, dédale m
MD n abbr (= Doctor of Medicine) titre universitaire;

(Comm) = **managing director** ▷ abbr (US) = **Maryland**
me [mi:] pron me, m' + vowel or h mute; (stressed, after prep) moi; **it's me** c'est moi; **he heard me** il m'a entendu; **give me a book** donnez-moi un livre; **it's for me** c'est pour moi
meadow ['mɛdəu] n prairie f, pré m
meagre, (US) **meager** ['mi:gəʳ] adj maigre
meal [mi:l] n repas m; (flour) farine f; **to go out for a** ~ sortir manger
mealtime ['mi:ltaɪm] n heure f du repas
mean [mi:n] adj (with money) avare, radin(e); (unkind) mesquin(e), méchant(e); (shabby) misérable; (US inf: animal) méchant, vicieux(-euse); (: person) vache; (average) moyen(ne) ▷ vt (pt, pp -t) [mɛnt] (signify) signifier, vouloir dire; (refer to) faire allusion à, parler de; (intend): **to** ~ **to do** avoir l'intention de faire ▷ n moyenne f; **means** npl (way, money) moyens mpl; **by** ~**s of** (instrument) au moyen de; **by all** ~s je vous en prie; **to be** ~**t for** être destiné(e) à; **do you** ~ **it?** vous êtes sérieux?; **what do you** ~? que voulez-vous dire?
meander [mɪ'ændəʳ] vi faire des méandres; (fig) flâner
meaning ['mi:nɪŋ] n signification f, sens m
meaningful ['mi:nɪŋful] adj significatif(-ive); (relationship) valable
meaningless ['mi:nɪŋlɪs] adj dénué(e) de sens
meanness ['mi:nnɪs] n avarice f; mesquinerie f
meant [mɛnt] pt, pp of **mean**
meantime ['mi:ntaɪm] adv (also: **in the meantime**) pendant ce temps
meanwhile ['mi:nwaɪl] adv = **meantime**
measles ['mi:zlz] n rougeole f
measure ['mɛʒəʳ] vt, vi mesurer ▷ n mesure f; (ruler) règle (graduée); **a litre** ~ un litre; **some** ~ **of success** un certain succès; **to take** ~**s to do sth** prendre les mesures pour faire qch
▶ **measure up** vi: **to** ~ **up (to)** être à la hauteur (de)
measurements ['mɛʒəməntz] npl mesures fpl; **chest/hip** ~ tour m de poitrine/hanches; **to take sb's** ~ prendre les mesures de qn
meat [mi:t] n viande f; **I don't eat** ~ je ne mange pas de viande; **cold** ~**s** (Brit) viandes froides; **crab** ~ crabe f
meatball ['mi:tbɔ:l] n boulette f de viande
Mecca ['mɛkə] n la Mecque; (fig): **a** ~ **(for)** la Mecque (de)
mechanic [mɪ'kænɪk] n mécanicien m; **can you send a** ~? pouvez-vous nous envoyer un mécanicien?
mechanical [mɪ'kænɪkl] adj mécanique
mechanics [mə'kænɪks] n mécanique f ▷ npl mécanisme m
mechanism ['mɛkənɪzəm] n mécanisme m
medal ['mɛdl] n médaille f
medallion [mɪ'dælɪən] n médaillon m
medallist, (US) **medalist** ['mɛdlɪst] n (Sport) médaillé(e)
meddle ['mɛdl] vi: **to** ~ **in** se mêler de, s'occuper

de; **to ~ with** toucher à
media ['miːdɪə] *npl* media *mpl* ▷ *npl of* **medium**
mediaeval [mɛdɪ'iːvl] *adj* = **medieval**
median ['miːdɪən] *n* (US: also: **median strip**)
bande médiane
mediate ['miːdɪeɪt] *vi* servir d'intermédiaire
Medicaid ['mɛdɪkeɪd] *n* (US) *assistance médicale aux indigents*
medical ['mɛdɪkl] *adj* médical(e) ▷ *n* (also:
medical examination) visite médicale; (*private*)
examen médical
medical certificate *n* certificat médical
Medicare ['mɛdɪkɛəʳ] *n* (US) *régime d'assurance maladie*
medicated ['mɛdɪkeɪtɪd] *adj* traitant(e),
médicamenteux(-euse)
medication [mɛdɪ'keɪʃən] *n* (*drugs etc*)
médication *f*
medicine ['mɛdsɪn] *n* médecine *f*; (*drug*)
médicament *m*
medieval [mɛdɪ'iːvl] *adj* médiéval(e)
mediocre [miːdɪ'əʊkəʳ] *adj* médiocre
meditate ['mɛdɪteɪt] *vi*: **to ~ (on)** méditer (sur)
meditation [mɛdɪ'teɪʃən] *n* méditation *f*
Mediterranean [mɛdɪtə'reɪnɪən] *adj*
méditerranéen(ne); **the ~ (Sea)** la (mer)
Méditerranée
medium ['miːdɪəm] *adj* moyen(ne) ▷ *n* (*pl* **media**)
(*means*) moyen *m* (*pl* -**s**) (*person*) médium *m*; **the
happy ~** le juste milieu
medium-sized ['miːdɪəm'saɪzd] *adj* de taille
moyenne
medium wave *n* (*Radio*) ondes moyennes, petites
ondes
medley ['mɛdlɪ] *n* mélange *m*
meek [miːk] *adj* doux (douce), humble
meet (*pt, pp* **met**) [miːt, mɛt] *vt* rencontrer; (*by
arrangement*) retrouver, rejoindre; (*for the first
time*) faire la connaissance de; (*go and fetch*): **I'll
~ you at the station** j'irai te chercher à la gare;
(*opponent, danger, problem*) faire face à; (*requirements*)
satisfaire à, répondre à; (*bill, expenses*) régler,
honorer ▷ *vi* (*friends*) se rencontrer; se retrouver;
(*in session*) se réunir; (*join: lines, roads*) se joindre
▷ *n* (*Brit Hunting*) rendez-vous *m* de chasse; (*US
Sport*) rencontre *f*, meeting *m*; **pleased to ~ you!**
enchanté!; **nice ~ing you** ravi d'avoir fait votre
connaissance
▶ **meet up** *vi*: **to ~ up with sb** rencontrer qn
▶ **meet with** *vt fus* (*difficulty*) rencontrer; **to ~
with success** être couronné(e) de succès
meeting ['miːtɪŋ] *n* (*of group of people*) réunion
f; (*between individuals*) rendez-vous *m*; (*formal*)
assemblée *f*; (*Sport: rally*) rencontre, meeting *m*;
(*interview*) entrevue *f*; **she's at** or **in a ~** (*Comm*)
elle est en réunion; **to call a ~** convoquer une
réunion
meeting place *n* lieu *m* de (la) réunion; (*for
appointment*) lieu de rendez-vous
mega ['mɛgə] (*inf*) *adv*: **he's ~ rich** il est hyper-
riche
megabyte ['mɛgəbaɪt] *n* (*Comput*) méga-octet *m*

megaphone ['mɛgəfəʊn] *n* porte-voix *m inv*
megapixel ['mɛgəpɪksl] *n* mégapixel *m*
melancholy ['mɛlənkəlɪ] *n* mélancolie *f* ▷ *adj*
mélancolique
mellow ['mɛləʊ] *adj* velouté(e), doux (douce);
(*colour*) riche et profond(e); (*fruit*) mûr(e) ▷ *vi*
(*person*) s'adoucir
melody ['mɛlədɪ] *n* mélodie *f*
melon ['mɛlən] *n* melon *m*
melt [mɛlt] *vi* fondre; (*become soft*) s'amollir; (*fig*)
s'attendrir ▷ *vt* faire fondre
▶ **melt away** *vi* fondre complètement
▶ **melt down** *vt* fondre
meltdown ['mɛltdaʊn] *n* fusion *f* (du cœur d'un
réacteur nucléaire)
melting pot ['mɛltɪŋ-] *n* (*fig*) creuset *m*; **to be in
the ~** être encore en discussion
member ['mɛmbəʳ] *n* membre *m*; (*of club, political
party*) membre, adhérent(e) ▷ *cpd*: **~ country/
state** *n* pays *m*/état *m* membre
membership ['mɛmbəʃɪp] *n* (*becoming a member*)
adhésion *f*; admission *f*; (*being a member*) qualité
f de membre, fait *m* d'être membre; (*members*)
membres *mpl*, adhérents *mpl*; (*number of members*)
nombre *m* des membres or adhérents
membership card *n* carte *f* de membre
memento [mə'mɛntəʊ] *n* souvenir *m*
memo ['mɛməʊ] *n* note *f* (de service)
memoir ['mɛmwaːʳ] *n* mémoire *m*, étude *f*;
memoirs *npl* mémoires
memorable ['mɛmərəbl] *adj* mémorable
memorandum (*pl* **memoranda**)
[mɛmə'rændəm, -də] *n* note *f* (de service);
(*Diplomacy*) mémorandum *m*
memorial [mɪ'mɔːrɪəl] *n* mémorial *m* ▷ *adj*
commémoratif(-ive)
memorize ['mɛməraɪz] *vt* apprendre or retenir
par cœur
memory ['mɛmərɪ] *n* (*also Comput*) mémoire *f*;
(*recollection*) souvenir *m*; **to have a good/bad ~**
avoir une bonne/mauvaise mémoire; **loss of ~**
perte *f* de mémoire; **in ~ of** à la mémoire de
memory card *n* (*for digital camera*) carte *f* mémoire
men [mɛn] *npl of* **man**
menace ['mɛnɪs] *n* menace *f*; (*inf: nuisance*) peste
f, plaie *f* ▷ *vt* menacer; **a public ~** un danger
public
menacing ['mɛnɪsɪŋ] *adj* menaçant(e)
mend [mɛnd] *vt* réparer; (*darn*) raccommoder,
repriser ▷ *n* reprise *f*; **on the ~** en voie de
guérison; **to ~ one's ways** s'amender
mending ['mɛndɪŋ] *n* raccommodages *mpl*
menial ['miːnɪəl] *adj* de domestique, inférieur(e);
subalterne
meningitis [mɛnɪn'dʒaɪtɪs] *n* méningite *f*
menopause ['mɛnəʊpɔːz] *n* ménopause *f*
men's room (US) *n*: **the men's room** les
toilettes *fpl* pour hommes
menstruation [mɛnstru'eɪʃən] *n* menstruation *f*
menswear ['mɛnzwɛəʳ] *n* vêtements *mpl*
d'hommes
mental ['mɛntl] *adj* mental(e); **~ illness** maladie

mentale
mental hospital n hôpital m psychiatrique
mentality [mɛn'tælɪtɪ] n mentalité f
mentally ['mɛntlɪ] adv: **to be ~ handicapped**
être handicapé(e) mental(e); **the ~ ill** les
malades mentaux
menthol ['mɛnθɔl] n menthol m
mention ['mɛnʃən] n mention f ▷ vt
mentionner, faire mention de; **don't ~ it!** je
vous en prie, il n'y a pas de quoi!; **I need hardly
~ that** ... est-il besoin de rappeler que ...?; **not
to ~ ..., without ~ing ...** sans parler de ..., sans
compter ...
menu ['mɛnju:] n (set menu, Comput) menu m; (list
of dishes) carte f; **could we see the ~?** est-ce qu'on
peut voir la carte?
MEP n abbr = **Member of the European
Parliament**
mercenary ['mɜːsɪnərɪ] adj (person) intéressé(e),
mercenaire ▷ n mercenaire m
merchandise ['mɜːtʃəndaɪz] n marchandises fpl
▷ vt commercialiser
merchant ['mɜːtʃənt] n négociant m, marchand
m; **timber/wine ~** négociant en bois/vins,
marchand de bois/vins
merchant bank n (Brit) banque f d'affaires
merchant navy, (US) **merchant marine** n
marine marchande
merciful ['mɜːsɪful] adj miséricordieux(-euse),
clément(e)
merciless ['mɜːsɪlɪs] adj impitoyable, sans pitié
mercury ['mɜːkjurɪ] n mercure m
mercy ['mɜːsɪ] n pitié f, merci f; (Rel) miséricorde
f; **to have ~ on sb** avoir pitié de qn; **at the ~ of** à
la merci de
mere [mɪəʳ] adj simple; (chance) pur(e); **a ~ two
hours** seulement deux heures
merely ['mɪəlɪ] adv simplement, purement
merge [mɜːdʒ] vt unir; (Comput) fusionner,
interclasser ▷ vi (colours, shapes, sounds) se mêler;
(roads) se joindre; (Comm) fusionner
merger ['mɜːdʒəʳ] n (Comm) fusion f
meringue [mə'ræŋ] n meringue f
merit ['mɛrɪt] n mérite m, valeur f ▷ vt mériter
mermaid ['mɜːmeɪd] n sirène f
merry ['mɛrɪ] adj gai(e); **M~ Christmas!** joyeux
Noël!
merry-go-round ['mɛrɪgəuraund] n manège m
mesh [mɛʃ] n mailles fpl ▷ vi (gears) s'engrener;
wire ~ grillage m (métallique), treillis m
(métallique)
mesmerize ['mezməraɪz] vt hypnotiser; fasciner
mess [mɛs] n désordre m, fouillis m, pagaille f;
(muddle: of life) gâchis m; (: of economy) pagaille f;
(dirt) saleté f; (Mil) mess m, cantine f; **to be (in) a
~** être en désordre; **to be/get o.s. in a ~** (fig) être/
se mettre dans le pétrin
▸ **mess about** or **around** (inf) vi perdre son temps
▸ **mess about** or **around with** vt fus (inf)
chambarder, tripoter
▸ **mess up** vt (dirty) salir; (spoil) gâcher
▸ **mess with** (inf) vt fus (challenge, confront) se

frotter à; (interfere with) toucher à
message ['mɛsɪdʒ] n message m; **can I leave
a ~?** est-ce que je peux laisser un message?;
are there any ~s for me? est-ce que j'ai des
messages?; **to get the ~** (fig: inf) saisir, piger
messenger ['mɛsɪndʒəʳ] n messager m
Messrs, Messrs. ['mɛsəz] abbr (on letters:
= messieurs) MM
messy ['mɛsɪ] adj (dirty) sale; (untidy) en désordre
met [mɛt] pt, pp of **meet** ▷ adj abbr (= meteorological)
météo inv
metabolism [mɛ'tæbəlɪzəm] n métabolisme m
metal ['mɛtl] n métal m ▷ cpd en métal ▷ vt
empierrer
metallic [mɛ'tælɪk] adj métallique
metaphor ['mɛtəfəʳ] n métaphore f
meteor ['mi:tɪəʳ] n météore m
meteorite ['mi:tɪəraɪt] n météorite m or f
meteorology [mi:tɪə'rɔlədʒɪ] n météorologie f
meter ['mi:təʳ] n (instrument) compteur m; (also:
parking meter) parc(o)mètre m; (US: unit) =
metre ▷ vt (US Post) affranchir à la machine
method ['mɛθəd] n méthode f; **~ of payment**
mode m or modalité f de paiement
methodical [mɪ'θɔdɪkl] adj méthodique
Methodist ['mɛθədɪst] adj, n méthodiste (m/f)
methylated spirit ['mɛθɪleɪtɪd-] n (Brit: also:
meths) alcool m à brûler
meticulous [mɛ'tɪkjuləs] adj méticuleux(-euse)
metre, (US) **meter** ['mi:təʳ] n mètre m
metric ['mɛtrɪk] adj métrique; **to go ~** adopter le
système métrique
metro ['mɛtrəu] n métro m
metropolitan [mɛtrə'pɔlɪtən] adj
métropolitain(e); **the M~ Police** (Brit) la police
londonienne
mettle ['mɛtl] n courage m
mew [mju:] vi (cat) miauler
mews [mju:z] n (Brit): **~ cottage** maisonnette
aménagée dans une ancienne écurie ou remise
Mexican ['mɛksɪkən] adj mexicain(e) ▷ n
Mexicain(e)
Mexico ['mɛksɪkəu] n Mexique m
mg abbr (= milligram) mg
miaow [mi:'au] vi miauler
mice [maɪs] npl of **mouse**
micro ['maɪkrəu] n (also: **microcomputer**)
micro(-ordinateur) m
micro... [maɪkrəu] prefix
microchip ['maɪkrəutʃɪp] n (Elec) puce f
microcomputer ['maɪkrəukəm'pju:təʳ] n micro-
ordinateur m
microphone ['maɪkrəfəun] n microphone m
microscope ['maɪkrəskəup] n microscope m;
under the ~ au microscope n
mid [mɪd] adj: **~ May** la mi-mai; **~ afternoon** le
milieu de l'après-midi; **in ~ air** en plein ciel;
he's in his ~ thirties il a dans les trente-cinq
ans
midday [mɪd'deɪ] n midi m
middle ['mɪdl] n milieu m; (waist) ceinture f,
taille f ▷ adj du milieu; (average) moyen(ne); **in**

the ~ of the night au milieu de la nuit; **I'm in the ~ of reading it** je suis (justement) en train de le lire

middle-aged [mɪdl'eɪdʒd] *adj* d'un certain âge, ni vieux ni jeune; (*pej: values, outlook*) conventionnel(le), rassis(e)

Middle Ages *npl*: **the ~** le moyen âge

middle-class [mɪdl'klɑːs] *adj* bourgeois(e)

middle class *n*, **middle classes** *npl*: **the ~(es)** ≈ les classes moyennes

Middle East *n*: **the ~** le Proche-Orient, le Moyen-Orient

middleman ['mɪdlmæn] (*irreg*) *n* intermédiaire *m*

middle name *n* second prénom

middle-of-the-road ['mɪdləvðə'rəud] *adj* (*policy*) modéré(e), du juste milieu; (*music etc*) plutôt classique, assez traditionnel(le)

middle school *n* (*US*) école pour les enfants de 12 à 14 ans, ≈ collège *m*; (*Brit*) école pour les enfants de 8 à 14 ans

middleweight ['mɪdlweɪt] *n* (*Boxing*) poids moyen

middling ['mɪdlɪŋ] *adj* moyen(ne)

midge [mɪdʒ] *n* moucheron *m*

midget ['mɪdʒɪt] *n* nain(e) ▷ *adj* minuscule

Midlands ['mɪdləndz] *npl* comtés du centre de l'Angleterre

midnight ['mɪdnaɪt] *n* minuit *m*; **at ~** à minuit

midriff ['mɪdrɪf] *n* estomac *m*, taille *f*

midst [mɪdst] *n*: **in the ~ of** au milieu de

midsummer [mɪd'sʌmər] *n* milieu *m* de l'été

midway [mɪd'weɪ] *adj*, *adv*: **~ (between)** à mi-chemin (entre); **~ through ...** au milieu de ..., en plein(e) ...

midweek [mɪd'wiːk] *adj* du milieu de la semaine ▷ *adv* au milieu de la semaine, en pleine semaine

midwife (*pl* **midwives**) ['mɪdwaɪf, -vz] *n* sage-femme *f*

midwinter [mɪd'wɪntər] *n* milieu *m* de l'hiver

might [maɪt] *vb see* **may** ▷ *n* puissance *f*, force *f*

mighty ['maɪtɪ] *adj* puissant(e) ▷ *adv* (*inf*) rudement

migraine ['miːgreɪn] *n* migraine *f*

migrant ['maɪɡrənt] *n* (*bird, animal*) migrateur *m*; (*person*) migrant(e); nomade *m/f* ▷ *adj* migrateur(-trice); migrant(e); nomade; (*worker*) saisonnier(-ière)

migrate [maɪ'ɡreɪt] *vi* migrer

migration [maɪ'ɡreɪʃən] *n* migration *f*

mike [maɪk] *n abbr* (= *microphone*) micro *m*

mild [maɪld] *adj* doux (douce); (*reproach, infection*) léger(-ère); (*illness*) bénin(-igne); (*interest*) modéré(e); (*taste*) peu relevé(e) ▷ *n* bière légère

mildly ['maɪldlɪ] *adv* doucement; légèrement; **to put it ~** (*inf*) c'est le moins qu'on puisse dire

mile [maɪl] *n* mil(l)e *m* (= 1609 *m*); **to do 30 ~s per gallon** ≈ faire 9, 4 litres aux cent

mileage ['maɪlɪdʒ] *n* distance *f* en milles, ≈ kilométrage *m*

mileometer [maɪ'lɔmɪtər] *n* compteur *m* kilométrique

milestone ['maɪlstəun] *n* borne *f*; (*fig*) jalon *m*

militant ['mɪlɪtnt] *adj*, *n* militant(e)

military ['mɪlɪtərɪ] *adj* militaire ▷ *n*: **the ~** l'armée *f*, les militaires *mpl*

militia [mɪ'lɪʃə] *n* milice *f*

milk [mɪlk] *n* lait *m* ▷ *vt* (*cow*) traire; (*fig: person*) dépouiller, plumer; (: *situation*) exploiter à fond

milk chocolate *n* chocolat *m* au lait

milkman ['mɪlkmən] (*irreg*) *n* laitier *m*

milk shake *n* milk-shake *m*

milky ['mɪlkɪ] *adj* (*drink*) au lait; (*colour*) laiteux(-euse)

Milky Way *n* Voie lactée

mill [mɪl] *n* moulin *m*; (*factory*) usine *f*, fabrique *f*; (*spinning mill*) filature *f*; (*flour mill*) minoterie *f*; (*steel mill*) aciérie *f* ▷ *vt* moudre, broyer ▷ *vi* (*also*: **mill about**) grouiller

millennium (*pl* **-s** *or* **millennia**) [mɪ'lɛnɪəm, -'lɛnɪə] *n* millénaire *m*

millennium bug [mɪ'lɛnɪəm-] *n* bogue *m or* bug *m* de l'an 2000

miller ['mɪlər] *n* meunier *m*

milli... ['mɪlɪ] *prefix* milli...

milligram, milligramme ['mɪlɪɡræm] *n* milligramme *m*

millilitre, (*US*) **milliliter** ['mɪlɪliːtər] *n* millilitre *m*

millimetre, (*US*) **millimeter** ['mɪlɪmiːtər] *n* millimètre *m*

million ['mɪljən] *n* million *m*; **a ~ pounds** un million de livres sterling

millionaire [mɪljə'nɛər] *n* millionnaire *m*

millionth [-θ] *num* millionième

milometer [maɪ'lɔmɪtər] *n* = **mileometer**

mime [maɪm] *n* mime *m* ▷ *vt*, *vi* mimer

mimic ['mɪmɪk] *n* imitateur(-trice) ▷ *vt*, *vi* imiter, contrefaire

min. *abbr* (= *minute(s)*) mn.; (= *minimum*) min.

mince [mɪns] *vt* hacher ▷ *vi* (*in walking*) marcher à petits pas maniérés ▷ *n* (*Brit Culin*) viande hachée, hachis *m*; **he does not ~ (his) words** il ne mâche pas ses mots

mincemeat ['mɪnsmiːt] *n* hachis de fruits secs utilisés en pâtisserie; (*US*) viande hachée, hachis *m*

mince pie *n* sorte de tarte aux fruits secs

mincer ['mɪnsər] *n* hachoir *m*

mind [maɪnd] *n* esprit *m* ▷ *vt* (*attend to, look after*) s'occuper de; (*be careful*) faire attention à; (*object to*): **I don't ~ the noise** je ne crains pas le bruit, le bruit ne me dérange pas; **it is on my ~** cela me préoccupe; **to change one's ~** changer d'avis; **to be in two ~s about sth** (*Brit*) être indécis(e) *or* irrésolu(e) en ce qui concerne qch; **to my ~** à mon avis, selon moi; **to be out of one's ~** ne plus avoir toute sa raison; **to keep sth in ~** ne pas oublier qch; **to bear sth in ~** tenir compte de qch; **to have sb/sth in ~** avoir qn/qch en tête; **to have in ~ to do** avoir l'intention de faire; **it went right out of my ~** ça m'est complètement sorti de la tête; **to bring** *or* **call sth to ~** se rappeler qch; **to make up one's ~** se décider; **do you ~ if ...?** est-ce que cela vous gêne si ...?; **I don't ~** cela ne me dérange pas; (*don't care*) ça m'est égal; **~ you**, ... remarquez, ...; **never ~** peu importe, ça ne fait rien; (*don't worry*) ne vous en faîtes pas; **"~ the step"** "attention à la marche"

minder ['maɪndə^r] *n* (*child minder*) gardienne *f*; (*bodyguard*) ange gardien (*fig*)

mindful ['maɪndful] *adj*: **~ of** attentif(-ive) à, soucieux(-euse) de

mindless ['maɪndlɪs] *adj* irréfléchi(e); (*violence, crime*) insensé(e); (*boring: job*) idiot(e)

mine¹ [maɪn] *pron* le (la) mien(ne), les miens (miennes); **a friend of ~** un de mes amis, un ami à moi; **this book is ~** ce livre est à moi

mine² [maɪn] *n* mine *f* ▷ *vt* (*coal*) extraire; (*ship, beach*) miner

minefield ['maɪnfiːld] *n* champ *m* de mines

miner ['maɪnə^r] *n* mineur *m*

mineral ['mɪnərəl] *adj* minéral(e) ▷ *n* minéral *m*; **minerals** *npl* (*Brit: soft drinks*) boissons gazeuses (sucrées)

mineral water *n* eau minérale

mingle ['mɪŋgl] *vt* mêler, mélanger ▷ *vi*: **to ~ with** se mêler à

miniature ['mɪnətʃə^r] *adj* (en) miniature ▷ *n* miniature *f*

minibar ['mɪnɪbɑː^r] *n* minibar *m*

minibus ['mɪnɪbʌs] *n* minibus *m*

minicab ['mɪnɪkæb] *n* (*Brit*) taxi *m* indépendant

minimal ['mɪnɪml] *adj* minimal(e)

minimize ['mɪnɪmaɪz] *vt* (*reduce*) réduire au minimum; (*play down*) minimiser

minimum ['mɪnɪməm] *n* (*pl* **minima**) [-mə] minimum *m* ▷ *adj* minimum; **to reduce to a ~** réduire au minimum

mining ['maɪnɪŋ] *n* exploitation minière ▷ *adj* minier(-ière); de mineurs

miniskirt ['mɪnɪskəːt] *n* mini-jupe *f*

minister ['mɪnɪstə^r] *n* (*Brit Pol*) ministre *m*; (*Rel*) pasteur *m* ▷ *vi*: **to ~ to sb** donner ses soins à qn; **to ~ to sb's needs** pourvoir aux besoins de qn

ministerial [mɪnɪs'tɪərɪəl] *adj* (*Brit Pol*) ministériel(le)

ministry ['mɪnɪstrɪ] *n* (*Brit Pol*) ministère *m*; (*Rel*): **to go into the ~** devenir pasteur

mink [mɪŋk] *n* vison *m*

minor ['maɪnə^r] *adj* petit(e), de peu d'importance; (*Mus, poet, problem*) mineur(e) ▷ *n* (*Law*) mineur/e

minority [maɪ'nɔrɪtɪ] *n* minorité *f*; **to be in a ~** être en minorité

mint [mɪnt] *n* (*plant*) menthe *f*; (*sweet*) bonbon *m* à la menthe ▷ *vt* (*coins*) battre; **the (Royal) M~**, **the (US) M~** ≈ l'hôtel *m* de la Monnaie; **in ~ condition** à l'état de neuf

minus ['maɪnəs] *n* (*also*: **minus sign**) signe *m* moins ▷ *prep* moins; **12 ~ 6 equals 6** 12 moins 6 égal 6; **~ 24°C** moins 24°C

minute¹ *n* ['mɪnɪt] minute *f*; (*official record*) procès-verbal *m*, compte rendu; **minutes** *npl* (*of meeting*) procès-verbal *m*, compte rendu; **it is 5 ~s past 3** il est 3 heures 5; **wait a ~!** (*attendez*) un instant!; **at the last ~** à la dernière minute; **up to the ~** (*fashion*) dernier cri; (*news*) de dernière minute;

(*machine, technology*) de pointe

minute² *adj* [maɪ'njuːt] minuscule; (*detailed*) minutieux(-euse); **in ~ detail** par le menu

miracle ['mɪrəkl] *n* miracle *m*

miraculous [mɪ'rækjuləs] *adj* miraculeux(-euse)

mirage ['mɪrɑːʒ] *n* mirage *m*

mirror ['mɪrə^r] *n* miroir *m*, glace *f*; (*in car*) rétroviseur *m* ▷ *vt* refléter

mirth [məːθ] *n* gaieté *f*

misadventure [mɪsəd'vɛntʃə^r] *n* mésaventure *f*; **death by ~** (*Brit*) décès accidentel

misapprehension ['mɪsæprɪ'hɛnʃən] *n* malentendu *m*, méprise *f*

misappropriate [mɪsə'prəuprɪeɪt] *vt* détourner

misbehave [mɪsbɪ'heɪv] *vi* mal se conduire

misc. *abbr* = **miscellaneous**

miscalculate [mɪs'kælkjuleɪt] *vt* mal calculer

miscarriage ['mɪskærɪdʒ] *n* (*Med*) fausse couche; **~ of justice** erreur *f* judiciaire

miscellaneous [mɪsɪ'leɪnɪəs] *adj* (*items, expenses*) divers(es); (*selection*) varié(e)

mischief ['mɪstʃɪf] *n* (*naughtiness*) sottises *fpl*; (*fun*) farce *f*; (*playfulness*) espièglerie *f*; (*harm*) mal *m*, dommage *m*; (*maliciousness*) méchanceté *f*

mischievous ['mɪstʃɪvəs] *adj* (*playful, naughty*) coquin(e), espiègle; (*harmful*) méchant(e)

misconception ['mɪskən'sɛpʃən] *n* idée fausse

misconduct [mɪs'kɔndʌkt] *n* inconduite *f*; **professional ~** faute professionnelle

misdemeanour, (*US*) **misdemeanor** [mɪsdɪ'miːnə^r] *n* écart *m* de conduite; infraction *f*

miser ['maɪzə^r] *n* avare *m/f*

miserable ['mɪzərəbl] *adj* (*person, expression*) malheureux(-euse); (*conditions*) misérable; (*weather*) maussade; (*offer, donation*) minable; (*failure*) pitoyable; **to feel ~** avoir le cafard

miserly ['maɪzəlɪ] *adj* avare

misery ['mɪzərɪ] *n* (*unhappiness*) tristesse *f*; (*pain*) souffrances *fpl*; (*wretchedness*) misère *f*

misfire [mɪs'faɪə^r] *vi* rater; (*car engine*) avoir des ratés

misfit ['mɪsfɪt] *n* (*person*) inadapté(e)

misfortune [mɪs'fɔːtʃən] *n* malchance *f*, malheur *m*

misgiving [mɪs'gɪvɪŋ] *n* (*apprehension*) craintes *fpl*; **to have ~s about sth** avoir des doutes quant à qch

misguided [mɪs'gaɪdɪd] *adj* malavisé(e)

mishandle [mɪs'hændl] *vt* (*treat roughly*) malmener; (*mismanage*) mal s'y prendre pour faire *or* résoudre *etc*

mishap ['mɪshæp] *n* mésaventure *f*

misinform [mɪsɪn'fɔːm] *vt* mal renseigner

misinterpret [mɪsɪn'təːprɪt] *vt* mal interpréter

misjudge [mɪs'dʒʌdʒ] *vt* méjuger, se méprendre sur le compte de

mislay [mɪs'leɪ] *vt* (*irreg: like* **lay**) égarer

mislead [mɪs'liːd] *vt* (*irreg: like* **lead**) induire en erreur

misleading [mɪs'liːdɪŋ] *adj* trompeur(-euse)

mismanage [mɪs'mænɪdʒ] *vt* mal gérer; mal s'y prendre pour faire *or* résoudre *etc*

misplace [mɪs'pleɪs] vt égarer; **to be ~d** (trust etc) être mal placé(e)

misprint ['mɪsprɪnt] n faute f d'impression

misrepresent [mɪsreprɪ'zent] vt présenter sous un faux jour

Miss [mɪs] n Mademoiselle; **Dear ~ Smith** Chère Mademoiselle Smith

miss [mɪs] vt (fail to get, attend, see) manquer, rater; (appointment, class) manquer; (escape, avoid) échapper à, éviter; (notice loss of: money etc) s'apercevoir de l'absence de; (regret the absence of): **I ~ him/it** il/cela me manque ▷ vi manquer ▷ n (shot) coup manqué; **we ~ed our train** nous avons raté notre train; **the bus just ~ed the wall** le bus a évité le mur de justesse; **you're ~ing the point** vous êtes à côté de la question; **you can't ~ it** vous ne pouvez pas vous tromper
  ▶ **miss out** vt (Brit) oublier
  ▶ **miss out on** vt fus (fun, party) rater, manquer; (chance, bargain) laisser passer

misshapen [mɪs'ʃeɪpən] adj difforme

missile ['mɪsaɪl] n (Aviat) missile m; (object thrown) projectile m

missing ['mɪsɪŋ] adj manquant(e); (after escape, disaster: person) disparu(e); **to go ~** disparaître; **~ person** personne disparue, disparu(e); **~ in action** (Mil) porté(e) disparu(e)

mission ['mɪʃən] n mission f; **on a ~ to sb** en mission auprès de qn

missionary ['mɪʃənrɪ] n missionnaire m/f

mission statement n déclaration f d'intention

misspell ['mɪs'spel] vt (irreg: like **spell**) mal orthographier

mist [mɪst] n brume f ▷ vi (also: **mist over, mist up**) devenir brumeux(-euse); (Brit: windows) s'embuer

mistake [mɪs'teɪk] n erreur f, faute f ▷ vt (irreg: like **take**); (meaning) mal comprendre; (intentions) se méprendre sur; **to ~ for** prendre pour; **by ~** par erreur, par inadvertance; **to make a ~** (in writing) faire une faute; (in calculating etc) faire une erreur; **there must be some ~** il doit y avoir une erreur, se tromper; **to make a ~ about sb/ sth** se tromper sur le compte de qn/sur qch

mistaken [mɪs'teɪkən] pp of **mistake** ▷ adj (idea etc) erroné(e); **to be ~** faire erreur, se tromper

mister ['mɪstə'] n (inf) Monsieur m; see **Mr**

mistletoe ['mɪsltəu] n gui m

mistook [mɪs'tuk] pt of **mistake**

mistress ['mɪstrɪs] n maîtresse f; (Brit: in primary school) institutrice f; (: in secondary school) professeur m

mistrust [mɪs'trʌst] vt se méfier de ▷ n: **~ (of)** méfiance f (à l'égard de)

misty ['mɪstɪ] adj brumeux(-euse); (glasses, window) embué(e)

misunderstand [mɪsʌndə'stænd] vt, vi (irreg: like **stand**) mal comprendre

misunderstanding ['mɪsʌndə'stændɪŋ] n méprise f, malentendu m; **there's been a ~** il y a eu un malentendu

misunderstood [mɪsʌndə'stud] pt, pp of

misunderstand ▷ adj (person) incompris(e)

misuse n [mɪs'juːs] mauvais emploi; (of power) abus m ▷ vt [mɪs'juːz] mal employer; abuser de

mitigate ['mɪtɪgeɪt] vt atténuer; **mitigating circumstances** circonstances atténuantes

mitt ['mɪt], **mitten** ['mɪtn] n moufle f; (fingerless) mitaine f

mix [mɪks] vt mélanger; (sauce, drink etc) préparer ▷ vi se mélanger; (socialize): **he doesn't ~ well** il est peu sociable ▷ n mélange m; **to ~ sth with sth** mélanger qch à qch; **to ~ business with pleasure** unir l'utile à l'agréable; **cake ~** préparation f pour gâteau
  ▶ **mix in** vt incorporer, mélanger
  ▶ **mix up** vt mélanger; (confuse) confondre; **to be ~ed up in sth** être mêlé(e) à qch or impliqué(e) dans qch

mixed [mɪkst] adj (feelings, reactions) contradictoire; (school, marriage) mixte

mixed grill n (Brit) assortiment m de grillades

mixed salad n salade f de crudités

mixed-up [mɪkst'ʌp] adj (person) désorienté(e), embrouillé(e)

mixer ['mɪksə'] n (for food) batteur m, mixeur m; (drink) boisson gazeuse (servant à couper un alcool); (person): **he is a good ~** il est très sociable

mixture ['mɪkstʃə'] n assortiment m, mélange m; (Med) préparation f

mix-up ['mɪksʌp] n: **there was a ~** il y a eu confusion

ml abbr (= millilitre(s)) ml

mm abbr (= millimetre) mm

moan [məun] n gémissement m ▷ vi gémir; (inf: complain): **to ~ (about)** se plaindre (de)

moat [məut] n fossé m, douves fpl

mob [mɔb] n foule f; (disorderly) cohue f; (pej): **the ~** la populace ▷ vt assaillir

mobile ['məubaɪl] adj mobile ▷ n (Art) mobile m; (Brit inf: mobile phone) (téléphone m) portable m, mobile m; **applicants must be ~** (Brit) les candidats devront être prêts à accepter tout déplacement

mobile home n caravane f

mobile phone n (téléphone m) portable m, mobile m

mobility [məu'bɪlɪtɪ] n mobilité f

mobilize ['məubɪlaɪz] vt, vi mobiliser

mock [mɔk] vt ridiculiser; (laugh at) se moquer de ▷ adj faux (fausse); **mocks** npl (Brit: Scol) examens blancs

mockery ['mɔkərɪ] n moquerie f, raillerie f; **to make a ~ of** ridiculiser, tourner en dérision

mock-up ['mɔkʌp] n maquette f

mod [mɔd] adj see **convenience**

mod cons ['mɔd'kɔnz] npl abbr (Brit) = **modern conveniences**; see **convenience**

mode [məud] n mode m; (of transport) moyen m

model ['mɔdl] n modèle m; (person: for fashion) mannequin m; (: for artist) modèle ▷ vt (with clay etc) modeler ▷ vi travailler comme mannequin ▷ adj (railway: toy) modèle réduit inv; (child, factory) modèle; **to ~ clothes** présenter des vêtements;

to ~ o.s. on imiter; **to ~ sb/sth on** modeler qn/qch sur

modem ['məudɛm] n modem m

moderate [adj, n 'mɔdərət, vb 'mɔdəreɪt] adj modéré(e); (amount, change) peu important(e) ▷ n (Pol) modéré(e) ▷ vi se modérer, se calmer ▷ vt modérer

moderation [mɔdə'reɪʃən] n modération f, mesure f; **in ~** à dose raisonnable, pris(e) or pratiqué(e) modérément

modern ['mɔdən] adj moderne

modernize ['mɔdənaɪz] vt moderniser

modern languages npl langues vivantes

modest ['mɔdɪst] adj modeste

modesty ['mɔdɪstɪ] n modestie f

modification [mɔdɪfɪ'keɪʃən] n modification f; **to make ~s** faire or apporter des modifications

modify ['mɔdɪfaɪ] vt modifier

module ['mɔdju:l] n module m

mogul ['məugl] n (fig) nabab m; (Ski) bosse f

mohair ['məuhɛər] n mohair m

Mohammed [mə'hæmɛd] n Mahomet m

moist [mɔɪst] adj humide, moite

moisten ['mɔɪsn] vt humecter, mouiller légèrement

moisture ['mɔɪstʃər] n humidité f; (on glass) buée f

moisturizer ['mɔɪstʃəraɪzər] n crème hydratante

molar ['məulər] n molaire f

molasses [məu'læsɪz] n mélasse f

mold etc [məuld] (US) = **mould** etc

mole [məul] n (animal, spy) taupe f; (spot) grain m de beauté

molecule ['mɔlɪkju:l] n molécule f

molest [məu'lɛst] vt (assault sexually) attenter à la pudeur de; (attack) molester; (harass) tracasser

mollycoddle ['mɔlɪkɔdl] vt chouchouter, couver

molt [məult] vi (US) = **moult**

molten ['məultən] adj fondu(e); (rock) en fusion

mom [mɔm] n (US) = **mum**

moment ['məumənt] n moment m, instant m; (importance) importance f; **at the ~** en ce moment; **for the ~** pour l'instant; **in a ~** dans un instant; **"one ~ please"** (Tel) "ne quittez pas"

momentarily ['məuməntrɪlɪ] adv momentanément; (US: soon) bientôt

momentary ['məuməntərɪ] adj momentané(e), passager(-ère)

momentous [məu'mɛntəs] adj important(e), capital(e)

momentum [məu'mɛntəm] n élan m, vitesse acquise; (fig) dynamique f; **to gather ~** prendre de la vitesse; (fig) gagner du terrain

mommy ['mɔmɪ] n (US: mother) maman f

Monaco ['mɔnəkəu] n Monaco f

monarch ['mɔnək] n monarque m

monarchy ['mɔnəkɪ] n monarchie f

monastery ['mɔnəstərɪ] n monastère m

Monday ['mʌndɪ] n lundi m; for phrases see also **Tuesday**

monetary ['mʌnɪtərɪ] adj monétaire

money ['mʌnɪ] n argent m; **to make ~** (person) gagner de l'argent; (business) rapporter; **I've got**

no ~ left je n'ai plus d'argent, je n'ai plus un sou

money belt n ceinture-portefeuille f

money order n mandat m

money-spinner ['mʌnɪspɪnər] n (inf) mine f d'or (fig)

mongrel ['mʌŋgrəl] n (dog) bâtard m

monitor ['mɔnɪtər] n (TV, Comput) écran m, moniteur m; (Brit Scol) chef m de classe; (US Scol) surveillant m (d'examen) ▷ vt contrôler; (foreign station) être à l'écoute de; (progress) suivre de près

monk [mʌŋk] n moine m

monkey ['mʌŋkɪ] n singe m

monkey nut n (Brit) cacahuète f

monologue ['mɔnəlɔg] n monologue m

monopoly [mə'nɔpəlɪ] n monopole m; **Monopolies and Mergers Commission** (Brit) commission britannique d'enquête sur les monopoles

monosodium glutamate [mɔnə'səudiəm 'glu:təmeɪt] n glutamate m de sodium

monotone ['mɔnətəun] n ton m (or voix f) monocorde; **to speak in a ~** parler sur un ton monocorde

monotonous [mə'nɔtənəs] adj monotone

monsoon [mɔn'su:n] n mousson f

monster ['mɔnstər] n monstre m

monstrous ['mɔnstrəs] adj (huge) gigantesque; (atrocious) monstrueux(-euse), atroce

month [mʌnθ] n mois m; **every ~** tous les mois; **300 dollars a ~** 300 dollars par mois

monthly ['mʌnθlɪ] adj mensuel(le) ▷ adv mensuellement ▷ n (magazine) mensuel m, publication mensuelle; **twice ~** deux fois par mois

Montreal [mɔntrɪ'ɔ:l] n Montréal

monument ['mɔnjumənt] n monument m

moo [mu:] vi meugler, beugler

mood [mu:d] n humeur f, disposition f; **to be in a good/bad ~** être de bonne/mauvaise humeur; **to be in the ~ for** être d'humeur à, avoir envie de

moody ['mu:dɪ] adj (variable) d'humeur changeante, lunatique; (sullen) morose, maussade

moon [mu:n] n lune f

moonlight ['mu:nlaɪt] n clair m de lune ▷ vi travailler au noir

moonlighting ['mu:nlaɪtɪŋ] n travail m au noir

moonlit ['mu:nlɪt] adj éclairé(e) par la lune; **a ~ night** une nuit de lune

moor [muər] n lande f ▷ vt (ship) amarrer ▷ vi mouiller

moorland ['muələnd] n lande f

moose [mu:s] n (pl inv) élan m

mop [mɔp] n balai m à laver; (for dishes) lavette f à vaisselle ▷ vt éponger, essuyer; **~ of hair** tignasse f

▶ **mop up** vt éponger

mope [məup] vi avoir le cafard, se morfondre

▶ **mope about, mope around** vi broyer du noir, se morfondre

moped ['məupɛd] n cyclomoteur m

moral ['mɔrl] adj moral(e) ▷ n morale f; **morals**

npl moralité *f*

morale [mɔ'rɑːl] *n* moral *m*

morality [mə'rælɪtɪ] *n* moralité *f*

morass [mə'ræs] *n* marais *m*, marécage *m*

morbid ['mɔːbɪd] *adj* morbide

more [mɔːʳ] *adj* **1** (*greater in number etc*) plus (de), davantage (de); ~ **people/work (than)** plus de gens/de travail (que)

2 (*additional*) encore (de); **do you want (some) ~ tea?** voulez-vous encore du thé?; **is there any ~ wine?** reste-t-il du vin?; **I have no** or **I don't have any ~ money** je n'ai plus d'argent; **it'll take a few ~ weeks** ça prendra encore quelques semaines

▷ *pron* plus, davantage; ~ **than 10** plus de 10; **it cost ~ than we expected** cela a coûté plus que prévu; **I want ~** j'en veux plus or davantage; **is there any ~?** est-ce qu'il en reste?; **there's no ~** il n'y en a plus; **a little ~** un peu plus; **many/much ~** beaucoup plus, bien davantage

▷ *adv* plus; ~ **dangerous/easily (than)** plus dangereux/facilement (que); ~ **and ~ expensive** de plus en plus cher; ~ **or less** plus ou moins; ~ **than ever** plus que jamais; **once ~** encore une fois, une fois de plus; **and what's ~** ... et de plus ..., et qui plus est ...

moreover [mɔː'rəuvəʳ] *adv* de plus

morgue [mɔːg] *n* morgue *f*

morning ['mɔːnɪŋ] *n* matin *m*; (*as duration*) matinée *f* ▷ *cpd* matinal(e); (*paper*) du matin; **in the ~** le matin; **7 o'clock in the ~** 7 heures du matin; **this ~** ce matin

morning sickness *n* nausées matinales

Moroccan [mə'rɔkən] *adj* marocain(e) ▷ *n* Marocain(e)

Morocco [mə'rɔkəu] *n* Maroc *m*

moron ['mɔːrɔn] *n* idiot(e), minus *m/f*

morphine ['mɔːfiːn] *n* morphine *f*

morris dancing ['mɔrɪs-] *n* (*Brit*) *danses folkloriques anglaises*

Morse [mɔːs] *n* (*also*: **Morse code**) morse *m*

morsel ['mɔːsl] *n* bouchée *f*

mortal ['mɔːtl] *adj*, *n* mortel(le)

mortar ['mɔːtəʳ] *n* mortier *m*

mortgage ['mɔːgɪdʒ] *n* hypothèque *f*; (*loan*) prêt *m* (or crédit *m*) hypothécaire ▷ *vt* hypothéquer; **to take out a ~** prendre une hypothèque, faire un emprunt

mortgage company *n* (*US*) société *f* de crédit immobilier

mortician [mɔː'tɪʃən] *n* (*US*) entrepreneur *m* de pompes funèbres

mortified ['mɔːtɪfaɪd] *adj* mort(e) de honte

mortuary ['mɔːtjuərɪ] *n* morgue *f*

mosaic [məu'zeɪɪk] *n* mosaïque *f*

Moscow ['mɔskəu] *n* Moscou

Moslem ['mɔzləm] *adj*, *n* = **Muslim**

mosque [mɔsk] *n* mosquée *f*

mosquito (*pl* **-es**) [mɔs'kiːtəu] *n* moustique *m*

moss [mɔs] *n* mousse *f*

most [məust] *adj* (*majority of*) la plupart de; (*greatest amount of*) le plus de ▷ *pron* la plupart

▷ *adv* le plus; (*very*) très, extrêmement; **the ~** le plus; ~ **fish** la plupart des poissons; **the ~ beautiful woman in the world** la plus belle femme du monde; ~ **of** (*with plural*) la plupart de; (*with singular*) la plus grande partie de; ~ **of them** la plupart d'entre eux; ~ **of the time** la plupart du temps; **I saw ~** (*a lot but not all*) j'en ai vu la plupart; (*more than anyone else*) c'est moi qui en ai vu le plus; **at the (very) ~** au plus; **to make the ~ of** profiter au maximum de

mostly ['məustlɪ] *adv* (*chiefly*) surtout, principalement; (*usually*) généralement

MOT *n abbr* (*Brit*) = **Ministry of Transport**; **the ~ (test)** *visite technique (annuelle) obligatoire des véhicules à moteur*

motel [məu'tel] *n* motel *m*

moth [mɔθ] *n* papillon *m* de nuit; (*in clothes*) mite *f*

mother ['mʌðəʳ] *n* mère *f* ▷ *vt* (*pamper, protect*) dorloter

motherhood ['mʌðəhud] *n* maternité *f*

mother-in-law ['mʌðərɪnlɔː] *n* belle-mère *f*

motherly ['mʌðəlɪ] *adj* maternel(le)

mother-of-pearl ['mʌðərəv'pəːl] *n* nacre *f*

Mother's Day *n* fête *f* des Mères

mother-to-be ['mʌðətə'biː] *n* future maman

mother tongue *n* langue maternelle

motif [məu'tiːf] *n* motif *m*

motion ['məuʃən] *n* mouvement *m*; (*gesture*) geste *m*; (*at meeting*) motion *f*; (*Brit: also*: **bowel motion**) selles *fpl* ▷ *vt*, *vi*: **to ~ (to) sb to do** faire signe à qn de faire; **to be in ~** (*vehicle*) être en marche; **to set in ~** mettre en marche; **to go through the ~s of doing sth** (*fig*) faire qch machinalement or sans conviction

motionless ['məuʃənlɪs] *adj* immobile, sans mouvement

motion picture *n* film *m*

motivate ['məutɪveɪt] *vt* motiver

motivated ['məutɪveɪtɪd] *adj* motivé(e)

motivation [məutɪ'veɪʃən] *n* motivation *f*

motive ['məutɪv] *n* motif *m*, mobile *m* ▷ *adj* moteur(-trice); **from the best (of) ~s** avec les meilleures intentions (du monde)

motley ['mɔtlɪ] *adj* hétéroclite; bigarré(e), bariolé(e)

motor ['məutəʳ] *n* moteur *m*; (*Brit inf: vehicle*) auto *f* ▷ *adj* moteur(-trice)

motorbike ['məutəbaɪk] *n* moto *f*

motorboat ['məutəbəut] *n* bateau *m* à moteur

motorcar ['məutəkɑː] *n* (*Brit*) automobile *f*

motorcycle ['məutəsaɪkl] *n* moto *f*

motorcycle racing *n* course *f* de motos

motorcyclist ['məutəsaɪklɪst] *n* motocycliste *m/f*

motoring ['məutərɪŋ] (*Brit*) *n* tourisme *m* automobile ▷ *adj* (*accident*) de voiture, de la route; ~ **holiday** vacances *fpl* en voiture; ~ **offence** infraction *f* au code de la route

motorist ['məutərɪst] *n* automobiliste *m/f*

motor mechanic *n* mécanicien *m* garagiste

motor racing *n* (*Brit*) course *f* automobile

motor trade *n* secteur *m* de l'automobile

motorway ['məutəweɪ] *n* (*Brit*) autoroute *f*

mottled ['mɒtld] *adj* tacheté(e), marbré(e)
motto (*pl* -**es**) ['mɒtəu] *n* devise *f*
mould, (*US*) **mold** [məuld] *n* moule *m*; (*mildew*) moisissure *f* ▷ *vt* mouler, modeler; (*fig*) façonner
mouldy, (*US*) **moldy** ['məuldɪ] *adj* moisi(e); (*smell*) de moisi
moult, (*US*) **molt** [məult] *vi* muer
mound [maund] *n* monticule *m*, tertre *m*
mount [maunt] *n* (*hill*) mont *m*, montagne *f*; (*horse*) monture *f*; (*for picture*) carton *m* de montage; (*for jewel etc*) monture ▷ *vt* monter; (*horse*) monter à; (*bike*) monter sur; (*exhibition*) organiser, monter; (*picture*) monter sur carton; (*stamp*) coller dans un album ▷ *vi* (*inflation, tension*) augmenter
   ▶ **mount up** *vi* s'élever, monter; (*bills, problems, savings*) s'accumuler
mountain ['mauntɪn] *n* montagne *f* ▷ *cpd* de (la) montagne; **to make a ~ out of a molehill** (*fig*) se faire une montagne d'un rien
mountain bike *n* VTT *m*, vélo *m* tout terrain
mountaineer [mauntɪ'nɪəʳ] *n* alpiniste *m/f*
mountaineering [mauntɪ'nɪərɪŋ] *n* alpinisme *m*; **to go ~** faire de l'alpinisme
mountainous ['mauntɪnəs] *adj* montagneux(-euse)
mountain range *n* chaîne *f* de montagnes
mountain rescue team *n* colonne *f* de secours
mountainside ['mauntɪnsaɪd] *n* flanc *m* or versant *m* de la montagne
mourn [mɔːn] *vt* pleurer ▷ *vi*: **to ~ for sb** pleurer qn; **to ~ for sth** se lamenter sur qch
mourner ['mɔːnəʳ] *n* parent(e) or ami(e) du défunt; personne *f* en deuil or venue rendre hommage au défunt
mourning ['mɔːnɪŋ] *n* deuil *m* ▷ *cpd* (*dress*) de deuil; **in ~** en deuil
mouse (*pl* **mice**) [maus, maɪs] *n* (*also Comput*) souris *f*
mouse mat *n* (*Comput*) tapis *m* de souris
mousetrap ['maustræp] *n* souricière *f*
moussaka [mu'sɑːkə] *n* moussaka *f*
mousse [muːs] *n* mousse *f*
moustache, (*US*) **mustache** [məs'tɑːʃ] *n* moustache(s) *f(pl)*
mousy ['mausɪ] *adj* (*person*) effacé(e); (*hair*) d'un châtain terne
mouth [mauθ, *pl* mauðz] *n* bouche *f*; (*of dog, cat*) gueule *f*; (*of river*) embouchure *f*; (*of hole, cave*) ouverture *f*; (*of bottle*) goulot *m*; (*opening*) orifice *m*
mouthful ['mauθful] *n* bouchée *f*
mouth organ *n* harmonica *m*
mouthpiece ['mauθpiːs] *n* (*of musical instrument*) bec *m*, embouchure *f*; (*spokesperson*) porte-parole *m inv*
mouthwash ['mauθwɒʃ] *n* eau *f* dentifrice
mouth-watering ['mauθwɔːtərɪŋ] *adj* qui met l'eau à la bouche
movable ['muːvəbl] *adj* mobile
move [muːv] *n* (*movement*) mouvement *m*; (*in game*) coup *m*; (*: turn to play*) tour *m*; (*change of house*) déménagement *m*; (*change of job*)

changement *m* d'emploi ▷ *vt* déplacer, bouger; (*emotionally*) émouvoir; (*Pol: resolution etc*) proposer ▷ *vi* (*gen*) bouger, remuer; (*traffic*) circuler; (*also*: **move house**) déménager; (*in game*) jouer; **can you ~ your car, please?** pouvez-vous déplacer votre voiture, s'il vous plaît?; **to ~ towards** se diriger vers; **to ~ sb to do sth** pousser *or* inciter qn à faire qch; **to get a ~ on** se dépêcher, se remuer
   ▶ **move about**, **move around** *vi* (*fidget*) remuer; (*travel*) voyager, se déplacer
   ▶ **move along** *vi* se pousser
   ▶ **move away** *vi* s'en aller, s'éloigner
   ▶ **move back** *vi* revenir, retourner
   ▶ **move forward** *vi* avancer ▷ *vt* avancer; (*people*) faire avancer
   ▶ **move in** *vi* (*to a house*) emménager; (*police, soldiers*) intervenir
   ▶ **move off** *vi* s'éloigner, s'en aller
   ▶ **move on** *vi* se remettre en route ▷ *vt* (*onlookers*) faire circuler
   ▶ **move out** *vi* (*of house*) déménager
   ▶ **move over** *vi* se pousser, se déplacer
   ▶ **move up** *vi* avancer; (*employee*) avoir de l'avancement; (*pupil*) passer dans la classe supérieure
moveable ['muːvəbl] *adj* = **movable**
movement ['muːvmənt] *n* mouvement *m*; **~ (of the bowels)** (*Med*) selles *fpl*
movie ['muːvɪ] *n* film *m*; **movies** *npl*: **the ~s** le cinéma
movie theater (*US*) *n* cinéma *m*
moving ['muːvɪŋ] *adj* en mouvement; (*touching*) émouvant(e) ▷ *n* (*US*) déménagement *m*
mow (*pt* -**ed**, *pp* -**ed** *or* -**n**) [məu, -d, -n] *vt* faucher; (*lawn*) tondre
   ▶ **mow down** *vt* faucher
mower ['məuəʳ] *n* (*also*: **lawnmower**) tondeuse *f* à gazon
mown [məun] *pp of* **mow**
Mozambique [məuzəm'biːk] *n* Mozambique *m*
MP *n abbr* (= *Military Police*) PM; (*Brit*) = **Member of Parliament**; (*Canada*) = **Mounted Police**
MP3 *n* mp3 *m*
MP3 player *n* baladeur *m* numérique, lecteur *m* mp3
mpg *n abbr* (= *miles per gallon*) (*30 mpg = 9,4 l. aux 100 km*)
m.p.h. *abbr* (= *miles per hour*) (*60 mph = 96 km/h*)
Mr, (*US*) **Mr.** ['mɪstəʳ] *n*: **Mr X** Monsieur X, M. X
Mrs, (*US*) **Mrs.** ['mɪsɪz] *n*: **~ X** Madame X, Mme X
Ms, (*US*) **Ms.** [mɪz] *n* (*Miss or Mrs*): **Ms X** Madame X, Mme X; *voir article*
MSc *n abbr* = **Master of Science**
MSP *n abbr* (= *Member of the Scottish Parliament*) député *m* au Parlement écossais
Mt *abbr* (*Geo*: = *mount*) Mt
much [mʌtʃ] *adj* beaucoup de ▷ *adv*, *n or pron* beaucoup; **~ milk** beaucoup de lait; **we don't have ~ time** nous n'avons pas beaucoup de temps; **how ~ is it?** combien est-ce que ça coûte?; **it's not ~** ce n'est pas beaucoup; **too**

~ trop (de); **so ~** tant (de); **I like it very/so ~** j'aime beaucoup/tellement ça; **as ~ as** autant de; **thank you very ~** merci beaucoup; **that's ~ better** c'est beaucoup mieux; **~ to my amazement ...** à mon grand étonnement ...

muck [mʌk] *n* (*mud*) boue *f*; (*dirt*) ordures *fpl*
  ▸ **muck about** *vi* (*inf*) faire l'imbécile; (: *waste time*) traînasser; (: *tinker*) bricoler; tripoter
  ▸ **muck in** *vi* (*Brit inf*) donner un coup de main
  ▸ **muck out** *vt* (*stable*) nettoyer
  ▸ **muck up** *vt* (*inf: ruin*) gâcher, esquinter; (: *dirty*) salir; (: *exam, interview*) se planter à

mucky ['mʌkɪ] *adj* (*dirty*) boueux(-euse), sale
mucus ['mju:kəs] *n* mucus *m*
mud [mʌd] *n* boue *f*
muddle ['mʌdl] *n* (*mess*) pagaille *f*, fouillis *m*; (*mix-up*) confusion *f* ▸ *vt* (*also*: **muddle up**) brouiller, embrouiller; **to be in a ~** (*person*) ne plus savoir où l'on en est; **to get in a ~** (*while explaining etc*) s'embrouiller
  ▸ **muddle along** *vi* aller son chemin tant bien que mal
  ▸ **muddle through** *vi* se débrouiller

muddy ['mʌdɪ] *adj* boueux(-euse)
mudguard ['mʌdgɑːd] *n* garde-boue *m inv*
muesli ['mju:zlɪ] *n* muesli *m*
muffin ['mʌfɪn] *n* (*roll*) petit pain rond et plat; (*cake*) petit gâteau au chocolat ou aux fruits
muffle ['mʌfl] *vt* (*sound*) assourdir, étouffer; (*against cold*) emmitoufler
muffled ['mʌfld] *adj* étouffé(e), voilé(e)
muffler ['mʌflər] *n* (*scarf*) cache-nez *m inv*; (*US Aut*) silencieux *m*
mug [mʌg] *n* (*cup*) tasse *f* (*sans soucoupe*); (: *for beer*) chope *f*; (*inf: face*) bouille *f*; (: *fool*) poire *f* ▸ *vt* (*assault*) agresser; **it's a ~'s game** (*Brit*) c'est bon pour les imbéciles
  ▸ **mug up** *vt* (*Brit inf: also*: **mug up on**) bosser, bûcher

mugger ['mʌgər] *n* agresseur *m*
mugging ['mʌgɪŋ] *n* agression *f*
muggy ['mʌgɪ] *adj* lourd(e), moite
mule [mju:l] *n* mule *f*
multicoloured, (*US*) **multicolored** ['mʌltɪkʌləd] *adj* multicolore
multi-level ['mʌltɪlɛvl] *adj* (*US*) = **multistorey**
multimedia ['mʌltɪ'mi:dɪə] *adj* multimédia *inv*
multinational [mʌltɪ'næʃənl] *n* multinationale *f* ▸ *adj* multinational(e)
multiple ['mʌltɪpl] *adj* multiple ▸ *n* multiple *m*; (*Brit: also*: **multiple store**) magasin *m* à succursales (multiples)
multiple choice, multiple choice test *n* QCM *m*, questionnaire *m* à choix multiple
multiple sclerosis [-sklɪ'rəʊsɪs] *n* sclérose *f* en plaques
multiplex ['mʌltɪplɛks], **multiplex cinema** *n* (cinéma *m*) multisalles *m*
multiplication [mʌltɪplɪ'keɪʃən] *n* multiplication *f*
multiply ['mʌltɪplaɪ] *vt* multiplier ▸ *vi* se multiplier

173 | mutual

multistorey ['mʌltɪ'stɔːrɪ] *adj* (*Brit: building*) à étages; (: *car park*) à étages *or* niveaux multiples
mum [mʌm] *n* (*Brit*) maman *f* ▸ *adj*: **to keep ~** ne pas souffler mot; **~'s the word!** motus et bouche cousue!
mumble ['mʌmbl] *vt, vi* marmotter, marmonner
mummy ['mʌmɪ] *n* (*Brit: mother*) maman *f*; (*embalmed*) momie *f*
mumps [mʌmps] *n* oreillons *mpl*
munch [mʌntʃ] *vt, vi* mâcher
mundane [mʌn'deɪn] *adj* banal(e), terre à terre *inv*
municipal [mju:'nɪsɪpl] *adj* municipal(e)
mural ['mjuərl] *n* peinture murale
murder ['mɜːdər] *n* meurtre *m*, assassinat *m* ▸ *vt* assassiner; **to commit ~** commettre un meurtre
murderer ['mɜːdərər] *n* meurtrier *m*, assassin *m*
murderous ['mɜːdərəs] *adj* meurtrier(-ière)
murky ['mɜːkɪ] *adj* sombre, ténébreux(-euse); (*water*) trouble
murmur ['mɜːmər] *n* murmure *m* ▸ *vt, vi* murmurer; **heart ~** (*Med*) souffle *m* au cœur
muscle ['mʌsl] *n* muscle *m*; (*fig*) force *f*
  ▸ **muscle in** *vi* s'imposer, s'immiscer
muscular ['mʌskjulər] *adj* musculaire; (*person, arm*) musclé(e)
muse [mju:z] *vi* méditer, songer ▸ *n* muse *f*
museum [mju:'zɪəm] *n* musée *m*
mushroom ['mʌʃrum] *n* champignon *m* ▸ *vi* (*fig*) pousser comme un (*or des*) champignon(s)
music ['mju:zɪk] *n* musique *f*
musical ['mju:zɪkl] *adj* musical(e); (*person*) musicien(ne) ▸ *n* (*show*) comédie musicale
musical instrument *n* instrument *m* de musique
music centre *n* chaîne compacte
musician [mju:'zɪʃən] *n* musicien(ne)
Muslim ['mʌzlɪm] *adj, n* musulman(e)
muslin ['mʌzlɪn] *n* mousseline *f*
mussel ['mʌsl] *n* moule *f*
must [mʌst] *aux vb* (*obligation*): **I ~ do it** je dois le faire, il faut que je le fasse; (*probability*): **he ~ be there by now** il doit y être maintenant, il est probablement maintenant; (*suggestion, invitation*): **you ~ come and see me** il faut que vous veniez me voir ▸ *n* nécessité *f*, impératif *m*; **it's a ~** c'est indispensable; **I ~ have made a mistake** j'ai dû me tromper
mustache ['mʌstæʃ] *n* (*US*) = **moustache**
mustard ['mʌstəd] *n* moutarde *f*
muster ['mʌstər] *vt* rassembler; (*also*: **muster up**: *strength, courage*) rassembler
mustn't ['mʌsnt] = **must not**
mute [mju:t] *adj, n* muet(te)
muted ['mju:tɪd] *adj* (*noise*) sourd(e), assourdi(e); (*criticism*) voilé(e); (*Mus*) en sourdine; (: *trumpet*) bouché(e)
mutilate ['mju:tɪleɪt] *vt* mutiler
mutiny ['mju:tɪnɪ] *n* mutinerie *f* ▸ *vi* se mutiner
mutter ['mʌtər] *vt, vi* marmonner, marmotter
mutton ['mʌtn] *n* mouton *m*
mutual ['mju:tʃuəl] *adj* mutuel(le), réciproque;

(*benefit, interest*) commun(e)
mutually ['mju:tʃuəlɪ] *adv* mutuellement,
réciproquement
muzzle ['mʌzl] *n* museau *m*; (*protective device*)
muselière *f*; (*of gun*) gueule *f* ▷ *vt* museler
my [maɪ] *adj* mon (ma), mes *pl*; **my house/car/
gloves** ma maison/ma voiture/mes gants; **I've
washed my hair/cut my finger** je me suis lavé
les cheveux/coupé le doigt; **is this my pen or
yours?** c'est mon stylo ou c'est le vôtre?

myself [maɪ'sɛlf] *pron* (*reflexive*) me; (*emphatic*)
moi-même; (*after prep*) moi; *see also* **oneself**
mysterious [mɪs'tɪərɪəs] *adj* mystérieux(-euse)
mystery ['mɪstərɪ] *n* mystère *m*
mystical ['mɪstɪkl] *adj* mystique
mystify ['mɪstɪfaɪ] *vt* (*deliberately*) mystifier;
(*puzzle*) ébahir
myth [mɪθ] *n* mythe *m*
mythology [mɪ'θɔlədʒɪ] *n* mythologie *f*

Nn

n/a *abbr* (= *not applicable*) n.a.; (*Comm etc*) = **no account**

naff [næf] (*Brit*: *inf*) *adj* nul(le)

nag [næg] *vt* (*scold*) être toujours après, reprendre sans arrêt ▷ *n* (*pej*: *horse*) canasson *m*; (*person*): **she's an awful ~** elle est constamment après lui (*or* eux *etc*), elle est très casse-pieds

nagging ['nægɪŋ] *adj* (*doubt, pain*) persistant(e) ▷ *n* remarques continuelles

nail [neɪl] *n* (*human*) ongle *m*; (*metal*) clou *m* ▷ *vt* clouer; **to ~ sth to sth** clouer qch à qch; **to ~ sb down to a date/price** contraindre qn à accepter *or* donner une date/un prix; **to pay cash on the ~** (*Brit*) payer rubis sur l'ongle

nailbrush ['neɪlbrʌʃ] *n* brosse *f* à ongles

nailfile ['neɪlfaɪl] *n* lime *f* à ongles

nail polish *n* vernis *m* à ongles

nail polish remover *n* dissolvant *m*

nail scissors *npl* ciseaux *mpl* à ongles

nail varnish *n* (*Brit*) = **nail polish**

naïve [naɪˈiːv] *adj* naïf(-ïve)

naked ['neɪkɪd] *adj* nu(e); **with the ~ eye** à l'œil nu

name [neɪm] *n* nom *m*; (*reputation*) réputation *f* ▷ *vt* nommer; (*identify*: *accomplice etc*) citer; (*price, date*) fixer, donner; **by ~** par son nom; de nom; **in the ~ of** au nom de; **what's your ~?** comment vous appelez-vous?, quel est votre nom?; **my ~ is Peter** je m'appelle Peter; **to take sb's ~ and address** relever l'identité de qn *or* les nom et adresse de qn; **to make a ~ for o.s.** se faire un nom; **to get (o.s.) a bad ~** se faire une mauvaise réputation; **to call sb ~s** traiter qn de tous les noms

nameless ['neɪmlɪs] *adj* sans nom; (*witness, contributor*) anonyme

namely ['neɪmlɪ] *adv* à savoir

namesake ['neɪmseɪk] *n* homonyme *m*

nanny ['nænɪ] *n* bonne *f* d'enfants

nap [næp] *n* (*sleep*) (petit) somme ▷ *vi*: **to be caught ~ping** être pris(e) à l'improviste *or* en défaut

nape [neɪp] *n*: **~ of the neck** nuque *f*

napkin ['næpkɪn] *n* serviette *f* (de table)

nappy ['næpɪ] *n* (*Brit*) couche *f*

nappy rash *n*: **to have ~** avoir les fesses rouges

narcissus (*pl* **narcissi**) [nɑːˈsɪsəs, -saɪ] *n* narcisse *m*

narcotic [nɑːˈkɔtɪk] *n* (*Med*) narcotique *m*

narcotics [nɑːˈkɔtɪkz] *npl* (*illegal drugs*) stupéfiants *mpl*

narrative ['nærətɪv] *n* récit *m* ▷ *adj* narratif(-ive)

narrator [nəˈreɪtəʳ] *n* narrateur(-trice)

narrow ['nærəu] *adj* étroit(e); (*fig*) restreint(e), limité(e) ▷ *vi* (*road*) devenir plus étroit, se rétrécir; (*gap, difference*) se réduire; **to have a ~ escape** l'échapper belle
  ▶ **narrow down** *vt* restreindre

narrowly ['nærəulɪ] *adv*: **he ~ missed injury/the tree** il a failli se blesser/rentrer dans l'arbre; **he only ~ missed the target** il a manqué la cible de peu *or* de justesse

narrow-minded [nærəuˈmaɪndɪd] *adj* à l'esprit étroit, borné(e); (*attitude*) borné(e)

nasal ['neɪzl] *adj* nasal(e)

nasty ['nɑːstɪ] *adj* (*person*: *malicious*) méchant(e); (: *rude*) très désagréable; (*smell*) dégoûtant(e); (*wound, situation*) mauvais(e), vilain(e); (*weather*) affreux(-euse); **to turn ~** (*situation*) mal tourner; (*weather*) se gâter; (*person*) devenir méchant; **it's a ~ business** c'est une sale affaire

nation ['neɪʃən] *n* nation *f*

national ['næʃənl] *adj* national(e) ▷ *n* (*abroad*) ressortissant(e); (*when home*) national(e)

national anthem *n* hymne national

national dress *n* costume national

National Health Service *n* (*Brit*) *service national de santé*, ≈ Sécurité Sociale

National Insurance *n* (*Brit*) ≈ Sécurité Sociale

nationalism ['næʃnəlɪzəm] *n* nationalisme *m*

nationalist ['næʃnəlɪst] *adj, n* nationaliste *m/f*

nationality [næʃəˈnælɪtɪ] *n* nationalité *f*

nationalize ['næʃnəlaɪz] *vt* nationaliser

nationally ['næʃnəlɪ] *adv* du point de vue national; dans le pays entier

national park *n* parc national

National Trust *n* (*Brit*) ≈ Caisse *f* nationale des monuments historiques et des sites; *voir article*

nationwide ['neɪʃənwaɪd] *adj* s'étendant à l'ensemble du pays; (*problem*) à l'échelle du pays entier ▷ *adv* à travers *or* dans tout le pays

native ['neɪtɪv] *n* habitant(e) du pays, autochtone *m/f*; (*in colonies*) indigène *m/f* ▷ *adj* du pays, indigène; (*country*) natal(e); (*language*) maternel(le); (*ability*) inné(e); **a ~ of Russia** une personne originaire de Russie; **a ~ speaker of French** une personne de langue maternelle française

Native American *n* Indien(ne) d'Amérique ▷ *adj* amérindien(ne)

native speaker *n* locuteur natif

NATO ['neɪtəʊ] *n abbr* (= *North Atlantic Treaty Organization*) OTAN *f*

natural ['nætʃrəl] *adj* naturel(le); **to die of ~ causes** mourir d'une mort naturelle

natural gas *n* gaz naturel

natural history *n* histoire naturelle

naturalist ['nætʃrəlɪst] *n* naturaliste *m/f*

naturally ['nætʃrəlɪ] *adv* naturellement

natural resources *npl* ressources naturelles

nature ['neɪtʃə'] *n* nature *f*; **by ~** par tempérament, de nature; **documents of a confidential ~** documents à caractère confidentiel

nature reserve *n* (*Brit*) réserve naturelle

naught [nɔːt] *n* = **nought**

naughty ['nɔːtɪ] *adj* (*child*) vilain(e), pas sage; (*story, film*) grivois(e)

nausea ['nɔːsɪə] *n* nausée *f*

naval ['neɪvl] *adj* naval(e)

naval officer *n* officier *m* de marine

nave [neɪv] *n* nef *f*

navel ['neɪvl] *n* nombril *m*

navigate ['nævɪgeɪt] *vt* (*steer*) diriger, piloter ▷ *vi* naviguer; (*Aut*) indiquer la route à suivre

navigation [nævɪ'geɪʃən] *n* navigation *f*

navvy ['nævɪ] *n* (*Brit*) terrassier *m*

navy ['neɪvɪ] *n* marine *f*; **Department of the N~** (*US*) ministère *m* de la Marine

navy-blue ['neɪvɪ'bluː] *adj* bleu marine *inv*

Nazi ['nɑːtsɪ] *adj* nazi(e) ▷ *n* Nazi(e)

NB *abbr* (= *nota bene*) NB; (*Canada*) = **New Brunswick**

near [nɪə'] *adj* proche ▷ *adv* près ▷ *prep* (*also:* **near to**) près de ▷ *vt* approcher de; **~ here/there** près d'ici/non loin de là; **£25,000 or ~est offer** (*Brit*) 25 000 livres à débattre; **in the ~ future** dans un proche avenir; **to come ~** *vi* s'approcher

nearby [nɪə'baɪ] *adj* proche ▷ *adv* tout près, à proximité

nearly ['nɪəlɪ] *adv* presque; **I ~ fell** j'ai failli tomber; **it's not ~ big enough** ce n'est vraiment pas assez grand, c'est loin d'être assez grand

near miss *n* collision évitée de justesse; (*when aiming*) coup manqué de peu or de justesse

nearside ['nɪəsaɪd] (*Aut*) *n* (*right-hand drive*) côté *m* gauche; (*left-hand drive*) côté droit ▷ *adj* de gauche; de droite

near-sighted [nɪə'saɪtɪd] *adj* myope

neat [niːt] *adj* (*person, work*) soigné(e); (*room etc*) bien tenu(e) or rangé(e); (*solution, plan*) habile; (*spirits*) pur(e); **I drink it ~** je le bois sec or sans eau

neatly ['niːtlɪ] *adv* avec soin or ordre; (*skilfully*) habilement

necessarily ['nɛsɪsrɪlɪ] *adv* nécessairement; **not**

~ pas nécessairement or forcément

necessary ['nɛsɪsrɪ] *adj* nécessaire; **if ~** si besoin est, le cas échéant

necessity [nɪ'sɛsɪtɪ] *n* nécessité *f*; chose nécessaire or essentielle; **in case of ~** en cas d'urgence

neck [nɛk] *n* cou *m*; (*of horse, garment*) encolure *f*; (*of bottle*) goulot *m* ▷ *vi* (*inf*) se peloter; **~ and ~** à égalité; **to stick one's ~ out** (*inf*) se mouiller

necklace ['nɛklɪs] *n* collier *m*

neckline ['nɛklaɪn] *n* encolure *f*

necktie ['nɛktaɪ] *n* (*esp US*) cravate *f*

nectarine ['nɛktərɪn] *n* brugnon *m*, nectarine *f*

need [niːd] *n* besoin *m* ▷ *vt* avoir besoin de; **to ~ to do** devoir faire; avoir besoin de faire; **you don't ~ to go** vous n'avez pas besoin or vous n'êtes pas obligé de partir; **a signature is ~ed** il faut une signature; **to be in ~ of** or **have ~ of** avoir besoin de; **£10 will meet my immediate ~s** 10 livres suffiront pour mes besoins immédiats; **in case of ~** en cas de besoin, au besoin; **there's no ~ to do ....** il n'y a pas lieu de faire ..., il n'est pas nécessaire de faire ...; **there's no ~ for that** ce n'est pas la peine, cela n'est pas nécessaire

needle ['niːdl] *n* aiguille *f*; (*on record player*) saphir *m* ▷ *vt* (*inf*) asticoter, tourmenter

needless ['niːdlɪs] *adj* inutile; **~ to say, ...** inutile de dire que ...

needlework ['niːdlwəːk] *n* (*activity*) travaux *mpl* d'aiguille; (*object*) ouvrage *m*

needn't ['niːdnt] = **need not**

needy ['niːdɪ] *adj* nécessiteux(-euse)

negative ['nɛgətɪv] *n* (*Phot, Elec*) négatif *m*; (*Ling*) terme *m* de négation ▷ *adj* négatif(-ive); **to answer in the ~** répondre par la négative

neglect [nɪ'glɛkt] *vt* négliger; (*garden*) ne pas entretenir; (*duty*) manquer à ▷ *n* (*of person, duty, garden*) le fait de négliger; (*state of*) ~ abandon *m*; **to ~ to do sth** négliger or omettre de faire qch; **to ~ one's appearance** se négliger

neglected [nɪ'glɛktɪd] *adj* négligé(e), à l'abandon

negligee ['nɛglɪʒeɪ] *n* déshabillé *m*

negotiate [nɪ'gəʊʃɪeɪt] *vi* négocier ▷ *vt* négocier; (*Comm*) négocier; (*obstacle*) franchir, négocier; (*bend in road*) négocier; **to ~ with sb for sth** négocier avec qn en vue d'obtenir qch

negotiation [nɪgəʊʃɪ'eɪʃən] *n* négociation *f*, pourparlers *mpl*; **to enter into ~s with sb** engager des négociations avec qn

negotiator [nɪ'gəʊʃɪeɪtə'] *n* négociateur(-trice)

neigh [neɪ] *vi* hennir

neighbour, (*US*) **neighbor** ['neɪbə'] *n* voisin(e)

neighbourhood, (*US*) **neighborhood** ['neɪbəhʊd] *n* (*place*) quartier *m*; (*people*) voisinage *m*

neighbouring, (*US*) **neighboring** ['neɪbərɪŋ] *adj* voisin(e), avoisinant(e)

neighbourly, (*US*) **neighborly** ['neɪbəlɪ] *adj* obligeant(e); (*relations*) de bon voisinage

neither ['naɪðə'] *adj, pron* aucun(e) (des deux), ni

l'un(e) ni l'autre ▷ *conj*: ~ **do I** moi non plus; **I didn't move and ~ did Claude** je n'ai pas bougé, (et) Claude non plus ▷ *adv*: ~ **good nor bad** ni bon ni mauvais; ~ **did I refuse** (et *or* mais) je n'ai pas non plus refusé; ~ **of them** ni l'un ni l'autre

neon ['niːɔn] *n* néon *m*

neon light *n* lampe *f* au néon

Nepal [nɪ'pɔːl] *n* Népal *m*

nephew ['nɛvjuː] *n* neveu *m*

nerve [nəːv] *n* nerf *m*; (*bravery*) sang-froid *m*, courage *m*; (*cheek*) aplomb *m*, toupet *m*; **nerves** *npl* (*nervousness*) nervosité *f*; **he gets on my ~s** il m'énerve; **to have a fit of ~s** avoir le trac; **to lose one's ~** (*self-confidence*) perdre son sang-froid

nerve-racking ['nəːvrækɪŋ] *adj* angoissant(e)

nervous ['nəːvəs] *adj* nerveux(-euse); (*anxious*) inquiet(-ète), plein(e) d'appréhension; (*timid*) intimidé(e)

nervous breakdown *n* dépression nerveuse

nest [nɛst] *n* nid *m* ▷ *vi* (se) nicher, faire son nid; ~ **of tables** table *f* gigogne

nest egg *n* (*fig*) bas *m* de laine, magot *m*

nestle ['nɛsl] *vi* se blottir

Net [nɛt] *n* (*Comput*): **the ~** (*Internet*) le Net

net [nɛt] *n* filet *m*; (*fabric*) tulle *f* ▷ *adj* net(te) ▷ *vt* (*fish etc*) prendre au filet; (*money: person*) toucher; (*: deal, sale*) rapporter; ~ **of tax** net d'impôt; **he earns £10,000 ~ per year** il gagne 10 000 livres net par an

netball ['nɛtbɔːl] *n* netball *m*

Netherlands ['nɛðələndz] *npl*: **the ~** les Pays-Bas *mpl*

nett [nɛt] *adj* = **net**

netting ['nɛtɪŋ] *n* (*for fence etc*) treillis *m*, grillage *m*; (*fabric*) voile *m*

nettle ['nɛtl] *n* ortie *f*

network ['nɛtwəːk] *n* réseau *m* ▷ *vt* (*Radio, TV*) diffuser sur l'ensemble du réseau; (*computers*) interconnecter; **there's no ~ coverage here** (*Tel*) il n'y a pas de réseau ici

neurotic [njuə'rɔtɪk] *adj*, *n* névrosé(e)

neuter ['njuːtəʳ] *adj* neutre ▷ *n* neutre *m* ▷ *vt* (*cat etc*) châtrer, couper

neutral ['njuːtrəl] *adj* neutre ▷ *n* (*Aut*) point mort

neutralize ['njuːtrəlaɪz] *vt* neutraliser

never ['nɛvəʳ] *adv* (ne ...) jamais; **I ~ went** je n'y suis pas allé; **I've ~ been to Spain** je ne suis jamais allé en Espagne; ~ **again** plus jamais; ~ **in my life** jamais de ma vie; *see also* **mind**

never-ending [nɛvər'ɛndɪŋ] *adj* interminable

nevertheless [nɛvəðə'lɛs] *adv* néanmoins, malgré tout

new [njuː] *adj* nouveau (nouvelle); (*brand new*) neuf (neuve); **as good as ~** comme neuf

New Age *n* New Age *m*

newborn ['njuːbɔːn] *adj* nouveau-né(e)

newcomer ['njuːkʌməʳ] *n* nouveau venu (nouvelle venue)

new-fangled ['njuːfæŋgld] *adj* (*pej*) ultramoderne (et farfelu(e))

new-found ['njuːfaund] *adj* de fraîche date; (*friend*) nouveau (nouvelle)

newly ['njuːlɪ] *adv* nouvellement, récemment

newly-weds ['njuːlɪwɛdz] *npl* jeunes mariés *mpl*

news [njuːz] *n* nouvelle(s) *f(pl)*; (*Radio, TV*) informations *fpl*, actualités *fpl*; **a piece of ~** une nouvelle; **good/bad ~** bonne/mauvaise nouvelle; **financial ~** (*Press, Radio, TV*) page financière

news agency *n* agence *f* de presse

newsagent ['njuːzeɪdʒənt] *n* (*Brit*) marchand *m* de journaux

newscaster ['njuːzkaːstəʳ] *n* (*Radio, TV*) présentateur(-trice)

news flash *n* flash *m* d'information

newsletter ['njuːzlɛtəʳ] *n* bulletin *m*

newspaper ['njuːzpeɪpəʳ] *n* journal *m*; **daily ~** quotidien *m*; **weekly ~** hebdomadaire *m*

newsprint ['njuːzprɪnt] *n* papier *m* (de) journal

newsreader ['njuːzriːdəʳ] *n* = **newscaster**

newsreel ['njuːzriːl] *n* actualités (filmées)

news stand *n* kiosque *m* à journaux

newt [njuːt] *n* triton *m*

New Year *n* Nouvel An; **Happy ~!** Bonne Année!; **to wish sb a happy ~** souhaiter la Bonne Année à qn

New Year's Day *n* le jour de l'An

New Year's Eve *n* la Saint-Sylvestre

New York [-'jɔːk] *n* New York; (*also*: **New York State**) New York *m*

New Zealand [-'ziːlənd] *n* Nouvelle-Zélande *f* ▷ *adj* néo-zélandais(e)

New Zealander [-'ziːləndəʳ] *n* Néo-Zélandais(e)

next [nɛkst] *adj* (*in time*) prochain(e); (*seat, room*) voisin(e), d'à côté; (*meeting, bus stop*) suivant(e) ▷ *adv* la fois suivante; la prochaine fois; (*afterwards*) ensuite; ~ **to** (*prep*) à côté de; ~ **to nothing** presque rien; ~ **time** (*adv*) la prochaine fois; **the ~ day** le lendemain, le jour suivant *or* d'après; ~ **week** la semaine prochaine; **the ~ week** la semaine suivante; ~ **year** l'année prochaine; **"turn to the ~ page"** "voir page suivante"; ~ **please!** (*at doctor's etc*) au suivant!; **who's ~?** c'est à qui?; **the week after ~** dans deux semaines; **when do we meet ~?** quand nous revoyons-nous?

next door *adv* à côté ▷ *adj* (*neighbour*) d'à côté

next-of-kin ['nɛkstəv'kɪn] *n* parent *m* le plus proche

NHS *n abbr* (*Brit*) = **National Health Service**

nib [nɪb] *n* (*of pen*) (bec *m* de) plume *f*

nibble ['nɪbl] *vt* grignoter

nice [naɪs] *adj* (*holiday, trip, taste*) agréable; (*flat, picture*) joli(e); (*person*) gentil(le); (*distinction, point*) subtil(e)

nicely ['naɪslɪ] *adv* agréablement; joliment; gentiment; subtilement; **that will do ~** ce sera parfait

niceties ['naɪsɪtɪz] *npl* subtilités *fpl*

niche [niːʃ] *n* (*Archit*) niche *f*

nick [nɪk] *n* (*indentation*) encoche *f*; (*wound*) entaille *f*; (*Brit inf*): **in good ~** en bon état ▷ *vt* (*cut*): **to ~ o.s.** se couper; (*inf: steal*) faucher, piquer; (*: Brit: arrest*) choper, pincer; **in the ~ of time** juste à temps

nickel ['nɪkl] n nickel m; (US) pièce f de 5 cents
nickname ['nɪkneɪm] n surnom m ▷ vt
surnommer
nicotine ['nɪkəti:n] n nicotine f
nicotine patch n timbre m anti-tabac, patch m
niece [ni:s] n nièce f
Nigeria [naɪ'dʒɪərɪə] n Nigéria m or f
niggling ['nɪglɪŋ] adj tatillon(ne); (detail)
insignifiant(e); (doubt, pain) persistant(e)
night [naɪt] n nuit f; (evening) soir m; **at ~** la nuit;
by ~ de nuit; **in the ~, during the ~** pendant la
nuit; **last ~** (evening) hier soir; (night-time) la nuit
dernière; **the ~ before last** avant-hier soir
nightcap ['naɪtkæp] n boisson prise avant le coucher
night club n boîte f de nuit
nightdress ['naɪtdrɛs] n chemise f de nuit
nightfall ['naɪtfɔ:l] n tombée f de la nuit
nightie ['naɪtɪ] n chemise f de nuit
nightingale ['naɪtɪŋgeɪl] n rossignol m
nightlife ['naɪtlaɪf] n vie f nocturne
nightly ['naɪtlɪ] adj (news) du soir; (by night)
nocturne ▷ adv (every evening) tous les soirs; (every
night) toutes les nuits
nightmare ['naɪtmɛəʳ] n cauchemar m
night porter n gardien m de nuit, concierge m de
service la nuit
night school n cours mpl du soir
night shift ['naɪtʃɪft] n équipe f de nuit
night-time ['naɪttaɪm] n nuit f
night watchman (irreg) n veilleur m de nuit;
poste m de nuit
nil [nɪl] n rien m; (Brit Sport) zéro m
Nile [naɪl] n: **the ~** le Nil
nimble ['nɪmbl] adj agile
nine [naɪn] num neuf
nineteen ['naɪn'ti:n] num dix-neuf
nineteenth [naɪn'ti:nθ] num dix-neuvième
ninetieth ['naɪntɪɪθ] num quatre-vingt-dixième
ninety ['naɪntɪ] num quatre-vingt-dix
ninth [naɪnθ] num neuvième
nip [nɪp] vt pincer ▷ vi (Brit inf): **to ~ out/down/
up** sortir/descendre/monter en vitesse ▷ n
pincement m; (drink) petit verre; **to ~ into a
shop** faire un saut dans un magasin
nipple ['nɪpl] n (Anat) mamelon m, bout m du sein
nitrogen ['naɪtrədʒən] n azote m
no [nəu] (pl **noes**) adv (opposite of "yes") non; **are
you coming?** — **no (I'm not)** est-ce que vous
venez? — non; **would you like some more?**
— **no thank you** vous en voulez encore? — non
merci
▷ adj (not any) (ne ...) pas de, (ne ...) aucun(e); **I
have no money/books** je n'ai pas d'argent/de
livres; **no student would have done it** aucun
étudiant ne l'aurait fait; **"no smoking"**
"défense de fumer"; **"no dogs"** "les chiens ne
sont pas admis"
▷ n non m; **I won't take no for an answer** il
n'est pas question de refuser
nobility [nəu'bɪlɪtɪ] n noblesse f
noble ['nəubl] adj noble
nobody ['nəubədɪ] pron (ne ...) personne

nod [nɔd] vi faire un signe de (la) tête (affirmatif
ou amical); (sleep) somnoler ▷ vt: **to ~ one's head**
faire un signe de (la) tête; (in agreement) faire
signe que oui ▷ n signe m de (la) tête; **they ~ded
their agreement** ils ont acquiescé d'un signe
de la tête
▷ **nod off** vi s'assoupir
noise [nɔɪz] n bruit m; **I can't sleep for the ~** je
n'arrive pas à dormir à cause du bruit
noisy ['nɔɪzɪ] adj bruyant(e)
nominal ['nɔmɪnl] adj (rent, fee) symbolique;
(value) nominal(e)
nominate ['nɔmɪneɪt] vt (propose) proposer;
(appoint) nommer
nomination [nɔmɪ'neɪʃən] n nomination f
nominee [nɔmɪ'ni:] n candidat agréé; personne
nommée
non- [nɔn] prefix non-
nonalcoholic [nɔnælkə'hɔlɪk] adj non
alcoolisé(e)
noncommittal [nɔnkə'mɪtl] adj évasif(-ive)
nondescript ['nɔndɪskrɪpt] adj quelconque,
indéfinissable
none [nʌn] pron aucun(e); **~ of you** aucun
d'entre vous, personne parmi vous; **I have ~**
je n'en ai pas; **I have ~ left** je n'en ai plus; **~ at
all** (not one) aucun(e); **how much milk?** — **~ at
all** combien de lait? — pas du tout; **he's ~ the ~
worse for it** il ne s'en porte pas plus mal
nonentity [nɔ'nɛntɪtɪ] n personne insignifiante
nonetheless ['nʌnðə'lɛs] adv néanmoins
nonexistent [nɔnɪg'zɪstənt] adj inexistant(e)
non-fiction [nɔn'fɪkʃən] n littérature f non
romanesque
nonplussed [nɔn'plʌst] adj perplexe
nonsense ['nɔnsəns] n absurdités fpl, idioties fpl;
~! ne dites pas d'idioties!; **it is ~ to say that ...** il
est absurde de dire que ....
non-smoker ['nɔn'sməukəʳ] n non-fumeur m
non-smoking ['nɔn'sməukɪŋ] adj non-fumeur
non-stick ['nɔn'stɪk] adj qui n'attache pas
nonstop ['nɔn'stɔp] adj direct(e), sans arrêt (or
escale) ▷ adv sans arrêt
noodles ['nu:dlz] npl nouilles fpl
nook [nuk] n: **~s and crannies** recoins mpl
noon [nu:n] n midi m
no-one ['nəuwʌn] pron = **nobody**
noose [nu:s] n nœud coulant; (hangman's) corde f
nor [nɔ:ʳ] conj = **neither** ▷ adv see **neither**
norm [nɔ:m] n norme f
normal ['nɔ:ml] adj normal(e) ▷ n: **to return to
~** redevenir normal(e)
normally ['nɔ:məlɪ] adv normalement
Normandy ['nɔ:məndɪ] n Normandie f
north [nɔ:θ] n nord m ▷ adj nord inv; (wind) du
nord ▷ adv au or vers le nord
North Africa n Afrique f du Nord
North African adj nord-africain(e), d'Afrique du
Nord ▷ n Nord-Africain(e)
North America n Amérique f du Nord
North American n Nord-Américain(e) ▷ adj
nord-américain(e), d'Amérique du Nord

northbound ['nɔːθbaund] *adj* (*traffic*) en direction du nord; (*carriageway*) nord *inv*

north-east [nɔːθ'iːst] *n* nord-est *m*

northerly ['nɔːðəlɪ] *adj* (*wind, direction*) du nord

northern ['nɔːðən] *adj* du nord, septentrional(e)

Northern Ireland *n* Irlande *f* du Nord

North Korea *n* Corée *f* du Nord

North Pole *n*: **the ~** le pôle Nord

North Sea *n*: **the ~** la mer du Nord

northward ['nɔːθwəd], **northwards** ['nɔːθwədz] *adv* vers le nord

north-west [nɔːθ'wɛst] *n* nord-ouest *m*

Norway ['nɔːweɪ] *n* Norvège *f*

Norwegian [nɔː'wiːdʒən] *adj* norvégien(ne) ▷ *n* Norvégien(ne); (*Ling*) norvégien *m*

nose [nəuz] *n* nez *m*; (*of dog, cat*) museau *m*; (*fig*) flair *m* ▷ *vi* (*also:* **nose one's way**) avancer précautionneusement; **to pay through the ~ (for sth)** (*inf*) payer un prix excessif (pour qch)
  ▶ **nose about, nose around** *vi* fouiner *or* fureter (partout)

nosebleed ['nəuzbliːd] *n* saignement *m* de nez

nose-dive ['nəuzdaɪv] *n* (*descente f en*) piqué *m*

nosey ['nəuzɪ] *adj* (*inf*) curieux(-euse)

nostalgia [nɔs'tældʒɪə] *n* nostalgie *f*

nostalgic [nɔs'tældʒɪk] *adj* nostalgique

nostril ['nɔstrɪl] *n* narine *f*; (*of horse*) naseau *m*

nosy ['nəuzɪ] (*inf*) *adj* = **nosey**

not [nɔt] *adv* (ne ...) pas; **he is ~** *or* **isn't here** il n'est pas ici; **you must ~** *or* **mustn't do that** tu ne dois pas faire ça; **I hope ~** j'espère que non; **~ at all** pas du tout; (*after thanks*) de rien; **it's too late, isn't it?** c'est trop tard, n'est-ce pas?; **~ yet/ now** pas encore/maintenant; *see also* **only**

notable ['nəutəbl] *adj* notable

notably ['nəutəblɪ] *adv* (*particularly*) en particulier; (*markedly*) spécialement

notary ['nəutərɪ] *n* (*also:* **notary public**) notaire *m*

notch [nɔtʃ] *n* encoche *f*
  ▶ **notch up** *vt* (*score*) marquer; (*victory*) remporter

note [nəut] *n* note *f*; (*letter*) mot *m*; (*banknote*) billet *m* ▷ *vt* (*also:* **note down**) noter; (*notice*) constater; **just a quick ~ to let you know ...** juste un mot pour vous dire ...; **to take ~s** prendre des notes; **to compare ~s** (*fig*) échanger des (*or leurs etc*) impressions; **to take ~ of** prendre note de; **a person of ~** une personne éminente

notebook ['nəutbuk] *n* carnet *m*; (*for shorthand etc*) bloc-notes *m*

noted ['nəutɪd] *adj* réputé(e)

notepad ['nəutpæd] *n* bloc-notes *m*

notepaper ['nəutpeɪpəʳ] *n* papier *m* à lettres

nothing ['nʌθɪŋ] *n* rien *m*; **he does ~** il ne fait rien; **~ new** de nouveau, rien de nouveau; **for ~** (*free*) pour rien, gratuitement; (*in vain*) pour rien; **~ at all** rien du tout; **~ much** pas grand-chose

notice ['nəutɪs] *n* (*announcement, warning*) avis *m*; (*of leaving*) congé *m*; (*Brit: review: of play etc*) critique *f*, compte rendu *m* ▷ *vt* remarquer, s'apercevoir de; **without ~** sans préavis; **advance ~** préavis *m*; **to give sb ~ of sth** notifier qn de qch; **at**

short ~ dans un délai très court; **until further ~** jusqu'à nouvel ordre; **to give ~, hand in one's ~** (*employee*) donner sa démission, démissionner; **to take ~ of** prêter attention à; **to bring sth to sb's ~** porter qch à la connaissance de qn; **it has come to my ~ that ...** on m'a signalé que ...; **to escape** *or* **avoid ~** (essayer de) passer inaperçu *or* ne pas se faire remarquer

noticeable ['nəutɪsəbl] *adj* visible

notice board *n* (*Brit*) panneau *m* d'affichage

notify ['nəutɪfaɪ] *vt*: **to ~ sth to sb** notifier qch à qn; **to ~ sb of sth** avertir qn de qch

notion ['nəuʃən] *n* idée *f*; (*concept*) notion *f*; **notions** *npl* (*US: haberdashery*) mercerie *f*

notorious [nəu'tɔːrɪəs] *adj* notoire (*souvent en mal*)

notwithstanding [nɔtwɪθ'stændɪŋ] *adv* néanmoins ▷ *prep* en dépit de

nought [nɔːt] *n* zéro *m*

noun [naun] *n* nom *m*

nourish ['nʌrɪʃ] *vt* nourrir

nourishing ['nʌrɪʃɪŋ] *adj* nourrissant(e)

nourishment ['nʌrɪʃmənt] *n* nourriture *f*

Nov. *abbr* (= *November*) nov

novel ['nɔvl] *n* roman *m* ▷ *adj* nouveau (nouvelle), original(e)

novelist ['nɔvəlɪst] *n* romancier *m*

novelty ['nɔvəltɪ] *n* nouveauté *f*

November [nəu'vɛmbəʳ] *n* novembre *m*; *for phrases see also* **July**

novice ['nɔvɪs] *n* novice *m/f*

now [nau] *adv* maintenant ▷ *conj*: **~ (that)** maintenant (que); **right ~** tout de suite; **by ~** à l'heure qu'il est; **just ~: that's the fashion just now** c'est la mode en ce moment *or* maintenant; **I saw her just ~** je viens de la voir, je l'ai vue à l'instant; **I'll read it just ~** je vais le lire à l'instant *or* dès maintenant; **~ and then, ~ and again** de temps en temps; **from ~ on** dorénavant; **in 3 days from ~** dans *or* d'ici trois jours; **between ~ and Monday** d'ici (à) lundi; **that's all for ~** c'est tout pour l'instant

nowadays ['nauədeɪz] *adv* de nos jours

nowhere ['nəuwɛəʳ] *adv* (ne ...) nulle part; **~ else** nulle part ailleurs

nozzle ['nɔzl] *n* (*of hose*) jet *m*, lance *f*; (*of vacuum cleaner*) suceur *m*

nr *abbr* (*Brit*) = **near**

nuclear ['njuːklɪəʳ] *adj* nucléaire

nucleus (*pl* **nuclei**) ['njuːklɪəs, 'njuːklɪaɪ] *n* noyau *m*

nude [njuːd] *adj* nu(e) ▷ *n* (*Art*) nu *m*; **in the ~** (tout(e)) nu(e)

nudge [nʌdʒ] *vt* donner un (petit) coup de coude à

nudist ['njuːdɪst] *n* nudiste *m/f*

nudity ['njuːdɪtɪ] *n* nudité *f*

nuisance ['njuːsns] *n*: **it's a ~** c'est (très) ennuyeux *or* gênant; **he's a ~** il est assommant *or* casse-pieds; **what a ~!** quelle barbe!

null [nʌl] *adj*: **~ and void** nul(le) et non avenu(e)

numb [nʌm] *adj* engourdi(e); (*with fear*) paralysé(e) ▷ *vt* engourdir; **~ with cold**

engourdi(e) par le froid, transi(e) (de froid); ~
with fear transi de peur, paralysé(e) par la peur
number ['nʌmbə^r] n nombre m; (*numeral*) chiffre
m; (*of house, car, telephone, newspaper*) numéro m
▷ vt numéroter; (*amount to*) compter; **a ~ of** un
certain nombre de; **they were seven in ~** ils
étaient (au nombre de) sept; **to be ~ed among**
compter parmi; **the staff ~s 20** le nombre
d'employés s'élève à or est de 20; **wrong ~** (*Tel*)
mauvais numéro
number plate n (*Brit Aut*) plaque f minéralogique
or d'immatriculation
Number Ten n (*Brit: 10 Downing Street*) *résidence du
Premier ministre*
numeral ['nju:mərəl] n chiffre m
numerate ['nju:mərɪt] adj (*Brit*): **to be ~** avoir des
notions d'arithmétique
numerical [nju:'mɛrɪkl] adj numérique
numerous ['nju:mərəs] adj nombreux(-euse)
nun [nʌn] n religieuse f, sœur f
nurse [nə:s] n infirmière f, (*also:* **nursemaid**)
bonne f d'enfants ▷ vt (*patient, cold*) soigner;
(*baby: Brit*) bercer (dans ses bras); (*: US*) allaiter,
nourrir; (*hope*) nourrir
nursery ['nə:sərɪ] n (*room*) nursery f; (*institution*)
crèche f, garderie f; (*for plants*) pépinière f
nursery rhyme n comptine f, chansonnette f
pour enfants
nursery school n école maternelle
nursery slope n (*Brit Ski*) piste f pour débutants

nursing ['nə:sɪŋ] n (*profession*) profession f
d'infirmière; (*care*) soins mpl ▷ adj (*mother*) qui
allaite
nursing home n clinique f; (*for convalescence*)
maison f de convalescence or de repos; (*for old
people*) maison de retraite
nurture ['nə:tʃə^r] vt élever
nut [nʌt] n (*of metal*) écrou m; (*fruit: walnut*) noix
f; (*: hazelnut*) noisette f; (*: peanut*) cacahuète f
(*terme générique en anglais*) ▷ adj (*chocolate etc*) aux
noisettes; **he's ~s** (*inf*) il est dingue
nutcrackers ['nʌtkrækəz] npl casse-noix m inv,
casse-noisette(s) m
nutmeg ['nʌtmɛg] n (*noix f*) muscade f
nutrient ['nju:trɪənt] adj nutritif(-ive) ▷ n
substance nutritive
nutrition [nju:'trɪʃən] n nutrition f,
alimentation f
nutritious [nju:'trɪʃəs] adj nutritif(-ive),
nourrissant(e)
nuts [nʌts] (*inf*) adj dingue
nutshell ['nʌtʃɛl] n coquille f de noix; **in a ~** en
un mot
nutter ['nʌtə^r] (*Brit: inf*) n: **he's a complete ~** il
est complètement cinglé
NVQ n abbr (*Brit*) = **National Vocational
Qualification**
nylon ['naɪlɔn] n nylon m ▷ adj de or en nylon;
nylons npl bas mpl nylon

Oo

oak [əuk] *n* chêne *m* ▷ *cpd* de *or* en (bois de) chêne

O.A.P. *n abbr* (*Brit*) = **old age pensioner**

oar [ɔː^r] *n* aviron *m*, rame *f*; **to put** *or* **shove one's ~ in** (*fig: inf*) mettre son grain de sel

oasis (*pl* **oases**) [əu'eısıs, əu'eısiːz] *n* oasis *f*

oath [əuθ] *n* serment *m*; (*swear word*) juron *m*; **to take the ~** prêter serment; **on** (*Brit*) *or* **under ~** sous serment; assermenté(e)

oatmeal ['əutmiːl] *n* flocons *mpl* d'avoine

oats [əuts] *n* avoine *f*

obedience [ə'biːdıəns] *n* obéissance *f*; **in ~ to** conformément à

obedient [ə'biːdıənt] *adj* obéissant(e); **to be ~ to sb/sth** obéir à qn/qch

obese [əu'biːs] *adj* obèse

obesity [əu'biːsıtı] *n* obésité *f*

obey [ə'beı] *vt* obéir à; (*instructions, regulations*) se conformer à ▷ *vi* obéir

obituary [ə'bıtjuərı] *n* nécrologie *f*

object *n* ['ɔbdʒıkt] objet *m*; (*purpose*) but *m*, objet, (*Ling*) complément *m* d'objet ▷ *vi* [əb'dʒɛkt]: **to ~ to** (*attitude*) désapprouver; (*proposal*) protester contre, élever une objection contre; **I ~!** je proteste!; **he ~ed that ...** il a fait valoir *or* a objecté que ...; **do you ~ to my smoking?** est-ce que cela vous gêne si je fume?; **what's the ~ of doing that?** quel est l'intérêt de faire cela?; **money is no ~** l'argent n'est pas un problème

objection [əb'dʒɛkʃən] *n* objection *f*; (*drawback*) inconvénient *m*; **if you have no ~** si vous n'y voyez pas d'inconvénient; **to make** *or* **raise an ~** élever une objection

objectionable [əb'dʒɛkʃənəbl] *adj* très désagréable; choquant(e)

objective [əb'dʒɛktıv] *n* objectif *m* ▷ *adj* objectif(-ive)

obligation [ɔblı'geıʃən] *n* obligation *f*, devoir *m*; (*debt*) dette *f* (de reconnaissance); **"without ~"** "sans engagement"

obligatory [ə'blıgətərı] *adj* obligatoire

oblige [ə'blaıdʒ] *vt* (*force*): **to ~ sb to do** obliger *or* forcer qn à faire; (*do a favour*) rendre service à, obliger; **to be ~d to sb for sth** être obligé(e) à qn de qch; **anything to ~!** (*inf*) (toujours prêt à rendre) service!

obliging [ə'blaıdʒıŋ] *adj* obligeant(e), serviable

oblique [ə'bliːk] *adj* oblique; (*allusion*) indirect(e)

▷ *n* (*Brit Typ*): **~ (stroke)** barre *f* oblique

obliterate [ə'blıtəreıt] *vt* effacer

oblivion [ə'blıvıən] *n* oubli *m*

oblivious [ə'blıvıəs] *adj*: **~ of** oublieux(-euse) de

oblong ['ɔblɔŋ] *adj* oblong(ue) ▷ *n* rectangle *m*

obnoxious [əb'nɔkʃəs] *adj* odieux(-euse); (*smell*) nauséabond(e)

oboe ['əubəu] *n* hautbois *m*

obscene [əb'siːn] *adj* obscène

obscure [əb'skjuə^r] *adj* obscur(e) ▷ *vt* obscurcir; (*hide: sun*) cacher

observant [əb'zəːvnt] *adj* observateur(-trice)

observation [ɔbzə'veıʃən] *n* observation *f*; (*by police etc*) surveillance *f*

observatory [əb'zəːvətrı] *n* observatoire *m*

observe [əb'zəːv] *vt* observer; (*remark*) faire observer *or* remarquer

observer [əb'zəːvə^r] *n* observateur(-trice)

obsess [əb'sɛs] *vt* obséder; **to be ~ed by** *or* **with sb/sth** être obsédé(e) par qn/qch

obsession [əb'sɛʃən] *n* obsession *f*

obsessive [əb'sɛsıv] *adj* obsédant(e)

obsolete ['ɔbsəliːt] *adj* dépassé(e), périmé(e)

obstacle ['ɔbstəkl] *n* obstacle *m*

obstacle race *n* course *f* d'obstacles

obstinate ['ɔbstınıt] *adj* obstiné(e); (*pain, cold*) persistant(e)

obstruct [əb'strʌkt] *vt* (*block*) boucher, obstruer; (*halt*) arrêter; (*hinder*) entraver

obstruction [əb'strʌkʃən] *n* obstruction *f*; (*to plan, progress*) obstacle *m*

obtain [əb'teın] *vt* obtenir ▷ *vi* avoir cours

obvious ['ɔbvıəs] *adj* évident(e), manifeste

obviously ['ɔbvıəslı] *adv* manifestement; (*of course*): **~, he ... or he ~ ...** il est bien évident qu'il ...; **~!** bien sûr!; **~ not!** évidemment pas!, bien sûr que non!

occasion [ə'keıʒən] *n* occasion *f*; (*event*) événement *m* ▷ *vt* occasionner, causer; **on that ~** à cette occasion; **to rise to the ~** se montrer à la hauteur de la situation

occasional [ə'keıʒənl] *adj* pris(e) (*or* fait(e) *etc*) de temps en temps; (*worker, spending*) occasionnel(le)

occasionally [ə'keıʒənəlı] *adv* de temps en temps, quelquefois; **very ~** (assez) rarement

occult [ɔ'kʌlt] *adj* occulte ▷ *n*: **the ~** le surnaturel

occupant ['ɔkjupənt] *n* occupant *m*

occupation [ɔkjuˈpeɪʃən] n occupation f; (job)
métier m, profession f; **unfit for ~** (house)
impropre à l'habitation

occupational hazard n risque m du métier

occupier [ˈɔkjupaɪəʳ] n occupant(e)

occupy [ˈɔkjupaɪ] vt occuper; **to ~ o.s. with** or **by
doing** s'occuper à faire; **to be occupied with
sth** être occupé avec qch

occur [əˈkəːʳ] vi se produire; (difficulty, opportunity)
se présenter; (phenomenon, error) se rencontrer; **to
~ to sb** venir à l'esprit de qn

occurrence [əˈkʌrəns] n (existence) présence f,
existence f; (event) cas m, fait m

ocean [ˈəuʃən] n océan m; **~s of** (inf) des masses de

o'clock [əˈklɔk] adv: **it is 5 o'clock** il est 5 heures

OCR n abbr = **optical character reader; optical
character recognition**

Oct. abbr (= October) oct

October [ɔkˈtəubəʳ] n octobre m; for phrases see
also **July**

octopus [ˈɔktəpəs] n pieuvre f

odd [ɔd] adj (strange) bizarre, curieux(-euse);
(number) impair(e); (left over) qui reste, en plus;
(not of a set) dépareillé(e); **60-~** 60 et quelques;
at ~ times de temps en temps; **the ~ one out**
l'exception f

oddity [ˈɔdɪtɪ] n bizarrerie f; (person) excentrique
m/f

odd-job man [ɔdˈdʒɔb-] (irreg) n homme m à tout
faire

odd jobs npl petits travaux divers

oddly [ˈɔdlɪ] adv bizarrement, curieusement

oddments [ˈɔdmənts] npl (Brit Comm) fins fpl de
série

odds [ɔdz] npl (in betting) cote f; **the ~ are against
his coming** il y a peu de chances qu'il vienne;
it makes no ~ cela n'a pas d'importance; **to
succeed against all the ~** réussir contre toute
attente; **~ and ends** de petites choses; **at ~** en
désaccord

odometer [ɔˈdɔmɪtəʳ] n (US) odomètre m

odour, (US) **odor** [ˈəudəʳ] n odeur f

of [ɔv, əv] prep **1** (gen) de; **a friend of ours** un de
nos amis; **a boy of 10** un garçon de 10 ans; **that
was kind of you** c'était gentil de votre part
2 (expressing quantity, amount, dates etc) de; **a kilo
of flour** un kilo de farine; **how much of this
do you need?** combien vous en faut-il?; **there
were three of them** (people) ils étaient 3; (objects)
il y en avait 3; **three of us went** 3 d'entre nous
y sont allé(e)s; **the 5th of July** le 5 juillet; **a
quarter of 4** (US) 4 heures moins le quart
3 (from, out of) en, de; **a statue of marble** une
statue de or en marbre; **made of wood** (fait) en
bois

off [ɔf] adj, adv (engine) coupé(e); (light, TV)
éteint(e); (tap) fermé(e); (Brit: food) mauvais(e),
avancé(e); (: milk) tourné(e); (absent) absent(e);
(cancelled) annulé(e); (removed): **the lid was ~** le
couvercle était retiré or n'était pas mis; (away):
to run/drive ~ partir en courant/en voiture
▷ prep de; **to be ~** (to leave) partir, s'en aller; **I

must be ~** il faut que je file; **to be ~ sick** être
absent pour cause de maladie; **a day ~** un jour
de congé; **to have an ~ day** n'être pas en forme;
he had his coat ~ il avait enlevé son manteau;
the hook is ~ le crochet s'est détaché; le crochet
n'est pas mis; **10% ~** (Comm) 10% de rabais; **5 km
~ (the road)** à 5 km (de la route); **~ the coast** au
large de la côte; **a house ~ the main road** une
maison à l'écart de la grand-route; **it's a long
way ~** c'est loin (d'ici); **I'm ~ meat** je ne mange
plus de viande; je n'aime plus la viande; **on the
~ chance** à tout hasard; **to be well/badly ~** être
bien/mal loti; (financially) être aisé/dans la gêne;
~ and on, on and ~ de temps à autre; **I'm afraid
the chicken is ~** (Brit: not available) je regrette, il
n'y a plus de poulet; **that's a bit ~** (fig: inf) c'est
un peu fort

offal [ˈɔfl] n (Culin) abats mpl

off-colour [ˈɔfˈkʌləʳ] adj (Brit: ill) malade, mal
fichu(e); **to feel ~** être mal fichu

offence, (US) **offense** [əˈfɛns] n (crime) délit m,
infraction f; **to give ~ to** blesser, offenser; **to
take ~ at** se vexer de, s'offenser de; **to commit
an ~** commettre une infraction

offend [əˈfɛnd] vt (person) offenser, blesser ▷ vi:
to ~ against (law, rule) contrevenir à, enfreindre

offender [əˈfɛndəʳ] n délinquant(e); (against
regulations) contrevenant(e)

offense [əˈfɛns] n (US) = **offence**

offensive [əˈfɛnsɪv] adj offensant(e),
choquant(e); (smell etc) très déplaisant(e);
(weapon) offensif(-ive) ▷ n (Mil) offensive f

offer [ˈɔfəʳ] n offre f, proposition f ▷ vt offrir,
proposer; **to make an ~ for sth** faire une offre
pour qch; **to ~ sth to sb, ~ sb sth** offrir qch à
qn; **to ~ to do sth** proposer de faire qch; **"on ~"**
(Comm) "en promotion"

offering [ˈɔfərɪŋ] n offrande f

offhand [ˈɔfˈhænd] adj désinvolte ▷ adv
spontanément; **I can't tell you ~** je ne peux pas
vous le dire comme ça

office [ˈɔfɪs] n (place) bureau m; (position) charge f,
fonction f; **doctor's ~** (US) cabinet (médical); **to
take ~** entrer en fonctions; **through his good ~s**
(fig) grâce à ses bons offices; **O~ of Fair Trading**
(Brit) organisme de protection contre les pratiques
commerciales abusives

office automation n bureautique f

office block, (US) **office building** n immeuble m
de bureaux

office hours npl heures fpl de bureau; (US Med)
heures de consultation

officer [ˈɔfɪsəʳ] n (Mil etc) officier m; (also: **police
officer**) agent m (de police); (of organization)
membre m du bureau directeur

office worker n employé(e) de bureau

official [əˈfɪʃl] adj (authorized) officiel(le) ▷ n
officiel m; (civil servant) fonctionnaire m/f; (of
railways, post office, town hall) employé(e)

officiate [əˈfɪʃɪeɪt] vi (Rel) officier; **to ~ as
Mayor** exercer les fonctions de maire; **to ~ at a
marriage** célébrer un mariage

officious [əˈfɪʃəs] *adj* trop empressé(e)
offing [ˈɔfɪŋ] *n*: **in the ~** (*fig*) en perspective
off-licence [ˈɔflaɪsns] *n* (*Brit: shop*) débit *m* de vins et de spiritueux
off-line [ɔfˈlaɪn] *adj* (*Comput*) (en mode) autonome; (: *switched off*) non connecté(e)
off-peak [ɔfˈpiːk] *adj* aux heures creuses; (*electricity, ticket*) au tarif heures creuses
off-putting [ˈɔfputɪŋ] *adj* (*Brit: remark*) rébarbatif(-ive); (*person*) rebutant(e), peu engageant(e)
off-road vehicle [ˈɔfrəud-] *n* véhicule *m* tout-terrain
off-season [ˈɔfsiːzn] *adj, adv* hors-saison *inv*
offset [ˈɔfsɛt] *vt* (*irreg: like* **set**); (*counteract*) contrebalancer, compenser ▷ *n* (*also*: **offset printing**) offset *m*
offshoot [ˈɔfʃuːt] *n* (*fig*) ramification *f*, antenne *f*; (: *of discussion etc*) conséquence *f*
offshore [ɔfˈʃɔːʳ] *adj* (*breeze*) de terre; (*island*) proche du littoral; (*fishing*) côtier(-ière); **~ oilfield** gisement *m* pétrolifère en mer
offside [ˈɔfsaɪd] *n* (*Aut: with right-hand drive*) côté droit; (: *with left-hand drive*) côté gauche ▷ *adj* (*Sport*) hors jeu; (*Aut: in Britain*) de droite; (: *in US, Europe*) de gauche
offspring [ˈɔfsprɪŋ] *n* progéniture *f*
offstage [ɔfˈsteɪdʒ] *adv* dans les coulisses
off-the-peg [ˈɔfðəˈpɛg], (*US*) **off-the-rack** [ˈɔfðəˈræk] *adv* en prêt-à-porter
off-white [ˈɔfwaɪt] *adj* blanc cassé *inv*
often [ˈɔfn] *adv* souvent; **how ~ do you go?** vous y allez tous les combien?; **every so ~** de temps en temps, de temps à autre; **as ~ as not** la plupart du temps
Ofwat [ˈɔfwɔt] *n abbr* (*Brit*: = *Office of Water Services*) *organisme qui surveille les activités des compagnies des eaux*
oh [əu] *excl* ô!, oh!, ah!
oil [ɔɪl] *n* huile *f*; (*petroleum*) pétrole *m*; (*for central heating*) mazout *m* ▷ *vt* (*machine*) graisser
oilcan [ˈɔɪlkæn] *n* burette *f* de graissage; (*for storing*) bidon *m* à huile
oilfield [ˈɔɪlfiːld] *n* gisement *m* de pétrole
oil filter *n* (*Aut*) filtre *m* à huile
oil painting *n* peinture *f* à l'huile
oil refinery *n* raffinerie *f* de pétrole
oil rig *n* derrick *m*; (*at sea*) plate-forme pétrolière
oil slick *n* nappe *f* de mazout
oil tanker *n* (*ship*) pétrolier *m*; (*truck*) camion-citerne *m*
oil well *n* puits *m* de pétrole
oily [ˈɔɪlɪ] *adj* huileux(-euse); (*food*) gras(se)
ointment [ˈɔɪntmənt] *n* onguent *m*
O.K., okay [ˈəuˈkeɪ] (*inf*) *excl* d'accord! ▷ *vt* approuver, donner son accord à ▷ *n*: **to give sth one's O.K.** donner son accord à qch ▷ *adj* (*not bad*) pas mal, en règle; en bon état; sain et sauf; acceptable; **is it O.K.?**, **are you O.K.?** ça va?; **are you O.K. for money?** ça va *or* ira question argent?; **it's O.K. with** *or* **by me** ça me va, c'est d'accord en ce qui me concerne

old [əuld] *adj* vieux (vieille); (*person*) vieux, âgé(e); (*former*) ancien(ne), vieux; **how ~ are you?** quel âge avez-vous?; **he's 10 years ~** il a 10 ans, il est âgé de 10 ans; **~er brother/sister** frère/sœur aîné(e); **any ~ thing will do** n'importe quoi fera l'affaire
old age *n* vieillesse *f*
old-age pensioner *n* (*Brit*) retraité(e)
old-fashioned [ˈəuldˈfæʃnd] *adj* démodé(e); (*person*) vieux jeu *inv*
old people's home *n* (*esp Brit*) maison *f* de retraite
olive [ˈɔlɪv] *n* (*fruit*) olive *f*; (*tree*) olivier *m* ▷ *adj* (*also*: **olive-green**) (vert) olive *inv*
olive oil *n* huile *f* d'olive
Olympic [əuˈlɪmpɪk] *adj* olympique; **the ~ Games, the ~s** les Jeux *mpl* olympiques
omelette, omelet [ˈɔmlɪt] *n* omelette *f*; **ham/cheese omelet(te)** omelette au jambon/fromage
omen [ˈəumən] *n* présage *m*
ominous [ˈɔmɪnəs] *adj* menaçant(e), inquiétant(e); (*event*) de mauvais augure
omit [əuˈmɪt] *vt* omettre; **to ~ to do sth** négliger de faire qch
on [ɔn] *prep* **1** (*indicating position*) sur; **on the table** sur la table; **on the wall** sur le *or* au mur; **on the left** à gauche; **I haven't any money on me** je n'ai pas d'argent sur moi
2 (*indicating means, method, condition etc*): **on foot** à pied; **on the train/plane** (*be*) dans le train/l'avion; (*go*) en train/avion; **on the telephone/radio/television** au téléphone/à la radio/à la télévision; **to be on drugs** se droguer; **on holiday** (*Brit*): **on vacation** (*US*) en vacances; **on the continent** sur le continent
3 (*referring to time*): **on Friday** vendredi; **on Fridays** le vendredi; **on June 20th** le 20 juin; **a week on Friday** vendredi en huit; **on arrival** à l'arrivée; **on seeing this** en voyant cela
4 (*about, concerning*) sur, de; **a book on Balzac/physics** un livre sur Balzac/de physique
5 (*at the expense of*): **this round is on me** c'est ma tournée
▷ *adv* **1** (*referring to dress*): **to have one's coat on** avoir (mis) son manteau; **to put one's coat on** mettre son manteau; **what's she got on?** qu'est-ce qu'elle porte?
2 (*referring to covering*): **screw the lid on tightly** vissez bien le couvercle
3 (*further, continuously*): **to walk** *etc* **on** continuer à marcher *etc*; **on and off** de temps à autre; **from that day on** depuis ce jour
▷ *adj* **1** (*in operation: machine*) en marche; (: *radio, TV, light*) allumé(e); (: *tap, gas*) ouvert(e); (: *brakes*) mis(e); **is the meeting still on?** (*not cancelled*) est-ce que la réunion a bien lieu?; **it was well on in the evening** c'était tard dans la soirée; **when is this film on?** quand passe ce film?
2 (*inf*): **that's not on!** (*not acceptable*) cela ne se fait pas!; (*not possible*) pas question!
once [wʌns] *adv* une fois; (*formerly*) autrefois

▷ *conj* une fois que + *sub*; **~ he had left/it was done** une fois qu'il fut parti/ que ce fut terminé; **at ~** tout de suite, immédiatement; (*simultaneously*) à la fois; **all at ~** (*adv*) tout d'un coup; **~ a week** une fois par semaine; **~ more** encore une fois; **I knew him ~** je l'ai connu autrefois; **~ and for all** une fois pour toutes; **~ upon a time there was …** il y avait une fois …, il était une fois …

oncoming ['ɔnkʌmɪŋ] *adj* (*traffic*) venant en sens inverse

one [wʌn] *num* un(e); **~ hundred and fifty** cent cinquante; **~ by ~** un(e) à *or* par un(e); **~ day** un jour

▷ *adj* **1** (*sole*) seul(e), unique; **the ~ book which** l'unique *or* le seul livre qui; **the ~ man who** le seul (homme) qui

2 (*same*) même; **they came in the ~ car** ils sont venus dans la même voiture

▷ *pron* **1**: **this ~** celui-ci (celle-ci); **that ~** celui-là (celle-là); **I've already got ~/a red ~** j'en ai déjà un(e)/un(e) rouge; **which ~ do you want?** lequel voulez-vous?

2: **another ~** l'un(e) l'autre; **to look at ~ another** se regarder

3 (*impersonal*) on; **~ never knows** on ne sait jamais; **to cut ~'s finger** se couper le doigt; **~ needs to eat** il faut manger

4 (*phrases*): **to be ~ up on sb** avoir l'avantage sur qn; **to be at ~ (with sb)** être d'accord (avec qn)

one-day excursion ['wʌndeɪ-] *n* (US) billet *m* d'aller-retour (valable pour la journée)

one-man ['wʌn'mæn] *adj* (*business*) dirigé(e) *etc* par un seul homme

one-man band *n* homme-orchestre *m*

one-off ['wʌn'ɔf] *n* (*Brit inf*) exemplaire *m* unique ▷ *adj* unique

oneself [wʌn'sɛlf] *pron* se; (*after prep, also emphatic*) soi-même; **to hurt ~** se faire mal; **to keep sth for ~** garder qch pour soi; **to talk to ~** se parler à soi-même; **by ~** tout seul

one-shot [wʌn'ʃɔt] (US) *n* = **one-off**

one-sided [wʌn'saɪdɪd] *adj* (*argument, decision*) unilatéral(e); (*judgment, account*) partial(e); (*contest*) inégal(e)

one-to-one ['wʌntəwʌn] *adj* (*relationship*) univoque

one-way ['wʌnweɪ] *adj* (*street, traffic*) à sens unique

ongoing ['ɔngəʊɪŋ] *adj* en cours; (*relationship*) suivi(e)

onion ['ʌnjən] *n* oignon *m*

on-line ['ɔnlaɪn] *adj* (*Comput*) en ligne; (: *switched on*) connecté(e)

onlooker ['ɔnlukə'] *n* spectateur(-trice)

only ['əʊnlɪ] *adv* seulement ▷ *adj* seul(e), unique ▷ *conj* seulement, mais; **an ~ child** un enfant unique; **not ~ … but also** non seulement … mais aussi; **I ~ took one** j'en ai seulement pris un, je n'en ai pris qu'un; **I saw her ~ yesterday** je l'ai vue hier encore; **I'd be ~ too pleased to help** je ne serais que trop content de vous aider;

I would come, ~ I'm very busy je viendrais bien mais j'ai beaucoup à faire

on-screen [ɔn'skriːn] *adj* à l'écran

onset ['ɔnsɛt] *n* début *m*; (*of winter, old age*) approche *f*

onshore ['ɔnʃɔː'] *adj* (*wind*) du large

onslaught ['ɔnslɔːt] *n* attaque *f*, assaut *m*

onto ['ɔntu] *prep* = **on to**

onward ['ɔnwəd], **onwards** ['ɔnwədz] *adv* (*move*) en avant; **from that time ~s** à partir de ce moment

oops [ups] *excl* houp!; **~-a-daisy!** houp-là!

ooze [uːz] *vi* suinter

opaque [əʊ'peɪk] *adj* opaque

OPEC ['əʊpɛk] *n abbr* (= *Organization of Petroleum-Exporting Countries*) OPEP *f*

open ['əʊpn] *adj* ouvert(e); (*car*) découvert(e); (*road, view*) dégagé(e); (*meeting*) public(-ique); (*admiration*) manifeste; (*question*) non résolu(e); (*enemy*) déclaré(e) ▷ *vt* ouvrir ▷ *vi* (*flower, eyes, door, debate*) s'ouvrir; (*shop, bank, museum*) ouvrir; (*book etc: commence*) commencer, débuter; **is it ~ to public?** est-ce ouvert au public?; **what time do you ~?** à quelle heure ouvrez-vous?; **in the ~ (air)** en plein air; **the ~ sea** le large; **~ ground** (*among trees*) clairière *f*; (*waste ground*) terrain *m* vague; **to have an ~ mind (on sth)** avoir l'esprit ouvert (sur qch)

▶ **open on to** *vt fus* (*room, door*) donner sur

▶ **open out** *vt* ouvrir ▷ *vi* s'ouvrir

▶ **open up** *vt* ouvrir; (*blocked road*) dégager ▷ *vi* s'ouvrir

open-air [əʊpn'ɛə'] *adj* en plein air

opening ['əʊpnɪŋ] *n* ouverture *f*; (*opportunity*) occasion *f*; (*work*) débouché *m*; (*job*) poste vacant

opening hours *npl* heures *fpl* d'ouverture

open learning *n* enseignement universitaire à la carte, notamment par correspondance; (*distance learning*) télé-enseignement *m*

openly ['əʊpnlɪ] *adv* ouvertement

open-minded [əʊpn'maɪndɪd] *adj* à l'esprit ouvert

open-necked ['əʊpnnɛkt] *adj* à col ouvert

open-plan ['əʊpn'plæn] *adj* sans cloisons

Open University *n* (*Brit*) cours universitaires par correspondance

opera ['ɔpərə] *n* opéra *m*

opera house *n* opéra *m*

opera singer *n* chanteur(-euse) d'opéra

operate ['ɔpəreɪt] *vt* (*machine*) faire marcher, faire fonctionner; (*system*) pratiquer ▷ *vi* fonctionner; (*drug*) faire effet; **to ~ on sb (for)** (*Med*) opérer qn (de)

operatic [ɔpə'rætɪk] *adj* d'opéra

operating ['ɔpəreɪtɪŋ] *adj* (*Comm: costs, profit*) d'exploitation; (*Med*): **~ table** table *f* d'opération

operating room *n* (US: *Med*) salle *f* d'opération

operating theatre *n* (*Brit: Med*) salle *f* d'opération

operation [ɔpə'reɪʃən] *n* opération *f*; (*of machine*) fonctionnement *m*; **to have an ~ (for)** se faire opérer (de); **to be in ~** (*machine*) être en service;

(system) être en vigueur
operational [ɔpəˈreɪʃənl] adj opérationnel(le); (ready for use) en état de marche; **when the service is fully ~** lorsque le service fonctionnera pleinement
operative [ˈɔpərətɪv] adj (measure) en vigueur ▷ n (in factory) ouvrier(-ière); **the ~ word** le mot clef
operator [ˈɔpəreɪtəʳ] n (of machine) opérateur(-trice); (Tel) téléphoniste m/f
opinion [əˈpɪnjən] n opinion f, avis m; **in my ~** à mon avis; **to seek a second ~** demander un deuxième avis
opinionated [əˈpɪnjəneɪtɪd] adj aux idées bien arrêtées
opinion poll n sondage m d'opinion
opponent [əˈpəunənt] n adversaire m/f
opportunity [ɔpəˈtjuːnɪtɪ] n occasion f; **to take the ~ to do** or **of doing** profiter de l'occasion pour faire
oppose [əˈpəuz] vt s'opposer à; **to be ~d to sth** être opposé(e) à qch; **as ~d to** par opposition à
opposing [əˈpəuzɪŋ] adj (side) opposé(e)
opposite [ˈɔpəzɪt] adj opposé(e); (house etc) d'en face ▷ adv en face ▷ prep en face de ▷ n opposé m, contraire m; (of word) contraire; **"see ~ page"** "voir ci-contre"
opposition [ɔpəˈzɪʃən] n opposition f
oppress [əˈprɛs] vt opprimer
oppressive [əˈprɛsɪv] adj oppressif(-ive)
opt [ɔpt] vi: **to ~ for** opter pour; **to ~ to do** choisir de faire
 ▶ **opt out** vi (school, hospital) devenir autonome; (health service) devenir privé(e); **to ~ out of** choisir de ne pas participer à or de ne pas faire
optical [ˈɔptɪkl] adj optique; (instrument) d'optique
optical character reader n lecteur m optique
optical character recognition n lecture f optique
optician [ɔpˈtɪʃən] n opticien(ne)
optimism [ˈɔptɪmɪzəm] n optimisme m
optimist [ˈɔptɪmɪst] n optimiste m/f
optimistic [ɔptɪˈmɪstɪk] adj optimiste
optimum [ˈɔptɪməm] adj optimum
option [ˈɔpʃən] n choix m, option f; (Scol) matière f à option; (Comm) option; **to keep one's ~s open** (fig) ne pas s'engager; **I have no ~** je n'ai pas le choix
optional [ˈɔpʃnl] adj facultatif(-ive); (Comm) en option; **~ extras** accessoires mpl en option, options fpl
or [ɔːʳ] conj ou; (with negative): **he hasn't seen or heard anything** il n'a rien vu ni entendu; **or else** sinon; ou bien
oral [ˈɔːrəl] adj oral(e) ▷ n oral m
orange [ˈɔrɪndʒ] n (fruit) orange f ▷ adj orange inv
orange juice n jus m d'orange
orbit [ˈɔːbɪt] n orbite f ▷ vt graviter autour de; **to be in/go into ~ (round)** être/entrer en orbite (autour de)
orchard [ˈɔːtʃəd] n verger m; **apple ~** verger de pommiers

orchestra [ˈɔːkɪstrə] n orchestre m; (US: seating) (fauteuils mpl d')orchestre
orchid [ˈɔːkɪd] n orchidée f
ordain [ɔːˈdeɪn] vt (Rel) ordonner; (decide) décréter
ordeal [ɔːˈdiːl] n épreuve f
order [ˈɔːdəʳ] n ordre m; (Comm) commande f ▷ vt ordonner; (Comm) commander; **in ~** en ordre; (of document) en règle; **out of ~** (not in correct order) en désordre; (machine) hors service; (telephone) en dérangement; **a machine in working ~** une machine en état de marche; **in ~ of size** par ordre de grandeur; **in ~ to do/that** pour faire/que + sub; **to place an ~ for sth with sb** commander qch auprès de qn, passer commande de qch à qn; **could I ~ now, please?** je peux commander, s'il vous plaît?; **to be on ~** être en commande; **made to ~** fait sur commande; **to be under ~s to do sth** avoir ordre de faire qch; **a point of ~** un point de procédure; **to the ~ of** (Banking) à l'ordre de; **to ~ sb to do** ordonner à qn de faire
order form n bon m de commande
orderly [ˈɔːdəlɪ] n (Mil) ordonnance f; (Med) garçon m de salle ▷ adj (room) en ordre; (mind) méthodique; (person) qui a de l'ordre
ordinary [ˈɔːdnrɪ] adj ordinaire, normal(e); (pej) ordinaire, quelconque; **out of the ~** exceptionnel(le)
Ordnance Survey map n (Brit) ≈ carte f d'État-major
ore [ɔːʳ] n minerai m
oregano [ɔrɪˈgɑːnəu] n origan m
organ [ˈɔːgən] n organe m; (Mus) orgue m, orgues fpl
organic [ɔːˈgænɪk] adj organique; (crops etc) biologique, naturel(le)
organism [ˈɔːgənɪzəm] n organisme m
organization [ɔːgənaɪˈzeɪʃən] n organisation f
organize [ˈɔːgənaɪz] vt organiser; **to get ~d** s'organiser
organized [ˈɔːgənaɪzd] adj (planned) organisé(e); (efficient) bien organisé
organizer [ˈɔːgənaɪzəʳ] n organisateur(-trice)
orgasm [ˈɔːgæzəm] n orgasme m
orgy [ˈɔːdʒɪ] n orgie f
Orient [ˈɔːrɪənt] n: **the ~** l'Orient m
oriental [ɔːrɪˈɛntl] adj oriental(e) ▷ n Oriental(e)
orientation [ɔːrɪɛnˈteɪʃən] n (attitudes) tendance f; (in job) orientation f; (of building) orientation, exposition f
origin [ˈɔrɪdʒɪn] n origine f; **country of ~** pays m d'origine
original [əˈrɪdʒɪnl] adj original(e); (earliest) originel(le) ▷ n original m
originally [əˈrɪdʒɪnəlɪ] adv (at first) à l'origine
originate [əˈrɪdʒɪneɪt] vi: **to ~ from** être originaire de; (suggestion) provenir de; **to ~ in** (custom) prendre naissance dans, avoir son origine dans
Orkney [ˈɔːknɪ] n (also: **the Orkneys, the Orkney Islands**) les Orcades fpl
ornament [ˈɔːnəmənt] n ornement m; (trinket)

bibelot *m*

ornamental [ɔːnəˈmɛntl] *adj* décoratif(-ive);
  (*garden*) d'agrément

ornate [ɔːˈneɪt] *adj* très orné(e)

orphan [ˈɔːfn] *n* orphelin(e) ▷ *vt*: **to be ~ed**
  devenir orphelin

orthodox [ˈɔːθədɔks] *adj* orthodoxe

orthopaedic, (*US*) **orthopedic** [ɔːθəˈpiːdɪk] *adj*
  orthopédique

ostensibly [ɔsˈtɛnsɪblɪ] *adv* en apparence

ostentatious [ɔstɛnˈteɪʃəs] *adj*
  prétentieux(-euse); ostentatoire

osteopath [ˈɔstɪəpæθ] *n* ostéopathe *m/f*

ostracize [ˈɔstrəsaɪz] *vt* frapper d'ostracisme

ostrich [ˈɔstrɪtʃ] *n* autruche *f*

other [ˈʌðəʳ] *adj* autre ▷ *pron*: **the ~ (one)** l'autre;
  ~s (*other people*) d'autres ▷ *adv*: **~ than** autrement
  que; à part; **some actor or ~** un certain acteur, je
  ne sais quel acteur; **somebody or ~** quelqu'un;
  some ~ people have still to arrive on attend
  encore quelques personnes; **the ~ day** l'autre
  jour; **the car was none ~ than John's** la voiture
  n'était autre que celle de John

otherwise [ˈʌðəwaɪz] *adv, conj* autrement; **an ~
  good piece of work** par ailleurs, un beau travail

Ottawa [ˈɔtəwə] *n* Ottawa

otter [ˈɔtəʳ] *n* loutre *f*

ouch [autʃ] *excl* aïe!

ought (*pt ~*) [ɔːt] *aux vb*: **I ~ to do it** je devrais le
  faire, il faudrait que je le fasse; **this ~ to have
  been corrected** cela aurait dû être corrigé; **he ~
  to win** (*probability*) il devrait gagner; **you ~ to go
  and see it** vous devriez aller le voir

ounce [auns] *n* once *f* (*28.35g; 16 in a pound*)

our [ˈauəʳ] *adj* notre, nos *pl*; *see also* **my**

ours [auəz] *pron* le (la) nôtre, les nôtres; *see also*
  mine¹

ourselves [auəˈsɛlvz] *pron pl* (*reflexive, after
  preposition*) nous; (*emphatic*) nous-mêmes; **we did
  it (all) by ~** nous avons fait ça tout seuls; *see also*
  oneself

oust [aust] *vt* évincer

out [aut] *adv* dehors; (*published, not at home etc*)
  sorti(e); (*light, fire*) éteint(e); (*on strike*) en grève
  ▷ *vt*: **to ~ sb** révéler l'homosexualité de qn; **~
  here** ici; **~ there** là-bas; **he's ~** (*absent*) il est
  sorti; (*unconscious*) il est sans connaissance;
  to be ~ in one's calculations s'être trompé
  dans ses calculs; **to run/back** *etc* **~** sortir en
  courant/en reculant *etc*; **to be ~ and about**
  or (*US*) **around again** être de nouveau sur
  pied; **before the week was ~** avant la fin de
  la semaine; **the journey ~** l'aller *m*; **the boat
  was 10 km ~** le bateau était à 10 km du rivage;
  ~ loud (*adv*) à haute voix; **~ of** (*prep: outside*) en
  dehors de; (*because of: anger etc*) par; (*from among*):
  10 ~ of 10 10 sur 10; (*without*): **~ of petrol** sans
  essence, à court d'essence; **made ~ of wood** en
  or de bois; **~ of order** (*machine*) en panne; (*Tel:
  line*) en dérangement; **~ of stock** (*Comm: article*)
  épuisé(e); (*: shop*) en rupture de stock

out-and-out [ˈautəndaut] *adj* véritable

outback [ˈautbæk] *n* campagne isolée; (*in
  Australia*) intérieur *m*

outboard [ˈautbɔːd] *n*: **~ (motor)** (moteur *m*)
  hors-bord *m*

outbound [ˈautbaund] *adj*: **~ (from/for)** en
  partance (de/pour)

outbreak [ˈautbreɪk] *n* (*of violence*) éruption *f*,
  explosion *f*; (*of disease*) de nombreux cas; **the ~
  of war south of the border** la guerre qui s'est
  déclarée au sud de la frontière

outburst [ˈautbəːst] *n* explosion *f*, accès *m*

outcast [ˈautkɑːst] *n* exilé(e); (*socially*) paria *m*

outcome [ˈautkʌm] *n* issue *f*, résultat *m*

outcrop [ˈautkrɔp] *n* affleurement *m*

outcry [ˈautkraɪ] *n* tollé (général)

outdated [autˈdeɪtɪd] *adj* démodé(e)

outdo [autˈduː] *vt* (*irreg: like* **do**) surpasser

outdoor [autˈdɔːʳ] *adj* de *or* en plein air

outdoors [autˈdɔːz] *adv* dehors; au grand air

outer [ˈautəʳ] *adj* extérieur(e); **~ suburbs** grande
  banlieue

outer space *n* espace *m* cosmique

outfit [ˈautfɪt] *n* équipement *m*; (*clothes*) tenue *f*;
  (*inf: Comm*) organisation *f*, boîte *f*

outgoing [ˈautgəuɪŋ] *adj* (*president, tenant*)
  sortant(e); (*character*) ouvert(e), extraverti(e)

outgoings [ˈautgəuɪŋz] *npl* (*Brit: expenses*)
  dépenses *fpl*

outgrow [autˈgrəu] *vt* (*irreg: like* **grow**); (*clothes*)
  devenir trop grand(e) pour

outhouse [ˈauthaus] *n* appentis *m*, remise *f*

outing [ˈautɪŋ] *n* sortie *f*; excursion *f*

outlaw [ˈautlɔː] *n* hors-la-loi *m inv* ▷ *vt* (*person*)
  mettre hors la loi; (*practice*) proscrire

outlay [ˈautleɪ] *n* dépenses *fpl*; (*investment*) mise *f*
  de fonds

outlet [ˈautlɛt] *n* (*for liquid etc*) issue *f*, sortie *f*; (*for
  emotion*) exutoire *m*; (*for goods*) débouché *m*; (*also:
  retail outlet) point *m* de vente; (*US: Elec*) prise *f*
  de courant

outline [ˈautlaɪn] *n* (*shape*) contour *m*; (*summary*)
  esquisse *f*, grandes lignes ▷ *vt* (*fig: theory, plan*)
  exposer à grands traits

outlive [autˈlɪv] *vt* survivre à

outlook [ˈautluk] *n* perspective *f*; (*point of view*)
  attitude *f*

outlying [ˈautlaɪɪŋ] *adj* écarté(e)

outmoded [autˈməudɪd] *adj* démodé(e),
  dépassé(e)

outnumber [autˈnʌmbəʳ] *vt* surpasser en
  nombre

out-of-date [autəvˈdeɪt] *adj* (*passport, ticket*)
  périmé(e); (*theory, idea*) dépassé(e); (*custom*)
  désuet(-ète); (*clothes*) démodé(e)

out-of-doors [autəvˈdɔːz] *adv* = **outdoors**

out-of-the-way [ˈautəvðəˈweɪ] *adj* loin de tout;
  (*fig*) insolite

out-of-town [autəvˈtaun] *adj* (*shopping centre etc*)
  en périphérie

outpatient [ˈautpeɪʃənt] *n* malade *m/f* en
  consultation externe

outpost [ˈautpəust] *n* avant-poste *m*

output ['autput] n rendement m, production f;
(Comput) sortie f ▷ vt (Comput) sortir

outrage ['autreɪdʒ] n (anger) indignation f;
(violent act) atrocité f, acte m de violence; (scandal)
scandale m ▷ vt outrager

outrageous [aut'reɪdʒəs] adj atroce; (scandalous)
scandaleux(-euse)

outright adv [aut'raɪt] complètement; (deny,
refuse) catégoriquement; (ask) carrément;
(kill) sur le coup ▷ adj ['autraɪt] complet(-ète);
catégorique

outset ['autset] n début m

outside [aut'saɪd] n extérieur m ▷ adj
extérieur(e); (remote, unlikely): **an ~ chance**
une (très) faible chance ▷ adv (au) dehors,
à l'extérieur ▷ prep hors de, à l'extérieur
de; (in front of) devant; **at the ~** (fig) au plus
or maximum; **~ left/right** n (Football) ailier
gauche/droit

outside lane n (Aut: in Britain) voie f de droite; (: in
US, Europe) voie de gauche

outside line n (Tel) ligne extérieure

outsider [aut'saɪdə^r] n (in race etc) outsider m;
(stranger) étranger(-ère)

outsize ['autsaɪz] adj énorme; (clothes) grande
taille inv

outskirts ['autskə:ts] npl faubourgs mpl

outspoken [aut'spəukən] adj très franc
(franche)

outstanding [aut'stændɪŋ] adj remarquable,
exceptionnel(le); (unfinished: work, business)
en suspens, en souffrance; (debt) impayé(e);
(problem) non réglé(e); **your account is still ~**
vous n'avez pas encore tout remboursé

outstay [aut'steɪ] vt: **to ~ one's welcome** abuser
de l'hospitalité de son hôte

outstretched [aut'stretʃt] adj (hand) tendu(e);
(body) étendu(e)

outstrip [aut'strɪp] vt (also fig) dépasser

out-tray ['auttreɪ] n courrier m "départ"

outward ['autwəd] adj (sign, appearances)
extérieur(e); (journey) (d')aller

outwards ['autwədz] adv (esp Brit) = **outward**

outweigh [aut'weɪ] vt l'emporter sur

outwit [aut'wɪt] vt se montrer plus malin que

oval ['əuvl] adj, n ovale m

Oval Office n (US: Pol) voir article

ovary ['əuvərɪ] n ovaire m

oven ['ʌvn] n four m

oven glove n gant m de cuisine

ovenproof ['ʌvnpru:f] adj allant au four

oven-ready ['ʌvnredɪ] adj prêt(e) à cuire

over ['əuvə^r] adv (par-)dessus; (excessively) trop
▷ adj (or adv) (finished) fini(e), terminé(e); (too
much) en plus ▷ prep sur; par-dessus; (above)
au-dessus de; (on the other side of) de l'autre côté
de; (more than) plus de; (during) pendant; (about,
concerning): **they fell out ~ money/her** ils se
sont brouillés pour des questions d'argent/à
cause d'elle; **~ here** ici; **~ there** là-bas; **all ~**
(everywhere) partout; (finished) fini(e); **~ and ~**
(again) à plusieurs reprises; **~ and above** en

plus de; **to ask sb ~** inviter qn (à passer); **to go
~ to sb's** passer chez qn; **to fall ~** tomber; **to
turn sth ~** retourner qch; **now ~ to our Paris
correspondent** nous passons l'antenne à notre
correspondant à Paris; **the world ~** dans le
monde entier; **she's not ~ intelligent** (Brit) elle
n'est pas particulièrement intelligente

overall ['əuvərɔ:l] adj (length) total(e); (study,
impression) d'ensemble ▷ n (Brit) blouse f ▷ adv
[əuvər'ɔ:l] dans l'ensemble, en général; **overalls**
npl (boiler suit) bleus mpl (de travail)

overawe [əuvər'ɔ:] vt impressionner

overbalance [əuvə'bæləns] vi basculer

overboard ['əuvəbɔ:d] adv (Naut) par-dessus
bord; **to go ~ for sth** (fig) s'emballer (pour qch)

overbook [əuvə'buk] vi faire du surbooking

overcame [əuvə'keɪm] pt of **overcome**

overcast ['əuvəkɑ:st] adj couvert(e)

overcharge [əuvə'tʃɑ:dʒ] vt: **to ~ sb for sth** faire
payer qch trop cher à qn

overcoat ['əuvəkəut] n pardessus m

overcome [əuvə'kʌm] vt (irreg: like **come**);
(defeat) triompher de; (difficulty) surmonter
▷ adj (emotionally) bouleversé(e); **~ with grief**
accablé(e) de douleur

overcrowded [əuvə'kraudɪd] adj bondé(e); (city,
country) surpeuplé(e)

overdo [əuvə'du:] vt (irreg: like **do**) exagérer;
(overcook) trop cuire; **to ~ it, to ~ things** (work too
hard) en faire trop, se surmener

overdone [əuvə'dʌn] adj (vegetables, steak) trop
cuit(e)

overdose ['əuvədəus] n dose excessive

overdraft ['əuvədrɑ:ft] n découvert m

overdrawn [əuvə'drɔ:n] adj (account) à découvert

overdue [əuvə'dju:] adj en retard; (bill)
impayé(e); (change) qui tarde; **that change was
long ~** ce changement n'avait que trop tardé

overestimate [əuvər'estɪmeɪt] vt surestimer

overflow vi [əuvə'fləu] déborder ▷ n ['əuvəfləu]
trop-plein m; (also: **overflow pipe**) tuyau m
d'écoulement, trop-plein m

overgrown [əuvə'grəun] adj (garden) envahi(e)
par la végétation; **he's just an ~ schoolboy** (fig)
c'est un écolier attardé

overhaul vt [əuvə'hɔ:l] réviser ▷ n ['əuvəhɔ:l]
révision f

overhead adv [əuvə'hed] au-dessus ▷ adj, n
['əuvəhed] ▷ adj aérien(ne); (lighting) vertical(e)
▷ n (US) = **overheads**

overhead projector n rétroprojecteur m

overheads ['əuvəhedz] npl (Brit) frais généraux

overhear [əuvə'hɪə^r] vt (irreg: like **hear**) entendre
(par hasard)

overheat [əuvə'hi:t] vi devenir surchauffé(e);
(engine) chauffer

overjoyed [əuvə'dʒɔɪd] adj ravi(e), enchanté(e)

overland ['əuvəlænd] adj, adv par voie de terre

overlap vi [əuvə'læp] se chevaucher ▷ n
['əuvəlæp] chevauchement m

overleaf [əuvə'li:f] adv au verso

overload [əuvə'ləud] vt surcharger

overlook [əuvə'luk] *vt* (*have view of*) donner sur; (*miss*) oublier, négliger; (*forgive*) fermer les yeux sur

overnight *adv* [əuvə'naɪt] (*happen*) durant la nuit; (*fig*) soudain ▷ *adj* ['əuvənaɪt] d'une (*or* de) nuit; soudain(e); **to stay ~ (with sb)** passer la nuit (chez qn); **he stayed there ~** il y a passé la nuit; **if you travel ~ ...** si tu fais le voyage de nuit ...; **he'll be away ~** il ne rentrera pas ce soir

overnight bag *n* nécessaire *m* de voyage

overpass ['əuvəpɑ:s] *n* (*US: for cars*) pont autoroutier; (*: for pedestrians*) passerelle *f*, pont *m*

overpower [əuvə'pauəʳ] *vt* vaincre; (*fig*) accabler

overpowering [əuvə'pauərɪŋ] *adj* irrésistible; (*heat, stench*) suffocant(e)

overrate [əuvə'reɪt] *vt* surestimer

overreact [əuvəri:'ækt] *vi* réagir de façon excessive

override [əuvə'raɪd] *vt* (*irreg: like* **ride**); (*order, objection*) passer outre à; (*decision*) annuler

overriding [əuvə'raɪdɪŋ] *adj* prépondérant(e)

overrule [əuvə'ru:l] *vt* (*decision*) annuler; (*claim*) rejeter; (*person*) rejeter l'avis de

overrun [əuvə'rʌn] *vt* (*irreg: like* **run**); (*Mil: country etc*) occuper; (*time limit etc*) dépasser ▷ *vi* dépasser le temps imparti; **the town is ~ with tourists** la ville est envahie de touristes

overseas [əuvə'si:z] *adv* outre-mer; (*abroad*) à l'étranger ▷ *adj* (*trade*) extérieur(e); (*visitor*) étranger(-ère)

oversee [əuvə'si:] *vt* (*irreg: like* **see**) surveiller

overshadow [əuvə'ʃædəu] *vt* (*fig*) éclipser

oversight ['əuvəsaɪt] *n* omission *f*, oubli *m*; **due to an ~** par suite d'une inadvertance

oversleep [əuvə'sli:p] *vi* (*irreg: like* **sleep**) se réveiller (trop) tard

overspend [əuvə'spɛnd] *vi* (*irreg: like* **spend**) dépenser de trop; **we have overspent by 5,000 dollars** nous avons dépassé notre budget de 5 000 dollars, nous avons dépensé 5 000 dollars de trop

overstep [əuvə'stɛp] *vt*: **to ~ the mark** dépasser la mesure

overt [əu'və:t] *adj* non dissimulé(e)

overtake [əuvə'teɪk] *vt* (*irreg: like* **take**) dépasser; (*Brit: Aut*) dépasser, doubler

overthrow [əuvə'θrəu] *vt* (*irreg: like* **throw**); (*government*) renverser

overtime ['əuvətaɪm] *n* heures *fpl* supplémentaires; **to do** *or* **work ~** faire des heures supplémentaires

overtone ['əuvətəun] *n* (*also:* **overtones**) note *f*, sous-entendus *mpl*

overtook [əuvə'tuk] *pt of* **overtake**

overture ['əuvətʃuəʳ] *n* (*Mus, fig*) ouverture *f*

overturn [əuvə'tə:n] *vt* renverser; (*decision, plan*) annuler ▷ *vi* se retourner

overweight [əuvə'weɪt] *adj* (*person*) trop gros(se); (*luggage*) trop lourd(e)

overwhelm [əuvə'wɛlm] *vt* (*subj: emotion*) accabler, submerger; (*enemy, opponent*) écraser

overwhelming [əuvə'wɛlmɪŋ] *adj* (*victory, defeat*) écrasant(e); (*desire*) irrésistible; **one's ~ impression is of heat** on a une impression dominante de chaleur

overwrought [əuvə'rɔ:t] *adj* excédé(e)

owe [əu] *vt* devoir; **to ~ sb sth, to ~ sth to sb** devoir qch à qn; **how much do I ~ you?** combien est-ce que je vous dois?

owing to ['əuɪŋtu:] *prep* à cause de, en raison de

owl [aul] *n* hibou *m*

own [əun] *vt* posséder ▷ *vi* (*Brit*): **to ~ to sth** reconnaître or avouer qch; **to ~ to having done sth** avouer avoir fait qch ▷ *adj* propre; **a room of my ~** une chambre à moi, ma propre chambre; **can I have it for my (very) ~?** puis-je l'avoir pour moi (tout) seul?; **to get one's ~ back** prendre sa revanche; **on one's ~** tout(e) seul(e); **to come into one's ~** trouver sa voie; trouver sa justification

▶ **own up** *vi* avouer

owner ['əunəʳ] *n* propriétaire *m/f*

ownership ['əunəʃɪp] *n* possession *f*; **it's under new ~** (*shop etc*) il y a eu un changement de propriétaire

ox (*pl* **oxen**) [ɔks, 'ɔksn] *n* bœuf *m*

Oxbridge ['ɔksbrɪdʒ] *n* (*Brit*) *les universités d'Oxford et de Cambridge*; *voir article*

oxen ['ɔksən] *npl of* **ox**

oxtail ['ɔksteɪl] *n*: **~ soup** soupe *f* à la queue de bœuf

oxygen ['ɔksɪdʒən] *n* oxygène *m*

oyster ['ɔɪstəʳ] *n* huître *f*

oz. *abbr* = **ounce; ounces**

ozone ['əuzəun] *n* ozone *m*

ozone friendly ['əuzəunfrɛndlɪ] *adj* qui n'attaque pas or qui préserve la couche d'ozone

ozone hole *n* trou *m* d'ozone

ozone layer *n* couche *f* d'ozone

Pp

p *abbr* (= *page*) p; (*Brit*) = **penny; pence**
P.A. *n abbr* = **personal assistant; public address
system** ▷ *abbr* (*US*) = **Pennsylvania**
pa [pɑ:] *n* (*inf*) papa *m*
p.a. *abbr* = **per annum**
pace [peɪs] *n* pas *m*; (*speed*) allure *f*; vitesse *f* ▷ *vi*:
to ~ up and down faire les cent pas; **to keep
~ with** aller à la même vitesse que; (*events*) se
tenir au courant de; **to set the ~** (*running*) donner
l'allure; (*fig*) donner le ton; **to put sb through
his ~s** (*fig*) mettre qn à l'épreuve
pacemaker ['peɪsmeɪkər] *n* (*Med*) stimulateur
m cardiaque; (*Sport*: *also*: **pacesetter**)
meneur(-euse) de train
Pacific [pə'sɪfɪk] *n*: **the ~ (Ocean)** le Pacifique,
l'océan *m* Pacifique
pacifier ['pæsɪfaɪər] *n* (*US*: *dummy*) tétine *f*
pack [pæk] *n* paquet *m*; (*bundle*) ballot *m*; (*of
hounds*) meute *f*; (*of thieves, wolves etc*) bande *f*; (*of
cards*) jeu *m*; (*US*: *of cigarettes*) paquet; (*back pack*)
sac *m* à dos ▷ *vt* (*goods*) empaqueter, emballer;
(*in suitcase etc*) emballer; (*box*) remplir; (*cram*)
entasser; (*press down*) tasser; damer; (*Comput*)
grouper, tasser ▷ *vi*: **to ~ into** (*room, stadium*) s'entasser
dans; **to send sb ~ing** (*inf*) envoyer promener qn
▶ **pack in** (*Brit inf*) *vi* (*machine*) tomber en panne
▷ *vt* (*boyfriend*) plaquer; **~ it in!** laisse tomber!
▶ **pack off** *vt*: **to ~ sb off to** expédier qn à
▶ **pack up** *vi* (*Brit inf*: *machine*) tomber en panne;
(: *person*) se tirer ▷ *vt* (*belongings*) ranger; (*goods,
presents*) empaqueter, emballer
package ['pækɪdʒ] *n* paquet *m*; (*of goods*)
emballage *m*, conditionnement *m*; (*also*:
package deal: *agreement*) marché global;
(: *purchase*) forfait *m*; (*Comput*) progiciel *m* ▷ *vt*
(*goods*) conditionner
package holiday *n* (*Brit*) vacances organisées
package tour *n* voyage organisé
packaging ['pækɪdʒɪŋ] *n* (*wrapping materials*)
emballage *m*; (*of goods*) conditionnement *m*
packed [pækt] *adj* (*crowded*) bondé(e)
packed lunch (*Brit*) *n* repas froid
packet ['pækɪt] *n* paquet *m*
packing ['pækɪŋ] *n* emballage *m*
packing case *n* caisse *f* (d'emballage)
pact [pækt] *n* pacte *m*, traité *m*

pad [pæd] *n* bloc(-notes *m*) *m*; (*to prevent friction*)
tampon *m*; (*for inking*) tampon *m* encreur; (*inf*:
flat) piaule *f* ▷ *vt* rembourrer ▷ *vi*: **to ~ in/about**
etc entrer/aller et venir *etc* à pas feutrés
padded ['pædɪd] *adj* (*jacket*) matelassé(e); (*bra*)
rembourré(e); **~ cell** cellule capitonnée
padding ['pædɪŋ] *n* rembourrage *m*; (*fig*)
délayage *m*
paddle ['pædl] *n* (*oar*) pagaie *f*; (*US*: *for table tennis*)
raquette *f* de ping-pong ▷ *vi* (*with feet*) barboter,
faire trempette ▷ *vt*: **to ~ a canoe** *etc* pagayer
paddling pool ['pædlɪŋ-] *n* petit bassin
paddock ['pædək] *n* enclos *m*; (*Racing*) paddock *m*
padlock ['pædlɔk] *n* cadenas *m* ▷ *vt* cadenasser
paediatrics, (*US*) **pediatrics** [pi:dɪ'ætrɪks] *n*
pédiatrie *f*
paedophile, (*US*) **pedophile** ['pi:dəufaɪl] *n*
pédophile *m*
pagan ['peɪgən] *adj*, *n* païen(ne)
page [peɪdʒ] *n* (*of book*) page *f*; (*also*: **page boy**)
groom *m*, chasseur *m*; (*at wedding*) garçon *m*
d'honneur ▷ *vt* (*in hotel etc*) (faire) appeler
pageant ['pædʒənt] *n* spectacle *m* historique;
grande cérémonie
pageantry ['pædʒəntrɪ] *n* apparat *m*, pompe *f*
pager ['peɪdʒər] *n* bip *m* (*inf*), Alphapage® *m*
paid [peɪd] *pt*, *pp* *of* **pay** ▷ *adj* (*work, official*)
rémunéré(e); (*holiday*) payé(e); **to put ~ to** (*Brit*)
mettre fin à, mettre par terre
pail [peɪl] *n* seau *m*
pain [peɪn] *n* douleur *f*; (*inf*: *nuisance*) plaie *f*; **to
be in ~** souffrir, avoir mal; **to have a ~ in** avoir
mal *or* une douleur à *or* dans; **to take ~s to do**
se donner du mal pour faire; **on ~ of death** sous
peine de mort
pained [peɪnd] *adj* peiné(e), chagrin(e)
painful ['peɪnful] *adj* douloureux(-euse);
(*difficult*) difficile, pénible
painfully ['peɪnfəlɪ] *adv* (*fig*: *very*) terriblement
painkiller ['peɪnkɪlər] *n* calmant *m*,
analgésique *m*
painless ['peɪnlɪs] *adj* indolore
painstaking ['peɪnzteɪkɪŋ] *adj* (*person*)
soigneux(-euse); (*work*) soigné(e)
paint [peɪnt] *n* peinture *f* ▷ *vt* peindre; (*fig*)
dépeindre; **to ~ the door blue** peindre la porte
en bleu; **to ~ in oils** faire de la peinture à l'huile

paintbrush ['peɪntbrʌʃ] n pinceau m
painter ['peɪntə^r] n peintre m
painting ['peɪntɪŋ] n peinture f; (picture)
tableau m
paintwork ['peɪntwə:k] n (Brit) peintures fpl; (: of
car) peinture f
pair [peə^r] n (of shoes, gloves etc) paire f; (of people)
couple m; (twosome) duo m; ~ **of scissors** (paire
de) ciseaux mpl; ~ **of trousers** pantalon m
  ▶ **pair off** vi se mettre par deux
pajamas [pə'dʒɑːməz] npl (US) pyjama(s) m(pl)
Pakistan [pɑːkɪ'stɑːn] n Pakistan m
Pakistani [pɑːkɪ'stɑːnɪ] adj pakistanais(e) ▷ n
Pakistanais(e)
pal [pæl] n (inf) copain (copine)
palace ['pæləs] n palais m
palatable ['pælɪtəbl] adj bon (bonne), agréable
au goût
palate ['pælɪt] n palais m (Anat)
pale [peɪl] adj pâle ▷ vi pâlir ▷ n: **to be beyond
the** ~ être au ban de la société; **to grow** or **turn**
~ (person) pâlir; ~ **blue** (adj) bleu pâle inv; **to** ~
into insignificance (beside) perdre beaucoup
d'importance (par rapport à)
Palestine ['pælɪstaɪn] n Palestine f
Palestinian [pælɪs'tɪnɪən] adj palestinien(ne)
▷ n Palestinien(ne)
palette ['pælɪt] n palette f
pall [pɔːl] n (of smoke) voile m ▷ vi: **to** ~ **(on)**
devenir lassant (pour)
pallet ['pælɪt] n (for goods) palette f
pallid ['pælɪd] adj blême
palm [pɑːm] n (Anat) paume f; (also: **palm tree**)
palmier m; (leaf, symbol) palme f ▷ vt: **to** ~ **sth off
on sb** (inf) refiler qch à qn
Palm Sunday n le dimanche des Rameaux
paltry ['pɔːltrɪ] adj dérisoire; piètre
pamper ['pæmpə^r] vt gâter, dorloter
pamphlet ['pæmflət] n brochure f; (political etc)
tract m
pan [pæn] n (also: **saucepan**) casserole f; (also:
frying pan) poêle f; (of lavatory) cuvette f ▷ vi
(Cine) faire un panoramique ▷ vt (inf: book, film)
éreinter; **to** ~ **for gold** laver du sable aurifère
pancake ['pænkeɪk] n crêpe f
panda ['pændə] n panda m
pandemonium [pændɪ'məunɪəm] n tohu-
bohu m
pander ['pændə^r] vi: **to** ~ **to** flatter bassement;
obéir servilement à
pane [peɪn] n carreau m (de fenêtre), vitre f
panel ['pænl] n (of wood, cloth etc) panneau m;
(Radio, TV) panel m, invités mpl; (for interview,
exams) jury m; (official: of experts) table ronde,
comité m
panelling, (US) **paneling** ['pænəlɪŋ] n boiseries
fpl
pang [pæŋ] n: ~s **of remorse** pincements
mpl de remords; ~s **of hunger/conscience**
tiraillements mpl d'estomac/de la conscience
panhandler ['pænhændlə^r] n (US inf)
mendiant(e)

panic ['pænɪk] n panique f, affolement m ▷ vi
s'affoler, paniquer
panicky ['pænɪkɪ] adj (person) qui panique or
s'affole facilement
panic-stricken ['pænɪkstrɪkən] adj affolé(e)
panorama [pænə'rɑːmə] n panorama m
pansy ['pænzɪ] n (Bot) pensée f; (inf) tapette f,
pédé m
pant [pænt] vi haleter
panther ['pænθə^r] n panthère f
panties ['pæntɪz] npl slip m, culotte f
pantihose ['pæntɪhəuz] n (US) collant m
pantomime ['pæntəmaɪm] n (Brit) spectacle m
de Noël
pantry ['pæntrɪ] n garde-manger m inv; (room)
office m
pants [pænts] n (Brit: woman's) culotte f, slip m;
(: man's) slip m, caleçon m; (US: trousers) pantalon m
pantyhose ['pæntɪhəuz] (US) npl collant m
paper ['peɪpə^r] n papier m; (also: **wallpaper**)
papier peint; (also: **newspaper**) journal m;
(academic essay) article m; (exam) épreuve écrite
▷ adj en or de papier ▷ vt tapisser (de papier
peint); **papers** npl (also: **identity papers**) papiers
mpl (d'identité); **a piece of** ~ (odd bit) un bout de
papier; (sheet) une feuille de papier; **to put sth
down on** ~ mettre qch par écrit
paperback ['peɪpəbæk] n livre broché or non
relié; (small) livre m de poche ▷ adj: ~ **edition**
édition brochée
paper bag n sac m en papier
paper clip n trombone m
paper handkerchief n, **paper hankie** (inf)
mouchoir m en papier
paper shop n (Brit) marchand m de journaux
paperweight ['peɪpəweɪt] n presse-papiers m inv
paperwork ['peɪpəwə:k] n papiers mpl; (pej)
paperasserie f
paprika ['pæprɪkə] n paprika m
par [pɑː^r] n pair m; (Golf) normale f du parcours;
on a ~ **with** à égalité avec, au même niveau
que; **at** ~ au pair; **above/below** ~ au-dessus/au-
dessous du pair; **to feel below** or **under** or **not
up to** ~ ne pas se sentir en forme
paracetamol [pærə'siːtəmɔl] (Brit) n
paracétamol m
parachute ['pærəʃuːt] n parachute m ▷ vi sauter
en parachute
parade [pə'reɪd] n défilé m; (inspection) revue f;
(street) boulevard m ▷ vt (fig) faire étalage de ▷ vi
défiler; **a fashion** ~ (Brit) un défilé de mode
paradise ['pærədaɪs] n paradis m
paradox ['pærədɔks] n paradoxe m
paradoxically [pærə'dɔksɪklɪ] adv
paradoxalement
paraffin ['pærəfɪn] n (Brit): ~ **(oil)** pétrole
(lampant); **liquid** ~ huile f de paraffine
paragon ['pærəgən] n parangon m
paragraph ['pærəgrɑːf] n paragraphe m; **to
begin a new** ~ aller à la ligne
parallel ['pærəlɛl] adj: ~ **(with** or **to)** parallèle (à);
(fig) analogue (à) ▷ n (line) parallèle f; (fig, Geo)

parallèle *m*

paralysed ['pærəlaɪzd] *adj* paralysé(e)

paralysis (*pl* **paralyses**) [pə'rælɪsɪs, -si:z] *n*
paralysie *f*

paralyze ['pærəlaɪz] *vt* paralyser

paramedic [pærə'mɛdɪk] *n* auxiliaire *m/f*
médical(e)

paramount ['pærəmaunt] *adj*: **of ~ importance**
de la plus haute *or* grande importance

paranoid ['pærənɔɪd] *adj* (*Psych*) paranoïaque;
(*neurotic*) paranoïde

paraphernalia [pærəfə'neɪlɪə] *n* attirail *m*,
affaires *fpl*

parasite ['pærəsaɪt] *n* parasite *m*

parasol ['pærəsɔl] *n* ombrelle *f*; (*at café etc*)
parasol *m*

paratrooper ['pærətru:pə'] *n* parachutiste *m*
(*soldat*)

parcel ['pɑ:sl] *n* paquet *m*, colis *m* ▷ *vt* (*also*:
parcel up) empaqueter
  ▶ **parcel out** *vt* répartir

parchment ['pɑ:tʃmənt] *n* parchemin *m*

pardon ['pɑ:dn] *n* pardon *m*; (*Law*) grâce *f* ▷ *vt*
pardonner à; (*Law*) gracier; **~! pardon!; ~ me!**
(*after burping etc*) excusez-moi!; **I beg your ~!** (*I'm
sorry*) pardon!, je suis désolé!; (**I beg your**) **~?**
(*US*): **~ me?** (*what did you say?*) pardon?

parent ['pɛərənt] *n* (*father*) père *m*; (*mother*) mère
f; **parents** *npl* parents *mpl*

parental [pə'rɛntl] *adj* parental(e), des parents

Paris ['pærɪs] *n* Paris

parish ['pærɪʃ] *n* paroisse *f*; (*Brit*: *civil*) ≈ commune
f ▷ *adj* paroissial(e)

Parisian [pə'rɪzɪən] *adj* parisien(ne), de Paris ▷ *n*
Parisien(ne)

park [pɑ:k] *n* parc *m*, jardin public ▷ *vt* garer ▷ *vi*
se garer; **can I ~ here?** est-ce que je peux me
garer ici?

parking ['pɑ:kɪŋ] *n* stationnement *m*; **"no ~"**
"stationnement interdit"

parking lot *n* (*US*) parking *m*, parc *m* de
stationnement

parking meter *n* parc(o)mètre *m*

parking ticket *n* P.-V. *m*

parkway ['pɑ:kweɪ] *n* (*US*) route *f* express (*en site
vert ou aménagé*)

parliament ['pɑ:ləmənt] *n* parlement *m*

parliamentary [pɑ:lə'mɛntərɪ] *adj*
parlementaire

parlour, (*US*) **parlor** ['pɑ:lə'] *n* salon *m*

Parmesan [pɑ:mɪ'zæn] *n* (*also*: **Parmesan
cheese**) Parmesan *m*

parochial [pə'rəukɪəl] *adj* paroissial(e); (*pej*) à
l'esprit de clocher

parole [pə'rəul] *n*: **on ~** en liberté conditionnelle

parrot ['pærət] *n* perroquet *m*

parry ['pærɪ] *vt* esquiver, parer à

parsley ['pɑ:slɪ] *n* persil *m*

parsnip ['pɑ:snɪp] *n* panais *m*

parson ['pɑ:sn] *n* ecclésiastique *m*; (*Church of
England*) pasteur *m*

part [pɑ:t] *n* partie *f*; (*of machine*) pièce *f*; (*Theat*)

rôle *m*; (*Mus*) voix *f*; partie; (*of serial*) épisode *m*;
(*US*: *in hair*) raie *f* ▷ *adj* partiel(le) ▷ *adv* = **partly**
▷ *vt* séparer ▷ *vi* (*people*) se séparer; (*crowd*)
s'ouvrir; (*roads*) se diviser; **to take ~** participer
à, prendre part à; **to take sb's ~** prendre le parti
de qn, prendre parti pour qn; **on his ~** de sa part;
for my ~ en ce qui me concerne; **for the most
~** en grande partie; dans la plupart des cas; **for
the better ~ of the day** pendant la plus grande
partie de la journée; **to be ~ and parcel of** faire
partie de; **in ~** en partie; **to take sth in good/
bad ~** prendre qch du bon/mauvais côté
  ▶ **part with** *vt fus* (*person*) se séparer de;
(*possessions*) se défaire de

part exchange *n* (*Brit*): **in ~** en reprise

partial ['pɑ:ʃl] *adj* (*incomplete*) partiel(le); (*unjust*)
partial(e); **to be ~ to** aimer, avoir un faible pour

participant [pɑ:'tɪsɪpənt] *n* (*in competition*,
campaign) participant(e)

participate [pɑ:'tɪsɪpeɪt] *vi*: **to ~ (in)** participer
(à), prendre part (à)

participation [pɑ:tɪsɪ'peɪʃən] *n* participation *f*

participle ['pɑ:tɪsɪpl] *n* participe *m*

particle ['pɑ:tɪkl] *n* particule *f*; (*of dust*) grain *m*

particular [pə'tɪkjulə'] *adj* (*specific*)
particulier(-ière); (*special*) particulier,
spécial(e); (*fussy*) difficile, exigeant(e); (*careful*)
méticuleux(-euse); **in ~** en particulier, surtout

particularly [pə'tɪkjuləlɪ] *adv* particulièrement;
(*in particular*) en particulier

particulars [pə'tɪkjuləz] *npl* détails *mpl*;
(*information*) renseignements *mpl*

parting ['pɑ:tɪŋ] *n* séparation *f*; (*Brit*: *in hair*) raie
f ▷ *adj* d'adieu; **his ~ shot was ...** il lança en
partant ....

partisan [pɑ:tɪ'zæn] *n* partisan(e) ▷ *adj*
partisan(e); de parti

partition [pɑ:'tɪʃən] *n* (*Pol*) partition *f*, division *f*;
(*wall*) cloison *f*

partly ['pɑ:tlɪ] *adv* en partie, partiellement

partner ['pɑ:tnə'] *n* (*Comm*) associé(e); (*Sport*)
partenaire *m/f*; (*spouse*) conjoint(e); (*lover*) ami(e);
(*at dance*) cavalier(-ière) ▷ *vt* être l'associé *or* le
partenaire *or* le cavalier de

partnership ['pɑ:tnəʃɪp] *n* association *f*; **to go
into ~ (with), form a ~ (with)** s'associer (avec)

partridge ['pɑ:trɪdʒ] *n* perdrix *f*

part-time ['pɑ:t'taɪm] *adj*, *adv* à mi-temps, à
temps partiel

party ['pɑ:tɪ] *n* (*Pol*) parti *m*; (*celebration*) fête *f*;
(: *formal*) réception *f*; (: *in evening*) soirée *f*; (*team*)
équipe *f*; (*group*) groupe *m*; (*Law*) partie *f*; **dinner
~ dîner *m*; **to give** *or* **throw a ~** donner une
réception; **we're having a ~ next Saturday**
nous organisons une soirée *or* réunion entre
amis samedi prochain; **it's for our son's
birthday ~** c'est pour la fête (*or* le goûter)
d'anniversaire de notre garçon; **to be a ~ to a
crime** être impliqué(e) dans un crime

party dress *n* robe habillée

pass [pɑ:s] *vt* (*time, object*) passer; (*place*) passer
devant; (*friend*) croiser; (*exam*) être reçu(e) à,

réussir; (candidate) admettre; (overtake) dépasser; (approve) approuver, accepter; (law) promulguer ▷ vi passer; (Scol) être reçu(e) or admis(e), réussir ▷ n (permit) laissez-passer m inv; (membership card) carte f d'accès or d'abonnement; (in mountains) col m; (Sport) passe f; (Scol: also: **pass mark**): **to get a ~** être reçu(e) (sans mention); **to ~ sb sth** passer qch à qn; **could you ~ the salt/oil, please?** pouvez-vous me passer le sel/l'huile, s'il vous plaît?; **she could ~ for 25** on lui donnerait 25 ans; **to ~ sth through a ring** etc (faire) passer qch dans un anneau etc; **could you ~ the vegetables round?** pourriez-vous faire passer les légumes?; **things have come to a pretty ~** (Brit) voilà où on en est!; **to make a ~ at sb** (inf) faire des avances à qn

▸ **pass away** vi mourir
▸ **pass by** vi passer ▷ vt (ignore) négliger
▸ **pass down** vt (customs, inheritance) transmettre
▸ **pass on** vi (die) s'éteindre, décéder ▷ vt (hand on): **to ~ on (to)** transmettre (à); (: illness) passer (à); (: price rises) répercuter (sur)
▸ **pass out** vi s'évanouir; (Brit Mil) sortir (d'une école militaire)
▸ **pass over** vt (ignore) passer sous silence
▸ **pass up** vt (opportunity) laisser passer

passable ['pɑːsəbl] adj (road) praticable; (work) acceptable
passage ['pæsɪdʒ] n (also: **passageway**) couloir m; (gen, in book) passage m; (by boat) traversée f
passbook ['pɑːsbuk] n livret m
passenger ['pæsɪndʒəʳ] n passager(-ère)
passer-by [pɑːsə'baɪ] n passant(e)
passing ['pɑːsɪŋ] adj (fig) passager(-ère); **in ~** en passant
passing place n (Aut) aire f de croisement
passion ['pæʃən] n passion f; **to have a ~ for sth** avoir la passion de qch
passionate ['pæʃənɪt] adj passionné(e)
passion fruit n fruit m de la passion
passive ['pæsɪv] adj (also Ling) passif(-ive)
passive smoking n tabagisme passif
Passover ['pɑːsəuvəʳ] n Pâque juive
passport ['pɑːspɔːt] n passeport m
passport control n contrôle m des passeports
passport office n bureau m de délivrance des passeports
password ['pɑːswɑːd] n mot m de passe
past [pɑːst] prep (in front of) devant; (further than) au delà de, plus loin que; après; (later than) après ▷ adv: **to run ~** passer en courant ▷ adj passé(e); (president etc) ancien(ne) ▷ n passé m; **he's ~ forty** il a dépassé la quarantaine, il a plus de or passé quarante ans; **ten/quarter ~ eight** huit heures dix/un or et quart; **it's ~ midnight** il est plus de minuit, il est passé minuit; **he ran ~ me** il m'a dépassé en courant, il a passé devant moi en courant; **for the ~ few/3 days** depuis quelques/3 jours; ces derniers/3 derniers jours; **in the ~** (gen) dans le temps, autrefois; (Ling) au passé; **I'm ~ caring** je ne m'en fais plus; **to be ~ it** (Brit inf: person) avoir passé l'âge

pasta ['pæstə] n pâtes fpl
paste [peɪst] n pâte f; (Culin: meat) pâté m (à tartiner); (: tomato) purée f, concentré m; (glue) colle f (de pâte); (jewellery) strass m ▷ vt coller
pastel ['pæstl] adj pastel inv ▷ n (Art: pencil) (crayon m) pastel m; (: drawing) (dessin m au) pastel; (colour) ton m pastel inv
pasteurized ['pæstəraɪzd] adj pasteurisé(e)
pastille ['pæstl] n pastille f
pastime ['pɑːstaɪm] n passe-temps m inv, distraction f
pastor ['pɑːstəʳ] n pasteur m
pastry ['peɪstrɪ] n pâte f; (cake) pâtisserie f
pasture ['pɑːstʃəʳ] n pâturage m
pasty[1] ['pæstɪ] petit pâté (en croûte)
pasty[2] ['peɪstɪ] adj pâteux(-euse); (complexion) terreux(-euse)
pat [pæt] vt donner une petite tape à; (dog) caresser ▷ n: **a ~ of butter** une noisette de beurre; **to give sb/o.s. a ~ on the back** (fig) congratuler qn/se congratuler; **he knows it (off) ~** (US): **he has it down ~** il sait cela sur le bout des doigts
patch [pætʃ] n (of material) pièce f; (eye patch) cache m; (spot) tache f; (of land) parcelle f; (on tyre) rustine f ▷ vt (clothes) rapiécer; **a bad ~** (Brit) une période difficile
▸ **patch up** vt réparer
patchy ['pætʃɪ] adj inégal(e); (incomplete) fragmentaire
pâté ['pæteɪ] n pâté m, terrine f
patent ['peɪtnt] n brevet m (d'invention) ▷ vt faire breveter ▷ adj patent(e), manifeste
patent leather n cuir verni
paternal [pə'tɜːnl] adj paternel(le)
paternity leave [pə'tɜːnɪtɪ-] n congé m de paternité
path [pɑːθ] n chemin m, sentier m; (in garden) allée f; (of planet) course f; (of missile) trajectoire f
pathetic [pə'θetɪk] adj (pitiful) pitoyable; (very bad) lamentable, minable; (moving) pathétique
pathological [pæθə'lɒdʒɪkl] adj pathologique
pathway ['pɑːθweɪ] n chemin m, sentier m; (in garden) allée f
patience ['peɪʃns] n patience f; (Brit: Cards) réussite f; **to lose (one's) ~** perdre patience
patient ['peɪʃnt] n malade m/f; (of dentist etc) patient(e) ▷ adj patient(e)
patio ['pætɪəu] n patio m
patriotic [pætrɪ'ɒtɪk] adj patriotique; (person) patriote
patrol [pə'trəul] n patrouille f ▷ vt patrouiller dans; **to be on ~** être de patrouille
patrol car n voiture f de police
patrolman [pə'trəulmən] (irreg) n (US) agent m de police
patron ['peɪtrən] n (in shop) client(e); (of charity) patron(ne); **~ of the arts** mécène m
patronize ['pætrənaɪz] vt être (un) client or un habitué de; (fig) traiter avec condescendance
patronizing ['pætrənaɪzɪŋ] adj condescendant(e)

patter ['pætə'] n crépitement m, tapotement m; (sales talk) boniment m ▷ vi crépiter, tapoter
pattern ['pætən] n modèle m; (Sewing) patron m; (design) motif m; (sample) échantillon m; **behaviour ~** mode m de comportement
patterned ['pætənd] adj à motifs
pauper ['pɔ:pə'] n indigent(e); **~'s grave** fosse commune
pause [pɔ:z] n pause f, arrêt m; (Mus) silence m ▷ vi faire une pause, s'arrêter; **to ~ for breath** reprendre son souffle; (fig) faire une pause
pave [peɪv] vt paver, daller; **to ~ the way for** ouvrir la voie à
pavement ['peɪvmənt] n (Brit) trottoir m; (US) chaussée f
pavilion [pə'vɪlɪən] n pavillon m; tente f; (Sport) stand m
paving ['peɪvɪŋ] n (material) pavé m, dalle f; (area) pavage m, dallage m
paving stone n pavé m
paw [pɔ:] n patte f ▷ vt donner un coup de patte à; (person: pej) tripoter
pawn [pɔ:n] n gage m; (Chess, also fig) pion m ▷ vt mettre en gage
pawnbroker ['pɔ:nbrəukə'] n prêteur m sur gages
pawnshop ['pɔ:nʃɔp] n mont-de-piété m
pay [peɪ] (pt, pp **paid**) [peɪd] n salaire m; (of manual worker) paie f ▷ vt payer; (be profitable to: also fig) rapporter à ▷ vi payer; (be profitable) être rentable; **how much did you ~ for it?** combien l'avez-vous payé?, vous l'avez payé combien?; **I paid £5 for that ticket** j'ai payé ce billet 5 livres; **can I ~ by credit card?** est-ce que je peux payer par carte de crédit?; **to ~ one's way** payer sa part; (company) couvrir ses frais; **to ~ dividends** (fig) porter ses fruits, s'avérer rentable; **it won't ~ you to do that** vous ne gagnerez rien à faire cela; **to ~ attention (to)** prêter attention (à); **to ~ sb a visit** rendre visite à qn; **to ~ one's respects to sb** présenter ses respects à qn
▶ **pay back** vt rembourser
▶ **pay for** vt fus payer
▶ **pay in** vt verser
▶ **pay off** vt (debts) régler, acquitter; (person) rembourser; (workers) licencier ▷ vi (scheme, decision) se révéler payant(e); **to ~ sth off in instalments** payer qch à tempérament
▶ **pay out** vt (money) payer, sortir de sa poche; (rope) laisser filer
▶ **pay up** vt (debts) régler; (amount) payer
payable ['peɪəbl] adj payable; **to make a cheque ~ to sb** établir un chèque à l'ordre de qn
pay-as-you-go [,peɪəzjə'gəu] adj (mobile phone) à carte prépayée
pay day n jour m de paie
payee [peɪ'i:] n bénéficiaire m/f
pay envelope n (US) paie f
payment ['peɪmənt] n paiement m; (of bill) règlement m; (of deposit, cheque) versement m; **advance ~** (part sum) acompte m; (total sum) paiement anticipé; **deferred ~, ~ by**

instalments paiement par versements échelonnés; **monthly ~** mensualité f; **in ~ for**, **in ~ of** en règlement de; **on ~ of £5** pour 5 livres
payout ['peɪaut] n (from insurance) dédommagement m; (in competition) prix m
pay packet n (Brit) paie f
pay phone n cabine f téléphonique, téléphone public
pay raise n (US) = **pay rise**
pay rise n (Brit) augmentation f (de salaire)
payroll ['peɪrəul] n registre m du personnel; **to be on a firm's ~** être employé par une entreprise
pay slip n (Brit) bulletin m de paie, feuille f de paie
pay television n chaînes fpl payantes
PC n abbr = **personal computer**; (Brit) = **police constable** ▷ adj abbr = **politically correct** ▷ abbr (Brit) = **Privy Councillor**
p.c. abbr = **per cent**; **postcard**
pcm n abbr (= per calender month) par mois
PDA n abbr (= personal digital assistant) agenda m électronique
PE n abbr (= physical education) EPS f ▷ abbr (Canada) = **Prince Edward Island**
pea [pi:] n (petit) pois
peace [pi:s] n paix f; (calm) calme m, tranquillité f; **to be at ~ with sb/sth** être en paix avec qn/qch; **to keep the ~** (policeman) assurer le maintien de l'ordre; (citizen) ne pas troubler l'ordre
peaceful ['pi:sful] adj paisible, calme
peach [pi:tʃ] n pêche f
peacock ['pi:kɔk] n paon m
peak [pi:k] n (mountain) pic m, cime f; (of cap) visière f; (fig: highest level) maximum m; (: of career, fame) apogée m
peak hours npl heures fpl d'affluence or de pointe
peal [pi:l] n (of bells) carillon m; **~s of laughter** éclats mpl de rire
peanut ['pi:nʌt] n arachide f, cacahuète f
peanut butter n beurre m de cacahuète
pear [pɛə'] n poire f
pearl [pə:l] n perle f
peasant ['pɛznt] n paysan(ne)
peat [pi:t] n tourbe f
pebble ['pɛbl] n galet m, caillou m
peck [pɛk] vt (also: **peck at**) donner un coup de bec à; (food) picorer ▷ n coup m de bec; (kiss) bécot m
pecking order ['pɛkɪŋ-] n ordre m hiérarchique
peckish ['pɛkɪʃ] adj (Brit inf): **I feel ~** je mangerais bien quelque chose, j'ai la dent
peculiar [pɪ'kju:lɪə'] adj (odd) étrange, bizarre, curieux(-euse); (particular) particulier(-ière); **~ to** particulier à
pedal ['pɛdl] n pédale f ▷ vi pédaler
pedantic [pɪ'dæntɪk] adj pédant(e)
peddler ['pɛdlə'] n colporteur m; camelot m
pedestal ['pɛdəstl] n piédestal m
pedestrian [pɪ'dɛstrɪən] n piéton m ▷ adj piétonnier(-ière); (fig) prosaïque, terre à terre inv
pedestrian crossing n (Brit) passage clouté
pedestrianized [pɪ'dɛstrɪənaɪzd] adj: **a ~ street**

une rue piétonne

pedestrian precinct, (US) **pedestrian zone** n
(Brit) zone piétonne

pediatrics [piːdɪˈætrɪks] n (US) = **paediatrics**

pedigree [ˈpɛdɪgriː] n ascendance f; (of animal)
pedigree m ▷ cpd (animal) de race

pedophile [ˈpiːdəʊfaɪl] (US) n = **paedophile**

pee [piː] vi (inf) faire pipi, pisser

peek [piːk] vi jeter un coup d'œil (furtif)

peel [piːl] n pelure f, épluchure f; (of orange,
lemon) écorce f ▷ vt peler, éplucher ▷ vi (paint etc)
s'écailler; (wallpaper) se décoller; (skin) peler
▶ **peel back** vt décoller

peep [piːp] n (Brit: look) coup d'œil furtif; (sound)
pépiement m ▷ vi (Brit) jeter un coup d'œil
(furtif)
▶ **peep out** vi (Brit) se montrer (furtivement)

peephole [ˈpiːphəʊl] n judas m

peer [pɪəʳ] vi: **to ~ at** regarder attentivement,
scruter ▷ n (noble) pair m; (equal) pair, égal(e)

peerage [ˈpɪərɪdʒ] n pairie f

peeved [piːvd] adj irrité(e), ennuyé(e)

peg [pɛg] n cheville f; (for coat etc) patère f; (Brit:
also: **clothes peg**) pince f à linge ▷ vt (clothes)
accrocher; (Brit: groundsheet) fixer (avec des
piquets); (fig: prices, wages) contrôler, stabiliser

Pekinese, Pekingese [piːkɪˈniːz] n pékinois m

pelican [ˈpɛlɪkən] n pélican m

pelican crossing n (Brit Aut) feu m à commande
manuelle

pellet [ˈpɛlɪt] n boulette f; (of lead) plomb m

pelt [pɛlt] vt: **to ~ sb (with)** bombarder qn (de)
▷ vi (rain) tomber à seaux; (inf: run) courir à toutes
jambes ▷ n peau f

pelvis [ˈpɛlvɪs] n bassin m

pen [pɛn] n (for writing) stylo m; (for sheep) parc m;
(US inf: prison) taule f; **to put ~ to paper** prendre
la plume

penal [ˈpiːnl] adj pénal(e)

penalize [ˈpiːnəlaɪz] vt pénaliser; (fig)
désavantager

penalty [ˈpɛnltɪ] n pénalité f; sanction f; (fine)
amende f; (Sport) pénalisation f; (also: **penalty
kick**: Football) penalty m; (: Rugby) pénalité f; **to
pay the ~ for** être pénalisé(e) pour

penance [ˈpɛnəns] n pénitence f

pence [pɛns] npl of **penny**

pencil [ˈpɛnsl] n crayon m
▶ **pencil in** vt noter provisoirement

pencil case n trousse f (d'écolier)

pencil sharpener n taille-crayon(s) m inv

pendant [ˈpɛndnt] n pendentif m

pending [ˈpɛndɪŋ] prep en attendant ▷ adj en
suspens

pendulum [ˈpɛndjʊləm] n pendule m; (of clock)
balancier m

penetrate [ˈpɛnɪtreɪt] vt pénétrer dans; (enemy
territory) entrer en; (sexually) pénétrer

penfriend [ˈpɛnfrɛnd] n (Brit) correspondant(e)

penguin [ˈpɛŋgwɪn] n pingouin m

penicillin [pɛnɪˈsɪlɪn] n pénicilline f

peninsula [pəˈnɪnsjʊlə] n péninsule f

penis [ˈpiːnɪs] n pénis m, verge f

penitentiary [pɛnɪˈtɛnʃərɪ] n (US) prison f

penknife [ˈpɛnnaɪf] n canif m

pen name n nom m de plume, pseudonyme m

penniless [ˈpɛnɪlɪs] adj sans le sou

penny (pl **pennies** or **pence**) [ˈpɛnɪ, ˈpɛnɪz, pɛns] n
(Brit) penny m; (US) cent m

penpal [ˈpɛnpæl] n correspondant(e)

pension [ˈpɛnʃən] n (from company) retraite f; (Mil)
pension f
▶ **pension off** vt mettre à la retraite

pensioner [ˈpɛnʃənəʳ] n (Brit) retraité(e)

pension fund n caisse f de retraite

pension plan n plan m de retraite

pentagon [ˈpɛntəgən] n pentagone m; **the P~**
(US Pol) le Pentagone; voir article

pentathlon [pɛnˈtæθlən] n pentathlon m

Pentecost [ˈpɛntɪkɒst] n Pentecôte f

penthouse [ˈpɛnthaʊs] n appartement m (de
luxe) en attique

pent-up [ˈpɛntʌp] adj (feelings) refoulé(e)

penultimate [pɪˈnʌltɪmət] adj pénultième,
avant-dernier(-ière)

people [ˈpiːpl] npl gens mpl; personnes fpl;
(inhabitants) population f; (Pol) peuple m ▷ n
(nation, race) peuple m ▷ vt peupler; **I know ~
who ...** je connais des gens qui ...; **the room
was full of ~** la salle était pleine de monde or de
gens; **several ~ came** plusieurs personnes sont
venues; **~ say that ...** on dit or les gens disent
que ...; **old ~** les personnes âgées; **young ~** les
jeunes; **a man of the ~** un homme du peuple

pepper [ˈpɛpəʳ] n poivre m; (vegetable) poivron m
▷ vt (Culin) poivrer

pepper mill n moulin m à poivre

peppermint [ˈpɛpəmɪnt] n (plant) menthe
poivrée; (sweet) pastille f de menthe

pep talk [ˈpɛptɔːk] n (inf) (petit) discours
d'encouragement

per [pəːʳ] prep par; **~ hour** (miles etc) à l'heure; (fee)
(de) l'heure; **~ kilo** etc le kilo etc; **~ day/person**
par jour/personne; **~ annum** per an; **as ~ your
instructions** conformément à vos instructions

perceive [pəˈsiːv] vt percevoir; (notice)
remarquer, s'apercevoir de

per cent adv pour cent; **a 20 ~ discount** une
réduction de 20 pour cent

percentage [pəˈsɛntɪdʒ] n pourcentage m; **on a ~
basis** au pourcentage

perception [pəˈsɛpʃən] n perception f; (insight)
sensibilité f

perceptive [pəˈsɛptɪv] adj (remark, person)
perspicace

perch [pəːtʃ] n (fish) perche f; (for bird) perchoir m
▷ vi (se) percher

percolator [ˈpəːkəleɪtəʳ] n percolateur m;
cafetière f électrique

percussion [pəˈkʌʃən] n percussion f

perennial [pəˈrɛnɪəl] adj perpétuel(le); (Bot)
vivace ▷ n (Bot) (plante f) vivace f, plante
pluriannuelle

perfect [ˈpəːfɪkt] adj parfait(e) ▷ n (also: **perfect**

tense) parfait *m* ▷ *vt* [pə'fɛkt] (*technique, skill, work of art*) parfaire; (*method, plan*) mettre au point; **he's a ~ stranger to me** il m'est totalement inconnu

perfection [pə'fɛkʃən] *n* perfection *f*

perfectly ['pə:fɪktlɪ] *adv* parfaitement; **I'm ~ happy with the situation** cette situation me convient parfaitement; **you know ~ well** vous le savez très bien

perforate ['pə:fəreɪt] *vt* perforer, percer

perforation [pə:fə'reɪʃən] *n* perforation *f*; (*line of holes*) pointillé *m*

perform [pə'fɔ:m] *vt* (*carry out*) exécuter, remplir; (*concert etc*) jouer, donner ▷ *vi* (*actor, musician*) jouer; (*machine, car*) marcher, fonctionner; (*company, economy*): **to ~ well/badly** produire de bons/mauvais résultats

performance [pə'fɔ:məns] *n* représentation *f*, spectacle *m*; (*of an artist*) interprétation *f*; (*Sport: of car, engine*) performance *f*; (*of company, economy*) résultats *mpl*; **the team put up a good ~** l'équipe a bien joué

performer [pə'fɔ:mə*r*] *n* artiste *m/f*

perfume ['pə:fju:m] *n* parfum *m* ▷ *vt* parfumer

perhaps [pə'hæps] *adv* peut-être; **~ he'll ...** peut-être qu'il ...; **~ so/not** peut-être que oui/que non

peril ['pɛrɪl] *n* péril *m*

perimeter [pə'rɪmɪtə*r*] *n* périmètre *m*

period ['pɪərɪəd] *n* période *f*; (*History*) époque *f*; (*Scol*) cours *m*; (*full stop*) point *m*; (*Med*) règles *fpl* ▷ *adj* (*costume, furniture*) d'époque; **for a ~ of three weeks** pour (une période de) trois semaines; **the holiday ~** (*Brit*) la période des vacances

periodical [pɪərɪ'ɔdɪkl] *adj* périodique ▷ *n* périodique *m*

periodically [pɪərɪ'ɔdɪklɪ] *adv* périodiquement

peripheral [pə'rɪfərəl] *adj* périphérique ▷ *n* (*Comput*) périphérique *m*

perish ['pɛrɪʃ] *vi* périr, mourir; (*decay*) se détériorer

perishable ['pɛrɪʃəbl] *adj* périssable

perjury ['pə:dʒərɪ] *n* (*Law: in court*) faux témoignage; (*breach of oath*) parjure *m*

perk [pə:k] *n* (*inf*) avantage *m*, à-côté *m* ▷ **perk up** *vi* (*inf: cheer up*) se ragaillardir

perky ['pə:kɪ] *adj* (*cheerful*) guilleret(te), gai(e)

perm [pə:m] *n* (*for hair*) permanente *f* ▷ *vt*: **to have one's hair ~ed** se faire faire une permanente

permanent ['pə:mənənt] *adj* permanent(e); (*job, position*) permanent, fixe; (*dye, ink*) indélébile; **I'm not ~ here** je ne suis pas ici à titre définitif; **~ address** adresse habituelle

permanently ['pə:mənəntlɪ] *adv* de façon permanente; (*move abroad*) définitivement; (*open, closed*) en permanence; (*tired, unhappy*) constamment

permeate ['pə:mɪeɪt] *vi* s'infiltrer ▷ *vt* s'infiltrer dans; pénétrer

permissible [pə'mɪsɪbl] *adj* permis(e), acceptable

permission [pə'mɪʃən] *n* permission *f*, autorisation *f*; **to give sb ~ to do sth** donner à qn la permission de faire qch

permissive [pə'mɪsɪv] *adj* tolérant(e); **the ~ society** la société de tolérance

permit *n* ['pə:mɪt] permis *m*; (*entrance pass*) autorisation *f*, laissez-passer *m*; (*for goods*) licence *f* ▷ *vt* [pə'mɪt] permettre; **to ~ sb to do** autoriser qn à faire, permettre à qn de faire; **weather ~ting** si le temps le permet

perpendicular [pə:pən'dɪkjulə*r*] *adj, n* perpendiculaire *f*

perplex [pə'plɛks] *vt* (*person*) rendre perplexe; (*complicate*) embrouiller

persecute ['pə:sɪkju:t] *vt* persécuter

persecution [pə:sɪ'kju:ʃən] *n* persécution *f*

persevere [pə:sɪ'vɪə*r*] *vi* persévérer

Persian ['pə:ʃən] *adj* persan(e) ▷ *n* (*Ling*) persan *m*; **the ~ Gulf** le golfe Persique

persist [pə'sɪst] *vi*: **to ~ (in doing)** persister (à faire), s'obstiner (à faire)

persistent [pə'sɪstənt] *adj* persistant(e), tenace; (*lateness, rain*) persistant; **~ offender** (*Law*) multirécidiviste *m/f*

person ['pə:sn] *n* personne *f*; **in ~** en personne; **on** *or* **about one's ~** sur soi; **~ to ~ call** (*Tel*) appel *m* avec préavis

personal ['pə:snl] *adj* personnel(le); **~ belongings, ~ effects** effets personnels; **~ hygiene** hygiène *f* intime; **a ~ interview** un entretien

personal assistant *n* secrétaire personnel(le)

personal column *n* annonces personnelles

personal computer *n* ordinateur individuel, PC *m*

personality [pə:sə'nælɪtɪ] *n* personnalité *f*

personally ['pə:snlɪ] *adv* personnellement; **to take sth ~** se sentir visé(e) par qch

personal organizer *n* agenda (personnel); (*electronic*) agenda électronique

personal stereo *n* Walkman® *m*, baladeur *m*

personnel [pə:sə'nɛl] *n* personnel *m*

perspective [pə'spɛktɪv] *n* perspective *f*; **to get sth into ~** ramener qch à sa juste mesure

perspex® ['pə:spɛks] *n* (*Brit*) Plexiglas® *m*

perspiration [pə:spɪ'reɪʃən] *n* transpiration *f*

persuade [pə'sweɪd] *vt*: **to ~ sb to do sth** persuader qn de faire qch, amener *or* décider qn à faire qch; **to ~ sb of sth/that** persuader qn de qch/que

persuasion [pə'sweɪʒən] *n* persuasion *f*; (*creed*) conviction *f*

persuasive [pə'sweɪsɪv] *adj* persuasif(-ive)

perverse [pə'və:s] *adj* pervers(e); (*contrary*) entêté(e), contrariant(e)

pervert *n* ['pə:və:t] perverti(e) ▷ *vt* [pə'və:t] pervertir; (*words*) déformer

pessimism ['pɛsɪmɪzəm] *n* pessimisme *m*

pessimist ['pɛsɪmɪst] *n* pessimiste *m/f*

pessimistic [pɛsɪ'mɪstɪk] *adj* pessimiste

pest [pɛst] *n* animal *m* (or insecte *m*) nuisible; (*fig*) fléau *m*

pester ['pɛstə*r*] *vt* importuner, harceler

pesticide ['pɛstɪsaɪd] *n* pesticide *m*

pet [pɛt] n animal familier; (favourite) chouchou m ▷ cpd (favourite) favori(e) ▷ vt choyer; (stroke) caresser, câliner ▷ vi (inf) se peloter; **~ lion** etc lion etc apprivoisé; **teacher's ~** chouchou m du professeur; **~ hate** bête noire

petal ['pɛtl] n pétale m

peter ['pi:tər]: **to ~ out** vi s'épuiser; s'affaiblir

petite [pə'ti:t] adj menu(e)

petition [pə'tɪʃən] n pétition f ▷ vt adresser une pétition à ▷ vi: **to ~ for divorce** demander le divorce

petrified ['pɛtrɪfaɪd] adj (fig) mort(e) de peur

petrol ['pɛtrəl] n (Brit) essence f; **I've run out of ~** je suis en panne d'essence

petrol can n (Brit) bidon m à essence

petroleum [pə'trəʊlɪəm] n pétrole m

petrol pump n (Brit: in car, at garage) pompe f à essence

petrol station n (Brit) station-service f

petrol tank n (Brit) réservoir m d'essence

petticoat ['pɛtɪkəʊt] n jupon m

petty ['pɛtɪ] adj (mean) mesquin(e); (unimportant) insignifiant(e), sans importance

petty cash n caisse f des dépenses courantes, petite caisse

petty officer n second-maître m

petulant ['pɛtjʊlənt] adj irritable

pew [pju:] n banc m (d'église)

pewter ['pju:tər] n étain m

phantom ['fæntəm] n fantôme m; (vision) fantasme m

pharmacist ['fɑ:məsɪst] n pharmacien(ne)

pharmacy ['fɑ:məsɪ] n pharmacie f

phase [feɪz] n phase f, période f
  ▷ **phase in** vt introduire progressivement
  ▷ **phase out** vt supprimer progressivement

Ph.D. abbr = **Doctor of Philosophy**

pheasant ['fɛznt] n faisan m

phenomena [fə'nɔmɪnə] npl of **phenomenon**

phenomenal [fɪ'nɔmɪnl] adj phénoménal(e)

phenomenon (pl **phenomena**) [fə'nɔmɪnən, -nə] n phénomène m

Philippines ['fɪlɪpi:nz] npl (also: **Philippine Islands**): **the ~** les Philippines fpl

philosopher [fɪ'lɔsəfər] n philosophe m

philosophical [fɪlə'sɔfɪkl] adj philosophique

philosophy [fɪ'lɔsəfɪ] n philosophie f

phlegm [flɛm] n flegme m

phobia ['fəʊbjə] n phobie f

phone [fəʊn] n téléphone m ▷ vt téléphoner à ▷ vi téléphoner; **to be on the ~** avoir le téléphone; (be calling) être au téléphone
  ▷ **phone back** vt, vi rappeler
  ▷ **phone up** vt téléphoner à ▷ vi téléphoner

phone bill n facture f de téléphone

phone book n annuaire m

phone box, (US) **phone booth** n cabine f téléphonique

phone call n coup m de fil or de téléphone

phonecard ['fəʊnkɑ:d] n télécarte f

phone-in ['fəʊnɪn] n (Brit Radio, TV) programme m à ligne ouverte

phone number n numéro m de téléphone

phonetics [fə'nɛtɪks] n phonétique f

phoney ['fəʊnɪ] adj faux (fausse), factice; (person) pas franc (franche) ▷ n (person) charlatan m; fumiste m/f

photo ['fəʊtəʊ] n photo f; **to take a ~ of** prendre en photo

photo album n album m de photos

photocopier ['fəʊtəʊkɔpɪər] n copieur m

photocopy ['fəʊtəʊkɔpɪ] n photocopie f ▷ vt photocopier

photograph ['fəʊtəgræf] n photographie f ▷ vt photographier; **to take a ~ of sb** prendre qn en photo

photographer [fə'tɔgrəfər] n photographe m/f

photography [fə'tɔgrəfɪ] n photographie f

phrase [freɪz] n expression f; (Ling) locution f ▷ vt exprimer; (letter) rédiger

phrase book n recueil m d'expressions (pour touristes)

physical ['fɪzɪkl] adj physique; **~ examination** examen médical; **~ exercises** gymnastique f

physical education n éducation f physique

physically ['fɪzɪklɪ] adv physiquement

physician [fɪ'zɪʃən] n médecin m

physicist ['fɪzɪsɪst] n physicien(ne)

physics ['fɪzɪks] n physique f

physiotherapist [fɪzɪəʊ'θɛrəpɪst] n kinésithérapeute m/f

physiotherapy [fɪzɪəʊ'θɛrəpɪ] n kinésithérapie f

physique [fɪ'zi:k] n (appearance) physique m; (health etc) constitution f

pianist ['pi:ənɪst] n pianiste m/f

piano [pɪ'ænəʊ] n piano m

pick [pɪk] n (tool: also: **pick-axe**) pic m, pioche f ▷ vt choisir; (gather) cueillir; (remove) prendre; (lock) forcer; (scab, spot) gratter, écorcher; **take your ~** faites votre choix; **the ~ of** le (la) meilleur(e) de; **to ~ a bone** ronger un os; **to ~ one's nose** se mettre les doigts dans le nez; **to ~ one's teeth** se curer les dents; **to ~ sb's brains** faire appel aux lumières de qn; **to ~ pockets** pratiquer le vol à la tire; **to ~ a quarrel with sb** chercher noise à qn
  ▷ **pick at** vt fus: **to ~ at one's food** manger du bout des dents, chipoter
  ▷ **pick off** vt (kill) (viser soigneusement et) abattre
  ▷ **pick on** vt fus (person) harceler
  ▷ **pick out** vt choisir; (distinguish) distinguer
  ▷ **pick up** vi (improve) remonter, s'améliorer ▷ vt ramasser; (telephone) décrocher; (collect) passer prendre; (Aut: give lift to) prendre; (learn) apprendre; (Radio) capter; **to ~ up speed** prendre de la vitesse; **to ~ o.s. up** se relever; **to ~ up where one left off** reprendre là où l'on s'est arrêté

picket ['pɪkɪt] n (in strike) gréviste m/f participant à un piquet de grève; piquet m de grève ▷ vt mettre un piquet de grève devant

pickle ['pɪkl] n (also: **pickles**: as condiment) pickles mpl ▷ vt conserver dans du vinaigre or dans de la saumure; **in a ~** (fig) dans le pétrin

pickpocket ['pɪkpɒkɪt] n pickpocket m
pick-up ['pɪkʌp] n (also: **pick-up truck**) pick-up m
inv; (Brit: on record player) bras m pick-up
picnic ['pɪknɪk] n pique-nique m ▷ vi pique-
niquer
picnic area n aire f de pique-nique
picture ['pɪktʃə'] n (also TV) image f;
(painting) peinture f, tableau m; (photograph)
photo(graphie) f; (drawing) dessin m; (film) film
m; (fig: description) description f ▷ vt (imagine) se
représenter; (describe) dépeindre, représenter;
pictures npl: **the ~s** (Brit) le cinéma; **to take a**
~ of sb/sth prendre qn/qch en photo; **would**
you take a ~ of us, please? pourriez-vous nous
prendre en photo, s'il vous plaît?; **the overall ~**
le tableau d'ensemble; **to put sb in the ~** mettre
qn au courant
picture book n livre m d'images
picture frame n cadre m
picture messaging n picture messaging m,
messagerie f d'images
picturesque [pɪktʃə'resk] adj pittoresque
pie [paɪ] n tourte f; (of fruit) tarte f; (of meat) pâté m
en croûte
piece [pi:s] n morceau m; (of land) parcelle f;
(item): **a ~ of furniture/advice** un meuble/
conseil; (Draughts) pion m ▷ vt: **to ~ together**
rassembler; **in ~s** (broken) en morceaux, en
miettes; (not yet assembled) en pièces détachées;
to take to ~s démonter; **in one ~** (object)
intact(e); **to get back all in one ~** (person)
rentrer sain et sauf; **a 1op ~** (Brit) une pièce de
1op; **~ by ~** morceau par morceau; **a six-~ band**
un orchestre de six musiciens; **to say one's ~**
réciter son morceau
piecemeal ['pi:smi:l] adv par bouts
piecework ['pi:swə:k] n travail m aux pièces or
à la pièce
pie chart n graphique m à secteurs,
camembert m
pier [pɪə'] n jetée f; (of bridge etc) pile f
pierce [pɪəs] vt percer, transpercer; **to have**
one's ears ~d se faire percer les oreilles
pierced [pɪəst] adj (ears) percé(e)
pig [pɪg] n cochon m, porc m; (pej: unkind person)
mufle m; (: greedy person) goinfre m
pigeon ['pɪdʒən] n pigeon m
pigeonhole ['pɪdʒənhəul] n casier m
piggy bank ['pɪgɪ-] n tirelire f
pigheaded ['pɪg'hedɪd] adj entêté(e), têtu(e)
piglet ['pɪglɪt] n petit cochon, porcelet m
pigskin ['pɪgskɪn] n (peau f de) porc m
pigsty ['pɪgstaɪ] n porcherie f
pigtail ['pɪgteɪl] n natte f, tresse f
pike [paɪk] n (spear) pique f; (fish) brochet m
pilchard ['pɪltʃəd] n pilchard m (sorte de sardine)
pile [paɪl] n (pillar, of books) pile f; (heap) tas m; (of
carpet) épaisseur f; **in a ~** en tas
▶ **pile on** vt: **to ~ it on** (inf) exagérer
▶ **pile up** vi (accumulate) s'entasser, s'accumuler
▷ vt (put in heap) empiler, entasser; (accumulate)
accumuler

piles [paɪlz] npl hémorroïdes fpl
pile-up ['paɪlʌp] n (Aut) télescopage m, collision f
en série
pilfering ['pɪlfərɪŋ] n chapardage m
pilgrim ['pɪlgrɪm] n pèlerin m; voir article
pilgrimage ['pɪlgrɪmɪdʒ] n pèlerinage m
pill [pɪl] n pilule f; **the ~** la pilule; **to be on the ~**
prendre la pilule
pillage ['pɪlɪdʒ] vt piller
pillar ['pɪlə'] n pilier m
pillar box n (Brit) boîte f aux lettres (publique)
pillion ['pɪljən] n (of motor cycle) siège m arrière; **to**
ride ~ être derrière; (on horse) être en croupe
pillow ['pɪləu] n oreiller m
pillowcase ['pɪləukeɪs], **pillowslip** ['pɪləuslɪp] n
taie f d'oreiller
pilot ['paɪlət] n pilote m ▷ cpd (scheme etc) pilote,
expérimental(e) ▷ vt piloter
pilot light n veilleuse f
pimp [pɪmp] n souteneur m, maquereau m
pimple ['pɪmpl] n bouton m
PIN n abbr (= personal identification number) code m
confidentiel
pin [pɪn] n épingle f; (Tech) cheville f; (Brit: drawing
pin) punaise f; (in grenade) goupille f; (Brit Elec:
of plug) broche f ▷ vt épingler; **~s and needles**
fourmis fpl; **to ~ sb against/to** clouer qn contre/
à; **to ~ sb down** (fig) coincer qn; **to ~ sth on sb**
(fig) mettre qch sur le dos de qn
▶ **pin down** vt (fig): **to ~ sb down** obliger qn à
répondre; **there's something strange here**
but I can't quite ~ it down il y a quelque chose
d'étrange ici, mais je n'arrive pas exactement à
savoir quoi
pinafore ['pɪnəfɔ:'] n tablier m
pinball ['pɪnbɔ:l] n flipper m
pincers ['pɪnsəz] npl tenailles fpl
pinch [pɪntʃ] n pincement m; (of salt etc) pincée
f ▷ vt pincer; (inf: steal) piquer, chiper ▷ vi (shoe)
serrer; **at a ~** à la rigueur; **to feel the ~** (fig) se
ressentir des restrictions (or de la récession etc)
pincushion ['pɪnkuʃən] n pelote f à épingles
pine [paɪn] n (also: **pine tree**) pin m ▷ vi: **to ~ for**
aspirer à, désirer ardemment
▶ **pine away** vi dépérir
pineapple ['paɪnæpl] n ananas m
ping [pɪŋ] n (noise) tintement m
ping-pong® ['pɪŋpɒŋ] n ping-pong® m
pink [pɪŋk] adj rose ▷ n (colour) rose m; (Bot) œillet
m, mignardise f
pinpoint ['pɪnpɔɪnt] vt indiquer (avec précision)
pint [paɪnt] n pinte f (Brit = 0,57 l; US = 0,47 l); (Brit
inf) ≈ demi m, ≈ pot m
pioneer [paɪə'nɪə'] n explorateur(-trice); (early
settler) pionnier m; (fig) pionnier, précurseur m
▷ vt être un pionnier de
pious ['paɪəs] adj pieux(-euse)
pip [pɪp] n (seed) pépin m; **pips** npl: **the ~s** (Brit:
time signal on radio) le top
pipe [paɪp] n tuyau m, conduite f; (for smoking)
pipe f; (Mus) pipeau m ▷ vt amener par tuyau;
pipes npl (also: **bagpipes**) cornemuse f

▸ **pipe down** vi (inf) se taire

pipe cleaner n cure-pipe m

pipe dream n chimère f, utopie f

pipeline ['paɪplaɪn] n (for gas) gazoduc m, pipeline m; (for oil) oléoduc m, pipeline m; **it is in the ~** (fig) c'est en route, ça va se faire

piper ['paɪpəʳ] n (flautist) joueur(-euse) de pipeau; (of bagpipes) joueur(-euse) de cornemuse

piping ['paɪpɪŋ] adv: ~ **hot** très chaud(e)

pique [pi:k] n dépit m

pirate ['paɪərət] n pirate m ▷ vt (CD, video, book) pirater

pirated ['paɪərətɪd] adj pirate

Pisces ['paɪsiːz] n les Poissons mpl; **to be ~** être des Poissons

piss [pɪs] vi (inf!) pisser (!); **~ off!** tire-toi! (!)

pissed [pɪst] (inf!) adj (Brit: drunk) bourré(e); (US: angry) furieux(-euse)

pistol ['pɪstl] n pistolet m

piston ['pɪstən] n piston m

pit [pɪt] n trou m, fosse f; (also: **coal pit**) puits m de mine; (also: **orchestra pit**) fosse d'orchestre; (US: fruit stone) noyau m ▷ vt: **to ~ sb against sb** opposer qn à qn; **to ~ o.s. against** se mesurer à; **pits** npl (in motor racing) aire f de service

pitch [pɪtʃ] n (Brit Sport) terrain m; (throw) lancement m; (Mus) ton m; (of voice) hauteur f; (fig: degree) degré m; (also: **sales pitch**) baratin m, boniment m; (Naut) tangage m; (tar) poix f ▷ vt (throw) lancer; (tent) dresser; (set: price, message) adapter, positionner ▷ vi (Naut) tanguer; (fall): **to ~ into/off** tomber dans/de; **to be ~ed forward** être projeté(e) en avant; **at this ~** à ce rythme

pitch-black ['pɪtʃ'blæk] adj noir(e) comme poix

pitched battle [pɪtʃt-] n bataille rangée

pitfall ['pɪtfɔːl] n trappe f, piège m

pith [pɪθ] n (of plant) moelle f; (of orange etc) intérieur m de l'écorce; (fig) essence f; vigueur f

pithy ['pɪθɪ] adj piquant(e); vigoureux(-euse)

pitiful ['pɪtɪful] adj (touching) pitoyable; (contemptible) lamentable

pitiless ['pɪtɪlɪs] adj impitoyable

pittance ['pɪtns] n salaire m de misère

pity ['pɪtɪ] n pitié f ▷ vt plaindre; **what a ~!** quel dommage!; **it is a ~ that you can't come** c'est dommage que vous ne puissiez venir; **to have** or **take ~ on sb** avoir pitié de qn

pizza ['piːtsə] n pizza f

placard ['plækɑːd] n affiche f; (in march) pancarte f

placate [plə'keɪt] vt apaiser, calmer

place [pleɪs] n endroit m, lieu m; (proper position, job, rank, seat) place f; (house) maison f, logement m; (in street names): **Laurel ~** ≈ rue des Lauriers; (home): **at/to his ~** chez lui ▷ vt (position) placer, mettre; (identify) situer; reconnaître; **to take ~** avoir lieu; (occur) se produire; **to take sb's ~** remplacer qn; **to change ~s with sb** changer de place avec qn; **from ~ to ~** d'un endroit à l'autre; **all over the ~** partout; **out of ~** (not

suitable) déplacé(e), inopportun(e); **I feel out of ~ here** je ne me sens pas à ma place ici; **in the first ~** d'abord, en premier; **to put sb in his ~** (fig) remettre qn à sa place; **he's going ~s** (fig: inf) il fait son chemin; **it is not my ~ to do it** ce n'est pas à moi de le faire; **to ~ an order with sb (for)** (Comm) passer commande à qn (de); **to be ~d** (in race, exam) se placer; **how are you ~d next week?** comment ça se présente pour la semaine prochaine?

place mat n set m de table; (in linen etc) napperon m

placement ['pleɪsmənt] n placement m; (during studies) stage m

placid ['plæsɪd] adj placide

plague [pleɪg] n fléau m; (Med) peste f ▷ vt (fig) tourmenter; **to ~ sb with questions** harceler qn de questions

plaice [pleɪs] n (pl inv) carrelet m

plaid [plæd] n tissu écossais

plain [pleɪn] adj (in one colour) uni(e); (clear) clair(e), évident(e); (simple) simple, ordinaire; (frank) franc (franche); (not handsome) quelconque, ordinaire; (cigarette) sans filtre; (without seasoning etc) nature inv ▷ adv franchement, carrément ▷ n plaine f; **in ~ clothes** (police) en civil; **to make sth ~ to sb** faire clairement comprendre qch à qn

plain chocolate n chocolat m à croquer

plainly ['pleɪnlɪ] adv clairement; (frankly) carrément, sans détours

plaintiff ['pleɪntɪf] n plaignant(e)

plait [plæt] n tresse f, natte f ▷ vt tresser, natter

plan [plæn] n plan m; (scheme) projet m ▷ vt (think in advance) projeter; (prepare) organiser ▷ vi faire des projets; **to ~ to do** projeter de faire; **how long do you ~ to stay?** combien de temps comptez-vous rester?

plane [pleɪn] n (Aviat) avion m; (also: **plane tree**) platane m; (tool) rabot m; (Art, Math etc) plan m; (fig) niveau m, plan ▷ adj plan(e); plat(e) ▷ vt (with tool) raboter

planet ['plænɪt] n planète f

plank [plæŋk] n planche f; (Pol) point m d'un programme

planner ['plænəʳ] n planificateur(-trice); (chart) planning m; **town** or (US) **city ~** urbaniste m/f

planning ['plænɪŋ] n planification f; **family ~** planning familial

planning permission n (Brit) permis m de construire

plant [plɑːnt] n plante f; (machinery) matériel m; (factory) usine f ▷ vt planter; (bomb) déposer, poser; (microphone, evidence) cacher

plantation [plæn'teɪʃən] n plantation f

plaque [plæk] n plaque f

plaster ['plɑːstəʳ] n plâtre m; (also: **plaster of Paris**) plâtre à mouler; (Brit: also: **sticking plaster**) pansement adhésif ▷ vt plâtrer; (cover): **to ~ with** couvrir de; **in ~** (Brit: leg etc) dans le plâtre

plaster cast n (Med) plâtre m; (model, statue)

moule m

plastered ['plɑːstəd] adj (inf) soûl(e)

plastic ['plæstɪk] n plastique m ▷ adj (made of plastic) en plastique; (flexible) plastique, malléable; (art) plastique

plastic bag n sac m en plastique

plasticine® ['plæstɪsiːn] n pâte f à modeler

plastic surgery n chirurgie f esthétique

plate [pleɪt] n (dish) assiette f; (sheet of metal, on door: Phot) plaque f; (Typ) cliché m; (in book) gravure f; (dental) dentier m; (Aut: number plate) plaque minéralogique; **gold/silver ~** (dishes) vaisselle f d'or/d'argent

plateau (pl **-s** or **-x**) ['plætəu, -z] n plateau m

plate glass n verre m à vitre, vitre f

platform ['plætfɔːm] n (at meeting) tribune f; (Brit: of bus) plate-forme f; (stage) estrade f; (Rail) quai m; (Pol) plateforme f; **the train leaves from ~ 7** le train part de la voie 7

platinum ['plætɪnəm] n platine m

platoon [plə'tuːn] n peloton m

platter ['plætər] n plat m

plausible ['plɔːzɪbl] adj plausible; (person) convaincant(e)

play [pleɪ] n jeu m; (Theat) pièce f (de théâtre) ▷ vt (game) jouer à; (team, opponent) jouer contre; (instrument) jouer de; (part, piece of music, note) jouer; (CD etc) passer ▷ vi jouer; **to bring** or **call into ~** faire entrer en jeu; **~ on words** jeu de mots; **to ~ safe** ne prendre aucun risque; **to ~ a trick on sb** jouer un tour à qn; **they're ~ing at soldiers** ils jouent aux soldats; **to ~ for time** (fig) chercher à gagner du temps; **to ~ into sb's hands** (fig) faire le jeu de qn

▸ **play about, play around** vi (person) s'amuser

▸ **play along** vi (fig): **to ~ along with** (person) entrer dans le jeu de ▷ vt (fig): **to ~ sb along** faire marcher qn

▸ **play back** vt repasser, réécouter

▸ **play down** vt minimiser

▸ **play on** vt fus (sb's feelings, credulity) jouer sur; **to ~ on sb's nerves** porter sur les nerfs de qn

▸ **play up** vi (cause trouble) faire des siennes

playboy ['pleɪbɔɪ] n playboy m

player ['pleɪər] n joueur(-euse); (Theat) acteur(-trice); (Mus) musicien(ne)

playful ['pleɪful] adj enjoué(e)

playground ['pleɪɡraund] n cour f de récréation; (in park) aire f de jeux

playgroup ['pleɪɡruːp] n garderie f

playing card ['pleɪɪŋ-] n carte f à jouer

playing field ['pleɪɪŋ-] n terrain m de sport

playmate ['pleɪmeɪt] n camarade m/f, copain (copine)

play-off ['pleɪɔf] n (Sport) belle f

playpen ['pleɪpɛn] n parc m (pour bébé)

playschool ['pleɪskuːl] n = **playgroup**

plaything ['pleɪθɪŋ] n jouet m

playtime ['pleɪtaɪm] n (Scol) récréation f

playwright ['pleɪraɪt] n dramaturge m

plc abbr (Brit: = public limited company) ≈ SARL f

plea [pliː] n (request) appel m; (excuse) excuse f;

(Law) défense f

plead [pliːd] vt plaider; (give as excuse) invoquer ▷ vi (Law) plaider; (beg): **to ~ with sb (for sth)** implorer qn (d'accorder qch); **to ~ for sth** implorer qch; **to ~ guilty/not guilty** plaider coupable/non coupable

pleasant ['plɛznt] adj agréable

pleasantry ['plɛzntrɪ] n (joke) plaisanterie f; **pleasantries** npl (polite remarks) civilités fpl

please [pliːz] excl s'il te (or vous) plaît ▷ vt plaire à ▷ vi (think fit): **do as you ~** faites comme il vous plaira; **my bill, ~** l'addition, s'il vous plaît; **~ don't cry!** je t'en prie, ne pleure pas!; **~ yourself!** (inf) (faites) comme vous voulez!

pleased [pliːzd] adj: **~ (with)** content(e) (de); **~ to meet you** enchanté (de faire votre connaissance); **we are ~ to inform you that ...** nous sommes heureux de vous annoncer que ...

pleasing ['pliːzɪŋ] adj plaisant(e), qui fait plaisir

pleasure ['plɛʒər] n plaisir m; **"it's a ~"** "je vous en prie"; **with ~** avec plaisir; **is this trip for business or ~?** est-ce un voyage d'affaires ou d'agrément?

pleat [pliːt] n pli m

pledge [plɛdʒ] n gage m; (promise) promesse f ▷ vt engager; promettre; **to ~ support for sb** s'engager à soutenir qn; **to ~ sb to secrecy** faire promettre à qn de garder le secret

plentiful ['plɛntɪful] adj abondant(e), copieux(-euse)

plenty ['plɛntɪ] n abondance f; **~ of** beaucoup de; (sufficient) (bien) assez de; **we've got ~ of time** nous avons largement le temps

pliable ['plaɪəbl] adj flexible; (person) malléable

pliers ['plaɪəz] npl pinces fpl

plight [plaɪt] n situation f critique

plimsolls ['plɪmsəlz] npl (Brit) (chaussures fpl) tennis fpl

plinth [plɪnθ] n socle m

PLO n abbr (= Palestine Liberation Organization) OLP f

plod [plɔd] vi avancer péniblement; (fig) peiner

plonk [plɔŋk] (inf) n (Brit: wine) pinard m, piquette f ▷ vt: **to ~ sth down** poser brusquement qch

plot [plɔt] n complot m, conspiration f; (of story, play) intrigue f; (of land) lot m de terrain, lopin m ▷ vt (mark out) tracer point par point; (Naut) pointer; (make graph of) faire le graphique de; (conspire) comploter ▷ vi comploter; **a vegetable ~** (Brit) un carré de légumes

plough, (US) **plow** [plau] n charrue f ▷ vt (earth) labourer; **to ~ money into** investir dans

▸ **plough back** vt (Comm) réinvestir

▸ **plough through** vt fus (snow etc) avancer péniblement dans

ploughman, (US) **plowman** ['plaumən] (irreg) n laboureur m

plow [plau] (US) = **plough**

ploy [plɔɪ] n stratagème m

pls abbr (= please) SVP m

pluck [plʌk] vt (fruit) cueillir; (musical instrument) pincer; (bird) plumer ▷ n courage m, cran m; **to ~ one's eyebrows** s'épiler les sourcils; **to ~ up**

courage prendre son courage à deux mains

plug [plʌg] n (stopper) bouchon m, bonde f; (Elec) prise f de courant; (Aut: also: **spark(ing) plug**) bougie f ▷ vt (hole) boucher; (inf: advertise) faire du battage pour, matraquer; **to give sb/sth a ~** (inf) faire de la pub pour qn/qch
▶ **plug in** vt (Elec) brancher ▷ vi (Elec) se brancher

plughole ['plʌɡhəul] n (Brit) trou m (d'écoulement)

plum [plʌm] n (fruit) prune f ▷ adj: **~ job** (inf) travail m en or

plumb [plʌm] adj vertical(e) ▷ n plomb m ▷ adv (exactly) en plein ▷ vt sonder
▶ **plumb in** vt (washing machine) faire le raccordement sur

plumber ['plʌmə^r] n plombier m

plumbing ['plʌmɪŋ] n (trade) plomberie f; (piping) tuyauterie f

plummet ['plʌmɪt] vi (person, object) plonger; (sales, prices) dégringoler

plump [plʌmp] adj rondelet(te), dodu(e), bien en chair ▷ vt: **to ~ sth (down) on** laisser tomber qch lourdement sur
▶ **plump for** vt fus (inf: choose) se décider pour
▶ **plump up** vt (cushion) battre (pour lui redonner forme)

plunder ['plʌndə^r] n pillage m ▷ vt piller

plunge [plʌndʒ] n plongeon m; (fig) chute f ▷ vt plonger ▷ vi (fall) tomber, dégringoler; (dive) plonger; **to take the ~** se jeter à l'eau

plunging ['plʌndʒɪŋ] adj (neckline) plongeant(e)

pluperfect [plu:'pə:fɪkt] n (Ling) plus-que-parfait m

plural ['pluərl] adj pluriel(le) ▷ n pluriel m

plus [plʌs] n (also: **plus sign**) signe m plus; (advantage) atout m ▷ prep plus; **ten/twenty ~** plus de dix/vingt; **it's a ~** c'est un atout

plush [plʌʃ] adj somptueux(-euse) ▷ n peluche f

ply [plaɪ] n (of wool) fil m; (of wood) feuille f, épaisseur f ▷ vt (tool) manier; (a trade) exercer ▷ vi (ship) faire la navette; **three ~ (wool)** n laine f trois fils; **to ~ sb with drink** donner continuellement à boire à qn

plywood ['plaɪwud] n contreplaqué m

P.M. n abbr (Brit) = **prime minister**

p.m. adv abbr (= post meridiem) de l'après-midi

PMS n abbr (= premenstrual syndrome) syndrome prémenstruel

PMT n abbr (= premenstrual tension) syndrome prémenstruel

pneumatic [nju:'mætɪk] adj pneumatique

pneumatic drill [nju:'mætɪk-] n marteau-piqueur m

pneumonia [nju:'məunɪə] n pneumonie f

poach [pəutʃ] vt (cook) pocher; (steal) pêcher (or chasser) sans permis ▷ vi braconner

poached [pəutʃt] adj (egg) poché(e)

poacher ['pəutʃə^r] n braconnier m

P.O. Box n abbr = **post office box**

pocket ['pɔkɪt] n poche f ▷ vt empocher; **to be (£5) out of ~** (Brit) en être de sa poche (pour 5 livres)

pocketbook ['pɔkɪtbuk] n (notebook) carnet m; (US: wallet) portefeuille m; (: handbag) sac m à main

pocket knife n canif m

pocket money n argent m de poche

pod [pɔd] n cosse f ▷ vt écosser

podcast n podcast m

podgy ['pɔdʒɪ] adj rondelet(te)

podiatrist [pɔ'di:ətrɪst] n (US) pédicure m/f

podium ['pəudɪəm] n podium m

poem ['pəuɪm] n poème m

poet ['pəuɪt] n poète m

poetic [pəu'etɪk] adj poétique

poetry ['pəuɪtrɪ] n poésie f

poignant ['pɔɪnjənt] adj poignant(e); (sharp) vif (vive)

point [pɔɪnt] n (Geom, Scol, Sport, on scale) point m; (tip) pointe f; (in time) moment m; (in space) endroit m; (subject, idea) point, sujet m; (purpose) but m; (also: **decimal point**): **2 ~ 3 (2.3)** 2 virgule 3 (2,3); (Brit Elec: also: **power point**) prise f (de courant) ▷ vt (show) indiquer; (wall, window) jointoyer; (gun etc): **to ~ sth at** braquer or diriger qch sur ▷ vi: **to ~ at** montrer du doigt; **points** npl (Aut) vis platinées; (Rail) aiguillage m; **good ~s** qualités fpl; **the train stops at Carlisle and all ~s south** le train dessert Carlisle et toutes les gares vers le sud; **to make a ~** faire une remarque; **to make a ~ of doing sth** ne pas manquer de faire qch; **to make one's ~** se faire comprendre; **to get/miss the ~** comprendre/ne pas comprendre; **to come to the ~** en venir au fait; **when it comes to the ~** le moment venu; **there's no ~ (in doing)** cela ne sert à rien (de faire); **what's the ~?** à quoi ça sert?; **to be on the ~ of doing sth** être sur le point de faire qch; **that's the whole ~!** précisément!; **to be beside the ~** être à côté de la question; **you've got a ~ there!** (c'est) juste!; **in ~ of fact** en fait, en réalité; **~ of departure** (also fig) point de départ; **~ of order** point de procédure; **~ of sale** (Comm) point de vente; **to ~ to sth** (fig) signaler
▶ **point out** vt (show) montrer, indiquer; (mention) faire remarquer, souligner

point-blank ['pɔɪnt'blæŋk] adv (fig) catégoriquement; (also: **at point-blank range**) à bout portant ▷ adj (fig) catégorique

pointed ['pɔɪntɪd] adj (shape) pointu(e); (remark) plein(e) de sous-entendus

pointer ['pɔɪntə^r] n (stick) baguette f; (needle) aiguille f; (dog) chien m d'arrêt; (clue) indication f; (advice) tuyau m

pointless ['pɔɪntlɪs] adj inutile, vain(e)

point of view n point m de vue

poise [pɔɪz] n (balance) équilibre m; (of head, body) port m; (calmness) calme m ▷ vt placer en équilibre; **to be ~d for** (fig) être prêt à

poison ['pɔɪzn] n poison m ▷ vt empoisonner

poisonous ['pɔɪznəs] adj (snake) venimeux(-euse); (substance, plant) vénéneux(-euse); (fumes) toxique; (fig) pernicieux(-euse)

poke [pəuk] vt (fire) tisonner; (jab with finger, stick etc) piquer; pousser du doigt; (put): **to ~ sth in(to)** fourrer or enfoncer qch dans ▷ n (jab) (petit) coup; (to fire) coup m de tisonnier; **to ~ fun at sb** se moquer de qn
▶ **poke about** vi fureter
▶ **poke out** vi (stick out) sortir ▷ vt: **to ~ one's head out of the window** passer la tête par la fenêtre
poker ['pəukə'] n tisonnier m; (Cards) poker m
poky ['pəukı] adj exigu(ë)
Poland ['pəulənd] n Pologne f
polar ['pəulə'] adj polaire
polar bear n ours blanc
Pole [pəul] n Polonais(e)
pole [pəul] n (of wood) mât m, perche f; (Elec) poteau m; (Geo) pôle m
pole bean n (US) haricot m (à rames)
pole vault ['pəulvɔ:lt] n saut m à la perche
police [pə'li:s] npl police f ▷ vt maintenir l'ordre dans; **a large number of ~ were hurt** de nombreux policiers ont été blessés
police car n voiture f de police
police constable n (Brit) agent m de police
police force n police f, forces fpl de l'ordre
policeman [pə'li:smən] (irreg) n agent m de police, policier m
police officer n agent m de police
police station n commissariat m de police
policewoman [pə'li:swumən] (irreg) n femme-agent f
policy ['pɔlısı] n politique f; (also: **insurance policy**) police f (d'assurance); (of newspaper, company) politique générale; **to take out a ~** (Insurance) souscrire une police d'assurance
polio ['pəuliəu] n polio f
Polish ['pəulıʃ] adj polonais(e) ▷ n (Ling) polonais m
polish ['pɔlıʃ] n (for shoes) cirage m; (for floor) cire f, encaustique f; (for nails) vernis m; (shine) éclat m, poli m; (fig: refinement) raffinement m ▷ vt (put polish on: shoes, wood) cirer; (make shiny) astiquer, faire briller; (fig: improve) perfectionner
▶ **polish off** vt (work) expédier; (food) liquider
polished ['pɔlıʃt] adj (fig) raffiné(e)
polite [pə'laıt] adj poli(e); **it's not ~ to do that** ça ne se fait pas
politely [pə'laıtlı] adv poliment
politeness [pə'laıtnıs] n politesse f
political [pə'lıtıkl] adj politique
politically [pə'lıtıklı] adv politiquement; **~ correct** politiquement correct(e)
politician [pɔlı'tıʃən] n homme/femme politique, politicien(ne)
politics ['pɔlıtıks] n politique f
poll [pəul] n scrutin m, vote m; (also: **opinion poll**) sondage m (d'opinion) ▷ vt (votes) obtenir; **to go to the ~s** (voters) aller aux urnes; (government) tenir des élections
pollen ['pɔlən] n pollen m
polling day n (Brit) jour m des élections
polling station n (Brit) bureau m de vote

pollute [pə'lu:t] vt polluer
pollution [pə'lu:ʃən] n pollution f
polo ['pəuləu] n polo m
polo-neck ['pəuləunek] adj à col roulé ▷ n (sweater) pull m à col roulé
polo shirt n polo m
polyester [pɔlı'ɛstə'] n polyester m
polystyrene [pɔlı'staıri:n] n polystyrène m
polythene ['pɔlıθi:n] n (Brit) polyéthylène m
polythene bag n sac m en plastique
pomegranate ['pɔmıgrænıt] n grenade f
pomp [pɔmp] n pompe f, faste f, apparat m
pompous ['pɔmpəs] adj pompeux(-euse)
pond [pɔnd] n étang m; (stagnant) mare f
ponder ['pɔndə'] vi réfléchir ▷ vt considérer, peser
ponderous ['pɔndərəs] adj pesant(e), lourd(e)
pong [pɔŋ] (Brit inf) n puanteur f ▷ vi schlinguer
pony ['pəunı] n poney m
ponytail ['pəunıteıl] n queue f de cheval
pony trekking [-trekıŋ] n (Brit) randonnée f équestre or à cheval
poodle ['pu:dl] n caniche m
pool [pu:l] n (of rain) flaque f; (pond) mare f; (artificial) bassin m; (also: **swimming pool**) piscine f; (sth shared) fonds commun; (money at cards) cagnotte f; (billiards) poule f; (Comm: consortium) pool m; (US: monopoly trust) trust m ▷ vt mettre en commun; **pools** npl (football) ≈ loto sportif; **typing ~** (US): **secretary ~ pool** m dactylographique; **to do the (football) ~s** (Brit) ≈ jouer au loto sportif; see also **football pools**
poor [puə'] adj pauvre; (mediocre) médiocre, faible, mauvais(e) ▷ npl: **the ~** les pauvres mpl
poorly ['puəlı] adv pauvrement; (badly) mal, médiocrement ▷ adj souffrant(e), malade
pop [pɔp] n (noise) bruit sec; (Mus) musique f pop; (inf: drink) soda m; (US inf: father) papa m ▷ vt (put) fourrer, mettre (rapidement) ▷ vi éclater; (cork) sauter; **she ~ped her head out of the window** elle passa la tête par la fenêtre
▶ **pop in** vi entrer en passant
▶ **pop out** vi sortir
▶ **pop up** vi apparaître, surgir
popcorn ['pɔpkɔ:n] n pop-corn m
pope [pəup] n pape m
poplar ['pɔplə'] n peuplier m
popper ['pɔpə'] n (Brit) bouton-pression m
poppy ['pɔpı] n (wild) coquelicot m; (cultivated) pavot m
Popsicle® ['pɔpsıkl] n (US) esquimau m (glace)
pop star n pop star f
popular ['pɔpjulə'] adj populaire; (fashionable) à la mode; **to be ~ (with)** (person) avoir du succès (auprès de); (decision) être bien accueilli(e) (par)
popularity [pɔpju'lærıtı] n popularité f
population [pɔpju'leıʃən] n population f
pop-up adj (Comput: menu, window) pop up inv ▷ n pop up m inv, fenêtre f pop up
porcelain ['pɔ:slın] n porcelaine f
porch [pɔ:tʃ] n porche m; (US) véranda f
porcupine ['pɔ:kjupaın] n porc-épic m

pore [pɔːʳ] n pore m ▷ vi: **to ~ over** s'absorber dans, être plongé(e) dans

pork [pɔːk] n porc m

pork chop n côte f de porc

pork pie n pâté m de porc en croûte

porn [pɔːn] adj (inf) porno ▷ n (inf) porno m

pornographic [pɔːnəˈgræfɪk] adj pornographique

pornography [pɔːˈnɔgrəfɪ] n pornographie f

porpoise [ˈpɔːpəs] n marsouin m

porridge [ˈpɔrɪdʒ] n porridge m

port [pɔːt] n (harbour) port m; (opening in ship) sabord m; (Naut: left side) bâbord m; (wine) porto m; (Comput) port m, accès m ▷ cpd portuaire, du port; **to ~** (Naut) à bâbord; **~ of call** (port d')escale f

portable [ˈpɔːtəbl] adj portatif(-ive)

porter [ˈpɔːtəʳ] n (for luggage) porteur m; (doorkeeper) gardien(ne); portier m

portfolio [pɔːtˈfəulɪəu] n portefeuille m; (of artist) portfolio m

porthole [ˈpɔːthəul] n hublot m

portion [ˈpɔːʃən] n portion f, part f

portrait [ˈpɔːtreɪt] n portrait m

portray [pɔːˈtreɪ] vt faire le portrait de; (in writing) dépeindre, représenter; (subj: actor) jouer

Portugal [ˈpɔːtjugl] n Portugal m

Portuguese [pɔːtjuˈgiːz] adj portugais(e) ▷ n (pl inv) Portugais(e); (Ling) portugais m

pose [pəuz] n pose f; (pej) affectation f ▷ vi poser; (pretend): **to ~ as** se faire passer pour ▷ vt poser; (problem) créer; **to strike a ~** poser (pour la galerie)

posh [pɔʃ] adj (inf) chic inv; **to talk ~** parler d'une manière affectée

position [pəˈzɪʃən] n position f; (job, situation) situation f ▷ vt mettre en place or en position; **to be in a ~ to do sth** être en mesure de faire qch

positive [ˈpɔzɪtɪv] adj positif(-ive); (certain) sûr(e), certain(e); (definite) formel(le), catégorique; (clear) indéniable, réel(le)

positively [ˈpɔzɪtɪvlɪ] adv (affirmatively, enthusiastically) de façon positive; (inf: really) carrément; **to think ~** être positif(-ive)

possess [pəˈzɛs] vt posséder; **like one ~ed** comme un fou; **whatever can have ~ed you?** qu'est-ce qui vous a pris?

possession [pəˈzɛʃən] n possession f; **possessions** npl (belongings) affaires fpl; **to take ~ of sth** prendre possession de qch

possessive [pəˈzɛsɪv] adj possessif(-ive)

possibility [pɔsɪˈbɪlɪtɪ] n possibilité f; (event) éventualité f; **he's a ~ for the part** c'est un candidat possible pour le rôle

possible [ˈpɔsɪbl] adj possible; (solution) envisageable, éventuel(le); **it is ~ to do it** il est possible de le faire; **as far as ~** dans la mesure du possible, autant que possible; **if ~** si possible; **as big as ~** aussi gros que possible

possibly [ˈpɔsɪblɪ] adv (perhaps) peut-être; **if you can** si cela vous est possible; **I cannot ~ come** il m'est impossible de venir

post [pəust] n (Brit: mail) poste f; (: collection)

levée f; (: letters, delivery) courrier m; (job, situation) poste m; (pole) poteau m; (trading post) comptoir (commercial) ▷ vt (Brit: send by post, Mil) poster; (: appoint): **to ~ to** affecter à; (notice) afficher; **by ~** (Brit) par la poste; **by return of ~** (Brit) par retour du courrier; **where can I ~ these cards?** où est-ce que je peux poster ces cartes postales?; **to keep sb ~ed** tenir qn au courant

postage [ˈpəustɪdʒ] n tarifs mpl d'affranchissement; **~ paid** port payé; **~ prepaid** (US) franco (de port)

postal [ˈpəustl] adj postal(e)

postal order n mandat(-poste m) m

postbox [ˈpəustbɔks] n (Brit) boîte f aux lettres (publique)

postcard [ˈpəustkaːd] n carte postale

postcode [ˈpəustkəud] n (Brit) code postal

poster [ˈpəustəʳ] n affiche f

poste restante [pəustˈrɛstaːnt] n (Brit) poste restante

postgraduate [ˈpəustˈgrædjuət] n ≈ étudiant(e) de troisième cycle

posthumous [ˈpɔstjuməs] adj posthume

postman [ˈpəustmən] (Brit: irreg) n facteur m

postmark [ˈpəustmaːk] n cachet m (de la poste)

post-mortem [pəustˈmɔːtəm] n autopsie f

post office n (building) poste f; (organization): **the Post Office** les postes fpl

post office box n boîte postale

postpone [pəsˈpəun] vt remettre (à plus tard), reculer

posture [ˈpɔstʃəʳ] n posture f; (fig) attitude f ▷ vi poser

postwar [pəustˈwɔːʳ] adj d'après-guerre

postwoman [pəustˈwumən] (Brit: irreg) n factrice f

posy [ˈpəuzɪ] n petit bouquet

pot [pɔt] n (for cooking) marmite f; casserole f; (teapot) théière f; (for coffee) cafetière f; (for plants, jam) pot m; (piece of pottery) poterie f; (inf: marijuana) herbe f ▷ vt (plant) mettre en pot; **to ~** (inf) aller à vau-l'eau; **~s of** (Brit inf) beaucoup de, plein de

potato (pl **-es**) [pəˈteɪtəu] n pomme f de terre

potato peeler n épluche-légumes m

potent [ˈpəutnt] adj puissant(e); (drink) fort(e), très alcoolisé(e); (man) viril

potential [pəˈtɛnʃl] adj potentiel(le) ▷ n potentiel m; **to have ~** être prometteur(-euse); ouvrir des possibilités

pothole [ˈpɔthəul] n (in road) nid m de poule; (Brit: underground) gouffre m, caverne f

potholing [ˈpɔthəulɪŋ] n (Brit): **to go ~** faire de la spéléologie

potluck [pɔtˈlʌk] n: **to take ~** tenter sa chance

pot plant n plante f d'appartement

potted [ˈpɔtɪd] adj (food) en conserve; (plant) en pot; (fig: shortened) abrégé(e)

potter [ˈpɔtəʳ] n potier m ▷ vi (Brit): **to ~ around** or **about** bricoler; **~'s wheel** tour m de potier

pottery [ˈpɔtərɪ] n poterie f; **a piece of ~** une poterie

potty ['pɒtɪ] adj (Brit inf: mad) dingue ▷ n (child's) pot m

pouch [pautʃ] n (Zool) poche f; (for tobacco) blague f; (for money) bourse f

poultry ['pəultrɪ] n volaille f

pounce [pauns] vi: **to ~ (on)** bondir (sur), fondre (sur) ▷ n bond m, attaque f

pound [paund] n livre f (weight = 453g, 16 ounces; money = 100 pence); (for dogs, cars) fourrière f ▷ vt (beat) bourrer de coups, marteler; (crush) piler, pulvériser; (with guns) pilonner ▷ vi (heart) battre violemment, taper; **half a ~ (of)** une demi-livre (de); **a five-~ note** un billet de cinq livres

pound sterling n livre f sterling

pour [pɔːʳ] vt verser ▷ vi couler à flots; (rain) pleuvoir à verse; **to ~ sb a drink** verser or servir à boire à qn; **to come ~ing in** (water) entrer à flots; (letters) arriver par milliers; (cars, people) affluer
  ▸ **pour away, pour off** vt vider
  ▸ **pour in** vi (people) affluer, se précipiter; (news, letters) arriver en masse
  ▸ **pour out** vi (people) sortir en masse ▷ vt vider; (fig) déverser; (serve: a drink) verser

pouring ['pɔːrɪŋ] adj: **~ rain** pluie torrentielle

pout [paut] n moue f ▷ vi faire la moue

poverty ['pɒvətɪ] n pauvreté f, misère f

poverty-stricken ['pɒvətɪstrɪkn] adj pauvre, déshérité(e)

powder ['paudəʳ] n poudre f ▷ vt poudrer; **to ~ one's nose** se poudrer; (euphemism) aller à la salle de bain

powder compact n poudrier m

powdered milk n lait m en poudre

powder room n toilettes fpl (pour dames)

power ['pauəʳ] n (strength, nation) puissance f, force f; (ability, Pol: of party, leader) pouvoir m; (Math) puissance; (of speech, thought) faculté f; (Elec) courant m ▷ vt faire marcher, actionner; **to do all in one's ~ to help sb** faire tout ce qui est en son pouvoir pour aider qn; **the world ~s** les grandes puissances; **to be in ~** être au pouvoir

power cut n (Brit) coupure f de courant

powered ['pauəd] adj: **~ by** actionné(e) par, fonctionnant à; **nuclear-~ submarine** sous-marin m (à propulsion) nucléaire

power failure n panne f de courant

powerful ['pauəful] adj puissant(e); (performance etc) très fort(e)

powerless ['pauəlɪs] adj impuissant(e)

power point n (Brit) prise f de courant

power station n centrale f électrique

power struggle n lutte f pour le pouvoir

p.p. abbr (= per procurationem: by proxy) p.p.

PR n abbr = **proportional representation; public relations** ▷ abbr (US) = **Puerto Rico**

practical ['præktɪkl] adj pratique

practicality [præktɪ'kælɪtɪ] n (of plan) aspect m pratique; (of person) sens m pratique; **practicalities** npl détails mpl pratiques

practical joke n farce f

practically ['præktɪklɪ] adv (almost) pratiquement

practice ['præktɪs] n pratique f; (of profession) exercice m; (at football etc) entraînement m; (business) cabinet m; clientèle f ▷ vt, vi (US) = **practise; in ~** (in reality) en pratique; **out of ~** rouillé(e); **2 hours' piano ~** 2 heures de travail or d'exercices au piano; **target ~** exercices de tir; **it's common ~** c'est courant, ça se fait couramment; **to put sth into ~** mettre qch en pratique

practise, (US) **practice** ['præktɪs] vt (work at: piano, backhand etc) s'exercer à, travailler; (train for: sport) s'entraîner à; (a sport, religion, method) pratiquer; (profession) exercer ▷ vi s'exercer, travailler; (train) s'entraîner; (lawyer, doctor) exercer; **to ~ for a match** s'entraîner pour un match

practising, (US) **practicing** ['præktɪsɪŋ] adj (Christian etc) pratiquant(e); (lawyer) en exercice; (homosexual) déclaré

practitioner [præk'tɪʃənəʳ] n praticien(ne)

pragmatic [præg'mætɪk] adj pragmatique

prairie ['prɛərɪ] n savane f; (US): **the ~s** la Prairie

praise [preɪz] n éloge(s) m(pl), louange(s) f(pl) ▷ vt louer, faire l'éloge de

praiseworthy ['preɪzwəːðɪ] adj digne de louanges

pram [præm] n (Brit) landau m, voiture f d'enfant

prance [prɑːns] vi (horse) caracoler

prank [præŋk] n farce f

prawn [prɔːn] n crevette f (rose)

prawn cocktail n cocktail m de crevettes

pray [preɪ] vi prier

prayer [prɛəʳ] n prière f

preach [priːtʃ] vt, vi prêcher; **to ~ at sb** faire la morale à qn

preacher ['priːtʃəʳ] n prédicateur m; (US: clergyman) pasteur m

precarious [prɪ'kɛərɪəs] adj précaire

precaution [prɪ'kɔːʃən] n précaution f

precede [prɪ'siːd] vt, vi précéder

precedent ['presɪdənt] n précédent m; **to establish** or **set a ~** créer un précédent

preceding [prɪ'siːdɪŋ] adj qui précède (or précédait)

precinct ['priːsɪŋkt] n (round cathedral) pourtour m, enceinte f; (US: district) circonscription f, arrondissement m; **precincts** npl (neighbourhood) alentours mpl, environs mpl; **pedestrian ~** (Brit) zone piétonnière; **shopping ~** (Brit) centre commercial

precious ['preʃəs] adj précieux(-euse) ▷ adv (inf): **~ little** or **few** fort peu; **your ~ dog** (ironic) ton chien chéri, ton chéri chien

precipitate [prɪ'sɪpɪtɪt] adj (hasty) précipité(e) ▷ vt [prɪ'sɪpɪteɪt] précipiter

precise [prɪ'saɪs] adj précis(e)

precisely [prɪ'saɪslɪ] adv précisément

precision [prɪ'sɪʒən] n précision f

precocious [prɪ'kəuʃəs] adj précoce

precondition ['priːkən'dɪʃən] n condition f nécessaire

predator ['prɛdətəʳ] n prédateur m, rapace m

predecessor ['pri:dısɛsəʳ] n prédécesseur m

predicament [prɪ'dɪkəmənt] n situation f difficile

predict [prɪ'dɪkt] vt prédire

predictable [prɪ'dɪktəbl] adj prévisible

prediction [prɪ'dɪkʃən] n prédiction f

predominantly [prɪ'dɒmɪnəntlɪ] adv en majeure partie; (especially) surtout

pre-empt [priː'ɛmt] vt (Brit) acquérir par droit de préemption; (fig) anticiper sur; **to ~ the issue** conclure avant même d'ouvrir les débats

preen [priːn] vt: **to ~ itself** (bird) se lisser les plumes; **to ~ o.s.** s'admirer

prefab ['priːfæb] n abbr (= prefabricated building) bâtiment préfabriqué

preface ['prɛfəs] n préface f

prefect ['priːfɛkt] n (Brit: in school) élève chargé de certaines fonctions de discipline; (in France) préfet m

prefer [prɪ'fəːʳ] vt préférer; (Law): **to ~ charges** procéder à une inculpation; **to ~ coffee to tea** préférer le café au thé; **to ~ doing** or **to do sth** préférer faire qch

preferable ['prɛfrəbl] adj préférable

preferably ['prɛfrəblɪ] adv de préférence

preference ['prɛfrəns] n préférence f; **in ~ to sth** plutôt que qch, de préférence à qch

preferential [prɛfə'rɛnʃəl] adj préférentiel(le); **~ treatment** traitement m de faveur

prefix ['priːfɪks] n préfixe m

pregnancy ['prɛgnənsɪ] n grossesse f

pregnant ['prɛgnənt] adj enceinte adj f; (animal) pleine; **3 months ~** enceinte de 3 mois

prehistoric ['priːhɪs'tɔrɪk] adj préhistorique

prejudice ['prɛdʒudɪs] n préjugé m; (harm) tort m, préjudice m ▷ vt porter préjudice à; (bias): **to ~ sb in favour of/against** prévenir qn en faveur de/contre; **racial ~** préjugés raciaux

prejudiced ['prɛdʒudɪst] adj (person) plein(e) de préjugés; (in a matter) partial(e); (view) préconçu(e), partial(e); **to be ~ against sb/sth** avoir un parti-pris contre qn/qch; **to be racially ~** avoir des préjugés raciaux

preliminary [prɪ'lɪmɪnərɪ] adj préliminaire

prelude ['prɛljuːd] n prélude m

premarital ['priː'mærɪtl] adj avant le mariage; **~ contract** contrat m de mariage

premature ['prɛmətʃuəʳ] adj prématuré(e); **to be ~ (in doing sth)** aller un peu (trop) vite (en faisant qch)

premier ['prɛmɪəʳ] adj premier(-ière), principal(e) ▷ n (Pol: Prime Minister) premier ministre; (Pol: President) chef m de l'État

premiere ['prɛmɪɛəʳ] n première f

Premier League n première division

premise ['prɛmɪs] n prémisse f

premises ['prɛmɪsɪz] npl locaux mpl; **on the ~** sur les lieux; sur place; **business ~** locaux commerciaux

premium ['priːmɪəm] n prime f; **to be at a ~** (fig: housing etc) être très demandé(e), être rarissime; **to sell at a ~** (shares) vendre au-dessus du pair

premium bond n (Brit) obligation f à prime, bon m à lots

premonition [prɛmə'nɪʃən] n prémonition f

preoccupied [priː'ɔkjupaɪd] adj préoccupé(e)

prep [prɛp] adj abbr: **~ school**; = **preparatory school** ▷ n abbr (Scol: = preparation) étude f

prepaid [priː'peɪd] adj payé(e) d'avance

preparation [prɛpə'reɪʃən] n préparation f; **preparations** npl (for trip, war) préparatifs mpl; **in ~ for** en vue de

preparatory [prɪ'pærətərɪ] adj préparatoire; **~ to sth/to doing sth** en prévision de qch/avant de faire qch

preparatory school n (Brit) école primaire privée; (US) lycée privé; voir article

prepare [prɪ'pɛəʳ] vt préparer ▷ vi: **to ~ for** se préparer à

prepared [prɪ'pɛəd] adj: **~ for** préparé(e) à; **~ to** prêt(e) à

preposition [prɛpə'zɪʃən] n préposition f

preposterous [prɪ'pɒstərəs] adj ridicule, absurde

prep school n = **preparatory school**

prerequisite [priː'rɛkwɪzɪt] n condition f préalable

presbyterian [prɛzbɪ'tɪərɪən] adj, n presbytérien(ne)

preschool ['priː'skuːl] adj préscolaire; (child) d'âge préscolaire

prescribe [prɪ'skraɪb] vt prescrire; **~d books** (Brit Scol) œuvres fpl au programme

prescription [prɪ'skrɪpʃən] n prescription f; (Med) ordonnance f; (: medicine) médicament m (obtenu sur ordonnance); **to make up** or (US) **fill a ~** faire une ordonnance; **could you write me a ~?** pouvez-vous me faire une ordonnance?; **"only available on ~"** "uniquement sur ordonnance"

presence ['prɛzns] n présence f; **in sb's ~** en présence de qn; **~ of mind** présence d'esprit

present ['prɛznt] adj présent(e); (current) présent, actuel(le) ▷ n cadeau m; (actuality, also: **present tense**) présent m ▷ vt [prɪ'zɛnt] présenter; (prize, medal) remettre; (give): **to ~ sb with sth** offrir qch à qn; **to be ~ at** assister à; **those ~** les présents; **at ~** en ce moment; **to give sb a ~** offrir un cadeau à qn; **to ~ sb (to sb)** présenter qn (à qn)

presentable [prɪ'zɛntəbl] adj présentable

presentation [prɛzn'teɪʃən] n présentation f; (gift) cadeau m, présent m; (ceremony) remise f du cadeau (or de la médaille etc); **on ~ of** (voucher etc) sur présentation de

present-day ['prɛzntdeɪ] adj contemporain(e), actuel(le)

presenter [prɪ'zɛntəʳ] n (Brit Radio, TV) présentateur(-trice)

presently ['prɛzntlɪ] adv (soon) tout à l'heure, bientôt; (with verb in past) peu après; (at present) en ce moment; (US: now) maintenant

preservation [prɛzə'veɪʃən] n préservation f, conservation f

preservative [prɪ'zəːvətɪv] n agent m de

conservation

preserve [prɪˈzəːv] *vt* (*keep safe*) préserver, protéger; (*maintain*) conserver, garder; (*food*) mettre en conserve ▷ *n* (*for game, fish*) réserve *f*; (*often pl: jam*) confiture *f*; (*: fruit*) fruits *mpl* en conserve

preside [prɪˈzaɪd] *vi* présider

president [ˈprɛzɪdənt] *n* président(e); (US: *of company*) président-directeur général, PDG *m*

presidential [prɛzɪˈdɛnʃl] *adj* présidentiel(le)

press [prɛs] *n* (*tool, machine, newspapers*) presse *f*; (*for wine*) pressoir *m*; (*crowd*) cohue *f*, foule *f* ▷ *vt* (*push*) appuyer sur; (*squeeze*) presser, serrer; (*clothes: iron*) repasser; (*pursue*) talonner; (*insist*): **to ~ sth on sb** presser qn d'accepter qch; (*urge, entreat*): **to ~ sb to do** *or* **into doing sth** pousser qn à faire qch ▷ *vi* appuyer, peser; se presser; **we are ~ed for time** le temps nous manque; **to ~ for sth** faire pression pour obtenir qch; **to ~ sb for an answer** presser qn de répondre; **to ~ charges against sb** (*Law*) engager des poursuites contre qn; **to go to ~** (*newspaper*) aller à l'impression; **to be in the ~** (*being printed*) être sous presse; (*in the newspapers*) être dans le journal

▸ **press ahead** *vi* = **press on**

▸ **press on** *vi* continuer

press conference *n* conférence *f* de presse

pressing [ˈprɛsɪŋ] *adj* urgent(e), pressant(e) ▷ *n* repassage *m*

press stud *n* (Brit) bouton-pression *m*

press-up [ˈprɛsʌp] *n* (Brit) traction *f*

pressure [ˈprɛʃəʳ] *n* pression *f*; (*stress*) tension *f* ▷ *vt* = **to put pressure on**; **to put ~ on sb (to do sth)** faire pression sur qn (pour qu'il fasse qch)

pressure cooker *n* cocotte-minute *f*

pressure gauge *n* manomètre *m*

pressure group *n* groupe *m* de pression

prestige [prɛsˈtiːʒ] *n* prestige *m*

prestigious [prɛsˈtɪdʒəs] *adj* prestigieux(-euse)

presumably [prɪˈzjuːməblɪ] *adv* vraisemblablement; **~ he did it** c'est sans doute lui (qui a fait cela)

presume [prɪˈzjuːm] *vt* présumer, supposer; **to ~ to do** (*dare*) se permettre de faire

pretence, (US) **pretense** [prɪˈtɛns] *n* (*claim*) prétention *f*; (*pretext*) prétexte *m*; **she is devoid of all ~** elle n'est pas du tout prétentieuse; **to make a ~ of doing** faire semblant de faire; **on** *or* **under the ~ of doing sth** sous prétexte de faire qch; **under false ~s** sous des prétextes fallacieux

pretend [prɪˈtɛnd] *vt* (*feign*) feindre, simuler ▷ *vi* (*feign*) faire semblant; (*claim*): **to ~ to sth** prétendre à qch; **to ~ to do** faire semblant de faire

pretense [prɪˈtɛns] *n* (US) = **pretence**

pretentious [prɪˈtɛnʃəs] *adj* prétentieux(-euse)

pretext [ˈpriːtɛkst] *n* prétexte *m*; **on** *or* **under the ~ of doing sth** sous prétexte de faire qch

pretty [ˈprɪtɪ] *adj* joli(e) ▷ *adv* assez

prevail [prɪˈveɪl] *vi* (*win*) l'emporter, prévaloir; (*be*

usual) avoir cours; (*persuade*): **to ~ (up)on sb to do** persuader qn de faire

prevailing [prɪˈveɪlɪŋ] *adj* (*widespread*) courant(e), répandu(e); (*wind*) dominant(e)

prevalent [ˈprɛvələnt] *adj* répandu(e), courant(e); (*fashion*) en vogue

prevent [prɪˈvɛnt] *vt*: **to ~ (from doing)** empêcher (de faire)

preventative [prɪˈvɛntətɪv] *adj* préventif(-ive)

prevention [prɪˈvɛnʃən] *n* prévention *f*

preventive [prɪˈvɛntɪv] *adj* préventif(-ive)

preview [ˈpriːvjuː] *n* (*of film*) avant-première *f*; (*fig*) aperçu *m*

previous [ˈpriːvɪəs] *adj* (*last*) précédent(e); (*earlier*) antérieur(e); (*question, experience*) préalable; **I have a ~ engagement** je suis déjà pris(e); **~ to doing** avant de faire

previously [ˈpriːvɪəslɪ] *adv* précédemment, auparavant

prewar [priːˈwɔːʳ] *adj* d'avant-guerre

prey [preɪ] *n* proie *f* ▷ *vi*: **to ~ on** s'attaquer à; **it was ~ing on his mind** ça le rongeait *or* minait

price [praɪs] *n* prix *m*; (*Betting: odds*) cote *f* ▷ *vt* (*goods*) fixer le prix de; tarifer; **what is the ~ of ...?** combien coûte ...?, quel est le prix de ...?; **to go up** *or* **rise in ~** augmenter; **to put a ~ on sth** chiffrer qch; **to be ~d out of the market** (*article*) être trop cher pour soutenir la concurrence; (*producer, nation*) ne pas pouvoir soutenir la concurrence; **what ~ his promises now?** (Brit) que valent maintenant toutes ses promesses?; **he regained his freedom, but at a ~** il a retrouvé sa liberté, mais cela lui a coûté cher

priceless [ˈpraɪslɪs] *adj* sans prix, inestimable; (*inf: amusing*) impayable

price list *n* tarif *m*

prick [prɪk] *n* (*sting*) piqûre *f*; (*inf!*) bitte *f* (!); connard *m* (!) ▷ *vt* piquer; **to ~ up one's ears** dresser *or* tendre l'oreille

prickle [ˈprɪkl] *n* (*of plant*) épine *f*; (*sensation*) picotement *m*

prickly [ˈprɪklɪ] *adj* piquant(e), épineux(-euse); (*fig: person*) irritable

prickly heat *n* fièvre *f* miliaire

pride [praɪd] *n* (*feeling proud*) fierté *f*; (*pej*) orgueil *m*; (*self-esteem*) amour-propre *m* ▷ *vt*: **to ~ o.s. on** se flatter de; s'enorgueillir de; **to take (a) ~ in** être (très) fier(-ère) de; **to take a ~ in doing** mettre sa fierté à faire; **to have ~ of place** (Brit) avoir la place d'honneur

priest [priːst] *n* prêtre *m*

priesthood [ˈpriːsthud] *n* prêtrise *f*, sacerdoce *m*

prim [prɪm] *adj* collet monté *inv*, guindé(e)

primarily [ˈpraɪmərɪlɪ] *adv* principalement, essentiellement

primary [ˈpraɪmərɪ] *adj* primaire; (*first in importance*) premier(-ière), primordial(e) ▷ *n* (US: *election*) (élection *f*) primaire *f*

primary school *n* (Brit) école *f* primaire; *voir article*

prime [praɪm] *adj* primordial(e), fondamental(e); (*excellent*) excellent(e) ▷ *vt* (*gun,* *pump*) amorcer; (*fig*) mettre au courant ▷ *n*: **in the ~ of life** dans la fleur de l'âge

Prime Minister *n* Premier ministre

primeval [praɪˈmiːvl] *adj* primitif(-ive)

primitive [ˈprɪmɪtɪv] *adj* primitif(-ive)

primrose [ˈprɪmrəuz] *n* primevère *f*

primus® [ˈpraɪməs], **primus® stove** *n* (*Brit*) réchaud *m* de camping

prince [prɪns] *n* prince *m*

princess [prɪnˈses] *n* princesse *f*

principal [ˈprɪnsɪpl] *adj* principal(e) ▷ *n* (*head teacher*) directeur *m*, principal *m*; (*in play*) rôle principal; (*money*) principal *m*

principally [ˈprɪnsɪplɪ] *adv* principalement

principle [ˈprɪnsɪpl] *n* principe *m*; **in ~** en principe; **on ~** par principe

print [prɪnt] *n* (*mark*) empreinte *f*; (*letters*) caractères *mpl*; (*fabric*) imprimé *m*; (*Art*) gravure *f*, estampe *f*; (*Phot*) épreuve *f* ▷ *vt* imprimer; (*publish*) publier; (*write in capitals*) écrire en majuscules; **out of ~** épuisé(e)
  ▸ **print out** *vt* (*Comput*) imprimer

printed matter [ˈprɪntɪd-] *n* imprimés *mpl*

printer [ˈprɪntə^r] *n* (*machine*) imprimante *f*; (*person*) imprimeur *m*

printing [ˈprɪntɪŋ] *n* impression *f*

printout [ˈprɪntaut] *n* (*Comput*) sortie *f* imprimante

prior [ˈpraɪə^r] *adj* antérieur(e), précédent(e); (*more important*) prioritaire ▷ *n* (*Rel*) prieur *m* ▷ *adv*: **~ to doing** avant de faire; **without ~ notice** sans préavis; **to have a ~ claim to sth** avoir priorité pour qch

priority [praɪˈɔrɪtɪ] *n* priorité *f*; **to have** *or* **take ~ over sth/sb** avoir la priorité sur qch/qn

prise [praɪz] *vt*: **to ~ open** forcer

prison [ˈprɪzn] *n* prison *f* ▷ *cpd* pénitentiaire

prisoner [ˈprɪznə^r] *n* prisonnier(-ière); **the ~ at the bar** l'accusé(e); **to take sb ~** faire qn prisonnier

prisoner of war *n* prisonnier(-ière) de guerre

pristine [ˈprɪstiːn] *adj* virginal(e)

privacy [ˈprɪvəsɪ] *n* intimité *f*, solitude *f*

private [ˈpraɪvɪt] *adj* (*not public*) privé(e); (*personal*) personnel(le); (*house, car, lesson*) particulier(-ière); (*quiet: place*) tranquille ▷ *n* soldat *m* de deuxième classe; **"~"** (*on envelope*) "personnelle"; (*on door*) "privé"; **in ~** en privé; **in (his) ~ life** dans sa vie privée; **he is a very ~ person** il est très secret; **to be in ~ practice** être médecin (*or* dentiste *etc*) non conventionné; **~ hearing** (*Law*) audience *f* à huis-clos

private detective *n* détective privé

private enterprise *n* entreprise privée

privately [ˈpraɪvɪtlɪ] *adv* en privé; (*within oneself*) intérieurement

private property *n* propriété privée

private school *n* école privée

privatize [ˈpraɪvɪtaɪz] *vt* privatiser

privet [ˈprɪvɪt] *n* troène *m*

privilege [ˈprɪvɪlɪdʒ] *n* privilège *m*

privy [ˈprɪvɪ] *adj*: **to be ~ to** être au courant de

prize [praɪz] *n* prix *m* ▷ *adj* (*example, idiot*) parfait(e); (*bull, novel*) primé(e) ▷ *vt* priser, faire grand cas de

prize-giving [ˈpraɪzgɪvɪŋ] *n* distribution *f* des prix

prizewinner [ˈpraɪzwɪnə^r] *n* gagnant(e)

pro [prəu] *n* (*inf: Sport*) professionnel(le) ▷ *prep* pro; **pros** *npl*: **the ~s and cons** le pour et le contre

probability [prɔbəˈbɪlɪtɪ] *n* probabilité *f*; **in all ~** très probablement

probable [ˈprɔbəbl] *adj* probable; **it is ~/hardly ~ that ...** il est probable/peu probable que ...

probably [ˈprɔbəblɪ] *adv* probablement

probation [prəˈbeɪʃən] *n* (*in employment*) (période *f* d')essai *m*; (*Law*) liberté surveillée; (*Rel*) noviciat *m*, probation *f*; **on ~** (*employee*) à l'essai; (*Law*) en liberté surveillée

probe [prəub] *n* (*Med, Space*) sonde *f*; (*enquiry*) enquête *f*, investigation *f* ▷ *vt* sonder, explorer

problem [ˈprɔbləm] *n* problème *m*; **to have ~s with the car** avoir des ennuis avec la voiture; **what's the ~?** qu'y a-t-il?, quel est le problème?; **I had no ~ in finding her** je n'ai pas eu de mal à la trouver; **no ~!** pas de problème!

procedure [prəˈsiːdʒə^r] *n* (*Admin, Law*) procédure *f*; (*method*) marche *f* à suivre, façon *f* de procéder

proceed [prəˈsiːd] *vi* (*go forward*) avancer; (*act*) procéder; (*continue*): **to ~ (with)** continuer, poursuivre; **to ~ to** aller à; passer à; **to ~ to do** se mettre à faire; **I am not sure how to ~** je ne sais pas exactement comment m'y prendre; **to ~ against sb** (*Law*) intenter des poursuites contre qn

proceedings [prəˈsiːdɪŋz] *npl* (*measures*) mesures *fpl*; (*Law: against sb*) poursuites *fpl*; (*meeting*) réunion *f*, séance *f*; (*records*) compte rendu; actes *mpl*

proceeds [ˈprəusiːdz] *npl* produit *m*, recette *f*

process [ˈprəuses] *n* processus *m*; (*method*) procédé *m* ▷ *vt* traiter ▷ *vi* [prəˈses] (*Brit formal: go in procession*) défiler; **in ~** en cours; **we are in the ~ of doing** nous sommes en train de faire

processing [ˈprəusesɪŋ] *n* traitement *m*

procession [prəˈseʃən] *n* défilé *m*, cortège *m*; **funeral ~** (*on foot*) cortège funèbre; (*in cars*) convoi *m* mortuaire

proclaim [prəˈkleɪm] *vt* déclarer, proclamer

procrastinate [prəuˈkræstɪneɪt] *vi* faire traîner les choses, vouloir tout remettre au lendemain

procure [prəˈkjuə^r] *vt* (*for o.s.*) se procurer; (*for sb*) procurer

prod [prɔd] *vt* pousser ▷ *n* (*push, jab*) petit coup, poussée *f*

prodigal [ˈprɔdɪgl] *adj* prodigue

prodigy [ˈprɔdɪdʒɪ] *n* prodige *m*

produce *n* [ˈprɔdjuːs] (*Agr*) produits *mpl* ▷ *vt* [prəˈdjuːs] produire; (*show*) présenter; (*cause*) provoquer, causer; (*Theat*) monter, mettre en scène; (*TV: programme*) réaliser; (*: play, film*) mettre en scène; (*Radio: programme*) réaliser; (*: play*) mettre en ondes

producer [prə'dju:sə'] n (Theat) metteur m en scène; (Agr, Comm, Cine) producteur m; (TV: of programme) réalisateur m; (: of play, film) metteur en scène; (Radio: of programme) réalisateur; (: of play) metteur en ondes

product ['prɔdʌkt] n produit m

production [prə'dʌkʃən] n production f; (Theat) mise f en scène; **to put into ~** (goods) entreprendre la fabrication de

production line n chaîne f (de fabrication)

productive [prə'dʌktɪv] adj productif(-ive)

productivity [prɔdʌk'tɪvɪtɪ] n productivité f

Prof. [prɔf] abbr (= professor) Prof

profession [prə'fɛʃən] n profession f; **the ~s** les professions libérales

professional [prə'fɛʃənl] n professionnel(le) ▷ adj professionnel(le); (work) de professionnel; **he's a ~ man** il exerce une profession libérale; **to take ~ advice** consulter un spécialiste

professionally [prə'fɛʃnəlɪ] adv professionnellement; (Sport: play) en professionnel; **I only know him ~** je n'ai avec lui que des relations de travail

professor [prə'fɛsə'] n professeur m (titulaire d'une chaire); (US: teacher) professeur m

proficiency [prə'fɪʃənsɪ] n compétence f, aptitude f

profile ['prəʊfaɪl] n profil m; **to keep a high/low ~** (fig) rester or être très en évidence/discret(-ète)

profit ['prɔfɪt] n (from trading) bénéfice m; (advantage) profit m ▷ vi: **to ~ (by or from)** profiter (de); **~ and loss account** compte m de profits et pertes; **to make a ~** faire un or des bénéfice(s); **to sell sth at a ~** vendre qch à profit

profitable ['prɔfɪtəbl] adj lucratif(-ive), rentable; (fig: beneficial) avantageux(-euse); (: meeting) fructueux(-euse)

profound [prə'faʊnd] adj profond(e)

profusely [prə'fju:slɪ] adv abondamment; (thank etc) avec effusion

prognosis [prɔg'nəʊsɪs] (pl **prognoses**) n pronostic m

programme, (US) **program** ['prəʊgræm] n (Comput: also Brit) programme m; (Radio, TV) émission f ▷ vt programmer

programmer ['prəʊgræmə'] n programmeur(-euse)

programming, (US) **programing** ['prəʊgræmɪŋ] n programmation f

progress n ['prəʊgrɛs] progrès m(pl) ▷ vi [prə'grɛs] progresser, avancer; **in ~** en cours; **to make ~** progresser, faire des progrès, être en progrès; **as the match ~ed** au fur et à mesure que la partie avançait

progressive [prə'grɛsɪv] adj progressif(-ive); (person) progressiste

prohibit [prə'hɪbɪt] vt interdire, défendre; **to ~ sb from doing sth** défendre or interdire à qn de faire qch; **"smoking ~ed"** "défense de fumer"

project [n 'prɔdʒɛkt, vb prə'dʒɛkt] n (plan) projet m, plan m; (venture) opération f, entreprise f; (Scol: research) étude f, dossier m ▷ vt projeter ▷ vi (stick out) faire saillie, s'avancer

projection [prə'dʒɛkʃən] n projection f; (overhang) saillie f

projector [prə'dʒɛktə'] n (Cine etc) projecteur m

prolific [prə'lɪfɪk] adj prolifique

prolong [prə'lɔŋ] vt prolonger

prom [prɔm] n abbr = **promenade**; **promenade concert**; (US: ball) bal m d'étudiants; **the P~s** série de concerts de musique classique; voir article

promenade [prɔmə'nɑːd] n (by sea) esplanade f, promenade f

promenade concert n concert m (de musique classique)

prominent ['prɔmɪnənt] adj (standing out) proéminent(e); (important) important(e); **he is ~ in the field of ...** il est très connu dans le domaine de ...

promiscuous [prə'mɪskjuəs] adj (sexually) de mœurs légères

promise ['prɔmɪs] n promesse f ▷ vt, vi promettre; **to make sb a ~** faire une promesse à qn; **a young man of ~** un jeune homme plein d'avenir; **to ~ well** vi promettre

promising ['prɔmɪsɪŋ] adj prometteur(-euse)

promote [prə'məʊt] vt promouvoir; (venture, event) organiser, mettre sur pied; (new product) lancer; **the team was ~d to the second division** (Brit Football) l'équipe est montée en 2e division

promoter [prə'məʊtə'] n (of event) organisateur(-trice)

promotion [prə'məʊʃən] n promotion f

prompt [prɔmpt] adj rapide ▷ n (Comput) message m (de guidage) ▷ vt inciter; (cause) entraîner, provoquer; (Theat) souffler (son rôle or ses répliques) à; **they're very ~** (punctual) ils sont ponctuels; **at 8 o'clock ~** à 8 heures précises; **he was ~ to accept** il a tout de suite accepté; **to ~ sb to do** inciter or pousser qn à faire

promptly ['prɔmptlɪ] adv (quickly) rapidement, sans délai; (on time) ponctuellement

prone [prəʊn] adj (lying) couché(e) (face contre terre); (liable): **~ to** enclin(e) à; **to be ~ to illness** être facilement malade; **to be ~ to an illness** être sujet à une maladie; **she is ~ to burst into tears if ...** elle a tendance à tomber en larmes si ...

prong [prɔŋ] n pointe f; (of fork) dent f

pronoun ['prəʊnaʊn] n pronom m

pronounce [prə'naʊns] vt prononcer ▷ vi: **to ~ (up)on** se prononcer sur; **how do you ~ it?** comment est-ce que ça se prononce?; **they ~d him unfit to drive** ils l'ont déclaré inapte à la conduite

pronunciation [prənʌnsɪ'eɪʃən] n prononciation f

proof [pru:f] n preuve f; (test, of book, Phot) épreuve f; (of alcohol) degré m ▷ adj: **~ against** à l'épreuve de ▷ vt (Brit: tent, anorak) imperméabiliser; **to be 70° ~** ≈ titrer 40 degrés

prop [prɔp] n support m, étai m; (fig) soutien m ▷ vt (also: **prop up**) étayer, soutenir; **props** npl

accessoires *mpl*; (*lean*): **to ~ sth against** appuyer qch contre *or* à
propaganda [prɔpə'gændə] *n* propagande *f*
propel [prə'pɛl] *vt* propulser, faire avancer
propeller [prə'pɛləʳ] *n* hélice *f*
propensity [prə'pɛnsɪtɪ] *n* propension *f*
proper ['prɔpəʳ] *adj* (*suited, right*) approprié(e), bon (bonne); (*seemly*) correct(e), convenable; (*authentic*) vrai(e), (*land*) véritable; (*inf: real*) fini(e), vrai(e); (*referring to place*): **the village ~** le village proprement dit; **to go through the ~ channels** (*Admin*) passer par la voie officielle
properly ['prɔpəlɪ] *adv* correctement, convenablement; (*really*) bel et bien
proper noun *n* nom *m* propre
property ['prɔpətɪ] *n* (*possessions*) biens *mpl*; (*house etc*) propriété *f*; (*land*) terres *fpl*, domaine *m*; (*Chem etc: quality*) propriété *f*; **it's their ~** cela leur appartient, c'est leur propriété
prophecy ['prɔfɪsɪ] *n* prophétie *f*
prophesy ['prɔfɪsaɪ] *vt* prédire ▷ *vi* prophétiser
prophet ['prɔfɪt] *n* prophète *m*
proportion [prə'pɔːʃən] *n* proportion *f*; (*share*) part *f*; partie *f* ▷ *vt* proportionner; **proportions** *npl* (*size*) dimensions *fpl*; **to be in/out of ~ to** *or* **with sth** être à la mesure de/hors de proportion avec qch; **to see sth in ~** (*fig*) ramener qch à de justes proportions
proportional [prə'pɔːʃənl], **proportionate** [prə'pɔːʃənɪt] *adj* proportionnel(le)
proposal [prə'pəuzl] *n* proposition *f*, offre *f*; (*plan*) projet *m*; (*of marriage*) demande *f* en mariage
propose [prə'pəuz] *vt* proposer, suggérer; (*have in mind*): **to ~ sth/to do** *or* **doing sth** envisager qch/de faire qch ▷ *vi* faire sa demande en mariage; **to ~ to do** avoir l'intention de faire
proposition [prɔpə'zɪʃən] *n* proposition *f*; **to make sb a ~** faire une proposition à qn
proprietor [prə'praɪətəʳ] *n* propriétaire *m/f*
propriety [prə'praɪətɪ] *n* (*seemliness*) bienséance *f*, convenance *f*
prose [prəuz] *n* prose *f*; (*Scol: translation*) thème *m*
prosecute ['prɔsɪkjuːt] *vt* poursuivre
prosecution [prɔsɪ'kjuːʃən] *n* poursuites *fpl* judiciaires; (*accusing side: in criminal case*) accusation *f*; (*: in civil case*) la partie plaignante
prosecutor ['prɔsɪkjuːtəʳ] *n* (*lawyer*) procureur *m*; (*also*: **public prosecutor**) ministère public; (*US: plaintiff*) plaignant(e)
prospect *n* ['prɔspɛkt] perspective *f*; (*hope*) espoir *m*, chances *fpl* ▷ *vt*, *vi* [prə'spɛkt] prospecter; **prospects** *npl* (*for work etc*) possibilités *fpl* d'avenir, débouchés *mpl*; **we are faced with the ~ of leaving** nous risquons de devoir partir; **there is every ~ of an early victory** tout laisse prévoir une victoire rapide
prospecting [prə'spɛktɪŋ] *n* prospection *f*
prospective [prə'spɛktɪv] *adj* (*possible*) éventuel(le); (*future*) futur(e)
prospectus [prə'spɛktəs] *n* prospectus *m*
prosper ['prɔspəʳ] *vi* prospérer

prosperity [prɔ'spɛrɪtɪ] *n* prospérité *f*
prosperous ['prɔspərəs] *adj* prospère
prostitute ['prɔstɪtjuːt] *n* prostituée *f*; **male ~** prostitué *m*
protect [prə'tɛkt] *vt* protéger
protection [prə'tɛkʃən] *n* protection *f*; **to be under sb's ~** être sous la protection de qn
protective [prə'tɛktɪv] *adj* protecteur(-trice); (*clothing*) de protection; **~ custody** (*Law*) détention préventive
protein ['prəutiːn] *n* protéine *f*
protest [*n* 'prəutɛst, *vb* prə'tɛst] *n* protestation *f* ▷ *vi*: **to ~ against/about** protester contre/à propos de ▷ *vt* protester de; **to ~ (that)** protester que
Protestant ['prɔtɪstənt] *adj*, *n* protestant(e)
protester, protestor [prə'tɛstəʳ] *n* (*in demonstration*) manifestant(e)
protracted [prə'træktɪd] *adj* prolongé(e)
protractor [prə'træktəʳ] *n* (*Geom*) rapporteur *m*
protrude [prə'truːd] *vi* avancer, dépasser
proud [praud] *adj* fier(-ère); (*pej*) orgueilleux(-euse); **to be ~ to do sth** être fier de faire qch; **to do sb ~** (*inf*) faire honneur à qn; **to do o.s. ~** (*inf*) ne se priver de rien
prove [pruːv] *vt* prouver, démontrer ▷ *vi*: **to ~ correct** *etc* s'avérer juste *etc*; **to ~ o.s.** montrer ce dont on est capable; **to ~ o.s./itself (to be) useful** *etc* se montrer *or* se révéler utile *etc*; **he was ~d right in the end** il s'est avéré qu'il avait raison
proverb ['prɔvəːb] *n* proverbe *m*
provide [prə'vaɪd] *vt* fournir; **to ~ sb with sth** fournir qch à qn; **to be ~d with** (*person*) disposer de; (*thing*) être équipé(e) *or* muni(e) de
  ▶ **provide for** *vt fus* (*person*) subvenir aux besoins de; (*future event*) prévoir
provided [prə'vaɪdɪd] *conj*: **~ (that)** à condition que + *sub*
providing [prə'vaɪdɪŋ] *conj* à condition que + *sub*
province ['prɔvɪns] *n* province *f*; (*fig*) domaine *m*
provincial [prə'vɪnʃəl] *adj* provincial(e)
provision [prə'vɪʒən] *n* (*supply*) provision *f*; (*supplying*) fourniture *f*; approvisionnement *m*; (*stipulation*) disposition *f*; **provisions** *npl* (*food*) provisions *fpl*; **to make ~ for** (*one's future*) assurer; (*one's family*) assurer l'avenir de; **there's no ~ for this in the contract** le contrat ne prévoit pas cela
provisional [prə'vɪʒənl] *adj* provisoire ▷ *n*: **P~** (*Irish Pol*) Provisional *m* (*membre de la tendance activiste de l'IRA*)
proviso [prə'vaɪzəu] *n* condition *f*; **with the ~ that** à la condition (expresse) que
provocative [prə'vɔkətɪv] *adj* provocateur(-trice), provocant(e)
provoke [prə'vəuk] *vt* provoquer; **to ~ sb to sth/to do** *or* **into doing sth** pousser qn à qch/à faire qch
prowess ['prauɪs] *n* prouesse *f*
prowl [praul] *vi* (*also*: **prowl about, prowl around**) rôder ▷ *n*: **to be on the ~** rôder

prowler ['praulə'] n rôdeur(-euse)
proximity [prɔk'sɪmɪtɪ] n proximité f
proxy ['prɔksɪ] n procuration f; **by** ~ par
procuration
prudent ['pru:dnt] adj prudent(e)
prune [pru:n] n pruneau m ▷ vt élaguer
pry [praɪ] vi: **to** ~ **into** fourrer son nez dans
PS n abbr (= postscript) PS m
psalm [sɑ:m] n psaume m
pseudonym ['sju:dənɪm] n pseudonyme m
PSHE n abbr (Brit: Scol: = personal, social and health
education) cours d'éducation personnelle, sanitaire et
sociale préparant à la vie adulte
psyche ['saɪkɪ] n psychisme m
psychiatric [saɪkɪ'ætrɪk] adj psychiatrique
psychiatrist [saɪ'kaɪətrɪst] n psychiatre m/f
psychic ['saɪkɪk] adj (also: **psychical**)
(méta)psychique; (person) doué(e) de télépathie
or d'un sixième sens
psychoanalysis (pl **-ses**) [saɪkəuə'nælɪsɪs, -si:z]
n psychanalyse f
psychoanalyst [saɪkəu'ænəlɪst] n
psychanalyste m/f
psychological [saɪkə'lɔdʒɪkl] adj psychologique
psychologist [saɪ'kɔlədʒɪst] n psychologue m/f
psychology [saɪ'kɔlədʒɪ] n psychologie f
psychotherapy [saɪkəu'θɛrəpɪ] n
psychothérapie f
pt abbr = **pint; pints; point; points**
PTO abbr (= please turn over) TSVP
PTV abbr (US) = **pay television**
pub [pʌb] n abbr (= public house) pub m
puberty ['pju:bətɪ] n puberté f
public ['pʌblɪk] adj public(-ique) ▷ n public m; **in**
~ en public; **the general** ~ le grand public; **to**
be ~ **knowledge** être de notoriété publique; **to**
go ~ (Comm) être coté(e) en Bourse; **to make** ~
rendre public
public address system n (système m de)
sonorisation f, sono f (col)
publican ['pʌblɪkən] n patron m or gérant m de
pub
publication [pʌblɪ'keɪʃən] n publication f
public company n société f anonyme
public convenience n (Brit) toilettes fpl
public holiday n (Brit) jour férié
public house n (Brit) pub m
publicity [pʌb'lɪsɪtɪ] n publicité f
publicize ['pʌblɪsaɪz] vt (make known) faire
connaître, rendre public; (advertise) faire de la
publicité pour
public limited company n = société f anonyme
(SA) (cotée en Bourse)
publicly ['pʌblɪklɪ] adv publiquement, en public
public opinion n opinion publique
public relations n or npl relations publiques (RP)
public school n (Brit) école privée; (US) école
publique; voir article
public-spirited [pʌblɪk'spɪrɪtɪd] adj qui fait
preuve de civisme
public transport, (US) **public transportation** n
transports mpl en commun

publish ['pʌblɪʃ] vt publier
publisher ['pʌblɪʃə'] n éditeur m
publishing ['pʌblɪʃɪŋ] n (industry) édition f; (of a
book) publication f
pub lunch n repas m de bistrot
pucker ['pʌkə'] vt plisser
pudding ['pudɪŋ] n (Brit: dessert) dessert m,
entremets m; (sweet dish) pudding m, gâteau m;
(sausage) boudin m; **rice** ~ = riz m au lait; **black** ~
(US): **blood** ~ boudin (noir)
puddle ['pʌdl] n flaque f d'eau
puff [pʌf] n bouffée f ▷ vt: **to** ~ **one's pipe** tirer
sur sa pipe; (also: **puff out**: sails, cheeks) gonfler
▷ vi sortir par bouffées; (pant) haleter; **to** ~ **out**
smoke envoyer des bouffées de fumée
puff pastry, (US) **puff paste** n pâte feuilletée
puffy ['pʌfɪ] adj bouffi(e), boursouflé(e)
pull [pul] n (tug): **to give sth a** ~ tirer sur qch;
(of moon, magnet, the sea etc) attraction f; (fig)
influence f ▷ vt tirer; (trigger) presser; (strain:
muscle, tendon) se claquer ▷ vi tirer; **to** ~ **a face**
faire une grimace; **to** ~ **to pieces** mettre en
morceaux; **to** ~ **one's punches** (also fig) ménager
son adversaire; **to** ~ **one's weight** y mettre du
sien; **to** ~ **o.s. together** se ressaisir; **to** ~ **sb's**
leg (fig) faire marcher qn; **to** ~ **strings** (for sb)
intervenir (en faveur de qn)
  ▶ **pull about** vt (Brit: handle roughly: object)
maltraiter; (: person) malmener
  ▶ **pull apart** vt séparer; (break) mettre en pièces,
démantibuler
  ▶ **pull away** vi (vehicle: move off) partir; (draw back)
s'éloigner
  ▶ **pull back** vt (lever etc) tirer sur; (curtains) ouvrir
▷ vi (refrain) s'abstenir; (Mil: withdraw) se retirer
  ▶ **pull down** vt baisser, abaisser; (house) démolir;
(tree) abattre
  ▶ **pull in** vi (Aut) se ranger; (Rail) entrer en gare
  ▶ **pull off** vt enlever, ôter; (deal etc) conclure
  ▶ **pull out** vi démarrer, partir; (withdraw) se
retirer; (Aut: come out of line) déboîter ▷ vt (from
bag, pocket) sortir; (remove) arracher; (withdraw)
retirer
  ▶ **pull over** vi (Aut) se ranger
  ▶ **pull round** vi (unconscious person) revenir à soi;
(sick person) se rétablir
  ▶ **pull through** vi s'en sortir
  ▶ **pull up** vi (stop) s'arrêter ▷ vt remonter;
(uproot) déraciner, arracher; (stop) arrêter
pulley ['pulɪ] n poulie f
pullover ['puləuvə'] n pull-over m, tricot m
pulp [pʌlp] n (of fruit) pulpe f; (for paper) pâte f à
papier; (pej: also: **pulp magazines** etc) presse f à
sensation or de bas étage; **to reduce sth to (a)** ~
réduire qch en purée
pulpit ['pulpɪt] n chaire f
pulsate [pʌl'seɪt] vi battre, palpiter; (music)
vibrer
pulse [pʌls] n (of blood) pouls m; (of heart)
battement m; (of music, engine) vibrations fpl;
pulses npl (Culin) légumineuses fpl; **to feel** or
take sb's ~ prendre le pouls à qn

puma ['pju:mə] n puma m
pump [pʌmp] n pompe f; (shoe) escarpin m ▷ vt pomper; (fig: inf) faire parler; **to ~ sb for information** essayer de soutirer des renseignements à qn
▶ **pump up** vt gonfler
pumpkin ['pʌmpkɪn] n potiron m, citrouille f
pun [pʌn] n jeu m de mots, calembour m
punch [pʌntʃ] n (blow) coup m de poing; (fig: force) vivacité f, mordant m; (tool) poinçon m; (drink) punch m ▷ vt (make a hole in) poinçonner, perforer; (hit): **to ~ sb/sth** donner un coup de poing à qn/sur qch; **to ~ a hole (in)** faire un trou (dans)
▶ **punch in** vi (US) pointer (en arrivant)
▶ **punch out** vi (US) pointer (en partant)
punch line n (of joke) conclusion f
punch-up ['pʌntʃʌp] n (Brit inf) bagarre f
punctual ['pʌŋktjuəl] adj ponctuel(le)
punctuation [pʌŋktju'eɪʃən] n ponctuation f
puncture ['pʌŋktʃəʳ] n (Brit) crevaison f ▷ vt crever; **I have a ~** (Aut) j'ai (un pneu) crevé
pundit ['pʌndɪt] n individu m qui pontifie, pontife m
pungent ['pʌndʒənt] adj piquant(e); (fig) mordant(e), caustique
punish ['pʌnɪʃ] vt punir; **to ~ sb for sth/for doing sth** punir qn de qch/d'avoir fait qch
punishment ['pʌnɪʃmənt] n punition f, châtiment m; (fig: inf): **to take a lot of ~** (boxer) encaisser; (car, person etc) être mis(e) à dure épreuve
punk [pʌŋk] n (person: also: **punk rocker**) punk m/f; (music: also: **punk rock**) le punk; (US inf: hoodlum) voyou m
punt [pʌnt] n (boat) bachot m; (Irish) livre irlandaise ▷ vi (Brit: bet) parier
punter ['pʌntəʳ] n (Brit: gambler) parieur(-euse); (: inf) Monsieur m tout le monde; type m
puny ['pju:nɪ] adj chétif(-ive)
pup [pʌp] n chiot m
pupil ['pju:pl] n élève m/f; (of eye) pupille f
puppet ['pʌpɪt] n marionnette f, pantin m
puppy ['pʌpɪ] n chiot m, petit chien
purchase ['pə:tʃɪs] n achat m; (grip) prise f ▷ vt acheter; **to get a ~ on** trouver appui sur
purchaser ['pə:tʃɪsəʳ] n acheteur(-euse)
pure [pjuəʳ] adj pur(e); **a ~ wool jumper** un pull en pure laine; **~ and simple** pur(e) et simple
purely ['pjuəlɪ] adv purement
purge [pə:dʒ] n (Med) purge f; (Pol) épuration f, purge ▷ vt purger; (fig) épurer, purger
purify ['pjuərɪfaɪ] vt purifier, épurer
purity ['pjuərɪtɪ] n pureté f
purple ['pə:pl] adj violet(te); (face) cramoisi(e)
purpose ['pə:pəs] n intention f, but m; **on ~** exprès; **for illustrative ~s** à titre d'illustration; **for teaching ~s** dans un but pédagogique; **for the ~s of this meeting** pour cette réunion; **to no ~** en pure perte
purposeful ['pə:pəsful] adj déterminé(e), résolu(e)

purr [pə:ʳ] n ronronnement m ▷ vi ronronner
purse [pə:s] n (Brit: for money) porte-monnaie m inv, bourse f; (US: handbag) sac m (à main) ▷ vt serrer, pincer
purser ['pə:səʳ] n (Naut) commissaire m du bord
pursue [pə'sju:] vt poursuivre; (pleasures) rechercher; (inquiry, matter) approfondir
pursuit [pə'sju:t] n poursuite f; (occupation) occupation f, activité f; **scientific ~s** recherches fpl scientifiques; **in (the) ~ of sth** à la recherche de qch
pus [pʌs] n pus m
push [puʃ] n poussée f; (effort) gros effort; (drive) énergie f ▷ vt pousser; (button) appuyer sur; (thrust): **to ~ sth (into)** enfoncer qch (dans); (fig: product) mettre en avant, faire de la publicité pour ▷ vi pousser; appuyer; **to ~ a door open/shut** pousser une porte (pour l'ouvrir/pour la fermer); **"~"** (on door) "pousser"; (on bell) "appuyer"; **to ~ for** (better pay, conditions) réclamer; **to be ~ed for time/money** être à court de temps/d'argent; **she is ~ing fifty** (inf) elle frise la cinquantaine; **at a ~** (Brit inf) à la limite, à la rigueur
▶ **push aside** vt écarter
▶ **push in** vi s'introduire de force
▶ **push off** vi (inf) filer, ficher le camp
▶ **push on** vi (continue) continuer
▶ **push over** vt renverser
▶ **push through** vt (measure) faire voter ▷ vi (in crowd) se frayer un chemin
▶ **push up** vt (total, prices) faire monter
pushchair ['puʃtʃɛəʳ] n (Brit) poussette f
pusher ['puʃəʳ] n (also: **drug pusher**) revendeur(-euse) (de drogue), ravitailleur(-euse) (en drogue)
pushover ['puʃəuvəʳ] n (inf): **it's a ~** c'est un jeu d'enfant
push-up ['puʃʌp] n (US) traction f
pushy ['puʃɪ] adj (pej) arriviste
pussy ['pusɪ], **pussy-cat** n (inf) minet m
put (pt, pp **~**) [put] vt mettre; (place) poser, placer; (say) dire, exprimer; (a question) poser; (case, view) exposer, présenter; (estimate) estimer; **to ~ sb in a good/bad mood** mettre qn de bonne/ mauvaise humeur; **to ~ sb to bed** mettre qn au lit, coucher qn; **to ~ sb to a lot of trouble** déranger qn; **how shall I ~ it?** comment dirais-je?, comment dire?; **to ~ a lot of time into sth** passer beaucoup de temps à qch; **to ~ money on a horse** miser sur un cheval; **I ~ it to you that ...** (Brit) je (vous) suggère que ..., je suis d'avis que ...; **to stay ~** ne pas bouger
▶ **put about** vi (Naut) virer de bord ▷ vt (rumour) faire courir
▶ **put across** vt (ideas etc) communiquer; faire comprendre
▶ **put aside** vt mettre de côté
▶ **put away** vt (store) ranger
▶ **put back** vt (replace) remettre, replacer; (postpone) remettre; (delay, watch, clock) retarder; **this will ~ us back ten years** cela nous

ramènera dix ans en arrière

▶ **put by** vt (money) mettre de côté, économiser

▶ **put down** vt (parcel etc) poser, déposer; (pay) verser; (in writing) mettre par écrit, inscrire; (suppress: revolt etc) réprimer, écraser; (attribute) attribuer; (animal) abattre; (cat, dog) faire piquer

▶ **put forward** vt (ideas) avancer, proposer; (date, watch, clock) avancer

▶ **put in** vt (gas, electricity) installer; (complaint) soumettre; (time, effort) consacrer

▶ **put in for** vt fus (job) poser sa candidature pour; (promotion) solliciter

▶ **put off** vt (light etc) éteindre; (postpone) remettre à plus tard, ajourner; (discourage) dissuader

▶ **put on** vt (clothes, lipstick, CD) mettre; (light etc) allumer; (play etc) monter; (extra bus, train etc) mettre en service; (food, meal: provide) servir; (: cook) mettre à cuire or à chauffer; (weight) prendre; (assume: accent, manner) prendre; (: airs) se donner, prendre; (inf: tease) faire marcher; (inform, indicate): **to ~ sb on to sb/sth** indiquer qn/qch à qn; **to ~ the brakes on** freiner

▶ **put out** vt (take outside) mettre dehors; (one's hand) tendre; (news, rumour) faire courir, répandre; (light etc) éteindre; (person: inconvenience) déranger, gêner; (Brit: dislocate) se démettre ▷ vi (Naut): **to ~ out to sea** prendre le large; **to ~ out from Plymouth** quitter Plymouth

▶ **put through** vt (Tel: caller) mettre en communication; (: call) passer; (plan) faire accepter; **~ me through to Miss Blair** passez-moi Miss Blair

▶ **put together** vt mettre ensemble; (assemble: furniture) monter, assembler; (meal) préparer

▶ **put up** vt (raise) lever, relever, remonter; (pin up) afficher; (hang) accrocher; (build) construire, ériger; (tent) monter; (umbrella) ouvrir; (increase) augmenter; (accommodate) loger; (incite): **to ~ sb up to doing sth** pousser qn à faire qch; **to ~ sth up for sale** mettre qch en vente

▶ **put upon** vt fus: **to be ~ upon** (imposed on) se laisser faire

▶ **put up with** vt fus supporter

putt [pʌt] vt, vi putter ▷ n putt m

putting green ['pʌtɪŋ-] n green m

putty ['pʌtɪ] n mastic m

put-up ['putʌp] adj: **~ job** coup monté

puzzle ['pʌzl] n énigme f, mystère m; (game) jeu m, casse-tête m; (jigsaw) puzzle m; (also: **crossword puzzle**) mots croisés ▷ vt intriguer, rendre perplexe ▷ vi se creuser la tête; **to ~ over** chercher à comprendre

puzzled ['pʌzld] adj perplexe; **to be ~ about sth** être perplexe au sujet de qch

puzzling ['pʌzlɪŋ] adj déconcertant(e), inexplicable

pyjamas [pɪ'dʒɑːməz] npl (Brit) pyjama m; **a pair of ~** un pyjama

pylon ['paɪlən] n pylône m

pyramid ['pɪrəmɪd] n pyramide f

Pyrenees [pɪrə'niːz] npl Pyrénées fpl

Qq

quack [kwæk] *n* (*of duck*) coin-coin *m inv*; (*pej: doctor*) charlatan *m* ▷ *vi* faire coin-coin

quad [kwɔd] *n abbr* = **quadruplet; quadrangle**

quadrangle ['kwɔdræŋgl] *n* (*Math*) quadrilatère *m*; (*courtyard: abbr: quad*) cour *f*

quadruple [kwɔ'dru:pl] *adj, n* quadruple *m* ▷ *vt, vi* quadrupler

quadruplet [kwɔ'dru:plɪt] *n* quadruplé(e)

quail [kweɪl] *n* (*Zool*) caille *f* ▷ *vi*: **to ~ at** *or* **before** reculer devant

quaint [kweɪnt] *adj* bizarre; (*old-fashioned*) désuet(-ète); (*picturesque*) au charme vieillot, pittoresque

quake [kweɪk] *vi* trembler ▷ *n abbr* = **earthquake**

qualification [kwɔlɪfɪ'keɪʃən] *n* (*often pl: degree etc*) diplôme *m*; (*training*) qualification(s) *f(pl)*; (*ability*) compétence(s) *f(pl)*; (*limitation*) réserve *f*, restriction *f*; **what are your ~s?** qu'avez-vous comme diplômes?; quelles sont vos qualifications?

qualified ['kwɔlɪfaɪd] *adj* (*trained*) qualifié(e); (*professionally*) diplômé(e); (*fit, competent*) compétent(e), qualifié(e); (*limited*) conditionnel(le); **it was a ~ success** ce fut un succès mitigé; **~ for/to do** qui a les diplômes requis pour/pour faire; qualifié pour/pour faire

qualify ['kwɔlɪfaɪ] *vt* qualifier; (*modify*) atténuer, nuancer; (*limit: statement*) apporter des réserves à ▷ *vi*: **to ~ (as)** obtenir son diplôme (de); **to ~ (for)** remplir les conditions requises (pour); (*Sport*) se qualifier (pour)

quality ['kwɔlɪtɪ] *n* qualité *f* ▷ *cpd* de qualité; **of good/poor ~** de bonne/mauvaise qualité

quality time *n* moments privilégiés

qualm [kwɑ:m] *n* doute *m*; scrupule *m*; **to have ~s about sth** avoir des doutes sur qch; éprouver des scrupules à propos de qch

quandary ['kwɔndrɪ] *n*: **in a ~** devant un dilemme, dans l'embarras

quantify ['kwɔntɪfaɪ] *vt* quantifier

quantity ['kwɔntɪtɪ] *n* quantité *f*; **in ~** en grande quantité

quantity surveyor *n* (*Brit*) métreur vérificateur

quarantine ['kwɔrntiːn] *n* quarantaine *f*

quarrel ['kwɔrl] *n* querelle *f*, dispute *f* ▷ *vi* se disputer, se quereller; **to have a ~ with sb** se quereller avec qn; **I've no ~ with him** je n'ai rien contre lui; **I can't ~ with that** je ne vois rien à redire à cela

quarry ['kwɔrɪ] *n* (*for stone*) carrière *f*; (*animal*) proie *f*, gibier *m* ▷ *vt* (*marble etc*) extraire

quart [kwɔ:t] *n* ≈ litre *m*

quarter ['kwɔ:tə^r] *n* quart *m*; (*of year*) trimestre *m*; (*district*) quartier *m*; (*US, Canada: 25 cents*) (*pièce f de*) vingt-cinq cents *mpl* ▷ *vt* partager en quartiers *or* en quatre; (*Mil*) caserner, cantonner; **quarters** *npl* logement *m*; (*Mil*) quartiers *mpl*, cantonnement *m*; **a ~ of an hour** un quart d'heure; **it's a ~ to 3** (*US*): **it's a ~ of 3** il est 3 heures moins le quart; **it's a ~ past 3** (*US*): **it's a ~ after 3** il est 3 heures et quart; **from all ~s** de tous côtés

quarter final *n* quart *m* de finale

quarterly ['kwɔ:təlɪ] *adj* trimestriel(le) ▷ *adv* tous les trois mois ▷ *n* (*Press*) revue trimestrielle

quartet, quartette [kwɔ:'tɛt] *n* quatuor *m*; (*jazz players*) quartette *m*

quartz [kwɔ:ts] *n* quartz *m* ▷ *cpd* de *or* en quartz; (*watch, clock*) à quartz

quash [kwɔʃ] *vt* (*verdict*) annuler, casser

quaver ['kweɪvə^r] *n* (*Brit Mus*) croche *f* ▷ *vi* trembler

quay [ki:] *n* (*also*: **quayside**) quai *m*

queasy ['kwi:zɪ] *adj* (*stomach*) délicat(e); **to feel ~** avoir mal au cœur

Quebec [kwɪ'bɛk] *n* (*city*) Québec; (*province*) Québec *m*

queen [kwi:n] *n* (*gen*) reine *f*; (*Cards etc*) dame *f*

queen mother *n* reine mère *f*

queer [kwɪə^r] *adj* étrange, curieux(-euse); (*suspicious*) louche; (*Brit: sick*): **I feel ~** je ne me sens pas bien ▷ *n* (*inf: highly offensive*) homosexuel *m*

quell [kwɛl] *vt* réprimer, étouffer

quench [kwɛntʃ] *vt* (*flames*) éteindre; **to ~ one's thirst** se désaltérer

query ['kwɪərɪ] *n* question *f*; (*doubt*) doute *m*; (*question mark*) point *m* d'interrogation ▷ *vt* (*disagree with, dispute*) mettre en doute, questionner

quest [kwɛst] *n* recherche *f*, quête *f*

question ['kwɛstʃən] *n* question *f* ▷ *vt* (*person*) interroger; (*plan, idea*) mettre en question *or* en doute; **to ask sb a ~, to put a ~ to sb** poser une question à qn; **to bring** or **call sth into** ~ remettre qch en question; **the ~ is ...** la question est de savoir ...; **it's a ~ of doing** il s'agit de faire; **there's some ~ of doing** il est question de faire; **beyond** ~ sans aucun doute; **out of the ~** hors de question

questionable ['kwɛstʃənəbl] *adj* discutable

question mark *n* point *m* d'interrogation

questionnaire [kwɛstʃə'nɛəʳ] *n* questionnaire *m*

queue [kju:] (*Brit*) *n* queue *f*, file *f* ▷ *vi* (*also:* **queue up**) faire la queue; **to jump the ~** passer avant son tour

quibble ['kwɪbl] *vi* ergoter, chicaner

quiche [ki:ʃ] *n* quiche *f*

quick [kwɪk] *adj* rapide; (*reply*) prompt(e), rapide; (*mind*) vif (vive); (*agile*) agile, vif (vive), rapidement ▷ *n*: **cut to the ~** (*fig*) touché(e) au vif; **be ~!** dépêche-toi!; **to be ~ to act** agir tout de suite

quicken ['kwɪkən] *vt* accélérer, presser; (*rouse*) stimuler ▷ *vi* s'accélérer, devenir plus rapide

quickly ['kwɪklɪ] *adv* (*fast*) vite, rapidement; (*immediately*) tout de suite

quicksand ['kwɪksænd] *n* sables mouvants

quick-witted [kwɪk'wɪtɪd] *adj* à l'esprit vif

quid [kwɪd] *n* (*pl inv*: *Brit inf*) livre *f*

quiet ['kwaɪət] *adj* tranquille, calme; (*not noisy: engine*) silencieux(-euse); (*reserved*) réservé(e); (*voice*) bas(se); (*not busy: day, business*) calme; (*ceremony, colour*) discret(-ète) ▷ *n* tranquillité *f*, calme *m*; (*silence*) silence *m* ▷ *vt, vi* (*US*) = **quieten**; **keep ~!** tais-toi!; **on the ~** en secret, discrètement; **I'll have a ~ word with him** je lui en parlerai discrètement

quieten ['kwaɪətn] (*also:* **quieten down**) *vi* se calmer, s'apaiser ▷ *vt* calmer, apaiser

quietly ['kwaɪətlɪ] *adv* tranquillement; (*silently*) silencieusement; (*discreetly*) discrètement

quietness ['kwaɪətnɪs] *n* tranquillité *f*, calme *m*; silence *m*

quilt [kwɪlt] *n* édredon *m*; (*continental quilt*) couette *f*

quin [kwɪn] *n abbr* = **quintuplet**

quintuplet [kwɪn'tju:plɪt] *n* quintuplé(e)

quip [kwɪp] *n* remarque piquante or spirituelle, pointe *f* ▷ *vt*: **... he ~ped ...** lança-t-il

quirk [kwə:k] *n* bizarrerie *f*; **by some ~ of fate** par un caprice du hasard

quirky ['kwɜːkɪ] *adj* singulier(-ère)

quit [kwɪt] (*pt, pp* ~ or **-ted**) *vt* quitter ▷ *vi* (*give up*) abandonner, renoncer; (*resign*) démissionner; **to ~ doing** arrêter de faire; **~ stalling!** (*US inf*) arrête de te dérober!; **notice to ~** (*Brit*) congé *m* (*signifié au locataire*)

quite [kwaɪt] *adv* (*rather*) assez, plutôt; (*entirely*) complètement, tout à fait; **~ new** plutôt neuf; tout à fait neuf; **she's ~ pretty** elle est plutôt jolie; **I ~ understand** je comprends très bien; **~ a few of them** un assez grand nombre d'entre eux; **that's not ~ right** ce n'est pas tout à fait juste; **not ~ as many as last time** pas tout à fait autant que la dernière fois; **~ (so)!** exactement!

quits [kwɪts] *adj*: **~ (with)** quitte (envers); **let's call it ~** restons-en là

quiver ['kwɪvəʳ] *vi* trembler, frémir ▷ *n* (*for arrows*) carquois *m*

quiz [kwɪz] *n* (*on TV*) jeu-concours *m* (télévisé); (*in magazine etc*) test *m* de connaissances ▷ *vt* interroger

quizzical ['kwɪzɪkl] *adj* narquois(e)

quota ['kwəutə] *n* quota *m*

quotation [kwəu'teɪʃən] *n* citation *f*; (*of shares etc*) cote *f*, cours *m*; (*estimate*) devis *m*

quotation marks *npl* guillemets *mpl*

quote [kwəut] *n* citation *f*; (*estimate*) devis *m* ▷ *vt* (*sentence, author*) citer; (*price*) donner, soumettre; (*shares*) coter ▷ *vi*: **to ~ from** citer; **to ~ for a job** établir un devis pour des travaux; **quotes** *npl* (*inverted commas*) guillemets *mpl*; **in ~s** entre guillemets; **~ ... unquote** (*in dictation*) ouvrez les guillemets ... fermez les guillemets

Rr

Rabat [rə'bɑːt] n Rabat
rabbi ['ræbaɪ] n rabbin m
rabbit ['ræbɪt] n lapin m ▷ vi: **to ~ (on)** (Brit)
parler à n'en plus finir
rabbit hutch n clapier m
rabble ['ræbl] n (pej) populace f
rabies ['reɪbiːz] n rage f
RAC n abbr (Brit: = Royal Automobile Club) ≈ ACF m
raccoon, racoon [rə'kuːn] n raton m laveur
race [reɪs] n (species) race f; (competition, rush)
course f ▷ vt (person) faire la course avec; (horse)
faire courir; (engine) emballer ▷ vi (compete) faire
la course, courir; (hurry) aller à toute vitesse,
courir; (engine) s'emballer; (pulse) battre très vite;
the human ~ la race humaine; **to ~ in/out** etc
entrer/sortir etc à toute vitesse
race car n (US) = **racing car**
race car driver n (US) = **racing driver**
racecourse ['reɪskɔːs] n champ m de courses
racehorse ['reɪshɔːs] n cheval m de course
racer ['reɪsə'] n (bike) vélo m de course
racetrack ['reɪstræk] n piste f
racial ['reɪʃl] adj racial(e)
racing ['reɪsɪŋ] n courses fpl
racing car n (Brit) voiture f de course
racing driver n (Brit) pilote m de course
racism ['reɪsɪzəm] n racisme m
racist ['reɪsɪst] adj, n raciste m/f
rack [ræk] n (for guns, tools) râtelier m; (for clothes)
portant m; (for bottles) casier m; (also: **luggage
rack**) filet m à bagages; (also: **roof rack**) galerie
f; (also: **dish rack**) égouttoir m ▷ vt tourmenter;
magazine ~ porte-revues m inv; **shoe ~** étagère f
à chaussures; **toast ~** porte-toast m; **to ~ one's
brains** se creuser la cervelle; **to go to ~ and ruin**
(building) tomber en ruine; (business) péricliter
▶ **rack up** vt accumuler
racket ['rækɪt] n (for tennis) raquette f; (noise)
tapage m, vacarme m; (swindle) escroquerie f;
(organized crime) racket m
racquet ['rækɪt] n raquette f
racy ['reɪsɪ] adj plein(e) de verve, osé(e)
radar ['reɪdɑː'] n radar m ▷ cpd radar inv
radial ['reɪdɪəl] adj (also: **radial-ply**) à carcasse
radiale
radiant ['reɪdɪənt] adj rayonnant(e); (Physics)
radiant(e)

radiate ['reɪdɪeɪt] vt (heat) émettre, dégager ▷ vi
(lines) rayonner
radiation [reɪdɪ'eɪʃən] n rayonnement m;
(radioactive) radiation f
radiator ['reɪdɪeɪtə'] n radiateur m
radical ['rædɪkl] adj radical(e)
radii ['reɪdɪaɪ] npl of **radius**
radio ['reɪdɪəu] n radio f ▷ vi: **to ~ to sb** envoyer
un message radio à qn ▷ vt (information)
transmettre par radio; (one's position) signaler
par radio; (person) appeler par radio; **on the ~** à
la radio
radioactive ['reɪdɪəu'æktɪv] adj radioactif(-ive)
radio cassette n radiocassette m
radio-controlled ['reɪdɪəukən'trəuld] adj
radioguidé(e)
radio station n station f de radio
radish ['rædɪʃ] n radis m
radius (pl **radii**) ['reɪdɪəs, -ɪaɪ] n rayon m; (Anat)
radius m; **within a ~ of 50 miles** dans un rayon
de 50 milles
RAF n abbr (Brit) = **Royal Air Force**
raffle ['ræfl] n tombola f ▷ vt mettre comme lot
dans une tombola
raft [rɑːft] n (craft: also: **life raft**) radeau m; (logs)
train m de flottage
rafter ['rɑːftə'] n chevron m
rag [ræg] n chiffon m; (pej: newspaper) feuille f,
torchon m; (for charity) attractions organisées par
les étudiants au profit d'œuvres de charité ▷ vt (Brit)
chahuter, mettre en boîte; **rags** npl haillons mpl;
in ~s (person) en haillons; (clothes) en lambeaux
rag doll n poupée f de chiffon
rage [reɪdʒ] n (fury) rage f, fureur f ▷ vi (person)
être fou (folle) de rage; (storm) faire rage, être
déchaîné(e); **to fly into a ~** se mettre en rage;
it's all the ~ cela fait fureur
ragged ['rægɪd] adj (edge) inégal(e), qui accroche;
(clothes) en loques; (cuff) effiloché(e); (appearance)
déguenillé(e)
raid [reɪd] n (Mil) raid m; (criminal) hold-up m inv;
(by police) descente f, rafle f ▷ vt faire un raid sur
or un hold-up dans or une descente dans
rail [reɪl] n (on stair) rampe f; (on bridge, balcony)
balustrade f; (of ship) bastingage m; (for train) rail
m; **rails** npl rails mpl, voie ferrée; **by ~** en train,
par le train

railcard ['reɪlkɑːd] n (Brit) carte f de chemin de fer; **young person's** ~ carte f jeune

railing ['reɪlɪŋ] n, **railings** ['reɪlɪŋz] ▷ npl grille f

railway ['reɪlweɪ], (US) **railroad** ['reɪlrəʊd] n chemin m de fer; (track) voie f ferrée

railway line n (Brit) ligne f de chemin de fer; (track) voie ferrée

railwayman ['reɪlweɪmən] (irreg) n cheminot m

railway station n (Brit) gare f

rain [reɪn] n pluie f ▷ vi pleuvoir; **in the** ~ sous la pluie; **it's ~ing** il pleut; **it's ~ing cats and dogs** il pleut à torrents

rainbow ['reɪnbəʊ] n arc-en-ciel m

raincoat ['reɪnkəʊt] n imperméable m

raindrop ['reɪndrɒp] n goutte f de pluie

rainfall ['reɪnfɔːl] n chute f de pluie; (measurement) hauteur f des précipitations

rainforest ['reɪnfɒrɪst] n forêt tropicale

rainy ['reɪnɪ] adj pluvieux(-euse)

raise [reɪz] n augmentation f ▷ vt (lift) lever; hausser; (end: siege, embargo) lever; (build) ériger; (increase) augmenter; (morale) remonter; (standards) améliorer; (a protest, doubt) provoquer, causer; (a question) soulever; (cattle, family) élever; (crop) faire pousser; (army, funds) rassembler; (loan) obtenir; **to ~ one's glass to sb/sth** porter un toast en l'honneur de qn/qch; **to ~ one's voice** élever la voix; **to ~ sb's hopes** donner de l'espoir à qn; **to ~ a laugh/a smile** faire rire/sourire

raisin ['reɪzn] n raisin sec

rake [reɪk] n (tool) râteau m; (person) débauché m ▷ vt (garden) ratisser; (fire) tisonner; (with machine gun) balayer ▷ vi: **to ~ through** (fig: search) fouiller (dans)

rally ['rælɪ] n (Pol etc) meeting m, rassemblement m; (Aut) rallye m; (Tennis) échange m ▷ vt rassembler, rallier; (support) gagner ▷ vi se rallier; (sick person) aller mieux; (Stock Exchange) reprendre
▸ **rally round** vi venir en aide ▷ vt fus se rallier à; venir en aide à

RAM [ræm] n abbr (Comput: = random access memory) mémoire vive

ram [ræm] n bélier m ▷ vt (push) enfoncer; (soil) tasser; (crash into: vehicle) emboutir; (: lamppost etc) percuter; (in battle) éperonner

Ramadan [ræmə'dæn] n Ramadan m

ramble ['ræmbl] n randonnée f ▷ vi (walk) se promener, faire une randonnée; (pej: also: **ramble on**) discourir

rambler ['ræmblər] n promeneur(-euse), randonneur(-euse); (Bot) rosier grimpant

rambling ['ræmblɪŋ] adj (speech) décousu(e); (house) plein(e) de coins et de recoins; (Bot) grimpant(e)

ramp [ræmp] n (incline) rampe f; (Aut) dénivellation f; (in garage) pont m; **on/off** ~ (US Aut) bretelle f d'accès

rampage [ræm'peɪdʒ] n: **to be on the** ~ se déchaîner ▷ vi: **they went rampaging through the town** ils ont envahi les rues et ont tout saccagé sur leur passage

rampant ['ræmpənt] adj (disease etc) qui sévit

ram raiding [-reɪdɪŋ] n pillage d'un magasin en enfonçant la vitrine avec une voiture volée

ramshackle ['ræmʃækl] adj (house) délabré(e); (car etc) déglingué(e)

ran [ræn] pt of **run**

ranch [rɑːntʃ] n ranch m

rancher ['rɑːntʃər] n (owner) propriétaire m de ranch; (ranch hand) cowboy m

rancid ['rænsɪd] adj rance

rancour, (US) **rancor** ['ræŋkər] n rancune f, rancœur f

random ['rændəm] adj fait(e) or établi(e) au hasard; (Comput, Math) aléatoire ▷ n: **at** ~ au hasard

random access memory n (Comput) mémoire vive, RAM f

randy ['rændɪ] adj (Brit inf) excité(e); lubrique

rang [ræŋ] pt of **ring**

range [reɪndʒ] n (of mountains) chaîne f; (of missile, voice) portée f; (of products) choix m, gamme f; (also: **shooting range**) champ m de tir; (: indoor) stand m de tir; (also: **kitchen range**) fourneau m (de cuisine) ▷ vt (place) mettre en rang, placer; (roam) parcourir ▷ vi: **to ~ over** couvrir; **to ~ from ... to** aller de ... à; **price ~** éventail m des prix; **do you have anything else in this price ~?** avez-vous autre chose dans ces prix?; **within (firing)** ~ à portée (de tir); **~d left/right** (text) justifié à gauche/à droite

ranger ['reɪndʒər] n garde m forestier

rank [ræŋk] n rang m; (Mil) grade m; (Brit: also: **taxi rank**) station f de taxis ▷ vi: **to ~ among** compter or se classer parmi ▷ vt: **I ~ him sixth** je le place sixième ▷ adj (smell) nauséabond(e); (hypocrisy, injustice etc) flagrant(e); **he's a ~ outsider** il n'est vraiment pas dans la course; **the ~s** (Mil) la troupe; **the ~ and file** (fig) la masse, la base; **to close ~s** (Mil: fig) serrer les rangs

ransack ['rænsæk] vt fouiller (à fond); (plunder) piller

ransom ['rænsəm] n rançon f; **to hold sb to** ~ (fig) exercer un chantage sur qn

rant [rænt] vi fulminer

rap [ræp] n petit coup sec; tape f; (music) rap m ▷ vt (door) frapper sur or à; (table etc) taper sur

rape [reɪp] n viol m; (Bot) colza m ▷ vt violer

rape oil, rapeseed oil ['reɪp(siːd)] n huile f de colza

rapid ['ræpɪd] adj rapide

rapidly ['ræpɪdlɪ] adv rapidement

rapids ['ræpɪdz] npl (Geo) rapides mpl

rapist ['reɪpɪst] n auteur m d'un viol

rapport [ræ'pɔːr] n entente f

rapturous ['ræptʃərəs] adj extasié(e); frénétique

rare [reər] adj rare; (Culin: steak) saignant(e)

rarely ['reəlɪ] adv rarement

raring ['reərɪŋ] adj: **to be ~ to go** (inf) être très impatient(e) de commencer

rascal ['rɑːskl] n vaurien m

rash [ræʃ] *adj* imprudent(e), irréfléchi(e) ▷ *n*
(*Med*) rougeur *f*, éruption *f*; (*of events*) série *f*
(noire); **to come out in a ~** avoir une éruption
rasher ['ræʃə'] *n* fine tranche (de lard)
raspberry ['rɑːzbərɪ] *n* framboise *f*
raspberry bush *n* framboisier *m*
rasping ['rɑːspɪŋ] *adj*: **~ noise** grincement *m*
rat [ræt] *n* rat *m*
rate [reɪt] *n* (*ratio*) taux *m*, pourcentage *m*; (*speed*)
vitesse *f*, rythme *m*; (*price*) tarif *m* ▷ *vt* (*price*)
évaluer, estimer; (*people*) classer; (*deserve*)
mériter; **rates** *npl* (*Brit: property tax*) impôts
locaux; **to ~ sb/sth as** considérer qn/qch
comme; **to ~ sb/sth among** classer qn/qch
parmi; **to ~ sb/sth highly** avoir une haute
opinion de qn/qch; **at a ~ of 60 kph** à une vitesse
de 60 km/h; **at any ~** en tout cas; **~ of exchange**
taux *or* cours *m* du change; **~ of flow** débit *m*;
~ of return (taux de) rendement *m*; **pulse ~**
fréquence *f* des pulsations
rateable value ['reɪtəbl-] *n* (*Brit*) valeur locative
imposable
ratepayer ['reɪtpeɪə'] *n* (*Brit*) contribuable *m/f*
(*payant les impôts locaux*)
rather ['rɑːðə'] *adv* (*somewhat*) assez, plutôt; (*to
some extent*) un peu; **it's ~ expensive** c'est assez
cher; (*too much*) c'est un peu cher; **there's ~
a lot** il y en a beaucoup; (*more*) **I would** *or* **I'd ~ go**
j'aimerais mieux *or* je préférerais partir; **I had
~ go** il vaudrait mieux que je parte; **I'd ~ not
leave** j'aimerais mieux ne pas partir; **or ~** (*more
accurately*) ou plutôt; **I ~ think he won't come** je
crois bien qu'il ne viendra pas
rating ['reɪtɪŋ] *n* (*assessment*) évaluation *f*; (*score*)
classement *m*; (*Finance*) cote *f*; (*Naut: category*)
classe *f*; (: *sailor: Brit*) matelot *m*; **ratings** *npl*
(*Radio*) indice(s) *m(pl)* d'écoute; (*TV*) Audimat® *m*
ratio ['reɪʃɪəu] *n* proportion *f*; **in the ~ of 100 to 1**
dans la proportion de 100 contre 1
ration ['ræʃən] *n* ration *f* ▷ *vt* rationner; **rations**
npl (*food*) vivres *mpl*
rational ['ræʃənl] *adj* raisonnable, sensé(e);
(*solution, reasoning*) logique; (*Med: person*) lucide
rationale [ræʃə'nɑːl] *n* raisonnement *m*;
justification *f*
rationalize ['ræʃnəlaɪz] *vt* rationaliser; (*conduct*)
essayer d'expliquer *or* de motiver
rat race *n* foire *f* d'empoigne
rattle ['rætl] *n* (*of door, window*) battement *m*; (*of
coins, chain*) cliquetis *m*; (*of train, engine*) bruit *m*
de ferraille; (*for baby*) hochet *m*; (*of sports fan*)
crécelle *f* ▷ *vi* cliqueter; (*car, bus*): **to ~ along**
rouler en faisant un bruit de ferraille ▷ *vt* agiter
(bruyamment); (*inf: disconcert*) décontenancer;
(: *annoy*) embêter
rattlesnake ['rætlsneɪk] *n* serpent *m* à sonnettes
raucous ['rɔːkəs] *adj* rauque
rave [reɪv] *vi* (*in anger*) s'emporter; (*with
enthusiasm*) s'extasier; (*Med*) délirer ▷ *n* (*inf:
party*) rave *f*, soirée *f* techno ▷ *adj* (*scene, culture,
music*) rave, techno ▷ *cpd*: **~ review** (*inf*) critique *f*
dithyrambique

raven ['reɪvən] *n* grand corbeau
ravenous ['rævənəs] *adj* affamé(e è)
ravine [rə'viːn] *n* ravin *m*
raving ['reɪvɪŋ] *adj*: **he's ~ mad** il est
complètement cinglé
ravishing ['rævɪʃɪŋ] *adj* enchanteur(-eresse)
raw [rɔː] *adj* (*uncooked*) cru(e); (*not processed*)
brut(e); (*sore*) à vif, irrité(e); (*inexperienced*)
inexpérimenté(e); (*weather, day*) froid(e) et
humide; **~ deal** (*inf: bad bargain*) sale coup *m*;
(: *unfair treatment*): **to get a ~ deal** être traité(e)
injustement; **~ materials** matières premières
raw material *n* matière première
ray [reɪ] *n* rayon *m*; **~ of hope** lueur *f* d'espoir
raze [reɪz] *vt* (*also*: **raze to the ground**) raser
razor ['reɪzə'] *n* rasoir *m*
razor blade *n* lame *f* de rasoir
Rd *abbr* = **road**
RE *n abbr* (*Brit*) = **religious education**; (*Brit Mil*)
= **Royal Engineers**
re [riː] *prep* concernant
reach [riːtʃ] *n* portée *f*, atteinte *f*; (*of river etc*)
étendue *f* ▷ *vt* atteindre, arriver à; (*conclusion,
decision*) parvenir à ▷ *vi* s'étendre; (*stretch out
hand*): **to ~ up/down** *etc* (**for sth**) lever/baisser
etc le bras (pour prendre qch); **to ~ sb by phone**
joindre qn par téléphone; **out of/within ~**
(*object*) hors de/à portée; **within easy ~ (of)**
(*place*) à proximité (de), proche (de)
▶ **reach out** *vt* tendre ▷ *vi*: **to ~ out (for)**
allonger le bras (pour prendre)
react [riː'ækt] *vi* réagir
reaction [riː'ækʃən] *n* réaction *f*
reactor [riː'æktə'] *n* réacteur *m*
read (*pt, pp* ~) [riːd, rɛd] *vi* lire ▷ *vt* lire;
(*understand*) comprendre, interpréter; (*study*)
étudier; (*meter*) relever; (*subj: instrument etc*)
indiquer, marquer; **to take sth as ~** (*fig*)
considérer qch comme accepté; **do you ~ me?**
(*Tel*) est-ce que vous me recevez?
▶ **read out** *vt* lire à haute voix
▶ **read over** *vt* relire
▶ **read through** *vt* (*quickly*) parcourir; (*thoroughly*)
lire jusqu'au bout
▶ **read up** *vt*, **read up on** *vt fus* étudier
readable ['riːdəbl] *adj* facile *or* agréable à lire
reader ['riːdə'] *n* lecteur(-trice); (*book*) livre
m de lecture; (*Brit: at university*) maître *m* de
conférences
readership ['riːdəʃɪp] *n* (*of paper etc*) (nombre *m*
de) lecteurs *mpl*
readily ['rɛdɪlɪ] *adv* volontiers, avec
empressement; (*easily*) facilement
readiness ['rɛdɪnɪs] *n* empressement *m*; **in ~**
(*prepared*) prêt(e)
reading ['riːdɪŋ] *n* lecture *f*; (*understanding*)
interprétation *f*; (*on instrument*) indications *fpl*
ready ['rɛdɪ] *adj* prêt(e); (*willing*) prêt, disposé(e);
(*quick*) prompt(e); (*available*) disponible ▷ *n*: **at
the ~** (*Mil*) prêt à faire feu; (*fig*) tout(e) prêt(e); **~
for use** prêt à l'emploi; **to be ~ to do sth** être
prêt à faire qch; **when will my photos be ~?**

quand est-ce que mes photos seront prêtes?; **to get ~** *(as vi)* se préparer; *(as vt)* préparer

ready-cooked ['rɛdɪ'kukd] *adj* précuit(e)

ready-made ['redɪ'meɪd] *adj* tout(e) faite(e)

ready-to-wear ['redɪtə'wɛəʳ] *adj* (en) prêt-à-porter

real [rɪəl] *adj* *(world, life)* réel(le); *(genuine)* véritable; *(proper)* vrai(e) ▷ *adv (US inf: very)* vraiment; **in ~ life** dans la réalité

real ale *n* bière traditionnelle

real estate *n* biens fonciers *or* immobiliers

realistic [rɪə'lɪstɪk] *adj* réaliste

reality [riː'ælɪtɪ] *n* réalité *f*; **in ~** en réalité, en fait

realityTV *n* téléréalité *f*

realization [rɪəlaɪ'zeɪʃən] *n (awareness)* prise *f* de conscience; *(fulfilment: also: of asset)* réalisation *f*

realize ['rɪəlaɪz] *vt (understand)* se rendre compte de, prendre conscience de; *(a project, Comm: asset)* réaliser

really ['rɪəlɪ] *adv* vraiment; **~?** vraiment?, c'est vrai?

realm [rɛlm] *n* royaume *m*; *(fig)* domaine *m*

realtor ['rɪəltɔːʳ] *n (US)* agent immobilier

reap [riːp] *vt* moissonner; *(fig)* récolter

reappear [riːə'pɪəʳ] *vi* réapparaître, reparaître

rear [rɪəʳ] *adj* de derrière, arrière *inv*; *(Aut: wheel etc)* arrière ▷ *n* arrière *m*, derrière *m* ▷ *vt (cattle, family)* élever ▷ *vi (also: rear up: animal)* se cabrer

rearguard ['rɪəgɑːd] *n* arrière-garde *f*

rearrange [riːə'reɪndʒ] *vt* réarranger

rear-view mirror *n (Aut)* rétroviseur *m*

rear-wheel drive *n (Aut)* traction *f* arrière

reason ['riːzn] *n* raison *f* ▷ *vi*: **to ~ with sb** raisonner qn, faire entendre raison à qn; **the ~ for/why** la raison de/pour laquelle; **to have ~ to think** avoir lieu de penser; **it stands to ~ that** il va sans dire que; **she claims with good ~ that** ... elle affirme à juste titre que ...; **all the more ~ why** raison de plus pour + *infinitive or* pour que + *sub*; **within ~** dans les limites du raisonnable

reasonable ['riːznəbl] *adj* raisonnable; *(not bad)* acceptable

reasonably ['riːznəblɪ] *adv (behave)* raisonnablement; *(fairly)* assez; **one can ~ assume that** ... on est fondé à *or* il est permis de supposer que ...

reasoning ['riːznɪŋ] *n* raisonnement *m*

reassurance [riːə'ʃuərəns] *n (factual)* assurance *f*, garantie *f*; *(emotional)* réconfort *m*

reassure [riːə'ʃuəʳ] *vt* rassurer; **to ~ sb of** donner à qn l'assurance répétée de

rebate ['riːbeɪt] *n (on product)* rabais *m*; *(on tax etc)* dégrèvement *m*; *(repayment)* remboursement *m*

rebel *n* ['rɛbl] rebelle *m/f* ▷ *vi* [rɪ'bɛl] se rebeller, se révolter

rebellion [rɪ'bɛljən] *n* rébellion *f*, révolte *f*

rebellious [rɪ'bɛljəs] *adj* rebelle

rebound *vi* [rɪ'baund] *(ball)* rebondir ▷ *n* ['riː: baund] rebond *m*

rebuff [rɪ'bʌf] *n* rebuffade *f* ▷ *vt* repousser

rebuild [riː'bɪld] *vt (irreg: like* **build***)* reconstruire

rebuke [rɪ'bjuːk] *n* réprimande *f*, reproche *m* ▷ *vt* réprimander

rebut [rɪ'bʌt] *vt* réfuter

recall *vt* [rɪ'kɔːl] rappeler; *(remember)* se rappeler, se souvenir de ▷ *n* ['riː:kɔːl] rappel *m*; *(ability to remember)* mémoire *f*; **beyond ~** *adj* irrévocable

recant [rɪ'kænt] *vi* se rétracter; *(Rel)* abjurer

recap ['riː:kæp] *n* récapitulation *f* ▷ *vt, vi* récapituler

recede [rɪ'siːd] *vi* s'éloigner; reculer

receding [rɪ'siːdɪŋ] *adj (forehead, chin)* fuyant(e); **~ hairline** front dégarni

receipt [rɪ'siːt] *n (document)* reçu *m*; *(for parcel etc)* accusé *m* de réception; *(act of receiving)* réception *f*; **receipts** *npl (Comm)* recettes *fpl*; **to acknowledge ~ of** accuser réception de; **we are in ~ of** ... nous avons reçu ...; **can I have a ~, please?** je peux avoir un reçu, s'il vous plaît?

receive [rɪ'siːv] *vt* recevoir; *(guest)* recevoir, accueillir; **"~d with thanks"** *(Comm)* "pour acquit"; **R~d Pronunciation** *voir article*

receiver [rɪ'siːvəʳ] *n (Tel)* récepteur *m*, combiné *m*; *(Radio)* récepteur; *(of stolen goods)* receleur *m*; *(for bankruptcies)* administrateur *m* judiciaire

recent ['riː:snt] *adj* récent(e); **in ~ years** au cours de ces dernières années

recently ['riː:sntlɪ] *adv* récemment; **as ~ as** pas plus tard que; **until ~** jusqu'à il y a peu de temps encore

receptacle [rɪ'sɛptɪkl] *n* récipient *m*

reception [rɪ'sɛpʃən] *n* réception *f*; *(welcome)* accueil *m*, réception

reception desk *n* réception *f*

receptionist [rɪ'sɛpʃnɪst] *n* réceptionniste *m/f*

recess [rɪ'sɛs] *n (in room)* renfoncement *m*; *(for bed)* alcôve *f*; *(secret place)* recoin *m*; *(Pol etc: holiday)* vacances *fpl*; *(US Law: short break)* suspension *f* d'audience; *(Scol: esp US)* récréation *f*

recession [rɪ'sɛʃən] *n (Econ)* récession *f*

recharge [riː'tʃɑːdʒ] *vt (battery)* recharger

recipe ['rɛsɪpɪ] *n* recette *f*

recipient [rɪ'sɪpɪənt] *n (of payment)* bénéficiaire *m/f*; *(of letter)* destinataire *m/f*

recital [rɪ'saɪtl] *n* récital *m*

recite [rɪ'saɪt] *vt (poem)* réciter; *(complaints etc)* énumérer

reckless ['rɛkləs] *adj (driver etc)* imprudent(e); *(spender etc)* insouciant(e)

reckon ['rɛkən] *vt (count)* calculer, compter; *(consider)* considérer, estimer; *(think)*: **I ~ (that)** ... je pense (que) ..., j'estime (que) ... ▷ *vi*: **he is somebody to be ~ed with** il ne faut pas le sous-estimer; **to ~ without sb/sth** ne pas tenir compte de qn/qch

▶ **reckon on** *vt fus* compter sur, s'attendre à

reckoning ['rɛknɪŋ] *n* compte *m*, calcul *m*; estimation *f*; **the day of ~** le jour du Jugement

reclaim [rɪ'kleɪm] *vt (land: from sea)* assécher; *(: from forest)* défricher; *(: with fertilizer)* amender; *(demand back)* réclamer (le remboursement *or* la restitution de); *(waste materials)* récupérer

recline [rɪ'klaɪn] *vi* être allongé(e) *or* étendu(e)

reclining [rɪ'klaɪnɪŋ] *adj (seat)* à dossier réglable

recluse [rɪ'kluːs] n reclus(e), ermite m
recognition [rɛkəg'nɪʃən] n reconnaissance f; **in ~ of** en reconnaissance de; **to gain ~** être reconnu(e); **transformed beyond ~** méconnaissable
recognizable ['rɛkəgnaɪzəbl] adj: **~ (by)** reconnaissable (à)
recognize ['rɛkəgnaɪz] vt: **to ~ (by/as)** reconnaître (à/comme étant)
recoil [rɪ'kɔɪl] vi (person): **to ~ (from)** reculer (devant) ▷ n (of gun) recul m
recollect [rɛkə'lɛkt] vt se rappeler, se souvenir de
recollection [rɛkə'lɛkʃən] n souvenir m; **to the best of my ~** autant que je m'en souvienne
recommend [rɛkə'mɛnd] vt recommander; **can you ~ a good restaurant?** pouvez-vous me conseiller un bon restaurant?; **she has a lot to ~ her** elle a beaucoup de choses en sa faveur
recommendation [rɛkəmɛn'deɪʃən] n recommandation f
reconcile ['rɛkənsaɪl] vt (two people) réconcilier; (two facts) concilier, accorder; **to ~ o.s. to** se résigner à
recondition [riːkən'dɪʃən] vt remettre à neuf; réviser entièrement
reconnoitre, (US) **reconnoiter** [rɛkə'nɔɪtər] (Mil) vt reconnaître ▷ vi faire une reconnaissance
reconsider [riːkən'sɪdər] vt reconsidérer
reconstruct [riːkən'strʌkt] vt (building) reconstruire; (crime, system) reconstituer
record n ['rɛkɔːd] rapport m, récit m; (of meeting etc) procès-verbal m; (register) registre m; (file) dossier m; (Comput) article m; (also: **police record**) casier m judiciaire; (Mus: disc) disque m; (Sport) record m ▷ adj record inv ▷ vt [rɪ'kɔːd] (set down) noter; (relate) rapporter; (Mus: song etc) enregistrer; **public ~s** archives fpl; **to keep a ~ of** noter; **to keep the ~ straight** (fig) mettre les choses au point; **he is on ~ as saying that ...** il a déclaré en public que ...; **Italy's excellent ~** les excellents résultats obtenus par l'Italie; **off the ~** adj officieux(-euse) ▷ adv officieusement; **in ~ time** dans un temps record
record card n (in file) fiche f
recorded delivery [rɪ'kɔːdɪd-] n (Brit Post): **to send sth ~** = envoyer qch en recommandé
recorded delivery letter [rɪ'kɔːdɪd-] n (Brit Post) = lettre recommandée
recorder [rɪ'kɔːdər] n (Law) avocat nommé à la fonction de juge; (Mus) flûte f à bec
record holder n (Sport) détenteur(-trice) du record
recording [rɪ'kɔːdɪŋ] n (Mus) enregistrement m
record player n tourne-disque m
recount [rɪ'kaunt] vt raconter
re-count n ['riːkaunt] (Pol: of votes) nouveau décompte (des suffrages) ▷ vt [riː'kaunt] recompter
recoup [rɪ'kuːp] vt: **to ~ one's losses** récupérer ce qu'on a perdu, se refaire
recourse [rɪ'kɔːs] n recours m; expédient m; **to have ~ to** recourir à, avoir recours à

recover [rɪ'kʌvər] vt récupérer ▷ vi (from illness) se rétablir; (from shock) se remettre; (country) se redresser
recovery [rɪ'kʌvərɪ] n récupération f; rétablissement m; (Econ) redressement m
recreate [riːkrɪ'eɪt] vt recréer
recreation [rɛkrɪ'eɪʃən] n (leisure) récréation f, détente f
recreational [rɛkrɪ'eɪʃənl] adj pour la détente, récréatif(-ive)
recreational drug [rɛkrɪ'eɪʃənl-] n drogue récréative
recreational vehicle [rɛkrɪ'eɪʃənl-] n (US) camping-car m
recruit [rɪ'kruːt] n recrue f ▷ vt recruter
recruitment [rɪ'kruːtmənt] n recrutement m
rectangle ['rɛktæŋgl] n rectangle m
rectangular [rɛk'tæŋgjulər] adj rectangulaire
rectify ['rɛktɪfaɪ] vt (error) rectifier, corriger; (omission) réparer
rector ['rɛktər] n (Rel) pasteur m; (in Scottish universities) personnalité élue par les étudiants pour les représenter
recuperate [rɪ'kjuːpəreɪt] vi (from illness) se rétablir
recur [rɪ'kəːr] vi se reproduire; (idea, opportunity) se retrouver; (symptoms) réapparaître
recurrence [rɪ'kəːrns] n répétition f; réapparition f
recurrent [rɪ'kəːrnt] adj périodique, fréquent(e)
recurring [rɪ'kəːrɪŋ] adj (problem) périodique, fréquent(e); (Math) périodique
recyclable [riː'saɪkləbl] adj recyclable
recycle [riː'saɪkl] vt, vi recycler
recycling [riː'saɪklɪŋ] n recyclage m
red [rɛd] n rouge m; (Pol: pej) rouge m/f ▷ adj rouge; (hair) roux (rousse); **in the ~** (account) à découvert; (business) en déficit
red carpet treatment n réception f en grande pompe
Red Cross n Croix-Rouge f
redcurrant ['rɛdkʌrənt] n groseille f (rouge)
redden ['rɛdn] vt, vi rougir
redecorate [riː'dɛkəreɪt] vt refaire à neuf, repeindre et retapisser
redeem [rɪ'diːm] vt (debt) rembourser; (sth in pawn) dégager; (fig, also Rel) racheter
redeeming [rɪ'diːmɪŋ] adj (feature) qui sauve, qui rachète (le reste)
redeploy [riːdɪ'plɔɪ] vt (Mil) redéployer; (staff, resources) reconvertir
red-haired [rɛd'hɛəd] adj roux (rousse)
red-handed [rɛd'hændɪd] adj: **to be caught ~** être pris(e) en flagrant délit or la main dans le sac
redhead ['rɛdhɛd] n roux (rousse)
red herring n (fig) diversion f, fausse piste
red-hot [rɛd'hɔt] adj chauffé(e) au rouge, brûlant(e)
redirect [riːdaɪ'rɛkt] vt (mail) faire suivre
red light n: **to go through a ~** (Aut) brûler un feu rouge

red-light district ['rɛdlaɪt-] n quartier mal famé
red meat n viande f rouge
redo [ri:'du:] vt (irreg: like **do**) refaire
redress [rɪ'drɛs] n réparation f ▷ vt redresser; **to ~ the balance** rétablir l'équilibre
Red Sea n: **the ~** la mer Rouge
redskin ['rɛdskɪn] n Peau-Rouge m/f
red tape n (fig) paperasserie (administrative)
reduce [rɪ'dju:s] vt réduire; (lower) abaisser; **"~ speed now"** (Aut) "ralentir"; **to ~ sth by/to** réduire qch de/à; **to ~ sb to tears** faire pleurer qn
reduced [rɪ'dju:st] adj réduit(e); **"greatly ~ prices"** "gros rabais"; **at a ~ price** (goods) au rabais; (ticket etc) à prix réduit
reduction [rɪ'dʌkʃən] n réduction f; (of price) baisse f; (discount) rabais m; réduction; **is there a ~ for children/students?** y a-t-il une réduction pour les enfants/les étudiants?
redundancy [rɪ'dʌndənsɪ] n (Brit) licenciement m, mise f au chômage; **compulsory ~** licenciement; **voluntary ~** départ m volontaire
redundant [rɪ'dʌndnt] adj (Brit: worker) licencié(e), mis(e) au chômage; (detail, object) superflu(e); **to be made ~** (worker) être licencié, être mis au chômage
reed [ri:d] n (Bot) roseau m; (Mus: of clarinet etc) anche f
reef [ri:f] n (at sea) récif m, écueil m
reek [ri:k] vi: **to ~ (of)** puer, empester
reel [ri:l] n bobine f; (Tech) dévidoir m; (Fishing) moulinet m; (Cine) bande f; (dance) quadrille écossais ▷ vt (Tech) bobiner; (also: **reel up**) enrouler ▷ vi (sway) chanceler; **my head is ~ing** j'ai la tête qui tourne
▶ **reel in** vt (fish, line) ramener
▶ **reel off** vt (say) énumérer, débiter
ref [rɛf] n abbr (inf: = referee) arbitre m
refectory [rɪ'fɛktərɪ] n réfectoire m
refer [rɪ'fə:ʳ] vt: **to ~ sth to** (dispute, decision) soumettre qch à; **to ~ sb to** (inquirer, patient) adresser qn à; (reader: to text) renvoyer qn à ▷ vi: **to ~ to** (allude to) parler de, faire allusion à; (consult) se reporter à; (apply to) s'appliquer à; **~ring to your letter** (Comm) en réponse à votre lettre; **he ~red me to the manager** il m'a dit de m'adresser au directeur
referee [rɛfə'ri:] n arbitre m; (Tennis) juge-arbitre m; (Brit: for job application) répondant(e) ▷ vt arbitrer
reference ['rɛfrəns] n référence f, renvoi m; (mention) allusion f, mention f; (for job application: letter) références; lettre f de recommandation; (: person) répondant(e); (Comm: in letter) me référant à; **"please quote this ~"** (Comm) "prière de rappeler cette référence"
reference book n ouvrage m de référence
reference number n (Comm) numéro m de référence
refill vt [ri:'fɪl] remplir à nouveau; (pen, lighter etc) recharger ▷ n ['ri:fɪl] (for pen etc) recharge f

refine [rɪ'faɪn] vt (sugar, oil) raffiner; (taste) affiner; (idea, theory) peaufiner
refined [rɪ'faɪnd] adj (person, taste) raffiné(e)
refinery [rɪ'faɪnərɪ] n raffinerie f
reflect [rɪ'flɛkt] vt (light, image) réfléchir, refléter; (fig) refléter ▷ vi (think) réfléchir, méditer; **it ~s badly on him** cela le discrédite; **it ~s well on him** c'est tout à son honneur
reflection [rɪ'flɛkʃən] n réflexion f; (image) reflet m; (criticism): **~ on** critique f de; atteinte f à; **on ~** réflexion faite
reflex ['ri:flɛks] adj, n réflexe (m)
reflexive [rɪ'flɛksɪv] adj (Ling) réfléchi(e)
reform [rɪ'fɔ:m] n réforme f ▷ vt réformer
reformatory [rɪ'fɔ:mətərɪ] n (US) centre m d'éducation surveillée
refrain [rɪ'freɪn] vi: **to ~ from doing** s'abstenir de faire ▷ n refrain m
refresh [rɪ'frɛʃ] vt rafraîchir; (subj: food, sleep etc) redonner des forces à
refresher course [rɪ'frɛʃə-] n (Brit) cours m de recyclage
refreshing [rɪ'frɛʃɪŋ] adj (drink) rafraîchissant(e); (sleep) réparateur(-trice); (fact, idea etc) qui réjouit par son originalité or sa rareté
refreshment [rɪ'frɛʃmənt] n: **for some ~** (eating) pour se restaurer ou sustenter; **in need of ~** (resting etc) ayant besoin de refaire ses forces
refreshments [rɪ'frɛʃmənts] npl rafraîchissements mpl
refrigerator [rɪ'frɪdʒəreɪtəʳ] n réfrigérateur m, frigidaire m
refuel [ri:'fjuəl] vt ravitailler en carburant ▷ vi se ravitailler en carburant
refuge ['rɛfju:dʒ] n refuge m; **to take ~ in** se réfugier dans
refugee [rɛfju'dʒi:] n réfugié(e)
refund n ['ri:fʌnd] remboursement m ▷ vt [ri'fʌnd] rembourser
refurbish [ri:'fə:bɪʃ] vt remettre à neuf
refusal [rɪ'fju:zəl] n refus m; **to have first ~ on sth** avoir droit de préemption sur qch
refuse¹ ['rɛfju:s] n ordures fpl, détritus mpl
refuse² [rɪ'fju:z] vt, vi refuser; **to ~ to do sth** refuser de faire qch
refuse collection n ramassage m d'ordures
regain [rɪ'geɪn] vt (lost ground) regagner; (strength) retrouver
regal ['ri:gl] adj royal(e)
regard [rɪ'gɑ:d] n respect m, estime f, considération f ▷ vt considérer; **to give one's ~s to** faire ses amitiés à; **"with kindest ~s"** "bien amicalement"; **as ~s, with ~ to** en ce qui concerne
regarding [rɪ'gɑ:dɪŋ] prep en ce qui concerne
regardless [rɪ'gɑ:dlɪs] adv quand même; **~ of** sans se soucier de
regenerate [rɪ'dʒɛnəreɪt] vt régénérer ▷ vi se régénérer
reggae ['rɛgeɪ] n reggae m
régime [reɪ'ʒi:m] n régime m
regiment ['rɛdʒɪmənt] n régiment m ▷ vt

['rɛdʒɪmɛnt] imposer une discipline trop stricte à

regimental [rɛdʒɪ'mɛntl] *adj* d'un régiment

region ['riːdʒən] *n* région *f*; **in the ~ of** (*fig*) aux alentours de

regional ['riːdʒənl] *adj* régional(e)

register ['rɛdʒɪstəʳ] *n* registre *m*; (*also*: **electoral register**) liste électorale ▷ *vt* enregistrer, inscrire; (*birth*) déclarer; (*vehicle*) immatriculer; (*luggage*) enregistrer; (*letter*) envoyer en recommandé; (*subj: instrument*) marquer ▷ *vi* s'inscrire; (*at hotel*) signer le registre; (*make impression*) être (bien) compris(e); **to ~ for a course** s'inscrire à un cours; **to ~ a protest** protester

registered ['rɛdʒɪstəd] *adj* (*design*) déposé(e); (*Brit: letter*) recommandé(e); (*student, voter*) inscrit(e)

registered trademark *n* marque déposée

registrar ['rɛdʒɪstrɑːʳ] *n* officier *m* de l'état civil; secrétaire *m/f* général

registration [rɛdʒɪs'treɪʃən] *n* (*act*) enregistrement *m*; (*of student*) inscription *f*; (*Brit Aut: also*: **registration number**) numéro *m* d'immatriculation

registry ['rɛdʒɪstrɪ] *n* bureau *m* de l'enregistrement

registry office ['rɛdʒɪstrɪ-] *n* (*Brit*) bureau *m* de l'état civil; **to get married in a ~** ≈ se marier à la mairie

regret [rɪ'grɛt] *n* regret *m* ▷ *vt* regretter; **to ~ that** regretter que + *sub*; **we ~ to inform you that** ... nous sommes au regret de vous informer que ...

regretfully [rɪ'grɛtfəlɪ] *adv* à or avec regret

regrettable [rɪ'grɛtəbl] *adj* regrettable, fâcheux(-euse)

regular ['rɛgjuləʳ] *adj* régulier(-ière); (*usual*) habituel(le), normal(e); (*listener, reader*) fidèle; (*soldier*) de métier; (*Comm: size*) ordinaire ▷ *n* (*client etc*) habitué(e)

regularly ['rɛgjuləlɪ] *adv* régulièrement

regulate ['rɛgjuleɪt] *vt* régler

regulation [rɛgju'leɪʃən] *n* (*rule*) règlement *m*; (*adjustment*) réglage *m* ▷ *cpd* réglementaire

rehabilitation ['riːəbɪlɪ'teɪʃən] *n* (*of offender*) réhabilitation *f*; (*of addict*) réadaptation *f*; (*of disabled*) rééducation *f*, réadaptation *f*

rehearsal [rɪ'həːsəl] *n* répétition *f*; **dress ~** (*répétition*) générale *f*

rehearse [rɪ'həːs] *vt* répéter

reign [reɪn] *n* règne *m* ▷ *vi* régner

reimburse [riːɪm'bəːs] *vt* rembourser

rein [reɪn] *n* (*for horse*) rêne *f*; **to give sb free ~** (*fig*) donner carte blanche à qn

reincarnation [riːɪnkɑː'neɪʃən] *n* réincarnation *f*

reindeer ['reɪndɪəʳ] *n* (*pl inv*) renne *m*

reinforce [riːɪn'fɔːs] *vt* renforcer

reinforced concrete [riːɪn'fɔːst-] *n* béton armé

reinforcement [riːɪn'fɔːsmənt] *n* (*action*) renforcement *m*

reinforcements [riːɪn'fɔːsmənts] *npl* (*Mil*) renfort(s) *m(pl)*

reinstate [riːɪn'steɪt] *vt* rétablir, réintégrer

reject *n* ['riːdʒɛkt] (*Comm*) article *m* de rebut ▷ *vt* [rɪ'dʒɛkt] refuser; (*Comm: goods*) mettre au rebut; (*idea*) rejeter

rejection [rɪ'dʒɛkʃən] *n* rejet *m*, refus *m*

rejoice [rɪ'dʒɔɪs] *vi*: **to ~ (at or over)** se réjouir (de)

rejuvenate [rɪ'dʒuːvəneɪt] *vt* rajeunir

relapse [rɪ'læps] *n* (*Med*) rechute *f*

relate [rɪ'leɪt] *vt* (*tell*) raconter; (*connect*) établir un rapport entre ▷ *vi*: **to ~ to** (*connect*) se rapporter à; **to ~ to sb** (*interact*) entretenir des rapports avec qn

related [rɪ'leɪtɪd] *adj* apparenté(e); **~ to** (*subject*) lié(e) à

relating to [rɪ'leɪtɪŋ-] *prep* concernant

relation [rɪ'leɪʃən] *n* (*person*) parent(e); (*link*) rapport *m*, lien *m*; **relations** *npl* (*relatives*) famille *f*; **diplomatic/international ~s** relations diplomatiques/internationales; **in ~ to** en ce qui concerne; par rapport à; **to bear no ~ to** être sans rapport avec

relationship [rɪ'leɪʃənʃɪp] *n* rapport *m*, lien *m*; (*personal ties*) relations *fpl*, rapports; (*also*: **family relationship**) lien de parenté; (*affair*) liaison *f*; **they have a good ~** ils s'entendent bien

relative ['rɛlətɪv] *n* parent(e) ▷ *adj* relatif(-ive); (*respective*) respectif(-ive); **all her ~s** toute sa famille

relatively ['rɛlətɪvlɪ] *adv* relativement

relax [rɪ'læks] *vi* (*muscle*) se relâcher; (*person: unwind*) se détendre; (*calm down*) se calmer ▷ *vt* relâcher; (*mind, person*) détendre

relaxation [riːlæk'seɪʃən] *n* relâchement *m*; (*of mind*) détente *f*; (*recreation*) détente, délassement *m*; (*entertainment*) distraction *f*

relaxed [rɪ'lækst] *adj* relâché(e); détendu(e)

relaxing [rɪ'læksɪŋ] *adj* délassant(e)

relay ['riːleɪ] *n* (*Sport*) course *f* de relais ▷ *vt* (*message*) retransmettre, relayer

release [rɪ'liːs] *n* (*from prison, obligation*) libération *f*; (*of gas etc*) émission *f*; (*of film etc*) sortie *f*; (*new recording*) disque *m*; (*device*) déclencheur *m* ▷ *vt* (*prisoner*) libérer; (*book, film*) sortir; (*report, news*) rendre public, publier; (*gas etc*) émettre, dégager; (*free: from wreckage etc*) dégager; (*Tech: catch, spring etc*) déclencher; (*let go: person, animal*) relâcher; (*: hand, object*) lâcher; (*: grip, brake*) desserrer; **to ~ one's grip or hold** lâcher prise; **to ~ the clutch** (*Aut*) débrayer

relegate ['rɛləgeɪt] *vt* reléguer; (*Brit Sport*): **to be ~d** descendre dans une division inférieure

relent [rɪ'lɛnt] *vi* se laisser fléchir

relentless [rɪ'lɛntlɪs] *adj* implacable; (*non-stop*) continuel(le)

relevant ['rɛləvənt] *adj* (*question*) pertinent(e); (*corresponding*) approprié(e); (*fact*) significatif(-ive); (*information*) utile; **~ to** ayant rapport à, approprié à

reliable [rɪ'laɪəbl] *adj* (*person, firm*) sérieux(-euse), fiable; (*method, machine*) fiable; (*news, information*) sûr(e)

reliably [rɪ'laɪəblɪ] *adv*: **to be ~ informed** savoir de source sûre

reliance [rɪ'laɪəns] n: **~ (on)** (trust) confiance f (en); (dependence) besoin m (de), dépendance f (de)

relic ['rɛlɪk] n (Rel) relique f; (of the past) vestige m

relief [rɪ'liːf] n (from pain, anxiety) soulagement m; (help, supplies) secours m (pl); (of guard) relève f; (Art, Geo) relief m; **by way of light ~** pour faire diversion

relieve [rɪ'liːv] vt (pain, patient) soulager; (fear, worry) dissiper; (bring help) secourir; (take over from: gen) relayer; (: guard) relever; **to ~ sb of sth** débarrasser qn de qch; **to ~ sb of his command** (Mil) relever qn de ses fonctions; **to ~ o.s.** (euphemism) se soulager, faire ses besoins

relieved [rɪ'liːvd] adj soulagé(e); **to be ~ that** ... être soulagé que ...; **I'm ~ to hear it** je suis soulagé de l'entendre

religion [rɪ'lɪdʒən] n religion f

religious [rɪ'lɪdʒəs] adj religieux(-euse); (book) de piété

religious education n instruction religieuse

relinquish [rɪ'lɪŋkwɪʃ] vt abandonner; (plan, habit) renoncer à

relish ['rɛlɪʃ] n (Culin) condiment m; (enjoyment) délectation f ▷ vt (food etc) savourer; **to ~ doing** se délecter à faire

relocate [riː'ləʊ'keɪt] vt (business) transférer ▷ vi se transférer, s'installer or s'établir ailleurs; **to ~ in** (déménager et) s'installer or s'établir à, se transférer à

reluctance [rɪ'lʌktəns] n répugnance f

reluctant [rɪ'lʌktənt] adj peu disposé(e), qui hésite; **to be ~ to do sth** hésiter à faire qch

reluctantly [rɪ'lʌktəntlɪ] adv à contrecœur, sans enthousiasme

rely on [rɪ'laɪ-] vt fus (be dependent on) dépendre de; (trust) compter sur

remain [rɪ'meɪn] vi rester; **to ~ silent** garder le silence; **I ~, yours faithfully** (Brit: in letters) je vous prie d'agréer, Monsieur etc l'assurance de mes sentiments distingués

remainder [rɪ'meɪndəʳ] n reste m; (Comm) fin f de série

remaining [rɪ'meɪnɪŋ] adj qui reste

remains [rɪ'meɪnz] npl restes mpl

remake ['riːmeɪk] n (Cine) remake m

remand [rɪ'mɑːnd] n: **~ on** en détention préventive ▷ vt: **to be ~ed in custody** être placé(e) en détention préventive

remark [rɪ'mɑːk] n remarque f, observation f ▷ vt (faire) remarquer, dire; (notice) remarquer; **to ~ on sth** faire une or des remarque(s) sur qch

remarkable [rɪ'mɑːkəbl] adj remarquable

remarkably [rɪ'mɑːkəblɪ] adv remarquablement

remarry [riː'mærɪ] vi se remarier

remedial [rɪ'miːdɪəl] adj (tuition, classes) de rattrapage

remedy ['rɛmədɪ] n: **~ (for)** remède m (contre or à) ▷ vt remédier à

remember [rɪ'mɛmbəʳ] vt se rappeler, se souvenir de; (send greetings): **~ me to him** saluez-le de ma part; **I ~ seeing it, I ~ having seen it** je

me rappelle l'avoir vu or que je l'ai vu; **she ~ed to do it** elle a pensé à le faire; **~ me to your wife** rappelez-moi au bon souvenir de votre femme

remembrance [rɪ'mɛmbrəns] n souvenir m; mémoire f

Remembrance Day [rɪ'mɛmbrəns-] n (Brit) ≈ (le jour de) l'Armistice m, ≈ le 11 novembre; voir article

remind [rɪ'maɪnd] vt: **to ~ sb of sth** rappeler qch à qn; **to ~ sb to do** faire penser à qn à faire, rappeler à qn qu'il doit faire; **that ~s me!** j'y pense!

reminder [rɪ'maɪndəʳ] n (Comm: letter) rappel m; (note etc) pense-bête m; (souvenir) souvenir m

reminisce [rɛmɪ'nɪs] vi: **to ~ (about)** évoquer ses souvenirs (de)

reminiscent [rɛmɪ'nɪsnt] adj: **~ of** qui rappelle, qui fait penser à

remiss [rɪ'mɪs] adj négligent(e); **it was ~ of me** c'était une négligence de ma part

remission [rɪ'mɪʃən] n rémission f; (of debt, sentence) remise f; (of fee) exemption f

remit [rɪ'mɪt] vt (send: money) envoyer

remittance [rɪ'mɪtns] n envoi m, paiement m

remnant ['rɛmnənt] n reste m, restant m; (of cloth) coupon m; **remnants** npl (Comm) fins fpl de série

remorse [rɪ'mɔːs] n remords m

remorseful [rɪ'mɔːsful] adj plein(e) de remords

remorseless [rɪ'mɔːslɪs] adj (fig) impitoyable

remote [rɪ'məʊt] adj éloigné(e), lointain(e); (person) distant(e); (possibility) vague; **there is a ~ possibility that ...** il est tout juste possible que ...

remote control n télécommande f

remotely [rɪ'məʊtlɪ] adv au loin; (slightly) très vaguement

remould ['riːməʊld] n (Brit: tyre) pneu m rechapé

removable [rɪ'muːvəbl] adj (detachable) amovible

removal [rɪ'muːvəl] n (taking away) enlèvement m; suppression f; (Brit: from house) déménagement m; (from office: dismissal) renvoi m; (of stain) nettoyage m; (Med) ablation f

removal man (irreg) n (Brit) déménageur m

removal van n (Brit) camion m de déménagement

remove [rɪ'muːv] vt enlever, retirer; (employee) renvoyer; (stain) faire partir; (abuse) supprimer; (doubt) chasser; **first cousin once ~d** cousin(e) au deuxième degré

Renaissance [rɪ'neɪsɑ̃s] n: **the ~** la Renaissance

rename [riː'neɪm] vt rebaptiser

render ['rɛndəʳ] vt rendre; (Culin: fat) clarifier

rendering ['rɛndərɪŋ] n (Mus etc) interprétation f

rendezvous ['rɔndɪvuː] n rendez-vous m inv ▷ vi opérer une jonction, se rejoindre; **to ~ with sb** rejoindre qn

renew [rɪ'njuː] vt renouveler; (negotiations) reprendre; (acquaintance) renouer

renewable [rɪ'njuːəbl] adj renouvelable; **~ energy, ~s** énergies renouvelables

renewal [rɪ'njuːəl] n renouvellement m; reprise f

renounce [rɪ'naʊns] vt renoncer à; (disown)

renier

renovate ['rɛnəveɪt] *vt* rénover; (*work of art*) restaurer

renown [rɪ'naun] *n* renommée *f*

renowned [rɪ'naund] *adj* renommé(e)

rent [rɛnt] *pt, pp of* **rend** ▷ *n* loyer *m* ▷ *vt* louer; (*car, TV*) louer, prendre en location; (*also:* **rent out**: *car, TV*) louer, donner en location

rental ['rɛntl] *n* (*for television, car*) (prix *m* de) location *f*

reorganize [ri:'ɔ:gənaɪz] *vt* réorganiser

rep [rɛp] *n abbr* (*Comm*) = **representative**; (*Theat*) = **repertory**

repair [rɪ'pɛəʳ] *n* réparation *f* ▷ *vt* réparer; **in good/bad** ~ en bon/mauvais état; **under** ~ en réparation; **where can I get this ~ed?** où est-ce que je peux faire réparer ceci?

repair kit *n* trousse *f* de réparations

repatriate [ri:'pætrɪeɪt] *vt* rapatrier

repay [ri:'peɪ] *vt* (*irreg: like* **pay**); (*money, creditor*) rembourser; (*sb's efforts*) récompenser

repayment [ri:'peɪmənt] *n* remboursement *m*; récompense *f*

repeal [rɪ'pi:l] *n* (*of law*) abrogation *f*; (*of sentence*) annulation *f* ▷ *vt* abroger; annuler

repeat [rɪ'pi:t] *n* (*Radio, TV*) reprise *f* ▷ *vt* répéter; (*pattern*) reproduire; (*promise, attack, also Comm*: *order*) renouveler; (*Scol: a class*) redoubler ▷ *vi* répéter; **can you ~ that, please?** pouvez-vous répéter, s'il vous plaît?

repeatedly [rɪ'pi:tɪdlɪ] *adv* souvent, à plusieurs reprises

repeat prescription *n* (*Brit*): **I'd like a ~** je voudrais renouveler mon ordonnance

repel [rɪ'pɛl] *vt* repousser

repellent [rɪ'pɛlənt] *adj* repoussant(e) ▷ *n*: **insect ~** insectifuge *m*; **moth ~** produit *m* antimite(s)

repent [rɪ'pɛnt] *vi*: **to ~ (of)** se repentir (de)

repentance [rɪ'pɛntəns] *n* repentir *m*

repercussions [ri:pə'kʌʃənz] *npl* répercussions *fpl*

repertory ['rɛpətərɪ] *n* (*also:* **repertory theatre**) théâtre *m* de répertoire

repetition [rɛpɪ'tɪʃən] *n* répétition *f*

repetitive [rɪ'pɛtɪtɪv] *adj* (*movement, work*) répétitif(-ive); (*speech*) plein(e) de redites

replace [rɪ'pleɪs] *vt* (*put back*) remettre, replacer; (*take the place of*) remplacer; (*Tel*): **"~ the receiver"** "raccrochez"

replacement [rɪ'pleɪsmənt] *n* replacement *m*; (*substitution*) remplacement *m*; (*person*) remplaçant(e)

replay ['ri:pleɪ] *n* (*of match*) match rejoué; (*of tape, film*) répétition *f*

replenish [rɪ'plɛnɪʃ] *vt* (*glass*) remplir (de nouveau); (*stock etc*) réapprovisionner

replica ['rɛplɪkə] *n* réplique *f*, copie exacte

reply [rɪ'plaɪ] *n* réponse *f* ▷ *vi* répondre; **in ~ (to)** en réponse (à); **there's no ~** (*Tel*) ça ne répond pas

report [rɪ'pɔ:t] *n* rapport *m*; (*Press etc*) reportage

m; (*Brit: also*: **school report**) bulletin *m* (scolaire); (*of gun*) détonation *f* ▷ *vt* rapporter, faire un compte rendu de; (*Press etc*) faire un reportage sur; (*notify: accident*) signaler; (: *culprit*) dénoncer ▷ *vi* (*make a report*) faire un rapport; (*for newspaper*) faire un reportage (sur); **I'd like to ~ a theft** je voudrais signaler un vol; (*present o.s.*): **to ~ (to sb)** se présenter (chez qn); **it is ~ed that** on dit *or* annonce que; **it is ~ed from Berlin that** on nous apprend de Berlin que

report card *n* (*US, Scottish*) bulletin *m* (scolaire)

reportedly [rɪ'pɔ:tɪdlɪ] *adv*: **she is ~ living in Spain** elle habiterait en Espagne; **he ~ told them to ...** il leur aurait dit de ...

reporter [rɪ'pɔ:təʳ] *n* reporter *m*

repose [rɪ'pəuz] *n*: **in ~** en *or* au repos

represent [rɛprɪ'zɛnt] *vt* représenter; (*view, belief*) présenter, expliquer; (*describe*): **to ~ sth as** présenter *or* décrire qch comme; **to ~ to sb that** expliquer à qn que

representation [rɛprɪzɛn'teɪʃən] *n* représentation *f*; **representations** *npl* (*protest*) démarche *f*

representative [rɛprɪ'zɛntətɪv] *n* représentant(e); (*Comm*) représentant(e) (de commerce); (*US Pol*) député *m* ▷ *adj* représentatif(-ive), caractéristique

repress [rɪ'prɛs] *vt* réprimer

repression [rɪ'prɛʃən] *n* répression *f*

reprieve [rɪ'pri:v] *n* (*Law*) grâce *f*; (*fig*) sursis *m*, délai *m* ▷ *vt* gracier; accorder un sursis *or* un délai à

reprimand ['rɛprɪmɑ:nd] *n* réprimande *f* ▷ *vt* réprimander

reprisal [rɪ'praɪzl] *n* représailles *fpl*; **to take ~s** user de représailles

reproach [rɪ'prəutʃ] *n* reproche *m* ▷ *vt*: **to ~ sb with sth** reprocher qch à qn; **beyond ~** irréprochable

reproachful [rɪ'prəutʃful] *adj* de reproche

reproduce [ri:prə'dju:s] *vt* reproduire ▷ *vi* se reproduire

reproduction [ri:prə'dʌkʃən] *n* reproduction *f*

reproof [rɪ'pru:f] *n* reproche *m*

reptile ['rɛptaɪl] *n* reptile *m*

republic [rɪ'pʌblɪk] *n* république *f*

republican [rɪ'pʌblɪkən] *adj, n* républicain(e)

repudiate [rɪ'pju:dɪeɪt] *vt* (*ally, behaviour*) désavouer; (*accusation*) rejeter; (*wife*) répudier

repulsive [rɪ'pʌlsɪv] *adj* repoussant(e), répulsif(-ive)

reputable ['rɛpjutəbl] *adj* de bonne réputation; (*occupation*) honorable

reputation [rɛpju'teɪʃən] *n* réputation *f*; **to have a ~ for** être réputé(e) pour; **he has a ~ for being awkward** il a la réputation de ne pas être commode

reputed [rɪ'pju:tɪd] *adj* réputé(e); **he is ~ to be rich/intelligent** *etc* on dit qu'il est riche/intelligent *etc*

reputedly [rɪ'pju:tɪdlɪ] *adv* d'après ce qu'on dit

request [rɪ'kwɛst] *n* demande *f*; (*formal*) requête ▷

▷ vt: **to ~ (of** or **from sb)** demander (à qn); **at the ~ of** à la demande de

request stop n (Brit: for bus) arrêt facultatif

require [rɪˈkwaɪəʳ] vt (need: subj: person) avoir besoin de; (: thing, situation) nécessiter, demander; (want) exiger; (order): **to ~ sb to do sth/sth of sb** exiger que qn fasse qch/qch de qn; **if ~d** s'il le faut; **what qualifications are ~d?** quelles sont les qualifications requises?; **~d by law** requis par la loi

requirement [rɪˈkwaɪəmənt] n (need) exigence f; besoin m; (condition) condition f (requise)

requisition [rɛkwɪˈzɪʃən] n: **~ (for)** demande f (de) ▷ vt (Mil) réquisitionner

resat [riːˈsæt] pt, pp of **resit**

rescue [ˈrɛskjuː] n (from accident) sauvetage m; (help) secours mpl ▷ vt sauver; **to come to sb's ~** venir au secours de qn

rescue party n équipe f de sauvetage

rescuer [ˈrɛskjuəʳ] n sauveteur m

research [rɪˈsəːtʃ] n recherche(s) f(pl) ▷ vt faire des recherches sur ▷ vi: **to ~ (into sth)** faire des recherches (sur qch); **a piece of ~** un travail de recherche; **~ and development (R & D)** recherche-développement (R-D)

resemblance [rɪˈzɛmbləns] n ressemblance f; **to bear a strong ~ to** ressembler beaucoup à

resemble [rɪˈzɛmbl] vt ressembler à

resent [rɪˈzɛnt] vt éprouver du ressentiment de, être contrarié(e) par

resentful [rɪˈzɛntful] adj irrité(e), plein(e) de ressentiment

resentment [rɪˈzɛntmənt] n ressentiment m

reservation [rɛzəˈveɪʃən] n (booking) réservation f; (doubt, protected area) réserve f; (Brit Aut: also: **central reservation**) bande médiane; **to make a ~ (in an hotel/a restaurant/on a plane)** réserver or retenir une chambre/une table/une place; **with ~s** (doubts) avec certaines réserves

reservation desk n (US: in hotel) réception f

reserve [rɪˈzəːv] n réserve f; (Sport) remplaçant(e) ▷ vt (seats etc) réserver, retenir; **reserves** npl (Mil) réservistes mpl; **in ~** en réserve

reserved [rɪˈzəːvd] adj réservé(e)

reservoir [ˈrɛzəvwɑːʳ] n réservoir m

reshuffle [riːˈʃʌfl] n: **Cabinet ~** (Pol) remaniement ministériel

residence [ˈrɛzɪdəns] n résidence f; **to take up ~** s'installer; **in ~** (queen etc) en résidence; (doctor) résidant(e)

residence permit n (Brit) permis m de séjour

resident [ˈrɛzɪdənt] n (of country) résident(e); (of area, house) habitant(e); (in hotel) pensionnaire ▷ adj résidant(e)

residential [rɛzɪˈdɛnʃəl] adj de résidence; (area) résidentiel(le); (course) avec hébergement sur place

residential school n internat m

residue [ˈrɛzɪdjuː] n reste m; (Chem, Physics) résidu m

resign [rɪˈzaɪn] vt (one's post) se démettre de ▷ vi démissionner; **to ~ o.s. to** (endure) se résigner à

resignation [rɛzɪgˈneɪʃən] n (from post) démission f; (state of mind) résignation f; **to tender one's ~** donner sa démission

resigned [rɪˈzaɪnd] adj résigné(e)

resilient [rɪˈzɪlɪənt] adj (person) qui réagit, qui a du ressort

resin [ˈrɛzɪn] n résine f

resist [rɪˈzɪst] vt résister à

resistance [rɪˈzɪstəns] n résistance f

resit vt [riːˈsɪt] (Brit) (pt, pp **resat**) (exam) repasser ▷ n [ˈriːsɪt] deuxième session f (d'un examen)

resolution [rɛzəˈluːʃən] n résolution f; **to make a ~** prendre une résolution

resolve [rɪˈzɔlv] n résolution f ▷ vt (decide): **to ~ to do** résoudre or décider de faire; (problem) résoudre

resort [rɪˈzɔːt] n (seaside town) station f balnéaire; (for skiing) station de ski; (recourse) recours m ▷ vi: **to ~ to** avoir recours à; **in the last ~** en dernier ressort

resounding [rɪˈzaundɪŋ] adj retentissant(e)

resource [rɪˈsɔːs] n ressource f; **resources** npl ressources; **natural ~s** ressources naturelles; **to leave sb to his** (or **her) own ~s** (fig) livrer qn à lui-même (or elle-même)

resourceful [rɪˈsɔːsful] adj ingénieux(-euse), débrouillard(e)

respect [rɪsˈpɛkt] n respect m; (point, detail): **in some ~s** à certains égards ▷ vt respecter; **respects** npl respects, hommages mpl; **to have** or **show ~ for sb/sth** respecter qn/qch; **out of ~ for** par respect pour; **with ~ to** en ce qui concerne; **in ~ of** sous le rapport de, quant à; **in this ~** sous ce rapport, à cet égard; **with due ~ I** ... malgré le respect que je vous dois, je ...

respectable [rɪsˈpɛktəbl] adj respectable; (quite good: result etc) honorable; (player) assez bon (bonne)

respectful [rɪsˈpɛktful] adj respectueux(-euse)

respective [rɪsˈpɛktɪv] adj respectif(-ive)

respectively [rɪsˈpɛktɪvlɪ] adv respectivement

respite [ˈrɛspaɪt] n répit m

respond [rɪsˈpɔnd] vi répondre; (react) réagir

response [rɪsˈpɔns] n réponse f; (reaction) réaction f; **in ~ to** en réponse à

responsibility [rɪspɔnsɪˈbɪlɪtɪ] n responsabilité f; **to take ~ for sth/sb** accepter la responsabilité de qch/d'être responsable de qn

responsible [rɪsˈpɔnsɪbl] adj (liable): **~ (for)** responsable (de); (person) digne de confiance; (job) qui comporte des responsabilités; **to be ~ to sb (for sth)** être responsable devant qn (de qch)

responsibly [rɪsˈpɔnsɪblɪ] adv avec sérieux

responsive [rɪsˈpɔnsɪv] adj (student, audience) réceptif(-ive); (brakes, steering) sensible

rest [rɛst] n repos m; (stop) arrêt m, pause f; (Mus) silence m; (support) support m, appui m; (remainder) reste m, restant m ▷ vi se reposer; (be supported): **to ~ on** appuyer or reposer sur; (remain) rester ▷ vt (lean): **to ~ sth on/against** appuyer qch sur/contre; **the ~ of them** les autres; **to set sb's mind at ~** tranquilliser qn; **it ~s with him**

to c'est à lui de; **~ assured that ...** soyez assuré que ...

restaurant ['rɛstərɔ̃ŋ] n restaurant m

restaurant car n (Brit Rail) wagon-restaurant m

restful ['rɛstful] adj reposant(e)

restive ['rɛstɪv] adj agité(e), impatient(e); (horse) rétif(-ive)

restless ['rɛstlɪs] adj agité(e); **to get ~** s'impatienter

restoration [rɛstə'reɪʃən] n (of building) restauration f; (of stolen goods) restitution f

restore [rɪ'stɔːʳ] vt (building) restaurer; (sth stolen) restituer; (peace, health) rétablir; **to ~ to** (former state) ramener à

restrain [rɪs'treɪn] vt (feeling) contenir; (person): **to ~ (from doing)** retenir (de faire)

restrained [rɪs'treɪnd] adj (style) sobre; (manner) mesuré(e)

restraint [rɪs'treɪnt] n (restriction) contrainte f; (moderation) retenue f; (of style) sobriété f; **wage ~** limitations salariales

restrict [rɪs'trɪkt] vt restreindre, limiter

restriction [rɪs'trɪkʃən] n restriction f, limitation f

rest room n (US) toilettes fpl

restructure [riː'strʌktʃəʳ] vt restructurer

result [rɪ'zʌlt] n résultat m ▷ vi: **to ~ (from)** résulter (de); **to ~ in** aboutir à, se terminer par; **as a ~ it is too expensive** il en résulte que c'est trop cher; **as a ~ of** à la suite de

resume [rɪ'zjuːm] vt (work, journey) reprendre; (sum up) résumer ▷ vi (work etc) reprendre

résumé ['reɪzjuːmeɪ] n (summary) résumé m; (US: curriculum vitae) curriculum vitae m inv

resumption [rɪ'zʌmpʃən] n reprise f

resurgence [rɪ'səːdʒəns] n réapparition f

resurrection [rɛzə'rɛkʃən] n résurrection f

resuscitate [rɪ'sʌsɪteɪt] vt (Med) réanimer

retail ['riːteɪl] n (vente f au) détail m ▷ adj de or au détail ▷ adv au détail ▷ vt vendre au détail ▷ vi: **to ~ at 10 euros** se vendre au détail à 10 euros

retailer ['riːteɪləʳ] n détaillant(e)

retail price n prix m de détail

retain [rɪ'teɪn] vt (keep) garder, conserver; (employ) engager

retainer [rɪ'teɪnəʳ] n (servant) serviteur m; (fee) acompte m, provision f

retaliate [rɪ'tælɪeɪt] vi: **to ~ (against)** se venger (de); **to ~ (on sb)** rendre la pareille (à qn)

retaliation [rɪtælɪ'eɪʃən] n représailles fpl, vengeance f; **in ~ for** par représailles pour

retarded [rɪ'tɑːdɪd] adj retardé(e)

retch [rɛtʃ] vi avoir des haut-le-cœur

retentive [rɪ'tɛntɪv] adj: **~ memory** excellente mémoire

retina ['rɛtɪnə] n rétine f

retire [rɪ'taɪəʳ] vi (give up work) prendre sa retraite; (withdraw) se retirer, partir; (go to bed) (aller) se coucher

retired [rɪ'taɪəd] adj (person) retraité(e)

retirement [rɪ'taɪəmənt] n retraite f

retiring [rɪ'taɪərɪŋ] adj (person) réservé(e);

(chairman etc) sortant(e)

retort [rɪ'tɔːt] n (reply) riposte f; (container) cornue f ▷ vi riposter

retrace [riː'treɪs] vt reconstituer; **to ~ one's steps** revenir sur ses pas

retract [rɪ'trækt] vt (statement, claws) rétracter; (undercarriage, aerial) rentrer, escamoter ▷ vi se rétracter; rentrer

retrain [riː'treɪn] vt recycler ▷ vi se recycler

retread vt [riː'trɛd] (Aut: tyre) rechaper ▷ n ['riː'trɛd] pneu rechapé

retreat [rɪ'triːt] n retraite f ▷ vi battre en retraite; (flood) reculer; **to beat a hasty ~** (fig) partir avec précipitation

retribution [rɛtrɪ'bjuːʃən] n châtiment m

retrieval [rɪ'triːvəl] n récupération f; réparation f; recherche f et extraction f

retrieve [rɪ'triːv] vt (sth lost) récupérer; (situation, honour) sauver; (error, loss) réparer; (Comput) rechercher

retriever [rɪ'triːvəʳ] n chien m d'arrêt

retrospect ['rɛtrəspɛkt] n: **in ~** rétrospectivement, après coup

retrospective [rɛtrə'spɛktɪv] adj rétrospectif(-ive); (law) rétroactif(-ive) ▷ n (Art) rétrospective f

return [rɪ'təːn] n (going or coming back) retour m; (of sth stolen etc) restitution f; (recompense) récompense f; (Finance: from land, shares) rapport m; (report) relevé m, rapport ▷ cpd (journey) de retour; (Brit: ticket) aller et retour; (match) retour ▷ vi (person etc: come back) revenir; (: go back) retourner ▷ vt rendre; (bring back) rapporter; (send back) renvoyer; (put back) remettre; (Pol: candidate) élire; **returns** npl (Comm) recettes fpl; (Finance) bénéfices mpl; (: returned goods) marchandises renvoyées; **many happy ~s (of the day)!** bon anniversaire!; **by ~ (of post)** par retour (du courrier); **in ~ (for)** en échange (de); **a ~ (ticket) for ...** un billet aller et retour pour ...

return ticket n (esp Brit) billet m aller-retour

reunion [riː'juːnɪən] n réunion f

reunite [riːju'naɪt] vt réunir

reuse [riː'juːz] vt réutiliser

rev [rɛv] n abbr = **revolution**; (Aut) tour m ▷ vt (also: **rev up**) emballer ▷ vi (also: **rev up**) s'emballer

revamp [riː'væmp] vt (house) retaper; (firm) réorganiser

reveal [rɪ'viːl] vt (make known) révéler; (display) laisser voir

revealing [rɪ'viːlɪŋ] adj révélateur(-trice); (dress) au décolleté généreux or suggestif

revel ['rɛvl] vi: **to ~ in sth/in doing** se délecter de qch/à faire

revelation [rɛvə'leɪʃən] n révélation f

revenge [rɪ'vɛndʒ] n vengeance f; (in game etc) revanche f ▷ vt venger; **to take ~ (on)** se venger (sur)

revenue ['rɛvənjuː] n revenu m

reverberate [rɪ'vəːbəreɪt] vi (sound) retentir, se répercuter; (light) se réverbérer

reverence ['revərəns] n vénération f, révérence f

Reverend ['revərənd] adj vénérable; (in titles): **the ~ John Smith** (Anglican) le révérend John Smith; (Catholic) l'abbé (John) Smith; (Protestant) le pasteur (John) Smith

reversal [rɪ'və:sl] n (of opinion) revirement m; (of order) renversement m; (of direction) changement m

reverse [rɪ'və:s] n contraire m, opposé m; (back) dos m, envers m; (of paper) verso m; (of coin) revers m; (Aut: also: **reverse gear**) marche f arrière ▷ adj (order, direction) opposé(e), inverse ▷ vt (order, position) changer, inverser; (direction, policy) changer complètement de; (decision) annuler; (roles) renverser; (car) faire marche arrière avec; (Law: judgment) réformer ▷ vi (Brit Aut) faire marche arrière; **to go into ~** faire marche arrière; **in ~ order** en ordre inverse

reversing lights [rɪ'və:sɪŋ-] npl (Brit Aut) feux mpl de marche arrière or de recul

revert [rɪ'və:t] vi: **to ~ to** revenir à, retourner à

review [rɪ'vju:] n revue f; (of book, film) critique f; (of situation, policy) examen m, bilan m; (US: examination) examen ▷ vt passer en revue; faire la critique de; examiner; **to come under ~** être révisé(e)

reviewer [rɪ'vju:əʳ] n critique m

revise [rɪ'vaɪz] vt réviser, modifier; (manuscript) revoir, corriger ▷ vi (study) réviser; **~d edition** édition revue et corrigée

revision [rɪ'vɪʒən] n révision f; (revised version) version corrigée

revival [rɪ'vaɪvəl] n reprise f; (recovery) rétablissement m; (of faith) renouveau m

revive [rɪ'vaɪv] vt (person) ranimer; (custom) rétablir; (economy) relancer; (hope, courage) raviver, faire renaître; (play, fashion) reprendre ▷ vi (person) reprendre connaissance; (: from ill health) se rétablir; (hope etc) renaître; (activity) reprendre

revoke [rɪ'vəuk] vt révoquer; (promise, decision) revenir sur

revolt [rɪ'vəult] n révolte f ▷ vi se révolter, se rebeller ▷ vt révolter, dégoûter

revolting [rɪ'vəultɪŋ] adj dégoûtant(e)

revolution [revə'lu:ʃən] n révolution f; (of wheel etc) tour m, révolution

revolutionary [revə'lu:ʃənrɪ] adj, n révolutionnaire (m/f)

revolve [rɪ'vɔlv] vi tourner

revolver [rɪ'vɔlvəʳ] n revolver m

revolving [rɪ'vɔlvɪŋ] adj (chair) pivotant(e); (light) tournant(e)

revolving door n (porte f à) tambour m

revulsion [rɪ'vʌlʃən] n dégoût m, répugnance f

reward [rɪ'wɔ:d] n récompense f ▷ vt: **to ~ (for)** récompenser (de)

rewarding [rɪ'wɔ:dɪŋ] adj (fig) qui (en) vaut la peine, gratifiant(e); **financially ~** financièrement intéressant(e)

rewind [ri:'waɪnd] vt (irreg: like **wind**); (watch) remonter; (tape) réembobiner

rewire [ri:'waɪəʳ] vt (house) refaire l'installation électrique de

rewritable [ri:'raɪtəbl] adj (CD, DVD) réinscriptible

rewrite [ri:'raɪt] (pt **rewrote**, pp **rewritten**) vt récrire

rheumatism ['ru:mətɪzəm] n rhumatisme m

Rhine [raɪn] n: **the (River) ~** le Rhin

rhinoceros [raɪ'nɔsərəs] n rhinocéros m

rhubarb ['ru:ba:b] n rhubarbe f

rhyme [raɪm] n rime f; (verse) vers mpl ▷ vi: **to ~ (with)** rimer (avec); **without ~ or reason** sans rime ni raison

rhythm ['rɪðm] n rythme m

rib [rɪb] n (Anat) côte f ▷ vt (mock) taquiner

ribbon ['rɪbən] n ruban m; **in ~s** (torn) en lambeaux

rice [raɪs] n riz m

rice pudding n riz m au lait

rich [rɪtʃ] adj riche; (gift, clothes) somptueux(-euse); **the ~** (npl) les riches mpl; **riches** npl richesses fpl; **to be ~ in sth** être riche en qch

richly ['rɪtʃlɪ] adv richement; (deserved, earned) largement, grandement

rickets ['rɪkɪts] n rachitisme m

rid [rɪd] (pt, pp **~**) vt: **to ~ sb of** débarrasser qn de; **to get ~ of** se débarrasser de

riddle ['rɪdl] n (puzzle) énigme f ▷ vt: **to be ~d with** être criblé(e) de; (fig) être en proie à

ride [raɪd] (pt **rode**, pp **ridden**) [rəud, 'rɪdn] n promenade f, tour m; (distance covered) trajet m ▷ vi (as sport) monter (à cheval), faire du cheval; (go somewhere: on horse, bicycle) aller (à cheval or à bicyclette etc); (travel: on bicycle, motor cycle, bus) rouler ▷ vt (a horse) monter; (distance) parcourir, faire; **we rode all day/all the way** nous sommes restés toute la journée en selle/avons fait tout le chemin en selle or à cheval; **to ~ a horse/bicycle** monter à cheval/à bicyclette; **can you ~ a bike?** est-ce que tu sais monter à bicyclette?; **to ~ at anchor** (Naut) être à l'ancre; **horse/car ~** promenade or tour à cheval/en voiture; **to go for a ~** faire une promenade (en voiture or à bicyclette etc); **to take sb for a ~** (fig) faire marcher qn; (cheat) rouler qn

▶ **ride out** vt: **to ~ out the storm** (fig) surmonter les difficultés

rider ['raɪdəʳ] n cavalier(-ière) n; (in race) jockey m; (on bicycle) cycliste m/f; (on motorcycle) motocycliste m/f; (in document) annexe f, clause additionnelle

ridge [rɪdʒ] n (of hill) faîte m; (of roof, mountain) arête f; (on object) strie f

ridicule ['rɪdɪkju:l] n ridicule m; dérision f ▷ vt ridiculiser, tourner en dérision; **to hold sb/sth up to ~** tourner qn/qch en ridicule

ridiculous [rɪ'dɪkjuləs] adj ridicule

riding ['raɪdɪŋ] n équitation f

riding school n manège m, école f d'équitation

rife [raɪf] adj répandu(e); **~ with** abondant(e) en

riffraff ['rɪfræf] n racaille f

rifle ['raɪfl] n fusil m (à canon rayé) ▷ vt vider,

dévaliser
▶ **rifle through** vt fus fouiller dans
rifle range n champ m de tir; (indoor) stand m
de tir
rift [rɪft] n fente f, fissure f; (fig: disagreement)
désaccord m
rig [rɪg] n (also: **oil rig**: on land) derrick m; (: at sea)
plate-forme pétrolière ▷ vt (election etc) truquer
▶ **rig out** vt (Brit) habiller; (: pej) fringuer, attifer
▶ **rig up** vt arranger, faire avec des moyens de
fortune
rigging ['rɪgɪŋ] n (Naut) gréement m
right [raɪt] adj (true) juste, exact(e); (correct) bon
(bonne); (suitable) approprié(e), convenable;
(just) juste, équitable; (morally good) bien inv;
(not left) droit(e) ▷ n (moral good) bien m; (title,
claim) droit m; (not left) droite f ▷ adv (answer)
correctement; (treat) bien, comme il faut; (not on
the left) à droite ▷ vt redresser ▷ excl bon!; **rights**
npl (Comm) droits mpl; **the ~ time** (precise) l'heure
exacte; (not wrong) la bonne heure; **do you have
the ~ time?** avez-vous l'heure juste or exacte?;
to be ~ (person) avoir raison; (answer) être juste
or correct(e); **to get sth ~** ne pas se tromper sur
qch; **let's get it ~ this time!** essayons de ne
pas nous tromper cette fois-ci!; **you did the ~
thing** vous avez bien fait; **to put a mistake ~**
(Brit) rectifier une erreur; **by ~s** en toute justice;
on the ~ à droite; **~ and wrong** le bien et le
mal; **to be in the ~** avoir raison; **film ~s** droits
d'adaptation cinématographique; **~ now** en ce
moment même; (immediately) tout de suite; **~
before/after** juste avant/après; **~ against the
wall** tout contre le mur; **~ ahead** tout droit; droit
devant; **~ in the middle** en plein milieu; **~ away**
immédiatement; **to go ~ to the end of sth** aller
jusqu'au bout de qch
right angle n (Math) angle droit
righteous ['raɪtʃəs] adj droit(e), vertueux(-euse);
(anger) justifié(e)
rightful ['raɪtful] adj (heir) légitime
right-hand ['raɪthænd] adj: **the ~ side** la droite
right-hand drive n (Brit) conduite f à droite;
(vehicle) véhicule m avec la conduite à droite
right-handed [raɪt'hændɪd] adj (person)
droitier(-ière)
right-hand man ['raɪthænd-] (irreg) n bras droit
(fig)
rightly ['raɪtlɪ] adv bien, correctement; (with
reason) à juste titre; **if I remember ~** (Brit) si je
me souviens bien
right of way n (on path etc) droit m de passage;
(Aut) priorité f
right wing n (Mil, Sport) aile droite; (Pol) droite f
right-wing [raɪt'wɪŋ] adj (Pol) de droite
rigid ['rɪdʒɪd] adj rigide; (principle, control) strict(e)
rigmarole ['rɪgmərəʊl] n galimatias m, comédie f
rigorous ['rɪgərəs] adj rigoureux(-euse)
rile [raɪl] vt agacer
rim [rɪm] n bord m; (of spectacles) monture f; (of
wheel) jante f
rind [raɪnd] n (of bacon) couenne f; (of lemon etc)

écorce f, zeste m; (of cheese) croûte f
ring [rɪŋ] (pt **rang**, pp **rung**) [ræŋ, rʌŋ] n anneau
m; (on finger) bague f; (also: **wedding ring**) alliance
f; (for napkin) rond m; (of people, objects) cercle m;
(of spies) réseau m; (of smoke etc) rond m; (arena)
piste f, arène f; (for boxing) ring m; (sound of bell)
sonnerie f; (telephone call) coup m de téléphone
▷ vi (telephone, bell) sonner; (person: by telephone)
téléphoner; (ears) bourdonner; (also: **ring out**:
voice, words) retentir ▷ vt (Brit Tel: also: **ring up**)
téléphoner à, appeler; **to ~ the bell** sonner; **to
give sb a ~** (Tel) passer un coup de téléphone or
de fil à qn; **that has the ~ of truth about it** cela
sonne vrai; **the name doesn't ~ a bell (with
me)** ce nom ne me dit rien
▶ **ring back** vt, vi (Brit Tel) rappeler
▶ **ring off** vi (Brit Tel) raccrocher
▶ **ring up** (Brit) vt (Tel) téléphoner à, appeler
ring binder n classeur m à anneaux
ringing ['rɪŋɪŋ] n (of bell) tintement m;
(louder: also: **of telephone**) sonnerie f; (in ears)
bourdonnement m
ringing tone n (Brit Tel) tonalité f d'appel
ringleader ['rɪŋliːdəʳ] n (of gang) chef m,
meneur m
ringlets ['rɪŋlɪts] npl anglaises fpl
ring road n (Brit) rocade f; (motorway)
périphérique m
ring tone ['rɪŋtəʊn] n (on mobile) sonnerie f (de
téléphone portable)
rink [rɪŋk] n (also: **ice rink**) patinoire f; (for roller-
skating) skating m
rinse [rɪns] n rinçage m ▷ vt rincer
riot ['raɪət] n émeute f, bagarres fpl ▷ vi
(demonstrators) manifester avec violence;
(population) se soulever, se révolter; **a ~ of colours**
une débauche or orgie de couleurs; **to run ~** se
déchaîner
riotous ['raɪətəs] adj tapageur(-euse); tordant(e)
rip [rɪp] n déchirure f ▷ vt déchirer ▷ vi se
déchirer
▶ **rip off** vt (inf: cheat) arnaquer
▶ **rip up** vt déchirer
ripcord ['rɪpkɔːd] n poignée f d'ouverture
ripe [raɪp] adj (fruit) mûr(e); (cheese) fait(e)
ripen ['raɪpn] vt mûrir ▷ vi mûrir; se faire
rip-off ['rɪpɔf] n (inf): **it's a ~!** c'est du vol
manifeste!, c'est de l'arnaque!
ripple ['rɪpl] n ride f, ondulation f; (of applause,
laughter) cascade f ▷ vi se rider, onduler ▷ vt
rider, faire onduler
rise [raɪz] n (slope) côte f, pente f; (hill) élévation f;
(increase: in wages: Brit) augmentation f; (: in prices,
temperature) hausse f, augmentation; (fig: to power
etc) ascension f ▷ vi (pt **rose**, pp **-n**) [rəʊz, rɪzn]
s'élever, monter; (prices, numbers) augmenter,
monter; (waters, river) monter; (sun, wind, person:
from chair, bed) se lever; (also: **rise up**: tower, building)
s'élever; (: rebel) se révolter, se rebeller; (in rank)
s'élever; **~ to power** montée f au pouvoir; **to
give ~ to** donner lieu à; **to ~ to the occasion** se
montrer à la hauteur

risen ['rɪzn] *pp of* **rise**

rising ['raɪzɪŋ] *adj* (*increasing: number, prices*) en hausse; (*tide*) montant(e); (*sun, moon*) levant(e) ▷ *n* (*uprising*) soulèvement *m*, insurrection *f*

risk [rɪsk] *n* risque *m*, danger *m*; (*deliberate*) risque *m* ▷ *vt* risquer; **to take** *or* **run the ~ of doing** courir le risque de faire; **at ~** en danger; **at one's own ~** à ses risques et périls; **it's a fire/health ~** cela présente un risque d'incendie/pour la santé; **I'll ~ it** je vais risquer le coup

risky ['rɪskɪ] *adj* risqué(e)

rissole ['rɪsəul] *n* croquette *f*

rite [raɪt] *n* rite *m*; **the last ~s** les derniers sacrements

ritual ['rɪtjuəl] *adj* rituel(le) ▷ *n* rituel *m*

rival ['raɪvl] *n* rival(e); (*in business*) concurrent(e) ▷ *adj* rival(e); qui fait concurrence ▷ *vt* (*match*) égaler; (*compete with*) être en concurrence avec; **to ~ sb/sth in** rivaliser avec qn/qch de

rivalry ['raɪvlrɪ] *n* rivalité *f*; (*in business*) concurrence *f*

river ['rɪvəʳ] *n* rivière *f*; (*major: also fig*) fleuve *m* ▷ *cpd* (*port, traffic*) fluvial(e); **up/down ~** en amont/aval

riverbank ['rɪvəbæŋk] *n* rive *f*, berge *f*

riverbed ['rɪvəbɛd] *n* lit *m* (de rivière *or* de fleuve)

rivet ['rɪvɪt] *n* rivet *m* ▷ *vt* riveter; (*fig*) river, fixer

Riviera [rɪvɪ'ɛərə] *n*: **the (French) ~** la Côte d'Azur; **the Italian ~** la Riviera (italienne)

road [rəud] *n* route *f*; (*in town*) rue *f*; (*fig*) chemin, voie *f* ▷ *cpd* (*accident*) de la route; **main ~** grande route; **major/minor ~** route principale *or* à priorité/voie secondaire; **it takes four hours by ~** il y a quatre heures de route; **which ~ do I take for …?** quelle route dois-je prendre pour aller à …?; **"~ up"** (*Brit*) "attention travaux"

road accident *n* accident *m* de la circulation

roadblock ['rəudblɔk] *n* barrage routier

roadhog ['rəudhɔg] *n* chauffard *m*

road map *n* carte routière

road rage *n* comportement très agressif de certains usagers de la route

road safety *n* sécurité routière

roadside ['rəudsaɪd] *n* bord *m* de la route, bas-côté *m* ▷ *cpd* (*situé(e) etc*) au bord de la route; **by the ~** au bord de la route

road sign ['rəudsaɪn] *n* panneau *m* de signalisation

road tax *n* (*Brit Aut*) taxe *f* sur les automobiles

roadway ['rəudweɪ] *n* chaussée *f*

roadworks ['rəudwə:ks] *npl* travaux *mpl* (de réfection des routes)

roadworthy ['rəudwə:ðɪ] *adj* en bon état de marche

roam [rəum] *vi* errer, vagabonder ▷ *vt* parcourir, errer par

roar [rɔ:ʳ] *n* rugissement *m*; (*of crowd*) hurlements *mpl*; (*of vehicle, thunder, storm*) grondement *m* ▷ *vi* rugir; hurler; gronder; **to ~ with laughter** rire à gorge déployée

roast [rəust] *n* rôti *m* ▷ *vt* (*meat*) (faire) rôtir; (*coffee*) griller, torréfier

roast beef *n* rôti *m* de bœuf, rosbif *m*

rob [rɔb] *vt* (*person*) voler; (*bank*) dévaliser; **to ~ sb of sth** voler *or* dérober qch à qn; (*fig: deprive*) priver qn de qch

robber ['rɔbəʳ] *n* bandit *m*, voleur *m*

robbery ['rɔbərɪ] *n* vol *m*

robe [rəub] *n* (*for ceremony etc*) robe *f*; (*also:* **bathrobe**) peignoir *m*; (*US: rug*) couverture *f* ▷ *vt* revêtir (d'une robe)

robin ['rɔbɪn] *n* rouge-gorge *m*

robot ['rəubɔt] *n* robot *m*

robust [rəu'bʌst] *adj* robuste; (*material, appetite*) solide

rock [rɔk] *n* (*substance*) roche *f*, roc *m*; (*boulder*) rocher *m*, roche; (*US: small stone*) caillou *m*; (*Brit: sweet*) ≈ sucre d'orge ▷ *vt* (*swing gently: cradle*) balancer; (: *child*) bercer; (*shake*) ébranler, secouer ▷ *vi* se balancer, être ébranlé(e) *or* secoué(e); **on the ~s** (*drink*) avec des glaçons; (*ship*) sur les écueils; (*marriage etc*) en train de craquer; **to ~ the boat** (*fig*) jouer les trouble-fête

rock and roll *n* rock (and roll) *m*, rock'n'roll *m*

rock-bottom ['rɔk'bɔtəm] *n* (*fig*) niveau le plus bas ▷ *adj* (*fig: prices*) sacrifié(e); **to reach** *or* **touch ~** (*price, person*) tomber au plus bas

rock climbing *n* varappe *f*

rockery ['rɔkərɪ] *n* (*jardin m de*) rocaille *f*

rocket ['rɔkɪt] *n* fusée *f*; (*Mil*) fusée, roquette *f*; (*Culin*) roquette ▷ *vi* (*prices*) monter en flèche

rocking chair ['rɔkɪŋ-] *n* fauteuil *m* à bascule

rocking horse ['rɔkɪŋ-] *n* cheval *m* à bascule

rocky ['rɔkɪ] *adj* (*hill*) rocheux(-euse); (*path*) rocailleux(-euse); (*unsteady: table*) branlant(e)

rod [rɔd] *n* (*metallic*) tringle *f*; (*Tech*) tige *f*; (*wooden*) baguette *f*; (*also:* **fishing rod**) canne *f* à pêche

rode [rəud] *pt of* **ride**

rodent ['rəudnt] *n* rongeur *m*

rodeo ['rəudɪəu] *n* rodéo *m*

roe [rəu] *n* (*species: also:* **roe deer**) chevreuil *m*; (*of fish: also:* **hard roe**) œufs *mpl* de poisson; **soft ~** laitance *f*

rogue [rəug] *n* coquin(e)

role [rəul] *n* rôle *m*

role-model ['rəulmɔdl] *n* modèle *m* à émuler

role play, role playing *n* jeu *m* de rôle

roll [rəul] *n* rouleau *m*; (*of banknotes*) liasse *f*; (*also:* **bread roll**) petit pain; (*register*) liste *f*; (*sound: of drums etc*) roulement *m*; (*movement: of ship*) roulis *m* ▷ *vt* rouler; (*also:* **roll up**: *string*) enrouler; (*cigarettes*) rouler; **roll out**: *pastry*) étendre au rouleau, abaisser ▷ *vi* rouler; (*wheel*) tourner; **cheese ~** = sandwich *m* au fromage (*dans un petit pain*)

▶ **roll about, roll around** *vi* rouler çà et là; (*person*) se rouler par terre

▶ **roll by** *vi* (*time*) s'écouler, passer

▶ **roll in** *vi* (*mail, cash*) affluer

▶ **roll over** *vi* se retourner

▶ **roll up** *vi* (*inf: arrive*) arriver, s'amener ▷ *vt* (*carpet, cloth, map*) rouler; (*sleeves*) retrousser; **to ~ o.s. up into a ball** se rouler en boule

roll call *n* appel *m*

roller ['rəʊləʳ] n rouleau m; (wheel) roulette f; (for road) rouleau compresseur; (for hair) bigoudi m
Rollerblades® ['rəʊləʳbleɪdz] npl patins mpl en ligne
roller coaster n montagnes fpl russes
roller skates npl patins mpl à roulettes
roller-skating ['rəʊləʳskeɪtɪŋ] n patin m à roulettes; **to go ~** faire du patin à roulettes
rolling ['rəʊlɪŋ] adj (landscape) onduleux(-euse)
rolling pin n rouleau m à pâtisserie
rolling stock n (Rail) matériel roulant
ROM [rɔm] n abbr (Comput: = read-only memory) mémoire morte, ROM f
Roman ['rəʊmən] adj romain(e) ▷ n Romain(e)
Roman Catholic adj, n catholique (m/f)
romance [rə'mæns] n (love affair) idylle f; (charm) poésie f; (novel) roman m à l'eau de rose
Romania [rəʊ'meɪnɪə] = **Rumania**
Romanian [rəʊ'meɪnɪən] adj, n see **Rumanian**
Roman numeral n chiffre romain
romantic [rə'mæntɪk] adj romantique; (novel, attachment) sentimental(e)
Rome [rəʊm] n Rome
romp [rɔmp] n jeux bruyants ▷ vi (also: **romp about**) s'ébattre, jouer bruyamment; **to ~ home** (horse) arriver bon premier
rompers ['rɔmpəz] npl barboteuse f
roof [ru:f] n toit m; (of tunnel, cave) plafond m ▷ vt couvrir (d'un toit); **the ~ of the mouth** la voûte du palais
roofing ['ru:fɪŋ] n toiture f
roof rack n (Aut) galerie f
rook [ruk] n (bird) freux m; (Chess) tour f ▷ vt (inf: cheat) rouler, escroquer
room [ru:m] n (in house) pièce f; (also: **bedroom**) chambre f (à coucher); (in school etc) salle f; (space) place f; **rooms** npl (lodging) meublé m; **"~s to let"** (US): **"~s for rent"** "chambres à louer"; **is there ~ for this?** est-ce qu'il y a de la place pour ceci?; **to make ~ for sb** faire de la place à qn; **there is ~ for improvement** on peut faire mieux
rooming house ['ru:mɪŋ-] n (US) maison f de rapport
roommate ['ru:mmeɪt] n camarade m/f de chambre
room service n service m des chambres (dans un hôtel)
roomy ['ru:mɪ] adj spacieux(-euse); (garment) ample
roost [ru:st] n juchoir m ▷ vi se jucher
rooster ['ru:stəʳ] n coq m
root [ru:t] n (Bot, Math) racine f; (fig: of problem) origine f, fond m ▷ vi (plant) s'enraciner; **to take ~** (plant, idea) prendre racine
▷ **root about** vi (fig) fouiller
▷ **root for** vt fus (inf) applaudir
▷ **root out** vt extirper
rope [rəʊp] n corde f; (Naut) cordage m ▷ vt (box) corder; (tie up or together) attacher; (climbers: also: **rope together**) encorder; (area: also: **rope off**) interdire l'accès de; (: divide off) séparer; **to ~ sb in** (fig) embringuer qn; **to know the ~s** (fig) être

au courant, connaître les ficelles
rosary ['rəʊzərɪ] n chapelet m
rose [rəʊz] pt of **rise** ▷ n rose f; (also: **rosebush**) rosier m; (on watering can) pomme f ▷ adj rose
rosé ['rəʊzeɪ] n rosé m
rosebud ['rəʊzbʌd] n bouton m de rose
rosemary ['rəʊzmərɪ] n romarin m
roster ['rɔstəʳ] n: **duty ~** tableau m de service
rostrum ['rɔstrəm] n tribune f (pour un orateur etc)
rosy ['rəʊzɪ] adj rose; **a ~ future** un bel avenir
rot [rɔt] n (decay) pourriture f; (fig: pej: nonsense) idioties fpl, balivernes fpl ▷ vt, vi pourrir; **to stop the ~** (Brit fig) rétablir la situation; **dry ~** pourriture sèche (du bois); **wet ~** pourriture (du bois)
rota ['rəʊtə] n liste f, tableau m de service; **on a ~ basis** par roulement
rotary ['rəʊtərɪ] adj rotatif(-ive)
rotate [rəʊ'teɪt] vt (revolve) faire tourner; (change round: crops) alterner; (: jobs) faire à tour de rôle ▷ vi (revolve) tourner
rotating [rəʊ'teɪtɪŋ] adj (movement) tournant(e)
rotten ['rɔtn] adj (decayed) pourri(e); (dishonest) corrompu(e); (inf: bad) mauvais(e), moche; **to feel ~** (ill) être mal fichu(e)
rotund [rəʊ'tʌnd] adj rondelet(te); arrondi(e)
rough [rʌf] adj (cloth, skin) rêche, rugueux(-euse); (terrain) accidenté(e); (path) rocailleux(-euse); (voice) rauque, rude; (person, manner: coarse) rude, fruste; (: violent) brutal(e); (district, weather) mauvais(e); (sea) houleux(-euse); (plan) ébauché(e); (guess) approximatif(-ive) ▷ n (Golf) rough m ▷ vt: **to ~ it** vivre à la dure; **the sea is ~ today** la mer est agitée aujourd'hui; **to have a ~ time (of it)** en voir de dures; **~ estimate** approximation f; **to play ~** jouer avec brutalité; **to sleep ~** (Brit) coucher à la dure; **to feel ~** (Brit) être mal fichu(e)
▷ **rough out** vt (draft) ébaucher
roughage ['rʌfɪdʒ] n fibres fpl diététiques
rough-and-ready ['rʌfən'redɪ] adj (accommodation, method) rudimentaire
rough copy, rough draft n brouillon m
roughly ['rʌflɪ] adv (handle) rudement, brutalement; (speak) avec brusquerie; (make) grossièrement; (approximately) à peu près, en gros; **~ speaking** en gros
roulette [ru:'lɛt] n roulette f
Roumania etc [ru:'meɪnɪə] = **Romania** etc
round [raʊnd] adj rond(e) ▷ n rond m, cercle m; (Brit: of toast) tranche f; (duty: of policeman, milkman etc) tournée f; (: of doctor) visites fpl; (game: of cards, in competition) partie f; (Boxing) round m; (of talks) série f ▷ vt (corner) tourner; (bend) prendre; (cape) doubler ▷ prep autour de ▷ adv: **right ~, all ~** tout autour; **in ~ figures** en chiffres ronds; **to go the ~s** (disease, story) circuler; **the daily ~** (fig) la routine quotidienne; **~ of ammunition** cartouche f; **~ of applause** applaudissements mpl; **~ of drinks** tournée f; **~ of sandwiches** (Brit) sandwich m; **the long way ~** (par) le chemin le plus long; **all (the) year ~** toute l'année; **it's**

just ~ **the corner** c'est juste après le coin; (fig) c'est tout près; **to ask sb** ~ inviter qn (chez soi); **I'll be** ~ **at 6 o'clock** je serai là à 6 heures; **to go** ~ faire le tour or un détour; **to go** ~ **to sb's (house)** aller chez qn; **to go** ~ **an obstacle** contourner un obstacle; **go** ~ **the back** passez par derrière; **to go** ~ **a house** visiter une maison, faire le tour d'une maison; **enough to go** ~ assez pour tout le monde; **she arrived** ~ **(about) noon** (Brit) elle est arrivée vers midi; ~ **the clock** 24 heures sur 24

▸ **round off** vt (speech etc) terminer

▸ **round up** vt rassembler; (criminals) effectuer une rafle de; (prices) arrondir (au chiffre supérieur)

roundabout ['raundəbaut] n (Brit Aut) rond-point m (à sens giratoire); (at fair) manège m (de chevaux de bois) ▷ adj (route, means) détourné(e)

rounders ['raundəz] npl (game) ≈ balle f au camp

roundly ['raundlɪ] adv (fig) tout net, carrément

round trip n (voyage m) aller et retour m

roundup ['raundʌp] n rassemblement m; (of criminals) rafle f; **a** ~ **of the latest news** un rappel des derniers événements

rouse [rauz] vt (wake up) réveiller; (stir up) susciter, provoquer; (interest) éveiller; (suspicions) susciter, éveiller

rousing ['rauzɪŋ] adj (welcome) enthousiaste

route [ru:t] n itinéraire m; (of bus) parcours m; (of trade, shipping) route f; **"all ~s"** (Aut) "toutes directions"; **the best** ~ **to London** le meilleur itinéraire pour aller à Londres

routine [ru:'ti:n] adj (work) ordinaire, courant(e); (procedure) d'usage ▷ n (habits) habitudes fpl; (pej) train-train m; (Theat) numéro m; **daily** ~ occupations journalières

row[1] [rəu] n (line) rangée f; (of people, seats, Knitting) rang m; (behind one another: of cars, people) file f ▷ vi (in boat) ramer; (as sport) faire de l'aviron ▷ vt (boat) faire aller à la rame or à l'aviron; **in a** ~ (fig) d'affilée

row[2] [rau] n (noise) vacarme m; (dispute) dispute f, querelle f; (scolding) réprimande f, savon m ▷ vi (also: **to have a row**) se disputer, se quereller

rowboat ['rəubəut] n (US) canot m (à rames)

rowdy ['raudɪ] adj chahuteur(-euse); bagarreur(-euse) ▷ n voyou m

rowing ['rəuɪŋ] n canotage m; (as sport) aviron m

rowing boat n (Brit) canot m (à rames)

royal ['rɔɪəl] adj royal(e)

Royal Air Force n (Brit) armée de l'air britannique

royalty ['rɔɪəltɪ] n (royal persons) (membres mpl de la) famille royale; (payment: to author) droits mpl d'auteur; (: to inventor) royalties fpl

rpm abbr (= revolutions per minute) t/mn (= = tours/minute)

R.S.V.P. abbr (= répondez s'il vous plaît) RSVP

Rt. Hon. abbr (Brit: = Right Honourable) titre donné aux députés de la Chambre des communes

rub [rʌb] n (with cloth) coup m de chiffon or de torchon; (on person) friction f; **to give sth a** ~ donner un coup de chiffon or de torchon à qch ▷ vt frotter; (person) frictionner; (hands) se frotter; **to** ~ **sb up** (Brit) or **to** ~ **sb** (US) **the wrong way** prendre qn à rebrousse-poil

▸ **rub down** vt (body) frictionner; (horse) bouchonner

▸ **rub in** vt (ointment) faire pénétrer

▸ **rub off** vi partir; **to** ~ **off on** déteindre sur

▸ **rub out** vt effacer ▷ vi s'effacer

rubber ['rʌbə[r]] n caoutchouc m; (Brit: eraser) gomme f (à effacer)

rubber band n élastique m

rubber gloves npl gants mpl en caoutchouc

rubber plant n caoutchouc m (plante verte)

rubbish ['rʌbɪʃ] n (from household) ordures fpl; (fig: pej) choses fpl sans valeur; camelote f; (nonsense) bêtises fpl, idioties fpl ▷ vt (Brit inf) dénigrer, rabaisser; **what you've just said is** ~ tu viens de dire une bêtise

rubbish bin n (Brit) boîte f à ordures, poubelle f

rubbish dump n (Brit: in town) décharge publique, dépotoir m

rubble ['rʌbl] n décombres mpl; (smaller) gravats mpl; (Constr) blocage m

ruby ['ru:bɪ] n rubis m

rucksack ['rʌksæk] n sac m à dos

rudder ['rʌdə[r]] n gouvernail m

ruddy ['rʌdɪ] adj (face) coloré(e); (inf: damned) sacré(e), fichu(e)

rude [ru:d] adj (impolite: person) impoli(e); (: word, manners) grossier(-ière); (shocking) indécent(e), inconvenant(e); **to be** ~ **to sb** être grossier envers qn

ruffle ['rʌfl] vt (hair) ébouriffer; (clothes) chiffonner; (water) agiter; (fig: person) émouvoir, faire perdre son flegme à; **to get** ~**d** s'énerver

rug [rʌg] n petit tapis; (Brit: blanket) couverture f

rugby ['rʌgbɪ] n (also: **rugby football**) rugby m

rugged ['rʌgɪd] adj (landscape) accidenté(e); (features, character) rude; (determination) farouche

ruin ['ru:ɪn] n ruine f ▷ vt ruiner; (spoil: clothes) abîmer; (: event) gâcher; **ruins** npl (of building) ruine(s) m; **in** ~**s** en ruine

rule [ru:l] n règle f; (regulation) règlement m; (government) autorité f, gouvernement m; (dominion etc): **under British** ~ sous l'autorité britannique ▷ vt (country) gouverner; (person) dominer; (decide) décider ▷ vi commander; décider; (Law): **to** ~ **against/in favour of/on** statuer contre/en faveur de/sur; **to** ~ **that** (umpire, judge etc) décider que; **it's against the** ~**s** c'est contraire au règlement; **by** ~ **of thumb** à vue de nez; **as a** ~ normalement, en règle générale

▸ **rule out** vt exclure; **murder cannot be** ~**d out** l'hypothèse d'un meurtre ne peut être exclue

ruled [ru:ld] adj (paper) réglé(e)

ruler ['ru:lə[r]] n (sovereign) souverain(e); (leader) chef m (d'État); (for measuring) règle f

ruling ['ru:lɪŋ] adj (party) au pouvoir; (class) dirigeant(e) ▷ n (Law) décision f

rum [rʌm] n rhum m ▷ adj (Brit inf) bizarre

Rumania [ru:'meɪnɪə] n Roumanie f

Rumanian [ruːˈmeɪnɪən] adj roumain(e) ▷ n Roumain(e); (Ling) roumain m

rumble [ˈrʌmbl] n grondement m; (of stomach, pipe) gargouillement m ▷ vi gronder; (stomach, pipe) gargouiller

rummage [ˈrʌmɪdʒ] vi fouiller

rumour, (US) **rumor** [ˈruːməʳ] n rumeur f, bruit m (qui court) ▷ vt: **it is ~ed that** le bruit court que

rump [rʌmp] n (of animal) croupe f

rump steak n romsteck m

rumpus [ˈrʌmpəs] n (inf) tapage m, chahut m; (quarrel) prise f de bec; **to kick up a ~** faire toute une histoire

run [rʌn] (pt **ran**, pp **~**) [ræn, rʌn] n (race) course f; (outing) tour m or promenade f (en voiture); (distance travelled) parcours m, trajet m; (series) suite f, série f; (Theat) série de représentations; (Ski) piste f; (Cricket, Baseball) point m; (in tights, stockings) maille filée, échelle f ▷ vt (business) diriger; (competition, course) organiser; (hotel, house) tenir; (race) participer à; (Comput: program) exécuter; (force through: rope, pipe): **to ~ sth through** faire passer qch à travers; (to pass: hand, finger): **to ~ sth over** promener or passer qch sur; (water, bath) faire couler; (Press: feature) publier ▷ vi courir; (pass: road etc) passer; (work: machine, factory) marcher; (bus, train) circuler; (continue: play) se jouer, être à l'affiche; (: contract) être valide or en vigueur; (slide: drawer etc) glisser; (flow: river, bath, nose) couler; (colours, washing) déteindre; (in election) être candidat, se présenter; **at a ~** au pas de course; **to go for a ~** aller courir or faire un peu de course à pied; (in car) faire un tour or une promenade (en voiture); **to break into a ~** se mettre à courir; **a ~ of luck** une série de coups de chance; **to have the ~ of sb's house** avoir la maison de qn à sa disposition; **there was a ~ on** (meat, tickets) les gens se sont rués sur; **in the long ~** à la longue, à longue échéance; **in the short ~** à brève échéance, à court terme; **on the ~** en fuite; **to make a ~ for it** s'enfuir; **I'll ~ you to the station** je vais vous emmener or conduire à la gare; **to ~ errands** faire des commissions; **the train ~s between Gatwick and Victoria** le train assure le service entre Gatwick et Victoria; **the bus ~s every 20 minutes** il y a un autobus toutes les 20 minutes; **it's very cheap to ~** (car, machine) c'est très économique; **to ~ on petrol** or (US) **gas/on diesel/off batteries** marcher à l'essence/au diesel/sur piles; **to ~ for president** être candidat à la présidence; **to ~ a risk** courir un risque; **their losses ran into millions** leurs pertes se sont élevées à plusieurs millions; **to be ~ off one's feet** (Brit) ne plus savoir où donner de la tête

▸ **run about** vi (children) courir çà et là

▸ **run across** vt fus (find) trouver par hasard

▸ **run after** vt fus (to catch up) courir après; (chase) poursuivre

▸ **run around** vi = **run about**

▸ **run away** vi s'enfuir

▸ **run down** vi (clock) s'arrêter (faute d'avoir été remonté) ▷ vt (Aut: knock over) renverser; (Brit: reduce: production) réduire progressivement; (: factory/shop) réduire progressivement la production/l'activité de; (criticize) critiquer, dénigrer; **to be ~ down** (tired) être fatigué(e) or à plat

▸ **run in** vt (Brit: car) roder

▸ **run into** vt fus (meet: person) rencontrer par hasard; (: trouble) se heurter à; (collide with) heurter; **to ~ into debt** contracter des dettes

▸ **run off** vi s'enfuir ▷ vt (water) laisser s'écouler; (copies) tirer

▸ **run out** vi (person) sortir en courant; (liquid) couler; (lease) expirer; (money) être épuisé(e)

▸ **run out of** vt fus se trouver à court de; **I've ~ out of petrol** or (US) **gas** je suis en panne d'essence

▸ **run over** vt (Aut) écraser ▷ vt fus (revise) revoir, reprendre

▸ **run through** vt fus (recap) reprendre, revoir; (play) répéter

▸ **run up** vi: **to ~ up against** (difficulties) se heurter à ▷ vt: **to ~ up a debt** s'endetter

runaway [ˈrʌnəweɪ] adj (horse) emballé(e); (truck) fou (folle); (person) fugitif(-ive); (child) fugueur(-euse); (inflation) galopant(e)

rung [rʌŋ] pp of **ring** ▷ n (of ladder) barreau m

runner [ˈrʌnəʳ] n (in race: person) coureur(-euse); (: horse) partant m; (on sledge) patin m; (for drawer etc) coulisseau m; (carpet: in hall etc) chemin m

runner bean n (Brit) haricot m (à rames)

runner-up [rʌnərˈʌp] n second(e)

running [ˈrʌnɪŋ] n (in race etc) course f; (of business, organization) direction f, gestion f; (of event) organisation f; (of machine etc) marche f, fonctionnement m ▷ adj (water) courant(e); (commentary) suivi(e); **6 days ~** 6 jours de suite; **to be in/out of the ~ for sth** être/ne pas être sur les rangs pour qch

running commentary n commentaire détaillé

running costs npl (of business) frais mpl de gestion; (of car): **the ~ are high** elle revient cher

runny [ˈrʌnɪ] adj qui coule

run-of-the-mill [ˈrʌnəvðəˈmɪl] adj ordinaire, banal(e)

runt [rʌnt] n avorton m

run-up [ˈrʌnʌp] n (Brit): **~ to sth** période f précédant qch

runway [ˈrʌnweɪ] n (Aviat) piste f (d'envol or d'atterrissage)

rupture [ˈrʌptʃəʳ] n (Med) hernie f ▷ vt: **to ~ o.s.** se donner une hernie

rural [ˈruərl] adj rural(e)

rush [rʌʃ] n course précipitée; (of crowd, Comm: sudden demand) ruée f; (hurry) hâte f; (of anger, joy) accès m; (current) flot m; (Bot) jonc m; (for chair) paille f ▷ vt (hurry) transporter or envoyer d'urgence; (attack: town etc) prendre d'assaut; (Brit inf: overcharge) estamper; faire payer ▷ vi se précipiter; **don't ~ me!** laissez-moi le temps de souffler!; **to ~ sth off** (do quickly) faire qch à

la hâte; (*send*) envoyer qch d'urgence; **is there any ~ for this?** est-ce urgent?; **we've had a ~ of orders** nous avons reçu une avalanche de commandes; **I'm in a ~ (to do)** je suis vraiment pressé (de faire); **gold ~** ruée vers l'or
▶ **rush through** *vt fus* (*work*) exécuter à la hâte
▷ *vt* (*Comm: order*) exécuter d'urgence

rush hour *n* heures *fpl* de pointe *or* d'affluence

rusk [rʌsk] *n* biscotte *f*

Russia ['rʌʃə] *n* Russie *f*

Russian ['rʌʃən] *adj* russe ▷ *n* Russe *m/f*; (*Ling*) russe *m*

rust [rʌst] *n* rouille *f* ▷ *vi* rouiller

rustic ['rʌstɪk] *adj* rustique ▷ *n* (*pej*) rustaud(e)

rustle ['rʌsl] *vi* bruire, produire un bruissement ▷ *vt* (*paper*) froisser; (*US: cattle*) voler

rustproof ['rʌstpruːf] *adj* inoxydable

rusty ['rʌstɪ] *adj* rouillé(e)

rut [rʌt] *n* ornière *f*; (*Zool*) rut *m*; **to be in a ~** (*fig*) suivre l'ornière, s'encroûter

ruthless ['ruːθlɪs] *adj* sans pitié, impitoyable

RV *abbr* (= *revised version*) traduction anglaise de la Bible de 1885 ▷ *n abbr* (*US*) = **recreational vehicle**

rye [raɪ] *n* seigle *m*

Ss

Sabbath ['sæbəθ] *n* (*Jewish*) sabbat *m*; (*Christian*) dimanche *m*

sabotage ['sæbətɑːʒ] *n* sabotage *m* ▷ *vt* saboter

saccharin, saccharine ['sækərɪn] *n* saccharine *f*

sachet ['sæʃeɪ] *n* sachet *m*

sack [sæk] *n* (*bag*) sac *m* ▷ *vt* (*dismiss*) renvoyer, mettre à la porte; (*plunder*) piller, mettre à sac; **to give sb the ~** renvoyer qn, mettre qn à la porte; **to get the ~** être renvoyé(e) *or* mis(e) à la porte

sacking ['sækɪŋ] *n* toile *f* à sac; (*dismissal*) renvoi *m*

sacrament ['sækrəmənt] *n* sacrement *m*

sacred ['seɪkrɪd] *adj* sacré(e)

sacrifice ['sækrɪfaɪs] *n* sacrifice *m* ▷ *vt* sacrifier; **to make ~s (for sb)** se sacrifier *or* faire des sacrifices (pour qn)

sad [sæd] *adj* (*unhappy*) triste; (*deplorable*) triste, fâcheux(-euse); (*inf: pathetic: thing*) triste, lamentable; (: *person*) minable

saddle ['sædl] *n* selle *f* ▷ *vt* (*horse*) seller; **to be ~d with sth** (*inf*) avoir qch sur les bras

saddlebag ['sædlbæg] *n* sacoche *f*

sadistic [sə'dɪstɪk] *adj* sadique

sadly ['sædlɪ] *adv* tristement; (*unfortunately*) malheureusement; (*seriously*) fort

sadness ['sædnɪs] *n* tristesse *f*

s.a.e. *n abbr* (*Brit*: = *stamped addressed envelope*) enveloppe affranchie pour la réponse

safari [sə'fɑːrɪ] *n* safari *m*

safe [seɪf] *adj* (*out of danger*) hors de danger, en sécurité; (*not dangerous*) sans danger; (*cautious*) prudent(e); (*sure: bet*) assuré(e) ▷ *n* coffre-fort *m*; **~ from** à l'abri de; **~ and sound** sain(e) et sauf (sauve); **(just) to be on the ~ side** pour plus de sûreté, par précaution; **to play ~** ne prendre aucun risque; **it is ~ to say that ...** on peut dire sans crainte que ...; **~ journey!** bon voyage!

safe-conduct [seɪf'kɔndʌkt] *n* sauf-conduit *m*

safe-deposit ['seɪfdɪpɔzɪt] *n* (*vault*) dépôt *m* de coffres-forts; (*box*) coffre-fort *m*

safeguard ['seɪfgɑːd] *n* sauvegarde *f*, protection *f* ▷ *vt* sauvegarder, protéger

safekeeping ['seɪf'kiːpɪŋ] *n* bonne garde

safely ['seɪflɪ] *adv* (*assume, say*) sans risque d'erreur; (*drive, arrive*) sans accident; **I can ~ say ...** je peux dire à coup sûr ...

safe sex *n* rapports sexuels protégés

safety ['seɪftɪ] *n* sécurité *f*; **~ first!** la sécurité d'abord!

safety belt *n* ceinture *f* de sécurité

safety pin *n* épingle *f* de sûreté *or* de nourrice

safety valve *n* soupape *f* de sûreté

saffron ['sæfrən] *n* safran *m*

sag [sæg] *vi* s'affaisser, fléchir; (*hem, breasts*) pendre

sage [seɪdʒ] *n* (*herb*) sauge *f*; (*person*) sage *m*

Sagittarius [sædʒɪ'tɛərɪəs] *n* le Sagittaire; **to be ~** être du Sagittaire

Sahara [sə'hɑːrə] *n*: **the ~ (Desert)** le (désert du) Sahara *m*

said [sed] *pt, pp of* **say**

sail [seɪl] *n* (*on boat*) voile *f*; (*trip*): **to go for a ~** faire un tour en bateau ▷ *vt* (*boat*) manœuvrer, piloter ▷ *vi* (*travel: ship*) avancer, naviguer; (: *passenger*) aller *or* se rendre (en bateau); (*set off*) partir, prendre la mer; (*Sport*) faire de la voile; **they ~ed into Le Havre** ils sont entrés dans le port du Havre

▷ **sail through** *vi, vt fus* (*fig*) réussir haut la main

sailboat ['seɪlbəut] *n* (*US*) bateau *m* à voiles, voilier *m*

sailing ['seɪlɪŋ] *n* (*Sport*) voile *f*; **to go ~** faire de la voile

sailing boat *n* bateau *m* à voiles, voilier *m*

sailing ship *n* grand voilier

sailor ['seɪlə*] *n* marin *m*, matelot *m*

saint [seɪnt] *n* saint(e)

sake [seɪk] *n*: **for the ~ of** (*out of concern for*) pour (l'amour de), dans l'intérêt de; (*out of consideration for*) par égard pour; (*in order to achieve*) pour plus de, par souci de; **arguing for arguing's ~** discuter pour (le plaisir de) discuter; **for heaven's ~!** pour l'amour du ciel!; **for the ~ of argument** à titre d'exemple

salad ['sæləd] *n* salade *f*; **tomato ~** salade de tomates

salad bowl *n* saladier *m*

salad cream *n* (*Brit*) (sorte *f* de) mayonnaise *f*

salad dressing *n* vinaigrette *f*

salami [sə'lɑːmɪ] *n* salami *m*

salary ['sælərɪ] *n* salaire *m*, traitement *m*

sale [seɪl] *n* vente *f*; (*at reduced prices*) soldes *mpl*; **sales** *npl* (*total amount sold*) chiffre *m* de ventes;

"for ~" "à vendre"; **on ~** en vente; **on ~ or return** vendu(e) avec faculté de retour; **closing-down** or **liquidation ~** (US) liquidation f (avant fermeture); **~ and lease back** n cession-bail f

saleroom ['seɪlruːm] n salle f des ventes

sales assistant, (US) **sales clerk** n vendeur(-euse)

salesman ['seɪlzmən] (irreg) n (in shop) vendeur m; (representative) représentant m de commerce

salesperson ['seɪlzpəːsn] (irreg) n (in shop) vendeur(-euse)

sales rep n (Comm) représentant(e) m/f

saleswoman ['seɪlzwumən] (irreg) n (in shop) vendeuse f

saline ['seɪlaɪn] adj salin(e)

saliva [sə'laɪvə] n salive f

salmon ['sæmən] n (pl inv) saumon m

salon ['sælɔn] n salon m

saloon [sə'luːn] n (US) bar m; (Brit Aut) berline f; (ship's lounge) salon m

salt [sɔːlt] n sel m ▷ vt saler ▷ cpd de sel; (Culin) salé(e); **an old ~** un vieux loup de mer
  ▶ **salt away** vt mettre de côté

salt cellar n salière f

saltwater ['sɔːltˈwɔːtər] adj (fish etc) (d'eau) de mer

salty ['sɔːltɪ] adj salé(e)

salute [sə'luːt] n salut m; (of guns) salve f ▷ vt saluer

salvage ['sælvɪdʒ] n (saving) sauvetage m; (things saved) biens sauvés or récupérés ▷ vt sauver, récupérer

salvation [sæl'veɪʃən] n salut m

Salvation Army [sæl'veɪʃən-] n Armée f du Salut

same [seɪm] adj même ▷ pron: **the ~** le (la) même, les mêmes; **the ~ book as** le même livre que; **on the ~ day** le même jour; **at the ~ time** en même temps; (yet) néanmoins; **all** or **just the ~** tout de même, quand même; **they're one and the ~** (person/thing) c'est une seule et même personne/chose; **to do the ~** faire de même, en faire autant; **to do the ~ as sb** faire comme qn; **and the ~ to you!** et à vous de même!; (after insult) toi-même!; **~ here!** moi aussi!; **the ~ again!** (in bar etc) la même chose!

sample ['saːmpl] n échantillon m; (Med) prélèvement m ▷ vt (food, wine) goûter; **to take a ~** prélever un échantillon; **free ~** échantillon gratuit

sanction ['sæŋkʃən] n approbation f, sanction f ▷ vt cautionner, sanctionner; **sanctions** npl (Pol) sanctions; **to impose economic ~s on** or **against** prendre des sanctions économiques contre

sanctity ['sæŋktɪtɪ] n sainteté f, caractère sacré

sanctuary ['sæŋktjuərɪ] n (holy place) sanctuaire m; (refuge) asile m; (for wildlife) réserve f

sand [sænd] n sable m ▷ vt sabler; (also: **sand down**: wood etc) poncer

sandal ['sændl] n sandale f

sandbox ['sændbɔks] n (US: for children) tas m de sable

sand castle ['sændkɑːsl] n château m de sable

sand dune n dune f de sable

sandpaper ['sændpeɪpər] n papier m de verre

sandpit ['sændpɪt] n (Brit: for children) tas m de sable

sands [sændz] npl plage f (de sable)

sandstone ['sændstəun] n grès m

sandwich ['sændwɪtʃ] n sandwich m ▷ vt (also: **sandwich in**) intercaler; **~ed between** pris en sandwich entre; **cheese/ham ~** sandwich au fromage/jambon

sandwich course n (Brit) cours m de formation professionnelle

sandy ['sændɪ] adj sablonneux(-euse); couvert(e) de sable; (colour) sable inv, blond roux inv

sane [seɪn] adj (person) sain(e) d'esprit; (outlook) sensé(e), sain(e)

sang [sæŋ] pt of **sing**

sanitary ['sænɪtərɪ] adj (system, arrangements) sanitaire; (clean) hygiénique

sanitary towel, (US) **sanitary napkin** ['sænɪtərɪ-] n serviette f hygiénique

sanitation [sænɪ'teɪʃən] n (in house) installations fpl sanitaires; (in town) système m sanitaire

sanitation department n (US) service m de voirie

sanity ['sænɪtɪ] n santé mentale; (common sense) bon sens

sank [sæŋk] pt of **sink**

Santa Claus [sæntə'klɔːz] n le Père Noël

sap [sæp] n (of plants) sève f ▷ vt (strength) saper, miner

sapling ['sæplɪŋ] n jeune arbre m

sapphire ['sæfaɪər] n saphir m

sarcasm ['sɑːkæzm] n sarcasme m, raillerie f

sarcastic [sɑː'kæstɪk] adj sarcastique

sardine [sɑː'diːn] n sardine f

Sardinia [sɑː'dɪnɪə] n Sardaigne f

SASE n abbr (US: = self-addressed stamped envelope) enveloppe affranchie pour la réponse

sash [sæʃ] n écharpe f

sat [sæt] pt, pp of **sit**

Sat. abbr (= Saturday) sa

satchel ['sætʃl] n cartable m

satellite ['sætəlaɪt] adj, n satellite m

satellite dish n antenne f parabolique

satellite navigation system n système m de navigation par satellite

satellite television n télévision f par satellite

satin ['sætɪn] n satin m ▷ adj en or de satin, satiné(e); **with a ~ finish** satiné(e)

satire ['sætaɪər] n satire f

satisfaction [sætɪs'fækʃən] n satisfaction f

satisfactory [sætɪs'fæktərɪ] adj satisfaisant(e)

satisfied ['sætɪsfaɪd] adj satisfait(e); **to be ~ with sth** être satisfait de qch

satisfy ['sætɪsfaɪ] vt satisfaire, contenter; (convince) convaincre, persuader; **to ~ the requirements** remplir les conditions; **to ~ sb (that)** convaincre qn (que); **to ~ o.s. of sth** vérifier qch, s'assurer de qch

satisfying ['sætɪsfaɪɪŋ] adj satisfaisant(e)

Saturday ['sætədɪ] n samedi m; for phrases see also
  Tuesday
sauce [sɔːs] n sauce f
saucepan ['sɔːspən] n casserole f
saucer ['sɔːsəʳ] n soucoupe f
Saudi Arabia n Arabie f Saoudite
Saudi (Arabian) ['saudɪ] adj saoudien(ne) ▷ n
  Saoudien(ne)
sauna ['sɔːnə] n sauna m
saunter ['sɔːntəʳ] vi: **to ~ to** aller en flânant or se
  balader jusqu'à
sausage ['sɔsɪdʒ] n saucisse f; (salami etc)
  saucisson m
sausage roll n friand m
sautéed ['səuteɪd] adj sauté(e)
savage ['sævɪdʒ] adj (cruel, fierce) brutal(e), féroce;
  (primitive) primitif(-ive), sauvage ▷ n sauvage m/f
  ▷ vt attaquer férocement
save [seɪv] vt (person, belongings) sauver; (money)
  mettre de côté, économiser; (time) (faire) gagner;
  (keep) garder; (Comput) sauvegarder; (Sport: stop)
  arrêter; (avoid: trouble) éviter ▷ vi (also: **save up**)
  mettre de l'argent de côté ▷ n (Sport) arrêt m (du
  ballon) ▷ prep sauf, à l'exception de; **it will ~ me
  an hour** ça me fera gagner une heure; **to ~ face**
  sauver la face; **God ~ the Queen!** vive la Reine!
saving ['seɪvɪŋ] n économie f ▷ adj: **the ~ grace
  of** ce qui rachète; **savings** npl économies fpl; **to
  make ~s** faire des économies
savings account n compte m d'épargne
savings and loan association (US) n ≈ société f
  de crédit immobilier
savings bank n caisse f d'épargne
saviour, (US) **savior** ['seɪvjəʳ] n sauveur m
savour, (US) **savor** ['seɪvəʳ] n saveur f, goût m ▷ vt
  savourer
savoury, (US) **savory** ['seɪvərɪ] adj
  savoureux(-euse); (dish: not sweet) salé(e)
saw [sɔː] pt of **see** ▷ n (tool) scie f ▷ vt (pt -**ed**, pp
  -**ed** or -**n**) [sɔːn] scier; **to ~ sth up** débiter qch à
  la scie
sawdust ['sɔːdʌst] n sciure f
sawmill ['sɔːmɪl] n scierie f
sawn [sɔːn] pp of **saw**
sawn-off ['sɔːnɔf], (US) **sawed-off** ['sɔːdɔf] adj: ~
  shotgun carabine f à canon scié
sax [sæks] (inf) n saxo m
saxophone ['sæksəfəun] n saxophone m
say [seɪ] n: **to have one's ~** dire ce qu'on a à dire
  ▷ vt (pt, pp **said**) [sɛd] dire; **to have a ~** avoir voix
  au chapitre; **could you ~ that again?** pourriez-
  vous répéter ce que vous venez de dire?; **to ~
  yes/no** dire oui/non; **she said (that) I was to
  give you this** elle m'a chargé de vous remettre
  ceci; **my watch ~s 3 o'clock** ma montre indique
  3 heures, il est 3 heures à ma montre; **shall we ~
  Tuesday?** disons mardi?; **that doesn't ~ much
  for him** ce n'est pas vraiment à son honneur;
  when all is said and done en fin de compte,
  en définitive; **there is something** or **a lot to
  be said for it** cela a des avantages; **that is to
  ~** c'est-à-dire; **to ~ nothing of** sans compter;

~ that ... mettons or disons que ...; **that goes
  without ~ing** cela va sans dire, cela va de soi
saying ['seɪɪŋ] n dicton m, proverbe m
scab [skæb] n croûte f; (pej) jaune m
scaffold ['skæfəld] n échafaud m
scaffolding ['skæfəldɪŋ] n échafaudage m
scald [skɔːld] n brûlure f ▷ vt ébouillanter
scale [skeɪl] n (of fish) écaille f; (Mus) gamme
  f; (of ruler, thermometer etc) graduation f, échelle
  (graduée); (of salaries, fees etc) barème m; (of map,
  also size, extent) échelle ▷ vt (mountain) escalader;
  (fish) écailler; **scales** npl balance f; (larger)
  bascule f; (also: **bathroom scales**) pèse-personne
  m inv; **pay ~** échelle des salaires; **~ of charges**
  tableau m des tarifs; **on a large ~** sur une grande
  échelle, en grand; **to draw sth to ~** dessiner qch
  à l'échelle; **small-~ model** modèle réduit
  ▶ **scale down** vt réduire
scallion ['skæljən] n oignon m; (US: salad onion)
  ciboule f; (: shallot) échalote f; (: leek) poireau m
scallop ['skɔləp] n coquille f Saint-Jacques;
  (Sewing) feston m
scalp [skælp] n cuir chevelu ▷ vt scalper
scalpel ['skælpl] n scalpel m
scam [skæm] n (inf) arnaque f
scampi ['skæmpɪ] npl langoustines (frites),
  scampi mpl
scan [skæn] vt (examine) scruter, examiner;
  (glance at quickly) parcourir; (poetry) scander; (TV,
  Radar) balayer ▷ n (Med) scanographie f
scandal ['skændl] n scandale m; (gossip) ragots
  mpl
Scandinavia [skændɪ'neɪvɪə] n Scandinavie f
Scandinavian [skændɪ'neɪvɪən] adj scandinave
  ▷ n Scandinave m/f
scanner ['skænəʳ] n (Radar, Med) scanner m,
  scanographe m; (Comput) scanner
scant [skænt] adj insuffisant(e)
scanty ['skæntɪ] adj peu abondant(e),
  insuffisant(e), maigre
scapegoat ['skeɪpgəut] n bouc m émissaire
scar [skɑːʳ] n cicatrice f ▷ vt laisser une cicatrice
  or une marque à
scarce [skeəs] adj rare, peu abondant(e); **to
  make o.s. ~** (inf) se sauver
scarcely ['skeəslɪ] adv à peine, presque pas;
  ~ anybody pratiquement personne; **I can ~
  believe it** j'ai du mal à le croire
scarcity ['skeəsɪtɪ] n rareté f, manque m,
  pénurie f
scare [skeəʳ] n peur f, panique f ▷ vt effrayer,
  faire peur à; **to ~ sb stiff** faire une peur bleue à
  qn; **bomb ~** alerte f à la bombe
  ▶ **scare away**, **scare off** vt faire fuir
scarecrow ['skeəkrəu] n épouvantail m
scared ['skeəd] adj: **to be ~** avoir peur
scarf (pl **scarves**) [skɑːf, skɑːvz] n (long) écharpe f;
  (square) foulard m
scarlet ['skɑːlɪt] adj écarlate
scarlet fever n scarlatine f
scarves [skɑːvz] npl of **scarf**
scary ['skeərɪ] adj (inf) effrayant(e); (film) qui fait

peur

scathing ['skeɪðɪŋ] *adj* cinglant(e), acerbe; **to be ~ about sth** être très critique vis-à-vis de qch

scatter ['skætəʳ] *vt* éparpiller, répandre; *(crowd)* disperser ▷ *vi* se disperser

scatterbrained ['skætəbreɪnd] *adj* écervelé(e), étourdi(e)

scavenger ['skævəndʒəʳ] *n* éboueur *m*

scenario [sɪ'nɑːrɪəu] *n* scénario *m*

scene [siːn] *n* (Theat, fig etc) scène *f*; *(of crime, accident)* lieu(x) *m(pl)*, endroit *m*; *(sight, view)* spectacle *m*, vue *f*; **behind the ~s** *(also fig)* dans les coulisses; **to make a ~** *(inf: fuss)* faire une scène *or* toute une histoire; **to appear on the ~** *(also fig)* faire son apparition, arriver; **the political ~** la situation politique

scenery ['siːnərɪ] *n* (Theat) décor(s) *m(pl)*; *(landscape)* paysage *m*

scenic ['siːnɪk] *adj* scénique; offrant de beaux paysages *or* panoramas

scent [sɛnt] *n* parfum *m*, odeur *f*; *(fig: track)* piste *f*; *(sense of smell)* odorat *m* ▷ *vt* parfumer; *(smell: also fig)* flairer; *(also:* **to put** *or* **throw sb off the scent:** *fig)* mettre qn sur une mauvaise piste

sceptical, *(US)* **skeptical** ['skɛptɪkl] *adj* sceptique

schedule ['ʃɛdjuːl] *(US)* ['skɛdjuːl] *n* programme *m*, plan *m*; *(of trains)* horaire *m*; *(of prices etc)* barème *m*, tarif *m* ▷ *vt* prévoir; **as ~d** comme prévu; **on ~** à l'heure (prévue); à la date prévue; **to be ahead of/behind ~** avoir de l'avance/du retard; **we are working to a very tight ~** notre programme de travail est très serré *or* intense; **everything went according to ~** tout s'est passé comme prévu

scheduled flight *n* vol régulier

scheme [skiːm] *n* plan *m*, projet *m*; *(method)* procédé *m*; *(plot)* complot *m*, combine *f*; *(arrangement)* arrangement *m*, classification *f*; *(pension scheme etc)* régime *m* ▷ *vt, vi* comploter, manigancer; **colour ~** combinaison *f* de(s) couleurs

scheming ['skiːmɪŋ] *adj* rusé(e), intrigant(e) ▷ *n* manigances *fpl*, intrigues *fpl*

schizophrenic [skɪtsə'frɛnɪk] *adj* schizophrène

scholar ['skɔləʳ] *n* érudit(e); *(pupil)* boursier(-ère)

scholarship ['skɔləʃɪp] *n* érudition *f*; *(grant)* bourse *f* (d'études)

school [skuːl] *n* (gen) école *f*; *(secondary school)* collège *m*; lycée *m*; *(in university)* faculté *f*; *(US: university)* université *f*; *(of fish)* banc *m* ▷ *cpd* scolaire ▷ *vt* (animal) dresser

schoolbook ['skuːlbuk] *n* livre *m* scolaire *or* de classe

schoolboy ['skuːlbɔɪ] *n* écolier *m*; *(at secondary school)* collégien *m*; lycéen *m*

schoolchildren ['skuːltʃɪldrən] *npl* écoliers *mpl*; *(at secondary school)* collégiens *mpl*; lycéens *mpl*

schoolgirl ['skuːlgəːl] *n* écolière *f*; *(at secondary school)* collégienne *f*; lycéenne *f*

schooling ['skuːlɪŋ] *n* instruction *f*, études *fpl*

schoolmaster ['skuːlmɑːstəʳ] *n* (primary)

instituteur *m*; *(secondary)* professeur *m*

schoolmistress ['skuːlmɪstrɪs] *n* (primary) institutrice *f*; *(secondary)* professeur *m*

schoolteacher ['skuːltiːtʃəʳ] *n* (primary) instituteur(-trice); *(secondary)* professeur *m*

science ['saɪəns] *n* science *f*; **the ~s** les sciences; *(Scol)* les matières *fpl* scientifiques

science fiction *n* science-fiction *f*

scientific [saɪən'tɪfɪk] *adj* scientifique

scientist ['saɪəntɪst] *n* scientifique *m/f*; *(eminent)* savant *m*

sci-fi ['saɪfaɪ] *n abbr* (inf: = science fiction) SF *f*

scissors ['sɪzəz] *npl* ciseaux *mpl*; **a pair of ~** une paire de ciseaux

scoff [skɔf] *vt* (Brit inf: eat) avaler, bouffer ▷ *vi:* **to ~ (at)** (mock) se moquer (de)

scold [skəuld] *vt* gronder, attraper, réprimander

scone [skɔn] *n* sorte de petit pain rond au lait

scoop [skuːp] *n* pelle *f* (à main); *(for ice cream)* boule *f* à glace; *(Press)* reportage exclusif *or* à sensation

▶ **scoop out** *vt* évider, creuser

▶ **scoop up** *vt* ramasser

scooter ['skuːtəʳ] *n* (motor cycle) scooter *m*; *(toy)* trottinette *f*

scope [skəup] *n* (capacity: of plan, undertaking) portée *f*, envergure *f*; *(: of person)* compétence *f*, capacités *fpl*; *(opportunity)* possibilités *fpl*; **within the ~ of** dans les limites de; **there is plenty of ~ for improvement** (Brit) cela pourrait être beaucoup mieux

scorch [skɔːtʃ] *vt* (clothes) brûler (légèrement), roussir; *(earth, grass)* dessécher, brûler

scorching ['skɔːtʃɪŋ] *adj* torride, brûlant(e)

score [skɔːʳ] *n* score *m*, décompte *m* des points; *(Mus)* partition *f* ▷ *vt* (goal, point) marquer; *(success)* remporter; *(cut: leather, wood, card)* entailler, inciser ▷ *vi* marquer des points; *(Football)* marquer un but; *(keep score)* compter les points; **on that ~** sur ce chapitre, à cet égard; **to have an old ~ to settle with sb** (fig) avoir un (vieux) compte à régler avec qn; **a ~ of** (twenty) vingt; **~s of** (fig) des tas de; **to ~ 6 out of 10** obtenir 6 sur 10

▶ **score out** *vt* rayer, barrer, biffer

scoreboard ['skɔːbɔːd] *n* tableau *m*

scorer ['skɔːrəʳ] *n* (Football) auteur *m* du but; buteur *m*; *(keeping score)* marqueur *m*

scorn [skɔːn] *n* mépris *m*, dédain *m* ▷ *vt* mépriser, dédaigner

Scorpio ['skɔːpɪəu] *n* le Scorpion; **to be ~** être du Scorpion

scorpion ['skɔːpɪən] *n* scorpion *m*

Scot [skɔt] *n* Écossais(e)

Scotch [skɔtʃ] *n* whisky *m*, scotch *m*

scotch [skɔtʃ] *vt* faire échouer; enrayer; étouffer

Scotch tape® *(US) n* scotch® *m*, ruban adhésif

scot-free ['skɔt'friː] *adj:* **to get off ~** s'en tirer sans être puni(e); s'en sortir indemne

Scotland ['skɔtlənd] *n* Écosse *f*

Scots [skɔts] *adj* écossais(e)

Scotsman ['skɔtsmən] *(irreg) n* Écossais *m*

Scotswoman ['skɔtswumən] (irreg) n Écossaise f
Scottish ['skɔtɪʃ] adj écossais(e); **the ~ National Party** le parti national écossais; **the ~ Parliament** le Parlement écossais
scoundrel ['skaundrl] n vaurien m
scour ['skauəʳ] vt (clean) récurer; frotter; décaper; (search) battre, parcourir
scout [skaut] n (Mil) éclaireur m; (also: **boy scout**) scout m; **girl ~** (US) guide f
▶ **scout around** vi chercher
scowl [skaul] vi se renfrogner, avoir l'air maussade; **to ~ at** regarder de travers
scrabble ['skræbl] vi (claw): **to ~ (at)** gratter; **to ~ about** or **around for sth** chercher qch à tâtons ▷ n: **S~®** Scrabble® m
scram [skræm] vi (inf) ficher le camp
scramble ['skræmbl] n (rush) bousculade f, ruée f ▷ vi grimper/descendre tant bien que mal; **to ~ for** se bousculer or se disputer pour (avoir); **to go scrambling** (Sport) faire du trial
scrambled eggs ['skræmbld-] npl œufs brouillés
scrap [skræp] n bout m, morceau m; (fight) bagarre f; (also: **scrap iron**) ferraille f ▷ vt jeter, mettre au rebut; (fig) abandonner, laisser tomber ▷ vi se bagarrer; **scraps** npl (waste) déchets mpl; **to sell sth for ~** vendre qch à la casse or à la ferraille
scrapbook ['skræpbuk] n album m
scrap dealer n marchand m de ferraille
scrape [skreɪp] vt, vi gratter, racler ▷ n: **to get into a ~** s'attirer des ennuis
▶ **scrape through** vi (exam etc) réussir de justesse
▶ **scrape together** vt (money) racler ses fonds de tiroir pour réunir
scrap heap n tas m de ferraille; (fig): **on the ~** au rancart or rebut
scrap merchant n (Brit) marchand m de ferraille
scrap paper n papier m brouillon
scratch [skrætʃ] n égratignure f, rayure f; (on paint) éraflure f; (from claw) coup m de griffe ▷ adj: **~ team** équipe de fortune or improvisée ▷ vt (rub) (se) gratter; (record) rayer; (paint etc) érafler; (with claw, nail) griffer; (Comput) effacer ▷ vi (se) gratter; **to start from ~** partir de zéro; **to be up to ~** être à la hauteur
scratch card n carte f à gratter
scrawl [skrɔ:l] n gribouillage m ▷ vi gribouiller
scrawny ['skrɔ:nɪ] adj décharné(e)
scream [skri:m] n cri perçant, hurlement m ▷ vi crier, hurler; **to be a ~** (inf) être impayable; **to ~ at sb to do sth** crier or hurler à qn de faire qch
screech [skri:tʃ] n cri strident, hurlement m; (of tyres, brakes) crissement m, grincement m ▷ vi hurler; crisser, grincer
screen [skri:n] n écran m; (in room) paravent m; (Cine, TV) écran m; (fig) écran, rideau m ▷ vt masquer, cacher; (from the wind etc) abriter, protéger; (film) projeter; (candidates etc) filtrer; (for illness): **to ~ sb for sth** faire subir un test de dépistage de qch à qn
screening ['skri:nɪŋ] n (of film) projection f; (Med) test m (or tests) de dépistage; (for security) filtrage m
screenplay ['skri:npleɪ] n scénario m
screen saver n (Comput) économiseur m d'écran
screw [skru:] n vis f; (propeller) hélice f ▷ vt (also: **screw in**) visser; (inf!: woman) baiser (!); **to ~ sth to the wall** visser qch au mur; **to have one's head ~ed on** (fig) avoir la tête sur les épaules
▶ **screw up** vt (paper etc) froisser; (inf: ruin) bousiller; **to ~ up one's eyes** se plisser les yeux; **to ~ up one's face** faire la grimace
screwdriver ['skru:draɪvəʳ] n tournevis m
scribble ['skrɪbl] n gribouillage m ▷ vt gribouiller, griffonner; **to ~ sth down** griffonner qch
script [skrɪpt] n (Cine etc) scénario m, texte m; (in exam) copie f; (writing) (écriture f) script m
Scripture ['skrɪptʃəʳ] n Écriture sainte
scroll [skrəul] n rouleau m ▷ vt (Comput) faire défiler (sur l'écran)
scrounge [skraundʒ] (inf) vt: **to ~ sth (off** or **from sb)** se faire payer qch (par qn), emprunter qch (à qn) ▷ vi: **to ~ on sb** vivre aux crochets de qn
scrounger ['skraundʒəʳ] n parasite m
scrub [skrʌb] n (clean) nettoyage m (à la brosse); (land) broussailles fpl ▷ vt (floor) nettoyer à la brosse; (pan) récurer; (washing) frotter; (reject) annuler
scruff [skrʌf] n: **by the ~ of the neck** par la peau du cou
scruffy ['skrʌfɪ] adj débraillé(e)
scrum [skrʌm], **scrummage** ['skrʌmɪdʒ] n mêlée f
scruple ['skru:pl] n scrupule m; **to have no ~s about doing sth** n'avoir aucun scrupule à faire qch
scrutiny ['skru:tɪnɪ] n examen minutieux; **under the ~ of sb** sous la surveillance de qn
scuba diving ['sku:bə-] n plongée sous-marine
scuff [skʌf] vt érafler
scuffle ['skʌfl] n échauffourée f, rixe f
sculptor ['skʌlptəʳ] n sculpteur m
sculpture ['skʌlptʃəʳ] n sculpture f
scum [skʌm] n écume f, mousse f; (pej: people) rebut m, lie f
scurry ['skʌrɪ] vi filer à toute allure; **to ~ off** détaler, se sauver
scuttle ['skʌtl] n (Naut) écoutille f; (also: **coal scuttle**) seau m (à charbon) ▷ vt (ship) saborder ▷ vi (scamper): **to ~ away, ~ off** détaler
scythe [saɪð] n faux f
sea [si:] n mer f ▷ cpd marin(e), de (la) mer, maritime; **on the ~** (boat) en mer; (town) au bord de la mer; **by** or **beside the ~** (holiday, town) au bord de la mer; **by ~** par mer, en bateau; **out to ~** au large; **(out) at ~** en mer; **heavy** or **rough ~(s)** grosse mer, mer agitée; **a ~ of faces** (fig) une multitude de visages; **to be all at ~** (fig) nager complètement
seaboard ['si:bɔ:d] n côte f
seafood ['si:fu:d] n fruits mpl de mer
sea front ['si:frʌnt] n bord m de mer

seagoing ['siːgəʊɪŋ] *adj* (*ship*) de haute mer
seagull ['siːgʌl] *n* mouette *f*
seal [siːl] *n* (*animal*) phoque *m*; (*stamp*) sceau *m*, cachet *m*; (*impression*) cachet, estampille *f* ▷ *vt* sceller; (*envelope*) coller; (: *with seal*) cacheter; (*decide: sb's fate*) décider (de); (: *bargain*) conclure; ~ **of approval** approbation *f*
  ▶ **seal off** *vt* (*close*) condamner; (*forbid entry to*) interdire l'accès to
sea level *n* niveau *m* de la mer
sea lion *n* lion *m* de mer
seam [siːm] *n* couture *f*; (*of coal*) veine *f*, filon *m*; **the hall was bursting at the ~s** la salle était pleine à craquer
seaman ['siːmən] (*irreg*) *n* marin *m*
seance ['seɪɒns] *n* séance *f* de spiritisme
seaplane ['siːpleɪn] *n* hydravion *m*
search [səːtʃ] *n* (*for person, thing, Comput*) recherche(s) *f(pl)*; (*of drawer, pockets*) fouille *f*; (*Law: at sb's home*) perquisition *f* ▷ *vt* fouiller; (*examine*) examiner minutieusement; scruter ▷ *vi*: **to ~ for** chercher; **in ~ of** à la recherche de
  ▶ **search through** *vt fus* fouiller
search engine *n* (*Comput*) moteur *m* de recherche
searching ['səːtʃɪŋ] *adj* (*look, question*) pénétrant(e); (*examination*) minutieux(-euse)
searchlight ['səːtʃlaɪt] *n* projecteur *m*
search party *n* expédition *f* de secours
search warrant *n* mandat *m* de perquisition
seashore ['siːʃɔːʳ] *n* rivage *m*, plage *f*, bord *m* de (la) mer; **on the ~** sur le rivage
seasick ['siːsɪk] *adj*: **to be ~** avoir le mal de mer
seaside ['siːsaɪd] *n* bord *m* de mer
seaside resort *n* station *f* balnéaire
season ['siːzn] *n* saison *f* ▷ *vt* assaisonner, relever; **to be in/out of ~** être/ne pas être de saison; **the busy ~** (*for shops*) la période de pointe; (*for hotels etc*) la pleine saison; **the open ~** (*Hunting*) la saison de la chasse
seasonal ['siːznl] *adj* saisonnier(-ière)
seasoned ['siːznd] *adj* (*wood*) séché(e); (*fig: worker, actor, troops*) expérimenté(e); **a ~ campaigner** un vieux militant, un vétéran
seasoning ['siːznɪŋ] *n* assaisonnement *m*
season ticket *n* carte *f* d'abonnement
seat [siːt] *n* siège *m*; (*in bus, train: place*) place *f*; (*Parliament*) siège; (*buttocks*) postérieur *m*; (*of trousers*) fond *m* ▷ *vt* faire asseoir, placer; (*have room for*) avoir des places assises pour, pouvoir accueillir; **are there any ~s left?** est-ce qu'il reste des places?; **to take one's ~** prendre place; **to be ~ed** être assis; **please be ~ed** veuillez vous asseoir
seat belt *n* ceinture *f* de sécurité
seating ['siːtɪŋ] *n* sièges *fpl*, places assises
sea water *n* eau *f* de mer
seaweed ['siːwiːd] *n* algues *fpl*
seaworthy ['siːwəːðɪ] *adj* en état de naviguer
sec. *abbr* (= *second*) sec
secluded [sɪ'kluːdɪd] *adj* retiré(e), à l'écart
seclusion [sɪ'kluːʒən] *n* solitude *f*
second¹ ['sekənd] *num* deuxième, second(e) ▷ *adv*

(*in race etc*) en seconde position ▷ *n* (*unit of time*) seconde *f*; (*Aut: also*: **second gear**) seconde; (*in series, position*) deuxième *m/f*, second(e); (*Comm: imperfect*) article *m* de second choix; (*Brit Scol*) ≈ licence *f* avec mention ▷ *vt* (*motion*) appuyer; **seconds** *npl* (*inf: food*) rab *m* (*inf*); **Charles the S~** Charles II; **just a ~!** une seconde!, un instant!; (*stopping sb*) pas si vite!; ~ **floor** (*Brit*) deuxième (étage) *m*; (*US*) premier (étage) *m*; **to ask for a ~ opinion** (*Med*) demander l'avis d'un autre médecin
second² [sɪ'kɒnd] *vt* (*employee*) détacher, mettre en détachement
secondary ['sekəndərɪ] *adj* secondaire
secondary school *n* (*age 11 to 15*) collège *m*; (*age 15 to 18*) lycée *m*
second-class ['sekənd'klɑːs] *adj* de deuxième classe; (*Rail*) de seconde (classe); (*Post*) au tarif réduit; (*pej*) de qualité inférieure ▷ *adv* (*Rail*) en seconde; (*Post*) au tarif réduit; ~ **citizen** citoyen(ne) de deuxième classe
second hand *n* (*on clock*) trotteuse *f*
secondhand ['sekənd'hænd] *adj* d'occasion; (*information*) de seconde main ▷ *adv* (*buy*) d'occasion; **to hear sth ~** apprendre qch indirectement
secondly ['sekəndlɪ] *adv* deuxièmement; **firstly ... ~ ...** d'abord ... ensuite ... or de plus ...
secondment [sɪ'kɒndmənt] *n* (*Brit*) détachement *m*
second-rate ['sekənd'reɪt] *adj* de deuxième ordre, de qualité inférieure
second thoughts *npl*: **to have ~** changer d'avis; **on ~** *or* **thought** (*US*) à la réflexion
secrecy ['siːkrəsɪ] *n* secret *m*; **in ~** en secret
secret ['siːkrɪt] *adj* secret(-ète) ▷ *n* secret *m*; **in ~** (*adv*) en secret, secrètement, en cachette; **to keep sth ~ from sb** cacher qch à qn, ne pas révéler qch à qn; **to make no ~ of sth** ne pas cacher qch; **keep it ~** n'en parle à personne
secretary ['sekrətrɪ] *n* secrétaire *m/f*; (*Comm*) secrétaire général; **S~ of State** (*US Pol*) ≈ ministre *m* des Affaires étrangères; **S~ of State (for)** (*Brit Pol*) ministre *m* (de)
secretive ['siːkrətɪv] *adj* réservé(e); (*pej*) cachottier(-ière), dissimulé(e)
secretly ['siːkrɪtlɪ] *adv* en secret, secrètement, en cachette
secret service *n* services secrets
sect [sekt] *n* secte *f*
sectarian [sek'teərɪən] *adj* sectaire
section ['sekʃən] *n* section *f*; (*department*) section; (*Comm*) rayon *m*; (*of document*) section, article *m*, paragraphe *m*; (*cut*) coupe *f* ▷ *vt* sectionner; **the business** *etc* ~ (*Press*) la page des affaires *etc*
sector ['sektəʳ] *n* secteur *m*
secular ['sekjʊləʳ] *adj* laïque
secure [sɪ'kjuəʳ] *adj* (*free from anxiety*) sans inquiétude, sécurisé(e); (*firmly fixed*) solide, bien attaché(e) (*or* fermé(e) *etc*); (*in safe place*) en lieu sûr, en sûreté ▷ *vt* (*fix*) fixer, attacher; (*get*) obtenir, se procurer; (*Comm: loan*) garantir; **to**

make sth ~ bien fixer or attacher qch; **to ~ sth for sb** obtenir qch pour qn, procurer qch à qn

security [sɪ'kjʊərɪtɪ] n sécurité f, mesures fpl de sécurité; (for loan) caution f, garantie f; **securities** npl (Stock Exchange) valeurs fpl, titres mpl; **to increase** or **tighten ~** renforcer les mesures de sécurité; **~ of tenure** stabilité f d'un emploi, titularisation f

security guard n garde chargé de la sécurité; (transporting money) convoyeur m de fonds

sedan [sə'dæn] n (US Aut) berline f

sedate [sɪ'deɪt] adj calme; posé(e) ▷ vt donner des sédatifs à

sedative ['sedɪtɪv] n calmant m, sédatif m

seduce [sɪ'dju:s] vt séduire

seduction [sɪ'dʌkʃən] n séduction f

seductive [sɪ'dʌktɪv] adj séduisant(e); (smile) séducteur(-trice); (fig: offer) alléchant(e)

see [si:] (pt **saw**, pp **-n**) [sɔː, si:n] vt (gen) voir; (accompany): **to ~ sb to the door** reconduire or raccompagner qn jusqu'à la porte ▷ vi voir ▷ n évêché m; **to ~ that** (ensure) veiller à ce que + sub, faire en sorte que + sub, s'assurer que; **there was nobody to be ~n** il n'y avait pas un chat; **let me ~** (show me) fais-(moi) voir; (let me think) voyons (un peu); **to go and ~ sb** aller voir qn; **~ for yourself** voyez vous-même; **I don't know what she ~s in him** je ne sais pas ce qu'elle lui trouve; **as far as I can ~** pour autant que je puisse en juger; **~ you!** au revoir!, à bientôt!; **~ you soon/ later/tomorrow!** à bientôt/plus tard/demain!

▸ **see about** vt fus (deal with) s'occuper de

▸ **see off** vt accompagner (à l'aéroport etc)

▸ **see out** vt (take to door) raccompagner à la porte

▸ **see through** vt mener à bonne fin ▷ vt fus voir clair dans

▸ **see to** vt fus s'occuper de, se charger de

seed [si:d] n graine f; (fig) germe m; (Tennis etc) tête f de série; **to go to ~** (plant) monter en graine; (fig) se laisser aller

seedling ['si:dlɪŋ] n jeune plant m, semis m

seedy ['si:dɪ] adj (shabby) minable, miteux(-euse)

seeing ['si:ɪŋ] conj: **~ (that)** vu que, étant donné que

seek [si:k] (pt, pp **sought**) [sɔːt] vt chercher, rechercher; **to ~ advice/help from sb** demander conseil/de l'aide à qn

▸ **seek out** vt (person) chercher

seem [si:m] vi sembler, paraître; **there ~s to be ...** il semble qu'il y a ..., on dirait qu'il y a ...; **it ~s (that)** ... il semble que ...; **what ~s to be the trouble?** qu'est-ce qui ne va pas?

seemingly ['si:mɪŋlɪ] adv apparemment

seen [si:n] pp of **see**

seep [si:p] vi suinter, filtrer

seesaw ['si:sɔː] n (jeu m de) bascule f

seethe [si:ð] vi être en effervescence; **to ~ with anger** bouillir de colère

see-through ['si:θru:] adj transparent(e)

segment ['segmənt] n segment m; (of orange) quartier m

segregate ['segrɪgeɪt] vt séparer, isoler

Seine [seɪn] n: **the (River) ~** la Seine

seize [si:z] vt (grasp) saisir, attraper; (take possession of) s'emparer de; (opportunity) saisir; (Law) saisir

▸ **seize on** vt fus saisir, sauter sur

▸ **seize up** vi (Tech) se gripper

▸ **seize upon** vt fus = **seize on**

seizure ['si:ʒər] n (Med) crise f, attaque f; (of power) prise f; (Law) saisie f

seldom ['seldəm] adv rarement

select [sɪ'lekt] adj choisi(e), d'élite; (hotel, restaurant, club) chic inv, sélect inv ▷ vt sélectionner, choisir; **a ~ few** quelques privilégiés

selection [sɪ'lekʃən] n sélection f, choix m

selective [sɪ'lektɪv] adj sélectif(-ive); (school) à recrutement sélectif

self [self] n (pl **selves**) [selvz]: **the ~** le moi inv ▷ prefix auto-

self-assured [selfə'ʃuəd] adj sûr(e) de soi, plein(e) d'assurance

self-catering [self'keɪtərɪŋ] adj (Brit: flat) avec cuisine, où l'on peut faire sa cuisine; (: holiday) en appartement (or chalet etc) loué

self-centred, (US) **self-centered** [self'sentəd] adj égocentrique

self-confidence [self'kɔnfɪdns] n confiance f en soi

self-confident [self'kɔnfɪdnt] adj sûr(e) de soi, plein(e) d'assurance

self-conscious [self'kɔnʃəs] adj timide, qui manque d'assurance

self-contained [selfkən'teɪnd] adj (Brit: flat) avec entrée particulière, indépendant(e)

self-control [selfkən'trəul] n maîtrise f de soi

self-defence, (US) **self-defense** [selfdɪ'fens] n autodéfense f; (Law) légitime défense f

self-discipline [self'dɪsɪplɪn] n discipline personnelle

self-drive [self'draɪv] adj (Brit): **~ car** voiture f de location

self-employed [selfɪm'plɔɪd] adj qui travaille à son compte

self-esteem [selfɪ'sti:m] n amour-propre m

self-evident [self'evɪdnt] adj évident(e), qui va de soi

self-governing [self'gʌvənɪŋ] adj autonome

self-indulgent [selfɪn'dʌldʒənt] adj qui ne se refuse rien

self-interest [self'ɪntrɪst] n intérêt personnel

selfish ['selfɪʃ] adj égoïste

selfishness ['selfɪʃnɪs] n égoisme m

selfless ['selflɪs] adj désintéressé(e)

self-pity [self'pɪtɪ] n apitoiement m sur soi-même

self-possessed [selfpə'zest] adj assuré(e)

self-preservation ['selfprezə'veɪʃən] n instinct m de conservation

self-raising [self'reɪzɪŋ], (US) **self-rising** [self'raɪzɪŋ] adj: **~ flour** farine f pour gâteaux (avec levure incorporée)

self-respect [selfrɪs'pekt] n respect m de soi,

amour-propre m

self-righteous [sɛlfˈraɪtʃəs] adj satisfait(e) de soi, pharisaïque

self-sacrifice [sɛlfˈsækrɪfaɪs] n abnégation f

self-satisfied [sɛlfˈsætɪsfaɪd] adj content(e) de soi, suffisant(e)

self-service [sɛlfˈsəːvɪs] adj, n libre-service (m), self-service (m)

self-sufficient [sɛlfsəˈfɪʃənt] adj indépendant(e)

self-taught [sɛlfˈtɔːt] adj autodidacte

sell (pt, pp **sold**) [sɛl, səuld] vt vendre ▷ vi se vendre; **to ~ at** or **for 10 euros** se vendre 10 euros; **to ~ sb an idea** (fig) faire accepter une idée à qn

▶ **sell off** vt liquider

▶ **sell out** vi: **to ~ out (of sth)** (use up stock) vendre tout son stock (de qch); **to ~ out (to)** (Comm) vendre son fonds or son affaire (à) ▷ vt vendre tout son stock de; **the tickets are all sold out** il ne reste plus de billets

▶ **sell up** vi vendre son fonds or son affaire

sell-by date [ˈsɛlbaɪ-] n date f limite de vente

seller [ˈsɛləʳ] n vendeur(-euse), marchand(e); **~'s market** marché m à la hausse

selling price [ˈsɛlɪŋ-] n prix m de vente

Sellotape® [ˈsɛləuteɪp] n (Brit) scotch® m

selves [sɛlvz] npl of **self**

semblance [ˈsɛmbləns] n semblant m

semen [ˈsiːmən] n sperme m

semester [sɪˈmɛstəʳ] n (esp US) semestre m

semi... [ˈsɛmɪ] prefix semi-, demi-; à demi, à moitié ▷ n: **semi;** = **semidetached house**

semicircle [ˈsɛmɪsəːkl] n demi-cercle m

semicolon [sɛmɪˈkəulən] n point-virgule m

semidetached [sɛmɪdɪˈtætʃt], **semidetached house** n (Brit) maison jumelée or jumelle

semi-final [sɛmɪˈfaɪnl] n demi-finale f

seminar [ˈsɛmɪnɑːʳ] n séminaire m

seminary [ˈsɛmɪnərɪ] n (Rel: for priests) séminaire m

semiskilled [sɛmɪˈskɪld] adj: **~ worker** ouvrier(-ière) spécialisé(e)

semi-skimmed [ˈsɛmɪˈskɪmd] adj demi-écrémé(e)

senate [ˈsɛnɪt] n sénat m; (US): **the S~** le Sénat; voir article

senator [ˈsɛnɪtəʳ] n sénateur m

send (pt, pp **sent**) [sɛnd, sɛnt] vt envoyer; **to ~ by post** or (US) **mail** envoyer or expédier par la poste; **to ~ sb for sth** envoyer qn chercher qch; **to ~ word that ...** faire dire que ...; **she ~s (you) her love** elle vous adresse ses amitiés; **to ~ sb to Coventry** (Brit) mettre qn en quarantaine; **to ~ sb to sleep** endormir qn; **to ~ sb into fits of laughter** faire rire qn aux éclats; **to ~ sth flying** envoyer valser qch

▶ **send away** vt (letter, goods) envoyer, expédier

▶ **send away for** vt fus commander par correspondance, se faire envoyer

▶ **send back** vt renvoyer

▶ **send for** vt fus envoyer chercher; faire venir; (by post) se faire envoyer, commander par correspondance

▶ **send in** vt (report, application, resignation) remettre

▶ **send off** vt (goods) envoyer, expédier; (Brit Sport: player) expulser or renvoyer du terrain

▶ **send on** vt (Brit: letter) faire suivre; (luggage etc: in advance) (faire) expédier à l'avance

▶ **send out** vt (invitation) envoyer (par la poste); (emit: light, heat, signal) émettre

▶ **send round** vt (letter, document etc) faire circuler

▶ **send up** vt (person, price) faire monter; (Brit: parody) mettre en boîte, parodier

sender [ˈsɛndəʳ] n expéditeur(-trice)

send-off [ˈsɛndɔf] n: **a good ~** des adieux chaleureux

senile [ˈsiːnaɪl] adj sénile

senior [ˈsiːnɪəʳ] adj (older) aîné(e), plus âgé(e); (high-ranking) de haut niveau; (of higher rank): **to be ~ to sb** être le supérieur de qn ▷ n (older): **she is 15 years his ~** elle est son aînée de 15 ans, elle est plus âgée que lui de 15 ans; (in service) personne f qui a plus d'ancienneté; **P. Jones ~** P. Jones père

senior citizen n personne f du troisième âge

senior high school n (US) ≈ lycée m

seniority [siːnɪˈɔrɪtɪ] n priorité f d'âge, ancienneté f; (in rank) supériorité f (hiérarchique)

sensation [sɛnˈseɪʃən] n sensation f; **to create a ~** faire sensation

sensational [sɛnˈseɪʃənl] adj qui fait sensation; (marvellous) sensationnel(le)

sense [sɛns] n sens m; (feeling) sentiment m; (meaning) sens, signification f; (wisdom) bon sens ▷ vt sentir, pressentir; **senses** npl raison f; **it makes ~** c'est logique; **there is no ~ in (doing) that** cela n'a pas de sens; **to come to one's ~s** (regain consciousness) reprendre conscience; (become reasonable) revenir à la raison; **to take leave of one's ~s** perdre la tête

senseless [ˈsɛnslɪs] adj insensé(e), stupide; (unconscious) sans connaissance

sense of humour, (US) **sense of humor** n sens m de l'humour

sensible [ˈsɛnsɪbl] adj sensé(e), raisonnable; (shoes etc) pratique

sensitive [ˈsɛnsɪtɪv] adj: **~ (to)** sensible (à); **he is very ~ about it** c'est un point très sensible (chez lui)

sensual [ˈsɛnsjuəl] adj sensuel(le)

sensuous [ˈsɛnsjuəs] adj voluptueux(-euse), sensuel(le)

sent [sɛnt] pt, pp of **send**

sentence [ˈsɛntns] n (Ling) phrase f; (Law: judgment) condamnation f, sentence f; (: punishment) peine f ▷ vt: **to ~ sb to death/to 5 years** condamner qn à mort/à 5 ans; **to pass ~ on sb** prononcer une peine contre qn

sentiment [ˈsɛntɪmənt] n sentiment m; (opinion) opinion f, avis m

sentimental [sɛntɪˈmɛntl] adj sentimental(e)

sentry [ˈsɛntrɪ] n sentinelle f, factionnaire m

separate [adj 'sɛprɪt, vb 'sɛpəreɪt] adj séparé(e); (organization) indépendant(e); (day, occasion, issue) différent(e) ▷ vt séparer; (distinguish) distinguer ▷ vi se séparer; ~ **from** distinct(e) de; **under ~ cover** (Comm) sous pli séparé; **to ~ into** diviser en

separately ['sɛprɪtlɪ] adv séparément

separates ['sɛprɪts] npl (clothes) coordonnés mpl

separation [sɛpə'reɪʃən] n séparation f

September [sɛp'tɛmbə'] n septembre m; for phrases see also **July**

septic ['sɛptɪk] adj septique; (wound) infecté(e); **to go ~** s'infecter

septic tank n fosse f septique

sequel ['si:kwl] n conséquence f; séquelles fpl; (of story) suite f

sequence ['si:kwəns] n ordre m, suite f; (in film) séquence f; (dance) numéro m; **in ~** par ordre, dans l'ordre, les uns après les autres; **~ of tenses** concordance f des temps

sequin ['si:kwɪn] n paillette f

Serb [sə:b] adj, n = **Serbian**

Serbia ['sə:bɪə] n Serbie f

Serbian ['sə:bɪən] adj serbe ▷ n Serbe m/f; (Ling) serbe m

serene [sɪ'ri:n] adj serein(e), calme, paisible

sergeant ['sɑ:dʒənt] n sergent m; (Police) brigadier m

serial ['sɪərɪəl] n feuilleton m ▷ adj (Comput: interface, printer) série inv; (: access) séquentiel(le)

serial killer n meurtrier m tuant en série

serial number n numéro m de série

series ['sɪərɪz] n série f; (Publishing) collection f

serious ['sɪərɪəs] adj sérieux(-euse); (accident etc) grave; **are you ~ (about it)?** parlez-vous sérieusement?

seriously ['sɪərɪəslɪ] adv sérieusement; (hurt) gravement; **~ rich/difficult** (inf: extremely) drôlement riche/difficile; **to take sth/sb ~** prendre qch/qn au sérieux

sermon ['sə:mən] n sermon m

serrated [sɪ'reɪtɪd] adj en dents de scie

servant ['sə:vənt] n domestique m/f; (fig) serviteur (servante)

serve [sə:v] vt (employer etc) servir, être au service de; (purpose) servir à; (customer, food, meal) servir; (subj: train) desservir; (apprenticeship) faire, accomplir; (prison term) faire; purger ▷ vi (Tennis) servir; (be useful): **to ~ as/for/to do** servir de/à/à faire ▷ n (Tennis) service m; **are you being ~d?** est-ce qu'on s'occupe de vous?; **to ~ on a committee/jury** faire partie d'un comité/jury; **it ~s him right** c'est bien fait pour lui; **it ~s my purpose** cela fait mon affaire

▸ **serve out, serve up** vt (food) servir

server [sə:və'] n (Comput) serveur m

service ['sə:vɪs] n (gen) service m; (Aut) révision f; (Rel) office m ▷ vt (car etc) réviser; **services** npl (Econ: tertiary sector) (secteur m) tertiaire m, secteur des services; (Brit: on motorway) station-service f; (Mil): **the S~s** (npl) les forces armées; **to be of ~ to sb, to do sb a ~** rendre service à qn;

~ included/not included service compris/non compris; **to put one's car in for ~** donner sa voiture à réviser; **dinner ~** service de table

serviceable ['sə:vɪsəbl] adj pratique, commode

service area n (on motorway) aire f de services

service charge n (Brit) service m

serviceman ['sə:vɪsmən] (irreg) n militaire m

service station n station-service f

serviette [sə:vɪ'ɛt] n (Brit) serviette f (de table)

session ['sɛʃən] n (sitting) séance f; (Scol) année f scolaire (or universitaire); **to be in ~** siéger, être en session or en séance

set [sɛt] (pt, pp ~) n série f, assortiment m; (of tools etc) jeu m; (Radio, TV) poste m; (Tennis) set m; (group of people) cercle m, milieu m; (Cine) plateau m; (Theat: stage) scène f; (: scenery) décor m; (Math) ensemble m; (Hairdressing) mise f en plis ▷ adj (fixed) fixe, déterminé(e); (ready) prêt(e) ▷ vt (place) mettre, poser, placer; (fix, establish) fixer; (: record) établir; (assign: task, homework) donner; (exam) composer; (adjust) régler; (decide: rules etc) fixer, choisir; (Typ) composer ▷ vi (sun) se coucher; (jam, jelly, concrete) prendre; (bone) se ressouder; **to be ~ on doing** être résolu(e) à faire; **to be all ~ to do** être (fin) prêt(e) pour faire; **to be (dead) ~ against** être (totalement) opposé à; **he's ~ in his ways** il n'est pas très souple; il tient à ses habitudes; **to ~ to music** mettre en musique; **to ~ on fire** mettre le feu à; **to ~ free** libérer; **to ~ sth going** déclencher qch; **to ~ the alarm clock for seven o'clock** mettre le réveil à sonner à sept heures; **to ~ sail** partir, prendre la mer; **a ~ phrase** une expression toute faite, une locution; **a ~ of false teeth** un dentier; **a ~ of dining-room furniture** une salle à manger

▸ **set about** vt fus (task) entreprendre, se mettre à; **to ~ about doing sth** se mettre à faire qch

▸ **set aside** vt mettre de côté; (time) garder

▸ **set back** vt (in time): **to ~ back (by)** retarder (de); (place): **a house ~ back from the road** une maison située en retrait de la route

▸ **set down** vt (subj: bus, train) déposer

▸ **set in** vi (infection, bad weather) s'installer; (complications) survenir, surgir; **the rain has ~ in for the day** c'est parti pour qu'il pleuve toute la journée

▸ **set off** vi se mettre en route, partir ▷ vt (bomb) faire exploser; (cause to start) déclencher; (show up well) mettre en valeur, faire valoir

▸ **set out** vi: **to ~ out (from)** partir (de) ▷ vt (arrange) disposer; (state) présenter, exposer; **to ~ out to do** entreprendre de faire; avoir pour but or intention de faire

▸ **set up** vt (organization) fonder, créer; (monument) ériger; **to ~ up shop** (fig) s'établir, s'installer

setback ['sɛtbæk] n (hitch) revers m, contretemps m; (in health) rechute f

set menu n menu m

settee [sɛ'ti:] n canapé m

setting ['sɛtɪŋ] n cadre m; (of jewel) monture f; (position: of controls) réglage m

settle ['sɛtl] vt (argument, matter, account) régler; (problem) résoudre; (Med: calm) calmer; (colonize: land) coloniser ▷ vi (bird, dust etc) se poser; (sediment) se déposer; **to ~ to sth** se mettre sérieusement à qch; **to ~ for sth** accepter qch, se contenter de qch; **to ~ on sth** opter or se décider pour qch; **that's ~d then** alors, c'est d'accord!; **to ~ one's stomach** calmer les maux d'estomac
▶ **settle down** vi (get comfortable) s'installer; (become calmer) se calmer; se ranger
▶ **settle in** vi s'installer
▶ **settle up** vi: **to ~ up with sb** régler (ce que l'on doit à) qn

settlement ['sɛtlmənt] n (payment) règlement m; (agreement) accord m; (colony) colonie f; (village etc) village m, hameau m; **in ~ of our account** (Comm) en règlement de notre compte

settler ['sɛtlə'] n colon m

setup ['sɛtʌp] n (arrangement) manière f dont les choses sont organisées; (situation) situation f, allure f des choses

seven ['sɛvn] num sept

seventeen [sɛvn'ti:n] num dix-sept

seventeenth [sɛvn'ti:nθ] num dix-septième

seventh ['sɛvnθ] num septième

seventieth ['sɛvntɪɪθ] num soixante-dixième

seventy ['sɛvntɪ] num soixante-dix

sever ['sɛvə'] vt couper, trancher; (relations) rompre

several ['sɛvərl] adj, pron plusieurs pl; **~ of us** plusieurs d'entre nous; **~ times** plusieurs fois

severance ['sɛvərəns] n (of relations) rupture f

severance pay n indemnité f de licenciement

severe [sɪ'vɪə'] adj (stern) sévère, strict(e); (serious) grave, sérieux(-euse); (hard) rigoureux(-euse), dur(e); (plain) sévère, austère

severity [sɪ'vɛrɪtɪ] n sévérité f; gravité f; rigueur f

sew (pt **-ed**, pp **-n**) [səu], vt, vi coudre
▶ **sew up** vt (re)coudre; **it is all ~n up** (fig) c'est dans le sac or dans la poche

sewage ['su:ɪdʒ] n vidange(s) f(pl)

sewer ['su:ə'] n égout m

sewing ['səuɪŋ] n couture f; (item(s)) ouvrage m

sewing machine n machine f à coudre

sewn [səun] pp of **sew**

sex [sɛks] n sexe m; **to have ~ with** avoir des rapports (sexuels) avec

sexism ['sɛksɪzəm] n sexisme m

sexist ['sɛksɪst] adj sexiste

sexual ['sɛksjuəl] adj sexuel(le); **~ assault** attentat m à la pudeur; **~ harassment** harcèlement sexuel

sexual intercourse n rapports sexuels

sexuality [sɛksju'ælɪtɪ] n sexualité f

sexy ['sɛksɪ] adj sexy inv

shabby ['ʃæbɪ] adj miteux(-euse); (behaviour) mesquin(e), méprisable

shack [ʃæk] n cabane f, hutte f

shackles ['ʃæklz] npl chaînes fpl, entraves fpl

shade [ʃeɪd] n ombre f; (for lamp) abat-jour m inv; (of colour) nuance f, ton m; (US: window shade) store m; (small quantity): **a ~ of** un soupçon de
▷ vt abriter du soleil, ombrager; **shades** npl (US: sunglasses) lunettes fpl de soleil; **in the ~** à l'ombre; **a ~ smaller** un tout petit peu plus petit

shadow ['ʃædəu] n ombre f ▷ vt (follow) filer; **without** or **beyond a ~ of doubt** sans l'ombre d'un doute

shadow cabinet n (Brit Pol) cabinet parallèle formé par le parti qui n'est pas au pouvoir

shadowy ['ʃædəuɪ] adj ombragé(e); (dim) vague, indistinct(e)

shady ['ʃeɪdɪ] adj ombragé(e); (fig: dishonest) louche, véreux(-euse)

shaft [ʃɑ:ft] n (of arrow, spear) hampe f; (Aut, Tech) arbre m; (of mine) puits m; (of lift) cage f; (of light) rayon m, trait m; **ventilator ~** conduit m d'aération or de ventilation

shaggy ['ʃægɪ] adj hirsute; en broussaille

shake [ʃeɪk] (pt **shook**, pp **-n**) [ʃuk, 'ʃeɪkn] vt secouer; (bottle, cocktail) agiter; (house, confidence) ébranler ▷ vi trembler ▷ n secousse f; **to ~ one's head** (in refusal etc) dire or faire non de la tête; (in dismay) secouer la tête; **to ~ hands with sb** serrer la main à qn
▶ **shake off** vt secouer; (pursuer) se débarrasser de
▶ **shake up** vt secouer

shaky ['ʃeɪkɪ] adj (hand, voice) tremblant(e); (building) branlant(e), peu solide; (memory) chancelant(e); (knowledge) incertain(e)

shall [ʃæl] aux vb: **I ~ go** j'irai; **~ I open the door?** j'ouvre la porte?; **I'll get the coffee, ~ I?** je vais chercher le café, d'accord?

shallow ['ʃæləu] adj peu profond(e); (fig) superficiel(le), qui manque de profondeur

sham [ʃæm] n frime f; (jewellery, furniture) imitation f ▷ adj feint(e), simulé(e) ▷ vt feindre, simuler

shambles ['ʃæmblz] n confusion f, pagaïe f, fouillis m; **the economy is (in) a complete ~** l'économie est dans la confusion la plus totale

shame [ʃeɪm] n honte f ▷ vt faire honte à; **it is a ~ (that/to do)** c'est dommage (que + sub/de faire); **what a ~!** quel dommage!; **to put sb/sth to ~** (fig) faire honte à qn/qch

shameful ['ʃeɪmful] adj honteux(-euse), scandaleux(-euse)

shameless ['ʃeɪmlɪs] adj éhonté(e), effronté(e); (immodest) impudique

shampoo [ʃæm'pu:] n shampooing m ▷ vt faire un shampooing à; **~ and set** shampooing et mise f en plis

shamrock ['ʃæmrɔk] n trèfle m (emblème national de l'Irlande)

shandy ['ʃændɪ] n bière panachée

shan't [ʃɑ:nt] = **shall not**

shantytown ['ʃæntɪtaun] n bidonville m

shape [ʃeɪp] n forme f ▷ vt façonner, modeler; (clay, stone) donner forme à; (statement) formuler; (sb's ideas, character) former; (sb's life) déterminer; (course of events) influer sur le cours de ▷ vi (also: **shape up**: events) prendre tournure; (: person) faire des progrès, s'en sortir; **to take ~** prendre forme or tournure; **in the ~ of a heart** en forme de cœur; **I can't bear gardening in any ~ or form** je déteste le jardinage sous quelque forme que ce soit; **to get o.s. into ~** (re)trouver la forme

-shaped [ʃeɪpt] *suffix*: **heart~** en forme de cœur

shapeless ['ʃeɪplɪs] *adj* informe, sans forme

shapely ['ʃeɪplɪ] *adj* bien proportionné(e), beau (belle)

share [ʃɛəʳ] *n* (*thing received, contribution*) part *f*; (*Comm*) action *f* ▷ *vt* partager; (*have in common*) avoir en commun; **to ~ out** (*among or between*) partager (entre); **to ~ in** (*joy, sorrow*) prendre part à; (*profits*) participer à, avoir part à; (*work*) partager

shareholder ['ʃɛəhəʊldəʳ] *n* (*Brit*) actionnaire *m/f*

shark [ʃɑːk] *n* requin *m*

sharp [ʃɑːp] *adj* (*razor, knife*) tranchant(e), bien aiguisé(e); (*point, voice*) aigu(ë); (*nose, chin*) pointu(e); (*outline, increase*) net(te); (*curve, bend*) brusque; (*cold, pain*) vif (vive); (*taste*) piquant(e), âcre; (*Mus*) dièse; (*person: quick-witted*) vif (vive), éveillé(e); (: *unscrupulous*) malhonnête ▷ *n* (*Mus*) dièse *m* ▷ *adv*: **at 2 o'clock ~** à 2 heures pile or tapantes; **turn ~ left** tournez immédiatement à gauche; **to be ~ with sb** être brusque avec qn; **look ~!** dépêche-toi!

sharpen ['ʃɑːpn] *vt* aiguiser; (*pencil*) tailler; (*fig*) aviver

sharpener ['ʃɑːpnəʳ] *n* (*also*: **pencil sharpener**) taille-crayon(s) *m inv*; (*also*: **knife sharpener**) aiguisoir *m*

sharp-eyed [ʃɑːp'aɪd] *adj* à qui rien n'échappe

sharply ['ʃɑːplɪ] *adv* (*turn, stop*) brusquement; (*stand out*) nettement; (*criticize, retort*) sèchement, vertement

shatter ['ʃætəʳ] *vt* fracasser, briser, faire voler en éclats; (*fig: upset*) bouleverser; (: *ruin*) briser, ruiner ▷ *vi* voler en éclats, se briser, se fracasser

shattered ['ʃætəd] *adj* (*overwhelmed, grief-stricken*) bouleversé(e); (*inf: exhausted*) éreinté(e)

shave [ʃeɪv] *vt* raser ▷ *vi* se raser ▷ *n*: **to have a ~** se raser

shaver ['ʃeɪvəʳ] *n* (*also*: **electric shaver**) rasoir *m* électrique

shaving ['ʃeɪvɪŋ] *n* (*action*) rasage *m*

shaving brush *n* blaireau *m*

shaving cream *n* crème *f* à raser

shaving foam *n* mousse *f* à raser

shavings ['ʃeɪvɪŋz] *npl* (*of wood etc*) copeaux *mpl*

shawl [ʃɔːl] *n* châle *m*

she [ʃiː] *pron* elle; **there ~ is** la voilà; **~-elephant** *etc* éléphant *m etc* femelle

sheaf (*pl* **sheaves**) [ʃiːf, ʃiːvz] *n* gerbe *f*

shear [ʃɪəʳ] *vt* (*pt* **-ed**, *pp* **-ed** or **shorn**) [ʃɔːn] (*sheep*) tondre

▶ **shear off** *vt* tondre; (*branch*) élaguer

shears ['ʃɪəz] *npl* (*for hedge*) cisaille(s) *f(pl)*

sheath [ʃiːθ] *n* gaine *f*, fourreau *m*, étui *m*; (*contraceptive*) préservatif *m*

shed [ʃed] *n* remise *f*, resserre *f*; (*Industry, Rail*) hangar *m* ▷ *vt* (*pt, pp* **~**) (*leaves, fur etc*) perdre; (*tears*) verser, répandre; (*workers*) congédier; **to ~**

light on (*problem, mystery*) faire la lumière sur

she'd [ʃiːd] = **she had; she would**

sheen [ʃiːn] *n* lustre *m*

sheep [ʃiːp] *n* (*pl inv*) mouton *m*

sheepdog ['ʃiːpdɔɡ] *n* chien *m* de berger

sheepskin ['ʃiːpskɪn] *n* peau *f* de mouton

sheer [ʃɪəʳ] *adj* (*utter*) pur(e), pur et simple; (*steep*) à pic, abrupt(e); (*almost transparent*) extrêmement fin(e) ▷ *adv* à pic, abruptement; **by ~ chance** par pur hasard

sheet [ʃiːt] *n* (*on bed*) drap *m*; (*of paper*) feuille *f*; (*of glass, metal etc*) feuille *f*, plaque *f*

sheik, sheikh [ʃeɪk] *n* cheik *m*

shelf (*pl* **shelves**) [ʃelf, ʃelvz] *n* étagère *f*, rayon *m*; **set of shelves** rayonnage *m*

shell [ʃel] *n* (*on beach*) coquillage *m*; (*of egg, nut etc*) coquille *f*; (*explosive*) obus *m*; (*of building*) carcasse *f* ▷ *vt* (*crab, prawn etc*) décortiquer; (*peas*) écosser; (*Mil*) bombarder (d'obus)

▶ **shell out** *vi* (*inf*): **to ~ out (for)** casquer (pour)

she'll [ʃiːl] = **she will; she shall**

shellfish ['ʃelfɪʃ] *n* (*pl inv: crab etc*) crustacé *m*; (: *scallop etc*) coquillage *m* ▷ *npl* (*as food*) fruits *mpl* de mer

shell suit *n* survêtement *m*

shelter ['ʃeltəʳ] *n* abri *m*, refuge *m* ▷ *vt* abriter, protéger; (*give lodging to*) donner asile à ▷ *vi* s'abriter, se mettre à l'abri; **to take ~ (from)** s'abriter (de)

sheltered ['ʃeltəd] *adj* (*life*) retiré(e), à l'abri des soucis; (*spot*) abrité(e)

sheltered housing *n* foyers *mpl* (pour personnes âgées ou handicapées)

shelve [ʃelv] *vt* (*fig*) mettre en suspens or en sommeil

shelves ['ʃelvz] *npl of* **shelf**

shelving ['ʃelvɪŋ] *n* (*shelves*) rayonnage(s) *m(pl)*

shepherd ['ʃepəd] *n* berger *m* ▷ *vt* (*guide*) guider, escorter

shepherd's pie ['ʃepədz-] *n* ≈ hachis *m* Parmentier

sheriff ['ʃerɪf] (*US*) *n* shérif *m*

sherry ['ʃerɪ] *n* xérès *m*, sherry *m*

she's [ʃiːz] = **she is; she has**

Shetland ['ʃetlənd] *n* (*also*: **the Shetlands, the Shetland Isles** or **Islands**) les îles *fpl* Shetland

shield [ʃiːld] *n* bouclier *m*; (*protection*) écran *m* de protection ▷ *vt*: **to ~ (from)** protéger (de or contre)

shift [ʃɪft] *n* (*change*) changement *m*; (*work period*) période *f* de travail; (*of workers*) équipe *f*, poste *m* ▷ *vt* déplacer, changer de place; (*remove*) enlever ▷ *vi* changer de place, bouger; **the wind has ~ed to the south** le vent a tourné au sud; **a ~ in demand** (*Comm*) un déplacement de la demande

shift work *n* travail *m* par roulement; **to do ~** travailler par roulement

shifty ['ʃɪftɪ] *adj* sournois(e); (*eyes*) fuyant(e)

shimmer ['ʃɪməʳ] *n* miroitement *m*, chatoiement *m* ▷ *vi* miroiter, chatoyer

shin [ʃɪn] *n* tibia *m* ▷ *vi*: **to ~ up/down a tree** grimper dans un/descendre d'un arbre

shine [ʃaɪn] (pt, pp **shone**) [ʃɔn] n éclat m, brillant m ▷ vi briller ▷ vt (torch): **to ~ on** braquer sur; (polish) (pt, pp **-d**) faire briller or reluire

shingle [ˈʃɪŋgl] n (on beach) galets mpl; (on roof) bardeau m

shingles [ˈʃɪŋglz] n (Med) zona m

shiny [ˈʃaɪnɪ] adj brillant(e)

ship [ʃɪp] n bateau m; (large) navire m ▷ vt transporter (par mer); (send) expédier (par mer); (load) charger, embarquer; **on board** ~ à bord

shipbuilding [ˈʃɪpbɪldɪŋ] n construction navale

shipment [ˈʃɪpmənt] n cargaison f

shipping [ˈʃɪpɪŋ] n (ships) navires mpl; (traffic) navigation f; (the industry) industrie navale; (transport) transport m

shipwreck [ˈʃɪprɛk] n épave f; (event) naufrage m ▷ vt: **to be ~ed** faire naufrage

shipyard [ˈʃɪpjɑːd] n chantier naval

shire [ˈʃaɪəʳ] n (Brit) comté m

shirt [ʃəːt] n chemise f; (woman's) chemisier m; **in ~ sleeves** en bras de chemise

shit [ʃɪt] excl (inf!) merde (!)

shiver [ˈʃɪvəʳ] n frisson m ▷ vi frissonner

shoal [ʃəul] n (of fish) banc m

shock [ʃɔk] n (impact) choc m, heurt m; (Elec) secousse f, décharge f; (emotional) choc; (Med) commotion f, choc ▷ vt (scandalize) choquer, scandaliser; (upset) bouleverser; **suffering from ~** (Med) commotionné(e); **it gave us a ~** ça nous a fait un choc; **it came as a ~ to hear that …** nous avons appris avec stupeur que …

shock absorber [-əbzɔːbəʳ] n amortisseur m

shocking [ˈʃɔkɪŋ] adj (outrageous) choquant(e), scandaleux(-euse); (awful) épouvantable

shoddy [ˈʃɔdɪ] adj de mauvaise qualité, mal fait(e)

shoe [ʃuː] n chaussure f, soulier m; (also: **horseshoe**) fer m à cheval; (also: **brake shoe**) mâchoire f de frein ▷ vt (pt, pp **shod**) [ʃɔd] (horse) ferrer

shoelace [ˈʃuːleɪs] n lacet m (de soulier)

shoe polish n cirage m

shoeshop [ˈʃuːʃɔp] n magasin m de chaussures

shoestring [ˈʃuːstrɪŋ] n: **on a ~** (fig) avec un budget dérisoire; avec des moyens très restreints

shone [ʃɔn] pt, pp of **shine**

shook [ʃuk] pt of **shake**

shoot [ʃuːt] (pt, pp **shot**) [ʃɔt] n (on branch, seedling) pousse f; (shooting party) partie f de chasse ▷ vt (game: hunt) chasser; (: aim at) tirer; (: kill) abattre; (person) blesser/tuer d'un coup de fusil (or de revolver); (execute) fusiller; (arrow) tirer; (gun) tirer un coup de; (Cine) tourner ▷ vi (with gun, bow): **to ~ (at)** tirer (sur); (Football) shooter, tirer; **to ~ past sb** passer en flèche devant qn; **to ~ in/out** entrer/sortir comme une flèche

▶ **shoot down** vt (plane) abattre

▶ **shoot up** vi (fig: prices etc) monter en flèche

shooting [ˈʃuːtɪŋ] n (shots) coups mpl de feu; (attack) fusillade f; (murder) homicide m (à l'aide d'une arme à feu); (Hunting) chasse f; (Cine) tournage m

shooting star n étoile filante

shop [ʃɔp] n magasin m; (workshop) atelier m ▷ vi (also: **go shopping**) faire ses courses or ses achats; **repair ~** atelier de réparations; **to talk ~** (fig) parler boutique

▶ **shop around** vi faire le tour des magasins (pour comparer les prix); (fig) se renseigner avant de choisir or décider

shop assistant n (Brit) vendeur(-euse)

shop floor n (Brit: fig) ouvriers mpl

shopkeeper [ˈʃɔpkiːpəʳ] n marchand(e), commerçant(e)

shoplifting [ˈʃɔplɪftɪŋ] n vol m à l'étalage

shopper [ˈʃɔpəʳ] n personne f qui fait ses courses, acheteur(-euse)

shopping [ˈʃɔpɪŋ] n (goods) achats mpl, provisions fpl

shopping bag n sac m (à provisions)

shopping centre, (US) **shopping center** n centre commercial

shopping mall n centre commercial

shopping trolley n (Brit) Caddie® m

shop-soiled [ˈʃɔpsɔɪld] adj défraîchi(e), qui a fait la vitrine

shop window n vitrine f

shore [ʃɔːʳ] n (of sea, lake) rivage m, rive f ▷ vt: **to ~ (up)** étayer; **on ~** à terre

shorn [ʃɔːn] pp of **shear** ▷ adj: **~ of** dépouillé(e) de

short [ʃɔːt] adj (not long) court(e); (soon finished) court, bref (brève); (person, step) petit(e); (curt) brusque, sec (sèche); (insufficient) insuffisant(e) ▷ n (also: **short film**) court métrage; (Elec) court-circuit m; **to be ~ of sth** être à court de or manquer de qch; **to be in ~ supply** manquer, être difficile à trouver; **I'm ~ of 3** il m'en manque 3; **in ~** bref; en bref; **~ of doing** à moins de faire; **everything ~ of** tout sauf; **it is ~ for** c'est l'abréviation or le diminutif de; **a ~ time ago** il y a peu de temps; **in the ~ term** à court terme; **to cut ~** (speech, visit) abréger, écourter; (person) couper la parole à; **to fall ~ of** ne pas être à la hauteur de; **to run ~ of** arriver à court de, venir à manquer de; **to stop ~** s'arrêter net; **to stop ~ of** ne pas aller jusqu'à

shortage [ˈʃɔːtɪdʒ] n manque m, pénurie f

shortbread [ˈʃɔːtbrɛd] n ≈ sablé m

short-change [ʃɔːtˈtʃeɪndʒ] vt: **to ~ sb** ne pas rendre assez à qn

short-circuit [ʃɔːtˈsəːkɪt] n court-circuit m ▷ vt court-circuiter ▷ vi se mettre en court-circuit

shortcoming [ˈʃɔːtkʌmɪŋ] n défaut m

shortcrust pastry [ˈʃɔːtkrʌst-], **short pastry** n (Brit) pâte brisée

shortcut [ˈʃɔːtkʌt] n raccourci m

shorten [ˈʃɔːtn] vt raccourcir; (text, visit) abréger

shortfall [ˈʃɔːtfɔːl] n déficit m

shorthand [ˈʃɔːthænd] n (Brit) sténo(graphie) f; **to take sth down in ~** prendre qch en sténo

shorthand typist n (Brit) sténodactylo m/f

shortlist [ˈʃɔːtlɪst] n (Brit: for job) liste f des candidats sélectionnés

short-lived [ˈʃɔːtˈlɪvd] adj de courte durée

shortly ['ʃɔːtlɪ] adv bientôt, sous peu
short notice n: **at ~** au dernier moment
shorts [ʃɔːts] npl: **(a pair of) ~** un short
short-sighted [ʃɔːt'saɪtɪd] adj (Brit) myope; (fig) qui manque de clairvoyance
short-sleeved [ʃɔːt'sliːvd] adj à manches courtes
short-staffed [ʃɔːt'stɑːft] adj à court de personnel
short-stay [ʃɔːt'steɪ] adj (car park) de courte durée
short story n nouvelle f
short-tempered [ʃɔːt'tɛmpəd] adj qui s'emporte facilement
short-term ['ʃɔːttəːm] adj (effect) à court terme
short wave n (Radio) ondes courtes
shot [ʃɔt] pt, pp of **shoot** ▷ n coup m (de feu); (shotgun pellets) plombs mpl; (try) coup, essai m; (injection) piqûre f; (Phot) photo f; **to be a good/ poor ~** (person) tirer bien/mal; **to fire a ~ at sb/ sth** tirer sur qn/qch; **to have a ~ at (doing) sth** essayer de faire qch; **like a ~** comme une flèche; (very readily) sans hésiter; **to get ~ of sb/sth** (inf) se débarrasser de qn/qch; **a big ~** (inf) un gros bonnet
shotgun ['ʃɔtgʌn] n fusil m de chasse
should [ʃud] aux vb: **I ~ go now** je devrais partir maintenant; **he ~ be there now** il devrait être arrivé maintenant; **I ~ go if I were you** si j'étais vous j'irais; **I ~ like to** volontiers, j'aimerais bien; **~ he phone ...** si jamais il téléphone ...
shoulder ['ʃəuldə'] n épaule f; (Brit: of road): **hard ~** accotement m ▷ vt (fig) endosser, se charger de; **to look over one's ~** regarder derrière soi (en tournant la tête); **to rub ~s with sb** (fig) côtoyer qn; **to give sb the cold ~** (fig) battre froid à qn
shoulder bag n sac m à bandoulière
shoulder blade n omoplate f
shouldn't ['ʃudnt] = **should not**
shout [ʃaut] n cri m ▷ vt crier ▷ vi crier, pousser des cris; **to give sb a ~** appeler qn
▶ **shout down** vt huer
shouting ['ʃautɪŋ] n cris mpl
shove [ʃʌv] vt pousser; (inf: put): **to ~ sth in** fourrer or ficher qch dans ▷ n poussée f; **he ~d me out of the way** il m'a écarté en me poussant
▶ **shove off** vi (Naut) pousser au large; (fig: col) ficher le camp
shovel ['ʃʌvl] n pelle f ▷ vt pelleter, enlever (or enfourner) à la pelle
show [ʃəu] (pt **-ed**, pp **-n**) [ʃəun] n (of emotion) manifestation f, démonstration f; (semblance) semblant m, apparence f; (exhibition) exposition f, salon m; (Theat, TV) spectacle m; (Cine) séance f ▷ vt montrer; (film) passer; (courage etc) faire preuve de, manifester; (exhibit) exposer ▷ vi se voir, être visible; **can you ~ me where it is, please?** pouvez-vous me montrer où c'est?; **to ask for a ~ of hands** demander que l'on vote à main levée; **to be on ~** être exposé(e); **it's just for ~** c'est juste pour l'effet; **who's running the ~ here?** (inf) qui est-ce qui commande ici?; **to ~ sb to his seat/to the door** accompagner qn jusqu'à sa place/la porte; **to ~ a profit/loss**

(Comm) indiquer un bénéfice/une perte; **it just goes to ~ that ...** ça prouve bien que ...
▶ **show in** vt faire entrer
▶ **show off** vi (pej) crâner ▷ vt (display) faire valoir; (pej) faire étalage de
▶ **show out** vt reconduire à la porte
▶ **show up** vi (stand out) ressortir; (inf: turn up) se montrer ▷ vt démontrer; (unmask) démasquer, dénoncer; (flaw) faire ressortir
show business n le monde du spectacle
showdown ['ʃəudaun] n épreuve f de force
shower ['ʃauə'] n (for washing) douche f; (rain) averse f; (of stones etc) pluie f, grêle f; (US: party) réunion organisée pour la remise de cadeaux ▷ vi prendre une douche, se doucher ▷ vt: **to ~ sb with** (gifts etc) combler qn de; (abuse etc) accabler qn de; (missiles) bombarder qn de; **to have or take a ~** prendre une douche, se doucher
shower cap n bonnet m de douche
shower gel n gel m douche
showerproof ['ʃauəpruːf] adj imperméable
showing ['ʃəuɪŋ] n (of film) projection f
show jumping [-dʒʌmpɪŋ] n concours m hippique
shown [ʃəun] pp of **show**
show-off ['ʃəuɔf] n (inf: person) crâneur(-euse), m'as-tu-vu(e)
showpiece ['ʃəupiːs] n (of exhibition etc) joyau m, clou m; **that hospital is a ~** cet hôpital est un modèle du genre
showroom ['ʃəurum] n magasin m or salle f d'exposition
shrank [ʃræŋk] pt of **shrink**
shrapnel ['ʃræpnl] n éclats mpl d'obus
shred [ʃrɛd] n (gen pl) lambeau m, petit morceau; (fig: of truth, evidence) parcelle f ▷ vt mettre en lambeaux, déchirer; (documents) détruire; (Culin: grate) râper; (: lettuce etc) couper en lanières
shredder ['ʃrɛdə'] n (for vegetables) râpeur m; (for documents, papers) déchiqueteuse f
shrewd [ʃruːd] adj astucieux(-euse), perspicace; (business person) habile
shriek [ʃriːk] n cri perçant or aigu, hurlement m ▷ vt, vi hurler, crier
shrill [ʃrɪl] adj perçant(e), aigu(ë), strident(e)
shrimp [ʃrɪmp] n crevette grise
shrine [ʃraɪn] n châsse f; (place) lieu m de pèlerinage
shrink (pt **shrank**, pp **shrunk**) [ʃrɪŋk, ʃræŋk, ʃrʌŋk] vi rétrécir; (fig) diminuer; (also: **shrink away**) reculer ▷ vt (wool) (faire) rétrécir ▷ n (inf: pej) psychanalyste m/f; **to ~ from (doing) sth** reculer devant (la pensée de faire) qch
shrink-wrap ['ʃrɪŋkræp] vt emballer sous film plastique
shrivel ['ʃrɪvl] (also: **shrivel up**) vt ratatiner, flétrir ▷ vi se ratatiner, se flétrir
shroud [ʃraud] n linceul m ▷ vt: **~ed in mystery** enveloppé(e) de mystère
Shrove Tuesday ['ʃrəuv-] n (le) Mardi gras
shrub [ʃrʌb] n arbuste m
shrubbery ['ʃrʌbərɪ] n massif m d'arbustes

shrug [ʃrʌg] n haussement m d'épaules ▷ vt, vi:
to ~ (one's shoulders) hausser les épaules
▶ **shrug off** vt faire fi de; (cold, illness) se
débarrasser de

shrunk [ʃrʌŋk] pp of **shrink**

shudder ['ʃʌdə'] n frisson m, frémissement m ▷ vi
frissonner, frémir

shuffle ['ʃʌfl] vt (cards) battre; **to ~ (one's feet)**
traîner les pieds

shun [ʃʌn] vt éviter, fuir

shunt [ʃʌnt] vt (Rail: direct) aiguiller; (: divert)
détourner ▷ vi: **to ~ (to and fro)** faire la navette

shut (pt, pp-) [ʃʌt] vt fermer ▷ vi (se) fermer
▶ **shut down** vt fermer définitivement;
(machine) arrêter ▷ vi fermer définitivement
▶ **shut off** vt couper, arrêter
▶ **shut out** vt (person, cold) empêcher d'entrer;
(noise) éviter d'entendre; (block: view) boucher;
(: memory of sth) chasser de son esprit
▶ **shut up** vi (inf: keep quiet) se taire ▷ vt (close)
fermer; (silence) faire taire qch

shutter ['ʃʌtə'] n volet m; (Phot) obturateur m

shuttle ['ʃʌtl] n navette f; (also: **shuttle service**)
(service m de) navette f ▷ vi (vehicle, person) faire
la navette ▷ vt (passengers) transporter par un
système de navette

shuttlecock ['ʃʌtlkɔk] n volant m (de badminton)

shuttle diplomacy n navettes fpl diplomatiques

shy [ʃaɪ] adj timide; **to fight ~ of** se dérober
devant; **to be ~ of doing sth** hésiter à faire qch,
ne pas oser faire qch ▷ vi: **to ~ away from doing
sth** (fig) craindre de faire qch

Siberia [saɪ'bɪərɪə] n Sibérie f

siblings ['sɪblɪŋz] npl (formal) frères et sœurs mpl
(de mêmes parents)

Sicily ['sɪsɪlɪ] n Sicile f

sick [sɪk] adj (ill) malade; (Brit: vomiting): **to be ~**
vomir; (humour) noir(e), macabre; **to feel ~** avoir
envie de vomir, avoir mal au cœur; **to fall ~**
tomber malade; **to be (off) ~** être absent(e) pour
cause de maladie; **a ~ person** un(e) malade; **to
be ~ of** (fig) en avoir assez de

sick bay n infirmerie f

sicken ['sɪkn] vt écœurer ▷ vi: **to be ~ing for sth**
(cold, flu etc) couver qch

sickening ['sɪknɪŋ] adj (fig) écœurant(e),
révoltant(e), répugnant(e)

sickle ['sɪkl] n faucille f

sick leave n congé m de maladie

sickly ['sɪklɪ] adj maladif(-ive),
souffreteux(-euse); (causing nausea) écœurant(e)

sickness ['sɪknɪs] n maladie f; (vomiting)
vomissement(s) m(pl)

sick note n (from parents) mot m d'absence; (from
doctor) certificat médical

sick pay n indemnité f de maladie (versée par
l'employeur)

side [saɪd] n côté m; (of animal) flanc m; (of lake,
road) bord m; (of mountain) versant m; (fig: aspect)
côté, aspect m; (team: Sport) équipe f; (TV: channel)
chaîne f ▷ adj (door, entrance) latéral(e) ▷ vi: **to
~ with sb** prendre le parti de qn, se ranger du

côté de qn; **by the ~ of** au bord de; **~ by ~** côte à
côte; **the right/wrong ~** le bon/mauvais côté,
l'endroit/l'envers m; **they are on our ~** ils sont
avec nous; **from all ~s** de tous côtés; **to rock
from ~ to ~** se balancer; **to take ~s (with)**
prendre parti (pour); **a ~ of beef** ≈ un quartier
de bœuf

sideboard ['saɪdbɔːd] n buffet m

sideboards (Brit) ['saɪdbɔːdz], **sideburns**
['saɪdbə:nz] npl (whiskers) pattes fpl

side drum n (Mus) tambour plat, caisse claire

side effect n effet m secondaire

sidelight ['saɪdlaɪt] n (Aut) veilleuse f

sideline ['saɪdlaɪn] n (Sport) (ligne f de) touche f;
(fig) activité f secondaire

sidelong ['saɪdlɔŋ] adj: **to give sb a ~ glance**
regarder qn du coin de l'œil

side order n garniture f

side road n petite route, route transversale

sideshow ['saɪdʃəu] n attraction f

sidestep ['saɪdstɛp] vt (question) éluder; (problem)
éviter ▷ vi (Boxing etc) esquiver

side street n rue transversale

sidetrack ['saɪdtræk] vt (fig) faire dévier de son
sujet

sidewalk ['saɪdwɔːk] n (US) trottoir m

sideways ['saɪdweɪz] adv de côté

siding ['saɪdɪŋ] n (Rail) voie f de garage

siege [siːdʒ] n siège m; **to lay ~ to** assiéger

sieve [sɪv] n tamis m, passoire f ▷ vt tamiser,
passer (au tamis)

sift [sɪft] vt passer au tamis or au crible; (fig)
passer au crible ▷ vi (fig): **to ~ through** passer
en revue

sigh [saɪ] n soupir m ▷ vi soupirer, pousser un
soupir

sight [saɪt] n (faculty) vue f; (spectacle) spectacle m;
(on gun) mire f ▷ vt apercevoir; **in ~** visible; (fig)
en vue; **out of ~** hors de vue; **at ~** (Comm) à vue;
at first ~ à première vue, au premier abord; **I
know her by ~** je la connais de vue; **to catch ~
of sb/sth** apercevoir qn/qch; **to lose ~ of sb/sth**
perdre qn/qch de vue; **to set one's ~s on sth**
jeter son dévolu sur qch

sightseeing ['saɪtsiːɪŋ] n tourisme m; **to go ~**
faire du tourisme

sign [saɪn] n (gen) signe m; (with hand etc) signe,
geste m; (notice) panneau m, écriteau m; (also:
road sign) panneau de signalisation ▷ vt signer;
as a ~ of en signe de; **it's a good/bad ~** c'est bon/
mauvais signe; **plus/minus ~** signe plus/moins;
there's no ~ of a change of mind rien ne laisse
présager un revirement; **he was showing ~s
of improvement** il commençait visiblement
à faire des progrès; **to ~ one's name** signer;
where do I ~? où dois-je signer?
▶ **sign away** vt (rights etc) renoncer
officiellement à
▶ **sign for** vt fus (item) signer le reçu pour
▶ **sign in** vi signer le registre (en arrivant)
▶ **sign off** vi (Radio, TV) terminer l'émission
▶ **sign on** vi (Mil) s'engager; (Brit: as unemployed)

s'inscrire au chômage; (*enrol*) s'inscrire ▷ *vt*
(*Mil*) engager; (*employee*) embaucher; **to ~ on for
a course** s'inscrire pour un cours
▸ **sign out** *vt* signer le registre (en partant)
▸ **sign over** *vt*: **to ~ sth over to sb** céder qch par
écrit à qn
▸ **sign up** *vt* (*Mil*) engager ▷ *vi* (*Mil*) s'engager;
(*for course*) s'inscrire

signal ['sɪɡnl] *n* signal *m* ▷ *vi* (*Aut*) mettre son
clignotant ▷ *vt* (*person*) faire signe à; (*message*)
communiquer par signaux; **to ~ a left/right
turn** (*Aut*) indiquer *or* signaler que l'on tourne à
gauche/droite; **to ~ to sb (to do sth)** faire signe
à qn (de faire qch)

signalman ['sɪɡnlmən] *n* (*Rail*) aiguilleur *m*
signature ['sɪɡnətʃəᵣ] *n* signature *f*
signature tune *n* indicatif musical
signet ring ['sɪɡnət-] *n* chevalière *f*
significance [sɪɡ'nɪfɪkəns] *n* signification
f; importance *f*; **that is of no ~** ceci n'a pas
d'importance
significant [sɪɡ'nɪfɪkənt] *adj* significatif(-ive);
(*important*) important(e), considérable
signify ['sɪɡnɪfaɪ] *vt* signifier
sign language *n* langage *m* par signes
signpost ['saɪnpəust] *n* poteau indicateur
Sikh [siːk] *adj, n* Sikh *m/f*
silence ['saɪləns] *n* silence *m* ▷ *vt* faire taire,
réduire au silence
silencer ['saɪlənsəᵣ] *n* (*Brit: on gun, Aut*)
silencieux *m*
silent ['saɪlnt] *adj* silencieux(-euse); (*film*)
muet(te); **to keep** *or* **remain ~** garder le silence,
ne rien dire
silent partner *n* (*Comm*) bailleur *m* de fonds,
commanditaire *m*
silhouette [sɪluː'et] *n* silhouette *f* ▷ *vt*: **~d
against** se profilant sur, se découpant contre
silicon chip ['sɪlɪkən-] *n* puce *f* électronique
silk [sɪlk] *n* soie *f* ▷ *cpd* de *or* en soie
silky ['sɪlkɪ] *adj* soyeux(-euse)
silly ['sɪlɪ] *adj* stupide, sot(te), bête; **to do
something ~** faire une bêtise
silt [sɪlt] *n* vase *f*; limon *m*
silver ['sɪlvəᵣ] *n* argent *m*; (*money*) monnaie *f* (en
pièces d'argent); (*also*: **silverware**) argenterie *f*
▷ *adj* (*made of silver*) d'argent, en argent; (*in colour*)
argenté(e); (*car*) gris métallisé *inv*
silver-plated [sɪlvə'pleɪtɪd] *adj* plaqué(e) argent
silversmith ['sɪlvəsmɪθ] *n* orfèvre *m/f*
silvery ['sɪlvrɪ] *adj* argenté(e)
similar ['sɪmɪləᵣ] *adj*: **~ (to)** semblable (à)
similarity [sɪmɪ'lærɪtɪ] *n* ressemblance *f*,
similarité *f*
similarly ['sɪmɪləlɪ] *adv* de la même façon, de
même
simmer ['sɪməᵣ] *vi* cuire à feu doux, mijoter
▸ **simmer down** *vi* (*fig: inf*) se calmer
simple ['sɪmpl] *adj* simple; **the ~ truth** la vérité
pure et simple
simplicity [sɪm'plɪsɪtɪ] *n* simplicité *f*
simplify ['sɪmplɪfaɪ] *vt* simplifier

simply ['sɪmplɪ] *adv* simplement; (*without fuss*)
avec simplicité; (*absolutely*) absolument
simulate ['sɪmjuleɪt] *vt* simuler, feindre
simultaneous [sɪməl'teɪnɪəs] *adj* simultané(e)
simultaneously [sɪməl'teɪnɪəslɪ] *adv*
simultanément
sin [sɪn] *n* péché *m* ▷ *vi* pécher
since [sɪns] *adv, prep* depuis ▷ *conj* (*time*) depuis
que; (*because*) puisque, étant donné que, comme;
~ then, ever ~ depuis ce moment-là; **~ Monday**
depuis lundi; (*ever*) **~ I arrived** depuis mon
arrivée, depuis que je suis arrivé
sincere [sɪn'sɪəᵣ] *adj* sincère
sincerely [sɪn'sɪəlɪ] *adv* sincèrement; **Yours
~** (*at end of letter*) veuillez agréer, Monsieur (*or*
Madame) l'expression de mes sentiments
distingués *or* les meilleurs
sincerity [sɪn'serɪtɪ] *n* sincérité *f*
sinew ['sɪnjuː] *n* tendon *m*; **sinews** *npl* muscles
mpl
sing (*pt* **sang**, *pp* **sung**) [sɪŋ, sæŋ, sʌŋ] *vt, vi*
chanter
Singapore [sɪŋɡə'pɔːᵣ] *n* Singapour *m*
singe [sɪndʒ] *vt* brûler légèrement; (*clothes*)
roussir
singer ['sɪŋəᵣ] *n* chanteur(-euse)
singing ['sɪŋɪŋ] *n* (*of person, bird*) chant *m*; façon *f*
de chanter; (*of kettle, bullet, in ears*) sifflement *m*
single ['sɪŋɡl] *adj* seul(e), unique; (*unmarried*)
célibataire; (*not double*) simple ▷ *n* (*Brit: also*:
single ticket) aller *m* (simple); (*record*) 45 tours
m; **singles** *npl* (*Tennis*) simple *m*; (*US: single people*)
célibataires *m/fpl*; **not a ~ one was left** il n'en est
pas resté un(e), seul(e); **every ~ day** chaque jour
sans exception
▸ **single out** *vt* choisir; (*distinguish*) distinguer
single bed *n* lit *m* d'une personne *or* à une place
single-breasted ['sɪŋɡlbrestɪd] *adj* droit(e)
single file *n*: **in ~** en file indienne
single-handed [sɪŋɡl'hændɪd] *adv* tout(e)
seul(e), sans (aucune) aide
single-minded [sɪŋɡl'maɪndɪd] *adj* résolu(e),
tenace
single parent *n* parent unique (*or* célibataire);
single-parent family famille monoparentale
single room *n* chambre *f* à un lit *or* pour une
personne
single-track road [sɪŋɡl'træk-] *n* route *f* à voie
unique
singly ['sɪŋɡlɪ] *adv* séparément
singular ['sɪŋɡjuləᵣ] *adj* singulier(-ière); (*odd*)
singulier, étrange; (*outstanding*) remarquable;
(*Ling*) (au) singulier, du singulier ▷ *n* (*Ling*)
singulier *m*; **in the feminine ~** au féminin
singulier
sinister ['sɪnɪstəᵣ] *adj* sinistre
sink [sɪŋk] (*pt* **sank**, *pp* **sunk**) [sæŋk, sʌŋk] *n*
évier *m*; (*washbasin*) lavabo *m* ▷ *vt* (*ship*) (faire)
couler, faire sombrer; (*foundations*) creuser;
(*piles etc*): **to ~ sth into** enfoncer qch dans ▷ *vi*
couler, sombrer; (*ground etc*) s'affaisser; **to ~
into sth** (*chair*) s'enfoncer dans qch; **he sank**

into a chair/the mud il s'est enfoncé dans un fauteuil/la boue; **a ~ing feeling** un serrement de cœur
 ▶ **sink in** vi s'enfoncer, pénétrer; (explanation) rentrer (inf), être compris; **it took a long time to ~ in** il a fallu longtemps pour que ça rentre

sinner ['sɪnə^r] n pécheur(-eresse)

sinus ['saɪnəs] n (Anat) sinus m inv

sip [sɪp] n petite gorgée ▷ vt boire à petites gorgées

siphon ['saɪfən] n siphon m ▷ vt (also: **siphon off**) siphonner; (: fig: funds) transférer; (: illegally) détourner

sir [sə^r] n monsieur m; **S~ John Smith** sir John Smith; **yes ~** oui Monsieur; **Dear S~** (in letter) Monsieur

siren ['saɪərn] n sirène f

sirloin ['sə:lɔɪn] n (also: **sirloin steak**) aloyau m

sissy ['sɪsɪ] n (inf: coward) poule mouillée

sister ['sɪstə^r] n sœur f; (nun) religieuse f, (bonne) sœur; (Brit: nurse) infirmière f en chef ▷ cpd: **~ organization** organisation f sœur; **~ ship** sister(-)ship m

sister-in-law ['sɪstərɪnlɔ:] n belle-sœur f

sit (pt, pp **sat**) [sɪt, sæt] vi s'asseoir; (be sitting) être assis(e); (assembly) être en séance, siéger; (for painter) poser; (dress etc) tomber ▷ vt (exam) passer, se présenter à; **to ~ tight** ne pas bouger
 ▶ **sit about, sit around** vi être assis(e) or rester à ne rien faire
 ▶ **sit back** vi (in seat) bien s'installer, se carrer
 ▶ **sit down** vi s'asseoir; **to be ~ting down** être assis(e)
 ▶ **sit in** vi: **to ~ in on a discussion** assister à une discussion
 ▶ **sit on** vt fus (jury, committee) faire partie de
 ▶ **sit up** vi s'asseoir; (straight) se redresser; (not go to bed) rester debout, ne pas se coucher

sitcom ['sɪtkɔm] n abbr (TV: = situation comedy) sitcom f, comédie f de situation

site [saɪt] n emplacement m, site m; (also: **building site**) chantier m ▷ vt placer

sit-in ['sɪtɪn] n (demonstration) sit-in m inv, occupation f de locaux

sitting ['sɪtɪŋ] n (of assembly etc) séance f; (in canteen) service m

sitting room n salon m

situated ['sɪtjueɪtɪd] adj situé(e)

situation [sɪtju'eɪʃən] n situation f; **"~s vacant/wanted"** (Brit) "offres/demandes d'emploi"

six [sɪks] num six

sixteen [sɪks'ti:n] num seize

sixteenth [sɪks'ti:nθ] num seizième

sixth [sɪksθ] num sixième ▷ n: **the upper/lower ~** (Brit Scol) la terminale/la première

sixth form n (Brit) ≈ classes fpl de première et de terminale

sixth-form college n lycée n'ayant que des classes de première et de terminale

sixtieth ['sɪkstɪθ] num soixantième

sixty ['sɪkstɪ] num soixante

size [saɪz] n dimensions fpl; (of person) taille f; (of

clothing) taille; (of shoes) pointure f; (of estate, area) étendue f; (of problem) ampleur f; (of company) importance f; (glue) colle f; **I take ~ 14** (of dress etc) ≈ je prends du 42 or la taille 42; **the small/large ~** (of soap powder etc) le petit/grand modèle; **it's the ~ of ...** c'est de la taille (or grosseur) de ..., c'est grand (or gros) comme ...; **cut to ~** découpé(e) aux dimensions voulues
 ▶ **size up** vt juger, jauger

sizeable ['saɪzəbl] adj (object, building, estate) assez grand(e); (amount, problem, majority) assez important(e)

sizzle ['sɪzl] vi grésiller

skate [skeɪt] n patin m; (fish: pl inv) raie f ▷ vi patiner
 ▶ **skate over, skate around** vt (problem, issue) éluder

skateboard ['skeɪtbɔ:d] n skateboard m, planche f à roulettes

skateboarding ['skeɪtbɔ:dɪŋ] n skateboard m

skater ['skeɪtə^r] n patineur(-euse)

skating ['skeɪtɪŋ] n patinage m

skating rink n patinoire f

skeleton ['skɛlɪtn] n squelette m; (outline) schéma m

skeleton staff n effectifs réduits

skeptical ['skɛptɪkl] (US) = **sceptical**

sketch [skɛtʃ] n (drawing) croquis m, esquisse f; (outline plan) aperçu m; (Theat) sketch m, saynète f ▷ vt esquisser, faire un croquis or une esquisse de; (plan etc) esquisser

sketch book n carnet m à dessin

sketchy ['skɛtʃɪ] adj incomplet(-ète), fragmentaire

skewer ['skju:ə^r] n brochette f

ski [ski:] n ski m ▷ vi skier, faire du ski

ski boot n chaussure f de ski

skid [skɪd] n dérapage m ▷ vi déraper; **to go into a ~** déraper

skier ['ski:ə^r] n skieur(-euse)

skiing ['ski:ɪŋ] n ski m; **to go ~** (aller) faire du ski

ski jump n (ramp) tremplin m; (event) saut m à skis

skilful, (US) **skillful** ['skɪlful] adj habile, adroit(e)

ski lift n remonte-pente m inv

skill [skɪl] n (ability) habileté f, adresse f, talent m; (requiring training) compétences fpl

skilled [skɪld] adj habile, adroit(e); (worker) qualifié(e)

skim [skɪm] vt (milk) écrémer; (soup) écumer; (glide over) raser, effleurer ▷ vi: **to ~ through** (fig) parcourir

skimmed milk [skɪmd-], (US) **skim milk** n lait écrémé

skimp [skɪmp] vt (work) bâcler, faire à la va-vite; (cloth etc) lésiner sur

skimpy ['skɪmpɪ] adj étriqué(e); maigre

skin [skɪn] n peau f ▷ vt (fruit etc) éplucher; (animal) écorcher; **wet or soaked to the ~** trempé(e) jusqu'aux os

skin cancer n cancer m de la peau

skin-deep ['skɪn'di:p] adj superficiel(le)

skin diving n plongée sous-marine

skinhead ['skɪnhɛd] *n* skinhead *m*

skinny ['skɪnɪ] *adj* maigre, maigrichon(ne)

skintight ['skɪntaɪt] *adj* (*dress etc*) collant(e), ajusté(e)

skip [skɪp] *n* petit bond *or* saut; (*Brit: container*) benne *f* ▷ *vi* gambader, sautiller; (*with rope*) sauter à la corde ▷ *vt* (*pass over*) sauter; **to ~ school** (*esp US*) faire l'école buissonnière

ski pass *n* forfait-skieur(s) *m*

ski pole *n* bâton *m* de ski

skipper ['skɪpə'] *n* (*Naut, Sport*) capitaine *m*; (*in race*) skipper *m* ▷ *vt* (*boat*) commander; (*team*) être le chef de

skipping rope ['skɪpɪŋ-], (*US*) **skip rope** *n* corde *f* à sauter

skirmish ['skə:mɪʃ] *n* escarmouche *f*, accrochage *m*

skirt [skə:t] *n* jupe *f* ▷ *vt* longer, contourner

skirting board ['skə:tɪŋ-] *n* (*Brit*) plinthe *f*

ski slope *n* piste *f* de ski

ski suit *n* combinaison *f* de ski

ski tow *n* = **ski lift**

skittle ['skɪtl] *n* quille *f*; **skittles** (*game*) (jeu *m* de) quilles *fpl*

skive [skaɪv] *vi* (*Brit inf*) tirer au flanc

skull [skʌl] *n* crâne *m*

skunk [skʌŋk] *n* mouffette *f*; (*fur*) sconse *m*

sky [skaɪ] *n* ciel *m*; **to praise sb to the skies** porter qn aux nues

skylight ['skaɪlaɪt] *n* lucarne *f*

skyscraper ['skaɪskreɪpə'] *n* gratte-ciel *m inv*

slab [slæb] *n* plaque *f*; (*of stone*) dalle *f*; (*of wood*) bloc *m*; (*of meat, cheese*) tranche épaisse

slack [slæk] *adj* (*loose*) lâche, desserré(e); (*slow*) stagnant(e); (*careless*) négligent(e), peu sérieux(-euse) *or* consciencieux(-euse); (*Comm: market*) peu actif(-ive); (*: demand*) faible; (*period*) creux(-euse) ▷ *n* (*in rope etc*) mou *m*; **business is ~** les affaires vont mal

slacken ['slækn] (*also*: **slacken off**) *vi* ralentir, diminuer ▷ *vt* relâcher

slacks [slæks] *npl* pantalon *m*

slag heap *n* crassier *m*

slag off (*Brit: inf*) *vt* dire du mal de

slain [sleɪn] *pp of* **slay**

slam [slæm] *vt* (*door*) (faire) claquer; (*throw*) jeter violemment, flanquer; (*inf: criticize*) éreinter, démolir ▷ *vi* claquer

slander ['slɑ:ndə'] *n* calomnie *f*; (*Law*) diffamation *f* ▷ *vt* calomnier; diffamer

slang [slæŋ] *n* argot *m*

slant [slɑ:nt] *n* inclinaison *f*; (*fig*) angle *m*, point *m* de vue

slanted ['slɑ:ntɪd] *adj* tendancieux(-euse)

slanting ['slɑ:ntɪŋ] *adj* en pente, incliné(e); couché(e)

slap [slæp] *n* claque *f*, gifle *f*; (*on the back*) tape *f* ▷ *vt* donner une claque *or* une gifle (*or* une tape) à; **to ~ on** (*paint*) appliquer rapidement ▷ *adv* (*directly*) tout droit, en plein

slapdash ['slæpdæʃ] *adj* (*work*) fait(e) sans soin *or* à la va-vite; (*person*) insouciant(e), négligent(e)

slapstick ['slæpstɪk] *n* (*comedy*) grosse farce (*style tarte à la crème*)

slap-up ['slæpʌp] *adj* (*Brit*): **a ~ meal** un repas extra *or* fameux

slash [slæʃ] *vt* entailler, taillader; (*fig: prices*) casser

slat [slæt] *n* (*of wood*) latte *f*, lame *f*

slate [sleɪt] *n* ardoise *f* ▷ *vt* (*fig: criticize*) éreinter, démolir

slaughter ['slɔ:tə'] *n* carnage *m*, massacre *m*; (*of animals*) abattage *m* ▷ *vt* (*animal*) abattre; (*people*) massacrer

slaughterhouse ['slɔ:təhaus] *n* abattoir *m*

Slav [slɑ:v] *adj* slave

slave [sleɪv] *n* esclave *m/f* ▷ *vi* (*also*: **slave away**) trimer, travailler comme un forçat; **to ~ (away) at sth/at doing sth** se tuer à qch/à faire qch

slavery ['sleɪvərɪ] *n* esclavage *m*

slay [sleɪ] (*pt* **slew**, *pp* **slain**) [sleɪ, slu:, sleɪn] *vt* (*literary*) tuer

sleazy ['sli:zɪ] *adj* miteux(-euse), minable

sled [slɛd] (*US*) = **sledge**

sledge [slɛdʒ] *n* luge *f*

sledgehammer ['slɛdʒhæmə'] *n* marteau *m* de forgeron

sleek [sli:k] *adj* (*hair, fur*) brillant(e), luisant(e); (*car, boat*) aux lignes pures *or* élégantes

sleep [sli:p] *n* sommeil *m* ▷ *vi* (*pt, pp* **slept**) [slɛpt] dormir; (*spend night*) dormir, coucher ▷ *vt*: **we can ~ 4** on peut coucher *or* loger 4 personnes; **to go to ~** s'endormir; **to have a good night's ~** passer une bonne nuit; **to put to ~** (*patient*) endormir; (*animal: euphemism: kill*) piquer; **to ~ lightly** avoir le sommeil léger; **to ~ with sb** (*have sex*) coucher avec qn

▸ **sleep around** *vi* coucher à droite et à gauche

▸ **sleep in** *vi* (*oversleep*) se réveiller trop tard; (*on purpose*) faire la grasse matinée

▸ **sleep together** *vi* (*have sex*) coucher ensemble

sleeper ['sli:pə'] *n* (*person*) dormeur(-euse); (*Brit Rail: on track*) traverse *f*; (*: train*) train-couchettes *m*; (*: carriage*) wagon-lits *m*, voiture-lits *f*; (*: berth*) couchette *f*

sleeping bag *n* sac *m* de couchage

sleeping car *n* wagon-lits *m*, voiture-lits *f*

sleeping partner *n* (*Brit Comm*) = **silent partner**

sleeping pill *n* somnifère *m*

sleepless ['sli:plɪs] *adj*: **a ~ night** une nuit blanche

sleepover ['sli:pəuvə'] *n* nuit *f* chez un copain *or* une copine; **we're having a ~ at Jo's** nous allons passer la nuit chez Jo

sleepwalk ['sli:pwɔ:k] *vi* marcher en dormant

sleepwalker ['sli:pwɔ:kə'] *n* somnambule *m/f*

sleepy ['sli:pɪ] *adj* qui a envie de dormir; (*fig*) endormi(e); **to be** *or* **feel ~** avoir sommeil, avoir envie de dormir

sleet [sli:t] *n* neige fondue

sleeve [sli:v] *n* manche *f*; (*of record*) pochette *f*

sleeveless ['sli:vlɪs] *adj* (*garment*) sans manches

sleigh [sleɪ] *n* traîneau *m*

sleight [slaɪt] *n*: **~ of hand** tour *m* de passe-passe

slender ['slɛndə'] adj svelte, mince; (fig) faible, ténu(e)

slept [slɛpt] pt, pp of **sleep**

slew [slu:] vi (also: **slew round**) virer, pivoter ▷ pt of **slay**

slice [slaɪs] n tranche f; (round) rondelle f; (utensil) spatule f; (also: **fish slice**) pelle f à poisson ▷ vt couper en tranches (or en rondelles); **~d bread** pain m en tranches

slick [slɪk] adj (skilful) bien ficelé(e); (salesperson) qui a du bagout, mielleux(-euse) ▷ n (also: **oil slick**) nappe f de pétrole, marée noire

slide [slaɪd] (pt, pp slid) [slɪd] n (in playground) toboggan m; (Phot) diapositive f; (Brit: also: **hair slide**) barrette f; (microscope slide) lame f) porte-objet m; (in prices) chute f, baisse f ▷ vt (faire) glisser ▷ vi glisser; **to let things ~** (fig) laisser les choses aller à la dérive

sliding ['slaɪdɪŋ] adj (door) coulissant(e); **~ roof** (Aut) toit ouvrant

sliding scale n échelle f mobile

slight [slaɪt] adj (slim) mince, menu(e); (frail) frêle; (trivial) faible, insignifiant(e); (small) petit(e), léger(-ère); (before n) ▷ n offense f, affront m ▷ vt (offend) blesser, offenser; **the ~est** le (or la) moindre; **not in the ~est** pas le moins du monde, pas du tout

slightly ['slaɪtlɪ] adv légèrement, un peu; **~ built** fluet(te)

slim [slɪm] adj mince ▷ vi maigrir; (diet) suivre un régime amaigrissant

slime [slaɪm] n vase f; substance visqueuse

slimming ['slɪmɪŋ] n amaigrissement m ▷ adj (diet, pills) amaigrissant(e), pour maigrir; (food) qui ne fait pas grossir

slimy ['slaɪmɪ] adj visqueux(-euse), gluant(e); (covered with mud) vaseux(-euse)

sling [slɪŋ] n (Med) écharpe f; (for baby) porte-bébé m; (weapon) fronde f, lance-pierre m ▷ vt (pt, pp slung) [slʌŋ] lancer, jeter; **to have one's arm in a ~** avoir le bras en écharpe

slip [slɪp] n faux pas; (mistake) erreur f, bévue f; (underskirt) combinaison f; (of paper) petite feuille, fiche f ▷ vt (slide) glisser ▷ vi (slide) glisser; (decline) baisser; (move smoothly): **to ~ into/out of** se glisser or se faufiler dans/hors de; **to let a chance ~ by** laisser passer une occasion; **to ~ sth on/off** enfiler/enlever qch; **it ~ped from her hand** cela lui a glissé des mains; **to give sb the ~** fausser compagnie à qn; **a ~ of the tongue** un lapsus

▶ **slip away** vi s'esquiver

▶ **slip in** vt glisser

▶ **slip out** vi sortir

▶ **slip up** vi faire une erreur, gaffer

slipped disc [slɪpt-] n déplacement m de vertèbre

slipper ['slɪpə'] n pantoufle f

slippery ['slɪpərɪ] adj glissant(e); (fig: person) insaisissable

slip road n (Brit: to motorway) bretelle f d'accès

slip-up ['slɪpʌp] n bévue f

slipway ['slɪpweɪ] n cale f (de construction or de lancement)

slit [slɪt] n fente f; (cut) incision f; (tear) déchirure f ▷ vt (pt, pp ~) fendre; couper, inciser; déchirer; **to ~ sb's throat** trancher la gorge à qn

slither ['slɪðə'] vi glisser, déraper

sliver ['slɪvə'] n (of glass, wood) éclat m; (of cheese, sausage) petit morceau

slob [slɔb] n (inf) rustaud(e)

slog [slɔg] n (Brit: effort) gros effort; (: work) tâche fastidieuse ▷ vi travailler très dur

slogan ['sləugən] n slogan m

slope [sləup] n pente f, côte f; (side of mountain) versant m; (slant) inclinaison f ▷ vi: **to ~ down** être or descendre en pente; **to ~ up** monter

sloping ['sləupɪŋ] adj en pente, incliné(e); (handwriting) penché(e)

sloppy ['slɔpɪ] adj (work) peu soigné(e), bâclé(e); (appearance) négligé(e), débraillé(e); (film etc) sentimental(e)

slot [slɔt] n fente f; (fig: in timetable, Radio, TV) créneau m, plage f ▷ vt: **to ~ sth into** encastrer or insérer qch dans ▷ vi: **to ~ into** s'encastrer or s'insérer dans

sloth [sləuθ] n (vice) paresse f; (Zool) paresseux m

slot machine n (Brit: vending machine) distributeur m (automatique), machine f à sous; (for gambling) appareil m or machine à sous

slouch [slautʃ] vi avoir le dos rond, être voûté(e)

▶ **slouch about, slouch around** vi traîner à ne rien faire

Slovakia [sləu'vækɪə] n Slovaquie f

Slovene [sləu'vi:n] adj slovène ▷ n Slovène m/f; (Ling) slovène m

Slovenia [sləu'vi:nɪə] n Slovénie f

Slovenian [sləu'vi:nɪən] adj, n = **Slovene**

slovenly ['slʌvənlɪ] adj sale, débraillé(e), négligé(e)

slow [sləu] adj lent(e); (watch): **to be ~** retarder ▷ adv lentement ▷ vt, vi ralentir; **"~"** (road sign) "ralentir"; **at a ~ speed** à petite vitesse; **to be ~ to act/decide** être lent à agir/décider; **my watch is 20 minutes ~** ma montre retarde de 20 minutes; **business is ~** les affaires marchent au ralenti; **to go ~** (driver) rouler lentement; (in industrial dispute) faire la grève perlée

▶ **slow down** vi ralentir

slowly ['sləulɪ] adv lentement

slow motion n: **in ~** au ralenti

sludge [slʌdʒ] n boue f

slug [slʌg] n limace f; (bullet) balle f

sluggish ['slʌgɪʃ] adj (person) mou (molle), lent(e); (stream, engine, trading) lent(e); (business, sales) stagnant(e)

sluice [slu:s] n écluse f; (also: **sluice gate**) vanne f ▷ vt: **to ~ down** or **out** laver à grande eau

slum [slʌm] n (house) taudis m; **slums** npl (area) quartiers mpl pauvres

slump [slʌmp] n baisse soudaine, effondrement m; (Econ) crise f ▷ vi s'effondrer, s'affaisser

slung [slʌŋ] pt, pp of **sling**

slur [slə:'] n bredouillement m; (smear): **~ (on)** atteinte f (à); insinuation f (contre) ▷ vt mal articuler; **to be a ~ on** porter atteinte à

slush [slʌʃ] n neige fondue

slut [slʌt] n souillon f

sly [slaɪ] adj (person) rusé(e); (smile, expression, remark) sournois(e); **on the ~** en cachette

smack [smæk] n (slap) tape f; (on face) gifle f ▷ vt donner une tape à; (on face) gifler; (on bottom) donner la fessée à ▷ vi: **to ~ of** avoir des relents de, sentir ▷ adv (inf): **it fell ~ in the middle** c'est tombé en plein milieu or en plein dedans; **to ~ one's lips** se lécher les babines

small [smɔːl] adj petit(e); (letter) minuscule ▷ n: **the ~ of the back** le creux des reins; **to get** or **grow ~er** diminuer; **to make ~er** (amount, income) diminuer; (object, garment) rapetisser; **a ~ shopkeeper** un petit commerçant

small ads npl (Brit) petites annonces

small change n petite or menue monnaie

smallholder ['smɔːlhəuldər] n (Brit) petit cultivateur

small hours npl: **in the ~** au petit matin

smallpox ['smɔːlpɔks] n variole f

small talk n menus propos

smart [smɑːt] adj élégant(e), chic inv; (clever) intelligent(e); (pej) futé(e); (quick) vif (vive), prompt(e) ▷ vi faire mal, brûler; **the ~ set** le beau monde; **to look ~** être élégant(e); **my eyes are ~ing** j'ai les yeux irrités or qui me piquent

smart card ['smɑːtkɑːd] n carte f à puce

smarten up ['smɑːtn-] vi devenir plus élégant(e), se faire beau (belle) ▷ vt rendre plus élégant(e)

smash [smæʃ] n (also: **smash-up**) collision f, accident m; (Mus) succès foudroyant; (sound) fracas m ▷ vt casser, briser, fracasser; (opponent) écraser; (hopes) ruiner, détruire; (Sport: record) pulvériser ▷ vi se briser, se fracasser; s'écraser
▶ **smash up** vt (car) bousiller; (room) tout casser dans

smashing ['smæʃɪŋ] adj (inf) formidable

smattering ['smætərɪŋ] n: **a ~ of** quelques notions de

smear [smɪər] n (stain) tache f; (mark) trace f; (Med) frottis m; (insult) calomnie f ▷ vt enduire; (make dirty) salir; (fig) porter atteinte à; **his hands were ~ed with oil/ink** il avait les mains maculées de cambouis/d'encre

smear campaign n campagne f de dénigrement

smear test n (Brit Med) frottis m

smell [smɛl] (pt, pp **smelt** or **-ed**) [smɛlt, smɛld] n odeur f; (sense) odorat m ▷ vt sentir ▷ vi (pej) sentir mauvais; (food etc): **to ~ (of)** sentir; **it ~s good** ça sent bon

smelly ['smɛlɪ] adj qui sent mauvais, malodorant(e)

smelt [smɛlt] pt, pp of **smell** ▷ vt (ore) fondre

smile [smaɪl] n sourire m ▷ vi sourire

smirk [sməːk] n petit sourire suffisant or affecté

smock [smɔk] n blouse f, sarrau m

smog [smɔg] n brouillard mêlé de fumée

smoke [sməuk] n fumée f ▷ vt, vi fumer; **to have a ~** fumer une cigarette; **do you ~?** est-ce que

vous fumez?; **do you mind if I ~?** ça ne vous dérange pas que je fume?; **to go up in ~** (house etc) brûler; (fig) partir en fumée

smoke alarm n détecteur m de fumée

smoked ['sməukt] adj (bacon, glass) fumé(e)

smoker ['sməukər] n (person) fumeur(-euse); (Rail) wagon m fumeurs

smoke screen n rideau m or écran m de fumée; (fig) paravent m

smoking ['sməukɪŋ] n: **"no ~"** (sign) "défense de fumer"; **to give up ~** arrêter de fumer

smoking compartment, (US) **smoking car** n wagon m fumeurs

smoky ['sməukɪ] adj enfumé(e); (taste) fumé(e)

smolder ['sməuldər] vi (US) = **smoulder**

smooth [smuːð] adj lisse; (sauce) onctueux(-euse); (flavour, whisky) moelleux(-euse); (cigarette) doux (douce); (movement) régulier(-ière), sans à-coups or heurts; (landing, takeoff) en douceur; (flight) sans secousses, (pej: person) doucereux(-euse), mielleux(-euse) ▷ vt (also: **smooth out**) lisser, défroisser; (creases, difficulties) faire disparaître
▶ **smooth over** vt: **to ~ things over** (fig) arranger les choses

smother ['smʌðər] vt étouffer

smoulder, (US) **smolder** ['sməuldər] vi couver

SMS n abbr (= short message service) SMS m

SMS message n (message m) SMS m

smudge [smʌdʒ] n tache f, bavure f ▷ vt salir, maculer

smug [smʌg] adj suffisant(e), content(e) de soi

smuggle ['smʌgl] vt passer en contrebande or en fraude; **to ~ in/out** (goods etc) faire entrer/sortir clandestinement or en fraude

smuggler ['smʌglər] n contrebandier(-ière)

smuggling ['smʌglɪŋ] n contrebande f

smutty ['smʌtɪ] adj (fig) grossier(-ière), obscène

snack [snæk] n casse-croûte m inv; **to have a ~** prendre un en-cas, manger quelque chose (de léger)

snack bar n snack(-bar) m

snag [snæg] n inconvénient m, difficulté f

snail [sneɪl] n escargot m

snake [sneɪk] n serpent m

snap [snæp] n (sound) claquement m, bruit sec; (photograph) photo f, instantané m; (game) sorte de jeu de bataille ▷ adj subit(e), fait(e) sans réfléchir ▷ vt (fingers) faire claquer; (break) casser net; (photograph) prendre un instantané de ▷ vi se casser net or avec un bruit sec; (fig: person) craquer; (speak sharply) parler d'un ton brusque; **to ~ open/shut** s'ouvrir/se refermer brusquement; **to ~ one's fingers at** (fig) se moquer de; **a cold ~** (of weather) un refroidissement soudain de la température
▶ **snap at** vt fus (subj: dog) essayer de mordre
▶ **snap off** vt (break) casser net
▶ **snap up** vt sauter sur, saisir

snappy ['snæpɪ] adj prompt(e); (slogan) qui a du punch; **make it ~!** (inf: hurry up) grouille-toi!, magne-toi!

snapshot ['snæpʃɒt] *n* photo *f*, instantané *m*

snare [snɛəʳ] *n* piège *m* ▷ *vt* attraper, prendre au piège

snarl [snɑːl] *n* grondement *m or* grognement *m* féroce ▷ *vi* gronder ▷ *vt*: **to get ~ed up** (*wool, plans*) s'emmêler; (*traffic*) se bloquer

snatch [snætʃ] *n* (*fig*) vol *m*; (*small amount*): **~es of** des fragments *mpl or* bribes *fpl* de ▷ *vt* saisir (*d'un geste vif*); (*steal*) voler ▷ *vi*: **don't ~!** doucement!; **to ~ a sandwich** manger *or* avaler un sandwich à la hâte; **to ~ some sleep** arriver à dormir un peu ▶ **snatch up** *vt* saisir, s'emparer de

sneak [sniːk] (*US*) (*pt* **snuck**) *vi*: **to ~ in/out** entrer/sortir furtivement *or* à la dérobée ▷ *vt*: **to ~ a look at sth** regarder furtivement qch ▷ *n* (*inf: pej: informer*) faux jeton; **to ~ up on sb** s'approcher de qn sans faire de bruit

sneakers ['sniːkəz] *npl* tennis *mpl*, baskets *fpl*

sneer [snɪəʳ] *n* ricanement *m* ▷ *vi* ricaner, sourire d'un air sarcastique; **to ~ at sb/sth** se moquer de qn/qch avec mépris

sneeze [sniːz] *n* éternuement *m* ▷ *vi* éternuer

sniff [snɪf] *n* reniflement *m* ▷ *vi* renifler ▷ *vt* renifler, flairer; (*glue, drug*) sniffer, respirer ▶ **sniff at** *vt fus*: **it's not to be ~ed at** il ne faut pas cracher dessus, ce n'est pas à dédaigner

snigger ['snɪgəʳ] *n* ricanement *m*; rire moqueur ▷ *vi* ricaner

snip [snɪp] *n* (*cut*) entaille *f*; (*piece*) petit bout; (*Brit: inf: bargain*) (bonne) occasion *or* affaire ▷ *vt* couper

sniper ['snaɪpəʳ] *n* (*marksman*) tireur embusqué

snippet ['snɪpɪt] *n* bribes *fpl*

snob [snɒb] *n* snob *m/f*

snobbish ['snɒbɪʃ] *adj* snob *inv*

snooker ['snuːkəʳ] *n* sorte de jeu de billard

snoop [snuːp] *vi*: **to ~ on sb** espionner qn; **to ~ about** fureter

snooze [snuːz] *n* petit somme ▷ *vi* faire un petit somme

snore [snɔːʳ] *vi* ronfler ▷ *n* ronflement *m*

snorkel ['snɔːkl] *n* (*of swimmer*) tuba *m*

snort [snɔːt] *n* grognement *m* ▷ *vi* grogner; (*horse*) renâcler ▷ *vt* (*inf: drugs*) sniffer

snout [snaut] *n* museau *m*

snow [snəu] *n* neige *f* ▷ *vi* neiger ▷ *vt*: **to be ~ed under with work** être débordé(e) de travail

snowball ['snəubɔːl] *n* boule *f* de neige

snowbound ['snəubaund] *adj* enneigé(e), bloqué(e) par la neige

snowdrift ['snəudrɪft] *n* congère *f*

snowdrop ['snəudrɒp] *n* perce-neige *m*

snowfall ['snəufɔːl] *n* chute *f* de neige

snowflake ['snəufleɪk] *n* flocon *m* de neige

snowman ['snəumæn] (*irreg*) *n* bonhomme *m* de neige

snowplough, (*US*) **snowplow** ['snəuplau] *n* chasse-neige *m inv*

snowshoe ['snəuʃuː] *n* raquette *f* (*pour la neige*)

snowstorm ['snəustɔːm] *n* tempête *f* de neige

snub [snʌb] *vt* repousser, snober ▷ *n* rebuffade *f*

snub-nosed [snʌb'nəuzd] *adj* au nez retroussé

snuck [snʌk] (*US*) *pt, pp of* **sneak**

snuff [snʌf] *n* tabac *m* à priser ▷ *vt* (*also*: **snuff out**: *candle*) moucher

snug [snʌg] *adj* douillet(te), confortable; (*person*) bien au chaud; **it's a ~ fit** c'est bien ajusté(e)

snuggle ['snʌgl] *vi*: **to ~ down in bed/up to sb** se pelotonner dans son lit/contre qn

so [səu] *adv* **1** (*thus, likewise*) ainsi, de cette façon; **if so** si oui; **so do** *or* **have I** moi aussi; **it's 5 o'clock — so it is!** il est 5 heures — en effet! *or* c'est vrai!; **I hope/think so** je l'espère/le crois; **so far** jusqu'ici, jusqu'à maintenant; (*in past*) jusque-là; **quite so!** exactement!, c'est bien ça!; **even so** quand même, tout de même

2 (*in comparisons etc: to such a degree*) si, tellement; **so big (that)** si *or* tellement grand (que); **she's not so clever as her brother** elle n'est pas aussi intelligente que son frère

3: **so much** (*adj, adv*) tant (de); **I've got so much work** j'ai tant de travail; **I love you so much** je vous aime tant; **so many** tant (de)

4 (*phrases*): **10 or so** à peu près *or* environ 10; **so long!** (*inf: goodbye*) au revoir!, à un de ces jours!; **so to speak** pour ainsi dire; **so (what)?** (*inf*) (bon) et alors?, et après?

▷ *conj* **1** (*expressing purpose*): **so as to do** pour faire, afin de faire; **so (that)** pour que *or* afin que + *sub*

2 (*expressing result*) donc, par conséquent; **so that** si bien que, de (telle) sorte que; **so that's the reason!** c'est donc (pour) ça!; **so you see, I could have gone** alors tu vois, j'aurais pu y aller

soak [səuk] *vt* faire *or* laisser tremper; (*drench*) tremper ▷ *vi* tremper; **to be ~ed through** être trempé jusqu'aux os ▶ **soak in** *vi* pénétrer, être absorbé(e) ▶ **soak up** *vt* absorber

soaking ['səukɪŋ] *adj* (*also*: **soaking wet**) trempé(e)

so-and-so ['səuənsəu] *n* (*somebody*) un(e) tel(le)

soap [səup] *n* savon *m*

soapflakes ['səupfleɪks] *npl* paillettes *fpl* de savon

soap opera *n* feuilleton télévisé (*quotidienneté réaliste ou embellie*)

soap powder *n* lessive *f*, détergent *m*

soapy ['səupɪ] *adj* savonneux(-euse)

soar [sɔːʳ] *vi* monter (en flèche), s'élancer; (*building*) s'élancer; **~ing prices** prix qui grimpent

sob [sɒb] *n* sanglot *m* ▷ *vi* sangloter

sober ['səubəʳ] *adj* qui n'est pas (*or* plus) ivre; (*serious*) sérieux(-euse), sensé(e); (*moderate*) mesuré(e); (*colour, style*) sobre, discret(-ète) ▶ **sober up** *vt* dégriser ▷ *vi* se dégriser

so-called ['səu'kɔːld] *adj* soi-disant *inv*

soccer ['sɒkəʳ] *n* football *m*

sociable ['səuʃəbl] *adj* sociable

social ['səuʃl] *adj* social(e); (*sociable*) sociable ▷ *n* (petite) fête

social club *n* amicale *f*, foyer *m*

socialism ['səuʃəlɪzəm] *n* socialisme *m*

socialist ['səuʃəlɪst] *adj, n* socialiste (*m/f*)

socialize ['səʊʃəlaɪz] vi voir or rencontrer des gens, se faire des amis; **to ~ with** (meet often) fréquenter; (get to know) lier connaissance or parler avec

social life n vie sociale; **how's your ~?** est-ce que tu sors beaucoup?

socially ['səʊʃəlɪ] adv socialement, en société

social security n aide sociale

social services npl services sociaux

social work n assistance sociale

social worker n assistant(e) sociale(e)

society [sə'saɪətɪ] n société f; (club) société, association f; (also: **high society**) (haute) société, grand monde ▷ cpd (party) mondain(e)

sociology [səʊsɪ'ɒlədʒɪ] n sociologie f

sock [sɒk] n chaussette f ▷ vt (inf: hit) flanquer un coup à; **to pull one's ~s up** (fig) se secouer (les puces)

socket ['sɒkɪt] n cavité f; (Elec: also: **wall socket**) prise f de courant; (: for light bulb) douille f

sod [sɒd] n (of earth) motte f; (Brit inf!) con m (!), salaud m (!)

  ▷ **sod off** vi: ~ **off!** (Brit inf!) fous le camp!, va te faire foutre! (!)

soda ['səʊdə] n (Chem) soude f; (also: **soda water**) eau f de Seltz; (US: also: **soda pop**) soda m

sodium ['səʊdɪəm] n sodium m

sofa ['səʊfə] n sofa m, canapé m

sofa bed n canapé-lit m

soft [sɒft] adj (not rough) doux (douce); (not hard) doux, mou (molle); (not loud) doux, léger(-ère); (kind) doux, gentil(le); (weak) indulgent(e); (stupid) stupide, débile

soft drink n boisson non alcoolisée

soft drugs npl drogues douces

soften ['sɒfn] vt (r)amollir; (fig) adoucir ▷ vi se ramollir; (fig) s'adoucir

softly ['sɒftlɪ] adv doucement; (touch) légèrement; (kiss) tendrement

softness ['sɒftnɪs] n douceur f

software ['sɒftwɛəʳ] n (Comput) logiciel m, software m

soggy ['sɒgɪ] adj (clothes) trempé(e); (ground) détrempé(e)

soil [sɔɪl] n (earth) sol m, terre f ▷ vt salir; (fig) souiller

solar ['səʊləʳ] adj solaire

solar panel n panneau m solaire

solar power n énergie f solaire

solar system n système m solaire

sold [səʊld] pt, pp of **sell**

solder ['səʊldəʳ] vt souder (au fil à souder) ▷ n soudure f

soldier ['səʊldʒəʳ] n soldat m, militaire m ▷ vi: **to ~ on** persévérer, s'accrocher; **toy ~** petit soldat

sold out adj (Comm) épuisé(e)

sole [səʊl] n (of foot) plante f; (of shoe) semelle f; (fish: pl inv) sole f ▷ adj seul(e), unique; **the ~ reason** la seule et unique raison

solely ['səʊllɪ] adv seulement, uniquement; **I will hold you ~ responsible** je vous en tiendrai pour seul responsable

solemn ['sɒləm] adj solennel(le); (person) sérieux(-euse), grave

sole trader n (Comm) chef m d'entreprise individuelle

solicit [sə'lɪsɪt] vt (request) solliciter ▷ vi (prostitute) racoler

solicitor [sə'lɪsɪtəʳ] n (Brit: for wills etc) ≈ notaire m; (: in court) ≈ avocat m

solid ['sɒlɪd] adj (strong, sound, reliable; not liquid) solide; (not hollow: mass) compact(e); (: metal, rock, wood) massif(-ive); (meal) consistant(e), substantiel(le); (vote) unanime ▷ n solide m; **to be on ~ ground** être sur la terre ferme; (fig) être en terrain sûr; **we waited two ~ hours** nous avons attendu deux heures entières

solidarity [sɒlɪ'dærɪtɪ] n solidarité f

solitary ['sɒlɪtərɪ] adj solitaire

solitary confinement n (Law) isolement m (cellulaire)

solitude ['sɒlɪtjuːd] n solitude f

solo ['səʊləʊ] n solo m ▷ adv (fly) en solitaire

soloist ['səʊləʊɪst] n soliste m/f

soluble ['sɒljubl] adj soluble

solution [sə'luːʃən] n solution f

solve [sɒlv] vt résoudre

solvent ['sɒlvənt] adj (Comm) solvable ▷ n (Chem) (dis)solvant m

sombre, (US) **somber** ['sɒmbəʳ] adj sombre, morne

some [sʌm] adj **1** (a certain amount or number of): ~ **tea/water/ice cream** du thé/de l'eau/de la glace; ~ **children/apples** des enfants/pommes; **I've got ~ money but not much** j'ai de l'argent mais pas beaucoup

2 (certain: in contrasts): ~ **people say that ...** il y a des gens qui disent que ...; ~ **films were excellent, but most were mediocre** certains films étaient excellents, mais la plupart étaient médiocres

3 (unspecified): ~ **woman was asking for you** il y avait une dame qui vous demandait; **he was asking for ~ book** (or other) il demandait un livre quelconque; ~ **day** un de ces jours; ~ **day next week** un jour la semaine prochaine; **after ~ time** après un certain temps; **at ~ length** assez longuement; **in ~ form or other** sous une forme ou une autre, sous une forme quelconque

  ▷ pron **1** (a certain number) quelques-un(e)s, certain(e)s; **I've got ~** (books etc) j'en ai (quelques-uns); ~ **(of them) have been sold** certains ont été vendus

2 (a certain amount) un peu; **I've got ~** (money, milk) j'en ai (un peu); **would you like ~?** est-ce que vous en voulez?, en voulez-vous?; **could I have ~ of that cheese?** pourrais-je avoir un peu de ce fromage?; **I've read ~ of the book** j'ai lu une partie du livre

  ▷ adv: ~ **10 people** quelque 10 personnes, 10 personnes environ

somebody ['sʌmbədɪ] pron = **someone**

somehow ['sʌmhaʊ] adv d'une façon ou d'une autre; (for some reason) pour une raison ou une autre

someone ['sʌmwʌn] *pron* quelqu'un; ~ **or other** quelqu'un, je ne sais qui

someplace ['sʌmpleɪs] *adv* (US) = **somewhere**

somersault ['sʌməsɔːlt] *n* culbute *f*, saut périlleux ▷ *vi* faire la culbute *or* un saut périlleux; *(car)* faire un tonneau

something ['sʌmθɪŋ] *pron* quelque chose *m*; ~ **interesting** quelque chose d'intéressant; ~ **to do** quelque chose à faire; **he's ~ like me** il est un peu comme moi; **it's ~ of a problem** il y a là un problème

sometime ['sʌmtaɪm] *adv* (*in future*) un de ces jours, un jour ou l'autre; (*in past*): ~ **last month** au cours du mois dernier

sometimes ['sʌmtaɪmz] *adv* quelquefois, parfois

somewhat ['sʌmwɔt] *adv* quelque peu, un peu

somewhere ['sʌmwɛəʳ] *adv* quelque part; ~ **else** ailleurs, autre part

son [sʌn] *n* fils *m*

song [sɔŋ] *n* chanson *f*; (*of bird*) chant *m*

son-in-law ['sʌnɪnlɔː] *n* gendre *m*, beau-fils *m*

soon [suːn] *adv* bientôt; (*early*) tôt; ~ **afterwards** peu après; **quite** ~ sous peu; **how** ~ **can you do it?** combien de temps vous faut-il pour le faire, au plus pressé?; **how** ~ **can you come back?** quand *or* dans combien de temps pouvez-vous revenir, au plus tôt?; **see you** ~! à bientôt!; *see also* **as**

sooner ['suːnəʳ] *adv* (*time*) plus tôt; (*preference*): **I would ~ do that** j'aimerais autant *or* je préférerais faire ça; ~ **or later** tôt ou tard; **no ~ said than done** sitôt dit, sitôt fait; **the ~ the better** le plus tôt sera le mieux; **no ~ had we left than** ... à peine étions-nous partis que ...

soot [sut] *n* suie *f*

soothe [suːð] *vt* calmer, apaiser

sophisticated [sə'fɪstɪkeɪtɪd] *adj* raffiné(e), sophistiqué(e); (*machinery*) hautement perfectionné(e), très complexe; (*system etc*) très perfectionné(e), sophistiqué

sophomore ['sɔfəmɔːʳ] *n* (US) étudiant(e) de seconde année

sopping ['sɔpɪŋ] *adj* (*also*: **sopping wet**) tout(e) trempé(e)

soppy ['sɔpɪ] *adj* (*pej*) sentimental(e)

soprano [sə'prɑːnəu] *n* (*voice*) soprano *m*; (*singer*) soprano *m/f*

sorbet ['sɔːbeɪ] *n* sorbet *m*

sorcerer ['sɔːsərəʳ] *n* sorcier *m*

sordid ['sɔːdɪd] *adj* sordide

sore [sɔːʳ] *adj* (*painful*) douloureux(-euse), sensible; (*offended*) contrarié(e), vexé(e) ▷ *n* plaie *f*; **to have a ~ throat** avoir mal à la gorge; **it's a ~ point** (*fig*) c'est un point délicat

sorely ['sɔːlɪ] *adv* (*tempted*) fortement

sorrow ['sɔrəu] *n* peine *f*, chagrin *m*

sorry ['sɔrɪ] *adj* désolé(e); (*condition, excuse, tale*) triste, déplorable; (*sight*) désolant(e); ~! pardon!, excusez-moi!; ~? pardon?; **to feel ~ for sb** plaindre qn; **I'm ~ to hear that** ... je suis désolé(e) *or* navré(e) d'apprendre que ...; **to be ~ about sth** regretter qch

sort [sɔːt] *n* genre *m*, espèce *f*, sorte *f*; (*make: of coffee, car etc*) marque *f* ▷ *vt* (*also*: **sort out**: *select which to keep*) trier; (*classify*) classer; (*tidy*) ranger; (*letters etc*) trier; (*Comput*) trier; **what ~ do you want?** quelle sorte *or* quel genre voulez-vous?; **what ~ of car?** quelle marque de voiture?; **I'll do nothing of the ~!** je ne ferai rien de tel!; **it's ~ of awkward** (*inf*) c'est plutôt gênant

▷ **sort out** *vt* (*problem*) résoudre, régler

sorting office ['sɔːtɪŋ-] *n* (*Post*) bureau *m* de tri

SOS *n* SOS *m*

so-so ['səusəu] *adv* comme ci comme ça

sought [sɔːt] *pt*, *pp* of **seek**

soul [səul] *n* âme *f*; **the poor ~ had nowhere to sleep** le pauvre n'avait nulle part où dormir; **I didn't see a ~** je n'ai vu (absolument) personne

soulful ['səulful] *adj* plein(e) de sentiment

sound [saund] *adj* (*healthy*) en bonne santé, sain(e); (*safe, not damaged*) solide, en bon état; (*reliable, not superficial*) sérieux(-euse), solide; (*sensible*) sensé(e) ▷ *adv*: ~ **asleep** profondément endormi(e) ▷ *n* (*noise, volume*) son *m*; (*louder*) bruit *m*; (*Geo*) détroit *m*, bras *m* de mer ▷ *vt* (*alarm*) sonner; (*also*: **sound out**: *opinions*) sonder ▷ *vi* sonner, retentir; (*fig: seem*) sembler (être); **to be of ~ mind** être sain(e) d'esprit; **I don't like the ~ of it** ça ne me dit rien qui vaille; **to ~ one's horn** (*Aut*) klaxonner, actionner son avertisseur; **to ~ like** ressembler à; **it ~s as if** ... il semblerait que ..., j'ai l'impression que ...

▷ **sound off** *vi* (*inf*): **to ~ off (about)** la ramener (sur)

sound barrier *n* mur *m* du son

sound bite *n* phrase toute faite (*pour être citée dans les médias*)

sound effects *npl* bruitage *m*

soundly ['saundlɪ] *adv* (*sleep*) profondément; (*beat*) complètement, à plate couture

soundproof ['saundpruːf] *vt* insonoriser ▷ *adj* insonorisé(e)

soundtrack ['saundtræk] *n* (*of film*) bande *f* sonore

soup [suːp] *n* soupe *f*, potage *m*; **in the ~** (*fig*) dans le pétrin

soup plate *n* assiette creuse *or* à soupe

soupspoon ['suːpspuːn] *n* cuiller *f* à soupe

sour ['sauəʳ] *adj* aigre, acide; (*milk*) tourné(e), aigre; (*fig*) acerbe, aigre; revêche; **to go** *or* **turn ~** (*milk, wine*) tourner; (*fig: relationship, plans*) mal tourner; **it's ~ grapes** c'est du dépit

source [sɔːs] *n* source *f*; **I have it from a reliable ~ that** je sais de source sûre que

south [sauθ] *n* sud *m* ▷ *adj* sud *inv*; (*wind*) du sud ▷ *adv* au sud, vers le sud; **(to the) ~ of** au sud de; **to travel ~** aller en direction du sud

South Africa *n* Afrique *f* du Sud

South African *adj* sud-africain(e) ▷ *n* Sud-Africain(e)

South America *n* Amérique *f* du Sud

South American *adj* sud-américain(e) ▷ *n* Sud-Américain(e)

southbound ['sauθbaund] *adj* en direction du

sud; (*carriageway*) sud *inv*

south-east [sauθ'i:st] *n* sud-est *m*

southerly ['sʌðəlɪ] *adj* du sud; au sud

southern ['sʌðən] *adj* (du) sud; méridional(e); **with a ~ aspect** orienté(e) *or* exposé(e) au sud; **the ~ hemisphere** l'hémisphère sud *or* austral

South Korea *n* Corée *f* du Sud

South of France *n*: **the ~** le Sud de la France, le Midi

South Pole *n* Pôle *m* Sud

South Wales *n* sud *m* du Pays de Galles

southward ['sauθwəd], **southwards** ['sauθwədz] *adv* vers le sud

south-west [sauθ'wɛst] *n* sud-ouest *m*

souvenir [su:və'nɪəʳ] *n* souvenir *m* (*objet*)

sovereign ['sɔvrɪn] *adj, n* souverain(e)

soviet ['səuvɪət] *adj* soviétique

sow¹ [səu] (*pt* **-ed**, *pp* **-n**) [səun] *vt* semer

sow² *n* [sau] truie *f*

soya ['sɔɪə], (*US*) **soy** [sɔɪ] *n*: **~ bean** graine *f* de soja; **~ sauce** sauce *f* au soja

spa [spa:] *n* (*town*) station thermale; (*US: also*: **health spa**) établissement *m* de cure de rajeunissement

space [speɪs] *n* (*gen*) espace *m*; (*room*) place *f*; espace; (*length of time*) laps *m* de temps ▷ *cpd* spatial(e) ▷ *vt* (*also*: **space out**) espacer; **to clear a ~ for sth** faire de la place pour qch; **in a confined ~** dans un espace réduit *or* restreint; **in a short ~ of time** dans peu de temps; **(with)in the ~ of an hour** en l'espace d'une heure

spacecraft ['speɪskra:ft] *n* engin *or* vaisseau spatial

spaceman ['speɪsmæn] (*irreg*) *n* astronaute *m*, cosmonaute *m*

spaceship ['speɪsʃɪp] *n* = **spacecraft**

spacing ['speɪsɪŋ] *n* espacement *m*; **single/double ~** (*Typ etc*) interligne *m* simple/double

spacious ['speɪʃəs] *adj* spacieux(-euse), grand(e)

spade [speɪd] *n* (*tool*) bêche *f*, pelle *f*; (*child's*) pelle; **spades** *npl* (*Cards*) pique *m*

spaghetti [spə'gɛtɪ] *n* spaghetti *mpl*

Spain [speɪn] *n* Espagne *f*

spam [spæm] *n* (*Comput*) spam *m*

span [spæn] *n* (*of bird, plane*) envergure *f*; (*of arch*) portée *f*; (*in time*) espace *m* de temps, durée *f* ▷ *vt* enjamber, franchir; (*fig*) couvrir, embrasser

Spaniard ['spænjəd] *n* Espagnol(e)

spaniel ['spænjəl] *n* épagneul *m*

Spanish ['spænɪʃ] *adj* espagnol(e), d'Espagne ▷ *n* (*Ling*) espagnol *m*; **the Spanish** *npl* les Espagnols; **~ omelette** omelette *f* à l'espagnole

spank [spæŋk] *vt* donner une fessée à

spanner ['spænəʳ] *n* (*Brit*) clé *f* (de mécanicien)

spare [spɛəʳ] *adj* de réserve, de rechange; (*surplus*) de *or* en trop, de reste ▷ *n* (*part*) pièce *f* de rechange, pièce détachée ▷ *vt* (*do without*) se passer de; (*afford to give*) donner, accorder, passer; (*not hurt*) épargner; (*not use*) ménager; **to ~ (*surplus*)** en surplus, de trop; **there are 2 going ~ (*Brit*)** il y en a 2 de disponible; **to ~ no expense** ne pas reculer devant la dépense; **can you ~ the**

time? est-ce que vous avez le temps?; **there is no time to ~** il n'y a pas de temps à perdre; **I've a few minutes to ~** je dispose de quelques minutes

spare part *n* pièce *f* de rechange, pièce détachée

spare room *n* chambre *f* d'ami

spare time *n* moments *mpl* de loisir

spare tyre, (*US*) **spare tire** *n* (*Aut*) pneu *m* de rechange

spare wheel *n* (*Aut*) roue *f* de secours

sparingly ['spɛərɪŋlɪ] *adv* avec modération

spark [spa:k] *n* étincelle *f*; (*fig*) étincelle, lueur *f*

sparkle ['spa:kl] *n* scintillement *m*, étincellement *m*, éclat *m* ▷ *vi* étinceler, scintiller; (*bubble*) pétiller

sparkling ['spa:klɪŋ] *adj* étincelant(e), scintillant(e); (*wine*) mousseux(-euse), pétillant(e); (*water*) pétillant(e), gazeux(-euse)

spark plug *n* bougie *f*

sparrow ['spærəu] *n* moineau *m*

sparse [spa:s] *adj* clairsemé(e)

spartan ['spa:tən] *adj* (*fig*) spartiate

spasm ['spæzəm] *n* (*Med*) spasme *m*; (*fig*) accès *m*

spasmodic [spæz'mɔdɪk] *adj* (*fig*) intermittent(e)

spastic ['spæstɪk] *n* handicapé(e) moteur

spat [spæt] *pt, pp of* **spit** ▷ *n* (*US*) prise *f* de bec

spate [speɪt] *n* (*fig*): **~ of** avalanche *f* or torrent *m* de; **in ~** (*river*) en crue

spatula ['spætjulə] *n* spatule *f*

spawn [spɔ:n] *vt* pondre; (*pej*) engendrer ▷ *vi* frayer ▷ *n* frai *m*

speak (*pt* **spoke**, *pp* **spoken**) [spi:k, spəuk, 'spəukn] *vt* (*language*) parler; (*truth*) dire ▷ *vi* parler; (*make a speech*) prendre la parole; **to ~ to sb/of *or* about sth** parler à qn/de qch; **I don't ~ French** je ne parle pas français; **do you ~ English?** parlez-vous anglais?; **can I ~ to ...?** est-ce que je peux parler à ...?; **~ing!** (*on telephone*) c'est moi-même!; **to ~ one's mind** dire ce que l'on pense; **it ~s for itself** c'est évident; **~ up!** parle plus fort!; **he has no money to ~ of** il n'a pas d'argent

▷ **speak for** *vt fus*: **to ~ for sb** parler pour qn; **that picture is already spoken for** (*in shop*) ce tableau est déjà réservé

speaker ['spi:kəʳ] *n* (*in public*) orateur *m*; (*also*: **loudspeaker**) haut-parleur *m*; (*for stereo etc*) baffle *m*, enceinte *f*; (*Pol*): **the S~** (*Brit*) le président de la Chambre des communes *or* des représentants; (*US*) le président de la Chambre; **are you a Welsh ~?** parlez-vous gallois?

spear [spɪəʳ] *n* lance *f* ▷ *vt* transpercer

spearhead ['spɪəhɛd] *n* fer *m* de lance; (*Mil*) colonne *f* d'attaque ▷ *vt* (*attack etc*) mener

spec [spɛk] *n* (*Brit inf*): **on ~** à tout hasard; **to buy on ~** acheter avec l'espoir de faire une bonne affaire

special ['spɛʃl] *adj* spécial(e) ▷ *n* (*train*) train spécial; **take ~ care** soyez particulièrement prudents; **nothing ~** rien de spécial; **today's ~** (*at restaurant*) le plat du jour

special delivery *n* (*Post*): **by ~** en express

special effects npl (Cine) effets spéciaux
specialist ['spɛʃəlɪst] n spécialiste m/f; **heart ~** cardiologue m/f
speciality [spɛʃɪ'ælɪtɪ] n (Brit) spécialité f
specialize ['spɛʃəlaɪz] vi: **to ~ (in)** se spécialiser (dans)
specially ['spɛʃlɪ] adv spécialement, particulièrement
special needs npl (Brit) difficultés fpl d'apprentissage scolaire
special offer n (Comm) réclame f
special school n (Brit) établissement m d'enseignement spécialisé
specialty ['spɛʃəltɪ] n (US) = **speciality**
species ['spiːʃiːz] n (pl inv) espèce f
specific [spə'sɪfɪk] adj (not vague) précis(e), explicite; (particular) particulier(-ière); (Bot, Chem etc) spécifique; **to be ~** être particulier à, être le or un caractère (or les caractères) spécifique(s) de
specifically [spə'sɪfɪklɪ] adv explicitement, précisément; (intend, ask, design) expressément, spécialement; (exclusively) exclusivement, spécifiquement
specification [spɛsɪfɪ'keɪʃən] n spécification f; stipulation f; **specifications** npl (of car, building etc) spécification
specify ['spɛsɪfaɪ] vt spécifier, préciser; **unless otherwise specified** sauf indication contraire
specimen ['spɛsɪmən] n spécimen m, échantillon m; (Med: of blood) prélèvement m; (: of urine) échantillon m
speck [spɛk] n petite tache, petit point; (particle) grain m
speckled ['spɛkld] adj tacheté(e), moucheté(e)
specs [spɛks] npl (inf) lunettes fpl
spectacle ['spɛktəkl] n spectacle m; **spectacles** npl (Brit) lunettes fpl
spectacular [spɛk'tækjulər] adj spectaculaire ▷ n (Cine etc) superproduction f
spectator [spɛk'teɪtər] n spectateur(-trice)
spectrum (pl **spectra**) ['spɛktrəm, -rə] n spectre m; (fig) gamme f
speculate ['spɛkjuleɪt] vi spéculer; (try to guess): **to ~ about** s'interroger sur
speculation [spɛkju'leɪʃən] n spéculation f; conjectures fpl
sped [spɛd] pt, pp of **speed**
speech [spiːtʃ] n (faculty) parole f; (talk) discours m, allocution f; (manner of speaking) façon f de parler, langage m; (language) langage m; (enunciation) élocution f
speechless ['spiːtʃlɪs] adj muet(te)
speed [spiːd] n vitesse f; (promptness) rapidité f ▷ vi (pt, pp **sped**) [spɛd] (Aut: exceed speed limit) faire un excès de vitesse; **to ~ along/by** etc aller/ passer etc à toute vitesse; **at ~** (Brit) rapidement; **at full** or **top ~** à toute vitesse or allure; **at a ~ of 70 km/h** à une vitesse de 70 km/h; **shorthand/ typing ~s** nombre m de mots à la minute en sténographie/dactylographie; **a five-~ gearbox** une boîte cinq vitesses

▶ **speed up** (pt, pp **-ed up**) vi aller plus vite, accélérer ▷ vt accélérer
speedboat ['spiːdbəut] n vedette f, hors-bord m inv
speedily ['spiːdɪlɪ] adv rapidement, promptement
speeding ['spiːdɪŋ] n (Aut) excès m de vitesse
speed limit n limitation f de vitesse, vitesse maximale permise
speedometer [spɪ'dɔmɪtər] n compteur m (de vitesse)
speedway n (Sport) piste f de vitesse pour motos; (also: **speedway racing**) épreuve(s) f(pl) de vitesse de motos
speedy [spiːdɪ] adj rapide, prompt(e)
spell [spɛl] n (also: **magic spell**) sortilège m, charme m; (period of time) (courte) période ▷ vt (pt, pp **spelt** or **-ed**) [spɛlt, spɛld] (in writing) écrire, orthographier; (aloud) épeler; (fig) signifier; **to cast a ~ on sb** jeter un sort à qn; **he can't ~** il fait des fautes d'orthographe; **how do you ~ your name?** comment écrivez-vous votre nom?; **can you ~ it for me?** pouvez-vous me l'épeler?
▶ **spell out** vt (explain): **to ~ sth out for sb** expliquer qch clairement à qn
spellbound ['spɛlbaund] adj envoûté(e), subjugué(e)
spellchecker ['spɛltʃekər] n (Comput) correcteur m or vérificateur m orthographique
spelling ['spɛlɪŋ] n orthographe f
spelt [spɛlt] pt, pp of **spell**
spend (pt, pp **spent**) [spɛnd, spɛnt] vt (money) dépenser; (time, life) passer; (devote) consacrer; **to ~ time/money/effort on sth** consacrer du temps/de l'argent/de l'énergie à qch
spending ['spɛndɪŋ] n dépenses fpl; **government ~** les dépenses publiques
spendthrift ['spɛndθrɪft] n dépensier(-ière)
spent [spɛnt] pt, pp of **spend** ▷ adj (patience) épuisé(e), à bout; (cartridge, bullets) vide; **~ matches** vieilles allumettes
sperm [spəːm] n spermatozoïde m; (semen) sperme m
sphere [sfɪər] n sphère f; (fig) sphère, domaine m
spice [spaɪs] n épice f ▷ vt épicer
spicy ['spaɪsɪ] adj épicé(e), relevé(e); (fig) piquant(e)
spider ['spaɪdər] n araignée f; **~'s web** toile f d'araignée
spike [spaɪk] n pointe f; (Elec) pointe de tension; (Bot) épi m; **spikes** npl (Sport) chaussures fpl à pointes
spill (pt, pp **spilt** or **-ed**) [spɪl, -t, -d] vt renverser; répandre ▷ vi se répandre; **to ~ the beans** (inf) vendre la mèche; (: confess) lâcher le morceau
▶ **spill out** vi sortir à flots, se répandre
▶ **spill over** vi déborder
spilt [spɪlt] pt, pp of **spill**
spin [spɪn] (pt, pp **spun**) [spʌn] n (revolution of wheel) tour m; (Aviat) (chute f en) vrille f; (trip in car) petit tour, balade f; (on ball) effet m ▷ vt (wool etc) filer; (wheel) faire tourner; (Brit: clothes)

essorer ▷ vi (*turn*) tourner, tournoyer; **to ~ a yarn** débiter une longue histoire; **to ~ a coin** (*Brit*) jouer à pile ou face
▶ **spin out** vt faire durer

spinach ['spɪnɪtʃ] n épinard m; (*as food*) épinards mpl

spinal ['spaɪnl] adj vertébral(e), spinal(e)

spinal cord n moelle épinière

spin doctor n (*inf*) personne employée pour présenter un parti politique sous un jour favorable

spin-dryer [spɪn'draɪəʳ] n (*Brit*) essoreuse f

spine [spaɪn] n colonne vertébrale; (*thorn*) épine f, piquant m

spineless ['spaɪnlɪs] adj invertébré(e); (*fig*) mou (molle), sans caractère

spinning ['spɪnɪŋ] n (*of thread*) filage m; (*by machine*) filature f

spinning top n toupie f

spin-off ['spɪnɔf] n sous-produit m; avantage inattendu

spinster ['spɪnstəʳ] n célibataire f; vieille fille

spiral ['spaɪərl] n spirale f ▷ adj en spirale ▷ vi (*fig: prices etc*) monter en flèche; **the inflationary ~** la spirale inflationniste

spiral staircase n escalier m en colimaçon

spire ['spaɪəʳ] n flèche f, aiguille f

spirit ['spɪrɪt] n (*soul*) esprit m, âme f; (*ghost*) esprit, revenant m; (*mood*) esprit, état m d'esprit; (*courage*) courage m, énergie f; **spirits** npl (*drink*) spiritueux mpl, alcool m; **in good ~s** de bonne humeur; **in low ~s** démoralisé(e); **community ~** solidarité f; **public ~** civisme m

spirited ['spɪrɪtɪd] adj vif (vive), fougueux(-euse), plein(e) d'allant

spiritual ['spɪrɪtjuəl] adj spirituel(le); (*religious*) religieux(-euse) ▷ n (*also*: **Negro spiritual**) spiritual m

spit [spɪt] n (*for roasting*) broche f; (*spittle*) crachat m; (*saliva*) salive f ▷ vi (*pt, pp* **spat**) [spæt] cracher; (*sound*) crépiter; (*rain*) crachiner

spite [spaɪt] n rancune f, dépit m ▷ vt contrarier, vexer; **in ~ of** en dépit de, malgré

spiteful ['spaɪtful] adj malveillant(e), rancunier(-ière)

spittle ['spɪtl] n salive f; bave f; crachat m

splash [splæʃ] n (*sound*) plouf m; (*of colour*) tache f ▷ vt éclabousser ▷ vi (*also*: **splash about**) barboter, patauger
▶ **splash out** vi (*Brit*) faire une folie

spleen [spli:n] n (*Anat*) rate f

splendid ['splendɪd] adj splendide, superbe, magnifique

splint [splɪnt] n attelle f, éclisse f

splinter ['splɪntəʳ] n (*wood*) écharde f; (*metal*) éclat m ▷ vi (*wood*) se briser

split [splɪt] (*pt, pp* **-**) n fente f, déchirure f; (*fig: Pol*) scission f ▷ vt fendre, déchirer; (*party*) diviser; (*work, profits*) partager, répartir ▷ vi (*break*) se fendre, se briser; (*divide*) se diviser; **let's ~ the difference** coupons la poire en deux; **to do the ~s** faire le grand écart
▶ **split up** vi (*couple*) se séparer, rompre; (*meeting*)

se disperser

spoil (*pt, pp* **-ed** or **-t**) [spɔɪl, -d, -t] vt (*damage*) abîmer; (*mar*) gâcher; (*child*) gâter; (*ballot paper*) rendre nul ▷ vi: **to be ~ing for a fight** chercher la bagarre

spoils [spɔɪlz] npl butin m

spoilsport ['spɔɪlspɔ:t] n trouble-fête m/f inv, rabat-joie m inv

spoilt [spɔɪlt] pt, pp of **spoil** ▷ adj (*child*) gâté(e); (*ballot paper*) nul(le)

spoke [spəuk] pt of **speak** ▷ n rayon m

spoken ['spəukn] pp of **speak**

spokesman ['spəuksmən] (*irreg*) n porte-parole m inv

spokesperson ['spəukspə:sn] (*irreg*) n porte-parole m inv

spokeswoman ['spəukswumən] (*irreg*) n porte-parole m inv

sponge [spʌndʒ] n éponge f; (*Culin: also*: **sponge cake**) ≈ biscuit m de Savoie ▷ vt éponger ▷ vi: **to ~ off** or **on** vivre aux crochets de

sponge bag n (*Brit*) trousse f de toilette

sponsor ['spɔnsəʳ] n (*Radio, TV, Sport*) sponsor m; (*for application*) parrain m, marraine f; (*Brit: for fund-raising event*) donateur(-trice) ▷ vt (*programme, competition etc*) parrainer, patronner, sponsoriser; (*Pol: bill*) présenter; (*new member*) parrainer; (*fund-raiser*) faire un don à; **I ~ed him at 3p a mile** (*in fund-raising race*) je me suis engagé à lui donner 3p par mile

sponsorship ['spɔnsəʃɪp] n sponsoring m; patronage m, parrainage m; dons mpl

spontaneous [spɔn'teɪnɪəs] adj spontané(e)

spooky ['spu:kɪ] adj (*inf*) qui donne la chair de poule

spool [spu:l] n bobine f

spoon [spu:n] n cuiller f

spoon-feed ['spu:nfi:d] vt nourrir à la cuiller; (*fig*) mâcher le travail à

spoonful ['spu:nful] n cuillerée f

sport [spɔ:t] n sport m; (*amusement*) divertissement m; (*person*) chic type m/chic fille f ▷ vt (*wear*) arborer; **indoor/outdoor ~s** sports en salle/de plein air; **to say sth in ~** dire qch pour rire

sporting ['spɔ:tɪŋ] adj sportif(-ive); **to give sb a ~ chance** donner sa chance à qn

sport jacket n (*US*) = **sports jacket**

sports car n voiture f de sport

sports centre (*Brit*) n centre sportif

sports jacket (*Brit*) n veste f de sport

sportsman ['spɔ:tsmən] (*irreg*) n sportif m

sportsmanship ['spɔ:tsmənʃɪp] n esprit sportif, sportivité f

sports utility vehicle n véhicule m de loisirs (*de type SUV*)

sportswear ['spɔ:tswɛəʳ] n vêtements mpl de sport

sportswoman ['spɔ:tswumən] (*irreg*) n sportive f

sporty ['spɔ:tɪ] adj sportif(-ive)

spot [spɔt] n tache f; (*dot: on pattern*) pois m; (*pimple*) bouton m; (*place*) endroit m, coin m; (*also*:

spot advertisement) message *m* publicitaire; (*small amount*): **a ~ of** un peu de ▷ *vt* (*notice*) apercevoir, repérer; **on the ~** sur place, sur les lieux; (*immediately*) sur le champ; **to put sb on the ~** (*fig*) mettre qn dans l'embarras; **to come out in ~s** se couvrir de boutons, avoir une éruption de boutons

spot check *n* contrôle intermittent

spotless ['spɔtlɪs] *adj* immaculé(e)

spotlight ['spɔtlaɪt] *n* projecteur *m*; (*Aut*) phare *m* auxiliaire

spotted ['spɔtɪd] *adj* tacheté(e), moucheté(e); à pois; **~ with** tacheté(e) de

spotty ['spɔtɪ] *adj* (*face*) boutonneux(-euse)

spouse [spauz] *n* époux (épouse)

spout [spaut] *n* (*of jug*) bec *m*; (*of liquid*) jet *m* ▷ *vi* jaillir

sprain [spreɪn] *n* entorse *f*, foulure *f* ▷ *vt*: **to ~ one's ankle** se fouler *or* se tordre la cheville

sprang [spræŋ] *pt of* **spring**

sprawl [sprɔ:l] *vi* s'étaler ▷ *n*: **urban ~** expansion urbaine; **to send sb ~ing** envoyer qn rouler par terre

spray [spreɪ] *n* jet *m* (en fines gouttelettes); (*from sea*) embruns *mpl*; (*aerosol*) vaporisateur *m*, bombe *f*; (*for garden*) pulvérisateur *m*; (*of flowers*) petit bouquet ▷ *vt* vaporiser, pulvériser; (*crops*) traiter ▷ *cpd* (*deodorant etc*) en bombe *or* atomiseur

spread [spred] (*pt, pp* **~**) *n* (*distribution*) répartition *f*; (*Culin*) pâte *f* à tartiner; (*inf: meal*) festin *m*; (*Press, Typ: two pages*) double page *f* ▷ *vt* (*paste, contents*) étendre, étaler; (*rumour, disease*) répandre, propager; (*repayments*) échelonner, étaler; (*wealth*) répartir ▷ *vi* s'étendre; se répandre; se propager; (*stain*) s'étaler; **middle-age ~** embonpoint *m* (pris avec l'âge)

▶ **spread out** *vi* (*people*) se disperser

spread-eagled ['spredɪ:gld] *adj*: **to be** *or* **lie ~** être étendu(e) bras et jambes écartés

spreadsheet ['spredʃi:t] *n* (*Comput*) tableur *m*

spree [spri:] *n*: **to go on a ~** faire la fête

sprightly ['spraɪtlɪ] *adj* alerte

spring [sprɪŋ] (*pt* **sprang**, *pp* **sprung**) [spræŋ, sprʌŋ] *n* (*season*) printemps *m*; (*leap*) bond *m*, saut *m*; (*coiled metal*) ressort *m*; (*bounciness*) élasticité *f*; (*of water*) source *f* ▷ *vi* bondir, sauter ▷ *vt*: **to ~ a leak** (*pipe etc*) se mettre à fuir; **he sprang the news on me** il m'a annoncé la nouvelle de but en blanc; **in ~, in the ~** au printemps; **to ~ from** provenir de; **to ~ into action** passer à l'action; **to walk with a ~ in one's step** marcher d'un pas souple

▶ **spring up** *vi* (*problem*) se présenter, surgir; (*plant, buildings*) surgir de terre

springboard ['sprɪŋbɔ:d] *n* tremplin *m*

spring-clean [sprɪŋ'kli:n] *n* (*also*: **spring-cleaning**) grand nettoyage de printemps

spring onion *n* (*Brit*) ciboule *f*, cive *f*

springtime ['sprɪŋtaɪm] *n* printemps *m*

sprinkle ['sprɪŋkl] *vt* (*pour*) répandre; verser; **to ~ water etc on, ~ with water etc** asperger d'eau *etc*; **to ~ sugar etc on, ~ with sugar etc** saupoudrer de

sucre *etc*; **~d with** (*fig*) parsemé(e) de

sprinkler ['sprɪŋklə^r] *n* (*for lawn etc*) arroseur *m*; (*to put out fire*) diffuseur *m* d'extincteur automatique d'incendie

sprint [sprɪnt] *n* sprint *m* ▷ *vi* courir à toute vitesse; (*Sport*) sprinter

sprinter ['sprɪntə^r] *n* sprinteur(-euse)

sprout [spraut] *vi* germer, pousser

sprouts [sprauts] *npl* (*also*: **Brussels sprouts**) choux *mpl* de Bruxelles

spruce [spru:s] *n* épicéa *m* ▷ *adj* net(te), pimpant(e)

▶ **spruce up** *vt* (*smarten up: room etc*) apprêter; **to ~ o.s. up** se faire beau (belle)

sprung [sprʌŋ] *pp of* **spring**

spun [spʌn] *pt, pp of* **spin**

spur [spə:^r] *n* éperon *m*; (*fig*) aiguillon *m* ▷ *vt* (*also*: **spur on**) éperonner; aiguillonner; **on the ~ of the moment** sous l'impulsion du moment

spurious ['spjuərɪəs] *adj* faux (fausse)

spurn [spə:n] *vt* repousser avec mépris

spurt [spə:t] *n* jet *m*; (*of blood*) jaillissement *m*; (*of energy*) regain *m*, sursaut *m* ▷ *vi* jaillir, gicler; **to put in** *or* **on a ~** (*runner*) piquer un sprint; (*fig: in work etc*) donner un coup de collier

spy [spaɪ] *n* espion(ne) ▷ *vi*: **to ~ on** espionner, épier ▷ *vt* (*see*) apercevoir ▷ *cpd* (*film, story*) d'espionnage

spying ['spaɪɪŋ] *n* espionnage *m*

sq. *abbr* (*Math etc*) = **square**

squabble ['skwɔbl] *n* querelle *f*, chamaillerie *f* ▷ *vi* se chamailler

squad [skwɔd] *n* (*Mil, Police*) escouade *f*, groupe *m*; (*Football*) contingent *m*; **flying ~** (*Police*) brigade volante

squadron ['skwɔdrn] *n* (*Mil*) escadron *m*; (*Aviat, Naut*) escadrille *f*

squalid ['skwɔlɪd] *adj* sordide, ignoble

squall [skwɔ:l] *n* rafale *f*, bourrasque *f*

squalor ['skwɔlə^r] *n* conditions *fpl* sordides

squander ['skwɔndə^r] *vt* gaspiller, dilapider

square [skweə^r] *n* carré *m*; (*in town*) place *f*; (*US: block of houses*) îlot *m*, pâté *m* de maisons; (*instrument*) équerre *f* ▷ *adj* carré(e); (*honest*) honnête, régulier(-ière); (*inf: ideas, tastes*) vieux jeu *inv*, qui retarde ▷ *vt* (*arrange*) régler; arranger; (*Math*) élever au carré; (*reconcile*) concilier ▷ *vi* (*agree*) cadrer, s'accorder; **all ~** quitte; à égalité; **a ~ meal** un repas convenable; **2 metres ~** (de) 2 mètres sur 2; **1 ~ metre** 1 mètre carré; **we're back to ~ one** (*fig*) on se retrouve à la case départ

▶ **square up** *vi* (*Brit: settle*) régler; **to ~ up with sb** régler ses comptes avec qn

squarely ['skweəlɪ] *adv* carrément; (*honestly, fairly*) honnêtement, équitablement

square root *n* racine carrée

squash [skwɔʃ] *n* (*Brit: drink*): **lemon/orange ~** citronnade *f*/orangeade *f*; (*Sport*) squash *m*; (*US: vegetable*) courge *f* ▷ *vt* écraser

squat [skwɔt] *adj* petit(e) et épais(se), ramassé(e) ▷ *vi* (*also*: **squat down**) s'accroupir; (*on property*) squatter, squattériser

squatter ['skwɔtə^r] n squatter m
squeak [skwi:k] n (of hinge, wheel etc) grincement m; (of shoes) craquement m; (of mouse etc) petit cri aigu ▷ vi (hinge, wheel) grincer; (mouse) pousser un petit cri
squeal [skwi:l] vi pousser un or des cri(s) aigu(s) or perçant(s); (brakes) grincer
squeamish ['skwi:mɪʃ] adj facilement dégoûté(e); facilement scandalisé(e)
squeeze [skwi:z] n pression f; (also: **credit squeeze**) encadrement m du crédit, restrictions fpl de crédit ▷ vt presser; (hand, arm) serrer ▷ vi: **to ~ past/under sth** se glisser avec (beaucoup de) difficulté devant/sous qch; **a ~ of lemon** quelques gouttes de citron
▶ **squeeze out** vt exprimer; (fig) soutirer
squelch [skwɛltʃ] vi faire un bruit de succion; patauger
squid [skwɪd] n calmar m
squiggle ['skwɪgl] n gribouillis m
squint [skwɪnt] vi loucher ▷ n: **he has a ~** il louche, il souffre de strabisme; **to ~ at sth** regarder qch du coin de l'œil; (quickly) jeter un coup d'œil à qch
squirm [skwə:m] vi se tortiller
squirrel ['skwɪrəl] n écureuil m
squirt [skwə:t] n jet m ▷ vi jaillir, gicler ▷ vt faire gicler
Sr abbr = **senior** (Rel); = **sister**
Sri Lanka [srɪ'læŋkə] n Sri Lanka m
St abbr = **saint**; **street**
stab [stæb] n (with knife etc) coup m (de couteau etc); (of pain) lancée f; (inf: try): **to have a ~ at (doing) sth** s'essayer à (faire) qch ▷ vt poignarder; **to ~ sb to death** tuer qn à coups de couteau
stability [stə'bɪlɪtɪ] n stabilité f
stable ['steɪbl] n écurie f ▷ adj stable; **riding ~s** centre m d'équitation
stack [stæk] n tas m, pile f ▷ vt empiler, entasser; **there's ~s of time** (Brit inf) on a tout le temps
stadium ['steɪdɪəm] n stade m
staff [stɑːf] n (work force) personnel m; (Brit Scol: also: **teaching staff**) professeurs mpl, enseignants mpl, personnel enseignant; (servants) domestiques mpl; (Mil) état-major m; (stick) perche f, bâton m ▷ vt pourvoir en personnel
stag [stæg] n cerf m; (Brit Stock Exchange) loup m
stage [steɪdʒ] n scène f; (platform) estrade f; (point) étape f, stade m; (profession): **the ~** le théâtre ▷ vt (play) monter, mettre en scène; (demonstration) organiser; (fig: recovery etc) effectuer; **in ~s** par étapes, par degrés; **to go through a difficult ~** traverser une période difficile; **in the early ~s** au début; **in the final ~s** à la fin
stagecoach ['steɪdʒkəutʃ] n diligence f
stage manager n régisseur m
stagger ['stægə^r] vi chanceler, tituber ▷ vt (person: amaze) stupéfier; bouleverser; (hours, holidays) étaler, échelonner
staggering ['stægərɪŋ] adj (amazing)

stupéfiant(e), renversant(e)
stagnant ['stægnənt] adj stagnant(e)
stagnate [stæg'neɪt] vi stagner, croupir
stag night, stag party n enterrement m de vie de garçon
staid [steɪd] adj posé(e), rassis(e)
stain [steɪn] n tache f; (colouring) colorant m ▷ vt tacher; (wood) teindre
stained glass [steɪnd-] n (decorative) verre coloré; (in church) vitraux mpl; **~ window** vitrail m
stainless ['steɪnlɪs] adj (steel) inoxydable
stainless steel n inox m, acier m inoxydable
stain remover n détachant m
stair [stɛə^r] n (step) marche f
staircase ['stɛəkeɪs] n = **stairway**
stairs [stɛəz] npl escalier m; **on the ~** dans l'escalier
stairway ['stɛəweɪ] n escalier m
stake [steɪk] n pieu m, poteau m; (Comm: interest) intérêts mpl; (Betting) enjeu m ▷ vt risquer, jouer; (also: **stake out**: area) marquer, délimiter; **to be at ~** être en jeu; **to have a ~ in sth** avoir des intérêts (en jeu) dans qch; **to ~ a claim (to sth)** revendiquer (qch)
stale [steɪl] adj (bread) rassis(e); (food) pas frais (fraîche); (beer) éventé(e); (smell) de renfermé; (air) confiné(e)
stalemate ['steɪlmeɪt] n pat m; (fig) impasse f
stalk [stɔːk] n tige f ▷ vt traquer ▷ vi: **to ~ out/off** sortir/partir d'un air digne
stall [stɔːl] n (Brit: in street, market etc) éventaire m, étal m; (in stable) stalle f ▷ vt (Aut) caler; (fig: delay) retarder ▷ vi (Aut) caler; (fig) essayer de gagner du temps; **stalls** npl (Brit: in cinema, theatre) orchestre m; **a newspaper/flower ~** un kiosque à journaux/de fleuriste
stallion ['stæljən] n étalon m (cheval)
stamina ['stæmɪnə] n vigueur f, endurance f
stammer ['stæmə^r] n bégaiement m ▷ vi bégayer
stamp [stæmp] n timbre m; (also: **rubber stamp**) tampon m; (mark, also fig) empreinte f; (on document) cachet m ▷ vi (also: **stamp one's foot**) taper du pied ▷ vt (letter) timbrer; (with rubber stamp) tamponner
▶ **stamp out** vt (fire) piétiner; (crime) éradiquer; (opposition) éliminer
stamp album n album m de timbres(-poste)
stamp collecting [-kəlektɪŋ] n philatélie f
stamped addressed envelope n (Brit) enveloppe affranchie pour la réponse
stampede [stæm'piːd] n ruée f; (of cattle) débandade f
stance [stæns] n position f
stand [stænd] (pt, pp **stood**) [stud] n (position) position f; (for taxis) station f (de taxis); (Mil) résistance f; (structure) guéridon m; support m; (Comm) étalage m, stand m; (Sport: also: **stands**) tribune f; (also: **music stand**) pupitre m ▷ vi être or se tenir (debout); (rise) se lever, se mettre debout; (be placed) se trouver; (remain: offer etc) rester valable ▷ vt (place) mettre, poser; (tolerate, withstand) supporter; (treat, invite) offrir, payer;

to make a ~ prendre position; **to take a ~ on an issue** prendre position sur un problème; **to ~ for parliament** (*Brit*) se présenter aux élections (*comme candidat à la députation*); **to ~ guard** or **watch** (*Mil*) monter la garde; **it ~s to reason** c'est logique; cela va de soi; **as things ~** dans l'état actuel des choses; **to ~ sb a drink/meal** payer à boire/à manger à qn; **I can't ~ him** je ne peux pas le voir

▶ **stand aside** *vi* s'écarter

▶ **stand back** *vi* (*move back*) reculer, s'écarter

▶ **stand by** *vi* (*be ready*) se tenir prêt(e) ▷ *vt fus* (*opinion*) s'en tenir à; (*person*) ne pas abandonner, soutenir

▶ **stand down** *vi* (*withdraw*) se retirer; (*Law*) renoncer à ses droits

▶ **stand for** *vt fus* (*signify*) représenter, signifier; (*tolerate*) supporter, tolérer

▶ **stand in for** *vt fus* remplacer

▶ **stand out** *vi* (*be prominent*) ressortir

▶ **stand up** *vi* (*rise*) se lever, se mettre debout

▶ **stand up for** *vt fus* défendre

▶ **stand up to** *vt fus* tenir tête à, résister à

standard ['stændəd] *n* (*norm*) norme *f*, étalon *m*; (*level*) niveau *m* (voulu); (*criterion*) critère *m*; (*flag*) étendard *m* ▷ *adj* (*size etc*) ordinaire, normal(e); (*model, feature*) standard *inv*; (*practice*) courant(e); (*text*) de base; **standards** *npl* (*morals*) morale *f*, principes *mpl*; **to be** or **come up to ~** être du niveau voulu or à la hauteur; **to apply a double ~** avoir or appliquer deux poids deux mesures

standard lamp *n* (*Brit*) lampadaire *m*

standard of living *n* niveau *m* de vie

stand-by ['stændbaɪ] *n* remplaçant(e) ▷ *adj* (*provisions*) de réserve; **to be on ~** se tenir prêt(e) (à intervenir); (*doctor*) être de garde

stand-by ticket *n* (*Aviat*) billet *m* stand-by

stand-in ['stændɪn] *n* remplaçant(e); (*Cine*) doublure *f*

standing ['stændɪŋ] *adj* debout *inv*; (*permanent*) permanent(e); (*rule*) immuable; (*army*) de métier; (*grievance*) constant(e), de longue date ▷ *n* réputation *f*, rang *m*, standing *m*; (*duration*): **of 6 months' ~** qui dure depuis 6 mois; **of many years' ~** qui dure or existe depuis longtemps; **he was given a ~ ovation** on s'est levé pour l'acclamer; **it's a ~ joke** c'est un vieux sujet de plaisanterie; **a man of some ~** un homme estimé

standing order *n* (*Brit: at bank*) virement *m* automatique, prélèvement *m* bancaire; **standing orders** *npl* (*Mil*) règlement *m*

standing room *n* places *fpl* debout

standpoint ['stændpɔɪnt] *n* point *m* de vue

standstill ['stændstɪl] *n*: **at a ~** à l'arrêt; (*fig*) au point mort; **to come to a ~** s'immobiliser, s'arrêter

stank [stæŋk] *pt of* **stink**

staple ['steɪpl] *n* (*for papers*) agrafe *f*; (*chief product*) produit *m* de base ▷ *adj* (*food, crop, industry etc*) de base principal(e) ▷ *vt* agrafer

stapler ['steɪplə'] *n* agrafeuse *f*

star [stɑː'] *n* étoile *f*; (*celebrity*) vedette *f* ▷ *vi*: **to ~ (in)** être la vedette (de) ▷ *vt* (*Cine*) avoir pour vedette; **4-~ hotel** hôtel *m* 4 étoiles; **2-~ petrol** (*Brit*) essence *f* ordinaire; **4-~ petrol** (*Brit*) super *m*; **stars** *npl*: **the ~s** (*Astrology*) l'horoscope *m*

starboard ['stɑːbəd] *n* tribord *m*; **to ~** à tribord

starch [stɑːtʃ] *n* amidon *m*; (*in food*) fécule *f*

stardom ['stɑːdəm] *n* célébrité *f*

stare [stɛə'] *n* regard *m* fixe ▷ *vi*: **to ~ at** regarder fixement

starfish ['stɑːfɪʃ] *n* étoile *f* de mer

stark [stɑːk] *adj* (*bleak*) désolé(e), morne; (*simplicity, colour*) austère; (*reality, poverty*) nu(e) ▷ *adv*: **~ naked** complètement nu(e)

starling ['stɑːlɪŋ] *n* étourneau *m*

starry ['stɑːrɪ] *adj* étoilé(e)

starry-eyed [stɑːrɪ'aɪd] *adj* (*innocent*) ingénu(e)

start [stɑːt] *n* commencement *m*, début *m*; (*of race*) départ *m*; (*sudden movement*) sursaut *m*; (*advantage*) avance *f*, avantage *m* ▷ *vt* commencer; (*cause: fight*) déclencher; (*rumour*) donner naissance à; (*fashion*) lancer; (*found: business, newspaper*) lancer, créer; (*engine*) mettre en marche ▷ *vi* (*begin*) commencer; (*begin journey*) partir, se mettre en route; (*jump*) sursauter; **when does the film ~?** à quelle heure est-ce que le film commence?; **at the ~** au début; **for a ~** d'abord, pour commencer; **to make an early ~** partir or commencer de bonne heure; **to ~ doing** or **to do sth** se mettre à faire qch; **to ~ (off) with ...** (*firstly*) d'abord ...; (*at the beginning*) au commencement ...

▶ **start off** *vi* commencer; (*leave*) partir

▶ **start out** *vi* (*begin*) commencer; (*set out*) partir

▶ **start over** *vi* (*US*) recommencer

▶ **start up** *vi* commencer; (*car*) démarrer ▷ *vt* (*fight*) déclencher; (*business*) créer; (*car*) mettre en marche

starter ['stɑːtə'] *n* (*Aut*) démarreur *m*; (*Sport: official*) starter *m*; (: *runner, horse*) partant *m*; (*Brit Culin*) entrée *f*

starting point ['stɑːtɪŋ-] *n* point *m* de départ

startle ['stɑːtl] *vt* faire sursauter; donner un choc à

startling ['stɑːtlɪŋ] *adj* surprenant(e), saisissant(e)

starvation [stɑː'veɪʃən] *n* faim *f*, famine *f*; **to die of ~** mourir de faim or d'inanition

starve [stɑːv] *vi* mourir de faim ▷ *vt* laisser mourir de faim; **I'm starving** je meurs de faim

state [steɪt] *n* état *m*; (*Pol*) État; (*pomp*): **in ~** en grande pompe ▷ *vt* (*declare*) déclarer, affirmer; (*specify*) indiquer, spécifier; **States** *npl*: **the S~s** les États-Unis; **to be in a ~** être dans tous ses états; **~ of emergency** état d'urgence; **~ of mind** état d'esprit; **the ~ of the art** l'état actuel de la technologie (*or des connaissances*)

stately ['steɪtlɪ] *adj* majestueux(-euse), imposant(e)

stately home ['steɪtlɪ-] *n* manoir *m* or château *m* (*ouvert au public*)

statement ['steɪtmənt] *n* déclaration *f*;

(*Law*) déposition *f*; (*Econ*) relevé *m*; **official ~** communiqué officiel; **~ of account, bank ~** relevé de compte

state school *n* école publique

statesman ['steɪtsmən] (*irreg*) *n* homme *m* d'État

static ['stætɪk] *n* (*Radio*) parasites *mpl*; (*also:* **static electricity**) électricité *f* statique ▷ *adj* statique

station ['steɪʃən] *n* gare *f*; (*also:* **police station**) poste *m or* commissariat *m* (de police); (*Mil*) poste *m* (militaire); (*rank*) condition *f*, rang *m* ▷ *vt* placer, poster; **action ~s** postes de combat; **to be ~ed in** (*Mil*) être en garnison à

stationary ['steɪʃnərɪ] *adj* à l'arrêt, immobile

stationer ['steɪʃənər] *n* papetier(-ière)

stationer's, stationer's shop *n* (*Brit*) papeterie *f*

stationery ['steɪʃnərɪ] *n* papier *m* à lettres, petit matériel de bureau

station wagon *n* (*US*) break *m*

statistic [stə'tɪstɪk] *n* statistique *f*

statistics [stə'tɪstɪks] *n* (*science*) statistique *f*

statue ['stætjuː] *n* statue *f*

stature ['stætʃər] *n* stature *f*; (*fig*) envergure *f*

status ['steɪtəs] *n* position *f*, situation *f*; (*prestige*) prestige *m*; (*Admin, official position*) statut *m*

status quo [-'kwəu] *n*: **the ~** le statu quo

status symbol *n* marque *f* de standing, signe extérieur de richesse

statute ['stætjuːt] *n* loi *f*; **statutes** *npl* (*of club etc*) statuts *mpl*

statutory ['stætjutrɪ] *adj* statutaire, prévu(e) par un article de loi; **~ meeting** assemblée constitutive *or* statutaire

staunch [stɔːntʃ] *adj* sûr(e), loyal(e) ▷ *vt* étancher

stay [steɪ] *n* (*period of time*) séjour *m*; (*Law*): **~ of execution** sursis *m* à statuer ▷ *vi* rester; (*reside*) loger; (*spend some time*) séjourner; **to ~ put** ne pas bouger; **to ~ with friends** loger chez des amis; **to ~ the night** passer la nuit

  ▶ **stay away** *vi* (*from person, building*) ne pas s'approcher; (*from event*) ne pas venir

  ▶ **stay behind** *vi* rester en arrière

  ▶ **stay in** *vi* (*at home*) rester à la maison

  ▶ **stay on** *vi* rester

  ▶ **stay out** *vi* (*of house*) ne pas rentrer; (*strikers*) rester en grève

  ▶ **stay up** *vi* (*at night*) ne pas se coucher

staying power ['steɪɪŋ-] *n* endurance *f*

stead [stɛd] *n* (*Brit*): **in sb's ~** à la place de qn; **to stand sb in good ~** être très utile *or* servir beaucoup à qn

steadfast ['stɛdfɑːst] *adj* ferme, résolu(e)

steadily ['stɛdɪlɪ] *adv* progressivement; (*firmly*) fermement; (*walk*) d'un pas ferme; (*fixedly: look*) sans détourner les yeux

steady ['stɛdɪ] *adj* stable, solide, ferme; (*regular*) constant(e), régulier(-ière); (*person*) calme, pondéré(e) ▷ *vt* assurer, stabiliser; (*nerves*) calmer; (*voice*) assurer; **a ~ boyfriend** un petit ami; **to ~ oneself** reprendre son aplomb

steak [steɪk] *n* (*meat*) bifteck *m*, steak *m*; (*fish, pork*) tranche *f*

steal (*pt* **stole**, *pp* **stolen**) [stiːl, stəul, 'stəuln] *vt*, *vi* voler; (*move*) se faufiler, se déplacer furtivement; **my wallet has been stolen** on m'a volé mon portefeuille

  ▶ **steal away, steal off** *vi* s'esquiver

stealth [stɛlθ] *n*: **by ~** furtivement

steam [stiːm] *n* vapeur *f* ▷ *vt* passer à la vapeur; (*Culin*) cuire à la vapeur ▷ *vi* fumer; (*ship*): **to ~ along** filer; **under one's own ~** (*fig*) par ses propres moyens; **to run out of ~** (*fig: person*) caler; être à bout; **to let off ~** (*fig: inf*) se défouler

  ▶ **steam up** *vi* (*window*) se couvrir de buée; **to get ~ed up about sth** (*fig: inf*) s'exciter à propos de qch

steam engine *n* locomotive *f* à vapeur

steamer ['stiːmər] *n* (*bateau m à*) vapeur *m*; (*Culin*) ≈ couscoussier *m*

steamship ['stiːmʃɪp] *n* = **steamer**

steamy ['stiːmɪ] *adj* humide; (*window*) embué(e); (*sexy*) torride

steel [stiːl] *n* acier *m* ▷ *cpd* d'acier

steelworks ['stiːlwəːks] *n* aciérie *f*

steep [stiːp] *adj* raide, escarpé(e); (*price*) très élevé(e), excessif(-ive) ▷ *vt* (faire) tremper

steeple ['stiːpl] *n* clocher *m*

steer [stɪər] *n* bœuf *m* ▷ *vt* diriger; (*boat*) gouverner; (*lead: person*) guider, conduire ▷ *vi* tenir le gouvernail; **to ~ clear of sb/sth** (*fig*) éviter qn/qch

steering ['stɪərɪŋ] *n* (*Aut*) conduite *f*

steering wheel *n* volant *m*

stem [stɛm] *n* (*of plant*) tige *f*; (*of leaf, fruit*) queue *f*; (*of glass*) pied *m* ▷ *vt* contenir, endiguer; (*attack, spread of disease*) juguler

  ▶ **stem from** *vt fus* provenir de, découler de

stench [stɛntʃ] *n* puanteur *f*

stencil ['stɛnsl] *n* stencil *m*; pochoir *m* ▷ *vt* polycopier

stenographer [stɛ'nɔɡrəfər] *n* (*US*) sténographe *m/f*

step [stɛp] *n* pas *m*; (*stair*) marche *f*; (*action*) mesure *f*, disposition *f* ▷ *vi*: **to ~ forward/back** faire un pas en avant/arrière, avancer/reculer; **steps** *npl* (*Brit*) = **stepladder**; **~ by ~** pas à pas; (*fig*) petit à petit; **to be in/out of ~ (with)** (*fig*) aller dans le sens (de)/être déphasé(e) (par rapport à)

  ▶ **step down** *vi* (*fig*) se retirer, se désister

  ▶ **step in** *vi* (*fig*) intervenir

  ▶ **step off** *vt fus* descendre de

  ▶ **step over** *vt fus* enjamber

  ▶ **step up** *vt* (*production, sales*) augmenter; (*campaign, efforts*) intensifier

stepbrother ['stɛpbrʌðər] *n* demi-frère *m*

stepchild ['stɛptʃaɪld] (*pl* **-ren**) *n* beau-fils *m*, belle-fille *f*

stepdaughter ['stɛpdɔːtər] *n* belle-fille *f*

stepfather ['stɛpfɑːðər] *n* beau-père *m*

stepladder ['stɛplædər] *n* (*Brit*) escabeau *m*

stepmother ['stɛpmʌðər] *n* belle-mère *f*

stepping stone ['stɛpɪŋ-] n pierre f de gué; (fig) tremplin m

stepsister ['stɛpsɪstər] n demi-sœur f

stepson ['stɛpsʌn] n beau-fils m

stereo ['stɛrɪəu] n (sound) stéréo f; (hi-fi) chaîne f stéréo ▷ adj (also: **stereophonic**) stéréo(phonique); **in ~** en stéréo

stereotype ['stɪərɪətaɪp] n stéréotype m ▷ vt stéréotyper

sterile ['stɛraɪl] adj stérile

sterilize ['stɛrɪlaɪz] vt stériliser

sterling ['stə:lɪŋ] adj sterling inv; (silver) de bon aloi, fin(e); (fig) à toute épreuve, excellent(e) ▷ n (currency) livre f sterling inv; **a pound ~** une livre sterling

stern [stə:n] adj sévère ▷ n (Naut) arrière m, poupe f

steroid ['stɪərɔɪd] n stéroïde m

stew [stju:] n ragoût m ▷ vt, vi cuire à la casserole; **~ed tea** thé trop infusé; **~ed fruit** fruits cuits or en compote

steward ['stju:əd] n (Aviat, Naut, Rail) steward m; (in club etc) intendant m; (also: **shop steward**) délégué syndical

stewardess ['stju:ədɛs] n hôtesse f

stick [stɪk] (pt, pp **stuck**) [stʌk] n bâton m; (for walking) canne f; (of chalk etc) morceau m ▷ vt (glue) coller; (thrust): **to ~ sth into** piquer or planter or enfoncer qch dans; (inf: put) mettre, fourrer; (: tolerate) supporter ▷ vi (adhere) tenir, coller; (remain) rester; (get jammed: door, lift) se bloquer; **to get hold of the wrong end of the ~** (Brit fig) comprendre de travers; **to ~ to** (one's promise) s'en tenir à; (principles) rester fidèle à

▶ **stick around** vi (inf) rester (dans les parages)

▶ **stick out** vi dépasser, sortir ▷ vt: **to ~ it out** (inf) tenir le coup

▶ **stick up** vi dépasser, sortir

▶ **stick up for** vt fus défendre

sticker ['stɪkər] n auto-collant m

sticking plaster ['stɪkɪŋ-] n sparadrap m, pansement adhésif

stick insect n phasme m

stick shift n (US Aut) levier m de vitesses

stick-up ['stɪkʌp] n (inf) braquage m, hold-up m

sticky ['stɪkɪ] adj poisseux(-euse); (label) adhésif(-ive); (fig: situation) délicat(e)

stiff [stɪf] adj (gen) raide, rigide; (door, brush) dur(e); (difficult) difficile, ardu(e); (cold) froid(e), distant(e); (strong, high) fort(e), élevé(e) ▷ adv: **to be bored/scared/frozen ~** s'ennuyer à mourir/être mort(e) de peur/froid; **to be** or **feel ~** (person) avoir des courbatures; **to have a ~ back** avoir mal au dos; **~ upper lip** (Brit: fig) flegme m (typiquement britannique)

stiffen ['stɪfn] vt raidir, renforcer ▷ vi se raidir; se durcir

stiff neck n torticolis m

stifle ['staɪfl] vt étouffer, réprimer

stifling ['staɪflɪŋ] adj (heat) suffocant(e)

stigma ['stɪgmə] (Bot, Med, Rel) (pl **-ta**) [stɪg'mɑ:tə] (fig), **stigmas** n stigmate m

stile [staɪl] n échalier m

stiletto [stɪ'lɛtəu] n (Brit: also: **stiletto heel**) talon m aiguille

still [stɪl] adj (motionless) immobile; (calm) calme, tranquille; (Brit: mineral water etc) non gazeux(-euse) ▷ adv (up to this time) encore, toujours; (even) encore; (nonetheless) quand même, tout de même ▷ n (Cine) photo f; **to stand ~** rester immobile, ne pas bouger; **keep ~!** ne bouge pas!; **he ~ hasn't arrived** il n'est pas encore arrivé, il n'est pas toujours pas arrivé

stillborn ['stɪlbɔ:n] adj mort-né(e)

still life n nature morte

stilt [stɪlt] n échasse f; (pile) pilotis m

stilted ['stɪltɪd] adj guindé(e), emprunté(e)

stimulate ['stɪmjuleɪt] vt stimuler

stimulus (pl **stimuli**) ['stɪmjuləs, 'stɪmjulaɪ] n stimulant m; (Biol, Psych) stimulus m

sting [stɪŋ] n piqûre f; (organ) dard m; (inf: confidence trick) arnaque m ▷ vt, vi (pt, pp **stung**) [stʌŋ] piquer; **my eyes are ~ing** j'ai les yeux qui piquent

stingy ['stɪndʒɪ] adj avare, pingre, chiche

stink [stɪŋk] n puanteur f ▷ vi (pt **stank**, pp **stunk**) [stæŋk, stʌŋk] puer, empester

stinking ['stɪŋkɪŋ] adj (fig: inf) infect(e); **~ rich** bourré(e) de pognon

stint [stɪnt] n part f de travail ▷ vi: **to ~ on** lésiner sur, être chiche de

stir [stə:r] n agitation f, sensation f ▷ vt remuer ▷ vi remuer, bouger; **to give sth a ~** remuer qch; **to cause a ~** faire sensation

▶ **stir up** vt exciter; (trouble) fomenter, provoquer

stir-fry ['stə:'fraɪ] vt faire sauter ▷ n: **vegetable ~** légumes sautés à la poêle

stirrup ['stɪrəp] n étrier m

stitch [stɪtʃ] n (Sewing) point m; (Knitting) maille f; (Med) point de suture; (pain) point de côté ▷ vt coudre, piquer; (Med) suturer

stoat [stəut] n hermine f (avec son pelage d'été)

stock [stɔk] n réserve f, provision f; (Comm) stock m; (Agr) cheptel m, bétail m; (Culin) bouillon m; (Finance) valeurs fpl, titres mpl; (Rail: also: **rolling stock**) matériel roulant; (descent, origin) souche f ▷ adj (fig: reply etc) courant(e); classique ▷ vt (have in stock) avoir, vendre; **well-~ed** bien approvisionné(e) or fourni(e); **in ~** en stock, en magasin; **out of ~** épuisé(e); **to take ~** (fig) faire le point; **~s and shares** valeurs (mobilières), titres; **government ~** fonds publics

▶ **stock up** vi: **to ~ up (with)** s'approvisionner (en)

stockbroker ['stɔkbrəukər] n agent m de change

stock cube n (Brit Culin) bouillon-cube m

stock exchange n Bourse f (des valeurs)

stockholder ['stɔkhəuldər] n (US) actionnaire m/f

stocking ['stɔkɪŋ] n bas m

stock market n Bourse f, marché financier

stockpile ['stɔkpaɪl] n stock m, réserve f ▷ vt stocker, accumuler

stocktaking ['stɔkteɪkɪŋ] n (Brit Comm)

inventaire *m*

stocky ['stɔkɪ] *adj* trapu(e), râblé(e)

stodgy ['stɔdʒɪ] *adj* bourratif(-ive), lourd(e)

stoke [stəuk] *vt* garnir, entretenir; chauffer

stole [stəul] *pt of* **steal** ⊳ *n* étole *f*

stolen ['stəuln] *pp of* **steal**

stomach ['stʌmək] *n* estomac *m*; (*abdomen*) ventre *m* ⊳ *vt* supporter, digérer

stomachache ['stʌməkeɪk] *n* mal *m* à l'estomac *or* au ventre

stone [stəun] *n* pierre *f*; (*pebble*) caillou *m*, galet *m*; (*in fruit*) noyau *m*; (*Med*) calcul *m*; (*Brit: weight*) = 6.348 kg; 14 pounds ⊳ *cpd* de or en pierre ⊳ *vt* (*person*) lancer des pierres sur, lapider; (*fruit*) dénoyauter; **within a ~'s throw of the station** à deux pas de la gare

stone-cold ['stəun'kəuld] *adj* complètement froid(e)

stone-deaf ['stəun'dɛf] *adj* sourd(e) comme un pot

stonework ['stəunwə:k] *n* maçonnerie *f*

stood [stud] *pt, pp of* **stand**

stool [stu:l] *n* tabouret *m*

stoop [stu:p] *vi* (*also:* **have a stoop**) être voûté(e); (*also:* **stoop down:** *bend*) se baisser, se courber; (*fig*): **to ~ to sth/doing sth** s'abaisser jusqu'à qch/jusqu'à faire qch

stop [stɔp] *n* arrêt *m*; (*short stay*) halte *f*; (*in punctuation*) point *m* ⊳ *vt* arrêter; (*break off*) interrompre; (*also:* **put a stop to**) mettre fin à; (*prevent*) empêcher ⊳ *vi* s'arrêter; (*rain, noise etc*) cesser, s'arrêter; **could you ~ here/at the corner?** arrêtez-vous ici/au coin, s'il vous plaît; **to ~ doing sth** cesser *or* arrêter de faire qch; **to ~ sb (from) doing sth** empêcher qn de faire qch; **to ~ dead** *vi* s'arrêter net; **~ it!** arrête!

▸ **stop by** *vi* s'arrêter (au passage)

▸ **stop off** *vi* faire une courte halte

▸ **stop up** *vt* (*hole*) boucher

stopgap ['stɔpgæp] *n* (*person*) bouche-trou *m*; (*also:* **stopgap measure**) mesure *f* intérimaire

stopover ['stɔpəuvər] *n* halte *f*; (*Aviat*) escale *f*

stoppage ['stɔpɪdʒ] *n* arrêt *m*; (*of pay*) retenue *f*; (*strike*) arrêt *m* de travail; (*obstruction*) obstruction *f*

stopper ['stɔpər] *n* bouchon *m*

stop press *n* nouvelles *fpl* de dernière heure

stopwatch ['stɔpwɔtʃ] *n* chronomètre *m*

storage ['stɔ:rɪdʒ] *n* emmagasinage *m*; (*of nuclear waste etc*) stockage *m*; (*in house*) rangement *m*; (*Comput*) mise *f* en mémoire *or* réserve

storage heater *n* (*Brit*) radiateur *m* électrique par accumulation

store [stɔ:r] *n* (*stock*) provision *f*, réserve *f*; (*depot*) entrepôt *m*; (*Brit: large shop*) grand magasin; (*US: shop*) magasin *m* ⊳ *vt* emmagasiner; (*nuclear waste etc*) stocker; (*information*) enregistrer; (*in filing system*) classer, ranger; (*Comput*) mettre en mémoire; **stores** *npl* (*food*) provisions; **who knows what is in ~ for us?** qui sait ce que l'avenir nous réserve *or* ce qui nous attend?; **to set great/little ~ by sth** faire grand cas/peu de

cas de qch

▸ **store up** *vt* mettre en réserve, emmagasiner

storekeeper ['stɔ:ki:pər] *n* (*US*) commerçant(e)

storeroom ['stɔ:ru:m] *n* réserve *f*, magasin *m*

storey, (*US*) **story** ['stɔ:rɪ] *n* étage *m*

stork [stɔ:k] *n* cigogne *f*

storm [stɔ:m] *n* tempête *f*; (*thunderstorm*) orage *m* ⊳ *vi* (*fig*) fulminer ⊳ *vt* prendre d'assaut

stormy ['stɔ:mɪ] *adj* orageux(-euse)

story ['stɔ:rɪ] *n* histoire *f*; récit *m*; (*Press: article*) article *m*; (*: subject*) affaire *f*; (*US*) = **storey**

storybook ['stɔ:rɪbuk] *n* livre *m* d'histoires *or* de contes

stout [staut] *adj* (*strong*) solide; (*brave*) intrépide; (*fat*) gros(se), corpulent(e) ⊳ *n* bière brune

stove [stəuv] *n* (*for cooking*) fourneau *m*; (*: small*) réchaud *m*; (*for heating*) poêle *m*; **gas/electric ~** (*cooker*) cuisinière *f* à gaz/électrique

stow [stəu] *vt* ranger; cacher

stowaway ['stəuəweɪ] *n* passager(-ère) clandestin(e)

straddle ['strædl] *vt* enjamber, être à cheval sur

straggle ['strægl] *vi* être (*or* marcher) en désordre; **~d along the coast** disséminé(e) tout au long de la côte

straight [streɪt] *adj* droit(e); (*hair*) raide; (*frank*) honnête, franc (franche); (*simple*) simple; (*Theat: part, play*) sérieux(-euse); (*inf: heterosexual*) hétéro *inv* ⊳ *adv* (tout) droit; (*drink*) sec, sans eau ⊳ *n*: **the ~** (*Sport*) la ligne droite; **to put** *or* **get ~** mettre en ordre, mettre de l'ordre dans; (*fig*) mettre au clair; **let's get this ~** mettons les choses au point; **10 ~ wins** 10 victoires d'affilée; **to go ~ home** rentrer directement à la maison; **~ away, ~ off** (*at once*) tout de suite; **~ off, ~ out** sans hésiter

straighten ['streɪtn] *vt* ajuster; (*bed*) arranger

▸ **straighten out** *vt* (*fig*) débrouiller; **to ~ things out** arranger les choses

▸ **straighten up** *vi* (*stand up*) se redresser; (*tidy*) ranger

straight-faced [streɪt'feɪst] *adj* impassible ⊳ *adv* en gardant son sérieux

straightforward [streɪt'fɔ:wəd] *adj* simple; (*frank*) honnête, direct(e)

strain [streɪn] *n* (*Tech*) tension *f*; pression *f*; (*physical*) effort *m*; (*mental*) tension (nerveuse); (*Med*) entorse *f*; (*streak, trace*) tendance *f*; élément *m*; (*breed: of plants*) variété *f*; (*: of animals*) race *f*; (*of virus*) souche *f* ⊳ *vt* (*stretch*) tendre fortement; (*fig: resources etc*) mettre à rude épreuve, grever; (*hurt: back etc*) se faire mal à; (*filter*) passer, filtrer; (*vegetables*) égoutter ⊳ *vi* peiner, fournir un gros effort; **strains** *npl* (*Mus*) accords *mpl*, accents *mpl*; **he's been under a lot of ~** il a traversé des moments difficiles, il est très éprouvé nerveusement

strained [streɪnd] *adj* (*muscle*) froissé(e); (*laugh etc*) forcé(e), contraint(e); (*relations*) tendu(e)

strainer ['streɪnər] *n* passoire *f*

strait [streɪt] *n* (*Geo*) détroit *m*; **straits** *npl*: **to be in dire ~s** (*fig*) avoir de sérieux ennuis

straitjacket ['streɪtdʒækɪt] *n* camisole *f* de force
strait-laced [streɪt'leɪst] *adj* collet monté *inv*
strand [strænd] *n* (*of thread*) fil *m*, brin *m*; (*of rope*) toron *m*; (*of hair*) mèche *f* ▷ *vt* (*boat*) échouer
stranded ['strændɪd] *adj* en rade, en plan
strange [streɪndʒ] *adj* (*not known*) inconnu(e); (*odd*) étrange, bizarre
strangely ['streɪndʒlɪ] *adv* étrangement, bizarrement; *see also* **enough**
stranger ['streɪndʒəʳ] *n* (*unknown*) inconnu(e); (*from somewhere else*) étranger(-ère); **I'm a ~ here** je ne suis pas d'ici
strangle ['stræŋgl] *vt* étrangler
stranglehold ['stræŋglhəuld] *n* (*fig*) emprise totale, mainmise *f*
strap [stræp] *n* lanière *f*, courroie *f*, sangle *f*; (*of slip, dress*) bretelle *f* ▷ *vt* attacher (avec une courroie *etc*)
strappy ['stræpɪ] *adj* (*dress*) à bretelles; (*sandals*) à lanières
strategic [strə'tiːdʒɪk] *adj* stratégique
strategy ['strætɪdʒɪ] *n* stratégie *f*
straw [strɔː] *n* paille *f*; **that's the last ~!** ça c'est le comble!
strawberry ['strɔːbərɪ] *n* fraise *f*; (*plant*) fraisier *m*
stray [streɪ] *adj* (*animal*) perdu(e), errant(e); (*scattered*) isolé(e) ▷ *vi* s'égarer; **~ bullet** balle perdue
streak [striːk] *n* bande *f*, filet *m*; (*in hair*) raie *f*; (*fig: of madness etc*): **a ~ of** une *or* des tendance(s) à ▷ *vt* zébrer, strier ▷ *vi*: **to ~ past** passer à toute allure; **to have ~s in one's hair** s'être fait faire des mèches; **a winning/losing ~** une bonne/ mauvaise série *or* période
stream [striːm] *n* (*brook*) ruisseau *m*; (*current*) courant *m*, flot *m*; (*of people*) défilé ininterrompu, flot ▷ *vt* (*Scol*) répartir par niveau ▷ *vi* ruisseler; **to ~ in/out** entrer/sortir à flots; **against the ~** à contre courant; **on ~** (*new power plant etc*) en service
streamer ['striːməʳ] *n* serpentin *m*, banderole *f*
streamlined ['striːmlaɪnd] *adj* (*Aviat*) fuselé(e), profilé(e); (*Aut*) aérodynamique; (*fig*) rationalisé(e)
street [striːt] *n* rue *f*; **the back ~s** les quartiers pauvres; **to be on the ~s** (*homeless*) être à la rue *or* sans abri
streetcar ['striːtkɑːʳ] *n* (*US*) tramway *m*
street lamp *n* réverbère *m*
street light *n* réverbère *m*
street map, street plan *n* plan *m* des rues
streetwise ['striːtwaɪz] *adj* (*inf*) futé(e), réaliste
strength [strɛŋθ] *n* force *f*; (*of girder, knot etc*) solidité *f*; (*of chemical solution*) titre *m*; (*of wine*) degré *m* d'alcool; **on the ~ of** en vertu de; **at full ~** au grand complet; **below ~** à effectifs réduits
strengthen ['strɛŋθn] *vt* renforcer; (*muscle*) fortifier; (*building, fig*) consolider
strenuous ['strɛnjuəs] *adj* vigoureux(-euse), énergique; (*tiring*) ardu(e), fatigant(e)
stress [strɛs] *n* (*force, pressure*) pression *f*; (*mental strain*) tension (nerveuse), stress *m*; (*accent*) accent *m*; (*emphasis*) insistance *f* ▷ *vt* insister sur, souligner; (*syllable*) accentuer; **to lay great ~ on sth** insister beaucoup sur qch; **to be under ~** être stressé(e)
stressed [strɛst] *adj* (*tense*) stressé(e); (*syllable*) accentué(e)
stressful ['strɛsful] *adj* (*job*) stressant(e)
stretch [strɛtʃ] *n* (*of sand etc*) étendue *f*; (*of time*) période *f* ▷ *vi* s'étirer; (*extend*): **to ~ to** *or* **as far as** s'étendre jusqu'à; (*be enough: money, food*): **to ~ to** aller pour ▷ *vt* tendre, étirer; (*spread*) étendre; (*fig*) pousser (au maximum); **at a ~** d'affilée; **to ~ a muscle** se distendre un muscle; **to ~ one's legs** se dégourdir les jambes
  ▶ **stretch out** *vi* s'étendre ▷ *vt* (*arm etc*) allonger, tendre; (*to spread*) étendre; **to ~ out for sth** allonger la main pour prendre qch
stretcher ['strɛtʃəʳ] *n* brancard *m*, civière *f*
stretchy ['strɛtʃɪ] *adj* élastique
strewn [struːn] *adj*: **~ with** jonché(e) de
stricken ['strɪkən] *adj* très éprouvé(e); dévasté(e); (*ship*) très endommagé(e); **~ with** frappé(e) *or* atteint(e) de
strict [strɪkt] *adj* strict(e); **in ~ confidence** tout à fait confidentiellement
strictly ['strɪktlɪ] *adv* strictement; **~ confidential** strictement confidentiel(le); **~ speaking** à strictement parler
stride [straɪd] *n* grand pas, enjambée *f* ▷ *vi* (*pt* **strode**) [strəud] marcher à grands pas; **to take in one's ~** (*fig: changes etc*) accepter sans sourciller
strife [straɪf] *n* conflit *m*, dissensions *fpl*
strike [straɪk] (*pt, pp* **struck**) [strʌk] *n* grève *f*; (*of oil etc*) découverte *f*; (*attack*) raid *m* ▷ *vt* frapper; (*oil etc*) trouver, découvrir; (*make: agreement, deal*) conclure ▷ *vi* faire grève; (*attack*) attaquer; (*clock*) sonner; **to go on** *or* **come out on ~** se mettre en grève, faire grève; **to ~ a match** frotter une allumette; **to ~ a balance** (*fig*) trouver un juste milieu
  ▶ **strike back** *vi* (*Mil, fig*) contre-attaquer
  ▶ **strike down** *vt* (*fig*) terrasser
  ▶ **strike off** *vt* (*from list*) rayer; (: *doctor etc*) radier
  ▶ **strike out** *vt* rayer
  ▶ **strike up** *vt* (*Mus*) se mettre à jouer; **to ~ up a friendship with** se lier d'amitié avec
striker ['straɪkəʳ] *n* gréviste *m/f*; (*Sport*) buteur *m*
striking ['straɪkɪŋ] *adj* frappant(e), saisissant(e); (*attractive*) éblouissant(e)
string [strɪŋ] *n* ficelle *f*, fil *m*; (*row: of beads*) rang *m*; (: *of onions, excuses*) chapelet *m*; (: *of people, cars*) file *f*; (*Mus*) corde *f*; (*Comput*) chaîne *f* ▷ *vt* (*pt, pp* **strung**) [strʌŋ]: **to ~ out** échelonner; **to ~ together** enchaîner; **the strings** *npl* (*Mus*) les instruments *mpl* à cordes; **to pull ~s** (*fig*) faire jouer le piston; **to get a job by pulling ~s** obtenir un emploi en faisant jouer le piston; **with no ~s attached** (*fig*) sans conditions
stringed instrument [strɪŋ(d)-], **string instrument** *n* (*Mus*) instrument *m* à cordes
stringent ['strɪndʒənt] *adj* rigoureux(-euse);

(*need*) impérieux(-euse)

strip [strɪp] *n* bande *f*; (*Sport*) tenue *f* ▷ *vt* (*undress*) déshabiller; (*paint*) décaper; (*fig*) dégarnir, dépouiller; (*also*: **strip down**: *machine*) démonter ▷ *vi* se déshabiller; **wearing the Celtic ~** en tenue du Celtic

▶ **strip off** *vt* (*paint etc*) décaper ▷ *vi* (*person*) se déshabiller

strip cartoon *n* bande dessinée

stripe [straɪp] *n* raie *f*, rayure *f*; (*Mil*) galon *m*

striped ['straɪpt] *adj* rayé(e), à rayures

stripper ['strɪpə'] *n* strip-teaseuse *f*

strip-search ['strɪpsə:tʃ] *n* fouille corporelle (*en faisant se déshabiller la personne*) ▷ *vt*: **to ~ sb** fouiller qn (*en le faisant se déshabiller*)

stripy ['straɪpɪ] *adj* rayé(e)

strive (*pt* **strove**, *pp* **-n**) [straɪv, strəuv, 'strɪvn] *vi*: **to ~ to do/for sth** s'efforcer de faire/d'obtenir qch

strode [strəud] *pt of* **stride**

stroke [strəuk] *n* coup *m*; (*Med*) attaque *f*; (*caress*) caresse *f*; (*Swimming*: *style*) (sorte *f* de) nage *f*; (*of piston*) course *f* ▷ *vt* caresser; **at a ~** d'un (seul) coup; **on the ~ of 5** à 5 heures sonnantes; **a ~ of luck** un coup de chance; **a 2-~ engine** un moteur à 2 temps

stroll [strəul] *n* petite promenade ▷ *vi* flâner, se promener nonchalamment; **to go for a ~** aller se promener *or* faire un tour

stroller ['strəulə'] *n* (*US: for child*) poussette *f*

strong [strɔŋ] *adj* (*gen*) fort(e); (*healthy*) vigoureux(-euse); (*heart, nerves*) solide; (*distaste, desire*) vif (vive); (*drugs, chemicals*) puissant(e) ▷ *adv*: **to be going ~** (*company*) marcher bien; (*person*) être toujours solide; **they are 50 ~** ils sont au nombre de 50

stronghold ['strɔŋhəuld] *n* forteresse *f*, fort *m*; (*fig*) bastion *m*

strongly ['strɔŋlɪ] *adv* fortement, avec force; vigoureusement; solidement; **I feel ~ about it** c'est une question qui me tient particulièrement à cœur; (*negatively*) j'y suis profondément opposé(e)

strongroom ['strɔŋru:m] *n* chambre forte

strove [strəuv] *pt of* **strive**

struck [strʌk] *pt, pp of* **strike**

structural ['strʌktʃrəl] *adj* structural(e); (*Constr*) de construction; affectant les parties portantes

structure ['strʌktʃə'] *n* structure *f*; (*building*) construction *f*

struggle ['strʌgl] *n* lutte *f* ▷ *vi* lutter, se battre; **to have a ~ to do sth** avoir beaucoup de mal à faire qch

strum [strʌm] *vt* (*guitar*) gratter de

strung [strʌŋ] *pt, pp of* **string**

strut [strʌt] *n* étai *m*, support *m* ▷ *vi* se pavaner

stub [stʌb] *n* (*of cigarette*) bout *m*, mégot *m*; (*of ticket etc*) talon *m* ▷ *vt*: **to ~ one's toe (on sth)** se heurter le doigt de pied (contre qch)

▶ **stub out** *vt* écraser

stubble ['stʌbl] *n* chaume *m*; (*on chin*) barbe *f* de plusieurs jours

stubborn ['stʌbən] *adj* têtu(e), obstiné(e), opiniâtre

stuck [stʌk] *pt, pp of* **stick** ▷ *adj* (*jammed*) bloqué(e), coincé(e); **to get ~** se bloquer *or* coincer

stuck-up [stʌk'ʌp] *adj* prétentieux(-euse)

stud [stʌd] *n* (*on boots etc*) clou *m*; (*collar stud*) bouton *m* de col; (*earring*) petite boucle d'oreille; (*of horses*: *also*: **stud farm**) écurie *f*, haras *m*; (*also*: **stud horse**) étalon *m* ▷ *vt* (*fig*): **~ded with** parsemé(e) *or* criblé(e) de

student ['stju:dənt] *n* étudiant(e) ▷ *adj* (*life*) estudiantin(e), étudiant(e), d'étudiant; (*residence, restaurant*) universitaire; (*loan, movement*) étudiant, universitaire d'étudiant; **law/medical ~** étudiant en droit/ médecine

student driver *n* (*US*) (conducteur(-trice)) débutant(e)

students' union *n* (*Brit*: *association*) ≈ union *f* des étudiants; (: *building*) ≈ foyer *m* des étudiants

studio ['stju:dɪəu] *n* studio *m*, atelier *m*; (*TV etc*) studio

studio flat, (*US*) **studio apartment** *n* studio *m*

studious ['stju:dɪəs] *adj* studieux(-euse), appliqué(e); (*studied*) étudié(e)

studiously ['stju:dɪəslɪ] *adv* (*carefully*) soigneusement

study ['stʌdɪ] *n* étude *f*; (*room*) bureau *m* ▷ *vt* étudier; (*examine*) examiner ▷ *vi* étudier, faire ses études; **to make a ~ of sth** étudier qch, faire une étude de qch; **to ~ for an exam** préparer un examen

stuff [stʌf] *n* (*gen*) chose(s) *f(pl)*, truc *m*; (*belongings*) affaires *fpl*, trucs; (*substance*) substance *f* ▷ *vt* rembourrer; (*Culin*) farcir; (*inf*: *push*) fourrer; (*animal*: *for exhibition*) empailler; **my nose is ~ed up** j'ai le nez bouché; **get ~ed!** (*inf!*) va te faire foutre! (*!*); **~ed toy** jouet *m* en peluche

stuffing ['stʌfɪŋ] *n* bourre *f*, rembourrage *m*; (*Culin*) farce *f*

stuffy ['stʌfɪ] *adj* (*room*) mal ventilé(e) *or* aéré(e); (*ideas*) vieux jeu *inv*

stumble ['stʌmbl] *vi* trébucher; **to ~ across** *or* **on** (*fig*) tomber sur

stumbling block ['stʌmblɪŋ-] *n* pierre *f* d'achoppement

stump [stʌmp] *n* souche *f*; (*of limb*) moignon *m* ▷ *vt*: **to be ~ed** sécher, ne pas savoir que répondre

stun [stʌn] *vt* (*blow*) étourdir; (*news*) abasourdir, stupéfier

stung [stʌŋ] *pt, pp of* **sting**

stunk [stʌŋk] *pp of* **stink**

stunned [stʌnd] *adj* assommé(e); (*fig*) sidéré(e)

stunning ['stʌnɪŋ] *adj* (*beautiful*) étourdissant(e); (*news etc*) stupéfiant(e)

stunt [stʌnt] *n* tour *m* de force; (*in film*) cascade *f*, acrobatie *f*; (*publicity*) truc *m* publicitaire; (*Aviat*) acrobatie *f* ▷ *vt* retarder, arrêter

stuntman ['stʌntmæn] (*irreg*) *n* cascadeur *m*

stupendous [stju:'pɛndəs] *adj* prodigieux(-euse), fantastique

stupid ['stju:pɪd] *adj* stupide, bête

stupidity [stju:'pɪdɪtɪ] n stupidité f, bêtise f
sturdy ['stə:dɪ] adj (person, plant) robuste, vigoureux(-euse); (object) solide
stutter ['stʌtəʳ] n bégaiement m ▷ vi bégayer
sty [staɪ] n (of pigs) porcherie f
stye [staɪ] n (Med) orgelet m
style [staɪl] n style m; (of dress etc) genre m; (distinction) allure f, cachet m, style; (design) modèle m; **in the latest ~** à la dernière mode; **hair ~** coiffure f
stylish ['staɪlɪʃ] adj élégant(e), chic inv
stylist ['staɪlɪst] n (hair stylist) coiffeur(-euse); (literary stylist) styliste m/f
stylus (pl styli or -es) ['staɪləs, -laɪ] n (of record player) pointe f de lecture
suave [swɑ:v] adj doucereux(-euse), onctueux(-euse)
sub... [sʌb] prefix sub..., sous-
subconscious [sʌb'kɒnʃəs] adj subconscient(e) ▷ n subconscient m
subcontract n ['sʌb'kɒntrækt] contrat m de sous-traitance ▷ vt [sʌbkən'trækt] sous-traiter
subdue [səb'dju:] vt subjuguer, soumettre
subdued [səb'dju:d] adj contenu(e), atténué(e); (light) tamisé(e); (person) qui a perdu de son entrain
subject n ['sʌbdʒɪkt] sujet m; (Scol) matière f ▷ vt [səb'dʒɛkt]: **to ~ to** soumettre à; exposer à; **to be ~ to** (law) être soumis(e) à; (disease) être sujet(te) à; **~ to confirmation in writing** sous réserve de confirmation écrite; **to change the ~** changer de conversation
subjective [səb'dʒɛktɪv] adj subjectif(-ive)
subject matter n sujet m; (content) contenu m
subjunctive [səb'dʒʌŋktɪv] adj subjonctif(-ive) ▷ n subjonctif m
sublet [sʌb'lɛt] vt sous-louer
submarine [sʌbmə'ri:n] n sous-marin m
submerge [səb'mə:dʒ] vt submerger; immerger ▷ vi plonger
submission [səb'mɪʃən] n soumission f; (to committee etc) présentation f
submissive [səb'mɪsɪv] adj soumis(e)
submit [səb'mɪt] vt soumettre ▷ vi se soumettre
subnormal [sʌb'nɔ:ml] adj au-dessous de la normale; (person) arriéré(e)
subordinate [sə'bɔ:dɪnət] adj (junior) subalterne; (Grammar) subordonné(e) ▷ n subordonné(e)
subpoena [səb'pi:nə] (Law) n citation f, assignation f ▷ vt citer or assigner (à comparaître)
subscribe [səb'skraɪb] vi cotiser; **to ~ to** (opinion, fund) souscrire à; (newspaper) s'abonner à; être abonné(e) à
subscriber [səb'skraɪbəʳ] n (to periodical, telephone) abonné(e)
subscription [səb'skrɪpʃən] n (to fund) souscription f; (to magazine etc) abonnement m; (membership dues) cotisation f; **to take out a ~ to** s'abonner à
subsequent ['sʌbsɪkwənt] adj ultérieur(e), suivant(e); **~ to** prep à la suite de

subsequently ['sʌbsɪkwəntlɪ] adv par la suite
subside [səb'saɪd] vi (land) s'affaisser; (flood) baisser; (wind, feelings) tomber
subsidence [səb'saɪdns] n affaissement m
subsidiary [səb'sɪdɪərɪ] adj subsidiaire; accessoire; (Brit Scol: subject) complémentaire ▷ n filiale f
subsidize ['sʌbsɪdaɪz] vt subventionner
subsidy ['sʌbsɪdɪ] n subvention f
substance ['sʌbstəns] n substance f; (fig) essentiel m; **a man of ~** un homme jouissant d'une certaine fortune; **to lack ~** être plutôt mince (fig)
substantial [səb'stænʃl] adj substantiel(le); (fig) important(e)
substantially [səb'stænʃəlɪ] adv considérablement; en grande partie
substantiate [səb'stænʃɪeɪt] vt étayer, fournir des preuves à l'appui de
substitute ['sʌbstɪtju:t] n (person) remplaçant(e); (thing) succédané m ▷ vt: **to ~ sth/sb for** substituer qch/qn à, remplacer par qch/qn
substitution [sʌbstɪ'tju:ʃən] n substitution f
subterranean [sʌbtə'reɪnɪən] adj souterrain(e)
subtitled ['sʌbtaɪtld] adj sous-titré(e)
subtitles ['sʌbtaɪtlz] npl (Cine) sous-titres mpl
subtle ['sʌtl] adj subtil(e)
subtotal [sʌb'təutl] n total partiel
subtract [səb'trækt] vt soustraire, retrancher
subtraction [səb'trækʃən] n soustraction f
suburb ['sʌbə:b] n faubourg m; **the ~s** la banlieue
suburban [sə'bə:bən] adj de banlieue, suburbain(e)
suburbia [sə'bə:bɪə] n la banlieue
subway ['sʌbweɪ] n (Brit: underpass) passage souterrain; (US: railway) métro m
succeed [sək'si:d] vi réussir ▷ vt succéder à; **to ~ in doing** réussir à faire
succeeding [sək'si:dɪŋ] adj suivant(e), qui suit (or suivent or suivront etc)
success [sək'sɛs] n succès m; réussite f
successful [sək'sɛsful] adj qui a du succès; (candidate) choisi(e), agréé(e); (business) prospère, qui réussit; (attempt) couronné(e) de succès; **to be ~ (in doing)** réussir (à faire)
successfully [sək'sɛsfəlɪ] adv avec succès
succession [sək'sɛʃən] n succession f; **in ~** successivement; **3 years in ~** 3 ans de suite
successive [sək'sɛsɪv] adj successif(-ive); **on 3 ~ days** 3 jours de suite or consécutifs
successor [sək'sɛsəʳ] n successeur m
succumb [sə'kʌm] vi succomber
such [sʌtʃ] adj tel (telle); (of that kind): **~ a book** un livre de ce genre or pareil, un tel livre; (so much): **~ courage** un tel courage ▷ adv si; **~ books** des livres de ce genre or pareils, de tels livres; **~ a long trip** un si long voyage; **~ good books** de si bons livres; **~ a long trip that** un voyage si or tellement long que; **~ a lot of** tellement or tant de; **making ~ a noise that** faisant un tel bruit que or tellement de bruit que; **~ a long time ago** il y a si or tellement longtemps; **~ as**

(*like*) tel (telle) que, comme; **a noise ~ as to** un bruit de nature à; **~ books as I have** les quelques livres que j'ai; **as ~** (*adv*) en tant que tel (telle), à proprement parler

such-and-such ['sʌtʃənsʌtʃ] *adj* tel ou tel (telle ou telle)

suck [sʌk] *vt* sucer; (*breast, bottle*) téter; (*pump, machine*) aspirer

sucker ['sʌkər] *n* (*Bot, Zool, Tech*) ventouse *f*; (*inf*) naïf(-ïve), poire *f*

suction ['sʌkʃən] *n* succion *f*

Sudan [su'dɑːn] *n* Soudan *m*

sudden ['sʌdn] *adj* soudain(e), subit(e); **all of a ~** soudain, tout à coup

suddenly ['sʌdnlı] *adv* brusquement, tout à coup, soudain

sudoku [sʊ'dəʊkuː] *n* sudoku *m*

suds [sʌdz] *npl* eau savonneuse

sue [suː] *vt* poursuivre en justice, intenter un procès à ▷ *vi*: **to ~ (for)** intenter un procès (pour); **to ~ for divorce** engager une procédure de divorce; **to ~ sb for damages** poursuivre qn en dommages-intérêts

suede [sweɪd] *n* daim *m*, cuir suédé ▷ *cpd* de daim

suet ['suɪt] *n* graisse *f* de rognon *or* de bœuf

suffer ['sʌfər] *vt* souffrir, subir; (*bear*) tolérer, supporter, subir ▷ *vi* souffrir; **to ~ from** (*illness*) souffrir de, avoir; **to ~ from the effects of alcohol/a fall** se ressentir des effets de l'alcool/des conséquences d'une chute

sufferer ['sʌfərər] *n* malade *m/f*; victime *m/f*

suffering ['sʌfərɪŋ] *n* souffrance(s) *f(pl)*

suffice [sə'faɪs] *vi* suffire

sufficient [sə'fɪʃənt] *adj* suffisant(e); **~ money** suffisamment d'argent

sufficiently [sə'fɪʃəntlı] *adv* suffisamment, assez

suffocate ['sʌfəkeɪt] *vi* suffoquer; étouffer

sugar ['ʃʊgər] *n* sucre *m* ▷ *vt* sucrer

sugar beet *n* betterave sucrière

sugar cane *n* canne *f* à sucre

suggest [sə'dʒɛst] *vt* suggérer, proposer; (*indicate*) sembler indiquer; **what do you ~ I do?** que vous me suggérez de faire?

suggestion [sə'dʒɛstʃən] *n* suggestion *f*

suicide ['suɪsaɪd] *n* suicide *m*; **to commit ~** se suicider; **~ bombing** attentat *m* suicide; *see also* **commit**

suicide bomber *n* kamikaze *m/f*

suit [suːt] *n* (*man's*) costume *m*, complet *m*; (*woman's*) tailleur *m*, ensemble *m*; (*Cards*) couleur *f*; (*lawsuit*) procès *m* ▷ *vt* (*subj: clothes, hairstyle*) aller à; (*be convenient for*) convenir à; (*adapt*): **to ~ sth to** adapter *or* approprier qch à; **to be ~ed to sth** (*suitable for*) être adapté(e) *or* approprié(e) à qch; **well ~ed** (*couple*) faits l'un pour l'autre, très bien assortis; **to bring a ~ against sb** intenter un procès contre qn; **to follow ~** (*fig*) faire de même

suitable ['suːtəbl] *adj* qui convient; approprié(e), adéquat(e); **would tomorrow be ~?** est-ce que demain vous conviendrait?; **we found**

somebody ~ nous avons trouvé la personne qu'il nous faut

suitably ['suːtəblı] *adv* comme il se doit (*or* se devait *etc*), convenablement

suitcase ['suːtkeɪs] *n* valise *f*

suite [swiːt] *n* (*of rooms, also Mus*) suite *f*; (*furniture*): **bedroom/dining room ~** (ensemble *m* de) chambre *f* à coucher/salle *f* à manger; **a three-piece ~** un salon (canapé et deux fauteuils)

suitor ['suːtər] *n* soupirant *m*, prétendant *m*

sulfur ['sʌlfər] (*US*) *n* = **sulphur**

sulk [sʌlk] *vi* bouder

sulky ['sʌlkı] *adj* boudeur(-euse), maussade

sullen ['sʌlən] *adj* renfrogné(e), maussade; morne

sulphur, (*US*) **sulfur** ['sʌlfər] *n* soufre *m*

sultana [sʌl'tɑːnə] *n* (*fruit*) raisin (sec) de Smyrne

sultry ['sʌltrı] *adj* étouffant(e)

sum [sʌm] *n* somme *f*; (*Scol etc*) calcul *m*
▶ **sum up** *vt* résumer; (*evaluate rapidly*) récapituler ▷ *vi* résumer

summarize ['sʌməraɪz] *vt* résumer

summary ['sʌmərı] *n* résumé *m* ▷ *adj* (*justice*) sommaire

summer ['sʌmər] *n* été *m* ▷ *cpd* d'été, estival(e); **in (the) ~** en été, pendant l'été

summer holidays *npl* grandes vacances

summerhouse ['sʌməhaus] *n* (*in garden*) pavillon *m*

summertime ['sʌmətaɪm] *n* (*season*) été *m*

summer time *n* (*by clock*) heure *f* d'été

summit ['sʌmɪt] *n* sommet *m*; (*also:* **summit conference**) (conférence *f* au) sommet *m*

summon ['sʌmən] *vt* appeler, convoquer; **to ~ a witness** citer *or* assigner un témoin
▶ **summon up** *vt* rassembler, faire appel à

summons ['sʌmənz] *n* citation *f*, assignation *f*
▷ *vt* citer, assigner; **to serve a ~ on sb** remettre une assignation à qn

Sun. *abbr* (= *Sunday*) dim

sun [sʌn] *n* soleil *m*; **in the ~** au soleil; **to catch the ~** prendre le soleil; **everything under the ~** absolument tout

sunbathe ['sʌnbeɪð] *vi* prendre un bain de soleil

sunbed ['sʌnbed] *n* lit pliant; (*with sun lamp*) lit à ultra-violets

sunblock ['sʌnblɔk] *n* écran *m* total

sunburn ['sʌnbəːn] *n* coup *m* de soleil

sunburned ['sʌnbəːnd], **sunburnt** ['sʌnbəːnt] *adj* bronzé(e), hâlé(e); (*painfully*) brûlé(e) par le soleil

Sunday ['sʌndı] *n* dimanche *m*; *for phrases see also* **Tuesday**

Sunday school *n* ≈ catéchisme *m*

sundial ['sʌndaɪəl] *n* cadran *m* solaire

sundown ['sʌndaun] *n* coucher *m* du soleil

sundries ['sʌndrɪz] *npl* articles divers

sundry ['sʌndrı] *adj* divers(e), différent(e); **all and ~** tout le monde, n'importe qui

sunflower ['sʌnflauər] *n* tournesol *m*

sung [sʌŋ] *pp of* **sing**

sunglasses ['sʌnglɑːsɪz] *npl* lunettes *fpl* de soleil

sunk [sʌŋk] *pp of* **sink**

sunlight ['sʌnlaɪt] *n* (lumière *f* du) soleil *m*

sunlit ['sʌnlɪt] *adj* ensoleillé(e)

sun lounger *n* chaise longue

sunny ['sʌnɪ] *adj* ensoleillé(e); *(fig)* épanoui(e), radieux(-euse); **it is ~** il fait (du) soleil, il y a du soleil

sunrise ['sʌnraɪz] *n* lever *m* du soleil

sun roof *n* (Aut) toit ouvrant

sunscreen ['sʌnskriːn] *n* crème *f* solaire

sunset ['sʌnsɛt] *n* coucher *m* du soleil

sunshade ['sʌnʃeɪd] *n* (lady's) ombrelle *f*; (over table) parasol *m*

sunshine ['sʌnʃaɪn] *n* (lumière *f* du) soleil *m*

sunstroke ['sʌnstrəʊk] *n* insolation *f*, coup *m* de soleil

suntan ['sʌntæn] *n* bronzage *m*

suntan lotion *n* lotion *f* or lait *m* solaire

suntan oil *n* huile *f* solaire

super ['suːpə'] *adj* (inf) formidable

superannuation [suːpərænjuˈeɪʃən] *n* cotisations *fpl* pour la pension

superb [suːˈpəːb] *adj* superbe, magnifique

supercilious [suːpəˈsɪlɪəs] *adj* hautain(e), dédaigneux(-euse)

superficial [suːpəˈfɪʃəl] *adj* superficiel(le)

superimpose ['suːpərɪmˈpəʊz] *vt* superposer

superintendent [suːpərɪnˈtɛndənt] *n* directeur(-trice); (Police) ≈ commissaire *m*

superior [suˈpɪərɪə'] *adj* supérieur(e); *(Comm: goods, quality)* de qualité supérieure; *(smug)* condescendant(e), méprisant(e) ▷ *n* supérieur(e); **Mother S~** (Rel) Mère supérieure

superiority [supɪərɪˈɒrɪtɪ] *n* supériorité *f*

superlative [suˈpəːlətɪv] *adj* sans pareil(le), suprême ▷ *n* (Ling) superlatif *m*

superman ['suːpəmæn] *(irreg)* *n* surhomme *m*

supermarket ['suːpəmɑːkɪt] *n* supermarché *m*

supernatural [suːpəˈnætʃərəl] *adj* surnaturel(le) ▷ *n*: **the ~** le surnaturel

superpower ['suːpəpaʊə'] *n* (Pol) superpuissance *f*

supersede [suːpəˈsiːd] *vt* remplacer, supplanter

superstition [suːpəˈstɪʃən] *n* superstition *f*

superstitious [suːpəˈstɪʃəs] *adj* superstitieux(-euse)

superstore ['suːpəstɔː'] *n* (Brit) hypermarché *m*, grande surface

supervise ['suːpəvaɪz] *vt* (children etc) surveiller; *(organization, work)* diriger

supervision [suːpəˈvɪʒən] *n* surveillance *f*; *(monitoring)* contrôle *m*; *(management)* direction *f*; **under medical ~** sous contrôle du médecin

supervisor ['suːpəvaɪzə'] *n* surveillant(e); (in shop) chef *m* de rayon; (Scol) directeur(-trice) de thèse

supper ['sʌpə'] *n* dîner *m*; *(late)* souper *m*; **to have ~** dîner; souper

supple ['sʌpl] *adj* souple

supplement *n* ['sʌplɪmənt] supplément *m* ▷ *vt* [sʌplɪˈmɛnt] ajouter à, compléter

supplementary [sʌplɪˈmɛntərɪ] *adj* supplémentaire

supplementary benefit *n* (Brit) allocation *f* supplémentaire d'aide sociale

supplier [səˈplaɪə'] *n* fournisseur *m*

supply [səˈplaɪ] *vt* *(provide)* fournir; *(equip)*: **to ~ (with)** approvisionner *or* ravitailler (en); fournir (en); *(system, machine)*: **to ~ sth (with sth)** alimenter qch (en qch); *(a need)* répondre à ▷ *n* provision *f*, réserve *f*; *(supplying)* approvisionnement *m*; (Tech) alimentation *f*; **supplies** *npl* *(food)* vivres *mpl*; (Mil) subsistances *fpl*; **office supplies** fournitures *fpl* de bureau; **to be in short ~** être rare, manquer; **the electricity/water/gas ~** l'alimentation *f* en électricité/eau/gaz; **~ and demand** l'offre *f* et la demande; **it comes supplied with an adaptor** il (*or* elle) est pourvu(e) d'un adaptateur

supply teacher *n* (Brit) suppléant(e)

support [səˈpɔːt] *n* (moral, financial etc) soutien *m*, appui *m*; (Tech) support *m*, soutien ▷ *vt* soutenir, supporter; *(financially)* subvenir aux besoins de; *(uphold)* être pour, être partisan de, appuyer; *(Sport: team)* être pour; **to ~ o.s.** *(financially)* gagner sa vie

supporter [səˈpɔːtə'] *n* (Pol etc) partisan(e); *(Sport)* supporter *m*

suppose [səˈpəʊz] *vt*, *vi* supposer; imaginer; **to be ~d to do/be** être censé(e) faire/être; **I don't ~ she'll come** je suppose qu'elle ne viendra pas, cela m'étonnerait qu'elle vienne

supposedly [səˈpəʊzɪdlɪ] *adv* soi-disant

supposing [səˈpəʊzɪŋ] *conj* si, à supposer que + *sub*

suppress [səˈprɛs] *vt* (revolt, feeling) réprimer; *(information)* faire disparaître; *(scandal, yawn)* étouffer

supreme [suˈpriːm] *adj* suprême

surcharge ['səːtʃɑːdʒ] *n* surcharge *f*; (extra tax) surtaxe *f*

sure [ʃuə'] *adj* (gen) sûr(e); *(definite, convinced)* sûr, certain(e) ▷ *adv* (inf: US): **that ~ is pretty, that's ~ pretty** c'est drôlement joli(e); **~!** *(of course)* bien sûr!; **~ enough** effectivement; **I'm not ~ how/ why/when** je ne sais pas très bien comment/ pourquoi/quand; **to be ~ of o.s.** être sûr de soi; **to make ~ of sth/that** s'assurer de qch/que, vérifier qch/que

surely ['ʃuəlɪ] *adv* sûrement; certainement; **~ you don't mean that!** vous ne parlez pas sérieusement!

surf [səːf] *n* (waves) ressac *m* ▷ *vt*: **to ~ the Net** surfer sur Internet, surfer sur le net

surface ['səːfɪs] *n* surface *f* ▷ *vt* (road) poser un revêtement sur ▷ *vi* remonter à la surface; *(fig)* faire surface; **on the ~** (fig) au premier abord; **by ~ mail** par voie de terre; *(by sea)* par voie maritime

surface mail *n* courrier *m* par voie de terre (*or* maritime)

surfboard ['səːfbɔːd] *n* planche *f* de surf

surfeit ['səːfɪt] *n*: **a ~ of** un excès de; une indigestion de

surfer ['sə:fə^r] n (in sea) surfeur(-euse); **web** or **net** ~ internaute m/f

surfing ['sə:fɪŋ] n surf m

surge [sə:dʒ] n (of emotion) vague f; (Elec) pointe f de courant ▷ vi déferler; **to ~ forward** se précipiter (en avant)

surgeon ['sə:dʒən] n chirurgien m

surgery ['sə:dʒərɪ] n chirurgie f; (Brit: room) cabinet m (de consultation); (also: **surgery hours**) heures fpl de consultation; (of MP etc) permanence f (où le député etc reçoit les électeurs etc); **to undergo ~** être opéré(e)

surgical ['sə:dʒɪkl] adj chirurgical(e)

surgical spirit n (Brit) alcool m à 90°

surname ['sə:neɪm] n nom m de famille

surpass [sə:'pɑ:s] vt surpasser, dépasser

surplus ['sə:pləs] n surplus m, excédent m ▷ adj en surplus, de trop; (Comm) excédentaire; **it is ~ to our requirements** cela dépasse nos besoins; **~ stock** surplus m

surprise [sə'praɪz] n (gen) surprise f; (astonishment) étonnement m ▷ vt surprendre, étonner; **to take by ~** (person) prendre au dépourvu; (Mil: town, fort) prendre par surprise

surprised [sə'praɪzd] adj (look, smile) surpris(e), étonné(e); **to be ~** être surpris

surprising [sə'praɪzɪŋ] adj surprenant(e), étonnant(e)

surprisingly [sə'praɪzɪŋlɪ] adv (easy, helpful) étonnamment, étrangement; **(somewhat) ~, he agreed** curieusement, il a accepté

surrender [sə'rɛndə^r] n reddition f, capitulation f ▷ vi se rendre, capituler ▷ vt (claim, right) renoncer à

surreptitious [sʌrəp'tɪʃəs] adj subreptice, furtif(-ive)

surrogate ['sʌrəgɪt] n (Brit: substitute) substitut m ▷ adj de substitution, de remplacement; **a food ~** un succédané alimentaire; **~ coffee** ersatz m or succédané m de café

surrogate mother n mère porteuse or de substitution

surround [sə'raund] vt entourer; (Mil etc) encercler

surrounding [sə'raundɪŋ] adj environnant(e)

surroundings [sə'raundɪŋz] npl environs mpl, alentours mpl

surveillance [sə:'veɪləns] n surveillance f

survey n ['sə:veɪ] enquête f, étude f; (in house buying etc) inspection f, (rapport m d')expertise f; (of land) levé m; (comprehensive view: of situation etc) vue f d'ensemble ▷ vt [sə:'veɪ] (situation) passer en revue; (examine carefully) inspecter; (building) expertiser; (land) faire le levé de; (look at) embrasser du regard

surveyor [sə'veɪə^r] n (of building) expert m; (of land) (arpenteur m) géomètre m

survival [sə'vaɪvl] n survie f; (relic) vestige m ▷ cpd (course, kit) de survie

survive [sə'vaɪv] vi survivre; (custom etc) subsister ▷ vt (accident etc) survivre à, réchapper de; (person) survivre à

survivor [sə'vaɪvə^r] n survivant(e)

susceptible [sə'sɛptəbl] adj: ~ **(to)** sensible (à); (disease) prédisposé(e) (à)

suspect adj, n ['sʌspɛkt] suspect(e) ▷ vt [səs'pɛkt] soupçonner, suspecter

suspend [səs'pɛnd] vt suspendre

suspended sentence [səs'pɛndɪd-] n (Law) condamnation f avec sursis

suspender belt [səs'pɛndə-] n (Brit) porte-jarretelles m inv

suspenders [səs'pɛndəz] npl (Brit) jarretelles fpl; (US) bretelles fpl

suspense [səs'pɛns] n attente f, incertitude f; (in film etc) suspense m; **to keep sb in ~** tenir qn en suspens, laisser qn dans l'incertitude

suspension [səs'pɛnʃən] n (gen, Aut) suspension f; (of driving licence) retrait m provisoire

suspension bridge n pont suspendu

suspicion [səs'pɪʃən] n soupçon(s) m(pl); **to be under ~** être considéré(e) comme suspect(e), être suspecté(e); **arrested on ~ of murder** arrêté sur présomption de meurtre

suspicious [səs'pɪʃəs] adj (suspecting) soupçonneux(-euse), méfiant(e); (causing suspicion) suspect(e); **to be ~ of** or **about sb/sth** avoir des doutes à propos de qn/sur qch, trouver qn/qch suspect(e)

sustain [səs'teɪn] vt soutenir; supporter; corroborer; (subj: food) nourrir, donner des forces à; (damage) subir; (injury) recevoir

sustainable [səs'teɪnəbl] adj (rate, growth) qui peut être maintenu(e); (development) durable

sustained [səs'teɪnd] adj (effort) soutenu(e), prolongé(e)

sustenance ['sʌstɪnəns] n nourriture f; moyens mpl de subsistance

SUV n abbr (esp US: = sports utility vehicle) SUV m, véhicule m de loisirs

swab [swɔb] n (Med) tampon m; prélèvement m ▷ vt (Naut: also: **swab down**) nettoyer

swagger ['swægə^r] vi plastronner, parader

swallow ['swɔləu] n (bird) hirondelle f; (of food etc) gorgée f ▷ vt avaler; (fig: story) gober
▶ **swallow up** vt engloutir

swam [swæm] pt of **swim**

swamp [swɔmp] n marais m, marécage m ▷ vt submerger

swan [swɔn] n cygne m

swap [swɔp] n échange m, troc m ▷ vt: **to ~ (for)** échanger (contre), troquer (contre)

swarm [swɔ:m] n essaim m ▷ vi (bees) essaimer; (people) grouiller; **to be ~ing with** grouiller de

swastika ['swɔstɪkə] n croix gammée

swat [swɔt] vt écraser ▷ n (Brit: also: **fly swat**) tapette f

sway [sweɪ] vi se balancer, osciller; tanguer ▷ vt (influence) influencer ▷ n (rule, power): ~ **(over)** emprise f (sur); **to hold ~ over sb** avoir de l'emprise sur qn

swear [swɛə^r] (pt **swore**, pp **sworn**) [swɔ:^r, swɔ:n] vt, vi jurer; **to ~ to sth** jurer de qch; **to ~ an oath** prêter serment

▶ **swear in** vt assermenter

swearword ['swεəwəːd] n gros mot, juron m

sweat [swεt] n sueur f, transpiration f ▷ vi suer;
in a ~ en sueur

sweater ['swεtəʳ] n tricot m, pull m

sweatshirt ['swεtʃəːt] n sweat-shirt m

sweaty ['swεtɪ] adj en sueur, moite or mouillé(e)
de sueur

Swede [swiːd] n Suédois(e)

swede [swiːd] n (Brit) rutabaga m

Sweden ['swiːdn] n Suède f

Swedish ['swiːdɪʃ] adj suédois(e) ▷ n (Ling)
suédois m

sweep [swiːp] (pt, pp **swept**) [swεpt] n coup m de
balai; (curve) grande courbe; (range) champ m;
(also: **chimney sweep**) ramoneur m ▷ vt balayer;
(subj: current) emporter; (subj: fashion, craze) se
répandre dans ▷ vi avancer majestueusement or
rapidement; s'élancer; s'étendre
▶ **sweep away** vt balayer; entraîner; emporter
▶ **sweep past** vi passer majestueusement or
rapidement
▶ **sweep up** vt, vi balayer

sweeping ['swiːpɪŋ] adj (gesture) large; circulaire;
(changes, reforms) radical(e); **a ~ statement** une
généralisation hâtive

sweet [swiːt] n (Brit: pudding) dessert m; (candy)
bonbon m ▷ adj doux (douce); (not savoury)
sucré(e); (fresh) frais (fraîche), pur(e); (kind)
gentil(le); (baby) mignon(ne) ▷ adv: **to smell ~**
sentir bon; **to taste ~** avoir un goût sucré; **~ and
sour** adj aigre-doux (douce)

sweetcorn ['swiːtkɔːn] n maïs doux

sweeten ['swiːtn] vt sucrer; (fig) adoucir

sweetener ['swiːtnəʳ] n (Culin) édulcorant m

sweetheart ['swiːthɑːt] n amoureux(-euse)

sweetness ['swiːtnɪs] n douceur f; (of taste) goût
sucré

sweet pea n pois m de senteur

sweetshop ['swiːtʃɔp] n (Brit) confiserie f

swell [swεl] (pt **-ed**, pp **swollen** or **-ed**) ['swəulən]
n (of sea) houle f ▷ adj (US: inf: excellent) chouette
▷ vt (increase) grossir, augmenter ▷ vi (increase)
grossir, augmenter; (sound) s'enfler; (Med: also:
swell up) enfler

swelling ['swεlɪŋ] n (Med) enflure f; (: lump)
grosseur f

sweltering ['swεltərɪŋ] adj étouffant(e),
oppressant(e)

swept [swεpt] pt, pp of **sweep**

swerve [swəːv] vi (to avoid obstacle) faire une
embardée or un écart; (off the road) dévier

swift [swɪft] n (bird) martinet m ▷ adj rapide,
prompt(e)

swig [swɪg] n (inf: drink) lampée f

swill [swɪl] n pâtée f ▷ vt (also: **swill out, swill
down**) laver à grande eau

swim [swɪm] (pt **swam**, pp **swum**) [swæm, swʌm]
n: **to go for a ~** aller nager or se baigner ▷ vi
nager; (Sport) faire de la natation; (fig: head, room)
tourner ▷ vt traverser (à la nage); (distance) faire
(à la nage); **to ~ a length** nager une longueur;

to go ~ming aller nager

swimmer ['swɪməʳ] n nageur(-euse)

swimming ['swɪmɪŋ] n nage f, natation f

swimming cap n bonnet m de bain

swimming costume n (Brit) maillot m (de bain)

swimming pool n piscine f

swimming trunks npl maillot m de bain

swimsuit ['swɪmsuːt] n maillot m (de bain)

swindle ['swɪndl] n escroquerie f ▷ vt escroquer

swine [swaɪn] n (pl inv) pourceau m, porc m; (inf!)
salaud m (!)

swing [swɪŋ] (pt, pp **swung**) [swʌŋ] n (in
playground) balançoire f; (movement) balancement
m, oscillations fpl; (change in opinion etc)
revirement m; (Mus) swing m; rythme m ▷ vt
balancer, faire osciller; (also: **swing round**)
tourner, faire virer ▷ vi se balancer, osciller;
(also: **swing round**) virer, tourner; **a ~ to the left**
(Pol) un revirement en faveur de la gauche; **to
be in full ~** battre son plein; **to get into the ~
of things** se mettre dans le bain; **the road ~s
south** la route prend la direction sud

swing bridge n pont tournant

swing door n (Brit) porte battante

swingeing ['swɪndʒɪŋ] adj (Brit) écrasant(e);
considérable

swipe [swaɪp] n grand coup; gifle f ▷ vt (hit)
frapper à toute volée; gifler; (inf: steal) piquer;
(credit card etc) faire passer (dans la machine)

swipe card n carte f magnétique

swirl [swəːl] n tourbillon m ▷ vi tourbillonner,
tournoyer

Swiss [swɪs] adj suisse ▷ n (pl inv) Suisse(-esse)

switch [swɪtʃ] n (for light, radio etc) bouton m;
(change) changement m, revirement m ▷ vt
(change) changer; (exchange) intervertir; (invert):
to ~ (round or **over)** changer de place
▶ **switch off** vt éteindre; (engine, machine) arrêter;
could you ~ off the light? pouvez-vous éteindre
la lumière?
▶ **switch on** vt allumer; (engine, machine) mettre
en marche; (Brit: water supply) ouvrir

switchboard ['swɪtʃbɔːd] n (Tel) standard m

Switzerland ['swɪtsələnd] n Suisse f

swivel ['swɪvl] vi (also: **swivel round**) pivoter,
tourner

swollen ['swəulən] pp of **swell** ▷ adj (ankle etc)
enflé(e)

swoon [swuːn] vi se pâmer

swoop [swuːp] n (by police etc) rafle f, descente
f; (of bird etc) descente f en piqué ▷ vi (bird: also:
swoop down) descendre en piqué, piquer

swop [swɔp] n, vt = **swap**

sword [sɔːd] n épée f

swordfish ['sɔːdfɪʃ] n espadon m

swore [swɔːʳ] pt of **swear**

sworn [swɔːn] pp of **swear** ▷ adj (statement,
evidence) donné(e) sous serment; (enemy) juré(e)

swot [swɔt] vt, vi bûcher, potasser

swum [swʌm] pp of **swim**

swung [swʌŋ] pt, pp of **swing**

syllable ['sɪləbl] n syllabe f

syllabus ['sɪləbəs] n programme m; **on the ~** au programme
symbol ['sɪmbl] n symbole m
symbolic [sɪm'bɔlɪk], **symbolical** [sɪm'bɔlɪkl] adj symbolique
symmetrical [sɪ'metrɪkl] adj symétrique
symmetry ['sɪmɪtrɪ] n symétrie f
sympathetic [sɪmpə'θetɪk] adj (showing pity) compatissant(e); (understanding) bienveillant(e), compréhensif(-ive); **~ towards** bien disposé(e) envers
sympathize ['sɪmpəθaɪz] vi: **to ~ with sb** plaindre qn; (in grief) s'associer à la douleur de qn; **to ~ with sth** comprendre qch
sympathizer ['sɪmpəθaɪzə'] n (Pol) sympathisant(e)
sympathy ['sɪmpəθɪ] n (pity) compassion f; **sympathies** npl (support) soutien m; **in ~ with** en accord avec; (strike) en or par solidarité avec; **with our deepest ~** en vous priant d'accepter nos sincères condoléances
symphony ['sɪmfənɪ] n symphonie f

symptom ['sɪmptəm] n symptôme m; indice m
synagogue ['sɪnəgɔg] n synagogue f
syndicate ['sɪndɪkɪt] n syndicat m, coopérative f; (Press) agence f de presse
syndrome ['sɪndrəum] n syndrome m
synonym ['sɪnənɪm] n synonyme m
synopsis (pl **synopses**) [sɪ'nɔpsɪs, -siːz] n résumé m, synopsis m or f
synthetic [sɪn'θetɪk] adj synthétique ▷ n matière f synthétique; **synthetics** npl textiles artificiels
syphon ['saɪfən] n, vb = **siphon**
Syria ['sɪrɪə] n Syrie f
syringe [sɪ'rɪndʒ] n seringue f
syrup ['sɪrəp] n sirop m; (Brit: also: **golden syrup**) mélasse raffinée
system ['sɪstəm] n système m; (order) méthode f; (Anat) organisme m
systematic [sɪstə'mætɪk] adj systématique; méthodique
system disk n (Comput) disque m système
systems analyst n analyste-programmeur m/f

Tt

ta [tɑ:] *excl* (*Brit inf*) merci!

tab [tæb] *n abbr* = **tabulator** ▷ *n* (*loop on coat etc*) attache *f*; (*label*) étiquette *f*; (*on drinks can etc*) languette *f*; **to keep ~s on** (*fig*) surveiller

tabby ['tæbɪ] *n* (*also:* **tabby cat**) chat(te) tigré(e)

table ['teɪbl] *n* table *f* ▷ *vt* (*Brit: motion etc*) présenter; **to lay** *or* **set the ~** mettre le couvert *or* la table; **to clear the ~** débarrasser la table; **~ league** ~ (*Brit Football, Rugby*) classement *m* (du championnat); **~ of contents** table des matières

tablecloth ['teɪblklɔθ] *n* nappe *f*

table d'hôte [tɑ:bl'dəut] *adj* (*meal*) à prix fixe

table lamp *n* lampe décorative *or* de table

tablemat ['teɪblmæt] *n* (*for plate*) napperon *m*, set *m*; (*for hot dish*) dessous-de-plat *m inv*

tablespoon ['teɪblspu:n] *n* cuiller *f* de service; (*also:* **tablespoonful:** *as measurement*) cuillerée *f* à soupe

tablet ['tæblɪt] *n* (*Med*) comprimé *m*; (: *for sucking*) pastille *f*; (*of stone*) plaque *f*; **~ of soap** (*Brit*) savonnette *f*

table tennis *n* ping-pong *m*, tennis *m* de table

table wine *n* vin *m* de table

tabloid ['tæblɔɪd] *n* (*newspaper*) quotidien *m* populaire; *voir article*

taboo [tə'bu:] *adj, n* tabou (*m*)

tack [tæk] *n* (*nail*) petit clou; (*stitch*) point *m* de bâti; (*Naut*) bord *m*, bordée *f*; (*fig*) direction *f* ▷ *vt* (*nail*) clouer; (*sew*) bâtir ▷ *vi* (*Naut*) tirer un *or* des bord(s); **to change ~** virer de bord; **on the wrong ~** (*fig*) sur la mauvaise voie; **to ~ sth on to (the end of) sth** (*of letter, book*) rajouter qch à la fin de qch

tackle ['tækl] *n* matériel *m*, équipement *m*; (*for lifting*) appareil *m* de levage; (*Football, Rugby*) plaquage *m* ▷ *vt* (*difficulty, animal, burglar*) s'attaquer à; (*person: challenge*) s'expliquer avec; (*Football, Rugby*) plaquer

tacky ['tækɪ] *adj* collant(e); (*paint*) pas sec (sèche); (*inf: shabby*) moche; (*pej: poor-quality*) minable; (: *showing bad taste*) ringard(e)

tact [tækt] *n* tact *m*

tactful ['tæktful] *adj* plein(e) de tact

tactical ['tæktɪkl] *adj* tactique; **~ error** erreur *f* de tactique

tactics ['tæktɪks] *n, npl* tactique *f*

tactless ['tæktlɪs] *adj* qui manque de tact

tadpole ['tædpəul] *n* têtard *m*

taffy ['tæfɪ] *n* (*US*) (bonbon *m* au) caramel *m*

tag [tæg] *n* étiquette *f*; **price/name ~** étiquette (portant le prix/le nom)
  ▶ **tag along** *vi* suivre

tail [teɪl] *n* queue *f*; (*of shirt*) pan *m* ▷ *vt* (*follow*) suivre, filer; **tails** *npl* (*suit*) habit *m*; **to turn ~** se sauver à toutes jambes; *see also* **head**
  ▶ **tail away**
  ▶ **tail off** *vi* (*in size, quality etc*) baisser peu à peu

tailback ['teɪlbæk] *n* (*Brit*) bouchon *m*

tail end *n* bout *m*, fin *f*

tailgate ['teɪlgeɪt] *n* (*Aut*) hayon *m* arrière

tailor ['teɪlə*r*] *n* tailleur *m* (*artisan*) ▷ *vt*: **to ~ sth (to)** adapter qch exactement (à); **~'s (shop)** (boutique *f* de) tailleur *m*

tailoring ['teɪlərɪŋ] *n* (*cut*) coupe *f*

tailor-made ['teɪlə'meɪd] *adj* fait(e) sur mesure; (*fig*) conçu(e) spécialement

tailwind ['teɪlwɪnd] *n* vent *m* arrière *inv*

tainted ['teɪntɪd] *adj* (*food*) gâté(e); (*water, air*) infecté(e); (*fig*) souillé(e)

Taiwan ['taɪ'wɑ:n] *n* Taïwan (*no article*)

Taiwanese [taɪwə'ni:z] *adj* taïwanais(e) ▷ *n inv* Taïwanais(e)

take [teɪk] (*pt* **took**, *pp* **~n**) [tuk, 'teɪkn] *vt* prendre; (*gain: prize*) remporter; (*require: effort, courage*) demander; (*tolerate*) accepter, supporter; (*hold: passengers etc*) contenir; (*accompany*) emmener, accompagner; (*bring, carry*) apporter, emporter; (*exam*) passer, se présenter à; (*conduct: meeting*) présider ▷ *vi* (*dye, fire etc*) prendre ▷ *n* (*Cine*) prise *f* de vues; **to ~ sth from** (*drawer etc*) prendre qch dans; (*person*) prendre qch à; **I ~ it that** je suppose que; **I took him for a doctor** je l'ai pris pour un docteur; **to ~ sb's hand** prendre qn par la main; **to ~ for a walk** (*child, dog*) emmener promener; **to be ~n ill** tomber malade; **to ~ it upon o.s. to do sth** prendre sur soi de faire qch; **~ the first (street) on the left** prenez la première à gauche; **it won't ~ long** ça ne prendra pas longtemps; **I was quite ~n with her/it** elle/cela m'a beaucoup plu
  ▶ **take after** *vt fus* ressembler à
  ▶ **take apart** *vt* démonter
  ▶ **take away** *vt* (*carry off*) emporter; (*remove*) enlever; (*subtract*) soustraire ▷ *vi*: **to ~ away**

▶ **take back** vt (return) rendre, rapporter; (one's words) retirer

▶ **take down** vt (building) démolir; (dismantle: scaffolding) démonter; (letter etc) prendre, écrire

▶ **take in** vt (deceive) tromper, rouler; (understand) comprendre, saisir; (include) couvrir, inclure; (lodger) prendre; (orphan, stray dog) recueillir; (dress, waistband) reprendre

▶ **take off** vi (Aviat) décoller ▷ vt (remove) enlever; (imitate) imiter, pasticher

▶ **take on** vt (work) accepter, se charger de; (employee) prendre, embaucher; (opponent) accepter de se battre contre

▶ **take out** vt sortir; (remove) enlever; (invite) sortir avec; (licence) prendre, se procurer; **to ~ sth out of** enlever qch de; (out of drawer etc) prendre qch dans; **don't ~ it out on me!** ne t'en prends pas à moi!; **to ~ sb out to a restaurant** emmener qn au restaurant

▶ **take over** vt (business) reprendre ▷ vi: **to ~ over from sb** prendre la relève de qn

▶ **take to** vt fus (person) se prendre d'amitié pour; (activity) prendre goût à; **to ~ to doing sth** prendre l'habitude de faire qch

▶ **take up** vt (one's story) reprendre; (dress) raccourcir; (occupy: time, space) prendre, occuper; (engage in: hobby etc) se mettre à; (accept: offer, challenge) accepter; (absorb: liquids) absorber ▷ vi: **to ~ up with sb** se lier d'amitié avec qn

takeaway ['teɪkəweɪ] (Brit) adj (food) à emporter ▷ n (shop, restaurant) ≈ magasin m qui vend des plats à emporter

taken ['teɪkən] pp of **take**

takeoff ['teɪkɔf] n (Aviat) décollage m

takeout ['teɪkaut] adj, n (US) = **takeaway**

takeover ['teɪkəuvər] n (Comm) rachat m

takings ['teɪkɪŋz] npl (Comm) recette f

talc [tælk] n (also: **talcum powder**) talc m

tale [teɪl] n (story) conte m, histoire f; (account) récit m; (pej) histoire; **to tell ~s** (fig) rapporter

talent ['tælnt] n talent m, don m

talented ['tæləntɪd] adj doué(e), plein(e) de talent

talk [tɔːk] n (a speech) causerie f, exposé m; (conversation) discussion f; (interview) entretien m, propos mpl; (gossip) racontars mpl (pej) ▷ vi parler; (chatter) bavarder; **talks** npl (Pol etc) entretiens mpl; conférence f; **to give a ~** faire un exposé; **to ~ about** parler de; (converse) s'entretenir or parler de; **~ing of films, have you seen ...?** à propos de films, as-tu vu ...?; **to ~ sb out of/into doing** persuader qn de ne pas faire/de faire; **to ~ shop** parler métier or affaires

▶ **talk over** vt discuter (de)

talkative ['tɔːkətɪv] adj bavard(e)

talk show n (TV, Radio) émission-débat f

tall [tɔːl] adj (person) grand(e); (building, tree) haut(e); **to be 6 feet ~** ≈ mesurer 1 mètre 80; **how ~ are you?** combien mesurez-vous?

tall story n histoire f invraisemblable

tally ['tælɪ] n compte m ▷ vi: **to ~ (with)**

correspondre (à); **to keep a ~ of sth** tenir le compte de qch

talon ['tælən] n griffe f; (of eagle) serre f

tambourine [tæmbə'riːn] n tambourin m

tame [teɪm] adj apprivoisé(e); (fig: story, style) insipide

tamper ['tæmpər] vi: **to ~ with** toucher à (en cachette ou sans permission)

tampon ['tæmpən] n tampon m hygiénique or périodique

tan [tæn] n (also: **suntan**) bronzage m ▷ vt, vi bronzer, brunir ▷ adj (colour) marron clair inv; **to get a ~** bronzer

tandem ['tændəm] n tandem m

tang [tæŋ] n odeur (or saveur) piquante

tangent ['tændʒənt] n (Math) tangente f; **to go off at a ~** (fig) partir dans une digression

tangerine [tændʒə'riːn] n mandarine f

tangle ['tæŋgl] n enchevêtrement m ▷ vt enchevêtrer; **to get in(to) a ~** s'emmêler

tank [tæŋk] n réservoir m; (for processing) cuve f; (for fish) aquarium m; (Mil) char m d'assaut, tank m

tanker ['tæŋkər] n (ship) pétrolier m, tanker m; (truck) camion-citerne m; (Rail) wagon-citerne m

tanned [tænd] adj bronzé(e)

tantalizing ['tæntəlaɪzɪŋ] adj (smell) extrêmement appétissant(e); (offer) terriblement tentant(e)

tantamount ['tæntəmaunt] adj: **~ to** qui équivaut à

tantrum ['tæntrəm] n accès m de colère; **to throw a ~** piquer une colère

Tanzania [tænzə'nɪə] n Tanzanie f

tap [tæp] n (on sink etc) robinet m; (gentle blow) petite tape ▷ vt frapper or taper légèrement; (resources) exploiter, utiliser; (telephone) mettre sur écoute; **on ~** (beer) en tonneau; (fig: resources) disponible

tap dancing ['tæpdɑːnsɪŋ] n claquettes fpl

tape [teɪp] n (for tying) ruban m; (also: **magnetic tape**) bande f (magnétique); (cassette) cassette f; (sticky) Scotch® ▷ vt (record) enregistrer (au magnétoscope or sur cassette); (stick) coller avec du Scotch®; **on ~** (song etc) enregistré(e)

tape deck n platine f d'enregistrement

tape measure n mètre m à ruban

taper ['teɪpər] n cierge m ▷ vi s'effiler

tape recorder n magnétophone m

tapestry ['tæpɪstrɪ] n tapisserie f

tar [tɑː] n goudron m; **low-/middle-~ cigarettes** cigarettes fpl à faible/moyenne teneur en goudron

target ['tɑːgɪt] n cible f; (fig: objective) objectif m; **to be on ~** (project) progresser comme prévu

tariff ['tærɪf] n (Comm) tarif m; (taxes) tarif douanier

tarmac ['tɑːmæk] n (Brit: on road) macadam m; (Aviat) aire f d'envol ▷ vt (Brit) goudronner

tarnish ['tɑːnɪʃ] vt ternir

tarpaulin [tɑː'pɔːlɪn] n bâche goudronnée

tarragon ['tærəgən] n estragon m

art [tɑːt] n (Culin) tarte f; (Brit inf: pej: prostitute) poule f ▷ adj (flavour) âpre, aigrelet(te)
▶ **tart up** vt (inf): **to ~ o.s. up** se faire beau (belle); (: pej) s'attifer

artan ['tɑːtn] n tartan m ▷ adj écossais(e)

artar ['tɑːtə^r] n (on teeth) tartre m

artar sauce, tartare sauce n sauce f tartare

ask [tɑːsk] n tâche f; **to take to ~** prendre à partie

ask force n (Mil, Police) détachement spécial

assel ['tæsl] n gland m; pompon m

aste [teɪst] n goût m; (fig: glimpse, idea) idée f, aperçu m ▷ vt goûter ▷ vi: **to ~ of** (fish etc) avoir le or un goût de; **it ~s like fish** ça a un or le goût de poisson, on dirait du poisson; **what does it ~ like?** quel goût ça a?; **you can ~ the garlic (in it)** on sent bien l'ail; **to have a ~ of sth** goûter (à) qch; **can I have a ~?** je peux goûter?; **to have a ~ for sth** aimer qch, avoir un penchant pour qch; **to be in good/bad** or **poor ~** être de bon/mauvais goût

asteful ['teɪstful] adj de bon goût

asteless ['teɪstlɪs] adj (food) insipide; (remark) de mauvais goût

asty ['teɪstɪ] adj savoureux(-euse), délicieux(-euse)

atters ['tætəz] npl: **in ~** (also: **tattered**) en lambeaux

attoo [tə'tuː] n tatouage m; (spectacle) parade f militaire ▷ vt tatouer

atty ['tætɪ] adj (Brit inf) défraîchi(e), en piteux état

aught [tɔːt] pt, pp of **teach**

aunt [tɔːnt] n raillerie f ▷ vt railler

aurus ['tɔːrəs] n le Taureau; **to be ~** être du Taureau

aut [tɔːt] adj tendu(e)

ax [tæks] n (on goods etc) taxe f; (on income) impôts mpl, contributions fpl ▷ vt taxer; imposer; (fig: patience etc) mettre à l'épreuve; **before/after ~** avant/après l'impôt; **free of ~** exonéré(e) d'impôt

axable ['tæksəbl] adj (income) imposable

axation [tæk'seɪʃən] n taxation f; impôts mpl, contributions fpl; **system of ~** système fiscal

ax avoidance n évasion fiscale

ax disc n (Brit Aut) vignette f (automobile)

ax evasion n fraude fiscale

ax-free ['tæksfriː] adj exempt(e) d'impôts

axi ['tæksɪ] n taxi m ▷ vi (Aviat) rouler (lentement) au sol

axi driver n chauffeur m de taxi

axi rank, (Brit) **taxi stand** n station f de taxis

ax payer [-peɪə^r] n contribuable m/f

ax relief n dégrèvement or allègement fiscal, réduction f d'impôt

ax return n déclaration f d'impôts or de revenus

⊕B n abbr = **tuberculosis**

bc abbr = **to be confirmed**

ea [tiː] n thé m; (Brit: snack: for children) goûter m; **high ~** (Brit) collation combinant goûter et dîner

ea bag n sachet m de thé

---

tea break n (Brit) pause-thé f

teach (pt, pp **taught**) [tiːtʃ, tɔːt] vt: **to ~ sb sth, to ~ sth to sb** apprendre qch à qn; (in school etc) enseigner qch à qn ▷ vi enseigner; **it taught him a lesson** (fig) ça lui a servi de leçon

teacher ['tiːtʃə^r] n (in secondary school) professeur m; (in primary school) instituteur(-trice); **French ~** professeur de français

teaching ['tiːtʃɪŋ] n enseignement m

tea cosy n couvre-théière m

teacup ['tiːkʌp] n tasse f à thé

teak [tiːk] n teck m ▷ adj en or de teck

tea leaves npl feuilles fpl de thé

team [tiːm] n équipe f; (of animals) attelage m
▶ **team up** vi: **to ~ up (with)** faire équipe (avec)

teamwork ['tiːmwəːk] n travail m d'équipe

teapot ['tiːpɔt] n théière f

tear¹ ['tɪə^r] n larme f; **in ~s** en larmes; **to burst into ~s** fondre en larmes

tear² [tɛə^r] (pt **tore**, pp **torn**) [tɔː^r, tɔːn] n déchirure f ▷ vt déchirer ▷ vi se déchirer; **to ~ to pieces** or **to bits** or **to shreds** mettre en pièces; (fig) démolir
▶ **tear along** vi (rush) aller à toute vitesse
▶ **tear apart** vt (also fig) déchirer
▶ **tear away** vt: **to ~ o.s. away (from sth)** (fig) s'arracher (de qch)
▶ **tear down** vt (building, statue) démolir; (poster, flag) arracher
▶ **tear off** vt (sheet of paper etc) arracher; (one's clothes) enlever à toute vitesse
▶ **tear out** vt (sheet of paper, cheque) arracher
▶ **tear up** vt (sheet of paper etc) déchirer, mettre en morceaux or pièces

tearful ['tɪəful] adj larmoyant(e)

tear gas ['tɪə-] n gaz m lacrymogène

tearoom ['tiːruːm] n salon m de thé

tease [tiːz] n taquin(e) ▷ vt taquiner; (unkindly) tourmenter

tea set n service m à thé

teaspoon ['tiːspuːn] n petite cuiller; (also: **teaspoonful**: as measurement) ≈ cuillerée f à café

teat [tiːt] n tétine f

teatime ['tiːtaɪm] n l'heure f du thé

tea towel n (Brit) torchon m (à vaisselle)

technical ['tɛknɪkl] adj technique

technicality [tɛknɪ'kælɪtɪ] n technicité f; (detail) détail m technique; **on a legal ~** à cause de (or grâce à) l'application à la lettre d'une subtilité juridique; pour vice de forme

technically ['tɛknɪklɪ] adv techniquement; (strictly speaking) en théorie, en principe

technician [tɛk'nɪʃən] n technicien(ne)

technique [tɛk'niːk] n technique f

techno ['tɛknəu] n (Mus) techno f

technological [tɛknə'lɔdʒɪkl] adj technologique

technology [tɛk'nɔlədʒɪ] n technologie f

teddy ['tɛdɪ], **teddy bear** n ours m (en peluche)

tedious ['tiːdɪəs] adj fastidieux(-euse)

tee [tiː] n (Golf) tee m

teem [tiːm] vi: **to ~ (with)** grouiller (de); **it is ~ing (with rain)** il pleut à torrents

teen [ti:n] adj = **teenage** ▷ n (US) = **teenager**

teenage ['ti:neɪdʒ] adj (fashions etc) pour jeunes, pour adolescents; (child) qui est adolescent(e)

teenager ['ti:neɪdʒə'] n adolescent(e)

teens [ti:nz] npl: **to be in one's** ~ être adolescent(e)

tee-shirt ['ti:ʃə:t] n = **T-shirt**

teeter ['ti:tə'] vi chanceler, vaciller

teeth [ti:θ] npl of **tooth**

teethe [ti:ð] vi percer ses dents

teething troubles ['ti:ðɪŋ-] npl (fig) difficultés initiales

teetotal ['ti:'təutl] adj (person) qui ne boit jamais d'alcool

telecommunications ['tɛlɪkəmju:nɪ'keɪʃənz] n télécommunications fpl

teleconferencing [tɛlɪ'kɔnfərənsɪŋ] n téléconférence(s) f(pl)

telegram ['tɛlɪgræm] n télégramme m

telegraph ['tɛlɪgrɑ:f] n télégraphe m

telegraph pole ['tɛlɪgrɑ:f-] n poteau m télégraphique

telephone ['tɛlɪfəun] n téléphone m ▷ vt (person) téléphoner à; (message) téléphoner; **to have a** ~ (Brit): **to be on the** ~ (subscriber) être abonné(e) au téléphone; **to be on the** ~ (be speaking) être au téléphone

telephone book n = **telephone directory**

telephone booth, (Brit) **telephone box** n cabine f téléphonique

telephone call n appel m téléphonique

telephone directory n annuaire m (du téléphone)

telephone number n numéro m de téléphone

telephonist [tə'lɛfənɪst] n (Brit) téléphoniste m/f

telesales ['tɛlɪseɪlz] npl télévente f

telescope ['tɛlɪskəup] n télescope m ▷ vi se télescoper ▷ vt télescoper

televise ['tɛlɪvaɪz] vt téléviser

television ['tɛlɪvɪʒən] n télévision f; **on** ~ à la télévision

television programme n émission f de télévision

television set n poste m de télévision, téléviseur m

telex ['tɛlɛks] n télex m ▷ vt (message) envoyer par télex; (person) envoyer un télex à ▷ vi envoyer un télex

tell (pt, pp **told**) [tɛl, təuld] vt dire; (relate: story) raconter; (distinguish): **to** ~ **sth from** distinguer qch de ▷ vi (talk): **to** ~ **of** parler de; (have effect) se faire sentir, se voir; **to** ~ **sb to do** dire à qn de faire; **to** ~ **sb about sth** (place, object etc) parler de qch à qn; (what happened etc) raconter qch à qn; **to** ~ **the time** (know how to) savoir lire l'heure; **can you** ~ **me the time?** pourriez-vous me dire l'heure?; **(I)** ~ **you what, ...** écoute, ...; **I can't** ~ **them apart** je n'arrive pas à les distinguer

▸ **tell off** vt réprimander, gronder

▸ **tell on** vt fus (inform against) dénoncer, rapporter contre

teller ['tɛlə'] n (in bank) caissier(-ière)

telling ['tɛlɪŋ] adj (remark, detail) révélateur(-trice

telltale ['tɛlteɪl] n rapporteur(-euse) ▷ adj (sign) éloquent(e), révélateur(-trice)

telly ['tɛlɪ] n abbr (Brit inf: = television) télé f

temp [tɛmp] n abbr (Brit: = temporary worker) intérimaire m/f ▷ vi travailler comme intérimaire

temper ['tɛmpə'] n (nature) caractère m; (mood) humeur f; (fit of anger) colère f ▷ vt (moderate) tempérer, adoucir; **to be in a** ~ être en colère; **t** **lose one's** ~ se mettre en colère; **to keep one's** ~ rester calme

temperament ['tɛmprəmənt] n (nature) tempérament m

temperamental [tɛmprə'mɛntl] adj capricieux(-euse)

temperate ['tɛmprət] adj modéré(e); (climate) tempéré(e)

temperature ['tɛmprətʃə'] n température f; **to have** or **run a** ~ avoir de la fièvre

temple ['tɛmpl] n (building) temple m; (Anat) tempe f

temporary ['tɛmpərəri] adj temporaire, provisoire; (job, worker) temporaire; ~ **secretary** (secrétaire f) intérimaire f; **a** ~ **teacher** un professeur remplaçant or suppléant

tempt [tɛmpt] vt tenter; **to** ~ **sb into doing** induire qn à faire; **to be ~ed to do sth** être tenté(e) de faire qch

temptation [tɛmp'teɪʃən] n tentation f

tempting ['tɛmptɪŋ] adj tentant(e); (food) appétissant(e)

ten [tɛn] num dix ▷ n: ~**s of thousands** des dizaines fpl de milliers

tenacity [tə'næsɪtɪ] n ténacité f

tenancy ['tɛnənsɪ] n location f; état m de locataire

tenant ['tɛnənt] n locataire m/f

tend [tɛnd] vt s'occuper de; (sick etc) soigner ▷ vi: **to** ~ **to do** avoir tendance à faire; (colour): **to** ~ **to** tirer sur

tendency ['tɛndənsɪ] n tendance f

tender ['tɛndə'] adj tendre; (delicate) délicat(e); (sore) sensible; (affectionate) tendre, doux (douce) ▷ n (Comm: offer) soumission f; (money): **legal** ~ cours légal ▷ vt offrir; **to** ~ **one's resignation** donner sa démission; **to put in a** ~ **(for)** faire une soumission (pour); **to put work out to** ~ (Brit) mettre un contrat en adjudication

tendon ['tɛndən] n tendon m

tenement ['tɛnəmənt] n immeuble m (de rapport)

tenner ['tɛnə'] n (Brit inf) billet m de dix livres

tennis ['tɛnɪs] n tennis m ▷ cpd (club, match, racket player) de tennis

tennis ball n balle f de tennis

tennis court n (court m de) tennis m

tennis match n match m de tennis

tennis player n joueur(-euse) de tennis

tennis racket n raquette f de tennis

tennis shoes npl (chaussures fpl de) tennis mpl

tenor ['tɛnə'] n (Mus) ténor m; (of speech etc) sens

général

tenpin bowling ['tɛnpɪn-] n (Brit) bowling m (à 10 quilles)
tense [tɛns] adj tendu(e); (person) tendu, crispé(e) ▷ n (Ling) temps m ▷ vt (tighten: muscles) tendre
tension ['tɛnʃən] n tension f
tent [tɛnt] n tente f
tentative ['tɛntətɪv] adj timide, hésitant(e); (conclusion) provisoire
tenterhooks ['tɛntəhuks] npl: **on ~** sur des charbons ardents
tenth [tɛnθ] num dixième
tent peg n piquet m de tente
tent pole n montant m de tente
tenuous ['tɛnjuəs] adj ténu(e)
tenure ['tɛnjuəʳ] n (of property) bail m; (of job) période f de jouissance; statut m de titulaire
tepid ['tɛpɪd] adj tiède
term [təːm] n (limit) terme m; (word) terme, mot m; (Scol) trimestre m; (Law) session f ▷ vt appeler; **terms** npl (conditions) conditions fpl; (Comm) tarif m; **~ of imprisonment** peine f de prison; **his ~ of office** la période où il était en fonction; **in the short/long ~** à court/long terme; **"easy ~s"** (Comm) "facilités de paiement"; **to come to ~s with** (problem) faire face à; **to be on good ~s with** bien s'entendre avec, être en bons termes avec
terminal ['təːmɪnl] adj terminal(e); (disease) dans sa phase terminale; (patient) incurable ▷ n (Elec) borne f; (for oil, ore etc, also Comput) terminal m; (also: **air terminal**) aérogare f; (Brit: also: **coach terminal**) gare routière
terminally ['təːmɪnlɪ] adv: **to be ~ ill** être condamné(e)
terminate ['təːmɪneɪt] vt mettre fin à; (pregnancy) interrompre ▷ vi: **to ~ in** finir en or par
termini ['təːmɪnaɪ] npl of **terminus**
terminology [təːmɪ'nɔlədʒɪ] n terminologie f
terminus (pl **termini**) ['təːmɪnəs, 'təːmɪnaɪ] n terminus m inv
terrace ['tɛrəs] n terrasse f; (Brit: row of houses) rangée f de maisons (attenantes les unes aux autres); **the ~s** (Brit Sport) les gradins mpl
terraced ['tɛrəst] adj (garden) en terrasses; (in a row: house) attenant(e) aux maisons voisines
terracotta ['tɛrə'kɔtə] n terre cuite
terrain [tɛ'reɪn] n terrain m (sol)
terrestrial [tɪ'rɛstrɪəl] adj terrestre
terrible ['tɛrɪbl] adj terrible, atroce; (weather, work) affreux(-euse), épouvantable
terribly ['tɛrɪblɪ] adv terriblement; (very badly) affreusement mal
terrier ['tɛrɪəʳ] n terrier m (chien)
terrific [tə'rɪfɪk] adj (very great) fantastique, incroyable, terrible; (wonderful) formidable, sensationnel(le)
terrified ['tɛrɪfaɪd] adj terrifié(e); **to be ~ of sth** avoir très peur de qch
terrify ['tɛrɪfaɪ] vt terrifier
terrifying ['tɛrɪfaɪɪŋ] adj terrifiant(e)
territorial [tɛrɪ'tɔːrɪəl] adj territorial(e)

territory ['tɛrɪtərɪ] n territoire m
terror ['tɛrəʳ] n terreur f
terrorism ['tɛrərɪzəm] n terrorisme m
terrorist ['tɛrərɪst] n terroriste m/f
terrorist attack n attentat m terroriste
test [tɛst] n (trial, check) essai m; (: of goods in factory) contrôle m; (of courage etc) épreuve f; (Med) examen m; (Chem) analyse f; (exam: of intelligence etc) test m (d'aptitude); (Scol) interrogation f de contrôle; (also: **driving test**) (examen du) permis m de conduire ▷ vt essayer; contrôler; mettre à l'épreuve; examiner; analyser; tester; faire subir une interrogation à; **to put sth to the ~** mettre qch à l'épreuve
testament ['tɛstəmənt] n testament m; **the Old/New T~** l'Ancien/le Nouveau Testament
testicle ['tɛstɪkl] n testicule m
testify ['tɛstɪfaɪ] vi (Law) témoigner, déposer; **to ~ to sth** (Law) attester qch; (gen) témoigner de qch
testimony ['tɛstɪmənɪ] n (Law) témoignage m, déposition f
test match n (Cricket, Rugby) match international
test tube n éprouvette f
tetanus ['tɛtənəs] n tétanos m
tether ['tɛðəʳ] vt attacher ▷ n: **at the end of one's ~** à bout (de patience)
text [tɛkst] n texte m; (on mobile phone) texto m, SMS m inv ▷ vt (inf) envoyer un texto or SMS à
textbook ['tɛkstbuk] n manuel m
textile ['tɛkstaɪl] n textile m
text message n texto m, SMS m inv
text messaging [-'mɛsɪdʒɪŋ] n messagerie textuelle
texture ['tɛkstʃəʳ] n texture f; (of skin, paper etc) grain m
Thai [taɪ] adj thaïlandais(e) ▷ n Thaïlandais(e); (Ling) thaï m
Thailand ['taɪlænd] n Thaïlande f
Thames [tɛmz] n: **the (River) ~** la Tamise
than [ðæn, ðən] conj que; (with numerals): **more ~ 10/once** plus de 10/d'une fois; **I have more/less ~ you** j'en ai plus/moins que toi; **she has more apples ~ pears** elle a plus de pommes que de poires; **it is better to phone ~ to write** il vaut mieux téléphoner (plutôt) qu'écrire; **she is older ~ you think** elle est plus âgée que tu le crois; **no sooner did he leave ~ the phone rang** il venait de partir quand le téléphone a sonné
thank [θæŋk] vt remercier, dire merci à; **thanks** npl remerciements mpl ▷ excl merci!; **~ you (very much)** merci (beaucoup); **~ heavens**, **~ God** Dieu merci; **~s to** (prep) grâce à
thankful ['θæŋkful] adj: **~ (for)** reconnaissant(e) (de); **~ for/that** (relieved) soulagé(e) de/que
thankfully ['θæŋkfəlɪ] adv avec reconnaissance; avec soulagement; (fortunately) heureusement; **~ there were few victims** il y eut fort heureusement peu de victimes
thankless ['θæŋklɪs] adj ingrat(e)
Thanksgiving ['θæŋksgɪvɪŋ], **Thanksgiving Day** n jour m d'action de grâce

that [ðæt] *adj* (*demonstrative*) (*pl* **those**) ce, cet + *vowel or* h mute, cette *f*; ~ **man/woman/book** cet homme/cette femme/ce livre; (*not this*) cet homme-là/cette femme-là/ce livre-là; ~ **one** celui-là
▷ *pron* **1** (*demonstrative*) (*pl* **those**) ce; (*not this one*) cela, ça; (*that one*) celui (celle); **who's ~?** qui est-ce?; **what's ~?** qu'est-ce que c'est?; **is ~ you?** c'est toi?; **I prefer this to ~** je préfère ceci à cela *or* ça; **~'s what he said** c'est *or* voilà ce qu'il a dit; **will you eat all ~?** tu vas manger tout ça?; **~ is (to say)** c'est-à-dire, à savoir; **at** *or* **with ~, he ...** là-dessus, il ...; **do it like ~** fais-le comme ça **2** (*relative: subject*) qui; (*: object*) que; (*: after prep*) lequel (laquelle), lesquels (lesquelles) *pl*; **the book ~ I read** le livre que j'ai lu; **the books ~ are in the library** les livres qui sont dans la bibliothèque; **all ~ I have** tout ce que j'ai; **the box ~ I put it in** la boîte dans laquelle je l'ai mis; **the people ~ I spoke to** les gens auxquels *or* à qui j'ai parlé; **not ~ I know of** pas à ma connaissance
3 (*relative: of time*) où; **the day ~ he came** le jour où il est venu
▷ *conj* que; **he thought ~ I was ill** il pensait que j'étais malade
▷ *adv* (*demonstrative*): **I don't like it ~ much** ça ne me plaît pas tant que ça; **I didn't know it was ~ bad** je ne savais pas que c'était si *or* aussi mauvais; **~ high** aussi haut; si haut; **it's about ~ high** c'est à peu près de cette hauteur

thatched [θætʃt] *adj* (*roof*) de chaume; **~ cottage** chaumière *f*

thaw [θɔː] *n* dégel *m* ▷ *vi* (*ice*) fondre; (*food*) dégeler ▷ *vt* (*food*) (faire) dégeler; **it's ~ing** (*weather*) il dégèle

the [ðiː, ðə] *def art* **1** (*gen*) le, la *f*, l' + *vowel or* h mute, les *pl* (NB: à + le(s) = **au(x)**; de + le = **du**; de + les = **des**); ~ **boy/girl/ink** le garçon/la fille/l'encre; ~ **children** les enfants; ~ **history of ~ world** l'histoire du monde; **give it to ~ postman** donne-le au facteur; **to play ~ piano/flute** jouer du piano/de la flûte
2 (+ *adj to form n*) le, la *f*, l' + *vowel or* h mute, les *pl*; ~ **rich and ~ poor** les riches et les pauvres; **to attempt ~ impossible** tenter l'impossible
3 (*in titles*): **Elizabeth ~ First** Elisabeth première; **Peter ~ Great** Pierre le Grand
4 (*in comparisons*): ~ **more he works, ~ more he earns** plus il travaille, plus il gagne de l'argent; ~ **sooner ~ better** le plus tôt sera le mieux

theatre, (US) **theater** ['θɪətə'] *n* théâtre *m*; (*also*: **lecture theatre**) amphithéâtre *m*, amphi *m* (*inf*); (*Med: also*: **operating theatre**) salle *f* d'opération

theatre-goer, (US) **theater-goer** ['θɪətəgəʊə'] *n* habitué(e) du théâtre

theatrical [θɪ'ætrɪkl] *adj* théâtral(e); ~ **company** troupe *f* de théâtre

theft [θɛft] *n* vol *m* (*larcin*)

their [ðɛə'] *adj* leur, leurs *pl*; *see also* **my**

theirs [ðɛəz] *pron* le (la) leur, les leurs; **it is ~** c'est à eux; **a friend of ~** un de leurs amis; *see*

also **mine¹**

them [ðɛm, ðəm] *pron* (*direct*) les; (*indirect*) leur; (*stressed, after prep*) eux (elles); **I see ~** je les vois; **give ~ the book** donne-leur le livre; **give me a few of ~** donnez m'en quelques uns (*or* quelques unes); *see also* **me**

theme [θiːm] *n* thème *m*

theme park *n* parc *m* à thème

theme song *n* chanson principale

themselves [ðəm'sɛlvz] *pl pron* (*reflexive*) se; (*emphatic, after prep*) eux-mêmes (elles-mêmes); **between ~** entre eux (elles); *see also* **oneself**

then [ðɛn] *adv* (*at that time*) alors, à ce moment-là; (*next*) puis, ensuite; (*and also*) et puis
▷ *conj* (*therefore*) alors, dans ce cas ▷ *adj*: **the ~ president** le président d'alors *or* de l'époque; **by ~** (*past*) à ce moment-là; (*future*) d'ici là; **from ~ on** dès lors; **before ~** avant; **until ~** jusqu'à ce moment-là, jusque-là; **and ~ what?** et puis après?; **what do you want me to do ~?** (*afterwards*) que veux-tu que je fasse ensuite?; (*in that case*) bon alors, qu'est-ce que je fais?

theology [θɪ'ɔlədʒɪ] *n* théologie *f*

theoretical [θɪə'rɛtɪkl] *adj* théorique

theory ['θɪərɪ] *n* théorie *f*

therapist ['θɛrəpɪst] *n* thérapeute *m/f*

therapy ['θɛrəpɪ] *n* thérapie *f*

there [ðɛə'] *adv* **1**: ~ **is, ~ are** il y a; ~ **are 3 of them** (*people, things*) il y en a 3; ~ **is no-one here/no bread left** il n'y a personne/il n'y a plus de pain; ~ **has been an accident** il y a eu un accident
2 (*referring to place*) là, là-bas; **it's ~** c'est là(-bas); **in/on/up/down ~** là-dedans/là-dessus/là-haut/en bas; **he went ~ on Friday** il y est allé vendredi; **to go ~ and back** faire l'aller-retour; **I want that book ~** je veux ce livre-là; ~ **he is!** le voilà!
3: ~, ~, (*esp to child*) allons, allons!

thereabouts ['ðɛərə'baʊts] *adv* (*place*) par là, près de là; (*amount*) environ, à peu près

thereafter [ðɛər'ɑːftə'] *adv* par la suite

thereby ['ðɛəbaɪ] *adv* ainsi

therefore ['ðɛəfɔː'] *adv* donc, par conséquent

there's ['ðɛəz] = **there is; there has**

thermal ['θəːml] *adj* thermique; ~ **paper/printer** papier *m*/imprimante *f* thermique; ~ **underwear** sous-vêtements *mpl* en Thermolactyl®

thermometer [θə'mɔmɪtə'] *n* thermomètre *m*

Thermos® ['θəːməs] *n* (*also*: **Thermos flask**) thermos® *m or f inv*

thermostat ['θəːməʊstæt] *n* thermostat *m*

thesaurus [θɪ'sɔːrəs] *n* dictionnaire *m* synonymique

these [ðiːz] *pl pron* ceux-ci (celles-ci) ▷ *pl adj* ces; (*not those*): ~ **books** ces livres-ci

thesis (*pl* **theses**) ['θiːsɪs, 'θiːsiːz] *n* thèse *f*

they [ðeɪ] *pl pron* ils (elles); (*stressed*) eux (elles); ~ **say that ...** (*it is said that*) on dit que ...

they'd [ðeɪd] = **they had; they would**

they'll [ðeɪl] = **they shall; they will**

they're [ðεəʳ] = **they are**
they've [ðeɪv] = **they have**
thick [θɪk] adj épais(se); (crowd) dense; (stupid)
bête, borné(e) ▷ n: **in the ~ of** au beau milieu
de, en plein cœur de; **it's 20 cm ~** ça a 20 cm
d'épaisseur
thicken ['θɪkn] vi s'épaissir ▷ vt (sauce etc)
épaissir
thickness ['θɪknɪs] n épaisseur f
thickset [θɪk'sεt] adj trapu(e), costaud(e)
thief (pl **thieves**) [θi:f, θi:vz] n voleur(-euse)
thigh [θaɪ] n cuisse f
thimble ['θɪmbl] n dé m (à coudre)
thin [θɪn] adj mince; (skinny) maigre; (soup)
peu épais(se); (hair, crowd) clairsemé(e); (fog)
léger(-ère) ▷ vt (hair) éclaircir; (also: **thin down**:
sauce, paint) délayer ▷ vi (fog) s'éclaircir; (also: **thin
out**: crowd) se disperser; **his hair is ~ning** il se
dégarnit
thing [θɪŋ] n chose f; (object) objet m; (contraption)
truc m; **things** npl (belongings) affaires fpl; **first
~ (in the morning)** à la première heure, tout de
suite (le matin); **last ~ (at night), he ...** juste
avant de se coucher, il ...; **the ~ is ...** c'est que
...; **for one ~** d'abord; **the best ~ would be to** le
mieux serait de; **how are ~s?** comment ça va?;
to have a ~ about (be obsessed by) être obsédé(e)
par; (hate) détester; **poor ~!** le (or la) pauvre!
think (pt, pp **thought**) [θɪŋk, θɔ:t] vi penser,
réfléchir ▷ vt penser, croire; (imagine)
s'imaginer; **to ~ of** penser à; **what do you ~
of it?** qu'en pensez-vous?; **what did you ~ of
them?** qu'avez-vous pensé d'eux?; **to ~ about
sth/sb** penser à qch/qn; **I'll ~ about it** je vais y
réfléchir; **to ~ of doing** avoir l'idée de faire; **I ~
so/not** je crois or pense que oui/non; **to ~ well of**
avoir une haute opinion de; **~ again!** attention,
réfléchis bien!; **to ~ aloud** penser tout haut
▶ **think out** vt (plan) bien réfléchir à; (solution)
trouver
▶ **think over** vt bien réfléchir à; **I'd like to ~
things over** (offer, suggestion) j'aimerais bien y
réfléchir un peu
▶ **think through** vt étudier dans tous les détails
▶ **think up** vt inventer, trouver
think tank n groupe m de réflexion
thinly ['θɪnlɪ] adv (cut) en tranches fines; (spread)
en couche mince
third [θə:d] num troisième ▷ n troisième m/f;
(fraction) tiers m; (Aut) troisième (vitesse) f; (Brit
Scol: degree) ≈ licence f avec mention passable; **a ~
of** le tiers de
thirdly ['θə:dlɪ] adv troisièmement
third party insurance n (Brit) assurance f au tiers
third-rate ['θə:d'reɪt] adj de qualité médiocre
Third World n: **the ~** le Tiers-Monde
thirst [θə:st] n soif f
thirsty ['θə:stɪ] adj qui a soif, assoiffé(e); (work)
qui donne soif; **to be ~** avoir soif
thirteen [θə:'ti:n] num treize
thirteenth [-'ti:nθ] num treizième
thirtieth ['θə:tɪɪθ] num trentième

thirty ['θə:tɪ] num trente
this [ðɪs] adj (demonstrative) (pl **these**) ce, cet +
vowel or h mute, cette f; **~ man/woman/book**
cet homme/cette femme/ce livre; (not that) cet
homme-ci/cette femme-ci/ce livre-ci; **~ one**
celui-ci (celle-ci); **~ time** cette fois-ci; **~ time
last year** l'année dernière à la même époque; **~
way** (in this direction) par ici; (in this fashion) de cette
façon, ainsi
▷ pron (demonstrative) (pl **these**) ce; (not that one)
celui-ci (celle-ci), ceci; **who's ~?** qui est-ce?;
what's ~? qu'est-ce que c'est?; **I prefer ~ to that**
je préfère ceci à cela; **they were talking of ~
and that** ils parlaient de choses et d'autres; **~
is where I live** c'est ici que j'habite; **~ is what
he said** voici ce qu'il a dit; **~ is Mr Brown** (in
introductions) je vous présente Mr Brown; (in photo)
c'est Mr Brown; (on telephone) ici Mr Brown
▷ adv (demonstrative): **it was about ~ big** c'était à
peu près de cette grandeur or grand comme ça;
I didn't know it was ~ bad je ne savais pas que
c'était si or aussi mauvais
thistle ['θɪsl] n chardon m
thorn [θɔ:n] n épine f
thorough ['θʌrə] adj (search) minutieux(-euse);
(knowledge, research) approfondi(e); (work, person)
consciencieux(-euse); (cleaning) à fond
thoroughbred ['θʌrəbrεd] n (horse) pur-sang m inv
thoroughfare ['θʌrəfεəʳ] n rue f; **"no ~"** (Brit)
"passage interdit"
thoroughly ['θʌrəlɪ] adv (search)
minutieusement; (study) en profondeur; (clean)
à fond; (very) tout à fait; **he ~ agreed** il était tout
à fait d'accord
those [ðəuz] pl pron ceux-là (celles-là) ▷ pl adj ces;
(not these): **~ books** ces livres-là
though [ðəu] conj bien que + sub, quoique + sub
▷ adv pourtant; **even ~** quand bien même +
conditional; **it's not easy, ~** pourtant, ce n'est
pas facile
thought [θɔ:t] pt, pp of **think** ▷ n pensée f; (idea)
idée f; (opinion) avis m; (intention) intention f;
after much ~ après mûre réflexion; **I've just
had a ~** je viens de penser à quelque chose; **to
give sth some ~** réfléchir à qch
thoughtful ['θɔ:tful] adj (deep in thought)
pensif(-ive); (serious) réfléchi(e); (considerate)
prévenant(e)
thoughtless ['θɔ:tlɪs] adj qui manque de
considération
thousand ['θauzənd] num mille; **one ~** mille;
two ~ deux mille; **~s of** des milliers de
thousandth ['θauzəntθ] num millième
thrash [θræʃ] vt rouer de coups; (as punishment)
donner une correction à; (inf: defeat) battre à
plate(s) couture(s)
▶ **thrash about** vi se débattre
▶ **thrash out** vt débattre de
thread [θrεd] n fil m; (of screw) pas m, filetage m
▷ vt (needle) enfiler; **to ~ one's way between** se
faufiler entre
threadbare ['θrεdbεəʳ] adj râpé(e), élimé(e)

threat [θrɛt] n menace f; **to be under ~ of** être menacé(e) de

threaten ['θrɛtn] vi (storm) menacer ▷ vt: **to ~ sb with sth/to do** menacer qn de qch/de faire

threatening ['θrɛtnɪŋ] adj menaçant(e)

three [θriː] num trois

three-dimensional [θriːdɪ'mɛnʃənl] adj à trois dimensions; (film) en relief

three-piece suit ['θriːpiːs-] n complet m (avec gilet)

three-piece suite n salon m (canapé et deux fauteuils)

three-ply [θriː'plaɪ] adj (wood) à trois épaisseurs; (wool) trois fils inv

three-quarters [θriː'kwɔːtəz] npl trois-quarts mpl; **~ full** aux trois-quarts plein

threshold ['θrɛʃhəuld] n seuil m; **to be on the ~ of** (fig) être au seuil de

threw [θruː] pt of **throw**

thrifty ['θrɪftɪ] adj économe

thrill [θrɪl] n (excitement) émotion f, sensation forte; (shudder) frisson m ▷ vi tressaillir, frissonner ▷ vt (audience) électriser

thrilled [θrɪld] adj: **~ (with)** ravi(e) de

thriller ['θrɪlər] n film m (or roman m or pièce f) à suspense

thrilling ['θrɪlɪŋ] adj (book, play etc) saisissant(e); (news, discovery) excitant(e)

thrive (pt -**d** or **throve**, pp -**d** or -**n**) [θraɪv, θrəuv, 'θrɪvn] vi pousser or se développer bien; (business) prospérer; **he ~s on it** cela lui réussit

thriving ['θraɪvɪŋ] adj vigoureux(-euse); (business, community) prospère

throat [θrəut] n gorge f; **to have a sore ~** avoir mal à la gorge

throb [θrɔb] n (of heart) pulsation f; (of engine) vibration f; (of pain) élancement m ▷ vi (heart) palpiter; (engine) vibrer; (pain) lanciner; (wound) causer des élancements; **my head is ~bing** j'ai des élancements dans la tête

throes [θrəuz] npl: **in the ~ of** au beau milieu de; en proie à; **in the ~ of death** à l'agonie

throne [θrəun] n trône m

throng ['θrɔŋ] n foule f ▷ vt se presser dans

throttle ['θrɔtl] n (Aut) accélérateur m ▷ vt étrangler

through [θruː] prep à travers; (time) pendant, durant; (by means of) par, par l'intermédiaire de; (owing to) à cause de ▷ adj (ticket, train, passage) direct(e) ▷ adv à travers; **(from) Monday ~ Friday** (US) de lundi à vendredi; **to let sb ~** laisser passer qn; **to put sb ~ to sb** (Tel) passer qn à qn; **to be ~** (Brit: Tel) avoir la communication; (esp US: have finished) avoir fini; **"no ~ traffic"** (US) "passage interdit"; **"no ~ road"** (Brit) "impasse"

throughout [θruː'aut] prep (place) partout dans; (time) durant tout(e) le (la) ▷ adv partout

throw [θrəu] n jet m; (Sport) lancer m ▷ vt (pt **threw**, pp -**n**) [θruː, θrəun] lancer, jeter; (Sport) lancer; (rider) désarçonner; (fig) décontenancer; (pottery) tourner; **to ~ a party** donner une réception

▶ **throw about**

▶ **throw around** vt (litter etc) éparpiller

▶ **throw away** vt jeter; (money) gaspiller

▶ **throw in** vt (Sport: ball) remettre en jeu; (include) ajouter

▶ **throw off** vt se débarrasser de

▶ **throw out** vt jeter; (reject) rejeter; (person) mettre à la porte

▶ **throw together** vt (clothes, meal etc) assembler à la hâte; (essay) bâcler

▶ **throw up** vi vomir

throwaway ['θrəuəweɪ] adj à jeter

throw-in ['θrəuɪn] n (Sport) remise f en jeu

thrown [θrəun] pp of **throw**

thru [θruː] (US) = **through**

thrush [θrʌʃ] n (Zool) grive f; (Med: esp in children) muguet m; (: in women: Brit) muguet vaginal

thrust [θrʌst] n (Tech) poussée f ▷ vt (pt, pp -) pousser brusquement; (push in) enfoncer

thud [θʌd] n bruit sourd

thug [θʌg] n voyou m

thumb [θʌm] n (Anat) pouce m ▷ vt (book) feuilleter; **to ~ a lift** faire de l'auto-stop, arrêter une voiture; **to give sb/sth the ~s up/~s down** donner/refuser de donner le feu vert à qn/qch

▶ **thumb through** vt (book) feuilleter

thumbtack ['θʌmtæk] n (US) punaise f (clou)

thump [θʌmp] n grand coup; (sound) bruit sourd ▷ vt cogner sur ▷ vi cogner, frapper

thunder ['θʌndər] n tonnerre m ▷ vi tonner; (train etc): **to ~ past** passer dans un grondement or un bruit de tonnerre

thunderbolt ['θʌndəbəult] n foudre f

thunderclap ['θʌndəklæp] n coup m de tonnerre

thunderstorm ['θʌndəstɔːm] n orage m

thundery ['θʌndərɪ] adj orageux(-euse)

Thursday ['θəːzdɪ] n jeudi m; see also **Tuesday**

thus [ðʌs] adv ainsi

thwart [θwɔːt] vt contrecarrer

thyme [taɪm] n thym m

tiara [tɪ'ɑːrə] n (woman's) diadème m

Tibet [tɪ'bɛt] n Tibet m

tick [tɪk] n (sound: of clock) tic-tac m; (mark) coche f; (Zool) tique f; (Brit inf): **in a ~** dans un instant; (Brit inf: credit): **to buy sth on ~** acheter qch à crédit ▷ vi faire tic-tac ▷ vt (item on list) cocher; **to put a ~ against sth** cocher qch

▶ **tick off** vt (item on list) cocher; (person) réprimander, attraper

▶ **tick over** vi (Brit: engine) tourner au ralenti; (: fig) aller or marcher doucettement

ticket ['tɪkɪt] n billet m; (for bus, tube) ticket m; (in shop: on goods) étiquette f; (: from cash register) reçu m, ticket; (for library) carte f; (also: **parking ticket**) contravention f, p.-v. m; (US Pol) liste électorale (soutenue par un parti); **to get a (parking) ~** (Aut) attraper une contravention (pour stationnement illégal)

ticket barrier n (Brit: Rail) portillon m automatique

ticket collector n contrôleur(-euse)

ticket inspector n contrôleur(-euse)

ticket machine n billetterie f automatique

ticket office n guichet m, bureau m de vente des billets

tickle ['tɪkl] n chatouillement m ▷ vi chatouiller ▷ vt chatouiller; (fig) plaire à; faire rire

ticklish ['tɪklɪʃ] adj (person) chatouilleux(-euse); (which tickles: blanket) qui chatouille; (: cough) qui irrite; (problem) épineux(-euse)

tidal ['taɪdl] adj à marée

tidal wave n raz-de-marée m inv

tidbit ['tɪdbɪt] n (esp US) = **titbit**

tiddlywinks ['tɪdlɪwɪŋks] n jeu m de puce

tide [taɪd] n marée f; (fig: of events) cours m ▷ vt: **to ~ sb over** dépanner qn; **high/low ~** marée haute/basse

tidy ['taɪdɪ] adj (room) bien rangé(e); (dress, work) net (nette), soigné(e); (person) ordonné(e), qui a de l'ordre; (: in character) soigneux(-euse); (mind) méthodique ▷ vt (also: **tidy up**) ranger; **to ~ o.s. up** s'arranger

tie [taɪ] n (string etc) cordon m; (Brit: also: **necktie**) cravate f; (fig: link) lien m; (Sport: draw) égalité f de points; match nul; (: match) rencontre f; (US Rail) traverse f ▷ vt (parcel) attacher; (ribbon) nouer ▷ vi (Sport) faire match nul; finir à égalité de points; **"black/white ~"** "smoking/habit de rigueur"; **family ~s** liens de famille; **to ~ sth in a bow** faire un nœud à or avec qch; **to ~ a knot in sth** faire un nœud à qch

▶ **tie down** vt attacher; (fig): **to ~ sb down to** contraindre qn à accepter; **to feel ~d down** (by relationship) se sentir coincé(e)

▶ **tie in** vi: **to ~ in (with)** (correspond) correspondre (à)

▶ **tie on** vt (Brit: label etc) attacher (avec une ficelle)

▶ **tie up** vt (parcel) ficeler; (dog, boat) attacher; (prisoner) ligoter; (arrangements) conclure; **to be ~d up** (busy) être pris(e) or occupé(e)

tier [tɪər] n gradin m; (of cake) étage m

tiger ['taɪgər] n tigre m

tight [taɪt] adj (rope) tendu(e), raide; (clothes) étroit(e), très juste; (budget, programme, bend) serré(e); (control) strict(e), sévère; (inf: drunk) ivre, rond(e) ▷ adv (squeeze) très fort; (shut) à bloc, hermétiquement; **to be packed ~** (suitcase) être bourré(e); (people) être serré(e); **hold ~!** accrochez-vous bien!

tighten ['taɪtn] vt (rope) tendre; (screw) resserrer; (control) renforcer ▷ vi se tendre; se resserrer

tightfisted [taɪt'fɪstɪd] adj avare

tightly ['taɪtlɪ] adv (grasp) bien, très fort

tightrope ['taɪtrəup] n corde f raide

tights [taɪts] npl (Brit) collant m

tile [taɪl] n (on roof) tuile f; (on wall or floor) carreau m ▷ vt (floor, bathroom etc) carreler

tiled [taɪld] adj en tuiles; carrelé(e)

till [tɪl] n caisse (enregistreuse) ▷ vt (land) cultiver ▷ prep, conj = **until**

tiller ['tɪlər] n (Naut) barre f (du gouvernail)

tilt [tɪlt] vt pencher, incliner ▷ vi pencher, être incliné(e) ▷ n (slope) inclinaison f; **to wear one's hat at a ~** porter son chapeau incliné sur le côté; **(at) full ~** à toute vitesse

timber ['tɪmbər] n (material) bois m de construction; (trees) arbres mpl

time [taɪm] n temps m; (epoch: often pl) époque f, temps; (by clock) heure f; (moment) moment m; (occasion, also Math) fois f; (Mus) mesure f ▷ vt (race) chronométrer; (programme) minuter; (visit) fixer; (remark etc) choisir le moment de; **a long ~** un long moment, longtemps; **four at a ~** quatre à la fois; **for the ~ being** pour le moment; **from ~ to ~** de temps en temps; **~ after ~, ~ and again** bien des fois; **at ~s** parfois; **in ~** (soon enough) à temps; (after some time) avec le temps, à la longue; (Mus) en mesure; **in a week's ~** dans une semaine; **in no ~** en un rien de temps; **any ~** n'importe quand; **on ~** à l'heure; **to be 30 minutes behind/ahead of** ~ avoir 30 minutes de retard/d'avance; **by the ~ he arrived** quand il est arrivé, le temps qu'il arrive + sub; **5 ~s 5** 5 fois 5; **what ~ is it?** quelle heure est-il?; **what ~ do you make it?** quelle heure avez-vous?; **what ~ is the museum/shop open?** à quelle heure ouvre le musée/magasin?; **to have a good ~** bien s'amuser; **we (or they etc) had a hard ~** ça a été difficile or pénible; **~'s up!** c'est l'heure!; **I've no ~ for it** (fig) cela m'agace; **he'll do it in his own (good) ~** (without being hurried) il le fera quand il en aura le temps; **he'll do it in** or (US) **on his own ~** (out of working hours) il le fera à ses heures perdues; **to be behind the ~s** retarder (sur son temps)

time bomb n bombe f à retardement

time lag n (Brit) décalage m; (: in travel) décalage horaire

timeless ['taɪmlɪs] adj éternel(le)

time limit n limite f de temps, délai m

timely ['taɪmlɪ] adj opportun(e)

time off n temps m libre

timer ['taɪmər] n (in kitchen) compte-minutes m inv; (Tech) minuteur m

timescale ['taɪmskeɪl] n délais mpl

time-share ['taɪmʃɛər] n maison f/ appartement m en multipropriété

time switch n (Brit) minuteur m; (: for lighting) minuterie f

timetable ['taɪmteɪbl] n (Rail) (indicateur m) horaire m; (Scol) emploi m du temps; (programme of events etc) programme m

time zone n fuseau m horaire

timid ['tɪmɪd] adj timide; (easily scared) peureux(-euse)

timing ['taɪmɪŋ] n minutage m; (Sport) chronométrage m; **the ~ of his resignation** le moment choisi pour sa démission

timpani ['tɪmpənɪ] npl timbales fpl

tin [tɪn] n étain m; (also: **tin plate**) fer-blanc m; (Brit: can) boîte f (de conserve); (: for baking) moule m (à gâteau); (for storage) boîte f; **a ~ of paint** un pot de peinture

tinfoil ['tɪnfɔɪl] n papier m d'étain or d'aluminium

tinge [tɪndʒ] *n* nuance *f* ▷ *vt*: **~d with** teinté(e) de

tingle ['tɪŋgl] *n* picotement *m*; frisson *m* ▷ *vi* picoter; (*person*) avoir des picotements

tinker ['tɪŋkə'] *n* rétameur ambulant; (*gipsy*) romanichel *m*
▶ **tinker with** *vt fus* bricoler, rafistoler

tinkle ['tɪŋkl] *vi* tinter ▷ *n* (*inf*): **to give sb a ~** passer un coup de fil à qn

tinned [tɪnd] *adj* (*Brit: food*) en boîte, en conserve

tin opener [-'əupnə'] *n* (*Brit*) ouvre-boîte(s) *m*

tinsel ['tɪnsl] *n* guirlandes *fpl* de Noël (*argentées*)

tint [tɪnt] *n* teinte *f*; (*for hair*) shampooing colorant ▷ *vt* (*hair*) faire un shampooing colorant à

tinted ['tɪntɪd] *adj* (*hair*) teint(e); (*spectacles, glass*) teinté(e)

tiny ['taɪnɪ] *adj* minuscule

tip [tɪp] *n* (*end*) bout *m*; (*protective: on umbrella etc*) embout *m*; (*gratuity*) pourboire *m*; (*Brit: for coal*) terril *m*; (*Brit: for rubbish*) décharge *f*; (*advice*) tuyau *m* ▷ *vt* (*waiter*) donner un pourboire à; (*tilt*) incliner; (*overturn: also:* **tip over**) renverser; (*empty: also:* **tip out**) déverser; (*predict: winner etc*) pronostiquer; **he ~ped out the contents of the box** il a vidé le contenu de la boîte; **how much should I ~?** combien de pourboire est-ce qu'il faut laisser?
▶ **tip off** *vt* prévenir, avertir

tip-off ['tɪpɔf] *n* (*hint*) tuyau *m*

tipped ['tɪpt] *adj* (*Brit: cigarette*) (à bout) filtre *inv*; **steel-~** à bout métallique, à embout de métal

tipsy ['tɪpsɪ] *adj* un peu ivre, éméché(e)

tiptoe ['tɪptəu] *n*: **on ~** sur la pointe des pieds

tiptop ['tɪptɔp] *adj*: **in ~ condition** en excellent état

tire ['taɪə'] *n* (*US*) = **tyre** ▷ *vt* fatiguer ▷ *vi* se fatiguer
▶ **tire out** *vt* épuiser

tired ['taɪəd] *adj* fatigué(e); **to be/feel/look ~** être/se sentir/avoir l'air fatigué; **to be ~ of** en avoir assez de, être las (lasse) de

tireless ['taɪəlɪs] *adj* infatigable, inlassable

tire pressure (*US*) = **tyre pressure**

tiresome ['taɪəsəm] *adj* ennuyeux(-euse)

tiring ['taɪərɪŋ] *adj* fatigant(e)

tissue ['tɪʃuː] *n* tissu *m*; (*paper handkerchief*) mouchoir *m* en papier, kleenex® *m*

tissue paper *n* papier *m* de soie

tit [tɪt] *n* (*bird*) mésange *f*; (*inf: breast*) nichon *m*; **to give ~ for tat** rendre coup pour coup

titbit ['tɪtbɪt] *n* (*food*) friandise *f*; (*before meal*) amuse-gueule *m inv*; (*news*) potin *m*

title ['taɪtl] *n* titre *m*; (*Law: right*): **~ (to)** droit *m* (à)

title deed *n* (*Law*) titre (constitutif) de propriété

title role *n* rôle principal

T-junction ['tiː'dʒʌŋkʃən] *n* croisement *m* en T

TM *n abbr* = **trademark; transcendental meditation**

to [tuː, tə] *prep* (*with noun/pronoun*) **1** (*direction*) à; (*towards*) vers; envers; **to go to France/ Portugal/London/school** aller en France/au Portugal/à Londres/à l'école; **to go to Claude's/**
the doctor's aller chez Claude/le docteur; **the road to Edinburgh** la route d'Édimbourg
2 (*as far as*) (jusqu')à; **to count to 10** compter jusqu'à 10; **from 40 to 50 people** de 40 à 50 personnes
3 (*with expressions of time*): **a quarter to 5** 5 heures moins le quart; **it's twenty to 3** il est 3 heures moins vingt
4 (*for, of*) de; **the key to the front door** la clé de la porte d'entrée; **a letter to his wife** une lettre (adressée) à sa femme
5 (*expressing indirect object*) à; **to give sth to sb** donner qch à qn; **to talk to sb** parler à qn; **it belongs to him** cela lui appartient, c'est à lui; **to be a danger to sb** être dangereux(-euse) pour qn
6 (*in relation to*) à; **3 goals to 2** 3 (buts) à 2; **30 miles to the gallon** ≈ 9,4 litres aux cent (km)
7 (*purpose, result*): **to come to sb's aid** venir au secours de qn, porter secours à qn; **to sentence sb to death** condamner qn à mort; **to my surprise** à ma grande surprise
▷ *prep* (*with vb*) **1** (*simple infinitive*): **to go/eat** aller/ manger
2 (*following another vb*): **to want/try/start to do** vouloir/essayer de/commencer à faire
3 (*with vb omitted*): **I don't want to** je ne veux pas
4 (*purpose, result*): **I did it to help you** je l'ai fait pour vous aider
5 (*equivalent to relative clause*): **I have things to do** j'ai des choses à faire; **the main thing is to try** l'important est d'essayer
6 (*after adjective etc*): **ready to go** prêt(e) à partir; **too old/young to ...** trop vieux/jeune pour ...
▷ *adv*: **push/pull the door to** tirez/poussez la porte; **to go to and fro** aller et venir

toad [təud] *n* crapaud *m*

toadstool ['təudstuːl] *n* champignon (vénéneux)

toast [təust] *n* (*Culin*) pain grillé, toast *m*; (*drink, speech*) toast ▷ *vt* (*Culin*) faire griller; (*drink to*) porter un toast à; **a piece** *or* **slice of ~** un toast

toaster ['təustə'] *n* grille-pain *m inv*

tobacco [tə'bækəu] *n* tabac *m*; **pipe ~** tabac à pipe

tobacconist [tə'bækənɪst] *n* marchand(e) de tabac; **~'s (shop)** (bureau *m* de) tabac *m*

toboggan [tə'bɔgən] *n* toboggan *m*; (*child's*) luge *f*

today [tə'deɪ] *adv, n* (*also fig*) aujourd'hui (*m*); **what day is it ~?** quel jour sommes-nous aujourd'hui?; **what date is it ~?** quelle est la date aujourd'hui?; **~ is the 4th of March** aujourd'hui nous sommes le 4 mars; **a week ago ~** il y a huit jours aujourd'hui

toddler ['tɔdlə'] *n* enfant *m/f* qui commence à marcher, bambin *m*

toe [təu] *n* doigt *m* de pied, orteil *m*; (*of shoe*) bout *m* ▷ *vt*: **to ~ the line** (*fig*) obéir, se conformer; **big ~** gros orteil; **little ~** petit orteil

toenail ['təuneɪl] *n* ongle *m* de l'orteil

toffee ['tɔfɪ] *n* caramel *m*

toffee apple *n* (*Brit*) pomme caramélisée

together [tə'gɛðə'] *adv* ensemble; (*at same time*)

en même temps; **~ with** (prep) avec

toil [tɔɪl] n dur travail, labeur m ▷ vi travailler dur; peiner

toilet ['tɔɪlət] n (Brit: lavatory) toilettes fpl, cabinets mpl ▷ cpd (bag, soap etc) de toilette; **to go to the ~** aller aux toilettes; **where's the ~?** où sont les toilettes?

toilet bag n (Brit) nécessaire m de toilette

toilet paper n papier m hygiénique

toiletries ['tɔɪlətrɪz] npl articles mpl de toilette

toilet roll n rouleau m de papier hygiénique

token ['təukən] n (sign) marque f, témoignage m; (metal disc) jeton m; (voucher) bon m, coupon m ▷ adj (fee, strike) symbolique; **by the same ~** (fig) de même; **book/record ~** (Brit) chèque-livre/-disque m

Tokyo ['təukjəu] n Tokyo

told [təuld] pt, pp of **tell**

tolerable ['tɔlərəbl] adj (bearable) tolérable; (fairly good) passable

tolerant ['tɔlərnt] adj: **~ (of)** tolérant(e) (à l'égard de)

tolerate ['tɔləreɪt] vt supporter; (Med,: Tech) tolérer

toll [təul] n (tax, charge) péage m ▷ vi (bell) sonner; **the accident ~ on the roads** le nombre des victimes de la route

toll call n (US Tel) appel m (à) longue distance

toll-free ['təul'fri:] adj (US) gratuit(e) ▷ adv gratuitement

tomato [tə'mɑːtəu] (pl **-es**) n tomate f

tomato sauce n sauce f tomate

tomb [tu:m] n tombe f

tomboy ['tɔmbɔɪ] n garçon manqué

tombstone ['tu:mstəun] n pierre tombale

tomcat ['tɔmkæt] n matou m

tomorrow [tə'mɔrəu] adv, n (also fig) demain (m); **the day after ~** après-demain; **a week ~** demain en huit; **~ morning** demain matin

ton [tʌn] n tonne f (Brit: = 1016 kg; US = 907 kg; metric = 1000 kg); (Naut: also: **register ton**) tonneau m (= 2.83 cu.m); **~s of** (inf) des tas de

tone [təun] n ton m; (of radio, Brit Tel) tonalité f ▷ vi (also: **tone in**) s'harmoniser

▶ **tone down** vt (colour, criticism) adoucir; (sound) baisser

▶ **tone up** vt (muscles) tonifier

tone-deaf [təun'dɛf] adj qui n'a pas d'oreille

tongs [tɔŋz] npl pinces fpl; (for coal) pincettes fpl; (for hair) fer m à friser

tongue [tʌŋ] n langue f; **~ in cheek** (adv) ironiquement

tongue-tied ['tʌŋtaɪd] adj (fig) muet(te)

tonic ['tɔnɪk] n (Med) tonique m; (Mus) tonique f; (also: **tonic water**) Schweppes® m

tonight [tə'naɪt] adv, n cette nuit; (this evening) ce soir; **(I'll) see you ~!** à ce soir!

tonne [tʌn] n (Brit: metric ton) tonne f

tonsil ['tɔnsl] n amygdale f; **to have one's ~s out** se faire opérer des amygdales

tonsillitis [tɔnsɪ'laɪtɪs] n amygdalite f; **to have ~** avoir une angine or une amygdalite

too [tu:] adv (excessively) trop; (also) aussi; **it's ~ sweet** c'est trop sucré; **I went ~** moi aussi, j'y suis allé; **~ much** (as adv) trop; (as adj) trop de; **~ many** (adj) trop de; **~ bad!** tant pis!

took [tuk] pt of **take**

tool [tu:l] n outil m; (fig) instrument m ▷ vt travailler, ouvrager

tool box n boîte f à outils

tool kit n trousse f à outils

toot [tu:t] n coup m de sifflet (or de klaxon) ▷ vi siffler; (with car-horn) klaxonner

tooth (pl **teeth**) [tu:θ, ti:θ] n (Anat, Tech) dent f; **to have a ~ out** or (US) **pulled** se faire arracher une dent; **to brush one's teeth** se laver les dents; **by the skin of one's teeth** (fig) de justesse

toothache ['tu:θeɪk] n mal m de dents; **to have ~** avoir mal aux dents

toothbrush ['tu:θbrʌʃ] n brosse f à dents

toothpaste ['tu:θpeɪst] n pâte f dentifrice m

toothpick ['tu:θpɪk] n cure-dent m

top [tɔp] n (of mountain, head) sommet m; (of page, ladder) haut m; (of list, queue) commencement m; (of box, cupboard, table) dessus m; (lid: of box, jar) couvercle m; (: of bottle) bouchon m; (toy) toupie f; (Dress: blouse etc) haut m; (: of pyjamas) veste f ▷ adj du haut; (in rank) premier(-ière); (best) meilleur(e) ▷ vt (exceed) dépasser; (be first in) être en tête de; **the ~ of the milk** (Brit) la crème du lait; **at the ~ of the stairs/page/street** en haut de l'escalier/de la page/de la rue; **from ~ to bottom** de fond en comble; **on ~ of** sur; (in addition to) en plus de; **from ~ to toe** (Brit) de la tête aux pieds; **at the ~ of the list** en tête de liste; **at the ~ of one's voice** à tue-tête; **at ~ speed** à toute vitesse; **over the ~** (inf: behaviour etc) qui dépasse les limites

▶ **top up** (US)

▶ **top off** vt (bottle) remplir; (salary) compléter; **to ~ up one's mobile (phone)** recharger son compte

top floor n dernier étage

top hat n haut-de-forme m

top-heavy [tɔp'hɛvɪ] adj (object) trop lourd(e) du haut

topic ['tɔpɪk] n sujet m, thème m

topical ['tɔpɪkl] adj d'actualité

topless ['tɔplɪs] adj (bather etc) aux seins nus; **~ swimsuit** monokini m

top-level ['tɔplɛvl] adj (talks) à l'échelon le plus élevé

topmost ['tɔpməust] adj le (la) plus haut(e)

topping ['tɔpɪŋ] n (Culin) couche de crème, fromage etc qui recouvre un plat

topple ['tɔpl] vt renverser, faire tomber ▷ vi basculer; tomber

top-secret ['tɔp'si:krɪt] adj ultra-secret(-ète)

topsy-turvy ['tɔpsɪ'tə:vɪ] adj, adv sens dessus-dessous

top-up ['tɔpʌp] n (for mobile phone) recharge f, minutes fpl; **would you like a ~?** je vous en remets or rajoute?

top-up card n (for mobile phone) recharge f

torch [tɔ:tʃ] n torche f; (Brit: electric) lampe f de

poche

tore [tɔːʳ] *pt of* **tear²**

torment *n* ['tɔːmɛnt] tourment *m* ▷ *vt* [tɔːˈmɛnt] tourmenter; (*fig: annoy*) agacer

torn [tɔːn] *pp of* **tear²** ▷ *adj*: **~ between** (*fig*) tiraillé(e) entre

tornado [tɔːˈneɪdəʊ] (*pl* **-es**) *n* tornade *f*

torpedo [tɔːˈpiːdəʊ] (*pl* **-es**) *n* torpille *f*

torrent ['tɔrnt] *n* torrent *m*

torrential [tɔˈrɛnʃl] *adj* torrentiel(le)

tortoise ['tɔːtəs] *n* tortue *f*

tortoiseshell ['tɔːtəʃɛl] *adj* en écaille

torture ['tɔːtʃəʳ] *n* torture *f* ▷ *vt* torturer

Tory ['tɔːrɪ] *adj, n* (*Brit Pol*) tory *m/f*, conservateur(-trice)

toss [tɔs] *vt* lancer, jeter; (*Brit: pancake*) faire sauter; (*head*) rejeter en arrière ▷ *vi*: **to ~ up for sth** (*Brit*) jouer qch à pile ou face ▷ *n* (*movement: of head etc*) mouvement soudain; (*of coin*) tirage *m* à pile ou face; **to ~ a coin** jouer à pile ou face; **to ~ and turn** (*in bed*) se tourner et se retourner; **to win/lose the ~** gagner/perdre à pile ou face; (*Sport*) gagner/perdre le tirage au sort

tot [tɔt] *n* (*Brit: drink*) petit verre; (*child*) bambin *m*
▶ **tot up** *vt* (*Brit: figures*) additionner

total ['təʊtl] *adj* total(e) ▷ *n* total *m* ▷ *vt* (*add up*) faire le total de, additionner; (*amount to*) s'élever à; **in ~** au total

totalitarian [təʊtælɪˈtɛərɪən] *adj* totalitaire

totally ['təʊtəlɪ] *adv* totalement

totter ['tɔtəʳ] *vi* chanceler; (*object, government*) être chancelant(e)

touch [tʌtʃ] *n* contact *m*, toucher *m*; (*sense, skill: of pianist etc*) toucher; (*fig: note, also Football*) touche *f* ▷ *vt* (*gen*) toucher; (*tamper with*) toucher à; **the personal ~** la petite note personnelle; **to put the finishing ~es to sth** mettre la dernière main à qch; **a ~ of** (*fig*) un petit peu de; une touche de; **in ~ with** en contact or rapport avec; **to get in ~ with** prendre contact avec; **I'll be in ~** je resterai en contact; **to lose ~** (*friends*) se perdre de vue; **to be out of ~ with events** ne pas être au courant de ce qui se passe
▶ **touch down** *vi* (*Aviat*) atterrir; (*on sea*) amerrir
▶ **touch on** *vt fus* (*topic*) effleurer, toucher
▶ **touch up** *vt* (*paint*) retoucher

touch-and-go ['tʌtʃən'gəʊ] *adj* incertain(e); **it was ~ whether we did it** nous avons failli ne pas le faire

touchdown ['tʌtʃdaʊn] *n* (*Aviat*) atterrissage *m*; (*on sea*) amerrissage *m*; (*US Football*) essai *m*

touched [tʌtʃt] *adj* (*moved*) touché(e); (*inf*) cinglé(e)

touching ['tʌtʃɪŋ] *adj* touchant(e), attendrissant(e)

touchline ['tʌtʃlaɪn] *n* (*Sport*) (ligne *f* de) touche *f*

touch-sensitive ['tʌtʃsɛnsɪtɪv] *adj* (*keypad*) à effleurement; (*screen*) tactile

touchy ['tʌtʃɪ] *adj* (*person*) susceptible

tough [tʌf] *adj* dur(e); (*resistant*) résistant(e), solide; (*meat*) dur, coriace; (*firm*) inflexible; (*journey*) pénible; (*task, problem, situation*) difficile;
(*rough*) dur ▷ *n* (*gangster etc*) dur *m*; **~ luck!** pas de chance!; tant pis!

toughen ['tʌfn] *vt* rendre plus dur(e) (*or* plus résistant(e) *or* plus solide)

toupee ['tuːpeɪ] *n* postiche *m*

tour ['tʊəʳ] *n* voyage *m*; (*also:* **package tour**) voyage organisé; (*of town, museum*) tour *m*, visite *f*; (*by band*) tournée *f* ▷ *vt* visiter; **to go on a ~ of** (*museum, region*) visiter; **to go on ~** partir en tournée

tour guide *n* (*person*) guide *m/f*

tourism ['tʊərɪzm] *n* tourisme *m*

tourist ['tʊərɪst] *n* touriste *m/f* ▷ *adv* (*travel*) en classe touriste ▷ *cpd* touristique; **the ~ trade** le tourisme

tourist office *n* syndicat *m* d'initiative

tournament ['tʊənəmənt] *n* tournoi *m*

tour operator *n* (*Brit*) organisateur *m* de voyages, tour-opérateur *m*

tousled ['taʊzld] *adj* (*hair*) ébouriffé(e)

tout [taʊt] *vi*: **to ~ for** essayer de raccrocher, racoler; **to ~ sth (around)** (*Brit*) essayer de placer *or* (re)vendre qch ▷ *n* (*Brit: ticket tout*) revendeur *m* de billets

tow [təʊ] *n*: **to give sb a ~** (*Aut*) remorquer qn ▷ *vt* remorquer; (*caravan, trailer*) tracter; **"on ~"** (*US*): **"in ~"** (*Aut*) "véhicule en remorque"
▶ **tow away** *vt* (*subj: police*) emmener à la fourrière; (*: breakdown service*) remorquer

toward [təˈwɔːd], **towards** [təˈwɔːdz] *prep* vers; (*of attitude*) envers, à l'égard de; (*of purpose*) pour; **~(s) noon/the end of the year** vers midi/la fin de l'année; **to feel friendly ~(s) sb** être bien disposé envers qn

towel ['taʊəl] *n* serviette *f* (de toilette); (*also:* **tea towel**) torchon *m*; **to throw in the ~** (*fig*) jeter l'éponge

towelling ['taʊəlɪŋ] *n* (*fabric*) tissu-éponge *m*

towel rail, (*US*) **towel rack** *n* porte-serviettes *m inv*

tower ['taʊəʳ] *n* tour *f* ▷ *vi* (*building, mountain*) se dresser (majestueusement); **to ~ above** *or* **over sb/sth** dominer qn/qch

tower block *n* (*Brit*) tour *f* (d'habitation)

towering ['taʊərɪŋ] *adj* très haut(e), imposant(e)

town [taʊn] *n* ville *f*; **to go to ~** aller en ville; (*fig*) y mettre le paquet; **in the ~** dans la ville, en ville; **to be out of ~** (*person*) être en déplacement

town centre *n* (*Brit*) centre *m* de la ville, centre-ville *m*

town council *n* conseil municipal

town hall *n* ≈ mairie *f*

town plan *n* plan *m* de ville

town planning *n* urbanisme *m*

towrope ['təʊrəʊp] *n* (câble *m* de) remorque *f*

tow truck *n* (*US*) dépanneuse *f*

toxic ['tɔksɪk] *adj* toxique

toy [tɔɪ] *n* jouet *m*
▶ **toy with** *vt fus* jouer avec; (*idea*) caresser

toyshop ['tɔɪʃɔp] *n* magasin *m* de jouets

trace [treɪs] *n* trace *f* ▷ *vt* (*draw*) tracer, dessiner; (*follow*) suivre la trace de; (*locate*) retrouver;

without ~ (*disappear*) sans laisser de traces;
there was no ~ **of it** il n'y en avait pas trace
tracing paper ['treısıŋ-] *n* papier-calque *m*
track [træk] *n* (*mark*) trace *f*; (*path: gen*) chemin
m, piste *f*; (: *of bullet etc*) trajectoire *f*; (: *of suspect*,
animal) piste; (*Rail*) voie ferrée, rails *mpl*; (*on tape*,
Comput, *Sport*) piste; (*on CD*) piste *f*; (*on record*)
plage *f* ▷ *vt* suivre la trace or la piste de; **to keep**
~ **of** suivre; **to be on the right** ~ (*fig*) être sur la
bonne voie
  ▶ **track down** *vt* (*prey*) trouver et capturer; (*sth
  lost*) finir par retrouver
tracksuit ['træksuːt] *n* survêtement *m*
tract [trækt] *n* (*Geo*) étendue *f*, zone *f*; (*pamphlet*)
tract *m*; **respiratory** ~ (*Anat*) système *m*
respiratoire
traction ['trækʃən] *n* traction *f*
tractor ['træktəʳ] *n* tracteur *m*
trade [treıd] *n* commerce *m*; (*skill, job*) métier *m*
▷ *vi* faire du commerce ▷ *vt* (*exchange*): **to** ~ **sth**
(for sth) échanger qch (contre qch); **to** ~ **with/**
in faire du commerce avec/le commerce de;
foreign ~ commerce extérieur; **Department**
of T~ and Industry (DTI) (*Brit*) ministère *m* du
Commerce et de l'Industrie
  ▶ **trade in** *vt* (*old car etc*) faire reprendre
trade fair *n* foire(-exposition) commerciale
trade-in price *n* prix *m* à la reprise
trademark ['treıdmaːk] *n* marque *f* de fabrique
trade name *n* marque déposée
trader ['treıdəʳ] *n* commerçant(e), négociant(e)
tradesman ['treıdzmən] (*irreg*) *n* (*shopkeeper*)
commerçant *m*; (*skilled worker*) ouvrier qualifié
trade union *n* syndicat *m*
trade unionist [-'juːnjənıst] *n* syndicaliste *m/f*
trading ['treıdıŋ] *n* affaires *fpl*, commerce *m*
tradition [trə'dıʃən] *n* tradition *f*; **traditions** *npl*
coutumes *fpl*, traditions
traditional [trə'dıʃənl] *adj* traditionnel(le)
traffic ['træfık] *n* trafic *m*; (*cars*) circulation *f* ▷ *vi*:
to ~ **in** (*pej: liquor, drugs*) faire le trafic de
traffic calming [-'kaːmıŋ] *n* ralentissement *m*
de la circulation
traffic circle *n* (*US*) rond-point *m*
traffic island *n* refuge *m* (pour piétons)
traffic jam *n* embouteillage *m*
traffic lights *npl* feux *mpl* (de signalisation)
traffic warden *n* contractuel(le)
tragedy ['trædʒədı] *n* tragédie *f*
tragic ['trædʒık] *adj* tragique
trail [treıl] *n* (*tracks*) trace *f*, piste *f*; (*path*) chemin
m, piste; (*of smoke etc*) traînée *f* ▷ *vt* (*drag*) traîner,
tirer; (*follow*) suivre ▷ *vi* traîner; (*in game, contest*)
être en retard; **to be on sb's** ~ être sur la piste
de qn
  ▶ **trail away**
  ▶ **trail off** *vi* (*sound, voice*) s'évanouir; (*interest*)
  disparaître
  ▶ **trail behind** *vi* traîner, être à la traîne
trailer ['treıləʳ] *n* (*Aut*) remorque *f*; (*US*) caravane
f; (*Cine*) bande-annonce *f*
trailer truck *n* (*US*) (camion *m*) semi-remorque *m*

train [treın] *n* train *m*; (*in underground*) rame *f*;
(*of dress*) traîne *f*; (*Brit: series*): ~ **of events** série *f*
d'événements ▷ *vt* (*apprentice, doctor etc*) former;
(*Sport*) entraîner; (*dog*) dresser; (*memory*) exercer;
(*point: gun etc*): **to** ~ **sth on** braquer qch sur ▷ *vi*
recevoir sa formation; (*Sport*) s'entraîner; **one's**
~ **of thought** le fil de sa pensée; **to go by** ~
voyager par le train or en train; **what time does**
the ~ **from Paris get in?** à quelle heure arrive le
train de Paris?; **is this the** ~ **for ...?** c'est bien le
train pour ...?; **to** ~ **sb to do sth** apprendre à qn à
faire qch; (*employee*) former qn à faire qch
trained [treınd] *adj* qualifié(e), qui a reçu une
formation; dressé(e)
trainee [treı'niː] *n* stagiaire *m/f*; (*in trade*)
apprenti(e)
trainer ['treınəʳ] *n* (*Sport*) entraîneur(-euse); (*of
dogs etc*) dresseur(-euse); **trainers** *npl* (*shoes*)
chaussures *fpl* de sport
training ['treınıŋ] *n* formation *f*; (*Sport*)
entraînement *m*; (*of dog etc*) dressage *m*; **in** ~
(*Sport*) à l'entraînement; (*fit*) en forme
training college *n* école professionnelle; (*for
teachers*) ≈ école normale
training course *n* cours *m* de formation
professionnelle
training shoes *npl* chaussures *fpl* de sport
trait [treıt] *n* trait *m* (de caractère)
traitor ['treıtəʳ] *n* traître *m*
tram [træm] *n* (*Brit: also:* **tramcar**) tram(way) *m*
tramp [træmp] *n* (*person*) vagabond(e),
clochard(e); (*inf: pej: woman*): **to be a** ~ être
coureuse ▷ *vi* marcher d'un pas lourd ▷ *vt* (*walk
through: town, streets*) parcourir à pied
trample ['træmpl] *vt*: **to** ~ **(underfoot)** piétiner;
(*fig*) bafouer
trampoline ['træmpəliːn] *n* trampoline *m*
tranquil ['træŋkwıl] *adj* tranquille
tranquillizer, (*US*) **tranquilizer** ['træŋkwılaızəʳ]
n (*Med*) tranquillisant *m*
transact [træn'zækt] *vt* (*business*) traiter
transaction [træn'zækʃən] *n* transaction *f*;
transactions *npl* (*minutes*) actes *mpl*; **cash** ~
transaction au comptant
transatlantic ['trænzət'læntık] *adj*
transatlantique
transcript ['trænskrıpt] *n* transcription *f* (*texte*)
transfer *n* ['trænsfəʳ] (*gen, also Sport*) transfert
m; (*Pol: of power*) passation *f*; (*of money*) virement
m; (*picture, design*) décalcomanie *f*; (: *stick-on*)
autocollant *m* ▷ *vt* [træns'fəːʳ] transférer; passer;
virer; décalquer; **to** ~ **the charges** (*Brit Tel*)
téléphoner en P.C.V.; **by bank** ~ par virement
bancaire
transfer desk *n* (*Aviat*) guichet *m* de transit
transform [træns'fɔːm] *vt* transformer
transformation [trænsfə'meıʃən] *n*
transformation *f*
transfusion [træns'fjuːʒən] *n* transfusion *f*
transient ['trænzıənt] *adj* transitoire, éphémère
transistor [træn'zıstəʳ] *n* (*Elec: also:* **transistor
radio**) transistor *m*

transit ['trænzɪt] n: **in ~** en transit

transition [træn'zɪʃən] n transition f

transitive ['trænzɪtɪv] adj (Ling) transitif(-ive)

transit lounge n (Aviat) salle f de transit

translate [trænz'leɪt] vt: **to ~ (from/into)** traduire (du/en); **can you ~ this for me?** pouvez-vous me traduire ceci?

translation [trænz'leɪʃən] n traduction f; (Scol: as opposed to prose) version f

translator [trænz'leɪtəʳ] n traducteur(-trice)

transmission [trænz'mɪʃən] n transmission f

transmit [trænz'mɪt] vt transmettre; (Radio, TV) émettre

transmitter [trænz'mɪtəʳ] n émetteur m

transparency [træns'pɛərnsɪ] n (Brit Phot) diapositive f

transparent [træns'pærnt] adj transparent(e)

transpire [træns'paɪəʳ] vi (become known): **it finally ~d that ...** on a finalement appris que ...; (happen) arriver

transplant vt [træns'plɑːnt] transplanter; (seedlings) repiquer ▷ n ['trænsplɑːnt] (Med) transplantation f; **to have a heart ~** subir une greffe du cœur

transport n ['trænspɔːt] transport m ▷ vt [træns'pɔːt] transporter; **public ~** transports en commun; **Department of T~** (Brit) ministère m des Transports

transportation [trænspɔː'teɪʃən] n (moyen m de) transport m; (of prisoners) transportation f; **Department of T~** (US) ministère m des Transports

transport café n (Brit) ≈ routier m

transvestite [trænz'vɛstaɪt] n travesti(e)

trap [træp] n (snare, trick) piège m; (carriage) cabriolet m ▷ vt prendre au piège; (immobilize) bloquer; (confine) coincer; **to set** or **lay a ~ (for sb)** tendre un piège (à qn); **to shut one's ~** (inf) la fermer

trap door n trappe f

trapeze [trə'piːz] n trapèze m

trappings ['træpɪŋz] npl ornements mpl; attributs mpl

trash [træʃ] n (pej: goods) camelote f; (: nonsense) sottises fpl; (US: rubbish) ordures fpl

trash can n (US) poubelle f

trashy ['træʃɪ] adj (inf) de camelote, qui ne vaut rien

trauma ['trɔːmə] n traumatisme m

traumatic [trɔː'mætɪk] adj traumatisant(e)

travel ['trævl] n voyage(s) m(pl) ▷ vi voyager; (move) aller, se déplacer; (news, sound) se propager ▷ vt (distance) parcourir; **this wine doesn't ~ well** ce vin voyage mal

travel agency n agence f de voyages

travel agent n agent m de voyages

travel insurance n assurance-voyage f

traveller, (US) **traveler** ['trævləʳ] n voyageur(-euse); (Comm) représentant m de commerce

traveller's cheque, (US) **traveler's check** n chèque m de voyage

travelling, (US) **traveling** ['trævlɪŋ] n voyage(s) m(pl) ▷ adj (circus, exhibition) ambulant(e) ▷ cpd (bag, clock) de voyage; (expenses) de déplacement

travel-sick ['trævlsɪk] adj: **to get ~** avoir le mal de la route (or de mer or de l'air)

travel sickness n mal m de la route (or de mer or de l'air)

trawler ['trɔːləʳ] n chalutier m

tray [treɪ] n (for carrying) plateau m; (on desk) corbeille f

treacherous ['trɛtʃərəs] adj traître(sse); (ground, tide) dont il faut se méfier; **road conditions are ~** l'état des routes est dangereux

treacle ['triːkl] n mélasse f

tread [trɛd] n (step) pas m; (sound) bruit m de pas; (of tyre) chape f, bande f de roulement ▷ vi (pt **trod**, pp **trodden**) [trɔd, 'trɔdn] marcher
▷ **tread on** vt fus marcher sur

treason ['triːzn] n trahison f

treasure ['trɛʒəʳ] n trésor m ▷ vt (value) tenir beaucoup à; (store) conserver précieusement

treasurer ['trɛʒərəʳ] n trésorier(-ière)

treasury ['trɛʒərɪ] n trésorerie f; **the T~** (US): **the T~ Department** le ministère des Finances

treat [triːt] n petit cadeau, petite surprise ▷ vt traiter; **it was a ~** ça m'a (or nous a etc) vraiment fait plaisir; **to ~ sb to sth** offrir qch à qn; **to ~ sth as a joke** prendre qch à la plaisanterie

treatment ['triːtmənt] n traitement m; **to have ~ for sth** (Med) suivre un traitement pour qch

treaty ['triːtɪ] n traité m

treble ['trɛbl] adj triple ▷ n (Mus) soprano m ▷ vt, vi tripler

treble clef n clé f de sol

tree [triː] n arbre m

trek [trɛk] n (long walk) randonnée f; (tiring walk) longue marche, trotte f ▷ vi (as holiday) faire de la randonnée

tremble ['trɛmbl] vi trembler

tremendous [trɪ'mɛndəs] adj (enormous) énorme; (excellent) formidable, fantastique

tremor ['trɛməʳ] n tremblement m; (also: **earth tremor**) secousse f sismique

trench [trɛntʃ] n tranchée f

trend [trɛnd] n (tendency) tendance f; (of events) cours m; (fashion) mode f; **~ towards/away from doing** tendance à faire/à ne pas faire; **to set the ~** donner le ton; **to set a ~** lancer une mode

trendy ['trɛndɪ] adj (idea, person) dans le vent; (clothes) dernier cri inv

trespass ['trɛspəs] vi: **to ~ on** s'introduire sans permission dans; (fig) empiéter sur; **"no ~ing"** "propriété privée", "défense d'entrer"

trestle ['trɛsl] n tréteau m

trial ['traɪəl] n (Law) procès m, jugement m; (test: of machine etc) essai m; (worry) souci m; **trials** npl (unpleasant experiences) épreuves fpl; (Sport) épreuves éliminatoires; **horse ~s** concours m hippique; **by jury** jugement par jury; **to be sent for ~** être traduit(e) en justice; **to be on ~** passer en jugement; **by ~ and error** par tâtonnements

trial period n période f d'essai
triangle ['traɪæŋgl] n (Math, Mus) triangle m
triangular [traɪ'æŋgjulə'] adj triangulaire
tribe [traɪb] n tribu f
tribesman ['traɪbzmən] n membre m de la tribu
tribunal [traɪ'bju:nl] n tribunal m
tributary ['trɪbjutərɪ] n (river) affluent m
tribute ['trɪbju:t] n tribut m, hommage m; **to pay ~ to** rendre hommage à
trick [trɪk] n (magic) tour m; (joke, prank) tour, farce f; (skill, knack) astuce f; (Cards) levée f ▷ vt attraper, rouler; **to play a ~ on sb** jouer un tour à qn; **to ~ sb into doing sth** persuader qn par la ruse de faire qch; **to ~ sb out of sth** obtenir qch de qn par la ruse; **it's a ~ of the light** c'est une illusion d'optique causée par la lumière; **that should do the ~** (fam) ça devrait faire l'affaire
trickery ['trɪkərɪ] n ruse f
trickle ['trɪkl] n (of water etc) filet m ▷ vi couler en un filet or goutte à goutte; **to ~ in/out** (people) entrer/sortir par petits groupes
tricky ['trɪkɪ] adj difficile, délicat(e)
tricycle ['traɪsɪkl] n tricycle m
trifle ['traɪfl] n bagatelle f; (Culin) ≈ diplomate m ▷ adv: **a ~ long** un peu long ▷ vi: **to ~ with** traiter à la légère
trifling ['traɪflɪŋ] adj insignifiant(e)
trigger ['trɪgə'] n (of gun) gâchette f
▶ **trigger off** vt déclencher
trim [trɪm] adj net(te); (house, garden) bien tenu(e); (figure) svelte ▷ n (haircut etc) légère coupe; (embellishment) finitions fpl; (on car) garnitures fpl ▷ vt (cut) couper légèrement; (decorate): **to ~ (with)** décorer (de); (Naut: a sail) gréer; **to keep in (good) ~** maintenir en (bon) état
trimmings ['trɪmɪŋz] npl décorations fpl; (extras: gen Culin) garniture f
trinket ['trɪŋkɪt] n bibelot m; (piece of jewellery) colifichet m
trio ['tri:əʊ] n trio m
trip [trɪp] n voyage m; (excursion) excursion f; (stumble) faux pas ▷ vi faire un faux pas, trébucher; (go lightly) marcher d'un pas léger; **on a ~** en voyage
▶ **trip up** vi trébucher ▷ vt faire un croc-en-jambe à
tripe [traɪp] n (Culin) tripes fpl; (pej: rubbish) idioties fpl
triple ['trɪpl] adj triple ▷ adv: **~ the distance/the speed** trois fois la distance/la vitesse
triplets ['trɪplɪts] npl triplés(-ées)
triplicate ['trɪplɪkət] n: **in ~** en trois exemplaires
tripod ['traɪpɔd] n trépied m
trite [traɪt] adj banal(e)
triumph ['traɪʌmf] n triomphe m ▷ vi: **to ~ (over)** triompher (de)
triumphant [traɪ'ʌmfənt] adj triomphant(e)
trivia ['trɪvɪə] npl futilités fpl
trivial ['trɪvɪəl] adj insignifiant(e); (commonplace) banal(e)
trod [trɔd] pt of **tread**

trodden ['trɔdn] pp of **tread**
trolley ['trɔlɪ] n chariot m
trombone [trɔm'bəʊn] n trombone m
troop [tru:p] n bande f, groupe m ▷ vi: **to ~ in/out** entrer/sortir en groupe; **troops** npl (Mil) troupes fpl; (: men) hommes mpl, soldats mpl; **~ing the colour** (Brit: ceremony) le salut au drapeau
trophy ['trəʊfɪ] n trophée m
tropic ['trɔpɪk] n tropique m; **in the ~s** sous les tropiques; **T~ of Cancer/Capricorn** tropique du Cancer/Capricorne
tropical ['trɔpɪkl] adj tropical(e)
trot [trɔt] n trot m ▷ vi trotter; **on the ~** (Brit: fig) d'affilée
▶ **trot out** vt (excuse, reason) débiter; (names, facts) réciter les uns après les autres
trouble ['trʌbl] n difficulté(s) f(pl), problème(s) m(pl); (worry) ennuis mpl, soucis mpl; (bother, effort) peine f; (Pol) conflit(s) m(pl), troubles mpl; (Med): **stomach etc ~** troubles gastriques etc ▷ vt (disturb) déranger, gêner; (worry) inquiéter ▷ vi: **to ~ to do** prendre la peine de faire; **troubles** npl (Pol etc) troubles; (personal) ennuis mpl, soucis; **to be in ~** avoir des ennuis; (ship, climber etc) être en difficulté; **to have ~ doing sth** avoir du mal à faire qch; **to go to the ~ of doing** se donner le mal de faire; **it's no ~!** je vous en prie!; **please don't ~ yourself** je vous en prie, ne vous dérangez pas!; **the ~ is ...** le problème, c'est que ...; **what's the ~?** qu'est-ce qui ne va pas?
troubled ['trʌbld] adj (person) inquiet(-ète); (times, life) agité(e)
troublemaker ['trʌblmeɪkə'] n élément perturbateur, fauteur m de troubles
troubleshooter ['trʌblʃu:tə'] n (in conflict) conciliateur m
troublesome ['trʌblsəm] adj (child) fatigant(e), difficile; (cough) gênant(e)
trough [trɔf] n (also: **drinking trough**) abreuvoir m; (also: **feeding trough**) auge f; (depression) creux m; (channel) chenal m; **~ of low pressure** (Meteorology) dépression f
trousers ['traʊzəz] npl pantalon m; **short ~** (Brit) culottes courtes
trout [traʊt] n (pl inv) truite f
trowel ['traʊəl] n truelle f; (garden tool) déplantoir m
truant ['truənt] n: **to play ~** (Brit) faire l'école buissonnière
truce [tru:s] n trêve f
truck [trʌk] n camion m; (Rail) wagon m à plate-forme; (for luggage) chariot m (à bagages)
truck driver n camionneur m
truck farm n (US) jardin m maraîcher
true [tru:] adj vrai(e); (accurate) exact(e); (genuine) vrai, véritable; (faithful) fidèle; (wall) d'aplomb; (beam) droit(e); (wheel) dans l'axe; **to come ~** se réaliser; **~ to life** réaliste
truffle ['trʌfl] n truffe f
truly ['tru:lɪ] adv vraiment, réellement; (truthfully) sans mentir; (faithfully) fidèlement; **yours ~** (in letter) je vous prie d'agréer, Monsieur

(*or* Madame *etc*), l'expression de mes sentiments respectueux

trump [trʌmp] *n* atout *m*; **to turn up ~s** (*fig*) faire des miracles

trumpet ['trʌmpɪt] *n* trompette *f*

truncheon ['trʌntʃən] *n* bâton *m* (d'agent de police); matraque *f*

trundle ['trʌndl] *vt, vi*: **to ~ along** rouler bruyamment

trunk [trʌŋk] *n* (*of tree, person*) tronc *m*; (*of elephant*) trompe *f*; (*case*) malle *f*; (*US Aut*) coffre *m*; **trunks** *npl* (*also*: **swimming trunks**) maillot *m or* slip *m* de bain

truss [trʌs] *n* (*Med*) bandage *m* herniaire ▷ *vt*: **to ~ (up)** (*Culin*) brider

trust [trʌst] *n* confiance *f*; (*responsibility*): **to place sth in sb's ~** confier la responsabilité de qch à qn; (*Law*) fidéicommis *m*; (*Comm*) trust *m* ▷ *vt* (*rely on*) avoir confiance en; (*entrust*): **to ~ sth to sb** confier qch à qn; (*hope*): **to ~ (that)** espérer (que); **to take sth on ~** accepter qch les yeux fermés; **in ~** (*Law*) par fidéicommis

trusted ['trʌstɪd] *adj* en qui l'on a confiance

trustee [trʌs'tiː] *n* (*Law*) fidéicommissaire *m/f*; (*of school etc*) administrateur(-trice)

trustful ['trʌstful] *adj* confiant(e)

trustworthy ['trʌstwəːðɪ] *adj* digne de confiance

truth [truːθ, *pl* truːðz] *n* vérité *f*

truthful ['truːθful] *adj* (*person*) qui dit la vérité; (*answer*) sincère; (*description*) exact(e), vrai(e)

try [traɪ] *n* essai *m*, tentative *f*; (*Rugby*) essai ▷ *vt* (*attempt*) essayer, tenter; (*test: sth new: also*: **try out**) essayer, tester; (*Law: person*) juger; (*strain*) éprouver ▷ *vi* essayer; **to ~ to do** essayer de faire; (*seek*) chercher à faire; **to ~ one's (very) best** *or* **one's (very) hardest** faire de son mieux; **to give sth a ~** essayer qch

▸ **try on** *vt* (*clothes*) essayer; **to ~ it on** (*fig*) tenter le coup, bluffer

▸ **try out** *vt* essayer, mettre à l'essai

trying ['traɪɪŋ] *adj* pénible

T-shirt ['tiːʃəːt] *n* tee-shirt *m*

tsunami [tsʊ'nɑːmɪ] *n* tsunami *m*

T-square ['tiːskwɛəʳ] *n* équerre *f* en T

tub [tʌb] *n* cuve *f*; (*for washing clothes*) baquet *m*; (*bath*) baignoire *f*

tubby ['tʌbɪ] *adj* rondelet(te)

tube [tjuːb] *n* tube *m*; (*Brit: underground*) métro *m*; (*for tyre*) chambre *f* à air; (*inf: television*): **the ~** la télé

tuberculosis [tjubəːkju'ləusɪs] *n* tuberculose *f*

tube station *n* (*Brit*) station *f* de métro

TUC *n abbr* (*Brit*: = *Trades Union Congress*) confédération *f* des syndicats britanniques

tuck [tʌk] *n* (*Sewing*) pli *m*, rempli *m* ▷ *vt* (*put*) mettre

▸ **tuck away** *vt* cacher, ranger; (*money*) mettre de côté; (*building*): **to be ~ed away** être caché(e)

▸ **tuck in** *vt* rentrer; (*child*) border ▷ *vi* (*eat*) manger de bon appétit; attaquer le repas

▸ **tuck up** *vt* (*child*) border

tuck shop *n* (*Brit Scol*) boutique *f* à provisions

Tuesday ['tjuːzdɪ] *n* mardi *m*; **(the date) today is ~ 23rd March** nous sommes aujourd'hui le mardi 23 mars; **on ~** mardi; **on ~s** le mardi; **every ~** tous les mardis, chaque mardi; **every other ~** un mardi sur deux; **last/next ~** mardi dernier/prochain; **~ next** mardi qui vient; **the following ~** le mardi suivant; **a week/fortnight on ~**, **~ week/fortnight** mardi en huit/quinze; **the ~ before last** l'autre mardi; **the ~ after next** mardi en huit; **~ morning/lunchtime/afternoon/evening** mardi matin/midi/après-midi/soir; **~ night** mardi soir; (*overnight*) la nuit de mardi (à mercredi); **~'s newspaper** le journal de mardi

tuft [tʌft] *n* touffe *f*

tug [tʌg] *n* (*ship*) remorqueur *m* ▷ *vt* tirer (sur)

tug-of-war [tʌgəv'wɔːʳ] *n* lutte *f* à la corde

tuition [tjuː'ɪʃən] *n* (*Brit: lessons*) leçons *fpl*; (: *private*) cours particuliers; (*US: fees*) frais *mpl* de scolarité

tulip ['tjuːlɪp] *n* tulipe *f*

tumble ['tʌmbl] *n* (*fall*) chute *f*, culbute *f* ▷ *vi* tomber, dégringoler; (*somersault*) faire une *or* des culbute(s) ▷ *vt* renverser, faire tomber; **to ~ to sth** (*inf*) réaliser qch

tumbledown ['tʌmbldaun] *adj* délabré(e)

tumble dryer *n* (*Brit*) séchoir *m* (à linge) à air chaud

tumbler ['tʌmbləʳ] *n* verre (droit), gobelet *m*

tummy ['tʌmɪ] *n* (*inf*) ventre *m*

tumour, (*US*) **tumor** ['tjuːməʳ] *n* tumeur *f*

tuna ['tjuːnə] *n* (*pl inv*: **tuna**; *also*: **tuna fish**) thon *m*

tune [tjuːn] *n* (*melody*) air *m* ▷ *vt* (*Mus*) accorder; (*Radio, TV, Aut*) régler, mettre au point; **to be in/out of ~** (*instrument*) être accordé/désaccordé; (*singer*) chanter juste/faux; **to be in/out of ~ with** (*fig*) être en accord/désaccord avec; **she was robbed to the ~ of £30,000** (*fig*) on lui a volé la jolie somme de 10 000 livres

▸ **tune in** *vi* (*Radio, TV*): **to ~ in (to)** se mettre à l'écoute (de)

▸ **tune up** *vi* (*musician*) accorder son instrument

tuneful ['tjuːnful] *adj* mélodieux(-euse)

tuner ['tjuːnəʳ] *n* (*radio set*) tuner *m*; **piano ~** accordeur *m* de pianos

tunic ['tjuːnɪk] *n* tunique *f*

Tunis ['tjuːnɪs] *n* Tunis

Tunisia [tjuː'nɪzɪə] *n* Tunisie *f*

Tunisian [tjuː'nɪzɪən] *adj* tunisien(ne) ▷ *n* Tunisien(ne)

tunnel ['tʌnl] *n* tunnel *m*; (*in mine*) galerie *f* ▷ *vi* creuser un tunnel (*or* une galerie)

turbulence ['təːbjuləns] *n* (*Aviat*) turbulence *f*

tureen [tə'riːn] *n* soupière *f*

turf [təːf] *n* gazon *m*; (*clod*) motte *f* (de gazon) ▷ *vt* gazonner; **the T~** le turf, les courses *fpl*

▸ **turf out** *vt* (*inf*) jeter; jeter dehors

Turk [təːk] *n* Turc (Turque)

Turkey ['təːkɪ] *n* Turquie *f*

turkey ['təːkɪ] *n* dindon *m*, dinde *f*

Turkish ['təːkɪʃ] *adj* turc (turque) ▷ *n* (*Ling*) turc *m*

turmoil ['təːmɔɪl] *n* trouble *m*, bouleversement *m*

turn [tə:n] n tour m; (in road) tournant m; (tendency: of mind, events) tournure f; (performance) numéro m; (Med) crise f, attaque f ▷ vt tourner; (collar, steak) retourner; (age) atteindre; (shape: wood, metal) tourner; (milk) faire tourner; (change): **to ~ sth into** changer qch en ▷ vi (object, wind, milk) tourner; (person: look back) se (re)tourner; (reverse direction) faire demi-tour; (change) changer; (become) devenir; **to ~ into** se changer en, se transformer en; **a good ~** un service; **a bad ~** un mauvais tour; **it gave me quite a ~** ça m'a fait un coup; **"no left ~"** (Aut) "défense de tourner à gauche"; **~ left/right at the next junction** tournez à gauche/droite au prochain carrefour; **it's your ~** c'est (à) votre tour; **in ~** à son tour; **à tour de rôle**; **to take ~s** se relayer; **to take ~s at** faire à tour de rôle; **at the ~ of the year/century** à la fin de l'année/du siècle; **to take a ~ for the worse** (situation, events) empirer; **his health** or **he has taken a ~ for the worse** son état s'est aggravé
▶ **turn about** vi faire demi-tour; faire un demi-tour
▶ **turn around** vi (person) se retourner ▷ vt (object) tourner
▶ **turn away** vi se détourner, tourner la tête ▷ vt (reject: person) renvoyer; (: business) refuser
▶ **turn back** vi revenir, faire demi-tour
▶ **turn down** vt (refuse) rejeter, refuser; (reduce) baisser; (fold) rabattre
▶ **turn in** vi (inf: go to bed) aller se coucher ▷ vt (fold) rentrer
▶ **turn off** vi (from road) tourner ▷ vt (light, radio etc) éteindre; (tap) fermer; (engine) arrêter; **I can't ~ the heating off** je n'arrive pas à éteindre le chauffage
▶ **turn on** vt (light, radio etc) allumer; (tap) ouvrir; (engine) mettre en marche; **I can't ~ the heating on** je n'arrive pas à allumer le chauffage
▶ **turn out** vt (light, gas) éteindre; (produce: goods, novel, good pupils) produire ▷ vi (voters, troops) se présenter; **to ~ out to be ...** s'avérer ..., se révéler ...
▶ **turn over** vi (person) se retourner ▷ vt (object) retourner; (page) tourner
▶ **turn round** vi faire demi-tour; (rotate) tourner
▶ **turn to** vt fus: **to ~ to sb** s'adresser à qn
▶ **turn up** vi (person) arriver, se pointer (inf); (lost object) être retrouvé(e) ▷ vt (collar) remonter; (radio, heater) mettre plus fort

turning ['tə:nɪŋ] n (in road) tournant m; **the first ~ on the right** la première (rue or route) à droite
turning point n (fig) tournant m, moment décisif
turnip ['tə:nɪp] n navet m
turnout ['tə:naut] n (nombre m de personnes dans l')assistance f; (of voters) taux m de participation
turnover ['tə:nəuvəʳ] n (Comm: amount of money) chiffre m d'affaires; (: of goods) roulement m; (of staff) renouvellement m, changement m; (Culin) sorte de chausson; **there is a rapid ~ in staff** le personnel change souvent

turnpike ['tə:npaɪk] n (US) autoroute f à péage
turnstile ['tə:nstaɪl] n tourniquet m (d'entrée)
turntable ['tə:nteɪbl] n (on record player) platine f
turn-up ['tə:nʌp] n (Brit: on trousers) revers m
turpentine ['tə:pəntaɪn] n (also: **turps**) (essence f de) térébenthine f
turquoise ['tə:kwɔɪz] n (stone) turquoise f ▷ adj turquoise inv
turret ['tʌrɪt] n tourelle f
turtle ['tə:tl] n tortue marine
turtleneck ['tə:tlnɛk], **turtleneck sweater** n pullover m à col montant
tusk [tʌsk] n défense f (d'éléphant)
tutor ['tju:təʳ] n (Brit Scol: in college) directeur(-trice) d'études; (private teacher) précepteur(-trice)
tutorial [tju:'tɔ:rɪəl] n (Scol) (séance f de) travaux mpl pratiques
tuxedo [tʌk'si:dəu] n (US) smoking m
TV [ti:'vi:] n abbr (= television) télé f, TV f
twang [twæŋ] n (of instrument) son vibrant; (of voice) ton nasillard ▷ vi vibrer ▷ vt (guitar) pincer les cordes de
tweed [twi:d] n tweed m
tweezers ['twi:zəz] npl pince f à épiler
twelfth [twelfθ] num douzième
twelve [twelv] num douze; **at ~ (o'clock)** à midi; (midnight) à minuit
twentieth ['twentɪɪθ] num vingtième
twenty ['twentɪ] num vingt
twice [twaɪs] adv deux fois; **~ as much** deux fois plus; **~ a week** deux fois par semaine; **she is ~ your age** elle a deux fois ton âge
twiddle ['twɪdl] vt, vi: **to ~ (with) sth** tripoter qch; **to ~ one's thumbs** (fig) se tourner les pouces
twig [twɪg] n brindille f ▷ vt, vi (inf) piger
twilight ['twaɪlaɪt] n crépuscule m; (morning) aube f; **in the ~** dans la pénombre
twin [twɪn] adj, n jumeau(-elle) ▷ vt jumeler
twin-bedded room ['twɪn'bedɪd-] n = **twin room**
twin beds npl lits mpl jumeaux
twine [twaɪn] n ficelle f ▷ vi (plant) s'enrouler
twinge [twɪndʒ] n (of pain) élancement m; (of conscience) remords m
twinkle ['twɪŋkl] n scintillement m; pétillement m ▷ vi scintiller; (eyes) pétiller
twin room n chambre f à deux lits
twirl [twə:l] n tournoiement m ▷ vt faire tournoyer ▷ vi tournoyer
twist [twɪst] n torsion f, tour m; (in wire, flex) tortillon m; (bend: in road) tournant m; (in story) coup m de théâtre ▷ vt tordre; (weave) entortiller; (roll around) enrouler; (fig) déformer ▷ vi s'entortiller; s'enrouler; (road, river) serpenter; **to ~ one's ankle/wrist** (Med) se tordre la cheville/le poignet
twit [twɪt] n (inf) crétin(e)
twitch [twɪtʃ] n (pull) coup sec, saccade f; (nervous) tic m ▷ vi se convulser; avoir un tic
two [tu:] num deux; **~ by ~, in ~s** par deux; **to put ~ and ~ together** (fig) faire le rapprochement

two-door [tuː'dɔːʳ] *adj* (*Aut*) à deux portes
two-faced [tuː'feɪst] *adj* (*pej: person*) faux (fausse)
twofold ['tuːfəʊld] *adv*: **to increase** ~ doubler
▷ *adj* (*increase*) de cent pour cent; (*reply*) en deux parties
two-piece ['tuː'piːs] *n* (*also*: **two-piece suit**) (costume *m*) deux-pièces *m inv*; (*also*: **two-piece swimsuit**) (maillot *m* de bain) deux-pièces
twosome ['tuːsəm] *n* (*people*) couple *m*
two-way ['tuːweɪ] *adj* (*traffic*) dans les deux sens; ~ **radio** émetteur-récepteur *m*
tycoon [taɪ'kuːn] *n*: (**business**) ~ gros homme d'affaires
type [taɪp] *n* (*category*) genre *m*, espèce *f*; (*model*) modèle *m*; (*example*) type *m*; (*Typ*) type, caractère *m* ▷ *vt* (*letter etc*) taper (à la machine); **what ~ do you want?** quel genre voulez-vous?; **in bold/**
italic ~ en caractères gras/en italiques
typecast ['taɪpkɑːst] *adj* condamné(e) à toujour jouer le même rôle
typeface ['taɪpfeɪs] *n* police *f* (de caractères)
typescript ['taɪpskrɪpt] *n* texte dactylographié
typewriter ['taɪpraɪtəʳ] *n* machine *f* à écrire
typewritten ['taɪprɪtn] *adj* dactylographié(e)
typhoid ['taɪfɔɪd] *n* typhoïde *f*
typhoon [taɪ'fuːn] *n* typhon *m*
typical ['tɪpɪkl] *adj* typique, caractéristique
typically ['tɪpɪklɪ] *adv* (*as usual*) comme d'habitude; (*characteristically*) typiquement
typing ['taɪpɪŋ] *n* dactylo(graphie) *f*
typist ['taɪpɪst] *n* dactylo *m/f*
tyrant ['taɪrənt] *n* tyran *m*
tyre, (*US*) **tire** ['taɪəʳ] *n* pneu *m*
tyre pressure *n* (*Brit*) pression *f* (de gonflage)

Uu

U-bend ['juːbɛnd] n (Brit Aut) coude m, virage m en épingle à cheveux; (in pipe) coude

ubiquitous [juːˈbɪkwɪtəs] adj doué(e) d'ubiquité, omniprésent(e)

udder ['ʌdəʳ] n pis m, mamelle f

UFO ['juːfəu] n abbr (= unidentified flying object) ovni m

Uganda [juːˈgændə] n Ouganda m

ugh [əːh] excl pouah!

ugly ['ʌglɪ] adj laid(e), vilain(e); (fig) répugnant(e)

UHT adj abbr = **ultra-heat treated**; ~ **milk** lait m UHT or longue conservation

UK n abbr = **United Kingdom**

ulcer ['ʌlsəʳ] n ulcère m; **mouth** ~ aphte f

Ulster ['ʌlstəʳ] n Ulster m

ulterior [ʌlˈtɪərɪəʳ] adj ultérieur(e); ~ **motive** arrière-pensée f

ultimate ['ʌltɪmət] adj ultime, final(e); (authority) suprême ⊳ n: **the** ~ **in luxury** le summum du luxe

ultimately ['ʌltɪmətlɪ] adv (at last) en fin de compte; (fundamentally) finalement; (eventually) par la suite

ultimatum (pl **-s** or **ultimata**) [ʌltɪˈmeɪtəm, -tə] n ultimatum m

ultrasound ['ʌltrəsaund] n (Med) ultrason m

ultraviolet ['ʌltrəˈvaɪəlɪt] adj ultraviolet(te)

umbilical [ʌmbɪˈlaɪkl] adj: ~ **cord** cordon ombilical

umbrella [ʌmˈbrɛlə] n parapluie m; (for sun) parasol m; (fig): **under the** ~ **of** sous les auspices de; chapeauté(e) par

umpire ['ʌmpaɪəʳ] n arbitre m; (Tennis) juge m de chaise ⊳ vt arbitrer

umpteen [ʌmpˈtiːn] adj je ne sais combien de; **for the** ~**th time** pour la nième fois

UN n abbr = **United Nations**

unable [ʌnˈeɪbl] adj: **to be** ~ **to** ne (pas) pouvoir, être dans l'impossibilité de; (not capable) être incapable de

unacceptable [ʌnəkˈsɛptəbl] adj (behaviour) inadmissible; (price, proposal) inacceptable

unaccompanied [ʌnəˈkʌmpənɪd] adj (child, lady) non accompagné(e); (singing, song) sans accompagnement

unaccustomed [ʌnəˈkʌstəmd] adj inaccoutumé(e), inhabituel(le); **to be** ~ **to sth** ne pas avoir l'habitude de qch

unanimous [juːˈnænɪməs] adj unanime

unanimously [juːˈnænɪməslɪ] adv à l'unanimité

unarmed [ʌnˈɑːmd] adj (person) non armé(e); (combat) sans armes

unattached [ʌnəˈtætʃt] adj libre, sans attaches

unattended [ʌnəˈtɛndɪd] adj (car, child, luggage) sans surveillance

unattractive [ʌnəˈtræktɪv] adj peu attrayant(e); (character) peu sympathique

unauthorized [ʌnˈɔːθəraɪzd] adj non autorisé(e), sans autorisation

unavailable [ʌnəˈveɪləbl] adj (article, room, book) (qui n'est) pas disponible; (person) (qui n'est) pas libre

unavoidable [ʌnəˈvɔɪdəbl] adj inévitable

unaware [ʌnəˈwɛəʳ] adj: **to be** ~ **of** ignorer, ne pas savoir, être inconscient(e) de

unawares [ʌnəˈwɛəz] adv à l'improviste, au dépourvu

unbalanced [ʌnˈbælənst] adj déséquilibré(e)

unbearable [ʌnˈbɛərəbl] adj insupportable

unbeatable [ʌnˈbiːtəbl] adj imbattable

unbeknown [ʌnbɪˈnəun], **unbeknownst** [ʌnbɪˈnəunst] adv: ~ **to** à l'insu de

unbelievable [ʌnbɪˈliːvəbl] adj incroyable

unbend [ʌnˈbɛnd] (irreg: like **bend**) vi se détendre ⊳ vt (wire) redresser, détordre

unbiased, unbiassed [ʌnˈbaɪəst] adj impartial(e)

unborn [ʌnˈbɔːn] adj à naître

unbreakable [ʌnˈbreɪkəbl] adj incassable

unbroken [ʌnˈbrəukn] adj intact(e); (line) continu(e); (record) non battu(e)

unbutton [ʌnˈbʌtn] vt déboutonner

uncalled-for [ʌnˈkɔːldfɔːʳ] adj déplacé(e), injustifié(e)

uncanny [ʌnˈkænɪ] adj étrange, troublant(e)

unceremonious [ʌnsɛrɪˈməunɪəs] adj (abrupt, rude) brusque

uncertain [ʌnˈsəːtn] adj incertain(e); (hesitant) hésitant(e); **we were** ~ **whether ...** nous ne savions pas vraiment si ...; **in no** ~ **terms** sans équivoque possible

uncertainty [ʌnˈsəːtntɪ] n incertitude f, doutes mpl

unchanged [ʌn'tʃeɪndʒd] adj inchangé(e)

uncivilized [ʌn'sɪvɪlaɪzd] adj non civilisé(e); (fig) barbare

uncle ['ʌŋkl] n oncle m

unclear [ʌn'klɪəʳ] adj (qui n'est) pas clair(e) or évident(e); **I'm still ~ about what I'm supposed to do** je ne sais pas encore exactement ce que je dois faire

uncomfortable [ʌn'kʌmfətəbl] adj inconfortable, peu confortable; (uneasy) mal à l'aise, gêné(e); (situation) désagréable

uncommon [ʌn'kɔmən] adj rare, singulier(-ière), peu commun(e)

uncompromising [ʌn'kɔmprəmaɪzɪŋ] adj intransigeant(e), inflexible

unconcerned [ʌnkən'sə:nd] adj (unworried): **to be ~ (about)** ne pas s'inquiéter (de)

unconditional [ʌnkən'dɪʃənl] adj sans conditions

unconscious [ʌn'kɔnʃəs] adj sans connaissance, évanoui(e); (unaware): **~ (of)** inconscient(e) (de) ▷ n: **the ~** l'inconscient m; **to knock sb ~** assommer qn

unconsciously [ʌn'kɔnʃəslɪ] adv inconsciemment

uncontrollable [ʌnkən'trəuləbl] adj (child, dog) indiscipliné(e); (temper, laughter) irrépressible

unconventional [ʌnkən'vɛnʃənl] adj peu conventionnel(le)

uncouth [ʌn'ku:θ] adj grossier(-ière), fruste

uncover [ʌn'kʌvəʳ] vt découvrir

undecided [ʌndɪ'saɪdɪd] adj indécis(e), irrésolu(e)

undeniable [ʌndɪ'naɪəbl] adj indéniable, incontestable

under ['ʌndəʳ] prep sous; (less than) (de) moins de; au-dessous de; (according to) selon, en vertu de ▷ adv au-dessous; en dessous; **from ~ sth** de dessous or de sous qch; **~ there** là-dessous; **in ~ 2 hours** en moins de 2 heures; **~ anaesthetic** sous anesthésie; **~ discussion** en discussion; **~ the circumstances** étant donné les circonstances; **~ repair** en (cours de) réparation

underage [ʌndər'eɪdʒ] adj qui n'a pas l'âge réglementaire

undercarriage ['ʌndəkærɪdʒ] n (Brit Aviat) train m d'atterrissage

undercharge [ʌndə'tʃɑ:dʒ] vt ne pas faire payer assez à

undercoat ['ʌndəkəut] n (paint) couche f de fond

undercover [ʌndə'kʌvəʳ] adj secret(-ète), clandestin(e)

undercurrent ['ʌndəkʌrnt] n courant sous-jacent

undercut [ʌndə'kʌt] vt (irreg: like **cut**) vendre moins cher que

underdog ['ʌndədɔg] n opprimé m

underdone [ʌndə'dʌn] adj (Culin) saignant(e); (: pej) pas assez cuit(e)

underestimate ['ʌndər'ɛstɪmeɪt] vt sous-estimer, mésestimer

underfed [ʌndə'fɛd] adj sous-alimenté(e)

underfoot [ʌndə'fut] adv sous les pieds

undergo [ʌndə'gəu] vt (irreg: like **go**) subir; (treatment) suivre; **the car is ~ing repairs** la voiture est en réparation

undergraduate [ʌndə'grædjuɪt] n étudiant(e) (qui prépare la licence) ▷ cpd: **~ courses** cours mpl préparant à la licence

underground ['ʌndəgraund] adj souterrain(e); (fig) clandestin(e) ▷ n (Brit: railway) métro m; (Pol) clandestinité f

undergrowth ['ʌndəgrəuθ] n broussailles fpl, sous-bois m

underhand [ʌndə'hænd], **underhanded** [ʌndə'hændɪd] adj (fig) sournois(e), en dessous

underlie [ʌndə'laɪ] vt (irreg: like **lie**) être à la base de; **the underlying cause** la cause sous-jacente

underline [ʌndə'laɪn] vt souligner

undermine [ʌndə'maɪn] vt saper, miner

underneath [ʌndə'ni:θ] adv (en) dessous ▷ prep sous, au-dessous de

underpaid [ʌndə'peɪd] adj sous-payé(e)

underpants ['ʌndəpænts] npl caleçon m, slip m

underpass ['ʌndəpɑ:s] n (Brit: for pedestrians) passage souterrain; (: for cars) passage inférieur

underprivileged [ʌndə'prɪvɪlɪdʒd] adj défavorisé(e)

underrate [ʌndə'reɪt] vt sous-estimer, mésestimer

underscore [ʌndə'skɔ:ʳ] vt souligner (irreg: like **sell**)

undershirt ['ʌndəʃə:t] n (US) tricot m de corps

undershorts ['ʌndəʃɔ:ts] npl (US) caleçon m, slip m

underside ['ʌndəsaɪd] n dessous m

underskirt ['ʌndəskə:t] n (Brit) jupon m

understand [ʌndə'stænd] vt, vi (irreg: like **stand**) comprendre; **I don't ~** je ne comprends pas; **I ~ that ...** je me suis laissé dire que ..., je crois comprendre que ...; **to make o.s. understood** se faire comprendre

understandable [ʌndə'stændəbl] adj compréhensible

understanding [ʌndə'stændɪŋ] adj compréhensif(-ive) ▷ n compréhension f; (agreement) accord m; **to come to an ~ with sb** s'entendre avec qn; **on the ~ that ...** à condition que ...

understatement ['ʌndəsteɪtmənt] n: **that's an ~** c'est (bien) peu dire, le terme est faible

understood [ʌndə'stud] pt, pp of **understand** ▷ adj entendu(e); (implied) sous-entendu(e)

understudy ['ʌndəstʌdɪ] n doublure f

undertake [ʌndə'teɪk] vt (irreg: like **take**); (job, task) entreprendre; (duty) se charger de; **to ~ to do sth** s'engager à faire qch

undertaker ['ʌndəteɪkəʳ] n (Brit) entrepreneur m des pompes funèbres, croque-mort m

undertaking ['ʌndəteɪkɪŋ] n entreprise f; (promise) promesse f

undertone ['ʌndətəun] n (low voice): **in an ~** à mi-voix; (of criticism etc) nuance cachée

underwater [ʌndə'wɔ:təʳ] adv sous l'eau ▷ adj

sous-marin(e)

underway [ˌʌndə'weɪ] *adj*: **to be** ~ (*meeting, investigation*) être en cours

underwear ['ʌndəwɛəʳ] *n* sous-vêtements *mpl*; (*women's only*) dessous *mpl*

underwent [ˌʌndə'wɛnt] *pt of* **undergo**

underworld ['ʌndəwə:ld] *n* (*of crime*) milieu *m*, pègre *f*

underwrite [ˌʌndə'raɪt] *vt* (*Finance*) garantir; (*Insurance*) souscrire

undesirable [ˌʌndɪ'zaɪərəbl] *adj* peu souhaitable; (*person, effect*) indésirable

undies ['ʌndɪz] *npl* (*inf*) dessous *mpl*, lingerie *f*

undiplomatic ['ʌndɪplə'mætɪk] *adj* peu diplomatique, maladroit(e)

undisputed ['ʌndɪs'pju:tɪd] *adj* incontesté(e)

undo [ʌn'du:] *vt* (*irreg: like* **do**) défaire

undoing [ʌn'du:ɪŋ] *n* ruine *f*, perte *f*

undone [ʌn'dʌn] *pp of* **undo** ▷ *adj*: **to come** ~ se défaire

undoubted [ʌn'dautɪd] *adj* indubitable, certain(e)

undoubtedly [ʌn'dautɪdlɪ] *adv* sans aucun doute

undress [ʌn'drɛs] *vi* se déshabiller ▷ *vt* déshabiller

undue [ʌn'dju:] *adj* indu(e), excessif(-ive)

undulating ['ʌndjuleɪtɪŋ] *adj* ondoyant(e), onduleux(-euse)

unduly [ʌn'dju:lɪ] *adv* trop, excessivement

unearth [ʌn'ə:θ] *vt* déterrer; (*fig*) dénicher

unearthly [ʌn'ə:θlɪ] *adj* surnaturel(le); (*hour*) indu(e), impossible

uneasy [ʌn'i:zɪ] *adj* mal à l'aise, gêné(e); (*worried*) inquiet(-ète); (*feeling*) désagréable; (*peace, truce*) fragile; **to feel** ~ **about doing sth** se sentir mal à l'aise à l'idée de faire qch

uneconomic ['ʌni:kə'nɔmɪk], **uneconomical** ['ʌni:kə'nɔmɪkl] *adj* peu économique; peu rentable

uneducated [ʌn'ɛdjukeɪtɪd] *adj* sans éducation

unemployed [ʌnɪm'plɔɪd] *adj* sans travail, au chômage ▷ *n*: **the** ~ les chômeurs *mpl*

unemployment [ʌnɪm'plɔɪmənt] *n* chômage *m*

unemployment benefit, (*US*) **unemployment compensation** *n* allocation *f* de chômage

unending [ʌn'ɛndɪŋ] *adj* interminable

unequal [ʌn'i:kwəl] *adj* inégal(e)

unerring [ʌn'ə:rɪŋ] *adj* infaillible, sûr(e)

uneven [ʌn'i:vn] *adj* inégal(e); (*quality, work*) irrégulier(-ière)

unexpected [ʌnɪk'spɛktɪd] *adj* inattendu(e), imprévu(e)

unexpectedly [ʌnɪk'spɛktɪdlɪ] *adv* (*succeed*) contre toute attente; (*arrive*) à l'improviste

unfailing [ʌn'feɪlɪŋ] *adj* inépuisable; infaillible

unfair [ʌn'fɛəʳ] *adj*: ~ **(to)** injuste (envers); **it's** ~ **that** ... il n'est pas juste que ...

unfaithful [ʌn'feɪθful] *adj* infidèle

unfamiliar [ʌnfə'mɪlɪəʳ] *adj* étrange, inconnu(e); **to be** ~ **with sth** mal connaître qch

unfashionable [ʌn'fæʃnəbl] *adj* (*clothes*) démodé(e); (*place*) peu chic *inv*; (*district*) déshérité(e), pas à la mode

unfasten [ʌn'fɑ:sn] *vt* défaire; (*belt, necklace*) détacher; (*open*) ouvrir

unfavourable, (*US*) **unfavorable** [ʌn'feɪvrəbl] *adj* défavorable

unfeeling [ʌn'fi:lɪŋ] *adj* insensible, dur(e)

unfinished [ʌn'fɪnɪʃt] *adj* inachevé(e)

unfit [ʌn'fɪt] *adj* (*physically: ill*) en mauvaise santé; (: *out of condition*) pas en forme; (*incompetent*): ~ **(for)** impropre (à); (*work, service*) inapte (à)

unfold [ʌn'fəuld] *vt* déplier; (*fig*) révéler, exposer ▷ *vi* se dérouler

unforeseen ['ʌnfɔ:'si:n] *adj* imprévu(e)

unforgettable [ʌnfə'gɛtəbl] *adj* inoubliable

unfortunate [ʌn'fɔ:tʃnət] *adj* malheureux(-euse); (*event, remark*) malencontreux(-euse)

unfortunately [ʌn'fɔ:tʃnətlɪ] *adv* malheureusement

unfounded [ʌn'faundɪd] *adj* sans fondement

unfriendly [ʌn'frɛndlɪ] *adj* peu aimable, froid(e), inamical(e)

unfurnished [ʌn'fə:nɪʃt] *adj* non meublé(e)

ungainly [ʌn'geɪnlɪ] *adj* gauche, dégingandé(e)

ungodly [ʌn'gɔdlɪ] *adj* impie; **at an** ~ **hour** à une heure indue

ungrateful [ʌn'greɪtful] *adj* qui manque de reconnaissance, ingrat(e)

unhappiness [ʌn'hæpɪnɪs] *n* tristesse *f*, peine *f*

unhappy [ʌn'hæpɪ] *adj* triste, malheureux(-euse); (*unfortunate: remark etc*) malheureux(-euse); (*not pleased*): ~ **with** mécontent(e) de, peu satisfait(e) de

unharmed [ʌn'hɑ:md] *adj* indemne, sain(e) et sauf (sauve)

UNHCR *n abbr* (= *United Nations High Commission for Refugees*) HCR *m*

unhealthy [ʌn'hɛlθɪ] *adj* (*gen*) malsain(e); (*person*) maladif(-ive)

unheard-of [ʌn'hə:dɔv] *adj* inouï(e), sans précédent

unhelpful [ʌn'hɛlpful] *adj* (*person*) peu serviable; (*advice*) peu utile

unhurt [ʌn'hə:t] *adj* indemne, sain(e) et sauf (sauve)

unidentified [ʌnaɪ'dɛntɪfaɪd] *adj* non identifié(e); *see also* **UFO**

uniform ['ju:nɪfɔ:m] *n* uniforme *m* ▷ *adj* uniforme

unify ['ju:nɪfaɪ] *vt* unifier

unimportant [ʌnɪm'pɔ:tənt] *adj* sans importance

uninhabited [ʌnɪn'hæbɪtɪd] *adj* inhabité(e)

unintentional [ʌnɪn'tɛnʃənəl] *adj* involontaire

union ['ju:njən] *n* union *f*; (*also*: **trade union**) syndicat *m* ▷ *cpd* du syndicat, syndical(e)

Union Jack *n* drapeau du Royaume-Uni

unique [ju:'ni:k] *adj* unique

unisex ['ju:nɪsɛks] *adj* unisexe

unison ['ju:nɪsn] *n*: **in** ~ à l'unisson, en chœur

unit ['ju:nɪt] *n* unité *f*; (*section: of furniture etc*) élément *m*, bloc *m*; (*team, squad*) groupe *m*, service m; **production** ~ atelier m de fabrication; **kitchen** ~ élément de cuisine; **sink** ~ bloc-évier m

unite [juːˈnaɪt] vt unir ▷ vi s'unir

united [juːˈnaɪtɪd] adj uni(e); (country, party) unifié(e); (efforts) conjugué(e)

United Kingdom n Royaume-Uni m

United Nations, United Nations Organization n (Organisation f des) Nations unies

United States, United States of America n États-Unis mpl

unit trust n (Brit Comm) fonds commun de placement, FCP m

unity [ˈjuːnɪtɪ] n unité f

universal [juːnɪˈvɜːsl] adj universel(le)

universe [ˈjuːnɪvɜːs] n univers m

university [juːnɪˈvɜːsɪtɪ] n université f ▷ cpd (student, professor) d'université; (education, year, degree) universitaire

unjust [ʌnˈdʒʌst] adj injuste

unkempt [ʌnˈkɛmpt] adj mal tenu(e), débraillé(e); mal peigné(e)

unkind [ʌnˈkaɪnd] adj peu gentil(le), méchant(e)

unknown [ʌnˈnəʊn] adj inconnu(e); ~ **to me** sans que je le sache; ~ **quantity** (Math, fig) inconnue f

unlawful [ʌnˈlɔːful] adj illégal(e)

unleaded [ʌnˈlɛdɪd] n (also: **unleaded petrol**) essence f sans plomb

unleash [ʌnˈliːʃ] vt détacher; (fig) déchaîner, déclencher

unless [ʌnˈlɛs] conj: ~ **he leaves** à moins qu'il (ne) parte; ~ **we leave** à moins de partir, à moins que nous (ne) partions; ~ **otherwise stated** sauf indication contraire; ~ **I am mistaken** si je ne me trompe

unlike [ʌnˈlaɪk] adj dissemblable, différent(e) ▷ prep à la différence de, contrairement à

unlikely [ʌnˈlaɪklɪ] adj (result, event) improbable; (explanation) invraisemblable

unlimited [ʌnˈlɪmɪtɪd] adj illimité(e)

unlisted [ˈʌnˈlɪstɪd] adj (US Tel) sur la liste rouge; (Stock Exchange) non coté(e) en Bourse

unload [ʌnˈləʊd] vt décharger

unlock [ʌnˈlɔk] vt ouvrir

unlucky [ʌnˈlʌkɪ] adj (person) malchanceux(-euse); (object, number) qui porte malheur; **to be** ~ (person) ne pas avoir de chance

unmarried [ʌnˈmærɪd] adj célibataire

unmistakable, unmistakeable [ʌnmɪsˈteɪkəbl] adj indubitable; qu'on ne peut pas ne pas reconnaître

unmitigated [ʌnˈmɪtɪgeɪtɪd] adj non mitigé(e), absolu(e), pur(e)

unnatural [ʌnˈnætʃrəl] adj non naturel(le); (perversion) contre nature

unnecessary [ʌnˈnɛsəsərɪ] adj inutile, superflu(e)

unnoticed [ʌnˈnəʊtɪst] adj inaperçu(e); **to go** ~ passer inaperçu

UNO [ˈjuːnəʊ] n abbr = **United Nations Organization**

unobtainable [ʌnəbˈteɪnəbl] adj (Tel) impossible à obtenir

unobtrusive [ʌnəbˈtruːsiv] adj discret(-ète)

unofficial [ʌnəˈfɪʃl] adj (news) officieux(-euse), non officiel(le); (strike) ≈ sauvage

unorthodox [ʌnˈɔːθədɔks] adj peu orthodoxe

unpack [ʌnˈpæk] vi défaire sa valise, déballer ses affaires ▷ vt (suitcase) défaire; (belongings) déballer

unpaid [ʌnˈpeɪd] adj (bill) impayé(e); (holiday) non-payé(e), sans salaire; (work) non rétribué(e); (worker) bénévole

unpalatable [ʌnˈpælətəbl] adj (truth) désagréable (à entendre)

unparalleled [ʌnˈpærəlɛld] adj incomparable, sans égal

unpleasant [ʌnˈplɛznt] adj déplaisant(e), désagréable

unplug [ʌnˈplʌg] vt débrancher

unpopular [ʌnˈpɔpjʊləˈ] adj impopulaire; **to make o.s.** ~ **(with)** se rendre impopulaire (auprès de)

unprecedented [ʌnˈprɛsɪdɛntɪd] adj sans précédent

unpredictable [ʌnprɪˈdɪktəbl] adj imprévisible

unprofessional [ʌnprəˈfɛʃənl] adj (conduct) contraire à la déontologie

UNPROFOR [ʌnˈprəʊfɔːˈ] n abbr (= United Nations Protection Force) FORPRONU f

unprotected [ˈʌnprəˈtɛktɪd] adj (sex) non protégé(e)

unqualified [ʌnˈkwɔlɪfaɪd] adj (teacher) non diplômé(e), sans titres; (success) sans réserve, total(e); (disaster) total(e)

unquestionably [ʌnˈkwɛstʃənəblɪ] adv incontestablement

unravel [ʌnˈrævl] vt démêler

unreal [ʌnˈrɪəl] adj irréel(le); (extraordinary) incroyable

unrealistic [ˈʌnrɪəˈlɪstɪk] adj (idea) irréaliste; (estimate) peu réaliste

unreasonable [ʌnˈriːznəbl] adj qui n'est pas raisonnable; **to make** ~ **demands on sb** exiger trop de qn

unrelated [ʌnrɪˈleɪtɪd] adj sans rapport; (people) sans lien de parenté

unreliable [ʌnrɪˈlaɪəbl] adj sur qui (or quoi) on ne peut pas compter, peu fiable

unremitting [ʌnrɪˈmɪtɪŋ] adj inlassable, infatigable, acharné(e)

unreservedly [ʌnrɪˈzɜːvɪdlɪ] adv sans réserve

unrest [ʌnˈrɛst] n agitation f, troubles mpl

unroll [ʌnˈrəʊl] vt dérouler

unruly [ʌnˈruːlɪ] adj indiscipliné(e)

unsafe [ʌnˈseɪf] adj (in danger) en danger; (journey, car) dangereux(-euse); (method) hasardeux(-euse); ~ **to drink/eat** non potable/comestible

unsaid [ʌnˈsɛd] adj: **to leave sth** ~ passer qch sous silence

unsatisfactory [ˈʌnsætɪsˈfæktərɪ] adj peu satisfaisant(e), qui laisse à désirer

unsavoury, (US) **unsavory** [ʌn'seɪvərɪ] *adj* (*fig*) peu recommandable, répugnant(e)

unscathed [ʌn'skeɪðd] *adj* indemne

unscrew [ʌn'skru:] *vt* dévisser

unscrupulous [ʌn'skru:pjuləs] *adj* sans scrupules

unsettled [ʌn'sɛtld] *adj* (*restless*) perturbé(e); (*unpredictable*) instable; incertain(e); (*not finalized*) non résolu(e)

unsettling [ʌn'sɛtlɪŋ] *adj* qui a un effet perturbateur

unshaven [ʌn'ʃeɪvn] *adj* non or mal rasé(e)

unsightly [ʌn'saɪtlɪ] *adj* disgracieux(-euse), laid(e)

unskilled [ʌn'skɪld] *adj*: ~ **worker** manœuvre *m*

unspeakable [ʌn'spi:kəbl] *adj* indicible; (*awful*) innommable

unspoiled ['ʌn'spɔɪld], **unspoilt** ['ʌn'spɔɪlt] *adj* (*place*) non dégradé(e)

unstable [ʌn'steɪbl] *adj* instable

unsteady [ʌn'stɛdɪ] *adj* mal assuré(e), chancelant(e), instable

unstuck [ʌn'stʌk] *adj*: **to come** ~ se décoller; (*fig*) faire fiasco

unsuccessful [ʌnsək'sɛsful] *adj* (*attempt*) infructueux(-euse); (*writer, proposal*) qui n'a pas de succès; (*marriage*) malheureux(-euse), qui ne réussit pas; **to be** ~ (*in attempting sth*) ne pas réussir; ne pas avoir de succès; (*application*) ne pas être retenu(e)

unsuitable [ʌn'su:təbl] *adj* qui ne convient pas, peu approprié(e); (*time*) inopportun(e)

unsure [ʌn'ʃuəʳ] *adj* pas sûr(e); **to be ~ of o.s.** ne pas être sûr de soi, manquer de confiance en soi

unsuspecting [ʌnsə'spɛktɪŋ] *adj* qui ne se méfie pas

unsympathetic ['ʌnsɪmpə'θɛtɪk] *adj* hostile; (*unpleasant*) antipathique; ~ **to** indifférent(e) à

untapped [ʌn'tæpt] *adj* (*resources*) inexploité(e)

unthinkable [ʌn'θɪŋkəbl] *adj* impensable, inconcevable

untidy [ʌn'taɪdɪ] *adj* (*room*) en désordre; (*appearance, person*) débraillé(e); (*person: in character*) sans ordre, désordonné; débraillé; (*work*) peu soigné(e)

untie [ʌn'taɪ] *vt* (*knot, parcel*) défaire; (*prisoner, dog*) détacher

until [ən'tɪl] *prep* jusqu'à; (*after negative*) avant
▷ *conj* jusqu'à ce que + *sub*, en attendant que + *sub*; (*in past, after negative*) avant que + *sub*; ~ **he comes** jusqu'à ce qu'il vienne, jusqu'à son arrivée; ~ **now** jusqu'à présent, jusqu'ici; ~ **then** jusque-là; **from morning ~ night** du matin au soir or jusqu'au soir

untimely [ʌn'taɪmlɪ] *adj* inopportun(e); (*death*) prématuré(e)

untold [ʌn'təuld] *adj* incalculable; indescriptible

untoward [ʌntə'wɔ:d] *adj* fâcheux(-euse), malencontreux(-euse)

untrue [ʌn'tru:] *adj* (*statement*) faux (fausse)

unused[1] [ʌn'ju:zd] *adj* (*new*) neuf (neuve)

unused[2] [ʌn'ju:st] *adj*: **to be ~ to sth/to doing**

sth ne pas avoir l'habitude de qch/de faire qch

unusual [ʌn'ju:ʒuəl] *adj* insolite, exceptionnel(le), rare

unusually [ʌn'ju:ʒulɪ] *adv* exceptionnellement, particulièrement

unveil [ʌn'veɪl] *vt* dévoiler

unwanted [ʌn'wɔntɪd] *adj* (*child, pregnancy*) non désiré(e); (*clothes etc*) à donner

unwelcome [ʌn'wɛlkəm] *adj* importun(e); **to feel ~** se sentir de trop

unwell [ʌn'wɛl] *adj* indisposé(e), souffrant(e); **to feel ~** ne pas se sentir bien

unwieldy [ʌn'wi:ldɪ] *adj* difficile à manier

unwilling [ʌn'wɪlɪŋ] *adj*: **to be ~ to do** ne pas vouloir faire

unwillingly [ʌn'wɪlɪŋlɪ] *adv* à contrecœur, contre son gré

unwind [ʌn'waɪnd] (*irreg: like* **wind**) *vt* dérouler
▷ *vi* (*relax*) se détendre

unwise [ʌn'waɪz] *adj* imprudent(e), peu judicieux(-euse)

unwitting [ʌn'wɪtɪŋ] *adj* involontaire

unwittingly [ʌn'wɪtɪŋlɪ] *adv* involontairement

unworkable [ʌn'wə:kəbl] *adj* (*plan etc*) inexploitable

unworthy [ʌn'wə:ðɪ] *adj* indigne

unwrap [ʌn'ræp] *vt* défaire; ouvrir

unwritten [ʌn'rɪtn] *adj* (*agreement*) tacite

unzip [ʌn'zɪp] *vt* ouvrir (la fermeture éclair de); (*Comput*) dézipper

up [ʌp] *prep*: **he went up the stairs/the hill** il a monté l'escalier/la colline; **the cat was up a tree** le chat était dans un arbre; **they live further up the street** ils habitent plus haut dans la rue; **go up that road and turn left** remontez la rue et tournez à gauche
▷ *vi* (*inf*): **she upped and left** elle a fichu le camp sans plus attendre
▷ *adv* **1** en haut; en l'air; (*upwards, higher*): **up in the sky/the mountains** (là-haut) dans le ciel/ les montagnes; **put it a bit higher up** mettez-le un peu plus haut; **to stand up** (*get up*) se lever, se mettre debout; (*be standing*) être debout; **up there** là-haut; **up above** au-dessus; **"this side up"** "haut"
2: **to be up** (*out of bed*) être levé(e); (*prices*) avoir augmenté or monté; (*finished*): **when the year was up** à la fin de l'année; **time's up** c'est l'heure
3: **up to** (*as far as*) jusqu'à; **up to now** jusqu'à présent
4: **to be up to** (*depending on*): **it's up to you** c'est à vous de décider; (*equal to*): **he's not up to it** (*job, task etc*) il n'en est pas capable; (*inf: be doing*): **what is he up to?** qu'est-ce qu'il peut bien faire?
5 (*phrases*): **he's well up in** or **on ...** (*Brit: knowledgeable*) il s'y connaît en ...; **up with Leeds United!** vive Leeds United!; **what's up?** (*inf*) qu'est-ce qui ne va pas?; **what's up with him?** (*inf*) qu'est-ce qui lui arrive?
▷ *n*: **ups and downs** hauts et bas *mpl*

up-and-coming [ʌpənd'kʌmɪŋ] *adj* plein(e)

d'avenir *or* de promesses

upbringing ['ʌpbrɪŋɪŋ] *n* éducation *f*

update [ʌp'deɪt] *vt* mettre à jour

upfront [ʌp'frʌnt] *adj* (*open*) franc (franche) ▷ *adv* (*pay*) d'avance; **to be ~ about sth** ne rien cacher de qch

upgrade [ʌp'greɪd] *vt* (*person*) promouvoir; (*job*) revaloriser; (*property, equipment*) moderniser

upheaval [ʌp'hiːvl] *n* bouleversement *m*; (*in room*) branle-bas *m*; (*event*) crise *f*

uphill [ʌp'hɪl] *adj* qui monte; (*fig: task*) difficile, pénible ▷ *adv* (*face, look*) en amont, vers l'amont; (*go, move*) vers le haut, en haut; **to go ~** monter

uphold [ʌp'həuld] *vt* (*irreg: like* **hold**) maintenir; soutenir

upholstery [ʌp'həulstəri] *n* rembourrage *m*; (*cover*) tissu *m* d'ameublement; (*of car*) garniture *f*

upkeep ['ʌpkiːp] *n* entretien *m*

upmarket [ʌp'mɑːkɪt] *adj* (*product*) haut de gamme *inv*; (*area*) chic *inv*

upon [ə'pɔn] *prep* sur

upper ['ʌpəʳ] *adj* supérieur(e); du dessus ▷ *n* (*of shoe*) empeigne *f*

upper class *n*: **the ~** ≈ la haute bourgeoisie

upper-class [ʌpə'klɑːs] *adj* de la haute société, aristocratique; (*district*) élégant(e), huppé(e); (*accent, attitude*) caractéristique des classes supérieures

upper hand *n*: **to have the ~** avoir le dessus

uppermost ['ʌpəməust] *adj* le (la) plus haut(e), en dessus; **it was ~ in my mind** j'y pensais avant tout autre chose

upper sixth *n* terminale *f*

upright ['ʌpraɪt] *adj* droit(e); (*fig*) droit, honnête ▷ *n* montant *m*

uprising ['ʌpraɪzɪŋ] *n* soulèvement *m*, insurrection *f*

uproar ['ʌprɔːʳ] *n* tumulte *m*, vacarme *m*; (*protests*) protestations *fpl*

uproot [ʌp'ruːt] *vt* déraciner

upset *n* ['ʌpsɛt] dérangement *m* ▷ *vt* [ʌp'sɛt] (*irreg: like* **set**); (*glass etc*) renverser; (*plan*) déranger; (*person: offend*) contrarier; (*: grieve*) faire de la peine à; bouleverser ▷ *adj* [ʌp'sɛt] contrarié(e); peiné(e); (*stomach*) détraqué(e), dérangé(e); **to get ~** (*sad*) devenir triste; (*offended*) se vexer; **to have a stomach ~** (*Brit*) avoir une indigestion

upshot ['ʌpʃɔt] *n* résultat *m*; **the ~ of it all was that ...** il a résulté de tout cela que ...

upside down ['ʌpsaɪd-] *adv* à l'envers; **to turn sth ~** (*fig: place*) mettre sens dessus dessous

upstairs [ʌp'stɛəz] *adv* en haut ▷ *adj* (*room*) du dessus, d'en haut ▷ *n*: **the ~** l'étage *m*; **there's no ~** il n'y a pas d'étage

upstart ['ʌpstɑːt] *n* parvenu(e)

upstream [ʌp'striːm] *adv* en amont

uptake ['ʌpteɪk] *n*: **he is quick/slow on the ~** il comprend vite/est lent à comprendre

uptight [ʌp'taɪt] *adj* (*inf*) très tendu(e), crispé(e)

up-to-date ['ʌptə'deɪt] *adj* moderne; (*information*) très récent(e)

upturn ['ʌptəːn] *n* (*in economy*) reprise *f*

upward ['ʌpwəd] *adj* ascendant(e); vers le haut ▷ *adv* vers le haut; (*more than*): **~ of** plus de; **and ~** et plus, et au-dessus

upwards ['ʌpwədz] *adv* vers le haut; (*more than*): **~ of** plus de; **and ~** et plus, et au-dessus

uranium [juə'reɪnɪəm] *n* uranium *m*

Uranus [juə'reɪnəs] *n* Uranus *f*

urban ['əːbən] *adj* urbain(e)

urban clearway *n* rue *f* à stationnement interdit◆

urbane [əː'beɪn] *adj* urbain(e), courtois(e)

urchin ['əːtʃɪn] *n* gosse *m*, garnement *m*

urge [əːdʒ] *n* besoin (impératif), envie (pressante) ▷ *vt* (*caution etc*) recommander avec insistance; (*person*): **to ~ sb to do** exhorter qn à faire, pousser qn à faire, recommander vivement à qn de faire

▶ **urge on** *vt* pousser, presser

urgency ['əːdʒənsɪ] *n* urgence *f*; (*of tone*) insistance *f*

urgent ['əːdʒənt] *adj* urgent(e); (*plea, tone*) pressant(e)

urinal ['juərɪnl] *n* (*Brit: place*) urinoir *m*

urinate ['juərɪneɪt] *vi* uriner

urine ['juərɪn] *n* urine *f*

URL *abbr* (= *uniform resource locator*) URL *f*

urn [əːn] *n* urne *f*; (*also*: **tea urn**) fontaine *f* à thé

US *n abbr* = **United States**

us [ʌs] *pron* nous; *see also* **me**

USA *n abbr* = **United States of America**; (*Mil*) = **United States Army**

use *n* [juːs] emploi *m*, utilisation *f*; usage *m*; (*usefulness*) utilité *f* ▷ *vt* [juːz] se servir de, utiliser, employer; **in ~** en usage; **out of ~** hors d'usage; **to be of ~** servir, être utile; **to make ~ of sth** utiliser qch; **ready for ~** prêt à l'emploi; **it's no ~** ça ne sert à rien; **to have the ~ of** avoir l'usage de; **what's this ~d for?** à quoi est-ce que ça sert?; **she ~d to do it** elle le faisait (autrefois), elle avait coutume de le faire; **to be ~d to** avoir l'habitude de, être habitué(e) à; **to get ~d to** s'habituer à

▶ **use up** *vt* finir, épuiser; (*food*) consommer

used [juːzd] *adj* (*car*) d'occasion

useful ['juːsful] *adj* utile; **to come in ~** être utile

usefulness ['juːsfəlnɪs] *n* utilité *f*

useless ['juːslɪs] *adj* inutile; (*inf: person*) nul(le)

user ['juːzəʳ] *n* utilisateur(-trice), usager *m*

user-friendly ['juːzə'frɛndlɪ] *adj* convivial(e), facile d'emploi

usher ['ʌʃəʳ] *n* placeur *m* ▷ *vt*: **to ~ sb in** faire entrer qn

usherette [ʌʃə'rɛt] *n* (*in cinema*) ouvreuse *f*

usual ['juːʒuəl] *adj* habituel(le); **as ~** comme d'habitude

usually ['juːʒuəlɪ] *adv* d'habitude, d'ordinaire

utensil [juː'tɛnsl] *n* ustensile *m*; **kitchen ~s** batterie *f* de cuisine

uterus ['juːtərəs] *n* utérus *m*

utility [juː'tɪlɪtɪ] *n* utilité *f*; (*also*: **public utility**) service public

utility room *n* buanderie *f*

utilize ['juːtɪlaɪz] *vt* utiliser; (*make good use of*) exploiter

utmost ['ʌtməust] *adj* extrême, le (la) plus grand(e) ▷ *n*: **to do one's ~** faire tout son possible; **of the ~ importance** d'une importance capitale, de la plus haute importance

utter ['ʌtəʳ] *adj* total(e), complet(-ète) ▷ *vt* prononcer, proférer; (*sounds*) émettre

utterance ['ʌtrns] *n* paroles *fpl*

utterly ['ʌtəlɪ] *adv* complètement, totalement

U-turn ['juːˈtəːn] *n* demi-tour *m*; (*fig*) volte-face *f inv*

Vv

v. *abbr* = **verse**; (= *vide*) v.; (= *versus*) vs; (= *volt*) V

vacancy ['veɪkənsɪ] *n* (*Brit: job*) poste vacant; (*room*) chambre *f* disponible; **"no vacancies"** "complet"

vacant ['veɪkənt] *adj* (*post*) vacant(e); (*seat etc*) libre, disponible; (*expression*) distrait(e)

vacate [və'keɪt] *vt* quitter

vacation [və'keɪʃən] *n* (*esp US*) vacances *fpl*; **to take a ~** prendre des vacances; **on ~** en vacances

vacationer [və'keɪʃənəʳ], (*US*) **vacationist** [və'keɪʃənɪst] *n* vacancier(-ière)

vaccinate ['væksɪneɪt] *vt* vacciner

vaccination [væksɪ'neɪʃən] *n* vaccination *f*

vaccine ['væksiːn] *n* vaccin *m*

vacuum ['vækjum] *n* vide *m*

vacuum cleaner *n* aspirateur *m*

vacuum-packed ['vækjumpækt] *adj* emballé(e) sous vide

vagina [və'dʒaɪnə] *n* vagin *m*

vagrant ['veɪɡrənt] *n* vagabond(e), mendiant(e)

vague [veɪɡ] *adj* vague, imprécis(e); (*blurred: photo, memory*) flou(e); **I haven't the ~st idea** je n'en ai pas la moindre idée

vaguely ['veɪɡlɪ] *adv* vaguement

vain [veɪn] *adj* (*useless*) vain(e); (*conceited*) vaniteux(-euse); **in ~** en vain

valentine ['væləntaɪn] *n* (*also*: **valentine card**) carte *f* de la Saint-Valentin

Valentine's Day ['væləntaɪnz-] *n* Saint-Valentin *f*

valiant ['vælɪənt] *adj* vaillant(e), courageux(-euse)

valid ['vælɪd] *adj* (*document*) valide, valable; (*excuse*) valable

valley ['vælɪ] *n* vallée *f*

valour, (*US*) **valor** ['væləʳ] *n* courage *m*

valuable ['væljuəbl] *adj* (*jewel*) de grande valeur; (*time, help*) précieux(-euse)

valuables ['væljuəblz] *npl* objets *mpl* de valeur

valuation [vælju'eɪʃən] *n* évaluation *f*, expertise *f*

value ['væljuː] *n* valeur *f* ▷ *vt* (*fix price*) évaluer, expertiser; (*appreciate*) apprécier; (*cherish*) tenir à; **values** *npl* (*principles*) valeurs *fpl*; **you get good ~ (for money) in that shop** vous en avez pour votre argent dans ce magasin; **to lose (in) ~** (*currency*) baisser; (*property*) se déprécier; **to gain (in) ~** (*currency*) monter; (*property*) prendre de la

valeur; **to be of great ~ to sb** (*fig*) être très utile à qn

value added tax [-'ædɪd-] *n* (*Brit*) taxe *f* à la valeur ajoutée

valued ['væljuːd] *adj* (*appreciated*) estimé(e)

valve [vælv] *n* (*in machine*) soupape *f*; (*on tyre*) valve *f*; (*in radio*) lampe *f*; (*Med*) valve, valvule *f*

vampire ['væmpaɪəʳ] *n* vampire *m*

van [væn] *n* (*Aut*) camionnette *f*; (*Brit Rail*) fourgon *m*

vandal ['vændl] *n* vandale *m/f*

vandalism ['vændəlɪzəm] *n* vandalisme *m*

vandalize ['vændəlaɪz] *vt* saccager

vanguard ['vænɡɑːd] *n* avant-garde *m*

vanilla [və'nɪlə] *n* vanille *f* ▷ *cpd* (*ice cream*) à la vanille

vanish ['vænɪʃ] *vi* disparaître

vanity ['vænɪtɪ] *n* vanité *f*

vantage ['vɑːntɪdʒ] *n*: **~ point** bonne position

vapour, (*US*) **vapor** ['veɪpəʳ] *n* vapeur *f*; (*on window*) buée *f*

variable ['veərɪəbl] *adj* variable; (*mood*) changeant(e) ▷ *n* variable *f*

variance ['veərɪəns] *n*: **to be at ~ (with)** être en désaccord (avec); (*facts*) être en contradiction (avec)

variant ['veərɪənt] *n* variante *f*

variation [veərɪ'eɪʃən] *n* variation *f*; (*in opinion*) changement *m*

varicose ['værɪkəus] *adj*: **~ veins** varices *fpl*

varied ['veərɪd] *adj* varié(e), divers(e)

variety [və'raɪətɪ] *n* variété *f*; (*quantity*) nombre *m*, quantité *f*; **a wide ~ of ...** une quantité *or* un grand nombre de ... (différent(e)s *or* divers(es)); **for a ~ of reasons** pour diverses raisons

variety show *n* (spectacle *m* de) variétés *fpl*

various ['veərɪəs] *adj* divers(e), différent(e); (*several*) divers, plusieurs; **at ~ times** (*different*) en diverses occasions; (*several*) à plusieurs reprises

varnish ['vɑːnɪʃ] *n* vernis *m*; (*for nails*) vernis (à ongles) ▷ *vt* vernir; **to ~ one's nails** se vernir les ongles

vary ['veərɪ] *vt, vi* varier, changer; **to ~ with** *or* **according to** varier selon

vase [vɑːz] *n* vase *m*

Vaseline® ['væsɪliːn] *n* vaseline *f*

vast [vɑːst] *adj* vaste, immense; (*amount, success*)

VAT [væt] *n abbr* (*Brit*: = *value added tax*) TVA *f*

vat [væt] *n* cuve *f*

vault [vɔ:lt] *n* (*of roof*) voûte *f*; (*tomb*) caveau *m*; (*in bank*) salle *f* des coffres; chambre forte; (*jump*) saut *m* ▷ *vt* (*also*: **vault over**) sauter (d'un bond)

vaunted ['vɔ:ntɪd] *adj*: **much-~** tant célébré(e)

VCR *n abbr* = **video cassette recorder**

VD *n abbr* = **venereal disease**

VDU *n abbr* = **visual display unit**

veal [vi:l] *n* veau *m*

veer [vɪəʳ] *vi* tourner; (*car, ship*) virer

vegan ['vi:gən] *n* végétalien(ne)

vegeburger ['vɛdʒɪbə:gəʳ] *n* burger végétarien

vegetable ['vɛdʒtəbl] *n* légume *m* ▷ *adj* végétal(e)

vegetarian [vɛdʒɪ'tɛərɪən] *adj, n* végétarien(ne); **do you have any ~ dishes?** avez-vous des plats végétariens?

vegetation [vɛdʒɪ'teɪʃən] *n* végétation *f*

vehement ['vi:ɪmənt] *adj* violent(e), impétueux(-euse); (*impassioned*) ardent(e)

vehicle ['vi:ɪkl] *n* véhicule *m*

veil [veɪl] *n* voile *m* ▷ *vt* voiler; **under a ~ of secrecy** (*fig*) dans le plus grand secret

vein [veɪn] *n* veine *f*; (*on leaf*) nervure *f*; (*fig: mood*) esprit *m*

Velcro® ['vɛlkrəu] *n* velcro® *m*

velocity [vɪ'lɔsɪtɪ] *n* vitesse *f*, vélocité *f*

velvet ['vɛlvɪt] *n* velours *m*

vending machine ['vɛndɪŋ-] *n* distributeur *m* automatique

vendor ['vɛndəʳ] *n* vendeur(-euse); **street ~** marchand ambulant

veneer [və'nɪəʳ] *n* placage *m* de bois; (*fig*) vernis *m*

venereal [vɪ'nɪərɪəl] *adj*: **~ disease** maladie vénérienne

Venetian blind [vɪ'ni:ʃən-] *n* store vénitien

vengeance ['vɛndʒəns] *n* vengeance *f*; **with a ~** (*fig*) vraiment, pour de bon

venison ['vɛnɪsn] *n* venaison *f*

venom ['vɛnəm] *n* venin *m*

vent [vɛnt] *n* conduit *m* d'aération; (*in dress, jacket*) fente *f* ▷ *vt* (*fig: one's feelings*) donner libre cours à

ventilation [vɛntɪ'leɪʃən] *n* ventilation *f*, aération *f*

ventilator ['vɛntɪleɪtəʳ] *n* ventilateur *m*

ventriloquist [vɛn'trɪləkwɪst] *n* ventriloque *m/f*

venture ['vɛntʃəʳ] *n* entreprise *f* ▷ *vt* risquer, hasarder ▷ *vi* s'aventurer, se risquer; **a business ~** une entreprise commerciale; **to ~ to do sth** se risquer à faire qch

venue ['vɛnju:] *n* lieu *m*; (*of conference etc*) lieu de la réunion (*or* manifestation *etc*); (*of match*) lieu de la rencontre

Venus ['vi:nəs] *n* (*planet*) Vénus *f*

verb [və:b] *n* verbe *m*

verbal ['və:bl] *adj* verbal(e); (*translation*) littéral(e)

verbatim [və:'beɪtɪm] *adj, adv* mot pour mot

verdict ['və:dɪkt] *n* verdict *m*; **~ of guilty/not guilty** verdict de culpabilité/de non-culpabilité

verge [və:dʒ] *n* bord *m*; **"soft ~s"** (*Brit*) "accotements non stabilisés"; **on the ~ of doing** sur le point de faire
  ▶ **verge on** *vt fus* approcher de

verify ['vɛrɪfaɪ] *vt* vérifier

vermin ['və:mɪn] *npl* animaux *mpl* nuisibles; (*insects*) vermine *f*

vermouth ['və:məθ] *n* vermouth *m*

versatile ['və:sətaɪl] *adj* polyvalent(e)

verse [və:s] *n* vers *mpl*; (*stanza*) strophe *f*; (*in Bible*) verset *m*; **in ~** en vers

version ['və:ʃən] *n* version *f*

versus ['və:səs] *prep* contre

vertical ['və:tɪkl] *adj* vertical(e) ▷ *n* verticale *f*

vertigo ['və:tɪgəu] *n* vertige *m*; **to suffer from ~** avoir des vertiges

verve [və:v] *n* brio *m*; enthousiasme *m*

very ['vɛrɪ] *adv* très ▷ *adj*: **the ~ book which** le livre même que; **the ~ thought (of it)** ... rien que d'y penser ...; **at the ~ end** tout à la fin; **the ~ last** le tout dernier; **at the ~ least** au moins; **~ well** très bien; **~ little** très peu; **~ much** beaucoup

vessel ['vɛsl] *n* (*Anat, Naut*) vaisseau *m*; (*container*) récipient *m*; *see also* **blood**

vest [vɛst] *n* (*Brit: underwear*) tricot *m* de corps; (*US: waistcoat*) gilet *m* ▷ *vt*: **to ~ sb with sth, to ~ sth in sb** investir qn de qch

vested interest *n*: **to have a ~ in doing** avoir tout intérêt à faire; **vested interests** *npl* (*Comm*) droits acquis

vet [vɛt] *n abbr* (*Brit*: = *veterinary surgeon*) vétérinaire *m/f*; (*US*: = *veteran*) ancien(ne) combattant(e) ▷ *vt* examiner minutieusement; (*text*) revoir; (*candidate*) se renseigner soigneusement sur, soumettre à une enquête approfondie

veteran ['vɛtərn] *n* vétéran *m*; (*also*: **war veteran**) ancien combattant ▷ *adj*: **she's a ~ campaigner for** ... cela fait très longtemps qu'elle lutte pour ...

veterinary surgeon ['vɛtrɪnərɪ-] (*Brit*) *n* vétérinaire *m/f*

veto ['vi:təu] *n* (*pl* **-es**) veto *m* ▷ *vt* opposer son veto à; **to put a ~ on** mettre (*or* opposer) son veto à

vex [vɛks] *vt* fâcher, contrarier

vexed [vɛkst] *adj* (*question*) controversé(e)

via ['vaɪə] *prep* par, via

viable ['vaɪəbl] *adj* viable

vibrate [vaɪ'breɪt] *vi*: **to ~ (with)** vibrer (de); (*resound*) retentir (de)

vibration [vaɪ'breɪʃən] *n* vibration *f*

vicar ['vɪkəʳ] *n* pasteur *m* (*de l'Église anglicane*)

vicarage ['vɪkərɪdʒ] *n* presbytère *m*

vicarious [vɪ'kɛərɪəs] *adj* (*pleasure, experience*) indirect(e)

vice [vaɪs] *n* (*evil*) vice *m*; (*Tech*) étau *m*

vice- [vaɪs] *prefix* vice-

vice-chairman [vaɪs'tʃɛəmən] (*irreg*) *n* vice-président(e)

vice squad *n* ≈ brigade mondaine

vice versa ['vaɪsɪ'və:sə] *adv* vice versa

vicinity [vɪˈsɪnɪtɪ] n environs mpl, alentours mpl

vicious [ˈvɪʃəs] adj (remark) cruel(le), méchant(e); (blow) brutal(e); (dog) méchant(e), dangereux(-euse); **a ~ circle** un cercle vicieux

victim [ˈvɪktɪm] n victime f; **to be the ~ of** être victime de

victor [ˈvɪktəʳ] n vainqueur m

Victorian [vɪkˈtɔːrɪən] adj victorien(ne)

victorious [vɪkˈtɔːrɪəs] adj victorieux(-euse)

victory [ˈvɪktərɪ] n victoire f; **to win a ~ over sb** remporter une victoire sur qn

video [ˈvɪdɪəu] n (video film) vidéo f; (also: **video cassette**) vidéocassette f; (also: **video cassette recorder**) magnétoscope m ▷ vt (with recorder) enregistrer; (with camera) filmer ▷ cpd vidéo inv

video camera n caméra f vidéo inv

video cassette recorder n = **video recorder**

video game n jeu m vidéo inv

video recorder n magnétoscope m

video shop n vidéoclub m

video tape n bande f vidéo inv; (cassette) vidéocassette f

video wall n mur m d'images vidéo

vie [vaɪ] vi: **to ~ with** lutter avec, rivaliser avec

Vienna [vɪˈɛnə] n Vienne

Vietnam, Viet Nam [ˈvjɛtˈnæm] n Viêt-nam or Vietnam m

Vietnamese [vjɛtnəˈmiːz] adj vietnamien(ne) ▷ n (pl inv) Vietnamien(ne); (Ling) vietnamien m

view [vjuː] n vue f; (opinion) avis m, vue ▷ vt voir, regarder; (situation) considérer; (house) visiter; **on ~** (in museum etc) exposé(e); **in full ~ of sb** sous les yeux de qn; **to be within ~ (of sth)** être à portée de vue (de qch); **an overall ~ of the situation** une vue d'ensemble de la situation; **in my ~** à mon avis; **in ~ of the fact that** étant donné que; **with a ~ to doing sth** dans l'intention de faire qch

viewer [ˈvjuːəʳ] n (viewfinder) viseur m; (small projector) visionneuse f; (TV) téléspectateur(-trice)

viewfinder [ˈvjuːfaɪndəʳ] n viseur m

viewpoint [ˈvjuːpɔɪnt] n point m de vue

vigilant [ˈvɪdʒɪlənt] adj vigilant(e)

vigorous [ˈvɪgərəs] adj vigoureux(-euse)

vile [vaɪl] adj (action) vil(e); (smell, food) abominable; (temper) massacrant(e)

villa [ˈvɪlə] n villa f

village [ˈvɪlɪdʒ] n village m

villager [ˈvɪlɪdʒəʳ] n villageois(e)

villain [ˈvɪlən] n (scoundrel) scélérat m; (Brit: criminal) bandit m; (in novel etc) traître m

vinaigrette [vɪneɪˈgrɛt] n vinaigrette f

vindicate [ˈvɪndɪkeɪt] vt défendre avec succès; justifier

vindictive [vɪnˈdɪktɪv] adj vindicatif(-ive), rancunier(-ière)

vine [vaɪn] n vigne f; (climbing plant) plante grimpante

vinegar [ˈvɪnɪgəʳ] n vinaigre m

vineyard [ˈvɪnjɑːd] n vignoble m

vintage [ˈvɪntɪdʒ] n (year) année f, millésime m ▷ cpd (car) d'époque; (wine) de grand cru; **the 1970 ~** le millésime 1970

vinyl [ˈvaɪnl] n vinyle m

viola [vɪˈəulə] n alto m

violate [ˈvaɪəleɪt] vt violer

violation [vaɪəˈleɪʃən] n violation f; **in ~ of** (rule, law) en infraction à, en violation de

violence [ˈvaɪələns] n violence f; (Pol etc) incidents violents

violent [ˈvaɪələnt] adj violent(e); **a ~ dislike of sb/sth** une aversion profonde pour qn/qch

violet [ˈvaɪələt] adj (colour) violet(te) ▷ n (plant) violette f

violin [vaɪəˈlɪn] n violon m

violinist [vaɪəˈlɪnɪst] n violoniste m/f

VIP n abbr (= very important person) VIP m

virgin [ˈvəːdʒɪn] n vierge f ▷ adj vierge; **she is a ~** elle est vierge; **the Blessed V~** la Sainte Vierge

Virgo [ˈvəːgəu] n la Vierge; **to be ~** être de la Vierge

virile [ˈvɪraɪl] adj viril(e)

virtual [ˈvəːtjuəl] adj (Comput, Physics) virtuel(le); (in effect): **it's a ~ impossibility** c'est quasiment impossible; **the ~ leader** le chef dans la pratique

virtually [ˈvəːtjuəlɪ] adv (almost) pratiquement; **it is ~ impossible** c'est quasiment impossible

virtual reality n (Comput) réalité virtuelle

virtue [ˈvəːtjuː] n vertu f; (advantage) mérite m, avantage m; **by ~ of** en vertu or raison de

virtuous [ˈvəːtjuəs] adj vertueux(-euse)

virus [ˈvaɪərəs] n (Med, Comput) virus m

visa [ˈviːzə] n visa m

vise [vaɪs] n (US Tech) = **vice**

visibility [vɪzɪˈbɪlɪtɪ] n visibilité f

visible [ˈvɪzəbl] adj visible; **~ exports/imports** exportations/importations fpl visibles

vision [ˈvɪʒən] n (sight) vue f, vision f; (foresight, in dream) vision

visit [ˈvɪzɪt] n visite f; (stay) séjour m ▷ vt (person: US: also: **visit with**) rendre visite à; (place) visiter; **on a private/official ~** en visite privée/officielle

visiting hours npl heures fpl de visite

visitor [ˈvɪzɪtəʳ] n visiteur(-euse); (to one's house) invité(e); (in hotel) client(e)

visitor centre, (US) **visitor center** n hall m or centre m d'accueil

visor [ˈvaɪzəʳ] n visière f

vista [ˈvɪstə] n vue f, perspective f

visual [ˈvɪzjuəl] adj visuel(le)

visual aid n support visuel (pour l'enseignement)

visual display unit n console f de visualisation, visuel m

visualize [ˈvɪzjuəlaɪz] vt se représenter; (foresee) prévoir

visually-impaired [ˈvɪzjuəlɪmˈpeəʳd] adj malvoyant(e)

vital [ˈvaɪtl] adj vital(e); **of ~ importance (to sb/sth)** d'une importance capitale (pour qn/qch)

vitality [vaɪˈtælɪtɪ] n vitalité f

vitally [ˈvaɪtəlɪ] adv extrêmement

vital statistics npl (of population) statistiques fpl

démographiques; (*inf: woman's*) mensurations *fpl*
vitamin ['vɪtəmɪn] *n* vitamine *f*
vivacious [vɪ'veɪʃəs] *adj* animé(e), qui a de la vivacité
vivid ['vɪvɪd] *adj* (*account*) frappant(e), vivant(e); (*light, imagination*) vif (vive)
vividly ['vɪvɪdlɪ] *adv* (*describe*) d'une manière vivante; (*remember*) de façon précise
V-neck ['viːnɛk] *n* décolleté *m* en V
vocabulary [vəu'kæbjulərɪ] *n* vocabulaire *m*
vocal ['vəukl] *adj* vocal(e); (*articulate*) qui n'hésite pas à s'exprimer, qui sait faire entendre ses opinions; **vocals** *npl* voix *fpl*
vocal cords *npl* cordes vocales
vocation [vəu'keɪʃən] *n* vocation *f*
vocational [vəu'keɪʃənl] *adj* professionnel(le); **~ guidance/training** orientation/formation professionnelle
vociferous [və'sɪfərəs] *adj* bruyant(e)
vodka ['vɔdkə] *n* vodka *f*
vogue [vəug] *n* mode *f*; (*popularity*) vogue *f*; **to be in ~** être en vogue *or* à la mode
voice [vɔɪs] *n* voix *f*; (*opinion*) avis *m* ▷ *vt* (*opinion*) exprimer, formuler; **in a loud/soft ~** à voix haute/basse; **to give ~ to** exprimer
voice mail *n* (*system*) messagerie *f* vocale; (*device*) boîte *f* vocale
void [vɔɪd] *n* vide *m* ▷ *adj* (*invalid*) nul(le); (*empty*): **~ of** vide de, dépourvu(e) de
volatile ['vɔlətaɪl] *adj* volatil(e); (*fig: person*) versatile; (: *situation*) explosif(-ive)
volcano (*pl* **-es**) [vɔl'keɪnəu] *n* volcan *m*
volition [və'lɪʃən] *n*: **of one's own ~** de son propre gré
volley ['vɔlɪ] *n* (*of gunfire*) salve *f*; (*of stones etc*) pluie *f*, volée *f*; (*Tennis etc*) volée *f*
volleyball ['vɔlɪbɔːl] *n* volley(-ball) *m*
volt [vəult] *n* volt *m*

voltage ['vəultɪdʒ] *n* tension *f*, voltage *m*; **high/low ~** haute/basse tension
volume ['vɔljuːm] *n* volume *m*; (*of tank*) capacité *f*; **~ one/two** (*of book*) tome un/deux; **his expression spoke ~s** son expression en disait long
voluntarily ['vɔləntrɪlɪ] *adv* volontairement; bénévolement
voluntary ['vɔləntərɪ] *adj* volontaire; (*unpaid*) bénévole
volunteer [vɔlən'tɪə'] *n* volontaire *m/f* ▷ *vt* (*information*) donner spontanément ▷ *vi* (*Mil*) s'engager comme volontaire; **to ~ to do** se proposer pour faire
vomit ['vɔmɪt] *n* vomissure *f* ▷ *vt, vi* vomir
vote [vəut] *n* vote *m*, suffrage *m*; (*votes cast*) voix *f*, vote; (*franchise*) droit *m* de vote ▷ *vt* (*bill*) voter; (*chairman*) élire; (*propose*): **to ~ that** proposer que + *sub* ▷ *vi* voter; **to put sth to the ~, to take a ~ on sth** mettre qch aux voix, procéder à un vote sur qch; **~ for** *or* **in favour of/against** vote pour/contre; **to ~ to do sth** voter en faveur de faire qch; **~ of censure** motion *f* de censure; **~ of thanks** discours *m* de remerciement
voter ['vəutə'] *n* électeur(-trice)
voting ['vəutɪŋ] *n* scrutin *m*, vote *m*
vouch [vautʃ]: **to ~ for** *vt fus* se porter garant de
voucher ['vautʃə'] *n* (*for meal, petrol, gift*) bon *m*; (*receipt*) reçu *m*; **travel ~** bon *m* de transport
vow [vau] *n* vœu *m*, serment *m* ▷ *vi* jurer; **to take** *or* **make a ~ to do sth** faire le vœu de faire qch
vowel ['vauəl] *n* voyelle *f*
voyage ['vɔɪɪdʒ] *n* voyage *m* par mer, traversée *f*; (*by spacecraft*) voyage
vulgar ['vʌlgə'] *adj* vulgaire
vulnerable ['vʌlnərəbl] *adj* vulnérable
vulture ['vʌltʃə'] *n* vautour *m*

Ww

wad [wɔd] *n* (*of cotton wool, paper*) tampon *m*; (*of banknotes etc*) liasse *f*

waddle ['wɔdl] *vi* se dandiner

wade [weɪd] *vi*: **to ~ through** marcher dans, patauger dans; (*fig: book*) venir à bout de ▷ *vt* passer à gué

wafer ['weɪfə^r] *n* (*Culin*) gaufrette *f*; (*Rel*) pain *m* d'hostie; (*Comput*) tranche *f* (de silicium)

waffle ['wɔfl] *n* (*Culin*) gaufre *f*; (*inf*) rabâchage *m*; remplissage *m* ▷ *vi* parler pour ne rien dire; faire du remplissage

waft [wɔft] *vt* porter ▷ *vi* flotter

wag [wæg] *vt* agiter, remuer ▷ *vi* remuer; **the dog ~ged its tail** le chien a remué la queue

wage [weɪdʒ] *n* (*also*: **wages**) salaire *m*, paye *f* ▷ *vt*: **to ~ war** faire la guerre; **a day's ~s** un jour de salaire

wage earner [-əːnə^r] *n* salarié(e); (*breadwinner*) soutien *m* de famille

wage packet *n* (*Brit*) (enveloppe *f* de) paye *f*

wager ['weɪdʒə^r] *n* pari *m* ▷ *vt* parier

wagon, waggon ['wægən] *n* (*horse-drawn*) chariot *m*; (*Brit Rail*) wagon *m* (de marchandises)

wail [weɪl] *n* gémissement *m*; (*of siren*) hurlement *m* ▷ *vi* gémir; (*siren*) hurler

waist [weɪst] *n* taille *f*, ceinture *f*

waistcoat ['weɪskəut] *n* (*Brit*) gilet *m*

waistline ['weɪstlaɪn] *n* (tour *m* de) taille *f*

wait [weɪt] *n* attente *f* ▷ *vi* attendre; **to ~ for sb/sth** attendre qn/qch; **to keep sb ~ing** faire attendre qn; **~ for me, please** attendez-moi, s'il vous plaît; **~ a minute!** un instant!; **"repairs while you ~"** "réparations minute"; **I can't ~ to ...** (*fig*) je meurs d'envie de ...; **to lie in ~ for** guetter

▶ **wait behind** *vi* rester (à attendre)

▶ **wait on** *vt fus* servir

▶ **wait up** *vi* attendre, ne pas se coucher; **don't ~ up for me** ne m'attendez pas pour aller vous coucher

waiter ['weɪtə^r] *n* garçon *m* (de café), serveur *m*

waiting ['weɪtɪŋ] *n*: **"no ~"** (*Brit Aut*) "stationnement interdit"

waiting list *n* liste *f* d'attente

waiting room *n* salle *f* d'attente

waitress ['weɪtrɪs] *n* serveuse *f*

waive [weɪv] *vt* renoncer à, abandonner

wake [weɪk] (*pt* **woke** *or* **-d**, *pp* **woken** *or* **-d**) [wəuk, 'wəukn] *vt* (*also*: **wake up**) réveiller ▷ *vi* (*also*: **wake up**) se réveiller ▷ *n* (*for dead person*) veillée *f* mortuaire; (*Naut*) sillage *m*; **to ~ up to sth** (*fig*) se rendre compte de qch; **in the ~ of** (*fig*) à la suite de; **to follow in sb's ~** (*fig*) marcher sur les traces de qn

Wales [weɪlz] *n* pays *m* de Galles; **the Prince of ~** le prince de Galles

walk [wɔːk] *n* promenade *f*; (*short*) petit tour; (*gait*) démarche *f*; (*path*) chemin *m*; (*in park etc*) allée *f*; (*pace*): **at a quick ~** d'un pas rapide ▷ *vi* marcher; (*for pleasure, exercise*) se promener ▷ *vt* (*distance*) faire à pied; (*dog*) promener; **10 minutes' ~ from** à 10 minutes de marche de; **to go for a ~** se promener; faire un tour; **from all ~s of life** de toutes conditions sociales; **I'll ~ you home** je vais vous raccompagner chez vous

▶ **walk out** *vi* (*go out*) sortir; (*as protest*) partir (en signe de protestation); (*strike*) se mettre en grève; **to ~ out on sb** quitter qn

walker ['wɔːkə^r] *n* (*person*) marcheur(-euse)

walkie-talkie ['wɔːkɪ'tɔːkɪ] *n* talkie-walkie *m*

walking ['wɔːkɪŋ] *n* marche *f* à pied; **it's within ~ distance** on peut y aller à pied

walking shoes *npl* chaussures *fpl* de marche

walking stick *n* canne *f*

Walkman® ['wɔːkmən] *n* Walkman® *m*

walkout ['wɔːkaut] *n* (*of workers*) grève-surprise *f*

walkover ['wɔːkəuvə^r] *n* (*inf*) victoire *f* or examen *m etc* facile

walkway ['wɔːkweɪ] *n* promenade *f*, cheminement piéton

wall [wɔːl] *n* mur *m*; (*of tunnel, cave*) paroi *f*; **to go to the ~** (*fig: firm etc*) faire faillite

▶ **wall in** *vt* (*garden etc*) entourer d'un mur

walled [wɔːld] *adj* (*city*) fortifié(e)

wallet ['wɔlɪt] *n* portefeuille *m*; **I can't find my ~** je ne retrouve plus mon portefeuille

wallflower ['wɔːlflauə^r] *n* giroflée *f*; **to be a ~** (*fig*) faire tapisserie

wallow ['wɔləu] *vi* se vautrer; **to ~ in one's grief** se complaire à sa douleur

wallpaper ['wɔːlpeɪpə^r] *n* papier peint ▷ *vt* tapisser

walnut ['wɔːlnʌt] *n* noix *f*; (*tree, wood*) noyer *m*

walrus (*pl* **-** *or* **-es**) ['wɔːlrəs] *n* morse *m*

waltz [wɔ:lts] *n* valse *f* ▷ *vi* valser

wand [wɒnd] *n* (*also*: **magic wand**) baguette *f* (magique)

wander ['wɒndə^r] *vi* (*person*) errer, aller sans but; (*thoughts*) vagabonder; (*river*) serpenter ▷ *vt* errer dans

wane [weɪn] *vi* (*moon*) décroître; (*reputation*) décliner

wangle ['wæŋgl] (*Brit inf*) *vt* se débrouiller pour avoir; carotter ▷ *n* combine *f*, magouille *f*

want [wɒnt] *vt* vouloir; (*need*) avoir besoin de; (*lack*) manquer de ▷ *n* (*poverty*) pauvreté *f*, besoin *m*; **wants** *npl* (*needs*) besoins *mpl*; **to ~ to do** vouloir faire; **to ~ sb to do** vouloir que qn fasse; **you're ~ed on the phone** on vous demande au téléphone; **"cook ~ed"** "on demande un cuisinier"; **for ~ of** par manque de, faute de

wanted ['wɒntɪd] *adj* (*criminal*) recherché(e) par la police

wanting ['wɒntɪŋ] *adj*: **to be ~ (in)** manquer (de); **to be found ~** ne pas être à la hauteur

war [wɔ:^{r}] *n* guerre *f*; **to go to ~** se mettre en guerre; **to make ~ (on)** faire la guerre (à)

ward [wɔ:d] *n* (*in hospital*) salle *f*; (*Pol*) section électorale; (*Law: child: also*: **ward of court**) pupille *m/f*

▶ **ward off** *vt* parer, éviter

warden ['wɔ:dn] *n* (*Brit: of institution*) directeur(-trice); (*of park, game reserve*) gardien(ne); (*Brit: also*: **traffic warden**) contractuel(le); (*of youth hostel*) responsable *m/f*

warder ['wɔ:də^r] *n* (*Brit*) gardien *m* de prison

wardrobe ['wɔ:drəub] *n* (*cupboard*) armoire *f*; (*clothes*) garde-robe *f*; (*Theat*) costumes *mpl*

warehouse ['wɛəhaus] *n* entrepôt *m*

wares [wɛəz] *npl* marchandises *fpl*

warfare ['wɔ:fɛə^r] *n* guerre *f*

warhead ['wɔ:hed] *n* (*Mil*) ogive *f*

warily ['wɛərɪlɪ] *adv* avec prudence, avec précaution

warm [wɔ:m] *adj* chaud(e); (*person, thanks, welcome, applause*) chaleureux(-euse); (*supporter*) ardent(e), enthousiaste; **it's ~** il fait chaud; **I'm ~** j'ai chaud; **to keep sth ~** tenir qch au chaud; **with my ~est thanks/congratulations** avec mes remerciements/mes félicitations les plus sincères

▶ **warm up** *vi* (*person, room*) se réchauffer; (*water*) chauffer; (*athlete, discussion*) s'échauffer ▷ *vt* (*food*) (faire) réchauffer; (*water*) (faire) chauffer; (*engine*) faire chauffer

warm-hearted [wɔ:m'hɑ:tɪd] *adj* affectueux(-euse)

warmly ['wɔ:mlɪ] *adv* (*dress*) chaudement; (*thank, welcome*) chaleureusement

warmth [wɔ:mθ] *n* chaleur *f*

warn [wɔ:n] *vt* avertir, prévenir; **to ~ sb (not) to do** conseiller à qn de (ne pas) faire

warning ['wɔ:nɪŋ] *n* avertissement *m*; (*notice*) avis *m*; (*signal*) avertisseur *m*; **without (any) ~** (*suddenly*) inopinément; (*without notifying*) sans prévenir; **gale ~** (*Meteorology*) avis de grand vent

warning light *n* avertisseur lumineux

warning triangle *n* (*Aut*) triangle *m* de présignalisation

warp [wɔ:p] *n* (*Textiles*) chaîne *f* ▷ *vi* (*wood*) travailler, se voiler *or* gauchir ▷ *vt* voiler; (*fig*) pervertir

warrant ['wɔrnt] *n* (*guarantee*) garantie *f*; (*Law: to arrest*) mandat *m* d'arrêt; (: *to search*) mandat de perquisition ▷ *vt* (*justify, merit*) justifier

warranty ['wɔrəntɪ] *n* garantie *f*; **under ~** (*Comm*) sous garantie

warren ['wɔrən] *n* (*of rabbits*) terriers *mpl*, garenne *f*

warrior ['wɔrɪə^r] *n* guerrier(-ière)

Warsaw ['wɔ:sɔ:] *n* Varsovie

warship ['wɔ:ʃɪp] *n* navire *m* de guerre

wart [wɔ:t] *n* verrue *f*

wartime ['wɔ:taɪm] *n*: **in ~** en temps de guerre

wary ['wɛərɪ] *adj* prudent(e); **to be ~ about** *or* **of doing sth** hésiter beaucoup à faire qch

was [wɒz] *pt of* **be**

wash [wɒʃ] *vt* laver; (*sweep, carry: sea etc*) emporter, entraîner; (: *ashore*) rejeter ▷ *vi* se laver; (*sea*): **to ~ over/against sth** inonder/baigner qch ▷ *n* (*paint*) badigeon *m*; (*clothes*) lessive *f*; (*washing programme*) lavage *m*; (*of ship*) sillage *m*; **to give sth a ~** laver qch; **to have a ~** se laver, faire sa toilette; **he was ~ed overboard** il a été emporté par une vague

▶ **wash away** *vt* (*stain*) enlever au lavage; (*subj: river etc*) emporter

▶ **wash down** *vt* laver; laver à grande eau

▶ **wash off** *vi* partir au lavage

▶ **wash up** *vi* (*Brit*) faire la vaisselle; (*US: have a wash*) se débarbouiller

washable ['wɒʃəbl] *adj* lavable

washbasin ['wɒʃbeɪsn] *n* lavabo *m*

washer ['wɒʃə^r] *n* (*Tech*) rondelle *f*, joint *m*

washing ['wɒʃɪŋ] *n* (*Brit: linen etc: dirty*) linge *m*; (: *clean*) lessive *f*

washing line *n* (*Brit*) corde *f* à linge

washing machine *n* machine *f* à laver

washing powder *n* (*Brit*) lessive *f* (en poudre)

Washington ['wɒʃɪŋtən] *n* (*city, state*) Washington *m*

washing-up [wɒʃɪŋ'ʌp] *n* (*Brit*) vaisselle *f*

washing-up liquid *n* (*Brit*) produit *m* pour la vaisselle

wash-out ['wɒʃaut] *n* (*inf*) désastre *m*

washroom ['wɒʃrum] *n* (*US*) toilettes *fpl*

wasn't ['wɒznt] = **was not**

wasp [wɒsp] *n* guêpe *f*

wastage ['weɪstɪdʒ] *n* gaspillage *m*; (*in manufacturing, transport etc*) déchet *m*

waste [weɪst] *n* gaspillage *m*; (*of time*) perte *f*; (*rubbish*) déchets *mpl*; (*also*: **household waste**) ordures *fpl* ▷ *adj* (*energy, heat*) perdu(e); (*food*) inutilisé(e); (*land, ground: in city*) à l'abandon; (: *in country*) inculte, en friche; (*leftover*): **~ material** déchets ▷ *vt* gaspiller; (*time, opportunity*) perdre; **wastes** *npl* étendue *f* désertique; **it's a ~ of money** c'est de l'argent jeté en l'air; **to go to ~**

être gaspillé(e); **to lay ~** (*destroy*) dévaster
▶ **waste away** vi dépérir
waste disposal, waste disposal unit n (Brit)
broyeur m d'ordures
wasteful ['weɪstful] adj gaspilleur(-euse);
(*process*) peu économique
waste ground n (Brit) terrain m vague
wastepaper basket ['weɪstpeɪpə-] n corbeille f
à papier
watch [wɔtʃ] n montre f; (*act of watching*)
surveillance f; (*guard: Mil*) sentinelle f; (: Naut)
homme m de quart; (*Naut: spell of duty*) quart
m ▷ vt (*look at*) observer; (: *match, programme*)
regarder; (*spy on, guard*) surveiller; (*be careful
of*) faire attention à ▷ vi regarder; (*keep guard*)
monter la garde; **to keep a close ~ on sb/sth**
surveiller qn/qch de près; **to keep ~** faire le guet;
~ what you're doing fais attention à ce que tu
fais
▶ **watch out** vi faire attention
watchdog ['wɔtʃdɔg] n chien m de garde; (*fig*)
gardien(ne)
watchful ['wɔtʃful] adj attentif(-ive), vigilant(e)
watchmaker ['wɔtʃmeɪkə'] n horloger(-ère)
watchman ['wɔtʃmən] (*irreg*) n gardien m; (*also:*
night watchman) veilleur m de nuit
watch strap ['wɔtʃstræp] n bracelet m de montre
water ['wɔːtə'] n eau f ▷ vt (*plant, garden*) arroser
▷ vi (*eyes*) larmoyer; **a drink of ~** un verre
d'eau; **in British ~s** dans les eaux territoriales
Britanniques; **to pass ~** uriner; **to make sb's
mouth ~** mettre l'eau à la bouche de qn
▶ **water down** vt (*milk etc*) couper avec de l'eau;
(*fig: story*) édulcorer
watercolour, (US) **watercolor** ['wɔːtəkʌlə'] n
aquarelle f; **watercolours** npl couleurs fpl pour
aquarelle
watercress ['wɔːtəkrɛs] n cresson m (de
fontaine)
waterfall ['wɔːtəfɔːl] n chute f d'eau
water heater n chauffe-eau m
watering can ['wɔːtərɪŋ-] n arrosoir m
water lily n nénuphar m
waterline ['wɔːtəlaɪn] n (Naut) ligne f de
flottaison
waterlogged ['wɔːtələgd] adj détrempé(e);
imbibé(e) d'eau
water main n canalisation f d'eau
watermelon ['wɔːtəmɛlən] n pastèque f
waterproof ['wɔːtəpruːf] adj imperméable
watershed ['wɔːtəʃɛd] n (Geo) ligne f de partage
des eaux; (*fig*) moment m critique, point décisif
water-skiing ['wɔːtəskiːɪŋ] n ski m nautique
watertight ['wɔːtətaɪt] adj étanche
waterway ['wɔːtəweɪ] n cours m d'eau navigable
waterworks ['wɔːtəwəːks] npl station f
hydraulique
watery ['wɔːtərɪ] adj (*colour*) délavé(e); (*coffee*)
trop faible
watt [wɔt] n watt m
wave [weɪv] n vague f; (*of hand*) geste m, signe
m; (Radio) onde f; (*in hair*) ondulation f; (*fig: of*

enthusiasm, strikes etc) vague ▷ vi faire signe de
la main; (*flag*) flotter au vent; (*grass*) ondoyer
▷ vt (*handkerchief*) agiter; (*stick*) brandir; (*hair*)
onduler; **short/medium ~** (Radio) ondes
courtes/moyennes; **long ~** (Radio) grandes
ondes; **the new ~** (Cine, Mus) la nouvelle vague;
to ~ goodbye to sb dire au revoir de la main à qn
▶ **wave aside**
▶ **wave away** vt (*fig: suggestion, objection*) rejeter,
repousser; (: *doubts*) chasser; (*person*): **to ~ sb
aside** faire signe à qn de s'écarter
wavelength ['weɪvlɛŋθ] n longueur f d'ondes
waver ['weɪvə'] vi vaciller; (*voice*) trembler;
(*person*) hésiter
wavy ['weɪvɪ] adj (*hair, surface*) ondulé(e); (*line*)
onduleux(-euse)
wax [wæks] n cire f; (*for skis*) fart m ▷ vt cirer;
(*car*) lustrer; (*skis*) farter ▷ vi (*moon*) croître
waxworks ['wækswəːks] npl personnages mpl de
cire; musée m de cire
way [weɪ] n chemin m, voie f; (*path, access*)
passage m; (*distance*) distance f; (*direction*)
chemin, direction f; (*manner*) façon f, manière f;
(*habit*) habitude f, façon; (*condition*) état m; **which
~? — this ~/that** ~ par où or de quel côté? — par
ici/par là; **to crawl one's ~ to ...** ramper jusqu'à
...; **to lie one's ~ out of it** s'en sortir par un
mensonge; **to lose one's ~** perdre son chemin;
on the ~ (to) en route (pour); **to be on one's ~**
être en route; **to be in the ~** bloquer le passage;
(*fig*) gêner; **to keep out of sb's ~** éviter qn; **it's
a long ~ away** c'est loin d'ici; **the village is
rather out of the ~** le village est plutôt à l'écart
or isolé; **to go out of one's ~ to do** (*fig*) se donner
beaucoup de mal pour faire; **to be under ~** (*work,
project*) être en cours; **to make ~ (for sb/sth)**
faire place (à qn/qch), s'écarter pour laisser
passer (qn/qch); **to get one's own ~** arriver à
ses fins; **put it the right ~ up** (Brit) mettez-le
dans le bon sens; **to be the wrong ~ round** être
à l'envers, ne pas être dans le bon sens; **he's in
a bad ~** il va mal; **in a ~** dans un sens; **by the ~** à
propos; **in some ~s** à certains égards; d'un côté;
in the ~ of en fait de, comme; **by ~ of** (*through*) en
passant par, via; (*as a sort of*) en guise de; **"~ in"**
(Brit) "entrée"; **"~ out"** (Brit) "sortie"; **the ~ back**
le chemin du retour; **this ~ and that** par-ci par-
là; **"give ~"** (Brit Aut) "cédez la priorité"; **no ~!**
(*inf*) pas question!
waylay [weɪ'leɪ] vt (*irreg: like* **lay**) attaquer; (*fig*): **I
got waylaid** quelqu'un m'a accroché
wayward ['weɪwəd] adj capricieux(-euse),
entêté(e)
W.C. n abbr (Brit: = water closet) w.-c. mpl, waters mpl
we [wiː] pl pron nous
weak [wiːk] adj faible; (*health*) fragile; (*beam etc*)
peu solide; (*tea, coffee*) léger(-ère); **to grow ~(er)**
s'affaiblir, faiblir
weaken ['wiːkn] vi faiblir ▷ vt affaiblir
weakling ['wiːklɪŋ] n gringalet m; faible m/f
weakness ['wiːknɪs] n faiblesse f; (*fault*) point m
faible

wealth [wɛlθ] n (money, resources) richesse(s) f(pl); (of details) profusion f

wealthy ['wɛlθɪ] adj riche

wean [wi:n] vt sevrer

weapon ['wɛpən] n arme f; **~s of mass destruction** armes fpl de destruction massive

wear [wɛəʳ] (pt **wore**, pp **worn**) [wɔːʳ, wɔːn] n (use) usage m; (deterioration through use) usure f ▷ vt (clothes) porter; (put on) mettre; (beard etc) avoir; (damage: through use) user ▷ vi (last) faire de l'usage; (rub etc through) s'user; **sports/baby~** vêtements mpl de sport/pour bébés; **evening ~** tenue f de soirée; **~ and tear** usure f; **to ~ a hole in sth** faire (à la longue) un trou dans qch
  ▶ **wear away** vt user, ronger ▷ vi s'user, être rongé(e)
  ▶ **wear down** vt user; (strength) épuiser
  ▶ **wear off** vi disparaître
  ▶ **wear on** vi se poursuivre; passer
  ▶ **wear out** vt user; (person, strength) épuiser

weary ['wɪərɪ] adj (tired) épuisé(e); (dispirited) las (lasse); abattu(e) ▷ vt lasser ▷ vi: **to ~ of** se lasser de

weasel ['wi:zl] n (Zool) belette f

weather ['wɛðəʳ] n temps m ▷ vt (wood) faire mûrir; (storm: lit, fig) essuyer; (crisis) survivre à; **what's the ~ like?** quel temps fait-il?; **under the ~** (fig: ill) mal fichu(e)

weather-beaten ['wɛðəbi:tn] adj (person) hâlé(e); (building) dégradé(e) par les intempéries

weather forecast n prévisions fpl météorologiques, météo f

weatherman ['wɛðəmæn] (irreg) n météorologue m

weather vane [-veɪn] n = **weather cock**

weave (pt **wove**, pp **woven**) [wi:v, wəuv, 'wəuvn] vt (cloth) tisser; (basket) tresser ▷ vi (fig) (pt, pp **-d**) (move in and out) se faufiler

weaver ['wi:vəʳ] n tisserand(e)

web [wɛb] n (of spider) toile f; (on duck's foot) palmure f; (fig) tissu m; (Comput): **the (World-Wide) W~** le Web

web address n adresse f Web

webcam ['wɛbkæm] n webcam f

weblog ['wɛblɔg] n blog m, blogue m

web page n (Comput) page f Web

website ['wɛbsaɪt] n (Comput) site m web

wed [wɛd] (pt, pp **-ded**) vt épouser ▷ vi se marier ▷ n: **the newly-~s** les jeunes mariés

we'd [wi:d] = **we had**; **we would**

wedding ['wɛdɪŋ] n mariage m

wedding anniversary n anniversaire m de mariage; **silver/golden ~** noces fpl d'argent/d'or

wedding day n jour m du mariage

wedding dress n robe f de mariée

wedding ring n alliance f

wedge [wɛdʒ] n (of wood etc) coin m; (under door etc) cale f; (of cake) part f ▷ vt (fix) caler; (push) enfoncer, coincer

Wednesday ['wɛdnzdɪ] n mercredi m; for phrases see also **Tuesday**

wee [wi:] adj (Scottish) petit(e); tout(e) petit(e)

weed [wi:d] n mauvaise herbe ▷ vt désherber
  ▶ **weed out** vt éliminer

weedkiller ['wi:dkɪləʳ] n désherbant m

weedy ['wi:dɪ] adj (man) gringalet

week [wi:k] n semaine f; **once/twice a ~** une fois/deux fois par semaine; **in two ~s' time** dans quinze jours; **a ~ today/on Tuesday** aujourd'hui/mardi en huit

weekday ['wi:kdeɪ] n jour m de semaine; (Comm) jour ouvrable; **on ~s** en semaine

weekend [wi:k'ɛnd] n week-end m

weekly ['wi:klɪ] adv une fois par semaine, chaque semaine ▷ adj, n hebdomadaire (m)

weep [wi:p] (pt, pp **wept**) [wɛpt] vi (person) pleurer; (Med: wound etc) suinter

weeping willow ['wi:pɪŋ-] n saule pleureur

weigh [weɪ] vt, vi peser; **to ~ anchor** lever l'ancre; **to ~ the pros and cons** peser le pour et le contre
  ▶ **weigh down** vt (branch) faire plier; (fig: with worry) accabler
  ▶ **weigh out** vt (goods) peser
  ▶ **weigh up** vt examiner

weight [weɪt] n poids m ▷ vt alourdir; (fig: factor) pondérer; **sold by ~** vendu au poids; **to put on/ lose ~** grossir/maigrir; **~s and measures** poids et mesures

weighting ['weɪtɪŋ] n: **~ allowance** indemnité f de résidence

weightlifter ['weɪtlɪftəʳ] n haltérophile m

weightlifting ['weɪtlɪftɪŋ] n haltérophilie f

weighty ['weɪtɪ] adj lourd(e)

weir [wɪəʳ] n barrage m

weird [wɪəd] adj bizarre; (eerie) surnaturel(le)

welcome ['wɛlkəm] adj bienvenu(e) ▷ n accueil m ▷ vt accueillir; (also: **bid welcome**) souhaiter la bienvenue à; (be glad of) se réjouir de; **to be ~** être le (la) bienvenu(e); **to make sb ~** faire bon accueil à qn; **you're ~** to try vous pouvez essayer si vous voulez; **you're ~!** (after thanks) de rien, il n'y a pas de quoi

weld [wɛld] n soudure f ▷ vt souder

welder ['wɛldəʳ] n (person) soudeur m

welfare ['wɛlfɛəʳ] n (wellbeing) bien-être m; (social aid) assistance sociale

welfare state n État-providence m

well [wɛl] n puits m ▷ adv bien ▷ adj: **to be ~** aller bien ▷ excl eh bien!; (relief also) bon!; (resignation) enfin!; **~ done!** bravo!; **I don't feel ~** je ne me sens pas bien; **get ~ soon!** remets-toi vite!; **to do ~** bien réussir; (business) prospérer; **to think ~ of sb** penser du bien de qn; **as ~** (in addition) aussi, également; **you might as ~ tell me** tu ferais aussi bien de me le dire; **as ~ as** aussi bien que or de; en plus de; **~, as I was saying ...** donc, comme je disais ...
  ▶ **well up** vi (tears, emotions) monter

we'll [wi:l] = **we will**; **we shall**

well-behaved ['wɛlbɪ'heɪvd] adj sage, obéissant(e)

well-being ['wɛl'bi:ɪŋ] n bien-être m

well-built ['wɛl'bɪlt] adj (house) bien construit(e);

(*person*) bien bâti(e)
well-deserved ['wɛldɪ'zə:vd] *adj* (bien) mérité(e)
well-dressed ['wɛl'drɛst] *adj* bien habillé(e), bien vêtu(e)
well-groomed [-'gru:md] *adj* très soigné(e)
well-heeled ['wɛl'hi:ld] *adj* (*inf: wealthy*) fortuné(e), riche
wellies ['wɛlɪz] (*inf*) *npl* (*Brit*) = **wellingtons**
wellingtons ['wɛlɪŋtənz] *npl* (*also: **wellington boots***) bottes *fpl* en caoutchouc
well-known ['wɛl'nəun] *adj* (*person*) bien connu(e)
well-mannered ['wɛl'mænəd] *adj* bien élevé(e)
well-meaning ['wɛl'mi:nɪŋ] *adj* bien intentionné(e)
well-off ['wɛl'ɔf] *adj* aisé(e), assez riche
well-paid [wɛl'peɪd] *adj* bien payé(e)
well-read ['wɛl'rɛd] *adj* cultivé(e)
well-to-do ['wɛltə'du:] *adj* aisé(e), assez riche
well-wisher ['wɛlwɪʃəʳ] *n* ami(e), admirateur(-trice); **scores of ~s had gathered** de nombreux amis et admirateurs s'étaient rassemblés; **letters from ~s** des lettres d'encouragement
Welsh [wɛlʃ] *adj* gallois(e) ▷ *n* (*Ling*) gallois *m*; **the Welsh** *npl* (*people*) les Gallois
Welsh Assembly *n* Parlement gallois
Welshman ['wɛlʃmən] (*irreg*) *n* Gallois *m*
Welshwoman ['wɛlʃwumən] (*irreg*) *n* Galloise *f*
went [wɛnt] *pt of* **go**
wept [wɛpt] *pt, pp of* **weep**
were [wə:ʳ] *pt of* **be**
we're [wɪəʳ] = **we are**
weren't [wə:nt] = **were not**
west [wɛst] *n* ouest *m* ▷ *adj* (*wind*) d'ouest; (*side*) ouest *inv* ▷ *adv* à or vers l'ouest; **the W~** l'Occident *m*, l'Ouest
westbound ['wɛstbaund] *adj* en direction de l'ouest; (*carriageway*) ouest *inv*
westerly ['wɛstəlɪ] *adj* (*situation*) à l'ouest; (*wind*) d'ouest
western ['wɛstən] *adj* occidental(e), de or à l'ouest ▷ *n* (*Cine*) western *m*
West Indian *adj* antillais(e) ▷ *n* Antillais(e)
West Indies [-'ɪndɪz] *npl* Antilles *fpl*
westward ['wɛstwəd], **westwards** ['wɛstwədz] *adv* vers l'ouest
wet [wɛt] *adj* mouillé(e); (*damp*) humide; (*soaked: also: **wet through***) trempé(e); (*rainy*) pluvieux(-euse) ▷ *vt*: **to ~ one's pants** *or* **o.s.** mouiller sa culotte, faire pipi dans sa culotte; **to get ~** se mouiller; **"~ paint"** "attention peinture fraîche"
wetsuit ['wɛtsu:t] *n* combinaison *f* de plongée
we've [wi:v] = **we have**
whack [wæk] *vt* donner un grand coup à
whale [weɪl] *n* (*Zool*) baleine *f*
wharf (*pl* **wharves**) [wɔ:f, wɔ:vz] *n* quai *m*
what [wɔt] *adj* **1** (*in questions*) quel(le); **~ size is he?** quelle taille fait-il?; **~ colour is it?** de quelle couleur est-ce?; **~ books do you need?** quels livres vous faut-il?

2 (*in exclamations*): **~ a mess!** quel désordre!; **~ a fool I am!** que je suis bête!
▷ *pron* **1** (*interrogative*) que; de/à/en *etc* quoi; **~ are you doing?** que faites-vous?, qu'est-ce que vous faites?; **~ is happening?** qu'est-ce qui se passe?, que se passe-t-il?; **~ are you talking about?** de quoi parlez-vous?; **~ are you thinking about?** à quoi pensez-vous?; **~ is it called?** comment est-ce que ça s'appelle?; **~ about me?** et moi?; **~ about doing ...?** et si on faisait ...?
2 (*relative: subject*) ce qui; (: *direct object*) ce que; (: *indirect object*) ce à quoi, ce dont; **I saw ~ you did/was on the table** j'ai vu ce que vous avez fait/ce qui était sur la table; **tell me ~ you remember** dites-moi ce dont vous vous souvenez; **~ I want is a cup of tea** ce que je veux, c'est une tasse de thé
▷ *excl* (*disbelieving*) quoi!, comment!
whatever [wɔt'ɛvəʳ] *adj*: **take ~ book you prefer** prenez le livre que vous préférez, peu importe lequel; **~ book you take** quel que soit le livre que vous preniez ▷ *pron*: **do ~ is necessary** faites (tout) ce qui est nécessaire; **~ happens** quoi qu'il arrive; **no reason ~** *or* **whatsoever** pas la moindre raison; **nothing ~** *or* **whatsoever** rien du tout
whatsoever [wɔtsəu'ɛvəʳ] *adj see* **whatever**
wheat [wi:t] *n* blé *m*, froment *m*
wheedle ['wi:dl] *vt*: **to ~ sb into doing sth** cajoler *or* enjôler qn pour qu'il fasse qch; **to ~ sth out of sb** obtenir qch de qn par des cajoleries
wheel [wi:l] *n* roue *f*; (*Aut: also: **steering wheel***) volant *m*; (*Naut*) gouvernail *m* ▷ *vt* (*pram etc*) pousser, rouler ▷ *vi* (*birds*) tournoyer; (*also: **wheel round***: *person*) se retourner, faire volte-face
wheelbarrow ['wi:lbærəu] *n* brouette *f*
wheelchair ['wi:ltʃɛəʳ] *n* fauteuil roulant
wheel clamp *n* (*Aut*) sabot *m* (de Denver)
wheeze [wi:z] *n* respiration bruyante (*d'asthmatique*) ▷ *vi* respirer bruyamment
when [wɛn] *adv* quand; **~ did he go?** quand est-ce qu'il est parti?
▷ *conj* **1** (*at, during, after the time that*) quand, lorsque; **she was reading ~ I came in** elle lisait quand *or* lorsque je suis entré
2 (*on, at which*): **on the day ~ I met him** le jour où je l'ai rencontré
3 (*whereas*) alors que; **I thought I was wrong ~ in fact I was right** j'ai cru que j'avais tort alors qu'en fait j'avais raison
whenever [wɛn'ɛvəʳ] *adv* quand donc ▷ *conj* quand; (*every time that*) chaque fois que; **I go ~ I can** j'y vais quand *or* chaque fois que je le peux
where [wɛəʳ] *adv, conj* où; **this is ~** c'est là que; **~ are you from?** d'où venez-vous?
whereabouts ['wɛərəbauts] *adv* où donc ▷ *n*: **nobody knows his ~** personne ne sait où il se trouve
whereas [wɛər'æz] *conj* alors que
whereby [wɛə'baɪ] *adv* (*formal*) par lequel (*or* laquelle *etc*)
wherever [wɛər'ɛvəʳ] *adv* où donc ▷ *conj* où que

+*sub*; **sit ~ you like** asseyez-vous (là) où vous
voulez

wherewithal ['wɛəwɪðɔːl] *n*: **the ~ (to do sth)**
les moyens *mpl* (de faire qch)

whether ['wɛðəʳ] *conj* si; **I don't know ~ to
accept or not** je ne sais pas si je dois accepter ou
non; **it's doubtful ~** il est peu probable que + *sub*;
~ you go or not que vous y alliez ou non

which [wɪtʃ] *adj* **1** (*interrogative: direct, indirect*)
quel(le); **~ picture do you want?** quel tableau
voulez-vous?; **~ one?** lequel (laquelle)?

2: **in ~ case** auquel cas; **we got there at 8pm,
by ~ time the cinema was full** quand nous
sommes arrivés à 20h, le cinéma était complet
▷ *pron* **1** (*interrogative*) lequel (laquelle), lesquels
(lesquelles) *pl*; **I don't mind ~** peu importe
lequel; **~ (of these) are yours?** lesquels sont à
vous?; **tell me ~ you want** dites-moi lesquels *or*
ceux que vous voulez

2 (*relative: subject*) qui; (: *object*) que; sur/vers *etc*
lequel (laquelle) (NB: *à + lequel = auquel; de + lequel
= duquel*); **the apple ~ you ate/~ is on the table**
la pomme que vous avez mangée/qui est sur la
table; **the chair on ~ you are sitting** la chaise
sur laquelle vous êtes assis; **the book of ~ you
spoke** le livre dont vous avez parlé; **he said he
knew, ~ is true/I was afraid of** il a dit qu'il le
savait, ce qui est vrai/ce que je craignais; **after
~** après quoi

whichever [wɪtʃ'ɛvəʳ] *adj*: **take ~ book you
prefer** prenez le livre que vous préférez, peu
importe lequel; **~ book you take** quel que soit
le livre que vous preniez; **~ way you** de quelque
façon que vous + *sub*

while [waɪl] *n* moment *m* ▷ *conj* pendant que; (*as
long as*) tant que; (*as, whereas*) alors que; (*though*)
bien que + *sub*, quoique + *sub*; **for a ~** pendant
quelque temps; **in a ~** dans un moment; **all
the ~** pendant tout ce temps-là; **we'll make it
worth your ~** nous vous récompenserons de
votre peine

▷ **while away** *vt* (*time*) (faire) passer

whilst [waɪlst] *conj* = **while**

whim [wɪm] *n* caprice *m*

whimper ['wɪmpəʳ] *n* geignement *m* ▷ *vi* geindre

whimsical ['wɪmzɪkl] *adj* (*person*)
capricieux(-euse); (*look*) étrange

whine [waɪn] *n* gémissement *m*; (*of engine,
siren*) plainte stridente ▷ *vi* gémir, geindre,
pleurnicher; (*dog, engine, siren*) gémir

whip [wɪp] *n* fouet *m*; (*for riding*) cravache *f*; (Pol:
person) chef *m* de file (*assurant la discipline dans son
groupe parlementaire*) ▷ *vt* fouetter; (*snatch*) enlever
(*or sortir*) brusquement

▷ **whip up** *vt* (*cream*) fouetter; (*inf: meal*) préparer
en vitesse; (*stir up: support*) stimuler; (: *feeling*)
attiser, aviver; *voir article*

whipped cream [wɪpt-] *n* crème fouettée

whip-round ['wɪpraund] *n* (Brit) collecte *f*

whirl [wəːl] *n* tourbillon *m* ▷ *vi* tourbillonner;
(*dancers*) tournoyer ▷ *vt* faire tourbillonner; faire
tournoyer

whirlpool ['wəːlpuːl] *n* tourbillon *m*

whirlwind ['wəːlwɪnd] *n* tornade *f*

whirr [wəːʳ] *vi* bruire; ronronner; vrombir

whisk [wɪsk] *n* (Culin) fouet *m* ▷ *vt* (*eggs*) fouetter,
battre; **to ~ sb away** *or* **off** emmener qn
rapidement

whiskers ['wɪskəz] *npl* (*of animal*) moustaches *fpl*;
(*of man*) favoris *mpl*

whisky, (*Irish, US*) **whiskey** ['wɪskɪ] *n* whisky *m*

whisper ['wɪspəʳ] *n* chuchotement *m*; (*fig: of
leaves*) bruissement *m*; (*rumour*) rumeur *f* ▷ *vt*, *vi*
chuchoter

whistle ['wɪsl] *n* (*sound*) sifflement *m*; (*object*)
sifflet *m* ▷ *vi* siffler ▷ *vt* siffler, siffloter

white [waɪt] *adj* blanc (blanche); (*with fear*)
blême ▷ *n* blanc *m*; (*person*) blanc (blanche); **to
turn** *or* **go ~** (*person*) pâlir, blêmir; (*hair*) blanchir;
the ~s (*washing*) le linge blanc; **tennis ~s** tenue *f*
de tennis

whiteboard ['waɪtbɔːd] *n* tableau *m* blanc;
interactive ~ tableau *m* (blanc) interactif

white coffee *n* (Brit) café *m* au lait, (café) crème *m*

white-collar worker ['waɪtkɔlə-] *n* employé(e)
de bureau

white elephant *n* (*fig*) objet dispendieux et
superflu

White House *n* (US): **the ~** la Maison-Blanche;
voir article

white lie *n* pieux mensonge

white paper *n* (Pol) livre blanc

whitewash ['waɪtwɔʃ] *n* (*paint*) lait *m* de chaux
▷ *vt* blanchir à la chaux; (*fig*) blanchir

whiting ['waɪtɪŋ] *n* (*pl inv: fish*) merlan *m*

Whitsun ['wɪtsn] *n* la Pentecôte

whittle ['wɪtl] *vt*: **to ~ away, to ~ down** (*costs*)
réduire, rogner

whizz [wɪz] *vi* aller (*or* passer) à toute vitesse

whizz kid *n* (*inf*) petit prodige

who [huː] *pron* qui

whodunit [huː'dʌnɪt] *n* (*inf*) roman policier

whoever [huː'ɛvəʳ] *pron*: **~ finds it** celui (celle)
qui le trouve (, qui que ce soit), quiconque le
trouve; **ask ~ you like** demandez à qui vous
voulez; **~ he marries** qui que ce soit *or* quelle
que soit la personne qu'il épouse; **~ told you
that?** qui a bien pu vous dire ça?, qui donc vous
a dit ça?

whole [həul] *adj* (*complete*) entier(-ière), tout(e);
(*not broken*) intact(e), complet(-ète) ▷ *n* (*entire
unit*) tout *m*; (*all*): **the ~ of** la totalité de, tout(e)
le (la); **the ~ lot (of it)** tout; **the ~ lot (of them)**
tous (sans exception); **the ~ of the time** tout le
temps; **the ~ of the town** la ville tout entière;
on the ~, **as a ~** dans l'ensemble

wholefood ['həulfuːd] *n*, **wholefoods** ['həulfuː
dz] ▷ *npl* aliments complets

wholehearted [həul'hɑːtɪd] *adj* sans réserve(s),
sincère

wholeheartedly [həul'hɑːtɪdlɪ] *adv* sans
réserve; **to agree ~** être entièrement d'accord

wholemeal ['həulmiːl] *adj* (Brit: *flour, bread*)
complet(-ète)

wholesale ['həulseɪl] n (vente f en) gros m ▷ adj (price) de gros; (destruction) systématique
wholesaler ['həulseɪlə'] n grossiste m/f
wholesome ['həulsəm] adj sain(e); (advice) salutaire
wholewheat ['həulwi:t] adj = **wholemeal**
wholly ['həulɪ] adv entièrement, tout à fait
whom [hu:m] pron 1 (interrogative) qui; ~ did you see? qui avez-vous vu?; to ~ did you give it? à qui l'avez-vous donné?
2 (relative) que; à/de etc qui; the man ~ I saw/to ~ I spoke l'homme que j'ai vu/à qui j'ai parlé
whooping cough ['hu:pɪŋ-] n coqueluche f
whore [hɔː'] n (inf: pej) putain f
whose [hu:z] adj 1 (possessive: interrogative): ~ book is this?, ~ is this book? à qui est ce livre?; ~ pencil have you taken? à qui est le crayon que vous avez pris?, c'est le crayon de qui que vous avez pris?; ~ daughter are you? de qui êtes-vous la fille?
2 (possessive: relative): the man ~ son you rescued l'homme dont or de qui vous avez sauvé le fils; the girl ~ sister you were speaking to la fille à la sœur de qui or de laquelle vous parliez; the woman ~ car was stolen la femme dont la voiture a été volée
▷ pron à qui; ~ is this? à qui est ceci?; I know ~ it is je sais à qui c'est
why [waɪ] adv pourquoi; ~ is he late? pourquoi est-il en retard?; ~ not? pourquoi pas?
▷ conj: I wonder ~ he said that je me demande pourquoi il a dit ça; that's not ~ I'm here ce n'est pas pour ça que je suis là; the reason ~ la raison pour laquelle
▷ excl eh bien!, tiens!; ~, it's you! tiens, c'est vous!; ~, that's impossible! voyons, c'est impossible!
wicked ['wɪkɪd] adj méchant(e); (mischievous: grin, look) espiègle, malicieux(-euse); (crime) pervers(e); (terrible: prices, weather) épouvantable; (inf: very good) génial(e) (inf)
wicket ['wɪkɪt] n (Cricket: stumps) guichet m; (: grass area) espace compris entre les deux guichets
wide [waɪd] adj large; (area, knowledge) vaste, très étendu(e); (choice) grand(e) ▷ adv: to open ~ ouvrir tout grand; to shoot ~ tirer à côté; it is 3 metres ~ cela fait 3 mètres de large
wide-awake [waɪdə'weɪk] adj bien éveillé(e)
widely ['waɪdlɪ] adv (different) radicalement; (spaced) sur une grande étendue; (believed) généralement; (travel) beaucoup; to be ~ read (author) être beaucoup lu(e); (reader) avoir beaucoup lu, être cultivé(e)
widen ['waɪdn] vt élargir ▷ vi s'élargir
wide open adj grand(e) ouvert(e)
widespread ['waɪdspred] adj (belief etc) très répandu(e)
widow ['wɪdəu] n veuve f
widowed ['wɪdəud] adj (qui est devenu(e)) veuf (veuve)
widower ['wɪdəuə'] n veuf m

width [wɪdθ] n largeur f; it's 7 metres in ~ cela fait 7 mètres de large
wield [wi:ld] vt (sword) manier; (power) exercer
wife (pl wives) [waɪf, waɪvz] n femme f, épouse f
wig [wɪg] n perruque f
wiggle ['wɪgl] vt agiter, remuer ▷ vi (loose screw etc) branler; (worm) se tortiller
wild [waɪld] adj sauvage; (sea) déchaîné(e); (idea, life) fou (folle); (behaviour) déchaîné(e), extravagant(e); (inf: angry) hors de soi, furieux(-euse); (: enthusiastic): to be ~ about être fou (folle) or dingue de ▷ n: the ~ la nature; wilds npl régions fpl sauvages
wild card n (Comput) caractère m de remplacement
wilderness ['wɪldənɪs] n désert m, région f sauvage
wildlife ['waɪldlaɪf] n faune f (et flore f)
wildly ['waɪldlɪ] adv (behave) de manière déchaînée; (applaud) frénétiquement; (hit, guess) au hasard; (happy) follement
wilful, (US) **willful** ['wɪlful] adj (person) obstiné(e); (action) délibéré(e); (crime) prémédité(e)
will [wɪl] aux vb 1 (forming future tense): I ~ finish it tomorrow je le finirai demain; I ~ have finished it by tomorrow je l'aurai fini d'ici demain; ~ you do it? — yes I ~/no I won't le ferez-vous? — oui/non; you won't lose it, ~ you? vous ne le perdrez pas, n'est-ce pas?
2 (in conjectures, predictions): he ~ or he'll be there by now il doit être arrivé à l'heure qu'il est; that ~ be the postman ça doit être le facteur
3 (in commands, requests, offers): ~ you be quiet! voulez-vous bien vous taire!; ~ you help me? est-ce que vous pouvez m'aider?; ~ you have a cup of tea? voulez-vous une tasse de thé?; I won't put up with it! je ne le tolérerai pas!
▷ vt (pt, pp -ed): to ~ sb to do souhaiter ardemment que qn fasse; he ~ed himself to go on par un suprême effort de volonté, il continua
▷ n volonté f; (document) testament m; to do sth of one's own free ~ faire qch de son propre gré; against one's ~ à contre-cœur
willing ['wɪlɪŋ] adj de bonne volonté, serviable
▷ n: to show ~ faire preuve de bonne volonté; he's ~ to do it il est disposé à le faire, il veut bien le faire
willingly ['wɪlɪŋlɪ] adv volontiers
willingness ['wɪlɪŋnɪs] n bonne volonté
willow ['wɪləu] n saule m
willpower ['wɪl'pauə'] n volonté f
willy-nilly ['wɪlɪ'nɪlɪ] adv bon gré mal gré
wilt [wɪlt] vi dépérir
win [wɪn] (pt, pp won) [wʌn] n (in sports etc) victoire f ▷ vt (battle, money) gagner; (prize, contract) remporter; (popularity) acquérir ▷ vi gagner
▶ **win over** vt convaincre
▶ **win round** vt gagner, se concilier
wince [wɪns] n tressaillement m ▷ vi tressaillir
winch [wɪntʃ] n treuil m
wind¹ [wɪnd] n (also Med) vent m; (breath) souffle

m ▷ vt (take breath away) couper le souffle à; **the ~(s)** (Mus) les instruments mpl à vent; **into** or **against the ~** contre le vent; **to get ~ of sth** (fig) avoir vent de qch; **to break ~** avoir des gaz

wind² (pt, pp **wound**) [waɪnd, waʊnd] vt enrouler; (wrap) envelopper; (clock, toy) remonter ▷ vi (road, river) serpenter

▶ **wind down** vt (car window) baisser; (fig: production, business) réduire progressivement

▶ **wind up** vt (clock) remonter; (debate) terminer, clôturer

windfall ['wɪndfɔːl] n coup m de chance

winding ['waɪndɪŋ] adj (road) sinueux(-euse); (staircase) tournant(e)

wind instrument n (Mus) instrument m à vent

windmill ['wɪndmɪl] n moulin m à vent

window ['wɪndəu] n fenêtre f; (in car, train: also: **windowpane**) vitre f; (in shop etc) vitrine f

window box n jardinière f

window cleaner n (person) laveur(-euse) de vitres

window ledge n rebord m de la fenêtre

window pane n vitre f, carreau m

window seat n (in vehicle) place f côté fenêtre

window-shopping ['wɪndəuʃɔpɪŋ] n: **to go ~** faire du lèche-vitrines

windowsill ['wɪndəusɪl] n (inside) appui m de la fenêtre; (outside) rebord m de la fenêtre

windpipe ['wɪndpaɪp] n gosier m

wind power n énergie éolienne

windscreen ['wɪndskriːn] n pare-brise m inv

windscreen washer n lave-glace m inv

windscreen wiper, (US) **windshield wiper** [-waɪpəʳ] n essuie-glace m inv

windshield ['wɪndʃiːld] (US) n = **windscreen**

windsurfing ['wɪndsəːfɪŋ] n planche f à voile

windswept ['wɪndswɛpt] adj balayé(e) par le vent

windy ['wɪndɪ] adj (day) de vent, venteux(-euse); (place, weather) venteux; **it's ~** il y a du vent

wine [waɪn] n vin m ▷ vt: **to ~ and dine sb** offrir un dîner bien arrosé à qn

wine bar n bar m à vin

wine cellar n cave f à vins

wine glass n verre m à vin

wine list n carte f des vins

wine tasting [-teɪstɪŋ] n dégustation f (de vins)

wine waiter n sommelier m

wing [wɪŋ] n aile f; (in air force) groupe m d'escadrilles; **wings** npl (Theat) coulisses fpl

winger ['wɪŋəʳ] n (Sport) ailier m

wing mirror n (Brit) rétroviseur latéral

wink [wɪŋk] n clin m d'œil ▷ vi faire un clin d'œil; (blink) cligner des yeux

winner ['wɪnəʳ] n gagnant(e)

winning ['wɪnɪŋ] adj (team) gagnant(e); (goal) décisif(-ive); (charming) charmeur(-euse)

winnings ['wɪnɪŋz] npl gains mpl

winter ['wɪntəʳ] n hiver m ▷ vi hiverner; **in ~** en hiver

winter sports npl sports mpl d'hiver

wintertime ['wɪntətaɪm] n hiver m

wintry ['wɪntrɪ] adj hivernal(e)

wipe [waɪp] n coup m de torchon (or de chiffon or d'éponge); **to give sth a ~** donner un coup de torchon/de chiffon/d'éponge à qch ▷ vt essuyer; (erase: tape) effacer; **to ~ one's nose** se moucher

▶ **wipe off** vt essuyer

▶ **wipe out** vt (debt) éteindre, amortir; (memory) effacer; (destroy) anéantir

▶ **wipe up** vt essuyer

wire ['waɪəʳ] n fil m (de fer); (Elec) fil électrique; (Tel) télégramme m ▷ vt (fence) grillager; (house) faire l'installation électrique de; (also: **wire up**) brancher; (person: send telegram to) télégraphier à

wireless ['waɪəlɪs] n (Brit) télégraphie f sans fil; (set) T.S.F. f

wiring ['waɪərɪŋ] n (Elec) installation f électrique

wiry ['waɪərɪ] adj noueux(-euse), nerveux(-euse)

wisdom ['wɪzdəm] n sagesse f; (of action) prudence f

wisdom tooth n dent f de sagesse

wise [waɪz] adj sage, prudent(e); (remark) judicieux(-euse); **I'm none the ~r** je ne suis pas plus avancé(e) pour autant

▶ **wise up** vi (inf): **to ~ up to** commencer à se rendre compte de

wish [wɪʃ] n (desire) désir m; (specific desire) souhait m, vœu m ▷ vt souhaiter, désirer, vouloir; **best ~es** (on birthday etc) meilleurs vœux; **with best ~es** (in letter) bien amicalement; **give her my best ~es** faites-lui mes amitiés; **to ~ sb goodbye** dire au revoir à qn; **he ~ed me well** il m'a souhaité bonne chance; **to ~ to do/sb to do** désirer or vouloir faire/que qn fasse; **to ~ for** souhaiter; **to ~ sth on sb** souhaiter qch à qn

wishful ['wɪʃful] adj: **it's ~ thinking** c'est prendre ses désirs pour des réalités

wistful ['wɪstful] adj mélancolique

wit [wɪt] n (also: **wits**: intelligence) intelligence f, esprit m; (presence of mind) présence f d'esprit; (wittiness) esprit; (person) homme/femme d'esprit; **to be at one's ~s' end** (fig) ne plus savoir que faire; **to have one's ~s about one** avoir toute sa présence d'esprit, ne pas perdre la tête; **to ~** adv à savoir

witch [wɪtʃ] n sorcière f

witchcraft ['wɪtʃkrɑːft] n sorcellerie f

with [wɪð, wɪθ] prep **1** (in the company of) avec; (at the home of) chez; **we stayed ~ friends** nous avons logé chez des amis; **I'll be ~ you in a minute** je suis à vous dans un instant

2 (descriptive): **a room ~ a view** une chambre avec vue; **the man ~ the grey hat/blue eyes** l'homme au chapeau gris/aux yeux bleus

3 (indicating manner, means, cause): **~ tears in her eyes** les larmes aux yeux; **to walk ~ a stick** marcher avec une canne; **red ~ anger** rouge de colère; **to shake ~ fear** trembler de peur; **to fill sth ~ water** remplir qch d'eau

4 (in phrases): **I'm ~ you** (I understand) je vous suis; **to be ~ it** (inf: up-to-date) être dans le vent

withdraw [wɪθ'drɔː] vt (irreg: like **draw**) retirer ▷ vi se retirer; (go back on promise) se rétracter; **to ~ into o.s.** se replier sur soi-même

withdrawal [wɪθ'drɔːəl] n retrait m; (Med) état m de manque

withdrawal symptoms npl: **to have ~** être en état de manque, présenter les symptômes mpl de sevrage

withdrawn [wɪθ'drɔːn] pp of **withdraw** ▷ adj (person) renfermé(e)

withdrew [wɪθ'druː] pt of **withdraw**

wither ['wɪðəʳ] vi se faner

withhold [wɪθ'həʊld] vt (irreg: like **hold**); (money) retenir; (decision) remettre; **to ~ (from)** (permission) refuser (à); (information) cacher (à)

within [wɪð'ɪn] prep à l'intérieur de ▷ adv à l'intérieur; **~ his reach** à sa portée; **~ sight of** en vue de; **~ a mile of** à moins d'un mille de; **~ the week** avant la fin de la semaine; **~ an hour from now** d'ici une heure; **to be ~ the law** être légal(e) or dans les limites de la légalité

without [wɪð'aʊt] prep sans; **~ a coat** sans manteau; **~ speaking** sans parler; **~ anybody knowing** sans que personne le sache; **to go** or **do ~ sth** se passer de qch

withstand [wɪθ'stænd] vt (irreg: like **stand**) résister à

witness ['wɪtnɪs] n (person) témoin m; (evidence) témoignage m ▷ vt (event) être témoin de; (document) attester l'authenticité de; **to bear ~ to sth** témoigner de qch; **~ for the prosecution/defence** témoin à charge/à décharge; **to ~ to sth/having seen sth** témoigner de qch/d'avoir vu qch

witness box, (US) **witness stand** n barre f des témoins

witty ['wɪtɪ] adj spirituel(le), plein(e) d'esprit

wives [waɪvz] npl of **wife**

wizard ['wɪzəd] n magicien m

wk abbr = **week**

wobble ['wɔbl] vi trembler; (chair) branler

woe [wəʊ] n malheur m

woke [wəʊk] pt of **wake**

woken ['wəʊkn] pp of **wake**

wolf (pl **wolves**) [wulf, wulvz] n loup m

woman (pl **women**) ['wumən, 'wɪmɪn] n femme f ▷ cpd: **~ doctor** femme f médecin; **~ friend** amie f; **~ teacher** professeur m femme; **young ~** jeune femme; **women's page** (Press) page f des lectrices

womanly ['wumənlɪ] adj féminin(e)

womb [wuːm] n (Anat) utérus m

women ['wɪmɪn] npl of **woman**

won [wʌn] pt, pp of **win**

wonder ['wʌndəʳ] n merveille f, miracle m; (feeling) émerveillement m ▷ vi: **to ~ whether/why** se demander si/pourquoi; **to ~ at** (surprise) s'étonner de; (admiration) s'émerveiller de; **to ~ about** songer à; **it's no ~ that** il n'est pas étonnant que + sub

wonderful ['wʌndəful] adj merveilleux(-euse)

won't [wəʊnt] = **will not**

wood [wud] n (timber, forest) bois m ▷ cpd de bois, en bois

wood carving n sculpture f en or sur bois

wooded ['wudɪd] adj boisé(e)

wooden ['wudn] adj en bois; (fig: actor) raide; (: performance) qui manque de naturel

woodpecker ['wudpekəʳ] n pic m (oiseau)

woodwind ['wudwɪnd] n (Mus) bois m; **the ~** les bois mpl

woodwork ['wudwəːk] n menuiserie f

woodworm ['wudwəːm] n ver m du bois; **the table has got ~** la table est piquée des vers

wool [wul] n laine f; **to pull the ~ over sb's eyes** (fig) en faire accroire à qn

woollen, (US) **woolen** ['wulən] adj de or en laine; (industry) lainier(-ière) ▷ n: **~s** lainages mpl

woolly, (US) **wooly** ['wulɪ] adj laineux(-euse); (fig: ideas) confus(e)

word [wəːd] n mot m; (spoken) mot, parole f; (promise) parole; (news) nouvelles fpl ▷ vt rédiger, formuler; **~ for ~** (repeat) mot pour mot; (translate) mot à mot; **what's the ~ for "pen" in French?** comment dit-on "pen" en français?; **to put sth into ~s** exprimer qch; **in other ~s** en d'autres termes; **to have a ~ with sb** toucher un mot à qn; **to have ~s with sb** (quarrel with) avoir des mots avec qn; **to break/keep one's ~** manquer à sa parole/tenir (sa) parole; **I'll take your ~ for it** je vous crois sur parole; **to send ~ of** prévenir de; **to leave ~ (with sb/for sb) that** ... laisser un mot (à qn/pour qn) disant que ...

wording ['wəːdɪŋ] n termes mpl, langage m; (of document) libellé m

word processing n traitement m de texte

word processor [-prəʊsesəʳ] n machine f de traitement de texte

wore [wɔːʳ] pt of **wear**

work [wəːk] n travail m; (Art, Literature) œuvre f ▷ vi travailler; (mechanism) marcher, fonctionner; (plan etc) marcher; (medicine) agir ▷ vt (clay, wood etc) travailler; (mine etc) exploiter; (machine) faire marcher or fonctionner; (miracles etc) faire; **works** n (Brit: factory) usine f ▷ npl (of clock, machine) mécanisme m; **how does this ~?** comment est-ce que ça marche?; **the TV isn't ~ing** la télévision est en panne or ne marche pas; **to go to ~** aller travailler; **to set to ~, to start ~** se mettre à l'œuvre; **to be at ~ (on sth)** travailler (sur qch); **to be out of ~** être au chômage or sans emploi; **to ~ hard** travailler dur; **to ~ loose** se défaire, se desserrer; **road ~s** travaux mpl (d'entretien des routes)

▶ **work on** vt fus travailler à; (principle) se baser sur

▶ **work out** vi (plans etc) marcher; (Sport) s'entraîner ▷ vt (problem) résoudre; (plan) élaborer; **it ~s out at £100** ça fait 100 livres

▶ **work up** vt: **to get ~ed up** se mettre dans tous ses états

workable ['wəːkəbl] adj (solution) réalisable

workaholic [wəːkə'hɔlɪk] n bourreau m de travail

worker ['wəːkəʳ] n travailleur(-euse), ouvrier(-ière); **office ~** employé(e) de bureau

work experience n stage m

workforce ['wəːkfɔːs] n main-d'œuvre f

working ['wə:kɪŋ] adj (day, tools etc, conditions) de travail; (wife) qui travaille; (partner, population) actif(-ive); **in ~ order** en état de marche; **a ~ knowledge of English** une connaissance toute pratique de l'anglais

working class n classe ouvrière ▷ adj: **working-class** ouvrier(-ière), de la classe ouvrière

working week n semaine f de travail

workman ['wə:kmən] (irreg) n ouvrier m

workmanship ['wə:kmənʃɪp] n métier m, habileté f; facture f

work of art n œuvre f d'art

workout ['wə:kaut] n (Sport) séance f d'entraînement

work permit n permis m de travail

workplace ['wə:kpleɪs] n lieu m de travail

worksheet ['wə:kʃi:t] n (Scol) feuille f d'exercices; (Comput) feuille f de programmation

workshop ['wə:kʃɔp] n atelier m

work station n poste m de travail

work surface n plan m de travail

worktop ['wə:ktɔp] n plan m de travail

work-to-rule ['wə:ktə'ru:l] n (Brit) grève f du zèle

world [wə:ld] n monde m ▷ cpd (champion) du monde; (power, war) mondial(e); **all over the ~** dans le monde entier, partout dans le monde; **to think the ~ of sb** (fig) ne jurer que par qn; **what in the ~ is he doing?** qu'est-ce qu'il peut bien être en train de faire?; **to do sb a ~ of good** faire le plus grand bien à qn; **W~ War One/Two, the First/Second W~ War** la Première/Deuxième Guerre mondiale; **out of this ~** adj extraordinaire

World Cup n: **the ~** (Football) la Coupe du monde

worldly ['wə:ldlɪ] adj de ce monde

world-wide ['wə:ld'waɪd] adj universel(le) ▷ adv dans le monde entier

World-Wide Web n: **the ~** le Web

worm [wə:m] n (also: **earthworm**) ver m

worn [wɔ:n] pp of **wear** ▷ adj usé(e)

worn-out ['wɔ:naut] adj (object) complètement usé(e); (person) épuisé(e)

worried ['wʌrɪd] adj inquiet(-ète); **to be ~ about sth** être inquiet au sujet de qch

worry ['wʌrɪ] n souci m ▷ vt inquiéter ▷ vi s'inquiéter, se faire du souci; **to ~ about** or **over sth/sb** se faire du souci pour or à propos de qch/qn

worrying ['wʌrɪɪŋ] adj inquiétant(e)

worse [wə:s] adj pire, plus mauvais(e) ▷ adv plus mal ▷ n pire m; **to get ~** (condition, situation) empirer, se dégrader; **a change for the ~** une détérioration; **he is none the ~ for it** il ne s'en porte pas plus mal; **so much the ~ for you!** tant pis pour vous!

worsen ['wə:sn] vt, vi empirer

worse off adj moins à l'aise financièrement; (fig): **you'll be ~ this way** ça ira moins bien de cette façon; **he is now ~ than before** il se retrouve dans une situation pire qu'auparavant

worship ['wə:ʃɪp] n culte m ▷ vt (God) rendre un culte à; (person) adorer; **Your W~** (Brit: to mayor)

Monsieur le Maire; (: to judge) Monsieur le Juge

worst [wə:st] adj le (la) pire, le (la) plus mauvais(e) ▷ adv le plus mal ▷ n pire m; **at ~** au pis aller; **if the ~ comes to the ~** si le pire doit arriver

worth [wə:θ] n valeur f ▷ adj: **to be ~** valoir; **how much is it ~?** ça vaut combien?; **it's ~ it** cela en vaut la peine, ça vaut la peine; **it is ~ one's while (to do)** ça vaut le coup (inf) (de faire); **50 pence ~ of apples** (pour) 50 pence de pommes

worthless ['wə:θlɪs] adj qui ne vaut rien

worthwhile ['wə:θ'waɪl] adj (activity) qui en vaut la peine; (cause) louable; **a ~ book** un livre qui vaut la peine d'être lu

worthy ['wə:ðɪ] adj (person) digne; (motive) louable; **~ of** digne de

would [wud] aux vb **1** (conditional tense): **if you asked him he ~ do it** si vous le lui demandiez, il le ferait; **if you had asked him he ~ have done it** si vous le lui aviez demandé, il l'aurait fait

2 (in offers, invitations, requests): **~ you like a biscuit?** voulez-vous un biscuit?; **~ you close the door please?** voulez-vous fermer la porte, s'il vous plaît?

3 (in indirect speech): **I said I ~ do it** j'ai dit que je le ferais

4 (emphatic): **it ~ have to snow today!** naturellement il neige aujourd'hui! or il fallait qu'il neige aujourd'hui!

5 (insistence): **she ~n't do it** elle n'a pas voulu or elle a refusé de le faire

6 (conjecture): **it ~ have been midnight** il devait être minuit; **it ~ seem so** on dirait bien

7 (indicating habit): **he ~ go there on Mondays** il y allait le lundi

would-be ['wudbi:] adj (pej) soi-disant

wouldn't ['wudnt] = **would not**

wound¹ [wu:nd] n blessure f ▷ vt blesser; **~ed in the leg** blessé à la jambe

wound² [waund] pt, pp of **wind²**

wove [wəuv] pt of **weave**

woven ['wəuvn] pp of **weave**

wrap [ræp] n (stole) écharpe f; (cape) pèlerine f ▷ vt (also: **wrap up**) envelopper; (parcel) emballer; (wind) enrouler; **under ~s** (fig: plan, scheme) secret(-ète)

wrapper ['ræpə'] n (on chocolate etc) papier m; (Brit: of book) couverture f

wrapping ['ræpɪŋ] n (of sweet, chocolate) papier m; (of parcel) emballage m

wrapping paper n papier m d'emballage; (for gift) papier cadeau

wreak [ri:k] vt (destruction) entraîner; **to ~ havoc** faire des ravages; **to ~ vengeance on** se venger de, exercer sa vengeance sur

wreath [ri:θ, pl ri:ðz] n couronne f

wreck [rɛk] n (sea disaster) naufrage m; (ship) épave f; (vehicle) véhicule accidentée; (pej: person) loque (humaine) ▷ vt démolir; (ship) provoquer le naufrage de; (fig) briser, ruiner

wreckage ['rɛkɪdʒ] n débris mpl; (of building) décombres mpl; (of ship) naufrage m

wren [rɛn] n (Zool) troglodyte m
wrench [rɛntʃ] n (Tech) clé f (à écrous);
(tug) violent mouvement de torsion; (fig)
déchirement m ⊳ vt tirer violemment
sur, tordre; **to ~ sth from** arracher qch
(violemment) à or de
wrestle ['rɛsl] vi: **to ~ (with sb)** lutter (avec qn);
to ~ with (fig) se débattre avec, lutter contre
wrestler ['rɛslə'] n lutteur(-euse)
wrestling ['rɛslɪŋ] n lutte f; (also: **all-in
wrestling**: Brit) catch m
wretched ['rɛtʃɪd] adj misérable; (inf) maudit(e)
wriggle ['rɪgl] n tortillement m ⊳ vi (also: **wriggle
about**) se tortiller
wring (pt, pp **wrung**) [rɪŋ, rʌŋ] vt tordre; (wet
clothes) essorer; (fig): **to ~ sth out of** arracher
qch à
wrinkle ['rɪŋkl] n (on skin) ride f; (on paper etc) pli m
⊳ vt rider, plisser ⊳ vi se plisser
wrinkled ['rɪŋkld], **wrinkly** ['rɪŋklɪ] adj (fabric,
paper) froissé(e), plissé(e); (surface) plissé; (skin)
ridé(e), plissé
wrist [rɪst] n poignet m
wrist watch ['rɪstwɔtʃ] n montre-bracelet f
writ [rɪt] n acte m judiciaire; **to issue a ~ against
sb, to serve a ~ on sb** assigner qn en justice
write (pt **wrote**, pp **written**) [raɪt, rəut, 'rɪtn] vt,
vi écrire; (prescription) rédiger; **to ~ sb a letter**
écrire une lettre à qn
  ▶ **write away** vi: **to ~ away for** (information)
(écrire pour) demander; (goods) (écrire pour)
commander
  ▶ **write down** vt noter; (put in writing) mettre
par écrit
  ▶ **write off** vt (debt) passer aux profits et pertes;
(project) mettre une croix sur; (depreciate) amortir;
(smash up: car etc) démolir complètement

  ▶ **write out** vt écrire; (copy) recopier
  ▶ **write up** vt rédiger
write-off ['raɪtɔf] n perte totale; **the car is a ~** la
voiture est bonne pour la casse
writer ['raɪtə'] n auteur m, écrivain m
writhe [raɪð] vi se tordre
writing ['raɪtɪŋ] n écriture f; (of author) œuvres fpl;
in ~ par écrit; **in my own ~** écrit(e) de ma main
writing paper n papier m à lettres
written ['rɪtn] pp of **write**
wrong [rɔŋ] adj (incorrect) faux (fausse); (incorrectly
chosen: number, road etc) mauvais(e); (not suitable)
qui ne convient pas; (wicked) mal; (unfair) injuste
⊳ adv mal ⊳ n tort m ⊳ vt faire du tort à, léser; **to
be ~** (answer) être faux (fausse); (in doing/saying)
avoir tort (de dire/faire); **you are ~ to do it** tu
as tort de le faire; **it's ~ to steal, stealing is ~**
c'est mal de voler; **you are ~ about that, you've
got it ~** tu te trompes; **to be in the ~** avoir tort;
what's ~? qu'est-ce qui ne va pas?; **there's
nothing ~** tout va bien; **what's ~ with the car?**
qu'est-ce qu'elle a, la voiture?; **to go ~** (person)
se tromper; (plan) mal tourner; (machine) se
détraquer; **I took a ~ turning** je me suis trompé
de route
wrongful ['rɔŋful] adj injustifié(e); **~ dismissal**
(Industry) licenciement abusif
wrongly ['rɔŋlɪ] adv à tort; (answer, do, count) mal,
incorrectement; (treat) injustement
wrong number n (Tel): **you have the ~** vous vous
êtes trompé de numéro
wrong side n (of cloth) envers m
wrote [rəut] pt of **write**
wrought [rɔːt] adj: **~ iron** fer forgé
wrung [rʌŋ] pt, pp of **wring**
wt. abbr (= weight) pds.
WWW n abbr = **World-Wide Web**

XL *abbr* (= *extra large*) XL
Xmas ['ɛksməs] *n abbr* = **Christmas**
X-ray ['ɛksreɪ] *n* (*ray*) rayon *m* X; (*photograph*)

radio(graphie) *f* ▷ *vt* radiographier
xylophone ['zaɪləfəun] *n* xylophone *m*

Yy

yacht [jɔt] n voilier m; (motor, luxury yacht) yacht m
yachting ['jɔtɪŋ] n yachting m, navigation f de plaisance
yachtsman ['jɔtsmən] (irreg) n yacht(s)man m
Yank [jæŋk], **Yankee** ['jæŋkɪ] n (pej) Amerloque m/f, Ricain(e)
yank [jæŋk] vt tirer d'un coup sec
yap [jæp] vi (dog) japper
yard [jɑːd] n (of house etc) cour f; (US: garden) jardin m; (measure) yard m (= 914 mm; 3 feet); **builder's ~** chantier m
yard sale n (US) brocante f (dans son propre jardin)
yardstick ['jɑːdstɪk] n (fig) mesure f, critère m
yarn [jɑːn] n fil m; (tale) longue histoire
yawn [jɔːn] n bâillement m ▷ vi bâiller
yawning ['jɔːnɪŋ] adj (gap) béant(e)
yd. abbr = **yard; yards**
yeah [jɛə] adv (inf) ouais
year [jɪəʳ] n an m, année f; (Scol etc) année; **every ~** tous les ans, chaque année; **this ~** cette année; **a** or **per ~** par an; **~ in, ~ out** année après année; **to be 8 ~s old** avoir 8 ans; **an eight-~-old child** un enfant de huit ans
yearly ['jɪəlɪ] adj annuel(le) ▷ adv annuellement; **twice ~** deux fois par an
yearn [jəːn] vi: **to ~ for sth/to do** aspirer à qch/à faire
yeast [jiːst] n levure f
yell [jɛl] n hurlement m, cri m ▷ vi hurler
yellow ['jɛləu] adj, n jaune (m)
Yellow Pages® npl (Tel) pages fpl jaunes
yelp [jɛlp] n jappement m; glapissement m ▷ vi japper; glapir
yes [jɛs] adv oui; (answering negative question) si ▷ n oui m; **to say ~ (to)** dire oui (à)
yesterday ['jɛstədɪ] adv, n hier (m); **~ morning/evening** hier matin/soir; **the day before ~** avant-hier; **all day ~** toute la journée d'hier
yet [jɛt] adv encore; (in questions) déjà ▷ conj pourtant, néanmoins; **it is not finished ~** ce n'est pas encore fini or toujours pas fini; **must you go just ~?** dois-tu déjà partir?; **have you eaten ~?** vous avez déjà mangé?; **the best ~** le meilleur jusqu'ici or jusque-là; **as ~** jusqu'ici, encore; **a few days ~** encore quelques jours; **~ again** une fois de plus

yew [juː] n if m
Yiddish ['jɪdɪʃ] n yiddish m
yield [jiːld] n production f, rendement m; (Finance) rapport m ▷ vt produire, rendre, rapporter; (surrender) céder ▷ vi céder; (US Aut) céder la priorité; **a ~ of 5%** un rendement de 5%
YMCA n abbr (= Young Men's Christian Association) ≈ union chrétienne de jeunes gens (UCJG)
yob ['jɔb], **yobbo** ['jɔbəu] n (Brit inf) loubar(d) m
yoga ['jəugə] n yoga m
yoghurt, yogurt ['jɔgət] n yaourt m
yoke [jəuk] n joug m ▷ vt (also: **yoke together**: oxen) accoupler
yolk [jəuk] n jaune m (d'œuf)
you [juː] pron **1** (subject) tu; (polite form) vous; (plural) vous; **~ are very kind** vous êtes très gentil; **~ French enjoy ~r food** vous autres Français, vous aimez bien manger; **~ and I will go** toi et moi or vous et moi, nous irons; **there ~ are!** vous voilà!
2 (object: direct, indirect) te, t' +vowel; vous; **I know ~** je te or vous connais; **I gave it to ~** je te l'ai donné, je vous l'ai donné
3 (stressed) toi; vous; **I told ~ to do it** c'est à toi or vous que j'ai dit de le faire
4 (after prep, in comparisons) toi; vous; **it's for ~** c'est pour toi or vous; **she's ~nger than ~** elle est plus jeune que toi or vous
5 (impersonal: one) on; **fresh air does ~ good** l'air frais fait du bien; **~ never know** on ne sait jamais; **~ can't do that!** ça ne se fait pas!
you'd [juːd] = **you had; you would**
you'll [juːl] = **you will; you shall**
young [jʌŋ] adj jeune ▷ npl (of animal) petits mpl; (people): **the ~** les jeunes, la jeunesse; **a ~ man** un jeune homme; **a ~ lady** (unmarried) une jeune fille, une demoiselle; (married) une jeune femme or dame; **my ~er brother** mon frère cadet; **the ~er generation** la jeune génération
younger [jʌŋgəʳ] adj (brother etc) cadet(te)
youngster ['jʌŋstəʳ] n jeune m/f; (child) enfant m/f
your [jɔːʳ] adj ton (ta), tes pl; (polite form, pl) votre, vos pl; see also **my**
you're [juəʳ] = **you are**
yours [jɔːz] pron le (la) tien(ne), les tiens (tiennes); (polite form, pl) le (la) vôtre, les vôtres; **is**

it ~? c'est à toi (*or* à vous)?; **a friend of** ~ un(e) de tes (*or* de vos) amis; *see also* **faithfully; sincerely**
yourself [jɔːˈsɛlf] *pron* (*reflexive*) te; (: *polite form*) vous; (*after prep*) toi; vous; (*emphatic*) toi-même; vous-même; **you** ~ **told me** c'est vous qui me l'avez dit, vous me l'avez dit vous-même; *see also* **oneself**
yourselves [jɔːˈsɛlvz] *pl pron* vous; (*emphatic*) vous-mêmes; *see also* **oneself**
youth [juːθ] *n* jeunesse *f*; (*young man*) (*pl* **-s**) [juːðz] jeune homme *m*; **in my** ~ dans ma jeunesse, quand j'étais jeune

youth club *n* centre *m* de jeunes
youthful [ˈjuːθful] *adj* jeune; (*enthusiasm etc*) juvénile; (*misdemeanour*) de jeunesse
youth hostel *n* auberge *f* de jeunesse
you've [juːv] = **you have**
Yugoslav [ˈjuːɡəuslɑːv] *adj* (*Hist*) yougoslave ▷ *n* Yougoslave *m/f*
Yugoslavia [juːɡəuˈslɑːvɪə] *n* (*Hist*) Yougoslavie *f*
yuppie [ˈjʌpɪ] *n* yuppie *m/f*
YWCA *n abbr* (= *Young Women's Christian Association*) union chrétienne féminine

Zz

zany ['zeɪnɪ] *adj* farfelu(e), loufoque

zap [zæp] *vt* (*Comput*) effacer

zeal [ziːl] *n* (*revolutionary etc*) ferveur *f*; (*keenness*) ardeur *f*, zèle *m*

zebra ['ziːbrə] *n* zèbre *m*

zebra crossing *n* (*Brit*) passage clouté *or* pour piétons

zero ['zɪərəu] *n* zéro *m* ▷ *vi*: **to ~ in on** (*target*) se diriger droit sur; **5° below ~** 5 degrés au-dessous de zéro

zest [zɛst] *n* entrain *m*, élan *m*; (*of lemon etc*) zeste *m*

zigzag ['zɪgzæg] *n* zigzag *m* ▷ *vi* zigzaguer, faire des zigzags

Zimbabwe [zɪm'bɑːbwɪ] *n* Zimbabwe *m*

Zimmer® ['zɪmə^r] *n* (*also*: **Zimmer frame**) déambulateur *m*

zinc [zɪŋk] *n* zinc *m*

zip [zɪp] *n* (*also*: **zip fastener**) fermeture *f* éclair® *or* à glissière; (*energy*) entrain *m* ▷ *vt* (*file*) zipper; (*also*: **zip up**) fermer (avec une fermeture éclair®)

zip code *n* (*US*) code postal

zip file *n* (*Comput*) fichier *m* zip *inv*

zipper ['zɪpə^r] *n* (*US*) = **zip**

zit [zɪt] (*inf*) *n* bouton *m*

zodiac ['zəudɪæk] *n* zodiaque *m*

zone [zəun] *n* zone *f*

zoo [zuː] *n* zoo *m*

zoology [zuːˈɔlədʒɪ] *n* zoologie *f*

zoom [zuːm] *vi*: **to ~ past** passer en trombe; **to ~ in (on sb/sth)** (*Phot, Cine*) zoomer (sur qn/qch)

zoom lens *n* zoom *m*, objectif *m* à focale variable

zucchini [zuːˈkiːnɪ] *n* (*US*) courgette *f*